VARIETY'S®
FILM
REVIEWS

Contents

Variety's® FILM REVIEWS

1991-1992

VOLUME 22

R.R. Bowker
A Reed Reference Publishing Company
New Providence, New Jersey

Volume 22, 1991-1992 of Variety's Film Reviews
was prepared by the R. R. Bowker's Bibliographic Group

Albert Simmonds, Managing Director, Bibliographic Group

Doreen Gravesande, Senior Managing Editor,
Barbara Holton, Senior Editor,
Megan Roxberry, Senior Associate Editor

Published by R. R. Bowker, A Reed Reference Publishing Company
121 Chanlon Road, New Providence, NJ 07974

R. R. Bowker has used its best efforts in preparing **Variety's Film Reviews**, but does not warrant that the information herein is complete or accurate, and does not assume, and hereby disclaims, any liability to any person for any loss or damage caused by errors or omissions herein, whether such errors or omissions result from negligence, accident, or any other cause.

Volume Twenty-Two, 1991-1992

PRINTED AND BOUND IN THE UNITED STATES OF AMERICA

Library of Congress Serial Data

Variety's Film Reviews, 1991-1992
Volume 22

ISSN 0897-4373

ISBN 0-8352-3273-5

Manufactured in the United States of America

ISBN 0-8352-3273-5

9 780835 232739

Preface

The reviews contained in this volume are complete and comprehensive reproductions of the original reviews printed in *Variety*. Only full-length feature films are included. Short subjects and made for television films are not included.

User's Guide

The reviews in this collection are published in chronological order, by the date on which the original review appeared. The date of each issue appears at the top of the column where the reviews for that issue begin. The reviews continue through that column and all following columns, until a new date appears at the top of the page. Where blank spaces occur at the end of a column, this indicates the end of that particular week's reviews.

There are separate indexes for 1991 and 1992 film titles. As an added enhancement to this volume, the director's name follows each film's original-language title. The film's review date is also included. An English translation of each foreign-language title accompanies that title in parentheses, and is also shown separately in the alphabetical listings. Reviews for film titles marked with an asterisk can be found in the Addendum, which appears after the 1992 reviews.

1991

NAKED OBSESSION

A Concorde Pictures release. Produced by Ron Zwang. Executive producer, Rodman Flender. Directed by Dan Golden. Screenplay, Robert Dodson, based on a story by Golden, Dodson; camera (color), Dick Buckley; editor, Gabrielle Gilbert-Reeves; music, Scott Singer; sound, Cameron Hamza; production design, Johan Le Tenoux; art direction, Mark Walters, Hayden de M. Yates; costume design, Paris Libby; assistant director, Charles Philip Moore; casting, Steve Rabiner. Reviewed at Foto-Kem Studios, Burbank, Calif., Dec. 18, 1990. MPAA Rating: R. Running time: 80 MIN.
Franklin Carlyle . . . . . William Katt
Sam Silver . . . . Rick Dean
Lynne . . . . Maria Ford
Becky . . . . Elena Sahagun
Mitch . . . . Tommy Hinkley
Saundra . . . . . . Wendy MacDonald
Det. Ludlow . . . . Roger Craig

A low-budget soft-porn thriller with a reasonably entertaining plot, "Naked Obsession" supplies enough titillation and lurid plot twists to satisfy viewers whose expectations are appropriately low. Concorde plans a regional sendout starting Jan. 11.

William Katt plays an uptight city councilman who unexpectedly takes a walk on the wild side when he's mugged while exploring a rundown urban area he's targeted for redevelopment.

Banged up and minus his wallet and car, he's befriended by a tall, peculiar wino (Rick Dean) who takes him into a strip club to make a phone call. Katt gets distracted by the teasing antics of a gorgeous blonde stripper (Maria Ford) and winds up returning the next night for a kinky tryst at her apartment.

When she's found dead the next day, the married councilman's reputation is in big trouble. As he tries to cover his tracks he gets in deeper.

First-time director Dan Golden builds in a fantasy-horror atmosphere that makes Katt's wino friend seem like a satanic emissary out to bring him down. Golden demonstrates a flair for the fantastic in pic's lurid dream scenes, but is not as lucky with actors.

Katt in particular does a wooden walk-through, looking pained whenever someone tries to seduce him. Pic's main attraction will be the glossy strip scenes, well-choreographed and seductively cast. Ford looks destined to have all the work she wants in this genre.

Screenplay by Golden and Robert Dodson unravels with holes big enough to drive a police van through, particularly toward the end when the councilman doesn't report his wife's murder in their home. But its kinky developments should interest a fringe audience.

Tommy Hinkley brings a burst of energy to the screen as the randy, corrupt lobbyist, and looks headed for bigger roles. — *Daws.*

CRACKDOWN

A Concorde release. Produced by Luis Llosa. Executive producer, Kevin Reidy. Directed by Louis Morneau. Screenplay, Ross Bell, Daryl Haney; camera (color), Pili Flores Guerra; editor, Eric L. Beason; music, Terry Plumeri; sound, Edgard Lostaunau; costume design, Greg LaVoi; art direction, Jaime Gonzales; assistant director, Ramsay Ross; casting, Reidy, Steve Rabiner. Reviewed at Foto-Kem screening room, Burbank, Calif., Dec. 19, 1990. MPAA Rating: Running time: 88 MIN.
Shaun Broderick . . . . Cliff De Young
Lt. Delgado . . . . . . Robert Beltran
Constance Bigelow . . . . . Jamie Rose
Castillo . . . . Orlando Sacha
Cowley . . . . Kevin Reidy
Thurmond . . . . . . Gerald Anthony

This sprawling drug actioner has an ambitious scope, given its obvious time and budget constraints, but it ends up skating clumsily over familiar territory. Abundant gunfire and explosions should satisfy action fans at the lowest rungs, but overall b.o. prospects in Concorde's regional release look minimal.

Producer Luis Llosa, cousin of Peruvian author/politico Mario Vargas Llosa and an accomplished journalist/documentarian, apparently set his sights on creating a large-scale Latin American crime saga.

Money for the lensed-in-Peru pic went to glitzy surroundings and extras, abundant locales, chase scenes, bullets and explosions at the expense of a compelling script, a supporting cast that doesn't embarrass, and time for rehearsal, retakes and postproduction values.

Cliff De Young borrows his style from early Jack Nicholson pics to play an obnoxious U.S. Drug Enforcement Agency agent who's teamed with Robert Beltran, a by-the-book Peruvian cop, to extradite a drug kingpin (Orlando Sacha) to a jail cell in Miami.

They bungle it and spend the rest of the pic trying to recapture their prey while each cop's style has its inevitable influence on the other.

De Young's I'm-so-crazy-I'm-dangerous routine begins as a rushed and sloppy piece of acting, but it warms up and provides pic's only memorable peg.

Beltran is solid as the straightman, and Sacha is fine as the unruffled prisoner, but other players are dismal. Debuting director Louis Morneau has better luck handling bullets and gunpowder, but even pic's abundant action is unexciting, given the routine nature of the story.

Camera flits all over the place with a maddening absence of purpose, and editing is often rough.

Local Latin color provides some fringe interest in scenes of cockfights, street musicians, etc., and pic has no lack of new setups as it moves hurriedly across more ground than it can properly cover. — *Daws.*

HUSH-A-BYE-BABY
(BRITISH-16M)

A Derry Film and Video Workshop production in association with Channel Four and British Screen. (Intl. sales: Jane Balfour Films, London.) Exec producer, Simon Relph. Produced by Tom Collins. Directed by Margo Harkin. Screenplay, Harkin, Stephanie English; camera (color, 16m), Breffni Byrne; editor, Martin Duffy; music, Sinead O'Connor; sound, Liam Saurin. Reviewed at the Toronto Festival of Festivals, Sept. 11, 1990. Running time: 72 MIN.
With: Emer McCourt, Michael Liebman, Cathy Casaey, Julie Marie Reynolds, Sinead O'Connor.

Director Margo Harkin makes a notable debut with this bittersweet tale of young love during troubled times in her home base of Derry, Northern Ireland. Reminiscent of Bill Forsyth's early films, but bleaker, "Hush-A-Bye-Baby" is a bit too unpolished for commercial release but could interest adventurous public tv programmers.

The film unfolds at a casual pace as it follows the everyday lives of a group of Derry Catholic high school students. Like teens everywhere, they're concerned with clique status and the opposite sex. While the presence of British soldiers on the streets lends a subtle tension to the atmosphere, the students and their families subsume their resentment of the occupation in daily routine.

Cultural nationalism is expressed through the study of Gallic, a tongue-twisting challenge which at least one British soldier meets more easily than the students.

When 15-year-old Goretti (Emer McCourt) falls in love with her boyfriend, she falls hard. In a land where contraception and abortion are forbidden, nature takes its course with only one consequence. Initially whimsical and low-key about her pregnancy, Goretti soon feels she's carrying "the weight of the world," when her b.f., wrongly imprisoned by the British, begs off responsibility in a letter from jail.

Despite the loyalty of a steadfast friend, Goretti is unable to face her family with her secret. Instead she grows increasingly terrified and withdrawn, until she becomes a tragic victim of rigid societal mores that the filmmaker explicitly condemns.

Its downbeat denouement notwithstanding "Hush-A-Bye-Baby" affectionately illuminates its small corner of the world. Performances are fresh and unstudied, although the actors' thick Ulster accents are occasionally impenetrable. — *Rich.*

NOT WITHOUT MY DAUGHTER

An MGM release of a Pathé Entertainment presentation of an Ufland production. Produced by Harry J. Ufland, Mary Jane Ufland. Directed by Brian Gilbert. Screenplay, David W. Rintels, based on the book by Betty Mahmoody with William Hoffer; camera (Fuji color), Peter Hannan; editor, Terry Rawlings; music, Jerry Goldsmith; sound (Dolby), Eli Yarkoni, Jim Hawkins (Atlanta); production design, Anthony Pratt; art direction, Desmond Crowe, Avi Avivi; set decoration, Shlomo Zafir, Joe Litsch (Atlanta); costume design, Nic Ede; associate producer, Anthony Waye; assistant directors, Adi Shoval, Dick Feury (Atlanta); casting, Mike Fenton, Judy Taylor, Joyce Gallie, Shay Griffin. Reviewed at the Embassy Theater, N.Y., Jan. 3, 1991. MPAA Rating: PG-13. Running time: 114 MIN.
Betty Mahmoody . . . . . . Sally Field
Moody . . . . Alfred Molina
Mahtob . . . . Sheila Rosenthal
Houssein . . . . Roshan Seth
Nicole . . . . Sarah Badel
Ameh Bozorg . . . . Mony Rey
Mohsen . . . . . . Georges Corraface

A horror story about being trapped in Iran, "Not Without My Daughter" hits the screen at the most fortuitous possible time, when U.S. audiences might be most receptive to being whipped into an anti-Islamic frenzy. It is certainly as propaganda that the film is most successful, for its artlessness in all other respects will be noticeable even to those who may be convulsed by the central dilemma.

A tv film in feel and substance, pic has possible sleeper potential, especially with women, and political aspects will prompt off-entertainment pages commentary.

True story of Betty Mahmoody is a harrowing one by any standard. Married to an Iranian doctor who has lived in the U.S. for 20 years, she reluctantly agrees to accompany him back to Teheran in 1984 to visit his family. With her four-year-old daughter in tow, she endures the annoyance of wearing a chador and the hateful looks of Moody's fanatical relatives, only to be told at the end of two weeks that they are going to remain in Iran.

As related in David W. Rintels' by-the-numbers screenplay, Iran turns Moody from a civilized, sophisticated gent into an intolerant monster within a fortnight. Not only is Betty restricted to the home, but she can't use the phone, has her passport and credit cards taken away, and is told that her daughter will be raised as a Muslim.

For awhile, all looks hopeless. Sneaking into the American Interests Section at the Swiss Embassy, Betty is informed she is now an Iranian citizen and, as a woman, has no rights whatsoever. The penalty for trying to escape is execution, and her husband, discovering her stunt, threatens to kill her should she try anything like it again.

After nearly two years of staggering suffering, Betty finally manages to make contact with an underground of helpful Iranians who offer to try to smuggle her and little Mahtob over the mountains into Turkey, a perilous episode in itself.

With Israel, of all places, standing in for Iran, film manages to strongly convey how strange and off-putting a truly alien culture can be to an average American. Arriving at the Teheran Airport straight from Michigan, Betty is assaulted by armed militia, wailing women and endless portraits of the Ayatollah.

Overall treatment plays upon those aspects of Islam that seem most horrific to Westerners, notably its treatment of women, to the point that virtually all the Iranians come off as vicious fiends.

Dramatically, the biggest problem is Moody's abrupt transition from sensitive husband to violent tyrant. Only motivation given is his sudden reawakening to the values of his religion. "Islam's the greatest gift I can give my child," he insists at one point, and there is little the gifted actor Alfred Molina can do to clarify psychological issues ignored by the script.

Unfortunately, pic makes no effort to portray anyone but Betty in more than a one-dimensional manner. Sally Field, therefore, has the stage to herself to engage the audience's sympathy, and this she does with an earnest, suitably emotional performance as a rather typically sincere, middle-class American who eventually outwits her jailer of a husband and his repressive country.

A couple of air attacks sharply remind one of the war going on in Iran in the mid-1980s, and Moody pointedly informs his wife that the U.S. was principally responsible for arming and backing Iraq at the time.

Sheila Rosenthal is suitably adorable as the couple's unfortunate daughter, and Indian actor Roshan Seth warmly inspires confidence as a "good" Iranian.

Anthony Pratt's production design contributes appropriately to the claustrophobic feel, and Jerry Goldsmith's score is varied and effectively dramatic. — *Cart.*

NIETS VOOR DE EEUWIGHEID
(NOTHING IS FOREVER)
(DUTCH-DOCU-COLOR/B&W-16M)

A NFI (Hilversum) release of a René Scholten-Studio Nieuwe Gronden production, in association with NOS-Television. Produced by René Scholten. Written and directed by Digna Sinke. Camera (color, b&w, 16m), Goert Giltay; editor-sound, Jan Wouter van Reijen. Reviewed at the Movies, Amsterdam, Sept. 10, 1990. Running time: **74 MIN.**

This celebration of industrial monuments neither drowns in nostalgia nor runs dry on facts and figures. Notwithstanding her thorough research in all corners of Holland, filmmaker Digna Sinke came up with a nimble, sparkling docu on "industrial archaeology."

That fairly novel science usually takes the Industrial Revolution as its starting point, but it also could include Roman lead mines or medieval shipyards. "Nothing Is Forever," however, concentrates on remnants of 19th and 20th century industrial activity.

Intent on presenting surprising structures and clear meanings, Sinke tells her story with extant industrial objects: steam engine, railway bridge, electrical power plant.

She also uses drawings, photos and film from the recent past, topical interviews and sparse commentary. Old and new images are framed to full effect. Editor Jan Wouter van Reijen keeps things moving at a fast pace.

A sensitive use of sound gives "Nothing Is Forever" its remarkable impact. Heard from time to time are two female voices: a prosaic voice that informs briskly, like a determined schoolteacher, and a poetic voice that informs darkly, pensively.

Composed with great care, the film's impressive coda has houses collapsing in quick succession, with a little Mozart alongside the dull sounds of demolition. — *Ewa.*

ROSA ROSA
(DUTCH-16M)

A Cor Koppies Filmdistribution release of a Meatball production. Produced by Cesar Messemaker. Written and directed by Martin Uitvlugt. Camera (color, 16m), Piotr Kukla; editor, Arno Hagers; music, Robert Jan Stips; sound, Bert Koops; art direction, Rob Vermeulen, Diana van den Vossenberg. Reviewed at the Movies, Amsterdam, Sept. 14, 1990. Running time: **90 MIN.**
Rosa . . . . Guusje van Tilborgh
Heinz/Herman . . . . . Johan Leysen
Also with: Marieke van der Pol, Herbert Flack, Sanderien van Rooij.

Timely thriller and smoldering love story "Rosa Rosa" is tied together with an ingenious plotline, but pic's setup promises more tension than it generates.

This feature debut from a screenwriter-director with tv and video experience thrills only intermittently. Scenes tend to linger over a beautiful shot, an amusing situation or a choice bit of character acting while audiences want to go on with the heroine's hunt for her mystery man.

The long gestation of "Rosa Rosa" (four years) and dearth of coin (less than $250,000) may have a lot to do with the picture's lack of rhythm.

Individual sequences, however, are entertaining, thanks to the spirited acting of Guusje van Tilborgh. Her Rosa, an attractive, vivacious divorcée recalling the exciting protest movements and amorous pursuits of her rebellious youth, is bored stiff in her small hairdressing salon in the Hague.

One evening a bearded, long-haired stranger arrives with a letter from her ex, who asks Rosa to change the stranger's appearance without asking questions. She complies with gusto. It's tempestuous love at first sight, but in the morning, the stranger disappears.

Rosa starts searching furiously for her lost heartthrob. She finds him, but is it really him? Can this well-dressed man with his smart bungalow and his yacht be the mysterious fugitive? Or is he a lookalike? Why does he, too, vanish without a trace? All questions are answered in pic's last seconds.

Johan Leysen shines both as terrorist on the run and as debonair lover. Acting on the whole is a big plus, as is director Martin Uitvlugt's light touch. — *Ewa.*

LOVE YOUR MAMA

A Ruby L. Oliver production. Written, produced and directed by Oliver. Camera (color), Ronald Courtney; editor, Joy L. Rencher; music, John Van Allen Jr., Markan Fedorowycz; production design, Oliver. Reviewed at Toronto Festival of Festivals, Sept. 14, 1990. Running time: **100 MIN.**
Leola . . . . Carol E. Hall
Mama . . . . Audrey Morgan
Wren . . . . Andre Robinson
Sam . . . . Earnest III Rayford
Willie . . . . Keard Johnson
Lois . . . . Artavia Wright

If spirit, grasp of story and understanding of characters count, Ruby L. Oliver is a comer. Her first feature, "Love Your Mama," focusing on an indomitable black mother, is best-suited for public tv.

Mama is married to a drunk and philanderer. Her eldest and youngest sons steal cars, and her teen daughter, though wanting to go to college and open a day care center, becomes pregnant out of wedlock.

That's a bit more than Mama

and the plot can bear, but she shoulders on, keeping the family together so they can all resolve their problems by fadeout.

Audrey Morgan is a terrific mama, handling an almost saintly role with earthy style and grace. Daughter Carol E. Hall, father Earnest III Rayford and sons Andre Robinson and Keard Johnson play to the hilt.

Oliver's script, which has some delightfully tart lines, deals goodnaturedly with harsh realities in this black family composite. But happy resolutions, one right after another, collapse the pic into melodrama.

Obvious low budget works to pic's advantage. In its unidentified eastern U.S. suburban setting, it always seems like July despite passage of months indicated by plot. Production values and music are good. — *Adil.*

PAPIRPETER
(PAPER PETER)
(ICELANDIC)

A HRIF Kvikmyndagerd Film presentation of HRIF production with RUV-TV (Iceland), WDR-TV (Germany) and VPRO (Holland). Produced by Vilhjalmur Ragnarsson. Directed by Ari R. Kristinsson. Screenplay, Kristinsson, Herdis Egilsdottir, based on Egilsdottir's novel; camera (color) Tony Forsberg; editor, uncredited; music, Michael Elers, Hjörtur Howser; animation-puppet handling, Bernd Ogrodnik. Reviewed at private screening, Copenhagen, Denmark, Nov. 28, 1990. Running time: **80 MIN.**
Mark . . . . Kristmann Oskarsson
The cobbler . . . . . . Arni Tryggvason
Sally . . . . Ranveig Jonsdottir
Tom . . . . Ingolfur Gudvardsson

Assured of tv serialization via co-production deals with services at home and in Germany and Holland, Ari Kristinsson's kiddie comedy "Paper Peter" could pass muster as matinee programming in offshore theaters as well.

A little boy beating the boredom of being home alone draws a lifesize companion on a huge piece of paper. Miraculously, the drawing starts moving about, although it retains its one-dimensionality.

The boy and Paper Peter soon join other kids on the suburban block. They all find Peter a great ally in combatting and outsmarting the local grown-up sourpuss, a fat man who steps into every imaginable pitfall. Being flat and lightweight gets Peter out of all scrapes.

Kristinsson directs amateur kid actors with vigor and works in

fine rhythm with animator-puppeteer Bernd Ogrodnik, who also on occasion dresses up Peter like a hilarious takeoff of Charles Schulz' Snoopy as the Red Baron.

Lively soft-rock vocalizing on the soundtrack fits in well. Pic's Reykjavik b.o. has been impressive. — *Kell.*

THE ANNA ACHMATOVA FILE
(SOVIET-DOCU-COLOR/B&W)

A Lenfilms Studio production. Directed by Semeon Aranovitch. Screenplay, Aranovitch, E. Ignatova; camera (color, black & white), V. Mulgaut. Reviewed at Toronto Festival of Festivals, Sept. 11, 1990. Running time: **65 MIN.**

At once a personal and grandly political biography, "The Anna Achmatova File" provides a compelling portrait of a beloved Soviet poet who suffered under Stalinism. Veteran docu director Semeon Aranovitch can expect great interest from fest programmers as well as educational webs, for whom the pic's 65-minute running time is suited.

Using Achmatova's own voice from recorded interviews, docu footage of political events, personal photographs and clips from the poet's funeral, Aranovitch seamlessly weaves the elements together and supports them with an intimate and dramatic score to delineate the difficulties she endured as a lyric poet.

Docu uses Achmatova's voice to provide biographical details. Born "the same year as Charlie Chaplin and the Eiffel Tower," she had to endure the shame of her father when she announced she would be a poet. She married childhood friend Nikolai Gumliyov, who fully supported her work, and she published her first poetry book in 1912.

As her life unfolds and her poetry becomes more sensitive, it's clear to Stalin that her choices for subject matter are not politically correct and that she cannot be reformed. She was told her poetry was empty and had nothing in common with the national interest.

Interspersed are clips of Stalin making public speeches, people being carted off to labor camps and Khrushchev taking a playful sleigh ride.

In readings from Achmatova's diaries, she reminisces about her encounters with the literary

heavyweights of her day: Boris Pasternak, Vladimir Mayakovsky, Alexander Solzhenitsyn and Mikhail Bostchenko. She was expelled from the Writers Union in 1966, and was no longer published until 1987.

But Achmatova has become a national heroine for writing inspiring testaments to those who survived under Stalin. She said she could not put into words the sinister news which descended on every family.

The black & white docu footage is preserved beautifully, and Aranovitch also plays with the still photos by shifting his camera over the images and creating movement.

Docu is somber, one-sided and reverential, but pays homage to a vital Soviet literary figure whose works are now readily available. For much of the time "The Anna Achmatova File" really is poetry. — *Devo.*

LES DERNIERS MARRANES
(THE LAST MARRANOS)
(FRENCH-DOCU)

A Film d'ICI release of a Film d'ICI-La Sept-Assn. Memoires et Histoires-Canaan Prods. co-production. Directed by Stan Neumann. Camera (color), Robert Alazraki, Ned Burgess, Richard Copans, Roberto Venturi; editor, Neumann, Daniela Abadi; sound, Jean Umansky. Reviewed at Festival dei Popoli, Florence, Dec. 7, 1990. Running time: **65 MIN.**

Czech director Stan Neumann, working in the best tradition of French documentary filmmaking, has filmed rituals and given full account of *marranos* in a Portuguese village.

Marranos are Jews in Spain and Portugal who converted to Catholicism to avoid persecution but secretly practiced Judaism. The 100 who live in a village 150 miles north of Lisbon have been separated from their culture since 1497.

The *marranos* would go to church on Sundays and practice their Judaism in the closet (literally, as the Sabbath candle still is traditionally hidden in a cupboard even though there's no danger).

While one community member went to Lisbon to become a "real" Jew after the making of the film, many go to the synagogue but come home for "real"

prayer.

One condition for making the film was that it would not be distributed in Spain or Portugal.

Lensing is clean and clear even though subjects are not always willing, and lighting conditions often are inadequate. Panoramas of Portuguese countryside are pretty. Interviews, rather than voiceovers, carry the narrative. — *Wals.*

IT'S A BLUE WORLD
(DANISH)

A Man Overboard Film release of Torben Skjödt Jensen Film production in association with the Danish Film Workshop, State Film Central and Danish Film Institute. Written, produced and directed by Torben Skjödt Jensen; camera (Eastmancolor), Jens Tang and (black & white video), Anders Askegard, Henrik Örslev; editor, Jensen; music, Chet Baker, Lis Damm; sound, Torsten Bolvig; production design, Sören A. Olsen; costume design, Mette Thelim; special effects, Govert Lund; production manager, Christine Tharup, Gitte Randlöv. Reviewed at the Grand, Copenhagen, Sept. 17, 1990. Running time: **65 MIN.**
As himself . . . . Hans Henrik Lerfeldt
The boy . Mikkel Rievers Christensen
The model . . . . Birgitte Braidensten
Cinema manager . . . . Jens Tang
Also with: Anine Boisen, Cerry Ribel, Annette Sveinsson, Patricia Nielsen.

Cleanly executed semi-fiction and blurry black & white docu material is efficiently mixed in "It's A Blue World," a stubbornly offbeat item that will catch attention at smaller festivals. Nudity, sometimes a b.o. enhancer, is abundant here, but general commercial prospects appear dim.

Filmmaker Torben Skjödt Jensen videotaped controversial painter Hans Henrik Lerfeldt in Copenhagen during the last two years of the artist's life. Afterward, he reconstructed Lerfeldt's early life on color film.

When Lerfeldt died in 1989 at age 43, he enjoyed a modicum of world renown as an explorer in the super realism style, painting mostly nudes in black garterbelts and hats. His garish pop-art colored works had supreme technical gloss. The paintings often featured minimalist surrealism (like a fly on a bare thigh) and the paraphernalia of sado-masochistic sex.

Blurrily recorded on video, Lerfeldt is heard mumbling about Nordic sexual repression vs. Southern freedom of expression. In the filmed color inserts, a shy little boy wanders mutely in an apartment where a woman constantly is dressing up or down for kinky sex, revealing the artist's introduction to the love life of adults.

Recalling the influence on Lerfeldt of his boyhood experiences in war-ravaged Berlin, much newsreel footage from that city is provided. In contrast, clips of Marilyn Monroe photos and porno flicks in the artist's personal collection are included.

The artist also collected kitchy erotic statues and a number of jazz recordings, many by Lerfeldt's friend Chet Baker, who appears in filmclips singing and playing the trumpet. Lerfeldt's apartment was as crowded as the spaces of his paintings are empty except for their central character.

Lerfeldt was what might be termed an extroverted loner. He was more or less imprisoned not only in his apartment but also in his vast body.

He is seen consorting with calm ease with his unclad models, but, curiously, never is seen painting. He subsisted mostly on ice cream and soda.

Toward the end of the film, Jensen's personal visions of Lerfeldt's art take over as the little boy emerges in a sunlit garden wearing the makeup of a Joel Grey-style cabaret emcee, obviously ready to enter adult life as an observer/recorder rather than as a participant. — *Kell.*

MAMA CALLE
(DUTCH-DOCU-16M)

A NFI (Hilversum) release of a Moving Image production. Produced by Kale Klaassen. Written and directed by Arjanna Laan. Camera (Fuji color, 16m), Melle van Essen; editor, Jan Dop; music, Patricio Wang; sound, Jesus Sanchez. Reviewed at the Movies, Amsterdam, Sept. 4, 1990. Running time: **62 MIN.**

"**M**ama Calle," a stirring documentary about destitute street kids in Mexico City, should do well on television and at film festivals, and possibly in special theatrical situations.

Marked contrast between the picture's subject and its strikingly beautiful imagery is disconcerting at first, but gradually the recurring images of an immense star-studded sky, a faraway moon with its evening star and the unending stream of golden lights on the highway fall into place.

Far from an exercise in cinema aesthetics, the filmmaker surrounds the abandoned youngsters with a vast area of indifference. Though the world does not care for these kids, the film makes the audience care.

Four boys living on the roof of a subway station swoop down on the highway each morning to beg for a few pesos from motorists. They hurriedly wash windows and perform tricks before the traffic moves on. If they're lucky, a window carefully opens and a coin appears.

Survival is difficult, at times violent work, but the picture shows little violence. Instead, it depicts at length the kids' yearning for relaxation.

As they sniff glue from plastic bags, their faces slowly age into blissful, deathlike oblivion. Neither does "Mama Calle" wallow in misery, instead celebrating the children's resilience and playfulness.

Dutch documentary filmmaker Arjanna Laan first saw the kids a few years ago while in Mexico on an editing assignment. She returned to watch them at work and play, hear their stories, win their confidence and, finally, come up with in-depth portraits.

Immediately impressive to the filmmaker was the flinty, grownup expression of their eyes. These kids find it difficult to smile, but they relish adventure, such as hopping on a train for a breather in the countryside they once left to escape prison sentences, broken homes or parental beatings. The country sequence is a lyrical interlude before the struggle in the urban jungle resumes.

Laan's choice of scenes and snatches of dialog, Melle van Essen's outstanding cinematography and Jan Dop's to-the-point editing combine to stress the nature of this moving pastoral break. — *Ewa.*

IN NECUEPALIZTLI IN AZTLÁN—RETORNO A AZTLÁN
(RETURN TO AZTLÁN)
(MEXICAN)

A Juan Mora Catlett-FFCC-UNAM Prods. Volcán production. Executive producer, Jorge Prior. Written and directed by Juan Mora Catlett. Camera (color), Toni Kuhn; editor, Jorge Vargas; music, Antonio Zepeda; sound, Ernesto Estrada; choreography, Rodolfo Reyes; art direction, Gabriel Pascual. Reviewed at Sala José Reveultas, Mexico City, Nov. 6, 1990. Running time: **92 MIN.**
With: Rodrigo Puebla, Rafael Cortés, Amado Sumaya, Socorro Avelar, Soledad Ruíz, José Chávez Trowe, Marco Antonio Novelo, Roberto Ruy, Martín Palomares, Marcial Salinas, María Luisa Avila, Jairo Márques Padilla.

Touting dialog delivered entirely in classic Nahuatl (language of the Aztecs), "Return To Aztlán" attempts to follow the same path as such anthropological films as "Quest For Fire," except this meandering journey may fall short of b.o. expectations. Pic's premise lands it squarely in the arthouse market.

First feature by Juan Mora Catlett, who studied film in Czechoslovakia, boasts ambitious lensing, stunning art direction and beautifully designed tribal makeup and body painting. Novelty selling point (use of classical Nahuatl) overemphasizes the literary text, which dominates much of the screentime.

Film begins in the year of the fifth sun (69 years before the 1519 conquest by Cortes) and follows the travails of Ollín (Rodrigo Puebla) on his mystical journey to Aztlán, the tribal homeland of the Aztecs, to petition the gods to end a four-year drought.

Although full of magic, film fails to establish a personality for Ollín. Viewers follow his actions but never get a glimpse into his humanity or personality, and in the end, lose interest in the quest. A flat visual tone also renders the magical commonplace.

As a curiosity, "Return To Aztlán" will find some international interest. Also, beautiful score by well-known anthropological musician Antonio Zepeda is effective in establishing a bygone era. — *Lent.*

DER BERG
(THE MOUNTAIN)
(SWISS-GERMAN-AUSTRIAN)

A Bernard Lang AG Zurich release and production in association with Markus Imhoof, Ulrich Bär, Werner Merzbacher, SRG, ZDF and ORF. Directed by Imhoof. Screenplay, Thomas Hürlimann, Imhoof, from a story by Hürlimann; camera (Eastmancolor), Lukas Strebel; editor, Daniela Roderer; music, Nicola Piovani; sound, Barbara Flückiger; production managers, Peter Spörri, Anne-Catherine Lang; art direction, Uli Bergfelder; assistant directors, Judith Kennel, Marcel Just, Christof Vorster. Reviewed at Cinema Frosch, Zurich, Nov. 7, 1990. Running time: **103 MIN.**
Lena . . . . Susanne Lothar
Manser . . . . Mathias Gnädinger
Kreuzpointner . . . Peter Simonischek
Manser's mother . . . . . . Anges Fink
Direktor . . . . Jürgen Cziesla
Colonel . . . . Adolf Laimböck
Parson . . . . Heinrich Beens
Railway man . . . . Ingold Wildenauer
(Swiss-German soundtrack)

With his latest pic, Swiss helmer Markus Imhoof stands a better chance of matching the native b.o. success of his "The Boat Is Full" (1980 foreign-film Oscar nominee) than his 1982 and '86 entries, "Via Scarlatti 20" and "Die Reise" (The Journey). Still, "The Mountain's" international outlook isn't as positive.

Thomas Hürlimann and Imhoof's script is based on an actual 1922 murder in the Swiss Alps. A weather observer and his wife were killed in their mountain cabin by a rival for the man's job. The murderer later took his own life. In the film, the tragic real-life outcome was changed to a less gloomy ending.

Even so, "The Mountain" is a dark and brooding film about a claustrophobic situation, relieved by few patches of brightness.

The intruder, an Austrian, makes a pass at the wife, who seems to respond. The men become rivals not only for the job, but for the woman. A violent ending is unavoidable.

Pic's subject matter and predominantly bleak locale may not be everyone's idea of entertainment, but "The Mountain" is a quality film with intelligent scripting and tight direction. Lensing by Lukas Strebel is exceptional.

Main asset, however, is the cast. Susanne Lothar as the initially timid and restrained wife, Mathias Gnädinger as the weatherman overcome by violence and Peter Simonischek as the charming but overambitious Austrian, are all excellent. Technical credits are all pro. — *Mezo.*

MDGMUREBI
(LODGERS)
(SOVIET)

A Gruzia Filmstudio production, in association with Lileo Arts. Directed by Dato Janelidze. Screenplay, Mamuka Dolidze, Janelidze; camera (Sovcolor), Leri Machaidze; editor, Kaha Tolordova; music, David Mirzashvili; sound, Imeri Manjgaiadze; production design, Jemal Mirzshvili. Reviewed at Montreal World Film Festival (Cinema of Today & Tomorrow), Sept. 3, 1990. Running time: **81 MIN.**

With: Buba Kotivari, Michael Shonia, Nino Koberitze, Michael Jojua, Shota Kristesashvili, Lia Gudadze, Otar Bagaturia, Lado Mekvarishvili.

A grimly funny comedy-of-the-absurd, "Lodgers" is presumably intended as an allegory of the absorption of Georgia into the Soviet Union. That's one interpretation, at least, for a pic could play the festival route where its offbeat humor will be appreciated.

It begins with its central character, Amiran, living alone in his apartment and thinking of the past (he's been studying old photographs). Suddenly, an old man knocks at the door, then collapses. Amiran takes him in, and soon the old man's two nubile daughters turn up and simply move in. The first night, these young women paint flowers on their faces, oil their bodies and join Amiran in bed.

But the next day, more relatives arrive who are less seductive. They gradually take over the apartment, shifting the furniture, bringing in a large cage full of doves and junking Amiran's possessions.

He seems just too weak and slothful to protest, and just goes along with the takeover, gradually losing more and more of his space until he becomes, literally, a prisoner of the "lodgers," who restrict his movements and put him in the bird cage.

All this is done with a fine comic touch yet played just seriously enough to make it convincing. An added touch of surrealism is that the view from the apartment window actually consists of back-projected street scenes.

The print caught was very dark, with some of the nighttime action obscured as a result. Also, presumably important intro titles were untranslated. — *Strat.*

YO SOY ESA
(I'M THE ONE)
(SPANISH)

An Ion Films production, in association with Spanish Television (TVE). Executive producer, José Luis García Sánchez. Written and directed by Luis Sanz. Camera (Eastmancolor), Juan Amorós; editor, Carmen Frías; music, Luis Cobos; sound (Dolby), Gilles Ortión; production manager, Andrés Santana; sets, Julio Esteban; choreography, Eduardo Montero. Reviewed at Cine Luna, Madrid, Jan. 8, 1991. Running time: **95 MIN.**
Carmen Torres/Ana Montes . . . . . .
. . . . Isabel Pantoja
Ramón . . . . José Coronado
Marquis . . . . Juan Echanove
Also with: Loles León, Alberto Alonso, Elisa Matilla, Magui Mira, Juan Luis Galiardo, María Asquerino, Pedro Diez de Coral, Martías Prats.

Minimal storyline and rudimentary production values did not prevent "I'm The One" from becoming a b.o. hit in Spain for the pre-Christmas period. The reason mass audiences flocked to see this tuner was the presence of the well-endowed Isabel Pantoja belting out folkloric flamenco songs.

Pic could garner considerable interest in less sophisticated markets, particularly in Latin America and perhaps U.S. Hispano sites.

This is Pantoja's celluloid bow. In the past she was known as a songstress on records and tv, but above all her vows of virtue and fidelity after the death of her bullfighter husband Paquirri raised her profile.

Pic is a film within a film. The star Ana Montes arrives at the theater where a gala preem of her film will be shown. She takes her seat in a loge, accompanied by her leading man. Ana is voluptuously overweight, the leading man is thin and haggard.

In the film within the film, Pantoja plays the part of a stage singer. Two rivals are smitten by her adipose charms: a nobleman and a sleek but impecunious admirer with pencil mustache and brillantined hair.

Most of pic consists of Pantoja doing musical numbers on a stage or in outdoor sets. Every now and then the scene shifts back to the less idyllic present. During the screening the leading man ducks out to engage in a high-stakes poker game.

The film within the film ends happily; the real story ends with the leading man dying of an overdose.

Pantoja has a good, raucous voice and her physical attractions are considerable. Supporting cast is adequate, as are production values. Other than Pantoja's decollete, pic is lily white. — *Besa.*

VERSO SERA
(TOWARDS EVENING)
(ITALIAN-FRENCH)

A IIF Distribuzione release of an Ellepi Film (Rome)-Paradis Films (Paris) coproduction, in association with RAI-TV Channel 1. Produced by Leo Pescarolo and Guido De Laurentiis. Directed by Francesca Archibugi. Screenplay, Archibugi, Gloria Malatesta, Claudia Sbarigia; camera (color), Paolo Carnera; editor, Roberto Missiroli; music, Roberto Gatto, Battista Lena; production design, Osvaldo Desideri. Reviewed at Etoile Cinema, Rome, Dec. 26, 1990. Running time: **97 MIN.**
Prof. Bruschi . . Marcello Mastroianni
Stella . . . . Sandrine Bonnaire
Papere . . . . Lara Pranzoni
Elvira . . . . Zoe Incrocci
Oliviero . . . . Giorgio Tirabassi
Also with: Victor Cavallo, Veronica Lazar, Paolo Panelli, Giovanna Ralli, Gisella Burinato, Pupo De Luca, Dante Biagioni.

"Towards Evening," a bittersweet and delightful trip back to 1977 Rome, hasn't gone far at local wickets, but it confirms the promise of 29-year-old director Francesca Archibugi ("Mignon Has Gone Away") and is a good candidate for foreign arthouse exposure.

Marcello Mastroianni's presence as aging Prof. Bruschi, cultured, aristocratic and communist, is the hook that draws viewers into the film. He has strong competition, however, from the two aptly cast femme leads: Lara Pranzoni as a 4-year-old who thinks she's two kids in one, and Sandrine Bonnaire as her tough, disorderly hippie mother.

The widowed prof's rigidly programmed life, split between teaching Russian at the university, playing in a chamber orchestra and tending his garden, is brusquely capsized when granddaughter Pranzoni gets dumped on the household. He launches into a retraining program to civilize the child, and he succeeds.

Next it's Bonnaire's turn for re-education. She proves a much harder nut to crack, but while laid up with a broken leg in the prof's house, she too falls under the spell of order and culture.

The comic live-in maid, played by the excellent Zoe Incrocci, joins forces with the mother and daughter waifs. The professor's son (a finely fragile Giorgio Tirabassi) is off tending goats in the country, and all looks comfortably settled.

But the spirit of '77, at the height of the chaotic student movement but before the Red Brigades and terrorism, penetrates into even the most protected homes. Bonnaire and Pranzoni leave (forever) for a weekend demonstration in Bologna, and the prof is left writing a yearning letter for his granddaughter to read when she grows up.

Archibugi proves she is a subtle if ambitious storyteller, usually successful in balancing social and private sentiments and shifting gears from comic to tragic to banal.

To quibble, a few of "Evening's" stereotypes feel more like '68 than the decade that follows. Despite Bonnaire's naturalness as an mixed-up Italian girl in search of herself, and Mastroianni's letter-perfect portrait of the gentleman communist, the generational conflict becomes a little predictable.

Still, a few out-of-focus moments don't tip the scales against a film so fresh, well-acted and well-scripted (by Gloria Malatesta and Claudia Sbarigia, along with the helmer).

Paolo Carnera's crisp camerawork is a pleasure, as are Osvaldo Desideri's refined sets and the tuneful score by Roberto Gatto and Battista Lena. The suspicion nevertheless remains that the pic is missing a small dose of ugliness to bring out the reality laying on the other side of the prof's garden walls. — *Yung.*

THE LAST ISLAND
(DUTCH)

A President Films (Paris) release of a First Floor Features production. Produced by Laurens Geels, Dick Maas. Written and directed by Marleen Gorris. Camera (color), Marc Felperlaan; editor, Hans van Dongen; sound, Bert Flantua; art director, Harry Ammerlaan. Reviewed at Tuschinski theater, Amsterdam, Nov. 25, 1990. Running time: **90 MIN.**
With: Paul Freeman, Shelagh McLeod, Patricia Hayes, Kenneth Colley, Mark Hembrow, Marc Berman, Ian Tracey.

Despite an unusually large budget for a Dutch film (about $4 million), Marleen Gorris' "The Last Island" is destined mostly for fest fans and higher-brow, off-peak tube viewers.

Pic's pluses are a carefully thought-out and meticulously executed screenplay, a good Dutch crew and an international, English-speaking cast.

Thesps are typically supporting actors, but here they're without stars to support. Though clearly limned in the screenplay, characters never come to life. The blame is mainly the writer-helmer's; the actors perform to the limits of their capabilities. An airliner crashes on a desert island for no apparent reason. Only two women, five men and a dog survive. There's no radio to be heard anywhere, and one might think the human race ended at the same time their plane crashed.

Communal life is not easy, given the survivors' individual idiosyncrasies. There are the gun-toting, Bible-punching, macho military man; the rich, civilized homosexual Scotsman; his gay companion; the nice, inoffensive, ineffectual biologist, and the foul-mouthed juvenile with nothing much between the ears but plenty of urges between the legs.

And then there are the women: one youngish, self-assured; the other elderly, vaguely East European, respected by all, wise and even-tempered. The women stand for life to the extent that they refuse to participate in a mercy killing when one passenger is seriously wounded and in intense pain.

Tension mounts between the men, who, by pic's end, inflict painful and violent deaths on one another, leaving the women to carry on bravely.

Gorris ("A Question Of Silence," "Broken Mirrors") obviously takes a dim view of the human race, with women its only saving grace. The clearly enunciated dialog slows pic down to the level of a tract. In her next film, Gorris should liberate her cinematic talents from cerebral juggling with genders, despair and the alluring attraction of prankish brain waves. — *Wall.*

MACKEN
(THE GAS STATION)
(SWEDISH)

A Svensk release. Produced by Waldemar Bergendahl, Anne Otto. Written and directed by Claes Eriksson. Camera, Dan Myhrman; editor, Jan Persson; music, Eriksson; art direction, Rolf Allan Hakansson. Reviewed at Röda Kvarn cinema, Stockholm, Dec. 21, 1990. Running time: **97 MIN.**
With: Anders Eriksson, Jan Rippe, Knut Agnred, Hans Alfredson, Claes Eriksson, Per Fritzell, Kerstin Granlund, Sven Melander, Peter Rangmar, Magnus Härenstam, Hakan Johannesson, Charlotte Strandberg, Laila Westersund.

Although "Macken" is already a big boxoffice success in Sweden, it is highly unlikely this intermittently funny comedy adapted from a tv series will travel anywhere outside the Scandinavian countries.

In the wake of their late 1980s breakthrough, Claes Eriksson and his comedy group Galenskaparna joined forces with the musical group After Shave. The combined comedians and singers achieved a string of successes with stage shows, tv series and features. In "Macken," their latest bigscreen effort, they combine tv and cinema.

"Macken," a popular series some years back, consisted of six episodes, but this film known as "Episode 7" suggests that the group should have stuck to the smaller, and shorter, formula.

Two brothers (Anders Eriksson and Jan Rippe) run a rundown gas station in rural Sweden. They're not too bright, but their common sense and their naive world view always put them on the winning side. They never notice what's happening around them, and sometimes the events can border on the disastrous.

The tv series worked this way, and it was mostly very funny. The beginning of the feature version is especially comical as the brothers open their gas station early one summer morning. All the regulars from the tv series come in, with all the expected disastrous results.

Figuring a feature film has to have more than just faces and situations familiar from tv, the filmmakers developed a plot where the two brothers search for the father they never met. Search takes them out of their element, to Stockholm and Copenhagen, and it also leads the film astray.

The Copenhagen scenes, including the brothers' confused encounter with a crook who they falsely thought was their missing dad, are downright boring and bring the film to a standstill.

Speed picks up again when comedian/director Hans Alfredson as the real father introduces some inspired lunacy with a song-and-dance routine, but the film doesn't recover from the disastrous urban visit.

Eriksson and Rippe function well together, but too bad director Eriksson didn't use them in their natural (rural) environment. Also, the other actors from Galenskaparra/After Shave did not have the opportunity to develop their beloved characters.

Pic has a humorous, well-made opening and a ditto finale, but a boring middle. Still, Eriksson's "Leif," "The Shark That Knew Too Much" and now "Macken," show he has the potential to make a thoroughly good comedy.

Swedish audiences seem to enjoy "Macken" in feature film version. The first b.o. reports are positive, and Svensk apparently has a commercial winner on its hands. — *Gunn.*

NOORDEINDE—ZUIDEINDE
(NORTHSIDE—SOUTHSIDE)
(DUTCH-DOCU-16M)

A Cinemien release of a Yuce Film production. Executive producer, Suzanne van Voorst. Written and directed by Gerard d'Olivat. Camera, (16m), Peter Brugman; editor, Jan Wouter van Reijen; sound, Floor Kooij. Reviewed at the Movies, Amsterdam, Sept. 14, 1990. Running time: **104 MIN.**

A sociodocumentary with an intriguing theme, "Northside — Southside" suffers from impartiality and non-aggressiveness.

Helmer Gerard d'Olivat interviewed a group of high school grads before their final exam, and then at irregular intervals over the next five years. Main question: What do you expect from life?

Hailing from a small village of some 500 inhabitants (about 45 miles from Amsterdam), the youths are unsure of their aspirations. One boy says he definitely wants to be a farmer, but later recants.

Some stay at home. Some can't wait to move out. One boy and his girl immediately set out on a trip to the Far East. Some fit

into conventional slots of marriage and mortgage. Some have babies. Most of them study.

The young adults each are asked more or less the same questions. The film never pushes them, never tries to get under their skin. The interviewer's voice is devoid of emotion. — *Wall.*

PALM SPRINGS FEST

BLUE DESERT

A Neo Films production in association with First Look Films. Executive producers, Joel Soisson, Michael Murphey. Produced by David Andrew Peters. Directed by Brad Battersby. Screenplay, Arthur Collis, Battersby; camera (color), Paul Murphy; editor, Debra Bard; sound, Richard Schexnayder; production design, Michael Perry; costume design, Coleen Kelso; art direction, David Cannon, Dara L. Waxman; assistant director, Bill Barry; associate producer, Collis. Reviewed at Palm Springs Intl. Film Festival, Palm Springs, Calif., Jan. 9, 1991. No MPAA Rating. Running time: **98 MIN.**
Lisa Roberts . . . . . . Courtney Cox
Steve Smith . . . . D.B. Sweeney
Randall Atkins . . . . . . Craig Sheffer
Walter . . . . Sandy Ward

With a plot that has more twists and holes than a donut shop, most viewers won't buy "Blue Desert," but it's well-made enough to be a good candidate for regional theatrical release, with more potential in video via Academy Entertainment.

"Come On In" might be a better title for this bottom-rung thriller about a young woman who can't seem to keep her doors locked even with a rapist lurking around her isolated home.

First film under the Neo Pictures banner of exec producers Joel Soisson and Michael Murphey (who scored a hit with "Bill & Ted's Excellent Adventure") freshens up its approach to the genre by making heroine Lisa (Courteney Cox), a comic-book illustrator who strongly identifies with her most successful character, a fierce female gladiator called Iron Medusa.

Most inventive part of "Blue Desert" is the way Lisa's most harrowing experiences are transformed in her illustrations into fanciful adventures in which Iron Medusa triumphs. (Matthew Nelson renders the drawings.)

Plot has Lisa, a New Yorker who's been traumatized by a rape, moving to a remote desert town to try to heal her nerves and work in peace.

But in this isolated burg she finds she's more a target than ever. No sooner has she befriended Randall, a strung-out young desert rat (Craig Sheffer), than he makes a pass at her and she reacts violently, clouting him with a frying pan.

The police arrive and local lawman Steve Smith (D.B. Sweeney) also takes a strong interest in the fetching newcomer, spelling the end of Lisa's privacy and the beginning of her endless troubles.

Most offensive part of this pic — like so many other low-budgeters from today's young male screenwriters — is the way it purports to take an enlightened view of Lisa's right to live without harassment while at the same time using her as titillation in the most old-fashioned, exploitative way.

Costume department dresses her in scanty, fetching get-ups, and script has her displaying the haziest judgment, such as inviting the alienated Randall in at night when she barely knows him, and sending a flurry of mixed signals to her two male suitors throughout.

A script like this does more damage than good, while at the same time stroking itself for sympathy to Lisa. Meanwhile, the dialog is dull and the plot full of glaring illogic.

Steve tells Lisa that Randall is a convicted sex offender and wants her to pin assault charges on him, while Randall tells her the cop is a sicko who wants to kill her. With her nerves already frayed from past experience, she's left to sort out who's who.

Scripters Arthur Collis and Brad Battersby, who also directs, work hard to keep the viewer offguard, and sometime succeed, but the credibility of all the characters suffers.

Meanwhile, it's a good showcase for all three young actors, despite the script's offenses. Cox and Sweeney comport themselves winningly, and Sheffer struggles past a heavy load of Brad Dourif mannerisms to achieve an ultimately credible performance. It's a far cry from, say, Jason Patric as the desert drifter in "After Dark, My Sweet," but given the limitations of "Blue Desert," it's a bravura turn.

First-time director Battersby, whose pic world premieres at this festival, opens with a heavily stylized black & white assault sequence that carries plenty of menace but is cut puzzlingly

short. Most of the pic proceeds in competent fashion but with no particular flair, while an overloud, brooding synthesized score is relied on for suspense.

The producers have found a handy format for an inexpensive thriller, with most of the action centering on a mobile home in the desert and the three main characters.

Oddly, in a town where everyone knows everyone's business, it's the neighbors 50 feet away who seem most oblivious to Lisa's perils, and equally oddly, she never tells them. — Daws.

LA GLOIRE DE MON PÉRE
(MY FATHER'S GLORY)
(FRENCH)

A co-production of Gaumont, Prods. De La Gueville and TF1 Films. Produced by Alan Poire. Directed by Yves Robert. Screenplay, Jerome Tonnere, Louis Nucera, Robert, based on the novel by Marcel Pagnol; camera, Robert Alazraki; editor, Pierre Gillette; music, Vladimir Cosma; production design, Jacques Dugied; costumes, Agnes Negre. Reviewed at Palm Springs Intl. Film Festival, Palm Springs, Calif., Jan. 8, 1991. No MPAA rating. Running time: **110 MIN.**

Joseph	Philippe Caubere
Augustine	Nathalie Roussel
Uncle Jules	Didier Pain
Aunt Rose	Therese Liotard
Marcel	Julien Ciamaca
Paul	Victorian Delamare
Lili	Joris Molinas

"La Gloire de Mon Pèere," kickoff film of the second Palm Springs Intl. Film Festival, was a crowd-pleaser in a nearly soldout house, but the charming and sentimental tale, based on the reminiscences of beloved French author Marcel Pagnol, appears to have only mild commercial prospects for U.S. release.

A huge b.o. hit in France, where the Gaumont-distributed pic grossed nearly $33 million in the first 13 weeks after a September '90 launch, the rather ordinary story, given enchanting treatment in first-person (subtitled) narration throughout, is likely to prove less satisfying to hook-hungry U.S. audiences.

Its sequel, "Le Château De Ma Mère" (My Mother's Castle), released eight weeks after the first, set a similarly torrid pace in France, grossing nearly $18 million in its first five weeks. That pic, based on a second Pagnol book and featuring the same cast, will close the fest.

Pagnol's turn-of-the-century tale, based on his book of the same title, begins with his own birth in Aubagne to a pretty seamstress mother (Nathalie Roussel) and a dynamic, atheistic schoolteacher father (Philippe Caubere).

Whiling away his days in the rear of the schoolroom, the tot learns to read with astonishing speed, to the delight of his prideful father but the alarm of his sensitive mother, who keeps him away from books in an effort to preserve his childhood.

The cheeky scamp wanders about the house reading everything from soap wrappers to railway schedules, until she is forced to give up.

The father's teaching posts improve and the family moves to Marseilles, where little Marcel's Aunt Rose (Therese Liotard) is courted by a portly but ebullient government clerk (Didier Pain) who marries her and becomes part of the family. Marcel gains a younger brother, Paul, and his aunt and uncle have twin girls.

Major episode in "La Gloire" is when the family packs up to spend the summer in the hills near Aubagne, in Provence, where Marcel (played in boyhood by Julien Ciamaca) falls passionately in love with the outdoors and the simple, charmed life of the village.

Pic's major attraction to the French is apparently its storybook naivete and its affection for a simpler, seemingly enchanted life (in which well-prepared food was always present).

Narrated from the viewpoint of the clever young Marcel, tale contains enough self-mocking humor to keep it from becoming cloying, while its tone of discovery and wonder is irresistible.

One of the most memorable scenes shows Marcel and his newfound friend, Lili (Joris Molinas), a roughhewn hill country boy who shows him the secrets of the outdoors, watch a magnificent lightning storm explode over the valley from the safety of a cave, only to be chased into the rain by a giant owl who lives there.

Director Yves Robert ("Pardon Mon Affair," "The Tall Blond Man With One Black Shoe") infuses the pic with unabashed romance (such as the scene of Marcel's aunt and soon-to-be uncle waltzing in the rain at the Parc Borely) and laces its humor with deft visual touches of adult irony.

Scenes in the southern countryside are beautifully shot, and the performances of the story-

book villagers are a delight.

But with its episodic, novelistic structure, the pic loses pace, and suffers from an overlong buildup to its crowning episode, a hunting trip undertaken by Marcel's father. Credit the warm and involving tone of Robert's direction for holding it together despite a lack of dramatic thrust.

Pic's spirit also gains from a particularly stirring and sprightly score by Vladimir Cosma.

Despite its hearty homeland embrace, "La Gloire" probably features too commonplace a concept and too soft a tone to penetrate the U.S. market, where edgier pics like "Avalon," with more to say about Yanks' own evolution, better serve yearnings for the past. — Daws.

WHITE FANG

A Buena Vista release of a Walt Disney Pictures presentation of a Hybrid production, in association with Silver Screen Partners IV. Produced by Markay Powell. Executive producers, Mike Lobell, Andrew Bergman. Directed by Randal Kleiser. Screenplay, Jeanne Rosenberg, Nick Thiel, David Fallon, based on Jack London's novel; camera (Technicolor prints), Tony Pierce-Roberts; editor, Lisa Day; music, Basil Poledouris; additional music, Fiachra Trench; "The Bear" theme by Shirley Walker; sound (Dolby), David Kelson; production design, Michael Bolton; art direction, Sandy Cochrane; production managers, Robert Schneider, Richard H. Prince; assistant director, Doug Metzger; 2nd unit director-camera, Gary Capo; stunt coordinator, Rick Barker; casting, Michael Fenton, Judy Taylor, Valorie Massalas. Reviewed at Gotham Cinema, N.Y., Jan. 14, 1990. MPAA Rating: PG. Running time: **107 MIN.**

Alex Larson	Klaus Maria Brandauer
Jack Conroy	Ethan Hawke
Skunker	Seymour Cassel
Belinda	Susan Hogan
Beauty Smith	James Remar
Luke	Bill Moseley
Tinker	Clint B. Youngreen
Grey Beaver	Pius Savage
Heather	Suzanne Kent
White Fang	Jed
Bear	Bart the bear

Disney's workmanlike remake of Jack London's adventure "White Fang" boasts enough nature footage and a strong central performance by Ethan Hawke to win over small fry. It should do okay off-season business and has strong offshore possibilities.

Twentieth Century-Fox first filmed the book in 1936 as a programmer followup to its London-derived hit "Call Of The Wild," notable for John Carra-

Original film

Twentieth-Fox release of Bogart Rogers production. Features Michael Whalen, Jean Muir, Slim Summerville, Charles Winninger, John Carradine, Jane Darwell and Thomas Beck. Directed by David Butler. From Jack London novel of same name; adaptation, Gene Fowler, Hal Long and S.G. Duncan; film editor, Irene Morra; camera (b&w), Arthur Miller. Reviewed at Roxy, N.Y., week July 17, '36. Running time: **70 MIN.**

Weedon Scott	Michael Whalen
Sylvia Burgess	Jean Muir
Slats	Slim Summerville
Doc McFane	Charles Winninger
Beauty Smith	John Carradine
Maud Mahoney	Jane Darwell
Hal Burgess	Thomas Beck
Kobi	Joseph Herrick
Francois	George Ducount
Nomi	Marie Chorie
White Fang	Lightning

dine's performance as the villain. Italian horror maestro Lucio Fulci directed an excellent remake in 1973 topling Franco Nero and Virna Lisi that had only a brief U.S. run.

Oscar-winning cinematographer Chris Menges (who had turned to feature direction with "A World Apart") was originally slated to direct the Disney version, but Randal Kleiser took over the helm during advanced pre-production a year ago. The chronicler of rites of passage in "Grease" and "The Blue Lagoon" may have been the right pilot to guide young star Hawke's turn, but Menges' documentary background and grittiness could well have produced stronger results.

Hawke plays a would-be prospector who heads to the Alaska gold rush just before the turn of the century to find and work his late father's claim. After a scenic, "cast of 100s" climb up a mountain, Hawke teams up with veteran miner Klaus Maria Brandauer and his Gabby Hayes-esque sidekick Seymour Cassel to trek across the snow.

Brandauer is singleminded about toting his dead pal Dutch's casket to their claim to bury him. One of pic's best scenes occurs when the casket comes loose and Dutch's bluish-skinned corpse, clutching his dead dog, goes sliding across the ice followed by Hawke's harrowing fall into icy waters. This black humor combines with pic's best evocation of the survival theme, London's strongest suit.

Hampered by a choppy screenplay that reduces earthy star Brandauer's dialog to near Pidgin English, pic never adds up to more than a series of individual moments. The majestic beauty of Tony Pierce-Roberts' cinematography and Basil Poledouris' score are highlights.

Disney's success in the '50s with its wildlife adventure films was more recently mirrored by Carroll Ballard's excellent "Never Cry Wolf." French epic "The Bear" covers similar territory to "White Fang" minus most of the human element, and here that pic's animal star Bart the bear pops up in a cameo doing his growling routine to scare Hawke until wolf-dog White Fang (played by Jed) saves him.

Actually, White Fang's best scenes occur when he's just a pup tended to by his resourceful mother, providing some irresistible footage. As an adult, his developing relationship with Hawke, who wants to tame him, is unconvincingly presented as the animal is rescued from working in pit bull-type contests for hissable villain Beauty Smith (James Remar in a nothing performance).

Hawke, in a physically demanding role, builds audience sympathy while his bosom buddy Brandauer is hamstrung in an underwritten part unworthy of his talents. Cassel's welcome comic relief is inexplicably cut short when he's written out of the film after about three reels.

Susan Hogan, Canadian thesp who did a fine job in the recent "Narrow Margin" remake, exudes warmth as Brandauer's girlfriend. Sex is downplayed per Disney requirements, but her role is important in keeping the male bonding between Brandauer and Hawke down to a roar.

Given Kevin Costner's recent overwhelming success in bringing back such period adventures with "Dances With Wolves," it's unfortunate "White Fang" lacks the slow, deliberate build that can grab an audience. Instead, its series of short scenes add up to a tedious 107 minutes. Worse still, infinitely more pathos is drummed up for Costner's wolf playmate than the wounded adult Fang ever generates here.

— *Lor.*

EVE OF DESTRUCTION

An Orion Pictures release of a Nelson Entertainment presentation of an Interscope Communications production. Produced by David Madden. Executive producers, Robert W. Cort, Rick Finkelstein, Melinda Jason. Directed by Duncan Gibbins. Screenplay, Gibbins, Yale Udoff; camera (Deluxe color), Alan Hume; editor, Caroline Biggerstaff; music, Philippe Sarde; sound (Dolby), Jonathan Stein; production design, Peter Lamont; art direction, Matthew Jacobs; costume design, Deborah L. Scott; assistant director, Jules Lichtman; production manager, Jack Roe; prosthetics & special makeup effects, Art & Magic, R. Christopher Biggs; special effects coordinator, Steve Galich; visual effects supervisor, Dale Fay; stunt coordinator-2nd unit director, John Moio; 2nd unit camera, John M. Stephens; co-executive producer, Graham Henderson; casting, Marci Liroff; additional casting, Sally Stiner. Reviewed at Embassy 2 theater, N.Y., Jan. 17, 1990. MPAA Rating: R. Running time: **98 MIN.**

Jim McQuade	Gregory Hines
Dr. Eve Simmons/Eve VIII	Renée Soutendijk
Gen. Curtis	Michael Greene
Schneider	Kurt Fuller
Peter Arnold	John M. Jackson
Robot Steve	Loren Haynes
Timmy Arnold	Ross Malinger
Scientist/waiter	Nelson Mashita
Dr. Heller	Alan Haufrect

Also with: Kevin McCarthy, Jeff McCarthy, Nancy Locke, Bethany Richards.

Intense thesping by Renée Soutendijk in dual roles as "Eve Of Destruction" almost lifts this tasteless horror fantasy above the norm. Inconsistent scripting and direction reduce the

Orion release to a genre fan special with limited chances at finding a crossover audience.

That's a shame, because there are germs of interesting ideas in the screenplay by helmer Duncan Gibbins and Yale Udoff, latter the scripter of Nicolas Roeg's intriguing "Bad Timing."

Pic's basis is that most durable of sci-fi properties, Mary Shelley's "Frankenstein," which ranks second only to Bram Stoker's "Dracula" for inspiring motion pictures. "Eve" is the third recent pic to hark back to James Whale's classic "Bride Of Frankenstein," after last year's satire "Frankenhooker" as well as mad scientist Bruce Davison creating a female cyborg in "Steel & Lace."

Italian bombshell Rosalba Neri played "Lady Frankenstein" in 1971 and created male monsters, but "Eve" goes one logical step further in having Dutch actress Soutendijk as scientist Eve Simmons creating a robot in her own image.

Effective opening scenes show the robot, Eve VIII, on a test run in San Francisco being damaged by gunfire during a bank holdup. The man monitoring Eve is killed and the beautiful monster becomes a loose cannon.

Gung ho Jim McQuade (Gregory Hines), no relation to Orion's "Lone Wolf McQuade" of eight years ago, is called in from his anti-terrorist activities to find Eve and immobilize her with a shot through the eye. What he isn't told is that Eve was created as a robot/bomb with nuclear capability.

Since Eve is endowed with her creator's memories as well as good looks, the trail to track her down retraces Dr. Eve's childhood traumas and current relationships. Film's pseudo-feminist theme is bungled badly: the monster starts living out Simmons' unrealized sexual fantasies only to kill or maim the endless stream of male chauvinist pigs it teases.

Further, the doctor's unresolved problems with her estranged dad (Kevin McCarthy, in a brief uncredited role) who beat her mother and caused her death, leads to a contrived scene of robot revenge.

Aiming at the low-end audience, film's nadir is a tasteless scene of sexy Eve picking up a guy in a bar and then biting off his most prized possession in a hot sheets motel room. The audience is spared the visualization of this "Porky's" level horror motif, but the damage to the film's tone is irreversible.

Running motif of Eve going into her killing mode whenever some guy calls her "bitch!" is the worst sort of pandering to one's assumed target viewer.

Atmospheric climax of Hines chasing Eve (clutching Simmons' son she takes to be her own) through the Manhattan subway tunnels is clumsily directed by Gibbins with several anti-climaxes and a fake James Bond-style countdown as the activated robot is seconds away from a nuclear explosion (film coincidentally is lensed by Bond cinematographer Alan Hume). Much is made of the boy's safety during this sequence, but pic foolishly ignores him completely once the danger is over.

Soutendijk, a versatile thesp who has followed her Dutch triumphs like "Spetters" with several U.S. telefilms and two American features released by Shapiro Glickenhaus, brings utter conviction to both roles to carry the picture.

Hines, no stranger to action roles in "Wolfen" and "Off Limits," still seems out of place espousing Oliver North-style rhetoric in playing a shoot first, ask questions later hero. Supporting cast is weak in what plays like a 2½ hander.

Makeup effects are satisfying, notably Soutendijk's more than nude scenes as she peels away body tissue to make self-repairs on her robot body. French ace Philippe Sarde contributes an effective musical score. — Lor.

FLIGHT OF THE INTRUDER

A Paramount release of a Mace Neufeld and Robert Rehme production. Produced by Neufeld. Executive producer, Brian Frankish. Directed by John Milius. Screenplay, Robert Dillon, David Shaber, based on the novel by Stephen Coonts; camera (Technicolor, Panavision widescreen), Fred J. Koenekamp; editor, C. Timothy O'Mears, Steve Mirkovich, Peck Prior; music, Basil Poledouris; sound (Dolby), Jack Solomon; production design, Jack T. Collis; art direction, E. Albert Heschong; set design, Nick S. Navarro, Richard Franklin Mays, Joseph E. Hubbard; set decoration, Mickey S. Michaels; visual effects producer, Mark Vargo; assistant director, Steve Danton; 2nd unit director-stunt coordinator, Terry J. Leonard; 2nd unit camera, David B. Nowell; associate producer, Lis Kern; coexecutive producer, Ralph Winter; casting, Mindy Marin. Reviewed at the Paramount Theater, N.Y., Jan. 10, 1991. MPAA Rating: PG-13. Running time: **113 MIN.**
Frank Camparelli . . . . Danny Glover
Virgil Cole . . . . Willem Dafoe
Jake Grafton . . . . . . Brad Johnson
Callie . . . . Rosanna Arquette
Boxman . . . . Tom Sizemore
Cowboy Parker . J. Kenneth Campbell
Also with: Jared Chandler, Dann Florek, Madison Mason, Ving Rhames, Christopher Rich, Douglas Roberts.

"**F**light Of The Intruder" is the most boring Vietnam War pic since "The Green Berets," but lacks the benefit of the latter's political outrageousness to spark a little interest and humor. Leaden actioner can be promoted to some initial grosses, but fuel shortage will ground this one before long.

Director John Milius wrote "Apocalypse Now," one of the most memorable Vietnam epics, but any interesting take he may still have on the conflict is lost here amid a flotilla of banalities and clichés straight out of bloated 1950s service dramas.

Set mostly aboard a giant aircraft carrier, yarn unspools in 1972. Prevented from bombing Hanoi and other strategic spots while the Paris peace talks are in progress, fighter pilots are reduced to assaulting meaningless targets and facing the likelihood that the massive U.S. war effort will have been in vain.

Nonetheless, officers have to keep discipline and morale up, a task that falls to Danny Glover, the tough-talking but humorous squadron leader. Half of his scenes consist of chewing out subordinates in ways clearly meant to be funnier than they are, which is no fault of the actor. It's just that this stuff went out with Victor McLaglen and Ward Bond.

Title refers to the A-6, a small, low-altitude bomber designed for quick in-and-out strikes. Ace of the outfit is Brad Johnson, who loses a bombardier in an elaborate credit sequence and is thereafter interested in "payback."

Opportunity presents itself with the arrival of a vet bombardier (Willem Dafoe) not averse to hijinks. Johnson and Dafoe cook up a scheme to devastate People's Resistance Park in downtown Hanoi, a.k.a. SAM City, where captured U.S. artillery is on display.

This renegade mission is pic's major setpiece, and provides an opportunity for special effects wizards and model makers to strut their stuff. Sequence is the only thing that will bring audiences out of their torpor. Sole other exceptional element is a romantic subplot between Johnson and Rosanna Arquette that is possibly unprecedented in its feebleness.

Glover brings energy and glee to his reams of dialog. Dafoe puts a few cynical spins on his delivery, but his character pales next to his role in "Platoon." Johnson, again playing a flier, is even more lackluster than he was in "Always."

Military cooperation has provided many fighter jets to look at, but production values are pretty routine. Hawaiian locations, when viewed from the air, are too lushly recognizable to be an entirely credible Vietnam.

Except for echoing the disillusionment of pilots, film has a surprisingly ill-defined point-of-view about the war. Most pointed rhetoric, in fact, is directed toward Jane Fonda in a gratuitous throwaway. — Cart.

ONCE AROUND

A Universal release of a Universal and Cinecom Entertainment Group presentation of a Double Play production. Produced by Amy Robinson, Griffin Dunne. Executive producer, G. Mac Brown. Directed by Lasse Hallström. Screenplay, Malia Scotch Marmo; camera (Du Art processing, Deluxe color prints), Theo Van De Sande; editor, Andrew Mondshein; music, James Horner; sound (Dolby), Danny Michael; production design, David Gropman; art direction, Dan Davis, Michael Foxworthy (Boston); costume design, Renee Kalfus; assistant director, Louis D'Esposito; coproducer, Dreyfuss/James Prods.; casting, Meg Simon, Fran Kumin. Reviewed at the Avco Cinema, L.A., Jan. 14, 1991. (In Sundance Film Festival, Salt Lake City.) MPAA Rating R. Running time: **114 MIN.**
Sam Sharpe . . . . . Richard Dreyfuss
Renata Bella . . . . Holly Hunter
Joe Bella . . . . Danny Aiello
Jan Bella . . . . . Laura San Giacomo
Marilyn Bella . . . . . Gena Rowlands
Gail Bella . . . . Roxanne Hart
Tony Bella . . . . Danton Stone
Also with: Tim Guinee, Greg Germann, Griffin Dunne.

Vast opportunities for unbearable quantities of sentimentality are fortunately squelched in "Once Around," an intelligently engaging domestic comedy-drama. Universal ought to be able to milk some good early year returns from this well-observed mainstream release.

Auspicious U.S. debut by Lasse Hallström, director of the widely loved 1985 Swedish hit "My Life As A Dog," isn't really about anything other than such well-worn subjects as acceptance, forgiveness and grabbing life's chances when they appear, but the characters here are decidedly alive and the texture is rich.

Malia Scotch Marmo's original screenplay keenly delineates how a woman finding happiness with a man for the first time paradoxically involves the serious deterioration of relations within her close-knit family.

Viewer sympathies, along with reactions to the pic itself, are bound to be significantly divided, as the two main characters are often obnoxious to the point of insupportability, but filmmakers are cleverly able to use even this seeming liability to their ultimate advantage.

Story is hung upon numerous family rituals — weddings, dinners, birthdays, baptisms, funerals — and opening sees thirtysomething Holly Hunter being badgered about her marital prospects at the wedding of her sister, Laura San Giacomo.

Rebuffed by her b.f. (coproducer Griffin Dunne in a neat

cameo), Hunter flees chilly Boston for the Caribbean, where she instantly is swept off her feet by an irrepressible, vulgar, tireless, wealthy condominium salesman, Richard Dreyfuss.

Seemingly a specialist in human takeover schemes, Dreyfuss easily conquers Hunter. His conquest of her family would normally seem an easy matter, as the Bellas could scarcely be warmer or more civilized. Danny Aiello and Gena Rowlands present a portrait of dream parents. San Giacomo is an emotional, straight-talking sister. Her husband, Tim Guinee, is friendly, and brother Danton Stone and his wife, Roxanne Hart, are regular folk.

But Dreyfuss, always in a sales-pitching mode and impossible to silence, turns off the family in inverse ratio to his charming of Hunter. Aiello exclaims, "Could you imagine that guy on a day-to-day basis?"

Most people would answer a big no to that one, sending one's allegiance away from the couple in the direction of the family, and Aiello in particular. When the brash outsider abruptly announces he and Hunter are going to marry, all the rest of them can do is throw up their hands and accept him.

But after well-written scenes of difficulties escalating to breaking point, Aiello banishes the boor from the house. Joyful reconciliation and tragedy follow in short order, capped by a pat and calculatedly upbeat finale.

Brightest strategy worked out by Hallström and scripter Marmo is forcing the viewer to experience the Bella family's acceptance of Dreyfuss. A more conventional approach would have added "cute" touches to make the character more palatable and provide reassurance that the family will come around.

As it is, Dreyfuss' sheer relentlessness darkens the mood and thickens the complexity of the situation, removing the film from the realm of the feel-good Hollywood formula. Despite pic's commercial trappings, its origins clearly lie in real-life emotions and experiences, authenticated in the sharp-witted telling.

Downside of this approach is that Dreyfuss' Sam, for all the time he's onscreen, remains essentially one-dimensional.

But Hallström succeeds in bringing these New England Italians robustly alive just as he craftily steers clear of easy emotionalism. One of his methods for achieving the latter, disengaged high overhead shots, is overdone but still proves effective when it counts near the end.

Aiello, brightest in an excellent cast, invests all his scenes with evident emotional and mental deliberation. Hunter has many nice moments, but the childishness of her character and a wobbly Boston accent neither parent has irritate as well. San Giacomo and Rowlands are very much on the money. Theo Van De Sande's lensing is resourceful and involving. Andrew Mondshein's editing and James Horner's score are fine. — *Cart.*

LE CHATEAU DE MA MÈRE
(MY MOTHER'S CASTLE)
(FRENCH)

A co-production of Gaumont, Prods. de La Guéville and TF1 Films. (Intl. sales: Gaumont.) Produced by Alan Poire. Directed by Yves Robert. Screenplay, Jerome Tonnere, Robert, based on the novel by Marcel Pagnol; camera (color), Robert Alazraki; editor, Pierre Gillette; music, Vladimir Cosma; sound, Alain Sempé, production design, Jacques Dugied, costumes, Agnès Nègre. Reviewed at the Palm Springs Intl. Film Festival, Palm Springs, Calif., Jan. 13, 1991. No MPAA rating. Running time: **98 MIN.**
Marcel . . . . Julien Ciamaca
Joseph . . . . Philippe Caubère
Augustine . . . . Nathalie Roussel
Uncle Jules . . . . Didier Pain
Aunt Rose . . . . . . Thérèse Liotard
Paul . . . . Victorien Delamare
Lili . . . . Joris Molinas

As the closing event at the second annual Palm Springs Film Fest, "Le Chateau De Ma Mère," a near sellout with a $15 admission at the 800-seat Plaza Theater, drew hearty applause from the mostly local audience. But pic proceeds at a leisurely episodic pace and is unlikely to be a strong draw for general U.S. auds.

It's easy to see why the sequel to French director Yves Robert's "La Gloire De Mon Père" (which opened the Palm Springs fest) has proved as popular in its homeland as the first, as the two films are so similar in spirit.

Identical cast is featured in the continuation of the turn-of-the-century reminiscences of French author Marcel Pagnol's childhood, with young Marcel (Julien Ciamaca) now studying for scholarship exams.

Meanwhile, the family's trips to his beloved Provence hills have become a weekend ritual, with the main obstacle being the long trek for the baggage-laden pilgrims from the end of the tram line to the country abode.

Relief materializes in the form of a cheerful canal spiker who offers them a key to the gated paths along the waterway, a shortcut of more than two hours' walking. But to use the canals, they must trespass across the private lands fronting many expensive estates, a breach of procedure Marcel's schoolteacher father, Joseph, feels he simply cannot risk.

Director Yves Robert sets a delightful scene at a country tavern where the family and the canalman, a former student of Joseph's, all take turns talking the father into blurring his principles for their comfort.

Pagnol's marvelous embroidery of the trespassing incident, in which Joseph eventually ends up caught and fearing the worst, is storytelling of the first order.

But like the hunting adventure in "La Gloire," it goes on too long, proving to be the major episode in the picture. Pace drags, and all in all it's rather a slight hook on which to hang a theatrical feature.

Not quite as rich (or commercial) as the first episode, "Le Chateau" still benefits from Pagnol's delightful rendering of human behavior in a simpler time. Robert has his own little jokes with the deft visuals, and for those hooked on the Pagnol family after seeing part one, this will be a pleasurable enough second visit. — *Daws.*

BLOOD AND CONCRETE

An IRS Media production. Executive producers, Miles A. Copeland III, Paul Colichman, Harold Welb. Produced by Richard La Brie. Directed by Jeffrey Reiner. Screenplay, LaBrie, Reiner; camera, Declan Quinn; editor, LaBrie, Reiner; music, Vinny Golia; sound, Giovanni Di Simone; production design, Pamela Woodbridge; art direction, Wendy Guidery; set decoration, Robert Stover; wardrobe design, Jan Rowton; assistant director, Gregory Everage; casting, Don Pemrick. Reviewed at Palm Springs Intl. Film Festival, Palm Springs, Calif., Jan. 10, 1991. MPAA rating: R. Running time: **97 MIN.**
Joey Turks . . . . Billy Zane
Mona . . . . Jennifer Beals
Lance . . . . James Le Gros
Hank Dick . . . . Darren McGavin
Spunz . . . . Nicholas Worth
Bart . . . . Mark Pellegrino
Sammy . . . . Harry Shearer
Mort . . . . William Bastiani

A hip, funny whodunit set in seedy underground Hollywood, "Blood And Concrete" (world preemed at the Palm Springs Film Festival) is polished enough for theatrical profits and bound to find an enduring video following.

Director Jeff Reiner and producer Richard LaBrie, who also share writing and editing credit, sidestep the arty ennui common to many pics set in this offbeat milieu in favor of crude and rambunctious comedy.

Viewers who can get past the long torrent of exceedingly foul language unleashed in the first reel by the unlucky drug dealer Mort (William Bastiani) will settle in for a stylish, well-paced romp that scores high in entertainment value.

Good-looking, sensual Billy Zane ("Dead Calm") plays Joey Turks, a dimwitted car thief who has a knack for being in the wrong place at the wrong time.

Bleeding from a knife wound dealt him by Mort after he tries to steal the hood's tv, he runs into strung-out singer Mona (Jennifer Beals), who's about to slash her wrists, and the two of them manage to pull each other back from the brink.

But Mort is found floating dead in his pool and Joey's fingered for the murder, as well as the whereabouts of a big stash of designer love drugs Mort supposedly was holding. Pursued by a trigger-happy police detective (Darren McGavin) as well as by a fat, gay gangster (Nicholas Worth) who wants the drugs, Joey and Mona end up running in an ever-smaller circle as they try to elude danger and still score enough cash somewhere to get out of town.

Mona, who's none too keen on taking another loser into her shaky life, nonetheless tries to remain true to Joey while being pursued by her obnoxious ex-lover Lance (James Le Gros), a scummy trash-rock singer who's hot to resume their carnal relationship.

Pic's parameters have been oft-traveled before, but what's refreshing here is the gleeful energy and crack comic timing with which the filmmakers present their gallery of going-nowhere characters.

With the frames painted in garish neon colors by cinematographer Declan Quinn and production designer Pamela Woodbridge, pic captures the drug-heightened atmosphere of this seedy, comic nightworld in a way that recalls, on a more modest scale, Martin Scorsese's "After Hours."

Zane is on the mark as the hapless hood determined to figure a way out of his troubles, and Beals is impressive as the shrieking, morose Mona, who seems grounded only on stage, where she displays a strong, classy cabaret style.

Reiner's work with the supporting actors, both in script and direction, is particularly strong, as each and every one makes a potent contribution, particularly Le Gros ("Drugstore Cowboy") as the out-of-control rocker, Mark Pellegrino as the musclehead hustler and Harry Shearer as the supposedly cleaned-up drug dealer who sports a cooled-out new age demeanor.

Pic's frequently rude and crude sensibilities will likely limit it to a youthful urban audience, but all talent involved is likely to find new opportunities. — *Daws.*

GAVRE PRINCIP HIMMEL UNTER STEINEN
(DEATH OF A SCHOOLBOY)
(AUSTRIAN)

A production of Neue Studio Film GMBH in association with Miran Ltd., London, and Jadran Film, Zagreb. Produced by Peter Pochlatko. Executive producers, Eduard Meisel, Stipe Gurdulic. Directed by Peter Patzak. Screenplay, David Antony, Patzak, based on the book by Hans Konig; camera, Igor Luther; editor, Michou Hutter; music, Peter Ponger; costumes, Heidi Melinc. Reviewed at Palm Springs Intl. Film Festival, Palm Springs, Calif., Jan. 11, 1991. No MPAA rating. Running time: **93 MIN.**
With: Reuben Pillsbury, Christopher Chaplin, Robert Munic, Sinolicka Trpkova, Philippe Léotard.

A mere blue-eyed schoolboy assassinated the archduke of Austria, touching off World War I, and the story of how 17-year-old Gavre Princip came to fire the shot is the chief point of interest in "Death Of A Schoolboy."

Larger context of early 20th-century Euro political stage, however, is not fully addressed and may leave younger U.S. viewers shaking their heads. That, and pic's dreamy pace and anticlimactic structure, will limit it to festival play on these shores.

Austrian director Peter Patzak extensively researched the background and character of the

young Sarajevo assassin. Pic points up that, remarkably, this intelligent youth acted on his own and with a clear head.

Princip is revealed as a talented student and serious thinker who's disturbed by the monarchy's occupation of his city and by any act of bullying.

Expelled from school after a political demonstration, Princip and his schoolmates end up eager but penniless in free Belgrade, keenly tuned in to the political climate while struggling just for bread, coffee and a bed.

When they learn the monarchy plans a parade in Sarajevo on June 28, 1914, a national holiday in their homeland, they consider the insult too much to bear. Eager to prove his courage and sincerity, the strong-willed Princip decides he must kill Franz Ferdinand before he ascends the throne. After managing to get pistols and bombs from an ex-soldier friend, they set out for Sarajevo.

Patzak, a filmmaker for nearly 20 years, then runs the picture off course by intercutting scenes of the consequences of the deed — imprisonment in a dungeon — with the actions leading up to it.

Technique is confusing at first and seems employed merely to delay the climax, which, ironically, never comes, as the shooting of the archduke is not even shown. Rather, it's recounted by Princip to a kindly doctor in the prison. It's hard to understand why Patzak made this choice, except perhaps for budget limitations.

Pic also suffers from the lack of info on the domino effect of the assassination. "Austria, Serbia, Italy, France, Russia — the whole world is burning," the doctor tells the boy, who does not ask how it happened and never seems to grasp the historic significance of his deed.

Though "Schoolboy" stops short of its dramatic potential, it's attractively filmed with many graceful scenes. Patzak does a good job of establishing the tensions of the times. One scene has a businessman and a radical take to bashing each other on a train, only to then sit miserably together until the next stop.

Reuben Pillsbury, a novice with no other screen experience, is well-cast as Princip, projecting a compelling combination of innocence and maturity. Some of the cast is weak, including Sinolicka Trpkova, who, as Princip's teenage girlfriend, lacks presence or point of view. — *Daws.*

DELUSION

An IRS Media production. Produced by Daniel Hassid. Executive producers, Seth M. Willenson, Christoph Henkel. Directed by Carl Colpaert. Screenplay, Colpaert, Kurt Voss; camera, Geza Sinkovics; editor, Mark Allan Kaplan; music, Barry Adamson; sound, Al Samuels; production design, Ilkido Toth; costume design, Kimberly Tillman; assistant directors, Rodney Smith, Gregory K. Simmons; coproducers, William Ewart, Cevin Cathell; casting, Elisa Goodman. Reviewed at Courtyard Theater, Palm Springs, Jan. 12, 1991. No MPAA rating. Running time: **100 MIN.**
George O'Brien . . . . .Jim Metzler
Patti . . . . .Jennifer Rubin
Chevy . . . . .Kyle Secor
Larry . . . . .Jerry Orbach

Writer-director Carl Colpaert makes an auspicious debut in "Delusion," a stylish desert kidnap saga. Good performances and visuals compensate where the script gives out, and result is worth seeing for industryites scouting new talent. Theatrical payoff will be a struggle, given public indifference to no-profile indie efforts.

A novice white-collar criminal meets his hard-bitten alter ego in this mirage-like Death Valley scenario. George (Jim Metzler), a computer exec who's devastated because the company he built is vanishing in a post-'80s takeover, heads for a new start in Reno with nearly half a million in stolen cash.

Plan is to set up shop anew in Nevada, but George's course is changed when he stops to aid two travelers whose car has turned over.

Shaken out of the wreck like two tumbleweeds but barely affected, the two (Kyle Secor and Jennifer Rubin) wind up taking over the car and threatening to kill him.

Instead, George winds up witness to a contract murder, then beaten up and abandoned in the desert. Limping back to life with the aid of a loony desert femme, he sets out on their trail, trying to get back the car and his half-million dollar stash.

Belgium-born director Colpaert has an eye for the color and style of the American landscape, filling the simplest scenes with visual interest. His work with actors is remarkable, as Secor and Rubin deliver striking performances for a film at this budget level.

Screenplay, penned by Colpaert and Kurt Voss ("Border Radio," "The Horseplayer"), features rich, clever wordplay and a

strongly drawn love-hate relationship between Secor's compulsive gambler, always spinning toward disaster, and Rubin's part-time showgirl, who's hooked because he needs her.

Nonetheless pic has weaknesses, including narrative illogic and a general lack of sympathy for George, who seems to lack the will to save himself. His actions throughout indicate bad judgment and a perverse spiral toward ruin. No wonder his company went under.

The melodramatic struggle for survival between Chevy and George seems a mere theatrical ploy, given the solutions George keeps ignoring. Chevy dances while George is forced to dig his own grave; for some reason George doesn't crown him with the shovel.

Colpaert at least has the humor to mock the whole setup, staging a Sergio Leone-style showdown in a Death Valley vacant lot. It turns into an amusingly stalled standoff after Patti tosses the bag of cash between the two gunmen.

Whatever Colpaert may have wanted to say about post-'80s morality, however, is not clearly rendered. Metzler does a good job of putting across his underwritten character, and Secor and Rubin are impressive. Jerry Orbach is terrific as a gangster trying to bluster his way through his last hours. Barry Adamson contributes a sparse, spaghetti-western guitar score.
— *Daws.*

HANGFIRE

A Motion Picture Corp. of America release of a Brad Krevoy/Steve Stabler production. Produced by Krevoy, Stabler. Directed by Peter Maris. Screenplay, Brian D. Jeffries; camera (Foto-Kem color), Mark Norris; editor, Maris; music, Jim Price; sound (Ultra-Stereo), Gerald Wolfe; production design, Stephen Greenberg; costume design, Harold Evans; assistant director/co-producer, Randy Pope; production manager, Kevin Cathell; stunt coordinator, Peter Horak; special-effects coordinator, Donald Power; associate producer, Ann Narus; casting, Sharon Nederlander. Reviewed at Criterion 5 theater, N.Y., Jan. 12, 1990. MPAA Rating: R. Running time: **89 MIN.**
Sheriff Ike Slayton . . . . . Brad Davis
Maria . . . . Kim Delaney
Johnson . . . . . . Jan-Michael Vincent
Billy . . . . Ken Foree
Kuttner . . . . Lee de Broux
Warden . . . . George Kennedy
Patch . . . . James Tolkan
Lieutenant . . . . Yaphet Kotto
Also with: Blake Conway, Lyle Alzado, Lou Ferrigno, Robert Miano, Collin Bernsen, Peter Lupus, Nancy Schuster, Lawrence Rothschild, Myron Dubow.

"**H**angfire" is a tight little action thriller about a prison break that attempts to serve as a metaphor for the current Middle East crisis, but strains credibility.

Filmmaker Peter Maris had a rather silly actioner last year, "Ministry Of Vengeance," about a clergyman who goes to the Middle East as an avenger. Prior to that, he made two fascinating Bs about Libyan terrorism, "Terror Squad" and "Viper."

This time out, except for a wisecrack about Henry Kissinger-style shuttle diplomacy, the film is ostensibly all-American in content. Character actor Lee de Broux, in a bravura performance, plays a serial killer/rapist who leads a prison escape in New Mexico as the cons are being transported to safety to avoid toxic chemical clouds after a truck crash near the pen.

De Broux and his minions take over the town of Sonora and hold its 50 or so inhabitants prisoner. The National Guard is called in, led by gung ho Jan-Michael Vincent, who calls up helicopters and even a tank to do battle.

From the opening threat of dangerous chemicals to the emphasis on hostages during a confrontation, scripter Brian Jeffries is obviously shooting for bigger bear in this actioner. However, film succeeds on a literal level, with effective tension, solid thesping and good stunts.

Local sheriff Brad Davis and his Vietnam vet pal Ken Foree (who excels in Maris assignments such as "Viper") are the secret weapons who manage to defeat de Broux and rescue Davis' wife (Kim Delaney) while the military proves largely ineffectual.

De Broux' no-nonsense portrayal of a heinous villain deserves kudos for not romanticizing the character. Vincent's military man is a stereotype, but the rest of the cast, including Lyle Alzado and Lou Ferrigno for comic relief, is effective. — *Lor.*

ETT PARADIS UTAN BILJARD
(A PARADISE WITHOUT BILLIARDS)
(SWEDISH-ITALIAN)

A Börje Hansson production. Co-producers, Bo Christensen, Fulvio Lucisano. Written and directed by Carlo Barsotti. Camera, Göran Aslund; music, Kjell Westling; art direction, Staffan Erstam; editor, Susanne Linnman. Reviewed at Sandrews screening room, Stockholm, Jan. 14, 1991. Running time: **107 MIN.**
With: Paolo Migone, Gianluca Favilla, Giacomo Poretti, Giuseppe Nesi, Renzo Spinetti, Carlo Felicettti, Björn Granath, Carin Ödquist, Görel Crona, Carina Lidbom.

A comedy about Italian workers in Sweden in the 1950s, "A Paradise Without Billiards" might not pull the crowds in Sweden, but could perform okay in Italy and on the festival circuit.

In his feature film debut, actor-director-writer Carlo Barsotti, Sweden resident since the late '60s, focuses on Italian workers who emigrated to work in Sweden after the war. They could not find work in their homeland and were easy prey for stories about a golden future in Sweden.

Barsotti's film centers around Giuseppe, whose friend Franco previously moved to Sweden. In his many letters, Franco told Giuseppe about the wonderful life north of Europe. Giuseppe leaves his family, friends and (most important) daily billiards at the local cafe.

The Sweden he finds is not the Sweden he dreamed about. He soon encounters insensitivity as immigrants are de-liced at the border in a way that reminds them of the gas chambers during the war. When he and his comrades arrive in the rural town where they have factory jobs, they find their living quarters are barracks. He also discovers that the wages are not as big as Franco had said.

The Italians use their exotic appeal to invite some Swedish girls to the barracks for dinner and sex. Some of them are married, and this creates hostility toward the foreigners.

Giuseppe dreams about a blonde Swedish girl, but in the back of his mind is Maria, the girl Franco left behind in Italy and whom Giuseppe also loves. He meets Eva, a girl who is everything he has dreamed about, and sleeps with her.

In the morning he is rudely awakened by her drunken ex-husband and makes a hasty exit through the window. Disillusioned with Sweden and the Swedes, and the absence of billiards, he decides to move back to Italy.

Barsotti's appealing tone manages to combine Italian and Swedish sentiment. The contrast between the lively Italians and the moody, quiet Swedes often is strikingly portrayed.

The director overdoes the flashbacks depicting the difference between events in Sweden and similar events in Italy. Still, many immigrants in the Scandinavian countries probably will find a lot to laugh at.

The mainly Italian actors perform well, but lead Paolo Migone (Giuseppe) acts and looks like he belongs in Italian comedy, and thus seems out of place. From the beginning, it's clear Giuseppe never will feel at home in Sweden, and this robs the film of any suspense about whether he will stay or return to Italy.

Still, pic will appeal to Italians living in Sweden. Meanwhile, Italians in Italy can get a good look at the realities faced by their countrymen who have emigrated. — *Gunn.*

CEI CARE PLATESC CU VIATA
(THOSE WHO PAY WITH THEIR LIVES)
(ROMANIAN)

A Film Four Unit, Romaniafilm production. Produced by Radu Stegaroiu. Written and directed by Serban Marinescu, based on "Procust's Bed" and "Dance Of The Evil Fairies" by Camil Petrescu; camera (color), Vlad Paunescu; editor, Nita Chivulescu; music, Dan Stefanica; sound, Horea Murgu; production design, Lucian Nicolau. Reviewed at Montreal World Film Festival (Cinema of Today & Tomorrow), Sept. 2, 1990. Running time: **100 MIN.**
With: Stefan Tordache, Adrian Pintea, Gheorghe Visu, Ovidiu Ghinita, Marcel Iures, Maia Morgenstern, Julieta Ghiga, Mariana Mihut, Irina Petrescu.

A convoluted period melodrama of intrigue set among the world of politicians, publishers and the theater, "Those Who Pay With Their Lives" is a handsome picture but dramatically uninvolving.

The main plot involves a journalist who seeks to expose a suave politician in his newspaper, but various subplots clutter the narrative. One of them involves an impoverished young poet back from the war and hopelessly in love with a wealthy woman.

Visually, the picture, made in 1988, is attractive. The filmmakers make full use of some magnificent old Bucharest buildings. But dramatically it is less successful, perhaps because it attempts to cover too much ground with too many characters.

But the ambience of post-World War I Bucharest is intriguingly evoked and forms an interesting backdrop to the solemn goings-on. — *Strat.*

WELCOME TO OBLIVION

A Concorde Pictures release. Produced by Luis Llosa. Directed by Augusto Tamayo. Screenplay, Len Jenkin, Dan Kleinman; camera (Foto-Kem color), Cusi Barrio; editor, Tamayo, Dan Schalk; music, Kevin Klingler; sound, Edgar Lostaunau; assistant director, Pili Flores Guerra; stunt coordinator, Jose Luy; special makeup effects, Thom Schouse; co-producer, Sally Mattison; associate producer, Margarita Morales Macedo. Reviewed on Concorde vidcassette, N.Y., Dec. 30, 1990. MPAA Rating: R. Running time: **80 MIN.**
Kenner . . . . Dack Rambo
Grace . . . . Clare Beresford
Elijah . . . . Meshach Taylor
Big . . . . Mark Bringelson
Zig . . . . Charles Dougherty
Radio . . . . Diana Quijano
Shiela . . . . Emily Kreimer
Bishop . . . . Orlando Sacha
Also with: Ramsay Ross.

This threadbare sci-fi pic has the unusual locale of Peru to boast, but otherwise it's a forgettable effort released last year by Roger Corman's Concorde banner.

Dack Rambo brings little conviction to his reluctant hero role in another "Mad Max"-cloned universe. He's sent by The Company to a heavily irradiated district called Oblivion following World War III to secure zirconium mining rights.

Befriended by feisty mutant heroine Clare Beresford, he gradually begins to identify with the downtrodden inhabitants of Oblivion. By film's end he has thrown in his lot with them and maneuvered it so the outside world won't exploit them overmuch.

Corny pic involves a gladiatorial contest reminiscent of "Mad Max Beyond Thunderdome" but executed on a low budget. Film is far too tame for its target audience and has poor makeup effects, such as phony-looking false ears worn by the mutants.

Rambo's haircut is designed to remind us of Harrison Ford in "Blade Runner," but the resemblance ends there. Some of the local supporting cast is dubbed into English, which negates the impact of the villain played by Orlando Sacha. — *Lor.*

SUNDANCE FEST

CITY OF HOPE

An Esperanza Inc. production. Produced by Sarah Green, Maggie Renzi. Executive producers, John Sloss, Harold Welb. Written and directed by John Sayles. Camera, Robert Richardson; editor, Sayles; music, Mason Daring; sound, Scott Breindel; production design, Dan Bishop, Dianna Freas; art direction, Ohas. B. Plummer; set decoration, Carolyn Cartwright; costume design, John Dunn; assistant director, Steve Apicella; casting, Barbara Hewson Shapiro, Eve Battaglia. Reviewed at Egyptian Theater, Park City, Utah, Jan. 23, 1991. No MPAA rating. Running time: **129 MIN.**
Nick . . . . Vincent Spano
Wynn . . . . Joe Morton
Joe . . . . Tony LoBianco
Rizzo . . . . . . Anthony John Denison
Angela . . . . Barbara Williams
Carl . . . . John Sayles
Les . . . . Bill Raymond
Reesha . . . . Angela Bassett
Riggs . . . . Chris Cooper
Jeanette . . . . Gloria Foster
Mad Anthony . . . . Josh Mostel

Most notable as an experiment in form, John Sayles' "City Of Hope" should have no trouble finding distribution, but it's unlikely to make more than a minor boxoffice impact because of its diffused focus and challenging view.

Watching this very independent feature in its world premiere at the Sundance fest was like watching the first season feature-length pilot of "Twin Peaks" unspool at fests before it reached the tube. It is cinema or is it television?

Sayles' ambitious, wide-ranging study of corruption and community in a small Eastern city has as many parallel plots and characters as "Hill Street Blues," while at the same time having a richness of theme and specificity of vision more common to serious cinema. Perhaps this film, made with RCA/Columbia funding, will one day turn up in high school civics classes as an illustration of the way things really work.

A disturbingly dark view of community dynamics in which "everybody's a politician," as one cop says, and everyone's working a deal, "City" escapes total cynicism by allowing for the strength of individual will in maintaining some integrity.

Picture hinges on the opposite directions of two characters: Nick (Vincent Spano), disillusioned son of a well-connected builder, who has easy access to the system but only wants out of it, and Wynn (Joe Morton), a young black city councilman who's determined to work within the system but encounters hostility from his own constituents.

Nick, a good-looking but aimless man who lives in the shadow of his older brother, a local sports hero who died in the Marines, quits his no-work job on his father's construction project and hits the street, where he soon gets involved in a robbery to get money to pay off his gambling debts.

Meanwhile he's starting a romance with an old high school classmate Angela (Barbara Williams), which draws the wrath of her mad-dog ex-husband and cop (Anthony John Denison).

Wynn is trying to rally participation from the people in his ward to show the council they care about civic issues, but he is harshly derided by the quick-trigger mouth-offs at the African-American center for playing to the white man.

Then a racial crisis erupts when two black kids attack a white college teacher and then tells the cops that the prof had made homosexual advances on them. Wynn knows they're lying but must find a course that serves both his community and his conscience.

Meanwhile Nick's father (Tony LoBianco) is caught up in a city scheme to put a profitable development in place of a slum apartment he owns. Unable to get the tenants out, they resort to arson, with tragic results.

None of these plots offers clearly defined good and bad — everything's a gray area and blame for all incidents is shared by everyone. Indeed, the most pervasive theme here is the connectedness of community, with the actions of seemingly disconnected persons bouncing from one faction to another in a chain reaction.

Camera style particularly underscores this theme, with the very mobile, energetic eye of the picture bounding from one group of characters to another, sometimes literally turning on its heel to follow a new set of people moving through the frame from the opposite direction.

For much of the film, the restlessness of focus seems a liability. Audience gets snatches of this story and that, the situations of ordinary folk like teachers and cops, pols and construction workers, making it all seem too much like this week's episode of "L.A. Law" or, better yet, Sayles' own NBC series, "Shannon's Deal."

But when the camera stops long enough to put two characters together one-on-one, as in Nick's charming courtship of the edgy Angela, or in his anguished last scene with his father, quality of performance, dialog and emotional connection emerge.

As pic's many threads come together in the final reels, the payoff makes the film's technique best appreciated in retrospect. Sayles' darkly poetic stroke at the end sounds as both a warning and a cry for help. It's an abruptly confident ending that renders the pic a fully realized statement in itself — but not, one cannot fail to note, without the potential to launch a series in this climate of adventurous tv.

Most of the actors have been seen in other Sayles pics. Spano ("Baby It's You") and Morton ("The Brother From Another Planet") are both terrific in demanding roles, and Williams is particularly interesting in a nicely nuanced perf as the wary Angela.

Josh Mostel adds welcome levity as appliance store owner Mad Anthony. Sayles himself plays a grim, bullying blue-collar dealmaker who's got some sensitive goods on Nick's brother.

Pic's sensibilities overall seem somehow more suited to the '70s than today, perhaps because Eastern blue-collar communities like the fictional Hudson City have been somewhat left behind. Some kind of update could have given this picture a bit more tang in these times. — *Daws.*

HANGIN' WITH THE HOMEBOYS

A New Line Cinema production. Executive producer, Janet Grillo. Produced by Richard Brick. Written and directed by Joseph P. Vasquez. Camera (color), Anghel Decca; editor, Michael Schweitzer; music, Joel Sill, David Chackler; sound, William Sarokin; art direction, Isabel Bau Madden; set decoration, Anne Czerwatiuk; costume design, Mary Jane Fort; assistant director, Howard McMaster; casting, Deborah Aquila. Reviewed at Sundance Film Festival, Park City, Utah. MPAA rating: R. Running time: **88 MIN.**
Willie . . . . Doug E. Doug
Tom . . . . Mario Joyner
Johnny . . . . John Leguizamo
Vinnie . . . . Nestor Serrano
Vanessa . . . . Kimberly Russell
Luna . . . . Mary B. Ward

A party night in the Bronx becomes a night of revelation for the tragicomic heroes of "Hangin' With The Homeboys." Targeting urban males in selected cities, New Line should manage a tidy profit on this low-budget venture upon April release.

Writer-director Joe Vasquez brings unexpected dimension to his four distinct characters in this fresh, funny and clear-eyed portrait, world-premiered at the Sundance Film Festival.

"Homeboys" is a good example of what independents can bring to the party: a vibrant tale told at minimum cost (under $2 million), a focus on cultural minorities (ghetto blacks and Puerto Ricans) and access to the system for a talented minority director (Vasquez, who did "Street Story" and "The Bronx War").

Ensemble piece "Homeboys" follows the misadventures of four South Bronx youths from mid-morning Friday to Saturday dawn. It looks like it could be their last time together, as reality is bearing down.

Willie is a welfare sponger whose caseworker has run out of patience. Played as angry, lazy and dumb in an excellent performance by Doug E. Doug, he's the most hopeless of the bunch.

Tom (Mario Joyner) is a would-be actor with a telemarketing gig. Johnny (John Leguizamo), a shy, serious Puerto Rican supermarket stocker, ignores his boss' encouragement to try for a Hispanic college scholarship.

Vinnie (Nestor Serrano), a Puerto Rican (real name, Fernando) who pretends to be an Italian stud, sleeps all day and funds his party life by cajoling money from young girlfriends.

Sticking close to his characters all the way through, Vasquez creates an unflinchingly honest picture of what makes them tick as they set out for a loose ramble through the night. Slippery talk is their stock-in-trade, and when nobody falls for it, they're out of luck, as in a scene where they're hurled out of a Puerto Rican party they've crashed.

With plenty of tensions among themselves, they mostly pick on one another and get high on perpetual motion as they bounce from cruising to party-crashing to bars, cafes, peepshows, a billiards hall and a disco.

Two-thirds of the way through, Tom plows his Plymouth into a brick wall on a dead-end Manhattan street. The message is clear: They're going nowhere.

Vasquez doesn't exactly transcend negative stereotypes. The worst of these characters are perpetual liars and takers; the other two are just trying to survive. He adds humanity and distinction to their lives. Johnny clearly is not the same as Vinnie or Willie, and their fates lie in the difference.

In the pic's loveliest and most unexpected passage, Johnny is accosted in a crummy diner by a smooth and sophisticated femme (played nimbly by Mary B. Ward) who takes him to an upscale pool hall where she clues him in to the wide world he could be part of if only he'd open his eyes and leave his gawking friends behind.

Vasquez has a knack for setup and payoff. Several laugh lines are nicely exploited throughout the pic, while one of the best jokes, Fernando's insistence that he be called Vinnie, leads up to a savory encounter with the cops in which he's accused of having a fake i.d.

Film is infused with an aggressive and engaging street energy and plenty of humor (Vinnie's little clown act with the shaving cream is brilliant).

There's also a lot of edge here, as pic starts out seeming like merely a good-time ramble but winds up being quite incisive about the boundaries and frustrations of this limited world. The ugly language and ugly attitudes on display are used to reveal the characters more than to endorse them.

Pic is neither as stylized nor as accessible as Warrington and Reginald Hudlin's "House Party," another strong film with a minority

focus, which debuted at last year's Sundance fest. Nonetheless, it has many things in its favor, including Vasquez' terrific work with the actors.

Opening scene on a subway says a lot about what this filmmaker's up to: A violent fight breaks out among blacks and Puerto Ricans and turns out to be only a joke among friends. In his "ghetto theater," Vasquez is out to turn audience expectations upside down.

Lensed on location in the Bronx and Manhattan, pic benefits from an alternately vibrant and subdued color palette by cinematographer Anghel Decca in his best work yet, though lighting in this entirely night-lensed shoot is sometimes too bright. Costumes are terrific, and soundtrack is also an asset. — *Daws*.

SLACKER

An Orion Classics release of a Detour Filmproduction presentation. Produced, directed and written by Richard Linklater. Camera (Du Art color), Lee Daniel; editor, Scott Rhodes; sound (Ultra-Stereo), D. Montgomery; art direction, Debbie Pastor; casting, Anne Walker. Reviewed at Sundance Film Festival, Park City, Utah, Jan. 23, 1991. No MPAA rating. Running time: **97 MIN.**

"Slacker" is one of the freshest independent films to come along in some time, but because of its nonnarrative, non-characterization approach, film won't be to all tastes. It will, however, attract attention on the specialized circuit and could do well in college communities on its projected release this spring.

Highly idiosyncratic and original in approach, pic was produced on a shoestring budget in Austin, Tex., in the summer of 1989 and was seen in a slightly different version last year at festivals in Seattle, Dallas and Munich. Orion Classics picked it up last fall and provided funds for enhanced postproduction and transfer from 16m to 35m.

Producer-director-writer Richard Linklater has used his enormous cast of mostly nonpros from Austin like a cinematic relay team.

Set in one day, the action shifts fluidly from one character to another as people walk around town, hang out in cafes, speechify, lay raps on one another and generally go about their business in ways that determined-

ly avoid any hint of work or responsibility.

Title refers to a new species of beatnik or hippie that, from the evidence presented here, has some humor and wants to be committed to some ideal, although members could use a strong dose of reality along with their espresso to perk them up a bit.

People on display are nearly all white and in their 20s and appear to be doing extended postgraduate work in entropy.

There's the young man (Linklater himself) who opens the film by regaling a diffident cab driver with his theories of alternate realities. Arriving at his destination, he notices a woman who has been run over, whereupon the action switches to the woman's disturbed son, who apparently has committed the crime.

And on it goes with a population consisting of political conspiracy freaks, out-of-work musicians, car fanatics, anarchists, idle girls, would-be philosophers and proselytizers of many persuasions.

No one has any money, and few show any inclination to work for it, except, perhaps, for a goofy young woman who, in one of the film's most inspired sequences, tries to peddle what she claims is a genuine Madonna pap smear, straight from the lab. One of the picture's major strengths is its humor, which arrives unpredictably, directly from the characters and the ways in which they speak.

A conspiracy nut can speak about how the Americans and Russians jointly colonized the moon years ago, while another, a somewhat looped young man, can speculate about the religious implications of Smurfs.

The most disconcerting thing is that, more often than not, these people seem to be speaking for their own benefit, talking at, not with, others. How much communicating is going on as a result of all the talk is highly questionable, as very few meaningful connections appear to be made.

A surprising amount of the conversation involves political subject matter, while amazingly little concerns personal relationships, sex and routine gossip.

Linklater springs these seemingly random encounters together with a fluid, on-the-move style that easily picks up a new character when the previous one is dropped. Lee Daniel's lensing is strictly verite, although subtle,

sophisticated visual motifs surface periodically.

Basic problem, given the absence of a storyline, is that interest quickly rises and falls by virtue of who happens to be on screen. Many of the anecdotes and spiels are abundantly amusing, but when they are not, pic falls flat until someone new comes along to rescue it.

Still, "Slacker" is more stylistically ambitious, and successfully so, than most American films, and Linklater deserves high marks for originality. It remains to be seen what he can do with dramatic staging and pacing, but chances are he'll get an opportunity to demonstrate it on the strength of this film. — *Cart*.

TWENTY-ONE

An Anglo Intl. Films Ltd. production. Executive producers, Mike Curb, Lester Korn, Carole Curb. Produced by Morgan Mason and John Hardy. Directed by Don Boyd. Screenplay, Zoe Heller, Boyd, based on a story by Boyd; camera (color), Keith Goddard; editor, David Spiers; music, Phil Sawyer; production design, Roger Murray-Leach; art direction, Terrie Wixon; costume design, Susannah Buxton; assistant director-production manager, Waldo Roeg; casting, Suzanne Crowley, Gilly Poole. Reviewed at Sundance Film Festival, Park City, Utah, Jan. 18, 1991. No MPAA rating. Running time: **101 MIN.**
Katie . . . . Patsy Kensit
Kenneth . . . . Jack Shepherd
Jack . . . . Patrick Ryecart
Bobby . . . . Rufus Sewell
Francesca . . . . . . Sophie Thompson
Baldie . . . . Maynard Eziashi

"Twenty-one" mirrors the character of its cheeky protagonist: bored, cynical and operating chiefly for self-amusement. This RCA/Col-financed pic, lensed chiefly in London, will need more than a green card to thrive in Yank markets.

Director/co-writer Don Boyd depicts the uncensored experience of a worldly young Brit (Patsy Kensit) who ankles her life in London for a fresh start in New York.

Boyd employs a direct-to-camera technique in which the frank, salty-tongued heroine talks while having her facial, tending to nature's call and so on.

If only she were more compelling. This rather vapid lass hasn't much on her mind, and her intimate revelations are forgettable. Displaying tragically bad judgment in choosing her associates, she goes on and on about them and sticks to them to the bitter end.

Stepping back in time and across the ocean, Kensit tells the audience she was doing all right in London, bouncing from job to job and having an affair on the sly with a horrible married man (Patrick Ryecart) until she fell for a lovely Scot (Rufus Sewell). He proved to be a junkie, which didn't deter her interest. When that ended predictably and irrevocably, she was upset enough to head to the States.

But not before her other London friends are introed. Viewers might rather have passed the time with funny Francesca (Sophie Thompson, playing with Tracey Ullman-like aplomb). Nigerian musician friend (Maynard Eziashi) fears deportation until Kensit does him the favor of marrying him.

Meanwhile, Boyd (who produced "Aria") indulgently lays out the tale, constantly introducing segments with no setup or flow. One is left to wonder what one thing has to do with another, until eventually some fragile purpose is revealed.

Camera also operates in pic's spirit (with flash and style, and no real purpose). Tricks like sideways shots and speed-ups are thrown in to vary the pace. Whole affair is topped off with an unpleasant electronic score.

Certainly, fans of Kensit ("Lethal Weapon 2") get plenty of her; her lovely face and form are always the center of attention. The cool control with which she executes the role is admirable.

Meanwhile, one wonders how she managed to snag that swank New York apartment on a receptionist's salary and why it's decorated in those distracting Southwest motifs. Perhaps there's some sort of gap in cultural understanding at work here. — *Daws.*

QUEEN OF DIAMONDS

A Menkes Film production. Written, produced and directed by Nina Menkes. Camera (color), uncredited. Reviewed at Sundance Film Festival, Park City, Utah, Jan. 21, 1991. No MPAA rating. Running time: **77 MIN.**
Las Vegas dealer . . . . Tinka Menkes

What would an indie film showcase be without an unconventional entry as bold and masterful as this minimalist underground pic? Still, few will have the patience to join Nina Menkes' personal vision, and exhibition prospects for "Queen Of Diamonds" are limited to fests and specialized venues.

Pic, with its endless meditative shots forcing the viewer to see what's there even when there appears to be nothing, has value just for the integrity and singularity of its approach.

Pic's first image sets up its content. A woman is burrowed in bed with only her hand visible. Her red lacquered nails rake the pillow as if holding on desperately or ready to ward off attackers. The camera remains on this unsettling image while at least 45 seconds tick by uneventfully.

Lensed in and around Las Vegas and preoccupied with its bleakest, most desolate aspects, pic occasionally focuses on an alienated, methodical blackjack dealer, played with studied ennui by the filmmaker's sister, pale, raven-haired Tinka Menkes.

Thread of drama running through the film involves her lethargic concern about her missing husband and the activities of the mutually abusive couple next door, who eventually get married in a tacky lakeside wedding. An Elvis impersonator is one of the guests.

Menkes, internationally recognized as one of the U.S.' most challenging underground filmmakers (her previous film "Magdalena Viraga" won the Los Angeles Film Critics Award in 1986 for best independent/experimental film), finds images that stick in the mind and gain power as one dwells on them.

The film's seemingly disconnected images add up to an affecting portrait of desolation. Unfortunately, the point of the film and its techniques are easily grasped within 15 minutes. As the reels unspool without conflict or narrative, the experience becomes increasingly tedious.

This is essentially a short-film technique stretched into an indulgent feature length, and, at 77 minutes, "Queen Of Diamonds" deals a few more cards than necessary. — *Daws.*

IRON & SILK

A Prestige release. Produced and directed by Shirley Sun. Screenplay, Mark Salzman, Sun, based on the book by Salzman; camera (color), James Hayman; editor, Geraldine Peroni, James Y. Kwei; music, Michael Gibbs; sound, Pamela Yates; production design, Calvin Tsao; associate producer, Mei Kwong Franklin. Reviewed at Magno Review 1 screening room, N.Y., Dec. 6, 1990. Running time: **90 MIN.**
Teacher Mark . . . . . . Mark Salzman
Teacher Pan . . . . Pan Qingfu
Teacher Hei . . . . . Jeanette Lin Tsui
Ming . . . . Vivian Wu
Sinbad . . . . Sun Xudong
Mr. Song . . . . Zheng Guo

Film version of Mark Salzman's book about his experiences in China, "Iron & Silk" gives a fascinating inside look at China. Similar in many respects to Peter Wang's "A Great Wall," also produced and co-written by Shirley Sun, it should perform well on the arthouse circuit for Prestige, a new Miramax division.

In his autobiographical account of his two years as an English teacher in China, Salzman co-wrote the screenplay and stars as himself, though the name is changed to Mark Franklin. He may be criticized for doing the part, but how many actors can speak fluent Chinese and are also experts in martial arts? Besides, he has an engaging screen presence.

Salzman's love of kung fu movies got him interested in China as a child. Soon after arriving there, one of his Chinese students, dubbed the "middle-aged English teachers," takes him to see a legendary *wushu* instructor named Teacher Pan. He is nicknamed "iron fist" because he punches an iron plate a thousand times a day.

Pan is played by Salzman's actual teacher, Pan Qingfu. It is difficult to imagine anyone else in the part, as Qingfu makes him at once intimidating and sympathetic.

His other instructor is Teacher Hei (Jeanette Lin Tsui), who gives Salzman lessons in manners and social customs, as well as in Chinese and tai chi. Her husband, it turns out, was imprisoned during the cultural revolution.

Although China seemed to have opened up to foreigners in the early 1980s, it was not as open as Salzman expected. He starts a relationship with a Chinese doctor named Ming (Vivian Wu), who was punished for her appreciation of Western books. A foreign affairs officer catches them together and warns Salzman it could be dangerous for her because of the changing political situation.

Sure enough, it becomes clear to Salzman that he is not supposed to become too close to anyone in China. Naturally, he resents being considered a "foreign devil."

The script reveals much about China, but some dialog is stilted. When Salzman meets Ming, he tells her he learned Chinese because he wanted to communicate with a quarter of mankind. Ming has a better line later when she says, "It's not as free as it seems. I live in a very different world from yours."

In addition to its realistic Chinese characters, "Iron & Silk" also includes some stunning scenery. It was filmed in Hangzhou, a southern city with picturesque bridges and beautiful lakes. James Hayman's cinematography makes it look mysterious without omitting less photogenic locations.

Equally fine is Michael Gibbs' music, which reinforces the pic's bittersweet tone. Shirley Sun deserves credit for her direction of Chinese non-actors. The class members have a few touching scenes, including a farewell party when they sing "Jingle Bells."

Unfortunately, this may be the last U.S. film shot in China for some time. The day after wrapping, the military crushed the student movement in Tiananmen Square. At least the makers of "Iron & Silk" were able to document the relatively open period preceding that sad event. — *Stev.*

POPCORN
(U.S.-JAMAICAN)

A Studio Three release of a Movie Partners production, in association with Century Films (Jamaica) Ltd. Produced by Torben Johnke, Gary Goch, Ashok Amritraj. Executive producers, Howard Hurst, Karl Hendrickson, Howard Baldwin. Directed by Mark Herrier. Screenplay, "Tod Hackett" (Alan Ormsby), based on Mitchell Smith's story; camera (Spot Film and Continental color), Ronnie Taylor; editor, Stan Cole; music, Paul J. Zaza; sound (Dolby), Oscar Lawson; production design, Peter Murton; assistant director, Phil Dumont; production manager, Natalie Thompson; special makeup effects, Bob Clark; special effects supervisor, Georgia Ferrari; 2d unit camera, John Harris; co-producer, Sophie Hurst; casting, Joe D. Agosta. Reviewed at Magno Review 2 screening room, N.Y., Jan. 31, 1991. MPAA Rating: R. Running time: **91 MIN.**

Maggie	Jill Schoelen
Toby	Tom Villard
Suzanne	Dee Wallace Stone
Mark	Derek Rydall
Bud	Malcolm Danare
Leon	Elliott Hurst
Tina	Freddie Marie Simpson
Cheryl	Kelly Jo Minter
Joannie	Yvette Solar
Mr. Davis	Tony Roberts
Dr. Mnesyne	Ray Walston
Joy	Karen Witter
Vernon	Bruce Glover

"Popcorn" is just that, a commercial popcorn picture that veers wildly from effective '50s gimmick films homage to corny slasher footage. It should do fairly well at the boxoffice with nostalgic horror fans.

Though set in southern California, pic was filmed entirely on the island of Jamaica in autumn 1989. Checkered production history saw writer-director Alan Ormsby being replaced at the helm after three weeks of lensing by actor-turned director Mark Herrier (co-star of the "Porky's" pics). Also, leading lady Jill Schoelen replaced originally cast Amy O'Neill.

Ormsby, best known for scripting "My Bodyguard" but with many genre credits including "Deranged" and the remake of "Cat People," took his name off the film, which lists a pseudonymn in the credits. He's come up with plenty of knowing references to William Castle gimmickry as well as satire of B-pictures made over three decades ago, but his contemporary story framework falls apart miserably.

Tony Roberts gueststars uncomfortably as a U. of California, Oceanview, film prof who gets the bright idea of putting on an all-night horror movie show to raise funds for his fledgling department. Old-time impresario Ray Walston provides him the '50s and '60s movies complete with gimmicks like "Aromarama," electrified seats and a giant insect to fly across the Dreamland movie palace.

Gauche dialog and unfunny gags (notably hero Derek Rydall's slapstick) hurt the framing story. A mad killer is gruesomely murdering the leading players as revenge for the death of his mother at a movie theater 15 years ago in an incident involving a satanic cultist/filmmaker.

Schoelen and her aunt Dee Wallace Stone are involved, but it takes many reels and red herrings before plot details are sorted out.

In the meantime, "Popcorn" takes flight with excellent re-creations of cornball old features. "Mosquito" is a terrific imitation of the nuclear-energy-themed monster films, ranging from "Tarantula" to "Them!" Its hokey acting is very funny, as is Bruce Glover's performance in "Attack Of The Amazing Electrified Man," which occasions a revival of a variation of Castle's famed electrifed seats gimmick for "The Tingler."

"Popcorn" emphasizes that "Mosquito" is in 3-D, but fails to exploit that fact or obey the rules. Part of the audience watches the film without glasses and neither it nor we see a double image.

A third film, Japanese "The Stench," is shown only briefly as "Popcorn" degenerates into several anticlimaxes that pay homage to "The Phantom Of The Opera" (already better spoofed in Brian DePalma's "Phantom Of The Paradise") and a punishment poll lifted from Castle's classic "Mr. Sardonicus."

Finale has the teen audience relishing in the mayhem taking place on stage almost like denizens of ancient Rome. That's about as serious as pic ever gets.

Cast is stuck with unplayable material, causing Schoelen (so good in "The Stepfather") to become irritating, and Tom Villard as her classmate to overact to the hilt. Absence of sex or even a tease in a cast featuring many beautiful women is a serious miscalculation for this genre. Throughout, the camp performances of the pastiche films dominate the subpar contemporary routines.

Makeup effects by Bob Clark are very fine, especially for villain's transformations between various characters. (This Bob Clark is not the same Bob Clark who directed "Porky's" and has worked frequently with both Ormsby and Herrier.)

Tech credits are above average and the Jamaican locale adequately subs for all-American setting (though appearance of a reggae band is a hint that subterfuge is afoot). — *Lor.*

QUEENS LOGIC

A Seven Arts release through New Line Cinema of a New Visions Pictures presentation of a Stuart Oken/Russ Smith production. Produced by Oken, Smith. Executive producers, Taylor Hackford, Stuart Benjamin. Directed by Steve Rash. Screenplay, Tony Spiridakis; story, Spiridakis, Joe Savino; camera, Amir Mokri; editor, Patrick Kennedy; music, Joe Jackson; music supervisors, Gary Goetzman, Sharon Boyle; sound (Dolby), Tom Brandau; production design, Edward Pisoni; art direction, Okowita; set decoration, Marcie Dale; costume design, Linda Bass; assistant directors, Joel Tuber, Martha Elcan; associate producer, Patricia Churchill; casting, Julie Hutchinson, Barbara Shapiro. Reviewed at the UA Coronet Theater, Westwood, Jan. 28, 1991. MPAA Rating: R. Running time: **112 MIN.**

Dennis	Kevin Bacon
Carla	Linda Fiorentino
Elliot	John Malkovich
Al	Joe Mantegna
Ray	Ken Olin
Vinny	Tony Spiridakis
Monte	Tom Waits
Patricia	Chloe Webb

Also with: Jamie Lee Curtis, Michael Zelniker, Kelly Bishop, Terry Kinney, Ed Marinaro.

A warmed-over blend of "Diner" and "The Big Chill" with a Big Apple twist, "Queen's Logic" is verbose, too-rarely amusing romantic comedy that milks some good moments out of its ensemble cast but mostly proves tiresome and clichéd.

B.o. prospects, like the characters, seem destined for life in the 'burbs, not the big time.

Despite its sometimes-quirky humor, the film (opening in limited release) too often resembles one of those annoying Levi's Dockers commercials, with a group of men sharing meaningless insights. Then again, with Ken Olin among the cast and all the whining about "needs," some may just assume they've stumbled into a poor man's episode of "thirtysomething."

As in "Diner," the characters are forced to grapple with "growing up" by an imminent wedding, in this case that of Ray (Olin) to his live-in g.f. (Chloe Webb).

The twist is that the participants are past their formative years but still struggling with fear of commitment and success — especially Olin, stumbling toward the altar on cold feet, and his cousin (Joe Mantegna), whose reluctance to take on responsibility has led to estrangement from his wife (Linda Fiorentino).

Rounding out "da guys" are Eliot (John Malkovich), a repressed homosexual who resists making concessions to what he deems the gay lifestyle; Dennis (Kevin Bacon), a struggling musician living in Hollywood, and Vinny (Tony Spiridakis), an actor and the group's resident ladies man.

Events build toward the "will he or won't he" wedding ceremony as members of that quintet come to grips with their various problems and idiosyncracies, all of which come to a head at a bachelor party sequence that feels longer than the galas in all the "Godfather" films combined.

Aside from his supporting role, Spiridakis wrote the script, which too often makes its point by having characters launch into long explanatory speeches. The most dreadful is an unintentionally funny confession by a tearful Bacon at the party.

The only character whose head remains opaque is Olin's — a major shortcoming since his uncertainty regarding marriage is central to the film. He finally resolves that problem after listening to another lengthy speech, this one by Webb, though the message that "the neighborhood" remains in one's heart is tired at best.

Director Steve Rash fares better with the pic's oddball humor, derived largely from the peripheral female players. In the veritable gallery of eccentrics and nutcases, Jamie Lee Curtis may be the weirdest of all in a cameo as a psycho/guardian angel who helps Mantegna work through his own ill-defined marital foibles.

Mantegna, with his easygoing humor, and Malkovich, glowering with trademark intensity, are the only cast members able to rise above the hackneyed material. Spiridakis has built his story around predictable characters and situations.

Tech credits are okay, and Joe Jackson provides a breezy score that dovetails nicely with the obligatory shades-of-"The Big Chill" soundtrack.

The film pointedly incorporates a "Just say no" drug scene in a disco bathroom, ironic only in light of all the binge drinking that goes on. That sort of oversight reflects the lapses in logic that plague "Queens." — *Bril.*

CATCHFIRE

A Vestron Pictures presentation in association with Precision Films/Mack-Taylor Prods. of a Dick Clark Cinema production. Produced by Dick Clark, Dan Paulson. Executive producers, Steven Reuther, Mitchell Cannold. Directed by "Alan Smithee" (Dennis Hopper). Screenplay, Rachel Kronstadt Mann, Ann Louise Bardach, from a story by Mann; camera (CFI Color, Fuji Film), Ed Lachman; editor, David Rawlins; music, Curt Sobel; sound (Dolby), uncredited; production design, Ron Foreman; art director, Paul Marcotte; costume design, Nancy Cone; assistant director, Craig Beaudine; line producer, Paul Lewis; co-producer, Lisa Demberg. Reviewed at Cannon Haymarket Cinema, London, Jan. 25, 1991. Running time: **98 MIN.**
Milo . . . . Dennis Hopper
Anne Benton . . . . Jodie Foster
John Luponi . . . . . . Dean Stockwell
Lino Avoca . . . . Vincent Price
Pinella . . . . John Turturro
Pauling . . . . Fred Ward
Carelli . . . . Joe Pesci
Grace Carelli . . . . Helena Kalianiotes
Bob . . . . Charlie Sheen
Martha . . . . Julie Adams
Also with: G. Anthony Sirico, Sy Richardson, Frank Gio, Bob Dylan.

A quirky comedy-thriller about a hitman who falls for his femme target, "Catchfire" won't set many boxoffices alight, but name cast and okay entertainment values should score some hit-and-run biz before being sent down for a longer stretch on video shelves.

Scrambled pic has an L.A. artiste (Jodie Foster) accidentally witnessing a mob killing when her car breaks down one night. The cops (Fred Ward, Sy Richardson) want her to talk, and the hoods (Joe Pesci, Dean Stockwell, Vincent Price) want her dead. So she dons a blond wig and an alias and goes AWOL.

Meanwhile, Pesci hires a top-league hitman (Dennis Hopper) to do the job his own goons can't, and after months of tracking her around the States finally runs her aground in an ad agency. She gives him the slip, but is eventually traced in New Mexico. That's when the story really begins: Hopper "kidnaps" his quarry, possesses her for himself, and the dynamic duo set off on a weird road-movie-to-nowhere, with the mob and the law in hot pursuit.

Somewhere in here is a dark, sassy picture, but final product is more like a jigsaw with half the pieces missing. Pic was lensed in L.A., Seattle and Taos, N.M., in summer 1988 under Hopper's direction and the title "Backtrack." After postproduction squabbles (reportedly over Hopper's three-hour cut), he opted for the Director's Guild of America moniker "Alan Smithee." Recut, rescored version (with a 1989 copyright) runs a trim 98 minutes.

Credits and billing also are confused. Toplined mob boss Price is only in for three brief scenes. Pesci (with a bigger part) isn't billed at all. Charlie Sheen, who has a few seconds as Foster's boyfriend before being ventilated in bed, is way down the end roller. Bob Dylan is left with an uncredited walk-on.

On the tech side, posters credit music to Michel Colombier, music supervision to Gary Goetzman and Sharon Boyle, and editing to Wende Pheiffer Mate. None of these match with the final print, and script contribs from Stephen Cotler, Lanny Cotler, Alex Cox and Tod Davies don't get a mention.

Much of the recutting seems to have taken its toll in the first half. Pic starts jerkily, with no background on Foster other than her ritzy art gallery full of wall-socket displays. The art plays a major role in the first half, as Hopper jots down their messages (such as "Lack of charisma can be fatal") to get into her mind and find out where she's hiding. When he spots one ("Protect me . . . from what I want") in a mag ad, he tracks her down to an agency.

Most of this psychological game-playing is missing in (and weakens) the second half when Hopper's obsession turns to lust and then love. From a clutch of sexy Polaroids he finds, Foster is clearly more into scanties and suspenders than the average artist.

Pic needs more footage in order to explain abrupt swings between comedy and drama, joke hoods, Johnny-come-lately cops (Ward's always three steps behind everyone else), and the central burgeoning love story.

Apart from Foster, who's strong, shrewd and sexy, thesping is vaudeville all the way. Pesci rants and raves, Stockwell shows a nice line in low-key comedy, Ward looks like he hasn't been shown the whole script, and Hopper has a go at Humphrey Bogart in shades.

Overall, pic is an oddball cross between other Hopper items, "The Last Movie" (1971) and last year's "The Hot Spot."

Tech credits are generally okay. Ed Lachman's lensing has character, especially in the more serious, noir-ish moments, and the driving music score helps to corral the wandering storyline. The (uncredited) sound is so-so, with the Dolby stereo out of phase in a couple of sequences.
— *Drek.*

RUN

A Buena Vista release of a Hollywood Pictures presentation in association with Silver Screen Partners IV. Produced by Raymond Wagner. Directed by Geoff Burrowes. Screenplay, Dennis Shryack, Michael Blodgett; camera (Gastown Film color, Technicolor prints), Bruce Surtees; editor, Jack Hofstra; music, Phil Marshall; sound (Dolby), Rob Young, Eric Batut, Mark Holden; production design, John Willett; costume design, Trish Keating; art direction, Willie Heslup; set decoration, Elizabeth Wilcox; assistant director, Lee Knippelberg; coproducer, Fitch Cady; casting, Stuart Aikins. Reviewed at Avco Cinema, L.A., Calif., Jan. 29, 1991. MPAA Rating: R. Running time: **91 MIN.**
Charlie Farrow . . . Patrick Dempsey
Karen Landers . . . . . Kelly Preston
Halloran . . . . Ken Pogue
Denny Halloran . . . Alan C. Peterson
Martins . . . . . Christopher Lawford
Police Chief Travers . . . Marc Strange

"Run" might describe the scene in Disney offices as execs flee from responsibility for this turkey. With its hollow concept propped up by lavish production resources, pic is not likely to impress either belt-tightening studio chiefs or the public. Boxoffice won't make it past a 50-yard-dash.

Per production notes, scripters were inspired to pen this nonstop chase-a-thon after seeing a magazine piece about a down-on-his-luck punk who rips off a small-time casino and is hunted down and killed within the next 90 minutes.

With reliable mainstream blandness, the idea has been inverted to make the victim a happy-go-lucky law student (Patrick Dempsey), who wins fair and square in a small-time casino poker game. He then is attacked by an over-grown sore loser (Alan C. Peterson), who slips and hits his head during the scuffle and dies.

The goon turns out to be the son of a feared mob boss (Ken Pogue) who supposedly controls the whole town. Dempsey is accused of murder, and for the next 80 minutes he has to run, run, run to keep himself from being ground up for retribution.

Even the corrupt cops are after him, spurred on by the godfather's $50,000 reward. If Aussie director Geoff Burrowes had striven for a creepy sci-fi tone in which something was seriously amiss about this roadside burg from the moment Dempsey pulled off the highway, pic might have had the menace and suspense it requires.

As is, the idea that the town runs on fear of the cardboard thug or that everyone is willing to hunt down the innocent kid hasn't a shred of believability. Played straight, pic is merely an excuse to crash cars, destroy an amusement park and keep the camera racing over obstacle courses as Dempsey sweats bullets keeping one step ahead of doom.

Even the wishy-washy femme casino card dealer (Kelly Preston) doesn't want to help him, and with good reason, since she ends up getting shot for her trouble. Burrowes and scripters try to keep the tone light, with snappy one-liners punctuating the action, but with so many people dying in pursuit of Dempsey — some at his hands — this isn't exactly a college caper.

It's fitting that a mechanical rabbit at a greyhound track winds up becoming a murder weapon, since the whole pic operates much on the level of the rabbit and the dogs. "Rabbit" Dempsey has the cocky, wisecracking demeanor and physical agility to more or less carry the pic on his own.

Burrowes maintains an adrenalin-pumping pace and keeps the camera in close pursuit of the action through rocky courses. Lensed mostly at night in Toronto, pic is technically adept.
— *Daws.*

LA NIÑA EN LA PALOMERA
(THE GIRL IN THE DOVECOTE)
(CHILEAN)

An Arauco Film release of an Arauco production. Executive producer, Abdullah Ommidvar. Directed by Alfredo Rates. Screenplay, Rates based on a play by Fernendo Cuadra; camera, José Luis Arredondo; music, Eduardo Campos; production design, Oriana Gómez; costume design, Maréa Kluczynska, Mercedes Castro. Reviewed at Chile Films screening room, Santiago, Aug. 9, 1990. Running time: **98 MIN.**
Ana . . . . Marcela Osorio
Manuel . . . . Carlos Valenzuela
Luisa . . . . Miriam Palacios
Don René . . . . Mario Montilles
Elsa . . . . Mónica Carrasco
Also with: Coca Melnick, Rolando Valenzuela, Enrique Madiña, Aldo Bernales, Renato Munster.

A dated play of the '60s now becomes a dated film of the '90s and a melodrama lacking the courage of its convictions. Boxoffice outlook is dim.

In "La Niña En La Palomera," a first film by Alfredo Rates, a married and 40-ish busdriver falls for a 15-year-old schoolgirl. He seduces her, not quite against her will, and hides her in his attic at home. In the end, tears and violence explode, but it takes a long time to get there.

Film was shot in super-16 and blown up to 35m. Camerawork is square and rudimentary. Most of the actors have a theatrical background and show it, but Marcela Osorio (the teenager) appears natural, as long as the screenplay leaves her that option.

The film's strength lies in its choice of locations, sets and costumes which successfully recreate a lower middle class milieu of the '60s — except for a neighborhood bar with shelves displaying only Coke. — *Amig.*

SUNDANCE FEST

POISON
(COLOR/B&W)

A Zeitgeist Films release of a Bronze Eye production. Produced by Christine Vachon. Executive producers, James Schamus, Brian Greenbaum. Directed by Todd Haynes. Screenplay, Haynes, inspired by writings of Jean Genet; camera (color, 16m), Maryse Alberti, (b&w, 16m), Barry Ellsworth; editor, James Lyons, Haynes; music, James Bennett; sound, Neil Danziger; production design, Sarah Stollman; art direction (Baton), Chas Plummer; set design (Baton), John Hansen; costume design, Jessica Haston; associate producer, Laren Zalaznick; assistant director, Vachon; casting, Andrew Harpending, Kim Ainouz, Laura Barnett, John Kelly. Reviewed at Sundance Film Festival, Park City, Utah, Jan. 24, 1991. No MPAA rating. Running time: **85 MIN.**
"HERO"
Felicia Beacon . . . . Edith Meeks
Millie Sklar . . . . Millie White
Gregory Lazar . . . . Buck Smith
Evelyn McAlpert . . . . . Anne Giotta
"HORROR"
Dr. Graves . . . . Larry Maxwell
Nancy Olsen . . . . Susan Norman
Deputy Hansen . . . . . . Al Quagliata
Prostitute . . . . Michelle Sullivan
"HOMO"
John Broom . . . . Scott Renderer
Jack Bolton . . . . James Lyons
Rass . . . . John R. Lombardi
Young Broom . . . . . Tony Pemberton
Young Bolton . . Andrew Harpending

Winner of the top prize in the dramatic competition at the 1991 Sundance Film Festival, Todd Haynes' "Poison" is a conceptually bold, stylistically audacious first feature that will keep humming on the fest circuit for months to come.

Compelling study of different forms of deviance features some very upfront gays-in-prison material that provoked numerous fest walkouts and will be unpalatable to many mainstream viewers. But offbeat pic's supporters will be passionate in their advocacy, ensuring strong word-of-mouth in art circles where hipness to what's on the cutting edge is paramount.

Haynes is known in the film underground for his 1989 "Superstar: The Karen Carpenter Story," videocassettes of which are highly prized since the featurette, which has an all-doll cast, had to be pulled from release due to legal difficulties.

New film's point of departure is the works of the late French writer Jean Genet: "Our Lady Of The Flowers," "Miracle Of The Rose" and "Thief's Journal." With considerable cleverness and imagination, Haynes has composed three distinctive stories that constitute case studies of antisocial aberrations, shot them in three strikingly different styles and intercut them in surprisingly successful ways.

In experimenting so explicitly with genre, director pushes artificiality to the point of camp, but it is a serious, ambitious variety of camp that will have great resonance with film-wise audiences.

"Hero" takes up the case of a seven-year-old boy who, in blandest suburbia, murders his father. Arguably the weakest of the three story strands, but amusing enough withal, section features straight-on tv documentary-style interviews with the lad's mother, neighbors, teachers and classmates in an attempt to piece together the possible reasons for his misguided deed.

The vastly effective "Horror" uses a 1950s B pic sci-fi approach to relate the sad story of a scientist who isolates the source of human sex drive, but, upon drinking the fluid, becomes horribly disfigured and murderous.

A direct representation of the Genet universe, "Homo" scrutinizes an obsessive relationship between a hardened criminal and a new arrival in a 1940s French prison. Elegantly shot in sordid surroundings, segment builds a creepy but seductive mood shattered by a climax that could easily set Jesse Helms back on the rampage. (Project received funding from the National Endowment for the Arts.)

Haynes' ability to find and sustain each cinematic style is masterful and, with a couple of exceptions, his juggling of the three sections is adroitly judged. Both "Hero" and "Horror" are, in part, played for laughs, the former via its deadpan interviews in generally tacky surroundings, the latter for its knowing use of melodramatic devices, most notably a spiralling special effect to mark the doctor's transformation.

Done in earnest, the "Homo" sequence will throw more than a few unsuspecting viewers. A mood of seething, violent homoeroticism permeates the proceedings, as one prisoner stalks another in an episode spiked with multiple glimpses of rear-entry intercourse and one of genital fondling.

But the most explicit and sure to be most talked-about scene is a flashback in which several young men humiliate another by repeatedly spitting into his gaping mouth. Unpleasant is an understatement.

Through an original combination of means, Haynes has put together a provocative look at societal outcasts and twisted behavior that can be read in ways both artistic and political.

In this, he has been immeasurably helped by inspired work by his crew, which accomplished a lot under undoubtedly meager circumstances.

Barry Ellsworth's black & white lensing of the "Horror" sequence superbly reproduces the cheapo expressionism of the best B pics, while Maryse Alberti's color work in "Homo" artfully stokes the fires of a dingy hothouse. James Bennett's music, Sarah Stollman's production design and Jessica Haston's costumes are all critical in helping create the studied look essential to the film's success.

Performances in "Hero" and "Horror" work on a camp level due to their utter sincerity, while Scott Renderer, in "Homo," is taut and intense as the lovesick inmate. — *Cart.*

ONE CUP OF COFFEE

A Miramax Films release of a Bullpen Ltd./Open Road production. (Intl. sales: J&M Films.) Produced by Eric Tynan Young and Robin B. Armstrong. Directed by Armstrong. Screenplay, D.M. Eyre Jr.; camera, Tom Richmond; editor, Mark S. Westmore; music, Lee Holdridge; production design, David W. Ford; costume design, Kristine Brown; associate producer, Jonathan G. Chambers; coproducer, Geral R. Molen; casting, Deborah Barylski, Camille Patton. Reviewed at Sundance Film Festival, Park City, Utah, Jan. 22, 1991. No MPAA rating. Running time: **98 MIN.**
Roy Dean Bream . . . . . William Russ
Tyrone Debray . . . . Glenn Plummer
Clyde Bigby . . . . . Noble Willingham
Peter LaPorte . . . . . Jeffrey Tambor
Randy Keever . . . . Scott Plank
Inez Brice . . . . . . Dierdre O'Connell

The screenplay for "One Cup Of Coffee" was written 18 years ago, and if this baseball pic had come out ahead of "Bull Durham," its depiction of life in the downtrodden minor leagues might have been more notable.

Screening in the dramatic competition, pic is easily one of the most commercial in the Sundance Film Fest, but, for the most part, it feels too slight to generate real interest in theatrical release. It was acquired ahead of the fest by Miramax for domestic and J&M overseas.

Pic did generate strong audience response in Park City, where its affirmative nature and accessibility contrast sharply with the bleaker, more challenging tone of most of the offerings.

A broadly sentimental tale about an aging white pitcher and his generosity toward a talented black rookie, pic rounds the bases in too predictable a way but benefits from an immensely likable performance by William Russ.

Russ plays relief pitcher Roy Dean Bream, over-the-hill at 41 but still in love with the game despite teammate hostility incited by starting pitcher Keever (Scott Plank). With no one to talk to, Bream befriends 17-year-old rookie Tyrone (Glenn Plummer), also an outcast, and begins to refine the kid's raw pitching talent by teaching him everything he knows.

With a fond, rueful tone, pic renders the realities of minor league life: sparse attendance at games, a nervous owner (Jeffrey Tambor) who considers the team a financial liability, transportation so rickety that when the bus breaks down the players have to push it through the night.

Meanwhile, the kindly coach (Noble Willingham) is under pressure from the owner to sack Bream for being too old. When Bream flubs a big game, the ax comes down, and the devoted ballplayer is grief-stricken. Some good emotional suspense is developed around his firing and his reaction.

Pic's poignant ending is too easy and too sentimental. Story seems to end before it developed; the central relationship between Bream and Tyrone is set up but never really tested.

Tyrone, pushed toward submissiveness by first-time helmer Robin Armstrong, functions merely as receiver for Bream's kindness and wisdom. Pairing has neither conflict nor complexity.

Likewise, Dierdre O'Connell brings attractive qualities to the sympathetic barmaid, but the role is too one-note to add much dimension. The romantic relationship ends before it has begun.

It's left mostly to the Bream character to carry the pic, and he certainly comes across as the inspirational type. Having had just one three-week stint in the "bigs," a "cup of coffee" in baseball terms, he nonetheless retains his sunny attitude and generous spirit, sticking close to the game and devoting himself to cheering and helping others.

In a finely honed, sympathetic performance, Russ comes across as a genuine, affirmative man and keeps pic in balance by never playing to its sentimentality.

Armstong, who with partner Eric Tynan Young raised money for this pic from private investors, directs carefully and resourcefully but sometimes too sincerely. One scene, in which the good-looking Bream goes through elaborate contortions of shyness before asking a barmaid for a date, is played for laughs but strains credibility.

"Coffee" is attractively lensed and features cameos by former ballplayers Ernie Banks, Don Newcombe and Duke Snider. Music by Lee Holdridge is a bit too heavy on sentimentality in a film in which that element really needs no underscoring. — *Daws.*

NEW JACK CITY

A Warner Bros. presentation of a Jackson/McHenry production. Produced by Doug McHenry and George Jackson. Directed by Mario Van Peebles. Screenplay, Thomas Lee Wright, Barry Michael Cooper, based on a story by Wright; camera, Francis Kenny; editor, Steven Kemper; music, Michel Colombier; sound, Frank Stetner; production design, Charles C. Bennett; costume design, Bernard Johnson; associate producer, Fab Five Freddie; coproducer, Preston L. Holmes. Reviewed at Sundance Film Festival, Park City, Utah, Jan. 26, 1991. MPAA rating: R. Running time: **97 MIN.**
Nino Brown . . . . Wesley Snipes
Scotty Appleton . . . . Ice-T
Det. Stone . . . . . Mario Van Peebles
Gee Money . . . . Allen Payne
Nick Peretti . . . . Judd Nelson
Pookie . . . . Chris Rock

Filmmakers Mario Van Peebles and producers Doug McHenry and George Jackson pull off a provocative, pulsating update on gangster pics with this action-laden epic about the rise and fall of an inner city crack dealer. Powerful antidrug sen-

timent will pack a punch with urban audiences, making "New Jack City" a strong bet as a longterm moneymaker.

Producers say they slotted in the pic at the Sundance fest as a last-minute "special preview" to stimulate dialog about drug issues before its March release.

The film ventures controversial opinions about the drug problem, including the idea that drug laws have created modern-day gangsterism just as anti-liquor laws created violence and mayhem during Prohibition.

Strongest element is the anger and disgust directed squarely at drug dealers. Pic doesn't really have answers to the drug quagmire, but it's powerful enough to be a cultural bellwether signaling the time for change.

Drawn from articles about real drug kingpins in California magazine and the Wall Street Journal, pic presents the fictional story of Nino Brown (Wesley Snipes), who in 1986 foresees the potential of crack and by 1989 has built an empire around it.

Term "new jack" was coined by journalist Barry Michael Cooper, pic's co-writer, to describe modern urban street life.

Nino's success exposes him to heat from both the better-established Italian mob, which wants a cut of the action and is offended by his attitude, and his own community, where too many people have suffered crack's effects.

After Nino takes over an apartment building, brutally ejecting the tenants, police detective Stone (played by the director) recruits undercover cops Scotty (rap artist Ice-T) and Peretti (Judd Nelson) to bring him in.

Pookie (Chris Rock), a wretched young street hustler addicted to crack, is rehabilitated and sent in to infiltrate and collect evidence. But Pookie winds up succumbing to the drug, and when the operation is blown, Stone's team is forced to start over with bolder methods.

It's clear from the start the filmmakers are out to blow audiences away with pic's jacked-up, hyperactive pace. Camera style is restless and aggressive. Audacious opening seg (a foot and bicycle chase over a perilous city obstacle course) sets the tone for a blood-pumping actioner.

Moreover, the ambitious Van Peebles can't resist a few "Godfather"-style hits with mobs clashing in a spray of machine-gun fire and spurting blood. This is obviously not a tale with the richness and sweep of a Coppola

epic; its tone is more appropriate to the "new jack" culture from which it sprang. This is a commercial achievement, not an artistic one, with a mishmash of borrowed styles substituting for a signature vision.

Problems of narrative flow mar the second half, with events jumping around without setup. Nonetheless, pic, filmed on location mostly in Harlem and the Bronx for $8.5 million, has a seat-of-the-pants energy guaranteed to sweep its target audience along.

Snipes ("Mo' Better Blues") is commanding as the megalomaniacal Nino, adding interesting dimension to a standard villain. Ice-T carries the role of the avenging cop with no trouble, and casting the ex-gang member and influential rap artist will help carry the pic's message.

"New Jack" soundtrack is particularly strong, with music of Ice-T, 2 Live Crew, Troop and Levert, and Color Me Bad, among others, woven in artfully with live performances. Producers McHenry and Jackson, veterans of countless network tv, film and musicvideo projects, worked with Warner Bros. music chief Irving Azoff to compile the sounds.

— *Daws.*

IRON MAZE
(U.S.-JAPANESE)

An Edward R. Pressman and Oliver Stone presentation of a Trans-Tokyo production. Produced by Ilona Herzberg, Hidenori Ueki. Executive producers, Stone, Pressman. Co-executive producers, Hidenori Taga, Katsumi Kimura. Directed by Hiroaki Yoshida. Screenplay, Tim Metcalfe; screen story, Yoshida, Metcalfe, based on the short story "In The Grove" by Ryunosuke Akutagawa; camera (CFI color), Morio Saegusa; editor, Bonnie Koehler; music, Stanley Myers; sound (Dolby), Stephen Halbert; production design, Toby Corbett; art direction, Gary Kosko; set decoration, Diana Stoughton; costume design, Susie DeSanto; associate producers, Janet Yang, Taiichi Inoue; assistant director, Terence J. Edwards; 2d unit director, Dan Bradley; 2d unit camera, Peter Lyons Collister; casting, Elisabeth Leustig. Reviewed at Sundance Film Festival, Park City, Utah, Jan. 22, 1991. No MPAA rating. Running time: **104 MIN.**
Barry . . . . Jeff Fahey
Chris . . . . Bridget Fonda
Sugita . . . . Hiroaki Murakami
Jack Ruhle . . . . J.T. Walsh
Mikey . . . . Gabriel Damon
Mayor Peluso . . . . . . John Randolph
Eddie . . . . Peter Allas

A provocative notion has been tiresomely elaborated in "Iron Maze," a contemporary retelling of the "Rashomon" story in which misunderstandings between Japanese and

Americans are meant to compound the tale's inherent mysteries and ambiguities. This Japanese-U.S. coproduction will face an uphill struggle commercially.

With his odd new film, backed by Oliver Stone and Edward R. Pressman but as yet without a domestic distrib, long-time commercials director Hiroaki Yoshida has ambitiously tackled the intercultural suspicions and resentments inevitable when Japanese businessmen invade U.S. soil. Unfortunately, in failing to bring the characters to convincing life, Yoshida ("Twilight Of The Cockroaches") has done little to elucidate the situation.

Ryunosuke Akutagawa's 1927 short story "In The Grove" inspired Akira Kurosawa's celebrated 1950 drama "Rashomon," the title of which has virtually entered the English language as a way of indicating that there can be as many versions of a story or incident as there were witnesses to it.

And so it is here, as Sugita (Hiroaki Murakami), the son of a Japanese billionaire, is critically wounded in an abandoned steel mill he has just bought in a depressed Pennsylvania town.

At first, it appears to be an open-and-shut case, as longhaired biker Barry (Jeff Fahey) turns himself in to police chief Jack Ruhle (J.T. Walsh) and declares he killed the foreigner in self-defense. Although Sugita is not dead, intent and deed were the same, and the cop begins talking to others involved.

The local mayor (John Randolph) fills in much of the background. In flashbacks, Sugita is shown arriving in the once-thriving, Pittsburgh vicinity town, flaunting his Mercedes, trendy clothes and flashy blonde wife Chris (Bridget Fonda). He announced he intended to build a state-of-the-art amusement park on the site of the old mill.

Through the prisms afforded by Barry, Chris and, finally, Sugita himself, one is given different versions of events leading up to the bloody fight between the two men at the dilapidated mill.

Perhaps Barry, a former steelworker unhappily working as a bellhop, raped Chris, or perhaps she shamelessly came on to him. Possibly Barry clobbered Sugita over the head with a heavy pipe, or it could have been Chris trying to cause her husband's death. Or maybe it was all an accident.

Theoretically and thematically, the mix of this story with such a setting and set of characters would seem to offer multiple reverberations. Despite a solid cast, however, the characters' true natures and motivations remain remote and unknown, and the repetition of their actions wearing.

Tim Metcalfe's screenplay provides too little information about his subjects and in particular delivers no good scenes between the moody Japanese businessman and his feisty gaijin wife, which leaves Murakami and Fonda striking attitudes rather than fleshing out characters.

As the shifty malcontent, Fahey has a bit more to work with and manages to engage interest, if not sympathy, via an energetic portrayal. Walsh does a good job as the probing police officer, although his investigative techniques seem eccentric at best.

Lenser Morio Saegusa has cast a bluish haze over the proceedings, which unfold partly in an impressive rundown factory and on the decaying streets of Braddock, Pa.

Toby Corbett's production design and Stanley Myers' score help with what impact the film has, but story remains too distant and uninvolving to stir up much audience interest. — *Cart.*

LITTLE NOISES

A Monument Pictures production. Produced by Michael Spielberg, Brad Gilbert. Directed by Jane Spencer. Screenplay, Spencer, Jon Zeiderman; camera (color), Makoto Watanabe; editor, Ernie Fritz, music, Kurt Hoffman, Fritz van Orden; sound, Mathew Price; production design, Charles Lagola. Reviewed at Sundance Film Festival, Park City, Utah, Jan. 19, 1991. No MPAA rating. Running time: **110 MIN.**

Joey	Crispin Glover
Timmy	Steven Schub
Stella	Tatum O'Neal
Mathias	Rik Mayall
Stu	John McGinley
Elliott	Tate Donovan
Dolores	Nina Siemaszko
Marty	Matthew Hutton

The dysfunctional characters in "Little Noises," first-time director/co-writer Jane Spencer's poignant look at modern failure, are not making noises loud, clear or appealing enough to hold audiences. B.o. for Monument's first production is bound to be muted.

Spencer displays the kind of unabashed individuality and rueful comic sense that spawn pics like "Harold And Maude," but she also ignores audience needs for plot, pacing and sympathetic connection.

It's hard to tell whether this pic would have benefited from a more rigorous development process or collapsed under it. Nonetheless, product is just not as far along as it needs to be.

Crispin Glover plays a self-deluded shambles of a young writer who's never actually turned out a single page. His attention is sought by the only person more pathetic than him, an orphaned mute (Matthew Hutton, who is deaf), who happens to have a gift for poetry everyone ignores.

Glover ends up with Hutton's neatly typed poems and, desperate for cash and newly homeless, presents them to a prissy literary agent (Rik Mayall) as his own. Talent scout's belief that the stumbling Glover did the work is not nearly as amazing as his doling out of an advance as if poetry were the next best thing to legal tender.

Glover's life changes. He adopts a new sartorial style and finds new company while poor Hutton's fortunes wither. He finds the real poet homeless and has to confront his misdeed.

The story develops too late, after endless mucking around in Glover's purposeless life. Tackling tough territory, Spencer built her film around a character whose energy level is akin to a sinkhole. Her sensibilities at this point are neither funny nor dark enough to make it work. A streak of Tennessee Williams' romanticism runs through the whole affair, adding some poignance but further blurring the focus.

"Noises" displays strong detail, including lovely work with actors, but the big picture is weak. Scenes involving Hutton's brother and his thug friends trying to pull off a dangerous deal are badly lacking in verisimilitude, suggesting limited experience of the young helmer.

Glover, playing yet another weirdo, seems to get far more screen time than his simple character requires. Still, he makes good use of it in what is probably his best role since "River's Edge." Newcomer Steven Schub comes across exceptionally well as Glover's pathetic and aggressively annoying actor friend.

Tatum O'Neal, looking bony and sharp-faced, appears as a playwright friend of Glover's who's a good deal more together than he is. The role offers little to play, but she brings an interesting intensity to it.

Attractively lensed in New York, pic boasts a score exceptionally well matched to the emotional tenor of the piece and is probably the strongest presence in the film. Titles are also classy. — *Daws.*

STRAIGHT OUT OF BROOKLYN

An American Playhouse Theatrical Films presentation of a Blacks N' Progress production. Executive producers, Lindsay Law, Ira Deutchman. Written, produced and directed by Matty Rich. Camera (color), John Rosnell; editor, Jack Haigis; music, Harold Wheeler; sound, Donna Farnum, William Kozy; associate producer, Allen Black; casting, Dorise Black, Shirley Matthews. Reviewed at Sundance Film Festival, Park City, Utah, Jan. 21, 1991. No MPAA rating. Running time: **91 MIN.**

Ray Brown	George T. Odom
Frankie Brown	Ann D. Sanders
Dennis Brown	Lawrence Gilliard Jr.
Carolyn Brown	Barbara Sanon
Shirley	Reana Drummond
Larry	Matty Rich
Kevin	Mark Malone

Nineteen-year-old Matty Rich had the gumption to finance and produce his first film at the tender age of 19, but "Straight Out Of Brooklyn" is rudimentary in every way, from writing to acting to camerawork, and covers all-too-familiar ground with no particular flair.

This harsh, straightforward look at the causes of despair in Brooklyn's Red Hook housing projects is unlikely to hold audiences outside the nurturing atmosphere of festivals. (Pic was partially funded by American Playhouse Theatrical Films.)

Based on Rich's own experiences, "Brooklyn" describes a black family caught in a cycle of futility. The father (George T. Odom) blames white society for his dead-end job in a gas station and takes out his frustration by beating the mother and making the children miserable.

The mother (Ann D. Sanders) accepts the abuse, while teenage son Dennis (Lawrence Gilliard Jr.) plots to get the family out of this rut by pulling off a robbery.

Despite the pleadings of his g.f. (Reana Drummond) who tells him it takes time to earn a better life, Dennis and his friends (played by the filmmaker and Mark Malone) go ahead with a ludicrously boneheaded heist. The family suffers the predictably tragic consequences.

Much of the film is shot in the tight quarters of a drab, subsidized apartment, with the camera usually maintaining one vantage point during a scene. Actors are directed to shout at each other, as if anger can be expressed only in the volume of one's voice. Poor sound mix makes this approach no more bearable.

A production as no-frills as this one needed a script with some subtext or cleverness to hold interest, but pic is relentlessly blunt and repetitive. Talk-heavy scenes go on long after the point has been grasped. Screentime would have been better spent developing the characters, who come off as types rather than individuals, especially the stubborn son.

Perhaps the rawness of the situation presented will hold some power for viewers who have not been previously exposed to it, but it seems to have been covered repeatedly in pics or tv shows.

Rich, showing a sense of humor now and then, pulls off a funny, energetic scene in a grocery store in which the two pals are accused of flirting with someone else's girl. But the tone seems copied from Spike Lee pics, and the fast-talking, goofball character Rich portrays in "Brooklyn" is too reminiscent of the sad sacks Lee plays.

Rich displays traditional dramatic sensibilities that probably will grow more interesting with time and experience. Meanwhile, pic is more notable for its origins than its content.

Despite the budget constraints, film includes some nice aerial pans on the housing projects. Harold Wheeler's traditional score contributes some unearned sentimentality. — *Daws.*

WHORE

A Trimark Pictures release of a Trimark-Ronaldo Vasconcellos-Dan Ireland production. Produced by Ireland, Vasconcellos. Executive producer, Mark Amin. Line producer, Michael D. Pariser. Directed by Ken Russell. Screenplay, Russell, Deborah Dalton, based on the play "Bondage" by David Hines; camera (CFI color), Amir Mokri; editor, Brian Tagg; music, Michael Gibbs; sound (Dolby), Tom Brandau; production design, Richard Lewis; art direction, Naomi Shohan; set decoration, Amy Wells; costume design, Leonard Pollack; assistant directors, Aaron Barsky, Deborah A. Dell'Amico; casting, Linda Francis. Reviewed at Sundance Film Festival, Park City, Utah, Jan. 24, 1991. Running time: **84 MIN.**

Liz . . . . Theresa Russell
Blake . . . . Benjamin Mouton
Rasta . . . . Antonio Fargas
Indian . . . . Sanjay
Katie . . . . Elizabeth Morehead
First man . . . . . . Michael Crabtree
Derelict . . . . John Diehl
    Also with: Robert O'Reilly, Charles McCaulay, Jason Kristofer, Jack Nance, Frank Smith, Jason Saucier.

Given the infinite possibilities afforded by the subject matter, "Whore" features little of the kinkiness and bravura stylistics one normally expects from director Ken Russell, and no compensating psychological or documentary insight into the lead character or her lifestyle.

It looks like a quickie theatrically for this Trimark release, although video prospects could be good.

What promised on paper to be a hot companion piece to Ken Russell's provocative 1984 sex opus, "Crimes Of Passion," has instead turned out as a cartoonish look at the life of a hooker.

Project is based on a British play by David Hines, a London cabbie who nightly picked up prostitutes in Kings Cross and began writing down stories they told him about their work.

Due to financing requirements, Russell and co-scenarist Deborah Dalton have shifted the setting to Los Angeles, where the consummately vulgar Liz, played by Theresa Russell, plies her trade on thinly populated downtown streets.

Liz never meets Richard Gere, but instead takes on a sordid assortment of predatory and aggressive men in cars. Her companions are not so much sisters on the pavement as an odd collection of derelicts and street people who represent a mild freak show rather than an interesting cross-section of society's rejects.

Taking a cue from the play, Liz, from the outset, addresses the camera directly, offering a running commentary on her complaints and providing a springboard for her to ruminate about her past. Flashbacks make up a substantial portion of the brief running time, as Liz covers her initial tricks, hook-up with her pimp and sometime boyfriend, Blake (Benjamin Mouton), and failed marriage and hopeless stint as a mother.

Overriding problem is a pervasive feeling of utter inauthenticity. Hines' play was already a second-hand account of a way of life, and version here is one step removed from that. Perhaps if it had been filmed in London, "Whore" might have retained a sense of documentary realism, but the characters all seem false, disconnected from any time and place.

Liz's thin, vicious white pimp feels like a specifically British conception, and two other characters who drop in and out, Antonio Fargas' Rasta and Sanjay's Indian, look like they've come from another planet. To make claims for the universality of a hooker's life is not enough, as the basics of her day-to-day existence should be believable in a way that they are not here.

Actress Russell's strident, stops-out performance sets the tone for the entire picture. She's is all over the place, occasionally hitting a responsive note but more often flailing about in an unrestricted manner more grating than illuminating. Remainder of the cast makes little impression.

Director Russell, on the other hand, is in restrained form, offering negligible treats in both the stylistic and sexual areas. Sex scenes are emphatically unerotic and mostly perfunctory, befitting the subject, but display none of the outrageous imagination Russell has brought to bear on the innumerable such encounters he has created over the years.

Director puts in an unbilled cameo appearance as a waiter in a snooty restaurant and, with moustache and clipped hair, appears to be doing a sly impersonation of Laurence Olivier.

Pic is framed by hilarious reggae song called "I Want To Bang Her," and film has a certain spunkiness that keeps it moving briskly along. But as any kind of serious examination of the life of a sex-for-hire woman, this pales alongside something like Tony Garnett's powerful, neglected 1980 feature, "Prostitute."
— *Cart.*

THE SILENCE OF THE LAMBS

An Orion release of a Strong Heart/Demme production. Produced by Edward Saxon, Kenneth Utt, Ron Bozman. Executive producer, Gary Goetzman. Directed by Jonathan Demme. Screenplay, Ted Tally, based on the novel by Thomas Harris; camera (Technicolor; Deluxe prints), Tak Fujimoto; editor, Craig McKay; music, Howard Shore; sound (Dolby), Christopher Newman; production design, Kristi Zea; costume design, Colleen Atwood; art direction, Tim Galvin; set decoration, Karen O'Hara; sound design, Skip Lievsay; associate producer, Grace Blake; assistant director, Bozman; casting, Howard Feuer. Reviewed at the Century Plaza Cinema, L.A., Feb. 2, 1991. MPAA Rating: R. Running time: **118 MIN.**

Clarice Starling . . . . . Jodie Foster
Dr. Hannibal Lecter . Anthony Hopkins
Jack Crawford . . . . . . Scott Glenn
Jame Gumb . . . . Ted Levine
Dr. Frederick Chilton . Anthony Heald
Catherine Martin . . . . Brooke Smith
Senator Ruth Martin . . Diane Baker
Ardelia Mapp . . . . . Kasi Lemmons
    Also with: Charles Napier, Roger Corman, George A. Romero.

All creative hands are at the top of their form in "The Silence Of The Lambs," a mesmerizing thriller that will grip audiences from first scene to last and generate solid b.o.

Skillful adaptation of Thomas Harris' bestseller intelligently wallows in the fascination for aberrant psychology and perverse evil, delivering the goods in a way that should electrify critics and mainstream audiences.

The specifics of the murder case in question here — a serial killer who partially skins his female victims — are certainly gruesome, but are handled to generate maximum suspense without descending into the exploitative.

Thoughtful and not debasing, pic takes a compelling, upfront look at sociopathic behavior and government attempts, with varying success, to keep it in check.

Faithfully following the essentials of Harris' book, playwright Ted Tally's sharp script charts tenacious efforts of young FBI recruit Clarice Starling (Jodie Foster) to cope with the appalling challenges of her first case.

Confounded by a series of grotesque murders committed by someone known only as "Buffalo Bill," bureau special agent Jack Crawford (Scott Glenn) asks his female protégé to seek the help of the American prison system's No. 1 resident monster in fashioning a psychological profile of the killer.

Dr. Hannibal Lecter (Anthony Hopkins) is commonly known as "Hannibal the Cannibal" for the antisocial dining habits he took up upon abandoning his career as a brilliant psychiatrist to pursue his calling as a homicidal maniac.

Astonishingly insightful and brutally frank, Lecter has been kept in a dungeon-like cell for eight years, and while officious doctors and investigators can get nothing out of him, he is willing to play ball with his attractive new inquisitor.

On a quid pro quo basis, Lecter gives Starling clues as to the killer's identity in exchange for details about her past. Even though Lecter is known as an ingenious manipulator and Starling has been warned against getting personal with him, she must proceed, especially after the daughter of a U.S. senator becomes Buffalo Bill's latest captive.

Just as it seems the noose is tightening around the killer, Lecter, in an remarkably fine suspense sequence, manages an unthinkable escape. The FBI and, on her own, Starling must use all the info and guts they have to finally corner Buffalo Bill. But then, there is Lecter.

Harris' plot is as tight as a coiled rattler, and it has motivated Jonathan Demme to turn out his leanest, meanest work. Abandoning the colorful frills and offbeat mixed moods of "Something Wild" and "Married To The Mob," this always interesting director has devoted himself to relentless storytelling.

There is not a false note nor an extraneous moment as he establishes a vise-like hold almost immediately and doesn't let up even through the chilling final shot. In the second half of "Something Wild," Demme demonstrated a marked talent for rough suspense, something he sustains for two hours here.

At the outset, Demme and his longtime ace lenser, Tak Fujimoto, plunge the viewer directly into the p.o.v. of the novice investigator Starling, as she goes face to face with the diabolical Lecter and, as suggested by the title, is forced to confront her own childhood demons relating to the slaughter of animals. Film is omniscient, however, showing the activities of Buffalo Bill as well as those of Lecter later on.

In a strong performance, Foster fully registers the inner strength her character must summon up to meet the challenges and occasional humiliations her tough assignment entails.

Cast against type as a reserved man in glasses and a suit, Scott Glenn is a very agreeable surprise as the FBI agent who takes a chance by putting his young charge on the case.

The juiciest part is Hopkins,' and he makes the most of it. Helped by some highly dramatic lighting, actor makes the role the personification of brilliant, hypnotic evil, and the screen jolts with electricity whenever he is on. This is, without doubt, his most effective film appearance to date.

From the huge hall in which Lecter is eerily caged at one point to the dingy rooms of Buffalo Bill's house, Kristi Zea's production design is critical to the picture's mood. Editor Craig McKay keeps doesn't let a frame stay on too long, and Howard Shore's rather traditional score outstandingly amplifies the tension and psychological mystery.
— *Cart.*

L.A. STORY

A Tri-Star release from Carolco of a Mario Kassar presentation of a Daniel Melnick/Indieprod/L.A. Films production. Produced by Melnick, Michael Rachmil. Executive producers, Kassar, Steve Martin. Directed by Mick Jackson. Screenplay, Martin; camera (Technicolor), Andrew Dunn; editor, Richard A. Harris; music, Peter Melnick; sound (Dolby), Jim Webb; production design, Lawrence Miller; art direction, Charles Breen; set decoration, Chris Butler; costume design, Rudy Dillon; assistant director, Albert Shapiro; casting, Mindy Marin. Reviewed at the AMC Century 14 Theater, L.A., Feb. 5, 1991. MPAA Rating: PG-13. Running time: **95 MIN.**
Harris K. Telemacher . . Steve Martin
Sara McDowel . . . . Victoria Tennant
Roland Mackey . . . Richard E. Grant
Trudi . . . . Marilu Henner
SanDeE* . . . . . Sarah Jessica Parker
Ariel . . . . Susan Forristal
Frank Swan . . . . Kevin Pollak
Morris Frost . . . . . . Sam McMurray

Goofy and sweet, "L.A. Story" constitutes Steve Martin's satiric valentine to his hometown and a pretty funny comedy in the bargain. Even if as many gags miss their marks as hit, the amusement quotient reaches a pleasing level through accretion, and good b.o. should be the reward.

In his first screenplay since his Cyrano De Bergerac takeoff, "Roxanne," Martin displays the same penchant for mixing his patented wild and crazy zaniness with delirious, weak-in-the-knees romanticism.

He is still far from creating a credible narrative (his fertile imagination takes him in too many other directions), but this film touches home base with its social and sexual ribbing more often than most of his previous pics.

Although he doesn't play it with an arrow through his head, Martin is in typically nutty form as an L.A. tv meteorologist who doesn't hesitate to take the weekends off since the weather isn't bound to change.

What he can't predict, however, is the lightning bolt that hits him in the form of Brit journalist Victoria Tennant, who arrives on assignment to dish up the latest English assessment of America's new melting pot.

Martin's relationship with his snooty longtime g.f. Marilu Henner is essentially over and, convinced that nothing can ever happen with his dreamgirl, he stumblingly takes up with ditzy shopgirl Sarah Jessica Parker.

But, all the while, he receives odd, somewhat inscrutable messages on an electronic freeway sign about how the weather is going to change his life, little hints that something big is around the corner.

Even after Martin and Tennant have gotten together and he has declared the grandest of romantic intentions, the future looks impossible, as she has promised her ex, Richard E. Grant, to attempt a reconciliation.

In the film's extended comic highlight, the two reluctant couples, Martin/Parker and Grant/Tennant, separately check in for romantic weekends at a luxury Santa Barbara hotel and are coincidentally booked into adjacent rooms.

Martin's winning optimism carries the day both for his character and the film as a whole, although British director Mick Jackson stacks the odds against it for awhile. Even in this musicvideo age, seldom has the bigscreen had such an example of strenuous, needless and quickly unbearable overcutting as is on display through roughly the first third of "L.A. Story."

Jackson and editor Richard A. Harris clutter things up with far more shots than necessary, as if in mortal fear of leaving any image onscreen for more than five seconds. Maddening style, which turns editing into dicing, doesn't give the film a chance to breathe, or the viewer an opportunity to settle in comfortably with the characters.

Fortunately, situation im-

proves somewhat as the film progresses, although on his next pic Jackson should be denied use of a crane, which he employs here to wearying extent. He might also dispense with such lamentable ideas as taking one shot at the Hard Rock Cafe from the p.o.v. of a plate of food.

Still, despite the frantic style, the feeling behind Martin's view of life and love in L.A. comes through, helped by the eerie, quasimystical interludes with the freeway sign, as well as the seductively adoring treatment of Tennant, actually Martin's wife.

Star-scripter's rampant affection for women in all their guises is slobberingly apparent and infectious, and the actresses all come off well.

Henner gamely trots out all the mannerisms of a self-centered princess, while Parker proves a scene-stealer as a New Age bimbo, a constantly twirling top whose idea of a perfect date is a joint visit to a colonic center.

Tennant is completely captivating as the daffy Englishwoman who lights up Martin's life even more than the incessant sun. If anything, Martin the writer has somewhat slighted Martin the actor. Much of the time, he is simply a blubbering fool, not knowing what to do and issuing no recognizable reaction even upon being fired from his job. Character is little but an irrepressible, romance-sick vessel waiting to be filled.

Audiences ready to indulge in the national pastime of laughing at L.A.'s peculiarities will find plenty to provoke them here.

Martin constructs the ultimate trendy restaurant nightmare, in which a prospective customer must have his entire financial background investigated before getting a reservation and still then only at 5:30 or after 10. Here, even Chevy Chase, in a cameo, is banished to Siberia.

Good sex jokes abound, and another scene amusingly sets up a system of ritual robbery at an automatic bank teller. On the other hand, a sequence featuring random freeway shootings is utterly tasteless and unfunny.

Grant is right on the money as Tennant's still-flaming former mate, and vast array of bit players make amusing impressions from beginning to end. — *Cart.*

SIRI MEDURA
(THE MANSION)
(SRI LANKAN)

A Thamara Films production. Produced by Randule Gunawaeadana. Directed by Parakrama Niriella. Screenplay, Niriella, Saimon Newagaththegama; camera (color), Andrew Jayamanne; editor, Stanley Alwis; music, Presmasiri Khemadasa; sound, Lionel Gunaratne. Reviewed at Indian Film Festival, Madras, Jan. 11, 1991. Running time: **165 MIN.**
Nirmala . . . . Melanie Fonseka
Leela . . . . Anoja Weerasinghe
Cyril . . . . . . Ravindra Randeniya
Sampath . . . . Lake Das

Winner of both best film and best director prizes at last year's Sri Lankan awards, and seen in Europe at the Nantes film fest, "The Mansion" is an intriguing psychological melodrama burdened by excessive running time.

The simple plot revolves around sexual jealousy. Newlyweds Nirmala and Cyril move into the plush home of Cyril's brother, Sampath, who is hospitalized with severe injuries suffered in a car accident. When he returns, unable even to speak, Nirmala realizes he has been involved in an affair with Leela, his attractive servant and that, despite Sampath's incapacity, the affair is continuing.

At first outraged, then fiercely jealous, Nirmala gradually worms her way into her brother-in-law's affections, and takes Leela's place, whereupon the jealous Leela kills both her lover and Nirmala.

Padding out the story is a subplot involving Cyril's work as a lawyer involved in the union movement, but this aspect of the film remains unresolved. Co-scripter/director Parakrama Niriella is good with understated scenes of sexual tension. He gets solid performances from his cast, but he unfolds the narrative far too slowly for Western tastes. Production is, in every other respect, good.

Of interest to film buffs is the appearance of Anoja Weerasinghe, one of the stars of Paul Cox' "Island," as the passionate Leela. — *Strat.*

SLEEPING WITH THE ENEMY

A 20th Century Fox release. Produced by Leonard Goldberg. Executive producer, Jeffrey Chernov. Directed by Joseph Ruben. Screenplay, Ronald Bass, based on the novel by Nancy Price; camera, John W. Lindley; editor, George Bowers; music, Jerry Goldsmith; sound, Susumu Tokunow; production design, Doug Kraner; costume design, Richard Hornung; art direction, Joseph P. Lucky; set design, Stan Tropp; set decoration, Lee Poll; associate producers, C. Tad Devlin, Michael E. Steele; assistant director, Steele; casting, Karen Rea. Reviewed at Avco Cinema, L.A., Calif., Jan. 31, 1991. MPAA Rating: R. Running time: **98 MIN.**
Sara/Laura . . . . Julia Roberts
Martin . . . . Patrick Bergin
Ben . . . . Kevin Anderson
Chloe . . . . Elizabeth Lawrence
Also with: Kyle Secor, Claudette Nevins, Tony Abatemarco, Marita Geraghty, Harley Venton, Nancy Fish.

In "Sleeping With The Enemy," a chilling look at marital abuse gives way to a streamlined thriller delivering muchosympathy for imperiled heroine Julia Roberts and screams aplenty as she's stalked by her maniacal husband. Pic's likely to extend Fox' winning streak with a b.o. bull's-eye.

Less about social and marital issues than about chills and suspense, pic takes off from an interesting premise: A young woman is so desperate to escape her monstrous husband that she fakes her own death and strikes out anew.

In a lushly photographed beachside dreamscape, Laura (Roberts) appears to be a perfect doll wife dwelling in an isolated Cape Cod beach manse with successful financial consultant Martin (Patrick Bergin). In fact, he's an overbearing control freak who demands perfection and directs her every move, subjecting her to physical and emotional abuse at will.

Though she appears to be submissive, she's actually been plotting her escape for a long time. One night she gets her chance, slipping off a sailboat during a storm and swimming ashore while her husband believes she's drowned.

Certain lapses in logic fray the edges of this otherwise well-constructed tale: How did she know weather would be rough that night (the boat's skipper didn't)? Why did no one think it odd that her body doesn't wash up on the beach?

These quibbles are likely to be swept aside by audiences in a tide of sympathy for the fragile but determined Roberts as she sets out very much alone to save herself, leaving no trail.

But Martin comes up with enough peculiar clues to believe he's been had. Soon after Laura, who's renamed herself Sara Waters, is ensconced in an idyllic Iowa college town and forging a friendship with a sweet-natured drama teacher (Kevin Anderson), the menacing Martin is on the trail.

Director Joseph Ruben ("True Believer," "The Stepfather") creates an aura of true terror around Martin's hunt for Laura and, using fright-film techniques of suspense and payoff, will have audiences squirming in their seats.

Ironically, it's Laura's poor, blind, stroke-ridden mother (Elizabeth Lawrence) who points Martin toward her door, and once there he indulges in some unique forms of fetishistic terrorism.

So solidly is audience sympathy pitched with Laura that the ending will not even be controversial, shaping up as simply a defiant outcry against oppression, with feminist undertones.

Ruben dwells on the wedding ring as the final image, but it hasn't much resonance. This pic early on traded off any real male/female issues for the rewards of a solid, black & white thriller.

Roberts is terrific in a layered part in which she must act one role to survive her marriage, another to preserve her cover in her new life and another to convey her real self to the audience. The fear, vulnerability and fragile determination she registers so clearly on screen, along with her radiance, will have much to do with the audience's total immersion in her peril.

Anderson brings an edge to the nice-guy-next-door role, and the dark, dashing Bergin is chillingly twisted. Ron Bass' script is taut, down to the choice last line of dialog.

Considering its impact, pic is remarkably streamlined, involving only three main characters and a few major locations. A few parade and carnival sequences involving countless extras pad it out.

The beach at Wilmington, N.C., stood in for the New England coast, and Abbeville, S.C., supplied the Midwestern Americana setting of Sara's new home.

Production designer Doug Kraner and cinematographer Doug Lindley achieve a sharply etched sense of Martin's icy mindset in the granite, glass and water motifs of the beach house, and Jerry Goldsmith's score is particularly effective. — *Daws.*

THE LAST BUTTERFLY
(FRENCH-CZECHOSLOVAKIAN)

A Cine Classic release (in France) of a Cinema et Communication (Paris)-Studio Barrandov (Prague) co-production in association with HTV, CTE and Filmexport. Executive producers, Boudjemaa Dahmane, Jacques Methe, Patrick Dromgoole. Produced by Steven North. Directed by Karel Kachyna. Screenplay, Ota Hofman, Kachyna, from the novel by Michael Jacot; camera (color), Jiri Krejcik; editor, Jiri Brozek; music, Alex North; additional music, Milan Svoboda; sound, Jiri Moudry; production design, Zbynek Hloch; costumes, Ester Krumbachova; choreography, Radomil Cech; production manager, Jean-Pierre Fayer; assistant director, Milos Kohout. Reviewed at Intl. Film Festival of India, Madras, Jan. 10, 1991. Running time: **109 MIN.**
Antoine Moreau . . . . Tom Courtenay
Véra . . . . Brigitte Fossey
Karl Rheinberg . . . . . Freddie Jones
Michelle . . . . Ingrid Held
Stella . . . . Linda Jablonska
Stadler . . . . .Josef Kemr
Gruber . . . . Milan Knazko
Laub . . . . Lubek Kopriva
Samuel . . . . Daniel Margolius
(English soundtrack)

Despite a sterling performance from Tom Courtenay in the lead, "The Last Butterfly" adds nothing new to the territory it covers. The Franco-Czech pic made in English suffers from a blandness often resulting from awkward international productions. Boxoffice prospects aren't great.

Czech director Karel Kachyna, whose long-banned "The Ear" proved a highlight of last year's Cannes Film Festival, set his new pic in occupied France during World War II. Courtenay plays a famous mime artist reduced to alcoholism and playing the fool to German audiences in a nightclub.

His relationship with a pretty dancer (Ingrid Held) is strained because he suspects her of having an affair with someone else. Actually, she's an active member of the resistance.

When the Gestapo bursts into their apartment, Held is killed and Courtenay arrested. Recognized by the officer in charge, he's offered his freedom if he will go to Terezin, the town set aside by German authorities for Jews, and perform for the children there. The Intl. Red Cross is to visit the town and the German authorities want to put on a good front.

In Terezin, Courtenay befriends a schoolteacher (Brigitte Fossey) and a couple of moppets. Though his act is usually a solo one, he agrees to let the small fry join him onstage. Appalled by the cynicism of the Nazis, who, he discovers, plan to ship the inhabitants of Terezin off to concentration camps as soon as the Red Cross visit is over, he puts on an elaborate mime production of "Hansel And Gretel" in which the classic fairy tale becomes a parable for the extermination of the Jews.

Mime sequence, inventively conceived and beautifully executed, is the high point in an otherwise disappointingly conventional film, which adds nothing new to the Holocaust pic genre.

Part of the problem is the lack of conviction stemming from the English soundtrack and the uncomfortable dubbing of the Czech actors. No performance is inspired, though Courtenay tries hard. His relationship with Fossey, an actress who usually gives reliably good perfs, is sterile and lacks sparks.

Technically, the pic (shot in the Barrandov studios in Prague late last year when the "velvet" revolution against the Communist regime was taking place) is fine, and producer Steven North's father, Alex North, provides a solid music score. But b.o. prospects are doubtful for a basically familiar effort. — *Strat.*

KICKBOXER 2: THE ROAD BACK

An Entertainment Film Distributors release (U.K.) of a Kings Road Entertainment production. (Intl. sales: Vision Intl.) Produced by Tom Karnowski. Directed by Albert Pyun. Screenplay, David S. Goyer; camera (color), Mark Emery Moore; editor, Alan E. Baumgarten; music, Tony Riparetti, James Saad; sound (Ultra-Stereo), uncredited; art director, Nicholas T. Prevolos; costume design, Joseph A. Porro; assistant director, Robert Williams; associate producer, Goyer; fight choreographers, Jim Nickerson, Benny Urquidez. Reviewed at Cannon Oxford St. theater, London, Feb. 1, 1991. MPAA Rating: R. Running time **89 MIN.**
David Sloan . . . . Sasha Mitchell
Justin . . . . Peter Boyle
Xian Chow . . . . Dennis Chan
Sanga . . . . . Cary-Hiroyuki Tagawa
Accountant . . . . John Diehl
Tong Po . . . . Michel Qissi
Lisa . . . . Heather McComb
Brian Wagner . . . . . Vince Murducco
Vargas . . . . Matthias Hues

Sans hunky Jean-Claude Van Damme and picturesque Thai locations, this out-of-shape sequel to "Kickboxer" (1989) may even have trouble going the course on vidshelves (where it's headed fast). Theatrically, the sweatshirt brigade should give thumbs down.

Yarn is lean "Rocky" fare spiced with Oriental revenge. Clean-cut David (Sasha Mitchell), sole surviving Sloan brother, runs a kickboxing gym on the wrong side of L.A. Behind on his mortgage payments, he agrees to a big-money bout with the chief gorilla (Matthias Hues) of a crooked promoter (Peter Boyle). That pays the bills, so he retires.

Enter Thai heavy Sanga (Cary-Hiroyuki Tagawa), who lost plenty of face after David's big brother (Van Damme) beat the stuffing out of champ Tong Po (Michel Qissi) in Bangkok in part 1. To force David back into the ring, Sanga torches his gym. When that doesn't work, he has Tong Po kill David's cocky pupil (Vince Murducco) in a surprise bout. Segue to sub-"Rocky" finale.

Despite all the bone-crunching slo-mo, pic has all the faults of many Stateside chop-socky carbons: slow pacing, fortune-cookie philosophy and fight sequences shot from all the wrong angles. Humor and femme interest are as thin as the script. Ditto any sense of mounting climax.

Mitchell ("Spike Of Bensonhurst") has a Matt Dillon-like charm, but that's it. Boyle is okay in an easy part, young Heather McComb impresses as Mitchell's spunky tomboy aide and Dennis Chan encores his cynical Chinese coach from part 1. Atmospheric lensing is way above par. — *Drek*.

SUNDANCE FEST

BLOOD IN THE FACE
(DOCU)

A First Run Features release of a Right Thinking production. Produced and directed by Anne Bohlen, Kevin Rafferty, James Ridgeway. Conceived by Ridgeway; camera (Du Art color, 16m), Rafferty, Sandi Sissel; editor, Rafferty. Reviewed at Sundance Film Festival, Park City, Utah, Jan. 23, 1991. Running time: **77 MIN.**

The "Invisible Empire" comes willingly out of the closet in "Blood In The Face," a cautionary but surprisingly unalarming look at the American white supremacist movement. Pic should find ready acceptance wherever politically themed works are welcomed.

Although made from a liberal-left point-of-view, well-made documentary (which bows Feb. 27 at Film Forum in New York) gives racists a human face. While there is enough inflammatory material here to incense most rational people, the straightforward, unabashed presentation of their views may, ironically, make the film pleasing to its subjects as well.

Much of the original footage was shot at an Aryan movement conclave in Cohacta, Mich., which immediately helps break the stereotype that all such bigoted extremists are Southern white trash.

Even though some of those gathered wear Nazi uniforms and rant about Jews and blacks, the interviews clearly reveal that these are mostly poor working stiffs with chips on their shoulders whose biggest thrill is putting on a costume and firing off some rounds in target practice.

Filmmakers have caught some grotesque images, notably a nocturnal marriage ceremony conducted by the light of a burning cross, and have included just enough material of speakers making fools of themselves to let the viewer know where they stand.

It's amazing how open the subjects have been in allowing the camera to cover their activities and record their thoughts. One frank old man states upfront that they have "nothing to hide," a far cry from the usually secretive policies of his ilk.

This attitude leads to scary aspects of the agenda of the distant right, for whom Ronald Reagan and Jerry Falwell are as bad as communists due to their embrace of Jews and Israel.

In freely airing their views, the American Nazi Party and like-minded organizations are attempting to enter the legitimate political arena in the same manner as other minority groups.

Foremost exponent of this approach is David Duke, who has homogenized his past in the Ku Klux Klan in his bid for office in Louisiana.

Others indicate following his lead in shifting the movement away from the lunatic fringe and more toward the political mainstream. In this context, film is very useful.

Archival interviews with late American Nazi Party founder George Lincoln Rockwell are riveting. Interviews with "Christian Identity" ministers, whose racial purity opinions jibe with those of their political counterparts, are fascinating in light of other forms of religious fundamentalism rampant in different parts of the world.

Title refers to the racists' claim that one way in which whites are superior to other people is that they can blush, or show "blood in the face." — *Cart*.

A LITTLE STIFF
(B&W)

A Just Above The Ground production. Written, produced and directed by Greg Watkins, Caveh Zahedi. Camera (b&w, 16m), Watkins; editor, Watkins, Zahedi; music, Kath Bloom; sound, Arnold Barkus. Reviewed at Sundance Film Festival, Park City, Utah, Jan. 22, 1991. No MPAA rating. Running time: **85 MIN.**
Caveh . . . . Caveh Zahedi
Greg . . . . Greg Watkins
Erin . . . . Erin McKim
Patrick . . . . Patrick Park

Two UCLA film students create a subtle, witty and entertaining comedy in "A Little Stiff," a $10,000 black & white 16m production. Stretching a one-note plot to feature length, pic grows a bit precious and indulgent in last reels but still could prove popular in fest and arthouse bookings.

Caveh Zahedi plays a tentative, neurotic filmmaking student infatuated with art student Erin McKim after seeing her in an elevator. He begins a nervous courtship. She has a b.f. and her own preoccupations, and gives him mixed signals. Zahedi spends much of the film agonizing over the meaning of her ambiguity.

Some of the best of the improvised scenes involve Zahedi and friend/co-director Greg Watkins sitting against a brick wall mulling the meaning of events.

Watkins plays easygoing straight man to Zahedi's obsessive Woody Allen type, and the workings of Zahedi's original mind are consistently amusing.

Considering the actors are non-pro, the scenes have a remarkable naturalness and consistency of tone, a tribute to Zahedi's work with the cast. The audacity of re-creating such personal events using the actual participants, including the girl he was obsessed with and her b.f. (Patrick Park), speaks well for him as an artist.

Unfortunately, the pic has some sound problems associated with the 16m format that muffles a lot of the dialog, a particular problem in a climactic phone conversation between Zahedi and Erin.

Pic is attractively lensed in deep contrast black & white. Aside from some tight, dizzying handheld camerawork, most of the scenes are shot long and deep, with a savvy use of framing.

Zahedi creates an interesting persona in his sensitive, worried character, which could easily make a return appearance in a more ambitiously scripted pic. — *Daws*.

DAUGHTERS OF THE DUST

An American Playhouse in association with WMG presentation of a Geechee Girls production. Executive producer, Lindsay Law. Line producer, Steven Jones. Written, produced and directed by Julie Dash. Camera (Du Art color), A. Jafa Fielder; editor, Amy Carey, Joseph Burton; music, John Barnes; sound, Veda Campell; production design, Kerry Marshall; art direction, Michael Kelly Williams; costume design, Arline Burks; assistant directors, C.C. Barnes, Nandi Bowe; casting, Len Hunt. Reviewed at Sundance Film Festival, Park City, Utah, Jan. 24, 1991. No MPAA rating. Running time: **114 MIN.**
Nana Peazant . . . . . . Cora Lee Day
Eula Peazant . . . . Alva Rodgers
Eli Peazant . . . . . . Adisa Anderson
Haagar . . . . Kaycee Moore
Mellow Mary . . . . Barbara O
Myown . . . . . . Eartha D. Robinson
Iona . . . . Bahni Turpin
Viola . . . . Cheryl Lynn Bruce
Mr. Snead . . . . Tommy Hicks
Also with: Malik Farrakhan, Cornell (Kofi) Royal, Vertamae Grosvenor, Umar Abdurrahman, Sherry Jackson, Rev. Ervin Green.

Nobly intended as an investigation into a little known African-American culture, "Daughters Of The Dust" plays like a two-hour Laura Ashley commercial. Wildly indulgent and undisciplined as filmmaking, Julie Dash's feature does possess a unique look and feel that, in addition to its inherent ethnographic interest, will appeal to some people.

Picture's primary asset, its visual beauty, can be much better appreciated on the bigscreen than on the tube, but this American Playhouse production has no theatrical distributor as yet. Some specialized market possibilities exist, notably with women and blacks, and international fests are a natural.

Set in 1902, highly impressionistic work focuses upon the Gullah, descendants of slaves who lived on the islands off South Carolina and Georgia and had their own distinctive traditions and way of speaking in a Caribbean-like accent known as "Gullah" or "Geechee."

Ostensible event framing the action is the imminent departure of the large Peazant family from their Sea Island home to the mainland and the North. But the true preoccupation here has to do with cultural memory and ethnic preservation, admirable aims unfortunately undercut by Dash's stylistic gambits.

On view for reel after endless reel are countless silent shots of women — all but one dressed in impeccably clean outfits of the whitest white cotton and lace — gamboling on the beach, lying around and laughing with one another. Interspersed are several ear-piercing arguments about matters not entirely clear, some scenes with men, and many others featuring amiable group activities such as eating and taking photographs, all on the most exquisite of summer days.

Everyone's happy, everyone looks great and nearly everyone seems to be so pleased with the state of life on the island that one can only wonder what has motivated them to plan the crossing to what will assuredly be a confrontation with racism, poverty and misery.

"Progress" for their people is the alleged, and ironic, reason, but on this, as on so many other points, Dash displays an antihistorical, anti-informational bent that is highly frustrating in light of the waves of repetitive seaside footage. Island life is idealized to the point of illustrating it as a paradise, which makes their plan to leave look absurd.

Film is narrated by an as-yet unborn child, and it could be posited that the impressionist pic portrait constitutes a sort of collective memory of a lost way of life.

But for a work so heavily into its own ethnicity, one is left with any number of unanswered questions relating to Gullah history, their position vis à vis other former slaves, the degree of their isolation and their ultimate fate. Regardless of the extent of research, film refuses to satisfy on a documentary level.

Gorgeously shot in the style of a fashion layout by A. Jafa Fielder, pic is redolent with slow dissolves, languid camera moves and a jerky, experimental form of slow motion that makes one want to shun another camera trick for six months. Backdropping it all is John Barnes' resourceful, varied score, seductive and excessive by turns.

Huge cast is strong and very attractive, but fact remains that Dash either doesn't know how, or doesn't care, to develop scenes dramatically. Highly emotional moments are sometimes dropped in with no preparation. Other sequences are allowed to seriously wear out their welcome.

Talent is definitely on view here, and certain viewers will assuredly fall in with the slow rhythm and privileged mood Dash sets up. But on any serious level, two hours of visual lyricism do not substitute for good drama and historical substance.
— *Cart.*

KING RALPH

A Universal Pictures release of a Mirage/Jbro production. Produced by Jack Brodsky. Executive producers, Sydney Pollack, Mark Rosenberg. Directed by. David S. Ward. Screenplay, Ward, based on the novel "Headlong" by Emlyn Williams; camera (Rank color), Kenneth MacMillan; editor, John Jympson; music, James Newton Howard; sound (Dolby), Scott A. Hecker; production design, Simon Holland; art direction, Clinton Cavers; set decoration, Peter Walpole; costume design, Catherine Cook; assistant directors, Derek Cracknell, Melvin Lind, Julian Wall; coproducers, Julie Bergman, John Comfort; casting, Mary Selway. Reviewed at the Universal City 18 Cinemas, Universal City, Calif., Feb. 11, 1990. MPAA Rating: PG. Running time: **97 MIN.**

Ralph	John Goodman
Willingham	Peter O'Toole
Graves	John Hurt
Miranda	Camille Coduri
Phipps	Richard Griffiths
Gordon	Leslie Phillips
Hale	James Villiers
Princess Anna	Joely Richardson
McGuire	Niall O'Brien
King Gustav	Julian Glover

Also with: Judy Parfitt, Ed Stobart.

Crowned with John Goodman's lovable loutishness and a regally droll performance by Peter O'Toole, "King Ralph" could be anointed with a sizable share of the winter boxoffice treasury.

This genial comic fable, much like its title character, periodically shines brighter than its humble ambitions and roots.

The unknown factor is whether Goodman will be a strong enough initial draw, since the film's crowd-pleasing, old-fashioned story should generate positive word of mouth. As the best component of hit sitcom "Roseanne" and a supporting player in several pics, he appears to have the necessary heft.

"Ralph" itself doesn't carry much weight in the story department, though the wispy premise is handled deftly by writer-director David S. Ward, who brings a blend of sprightly comedy and sappy romance to the pic.

Britain's entire royal family dies in a precredit sequence, resulting in a boorish American nightclub entertainer — the product of a dalliance between a prince and the American's paternal grandmother — becoming king.

After that, it's a basic fish-out-of-water tale, with King Ralph (Goodman) adjusting to the perks and constraints of nobility, aided by a group of harried advisers including his mentor Willingham (O'Toole) and officious bureaucrat Phipps (Richard Griffiths).

John Hurt plays the Snidely Whiplash in the piece, almost literally, as a British lord seeking to bring the new king down so his own family can regain the throne. He facilitates a liaison between the king and a buxom lower-class British girl (Camille Coduri) in order to force his resignation. What could have been as dull as palace life largely works thanks to several factors — the foremost being Goodman, who fleshes out a thinly written role with his innate good-heartedness.

The character is invested with broad comic appeal, but it was clearly a challenge to make the corpulent king sympathetic and believable in terms of getting the girl. While unconventional as leading men go, Goodman generally pulls it off on both fronts.

O'Toole, meanwhile, perfectly counterbalances Goodman's amiable dunce as his stiff secretary, a juicy part reminiscent of John Gielgud's butler in "Arthur." Hurt is deliciously snide as the lord, while Coduri wrestles gamely with her clichéd role as poor-girl-turned-stripper-with-heart-of-gold.

Then again, Coduri is at least "cute," perhaps the most descriptive term for "King Ralph," which seeks, and largely achieves, the same tone as a '40s comedy.

First-rate production qualities add greatly to the fairy-tale quality, with lavish production and costume designs, respectively, by Simon Holland and Catherine Cook. Lensing was done on U.K. locations and at London's Pinewood Studios. — *Bril.*

THE JUNIPER TREE
(U.S.-ICELANDIC-B&W)

A Keene/Moyroud production. Written, produced and directed by Nietzchka Keene. Camera (b&w), Randy Sellars; editor, Keene; editing consultant, Chris Painter; music, Larry Lipkis; sound, Patrick Moyroud; art direction, Dominique Polain; associate producer, Moyroud. Reviewed at Sundance Film Festival, Park City, Utah, Jan. 24, 1991. No MPAA rating. Running time: **80 MIN.**

Margit	Bjork Gudmundsdottir
Katla	Bryndis Petra Bragadottir
Johann	Valdimar Orn Flygenring
Mother	Gudrun S. Gisladottir
Jonas	Geirlaug Sunna Pormar

A fairy tale is invested with the severity of a Carl Th. Dreyer film or an August Strindberg drama in "The Juniper

Tree." This emphatically arty effort could go over only with the most highbrow audiences, but it merits attention for the stoic purity of its approach.

Nietzchka Keene's adaptation of a Bros. Grimm story, shot in black & white on bleak Icelandic landscapes, is demanding, but its refined pleasures make up for those demands.

In her first feature, Keene sets up numerous barriers against easy viewer entry. Everything is cold and offputting — the T.S. Eliot quotation, the Middle Ages setting, the forbidding countryside, the impenetrable verses and the distant camera style.

Gradually, however, the disturbing power of the story, as well as Keene's telling of it, take hold. Altered significantly from the original, tale is of two sisters who flee their home after their mother is burned to death as a witch.

The older of the two, Katla, soon marries a widowed farmer whose young son, Jonas, is obsessed with his dead mother. Jonas quickly forms a deep friendship with the budding teenager Margit, who has visions of her own dead mother, but loathes his stepmother, whom he accuses of being a witch.

Katla tries to win the boy over for a while but ultimately feels compelled to spurn him brutally, confirming everything the kid said about her. Ending is exceedingly somber, quite unlike any fairy tale heard or read in childhood.

Keene's talents may not be anywhere near those of her acknowledged masters, Dreyer and Andrei Tarkovsky, but her methods are nearly as exacting and austere. Ignoring conventional storytelling niceties, she concentrates on moments of despair, confrontation, intense privation and mystical insights, all unfolded in measured meter and whispered tones.

While hard to accept at first, this disciplined style finally blossoms into the film's greatest strength. Decision to shoot in black & white can still be questioned, however, since the stark, steppe-like landscapes almost cry out to be seen in their full, harsh glory. Some of lenser Randy Sellars' images run too dark, but pic still cuts a striking visual profile. Larry Lipkis' medieval-tinged score is another plus.

Icelandic thesps, all of whom speak in accented English, are attractive and effective, most notably Bjork Gudmundsdottir, lead singer of the rock group Sug-

arcubes, who effectively holds centerscreen as Margit, 13.

Pic takes itself with such seriousness that it borders on the suffocating. But on its own terms, "The Juniper Tree" accomplishes its objectives and reminds one of the disturbing power Grimm stories can have. — *Cart.*

VIAGGIO D'AMORE
(JOURNEY OF LOVE)
(ITALIAN-FRENCH)

A Paravalley/Pari a Deux production, in association with Reteitalia. Produced and directed by Ottavio Fabbri. Screenplay, Tonino Guerra, based on the poem "Il Viaggio"; camera (color), Mauro Marchetti; editor, Mauro Bonanni; music, Andrea Guerra; sound (Dolby), François de Morant; production design, Tommaso Bordone; costume design, Gianna Gissi, Carolina Olcese; assistant director, Roberto Pariante. Reviewed at Preview 9, N.Y., Jan. 25, 1991. Running time: **102 MIN.**
Rico . . . . Omar Sharif
Zaira . . . . Léa Massari
Driana . . . . Florence Guérin
Truck driver . . . . . Stephane Bonnet
Priest . . . . Ciccio Ingrassia
Teamster . . . . Leopoldo Trieste

"**J**ourney Of Love" is a slow-moving drama about a simple, aging couple traveling to the Adriatic. An Italian-French co-production starring Omar Sharif (who is dubbed in Italian), this small film will have a hard time finding an audience.

Shown last year in Los Angeles for Academy Awards consideration, pic has not yet secured a distrib.

Sharif and Léa Massari are well cast as Rico and Zaira, who have been married for 40 years. Nearly three decades after Sharif became a star in "Lawrence Of Arabia," he makes a likable peasant barber. Massari, best known for "Murmur Of The Heart," is equally good as his frustrated, guilt-ridden wife.

Plot is uneventful, however. Abandoning Petrella Guidi, their picturesque but fading village, the couple sets out to visit the sea. As they follow a river on foot they relive old memories, both happy and sad.

Unfortunately, Ottavio Fabbri's leisurely pacing of the early scenes makes the trip seem just as long to the audience as it does to the couple. Fabbri shoots pretty sunsets and lovely waterfalls, but there's little action.

Fabbri's camera also tends to linger on the lovely Florence Guérin, who plays the lover of a trucker (Stephane Bonnet) engaged to another woman. The picture briefly comes to life when

Sharif and Massari wistfully eavesdrop on the young lovers.

For the wife, the trip brings back memories of an affair she had years before with a gypsy violinist. She confesses to a priest, admitting she's still tormented by her infidelity. There are no flashbacks, though, which might have made the couple's past more vivid.

As it turns out, Massari's indiscretion is the most dramatic event in the film — and it happened 40 years ago. Her arguments with Sharif amount only to domestic squabbling.

At last they reach their destination, but heavy fog makes the sea invisible. Although reminiscent of the hilarious visit to Lake Erie in "Stranger Than Paradise," the ending is a fitting affirmation of the marriage.

But by the time the credits roll, the audience may have been lulled to sleep by the soothing music and pleasant scenery. With a faster pace, tighter editing and some additional conflict, "Journey Of Love" would be a more worthwhile trip. — *Stev.*

FIREHEAD

A Pyramid Distribution release of an AIP Studios presentation of a Winters Group production, in association with Sovereign Investment. Executive producers, David Winters, Marc Winters. Produced and directed by Peter Yuval. Screenplay, Jeff Mandel, Yuval; camera (Image Transform color), Paul Maibaum; editor, Steve Nielson; music, Vladimir Horunzhy; sound, Palmer Norris; art direction, Buzz Crump; production manager, Rai Reynolds; assistant director, Larry Litton; stunt coordinator, Gary Beall; casting, Billy DaMota Casting. Reviewed on AIP vidcassette, N.Y., Jan. 6, 1991. MPAA Rating: R. Running time: **88 MIN.**
Col. Vaughn . . Christopher Plummer
Warren Hart . . . . . . Chris Lemmon
Adm. Pendleton . . . . Martin Landau
Ivan . . . . Brett Porter
Melia Buchanan . . . Gretchen Becker
   Also with: George Elliott, Ed Kearney, Douglas Simms, Lauren Levy.

"**F**irehead" is an unusual cold war thriller with sci-fi overtones. Mobile, Ala.-lensed indie opened recently in southern territories with springtime vid release to come.

Chris Lemmon, again mirroring dad Jack's mannerisms and delivery, is cast as a government science whiz whose latest experiment is out of control. He has converted Soviet defector Brett Porter into a sort of a superman with telekinetic powers who shoots deadly laser beams from his eyes (hence his nickname, "Firehead"). Porter is busily

destroying U.S. factories recently awarded defense contracts.

Lemmon is assigned by his slimy bureaucrat boss (Christopher Plummer) to stop the freak, and beautiful blond Gretchen Becker is made his teammate. Not surprisingly, Porter teams up with Lemmon to go after the *real* bad guys.

Screenplay by Jeff Mandel and helmer Peter Yuval does a good job of maintaining interest while convincingly extrapolating the reactions of hardliners to the current spirit of glasnost. A subplot involving biological warfare plans is timely but not pursued in depth.

A prolog set in Estonia but filmed in Mobile is unconvincing, but pic otherwise is technically up to par. Becker is a personable leading lady and even gets to sing the rather silly title song over the end credits.

As a retired admiral who helps Lemmon, Martin Landau proves that recent upscale stints with Francis Coppola and Woody Allen do not preclude a sincere B-movie performance. — *Lor.*

DA NACHT VAN
DE WILDE EZELS
(THE NIGHT OF
THE WILD DONKEYS)
(DUTCH)

An NFM/IAF release of an Emjay Rechsteiner production. Produced by Rechsteiner. Directed by Pim de la Parra. Screenplay, de la Parra, Paul Ruven, Steven van Galen; camera (color, b&w), Alejandro Agresti; editor, Marc van Fucht; sound, Elmer Leupen, Rob Duf; sound mixer, Mike Boom; assistant director, Eugenie Jansen. Reviewed at Rotterdam Film Festival, Jan. 30, 1990. Running time: **105 MIN.**
   With: Pim de la Parra, Liz Snoying, Camilla Braaksma, Kenneth Herdigein, Hans Dagelet, Manouk van der Meulen.

After the success of his minimal pic "Max & Laura & Henk & Willie," Pim de la Parra's third pic in a year, "The Night Of The Wild Donkeys," is disappointing.

A "minimal movie," in de la Parra's terms, is a film with a very low budget, few shooting days, no salaries and no scenario. Improvisation and enthusiasm must do the job. In "Max & Laura," cast and crew's zest jumped from the screen and grabbed the audience.

Here, the wild donkeys are a bit tired. The beginning is strong, but the middle sags and the ending drags. This film about making a picture is meant to spoof (Dutch) filmmaking, but the satire doesn't bite, and both the film and the film within the film peter out.

Alejandro Agresti's camerawork is an enormous asset, notwithstanding some puzzling jumps from color to black & white. The nudity and sex are more naughty than titillating.

Actors do their best, especially Liz Snoying, but choppy editing gives them no chance to build their characters. — *Wall.*

TASUMANIA MONOGATARI
(TASMANIA STORY)
(JAPANESE)

A Toho release of a Fuji Television production. Produced by Hisashi Hie. Executive producers, Koichi Murakami, Juichi Horiguchi. Directed by Yasuo Orihata. Screenplay, Naruto Kaneko; camera (color), Junichiro Hayashi; editor, Katsu Izuka; music, Shuji Inoue; sound, Yoshitaka Imai; art direction, Shu Yamaguchi; assistant director, Toshihiko Nakajima; production coordinator, Hiroaki Shikauchi, Ken Mitsui; assistant producers, Maya Kawaii, Seichi Ichiko. Reviewed at Shibuya Toho, Tokyo, Aug. 9, 1990. Running time: **110 MIN.**
Eiji Kawano . . . . Kunie Tanaka
Naoko . . . . Hiroko Yakushimaru
Shoichi Ishizawa . . . . . Tomoshi Taga
Haruo Totsuji . . . . . . Jinpachi Nezu

Japanese moviegoers in search of laughs at one time could count on Toho Studios pics putting Kunie Tanaka in a foreign country. He has once again been sent abroad in a Toho release, but the result is a disappointingly uninvolving tearjerker.

From 1961 to '71, Tanaka played bumbling sidekick to polished Yuzo Kayama in the first 17 of 18 films in Toho's enormously popular "Waka Daisho" (Young Champ) series. The duo enjoyed adventures in various locales, many of them overseas, and Tanaka provided many of the series' well-remembered comic moments, as he became discombobulated by unfamiliar languages and customs.

Tanaka, 28 when the "Young Champ" series debuted, turns 58 this year and apparently is too much the dignified thespian to go for the easy laugh. Now he becomes involved in issues of enormous importance not merely to the country where he lives, works and converses with the natives in phonetically learned English, but to the world at large.

In "Tasmania Story," ex-businessman Tanaka has turned against his former Japanese employer for its ecologically unsound practices on the Australian island he now calls home. In addition to fighting to preserve Tasmania's natural wonders, Tanaka must decide how best to eliminate the unnatural tension existing between him and his estranged son.

The plot will be familiar to anyone who has followed Toho releases of the past 15 years. The studio has enjoyed success with stories about children who leave home in search of fathers who went abroad for work: "Uaito Rabu" (White Love), "Good Luck Love" and "Aijo Monogatari."

"Tasmania Story" is part of the same predictable pattern. Tanaka's son leaves crowded Japan for a sparsely populated country celebrated for its natural wonders, where Papa devotes himself to the preservation of those natural wonders.

The Hollywood equivalent of these Toho features would be a succession of films in which virtually every American who takes up residence in Japan becomes either a Zen priest or a geisha.

"Tasmania Story" is produced by Fuji Television, which packed theaters with pics in which dogs and cats star: "Nankyoku Monogatari" (Antarctica) and "Koneko Monogatari" (The Adventures Of Milo And Otis). Like those films, "Tasmania Story" boasts lots of furry creatures, including wombats and Tasmanian devils. But they can't save the pic from going to the dogs.
— *Bail.*

DISHA
(THE IMMIGRANTS)
(INDIAN)

A San Paranjpye Films production. Written and directed by San Paranjpye. Camera (color), Madhu Ambat, G.S. Bhaskar; editor, Om Prakash Makkad; music, Anand Modak; sound, Narendra Singh. Reviewed at Indian Panorama, Madras, Jan. 13, 1991. Running time: **136 MIN.**
With: Shabana Azmi, Nana Patekar, Raghuvir Yadav, Om Puri, Nilu Phule, Rajshree Sawant.

The theme of poor villagers' migration to Bombay is given fresh treatment by femme director San Paranjpye in "The Immigrants" (a.k.a. "The Uprooted Ones"), but excessive length and abrupt changes in mood will prove liabilities for international success.

The film involves two friends (one newly married) who decide to try their luck in the big city, while the brother of one (played by popular Indian thesp Om Puri) stays in the village obsessively digging a well in an attempt to locate much-needed water.

In Bombay, the friends are forced to share one room with a crowd of other men living on the edge of poverty, and to bend the laws in order to get work. The married one gets brief use of a friend's apartment and is able to invite his wife for a visit, but their happiness is short-lived.

"The Immigrants" is a frustrating mixture of good and bad. There are some fine scenes in the film, and a handful of excellent performances, including Shabana Azmi as the wife of the well-digging brother. Their scenes together are quite touching.

All too often, however, Paranjpye mistakes irony for low comedy, and so cheapens her material. An excruciating song-and-dance routine performed by the workers in their one-room apartment looks as if it strayed in from a Z-grade musical, and is the film's low point. With some trimming, pic could play the fest route, as the good sequences are quite powerful. But as is, it's likely to prove more irritating than enlightening. — *Strat.*

DR. M
(CLUB EXTINCTION)
(GERMAN-ITALIAN-FRENCH)

A Prism Entertainment video release of an NEF Filmproduktion, Ellepi Film, Clea Prods. co-production, in association with Deutsches Fernsehen, La Sept, Telefilm GmbH. (Intl. sales, Cori Films.) Executive producers, François Duplat, Hans Brockmann. Produced by Ingrid Windisch. Directed by Claude Chabrol. Screenplay, Sollace Mitchell, adapted by Chabrol from Thomas Bauermeister's story, inspired by Norbert Jacques' novel "Mabuse der Spieler"; camera (Geyer-Werke color), Jean Rabier; editor, Monique Fardoulis; music, Paul Hindemith; sound (Dolby), Axel Arft; production design, Wolfgang Hundhammer, Dante Ferretti; art direction, Thomas Schappert; costume design, Egon Strasser; production manager, Gilbert Funke; 2nd unit director, Mitchell. Reviewed on Prism videocassette, N.Y., Jan. 19, 1990. MPAA Rating: R. Running time: **116 MIN.**
Dr. Marsfeldt/Guru . . . . . Alan Bates
Sonja Vogler . . . . . . .Jennifer Beals
Lt. Hartmann . . . . Jan Niklas
Moser . . . . Hanns Zischler
Stieglitz . . . . Benoit Régent
Engler . . . . Alexander Radszun
Veidt . . . . Peter Fitz
Kathi . . . . Daniela Poggi
Penck . . . . William Berger
Also with: Michael Degen, Wolfgang Preiss, Isolde Barth, Andrew McCarthy, Tobias Hoesl, Beatrice Macola.
(English-language soundtrack)

Claude Chabrol goes sci-fi with depressing results in "Dr. M," an already dated 1989 European production that opened in Paris last November but reaches the U.S. in vidstores and retitled "Club Extinction."

Film is inspired by Fritz Lang's classic "Dr. Mabuse" features, but Chabrol clearly is not comfortable with this form. The dialog is stilted, and many scenes are designed for somnambulist acting more suited to the expressionism of Robert Wiene's "Dr. Caligari" than Lang's work.

Bates plays two roles: the title Dr. Marsfeldt, head of a German media conglomerate, and (uncredited) a white bearded guru who lords it over a Marsfeldt-owned resort Club Theratos that's closer to Jim Jones' Jonestown than Club Med. As the guru, he talks in a funny voice and hams it up embarrassingly.

The Berlin Wall is used throughout "Dr. M" as a metaphor for

Original film
DR. MABUSE, DER SPIELER

A Decla-Bioscop melodrama, directed by Fritz Lang. Scenario, Thea von Harbou, from Norbert Jacques' novel. Reviewed at Ufa Palast am Zoo, Berlin, April 15, 1922.
Dr. Mabuse . . . . Rudolf Klein-Rogge
Countess Stolat . . . Gertrude Weicker
Cara . . . . Auge Neggede Nissen
Brother . . . . Alfred Abel
De Witt . . . . Bernhard Goetzke
Hull . . . . Paul Richter

modern malaise, its presence contaminating the story's Berliners in a way now hopelessly dated since the wall was torn down. Using tv spokesmodel Jennifer Beals as his main instrument, Dr. M is causing Berliners to commit suicide by sending out subliminal messages over the airwaves beneath broadcasts exhorting folks to escape for a vacation at Theratos.

Jan Niklas plays the dogged police investigator trying to make sense of the rash of suicides, all of which point at Beals' involvement. He predictably falls in love with her and ultimately accompanies her to Theratos for an anticlimactic ending.

Except for repetitious use of an annoying noise-song by Mekong Delta to suggest the anomie of folks at a local night club, "Dr. M" is easy to watch. Best performance is by Hanns Zischler, erstwhile co-star of Wim Wenders' "Kings Of The Road," who has honed his English dialog delivery to perfection.

Gueststar Andrew McCarthy, who toplined Chabrol's "Quiet Days In Clichy," pops up briefly as an assassin. — *Lor.*

MALINA
(GERMAN-AUSTRIAN)

> A Kuchenreuther production in conjunction with Neue Studio Film GmbH and German ZDF-TV and Austrian ORF-TV. Produced by Thomas Kuchenreuther. Directed by Werner Schroeter. Screenplay, Elfriede Jelinek, from a novel by Ingeborg Bachmann; camera, Elfi Mikesch; editor, Andrea Wenzhler; music, Giacomo Manzoni; art direction-costumes, Alberte Barsacq. Reviewed at Passage Kino, Hamburg, Feb. 2, 1991. Running time: **123 MIN.**
> With: Isabelle Huppert, Mathieu Carriere, Can Togay, Fritz Schediwy, Isolde Barth, Peter Kern.

Oopera director Werner Schroeter, a protégé of the late Rainer Werner Fassbinder, has come out with yet another visually fascinating, but thoroughly inscrutable film which will appeal to a small circle of German intellectuals — and to almost no one else.

Colors are vibrant, the sets and lighting are superb. Beyond that, pic has precious little to offer, and certainly nothing to say.

French actress Isabelle Huppert runs wild-eyed through this story based on an autobiographical novel by an Austrian writer who ultimately immolated herself some years ago.

Huppert portrays a stifled writer torn between two lovers, although it is hard to understand her turmoil as supporting actors Matthieu Carriere and Can Togay turn in lackluster performances as her boring husband and uncaring lover.

That is the main problem with this film. The dull screenplay and stiff acting leave the audience totally indifferent to the human tragedy which literally ends in a roaring inferno.

In the throes of melodrama, Huppert repeatedly drops writhing and quaking to the floor, rips up curtains and clothes, scratches with her bare fingernails at the door, vomits in her handbag, bangs her head against a wall until it is bleeding and finally sets a myriad of small fires around her home. This goes on for two hours.

Schroeter's first love is the opera. So, at the pic's fiery climax, with flames crackling up the walls of a formerly pristine Vienna apartment, an opera sing-er appears singing arias from "Fidelio," "Oberon" and "Antigone" as Huppert's character — and the audience — go on suffering. — *Gill.*

DEAD SLEEP
(AUSTRALIAN)

> A Roadshow release of a Village Roadshow Pictures production. Executive producers, Graham Burke, Gregory Coote. Produced by Stanley O'Toole. Directed by Alec Mills. Screenplay, Michael Rymer; camera (color), John Stokes; editor, David Halliday; music, Brian May; sound, Ian Grant; production design, Philip Warner; line producer, Vincent O'Toole; production manager, Rosemary Spokes; assistant director, Bruce Redman; casting, Judy Hamilton. Reviewed at Mosman screening room, Sydney, Feb. 5, 1991. Running time: **100 MIN.**
> Maggie Healey . . . . Linda Blair
> Dr. Jonathan Heckett . . Tony Bonner
> Hugh Clayton . . . . . . Andrew Booth
> Sister Kereby . . . . . Christine Amor
> Wendy . . . . Suzie MacKenzie
> Kaye . . . . Sueyan Cox
> Dr. Harry Larke . . . . . Craige Cronin
> Dr. Schamberg . . . . Brian Moll
> Thena Feury . . . . Vassy Gotsopoulos
> Jessica Sharp . . . . Peta Downes
> McCarthy . . . . Slim de Grey

Though it fails to work as a thriller, "Dead Sleep," inspired by a real-life medical scandal recently investigated by the government Down Under, has an interesting subject which warranted more thoughtful treatment. Too weak for theatrical release, pic should have a mild video career.

Linda Blair toplines as a Yank nurse who comes to Brisbane, Australia, to be with the Aussie guy (Andrew Booth) she'd met in Los Angeles. She drops him when he gets heavily into the drug scene, and she gets a job in a private hospital.

The doctor in charge (Tony Bonner), a suave charmer, is involved in experimental treatment for psychiatric, alcohol and drug-related illnesses, giving patients electronically induced deep sleep for days and weeks at a time.

When one patient dies, Blair starts probing and discovers that many patients have "accidentally" expired, or committed suicide after undergoing the dubious treatment. Next victim in line is, natch, her ex-boyfriend, placed in the hospital by his rich parents.

Blair ankles in disgust, but is persuaded by a radical reformer to get her job back and to expose the sinister doctor by getting inside info on his illegal practices. She nearly winds up a victim herself in the process.

Blair is adequate as the disillusioned nurse, and Bonner brings the necessary bedside manner to his role as the fanatical doc. Some supporting roles are less well acted, though Peta Downes, as an actress who undergoes sleep therapy and has an affair with the doctor in the bargain, and Sueyan Cox, as Blair's feisty roommate, both impress.

Michael Rymer's screenplay is more interesting than Alec Mills' rote direction. Mills, a camera operator on "Return Of The Jedi," also helmed "Bloodmoon," produced by the same team that made "Dead Sleep." The new film is a cut above that clinker, but could have made far more impact if the producers had taken more trouble with the cheap-looking production.

Pic looks to attract neither a serious audience nor the genre thriller audience. The only (mild) hook is the fact that most of the hospital patients are female, nubile and sleep in the nude. That won't be enough to save the film. — *Strat.*

BERLIN FEST

THE BALLAD OF THE SAD CAFE
(U.S.-BRITISH)

> An Angelika Films release of a Merchant Ivory production, in association with Film Four Intl. Produced by Ismail Merchant. Executive producer, Paul Bradley. Directed by Simon Callow. Screenplay, Michael Hirst, based on Carson McCullers' novella and Edward Albee's play; camera (Technicolor), Walter Lassally; editor, Andrew Marcus; music, Richard Robbins; sound (Dolby), Drew Kunin; production design, Bruno Santini; art direction, Michael T. Roberts; set decoration, Scott Hale; costume design, Marianna Elliott; assistant director, Gary Marcus; production manager, Mary Church; fight director, Randy Kovitz; 2nd unit camera, Briggs Palmer; associate producer, Donald Rosenfeld; casting, Shirley Rich. Reviewed at Broadway screening room, N.Y., Feb. 1, 1991. (Competing at Berlin Film Festival.) No MPAA Rating. Running time: **100 MIN.**
> Miss Amelia . . . . Vanessa Redgrave
> Marvin Macy . . . . . Keith Carradine
> Cousin Lymon . . . . . . Cork Hubbert
> Rev. Willin . . . . Rod Steiger
> Lawyer Taylor . . . . Austin Pendleton
> Mary Hale . . . . Beth Dixon
> Merlie Ryan . . . . . . Lanny Flaherty
> Stumpy McPhail . . . . . Mert Hatfield
> Henry Macy . . . . . . Earl Hindman
> Mrs. McPhail . . . . . . Anne Pitoniak

Simon Callow makes an assured feature directing debut adapting Carson McCullers' "The Ballad Of The Sad Cafe," a demanding, abstract fable for art audiences. Topliner Vanessa Redgrave's adventurous performance will be in line for acting honors when the Merchant Ivory production debuts at the Berlin Film Festival.

Callow, the distinguished British stage thesp and stager, wrote a book about Charles Laughton, and, in making his film helming bow, has tipped his hat to the atmospheric nature imagery of Laughton's classic film and only directorial assignment, "The Night Of The Hunter."

However, where the allegory "Hunter" had an engrossing thriller plotline adapted by James Agee from Davis Grubb's novel, Callow works with an abstract story peopled by strange, otherworldly characters whose motivations and actions often are baffling. Resulting intellectual film is difficult to respond to and probably will not engage mainstream audiences.

After her bravura assignment for Peter Hall on stage and for tv in Tennessee Williams' "Orpheus Descending," Redgrave has stretched her craft even further in personifying McCullers' character Amelia.

She's a violent, mannishly styled woman who threw out her husband (Keith Carradine) on their wedding night and has become a legendary figure in her little Southern town in the '30s. With cropped hair and unglamorous makeup, Redgrave throws herself into the role (created in 1963 by Colleen Dewhurst in Edward Albee's play adaptation) with uncensored force.

Carradine, who replaced Sam Shepard at the start of film's production last summer in Texas, brings a naturalism to his embittered role as the ex-con and spurned spouse. His direct-sound singing and slide guitar playing add an extra dimension.

Catalyst in the piece is the fantasy character of Cousin Lymon, a hunchbacked dwarf who pops up out of nowhere claiming to be Redgrave's cousin. That role, a career breakthrough in 1963 for the late Michael Dunn, here is essayed adequately but rather too pathetically by Cork Hubbert.

Hubbert gets Redgrave to convert her general store into a cafe, serving the moonshine she prepares at her still. He provides entertainment for the locals with an act combining sleight of hand, singing and jester-like moves.

Tale, told at once and twice removed via embedded flashbacks, takes a dramatic turn when Carradine shows up midway through the pic fresh out of the state pen. He's out to avenge himself against Redgrave while Hubbert ambiguously plays both sides against the middle in this brutal war of the sexes.

Original Play

Lewis Allen & Ben Edwards presentation of a drama without intermission by Edward Albee, based on the Carson McCullers novelet. Staged by Alan Schneider; scenery, Ben Edwards, lighting, Jean Rosenthal; music, William Flanagan; costumes, Jane Greenwood. Stars Colleen Dewhurst, William Prince; features Lou Antonio, Roscoe Lee Browne, Enid Markey, Michael Dunn, John C. Becher, Jenny Egan, Roberts Blossom, Deane Selmier, Louis Waldon. Opened Oct. 30, '63, at the Martin Beck Theatre, N.Y.; $6.90 top weeknights, $7.50 Friday-Saturday nights.
Narrator . . . . . . Roscoe Lee Browne
Rainey Brothers . . Louis W. Waldon, Deane Selmier
Stumphy MacPhail . . . John C. Becher
Henry Macy . . . . . . William Prince
Amelia Evans . . . . Colleen Dewhurst
Cousin Lymon . . . . . Michael Dunn
Emma Hale . . . . Enid Markey
Mrs. Peterson . . . . Jenny Egan
Merlie Ryan . . . . . Roberts Blossom
Horace Wells . . . . . . William Duell
Henry Ford Crimp . . . . David Clarke
Rosser Cline . . . . Griff Evans
Lucy Willins . . . . . . Nell Harrison
Mrs. Hasty Malone . . . Bette Henritze
Marvin Macy . . . . Lou Antonio
Henrietta Ford Crimp . Susan Dunfee
Townspeople . . . Ernest Austin, Alice Drummond, Jack Kehoe
Musicians: Raymond Crisara, trumpet; Stanley Drucker, clarinet; Laura Newell, harp; Julius Baker, flute; Herb Harris, percussion; Seymour Barab, cello. Conductor: Samuel Baron.

Film climaxes memorably in a bare-knuckles boxing match staged at the cafe between Carradine and Redgrave to settle their differences once and for all. The tall actress convincingly holds her own in the contest.

Probably not since Katharine Hepburn achieved mixed results in her oddest role as the backwoods religious fanatic in "Spitfire" in 1934 has an attractive star actress attempted such a primitive, rustic role. Redgrave's body English, strange accent and physical outbursts are a triumph of pure acting.

Carradine's more natural approach helps bring pic closer to reality. An intense supporting performance by Rod Steiger also provides exposition as the town preacher, since Callow and scenarist Michael Hirst have jettisoned narration of Albee's play.

However, the relationships here, notably those between alternately naive and devilish Hubbert and the other principals, are cryptic and at times off-putting. One easily can admire the quali-

ty of acting writ large, but it is nearly impossible to relate emotionally to this strange universe. In that respect, Callow is following a recent tradition of such countrymen as Derek Jarman and Peter Greenaway in creating highly rewarding but private cinemas.

Tech credits are fine, with lensing on a remote little town set originally built by Willie Nelson for one of his films. Walter Lassally's photography captures the stark beauty of the surroundings. — *Lor.*

WOSOBIPO
(SPRING)
(INDIAN)

A Wojaru Cine Trust-Karbi Anglong District Council production. Written and directed by Gautam Bora. Camera (color), Vivek Banerjee; editor, Sreekar Prasad; music, Sher Choudhuri; sound, Anup Mukhopadhyay; production design, Utpal Barua. Reviewed at Indian Panorama, Madras, Jan. 14, 1991. (Also at Berlin Film Festival, Forum section.) Running time: **138 MIN.**
With: Eilsa Hanse, Bubul Terang, Raman Rongpi, Langbiram Engti.

"**S**pring," a.k.a. "The Cuckoo's Call," is an ambitious, well-meaning hymn to nature, but the director's ambitions are ambushed by technical deficiencies, notably poor processing in the print caught.

Made in Karbi, near the Chinese border, pic revolves around Sarthe, a schoolteacher whose life has been shaped by an idyllic childhood with his beloved grandfather, who imbued in him a passionate love for the lush, green countryside.

With decent visuals, the long scenes in which the boy and the old man commune with nature might have been delightful, but the muddy, unattractive images and the unsuccessful attempts at soft focus critically diminish the film's charms.

Nor is the chronology any too clear. Pic opens in 1979, with the adult Sarthe about to leave for the city. Flashbacks show the death of the grandfather, whose body was discovered by his small grandson. Further flashbacks detail the relationship between the two, and there's talk of a war going on (resulting in an increase in the price of opium) which seems to refer to World War II. In that case, surely Sarthe should have looked much older in the framing scenes.

Director Gautam Bora studied film in (East) Germany, and "Spring" is his first feature. He obviously has ideas, but not yet the technical abilities to express them fully. — *Strat.*

O PSYLOS
(THE FLEA)
(GREEK)

A Greek Film Center-Dimitris Spyrou production. Written and directed by Spyrou. Camera (color), Prokopis Dafnos; editor, Christos Santatsoglou; music, Michalis Terzis; songs performed by Nena Venetsanou, Lina Gerardi; sound, Costas Poulantzas, Yannis Haralambidis; sets, Vayia Paggaia, Antonis Halkias; costumes, Vayia Paggaia. Reviewed at Thessaloniki Film Festival, Oct. 4, 1990. (Also in Berlin Festival, children's section.) Running time: **108 MIN.**
Ilias (The Flea) . . . . Pantelis Trivizas
Crinio . . . . Costoula Tsellou
Galaxias . . . . Dimitris Spyrou
Journalist . . . . . . Dimitra Hatoupi
Also with: Vassilis Kolovos, Amalia Giza, Dimitris Palailchoritis, Leonidas Vardaros, Michalis Theodorou, Alekos Petrides, Nikos Zoiopoulos, Fotis Karvelas.

"**T**he Flea" has an appeal that spans the generations and gives it legs beyond the fest circuit.

An insightful view of rural Greece, pic incorporates universal themes in a delightful, stunningly lensed drama about a determined 12-year-old who publishes his own newspaper in a small mountain village.

Ilias (Pantelis Trivizas) publishes The Flea by himself in the mountains near ancient Olympia. His efforts go largely unappreciated by his elders, who tease him and nickname him "The Flea." His concerned parents are convinced his preoccupation with his newspaper will distract him from more serious studies and forbid him to continue it.

Ilias' only allies are Galaxias (a quixotic eccentric played by the director in a cameo) and Crinio (Costoula Tsellou), a sensitive classmate whose support of Ilias' efforts creates a friendship that sprouts into romance.

The villagers' scoffing at Ilias' ambitions changes to admiration bordering on the obsequious when an Athenian journalist (Dimitra Hatoupi) shows up to do a story on Ilias and The Flea. Wearing a miniskirt and casually smoking and drinking with the men in the cafe, she is set apart from the local women who never would behave so boldly.

The simplistic myth of the kind-hearted peasant is exploded, re-

vealing a portrayal of well-intentioned but intolerant people such as Ilias' parents.

Ilias becomes disheartened just when it seems the townspeople finally are recognizing his accomplishment. He realizes much of their enthusiasm stems from hopes for increased tourism spurred by his fame, and he distrusts the journalist's motives as well. Ultimately, he opts for the road less traveled, much as he always has done. Technical credits are fine, with exceptional lensing of picturesque stone houses and mountain scenery.

The original and folkloric score, featuring clarinet, guitar and flute music, is delicately incorporated into the action. Performances are refreshing, especially those of the children. — *Sam.*

SCENES FROM A MALL

A Touchstone Pictures presentation in association with Silver Screen Partners IV. Produced and directed by Paul Mazursky. Screenplay, Roger L. Simon, Mazursky; camera (Du Art color, Technicolor prints), Fred Murphy; editor, Stuart Pappé; music, Marc Shaiman; sound (Dolby), Les Lezarowitz; production design, Pato Guzman; costume design, Albert Wolsky; art direction, Steven J. Jordan; set decoration, Les Bloom; assistant director, Henry J. Bronchtein; associate producer, Pappé; co-producers, Guzman, Patrick McCormick; casting, Joy Todd. Reviewed at Crest Theater, L.A., Feb. 19, 1991. MPAA rating: R. Running time: **87 MIN.**

Deborah	Bette Midler
Nick	Woody Allen
Mime	Bill Irwin
Sam	Daren Firestone
Jennifer	Rebecca Nickels
Dr. Hans Clava	Paul Mazursky

Paul Mazursky's 14th film as director is a cozy, insular middle-aged marital comedy that's about as deep and rewarding as a day of mall-cruising. Even the comfortable, older urban audience "Scenes From A Mall" presumably is aimed at is likely to merely browse before shopping for a more substantial value.

Talents of Bette Midler and Woody Allen seem misspent in roles as cuddly but squabbling spouses. In his first performance for another director since Martin Ritt's "The Front" (1976), Allen is cast as a ponytailed west coast parody of his neurotic New Yorker persona, a move typical of the self-referential in-jokes this comedy relies on.

Disney regular Bette Midler plays a role that's more grounded — and a lot less fun — than her parody of a rich wife in Mazursky's "Down And Out In Beverly Hills."

Pic's title, a takeoff on Ingmar Bergman's "Scenes From A Marriage," should be consumers' first clue as to what's in store, so to speak. Mall setting only reinforces story's superficiality and claustrophobic, self-absorbed approach.

Midler and Allen are a Hollywood Hills-dwelling twin-career couple of the '90s. He's a successful sports lawyer; she's a psychologist who's written a high-concept book on how to renew a marriage.

They pack their kids off for a ski weekend and head for the Beverly Center mall to spend their 16th anniversary indulging their every whim.

Expecting to clear his conscience and renew his commitment to his wife, per her own published advice, Allen drops the bombshell that he's just ended a six-month affair with a 25-year-old. Midler is stunned by the news, demands a divorce and soon they're dividing up property on cafe napkins.

They make up, the tables turn and she confesses to an ongoing affair with a Czechoslovakian colleague played by Mazursky. Allen throws a tantrum and declares their marriage over.

These emotional storms never achieve any veracity. They seem like just another indulgence on the part of the pampered, secure spouses.

Biggest letdown is that such a bland creation should come from the scripting team of Mazursky and Roger L. Simon. "Scenes From A Mall" is a picture of such lazy, limited scope one has to wonder for whom Mazursky made it — himself and his friends?

Allen, relying on his characteristic nervous speech and gestures, dominates the pic. Mazursky, with his second L.A. lifestyle comedy to star Midler, seems to be positioning himself as a west coast Woody Allen.

With Allen's declaration in pic's production notes that he wants to feature Mazursky in one of his films, it all begins to blur together in a snug circle. The only party left out is the audience.

Mazursky's "Down And Out" contained some wicked satirical jabs at its rich protagonists, but "Scenes" complacently accepts its characters as they graze from sushi bar to boutique, toting their expensive love gifts.

Pic does feature some amusing thrust-and-parry between the sexes, and at some point the pic's mall backdrop redeems itself as it turns on the rattled characters, overwhelming them with the chaos and excesses of their chosen lifestyle.

Other than that, the sole comment on their behavior is an obnoxious and persistent mime played convincingly by Bill Irwin, whose mimicry drives Allen to hostile distraction.

Set close to home at the Beverly Center, pic shot exteriors there and moved to a mall in Stamford, Conn., for two weeks of interior filming. For the remainder, a huge, two-story replica mall was constructed at Kaufman Astoria Studios, N.Y., and 2,600 New York extras were outfitted in L.A. garb.

Project was the last film of the late Pato Guzman, production designer and co-producer, and his 12th collaboration with Mazursky. Production values are typically high, and cinematographer Fred Murphy's chaotic, multisource lighting gives the pic some needed grounding.

Music by Marc Shaiman is a puzzler. What have Cole Porter and Marlene Dietrich tunes got to do with this story? Perhaps it's because Allen uses music from that period in his films. — *Daws.*

MY HEROES HAVE ALWAYS BEEN COWBOYS

A Samuel Goldwyn Co. release of an E.K Gaylord II/Martin Poll production. Produced by Poll, Gaylord. Directed by Stuart Rosenberg. Screenplay, Joel Don Humphreys; camera (color), Bernd Heinl; editor, Dennis M. Hill; music, James Horner; sound, John Pritchett; costume design, Rudy Dillon; assistant director, Benjamin Rosenberg; associate producer, Anthony Poll; casting, Hank McCann & Associates. Reviewed at Broadway Screening Room, N.Y., Jan. 9, 1991. MPAA Rating: PG. Running time: **106 MIN.**

H.D. Dalton	Scott Glenn
Jolie Meadows	Kate Capshaw
Jesse Dalton	Ben Johnson
Jud Meadows	Balthazar Getty
Cheryl Hornby	Tess Harper
Clint Hornby	Gary Busey

Also with: Mickey Rooney, Clarence Williams III, Dub Taylor, Clu Gulager, Dennis Fimple, Megan Parlen.

Over-the-hill rodeo riders will get a major morale boost from "My Heroes Have Always Been Cowboys," but most others are likely to be nonplussed by this tale of a veteran bull rider's last stand.

An earnest family drama of "Rocky"-esque inspirational values, independently produced modern oater might have scared up some interest and a little b.o. as a four-waller back in the 1970s, but represents an anomaly in today's market.

Screenwriter Joel Don Humphreys' predictable tale of an aging, aching cowpoke's shot at redemption bears many similarities to Sam Peckinpah's fine, neglected 1972 feature "Junior Bonner," which starred Steve McQueen as a small-timer on the rodeo circuit.

This time, it's Scott Glenn's turn out of the gate, playing H.D. Dalton, a journeyman rider who, in the credit sequence, is stomped into the dust while working as a rodeo clown. To recover from his injuries, he returns, after some years, from Texas to his family in Oklahoma, only to find it in a fractured state.

His father, Jesse (Ben Johnson), has begun acting a bit gaga and has been moved from the family farm to an old folks' home by sister Cheryl (Tess Harper) and brother-in-law Clint (Gary Busey), who hope to sell off the compound. H.D.'s former girlfriend Jolie (Kate Capshaw) has lost her husband and is faced with raising two children alone.

Upset with this state of affairs, H.D. spirits his dad back home, where the two men renew their lifelong tense, bickering relationship, and takes up once again with Jolie, who needs the emotional support but is understandably reluctant due to her beau's limited prospects.

When Jesse is injured, pressure mounts on H.D. to make some big bucks fast in order to save the old man, the farm and his hopes to finally win over Jolie. The only way he knows, of course, is the rodeo, so mangled body and all, he goes into heavy training, in "Rocky" and "Karate Kid" style, for Bullmania and a date with the meanest bull of all, the unridable Thunder Bolt.

Directed in straightforward fashion by Stuart Rosenberg, pic casts its lot with the underdog in true American fashion, but is bland and unexciting.

Co-produced by Oklahoma-based entrepreneur E.K. Gaylord II, who owns the cavernous Lazy E Arena, where the climactic competition was staged, this is one of those periodic family dramas from the hinterlands that aspires to make 'em like they used to. Unfortunately, makers of such films almost uniformly fail to refresh or reinvent the wholesome genre formats they employ, resulting in rehashes rather than rehabs.

There's nothing wrong with the performances, although the characters are all cut from familiar cloth. Glenn bittersweetly conveys H.D.'s twinkle of hope that faintly flickers from beneath the pain of bottoming out.

Johnson is his reliable self, except goofier, while Capshaw has standard notes to hit as H.D.'s vulnerable sweetheart back home (but looks great in fancy cowgirl duds). Harper and Busey have thankless roles as selfish, mean-spirited kin.

They have little to do, but it's good to see Mickey Rooney and such stalwart Western character actors as Clu Gulager, Dub Taylor and Dennis Fimple filling out the supporting cast.

Tech contributions are serviceable, although James Horner's synthesized score ladles out the inspirational soup to overflowing. — *Cart.*

BRIDE OF RE-ANIMATOR

A 50th St. Films release of a Wildstreet Pictures presentation of a Keith Walley/Paul White production. Executive producers, White, Walley, Hidetaka Konno. Produced and directed by Brian Yuzna. Screenplay, Woody Keith, Rick Fry, from a story by Yuzna, Keith, Fry, based on H.P. Lovecraft's "Herbert West — Re-Animator"; camera (Foto-Kem color), Rick Fichter; editor, Peter Teschner; music, Richard Band; sound (Ultra-Stereo), Mary Jo Deveney; production design, Philip J.C. Duffin; assistant director, Tony Lowe; production manager, Gary Schmoeller; special makeup & visual effects, Screaming Mad George, Magical Media Industries (supervisor, John Carl Buechler), Anthony Doublin, KNB EFX Group (Robert Kurtzman, Greg Nicotero, Howard Berger); stop-motion animation, David Allen; special mechanical effects, Wayne Beauchamp; stunt coordinator, Ken Lesco; co-producer, Michael Muscal; casting, Billy DaMota. Reviewed at Moviemakers screening room, N.Y., Feb. 19, 1991. MPAA Rating: R. Running time: **97 MIN.**
Herbert West . . . . . . Jeffrey Combs
Dan Cain . . . . Bruce Abbott
Lt. Chapham . . . . Claude Earl Jones
Francesca . . . . Fabiana Udenio
Dr. Hill . . . . David Gale
Gloria/The Bride . . Kathleen Kinmont
Dr. Wilbur Graves . . . . Mel Stewart
Nurse . . . . Irene Forrest
Also with: Michael Strasser, Johnny Legend.

Fans of Stuart Gordon's 1985 "Re-Animator" will probably dig this sequel directed by the original's producer, Brian Yuzna. Campy gorefest, not suitable for mainstream audiences, is a midnight attraction at N.Y.'s Waverly Theater and a Live video entry next April.

Jeffrey Combs returns in top form as H.P. Lovecraft's dotty scientist Herbert West, this time intent on joining the trendy club of would-be Dr. Frankensteins creating a female monster (à la "Frankenhooker," "Steel & Lace," "Eve Of Destruction").

Reluctantly assisting Combs again is fellow doctor Bruce Abbott, whose beautiful new Italian girlfriend Fabiana Udenio can't shake his grieving attachment to his true love Megan, who was killed in the first film. When Combs tells him that he's going to build his femme creation around Megan's preserved heart, Abbott joins the grisly experiment.

The over-the-top acting that Gordon encouraged in "Re-Animator" is continued here with Combs particularly adept at the darkly comic throwaway line. Overabundance of gore (an even more explicit unrated version will be made available to vidstores) will turn off mainstream viewers, however.

Tall actress Kathleen Kinmont is a good choice for the monster, with her stitched together, see-through torso well-executed by KNB EFX Group. Dave Allen provides clever stop-motion animation and black humor is encouraged by Anthony Doublin's oddball creature effects.

Screaming Mad George, who recently directed a feature for Yuzna, delivers his usual quota of grotesques made up of incompatible human body parts. Final reel, with strobe lighting and subliminal music and sound effects, is hard to watch but technically impressive.

Supporting Combs, Abbott is a solid hero who has long since graduated to more mainstream features. Udenio is a lovely starlet with mucho sex appeal.
— *Lor.*

NOTHING BUT TROUBLE

A Warner Bros. release of an Applied Action production. Produced by Robert K. Weiss. Directed by Dan Aykroyd. Screenplay, Aykroyd, from a story by Peter Aykroyd; camera (Technicolor), Dean Cundey; editor, Malcolm Campbell, James Symons; music, Michael Kamen; sound (Dolby), Lon E. Bender; production design, William Sandell; set decoration, Michael Taylor; set design, James Tocci; costume design, Deborah Nadoolman; special makeup, David B. Miller; associate producer, John D. Schofield; assistant directors, Jim Van Wyck, Princess McLean; casting, Marion Dougherty, Sharon Howard-Field. Reviewed at Mann Bruin Theater, L. A., Feb. 15, 1991. MPAA Rating: PG-13. Running time: **94 MIN.**
Chris Thorne . . . . Chevy Chase
J.P./Bôbo . . . . Dan Aykroyd
Dennis/Eldona . . . . John Candy
Diane Lightson . . . . . . Demi Moore
Miss Purdah . . . . . . Valri Bromfield
Fausto . . . . Taylor Negron
Renalda . . . . Bertila Damas

Title of this astonishingly poor effort sounds like an inside joke at Warner Bros.' marketing department, which should have plenty of trouble getting anyone to see it. If it is, the joke is funnier than anything in "Nothing But Trouble," which amounts to one of the longest 94 minutes on record.

First-time director Dan Aykroyd, in fact, might have once parodied this sort of wretched excess in his "bad-cinema" sketches on "Saturday Night Live." Based on the talent involved, it's all the more remarkable that the film lacks a shred of humor.

Premise, stripped to the bone, had potential: A faceless drive-through town, on the road from someplace to someplace else, seems to have no resident except the cop who miraculously appears to pinch unsuspecting drivers.

The one-joke starter is then taken to absurd extremes as four Manhattan yuppies get shanghaied to the village of Valkenvania, where a demented old judge (Aykroyd, in heavy makeup) metes out executioner-style justice over moving violations.

There are plenty of cinematic violations to be found here, though few are moving. It's a good bet a film is in trouble when the highlight comes from seeing John Candy in drag.

Essentially, the story turns into an extended maze with Chevy Chase and Demi Moore as the principal Nintendo-ized targets running through one tepid peril after another, while mouthing banal wisecracks.

What might have been either a screwball comedy or a dark "Twilight Zone"-inspired black comedy, however, takes its own wrong turn somewhere in between, with wasteful loads of gadgetry, special effects and heavy character makeup.

David B. Miller merits special credit for the repulsive character makeup, though that can't cover up the film's murky lensing and occasionally confusing edits, despite an apparently generous budget for this genre.

Rappers Digital Underground, of "Humpty Hump" fame, makes a bizarre cameo and provides songs for the soundtrack, though it's doubtful the group's fans will be inclined to witness the performance. It makes more sense to wait for the musicvideo.
— *Bril.*

HIGHLANDER II: THE QUICKENING

A Ziad El Khoury-Jean Luc Defait presentation, in association with Lam Bear Entertainment, of a Davis/Panzer production. Executive producers, Mario Sotela, Guy Collins. Produced by Peter S. Davis, William Panzer. Directed by Russell Mulcahy. Screenplay, Peter Bellwood, from a story by Brian Clemens, Panzer; camera (Widescreen, Eastmancolor), Phil Meheux; editor, Herbert C. de la Boullerie; music, Stewart Copeland; sound, Richard Shorr; production design, Roger Hall; special effects, John Richardson; 2d unit director-camera, Arthur Wooster; costumes, Deborah Everton; assistant director, Stephen Buck; stunts, Frank Orsatt; line producers, Jack Cummins, Chris Chrisafis; co-producers, Alejandro Sessa, Robin Clark; associate producer, Stephen Kaye; casting, Fern Champion. Reviewed at UGC Odeon, Paris, Feb. 13, 1991. Running time: **96 MIN.**
Connor MacLeod . Christophe Lambert
Ramirez . . . . Sean Connery
Louise Marcus . . . . Virginia Madsen
Katana . . . . Michael Ironside
David Blake . . . . . John C. McGinley
Alan Neyman . . . . Allan Rich
Hamlet . . . . Steven Grives

"Highlander II: The Quickening" echoes the formula of its moderately successful 1985 predecessor (time travel plus swordplay and slick special effects), but this time the formula wears thin.

Although sequel opened very strongly in France, b.o. prospects elsewhere look modest. A better video shelf life is probable.

Audiences unfamiliar with the first film will be hard put to follow the action as it incoherently hops about in time and place.

Peter Bellwood's clumsily written screenplay opens in 1994. After one scene, there's a "five years later" title and shortly thereafter a "25 years later" title — and that's all before the opening credits. Later, "500 years earlier" makes for an unduly scrappy opening.

Original topliners Christophe Lambert and Sean Connery are back (as is Aussie director Russell Mulcahy). Lambert plays immortal Connor MacLeod, who, despite his Scottish ancestry, hails from the planet Zeist. He and partner Ramirez (Connery) were banished to Earth for participating in a failed rebellion.

Bellwood's screenplay unfolds two basic storylines. One involves the assassins led by Michael Ironside, and the other concentrates on the disappearing ozone layer which has been so reduced people die of exposure to the sun, among them Connor's wife.

Connor joins with scientists to devise a sun shield projected into space. The shield is controlled by a large, untrustworthy (natch) corporation, which keeps the later renewal of the ozone layer a secret.

Lambert, transformed from a husky-voiced oldster into a youthful warrior, manages to decapitate the villains arrayed against him while teaming up with attractive environmental terrorist Virginia Madsen.

Connery, sporting long white

hair in a ponytail, occasionally appears wielding a broadsword. In pic's most mystifying scene, he arrives in a Scottish town onstage during a performance of "Hamlet."

"Highlander II" comes alive during the action scenes, including an unexplained but nail-biting segment in which deranged Ironside takes over a subway and drives it at 400 mph, sending its terrified passengers crashing through windows.

Still, Mulcahy, lumbered with a convoluted plot, makes heavy weather of the narrative.

Pic is a derivative mishmash of ideas borrowed from other (better) films ("The Quickening" is another name for "The Force") and lame attempts at humor. Special effects are acceptable, but some settings, especially those on Zeist, look tatty enough to belong to a 1950s sci-fi film.

None of the cast gives his best. Lambert sleepwalks through his hero role. Connery's presence is marginal at best. Ironside looks as if he's still playing his character from "Total Recall." Madsen deserves far better material than the nothing heroine role she gets here.

Pic was lensed in Argentina on an apparently generous budget, but has a tired, second-hand feeling to it. — Strat.

HE SAID, SHE SAID

A Paramount Pictures release of a Frank Mancuso Jr. production. Produced by Mancuso. Directed by Ken Kwapis ("He Said"), Marisa Silver ("She Said"). Screenplay, Brian Hohlfeld; camera (Technicolor), Stephen H. Burum; editor, Sidney Levin; music, Miles Goodman; sound (Dolby), Richard Bryce Goodman; production design, Michael Corenblith; art direction, David James Bomba; set design, Siobhan C. Roome, Bruton Jones; set decoration, Merideth Boswell; costume design, Deena Appel; assistant director, John Hockridge; additional editing, Rick Sparr; associate producer, Vikki Williams; casting, Carrie Frazier. Reviewed at Loews N.Y. Twin, N.Y., Feb. 11, 1991. MPAA Rating: PG-13. Running time: **115 MIN.**
Dan Hanson . . . . Kevin Bacon
Lorie Bryer . . . . . Elizabeth Perkins
Wally Thurman . . . . . . Nathan Lane
Mark . . . . Anthony LaPaglia
Linda . . . . Sharon Stone
Mr. Weller . . . . . . Stanley Anderson
Cindy . . . . Charlayne Woodard
Eric . . . . Danton Stone
Mr. Spepk . . . . Phil Leeds
Mrs. Spepk . . . . Rita Karin

"He Said, She Said" is two awful films rolled into one. The potentially provocative idea of having a male and female director take separate but in- terlocking looks at the same love story fizzles here in the hokiest, most contrived telling imaginable.

Auds will steer clear of this one unless a sudden demand surfaces for a lame update of innocuous, 1950s-style romantic pap.

Co-directors Ken Kwapis and Marisa Silver, who are engaged, have turned out segments that differ slightly in tone, pacing and lighting styles, but are equal in banality and obviousness. In this sense, the two directors complement each other perfectly.

Sitcom slickness of the enterprise is established at the outset, as tv news commentator team of Kevin Bacon and Elizabeth Perkins apparently breaks up on the air when she beans him with a coffee cup.

In a flashback from the man's p.o.v., playboy reporter Bacon and feisty newsroom cohort Perkins were rather implausibly assigned to the same story, then paired in regular "His/Hers" twin columns en route to falling in love, moving in together and becoming Baltimore tv celebs.

Pushed along at a frantic, wearying pace, initial hour is devoted to mirthless jokes about the young hotshot's womanizing, fear of marriage and need to feel professionally superior, just as it emphasizes his willingness to walk the straight and narrow once he's found the right woman.

Kwapis' high gloss garishness and antic staging contrasts with the slower, more subdued approach of Silver, who, in covering the same ground, underlines a sense of romance and optimism in Perkins' character to which the male has been oblivious. At first, the change represents a relief, until it becomes apparent that her style is merely conventional, not unusually reflective.

What's shocking is how impersonal and unfelt the film is on both sides. On a couple of occasions, subjective, vaguely surreal perspectives are thrown in to give some strength to a character's viewpoint. Pic would certainly have been more interesting if most of it had been more extreme, as Brian Hohlfeld's script differentiates the two outlooks only in the blandest terms.

On screen virtually throughout, Bacon and Perkins are unable to escape this collision. Bacon's boyish charm is given an extended workout here, to the point of diminishing returns, while Perkins makes her character more difficult and neurotic than interesting and alluring. Supporting performances are uniformly broad and one-dimensional.

Lenser Stephen H. Burum has thrown in a great deal of dappled lighting in an attempt to give pic some texture, but can't disguise the production's overall threadbare look. Capping things off is Miles Goodman's oppressive, old-fashioned score. — Cart.

MAKER
(SEAGULLS)
(NORWEGIAN)

An As Film release in association with the Swedish Film Institute. Produced by Terje Kristiansen. Directed by Vibeke Lökkeberg. Screenplay, Lökkeberg, Kristiansen; camera (color), Paul René Roestad; editor, Kristiansen, Gunnar Carlssen, music, Örnulf Boye Hansen; production design, Guy Krogh. Reviewed at Saga Cinema, Oslo, Feb. 2, 1991. Running time: **106 MIN.**
Kristina . . Marie Kleivdal Kristiansen
Leda . . . . Tonje Kleivdal Kristiansen
Johannes . . . . Helge Jordal
Anna . . . . Vibeke Lökkeberg
Even . . . . Keve Hjelm
Also with: Helga Urdahl, Marius Krogh, Klags Hagerup.

A stilted and pretentious costume spectacle, "Seagulls" will satisfy no one but admirers of Nordic summer light, well captured by cinematographer Paul René Roestad. Pic's Oslo b.o. has been poor, and lifeless direction plus a virtual absence of storyline total minimal commercial prospects elsewhere.

Set on the Norwegian seaboard in the late 19th century, the film deals with pressures put on an upper-middle class family by the husband's bankruptcy and the arrival of the wife's mentally disturbed sister.

In an all-in-the-family affair, Vibeke Lökkeberg directs as well as acts the worried wife of an ambitious shipping agent. Her two real-life daughters are reasonably convincing as her children, and pic is produced, co-written and co-edited by Lökkeberg spouse Terje Kristiansen.

The husband is played by Helge Jordal, normally a lively actor. For an unduly long period of the film, he is made to cough his way to a final deathbed. Reliable Swedish actor Keve Hjelm (as a neighbor) is given one brief scene and immediately displays his skills.

On the whole, Lökkeberg, considered a key Norwegian filmmaker, is at a low level of inspiration here. Her themes are recognizable from earlier works; namely, the ambitious schemes and desperate social climbing of her male characters. They see the economic possibilities of their times, but are blind to their shortcomings and the effect of their ambitions on family.

In particular, Lökkeberg is preoccupied with the gradual isolation and alienation of women and the neglect of children as effects of wildcat schemes.

All is treated too lightly in this sun-filled costume parade. Script allows no room for the characters to develop, and the narrative has no natural flow. — Olav.

FAJR FILM FEST

NOBAT-E ASHEGHI
(TIME OF LOVE)
(IRANIAN)

A Khaneh Film Sabz production. Produced by Khaneh Film Sabz and Shahed Exhibition Complex. Written and directed by Mohsen Makhmalbaf. Camera (color), Mahmud Kalari; editor, Makhmalbaf; sound, Jahaangir Mirshekari; set design, Mohammad Nasrollahi. Reviewed at Fajr Intl. Film Festival, Teheran, Feb. 12, 1991. Running time: **75 MIN.**
With: Shiva Gerde, Abdorahman Yalmai, Aken Tunc, Menderes Samanjelar.

"Time Of Love," an intriguing romantic trilogy, is the first postrevolutionary Iranian film about adultery. Pic should be a hit in Islamic territories where the subject of love is considered racy onscreen. Tv is its only Western window.

Considered a radical departure for fundamentalist helmer Mohsen Makhmalbaf, pic is pristine by Western standards. Characters never touch and the mandatory head scarf for women never shed. Lovemaking is implied but not shown.

Makhmalbaf reprises the tragic trilogy structure of his "The Peddler" to tell an adulterous married woman's story with three different endings ranging from revenge to sympathy. In each part, the lover is a shoeshine boy and the husband is a taxi driver.

Family, friends and a judge are mystified that the woman would risk her life to love a man from a lower social class.

Unlike traditional Iranian pics, love knows no boundary in this one, which is perhaps why Makhmalbaf shot the film in Turkey with Turkish actors and subtitled it in Persian for release in Teheran.

Part 1 begins when the lovers meet in a cemetery. Lovemaking is intimated with tight closeups of birds, flowers and the woman's mouth seductively biting the corner of her scarf. The husband finds out, kills the lover and stands before the judge without remorse. He must choose his own method of execution.

In part 2, the blond lover of the first part is the husband. Back in the cemetery, the husband attacks the lover, but the husband winds up dead. The judge is confused: "The woman's husband is more beautiful and he had a taxi, so why did she pick you?" The social order is questioned, but someone must pay. The lover is hung offscreen.

Act 3, by far the best, hinges on a traitor, an old man who sees the lovers in the graveyard and coaxes the husband to get revenge. After taking a belt to his wife, husband humiliates lover by forcing him to shine his shoes while smearing black polish on his face with a dagger.

Then surprisingly, the men talk and all is forgiven. The judge, now without a role, tells the husband actor, "You should have killed him so I could execute you, and the film would have had a bad ending." But it doesn't, a fact which signals looser government restrictions on Iranian filmmakers.

Tech credits are superior to other Iranian films and are quite good by international standards. Acting is as believable as any American soap, but pic's ultimate value is as a harbinger of future Iranian cinema. — *Suze.*

DANDAN-E MAR
(SNAKE FANG)
(IRANIAN)

A Cadre Film production. Produced by Majid Modaresi and M.M. Dadgoo. Directed by Masoud Kimiai. Screenplay, Kimiai, based on a story by Ahmad Talebinejad; camera (color), Iraj Sadeghpour; editor, Mehdi Rajaiyan; music, Fariborz Lachini; sound, Mehdi Rajaiyan; art direction, Masoud Kimiai; special effects, M. R. Sharaffoddin. Reviewed at Fajr Intl. Film Festival, Teheran, Feb. 12, 1991. (Also competing at Berlin Film Festival.) Running time: **110 MIN.**
Reza . . . . Faramarz Sedighi
Ahmad . . . . Ahmad Najafi
Zivar . . . . . . Golchehreh Sajjadieh
Fatemeh . . . . Fariba Kosari
Abdol . . . . Nersi Gorgia
Agha Jalal . . . . Jalal Moghadam

Stung by venomous postwar chaos in southern Iran, Masoud Kimiai paints a horrifying picture of corruption and physical abuse.

Slow pace of "Snake Fang" will limit foreign theatrical potential, but the world's current thirst for anti-Iraqi images should breathe life into tv sales.

Street-smart orphans, war refugees and abused women are as common as poverty in Khorramshahr, a town devastated during the eight-year Iran-Iraq war. This new melodrama is about the ensuing desperation of a no-win situation and the hope offered by two underdog heroes sick of slimy opportunists.

Shunning an overt political stance, pic simply sifts through postwar devastation via the main character, a writer named Reza, who hooks up with a second-rate black marketeer, Ahmad, a pivotal character who eventually makes good.

Ahmad is responsible for a band of orphans willing to steal or sell anything to survive. They often pickpocket Afghani refugees to get their food coupons to sell for cash. But the black marketeers rip them off, trying to pay the kids with German marks, essentially worthless to an orphan.

This is not a pretty picture. Women are treated as property and regularly beaten by their husbands (including Reza's sister who's desperately trying to get a divorce) or "owners" who rescued them from the clutches of Iraqis during the war.

The whole situation seems hopeless until Reza and Ahmad team up against black market kingpin Abdol. They burn his illegal stock and throw boxes of food coupons to the orphans, but there's no glorious happy ending. Ahmad gets killed and evil Abdol survives.

Tech credits are fine. The exceptional music is a computerized version of traditional southern Iranian percussion. Soundtrack sets the pace and signals both danger and action throughout the film.

Pic ultimately is a horror story with a ray of hope. Story's significance makes it the first Iranian film participating in an important international competition (Berlin Film Fest). It lacks the polish of a U.S. pic, but it's well worth screening. — *Suze.*

URANUS
(FRENCH)

A Renn Prods.-Films A2-DD Prods. co-production, in association with Soficas Sofi-ARP-Investimage. (Intl. sales: Roissy Film, Paris.) Executive producer, Pierre Grunstein. Produced and directed by Claude Berri. Screenplay, Berri, Arlette Langmann, from the novel by Marcel Aymé; camera (Eastmancolor), Renato Berta; editor, Herve de Luze; sound, Louis Gimel, Dominique Hennequin; production design, Bernard Vezat; costumes, Caroline de Vivaise; production manager, Patrick Bordier; assistant director, Eric Bartonio. Reviewed at Berlin Film Festival (competing), Feb. 15, 1991. Running time: **99 MIN.**
Leopold . . . . Gérard Depardieu
Watrin . . . . Philippe Noiret
Archambaud . . . Jean-Pierre Marielle
Geigneux . . . . Michel Blanc
Monglat . . . . Michel Galabru
Maxine Loin . . . . . Gerard Desarthe
Also with: Fabrice Luchini, Daniel Prevost, Florence Darel, Daniele Lebrun, Josiane Leveque.

For his first film since his international clicks "Jean De Florette" and "Manon Des Sources," Claude Berri has turned to subject matter that will prevent similar success outside France, but an audience should emerge for this superbly made pic containing another smash performance from Gérard Depardieu.

Problem for non-French auds is the all-important politics of the piece, based on a controversial 1947 novel by Marcel Aymé. When war ended, rival factions — Gaullists, Communists (many of them former resistance fighters) and supporters of the pro-German Vichy regime (arguably the majority) — vied for government control.

These passionate struggles are seen in microcosm in "Uranus," set in a small, badly damaged, town. A schoolteacher (Philippe Noiret), whose wife, house and school were destroyed in a bombing raid, is lodging with Jean-Pierre Marielle, a family man who, though by no means a Nazi, had gone along with the now discredited Vichy government.

Also living in Marielle's house is Michel Blanc, an avowed Communist, Gerard Desarthe, a collaborationist, and Michel Galabru, the town capitalist who's despised by just about everyone.

In this atmosphere of revenge and recrimination, the police, who also worked for the Vichy regime, play an ambivalent and sinister role.

No French feature in memory has depicted the faction-fighting during the Occupation as forthrightly as "Uranus," and Berri deserves credit for tackling an uncompromising theme. His direction is always interesting and intelligent. The production is extremely handsome, with topnotch lensing by Renato Berta.

Every member of the strong cast is in excellent form, but Depardieu steals the film with a formidable performance. When he's onscreen, he literally takes over the pic. His final scene is an extraordinary tour de force.

Unless word of mouth can be built around Depardieu, the strong supporting cast and first-class production, pic may not reach the wide audience it deserves. The different factions are too difficult to sort out despite efforts to make them clear.

Pic was a fine choice to open the 1991 Berlin Film Festival.
— *Strat.*

ULTRA
(ULTRAS)
(ITALIAN)

A Filmauro release of a Numero Uno production in association with RAI-2. Produced by Claudio Bonivento. Directed by Ricky Tognazzi. Screenplay, Graziano Diana, Simona Izzo, Giuseppe Manfridi; camera (color), Alessio Gelsini; editor, Carla Simoncelli; music, Antonello Venditti; art direction, Mariangela Capuano. Reviewed at Sacis screening room, Rome, Feb. 18, 1991. (Competing in Berlin Film Festival.) Running time: **90 MIN.**
Prince . . . . Claudio Amendola
Red . . . . Ricky Memphis
Ciafretta . . . . . Gianmarco Tognazzi
Cinzia . . . . Giuppy Izzo
Fabio . . . . Alessandro Tiberi
Also with: Fabrizio Vidale, Krum De Nicola, Antonello Morroni, Michele Comparino, Fabrizio Franceschi, Fabio Buttinelli, Fabio Maraschi.

Ghetto anger bursts from "Ultràs" with the unsentimental force of a stomach punch. Ricky Tognazzi's second helming effort is a bravura piece of filmmaking and acting, and its sustained pace and unmitigated violence mean a solid financial return, particularly where soccer is popular (and violent fringe fans are an issue).

Ultràs are the Italo hooligans who follow their soccer team around the country and often tumble with boosters of rival squads. Roma and Juventus supporters are shown without apology as a dangerous band of swaggering hoods.

Their proletarian background

is presented simply. If by the picture's end the trio of antiheroes — Prince, Red and Ciafretta — are deeply sympathetic, it's because they are human characters with personal problems.

Pack leader Prince (Claudio Amendola, the bullish delinquent in "Forever Mary") is fresh out of a two-year jail term. He has lost his girl to his best pal, Red (excellent newcomer Ricky Memphis), but doesn't know it yet.

Introspective Red has decided to settle down with ghetto girl Cinzia (Giuppy Izzo, a little too delicate to ring true). He spends most of the film steeling himself to have it out with Prince, but when he finally confesses his relationship, it turns out that his real sin is wanting to betray the gang for a steady job.

Scripters Graziano Diana, Simona Izzo and Giuseppe Manfridi (who loosely based the screenplay on their terse plays "Ultrà" and "Teppisti") charge the drama with mounting tension: from the slum where the boys live, through a nightmarish train ride north to the game, to the culminating free-for-all with the Juventus hooligans that resolves the drama.

Tognazzi does a remarkable job directing a host of actors who speak their lines in such powerful Roman dialect even some Italians have trouble understanding them.

Particularly noteworthy are Memphis and Alessandro Tiberi, who plays an 11-year-old ultrà of the future with an uncanny mix of innocence and knowledge that recalls the fat tyke in "The Bicycle Thief." Though all the characters are a little stylized, they come across believably.

Their language is obscene, and some of the scenes — such as the humiliating attempt to pull down the pants of the weakest boy, or the death of a knifed hooligan in a stadium lavatory — push the limits of tolerance. "Ultràs," however, avoids vulgarity.

Editor Carla Simoncelli gives the film a relentlessly fast pace. Antonello Venditti's soundtrack is pulsing.

Tognazzi dedicates the film to his "father, friend and master" Ugo, the Italian actor who recently died. — *Yung.*

RAMA DAMA
(GERMAN)

A Senator Film release of a Perathon Film production. Produced and directed by Joseph Vilsmaier. Screenplay, Martin Kluger, Vilsmaier; camera, Vilsmaier; editor, Ingrid Broszat; music, Norbert Juergen Schneider; sound, Hans R. Weiss. Reviewed at Kino Center Hauptbahnhof, Hamburg, Feb. 7, 1991. (In Berlin Film Festival, New German Films.) Running time: **110 MIN.**
With: Dana Vavrova, Werner Stocker, Hans Schuler, Ivana Chylkova, Josef Kemr, Renate Grosser, Elisabeth Bertram.

It took half a century, but the German film industry has finally produced its equivalent of "Mrs. Miniver." Riding on the success of "Herbstmilch" two years earlier, helmer Joseph Vilsmaier's sentimental "Rama Dama" might have b.o. potential abroad.

In purest Greer Garson-style, dauntless heroine (played with a suitably stiff upper lip by Dana Vavrova) bears two daughters while dodging bombs during World War II. After the war, she more or less single-handedly rebuilds war-battered Munich. Pic's title is derived from a postwar slogan in Bavarian dialect which means something like, "Let's get this place cleaned up."

The title and dialog are bathed in so much local color that even most German audiences will be thrown for a loop. Backwoodsy Bavarian Alpine accents abound in this film, as do tear-jerking clichés.

All in all, the film is well enough made, but the hokum is hard to take at times. In style and construction, pic looks like it came right out of the 1940s. — *Gill.*

DER TANGOSPIELER
(THE TANGO PLAYER)
(GERMAN)

A Defa (Film Studio Babelsberg) production, in association with CSM Film and WDR. Produced by Herbert Ehler. Directed by Roland Graf. Screenplay, Graf, from a novel by Christoph Hein; camera (color), Peter Ziesche; editor, Monika Schindler; music, Gunther Fischer, Julio C. Sanders; sound, Hans-Henning Tholert; production design, Alfred Hirschmeier; assistant director, Hanna Seydel. Reviewed at Berlin Film Festival (competing), Feb. 18, 1991. Running time: **96 MIN.**
Hans-Peter Dallow . Michael Gwisdek
Elke . . . . Corinna Harfouch
Dr. Berger . . . . Hermann Beyer
Roessler . . . . Peter Prager
Schulze . . . . Peter Sodann
Harry . . . . Jaecki Schwarz

One of the last films produced under the old East German regime, "The Tango Player" is a well-made, ironic pic dealing with injustice in the police state. It's too subdued to attract a large audience, but could win friends at films fests.

Protagonist is a historian (played with tired cynicism by Michael Gwisdek) who served a two-year prison sentence simply because he stood in for an ailing pianist and played the tango for students in a cabaret. East German authorities considered this an illegal act.

His life in tatters, he returns home to pick up the threads, but no one will give him a job. Sole bright spot on his horizon is a relationship with a single mother (Corinna Harfouch) whom he meets in a bar.

She welcomes him to her bed at first, but soon tires of his self-pity and self-righteousness. He's also harrassed by a couple of plainclothes cops who regularly turn up at his apartment and who know about everything he's doing. All this is played out while the Prague spring (1968) was taking place in neighboring Czechoslovakia.

The crushing of the liberal regime there by Warsaw Pact troops serves to further convince the historian that things won't change in his country.

Writer-director Graf handles this material with simplicity and style, making his points firmly but non-dogmatically. The result is a sympathetic portrait of the struggles of an intellectual in a police state, all handled in low-key fashion.

"The Tango Player" is technically crisp, with a bright music score deserving of a special nod.
— *Strat.*

ERFOLG
(SUCCESS)
(GERMAN)

A Seitz Filmproduktion production. Produced and directed by Franz Seitz. Screenplay, Seitz, from the novel by Lion Feuchtwanger; camera (Eastmancolor), Rudolf Blahacek; editor, Gisela Haller; music, Friedrich Meyer, Karl Amadeus Hartmann; sound, Gunther Stadelmann; production design, Rolf Zehetbauer; costumes, Monika Ludwig; production manager, Ferdinand Althoff. Reviewed at Berlin Film Festival (competing), Feb. 16, 1991. Running time: **122 MIN.**
Jacques Tuverlin . . . . . . Bruno Ganz
Johanna Krain . . . . Franziska Walser
Martin Kruger . . . Peter Simonischek
Erich Bornhaak . . . Matthieu Carriere
Anna Haider . . . . . . Gudrun Gabriel
Frau von Radolny . . . . Jutta Spiedel
Paul Hessreither . . . . . Gerd Anthoff
Dr. Bichler . . . . Bernhard Wicki

Franz Seitz tackles another famous German book and comes up with "Success," a handsome production that should generate good biz in German territories, but is too literary and stolid to find audiences elsewhere.

Seitz, who specializes in film versions of novels ("The Magic Mountain" in 1981 and "Doctor Faustus" in 1982 both were based on Thomas Mann works), here focuses on Munich in the early '20s as the Nazi Party was starting to emerge.

The theme is miscarriage of justice. Peter Simonischek plays the curator of an art gallery that exhibits controversial paintings. He champions the work of an eccentric woman artist, and one painting of a nude woman creates a scandal. The curator is unjustly accused of sleeping with the artist, who had committed suicide after he rejected her. He is found guilty and imprisoned.

His girlfriend, who marries him in prison, sets about trying to have him released, but encounters cynicism and hypocrisy from the Bavarian authorities. A Swiss writer (sympathetically played by Bruno Ganz) helps her, and they fall in love even as they continue badgering the powers-that-be to reopen the case.

Final scene depicts an armed encounter between Hitler and his followers and a German army unit, a seldom-remembered incident of great political importance at the time.

The depiction of Bavarian society during the period of hyperinflation and the rise of fascism is a fascinating one for those interested in European history, but most non-German audiences will find "Success" too long and too dialog-based.

However, the performances are solid down the line: Ganz, Franziska Walser, appealing as the woman fighting for justice, and Mathieu Carriere, hissable as a fanatical Nazi.

Veteran director Bernard Wicki has a scene as an exiled political party leader who, like most other influential people depicted in the film, is unwilling to help the unfortunate and ailing curator.

Seitz has mounted a handsome production with excellent camerawork (Rudolf Blahacek) and production design (Rolf Zehetbauer). — *Strat.*

GO, TRABI, GO
(GERMAN)

> A Neue Constantin Film release of a Bavaria Film production. Produced by Reinhard Kloos. Directed by Peter Timm. Screenplay, Kloos, Timm; camera, Axel Block; editor, Christel Suckow; music, Ekki Stein; art direction, Goetz Weidner. Reviewed at Kino Center Hauptbahnhof, Hamburg, Feb. 7, 1991. (In Berlin Film Festival, New German Films.) Running time: **96 MIN.**
> With: Wolfgang Stumph, Claudia Schmutzler, Marie Gruber, Ottfried Fischer, Billie Zoeckler, Dieter Hildebrandt, Barbara Valentin, Konstantin Wecker, Diether Krebs, Monika Baumgartner.

"**G**o, Trabi, Go," is the first German film to exploit the funny side of German unification. While the laughs may be few and far between, pic could rev up some coin for exhibs outside Germany.

Audiences in eastern Germany are bound to go for it, but Western auds will find it old-fashioned.

At times, pic resembles a vintage Ma and Pa Kettle knee-slapper about pore ole country folks a-takin' their first vacation abroad (translated into East Germans motoring in Italy).

Real star of the show is a Trabant 601, familiar, homely, two-cylinder East German cars. This "Trabi" has the task of carrying Ma and Pa Struutz (Wolfgang Stumph and Claudia Schmutzler) and their daughter (Marie Gruber) from grimy Leipzig all the way over the Alps and down to sunny Naples.

The Kettles never undertook a more treacherous journey. Stunt drivers went through a dozen Trabants making this film.

Corny dialog is helped along by the able comic talents of Stumph, a longtime regular on former East German tv. A strong supporting cast includes veteran West German funny man Dieter Hildebrandt as a garage mechanic who manages to get a laugh out of the hokey line, "After all, cars are only human."

Helmer Peter Timm, 41, was thrown out of his native East Germany in 1973, and only recently turned to filmmaking. This picture bodes well for his future ventures. — *Gill.*

AMELIA LOPES O'NEILL
(CHILEAN-FRENCH-SWISS)

> An Arion Prods.-Ariane Films-Thelma Film AG co-production. Executive producers, Leonard Kocking, Maria Enrica Ramos. Produced by Patrick Sandrin. Directed by Valèria Sarmiento. Screenplay, Sarmiento, Raul Ruiz; camera (color), Jean Penzer; editor, Rodolfo Wedeles; music, Jorge Arrigada; sound, Florian Eidenbenz; production design, Juan Carlos Castillo; costumes, Mario Franceschi; production manager, Catherine Jacques; assistant director, François Ede; co-producers, Pierre-Alaine Meier, Andres Santana. Reviewed at Berlin Film Festival (competing), Feb. 16, 1991. Running time: **93 MIN.**
> Amelia . . . . Laura del Sol
> Fernando . . . . Franco Nero
> Anna . . . . Laura Benson
> Ginette . . . . Valerie Mairesse
> Igor . . . . Sergio Hernandez
> Anwalt . . . . Jaime Vadell
> Fernando's wife . . Claudio di Girolamo
> Journalist . . . . . Roberto Navarrete

A romantic melodrama about two sisters in love with the same man, "Amelia Lopes O'Neill" may spark international interest thanks to its lead actors, sumptuous setting (it was filmed in the port city of Valparaiso, Chile) and mildly intriguing story.

Director Valèria Sarmiento is wife of prolific Chilean helmer Raul Ruiz and editor of many of his pics. Couple collaborated on the screenplay about two beautiful sisters who live in a magnificent house overlooking Valparaiso harbor.

Amelia (Laura del Sol) one night encounters a doctor (Franco Nero) who mistakes her for a prostitute. Though she is a virgin, she willingly goes with him and falls hopelessly in love with him. But she never tells him who she is, and he always pays for their sexual encounters.

Sister Anna (Laura Benson) is taken ill and the doctor attends her. Now, Amelia turns to prostitution in earnest and one night apparently is murdered by a client.

The story is told in flashback by a magician-cum-thief (Sergio Hernandez) who claims to have known Amelia and wants a journalist who wrote about her to know the truth. The pressbook cites "Rashomon," a pic in which different accounts of the same story are told, but "Amelia" is restricted to one view of its subject.

As a romantic melodrama, pic is modestly successful, but it should attract auds in Latino territories thanks to its name cast. Otherwise, this saga of mad love isn't mad or romantic enough to make much of an impact. The Valparaiso settings are lovingly photographed by Jean Penzer.
— *Strat.*

DER GRÜNE BERG
(THE GREEN MOUNTAIN)
(SWISS-DOCU)

> Produced by Fredi M. Murer and Pio Corradi. Directed by Murer. Camera (color, 16m), Corradi; editor, Corradi, Kathrin Plüss, Murer; music, Fritz Hauser; sound, Tobias Ineichen, Martin Witz, Hanspi Fischer. Reviewed at Berlin Film Festival (Forum), Feb. 17, 1991. Running time: **125 MIN.**

This docu on a Swiss government plan to dump radioactive waste underground in an idyllic, agrarian area in Switzerland makes a strong environmental and social case, but lengthiness and abundant talking heads will dampen theatrical prospects.

"The Green Mountain," follow-up to director Fredi Murer's "We The Mountain People" (shot in the Niwalder canton of Switzerland in 1974), deals with the intention of Nagra, a Swiss organization of radioactive waste producers and health officials, to hollow out the Wellenberg mountain in an agricultural town.

Interviews with 12 farm families dominate the film. Shown at home and at work, the local residents are bitter about the possible exposure of their region to toxic waste. They complain that although their local government generally voted against the proposed mountain dump, officials deliberately left them uninformed and treated them like ignorant peasants.

Their low-tech lifestyles — mucking stalls, chopping wood and building wooden fences — provide an effective contrast to the high-tech city slickers who want to sink barrels of waste under their land.

Film also uses some archival footage, "Atomic Cafe"-style, to show how to remove radioactive waste from horses (hose them down) and from the water supply (cover it with a tarpaulin). Interviews with Nagra officials claiming the low-level radioactive waste will be dangerous for only 300 years is effectively contrasted with shots of local kids.

Pic runs into problems of talkiness. Interviews in Swiss German, a little spoken dialect, run for almost the entire film, making it a marathon of subtitle reading for nonlocals and hindering even tv sales. Tech credits are fine. — *Reli.*

IM GLANZE DIESES GLÜCKES
(IN THE SPLENDOR OF HAPPINESS)
(GERMAN-DOCU)

> An Ex Picturis release of a WDR Television and Max Film co-production. Produced by Wolfgang Pfeiffer. Directed by Johann Feindt, Helga Reidemeister. Written by Feindt, Reidemeister, Tamara Trampe; camera (color, 16m), Feindt, Peter van den Reek; editor, Juliane Lorenz; music, Andi Brauer; sound, Jochen Hergersberg, Dietmar Klein, Paul Oberle. Reviewed at Berlin Film Festival (New German Films), Feb. 18, 1991. Running time: **85 MIN.**

This low-key documentary on the aftermath of the Berlin Wall's fall is a mildly interesting collection of interviews and clips. No commercial prospects lie beyond German public tv, which co-produced "In The Splendor Of Happiness."

With bits of election rhetoric, statements from former East German authorities and interviews with kids peddling pieces of the wall, the docu attempts to show how an ingrained way of thinking also fell with the wall.

Tech credits are weak, reflecting 16m format. — *Gill.*

HEUTE STERBEN IMMER NUR DIE ANDEREN
(NOWADAYS ONLY THE OTHERS DIE)
(GERMAN)

A Progress Film release of a Defa Studio Babelsberg production. Produced by Volkmar Leweck. Directed by Siegfried Kühn. Screenplay, Kühn; camera (wideframe, color), Andreas Köfer; editor, Eva-Maria Schumann; music, Simone Danay-Iowa; sound, Klaus Tolstorf. Reviewed at Berlin Film Festival (New German Films), Feb. 18, 1991. Running time: **78 MIN.**

With: Katrin Sass, Gudrun Ritter, Volker Ranisch, Friedhelm Eberle, Wolf-Dieter Rammler, Ulrike Krumbiegel.

Another well-crafted but plodding pic from former East Germany's Defa Studios, "Nowadays Only The Others Die" is a thoughtful story about death, but has no b.o. prospects here or elsewhere.

The acting and screenplay are far superior to much of what is screened in western Germany, but the filmmakers' old-fashioned approach makes the audience wish this pic finally would stop twitching.

Screenplay revolves around two thesp friends (Katrin Sass, Gudrun Ritter) and their struggle with the Ritter character's cancer.

In the Teutonic medical tradition, patients are kept in the dark about their illness. Sass plays a friend who feels the terminal nature of the illness must be made known to the patient. It's heavy going all the way.

Tech credits reflect good craftsmanship, Defa's hallmark. — *Gill.*

THE DOORS

A Tri-Star release from Carolco of a Mario Kassar presentation of a Sasha Harari/Bill Graham Films/Imagine Entertainment production. Produced by Graham, Harari, A. Kitman Ho. Executive producers, Kassar, Nicholas Clainos, Brian Grazer. Directed by Oliver Stone. Screenplay, J. Randal Johnson, Stone; camera (Deluxe color, Panavision), Robert Richardson; editor, David Brenner, Joe Hutshing; executive music producer, Budd Car; music producer, Paul A. Rothchild; sound (Dolby), Tod A. Maitland; production design, Barbara Ling; art direction, Larry Fulton; set design, Steve Arnold, Lisette Thomas; set decoration, Cricket Rowland; costume design, Marlene Stewart; special visual effects, Industrial Light & Magic; visual effects supervisor, Michael Owens; associate producers, Clayton Townsend, Joseph Reidy; assistant director, Reidy; 2nd unit camera, Tom Sigel, Toby Phillips; casting, Risa Bramon, Billy Hopkins. Reviewed at Todd-AO Screening Room, N.Y., Feb. 14, 1991. MPAA Rating: R. Running time: **141 MIN.**

Jim Morrison	Val Kilmer
Pamela Courson	Meg Ryan
John Densmore	Kevin Dillon
Ray Manzarek	Kyle MacLachlan
Robby Krieger	Frank Whaley
Tom Baker	Michael Madsen
Patricia Kennealy	Kathleen Quinlan
Paul Rothchild	Michael Wincott
Dog	Dennis Burkley
Bill Siddons	Josh Evans
Warhol p.r.	Paul Williams
Nico	Kristina Fulton
Andy Warhol	Crispin Glover

Also with: Billy Idol, Charlie Spradling.

"The Doors" is another trip into 1960s hell from Oliver Stone. This long-awaited look at Jim Morrison's short, wild ride through a rock idol life is everything one expects from the filmmaker — intense, overblown, riveting, humorless, evocative, self-important and impossible to ignore.

The hype machine has been working overtime to stir up fresh interest in Morrison, one of the psychedelic era's legendary casualties. Initial curiosity should be strong, but spending $40 million on such a venture stands as a heavy risk.

His charisma, looks and talent notwithstanding, Morrison was, by all accounts, a real handful, and Stone, despite his professed hero worship, has bluntly presented him as very hard to take.

As rendered with considerable physical accuracy by Val Kiler, Morrison is drunk and/or stoned practically from beginning to end, providing an acute case study of ruinous excess.

Except for some naive hippie-era euphoria early on, the period of the Doors' preeminence feels like a major bummer filled with bad drugs, bad sex, bad parties and horrible things happening in the world.

Stone rightly makes the times a major part of the tale, for, if Morrison had lived at any other moment, this would have been just a sad story of another drunken Irish poet in love with the notion of his own doom.

The singer's obsession with death and mysticism is rooted, via a sepia-tinged prolog, in a childhood experience in which he views the aftermath of a traffic accident involving some Indians. A tribesman sporadically appears to Morrison thereafter, as if beckoning him to "break on through to the other side."

Action proper begins in 1965, as Morrison the would-be poet and pretentious UCLA student filmmaker hooks up with flower child Pamela Courson (Meg Ryan) and launches a band in Venice with John Densmore, Ray Manzarek and Robby Krieger.

Within six months, the Doors, named after Aldous Huxley's "The Doors Of Perception" courtesy of William Blake, are creating a stir on the Sunset Strip.

Stone and co-scenarist J. Randal Johnson show the Doors being signed by Elektra immediately after getting kicked out of the Whisky a Go Go; their travels to San Francisco for the Summer of Love and to New York where they brush up against the Andy Warhol crowd; and recording sessions that become increasingly difficult because of the lead singer's unhinged state.

Outside of Morrison's abusive, drug-drenched relationship with Courson, only two of his innumerable sexual trysts are detailed — one with the exotic Velvet Underground star Nico, the other with the demonic Patricia Kennealy (Kathleen Quinlan).

In a picture loaded with extended concert sequences, two stand out. After an intense encounter with Kennealy in a bathroom, Morrison is forcibly removed from a New Haven stage for obscenity in 1968. A year later, the bloated crooner creates his debacle in Miami, stumbling recklessly through an appearance before famously exposing himself and being dragged into court.

It all ends a mere two years later in Paris, where Morrison has gone to put the Doors behind him and be a poet. Dead at 27, he joined the many other celebrated artists buried at Pere-Lachaise.

Despite his relentless irresponsibility and boorishness, Morri-son remains an intriguing figure over the course of the film's long running time. Stone's attitude toward him is problematic, however.

The muckraking journalist in Stone feels compelled to expose the singer's appalling behavior and deficient character. The artist in Stone, however, celebrates Morrison's taboo-breaking and defiance of authority.

Pic suffers from Stone's penchant for pounding away at his points when subtlety and understatement would be welcome. Relationship between Morrison and and Courson also is delineated poorly; she seems willing to take anything he dishes out, but why they stick together throughout six years and many other women is a mystery.

Kilmer is convincing in the lead role, although he never allows the viewer to share any emotions. Morrison's own vocals have been skillfully augmented by Kilmer in some sequences.

The usually engaging Ryan brings little to a vaguely conceived part, whereas Quinlan commands the screen.

Much fun has been had with the casting of some incidental roles. Crispin Glover appears as a suitably weird Andy Warhol; co-producer Bill Graham as the New Haven concert promoter; Mimi Rogers as a photographer; Kelly Leach as a "birthday girl"; William Kunstler as Morrison's Miami attorney; Sean Stone, the director's son, as the young Morrison; and Stone himself uncredited, as a UCLA film prof.

"The Doors" succeeds in conveying some idea of what made Jim Morrison a compelling personality, but it also creates the impression that the late 1960s were an awful time to be alive and young. — *Cart.*

THE HARD WAY

A Universal Pictures release of a Badham/Cohen Group-William Sackheim production. Produced by Sackheim, Rob Cohen. Directed by John Badham. Co-producer, Peter R. McIntosh. Screenplay, Daniel Pyne, Lem Dobbs; story by Dobbs, Michael Kozoll; camera (Deluxe color), Don McAlpine, Robert Primes; editor, Frank Morriss, Tony Lombardo; music, Arthur B. Rubinstein; sound (Dolby), William L. Manger; production design, Philip Harrison; art direction, John Kasarda; costume design, Mary Vogt; set decoration, Susan Bode; associate producers, Keith Rubinstein, D.J. Caruso; assistant directors, David Sosna, Tony Adler; second-unit director, Cohen; casting, Bonnie Timmermann. Reviewed at Universal Studios screening room, Universal City, Calif., March 1, 1991.

MPAA Rating: R. Running time: **111 MIN.**
Nick Lang . . . . Michael J. Fox
John Moss . . . . James Woods
Party crasher . . . . . Stephen Lang
Susan . . . . Annabella Sciorra
Grainy . . . . John Capodice
Pooley . . . . Luis Guzman
Billy . . . . LL Cool J
China . . . . Mary Mara
Captain Brix . . . . . . Delroy Lindo
Witherspoon . . . . . Conrad Roberts
Bonnie . . . . Christina Ricci
Angie . . . . Penny Marshall

After buddy cop films featuring dogs, aliens and robots, trying to mine the genre again using an actor lives up to the pic's title. Too bad there's more method in the acting than the script, as John Badham's tired action-comedy formula squanders its best moments during the film's first act and wastes the nifty pairing of James Woods and Michael J. Fox. Initial boxoffice could be okay thanks to hardcore fans of the stars and genre before more discriminating tastes shoot it down.

That was the pattern, at least, that held true with Badham's most recent directorial effort, "Bird On A Wire," of which this film is a stylistic remake: pair antagonistic stars, then run them through a gauntlet of chases, fights and one-liners, culminating in a ridiculously overproduced finale.

At the outset, the film possesses some spark thanks to the Fox character — a popular star of action fluff, like "Smoking Gunn II," who yearns for a leading role in a film "without a Roman numeral in it."

Determined to land a serious part playing a tough street cop, he decides to research the role by partnering with real New York cop John Moss (Woods), who's involved in hunting the by-now familiar crazed lunatic serial killer (Stephen Lang).

The film exhausts its best Hollywood in-jokes during the first 20 minutes, with a Penny Marshall cameo as Fox' agent and lots of lines about cappuccino, personal trainers and Mel Gibson.

After the initial meeting of Fox and Woods, however, the pic degenerates into a series of random melees that will bring the buddies together — and introduce a stale subplot that has the actor helping Moss woo his sort-of girlfriend (Annabella Sciorra) as an added bonus.

Woods is appropriately gruff and nasty as the cop, and his trademark intensity makes a broad target for Fox to play off — aping his mannerisms and gushing over his "real" street wisdom, at one point calling him "a Yoda among cops."

Still, Badham gives in to his recent penchant for splashy mayhem working from Daniel Pyne and Lem Dobbs' uneven script and puts more emphasis on the action than the character interaction. While that may be great fun for the second-unit crew, it proves a rollicking bore for everyone else, and the film ultimately feels flat and poorly paced.

In fact, when Fox' character imparts some of his own reel wisdom about the bad-guy showing up in the third act one has to wonder if it's already happened, since it feels like Acts 4, 5 and 6 must surely have come and gone. The irony, of course, is in watching a film that lightly mocks the wretched excess and sappiness of action fare which then from all those shortcomings itself. The final stunt-laden encounter, for example, could serve as the dictionary definition of the term "anticlimax."

Tech credits are characteristically firstrate, especially some of the stunt and second-unit work. The obligatory rap song graces the closing credits, and rapper LL Cool J turns up in a supporting role. — *Bril.*

BERLIN FEST

LA CASA DEL SORRISO
(HOUSE OF SMILES)
(ITALIAN)

A Titanus Distribuzione release of a Titanus Distribuzione-Scena Intl. production. Produced by Giovanna Romagnoli, Augusto Caminito. Executive producer, Pino Auriemma. Directed by Marco Ferreri. Screenplay, Ferreri, Liliana Betti, Antonino Marino; camera (Kodak color), Franco Di Giacomo; editor, Dominique B. Martin; music, Bruno Guarnera, Henri Aguel; art direction, Ferreri. Reviewed at Titanus screening room, Feb. 13, 1991. (Competing in Berlin Film Festival.) Running time: **100 MIN.**
Adelina . . . . Ingrid Thulin
Andrea . . . . Dado Ruspoli
Lawyer . . . . . . Vincenzo Cannavale
Rosy . . . . Francesca Antonelli
Dr. Peri . . . . Caterina Casini
Esmeralda . . . . Elisabeth Kaza
Elvira . . . . Maria Mercader
Also with: Nuccia Fumo, Nunzia Fumo, Lucia Vasini, Rosalina Neri, Mohamed Kamara, Mimi Felixine.

More restrained than many of Marco Ferreri's films, "House Of Smiles" has just enough transgression to alienate family audiences, while it lacks the blistering irony and bitterness of the director's best arthouse work. Theme of the 41st Berlin Film Festival Golden Bear winner probably will keep it from scoring at the domestic boxoffice.

A hot love affair between 70-year-olds in a rest home turns into an offbeat, well-intentioned, occasionally banal comedy, the kind of film in which everybody over 60 is cheerful and generous, and everybody under 40 grumpy and grasping.

Adelina, courageously portrayed with indomtable good humour by Swedish actress and director Ingrid Thulin, is an independent oldster. Her son (born out of wedlock) is dead, and her daughter-in-law has just got her hands on his inheritance, leaving Adelina a pauper.

Still an attractive woman, she cedes to the genteel courtship of another resident, Andrea (played with irresistible charm by playboy-prince Dado Ruspoli).

Lack of privacy in the home leads Adelina and Andrea to hold their (tastefully suggested) trysts in a brightly painted camper, the property of a community of black immigrant workers who live nearby. The blacks are portrayed as generous, amorously inclined and quick to dance.

Both Ruspoli and Thulin are very human presences and reasonably attractive, a fact that considerably mutes the shock value of sex over 60. Much more scandalous — but far too predictable — is the indifference and cruelty of the bored doctors and attendants, who gang up on the happy couple. To "calm them down," they steal Adelina's dentures. It doesn't matter to Andrea, but it's a tragedy for the vain lady.

She finally gets hold of a pair of vampire-fang teeth that bring her smile back, and the afternoons in the camper begin again. But the lovers soon decide to go separate ways with the same strained optimism they've always shown. Adelina drives off with her black friends for some unknown destination, and film ends on a note of puzzling fantasy.

Pic's best qualities are the details Ferreri spotlights, such as Andrea's dandyism or his skill at playing the "Arab guitar." Elizabeth Kaza has a splendid cameo as his chronically ill wife, a feisty old Hungarian countess.

A few characters even manage to burst through the pic's heavy-handed thesis that old age is dignified and lovable, and they become believable people. Technical credits are adequate.
— *Yung.*

LE PETIT CRIMINEL
(THE LITTLE GANGSTER)
(FRENCH)

An AMLF release of a Sara Films production. (Intl. sales: World Marketing Film, Paris.) Produced by Alain Sarde. Written and directed by Jacques Doillon. Camera (color), William Lubtchansky; editor, Catherine Quesemand; music, Philippe Sarde; sound, Jean-Claude Laureux; production design, J.J. Malderez; production manager, Veronique Gozlan. Reviewed at Berlin Film Festival (competing), Feb. 19, 1991. Running time: **100 MIN.**
The cop . . . . Richard Anconina
The boy . . . . . . Gérald Thomassin
The sister . . . . Clotilde Courau
The mother . . . . . . Jocelyn Perhirin
The saleswoman . . . . Cecile Reigher
The teacher . . . . Dominique Huchede

Already the winner of France's Prix Louis Delluc and nominated for five Césars, Jacques Doillon's new film is a prestige success in France but unlikely to travel well abroad. The excellent dialog is almost impossible to translate effectively, making "The Little Gangster" more routine than it actually is.

Doillon is an uneven director whose films alternate tension and subtlety with repetition and banality. This is one of his better films, and it contains a memorable performance from Gérald Thomassin as a boy on his way to becoming a criminal. (Pic received a special mention at the Berlin Film Festival.)

Set in a provincial seaside town, the simple story follows the boy as he plays hooky, resents his stepfather and his mother's drinking, and rebels. When he discovers he has an older sister, the boy uses his stepfather's gun to hold up a drugstore to get cash to track down his sister.

He's picked up by a cop (Richard Anconina), whom the armed boy takes hostage. The cop helps him find the sister, who seems not much older than the boy himself, and the rest of the film consists of agonized argument over what to do about the boy's crime.

All this is shot in the scope format by William Lubtchansky, who uses the wide screen with rare intelligence to posit his three characters in the frame. Unfortunately, despite the film's many qualities, the finale offers a predictable freeze-frame.

For non-French speakers, "The Little Gangster" will come across as a merely sympathetic portrait of a troubled teen, but it's more than that.

Clotilde Courau is a find as the sister who takes on her brother's cause with passion, and Jocelyn Perhirin is in for a couple of brief but effective scenes as the hopeless mother.

Technically, "The Little Gangster" is topnotch, with another subtle score by Philippe Sarde augmenting the rich visuals.

— *Strat.*

AMANTES
(LOVERS)
(SPANISH)

> A Pedro Costa PCSA production, with the participation of TVE. Produced by Pedro Costa Muste. Directed by Vicente Aranda. Screenplay, Aranda, Alvaro Del, Carlos Perez Merinero; camera (color), Jose Luis Alcaine; editor, Teresa Font; music, Jose Nieto; sound, Miguel Angel Polo; production design, Josep Rosell; costume design, Nereida Bonmati; production manager, Carlos Ramon Lluch. Reviewed at Berlin Film Festival (competing), Feb. 25, 1991. Running time: **103 MIN.**
> Luisa . . . . Victoria Abril
> Paco . . . . Jorge Sanz
> Trini . . . . Maribel Verdu

A passionate love affair leading to murder is the gist of this stylish and erotic new Spanish pic, based on an actual 1955 murder case. Though the plot is familiar, Vicente Aranda's film is gripping throughout and boasts another steamy performance from Victoria Abril ("Tie Me Up! Tie Me Down!"), who netted the Berlin fest's best actress award for this one.

The drama is rooted in the restricted moral code of the Franco era. Paco (Jorge Sanz) has just finished his military training and is engaged to marry the virginal Trini (Maribel Verdu), a maid for Paco's former commander and his wife.

Trini won't allow sex before marriage, and frustrated Paco rents a room in town from Luisa (Abril), an attractive young widow who soon has him in her bed. The sex scenes are pretty hot and include a few new variations on the way such sequences usually are handled.

Trini suspects something's up, and, encouraged by her mistress, is determined to fight back, finally allowing Paco to sleep with her. But by now, it's too late.

Paco is hopelessly in lust with Luisa and only wants Trini's savings. When Luisa suggests they kill the girl, she further reveals her husband didn't die of natural causes.

Aranda, best known for the "El Lute" films, has handled this tale of *amour fou* with brio. He wastes no time on inessentials, pushing the story forward to its tragic conclusion and eliciting excellent performances from all three leads.

Camerawork by Jose Luis Alcaine is beautiful, both in the warm scenes in Madrid, where most of the events occur, and in the snowbound provincial town where the characters converge for the final tragedy.

Though the film's poster somewhat unnervingly features an open razor, the murder scene actually is handled with great discretion and is all the more powerful for that. The plot belongs to a well-worn tradition, but Aranda injects freshness into it. Result should do well in Spanish territories, with wider international release also possible. It's technically superior in every department. — *Strat.*

KOMM IN DEN GARTEN
(COME INTO THE GARDEN)
(GERMAN-DOCU)

> A CON Film release of a Defa Studio production. Produced by Fritz Hartthaler. Written and directed by Heinz Brinkmann, Jochen Wisotzki. Camera (color), Michael Lösche; editor, Karin Schoning; sound, Ulrich Fengler, Ronald Guhlke. Reviewed at Berlin Film Festival (New German Films), Feb. 17, 1991. Running time: **93 MIN.**

This documentary about East German political prisons is admirable for its detailed look at the lives of three men incarcerated for bucking the system. But what a downer, both in content and in commercial prospects.

The point of "Come Into The Garden" seems to be that, if these guys were not schizo before they were thrown into jail, they certainly became that way before long.

On the plus side, docu dispenses with the moralizing voiceover so common to West German docus on similar issues. Tech credits are up to par for Defa productions. — *Gill.*

CABEZA DE VACA
(MEXICAN-SPANISH)

> A Producciones Iguana-Television Española co-production, in association with Channel 4 Television, American Playhouse Theatrical Films. (Intl. sales: Ventana Films/Robert Littmen Co., L.A.) Executive producer, Bertha Navarro. Produced by Rafael Cruz, Jorge Sanchez, Julio Solorzano Foppa. Directed by Nicolas Echevarria. Screenplay, Echevarria, Guillermo Sheridan, based on book "Shipwrecks" by Alvar Nuñez Cabeza de Vaca; camera (Eastmancolor), Guillermo Navarro; editor, Rafael Castandeo; music, Mario Lavista; production design, Jose Luis Aguilar; costumes, Totita Figueroa; special effects, Laurencio (Chovi) Cordero; special effects makeup, Guillermo del Toro; production manger, Rosina Rivas; assistant director, Sabastian Silva; choreography, Lidya Romero. Reviewed at Berlin Film Festival (competing), Feb. 23, 1991. Running time: **111 MIN.**
> Alvar Nuñez Cabeza
> de Vaca . . . . Juan Diego
> Dorantes . . . . Daniel Gimenez Cacho
> Cascabel/Araino . . . . . Roberto Sosa
> Castillo . . . . Carlos Castanon
> Estebanico . . . . . . Gerardo Villareal
> Lozoya . . . . Roberto Cobo
> Malacosa . . . . Jose Flores
> Hechicero . . Eli Machuca (Chupadera)
> Anciana Avavar . . Josefina Echanove
> Esquivel . . . . Oscar Yoldi

A kind of Mexican "Dances With Wolves," "Cabeza de Vaca" is good enough to attract discriminating arthouse patrons around the world.

A large-scale film set between 1528 and 1536, pic is based on the memoirs of the title character, Alvar Nuñez Cabeza de Vaca, who, during the Spanish conquest, was captured by Indian tribes living in what is now Florida.

After Cabeza de Vaca is shipwrecked on the Florida coast, most of his comrades, including a priest, are killed in Indian attacks soon after they set foot on land. Cabeza de Vaca is captured and handed over to a shaman, who has an armless dwarf assistant.

Unable to communicate with the Spaniard, the Indians treat him roughly at first. After an attempt to escape, which is thwarted by the shaman's magic, Cabeza de Vaca accepts his fate and starts to learn his captors' language and magical powers. Eventually, he's even able to cure a man who's been blinded (as a result of a spell), and at that point is allowed to go free. Touchingly, the dwarf weeps as Cabeza de Vaca departs.

He wanders through the hostile countryside until he's captured by another tribe, which has imprisoned other survivors from his expedition. During an attack by a rival tribe, Cabeza de Vaca demonstrates his new powers, and a friendlier tribe accepts him as a shaman. But his Spanish comrades are dismayed when they see him bring an apparently dead girl back to life, fearing they are watching heresy.

Eventually, the Spaniards are reunited with their own people, just as the destruction of the Indian tribes that Cabeza de Vaca has befriended gets underway.

Director Nicolas Echevarria, who hitherto has made documentaries, has convincingly re-created the world of the long gone Indian tribes of Florida and Louisiana and presented a powerful story of survival.

Most of the film is told without dialog, with the Indians speaking in their own language (untranslated). As a result, Echevarria is forced to tell his story visually, which he does with great success. The film fascinates with its documentary-style details of tribal life, traditions and customs, though violence in the Indian attacks is shown as brutal and unrelenting.

Juan Diego gives a strong performance as the captive who learns a great deal during the eight years he lives with the Indians. He is ably supported by a wholly convincing cast.

Guillermo Navarro's camerawork is extremely fine, and the film is firstrate in every technical department. Every attempt has been made to achieve authenticity. It's a demanding pic for audiences, but they will be well rewarded with a film that's exotic, mysterious, bizarre (shades of Alexandro Jodorowsky) and dramatic. Certainly "Cabeza de Vaca" is one of the best Mexican films produced in recent years. — *Strat.*

ISICHES MERES TOU AVGOUSTOU
(QUIET DAYS IN AUGUST)
(GREEK)

A Greek Film Center-Kineton production. Written, produced and directed by Pantelis Voulgaris. Camera (Eastmancolor)-editor, Dinos Katsouridis; music, Manos Hadjidakis; sound, Andreas Achiadis, Thanassis Georgiadis; production design, Pericles Hoursoghlou; costumes, Anastasia Arseni; production manager, Stavros Melieas. Reviewed at Berlin Film Festival (competing), Feb. 25, 1991. Running time: **108 MIN.**
Aleka . . . . Aleka Paizi
Elly . . . . Themis Bazaka
Nikos . . . . Thanassis Vengos
Maria . . . . Chrysoula Diavati
Man on phone . . . . Alekos Oudinotis
Woman on phone . . . . . Irene Iglessi

Pantelis Voulgaris has turned out one of his best films with "Quiet Days In August," a calm, meditative pic about lonely people enduring the stifling summer in an Athens emptied by vacationing citizens. It's an unfashionable subject, but with careful handling it should find an appreciative audience.

Lonely old Aleka (Aleka Paizi) lives with memories of the man she loved during the war. She telephones radio stations with record requests but otherwise has little to do until she meets a neighbor, a younger woman (Themis Bazaka) with whom she strikes up an instant rapport.

The culmination of this relationship, which combines betrayal and fulfillment, ends the film on a sublime moment of beauty and peace.

Nikos (Thanassis Vengos), a retired seaman forever dreaming of the exotic life he used to lead, lives with his wife in an empty relationship. One evening, he helps a woman who has fainted in a train station. Her husband died that day, which, ironically, was her birthday.

This chance encounter gives new meaning to Nikos' life, and popular comic actor Vengos plays the character compellingly.

Alekos Oudinotis plays a bank employee who, every afternoon at 4, gets an erotic phone call from an unknown woman. He becomes obsessed with identifying her, but when he finally does, the excitement of the relationship dissipates.

Voulgaris skillfully intercuts these tales of lonely and frustrated people into a gentle, touching and beautifully made film. Photography by Dinos Katsouridis is outstanding, with much of the shooting taking place inside apartments shuttered against the hot August sun. There's also a beautiful score by veteran Manos Hadjidakis, with apt use of old romantic songs for the scenes involving Aleka.

The pacing and understated style will make the film hard to market, but it should play the fest route successfully and garner specialized distribution in territories where Voulgaris' work ("The Engagement Of Anna" and "Stone Years") is known.

"Quiet Days In August," which garnered a mention by the Berlin Film Fest's Intl. Protestant Film Jury, is a feather in the cap for Greek cinema. — *Strat.*

CLASS ACTION

A 20th Century Fox release of an Interscope Communications production. Produced by Ted Field, Scott Kroopf and Robert W. Cort. Co-producers, Carolyn Shelby, Christopher Ames. Directed by Michael Apted. Screenplay, Shelby, Ames, Samantha Shad; camera (Deluxe color), Conrad L. Hall; editor, Ian Crafford; music, James Horner; sound (Dolby), Michael Evje; production design, Todd Hallowell; art direction, Mark Billerman; set design, Barbara Mesney; set decoration, Dan May; costume design, Rita Ryack; assistant director, Marty Ewing; associate producer/unit production manager, Kim Kurumada; casting, Lora Kennedy, Linda Lowy. Reviewed at Cineplex Odeon Century Plaza Theaters, L.A., Feb. 28, 1991. MPAA rating: R. Running time: **109 MIN.**
Jedediah Ward . . . . . Gene Hackman
Maggie . Mary Elizabeth Mastrantonio
Michael Grazier . . . . . . Colin Friels
Estelle Ward . . . . . . Joanna Merlin
Nick Holbrook . . . . Larry Fishburne
Quinn . . . . Donald Moffat
Pavel . . . . Jan Rubes
Dr. Getchell . . Fred Dalton Thompson
Brian . . . . .Jonathan Silverman

Winning performances by Gene Hackman and Mary Elizabeth Mastrantonio and potent direction by Michael Apted pump life into the sturdy courtroom drama formula once again, and "Class Action" should bring 20th Century Fox a solid settlement at the boxoffice.

Pic's parameters may be worn, but Apted's keen focus on its emotional core helps it transcend the everyday. The script's stance against corporate greed should please the public in the aftermath of various 1980s financial debacles.

Hackman plays Jed Ward, a veteran civil rights lawyer still dedicated to defending the underdog, though his track record, both professional and personal, is not without blotches.

Mastrantonio is his daughter Maggie, a ruthlessly effective corporate advocate and ladder-climber, whose disdain for her father has more to do with his amorous indiscretions than his politics.

They wind up on opposite sides of a class action suit filed against an auto company by the maimed survivors of crashes in which the cars exploded on impact.

Viewer sympathy accumulates quickly for Hackman, the charismatic, if flawed, man of the people, but Mastrantonio carves out her own turf and hangs on to it, truly taking on the senior actor.

She doesn't overplay the role of razor-edge professional, and she takes a girlish pleasure in her successes. She projects an integrity that guides her through a confusing and incestuous scenario.

Her grudge against her father, for the way he wounded her mother, is expressed with conviction, whether or not it's justified, and their scenes together have a locked-horns intensity as they hurl barbs at each another.

For the first half, much of the script is by the numbers, as characters deliver plodding dialog to lay out the situation, but things pick up.

"I'm a professional killer," Maggie tells a flirtatious bartender on a day when her father has made her truly chagrined at her own tactics.

At first convinced the class action suit has no merit, Maggie works up a cool fury when she finds she's on the wrong side of it and that she's being used by her own firm.

Pic's dark exposé of corporate thinking should prove rousing to an audience fed up with the S&L and junk bond fiascos.

Courtroom confrontation plays out in a reasonably engrossing and inventive way, and action is boosted by some fine supporting turns, particularly Colin Friels as Maggie's corporate higher-up and love interest, and Joanna Merlin as Maggie's mother.

Director Apted ("Gorillas In The Mist," "Coal Miner's Daughter") allowed for a three-week rehearsal with the actors, and it pays off in the crucial chemistry between Hackman and Mastrantonio. Apted's work on location in San Francisco with director of photography Conrad Hall adds up to a particularly well-shot film.

Production credits are pro and James Horner's score is subtle and effective. — *Daws.*

CLOSET LAND

A Universal Pictures release of an Imagine Entertainment presentation. Executive producers, Brian Grazer and Ron Howard. Produced by Janet Meyers. Directed and written by Radha Bharadwaj. Camera (color), Bill Pope; editor, Lisa Churgin; production design, Eiko Ishioka; costume design, Ishioka; original music, Richard Einhorn; music supervision, Philip Glass; sound, Stephan Von Hase-Milhalik; art direction, Kenneth A. Hardy; set decoration, Gary Matteson; assistant director, Karen Koch. Reviewed at Skywalker screening room, Los Angeles, Feb. 20, 1990. MPAA rating: R. Running time: **89 MIN.**
Woman . . . . Madeleine Stowe
Man . . . . Alan Rickman

MCA-backed Imagine Entertainment has taken the commendable step of putting its resources behind a project that addresses the horror of political torture, but this harrowing, focused two-character piece by first-time director Radha Bharadwaj is not an experience many filmgoers will want to put down money for.

The highly theatrical "Closet Land," imaginatively produced by Janet Meyers on a modest $2.5 million, cannot be faulted for its presentation.

Entire thing takes place in an interrogation room, with a man (Alan Rickman) trying to break the will of a woman (Madeleine Stowe). Despite the claustrophobic setup, a great deal occurs to hold one's interest.

First of all, this is no harshly lighted dungeon. It's a gleaming, stylish, high-tech chamber most film execs would covet as an office. Its automated gadgets and mix of classical and futuristic motifs (designed by Eiko Ishioka) make it a volatile third presence.

Richman as interrogator is no ordinary brute but a complex, highly civilized man who displays a range of emotions and talents, including the ability to voice-act other people to confuse his blindfolded victim.

Stowe is a physically captivating victim with a fierce attachment to justice. Given a chance early on to escape, she stays and demands an apology. It's a costly error.

Bharadwaj and cinematographer Bill Pope combine stage and filmic techniques to effect many changes of mood and tortured mind in a confined space, beginning with the intense opening, in which the situation unfolds in darkness, as perceived by the blindfolded victim.

But none of these skillful flourishes make up for the fact that Bharadwaj's script is not terribly entrancing, suffering mostly from a weak central metaphor and lack of specificity.

Attempting to be "universal," it offers neither enough information nor enough realism on which to focus outrage.

Story has Stowe, an author of children's books, dragged from her bed to face a servant of the government (Rickman) who accuses her of peddling subversive ideas to children in the guise of innocent stories.

At issue is her work in progress, "Closet Land," about a little girl whose mother leaves her locked in a closet. The child pretends that the clothes turn into animal friends and have a party with her until the parrot scarf, who is the lookout, warns of her mother's return.

According to the interrogator, this is a veiled attempt to sell children on the idea of having secret meetings against the government. He wants the woman to sign a confession, but she won't, prompting him to torture her.

The story, which in many ways would seem more appropriate on a stage, is about a contest of wills — she wants to reach his humanity and sense of decency and to break down his resolve with her courage.

This conflict reaches its pitch in hurled flurries of dialog that have a precision and force equivalent to serious theater, and perhaps it was the headiness of these clashes that sold producers on the work.

But the children's story at the core is a thin and abbreviated one, not rich enough to anchor this abstract political treatise, and the "closet land" metaphor becomes rather strained, as it's supposed to represent not only the refuge the victim escapes to in her imagination but the whole secretive business of oppression.

It's all further clouded by the relevation that the author as a child was sexually abused in a closet, making this a rather confused hybrid of political and sexual outcry.

Nonetheless, there is one very affecting idea at work — the belief in the power of resistance at any cost — and it does bring the picture its measure of triumphant uplift.

Bharadwaj has done fine work with the actors, and Rickman deserves a great deal of notice for his powerfully controlled, multifaceted performance. Stowe displays some flash and backbone, but not enough to make this a truly engaging match.

Musical contributions by Richard Einhorn and Philip Glass are highly sophisticated, in line with Ishioka's arresting set.

The achievement of Bharadwaj in getting such an unusual project produced by a mainstream company is inspiring. Still, it undeniably will be a hard sell to theater audiences, and one wonders if it could not have found a wider audience in another medium — public television, perhaps.

Amnesty Intl. served as consultant and is participating in the pic's marketing campaign.
— *Daws.*

BUDDY'S SONG
(BRITISH)

A Castle Premier release (in U.K.) of a Buddy Prods. presentation. Produced by Roy Baird, Bill Curbishley, Roger Daltrey. Co-producer, Ron Boreham. Directed by Claude Whatham. Screenplay, Nigel Hinton, from his novel; camera (color), John Hooper; editor, John Grover; music, Alan Shacklock, Daltrey; sound (Dolby), Alistair Crocker; production design, Grant Hicks; art director, Ray Corbett; costume design, Sheelagh Killeen; assistant director, Andrew Rothschild; associate producer, Brenda Baird. Reviewed at Cannon Oxford St. theater, London, March 5, 1991. Running time: **105 MIN.**
Terry . . . . Roger Daltrey
Carol . . . . Sharon Duce
Buddy . . . . Chesney Hawkes
Des King . . . . Michael Elphick
Brian Rosen . . . . . . Douglas Hodge

A British gorblimey version of "Harry And Son," with a rock retro background, "Buddy's Song" is breezy, anodyne fare better suited to the tube. Roger Daltrey (in a non-singing role) lacks the present-day teen appeal to keep "Buddy's Song" from zooming down the theatrical charts.

Daltrey plays Terry, a streetwise a.o.r. (aging old rocker) who's into petty crime and reckons decent music died with Buddy Holly — he even named his son after the singer. After his latest stint in stir, he decides to turn over a new leaf and mastermind Buddy's burgeoning music career.

Meanwhile, Terry's home life is going from bad to worse: Estranged wife Carol (Sharon Duce) is studying computers and being romanced by her smarmy boss, and Buddy (Chesney Hawkes) is caught in a tug-of-love between his parents.

Squeaky-clean pic is reminiscent of old-style Children's Film Foundation matinee items. Daltrey, who co-produced as well as "designed and directed" the soundtrack of songs (Holly standards, plus newer items), plays the chirpy Cockney at full tilt, complete with '50s sideburns and outré teddy-boy gear. Duce makes the most of her long-suffering mom role, and tv thesps Michael Elphick and Douglas Hodge score briefly as a fellow crook and smooth diskery exec. As Buddy, Hawkes is too winsome by half whenever he puts down the microphone.

Claude Whatham, who trod some of this territory in "That'll Be The Day" (1973), keeps the so-so script moving along, much helped by John Grover's brisk editing. All other credits are par. — *Drek.*

GUILTY BY SUSPICION

A Warner Bros. release of an Arnon Milchan production. Produced by Milchan. Executive producer, Steven Reuther. Co-producer, Alan C. Blomquist. Directed and written by Irwin Winkler. Camera (Deluxe color; Technicolor prints), Michael Ballhaus; editor, Priscilla Nedd; music, James Newton Howard; sound (Dolby), Richard Lightstone; production design, Leslie Dilley; art direction, Leslie McDonald; set decoration, Nancy Haigh; costume design, Richard Bruno; associate producer, Nelson McCormick; assistant director, Rob Cowan; casting, Marion Dougherty. Reviewed at Warner Bros. Studios, Burbank, Calif., Feb. 5, 1991. MPAA Rating: PG-13. Running time: **105 MIN.**
David Merrill . . . . . . Robert De Niro
Ruth Merrill . . . . . . Annette Bening
Bunny Baxter . . . . . . George Wendt
Dorothy Nolan . . . Patricia Wettig
Felix Graff . . . . . Sam Wanamaker
Paulie Merrill . . . . . . Luke Edwards
Larry Nolan . . . . Chris Cooper
Darryl Zanuck . . . . Ben Piazza
Joe Lesser . . . . Martin Scorsese
Bert Alan . . . . Barry Primus
Chairman Wood . . . . Gailard Sartain
Congressman
Tavenner . . . . Robin Gammell
Congressman Velde . . . Brad Sullivan
Ray Karlin . . . . Tom Sizemore
Felicia Barron . . . . . . Roxann Biggs
Abe Barron . . . . . . Stuart Margolin
Jerry Cooper . . . . Barry Tubb
Gene Woods . . . . . . Gene Kirkwood
Leta Rosen . . . . . . Margo Winkler
Leonard Marks . . . . Allan Rich
Nan . . . . Illeana Douglas

"Guilty By Suspicion" tackles one of the thorniest issues in contemporary American history — the Hollywood blacklist — with sympathetic but mixed results.

First writing-directing effort by vet producer Irwin Winkler squarely lays out the professional, ethical and moral dilemmas engendered by the insidious political pressures brought to bear on filmmakers in the early 1950s, and Robert De Niro is excellent as a top director brought down by reactionary paranoia. But the drama comes to life only fitfully, and the perennial b.o. problems posed by both Hollywood and political subjects make this one a challenge commercially.

Project started with blacklist victim Abraham Polonsky on board as writer and Bertrand Tavernier, for whom Winkler produced " 'Round Midnight," as director. After both departed, Winkler proceeded alone, enlisting the collaboration of longtime associates De Niro and Martin Scorsese, with the latter playing a director very much like Joseph

Losey. Several actual blacklistees and their relatives turn up in supporting roles.

De Niro portrays David Merrill, "Zanuck's golden boy," a director on a roll who lives only for his work. Arriving back in Hollywood in 1951 after a European sojourn, he soon finds the atmosphere changed, and much for the worse.

Charged by a colleague as having attended a couple of left-wing meetings years before, Merrill is asked by 20th Century Fox boss Darryl F. Zanuck to cooperate with the House Un-American Activities Committee before proceeding with his next big production.

After a disagreeable meeting with an attorney (Sam Wanamaker) and a HUAC rep, Merrill, refusing to cooperate, finds that the chill sets in almost immediately.

Merrill is yanked from the Fox film, listens to his agent demand back a $50,000 advance, looks to lose his house and hears his 10-year-old son doubting him. Worst of all, no one will return his calls.

A trip back to New York, where Merrill imagines he can find work in the theater, proves fruitless, so it's back to L.A., where the wife of a guilt-ridden informer commits suicide, a demeaning job directing a seventh-day Monogram Western ends in Merrill's firing and his best friend, a screenwriter (George Wendt), comes to him tearfully begging permission to name him in his own upcoming testimony.

Pic climaxes with Merrill's raucous, contentious hearing before the full committee in Washington, a scene that reveals a fair measure of HUAC's pettiness and evil.

There are certainly hundreds of ways in which the tragic ramifications of the witch hunt era could be dramatized, and Winkler has opted on focusing on a middle-of-the-road character who happens, through youthful "indiscretion" rather than any true conviction on his part, to get caught in the blacklist's vast net.

Downside of this tack, however, is the presence centerscreen of a mild-mannered man who keeps wondering for the longest time why all this is happening to him, who waffles on the issues and can't decide what to do. All he wants is to be able to earn big money making films again.

After a promising beginning, pic bogs down as the director trudges around looking for work and trying to figure out a strate-gy. Too many scenes are bland, relatively undramatic two-character exchanges, the accumulation of which makes one feel that more interesting and exciting things are happening elsewhere that aren't getting any attention.

Affiliation or sympathy with communism is essentially palmed off as "people caring about people" back in the 1930s. Nowhere are Stalin, union activities or varying degrees of politicization discussed, and script really could have used a scene in which Merrill met with others in the same boat to discuss all the issues and possible ploys. The only famous film world figure to be presented by name is Zanuck, and pic could have benefited from more of the same.

Overall, Winkler's storytelling lacks dramatic tension, and the disturbing events on view should have emerged as even more convulsive than is the case. Nevertheless, handsome production has significant qualities to recommend it, beginning with De Niro's performance.

Looking more raffish and trimmer than he has in a while, De Niro perfectly conveys a charming, quiet confidence at the outset. After his character's protracted confusion, he distills his true feelings during the extraordinary appearance before HUAC, finally blossoming into a man of conviction and passion. The actor pulls off this last-minute transformation beautifully.

Supporting performances, including those by Annette Bening as Merrill's ex-wife, Wendt and the once-blacklisted Wanamaker, are solid. Ben Piazza's Zanuck is physically right but a bit genteel. Buffs will be amused by a scene in which the mogul watches dailies from "Gentlemen Prefer Blondes" featuring Marilyn Monroe and calls up director Howard Hawks to berate him for shooting too many takes.

Lenser Michael Ballhaus has attractively grounded the film in earth tones, and production designer Leslie Dilley has not only succeeded in expertly evoking the Hollywood of 40 years ago, but has reproduced areas of New York and Washington with utter conviction. — Cart.

SHADOW OF CHINA
(JAPANESE-AMERICAN)

A New Line release of a Nippon Herald Films/Fuji Television Network/Marubeni/Nissh Iwai presentation of an S.H. Prods. and Elliott Lewitt Prods. production. Produced by Elliott Lewitt, Don Guest. Executive producer, Satoru Iseki. Directed by Mitsuo Yanagimachi. Screenplay, Richard Maxwell, Yanagimachi, based on the novel "Snake Head" by Masaaki Nishiki. Camera (Foto-Kem color), Toyomichi Kurita; supervising editor, Paul Seydor; editor, Sachiko Yamagi; music, Yasuaki Shimizu; sound, Xanichi Benitani, Susumu Tokunow; production design, Andrew McAlpine; art direction, Rod McLean, Jonathan Cheung, Dominique Lo; set decoration, Barbara Drake; costume design, Sandy Powell; associate producers, Ben Sakurai, Aimi O; assistant director, Jerry Grandey; casting, Mali Finn (U.S.), Patricia Pao (Hong Kong). Reviewed at Sunset Towers screening room, L.A., March 6, 1991. No MPAA rating. Running time: **100 MIN.**
Wu Chang/Henry Wong . . John Lone
Akira . . . . Koichi Sato
Katharine . . . . Sammi Davis
Moo-Ling . . . . Vivian Wu
Lee Hok Chow . . . . Roy Chiao
Jameson . . . . . Constantine Gregory
Burke . . . . Colin George

Visually arresting but dramatically lethargic and unfocused, "Shadow Of China" suffers from a script that can't decide whether it wants to explore Chinese/Japanese/Hong Kong politics or settle into a more conventional crime plot. Filmed mostly in Hong Kong by Japanese director Mitsuo Yanagimachi, the New Line release is a marginal U.S. market entry.

(Film was released in Japan last year with a 120-minute running time, but subsequently was cut by the producer without director Yanagimachi's participation. — Ed.)

John Lone and his second wife from "The Last Emperor," Vivian Wu, here play fervent Chinese radical youths who flee their homeland during the 1976 upheavals and settle separately in gaudily decadent Hong Kong, where Lone becomes a corrupt capitalist and Wu scrounges for a living singing in a brothel.

Yanagimachi and co-scripter Richard Maxwell, working from the novel "Snake Head" by Masaaki Nishiki, intend to deal with such complex themes as the transformation of radical idealism into cynicism, the lingering post-World War II animosities between the Japanese and the Chinese and the anxieties in Hong Kong over the British colony's 1997 reversion to China.

But the plot mechanics are clumsy, most of the running time is spent working out the logistics of a boring financial struggle between Lone and equally sinister Hong Kong capitalist Roy Chiao over a local newspaper and some adjoining property, and not enough attention is devoted to the complexities of Lone's character.

After the Chinese prolog, the dialog is mostly in English, and the flat dialog is further weighed down by stiff and awkward delivery by most of the cast. Wu's English-language songs are poorly synched.

Lone seems more depressed than intense, the alluring Wu is saddled with an ill-defined part, Koichi Sato is too diffident for his crusading-journalist role, and Lone's British mistress (Sammi Davis) acts ridiculously lubricious, but Chiao makes a suitably imposing villain.

Only the firstrate contributions of lenser Toyomichi Kurita and production designer Andrew McAlpine keep the film from being a total snooze. — Mac.

EUROPA EUROPA
(FRENCH-GERMAN)

A Les Films Du Losange (Paris)-CCC Filmkunst (Berlin) co-production, in association with Perspektywa Film Unit (Janusz Morgenstern), Warsaw. (Intl. sales: Roissy Film, Paris.) Produced by Margaret Menegoz, Artur Brauner. Directed by Agnieszka Holland. Screenplay, Holland, based on memoirs of Salomon Perel; camera (Eastmancolor), Jacek Petrycki; editor, Ewa Smal; music, Zbigniew Priesner; sound, Elisabeth Mondi; production design, Allan Starski; costume design, Wiesa Starska; production manager, Barbara Pec Slesicka; assistant director, Krstyna Grochowitz; casting, Margot Capelier. Reviewed at Roissy Films screening room, Paris, Feb. 14, 1991. Running time: **110 MIN.**
Salomon Perel . . Marco Hofschneider
Leni . . . . Julie Delpy
Kellerman . . . . Andre Wilms
Eric . . . . Aschley Wanninger
Capt. Von Lereneau . . Hanns Zischler
Schultz . . . . Klaus Kowatsch
Leni's mother . . . Hanna Labornaska
Inna Moisievna . . . . Delphine Forest
David Perel . . . . . Rene Hoschneider
Pfeiffer . . . . .Jorg Schnass
Basia . . . . Natalie Schmidt

In "Europa Europa," Agnieszka Holland tells an almost unbelievable but true story of a young Polish Jew who successfully posed as a loyal German Nazi to escape death during World War II. Filled with suspense and touches of humor, pic brings a fresh approach to familiar themes and should find appreciative arthouse audiences in many parts of the world.

Holland's screenplay is based on the memoirs of Salomon Perel, who appears in the final sequence to lend authenticity to this remarkable record of his adventures.

Born in Germany in 1925 of Polish-Jewish parents, Sally discovered the humiliation of anti-Semitism at an early age. His family relocated to Lodz, Poland, where he had his first romance (at 16) with the hunchbacked usherette at a cinema. Later, after the death of his sister in a Nazi riot, Sally and his older brother, David, were sent east to Russia (the rest of his family stayed behind and perished in the Lodz ghetto).

Separated from David, Sally was captured by the Russians and placed in an orphanage where he was indoctrinated as a member of the Communist Komsomol Youth Organization. When the Germans attack, his fluency in German fools them into thinking he is, indeed, German; because he speaks fluent Russian also, he's used as interpreter.

There follows a series of extraordinary adventures as Sally is "adopted" by a German officer and sent to Berlin to be trained in a Hitler Youth School. Here he lives in dread that he will be exposed and is unable to consummate a budding relationship with a pretty young Nazi for fear she will see that he's circumcised. With the fall of Berlin, he gives himself up to Russian troops and is about to be executed when he's reunited with his long-lost brother.

Holland creates considerable suspense and tension as she charts the dangerous life the teen is forced to lead during the turbulent war years. Marco Hofschneider is wholly convincing as Sally, who detests the role he has to maintain.

The handsomely staged production, shot in Germany and Poland, benefits from authentic settings and a little-known cast, with Hanns Zischler (from Wim Wenders' "Kings Of The Road"), who plays the German officer who befriends Sally, the most familiar of the supporting players.

Technically, pic is fine. And though the basic situations are familiar, the fascinating real-life story brings freshness to them.

Though a majority French co-production, dialog is mostly in German with a little Polish and Russian in some scenes. — *Strat.*

UNDERJORDENS HEMLIGHET
(THE SECRET OF THE UNDERGROUND)
(SWEDISH)

A Sandrew release of a Sandrew production in association with the Swedish Film Institute and Swedish TV Channel 1. Produced by Lennart Dunér. Directed by Clas Lindberg. Screenplay, Lindberg; camera, Andra Lasmanis; editor, Lindberg, Carina Hellberg; music, Thomas Lindahl; sound, Patrik Strömdahl, Ulrika Akander; production design, Eric Johnson; costume design, Cecilia Nohrborg; assistant director, Kerstin Hagström; associate producer, Peter Hald. Reviewed at the Astoria cinema, Stockholm, Feb. 15, 1991. Running time: **81 MIN.**

With: Max Vitali, Oliver Loftéen, Gösta Ekman, Kristina Törnqvist, Gunnel Fred, Hans Wigren, Ulf Eklund.

A moody and suspenseful pic about children and death, "The Secret Of The Underground" is a well-made film appealing to both kids and adults. Carefully handled, it could cross over to other countries.

Since director Clas Lindberg's debut "The Fox" flopped, he has worked in tv, which seems to have done him good. His return to the big screen should generate lots of interest.

In a mostly somber mood, the film tells the story of 10-year-old Nils, who tries to get to know his hospital roommates, Carson, an old and egocentric man with spasms, and 12-year-old Lelle, his daydreams and his love for a pretty nurse are what keep him going.

Kids will be hooked on the suspense in the boys' nightly expeditions, and adults will be captured by Lelle and his fears of getting close to another human being. This film takes children seriously.

However, some scenes depicting the boys spying on the hospital staff and stealing things stretch the limits of credibility. And a chase in a hospital corridor toward the end of the film feels out of place. The somber mood is broken by ill-fitting slapstick action.

Tech credits are fine. The photography gives an efficiently cold and futuristic look to the underground scenes, and the direction lets the actors excel. The noteworthy music is an important ingredient in creating the mood.

Lindberg's fine film should attract an audience in Sweden

(where it opened in late February) and abroad, but it will need careful handling that emphasizes the serious aspects more than the comedic touches. — *Gunn.*

ISHANOU
(THE CHOSEN ONE)
(INDIAN)

An A.S. Sharma production. Produced and directed by Aribam Syam Sharma. Screenplay, M.K. Binodini Devi; camera (color), Girish Padhiar; editor, Ujjal Nandi; music, Sharma; sound, Durga Das Mitra; production manager, G. Nirmalkuma Sharma; assistant director, Kishore Chand. Reviewed at Sou h Indian Film Chamber of Commerce screening room, Madras, Jan. 15, 1991. Running time: **95 MIN.**

With: Kiranmala, Tomba, Manbi, Dhiren, Baby Molly.

One of the best Indian films of the past year, "The Chosen One" looks as though it'll make its way on the international film festival circuit. Specialized arthouse release also is possible.

The strange, haunting tale about a young wife who joins a religious sect is set in Manipur, which borders Burma. A young couple live with their small daughter and the wife's mother. The husband is a petty bureaucrat with a secure job, and the family is happy. An early sequence has the child go through an ear-piercing ceremony, an event that appears to have the same importance as a bar mitzvah.

But the wife starts acting strangely, at first talking to flowers and singing strange songs, and then having fits so violent she must be tied to her bed. The woman is possessed by a benign spirit and has been "chosen" to join a religious sect, the Meibis.

One night she wanders off and finds her Meibi guru and begins a strange new lifestyle, leaving her grieving husband and child behind.

Producer-director-composer Aribam Syam Sharma handles this exotic material with a simple, direct freshness that makes it most appealing and includes a touching coda.

Scenes of religious dances in the second part of the film could be slightly trimmed, but otherwise this unsettling, visually beautiful film should be well received by Western audiences.

It's technially fine, apart from slightly washed-out color.
— *Strat.*

SOMETHING TO DO WITH THE WALL
(DOCU)

A First Run Features release. Written, produced and directed by Marilyn Levine and Ross McElwee. Camera (color), editing and sound, Levine, McElwee; editing assistant, Annie Ballard; archival research, Jean Kendall; production assistant, Rosalie Levine. Reviewed at the Brattle Theater, Cambridge, Mass., Jan. 18, 1991. No MPAA rating. Running time: **88 MIN.**

This fascinating and often moving documentary about the Berlin Wall focuses on the 25th anni of the barrier in 1986 and its fall in 1989. In limited specialty engagements, "Something To Do With The Wall" should attract strong notice.

Instead of history, filmmakers Marilyn Levine and Ross McElwee depict people, mostly West Berliners, living in the shadow of the wall. In a brief intro, they explain the wall's meaning to Americans growing up at the height of the cold war: It is *the* symbol of Communist tyranny.

As tourists in summer 1986, they view the wall, climb an observation deck to look at largely deserted streets on the other side and watch the goings-on at Checkpoint Charlie.

The audience soon becomes interested in the people for whom the wall is not a tourist attraction but a fact of life. The film moves from protesters to neighborhood residents to a man living as a squatter on a Berlin thoroughfare turned dead-end.

The East German authorities are seen as they maintain the wall. In one quietly chilling sequence, an armed guard stands watch over an East German grounds worker so he won't try to escape.

Pic was intended to end with the anniversary protests, but post-production was interrupted by real life: The East German government was tearing down the wall. Levine and McElwee hurried back to Berlin to track down their interview subjects for perspectives on what was unthinkable three years before.

The comic souvenir hunters seeking a "piece of the wall" are interspersed with people whose lives were changing around them: The squatter must move, and one couple welcomes East Berlin relatives into their home for the first time in 30 years.

In this simply made cinema verité-style film, Levine and McElwee succeed in pointing out that while history is about statesmen and great events, it's also about everyday people and the impact those events have on their lives.
— *Kimm.*

DIE MAUER
(THE WALL)
(GERMAN-DOCU)

A DEFA Studio für Dokumentarfilme production. Produced by Stephan Röder. Directed by Jürgen Böttcher. Screenplay, Böttcher, Thomas Plenert. Camera (Arri color), Plenert; editor, Gudrun Steinbrück; sound, Ronald Gohlke; assistant director, Gerd Kroske. Reviewed at Berlin Film Festival (Forum), Feb. 16, 1991. Running time: **99 MIN.**

One of the last films produced in East Germany, "The Wall" documents the last months of the Berlin Wall in a straightforward manner, unembellished with either music or narration. It should continue on the fest circuit as a historical document, but unwillingness to take a stance on the subject dim theatrical prospects.

The winner of a Berlin fest Fipresci prize for best film out of competition is a lingering meditation on the Berlin Wall in all its many guises: monument, tourist attraction, commodity, graffiti showplace and symbol of a divided Germany.

Helmer Jürgen Böttcher began shooting the wall shortly after it came down Nov. 9, 1989, concentrating primarily on the areas familiar to those who saw the event on the news: the Brandenburg Gate, Potsdamer Platz (once Europe's busiest intersection, now a wasteland) and the Reichstag building.

To the film's credit, it doesn't dwell on familiar images of euphoric Germans breaching the wall and quaffing champagne. But neither does the film tell a story or take a position on the meaning of the wall or Germans' feelings about it.

Böttcher's camera mainly looks at people looking at the wall, occasionally with humor: Giggling Japanese schoolgirls daintily chip off souvenir pieces. A Turkish boy gamely whacks off chunks of the solidly constructed cement.

Kids sell wall pieces to passersby.

The winning moments include a pretty West German girl and East German border guard flirting with each other in the no-man's land that formerly was mined and patrolled by jeeps and dogs. CNN correspondent Richard Bleystone tries to deliver an on-the-spot report, four takes in a row. Hare Krishnas dance and chant through the newly opened Brandenburg Gate.

Pic also delivers a moving look at Berlin Wall and Cold War history via images of archival footage projected onto the scarred surface of the wall itself.

Scenes of jubilant crowds and fireworks are filmed dispassionately, without a point of view. Shots are often well composed, but the photography has an overly grainy look in many sequences.

"The Wall" is just a look at the wall: straightforward, unadorned and objective to a fault. — *Reli.*

LA CONDANNA
(THE JUDGMENT)
(ITALIAN-FRENCH)

A Cineeuropa 92 SRL-Italnoleggio Cinematografica-RAI 2 (Rome)-Banfilm (Paris) co-production in association with Cactus Film (Zurich). (Intl. sales: Sacis, Rome.) Produced by Michele Placido, Pietro Valsecchi. Directed by Marco Bellocchio. Screenplay, Bellocchio, Massimo Fagioli; camera (Eastmancolor), Giuseppe Lanci; editor, Mirco Garrone; music, Carlo Crivelli; sound, Gianni Zampagni; production design, Giantito Burchiellaro; assistant director, Angelo Vicari; production manager, Federico Starace. Reviewed at Berlin Film Festival (competing), Feb. 21, 1991. Running time: **92 MIN.**
Lorenzo Colaianni . . . . Vittorio Mezzogiorno
Sandra . . . . Claire Nebout
Giovanni Malatesta . Andrzej Seweryn
Monica . . . . . Grazyna Szapolowska
Also with: Paolo Graziosi, Maria Sneider, Claudio Emeri.

Marco Bellocchio's new film about rape is likely to stir up controversy, especially in Italy (it's loosely based on a well-reported case there a few years ago). Unfortunately, the precious, mannered treatment and performances that don't work will reduce impact and international prospects for "La Condanna."

Pic, co-winner of a Berlin film fest Silver Bear (special jury prize) opens with a long sequence in a museum where a student (French thesp Claire Nebout) is left behind when the building closes. She finds herself locked

with a stranger, an architect (Vittorio Mezzogiorno).

He makes sexual advances to her, and she appears willing. There are three sexual encounters, and she complains when he stops before she's ready. He then reveals that he had the keys to the building all along.

Bellocchio then cuts abruptly to the trial where, in a courtroom crowded with women, Nebout accuses the architect of rape. Her tearful account of the incident doesn't correspond with what was seen, but the prosecutor (Andrzej Seweryn) pushes successfully for a conviction.

The third part of the film consists of a debate on rape without force. Seweryn's live-in woman friend (Grazyna Szapolowska) unexpectedly takes the convicted rapist's side, cooling toward the confused prosecutor.

Realism is abandoned in the final scenes. The tormented prosecutor is tempted by three women, including Nebout and a strange peasant woman he tries to protect from the seemingly violent assault of men in a field, though she claims she didn't need protection.

Bellocchio handles this touchy subject in a presumably artistic way, but the audience at the press screening in Berlin laughed frequently when laughter was not the intended response. This is partly because the director encouraged his actors, and especially the usually reliable Seweryn, to act like robots. Seweryn is forever gazing at the camera in a mournful/quizzical way, which at first is distracting and then downright irritating. Mezzogiorno's pained grin also is infuriating.

The two women actors are, however, very good, with Nebout as the sensual young woman who shows her feminist attitudes only in court, making a considerable impression. Bellocchio takes himself and his subject so seriously that he shoots himself in the foot, and international audiences aren't likely to be impressed with the pompous debating that punctuates the film.

Worst of all, the film tips from being serious into being silly, reducing its important theme to banality.

"La Condanna" is technically firstrate, with the lengthy take during the sex scene something of a tour de force for the film crew and the actors alike. It will be interesting to see how it's accepted by audiences when it opens in Italy shortly. — *Strat.*

SATANA
(SATAN)
(SOVIET)

A Lenfilm production, with Studio Uliss and Studio Tak-T. Produced by Sergei Avrutin, Valentina Goroschnikova. Written and directed by Viktor Aristov. Camera (Sovcolor), Juri Voronzov; editor, J. Vigdorshik; music, Arkady Gagulaschvili; sound, Nikolai Astachov; production design, Vladimir Bannich; assistant director, L. Schumjatchev; production manager, G. Matjuschin. Reviewed at Berlin Film Festival (competing), Feb. 20, 1991. Running time: **106 MIN.**
Vitali . . . . Sergei Kuprianov
Aljona . . . . Svetlana Bragarnik
Aljona's husband . . Veniamin Malotschevski
Armen . . . . Armen Nasikjan
Vera . . . . Maria Averbach
Also with: Anatoli Aristov, Zhanna Schipkova, Margarita Alekseva, Anna Sagalovitch, Mikhail Staroduboz.

Another bleak look at contemporary life in the Soviet Union, "Satan" depicts a child-murderer in ultra-grim and visually drab terms. Still, pic, co-winner of the Berlin fest Silver Bear (special jury prize), might get international arthouse interest in its theme and setting.

Around dawn on a winter morning in a big city, a mother prepares her 10-year-old daughter for school. Outside, a well-dressed man, apparently the lover of the girl's mother, offers the child a lift on his bicycle. Whistling cheerfully, the young man takes the girl to a quiet place and casually murders her, burying her body in a grave he's already dug.

He returns and calls the girl's home, saying the child has been kidnaped and demanding a ransom. He then spends his day pursuing a young woman who rejects him. He eventually climbs into her apartment at night and she allows him to stay. He attends a wedding and rapes the bride after luring her to a basement room.

Meanwhile, the mother, an important government functionary, is hysterical and bitter toward her husband, an actor who still has to go on stage despite his daughter's disappearance. It turns out the wife, unknown to her husband, has illegally socked away currency, and the killer knew about it.

Eventually, the woman goes to see the killer, who admits his crime but challenges her to expose him without revealing her own wrongdoing. Leaving her in his apartment, he wanders off into the streets and is last seen chatting to pretty girls on a tram and waving to the camera.

This Satanic character's motivations remain obscure, though it's suggested he killed the child because her mother rejected him rather than for the money.

Sergei Kuprianov is chilling as the handsome young killer, who appears to justify his horrendous crime by citing the wider injustice of officials fleecing the Russian public. Still, the viewer is left to make up his own mind about the characters and their puzzling lifestyles.

"Satan" is a provocative film, but it would have been a better one if not for the tiresomely familiar jerky Russian hand-held camera style, murky color and drab lighting. Pic should be in demand on the fest circuit, but could attract a wider audience because of its controversial subject-matter and chillingly matter-of-fact approach to its subject.
— *Strat.*

DAS DEUTSCHE KETTENSÄGENMASSAKER
(THE GERMAN CHAINSAW MASSACRE)
(GERMAN)

A Mega Film Verleih release of a DEM Film and Rhewes Filmproduktion production. Produced by Christian Fürst. Written and directed by Christoph Schlingensief. Camera (color), Schlingensief; editor, Ariane Traub; music, Jacques Arr; sound, Eki Kuchenbecker. Reviewed at Berlin Film Festival (New German Film), Feb. 17, 1991. Running time: 63 MIN.
With: Karina Fallenstein, Suzanne Bredehöft, Artur Albrecht, Volker Spengler, Alfred Edel, Brigitte Kausch, Dietrich Kuhlbrodt.

Incorporating a lot of John Waters' "Female Trouble" with a generous dash of "Desperate Living," "The German Chainsaw Massacre" is supposed to be a shlocky look at German unification, but it's not good schlock. It's just tacky, gross and unfunny.

Early on in "Female Trouble," Divine tears open a Christmas present from her parents, desperately hoping to get a pair of cha-cha heels. When they turn out to be boring school shoes instead, she screams "What's this?" and shoves her folks into the Christmas tree.

That's something like the letdown viewers feel after watching Christoph Schlingensief's latest foray into bad taste. It's a

shame too, since the title is so tantalizingly trashy.

An East German woman kills her husband and flees in a beat-up East Bloc car into West Germany and takes up with a vicious lesbian. After German unification, her husband comes after her, wielding a chainsaw, and he means business. Much of the cast gets ground into sausage.

Tech credits for "German Chainsaw" are appropriately wretched. — *Gill.*

DA TAIJIAN LI LIANYING
(LI LIANYING, THE IMPERIAL EUNUCH)
(HONG KONG-CHINESE)

A Skai Film Prods. (Hong Kong)-Beijing Film Studios co-production. Executive producers, Cai Rubin, Zhang Mengrui, Lang Yiu. Produced by Tam Wing-chuen, Cheng Zhigu. Directed by Tian Zhuangzhuang. Screenplay, Jiang Wen, Zhuangzhuang; camera (Scope color), Zhao Fei; editor, Qian Lengleng; music, Mo Fan; sound, Wu Ning; production design, Yang Yuhe, Yao Qing; production manager, Lang Yun; assistant director, Liu Xiaoding. Reviewed at Berlin Film Festival (competing), Feb. 17, 1991. Running time: 107 MIN.
Li Lianying . . . . .Jiang Wen
Dowager Empress Cixi . Liu Xiaoqing
Prince Yihuan . . . . .Zhu Yu
Emperor Guangxu . . . . Tian Xiaojun
Pearl Consort . . . . Hsu Fan
Old woman . . . . Lin Wei

Yet another lavish exploration of colorful characters in Chinese history, "Li Lianying" boasts handsome sets and costumes and an exotic storyline. Despite these pluses, including a special mention prize at the Berlin fest, mucho talk and lack of action will reduce pic's international b.o. impact.

Chinese director Tian Zhuangzhuang is best known for the visually magnificent "The Horse Thief" (1986), set in Tibet. The action in his latest film, a tale of intrigue and corruption co-produced with Hong Kong, is confined to the Chinese court. It's as much the story of the infamous dowager empress of turn-of-the-century China as it is of her favorite eunuch.

The Boxer Rebellion and the Forbidden City takeover by Western powers serve as backdrop to the drama, but these dramatic events are never seen. All there is of the foreign invasion is the sound of a few gunshots.

Li Lianying is played by Jiang Wen ("Hibiscus Town," "Red Sorghum," "Black Snow"), who also

co-wrote the screenplay. He makes the notorious real-life character a sympathetic one who genuinely tries to help and protect the crotchety dowager empress during a period of political instability. He gives a fine performance, ably supported by Liu Xiaoqing as the dowager empress.

Sets and costumes are ravishing, but pic is almost nonstop talk as the intrigues of the period are discussed rather than enacted. It's all fascinating, but a more cinematic approach would have greater impact.

Another effective sequence takes place when the foreigners have invaded the Forbidden City (off-screen) and the royal family takes to the countryside incognito. Here, the dowager takes shelter in the home of a 107-year-old woman who's full of gripes about the royal family. It's an amusing, sardonic sequence.

"Li Lianying" is absorbing drama Sinophiles and film festivals will relish, but it won't appeal to a wide international audience. Hong Kong and mainland Chinese filmmakers cooperated to place the best talents from both film industries into the seamless co-production. — *Strat.*

TRIPLE BOGEY ON A PAR 5 HOLE
(U.S.-B&W)

A Poe Prods.-Meridien Theatrical production. (Intl. sales: World Film Services. N.Y.) Written, produced and directed by Amos Poe. Camera (b&w), Joe De Salvo; editor, Dana Congdon; music, Mader, Michael Delory, Anna Domino, Chic Streetman; sound, Tom Szabolcs; co-producer-assistant director, Dolly Hall; line producer-production manager, Benjamin Gruberg; casting, Ellen Parks. Reviewed at Berlin Film Festival (Forum), Feb. 17, 1991. No MPAA rating. Running time: 85 MIN.
Remy Gravelle . . . . . . Eric Mitchell
Amanda Levy . . . . Daisy Hall
Satch Levy . . . . Jesse McBride
Bree Levy . . . . Angela Goethals
Nina Baccardi . . . . . . Alba Clemente
Steffano Baccardi . . . Robbie Coltrane
Freddy Arnstein . . . . . Tom Cohen

Indie filmmaker Amos Poe, whose last pic was "Alphabet City" in 1984, is back with "Triple Bogey On A Par 5 Hole," an amusing but basically insubstantial new pic, indicating limited arthouse exposure on the commercial front.

Premise is obviously inspired by "Citizen Kane," though the pic lacks the stylistic innovation of that masterpiece. Eric Mitchell, his face unseen until near the end, plays a screenwriter work-

ing for a Japanese-owned studio who's researching a script about a rich couple shot to death on a golf course 14 years earlier. Their three children reside on a yacht that is constantly steaming around New York City harbor ("Triple Bogey" is the name of the vessel).

Opening scenes have Mitchell interviewing the fast-talking agent (Tom Cohen) of the eldest sibling, Amanda (Daisy Hall), who has become a famous writer. He also talks to the family lawyer, played by that mascot of low-budget British cinema, Robbie Coltrane.

Most of the pic unfolds on the yacht, as Mitchell views grainy old home movies (the only color footage in the pic) taken by the long-dead mother, and talks to the precocious siblings, eventually becoming the lover of the hitherto virginal Amanda.

The film is amusing in a dry kind of way, but contains no great revelations, save for the disarming performance of young Angela Goethals, who is great as a worldly 14-year-old with plenty to say for herself. Other characters are routine, and the film's laid-back style becomes irritating after a while.

The monochrome images are sharply lensed by Joe De Salvo, and, apart from the home movies, color is seen only in the opening credits (in red) and closing credits (in green). If a satire on the idle rich was intended here, Poe never really makes much of an impact, but "Triple Bogey" is watchable for indulgent audiences. — *Strat.*

MY LOVELY MONSTER
(GERMAN)

A Xenon Film production in conjunction with WDR and SFB television. Produced and directed by Michel Bergmann. Screenplay, Bergmann with additional dialog by Forrest J. Ackerman; camera (color), Fernando Arguelles; editor, Ursula Höff; music, Jürgen Wolter; sound, Michael Sombetzki; art direction, Christian Bussmann; costumes, Sabine Jesse; makeup, Rolf Baumann. Reviewed at Berlin Film Festival (New German Films), Feb. 20, 1991. Running time: 84 MIN.
Maximilian . . . . Silvio Francesco
The Master . . . . Forrest J. Ackerman
Nina . . . . Nicole Fischer
Father . . . . Matthias Fuchs
Mother . . . . Marlen Diekhoff
Duke . . . . Peter Voss
Duchess . . . . Olivia Davis
Also with: Karen Boehne, Lincoln Bond, Desi A. Hines, Russell Reeves, Ferdinand Mayne, Bobbie Bresee, Sara Karloff.

"My Lovely Monster" is the surprise of the year from Germany. This spoof of low-budget horror pics, full of wit and gentle charm, is must programming for fantasy film fests or specialty theaters' fright-night lineup.

Americans of a certain age and ilk will be drawn to the pic by Forrest J. Ackerman, wacky publisher of the legendary 1960s horror fan mag Famous Monsters Of Filmland and its sci-fi sister publication Spacemen.

Ackerman contributed to the dialog; all of the puns, no doubt. One wonders how the characters can say their lines, what with tongue planted so firmly in cheek. Ackerman also makes a cameo appearance.

Silvio Francesco got kudos as the silent film ghoul who escapes a burning piece of nitrate celluloid and suddenly finds himself in a darkened theater in Germany. Francesco is made up to look like Lon Chaney Sr.'s vampire in the classic silent chiller "London After Midnight," one of numerous horror pic references.

A tip of the vampire's top hat also goes to lead female thesp Nicole Fischer as the young German who assists the miming ghoul (he's from a silent film, after all) to find his way back to his film — at Ackerman's horror film museum, of course.

The zany supporting cast includes Ferdie Mayne and Sara Karloff.

Producer-helmer Michel Bergmann, a former pizza delivery boy, real estate agent and freelance writer, has turned out his best film yet. — *Gil.*

EINE WAHNSINNSEHE
(A CRAZY COUPLE)
(GERMAN)

A ZDF tv release of a ZDF and Olga Film production. Produced by Harald Küger. Directed by Sönke Wortmann. Screenplay, Karlheinz Freznik; camera (color, 16m), Rolf Paulerberg; editor, Wolfgang Raabe; music, Rolf G. Wehmeier; sound, Marc Parisotto, Heino Herrenbrück. Reviewed at Berlin Film Festival (New German Films), Feb. 18, 1991. Running time: **97 MIN.**
With: Barbara Auer, Thomas Heinze, Heinrich Schafmeister, Katharine Müller-Elmau, Jan-Paul Biczycki, Barbara Lass.

First feature by Sönke Wortmann, 31, is fine for its intended audience, the latenight crowd watching German pubcaster ZDF, which co-produced the film. But provincial focus and 16m format will keep "A Crazy Couple" from traveling abroad.

Barbara Auer stands out in an otherwise unremarkable cast. She plays an educated woman for whom the late 1960s student movement gave way to the peace movement and the women's movement, and then to self-discovery therapy and New Age dabblings. Her long-suffering husband (Thomas Heinze) tolerates her fad interests but always seems at loose ends himself.

Pic presents the couple as somewhat unusual, although there's nothing unusual about it — certainly not in modern Germany, where people grow up uncomfortable with who they are as a nation. Opening up the pic to a more universal perspective would have helped rescue it from late-night tv.

Tech credits are adequate for a 16m production intended for a single airing. — *Gill.*

CAFE EUROPA
(GERMAN)

A Filmverlag der Autoren release of a Roxy Film production. Produced by Luggi Waldleitner. Directed by Franz X. Bogner. Screenplay, Ekkehard Ziedrich, Bogner; camera (color), Frank Brühne; editor, Norbert Herzner; music, Rainhard Fendrich; sound, Georg Krautheim. Reviewed at Berlin Film Festival (New German Films), Feb. 18, 1991. Running time: **91 MIN.**
With: Barbara Auer, Jacques Breuer, August Zirner, Elmar Wepper, Rudolf Wessely, Raimund Harmstorf, Walter Plathe, Ottfried Fischer, Thomas Holtzmann, Remo Girone, Mario Adorf.

Talented Barbara Auer heads a top-drawer supporting cast in this amusing first feature film by veteran German tv helmer Franz X. Bogner. "Cafe Europa" is a natural for European tv.

Backing up Auer are Jacques Breuer and August Zirner as two mismatched Munich cops whose careers are in a slide until they stumble onto a major protection racket involving a seedy restaurant. The plot could have been lifted from any American cop show, but it is done well and will please German tv audiences.

Most pleasing of all, Bogner has shunned the 16m format plaguing European tv for 35m and quality production values. This is the kind of work that should be standard on German tv but is woefully lacking. — *Gill.*

MADO, POSTE RESTANTE
(MADO, HOLD FOR COLLECTION)
(FRENCH)

A Barnaba Films production. (Intl. sales: Motion Média, Paris.) Written and directed by Alexandre Adabachian. Camera (color), Levan Paatachvili; editor, Pauline Leroy; music, Jean-Louis Valero. Reviewed at Berlin Film Festival (market), Feb. 18, 1991. Running time: **100 MIN.**
Mado . . . . Marianne Groves
Jean-Marie Zerlini . . Oleg Yankovsky
Germaine . . . . Isabelle Gelinas
Priest . . . . Bernard Freyd

A bittersweet comedy about a plain girl and her fruitless efforts to find love and romance, "Mado Poste Restante" is a minor entry but represents a fresh point of view from Georgian expatriates Alexandre Adabachian (writer-director) and Levan Paatachvili (cinematographer).

In a small town, Mado (Marianne Groves) delivers the mail and pastes notices on walls and trees seeking a lover, one who's Catholic and likes sunrises. So far, she's had no luck, just derision from the locals. Her only friend is Germaine, who's pretty but has dubious morals.

Mado gets excited when a film director (Oleg Yankovsky) arrives in town and checks into the Grand Hotel. He's a glamorous figure to her, even though a check in the library reveals he isn't listed in a film encyclopedia and prefers Germaine. Mado is destined to lose out again.

Adabachian has created a quietly appealing feature with great sensitivity and humor. In addition to sight gags, one running joke has Mado regularly stumbling on the postmaster's plump wife and her eager lover.

Groves is disarming as the ugly duckling who isn't as plain as she thinks she is. Yankovsky, star of several noted Soviet pics, is find as the elegant director who isn't the success he seems to be.

Camerawork is particularly fine and inventive, and the film has something of the same off-center sense of humor displayed by another Georgian helmer, Otar Iosselliani. "Mado" deserves international play, but is probably a bit too slight and seemingly uneventual to make the grade.
— *Strat.*

ALLE JUDEN RAUS!
(ALL JEWS OUT!)
(GERMAN-DOCU)

A Katrin Seybold Film production. Produced by Seybold. Directed by Emanuel Rund. Camera (color, 16m), Rund; editor, Annette Dorn; sound, Thomas Meyer, Reinhard Gloge. Reviewed at Berlin Film Festival (New German Films), Feb. 17, 1991. Running time: **82 MIN.**

Former CBS cameraman Emanuel Rund has crafted a compelling documentary on the persecution of Jews in one small German town during the Third Reich. "All Jews Out!" is required viewing for specialty audiences and a natural for the fest circuit. Tv buyers also would do well to check it out.

Rund's experience as a lenser for American tv and a film scholar (he taught in New York, Los Angeles and Jerusalem) comes to the fore here. He has assembled rare footage, on-camera interviews and background material to best advantage. No frame of film is wasted; every camera angle has been precisely planned.

The details are astounding. Few would have thought to interview the aging telephone switchboard operator from the Theresienstadt concentration camp or the local fire chief who stood by as synagogues burned.

Bereft of schoolmarmish voiceover, the pictures and the interviewees speak for themselves, a rarity in often-amateurish German documentaries. — *Gill.*

DANA LECH
(GERMAN)

A Deutsche Film und Fernschakademie Berlin production. Produced by Milanka Comfort. Directed by Frank-Guido Blasberg. Screenplay, Blasberg; camera (color), Stepan Benda; editor, Boris Wieland; music, Wolgang Thiel, Angelika Thiel; sound, Christoph Willems, Jürgen Wolter. Reviewed at Berlin Film Festival (New German Films), Feb. 17, 1991. Running time: **78 MIN.**
With: Brygida Mich, Pjotr Beluch, Mirella D'Angelo, René Hofschneider, Max Gertsch, Szymon Kusmider.

"Dana Lech," film school graduation project for fledgling helmer Frank-Guido Blasberg, is a promising debut work, although b.o. prospects are limited for this dark pic.

At the center of this film is a Polish refugee (broodingly

played by Brygida Mich) torn between two lovers, two countries and two ways of looking at the world. Blasberg does what he can to breathe life into this tired old theme, and with some success. Acting is generally adequate.

Tech credits are capable for a supervised academic project.

— *Gill.*

DAKOTA ROAD
(BRITISH)

A Film Four Intl. and British Screen presentation of a Working Title production. (Intl. sales: Manifesto Film Sales.) Executive producer, Sarah Radclyffe. Produced by Donna Grey. Written and directed by Nick Ward. Camera (Fujicolor), Ian Wilson; editor, William Diver; music, Paul Stacey; sound, Simon Okin; production design, Careen Hertzog; production manager, Barney Reisz; assistant director, A.J. Wands; casting, Sarah Bird. Reviewed at Berlin Film Festival (market), Feb. 18, 1991. Running time: **88 MIN.**

Maud Cross	Amelda Brown
Raif Benson	Jason Carter
Jen Cross	Charlotte Chatton
Alan Brandon	Alan Howard
Amy Cross	Rachel Scott
Bernard Cross	Matthew Scurfield
Joan Benson	Liz Smith
Rev. Douglas Stonea	David Warrilow

Talented new British writer-director Nick Ward makes a striking debut with "Dakota Road," an original though small-scale picture of considerable merit. Selling the pic to the public may be tough, but critical reactions should be positive.

Despite its title, the film is British in every sense. Set in the Fen country in Norfolk, in a tiny farming community close to a U.S. air base (hence the title), pic deals with the effects of recession and pollution on a small group of ordinary Brits. It's also about repressed emotions and the difficulties of communication.

None of these subjects make for popular cinema, but audiences worldwide should appreciate this understated but strongly emotional drama.

Only name actor here is Alan Howard (the lover in Peter Greenaway's "The Cook, The Thief, His Wife And Her Lover") who plays Alan Brandon, a widowed small-time landowner living a solitary existence and quietly lusting after the wife and teenage daughter of Bernard Cross (Matthew Scurfield), who works for him as a laborer.

Cross and his wife, Maud (Amelda Brown) exist in a sterile marriage punctuated by violence and desperate quarrels. They have two daughters: Teenage Jen (Charlotte Chatton) is involved in a loveless sexual liaison with Raif Benson (Jason Carter), an orphan who lives with the old lady who runs the local store and post office. The younger daughter, Amy (Rachel Scott) is a wide-eyed, old-beyond-her-years tyke who observes everything.

Brandon fires Cross, but hires Maud as a cleaning woman, partly to have a desirable woman around the house. Unable to cope with no longer being a breadwinner, Cross kills himself, but, by a quirk of fate, his body isn't found, and it's thought that he's just disappeared.

Meanwhile, Jen is pregnant, but can't face the thought of marriage to Raif (who, it's hinted, may be the illegitimate son of the local priest, Rev. Stonea). She has a vibrant, but possibly imagined, sexual encounter with an American flyer she meets in the woods.

These are the bare bones of an apparently grim little tale of wasted lives. Bleakness of the film, is alleviated by the freshness of Ward's approach, the extraordinary camerawork of Ian Wilson and the fine ensemble performances.

"Dakota Road" was made on a modest budget as one of the first pictures to emerge from the British film partnership established by former British Screen topper Simon Relph. It's an artistic winner, and the problem now will be to find the audience it deserves. More should be heard from Ward, already an established playwright, in the future. — *Strat.*

DIE ARCHITEKTEN
(THE ARCHITECTS)
(GERMAN)

A Progress Film-Verleih release of a DEFA Studio Babelsberg production. Produced by Herbert Ehler. Directed by Peter Kahane. Screenplay, Thomas Knauf, Kahane; camera (color), Andreas Köfer; editor, Ilse Peters; music, Tamás Kahane; sound, Andreass Kaufmann. Reviewed at Berlin Film Festival (New German Films), Feb. 16, 1991. Running time: **97 MIN.**
With: Kurt Naumann, Rita Feldmeier, Uta Eisold, Jürgen Watzke, Ute Lubosch, Catherine Stoyan, Andrea Meissner, Jörg Schüttlauf, Hans-Joachim Hegewald.

"The Architects," although well crafted and ably acted, is a slow-paced and minor East German film. Its b.o. prospects are virtually nil.

The story behind the making of East German helmer Peter Kahane's low-key tragedy is integral to understanding the pic itself. Shooting started in September 1989 as multitudes took to the streets throughout East Germany. By the time the film was finished, East Germany no longer existed.

Now, East German filmmakers are faced with unemployment. Many of the DEFA studio execs who initially approved this picture are unemployed.

This film is about that social upheaval, though in a very subtle way. Kahane uses as his metaphor a disillusioned architect who finally gets bureaucratic approval to design a major urban project, only to see his personal and professional aspirations swept aside by the tumultuous events that have transformed the political face of Europe.

Prague-born Kahane deftly shows the bureaucratic inner workings of the former East German centrally controlled economy. His protagonist (Kurt Naumann) assembles a team of irreverent architects who intentionally goad the powers that be. They want to see just how much they can get away with, and that turns out to be precious little.

Techical credits are good, reflecting the craftsmanly tradition of DEFA Studios. — *Gill.*

DAS MÄDCHEN AUS DEM FAHRSTUHL
(THE GIRL IN THE LIFT)
(GERMAN)

A Progress Film Verleih release of a DEFA Studio Babelsberg production. Produced by Ralph Retzlaff. Directed by Herrmann Zschoche. Camera (color), Dieter Chill; editor, Monika Schindler; music, Johannes Schlect; sound, Wolfgang Grossmann. Reviewed at Berlin Film Festival (New German Films), Feb. 20, 1991. Running time: **91 MIN.**
With: Rolf Lukoschek, Barbara Sommer, Karin Gregorek, Monika Lennartz, Rita Feldmeier, Hans-Jörn Weber.

Veteran East German helmer Herrmann Zschoche has fashioned another insightful analysis of human relationships, but now that the East German film market is no longer state-controlled, his slow-paced pic is destined for pre-primetime viewing on German pubcasters. That's if it gets picked up at all.

The ingredients are here for what in years past would have been a successful film in East Germany. Acting from the stable of DEFA thesps, is good and techical credits are up to the studio's standards of craftsmanship.

The old-fashioned story of a well-to-do youth who falls for the less fortunate neighbor girl is too tame, however. Zschoche has spiced up the story with a hint of excitement involving the boy's standing up for his girl at a communist youth group meeting. But that is only exciting in a totalitarian country where such depictions are banned from the screen.

Zschoche, who has directed quality human dramas for DEFA for 30 years, faces an uncertain future in unified Germany, as does the studio he has worked for so long. — *Gill.*

AMERICAN FRIENDS
(BRITISH)

An MCEG Virgin Vision release (in U.K.) of a British Screen in association with the BBC presentation of a Millennium Films/Mayday/Prominent Features production. (Intl. sales: Sales Co., London.) Produced by Patrick Cassavetti, Steve Abbott. Directed by Tristram Powell. Screenplay, Michael Palin, Powell, from a story by Palin; camera (Eastmancolor, Metrocolor prints), Philip Bonham-Carter; editor, George Akers; music, Georges Delerue; sound (Dolby), John Ireland; production design, Andrew McAlpine; art director, Chris Townsend; costume design, Bob Ringwood; assistant director, Chris Hall; casting, Irene Lamb (U.K.), Margie Simpkin (U.S.). Reviewed at New Crown preview theater, London, March 7, 1991. Running time: **95 MIN.**

Francis Ashby . . . . . . Michael Palin
Caroline Hartley . . . . . Connie Booth
Elinor Hartley . . . . . Trini Alvarado
Oliver Syme . . . . Alfred Molina
Pollitt . . . . David Calder
Anderson . . . . Simon James
Rushden . . . . Robert Eddison
Dr. Weeks . . . . . . Alun Armstrong
Mrs. Weeks . . . . Sheila Reid
John Weeks . . . . . Edward Rawle-Hicks
Also with: Jonathan Firth, Bryan Pringle, Ian Dunn, John Nettleton.

Easy on the eyes and on the emotions, "American Friends" is the kind of immaculate period drama Brit filmmakers can do in their sleep. This slim vignette about two Yank women who fall for a reserved Oxford don is likely to enjoy only a brief b.o. encounter. It's more suited to tube sales or limited outings.

Pic opens in the 1860s at a stuffy Oxford U. college where bachelor classics don Francis Ashby (Michael Palin) is setting off for a walking vacation in Switzerland. Atop the Alps, he meets two Americans, Caroline (Connie Booth) and her doe-eyed ward, Elinor (Trini Alvarado). Emotions are stirred, and Elinor gets the first kiss.

Back in Oxford, Ashby is one of two candidates lined up to take over as college president when the current, aged one dies. Ashby rival Oliver Syme (Alfred Molina) has hyperactive hormones, so if Ashby can stay respectably celibate, the job's virtually his. Enter, en route to Philadelphia, the two Yanks — and mucho trouble for Ashby.

Caroline has a cozy dinner à deux but gets nowhere. Then Ashby finds Elinor hiding in his chambers. She gets a strong dose of British reserve, too, but both women decide to stay for the summer at Syme's cottage hideaway. Syme finally scores with Elinor, but her heart's really with Ashby. The women wait as the rumors mount and the college election draws nigh.

There's a lot going on beneath the surface, but not much of it reaches the screen. The conflict between British and American emotions gets only a single workout, and the contest between Ashby and Syme never builds to anything substantial.

Lack of dramatic tension can be blamed, in part, on the ex-Monty Python trouper's performance. Although yarn is based on an actual event discovered in his great-grandfather Edward's travel diaries, Palin is too lightweight for such a key role. He slips too often into semicomic mannerisms, and his crusty, middle-aged bachelor doesn't ring true.

Thesping otherwise is crisp and reliable, especially Alvarado as the lovelorn ward. Booth is a fine older foil for Alvarado's ingenuousness. Molina shines briefly in an underwritten part.

Pic is feature debut of tv helmer Tristram Powell, son of British scribe Anthony. Despite the stop-and-go script, his direction is solid and starts to pay off in the final half-hour. Tech credits are all firstrate, notably Philip Bonham-Carter's sensitive lensing and Bob Ringwood's alert costuming. More of Georges Delerue's limpid score would have helped.

Production is the fourth from the Pythons' Prominent Features, after "A Fish Named Wanda," "The Adventures Of Baron Munchausen" and "Erik The Viking." — *Drek.*

TRUE COLORS

A Paramount release of a Laurence Mark production. Produced by Herbert Ross, Mark. Executive producer, Joseph M. Caracciolo. Directed by Ross. Screenplay, Kevin Wade; camera (Technicolor), Dante Spinotti; editor, Robert Reitano, Stephen A. Rotter; music, Trevor Jones; sound (Dolby), Al Overton; production design, Edward Pisoni; art direction, William Barclay; set decoration, Robert J. Franco; costume design, Joseph G. Aulisi; assistant director, Michael Haley; 2nd unit director, Andrew Stone; casting, Hank McCann. Reviewed at Beekman Theater, N.Y., March 11, 1991. MPAA Rating: R. Running time: **111 MIN.**

Peter Burton . . . . John Cusack
Tim Garrity . . . . . . James Spader
Diana Stiles . . . . . . Imogen Stubbs
John Palmeri . . . . . . Mandy Patinkin
Sen. Stiles . . . . . Richard Widmark
Joan Stiles . . . . Dina Merrill
Sen. Steubens . . . . . . Philip Bosco
John Lawry . . . . . . Paul Guilfoyle

"True Colors" represents a cloyingly schematic attempt to portray the political and moral bankruptcy of the 1980s in a neat little package. From a vantage point barely removed from the decade in question, pic condemns but doesn't begin to analyze the corrupted values of the Reagan years, leaving one feeling soiled but unenlightened. Commercial prospects are modest.

Despite a contrived "meet cute" in which future college roommates John Cusack and James Spader first encounter one another in a car accident, tale starts out with some promise. Paired off at law school at the U. of Virginia in 1983, Spader is a rich boy with the daughter of U.S. senator Richard Widmark as a girlfriend, while Cusack is pretender, a social climber whose lower-class roots are quickly exposed.

The deception forgiven, the two remain best friends, and Cusack, a bluffer and something of a charmer, resolves to be elected to Congress within 10 years. To that end, he quits school after a summer's internship in Washington to try to short-cut his way to the top.

Well written within numerous specific scenes, Kevin Wade's screenplay begins seriously derailing at this point. Flaunting his motto for the new America, "Don't get caught," Cusack launches a political career based upon trickery, blackmail and betrayal, and receives backing, not from the people, but from sleazy business interests represented by oily developer Mandy Patinkin.

Personal relationships fall by the wayside like roadkill. Having scooped Spader's g.f., Imogen Stubbs, out from under him, Cusack then loses her when he stupidly threatens her powerful father. With self-interest his only principle, he then betrays his best friend, setting himself up for a big fall on election night after his run for Congress in Connecticut.

The ruthlessness of Cusack's character is believable enough, but not that he could get as far as he does so fast within an inner circle and some sort of constituency. Although his character defects are palmed off on a deprived childhood, they are also far too baldly laid out as symptoms of a sick decade, a time when greed, expediency and the me-first ethic reigned supreme. Cusack does what he can, but the character is simply weighed down with too much symbolic baggage for it to play convincingly.

Yet again playing a privileged preppie type, Spader is likable but suffers from his character being pushed to the side midstream. More socially motivated than his friend, he is left by Stubbs when she decides his career plans are not ambitious enough, but finally rises to the occasion by going undercover in Cusack's campaign on behalf of the Justice Dept.

Other roles are one-dimensional, with Stubbs' English inflections breaking through at times, Patinkin projecting New Age nastiness and Widmark smartly sporting the wiles of a cagey veteran player.

Director Herbert Ross has mounted the action with no special insight into the milieu or characters. Shot on good Eastern seaboard locations, production looks fine. But it just doesn't feel like the time to look back culturally on the late, unlamented 1980s, at least not in this unilluminating way. — *Cart.*

ROBOT CARNIVAL
(JAPANESE-ANIMATED)

A Streamline Pictures release of an APPP Co. Ltd. production. Produced by Kazufumi Nomura, Carl Macek. Written, designed and directed by Katsuhiro Otomo, Atsuko Fukushima, Kouji Morimoto, Kiroyuki Kitazume, Mao Lamdo, Hidetoshi Ohmori, Yasuomi Umetsu, Hiroyuki Kitakubo, Takashi Nakamura. Camera (color), Toshiaki Morita, K. Torigoe, Yukio Sugiyama; editor, Naotoshi Ogata, Yukiko Itoh, Nao Toyosaki; music, Jo Hisaishi, Isaku Fujita, Yasunori Honda; sound effects, Arts Pro; special effects, Kashiwabara Toyohiko, Goh Abe, Shiji Teraoka; assistant director, Tetsu Kimura; associate producers, Michael Haller, Jerry Beck. Reviewed at Film Forum, March 12, 1991. No MPAA Rating. Running time: **91 MIN.**

(English-dubbed soundtrack)

A collection of eight short fantasy films, "Robot Carnival" showcases the skills of some of Japan's top animators. Technically, all the work is firstrate, but, in a few of the films, conventional plots and characters undo the high standards of the animation.

The filmmakers were asked to feature robots as central characters in their stories. The results range from the highly imaginative to the entirely predictable.

Kouji Morimoto's dazzling "Franken's Gears," one of the best entries, retells "Frankenstein" with dramatic flashes of lightning. When the robot/monster comes to life, tubes shatter and the creator is left awestruck.

Animation buffs will be impressed, too.

In "Presence," a longer study of an inventor who falls in love with his robot, Yasuomi Umetsu applies a more lyrical touch. The animation is so detailed that the backgrounds and shadows seem startlingly real. Unfortunately, the stilted English dialog and perfect-looking characters are less convincing.

The heroes who battle robots in Hidetoshi Ohmori's "Deprive" are even further idealized, with the same WASPy looks. And in Kiroyuki Kitazume's "Starlight Angel," heroines resembling Barbie dolls seek true love as saccharine music blares.

When there are Japanese leads, such as the insane inventor in Hiroyuki Kitakubo's "A Tale Of Two Robots," they are saddled with dumb-sounding Japanese accents. (The dialog was dubbed in English by U.S. distrib Streamline Pictures).

More inventive is Takashi Nakamura's "Nightmare," with its Ralph Steadman-inspired swarm of robots overrunning a city. "Cloud," which has the least to do with robots, has a dreamy feel to it as Mao Lamdo transforms clouds into fleeting images.

Even the opening and closing credits of "Robot Carnival" are beautifully animated (by Atsuko Fukushima and Katsuhiro Otomo, who directed "Akira"). Pic's title is a huge machine destroying everything in its path.

Like many of the pic's self-destructing robots, some of the segs themselves fall apart because plot isn't as well thought out as animation. "Robot Carnival" reveals that Japanese directors have mastered the technical side of the art form, if not the subtlety that would improve the narratives. — *Stev.*

DEFENDING YOUR LIFE

A Warner Bros. release of a Geffen Film Co. presentation. Produced by Michael Grillo. Executive producer, Herbert S. Nanas. Written and directed by Albert Brooks. Camera (Technicolor), Allen Daviau; editor, David Finfer; music, Michael Gore; sound (Dolby), Thomas Causey; production design, Ida Random; art direction, Richard Reynolds; set design, Martha Johnston; set decoration, Linda DeScenna; costume design, Deborah L. Scott; assistant director, Grillo; visual effects, Dream Quest Images; co-producer, Robert Grand; casting, Barbara Claman, Mark Saks. Reviewed at Warner Bros. Studios, Burbank, March 5, 1991. MPAA Rating: PG. Running time: **112 MIN.**
Daniel Miller . . . . . . .Albert Brooks
Julia . . . . Meryl Streep
Bob Diamond . . . . Rip Torn
Lena Foster . . . . Lee Grant
Dick Stanley . . . . Buck Henry
Shirley MacLaine . . . . Herself

"Defending Your Life" is an inventive and mild bit of whimsy from Albert Brooks. Pic will fill the bill for some members of the post-yuppie audience, resulting in some urban b.o., but yocks are too sporadic to make it a mass-audience hit.

In his first outing as a writer-director since "Lost In America" six years ago, the former stand-up comedian has a little fun with the "Liliom" idea of being judged in a fanciful afterlife, but he doesn't carry his conceit nearly far enough.

Brooks plays his familiar role of a neurotic, warm-hearted, insecure, bull-headed, upper-middle class mensch who, in the opening reel, dies after crashing his showroom-fresh BMW smack into a bus.

The unlucky fellow instantly finds himself being whisked off by tram to Judgment City, a white-bread sort of resort community in which the recently departed have their lives reviewed in order to determine their next destination.

This review consists of a prosecutor and defender presenting scenes from the life of the deceased to two judges. The scenes demonstrate the individual's worthiness to pass on to an advanced stage of being or, depressingly, his need to return to earth and try again.

Concept of this ontological pitstop as an idyllic corporate amusement park outfitted with free restaurants and impeccable grounds is not amusing, but Brooks takes forever to lay out the details and rules, which are funnier than one's first impressions.

Core of the tale, though, is the presentation of the cases for and against Brooks' character. Seated in the middle of a high-tech hearing room, the victim is forced to watch particularly embarrassing moments from his life while listening to a torrent of vilification from the prosecutor (Lee Grant) and just a measure of defense from his cheerleader (Rip Torn).

These sequences would seem to offer a perfect opportunity for some wild, daring humor. Conversely, these glimpses back to moments best forgotten also might have provided looks at the moral choices that determined the course of his life and defined his nature.

Unfortunately, Brooks has invented what are, at best, lightly humorous anecdotes merely designed to demonstrate that his character always has been something of a chicken. It would appear that Brooks has lived a life of terminal blandness, the worst sins of which were investing poorly and having helped a little classmate get expelled from school.

Lending all of this some meaning is his chance meeting with Meryl Streep, the dream woman who would be the love of his life if only they weren't dead.

The two have a tryst of sorts, and, in the film's funniest but still disappointing sequence, visit an attraction called Past Lives Pavilion, where the participant is able to view corporal reproductions of his or her previous incarnations.

Brooks earns few laughs for all the care and concern he clearly has put into this effort, and he just has not dared to take his notions far enough to raise this from an amiable to a dazzling level.

Concept and intermittent inspirations are enough to keep the viewer interested through most of the overlong running time, but Brooks the writer has let down Brooks the actor and director by playing it too safe.

Brooks plays his victim like a homeless dog, warily eager to please but not expecting favorable attention. Streep appears to have enjoyed herself, as she smiles and laughs her way through an effortless role.

Torn, in ripping form, and an elegant Grant ably embody courtroom adversaries, while Buck Henry is wasted in a pointless bit as a one-day substitute for Torn.

Production designer Ida Random and her team have made essential contributions to what benign humor there is here, fashioning a purgatory of surpassing banality that lenser Allen Daviau has bathed in an antiseptic warmth. Michael Gore's swelling score emphasizes the most predictable and conventional aspects of the frail tale. — *Cart.*

IF LOOKS COULD KILL

A Warner Bros. release of a Craig Zadan production. Produced by Zadan, Neil Meron. Executive producer, Elliot Schick. Directed by William Dear. Screenplay, Darren Star, from Fred Dekker's story; camera (Technicolor), Doug Milsome; editor, John F. Link; music, David Foster; sound (Dolby), Don Cohen; production design, Guy J. Comtois; art direction, Real Proulx; costume design, Mary McLeod; assistant director, Tony Lucibello; production manager-associate producer, David Coatsworth; additional editor, Mark Stevens; stunt coordinator-2nd unit director, Glenn Randall Jr.; 2nd unit camera, John Stephens; special effects coordinator, Martin Malivoire; special visual effects, Introvision Intl. — supervisor, William Mesa; casting, Marion Dougherty, Sharon Howard-Field; casting (Canada), Nadia Rona, Vera Miller. Reviewed at Murray Hill Quad theater, N.Y., March 10, 1991. MPAA Rating: PG-13. Running time: **88 MIN.**
Michael Corben . . . . . Richard Grieco
Ilsa Grunt . . . . Linda Hunt
Augustus Steranko . . . . Roger Rees
Mrs. Grober . . . . Robin Bartlett
Mariska . . . . Gabrielle Anwar
Vendetta Galante . . . Geraldine James
Richardson . . . . Michael Siberry
Areola Canasta . . . . . Carole Davis
 Also with: Frederick Coffin, Tom Rack, Roger Daltrey, Oliver Dear, Cyndy Preston.

Young tv star Richard Grieco barely survives silly first film vehicle "If Looks Could Kill," which spoofs the James Bond formula in tiresome fashion. Better suited to tv, pic is aimed at undiscriminating audiences only.

Compared with the scores of spy spoofs churned out in the '60s, William Dear's film plays more like a pastiche of the Ian Fleming series than satire. Darren Star's one-joke script, based on Fred Dekker's story, runs out of gas before the halfway mark in its mimicking of 007 gimmicks, characters and specific films.

Grieco plays a high school student who's headed for France with his French teacher (Robin Bartlett) and class. Coincidentally, a CIA spy with same name is booked on the same plane, and rest of the film stems from both villains and good guy spooks mistaking young Grieco for a secret agent.

With simple terms like "mother" and "the French teacher" carrying double meanings, pic bogs down with increasingly improbable slapstick situations for Grieco. Nominal plot has Roger Rees as the megalomaniacal chairman of the European Economic Community who plans to take over Europe and issue gold coinage bearing his own likeness.

At first, the film is pleasant enough as a wish-fulfillment exercise, with Grieco getting the fabulous sports car, weaponry and beautiful babes most adolescent males dream of. However, unlike Richard Franklin's similar but far more interesting pic "Cloak & Dagger," the pointlessness of the proceedings becomes overwhelming.

Grieco puts up with the silliness, including being clad only in his underpants during a lengthy segment opposite femme fatale Carole Davis. His swarthy good looks (as promised in the film's title) bear a precocious maturity when decked out in evening dress at the baccarat table, but his acting skills are not tested here. The requisite one-liner throwaways the script hands him are quite poor, even by latter-day Bond standards.

Linda Hunt has only intermittent success with the comic-strip role of Rees' chief enforcer, a bullwhip wielding heavy named Ilsa Grunt who doesn't hold a candle to Lotte Lenya's immortal Rosa Klebb character in the second Bond opus. Heroine Gabrielle Anwar as the vengeful daughter of Britain's late great top spy (played in a miscast, no-impact cameo by Roger Daltrey) looks too young on screen opposite Grieco, though they are probably the same age.

Best role goes to Bartlett, who starts off as an easy target, the imperious teacher one loves to hate, but evolves into a superhero by fadeout. Geraldine James plays a female version of Denis Llewellyn's "Q," and Davis is briefly alluring (within the confines of a PG-13 rating) as Areola Canasta, a punning name in the Fleming tradition.

Montreal locations are not convincing substitutes for Paris and environs. Film's stunts are okay until the set piece climax involving a helicopter with cheesy special effects (grainy or blank backdrops) that probably will be masked on tv but show up glaringly on the big screen. — Lor.

BEKHATERE HAMEH CHIZ
(FOR EVERYTHING)
(IRANIAN)

A production of R. Mohammadin, Amir Amirsoleimani and Reza Alipoor-Mota'alem. Directed by Rajab Mohammadin. Screenplay, Mohammadin; camera (color), Ataollah Hayati; editor, Sohrab Mirsepasi, Mohammadin; music, Susan Shakerin; sound, Mahmud Sammakbashi, Hashem Musavi, Yadollah Najafi; set design, A. Amirsoleimani; production managers, Mojtaba Motavali, Jamshid Jahanzadeh. Reviewed at Fajr Intl. Film Festival, Teheran, Feb. 10, 1991. Running time: **90 MIN.**
With: Elisa Johari, Granaz Musavi, Belghais Rabihavi, Ima Mashadizadeh, Fatemeh Gudarzi, Mahin Amirfazli, Maliheh Nikjumand, Mandana Aslani, Zohreh Saeedi, Hushang Ghavanloo, Ruhangiz Mohtadi.

Seamstresses ban together, sacrificing time and money to help a co-worker in need in "For Everything," a simple humanitarian story with universal appeal. It's ideal family fare for quality tv outlets in Western territories.

A feminist film directed by a man is rare anywhere, and this Persian version is a microcosm of working women in Teheran, reflecting social values in which folks stick together in a crisis. In this small group, each woman's problems reflect Iran's current social structure, and each finds a way to give cash and energy to the common cause.

The cause is an old woman who will die if she doesn't receive an operation. Her granddaughter cannot afford the medical care, and the young girl's colleagues persuade her to take time off and sit by her grandmother's bedside. Without her knowing (and behind the shop owner's back), the seamstresses work day and night to pay the hospital bills. The accountant risks her neck by "borrowing" cash from the shop's safe for the initial payment.

Another of the girls is a university student hoping to escape a life of poverty. One is pregnant and committed to the extended family structure, whatever the price. One is engaged, and she offers her dowry as well as her time. Another is a traitor, an opportunist who hopes for a better position if she tells the lady boss what's going on after hours.

This mini-soap (from a plain and poignant script) has a triumphant ending: The grandmother lives, the traitor repents and the girls keep their jobs when the boss finds out, mainly because few women would work so hard for such minuscule wages.

Tech credits are good. Vibrant colors are a nice change from the usually drab Iranian set and wardrobe designs. — Suze.

PARDEHE AKHAR
(THE LAST ACT)
(IRANIAN)

A Cadre Film production. Produced by Majid Modaresi and M.M. Dadgoo. Written and directed by Varuzh Karim-Masihi. Camera (color), Asghar Fafi'ie Jam; editor, V. Karim-Masihi; music, Babak Bayat; sound, Parviz Abnar; set design, Hassan Farsi; makeup, Masud Valadbeigi, Mozhdeh Shamsai; production manager, Ahmad Kashanchi; executive project manager, Mohammad Mehdi Dadgu. Reviewed at Fajr Intl. Film Festival, Teheran, Feb. 9, 1991. Running time: **105 MIN.**
With: Farimah Farjami, Dariush Arjomand, Jamshid Hashempoor, Saeed Poorsamimi, Niku Kheradmand, Mohaya Petrosian.

This slick murder mystery is the Iranian equivalent of an American Playhouse production with good tv potential worldwide. The $3.5 million budget for "The Last Act" (double the norm for Iranian pics) was put to good use: Tech credits are exceptional for a third world film, and the script clips along effortlessly, winding into a surprise ending.

The pre-World War II costumes provide a nice change from the Islamic dress seen in virtually all postrevolution Iranian pics.

The mystery revolves around a brother and sister who plot to kill their recently widowed sister-in-law to get her inheritance (including the big old house they live in). To frighten the poor widow witless, the siblings hire a band of gypsies to stage horrific events as part of a scheme to drive her mad.

The widow begs police for help, but the assigned investigator is convinced the woman is crazy because "evidence" of each "crime" vanishes before police arrive on the scene.

Suspecting foul play, the gypsies pack up and leave in the middle of the night, but not for long. The investigator forces them back into the house — for one last performance — to find out once and for all if the brother

and sister are really murderers. They're not.

In a tricky theatrical ending, the whole game turns out to be one extended stage show, and the joke's on the investigator, who joins in "the last act."

Supporting actress Mohaya Petrosian deserves kudos for her double-edged performance. She turns on the theatrical charm as loyal maid to the widow and displays a natural finesse for film acting as a behind-the-scenes "real" gypsy. The distinction between her two styles lends credibility to the overall story.

Outside Iran, pic will have trouble in theatrical venues because of pacing and content. Still, it's top-notch tv material. — Suze.

KASHTI-E ANGELICA
(THE SHIP ANGELICA)
(IRANIAN)

An Ayeneh Co. production. Produced by Ali Akbar Erfani. Directed by Mohammad Reza Bozorgnia. Screenplay, Bozorgnia, Hassan Gholizadeh, Bahman Dayyani; camera (color), Hassan Gholizadeh; editor, Abbas Ganjavi; music, Babak Bayat. Reviewed at Fajr Intl. Film Festival, Teheran, Feb. 10, 1991. Running time: **110 MIN.**
With: Dariush Arjomand, Jamid Mozaffari, Ezzatollah Entezami, Mehdi Fathi, Sogand Rahmani, Atila Pesiani, Parviz Poorhosseini.

Glossy "The Ship Angelica" has all the elements of a good historical miniseries: action, romance, sunken treasure, a dash of politics, a solid cast of good guys and bad guys and quality tech credits.

Circa 1870, a rebellious Iranian captain sets sail to find a sunken Portuguese treasure ship. The transient captain is a sort of John Wayne of the sea, loyal only to himself and his crew. But he must deal with two opposing forces of evil: the British colonialists and the two-faced Iranian dynasty in Shiraz.

Backed, in theory, by the governor of Shiraz, the captain sails with a crew of divers who believe they're hunting for pearls. The British are oblivious to the voyage, even though they forbid any movement in the gulf without their permission. Unfortunately, the captain trusts the governor not to inform the British. Though the governor's son is on board with ulterior motives, the captain triumphs in the end.

Script and editing contribute to film's quick pace. Photography and lighting credits are exceptionally good for an Iranian film. Altogether, it's an action-adventure pic that meets international tv standards. — *Suze.*

DO FILM BA YEK BELIT
(DOUBLE FEATURE)
(IRANIAN)

An Iranian Center for Film Industry Services production. Produced by Gholam-Reza Moayeri, Dariush Farhang. Written and directed by Farhang. Camera (color), Alireza Zarrindast; editor, Abbas Ganjavi; music, Babak Bayat; sound, Jahangir Mirshekari, Asghar Shahverdi; set design, Amir Esbati; makeup, Amir Eskandari; special effects, Nader Mirkiani, Mehdi Bahmanpoor; production manager, Habib Esmaili. Reviewed at Fajr Intl. Film Festival, Teheran, Feb. 8, 1991. Running time: **90 MIN.** With: Mehdi Hashemi, Dariush Farhang, Afsaneh Bayegan, Atila Pasayani, Siamak Atlasi, Akbar Sabet-Kasai, Shahla Riahi, Nilufar Mohammadi.

"**D**ouble Feature," Teheran's contribution to the film-within-a-film genre, reveals the pitfalls of the moviemaking process in Iran through a fictionalized account of a filmmaker's behind-the-scenes frustrations. Outside its country of origin, pic's main target will be industryites and other festivals.

Scripter and helmer Dariush Farhang plays the director who has just returned from a long stay in America with plans to make an action film. With a skeleton script, no storyboard and a timid actor, the director has his work cut out for him.

The actor, plagued by fear and vertigo, refuses to jump from a conveyor belt into a sand heap during a chase scene. But, there's no stuntman, there's no union to defend the actor's rights and the slab of sponge set up to break his fall is a joke by Western standards.

Predictably, the actor is hurt and the production grinds to a halt while the crew searches for a replacement.

Since there are no talent agencies, the helmer conducts his search by word-of-mouth and accidentally discovers a street peddler who resembles the original thesp. The peddler then soaks the production for every penny he can and turns the set into a comedy as he tries to run the show himself.

Farhang makes it seem like a miracle that the film ends up in the can. Pic is an interesting document on the foibles of filming in Iran. — *Suze.*

SANTA BARBARA FILM FEST

THE DARK BACKWARD

An Elwes/Wyman and Talmadge/L.A. Dreams production. Produced by Brad Wyman and Cassian Elwes. Executive producers, Randolf Turrow, William Talmadge. Written and directed by Adam Rifkin. Camera (color), Joey Forsyte; editor, Peter Schink; music, Marc David Decker; sound, Mary Jo Devenney; production design, Sherman Williams; art direction, Wendy Guidery; costume design, Alexandria Forster; special makeup effects, Tony Gardner, Alterion Studios; co-producer, Ronald J. Diamond; associate producers, Lucy Anne Buffett, Lisa Lange; assistant director, Chris Edmonds; casting, Tony Markes. Reviewed at Santa Barbara (Calif.) Film Festival, March 9, 1991. No MPAA rating. Running time: **97 MIN.**
Marty Malt . . . . .Judd Nelson
Gus . . . . .Bill Paxton
Jackie Chrome . . . . .Wayne Newton
Rosarita . . . . . . .Lara Flynn Boyle
Dr. Scurvy . . . . .James Caan
Dirk Delta . . . . .Rob Lowe
Twinkee Doodle . . . . . .King Moody

Writer-director Adam Rifkin ventures audaciously into early John Waters-David Lynch territory in this grotesque tale of a no-talent comic who finds notoriety when a third arm grows out of his back. Despite inspired bursts of lunacy, pic leaves the possibilities dangling. Still, pic is bound to win at least a moderate stint on the midnight film circuit and some cult admiration.

RCA/Columbia contributed to financing and has video rights to the pic, which world premiered at the Santa Barbara Film Fest.

Judd Nelson, with slicked-down hair and geeky glasses, plays the furtive would-be comic. A garbageman by day, he gets unqualified encouragement from his fellow trash-bagger, idiotically happy Gus (Bill Paxton), who eventually joins the act as an accordion player.

Marty's inert material doesn't much impress his waitress g.f. Rosarita (played well by Lara Flynn Boyle), and his murky upside-down world grows ever darker. When a peculiar bump on his back turns into a horrifying little human hand, Rosarita clears out in a panic of revulsion.

Rifkin has much fun with the central concept of this freakish occurrence, drawing it out in a series of blackly amusing scenes. Even in Marty's warped world, the intrusion of this ever-growing limb is the ultimate humiliation.

Pinnacle of the proceedings comes when Gus, who has a romantic penchant for circus-size fat ladies, brings three of the giggling girls by Marty's place late at night for a promised look at the aberrant arm. It's enough to silence the party noises of even these silly sideshow sisters.

But once the arm has been unveiled, Rifkin lets it hang there, taking the pic down a conventional road rather than pushing into the violent or horrific territory that could have made it truly fascinating.

Marty trundles into the well-traveled boulevard of broken dreams, hooking up with a formerly indifferent talent agent (Wayne Newton) and selling himself as a novelty act.

Pic descends into a formulaic story of a futile quest for Hollywood success, though it's not without a measure of poignance. Much of the third act drags.

Nelson and Paxton achieve some highly amusing scenes, but both perfs are rather one-dimensional. Paxton's over-the-top energy becomes wearing by the third act.

Low-budget project has some sterling elements, including casting by Tony Markes, who enlisted a carnival of Diane Arbus characters. Marty's grubby, garbage-strewn world is designed with whimsy by Sherman Williams and shot garishly (and aptly) by Joey Forsyte. Peter Schink's editing is deft.

James Caan is very funny in a brief role as a fraudulent, out-of-control M.D., but Rob Lowe, hard to recognize with a break-nose makeup job, is superfluous in a cameo as a Hollywood operative.

Pic marks the second collaboration for Rifkin and producers Brad Wyman and Cassian Elwes ("Never On Tuesday") — *Daws.*

THE CLOSER

An Ion Pictures release of a Nabeel Zahid and Joseph Medawar presentation. Produced by Zahid, Medawar. Executive producers, George Pappas, Tony Conforti. Directed by Dimitri Logothetis. Screenplay, Robert Keats, Louis La Russo II, based on La Russo's play "Wheelbarrow Closers"; camera (Foto-Kem color, Deluxe prints), Nicholas Von Sternberg; editor, Tracy S. Granger; music, Al Kasha, Joel Hirschhorn; sound (Dolby), John Coffey; visual consultant, Peter Paul Raubertas; costume design, Kay Morris; assistant director, Richard Hench; production manager, William Tasgal; co-executive producers, Mitchell Calder, Roy Medawar; supervising producers, F. Daniel Somrack, Michel Kossak; associate producers, James Gianulias, Hassan Alkabbani, Barney Nelson; casting, Rosemary Welden. Reviewed at Broadway screening room, N.Y., Jan. 22, 1990. (Also in Santa Barbara Film Festival.) No MPAA Rating. Running time: **86 MIN.**
Chester Grant . . . . . . .Danny Aiello
Larry Freede . . . . . .Michael Paré
John Mogen . . . . .Joe Cortese
Jessica Grant . . . . .Justine Bateman
Chet Grant . . . . .Tim Quill
Billy Grant . . . . .Rick Aiello
Beatrice Grant . . . . . . .Diane Baker
Ned Randall . . . . .James Karen
Doctor . . . . .Michael Lerner
Hustler . . . . .Michael Colyar

Danny Aiello's bravura performance gives some backbone to "The Closer," a trite tale of an overbearing salesman that betrays its theatrical origins. Film should face tough sledding in movie houses but is okay fodder for tv.

Aiello toplined in the 1976 Broadway play basis of this material, co-scripter Louis La Russo II's "Wheelbarrow Closers," and that property's producer Tony Conforti returns as an exec producer of the film. Unfortunately, the thematics have dated.

Aiello is "The Closer," author of a book of that title detailing his ascent to the top closing real estate deals for his CDC Corp. He's about to step down and has rounded up his two leading salesmen from out of town, street smart Michael Paré and by-the-book Joseph Cortese, to share his family Thanksgiving dinner in L.A. and compete for the prexy office.

That structure is similar to Jean Negulesco's excellent 1954 20th Century-Fox film "Woman's World," but that Cinemascope pic emphasized in equal time fashion the wives of the aspiring execs competing for boss Clifton Webb's approval.

Though Aiello's family is the center of the action here, the employees' families are not presented, a telling change from the '50s when such matters counted. Aiello browbeats and abuses employees and his family alike to dominate the piece.

There's not much suspense generated, since as Paré's character says at one of several third-act climaxes, Aiello really has no intention of stepping down and is merely playing mind games.

Film is interesting to watch in conjunction with the current Aiello release "Once Around," which he filmed just one month after doing "The Closer." The role of dominant family patriarch facing retirement is similar, while in "The Closer" Aiello also incorporates the super salesman persona and heart condition that Richard Dreyfuss carried in the Lasse Hallström opus.

What's fascinating is the different acting style Aiello adopts here, a cold, calculating performance that carefully denies the immense sympathy he generated in "Once Around." Both roles are career triumphs for the character actor.

Supporting cast does yeoman work to enliven one-dimensional roles, with Paré convincing at the pool table beating his boss (in a fine scene where Aiello pays homage to Jackie Gleason's cool-as-a-cucumber Minnesota Fats in "The Hustler"). Cortese is given less to work with and obviously would be more at home playing Paré's role.

Diane Baker, looking as beautiful as in her starlet days, makes a welcome return to film as Aiello's long-suffering wife. Tv star Justine Bateman is sexy and acid-tongued as their independent

Original play: WHEELBARROW CLOSERS

Tony Conforti, in association with Howard Efron & George Tunick, presentation of a play in two acts, by Louis La Russo II. Staged by Paul Sorvino; setting, Charles Carmello Jr.; supervision, Ken Billington; lighting, Leon Di Leone; costumes, Jan Wallace; supervision, Carol Luiken; production associates, David Silberg, Diane Matthews; associate producers, Michael Bash, Howard Wesson, Irving Warhaftig. Features Danny Aiello. Publicity, Max Eisen, Barbara Glenn, Irene Gandy; stage managers, Gary Stein, Jane Barish. Opened Oct. 11, '76, at the Bijou Theatre, N.Y.
Millie Grant . . . . Norah Foster
John Mogan . . . . Ray Serra
Larry Freede . . . . . . Harvey Siegel
Beatrice Grant . . . . . Frances Helm
Chet Grant . . . . James Allan Bartz
Chester Grant . . . . . . Danny Aiello
Wilfred Dee . . . . Tom Degidon

daughter. Tim Quill creates sympathy as Aiello's misunderstood artist son.

James Karen gives a solid performance as the business confidante passed over for the top job. Viewer will have to look at '50s classics "Patterns" and "Executive Suite" for the real lowdown on his character, however.

Subplot involving the death of Aiello's son (played by his real-life son Rick) is awkwardly presented in a series of flashbacks and fantasy "ghost" scenes that interrupt the action and inject unhelpful sentimentality. Dimitri Logothetis' direction is smooth, and film's tech credits are modest. — *Lor.*

BERLIN FEST

THE MIRACLE
(BRITISH)

A Miramax Films release (in U.S.) of a Palace Pictures-Promenade production, in association with Film Four Intl. and British Screen. (Intl. sales: Sales Co., London.) Executive producer, Nik Powell. Produced by Stephen Woolley, Redmond Morris. Written and directed by Neil Jordan. Camera (Technicolor), Philippe Rousselot; editor, Joke van Wijk; music, Anne Dudley; sound, Colin Nicholson; production design, Gemma Jackson; costumes, Sandy Powell; production manager, Gemma Fallon; assistant director, David Brown; casting, Susie Figgis. Reviewed at Berlin Film Festival (competition), Feb. 16, 1991. Running time: **96 MIN.**
Renee Baker . . . . Beverly D'Angelo
Sam . . . . Donal McCann
Jimmy . . . . Niall Byrne
Rose . . . . Lorraine Pilkington
Mr. Beausang . . . . J.G. Devlin
Miss Strange . . . . Kathleen Delaney
Tommy . . . . Tom Hickey
Jonner . . . . Mikkel Gaup

Following his disappointing studio picture "We're No Angels," Irish writer-director Neil Jordan returns to his home turf with the small-scale romantic drama "The Miracle." Uneven results promise modest returns.

Jordan's first feature, "Angel," was a thriller about a young musician involved in a series of killings. Similarly, Jimmy (Niall Byrne), the young hero of "The Miracle," is a musician and a dreamer who spends much of his time in the company of Rose (Lorraine Pilkington). Rose would like their relationship to become more intimate. Together they walk the streets of their small coastal town (Bray in County Wicklow), inventing romantic stories about the people who pass them by.

Jimmy never knew his mother and lives with his father (Donal McCann), a drunken musician. One day his eye is caught by an attractive American woman (Beverly D'Angelo) who's in town to perform in a local production of "Destry Rides Again." He fantasizes a romantic liaison with her, but there are no prizes for guessing that she's really his long-lost mother.

Like everything else in the film, the incest theme is tentatively handled. More interesting is Rose's relationship with a circus animal trainer (Mikkel Gaup). Seizing the opportunity to steal his keys while making love, Rose releases all the circus animals for

a liberating and cheerful climax.

For most of its length, "The Miracle" is insubstantial fare, with predictable situations and plotting. Scenes between the two teenagers come over best, and the two young thesps, both introduced here, are charming.

D'Angelo exudes mature sexuality as the stranger in town, but McCann makes heavy weather of his role as the perpetually drunken father. Very handsomely photographed by Philippe Rousselot, "The Miracle" is technically fine in every department. Particularly noteworthy are the fine sax solos by Courtney Pine.

Paucity and predictability of plot undermine the effort, even though there are charming sequences along the way. — *Strat.*

DGE
(THE DAY)
(SOVIET-B&W)

A Skartwelos Telefilmebis Studio (Tbilisi) production. Written and directed by Levan Glonti. Camera (b&w), Kacha Tschelidse, David Gudshabidse; music, Teimuras Bakuradse; production design, Gogi Tatischvili. Reviewed at Berlin Film Festival (Forum), Feb. 21, 1991. Running time: **65 MIN.**
With: Ilo Glonti, Gia Kankava, Giorgi Kvavilaschvili.

Newcomer Levan Glonti originally made this atmospheric little pic as his film school thesis, and Georgian tv gave him some coin to lengthen it to a feature. The result, while not likely to set cash registers jingling, is good enough for fest exposure. The film's style isn't new, but Glonti's quiet observations and the beautiful monochrome camerawork are major pluses.

It's just a day in the life of a Georgian student, who awakens in his girlfriend's bed, goes back to sleep at his grandparents' apartment, gets up, meets a friend, wanders the streets, goes to a party, and so on.

It ends on a dramatic note, but most of the film consists of seemingly off-hand observations of city life in Tbilisi, where, for example, police are quick to pick up a couple of drunks as they carouse in the early-morning streets.

Pic was a worthy choice for Berlin's Forum, which always is on the lookout for new talent. Glonti certainly should be heard from in the future. — *Strat.*

DAMES GALANTES
(GALLANT LADIES)
(FRENCH-ITALIAN)

A Gaumont release of a Gaumont Prod.-CFC-Cine Video (Paris)-Cecchi Gori Group-Tiger Cinematografica (Rome) co-production, with the participation of Telefilm Canada. Produced by Christian Charret. Directed by Jean-Charles Tacchella. Screenplay, Tacchella, Jacques Emmanuel; camera (Eastmancolor), Dominique Le Rigoleur; editor, Marie-Anne Debril; music, Raymond Allessandrini; production design, Georges Levy; costumes, Cristine Guegan; production manager, Alain Darbon; assistant director, Patrick Jaquillard; casting, Ginette Tacchella. Reviewed at Berlin Film Festival (market), Feb. 20, 1991. Running time: **99 MIN.**
Brantome . . . . . . Richard Bohringer
Victofre . . . . Isabella Rossellini
Margaret . . Marie-Christine Barrault
Catherine de Medici . . . . Laura Betti
Henry IV . . . . Robin Renucci
Louise . . . . Nathalie Mann
Also with: Alain Doutey, Eva Grimaldi.

Director Jean-Charles Tacchella, who never has matched the international success he achieved with "Cousin, Cousine," has turned in a surprisingly lifeless new pic with "Gallant Ladies," a 16th century comedy with narrow commercial prospects.

On paper, it sounds fine. Brantome, a soldier involved in the religious wars, is more interested in women ("the joy of [his] life"). He has mistresses galore among the ladies of the royal court, all of them beautiful and willing, but his heart belongs to the lovely Victofre, played with elegance by Isabella Rossellini.

Apart from brief battle scenes in the first reel, pic consists almost entirely of bedroom encounters. The wonder is that they are uniformly devoid of interest. Part of the problem is actor Richard Bohringer, who seems totally uninterested in his character. The film would have greatly benefited from the presence someone like Gérard Depardieu in this crucial role.

Bohringer's flaccid performance is matched by Tacchella's distant handling of what should have been a joyous celebration of sex and female beauty. There's a little nudity, but the love scenes are empty of passion or enjoyment, and boredom sets in early. It's a pity as Gaumont apparently has spared no expense on this splendid-looking production, with its rich sets and costumes.

The result is a sterile picture of limited potential, further hampered by a drab music score. It's already played at a few fests, presumably because of Tacchella's reputation. — *Strat.*

DER ZYNISCHE KÖRPER
(THE HOLY BUNCH)
(GERMAN)

A Pym Films production. Written and directed by Heinz Emigholz. Camera (color), Emigholz; editor, Renate Merck; music, Nikolaus Utermohlen; sound, Alfred Olbrich; production design, Ueli Etter. Reviewed at Berlin Film Festival (Forum), Feb. 17, 1991. Running time: **89 MIN.**

Roy . . . . Klaus Behnklen
Carl . . . . Eckhard Rhode
Fred . . . . Wolfgang Muller
Liza . . . . Kyle de Camp
Bela . . . . Carola Regnier
Jon . . . . John Erdman

This low-budgeter for specialized audiences only is about a small group of friends and their relationships. Commercial possibilities are limited for "The Holy Bunch," a precious, self-consciously arty effort.

Set in Hamburg, the story revolves around the dead Roy, an editor who has left thousands of notebooks behind. His friends — Carl, a writer; Jon, an architect into the gay scene; Liza, a photographer; Fred, an artist, and Bela, a translator — pore over the minutely written notes.

None of the characters is very interesting. As the story develops, Rob, a fictional character created by Carl, comes alive and starts "cloning" the thoughts of the bunch.

The film, with its off-center camera angles and pointless jokes, has a student feel to it, though it's technically adequate.

There's some (male) nudity, a little violence, but mostly a lot of rather dull talk. The film is strictly for those fest audiences on the hunt for something supposedly new, though this kind of pic was done better by the French 30 years ago. — *Strat.*

LE COLLIER PERDU DE LA COLOMBE
(THE DOVE'S LOST COLLAR)
(TUNISIAN-FRENCH-ITALIAN)

An RTT (Tunis)-Tunisian Ministry of Culture-Carthago Films-La Sept-Canal Plus co-production. Produced by Tarak Ben Ammar. Written and directed by Nacer Khemir. Camera (Eastmancolor), Georges Barsky; editor, Den-

ise de Casabianca, Kahina Attia, Catherine Bonnetat; music, Jean Claude Petit; sound, Faouzi Thabet, Gérard Rousseau; costumes, Maud Perl; production manager, Michel Choquet. Reviewed at Berlin Film Festival (Panorama), Feb. 21, 1991. Running time: **90 MIN.**

Hassan . . . . Navin Chowdhry
Zin . . . . Walid Araki
Aziz . . . . Ninar Esber
Leila . . . . Sonia Hochlaff
Myriam . . . . Chloe Rejon
Osman . . . . Jivane Karmaly
Girl in rose garden . . . . Leila Dakhly

A visually sumptuous fairy tale obviously inspired by "Thousand And One Nights," "The Dove's Lost Collar" is a high-quality film from Tunis. It could well find a niche in the children's film market, while adults should relish the beauty and serenity of this timeless tale.

The young hero, Hassan, who is studying calligraphy, comes across part of a manuscript. He believes that if he can find the rest of it, love's secrets will be revealed. He is helped by a moppet, Zin, who acts as a go-between for lovers and who has a monkey he believes to be a prince under a spell.

On his quest for love, Hassan meets Aziz, the beautiful woman of his dreams. Though they're separated by war, they're reunited for the fadeout.

Writer-helmer Nacer Khemir has filmed this on fabulous North African locations, and he tells his exotic fairy tale with simplicity and charm. Costumes are sumptuous, the characters delightful, and though the story is a bit slight, it picks up toward the end.

Tech credits are excellent, especially Georges Barsky's glorious camerawork. — *Strat.*

HOW TO SURVIVE A BROKEN HEART
(DUTCH-B&W)

A Minimal Movies Intl.-Schram Studio production. Produced by Pim de la Parra, Erik Luijten. Directed by Paul Ruven. Screenplay, Ruven, de la Parra, P.J. Vernu; camera (b&w), Jan Wich; editor, Herman P. Koerts; music, Marcel de Groot, Ake Danielson; sound, Peter Guyt; production design, Ans Guers, Valesca Meist; production manager, Bastiaan Anink; assistant director, Eugenie Jansen. Reviewed at Berlin Film Festival (Forum), Feb. 16, 1991. Running time: **84 MIN.**

With: Bonnie Williams, Erik de Bruyn, Alejandro Agresti, Jim Cook, Isabella van Rooy, Frank Sheppard, Kim Soepnel, Gerard Thoolen.

This low-budget pic with English and Dutch dialog concerns a group of lovesick losers in an unglamorous Amsterdam. Pic could make the fest circuit thanks to its raffish sense of humor and attractive characters, all neatly etched by director Paul Ruven.

The hero is D.C., who hasn't recovered from the fact that his girl has left him. He participates in "chicken races," in which cars are driven fast on the wrong side of the road; some of the so-called races are rigged. Other characters include D.C.'s friend, Clay; Gina, a pregnant taxi driver whose lover, Frank, wants no more to do with her, and Giro, a Russian who lives in his car.

Pic is amusingly divided into chapter headings based on an entirely new set of Ten Commandments, most of them obscene. One of the cleaner instructions reads: "Thou shalt not desperately lose thyself in pretending to be a hero of a new love affair."

Jan Wilch's black & white lensing is sharp, and the film is amusing and offbeat enough to garner cult audience, with late-night screenings possible. Thesping is adequate down the line. — *Strat.*

ALICIA EN EL PUEBLO DE MARAVILLAS
(ALICE IN WONDER TOWN)
(CUBAN)

An ICAIC production. Produced by Humberto Hernandez. Directed by Daniel Diaz Torres. Screenplay, Diaz Torres, Jesus Diaz; camera (color), Raul Perez Ureta; editor, Jorge Abello; music, Frank Delgado; sound, Ricardo Istueta. Reviewed at Berlin Film Festival (Forum), Feb. 19, 1991. Running time: **93 MIN.**

Alice . . . . Thais Valdes
Also with: Reinaldo Miravalles, Alberto Pujols, Carlos Cruz, Raul Pomares, Alina Rodriguez, Jorge Martinez, Enrique Molina.

"Alice In Wonder Town" is a fast-paced mélange of jokes and surreal images. It will have a place at fests, but commercial prospects are limited.

Pic opens with credits placed around drawings based on the original Tenniel illustrations in Lewis Carroll's "Alice In Wonderland" and "Through The Looking Glass." But the film really

has nothing to do with Carroll. It's a modern satire about a young cultural bureaucrat who's sent to a small town (called Maravilles, or Wonders) as part of her job.

She finds it a very strange place indeed. The medicine chest in her hotel bathroom opens onto a room next door where a man is shaving. There's a swarm of cockroaches in the night. Camels, monkeys, snakes and other creatures seem to wander around at will in the middle of town.

Everyone Alice meets has a strange story to tell, starting with a truck driver, who helps her eliminate the roaches and who describes how he arrived in town and has somehow never left. Director Daniel Diaz Torres has some political and social comment to make here, as many of the inhabitants of Wonder Town seem to be people who've been sacked from official positions.

The jokes and allusions likely will be better understood by a Cuban audience, but the film has enough sight gags and bizarre moments to please a wider audience. This exotic comedy, featuring an appealing central performance from Thais Valdes as Alice, is visually plush and briskly paced. Technically, pic is firstrate. — *Strat.*

TEENAGE MUTANT NINJA TURTLES II: THE SECRET OF OOZE

A New Line Cinema release of a Golden Harvest production in association with Gary Propper. Produced by Thomas K. Gray, Kim Dawson, David Chan. Executive producer, Raymond Chow. Directed by Michael Pressman. Screenplay, Todd W. Langen, based on characters created by Kevin Eastman, Peter Laird; camera (Technicolor), Shelly Johnson; editor, John Wright, Steve Mirkovich; music, John Du Prez; sound (Dolby), David Kirschner, Gregg Landaker, Steve Maslow, Rick Kline; production design, Roy Forge Smith; supervising art director, Mayne Schuyler Berke; art direction, Geoffrey S. Grimsman; set decoration, Brendan Smith, Kosmo Houlton-Vinyl (N.Y.); costume design, Dodie Shepard; stunt coordinator-martial arts choreographer, Pat Johnson; dance choreographer, Myrna Gawryn; animatronic characters, Jim Henson's Creature Shop (creative supervisor, John Stephenson; visual supervisor, Jane Gootnick; designers, Ray Scott, Nigel Booth, Vin Burnham, Pete Brooke, Jamie Courtier, Verner Gresty, Neal Scanlan); chief puppeteer, Mak Wilson; animatronic puppeteers, David Greenaway, Wilson, Robert Tygner, Robert Mills, Kevin Clash, Susan Dacre, Richard Boyd, Gordon Robertson, Rick Lyon; assistant director, Rob Corn; 2d unit directors, Terry Leonard, Newton Dennis Arnold; 2d unit camera, Jon Kranhouse; 2d unit assistant director, Gary M. Strangis; co-producer, Terry Morse; casting, Lynn Stalmaster. Reviewed at AMC Century 14, L.A., March 19, 1991. MPAA Rating: PG. Running time: **88 MIN.**

April O'Neil . . . . Paige Turco
Prof. Jordan Perry . . . David Warner
Michelangelo . . . . . . Michelan Sisti
Donatello . . . . Leif Tilden
Raphael . . . . Kenn Troum
Leonardo . . . . Mark Caso
Splinter . . . . Kevin Clash
Keno . . . . Ernie Reyes Jr.
Shredder . . . . François Chau
Also with: Toshishiro Obata, Raymond Serra, Mark Ginther, Kurt Bryant, Michael Pressman, Vanilla Ice.
Also with the voices of: Robbie Rist, Brian Tochi, Laurie Faso, Adam Carl, Clash, David McCharen, Michael McConnohie, Frank Welker.

Though "Teenage Mutant Ninja Turtles II: The Secret Of The Ooze" suffers from a lack of novelty and an aimless screenplay, the bottom line is that the pic won't disappoint its core subteen audience. A huge opening seems assured, although the sequel's legs look less green than the original's.

Those lean, green and mean reptilian superheroes who became screen superstars last year for Golden Harvest and New Line ($133 million domestic b.o.) encore in this more lighthearted, brightly colored pic.

Dedicated to the late Jim Henson, whose Creature Shop created the delightful animatronic characters for both pics, "Turtles II" gives more footage to Michelangelo, Donatello, Raphael, Leonardo and their giant rat master Splinter than the original did, and adds two hilarious childlike monsters, Rahzar and Tokka, who virtually steal the show.

Some aspects of the original reviewers and parents criticized — murky lighting, uninteresting human characters, violence — have been modified in the more amiable sequel, mostly to good effect.

Director Michael Pressman (Steve Barron helmed the first) opts for a cheerier look with new lenser Shelly Johnson and returning production designer Roy Forge Smith. The change is welcome, since the first film too often looked like a pretentious, badly shot rock video.

The staging of fight scenes here is less like a Steven Seagal film and more like the Three Stooges, with the turtles nonchalantly jumping and kicking rings around inept foes.

Though this change will assuage parents who found the original a bit too rough, downplaying the menace of the villainous Foot Clan also reduces the suspense element and makes the story less involving.

Todd Langen's turtle dialog doesn't have the goofy wit his and Bobby Herbeck's script for the first film had; too often settling for mild, unimaginative wisecracks that don't enhance their characters.

Subtitle's promise that the ooze secret will be revealed doesn't pay off, since the film adds precious little to the backstory of the turtles' transformation into superheroes by green radioactive glop. David Warner, as the sympathetic and eccentric scientist who invented the stuff and now is trying to dispose of it, doesn't have much to do. Some flashbacks might have helped.

Paige Turco (of tv soap "All My Children") takes over the lead human role of Gotham tv newswoman April O'Neil from Judith Hoag, and while Turco is more glamorous, the character still seems unfocused and overly ditzy. Perhaps it's impossible to find the spine of a character living with four giant turtles who have crushes on her.

Ernie Reyes Jr. has a winning role as a youthful pizza deliveryman/martial arts expert who wangles his way into the turtles' company and helps them in their neverending battle with the Foot Clan. His chopsocky exploits (credits make it clear he did them without a double) are among pic's many uncomplicated pleasures, as is Pat Johnson's graceful fight choreography and stunt coordination.

The wonderful mutated wolf (Rahzar) and snapping turtle (Tokka) characters, whose lumbering fighting style and mischievous personalities provide much of the humor, resemble giant gremlins escaped from a Joe Dante pic. They're sure to tickle both kids and parents.

The rapper Vanilla Ice appears in an inconsequential and somewhat silly number while the turtles are battling the monsters in a Gotham disco.

Tech credits are uniformly slick, although the editing by John Wright and Steve Mirkovich doesn't do enough to counteract the languid storyline. — *Mac.*

THE OBJECT OF BEAUTY
(U.S.-BRITISH)

An Avenue Pictures release of an Avenue Pictures, BBC Films presentation of a Jon S. Denny production. Executive producer, Cary Brokaw. Produced by Denny. Producer (BBC Films), Alex Gohar. Directed by Michael Lindsay-Hogg. Screenplay, Lindsay-Hogg; camera (Rank color), David Watkin; editor, Ruth Foster; music, Tom Bähler; sound, John Pritchard; production design, Derek Dodd; costume design, Les Lansdown; assistant director, Brett Fallis; associate producer, Richard Turner. Reviewed at Magno Preview 9 screening room, N.Y., March 7, 1991. MPAA Rating: R. Running time: **101 MIN.**

Jake . . . . John Malkovich
Tina . . . . Andie MacDowell
Joan . . . . Lolita Davidovich
Jenny . . . . Rudi Davies
Mr. Mercer . . . . Joss Ackland
Victor Swayle . . . . . . Bill Paterson
Steve . . . . Ricci Harnett
Larry . . . . Peter Riegert
Mr. Slaughter . . . . . Jack Shepherd
Also with: Rosemary Martin, Roger Lloyd Pack, Andrew Hawkins.

"The Object Of Beauty" is a throwback to the romantic comedies of Swinging London cinema, but lacks the punch of the best of that late '60s genre. It has only modest prospects among sophisticated theatrical audiences, with a much better outlook in ancillary exposure.

Following up his "The Sheltering Sky" performance with another drifting character, John Malkovich toplines as a ne'er-do-well holed up in a swank London hotel with his mate Andie MacDowell. Everyone assumes the two of them are married, but MacDowell is still hitched to estranged hubbie Peter Riegert.

With amiable comedy situations to sugarcoat the opening reels, not much happens as the duo dine in the hotel's expensive restaurant, Malkovich worries about his broker selling him out on dubious investments and he carefully dodges the hotel manager (Joss Ackland) with inquiries about paying a portion of their bill.

Plot concerns the title object, a small Henry Moore figurine that MacDowell received from Riegert as a present and which Malkovich desperately wants to sell or use for an insurance scam to cover his hotel tab and ongoing business reverses.

Key script contrivance has a deaf-mute maid (Rudi Davies), newly hired at the hotel, becoming obsessed with the Moore sculpture and stealing it for a keepsake. This sets into motion trite complications, notably developing a wedge (as corny as O. Henry's "The Gift Of The Magi") between Malkovich and MacDowell as each believes the other has pocketed the $50,000 art work.

A subplot involving Davies and her punk-styled brother strains heavily for pathos. Another unsuccessful side issue is Malkovich's selfish affair with MacDowell's best friend Lolita Davidovich, who makes the most of her one-dimensional part. (She replaced Elizabeth Perkins in the role.)

As in "Sheltering Sky," Malkovich ably brings out the unsympathetic nature of his antihero, but the script doesn't help him much in balancing that with any impelling reason for identification. It's hard to care about someone whose future lies in produce sitting on a dock in Sierra Leone.

The viewer will instantly side with MacDowell, whose natural beauty is augmented here by a feisty violent streak whenever Malkovich steps over the line (which is frequent). In addition to Davidovich, Davies, Ackland, officious hotel dick Bill Paterson and no-nonsense insurance inspector Jack Shepherd turn in pro turns.

Filmmaker Michael Lindsay-Hogg, whose diverse credits range from the Beatles' "Let It Be" to farce ("Nasty Habits"), develops effective individual scenes but fails to create a reason for sustained interest in his characters. Result is a mildly diverting but empty picture. David Watkin, whose experience in the genre dates back to Richard Lester's classic "The Knack," has photographed the deceptively carefree setting with aplomb.
— *Lor.*

MILIARDI
(BILLIONS)
(ITALIAN)

A Penta Distribuzione release of a Mario and Vittorio Cecchi Gori-Silvio Berlusconi Communications production. Produced by Cecchi Gori Group Tiger-Intl. Video 80 for Penta Film. Directed by Carlo Vanzina. Screenplay, Carlo and Enrico Vanzina, based on the novel by Renzo Barbieri; camera (color), Luigi Kuveiller; editor, Ruggero Mastroianni; sound, Carlo Palmieri; set design, Davide Bassan; costumes, Roberta Guidi di Bagno; production manager, Lucio Orlandini. Reviewed at VIP Cinema, Rome, March 3, 1991. Running time: **100 MIN.**

Betta . . . . Carol Alt
Cristina . . . . Lauren Hutton
Maurizio Ferretti . . . . . Billy Zane
Leo Ferretti . . . . Jean Sorel
Connie . . . . . . Catherine Hickland
Giulia . . . . Alexandra Paul
Piero Costa . . . . Cyros Elias
Ripa . . . . Donald Pleasence

Beautiful women in expensive lingerie, sleek cars, luxurious homes, designer-clad execs talking on cellular phones — all the clichés of high-society living are on parade in "Billions." Usually a reliable helmer of popular commercial entertaintment, Carlo Vanzina has struck out in this feature film equivalent of "Dallas."

Lensed on stunning locations in Rome, New York, Acapulco, the Bahamas and the Cote d'Azur, "Billions" offers a voyeuristic look at bedroom and business intrigues in the family of wealthy Italo industrialist Leo Ferretti (Jean Sorrel).

Not exciting enough to be a thriller nor amusing enough to pass for comedy, pic's attempt at subtle satire of the ruling class is undermined by director's undisguised celebration of the accoutrements of wealth and power.

Serviceable plot revolves around an ambitious young hotshot (Billy Zane) and his attempt to take control of his uncle's industrial empire after the latter is injured in a helicopter crash.

During his frenetic climb to the top, Zane blackmails his father and beds dad's scheming blond secretary (Catherine Hickland), his cocaine-snorting cousin (Carol Alt) and his social-climbing sister-in-law (Alexandra Paul).

Zane manages to secure a bank loan to take his company public but eventually is undone by his uncle, who has been nursed back to health by his loving wife (Lauren Hutton).

Action moves along at a brisk clip, but characters and situations are so stereotyped that capable and attractive cast resemble animated mannequins at times. Technical work is above average. — *Clrk.*

THICK AS THIEVES
(CANADIAN)

An Alliance Releasing release (in Canada) of a DiMarco Films production. Produced by Andrea Shaw, Steve DiMarco. Executive producers, Don Haig, Victor Loewy. Written and directed by DiMarco. Camera (color), Rick Maguire; editor, Miume Jan; music, David Schellenberg; art direction, Bruce McKenna; casting, Pierce Casting. Reviewed at Cineplex Odeon Eaton Center, Toronto, Feb. 22, 1991. Running time: **90 MIN.**

Al Hacker . . . . Gerry Quigley
Lisa Hacker . . . . Carolyn Dunn
Nikki . . . . Amber-Lea Weston
Hal . . . . Karl Pruner

Destined for a quick trip to homevideo, low-budget "Thick As Thieves" is an intended comedy that never gets off the ground.

Toronto scripter-director Steve DiMarco's first theatrical feature centers on adventures of a down-at-the-heels pickpocket duo. Their mark turns out to be, not a businessman as they thought, but an undercover cop.

In court, the brother gets time to raise a $5,000 fine or face 90 days in jail. The sister and the cop, who thinks she is innocent, fall in love, to the brother's anger. But eventually, the sibs are back on the streets together, and the cop's out of the picture.

DiMarco's script has comic possibilities, but his direction and most production credits are listless and cartoonish.

Against those negatives, performances, notably by Carolyn Dunn as the sister and Karl Pruner as the cop, have no chance.

Of interest to the Canadian trade are cameos by Eugene Amadeo, general manager of Universal Films Canada; tv drama series regulars Sara Botsford, Eric Peterson, C. David Johnson and Jonathan Welsh; and stage actress Susan Wright. — *Adil.*

FLIRTING
(AUSTRALIAN)

A Warner Bros.-Roadshow (Australia) release of a Kennedy-Miller production. Produced by George Miller, Terry Hayes, Doug Mitchell. Written and directed by John Duigan. Camera (color), Geoff Burton; editor, Robert Gibson; sound, Ross Linton; production design, Roger Ford; postproduction, Marcus D'Arcy; associate producer-production manager, Barbara Gibbs; assistant director, Charles Rotherham; casting, Liz Mullinar. Reviewed at Film and Tv School, Sydney, Aug. 19, 1990. Running time: **96 MIN.**

Danny Embling . . . . . . Noah Taylor
Thandiwe Adjewa . . Thandie Newton
Nicola Radcliffe . . . . . Nicole Kidman
Gilby Fryer . . . . . Bartholomew Rose
Slag Green . . . . Kiri Paramore
Melissa Miles . . . . Kym Wilson
Morris Cutts . . . . Jeff Truman
Rupert Elliott . . . . . Marshall Napier

Miles ahead of the average teen film, "Flirting" is a most agreeable sequel to John Duigan's pic "The Year My Voice Broke," an Australian hit screened worldwide. The new film doesn't pack the emotional wallop of the first, but it still charms.

Because of affection for "The Year. . ." Down Under, "Flirting" is poised for a successful release there. Modest to good returns in other territories also can be expected.

This depiction of well-to-do teens in sexually segregated schools also looks obliquely at latent racism at the time of the "white Australia" policy. Events that led to the Vietnam War already were in motion.

Noah Taylor reprises his character of Danny Embling from the first film (1987), which ended when he was parted from the slightly older girl he'd adored since they were children. It's 1965, and Danny's parents have sent him to a boys-only boarding school across the lake from a similar institution for girls.

Loner Danny hates sports, stutters and is mildly defiant of authority. Macho boys regularly harass him.

In the girls' school, a young Ugandan student, whose politician father is lecturing in Australia, suffers racial slurs. Thandiwe (Thandie Newton) and Danny meet and are attracted to each other. Eventually, the couple spend a night in a local motel before Thandiwe has to return with her family to Africa and an uncertain future.

Duigan handles this material with a great deal of humor and charm, demonstrating a sharp ear for contemporaneous teen dialog.

Compared to Yank teen pics, "Flirting" is innocent and naive, but realistically so. Scenes in the classroom, cafeteria, dormitory and locker room are all handled with a tart sense of humor and sympathy for the youngsters' hangups. Adults come across as mostly unsympathetic.

Newton, a London actress, is a real find, and brings youthful sensuality and a light touch to her role. Taylor is fine, though Danny seems to have undergone character changes since the first film. Supporting players, both adults and youngsters, are uniformly well etched.

A curiosity is Nicole Kidman's appearance as one of the girls' school students. "Flirting" was shot before she went to the States to appear in "Days Of Thunder," and her presence is a reminder that "Flirting" was finished months ago. It's been under wraps despite winning the best film accolade in the 1990 Australian Film Awards last October.

Pic, produced by the Kennedy Miller company, displays top technical qualities, particularly camera-work and production design.
— *Strat.*

LA MUJER DE BANJAMIN
(BENJAMIN'S WOMAN)
(MEXICAN)

A Centro de Capacitacion Cinematografica-Estudios Churubusco-Azteca-Instituto Mexicano de Cinematografica production. Executive producer, Gustavo Montiel Pages. Directed by Carlos Carrera. Screenplay, Carrera, Ignacio Ortiz; camera (color), Xavier Perez Grobet; editor, Sigfrido Barjau, Oscar Figueroa; music, Jose Amozurruita, Alejancro Giacoman; sound, Fernando Camara; production manager, Jorge Ramirez-Suarez; assistant director, Javier Fox. Reviewed at Berlin Film Festival (Forum), Feb. 25, 1991. Running time: **89 MIN.**

Benjamin . . . . Eduardo Lopez Rojas
Natividad . . . . Arcelia Ramirez
Micaela . . . . Malena Doria
Leandro . . . . Eduardo Palomo
Natividad's mother . Ana Bertha Espin

"Benjamin's Woman" is an exploitable melodrama set in a small Mexican village. Beauty and the beast tale boasts a bewitching performance from young Arcelia Ramirez as a girl desired by an old simpleton.

Benjamin, overweight and in his 50s, lives and runs a general store with his grouchy sister. He doesn't work much, however, and spends his time with drunken layabouts and lusts after Natividad, a fetching teen. She lives with her widowed mother and appears innocent but is actually carrying on a secret liaison with a trucker.

Egged on by his pals, Benjamin kidnaps the girl as she's on her way to meet her boyfriend, but once he gets her back to his room, he finds she's pretty tough, and the shy man does nothing to harm her.

Natividad decides she prefers Benjamin's home to her own, and refuses to return to her mother. She gradually takes over the household and steals money from Benjamin and his sister.

Ramirez is fine as the calculating girl. Eduardo Lopez Rojas makes Benjamin a touching figure. Details of the village are neatly sketched in, with some satire at the expense of the local priest, who gets his kicks from religious paintings with nudes.

Camerawork by Xavier Perez Grobet is very good, and the film is briskly paced. It's no world beater, but could arouse interest in Latino territories and other festivals. — Strat.

THE PERFECT WEAPON

A Paramount Pictures presentation of a DiSalle/David production. Produced by Mark DiSalle and Pierre David. Directed by DiSalle. Screenplay, David Campbell Wilson; camera (color), Russell Carpenter; editor, Wayne Wahrman; music, Gary Chang; sound, Bob Anderson; production design, Curtis Schnell; costume design, Joseph Porro; art direction, Colin D. Irwin; set decoration, Archie D'Amico; stunt fight coordinator, Rick Avery; 2nd unit stunt coordinator, Glenn Wilder; assistant director, Kelly Schroeder. Reviewed at Paramount Studios, Hollywood, March 15, 1991. MPAA rating: R. Running time: **112 MIN.**
Jeff . . . . Jeff Speakman
Adam . . . . John Dye
Kim . . . . Mako
Yung . . . . James Hong
Jimmy Ho . . . . Dante Bosco
Tanaka . . . . Prof. Toru Tanaka

Thanks to first-time celluloid warrior Jeff Speakman, "The Perfect Weapon" tumbles out of the routine martial arts actioner mold. Sexier than Van Damme and untroubled by any foreign accent, Speakman has the goods to give the genre a lift. Payoff should be steady for both distrib and star.

Debuting screenwriter David Campbell Wilson's script for the Mark DiSalle ("Kickboxer," "Death Warrant") and Pierre David production sets up the classic excuse for violence among martial arts disciples: avenging the death of a friend.

In this formulaic blueprint, Speakman, who fights in the fluid and explosive kenpo karate style, goes up against an Asian crime-lord who's bumped off a merchant in L.A.'s Chinatown who'd been like a father to him.

Between mobster Yung (James Hong) and Speakman, script inserts the Perfect Obstacle — bodyguard Tanaka, a 350-pound lethal weapon who gives Speakman an exhaustive workout throughout the pic and in its climactic sequence, shot at San Pedro Harbor.

Hero also has a mouthy young sidekick (Dante Bosco), who naturally reminds him of his young self.

Director DiSalle and fight coordinator Rick Avery do an engrossing job with the action scenes. Speakman, a fourth degree kenpo black belt, unleashes his moves like an explosive string of firecrackers in a showy display of the brutal system of nonstop motion.

Promoted as the first pure display of kenpo American filmgoers have seen, the punching and kicking combo of judo, jujitsu, karate and kung fu elements should enliven the genre for core fans. Speakman, with his dimples, chin stubble and comic-book hero physique, plus credible acting skills, has the charisma to carry it through more installments.

Multicamera master shots let Speakman dispatch his throngs of foes unassisted by cuts or stunt doubles. Pic also finds an excuse for a gritty car chase in oncoming traffic and pulls off an explosive ending.

Strictly predictable nature of the proceedings renders the film uninvolving emotionally. It's like a video game in which the action hero topples foe after foe, which is probably just the way hardcore fans like it.

Pic is rather dimly shot by Russell Carpenter and production values, aside from the elaborate car chase, are just routine.
— Daws.

SAKAT
(SUNDOWN)
(SOVIET)

A Filmstudio Slovo (division of Mosfilm) production. Directed by Alexander Seldovitsch. Screenplay, Pavel Finn, based on Isaak Babel's "Stories From Odessa"; camera (color), Alexander Knjashinski; music, Leonid Desyatnikov; choreography, Marina Beltova; costumes, J. Melkonjan; stunts, Alexei Lubny; assistant directors, I. Wassiljeva, N. Sokol-Mzjuk, M. Fotijeva, O. Komarova; assistant camera, W. Kurakin, W. Bit-Brajdo, A. Demidov. Reviewed at Berlin Film Festival (Forum), Feb. 8, 1991. Running time: **87 MIN.**
Mendel Krik . . . Ramaz Chkhikvadze
Benja Krik . . . . . Viktor Gvozditsky
Old man . . . . . . Zinovy Korogodsky
Marusia . . . . Marina Maiko
Potapovna . . . . Olga Wolkova
Nechama Krik . . . . . Irina Sokolova
Also with: Julia Rutberg, Igor Solotovizki, Jakov Javno, Samuli Gruschevski, G. Woropajev.

Brilliantly shot and highly experimental, "Sakat" should find itself comfortably ensconced in the fest circuit for some time because of its visual style and the fact that it is one of the first films out of the Soviet Union to deal with Jewish themes. But film's difficult-to-comprehend storyline does not bode well for b.o.

Thirty-one-year-old helmer Alexander Seldovitsch's ambitious first feature was adapted from Isaak Babel's "Stories From Odessa," material Sergei Eisenstein wanted to shoot but couldn't, Jewish themes being taboo.

The story interweaves the biblical legend of David and Absalom with a father-and-son conflict set in the Odessa of the '20s. Mendel Krik (Ramaz Chkhikvadze), an old Jew, has two grown sons and a daughter and runs a hauling business. He wants to leave Odessa with his young mistress, buy a piece of land and begin a new life.

His son, Benja (Viktor Gvozditsky) is the Al Capone of the Odessa underworld. His life is filled with bank heists and vaudeville-style shootouts with police. The Russian stage pogroms against the Jews, Mendel is beaten by his son and Benja is bloodily murdered on his wedding night. Scenes jump between biblical times and Odessa.

Helmer Seldovitsch, an assimilated Russian Jew, has said his ambition was to make the first film dealing with Jewish subject matter in the Soviet Union, where Jewish history has long been off-limits to artists.

Film's finest feature is Alexander Knjashinski's stunning cinematography (he shot Andrei Tarkovsky's "Stalker"). His work captures perfectly the director's quest for a stagy and theatrical look.

In passion play-like vignettes portraying biblical scenes, such as the building of the Tower of Babel, the camera pulls back to reveal the massive tower as a small prop supported behind actors on poles. A wounded gangster falling from a great height is suddenly suspended in space by a wire connected to the ceiling. Shots are meticulously composed in frames within frames, with the camera situated behind doorways and windows.

While the pic has a wealth of wonderful characters, a good score and extremely sensuous tango sequences, its screenplay runs into problems. Stunning images, interesting sequences and compelling dialog are left disjointed by a narrative structure complex to the point of being enigmatic. — Reli.

AMERICAN NINJA 4: THE ANNIHILATION

A Cannon Pictures release. Executive producer, Avi Lerner. Produced by Christopher Pearce. Directed by Cedric Sundstrom. Screenplay, David Geeves, based on characters created by Avi Kleinberger, Gideon Amir; camera (color), Joseph Wein; editor, Claudio Ytruc; music, Nicolas Tenbroek; sound (Ultra Stereo), Colin MacFarlane; production design, Ruth Stripling; martial arts choreography, Mike Stone. Reviewed at AMC Meyer Park 14, Houston, Tex., March 10, 1991. MPAA Rating: R. Running time: **95 MIN.**
Joe Armstrong . . . . Michael Dudikoff
Sean . . . . David Bradley
Mulgrew . . . . James Booth
Brackston . . . . . Dwayne Alexandre
Sarah . . . . Robin Stille
Dr. Tamba . . . . Ken Gampu

That scratchy noise one might hear in "American Ninja 4: The Annihilation" is the sound of the very bottom of the barrel being scraped. Low-budget, no-talent programmer from newly revived Cannon gets a regional theatrical release, apparently as a mere formality.

Pic is so obviously intended for homevid consumption that instead of opening credits it should begin with the FBI anti-piracy warning. First-billed Michael Dudikoff, who had the good sense to skip "American Ninja 3," sits out the first half of this latest sequel.

In the first 45 minutes or so, good guys David Bradley (top kicker of "Ninja 3") and Dwayne Alexandre try to rescue four commandoes who have been captured and held for ransom by a ninja army in a tiny African country.

The ninjas are employed by an Arab sheik who's developing a briefcase-sized nuclear weapon. But the most dangerous of the bad guys is the sheik's sadistic henchman, wildly overacted by James Booth.

Booth and his ninja flunkies capture Bradley, Alexandre and

Robin Stille (as a Peace Corps nurse who jiggles a lot whenever she runs toward the camera). It's up to Dudikoff to interrupt his peaceful retirement as a teacher, revert to his ninja ways, invade the bad guys' fortress and save the world from nuclear terrorism and hammy supporting players.

Chopsocky mayhem imbues "American Ninja 4," but even the genre's most devoted fans will be disappointed by the lack of imagination and energy in the fight scenes.

Working from a lame script by David Geeves, director Cedric Sundstrom (another veteran of "Ninja 3") generates little excitement. Worse, he allows Booth too much liberty to chew up the scenery, his lines and, occasionally, other actors.

Dudikoff is wooden, Bradley is bland and the tech credits are no better than they have to be. Ken Gampu costars as the leader of a penal colony turned rebel camp.

In clothing, vehicles and generally surly attitude, the rebels resemble bit players from "Mad Max Beyond Thunderdome." That's not enough to pump much life into "American Ninja 4."

— *Ley.*

SCISSORS

A DDM Film Corp. production. Produced by Mel Pearl, Don Levin and Hal Polaire. Directed by Frank De Felitta. Screenplay, De Felitta, based on a story by Joyce Selznick; camera (color), Tony Richmond; editor, John Schreyer; sound, Kim Ornitz; production design, Craig Stearns; costume design, Del Adey-Jones; art direction, Randy Moore; set decoration, Kara Lindstrom; assistant director, Daisy Gerber; casting, Jan Glaser. Reviewed at Laemmle's Royal theater, L.A., March 1, 1991. No MPAA rating. Running time: **105 MIN.**
Angie . . . . Sharon Stone
Alex/Cole . . . . Steve Railsback
Dr. Carter . . . . Ronny Cox
Ann . . . . Michelle Phillips

In "Scissors," the heroine is trapped in a room where nothing is real, futilely banging on the window while she slowly goes mad. Audiences at pic's weeklong four-walling at L.A.'s Laemmle Monica may feel the same way, but they can rest assured they'll be let out after 105 minutes. It will no doubt seem a lot longer.

Sharon Stone as a sexually traumatized young woman trying to cope with life alone in the city is the only exception to a generally lifeless production. She deserves kudos for the sequence in which she must hold the screen alone while trapped in a high-tech chamber of horrors.

Her predicament comes about by way of a particularly nasty campaign by one of the few other characters in this thinly populated mystery. Writer-helmer Frank De Felitta (author of "Audrey Rose" and director of "Trapped" and "Killed In The Mirror") gives the film a stale, irrelevant feel not connected to a particular time or place.

Perhaps the isolated tone helps convey the heroine's paranoid state, but it doesn't much engage an audience.

Stone plays a collector and mender of damaged antique dolls who occasionally does temp secretarial work. At the outset, she's followed and attacked by a would-be rapist. The trauma brings her soap actor neighbor (Steve Railsback) into her life. Also taking an interest in Stone is Railsback's brother, a wheelchair-bound artist. Her therapist (Ronny Cox) is one of her few other contacts.

Heavily plotted pic is about someone's campaign to drive the fragile Stone around the bend. Trapped in a lavish apartment where she's ostensibly been sent to work for a designer, she's confronted with some of her deepest fears.

This location is the production's coup: It's a stunning suite of rooms where the fixtures come to life in nightmarish fashion, but De Felitta overuses it. That anyone would go to this much trouble on Angie's account, particularly for the reason finally given, is ludicrous.

Despite its turgid pace, pic has enough cohesion to perhaps make a go of it in regional release, but is really a long shot for urban theatrical revenue.

Production values are uneven, ranging from excellent costume choices for Stone and fascinating props like the authentic dolls and puppets to a horrid makeup job on a dead man.

Railsback plays a split role as the two brothers; one decent, one evil. Scissors are a murder weapon, but are not used in an imaginative enough way to merit the title. — *Daws.*

ABSOLUTELY POSITIVE
(U.S.-DOCU)

An Adair & Armstrong production. Directed by Peter Adair. Camera (color), Adair, Janet Cole; editor, Veronica Selver; music, Michael Becker. Reviewed at Berlin Film Festival (Forum), Feb. 25, 1991. Running time: **89 MIN.**

Peter Adair, whose "Word Is Out" (1978) was something of a landmark docu about gay lifestyles, is in a somber mood with "Absolutely Positive."

The filmmaker himself has tested HIV positive, as have all the participants in the film, who come from various backgrounds and who contracted the virus in a number of ways.

Adair narrates the film himself, but mostly leaves it up to his 12 participants to tell their stories. Some are gay, but others contracted the virus from dirty hypodermic needles, tainted blood transfusions or heterosexual relationships. They include a young wife and mother, a middle-aged couple, a hospital worker and an ex-soldier.

Adair's approach is simple and direct, and all the better for it. Some of the testimony given by these people is extremely moving. All show evidence of their strength and courage.

"Absolutely Positive" will find an audience in many urban centers in the U.S. and abroad, with tv broadcasts also indicated. It received a warm reception at its Berlin Forum screenings.

— *Strat.*

HEADING HOME
(BRITISH)

A BBC production. Executive producer, Mark Shivas. Produced by Rick McCallum. Written and directed by David Hare. Camera (color), Oliver Stapleton; editor, Frances Parker; music, Stanley Myers; sound, Graham Ross; production design, Derek Dodd; costumes, Hazel Pethig; assistant director, Mervyn Dougherty. Reviewed at Berlin Film Festival (Panorama), Feb. 26, 1991. Running time: **92 MIN.**
Ian Tyson . . . . Gary Oldman
Janetta Wheatland . Joely Richardson
Leonard Meopham . . Stephen Dillane
Beryl James . . . . Stella Gonet
Derek Green . . . . . Michael Bryant
Juliusz Janowski . . . Eugene Lipinski
Mr. Everden . . . . John Moffat
Also with: Leon Eagles, Sandy McDade, Lollie May, Alan Pattison, Paul Reeves, Rowena Cooper.

Writer-director David Hare's talent for dissecting the British character is in fine form in "Heading Home," a modestly produced feature about a "modern" young woman and the two men she loved just after World War II.

A sensitive performance from Joely Richardson, whose mother, Vanessa Redgrave, was so good in Hare's first feature, "Wetherby," is one of the film's many assets.

The story is told in hindsight as Richardson's Jeanetta recalls the happiest time of her life. She had moved to London from the provinces and found a job as a librarian. She also met Leonard (Stephen Dillane) and, although he appears to be living with Beryl (Stella Gonet), an unmarried mother, Jeanetta moves into his tiny apartment. Beryl assures her that she isn't involved with Leonard, but later berates Jeanetta for believing an obvious lie.

Throughout the film, Jeanetta accepts as gospel truth everything she's told, even though common sense should have made clear she was hearing white lies. In a very British way, these people don't speak their feelings; instead leaving their deepest thoughts unspoken. And the seemingly naive Jeanetta takes advantage of those gaps in communication.

Although she loves Leonard, she soon becomes attracted to a different kind of man, Ian (Gary Oldman), a pushy young whealer-dealer involved in shady property deals. For a while, Jeanetta fools herself into thinking that the quiet and self-absorbed Leonard is unaware of her secret liaisons with Ian, but one day he simply leaves her, and in the end she loses both men.

Hare's plays and films are so rooted in British character that they sometimes don't travel well, or are misunderstood. That may be the case with "Heading Home;" still, it's beautifully written and acted and suffused with a nostalgic regret for a time when England was a greener, more pleasant land.

Though produced on a modest scale, the film is splendidly handled in all departments. — *Strat.*

THE FIVE HEARTBEATS

A 20th Century Fox release. Produced by Loretha C. Jones. Executive producer, Robert Townsend. Directed by Townsend. Screenplay, Townsend, Keenen Ivory Wayans; camera (Deluxe color), Bill Dill; editor, John Carter; music, Stanley Clarke; sound (Dolby), David Brownlow; supervising music producers, Steve Tyrell, George Duke; production design, Wynn Thomas; costume design, Ruthe Carter; art direction, Don Diers; set decoration, Samara Schaffer; choreography, Michael Peters; assistant director, Richard A. Wells; coproducer, Nancy Israel; casting, Jaki Brown. Reviewed at Avco Cinema Center, L.A., March 21, 1991. MPAA rating: R. Running time: **122 MIN.**

Duck . . . . Robert Townsend
Eddie . . . . Michael Wright
J.T . . . . Leon
Dresser . . . . Harry J. Lennix
Choirboy . . . . Tico Wells
Jimmy Potter . . . . . Chuck Patterson
Eleanor Potter . . . . Diahann Carroll
Big Red . . . . . . Hawthorne James
Sarge . . . . Harold Nicholas

Sweeping rhythm & blues canvas of "The Five Heartbeats" is an ambitious step for Robert Townsend, and the exec producer-director-cowriter-actor doesn't quite have a handle on it. Convincing only in its sweet and dazzling musical sequences, this overly sincere effort otherwise misses its mark. Film will require special handling for Fox to recoup.

Counteracting the negative black stereotyping he lampooned in his directorial debut, "Hollywood Shuffle," Townsend lays out a parade of positive role models in a clean, upbeat family-oriented entertainment that feels oddly square and inauthentic, especially after the offbeat irreverence of "Shuffle."

Story begins in 1965 when fictional group the Five Heartbeats begins to emerge among other black pop groups then combining harmonies and slick choreography.

Film follows the bouncing ball through the paces of every mediocre musicbiz story ever told, from talent contest to record deal to shoestring radio station support tour, racism, hit single, media blitz and superstardom. Only one character, lead singer Eddie (Michael Wright), succumbs to drug use, and his decline and fall is so swift he might as well be wearing a placard that says "I am a bad example."

Meanwhile, the pic, overlong at 122 minutes, tries to be too many things, from a naive storybook musical (songwriter Townsend and his little sister interrupt their household chores to belt out a song he's just come up with) to a melodramatic gangster film (record label boss Big Red, played by Hawthorne James, deals brutally with those who stand up to him).

Script renders characters in the big ensemble cast as little more than types, with a constantly shifting focus and no one to really follow, and Townsend's vision and direction are wildly schizophrenic, veering from tragic depths to manipulative, heart-tugging poignance.

Townsend seems most at home with the music, and there are scenes onstage in which the film really hits its stride.

One particularly fine moment occurs during a rigged talent contest in which the Five Heartbeats unseat a bad piano player to bang out their own fresh, driving rhythm and lead singer Eddie unleashes a bold, soaring note that blows the house away. If only the whole project had that verve and clarity.

Soundtrack features some delightful original songs, including the group's "hit single" "Nothing But Love," and choreography by Michael Peters is also a big plus.

Among the nearly all-black cast, Wright does good work as the troubled Eddie, and Harry J. Lennix merits more screen exposure based on his role as the smooth, self-possessed Dresser.

Harold Nicholas of the Nicholas Brothers '40s tap-dance team plays a feisty oldster who sharpens up group's choreography.

Diahann Carroll, in her first screen appearance since "Claudine" in 1974, has a lamentable role as the uptight, stick-figure wife of the group's manager (Chuck Patterson), and she does nothing much to improve it.

Film is attractively lighted and shot on locations in Southern California by cinematographer Bill Dill ("Sidewalk Stories").
— *Daws.*

IMPROMPTU

A Hemdale Films release (in U.S.; Sovereign elsewhere) of a Sovereign Pictures presentation, in association with Governor Prods. and Les Films Ariane, of a Stuart Oken/Daniel A. Sherkow production. Produced by Oken, Sherkow. Executive producer, Jean Nachbaur. Directed by James Lapine. Screenplay, Sarah Kernochan; camera (Eclair color), Bruno De Keyzer; editor, Michael Ellis; musical supervision & arrangements, John Strauss; sound (Dolby), Peter Glossop; art direction, Gérard Daoudal; costume design, Jenny Beavan; assistant director, Bernard Seitz; stunt coordinator, Mario Luraschi; casting, John Lyons, Joanna Merlin, Trish Twomey, Joyce Gallie (U.K.), Françoise Meniorey (France). Reviewed at Magno Preview 9 screening room, N.Y., Oct. 29, 1990. MPAA Rating: PG-13. Running time: **109 MIN.**

George Sand . . . . .Judy Davis
Frederic Chopin . . . . . . Hugh Grant
Alfred de Musset . . . Mandy Patinkin
Marie d'Agoult . . . Bernadette Peters
Franz Liszt . . . . .Julian Sands
Eugene Delacroix . . . . Ralph Brown
Felicien Mallefille . Georges Corraface
Duke d'Antan . . . . . Anton Rodgers
Duchess d'Antan . . Emma Thompson
George Sand's mother . . Anna Massey
Buloz . . . . John Savident
Baroness Laginsky . Elizabeth Spriggs

"Impromptu" is a retelling of the oft-filmed George Sand/Chopin story that's an entertaining comedy-drama. Class audiences of the "Room With A View"/"Dangerous Liaisons" period pieces should turn out for this well-acted piece.

First-time film director James Lapine, who's had Broadway successes ("Into The Woods"), makes the most of a terrific ensemble drawn from recent E.M. Forster films as well as legit musicals. Bright playing, a bit broad at times but fitting the material, is pic's strongest suit.

Aussie thesp Judy Davis, in her juiciest role since launched internationally in 1979's "My Brilliant Career," plays Sand, the strong-willed author who dresses mannishly, smokes cheroots and gets a maddening crush on composer Chopin (Hugh Grant at his most foppish).

Bulk of film is light-hearted, set at the royal mansion of Emma Thompson and Anton Rodgers, where Chopin, Liszt (Julian Sands in a Ken Russell "Gothic" mood), artist Delacroix (Ralph Brown) and an uninvited George Sand show up for vacation. With Liszt's frau Bernadette Peters and Sand's swarthy lover Georges Corraface also present, plus a surprise appearance by Sand's would-be romantic interest Mandy Patinkin, it's a roundelay of amorous encounters like Bergman's "Smiles Of A Summer Night."

Film's tone turns a bit darker in later reels as the duels and fights of the first half turn more serious. Some abrupt editing and overly contrived resolutions of plot threads (notably Peters' forging of a letter written by Davis) keep the finale from carrying much emotional force.

Lapine's ability to maximize the humorous content is laudable yet this material, penned by his wife Sarah Kernochan, is in no way as strong as the similar gamesmanship of "Les Liaisons Dangereuses." As a result, "Impromptu" will no doubt linger in the viewer's mind more for the spontaneous high spirits of the opening reels rather than the intended dramatic payoffs.

Format takes the traditional Hollywood/BBC approach to language: French characters have British accents while Eastern European denizens (Grant and Sands) affect slight mittel European twangs.

Directed by Lapine with a very long leash, Davis is terrific and a logical successor to Julie Christie for this type of role. Patinkin is adroitly used as plot catalyst, and Peters makes a good foil for Davis. Grant gets to show more vulnerability than in his previous Russell and James Ivory assignments.

While the stars dominate, there are scene-stealing turns from the rest of the cast, notably Thompson (Kenneth Branagh's wife and frequent co-star) as the most dithering hostess since Billie Burke. Anna Massey is quite affecting in a brief but telling turn as Davis' mother.

Bruno De Keyzer captures lovely French locations in realistic terms, not distracting from the protagonists. John Strauss' soundtrack, drawing heavily from Chopin and Liszt with piano performances by Emanuel Axt and others, is very supportive. — *Lor.*

THE RETURNING
(NEW ZEALAND)

An Echo Pictures production in association with the New Zealand Film Commission. Executive producer, David Hannay. Produced by Trishia Downie. Directed by John Day. Screenplay, Arthur Baysting, Day, from story by Simon Willisson; camera (color), Kevin Hayward; editor, Simon Clothier; music, Clive Cockburn; sound, Kit Rowlings; production designer, Michael Becroft. Reviewed at St. James Theater, Gore, New Zealand, Feb. 16, 1991. Running time: **97 MIN.**

Alan . . . . .Phillip Gordon
Jessica . . . . Alison Routledge
Donohue . . . . Max Cullen
George . . . . Jim Moriarty
Steadman Senior . . . . . . John Ewart
Dr. Pitts . . . . Grant Tilly
Charlotte . . . . Jenny Ryken

"The Returning" is a good-looking psychodrama that misses. It has style and pace, but lacks narrative skills and the ability to draw an audience into the emotional maelstrom of a "Don't Look Now." While it will find a place on vidshelves, sizable theatrical play may be problematic.

Billed as "an obsessive love story," pic marks the feature film debut of awardwinning commercials maker John Day.

A young lawyer (Phillip Gordon) is on the run — from the family law practice, his woman (Alison Routledge) and himself. He is drawn to a dilapidated mansion deep in the country where he is passionately seduced in his dreams by the ghost of a young woman who died a century earlier.

With the help of an anarchic priest (Max Cullen) and a local (Jim Moriarty), Gordon begins to piece together the woman's story. But the more he is consumed by her, the more his fate is destined to mirror hers.

Most of the film's problems lie in execution. Events are not handled deftly. Too much is unexplained in a way that annoys rather than intrigues. Good scenes too often are followed by scenes that are inadequately set up and explained.

While most of the cast delivers quality acting, an uneven style and size of performance suggests timidity on the part of the director-writer. Only Grant Tilly (as the very unlikely Dr. Pitts) appears able to fully capitalize on the story's gothic characteristics.

Gordon is skillful and energetic. Routledge, very affecting in Geoff Murphy's "The Quiet Earth" a few years back, is given too little to do. Cullen has some of the best moments. Clive Cockburn's lush and evocative score is a definite plus. — *Nic.*

PRAYER OF THE ROLLERBOYS

A Gaga Communications, Fox/Lorber and Academy Entertainment in association with JVC and TV Tokyo presentation of a Mickelson/King/Iliff production. Produced by Robert Mickelson. Executive producers, Tetsu Fujimara, Martin F. Gold, Richard Lorber, Robert Baruc. Directed by Rick King. Screenplay, W. Peter Iliff; camera (color), Phedon Papamichael; editor, Daniel Loewenthal; music, Stacy Widelitz; sound, Craig Felburg; production design, Thomas A. Walsh; costume design, Merrily Murray-Walsh; art direction, Jay Klein; set decoration, Natalie K. Pope; stunt coordinator, Dan Bradley; special effects coordinator, Marty Bresin; associate producer, Adam Moos; assistant director,

Jay Tobias, casting, Marcia Shulman. Reviewed at American Film Market, Cineplex Odeon Broadway theater, Santa Monica, March 6, 1991. No MPAA rating. Running time: **94 MIN.**

Griffin	Corey Haim
Casey	Patricia Arquette
Gary Lee	Christopher Collet
Jaworski	J.C. Quinn
Speedbagger	Julius Harris
Miltie	Devin Clark
Bango	Mark Pellegrino

A lower-rung "Blade Runner" with hot stunts and a teen idol lead, "Prayer Of The Rollerboys" offers blood-pumping entertainment in a pulpy, cartoonish mode. Stylish sci-fi/skating hybrid should make it highly marketable to teens, and built-in sequel potential could make it a profitable pickup.

W. Peter Iliff's screenplay offers a cynically comic vision of a crumbling, sold-out America that points the finger at the current generation. "They were consumed by greed," intones the teen supremo (Christopher Collet) of a villainous, racist drug-selling cult called the Rollerboys.

Corey Haim, his teen-idol looks polished to a new gloss, plays an orphaned street teen trying to make an honest living delivering pizzas while keeping his 13-year-old brother (Devin Clark) out of trouble.

Temptation beckons in the form of an invitation from Collet to join the Rollerboys, betting on Haim's w.k. rep as a terrif skater. Haim opts to stay straight until a rumpled cop (J.C. Quinn) persuades him to infiltrate the gang and help police find their drug-making h.q. for the sake of his younger brother and his peers.

Action picks up as Haim is initiated into the pack of ruthless, cold-blooded hyenas, while being both drawn to and repelled by a seductive teen drug seeker (Patricia Arquette), who proves to be a fellow undercover cop.

Pressure to bring down the Rollerboys mounts as young Clark begins succumbing to the lure of the drug, a smokable powder known as "mist," while Haim's father-figure black neighbor (Julius Harris) turns a cold shoulder to him for his perceived drug-selling activities.

Meanwhile, Collet and cohorts make the dire consequences of disloyalty to the Rollerboys all too clear.

Director Rick King and stunt coordinator Dan Bradley keep action thumping with a combo of inner-city action scenes and skate stunts. Haim does a sizable portion of his own blade work.

Pic, lensed mostly in the Venice beach area, has a strong visual hook in image of Rollerboys, with their long Gestapo-like trenchcoats flapping, skating en masse through the beach and canal byways like a flock of aggressive gulls.

Teens no doubt will want to imitate them, and in some ways it seems the pic's creators could have gotten more mileage from the idea if the Rollerboys had been a gang of good guys, battling to win back the wasted nation from corrupt powers.

Perhaps such a turnabout could occur in a sequel. As is, concept of a murderous drug-dealing gang feels stale, regardless of year.

Nonetheless, pic has been imaginatively produced, with filmmakers creating a darkly amusing vision of a new depression-era L.A., with much of the population living in numbered homeless camps and foreign currency more valued than U.S. dollars.

L.A., ostensibly plundered by foreign buyers who then more or less cleared out, resemble a mix of Skid Row, a Far East brothel district and the grounds of some berserk carnival.

Budget constraints are compensated for by sprinkling the script with wry jokes about the future geopolitical situation, as in a news broadcast about hordes of Americans being shipped back from Mexico after illegally seeking jobs there.

Haim does a good job of holding pic's center together. Arquette brings interesting qualities to the screen, and pair have good chemistry that should appeal to young viewers.

Much of the cast is uneven, though, particularly the too-eager Clark in the role of the empty-headed brother, a character who merits little sympathy as portrayed here. Music by Stacy Widelitz makes a pleasing and effective contribution. — *Daws.*

TURE SVENTON OCH FALLET ISABELLA
(TURE SVENTON AND THE CASE OF ISABELLA)
(SWEDISH)

A Sandrews release of a Swedish TV-1 and Sandrews production. Produced by Lars Säfström. Directed by Torbjörn Ehrnvall. Screenplay, Birgit Hageby, based on a novel by Ake Holmberg; camera, Ralph M. Evers; editor, Sigurd Hallman; music, Björn Linnman; sound, Bengt Wallman; production design, Anita Kajaste-Bennwik;

assistant director, Birgit Hageby. Reviewed at Sandrews screening room, Stockholm, March 6, 1991. Running time: **75 MIN.**

With: Helge Skoog, Nils Moritz, Johan Ulveson, Lena Nyman, Loa Falkman, Lena Strömdahl, Eskil Steenberg, Janni Lilja, Brita Borg, Thomas Roos, Peter Harrysson, Johan Rabaeus.

F ilm version of the popular children's book, "Ture Sventon And The Case Of Isabella" has all the right characters, but is mostly disappointing and lacks genuine suspense and humor. B.o. might be okay in Sweden, but not anywhere else.

Pic shows the difficulty of transforming Ake Holmberg to celluloid; the book's dry and witty language cannot be substituted with pictures. The only funny bits are the quotes from the novel read by a narrator. The story, in which Stockholm private detective Ture Sventon solves the case of a famous horse stolen from a circus, becomes dull and lifeless.

The film is made in a style lifted from silent movies. The acting is consciously slightly over the top, the gestures large. Some of the characters — particularly villain Ville Vessla (Johan Ulvesson) — look like something out of a Mack Sennet movie.

The effort to do something unusual disappears within the film's general sense of boredom and shortage of suspense. The filmmakers have also `stayed away from special effects, which is a pity since the novel's exciting magic carpet rides, for example, are reduced to almost nothing here.

The performances of Helge Skoog as Sventon and Lena Nyman as the secretary are assets. Unfortunately, the film doesn't give Nyman enough screen time, another letdown in a film that in no way lives up to expectations. — *Gunn.*

DIPLOMATIC IMMUNITY

A Fries Distribution Co. release of a Harry Shuster production. Executive producer, Shuster. Produced and directed by Peter Maris. Screenplay, Randall Frakes, Jim Trombetta, Richard Donn, based on Theodore Taylor's novel "The Stalker"; camera (Foto-Kem color), Gerald B. Wolfe; editor, Jack Tucker; music, John Massari; sound, Alan Wasserman; production design, Chris Edmonds; art direction, Guy Pierre Pepin; costume design, Virginia (Gini) Kramer; assistant director, Chris Edmonds; production manager, Cevin Cortney; stunt coordinator, Gary Jensen; special effects, Roy Downey; 2nd unit camera,

Art Adams; co-producer, William J. Males; associate producer, Sunny Vest; casting, Annelise Collins. Reviewed at Magno Review 2 screening room, N.Y., March 6, 1991. MPAA Rating: R. Running time: **95 MIN.**

Cole Hickel . . . . . . Bruce Boxleitner
Cowboy . . . . Billy Drago
Klaus Hermann . . . . Tom Breznahan
Stefan Noll . . . . Christopher Neame
Teresa Escobal . . . . Fabiana Udenio
Gephardt . . . . Matthias Hues
Gerta Hermann . . . . . . Meg Foster
Ellen Hickel . . . . . . Sharon L. Kase
Also with: Jay Marvin Campbell, Robert Do'Qui, Ken Foree, Kenneth Kimmons, Robert Forster, Lee DeBroux, Rozlyn Sorrell, Robert Miano.

"**D**iplomatic Immunity" is a superior B actioner. Its crowd-pleasing, ingenious trick ending will satisfy urban audiences in theatrical play this spring while video sales loom strong.

In his best feature since the minor classic "Viper" (starring Linda Purl) made three years earlier, filmmaker Peter Maris is blessed with a clever script and topnotch cast.

Bruce Boxleitner, fitting a mature role comfortably, toplines as a Marine training sergeant who goes over the top when his beautiful young daughter (Sharon L. Kase) is raped and murdered by her foreign b.f. (Tom Breznahan). Pic's title comes into play early when Breznahan and his evil henchman Christopher Neame are returned to their home turf, Paraguay, since both hold diplomatic passports.

His old Vietnam War teammate Robert Forster, now a CIA bigwig controlling Latin American operations, tells Boxleitner to cool it, but the gung-ho leatherneck takes matters in his own hands and heads to Paraguay. His contact there is cynical Billy Drago, offering him arms and information.

The picture gains momentum when Boxleitner teams up with Breznahan's dominatrix mistress, Fabiana Udenio, and later Drago to mount an assault on the villain's island fortress. Good stuntwork and frequent action scenes are a plus.

Supporting Boxleitner in solid turns are Drago, who invests a stock role with terrific "juice"; Breznahan, the all-American boy who starred recently in "Ski School" but is perfect here as a sadistic villain; Udenio, a statuesque beauty who confirms the good impression she made in "Bride Of Re-Animator"; and Meg Foster, delightfully heinous as Breznahan's incestuous mother. Most of the cast gets to ham it up in final-reel death scenes.

The tiger in the tail at film's fadeout (two delicious twists) is the kind of clever scripting that would benefit many a high-priced recent superstar actioner. — *Lor.*

COUNTDOWN
(GERMAN-DOCU)

Produced by Ulrike Ottinger Filmproduktion. Directed by Ulrike Ottinger. Screenplay-camera (color, 16m), Ottinger; editor, Eva Schlensag; sound, Margit Eschenbach. Reviewed at Berlin Film Festival (Forum), Feb. 25, 1991. Running time: **188 MIN.**

A three-hour look at the prolog to German monetary union, this docu may have some festival legs in Germany but has severely limited commercial potential — if any.

Pic takes the form of observations in East and West Germany between June 21 and July 1, 1990, the last 10 days before the monetary union of the two countries and the first major step toward total unification.

"Observations" is the operative word. Filmmaker Ulrike Ottinger does not become engaged in the events she portrays. She simply turns on the camera at the start of each day and lets it roll. The resulting screen version is a wearying experience that seems to go on for days and demands considerable viewer commitment.

At worst, "Countdown" sometimes looks like unedited raw footage one might discover in an attic. At best, the film is a personal, poetic document that meanders, unobserved, through an historic period in which ordinary German citizens try to come to terms with rapid change.

To call this film "Countdown" may be erroneous; the word denotes action, something this three hours of celluloid lack. The low-key approach may have been an attempt, however, by Ottinger to reflect the disappointment and anticlimactic sentiments Germans felt when their world was turned on its head, and as a counterbalance to the euphoria that accompanied the fall of the Berlin Wall.

Audiences will be less than euphoric after seeing this film. — *Keoh.*

DAS SERBISCHE MÄDCHEN
(THE SERBIAN GIRL)
(GERMAN)

A Filmverlag der Autoren release of a TPI Trebitsch Produktion, Hamburg, Bavarian Broadcasting, Munich, production in conjunction with Arbor TV Filmproduktion. Produced by Holger Schulz. Directed by Peter Sehr. Screenplay, Sehr from story by Siegfried Lenz; camera (color), Dietrich Lohmann; editor, Dagmar Hirtz; music, Goran Bregovic; sound, Reiner Levin. Reviewed at Berlin Film Festival (New German Films), Feb. 17, 1991. Running time: **90 MIN.**

With: Mirjana Jokovic, Ben Becker, Pascal Breuer, Vladimir Torbica, Joachim Regelin, Peter Carstens, Werner Awam, Axel Ganz, Volker Prechtl.

"**T**he Serbian Girl," an impressive first film for director Peter Sehr, has fair b.o. possibilities in Germany but no legs to travel very far from home.

Mirjana Jokovic ably handles her challenging role as the young Yugoslavian girl who follows a dream of romance and adventure through Germany, going home sadder but wiser. She encounters some rather scruffy characters, offering this young thesp a chance to shine in a varied role.

Sehr, 39, makes ample use of a good literary source to stitch together a tight screenplay. He is also backed up by good lensing and generally topnotch technical credits. — *Gill.*

DAR KUCHE-HAYE ESHGH
(IN THE ALLEYS OF LOVE)
(IRANIAN)

A Center for the Development of Experimental & Semi-Professional Filmmaking presentation. Produced and directed by Khosro Sinai. Screenplay, uncredited, based on the diaries of immigrant youths; camera (color), Ali Loghmani; editor, Sinai, A Loghmani; music, K. Sinai; sound, Mohammad Ali Abiri; production manager, Ghasem Gholipoor. Reviewed at Fajr Intl. Film Festival, Feb. 10, 1991. Running time: **87 MIN.**

With: Mehdi Ahmadi, Behnaz Rudani, Ali Galehdari, Reza Pezhuhu, Abdolreza Baghban, Lon Khangaldian, Bahram Zandi, Yusef Chukar, Hamid Farajnezhad.

In detail, in closeup and at length, Khosro Sinai's docufiction roams the deserted alleys of Abadan, a southern border town virtually flattened by Iraq during the eight-year conflict with Iran. Trimmed to an hour, "In The Alleys Of Love" would be ideal for specialty tv.

Pic opens with a young Abandani refugee returned home checking out headstones in a cemetery. Wandering through devastated streets, he has flashbacks of the city before Iraqi bombs.

The flashbacks also show the chaos during the air raids and the inevitable hunger, thirst and desertion. Palm trees die. Wildlife suffocates. Orphans play amidst the rubble. Survivors stalk streets and graveyards like the living dead.

A few townspeople resent those who fled. They talk to the refugee, who eventually decides to stay. They also address the camera with an earnest concern for the town's future, the absurdity of war and the preciousness of life.

An occasionally handheld camera adds to pic's home movie feel. Tech credits in general are poor. The lack of a script is compounded by crude editing. Serious cuts are needed to achieve a tight documentary format.

Townspeople play themselves, a touch of realism that gives pic its validity. A scene where the director advises locals how to act like themselves is misplaced. As authentic as pic may be, and as valid as the locals' arguments for peace may ring, this film needs work. — *Suze.*

ALL OUT
(SWISS-GERMAN-FRENCH)

A Columbus Film Zurich release of a Thomas Koerfer production in association with Crocodile Prods., Paris, Paul-Boris Lobadowsky and Stella Film, Munich. Written and directed by Koerfer. Camera (color), Lukas Strebel; editor, Nicole Lubtschansky; music, Jean-Claude Petit; sound, Jürg von Allmen; art direction, Hans Gloor; costume design, Monica Schmid; assistant director, Marcel Just; production manager, Rudolf Santschi. Reviewed at Cinema Plaza 3, Zurich, Jan. 30, 1991. Running time: **105 MIN.**

Angelo . . . . Dexter Fletcher
Julia . . . . Fabienne Babe
Paul . . . . Uwe Ochsenknecht
Ciccio . . . . Paolo de Giorgio
Robert Brunner . . . . . . Michel Voita
Schnyder . . . . Peter Fitz
Also with: Jean Hache, Teco Celio, Bernhard Bettermann, Karsten Dörr, Maja Stolle, Ingold Wildenauer, Nanni Tormen, Anna Recchimuzzi.
(English soundtrack)

Swiss helmer Thomas Koerfer's thriller "All Out" has a Swiss-Italian background, international appeal and English dialog, but stands little chance in the highly competitive action market. Lack of star names and an incoherent, jumpy script are no help.

A clumsily prepared holdup in a Zurich bank by a gang of three goes awry. One of them is shot and another gets cold feet and flees in the escape car. The third, a young Italian, manages to grab a briefcase full of dollar notes and escapes by forcing himself into a young woman's car and taking her hostage.

Hiding in his apartment with the girl, he learns that she is the banker's daughter. He now extorts a ransom for her release, but realizes he is not only sought by the police, but also by a gang of killers hired by the man he stole the briefcase from.

At a shootout, Angelo is cornered but manages to escape, leaving behind the briefcase. The girl goes with him — this time of her own will as a passionate romance has developed between the two. They flee to Genoa, hoping to raise enough money to cross the ocean. Angelo gets involved with drug dealers.

Pic, filmed in Zurich and on location in Genoa, is an odd mix of action, sex and romance that never jells. Dexter Fletcher ("Raggedy Rawney") fares best as the violent young hoodlum, but he, French actress Fabienne Babe ("Zanzibar") and Uwe Ochsenknecht ("Men"), fail to save the implausible script.

Jean-Claude Petit's music underlines the gloomy atmosphere effectively. Other technical credits are okay. — Mezo.

DER RADFAHRER
(THE CYCLIST)
(IRANIAN)

An Institute for the Cinematographic Affairs of Janbazan Foundation production. Written and directed by Mohsen Makhmalbaf. Camera (color), Ali Reza Zarrindast; editor, Makhmalbaf; music, Majid Entezami; art direction, Makhmalbaf. Reviewed at Fajr Intl. Film Festival, Teheran, Feb. 12, 1991. Running time: **75 MIN.**
Nasim . . . . . Moharram Zeynalzadeh
Showman . . . . Esmail Soltanian
Jomeh . . . . Mohammad Reza Maleki
Gypsy woman . . Mahshid Afsharzadeh
Motorcyclist . . . . Firooz Kiyani

"The Cyclist" raises many questions about Iran's inadequate economic structure, the nation's vicious circle of poverty and the absurd lengths financially desperate people will go to. Although helmer Mohsen Makhmalbaf's themes are universal, pic will find limited audiences outside Iran.

Title character is an Afghan refugee who accepts a mad gamble to ride a bicycle nonstop for seven days in order to raise money to pay his wife's hospital bills.

As with most Iranian films, an underdeveloped script and tight budget limit the scope. The single location where the cyclist incessantly rides in circles becomes monotonous.

Before the ride, pic establishes that the frustrated hero has few options. Digging wells, a job reserved for refugees, doesn't pay enough to meet the rising medical costs. An honest man, he rejects a black market smuggling job. When he attempts suicide, he's saved by his young, hopful son. So the ex-showman gambles his last ounce of energy to save his wife and family.

Charlatans and hucksters dig in, betting on his success or failure, and a crowd gathers steam as the week passes. Numerous dirty pranks are played to break his stride. Government officials believe he is a spy and unsuccessfully try to thwart his efforts.

Although Nasim cheats (he is replaced by a hooded friend for several hours after collapsing one night), he triumphs in the end. However, he doesn't stop riding. As the credits roll, Nasim peddles on. — Suze.

NAGHSH-E ESHGH
(PORTRAIT OF LOVE)
(IRANIAN)

A Cinematographic Affairs of Mostazafan & Janbazan Foundation production. Written and directed by Shahriar Parsipoor. Camera (color), Hossein Jafarian; editor, Yavar Turang; music, Rasul Najafian; sound, Hashem Musavi; set design, Kayhan Mortazavi; makeup, Farhang Moayeri; production manager, Mahvash Sheikholeslami. Reviewed at Fajr Intl. Film Festival, Teheran, Feb. 10, 1991. Running time: **100 MIN.**
With: Jahangir Almasi, Hosein Mahjub, Fariba Kosari, Eliza Johari, Hormoz Sirati, Reza Hamedi.

Script for "Portrait Of Love," an intense feature debut for Shahriar Parsipoor, is so loaded with religious references and icons, it will be difficult for Westerners to comprehend, even with background research and simultaneous translation.

Simple premise has two young artists searching for the painter of a multifaceted canvas dominated by a Mona Lisa-like face. Their task is to discover the painting's significance. En route, volumes of Muslim mythology are unearthed.

On the surface, pic also deals with poverty of artists. In one of many commerce vs. art references, a tile artist says to another: "We are thinking about art, but it does not meet the expenses of life."

Iranians considered the film profound and worthy of endless discussion, indicating that pic should score well at the b.o. in Islamic territories.

Muslim theologians would be required to analyze this fascinating pic's many levels. A thorough study would undoubtedly help to illuminate a world and religion that remain a mystery to the West. — Suze.

ALL OF ME
(GERMAN)

A Bettina Wilhelm production. Produced by Madeleine Remy. Directed by Bettina Wilhelm. Screenplay, Wilhelm, Georgette Dee; camera (color, 16m), Frank Grunert; editor, Bernd Euscher; music, Terry Truck; sound, Malgorzata Jaworsky. Reviewed at Berlin Film Festival (New German Films), Feb. 19, 1991. Running time: **76 MIN.**
With: Georgette Dee, Mechthild Grossmann, Miroslaw Baka, Tadeusz Lomnicki, Terry Truck, Anna Romantowska, Andrjez Blumenfeld.

"All Of Me" is a vehicle for German nightclub singer Georgette Dee, a self-dubbed hermaphrodite with a husky, Marlene Dietrich-like voice and a penchant for flat-bosomed cocktail dresses, French cigarets and champagne, all of which are gone through in quantity onstage.

Stage sequences with Dee's real-life accompanist, Terry Truck, are the best part of an otherwise weak debut feature by helmer Bettina Wilhelm. The plot, built around the musical segments, is tedious at best.

Dee plays an entertainer of unspecific gender torn between a man and a woman (actually a guy in drag). To complicate things unnecessarily, everyone is supposed to be Polish, although pic is set in Berlin for the most part and dialog is in German.

Dee's fans will sit through the boring parts just to see their star. But the audience would be better served by learning more about this enigmatic entertainer and just what exactly it means to be a hermaphrodite.

Tech credits are adequate for a 16m production. — Gill.

DIVING IN

A Skouras Pictures release of a Maurer/Shaw Prods. presentation of a Creative Edge Films production. Produced by Martin Wiley. Executive producers, Michael S. Maurer, Mark Shaw. Directed by Strathford Hamilton. Screenplay, Eric Edson; camera (color), Hanania Baer; editor, Marcy Hamilton; music, Guy Moon, Paul Buckmaster; music director, Steve Tyrell; sound (Ultra-Stereo), Don Scales; art direction, Marty Bercaw; production manager, Greg Malone; assistant director, Tom Roland; additional camera, Carl Pope; co-producer, Jeffrey Neuman; casting, Pam Rack. Reviewed on Paramount Home Video videcassette, N.Y., Jan. 11, 1990. MPAA Rating: PG-13. Running time: **92 MIN.**
Wayne Hopkins . . . . Matt Adler
Terry Hopkins . . . . . Kristy Swanson
Coach Mack . . . . Burt Young
Jerome . . . . Matt Lattanzi
Amanda Lansky . . . . . Yolanda Jilot
Richard Anthony . . . Richard Johnson
Ryes . . . . Carey Scott
Also with: Tom Callaway, Claire Malis, Jennifer Ivary, Jill Hardin.

"Diving In" is a preposterous but entertaining sports film about would-be Olympic divers. Released theatrically last fall by Skouras, it should generate some greenbacks for Paramount in video release.

Casting of Burt Young as the high school diving team coach hints at the clichés to come in yet another "Rocky"-inspired battle against the odds. Unfortunately, scripter Eric Edson has concocted some ridiculous motivations and untimely plot twists that reduce an otherwise competent production to silliness.

Matt Adler is the prototypical underdog who wants to prove himself as a diver to defeat Young's arrogant protégé Matt Lattanzi but is afraid of the high platform. He gets girls' swimming coach Yolanda Jilot (a European beauty) to train him after hours at her home, with the expected May/December romantic overtones.

So far so good, but Edson piles on the melodrama to ill effect. Not only is Adler running against Lattanzi for class president, but Adler's beautiful sister Kristy Swanson is sexually abused by the oversexed Lattanzi at a party, and her honor needs avenging.

As if this weren't enough, at the last minute Jilot brings in ace coach Richard Johnson (a comedown for the distinguished British actor) as Adler's tutor. At the state championship swimming meet, Adler is way behind when suddenly Johnson concocts a tough dive on the spot, asks the boy to do it and gets the judges to arbitrarily assign a 3.6 degree of difficulty. Adler nails it and is the victor.

Cast of hunks and 10s does a fine job, and pic benefits from a quite liberal PG-13 rating that includes a surprising number of nude scenes. Jilot in particular is convincing as an athlete, and elsewhere the cutaways to doubles for diving footage are well handled. — *Lor.*

ISKELMÄPRINSSI
(PRINCE OF THE HIT PARADE)
(FINNISH)

A Finnkino release of a Tulto Tuotanto production. Directed by Juha Tapaninen. Screenplay, Tapaninen, Harri Rinne, Jukka Alihanka; camera (color, b&w), Ulf Sundwall; editor, Arturas Pozdniakovas; music, Alihanka, Paul Anka, Pentti Lasanen, Ilpo Murtojärvi, Pera Pirkkola, Rinne, Jaakko Salo, Tapaninen, Mitja Tuurala. Reviewed Jan. 25, 1991, at Nordia Cinema, Tampere. Running time: **110 MIN.**
With: Tiina Isohanni, Saija Hakola, Mart Sander, Tarmo Ruubel, Pirkko Mannola, Umberto Marcato, Paul Anka.

"**P**rince Of The Hit Parade" is a lighthearted musical comedy and an excellent pastiche of Finnish films from the 1960s, directed in the happy-go-lucky style of old tv blurbs.

Director Juha Tapaninen's welcome feature debut is bright, funny and a little silly. Dealing with an innocent era and people with big dreams, pic conveys no message and no troubles. All that counts is the feathery visual style that easily carries the light plot.

Tapaninen, an experienced tv commercial maker, includes enjoyable make-believe blurbs, parodies of '60s tv advertising.

Title of this pop musical recalls a certain type of Finnish musical comedy from the 1950s and '60s, most memorably "The Great Hit Parade" (1959), a mixture of chart hits, loose plots and terrible characterization.

In an easygoing and natural manner, young unknowns play small-town youths with dreams of making the headlines by modeling, singing or racing. The actors have been cast along with true popstars (including Paul Anka) and princes of the Finnish '60s hit parades.

Pic's rhythm comes from repeating black & white flashes, which blur the borderline between reality and fantasy by imitating a '60s look. The film is faithful to small details without being merely a decorative display of old things.

"Prince. . ." reps a fresh approach in Finnish filmmaking. Tapaninen has blended a spoonful of postmodern irony with the nostalgic tone, but only seldom is he caught being too smart or pretentious.

Pic is fluently edited and mostly well-paced. Innocent, a little banal, but irresistible, it's an important and promising Finnish feature debut. — *Mapu.*

HOME LESS HOME
(DOCU)

Produced and directed by Bill Brand. Screenplay, Brand, Joanna Kiernan; camera (TVC color), Zoe Beloff; editor, Kiernan; sound, Jason Simon. Reviewed at New Directors/New Films, Museum of Modern Art, N.Y., March 22, 1991. Running time: **70 MIN.**

Although the subject matter may alienate some, Bill Brand's documentary about homelessness in New York City deserves to be seen. Distributors may shy away from a film confronting such a depressing issue, but with significant exposure on public tv and elsewhere, pic will blow the whistle on the underside of President Bush's "kinder and gentler America."

By talking to the poor instead of officials and politicians, Brand shows that the 80,000-plus homeless people in New York are not all mentally ill, drug-addicted or alcoholic. Rather, he concludes, the problem stems from insufficient government funding and housing.

Many of his subjects are quite articulate. A man who has been through the Byzantine housing bureaucracy states, "The system is designed for failure." A man in Grand Central Station says, "It's the city and state's fault. What is the government doing?"

Unlike Brand's approach, most tv coverage is from the point of view of inconvenienced passersby. The news segments included in the film show how public sentiment toward the homeless has

turned from sympathy to anger and annoyance. This change in attitude, Brand contends, is largely due to the media's portrayal of the problem.

The value of "Home Less Home" is that Brand treats the homeless as people, not as numbers or as "voiceless victims." He also disputes the perception that the poor are unwilling to work, since many of those interviewed have jobs but still cannot afford an apartment.

The director-producer also includes hard facts: Homeless individuals are eligible for just $92 a month. A family of four is asked to live on $270. NYC spent $500 million on services for the homeless in 1989. For every homeless person, four people live illegally doubled up in apartments.

Brand's thesis is deeply political. He points to Reagan-era politics for the decline in assistance to the poor, and in fact, blames capitalism in general for social inequities. Such a conclusion is bound to alienate some viewers, but others may well change their opinions about the homeless after seeing Brand's work.

Surprisingly, the film is not overly bleak or depressing. Although Brand offer no solutions, he reveals the causes in a thought-provoking way.

Technically, the sound quality is uneven and the camera often moves around excessively, cutting away from people who are still talking. On the other hand, Brand skillfully intercuts photographs, both current and historical, and scenes from Preston Sturges' film "Sullivan's Travels," in which Joel McCrea plays a spoiled director who tries to experience poverty firsthand.

Such diverse images, along with the interviews, keep "Home Less Home" from becoming boring. — *Stev.*

AH FEI ZHENG ZHUAN
(DAYS OF BEING WILD)
(HONG KONG)

A Rover Tang & Alan Tang In-Gear Film production. Produced by Rover Tang. Executive producer, Alan Tang. Written and directed by Wong Kar-wai. Camera (color), Christopher Doyle; editor, Kai Kit-wai; music, Chan Do-ming; sound, Steve Chan Wai-hung; production design, William Chang Suk-ping; assistant directors, Rosanna Ng Wai-san, Johnny Kong Yeuk-shing. Reviewed at New Directors/New Films, Museum of Modern Art, N.Y., March 13, 1991. Running Time: **100 MIN.**
With: Leslie Cheung Kwok-wing, Maggie Cheung Man-yuk, Tony Leung Chiu-wai, Karina Lau Kar-ling, Andy Lau Tak-wah, Jackie Cheung Hok-yau, Poon Dik-wah.
(In Cantonese/Chinese/Tagalog)

"**D**ays Of Being Wild" is a sensitive look at a group of lovelorn youth. Pic's final half hour and its denouement prove protracted and contrived, but not before director Wong Karwai has scored emotional and atmospheric points with his audience.

Wong's second feature film should prove acceptable fare for fests and limited arthouse runs.

His first film, the 1988 "As Tears Go By," was a flashy gangster film. Current opus, with its gallery of suffering protagonists, is more an incursion into Rainer Werner Fassbinder territory. Like Fassbinder, Wong uses his own distancing devices (stylized lighting, old pop ballads on the soundtrack) while his characters submit themselves to their entrapping quirks.

Romantic roundelay begins when Yuddy (Leslie Cheung) meets a young woman on two consecutive days just before three o'clock. Yuddy declares that the minute before three is their minute, and for the young girl, this becomes a romantic, if not metaphysical, commitment.

It takes many meetings and minutes before she learns that Yuddy is not interested in marrying her. Yuddy, meanwhile, is concerned with the aging woman who raised him when his parents abandoned him and who still supports him.

He pummels one of her suitors who has abused her, but after relieving him of earrings stolen from his "auntie," Yuddy promptly gives them to his next lover. Auntie points out to Yuddy that she doesn't mind if the men she dates are only seeking her money as long as she enjoys their company. Yuddy also has a young friend and acolyte who likes to slink through buildings and ogles Yuddy's car.

Hovering around these characters' tortuous pursuit of love and lovemaking is their sense of rootlessness. Yuddy's first lover (poignantly played by Maggie Cheung) says "Hong Kong is not my home" and tells a sympathetic cop how she left her native Macao to join a cousin in H.K.

The swaggering Yuddy likens himself to a bird that's always flying and lands only when he dies. He later learns that his real family left Hong Kong for the

Philippines, and the last part of the film is a somewhat strained quest for their whereabouts.

All of this may be in keeping with the diverse origins of Hong Kong's populace and apprehensions about the British colony's reversion to Chinese rule by the end of the decade. Like Tsui Hark's 1990 "A Better Tomorrow III" set in 1975, this film may disguise its anxieties by being set in an earlier time (1960).

Christopher Doyle's camerawork ably controls the ambience while other tech credits are similarly solid. — *Lomb.*

L'ARIA SERENA DELL'OUEST
(A PEACEFUL AIR OF THE WEST)
(ITALIAN)

A Monogatari-PIC Film with SSR-RTSI. Executive producer, Daniele Maggoini. Directed by Silvio Soldini. Screenplay, Soldini, Roberto Tiraboschi; camera (color), Luca Bigazzi; editor, Claudio Cormio; music, Giovanni Venosta; sound, Barbara Flüuckliger; art direction, Daniela Verdenelli; associate producer, Caterina Genni. Reviewed at New Directors/New Films, Museum of Modern Art, N.Y., March 22, 1991. Running time: **100 MIN.**
Cesare . . . . Fabrizio Bentivoglio
Irene . . . . Antonella Fattori
Tobia . . . . Ivano Marescotti
Veronica . . . . Patrizia Piccinini
Clara . . . . Silli Togni
Rosa . . . . Olga Durane
Mario . . . . Roberto Accorno
Cesare's friend . . . . . . Cesare Bocci

"A Peaceful Air Of The West" is an accomplished work recalling the spirit and style of 1960s European art films. This distinctive effort's elliptical narrative will be off-putting to mainstream viewers while specialized audiences may well be attracted by its novel approach.

Focus of the film is director Silvio Soldini's native Milan. His technique crosscuts between the crises of four couples and individuals as the narrative gradually establishes contacts between each party. The Milanese malaise of Soldini's characters is revealed in personal and career stagnations familiar to many U.S. and other foreign urbanites.

Recent similar overview of metropolitan angst is Wim Wenders' angelic eavesdropping on Berlin in "Wings Of Desire," but a more tangible influence over the film is Michelangelo Antonioni.

As in Antonioni's "L'Avventura," plot thrust is the search for a woman who is never ultimately found, at least not to the satisfaction of the first protagonist, Ce-

sare. The woman he's looking for identified herself as Olga in a taped interview for a perfume company marketing survey. Cesare is a frustrated ethnologist, as shown when he starts asking perfume users elaborate questions on world affairs.

His sole instrument for finding Olga is a datebook left with him from their tryst. It will pass through different hands and have different effects in the story.

Olga is really the name used by a woman named Veronica when she spends her evenings compiling one-night stands. Although she's a nurse and tells her dates she's a photographer, she refers to herself as a postal worker on the tape. This is something of a plot joke since the search for her provides the story strands to two other couples.

One of them has moved to Milan from Siena with the wife, Irene, suddenly suffering a profound questioning of her professional abilities as a translator. The other is an upper-class workaholic couple with the neglected husband gradually stumbling into an affair with Veronica.

Aside from Antonioni plot elements such as voyeurism and violence ("Blow Up") or substitutions of identity ("The Passenger"), Soldini's visual style, like Antonioni's, dwells on the role of objects and formal surfaces. In one visual joke, for example, the workaholic couple meet talking from their respective autos so often that an overhead shot of the two cars is enough to establish their presence.

But Soldini's less austere style rarely assumes the contemplation of Antonioni's long takes and from that standpoint should be more commercial. His long shots emphasize movement and occasionally missed opportunities or chances of contact that glide by his characters. The inexorability of that movement dramatizes the static plight of his characters while distracting from some of their banality.

Fabrizio Bentivoglio, Antonella Fattori and Ivano Marescotti effectively capture the dramatic and comic foibles of their characters while Patrizia Piccinini as Veronica registers a strong enough presence to serve as a credible catylst.

Luca Bigazzi's cinematography and Claudio Cormio's editing adeptly serve the framework for Soldini's artistic patterns.

This is the second feature film for Soldini, who studied film at New York U. — *Lomb.*

SWITCH

A Warner Bros. release of an HBO presentation in association with Cinema Plus, L.P. of a BECO production. Produced by Tony Adams. Written and directed by Blake Edwards. Camera (Technicolor; Panavision widescreen; Dick Bush; editor, Robert Pergament; music, Henry Mancini; sound (Dolby), Jerry Jost; production design, Rodger Maus; art direction, Sandy Getzler; set decoration, John Franco Jr.; costume design, Ellen Mirojnick; associate producer, Trish Caroselli Rintels; assistant directors, David C. Anderson, Ron Bozman (N.Y.); casting, Gail Levin, Lauren Lloyd. Reviewed at Warner Bros. screening room, N.Y., April 1, 1991. MPAA Rating: R. Running time: **103 MIN.**
Amanda Brooks . . . . . . Ellen Barkin
Walter Stone . . . . Jimmy Smits
Margo Brofman . . . . JoBeth Williams
Sheila Faxton . . . . . Lorraine Bracco
Arnold Friedkin . . . . . Tony Roberts
Steve Brooks . . . . Perry King
The Devil . . . . . Bruce Martyn Payne
Liz . . . . Lysette Anthony
Felicia . . . . Victoria Mahoney
Higgins . . . . Basil Hoffman
Steve's Secretary . . Catherine Keener
Dan Jones . . . . Kevin Kilner

"Switch" is a faint-hearted sex comedy that doesn't have the courage of its initially provocative convictions. Undemanding audiences will get a few laughs from the slapstick emanating from the notion of a man parading around in Ellen Barkin's body, but younger, more sophisticated viewers will no doubt reject the tired farcical conceits and resent the copouts of the second half.

As keen as ever to play with gender and put his characters through the sexual wringer, Blake Edwards sets up a fantastical situation rife with possibilities. Ladykiller Steve Brooks (Perry King) accepts an invitation for a hot tub frolic with three of his old girlfriends, only to be murdered by them for his innumerable emotional crimes against women over the years.

Delivered to purgatory, Steve is given a chance to escape a fiery fate by returning to Earth and finding just one woman who genuinely likes him. Only catch is that he will henceforth inhabit the body of a woman, and that of an uncommonly sexy one.

"Steve" first discovers that he's not what he used to be when he wakes up, heads for the bathroom and finds he no longer has his accustomed genital equipment. Humor proceeds along these lines for awhile, as "Steve" sprawls with legs open in a skirt at a business meeting, unaware of what's showing underneath, and tiresomely has endless troub-

le walking in high heels (whatever happened to flats?).

Masquerading as the disappeared man's long-lost half-sister, "Amanda," as "she" is now known, manages to hold on to Steve's old job at a high-powered ad agency, hangs out with Steve's best friend Jimmy Smits and intimidates the murder ringleader, JoBeth Williams, into assisting her in dressing for her new role in life.

Still very much possessed of Steve's lecherous mind, Amanda relishes her own hot bod, feeling her breasts (as well as those of unsuspecting shopgirls) whenever possible, and making conceited comments. She also packs a mean punch and a foul mouth when any man dares to make a pass at her, finally concluding that, "I'm sick and tired of being treated like a piece of meat."

Things look like they'll shift into high gear when Amanda meets cosmetics queen Lorraine Bracco, a lesbian, and decides to seduce her into transferring her big account to the agency. Unfortunately, pic chickens out from this point on, to dismaying ends. Uptight when the moment of truth arrives with Bracco, Amanda passes out in the bedroom and never pursues a woman again.

At the same time, Amanda is equally unreceptive to male attention, to the extent that Edwards feels forced to resort to the ridiculous gag of having Smits impregnate Amanda while she's asleep, so she doesn't remember it and doesn't have to deal with it. Wrap-up is unremittingly silly and equivocating.

In all events, Edwards has missed entirely a great chance to explore, even in comedic terms, the notions of how sexuality is perceived by the two sexes, how much of sex is in the head and how much is strictly of the body, and what does it all matter anyway. Somewhat straitjacketed from the start by the farcical construction, he fails in the end purely through lack of nerve.

Barkin is clearly game for anything the director wants her to do, including extensive physical clowning, but mugs and overdoes the grimacing and macho posturing. Smits and Bracco are smooth enough, but most actors, especially the secondary and bit players, have been encouraged to broad and obvious effects.

Tech contributions are okay, but less sparkling than in many of Edwards' previous outings. Anyone looking for a repeat of the sexual sophistication of "Victor/Victoria," among other films, will be disappointed with this one. — *Cart.*

THE MARRYING MAN

A Buena Vista Release of a Hollywood Pictures presentation, in association with Silver Screen Partners IV, Odyssey Entertainment, of a David Permut production. Produced by Permut. Directed by Jerry Rees. Screenplay, Neil Simon; camera (Technicolor), Donald E. Thorin; editor, Michael Jablow; music, David Newman; sound (Dolby); Tim Cooney, Jacob Goldstein (add'l shoot); production design, William F. Matthews; art direction, Mark Mansbridge, Dan Maltese (add'l shoot); set decoration, Jim Duffy, Jeff Haley (add'l shoot); costume design, Ruth Myers; assistant director, David Householter, Hope Goodwin (add'l shoot); production manager, Jerry Sobul, Sharon Mann (add'l shoot); choreography, Jeffrey Hornaday; 2nd unit director-stunt coordinator, John A. Moio; co-producer, David Streit; associate producer, Donald Kreiss; casting, Ronnie Yeskel. Reviewed at Beekman theater, N.Y., March 28, 1991. MPAA Rating: R. Running time: **115 MIN.**

Vicki Anderson . . . . . Kim Basinger
Charley Pearl . . . . Alec Baldwin
Lew Horner . . . . Robert Loggia
Adele Horner . . . . . . Elisabeth Shue
Bugsy Siegel . . . . . Armand Assante
Phil . . . . Paul Reiser
Sammy . . . . Fisher Stevens
Tony . . . . Peter Dobson
Also with: Steve Hytner, Jeremy Robert, Big John Studd, Tony Longo.

Just when audiences got over Disney's "Scenes From A Mall," the distrib is unleashing "The Marrying Man," a stillborn romantic comedy of staggering ineptitude. Industry bad-mouthing of the stars during production was just a preview of the terrible picture.

Author Neil Simon reportedly has disowned this film, which offers little in the way of comedy or diversion. An awkward flashback structure tells of egotistical toothpaste heir Alec Baldwin falling in love with chanteuse Kim Basinger on an outing in 1948 with his buddies to Las Vegas.

Instead of marrying his beautiful g.f. back in L.A., Elisabeth Shue, Baldwin is forced into a shotgun wedding with Basinger by Armand Assante as Bugsy Siegel, Basinger's main man. Key plot point that this is Bugsy's "revenge" for catching Baldwin in the sack with his g.f. is impossible to swallow. Also unbelievable are the duo's several breakups and remarriages.

Lack of chemistry between the two principals is only the first problem with "Marrying Man." Obvious re-shoots result in an unwieldy package that has the film climaxing with perhaps 30

minutes to go, making it play like an original and a sequel spliced together. Director Jerry Rees, who previously helmed the animated feature "The Brave Little Toaster," has the usually dependable cinematographer Donald Thorin light interiors as if for film noir rather than comedy.

He also shifts uncomfortably from big setpieces to utterly static, talkative exposition scenes in closeup sans background action. Result is grim and pointless.

Basinger, replete with vocal coach and choreography by no less than Jeffrey Hornaday, gives a mechanical impression of a competent singer, while grabbing herself during her numbers in a manner more like the animated Jessica Rabbit (of "Who Framed Roger Rabbit") than Mae West. Unlike her obvious inspiration, Michelle Pfeiffer in "The Fabulous Baker Boys," Basinger fails to integrate the singing stunt organically into her character.

Stuck with the role of a handsome cad, Baldwin mugs and poses in embarrassing fashion, resembling his recent "Saturday Night Live" hosting assignments. Nearly every laugh here is achieved by Fisher Stevens, given the brightest lines in Baldwin's circle of male kibitzers.

Casting ploy of having Assante and Robert Loggia portray, respectively, stereotyped Jewish gangster and studio chief instead of Italians will give little solace to groups unhappy with the portrayal of Italian Americans on screen. — *Lor.*

PARIS TROUT

A Viacom Pictures presentation of a Konigsberg/Sanitsky production. Executive producer, Diana Kerew. Produced by Frank Konigsberg and Larry Sanitsky. Directed by Stephen Gyllenhaal. Screenplay, Pete Dexter, based upon his novel; camera, Robert Elswit; editor, Harvey Rosenstock; music, David Shire; production design, Richard Sherman; costume design, Mary Rose; set decoration, Michael Warga; assistant director, David Womark; associate producer, Jayne Bieber; casting, Chez Casting. Reviewed at the American Film Market, Mann Criterion Theater, Santa Monica, Calif., March 5, 1991. No MPAA rating. Running time **100 MIN.**

Paris Trout . . . . Dennis Hopper
Hanna Trout . . . . . Barbara Hershey
Harry Seagraves . . . . Ed Harris
Carol Bonner . . . . . . Ray McKinnon
Mary Sayers . . . . Tina Lifford
Rosie Sayers . . . . . . Darnita Henry
Henry Ray Sayers . . . . . . Eric Ware

Pete Dexter's haunting novel about an unspeakable crime is brought masterfully to life in

"Paris Trout." Mesmerizing, morbidly fascinating tale, empowered by outstanding performances by Dennis Hopper, Barbara Hershey and Ed Harris, will not be enriching U.S. screens, however, as domestic exposure is exclusive to the Showtime cable channel via its output deal with Viacom.

Stronger on artistry than formulaic payoff, pic nonetheless should fill the bill for foreign buyers clamoring for A product. U.S. audiences, outside of Showtime subscribers, will have to wait for the Media Home Entertainment vid release (Aug. 8).

Rarely does a modest production succeed on all creative counts as roundly as "Paris Trout." Named for its protagonist, a mean-spirited Southern storekeeper who lends money at high interest rates to poor blacks, story is an unusually rich and complex one about the human need to reach back toward decency in the face of barbarism.

Adapting his own National Book Award-winning novel, Dexter proves a keen craftsman in the screen medium, stripping away the novel's excesses and distractions with an uncannily cool hand.

Trouble begins when a young black man (Eric Ware) signs a note to buy a used car from Trout (Hopper). When the worthless car is wrecked the same day, he drops it off at Trout's store, declaring he won't pay. Trout and a hired gun head out to "the hollow" to settle the debt. When the black man runs off, they enter the house and unload their pistols into his terrified mother and 12-year-old sister.

The racist Trout is certain he won't be prosecuted for an incident with "nigras" in the natural course of collecting a debt, but when the child dies he's arrested and charged with murder.

After his horrified wife (Hershey) visits the dying child at the clinic, Trout begins to humiliate and abuse her. He hires the town's crack lawyer (Ed Harris) to defend him, but the attorney becomes more and more disturbed by the case and Trout's lack of remorse, while at the same time becoming passionately drawn to Hershey.

Events in this downward spiralling tale grow more and more bizarre as Trout, confronted with rules he was sure did not apply to him, loses his hold on reality.

The courtroom scenes are some of the most deftly written in

memory, with flashes of artistry and cutting truth. Even after Trout is convicted of manslaughter, he pays a judge to sign him out of prison and continues to lash back violently at a community he feels has betrayed him.

Hopper, beefy and aged for the role and sporting a clipped redneck haircut, gives an extraordinary portrayal of the tortured madman, with his deeply worried blue eyes fixed on some far-off point of injustice only he can see.

Roundfaced and plug-necked, Hopper projects simultaneously the sorrowful confusion of a small child and the brutish rage of a man in a performance that is always subtly unpredictable and terrifying.

Hershey is marvelous in a mature, nuanced perf as the compassionate spouse struggling to maintain dignity, evidencing an acute understanding of what makes the character tick.

Harris, with his clear-eyed, sunny countenance, brings a needed lightness and clarity to the triangle, while at the same time being most convincing in the courtroom scenes.

Stephen Gyllenhaal, an Emmy winner for "Killing In A Small Town" (also starring Hershey) directs with a keen appreciation for the tension between the courtly manners of the civilized South and the horrific events of the story, creating a piece that is both hypnotizing and restrained.

Sultry, fragilely controlled atmosphere of a simple Southern town circa 1949 has been acutely rendered in Richard Sherman's production design. Lensing by Robert Elswit, with dim, dusky interiors and brightly lit pastoral exteriors, is exemplary.

— *Daws.*

ANTE YEIA
(TAKE CARE)
(GREEK)

A Yorgos Tseberopoulos-Greek Film Center-ET-1-Filmiki Eteireis co-production. Directed by Yorgos Tseberopoulos. Screenplay, Tseberopoulos, Vasilis Alexakis, based on the novel by Giovannas; camera (color), Yannis Daskelathannasis; music, Stamatis Spanoudakis; songs performed by Yannis Parios; sound, Marinos Anthanasopoulos; set design-costumes, Alexis Kyritsopoulos; makeup, Yannis Papadakis. Reviewed at Ideal Cinema, Athens, Jan. 19, 1991. Running time: **93 MIN.**
Marina . . . . Kaiti Papanika
Christos . . . . Alkis Kourkoulos
Michalis . . . . Nikos Dimitratos
Fani . . . . Tania Tripi
Roula . . . . Vana Barba
Menios . . . . Kostas Koklas
Yorgos . . . . Vangelis Liodakis
Alexis . . . . Spyros Drosos
Also with: Lina Triantafylou, Yorgos Sampanis, Stelios Lionakis, Michalis Yiannatos, Thomas Konstantinidis.

"Take Care," a likable portrait of an Athenian family, relies heavily on the topnotch cast's sensitive performances. Its subtle charm makes it a natural for ethnic fests. Proper handling, buttressed by word-of-mouth and helmer's previous boxoffice success, could spark wider appeal.

Handsome hunk Christos (Alkis Kourkoulos), a cryptic loner detached from his possessive g.f. Roula (Vana Barba), is intent on becoming an entertainer. He is humiliated in his bid to get an audition, which never comes off because the club owner hustles off a busty off-key chanteuse, leaving Christos stuck with an inflated bar tab.

In order to make ends meet, Christos gets a job in a butcher shop. Owner Michalis (Nikos Dimitratos) has had a quarrel with his son Yorgos (Vangelis Liodakis), who has no interest in the family business and heads for a village to find himself.

Christos soon proves himself to be an enthusiastic learner, and as the father relies more heavily on him, he becomes amorously involved with daughter Fani (talented newcomer Tania Tripi), a lively student and potential Olympic swimmer.

When a neighbor shows the father a newspaper article about his son's arrest at a party in which hashish was allegedly smoked, the shock is too much and he succumbs to a heart attack. Christos takes over the expansion of the shop and becomes cozy with the mother (Kaiti Papanika) in the process.

Spiteful former g.f. Roula reemerges to fill in mother on Christos' liaison with the daughter. Christos is placed in a bind which peaks at the opening of the new shop. Tragedy is averted and the participants seem a bit wiser, albeit sadder.

Established actress Papanika is a standout in a solid cast, proving she still has the talent that made her a tremendous b.o. draw in the '60s. Without resorting to soap opera tactics, she is alternately girlishly flirtatious and touchingly griefstricken.

The well-lensed glimpses of everyday Athenian life may be only too familiar to local audiences, which have eschewed native films in recent years, but present a realistic and sympathetic portrayal for offshore viewing.

Catchy score by composer Stamatis Spanoudakis, sung by popular singer Yannis Parios, is a big plus. — Sam.

CAREER OPPORTUNITIES

A Universal release of a Hughes Entertainment presentation. Produced by John Hughes, A. Hunt Lowry. Executive producer, Lora Lee. Directed by Bryan Gordon. Screenplay, John Hughes; camera (Deluxe color), Don McAlpine; editor, Glenn Farr, Peck Prior; music, Thomas Newman; sound (Dolby), Jim Alexander; production design, Paul Sylbert; art direction, Guy Barnes; set decoration, Kathe Klopp; costume design, Betsy Cox; associate producers, Andi Capoziello; Cliff T. E. Roseman; assistant director, David Sosna; casting, Pam Dixon. Reviewed at Hollywood Pacific Theater, L.A., March 29, 1991. MPAA rating: PG-13. Running time: **85 MIN.**
Jim Dodge . . . . Frank Whaley
Josie McClellan . . . Jennifer Connelly
Nestor Pyle . . . . . Dermot Mulroney
Gil Kinney . . . . . Kieran Mulroney
Bud Dodge . . . . . . John M. Jackson
Dotty Dodge . . . . . . Jenny O'Hara
Roger Roy McClellan . . . . Noble Willingham
Officer Don . . . . Barry Corbin
Store manager . . . . . . John Candy

Writer-producer John Hughes' followup to "Home Alone" lacks the spit-polish and magic of the blockbuster but still has plenty of absorbing characters, smart, snappy dialog and delightful stretches of comic foolery. Prospects for landing a steady audience of teens and Hughes buffs look fair to moderate for "Career Opportunities."

Like "Home Alone," story has a young man on his own to defend a fortress against bungling burglars, but in this case he's a 21-year-old trapped in a job he hates (night janitor at a discount store) and pitted against guntoting hoods out to clean out, not clean up, the store.

Jim (Frank Whaley) is a ne'er-do-well fast talker and nonstop liar bounced from as many dead-end jobs as his humble hometown of Monroe, Ill., has to offer. No sooner does he don uniform and nametag than he dissolves into delusions of professional grandeur, daydreaming more than working. On the night in question, he's been given his last chance to succeed by his blue-collar father — or get kicked out of the house.

Locked in the mammoth discount store all night, the young clean-up boy soon takes to eating, watching tv and rollerstaking the aisles dressed in funny underwear and a bridal veil — same kind of free-for-all funmaking that sustained "Home Alone."

That's when he discovers he's not alone. Darkly voluptuous Josie (Jennifer Connelly), princess daughter of the town land baron, is locked in after falling asleep during a shoplifting spree.

Trapped together, the misfits discover each other, and, in the type of scenes Hughes writes best, sort out their differences and common ground from their horrifying high school years. In a well-scripted scene full of bumbling dares and double dares, they plot their escape to Hollywood where their unique talents are bound to lead to lucrative careers.

But the guntoting hoods (Dermot and Kieran Mulroney) show up and they must turn their specialties to more immediate escape.

As usual, Hughes' script gives young people plenty of credit for brains and individuality. Whaley makes the most of the buoyant self-promoter in a funny, sympathetic and technically impressive perf that carries the film. Josie's situation has little credibility (story's biggest weakness), but Connelly manages to bring some depth and presence to the role.

Driven by Whaley's character, story is set up skillfully but gets mighty slippery. The far-fetched ending that's brought off lacks the savvy of some of Hughes' more solidly anchored work.

Nonetheless, first-time director Bryan Gordon does a terrifically inventive and resourceful job, getting sharp perfs from all actors. One of the best is a hilarious interview between Whaley and John Candy (in an uncredited cameo) as a store manager who mistakes Jim for an exec.

Deft and dynamic camerawork in some scenes, particularly the rollerskating segs, adds as much pizzazz as the soundtrack. Don McAlpine's choice of a washed-out look for the cinematography is just right for the banal environs.

Slipped into the marketplace by Universal with no press screenings, pic could have used a bigger vote of confidence from the distrib. — Daws.

BLACK MAGIC WOMAN

A Trimark Pictures release of a Marc Springer-Deryn Warren production. Produced by Springer, Warren. Executive producers, Mark Amin, Joan Baribeault. Directed by Warren. Screenplay, Gerry Daly, from story by Daly, Springer, Warren; camera (Foto-Kem color), Levie Isaacks; editor, Tony Miller; music, Randy Miller; sound, David Chornow; production design, Elliot Gilbert; costume design, Rene Richards; assistant director, Scott Thomson; 2nd unit camera, Steve Grass; line producer, Gary Schmoeller; casting, Sharon Nederlander. Reviewed on Vidmark vidcassette, N.Y., March 23, 1991. MPAA Rating: R. Running time: **91 MIN.**
Brad Travis . . . . Mark Hamill
Diane Abbott . . . . . . Amanda Wyss
Cassandra Perry . . . Apollonia Kotero
Dr. Yantos . . . . Victor Rivers
Carlita . . . . Abidah Viera
Arna . . . . Carmen Moré
Suzanne . . . . Bonnie Ebsen
Hank . . . . Larry Hankin
Dr. Reiss . . . . Alan Toy

"Black Magic Woman" is a welcome entry to the growing list of video-driven erotic thrillers. Blessed with an extremely surprising final twist, pic should entertain genre fans.

Vidmark distribs the video in April, after having briefly tested it in theatrical dates several months ago via its Trimark subsid.

"Star Wars" alumnus Mark Hamill follows in Marc Singer's footsteps as the macho hero, a cad who runs an art gallery with Amanda Wyss but selfishly won't marry her despite their lengthy romance.

His comeuppance begins when voluptuous Apollonia Kotero visits the gallery and quickly seduces Hamill. Their whirlwind relationship results in plenty of sack time, but the callous antihero drops her as soon as business picks up. Scorned woman Apollonia segues into familiar "Fatal

Attraction" territory, even destroying a valuable sculpture during one violent confrontation with Hamill at the gallery.

Pic moves into supernatural horror territory as Hamill becomes victimized by black magic and voodoo rites. All the evidence points against Apollonia as the villainess responsible, but the police keep an open mind.

Careful viewer may guess who the real baddie is, but final revelation still packs a wallop.

Use of Santana's hit title song helps film's atmospherics and punches up the sex scenes. Fans accustomed to uninhibited nude performances by Shannon Tweed and Tanya Roberts may be slightly disappointed, as Apollonia avoids nudity to emphasize the tease. Her scenes are steamy, however, and won't need editing for the tv broadcast version.

— *Lor.*

CLOSE MY EYES
(BRITISH)

A Film Four Intl. presentation of a Beambright production. Produced by Therese Pickard. Written and directed by Stephen Poliakoff. Camera (Metrocolor), Witold Stok; editor, Michael Parkinson; music, Michael Gibbs; sound, Peter Edwards; production design, Luciana Arrighi; production manager, Alison Barnett; assistant director, Ray Corbett; casting, Joyce Gallie. Reviewed at Berlin Film Festival (Panorama), Feb. 22, 1991. Running time: **105 MIN.**
Sinclair . . . . Alan Rickman
Richard Gillespie . . . . . . Clive Owen
Natalie . . . . Saskia Reeves
Colin . . . . Karl Johnson
Jessica . . . . Lesley Sharp
Paula . . . . Kate Gartside
Philippa . . . . Karen Knight
Geal . . . . Niall Buggy
Girl . . . . Helen FitzGerald

"**C**lose My Eyes" is a powerful new British film about incest. Word of mouth about the subject, topflight performances and writer-director Stephen Poliakoff's intense handling of the material should bring dividends on the arthouse circuits, with wider bookings also possible.

The early scenes somewhat awkwardly chart the relationship between Natalie (Saskia Reeves) and her younger brother Richard (Clive Owen) over a five-year period. They live in different British cities; Richard is a successful and ambitious young man who likes women, especially young women, and has no trouble getting them. Natalie seems constantly unhappy, with boring jobs and broken love affairs.

One night, Richard stays in his sister's apartment and both sense a new feeling of intimacy between them, though nothing happens. Five years later, Natalie is married to the wealthy Sinclair (Alan Rickman) and they live in a magnificent house beside the Thames.

Richard also is living in London, and working for an outfit referred to as "Urban Greenpeace." Natalie visits her brother in his apartment, and the hitherto unspoken passion between them erupts into a sexual encounter that is frankly presented and challenging in its implications.

Although Natalie, who precipitated the situation, insists "this is not an affair" and "this isn't you, it isn't me," Richard is bowled over by passionate love for his sister. They meet again over a weekend in an empty apartment and the sexual affair continues with more abandon than before.

Sinclair has got wind of his wife's involvement with someone, though he doesn't know whom, and Natalie starts to pull back from the relationship. Richard, now completely besotted, refuses to let her go, and the affair reaches a dramatic climax at a lunchtime party given by Sinclair and Natalie who have decided to go to live in America.

The central triangular relationship is supported by well-observed and biting scenes involving marginal characters, such as Richard's boss (Karl Johnson), who is quietly dying of AIDS, or the girl (Kate Gartside) he picks up to try to get over his passion for Natalie but finds he can't make love to.

"Close My Eyes" challenges its audience. The love scenes are so frankly and passionately presented that viewers almost forget that they're watching one of the great taboos.

Reeves and Owen give brave, strong, unstinting performances. Rickman has his best screen role to date as the pompous but kindly husband.

Writer-director Poliakoff with this (his second) feature makes a big advance over his first, the uneven "Hidden City" (1987). He has taken a challenging theme and handled it with great power and passion, and is likely to win critical kudos as a result.

Witold Stok's superior camerawork makes fine use of London locations and of the beautifully lit interiors where the illicit lovers meet. Luciana Arrighi's production design also is tops, and

Michael Gibbs' music score is very apt.

Despite the lack of stellar names, "Close My Eyes" should have a solid career ahead of it and is a major plus for all involved. — *Strat.*

LENSMAN
(JAPANESE)

A Streamline Pictures release of an MK Co. production. Produced by Akihito Ito, Mitsuru Kaneko, Michihiro Tomii, Tadami Watanabe. Executive producer, Hiroshi Suto. Directed by Yoshiaki Kawajiri and Kazuyuki Hirokawa. Screenplay, Soji Yoshikawa; camera (CFI color), Ban Yamaki; editor, Osamu Tonaka; music, Akira Inoue; sound, Susumu Aketagawa; animation directors, Kazuo Tomizawa, Kobuyuki Kitajaima; art direction, Katsushi Aoki; adaptation-production, Carl Macek; dialog writer-director, Steve Kramer. Reviewed at Film Forum, March 25, 1991. Running time: **107 MIN.**
With voices of: Kerrigan Mahan, Edie Mirman, Michale McConnohie, Steve Kramer, Greg Snegoff, Tom Wyner.

Based on the influential stories of Edward E. (Doc) Smith, "Lensman" will impress sci-fi buffs with its computer graphic animation. Much like "Star Wars," whose plot and characters may derive from Smith's, this pic ultimately goes on too long, as one high-tech chase scene follows another.

Picture is also saddled with an annoying New Age score, with some pounding disco music thrown in for bad measure. It sounds dated because it is: The ambitious film was begun in 1979 and was finally released in Japan in shortened form. Streamline Pictures has restored the cut footage and dubbed it in English for U.S. release.

The story, concerning war between the good Galactic Alliance and evil Bosconian War Lords, is entertaining for an hour or so. Young hero Kim has greatness thrust upon him when he is made a lensman, a warrior with special powers. He is put in one life-threatening situation after another, barely escaping each time.

Some of the dialog is hokey, but there are also witty lines. During one attack, Chris (the heroine) says, "I knew I should have taken those classes in crisis stress management." The voices are well suited to the characters, ranging from idealized heroes in slick spacecraft to the grotesque Bosconians in blob-like vessels.

The battles and last-minute escapes become tedious. Despite the combination of computer

graphics and cel animation, non-fans are bound to lose interest. The syrupy ending falls flat, and the awful music drones on.

Still, anyone who loves futuristic fiction will eat it up. Once they tire of the action, animation buffs can admire the painstaking work. The music may be out of date, but visually this overblown cartoon outclasses anything found on Saturday morning tv. — *Stev.*

IL GIOCO DELLE OMBRE
(THE SHADOW GAME)
(ITALIAN)

A Stalker Film production. Produced by Donatella Palermo. Directed by Stefano Gabrini. Screenplay, Gabrini, Roberto Marafante; camera (Technicolor), Raffaele Mertes; editor, Carlo Fonatan; music, Popol Vuh; art direction, Emita Frigato. Reviewed at Palaexpo, Rome, Dec. 16, 1990. Running time: **108 MIN.**
Luca . . . . Fabio Bussotti
Alice . . . . Mariella Valentini
Marta . . . . Fiammetta Carena
Isa . . . . Isa Gallinelli

"**T**he Shadow Game," a poetically melancholy ghost story rich in imagery but frustratingly repetitive, suggests Wim Wenders gone gothic. Stefano Gabrini's feature debut, based on his own prizewinning script, has been making inroads at Euro festivals while awaiting a local distributor. With astute trimming, pic could interest arthouse audiences.

As the mournful writer-hero, Fabio Bussotti is an aching loner beset by undeserved guilt because his lover (the beautiful but remote Fiammetta Carena) has committed suicide.

He rents an eerie apartment in a sleepy village and leads the life of a recluse, writing a novel. In a secret room upstairs, he is drawn to a frightening fresco of a woman who reminds him of his lost love.

As the house draws Bussotti deeper into an unreal, morbid world of shadow, a chance acquaintance with a tightrope walker (the sparkling Mariella Valentini) in a surreal, chic traveling circus pulls him toward sanity. For too long, the writer shifts between depressing flashbacks of his dead lover and close encounters with Valentini. The winner of the struggle is apparent early on.

Film will appeal most to lovers of symbols and magical relationships. In that dimension, pic remains original and intriguing for most of its running time.

But woe to realists who wonder why a successful novelist receiving regular advances from his editor and regular affection from a charming acrobat should choose the path to madness. On this plane, story is a puzzle not even the likable thesps can make convincing.

Though shot on a shoestring with help from the Entertainment Ministry, Gabrini's technical bravura leaves an impression of luxury behind: rich interiors, fine camerawork by Raffaele Mertes of mysterious off-season beaches. Popol Vuh's poignant music makes an appropriately haunting score, which is a little overused. — *Yung.*

ARCHIVE REVIEW

SYMBIOPSYCHOTAXI-PLASM: TAKE ONE

A Take One Prods. Ltd. production. Produced and directed by William Greaves. Camera (color), Terry Filgate, Stevan Larner, Greaves; editor, Greaves; music, Miles Davis, John Pearson, Joe Zawinul; sound, Jonathan Gordon; production manager, Robert Rosen; co-producer, Manuel Melamed. Reviewed at Magno Preview 9 screening room, N.Y., March 28, 1991. (In Brooklyn Museum's William Greaves retrospective.) No MPAA Rating. Running time: **69 MIN.**
With: Patricia Ree Gilbert, Don Fellows, Jonathan Gordon, Robert Rosen, William Greaves.

This fascinating experimental film, which combines fictional and documentary techniques in innovative fashion, was shot in 1967 but never released.

Like Michael Roemer's "The Plot Against Harry," similarly 20 years on the shelf, it's an artifact modern audiences could appreciate. It offers a fresh look at society and filmmaking trends of the adventurous '60s.

Making his first fiction feature, documentarist William Greaves chose the challenging assignment of becoming a filmmaker-provocateur: using a screenplay "Over The Cliff" as the basis to instigate a revolt among his actors and his crew against directorial tyranny.

This is set against the backdrop of auteur filmmaking, in which Jean-Luc Godard and especially John Cassavetes were using *cinéma vérité* techniques

in fictional formats. Greaves takes his crew to Manhattan's Central Park in springtime and repeatedly shoots the same scenes of a marital breakup, using a succession of five different couples in the roles.

"Take One" focuses on one thespian team, stage actors Patricia Ree Gilbert and Don Fellows (latter frequently seen as an American in British films of the '70s and '80s), who ultimately question the lack of direction Greaves is giving them. Hazard of the vérité technique occurs when Gilbert storms off in disgust as Greaves interrupts her big scene before the payoff, and his camera crew is unprepared to capture on film the remainder of this high point incident.

What makes "Take One" unique is a series of segments Greaves did not direct: After several days of shooting, crew clandestinely assembles and films their own bull sessions (with the director absent) criticizing Greaves and pondering what can be done to save the "Over The Cliff" feature. Their comments are fascinating, and Greaves leaves this material in as part and parcel of his freeform filmmaking design.

Especially effective is sound man Jonathan Gordon's later eruption in which he tells Greaves to "drop the euphemisms" and lectures the writer-director on how his banal dialog would benefit from unexpurgated contemporary jargon.

This house revolt is exactly what Greaves wanted and demonstrates realistically, rather than satirically, how even the lowliest crew member often could give valuable input to a foundering production if such collaboration were encouraged (or permitted).

Use of split-screen techniques presents simultaneous different angles of the same "Over The Cliff" scene being shot as well as views of the crew. Film also documents the intrusion onto the set of an alcoholic who takes center stage briefly to inject his nihilistic, post-Beatnik but anti-hippie stream of consciousness.

Much of this film is quite funny though Greaves' Machiavellian approach to bamboozling his cast and crew is a bit hard to take at times. He reportedly shot enough footage for several features (a "Take Two" sequel is promised in the end credits), and included among the casts not shown here is Susan Anspach in what would have been her film dèbut pre-"The Landlord." — *Lor.*

ISTANBUL FEST

DALI
(SPANISH-ITALIAN)

A Montornès Films-TVE3-Televisió de Catalunya/Freixenet-Vito & Riccardo Di Bari production. (Intl. sales: Catalan Films, Barcelona.) Executive producer, Jaume Behar. Directed by Antoni Ribas. Screenplay, Miquel Sanz, Enric Gomà, Ribas, Temistocles Lopez; camera (Eastmancolor), Macari Golferichs; editor, Emilio Ortiz; music, Antonio Sechi. Reviewed at 10th Istanbul Intl. Film Festival, March 26, 1991. Running time: **108 MIN.**
Salvador Dali . . . . . . Lorenzo Quinn
Gala . . . . Sarah Douglas
Tom . . . . Michael Catlin
Also with: Katherine Wallach, Rosa Novell, Emma Quer, Paco Guijar.

A colorful romp through the early career of the surrealist dauber, "Dali" is entertainingly packaged and played with gusto. But lightweight approach could work against the pic in the subtitled market, despite film buff appeal in part of the yarn.

Events kick off with Salvador Dali (Lorenzo Quinn) arriving in New York in 1940, with a loaf of bread on his head, fried eggs on his lapel and an ego the size of Mt. Rushmore. A Time reporter (Michael Catlin) nabs him for an interview, sparking a series of flashbacks to his childhood and scandal-strewn youth.

Episodes include pranks as a pesky kid, stirring the loins of poet Garcia Lorca, working with helmer Luis Buñuel (shown as more interested in t&a) on classics "Un Chien Andalou" and "L'Âge D'Or," and quitting Spain during the civil war for some *dolce vita* in Italy. Other w.k. names who provide comic shtick are Picasso and René Clair. Cavalcade climaxes with Dali taking Gotham by storm.

Quinn (son of Anthony) looks the part of the louche painter and is suitably eccentric within the script's comic limitations. British thesp Sarah Douglas is classily decorative as his wife, and Catlin is okay as obsequious journo, but Catalan dubbing robs them of real contributions.

All other credits are tops, and Antonio Sechi's fairground score (recalling Nino Rota's work for Fellini) gives a real lift to the glossy setpieces. — *Del.*

CAMDAN KALP
(A HEART OF GLASS)
(TURKISH)

A Moda Film production. Produced by Mustafa Karaman, Yücel Özgür, Fehmi Yasar. Written and directed by Yasar. Camera (color), Erdal Kahraman; music, Okay Temiz; sound, Atila Van; art directors, Pascal Defins, Meral Özen. Reviewed at 10th Istanbul Intl. Film Festival, March 28, 1991. Running time: **111 MIN.**
Kirpi . . . . Genco Erkal
Kiraz . . . . Serif Sezer
Naciye . . . . Deniz Gökcer

A black comedy about a longhair helmer who gets entangled in his maid's marital problems, "A Heart Of Glass" is a characterful debut by former scripter and Yilmaz Guney associate Fehmi Yasar. Despite problems with a rambling structure, pic has enough oddball appeal to click at fests.

Kirpi has a sharp-tongued wife who dubs Marilyn Monroe pics and a script that no producer in town will touch. The money men tell him to make a Turkish version of "The Last Emperor" instead. Meanwhile, his maid, a peasant who can't even work the phone, is being slapped around by her oafish husband.

After volunteering to visit the maid's family in remote southeast Anatolia, Kirpi finds that life outside the big city operates under a different set of rules. He brings two of her brothers back to sort out her problems. Peasant solidarity wins the day in a tragic finale.

Pic's underlying theme of bourgeois vs. feudal values, and misunderstandings on both sides, is slow to emerge from the lowkey, Czech-like comedy. Better subtitles are also needed to make some of the yocks and local references work. But thesping all round is fine, especially by the lead trio, and after the first half-hour, pic builds up a proper head of steam.

Apart from a few murky interiors, it's technically okay. Pic won best Turkish film award at the Istanbul fest, with Yasar sharing best director award as well, and it's one of the few local films in the past season to rack up good boxoffice. Yasar has since trimmed 10 minutes from above running time, mostly from pic's first half. — *Del.*

PIANO PIANO BACAKSIZ
(PIANO PIANO KID)
(TURKISH)

A Cicek Film production. Produced by Arif Keskiner. Directed by Tunc Basaran. Screenplay, Basaran, Ümit Ünal, Kemel Demirel; camera, Colin Moulnier; editor, Veli Akbasli; music, Can Kozlu; art direction, Jale Basaran. Reviewed at 10th Istanbul Intl. Film Festival (competition), March 27, 1991. Running time: **84 MIN.**
Kemal . . . . Emin Sivas
Mother . . . . Serap Aksoy
Uncle Kerim . . . . Rutkay Aziz
Feriha . . . . Aysegül Unsal

A tender portrait of the inhabitants of an old Istanbul house in the 1940s as seen through the eyes of a 9-year-old, "Piano Piano Kid" combines ethnic flavor with gentle charm and universal appeal. It could find a slot on the fest circuit.

Kemal (wide-eyed Emin Sivas, also in this year's foreign film Oscar-winner, "Journey Of Hope"), is growing up in the impoverished but warmly nurturing atmosphere of his extended family's rooming house.

Dad, whose cardplaying earned him the title of Gambler Hasan, and mother Layla (ballerina-turned-actress Serap Aksoy) often wrangle over his profligate ways, but their underlying affection is apparent. In one telling scene, Hasan rips up a down comforter after being criticized for taking it as payment for a gambling debt. Tension is defused when little Kemal is enchanted by the floating feathers.

A mellow cadence is established as vignettes unfold among the other boarders. Kemal has a crush on pretty blonde Feriha (Aysegül Unsal), who left her first husband after falling head over heels with current hubby Senai, a sweet-natured fruit vendor who picked up a philosophy degree and pot-smoking habit while living in Berlin.

Near tragedy is averted when Senai nearly burns down the house while stoned, but he's redeemed and elevated in Kemal's eyes when he is called into action as a Navy officer in preparation for Turkey's possible entry into the war. Blackouts during air attacks are the only other direct reference to the conflict.

Kemal idolizes his studious uncle Kerim (Rutkay Aziz), who tirelessly researches antique coins in hopes of ending his family's financial woes. Uncle gives nephew his philosophy in a nutshell when he advises him in Italian to take it slow and easy — "Piano piano kid."

Later developments back up the underlying contention that money doesn't insure happiness, but lack of conflict more serious than a shouting match over a stolen chicken, considering all the different personalities living in tight quarters, strains credibility.

Still, it's a heartwarming tale that captured a shared best director award at the Istanbul Film Festival for leading helmer Tunc Basaran, reaffirming his position as one of the most humanistic Turkish filmmakers.

Tech credits are fine, especially the lensing by Colin Moulnier and art direction by Jale Basaran. — *Sam.*

DARBE
(THE STROKE)
(TURKISH)

A Tug-Çen Film Video production. Directed by Ümit Efekan. Screenplay, Bekir Yildiz, from his own novel; camera (color), Ertunç Senkay; editor, Sedat Karadeniz; music, Cahit Berkay. Reviewed at 10th Istanbul Intl. Film Festival, March 27, 1991. Running time: **81 MIN.**
Hamdullah/Yavuz . . . . . Kadir Inanir
Narin . . . . Nilgün Akçaoglu

There's a familiar feel to "The Stroke" that Turkish film buffs may find resistible. General auds will remain unconvinced by this yarn of an ex-political prisoner who undergoes plastic surgery and reseduces his wife, despite solid direction and playing. Fest chances look slim.

Hamdullah (Karid Inanir) names names and gets a new face under the government's "repentance law." As Yavuz, he begins to stalk his wife (Nilgün Akçaoglu) and young son, who both think he's dead and venerate his memory as a political martyr. She still doesn't recogize him when they end up in the sack, and only when a former "comrade" of Hamdullah blabs does she kick him out.

Local star Inanir is reliable as the husband locked in a limbo of prison memories and an uncharted future. Akçaoglu is better as the wife who got back on her feet and made a life for herself. But the central love story (from a recent novel) lacks believability.

Helming by commercial journeyman Ümit Efekan is smooth throughout, with only the prison flashbacks too obviously introduced. Other credits are up to scratch. Anglo title is misleading, as original (which means "The Blow") is double-edged similar to French "coup." — *Del.*

BERDEL
(TURKISH)

A Tapov (Turkish Family Health & Planning Foundation) production. Produced by Gulseven G. Yaser. Directed by Atif Yilmaz. Screenplay, Yilmaz, Yildirim Turker, from the book by Esma Ocak; camera (Eastmancolor), Erdal Kahraman; editor, Mevlut Kocak; music, Selim Atakan; production design, Mustafa Ziya Ulkenciler. Reviewed at Berlin Film Festival (Panorama), Feb. 17, 1991. (Also in Istanbul Intl. Film Festival.) Running time: **86 MIN.**
Omer . . . . Tarik Akan
Hanim . . . . Turkan Soray
Beyaz . . . . Mine Cayiroglu
Second wife . . . . . . Fusan Demirel
Beyaz' husband . . . . . Taner Barlas

"Berdel," one of the best pics unveiled in the Berlin Film Festival's Panorama section, is a simple but emotionally devastating indictment of arcane customs persistent in some rural areas of Turkey. Continued fest screenings are conceivable, and specialized commercial engagements are also possible.

This production of Turkey's Family Health & Planning Foundation has a message to get across, but director Atif Yilmaz makes his points without undue propaganda.

Omer loves his wife Hanim, who has given him five daughters, but his macho image demands a son. When another baby girl is born, he reluctantly decides he must get a new wife, but since he can't afford a dowry, he decides to follow an age-old custom and exchange eldest daughter Beyaz for a wife.

The distraught teenager, in love with a man her own age, is forced to marry an elderly and important man who soon expires. Omer gets a new wife he doesn't really care for.

Ironically, the new wife gives birth to a daughter, while Hanim, with whom Omer still has sexual relations, finally has a son but dies in childbirth.

Director Yilmaz tells this sad little story without fuss, moving the narrative along briskly. As lives are destroyed because Omer's pride insists that he have a son, emotions in the film are very strong. The actors are convincing in their roles.

One amusing scene, possibly inserted at the insistence of the film's backers, shows the village women being shown a video about family planning while their men grumble in the local bar.

Technically, "Berdel," which refers to the barter system involved, is fine, with crisp color camerawork of the picturesque village. — *Strat.*

ÖLÜRAYAK
(SWAN SONG)
(TURKISH)

A Tele-Video production. Produced by Hüseyin Apaydin. Directed by Aydin Bagardi. Screenplay, Aysenur Arslan; camera (color), Serdar Servidal; editor, Fadime Bektas; music, Cem Küçümen; art director, Cem Yalin. Reviewed at 10th Istanbul Intl. Film Festival, March 26, 1991. Running time: **83 MIN.**
Ömer . . . . Haluk Bilginer
Ela . . . . Meral Oguz
Also with: Filiz Taçbas, Erol Demiröz.

A drama about the romantic ups and downs of cancer victims, "Swan Song" won't make it past local markets. Femme lead Meral Oguz brightens up this first pic by young director Aydin Bagardi, but so-so helming and slight script don't add up to much.

Couple, who met in a London hospital, renew their brief acquaintance back in Turkey. He takes the affair more seriously and leaves his wife to shack up with her. She already is separated and on the surface remains more carefree.

It's a likable pic but not much more than that. Oguz is highly photogenic and throws herself into her role. As the steadfast Ömer, Haluk Bilginer mostly relies on his matinee idol looks.

Tech credits are of a commercial standard, with attractively bright lensing. Lack of progressive coughing into handkerchiefs is a bonus. — *Del.*

ELINE VERE
(DUTCH-BELGIAN-FRENCH)

A Cannon Tuschinski release of a Sigma-Silent Sunset-Odessa Films production in association with AVRO TV (Netherlands) and BRT TV (Belgium). Produced by Matthijs van Heijningen. Directed by Harry Kümel. Screenplay, Jan Blokker, with Patrick Pesnot, based on novel by Louis Couperus; camera (Agfa color), Eduard van der Enden; editor, Ludo Troch; music, Laurens van Rooyen; sound, Bruno Tarrière; production design, Ben van Os, Jan Roelfs; set dresser, Constance Vos; costume design, Yan Tax; production supervisor, Guurtje Buddenberg; production manager, Gerard Vercruysse; associate producers, Paula Breuls, Yannick Bernard; casting, Hans Kemna. Reviewed at Bellevue Cinerama, Amsterdam, March 6, 1991. Running time: **130 MIN.**
Eline Vere . . . . . . Marianne Basler
Betsy . . . . . . Monique van de Ven
Vincent . . . . Thom Hoffman
Henk . . . . Johan Leysen
Aunt Elise . . . . . . Aurore Clément
Mrs. van Raat . . . . Mary Dresselhuys
Lawrence Claire . . . . . Michael York
Jeanne . . . . Miryanne Boom
Also with: Bernard Kruysen, Herman Gillis, Joop Admiraal.

Aesthetically enthralling but less compelling dramatically, "Eline Vere" suffers from fragmentary storytelling and inability of its tragic heroine to elicit empathy. Still, pic's sheer beauty might attract fests and arthouses.

Directed by Belgian Harry Kümel with an elegance akin to novel's stylish prose, project is arguably the biggest artistic and financial challenge recently undertaken in feature production in the Low Countries.

Poet Louis Couperus' "Eline Vere" was avidly read by the Hague's leisured ladies when it first appeared in 1898 as a serial in a dignified daily. It held up a mirror to their fashionable society and emotional hang-ups. High schoolers still choose the weighty tome for their studies. A sizable (minority) audience in Holland and Flanders should be eager to see "Eline Vere" as a movie.

In the Hague at the end of the 19th century, where solid mansions house a notable coterie of wealthy bourgeois families, well-fed, well-dressed and stodgily self-satisfied, young and beautiful orphan Eline Vere (Marianne Basler) lives with her stern sister Betsy (Monique van de Ven) and admiring brother-in-law (Johan Leysen) in comfort, if not in harmony.

The only people Eline feels close to are her impoverished friend Jeanne (Miryanne Boom in a gem of a bit part) and her cynical cousin Vincent (smartly acted by Thom Hoffman), the black sheep of the family, utterly charming and perennially sponging. The scene is set for the romantic perils of Eline. They begin lightheartedly and end in self-destruction.

The emotional heroine is prone to fatal attractions. Three times she falls in love with the wrong man: first, a flamboyant opera singer who's old, ugly and vulgar; second, a wealthy gentleman who proves too dull; finally, the best of the lot, a likable and protective American (Michael York), who, alas, turns out to be romantically attached to Eline's cousin Vincent. When her last dream of love is shattered, Eline dies in a frenzy of despair — to the strains of Wagner's "Liebestod."

Pic shows the smooth cooperation of the screenwriters (Jan Blokker, Patrick Pesnot) and director. While the screenplay necessarily condensed Couperus' teeming multitude of minor characters, Kümel's mise-en-scène and judicious framing suggest the bustle of fashionable throngs at the seaside resort of Scheveningen, in cluttered ballrooms and salons.

Where Blokker's dialog injects an extra dose of irony, Kümel suggests feelings with music. But enticing imagery makes the film shine. Cinematographer Eduard van der Enden's near-impressionistic seascapes are especially memorable.

Production designers Ben van Os and Jan Roelfs (best known for Peter Greenaway pics) created the perfect illusion of overstuffed dwellings in the Hague, airier surroundings in the worldly city of Brussels where Eline enjoys the free and more frivolous atmosphere when she stays with her aunt and uncle.

Acting is very good generally. Eline's failure to convince is not the fault of Swiss-French actress Marianne Basler, who gives her best. Introducing a vivacious beauty revolting against her stifling environment instead of the languorous, neurotic girl readers pitied for nearly a century may have seemed a bright new idea, but it does not prepare auds for Eline's hallucinating insanity later on.

Hints of cousin Vincent's baleful influence are too fleeting to establish him as a dramatically potent embodiment of Eline's dark fate. French actress Aurore Clément trips away with acting honors as spirited, mischievous Aunt Elise, the very antidote to Eline's depressions.
— *Ewa.*

KISS ME A KILLER

A Califilm release. Executive producer, Mike Elliott. Produced by Catherine Cyran. Directed by Marcus DeLeon. Screenplay, Christopher Wooden, DeLeon; camera (Foto-Kem color), Nancy Schreiber; editor, Glenn Garland; associate editor, Richard Gentner; music, Nigel Holton; songs, Marcos Loya; sound (Ultra-Stereo), Chris Taylor; production design, James R. Shumaker; art direction, Amy B. Ancona; costume design, Meta Jardine; assistant director, Michael Upton; production manager, Michelle Weisler; choreographer, Renée Victor; stunt coordinator, Patrick J. Statham; 2nd unit director, Louis Morneau; 2nd unit camera, Chris Faloona; associate producer, Craig Nevius; casting, Steven Rabiner. Reviewed on vidcassette, N.Y., April 6, 1991. MPAA Rating: R. Running time: **92 MIN.**
Teresa . . . . Julie Carmen
Tony . . . . Robert Beltran
Jake Bozman . . . . Guy Boyd
Ramon . . . . Ramon Franco
Lt. Dennehy . . . . . Charles Boswell
Father Dominguez . . . . . Sam Vlahos
Tom . . . . Brad Blaisell
Pedro . . . . A.C. Santos
Pancho Sanchez . . . . Himself

An effective variation on themes by James Cain, "Kiss Me A Killer" brings film noir into a Latino neighborhood. New release from Califilm, a company affiliated with Roger Corman's Concorde Pictures, should score with the growing audience for steamy thrillers.

Pic is notable as a well-made quickie: Lensing began in January and finished product was already in theaters at the beginning of April.

Debuting helmer Marcus DeLeon's most obvious source inspiration is Cain's venerable "The Postman Always Rings Twice." This time around, the triangle is set in East L.A. where Anglo proprietor Guy Boyd runs a night club whose clientele is Hispanic.

He pushes around his beautiful young wife/employee Julie Carmen and takes an alternately paternalistic and hostile attitude towards his customers, largely determined by age (youngsters are treated as troublemakers and often prove to be).

Ex-con Robert Beltran insinuates himself into this little world when his guitar playing and singing voice earn him a job as a singer in Boyd's club. Carmen resists at first but soon is embroiled in a torrid love affair with Beltran. It doesn't take too long for the duo to cook up a scheme to bump off Boyd and live happily ever after running his night club together.

Serviceable script by Christopher Wooden and the director is convincing up to this point, but the coincidences and interventions of fate are tough to believe. Ironic ending plus a bittersweet coda work well enough, however. Compensating for the film's stretch of credibility are its frequent passionate love scenes featuring Carmen and Beltran. Both performers do a fine job, though the way DeLeon frames his shots implies that a body double was probably used for the topless footage of Carmen's character.

Beltran singing of several tunes penned by Marcos Loya is impressive. As the heavy, Boyd brings considerable depth to his part without turning it into being a good guy. Songs and dance sequences are a plus. — *Lor.*

CLASS OF NUKE 'EM HIGH PART II:
SUBHUMANOID MELTDOWN

A Troma release of a Lloyd Kaufman/Michael Herz production. Produced by Herz, Kaufman. Creative consulting producer, Glenn Green. Executive producers, Masahiro Ebisawa, Sammy O. Masada, Tetsu Fujimura. Directed by Eric Louzil. Screenplay, Kaufman, Louzil, Carl Morano, Marcus Roling, Jeffrey W. Sass, Matt Unger, from story by Kaufman, Morano, Unger; additional material written by Andrew Osborne; camera (TVC color), Ron Chapman; editor, Gordon Grinberg; music, Bob Mithoff; sound, N. Bruce Hively; production manager, Cheryl Pitkin; assistant director, Laura Cunniffe; line producer, Sass; associate producers, David Greenspan, Morano, Mark Richardson. Reviewed on vidcassette, N.Y., March 30, 1991. MPAA Rating: R. Running time: **95 MIN.**
Roger Smith . . . . . . Brick Bronsky
Prof. Holt . . . . Lisa Gaye
Victoria . . . . Leesa Rowland
Yoke . . . . Michael Kurtz
Dean Okra . . . . Scott Resnick
Prof. Jones . . . . . . Shelby Shepard
Diane . . . . . . Jacquelyn Rene Moen

Troma will have a hard time booking this unwarranted sequel, an incoherent mess that plays more like a trailer than a feature. Curiosity seekers in vidstores represent the target audience.

Presskit ludicrously credits director Eric Louzil with discovering Kevin Costner. Actually he held back the thesp's career by hiring him for a couple of exploitation films a decade ago. Louzil demonstrates here that he has no feel for satire or comedy, absolute prerequisites for a Troma pic. Instead most scenes consist of people running around aimlessly.

Beefcake star Brick Bronsky narrates a film-long flashback, a necessity given the lack of exposition in the live action. He's writing for the campus paper at Tromaville Institute of Technology, a combination college/nuclear power plant. Mad scientist Prof. Holt (attractive Lisa Gaye wearing piled up hairdo exaggerated from John Waters' "Hairspray") has created a race of drone subhumanoid workers, including beautiful Victoria (Leesa Rowland).

Unfortunately, they are subject to an ailment that causes them to melt into green goo. While Holt is working on the antidote, a squirrel turns into a Godzilla-type monster and stomps on some obvious miniatures.

An unfunny running gag insists on the subhumanoids having mouths where their belly buttons should be. This is an excuse for plenty of topless footage of starlets, including porn star Trinity Loren. Production is so sloppy that a scene of bald subhumanoids has one of them portrayed by porn actress Sharon Mitchell with her normal hairdo.

Lead cast members have trouble reading lines and the dumb sound effects aren't very funny. Makeup and stop-motion effects are strictly amateurish. — *Lor.*

MUUTTOLINNUN AIKA
(KATYA'S AUTUMN)
(FINNISH)

A Gaudeamus release of a Reppufilmi production. Produced by Petra Tarjanne. Directed by Anssi Mänttäri. Screenplay, Anssi Mänttäri; camera, Heikki Katajisto; editor, Timo Linnasalo; music, Asko Mänttäri; sound, Jussi Väntänen. Reviewed at Nordia theater, Tampere, March 30, 1991. Running time: **89 MIN.**
Katja . . . . Hanna Manu
Ossi . . . . Antti Litja
Mirjami . . . . Tarja Markus
Also with: Kari Heiskanen, Liisa Halonen, Vieno Saaristo, Heikki Peltonen.

"**K**atya's Autumn" is a warm, human comedy about a divorced family and subsequent father-daughter reunion. Comic elements and a tragic subplot are well-balanced.

This is the 13th film of Anssi Mänttäri, 49, one of the most productive Finnish filmmakers in the '80s. Most of his films have been intimate family studies, especially of broken marriages and aftermaths of divorce.

Katya, 17, has not seen her father since her parents went through a tumultuous divorce years earlier. The girl wants to get to know her father better and moves to his place. Mänttäri often portrays children as active operators who take the first steps in behalf of their hesitating parents, and Katya is no exception.

The father is a well-off man, who has the habits of a settled single. He is selfish and no longer used to making compromises or explaining his actions. He is a clumsy figure who has hidden his feelings behind his career.

Dark tones emerge in a subplot of a young couple living next door whose baby dies of cancer, and Mänttäri does not let emotions boil over

The director approaches his characters with understanding and a scarcely noticeable touch of irony. "Katya's Autumn" is a modest, but sympathetic film. It is serious without being earnest though occasionally it freezes to a few dead moments. — *Mapu.*

THE HECK WITH HOLLYWOOD!
(DOCU)

A Blockbusters production in association with WGBH Boston. Produced and directed by Doug Block. Camera (color), Block; editor, Deborah Rosenberg; music, Janice Kollar, Dick Solberg; sound, Judy Karp, Bill Neely; associate producers, Margaret Bruen, Susan Carucio. Reviewed at Berlin Film Festival (market), Feb. 22, 1991. Running time: **61 MIN.**

A documentary about the making and marketing of indie American feature films, "The Heck With Hollywood!" should be seen by every aspiring filmmaker. Both funny and saddening, the film already has been invited to several fests and should have a good career on video and tv.

Producer-director-cameraman Doug Block has selected three feature films: "Personal Foul," made in Rockford, Ill., by local boy Ted Lichtenheld, "Beirut: The Last Home Movie," helmed by Jennifer Fox; and "Only A Buck," a comedy directed by Gerry Cook, who's usually seen in the company of his lead actor and his accountant — they make a zany, good-natured trio.

Block discusses with all three directors their backgrounds and their objectives in making their films. In the case of "Personal Foul," he also talks to some of the project's investors. He then follows the filmmakers to the Independent Feature Film Market in New York, where their product is exposed to buyers for the first time.

The scenes in which nervous filmmakers anxiously await reactions from potential distribs are most effective.

"If I see another film about coming of age in rural America, I'm gonna puke!" Sam Kitt of Universal Pictures says of "Personal Foul." Other distribs, such as Ben Barenholtz of Circle Releasing, Janet Grillo of New Line, Barbara Simon of Double Helix and Derek Hill of Channel Four are kinder, but the message is basically the same.

Block follows through on the careers of all three films. "Personal Foul" is taken on board by Double Helix, but doesn't sit well in their library (mostly schlock films) and opens only in Rockford itself, to modest reactions and returns.

"Beirut: The Last Home Movie" wins a prize at the Sundance fest and is acquired by Circle Releasing, but the returns are disappointing. Cook and his friends decide to market "Only A Buck" themselves, touring the country in a decorated van (the Brickmobile) and flogging vidcassettes to the public.

Crock of gold at the end of the rainbow eludes all three, though at the outset they point out that the Coen brothers made it (with "Blood Simple") and so did Spike Lee ("She's Gotta Have It").

At the end, Litchtenheld seems crushed by the fact that few people get to see the movie he cared so much about. Fox relates how the business of marketing her film took over her personal life. And Cook and his friends wind up with a broken-down Brickmobile.

These are not American success stories, but the experiences are cautionary tales for other indie filmmakers, and Block relates these filmmakers' experiences with humor and sympathy. "The Heck With Hollywood!" deserves to be widely seen.
— *Strat.*

KIKUCHI
(TOKYO CLEANING MAN)
(JAPANESE)

A Vortex Japan production. Executive producer, Suichi Ohi. Written and directed by Kenchi Iwamoto. Camera (color), Hidyeo Fukuda; editor, Keiichi Okada; sound, Hidetoshi Nonaka; sound effects, Kaou Nakamura. Reviewed at Berlin Film Festival (Forum), Feb. 17, 1991. Running time: **68 MIN.**
Kikuchi . . . . Jiro Yoshimura
Man . . . . Yasuhiro Oka
Woman . . . . Misa Fukuma

A stylish, spare drama about the alienation of a Tokyo laundry worker, "Kikuchi" could find an arthouse following among hip urbanites. First-time helmer Kenchi Iwamoto, 30-year-old cartoonist/illustrator who has a cult following in Japan, is a man to keep an eye on.

His minimalist film drama borders on experimentalism without being pretentious, hip or obtuse.

Laundromat worker Kikuchi (Jiro Yoshimura) spends his days mechanically loading and unloading sheets into a long bank of dryers. Bland and unremarkable, he's practically incapable of interaction, either with other people or his environment.

He is secretly in love with a local supermarket checkout girl (Misa Fukuma), but finds himself incapable of making meaningful contact with her, limiting his relationship to voyeurism.

When a new employee (Yasuhiro Oka) is hired to work with Kikuchi, Kikuchi is supposed to train him, but their monosyllabic conversations soon stop entirely. The new worker seems uninterested in either the job or Kikuchi, and the two men avoid interaction, even eye contact, in the small work room. When Kikuchi discovers his new co-worker lives with the checkout girl, he is finally impelled to action.

Film is shot in long takes from a stationary camera. The lighting is flat and often monochromatic, and cuts are abrupt. Sound effects are exaggerated to an extreme degree, with all recording having been done in postproduction. The purr of a kitten that wanders into Kikuchi's apartment sounds like a menacing tiger, and when the creature scratches a straw mat, the sound level is booted up to the point that it sounds like heavy machinery.

Dialog is kept to a minimum, and the only music heard in the film is supermarket muzak, making the sound effects a very effective device in underlining the alienation of the characters and the starkness of the visuals.

Director Iwamoto manages to pull off the pic's stylishness without phoniness, never resorting to avant-garde pretension for its own sake. For all its experimentation, pic is always accessible.

The film was shot on a low budget, financed entirely by the people involved in the production. Iwamoto limited his crew to eight professionals whose average age was 25 and a support staff of film students.

Despite the budget and relative inexperience of the crew, nothing is amateur or lacking on the tech level. — *Reli.*

INTIMO
(MIDNIGHT SEDUCTION)
(ITALIAN)

A U.S. Media release of a Real Film production. Written and directed by Bob J. Ross. Camera (Luciano Vittori color), Franco Delli Colli; editor, Emanuele Foglietti; music performed by Liquid Eyes; sound, Antonio Brancaleone; production design-costumes, Antonio Marcon; assistant director, Alessandro Ojetti; production manager, Vincenzo Gallo; casting, Alberto Tarallo. Reviewed on MCTV-Viewer's Choice pay-per-view, N.Y., March 8, 1991. MPAA Rating: R. Running time: 72 MIN.
Tea . . . . Eva Grimaldi
Karl . . . . Leonardo Treviglio
Philippe . . . . Gabriele Gori
Portiere . . . . Thomas Arana
Lora . . . . Marisa Parra
Vera . . . . Monica Peracino
Simba . . . . Hernani Moreira
(English-dubbed soundtrack)

The Italian feature "Midnight Seduction" offers okay diversion for voyeurs as a direct to pay-per-view release Stateside, not available in other media such as vidstores.

Made in 1987 as "Intimo," film belongs to a then-popular genre in Italy, the thriller set in the world of fashion. Such pics as "A Taste For Fear" and Serena Grandi in Lamberto Bava's "Delirium" set the scene for this Eva Grimaldi-topliner.

Grimaldi portrays a night club waitress who has started moonlighting as a lingerie fashion model. She is harassed at both jobs by Leonardo Treviglio, a sleazy guy who ultimately seduces her with his lame come-on lines, notably "You're missing the best."

Film's most cryptic element involves a devil figure played by Thomas Arana, who works as the porter at Treviglio's hotel and intones portentously from time to time as if controlling the action. Film resolves cornily as Grimaldi goes back to her boyfriend after a fling on the wild side.

Punched up by some decadent musical numbers performed by Liquid Eyes, film (especially the curvaceous Grimaldi) is easy to watch. The main drawback is evident re-cutting for the U.S. market and an R rating.

Pic is typical of the sort of product in use for a decade in closed-circuit hotel situations for the tired traveler to watch. That's a natural niche for the burgeoning pay-per-view market; a month later Spectradyne supplies the similar "Forbidden Passion" in this same mode. — *Lor.*

IKI BASLI DEV
(PURGATORY)
(TURKISH)

An EKS production. Produced by Eris Akman. Directed by Orhan Oguz. Screenplay, Nuray Oguz; camera (color), Orhan Ogus; editor, Nevzat Disiacik; music, Daghan Baydur, Paul Bluckmaster; art director, Kamile Dagdemiren. Reviewed at 10th Istanbul Intl. Film Festival, March 28, 1991. Running time: 92 MIN.
Cengiz . . . . Cüneyt Arkin
Hakan . . . . Fikret Kuskan
Asir . . . . Sedef Ecer

Despite the turn-off Anglo title, there's nothing grim about "Purgatory." Well-scripted drama about a battle of wills between a father and son, and a young femme student who comes between them, looks set for fest outings.

Openings scenes sketch the tight macho world of a rich exec (Cüneyt Arkin) and his puppy-dog son (Fikret Kuskan): After the early-morning gym workout, it's chauffeured limos, power dressing and showing the workers who's boss. For relaxation, there's horseback riding, archery and postprandial games of chess.

The son's mother died years earlier in a car accident that also left the exec father blind, but that doesn't stop him from throwing his weight around.

Trouble starts when the son shows interest in a willful looker (Sedef Ecer) unfazed by dad's bullying. She's soon inviting herself to stay at their mansion, and after bedding the son tries her luck with dad. Latter drags his son off to the country for a dose of family tradition, but when that fails, scene is set for tragedy.

Apart from wooden playing in the early stages, Arkin is impressive as the overprotective father, especially when it's later revealed that he's a wimp compared with his own father. Ecer is striking as the sexual catalyst, and newcomer Kuskan suitably moody as the worm on the turn.

This is the third pic by former lenser Orhan Oguz, who debuted strongly four years ago with "Despite Everything." All tech credits are good, with Oguz himself handling photography. Script as usual by his wife Nuray, is lean and succinct.

Pic copped the Turkish jury's special prize at the Istanbul fest. Original title means "Two-Headed Giant," which better describes what's going on. — *Del.*

STREET SOLDIERS

An Academy Entertainment release of a Curb/Esquire Films presentation of an Action Bros. production. Executive producers, Maria Lim, D.S. Kim. Produced by Jun Chong. Directed and edited by Lee Harry. Screenplay, Spencer Grendahl, Harry, from Chong's story; camera (Image Transform color; Foto-Kem prints), Dennis Peters; music, David Bergeaud; sound (Ultra-Stereo), Diana Flores; production design, Matthew Jacobs; art direction, David Koneff; costume design, Anett Murray; assistant director, Phil Robinson, Terry Benedict; production manager-co-producer, Eric A. Gage; fight choreography, Chong; 2nd unit director-stunt coordinator, Kim Kahana; 2nd unit camera, Bruce L. Finn; line producer, David Chong; associate producer, Sherry Martin. Reviewed on Academy vidcassette, N.Y., March 23, 1991. MPAA Rating: R. Running time: 98 MIN.
Master Han . . . . Jun Chong
Priest . . . . Jeff Rector
Troy . . . . David Homb
Max . . . . Johnathan Gorman
Charles . . . . Joon Kim
Julie . . . . . . Katherine Armstrong
Tok . . . . Jason Hwang
Spider . . . . Jude Gerard
Marie . . . . Deborah Newmark
Wheelchair Willie . . . Jay Richardson
Also with: Joel Weiss, Frank Novak.

"Street Soldiers" delivers the goods as a diverting gang picture. Recently opened theatrically in St. Louis, its lack of name talent marks it better suited for vid fans.

L.A.-set piece adheres to the successful formula of violence begetting violence. In this case, producer Jun Chong runs a karate school and trains the clean-cut Tigers gang to fight the nasty Pee-wees after latter kill his nephew Joon Kim.

Along the way heroine Deborah Newmark is gang-raped by evil Jeff Rector and his henchmen, while Rector stops at nothing to win back his g.f. Katherine Armstrong.

Punctuated by well-staged rumbles (with Chong also handling fight choreography), film sidesteps the usual whites vs. blacks vs. Hispanics content of this genre in favor of warring Caucasian gangs. The producers are Korean and their brand of martial arts informs the action.

With gruff voice and mannered thesping, Rector is too much under the sway of Mickey Rourke to be credible as lead villain. Rest of the cast is okay.

Pic benefits from a strong background score of songs (one contributed by director Lee Harry), tied into a soundtrack album on Curb Records (Curb/Esquire Films is pic's international sales outfit). — *Lor.*

MANGE FLAGG—
INGEN GRENSER
(MANY FLAGS—NO BORDERS)
(NORWEGIAN-DOCU)

A Kikki Engelbrektson and Svein Traelvik production in association with Norsk Filmstudio and the Norwegian Broadcasting Corp. Written and directed by Engelbrektson. Camera (color), Rolf Larsen; additional camera, Harald Paalgard; editor, Arne Johnny Karlsson; music, Egil Kapstad; sound, Engelbrektson, Tom Sassebo; model construction, Per Hjort. Reviewed at Saga Cinema, Oslo, Feb. 20, 1991. Running time: 97 MIN.

While dealing with the fourth Norwegian Antarctic expedition (1989-90), this docu-sometimes is more concerned with the participants' peculiarities than the continent they're exploring. This allows for some unpretentious comedy, but weakens pic's docu quality.

The scientists exude good humor and harbor no grandiose notions about their importance (no Amundsen and Scott heroics here). Mood is closer to a typical outing with the Norwegians treating the Antarctic as a colder, drier and bigger version of home.

The most impressive scenes concern a huge colony of birds situated so far inland they have to fly for days to find food, so the bird death rate is high. Pic assumes a tone of ghostly fascination in the carcasses of thousands of birds, which do not decompose in the dry, cold and microbe-free climate. Mummified, they stay alongside the living members of the colony forever.

Structuring the material around the ongoing introduction of new expedition members and new endeavors was a mistake. Pic tries to cover too many scientific disciplines to do any of them justice. The attempt at the history and politics of the Antarctic also is lacking.

Still, the impressive documentary provides fresh insights into the objectives and mentality of Antarctic explorers. — Olav.

BANDIDOS
(BANDITS)
(MEXICAN)

A Bandidos Films-Mexican Film Institute (Imcine)-FFCC-Televisión Española (TVE) production. Executive producers, Hugo Rodríguez, Emilia Arau. Directed by Luis Estrada. Screenplay, Estrada, Jaime Sanpietro; camera (color), Emmanuel Lubezki; editor, Estrada, Juan Carlos Martín; music, Santiago Ojeda; sound, Salvador de la Fuenta; art direction, Brigitte Brouch. Reviewed at Estudios Churubusco, Mexico City, March 15, 1991. Running time: **105 MIN.**
Luis . . . . Eduardo Toussaint
Miguel . . . . Jorge A. Poza Pérez
Martin . . . . Alan Gutiérrez
Priest . . . . . . Pedro Armendáriz Jr.
Cacho . . . . Daniel Jiménez
Bandit . . . . Ernesto Yánez

In essence a children's pic, Luis Estrada's second feature venture "Bandidos" is a well-developed film that should find crossover acceptance. Unfortunately, its frequent depiction of graphic violence may scare off some potential markets.

Set against the turbulence of the 1910 Mexican Revolution, story begins when young Luis (Eduardo Toussaint) is left alone after bandits plunder his rural boarding school, killing his teachers and classmates. He is later discovered by a trio of secondary bandits, who arrive to pick over the remains.

Led by Miguel (Jorge A. Poza Pérez), the trio ranges in ages from about 7 to 13. In an effort to return home, Luis joins them and soon the quartet fall into various picaresque adventures. A rivalry between Miguel and Luis is averted and the two become fast friends.

Their main enemies are the adult bandits, led by Cacho (Daniel Jiménez), a wild murderer who loves nothing more than a good slaughter. He taunts

young Miguel about his mother, claiming to be the boy's possible father.

But this is no father-son reunion, and an eventual shootout between groups leaves only Luis and Miguel to pursue a Butch Cassidy-Sundance Kid notoriety as they inflict terror to travelers, attracting the attention of both the national press and federal police.

Helmer Luis Estrada maintains a firm grip on the story, which is well handled and amusing throughout. Adult material, such as the violence depicted during the sacking of the school or when the two oldest boys lose their virginity at the hands of an itinerate hooker, may affect sales.

Emmanuel Lubezki's lush lensing provides a rich patina to the Mexican countryside, while Santiago Ojeda's mostly guitar-picking score has a nice down-home feel. Child actors Toussaint and Poza Pérez are always believable. — Lent.

BLOBERMOUTH

An L.A. Connection-Kent Skov production. Produced by Jack H. Harris. Directed by Kent Skov. Screenplay, Steven L. Rothman, Steve Pinto, Robert Bucholz, Skov, based on their play by the L.A. Connection; editor, Chris Roth; music editor, Jim Mandell; animation, Jean-Guy Jacque, Craig Berkos; coproducer, Judith Parker Harris. Reviewed at Florence Film Festival, Nov. 29, 1990. Running time: **86 MIN.**
With the voices of: Robert Bucholz (Steve McQueen), Frances Kelly (Vaccine), Stephen L. Rothman (the sheriff).

"Blobermouth," a revisitation of horror classic "The Blob," should be of more than passing interest to cult film fans, but the clever idea of redubbing the original pic with new dialog is interesting only until the novelty wears off — which takes about 10 minutes.

Jack H. Harris, producer of "The Blob," turned the cult classic over to helmer Kent Skov and the L.A. Connection, the group that redubbed old pics for a local tv series called "Mad Movies" in 1986. Dialog offers a few chuckles and smart lampoons of 1950s smalltown life in America, but the comic setup soon gets bogged down in an endless goo of juvenile gags.

This time around, Steve McQueen is "re-cast" as a strug-

gling, hopelessly nerdy comedian getting ready to debut in a one-man show. But the Blob hits town with a series of one-liners (credited to Henny Youngman) and quickly steals the show from Steve. Instead of trying to convince the authorities that the

Original Film
THE BLOB
(1958)

Paramount release of a Jack H. Harris production. Stars Steve McQueen; co-stars Aneta Corseaut, Earl Rowe. Directed by Írvin S. Yeaworth Jr. Screenplay, Theodore Simonson and Kate Phillips, from idea by Irvine H. Millgate; camera (DeLuxe Color), Thomas Spalding; music, Jean Yeaworth; song, Bert Bachrach, Mack David; editor, Alfred Hillmann. Tradeshown in N.Y., Sept. 4, '59. Running time: **85 MIN.**
Steve . . . . Steven McQueen
Judy . . . . Aneta Corseaut
Police Lieut. . . . . Earl Rowe
Old Man . . . . Olin Howlin

Blob menaces the town as per the original, Steve tries to rally townsfolk to come to see his show before the Blob can steal his audience.

The Blob issues his tacky one-liners from a little red animated mouth and at times is quite funny: It ends up with a spot on "The Tonight Show." When the Blob is not on screen (which is most of the time), however, action drags and wafer-thin plot has nowhere to go. Sound recording of new dialog is poor, but generally is matched to lip movements.
— Clrk.

COMO SER MUJER Y NO MORIR EN EL INTENTO
(HOW TO BE A WOMAN AND NOT DIE TRYING)
(SPANISH)

An Iberoamericana Films-Atrium-IDEA production in association with Televisión Española. Executive producer, Andrés Vicent Gómez. Directed by Ana Belén. Screenplay, Carmen Rico-Godoy, based on her book; camera (Eastmancolor), Juan Amorós; editor, Carmen Frías; music, Antonio García de Diego, Pancho Varona, Mariano Diaz; sound, Gilles Ortión; sets, Gerardo Vera; production supervisor, José G. Jacoste; production manager, Rafael Fernández. Reviewed at Cine Palafox, Madrid, April 4, 1991. Running time: **83 MIN.**
Carmen . . . . Carmen Maura
Antonio . . . . Antonio Resines
Mariano . . . . Juanjo Puigcorvé
Chelo . . . . Carmen Conesa
Emilia . . . . Tina Sainz

Also with: Paco Casares, Victor García, Olalla Aguirre, Juan Diego Botto, Luis Pérez Agua, Asunción Balaguer, Enriqueta Carballeira, Miguel Rellán, Mercedes Lezcano.

The packaging and even the title of this pic are redolent of Almodóvar, as is the presence of Carmen Maura in the title role. But there the similiarity ends in this clumsy directorial bow by singer-thesp Ana Belén.

Instead of wit and inventiveness, pic plods along heavyhandedly in a seemingly endless succession of marital bickering and nagging. There are elements espousing women's lib, and critiques of modern life, and even occasional touches of humor, but the script goes nowhere and the characters are drawn paper thin.

More pointedly, pic never explains "How To Be A Woman" or how to grapple with the multiple problems of womanhood, marriage and domestic life. From beginning to end, the relationship rings false and unbelievable, a case of miscasting more than mismarriage.

The non-story concerns a married couple bored of each other. They are eternally irked, resentful and ill-humored, but the nonstop bickering, surveyed through the four seasons of the year, never comes to a head and the relationship never develops or climaxes. By the end of the film their discontent is as vapid as it was at the beginning.

Antonio Resines is unconvincingly cast as a record producer, and Carmen Maura as a journalist: They might as well have been told to play a warrior and a nun. He is his usual wooden self, and even her ebullience can't save this misguided effort at humor and social comment from tedium.

As if the rambling script were not bad enough, Belén's direction is nonexistent, and the technical credits, ranging from flat camerawork and lighting to pointless music, are embarrassingly bad. — Besa.

HARUKANARU KOSHIEN
(ROAR OF THE CROWD)
(JAPANESE)

A Daiei Co. Ltd. production. Executive producer, Yasuyoshi Tokuma. Produced by Yo Yamamoto, Fumito Shimizu, Hideo Abe. Directed by Yutaka Osawa. Screenplay, Takeo Kunihiro, based on novel by Takuji Ohno and comic strip by Osamu Yamamoto, Yoshinari Tobe; camera (color), Shun Yamamoto; editor, Yoshio Sugano; music, Kensaku Tanigawa; sound, Kazuharu Urata; production design, Terumi Hosoishi; assistant director, Yuji Asakura. Reviewed at Berlin Film Festival (Panorama), Feb. 25, 1991. Running time: **100 MIN.**

With: Tomokazu Miura, Misako Tanaka, Mayumi Ogawa, Hitoshi Ueki, Shigeru Kohyama, Akira Emoto, Yasufumi Hayashi, Tomoko Ohtakara.

A formula pic about students at a school for the deaf and dumb who form a baseball team and enter a national event, "Roar Of The Crowd" is handled in routine style.

The true story already has been immortalized in a popular book and a comic strip. On screen, the obstacles facing the handicapped boys on their road to baseball glory are sympathetically but uninvolvingly presented.

A further dimension is given to the story in that the large number of deaf children near Okinawa, where the story is set, stemmed from an outbreak of German measles at the U.S. base there in 1964, which spread to the local population.

The youngsters, many of them obviously genuinely handicapped, enter into the spirit of the film with enthusiasm.

The numerous baseball sequences might give this film a limited chance Stateside, but a fresher approach on the part of director Yutaka Osawa would have lifted the ordinary goings-on to a more interesting level. — *Strat.*

ABRAXUS, GUARDIAN OF THE UNIVERSE
(CANADIAN)

A Cineplex Odeon Films release (in Canada) of a Rose & Ruby Production. Produced by Damien Lee, David Mitchell, Curtis Peterson. Executive producer, Alexander Ruge. Written and directed by Lee. Camera (color), Peterson; editor, Reid Dennison; music, Carlos Lopez; sound, Alban Streeter; art direction, Michael Borthwick; special effects, Ron Craig, Stan Zuwala. Reviewed at Cineplex Odeon Eaton Center, Toronto, March 6, 1991. MPAA Rating: PG. Running time: **90 MIN.**

Abraxus . . Jessie (The Body) Ventura
Sonja . . . . Marjorie Bransfield
Secundus . . . . Sven-Ole Thorsen
Tommy . . . . Francis Mitchell
Hite . . . . Jerry Levitan

Also with the voices of: Marilyn Lightstone, Moses Znaimer.

Limp script and direction, two-bit special effects and wooden acting all make "Abraxus, Guardian Of The Universe" a waste of everyone's time and money. The indie Canadian low-budgeter is an MCA Home Video release.

Sci-fi misadventure has two former friends, cops of the universe, alighting on a small town on Earth to play out their final battle. Bad cop (Scandinavian-born Sven-Ole Thorsen) impregnates a local by just touching her stomach. She gives birth in a few seconds because good cop (pro wrestler Jessie Ventura) is too sensitive to kill her as his inner computer directs him.

Guided by his own inner computer, Thorsen returns years later to wrest from the boy what's called an anti-life equation that "if unleashed could shatter worlds." Ventura's on his trail, but, deprived of his power source, must fight the villain like a human.

After many chases, and falling in love with the mother, he kills the more-powerful baddie. The boy (Francis Mitchell), too frightened by powers he doesn't understand to speak, mouths his first words at fadeout.

Ventura and his inner computer remain on Earth, presumably to forever protect mother and son. Only the separate internal gizmos display a spark of life. They are voiced by an unseen Marilyn Lightstone and Moses Znaimer, who heads Canada's Much Music and Musique Plus specialty tv services and also Toronto's UHFer CITY TV.
— *Adil.*

ATHINAYI
(ATHENIANS)
(GREEK)

A Greek Film Center-La Sept-V. Alexakis & Co. production. Executive producer, Nikos Yannopoulos. Written and directed by Vassilis Alexakis. Camera (color), Andreas Bellis; editor, Giorgos Mavropsaridis; music, Lucianos Kelaidonis; music performed by Vassilis Ginos; sound, Dimitris Galanopoulos; sound editing, Elvira Varela; sound mixing, Thanassis Arvanitis; sets, Damianos Zarifis; choreography, Yannis Flery; production manager, Dionyssis Samiotis; casting, Haris Papadopoulos. Reviewed at Amalia Theater, Athens, Feb. 26, 1991. Running time: **88 MIN.**

Panos . . . . Antonis Kafetzopoulos
Antigoni . . . . Nadia Marouzi
Menas . . . . Giorgos Constas
Mother . . . . . . Voula Zoumboulaki

Also with: Mania Papadimitriou, Athinodoros Proussalis, Costas Tsakonas, Takis Moschos, Giorgos Ninios.

Despite a rousing start, invigorating score and talented cast, "Athenians" essentially is the story of a tired city. It should have modest success on the homefront, based on appeal of in-jokes and popular thesps, but offshore prospects seem limited to small screens.

Menas (Giorgos Constas) and wife (Mania Papadimitriou) live in a cramped semi-basement apartment. Opening scenes of their awakening to the smell of exhaust fumes and the sight of an apple core thrown in their window are given added zest by the powerful orchestration of popular composer Lucianos Kelaidonis.

Menas is in cahoots with brother-in-law Panos (Antonis Kafetzopoulos), a nimble con man who masterminds a robbery scheme.

Much of the humor is provided by veteran actor Kafetzopoulos' facial expressions and body language as he pilfers his way around town, conning amorous couples and garrulous mothers in the process.

Constas also has his moments, as love-smitten Menas courts an exotic, discontented actress (Nadia Marouzi) indifferent to his advances. Another subplot, involving Panos' visits to his dying father, includes funny sight gags laden with black humor.

Unfortunately, pic's initial promise never is fulfilled. It becomes apparent midway through that little substance lies beneath the film's frills, and the many subplots simply don't cohere. The long-awaited heist, staged at a theater during a performance, proves to be anticlimactic.

Tech credits are impressive with outstanding lensing by Andreas Bellis. — *Sam.*

LA PARTITA
(THE GAMBLE)
(ITALIAN)

A Prism Entertainment release, distributed by Paramount Home Video, of a Cecchi Gori Group Tiger Cinematografica, Reteitalia presentation. Executive producer, Aldo Santarelli. Produced by Mario and Vittorio Cecchi Gori. Directed by Carlo Vanzina. Screenplay, Enrico Vanzina, Carlo Vanzina, Livia Giampalmo, based on Alberto Ongaro's novel; camera (Cinecittà color), Luigi Kuveiller; editor, Ruggero Mastroianni; music, Pino Donaggio; sound (Dolby), Carlo Palmieri, Piero Fondi; art direction, Paola Comencini; costumes, Roberto Guidi Di Bagno. Reviewed on Prism videcassette, N.Y., Jan. 19, 1990. MPAA Rating: R. Running time: **103 MIN.**

Francesco . . . . Matthew Modine
Olivia . . . . Jennifer Beals
Countess . . . . Faye Dunaway

Also with: Corinne Cléry, Federica Moro, Ana Obregon, Vernon Wells, Feodor Chaliapin, Gianfranco Barra, Karina Huff, Cyrus Elias, Ian Bannen, Marco Stefanelli, Claudia Lawrence, Nazareno Natale, Claudio Lorimer.

Matthew Modine's enthusiasm is the distinguishing feature of "The Gamble," a.k.a. "The Match," a lush-looking but empty Italian film aimed at the world market.

It probably would take a filmmaker of Stanley Kubrick's caliber, in a "Barry Lyndon" mood, to put across this stale material of a young rake in period dress gamboling across the Italian countryside with mean Faye Dunaway in pursuit. Casting Yank talent is not enough to crack the U.S. market, where pic recently bowed in vidstores.

Modine's tragic error is gambling with noblewoman Dunaway after she's cleaned out his dad (Ian Bannen). To make the wager interesting (they're gambling with spinning tops instead of dice), he has to bet himself and she wins.

Modine violently escapes the villainess' clutches, and "Gamble" turns into a medieval road movie. In Verona, he teams up with Jennifer Beals and duo is pursued by Dunaway's evil henchmen.

Along the way, Modine has sexual dalliances with many beautiful women, including French "Story Of O" star Corinne Cléry. When Dunaway finally catches up with him, the payoff is a throwback to her campy "The Wicked Lady" image as she bests him in a swordfight. Finale is very disappointing.

Modine is dashing, but like the other American lead players, he is not convincing in the role as they use no accents. Supporting cast is dubbed acceptably into English, but some convention should have been followed to develop convincing Italian roles. Dunaway and Beals are glamorous, and the locations an eyeful.
— *Lor.*

ARUS
(THE BRIDE)
(IRANIAN)

A Mahab Film production. Directed by Behruz Afkhami. Screenplay, Afkhami, Alireza Davudnezhad; camera (color),

Nemat Haghighi; editor, Mohammad-Reza Moini; music, Babak Bayat; sound, Es'hagh Khanzadi; set design, Abdolmajid Ghadirian; makeup, Abdollah Eskandari; special effects, Mehdi Bahmanpoor; production manager, Zia Hashemi. Reviewed at the Fajr Intl. Film Festival, Teheran, Feb. 8, 1991. Running time: **85 MIN.**

With: Abolfazl Poorarab, Niki Karimi, Abbas Amiri, Ali Sajjadi.

"Macbeth" meets "Romeo And Juliet" in this stinging portrait of rigid marriage rituals in Iran. "The Bride" has potential, but not in the West.

A young actor playing Macbeth in a university stage production realizes his thesp income does not impress his loved one's dad. So he quits theater to become a businessman, even if that means selling medicine on the black market during the Iran-Iraq war. All this is told in flashback.

Pic begins with a wedding and the newlyweds heading to the sea on their honeymoon. In a bizarre nuptial conversation, groom doesn't promise bride love or romance, but her own Mercedes. Doom is on the horizon.

Driving like a madman, the husband hits an old woman and flees. Begging him to return and accusing him of being inhuman, the bride begins to realize she's married a stranger, not the actor she fell in love with. He's unwilling to risk losing his possessions to save a nobody.

However, the bride (a liberated woman by Iranian standards) is willing to risk all to save the old woman. She sneaks off and cashes in her husband's life savings to pay for the woman's hospital bills.

The enraged hubbie gets violent with her in-laws while trying to find her, but he ends up disillusioned, even repentant. There's no happy ending as he finally drives alone (in his Mercedes) into a dark tunnel.

Pic is typical of this year's crop of Iranian pics, which question tradition, corruption, greed and love. Tech credits also are typical: Iranian equipment (as underlined by the Farabi Cinema foundation topper in a public speech) is outdated. Script is underdeveloped, but the moral of the story is steadfast and simple. Outside Islamic territories, the film's potential is limited to specialized venues. — *Suze.*

FANTOZZI COLPISCE ANCORA
(FANTOZZI STRIKES BACK)
(ITALIAN)

A Penta Distribuzione release of a Cecchi Gori Group-Maura Intl. Film production. Produced by Mario and Vittorio Cecchi Gori for Penta Film-Silvio Berlusconi Communications. Executive producers, Bruno Altissimi, Claudio Saraceni. Directed by Neri Parenti. Screenplay, Leo Benvenuti, Piero De Bernardi, Alessandro Bencivenni, Domenico Saverni, Neri Parenti, Paolo Villaggio; camera (color), Sando D'Eva; editor, Sergio Montanari; music, Bruno Zambrini; set decoration, Maria Stilde Ambruzzi; costumes, Fiamma Bedendo; production manager, Maurizio Pastrovich. Reviewed at Cassio theater, Rome, Jan. 29, 1991. Running time: **105 MIN.**
Fantozzi . . . . Paolo Villaggio
Pina . . . . Milena Vukotic
Mariangela . . . . . . Plinio Fernando
Filini . . . . Gigi Reder
Giudice . . . . . . Silvia Annichiarico
Sad man . . . . Paul Muller
Hooligan . . . . Piero Villaggio
Miss Silvani . . . . Anna Mazzamauro

Continuing popularity of Paolo Villaggio's perennial underdog put the seventh installment of the series among the Italo season's top-grossing films. The hapless hero is endearing as ever, but "Fantozzi Strikes Back," basically a compendium of gags strung together by pointed social satire, is strictly for local consumption.

Fantozzi has spent his life as a mistreated accountant in a huge, dehumanizing corporation. His dormant self-pride is finally roused when the company topper singles him out at the annual staff meeting as the perfect example of a "failed human being."

From then on, film chronicles Fantozzi's clumsy attempts to avenge himself and gain self-esteem.

One typical sequence has his painfully ugly daughter chosen to star in a film at Cinecittà (a takeoff on Visconti's classic "Bellissima"), making Fantozzi dream of becoming a famous agent. But the film turns out to be "The Planet Of The Apes," and Fantozzi's mousey wife Pina convinces him to take their primate-like daughter off the set.

Fantozzi tries to redeem himself by doing jury duty in a Mafia trial and resisting all attempts to corrupt him, but in the end, of course, he succumbs.

Not to be discouraged, he convinces a local soccer hooligan (played by Villaggio's son Piero) to teach him how to be a thug, but inevitably fails when he robs the wrong person.

Predictable series of situations conclude in the only way a Fantozzi film can — with Villaggio back where he started from, unavenged. Rome locations accurately mirror the boredom and claustrophobia of the capital's *petit bourgeois* suburbs, and technical credits are all sharp.
— *Clrk.*

SKI SCHOOL
(CANADIAN)

A Moviestore Entertainment release of a Rose & Ruby production. Executive producer, Jeff Sackman. Produced and directed by Damian Lee. Screenplay, David Mitchell; camera (color), Curtis Petersen (Canada), Roxanne Di Santo (L.A.); editor, Reid Dennison; supervising editor, Robert Gordon; music, Steven Hunter; music supervision, Dan Howell, Jill Starr; sound, Michael Williamson (Canada), Bill Robbins (L.A.); art direction, Craig MacMillan; costume design, Kate Healey (Canada), Madeline Kozlowski (L.A.); assistant director, Steven Janisch (Canada), Robert Lee (Portland), J.B. Rogers (L.A.); production manager, Armand Leon (Canada), Adam Moos (L.A.); 2nd unit director, Petersen (Canada), Dean Lyras (Portland), Steve Barnett (L.A.); 2nd unit camera, David Pelletier; casting, Fiona Jackson, Betsy Fels. Reviewed on HBO vidcassette, N.Y., March 4, 1991. MPAA Rating: R. Running time: **88 MIN.**
Dave . . . . Dean Cameron
Johnny Roland . . . . . Tom Breznahan
Ed . . . . Patrick Labyorteaux
Reid . . . . Mark Thomas Miller
Lori . . . . Darlene Vogel
Paulette . . . . Charlie Spradling
Victoria . . . . Ava Fabian
Derek . . . . Spencer Rochfort
Fitz . . . . Stuart Fratkin
Bridget . . . . Gaetana Korbin
Brice . . . . Mark High
Also with: Alison Dobie, Stacey Brink, Kate Healey, Karen Isaaks, Christina Marazzo.

Though it flopped at the boxoffice in January, "Ski School" looms as a hotsy home-video entry and has enough t&a content to qualify as a paycable latenight perennial.

Film is a by-the-numbers version of the successful teen comedy formula that has led to numerous spring break films set in Florida or Texas, as well as the very similar 1984 hit "Hot Dog . . . The Movie." It's not related to a never-realized 1988 Claudio Guzman project also titled "Ski School" that was slated to shoot in Chile.

Disjointed plotline pits hotshot skier Mark Thomas Miller (the hissable bad guy) and his crew against party animal Dean Cameron (the sort of good guy) and his boys at a ski school at Whistler mountain. Cameron's practical jokes are set off too early to develop the suspense of a "Revenge Of The Nerds"-style comedy.

Instead, well-executed ski stunt scenes alternate with party or sex footage. Pic's most dated aspect is a recurring gag mocking the lambada craze, which already seems like a relic from far longer than just a year ago.

Technical credits are fine, though Canadian filmmaker Damian Lee's structuring of the picture is quite haphazard. Except for dangerous-looking stuntwork, the final reels are anticlimactic.
— *Lor.*

UNTERGÅNGENS ARKITEKTUR
(THE ARCHITECTURE OF DOOM)
(SWEDISH-DOCU)

A Poj Filmproduktion AB-Schwedisches Filminstitut-Swedisches Fernsehen-Kanal 1-Sandrew Film & Theatre production. (Intl. sales: Swedish Film Institute.) Written, produced and directed by Peter Cohen. Camera (color, b&w), Mikael Cohen, Gerhard Fromm, Peter Östlund; sound, Klas Dykhoff; music performed by the Symphony Orchestra of Schwedische Rundfunk; German-language narration, Bruno Ganz. Reviewed at the Berlin Film Festival (Forum), Feb. 17, 1991. No MPAA rating: Running time: **119 MIN.**

A small masterpiece of scholarship and imagination comprised largely of long-lost archival images, "The Architecture Of Doom" takes an amazing look at the Third Reich from the point of view of aesthetics, particularly Hitler's. This fest circuit natural also should get arthouse play.

With shockingly accurate logic and a wealth of visual material, filmmaker Peter Cohen posits a strong new answer to the question of how it could have happened in the first place. He also shows how Germany's aesthetic ultimately proved suicidal.

As a young man in Austria, Adolf Hitler, a painter of postcard quality architectural views, was denied admittance to the Academy of Art and embarked upon another career path. "The Architecture Of Doom" examines how the Nazi aesthetic, informed by *petit bourgeois* values of kitsch, sentimentality and a pathological obsession with cleanliness led Germany into war with the world and paved the path to genocide.

Hitler's fixation with art and beauty spurred him to design Nazi uniforms and flags (his own sketches are shown), and mastermind parades and exhibitions. He often acquired paintings by the dozen for his personal collection, most reeking with cheap sentimentality.

Also crucial is what Hitler did not consider to be art or beauty. Pic displays one by one the pseudo-scientific comparisons Nazi Party doctors made between sufferers of real psychological and physical handicaps and figures painted by "degenerate" modern artists.

Such comparisons, argue the filmmaker, led to the massive euthanasia campaign in which thousands of the mentally handicapped were murdered in secret hospitals.

The status of the doctor as demigod and the eradication of filth was of primary importance. As Nazi propaganda films were literally comparing Jews with rats, the zyklon gas that would later be used in concentration camps was being used to rid factories of rats. All of this is illustrated in the film through archival footage. Cohen makes the complicated case that the Germans developed a notion of war as a way to cleanse the world, and thereby to make it beautiful.

The filmmaker spent four years making his case by systematically searching through archives and private collections throughout Europe, uncovering hitherto unknown and unpublished visual material which comprises much of the film. Otherwise, docu uses clips from films, photos and paintings of the time.

Musical score by Hector Berlioz and Nazi favorite Richard Wagner is effective. — *Reli.*

MENEKSE KOYU
(VIOLET BAY)
(TURKISH-SWEDISH)

Produced by Konsept Film (Istanbul), Oberon & Son and Film Teknik (Stockholm). (Intl. sales: Dünya Haklari.) Executive producer, Onat Kutlar. Directed by Barbro Karabuda. Screenplay, Karabuda, based on short story "Still Waters" by Yasar Kemal; camera (color), Gunes Karabuda; editor, Tord Paag; music, Alfons; sound (Dolby), Bengt Sall, Mikael Lundin, Gunnar Nilsson, Thomas Huhn; art direction, Gürel Yontan. Reviewed at 10th Istanbul Intl. Film Festival (competition), March 26, 1991. Running time: **87 MIN.**
Kerem . . . . Sven Wollter
Neriman . . . . Türkan Soray
Rustem . . . . Macit Koper
Hasan . . . . Yavuzer Cetinkaya
Karakiz . . . . Vildan Kara

Also with: Kadir Savun, Lale Oraloglu, Erol Günaydin, Ozan Bilen.

"**V**iolet Bay," adaptation of revered author Yasar Kemal's short story about a mysterious stranger's attempt to settle in a small fishing village, is initially fragmented but gains strength and coherence in the second half. Performances also improve as pic unfolds, but chances for offshore theatrical release are slim.

Kerem (convincingly portrayed by sexy Swede Sven Wollter) arrives in a rugged coastal settlement in a small caique and immediately stakes out a plot of land on a hill. Under cover of darkness, he earnestly fashions mortar and bricks into a house, thinking it would be allowed to remain under an ordinance protecting shanties built in one night on unincorporated land.

Off-camera inhabitants' disembodied voices, conveying the constant banter in provincial communities, reveals Kerem is building on state land. Soon his house is demolished, though he tries to block the bulldozer's path` la "Grapes Of Wrath."

Undaunted, Kerem builds another abode, paints it a cheerful shade of peach and adorns it with playful paintings, a fitting symbol for his renewed hope. He gains acceptance from the skeptical villagers by unselfishly helping neighbors with large and small tasks.

However, when he abandons repair of Hasan's hurdy-gurdy to save Karakiz, a mentally defective young woman who is drowning, he gains her puppy-like devotion but incenses sleazy Hasan who waits for revenge.

Plot begins to make sense as Kerem's voluptuous wife Neriman (popular star Türkan Soray) arrives with their two children. Ill at ease in the small community and instantly causing tongues to wag, she becomes short-tempered and critical of Kerem's constant efforts to aid neighbors.

Fed up, Neriman leaves Kerem to live in Germany. He falls apart and tries to drown his sorrow in wine, living in total disarray and almost completely ignoring the children. He initially disdains Karakiz' efforts to look after the kids. Eventually, they become lovers.

A confrontation occurs when Neriman returns with babe in arms. Per local gossip, she had

the baby by a villager who ran off with her, but she insists to Kerem it's his.

Tech credits are uneven in Swede documentarist Barbro Karabuda's feature debut. Husband Gunes Karabuda's camerawork is fine, but son Alphons' overbearing synthesizer score cheapens the total effect, essentially defeating the purpose of the first Turkish movie with Dolby sound. — *Sam.*

CHUJIA NÜ
(THE GIRLS TO BE MARRIED)
(CHINESE-HONG KONG)

A Pearl River Studio (China)-Sil-Metropole (H.K.) production. Produced by Zhao Qingqiang. Executive producers, Huang Lanjin, Zhang Xinyan. Directed by Wang Jin. Screenplay, He Mengfan, from a short story by Ye Weilin; camera (color), Zhao Xiaoshi; editor, Yan Xiuying, Zeng Shiwei; music, Wang Shi; sound, Deng Qinghua; art director, He Qun; costume design, Wang Jishu, Huang Jiakang; assistant director, Weng Yanmei. Reviewed on Pearl River vidcassette, London, March 10, 1991. (At Montpellier Film Festival, France.) Running time: **96 MIN.**
Ming Tao . . . . Shen Rong
Ai Yue . . . . Tao Huimin
He Xiang . . . . Ju Xue
Gui Juan . . . . Ji Xueping
Jin Mei . . . . Chi Huaqiong

A rural drama about the lot of women in pre-communist China, "The Girls To Be Married" scores low on originality but high on looks and atmosphere. Feminist angle makes it a contender for film weeks and fest outings.

Set in remote Hunan province prior to the 1949 revolution, yarn follows five pubescent friends who make a pact to hang themselves to escape arranged marriages. Another village girl has already lynched herself in her bridal carriage after advice from a local sorceress.

Pic settles down into five vignettes of the girls' background before a surprise finale.

The eldest, Ming Tao, has a nitpicking stepmother and is due to be paired off with a tubercular hubby. Ai Yue, queen of a local parade, sees her 70-year-old grandmother insulted by men at a meal in her honor.

Feisty He Xiang's sister-in-law is beaten in the streets for taking a lover. Docile Gui Juan watches as her sister is sacrificed for her boy child during a grisly birth. Cute Jin Mei hears she is to be hitched to a cousin so

her family can save money.

Picture ends ironically with girls' botched suicide (the barn roof collapses) and a montage of their faces over their mountain wedding procession.

Theme and treatment is familiar from several other mainland Chinese pics, but the leads' sharp playing gives it a fresh edge. Commercial-style dubbing, which sometimes overdoes the giggling and weeping, may tax Western auds. Still, topnotch lensing and careful direction give pic a suitably arty feel.

Helmer Wang Jin made his local rep with China's first "X-rated" pic, "Village Of Widows" (1988), and there's the same peekaboo quality to an early scene of the teens stripping in the sundrenched fields. For Western viewers, it's tame.

Pic, co-produced with Hong Kong's Mainland-funded outfit Sil-Metropole, bowed in China late last year. Current English title, which translates original Chinese, will need overhauling for wider showings. — *Del.*

MY FATHER IS
COMING
(U.S.-GERMAN)

A Hyaenyfilm production co-produced by NDR, Hamburg. Produced and directed by Monika Treut. Screenplay, Treut, Bruce Benderson; camera (color), Elfi Mikesch; editor, Steve Brown; music, David van Tieghem; sound, Neill Danzinger. Reviewed at Berlin Film Festival (Panorama), Feb. 23, 1991. Running time: **82 MIN.**
Hans . . . . Alfred Edel
Vicky . . . . Shelly Kaestner
Annie . . . . Annie Sprinkle
Joe . . . . Michael Massee
Dora . . . . Flora Gaspara

A wry, comic look at the life and loves of a struggling, young German actress in New York, "My Father Is Coming" has definite potential on the arthouse circuit and should do respectable tv sales.

Underground German filmmaker Monika Treut juxtaposes Germans and Yanks living on the edge in NYC to explore the sexuality of the characters and of the city in general, and Treut pretty much hits the nail on the head. Sexual content is never shocking and usually well in keeping with pic's subject matter.

There are some excellent comic moments in the film. In the opening scene, the heroine (Shelly Kaestner) auditions for a commercial and is told to imagine deutschmarks and Nazis to help her attain the arrogance needed for the part. Later, she attempts to prop up a facade of success when her father comes to visit from deepest Bavaria.

The actress' aspirations are further shattered when her not-so-dumb father inadvertently lands a part in a primetime commercial. As her world comes tumbling down, she is forced to face up to herself and her ambiguous sexuality.

With her father in tow, she trawls through the sexual and erotic underworld in search of some type of love and meets some pretty weird characters along the way, including a female-to-male transexual, a skin-piercing fakir and a New Age sex goddess who takes a shine to the father, convincingly played by Alfred Edel.

Film is considerably helped by some sterling performances from the supporting cast members, who look like they have just wandered in from the Gotham streets. Particularly noteworthy is Flora Gaspara, who gives a deadpan, sinister performance.

Except for minor pacing problems, this low-budget comedy gives an accurate portrayal of humanity in the rough-and-tumble N.Y. life and the ability of love to span any barrier. — *Keoh.*

EKRAN ASIKLARI
(LOVE VIA DISPLAY)
(TURKISH)

A Kasak Film production and release. Produced by Bulent Kazak. Written and directed by Omer Ugur. Camera (Renkli color), Aytekin Cakmakci; editor, Yusuf Aldirma; music, Cahit Berkay. Reviewed at Istanbul Film Festival (competition), March 29, 1991. Running time: **95 MIN.**
Nedim . . . . Tarik Tarcan
Ince . . . . Sahia Tekand
Also with: Nevra Serezli, Erdinc Ustan.

A poorly made low-budget effort based on a plot premise that might have had interest if handled properly, "Love Via Display" faces dismal local market possibilities, and chances of being exported in any overseas medium are nil.

Yuppieish Nedim's (Tarik Tarcan) obsession with computers led him to neglect his wife, who left him. His typically bourgeois environment, complete with a meddling sister who nags her tippling husband, suits his needs

and provides an extended family for his young son.

Yet his sister pushes him to find another wife, although he clearly is in his element working on his computer, always logical and predictable. Thus, Nedim becomes interested in dating only when his friend suggests he apply to a computerized marriage bureau.

In his meeting with the lovely computer mate Ince (Sahia Tekand) and subsequent (chaste) courtship, all the clichés are laid on thick, from the red rose she wears to their rendezvous to her tactful instructions on how to eat spaghetti.

Ince is a computer service's dream — comely, sweet and bright — so it is not surprising Nedim falls for her. In a typical move, he programs his computers to announce his declaration of love.

The plot twist is abruptly rendered and the film grinds to a sudden, depressing halt. Tech credits are fair to poor. The photography is unfocused with uneven colors. Too bad one of the few current Turkish pics to deal with contemporary life in Istanbul is a dud. — *Sam.*

MIRAKEL
(MIRACLE)
(AUSTRIAN-SWISS)

A Filmcooperative Zurich release of a Neue Studio Film (Vienna)-Limbo-Film (Zurich) co-production. Produced by Peter Pochlatko, Theres Scherer. Written and directed by Leopold Huber. camera (color), Christian Berger; editor, Helena Gerber; music, Werner Pirchner; art direction, Fritz Hollergschwandtner; assistant director, Ruth Deutschmann; production manager, Alfred Deutsch; costumes, Gerda Nuspel. Reviewed at Frosch Cinema, Zurich, Feb. 21, 1991. Running time: **99 MIN.**
Quartierer . . . . . Dietmar Schönherr
Andreas . . . . Philip Stadler
Teacher . . . . Astrid Keller
Post office clerk . . . . . Hilde Ziegler
Dorfer . . . . Bernd Spitzer
Dorferin . . . Sibille aus der Schmitten
Parson . . . . Georg Schuchter
Also with: Gerhard Dorfer, Erhard Koren, Luise Prasser, Yvonne Kupper.
(German soundtrack)

Swiss-based Austrian director Leopold Huber has sensitively filmed this story of a 9-year-old Austrian boy who withdraws into speechless isolation after his grandmother's death. Mixture of poetry and realism, however, may not be to everyone's taste. At best, a mixed b.o. reaction looms for

"Miracle."

Stubbornly rejecting approaches by his foster parents (an idealistic young teacher and an emotionally unstable parson), the boy flees into a fantasy world by building himself a "snow village" where all is pure and undaunted.

Only person able to break through to the boy is an elderly vagabond (Austrian actor Dietmar Schönherr) who winters in the real Alpine village. The appealing rogue, half miracle man, half pseudo-magician, manages to communicate with the youngster and makes him speak again by playing his game.

When the boy steals a golden chalice and a small icon from the church, the vagabond is suspected of the thefts. The villagers' search for him leads them to the boy's snow structure, which they destroy. When all is cleared up, the boy is saved by a high church official who takes him away to the priesthood.

Huber maintains a poetic style with ironic overtones, but the script lacks substance, glossing over too many aspects inherent in the story. The result is a likable, but uneven film, probably too special for general audiences.

Schönherr dominates the cast as the vagabond, offering a colorful, yet subdued, performance. Philip Stadler, a non-pro from East Tyrol where the picture was filmed, is refreshingly natural as the youth.

Christian Berger's lensing deserves special mention for some brilliant light-and-shadow shots and the subtle use of muted colors. Tech credits are pro. — *Mezo.*

BLOODFIST II

A Concorde Pictures release. Produced by Roger Corman. Directed by Andy Blumenthal. Screenplay, Catherine Cyran; camera (Foto-Kem color), Bruce Dorfman; editor, Karen Joseph; music, Nigel Holton; sound (Ultra-Stereo), Do Bulatano, Enteng Dona; production design, Joe Mari Avellana; art direction, Ronnie Cruz; assistant director, Jose Torres; production manager, Honorato Perez Jr.; 2nd unit camera, Joe Batac; additional camera, Robert Brinkman; line producer, Christopher R. Santiago; associate producer, Cyran; casting, Enrique Reyes. Reviewed on MGM/UA Home Video vidcassette, N.Y., Feb. 9, 1991. MPAA Rating: R. Running time: **84 MIN.**
Jake . . . . . Don (The Dragon) Wilson
Mariella . . . . Rina Reyes
Su . . . . Joe Mari Avellana
Dieter . . . . Robert Marius
Vinny . . . . Maurice Smith
Sal . . . . Timothy Baker
John Jones . . . . . James Warring

Bobby . . . . Richard Hill
Ernest . . . . Steve Rogers
Jake's girlfriend . . . . . . Liza David

Second of three Don Wilson martial arts vehicles made for Roger Corman, this perfunctory exercise did not perform as well as the original at the b.o. "Bloodfist II" is an MGM/UA vid release.

Known as the Dragon, Wilson is a diminutive high-kicker who has the titles and expertise to whip any action movie superstar from Schwarzenegger to Van Damme in a fair fight. However, his acting is stilted and screen presence nil, making his films strictly for the purists.

In fact, both films have opening credits listing only the male cast members with the unusual designation of all their kickboxing and karate titles on screen. That's about as interesting as these features get.

This time, Wilson is called out of bed (with a pretty, nude woman beside him) to fly to the Philippines and search for a missing buddy. There he's befriended by another beauty (Rina Reyes) who gets him shanghaied to participate in a gladiatorial contest run by evil Joe Mari Avellana.

The fight footage, some of it staged in a steel cage, looks about as real as wrestling and the cast is woefully short on character actors. Wilson's next film costars Richard Roundtree, so some attention has been paid to this failing.

Cornball script has Reyes switching sides and helping Wilson out by the later reels, while he has to fight the big match to the death against the friend he's been seeking. Climax is diluted by Wilson taking time out during the match to give an anti-drug lecture.

Tech credits are meager, including phony sounding crowd murmuring dubbed in during the fight sequences. — *Lor.*

STEAL AMERICA
(B&W)

A Seamless Pictures-Pacific Film Fund production. Executive producers, Susan O'Connell, Patricia Marshall. Produced by Liz Gazzano, Lucy Phillips. Directed by Phillips. Screenplay, Phillips, Glen Scantlebury; camera (b&w), Jim Barrett, Scantlebury; editor, Scantlebury; music, Gregory Jones; associate producer, Patsy Shorr; production manager-assistant director, Gazzano. Reviewed at Berlin Film Festival (market), Feb. 23, 1991. Running time: **94 MIN.**
Stella . . . . Clara Bellino

Maria . . . . Diviana Ingravallo
Jack . . . . Kevin Haley
Christophe . . . . Charlie Homo

"**S**teal America," a fresh low-budget feature from San Francisco, is about three illegal immigrants sans green cards, but the approach here is a long way from Peter Weir. Modest but engaging pic should crop up at fests and do limited business in urban locations. Specialized tv and video are also possible.

For Stella (Clara Bellino), from Switzerland, America is only a stop on the way to Japan, her destination. On the bus from New York to Frisco she met Christophe (Charlie Homo), a Frenchman, and they began a relationship, which is why Stella hasn't moved on.

She works in a postcard shop; he parks cars. They have a friend, Maria (Diviana Ingravalla), a bisexual Italian. Stella gets involved with Jack (Kevin Haley), a painter. Midway through the film, the three non-Americans pick up for New Orleans in an auto Christophe stole from a customer.

At this point, principal filmmakers Lucy Phillips, Glen Scantlebury and Liz Gazzano had spent $40,000 on the project, which they completed as a 45-minute film. The short was favorably received at a number of fests in the U.S. and abroad. The Pacific Film Fund subsequently came aboard in exec producer capacity to extend the film to feature length.

Christophe doesn't appear in the second half (he was arrested and deported), but the women are back in Frisco for a deeper exploration of relationships.

Pic's attractive youths, uniformly well acted by the sympathetic cast, are after a piece of the American Dream. Christophe says he came to see the Wild West, and none of them seems happy with big-city life. They miss Europe and yet seem unable to break away until the end: Stella at last gets to go to Japan, and Jack may even tag along with her.

It's an intimate film, but it completely eschews sex scenes to the point that the relationship between the two women has a question mark hanging over it. More information about the characters' background might have helped. At times, the film is too elliptical, and, in the first half

especially, some sequences end too abruptly.

Overall, "Steal America" is an attractive and appealing film which intros talented actors. Clara Bellino makes a particular impression as the clear-eyed traveler who never loses sight of her goal but is willing to be sidetracked by a new relationship.

The black & white camerawork by Jim Barrett and Glen Scantlebury is fine, and the use of Bay Area locations adept. — *Strat.*

MIMA
(FRENCH)

A Pathé Europa NV release of a Pathé Cinema-Paris New York Prods. co-production. (Intl. sales: Pathé.) Produced by Claude Kunetz. Directed by Philomène Esposito. Screenplay, Esposito, Lucien Lambert; camera (Agfacolor), Carlo Varini; editor, Marie-Josèphe Yoyette; music, Reinhardt Wagner; sound, Georges Prat; production design, Christian Marti; costumes, Olga Berlutti; production manager, Sylvie Barchet; assistant director, Alain Peyrollaz. Reviewed at Berlin Film Festival (Panorama), Feb. 23, 1991. Running time: **82 MIN.**
Mima . . . . Virginie Ledoyen
Grandfather . . . . . . Nina Manfredi
Grandmother . . . . Margarita Lozano
Mother . . . . . Vittorio Scognamiglio
Father . . . . Toni Cecchinato
Annunziata . . . . Laura Martel
Inspector . . . . . . Patrick Bouchitey
Alfredo . . . . Philippe Fretun
Salvatore . . . . . Arnaud Giovaninetti
Antonia . . . . Anne-Marie Pisani
Marcello . . . . Nicola Donato
(French and Italian soundtrack)

"**M**ima" is an attractive first feature that brings freshness to an autobiographical theme. International arthouse possibilities are indicated for this charming and, ultimately, suspenseful pic.

Set in the small port town of Sete, story unfolds during the period around Christmas 1966. Mima, 12, sweetly played by Virginie Ledoyen, and her small sister, Annunziata (ultracute Laura Martel) are of a Calabrian family who moved to France years before, but never have assimilated.

They cling together in separate houses close to that of the head of the family, Mimi's beloved grandfather (Nino Manfredi), who eats pasta and complains about the French.

Early scenes establish the sensitive Mima's life, which is complicated because she feels neither completely French nor Italian. She adores her grandfather, who takes her to the cinema (a Belmondo action film) and tells and retells her favorite stories.

But one night a couple of sinister young men arrive to take grandfather away, and Mima never sees him again. He's been murdered, apparently as a result of a long-standing Mafia feud. Gradually, Mima, who doesn't let on that she saw the killers, realizes that if her father can identify them, he and his brother will, as a matter of honor, avenge the old man. Drawn to a sympathetic police inspector from Paris, the young girl has to decide for herself how to cope with a frightening situation.

First-time director Philomène Esposito tells her simple story with clarity and feeling, and gets wonderful performances from her ensemble cast. Enlisting Italo star Manfredi to play the grandfather was a coup. He's only in for a few scenes, but his benevolent presence stays with the viewer long after his character has been killed.

The use of the small seaside town as the setting is fine, thanks to Carlo Varini's warm camerawork, and the film is technically very good. There are deep emotions at play here, and the film, which has opened to good reviews in Paris, should find distribution in other countries where it could be a sleeper. Dialog is partly in French, partly in Italian. — *Strat.*

PRINTEMPS PERDU
(LOST SPRINGTIME)
(FRENCH)

A Binome production. (Intl. sales: K-Films, Paris.) Produced by N.T. Binh. Directed by Alain Mazars. Screenplay, Mazars, Binh; camera (color), Hélène Louvart; editor, Mazars, Nguyen Minh Tam; music, Oliver Hutman; opera music, Tang Xianzu; sound, Yves Laisne, Gérard Lamps; assistant director, Ursula Gauthier. Reviewed at 10th Istanbul Intl. Film Festival, March 30, 1991. Running time: **83 MIN.**
Yan Yuejun . . . . . . Song Xiaochuan
Lingling . . . . Ru Ping
Fengfeng . . . . Ding Jiaqing
Also with: Zhang Jiqing, Xu Hua.
(Mandarin Chinese; French subtitles)

Too much scholarship and too little drama take the bloom out of "Lost Springtime," a delicate love story lensed in China by French sinophile Alain Mazars. It's a respectable fest item, but no more.

Yarn is told through the eyes of Yan Yuejun (Song Xiaochuan), a Soochow Opera performer who gets three years of "re-education" during the Cultural Revolution and in 1969 stays on

in wild and woolly Inner Mongolia to forge a living as a truck driver.

He marries the orphaned Lingling (Ru Ping) and soon discovers why she's so quiet: She has a longlost childhood sweetheart, Fengfeng (Ding Jiaqing), who one day rolls up on the doorstep.

Yan nobly agrees to a quickie divorce and the two lovebirds set up house opposite. He turns his attentions to re-staging Tang Xianzu's 16th century Soochow Opera "The Peony Pavilion" with local talent, and finally in 1979 succeeds. The lovebirds are among the first-night audience, but Fengfeng falls sick and dies. Lingling vanishes, and Yan is left alone again. Curtain.

All of this unrolls with mucho finesse and restraint, in both acting and lensing. Scenes and characters from the opera that obsesses Yan are interwoven with the ongoing tale, and parallels between the doomed lovers of both are repeatedly underlined. But one wishes that, just occasionally, someone would raise their voice or smash a bowl.

Thesping is okay within the limitations, and Mazars does technical wonders with a miniscule budget and tiny crew. It's several notches in authenticity above the other Franco-Chinese exercise, "Chine, Ma Douleur" (1989).

Pic was 30 months in production, and won the youth prize at last year's Cannes fest as well as awards at Montreal and Florence. — *Del.*

BUSTER'S BEDROOM
(GERMAN-CANADIAN-PORTUGUESE)

A George Reinhart presentation of a coproduction of Metropolis Filmproduktion (Berlin), Les Prods. du Verseau (Montreal), Prole Filme (Lisbon) in cooperation with Limbo Film (Zurich) and Westdeutscher Rundfunk (Cologne). Produced by Luciano Gloor. Executive Producer, George Reinhart. Directed by Rebecca Horn. Screenplay, Horn, Martin Mosebach; camera, Sven Nykvist; editor, Barbara von Weitershausen; music, Ingfried Hoffman; sound (Dolby), Uwe Kersken; assistant director, Gabriele Mattner, Sabine Eckhard; coproducer, Aimee Daniels, with Henrique Espirito Santo, Martin Wiebel. Reviewed at Lupe 2, Berlin, April 10, 1991. Running time: **104 MIN.**
O'Connor . . . . . Donald Sutherland
Diana Daniels . . . . Geraldine Chaplin
Serafina . . . . . . Valentine Cortese
Micha . . . . Amanda Ooms
Mr. Warlock . . . . . David Warrilow
James . . . . Taylor Meade
Lenny Silver . . . . Ari Snyder
Joe . . . . Martin Wuttke
Sue . . . . Nina Franoszek
Ellen . . . . Lena Lessing
Jane . . . . Mary Woronow
Friend . . . . Steve Olson

Mrs. Noah	Tilly Lauenstein
Dr. Jacoby	Abel Fernandes
Sister Fowler	Maria Dulce

European pubcasters will probably be the only buyers for "Buster's Bedroom," a muddled co-prod. Theatrical prospects look dim to nonexistent stateside.

In pic's opening scene Micha (Amanda Ooms), a young student obsessed with Buster Keaton, drives blindfolded down a California coastal road, zigzagging aimlessly across the median line. The film's narrative is about as aimless as Micha's joyride.

Micha arrives at Nirvana House, a private asylum where Keaton allegedly went through detox in the 1930s. The once elegant asylum has just been taken over by its inmates following the chief physician's death. The patients elect their comrade, O'Connor (Donald Sutherland), who maintains a serpentarium in the basement, to be their new "doctor." Micha, the victim of an accident, becomes the newest "patient."

Rest of film follows the idiosyncrasies of the inmates. Serafina collects butterflies and reenacts her old love with a legionnaire with men who look as he did. Mr. Warlock collects pollen and enjoys sitting in bed with Micha. Wheelchair-bound, whiskey-drinking Mrs. Daniels envies Micha. And Lenny, a pianist, methodically destroys his instrument. Taylor Mead gives an enthusiastic performance as the gardener who holds the house together and disposes of corpses.

Characters are interesting but don't mesh with each other. Despite Sven Nykvist's splendid cinematography and stunning visual images that one expects from director Rebecca Horn, who has an international reputation as a visual artist, pic goes nowhere.

Audiences who sit through the whole pic can look forward to seeing, for no apparent reason, an animated fork in the final scene. — *Reli.*

EL EXTENSIONISTA
(MEXICAN)

A Cinematográfica Filmex-Fondo de Fomento a la Calidad Cinematográfica (FFCC) production. Exec producers, Jorge Rojas, Alberto Pedret. Produced by Fernando and Arturo Pérez Gavilán M. Directed by J. Fernando Pérez Gavilán E. Screenplay, Pérez Gavilán E., Victor Ugaldi, based on play by Felipe Santander; camera (color), Arturo de la Rosa; editor, Rogelio Zuñiga; music, Armando Manzanera; sound, Samuel Ovilla. Reviewed at Cine Variadades I, Mexico City, March 16, 1991. Running time: **127 MIN.**

Cruz López	Eduardo Palomo
Benito Sánchez	José Carlos Ruiz
Manuela	Claudia Guzmán
Severo	Manuel Ojeda
Nasario	Ernesto Gómez Cruz
Nacho	Sergio Jiménez
Don Máximo	Alberto Pedret
Also with: Eduardo López Rojas, Leonardo Daniel, María Rojo.

Based on the popular legit work of the same name by Felipe Santander (the longest-running play in Mexican history) "El Extensionista" suffers from a simplistic ill-fated journey from stage to screen. Although pic features some of Mexico's top actors, they can't save this lumbering attempt at political pamphleteering.

Dialectical story centers on "extensionista" Cruz López (Eduardo Palomo), a young agro-engineer doing a one-year internship in the field. (Untranslatable title refers to this position.)

In the community of Tenochtlán, he finds farmers ill-trusting of outside help. Their lives are controlled by the political machinations of the local boss (Alberto Pedret) and his two henchmen, who dictate all policy.

Through sheer tenacity and goodwill, young Cruz gains the trust of the community leader (José Carlos Ruiz), while courting his daughter (Claudia Guzmán).

Deciding that the only way to achieve his goals is to work with the machiavellian don, Cruz convinces farmers to switch from growing staples to the more-profitable crop of cotton. Yet, when the cotton crop comes to harvest, Cruz and the farmers discover they have been duped: Cotton prices fall, while staples double. The ensuing confrontation is as obvious as it is manipulative.

The cast boasts some of Mexico's best thesping talents, including Ruiz, Manuel Ojeda, Ernesto Gómez Cruz, Sergio Jiménez and María Rojo. Yet director J. Fernando Pérez Gavilán's heavy-handed approach panders to the story's basic political melodrama at the expense of characterization.

Arturo de la Rosa's flat and unimaginative camerawork is coupled with an out-of-place musical score by Armando Manzanera, whose nerve-racking brightness distracts throughout. — *Lent.*

LES ENFANTS VOLANTS
(THE FLYING CHILDREN)
(FRENCH)

A Gramaphone Enterprise et Associes production. (Intl. sales: Gramaphone.) Produced by Jean-Paul Adam. Written and directed by Guillaume Nicloux. Camera (color), Jean Badal, Raoul Coutard; editor, Brigitte Bennard; music, Michael Nyman; sound, Gilles Bénéfice, Emmanuel Rouleau. Reviewed at Berlin Film Festival (Forum), Feb, 24, 1991. Running time: **85 MIN.**

Suzanne	Anémone
Gilbert	Didier Abot
Gilles	Michel Debrane

A strange and disturbing film, "The Flying Children" will intrigue some, infuriate others. Its controversial approach to its central character, a young madman on a killing spree, could attract marginal arthouse or cult interest.

Writer-director Guillaume Nicloux, a new talent worth watching, at first takes a cool approach to the character of Gilbert (Didier Abot), who has just left the hospital but who is obviously quite deranged. Everywhere he goes, violence seems to follow in his wake, whether or not he provokes it himself.

An encounter with Suzanne (Anémone), a woman who's almost equally strange, leads to more killings on the way to Gilbert's obsessive trek towards the sea.

All this is shot in remote style by two of France's top cameramen, Jean Badal and Raoul Coutard, and is accompanied by the seductively tuneful piano compositions of British composer Michael Nyman, best known for his work with Peter Greenaway.

It adds up to a very personal and disturbing vision of madness, obviously not to everyone's taste, but worth seeking out as an example of a new filmmaker with fresh, challenging ideas.
— *Strat.*

FORTUNE EXPRESS
(FRENCH)

An Altair-Androméde-Blue Films-Films A2 co-production. (Intl. sales: President Films, Paris.) Produced by Marie-France Tremege. Directed by Olivier Schatzky. Screenplay, Schatzky, Pierre Jolivet; camera (Agfacolor), Carlo Varini; editor, Jean-François Naudon; music, Serge Perathoner, Jannick Top; sound, Yves Osmu; production design, Laurent Allaire; production manager, Christian Paumier; assistant director, Philippe Berenger; casting, Shula Siegfried. Reviewed at Berlin Film Festival (competition), Feb. 24, 1991. Running time: **90 MIN.**

Pascal	Cris Campion
Gadouille	Thierry Fremont
Marko	Herve Laudiere
Corinne	Valeria Bruni Tedeschi
Bobo	Christian Bouillette
Also with: Luc Bernard, Richard Bean, Thierry Ravel, Arnaud Chevrier, Herve Langlois, Vincent de Bouard, Jean O'Cottrell.

This first feature film from director Olivier Schatzky is an uneven but mostly gripping tale about overcoming physical handicap, but the intrusion of an unnecessary thriller element in the last couple of reels reduces the pic's impact. Mixed results can be expected.

"Fortune Express" opens with a gripping sequence as mountain climber Pascal (Cris Campion, from Roman Polanski's "Pirates") reaches the top of an Alpine peak, only to slip and fall. He winds up a paraplegic, confined to a wheelchair.

He winds up in a rehab home and befriends a couple of other loners, Gadouille (Thierry Fremont) and Marko (Herve Laudiere). He gradually begins to regain confidence and even makes tentative approaches to a pretty young woman who seems to like him and not care about his incapacities.

All this is sympathetically handled, with a particularly convincing performance from Fremont (to be seen in Bertrand Blier's next film); Campion and Laudiere always remain actors essaying roles in wheelchairs.

The intrusion of a thriller plot to climax the film might have seemed like a shrewd commercial move, but doesn't help the drama, since the motivations are unbelievable. The three friends decide to rob the bank next to their institution by using Pascal's mountaineering skills to break in through the roof. The robbery is successful, but Pascal is trapped overnight when he falls down the elevator shaft. The friends have to find a way to help him escape.

Director Schatzky is a former scripter whose work includes "Uncontrollable Circumstances" ("Force Majeure," 1989), written in collaboration with Pierre Jolivet, who also co-scripted this pic. He also has a documentary background, which is evident from the detail of many scenes in "Fortune Express."

Pic could spark interest on the subject matter, on Fremont's smash performance, or even on the contrived combination of suspense thriller and a serious study of the disabled. It's technically slick, especially in the climbing scenes. — Strat.

ON THE WAVES OF THE ADRIATIC
(AUSTRALIAN-DOCU)

A Standard Films production. Produced and directed by Brian McKenzie. Camera (color), McKenzie; editor, Ken Sallows; sound, Mark Tarpey, Philip Healey. Reviewed at Mosman screening room, Sydney, March 10, 1991. Running time: **130 MIN.**
With: Graham Branch, Steve Kotis, Harold Woodhall.

This oddly and, as it turns out, obscurely titled docu is Aussie director Brian McKenzie's latest painstaking look at life's losers. Overlong but fascinating, "On The Waves Of The Adriatic" is getting an arthouse release after world preeming at last June's Melbourne film fest.

McKenzie, who made a two-and-a-half hour docu about winos and derelicts ("I'll Be Home For Christmas") seven years ago, has now come up with a two-hour-plus look at three mentally retarded men who live in the inner suburbs of a large city.

Graham, who's in his 20s, lives in a run-down house with his cousins and Harry, an older man he "found" on a garbage dump. Unable to read, write or hold a job, Graham and Harry spend their time cycling the streets or arguing about nothing much. The young man yearns to own a car and is happy for a while when the filmmaker's crew gives him the money to buy an old auto which never actually works.

The third member of the trio is Steve, who lives nearby with his Greek family. He has a menial factory job making nipples for baby bottles. Unlike Graham and

Harry, he has the warm support of family and sees less of his friends as the film progresses. Eventually, Steve goes off to Greece with his clan.

Nothing much happens in the film, which was shot over nearly three years, but thoughtful viewers have plenty to chew on. Particularly interesting is the way characters unbend before McKenzie's camera. Graham's surly, Slovenian-born father, for instance, initially orders his son not to allow the filming but later participates in an illuminating biographical monolog.

These are sad, lonely characters, but their humor and resilience will endear them to patient viewers. McKenzie could, however, have made his pic more accessible if he had trimmed the excessive running time and conveyed a bit more information, perhaps with explanatory titles at the start of the film. There's far more info in the press kit than in the film.

There's also a hint of voyeurism in the way the filmmaker relentlessly probes the stunted lives of his friendly, naive protagonists. — Strat.

COMODAS MENSUALIDADES
(COMFORTABLE MONTHLY PAYMENTS)
(MEXICAN)

A "C" Producciones-Mexican Film Institute (Imcine)-Fondo de Fomento de la Calidad Cinematográfica (FFCC) production. Executive producer, Gonzalo Infante C. Directed by Julián Pastor. Screenplay, Angeles Necoachea, Edna Necoachea; camera (color), Gonzalo Infante C.; editor, Edgar Diaz; music, Annette Fradera; sound, Oscar Mateos; art direction, Carmen Giménez Cacho. Reviewed at Estudios Churubusco, Mexico City, March 15, 1991. Running time: **91 MIN.**
José Díaz . . . . Dino García
Verónica . . . . . Claudia Fernández
Domínguez . . . . Juan Carlos Colombo
English teacher . . . . . Mercedes Olea
Verónica's mother . . . Nora Velázquez
Verónica's father . . Mauricio Davison

A commercial satire on Mexico's urban yuppie lifestyle. "Comfortable Monthly Payments" offers plenty of knowing chuckles. Full of pokes at postmodern living, pic should fare well at national wickets and enjoy fruitful travel to other Latino territories.

The promising protagonist José (Dino García) has a brilliant future ahead of him. His boss has

him pegged to ascend the ladder of success. Everything is roses until he receives a call from his g.f. (Claudia Fernández), informing him that she is pregnant.

Marriage and a family have their immediate demands as José takes his place in adult society. There is the new condominium, furniture, insurance, a savings plan, a new car, driving lessons, monthly parking payments and other "necessities" of modern living. He also discovers all needs become obtainable through comfortable monthly payments.

While José's fellow workers seem happy, his own life becomes more and more complicated. Payments endlessly multiply and by the time the baby arrives, José lacks sufficient funds to pay the hospital bill, and so the baby stays.

The film boasts many fun moments. Intelligent script by Angeles and Edna Necoachea bursts with gags, including as parodies of tv commercials, incomprehensible visiting Japanese businessmen, regular office exercise classes, an unbearably cheerful "Business English" course and the daily exodus of happy successful workers ready to seize the day.

Helmer Julián Pastor has a good feel for comedy and handles the material well. Tech credits are also okay. With careful handling, pic could find comfortable commercial acceptance.
— Lent.

SOGUKTU VE YAGMUR CISELIYORDU
(IT WAS COLD AND RAINING)
(TURKISH)

An Erka Film production. Produced by Erhan Erzurumlu. Written and directed by Engin Ayca. Camera (color), Ertunç Senkay; editor, Mevlüt Koçak; music, Melih Kibar; art director, Suna Ciftçi. Reviewed at Beyoglu Cinema, Istanbul, March 27, 1991. Running time: **92 MIN.**
With: Türkân Soray, Ekrem Bora, Gülsen Tuncer, Alev Koral, Tunca Yönder, Mehmet Atak, Bülent Ufak.

A sophisticated drama about the platonic love between a chanteuse and a strummer in her folklorico band, "It Was Cold And Raining" is an unusual Turkish item that evokes the films of Gallic helmer Claude Sautet. Multilayered script and subtle playing made pic worthy of fest dates, although preprogrammed no-

tions of Turkish cinema could hinder its chances abroad.

After the death of a veteran lutist (Ekrem Bora), a star songstress (Turkan Soray) calls on his relatives, and a long chat with his sister (Gulsen Tuncer) spurs the singer to reassess her friendship with the musician.

Flashbacks limn the duo's growing attraction, a love founded on mutual artistic interests. Story ends with the femme singer exorcising the ghost of her idealized love and returning to work in a nitery.

Confidently paced pic is in no hurry to lay all its cards on the table. But from the meeting of the two women it exerts a growing pull as the main characters develop depth and interest. Overlapping structure of past and present, with new light being shed on both, shows no strain.

Soray and Bora, both w.k. local thesps, make a fine pair, the former drawing a nice contrast between her glitzier youth and middle age. As the sister who stirs the re-evaluation, legit actress Tuncer (wife of pic's director) is excellent in a key role.

Engin Ayca, 50, a critic and tv helmer, is known for his previous "Rag Doll" (1987). "Raining" is several strides ahead of that on all fronts. Tech credits are tops, with music skillfully placed throughout, although folklorico numbers may tax some foreign tastes. (Pic was screened privately for foreign critics during the Istanbul fest, and is skedded to compete at local Antalya fest this fall.) — Del.

KUUTAMOSONAATTI 2: KADUNLAKAISIJAT
(MOONLIGHT SONATA 2: THE STREET SWEEPERS)
(FINNISH)

A Finnkino release of a Filminor production. Produced by Heikki Takkinen. Written and directed by Olli Soinio. Camera (color), Kari Sohlberg; editor, Irma Taina; music, Antti Hytti; sound, Paul Jyrälä; production design, Risto Karhula. Reviewed at Rex theater, Helsinki, March 18, 1991. Running time: **85 MIN.**
Arvo Kyyrölä . . . . Kari Sorvali
Sulo Kyyrölä . . . . . . Mikko Kivinen
Aitee Kyyrölä . . . . Soli Labbart
Kata Kärkkäinen . . Kata Kärkkäinen
Also with: Erkki Pajala, Matti Tuominen, Mikko Nousiainen, Vesa Vierikko.

"The Street Sweepers" is a grotesque horror comedy, but the sloppy storyline and slipshod directing destroy the few laughs. The screenplay creates some enjoyable ideas, but the jokes are more Finnish than finished to be understood elsewhere.

Olli Soinio's sequel to his "Moonlight Sonata" (1988), a subtle comedy using not-very-heavy horror material to comment on Finnish people and their peculiarity, lacks the cleverness of the first film. Result is a rough farce with some gory but not very scary effects.

A family with a strictly religious mother and her two grown, mentally retarded sons move from the countryside to Helsinki.

In "Moonlight Sonata," the mother was frozen and the older son Arvo burned to death, and here they are revived in a sauna in the film's most enjoyable sequence.

They are joined by a memorable bunch of zombie Red Guards, killed in the Finnish civil war in 1918 and dumped in a swamp. With the Kyyrölä boys they create chaos on the streets of Helsinki.

Pic's humor is carried by Arvo, a babbling sex maniac who speaks a meta-language that artifically compiles different dialects.

Most international audiences will miss the verbal fun, as well as the local political jokes, such as the mocking of the Finnish culture minister. — Mapu.

MILENA
(FRENCH-CANADIAN-GERMAN)

A UGC release (Shapiro Glickenhaus Entertainment in U.S.) of a Stephan Films-FR3 Films-Farena Films-Sofinergie France-les Films l'Amante (Canada), Bavaria Films in association with Bayerischer Rundfunk (Germany) co-production. Written, produced and directed by Vera Belmont. Screenplay, Marie-Geneviève Ripeau, Guy Konopnicky, Dan Frank, Lou Garfinkle; camera (color), Dietrich Lohmann; editor, Yves Langlois, Martine Giordano; music, Jean-Marie Senia; sound, Partis Rousseau; production design, Jacques Bufnoir, Karel Vacek; costumes, Olga Berlutti; casting, Schulla Siegfried. Reviewed at Cannon screening room, Paris, Dec. 4, 1990. Running time: **139 MIN.**
Milena . . . . Valérie Kaprisky
Jesenski . . . . Stacy Keach
Olga . . . . Gudrun Landgrebe
Jaromir . . . . Nick Mancuso
Polak . . . . Peter Gallagher
Franz Kafka . . . . . . Philip Anglim
Max Brod . . . . Yves Jacques
(In French and English)

Prolific producer turned writer-director Vera Belmont's lovingly made biopic is uneven and episodic, but the power of Milena Jesenska's true story outweighs the flaws in its telling. Though attractive enough for the big screen, international film's unsubtle storytelling techniques are best suited to television.

Because "Milena" (filmed with the title, "The Lover") telescopes key political and artistic trends of "the joyous apocalypse" in Vienna and Prague between the wars, it lacks the narrative continuity of Belmont's previous outing as director-screenwriter, "Rouge Baiser" (Red Kiss). Still, international English-speaking cast achieves a better than average unity of tone.

Milena (Valérie Kaprisky) lived a brief but inspiring life devoted to radical humanist causes. Told in flashback from 1945, the story begins in Prague in 1923. Milena's widower father (Stacy Keach) wants her to pursue a career in medicine, but she has already discovered her flair for writing, along with an urge to defend picked-upon Jewish classmates.

When she takes up with outspoken Jewish music and theater critic Ernst Polak (Peter Gallagher), domineering dad has her strait-jacketed and confined to an asylum, but she elopes to Vienna with Ernst all the same.

The critic's career is soon destroyed by institutionalized anti-Semitism, prompting (non-Jew) Milena to take up journalism to support them. Their marriage doesn't survive the strain. Milena embarks on translating the writings of fellow Czech Franz Kafka (suitably cadaverous Philip Anglim) and enters into a passionately supportive correspondence with him.

While covering a miners' strike, Milena meets a utopian architect (Nick Mancuso) whom she marries and bears a daughter. Film is abrupt and awkward at this juncture.

Following her husband's departure for Moscow to build a workers' palace, Milena is fired from her paper and left with her young daughter in harrowing circumstances. Rise of Nazism further complicates their situation.

Kaprisky is called upon to portray a spirited schoolgirl, a fearless reporter, a morphine addict and courageous resistance worker. She handles her demanding role well.

Like Emma Goldman, Rosa Luxembourg and Lou-Andreas Salomé, all of whom have gotten the cinematic treatment, Milena Jasenska moved among famous men and worked for justice despite her own problems. Kafka's letters to her survived because she entrusted them to Kafka's great friend and literary executor, Max Brod (here played by Yves Jacques).

The nicely costumed characters quote Brecht and Apollinaire and are forever taking trains to and from propitious encounters in exotic settings. The public reading at which Milena and Kafka first meet is nicely handled.

Filmmaker's judgment literally goes out the window, however, when grainy newsreel footage stands in for the "view" from Kafka's room to a demonstration in the streets below.

There are moments of genuine humor (Milena mixing up the location of the fallopian tubes and the eustachian tubes during a medical drill with her father; Milena's reaction when her no-nonsense colleagues fail to be amused by the Marx Bros. suing Karl Marx for usurping their name), but the occasionally trite dialog and depictions of workers' strikes and free-floating decadence are less convincing.

Despite sometimes choppy and didactic presentation, film is boosted by decent performances, pleasing art direction and the integrity of an undersung heroine whose efforts on behalf of Jews landed her in Auschwitz. — *Ness.*

VOYAGER
(GERMAN-FRENCH)

A Bioskop Film (Munich)-Action Films (Paris) production in association with Stefi 2 (Athens) and Home Video Hellas. Produced by Eberhard Junkersdorf. Directed by Volker Schlöndorff. Screenplay, Schlöndorff, Rudy Wurlitzer, based on novel "Homo Faber" by Max Frisch; camera (color), Yorgos Arvanitis, Pierre L'Homme; editor, Dagmar Hirtz; music, Stanley Myers; in Dolby Stereo; production design, Nicos Perakis; costumes, Barbara Baum; artistic advisor, Suzanne Baron; production manager, Alexander von Eschwege. Reviewed at the Delphi, Berlin, April 13, 1991. Running time: **117 MIN.**
Walter Faber . . . . Sam Shepard
Sabeth . . . . Julie Delpy
Hanna . . . . Barbara Sukowa
Herbert Hencke . Dieter Kirchlechner
Charlene . . . . Traci Lind
Ivy . . . . Deborah-Lee Furness
Joachim . . . . August Zirner
Kurt . . . . Thomas Heinze
Lewin . . . . Bill Dunn
(English soundtrack)

Equal parts road movie and Greek tragedy, Volker Schlöndorff's "Voyager" may well find itself a comfortable niche in U.S. urban markets. A wealth of international locations and an appealing cast take the edge off what otherwise could be deemed material too highbrow for Yank auds.

Schlöndorff's latest literary adaptation (of Max Frisch's German classic "Homo Faber") makes good use of fine material. In this moral tale without a moral, Walter Faber (Swiss in the book, Yank in pic) is an inveterate traveler who lives in departure lounges and on board ships, planes, taxis and trains.

An engineer and pragmatist approaching middle age in the not-yet-defined postwar Europe of the '50s, Faber is indifferent to events or people passing through his life as he efficiently dispatches his assignments for UNESCO.

With his laconic intelligence, Sam Shepard is ideal as Faber, the quintessentially cool cowboy-loner-businessman, both at ease in and aloof to foreign surroundings. He kisses the girls but goes home to his typewriter until a chain of coincidences and accidents launch him on a voyage of discovery and a collision with his past (or perhaps his fate).

Via black & white flashbacks, Faber recalls his days as a student in Zurich before the war. He was in love with Hanna, a German Jew pregnant with his child. Through misunderstanding and blunder, Faber left Hanna and Europe, assuming that medical student friend Joachim would perform an abortion.

Waiting for a flight to Venezuela, Faber meets a passenger, Herbert, who's on his way to visit his brother Joachim, now operating a tobacco plantation in South America. Faber learns that Joachim married Hanna, and they had a daughter but divorced shortly afterward. Faber decides to go with Herbert to see Joachim and learn what happened, but they arrive too late: Joachim has committed suicide.

Back in New York, more random decisions and coincidence set Faber further on his existential voyage toward destiny. He breaks with his g.f. (Deborah-Lee Furness) and decides to travel to Paris by ship.

On board he meets Sabeth (Julie Delpy), 20ish and returning home after studying in the States. She takes an interest in the older man, inventing excuses to run into him. Faber initially ignores her until her charm and almost unbearably fragile beauty begin to take effect.

There's too long a build of vacuous ocean liner time until Faber unexpectedly pops the question to Sabeth. Whether meant in earnest or not, she won't know because just then her friend interrupts and another chance encounter veers lives in other directions.

Faber and Sabeth bump into one another in Paris and he decides — is it love or a protective, paternal instinct? — to accompany her on her drive through France and Italy to meet her mother, an archaeologist living in Athens. Travelling, visiting historic sites and staying in country inns, Faber and Sabeth become lovers.

When Sabeth casually mentions to Faber that her parents were Hanna and Joachim, the picture becomes truly gripping. One's first instinct, like Faber's, is that she must be his daughter. The second is to root for the lovers, to find the shadow of the doubt, to prefer to be suspended in uncertainty than face the possible, horrible truth. They press on toward Athens, and he says nothing.

Sabeth is hurt in an accident and rushed to an Athenian hospital. Faber finds himself with Hanna (Barbara Sukowa, playing the mother like a lioness). Consumed with knotted fury and concern about Sabeth, she wants

to know everything about Faber's relationship with her daughter, but the archaeologist draws a veil across the past, refusing to divulge the identity of Sabeth's father until a very Athenian ending of revelation and tragedy.

A well-told tale, fine cast and good tech credits will probably make "Voyager" travel a bit further than the arthouse circuit.
— *Reli.*

TOY SOLDIERS

A Tri-Star Pictures release of a Jack E. Freedman production, in association with Island World. Produced by Freedman, Wayne S. Williams, Patricia Herskovic. Executive producers, Mark Burg, Chris Zarpas. Directed by Daniel Petrie Jr. Screenplay, David Koepp, Petrie, based on William P. Kennedy's novel; camera (Continental color, Technicolor prints), Thomas Burstyn; editor, Michael Kahn; music, Robert Folk; sound (Dolby), Russell Fager; production design, Chester Kaczenski; costume design, Betsy Cox; production manager-co-producer, Donald Klune; 2nd unit director, Mickey Moore; 2nd unit camera, Rexford Metz; stunt coordinator, Chuck Waters. Reviewed at Columbia screening room, N.Y., April 8, 1991. MPAA Rating: R. Running time: **112 MIN.**
Billy Tepper . . . . Sean Astin
Joey Trotta . . . . Wil Wheaton
Snuffy Bradberry . . . . Keith Coogan
Luis Cali . . . . Andrew Divoff
Edward Parker . . . . Louis Gossett Jr.
Dr. Robert Gould . . . Denholm Elliott
Hank Giles . . . . T.E. Russell
Ricardo Montoya . . . . . George Perez
Otis Brown . . . . Mason Adams
Jack Thorpe . . . . . Michael Champion
Gen. Kramer . . . . R. Lee Ermey
Albert Trotta . . . . . . Jerry Orbach

Tri-Star's "Toy Soldiers" **is a very entertaining action film that updates 1981's sleeper hit "Taps." No-brainer should duplicate that Fox film's b.o. success, especially with its timely gung-ho approach.**

Pic is unrelated to the 1984 New World release "Toy Soldiers," wherein Jason Miller and Cleavon Little led a bunch of Beverly Hills kids (including Tim Robbins in an early role) on a hostage rescue mission against terrorists in Colombia.

The new picture by Daniel Petrie Jr. (Oscar nominee for his "Beverly Hills Cop" script) presents the reverse situation of rich kids at a Virginia prep school who have to develop some backbone and defend themselves against Andrew Divoff's group of Colombian terrorists who take over their school and hold them hostage.

Divoff's dad is the leader of a drug cartel who's been taken to Florida to stand trial, so Divoff uses the hostages to demand dad's

release. While the FBI led by Mason Adams plays it cool, ne'er-do-well student Sean Astin on the inside organizes resistance and ultimately outsmarts Divoff and his heavily armed cohorts.

What makes this preposterous film work is the strong motivations developed along the way. As headmaster Lou Gossett sums up in film's campiest scene, "My boys have a real problem with authority — there's no telling what they'll do in this situation." Seeing Astin and his pranksters turn into commandos who wipe out the nasty invaders makes for purely escapist, crowd-pleasing pleasure.

In his feature directing debut, Petrie gets maximum mileage out of the derring-do of the final reels while emphasizing comic relief earlier on. His script, co-written with David Koepp, is littered with in-jokes among the character names, such as "Billy Tepper" (Astin's role here; actor-writer who starred in Jack Nicholson's first helming effort, "Drive, He Said") and other kids named after the exec producers.

Harold Becker's "Taps," set at a military school, had a similarly violent climax and launched the film careers of Sean Penn and Tom Cruise. This variation on a generic theme should catapult Astin (son of John Astin and Patty Duke) towards stardom with his very physical, instantly likable rebel without a cause. Perhaps a girls school will host the next Hollywood extension of the plotline.

Young villain Divoff is terrific at creating a brutal figure of hate, while Wil Wheaton and Keith Coogan make good impressions as Astin's partners in practical jokes/counterterrorism. Gossett is effective, though there's self-mockery in handling a role so close to his "Iron Eagle" and Oscar-winning "An Officer And A Gentleman" personas.

Least successful subplot (which could have profitably been jettisoned) has Wheaton's dad, Jerry Orbach, as head of New Jersey's Mafia who intercedes to try and get Wheaton released. Orbach subsequently had his name taken off the credits.

Remaining in the end credits is Tracy Brooks Swope, but she doesn't appear on screen; in fact there are no women's roles other than bit parts. Tech credits are strong for this Virginia-lensed picture. — *Lor.*

A WOMAN'S TALE
(AUSTRALIAN)

A Beyond Films release of an Illumination Films production in association with the Australian Film Finance Corp. (Intl. sales: Beyond Intl.) Executive producer, William Marshall. Produced by Paul Cox, Santhana Naidu. Directed by Cox. Screenplay, Cox, Barry Dickins; camera (Eastmancolor), Nino G. Martinetti; editor-sound, Russell Hurley; music, Paul Grabowski; production design, Neil Angwin; line producer-production manager, Paul Ammitzboll. Reviewed at Longford theater, Melbourne, March 8, 1991. Running time: **93 MIN.**
Martha . . . . Sheila Florance
Anna . . . . Gosia Dobrowolska
Billy . . . . Norman Kaye
Jonathan . . . . Chris Haywood
Miss Inchley . . . . . . Myrtle Woods
Peter . . . . Ernest Gray
Billy's daughter . . . Monica Maughan
Billy's son-in-law . . . Max Gillies
Cafe owner . . . . . Nino G. Martinetti
Also with: Bruce Myles, Alex Menglet, Maria Findlay.

Sensitive and controversial themes about treatment of the aged and terminally ill are tackled with distinction in Paul Cox' new "A Woman's Tale," which bears all the director's hallmarks, yet in many ways differs from his last pic, "Golden Braid."

"A Woman's Tale" is structured around one of Cox' favorite actresses, veteran Sheila Florance, who carries the film on her frail shoulders. Her Martha is terminally ill yet fiercely determined to hold on to her independence. She lives alone (theme of loneliness recurs in Cox' films) in a small city apartment with her cat, canary and memories.

A nurse visits her every day and has become the old woman's closest friend. Martha even lets the nurse use her apartment for afternoon trysts with her married lover.

Gosia Dobrowolska (the mistress in "Golden Braid") plays the nurse with sweetness and sensitivity, while the lead in the earlier film, Chris Haywood, plays Martha's son. He worries about her but doesn't have much time to spend with his mother, who, it transpires, doesn't get on with his wife.

Living in the next-door apartment is the equally old and even frailer Billy (played by another Cox regular, Norman Kaye, in a tremendously touching performance). Anna also visits Billy, but is unamused when he makes pathetic sexual advances towards her.

These characters, and others, are, however, marginal. As

Martha, Florance dominates the film and is in almost every scene. The fictional character is reportedly close to that of the actress who plays her, even to the extent it's no secret Florance herself was seriously ill during production.

Constantly puffing on cigarettes, the old woman lives on her memories, recalling the war years in Britain and the death of her child during a German bombing raid. She also is very free-spirited and open-minded, and despises hypocrisy and narrow thinking, which makes her an endearing character akin to (though not as eccentric as) Ruth Gordon in "Harold And Maude."

Though there are moments that are overwritten and times when Florance is too theatrical, this is, on balance, a generous, passionate and even surprisingly humorous performance, and one likely to be in the running for accolades Down Under. A scene in which Martha takes a bath was a brave one for the actress, whose old body is dispassionately observed by the camera.

The plot, broken up with characteristic Cox dream sequences (mostly involving fire and water), is simple enough, but becomes provocative in the final sequence when the euthanasia theme is naturally introed, and the nurse lovingly helps the sick old woman die peacefully. The scene is beautifully done, but could spark controversy.

Cinematographer Nino G. Martinetti, in charge of the camerawork for the second time on a Cox film, has done a superlative job with the mostly interior sequences, and has an amusing cameo. Neil Angwin's production design and Russell Hurley's sound and editing all are fine.

Cox usually augments his pics with snatches of classical music, but this time out has an original music score, which has been subtly composed by Paul Grabowski. All technical credits are firstrate on this sensitive, touching, challenging picture. — Strat.

OUT FOR JUSTICE

A Warner Bros. release of an Arnold Kopelson/Steven Seagal production. Produced by Seagal, Kopelson. Executive producer, Julius R. Nasso. Directed by John Flynn. Screenplay, David Lee Henry; camera (Technicolor), Ric Waite; editor, Robert A. Ferretti, Donald Brochu; music, David Michael Frank; sound (Dolby), Robert R. Rutledge; production design, Gene Rudolf; art direction, Stephen M. Berger; set decoration, Gary Moreno, Ronald R. Reiss; costume de-

sign, Richard Bruno; associate producer, Jacqueline George; assistant directors, Jerry Ziesmer, Michael-McCloud Thompson; coproducer, Peter Macgregor-Scott; casting, Pamela Baker, Sue Swan. Reviewed at Mann Chinese Theater, Hollywood, April 12, 1991. MPAA Rating: R. Running time: **91 MIN.**
Gino Felino . . . . Steven Seagal
Richie Madano . . . . William Forsythe
Ronnie Donziger . . . . . Jerry Orbach
Vicky Felino . . . . Jo Champa
Also with: Shareen Mitchell, Sal Richards, Gina Gershon, Jay Acovone.

Steven Seagal should snap off another hefty chunk of boxoffice with this latest lamebrained excuse to showcase his bone-breaking talents. "Out For Justice" harbors an incredibly simple vengeance plot loaded with enough macho sadism to satiate the action genre's bloodthirsty fans.

Since his impressive debut in 1988's "Above The Law," well-made pic capitalizing on his foreboding presence and martial arts skill, the ponytailed one-man demolition crew has simply remade the same pic three times, substituting a new three-word title ("Hard To Kill," "Marked For Death" and now this) and despicable villain on each slugfest.

This time Seagal plays an Italian cop pursuing the killer of his partner, who's gunned down in broad daylight just after the opening credits. The killer and cops all grew up in "da neighborhood," counting among their mutual friends organized-crime types as eager to dispatch the guy for breaking their code as Seagal is for his buddy's murder.

Seagal relentlessly pursues the murderous, drugged-out Richie (William Forsythe), dispatching his henchmen in brutal encounters in a butcher shop, pool hall and his own apartment that make the LAPD's brutality seem tame. The code of these films is that if the bad guy is bad enough, then the good guy can do pretty much whatever he wants and appear justified.

For the action crowd, formula is perfectly serviceable, and director John Flynn does a fair job of keeping the minimal storyline crawling along well enough to justify all the mayhem. Too bad the climactic confrontation doesn't justify the buildup.

The pic stumbles blatantly during the more tender moments. When Seagal tries to wax eloquent about his impoverished youth or court his estranged wife (Jo Champa), the film comes to a grinding halt. While Seagal's not necessarily a bad actor, his range

appears limited to simmering rage and throwaway lines.

The supporting cast is almost uniformly limited to grunts and shrieks of either terror or pain.

Tech credits are subpar compared with previous patrols, particularly the sound, which frequently seems muted. Pic is snappily edited but interiors too often are limited to murky club settings that cloud the camerawork. Stuntwork, however, is firstrate, and Seagal remains a convincing action figure. — Bril.

AUJOURD'HUI PEUT-ÊTRE ...
(A DAY TO REMEMBER)
(FRENCH)

An Agepro Cinema-MP Prods.-SEDPA production. Produced by Marie-Christine de Montbrial, Michel Frichet, Jo Siritzky. Directed by Jean-Louis Bertuccelli. Screenplay, Isabelle Mergault, Bertuccelli; camera (color), Bernard Lutic; music, Paul Misraki; sound, Jean-Pierre Ruh; set design, Jean-Jacques Gernolle; costumes, Annie Bodin; make-up, Sylvie Jouineau, Catherine Vrignaud, Gabriella Trani. Reviewed at Sept Parnassiens, Paris, April 11, 1991. Running time: **100 MIN.**
Bertille . . . . Giulietta Masina
Christiane . . . . . . Véronique Silver
Marie . . . . Eva Darlan
Marcel . . . . Jean Benguigui
Romain . . . . Jean-Paul Muel
Thérèse . . . . Muni
Gaby . . . . Jean Mercure
Also with: Michel Berto, Christina Rauth, Jacques Toja, Anna Gaylor, Georges Staquet, Véronique Delbourg, François Dyrek.

"A Day To Remember" is a small family film that lingers in the mind, if only because of Giulietta Masina's sensitive portrayal of a matriarch who throws a big reunion, hoping her fugitive son will show up. Pic should have middling appeal for arthouse audiences.

Widow Bertille (Masina) has decided to sell her homestead after 50 years in French countryside. On the day before her departure she invites all of her extended family. Her mind, though, is on her youngest son, a bankrobber who's been gone 15 years but might read her newspaper announcements of the reunion.

French director Jean-Louis Bertuccelli co-scripted with Isabelle Mergault in subtle homage to Fellini's "La Strada": Masina is again accompanied by a fool (a simpleton nephew named Romain) while holding onto her optimism despite cruelty all around

her (bickering family members).

The trouble with the storyline is that Masina's character does little more than twist in the wind until the predictable ending. She has no worthy counterpart to rub up against. And the episode of a little boy witnessing a goat's birth is an obvious filler.

Still, the screen lights up every time Masina's round face, dark eyes and wide mouth appear. She's lost none of her talent as a mime actress. Each time she answers the telephone, hope, worry and disappointment flit across her face.

In her best scene, she explains why she bought tabloid announcements. She admits being bitter and then moves past that anger to generous hope. In her moving farewell speech, she uses all her charm to plead with family members not to quarrel over their inheritance, to no avail. Throughout, her French accent has a charming trace of Italian.

Solid cast of 22 adults and five kids is at continual cross-purposes during long front-yard meal. If someone puts a pesky dog in a car, someone else later lets it out. A distracting climax throws the entire family into an uproar: Distant male and female cousins announce that she's pregnant and they will elope that evening.

Topnotch supporting cast includes Véronique Silver as daughter Christiane who's driven to distraction by philandering doctor husband; Jean Benguigui is Bertille's son and brutish father of a musical child prodigy; and Jean-Paul Muel plays sweet-tempered retarded Romain who secretly helps Bertille rendezvous with her black sheep.

Bernard Lutic's cinematography of French countryside is a plus, and intimate string score by Paul Misraki boosts key moments. — Lour.

VERRIEGELTE ZEIT
(LOCKED UP TIME)
(GERMAN-DOCU-B&W)

A co-production of Alert Film and DEFA in cooperation with SFB. Produced by Bernd Burkhardt and Alfred Hürmer. Directed by Sybille Schönemann. Camera (b&w), Thomas Plenert, with Michael Löwenberg; editor, Gudrun Steinbrück; music, Thomas Kahane; sound, Ronald Gohlke; mix, Ulrich Fengler; lighting, Wolfgang Hirschke; production director, Herbert Kruschke. Reviewed at Berlin Film Festival, Feb. 17, 1991. Running time: **90 MIN.**

Probably the best of the

flood of docus about ex-East Germany, "Locked Up Time" relates — with force, humor and compassion — filmmaker Sybille Schönemann's search for those responsible for her imprisonment in the GDR.

The ability to reduce the bureaucratic complexities of a totalitarian system to a human level bodes well for the pic on the fest and arthouse circuits.

In 1984, East German Schönemann and her husband, both employed at the DEFA film studios in Babelsberg, applied for an exit visa. The Stasi secret police immediately began to follow their every move, eventually arresting and jailing Schönemann. The West German government literally bought her freedom, a common practice under the old East German regime.

Shortly after the fall of the Berlin Wall, Schönemann returned east with a West German crew to question those involved in her arrest, conviction and imprisonment. Pic opens effectively with interviews with construction workers who built a massive checkpoint between East and West. They are now earning their living dismantling the same buildings they constructed earlier.

Schönemann was bused through this checkpoint into the West after being stripped of her East German citizenship and expelled from the GDR after a year in prison.

Through a series of interviews Schönemann conducted on and off camera, she tracks down one by one those who cost her job, home, health and family. She gets nothing but evasion and denials of personal responsibility.

When asked why she wasn't allowed to receive mail from her husband, her former warden, who withheld the letters, isn't sure, but offers to look up the statute. He complains that the job of censoring letters was stressful. The Stasi officer who nabbed Schönemann on the street doesn't remember her when she finds him hanging out his wash.

Judge who convicted her says her case was out of his hands and acquittal out of the question. A DEFA worker who had never met Schönemann admitted to signing a document officially damning her because of orders from studio bigwigs. The former studio head, also a member of the Communist Party's Central Committee, wouldn't talk.

The hunters are hunted, and the buck passing and naysaying of petty functionaries in the service of an evil system will remind viewers of another period in German history.

Film's strong point is that the interviews are full of humor. Schönemann's nonconfrontational tone lends a human, rather than pedantic, feel to the film. With a meticulous eye for detail, she re-enacts her arrest, having her mugshots taken by the same camera that shot the originals and comparing the two, stripping off her clothing and jewelry. She returns to her former cell (with her former cellmate), and she even brings her camera to the communal toilets she used. A woman allows her to climb the cherry tree she could once see from her cell.

Schönemann gracefully hands her victims the rope and lets them hang themselves, avoiding lapses into vindictiveness or sentimentality.

Technical credits are good, especially the well-framed, crisp black & white photography. — *Reli.*

LA LEYENDA DE UNA MASCARA
(THE LEGEND OF A MASK)
(MEXICAN)

A Conacine-Mexican Film Institute (Imcine) production. Written and directed by José Buil. Camera (color), Henner Hofmann; editor, Sigfrido García Case; music, Oscar Reynoso; sound, Fernando Cámera, René Ruiz Cerón; art direction, Patricia Eguía, Alfonso Morales; costumes, Clementina Esquivel. Reviewed at the VI Festival de Cine Mexicano, Guadalajara, March 11, 1991. Running time: **95 MIN.**
El Angel Enmascarado . Héctor Bonilla
Juan J. Luna . . . . Héctor Ortega
Emilia . . . . María Rojo
Lina Roma . . . . Gina Morett
López . . . . Pedro Armendáriz
Blanca . . . . Martha Papadimitriou
Jacinto . . . . Roberto Cobo
Olmo Robles . . . . . Damián Alcázar
Also with: Fernando Rubio, Gabriel Pingarrón.

Functioning as both a homage to and a satire of the low-budget Mexican wrestling pics of the '50s and '60s (notably films featuring El Santo), "The Legend Of A Mask" is a quirky camp treatment that should find cult status, despite those unfamiliar with the genre.

First feature by José Buil, maker of an earlier 1981 short tribute to "El Santo" (Adiós, Adiós, Idolo Mio), pic follows a '40s film noir approach. With a nod to "Citizen Kane," story takes off when the body of famed wrestling great "El Angel Enmascarado" (The Masked Angel, played by Héctor Bonilla) is found dead on the floor of his luxurious mansion.

Urged on by his hardboiled editor (Pedro Armendáriz), alcoholic chain-smoking journalist Olmo Robles (Damián Alcázar) sets out to uncover the story of a lifetime, even if it means the end of his troubled marriage: To discover the true identity of the masked wrestler.

The story has him wander the dark capital streets in pursuit of the wrestler's past. As a young wrestler, he forsook his true identity forever, to become the man without a face. The reporter encounters the gritty underworld of wrestlers, gangsters, film producers, nightclubs, his path stalked by an old black car bearing a solitary figure. He is warned off the case, he is sure the secret lies with the Angel's former wife, a nightclub singer (Gina Morett).

Uncharacteristic of Mexican cinema, the pic plays generously with the genre, including an animated section. Mocking '50s-style serials, film begins with a voice-over labeling this as episode 27.

Art direction by Patricia Eguía and Alfonso Morales captures the dark look of this nocturnal work, as does the able lensing of cameraman Henner Hofmann.

Despite a few excesses, film has enough invention and humor to capture some international interest, and should do well on the fest and arthouse circuit. — *Lent.*

GISELLE
(DANISH-DOCU-B&W)

A Danish Film Institute presentation of a Metronome production, in cooperation with DFI and TV2/Denmark. Produced by Mads Egmont Christensen. Written and directed by Anne Regitze Wivel. Camera (b&w), Dan Laustsen; editor, Ghita Leavens Beckendorff; music, Adolphe Adam; sound (Dolby), Jan Juhler; assistant director, Lennart Pasborg; production manager, Marianne Christensen; choreography, Jean Coralli, Jules Perot. Reviewed at Nordic Film Festival, Florence Gould Hall-French Institute, N.Y., April 14, 1991. Running time: **98 MIN.**
Director . . . . . Henning Kronstam
Giselle . . . . Heidi Ryom
Albrecht . . . . Lloyd Riggins
Hilarion . . . . . Peter Bo Bendixen
Moderen . . . . Sorella Englund
Pianist . . . . Julian Thurber
Also with: Mette-Ida Kirk, Christina Nilsson.

This educational documentary presents the rehearsals and performance of Adolphe Adam's ballet "Giselle" from the point-of-view of talented ballet master Henning Kronstam. Anne Wivel's film is so single-minded in focus that it is of limited interest, however.

In zeroing in on Kronstam, Wivel chooses to ignore the rest of his collaborators. Gaunt ballerina Heidi Ryom and her co-stars strain to fulfill the directions of taskmaster Kronstam, but the performers never make a suggestion or seem to have any input into their roles.

With Kronstam dancing, miming and acting out every little gesture and move, as well as describing in Danish or English exactly what each character is thinking, the film presents ballet as the closest lively art to puppetry. Ballet students will learn a lot about how this particular piece works, as well as being impressed with Kronstam's understanding of same, but that's about it.

Other than footage of a class of youngsters preparing for a life of dance and moodily lit shots of Kronstam in pensive mode, the film is fairly straightforward documentation of the maestro's creative process. Not enough footage of the final performance is included to be satisfying to "Giselle" fans, since Wivel's interest is in the preparation. A 1978 German film release starring Carla Fracci as "Giselle" exists to satisfy the die-hards.

Wivel's decision to shoot in black & white has its pluses in dramatic moments, but would have benefited from a reel or two bursting into color when the full-dress ballet is performed. Besides Julian Thurber's piano accompaniment, there is disconcerting use of background music from diverse sources including Mozart's "The Magic Flute." — *Lor.*

LA TRIBU
(THE TRIBE)
(FRENCH)

An AAA release of a Sara Films-Ciné Cinq co-production with the participation of Canal Plus. Produced by Alain Sarde. Executive producer, Christine Gozlan. Directed by Yves Boisset. Screenplay, Boisset, Alain Scott, based on Christian Lehman's book; camera (Panavision, color), Fabio Conversi; editor, Albert Jurgenson; music, Philippe Sarde; sound, Jean-Pierre Fenie; art direction, Claude Bouvard, Jean-Baptiste Poirot; costumes, Fanny Jukubowicz. Reviewed at UGC Normandie theater, Paris, April 15, 1991. Running time: **90 MIN.**
Olivier Rohan . . . . . Stephane Freiss
Laurence . . . . . Catherine Wilkening
François . . . . Maxime Leroux

Not terribly suspenseful tale of young doctor who stumbles upon political and medical machinations, "The Tribe" unfolds like a standard tv movie-of-the-week. Since well-intentioned pic is only slightly more interesting than spending time in a doctor's waiting room, a microscope is needed to see prospects in other markets.

An idealistic young cardiologist (Stephane Freiss) has just gone into private general practice, but has to remain on call at the regional hospital to make ends meet. (Non-French audiences may find it difficult to accept the fact that 10% of full-fledged physicians routinely earn less than $1,000 a month.)

A local hotshot doc (Jean-Pierre Bacri) asks Freiss to replace him on night call. When he gets a message that a "kid's taken a turn for the worse," the young doctor makes a house call to the home of an extreme right-wing politician (Georges Wilson) that will have serious consequences. The surprise is mutual when Freiss' distinguished colleague (Jean-Pierre Bisson) answers the door.

Freiss recommends that the patient, a 16-year-old boy, be taken to the hospital for observation, but Wilson and Bisson won't hear of it. The older men thank the young M.D. for stopping by, and Wilson stuffs 2,000 francs ($400) into his pocket.

Hours later the same boy turns up in the emergency room where, despite Freiss' efforts, he dies.

With unrequested help from a diligent intern (Kader Boukhanef) and live-in girlfriend (Catherine Wilkening), host of a freewheeling investigative radio show, Friess will discover the unsavory connection between the dead boy, the older doctors and the all-powerful pol.

When the g.f. dies in a freak automobile accident, Freiss sets out on the path of ethical revenge. He will literally turn in his badge at film's end and walk off into the sunset — in this case, a volunteer stint with a medical aid outfit in Burma.

Despite a pre-credits disclaimer disavowing any similarity to real persons, living or dead, the politician and his Nouvelle France party, with its anti-Semitic, anti-immigration platform, is clearly modeled on Jean-Marie Le Pen's National Front. Discrepancies between fees charged by the national health service and in privately owned medical facilities also closely reflect recent scandals in Marseilles.

Despite widescreen, helmer's 20th feature looks perfunctory. Performances never rise above adequate although medical details, including an autopsy, ring true. Plot doesn't kick in until 25 minutes into pic, by which time audience pulse is dangerously low. — *Ness.*

GÈNIAL, MES PARENTS DIVORCENT!
(GREAT, MY PARENTS ARE DIVORCING!)
(FRENCH)

An AFMD release of an ASCL production. Produced by Anne François. Written and directed by Patrick Braoudé. Camera (color), Thierry Arbogast; music, Jacques Davidovici; sound, Jean-Bernard Thomasson; set design, Emmanuel Sorin; costumes, Carine Sarfati; makeup, Irene Ottavis. Reviewed at Cinéma George V, Paris, April 10, 1991. Running time: **96 MIN.**

Victor	Patrick Braoudé
Estelle	Sonia Vollereaux
Julien's mother	Clementine Celarie
Julien	Adrien Dirand
Thomas	Volodia Serre
Christian	Gianni Giardinelli
Pénélope	Jennifer Lauret

Also with: Jean-Paul Lilienfeld, Joachim Mazeau, Stanislas Forlani-Crevillen, Frabice Mansanarez, Edouard Barazer, Canaan Marguerite.

Given its astute mix of family insight and smoothly flowing comedy, "Great, My Parents Are Divorcing!" should have long legs as dubbed family video, and it also may succeed as a theatrical release.

This exceptionally clever grammar school comedy starts out with an 11-year-old boy trying to cope with his parents' divorce at home while falling in love for the first time at school. In an unusually inventive twist by director and scripter Patrick Braoudé, material mushrooms into all-out war between kids with divorced parents and rest of the suburban class.

Film features Julien (Adrien Dirand), an easygoing class leader with the same straight-backed gait and small nose as Mowgli in "The Jungle Book." He's stunned when his parents announce their divorce and his father moves out.

At school he becomes increasingly isolated until he meets a new classmate (Volodia Serre) who, with several sets of parents, explains the stages that Julien's mom (Clementine Celarie) is going through, from endless tears to a new lease on life.

Julien tries to hide home breakup at school where he and another classmate (Gianni Giradinelli) compete for the attention of teacher's foxy daughter (Jennifer Lauret). But when an incriminating photo of his father appears on a screen before the class, Julien picks a fight that turns into a schoolyard brawl.

Class divides into kids with and without divorced parents. Julien, seeing that his minority is fast losing ground, ups the ante during Christmas break: His club creates serious mischief for the other kids' parents. The feud eventually gets out of hand when a classmate nearly commits suicide because of his parents' separation.

First-time director Braoudé is adept at leading into scenes and weaving storylines. Especially good are short sequences added for emotional weight, such as the cut from Julien plugging his ears to his mother weeping in a nearby bedroom. Familiar clichés of school films look spontaneous, even the shamelessly saccharine shot of boy's first kiss.

Braoudé, who scripted the hit "Black Mic-Mac," has a fine ear here for moppet dialog. And as a teacher, he begins the new school year a well-meaning intelligent adult and ends up outmaneuvered and laughably frustrated.

Cast of talented nonpros includes 7-year-old Stanislas Forlani-Crevillen as a wisecracking shrimp, Canaan Marguerite as an overly sensitive boy and Richard Romain as a chubby teamplayer. Bright cinematography by Thierry Arbogast suits fast-paced material. — *Lour.*

PUEBLO DE MADERA
(WOODEN TOWN)
(MEXICAN)

A Conacite Dos-Television Española (TVE) production. Directed by Juan Antonio de la Riva. Screenplay, de la Riva, Francisco Sánchez; camera (color), Leoncio Villarias; editor, Oscar Figueroa; music, Antonio Avitia, Grupo Tránsito; sound, Miguel Sandoval; art direction, Patricia Eguía. Reviewed at the VI Festival de Cine Mexicano, Guadalajara, March 10, 1991. Running time: **138 MIN.**

Aurelio	Alfonso Echánove
Marina	Gabriela Roel
Nino	Ignacio Guadalupe
José Luis	Jahir de Rubín
Juan José	Ernesto Jesús
Shopkeeper	Angélica Aragón
Don Pancho	José Carlos Ruiz
Mario Almada	Himself

Following in the path of his 1984 pic "Vidas Errantes" (Errant Lives), Juan Antonio de la Riva's latest work "Wooden Town" also finds a home within the lumber camps and pine forests of the mountains of Durango. This intimate film offers a view of Mexico seldom depicted in cinema and deserves international interest.

Rather than pursue the adventures of a central character (as in his earlier pic), Mexican helmer de la Riva's episodic handling presents a large cast, tracing the day-to-day lives of these small-town inhabitants. Those expecting to see Mexican deserts and bright serapes will be surprised.

Among the many stories told: Newcomer (Alfonso Echánove) is carrying on an affair with his landlady (Angélica Aragón), two adolescent friends are about to be separated as one begins work at the camp and the other moves to the state capital, a young couple are torn as the husband plans to go to the U.S. for work, and town punks rob the local store.

Actor José Carlos Ruiz reprises his "Vidas Errantes" role as the town's projectionist, whose future is doomed as satellite dishes intrude on the rural landscape. Thesping throughout is low-key and naturalistic as the inhabitants establish a daily rhythm.

Leoncio Villarias' cinematography highlights the natural setting, and keeps focus on the town itself as pic's central character.

Unfortunately, some repetitions, such as the third fantasy appearance of Mario Almada as a gunfighter, tend to mar his intimate portrait of a town in transition. — *Lent.*

ITT A SZABADSAGI
(VOILA LA LIBERTÉ!)
(HUNGARIAN)

A Hunnia Filmstudio production. Produced by Peter Vajda. Screenplay, Vajda, Andras Salamon; camera (Eastmancolor), Sandor Kardos; editor, Teri Losonci; music, Laszlo Des, Ando Drom; sound, Gyorgy Kovacs; production design, Gabor Bachman. Reviewed at Berlin Film Festival (Panorama), Feb. 24, 1991. Running time: **92 MIN.**

Imre	Peter Andorai
Russian prostitute	Evdokija Germanova

Also with: Sandor Fabri, Karoly Lowry.

Some of the huge problems of political freedom's arrival to central European Communist satellites are graphically presented in bleak, intensely sad "Voila La Liberté." In commercial terms, a more disciplined approach to the subject matter would have made for a more successful picture.

It's basically a day in the life of an ordinary Hungarian worker who, with three friends, takes a trip to Vienna, an impossibility under the old system. He plans to launder some black market money and pick up valuable items like a tv set and VCR. His friends spend the trip grumbling about past and present.

There are huge traffic jams at the border, and when Imre tries to jump the line, he's forced back by other drivers. Eventually the quartet get to Vienna, which seems to be peopled with Hungarians trying to exploit other Hungarians. (Pic was shot last winter when the sense of freedom was still new.)

In the end, Imre loses everything: money, purchases, car (towed away by the police), friends and even his self-respect. He winds up, drunk and defeated, with a Russian prostitute, and then has to cross the border back into Hungary illegally, as if the bad old days prevail.

Director Peter Vajda tells a tragic story of a man unable to accept newfound freedoms, and the film suggests that the painful events depicted are all too true. Peter Andorai gives a strong performance as the basically stupid man who finds himself shafted at every turn.

Unfortunately, the film's strong, if extremely downbeat, qualities are swamped by ugly visuals. The film is shot in a way some Magyar filmmakers love: with hand-held camera constantly finding odd and pretentious angles from which to shoot the most simple setup. This kind of style should disappear fast from Hungarian films. The music, at least, is jolly. — *Strat.*

TANZ AUF DER KIPPE
(DANCE ON THE DUMP)
(GERMAN)

A DEFA Studio, Babelsberg Group, production. Produced by Horst Hartwig. Written and directed by Jurgen Brauer, from the book "Eye Operation" by Jurij Koch; camera (color), Brauer; editor, Erika Lempuhl; music, Ralf Hoyer; sound, Wolfgang Hofer; production design, Harry Leupold; costumes, Inge Konicek; production manager, Dieter Albrecht; assistant director, Sylvia Burza. Reviewed at Berlin Film Festival (Panorama), Feb. 16, 1991. Running time: 96 MIN.
With: Frank Stieren, Dagmar Manzel, Winifried Glatzeder, Eberhard Kirchberg.

Produced at DEFA Studios as the wall was coming down, "Dancing On The Dump" is an interesting insight into East German attitudes of that time, but it's unlikely to travel outside home turf.

Pic, told in flashback, opens with the hero, an anguished and rebellious teen, being badly beaten on a (symbolic) garbage dump. His attackers include the husband of a teacher he likes. The boy is left almost blind from being dunked into a lime solution. Much of pic takes place at the hospital as he undergoes treatment.

By incorporating the extinction of the East German state, writer-director-cameraman Jurgen Brauer has added a powerful dimension to familiar teenage rebellion and frustration. Frank Stieren is a find as the teen. Pic is technically efficient in all departments. — *Strat.*

UP AGAINST THE WALL

An African American Image production. Executive producer, Dr. Jawanza Kunjufu. Produced by Chuck Colbert, Zuindi Colbert. Directed by Ron O'Neal. Screenplay, Emma Young, Songodina Ifatunji, Chuck Colbert, Zuindi Colbert, from story by Kunjufu; camera (color), LeRoy Patton; editor, Thomas Miller; music, Theodis Rodgers; sound, Jake Collins; associate producer, Nate Grant, Sasha Dalton, Zuindi Colbert. Reviewed at the Cinecenter, Chicago, April 11, 1991. MPAA rating: PG-13. Running time: 100 MIN.
Louise Bradley . . . . . . Marla Gibbs
George Wilkes . . . . Ron O'Neal
Jesse Bradley . . . . . Stoney Jackson
Sean Bradley . . Catero Alain Colbert

"Up Against The Wall" begins as a meager, mildly interesting story of a black youth making the transition from the projects to suburbs, devolves into half-baked soap opera, then unravels completely with a series of hilarious gaffes. Pic might pick up a few dollars initially from audiences interested in black independent films, but it's unlikely to linger.

Catero Alain Colbert (who fared better two years ago in another low-budget Chicago indie, "The Perfect Model") plays the youth in question, Sean, an incredibly naive West Sider pushed by his mother (Marla Gibbs) into attending a suburban high school that might lead him to college.

The high school track coach (Oscar Brown Jr. in a likable performance) wants Sean for his cross country team since he's supposedly a top runner in Chicago, but it's difficult to tell since he falls over half-dead after a couple of laps around the gym on his first day.

For a kid from the Rockwell Gardens housing project, Sean really does not know his way around. He could definitely use a course in remedial street smarts.

After moving into the deluxe digs of dope-dealing older brother Jesse (Stoney Jackson) so he won't have to travel so far to school, Sean also takes a job running errands for him.

Though he knows his brother's lavish apartment and expensive clothes are made possible by drug deals, it does not occur to him to wonder why he is always delivering sacks of dirty laundry to the same seedy-looking guy in the same crummy laundromat — until one sack falls over one day and something like a five-pound bag of cocaine tumbles out.

Stoney Jackson effortlessly steals this film (though why he would want to is unclear) and he is especially entertaining when Sean self-righteously attacks Jesse for selling drugs, despite the fact that Sean has been living in the fancy house, wearing the expensive clothes and spending the easy money.

Jesse responds with towering indignation, paces frantically, registers shock, scorn and amazement and sputters incoherently.

Around this time the unintentional hilarity begins to turn up pretty regularly. Sean manfully confronts an evildoer and socks him on the jaw — only the sound of the punch is heard before his fist makes contact.

When good guy George Wilkes (Ron O'Neal of "Superfly") is still reeling after learning that Sean is his love child — enough to upset anybody — and his wife of many years is threatening divorce, his kid looks off into the distance and asks: "Why can't black men respect their women?" O'Neal, still gamely emoting, murmurs: "Oh, that's . . . just an assumption."

Final surprise comes at the very end when the legend "To God Be The Glory" scrolls up for no apparent reason. Religion plays little or no part in the proceedings of this pic, though one song on the soundtrack seems to have a pious theme.

Perhaps the producers felt that they could hedge their bets by making an appeal to the church trade. If the film dies at the box office, perhaps it could enjoy eternal life at youth retreats and runaway shelters. Maybe it could become a more up-to-date substitute for "The Cross And The Switchblade." — *Brin.*

IL PORTABORSE
(THE FACTOTUM)
(ITALIAN-FRENCH)

A Titanus Distribuzione release of a Sacher Film-Eidoscope Prods.-Banfilm coproduction. Produced by Nanni Moretti, Angelo Barbagallo. Directed by Daniele Lucchetti. Screenplay, Sandro Petraglia, Stefano Rulli, with Lucchetti; camera (Technicolor), Alessandro Pesci; editor, Mirco Garrone; music, Dario Lucantoni; art direction, Giancarlo Basili, Leonardo Scarpa. Reviewed at Rivoli Cinema, Rome, April 15, 1991. Running time: **115 MIN.**
Luciano Sandulli . . . . . Silvio Orlando
Cesaro Botero . . . . . . Nanni Moretti
Francesco Sanna . . . . . . Giulio Brogi
Juliette . . . . Anne Roussel
Irene . . . . Angela Finocchiaro
Also with: Graziano Giusti, Lucio Allocca, Dario Cantarelli, Antonio Petrocelli, Gianna Paola Scaffidi, Guido Alberti, Renato Carpentieri, Silvia Cohen.

"**T**he Factotum" is an irresistible broadside against Italian politics, and both critics and audiences are finding it one of the most exciting Italo films in years. This outspoken but humorous portrait of a cynical, corrupt politician already shows signs of becoming a local cult classic. A runaway hit since it opened, pic's been especially appreciated in the Machiavellian capital, Rome.

While arthouse distribs line up for offshore rights, foreigners will get a taste of the pic's pungent wit when it unspools in competition at Cannes. Even if they don't get all the sly jokes, they'll enjoy the picture's continental sarcasm and lively, American-style pace.

Newcomer Silvio Orlandi plays an honest high school lit teacher whose historic home on the Amalfi coast is crumbling for lack of repairs. To earn money, he ghostwrites for a nutty political columnist. This brings him to the attention of the minister of government investment (Nanni Moretti).

Moretti's character here — perfect personification of the self-serving, lying, vote-tampering politician — is destined to be remembered in Italian cinema. Playing with hilarious over-the-top dryness, Moretti makes a delightful, if chilling, archvillain.

Though the pol's party is never stated, local auds have no trouble identifying him as an amalgamation of several real Socialist Party politicos. This has created one of the controversies surrounding the pic.

The film goes far beyond attacking one party, however.

Through wickedly clever comedy, it attacks the underhanded workings of an entire class of decadent modern politicians.

In the beginning, the teacher enjoys the thrill of hearing his words in the young minister's mouth. He basks in the privileges of being close to power: an apartment in old Rome, a red convertible, his g.f. (Angela Finocchiaro) transferred to a teaching post in Rome, his crumbling house declared a historical monument and restored at state expense. Audiences meet each new perk with laughs and groans.

He also falls for Moretti's pretty French assistant (a charming Anne Roussel). His sense of fidelity to Finocchiaro keeps him from temptation, and his naivete prevents him from realizing the assistant is Moretti's mistress.

Helmer Daniele Lucchetti casts himself as a director who shoots a hideous tv commercial for Moretti's electoral campaign. The minister's fury is one of pic's great moments, as he berates his staff for choosing a director proposed by his party.

In two lines, Moretti slams party-line hirings at pubcaster RAI-TV and disparages the supposed "gift" from the Socialists to Silvio Berlusconi of "half the country's tv networks."

If Moretti is a vampirish bloodsucker who will stop at nothing to win the elections, Orlando is a caricature, too — an innocent lamb in the lion's den who slowly awakens to the truth. With militant left-wing journalist Giulio Brogi, he attempts to thwart the minister from tampering with the vote. But it's too late. There's no more need to tamper with anything, because the soul of the electorate has already been corrupted into voting for the crooks.

As producer and star of "The Factotum," Moretti (who produced Lucchetti's first film, "It'll Happen Tomorrow") is a key element to its success. The other important ingredient is a leering, on-target script by Stefano Rulli and Sandro Petraglia, youthful masters at turning incisive social themes into popular entertainment (they did tv's "The Octopus"). They took over from earlier writers Franco Bernini and Angelo Pasquini (in a publicized dispute) and made the main character more naive and sympathetic.

Cinematography by Alessandro Pesci and cameraman Roberto Cimatti is simple and effective; so is Dario Lucantoni's ironic score. To single out one thesp from a fine cast, Antonio Petrocelli is a terrifically unctuous assistant, who gets a laugh just by being in the shot. — *Yung.*

MADAME BOVARY
(FRENCH)

An MK2 release of a Marin Karmitz-MK2-CED-FR3 co-production. Directed by Claude Chabrol. Screenplay, Chabrol, based on the novel by Gustave Flaubert; camera (color), Jean Rabier; editor, Monique Fardoulis; music, Matthieu Chabrol; sound, Jean-Bernard Thomasson; set design, Michèle Abbe; costumes, Corinne Jorry; makeup, Catherin Demesmaeker. Reviewed at Gaumont Convention, Paris, April 19, 1991. Running time: **140 MIN.**
Emma Bovary . . . . Isabelle Huppert
Charles Bovary . Jean-François Balmer
Rodolphe Boulanger . . . .
           Christophe Malavoy
M. Homais . . . . Jean Yanne
Leon Dupuis . . . . . . Lucas Belvaux
Also with: Christiane Minazzoli, Jean-Louis Maury, Florent Gibassier, Marie Mergey.

Highly critical of all social conventions, "Madame Bovary" is a small-town melodrama about a middle-class couple who comes to total ruin. Claude Chabrol's cool adaptation of the French classic is solid fare for arthouses and the foreign vid market but risky for wider release.

The picture, closely based on Flaubert's novel, opens with the first meeting of coltish country-bred Emma (Isabelle Huppert) and country doctor Charles Bovary (Jean-François Balmer), a disastrous couple in the making. She's pretty and quick-witted and self-absorbed; he's sweet, affectionate and dull as a dust bin.

Once married, Emma soon regrets her decision but takes comfort in her social status and the luxury gowns sold by a devilishly eager merchant (Jean-Louis Maury). She also encourages the advances of a notary clerk (Lucas Belvaux) while clinging to social convention, at least until Rodolphe (Christophe Malavoy), an aristocratic womanizer next door, seduces her.

When she presses her lover for a permanent out-of-town holiday, he skips town and she finds herself up to her petticoats in debt. So she comes to a bad end, dragging her stupefied spouse with her.

Hubbert, in a possibly award-winning performance, shifts from marital frustration, to clinical depression to gleeful passion. Early on she's pitiful as the emotionally and intellectually starved young wife. But mostly she carries the repellent air of a small-time egoist.

Chabrol, ever the broad social satirist, constrains Hubbert's performance by keeping scenes short and the camera at a distance. But at least her big speech and best scene, when she verbally assaults her ex-lover for turning down her plea for dough, is a wonderfully spirited self-reckoning.

Helmer also skillfully weaves social motifs — brief reappearances by the deformed beggar, a snooty nobleman and a crippled doorman. The Gallic tone is consistently wry and sometimes outright mocking.

After Emma's first romp in the extramarital hay, a violin note rings out overhead. Chabrol has a wary sympathy for his heroine up until the last scenes, when she turns suddenly desperate and suffers an excruciating death.

Topnotch performances by the rest of cast include Balmer's Bovary, bovine and pathetically uncomprehending; Belvaux as a clerk who shifts from cautious beau to determined lover; and Maury's convincingly oily merchant.

Lenser Jean Rabier chooses strong shadows for indoor sets, which suits the film's serious tone. Corinne Jorry deserves kudos for Emma's wardrobe, which becomes more opulent as her finances worsen.

Michèle Abbe's set design is expert on period detail, right down to the expensive riding whip that Emma gives her aristocrat, a symbol of Chabrol's key interest: socially refined plays for power and sex in a small city. — *Lour.*

OSCAR

A Buena Vista release of a Touchstone Pictures presentation in association with Silver Screen Partners IV of a Ponti/Vecchio production and a Landis/Belzberg production. Produced by Leslie Belzberg. Executive producers, Alex Pónti, Joseph S. Vecchio. Directed by John Landis. Screenplay, Michael Barrie, Jim Mulholland, based on the play by Claude Magnier; camera (Technicolor), Mac Ahlberg; editor, Dale Beldin; music, Elmer Bernstein; sound (Dolby), William B. Kaplan; production design, Bill Kenney; art direction, Wm. Ladd Skinner; set design, Nick Navarro, Sally Thornton, Richard F. Mays, Lawrence Hubbs, Steven Wolff; set decoration, Rick T. Gentz; costume design, Deborah Nadoolman; associate producer, Tony Munafo; assistant director, Frank Capra III; casting, Jackie Burch. Reviewed at Loews Tower East theater, N.Y., April 18, 1991. MPAA Rating: PG. Running time: **109 MIN.**

Angelo (Snaps) Provolone . . . .
. . . . Sylvester Stallone
Sofia Provolone . . . . . . Ornella Muti
Father Clemente . . . . . Don Ameche
Aldo . . . . Peter Riegert
Dr. Poole . . . . Tim Curry
Anthony Rossano . . . . Vincent Spano
Lisa Provolone . . . . . Marisa Tomei
Five Spot Charlie . . . . Eddie Bracken
Roxanne . . . . Linda Gray
Connie . . . . Chazz Palminteri
Lt. Toomey . . . . . . Kurtwood Smith
Aunt Rosa . . . . . . Yvonne DeCarlo
Kirkwood . . . . Ken Howard
Overton . . . . William Atherton
Luigi Finucci . . . . . . Martin Ferrero
Guido Finucci . . . . . . Harry Shearer
Van Leland . . . . Sam Chew Jr.
Milhous . . . . Mark Metcalf
Vendetti . . . . Richard Romanus
Ace . . . . Joey Travolta
Theresa . . . . . . Elizabeth Barondes
    Also with: Joycelyn O'Brien, Robert Lesser, Art La Fleur, Richard Foronjy, Paul Greco, Arleen Sorkin, Kai Wulff, Kirk Douglas.

"Oscar" is an intermittently amusing throwback to gangster comedies of the 1930s. While dominated by star Sylvester Stallone and heavy doses of production and costume design, pic is most distinguished by sterling turns by superb character actors that immediately conjure up memories of old Hollywood. Zany farce generates a fair share of laughs but still probably remains too creaky a conceit for modern audiences to go for in a big way.

Verbally adept script by tv comedy writers Michael Barrie and Jim Mulholland is based on a 1958 French play of the same name by Claude Magnier that was turned into a 1967 film starring Louis de Funes and directed by Edouard Molinaro.

Set virtually entirely in Stallone's mansion, antics have an inescapably stagebound feel, and story construction involves the kind of outrageous implausibilities and coincidences most identified with boulevard farce.

Manic proceedings unfold within a four-hour time period on the morning when legendary hood Angelo (Snaps) Provolone (Stallone), following through on a promise to his dying father, will officially go straight by entering the banking business.

Surrounded by an assortment of genial lugs and self-styled wiseguys straight out of Damon Runyon and Preston Sturges, Snaps is rudely awakened on his big day by his young accountant (Vincent Spano), who brashly announces he needs a big raise so he can afford to marry the gang-

ster's daughter (Marisa Tomei).

This sets into motion a domestic tempest involving two more potential husbands for the daughter, her surprise announcement she's pregnant, the arrival of another woman who claims to be Snaps' daughter and the mixing up of three identical black bags that separately contain valuable jewels, $50,000 in cash and some ladies lingerie.

The main challenge of such a project is in bringing conviction to artificial conventions so specifically rooted in a particular time and place. Filled with malapropisms and nutty wordplay, most of the dialog is in Italian tough-guy vernacular, and altogether too many of the gags have to do with Snaps and his henchmen trying to wash the thuggery out of their behavior and assume an aura of class.

Such are the concerns of the story that one could imagine being performed in, say, 1938, in black & white with a dream cast of Edward G. Robinson in the Stallone role and such other stalwarts as Akim Tamiroff, Ned Sparks, Joan Blondell, John Garfield, Edward Everett Horton, Franklin Pangborn, Edgar Kennedy and Eduardo Ciannelli supporting him.

As it happens, director John Landis has done rather better than one might have expected in making a 1930s comedy in 1991.

Fundamentally, pic is hollow at the core, a concoction in which Stallone undoubtedly has more lines to say than in all his Rambo films put together and does no more than a serviceable job in getting across the humor. More belligerence and genuine menace would have helped the performance considerably, as would have a mastery of feigned outrage and the double take.

But pic's a pleasure around the edges. Landis has established a nifty link with the old days through his casting of Don Ameche and Eddie Bracken, not to mention Yvonne DeCarlo and, in an opening scene cameo as Snaps' father, Kirk Douglas.

Several of the younger players conjure up the style of classical Hollywood farce with remarkable flair, making the most of limited screen time.

As Stallone's grinning, fastidious elocution teacher who becomes an unlikely match for his boss' daughter, Tim Curry utterly steals the film whenever he's on and generates the film's biggest laughs. Peter Riegert rings astonishingly true as Stallone's

low-keyed, sarcastic major domo, Chazz Palminteri is similarly right on the money as his dimwitted bodyguard and Martin Ferrero and Harry Shearer are pricelessly funny as Italian tailors inadvertently mistaken for hitmen. Tomei has her moves down as the big man's overly protected daughter.

Stuck with the straight roles are Spano, vigorous as the gutsy but frustrated suitor, and lovely Italian star Ornella Muti, properly emotional and domineering as the strong-willed wife. Just about everyone in the very large cast hits the right note of slightly crazed enthusiasm without going over the top.

When not appreciating the comic performances, one can't help but notice the film's elaborate sets and costumes. As designed by Bill Kenney, Stallone's mansion is a florid Victorian affair reeking of flowers and the aspiration to dignity. Deborah Nadoolman's wardrobe designs run to impeccable opulence and the most expensive of fabrics. Mac Ahlberg has shot it all brightly, if not garishly.

With a considerable boost from Rossini, Elmer Bernstein's score energetically moves things along, and Landis and editor Dale Beldin have tried to slide through the most implausible and boringly expository scenes as quickly as possible.

"Oscar" won't win Oscars, but it isn't quite the Golden Turkey it might have been either.
— *Cart.*

MORTAL THOUGHTS

A Columbia Pictures release of a New Visions Entertainment and Polar Entertainment production in association with Rufglen Film. Produced by John Fiedler and Mark Tarlov. Executive producers, Taylor Hackford, Stuart Benjamin. Directed by Alan Rudolph. Screenplay, William Reilly, Claude Kerven; camera (color), Elliot Davis; editor, Tom Walls; music, Mark Isham; sound (Dolby), Gary Alper; production design, Howard Cummings; costume design, Hope Hanafin; art direction, Robert K. Shaw, Jr.; set decoration, Beth Kushnick; assistant director, Robert Girolami; 2nd unit director, Greg Walker; co-producer, Demi Moore; casting, Donna Isaacson, John Lyons. Reviewed at Columbia Studios, Culver City, Calif., April 11, 1991. MPAA rating: R. Running time: **104 MIN.**
Cynthia Kellogg . . . . . . Demi Moore
Joyce Urbanski . . . . Glenne Headley
James Urbanski . . . . . . Bruce Willis
Arthur Kellogg . . . . . . John Pankow
Det. John Woods . . . . Harvey Keitel
Linda Nealon . . . . Billie Neal

Two gals make a murderous mess of a bad situation in

"Mortal Thoughts," and audiences are not likely to root for them. Played straight and for sympathy, tale of dark retaliation goes astray early on, despite the promise created at the outset by imaginative, energetic production and appealing performances.

Light b.o. prospects for the Columbia release won't bring much cheer to the production entity, financially troubled New Visions. Demi Moore and Glenne Headley play lifelong friends who run a blue-collar New Jersey beauty shop and remain closer to each other than to their husbands. Small wonder, since Moore's husband (John Pankow) is a boorish salesman, and Headley's wed to a thoroughly despicable, abusive lout (Bruce Willis).

Headley's running response is that he should die and she wants to kill him, but Moore never takes it seriously until Willis ends up with his throat cut and the two femmes have the blood on their hands.

What happens next has a lot to do with their dark and justified loathing of the out-of-control brute, but not much to do with logic or nobility or even savvy criminality — three things audiences would rather see than the disaster that ensues.

Scripters William Reilly and Claude Kerven play the whole thing out from a police interrogation room, where a detective (Harvey Keitel) hammers away at Moore to get at the real story, which unspools in flashbacks. Structure works fine, thanks to strong work by director Alan Rudolph and his cast, who infuse both the q&a's and the flashbacks with propulsive energy.

But pic can't decide whether it's about abusive relationships (audience doesn't learn enough about Headley for that to work), the boundaries of femme friendship and loyalty (it's not very stirring in that department) or crafty police interrogation techniques. It winds up being the latter since Keitel's the one who triumphs. This is not a very satisfying outcome.

Pic has plenty of character and compelling human strife up until the black deed occurs. After that it's a long uncomfortable sweat in the old police hot seat while waiting for things to make some sense.

Project is handsomely mounted, despite its scripted pitfalls. Rudolph coaxes strong perfs all around and gets highly charged interplay from the ill-fated trio of Moore, Headley and Willis.

The excellent Headley is particularly fine as the wily, hard-edged murder suspect in a difficult, shifting role, while Willis and Moore (who co-produced) do just fine onscreen together with plenty of authentic charge between them and no hint of winky inside nonsense. — *Daws.*

A KISS BEFORE DYING

A Universal Pictures release of an Initial Film/Robert Lawrence production. Produced by Lawrence. Executive producer, Eric Fellner. Directed by James Dearden. Screenplay, Dearden, based on novel by Ira Levin; camera (Technicolor), Mike Southon; editor, Michael Bradsell; music, Howard Shore; sound, Simon Okin (U.K.), Frank Stettner (Va.); production design, Jim Clay; costume design, Marit Allen; art direction, Rod McClean, Chris Seagers; associate producer, Chris Thompson; assistant director, Patrick Clayton; casting, Davis and Zimmerman (U.K.), Suzanne Smith (N.Y.). Reviewed at Avco Cinema Center, L.A., April 22, 1991. MPAA rating: R. Running time: **95 MIN.**
Jonathan Corliss . . . . . . Matt Dillon
Ellen/Dory Carlsson . . . . Sean Young
Thor Carlsson . . . . . Max Von Sydow
Dan Corelli . . . . James Russo
Mrs. Corliss . . . . Diane Ladd

Played with a satirical edge, this update on the pulpy 1956 thriller about a murderous social climber might have been good for a chill and a hoot, but played straight it's a real clunker. Writer-director James Dearden's ambitions for "A Kiss Before Dying" apparently blinded him to the material's true nature. Boxoffice is likely to dissolve quickly.

Based on Ira Levin's novel, Dearden's script gives us a brooding, wounded nobody (Matt Dillon) who grew up next to the Pennsylvania Railroad tracks, obsessed with the fortunes of the local industrial magnate (Max Von Sydow) whose Carlsson Copper cars rumble down the tracks.

At college he gets involved with the magnate's daughter, Dory (Sean Young), but throws her over (a ledge, that is) when he learns she's pregnant.

He then moves to New York and gets involved with her twin, social worker Ellen (Young again), passing himself off as her type and eventually marrying her and getting a job as right-hand man to Von Sydow. The only problem is Ellen's relentless interest in her sister's unsolved murder.

Dearden plays all of this bluntly for real, as if the modern world

is just a pushover for a man with a plan. As if a shrewd old businessman wouldn't see through this blankly polite young man, even on long idle fishing trips together.

As if Ellen, a rich and eligible young woman of some substance who's relentlessly demanding and suspicious of the police investigating her sister's so-called suicide, wouldn't turn her b.s. detector on the unpedigreed man who's courting her.

As a result, the scenes lack credibility to the point that the actors, apparently at a loss for an approach, seem to glaze over.

Young, in a blandly uncommitted perf, connects not at all with the Dillon's hunky young beau, and the two of them seem a cardboard couple, going through the paces of a false life. Not even their explicit sex scenes add excitement.

The killer, despite the glimpses of his upbringing Dearden provides early on, remains a mystery for most of the film. Had viewers been let in on his desperation and need, pic might have been compelling and tense. Dillon plays him with a noncharismatic mix of hard-headed cool and blank sincerity.

It's not hard to figure out why Dillon took this role after his "Drugstore Cowboy" breakthrough — it probably seemed a grown-up challenge that rested on menace and charisma — but the role doesn't deliver, any more than the pic delivers on the seamy promise of its title.

Dearden's visual approach is mostly a pastiche, from the bombastically arty opening, shot in a U.K. copper smelting plant, to the incongruous Hitchcock homages.

He finally hits it in the final seg, a tight, heart-pounding climax and chase when the lethal husband discovers his wife has found him out.

This taut passage, given an aptly nerve-fraying score by Howard Shore, is so satisfying it almost redeems the rest of the film. But given the wooden walk-through that led up to it, it comes a little too late. — *Daws.*

VAIKI IS 'AMERIKOS VIESBUCIO'
(THE CHILDREN OF 'HOTEL AMERICA')
(SOVIET)

A Lithuanian Film Studio production. Directed by Raimundas Banionis. Screenplay, Macej Drygas; camera (color), Jonas Tomasevicius; music, Faustas Latenas. Reviewed at Berlin Film Festival (Panorama), Feb. 18, 1991. Running time: **90 MIN.**
Rina . . . . Gabija Jaraminaite
Jagger . . . . Augustas Savelis
Also with: Jurga Kasciukaite, Rolandas Kaslas, Gediminas Karka.

Though technically a film from the Soviet Union, "The Children Of 'Hotel America'" is a Lithuanian production, and an angry one at that. Its timely assaults on Moscow's tough rule over the Baltic state, though couched in a story set in 1972, could spark international interest.

For teens in Vilnius, news of Woodstock has been immensely influential, and they decide to hold their own rock love-in. They set out for a campsite near a lake, and though there isn't a lot of music, they all have a good time skinny-dipping, lovemaking and talking peace.

In the morning, scores of police brutally attack the teens. The boys' heads are shaved, and they're returned in custody to their parents.

That's the background to a sweet love affair between cheerful, bespectacled Jagger (named after Mick, naturally) and Rina, a conventional girl whose family eventually emigrates to Israel. The couple make love at the campsite, but are separated later.

Title refers to an unofficial club to which these pro-Yank teens belong. Their fascination for all things American is really a rebellion against all things Russian. In light of current events, pic can be seen as an angry cry for freedom for Lithuania.

But it's a small-scale picture, technically rough at times, though appealingly acted by its earnest young cast. A symbolic earthquake in the final scene suggests that change may, after all, be on its way. — *Strat.*

THE CASTANET CLUB
(AUSTRALIAN-DOCU)

A Ronin Films release of a Central Park Films production in association with the Australian Film Commission. Produced by Glenys Rowe. Directed by Neil Armfield. Camera (color), Ray Argall; editor, Bill Russo; sound, David White; associate producer, Hilary Linstead. Reviewed at Mosman screening room, Sydney, April 12, 1991. Running time: **85 MIN.**
With: Angela Moore, Rodney Cambridge, Kylie Thomas, Penny Biggins, Peter

Mahoney, Stephen Abbott, Warren Coleman, Glenn Butcher, Kathy Bluff, Russell Cheek.

"The Castanet Club" is a performance film recording the antics of a 10-member group of musicians/comedians with a cult following in Australia. The Castanets are very much an acquired taste, and general audiences may not respond to the arch mixture of corny songs and low humor.

Locally, a quick theatrical release and then a useful video life is indicated; international success looks doubtful.

Stage director Neil Armfield used a top camera crew led by Ray Argall (director of "Return Home") to film three performances at a club at the famous Sydney beachside suburb of Bondi. Pic opens with the club manager urgently seeking a cheap act as a fill-in and deciding the Castanets is about the cheapest there is.

What follows is distinctively Australian, with songs like "Have A Few Drinks With Barnesy After A Gig" or "I've Been Everywhere" in which Peggy Biggins sings names of barely pronounceable Aussie towns at a lightning pace.

For comedy, a variation on wet t-shirt contests has three males dragged up from the audience and getting wet underpants, with the audience scoring the result. This might be a riot when seen live in a club after a few drinks, but is less likely to have cinema audiences rolling.

Pic's a creditable record of a popular phenomenon, lovingly filmed but lacking the impact of the real thing. At the 1984 Edinburgh Film Festival, group nabbed the "pick of the fringe" award. — *Strat.*

DANZON
(MEXICAN)

A Mexican Film Institute (Imcine)-Macondo Cine Video-Fondo de Fomento a la Calidad Cinematográfica (FFCC)-Television Española (TVE)-Tabasco Films-Gobierno del Estado de Veracruz production. Exec producer, Dulce Kuri. Produced by Jorge Sáanchez. Directed by María Novaro. Screenplay, María Novaro, Beatriz Novaro; camera (color), Rodrigo García; editor, Nelson Rodríguez, María Novaro; music, Danzonera Dimas de los Hnos. Pérez, Pepe Luis y Su Orquesta Universitaria, Danzonera Alma de Sotavento, Manzanita y el Son 4, Marimba "La Voz de Chiapas"; sound, Nerio Berberis; art direction, Marisa Pecanins, Norberto Sánchez. Reviewed at Estudios Churubusco, Mexi-

co City, March 15, 1991. Running time: **120 MIN.**
Julia . . . . María Rojo
Doña Ti . . . . Carmen Salinas
Silvia . . . . Margarita Isabel
Susy . . . . Tito Vasconcelos
La Colorada . . . . . . Blanca Guerra

Second feature by Mexican helmer **María Novaro**, "Danzón" shows an able hand in control of the material. Catchy danzón and bolero rhythms, imaginative lensing, able hoofing, a sympathetic heroine and a host of colorful characters should give this pic major crossover appeal.

Film features actress María Rojo as a Mexico City telephone operator whose one escape is ballroom dancing. When her partner of many years disappears one day, she decides to go to his native Veracruz to find him. Although there is no romantic link between the two, they had danced together for six years and had won several contests.

Her odyssey brings her into contact with a bevy of lively characters, such as a landlady played by veteran comic actress Carmen Salinas, a prostitute (Blanca Guerra) and a congenial transvestite nightclub performer (Tito Vasconcelos). The dancer also has a fling with a tugboat captain half her age.

Although the film is episodic, Rojo's infectious charm gives the film a solid center. And while acting all around is reliable, Guerra is the only one who makes an effort to use the distinctive Veracruz accent.

Rodrigo García's creative camerawork catches both the lingering intimate movements on the dance floor and the tropical bustling-port atmosphere of Veracruz.

Producers would be wise to issue a soundtrack disk. — *Lent.*

SWEET TALKER
(AUSTRALIAN)

A Seven Arts through New Line Cinema in U.S. release (Roadshow in Australia) of a New Visions Pictures presentation of a New Town film, in association with the Australian Film Finance Corp. Executive producers, Taylor Hackford, Stuart Benjamin. Produced by Ben Gannon. Directed by Michael Jenkins. Screenplay, Tony Morphett, from a story by Bryan Brown, Morphett; camera (Eastmancolor), Russell Boyd; supervising editor, Sheldon Kahn; editor, Neil Thumpston; music, Richard Thompson, with Peter Filleul; sound, Gary Wilkins; production design, John Stoddart; costumes, Terry Ryan; production manager, Adrienne Read;

assistant director, Chris Webb; casting, Liz Mulinar. Reviewed at Village Roadshow screening room, Sydney, April 15, 1991. MPAA Rating: PG. Running time: **89 MIN.**
Harry Reynolds . . . . . Bryan Brown
Julie . . . . Karen Allen
David . . . . Justin Rosniak
Bostock . . . . Chris Haywood
Cec . . . . Bill Kerr
Norman Foster . . . . . . Bruce Spence
Scraper . . . . Bruce Myles
Billy . . . . Paul Chubb
Giles . . . . Peter Hehir
Sgt. Watts . . . . Don Barker

"Sweet Talker" is a sweet, Capraesque romantic comedy with a positive feel to it. It's lightweight fare, but charming lead performances from Bryan Brown and Karen Allen, backed by a strong supporting cast of Aussie character actors, make it disarming entertainment.

Produced two years ago on location in South Australia by Taylor Hackford's New Visions outfit, pic underwent a lengthy postproduction period and some re-shooting, but emerges without a trace of difficulties.

In low-key style, screenplay by Tony Morphett (from a story written in collaboration with Brown) debunks the greed of the '80s in a simple tale of a conman who gets involved in an elaborate scam but then gives it all away because he grows to like his victims too much.

Brown is in excellent form as a swindler finishing a five-year prison term. As he leaves, he robs his cellmate (Bill Kerr) of plans to swindle the citizens of a seaside village out of their savings.

His ruse involves pretending a wrecked 15th century Portuguese galleon is buried in the sand dunes near town. Convincing local historian Bruce Spence, mayor Bruce Myles and other locals of the existence of the gold-laden ship, Brown proposes a theme park in which the locals willingly invest.

The investment also attracts local drug dealer Peter Hehir as a way to launder some cash, and Hehir has his dim-witted strong-arm man (Paul Chubb) watch over Brown and the cash.

Meanwhile, Brown befriends 10-year-old Justin Rosniak, a bright kid missing his father (who left home for another woman), and starts falling for the boy's Yank-born mother (Karen Allen). Rosniak gives a stand-out performance as the youngster.

With Russell Boyd's lovely photography evocatively capturing the beaches and vistas of the little seaside community, "Sweet

Talker" moves along gently to its satisfactory conclusion: The conman predictably has a change of heart and decides to stay on and live in Beachport, which he has helped change to a town with a future.

Brown also turns the tables on the drug dealer and a greedy property developer (Chris Haywood) who's presented as more of a conman than the conmen themselves.

Director Michael Jenkins has come up with his most relaxed and most successful pic to date, and producer Ben Gannon has mounted an attractive picture which should please family audiences. It's undeniably a small-scale picture, but it's a warm-hearted and honest one.

Tech credits are fine, including the jolly music score and songs provided by Richard Thompson and Peter Filleul. — *Strat.*

L'OPÉRATION CORNED BEEF
(OPERATION CORNED BEEF)
(FRENCH)

A Gaumont release of an Alter Films-Gaumont-Gaumont Prods.-TF1 Films Prods.-Alpilles Prods.-Amigo Prods. coproduction with the participation of Canal Plus. Produced by Alain Terzian. Directed by Jean-Marie Poiré. Screenplay, Poiré, Christian Clavier; camera (color), Jean-Yves Lemener; editor, Catherine Kelber; sound, Pierre Lenoir; production design, Hugues Tissandier; costumes, Sophie Marcou, Sylvie Marcou; production manager, Philippe Lievre; assistant director, Paul Gueu; casting, Françoise Menidrey. Reviewed at Gaumont Ambassade theater, Paris, April 13, 1991. Running time: **105 MIN.**
Jean-Jacques Granianski . . . .
. . . . Christian Clavier
Le Squale . . . . Jean Reno
Isabelle . . . . Isabelle Renauld
Marie Laurence Granianski . . . .
. . . . Valerie Lemercier
Masse . . . . Jacques François
Bibi . . . . Jacques Dacqmine
Burger . . . . Marc de Jonge
Garcia . . . . Mireille Rufel

"Operation Corned Beef" is a fast-paced comedy of errors that aims at and hits the lowest common denominator. Irreverent spoof of French secret service's clandestine activities has entertaining moments of pure farce, particularly in antagonistic pairing of he-man Jean Reno and schlemiel Christian Clavier, but pic, unless remade, has scant prospects outside of French-speaking territory.

Slapstick overkill of the opening sequence set in Bogota — a

nun gets hit by a speeding getaway car, bounces off the next few pursuit vehicles and survives without a scratch — gives way to pic's central premise.

To unmask high-level arms trafficking involving a French government official, undercover operatives have installed a microphone in the engagement ring of Madame Granianski (Valerie Lemercier), the Spanish-French interpreter at the German embassy in Paris. However, on crucial weekend when a Colombian general is due in town to clinch deal, Madame Granianski requests three days off to celebrate her wedding anniversary.

Since the presence of both interpreter and bugged ring is essential, Le Squale ("The Shark," Jean Reno), still stationed in Colombia, orders his counterespionage colleagues to assign a female agent to seduce Granianski (Christian Clavier) and take incriminating photos, thereby wrecking the couple's marriage so that the wife will report to work as required.

Slimy maneuver has desired effect and Le Squale returns to France to oversee sting operation. But what he doesn't know is that his own luscious g.f. (Isabelle Renauld) was drafted to do the seducing since other available femme agents were grossly overweight.

Granianski persists in trying to reconcile with his wife, jeopardizing entire operation which, incidentally, has been expressly vetoed by the president. Le Squale, whose surveillance truck masquerades as a medical vehicle, ends up stuck with Granianski, who believes him to be a real doctor. Duty requires Le Squale to encourage Granianski to run off to Venice with his g.f. but honor and jealousy gum up the works.

Fiercely virile Reno (Luc Besson stock player in "La Femme Nikita") struggles to remain professional as dorky Clavier obliviously rhapsodizes about Isabelle's sexual charms. Comic timing is good throughout, and pic, though often silly, is never dull.

Film spares no low blows including jokes based on fat women, the president's incontinent dog and a man in a wheelchair, but cheap shots seem to be there for benefit of viewers who may have lost track of the plot. Stunts are not impressive enough for fans of pure action.

Co-writer-director Poiré says title "is no more ridiculous than

"Operation Desert Shield."
— Ness.

THE UNBORN

A Califilm release. Executive producer, Mike Elliott. Produced and directed by Rodman Flender. Screenplay, Henry Dominic; camera (Foto-Kem color), Wally Pfister; editor, Patrick Rand; music, Gary Numan, Michael R. Smith; sound (Ultra-Stereo), Bill Robbins; production design, Gary Randall; costume design, Greg LaVoi; assistant director, Charles Philip Moore; special makeup effects & baby design, Joe Podnar; additional camera, Flavio Labiano; 2nd unit director, Karen Urbach; 2nd unit camera, Janusz Kaminski; stunt coordinator, Patrick J. Statham; line producer, Jonathan Winfrey; casting, Steve Rabiner. Reviewed on vidcassette, N.Y., April 13, 1991. MPAA Rating: R. Running time: **83 MIN.**
Virginia Marshall . . . . Brooke Adams
Brad Marshall . . . . . . Jeff Hayenga
Dr. Meyerling . . . . . . James Karen
Martha Wellington . . . . K Callan
Beth . . . . Jane Cameron
Connie . . . . Kathy Griffin
Gloria . . . . Wendy Kamenoff
Janet . . . . Laura Stockton
Mark . . . . .Jonathan Emerson
Also with: Janice Kent, Matt Roe.

Pregnancy fears make for an effective horror topic in "The Unborn," entertaining though tasteless shocker. Film is currently in regional theatrical release and will turn on vid fans.

Brooke Adams returns to the paranoid horror turf of "Invasion Of The Body Snatchers," portraying a young wife and author of children's books who has a history of miscarriages and turns to a mysterious doctor (James Karen) for help.

Unfortunately for her, he's your friendly neighborhood mad scientist, altering sperm (in this case from Brooke's sympathetic husband Jeff Hayenga) to create a master race of superintelligent babies who will supplant humans.

Manic-depressive Adams has a medical history that makes her suspect, so when she starts to cry wolf, beginning on a tv talkshow promoting her latest tome, no one believes her. Though well along in her pregnancy, she gets an abortion (illegally), but her worries aren't over.

The fetus lives on and debuting director Rodman Flender gets good mileage out of her ambivalent feelings towards the monstrous offspring. Film's open ending is quite unsettling.

With good performances, notably by Adams and Karen, film draws in the willing viewer. The monster baby, as created by Joe Podnar, is unconvincing, but Podnar's makeup effects are suitably gruesome. Flender's one misstep is the inclusion of an unnecessary subplot ridiculing two lesbians who run a natural childbirth class that excludes men.
— Lor.

LOS PASOS DE ANA
(THE PHASES OF ANA)
(MEXICAN)

A Canario Rojo-Feeling-Tragaluz-Mexican Film Institute (Imcine) production. Exec producers, Eduardo Carrasco Zinini, Héctor Cervera. Directed by Marysa Sistach. Screenplay, José Buil; camera (color), Emanuel Tacamba; editor, Buil; sound, Susana Garduño. Reviewed at the VI Festival de Cine Mexicano, Guadalajara, March 12, 1991. Running time: **90 MIN.**
Ana . . . . Guadalupe Sánchez
Vidal . . . . Emilio Echervarría
Clementina . . . . . Clementina Otero
Carlos . . . . David Beuchot
Drunk . . . . Roberto Cobo
Juan . . . . Valdiri Durand
Paula . . . . Pia Buil Sistach
Andrés . . . . Andrés Fonseca
Also with: Enrique Herranz, José Roberto Hill, Carlos García, Sergio Torres Cuesta, Juan Araizaga, Dhindra Cervantes.

First directorial effort by Marysa Sistach, "The Phases Of Ana" concerns the day-to-day life of a modern Mexican woman and her personal and professional relationships. Though this go-nowhere film is technically competent, interest level is so-so and may be limited to women's groups.

Hermetic story takes place over several months and covers the movements of a single mother in her 30s (Guadalupe Sánchez), with two children, whose ambition is to direct feature films. Besides working as an assistant director, she uses a video camera to record a visual diary of her life and her family.

She also is looking for love and none of the proposed candidates quite cuts the mustard. In fact, almost all of the male characters are portrayed unsympathetically. These include an insistent taxi driver (and unfortunate one-night-stand) and a rather ethereal long-haired neighbor, who watches her. The mother's ex-husband is so lackluster one wonders why she married him in the first place.

Video is skillfully used from time to time to vary visual texture. Realistic episodic script by José Buil and low-key acting are consistent with the overall treatment, but the effect throughout is numbing. — Lent.

DEADLY
(AUSTRALIAN)

A Hoyts release of a Moirstorm production, with the participation of the Australian Film Finance Corp. (Trust Fund). (Intl. sales: Beyond Intl. Films.) Produced by Richard Moir. Written and directed by Esben Storm. Camera (color), Geoffrey Simpson; editor, Ralph Strasser; music, Graeme Revell; sound, David Lee; production design, Peta Lawson; costumes, Terry Ryan; assistant director, Chris Webb; line producer, Antonia Barnard; production manager, Catherine Bishop; casting, Rae Davidson. Reviewed at Australian Film Commission screening room, Sydney, March 3, 1991. Running time: **99 MIN.**
Tony Bourke . . . . . Jerome Ehlers
Mick Thornton . . . . Frank Gallacher
Daphne . . . . Lydia Miller
Eddie . . . . John Moore
Irene . . . . Caz Lederman
Barry Blainey . . . . . Alan David Lee
Also with Tony Barry, Julie Nihill, Bill Hunter, Richard Moir, Martin Vaughan, Esben Storm.

"Deadly," a confident, fast-paced cop thriller, centers on an issue making headlines in Australia: high death rate among aboriginal prisoners in police custody. Solid business should be forthcoming for this stylish pic.

Handsomely made, intriguing and suspenseful, pic should break through Aussie filmgoers' resistance towards pics dealing with aborigines and may open a few eyes. International chances, in arthouse situations, are good.

White Australians still harbor strong elements of racism, especially in the remote country towns with large black populations. "Deadly" was mostly filmed in such a town, Wilcannia, in outback New South Wales, renamed Yabbabri in the film.

Sydney cop Jerome Ehlers is sent to investigate the apparent suicide hanging of a drunken aborigine in a police lock-up. Ehlers is a controversial choice to head the probe since he has only just been cleared in the killing of a young female drug addict who got caught in the crossfire during a confrontation with an armed man.

Yabbabri police, headed by Frank Gallacher, are confident Ehlers quickly will come up with a whitewash. It doesn't work out that way, as Ehlers is a more honest cop than anyone, including his superior (Tony Barry giving another subtle portrayal of genial evil), imagined.

He starts digging around, talking to the dead man's family and friends, and begins to suspect the victim couldn't possibly have
hanged himself. Pic develops into an intriguing whodunit. The violent climax is a bit overstated but provides a satisfying ending.

Writer-director Esben Storm, whose first feature this is since his comedy "Stanley" eight years ago, skillfully handles the potentially tricky subject, increasing suspense and tension as the film proceeds and staging a series of fierce gun battles for the final reel.

He also keeps at bay a potential romance between Ehlers and the aboriginal woman (Lydia Miller) who works at the motel where he's staying and who, like most other people in the town, has an angle on the case. Miller is effective in her role, as is Gallacher as the town's racist police chief, Caz Lederman as his distraught wife, who's hiding a guilty secret, John Moore as the dead man's angry brother and Bill Hunter as a racist bar owner.

In the lead, Ehlers gives a variable performance which is strong in some sequences but self-conscious in others. Producer Richard Moir, who played the lead in Storm's "In Search Of Anna," might have taken the lead role himself to good effect. He turns up as police doctor from Sydney. Storm himself turns up as an aggressive tv newsman.

"Deadly" has superlative camerawork from Geoffrey Simpson ("Green Card"). Use of the small-town location is very good. Ralph Strasser has done a brisk editing job and manages to bring clarity to a complex plot. Composer Graeme Revell ("Dead Calm") does a stand-out job with a brooding piano and percussion score.

Some may find the ending a shade over the top, but "Deadly" works both as a thriller and as an insight into racial tensions in rural Australia. — Strat.

JIDONG QIXIA
(THE ICEMAN COMETH)
(HONG KONG)

Produced by Golden Harvest Ltd. and Johnny Mak Prods. Directed by Fok Yiu-leung. Screenplay, Stephen Shiu; camera (color), Poon Hang-sang; editor, Poon Hung. Reviewed at Berlin Film Festival (Forum), Feb. 24, 1991. Running time: **114 MIN.**
With: Yuan Biao, Yuan Hua, Zhang Manyu, Maggie Cheung.

A rip-roaring ride through history with two ancient swordsmen, "The Iceman Cometh" delivers everything one expects from a Hong Kong martial arts film but expands the boundaries of the genre, making for strong theatrical and video potential.

Thriller-comedy's elements include historic settings in ancient China, promises to be kept to dying martial arts masters, honor to be upheld, special effects, time travel, street life in present-day Hong Kong, the prostitute with the golden heart, a little social comment and (surprise) good vs. evil.

Two ancient swordsmen locked in mortal combat are transported to Hong Kong where their frozen corpses are discovered by archaeologists. After a power failure in the cold storage room, they come to life and resume their historic struggle. Brilliant martial arts scenes stretch the imagination.

What lifts the film out of the ordinary is the excellent comic punctuation and a particularly good deadpan performance by Yuen Biao. His attempts to come to terms with the modern world and modern conveniences such as tv are comic high points.

Counterbalancing the existential soul of the chivalrous Yuan Biao, who wanders around Hong Kong bemoaning its loose morals and his own sorry state, is the superbly nasty killer Yuan Hua. Despite the predictability of their struggle, the plot has enough twists and turns to keep the audience's attention.

Maggie Cheung plays the call girl who inadvertently gets mixed up in the goings-on. The love that emerges between her and the good swordsmen makes her an honest woman.

The hero, in all his naivete, also can be seen as a symbol of mainland China refugees who face similar perplexing problems when they emigrate to Hong Kong, and director Fok Yiu-leung throws a sharp jab at the bureaucracy of communist China.

This possible future classic may well convert some nonbelievers to the chopsocky genre. — *Keoh.*

KED HVIEZDY BOLI CERVENE
(WHEN THE STARS WERE RED)
(CZECHOSLOVAKIAN-FRENCH)

A Slovenska Filmova Tvorba (Bratislava)-Constellation-UGC-Hachette Premiere (Paris) co-production. Produced by Claude Ossard, Cedomir Kolar. Directed by Dusan Trancik. Screenplay, Trancik, Eugen Gindl, Zuzana Tararova; camera (color), Vladimir Smutny; editor, Marus Cernak; music, Vaclav Kou-

bek; sound, Juraj Solan, Paul Bertault; production design, Milos Pietor; costumes, Milan Corba; production manager, Zuzana Ricotti; assistant director, Andrei Ludvid. Reviewed at Berlin Film Festival (competition), Feb. 23, 1991. Running time: **88 MIN.**
Jozef Brezik . . . . Vaclav Koubek
Count Szentirmai . . . . Dezso Garas
Heda . . . . Eva Salzmanova
Also with: Alena Ambrova, Jan Jasensky, Stanislav Harvan, Zuzana Kronerova, Jan Sedal, Frantisek Vyrostko, Miroslav Donutil, Matel Landl.

An ambitious pic with a story unfolding in a small Slovak village over 20 years, "When The Stars Were Red" is too familiar in theme (from countless other Eastern European pics over the years) and too confusing to make international impact.

Director Dusan Trancik sketches in a large group of characters, all with differing attitudes to events in their country. Though the types may be recognizable to East European audiences who lived through these times, they aren't well differentiated for foreign audiences.

Central character Jozef, first seen as a wide-eyed boy in 1950 as the Communists take over everything, including the home of the local count and amateur astronomer (Hungarian actor Dezso Garas), is one of those people who goes with the flow and tries to stay on the right side of whomever's in power.

This point is brought home sharply at the climax of the film, which takes place in 1968 when the village lies in the path of Russian tanks entering Slovakia from Hungary to crush the reformist regime in Prague.

Trancik makes heavy weather of the political allusions, but still creates a vibrant portrait of village life. Pic is pleasantly photographed in burnished colors, though a lot of it takes place at night in very subdued light.

With more clarity, Trancik could have made a moving film about families torn apart by political events. But the confusion that greeted the screening caught at Berlin seems likely to be repeated elsewhere. Worse, though time is obviously passing quickly during the film, there's little indication of year. — *Strat.*

LE BRASIER
(FRENCH)

A Flach Film-Films A2 production. Produced by Jean-François Lepetit. Directed by Eric Barbier. Screenplay, Eric Barbier, Jean-Pierre Barbier; camera (color), Thierry Arbogast; music, Frederic Talgorn; sound, Jean Garbonne; set design, Jacques Bufnoir; costumes, Pierre-Yves Gayraud; makeup, Joel Lavau. Reviewed at Cinoches, Paris, April 12, 1991. Running time: **124 MIN.**
Alice . . . . Maruschka Detmers
Victor . . . . Jean-Marc Barr
Pavlak . . Wladimir Kotliarov (Tolsty)
Emile . . . . Thierry Fortineau
Also with: François Hadji-Lazaro, Serge Merlin, Jean-Paul Roussillon, Arkadiusz Smolarczyk.

Packed with crowds and sketchy characters, "Le Braiser" fails to cut through a mountain of story material. As the history of an immigrant boxer's family, forbidden romance and conflicting ethnic communities, the picture's all over the map. At the French b.o., hoped-for blockbuster with $17.2 million budget sold 350,000 tickets before folding. Arthouse prospects are nil.

Fact-based mining town saga pic begins in the early 1930s in northern France. Pavlak (Wladimir Kotliarov), a stout Polish miner and winning boxer, has settled with wife and two sons. At local dance hall, son Victor (Jean-Marc Barr), heretofore a brawler and womanizer, falls for French Alice (Maruschka Detmers), but his chances are slim since the French resent the Poles. Besides, Alice's b.f. Emile (Thierry Fortineau) is determined to have his way even if that means raping her and coercing her into marriage.

At home, the son must face his father who insists he marry possibly pregnant Polish ex-girlfriend. After their falling out, Victor tries in vain to get Alice to flee with him.

Several years later, Alice has married Emile and the miners are feeling the pinch in a depressed economy. When a socialist demagogue seems ready to take over, Victor leads the Poles in takeover of the mine. While he and hostage Emile slug it out, Pavlak convinces Poles to release all French hostages.

But boss' promise of higher wages turns out to be a lie. Pic, whose title means inferno, nearly ends with a whimper as police deport Victor. Unsatisfying second ending has Pavlak beat a French boxer in a big match,

avenging son and community.

Barbier, who wrote the chaotic script with Jean-Pierre Barbier, lusts for shoulder-to-shoulder crowd scenes in dance palace, boxing arena, shopping district and political hall. But teeming social canvas gives short shrift to main characters, and Emile's fall to his death is a weak end to surprisingly brief fight.

Lenser also often uses Barr, the silent hunk in watery local hit "Le Grand Bleu," to drive home a message: love-struck lad stands in the rain staring up at the camera. Otherwise, Barr is convincing as hot-headed turk.

Clumsy inserts and confusing segues suggest desperate editing. Not even documentary footage tossed in at the end can save this narrative mishmash.
— *Lour.*

GOZAL
(IRANIAN)

An IRIB production. Directed by Mohammad Ali Sajjadi. Screenplay, Sajjadi, based on a script by Abdolijabbar Deldar; camera (color), Alireza Zarrindast; editor, M.A. Sajjadi; music, Nazarli Mahbub; sound, Freydun Khushabafar; set design, M.A. Sajjadi; makeup, Jalal Moayarian, Masud Valadbeigi; production manager, Nader Moghaddas. Reviewed at the Fajr Intl. Film Festival, Teheran, Feb. 10, 1991. Running time: **104 MIN.**
With: Mehdi Miami, Firuz Behjat-Mohammadi, Pardis Afkari, Mahmud Jafari, Reza Fayazi, Ruhangiz Mohtadi, Abdoljabbar Deldar.

Gozal is a champion racehorse. "Gozal," the film, has no theatrical prospects outside it's native Persia.

Melodrama is about Gozal's jockey, who lost his leg in the Iran/Iraq war. He returns home a war hero, but is devastated when he discovers his purebred companion has been sold to an old man, who refuses to return the horse to a one-legged rider.

The jockey's plight to get Gozal back is predictable to the end. Still, the love story which complicates his quest reveals historical and cultural tidbits about the harsh life on the Iranian/Soviet border.

The miserable old man shares a hut with his beautiful loyal daughter whom all believe to be his wife. When the jockey discovers the truth, he sets his sights on her as well as the horse, and a fierce competition develops between the two men.

A test of virility — a horse race — is called off when the daughter begs the jockey to have mercy on her failing old father, which he does. But his love for both woman and beast draws him back repeatedly to their desolate dwelling.

In the end, he gets both the woman and the horse when the old man dies. Tech credits are okay. Pic's interesting for details about life in a remote, backward no-man's land. If it wasn't for the reference to the Iran/Iraq war, pic could have been set 100 years ago. — *Suze.*

CIUDAD DE CIEGOS
(CITY OF THE BLIND)
(MEXICAN)

A Bataclán Cinematográfica-Mexican Film Institute (Imcine)-Fondo de Fomento a la Calidad Cinematográfica (FFCC)-Tabasco Films production. Executive producer, Rosina Rivas. Directed by Alberto Cortés. Screenplay, Cortés, Hernánn Bellinghaussen; camera (color), Carlos Marcovich; editor, Rafael Castañedo; music, José G. Elorza, Jaime López; sound, Sergio Zenteño; art direction, Homero Espinoza. Reviewed at Estudios Churubusco, Mexico City, March 15, 1991. Running time: **93 MIN.**
Socorro . . . . Gabriela Roel
Anselmo Sandoval . . . .
. . . . Fernando Balzaretti
Sra. Sandoval . . . . . . Silvia Mariscal
Mara (teen) . . . . . Arcelia Ramírez
Mara (adult) . . . . Macaria
Inés . . . . Blanca Guerra
Fabiola . . . . Elpidia Carrillo
Also with: Rita Guerrero, Benny Ibarra, Roberto Sosa, Enrique Rocha, Saúl Hernéndez, Juan Ibarra, Carmen Salinas, Claudia Fernández.

Firmly destined for the arthouse market, Mexican helmer Alberto Cortés' second feature "City Of The Blind" concerns the lives of various occupants of a Mexico City apartment over a three-decade span. With careful handling, pic may find some select interest, especially on the fest circuit.

While the apartment is the film's true central character, the only other bridge between the pic's disparate characters and episodes is that all 10 tales feature some sort of breakdown or separation in a relationship. Examples:

A gangster and his girlfriend hide out from police. A party between maids and chauffeurs takes place while the employers are away. And an updated version of Cocteau's "La Voix Humane" features an unexpected twist. Even Mexico City's 1985 earthquake features into this pic before the semi-destroyed apartment is taken over by a postmod-

ern new wave rock group.

Technically, pic is well crafted with able lensing by Carlos Marcovich, and Homero Espinoza's art direction offers some good period delineation. The director also supplies a visual nod to his first film "Amor a la Vuelta de la Esquina" (Love Around The Corner," 1985).

Exteriors come in only at the beginning and end when the viewer follows the footsteps of a woman into and away from the apartment. Rather than recap the characters, deconstructive final shots show the woman walking into Churubusco Studios and through the soundstages where the film was shot, ending with an aerial shot of the maze of sets.

While some stories are more interesting than others, "City Of The Blind" should generate some curiosity. — *Lent.*

CONDOMINIUM
(ITALIAN)

An Italian Intl. Film release of a Cooperative Immagininazione production in association with RAI-TV 1. Produced by Laura Cafiero, Giannandrea Pecorelli. Directed by Felice Farina. Screenplay, Paolo Virzi, Farina, with Francesco Bruni, Gianluca Greco; camera (Telecolor), Carlo Cerchio; editor, Roberto Schiavone, with Maddalena Colombo; music, Lamberto Macchi; art direction, Tonino Zera; costumes, Cinzia Lucchetti. Reviewed at Anica screening room, March 25, 1991. Running time: **100 MIN.**
Michele Marrone . . Carlo Delle Piane
Adelaide . . . . Ottavia Piccolo
Gaetano Scarfi . . . . . Ciccio Ingrassia
Roberto Sgorilon . . . . Roberto Citran
Lia Conticelli . . . . . Nicoletta Boris

Helmer Felice Farina's third film, "Condominium," is a bittersweet comedy about life in an overcrowded Roman housing development. Pic has festival potential and the kind of recognizable comedy that should help it float on a difficult Italo market.

Social themes are the strongest trend in this season's new Italian films (the violent "Ultrà," the nostalgic "Italy-Germany 4-3"). Farina and coscripter Paolo Virzi choose quirkish black humor to blame Italians for the stew they're in: They're selfish individualists totally lacking community spirit.

A broad cast of characters inhabits a low-income housing block in the depressing neighborhood of Magliana. When a new renter, the soft-spoken, good-hearted Carlo Delle Piane, turns up at a rough condo meeting in a suit

and tie, he is immediately appointed administrator.

But no one expects him to take the job seriously. Instead, with the help of a retired cop (Ciccio Ingrassia), he slowly wins his neighbors' respect and, against all odds, gets buzzers installed in the buildings: a giant victory over people's indifference to their environment and distrust of the next guy.

It may sound like a Frank Capra tale, but "Condominium" takes a sadder, more realistic approach. Many on the block are left isolated at pic's end; namely, an amiable telephone installer (Roberto Citran) whose romance with the lady upstairs (Nicoletta Boris) fizzles out.

Ingrassia, who turns in a remarkably moving perf, finds himself alone after his aged wife is run over on the highway they must cross to get to the market.

More fortunate is lonesome Alitalia employee Riccardo Pangallo, whose wife leaves him but who finds a new love in sultry hairdresser Ottavia Piccolo.

Farina fulfills the promise of his first two pics ("He Looks Dead But He's Only Fainted," "Special Affects"). He is stronger on ironic, offbeat humor than the few moments of dramatic emotion, awkwardly handled. The editing is less than seamless, tending to isolate scenes as if they were comic sketches and

ONE GOOD COP

A Hollywood Pictures presentation in association with Silver Screen Partners IV. Produced by Laurence Mark. Executive producer, Harry Colomby. Written and directed by Heywood Gould. Camera (Technicolor), Ralf Bode; editor, Richard Marks; music, David Foster, William Ross; sound (Dolby), Al Overton (L.A.); Tod Maitland (N.Y.); production design, Sandy Veneziano; costume design, Betsy Heimann; art direction, Daniel Maltese (L.A.), Rick Butler (N.Y.); set decoration, John Anderson (L.A.), Justin Scoppa Jr. (N.Y.); associate producer-unit production manager, Joan Bradshaw; assistant director, Marty Ewing; casting, Risa Bramon, Billy Hopkins, Heidi Levitt. Reviewed at Pacific Cinerama Dome, Hollywood, Calif., April 30, 1991. MPAA rating: R. Running time: **105 MIN.**
Artie Lewis . . . . . . Michael Keaton
Rita Lewis . . . . Rene Russo
Stevie Diroma . . . Anthony LaPaglia
Lt. Danny Quinn . . . . Kevin Conway
Grace . . . . Rachel Ticotin
Beniamino . . . . Tony Plana
Felix . . . . Benjamin Bratt
Cheryl Clark . . . Charlayne Woodard
Marian . . . . Grace Johnston
Barbara . . . . Rhea Silver-Smith
Carol . . . . Blair Swanson

Michael Keaton's impressive performance and writer-director Heywood Gould's smoothly orchestrated string-pulling should make "One Good Cop" a winner with mainstream audiences and bring at least a moderate b.o. return.

Underlying theme of this modest, skillful drama about an ethical NYPD detective who inherits the family of his slain partner is the struggle of modern man to balance the conflict between the cruel world of work and the comforting hearth.

Keaton plays a staunchly decent cop who's as close to his longtime partner (Anthony LaPaglia) as he is to his fashion designer wife (Rene Russo). When widowed LaPaglia gets killed in an heroic attempt to save a woman's life, Keaton and Russo take in his three orphaned little girls and decide they want to keep them.

But the authorities seem rather eager to take them away and Keaton's crowded digs can't accommodate a family, so he winds up a wrong-side-of-the law stunt to come up with enough money to be a hero at home. The plan backfires.

The drug-dealer villains and inner city skirmishes here are standard issue, and pic's basic parameters are only a cut above telefilm fare. Still, it's the skill with which the writer-director works the audience into the palm of his hand that makes this a crowd-pleaser. Characters and situations are strongly sympathetic here, and Gould, a first-time feature director but practiced writer ("Fort Apache, The Bronx," "Rolling Thunder") knows how to hook an audience and hold that focus.

Enjoyable light banter between Keaton and LaPaglia makes things fun, while the gritty, high-impact violence of Keaton's average day on the street offsets the tenderness and tension of domestic scenes.

At the pic's happy conclusion the precinct's cynical captain (J.E. Freeman) grumbles that he's got "heroes and martyrs" all around him, but it's good-natured grumbling, and even critical audiences are likely to feel the same, as there's not much complaint in being taken for a ride when it's as smooth as this one.

Keaton demonstrates remarkable range and dexterity, giving his best performance since "Clean And Sober," and soulful LaPaglia, in his short time on screen, projects a toned-down version of the same true-hearted qualities that made him so winning in "Betsy's Wedding."

The beguiling and flinty little girls are well cast, but one squirms in disbelief when confronted with as impossibly lovely and graceful a cop's wife as Russo in a pic whose basic tone is down-to-earth.

Cinematographer Ralf Bode gets high marks for the fluidly entertaining and grittily realistic camerawork, and the pleasing musical score by David Foster and William Ross sweetens the mix. — *Daws.*

NEVER LEAVE NEVADA

A Cabriolet release of a South of Canada production. Produced by Diane Campbell. Written and directed by Steve Swartz. Camera (Film Credit Lab, black & white), Lee Daniel; editor, Gordon A. Thomas; music, Ray Benson; sound, Randy Buck, Dee Montgomery; production managers, Cynthia Malley, Kate Bennett; assistant director, Ed Fuentes. Reviewed at Bleecker Street Cinema, April 30, 1991. No rating. Running time: **88 MIN.**
Sean Kaplan . . . . Steve Swartz
Luis Ramirez . . . . . . Rodney Rincon
Betty Gurling . . . . . Janelle Buchanan
Lou Ann . . . . . . Katherine Catmull

Steve Swartz wrote, directed and stars in this low-budget first feature, which imitates the deadpan satire of Jim Jarmusch's films but rarely manages to be funny. Even though it runs less than 90 minutes,

the contrived humor wears thin long before the ending. "Never Leave Nevada" is no sleeper; it's a snoozer.

Pic, shot in black & white, opens and closes with Swartz' annoyingly nasal narration. In long-winded fashion, it introduces us to two traveling salesmen (Swartz, Rodney Rincon) hawking tube socks and t-shirts.

Setting up shop in Beatty, Nev., a hick town whose only distinction is its proximity to a nuclear test site, they do a brisk business in t-shirts boasting slogans like "nuclear winter gives me the chills."

Swartz, who never stops talking, asks his quiet sidekick, "I'm bugging you?" Never mind Luis; what about the audience?

Eventually, the partners meet a pair of locals. Swartz becomes so fond of one of them he wants to settle down. Then he finds out she's married. Rincon initially hits it off with the other femme, but fears radiation sickness and prefers the open road.

So much for the plot. Most of the pic consists of intentionally silly dialog. Swartz condescends to his characters, giving them artificially cute things to say.

As the love interests, Janelle Buchanan and Katherine Catmull occasionally make the script convincing. As the former child star of "Mexican Mule Boy," Rincon has little to do, while Swartz gives himself a flashier part.

Due to poor sound quality and dim lighting, "Never Leave Nevada" resembles a home movie. But it lacks authenticity and always feels like an outsider's view of a small town. Swartz wants to be cool, like Jarmusch, but ends up being merely arch.

The director's other influence seems to be the road movie. Unfortunately, like its characters, "Never Leave Nevada" doesn't go anywhere. — *Stev.*

SCANNERS II:
THE NEW ORDER
(CANADIAN)

A Malofilm Group production and release (Triton Pictures in the U.S.). Produced by René Malo. Executive producers, Pierre David, Rénald Paré, Tom Berry. Directed by Christian Duguay. Screenplay, B.J. Nelson, based on the original characters created by David Cronenberg; camera (color), Rodney Gibbons; editor, Yves Langlois; music, Marty Simon; sound, Tim Archer, Rick Ellis; sound effects editor, Dan Sexton; production design, Richard Tassé; special

effects, Michael Smithson; coproducer, Franco Battista. Reviewed at Cineplex Odeon Cinema Dauphin, Montreal, April 19, 1991. MPAA Rating R. Running time: **104 MIN.**
David Kellum . . . . . David Hewlett
Wayne Forrester . . . . . Yvan Ponton
Julie Vale . . . . Deborah Raffin
Alice Leonardo . . . . . Isabelle Mejias
Peter Drak . . . . Raoul Trujillo
Dr. Morse . . . . Tom Butler
Lt. Gelson . . . . Vlasta Vrana
The Mayor . . . . Dorothée Berryman
Feck . . . . Michael Rudder
Gruner . . . . David Francis
Walter . . . . Stephan Zarov

It's not David Cronenberg but it's not bad. "Scanners II" marks a slick feature debut for helmer Christian Duguay with a first class imitation of the mind-blowing original. Zealots for schlock are in for a treat, and pic should do decent biz with sci-fi buffs. It'll make it to homevid moments before upcoming "Scanners III" is released.

For the uninitiated, scanners are people with powers to "scan" other people's minds, read their thoughts, control their actions or splatter their veins and brains. (The U.S. version is less graphic than the uncensored Quebec print, and the two exploding head scenes were "trimmed," not cut, to meet MPAA requirements for an R rating, per the producer).

True to form, in "The New Order," good eventually triumphs over evil after the virtuous and villainous scanners battle their brains out.

Script twist in the sequel comes from a seemingly moral, ultimately unethical police chief/politician Forrester (Yvan Ponton) turning unsuspecting scanners into junkies on EPH-2 (an addictive drug which sedates them) with the help of an amoral neuro scientist (played perfectly by the nondescript Tom Butler).

From the opening shot (a face bellowing a Neanderthal scream into darkness), sound is superb, lighting is eerily blue, and the stage is set for lethal scanner Peter Drak (Raoul Trujillo). He's escaped from the neurological research center where the mad scientist is conducting inhuman experiments on scanners, trying unsuccessfully to control them for Forrester. In Drak, they've created a monster only another scanner can conquer.

rester is merely a corrupt power-monger with a wicked vision he calls the "new order." When Kellum attempts to expose the truth, Forrester re-enlists Drak to kill him.

In the ensuing chase, Kellum's

love interest Alice Leonardo (played stiffly by Isabelle

Forrester's squeaky clean public image helps convince virgin scanner David Kellum (David Hewlett) that his unusual powers can help rid Montreal of evil (and Drak), but it's not long before Kellum realizes that For-Mejias) is held hostage by the cops and used as bait to find him. Cops kill Kellum's adopted parents but not before he discovers his long-lost sister Julie is another scanner, as were his natural parents (a major flaw in the plot).

Premise is that scanners' are a result of a pain-killing drug taken by their mothers during pregnancy, and not an inherited disorder. Nonetheless, the leap of logic shouldn't bother willing viewers. The re-united siblings predictably triumph, terminating both scientist and cop in explosive scenes which should satisfy serious schlock fans.

Aside from Mejias, thesps are well cast. Trujillo is terrific as villainous Drak. Tech credits and special effects are excellent.
— *Suze.*

CANNES FEST

A RAGE IN HARLEM
(BRITISH/U.S.)

A Miramax release of a Palace Woolley/Boyle production. Produced by Stephen Woolley, Kerry Boyle. Executive producers, Nik Powell, William Horberg, Terry Glinwood, Harvey Weinstein, Bob Weinstein. Directed by Bill Duke. Screenplay, John Toles-Bey, Bobby Crawford, from the novel by Chester Himes; camera (Deluxe color), Toyomichi Kurita; editor, Curtiss Clayton; music, Elmer Bernstein; sound (Dolby), Paul Cote; production design, Steven Legler; costume design, Nile Samples; assistant director, Warren D. Gray; line producer-production manager, Thomas A. Razzano; co-producers, Forest Whitaker, John Nicolella; casting, Aleta Chappelle. Reviewed at Filmland screening room, L.A., April 15, 1991. (In Cannes Film Festival, competing.) MPAA Rating: R. Running time: **108 MIN.**
Jackson . . . . Forest Whitaker
Goldy . . . . Gregory Hines
Imabelle . . . . Robin Givens
Big Kathy . . . . Zakes Mokae
Easy Money . . . . Danny Glover
Slim . . . . Badja Djola
Jodie . . . . John Toles-Bey
Hank . . . . Ron Taylor
Coffin Ed Johnson . . . . . Stack Pierce
Grave Digger Jones . . George Wallace
Claude X . . . . Willard E. Pugh
Screamin' Jay Hawkins . . . . Himself

Director Bill Duke has brought a stylish sheen to "A Rage In Harlem," but his mix of comedy and violence in the Chester Himes period crime tale is dubious. Many will be turned off by the excessive bloodshed, but the fine cast keeps the pic watchable. The Miramax release, competing at the Cannes Film Fest, looks like an only middling b.o. performer.

Though not promoted as such, "Rage" is a followup to the Himes film adaptations "Cotton Comes To Harlem" (1970) and "Come Back, Charleston Blue" (1972). Here the novelist's cynical police detective protagonists Coffin Ed Johnson and Grave Digger Jones are relegated to secondary parts as the criminals take centerstage.

The raffish humor that made "Cotton Comes To Harlem" so delightful is only fitfully present. Co-producer Forest Whitaker, as an innocent mortuary accountant sucked into a plot involving stolen gold transported to 1956 Harlem from Mississippi, provides amiable but overdone antics in the lead role.

Pudgy mama's boy Whitaker keeps large pictures of Jesus and his stolid mother framed over his bed, occasioning jokes that become progressively less funny. And when he falls for Southern siren Robin Givens, he falls predictably hard.

Givens turns in a winning portrayal of someone whose immersion in a life of thuggery and double dealing has not eradicated her better instincts. She holds the screen with assurance, though she works a bit too hard at the coy and sultry bits.

Duke, an actor whose directing credits include many tv shows and a feature, "The Killing Floor," that did not find a U.S. distrib, has a shrewd eye for casting.

There's raunchy con man Gregory Hines, transvestite brothel madame Zakes Mokae, feline crime lord Danny Glover and chillingly sadistic hood Badja Djola and his henchman, John Toles-Bey. Willard E. Pugh portrays a zealous and clean-cut Muslim, and Stack Pierce and George Wallace take the detective roles earlier played by the late Raymond St. Jacques and Godfrey Cambridge.

But the humor too often turns ugly, with sympathetic characters dispatched in prolonged agony and minor characters (including Glover's pet dog) squashed, sliced and shot with abandon.

The point of the story — those who maintain emotional openness (Whitaker and Givens) can

transcend the brutality of their surroundings — is submerged in the numbing and depressingly repetitive mayhem. Scripters Toles-Bey and Bobby Crawford don't do justice to the sardonic Himesian view of life.

Production values are excellent, particularly in light of the limited budget. Cincinnati locations stand in effectively for bygone Harlem, although someone should have spotted that late-model car visible through a train window in the last scene.

Toyomichi Kurita's lensing is attractively sepia-hued while not overdone. Production designer Steven Legler and costume designer Nile Samples capture the era with flair, and composer Elmer Bernstein contributes an evocative score featuring his trademark bluesy sax. — *Mac.*

VOLERE VOLARE
(I WANT TO FLY)
(ITALIAN)

A Penta Distribuzione release of a Bambu/Penta Film production. Produced by Ernesto di Sarro, Mario and Vittorio Cecchi Gori. Written and directed by Maurizio Nichetti and Guido Manuli. Camera (color), Mario Battistoni; editor, Rita Rossi; music, Manuel De Sica; art direction, Maria Pia Angelini; animation, Quick Sand. Reviewed at the Cola di Rienzo cinema, Rome, April 20, 1991. (Also in Cannes Film Festival, market.) Running time: **92 MIN.**
Maurizio . . . . . . Maurizio Nichetti
Martina . . . . Angela Finocchiaro
Brother . . . . Patrizio Roversi
Girlfriend . . . . . . Mariella Valentini

Roger Rabbit grows up: Milanese directors and animators Maurizio Nichetti and Guido Manuli mix live action with cartoons in "I Want to Fly," an offbeat fable for adults. Pic's expensive technical bravura is more impressive than the comedy, but it has performed briskly at local boxoffices and should have appeal for many other markets.

The wacky sense of humor that won Nichetti's "The Icicle Thief" fest prizes and worldwide release is recognizable in this impossible love story between a girl and a cartoon character.

Nichetti, the shy hero of this strange adventure, works as a cartoon sound engineer at a dubbing studio he runs with brother Patrizio Roversi. Always in search of new noises, he races around Milan like something out of a silent film, holding his mike up to wailing ambulances and pedestrians falling over trash

cans.

He meets Martina (bright new comic Angela Finocchiaro), whose job gets an even bigger laugh: She bills herself as a social assistant, but actually caters to clients' bizarre pseudosexual fantasies. Twin architects pay to watch her take a bath, and so on.

The two weirdoes are clearly meant for each other, and it's just a matter of time before they meet. But modern relationships are perilous business. As Maurizio gets close to Martina, he starts turning into a cartoon. First his hands become big yellow Mickey Mouse gloves with a will of their own. Then the rest of him undergoes a two-dimensional metamorphosis.

The bizarre last scene is a notable piece of animation technique, showing Maurizio as 100% drawn. As a cartoon, he can finally find the courage to make love to the undraped (live action) Martina, while a cartoon duck flaps around the room in excitement.

Few scenes can be called side-splitting, but the whole picture is pleasantly offbeat. The sporadic glimpses of female nudity are chaste and ironic, while Maurizio gets to appear in his birthday suit as a cartoon.

Performances by Finocchiaro, Roversi and friend Mariella Valentini are light and uninhibited. — *Yung.*

RIFF-RAFF
(BRITISH)

A British Film Institute release of a Parallax production for Channel Four. (Intl. sales: Film Four Intl., London.) Produced by Sally Hibbin. Directed by Ken Loach. Screenplay, Bill Jesse; camera (Metrocolor, 16m), Barry Ackroyd; editor, Jonathan Morris; music, Stewart Copeland; sound, Bob Withey; production design, Martin Johnson; costume design, Wendy Knowles; assistant director, Peter McLeese. Reviewed at British Film Institute screening room, London, April 16, 1991. (In Directors Fortnight, Cannes Film Festival.) Running time: **92 MIN.**
Stevie . . . . Robert Carlyle
Susan . . . . Emer McCourt
Shem . . . . Jimmy Coleman
Mo . . . . George Moss
Larry . . . . Ricky Tomlinson
Kevin . . . . David Finch
Kojo . . . . Richard Belgrave
Fiaman . . . . Ade Sapara
Desmonde . . . . Derek Young
Smurph . . . . Bill Moores
Ken Jones . . . . Luke Kelly
Mick . . . . Garrie J. Lammin
Gus . . . . Willie Ross

"Riff-Raff," a sprightly ensemble comedy about workers on a London building site, will surprise those who thought Brit

helmer Ken Loach could crank out only political items. Semi-improvised pic is strong on yocks and easy to digest, although local references and lingo will make it tough going for North Americans. Beyond fest and specialized outings, it's perfect for the tube.

Pic plays like a cross between films by Mike Leigh and early Bill Forsyth, with none of the portentousness of Loach's previous "Fatherland" and last year's "Hidden Agenda." There's an undercurrent of political irony, but it never gets in the way of the entertainment.

Central character is Stevie (Robert Carlyle), a young Glaswegian just out of stir, who's come south and got a job converting a closed-down hospital into luxury apartments. His co-workers are from all over — Liverpudlians, Geordies (natives of Newcastle), West Indians. They're breaking every regulation in the book and running scams on the side. Home is a squat in a dingy council block.

After Stevie meets Susan (Emer McCourt), a drifter from Belfast who's trying to make it as a singer, they move in together and make a go of it in the big city. Story yo-yos between their fragile relationship and the shenanigans on the building site.

Tone turns more serious in the latter half as Stevie is called back north for his mother's funeral. When he returns to London, he catches Susan shooting up and dumps her. When a laborer accidentally falls to his death, Stevie and a colleague take revenge on their lax employers by torching the apartments.

Fruity script by onetime laborer Bill Jesse (who died last year just before the pic was completed) catches the wisecracking flavor of navvy (Brit building site laborer) repartee. Comedic tone also spills over into the love story. Pic's abrupt ending leaves several plot strands in the air, but it's that sort of freewheeling movie.

Thesping by no-name cast is strong and clearly benefits from Loach's insistence that all actors have building-site experience. Carlyle is on the button as Stevie, and McCourt is quietly impressive as the ditzy g.f. Ricky Tomlinson is a standout as conscience, Willie Ross very funny as the hard-nosed site foreman Gus, and Derek Young breezy as the black laborer whose dream of visiting Africa is cut short.

Barry Ackroyd's 16m lensing

is astute within its limitations, and Stewart Copeland's bouncy score and Jonathan Morris' tight editing are real bonuses. Only weak tech credit is the sound, which makes the thick accents hard to penetrate, even for Brit ears.

"Riff-Raff" began life in 1987 as a David Puttnam commission during his stint at Columbia. With Channel 4 providing coin, it finally lensed last summer in London and Glasgow on a skimpy £750,000 ($1.3 million). Following a 10-day preem run at London's National Film Theater and limited regional release, pic is to air on Channel 4 in late June.

— *Del.*

UCIECZKA Z KINA WOLNOSC
(ESCAPE FROM THE LIBERTY CINEMA)
(POLISH-DANISH)

A Tor Studio-Poltel (Warsaw)-Crone Film (Copenhagen) co-production. Written and directed by Wojciech Marczewski. Camera (color), Jerzy Zielinski; editor, Elzbieta Kurkowska; music, Zygmunt Konieczny; production design, Andrzej Kowalczyk; production manager, Andrzej Soltyzik. Reviewed at Berlin Film Festival (market), Feb. 26, 1991. (In Cannes Film Festival, Un Certain Regard.) Running Time: **92 MIN.**

The censor . . . . Janusz Gajos
Deputy censor . . . .
        Zbigniew Zamachowski
Malgorzata . . . . Teresa Marczewska
Professor . . . . . Wladyslaw Kowalski
Cinema manager . . . . Jerzy Binczycki
Party secretary . . . Piotr Fronczewski
Film critic . . . . Michal Bajor
Malgorzata's husband . . . .
        Krzysztof Wakulinski
Projectionist . . . . Artur Barcis
Censor's ex-wife . . . Ewa Wisniewska
Censor's daughter . . . . Monika Bolly
American actor . . . Maciej Kozlowski

At first sight, "Escape From The Liberty Cinema" looks like a ripoff of Woody Allen's "The Purple Rose Of Cairo," but it turns out to have more going for it than that. However, the concerns here are very Polish, and international marketing looks difficult.

The film is set just before Poland's communist regime came to an end, and the central character is a provincial censor (Janusz Gajos), a tired, sloppy, lonely man whose wife has long since left him. For him, censorship is both an art and a game, but he doesn't seem to enjoy his work. Then the inexplicable occurs.

During the screening of a mawkish Polish melodrama called "Day-

break" at the Liberty Cinema across the road from the censor's office, the actors start to rebel and refuse to speak their lines. This is anarchy, of course, and when the censor is unable to control the situation, senior Communist Party officials are summoned.

Eventually a film critic notes that the situation smacks of "The Purple Rose Of Cairo," and brings along a reel of the film to demonstrate. The officials watch the Allen film with amusement until another mix-up occurs. The second projector accidentally is switched on and superimposes "Daybreak" over "Purple Rose," and the Jeff Daniels character in the American film suddenly finds himself in a hospital scene in the Polish film.

This is brilliantly done, with Daniels' stand-in thoroughly convincing (though his face is unshown). When he announces he'll have to call his agent, it's cause for hilarity among the Polish actors. Does he really expect to place a call to New York?

At its best, "Escape From The Liberty Cinema" is an exuberant attack on censorship which, a final title announces, was officially banned in Poland in May 1990. Writer-director Wojciech Marczewski knows all about the subject; his previous film, "Shivers," Silver Bear winner at Berlin 1982, was banned for many years by Polish authorities.

Marczewski makes surprisingly little of a promising idea, and pic comes across as gloomy when it should be bright and satirical. In the leading role, Gajos is very morose. It's technically good, and due acknowledgement is made in the end credits to Allen and Orion Pictures for their cooperation. — *Strat.*

TRUTH OR DARE: IN BED WITH MADONNA
(DOCU)

A Miramax release of a Propaganda Films production. Produced by Jay Roewe, Tim Clawson. Executive producer, Madonna. Directed by Alek Keshishian. Director of documentary photography, Robert Leacock (U.S./Europe), Doug Nichol (N.Y., Europe), Christophe Lanzenberg (U.S.), Marc Reshovsky (Japan), Daniel Pearl (Houston); director of concert photography, Toby Phillips; editor, Barry Alexander Brown; musical sequences editor, John Murray; sound supervisor, Lon E. Bender. Reviewed at Skywalker Sound screening rooms, L.A., Calif., May 1, 1991. MPAA rating: R. Running time: **118 MIN.**

Madonna's fans see mostly what she wants them to see, but the lengths to which the star is willing to go are extraordinary. With 26-year-old director Alek Keshishian proving himself as assured behind the camera as Madonna is in front of it, "Truth Or Dare" is destined to be an irresistible draw for a sizable segment of the filmgoing public.

"Dare," Madonna says decisively during a backstage game. And "dare" is both the message and the substance of this illusory yet revealing portrait.

Musicvideo director Kashishian landed the documaker's dream subject when CAA agents paired him with unfettered exhibitionist Madonna. "I have nothing to hide" seems to be her credo, and she's shown in acts ranging from humdrumly unglamorous to recklessly provocative.

Having her throat examined, talking gender-bent sex lives with pal Sandra Bernhard, cuddling near-naked in bed with her gay dancers (both black and white), or treating Warren Beatty like an aging girl toy to be pushed around her dressing room: What does she care who sees it?

It's the warily indulgent Beatty, clearly put out with the lack of privacy, who prods her with pic's most amusing jibe: "Why say anything if it's not on camera?"

Fortunately, there's a point to the shameless showing off, and it's both profitable and political. In the first place, Madonna has stayed in the media throne for nearly 10 years by showing the public something it hasn't seen before, in both her image and her stage shows. Second, she's got a message to send about sexuality and self-expression: Let everybody be who they are.

Visiting backstage post-concert, Madonna's papa wonders why she can't leave out some of the "arty" portions of her show, like the simulated masturbation in "Like A Virgin." "It's a journey, Dad. It's a catharsis," she responds.

In another scene, she stands up to Toronto cops when they threaten arrest if she doesn't excise the offending material. "I will not change my show . . . I'm an artist, and this is how I choose to express myself."

Keshishian includes just enough concert footage, all shot on the 1990 "Blond Ambition" tour, to make the importance of the stage time felt. Before each

grueling outing, Madonna leads her "family" of dancers in prayer, often praying for a voice to get her through the show.

Concert photography is dazzling, with as many as 22 35m cameras used at a show in Paris, and editing by Barry Alexander Brown ("Do The Right Thing") is superb.

Color is used for onstage sequences (to express theatricality), and a combination of hard and soft contrast black & white for offstage footage (to convey reality, such as it is here). All is rendered theatrical in Madonna's life. When she visits the grave of her mother — lays down beside it, in fact — one is surely seeing a performance.

Other times the "document" is refreshingly uncensored. Her mortification is real when she learns at a posh dinner party the man she's pursuing is married: "I'm going to stick my head in the toilet," she tells a girlfriend.

Keshishian, Brown and their team of d.p.'s seem to have every visual and audio technique at their command, and they blend them most skillfully. A few segs seem dispensable, but the crew's ability to eradicate privacy has to be admired, particularly in capturing the bawdy "truth or dare" game played at the end.

Portrait of this boundlessly nervy and vigorous young personage, with her spiritual faith, multiple family ties and political stance held high, could be revelatory to those who regard her as a calculating media magnet. Pic holds the right ingredients — celeb glitz and provocative content — to make a big stir when it's screened out of competition at the Cannes Film Fest.

— *Daws.*

HOUSTON FEST

GUILTY AS CHARGED

An IRS Media presentation of a Copeland/Colichman production. Executive producers, Miles A. Copeland III, Paul Colichman. Produced by Randolph Gale. Directed by Sam Irvin. Screenplay, Charles Gale; camera (Foto-Kem color), Richard Michalak; editor, Kevin Tent; music, Steve Bartek; sound (Dolby), Cameron Hamza; production design, Byrnadette DiSanto; execs in charge of production, Melissa Cobb, Toni Phillips, Steven Reich; co-producer, Adam Moos; casting, Debra Rubinstein. Reviewed at Houston Intl. Film Fest, April 19, 1991. Running time: **95 MIN.**

Ben Kallin . . . . Rod Steiger
Liz Stanford . . . . . . Lauren Hutton
Kimberly . . . . Heather Graham
Mark Stanford . . . . . . Lyman Ward
Aloysius . . . . Isaac Hayes

For his feature debut, Sam Irvin, one-time production associate of Brian De Palma, has directed a tongue-in-cheek melodrama with a darkly comical edge. "Guilty As Charged" looks iffy for long theatrical exposure, but it should generate considerable attention in video and pay-tv afterlife.

Rod Steiger gives a larger-than-life performance as a meatpacking tycoon who, with the aid of two loyal assistants (Isaac Hayes, Irwin Keyes), punishes murderers on early parole or those who have managed to avoid prison altogether with his very own electric chair.

The modern-day vigilante believes he has been ordered by God (with whom he frequently converses) to smite the wicked with a terrible swift charge of electricity. He keeps the evildoers in homemade cells and encourages them to repent before their execution. And if they refuse to repent, well, never mind — he fries them anyway.

And, no, Steiger doesn't do what a meatpacking tycoon might be expected do with the corpses.

All goes reasonably well in Charles Gale's inventive screenplay until Steiger and company capture a fugitive convicted killer (Michael Beach) who insists he was framed by an ambitious congressman (Lyman Ward) running for governor on a strong anti-crime platform. The congressman, who killed a secretary threatening to expose his dirty dealings, eagerly accepts Steiger's invite to the fugitive's execution.

Not surprisingly, helmer Irvin often evidences a strong De Palma influence: self-referential satirical touches, sweeping camera movements, cartoonish exaggeration. The style suits the subject matter.

The only real rough spot comes when Irvin (who also was a marketing exec for defunct U.S.-Canadian specialized distrib Spectrafilm) allows Steiger to tearfully explain why he became an avenging angel. It's not a bad scene; it's simply out of place in the middle of so much comic-book exaggeration.

Steiger is perfectly cast, playing his flamboyant role with unexpected restraint and giving it more character than caricature. Lauren Hutton has some deliciously slinky moments as the congressman's mocking wife. Heather Graham, late of tv's "Twin Peaks," is pert as a neophyte probation officer who discovers a lot of paroled murderers are missing.

Production values indicate the filmmakers made the most of a limited budget. Of particular note are Steve Bartek's lush score and Richard Michalak's fluid cinematography. The impressive electric chair is a rough wooden throne outfitted with angelic wings. Steiger explains the latter touch as an attempt "to give it more of an ethereal quality."
— *Ley*.

SGT. KABUKIMAN, N.Y.P.D.

A Troma release of a Michael Herz and Lloyd Kaufman production in association with Namco Ltd. and Gaga Communications. Executive producers, Masaya Nakamura, Tetsu Fujimura. Produced and directed by Kaufman, Herz. Screenplay, Kaufman, Andrew Osborne, Jeffrey W. Sass, with additional material by Robert Coffey, Cliff Hahn; camera (color), Bob Williams; editor, Ian Slater, Peter Novak; music, Bob Mithoff, inspired by Giacomo Puccini's "Madame Butterfly"; sound, Ron Kalish; art director, Michael Odell Green; special effects, Pericles Lewnes; character design; Fumio Furuya, Satoshi Kitahara; associate producer, David Greenspan, Andrew Wolk. Reviewed at Houston Intl. Film Festival, April 20, 1991. MPAA rating: PG-13. Running time: **90 MIN.**

Harry Griswold/Sgt. Kabukiman	Rick Gianasi
Lotus	Susan Byun
Reginald Stuart	Bill Weeden
Rembrandt	Thomas Crnkovich
Reverend Snipes	Larry Robinson
Captain Bender	Noble Lee Lester

Directed with coarse vigor by Troma toppers Lloyd Kaufman and Michael Herz, "Sgt. Kabukiman N.Y.P.D." is silly stuff, impure and simple, but fitfully hilarious. Pic has a reasonably good chance of appealing to mainstream audiences that ignore Troma's "Surf Nazis Must Die" or "Toxic Avenger" series. Video prospects are bright.

With this campy comic-book spoof about a N.Y. crimefighter armed with lethal chopsticks and suffocating sushi, Troma Inc. moves slightly upscale.

The screenplay, credited to five contributors, has a thick-witted Gotham cop (Rick Gianasi) transformed into a legendary Japanese superhero who dresses as his name, Kabukiman, suggests.

The cop just happens to be nearby when the previous Kabukiman is gunned down by agents of a villainous billionaire developer (Bill Weeden) who dabbles in black magic. The Kabukiman spirit enters the cop, but doesn't always reappear when needed. At one point, he tries to fight bad guys by turning into Kabukiman and becomes a circus clown instead. This leads to what's probably the first high-speed car-unicycle chase in film history.

Beautiful newcomer Susan Byun is the late Kabukiman's niece who resents that the Kabukiman spirit resides in someone who isn't Japanese and who's "a penis-wielding imbecile" to boot. (So much for the film's feminist subtext.)

But she winds up coaching the cop in the fine art of handling his superpowers, including flying, martial arts and the ability to transform himself into someone who looks like a garishly painted extra from "The Mikado."

Like most Troma product, "Sgt. Kabukiman" is ridiculously cheap-looking. When the hero flies, no attempt is made to hide the wires holding him aloft. The humor is broad and shameless, with punchlines not merely telegraphed, but sent via pony express so the audience sees them approaching from afar. But these elements are part of the method behind the madness. Pic's designed to make moviegoers laugh until they're thoroughly ashamed of themselves.

By and large, the performances are as broad as the material requires. Gianasi is a game chucklehead as the cop and only slightly brighter as Kabukiman. Weeden goes over the top early and edges into the stratosphere near the end when his character transforms into a dragonlike demon. (The special effects in this scene are surprisingly impressive for a Troma product.)

Byun has class and sass, and makes a strong impression in her straight-faced comic turn. Some Asian-American interest groups that might otherwise bristle at the stereotyping in "Kabukiman" may be appeased by Byun's performance. Clearly, hers is pic's brightest character.

Other pressure groups may be less pleased by Larry Robinson's very funny work as a black, bombastically corrupt inner-city minister, a character that appears to have wandered in from "The Bonfire Of The Vanities."

The co-production with two Japanese firms, Gaga Communications and Namco Ltd., has a few gross-out jokes, but the sex and violence elements are extremely tame. — *Ley*.

SON OF DARKNESS: TO DIE FOR II

A Trimark Pictures release of a Greg H. Sims presentation of an Arrowhead Entertainment-Lee Caplin production. Executive producers, Lee Caplin, Greg H. Sims. Produced by Richard Weinman. Directed by David F. Price. Screenplay, Leslie King; camera (color), Gerry Lively; editor, Barry Zetlin; music, Mark McKenzie; sound (Ultra-Stereo), Rick Waddel; special effects, John Buechler. Reviewed at Houston Intl. Film Festival, April 20, 1991. Running time: **96 MIN.**

Nina	Rosalind Allen
Tom	Steve Bond
Martin	Scott Jacoby
Max Schreck/Vlad Tepish	Michael Praed
Danny	Jay Underwood
Celia	Amanda Wyss
Jane	Remy O'Neill

Chalk up "Son of Darkness: To Die For II" as one of those rare sequels that's much better written, directed and acted than its predecessor. Unlike the thoroughly second-rate "To Die For," which received only minimal theatrical exposure, "Darkness" might actually haunt a respectable number of theaters before a long, profitable life on homevideo.

Like its 1989 precursor, "Darkness" is a tale of eternally youthful vampires in modern-day California. This time, the action moves from L.A. to the resort town of Lake Arrowhead (Lake Serenity here), where two hip, hot-blooded vampires from the first film (once again played by Amanda Wyss and Steve Bond) prey on victims.

A third vampire from "To Die For," Vlad Tepish (the "real" Count Dracula), is taking a far less aggressive approach to slaking his thirst for blood: He has assumed the identity of an emergency-room doctor and taps into the hospital blood bank.

Michael Praed of the British "Robin Hood" tv series takes over the Vlad role here (from Brendan Hughes of "To Die For"), and takes up a new alias — Max Schreck, which happens to be the name of the actor who played the vampire in the silent classic "Nosferatu."

Tepish/Schreck is content to hang up his cape and blend into the human world, but his past catches up with him. The beautiful owner of a local bed-and-breakfast (Rosalind Allen) has adopted a baby suffering from a strange malady. She brings the infant to Dr. Schreck who recognizes the infant is not only half vampire but the product of a union he enjoyed in the first film.

First-time director David F. Price (son of producer Frank Price) keeps things moving briskly, if not all that suspensefully. Scriptwriter Leslie King studiously ignores some basic tenets of vampire mythology and springs a few twists that don't quite jive with the information given in "To Die For." On the other hand, King's script for this one is a good deal wittier than his script for the original, and a great deal more coherent.

"Darkness" cheats a bit by bringing back two vampires decisively destroyed in "To Die For." Universal pretty much did the same thing in the 1940s when the studio kept bringing back Dracula and the Wolf Man. Fans of the genre are used to such logical inconsistencies.

The only real problem with "Son of Darkness" is that moviegoers who haven't seen the first pic will have a difficult time making sense of the plot in the opening reels.

Performances are fine, with standout work from Bond, Praed and Remy O'Neill as a slatternly vampire first bitten in the first pic. Vince Edwards makes a brief, unbilled appearance as a local police honcho who doesn't believe in vampires.

Special effects and other production values are just slick enough. The thunderous, lushly orchestrated musical score by Mark McKenzie is a definite asset, serving the pic while providing a smidgen of self-parody. — Ley.

METAMORPHOSIS:
THE ALIEN FACTOR

An Intl. Releasing Corp. presentation of a Petrified Films production. Executive producers, Steven Friedman, David Berson in association with Movie Moguls Inc. Produced by Ted A. Bohus, Scott Morette. Directed by Glenn Takakjian. Screenplay, Takakjian, with additional story material by Ted A. Bohus; camera (Technicolor), John A. Corso; additional cinematography, Phil Gries; editor, Janice Keunelian; music, John Gray; sound (Ultra Stereo), Steve and Dorielle Rogers; production design, John Piano; special visual effects, Dan Taylor; associate producers, Tony Grazia, Ron Giannotto; makeup-creature effects, R.S. Cole, Paul C. Reilly Jr., Brian Quinn, Patrick Shearn, Ken Walker. Reviewed at Houston Intl. Film Festival, April 20, 1991. MPAA rating: R. Running time: **97 MIN.**
Sherry Griffen . . . . Tara Leigh
Mitchell . . . . Tony Gigante
Kim Griffen . . . . . Dianna Flaherty
Nancy Kane . . . . Katherine Romaine

Dr. Viallini . . . . . . Marcus Powell
Dr. Stein . . . . Allen Lewis Rickman
Dr. Michael Foster . . . George Gerard
Jarrett . . . . Gregory Sullivan

"**M**etamorphosis: The Alien Factor" is a competently made but unexceptional sci-fi thriller best suited for home-video consumption.

Making the most of a limited budget, writer-director Glenn Takakjian keeps most of the action inside the hallways and labs of a high-security research center run by an autocratic doctor (Marcus Powell). Under Powell's direction, experiments are being conducted on a tissue sample rumored to be extraterrestrial. Actually, it's more than a rumor, something another doctor (George Gerard) finds out the hard way.

Using the sample, Gerard turns a frog into a mean-spirited mutation that bites him, transforming the scientist into first a mucus-coated slab of raw meat and then a big, nasty creature resembling the mate of the big mother in "Aliens."

The chief doctor tries to keep a lid on all this, and even calls in hitmen to make sure other scientists and the mutated doc don't spill the bad news. But neither Powell nor the hitmen count on the arrival of two perky teen-age girls hunting for their missing father, a security guard gobbled up by the mean mutation.

One of the teens (Tara Leigh) is a computer whiz who helps program the experimental weapon that eventually short-circuits the monster. The other (Dianna Flaherty) is a valley girl whose whining provides pic's few moments of intentional humor.

The special effects team makes okay use of stop-action animation for their big monster, and are gracious enough to pay tribute in the closing credits to Ray Harryhausen for "inspiration." Other production values are slick enough.

Most of the performances are inoffensively bland. The major exception is Powell's hammy superciliousness; he's shamelessly renders a bad imitation of Ray Milland in a mad scientist role, but he's undeniably amusing.

According to the producers, "Metamorphosis" started shooting in 1988 (year appearing several times on video monitors), but ended abruptly when money ran out.

By the time the producers raised sufficient coin to complete the film last year, one of the lead actors (Katharine Romaine, cast as Gerard's colleague and romantic interest) was no longer available. This entailed major rewriting, killing off of Romaine's character and rejuvenating another character (who, in the original script, was one of the monster's early victims).

Yet, "Metamorphosis" plays out seamlessly on screen. It may have its problems, but continuity isn't one of them. The producers would do well to write a book about their misadventures, if only to inspire other filmmakers who have to improvise their way out of tight corners and even tighter budgets. — Ley.

FRISCO FEST

AMAZONIA:
VOICES FROM THE RAIN FOREST
(DOCU)

An Amazonia Films release. Produced and directed by Monti Aguirre and Glenn Switkes. Screenplay, Aguirre, Switkes, Michael Rudnick; camera (color), Eduardo Poiano; editor, Michael Rudnick; music, Egberto Gismonti. Reviewed at San Francisco Film Festival, April 27, 1991. No MPAA rating. Running time: **70 MIN.**

"**A**mazonia: Voices From The Rain Forest" taps into current ecological concerns for the future of the South American jungle and its natives, winning a lot of attention from preservationists. But it has no answers for ancient problems.

Producer-directors Monti Aguirre and Glenn Switkes are clearly sensitive to the Indians, rubber tappers and farmers whose lives are being disrupted, maybe destroyed, by development of lands largely controlled by the wealthy. It's unclear, however, how much the people speaking really want to turn the clock back to simpler times or want to share in the spoils.

Much of the controversy is the old, old story of the rich getting richer and the poor getting poorer. But much of the discussion is overtoned with sympathetic admiration for how much the Indians cared for the forest before the coming of the white man.

Probably it's too much to tackle, but the filmmakers show only limited interest in the deeper complexities of how much modern benefits do the heirs want and how high a price are they willing to pay.

For example, watching a woman play drums for native dancing and yearning for the old ways makes a strong point. But she's also wearing eyeglasses. Would she give up the glasses and the technology they represent for a chance to keep the campfires while the menfolk hunt?

Historically, Indians resented the coming of rubber tappers, who resented farmers, who resented ranchers, etc. Everybody wants the land and the trees and a better life. It's a shame everybody is not going to get what they want. — Har.

GRANICA
(THE BORDER)
(YUGOSLAVIAN)

A TRZ Fit release of a Terra-CFS Avala Film-RTV Novi Sad co-production. (World sales: Jugoslavija Film.) Produced by Dragan Stamenkovic, Branko Baletic. Directed by Zoran Masirevic. Screenplay, Ferenc Deak with Zivojin Pavlovic, Masirevec; camera (color), Duran Ninkov; editor, Igor Spasov; music, Ivan Vrhunc; sound, Svetislav Ristic; art direction, Milenko Jeremic; makeup, Stanislava Zaric; costumes, Branka Petrovic; production manager, Ilija Basic. Reviewed at Istanbul Film Festival, March 28, 1991. (Also in San Francisco Film Festival). Running time: **98 MIN.**
Etel . . . . Mirjana Jokovic
Dani . . . . Marko Ratic
Marko . . . . Davor Janjic
Father . . . . Lajos Soltis
Rade Topic . . . . Lazar Ristovski
Also with: Miklos Korica, Zoran Cvijanovic, Branko Cvejic, Derd Fejes, Eva Ras, Istvan Bickel, Ljiljana Blagojevic, Stojan Arandelovic, Ema Doro, Katalin Ladik, Aleksandar Jovicic.

Zoran Maserivic's fine first feature is engrossing drama with a Balkanized Romeo-Juliet romance at its core. Timeless in scope but timely in theme, pic won the top award at last year's Pula fest and did well at home b.o.'s. "The Border" is a natural for fests and arthouse release.

Set in Vojvodina, Yugoslavia, a province on the Yugoslavian-Hungarian border, a microcosm of longtime inhabitants (mainly Hungarian plus recent transplants) reflects the turbulence and ethnic clashes of the post-World War II years.

Etel (played with understated grace by Mirjana Jokovic) and Dani (Marko Ratic), a Hungarian brother and sister, are interrupted in their idyllic playtime on the deserted border by sinister Russian soldiers. They grab

Etel and rape her as Dani desperately struggles to free himself while being held by other soldiers. Desperate looks exchanged between the siblings convey the scene's horror.

The brother seems most traumatized by the event and becomes an enigmatic loner, while the sister devotes herself to raising the child born as the result of the rape.

Meanwhile, the new communist regime relocates families from the rockier parts of the country to the fertile farmland of Vojvodina. As part of this "colonization," minorities such as Jews are labeled traitors and forced to leave the country.

A family of Serbs from Bosnia moves next door to Etel and Dani's family and begin to cultivate the vacant farm. The contrast between the Hungarian family's more refined European manners and the Serbs' earthy provincial nature is glaringly evident upon their first meeting. Language of Serb Rade Topic (played with gusto by veteran Lazar Ristovski) in the overly literal subtitles is laden with vulgarities.

Gentle pan pipe music and string arrangements signal the stirrings of infatuation between darkly handsome Marko Topic (Davor Janjic) and Etel. The prejudiced patriarchs of both families are opposed to their union.

When Topic stubbornly refuses to bow to the demands of agrarian reform, which include contributing a hefty portion of one's crops to the state, he and his family abandon the farm and set off to return to their former province. That seems to effectively seal the fate of the potential mates.

The border refers to the boundary arbitrarily drawn between nations as well as the inner barriers preventing individuals from opening themselves up to others of different backgrounds. The point is poignantly underscored by the violent events accompanying Yugoslavia's 1948 break with the USSR, events that finally break down the lingering hostility of the two fathers.

Technical credits are commendable in this promising debut that reveals the influence of helmer Masirevic's training at Prague's prestigious FAMU Academy. Lensing and lighting are excellent and the cast solid, especially the expressive youngsters.

The script is fresh and unpretentious, and one can't help but marvel at how history repeats itself, with Yugoslavia close to a violent division between the five provinces comprising the country. — *Sam.*

CHEB
(FRENCH-ALGERIAN)

An Artedis release of a 3B Prods. (France)-ENPA (Algeria)-Artedis-CRRAV co-production. Produced by Jean Bréhat. Directed by Rachid Bouchareb. Screenplay, Bouchareb, Abdelkrim Bahloul, Christian Zerbib; camera (color), Youcef Sahroui; editor, Guy Lecorne; music, Safy Boutella; sound, Fabien Ferreux, Olivier Schwob, Thierry Sabatier; casting, Nora Habib (France), Saïd Seghir (Algeria). Reviewed at Club de l'Etoile, Paris, April 5, 1991. (In San Francisco Film Festival and Cannes Film Festival, Perspectives on French Cinema.) Running time: **82 MIN.**
Merwan . . . . Mourad Bounaas
Malika . . . . Nozha Khouadra
Ceccaldi, the Frenchman . . . .
. . . . Pierre-Loup Rajot
The captain . . . . . Boualem Benani
Taxi driver . . . . . Yahia Benmabrouk
Also with: Faouzi Saichi, Mohamed Nacef, Nadji Beida, Cheik Doukouré, Houari Bellamou, Thameur.
(In French and Arabic)

"Cheb," which means "young" in Arabic, is a thought-provoking look at Western-style freedom vs. North African fundamentalism. Visually accomplished tale might have art-house potential, particularly with young audiences and fans of North African music.

Tackling the predicament of a teen born in Algeria, raised in France and expelled to Algeria, film kicks off with vivid documentary montage of racially motivated protest demonstrations and police violence.

It then cuts to a desert vista where 19-year-old Merwan hitches a ride across the sandy terrain. It's gradually learned that because of some legal infraction he has been stripped of his resident-alien status and deported from France, the only home he has ever known. Merwan is nabbed by customs authorities and conscripted into the Algerian army. A true misfit, he meets with disdain because he speaks only French, not Arabic.

He soon goes AWOL to join his girlfriend, Malika, an assertive French-born Arab whose uncle is keeping her sequestered after her own father tricked her into returning to Algeria for an alleged vacation visit. Uncle has confiscated her passport and intends to drum into her a woman's proper place in Algerian society.

Malika can't abide Algeria's restrictive family code. Merwan is an army deserter determined to escape from a country where he does not belong in order to return to a country that no longer wants him.

Pair set out to cross the border, encountering harsh administrative and cultural restrictions at every turn. They can't share a hotel room without a certificate proving they're married. No public displays of affection. Malika is reduced to cutting her hair and dressing as a boy in order to travel more freely.

Remainder of pic concerns young couple's often suspenseful efforts to elude capture and return to France although they have no travel documents, neither speaks Arabic and they have little knowledge of local customs. Despite their Arab heritage, both are pure products of a liberal French education, and they're stuck in hostile territory.

Helmer, whose first feature "Baton Rouge" toured the U.S. in 1986, skillfully exploits the fish out of water/man without a country angle. Nonprofessionals in two lead roles are touching and believable. Impressive lensing shows off landscape of sand and harsh shadows. — *Ness.*

FX2:
THE DEADLY ART OF ILLUSION

An Orion Pictures release of a Dodi Fayed-Jack Wiener production. Produced by Wiener, Fayed. Executive producers, Lee R. Mayes, Bryan Brown. Directed by Richard Franklin. Screenplay, Bill Condon, based on characters created by Robert T. Megginson, Gregory Fleeman; camera (DeLuxe color), Victor J. Kemper; editor, Andrew London; music, Lalo Schifrin; sound (Dolby), Ronald A. Jacobs, Jeff Watts; production design, John Jay Moore; art direction, Gregory P. Keen; set decoration, Gordon Sim; costume design, Linda Matheson; special effects, Eric Allard; assistant directors, Brian Cook, Carl Goldstein, Tom Quinn; casting, Lauren Lloyd, Gail Levin. Reviewed at Mann Bruin Theater, Westwood, Calif., May 7, 1991. MPAA Rating: PG-13. Running time: **109 MIN.**
Rollie Tyler . . . . Bryan Brown
Leo McCarthy . . . . . Brian Dennehy
Kim Brandon . . . . . . Rachel Ticotin
Liz Kennedy . . . . . . Joanna Gleason
Ray Silak . . . . Philip Bosco
Matt Neely . . . . . Kevin J. O'Connor
Mike Brandon . . . . Tom Mason
Chris Brandon . . Dominic Zamprogna
Velez . . . . .Josie DeGuzman
Rado . . . . John Walsh

With all the ingenuity that went into toys and gadgetry in this five-years-removed sequel, it's a shame no one bothered to hook a brain up to the plot. That said, the Bryan and Brian show should click with the undemanding, as "FX2" provides enough crowd-pleasing fun to hotwire initial b.o. receipts. Still, pic's primary allure, like its predecessor's, likely will remain in homevideo.

Beyond the engaging leads, there's little here on the level that made 1986's "F/X" so entertaining, as the sequel throttles a stale police-corruption setup loaded with genre clichés.

Structurally, pic also suffers from an annoying habit of introducing plot points and characters in willy-nilly fashion, in some cases late in the action. Even so, anyone who can't tap into the telegraphed twists must be watching through a light-refracting one-way mirror.

Because the pic's basic conceit is so simple — a film effects man using his "reel" skills to thwart dense public officials and criminals — the story actually gets off to a rather slow start, as the semiretired Rollie Tyler (Brown) is talked into participating in a police sting operation by his g.f.'s ex-husband (Tom Mason).

The operation goes haywire, the ex-husband is killed and Tyler starts looking into the intrigue behind it. In over his head, he recruits the help of Leo (Dennehy), the cop he teamed with at the end of the first pic.

Despite a few cute one-liners in Bill Condon's script, the ultimate appeal lies in the gadgets, which shine in a few moments. Most notable is a sequence in which Tyler uses a mannequin-sized robot clown as his surrogate in fending off a thug.

There's also a Mr. Wizard-like element to another encounter: Common products in a supermarket provide the tech ace's arsenal as he defends himself in increasingly absurd ways.

Still, director Richard Franklin doesn't maintain an even tone, leapfrogging between farcical, almost slapstick comedy and darker dramatic elements. As a result, the payoff seems particularly tepid, especially in light of the various people sacrificed on the road to short-circuiting the central conspiracy.

The lack of an interesting villain also hurts. Philip Bosco is more a comic foil than anything else, while other bad guys are merely shadowy mob types left on the film's fringe.

Dennehy remains one of the more effortlessly likable actors around, while Brown may be a little too self-assured this time in using his fantasy skills in life-or-death situations.

Scant effort is made to develop supporting players, although a few amusing throwaway lines do find their way into the mouths of Joanna Gleason and Josie DeGuzman, both solid in roles as Dennehy dames.

Tech credits are generally top-notch, though beyond the opening sequence the film offers few over-the-top illustrations of its title. Stuntwork is more impressive, while Lalo Schifrin's score is characteristically sprightly.

Film also merits mention for its absolutely gratuitous use of a single shot in Italy, no doubt welcomed by principals who picked up frequent-flyer miles off the 10-second sequence. — *Bril.*

HERDSMEN OF THE SUN
(FRENCH-DOCU)

An Interama release of an Arion Prods.-Antenne 2-Canal Plus co-production. Produced by Patrick Sandrin. Directed by Werner Herzog. Camera (color, 16m), Thomas Weber; editor, Rainer Standke; sound, Jacques Pietrobelli; assistant director, Walter Saxer. Reviewed at Film Forum, May 8, 1991. Running time: **52 MIN.**
(In English)

Werner Herzog has filmed exotic cultures before ("La Soufrière" and other documentaries), but none have been more unusual or fascinating than the nomads depicted in "Herdsmen Of The Sun." This 1988 portrait of a dwindling tribe in the southern Sahara is much more involving than the average anthropological pic.

The film opens with the bizarre image of seven-foot tribesmen in full regalia. Wearing bright makeup and jewelry, these tribal drag queens stand on their toes and flash the whites of their eyes and teeth.

They are, in fact, beauty contestants participating in a festival accurately described as a marriage market. The men spend hours beautifying themselves and then "radiate their charms" in order to attract a woman. In this culture, which dates back to the Stone Age, women get to choose men they find most beautiful.

Near the end of this short film comes the full ceremony. In the final round, all the men wear the same makeup and dress so as not to have an unfair advantage. After they preen for the crowd, a woman picks a winner who will spend the night with her.

The next morning, the winner asks the woman, "Do you love me because of my beauty or my charms?" The ritual resembles a role-reversed Miss America Pageant.

But Herzog does not neglect the Wodaabe's troubles. It's pointed out the festival was suspended during a four-year drought. Famine caused many families to lose their herds and their livelihood. As a result, the nomadic way of life is dying out.

Some have migrated to the city, where they are even hungrier. Herzog's final image is of a displaced tribesman walking a camel across a city bridge at twilight. It provides a poignant ending since the Wodaabe's culture, and their remarkable mating dance, may not endure.

Fortunately, Herzog has captured their rites in an enlightening, entertaining documentary.

On the same Film Forum bill is "Black Water," a more somber look at a Brazilian fishing village. Their livelihood is threatened, too, but in this case the problem is a factory polluting the water. Directed by Allen Moore, who produced the 28-minute film with Charlotte Cerf, "Black Water" conveys a powerful ecological message without becoming heavy-handed. — *Stev.*

CANTIQUE DES PIERRES/ NACHID EL-HAJAR
(CANTICLE OF STONES)
(BELGIAN-PALESTINIAN-GERMAN)

A Sourat Films-RTBF Television Belge-Centre de l'Audio-Visuel a Bruxelles-ZDF production in association with Channel Four. (Intl. sales: WMF, Paris.) Written and directed by Michel Khleifi. Camera (color), Raymond Fromont; editor, Moufida Tlatli; music, Jean-Marie Senia; sound, Ricardo Castro. Reviewed at 10th Istanbul Intl. Film Festival, March 27, 1991. (In Human Rights Watch Film Festival, Angelika Film Center, N.Y.) Running time: **106 MIN.**
With: Bushra Karaman, Makram Khouri.
(Arabic soundtrack; French subtitles)

An angry look at the condition of Palestinians in Israel, "Canticle Of Stones" grafts a florid romance onto docu-like footage. Uneasy fit grinds ill at times, but solid helming and political angles make this a natural for fests and specialized webs.

Fictional framing device recalls "Hiroshima, Mon Amour." Love story's he is an ex-political prisoner trying to finish a novel; she's just back from the U.S. after 18 years to do research in Jerusalem. The middle-aged couple re-kindle the affair they had in the 1960s and ruminate on what it means to be Palestinian.

Dialog is mostly of the French novella type ("he danced on the shadows of my dark hair"), intoned on balconies or in the sack. Pic's meat is in verismo segs of street fighting with Israelis and interviews with Palestinian vets.

The abrupt shifts in tone back and forth are occasionally effective, but the romantic baloney gets in the way later on as the pic moves to Gaza and the political engine shifts into top gear.

Brussels-based helmer Michel Khleifi, best known for "Wedding In Galilee," is a Palestinian of Christian-Arab parents. "Canticle" (which repped Belgium at last year's Cannes fest) has no pretense at balance, but carries an emotional charge nonetheless. Technically, pic is fine; thesping is routine. — *Del.*

WHITE LIGHT
(CANADIAN)

A Brightstar Films release in Canada of a Bellemonde Films presentation. (Intl. sales: Goldcrest Films and Television.) Produced by Anthony Kramreither. Executive producers, Don Haig, Alan Chapple, Michael Manley. Directed by Al Waxman. Screenplay, Ron Base; camera (color), Bert Dunk; editor, David Nicholson; music, Paul Zaza; production design, Ray Lorenz; associate producers, Base, Orval Fruitman; production supervisor, Susan Hart-Magee. Reviewed at Famous Players screening room, Toronto, April 29, 1991. Running time: **97 MIN.**
Sean Craig . . . . Martin Kove
Dr. Ella Wingwright . . Martha Henry
Debra Halifax . . . Heidi von Palleske
Bill Dockerty . . . . James Purcell
Clay Avery . . . . Bruce Boa
David Ramon . . . . George Sperdakos
Also with: Raoul Trujillo, Heath Lamberts, Allison Hossack.

"White Light," an efficient thriller/love story with a come-back-from-the-dead twist, should perform okay in theatrical, homevid and tv.

Cop Martin Kove blows his undercover pose in tense opening sequences and delivers mob boss George Sperdakos into the arms of rushing police. Left at home unprotected, Kove gets nailed by a mobster's bullet and is dead for five minutes in the hospital before regaining life.

While dead, he romances a loving blonde (Allison Hossack) whom he spends much of the pic trying to find again even though she tells him she, too, is dead. He dreams of her and relives those moments with the help of a doctor (Martha Henry) who gives him an experimental drug that helps patients recall their experiences while briefly dead.

Kove tracks his blonde through a mysterious poster campaign photographed by a partying Andy Warhol-type character (Heath Lamberts) to an abandoned rural house. Its owners, the girl and her parents, are said to have died three years before.

Ron Base's brisk script links the mob boss to the blonde, whom Kove finds still alive but who has no memory of him. Kove and Hossack celebrate their bond for real by the roaring fireplace, with nude vital parts not shown.

Next morning the mob boss shows up, shoots her and just before dying she shoots him. Crooked cops are thrown into the mix and bad-guy bodies pile up in various tasteful shootouts. Kove poses a lot in open neck shirts, but mostly delivers.

Henry is excellent as the wine-drinking, smoking doctor. Too bad she gets killed, too. Screen newcomer Hossack, a sweet woman of dreams, always filmed in refracted sunlight, is nothing more than pliant lover. And there are smoothly played character roles by Sperdakos, Lamberts, James Purcell as a bad cop and henchman Raoul Trujillo.

Al Waxman's direction is not as brisk as the plot. Tighter editing would help. Other tech credits, including Bert Dunk's camerawork, are thrifty. — *Adil.*

CANNES FEST

A CAPTIVE IN THE LAND

A Gloria Prods.-Gorky Film Studios-Soviet American films presentation of a John Berry-Stuart Phoenix production. Produced by Malcolm Stuart, Berry. Executive producer, Peter S. Gold. Directed by Berry. Screenplay, Lee Gold, based on the novel by James Aldridge; camera (Fuji color), Pierre William Glenn; editor, Georges Klotz; music, Bill Conti; sound (Dolby), Henri Roux, Jean-Michel Chauvet; production design, Yurih Konstantinov; art direction, Jacques Voizot; costumes, Eugenia Chervonskaya; special effects, Philippe Alleton; assistant director, Gilles Castera; 2nd unit camera, Alain Choquart. Reviewed at Vision Intl. screening room, L.A., April 26, 1991. (In Cannes Film Festival, Un Certain Regard.) Running time: **96 MIN.**
Royce . . . . Sam Waterston
Averyanov . . . . . Alexander Potapov

"A Captive In The Land" is a ruggedly effective allegorical survival tale from director John Berry. Shot on forbidding Arctic wastelands as well as in Russian studios, pic plays as a potent two-character piece about strangers forced to battle nature together, with the element of continued misunderstanding and mistrust between the U.S. and the USSR as a subtext.

Pic should be a saleable attraction in most markets, although very special handling would be required to build a proper profile for it Stateside.

Striking opening sequence (with one of the last title jobs by the late Maurice Binder, a longtime friend of the director's) economically presents the crash of a Soviet military plane in the polar region and the follow-up rescue jump by an American (Sam Waterston) who happens to be along for the ride in a transport that passes over the wreckage.

Finding just one Russian alive, Waterston drags him inside the broken fuselage and fashions makeshift quarters that will protect them until the U.S. Air Force comes to their expected rescue.

As the days wear on, however, no saviors appear on the bleak, white horizon, and Waterston and the survivor (Andrei Segueyvich) have no choice but to settle in for the long haul. With the Russian's injuries preventing him from walking, the Yank is saddled with all the work, mainly cooking and making the cabin livable.

Partly out of guilt for this state of affairs but mainly out of natural impulse, the talkative, outgoing Russian, who speaks fair English, pushes hard to strike up a friendship, but is rebuffed at every turn.

Refused of his offers to pass the time by reciting poetry and teaching his rescuer Russian, Potapov decides to clam up, only to break out of it by exclaiming, "It's not human to be silent! It's not cultural!" He adds his assessment that the Russian soul is "out in the open," while the American one is "locked in a box."

When the two do discuss literature, a strong message is delivered about the superiority of Russian to American education. Not only does the Russian speak English, but he can quote American poetry, analyze "The Sun Also Rises," which the Yank has not finished reading, and paraphrase Adm. Richard Byrd: It's difficult for two men to be isolated on the ice, whereas to be alone or three together is all right.

The Russian takes umbrage when Waterston casually dismisses communism as a failed system. While stating he's not a communist, Potapov admits his wife is, and allows, "It's tough to be a communist in my country today."

Shortly thereafter, he becomes enraged when the American passes uninformed judgment on his nation's politicos, insisting, "I can criticize them. You cannot."

Such exchanges represent the best sections of the tight screenplay by the late Lee Gold, while the least interesting is the allegorical, "Defiant Ones"-like international brotherhood theme. Fortunately, the latter is mostly downplayed by director Berry, who has expertly spared the audience undue claustrophobia during the relatively static first hour through highly mobile and probing use of the camera.

Once they realize they are unlikely to be rescued, the two men set out on an arduous journey, with Waterston pulling and rowing Potapov across ice, snow and water in search of possible civilization. Last third of the pic thus becomes an adventure tale, one with its share of absurdities and surprises.

Production might have been an arduous one for many filmmakers, but for a director of 73, it is notable. Berry, who has worked mostly overseas since being blacklisted more than 40 years ago, has made a lucid film that keeps moving in excellent fashion while offering issues to ponder.

He has elicited fine performances from the leads. Waterston strongly conveys the bitterness of a casual humanitarian whose life is put on the line in a seemingly futile attempt to save another. Potapov has the handicap of immobility but the advantage of a gregarious character, and brings him brimmingly to life.

Implicit in the personal/political exchanges is the notion that, while the American may think he's much freer than the disabled man he rescues, he's actually just as stuck as the Russian. What one is left with is that, even if the two men (nations) can't be great friends, they can at least get along and try to help each other out.

Pierre William Glenn's active camera contributes to the film's liveliness, and Georges Klotz' editing is tight and particularly good at matching action in close quarters. Bill Conti's score is rather overblown for a two-character drama. — *Cart.*

THELMA & LOUISE

A Pathé Entertainment presentation of a Percy Main production. Produced by Ridley Scott, Mimi Polk. Directed by Scott. Screenplay, Callie Khouri; camera (color), Adrian Biddle; editor, Thom Noble; music, Hans Zimmer; sound, Keith A. Wester; production design, Norris Spencer; costume design, Elizabeth McBride; art direction, Lisa Dean; set decoration, Anne Ahrens; set design, Alan Kaye; assistant director, Steve Danton; 2nd unit director-stunt coordinator, Bobby Bass; coproducers, Dean O'Brien, Khouri. Reviewed at Pathé screening room, L.A., May 2, 1991. (In Cannes Film Festival, noncompeting.) MPAA rating: R. Running time: **128 MIN.**
Louise . . . . Susan Sarandon
Thelma . . . . Geena Davis
Hal . . . . Harvey Keitel
Jimmy . . . . Michael Madsen
Darryl . . . . . Christopher McDonald
J.D . . . . Brad Pitt

"Thelma & Louise" is a thumpingly adventurous road pic about two regular gals who shoot down a would-be rapist and wind up on the lam in their '66 T-bird. Even those who don't rally to pic's fed-up feminist outcry will take to its comedy, momentum and dazzling visuals. This could be the pic that drags sidelined MGM/Pathé back out onto the road.

"I'd rather be a killer than a victim," decides reluctant cop Harrison Ford near the outset of Ridley Scott's "Blade Runner," and the director uses the same theme to kick off the saga of Arkansas housewife Thelma (Geena Davis) and waitress Louise (Susan Sarandon).

Setting out for a weekend fishing trip away from the drudgery of their lives and the indifference of their men, they stop at a roadside honkytonk to blow off steam, and things turn ugly. A guy tries to rape Thelma; Louise can't take it so she plugs the creep with a .38. Then they hit the highway, dazed and in trouble.

It's a tricky scene: She didn't have to kill him, but it's a welcome move. Shook-up Thelma wants to know why they don't just tell the police what happened. "Who's gonna believe you," retorts Louise. "We don't live in that kind of world."

Sarandon is the big sister; more feminine, more focused, smoldering with a quiet determination. The car's hers and she drives it. Davis is more loosely wrapped; she goes with the flow, follows her whims into trouble, but also discovers untapped capacities in herself. They're not man-haters; they can't seem to stay away from men.

They're just out for freedom and a good time, and though the trip quickly turns miserable and all seems ruined, the more trouble they get into, oddly enough, the more fun they have. The journey into recklessness is exhilarating, which gives the film its buoyant pull.

Scott, working from an original script by Callie Khouri, is also having fun — too much, now and then, in certain over-the-top scenes. But the helmer seems to be telling the audience this is just a movie. Don't expect to believe it, just get ready for the big finish.

It's big all right, and in an indelible final image, it maintains the sense of reckless exhilaration to the end, thus qualifying as a triumph.

This is a journey film where the characters find a whole lot more than they knew they were looking for when they started out. "I think I've found my calling," says Thelma at one point. "Something's crossed over in me. I can't go back."

Despite some delectably funny scenes between the sexes, Scott's latest pic isn't about women vs. men. It's about freedom, like any good road picture. In that sense, and in many others, it's a classic.

Visuals and music ride shotgun with the story here, and Scott, a Brit, has conjured more magic from the American Southwest landscape than any drug-free individual is likely to see.

California and southern Utah locales stand in for Arkansas, Oklahoma and Texas, but via Scott's vision and the superb Panavision lensing of cinematographer Adrian Biddle ("Alien"), the sites take on a mythic luster.

The screen yields them remarkable depth, space and clarity, and Scott fills it with savory images: A young cowboy (Brad Pitt) is seen through the T-bird's drop-spattered plastic rear window dancing in the rain.

Just as important is the music, whether it's country & western-tinged warbling from jukeboxes and bandstands or Hans Zimmer's twanging, shimmering score.

Sarandon and Davis have found a dream vehicle here, and they drive it. Davis, who starts out a ditz, blossoms into a stylish, take-charge criminal. "You be sweet to your wife," she tells a blubbering cop as she helps him into the trunk of his car. "My husband wasn't sweet to me, and look how I turned out."

Michael Madsen, a standout in a small part in "The Doors," puts in another strong bid for attention as Sarandon's bull-headed b.f. Pitt is sharp and beguiling as the young outlaw hitchhiker, and Harvey Keitel successfully sheds his Eastern edges for a soft Southern drawl and a sympathetic manner.

Delayed from an originally planned March opening by MGM/Pathé's merger-related financial troubles, pic is now set for nationwide release May 24. It screens out of competition at Cannes on closing night. — Daws.

PROOF
(AUSTRALIAN)

A House and Moorehouse production in association with the Australian Film Commission and Film Victoria. (Intl. sales: Kim Lewis Marketing.) Produced by Lynda House. Written and directed by Jocelyn Moorhouse. Camera (Eastmancolor), Martin McGrath; editor, Ken Sallows; music, Not Browning, Waving; sound, Lloyd Carrick; production design, Patrick Reardon; production manager, Catherine (Tatts) Bishop; assistant director, Tony Mahood; casting, Liz Millinar, Greg Apps. Reviewed at Walker Street theater, North Sydney, April 27, 1991. (In Cannes Film Festival, Directors Fortnight.) Running time: **86 MIN.**
Martin . . . . Hugo Weaving
Celia . . . . Genevieve Picot
Andy . . . . Russell Crowe
Martin's mother . . . Heather Mitchell
Young Martin . . . . . . Jeffrey Walker
Vet . . . . Frank Gallacher
Brian (policeman) . . Frankie J. Holden
Waitress . . . . Saskia Post

Opening the Directors Fortnight section of this year's Cannes fest, "Proof" is an intriguing psychological drama structured around the contradictory character of a blind photographer. International arthouse exposure is quite possible for this striking debut from writer-director Jocelyn Moorhouse.

Intriguing premise has a blind man required to rely on the information of others, and what if those people don't tell the truth? Blind from birth, Martin (Hugo Weaving) never really believed his mother (Heather Mitchell) was telling him the truth about the world around him. When she died, son was convinced that this was another lie; instead, she left him because she was ashamed of his blindness.

Now in his 30s, Martin lives alone, his only company a seeing-eye dog and Celia (Genevieve Picot), the young woman who comes to clean his house and do his shopping. She has become infatuated with Martin, but he keeps her firmly at arm's length, much to her frustration.

Enter Andy (Russell Crowe), a guileless young man who works in an Italian restaurant Martin frequents. Andy describes to Martin the photos he takes, and the blind man warns his new friend never to lie to him.

Celia, meanwhile, decides to get at Martin through Andy. She seduces the youth and persuades him to lie to Martin about the contents of one of his photos. Inevitably Martin discovers the lie, and also discovers Andy and Celia together in his apartment.

Moorhouse has constructed a clever screenplay, even though the story of the three characters seems to take place in a strange vacuum. Wouldn't a woman as attractive as Celia have some kind of life apart from her frustrating relationship with Martin? And not much is learned about Andy, who must have had friends before Martin.

Apart from that, Moorhouse builds up a good deal of sexual tension among the three characters, aided by a trio of excellent performances.

Not without humor, pic has a funny sequence in which Andy takes Martin to see a slasher movie at a drive-in (the recent Aussie release, "Blood Moon") and enthusiastically describes the grisly goings-on.

Moorhouse shows considerable promise with this first feature, which also has been invited to the upcoming Sydney Film Fest. More festival as well as arthouse berths await this intelligent variation on male bonding and themes of trust, friendship and betrayal. Technically, pic is first-class in all departments.
— Strat.

BIX
(ITALIAN)

An Artisti Associati release of a Duea Film-Union P.N. production in association with RAI-1, Artisti Associati, state of Iowa, city of Davenport, and Iowa Film Office. (Intl. sales: Sacis Intl.) Produced by Antonio Avati. Directed by Pupi Avati. Screenplay, Pupi Avati, Antonio Avati, Lino Patruno; camera (Telecolor), Pasquale Rachini; editor, Amedeo Salfa; music, Bix Beiderbecke, arranged by Bob Wilber; in Dolby Stereo; art direction, Carlo Simi. Reviewed at CDS screening room, Rome, May 2, 1991. (Competing in Cannes Film Festival.) Running time: **111 MIN.**
Bix . . . . Bryant Weeks
Bismark . . . . Ray Edelstein
Aggie . . . . Julia Ewing
Burnie . . . . Mark Coliver
Marie-Louise . . . . . . Barbara Wilder
Joe Venuti . . . . Emile Levisetti
Lisa . . . . Sally Groth
Hoagy Carmichael . . . .
. . . . Romano Luccio Orzari
With: Matthew Buzzell, Marc Sovei, Michael T. Henderson, Timothy L. Williams, Debbon Ayer, Darrell Bishop.
(In English)

Italian helmer Pupi Avati crossed the Atlantic to make an all-American biopic of legendary jazz cornetist Bix Beiderbecke. Lack of star cast will keep interest down in the U.S., but "Bix" could find playdates with careful handling.

Finicky jazz fans may take exception to Bob Wilber's arrangements of Beiderbecke's music.

Other picky viewers could question a curious lack of midwestern accents in Iowa. But pic's Italian twang shouldn't harm its chances at the family boxoffice, where this clean-cut tale seems likely to score.

Bryant Weeks (like much of the cast) makes his film debut in the complex role of an angel-faced musician tormented by the demon of music. Mom (the smotheringly maternal Julia Ewing, who bears an eerie resemblance to the late Agnes Moorehead) and pop want Bix to drudge away in the family lumberyard. So do his brother (Mark Coliver) and sister (Barbara Wilder), two nice, sentimental sticks-in-the-mud.

As much as Beiderbecke strives to please his family, talent will out. He runs away from a swanky boarding school to join a famous band, but papa drags him back to Davenport. He becomes the greatest white jazz cornetist of his time, yet time and again gets sucked back to stifling home life, either through his mother's emotional blackmail or bouts of alcoholism.

In this familiar portrait of an artist's rise and fall, Avati is drawn to the family drama more than the music (which is admittedly plentiful). The cornet is a joyful obsession for young Beiderbecke, compared to the embarrassment of his crippled private life.

Pic is framed by a heavy-handed storytelling device which only clicks in the last shot. In order to please his mother, Beiderbecke has sent her the photo of a stranger he claims he's going to marry. After Beiderbecke's death from alcohol, his brother and his best friend Joe Venuti (a winning Emile Levisetti as the Italo-American violinist) hunt down the girl in the picture and take her to visit Beiderbecke's mother, recounting Beiderbecke's life to her on the train.

Despite the drama of Beiderbecke's precocious rise and tragic self-destruction, film has little of the dark poignancy that seems a hallmark of doomed musician tales. Avati has a sunny, optimistic vision that comes through with every loving shot of Iowa and Illinois. Hailing from Emilia, one of Italy's only landlocked regions, he seems right at home in the American midwest.

Cinematographer Pasquale Rachini imparts a glossy sheen to the fresh faces of Beiderbecke's young fellow musicians. Technically "Bix" is the finest work Avati's team has ever put together, thanks also to convincing period decor by Carlo Simi.

Acting is uniformly acceptable, without standout performances (indeed, some of the look-alike faces blur together). As Beiderbecke, Weeks appeals but never opens up, hiding as many secrets from the audience behind his innocent stare as he does from his family and friends.

But this surface opaqueness is part of Avati's stylistic trademark as "naif" director, for whom the ensemble effect — often persuasive — counts more than individual revelation. It also marks "Bix'" basic limit as a biopic.

— Yung.

ASSASSIN OF THE TSAR
(BRITISH-SOVIET)

A Spectacor Entertainment Intl.-Mosfilm Studios production in association with Courier Studios. (Intl. sales: Spectacor Intl. Film Sales, London.) Produced by Christopher Gawor, Erik Vaisberg, Anthony Sloman. Executive producers, Benjamin Brahms, Vladimir Dostal. Directed by Karen Schakhnazarov. Screenplay, Alexander Borodyansky, Shakhnazarov; camera (Eastmancolor), Nikolai Nemolyaev; supervising editor, Sloman; editor, Lidia Milioti; music, John Altman, Vladimir Shut; sound (Dolby), Igor Mayorov, Paul Carr, Stan Fiferman; art direction, Ludmila Kusakova; set design, Alexander Petrov; special effects set artist, Albert Rudachenko; costume design, Vera Romanova; production managers, Valery Gandrabura, Evgeny Kharitonov; assistant director, Larissa Makhlayova; associate producer, Alexander Moody; special effects, John Evans, Vyatcheslav Stepanov, Jeff Clifford; special effects camera, Victor Zhanov; postproduction dialog supervisor, Constantine Gregory; casting, Natalya Polyakova. Reviewed at Century preview theater, London, May 2, 1991. (Russian version competing at Cannes Film Festival.) Running time: **104 MIN.**
Timofeyev/Yurovsky . . . .
                Malcolm McDowell
Smirnov/Nicholas II . Oleg Yankovsky
Alexander Yegorovich . . . .
                Armen Dzhigarkhanian
Kozlov . . . . Yuri Sherstnyov
Marina . . . . Angela Ptashuk
Voikov . . . . Victor Seferov
Empress Alexandra . . Olga Antonova
Princess Olga . . . . . Daria Mayorova
Princess Tatyana . Evgenia Kryukova
Princess Maria . . Alena Tememezova
Princess Anastasia . . Olga Borisova
Prince Alexei . . . . . Alexei Logunov
Dr. Botkin . . . . . Vyatcheslav Vdovin
Medvedev . . . . Vyatcheslav Mukhov
  Also with: Denis Dmitriev, Nadezhda Makeko, Anastasia Nemolyaeva, Dmitry Kurilenko, Natalya Kishova, Yuri Beliaev, Andrei Kritvitsky.
(English soundtrack)

Part historical drama, part psycho suspenser, "Assassin Of The Tsar" doesn't score clean hits on all its targets, but powerful playing by topper Malcolm McDowell and excellent all-round production values

could give this intriguing Anglo-Soviet item minor legs beyond the art circuit, with careful handling.

After a mysterioso pretitles sequence (female voiceover reciting the slaying of Belshazzar and fall of Babylon), pic kicks off with a tinted re-creation of Tsar Alexander II's assassination in 1881. It's the first of a series of delusions told to doctors by Timofeyev (McDowell), a schizo in a present-day Moscow hospital who thinks he singlehandedly wiped out the Russian royals.

Timofeyev thinks he was Yakov Yurovsky, in charge of icing Tsar Nicholas II and his family in 1918. Every year he develops the symptoms of a perforated ulcer from which the real Yurovsky died in 1938. Despite Timofeyev's claim that he's cured, new medico Smirnov (Oleg Yankovsky) reckons there's still a ghost to be exorcised.

Pic develops shape as the pair go head-on in their sessions, with Smirnov becoming obsessed with discovering the truth of the assassination and even taking on the role of Nicholas II in Timofeyev's fantasies.

Climax comes when the haggard Smirnov visits Svedlovsk (now Ekaterinburg, site of the '18 slayings) and joins minds with Timofeyev to relive the actual assassination. The doc finally snuffs it, and Timofeyev stays in his hospital lock-up.

Despite its complex structure and mass of historical references, pic's basically a doctor-patient two-hander. There's none of the megabuck pomp of Western exercises like "Nicholas And Alexandra" (1971) nor any overt political angles.

Pic fixes on the character of Yurovsky, the secret police functionary who aimed to become a "creator of history" by finishing off the most powerful dynasty in the world. There's also unstated a message for the present: Great changes in Russo history are always marked by bloodshed.

That's where the script, which draws on new sources like Yurovsky's actual reports, isn't quite up to the several themes. The historical "flashbacks" dilute the drama of the head-butting sessions. As the assassination yarn develops a momentum of its own in the final half-hour, the modern-day story slips out of focus. Smirnov's death is virtually an anticlimax. The two story strands don't quite mesh.

Director Karen Shakhnazarov, best known on the fest circuit for

the absurdist comedy "Zero City" (1989), brings intensity and visual beauty to individual sequences, but he blows the longer dramatic line to make the various strands coalesce.

McDowell papers over that crack most of the time with his best thesping in years. White-haired and craggy-faced as the wily loony, and dead-eyed as the secret police nobody, he's totally believable in both roles.

Soviet superstar Yankovsky is restricted in an underwritten part as the medico/tsar, but gives solid support. Other roles are mainly bits, apart from Armen Dzhigarkhanian's mellow elder colleague of Yankovsky, but the faces are well cast.

Tech credits are top-drawer, with special nods to Nikolai Nemolyaev's pristine lensing and British composer John Altman's multithemed orchestral score, which brings the pic alive and is sorely missed in several sequences.

Pic was lensed in Moscow and Leningrad in two language versions, virtually identical shot-for-shot. The $6 million coin came mostly from British-based affiliate of Soviet techno Spec Group, same source as for "Lost In Siberia" (in Directors Fortnight). Anglo version under review is for markets outside the USSR, with its own score and the soundtrack remixed (plus Dolby) in London. Dubbing of Soviet players is mostly okay.

Given superior tech credits and McDowell's *tour de force*, this seems the one to go for. Version competing at Cannes is in Russian, with McDowell dubbed.

— Del.

HOLIDAYS ON THE RIVER YARRA
(AUSTRALIAN)

A Ronin Film (Australia) release of a Jungle Pictures production in association with the Australian Film Commission and Film Victoria. (Intl. sales: Kim Lewis Marketing.) Produced by Fiona Cochrane. Written and directed by Leo Berkeley. Camera (Eastmancolor), Brendan Lavelle; editor, Berkeley; music, Sam Mallet; sound, Mark Tarpey; production design, Margaret Eastgate, Adele Flere; production manager, Peter Jordan; assistant director, Kate Stone. Reviewed at AFC screening room, North Sydney, March 4, 1991. (In Cannes Film Festival, Un Certain Regard.) Running time: **88 MIN.**
Eddie . . . . Craig Adams
Mick . . . . Luke Elliot
Big Mac . . . . Alex Menglet
Stewie . . . . Tahir Cambris
Elsa . . . . Claudia Karvan
  Also with: Ian Scott, Sheryl Munks.

Despite the cheerful title, "Holidays On The River Yarra" is a grim but honest picture about a teen trying to cope with unemployment, boredom and racism. Small-scale pic should get strong reviews prompting modest to good arthouses biz.

The Yarra, flowing through Melbourne (Australia's second largest city), is not the sort of place for a vacation. The title is one of the film's ironies as pic confounds expectations, starting out as another teen comedy and gradually changing moods until the bleak, pessimistic fadeout.

Eddie (Craig Adams) and Mick (Luke Elliot) are very different mates. The former is a bit of a wimp; the latter aggressive and macho. Pic opens with the pair, lacking funds and motivation, spending an idle Saturday night together. They earn some money by painting a racist slogan on a wall, apparently without caring about the significance of their action.

The seedy type who hired them (Tahir Cambris) introduces them to other racists who are plotting a wild adventure to sail to an island off the African coast and seize it by force of arms.

Mick seems keen to join the adventure, even though a $500 fee each is required. Eddie goes along with his mate, though with less enthusiasm. After all, they've nothing better to do. Eddie is deemed too wimpy to join the mercenaries unless he can prove he can cook. A black comic interlude at this point involves his vain attempts to produce something edible until his mother steps in and bakes him a cake.

The boys still need cash, however, and have one night to get it. Their efforts lead to escalating crime and a senseless and shocking killing committed by the guileless Eddie. The murder paves the way for the film's downbeat but strangely logical conclusion.

Leo Berkeley, a Melbourne film teacher, has made a distinguished debut here, subtly shifting audience perceptions as his mood gets darker. He's helped by extremely creative camerawork by Brendan Lavelle and winning performances from his two young leads, especially Adams, who makes the weaker mate genuinely tragic.

In supporting roles, Claudia Karvan ("The Big Steal") shines as a girl who tries to get through to Adams, though she has troubles of her own, and Alex Menglet proffers a chilling face of evil as the jocular leader of the gang of racists.

Pic has something of the same mood of black comedy mixed with despair as another fine Melbourne-based pic, "Death In Brunswick." Maybe it's too early to suggest a new school of filmmaking is coming from that city, but the development is intriguing.

This disturbing pic won't be easy to market, but should find a niche at fests and small, quality venues. Though obviously made on a modest budget, tech elements are fine. — *Strat.*

HOMICIDE

A Triumph release of an Edward R. Pressman-Cinehaus production. Produced by Michael Hausman, Pressman. Executive producer, Ron Rotholtz. Written and directed by David Mamet. Camera (color), Roger Deakins; editor, Barbara Tulliver; music, Aeric Jans; sound, John Pritchett; production design, Michael Merritt; costume design, Nan Cibula; art direction, Susan Kaufman; assistant director, Mathew Carlisle. Reviewed at Columbia Plaza screening room, Burbank, Calif., May 2, 1991. (Competing in Cannes Film Festival.) No MPAA rating. Running time: **100 MIN.**
Bobby Gold . . . . Joe Mantegna
Tim Sullivan . . . . . William H. Macy
Chava . . . . Natalija Nogulich
Randolph . . . . Ving Rhames
Miss Klein . . . . Rebecca Pidgeon
Senna . . . . . . Vincent Guastaferro
Olcott . . . . Lionel Mark Smith
Frank . . . . Jack Wallace

David Mamet's first-rate writing and boldly idiosyncratic directing redeem this story of a toughened Jewish cop torn between two worlds, but its narrow concerns and punishingly dark conclusions are likely to make it acceptable only to a small, serious audience.

Cineastes at Cannes will be kept busy taking sides on this Edward Pressman-Cinehaus production, which opens the fest.

The third collaboration for writer-director Mamet, producer Michael Hausman and actor Joe Mantegna, "Homicide" presents a uniquely brutal world — an urban hell — in which stoic survivor Bobby Gold (Mantegna) must negotiate through rotten politics, unpredictable violence and virulent racial tension just to get through a day of police work.

After an unduly harsh dressing down by a racist black superior, Gold sees a chance to regain his enthusiasm when he becomes a key player in a team effort to bring in a cop killer who's eluded

the FBI.

But no sooner is he immersed in what he does best than he's callously reassigned to a routine investigation of an elderly Jewish woman shot down in her candy store in a black ghetto.

Gold couldn't be more frustrated or less interested. He lets his resentment spill out in an anti-Semitic tirade on the phone. Overheard and confronted by one of the slain woman's well-to-do Jewish relatives (Natalija Nogulich), he's deeply embarrassed and disturbed at how he's disassociated himself from his own roots.

To the disgust of his cynical Irish partner (William H. Macy), Gold gets caught up in the family's claims that they are targets of a deep-rooted and violent anti-Semitic conspiracy.

As he plunges into the secret underworld of the Jewish defenders, pursuing arcane leads in dusty archives and begging his way into secret meetings, pic switches tracks onto a narrower, more personal course and its momentum lags. Story of the Jewish defense underground is no doubt rich, but as set up here it functions only as a perplexing detour.

Gold is clearly seeking redemption and late acceptance from his ethnic brethren, but his quest has a pathetic, desperate quality that meshes uncomfortably with the courage and competence he displays as a cop. When his fellow cops need him to help bring down the killer, he's busy with initiation rites into his new sect.

Trying to maintain tension in this oddball marriage of two different stories, Mamet has Gold dashing back and forth between conflicting interests like a man with two lovers.

One assumes the story will be about a man who finds meaning by demonstrating a different kind of courage than he's been accustomed to, but that isn't the case. Mamet isn't out to satisfy traditional expectations; he's charting a course that's true to a particular world he's created.

Nonetheless, pic's conclusions are so bleak it might well be renamed "Suicide." Some will embrace it on an intellectual level as an aberration strongly realized; others will reject it outright.

Mamet's direction gives much of the film a bracing, refreshing tone as he works to express the shattering tensions of Gold's world: Characters prod and provoke each other in unexpected ways, and group scenes are

played like passages of cacophonous music.

Excellent work by Mantegna does much to enlist sympathies and interest. Macy is also strong as the flinty partner. — *Daws.*

TA DONA
(FIRE!)
(MALIAN)

A Kora Films (Mali) production. (Intl. sales: Stand Afrique Noir.) Written and directed by Adama Drabo. Camera (color), Lionel Cousin; editor, Rose Evans Decraene; sound, Khalil Thera; art direction, Bekaye Traore; costumes-props, Ladji Diakite; 1st assistant director, Sidy Diabate. Reviewed at CNC screening room, Paris, April 26, 1991. (In Cannes Film Festival, Un Certain Regard.) Running time: **100 MIN.**
Sidy . . . . Fily Traore
Fabou . . . . Mamadou Fomba
Samou . . . . Djibril Kouyate
Bablé . . . . Arouna Diarra
Oumou . . . . Fatoumata Toure
Koro . . . . Djemba Diawara
Also with: Ballamousaa Keita, Amy Coulibaly, Samby Karambe.
(In Bambara)

Incorporating nice dashes of local color into a contempo tale of ancient mysticism and modern corruption, "Fire!" is acceptable fest fare. Earnest pic strikes an appealing balance between old ways and new, but it's far from distinctive enough to engage general auds.

Contrast between urban and village life is adequately portrayed by a mix of experienced and nonpro actors in this feature debut from self-taught Malian director-scripter Adama Drabo.

Sidy, a dedicated young forestry engineer, is disgusted by his money-grubbing superiors. Through field work with rural citizens, he has come to believe re-forestation should be a national priority. But government ministers are more interested in throwing their weight around than in providing for the future.

On his own time, Sidy tries to track down the elusive "seventh canari," a ritual clay pot containing a medicinal plant whose secret healing power is believed to have been lost.

Spirited verbal sex play permeates rural life. Although the men are in charge of tribal and government affairs, the women are far from submissive. (In one comic episode, a woman pours water directly into a sleeping man's ear because he was murmuring another woman's name in a dream.) Whether or not a given male is circumcised seems to be fair grounds for teasing.

With the dry season coming, tribal oracle predicts fire and other troubles. Film touches on post-independence (1960) disenchantment. Tribal elders discuss logistics of nourishing the village, paying taxes and deciding whether to obey the official edict forbidding the fires traditionally set to aid hunters.

Having fallen into disfavor with the administration, Sidy is transferred to a distant post. But his honesty and determination are rewarded when he unexpectedly comes across the seventh canari. Back in town, one of the most corrupt members of the government is named head of the anticorruption brigade.

Pic's most striking scenes include a seemingly endless line of men rhythmically tilling a field with their hands, a male dancer "leaving" his body during a celebration, the presentation of a ritual offering in hopes of rain.

In a chase sequence, the local biker/hood crashes through a market display, takes an infant hostage and threatens the crowd with a knife until he makes his getaway. "There you have the influence of the white man's films," remarks a bystander.

Apart from this self-conscious digression, film has distinctly African feel. — *Ness.*

HORS LA VIE
(FRENCH-ITALIAN-GERMAN)

A Bac Films release of a Galatee Films-Films A2 (Paris)-Filmalpha (Rome)-Lamy Films (Brussels) production with the participation of Canal Plus and Raidue. (Intl. sales: Président Films.) Produced by Jacques Perrin. Directed by Maroun Bagdadi. Screenplay, Bagdadi with Didier Decoin, Elias Khoury, inspired by the book by Roger Auque in collaboration with Patrick Forestier; camera (color), Patrick Blossier; editor, Luc Barnier; music, Nicola Piovani; sound, Guillaume Sciama, Chantal Quaglio, Dominique Hennequin; art direction, Dan Weil; costumes, Magali Guidasci, Frederique Santerre; assistant director, Elie Adabachi; production manager, Catherine Pierrat; production supervisor, Jacqueline Louis; associate producers, Mario Gallo, Benoit Lamy; executive producers, Hugues Nonn, Fabienne Tsai. Reviewed at Club 13 screening room, Paris, April 30, 1991. (Competing at Cannes Film Festival.) Running time: **97 MIN.**
Patrick . . . . Hippolyte Girardot
Walid . . . . Rafic Ali Ahmad
Omar . . . . Hussein Sbetty
Ali (Philippe) . . . . . Habib Hammoud
Moustapha . . . . . Magdi Machmouchi
Ahmed (Frankenstein) . Hassan Farhat
De Niro . . . . Hamzah Nasrullah
Khaled's mother . . . Nidal El Achkar
Also with: Hassan Zbib, Nabila Zeitoun, Sami Hawat, Sabrina Leurquin.
(French, Arabic and English soundtrack; French subtitles)

Harrowing and believable, "Hors La Vie" follows the life of a French photographer held hostage in Beirut, in the process personalizing the ongoing tragedy of Lebanon. Sober, uncompromising but never excessive treatment conveys the mental and physical horrors of detention while delineating delicate balance between captors and victim.

Chaotic and convincingly violent opening scenes of Beirut street warfare provide vivid contrast with the subsequent abduction of the French photographer (Hippolyte Girardot). In short order, film tips from the seemingly random violence of a war defined only as endless and incomprehensible to the focused, terrifically reduced circumstances of a prisoner.

Unflinching pic conveys the indignities of trying to maintain health and hygiene under frequently unbearable conditions. Girardot's sense of self — as photographer, French citizen, man — erodes in captivity.

His job as a photojournalist was to look at events and capture them for others. Once taken hostage, he is ordered to wear a blindfold whenever his captors approach. If he should see them, he's dead.

Captors, talking among themselves in Arabic, are not always translated, conveying the hostage's anxiety. Pic was shot in chronological order, and the cumulative dismay in the cowed photog's eyes is palpable.

Sinister comic relief is furnished by a captor who, speaking perfect English, says he lived in the U.S. for five years where he claims to have been "Bobby De Niro's bodyguard." He then launches into a serviceable rendition of "You talkin' to me?" complete with gun. Girardot, impressed, agrees to call him De Niro.

With a few notable exceptions, the torture is primarily mental. Distinctive ripping sound precedes visuals in a vividly disturbing scene in which the photojournalist is wrapped mummy-style in plastic packing tape. Limbs pinned, face sealed, there is no possibility of movement, sound or escape. He's also gagged and stuffed into the hollow bottom of a sofa and moved by truck.

Captors are thoughtfully portrayed. More than one is essentially decent. One believes ba-bysitting a prisoner is beneath him. One has pledged body and soul to an unnerving succession of ideological movements but now believes Islam is the ticket.

De Niro explains that their leader's brother is in prison in France for drug trafficking, and they hope to make a prisoner exchange, adding, "If you understand drugs, you understand Lebanon." Drug connection is not developed further, but it hardly needed to be. The reasons don't matter, only the reality.

Entire cast is fine. Lensing by Patrick Blossier, who shot the last two Costa Gavras films, makes the most of Beirut and substitute locations in Palermo and France. Composer Nicola Piovani, who has worked with the cream of Italian directors, also contributes the right touch: low-key, sinister and never overbearing. — *Ness*.

SPOTSWOOD
(AUSTRALIAN)

A Miramax release of a Meridien Films-Smiley Films production in association with the Australian Film Finance Corp. (Intl. sales: Beyond Films.) Produced by Richard Brennan, Timothy White. Directed by Mark Joffe. Screenplay, Max Dann, Andrew Knight; camera (Eastmancolor), Ellery Ryan; editor, Nicholas Beauman; music, Ricky Fataar; sound (Dolby), Lloyd Carrick; production design, Chris Kennedy; costumes, Tess Schofield; production manager, Bernadette O'Mahoney; assistant director, Euan Keddie; casting, Alison Barrett. Reviewed at Filmside, Sydney, April 23, 1991. (In Cannes Film Festival, market.) Running time: **97 MIN.**
Errol Wallace . . . . . Anthony Hopkins
Carey . . . . Ben Mendelsohn
Mr. Ball . . . . Alwyn Kurts
Robert Spencer . . . . Bruno Lawrence
Finn . . . . John Walton
Cheryl Ball . . . . Rebecca Rigg
Wendy . . . . Toni Collette
Kim Barrett . . . . Russell Crowe
Caroline Wallace . . . .
. . . . Angela Punch McGregor
Frank Fletcher . . . . Dan Wyllie
Gordon . . . . John Flaus
Ron . . . . Jeff Truman

In "Spotswood," a delightful new Aussie comedy, Anthony Hopkins plays a character far removed from that of "The Silence Of The Lambs." Reminiscent of the British Ealing comedies of the '40s and '50s, pic should charm discerning audiences worldwide.

Max Dann and Andrew Knight's amusing screenplay, set in the mid-'60s, also resembles a non-Ealing Peter Sellers comedy, "The Battle Of The Sexes." Made in 1959 by Charles Crichton, "Battle" was adapted from James Thurber's "The Catbird Seat." Premise of both films revolves around a time and motion study expert brought in to advise an ailing business concern.

Hopkins plays the t&m man whose suggestions have brought about wholesale layoffs at a Melbourne car manufacturing plant. Called in to help out at Ball's, which makes moccasins, he quickly discovers that the small family business needs all the help it can get. The woefully old-fashioned factory and offices are run by elderly Mr. Ball (Alwyn Kurts), and the company is losing alarming amounts of money.

Despite his track record of large-scale retrenchments, the remote, unhappily married consultant befriends the factory workers and begins to see his work in terms of the lives involved.

In times of worldwide recession and unemployment, pic's upbeat message is a welcome one convincingly charted by its warm-hearted screenplay. Mark Joffe, helming his second feature (after the good but little-seen "Grievous Bodily Harm"), proves he's adept at comedy, although this is the kind of pic that elicits constant chuckles rather than outloud laughter.

Hopkins, who gives another very professional performance, is backed by a fine Australian cast. Local heartthrob Ben Mendelsohn plays Hopkins' ally at the factory. Newcomer Tony Collette is a find as the plain-Jane girl he overlooks because of his attraction for the boss' flighty daughter (Rebecca Rigg). Russell Crowe is hissable as the unscrupulous employee.

First-class actors such as Bruno Lawrence, John Flaus and Jeff Truman enact key factory workers with great good humor, and Angela Punch McGregor is properly chilly as Wallace's unsympathetic wife.

Best of all is veteran Kurts, who came out of retirement to play the moccasin factory owner. He brings precise timing to the kindly old man who sees his staff as an extended family and who is touchingly determined to keep his crumbling business intact.

Visually, "Spotswood" (the Melbourne suburb where the factory is located) is first class, with a particularly fine production design by Chris Kennedy and inventive camerawork by Ellery Ryan. — *Strat*.

FEMME FATALE

A Republic Pictures Home Video release of a Gibraltar Entertainment production. Executive producer, Joel Levine. Produced by Andrew Lane, Nancy Rae Stone. Directed by André Guttfreund. Screenplay, Michael Ferris, John D. Brancato; camera (Foto-Kem color), Joey Forsyte; editor, Richard Candib; music, Parmer Fuller; sound, Giovanni di Simone; production design, Pam Warner; costume design, Mira Zavidowsky; assistant director, Rick Nakano; associate producer, Gregory Small; casting, Andrea Stone Guttfreund. Reviewed on Republic videcassette, N.Y., May 4, 1991. (In Cannes Film Festival, market.) MPAA Rating: R. Running time: **96 MIN.**
Joe Prince . . . . Colin Firth
Elizabeth/Cynthia/Maura . . . .
. . . . Lisa Zane
Elijah . . . . Billy Zane
Dr. Beaumont . . . . Scott Wilson
Jenny . . . . Lisa Blount
Andrea . . . . Suzanne Snyder
Ted . . . . Pat Skipper
Ed . . . . John Laviachielli
Dino . . . . Carmine Caridi

An intriguing premise remains stillborn in "Femme Fatale," a direct-to-video release that required thrills, not ennui. Tired blood offering is being shown to foreign distribs at this year's Cannes market and hits U.S. vid stores May 23.

Lisa Zane, whose slow-burning Hollywood career has encompassed the female leads in "Pucker Up And Bark Like A Dog" and "Bad Influence," is cast as a 1990s Sybil. Her multiple personalities come as a shock to husband Colin Firth, who wakes up one morning to find her gone.

Improbably cast as a forest ranger, the veddy British Firth heads south to L.A. in pursuit of wife Cynthia, but folks identify her from wedding pictures alternately as paralyzed Elizabeth or underground movie actress Maura Sade.

Zane turns out to be all three people and more. Eventually Firth finds out that her dad is shrink Scott Wilson, who sentimentally lets him take her home with him to the woods.

Idiotic climax is poorly scripted and awkwardly staged: Evil drug dealers catch up with the couple, obtain stolen drugs Zane has hidden in the woods and then let everyone go for a tentative, potentially happy ending that fails to address Zane's psychological problems.

Director André Guttfreund never creates the sense of danger needed in this story, preferring to take the viewer on a slumming tour of L.A.'s underground performance art scene.

Within this milieu Lisa Blount does a good job as an s&m movie director who's Zane's lesbian lover.

Zane remains an unusual-looking leading lady whose talents are still in search of a good role (the multiple personas here are all gimmick). The actress' real-life brother Billy Zane is diverting as an ultra-hip artist friend of Firth's. Oddly, script provides no scenes for the Zanes to play together.

Firth, who had a much juicier assignment in the quirky "Apartment Zero," is merely required to play straight in a world of weirdos. Suzanne Snyder, most often cast in horror pics, brings panache to an underwritten part as Billy Zane's frequently topless model. Film is enhanced by a moody keyboards score by Parmer Fuller. — *Lor.*

BACKSLIDING
(AUSTRALIAN-BRITISH)

A Target production in association with Film Four Intl., Itel and the Australian Film Finance Corp. (Intl. sales: Film Four Intl.) Executive producers, Charles and Simon Target. Produced by Sue Wild. Directed by Simon Target. Screenplay, Simon Target, Ross Wilson; camera (Eastmancolor), Tom Cowan; editor, Nicholas Holmes; music, Nigel Westlake; sound, Ross Linton; production design, Ross Major; production executive, Basil Appleby; production manager, Vanessa Brown; assistant director, Michael Bourchier; stunts, Glen Boswell; casting, Maizels and Associates. Reviewed at Roxy screening room, Film Australia, Sydney, April 14, 1991. (In Cannes Film Festival, market.) Running time: **91 MIN.**

Tom Whitton	Tim Roth
Jack Tyson	Jim Holt
Alison Tyson	Odile Le Clezio
The pastor	Ross McGregor

"Backsliding," the first feature film from director Simon Target (pronounced Tarjay) is a well produced, well-acted psychological thriller set in a remote part of the Australian desert. Despite a few rough edges, pic contains enough suspense and tension to please most audiences.

Jim Holt plays an ex-con with a violent past who's been converted to Christianity in prison. Born again, he and his devout wife (Odile Le Clezio) have found work looking after a compressor station on a gas pipeline located miles from anywhere.

Their simple but contented lifestyle is interrupted by the arrival of a standby electrician (British thesp Tim Roth) assigned to the station. It quickly becomes clear the mysterious visitor has lied about his qualifications and background. He doesn't have a clue how to operate the machinery, and the damage he causes triggers a series of emotional responses in the ex-con. He starts "backsliding" — reverting to violent behavior.

The script by Target and Ross Wilson contains a few improbabilities — Holt goes around the bend too quickly — but they are mostly offset by Target's robust direction and Tom Cowan's outstanding camerawork.

Thesping is fine, with Roth giving another solid performance as the mysterious interloper who winds up a near-victim. Holt convincingly portrays a religious nut trying to obliterate his violent past, and Le Clezio is both sensual and down-to-earth as the frightened wife. Only other significant character, neatly limned by Ross McGregor, is a priest who arrives by light plane to visit members of his flock.

Nicholas Holmes' editing doesn't entirely manage to cover up the gaps in the plot, and Nigel Westlake's music is over-emphatic at times. Still, pic is an entertaining effort which makes the most of a comparatively modest budget. — *Strat.*

LOVE-MOI
(CANADIAN)

An Aska Film Distribution release of a Production du Lundi Matin, Production Virage and National Film Board of Canada production. Produced by François Bouvier, Marcel Simard, Doris Girard. Directed by Simard. Screenplay, Simard, Lise Lemay-Rousseau; camera (color), Pierre Letarte; editor, Michel Arcand; music, Robert Léger; sound, Yvon Benoit; art direction, Jean-Baptiste Tard; costume design, Gaétanne Lévesque. Reviewed at Famous Players Parisien Cinema in Montreal, April 22, 1991. (In Cannes Film Festival, market.) Running time: **97 MIN.**

Charles	Germain Houde
Louise	Paule Baillargeon
Danielle	Lucie Laurier
Michelle	Sonia Laplante
Dolores	Dominique Leduc
Maryse	Lyne Durocher
Alain	Eric Brisebois
Jacques	Mario St.-Amand
La Piquette	Stephane Demers
Jerome	Yvon Roy
Philippe	Hugolin Chevrette-Landesque
The lawyer	Claire Pimpare
Mario Boivin	Denis Bouchard

Few films about troubled teens have the violent, gritty authenticity of "Love-Moi," fiction film based on real-life teen rapists, thieves and prostitutes. Not nearly as slick or conclusive as U.S. save-the-delinquent items ("Stand And Deliver," "Lean On Me"), pic has a realism and graininess that likely will limit release outside its native Quebec to specialized venues, tv and video.

Mercifully, director Marcel Simard, who works with delinquents in real life, avoids blaming society for the kids' crimes. He uses young actors instead of the actual delinquents (who no longer were teens by the time the film was shot), avoiding the docudrama route.

Here, the teens spill their tales of family violence and abuse into a theater piece, which the pic's main character, Charles, videotapes.

The scriptwriting sessions uncover the sad stories and the gritty results, sometimes via the camcorder's black & white eye, an effective technique. One of the most convincing stories comes from Lucie Laurier (Danielle) who writes poetry for the "play." "When they put me in an institution, they said it was to protect me from my mother's boyfriend, who raped me. I did his time," she says, resigned to her fate.

Jacques uses the exercise to talk about his obsession with suicide. During the production of the play, he hangs himself (as did one of Simard's own delinquent protégés). Another ends up in prison. One girl is beaten by her boyfriend, and another, a prostitute, is raped by cops.

Simard manages to work in a love story between Charles and his g.f. Louise (perhaps just to lighten up the film), but his message is pretty clear: Most kids in similar situations won't live to see 30. The ray of hope in this heavy pic comes from people like Charles and Simard, who never give up on them. — *Suze.*

OVO MALO DUSE
(A LITTLE BIT OF SOUL)
(YUGOSLAVIAN)

A Centar Film-Televizija Sarajevo production. Produced by Senad Zviz. Directed by Ademir Kenovic. Screenplay, Ranko Boxic; camera (color), Mustafa Mustafic; editor, Christel Tanovic; music, Esad Arnautalic; sound, Bogoljub Nikolic; production design, Kemal Hrustanovic; costumes, Sanja Dzeba. Reviewed at Berlin Film Festival (market), Feb. 26, 1991. (In Cannes Film Fest, Directors Fortnight.) Running time: **78 MIN.**
With: Branko Duric, Davor Janjic, Boro Stjepanovic, Zaim Muzaferija.

Life in a Muslim community in a small Bosnian village is lovingly depicted in "A Little Bit Of Soul," a beautifully observed picture made five years ago.

First feature of director Ademir Kenovic, whose subsequent "Kuduz" was shown at several fests last year, looks at the way ancient marriage customs still affect the way people live.

This simple story unfolds with economy and maximum emotional punch. Kenovic extracts natural and unforced performances from his cast. Pic confirms his talent as a humanist director who (like early Milos Forman) brings insight and humor to everyday lives and problems. — *Strat.*

WHAT ABOUT BOB?

A Buena Vista release of a Touchstone Pictures presentation in association with Touchstone Pacific Partners I of a Laura Ziskin production. Produced by Ziskin. Directed by Frank Oz. Screenplay, Tom Schulman, story by Alvin Sargent, Ziskin; camera (Technicolor), Michael Ballhaus; editor, Anne V. Coates; music, Miles Goodman; sound (Dolby), Bill Phillips; production design, Les Dilley; art direction, Jack Blackman; set decoration, Anne Kuljian; costume design, Bernie Pollack; assistant directors, James W. Skotchdopole, Donald J. Lee, Jr.; co-producer, Bernard Williams; casting, Glenn Daniels. Reviewed at Avco Center Cinema, Westwood, Calif., May 15, 1991. MPAA Rating: PG. Running time: **99 MIN.**
Bob Wiley . . . . Bill Murray
Dr. Leo Marvin . . . Richard Dreyfuss
Fay Marvin . . . . Julie Hagerty
Siggy Marvin . . . . . . Charlie Korsmo
Anna Marvin . . . . . . Kathryn Erbe
Mr. Guttman . . . . Tom Aldredge
Mrs. Guttman . . . . . . Susan Willis
Phil . . . . Roger Bowen
Lily . . . . Fran Brill

Bill Murray finds a real showcase for his oft-shackled talent in this manic comedy, a fun trip although it falls victim to its manic elements in the final reel. With Disney seemingly sneaking the film into theaters and the quick exit of Murray's last vehicle ("Quick Change"), "What About Bob?" seems to have a question mark hanging over its b.o. prospects as well as its title.

Originally discussed as a pairing of Murray and Woody Allen, pic ended up with Richard Dreyfuss in the role of the tightly wound, egotistical psychiatrist whose life is disrupted by "multiphobic" new patient Bob Wiley (Murray), the human equivalent of gum on the bottom of one's shoe.

Dreyfuss' Dr. Leo Marvin, author of a self-help book that's about to land him on that mecca of cultural achievement, "Good Morning America," gets irked when the persistent patient follows him to a rustic New Hampshire retreat, then grows increasingly outraged as Bob proceeds to win over his family. Despite his schizo persona, Bob proves remarkably resourceful when it comes to ingratiating himself with Marvin's brood, helping the doc's death-obsessed son (Charlie Korsmo, kid in "Dick Tracy") learn to enjoy life and showing compassion to his daughter (Kathryn Erbe) and unappreciated wife (Julie Hagerty).

Tom Schulman's screenplay is peppered with little gems, and Murray has a field day with the character, which allows him to act like a little kid while occasionally lapsing into other aspects from his "Saturday Night Live" days, from his smarmy lounge singer to the nerd.

Under Frank Oz' direction, Murray succeeds in creating a character, not merely the Murray-playing-Murray schmoozer of "Ghostbusters" or "Stripes," funny as that persona is. Even with some inconsistencies in his neuroses, it qualifies as an impressive performance.

Dreyfuss, by contrast, generally reprises the role he played in Disney's "Down And Out In Beverly Hills": domineering, nouveau riche family man whose stolid existence is turned upside down by unwelcome intruder.

The film's main structural flaw stems from Oz and Schulman's failure to let the audience off the rollercoaster, as Marvin — rather than seeing the error of his ways — instead escapes into a madness that starts to border on caricature. The dark comic twists still are fun, but the pic ultimately feels drawn out as it nears a slightly unsatisfying conclusion.

Oz has tilled the fields of black comedy before in "Little Shop Of Horrors" and knows the territory, sensing how far to push the limit without going over the edge. In that respect, "What About Bob?" is a much better version of a film like "Neighbors," which took a similar premise, then torched it with its own excesses.

Technically, Miles Goodman helps the film enormously with a comic, circuslike score. Other production values are firstrate in this modestly scaled effort, among them Michael Ballhaus' fine camerawork.

A central point of the film hinges on the prospect of Bob hanging around until Labor Day, but with summer fare on the way there's a chance people may have stopped asking about Bob soon after Memorial Day, a prospect for everyone associated with this well-above-average production to be legitimately phobic about.
— *Bril.*

ONLY THE LONELY

A 20th Century Fox release of a Hughes Entertainment production. Produced by John Hughes, Hunt Lowry. Executive producer, Tarquin Gotch. Written and directed by Chris Columbus. Camera (Deluxe color), Julio Macat; editor, Raja Gosnell; music, Maurice Jarre; sound (Dolby), Jim Alexander, Chris Carpenter, Rick Hart, Kevin Carpenter; production design, John Muto; art direction, Dan Webster; set design, Bill Arnold, Gary Baugh, Karen Fletcher-Trujillo; set decoration, Rosemary Brandenburg; costume design, Mary E. Vogt; assistant director, Radcliffe; 2nd unit camera, Bobby Byrne, Paul Vombrack, John Connor; 2nd unit assistant directors, Dennis White, Jacolyn Baker; coproducer, Mark Radcliffe; casting, Jane Jenkins, Janet Hirshenson. Reviewed at 20th Century Fox screening room, L.A., May 14, 1991. MPAA Rating: PG-13. Running time: **102 MIN.**
Danny Muldoon . . . . . . John Candy
Rose Muldoon . . . . . Maureen O'Hara
Theresa Luna . . . . Ally Sheedy
Patrick Muldoon . . . . Kevin Dunn
Doyle Ryan . . . . Milo O'Shea
Spats Shannon . . . . . . Bert Remsen
Nick Acropolis . . . . . Anthony Quinn
Sal Buonarte . . . . James Belushi
Johnny Luna . . . . Joe V. Greco
Father Strapovic . Marvin J. McIntyre
Billy . . . . Macaulay Culkin

A lower-key "Marty" for the '90s, "Only The Lonely" is a charming and well-observed romantic comedy about a single Chicago cop (John Candy) trying to break free from his smothering Irish mom (Maureen O'Hara, in her welcome return to the screen after 20 years). Performances are delightfully true and never descend into bathos or cheap sentiment. Chris Columbus pic should be a popular summer boxoffice entry.

O'Hara, who looks sensaysh and hardly changed since she last was seen in "Big Jake" with John Wayne in 1971, uses her native Dublin accent and her feistiest no-nonsense style to convey the mean-spirited, bigoted personality of Rose Muldoon. "Rose," says her priest, "I'm sure you realize it's the '90s. I'm not sure you realize it's the 1990s."

This flinty immigrant widow, who's bullied her son all his life and even objects to his eating "sissy food" like yogurt because he might slim down and leave her, also routinely spews out invective against Italians, Greeks, Poles and Jews. She's not kidding, and neither is the film, when she tells Candy, "I'm not so lovable."

A type unfortunately familiar both in Ireland and the U.S., she has inflicted her own narrow-minded misery on her son and selfishly kept him from settling down with another woman. She's the more down-to-earth Irish equivalent of Woody Allen's monstrous Jewish mother in "New York Stories."

Candy is a sweet-natured fellow who yearns for something more out of life but is afraid to ask for it. His mother belittles him as "nothing but a ball and chain of heartbreak and hurt." His best friend (James Belushi) and his brother (Kevin Dunn) want him to stay single and remain a convenient adjunct to their lives, and everyone treats him like an overgrown baby.

Candy's career-stretching, finely controlled role avoids the blubbering pitfalls other actors might have tumbled into, never begging for sympathy but evoking it through his unfailingly decent, quietly dignified and put-upon personality.

When he meets a shy mortuary cosmetician (Ally Sheedy) who's as lonely as he is, Candy begins to assert himself in ways that drive his mother to new lows of tart-tongued nastiness. "Where are her breasts?" O'Hara asks not so sotto voce when Sheedy shows up for their introductory dinner. "Is she anorexic or anything?"

Oddly handsome and graceful as only a big man can be graceful, looking more like Charles Laughton every day, Candy makes a surprisingly effective romantic lead. Sheedy is a good emotional match, likably conveying her character's flowering into self-assertion in reaction to O'Hara's insults and Candy's excessive passivity.

Weighed down with heavy doses of Catholic guilt, Candy can't enjoy an evening out with his Italian g.f. without having fantasies of his mother meeting luridly violent death because he's not there to protect her.

These amusingly visualized guilt trips also serve as images of his long-submerged anger, which eventually erupts in a powerful dramatic scene of Candy confronting O'Hara with his painful memories of how she hurt his father and announcing he's made up his mind to get married whether she likes it or not. The plot resolves itself in touching but not cloying fashion.

Julio Macat's attractively musty lighting and the traditional, old world Chi look of John Muto's production design create an unflashy atmosphere of repressive comfort, the kind that makes it particularly hard for someone to leave home. Maurice Jarre's score is romantic without being bombastic, and Roy Orbison's classic "Only The Lonely" suitably sets the mood.

The neighborhood is enjoyably populated with such serio-comic types as the silver-tongued denizens of O'Neill's pub, Bert Remsen and Milo O'Shea, and O'Hara's devastatingly sexy next-door neighbor, Anthony Quinn, whom she scorns as a "typical Greek" for besieging her with passion: "Come to my bed. You will never leave."

The sexiest moment in the film occurs when O'Hara unexpectedly succumbs to a kiss from Quinn that literally lifts her off the ground. If there's going to be a sequel, it would be fun to follow what happens to these older characters who bring such vigor and color to "Only The Lonely."

— *Mac.*

CANNES FEST

JACQUOT DE NANTES
(FRENCH)

An AMLF release of a Cine-Tamaris production with the participation of Canal Plus, La Sept, La Sofiarp. (Intl. sales: Les Films du Volcan.) Produced by Agnes Varda, Perrine Bauduin. Directed by Varda. Screenplay, Varda, based on the memoirs of Jacques Demy; camera (b&w, color), Patrick Blosier, Agnes Godard, Georges Strouve; editor, Marie-Jo Audiard; music, Joanna Bruzdowicz; sound, Jean-Pierre Duret, Nicolas Naegelen; production design, Robert Nardone, Olivier Radot; costumes, Françoise Disle; production manager, Danielle Vaugon; assistant director, Didier Rouget, Philippe Tourret. Reviewed at Cannes Film Festival (noncompeting), May 11, 1991. Running time: **119 MIN.**
Jacquot 1 . . . . Philippe Maron
Jacquot 2 . . . . . . Edouard Joubeaud
Jacquot 3 . . . . . Laurent Monnier
Marilou Demy (Mother) . . . .
. . . . Brigitte de Villepoix
Raymond Demy (Father) . . . .
. . . . Daniel Dublet
Joel . . . . Guillaume Navaud
Genevieve . . . . Fanny Lebreton
Grandmother . . Marie-Anne Emeriau

A touching farewell from Agnes Varda to her late husband, filmmaker Jacques Demy, "Jacquot De Nantes" is a delightful, if overlong, depiction of the formative years of a youngster determined to make films when he grows up. It will have great appeal for buffs and be a natural for fests, especially accompanying Demy retrospectives.

On another level, it's a tender study of growing up in a small French town in the pretelevision era. Demy's unfinished memoirs provide the basic material, and, looking far from well, he appears on camera from time to time providing part of the film's narration. (He died last October.)

There are also tantalizingly brief clips (frustratingly unidentified) from several of the late director's most famous pics, including "Lola," "The Bay Of An-

gels," "The Umbrellas Of Cherbourg," "The Young Girls Of Rochefort" and "Donkey Skin."

Varda and her crew shot the film in Nantes on the exact locations where young Jacquot, as he was called, grew up: in his father's old gas station, and in the home of the village clogmaker where the boy and his younger brother hid out during the darkest days of World War II.

The boy became fascinated by make-believe at an early age, seeing opera and puppet shows, later key French films of the periods and Disney's "Snow White And The Seven Dwarfs."

He constructed his own cardboard puppet theater and later managed to get hold of a 9.5m projector to screen a battered Chaplin film for family and friends. He also acquired a primitive 9.5m camera and filmed a live action short before deciding actors were too difficult and concentrating on animation.

Eventually he was able to show one of his animated films to visiting French director Christian-Jacque, who encouraged his career. Jacquot's working-class parents weren't so encouraging and constantly urged him to learn a "proper" trade.

Judicious trimming and brisker pacing would greatly enhance this sympathetic tale of a child with an all-consuming vocation.

The clips from Demy films bring back happy memories of some of the most delightful French pictures of the 1960s, but Demy's style of cinema went out of fashion in the 1970s and 1980s, and at the end he wryly notes that he ultimately became a painter.

Production values are firstrate for this expensive-looking pic, with wartime Nantes and its environs beautifully evoked. Performances by a no-name cast are perfect down the line, including the three youngsters playing Jacquot at various ages. Brigitte de Villepoix and Daniel Dublet are especially appealing as the boy's parents. — *Strat.*

HACHIGATSU NO KYOHSHIKYOKU
(RHAPSODY IN AUGUST)
(JAPANESE)

An Orion Classics release of a Kurosawa production, presented by Feature Film Enterprise 2. (Intl. sales: Odyssey Distributors.) Executive producer, Toru Okuyama. Produced by Hisao Kurosawa. Directed by Akira Kurosawa. Screenplay, Kurosawa, based on the novel "Nabe-No-Kaka" by Kiyoko Murata; camera (color), Takao Saito, Masaharu Ueda; music, Shinichiro Ikebe; sound, Kenichi Benitani; production design, Yoshiro Muraki; creative consultant, Ishiro Honda. Reviewed at Cannes Film Festival (noncompeting), May 12, 1991. Running time: **98 MIN.**
Clark . . . . Richard Gere
Grandmother . . . . . Sachiko Murase
Tami . . . . Tomoko Ohtakara
Shinjiro . . . . Mitsunori Isaki
Tateo . . . . Hidetaka Yoshioka
Minako . . . . Mie Suzuki

Now 81, Akira Kurosawa is in a mellow mood with his latest, "Rhapsody In August," a simple but at times very affecting family saga. The somewhat incongruous casting of Richard Gere as a Japanese-American Hawaiian will be a talking point. Whether his presence will be a plus or a minus for Orion Classics and international distribs is a toss-up.

Gere gets only about 20 minutes of screentime, appearing some 65 minutes into the picture as he flies into Nagasaki to visit his long-lost grandmother and her family. His father had emigrated from Japan in the '20s, and had lost touch with his family back home.

The first part of the film consists of a series of surprisingly static scenes in which four teens, whose parents have gone to America to meet Gere and his family, stay with their elderly grandmother and while away the time in her house in the country outside Nagasaki.

The old woman, whose husband died in 1945 when the atomic bomb razed the city, charms and sometimes frightens her grandchildren with her tall stories. She's a traditionalist who always wears a kimono, whereas the youngsters favor jeans and American t-shirts and spaghetti rather than grandma's Japanese fodder.

Surprisingly, the sum of their knowledge about America seems to be almost as miniscule as hers, though they try to persuade her

to join their parents in Hawaii to see her ailing brother (Gere's father) before he dies. But she never makes the trip, and Gere comes to Nagasaki instead.

The children are initially anxious about his visit, but he charms them all, as well as the old lady, and apologizes for the atomic attack 45 years ago. A scene in which he visits the Nagasaki monument to the dead is very touching. Gere plays his character in relaxed fashion, and delivers most of his lines in halting Japanese.

"Rhapsody In August" is very much an old man's film, and almost completely lacks the visual excitement Kurosawa once brought to the cinema. Scene after scene is flatly staged and shot, as characters just sit around and talk. It would be dull were it not for the evident sincerity with which Kurosawa is pushing his message of reconciliation between America and Japan for the past, though it almost seems a redundant message these days.

Occasionally, though, the film comes alive and the director's brilliance shines through, such as the final sequence in which the grandmother walks out into a violent storm. Sachiko Murase, 86, is splendid as the old woman, and easily overshadows her teen co-stars.

Those irritated by some of the more earnest sections of Kurosawa's previous film, "Dreams," will find a similar earnestness here, so that, despite the reverence with which the director is held, critical reaction may be spotty. The film is technically fine, except for one startlingly bad optical cloud effect, which should be cut pronto. — *Strat.*

EUROPA
(DANISH-FRENCH-GERMAN)

A Pathé-Nordisk release of a Nordisk Film & TV-Gunnar Obel-Gerard Mital production. Produced by Peter Aalbeck Jensen, Bo Christensen. Executive producers, Gerard Mital, Lars Kolvig, Gerard Corbiau, Philippe Guez. Directed by Lars Von Trier. Screenplay, Von Trier, Niels Vorsel; camera (Panavision, b&w, Kodak Pathé color), Henning Bendtsen, Edward Klosinky, Jean-Paul Meurisse; editor, Herve Schneid; music, Joakim Holbek; sound (Dolby), Per Streit Jensen; production design, Henning Bahs; costume design, Mann Rasmussen; special effects, Dansk Special Effekt Service; front-projection effects, Paul Witz; special makeup effects, Morten Jacobsen; assistant director, Tom Hedegaard; 2nd unit director, Tommy Gislason. Reviewed at Cannes Film Festival (competing), May 11, 1991. Running time: **114 MIN.**

Leopold Kessler	Jean-Marc Barr
Katharina Hartmann	Barbara Sukowa
Lawrence Hartmann	Udo Kier
Uncle Kessler	Ernst Hugo Jaregard
Pater	Erik Mork
Max	Jorgen Reenberg
Col. Harris	Eddie Constantine
Jew	Lars Von Trier
Narrator	Max Von Sydow

Bravura film technique doesn't hide an offputting, empty exercise in "Europa," Lars Von Trier's rumination on war guilt in the form of a low-voltage thriller. Distracting visuals only occasionally support the film's themes while mostly constituting an end in themselves.

In only his third feature, director of 1984's "The Element Of Crime" works on a vast canvas with all manner of special effects to tell the Kafkaesque story of young American Jean-Marc Barr working as an apprentice railroad conductor in occupied Germany, 1945.

His romance with cold, beautiful Barbara Sukowa, daughter of the trainline owner, plays second fiddle to Barr's surrealistic wanderings through a fantasy landscape. Beginning with Max Von Sydow's hypnotic voiceover narration, film creates a relentlessly artificial milieu that snuffs out believability or audience involvement with its characters.

Contrived plot involves Barr unwittingly with a gang of "were-wolves," namely partisan terrorists who chafe under Allied rule. Film's climax contains many elements of suspense but is drawn out too long and played off against the black humor of Barr failing a conductor test for visiting inspectors.

By the time he grabs a machine gun and starts threatening passengers rather than fawning over them, viewer's engagement with the material has been lost.

Along the way Von Trier mechanically conjures up numerous arresting images but lacks the poetry of a Jean Cocteau, whose "Orphée" remains the pinnacle of this vein of art film.

Bulk of widescreen footage is in black & white, with the director using front projection (usually obvious to spot) for shifting back and forth to muted color. This is done arbitrarily and pointlessly except in one fabulous shot in which color comes in to announce the result of Sukowa's dad's suicide, a bathtub filled with his blood.

Other amazing creations include a cathedral with parishioners covered in a light falling snow; an homage to "Citizen Kane" as the camera cranes up from a model train set through a hole in the roof and down into Barr's moving real train compartment; and final imagery of the star's corpse floating underwater down a river to the sea in dark poetry.

That the director has talent is proven in a spectacular and grueling climax.

Acting is on the lugubrious side. Barr does the best he can with often risible dialog, mostly in English but occasionally in German. Sukowa and Udo Kier stir memories of Rainer Werner Fassbinder with their stoic performances, while RWF's idol Douglas Sirk provides some influence as well, notably his widescreen adaptation of Erich Maria Remarque's "A Time To Love And A Time To Die."

Joakim Holbek's symphonic score is strong to the point of tongue-in-cheek and includes a credited riff from Bernard Herrmann's "Vertigo" soundtrack.

Technical credits are quite adventurous, though the film would have benefited from more invisible effects work. — *Lor.*

THE CLEARING
(U.S.-SOVIET)

A Kodiak Films presentation of a Babylon production in association with Odessa Studios and Sovampex. Executive producers, Robert Kaplan, Robert Martin. Produced and directed by Vladimir Alenikov. Screenplay, Alenikov, Katherine Martin, Yuri Petrov; camera (color), Anatoli Grishko; supervising editor, James Ruxin; editor, Ludmila Savina; music, Tamara Kline; sound, Dennis Carr; production design, V. Konovalov; line producer, Nicola Velminskin; costumes, Nina Zotkina; assistant director, Vitaly Vedenin. Reviewed at Cannes Film Fest (market), May 13, 1991. Running time: **91 MIN.**

Grigory	George Segal
Feofania	Tamara Tana
Father Agafangel	Nikolai Kochegarov
Nestor	Victor Repnikov
Also with: Natalia Silantyeva.

A tired exploitation item, this clinker might make it to video thanks to numerous scenes of attractive unclad damsels, many of whom fall victim to a mysterious killer. But 'The Clearing," made in Russia, lacks the basic values of even the most routine Yank slasher pictures.

Setting, in 11th century Siberia, is a valley where paganism and Christianity are at odds. Village elder George Segal (absurdly cast and seemingly dubbed with someone else's voice) is in favor of the old religion, especially when it means sexual orgies during full moon festivities. The Christian priest is seen by most villagers as a party pooper for opposing the sexual high jinks.

A year earlier, Segal's wife disappeared, and the film opens with the murder of a nubile, unclad femme by someone wearing a goat's head. Other murders occur, and the villagers begin to suspect the increasingly deranged cleric.

Not an ounce of suspense is to be found in Vladimir Alenikov's rote direction, and the pic ends with a giant cheat: The eventual killer proves to be heavily bearded, though the guy in the goat's head was clean-shaven.

The English dubbing is wayward, and the mostly femme cast seems to have been chosen for their looks, sans garments, rather than acting ability. — *Strat.*

THE CABINET OF DR. RAMIREZ
(U.S.-GERMAN)

A Mediascope production in association with Canal Plus Prods., Mod Films, Paladin Films, Thirteen/WNET, BBC, WDR. Produced by Rainer Mockert, Eberhard Scheele. Written and directed by Peter Sellars, in collaboration with Mikhail Baryshnikov, Joan Cusack, Peter Gallagher, Ron Vawter, loosely inspired by Robert Wiene's 1919 film "The Cabinet Of Dr. Caligari," written by Carl Mayer, Hans Janowitz; camera (Duart color), David Watkin; editor, Robert Estrin; music, John Adams; sound (Dolby), Milan Bor; production design, George Tsypin; art direction, John Magolin; set decoration, Gretchen Rau; costume design, Dunya Ramicova; assistant director, Katharina Wittich; stunt coordinator, Pete Bucossi; line producer, Charles Carroll; co-producers, George Ayoub, Jacques Kirsner, Hugh Simon, Yves Pasquier, Jac Venza; casting, Diane J. Malecki. Reviewed at Cannes Film Festival (Directors Fortnight), May 14, 1991. Running time: **111 MIN.**

Cesar	Mikhail Baryshnikov
Cathy	Joan Cusack
Matt	Peter Gallagher
Ramirez	Ron Vawter
Sue	Kate Valk
Bruce	Gregory Wallace
Also with: Werner Klemperer.

Legit director Peter Sellars' debut film is a pretentious silent feature that resembles a student film out of control. Tedious, often cryptic effort was shot using the old Academy 1.33 to 1 aspect ratio, making it suitable for public tv.

Using static camera throughout, Sellars begins fairly coherently with morose stockbroker Peter Gallagher witnessing his black co-worker and roommate Gregory Wallace gorily murdered at work by a disgruntled old guy. In a separate incident straight out of "Wall Street," their boss is taken away by undercover agents in handcuffs.

Gallagher's estranged g.f. Joan Cusack has a weird, traumatic encounter on the street with homeless derelict Mikhail Baryshnikov. She's soon having romantic nightmares about him that seem to come true, climaxing in her falling (apparently fatally) from a bridge.

Baryshnikov is under the power of another derelict, mysterious Ron Vawter, who looks like Italian star Gian Maria Volonte but has a snakelike scar down the middle of his face. Confusing later footage shows Baryshnikov apparently plummeting to his death (and possibly becoming re-animated by Vawter).

Coda resembles a stupid lift from "The Wizard Of Oz," as major and minor characters (like cops and the undercover agents) reappear in dual roles at a clinic run by Vawter (sans scar). Baryshnikov and Cusack's best friend Kate Valk are orderlies there; Cusack and Gallagher are patients.

Sellars finally turns off the music score for a boring 360-degree shot that ends the film on Gallagher, possibly implying that he imagined the whole thing.

Displaying little command of film technique, Sellars fails to organize his material in the rigorous fashion needed to convey information in silent format. Confusing crosscutting in the middle reels destroys continuity and has scenes contradicting each other.

Though the static compositions are classical, occasional use of skip-frame, time-lapse editing within a shot disrupts the viewer's concentration. Using business cards to make doggerel pronouncements (Wallace receives a "You have one day to live" message that comes true) is ridiculous.

John Adams' bombastic symphonic music is the dominant contrast throughout. It veers from the traditional romanticism of a Miklos Rozsa or Bronislau Kaper to the noisy lower-register blasts of John Corigliano's "Altered States" score whenever a horror scene is intended.

David Watkin's visuals are mainly mundane, looking like a well-shot 16m student short. Occasionally romantic tableaux of Cusack clash with the unflattering, no-makeup closeups she gets.

Despite his top billing, Baryshnikov has little to do in an ill-conceived role that pays homage to the somnambulist of Wiene's classic. Gallagher, often on the phone and looking like he stepped off the set of "Sex, Lies And Videotape," does a decent job when not encouraged to overact, but Cusack's silent hysteria holds no threat to the memory of classic divas.

David Lynch was listed as pic's exec producer during production, but his name does not appear in the final credits. — *Lor.*

LOST IN SIBERIA/
ZATYERYANNY V SIBRI
(BRITISH)

A Spectator Entertainment Intl. production. (Intl. sales: Spectator Intl. Film Sales, London.) Produced by Gagik Gasparyan, Alexander Moody. Executive producer, Benjamin Brahms. Directed by Alexander Mitta. Screenplay, Mitta, Valery Fried, Yuri Korotkov, James Brabazon; camera (Eastmancolor), Vladimir Shevtsik; editor, Anthony Sloman, N. Veselovskaya; music, Leonid Desyatnikov; sound (Dolby), Paul Carr; art directors, Valery Yurkevich, Vitali Klimenkov; set design, A. Schkelle, Y. Kharitonov, A. Bessolitsin; costume design, T. Lichmanova; assistant director, O. Kalymova; associate producers, Brabazon, Christopher Gawor; special effects, A. Yevmina, V. Klimenkov; post-production dialog supervisor, Constantine Gregory. Reviewed at Century preview theater, London, May 3, 1991. (In Cannes Film Festival, Directors Fortnight.) Running time: **107 MIN.**
Andrei Miller . . . . Anthony Andrews
Anna . . . . Yelena Mayorova
Capt. Malakhov . . . . . Vladimir Ilyin
Lilka . . . . Ira Mikhalyova
Volodya . . . . Yevgeni Mironov
Nikola . . . . Alexei Zharkov
Sgt. Konyaev . . . Alexander Bureyev
Charlie . . . . . . Vladimir Prozorov
Max Brunovich . . . . Hark Böhm
Lilka's father . . . . . . Albert Filozov
    Also with: Nikolai Pastukhov, Yuri Sherstnyov, Nicolas Chagrin.
(*In English, Russian; English subtitles*)

"Lost In Siberia" packs a powerful theatrical punch and could yank Soviet-lensed items out of the arthouse gulag and into more general arenas. Subtitled segs shouldn't be such a problem in the post-"Dances With Wolves" era. Anthony Andrews toplines strongly as a wrongly imprisoned Brit.

Trumpeted as the first warts-and-all look at the horrors of Soviet labor camps to be shot on Russo soil, yarn opens in 1945 in Persia where a British archaeologist (Andrews) is arrested as Soviet tanks roll in. Suspected of being a spy, he's carted off to Moscow, given the third degree, and thrown into a ramshackle Siberian camp.

Isolated from the other prisoners by language, he's initially befriended by a local 10-year-old girl (Ira Mikhalyova) and a student inmate (Yevgeni Mironov), who trades languages with him.

Two thugs enlist his aid as a map-reader in an escape plan, but when that goes bloodily wrong, the archaeologist's sentence is increased to 25 years. In hospital he becomes chummy with a femme medico (Yelena Mayorova), unwilling squeeze of the loutish camp captain (Vladimir Ilyin).

When the little girl almost dies of typhoid but for Andrews' intervention, a bond grows between them. But that in turn is threatened by her jealousy at his romance with the doctor. The threesome is finally broken up when the archaelogist, following a camp riot, is sent to a top-security pen at Kolyma, a Dantesque hell from which "no one ever returns."

Pic ends in 1950 with a sudden reprieve for the prisoner on the orders of a Communist Party hitman back in Moscow. In a jolting switch of tone, the Brit joins Persian high society, while back in Siberia "life" goes on for his former campmates.

Despite story similarities, this is no retread of the Tom Courtenay-starrer "One Day In The Life Of Ivan Denisovich," 1971 British-Norwegian coprod based on Alexander Solzhenitsyn's tome. For a start, the cast of "Siberia" is all-Russian, apart from Andrews and a disposable cameo by German thesp Hark Böhm as a doctor. The gain is realism and emotional clout is robust.

For another, Mitta's film is no dreary, one-note requiem. It's a real, fast-paced, multilayered pic, with sunshine as well as showers: The script (based on co-writer Valery Fried's 10-year stint in hard labor for supposedly conspiring to assassinate Stalin) draws a broad portrait of the camp community, mixing rough yocks with everyday violence, casual betrayals and sexual tensions. Pic's heartbeat is thoroughly Russian.

Andrews gives his best big-screen performance since "Under The Volcano" (1984). There's an unexpected depth to his progression from arrogant Brit to tough survivalist that goes far beyond his makeup. Plus, his scenes with the two femmes display real tenderness.

Mayorova as the doc is also standout, especially in the edgy sequences with Ilyin's piggish camp boss (neatly limned). The beautiful Russian thesp handles her several nude scenes with beguiling normality. Ditto the young Mikhalyova as the prepubescent Lilka, whose feisty playing etches a real character. Nudity here, though unblinking, also seems totally natural in the context.

Director Alexander Mitta's experience in various genres over the past 30 years pays dividends. Pic's range is broad, from operatic setpieces like the hell of Kolyma camp, through the inmates' riot and the two sickos' attempted rape of Mayorova to intimate moments between prisoners and the central threesome. Mobile camerawork and razor-sharp editing are major pluses.

Mitta, however, stumbles at the final fence. The Moscow scene with a lipsmackingly over-the-top hitman, and Andrews' return to Persia (complete with dreamlike waltz of prisoners mingling with the shah's guests), are clumsy and almost torpedo the enterprise. B-movie captions are no help, either.

Other credits are rich, with Leonid Desyatnikov's operatic score driving the action and Vladimir Shevtsik's handsome lensing. Subtitles for the Russian dialog are clear and idiomatic.

Unlike the same producers' "Assassin Of The Tsar," "Siberia" was made in one, mixed-language version. The $7 million tab was picked up by U.K.-based indie Spectator, affiliate of Soviet techno Spec Group. Mosfilm provided facilities, with postproduction in London. Pic technically rates as first U.K.-Soviet joint venture rather than true coprod. Gulag set was built near Yaroslavl, 200 miles northeast of Moscow. "Persia" exteriors were in Bukhara, Uzbekistan. — *Del.*

STASERA A
CASA DI ALICE
(TONIGHT AT ALICE'S)
(ITALIAN)

A Penta Film Distribuzione release of a Mario & Vittorio Cecchi Gori and Silvio Berlusconi Communications presentation of a CGG Tiger Cinematografica production. Produced by the Cecchi Goris. Directed by Carlo Verdone. Screenplay, Verdone, Piero Bernardi, Leo Benvenuti, Gianfillippo Asone; camera (Cinecitta color), Danilo Desidieri; editor, Antonoio Siciliano; music, Vasco Rossi; sound (Dolby), Benito Archimede; assistant director, Roberto Giandalia. Reviewed at Cannes Film Festival (market), May 10, 1991. Running time: **118 MIN.**
Saverio . . . . Carlo Verdone
Alice . . . . Ornella Muti
Filippo . . . . Sergio Castellitto
    Also with: Yvonne Scio, Beatrice Palme, Mariangela Giordano.

A top comedy hit recently on its home turf, Italian farce "Tonight At Alice's" combines irreverence and sentimentality in a manner unlikely to interest U.S. distribs.

Carlo Verdone, who broke into filmmaking over a decade ago sponsored by Sergio Leone, has fashioned a slim tale of infidelities that casts him and brother-in-law Sergio Castellitto as managers of a travel agency owned by their wives.

When Verdone finds out that company money is going to house Castellitto's mistress (Ornella Muti) in a warehouse converted to a loft, he's determined to throw her out. In the midst of one of her parties, he's won over by her beauty and a sob story about her depressed sister who lives with her.

Two hours of repetitive complications later, the bros-in-law have fought each other and come to an accommodation sharing Muti's favors. Twist is that while the viewer thinks she's a free-loving party girl she's never actually had sex with either Lothario.

Along the way Verdone gets in jabs at everything under the Roman sun: religion and would-be saints, abortion, glories of "freedom" when one's wife throws him out of the house, and even a funny but tasteless subplot about adopting a cute refugee kid from Romania.

What tags this property as a local effort is script's careless approach to character. In key scenes (Muti's comes early on), the leads are called upon to act quite unsympathetically with no justification. Their fans won't mind but the arm's length viewer might tune out. Least successful ploy is the depressed sister: She hangs around for many reels, suddenly commits suicide and then is promptly forgotten.

While Muti is too glamorous for the role of struggling model/actress, her charm and physical comedy talents work well here. A contrived nude scene for her is framed as if a double were used. Verdone is a believable everyman and plays well off Castellitto, latter a dead ringer for American-Italian thesp John Turturro. — *Lor.*

LA BELLE NOISEUSE
(FRENCH)

A Pierre Grise Distribution release (France) of an FR3 Film Prods.-Pierre Grise production. Produced by Martine Marignac. Directed by Jacques Rivette. Screenplay, Rivette, Pascal Bonitzer, Christine Laurent, based on Honore de Balzac's novel; camera (Kodak color), William Lubtchansky; editor, Nicole Lubtchansky; music, Igor Stravinsky; sound, Florian Eidenbenz; production design, Emmanuel de Chauvigny; costumes, Laurence Struz; associate producer, Maurice Tinchant. Reviewed at Cannes Film Festival (competing), May 13, 1991. Running time: **240 MIN.**
Edouard Frenhofer . . . Michel Piccoli
Liz . . . . Jane Birkin
Marianne . . . . . . Emmanuelle Béart
Julienne . . . . . Marianne Denicourt
Nicolas . . . . David Bursztein
Porbus . . . . Gilles Arbona
Françoise . . . . . Marie-Claude Roger
Hands of artist . . . . . Bernard Dufour

Jacques Rivette's four-hour dissection of the artistic impulse is a demanding film that has a leg up for French audiences' sampling, thanks to its star casting. Export possibilities are severely limited by the auteur's cold, humorless approach.

After numerous films using the legit theater as metaphor for creativity, Rivette turns here to Ken Russell territory of the self-divided painter. He arrives at the same conclusion as the British art specialist, but by using radically different tools.

In place of Russell's "dying flash" approach (actually discussed here by Jane Birkin in a speech about what a painting captures of one's life), Rivette painstakingly shows viewers, step by step, the creation of the painting "La Belle Noiseuse," an unfinished work by burnt-out artist Michel Piccoli. Young painter David Bursztein encourages Piccoli to complete it.

Birkin, Piccoli's wife, was the original model for the work 10 years back. Now Bursztein's girlfriend Emmanuelle Béart reluctantly takes over.

During the first half of the picture, Piccoli is the taskmaster treating Béart roughly as raw material for his work. After the intermission, the worm turns and she asserts her will, becoming his collaborator rather than merely contorted subject.

Payoff is quietly dramatic, as Piccoli violently brushes out Birkin's image to superimpose Béart's

nude form.

Morbid climax closely resembles the finale of Claude Chabrol's "Just Before Nightfall," with Birkin and Piccoli lying side by side in bed as if in a tomb, pondering their fates. A highly artificial coda, breezily tying up all the characters' relationships, is tacked on to ill effect.

At its best, "La Belle Noiseuse" presents in almost real-time fashion a painting being done on screen, similar to documentaries in which Pablo Picasso did start-to-finish art for the camera. With excellent shot matching, artist Bernard Dufour's hands in closeup do the sketching in pen and ink, charcoal and oil while Piccoli handles the emoting.

Due to a particularly flat performance by young Bursztein in a key role, the subplots involving his relationships with Béart and his possessive sister Marianne Denicourt are dead time. However, Béart has an impressive acting showcase in a physically demanding role.

Birkin is immensely sympathetic as a creative figure (her outlet is bird taxidermy) completely in the shadow of her husband. Piccoli is not given enough to work with by a facile script that billboards every thought and emotion, so he reverts to nearly comical acting shtick to fill the blanks.

With lovely locations at an ancient villa in the south of France, William Lubtchansky's 1.33 to 1 ratio visuals are on the money.
— *Lor.*

BOYZ N THE HOOD

A Columbia release of a New Deal production. Produced by Steve Nicolaides. Written and directed by John Singleton. Camera (Deluxe color; Technicolor prints), Charles Mills; editor, Bruce Cannon; music, Stanley Clarke; sound (Dolby), Veda Campbell; art direction, Bruce Bellamy; set decoration, Kathryn Peters; assistant director, Don Wilkerson; casting, Jaki Brown. Reviewed at Cannes Film Festival (Un Certain Regard), May 13, 1991. No MPAA rating. Running time: **111 MIN.**
Furious Styles . . . . Larry Fishburne
Doughboy . . . . Ice Cube
Tre Styles . . . . . . Cuba Gooding Jr.
Brandi . . . . Nia Long
Ricky Baker . . . . . . Morris Chestnut
Mrs. Baker . . . . Tyra Ferrell
Reva Styles . . . . Angela Bassett
Brandi's Mom . . . . Meta King
The old man . . . . . . Whitman Mayo
Tre (age 10) . . . . Desi Arnez Hines II
Doughboy (age 10) . . . . Baha Jackson
Ricky (age 10) . . . Donovan McCrary

If "Do The Right Thing" hadn't already been used, it

would have been the best title for "Boyz N The Hood," an absorbing, smartly made dramatic encyclopedia of problems and ethics in the black community, 1991.

An impressive debut by 23-year-old writer-director John Singleton, sincere pic is ultra socially responsible, sometimes to the point of playing like a laundry list of difficulties faced specifically by the urban black community. But the film clearly knows whereof it speaks and does so from an enlightened point of view that will command critical respect and generate good b.o.

Tale principally looks at the lives of three boys in south-central L.A., beginning in '84 and then jumping, after a half-hour, to the present, when the realities of violence hit the teens.

Along the way, however, a rich tapestry of diverse characters is painted, as is a picture of how much strength is required to break out of old patterns and change lives in a positive way.

Tre Styles is a bright but rather sullen and insolent kid who moves to his father's home when his mother decides he needs a man's discipline.

Dad, whose first name is Furious, is a walking lesson in how to live the right way, giving his son innumerable little lectures on when to resist the impulse to violence, why he should use condoms, how other ethnic groups keep blacks down and so on.

Tre's best friend is Ricky, who wants to be a football player, and they hang out with the latter's half-brother, Doughboy, a rough-houser with an unusually foul mouth, a generally bad attitude and no ambition. Furious is notably tough with Tre but advises him that in this he has a major advantage over his friends across the street, who are growing up with little guidance from their rowdy single mother.

Singleton constantly and effectively lays in the constant irritants and reminders of violence in the 'hood — the jets and choppers flying overhead, the ever-present dense smog, the random, easily provoked fights, the day-and-night wailing of police sirens, the nearby gunshots — all of which echo the opening title stating that one in 21 black males will end up murdered.

Contempo section opens with some bawdy sexual banter at a backyard barbeque, and some time is given over to a perfunctory and mild romance between Tre and his moralistic Catholic

g.f. But the between-the-sexes interludes take a back seat to the pressing social problems at hand, what it takes to become a man in this society and what that means.

Ricky becomes a father while still in high school, aspires to a football scholarship but, despairing of qualifying, decides to enlist in the Army (Furious, a Vietnam vet, has always advised Tre that black men don't belong in the white man's army).

Doughboy by now has taken to packing a pistol and cruising with his buddies in his low rider with lifts. Tre seems a bit more undecided and is preoccupied by the fact that his lady, Brandi, is forcing him to remain a virgin rather longer than he would like.

Senseless gang violence finally hits the neighborhood in tragic fashion, and pic fights the media's tendency to treat ghetto crime as a mere fact of life that doesn't need to be invested with the same seriousness as events in the white world or even overseas.

Treatment of the subject here underlines the fact that all such incidents are horrifying and tragic, with family and community consequences that need to be more deeply understood and felt by the nation.

Singleton's screenplay rambles from incident to incident, but appealingly so, and is quite convincing in its detailing of life in single-parent homes, as well as on the street.

Lively dialog embraces everything from Furious' righteous sermons to Doughboy's rough, sexist diatribes, and his direction is thoroughly confident and well-paced, if straightforward.

Director's skill clearly extends to handling actors, as leading players all do fine jobs of conveying various states of intensity.

Notable are Larry Fishburne as Furious, the father above reproach; Cuba Gooding Jr. as the conflicted but determined Tre; Morris Chestnut as the hopeful athlete Ricky, and Ice Cube as the violence-prone Doughboy.

Produced for $6 million, pic is simple from a technical p.o.v. but solid nonetheless. Soundtrack is sprinkled with modern sounds but also features more conventional scoring at times. — *Cart.*

LA DOUBLE VIE DE VERONIQUE
(THE DOUBLE LIFE OF WERONIKA)
(FRENCH/POLISH)

A Miramax release (in U.S.) of a Sideral Prods. (Paris)-Tor Prods. (Warsaw)-Le Studio Canal Plus (Paris) co-production in association with Norsk Film. Produced by Leonardo De La Fuente. Executive producer, Bernard P. Guiremand. Directed by Krzysztof Kieslowski. Screenplay, Kieslowski, Krzysztof Piesiewicz; camera (color), Slawomir Idziak; editor, Jacques Witta; music, Zbigniew Preisner; in Dolby Stereo; art direction, Patrice Mercier. Reviewed at Cannes Film Festival (competing), May 14, 1991. Running time: **90 MIN.**
Weronika/Veronique . . . Irene Jacob
Alexandre Fabbri . . . Philippe Volter
Veronique's father . . Claude Duneton
Weronika's father . . . .
. . . . Wladyslaw Kowalski
Antek . . . . Jerzy Gudejko
Also with: Halina Gryglaszewska, Kalina Jedrusik, Aleksander Bardini, Sandrine Dumas, Louis Ducreux.

"The Double Life Of Weronika" will have fans of Krzysztof Kieslowski, Poland's hottest director, taking sides. Despite pic's many-splendored outbursts of filmic creativity and intense emotion, final result remains a head-scratching cipher with blurred edges.

Presales to most major territories around the world assure a wide arthouse release and will allow audiences the pleasure of thrashing out the pic's meaning for themselves.

The opposite destinies of a Polish girl and a French girl who look alike and have the same name and tics appeal more to instinct than intellect. "Veronique" is unlikely to be as widely appreciated as the 10 jewels of "The Decalog," though it clearly belongs to the same family of human mystery tales.

Pic's first third takes place in Poland in an almost perfect confluence of shots, editing and dialog that holds the viewer rapt. Weronika (Irene Jacob in both roles) is a bubbly, happy girl in love with a young man (Jerzy Gudejko). While she's visiting her aunt in Krakow, her extraordinary voice is discovered by a music teacher.

Her passion shifts from love to singing. She continues despite a dangerous heart condition, and in a scene of overwhelming intensity, dies on stage during a recital.

After the tight, punchy open-er, film keeps its momentum for a little while into the French part. From a graveyard burial scene (eerily shot from the corpse's p.o.v.), story shifts to a passionate embrace between the French Veronique (also a singer) and her young lover.

Veronique feels no involvement with her b.f. What she does feel is an inexplicable urge to quit voice training. If the Polish girl asks herself what she wants, the French Veronique seems to "know" what she has to do, as though she had learned a lesson from a previous life. She follows her instincts unhesitatingly.

In one of Kieslowski's finest sequences, Veronique attends a puppet show about a ballerina who collapses while dancing. She is mesmerized by the handsome puppeteer, Alexandre Fabbri (Philippe Volter), a writer of children's books.

Veronique and Alexandre find each other, but the youth who initially seemed so intuitive fails to understand Veronique's anguished sensation that she has lived before. She retreats from him — a little — in a finale that leaves audience wondering.

Script by Kieslowski and Krzysztof Piesiewicz is incredibly rich with quasi-subliminal references and associations. A recurring image of distorting mirrors and lenses is coupled with special effects lensing from cinematographer Slawomir Idziak.

Soundtrack, as carefully composed as the images, jumps to the forefront when Alexandre sends Veronique a tape that's a symphony of noises. But it is Zbigniew Preisner's original score that sends chills down the spine. After Weronika's joyous, tragic recital, same haunting melody is judiciously dosed out to recall another time and place.

Jacob is a sparkling newcomer who imbues both roles with an innocent but powerful magic. Volter attracts as the shadowy puppeteer (a role originally offered to Italo actor-director Nanni Moretti). — *Yung.*

JUNGLE FEVER

A Universal release of a 40 Acres and a Mule Filmworks production. Written, produced and directed by Spike Lee. Camera (Duart color, Deluxe prints), Ernest Dickerson; editor, Sam Pollard; music, Stevie Wonder, Terence Blanchard; sound (Dolby), Russell Williams II; sound design, Skip Lievsay; production design, Wynn Thomas; set decoration, Ted Glass; costume design, Ruth E. Carter; assistant director, Randy Fletcher; line producer, Jon Kilik; co-producer, Monty Ross; casting, Robi Reed. Reviewed at Cannes Film Festival (competing), May 16, 1991. Running time: **132 MIN.**
Flipper Purify . . . . . . Wesley Snipes
Angie Tucci . . . . . Annabella Sciorra
Cyrus . . . . Spike Lee
The Good Rev. Dr. Purify . Ossie Davis
Lucinda Purify . . . . Ruby Dee
Gator Purify . . . . Samuel L. Jackson
Drew . . . . Lonette McKee
Paulie Carbone . . . . . John Turturro
Mike Tucci . . . . Frank Vincent
Also with: Anthony Quinn, Halle Berry, Tyra Ferrell, Veronica Webb, Veronica Timbers, David Dundara.

The jungle is decidedly present but the fever is notably missing in Spike Lee's latest exploration of racial tensions in urban America. Sure to spur plenty of talk and diverse critical views, "Jungle Fever" should generate biz at least in line with the director's top previous outings.

Exciting and frustrating by turns, this provocative, urgent work probes touchy issues in a way that will brace some viewers and disturb others. It also provides a platform for a myriad of pungent attitudes about race relations.

Subject of interracial romance has recurred periodically on-screen since the 1960s, when "sensitive" and mostly chaste approaches foreshadowed a day when enlightened integration would prevail. Lee tackles it from the unavoidable vantage point that, while things today are more open, they are also considerably more volatile and complex.

Script's surprising structural ploy is that little time is actually spent with the black man and white woman whose relationship is the core of the drama. Steering clear of conventional romantic scenes once the couple gets together, Lee instead uses the affair to detonate dozens of reactive sequences, showing how the blacks and Italians close to the principals deal with the developments.

Gambit has its pros and cons. Given the violent emotions triggered in others, it would have helped to see more of Flipper Purify (Wesley Snipes) and Angie Tucci's (Annabella Sciorra) feelings about each other as the surrounding fireworks go off. Dense structuring brings in a vast array of colorful, compelling characters but also provides too many outlets for political and philosophical grandstanding.

In an opening sequence as heartwarming as a 1950s family sitcom, if considerably raunchier, Flipper is presented as a terrific husband and father to a young daughter. A successful architect in a mainstream white firm, Flipper initially objects on racial grounds to the hiring of Angie as a new office temp but, as seen in an adroit series of short scenes, is soon spending late evenings with her in the office.

When the inevitable occurs, it constitutes Flipper's first infidelity and a major break for Angie, who lives with her father and two brothers in Bensonhurst and has been going out since high school with a rather gawky and awkward Italian boy (John Turturro).

Both Flipper and Angie seem quite taken with each other's "otherness," and knowledge of the affair is met with tremendously rough reactions at home. Flipper is unceremoniously kicked out his Harlem apartment and forced to move back in with his father (Ossie Davis), an ultra-righteous ex-preacher, and kindly mother (Ruby Dee). Angie is brutally beaten by her father and sent packing to a girlfriend's.

From this point on, little is seen of the couple together alone, and nothing that indicates their passion is worth the wrath of those around them.

Instead, viewer is treated to all manner of extremist racial diatribes: vicious outbursts of Paulie's father (Anthony Quinn) and his buddies; Flipper's wife (Lonette McKee) and her friends bluntly tackling many aspects of the racial aspects of sexuality; the attitudinizing of Flipper's best friend (Spike Lee); and the rigid moralizing of Flipper's father.

Granted, the story takes place on the Harlem-Bensonhurst axis of racial mistrust and hate (pic is dedicated to Yusef Hawkins, black teen killed by a white gang in Bensonhurst), but Lee takes advantage of this to essentially present only characters with extremist views. That a larger percentage of people are undoubtedly much more accepting of interracial love than was the case some years back is not acknowledged.

Lee is covering a lot of territory here, and for the first time in his films gets into the drug issue by way of Flipper's older brother, Gator, a crack addict constantly badgering his family for money. In an utterly stunning late sequence, Flipper goes looking for Gator in a crack house, and with one consummate stroke Lee says everything necessary about the bane that drugs represent to the community.

Like "Do The Right Thing," "Jungle Fever" is visually exciting at all times, thanks to the imaginative, often startling setups fashioned by the director and his perennial cinematographer, Ernest Dickerson. One device sure to be much discussed is used twice: Two characters walking down the street are photographed from below as if the camera and actors are on the same moving platform, creating an eerie effect.

Much of the score, which embraces Stevie Wonder's contributions as well as original music by Terence Blanchard, is excellent, but Lee's decision to lay music under nearly every scene proves irritating and distracting on numerous occasions.

A rather dreadful scene involves Flipper's quitting the architecture firm when his request to be made a partner is denied (bosses are played in cameos by Tim Robbins and Brad Dourif). This is compounded by the fact that Lee never follows up on Flipper's intention to open his own business. One never hears about his career again nor knows how he is paying for the pricey Greenwich Village apartment he eventually takes with Angie.

Performances are all pointed and emotionally edgy. Snipes and Sciorra make believable and likable leads, although they would have benefited from more screen time together. McKee is a powerhouse as the spurned wife, and Turturro, hitting more subtle notes than usual, is an offbeat surprise as a rejected suitor who appealingly grows from the experience.

At 132 minutes, film feels too long, but it ends powerfully, as the audience exits with the view that both the white and black communities are deeply troubled and have a very long way to go to resolve their differences, if such a result is even foreseen or desired by many people in the world the film presents. — *Cart.*

DIABLY DIABLY
(THE DEVILS, THE DEVILS)
(POLISH)

A Telewizja Polska-Indeks Film Studio production. (Intl. sales: Film Polski.) Written and directed by Dorota Kedzierzawska. Camera (color), Zdzislaw Najda; editor, Wanda Zeman; sound, Barbara Domaradzka; production design, Wojciech Jaworski; production manager, Pawel Rakowski. Reviewed at Cannes Film Festival (Intl. Critics Week), May 14, 1991. Running time: **86 MIN.**
Mala . . . . Justyna Ciemny

Grucha . . . . Pawel Chwedoruk
Karabin . . . . Grzegorz Karabin
Mother . . . . Monika Niemczyk
Witch . . . . Danuta Szaflarska
Teacher . . . . Krzysztof Plewka
Priest . . . . Jerzy Lapinski

"**T**he Devils, The Devils" is an attractively shot film set in a small Polish village in the '60s that deals with a young girl's awakening sexuality. Though this first feature from director Dorota Kedzierzawska is better suited for tv than theatrical internationally, it holds promise for her future.

Mala, about 13, lives with her unmarried mother and has a boyfriend her own age. The village is sent into a tizzy by the arrival of a clan of gypsies, who set up camp in a field. Damned as "devils" by the conservative villagers, the gypsies are ostracized.

Mala is attracted to them and is visiting the camp when the locals attack it with fire hoses. The gypsies move on, leaving Mala richer for having met them.

With a soundtrack made up of traditional gypsy songs and little dialog, "The Devils, The Devils" is a straightforward and sometimes naive mood piece. The gypsies are presented as being happy characters, always singing and dancing, and with beautiful children — a very rose-colored view.

Young Justyna Ciemny is a find as the budding teen, though more could have been made of her contact with the exotic gypsy world. Cinematography is attractive, and the music delightful.
— *Strat.*

LA CARNE
(THE FLESH)
(ITALIAN)

An MMD production. (Intl sales: Surf Film.) Produced by Giuseppe Auriemma. Directed by Marco Ferreri. Screenplay, Ferreri, Liliana Betti; camera (color), Ennio Guarnieri; editor, Ruggero Mastroianni; sound, Jean-Pierre Ruh; production design, Sergio Canevari. Reviewed at Cannes Film Festival (competing), May 13, 1991. Running time: **90 MIN.**
Paolo . . . . Sergio Castellitto
Francesca . . . . . Francesca Dellera
Also with: Philippe Leotard, Petra Reinhardt.

A mild scandal at this year's Cannes fest is Marco Ferreri's self-styled, indulgent exercise in absurdity, "La Carne." Meanderings over familiar Ferreri themes and fetishes is only fitfully amusing, with the Italian home audience its target.

Popular comic Sergio Castellitto plays a nightclub pianist/ singer whose marriage has broken up. He's a hypochondriac attached to his dog, and is a loving dad on visiting days with his two kids.

Castellitto's life is turned around when he meets fleshy sexpot Francesca Dellera while performing in the club. After she talks to him of sex with her young guru from India he closes the club early and takes her to his beach house for some of that mad love so many filmmakers dote on in lieu of a storyline.

Film drifts into arbitrary dialog and incident at this point, with Dellera reversing the roles and making Castellitto her rigid sex object after touching the proper pressure points on his neck.

Between rambling philosophical discussions, empty symbolism of storks and sunsets, Ferreri finds time for the duo to eat while making love. There is only brief nudity of both, but Dellera strolls around in push-up bras that show off enough decolletage to please a local sex comedy audience.

Final twist of arbitrary murder and cannibalism is a guaranteed turn-off, lacking the force of Ferreri's memorable Gérard Depardieu self-castration finale in "The Last Woman."

Castellitto provides the requisite laughs with his goofy reactions to Dellera's off-the-wall behavior. She is a pale-skinned, kewpie doll beauty that becomes tiresome under constant camera fixation after the supporting cast is dispensed with. Concentration on the two stars is relieved by interludes with a nursing mother on the beach, a lesbian who briefly joins the duo and a very funny visit from Castellitto's kids while he lies paralyzed on his back sporting an erection.

The director's intentional tastelessness has lost much of its shock value, so the off-screen death of Castellitto's dog from neglect is merely the pretext for a gag of Sergio literally in the doghouse where he tries out a new sexual position with Dellera.

Ennio Guarnieri's photography is mainly stark and functional, with the beach setting shot on sunny or overcast days at will. Other tech credits, including the direct sound recording, are pro.
— *Lor.*

BACKDRAFT

A Universal release of an Imagine Films Entertainment presentation of a Trilogy Entertainment Group-Brian Grazer production. Produced by Richard B. Lewis, Pen Densham, John Watson. Executive producers, Grazer, Raffaella DeLaurentiis. Directed by Ron Howard. Screenplay, Gregory Widen; camera (Deluxe color), Mikael Salomon; editor, Daniel Hanley, Michael Hill; music, Hans Zimmer; sound (Dolby), Glenn Williams; production design, Albert Brenner; art direction, Carol Winstead Wood; set design, Harold Fuhrman, William B. Fosser, Gary Baugh; set decoration, Garrett Lewis; costume design, Jodie Tillen; special effects & pyrotechnics, Allen Hall; special visual effects, Industrial Light & Magic; visual effects supervisor, Scott Farrar; visual effects producer, Suella Kennedy; visual effects art director, Paul Huston; stunt coordinator, Walter Scott; associate producer & 2nd unit director, Todd Hallowell; assistant director, Aldric La'Auli Porter; 2nd unit assistant director, Bruce Moriarty; 2nd. unit camera, Don Burgess; co-producer, Larry DeWaay; casting, Jane Jenkins, Janet Hirshenson, Jane Alderman (Chicago). Reviewed at AMPAS' Samuel Goldwyn Theater, L.A., May 16, 1991. MPAA Rating: R. Running time: **135 MIN.**
Stephen McCaffrey/Elder McCaffrey . . . . Kurt Russell
Brian McCaffrey . . . William Baldwin
Donald Rimgale . . . . Robert De Niro
Ronald Bartel . . . Donald Sutherland
Jennifer . . . . . . Jennifer Jason Leigh
John Adcox . . . . Scott Glenn
Helen . . . . Rebecca DeMornay
Tim Krizminski . . . . . Jason Gedrick
Martin Swayzak . . . . . . J.T. Walsh
Chief Fitzgerald . . . Tony Mockus Sr.
Grindle . . . . Cedric Young
Schmidt . . . . Jack McGee
Pengelly . . . . Mark Wheeler
Ricco . . . . Clint Howard
Brian (age 7) . . . . Ryan Todd
Stephen (age 12) . . . . . . John Duda

Laboring mightily to disprove the adage that a good film can't be made from a bad script, director Ron Howard torches off more thrilling scenes in "Backdraft" than any Saturday matinee serial ever dared. Visually, pic often is exhilarating, but it's shapeless and dragged down by corny, melodramatic characters and situations.

Release should generate its share of summer b.o. heat, but it doesn't feel like a blockbuster.

Ex-fireman Gregory Widen's script about Chicago smokeaters begins with the kind of clumsy character exposition that signals incipient narrative desperation. The scene of the two central characters as boys in 1971 provides shorthand for later formulaic conflicts between fire-fighting brothers Kurt Russell and William Baldwin.

Despite all the impressive pyrotechnics surrounding them and the verisimilitude Widen brings to the subject, the Russell-Baldwin relationship never rises above the repetitive, clichéd level of one of those old Warner Bros. B actioners about brawling blue-collar tough guys in a dangerous profession.

But the opening is still a stunner, with young Ryan Todd (the Baldwin character) watching with wide-eyed wonder and horror as his fireman father (also played by Russell) rescues a child but dies in an explosion. Howard, who (like Steven Spielberg) excels at bringing a sense of child-like awe to his material, conveys in a few powerful images both the romance and the risks of fire fighting.

Starting as overly gawky and callow but growing on the audience as his character matures, Baldwin is ambivalent about fire-fighting as a result of that experience. His older brother, the charismatic Russell, is a hard-boiled sort, even more recklessly heroic than the father. They discuss their differences with their fists whenever the narrative begins to slacken.

Widen uncertainly blends these tiresome family quarrels with a suspense plot involving fire department investigator Robert De Niro's search for a mysterious arsonist. His intense, obsessive characterization is a major plus for the film but isn't given enough screen time.

A rewrite focusing more on the arson plot might have been advisable, but the way it's worked out here is unsatisfying. Widen's heavy-handed casting of suspicion on one of the major characters and subsequent mechanical switcheroo amounts to offputting audience manipulation.

Though De Niro is portrayed as the Sherlock Holmes of arson investigators, script has him and Baldwin led to the truth by the airheaded assistant (Jennifer Jason Leigh) of a corrupt local alderman (J.T. Walsh) and, in an echo of "The Silence Of The Lambs," by an institutionalized pyromaniac played by Donald Sutherland with his customary glee.

The miscast Leigh, Baldwin's flame, is embarrassing in a ridiculous role that grinds "Backdraft" to a halt whenever she's around. Nor does the usually lively Rebecca DeMornay manage to do much with the dull, deglamorized and confusingly developed part of Russell's ex-wife.

Generally so good with family scenes, Howard seemingly became distracted by the technical challenges of the fire scenes, which keep "Backdraft" compellingly watchable despite its meandering structure and overlong running time.

"Backdraft" hardly is "the first motion picture that deals with the life-and-death struggles of fire fighters," as U publicity claims. What about the studio's own "Always," "Fahrenheit 451," "Hellfighters" and its 1931 serial "Heroes Of The Flames," or "The Towering Inferno," Humphrey Jennings' classic 1943 docu, "Fires Were Started," and Edwin S. Porter's "The Life Of An American Fireman" (1902)?

But "Backdraft" succeeds as no film has before in drawing the audience into the heart of a fire, showing it as a living, breathing "animal," as Sutherland calls it.

The spectacular fire scenes, whipped up by pyrotechnician Allen Hall and Industrial Light & Magic and lensed by Mikael Salomon, are done with terrifying believability (usually with the actors in the same shot as the fire effects) and a kind of sci-fi grandeur.

Evidently feeling a need to keep topping each action scene, Howard builds up to a ludicrously overdone conclusion, complete with a screaming expository confession scene on top of a burning chemical plant and a hokey climax inside the plant that would have been rejected as too far-fetched even by the makers of "Heroes Of The Flames."

Aside from the indulgent editing by Daniel Hanley and Michael Hill, tech credits are tops in this grippingly atmospheric film. It's the conception that makes "Backdraft" feel like a false alarm. — *Mac.*

WILD HEARTS CAN'T BE BROKEN

A Buena Vista release of a Walt Disney Pictures presentation in association with Silver Screen Partners IV of a Pegasus Prods. film. Produced by Matt Williams. Executive producer, Oley Sassone. Directed by Steve Miner. Screenplay, Williams, Sassone; camera (Continental color, Technicolor prints), Daryn Okada; editor, Jon Poll; music, Mason Daring; sound (Dolby), Steve Aaron, Glen Trew; production design, Randy Ser; art direction, Thomas Fichter; set design, Tony Fanning, James A. Kinney; set decoration, Jean Alan; costume design, Malissa Daniel; animal trainers, Corky Randall, Cherri Reiber; stunt coordinator, David B. Ellis; associate producer, Sarah Brock; assistant director, Matt Earl Beesley; co-producer, Robin S. Clark; casting, Mary Gale Artz. Reviewed at Avco Cinema Center, L.A., May 20, 1991. MPAA Rating: G. Running time: **88 MIN.**

Sonora Webster . . . Gabrielle Anwar
Al Carver . . . . . Michael Schoeffling
Dr. W. F. Carver . . . . Cliff Robertson
Clifford Henderson . . Dylan Kussman
Marie . . . . Kathleen York
Mr. Slater . . . . Frank Renzulli
Arnette Webster . . . .
Nancy Moore Atchison
Aunt Helen . . . . Lisa Norman

Disney's "Wild Hearts Can't Be Broken" is a sweet and unapologetically old-fashioned yarn about a Depression era girl who high-dives horses in a carnival act. When she goes blind, the dramatic development is surprisingly perfunctory, but this G-rated tearjerker still should please family audiences seeking a mild summer diversion.

Producer Matt Williams and exec producer Oley Sassone based their script on a real-life Atlantic City Steel Pier performer, Sonora Webster Carver, whom Sassone met while doing volunteer work with the blind. Her story is an interesting slice of offbeat Americana, but its improbable nature hasn't been made fully credible on screen.

With her live-wire energy, sauciness and fresh good looks, the British-born Gabrielle Anwar is a real comer as Carver. The 21-year-old actress effortlessly fits into the role of a 15-year-old Southern girl, enlivening this somewhat creaky low-budgeter, which resembles the kind of rustic romance Fox made in the early 1930s with Marian Nixon and Will Rogers. Anwar's rebellious, horse-fancying orphan runs away from her aunt's hardscrabble Georgia farm to join the carnival act run by seedy Buffalo Bill imitator Cliff Robertson. She starts as a stablehand but soon displaces Kathleen York, who is right on target as a bitchy second-rate performer.

Since it's a Disney film, there's no question of any overt Humbert Humbert behavior in the intimate but wholesome living arrangements on Robertson's ramshackle North Carolina farm, although the proximity of the lissome Anwar and the jealousy she inspires in York evidently help account for the boss' intense depression.

Also in the troupe are Dylan Kussman, a likably gawky groom who aspires to be a daredevil motorcycle rider, and Robertson's handsome and sensitive son, Michael Schoeffling, who ankles because of his father's domineering ways and writes love letters to Anwar that Robertson burns.

Taking an earnest, sincere approach that will be appreciated by the film's target subteen audience, director Steve Miner shows Anwar training strenuously with horses and overcoming her fears as she becomes adept at the outlandish stunt. Production designer Randy Ser skillfully recreates the tower, tank and other trappings of the carnival milieu.

Though the dialog is clunky in spots ("There's a Depression on," her aunt reminds Anwar before she kicks her out of the house) and more humor would have been welcome, "Wild Hearts" effectively limns the desperation and resourcefulness of characters driven by tawdry dreams.

Without having to verbalize it, Robertson conveys the sad, weary nature of a man who knows his life is a failure but keeps pushing on to the next town in search of an elusive future. His death scene is beautifully done, a subtle highlight of the film and Daryl Okada's overly romantic yet intermittently compelling photography.

The film falters when it reaches Atlantic City, the promised land of the carnies' aspirations. All too abruptly, Anwar is blinded in a jump, and the last 25 minutes turn into a rushed and utterly unmoving "inspirational" comeback-from-handicap story. Unusual as it is to say a film would benefit from running longer, spending another 15 minutes or so on this part could have made a vital difference.

The anguish of the young woman's blindness is scanted and the comeback happens so easily that it seems inadvertently slighting to the handicapped, implying that triumphing over physical disability so spectacularly is simply a matter of willpower.

"Wild Hearts'" effective horse stunts, a kind no longer performed in carnivals, were done with the aid of film magic that made 10-foot jumps look like 40-foot jumps. Veteran wrangler Corky Randall trained the horses with Cherri Reiber; David B. Ellis was stunt coordinator, with Shelley Peterson Boyle doubling Anwar and Reiber doubling York.

The film, shot in South Carolina, carries a commendation by the American Humane Assn. to the production company "for its care and concern in handling the horses and for the precautions taken to protect them." — *Mac.*

DROP DEAD FRED

A New Line Cinema release of a Polygram and Working Title production. Executive producers, Tim Bevan, Carlos Davis, Anthony Fingleton. Produced by Paul Webster. Directed by Ate De Jong. Screenplay, Davis, Fingleton, suggested by a story by Elizabeth Livingston; camera (CFI Color), Peter Deming; editor, Marshall Harvey; music, Randy Edelman; sound (Dolby), Michael Redbourn; production design, Joseph T. Garrity; art direction, Randall Schmook; set decoration, Colin Tugwell; costume design, Carol Wood; assistant directors, Michael Waxman, Dan Stillman; special makeup effects, Christopher Johnson; special effects, Bob Cooper; casting, Linn Kressel. Reviewed at UA Coronet Theater, Westwood, Calif., May 20, 1991. MPAA Rating: PG-13. Running time: **98 MIN.**

Elizabeth . . . . Phoebe Cates
Drop Dead Fred . . . . Rik Mayall
Polly . . . . Marsha Mason
Charles . . . . Tim Matheson
Janie . . . . Carrie Fisher
Murray . . . . Keith Charles
Young Elizabeth . . . . Ashley Peldon
Nigel . . . . Daniel Gerroll
Mickey Bunce . . . . Ron Eldard

Oscillating between long arid stretches, inspired explosions of slapstick and disarming warmth, "Drop Dead Fred" has an almost irresistible premise (kid's imaginary friend comes back to help the grown woman work out her problems), but it's probably too slow and mushy for kids and too sporadic in its rewards for adults.

Properly promoted, pic could show some early life signs at the boxoffice before meeting gradual demise.

At one point, the film seems to be sinking fast — just as heroine Elizabeth (Phoebe Cates) sinks the houseboat of her best friend (Carrie Fisher) — before it rights itself and basically breezes through a satisfying if predictable last 40 minutes.

By then, unfortunately, it may have used up most of its good will with many adults, as its "Beetlejuice"-inspired sight gags and literally snotty one-liners often prove frenetic but not particularly imaginative or funny.

Cates stars as a young wife who returns home to her domineering mother (Marsha Mason) after splitting up with her brazenly philandering husband (Tim Matheson).

At home she discovers a music box that contains her long-forgotten imaginary friend, Drop Dead Fred (British comic Rik Mayall in a red Beethoven fright wig), who explains that he's been released to wreak havoc until she's having fun again.

Elizabeth then sets out on a teeth-gnashingly unliberated quest to woo back her smarmy hubby, although it's patently obvious she'd be better off with the nice if rather boring childhood friend, Mickey (Ron Eldard), who conveniently re-emerges.

Director Ate De Jong has captured the silliness of childhood with their hyperactive title character but too often drill jokes deep into the pavement, until even children will have long stopped laughing.

When Elizabeth is taken to a doctor to cure her imaginary-friend syndrome, for example, the room is filled with the other kids' goofy-looking imaginary friends, a terrific initial jolt that fades as the group falls into a series of inane Three Stooges-like exchanges.

Cates is at her wide-eyed best as the painfully weak lead character and shows a real flair for physical comedy as well as the few dramatic elements. Too bad the script doesn't do a better job of fleshing out the role, pulling out a heartwarming but shamelessly manipulative twist to provide her final redemption.

Mason is okay as the overbearing mom, while Fisher has some of the pic's best lines in a small but showy role. Matheson, meanwhile, seems to be playing the grown version of his "Animal House" character, and Bridget Fonda turns up in an eye-catching-if-uncredited cameo as his mistress.

Mayall does his part as Fred, and kids may cotton to his antisocial tendencies. Still, it's doubtful this is the sort of character that will launch a thousand imitators, or even a line of action figures.

Visual effects lack inventiveness and budget, and animated shots of Fred bouncing around or his eyes bulging out look a little cheesy but don't detract from the fantasy.

The best moments, actually, come during "Harvey"-esque moments when Cates mimes reactions to the unseen Fred, especially a howlingly funny lunch scene that proves the film's best sequence.

Other tech credits are okay, though Randy Edelman's score is so drippingly sentimental at times that friends, real or imaginary, may have cause to snicker at it. Kudos to Carol Wood for Fred's outlandish costumes.

— *Bril.*

HUDSON HAWK

A Tri-Star Pictures release of a Silver Pictures-ABC Bone production. Executive producer, Robert Kraft. Produced by Joel Silver. Directed by Michael Lehmann. Screenplay, Steven E. de Souza, Daniel Waters, from a story by Bruce Willis, Kraft; camera (Technicolor), Dante Spinotti; editor, Chris Lebenzon, Michael Tronick; music, Michael Kamen, Kraft; sound (Dolby), Jerry Ross; production design, Jack DeGovia; art direction, John R. Jensen; costume design, Marilyn Vance-Straker; co-producer, Michael Dryhurst; associate producers, David Willis, Suzanne Todd; assistant directors, Michael Alan Kahn, Bob Girolami; 2nd unit director, Charles Picerni; casting, Jackie Burch. Reviewed at UA Coronet Theater, Westwood, Calif., May 22, 1991. MPAA Rating: R. Running time: **95 MIN.**

Hudson Hawk . . . . Bruce Willis
Tommy Five-Tone . . . . Danny Aiello
Anna Baragli . . . . Andie MacDowell
George Kaplan . . . . . James Coburn
Darwin Mayflower . Richard E. Grant
Minerva Mayflower . Sandra Bernhard
Alfred . . . . Donald Burton
Snickers . . . . Don Harvey
Kit Kat . . . . David Caruso
Butterfinger . . . . Andrew Bryniarski
Almond Joy . . . . Lorraine Toussaint

Ever wondered what a Three Stooges short would look like with a $40 million budget? Then meet "Hudson Hawk," a relentlessly annoying clay duck that crash-lands in a sea of wretched excess and silliness.

Those willing to check their brains at the door may find sparse amusement in pic's frenzied pace, but unless P.T. Barnum was right in spades, this bird should be grounded after one or two b.o. explosions.

Producer Joel Silver normally doesn't waste such extravagant pyrotechnics on a premise this thin. In fact, there's really no central plot to the film, which can't decide if it wants to be a live-action Warner Bros. cartoon or "Raiders Of The Lost Ark." Choosing neither, pic simply serves up one Bruce Willis-modeled gag after another and keeps laying on the mayhem, with every sound effect at cannon-shot level.

Willis plays just-released-from-prison cat burglar Hudson Hawk, who's immediately drawn into a plot to steal a bunch of Leonardo Da Vinci artifacts by, among others, a twisted billionaire couple (Richard E. Grant, Sandra Bernhard), a twisted CIA agent (James Coburn) and an agent for the Vatican (Andie MacDowell).

Mostly, though, Hawk hangs with his pal Tommy (Danny Aiel-lo), as the two croon old tunes to time their escapades. After a while it seems like they're humming the score from "War And Peace."

There's absolutely nothing subtle about this project, from naming the CIA agent George Kaplan (the fictitious agent in "North By Northwest") to conspicuous product placement for Tri-Star parent Sony.

Director Michael Lehmann, who made his feature debut with the deliciously subversive "Heathers," simply seems overwhelmed by the scale and banality of Steven E. de Souza and Daniel Waters' screenplay. Very few of the scenes actually seem connected, and the editing frequently leaves one puzzled (assuming one is thinking at this point) about the time lapse between them, including a sudden switch from day to night during the climactic action sequence.

The film primarily gives Willis a chance to toss off poor man's "Moonlighting" one-liners in the midst of utter chaos. While one or two laughs result, the stupidity quotient far outweighs the comedy.

Grant, Bernhard and Coburn do produce a few bursts of scatological humor based on the sheer energy of their over-the-top performances.

Still, the film suffers from a sense that it's all an inside joke — as if a college theater group were given unlimited resources to run hog wild — and the genuinely funny moments are too few and very far between.

Tech credits are characteristically firstrate, from the sound and special effects to the lavish globetrotting sets. All the more reason to be depressed by the magnitude of the waste, more likely to remind Tri-Star and Willis fans of his experience with "The Bonfire Of The Vanities" than "Die Hard." — *Bril.*

MANNEQUIN ON THE MOVE

A 20th Century Fox release of a Gladden Entertainment picture. Produced by Edward Rugoff. Directed by Stewart Raffill. Executive producer, John Foreman. Screenplay, Rugoff, David Isaacs, Ken Levine, Betsy Israel; camera (Duart color), Larry Pizer, editor, John Rosenberg, Joan Chapman; music, David McHugh; sound, Glenn Berkovitz, Morteza Rezvani, Thomas Brandau, Lawrence Hoff; production design, William J. Creber; art direction, Norman B. Dodge, Jr.; co-producer, Malcolm R. Harding; assistant director, Roger La Page; associate producer, Kate Bales; casting, Penny Perry, Annette Benson. Reviewed at Rowland Plaza Cinema, Navato, Calif., May 18, 1991. MPAA rating: PG. Running time: **95 MIN.**
Mr. Hollywood . . . . . Meshach Taylor
Jason . . . . William Ragsdale
Jessie . . . . Kristy Swanson
Count Spretzle . . . . Terry Kiser
Mr. James . . . . Stuart Pankin
Mom . . . . Cynthia Harris
Andy . . . . . . Andrew Hill Newman
Rolf . . . . John Edmonston
Egon . . . . Phil Latella
Arnold . . . . Mark Gray
Gail . . . . Julie Foreman

Twentieth Century Fox is putting "Mannequin On The Move" in the back of the store in a limited release, and if this stiff ever shows any life, it will be a wonder indeed.

By actual count, it took four writers to struggle with another idea of why a mannequin would come to life in a department store and what would happen if she did. Their solution: The dummy (Kristy Swanson) is actually a Bavarian peasant girl hexed a thousand years ago to prevent her marriage to the prince.

As part of a promotion, the legendary statue is displayed at a Philadelphia store under the care of William Ragsdale, who's the spitting image of the prince, and jealous eye of count Terry Kiser, a spit-on descendent of the sorcerer who bewitched her, now waiting for the spell to end so he can possess her.

The hex is in the necklace and when Ragsdale accidentally removes it, he suddenly has a date for the night with a wide-eyed blonde in a micro-miniskirt who still loves him after all this time. Since this is her first date in a thousand years, Ragsdale doesn't rush things.

Alas, Swanson gets stoned again while Ragsdale and Kiser fight for possession and director Stewart Raffill labors to breathe anything into the lot of them before he runs out of time.

The only real movement is offered by Meshach Taylor, a prancing decorator who returns from the original for more stereotyped fun. Working hard, Stuart Pankin earns a few smiles as the store manager, and, against all odds, Kiser makes some headway.

But the young lovers never conjure up the magic that would make this mess work. Credit Swanson for taking a part in which she would inevitably be compared to her plaster image. She's better than that. Ragsdale's role is written as if he's been asleep for several centuries himself.

It's not their fault. They never had a chance once the creative thinking stopped at adding "On The Move" to the title. — *Har.*

STONE COLD

A Columbia Pictures release of a Stone Group Pictures presentation of a Mace Neufeld-Yoram Ben Ami-Walter Doniger production. Produced by Ben Ami. Executive producers, Doniger, Gary Wichard. Directed by Craig R. Baxley. Screenplay, Doniger; camera (Deluxe color), Alexander Gruszynski; editor, Mark Helfrich; music, Sylvester Levay; sound (Dolby), Richard Shorr, Victor Iorillo; production design, John Mansbridge, Richard Johnson; set decoration, Phil Shirey; associate producer, Udi Nedivi; assistant directors, Benjamin Rosenberg, Michael Samson; stunt coordinator, Paul Baxley; co-producers, Andrew D.T. Pfeffer, Nick Grillo. Reviewed at Mann Chinese Theater, Hollywood, May 17, 1991. MPAA Rating: R. Running time: **93 MIN.**
Joe Huff/John Stone . Brian Bosworth
Chains . . . . Lance Henriksen
Ice . . . . William Forsythe
Nancy . . . . Arabella Holzbog
Lance . . . . San McMurray
Cunningham . . . . Richard Gant
Bolivian . . . . Paulo Tocha
Brent Whipperton . . . . . David Tress

Brian Bosworth certainly looks the part in this type of punch-and-shoot-'em-up, but it's doubtful "Stone Cold" has enough name recognition to tackle much boxoffice with what amounts to a Seagal/Norris/Van Damme wannabe.

Pic may inspire some curiosity among genre junkies, but the buzz-cutted linebacker may find it easier tackling halfbacks than filmgoers.

Actually, the budding star here is probably director Craig R. Baxley, who recently directed the sci-fi thriller "I Come In Peace." He shows a real flair for stuntwork and action sequences in both films.

Too bad the story is so mind-numbingly dense. Maverick cop Joe Huff (Bosworth) is drafted by the FBI to infiltrate a murderous motorcycle gang headed by the requisite psycho Chains (Lance Henriksen).

Ostensible reason for the undercover work is to gather evidence, but once the bad guys are all turned to Swiss cheese by the end à la "Raw Deal," one wonders why they don't just skip to the execution phase and forgo all the violent foreplay.

Huff's bloody triumph leaves behind a particularly hollow feeling since so many innocents are mowed down in the process. From that perspective, the film proffers the genre's pervasive and rather dubious morality: The hero's role is not to protect society but rather to indiscriminately sponge away its filth.

The early storyline tries hard to establish Huff as a rebel — a bruiser on suspension for insubordination who keeps a pet gila monster at home.

That image dovetails with Bosworth's own, dating back to his playing days at Oklahoma, and the physique and sneering demeanor are as on-target for a part as any of the Arnolds-come-lately.

From an acting standpoint, however, the Boz' range falls somewhere between Jim Brown and Bernie Casey on the former-footballer scale, perhaps with a little of Ben Davidson's snarl thrown in for good measure.

With that in mind it's fortunate he's surrounded by a reasonably seasoned cast. Even so he has trouble carrying the pic and might have been served better by starting out in a supporting role.

Henriksen continues to add to his impressive (if somewhat repetitive) stable of despicable bad guys, probably topped by his vampire in "Near Dark," while William Forsythe, last seen terrorizing Seagal's neighborhood in "Out For Justice," proves equally nasty.

Pic shies away from the prospect of a love interest, which is probably just as well since Arabella Holzbog comes off as stiff and stilted as Chains' remorseful "old lady."

Production values are commensurate with the better pics in the genre and suggest a reasonably high budget, with a number of topnotch explosions, crashes and stuntwork. Frequent fistfights also are well-choreographed, and despite the numerous shortcomings Baxley manages to keep "Cold's" pace on the warm side.
— *Bril.*

CANNES FEST

YOUNG SOUL REBELS
(BRITISH)

A British Film Institute production for Film Four Intl. in association with Sankofa, La Sept, Kinowelt, Iberoamericana. Executive producers, Colin MacCabe, Ben Gibson. Produced by Nadine Marsh-Edwards. Directed by Isaac Julien. Screenplay, Paul Hallam, Derrick McClintock, Julien; camera (Metrocolor), Nina Kellgren; editor, John Wilson; music, Simon Boswell; sound (Dolby), Ronald Bailey; production design, Derek Brown; art direction, Debra Overton; costume design, Annie Curtis Jones; production manager, Joanna Beresford; assistant director, Ian Ferguson; stunt coordinator, Clive Curtis; choreographer, Foster George. Reviewed at Cannes Film Festival (Intl. Critics Week), May 10, 1991. Running time: **105 MIN.**
Chris . . . . Valentine Nonyela
Caz . . . . Mo Sesay
Ken . . . . Dorian Healy
Ann . . . . Frances Barber
Tracy . . . . Sophie Okonedo
Billibud . . . . Jason Durr
Davis . . . . Gary McDonald
Jill . . . . Debra Gillett
Trish . . . . Danielle Scillitoe

Too many ingredients are mixed in the stew of Isaac Julien's debut pic "Young Soul Rebels," an intermittently entertaining saga of countercultures in 1977 London.

Picture's London black milieu and murder mystery plotline recall the classic Janet Green-scripted "Sapphire" over 30 years ago, but Julien keeps digressing from the main story to cover interesting yet tangential topics.

Theme, hammered away between musical or romantic interludes, concerns many forms of intolerance and stereotyping. Blacks and gays are the key protagonists, while other subgroups like punks, soul music fans in Britain, half-castes (a theme echoing "Sapphire") and even Scottish nationalists are given attention.

Chris (Valentine Nonyela) and Caz (Mo Sesay) are two fledgling deejays broadcasting from the pirate radio station WEFUNK a form of black-oriented disco music. Their friend Terry James is murdered by a white man during a homosexual tryst in the park. Chris accidentally obtains an audio tape of the murder from TJ's boombox.

Chris halfheartedly tries to break into the mainstream via Metropolitan Radio station, where he meets and romances a beautiful production assistant Tracy (Sophie Okonedo). Caz is revealed to be gay, and splits from his long-time partner to take up with a punk-styled white d.j. Billibud (Jason Durr).

With Queen Elizabeth's Silver Jubilee as a backdrop (and target for frequent satire of the establishment), pic establishes its thriller credentials at the outset but is poorly paced. Director Julien's inclusion of homoerotic love scenes is no longer a cinematic novelty, yet their placement distracts from the main narrative (especially a lengthy bed scene of Caz and Billibud late in the film).

Styling of aggressively androgynous Valentine Nonyela in the central heterosexual role misleads rather than adds to film's relentless attack on stereotypes.

Pic's most successful element is Nina Kellgren's high-contrast lighting that gives it a modern, futuristic look. Nostalgia content is covered by disco-era music ranging from Roy Ayers to War plus dancing to match. After the most obvious murder suspect is identified and in lameduck fashion disposed of, Julien adds a friendly ensemble dance scene for closure that doesn't ring true.

Young cast is attractive and enthusiastic, and Frances Barber guests in a droll turn as Chris' free-spirited white mom. Frequent male crotch (clothed) closeups à la Pasolini and the homosexual milieu should limit as well as define film's potential audience.

Some thick accents (French subtitles at Cannes definitely helped comprehension) are a drawback to Stateside acceptance.
— *Lor.*

LA BLANCA PALOMA
(THE WHITE DOVE)
(SPANISH)

A Cartel S.A. and Xaloc production in collaboration with Spanish Television (TVE). Executive producer, Eduardo Campoy. Directed by Juan Minon. Screenplay, Minon, Manuel Matji; camera (Agfa color), Jaume Peracaula; editor, Jose Salcedo; music, Louis Bague; sound, Goldstein & Steinberg S.A; sets, Javier Fernandez. Reviewed at Cannes Film Festival (market), May 12, 1991. Running time: **102 MIN.**
With: Francisco Rabal, Antonio Banderas, Emma Suarez, Mercedes Sampietro, Sonsoles Benedicto, Perla Cristal.

Opening of "The White Dove" serves up an apology for the Basque terrorists, with police playing the heavies. Although pic's background cen-

ters on the hatred and unrest in that part of Spain, it veers off to an inconclusive love story and various subplots. Pic is not apt to evoke much interest outside its own territory.

Despite sound direction and deft lensing, pic's plot meanders, and its central chararacter, Mario, remains ill-defined. The "White Dove" is the name of a bar where some of the local extremists hang out, though it is run by a tough, basically apolitical Andalusian. He has a daughter who goes sweet on one of the activists and who is having doubts about who the good guys are.

Pic's fast-paced start soon bogs down in unconvincing subplots concerning the bar owner's incest with his daughter, a suicidal mother and terrorists who spend their time playing jai alai, spewing revolutionary talk and calling anyone a fascist who doesn't sympathize with them.

Item terminates when the bar is blown up by Mario, who unwittingly kills not only owner but also daughter. — *Besa.*

DELICATESSEN
(FRENCH)

A UGC release of a Constellation-UGC-Hachette Premiere production. (Intl. sales: UGC.) Produced by Claudie Ossard. Directed by Jean-Pierre Jeunet, Marc Caro. Screenplay, Jeunet, Caro, Gilles Adrien; camera (color), Darius Khondji; editor, Herve Schneid; music, Carlos D'Alessio; sound, Jerome Thiault; production design, Jean-Philippe Carp; production manager, Michele Arnould; assistant director, Jean-Marc Tostivint; casting, Pierre-Jacques Benichon. Reviewed at Cannes Film Festival (market), May 13, 1991. Running time: **96 MIN.**
Louison . . . . Dominique Pinon
Julie . . . . Marie-Laure Dougnac
Butcher . . . . . Jean-Claude Dreyfus
Robert . . . . Rufus
Husband . . . . Ticky Holgado
Wife . . . . Anne-Marie Pisani
Also with: Silvie Laguna, Jean-François Perrier, Dominique Zardi, Karin Viard, Chick Ortega.

Beautifully textured, cleverly scripted and eerily shot (often with a wideangle lens making characters look even wierder), "Delicatessen" is a zany little film that should get terrific word of mouth, as it did at Cannes, and has terrific theatrical potential. This eclectic art pic also has a natural second life on video.

In a darkly bizarre, futuristic world where food shortages have led the butcher to serve up human flesh after murdering the locals, a bumbling group of Troglodins,

an underground force reminiscent of the government police in "Brazil," are engaged in a war on cannibal crime.

An excellent cast made up entirely of character actors provides a rich array of eccentrics who live in the building over the deli and the sewers used as tunnels by the Troglodins.

Brilliant opening has the big bad butcher sharpening his knives, then wielding a meat cleaver to lop off a hand: Slice to pic's title and pan to innovative credits scribbled on the deli walls. At this point, viewers can be sure they're in for something completely off-the-wall. Dozens of unique scenes paint a fascinating and morbid portrait of the darker side of human nature.

An unsuspecting comedian moves into the flat above the deli and falls in love with neighboring blind girl, who organizes a hilarious tea party for two.

Pic then quickly hooks viewers with an outrageous montage of rythmically edited visuals intiated by a sex scene between the butcher and his lover shot from under the bed (scene is similar to one in Rouben Mamoulian's 1932 "Love Me Tonight").

All other wacko characters are well-defined and carefully developed, including the armed postman who holds up people when delivering the mail and the snail eater whose flat is two inches deep in water and escargot shells.

Pic wears thin late in the pic, but it's still a startling and clever debut for co-helmers Jean-Pierre Jeunet and Marc Caro. Editing is superb. — *Suze.*

BARTON FINK

A 20th Century Fox release of a Circle Films presentation. Produced by Ethan Coen. Executive producers, Ben Barenholtz, Ted Pedas, Jim Pedas, Bill Durkin. Directed by Joel Coen. Screenplay, Ethan Coen, Joel Coen; camera (Duart color), Roger Deakins; editor, Roderick Jaynes; music, Carter Burwell; sound (Dolby), Allan Byer; production design, Dennis Gassner; costume design, Richard Hornung; associate producers, Leslie McDonald, Bob Goldstein; assistant director, Joe Camp III; co-producer, Graham Place; casting, Donna Isaacson, John Lyons. Reviewed at Cannes Film Festival (competition), May 17, 1991. No MPAA Rating. Running time: **116 MIN.**
Barton Fink . . . . John Turturro
Charlie Meadows . . . . John Goodman
Audrey Taylor . . . . Judy Davis
Jack Lipnick . . . . . Michael Lerner
W.P. Mayhew . . . . . John Mahoney
Ben Geisler . . . . Tony Shalhoub
Lou Breeze . . . . Jon Polito
Chet . . . . Steve Buscemi
Garland Stanford . . . David Warrilow
Det. Mastrionotti . . Richard Portnow
Det. Deutsch . . . Christopher Murney

"Barton Fink" is one of the most eccentric films to come out of, or take place in, Hollywood in many a moon. Accomplished on every artistic level, Joel and Ethan Coen's hermetic tale of a "genius" playwright's brief stint as a studio contract writer is a painstakingly miniaturist work that can be read any number of ways.

As with the Coens' previous pics, critical reaction should be strong, but the 1991 Golden Palm winner's circumscribed world and private meanings will limit commercial interest to the cognoscenti.

This new film will appeal to buffs at least as much as did the brothers' last, "Miller's Crossing," and for the same reasons: extraordinarily colorful period language spoken by superlative actors, leading of scenes into odd, unexpected places, and impeccable craftsmanship.

With the partial exception of "Raising Arizona," however, the Coens' films have proven elusive to a wide public, and that's likely to remain the case this time. Much of the action unfolds in a single dreary hotel room as a writer struggles to write.

Under this heavily constricted condition, the brothers generate some marvelous scenes in their engagingly surreal rumination on "the life of the mind," but don't provide a reliable key to entering their confidential world.

Title character, played with a creepily growing sense of dread by John Turturro, is a gravely serious New York dramatist who scores a soaring triumph on Broadway in 1941 with a deep-dish think piece about the working class. Fink gets to deliver a boilerplate anti-Hollywood speech before capitulating to a lucrative studio offer, but assures himself he will remain true to his ideals.

Before he can say proletarianism, however, he is assigned a Wallace Beery wrestling programmer and told to come up with something by the end of the week. He is coddled by studio chief Jack Lipnick (Michael Lerner) and, checking into a huge, slightly frayed and weirdly underpopulated hotel, becomes friendly with the hulking fellow bachelor next door, Charlie Meadows (John Goodman), an insurance salesman with a gift for gab.

Working at home, Fink suffers from intense writer's block, and shades of Kafka surface as scenes of the scribe staring at his blank page turn to such odd distractions as wallpaper peeling off walls and a mosquito buzzing about the room.

After a little more than an hour into the pic, one of those startling screen occurrences (like Janet Leigh's murder in "Psycho") takes place and throws the film in a wholly unexpected direction. There is a shocking murder, the presence of a mysterious box in Fink's room, the revelation of another's character's sinister true identity, three more killings, a truly weird hotel fire and the humiliation of the writer after he believes he's finally turned out a fine script. Ending is as lovely as it is enigmatic.

Scene after scene is filled with a ferocious strength and humor. Fink's encounters with the studio boss represent astounding displays of character domination and debasement. Lerner's performance as a Mayer-like overlord is sensational.

But much more of the action involves Fink and his friendly neighbor as Charlie expounds upon life, gives him a wrestling demonstration and invariably interrupts the writer just when he's about to get cracking.

It could plausibly be argued that the Meadows character actually doesn't exist, that he is simply a physical manifestation of extreme writer's block. He also stands in for the real working man that Fink idealizes and tries to write about, but in fact doesn't know at all.

The fat man has a thousand real-life stories he's willing to tell, but the writer is scarcely interested. Fink comes off as remote and difficult, with inflated notions of his work's importance, but hopeless as a social creature. Turturro invests this creative worm with convincing anxiety, sweat, desperation and inwardness.

Goodman is marvelous as the folksy neighbor, rolling his tongue around pages of wonderful dialog. Judy Davis nicely etches a woman who has a way with difficult writers, and John Mahoney turns up as a near dead ringer for William Faulkner in his Hollywood period.

Replacing Barry Sonnenfeld behind the camera for the Coens, Roger Deakins has created many brilliant images. Production designer Dennis Gassner's earth-toned sets, Roderick Jaynes' editing, Richard Hornung's costumes and Carter Burwell's score all contribute strongly in creat-

ing a Hollywood as it might have been sketched in a surrealist short story rather than a fleshed-out novel. — *Cart.*

BIAN ZHOU BIAN CHANG
(LIFE ON A STRING)
(GERMAN-BRITISH-CHINESE)

A Serene Prods. presentation of a Pandora Film-Beijing Film Studio-China Film co-production, in association with Herald Ace, Channel 4, Berlin Filmforderung. (Intl. sales: Cinepool, Munich.) Produced by Don Ranvaud. Executive co-producers, Cai Rubin, Karl Baumgartner. Directed by Chen Kaige. Screenplay, Kaige from a short story by Shi Tiesheng; camera (color), Gu Changwei; editor, Pei Xiaonan; music, Qu Xiaosong; sound (Dolby), Tao Jing; production design, Shao Ruigang; production manager, Yang Kebing, Xu Xiaoqing; assistant director, Zhang Jinzhan; associate producers, Hong Huang, Masato Hara; Berlin supervisors, Michael Bohme, Klaus Zimmermann; Hong Kong supervisor, Shu Kei. Reviewed at Cannes Film Festival (competition), May 15, 1991. Running time: **120 MIN.**

The saint . . . . Liu Zhongyuan
Shitou . . . . Huang Lei
Lanxiu . . . . Xu Qing
Noodleshop owner's wife . . . Ma Ling
(Mandarin soundtrack)

A visually superlative film poem, shot in spectacularly rugged scenery around Inner Mongolia, "Life On A String" is a rich film experience, but its length and lack of a conventional narrative will be factors to overcome in getting the film across to arthouse audiences.

The simple story tells of a blind boy whose dying master gives him a secret cure for his affliction. But before the prescription can be used, the boy is told, he must play his banjo until 1,000 strings have been broken. Sixty years later, all but five strings are gone, and the boy, now an old man revered as a saint, is wandering the countryside singing songs accompanied by his disciple, Shitou, a youth who's also blind.

They wind up in a village where Shitou falls in love with a local girl, but is attacked because the villagers don't want her to associate with the blind stranger. Meanwhile, the power of the old man's songs proves to be so great he can even prevent warring factions from fighting, but when the 1,000th string finally breaks, the result is unexpected.

On a basic level, the film is about the power of belief over logic and the ability of the blind to see better. But these simple

messages are conveyed in terms of powerful images and superb folk songs that at times give the film a rock opera quality.

Pic's locations are crucial elements in its success: mountain village, isolated temple and a noodle shop perched incongruously on the cliff above a crashing, spectacular waterfall, where spray and smoke combine to create a strange and awesome scene.

Chen's pacing is slow, and much is demanded of audiences who will have to accept the steady progression and gradual buildup of minor incidents. At times the film seems to be going nowhere, but it always gets back on track, moving inexorably to its sublime ending.

Film offers further proof of Chen's talents as a mythic filmmaker, whose work differs greatly from the realist style of his compatriot Zhang Yimou ("Ju Dou").

Liu Zhongyuan is a powerful presence as the old man, and overshadows other thesps. Gu Changwei's camerawork is simply stunning, and the Dolby sound mix is a magnificent achievement. Original Chinese title literally means "Walking, Singing." — *Strat.*

COMRADES IN ARMS

A Promark Entertainment Group presentation of a Cinema Sciences Corp. production. Produced and directed by Christian Ingvordsen. Screenplay, Ingvordsen, Steven Kaman, John Weiner; camera (color)-editor, Kaman; music, Paul Avgerinos; sound, Dan Leiner. Reviewed at Cannes Film Festival (market), May 10, 1991. No MPAA Rating. Running time: **88 MIN.**

With: Lance Henriksen, Lyle Alzado.

"Comrades In Arms" is a lame post-Cold War action pic in which CIA and KGB special forces team up to fight a drug cartel (so-called "third superpower"). Mindless action sequences and lack of a coherent plot make this a straight-to-video prospect.

The monosyllabic Lyle Alzado plays the intrepid hero who's ordered by boss Lance Henriksen to team up with his Russian counterpart to eliminate the Arab leader of the cartel. For some strange reason, the combined Yank-Russian forces train in Moscow, a cue for some stale stock shots and weird production design.

Pic is just a series of routine

shoot-'em-ups, with both sides blasting away at each other with automatic weapons; it's all pretty dull. Silliest scene has a blonde cartel assassin easily infiltrate CIA h.q. in Washington, shooting the only guard, and then wiping out half the attendees at a briefing given by Henriksen.

Technical credits for this cheapie are strictly ho-hum.
— *Strat.*

THE INDIAN RUNNER

A Universal release (in U.S.; Columbia Tri-Star elsewhere) of a Mount Film Group presentation in association with MICO/NHK Enterprises. Produced by Don Phillips. Executive producers, Thom Mount, Stephen K. Bannon, Mark Bisgeier. Written and directed by Sean Penn. Camera (Deluxe color), Anthony B. Richmond; editor, Jay Cassidy; music, Jack Nitzche, Gary Alper; sound (Dolby), Gary Alper; production design, Michael Haller; art direction, Bill Groom; set decoration, Derek Hill; costume design, Jill Ohanneson; assistant director, Artist Robinson; line producer, David S. Hamburger; co-producer, Patricia Morrison; casting, Deede Wehle. Reviewed at Cannes Film Festival (Directors Fortnight), May 17, 1991. MPAA Rating: R. Running time: **126 MIN.**

Joe Roberts . . . . David Morse
Frank Roberts . . . . Viggo Mortensen
Maria . . . . Valeria Golino
Dorothy . . . . . . Patricia Arquette
Father . . . . Charles Bronson
Mother . . . . Sandy Dennis
Caesar . . . . Dennis Hopper
Randall . . . . Jordan Rhodes

A tortured examination of the disintegration of a Midwestern family, "The Indian Runner" is very much actors' cinema. Rambling, indulgent and joltingly raw at times, Sean Penn's first outing as a director takes a fair amount of patience to get through but has an integrity that intermittently serves it well.

A downer from beginning to end, pic will struggle to find a commercial footing. Universal has first refusal rights for U.S. distribution, while Columbia Tri-Star is handling international.

Inspired by the Bruce Springsteen song "Highway Patrolman," overwrought piece looks at the muted tragedy of two brothers in the late 1960s. Joe Roberts (David Morse) is a small-town Nebraska cop who, in the opening scene, shoots to death a suspect after a high-speed car chase.

Living with his Mexican wife and small child, Joe tries to welcome his brother Frank (Viggo Mortensen) back into the fold after the latter returns from a stint in Vietnam, but Frank, a troublemaker dating back to childhood, immediately takes off and isn't heard from in six months.

Learning that Frank has been in prison, Joe goes to pick him up on his release but again is frustrated in his attempted reconciliation, as Frank shacks up with a blonde sprite named Dorothy. Along the way, traumas hit the family like clockwork. The brothers' mother dies and, a bit later, their father commits suicide.

Back in town and trying to work responsibly, the unpredictable Frank flakes out just as his wife is delivering their baby and commits an act of irrational violence, which leads to a potential showdown between siblings.

All this takes more than two hours to get through because Penn, as writer and director, lets his scenes play out at great length. Pic doesn't feel particularly improvised, but it shares in common with the work of John Cassavetes, for example, a sense of commitment to the actor's process above all else, a belief that truth will best emerge from the combustibility of emotions between performers.

Approach fosters a lack of discipline and rigor, as well as meandering sequences in which the points could have been made with infinitely greater economy. Occasionally, however, the method creates a lived-in quality, a texture of working class life that would be impossible with cinematic shorthand.

Penn mixes in some Indian mumbo jumbo about a man pursuing a deer which raises the pretention level, but doesn't push the Vietnam angle at all as a reason for Frank's antisocial behavior. Overall film has an aura of earnestness and conviction, but also of heaviness and self-indulgence.

Actors, notably Morse and Mortensen as the good and bad brothers, are given loads of room to work and come off to decent advantage. Charles Bronson puts in a supporting interp of repressed hysteria as the father, while Sandy Dennis and Dennis Hopper are in briefly as the mother and a local bartender, respectively. Valeria Golino and Patricia Arquette are vital as the women in the brothers' lives.

With much of the action set at night, Anthony B. Richmond's lensing is often on the murky side, and other production contributions are average. Overall, film marks a debut of incidental interest. — *Cart.*

LUNE FROIDE
(COLD MOON)
(FRENCH-B&W)

A Gaumont release of a Les Films du Dauphin-Studio Lavabo production, with the participation of Studio Canal Plus, Canal Plus. Produced by Luc Besson, Andree Martinez. Directed by Patrick Bouchitey. Screenplay, Bouchitey, Jacky Berroyer, based on "Copulating Mermaid Of Venice" and "Trouble With The Battery," by Charles Bukowski; camera (b&w), Jean-Jacques Bouhon; editor, Florence Bon; music, Didier Lockwood; sound, Guillaume Sciama; production design, Frank Lagache, Jean-Marc Pacaud; production manager, Jerome Chalou; assistant director, Vincent Canaple. Reviewed at Cannes Film Festival (competition), May 9, 1991. Running time: **92 MIN.**
Simon . . . . Jean-François Stevenin
Dede . . . . Patrick Bouchitey
Gerard . . . . Jean-Pierre Bisson
Nadine . . . . Laura Favali
Aunt Suzanne . . . . . Marie Mergey
The whore . . . . . . Sylvana de Faria
The blonde . . . Consuelo de Haviland
The mermaid . . . . Karin Nuris
Denis . . . . Alain Le Floch
Priest . . . . Jacky Berroyer

"Cold Moon," the latest adaptation of a work by Yank Charles Bukowski, is set in France, not the U.S., but still the writer's world of aimless boozing and loveless womanizing is instantly recognizable.

The main characters' unattractive activities won't appeal to a wide audience, though the picture will attract Bukowski fans and the curious.

European filmmakers previously have been inspired by Bukowski's dark, drink-sodden world, as evidenced by Marco Ferreri's "Tales Of Ordinary Madness" Barbet Schroder's "Barfly" and Dominique Deruddere's "Love Is A Dog From Hell."

First-time feature director Patrick Bouchitey expanded his earlier award winning short film (also called "Cold Moon") into this feature incorporating two Bukowski short stories. One of them, "Copulating Mermaid Of Venice," with its controversial necrophilia theme, also formed the basis of a Belgian Bukowski adaptation entitled "Crazy Love."

Helmer himself plays Dede, an out-of-work boozer who lives in a trailer parked outside his sister and brother-in-law's apartment. He spends most of his time in the company of Simon (Jean-François Stevenin), who works by night in a fish-packing plant.

With their beer guts, foul talk and their mindlessly sexist attitude towards women, these two are an unlovely pair. Simon is marginally the more sensitive of the two, but is haunted by a secret in his past involving "a mermaid."

The near-plotless film charts the adventures of these two who are first seen on a garbage-strewn beach. They listen to music (Procol Harum's "A Whiter Shade Of Pale" is described as "music for a lousy marriage"), get drunk in bars or discos, pick up women, visit prosties, even drink communion wine in church.

Simon takes time off to visit his aunt, who cares for a retarded man, but that's the one spark of decency he shows. He hires a svelte Spanish prostitute, and seems unfazed when her brother shares their room. Later, he picks up a woman in a bar, but allows his friend to have sex with her on a beach.

Climaxing these seemingly aimless incidents is a flashback to the time when the two pals stole the body of a dead girl from a morgue. Overcome by the beauty of the naked corpse, Simon made love to her, a gross act which, for him, became the discovery of genuine love. But the graphic scene isn't presented romantically as it was in "Crazy Love," but clinically and coldly.

Stevenin gives another fine performance as Simon, but Bouchitey is irritating and mannered as Dede. He does better work behind the camera, and Jean-Jacques Bouhon's moody black & white camerawork perfectly evokes Bukowski's miserable world.

Among the supporting cast, Alain Le Floch is touching as the retarded man and co-scripter Jacky Berroyer is briefly effective as a priest. Karin Nuris plays the beautiful corpse. Outside Europe, "Cold Moon" will probably get a chilly reception. The name of Bouchitey's production company, Studio Lavabo, got a laugh from the Cannes audience ("lavabo" means "lavatory"). — *Strat.*

LIFE STINKS

An MGM release (20th Century Fox internationally) of a Brooksfilms production in association with Le Studio Canal Plus. Executive producer, Ezra Swerdlow. Produced and directed by Mel Brooks. Screenplay, Brooks, Rudy De Luca, Steve Haberman, from story by Brooks, Ron Clark, De Luca, Haberman; camera (Deluxe color), Steven Poster; editor, David Rawlins, Anthony Redman, Michael Mulconery; music, John Morris; sound (Dolby), Willie D. Burton; production design, Peter Larkin; art direction, Josan Russo; set design, Carroll Johnston; set decoration, Marvin March; costume design, Mary Malin; associate producer, Kim Kurumada; assistant director, Mitchell Bock; casting, Bill Shepard, Todd Thaler. Reviewed at Cannes Film Festival (out of competition), May 15, 1991. No MPAA Rating. Running time: **95 MIN.**
Goddard Bolt (Pepto) . . . Mel Brooks
Molly . . . . Lesley Ann Warren
Vance Crasswell . . . . Jeffrey Tambor
Pritchard . . . . Stuart Pankin
Sailor . . . . Howard Morris
J. Paul Getty . . . . . . Rudy De Luca
Fumes . . . . Teddy Wilson
Knowles . . . . Michael Ensign
Stevens . . . . Matthew Faison
Willy . . . . Billy Barty
Mean Victor . . . . . . Brian Thompson
Yo . . . . Raymond O'Connor
Flophouse owner . . . . Carmine Caridi

Mel Brooks' "Life Stinks" is a fitfully funny vaudeville caricature about life on Skid Row. Screened at Cannes as a surprise entry, antic comedy has more laughs than the filmmaker's last couple of efforts, and presents an amiably sympathetic, if unreliable, look at the homeless.

But premise of a rich man who chooses to live among the poor for a spell feels sorely undeveloped, and suffers from the usual gross effects and exaggerations. Hoping for a big winner, MGM will more likely see middle-range b.o. results from this one.

Very much a poor man's "Sullivan's Travels," with elements of "Trading Places" and "It's A Mad, Mad, Mad, Mad World" thrown in, pic gets off to a good start with Brooks' callous billionaire Goddard Bolt informing his circle of yes-men of his plans to build a colossal futuristic development on the site of Los Angeles' worst slums, the plight of its residents be damned.

Green with jealousy over Bolt's potential profits, tycoon Jeffrey Tambor bets his rival that he can't last a month living out in the neighborhood he intends to buy. Accepting the wager, Bolt is shorn of his gold jewelry, credit cards and toupee and deposited on the streets, where he quickly learns that finding money for a meal isn't simple.

In a series of vignettes that play like blackout routines, Bolt, renamed Pepto by a local denizen, tries various survival tactics, such as dancing for donations and camping out under cardboard, only to discover the dangers of poaching on others' turf.

After being robbed of his shoes, he encounters baglady Lesley Ann Warren, a wildly gesticulating man-hater who slowly comes to admit Pepto is the only person she can stand. She takes him for a meal at the local mission and helps integrate him.

Although he gets beaten up and is sobered when an oldtimer friend dies, Pepto cruises through the remainder of the month and even develops a romance with the baglady. After an hour, it feels like the film is over, as the new couple returns to his mansion, only to discover that his lawyers and Tambor have used power of attorney to strip him of his holdings and are sending him back to the streets.

Action picks up at this point, as Pepto, in one of the film's funniest scenes, is hilariously overmedicated at a hospital before leading a revolt of the homeless against Tambor just as the latter breaks ground on his slum redevelopment. Climactic sequence has the two battling it out on huge caterpillar tractor cranes, shades of "Aliens."

Some effective bug-eyed, freewheeling comedy is scattered throughout, much of it descending to the Three Stooges level of sophistication. But distressingly little is done with the vast possibilities offered by the setting and the characters populating it. By giving a film a serious backdrop for a change, Brooks gave himself the chance for some reflective, social comedy, but doesn't seem remotely attracted to following through on it.

Brooks' notion of the homeless seems rooted in a comic caricature of a 1930s bum, not modern reality. Given the basic fantasy premise, this is not necessarily as offensive as it may seem, but the subject would still appear to be worthy of a bit of reflection, à la "Sullivan's Travels," or sufficient to raise the hero's consciousness more than superficially.

As it is, the humor here is less ethnic, sexual and film-derived than usual for Brooks (indeed, ethnic characters are given somewhat short shrift here). He even works in a relatively charming dance sequence for Warren and himself as they celebrate winning his bet.

As can be expected, acting is all over the top, which is fine when Brooks and Rudy De Luca go at each other in a funny running gag over which derelict is actually the richer, but not so good when Warren is flailing all over the place. Shot both on real locations and in the studio, film's tech credits are okay. — *Cart.*

THE BRIDGE
(BRITISH)

A British Screen and Film Four Intl. presentation of a Moonlight Film production. (Intl. sales: The Sales Co, London.) Produced by Lyn Goleby. Directed by Syd Macartney. Screenplay, Adrian Hodges; camera (Fujicolor), David Tattersall; editor, Michael Ellis; music, Richard G. Mitchell; production design, Terry Pritchard; costumes, Jenny Beavan; production manager, Nicky Kentish-Barnes; assistant director, Barry Wasserman. Reviewed at Cannes Film Festival (market), May 15, 1991. Running time: **99 MIN.**
Isobel Heatherington . . Saskia Reeves
Philip Wilson Steer . . . David O'Hara
Smithson . . . . Joss Ackland
Reg Heatherington . Anthony Higgins
Aunt Jude . . . . . Rosemary Harris
Mrs. Todd . . . . . . Geraldine James

Beautiful but inert, "The Bridge" firmly belongs in the Laura Ashley school of genteel British cinema. Story (set in 1887) of a summer romance between a married mother and a young artist will appeal to admirers of traditional British cinema and to incurable romantics. Tv transmission looms as a better bet than theatrical.

Saskia Reeves, effective in "Close My Eyes," goes through the motions here as the bored and restless wife of wealthy Anthony Higgins. While vacationing with her three daughters, she meets a painter (David O'Hara) who is so inspired by her beauty that he features her in his painting of a bridge where they meet. Admiration turns to love and a brief, secret afternoon liaison, followed by mutual guilt and torment.

There's nothing very original here, and director Syd Macartney brings nothing fresh to Adrian Hodges' familiar screenplay. O'Hara is an uninspiring lover, and the pic's best performance comes from Higgins as the jealous and powerful husband.

David Tattersall's cinematography is pretty but vapid. Ultimately, the pic is as hollow as the human relationships depicted, and is indistinguishable from countless telepics set in the past which deal with illicit relationships. David Lean's 55-year-old classic "Brief Encounter" is a far more incisive exploration of adultery than this vapid effort.

— *Strat.*

THE ADJUSTER
(CANADIAN)

An Alliance Releasing release (Canada) of an Alliance Communications presentation of an Ego Film Arts Production. Written and directed by Atom Egoyan. Camera (Cinemascope color), Paul Sarossy; editor, Susan Shipton; music, Mychael Danna; sound, Steven Munro; production design, Linda Del Rosario, Richard Paris; art direction, Kathleen Climie; set decorators, Richard Paris, Linda Del Rosario; costume design, Maya Mani; assistant director, David Webb; co-produced by Camelia Frieberg. Reviewed at Cannes Film Festival (Director's Fortnight), May 13, 1991. Running time: **102 MIN.**
Noah . . . . Elias Koteas
Hera . . . . Arsiné Khanjian
Bubba . . . . Maury Chaykin
Mimi . . . . Gabrielle Rose
Arianne . . . . Jennifer Dale
Censor . . . . David Hemblen
Sete . . . . Rose Sarkisyan
Simon . . . . Armen Kokorian
Also with: Jacqueline Samuda, Gerard Parkes, Patricia Collins, Don McKellar, Stephen Ouimette, Raoul Trujillo, John Gilbert.

Atom Egoyan's "The Adjuster" could arouse a following among commercial audiences in need of diversion. Visually stunning and suitably perverted, pic will have to be carefully targeted.

In an escalating quest for eccentricity, however, Egoyan's analysis of voyeurism is becoming profoundly shallow. Trying to streamline his radical and visionary "Family Viewing," Egoyan's follow-up pic "Speaking Parts" Xeroxed the theme and polished the images but lost its edge in the process.

Ditto for "The Adjuster," with its cast of superbly photographed, eclectic characters who take an aimless walk on the wild side. "Family Viewing" connoisseurs looking for added insight into baser voyeuristic instincts will be disappointed, however.

Story revolves around the unlikely meeting of a twisted, frigid couple and an amoral existential pair who live out absurd sexual fantasies. A vast supporting cast are all amorous desperados ranging from a bored married couple and a perverted film censor to a peeping Tom (a character which leads to pic's only surprising scene).

Noah (Elias Koteas), the insurance adjuster, heads a cast of eccentrics as a wedded philanderer who exploits the vulnerability of female clients who've lost their homes to fires. His mate Hera (played by Egoyan's mate, Arsiné Khanjian) is a film censor who secretly videotapes

porn flicks for her sister Sete (Rose Sarkisyan), a matron with betwixt desires.

These frigid spouses rent their model home to a couple who stiffly stage their sexual fantasies in absurd and eventually violent acts. Problem is, Egoyan creates fantasies which appear forced and unnatural so actors Maury Chaykin (as the fat, balding ex-football hero Bubba) and wild-eyed Gabrielle Rose (as kinky Mimi) try too hard to be weird. Their characters have potential that the script never develops.

The adjuster is an unsympathetic womanizer whose mate has warts on her feet. As in all other subplots, the provocative relationship she develops with her foot specialist never gets past zero. At no point does the viewer ever gain in-depth knowledge of any character in the film (a vast departure from the detailed caricatures in "Family Viewing").

Music is brilliantly haunting but editing is much weaker than the structural zapping cuts of "Viewing." Scenes linger unnecessarily.

Thesp David Hemblen shines as the admittedly suppressed censor board captain, but Egoyan should write new roles for actresses Khanjian and Rose who still play variations on their original tortured, neglected characters in "Viewing." Koteas resembles Robert DeNiro but should forget mimicking his facial movements. Visuals are gorgeous.

— *Suze.*

SANGO MALO
(TEACHER OF THE CANTON)
(CAMEROONIAN-BURKINA FASO)

A Les Films Terre Africaine-Fodic-Cameroon Radio and TV (Cameroon)-Diproci (Burkina Faso) coproduction in association with Ministry of Cooperation and Development (France), Channel 4 (U.K.), COE (Italy), Hubert Bals Foundation (Holland). Executive producer, Atriascop (Paris), Emmanuel Toko. Written and directed by Bassek Ba Kobhio, based on his novel. Camera (color), Joseph Guerin; editor, Marie Jeanne Kanyala; music, Francis Bebey; art direction, François Bollo. Reviewed at Cannes Film Festival (Un Certain Regard), May 11, 1991. Running time: **93 MIN.**
Bernard Malo . . . . . . Jerome Bolo
The director . . . . . Marcel Mvondo II
Ngo Bakang . Edwige Ntongon a Zock
Drunk . . . . Jean Minguele

A feature film from the Cameroon is a rarity, and "Sango Malo" offers a valuable look at the harsh realities of village life in this little-seen land. But despite a relatively lively script, pic is unable to sustain its initially fast pace, and audience will probably be limited to African film circuits.

Novelist-turned-helmer Bassek Ba Kobhio (a documaker and assistant to Claire Denis on "Chocolat") debuts with an idealistic tale of a young teacher who tries radical new methods on his first class of pupils, and pays for it. The subject is hardly original, but the emphasis is shifted from pedagogy per se to a giant ideological clash between characters' views of their country.

Malo (an intense, angry Jerome Bolo) arrives in the village convinced his young students need a practical education that will be useful to them in life. To the scandal of the school's pompous director (the enjoyable Marcel Mvondo II), the subversive Malo throws book-learning out the window and takes the class outdoors.

Watching the youngsters cutting down brush and flunk dictation, one wonders whether Malo's educational principles are on target. But his casual, liberating style includes lessons on sex education and politics.

Surprisingly, pic ends up taking a critical view of the fiery, but cocky, young teacher. He convinces the uneducated village men to band together in a cooperative rubber plantation, then attempts to run it over their protests. He marries fellow teacher Edwige Ntongon a Zock, but his stubborn refusal to follow tradition leads to her father committing suicide out of shame.

The director's writerly origins shine through in the characters, all complex, flawed human beings. He is on more uncertain ground directing, and there are repetitious slowdowns in the film that cause a certain attrition rate among audiences.

The portrait of the village of Lebamzip (a real place) is spiced up by a humorous description of the lazy, tyrannical local honchos. There is no sign of the idyllic family and tribal life depicted in, for example, West African films. From the comical school director to the nasty shop owner and the ridiculous village chief, "Sango Malo" shows locals as decadent and potentially dangerous. When they turn to the authorities against Malo, he is brutally arrested and jailed.

Lending an air of unreality to everything is the strained French spoken by everybody from school kids to local loafers.

The problem of shooting with actors repping Cameroon's 200 language groups appears insurmountable, and filmmakers chose to adopt the clumsy solution of quasi-universal French.

The film boasts an original, enjoyable score by composer Francis Bebey. There is plenty of tropical paradise scenery to look at, and technical work is acceptable. Four European countries contributed to the film's costs. — *Yung.*

PROM NIGHT IV—
DELIVER US FROM EVIL
(CANADIAN)

A Norstar Entertainment presentation of a Peter Simpson production. Produced by Ray Sager. Executive producer, Simpson. Directed by Clay Borris. Screenplay, Richard Beattie; camera (color), Rick Wincenty; editor, Stan Cole; music, Paul Zaza; production design, Ian Brock; production manager, Alice O'Neil. Reviewed at Cannes Film Festival (market), May 14, 1991. Running time: **95 MIN.**
Megan . . . . Nikki De Boer
Mark . . . . Alden Kane
Laura . . . . Joy Tanner
Jeff . . . . Alle Ghadban
Father Jonas . . . . . James Carver
Father Jaeger . . . . . Ken McGregor

Fourth installment of Peter Simpson's "Prom Night" horror offerings is an okay entry in the routine horror stakes, despite wafer thin credibility.

As with similar series, the original premise of the first installment seems a distant memory, but "Prom Night IV" has its moments, certainly enough for solid video returns.

This time out, mad monk James Carver terrorizes a group of four teens; two regular guys and two pubescent girls from a strict religious school. The church regards Carver as some form of evil incarnation after a slaying 30 years earlier. They subsequently keep him locked up in an underground cell on the rather flimsy premise that the church "protects its own."

Carver has a thing about sex and maintaining zealot-like faith. He escapes and returns to the monastery where he was kept and which naturally is now the summer house of Alden Kane's parents. Standard house-hunt procedure unfolds, with some good atmospherics but one too many backward and forward runs down corridors. Usual teen titillation is laced through pic's first half.

Borris builds some suspenseful moments without resorting to too much blood. Special mention goes to sound effects, used to solid advantage in some sequences. — *Doch.*

POGRZEB KARTOFLA
(BURIAL OF POTATOES)
(POLISH)

A K. Irzykwski Film Studio production. (Intl. sales: Film Polski.) Written and directed by Jan Jakub Kolski. Camera (color), Wojciech Todorow; music, Zygmunt Konieczny; sound, Norbert Medlewski; production design, Ewa Pakulska; production manager, Anna Gryczynska. Reviewed at Cannes Film Festival (Un Certain Regard), May 12, 1991. Running time: **100 MIN.**
Mateusz . . . . . . Franciszek Pieczka
Also with: Mariusz Saniternik, Grazyna Blecka-Kolska, Adam Ferency, Ewa Zukowska, Boguslaw Sochnacki.

"Burial Of Potatoes" is a somber picture set in 1946 about a Polish villager returning home after years in a concentration camp. A tough theme will limit the pic to marginal screenings, with the fest circuit a possible outlet.

Franciszek Pieczka plays the old-timer, a saddler, who finds nothing but hostility when he finally makes it home after years away. He's not a Jew, though the villagers brand him one and generally give him a hard time. They feel guilty about the death of his son during the latter stages of the war, and don't want the father around.

A similar theme to "Bad Day At Black Rock," but without that film's classic dramatic structure, this is a first feature from writer-director Jan Jakub Kolski. He makes rather heavy weather of it all, with the villagers as nasty a bunch of characters as you could hope to meet. Slow pacing and confused flashbacks are no help.

Pieczka gives a powerful performance as the old man, but the background, the beginning of the Communist regime in Poland, is more interesting than the foreground story. — *Strat.*

THE SEARCH FOR SIGNS
OF INTELLIGENT LIFE
IN THE UNIVERSE
(DOCU)

An Orion Classics release of a Tomlin & Wagner Theatricalz presentation. Produced by Paula Mazur. Executive producers, Lily Tomlin, Jane Wagner. Directed by John Bailey. Screenplay, Wagner, based on her play, camera (color), Bailey; editor, Carol Littleton; music, Jerry Goodman; art direction, Ed Richardson; costume design, David Pareles; associate producer, Janet Beroza. Reviewed at Cannes Film Festival (market), May 12, 1991. Running time: **106 MIN.**

This mostly effective screen adaptation of Lily Tomlin's "The Search For Signs Of Intelligent Life In The Universe" is a good bet for Orion Classics in limited theatrical engagements, and pic should thrive on Showtime cable dates and in eventual video release.

Originally performed at nearly three hours, the acclaimed one-woman show (which bowed on Broadway in 1985 and was the subject of a Nick Broomfield-Joan Churchill docu in '86) has been trimmed by a third. It also has been extensively elaborated with stylized sets and lighting to partially obliterate the proscenium effect.

Guiding principle of Tomlin, writer Jane Wagner, director-lenser John Bailey and editor Carol Littleton was to cut, in a variety of ways, between the simply clad Tomlin on a plain stage, and the performer decked out in full costumes and makeup.

After a strikingly designed opening descending upon a dark "Dick Tracy"-esque cityscape, camera settles upon what amounts to the evening's hostess, a bag lady who fancies herself a sort of adviser to an alien species and guide to the human race's assorted foibles and weirdnesses.

This framework provides a springboard to numerous other Tomlin creations, who are placed within stylized sets to vent their complaints and acerbic comments about the sorry state of society, human enlightenment, women's status in the world and the fulfillment of personal hopes and aspirations.

Show introduces such characters as a defensively hostile 15-year-old punkette, her bickering grandparents, a jaded high society lady, a hooker duo in a limo and a male body-builder.

Rather than outright hilarious (at least onscreen), most of the Wagner-Tomlin characters are wryly, ruefully humorous about how even their best efforts and intentions are thwarted in the face of what they can't know or control. Frantically, often hysterically seeking a measure of philosophical well-being, they are mocked by the cosmic context in which they are placed.

Film takes a little while to get on track, but gradually improves as it goes, reaching its highlight in an extended climactic mini-drama that effectively sketches in the history, aspirations, ironies and contradictions of American feminism since the late '60s.

Essaying several highly identifiable characters who bond in the first flowering of the movement, Tomlin concentrates on the personal story of a woman who graduates into a New Age marriage but, despite the couple's raised consciousness, can't avoid the age old pitfalls involving children, careerism, divorce and disillusionment.

Even on celluloid and at reduced length, Tomlin's performance is clearly a tour de force, although her hyperactivity nearly becomes exhausting even for the viewer. As has been the case throughout her career, she displays a brilliant talent for briefly detailing indelible characters, and fans will be grateful to add this to their home libraries.

As was the case onstage, use of sound effects is ingeniously effective, and debuting director Bailey, who also doubled in his usual role of cinematographer, as well as art director Ed Richardson, keep things interesting visually under the intensely concentrated circumstances.

Even though it is often sent up, the New Age terminology is so rampant as to be offputting, and also serves to pinpoint the work's origins in an early 1980s sensibility. But on balance, this is a solid job of transferring a unique piece of theater to the screen. — *Cart.*

AFGHAN BREAKDOWN
(ITALIAN-SOVIET)

A Clemi Cinematografica (Rome)-Lenfilm Studios (Leningrad)-Russkoe Video (Leningrad) co-production, in collaboration with Raidue. (Intl. sales, Sacis.) Produced by Giovanni di Clemente. Directed by Vladimir Bortko. Screenplay, Alexander Tchervinsky, adapted by Gino Capone; camera (Cinecitta color), Zasiadko Leomidovitch; editor, Bruno Micheli; music, Vladimir Draskovic. Reviewed at Cannes Film Festival (market), May 11, 1991. Running time: **108 MIN.**
Major Bandura . . . . . Michele Placido
Katya . . . . Tatiana Doghileva
Also with: Oleg Borisov, Iskander Giafarov, Boris Plotnikov, Nina Ruslanova, Alessandro Stefanelli.
(Italian soundtrack)

The Soviet withdrawal after nine years of war in Afghanistan is given a wacky pastiche treatment in "Afghan Breakdown." Downbeat pic has its darkly comic moments caused by dubbing virtually the entire picture into Italian.

Available in both tv miniseries and feature versions, pic, shot in Turkistan and Leningrad, avoids pretentiousness of such parallel-world films as "The Beast," in which all-American actors played Russians and Afghanis. Instead, Michele Placido is almost the only Italian in sight, but his Russo co-stars speak, and even gesture in, Italian.

He stoically walks through his role of a major sent by a cruel colonel on various missions to protect the Russian flank during the pullout. An air of gloom and defeat is sustained by helmer Vladimir Bortko. The Soviet involvement (never referred to explicitly as an invasion) is criticized heavily.

War horrors are treated here as a given rather than peculiar to the Afghan conflict. The career soldier's p.o.v. and the problems of a dogface are both presented.

Several corny subplots, seemingly truncated in the feature version, fail to arouse much interest. Though married, Placido is carrying on with blond nurse Tatiana Doghileva, who is constantly being hit on by the sex-starved colonel. Several visually impressive battle scenes punctuate the talkfest. Glum finale is a downer, as intended. — *Lor.*

INTIMATE STRANGER

A South Gate Entertainment presentation of a Yoram Pelman-Seiichi Hasumi production. Produced by Yoram Pelman and J.J. Lichauco Pelman. Directed by Allan Holzman. Screenplay, Rob Fresco; camera (color), Ilan Rosenberg; editor, Lorraine Salk; music, Jonathan Sheffer. Reviewed at Cannes Film Festival (market), May 11, 1991. Running time: **94 MIN.**
Cory Wheeler . . . . . Deborah Harry
Nick Ciccini . . . . James Russo
Malcolm Henthoff . . . Tim Thomerson
Meg Wheeler . . . . . . Paige French
D.P. Ashley . . . . . . Grace Zabriskie

This mediocre thriller has an interesting variation on a theme, but "Intimate Stranger" offers little else, apart from the curiosity factor of seeing Deborah Harry in front of the cameras again.

That's despite the film's intriguing beginning and premise: Harry plays a bar singer who earns extra money by taking calls for a sleazy phone sex firm.

Tim Thomerson, who likes to do "nasty" things to women, phones her and kills a prostitute during the call as a prelude to hunting her down. Harry finds the police unsympathetic, but ambitious young cop James Russo offers his help with an eye on promotion. The hunt begins.

Remainder of the pic is pacey enough, but some moments confuse and stretch credibility. Ending is very pedestrian. Russo's zealous behavior to catch his man doesn't ring true, and Thomerson's character and motives are disappointingly un-complex. Harry is fine, but she has some awkward moments with Russo. She also sings during the pic.

Glimpse of the weird world of phone sex is a nice variation — there's a voyeuristic attraction about Harry's calls, some of which are quite amusing — and with the success of "The Silence Of The Lambs," interest in pics dealing with psychopathic baddies might give the pic more mileage. Still, it's hard to imagine it rising above small-screen status.
— *Doch.*

SALE COMME UN ANGE
(DIRTY LIKE AN ANGEL)
(FRENCH)

A Pyramide release of a French Production-CB Films-Cine Manufacture-Veranfilm production. (Intl. sales: Pyramide Intl.) Executive producer, Pierre Sayag. Produced by Emmanuel Schlumberger. Written and directed by Catherine Breillat. Camera (color), Laurent Dailland; editor, Agnes Guillemaut; music, Olivier Manoury; sound, Georges Prat; production design, Olivier Paultre; costumes, Malika Brahim; assistant director, Richard Debuisne. Reviewed at Cannes Film Festival (market), May 15, 1991. Running time: **103 MIN.**
Georges Deblache . . Claude Brasseur
Barbara . . . . Lio
Didier Theron . . . . . Nils Tavernier
Manoni . . . . C.J. Philippe
Judy . . . . Lea Gabrielle
Arlette . . . . Lorella Di Cicco

Catherine Breillart's second feature, "Dirty Like An Angel," is a brutal look at sexual relationships featuring a shockingly frank liaison between a man in his 50s and a much younger woman. Pic will provoke controversy, but deserves film fest and arthouse exposure.

Pic, which bows in France mid-June, has a simple structure. Claude Brasseur plays Deblache, a 50-year-old police inspector who lives alone and basically hates women. His sex life involves joyless one-nighters with prosties. He's sickly, and fears he has cancer, but is so jaded and self-loathing that he hardly cares about his health.

His partner, Theron (well played by Nils Tavernier, son of director Bertrand Tavernier), has recently married Barbara (Lio), and though he regards her as sacred, it doesn't stop him sleeping around with Arab and black women he meets in the course of his work. Deblache's only other friend is a member of the underworld, an informer (C.J. Philippe) who's been quietly squealing on his pals. When they get wise, he realizes his number's up and goes into hiding. Deblache has Theron stake out the informer's home.

With his partner tied up on police business, Deblache starts moving in on the wife. Barbara resists at first, but in a long and harrowing scene finally submits to her husband's partner in a sex act which is part rape, part mutual lust. Though she later says she gave herself under protest, she goes to Deblache's apartment to resume the liaison the following day.

These sex scenes are presented with the same brutal frankness that marked Breillat's first film, "36 Fillettes" (a.k.a. "Virgin"). Femme director's honesty in dealing with sexual relationships is without parallel, but the scenes may be too confrontational and explicit for many audiences. They are not exploitative but incredibly candid in dealing with men and women's desires.

Pic concludes with several layers of irony, and the final freeze-frame will have audiences talking long after the film has ended. Brasseur gives one of his best screen performances as the jaded cop, and Tavernier is convincing as his partner. Both men show a contempt for women that's more shocking than any of the film's sex scenes.

Lio, a singer turned actress, gives a hot performance as the reluctant bride who succumbs to her husband's partner with a mixture of guilt and lust.

As Breillat favors long takes and allows scenes to go to the limit and beyond, the film will pose a marketing problem, and its frankness is possibly more than arthouse audiences may be willing to accept. Technically very good, pic's an important new French film from an interesting and original talent in French cinema. — *Strat.*

VAN GOGH
(FRENCH)

A Gaumont (France) release of an Erato Films-Les Films Canal Plus Films A2-Les Films du Livradois production. Produced by Daniel Toscan du Plantier, Sylvie Danton. Written and directed by Maurice Pialat. Camera (color), Emmanuel Machuel, Gilles Henri, Jacques Loiseleux; editor, Yann Dedet, Nathalie Hubert; sound, Jean-Pierre Duret; costumes, Edith Vesperini; production design, Philippe Pallut, Katia Vischkof; casting, Marie-Jeanne Pascal. Reviewed at Cannes Film Festival (competition), May 19, 1991. Running time: **175 MIN.**
Vincent Van Gogh . . Jacques Dutronc
Marguerite Gachet . Alexandra London
Dr. Gachet . . . . Gerard Sety
Theo Van Gogh . . . . Bernard Le Coq
Jo . . . . Corinne Bourdon
Cathy . . . . Elsa Zylberstein
Adeline Ravoux . . . . Leslie Azzoulai
Also with: Jacques Vidal, Lisa Lametrie, Chantal Barbarit, Claudine Ducret.

Maurice Pialat's long-awaited, expensive "Van Gogh" comes as a surprise because it takes a new slant on the great Dutch painter's life. This sumptuous production omits many of the staple elements of the Van Gogh story, including the famous ear-slashing incident, but still casts a magical spell.

"Van Gogh" opens with the artist's arrival by train in a small village where he visits the local doctor for an examination. Doc is something of an art lover and invites Van Gogh to stay in his house. Van Gogh uses the doctor's lovely young daughter as a model, and eventually they become lovers, to the kindly dad's consternation.

Meanwhile, Van Gogh's relationship with his brother, Theo, grows increasingly tense and bitter. Pialat suggests this was in part because of Vincent's attraction for his brother's wife.

Pialat (who follows directors Vincente Minnelli, Paul Cox and Robert Altman in filming the painter's life) lets scenes linger. A riverside picnic on a sunny Sunday afternoon, a visit to a Paris nightclub where the cancan is danced, or Theo's wife bathing herself in front of her admiring husband all are very relaxed and extended.

This method might irritate people who would prefer a more conventional narrative film about the artist's life (characters like Gauguin are totally omitted here), and yet the director successfully evokes a gentler, less frantic era via these elongated sequences.

The artist's suicidal shooting takes place off-screen, and is followed by a long and poignant death scene. Pic ends on a touching note between the doctor's daughter and an artist who arrives in the village. She tells him Van Gogh was her friend.

This "Van Gogh," estimated to have cost about $10 million, was halted during production when funds ran out. It is certainly visually stunning, but it's hard to see all the money on the screen.

Jacques Dutronc gives a fine performance as the suffering artist, with Alexandra London a delight as the sweet daughter who falls heavily for him. Indeed, playing is fine right down the line, and the film is technically outstanding.

The version screened in competition in Cannes was not quite finished, and lacked titles. Further trimming might make this ambitious picture more acceptable to a wider audience. — *Strat.*

VOICES FROM BEYOND
(ITALIAN)

A Scena Group and Exclusive Cine TV production. (Intl. sales, Wind Film.) Executive producer, Luigi Nannerini. Directed by Lucio Fulci. Screenplay, Fulci, Piero Regnoli, based on Fulci's story; camera (Fuji color), Sandro Grossi; editor, Vincenzo Tomassi; music, Stelvio Cipriani; assistant director, Camilla Fulci; makeup, Pino Ferranti. Reviewed at Cannes Film Festival (market), May 11, 1991. Running time: **89 MIN.**
With: Duilio Del Prete, Karina Huff, Pascal Persiano, Lorenzo Fromarty, Destina Giovannini, Frances Necman.
(English soundtrack)

Italian horror specialist Lucio Fulci takes a new tack with "Voices From Beyond," a stylish gothic thriller that features several novel scares. U.S. video play is in order.

Pic deals with the trendy topic of the afterlife from a horrific point-of-view. After a sexy nightmare prolog, Duilio Del Prete dies in the hospital, but his spirit lingers, anxious to find out who killed him.

When beautiful daughter Karina Huff returns home for the reading of the will, Del Prete appears to her and coaxes her to investigate. Film utilizes interesting flashbacks from various protagonists' viewpoints; almost everyone's a suspect.

What sets "Voices" apart are Fulci's ingenious stagings, which make every-day objects threatening or downright scary. Finale is extremely clever and exposes a new mode for murder.

Del Prete ("Daisy Miller") is droll as the dislikable victim. Huff shows off an impressive figure as the heroine. Articulation by the cast and postsynch in English is acceptable. — *Lor.*

SOAPDISH

A Paramount Pictures release of an Aaron Spelling/Alan Greisman production. Produced by Spelling, Greisman. Executive producer, Herbert Ross. Directed by Michael Hoffman. Screenplay, Robert Harling, Andrew Bergman, from a story by Harling; camera (Technicolor), Ueli Steiger; editor, Garth Craven; music, Alan Silvestri; sound (Dolby), Petur Hliddal, Tom Johnson, Jack Leahy, David Slusser; production design, Eugenio Zanetti; art direction, Jim Dultz; set decoration, Lee Poll; costume design, Nolan Miller; assistant director, John E. Hockridge; coproducers, Joel Freeman, Victoria White; casting, Lora Kennedy. Reviewed at Bruin Theater, L.A., May 21, 1991. MPAA Rating: PG-13. Running time: **95 MIN.**
Celeste Talbert . . . . Sally Field
Jeffrey Anderson . . . . . Kevin Kline
David Barnes . . . Robert Downey Jr.
Montana Moorehead . Cathy Moriarty
Rose Schwartz . . . . Whoopi Goldberg
Lori Craven . . . . Elisabeth Shue
Betsy Faye Sharon . . . Carrie Fisher
Edmund Edwards . . . Garry Marshall
Ariel Maloney . . . . Teri Hatcher
Bolt Brennan . . . . . . Paul Johansson
Also with: Leeza Gibbons, John Tesh, Stephen Nichols.

"Soapdish" aims at a satiric target as big as a Macy's float and intermittently hits it. Sally Field and Kevin Kline play a feuding pair of romantically involved soap opera stars in this broad but amiable sendup of daytime tv. Though it's never quite as outrageous as it thinks it is, or as pointed as it could be, pic should do okay at the boxoffice.

The setup is irresistible. Field, the reigning "queen of misery" on the sudser "The Sun Also Sets," is at the peak of her glory but is going to pieces emotionally. Her latest loser of a married b.f. has dumped her on the night of the Daytime Television Awards, and her life is taking more stomach-churning turns than "As The World Turns."

Amazonian harpy Cathy Moriarty is scheming to take over the show by using her sexual wiles to convince the slimy producer, Robert Downey Jr., to have Field's character destroy her popularity by committing some unspeakable crime, such as murdering a beautiful but mute homeless person played by the star's ambitious niece (Elisabeth Shue).

To drive Field even more off the edge, Downey surprises her by bringing back her long-ago flame, Kevin Kline, whom she had thrown off the show in 1973. Since then he's been languishing in actor's hell — defined here as hemorrhoid commercials and a hilariously awful Florida dinner theater production of "Death Of

A Salesman." Whoopi Goldberg, the show's jaded head writer, flips when told Kline is coming back because his character was written out by having him decapitated in a car crash. Downey helpfully suggests that his head was stitched back on in "a precedent-setting operation."

Also on board are such characters as the casting director with a leering eye for male hunks, Carrie Fisher; the bubble-brained sexpot with a Bride of Frankenstein hairdo, Teri Hatcher; the muscular young stud who improbably plays Field's tv husband, Paul Johansson; and a daytime programming chief who gives new meaning to the words "venal" and "lowbrow," Garry Marshall.

The cynicism of the makers of "The Sun Also Sets" toward their ludicrous product rings true, as does the suitably overripe color of the show's surroundings and the overemoting style that Field and her cohorts slip into both before the tv cameras and in what passes for their "real lives."

Director Michael Hoffman is an efficient ringmaster for this emotional circus, aided by Eugenio Zanetti's glittering circular set, Ueli Steiger's gaudy lensing and the wipes favored by Garth Craven's editing, backed by zingy music from Alan Silvestri.

Writers Robert Harling and Andrew Bergman wisely maintain a farcical rigor throughout, never succumbing to schmaltz, but their frequent amusing lines and situations are mixed in with too many flat or merely silly scenes. The film runs only 95 minutes, but seems longer because of the intermittent dry spots.

The paper-thin characters depend largely on casting to sustain interest. Field works hard and shows an expert sense of comic timing, but the grittily down-to-earth acting persona Field has developed since "Gidget" now makes her seem a bit too reasonable for the zany demands of this script. Nor does she seem glamorous enough to get the most out of a character that demands the screwball charm and offhand sexiness of a Carole Lombard.

Kline is utterly marvelous, though, as a sort of low-rent John Barrymore type, boozing and carousing his way through the ranks of worshipful young actresses but faltering when he's back in the big time and faced with sorting out his and Field's tangled past.

Moriarty, who acts as if she's been staying up late studying Mary Woronov pics, is a scream as Field's deep-voiced, hate-consumed rival, and Marshall distills his long experience in the tv medium into a poison arrow aimed straight into the cold hearts of programming execs.

But Goldberg, while pleasantly tart-tongued as always, isn't given enough to do; Fisher is hardly in the film; Downey mumbles too much for comedy; and Shue, though fielding Kline's pitches with aplomb, seems too unambiguously cute and perky for a role that could have had more grasping Eve Harrington overtones.

Most damaging is the smugness that too often creeps into "Soapdish." As an expression of mockery from a group of "real actors" and "real filmmakers" toward their daytime tv brethren, it misses some of the deeper insights and empathy for the subject that could have made it a more inspired farce.

Having the gushing, toothsome twosome from "Entertainment Tonight," Leeza Gibbons and John Tesh, around as a perpetually astonished Greek chorus provides an incestuous in-house crossplug for Par's film and tv operations, but at the cost of further blurring the satiric point.

The big revelation scene, while amusing enough in its implications for the Field-Kline-Shue triangle, doesn't pack enough seriocomic wallop — or what Mel Brooks once called "serious relief" — to sustain the weight of firstrate farce. — *Mac.*

CITY SLICKERS

A Columbia Pictures release of a Castle Rock Entertainment presentation, in association with Nelson Entertainment, of a Face production. Produced by Irby Smith. Executive producer, Billy Crystal. Directed by Ron Underwood. Screenplay, Lowell Ganz, Babaloo Mandel; camera (color), Dean Semler; editor, O. Nicholas Brown; music, Marc Shaiman; additional music, Hummie Mann; sound (Dolby), Robert Eber; production design, Lawrence G. Paull; art direction, Mark Mansbridge; set decoration, Rick Simpson; costume design, Judy Ruskin; assistant director, Jim Chory; production manager, Edward D. Markley; stunt coordinator, Mickey Gilbert; special effects coordinator, Kenneth D. Pepiot; mechanical animal effects, KNB EFX Group; 2nd unit director (Spain), Fraser Heston; 2nd unit camera, Martin Fuhrer; casting, Pam Dixon, Sally Jackson (New Mexico). Re-viewed at the Columbia Pictures Studios screening room, May 29, 1991. MPAA Rating: PG-13. Running time: **112 MIN.**

Mitch Robbins	Billy Crystal
Phil Berquist	Daniel Stern
Ed Furillo	Bruno Kirby
Barbara Robbins	Patricia Wettig
Bonnie Rayburn	Helen Slater
Curly	Jack Palance
Clay Stone	Noble Willingham
Cookie	Tracey Walter
Barry Shalowitz	Josh Mostel
Ira Shalowitz	David Paymer
Ben Jessup	Bill Henderson
Lou	Jeffrey Tambor
Steve Jessup	Phill Lewis

Also with: Kyle Secor, Dean Hallo, Karla Tamburrelli, Yeardley Smith, Jayne Meadows, Alan Charof.

Columbia should lasso a sizable portion of the boxoffice with this comedy adventure, a deft blend of wry humor and warmth (albeit with a little too much "thirtysomething"-esque angst for its own good). Still, firstrate performances and a strong premise overcome these sins, making "City Slickers" the comedy others may be seeking to catch up with all summer.

Writers Lowell Ganz and Babaloo Mandel manage to work a lot of the same preachy morals about the joys of family into this film that they did in "Parenthood," though they've again done so with enough catchy comic trappings that the medicine goes down with a lot of laughs.

There's also real strength in the relationship among the three principals, who work out their various midlife crises while affirming their friendship in a manner consistent with films like "Diner," which more directly tackled that terrain.

Perhaps most important, the pic provides a showcase for star-exec producer Billy Crystal for the wide range of his talent — from giddy comedy and reaction shots to his softer side that shone through in "When Harry Met Sally." Even with his shameless Oscarcast plug for the film, the comic's career looks to be riding into the sunlight, not the other way around.

The setup is sheer simplicity, as Crystal, coming to grips with the doldrums of midlife thanks to his 39th birthday, is convinced by his wife (Patricia Wettig) and two best friends (Daniel Stern, Bruno Kirby) to take off for two weeks on a ranch driving cattle across the west.

The childhood fantasy comes to life in a number of ways, perhaps foremost in the presence of gnarled trail boss Curly (Jack Palance), a figure always seemingly backlit in larger-than-life silhouettes.

The other cowboy wannabes include a father-and-son dentist team (Bill Henderson, Phill Lewis), fraternal ice-cream tycoons (David Paymer, Josh Mostel) and a beautiful woman (Bonnie Rayburn) who braved the trip on her own.

The latter proves a stab at letting the womenfolk in on the fun, but ultimately this is a game for the boys, as a series of increasingly absurd events lead the central trio toward an ultimate challenge that turns the vacation into a journey of self-discovery.

Still, the route is so well-traveled it's doubtful many will pause to question it. Crystal gets plenty of chance to crack wise while he, Stern and Kirby engage in playful and not-so-playful banter — Stern coming off a recently (and publicly) failed marriage while the womanizing Kirby grapples with his own fear of fidelity.

The film occasionally bogs down during these chattier moments, but director Ron Underwood (who made his feature debut on "Tremors") generally keeps the herd moving at a fine pace.

In addition, the fantasy elements of grown men getting to play cowboy are almost irresistible, and the comedy is often intelligent and nostalgic — especially Crystal's hilarious interaction with Palance's character, who makes the Marlboro man seem like a wimp.

As usual, Crystal skillfully capitalizes on seminal touches from his own tv-bred youth, such as the trio humming the "Bonanza" theme during their triumphant moment.

Stern continues to be one of the best sidekicks around, while Kirby is equally impressive as the sex-obsessed Ed. As a footnote, look for Yeardley Smith, the voice of Lisa Simpson, in a cameo as the object of Stern's own marital indiscretion.

Tech credits are terrific and heighten the film's western elements, from the camerawork of Dean Semler (Oscar-winner for "Dances With Wolves") to Marc Shaiman's lively score and Judy Ruskin's western getups.

Despite its few shortcomings, pic is aptly named: a slick, yet smart, bit of summer entertainment. — *Bril.*

RAW NERVE

A Pyramid Distribution release from AIP Studios release of a Winters Group production, in association with Sovereign Investment. Produced by Ruta K. Aras. Executive producers, David Winters, Marc Winters. Directed by David A. Prior. Screenplay, Prior, Lawrence L. Simeone; camera (Image Transform color), Andrew Parke; editor, Tony Malanowski; music, Greg Turner; sound, Palmer Norris; art direction, Betty (B.J.) Cline; production manager-associate producer, Robert Willoughby; assistant director, Teddy Lee; stunt coordinator, Bob Ivy; casting, Gerald Wolfe & Associates, Tanya Suzanne (Alabama). Reviewed on AIP videcassette, N.Y., May 24, 1991. MPAA Rating: R. Running time: **93 MIN.**
Capt. Gavin . . . . Glenn Ford
Gloria . . . . Sandahl Bergman
Blake Garrett . . . Randall (Tex) Cobb
Jimmy Clayton . . . . Ted Prior
Gina Clayton . . . . Traci Lords
Lt. Bruce Ellis . . Jan-Michael Vincent
Dave . . . . Red West
Lori . . . . Yvonne St. Ancil

Unusual casting perks up this perfunctory murder mystery. Released at regional theaters May 24, "Raw Nerve" is primarily a video title.

Eyebrows may be raised at a pic co-starring Hollywood icon Glenn Ford and Traci Lords, but pic proves to be a significant transitional film for the ex-porn queen. She handles dramatic scenes well in the first feature not to treat her as a caricature.

She plays the 18-year-old sister of Ted Prior, a young man troubled by nightmarish visions that prove to be accurate accounts of serial murders. He goes to the police with this info but is brushed aside as a kook by the captain, Ford, and detective on the case, Jan-Michael Vincent.

Vincent's ex-wife, Sandahl Bergman, is an aggressive reporter who listens to Prior and writes up his story. Of course Prior becomes the No. 1 suspect, but after a revelation of incest (à la "Chinatown") the killer is identified. A final twist comes as an anticlimax.

Acting is good, with action vet Prior showcased opposite Lords in a complicated central role. Name talent in support delivers pro turns.

Director David A. Prior makes good use of Mobile, Ala., locations but the film is too talky to qualify as an action pic, his prior specialty. A final reel stunt is well-done, however. — *Lor.*

TO METEORO VIMA TO PELARGOU
(THE SUSPENDED STEP OF THE STORK)
(GREEK-FRENCH-SWISS-ITALIAN)

A Theo Angelopoulos, Arena Films, Greek Film Center, Vega Film, Erre Produzioni co-production, with the participation of Canal Plus, ERT-1, RAI-2, Greek Ministry of Culture & Communication. (Intl. sales: Mainstream Films.) Produced by Bruno Pesery, Theo Angelopoulos. Directed by Angelopoulos. Screenplay, Angelopoulos, Tonino Guerra, Petros Markaris, Thanassis Valtinos; camera (Eastmancolor), Giorgos Arvanitis, Andreas Sinanos; editor, Giannis Tsitsopoulos; music, Helena Karaindrou; sound, Marinos Athanassopoulos; production design, Mikes Karapiperis; production manager, Phoebe Economopoulou; assistant director, Takis Katselis; co-producers, Ruth Waldburger, Angelo Rizzoli; casting, Charis Papadopoulos. Reviewed at Cannes Film Festival (competition), May 17, 1991. Running time: **151 MIN.**
The refugee . . . Marcello Mastroianni
The wife . . . . Jeanne Moreau
The journalist . . . . . . Gregory Karr
Dora . . . . Chrysikou
The colonel . . . . . . Ilias Logothetis

Up to the minute in its concerns and made with rigor and spare beauty, "The Suspended Step Of The Stork" finds leading Greek director Theo Angelopoulos in a somber mood. Long drama about refugees and separated families is a clarion call for the elimination of national boundaries.

Pic may find responsive audiences among those willing to go along with the director's slow pacing and demanding style. Top international stars Marcello Mastroianni and Jeanne Moreau, co-starring for the first time since Antonioni's "The Night" 31 years ago, have key but marginal roles.

Focus is on Gregory Karr, who plays a tv journalist covering a story about refugees from Albania, Kurdistan and Iran who are arriving in Greece by the trainload. In their own language, representatives from the three countries give vent to their anxiety, displacement and fear. These are timely scenes.

On one train, the journalist spots a middle-aged man he's certain was a Greek politician with a promising career who disappeared some years earlier. Karr finds the missing man's French wife (Moreau), who has remarried and has a new life, but who comes to the border to see the refugee who could be her missing husband. But she claims not to recognize him, though a videotape the journalist plays suggests that she is lying and that the man (played with quiet authority by Mastroianni) is, in fact, the missing politico.

Alongside this story is that of a young refugee woman (presumably Albanian) with whom the journalist has an affair. She is to marry a man stranded on the other side of the river that forms the border between Greece and their country. The film's climax consists of a bizarre wedding ceremony with the groom on one side of the frontier, the bride on the other, and the military keeping a watchful eye.

The film's title is derived from the step that takes one across the line between two countries. Angelopoulos savagely attacks the folly of such arbitrary international divisions. During production, the director was excommunicated by the bishop of Florina, the northern Greek city where the film was shot, because the traditionalist bishop considered the film anti-Greek.

Though the new film is beautifully shot, it is sometimes agonizingly slow. But Angelopoulos' regular cameraman, Giorgis Arvanitis, with assistant Andreas Sinanos, create stunning images of wintry landscapes and have once again devised the intricate crane and tracking shots that are the director's trademark.

This lengthy and slow film will be difficult to market, but interest in Angelopoulos' films seems to be growing around the world, and "Suspended Step" will be greeted with excitement by the director's supporters. However, those unprepared for the helmer's ultra-deliberate style will find the going rugged. Technically, pic is quite superb and the score is striking. Editing could have been tighter. — *Strat.*

YUMEJI
(JAPANESE)

A Genjiro Arato Pictures production. Produced by Genjiro Arato. Directed by Seijun Suzuki. Screenplay, Yozo Tanaka; camera (color), Junichi Fujisawa; editor, Akira Suzuki; music, Kaname Kawachi, Shigeru Umebayashi; art direction, Notiyoshi Ikeya. Reviewed at Cannes Film Festival (Un Certain Regard), May 18, 1991. Running time: **128 MIN.**
Yumeji Takehisa . . . . . Kenji Sawada
Also with: Tomoko Mariya, Yoshio Harada, Tamasaburo Bandoh, Masumi Miyazaki, Reona Hirota, Kazuhiko Hasegawa.

"Yumeji" is a flat biopic of the Japanese artist and poet Yumeji Takehisa, a playboy who apparently led a life of Western-style decadence from the 1920s until his death in 1934. Static, non-psychological, unerotic treatment offers nothing to the Western viewer.

Director Seijun Suzuki, now nearly 70, attained a certain celebrity under the name Suzuki Seitaro for his yakuza pictures in the 1960s. More recently, he has written books and directed for the big and small screens.

Given the personality of the subject, one might have hoped for something a bit spicy or analytical. Instead, Suzuki and his scenarist have concocted a story of surpassing blandness, a hodgepodge of symbolism, fantasy and random encounters.

Yumeji, imagining that he is involved in a duel, sets off for Kanazawa, where an intended assignation with one lover turns into an affair with another. Latter's husband, Wakiya, has been killed, but his ghost reappears to run roughshod over several people's lives, threaten Yumeji and take up entirely too much running time.

As an artist, Yumeji appears to have been a sort of poor man's Beardsley, tending toward delicate sketches of nubile women. As a character, he is entirely too ineffectual to anchor the film, his frequent couplings with women proving repetitive and unmemorable.

In the end, he comes off as a self-styled fashion follower of no particular interest, which can hardly have been filmmaker's intent.

Most interesting touches are some clever optical superimpositions and juxtapositions designed to relate his life to his work, but film overall is marked by a dull estheticism and a stylization that is more annoying than eye-catching. — *Cart.*

THE FALLS
(CANADIAN-DOCU)

A Primitive Features production in association with the National Film Board of Canada. Produced by Michael McMahon, Brian Dennis. Executive producers, George Flak, Clare Odgers. Written and directed by Kevin McMahon. Narrated by Rita McMahon. Camera (color), Douglas Koch; editor, Michael McMahon; music, Kurt Swinghammer; sound, Marvin Lawrence, Velcrow Ripper. Reviewed at Cannes Film Festival (market), May 19, 1991. Running time: **90 MIN.**

This comprehensive docu on Niagara Falls is loaded with stunning footage, revealing interviews and historical tidbits. A clever examination of the physical decay and moral corruption of a natural wonder, "The Falls" is definitely no promo reel.

Award-winning docu helmer Kevin McMahon ("The Zoo") hits all the tourist landmarks, from kitschy souvenir shops to wax museums, as pic's sharp narrative and ironic lens dissect the "honeymoon capital."

"Falls" also tackles the toxic waste issue via the environmental disaster at Love Canal. An interview with one of the Love Canal victims (a woman whose infant was born with birth defects) is strung throughout the film.

Unfortunately, pic doesn't adequately drive home the fact that Love Canal isn't over yet (the U.S. government has given developers the green light to build a new suburb on the toxic landfill site).

Pic's real strength is a poetic Laurie Anderson-style narrative. The powerful soundtrack is another asset.

But "Falls" isn't fare for general audiences. Distribs or tv programmers will have to target inquisitive audiences. Pic is an educational tool and an archivist's dream. — *Suze.*

HEARTS OF DARKNESS: A FILMMAKER'S APOCALYPSE
(DOCU)

A Showtime presentation of a ZM production in association with Zoetrope Studios. Produced by George Zaloom, Les Mayfield. Executive producers, Doug Claybourne, Fred Roos. Written and directed by Fax Bahr with George Hickenlooper. Documentary footage direct-ed by Eleanor Coppola. Editor, Michael Greer, Jay Miracle; music, Todd Boekelheide; music from "Apocalypse Now" by Carmine Coppola, Francis Coppola; percussion tracks from "Apocalypse Now," Mickey Hart. Reviewed at Cannes Film Festival (Un Certain Regard), May 17, 1991. Running time: **96 MIN.**

With: Francis Coppola, Eleanor Coppola, John Milius, George Lucas, Tom Sternberg, Dean Tavoularis, Martin Sheen, Vittorio Storaro, Robert Duvall, Larry Fishburne, Sam Bottoms, Frederic Forrest, Albert Hall, Monty Cox, Fred Roos, Doug Claybourne, Dennis Hopper.

Sixty hours of footage on the making of "Apocalypse Now" have been cut down and put to informative, enormously entertaining use in this feature documentary. Benefiting from full access to the Zoetrope archives, cooperation from nearly all key artistic personnel and a decade's hindsight, filmmakers have put together an incisive look at one of the most titanic, problem-plagued and, finally, memorable productions in film history.

The first documentary backed by Showtime, pic will be broadcast on the cable net this fall. In the meantime, it is a natural for fests and some theatrical dates. In exchange for its participation, Zoetrope holds all foreign rights.

At his Cannes Film Festival press conference 12 years ago, Francis Coppola said, "My film is not a movie about Vietnam. It is Vietnam. It is what it was really like. It was crazy.

"And the way we made it was very much like the Americans were in Vietnam. We were in the jungle; there were too many of us. We had access to too much money and too much equipment, and, little by little, we went insane."

Docu verifies that Coppola was not exaggerating. As an "officially approved" version of events, pic may tread a little lightly over the drug use and personal dramas played out during the 238 days of shooting, but the escalating insanity and surreal nature of the undertaking is made abundantly clear by the footage and commentary.

Cleverly beginning with a 1938 broadcast of Orson Welles' radio adaptation of "Heart Of Darkness" and an account of Welles' aborted attempt to film Joseph Conrad's classic novella, writer-directors Fax Bahr and George Hickenlooper then launch into George Lucas' original plans to shoot on location in Vietnam in the late 1960s.

"We probably would have been there in time for Tet," remarks John Milius, who wrote the script.

When Coppola, after his "Godfather" successes, took it on in 1975, the project had a $13 million budget and a 16-week shooting schedule. Footage covering the production, all of it shot by Coppola's wife, Eleanor, begins with an early reading of a scene and proceeds to early lensing in the Philippines. After a week, Harvey Keitel, cast as Willard, was let go and soon replaced by Martin Sheen.

In fresh, first-hand fashion, pic documents the disasters that befell the production — the diversion of needed helicopters to fight communist rebels in the mountains, Coppola's need to inject his own cash and guarantee overages with his personal holdings, Sheen's absence for five weeks after a heart attack, a typhoon that destroyed the elaborate sets, the soaring of the schedule and budget to more than $30 million, and the desperate search for an ending once an overweight Marlon Brando finally arrived.

For anyone interested in films, and "Apocalypse Now" in particular, docu is a feast. There are extraordinary glimpses of the typhoon, the French plantation sequence that was cut from the final film, Coppola's weight and beard changing dramatically throughout the lensing, the ironically festive celebrations marking the 100th, then 200th days of shooting, and the precarious sequence involving some of the actors and a huge tiger.

Also compelling are Sam Bottoms' admission of extensive drug consumption on the picture, dailies of Sheen's crazed freakout tug-of-war with the director over the fact that he hadn't learned his lines, and vivid depictions of the blood rites of the locals hired as extras for Kurtz' compound.

The whimsical nature of Marlon Brando's participation in various projects over the years has been much written about, but no number of words can ever match the insight into him provided by the glimpses of his work here. Proceeding "without a road map" and paying his star $1 million per week, Coppola indulged Brando with endless improvisations.

In fragments, the results could be brilliant, seemingly justifying the expense and exasperation. But it turned out that the actor hadn't even read the Conrad story and was basically groping for an approach, calling off work for the day when he didn't feel like continuing.

Coppola finally concluded, "He didn't give a shit," and Brando was the only major figure connected to the production who was unwilling to be interviewed.

Private tape recordings made at the time of unwitting participants also reveal the progressive dementia on the set, and Coppola's radical mood shifts are striking.

Ultimately, however, a portrait emerges of a filmmaker who, for reasons both foolish and daring, pushed himself through countless psychological, physical, financial and artistic barriers to arrive at a result that is arguably a work of art.

Nominally narrated by Eleanor Coppola, who years ago published "Notes," her diary of the shoot, this docu leaves the viewer wanting more. Expertly edited by Michael Greer and Jay Miracle, pic is an outstanding addition to the visual literature on the history of film. — *Cart.*

ANNA KARAMAZOVA
(FRENCH-SOVIET)

A UGC (France) release of a Mosfilm-Victoria Film Production-Parimedia-Mosmedia coproduction. Produced by Serge Silberman. Written and directed by Rustam Khamdamov. Camera (color, b&w), Yuri Klimenko; editor, Irina Brozkovskaya; music, Alexander Vustin; art direction, Vladimir Murzine; production manager, Gennadi Kovalenko. Reviewed at Cannes Film Festival (competing), May 15, 1991. Running time: **113 MIN.**

Woman	Jeanne Moreau
Natasha	Natasha Eble
Young man	Victor Sibilyov
Silent film star	Elena Solovei
Rich man	Yuri Solomine
His wife	Natalia Fateeva

Returning to filmmaking after years of inactivity, Soviet-born painter Rustam Khamdamov's visual flair gets lost in the pretentiousness of a tired exercise in avant-garde cinema. Long, slow and self-indulgent, the Serge Silberman/Mosfilm coprod "Anna Karamazova" has slim prospects post-Cannes beyond fest playdates.

Lest the familiar title raise expectations, the pic has nothing to do with "Anna Karenina" or "The Brothers Karamazov," except an undue affection for old Russia.

Story revolves around an aging woman (Jeanne Moreau) who gets out of Stalin's prison camps in the 1940s and realizes she has no place in the brave new Soviet world. Made up like an old crony for most of the film (except in one scene at the theater where she looks magnificent), Moreau is a spectral figure.

Khamdamov quickly casts aside storytelling to indulge his taste for the surreal. One such image features two Uzbek women in folk costumes pulling a spool of thread from a baby's mouth.

Then comes an overlong sequence in which a little girl claims to have poisoned her grandfather. The sequence is set in a spacious apartment littered with Malevich paintings and other arty paraphernalia of lost Russian culture, which, in this context, one mourns very little.

The film really belongs to cinematographer Yuri Klimenko, whose pyrotechnics reach their peak in the lengthy black & white midsection — a takeoff on silent films that isn't especially related to the Moreau story.

Interestingly, this segment is all that survives of Khamdamov's unfinished 1974 pic, "Slave of Love." Nikita Mikhalkov went on to direct the famous version with the same actress (Elena Solovei). Though inconsistent (the film starts out silent, then introduces sound), the tale of two silent film actresses overtaken by the revolution is unquestionably the most interesting part of "Anna Karamazova" — and the only part that really makes sense.

Moreau bravely walks through the role of the mysterious lady, contributing a strong presence but little in the way of a performance. Victor Sibilyov adds a spark of life as an eccentric young musician she beds.

Notable is Alexander Vustin's music, inspired by classical compositions. — *Yung.*

BLACK DEMONS
(ITALIAN)

A Filmakers production. (Intl. sales, the Film Co., Rome.) Produced by Giuseppe Garguilo. Directed by Umberto Lenzi. Screenplay, Olga Pehar, from Lenzi's story; camera (Technicolor), Maurizio Dell'Orco; editor, Varlo Amici; music, Franco Micalizzi; sound, Gianni D'Amico; assistant director, Frank Farrell; special makeup effects, Frank Casagni; casting, Paul Werner. Reviewed at Cannes Film Festival (market), May 16, 1991. Running time: **86 MIN.**
Dick . . . . Keith Van Hoven
Kevin . . . . Joe Balogh
Jessica . . . . Sonia Curtis
(English soundtrack)

Macumba-style black magic on location in Brazil

makes for a ho-hum Italian horror programmer. Some gory makeup effects and attractive locations are all this one has to offer. Prolific action director Umberto Lenzi has trouble padding this slim story out to feature length.

Keith Van Hoven, his sister Sonia Curtis and her British boyfriend Joe Balogh are in Rio where Van Hoven attends a ritual dance with killed-chicken and all the trimmings. He receives an amulet of Ogum and unwittingly becomes a force of evil.

When the youngsters' jeep breaks down on the road, they stay at a mansion inhabited by two youths and their black maid. Van Hoven is drawn mysteriously to a cemetery nearby where he plays back a tape of the Macumba ceremony and conjures up six black zombies from their graves.

It turns out the mansion is cursed and the blacks are runaway slaves who were recaptured, tortured and hung 100 years ago. Their revenge turns out to be killing six white people.

Direct sound recording of the English dialog is professionally executed. Heroine Curtis suffers through several verbose speeches that border on the comical. Cast is very weak, and it's often difficult to decipher if Van Hoven is acting like a zombie or simply a zombie-like actor.

Franco Micalizzi's score is an asset, making atmospheric use of marimba sounds. — *Lor.*

LIQUID DREAMS

A Fox/Elwes Corp. presentation of a Zeta Entertainment production. Produced by Zane W. Levitt, Diane Firestone. Executive producers, Ted Fox, Cassian Elwes. Directed by Mark Manos. Screenplay, Zack Davis, Manos; camera (color), Sven Kirsten; editor, Karen Joseph; music, Ed Tomney; production design, Pam Moffat; costume design, Merrie Lawson; choreography, Lexandre Magno; associate producer, Zack Davis. Reviewed at Cannes Film Festival (Intl. Critics Week), May 15, 1991. Running time: **91 MIN.**
Rodino . . . . Richard Steinmetz
Eve Black . . . . Candice Daly
The Major . . . . Barry Dennen
Juno . . . . Juan Fernandez
Cecil . . . . Tracey Walter
Paula . . . . Frankie Thorn
Maurice . . . . James Oseland
Felix . . . . Mink Stole
Violet . . . . Marilyn Tokuda
Cab driver . . . . John Doe

A strong array of new talent announces itself in "Liquid Dreams," a flashy ultra-low-

budget sci-fier edgy enough to attract a cult following. Hot direction, lensing, music and an even hotter new actress provide a healthy share of cheap thrills in a weird tale that wears thin only when conventional plotting takes the upper hand.

An adventurous small distributor could get some mileage out of this one, although brighter prospects loom in video.

A solicitous L.A. cabbie (rocker John Doe) drops gorgeous new Kansas arrival Eve Black (Candice Daly) at a dark, intimidating housing complex, where Eve finds her sister brutally murdered in her room. Dissatisfied with the dismissive attitude of the police, Eve moves in to launch her own investigation, which immerses her in the bizarre world of Neuro-Vid.

Violent, sexually degrading and mind-numbingly repetitive, NV is ceaselessly broadcast, "1984"-style, in all apartments, clearly with the intent of anesthetizing the citizenry. Despite the squalidness of the surroundings, Eve stays on to pursue her sister's killer, first by working as a taxi dance girl, then quickly rising through the ranks as an exotic video dancer and, finally, as a performer in a private show for the Major (Barry Dennen), the creator of NV.

Along the way, multiple killings are perpetrated by the Major's sadistic enforcer (Juan Fernandez), and a very tentative romance begins between Eve and a police detective (Richard Steinmetz). But first-time director Mark Manos rightly devotes most of his attention to the sex-and-violence turn-ons and the lurid atmospherics, exhibiting flair to spare in both areas.

Working on a few cheap sets, Manos, production designer Pam Moffat and cinematographer Sven Kirsten manage to convincingly create a whole world, a claustrophobic urban hell defined by the brutal domination of young women by warped men. Naturally, the film has it both ways, serving up a succession of titilating scenes just as it condemns the exploitation of sex.

But Manos clearly has some analytical smarts, and knows just what he wants to show and how long he should show it. Numerous sequences are hypnotic in their effect, and even if interest flags a bit during the perfunctory sleuthing of the climax, a genuinely sinister ambiance has been created here on the most limited of means.

Holding the film together through thick and thin is blonde leading lady Daly. The most stunning newcomer to arise from the exploitation ranks in recent memory, she is uncommonly sexy while managing to never take off all her clothes, but distinguishes herself through a projection of unusual poise and intelligence in dubious circumstances.

Reacting to almost continuous jeopardy, she keeps a check on hysteria and fear, registering instead a resourcefulness that is not too gung ho and a wary skepticism that is not unbelievably cool. In short, she's a knockout.

Fernandez is supremely evil as the cruel sergeant-at-arms, while Dennen proves suitably icy as the Major, who has created NV as a way to overcome a physical deficiency of an appalling (and explicitly seen) nature.

Ed Tomney's sensationally fine score aids the film tremendously, as does Karen Joseph's propulsive editing. Pic will serve as an effective calling card for many of its contributors. — *Cart.*

INDIO 2—THE REVOLT
(ITALIAN)

A Filiberto Bandini presentation of an RPA Intl. production. (Intl. sales, Sacis, in association with Adriana Chiesa Enterprises.) Produced by Bandini. Executive producer, Enrico Coletti. Directed by Anthony M. Dawson (Antonio Margheriti). Screenplay, Gianfranco Bucceri, Bandini, from Bandini's story; camera (Panavision, Technicolor), Roberto Benvenuti; editor, Angela Cipriani; music, Pino Donaggio; sound (Dolby), Umberto Montesanti; assistant director, Edoardo Margheriti; makeup, Franco Di Girolamo. Reviewed at Cannes Film Festival (market), May 10, 1991. Running time: **99 MIN.**
Sgt. Iron . . Marvelous Marvin Hagler
Indian guide . . . . Frank Cuervo
Vincent Van Eyck . . . . . Dirk Galuba
Mrs. Morrell . . . . . Tetchie Agbayani
Priest . . . . Maurizio Fardo
Mama Lou . . . . Jacqueline Carol
IMC president . . . . . Charles Napier
(Original English soundtrack)

With "Indio 2 — The Revolt," Italy provides an entertaining exploitation film with a message. Action specialist Antonio Margheriti reveals that a little gore never hurt a social conscience tract (see Gillo Pontecorvo's "Burn").

Ex-boxing champ Marvelous Marvin Hagler had a character part as a marine sergeant helping Francesco Quinn in the original pic. Quinn's character, a Brazilian Indian who's a U.S. marine, is killed at the beginning of the sequel, and Hagler (taking over the central role) vows revenge.

Hagler's line readings are flat, but his physical presence and ingratiating clowning are in context. After topically reciting the story of "Spartacus" to the Amazon Indians, he leads them cleverly in pitched battles with heinous South African villian Vincent Van Eyck (Dirk Galuba). Van Eyck is dropping acid defoliants on the forest and people alike while using the Indians as slave labor to clear the road for his mining company.

Sluggishly paced, film climaxes after an hour with explosions and a battle victory for the Indians. Remainder of the pic is repetitious though Hagler's mano-a-mano fight in an explosion pool of mud (straight out of Henri-Georges Clouzot's classic "Wages Of Fear") is worth waiting for. Margheriti's patented pyrotechnic scenes are also a plus.

Oddball cast is okay, with Filipino beauty Tetchie Agbayani looking a shade too glamorous as Quinn's widow. Widescreen lensing in Borneo, Brazil, Argentina and the Philippines is above average for an Italian-produced actioner. — *Lor.*

LA REVOLTE DES ENFANTS
(THE CHILDREN'S REBELLION)
(FRENCH)

A UGC release of a Blue Films-La Sept production. (Intl. sales: UGC Intl.) Produced by Raymond Blumenthal, Philippe Melenec. Written and directed by Gerard Poitou-Weber. Camera (color), Dominique Brenguier; editor, Colette Farrugia; music, René Aubry; sound, Dominique Duchatelle; production design, Claude Lenoir; production manager, Sylvie Barthet; assistant director, Antoine Santana; casting, Claude Martin. Reviewed at Unifrance screening room, Paris, May 6, 1991. (In Cannes Film Festival, market.) Running time: **127 MIN.**
Uncle . . . . Michel Aumont
M. Alexis . . . . André Wilms
Countess Marie D'Ozeray . . . .
. . . . Clementine Amouroux
Leon Astier . . . . Robinson Stevenin
Mme. Alexis . . . . . Nadia Strancar
Priest . . . . Daniel Laloux
Jeanne . . . . . Dominique Reymond

An intimate period drama about a revolt of child convicts at an isolated French prison is the subject of tv director Gerard Poitou-Weber's first feature. Despite some affecting moments, the pacing (especially in the first half) is too slow to provoke audience interest in theatrical. Tv exposure looms as a better bet internationally.

Pic also is available as a two-part tv miniseries.

During the Industrial Revolution, youngsters could be jailed just for stealing food. The film is set in 1847 in a prison for young offenders and run by a martinet (Michel Aumont) known derisively as Uncle.

A senior member of the prison staff (André Wilms) seeks reform and has invited a woman journalist (Clementine Amouroux) from Paris to help.

Events move slowly until, over an hour into the pic, the children (some in their late teens) finally rebel and capture the prison, putting Uncle and the more vicious guards in their own cells. Wilms seizes his chance to sign a pact with the rebel leaders for better conditions, but soldiers arrive triggering a battle in which Wilms and several young rebels die.

Events are routinely handled in a film that fails to make a great impression despite the care taken with production design and camerawork, and cast's best efforts.

Top-billed Aumont gives one of his less effective performances as the prison boss, but young Robinson Stevenin is good as the most prominent of the small fry. Technically, pic is up to par.
— *Strat.*

HOTEL OKLAHOMA

A European American Entertainment production. (Intl. sales: Eagle Entertainment.) Produced by Terry Kahn, Ed Elbert, Gregory Vanger. Executive producers, Lawrence Vanger, Martin Barab. Directed by Bobby Houston. Screenplay, Houston, Lisa Sutton, based on story by Elbert, Kahn, Houston; camera (Consolidated color), Alan Caso; editor, Erica Flaum; music, Toby Fitch; sound (Ultra-Stereo), David O'Daniel; production design, Clare Scarpulla; art direction, Mike Costanza; assistant director, Mike Dempsey; production manager-co-producer, Tony Payne; stunt coordinator, Bobby Sargent. Reviewed at Cannes Film Festival (market), May 17, 1991. MPAA Rating: R. Running time: **103 MIN.**
Tommy Lane . . . . David Keith
Deputy warden Charles . Deborah May
Warden Hayes . . . . . Ray Sharkey
Blanche . . . . Karen Black
Kristen Bell . . . . . . Kristen Cloke
Joy . . . . Charlie Spradling
Ray . . . . Rick Dean
Also with: Loretta Devine, Paddi Edwards.

The women's prison genre is sent way over the top in "Hotel Oklahoma," a feature long on silliness and short on exploitation footage. Paycable seems its logical outlet as a time killer.

Pic was titled "Chained Heat II" during production last year at Oklahoma State Penitentiary, but bears little resemblance to the 1983 Sybil Danning-Linda Blair hit.

Film begins in standard fashion with young innocent Kristen Cloke sent to prison as accomplice in lieu of her b.f. David Keith, after latter steals a wedding ring from an uppity jeweler. Director Bobby Houston rushes through the clichés: examination scene, shower scene, with no nudity in the entire pic.

Main subplot involves lesbianism in stir, with Cloke traumatized after being promoted to supervisor status when she unwittingly permits a murder involving a lesbian triangle. The head of prison security, Rick Dean, tries to rape Cloke early on, and succeeds in the final reel. As a camp bonus, Karen Black is on hand as a complete nut among the already fairly crazy prison population.

Parallel story is beyond farfetched: Chatting up Ray Sharkey in a bar, Keith blows his cover but lucks out when Sharkey has a fatal car crash chasing him. He steals the corpse's identity, and believe it or not, Sharkey is the new warden headed to take over the correctional facility where Cloke happens to be staying.

While retaining some of the violence of the pic's first half, latter section is played for laughs as Keith keeps dodging detection in his efforts to spring Cloke. Final reel is loaded with ludicrous twists that require most of the leads to step out of character. A happy ending for Cloke and Keith is thrown in out of left field.

Peppy cast almost makes this watchable, though plain-Jane Cloke doesn't fare well with her emotional breakdown scenes. Keith is breezy, and Deborah May as the nasty deputy warden is credible. Feminine pulchritude is provided by Charlie Spradling, vamping Keith as a trustee-prisoner who's allowed to violate the dress code.

On location lensing and mainly unglamorous casting of inmates provide the film's only nod to reality. — *Lor.*

THE SERVANTS OF TWILIGHT

A Trimark Pictures release. Produced by Jeffrey Obrow, Venetia Stevenson. Executive producers, Mark Amin, Andrew Lane, Joel Levine, Wayne Crawford. Directed by Obrow. Screenplay, Obrow, Stephen Carpenter, based on Dean R. Koontz' book "Twilight," camera (CFI, Deluxe color), Antonio Soriano; editor, Doug Ibold, Eric Ghaffari; music, Jim Manzie; sound (Ultra-Stereo), George Alch; assistant director, John E. Vohlers; production manager-associate producer, David Witz; stunt coordinator, Bud Davis; additional camera, Voya Mikulic, Paul Ryan; bat effects, Michael McCraken; co-producer, William Sachs; casting, Michelle Guillermin. Reviewed at Cannes Film Festival (market), May 10, 1991. MPAA Rating: R. Running time: **95 MIN.**
Charlie . . . . Bruce Greenwood
Christine Scavello . . . . Belinda Bauer
Grace Spivey . . . . . Grace Zabriskie
Henry Rankin . . . . Richard Bradford
Joey Scavello . . . . . Jarrett Lennon
Kyle . . . . Carel Struycken
Dr. Denton Boothe . . . . . Jack Kehoe
Sherri . . . . Kelli Maroney
Wilford . . . . Dale Dye
Also with: James Haner, Bruce Locke, Al White, Dante D'Andre.

Breathless suspense denotes this horror thriller, an unbelievable yet engrossing exercise in paranoia. Except for its B-picture lack of adequate production values, "The Servants Of Twilight" would stand a theatrical shot.

Invading "The Omen" territory minus special effects, this pic demonstrates that novelist Dean R. Koontz could be the next big-screen brand name in a genre dominated by Stephen King and Clive Barker. His plotting here is functional and elevated by director Jeffrey Obrow to a fever pitch.

Told in flashback by bearded private eye Bruce Greenwood to his shrink Jack Kehoe, story has the same feel as the classic "Invasion Of The Body Snatchers."

Months earlier, clean-shaven Greenwood decided to go back into the field after a year's layoff to help beautiful mom in distress Belinda Bauer. She and her young son (Jarrett Lennon) are being terrorized by religious fanatic Grace Zabriskie and her Church of the Twilight zealots.

They've tabbed Lennon as the young anti-Christ, and, before you can say Damien, they're making life for him and Bauer hell. When Greenwood's operatives are killed, he and the client duo take to the road, with Zabriskie's henchmen always hot on their tail.

The rapid succession of shoot-outs and narrow escapes is hard to believe but well staged for cliffhanger excitement.

Broad hints establish early on who's the fink among the good guys, and only a neophyte viewer won't suspect cute little Lennon of being too good to be true. Except for some pulsating bladders on the neck at the film's climax and some unimpressive bat effects, the film is not fantastic enough along the way to impress genre fans.

If the goal was to root the action in a routine policier format, success is without reward.

Zabriskie of "Twin Peaks" is perfectly cast as the fanatical villainess. Greenwood and Bauer are empathetic leads, and grotesque-looking Carel Struycken is the most frightening henchman since his role model, Michael Berryman of "The Hills Have Eyes." Visuals are mundane and mainly lack atmosphere.

Absent elsewhere is the poetry of an eerie overhead vista of Greenwood literally going crazy in a pet cemetery. — *Lor.*

CLEARCUT
(CANADIAN)

An Alliance Intl. release of a Cinexus production, with the participation of Telefilm Canada, Ontario FDC. Produced by Stephen J. Roth, Ian McDougall. Directed by Richard Bugajski. Screenplay, Rob Forsyth, based on the novel "A Dream Like Mine" by M.T. Kelly; camera (Eastmancolor), François Protat; editor, Michael Rea; music, Shane Harvey; sound, Clark McCarron; production design, Perri Gorrara; special effects, Ted Ross; 2nd unit director, McDougall; postproduction supervisor, Catherine Hunt; assistant director, Bill Spahic; casting, Deirdre Bowen. Reviewed at Cannes Film Festival (market), May 13, 1991. Running time: **96 MIN.**
Peter Maguire . . . . Ron Lea
Arthur . . . . Graham Greene
Bud Rickets . . . . Michael Hogan
Wilf . Floyd (Red Crow) Westerman
Journalist . . . . Rebecca Jenkins

A rugged outdoor pic featuring a topflight performance from Graham Greene ("Dances With Wolves"), "Clearcut" raises many issues within an entertaining kidnap drama format. This provocative Canadian pic could catch on in selected theaters and perhaps open wider unless the combination of serious subjects and grim violence prove commercially incompatible bedfellows.

Greene, rebelling against the white man's destruction of native lands, kidnaps the boss of a sawmill (Michael Hogan) as well as a liberal lawyer (Ron Lea) who has unsuccessfully repped Native American Canadians in suits against the loggers.

Pursued by police, the trio sets out across country, with Greene stopping along the way to "punish" the logging boss by skinning his legs (a very grueling scene). He also shoots a couple of cops who catch up with the fugitives.

Lea's particularly interesting character has always opposed the clearcutting of majestic forests and has done all he could to help the dispossessed natives, but, as Greene points out, he has also taken a nice fee for his trouble.

Now he finds himself agreeing with Greene's passionate opposition to the destruction of the environment, while deploring the violence heaped on the initially pompous but ultimately terrified Hogan. Though the climax is a bit thin, "Clearcut" generally works as both an outdoors adventure and as an issue raiser.

Richard Bugajski, whose last pic was the interior Polish drama, "The Interrogation" (a Cannes prizewinner last year), does a complete stylistic switch and handles the wide open spaces with flair.

Acting is fine, with Greene outstanding as the vengeful Indian. Rebecca Jenkins shines briefly in a marginal role as a journalist. François Protat's location shooting around Thunder Bay looks good on the Panavision screen, and the film is technically fine in every department.
— *Strat.*

PAPRIKA
(ITALIAN)

A Chance Film Distribuzione release of an Augusto Caminito presentation. (Intl. sales, Intra Films.) Executive producer, Giuseppe Auriemma. Directed by Giovanni Tinto Brass. Screenplay, Brass, Bernardino Zapponi; camera (Telecolor), Silvano Ippoliti; editor, Brass; music, Riz Ortolani; assistant director, Francesco Pscione; costumes, Just Jakob. Reviewed at Cannes Film Festival (market), May 15, 1991. Running time: **113 MIN.**
Mimma/Paprika . . . Debra Caprioglio
Madam Colette . . . Martine Brochard
Prince Brando . . . . John Steiner
Also with: Stephane Ferrara, Renzo Rinardi, Stephane Bonnet, Elizabeth Kaza.

Tinto Brass' "Paprika" is a failed attempt at Italian sex comedy. The maestro's patented "Caligula" brand of grossout is here in abundance, but where are the laughs?

Film introduces yet another zaftig Italian actress, Debra Caprioglio. As he did five years ago with Serena Grandi in the erotic hit "Miranda," Brass the talent scout has given Caprioglio an awesome undraped showcase that should win her repeat appearances in similar roles.

Caprioglio plays Mimma, an 18-year-old beauty from Pola who goes to work for 15 days in a brothel to earn money for her boyfriend. He turns out to be two-timing her, so she stays on in Madame Colette's establishment with a new name, Paprika.

Episodic feature set in the 1950s, way too long at nearly two hours, presents in amoral fashion the cheerful lass' misadventures as she's initiated into a world of libertines, much like the heroine of a Victorian porn novel. She takes up with a violent pimp, moves to brothels in Rome and Milan, and occasionally gets gigs at private parties.

Vulgar and sexist, "Paprika" hits its low point when hammy guest star John Steiner (as an aristocrat) invites the heroine and another prostitute to his mansion for some water sports. Brass had a similar scene in "Miranda," but here he outdoes that one for tastelessness.

Ultimately, Paprika marries a rich count, making for a happy ending that rings false. Brass' attempt to add social significance, pinning the story's climax to a law banning brothels in Italy, is lame.

Caprioglio's infectious smile and laugh bely the indignities she's put through here. While not hardcore pornography, Brass' highly explicit closeups and the Steiner episode make "Paprika" strictly NC-17 material.

Longtime Brass collaborator Silvano Ippoliti has attractively lit colorful art deco sets, but Brass' editing is atrocious. Riz Ortolani's period score is jaunty no matter how violent the action gets, and Brass has the gall to include classic songs by Edith Piaf and Leo Ferré during sex scenes. — *Lor.*

TREASURE ISLAND
(FRENCH-U.S.)

An Argos Films release of a Anatole Dauman presentation of a Les Films du Passage, Cannon Intl. production. Executive producer, Paolo Branco. Directed by Raul Ruiz. Screenplay, Ruiz, freely inspired by Robert Louis Stevenson's novel; camera (color), Acacio de Almeida; editor, Rodolfo Wedeles, Valeria Sarmiento; music, Georges Arriagada; sound, Joaquim Pinto; art direction, Maria-Jose Branco; costume design, Isabel Branco; assistant director, Philippe Grandrieux, Pierre Hodgson; line producer, Paulo de Sousa. Reviewed at Cannes Film Festival (Un Certain Regard), May 14, 1991. Running time: **115 MIN.**
Silver . . . . Vic Tayback
Jonathan/Jim Hawkins
. . . . Melvil Poupaud
Old captain . . . . . . Martin Landau
Doctor/father . . . . Lou Castell
Timothy . . . . Jeffrey Kime
Mother . . . . Anna Karina
Aunt Helen . . . . Sheila
Israel Hands . Jean-François Stevenin
Blind man . . . . . . Charles Schmidt
Midas/narrator . . . Jean-Pierre Léaud
French captain . . . . . Yves Afonso
Mendoza . . . . . Pedro Armendariz Jr.
Ben Gunn . . . . Tony Jessen
Crabb . . . . Michel Ferber

Raul Ruiz trashes adventure novels and films in his update of "Treasure Island," an incoherent assemblage of footage passed off as a feature film. It will confuse rather than amuse children.

Picture was produced in Portugal five years ago with Cannon backing. Financial problems of a co-production partner put the picture in limbo, and the release version, handled in France by Argos Films, looks unfinished with tons of voiceover narration covering up missing scenes.

Primarily in English, with some European cast members dubbed as U.S. leads speak their own dialog, screenplay is mainly non sequiturs, philosophical ramblings and satire of adventure clichés. Jean-Pierre Léaud hams it up as an author figure and narrator, ultimately revealed to be inventing the disconnected episodes.

Young hero Melvil Poupaud plays Jonathan, imagining a series of arbitrary and violent adventures inspired by a tv adventure show he watches and Stevenson's novel.

Quirky characters include old sea captain Martin Landau, Jonathan's mom Anna Karina and former captain/shoemaker Vic Tayback (an untraditional Long John Silver). Charles Schmidt is a blind man who delivers an eye to Landau, and Lou Castel plays a mysterious doctor who claims to be Jonathan's father.

Following Landau's hammy and much-mocked death scene, Ruiz abandons this tack and stages a new series of adventures at sea headed for an island of diamonds with some old cast members and some new ones.

Yves Afonso speaks in French as the captain who pilots the heroes. Film's most entertaining performance is provided by Pedro

Armendariz Jr. as a loquacious Mexican who stops the picture to tell the story of Herman Melville's novel "Benito Cereno."

Final reels become increasingly perverse as the games-playing of the characters is stripped bare. The late Tayback is embarrassing when called upon to step out of character and berate Jonathan's performance as Jim Hawkins. Léaud kills the kid off-screen as a particularly cynical finale.

Ruiz may amuse a small coterie of film buffs with his in-jokes, but the sloppy, half-baked work here is insulting in terms of craftsmanship. In addition to the use of distorting color filters, many scenes are murkily photographed, looking more like lab defects than stylization.

Dialog is shot in tight closeups and action scenes are awkwardly staged and skimpy. — *Lor.*

L'ENTRAINEMENT DU CHAMPION AVANT LA COURSE
(THE TRAINING OF THE CHAMPION BEFORE THE RACE)
(FRENCH)

A Production de Flandres production. Produced by Paul Giovanni. Directed by Bernard Favre. Screenplay, Favre, based on a play by Michel Deutsch. Camera (color), Michel Amathieu; editor, Emmanuelle Thibault; music, Patrick Ardan, Frederic Porte, Chants Slavons. Reviewed at Cannes Film Festival (Un Certain Regard), May 10, 1991. Running time: **80 MIN.**
Fabrice . . . . Richard Berry
Liliane . . . . Mireille Perrier
Loren . . . . Valerie Mairesse
Also with: Jef Odet Serfaty, Daniel Milgram, Daniel Schenmetzler, Yvon Bacq, Julia Maraval.

French star Richard Berry plays an unsavory provincial bully in "The Training Of The Champion Before The Race." His part-comic, mostly tragic portrait of a small-time fascist of the heart is the hypnotic center of this otherwise banal drama. Legs don't look long, and pic's tv career should outlast a few local runs.

A truck driver for a meat-packing plant, Fabrice (Berry) has only one passion in life — bicycle racing. He admits he's no champion and, in fact, nevers wins a race. In a series of inner monologs, he explains how the lonely sport affords him peace and escape from other people, whom he sees as threatening

and exploitative.

The bike scenes are lensed as a quasi-religious experience, accompanied by Michel Amathieu's slow-motion cinematography and a heavenly chorus from Chants Slavons. The sense of exaltation they convey is all too brief — for the audience as well as the paranoid hero.

The trouble is that people scare Fabrice. Being hard on people keeps them away, he reasons. So though it's distasteful, he is forced to act like a brute, mistreating everybody, especially a blowsy young widow (Valerie Mairesse) who owns a butcher shop and is in love with him.

In pic's most shocking scene, Fabrice forces the woman to choose between him and her large dog, which he absurdly claims she has performed unnatural acts with. Pushed to the limit, she stabs the beast to death with a butcher knife and is left with its head resting pathetically in her lap. Fabrice coldly peddles home for supper.

He doesn't show any more tenderness with his saintly wife (Mireille Perrier), a tired victim of beatings and domestic rapes. One day she bravely sets off to meet her rival, the butcher lady, who shows lots of solidarity but doesn't give up Fabrice. His wife, pregnant for the fourth time, has a lonely abortion against her husband's wishes. It's small wonder that she shows so little sorrow over his tragic end.

Somewhat like Fabrice, helmer Bernard Favre plays a double game with his characters, whom he professes to like but keeps at a safe distance. Fabrice, the most interesting, is so cruelly egocentric that his tantrums and one-liners are played for laughs.

As his tawdry, bleached-blonde mistress, Mairesse gives a mystical interpretation to the sex-crazed widow. Perrier's thin, beaten-up wife is the most clichéd figure of all, more the fault of the script than the actors, who all admirably go as far as their roles will take them.

Favre keeps the tale moving at a brisk and watchable pace, often buoyed by sudden passages of deafening rock music. Film is technically well made. — *Yung.*

BRAIN TWISTERS

A Crown Intl. Pictures Release of a Highlite Film Prods. picture. Produced by Dianne Sangiuliano. Executive producer, Frank Rasieleski. Written and directed by Jerry Sangiuliano. Camera (color), Tomasz Magierski; editor, Sandi

Gerling; music, Larry Gelb; line producer, Stan Bickman. Reviewed at Cannes Film Festival (market), May 12, 1991. Running time, **90 MIN.**
With: Terry Londeree, Farrah Forke, Joe Lombardo, Donna Bostany.

About as shocking as a stamp album, "Brain Twisters" is a particularly lame thriller destined for the tail end of video packages for unsuspecting markets.

Terry Londeree plays a professor conducting mind-altering experiments through audio-visual stimulation, using unsuspecting students.

Londeree is under orders from some mysterious software company that is trying to off-load destructive computer games to unsuspecting consumers.

As Londeree's patients become violent, the police take an interest in his experiments. Cop Joe Lombardo also takes a romantic interest in Londeree's assistant Farrah Forke.

Pedestrian ending is saved somewhat by an okay twist, but nothing can save the pic from general oblivion. — *Doch.*

DON'T TELL MOM THE BABYSITTER'S DEAD

A Warner Bros. release of a presentation of HBO in association with Cinema Plus L.P. and Mercury/Douglas Films of an Outlaw production. Produced by Robert Newmyer, Brian Reilly, Jeffrey Silver. Executive producer, Michael Phillips. Directed by Stephen Herek. Screenplay, Neil Landau, Tara Ison; camera (Deluxe color), Tim Suhrstedt; editor, Larry Bock; music, David Newman; additional music, Bruce Nazarian; sound (Dolby), Leslie Shatz; production design, Stephen Marsh; art direction, Patricia Klawonn; set decoration, Kara Lindstrom; costume design, Carol Ramsey; associate producers, Caroline Baron, Davis Guggenheim; assistant director, Bradley M. Gross; casting, Richard Pagano, Sharon Bialy. Reviewed at Mann's Westwood theater, Westwood, Calif., May 30, 1991. MPAA Rating: PG-13. Running time: **105 MIN.**
Sue Ellen Crandell . . . .
. . . . Christina Applegate
Rose Lindsey . . . . . . .Joanna Cassidy
Gus . . . . John Getz
Bryan . . . . Josh Charles
Kenny Crandell . . . . . Keith Coogan
Mrs. Crandell . . . . . Concetta Tomei
Bruce . . . . David Duchovny
Cathy . . . . Kimmy Robertson
Carolyn . . . . .Jayne Brook
Lil Sturak . . . . Eda Reiss Merin
Walter Crandell . . Robert Hy Gorman
Melissa Crandell . . . . Danielle Harris
Zach Crandell . . . Christopher Pettiet
Lizard . . . . Chris Claridge
Mole . . . . Jeff Bollow
Hellhound . . . . Michael Kopelow

"Don't Tell Mom The Babysitter's Dead" starts with the enjoyable, if crude, black comedy situation promised by the title, but then it turns into an incredibly dumb teenage girl's fantasy of making it in the business world. Even backward teenagers won't fall for this knuckleheaded release.

Christina Applegate of tv's "Married . . . With Children" has been unlucky in her film career to date. She previously starred as a homeless teen in last year's "Streets," a fine low-budgeter nobody saw. Now she's gone the teen exploitation route in a so-so perf that too many people will see before word of mouth dumps this pic into the vidstores.

Applegate and her four siblings (Keith Coogan, Robert Hy Gorman, Danielle Harris, Christopher Pettiet) are left by their ditzy vacationing mom (Concetta Tomei) in their suburban L.A. home with a seemingly sweet little old lady babysitter (Eda Reiss Merin), who turns out to be a "deranged Mary Poppins."

This babysitter-from-hell opening, followed by the old lady's death from a heart attack and the kids' ditching of her corpse on the doorstep of a local mortuary, is over all too quickly. Much more humor could have been milked from the situation, which looked like the setup for a raucous teen-comedy twist on Jack Clayton's 1967 masterpiece "Our Mother's House."

But Applegate has to earn money to support the kids so they won't have to ask mom to come home from Australia, and the leaden script by Neil Landau and Tara Ison turns mind-numbingly silly.

After a heavy-handed grossout interlude of Applegate working at a fast-food joint, where she starts a romance with charming Josh Charles, she improbably parlays a padded resume into a high-paying job as administrative assistant to glamorous L.A. garment industry exec Joanna Cassidy.

Cassidy's eager mentorship of Applegate, who's strikingly inept at her early assignments, is truly inexplicable, to the point that the viewer can be pardoned for wondering if the older woman has predatory sexual designs on her 17-year-old protégée. (Nothing that overt ever develops.)

No matter how outrageous, nothing Applegate does raises any questions in Cassidy's mind, whether it's pilfering petty cash, letting Cassidy's slimy b.f. John Getz come on to her or staging an elaborate fashion show at her house that blows her cover when mom returns yet still causes a sensation among the amazingly gullible buyers.

But then, this is a comedy that deals with a sweat shop industry and doesn't seem to realize, any more than the pampered Applegate character, that rows of Hispanic workers huddled over sewing machines are a depressing sight.

Though she has promise, Applegate is misused in a part making her seem more airheaded than shrewd (character thinks chainsmoking still looks sophisticated) and has her wearing surprisingly vulgar garb for a supposedly precocious fashion whiz.

Cassidy, whose mature sexiness livens the film for a while, is gradually made to act and look more and more ridiculous by the pic's clumsy director, Stephen Herek.

Adding some amusing moments are Coogan as Applegate's manically moronic oldest brother; Getz, as the right-on-target office sleazeball; and Jayne Brook, as a bitchy coworker of Applegate's.

Tech credits are okay. Tim Suhrstedt's lensing is appropriately gaudy, and David Newman's eclectic score thankfully avoids the ear-blasting clichés of teen pics. — *Mac.*

THE ROCKETEER

A Buena Vista release of a Walt Disney Pictures presentation of a Gordon Co. production in association with Silver Screen Partners IV. Produced by Lawrence Gordon, Charles Gordon, Lloyd Levin. Executive producer, Larry Franco. Directed by Joe Johnston. Screenplay, Danny Bilson, Paul De Meo; story by Bilson, De Meo, William Dear, based on the graphic novel by Dave Stevens; camera (Technicolor, Panavision widescreen), Hiro Narita; editor, Arthur Schmidt; film editor, Michael A. Stevenson; music, James Horner; sound (Dolby), Thomas Causey; production design, Jim Bissell; art direction, Christopher Burian-Mohr; set design, Carl J. Stensel, Paul Sonski, John Berger; set decoration, Linda DeScenna; costume design, Marilyn Vance-Straker; special visual effects, Industrial Light & Magic; visual effects supervisor, Ken Ralston; visual effects camera, Patrick Turner; associate producer, Lisa Bailey; assistant director, Betsy Magruder; 2nd unit directors, Ken Ralston, M. James Arnett; 2nd unit camera, Frank Holgate, Rexford Metz; Nazi animation director, Mark Dindal; coproducer, Dave Stevens; casting, Nancy Foy. Reviewed at the Gotham Theater, N.Y., June 6, 1991. MPAA Rating: PG. Running time: **108 MIN.**

Cliff Secord	Bill Campbell
Jenny Blake	Jennifer Connelly
Peevy	Alan Arkin
Neville Sinclair	Timothy Dalton
Eddie Valentine	Paul Sorvino
Howard Hughes	Terry O'Quinn
Fitch	Ed Lauter
Wooly	James Handy
Lothar	Tiny Ron
Spanish Johnny	Robert Guy Miranda
Rusty	John Lavachielli
Bigelow	Eddie Jones

Disney can chalk one up in the win column with "The Rocketeer." Considered a big-budget risk at $40 million under studio's fiscal conservatism, this high-octane, high-flying, live-action comic strip has been machine-tooled into agreeable lightweight summer fare, with plenty of action for kids and passably sophisticated humor for adults. Strong, if perhaps not blockbuster, b.o. looms ahead.

Based on a comic unveiled in 1981, this adventure fantasy puts a shiny polish on familiar elements: airborne hero, damsel in distress, Nazi villains, 1930s Hollywood glamor, dazzling special effects. There's nothing new or innovative here, which is why significant repeat biz may not be in the offing, and non-star leads were a calculated gamble. But the production accomplishes most of what it sets out to do, and fills

the bill as straight entertainment.

Slightly overinsistent in its thrills, elaborate opening sequence has an ace pilot (Bill Campbell) testing a new racing plane over L.A. skies in 1938 while, on the ground below, hoods and Feds in speeding cars shoot it out after robbery of a mysterious device.

Developed by none other than Howard Hughes, the invention makes its way into the pilot's hands, but it's coveted by a dashing star of swashbuckling films who also happens to be a dedicated Nazi (Timothy Dalton). Although he has hired thugs led by Paul Sorvino to recover the priceless device, Dalton has his own ideas about getting at Campbell through his gorgeous g.f. (Jennifer Connelly).

The object of intense interest is a portable rocket pack which, if strapped to one's back, can send its wearer zipping around almost as fast, if not as quietly, as Superman. After a humorous secret test, the Rocketeer, as Campbell is soon dubbed, makes his public debut saving a flyer in an air show emergency.

Redoubling efforts to snatch the prototype, Dalton kidnaps Connelly and Sorvino's goons put the squeeze on the pilots. It all ends up at a huge gunfight at the Griffith Observatory and a struggle to the death aboard a zeppelin above the Hollywood Hills.

Rather more convincing than Fred MacMurray's flying jalopy in Disney's "The Absent-Minded Professor" some 30 years ago, and most closely resembling "Commando Cody" in earlier screen lore, the Rocketeer takes to the air in state-of-the-art fashion thanks to another ace job by Industrial Light & Magic. Kids will delight at the hero's adept blast-offs and streaking trajectories, but a major bet was missed by not including more p.o.v. shots to convey the flyer's own thrills.

Younger viewers may not so keenly cotton to the numerous talky sequences, but these may please grownups. A number of the H'wood references and jokes are on the inside side, but should still go down easily with the general public.

Chief among these is the vastly entertaining use of an Errol Flynn-like character as a nasty Nazi. Flynn's own political propensities have been debated ever since Charles Higham first documented the actor's fascist leanings more than a decade ago, but the star's traditional image has

been fictionally debunked here in a humorously bracing manner.

In an on-the-set sequence, the art direction and staging of Flynn's "The Adventures Of Robin Hood" have even been reproduced to a remarkably faithful degree. Other fun derives from an arch villain who has been made up by the ever-inventive Rick Baker to look just like the '40s B character actor Rondo Hatton, some captured Nazi propaganda film that, ironically, has been done in the animation style of the "Why We Fight" series, and a novel explanation for what happened to the last four letters in what was once the "Hollywoodland" sign.

Contributing to the merriment is production designer Jim Bissell, who has created such fabulous sets as the mock-glamorous South Seas nightclub, Dalton's Wright-like abode and Hughes' all-white hangar.

Newcomer Campbell exhibits the requisite grit and all-American know-how, but the lead role is written with virtually no humor or subtext, leaving the actor with only predictable notes to hit, which he does adequately.

Those around him come off to better advantage, notably Dalton as the deliciously smooth, insidious Sinclair; Sorvino and Alan Arkin, with the latter as the Rocketeer's mentor; Terry O'Quinn as Hughes, and the lovely, voluptuous Connelly.

One-time ILM whiz, director Joe Johnston hit the jackpot with his first feature, "Honey, I Shrunk The Kids," and has effectively welded together effects, pace and dashing attitude in a seamless but not exactly inspired way. This could have ended up as camp, or just for kiddies, or too hip, but a happy medium has been nicely hit most of the time.

Danny Bilson and Paul De Meo's script has a pleasant nonchalant quality, and story leaves plenty of room for sequels. Enormous technical expertise has been applied in all departments, with Hiro Narita's sharp lensing, Arthur Schmidt's alert editing, Marilyn Vance-Straker's eye-catching costumes and James Horner's propulsive score all contributing importantly. — *Cart.*

FOREVER ACTIVISTS
(DOCU)

A Tara Releasing presentation of a Montell Associates production. Produced and directed by Judith Montell. Narration written by Yasha Aginsky, Phil Cousineau, Judith Montell. Camera (color), T. Robin Hirsh; editor, Yasha Aginsky; music, Bruce Barthol, Randy Craig; sound, Charles Dixson. Reviewed at Preview 9, June 4, 1991. Running time: **60 MIN.**
With: Ronnie Gilbert (narrator), Maury Colow, Ruth Davidow, Sam Gonshak, Steve Nelson, Hilda Roberts, Herman (Gabby) Rosenstein, Milt Wolff.

Nominated for a 1991 Academy Award for best documentary, "Forever Activists" is an engaging look at the Veterans of the Abraham Lincoln Brigade, volunteers in the Spanish Civil War who remain politically active. Picture quality is at times fuzzy, but interesting subject matter and illuminating interviews more than compensate for technical glitches.

Hour-long film opens with a montage of protest marches. With the credits, buzzwords like "Dissent," "Freedom" and "Justice" are flashed on screen. Fortunately, the remainder of the docu is less didactic. Through interviews, narration and old footage, it tells the story of the 3,000 Americans who fought the fascists in the George Washington-Abraham Lincoln Brigade in the '30s. After the war, the vets were considered a Communist front, and some members even did time in jail.

Over the years, brigade alums retained their principles, joining the civil rights and anti-Vietnam movements and, more recently, sending medical relief to Nicaragua. In 1986, the aging activists returned to Spain for the Spanish Civil War's 50th anni.

Judith Montell followed them as they revisited old battle sites and were warmly welcomed by the Spanish people. She also interviewed loyalist leader Dolores ("La Pasionaria") Ibarruri.

Helmer did make a few unfortunate choices. A clip of Ibarruri speaking to a crowd during the war is dubbed. And when two old friends reunite, the director superimposes an old photo of him rather than intercutting it.

Otherwise, Montell and her editor, Yasha Aginsky, skillfully interweave old and new footage, including everything from Depression-era clips to a Cold War propaganda film explaining how to spot a Communist.

Docu's greatest asset is the veterans themselves. Referring to Spain's socialist government, one says, "We didn't fight for nothing." In another moving scene, a man who lost an arm in the fighting says he gained more than he lost.

Even though its low budget sometimes shows, "Forever Activists" does justice to remarkable people. And while it is unlikely to score in theatrical release, pic should find a public tv audience. — *Stev.*

AMBITION

A Miramax release of a Spirit presentation of a Richard E. Johnson production. Produced by Johnson. Directed by Scott D. Goldstein. Screenplay, Lou Diamond Phillips; camera (Deluxe color), Jeff Jur; editor, Goldstein; music, Leonard Rosenman; sound (Dolby), Russel C. Fager; production design, Marek Dobrowolski; costume design, Diah Wymont; assistant director, Ian McVey; production manager, Tony To; co-producer, Gwen Field; casting, Amanda Mackey. Reviewed at 23rd St. West 1 theater, N.Y., June 1, 1991. MPAA Rating: R. Running time: **100 MIN.**
Mitchell Osgood . Lou Diamond Phillips
Albert Merrick. . . . . . Clancy Brown
Julie . . . . Cecilia Peck
Jordan . . . . Richard Bradford
Freddie . . . . Willard Pugh
Mrs. Merrick . . . . . Grace Zabriskie
Roseanne . . . . Katherine Armstrong
Jack . . . . J.D. Cullum
Tatay . . . . Haing S. Ngor
Also with: Maria Rangel, Teresa Bowman, Karen Landry, Chris Mulkey.

Lou Diamond Phillips wrote an indulgent vehicle for himself to play heavy in "Ambition." Poorly paced thriller is strictly for Phillips' vid fans, though Miramax is according it a theatrical release first.

Pic's original tag "Mind Game" better describes contents. Phillips portrays aspiring novelist Mitchell Osgood, whose first tome about his Filipino dad (Haing S. Ngor, Oscar-winner for "The Killing Fields") has gone unsold.

He wants to write about mass murderer Albert Merrick (Clancy Brown), but instead he hires the recent parolee to work in his L.A. bookstore.

Osgood is soon revealed as a no-good-nik, manipulating Merrick to bring back psychosis. Poorly paced film (edited by director Scott D. Goldstein) takes several reels to come to the point: Osgood is setting up Merrick to murder his kvetching dad (Ngor).

While watching a slime take over a weak-willed individual, à la Pinter's "The Servant," has some interest, this pic is too low-key to involve viewers. Scene of

Phillips reuniting Brown with his mom (Grace Zabriskie) in a restaurant is obviously "acted" rather than an organic extension of the story.

Phillips, unconvincing villain, most often seems to be an actor in a vanity production. Brown, a hulking actor born to play Lennie in "Of Mice And Men," is okay in the psycho role.

Cecilia Peck (Gregory Peck's daughter) is stuck with the nothing part of Osgood's g.f. Best acting is by Willard Pugh, providing comic relief as bookstore assistant. Cast, including Richard Bradford as parole officer and Katherine Armstrong as prostitute, is underutilized. Production values are meager.
— *Lor.*

PLAISIR D'AMOUR
(FRENCH)

A Cythere release of a Cythere-Boulogne-Pathé co-production. Produced by Claude Makovski. Directed by Nelly Kaplan. Screenplay, Kaplan, Jean Chapot; camera (color), Jean-François Robin; editor, Nicole Saunier; music, Claude Bolling; sound, Eric Devulder; set design, Philippe Chiffre; costumes, Serge Lutens; makeup, Judith Gayo; casting, Françoise Menidrey. Reviewed at Sept Parnassians theater, April 23, 1991. Running time: **105 MIN.**
Guillaume de Burlador . . . .
. . . . Pierre Arditi
Do . . . . Françoise Fabian
Clo . . . . Dominique Blanc
Jo . . . . Cécile Sanz de Alba
Raphaël . . . . Heinz Bennent
Cornelius . . . . Pierre Dux

Light-hearted and wryly feminist, "Plaisir d'Amour" is a tropical sex farce about a middle-aged Don Juan and the women who hire him as the family tutor with only his body in mind.

Fully clothed love pic should fare well with both arthouse audiences and fun-loving public.

The comic plot starts rolling when three rich, well-educated beauties hire a suave tutor named Willy (Pierre Arditi) for 13-year-old Flo, away on a vacation. The women, often standing together as a color-coordinated threesome, are entirely self-sufficient: Flo's mother Clo (Dominique Blanc) can repair radios and anything mechanical; sister Jo (Cécile Sanz de Alba) is a writer; and older relative Do (Françoise Fabian) is a world-class scientist.

Each woman encourages Willy to seduce her, which might look like heaven for this author of soupy romance novels except that

he's the supreme romantic: He longs for love as an elusive ideal, while all the ladies want is regular sex. Accusing his lovers of having imprisoned Flo, Willy is told that she simply was a lure.

Arditi, whether chatting at dinner in tux or fixing a fan in his boxers, is a top bedroom comic. He is occasionally upstaged by the offbeat male cast, starting with Heinz Bennent as an eccentric gay butler. Jean-Jacques Moreau, who specializes in a deep laugh, is convincing as a vulgarian.

Helmer Nelly Kaplan excels in smooth comic timing, and her directing has theatrical flare without being stagy. Co-scripters Kaplan and Jean Chapot adeptly pace telegrams, phone calls and letters from the fictional Flo.

The most memorable scene is Willy's second seduction: Jo feeds him in bed, stuffing his mouth with buttery white asparagus. Facial closeups of this erotic feasting are meant to be uncomfortably funny.

Yet the drollest feminist humor is the donkey's head on Willy's bedroom wall that blinks at his lovemaking, a parody of male voyeurism. It's no surprise, then, that sex scenes consist of clothed bodies wrestling madly in bed.

Tech credits are excellent with a sumptuous tropical villa setting in the flower-strewn jungle. Claude Bolling's mild jazz score keeps the mood light, along with the ever-popular 18th century song on which pic's title is based. — *Lour.*

RICH GIRL

A Studio Three release of a Film West presentation of a Michael B. London production. Produced by London. Executive producers, Mark Hoffman, Steven H. Parker. Directed by Joel Bender. Screenplay, Robert Elliot; camera (Foto-Kem color), Levie Isaacks; editor, Mark Helfrich, Richard Candib; music, Jay Chattaway; music supervision, Richard Mann, Arlene Matza; additional music, Joseph Smith; sound (Ultra-Stereo), Bo Franklin, Ken Segal; production design, Richard McGuire; costume design, Janet Sobel; assistant director, John E. Vohlers; production manager-line producer, Herb Linsey; 2nd unit camera, George Mooradian; associate producers, Carol Kottenbrook, Mann; casting, Robert MacDonald, Perry Bullington. Reviewed at Murray Hill theater, N.Y., May 4, 1991. MPAA Rating: R. Running time: **96 MIN.**
Courtney Wells . . . . . . Jill Schoelen
Rick . . . . Don Michael Paul
Rocco . . . . Ron Karabatsos
Jeff . . . . Sean Kanan
Marvin Wells . . . . . . Paul Gleason
Diane . . . . Melanie Tomlin

Showbiz and teen pic clichés mix incompatibly in "Rich Girl," a movie similar to drive-in fare of 15 years ago but really a throwback to early talkies. Studio Three's choice of wide theatrical release is not a shrewd move.

Pic coincidentally stars Jill Schoelen in the title role, after she toplined in Studio Three's debut pic "Popcorn," released in January. She filmed "Rich Girl" in October 1989 and immediately flew to Jamaica to replace the leading lady in "Popcorn." Both pics were made independently and acquired by the distrib.

Lame script credited to Robert Elliot (billing was Robert Havanna during production) is strictly by the numbers: Schoelen is a rich kid in L.A. who rebels against her dad (Paul Gleason) and fiancée who's a yuppie jerk (overplayed by Sean Kanan).

Out on her own, she gets a job as cocktail waitress in Ron Karabatsos' night club, where handsome hunk Don Michael Paul is lead singer of the house band. Inevitable Paul/Schoelen romance bridging class barriers, daddy and Kanan's attempts to break them up and Paul's attempt to make it in the music business supply dozens of stilted plot twists.

Absurd climax is a showcase night for record industry types in which Schoelen reluctantly debuts as replacement singer in Don's band, something Bessie Love or Ruby Keeler might have pulled off 60 years ago. Schoelen keeps her eyes tightly shut throughout the singing routine, but at least she attempts a warble; co-star Paul is dubbed in vocals by Jay Essess.

Joel Bender directs efficiently, but low-budget effort looks and plays like a direct-to-video feature. Numerous mediocre musical performances by groups including Precious Metal and Celebrity Skin just drag out the running time.

Schoelen, whose career peak thus far remains the lead role in "The Stepfather," is appealing but miscast as a rich brat — she looks folksy throughout.

Paul is convincing in leather jacket and on motorcycle (he subsequently wrote the screenplay for the Don Johnson-Mickey Rourke starrer "Harley Davidson And The Marlboro Man") though he looks uncomfortable doing a Michael Paré routine out of "Eddie And The Cruisers." Best acting is by Karabatsos, dead on as the friendly but tough club owner.
— *Lor.*

THE MISSION OF RAOUL WALLENBERG
(SOVIET-DOCU)

A Filmstudio Kievnauschfilm, Bul. L. Ukrainky, USSR-Kiew production, co-produced by Innova Film, Sovexportfilm, Swedish TV. Directed by Alexander Rodnjanski. Screenplay, Leonid Gurewitsch, Rodnjanski; camera (color, b&w), Wladimir Gujiewski, Igor Iwanow. Reviewed at Berlin Film Festival (Panorama), Feb. 21, 1991. Running time: **70 MIN.**

This disorganized, not very investigative attempt to get to the bottom of the disappearance of Raoul Wallenberg may have legs at specialized fests, but it has limited commercial possibilities.

Using archival footage, stills and interviews with Jewish survivors of Nazi persecution in Hungary during World War II, director Alexander Rodnjanski follows the recent attempts by Wallenberg's family and friends to get to the bottom of his disappearance.

Wallenberg, a Swedish diplomat stationed in Budapest in 1944, saved an estimated 100,000 Jews by issuing papers that put them under the protection of the Swedish diplomatic mission. After the capture of Budapest, Wallenberg was arrested by Soviet authorities. He died in a Soviet prison in 1947.

Wallenberg's death has been disputed in the intervening years, and family members have tracked down people who claim to have seen him alive after he reportedly died. Someone in the USSR claims to be Wallenberg's illegitimate son. Some family members say Wallenberg is still alive.

The film, which even suggests Brezhnev had a hand in the disappearance, reaches no conclusions. Just as the investigators lose their way among the reams of Soviet records and pursue a host of false leads, so does the film.

Loosely edited film never rises to the power of its subject matter. Pic is further neutralized by an overly sentimental soundtrack.

The most moving parts of the film are the interviews with the people who were saved from death by the heroic Wallenberg. But whatever the truth about

Wallenberg's fate, his life and deeds deserve a better, more thorough investigation than this documentary provides. — *Keoh.*

SEATTLE FEST

SON OF A GENERAL
(SOUTH KOREAN)

A Korean Motion Picture Promotion Corp. presentation. Produced by Lee Tae-won. Directed by Im Kwon-t'aek. Screenplay, Yun Sam-yuk; camera, Cheong Il-seong; editor, Park Soo-jin; music, Park Soon-deok. Reviewed at Seattle Intl. Film Festival, May 28, 1991. Running time: **108 MIN.**
With: Park Sang-min, Lee Il-jae, Sin Hyun-jun.

It's easy to understand why Im Kwon-t'aek's powerful "Son Of A General" has become the highest-grossing film ever in Korea. This brawling saga chronicling life of one of South Korea's leading statesmen offers an historical treatment in which the despised Japanese occupiers are humiliated and defeated by Koreans. Pic should provoke interest in cities with large Korean populations.

There is no love lost between South Korea and Japan, and this pic offers Koreans an opportunity to relish a small part of their history when one of their own actually came out on top.

"Son Of A General" focuses on the life of Kim Du-han, son of Gen. Kim Chwa-jin, who commanded the Korean independence army in Manchuria. Orphaned at the age of eight, his miserable childhood leads Kim first into joining a hooligan gang where he quickly ascends by virtue of his wit and fighting skills.

A Japanese colony at the time, Koreans were treated despicably by the occupiers, and Kim wins his greatest victory against the "yakusa" (Japanese gang), a triumph that sets him on the road to becoming one of South Korea's leading statesmen.

This action movie, calculated to attract local audiences seduced by Hong Kong productions, contains plenty of violence, yet lacks the exploitative nature of Hong Kong films. The fighting scenes are brutal, but not gratuitously violent. Camerawork is particularly good during such scenes.

While an American audience may be somewhat lost while the

various Korean gangs jockey for power (poorly written subtitles don't help), the overriding patriotic theme of "get the Japanese" helps hold this fast-paced pic together.

"Son Of A General" is a departure from Im's latest films, which are serious, meditative pieces. Yet Im, who actually began his career with action films, imbues his lead character (skillfully played by Park Sang-min) with a reflective self which makes this pic rise several notches above the standard action film, especially those from Hong Kong.
— *Magg.*

CROOKED HEARTS

An MGM release of an A&M Films production. Produced by Rick Stevenson, Dale Pollock and Gil Friesen. Directed by Michael Bortman. Screenplay, Bortman, based upon the novel by Robert Boswell; camera (color), Tak Fujimoto; editor, Richard Francis-Bruce; music, Mark Isham; production design, David Brisbin; costume design, Susan deLaval; associate producer, Lianne Halfon, Mark Bentley; casting, Lora Kennedy, Linda Lowy. Reviewed at Seattle Intl. Film Festival, May 16, 1991. Running time: **105 MIN.**
Charley . . . . . . Vincent D'Onofrio
Marriet . . . . . . Jennifer Jason Leigh
Tom . . . . Pete Berg
Edward . . . . Peter Coyote
Ask . . . . Noah Wyle
Jill . . . . Cindy Pickett
Cassie . . . . Juliette Lewis
Jenetta . . . . Marg Helgenberger

As a drama about a family stretched to the breaking point, "Crooked Hearts" also stretches events beyond believability, including an ending too tidy to accept. This lensed-in-the-Northwest film might draw a small following when it opens its exclusive run locally, but it's unlikely to incite much excitement elsewhere.

"Crooked Hearts" centers upon the Warren family, who project an outward image of peaceful harmony, but in reality, is largely dysfunctional as a family unit. In fact, nearly every character in the pic seems incapable of coping with life — except the affable, youngest son (Noah Wyle), who ends up getting killed.

The family tensions primarily spring from the love-hate relationship between the father (Peter Coyote) and the rebellious oldest son (Vincent D'Onofrio). Dad constantly harangues son about making something out of his life, but refuses to make the 26-year-old move out of the family home and fend for himself. Meanwhile, D'Onofrio feels smothered by those around him, yet is completely incapable of leaving the family. Mixed into this is his hatred of his father because he discovered his dad was having an affair with a waitress Charley wanted to date.

This long-running affair-by-post apparently was the basis for the son's decision to torch the family home (and finally run away). D'Onofrio leaves behind the love letters for his two younger brothers to discover and understand his motive. It was while the two younger brothers were burning the love letters that the youngest is accidentally hit and killed by a car, and D'Onofrio is blamed for that, as well.

The story is told through the eyes of the middle son (Pete Berg), who drops out of college and returns home struggling to understand himself. He strikes up an affair with a young woman (Jennifer Jason Leigh) trying to recover from a disastrous affair.

Despite what would seem like overwhelming odds, the family, following the funeral of the youngest son, all forgive D'Onofrio and each other, an event the audience is given little preparation to accept or believe.

Pic attempts to explore the family myth, the reality vs. the dream, and the consequences on the household. But it simply doesn't hold together. The audience has to make large leaps of casual relationships in order to accept the end results. Instead, the film presents a series of awkward moments which, strung together, make for very comfortable viewing.

Technically, the film is marred by an irregular sound system, making it difficult to understand all the dialog. It's hard to say if the problem rests with the film or with the venue. — *Magg.*

TO CROSS
THE RUBICON

A Lensman Co. production. Executive producer, Jim Clapp. Produced by Patricia Royce, Barry Caillier. Directed by Caillier. Screenplay, Lorraine Devon, Royce; camera (color), Christopher Tufty; editor, Patrick Barber; music, Paul Speer, David Lanz; production design, Michael Anderson; costumes, Ron Leamon; associate producer, Tom Hechim; unit production manager, Josh Conescu. Reviewed at Seattle Intl. Film Festival, May 21, 1991. Running time: **148 MIN.**
Kendall Byrne . . . . . Patricia Royce
Claire Runyan . . . . . Lorraine Devon
David Berry . . . . J.D. Souther
John Halpern . . . . . . Wade Madsen
James Bird . . . . Billy Burke

Lee Wilke . . . . . . Bruce P. Young

A tighter editing job could easily turn "To Cross The Rubicon," an engaging look at the contemporary lives of two women in their mid-30s, into a much stronger pic with serious b.o. potential. As it is, however, audience empathy for the characters as they struggle to understand and accept their lives is severely diluted as the pic drags on.

Personal insights become obvious statements; self-analyzing becomes incessant whining. The pic is remarkable, though, for its high production values achieved on a low, $1.4 million budget raised privately.

Lensed entirely in Seattle, pic is a slice-of-life comedy/drama that draws upon the experiences of the two writers, who also co-star in the production. Kendall Byrne (Patricia Royce) and Claire Runyan (Lorraine Devon) are at a major crossroads in their lives. They are successful, but personally unfulfilled career women searching for lasting and meaningful relationships with men who are not afraid of either commitment or the women's career successes. The situation should strike a responsive chord with many modern women.

Their close friendship becomes a forum in which to assess their choices in men, their careers and in the way they see and conduct themselves as independent yet "female" women. David Berry (J.D. Souther) is the mutual man in their lives. He is an ex-lover of them both, and a possible future lover for one.

Catching all three characters at a point of flux, the story follows them as they interact and influence each other through love, hate, jealousy, laughter, tears and ultimately, the knowledge that sometimes the best way to face life is to simply live it and allow it to unfold.

Part of the story's strength is that it is not a grand sociological study, not does it bite off more than it can chew.

One particularly sophomoric element which should be eliminated is shots of a lone Roman centurion to end particular scenes. The centurion apparently is to provide a not-so-subtle tie-in with the title. The Rubicon is the river Julius Caesar crossed under arms in 49 B.C., thus committing himself to civil war with Pompey.

Devon has particularly strong

appeal, while newcomer Billy Burke turns in a fine job as the young, misunderstood rock musician with whom Kendall tries to have an affair.

If the Lensman Co., a Seattle-based indie, can raise the capital to perform the necessary editing, "To Cross The Rubicon" (company's second full-length feature) shows future promise. — *Magg.*

CANNES FEST

ES MEGIS ...
(AFTER ALL ...)
(HUNGARIAN)

A Budapest Film Studio-Objektiv Film Studio production. (Intl. sales: Cinemagyar.) Written and directed by Zsolt Kezdi-Kovacs. Camera (Eastmancolor), Balazs Sara; editor, Eva Karmento; sound, Peter Kardos. Reviewed at Cannes Film Festival (Directors Fortnight), May 20, 1991. Running time: **94 MIN.**
Kristof Zeyk . . . . Andras Kozak
Ex-wife . . . . Lili Monori
Also with: Laszlo Mensaros, Iren Bordan, Laszlo Vajda, Eszter Karasz.

Focusing on the end of the Communist era in Hungary, "After All . . ." is a personal, emotional picture which will be deemed important in the historical context of Hungarian cinema. It's helmer Zsolt Kezdi-Kovacs best film in some time, and though arthouse exposure in the West looks doubtful, tv exposure is definitely indicated.

After 40 years of monolithic communism, Hungarians, the film suggests, found freedom hard to take at first. The central character is a journalist (Andras Kozak) who, like thousands of others, had gone along with the Communist system without ever privately agreeing with it. Now, people accuse him of being a Stalinist, which profoundly disturbs him.

He retreats into a private world and tries to make contact with his sprightly 14-year-old daughter, whom he hardly knew. Gradually he gathers the strength to start a new life at the age of 50, and the film ends as he drives towards the Rumanian border to cover the revolution there.

Pic's subject will have a powerful effect on audiences in the former communist countries of Europe, and Kezdi-Kovacs handles it with quiet distinction. Technically, film is very handsome,

with glowing color camerawork by Balazs Sara. It was a fine choice to close Cannes' Directors Fortnight sidebar. — *Strat.*

TRUMPET NUMBER
SEVEN

A Tainbreaker Films presentation. Produced by Crocker Coulson. Directed by Adrian Velicescu. Screenplay, Coulson; camera (Monaco color, b&w), Velicescu; sound, Jean-Luc Audy. Reviewed at Cannes Film Festival (Intl. Critics Week), May 15, 1991. Running time: **80 MIN.**
With: Ian McRae, Cheryl Bianchi, John Diehl.

Watching "Trumpet Number Seven" is the visual equivalent of listening to water slowly drip in the next room. Simultaneously pretentious and devoid of interest, this arty conceit will remain little seen.

Somnolent pacing, long-held abstract shots, industrial soundtrack and loser characters are employed to convey the angst-ridden existences of a former trumpet player and his aggravated mate.

Holed up in a filthy, dilapidated downtown L.A. loft, Ezzie (Ian McRae) does nothing but brood all day while Cinder (Cheryl Bianchi) rants about his slovenliness. As if this action — all shot in profound black & white — weren't enough, the viewer is treated to a gallery of urban wastescapes and images of fire, laughably reflecting the leading lady's name.

After an hour, the images suddenly jolt into color, for which director-cameraman Adrian Velicescu seems to possess a certain affinity. Some of the compositions in the desolate L.A. River embankment are striking, even if by this time there remains no hope for the film itself.

Only other plus is a rather ambitious, jazzy soundtrack, with interesting sound editing and effects.

But this study of terminal entropy is a classic example of bad avant-garde cinema. A half-baked attempt to inject quasi-religious meaning — by way of the title, the name of Ezzie's former band ("Dark Angels") and the succession of apocalyptic images — generates no coherent meaning, resulting in fully baked futility.
— *Cart.*

WHERE THE NIGHT BEGINS
(ITALIAN)

A Filmauro-Duea Film production, in association with RAI-1. (Intl. sales: Sacis.) Produced by Luigi and Aurelio De Laurentiis, Antonio Avati. Directed by Maurizio Zaccaro. Screenplay, Pupi Avati; camera (Telecolor), Pasquale Rachini; editor, Amedeo Salfa; music, Stefano Caprioli; sound (Dolby), Raffaele De Luca; production design, Carlo Simi. Reviewed at Cannes Film Festival (market), May 17, 1991. Running time: **94 MIN.**
Irving . . . . Tom Gallop
Nora . . . . Cara Wilder
Lee . . . . Don Pearson
Sybil . . . . Kim Mai Guest
Denny . . . . Blair Bybee
(English soundtrack)

This failed thriller plays like any other poor, unreleasable American film, but it turns out to be an Italian picture cranked out in Davenport, Iowa, last year by the production team already there to film "Bix." Meager results are strictly dullsville.

Screenplay is by "Bix" director Pupi Avati, who has fashioned "Where The Night Begins" as a talky shaggy-dog story with precious little action.

Tom Gallop plays a young man who has returned to his small hometown following the death of his estranged father. He's determined to set things right by giving the $300,000 mansion to the mother of a student who committed suicide 13 years earlier after becoming pregnant by his dad.

Overly detailed script provides dozens of clues that suggest the girl is still alive. A major subplot sets up the possibility of supernatural phenomena but is not properly followed up.

Revelation of what really happened to the girl is surprising but comes too late in the day. The fact that a key character (Gallop's mom) never shows up at all is evidence of the pic's slipshod production.

Gallop is earnest in the lead role, with squeaky-clean support from Cara Wilder and Kim Mai Guest. Best credit is title theme music by Stefano Caprioli, which weaves its way insidiously behind the action. — *Lor.*

TCHIN-TCHIN
(ITALIAN)

An Arturo La Pegna presentation of a Silvio Berlusconi Communications and Produzioni Cinematografiche CEP coproduction. Produced by Arturo and Massimiliano La Pegna. Directed by Gene Saks. Screenplay, Ronald Harwood; camera (color), Franco Di Giacomo; editor, Richard Nord, Anna Poscetti; music, Pino Donaggio; sets, Jean Michel Hugon, Michel Albournac; costumes, Gianni Versace; production manager, Serge Touboul. Reviewed at Cannes Film Festival (market), May 15, 1991. Running time: **98 MIN.**
Cesareo Gramaldi . . . .
. . . . Marcello Mastroianni
Pamela Piquet . . . . . Julie Andrews
Also with: Jonathan Cecil, Ian Fitzgibbon, Jean Pierre Castaldi.

About 10 minutes into "Tchin-Tchin," which strives vainly to be a comedy, a mantle of tedium settles in and never lifts. Julie Andrews and Marcello Mastroianni are made to perform their clichéd prim Englishwoman and clownish Italian, but the script goes nowhere, and at times seems like a Paris travelog.

Wafer-thin plot has an Italo construction engineer deserted by his Yank wife, and a priggish Englishwoman is abandoned by her doctor husband. The two decide to try to get their spouses back.

Mastroianni's character whines and moans in fractured English about the loss of his wife but is ready to take up with the standoffish Andrews. She, in turn, is at first repelled by his slobbering overtures, clumsy ebullience and embarrassing inebriation. But he presses his case and, ever so gradually and quite inexplicably, she starts to see his redeeming qualities.

Although in the story there is a rapprochement between the two, on screen the couple remain as distant as in their first meeting, even when they're in bed. The comedy never ignites, the dialog is flat and the attempted drollery is unconvincing.

A slight change of pace is introduced when the twosome visit a health spa and the Italian is urged to abstain from women and liquor. He breaks the rules, of course, but it's all rather tame and lacking in both wit and feeling. Pic lacks significant supporting parts or subplots to enliven the leaden pacing.

Some biz may be drummed up by the topbilling of Andrews and Mastroianni, but this tired Mastroianni almost mimics his own acting. — *Besa.*

SAM & ME
(CANADIAN)

A Sunrise Films Ltd. presentation of a Deepa Mehta Film production in association with Film Four Intl., ITC Distribution and Astral Film Enterprises. Executive producers, Paul Saltzman, Steve Levitan. Produced by Robert Wertheimer, Deepa Mehta. Directed by Mehta. Screenplay, Ranjit Chowdhry; camera (color), Guy Dufaux; editor, Boyd Bonitzke; music, Mark Korven; sound, Tony Gronick; production design, Linda Del Rosario, Richard Paris; costume design, Maya Mani. Reviewed at Cannes Film Festival (Intl. Critics Week), May 16, 1991. Running time: **92 MIN.**
Nikhil . . . . Ranjit Chowdhry
Sam Cohen . . . . . . Peter Boretski
Chetan Parikh . . . . Om Puri
Morris Cohen . . . . . Heath Lamberts
Baldev . . . . Kulbushan Kharbanda
Xavier . . . . Javed Jafri
Ali . . . . Jolly Bader
Keith Wong . . . . Leonard Chow
Hannah Cohen . . . . Marcia Diamond

A realistic slice-of-life drama, "Sam & Me" is a raw but sensitive story about a Canadian immigrant from India who refuses to compromise his morals at great personal cost. Deepa Mehta's debut pic should profit from good critical response but find a limited commercial audience.

Naughty opening scene (ushered in with a strong musical score) cools when accommodating Nik arrives in the land of the maple leaf, promising to be a good Muslim boy, which he is.

Sweet Nik (a character scripted and played with depth by Ranjit Chowdhry) is ingratiated to his sleazy uncle (Om Puri) who paid his ticket and got him a servant's job looking after crotchety old Sam.

Family feuds erupt when Nik helps Sam learn to live again, talking at length and hitting the town, adventures which include a visit to a Muslim transvestite party for kicks. When old Sam has too much fun, Nik is fired.

A melodrama develops when the two pals can no longer talk (even on the phone) and an unpredictable tragic event triggers Nik's indignation towards members of both the Jewish and Indian communities who are more concerned about cultural traditions than human contact.

As such, pic subtly slams immigrants' self-imposed racist tendencies while championing individual rights. Debut script by thesp Chowdhry is understated and accurate but meanders around racial issues.

Guy Dufaux' camerawork is dark and editing is amateur, but this tender story is a lovely aberration from stylized formula films with pat endings. Actors deliver a realistic portrayal of Indians in Canada. — *Suze.*

THE GOOD WOMAN OF BANGKOK
(AUSTRALIAN-DOCU)

An O'Rourke and Associates Filmmakers production in association with the Australian Film Commission and Channel 4. (Intl. sales: Kim Lewis Marketing.) Written, produced and directed by Dennis O'Rourke. Camera (color)-sound, O'Rourke; editor, Tim Litchfield; associate producer, Glenys Rowe. Reviewed at Cannes Film Festival (market), May 16, 1991. Running time: **79 MIN.**
Aoi . . . . . . Yaowalak Chonchanakun

Described as a documentary fiction film, "The Good Woman Of Bangkok" blurs the docu/fiction life in a personal study of a prostitute by a filmmaker who became emotionally involved with his subject. This frustrating mixture of the fascinating and the banal could spark interest on the arthouse circuit and tv.

Video also is a definite prospect (but pic isn't at all raunchy).

An opening title reveals that the 43-year-old Aussie filmmaker's marriage had ended and he came to Bangkok to meet a Thai prostie and make a film about her. Aoi (the name means "sweet" or "sugar cane") is the pseudonym of a young prostie who works the Patpong red light district of the Thai capital.

O'Rourke says he paid for the woman's services, and they shacked up at a seedy hotel where he filmed and videotaped her for hours. He also claims that he later fell in love with her.

This could obviously have been as intimate a story of a filmmaker as of his subject, but despite the candid commentary, O'Rourke stays out of the picture, with only his voice heard occasionally. Instead, Aoi talks about her life in a village, her marriage and how she was abandoned with a small baby to care for. She hates men, she says, and graphically describes how she handles her work.

O'Rourke also includes footage of nude girls dancing in a club while Western men ogle them. Towards the end, O'Rourke tries to persuade Aoi to start a new life, warning her about AIDS and other dangers. He offers to buy her a rice farm, and a title claims he did, but that a year later she was back in Bangkok working in a massage parlor.

From the film itself, it's hard to tell how close the filmmaker came to his "good woman," though the pressbook talks about "friendship and a kind of love" between them. Aoi is an articulate subject, but the film would have been stronger if O'Rourke had been willing to be more explicit about his relationship with her.

Technically, the film is variable with the video transfers to film typically grainy alongside the actual film footage. Aoi speaks in the Thai language, and the English subtitles are excellent. The film could find arthouse bookings, though in the end it doesn't really deliver the goods. O'Rourke's earlier docus ("Cannibal Tours," "Half Life") were on the whole more successful than this one. — *Strat.*

WISECRACKS
(CANADIAN-DOCU)

An Alliance release of a Zinger Films production in association with the National Film Board of Canada's Studio D. Executive producers, Rina Fraticelli, Ginny Stikeman, Susan Cavan. Produced by Gail Singer, Signe Johannson. Directed by Singer. Camera (color), Zoe Dirse, Bob Fresco; editor, Gordon McClellan. Reviewed at Cannes Film Festival (market), May 15, 1991. Running time: **90 MIN.**
With: Phyllis Diller, Whoopi Goldberg, Sandra Shamas, Jenny Lecoat, the Clichettes, Faking It Three, Feri Jewell, Jenny Jones, Ellen DeGeneres, Paula Poundstone.

Radical femmes wisecracking about premature ejaculation, married men, PMS and the "fat century"? "Wisecracks" sounds dicey and potentially vicious, but this comedy docu featuring America's top stand-up female comedians is downright hilarious.

Pic could make the fest circuit rounds and easily hold viewers through the closing credits on comedy tv outlets. (Profanity will limit possibilities on public tv.) Editing is excellent, and comics' timing is crackerjack, but the amateur camera will limit theatrical potential.

At its Cannes preem, audience was in stitches watching the transformation of taboo subjects into socially poignant material. Most of the femme comedians use traditionally no-nos — everything mothers told daughters never to mention in public — to shock audiences into laughter.

Interviews with a slew of comedians, including Whoopi Goldberg, add insight to the comedy biz. Vintage tv clips of Lucille Ball, Carole Burnett and Eve Arden add historical reference points.

Canadian comedian Jenny Jones, who has her own syndicated show in the U.S., delivers her usual "the girls must stick together" slant. On married men: "The liars. They tell you they're single, and then they come to pick you up in a Winnebago with a swing set on top."

Phyllis Diller, dressed "as a lampshade in a whorehouse," cleverly displays her usual self-deprecating style. However, in a backstage interview, her knowledge of the business defies her onstage persona.

"Wisecracks," refreshingly vulgar and witty, marks a return for National Film Board of Canada's women's Studio D. — *Suze.*

THE GIANT OF THUNDER MOUNTAIN

A Castle Hill Prods. release of a New Generation Entertainment presentation of a Herklotz-Kiel production. (Intl. sales, Intl. Creative Exchange.) Produced by Joseph Raffill. Executive producers, John Herklotz, Richard Kiel. Directed by James Roberson. Screenplay, Kiel, Tony Lozito; camera (Widescreen, Foto-Kem color), Stephen G. Shank; editor, Richard E. Rabjohn; music, Al Kasha, Joel Hirschhorn; sound (Ultra-Stereo), Trevor Black; production design, Phillip Thomas; art direction, Beau Petersen; stunt coordinator, Burt Marshall; line producers, Joan Weidman, Von Bernuth; casting, Ruth Conforte. Reviewed at Cannes Film Festival (market), May 11, 1991. MPAA Rating: PG. Running time: **101 MIN.**
Eli . . . . Richard Kiel
Hezekiah Crow . . . . . . Jack Elam
Alicia Wilson . . . . Marianne Rogers
Amy Wilson . . . . . . Noley Thornton
Bear . . . . Bart the Bear
Tommy . . . . Chance Michael Corbitt
Ben . . . . Ryan Todd
Agnes . . . . Ellen Crawford
Also with: William Sanderson, Foster Brooks, George (Buck) Flower.

Wholesome, square family entertainment returns with "The Giant Of Thunder Mountain." Well-mounted production offers nothing new but is nevertheless an entertaining package for old-fashioned audiences.

Actor Richard Kiel, best known for his toothy running role as Jaws in Roger Moore-led James Bond epics, is co-writer and executive producer of this wilderness adventure. He's also thoroughly sympathetic as a literal giant who's become a legend to nearby townsfolk.

A huge bear killed his parents, and Kiel has lived as a hermit ever since. When young siblings Chance Michael Corbitt, Ryan Todd and Noley Thornton find and befriend the big fellow, Kiel shaves off his beard and gets presentable to meet their widowed mom.

Unfortunately, crooked carnival man Jack Elam and his two sons are up to no good and Kiel gets blamed for their misdeeds. Pic effectively opposes vigilante justice and gets good mileage out of the small-town prejudices that mock and mistreat someone different, such as the 7-foot-plus Kiel.

Pic's high points are undoubtedly the scary fights involving guest star Bart the Bear, whose repertoire of moves is limited but effective. Script contrives to defeat Bart without killing him, a refreshing novelty for a usually bloody genre.

With Elam perfect as comic relief, Kiel carries the picture with an earnest performance in a tailor-made role. Cast of familiar good-ol'-boys is fine, and Marianne Rogers projects a mature beauty akin to Jennifer O'Neill as the romantic interest. The kids are cute but resistible.

Helmer James Roberson is experienced in this type of picture, and film scores high on Stephen Shank's widescreen visuals of beautiful, unspoiled locations. Robyn Smith's costumes ring true in conjuring up the right period feel. Sound effects for Bart or Kiel galumphing along the ground are overdone. — *Lor.*

LA MUJER DEL PUERTO
(WOMAN OF THE PORT)
(MEXICAN)

A Chariot 7 Prods. and Dos Prods. film. Executive producer, Hugo Scherer. Produced by Allen Persselin, Michael Donnelly. Directed by Arturo Ripstein. Screenplay, Paz Alicia Garciadiego, based on a story by Guy de Maupassant; camera (color), Angel Goded; editor, Carlos Puente; music, Lucia Alvarez; production design, Juan Jose Urbini; executives in charge of production, Richard Georges, Edwin R. Little Jr. Reviewed at Cannes Film Festival (Un Certain Regard), May 16, 1991. Running time: **110 MIN.**
Tomasa . . . . Patricia Reyes Spindola
Carmelo . . . . Alejandro Parodi
Perla . . . . Evangelina Sosa
Marro . . . . Damian Alcazar
Eneas . . . . Ernesto Yanez
Also with: Julian Pastor, Jorge Fegan, Alejandra Montoya, Fernando Soler.

This sordid pic retells a Guy de Maupassant story transposed to a Mexican port city. Ripstein's long shots, dim lighting and a script which lurches from the philosophically talky to the scatological makes for an unappealing film, tawdry and distant.

"Women Of The Port" involves a sailor who jumps ship, and who, sick and lonely, takes refuge in a bordello. The madame turns out to be his mother who is using her daughter for on- and off-stage prostitution. The sailor then falls in love with his sister, and soon the two are sexually entwined, waving aside compunctions about incest.

Instead of a straight telling of the story, Ripstein gives us various versions of the same events, seen from the different points of view of the main characters. The technique detracts rather than adds to the film, even though some new revelatory elements are added. Some moping secondary characters pull the film into still deeper mire.

Interest in this murky film will be limited to the fest circuit and to Ripstein admirers who may mistake pic's self-indulgence for profundity. — *Besa.*

TRANCERS II

A Full Moon Entertainment production. Produced and directed by Charles Band. Screenplay, Jackson Barr, from story by Barr, Band; camera (color), Adolfo Bartoli; editor, Ted Nicolaou, Andy Hornitch; music, Mark Ryder, Phil Davies; music supervision, Richard Band; sound (Ultra-Stereo), D.J. Ritchie; production design, Kathleen Coates; costume design, Angela Galog Calin; assistant director, Scott Thomson; special makeup effects, Palah Sandling; special effects supervisor, Kevin McCarthy; stunt coordinator, Chuck Borden; line producers, David DeCoteau, John Schouweiler; associate producer, Thomas Bradshaw; casting, Robert MacDonald, Perry Bullington. Reviewed at Cannes Film Festival (market), May 16, 1991. MPAA Rating: R. Running time: **87 MIN.**
Jack Deth . . . . Tim Thomerson
Lena Deth . . . . Helen Hunt
Alice Stillwell . . . . . . Megan Ward
Hap Ashby . . . . Biff Manard
Nurse Trotter . . . . Martine Beswicke

Dr. Pyle . . . . .Jeffrey Combs
McNulty . . . . Alyson Croft
Raines . . . . Telma Hopkins
Dr. Wardo . . . . .Richard Lynch
Sadie Brady . . . . Barbara Crampton
Rabbit . . . . Sonny Carl Davis

Some unintentional humor doesn't save this unnecessary sequel, a quickie that's all talk and no action. Sci-fi premise is wasted on standard shootouts.

Film is actually the second attempted sequel to 1985's comedy film noir "Future Cop," a.k.a. "Trancers," following a segment in Charles Band's unfinished 1987 three-part pic for his Empire Pictures banner, titled "Pulse Pounders."

New "Trancers II" is a talkfest that almost comically dwells on bringing the viewer up to date. Tim Thomerson returns as Jack Deth, an operative from 100 years in the future still assigned to protect Biff Manard, a former Cy Young Award-winning baseball pitcher who's now a rich commodities broker. He has to be kept alive to yield a descendant who's a top government leader in the future.

Zombies called trancers under the control of evil Richard Lynch (cast as the brother of the villain defeated in the original pic) are trying to kill Manard. Lynch runs an ecology organization as a front, recruiting homeless people to turn into more trancers.

Time paradoxes are lightly touched upon here, but other than the stupid gimmick of a watch that slows time for 15 seconds, there's precious little sci-fi content. The time-travel chamber looks like an aluminum foil prop whipped up over the weekend for a high school play.

Though Thomerson tries hard, he's given unfunny one-liners. Rest of the cast, including several cult thesps like Martine Beswicke and Jeffrey Combs, has little to do. Telma Hopkins, touted as co-star in the 1987 sequel, has only a tiny role here. Best performance is by Sonny Carl Davis (of "Last Night At The Alamo"), rather sympathetic as an asylum orderly.

Extremely poor production values give "Trancers II" a home movie look at times, and many scenes are shot in closeup with the actors looking directly at the camera. Special effects are meager and the dreaded trancers disappointingly put up no fight at all as the heroes calmly shoot them down. — *Lor.*

DE ONFATSOENLIJKE VROUW
(THE INDECENT WOMAN)
(DUTCH)

An MFP production. (Intl. sales: Capitol Films, London.) Produced by Chris Brouwer, Haig Balian. Directed by Ben Verbong. Screenplay, Verbong, Marianna Dikker, Jean Van de Velde, Peter Marthesheimer, Pea Frohlich; camera (Fujicolor), Lex Wertman; editor, Ton de Graaff; music, Nicola Piovani; line producer, Arnold Heslenfeld; production manager, Rens Oomens. Reviewed at Cannes Film Festival (market), May 17, 1991. Running time: **96 MIN.**
Emilia . . . . José Way
Leon . . . . Huub Stapel
Charles . . . .
Coen Van Vrijberghe de Coningh

A handsomely produced softcore erotic drama, Ben Verbong's new film could attract international arthouse audiences for its classy depiction of a bored wife's off-the-wall sexual adventures. A hot performance from José Way in the lead is a major plus of "The Indecent Woman."

Way plays Emilia, a 30-year-old wife and mother of a 6-year-old girl. She lives a comfortable life with Charles, her husband, and has no thought of having an extramarital affair until she meets Leon, who is purchasing the house owned by Emilia's late mother.

Something about the way they meet and the instant tension between them triggers a response in Emilia, and when Leon calls her later she goes along with his proposal that they play erotic games together, which quickly develop into a love affair based entirely on lust. They make love in the back of a car, and even in the washroom of a smart restaurant. There's always an element of danger to add spice to the erotic game-playing.

Verbong handles all this stylishly, eliciting a very sensual performance from his actress. The men are less interesting figures and more stereotypical. Inevitably, in the end, the lover changes the rules of the game, but one of the pic's flaws, especially given the five screenwriters, is the unsatisfactory conclusion.

Nevertheless, this looms as a possible arthouse entry where porno-chic is acceptable. It's technically fine, with an appropriate music score by Nicola Piovani.
— *Strat.*

ROBIN HOOD: PRINCE OF THIEVES

A Warner Bros. release of a James G. Robinson presentation of a Morgan Creek production. Produced by John Watson, Pen Densham, Richard B. Lewis. Executive producers, Robinson, David Nicksay, Gary Barber. Directed by Kevin Reynolds. Screenplay, Densham, Watson, from story by Densham; camera (Technicolor), Doug Milsome; editor, Peter Boyle; music, Michael Kamen; sound (Dolby), Chris Munro; production design, John Graysmark; supervising art director, Alan Tomkins; art direction, Fred Carter, John F. Ralph; set decoration, Peter Young; costume design, John Bloomfield; stunt coordinator, Paul Weston; assistant director, David Tringham; 2nd unit director, Mark Illsley; 2nd unit action sequence director, Max Kleven; 2nd unit camera, Egil Woxholt; coproducer, Michael J. Kagan; casting, Ilene Starger (U.S.), Davis and Zimmerman (U.K.). Reviewed at Ziegfeld Theater, N.Y., June 10, 1991. MPAA Rating PG-13. Running time: **138 MIN.**
Robin of Locksley . . . . Kevin Costner
Azeem . . . . Morgan Freeman
Marian . Mary Elizabeth Mastrantonio
Will Scarlett . . . . . . Christian Slater
Sheriff of Nottingham . Alan Rickman
Mortianna . . . . . Geraldine McEwan
Friar Tuck . . . . . . Michael McShane
Lord Locksley . . . . . . Brian Blessed
Guy of Gisborne . . . . Michael Wincott
Little John . . . . Nick Brimble
Fanny . . . . Soo Drouet
Wulf . . . . Daniel Newman
Bull . . . . Daniel Peacock
Duncan . . . . Walter Sparrow
Bishop . . . . Harold Innocent
Much . . . . Jack Wild
King Richard . . . . . . Sean Connery

Kevin Costner's "Robin Hood" is a Robin of wood. Murky and uninspired, this $50 million rendition of one of folklore's most perennially popular tales will do some major business due to its star's following, heavy want-see, the story's enduring appeal and the fact that this represents this generation's main chance to experience it. But no matter how much coin is raked in, total could have been a lot more had it been a good film.

Rather shoddy looking for such an expensive undertaking, this Morgan Creek production for Warner Bros. release bears evidence of the rushed and unpleasant production circumstances that have been much reported upon. Incoherent staging, bad matching, underlit photography, wildly disparate acting styles, and American leads whose accents don't conform to one another's, much less to those of the British supporting cast — these factors, among others, contribute to a far from satisfying film.

At the same time, the spirit of the underdog represented by Robin and his not-so-merry men, and the dramatic draw of the oppressed rising against an evil establishment, will provide something for audiences to latch onto, as will the numerous armed confrontations and spectacular displays of archery. This seriously intended, more realistically motivated revision of the Robin myth may have diminished the hero, but it hasn't destroyed him.

Trying to set the tale, which has debatable basis in reality, in historical context, lackluster script by Pen Densham and John Watson begins in the year 1194 in Jerusalem, where Robin leads a prison uprising and escapes with a Moor, Azeem (Morgan Freeman). Retreating from the Crusades, the pair head for England, where they find that Robin's father has been slain by the Sheriff of Nottingham (Alan Rickman), who is attempting to eliminate all resistance and perhaps make a play for the throne in the absence of King Richard.

To avenge his father's death, Robin joins up with Little John and the latter's band of outsiders in a safe enclave in Sherwood Forest. Film picks up a bit at this point, as the group takes to highway banditry to support their dissenting ways but see their popular support vastly increase as the overlord's repressive tactics become more brutal.

Major setpiece is the sheriff's attack on the outlaws' hippie-like compound, which decimates the group. But Robin is able to lead a counterattack on Nottingham Castle, ending with the inevitable duel between the two mortal enemies.

Script tries to invest the action and characters' behavior with psychological validity, however elementary, 1990s style, but from the outset what one notices is director Kevin Reynolds' frantic attempt to soup up every scene with visual distractions.

And distractions are what they are. In seemingly arbitrary fashion, Reynolds has used endless swooping crane shots, pointless handheld and Steadicam setups, grotesquely distorting closeups and nonsensical shot sequencing that combines to create an utter lack of visual stability and coherence.

Add to that cinematographer Doug Milsome's dim lighting of interior and night scenes, gloomy skies and considerable bad matching due to changeable weather conditions, and one has a surprisingly undistinguished looking picture for the money.

Things aren't a whole lot better on the acting side. Much comment will be devoted to Costner's faint-hearted attempt at an English accent, which is apparent initially but essentially disappears as the film progresses. In interviews, he has defensively complained that he didn't have enough time to master the accent and was deprived of his vocal coaches by the producers. He probably should have dropped the stab at it entirely and just spoken assertively.

But the best that can be said for his performance is that it is pleasant. At worst, it can be argued whether it is more properly described as wooden or cardboard. His displays with bow and arrow are strikingly impressive (but is he right or left-handed? He shoots from the left, but handles a sword with the right hand), and he does nicely swinging on ropes and fighting in battle. But he offers nothing comparable to the vigor and contagious enthusiasm of Douglas Fairbanks or Errol Flynn in rallying his men to the cause. Pic has little chance of coming electrifyingly to life as a result.

Looking beautiful and sporting an accent that comes and goes, Mary Elizabeth Mastrantonio makes a sprightly, appropriately feisty Marian who must literally fight off the unwanted advances of the sheriff before Robin intervenes to save her virtue literally at the last minute. Of the Americans, Christian Slater is most successful at putting on an English accent, and he has some spirited moments as Will Scarlett, Robin's combative and resentful half-brother.

As the "painted man" who accompanies Robin in gratitude for his life having been saved, Morgan Freeman is a constant, dominant presence, but the intriguingly anachronistic notion of a black Muslim cutting a swath through Olde England hasn't been fleshed out in any meaningful or subversive ways. Freeman gets to save the day on several occasions, delivering a baby at one point and introducing explosives into battle at another, but more often than not keeps to himself and regularly has to refuse invitations to drink due to his religion.

Given the opposition, it's Alan Rickman's film to steal if he wants to. But he gives the impression that just creating a memorably icy villain, as he did in "Die Hard," would be too easy. So he goes way over the top, emoting with facial and vocal leers and investing his treacherous tyrant with weirdly vulnerable qualities. It's a relief whenever this resourceful thesp is onscreen, such is the energy and brio he brings to the proceedings, and the brief scenes between him and Geraldine McEwan, who deliciously plays a witch who is his personal seer, are among the film's highlights.

Supporting actors, including Michael McShane as Friar Tuck and Nick Brimble as an appealing Little John, fill the bill adequately, but far from memorably. An unbilled Sean Connery shows up at the very end as King Richard to give his blessing to Robin and Marian's marriage.

John Bloomfield's costume designs are imaginative and more somber than usual for this sort of fare, while John Graysmark's production design is not shown to maximum advantage due to the visual approach. Michael Kamen's score is active but undistinguished by strong melodies, and is abetted by a useless pop song over the end credits.

Two curious credits are for Stuart Baird, an ace film editor, as project consultant, and for Costner as production consultant. One has no doubt he could consult without needing official billing to do so. — *Cart.*

CATTIVA
(WICKED)
(ITALIAN)

A Pietro & Mario Bregni presentation of a PAC production. (Intl. sales, Adriana Chiesa.) Directed by Carlo Lizzani. Screenplay, Furio Scarpelli, Francesca Archibugi, from Scarpelli's story; camera (Cinecittà color), Daniele Nannuzzi; editor, Franco Fraticelli; music, Armando Trovajoli; sound, Vittorio Melloni; costume design, Enrica Barbano. Reviewed at Cannes Film Festival (market), May 12, 1991. Running time: **93 MIN.**
Gustav . . . . Julian Sands
Amelia . . . . Giuliana De Sio
Dr. Bruckner . . . . Erland Josephson
Also with: Milena Vukotic, Flaminia Lizzani, Francesca Ventura, Arian Nijborg.
(English soundtrack)

An old-fashioned period drama, "Wicked" is a well-acted and well-mounted miniature, posing a woman's problems in a turn-of-the-century mental hospital.

Opening scene's lush settings and attractive costumes suggests an attempt to enter "A Room With A View" territory; and Julian Sands from that 1985 hit toplines as a dedicated young psychologist. Film jumps ahead seven years to heroine Giuliana De Sio's breakdown following the death of her daughter. She checks into a Swiss clinic run by old-fashioned Erland Josephson, who assigns Sands to her case. The eager young doctor is intent on trying out his new Freudian methods but runs into conflict with Josephson.

Sands even travels to Italy to interview relatives and friends in order to get to the bottom of De Sio's traumas. He helps her adjust, in a simply staged bittersweet finale. Film surprisingly does not develop a romance between Sands and De Sio.

With attractive lensing by Daniele Nannuzzi and a warm score by Armando Trovajoli, director Carlo Lizzani relies on a traditional approach to storytelling. Though the mature beauty of De Sio is displayed in tasteful nude scenes, film eschews the gross effects of modern cinema.

De Sio, whose English dialog is well-synched, does an excellent job of physical acting to suggest her unbalanced condition in subtle ways. Sands is a solid foil while comic relief is ably provided by De Sio's loyal servant Francesca Ventura.

All tech credits are above average in a pleasant but slight feature. — *Lor.*

KEDULDO URICHURUM
(THEY, LIKE US)
(SOUTH KOREAN)

A Korean Motion Pictures Promotion Corp. release. Produced by Lee Kwon-suk. Directed by Park Kwang-su. Screenplay, Park Kwang-su, Kim Sung-su; camera, You Young-kil; editor, Kim Hyun. Reviewed at San Francisco Film Festival, May 8, 1991. Running time: **100 MIN.**
With: Moon Sung-Keun, Shim Hye-jin, Park Joong-hoon.

There's not a lot to like about "They, Like Us," as love between a revolutionary loner and an unhappy hooker tries to take root in a dying South Korean coal town. But there's not a lot to dislike, either, and the story moves along well enough.

Apparently on the lam from trouble during the Seoul demonstrations (this is never too clear in flashbacks), the young man hides out in a menial job in a briquet factory. There he shares the discontent of the underpaid workers against the overbearing bosses, but he's not moved to take to the ramparts again.

Gradually, though, he's drawn into sympathy and lust for a "hostess" in a local dive, a favorite and mistreated plaything for a plant boss. Inevitably, this leads to a fight, and when it does, the newcomer is going to have to high-tail it once more. The girl, naturally, wants to go with him. Perhaps they'll meet again in a bar in Casablanca, and she will explain why she didn't make the train. — *Har.*

THE PIT AND THE PENDULUM

A Full Moon Entertainment production. Produced by Albert Band. Executive producer, Charles Band. Directed by Stuart Gordon. Screenplay, Dennis Paoli, based on the short story by Edgar Allan Poe; camera (color), Adolfo Bartoli; editor, Andy Horvitch; sound (Ultra-Stereo), Giuseppe Muratori; art director, Giovanni Natalucci; special effects, Giovanni Corridori; special effects makeup, Greg Connom. Reviewed at Houston Intl. Film Festival, April 25, 1991. MPAA Rating: R. Running time: **96 MIN.**
Torquemada . . . . . Lance Henriksen
Maria . . . . Rona De Ricci
Antonio . . . . Jonathan Fuller
Francisco . . . . Jeffrey Combs
Don Carlos . . . . Tom Towles
Gomez . . . . Stephen Lee
Esmerelda . . . . Frances Bay
Cardinal . . . . Oliver Reed

Stuart Gordon's "The Pit And The Pendulum" is a cold potato neither awful enough to qualify as camp nor sadistic and sexy enough to please the blood-and-breasts crowd. Lackadaisical pic is destined for quick video playoff.

Filmed on location in Giove, Italy, but set in 15th century Spain, this melodrama of lust and ungodly mayhem during the Spanish Inquisition stars Lance Henriksen as Torquemada. He makes a valiant effort to play the fanatical priest who wages a holy war against suspected witches and warlocks. With the help of some thick-witted assistants, he tortures confessions from suspects, then has them burned at the stake.

Torquemada's excesses move a visiting Italian cardinal (Oliver Reed) to complain: "The good Lord wants us to love our neighbor — not roast him." Torquemada responds by chaining the cardinal to a corner of his cellar, then burying him alive behind a brick wall.

Torquemada is distracted from his assorted torture devices and public executions only when he sights Maria (Rona De Ricci), a full-figured beauty who makes him regret his vow of chastity. He has her arrested on trumped-up charges of witchcraft, primarily so he can watch while she's strip-searched. Her baker husband, Antonio (Jonathan Fuller), objects. But it takes the help of a real witch in Torquemada's dungeon (Frances Bay) to save Maria from a fate worse than death.

For a pic dealing with premature burials, burnings at the stake, impalements, torture and tongue-slicing, "Pit" is remarkably unexciting.

Production values, particularly Giovanni Natalucci's evocative art direction, aren't half bad. But except for Henriksen's intense perf and Reed's juicily hammy cameo, the performances are bland.

The climax, which has Maria's husband tied beneath a slowly descending, razor-sharp pendulum, might look better on homevideo, which gives viewers access to a fast-forward button.

What this "Pit" really needs is for a member of the Monty Python gang to pop up and cry: "Aha! No one expects the Spanish Inquisition!" — *Ley.*

AMERICANO ROSSO
(RED AMERICAN)
(ITALIAN)

A Warner Bros. Italia release of a Videa-RAI-3 production. Produced by Sandro Parenzo. Directed by Alessandro D'Alatri. Screenplay, Enzo Monteleone from the novel by Gino Pugnetti; camera (color), Alessio Gelsini; editor, Cecilia Zanuso; music, Gabriele Ducros; sound, Remo Ugolinelli; set design, Maurizio Marchitelli; costumes, Paola Bonucci. Reviewed at Alcazar Cinema, Rome, April 25, 1991. Running time: **102 MIN.**
George Maniago . . . . . . Burt Young
Vittorio Benvegnu . Fabrizio Bentivoglio
Antonietta . . . . Valeria Milillo
Zaira . . . . Sabrina Ferilli
Irina . . . . Orsetta De Rossi
Santina . . . . Paola Lucentini
Elvira . . . . Tullia Alborghetti
Il questore . . . . Massimo Ghini

First-time helmer Alessan-dro D'Alatri turns out a stylish debut effort with "Red American," an engaging comedy set in the Fascist 1930s with a startling, film noirish ending. Pic will please local audiences looking for well-made entertainment and could appeal to festivals interested in new Italo cinema.

D'Alatri's advertising background is evident in the pic's lush photography, painstaking period detail and soundtrack of catchy 1930s tunes. But sketchy character development and lightweight story makes watching "Red American" seem like opening a nicely wrapped package with not much inside.

Well-paced and easy to watch, pic follows the adventures of womanizing provincial Fascist Vittorio Benvegnu (Fabrizio Bentivoglio), who works at his uncle's marriage agency, and wealthy Italo-American client George Maniago (Burt Young) in search of a wife who's "beautiful, Italian, virgin and big-breasted."

George is not the ideal catch. He's short, balding and claims to be an undertaker. The mismatched men set out for a posh beach resort. The search, at least for Vittorio, proves to be quite enjoyable as he manages to seduce each one of George's rejects (an aging but attractive widow, a sexy blond manhunter and a pretty deaf-mute peasant girl).

Plot continues along these amusing but somewhat repetitive lines until well into the second half, when the cynical Vittorio unexpectedly falls in love with the girl George has chosen as his bride.

Vittorio tries to convince her to come to Rome with him, where his ties with the Fascists offer him strong chances of a political career. She turns him down and sails for America with George.

Pic's violent ending catches the audience off guard when Vittorio suddenly discovers he's been framed for murder by his wealthy American client.

While Bentivolgio's good looks make him a natural choice as a detatched seducer, he's less effective when asked to put across real emotion. Young makes a good impression in an undeveloped role, and his pidgin Italian is quite funny. Technical credits are above average. — *Clrk.*

ZANDALEE

An Electric Pictures-ITC Entertainment Group production. Produced by William Blaylock, Eyal Rimmon. Executive producer, Nicole Seguin, Staffan Ahrenberg. Co-executive producer, Tom Eliasson. Directed by Sam Pillsbury. Screenplay, Mari Kornhauser; camera (CFI color), Walt Lloyd; editor, Michael Horton; music, Pray For Rain; sound, (Ultra-Stereo), Douglas Axtell; production design, Michael Corenblith; costume design, Deena Appel; assistant director, Pat Burns; paintings, James Mathers; co-producer, Kornhauser, Judge Reinhold. Reviewed at Cannon Haymarket, London, May 14, 1991. Running time: **103 MIN.**
Johnny Collins . . . . . Nicolas Cage
Thierry Martin . . . . . Judge Reinhold
Zandalee Martin . . . . Erika Anderson
Tatta . . . . Viveca Lindfors
Gerri . . . . Joe Pantoliano
Remy . . . . Marisa Toma
Also with: Aaron Neville.

An overheated New Orleans sex triangle let down by a laughable script, "Zandalee" is about par with other romps like "Two Moon Junction" and "Wild Orchid." Teaming of Nicolas Cage and Judge Reinhold could generate extra b.o. heat, but friskier biz is likely in video release.

Reinhold is a former poet who's inherited the family business and is having a hard time living up to his dad's local rep. Sexy young wife Zandalee (Erika Anderson) spends her time running a clothes shop and jogging through the streets in sweaty tank tops. Hubby is also not up to his marital duties between the sheets.

When former buddy Johnny (Cage) rolls into town, Reinhold hires him to do some paintings. Soon, lonesome Zandalee and the hobo are tangoing every which way — atop a washing machine, down an alley, in a church confessional, even a couple of times in bed.

Reinhold chooses to overlook matters, and he and Zandalee eventually try to make a trip out to bayou country. But Cage turns up there, too, and when Reinhold drowns in a boating accident/suicide, Zandalee calls it quits and Cage goes to pieces. Cue tragic finale.

Everyone concerned seems to think pic is some kind of "Nine 1/2 Weeks" Louisiana-style, but strip out the nudity and sack sessions, and all that's left is a script that pulls its punches and seems to

have been pasted together from subtitles on French movies.
— *Del.*

DO OR DIE

A Malibu Bay Films release. Produced by Arlene Sidaris. Written and directed by Andy Sidaris. Camera (Filmservice color), Mark Morris; editor, Michael Haight; music, Richard Lyons; sound (Ultra-Stereo), Mike Hall, Ken Segal; production design, Cherie Day Ledwith; costume design, Merrie Lawson; assistant director-production manager, Mike Freedman; special effects, Eddie Surkin, Etan Enterprises. Reviewed at Magno Review 1 screening room, N.Y., June 11, 1991. MPAA Rating: R. Running time: **97 MIN.**
Kaneshiro . . . . Pat Morita
Richard Estaban . . . . . Erik Estrada
Donna Hamilton . . . . . . Dona Speir
Nicole Justin . . . . . Roberta Vasquez
Bruce Christian . . . . . Bruce Penhall
Edy . . . . Cynthia Brimhall
Lucas . . . . William Bumiller
Shane Abilene . . . . . . Michael Shane
Atlanta Lee . . . . . . Stephanie Schick
Silk . . . . Carolyn Liu
Also with: Richard Cansino, Chu Chu Malave, Ava Cadell, Skip Ward, James Lew, Eric Chen.

Pat Morita switches to a heavy role with excellent results in "Do Or Die." Sixth entry in the "Malibu Express" series of campy actioners is a potent picture to titillate homevid and pay-cable audiences.

Due to a tough marketplace for smaller indies, this feature is getting only minimal theatrical exposure in Nashville ahead of RCA/Columbia's video release. It's a shame since voyeuristic action audiences would get a kick out of "Do Or Die" on the big screen.

Writer-director Andy Sidaris has a streamlined plotline this time, inspired by "The Most Dangerous Game." The pair of beautiful CIA undercover operatives in Hawaii, Dona Speir and Roberta Vasquez, are informed by international gangster Pat Morita that he has assigned six two-man death squads to hunt them down in fair combat. It's a trial run for his plan for world domination.

Aided by a crack team organized by their boss William Bumiller, the Molokai-based duo trek to Nevada, Louisiana and Texas with the mercenary assassins in hot pursuit. It's not surprising to fans of this pic series that the macha femmes handily dispose of the villains, even in hand-to-hand combat during a climactic ninja battle. Morita's underplaying, aided by moody lighting by Mark Morris, lends panache to his scheming role and the "Karate Kid" star also has fun in several scenes dallying romantically with his statuesque Asian-American assistant Carolyn Liu. Erik Estrada, the villain of the previous entry "Guns," is back in a new role as a good guy this time.

Full complement of movie veterans from this series is augmented by several impressive newcomers: notably Atlanta's extemely bosomy dancer Stephanie Schick who has a memorable, nearly NC-17 sex scene under a waterfall with handsome series regular Michael Shane; and Ava Cadell as a smug villainess quickly dispatched by Speir and Vasquez.

Sidaris changes the action series' balance by finding time for numerous sex and/or nude scenes no matter how perilous the situation. For action fans, excellent location work in atmospheric locales delivers the goods with motorcycle, speedboat and dune buggy chases. One highlight is a quarter-scale model airplane show in the Nevada desert to set the stage for model gimmickry à la James Bond flicks.

Tech credits are above average, giving this well-produced (by director's wife, Arlene Sidaris) picture a look and scale well beyond its modest budget.
— *Lor.*

A KARIM NA SALA
(KARIM AND SALA)
(BURKINA FASO)

An Arcadia Films production. Produced by Freddy Denaes. Written and directed by Idrissa Ouedraogo. Camera (color), Pierre-Laurent Chenieux, Dominique Perrier; editor, Dominique B. Martin, Emmanuelle Dehais; music, Myriam Makeba, Abdullah Ibrahim, Gwem, Ramon Cabera; sound, Christian Evanghelou, Arsene Ilboudo. Reviewed at Vues d'Afrique Film Festival, Montreal, April 25, 1991. Running time: **90 MIN.**
With: Noufou Ouedraogo, Roukietou Barry, Sibidou Ouedraogo, Hippolyte Wangrawa, Omar Coulibaly.

Idrissa Ouedraogo has created another beautifully simple story in "Karim And Sala," the tale of young love between two teens growing up in rural Burkina Faso. Tech credits are good and cinematography is lush. Pic is perfect for specialized venues.

As in "Yaaba" and "Tilai," Ouedraogo's trademark real-time pacing stops the clock for 90 minutes of sheer wonder. Helmer

gracefully transports the viewer into another world where emotion and personal interaction are life's most precious commodities. Without moralizing, Ouedraogo contrasts the honesty of youth with the callousness of adulthood via the perspective of children.

Karim initially wins Sala's respect by giving her — rather than selling her — a kid, even though her family has money and his doesn't. Sala is so thrilled with the baby goat, she and Karim become fast friends. However, all is not bliss: Karim has problems at home.

Karim's father is believed to be dead so his mean uncle has inherited both Karim's mom and the family hut. No matter how hard he works, Karim is rejected by his evil stepfather. One day when son and his mother have had enough, they up and leave without so much as a suitcase. Thanks to money provided by Sala, they relocate to another town and live with relatives.

They prosper in the village Bobo. Love develops between Karim and Sala. And the long-lost father reappears to provide a happy ending where the reunited family reclaim their hut and rid themselves of the uncle once and for all.

Fundamental values of survival, love and respect play a key role in script. Ouedraogo has a talent for turning basic themes into stories with universal appeal. — *Suze.*

BEGOTTEN

A Theater of Material production. Written, produced and directed by E. Elias Merhige. Story consultant, Tom Gunning; camera (Kin-O-Lux black & white, 16m), Merhige; editor, Noelle Penraat; sound, William Markle Associates; art direction-special effects, Harry Duggins; costumes, Celia Bryant, Duggins; assistant director, Timothy McCann. Reviewed at Film Forum, June 11, 1991. No MPAA rating. Running time: **78 MIN.**
God Killing Himself . . Brian Salzberg
Mother Earth . . . . . Donna Dempsey
Son of Earth-Flesh on Bone . . . . . .
Stephen Charles Barry

The characters' mythic names are a tipoff that E. Elias Merhige's experimental film is exceedingly artsy and pretentious. Although the director achieved a unique visual look, his slow-moving gore-fest will have all but the most ardent avant-garde buffs heading for the exits.

Besides a grainy, hazy look making it difficult to tell what exactly is going on, "Begotten" is notable for its unappetizing brutality. In the prolonged first scene, a god mutilates himself with a knife. Using his carcass, a mother impregnates herself and gives birth to a son. Eventually, both are captured, tortured and disemboweled by a nomadic tribe.

The glub-glub sounds as organs are pulled from their bodies are enough to make anyone become a vegetarian. There is no dialog and no music, just eerie sound effects to complement the tedious, pointless violence.

Although it has a mythological storyline, the film (made in 1989) has an anthropological look. By shooting in black & white reversal and then rephotographing it one frame at a time on a 16m negative, Merhige created a primitive, haunting mood.

When he shows Mother dragging her writhing son in the woods, the film is starkly beautiful. And his shots of a barren landscape look like something from another planet.

But technical achievement is not enough to sustain interest in the gruesome subject matter. Despite an abundance of blood and guts, camera lingers so long that the violence becomes boring.

Filmmakers and festival-goers interested in the painstaking creative process may want to take a look. Chances are they'll want to leave before the end, because this is one of the longest 78-minute films ever made. — *Stev.*

DEAD TO THE WORLD
(AUSTRALIAN)

A Huzzah Prods. P/L production in association with the Australian Film Commission. Produced by John Cruthers. Written and directed by Ross Gibson. Camera (Fujicolor), Jane Castle; editor, Andrew Plain; music, Gary Warner; production design, Edie Kurzer; production coordinator, Chris Johnson; assistant director, Carrie Soeterboek; co-producer, Adrienne Parr; casting, Alison Barrett. Reviewed at Roxy screening room, Film Australia, Sydney, March 13, 1991. Running time: **102 MIN.**
Johnny Tremain . . Richard Roxburgh
Alexandra Polonski . . . .
                        Agnieszka Perepeczko
Manny Alabaster . . . . Tibor Gyapjas
Pearl Elkington . . . . Lynette Curran
Mr. Keats . . . . John Doyle
Skip . . . . Noah Taylor
Lester . . . . Ghandi MacIntyre
Kogarah . . . . Paul Goddard
Sgt. Jack Grant . . . . . . Paul Chubb
Darcy . . . . John Hinde

An extremely ambitious

first feature using familiar plot devices to explore themes of loyalty, greed and betrayal, "Dead To The World" works on a number of levels. Fest outings could gain a reputation for this richly textured thriller, with arthouse prospects looking solid. It could also become a cult item.

Buffs instantly will recognize the many references to "Johnny Guitar" and "Force Of Evil," with elements of "Body And Soul" thrown in. The allusions are woven into the structure of the film to give it extra dimension, much like Jean-Luc Godard used Hollywood genres.

The setting here is the Sydney inner suburb of Newton, and a boxing gym run by Polish emigré Alexandra Polonski (played with sweaty, hard-bitten realism by Agnieska Perepeczko). The gym is located on real estate the ambitious Pearl (Lynette Curran) wants to develop into a site for yuppie apartments. Alexandra refuses to sell.

Pearl has another reason to hate Alex: Both women are personally involved with punk boxer Manny Alabaster (Tibor Gyapjas). Manny seems to favor Pearl, who's running in local council elections on a law and order ticket.

Enter Johnny Tremain (Richard Roxburgh), a former boxing champ and Alex' former lover. He returns to work at the gym as an odd-job man, but it's obvious Alex wants him around for protection. Before long, their old romance is rekindled.

When Pearl whips up the forces of law and order, including local cop (Paul Chubb) against Alex and Manny, matters start to get out of hand. Behind the scenes, and using all the principals in the drama to his own ends, is a mysterious "businessman" named Mr. Keats (John Doyle).

Not only does he know his old movies, but writer-director Ross Gibson also knows how to tell a story in fresh and exciting ways. Visually, with camerawork by first-timer Jane Castle, "Dead To The World" is extremely striking, using bold colors, off-center angles and extreme closeups.

The stylized soundtrack adds to the strange, oppressive mood. Use of locations, including an aquarium and a street with familiar cartoon characters painted on the walls, also testifies to a fresh and imaginative vision.

However, Gibson and his collaborators tread a knife-edge throughout the film, with florid dialog and literary as well as cinematic quotes. This is clearly not a thriller for the mainstream, but it deserves to find a receptive audience for its audacity.

Performances fit snugly into the mold Gibson has prepared for his actors, with Perepeczko convincing in her Joan Crawford-ish role, Roxburgh suitably heroic in the Sterling Hayden part, and Curran almost matching Mercedes McCambridge in sheer femme wickedness. As the enigmatic Mr. Keats, Doyle's role approximates Roy Roberts' Mr. Tucker in "Force Of Evil."

In support, Noah Taylor ("The Year My Voice Broke," "Flirting") is touching as an ineffectual member of the good guys, and Chubb makes his corrupt cop believably sleazy. There's also a neat cameo from local film critic John Hinde as one of Pearl's victims.

From its imaginative Huzzah Prods. opening logo until fadeout, "Dead To The World" looks and feels new. The problem will be to persuade audiences that this unusual approach to a genre pic is worth seeking out. — *Strat.*

THE RAPTURE

A Fine Line release of a New Line Cinema production in association with Wechsler/Tenenbaum/Parker. Produced by Nick Wechsler, Nancy Tenenbaum, Karen Koch. Executive producer, Laurie Parker. Written and directed by Michael Tolkin. Camera (Deluxe color, Metrocolor prints), Bojan Bazelli; editor, Suzanne Fenn; music, Thomas Newman; sound (Dolby), David Kelson; production design, Robin Standefer; art direction, Kathleen M. McKernin; set decoration, Susan Benjamin; costume design, Michael A. Jackson; assistant director, Josh King; casting, Deborah Aquila. Reviewed at Cannes Film Festival (market), May 12, 1991. MPAA Rating: R. Running time: **102 MIN.**
Sharon . . . . Mimi Rogers
Vic . . . . Patrick Bauchau
Randy . . . . David Duchovny
Mary . . . . Kimberly Cullum
Henry . . . . . Dick Anthony Williams
Sheriff Foster . . . . Will Patton
The boy . . . . De Vaughn Nixon
The older boy . . . . Christian Belnavis
Paula . . . . Terri Hanauer
Tattooed bartender . . . Marvin Elkins
Louis . . . . Douglas Roberts
Angie . . . . . . Carole Rachel Davis

An unexpectedly serious investigation into spiritual malaise and religious fanaticism, "The Rapture" has difficulty walking the line between profundity and pretentiousness. Rather too ambitious and solemn for its own good, film nev-

ertheless stands as a distinctively singular feature debut for writer-director Michael Tolkin, who demonstrates more talent than judgment.

Extremely talky and single-minded, bizarre drama has little to offer mainstream audiences. Specialized distrib Fine Line, taking pic on from parent New Line, can either send it out as wide as possible based on Mimi Rogers' name and the cult angle, or take the chance that critics will give it the boost necessary to create a profile in the semi-art market. It's a tough sell either way for the projected September release.

Rogers plays Sharon, a lost soul in a valueless society who goes to extremes in an effort to find herself. A beautiful young woman with no direction, she lives on the sexual edge in L.A. with her amoral b.f. (Patrick Bauchau), and in one of their group gropes meets Randy (David Duchovny).

Her hot affair with him pushes her to peer into the spiritual abyss, and odd encounters with fundamentalist evangelists and repeated revelations concerning a divine pearl lead her to the Bible, prayer and ultimate acceptance of the Lord.

Story's second half picks up six years later. Now a fervently devout married couple, Sharon and Randy are raising their daughter in the belief that the end is nigh. Indeed it is for Randy, who is killed in an office shooting spree by a fired employee.

Suddenly, Sharon absconds with her daughter to the desert, where she awaits the rapture, the ultimate fulfillment of her religious beliefs that will unite her with her husband and God. Already a modern-day Mary Magdalene after her reformation, Sharon now assumes the burden of Abraham, as she sacrifices her daughter but can't go through with killing herself.

Unsurprisingly, this lands her behind bars, but portents of the apocalypse are at hand. Amidst the arrival of horsemen and a furious storm, the prison walls literally come tumbling down. Still angry at God's cruelties, she is unable to love Him, and is thus adrift in the ruins of her life and the world.

At each turn of the plot, Tolkin surprises by how far he intends to take his highly concentrated drama. An utterly undistinguished personality, Sharon ex-

periences crises of conscience and moral struggles worthy of the most hallowed Biblical figures. Indeed, Tolkin lays on his religious meanings in a way that is both too dense and capricious, overloading the specific situations and characters with a symbolic weight they can't bear.

At the same time, the writer-director can be applauded, in a certain sense, for his audacity in grappling seriously with issues of belief that most modern artists would variously scoff at, satirize or ignore. Unfortunately, his treatment of heavy themes here lacks the clarity needed to make this a truly coherent, convincing film, rendering it easy to dismiss.

But there are some interesting things going on here. Aside from the often misguided adventurousness of Tolkin's dramaturgy, these include Rogers' wholehearted and intense performance. Centerscreen throughout, she reduces everyone else in range to pawns and delivers one of those soul-baring turns that is both impressive and almost too much.

Also notable is Bojan Bazelli's luminous lensing. Pic could profitably be cut by several minutes, particularly in the protracted desert section, when Rogers' desperate waiting and wondering become repetitive and, finally, irritating. — *Cart.*

FINAL APPROACH

An Intercontinental Releasing presentation, in association with Box Office Partners, of a Filmquest Pictures production. Produced and directed by Eric Steven Stahl. Screenplay, Stahl, Gerald Laurence; camera (Panavision, Deluxe color), Eric Goldstein; editor, Stefan Kut; music, Kirk Hunter; additional music, J. Eric Schmidt; sound (Cinema Digital Sound, Dolby), Jeff Vaughn, Keith W. Kresge, Lew Goldstein; production design, Ralph E. Stevic; costume design, Ruth A. Brown; assistant director, Michael Mahler; visual effects producer for Apogee, Denny Kelly; optical effects design, Filmquest Visual Effects Group; special effects animation, Harry Moreau; aerial unit director-camera, Robert Lee Mehnert; 2nd unit camera, Bruce L. Finn; 3rd unit camera, George B. Stephenson; casting, Tina Gordon, Carrie Deysher. Reviewed at Cannes Film Festival (market), May 18, 1991. MPAA Rating: R. Running time: **103 MIN.**
Col. Jason Halsey . . James B. Sikking
Dr. Gottlieb . . . . . . Hector Elizondo
Mrs. Halsey . . . . . . Madolyn Smith
Gen. Geller . . . . . . Kevin McCarthy
Brooke Halsey . . . . . Cameo Kneuer
Doug . . . . Wayne Duvall

"Final Approach" is a gimmicky, tedious sci-fi film, nota-

ble only for its pioneering use of digital sound recording and playback. Script's failure to involve the audience in its shaggy-dog story marks pic a dubious theatrical prospect.

Debuting director Eric Steven Stahl (a graduate of tv commercials) emphasizes technology over content with disastrous results. The touted Cinema Digital Sound provides crisp dialog (not noticeably better sounding than previous six-track stereo films) but is also used here for frequent noisy interruptions that recall the low-tech '70s Sensurround gimmick.

Annoying editing keeps interrupting the action with fleeting flashback shots that further distance the viewer.

While Stanley Kubrick's classic "2001: A Space Odyssey" is the obvious starting point for film's first-person aerial shots buzzing above pretty landscapes including Monument Valley, pic is really in the vein of Douglas Trumbull's would-be sci-fi breakthrough pic "Brainstorm."

"Approach" unsuccessfully attempts to present a roller coaster ride from the brain of air force pilot James B. Sikking. It becomes gradually evident that he was working for general Kevin McCarthy on a top-secret project to plastic-coat conventional aircraft and make them equivalent to Stealth bombers in terms of avoiding detection.

Awkward structure gives film the feel of a two-character play, as amnesiac Sikking is stuck for the duration in a large, antiseptic office questioned by unctuous Hector Elizondo, who appears to be a psychiatrist. Witless dialog leaves Elizondo on his own to provide some comic relief, but Sikking is colorless throughout, making the necessary viewer identification with him and his Kafka-esque plight nearly impossible.

It turns out this exercise is just another "dying flash" riff on Robert Enrico's classic adaptation of Ambrose Bierce's "Incident At Owl Creek Bridge," stretching a man's final moments into feature length trivia.

Supporting cast is virtually dispensed with, as Sikking's lovely wife Madolyn Smith gets just one meaningless scene and occasional flash cuts to work with. Genre vet McCarthy pops up only to bark out orders as Sikking's flashback commander.

Tech credits are pro but inspiration is sorely lacking. — *Lor.*

A ROW OF CROWS

A Propaganda Films production. Produced by Carol Kottenbrook. Executive producers, Steve Golin, Joni Sighvatsson. Directed and written by J.S. Cardone. Camera (color), Michael Cardone; editor, Tom Meshelski; music, Robert Folk; sound, Jan Brodin; production design, William Maynard; costume design, Kelly White; set decoration, Charlie Doane; assistant director, John Vohlers; 2nd unit director, David Womark. Reviewed at the American Film Institute, Warner Building screening room, L.A., April 27, 1991. MPAA Rating: R. Running time: **103 MIN.**

```
Kyle . . . . . . . . . . . . . . John Beck
Paul . . . . . . . . . . . . . Steven Bauer
Grace . . . . . . . . . . Katharine Ross
Click . . . . . . . . . . . . . Phil Brock
Elise . . . . . . . . . . . . . . Mia Sara
```

Time moves slowly in Yuma, Ariz., locale of this desultory, backpedaling tale about a new twist in a 16-year-old murder case. Most compelling mystery here is Propaganda Films' impetus to invest in this murky low-budgeter.

Screened in the U.S. independent section of the AFI/L.A. festival, "A Row Of Crows" (a.k.a. "A Climate For Killing"), even if it finds a distrib, is likely to flap off into the wild blue yonder with barely an audible cry.

John Beck plays a sheriff's captain who gets some puzzling info about a decapitated female body bearing the birthmark of a woman allegedly murdered 16 years earlier.

Since victim had been intimate with the town's feared and loathed land baron and his nutsy family, Beck has to tread carefully in his investigation and resort to unorthodox tactics.

That puts him at odds with "efficiency expert" Steven Bauer, who's been sent from Phoenix to bring the eccentric Yuma operation into line with procedures.

It also rubs wrong with the mayor, a puppet of the ruling family, who wants to keep everything copacetic during Rodeo Week and who threatens to pull Beck's badge.

None of this is very compelling, even to writer-director J.S. Cardone, who keeps veering away from the tensionless plot to linger on the quick-to-develop sexual relations between Bauer and Beck's daughter (Mia Sara).

Meanwhile, viewers may be musing on why the open-shirted, tousle-haired and lazily sensual Bauer character is an enforcer of efficiency. He looks like he'd rather be hoisting a brewski than forcing regulations.

Beck, as the lawman, starts out so laconic that when his doctor tells him to slow down on account of a heart condition, it's hard to believe the line is played straight.

To be fair, he eventually swings into action but the story never does, relying on flashbacks to churn up a turgid scenario of sordid goings-on in the town's richest family.

Even the gratuitous topless dancing scenes during a trip across the Mexican border, ostensibly in search of information, don't turn up the heat.

Producer Carol Kottenbrook, spouse of writer-director Cardone, tries resourcefully to wring some atmosphere from her native bordertown but the locale never takes on much character.

Katharine Ross is credible in a small role as a dedicated but alcoholic coroner, and Phil Brock, as a cheerful deputy, exudes the cocky charm.

Tech credits are merely serviceable on the modestly budgeted pic. — *Daws.*

STRIP JACK NAKED
(BRITISH-DOCU)

A Frameline release of a BFI production, in association with Channel 4 TV. (Intl. sales, BFI.) Executive producers, Kate Ogborn, Andy Powell. Produced and directed by Ron Peck. Screenplay, Peck, Paul Hallam; camera (color, 16m), Peck, Christopher Hughes; editor, Peck, Adrian James Carbott; music-sound, Carbott. Reviewed at Public Theater, N.Y., May 23, 1991. (In The New Festival.) Running time: **96 MIN.**

Subtitled "Nighthawks 2," this documentary gives a forthright account by British director Ken Peck about his filming of "Nighthawks" in 1978 and his experiences as a gay man in Britain over the past two decades.

Opening in June at N.Y.'s Public Theater in conjunction with a revival of "Nighthawks," pic is an effective consciousness raiser and highly personal approach to cinema.

Techically sub-par (its 16m transfer of video lensing comes off murky and dark), "Strip" relies heavily on Peck's ultraserious narration. Clips from "Nighthawks" plus outtakes from same are far more impressive than his impressionistic new video footage.

Peck explains how he had an unrequited love affair at age 14 with a classmate and went through many years at school before discovering an alternative gay lifestyle. The local Catacombs club became his headquarters for assignations, and Peck ultimately was driven to make a serious film (a genre breakthrough in Britain) about being gay and the problems in "coming out." Five-year effort, in collaboration with Paul Hallam, resulted in "Nighthawks."

Since "Nighthawks" was originally an unwieldy 3½ hours long feature, it was edited severely. Peck shows several scenes and characters who were cut, focusing on the late Colm Clifford who was one of the prime movers on the project.

Film moves smoothly back and forth between documenting social movements and personal events in Peck's life. With stills and other illustrative material, he explains how the magazine Films and Filming introduced him to serious treatment of cinema (as well as covers and photos highlighting many films' homoerotic content). Key icons are shown, notably the image of Dirk Bogarde's character tortured by his homosexual status in Basil Dearden's 1961 classic "Victim" and Joe Dallesandro in Paul Morrissey's 1968 "Flesh."

"Nighthawks" documented for Peck the rather frightening night world of the '70s when despite upbeat political activity the gay culture was often obsessed with sexual trysts (he cites John Rechy's boast of having had 7,000 different lovers in a decade as an example of misguided thinking). Peck himself got caught up in this mode, endlessly searching for "Mr. Right."

He ends the film on a bittersweet note of hope: The AIDS crisis has been met with heroism and, traditional stereotypes have been replaced even in the mainstream media by a multiplicity of voices. Peck wistfully accepts the pioneering mantle ("Nighthawks" was a breakthrough that is still influential in such films as "Young Soul Rebels") and believes the next generation will have an easier time coping. — *Lor.*

HALALUTAK ES ANGYALOK
(PATHS OF DEATH AND ANGELS)
(HUNGARIAN)

A Budapest Film Studio-Hungarian TV production. (Intl. sales: Cinemagyar.) Written and directed by Zoltan Kamondi. Camera (Eastmancolor), Gabor Medvigy; editor, Zsuzsa Posan; music, Laszlo Melis; sound, Peter Kardos; production design, Janos Rauschenberger, Sandor Kallai, Gyorgy Arvai; costumes, Maria Feher. Reviewed at Cannes Film Festival (Un Certain Regard), May 17, 1991. Running time: **96 MIN.**

```
Jozsef Schrevek . . . Rudolf Hrusinsky
Ilona . . . . . . . . . . Eniko Eszenyi
Ivan . . . . . . . . . . Grigory Gladiy
```

Visually sumptuous and mystifying, "Paths Of Death And Angels" is the first completed feature of short film maker Zoltan Kamondi whose 1988 production, "Subconscious Stop," was never finished. He seems to be treading Fellini territory with this inventive but frustrating film about an old man with mystical powers he wants to pass on to his son.

The old man is played by leading Czech actor Rudolf Hrusinsky, and he gives an imposing performance as the irascible character whose magic powers enable him to perform inexplicable feats. But he can't prevent his death, and his son, Ivan, seems more interested in dissolute cavortings in a nightclub than inheriting his father's powers.

Enter Ilona, a smart young woman who becomes a pawn in the game played between father and son. What follows isn't always clear, but Kamondi provides vivid and colorful imagery so that the film is always worth watching. It seems to be taking place in another world, certainly not the Hungary of today, but a place where the surreal is the norm.

Pic could get attention on the film fest circuit, and possibly segue into European arthouses and onto tv thanks to its visual elan. Performances are tuned to the director's unusual approach to the subject. — *Strat.*

LA PAGAILLE
(FRENCH)

A Pyramide-Vonier release of an R. Films-Films Français-Films A2 co-production. Produced by François Ravard. Directed by Pascal Thomas. Screenplay, Age and Pascal Thomas; camera (color), Renan Polles; editor, Helene Plemiannikov; music, Vladimir Cosma; sound, Michel Kharat; set design, Willy Holt; costumes, Florence Emir; make-up, Jasmine Nakache; casting, Romain Bremond. Reviewed at Gaumont Convention theater, April 24, 1991. Running time: **100 MIN.**

```
Martin . . . . . . . . . . Remy Girard
Brigitte . . . . . . . . . Coralie Seyrig
Gabriel . . . . . . . . François Périer
Clément . . . . . . . . Clément Thomas
Emilie . . . . . . . . . . Emilie Thomas
Patricia . . . . . . . . Sabine Haudepin
Jean-Jacques . . . . . Patrick Chesnais
  Also with: Nada Strancar, Jean-Marc
Roulot.
```

Despite a botched ending, "La Pagaille" is a thoroughly entertaining comedy about a contented post-divorce family turned upside-down when the father announces he wants the children's mother to return home. Pic, while destined for arthouses, also may find its way into general distribution.

Helmer Pascal Thomas takes the pulse of the contemporary family and finds an amusing irony: If, after seven years of divorce, the status quo is a happy household, it may seem irresponsible for a man to sleep with the mother of his children.

Pic opens one morning in a posh apartment where everyone gets along well. There's Martin, the father (Remy Girard); his lover Patricia (Sabine Haudepin), who's half his age; his actor son (Clément Thomas); his daughter (Emilie Thomas); and a gambling grandfather (François Perier).

Martin runs into classy ex-wife Brigitte (Coralie Seyrig) at an auction, takes her to dinner and they end up in bed together. When the adult kids and grandpa find out, they're wary of disturbing their comfy arrangement. But sometimes "la pagaille" (a mess) can't be avoided. Co-scripters Age and Pascal Thomas deserve credit for deft comic buildup as camera cuts between family pad, mother's apartment, dad's office and a romantic rundown cottage. Key family problem — how to face Dad's well-liked lover — is deliciously postponed as long as possible.

Among numerous entertaining complications are mother's wacko b.f. (wonderfully portrayed by Patrick Chesnais), and two hoods determined to collect on grandpa's gambling debt.

Convinced that Pakistani fundamentalists are out to kill him because he has translated a condemned book, Chesnais turns paranoid and begins noticing Muslims everywhere: among pedestrians, taxi drivers and carpet salesmen.

Acting is strong throughout, from portly Girard's eager lover and easygoing exec to Chesnais' farcical translator. Thomas shows real screen presence.

Helmer Thomas is amusingly inventive in comedy sketches. In the climactic (and cleverest) scene, Clément visits film dubber Patricia at work where she voices her anguish by reciting lines from the film within the film.

But overly long wrap-up diffuses the overall comic impact, and the script settles for easy plot solutions. Tech credits are topnotch. — *Lour.*

MONTREAL INTERDIT
(MONDO MONTREAL)
(CANADIAN-DOCU)

A Memphis production. Produced by Jean George. Directed by Vincent Ciambrone. Screenplay, Brenda Newman; camera (color), Roger Moride; editor, Alain Zaloum; music, Bat Taylor. Reviewed at Famous Players Complex Parisien, April 25, 1991. Running time: **90 MIN.**

"**M**ondo Montreal," a thoroughly absurd chapter in the unofficial Mondo series, promises love, business, uncensored films, "the most beautiful strippers in the world," drugs, voodoo, freak shows (including a man who keeps his tarantula in his mouth), folklore, hypnotists and daily visits from extraterrestials. Rather than raunchy, pic is so painfully bad, it's funny.**

Montreal strip clubs may have the most beautiful strippers in the world, but they aren't in this film. "Mondo Montreal" repeatedly shows the same two (thoroughly bored) dancers going through the motions.

"Montreal can satisfy your most sophisticated or primal desires," according to the pic, set principally in a cheap hotel room and an office with a desk and a water cooler. Acts of bondage and prostitution aren't graphic, and participants look more embarrassed than aroused. So much for the seedier side of Montreal.

There are endless scenes of everything from topless hairdressers to Haitian immigrants conducting voodoo "rituals" (a few dance numbers) beside the patio doors of a suburban condo. Pic drags through lingerie fashion shows and tarot card readings, but it goes into orbit with the scene about extraterrestials. Pathetic "E.T." lookalikes "prove" that extraterrestials "arrive in flying saucers on the south shore of Montreal. It's a daily event," per the narrator. Scene itself comes from outer space, but pic quickly cuts back to the two bored strippers, followed by a tourist boat ride on the St. Laurent river ("which pollutes whales.").

"Mondo Montreal" isn't edited; it's glued together. Tech credits are on the home-movie level. — *Suze.*

DE HOLLYWOOD
A TAMANRASSET
(FROM HOLLYWOOD
TO TAMANRASSET)
(ALGERIAN)

A Fennec Production. Written and directed by Mahmoud Zemmouri. Camera (color), Mustapha Belmihoub; editor, Youcef Tobni; music, Jean-Marie Seria; sound, Rachid Bouasia. Reviewed at the Vues d'Afrique Film Festival, Montreal, April 26, 1991. Running time: **90 MIN.**

J.R.	Mustapha Elanka
Kojak	Arezki Nebit
Colombo	Mostefa Stiti
Baretta	Driss Johoui
Clint Eastwood	Mazouz
Sue Ellen	Ouardia Hamtouche
Spock	Mustapha Zerguine
Rambo	Fawzi B. Saichi

In this slapstick comedy, everyone in Tamanrasset is so addicted to American tv shows that they become a Hollywood character and live their lives via manufactured dreams. Point is clearly that U.S. pics profoundly affect foreign cultures. Director Mahmoud Zemmouri targets all the appropriate characters but milks the concept to death without developing much of a story.**

In the opening scene, Spock almost gets himself beamed to another galaxy when he tunes the satellite dish into India rather than the U.S. for "Dallas." J.R. is a fat old man who tunes out of the show and into a daydream where he imagines he seduces a gorgeous secretary.

His lumpy wife Sue Ellen refuses to wear the Muslim veil because Brigitte Bardot didn't and "look where she got . . ." At bridge club, the women agree that in Dallas, "whiskey is the same price as lemonade." During prayers, Muslim men watch tv upside down between their legs.

Subplot revolves around a band of thieves who attack women and lop off a chunk of their hair. Detectives adopt American role models. The cop shop has an in-house hot dog stand. Baretta couldn't find a parrot so he parades around with a chicken on his arm. Rambo is inept. Colombo's trenchcoat is too clean. Kojak has trouble speaking with a lollypop in his mouth.

Even the children are hooked. The set for their school play is a cardboard television where talking heads mimic stars such as Rambo.

Everyone in town believes everything they see on tv and dreams of life in the land of milk 'n' honey. But even if this pic aptly nails a worldwide phenomena, it's too much caricature to carry a feature. — *Suze.*

TRABBI GOES TO HOLLYWOOD

A production of the Motion Picture Corp. of America. Producers, Brad Krevoy, Steven Stabler. Directed by Jon Turtletaub. Screenplay, Jon Turtletaub, David Tausik, John London; camera, Phedon Papamichael; editor, Nancy Richardson; production designer, Gary Randall; special effects, Don Power; stunts, Jeff Cadiente; costumes, Greg Lavoi. Reviewed at Marmorhaus Cinema, Berlin, May 22, 1991. Running time: **89 MIN.**

Gunther Schmidt	Thomas Gottschalk
Max	Billy Dee Williams
Ricki	Michelle Johnson
Vince	James Tolkan
Goodwyn	Steve Kanaly
Hotel Clerk	Milton Berle
Mr. B	Dom DeLuise
McCready	George Kennedy
Volvo Boss	Celeste Yarnell
Peugeot Boss	Aaron Heyman
Honda Boss	Ken Shinkai
Ford Boss	Michael Adler
Lee Iacocca	Roger Siegal

While it's doing some biz in Germany, "Trabbi Goes To Hollywood" looks like a straight-to-vid stateside. Thin script and jokes funny only to Germans won't make for legs in other markets.**

The Trabi (the title doesn't even get the spelling of the car's name right), the little stinker of an East German car, may currently be Germany's only boxoffice star, having been featured prominently in several post-Wall flicks. It's hard to figure why some bona fide Yank headliners agreed to participate in this lackluster, slapstick comedy which packs as much of a wallop as the Trabi's two-stroke lawnmower engine.

German tv luminary Thomas Gottschalk plays Gunther, an East German inventor who has souped up a Trabi which is fueled with turnip juice. Gunther takes his baby to an automotive convention in L.A. to sell the idea. Car is promptly nabbed by bad guys. Rest of the pic is Gunther's slapstick romp to get his wheels back.

Pic plays to the outsiders' view of the California lifestyle. Biggest yuks are derived from scenes where the hero tries on goofy sunglasses and Simpsons t-shirts on wacky Venice Beach. Billy Dee Williams is Gunther's parking lot attendent sidekick, and other celebs jump on and off the unfunny ride.

"Trabbi Goes to Hollywood" runs out of gas in a hurry.

— *Reli.*

LE CRI DES HOMMES
(THE CRY OF MEN)
(ALGERIAN)

A World Films Co. production. Produced by Kamel Hassen-Khokja and Mohamed Saim. Directed by Okacha Touita. Screenplay, Touita, Mohamed Bouchibi, Allel Yahyaoui; camera (color), Allel Yahyaoui; editor, Yamina Chouikh; music, Rachid Bahri; sound, Jean-Jacques Ferran. Reviewed at Vues d'Afrique Film Festival, Montreal, April 27, 1991. Running time: **105 MIN.**
With: Miloud Khetib, Jean-Yves Gauthier, Roland Blance.
(In Arabic with French subtitles)

"**T**he Cry Of Men" is the kind of sophisticated war drama that makes the hardest of hearts understand a minority struggle. It's a politically moderate action pic about Algeria's war with France, a battle which was to the French what Vietnam was to Americans.

Beautifully shot and superbly acted, pic is ideal for the small screen, especially in French-lingo territories. Tech credits are of high quality.

Story revolves around the French military occupation and the revolutionary FLN (Front de Liberation National), which eventually triumphed. French soldiers and Algerian cops (who comply with the occupation) are the villains, hassling families, arresting men almost at random, torturing them (off screen) and then shipping them off to the killing ground where many are shot.

A sly and subtle script puts viewer sympathies with a handsome Arab cop (smoothly acted by Miloud Khetib) and his French soldier colleague (Jean-Yves Gauthier). They participate in brutal raids and murders until they realize they're fighting for the wrong side. After they've witnessed all the atrocities they can handle, the two unconsciously begin protecting FLN members.

The Arab cop begins hiding truths from his superiors and eventually helps the FLN plan a raid on military headquarters. Realizing his French soldier pal also is torn (initially because he loves an Algerian woman who runs a brothel), he makes sure his buddy is not at h.q. the day of the raid. Suspect to both sides, they are the proverbial victims of circumstance who discover their morality only when faced with a life and death situation.

Plenty of action maintains a brisk pace right to the predictable but plausible ending. During a confrontation between the French army and the FLN, the Arab cop is gunned down by the military and the FLN retaliates by shooting his cohort. Pic is a very neat little package with a story well told.

Terrific acting make rich characters believable. Soundtrack (dotted with the "cries of men") is aptly used to spare viewers from witnessing torture scenes, but makes the message clear nonetheless. — *Suze.*

O DRAPETIS
(MASTER OF THE SHADOWS)
(GREEK)

A Xanthopoulos Co.-Greek Film Center-Greek Television ET 1 production. (Intl. sales: Greek Film Center.) Produced by Aglaia Latsiou, Nikos Moustakas. Directed by Lefteris Xanthopoulos. Screenplay, Xanthopoulos, Lefteris Kaponis; camera (color), Andreas Sinanos; editor, Kostas Iordanidis; music, Nikos Kypourgos; sound, Dinos Kittou; production design, Julia Stavridou; production manager, Nikos Moustakas. Reviewed at Cannes Film Festival (Directors Fortnight), May 19, 1991. Running time: **131 MIN.**
Antonis Barkas . . . . Kostas Kazakos
Theofanis . . . . . Stratos Tzortzoglou
Angelos . . . . Giorgos Ninios
Angela . . . . . . Dora Masklavanou
Simos . . . . Vlassis Bonatsos
Giorgos . . . . Patis Koutsaftis
Roula . . . . Nina Michalopoulou

An end-of-an-era pic, set in Athens in 1950, "Master Of The Shadows" features Kostas Kazakos as an old man who has long operated a traveling shadow-puppet show, but who finds this classical kind of theater out of favor with modern audiences who prefer movies.

In his first feature, Lefteris Xanthopoulos displays his documentary background in the detail of his relaxed and beautiful (but overlong) pic.

The old man knows time is running out for his shadow shows, and the anxiety he feels spills over into acrimonious relationships with the people around him, including his much younger sister (Dora Masklavanou), who's engaged to an unsympathetic seaman, and his young assistant (Stratos Tzortzoglou), who wants to move with the times.

Brisker pacing might have made the film more accessible, but it still could play the festival route and certainly indicates a new talent in this sensitive director. Performances are fine, with Nina Michalopoulou a standout as a bright young hairdresser and friend of the sister.

Andreas Sinanos' camerawork is glorious, and the music by Nikos Kypourgos lively and attractive. — *Strat.*

LANGITKU RUMAHKU
(MY SKY, MY HOME)
(INDONESIAN)

An Ekapraya Film release. Produced by Eros Djarot, Boy Salehuddin, Doddy Sukasah. Written and directed by Slamet Rahardjo Djarot. Camera, Soetomo Ganda Subrata; editor, Sentot Sahid. Reviewed at San Francisco Film Festival, May 4, 1991. No MPAA rating. Running time: **102 MIN.**
Andri . . . . Banyu Biru
Gempol . . . . Sunaryo

The chasm between wealth and poverty in modern Indonesia doesn't discourage writer-director Slamet Rahardjo Djarot, whose "My Sky, My Home" holds out some hope that the younger generation will narrow the gap.

While Djarot's optimism is admirable, his film is less convincing in its contrivances. From the start, the developing friendship between young rich kid, Banyu Biru, and impoverished Sunaryo falls under the "possible, but not likely" category, straining everything that follows.

When Sunaryo's shantytown home is bulldozed, the pair take off for the countryside in search of Sunaryo's grandmother (he never seems much interested in what happened to his father, mother and sister). The journey provides for some mild adventure and a first-hand introduction for Biru to the life of the poor. Poor Sunaryo, however, never gets equal time among the rich.

Eventually each boy returns to the life he's accustomed to. All along, the wealthy lad's father has expressed hope his son will one day be president. If he does, the film suggests, life will be better for the poor. Life might be better still if Sunaryo became president, but that doesn't come up in Djarot's equation. — *Har.*

WIZARDS OF THE DEMON SWORD

A Troma release of an American-Independent Prods. presentation of an Austin Enterprises production. Produced by Grant Austin Waldman. Co-produced and directed by Fred Olen Ray. Screenplay, Dan Golden, Ernest Farino; camera (color), Gary Graver; editor, Chris Roth; music, Anthony Jones; sound, Alexander Welles; art direction, Colin DeRouin; set design, Ildi Toth; assistant director, Waldman; production manager, Diana Jaffe; special effects animation, Bret Mixon; sword master, Dan Speaker; associate producer, Drew Waldman. Reviewed at Cannes Film Festival (market), May 17, 1991. Running time: **81 MIN.**
Lord Khoura . . . . . . Lyle Waggoner
Ulric . . . . Russ Tamblyn
Thane . . . . Blake Bahner
Malina . . . . Heidi Paine
Omar . . . . Jay Richardson
Selena . . . . Dawn Wildsmith
Damon . . . . Dan Speaker
Seer of Roebuck . . . . . Hoke Howell
Gorgon . . . . Dan Golden
Slave master . . . . Lawrence Tierney

Sword and sorcery was never cheaper looking than in "Wizards Of The Demon Sword," a poverty budget special by genre-meister Fred Olen Ray. Troma pickup is strictly a video title.

Filmed on terrain familiar from B westerns and Hollywood serials of yore, "Sword" is actually about the knife of Aktar, supposedly able to unlock evil forces. Russ Tamblyn and his beautiful daughter Heidi Paine have been entrusted with its safekeeping. Evil Lyle Waggoner has captured Tamblyn, but Paine is on the loose.

Macho warrior Blake Bahner accidentally teams up with Paine, and film limns their misadventures trying to spring Tamblyn. Slapstick and bad puns are attempted repeatedly without success (a wise man who helps out the duo is named Seer of Roebuck).

Hambone acting, especially by heavily made-up Waggoner and his chief enforcer, Amazonian warrior Dawn Wildsmith, is fun, but the swordplay here is unimpressive. Cheap sets, stock footage and silly insert sequences of crudely done stop motion animation of dinosaurs are serious drawbacks.

Dan Speaker, who devised the swordfights, is personable in the buddy role opposite Bahner.

— *Lor.*

PEGY PES BEGUSCHY KRAEM MIRA
(SPOTTED DOG RUNNING AT THE EDGE OF THE SEA)
(SOVIET)

A Goskino release. Executive producer, B. Rydvanova. Directed by Karen Gevorkian. Screenplay, Karen Gevorkian, Tolomush Okeev, based on novella by Chingiz Aitmatov; camera, A. Naida, A. Kuz'menko; editor, E. Lukashenko. Reviewed at San Francisco Film Festival, May 7, 1991. No MPAA rating. Running time: **124 MIN.**
With: Bayarto Dambaev, Aleksandr Saskykov, Doskhan Kholzhakcynov, Tokon Daiyrbekov.

"**S**potted Dog Running At The Edge Of The Sea" drags across the screen until it finally comes to a complete halt with another hour of running time still to go.

Like a lot of Soviet directors, Karen Gevorkian has an eye for grim existence, and about the only thing that could make the life of these Nyvkh villagers in Japan's frozen northlands more miserable would be a local theater showing films like these.

Huddled into smoky communal huts on the edge of the Arctic, the simple folk struggle for survival and try to have an occasional good time. A couple of guys have a fight to the death, but it's not clear why. A girl has a baby, and a bear gets killed and eaten and what seems to be a dead person gets dragged around by a rope. Then an equally dead white whale washes up on the beach and they build a house for it and sit around to watch it.

Grandfather goes into the woods and asks a tree "to have pity on me and let me cut you down — you'll make a fine boat." Unfortunately, the tree does not say no and before too long, grandpa, his two sons and grandson are lost in the fog at sea.

They are lost for a very long time while they argue the merits of rowing or not rowing while waiting for the fog to lift. Grandpa jumps overboard, then uncle jumps overboard, then dad jumps overboard and all that's left is the little boy, a sad situation, but at least they have stopped arguing about the rowing.

Just in time, the boat washes ashore and the little boy begins to crawl up the beach toward the village. He crawls. He crawls a bit farther. He crawls some more, with lots of pretty rocks along the way. Finally, he stands up. In Western filmmaking, that might be called the arc of the story. — *Har.*

THE BOY WHO CRIED BITCH

A Pilgrims 3 production. Executive producer, Catherine May Levin. Produced by Louis Tancredi. Directed by Juan Jose Campanella. Screenplay, Levin; camera (Duart color), Daniel Shulman; editor, Darren Kloomok; music, Wendy Blackstone; sound, Paul Cote; production design, Nancy Deren; costume design, Claudia Brown; assistant director, Gary Sales; stunt coordinator, Peter Hock; casting, Deborah Aquila, Alison Zimet. Reviewed at Cannes Film Festival (market), May 12, 1991. No MPAA Rating. Running time: **101 MIN.**
Dan Love . . . . Harley Cross
Candice Love . . . . Karen Young
Mike Love . . . . Jesse Bradford
Nick Love . . . . J.D. Daniels
Jim Cutler . . . . Gene Canfield
Jessica . . . . Moira Kelly
Eddie . . . . Adrien Brody
Also with: Dennis Boutsikaris, Reathel Bean, John Rothman, Samuel Wright, Perry Moore, Sean Ashby.

This hard-hitting drama deals unflinchingly with taboo subject matter: a 12-year-old psychotic boy threatening his mother and society. Bravura acting by young Harley Cross makes "The Boy Who Cried Bitch" riveting but disturbing.

With a more commercial title and specialized handling, pic could carve a niche for itself based on its intense, highly original approach.

Writer Catherine May Levin works in modern territory, far removed from the comfortable gothic horror of "The Bad Seed." Cross, as 12-year-old Dan Love, is all too real as a little terror who goads his younger brothers Jesse Bradford and J.D. Daniels to make life a hell for mom Karen Young.

She's estranged from her husband and trying to raise the boys while taking night classes in Manhattan. Money is not a problem; she's loaded from an inheritance, but it is soon obvious that Young is unbalanced and probably as crazy as her son.

Film reaches impressive dramatic heights early on as Cross' best friend at prep school, kindly janitor Gene Canfield, turns out to be a child molester haunted by his Vietnam War experiences. When the authorities drag Canfield away to lock him up after a violent incident, Cross goes crazy and is sent to a mental hospital for tests.

His uncontrollable behavior soon earns him a permanent stay there, but Cross' bad influence on the other youngsters builds to more violence and he's booted out. Young tries to find another institution but is rejected, and film climaxes with the two of them trapped together back home in a malevolent finish.

With precocious actor Cross' uncensored acting as the centerpiece, debuting Argentine director Juan Jose Campanella builds matters to a fever pitch. Lack of any hope for protagonists Young and Cross make this a tough one to watch, but canny promotion emphasizing lots of screenings could earn "Boy" a solid film festival and arthouse run.

Utilizing a convincing stammer, Cross delivers a stunning acting display, worthy of awards consideration up against any age bracket. In the trickier role, Young is a bit brittle at first times but overall provides the counterpoint to Cross while both Daniels and Bradford create differentiated characters as siblings in Cross' shadow.

Canfield makes the most of his early pivotal role. Sympathetic support is provided by Moira Kelly and Adrien Brody as two institutionalized youngsters who befriend Cross (at their own peril).

Tech credits are fine for this low-budget indie, with striking visuals by Daniel Shulman and a suspenseful score by Wendy Blackstone. — *Lor.*

PAYOFF

A Viacom Pictures presentation of an Aurora production. Produced by Andrew Sugarman, William Stuart. Executive producer, Douglas S. Cook. Directed by Stuart Cooper. Screenplay, David Weisberg, Cook, based on novel by Ronald T. Owen; camera (color), Steven Yaconelli; editor, Edward Abroms; music, Charles Bernstein; production design, Douglas Higgins; costumes, Mary E. McLeod; coproducer, Don Carmody; casting, Justine Jacoby. Reviewed at Cannes Film Festival (market), May 14, 1991. Running time: **115 MIN.**
Peter MacAllister . . . Keith Carradine
Justine Bates . . . . Kim Greist
Harvey Hook . . . Harry Dean Stanton
Rafael Concion . . . . . . John Saxon
Benny Cowan . . . . . . Robert Harper
Also with: Lawrence Monoson, Alan Blumenfeld, William S. Taylor, Suki Kaiser, Jeff Corey, Stephen E. Miller, Tom Heaton, Peter Radon, Don Crowe.

Despite over-familiar elements in this actioner's story line and occasional descents into bathos, perky thesping and a punchy script could boost "Payoff" beyond the tv movie arena.

Keith Carradine is cast as an ex-cop who chances upon the mafioso who sent a lethal bomb to his parents when he was a kid. The plot quickly thickens as the Feds, the Mafia, a pretty teller at a Lake Tahoe casino and a quirky killer get into the act.

Much of pic, which will be shown in the U.S. on Showtime June 22, involves Carradine trying to humble a Mafia boss (John Saxon). Some of the ploys resorted to are ingenious and droll: Carradine gets a casino job by losing a wad he had stolen from the mob; thereby impressing a guard who is watching.

The boss' pop, an old don, and the boss' son, a nasty, scheming viper nicely played by Lawrence Monoson, team up against Saxon after seeing incriminating tapes of him as a sexual deviant.

At moments the subplots entwine dizzyingly with a plan to rob the casino, but the plot remains clear and followable and the interaction of the wonderfully menacing Stanton, the fatuous Saxon, the hip and clever Carradine and the sexy Kim Greist add up to solid entertainment. — *Besa.*

LES SECRETS PROFESSIONELS DU DR. APFELGLÜCK
(FRENCH)

An AMLF release of a Son et Lumiere-Ice Films-Belt Prods.-Films A2 coproduction in association with Mistral Films Group, Canal Plus and Sofica. Produced by Louis Becker, Alain Clert, Thierry Lhermitte. Directed by Hervé Palud, Alessandro Capone, Mathias Ledoux, Stéphane Clavier, Lhermitte. Screenplay, Philippe Bruneau, Lhermitte; camera (color), Jean Jacques Tarbes, Roberto Girometti, Claude Agostini, Gérard Sterin; editor-sound, Pierre Lorrain, Massimo Loffredi, Bruno Charier, Jacques Pibarot; production design, Carlos Conti, Philippe Desert, Thérèse Ripaud; costume design, Martine Rapine, Marina Sciarelli, Friquette Thevenet; makeup, Jacques Clemente, Franco di Girolamo. Reviewed at Gaumont Convention, Paris, May 1, 1991. Running time: **85 MIN.**
Martineau . . . . Jacques Villeret
The old woman . . . . . Micha Bayard
The innkeeper . . . . . . Ticky Holgado
The innkeeper's wife . . Claire Nadeau
Dr. Apfelglück . . . Thierry Lhermitte
Lebeurk . . . . Roland Girard
Also with: Martin Lamotte, Philippe Bruneau, Christina Clavier, Ginette Garcin, Daniel Gélin.

Often dull and derivative, "Les Secrets Du Docteur Apfelglück" wastes top French comedians in five sketches about a young psychiatrist and his patients. Pic's big secret is that at best it belongs on Euro tv.

Not even Jacques Villeret's firstrate work as truck driver saves the opening number. On his way to Dr. Apfelglück's one stormy night, he stops at a remote country inn run by a one-eyed man (Ticky Holgado) and his exhibitionist wife (Claire Nadeau). Couple regularly beat their old servant (Micha Bayard) until the hag knocks them off and forces the driver to stay with her. Skit, with soggy homages to Mel Brooks and Hitchcock, wallows in gags such as Villeret's squeamish reaction to a dead rat.

Far more original is the fantasy of a tv gameshow where buxom model (Zabou) reads out questions of the grinning host who's trying to trip up brilliant blue-collar racist (Roland Giraud). After weeks of insults from arrogant winner, exasperated host flips out.

But the best sketch relies on an old gag. On a Franco-Italian film set in Rome, the prop man repeatedly fails to blow out a candle, which drives actors, crew and hot-tempered Italian helmer up the wall.

Scripters Philippe Bruneau and Thierry Lhermitte have loosely tied skits together with humdrum scenes of doctor's all-white office and a messy reception room run by insubordinate secretary. As for business-like doc with a weird neck beard (Lhermitte), he says little to his patients until his alarm clock rings and the session ends.

The final tv-worthy sketch is for French auds since it relies on a French party game that avoids the words "yes" and "no." Doc goes to heaven, a peaceful sunny village where anyone who says the words collapses instantly like a balloon and wakes up in a dangerous setting on earth. Skit slowly sets up amusing situations such as young doctor laying verbal traps for wrinkled old wife.

Varied styles and comic pacing feel like the work of different hands in sketches directed by Hervé Palud, Allesandro Capone, Mathias Ledoux, Stéphane Clavier and Lhermitte. Tech credits, however, are fine.

Press material says Lhermitte was inspired by Dostoyevsky's writings on dreams, which accounts for silly intellectualizing: "To hear is to be an accomplice." Too bad that fine French comics

were accomplices in this off-the-cuff work. — *Lour.*

AU PAIR

A Trans Atlantic Entertainment, Gel Prods. and Moviworld presentation of a William Shields production. Executive producers, Sandra Connoly, Shields. Produced by Paul Raleigh. Directed by Heinrich Dahms. Screenplay, Dahms, Richard Deynom; camera (Foto-Kem color), Paul Michelson; editor, Stephen Eichenberry; music, John Novello, David Haid; sound (Ultra-Stereo), Shaun Murdoch; production design, Marlene Prinsloo; associate producer, Robert B. Steuer; casting, Clair Sinnett, Jane Warren. Reviewed at Cannes Film Festival (market), May 12, 1991. No MPAA Rating. Running time: **92 MIN.**
Max . . . . Nicholas Guest
Rosa Marques . . . . Ana Padrao
Antonia . . . . . . Jocelyn Broderick
Daughter . . . . Kelly Westhof
  Also with: Jeremy Crutchley, Kevin Smith, John Carson.

Well-titled for the video market, "Au Pair" is a botched thriller that wastes a good premise: a killer nanny.

Nicholas Guest is miscast as a thriller writer who travels from London to Mozambique (actually South Africa, where bulk of pic was lensed) with wife Jocelyn Broderick and daughter when Broderick is assigned as a war correspondent there.

They hire an au pair girl, mysterious-looking Portuguese actress Ana Padrao, to take care of the kid while Broderick is away in the bush checking out military skirmishes. Predictably Guest and Padrao become romantically entwined making Broderick the odd woman out.

With too much foreshadowing that telegraphs to the viewer Padrao's psychotic tendencies, film is not very suspenseful. Lack of heat generated by the Guest-Padrao pairing robs the film of exploitation value in the crowded erotic thriller genre inspired by "Fatal Attraction."

Helmer Heinrich Dahms does a competent job of storytelling, but film suffers from inferior production values, most notable in a distracting, shabby-looking interior set for the climax. Both leads are bland, especially harmful as Padrao's vapid performance robs her role of the potential chills of a Bette Davis in "The Nanny."
— *Lor.*

DYING YOUNG

A 20th Century Fox release of a Fogwood Films production. Produced by Sally Field, Kevin McCormick. Directed by Joel Schumacher. Screenplay, Richard Friedenberg, based on Marti Leimbach's novel; camera (Deluxe color), Juan Ruiz Anchia; editor, Robert Brown; music, James Newton Howard; sound (Dolby), David MacMillan; production design, Guy J. Comtois; costume design, Susan Becker; art direction, Richard Johnson; set decoration, Cricket Rowland; associate producer, Mauri Gayton; assistant director, Stephen Dunn; coproducer, Duncan Henderson; casting, Mary Goldberg. Reviewed at 20th Century Fox studios, June 14, 1991. MPAA rating: R. Running time: **105 MIN.**
Hilary O'Neil . . . . . . Julia Roberts
Victor Geddes . . . . Campbell Scott
Gordon . . . . . . Vincent D'Onofrio
Estelle Whittier . . Colleen Dewhurst
Richard Geddes . . . . . David Selby
Mrs. O'Neil . . . . Ellen Burstyn

Julia's hot; "Dying Young" is lukewarm. Starpower should carry this rather thin and maudlin weeper through some heated weeks, but the only real legs likely to be shown are those amply exposed by the femme lead.

Toiling again for Fox, which released her recent thriller hit "Sleeping With The Enemy," Julia Roberts does little to extend her range in a performance that seems pieced together from aspects of previous roles.

Story's doomed love affair has a sudsy appeal that should capture a certain audience, but its contrived situation robs it of any real emotional veracity.

Campbell Scott ("The Sheltering Sky") plays Victor Geddes, an immensely wealthy young man, a kind of Richie Rich with a terminal illness, who at 28 has been battling leukemia for 10 years. He places an ad for an attractive young lady to nurse him through the bouts of violent illness that accompany chemotherapy.

Enter Julia Roberts as Hilary O'Neil, who in the interest of dramatic contrast is painted as a badly dressed, uneducated street-smart type from blue-collar Oakland. For the lonely, intellectual Victor, she's raw material to be shaped in his image — an irresistible draw.

He also has a romantic obsession with redheads, as evidenced by his Ph.D. dissertation work on German impressionist painter William Klimt, who was similarly inclined.

Roberts sports long scarlet tresses in this pic, so when Scott begins showing her slides of Klimt's voluptuous red-haired

nudes, his intentions are more than obvious.

Director Joel Schumacher ("Flatliners") apparently doubting an audience will stick around just out of concern for Victor's illness, turns a rather shabbily exploitative camera on Roberts, whose legs seem to play the lead role in the first act.

Much of the time pic operates on the level of a teaser sustained by the dangling question of Victor's unconsummated desire.

One shot — included in the trailer — slow-pans Roberts' coltish legs from spike heels to miniskirt, before she goes tottering off in her ill-fitting outfit for the job interview at Victor's palatial mansion.

In this and other aspects, pic smacks uncomfortably of a "Pretty Woman" repeat. Again Roberts plays a relatively powerless character who's getting paid for companionship and sexual allure. Her salary aside ($3 million this outing), one wonders how much progress this represents for actresses.

After Victor survives a wrenching bout of postchemo sickness, during which Hilary blossoms into a handy nurse and macrobiotic cook, story moves from his cold, pristine mansion to charming Mendocino, where the couple takes a beach house so Victor can recover his health (and hair).

Here, of course, they fall in love, and life seems charmed until Victor's illness rears its head again. New characters are introduced: Vincent D'Onofrio as a vigorous local handyman with eyes for Hilary, and Colleen Dewhurst as a wise, earthy vineyard owner. Still, the rather pedestrian script starts to run aground.

Schumacher compensates by restlessly adorning the story with all manner of decoration, from the dramatically austere interiors of Victor's San Francisco manse to the swimmingly romantic North Coast vistas.

In one mawkish shot, he even superimposes an art history text over the image of the couple gazing into each other's eyes on the beach, to imply the relationship has substance.

The fact that it continues to play as tenuous and circumstantial doesn't do much to aid pic's cause. Nor does the rather timid choice of ending, which negates Victor's self-chosen heroic quest. Pic winds up relying heavily on James Newton-Howard's string-heavy score to push it through its emotional paces.

Roberts, who displays the usual combo of flintily self-sufficient and winningly vulnerable traits, plus overdone reaction shots to Victor's humorous antics, seems to be showing the strain of two years of nonstop picture-making in a perf that's less affecting than usual. Her portrayal of a working-class character is not exactly chameleon-like.

Scott, in a beguiling and technically polished turn as the desparately lonely sufferer, should get a career boost from this high-exposure role.

The picture suffers from a general lack of credibility, from Victor's friendless isolation to the inability of his powerful father to locate him at his coastal retreat. Lush, high-tone production design and Roberts' array of fetching costumes (Hilary miraculously acquires good taste and a large wardrobe in a hurry) don't make it any more convincing.

Pic plays like a sentiment-soaked escapist fantasy for the bed-and-breakfast set. Only the public's appetite for Roberts will set it apart. — *Daws.*

DEAD SPACE

A Califilm release. Produced by Mike Elliott. Directed by Fred Gallo. Screenplay, Catherine Cyran; camera (Foto-Kem color), Mark Parry; editor, Lawrence Jordan; music, Daniel May; sound (Ultra-Stereo), Craig Feldburg; production design & 2nd unit director, Gary Randall; set design, Colin de Rouin; costume design, Greg Lavoi; assistant director, Chris Beckman; production manager, Michael E. Upton; special makeup effects, Gabe Bartalos; stunt coordinator, Patrick Statham; 2nd unit camera, Flavio Labiano; associate producer, Jonathan Winfrey; casting, Steve Rabiner. Reviewed on vidcassette, N.Y., June 14, 1991. MPAA Rating: R. Running time: **78 MIN.**
Steve Krieger . . . . . . Marc Singer
Marissa Salenger . . . . . Laura Tate
Darden . . . . Bryan Cranston
Stote . . . . Judith Chapman
Jill . . . . Lori Lively
Sal . . . . Frank Roman
Tim . . . . Randy Reinholz
Tinpan . . . . Rodger Hall
Joe . . . . Greg Blanchard
Devon . . . . Liz Rogers

An okay clone of "Alien," "Dead Space" has been in regional theatrical release since January but is mainly for sci-fi fans who haunt vidstores.

Debuting helmer Fred Gallo has carefully watched the Ridley Scott 1979 monster hit and has smoky sets, chest-bursting monsters and the other ingredients. Film was shot as "Biohazard," a

moniker used in 1983 by Fred Olen Ray.

Marc Singer toplines as a space jockey investigating a distress call from a research lab on the planet Phabon. Beautiful genetics researcher Laura Tate is worried after a research assistant died working on creating a new virus to combat the deadly Delta 5 virus. The other scientists, led by Judith Chapman and Bryan Cranston, want to hush up the incident and continue their research.

It turns out that the new virus is a "metamorphic mutant," changing its own genetic structure as it grows. Soon it gets loose, keeps changing form and starts killing people. Gabe Bartalos' makeup effects are okay in the gore department, but the little puppets representing the monster aren't scary. Full-grown monster resembles a huge praying mantis.

Leads Singer and Tate make an attractive team. Outer space scenes look like stock footage from "Battle Beyond The Stars," a 1980 production from Roger Corman who backed this one as well. — *Lor.*

TRANSIT
(FRENCH-GERMAN)

A Paris Classics-Action Films-FR3 Films-La Sept-SFPC (Paris)-ZDF (Germany) co-production. Produced by Humbert Balsan. Directed by René Allio. Screenplay, Allio, Jean Jourdeuil, from Anna Seghers' novel; camera (color), Richard Copans; editor, Marie-Hélène Quinton; music, George Boeuf; sound, Olivier Schwob; production design, Gisele Cavali, Sylvie Deldon; costumes, Gisela Storch; production manager, Malek Hamzaoui; assistant director, Christophe Marillier; associate producer, Klaus Hellwig. Reviewed at Unifrance screening room, Paris, May 6, 1991. Running time: **84 MIN.**
Gerhardt . . . . Sebastian Koch
Marie . . . . Claudia Messner
The doctor . . . . . . Rudiger Vögler
Nadine . . . . Magali Leris
Georges Binnet . . . . Paul Allio
Claudine . . . . Nicole Dogue
Strobel . . . . Ludwig Boettger
Heinz . . . . Hans Diehl
Mexican consul . . . . . Bob Facundo
U.S. consul . . . . . William Doherty

A wartime tale of intrigue centering on desperate attempts of European refugees to obtain transit visas to leave Vichy-occupied France will inevitably arouse comparisons with "Casablanca." René Allio's new film, though based on a much-praised novel by Anna Seghers, emerges as a disappointingly bland approach to

an exciting subject.

The film is set in Marseilles in 1941 and focuses on a group of people desperate to leave the country for a safer future in Mexico or the U.S. But Allio handles the subject without inspiration, rushing through the early scenes at breakneck speed (helped by a bland narration) and not making the most of the ironic ending.

Nor is he helped by his cast, with both Sebastian Koch and Claudia Messner giving rote lead performances, and only Rudiger Vögler bringing a touch of distinction to his role of a jaded doctor. Production design aptly captures the mood of the wartime city, and Allio has packed the film with an assortment of colorful characters, but, sadly, it all adds up to very little. — *Strat.*

DOU HAP
(GOD OF GAMBLERS II)
(HONG KONG)

A Wins' Movie production. Produced by Hueng Wa-sing. Written and directed by Wong Ching. Camera (color), David Chung; music, Lowell Lo; art director, Mok Siu-kei; costume design, Yee Chungman; associate producer, Lo Kwokkeung; action director, Wong Kwan. Reviewed at Metro 2 theater, London, April 20, 1991. Running time: **100 MIN.**
With Andy Lau, Stephen Chow, Ng Mang-dat, Sharla Chang, Heung Wasing, Chan Fat-yung. *(In Cantonese; English, Chinese subtitles)*

A deft sequel to the 1989 Hong Kong smash, "God Of Gamblers II" deals a better-balanced hand of yocks and action. Despite plethora of local references, this lively caper about two cardsharps will entertain fans of offshore Chinese commercial fare.

The original ended with master gambler Chow Yun-fat passing on his skills to disciple Andy Lau, now the big cheese in East Asia whose status is challenged by a heavy.

Enter Stephen Chow as a pushy kid who wants to study under Lau but whose psychokinetic powers only work when he's in love.

Pic's lure is the teaming of established superstar Lau with fast-rising Chow. Lau holds his own as the straight man and the gags are left up to Chow, who has a boyish charm and a nice line in deadpan and double-takes. Chow almost walks off with the pic until the all-stops-out finale,

but the combo works.

Experienced comedy helmer Wong Ching (who cameos in an outdoors john) encores as writer-director, and even works in send-ups of "Swordsman" and "A Terra-Cotta Warrior." Tech credits, including special effects, are all fine, with the usual speedy editing. Megastar Chow Yunfat, from the original, pops up briefly in a closing gag. — *Del.*

MAGYAR REKVIEM
(HUNGARIAN REQUIEM)
(HUNGARIAN)

A Dialóg Filmstudio-Clasart-Transatlatic Media Associates production. Produced by Péter Bacsó. Directed by Károly Makk. Screenplay, Makk, based on the novella by Mihály Kornis; camera (Eastmancolor), Miklós Bíró; editor, Maria Rigó; music, Kamilló Lendvay; sound, János Réti; production design, József Romvári. Reviewed at Hungarofilm screening room, Budapest, May 28, 1991. Running time: **102 MIN.**
With: György Cserhalmi, Károly Eperjes, Mathieu Carrière, Péter Andorai.

A starry cast doesn't save "Hungarian Requiem" from slowly dying on its feet. Sans name of w.k. helmer Károly Makk, this post-'56 Magyar prison drama wouldn't rate much of a chorus.

Story has a group of political prisoners waiting in a condemned cell two years after the abortive anti-Soviet uprising. They include a charismatic freedom fighter (György Cserhalmi), a former security officer (Károly Eperjes), a frightened idealist (Mathieu Carrière), a gypsy who's humiliated by the guards, and an aged professor.

Each one gets screen time before being carted off and lynched. Interviews with the prison governor (Péter Andorai), and occasional dream sequences and riots, break up the repetitive format. Pic ends with a final fantasy of the group horsing around on a seashore.

Flat dialog and downbeat direction take the clout out of the drama, with none of the characters registering in emotional terms. The dream sequences (one in a circus and another in a gypsy camp) trivialize the subject matter and seem spliced in from another movie.

From a strong cast, only Andorai as the compromised prison governor makes much impact. Cserhalmi has his moments in a flashback with a sexy girl guerrilla, but the hearts-and-flowers

tone grates badly. Tech credits are all fine. Pic bowed locally with much hoopla on Oct. 23 last, the 34th anni of the uprising.
— *Del.*

SZOBA KIÁLTÁSSAL
(CRUEL ESTATE)
(HUNGARIAN)

An Objektiv Filmstudio production. (Intl. sales: CineMagyar, Budapest.) Directed by János Xantus. Screenplay, Xantus, Sándor Sultz; camera (Eastmancolor), Tibor Klöpfler; editor, Katalin Kabdebó; sound, István Sipos; production design, Tamás Vayer; costume design, Andrea Flesch. Reviewed at Hungarofilm screening room, Budapest, May 28, 1991. Running time: **87 MIN.**
With: Zofia Rysiówna, Anikó Für, Andrzej Ferenc.

A Grand Guignol yarn with a darkly comic edge, "Cruel Estate" is a refreshingly different Magyar offering, with no historical or political baggage. Film fest dates could be in order.

A young couple, Jenö (Andrzej Ferenc) and Helén (Anikó Für), sign a contract with old biddy Szeréna (Zofia Rysiówna) to take over her snazzy Buda house when she dies. Under the deal (common in Hungary), they move in and take care of her.

It's soon clear that Szeréna doesn't have all her marbles. Terrified of being poisoned, she even refuses to eat fresh eggs. The house soon stinks of rotting food, and Szeréna becomes confined to a wheelchair.

Jenö, an architect, rigs up a sprung trapdoor to finish off the old dear; and while the couple are away having their baby, Szeréna ends up spliced to the wall on a coathook. All seems set fair until Szeréna's twin sister (supposedly dead) turns up one day and claims the property; and when Jenö checks Szeréna's coffin at the cemetery, it's empty.

Pic builds gradually and develops a Polanski-like atmosphere, with the wife going bananas and the old woman taking on a satanic edge. Chunks of Verdi on the soundtrack underline the operatic tone, and the bloody finale has an attractively surreal quality.

Thesping is on the button, especially Polish vet Rysiówna in the double role of the twin sisters. Technically pic is fine, with crisp lensing by Tibor Klöpfler and tight direction by young János Xantus, far more controlled here than in earlier efforts like

the 1984 "Eskimo Woman Feels Cold." — *Del.*

HOMO NOVUS
(HUNGARIAN-SOVIET)

A Budapest Filmstudio-Yunostfilm production. (Intl. sales: CineMagyar, Budapest.) Directed by Pál Erdöss. Screenplay, Zoya Kudriya; camera (b&w), Ferenc Pap, Vladimir Fridkin; editor, M. Kareva, Klára Majoros; music, Mikhail Tarivergiev; sound, Valentina Alexeyeva, György Fék; production design, Irina Kalashnikova; costume design, N. Kryuchkova. Reviewed at Hungarofilm screening room, Budapest, May 28, 1991. Running time: **91 MIN.**
With: Irina Kupchenko, Georgi Taratorkin, Anya Bazenkova, Olga Stulova, Igor Bukatko, Daniil Ivanov, Oleg Shpitalsky, Anton Bielov.

(Hungarian soundtrack)

A delinquent student drama with a preachy last act, "Homo Novus" gets by on unfussy direction and strong playing by Soviet thesp Irina Kupchenko, as the 30-something math teacher who's harrassed by her high school class.

Galina Alekseyevna (Kupchenko) is a divorcée who can't face her pupils and is also having a secret affair with fellow teacher Sasha (Georgi Taratorkin). The students lodge a complaint with the municipal party committee alleging she's incompetent — and anti-Semitic, to boot. They also spy on her affair and pin the photos up on the noticeboard.

With the school management twitchy and Galina close to cracking up, the pupils pull a final stunt, "kidnapping" her young son from nursery school. Galina calls in the cops and the students finally repent their wrongdoing.

Moralistic ending has a traditional Eastern Bloc feel; and though the students are hardly Ivy League, pic has little of the new nihilism of some recent Soviet items. Its real depth is in Kupchenko's sad, baggy-eyed performance, especially her wistful twosomes with Taratorkin.

Magyar helmer Pál Erdöss provides the same soft docudrama look as in "The Princess" (1983) and "Countdown" (1986). He's well served by characterful black & white lensing, especially in the night scenes, and solid playing down the line from the all-Soviet cast. Version caught was Hungarian dubbed, with Kupchenko expertly voiced by w.k. thesp Juli Básti. — *Del.*

GAWIN
(FRENCH)

A Gerard Louvin release of a Loco Corto Intl.-Soprofilms-TF-1 co-production. Produced by Gérard Louvin. Directed by Arnaud Selignac. Screenplay, Alexandre Jardin, Selignac; camera (color), Jean-Claude Larrieu; editor, Emmanuelle Castro; music, Jérome Soligny; sound, Rolly Heller-Selignac; makeup, Florence Fouquier; casting, Shula Siegfried. Reviewed at Forum Horizon, Paris, April 18, 1991. Running time: **95 MIN.**
Nicolas . . . . . Jean-Hugues Anglade
Xerkes . . . . Wojtek Pszoniak
Marthe . . . . Catherine Samie
Félix . . . . Bruno
The garage mechanic . . Yveds Afonso

Despite its rough edges, "Gawin" is an appealing variation on "E.T. The Extra-Terrestrial." Here, a father pretends to be a likable alien to fulfill the fantasy of his terminally ill 6-year-old. Pic has a slim chance at arthouses, but it should find a niche as a dubbed theatrical release or as a video for children and their parents.

Film's opening quickly runs through the "E.T." clichés: Cute boy with a roomful of toys and a dog hears spaceship land and meets extra-terrestial named Gawin. In an early scene, a doctor tells Nicolas (Jean-Hugues Anglade) that only a miracle can save his ailing son, Félix (Bruno). So dad borrows a circus spaceship and dons a gold lamé suit and crusty silver sea helmet (think Jules Verne).

Father then decides to risk the boy's health on the ultimate camping trip. Gawin invites Félix to blast off for his home planet. In reality, father hauls spaceship and doped son to a remote snow-covered summit.

The plastic mask for Gawin, a Humpty Dumpty face with three chins and spark plugs for ears, is surprisingly expressive while intentionally fake. Unlike Nicolas, a immature widower who lives with his mother, Gawin is the perfect papa: He's entertaining and emotionally responsive (his spark plugs wiggle) and always nonthreatening. Still, Félix' dad has potential — as a zoo veterinarian, he's a nurturing guy.

Co-scripters Alexandre Jardin and Arnaud Selignac (who helmed) fiddle awkwardly with paternal immaturity when dimwit dad leaves son alone for hours while he buys milk. Technical flaws don't help: Segues can be awkward, and lighting shifts from glacial brightness to dark cabin

interiors.

Helmer was wise to limit special effects to the boy's brief fantasy of travel at light speed. After all, this is a down-to-earth tale.

Not surprisingly, pic's biggest problem is the hermit Xerkes (Wojtek Pszoniak), a weirdo who investigates mountain rock and sulight from his summit cabin. He limps into pic's last half-hour to cure the boy with crystals. Only 6-year-olds will swallow this hocus-pocus.

Thankfully, helmer ends with an ordinary father-and-son scene and a casually inserted moral: Real fathers don't need masks to devote time to their son. — *Lour.*

UN COEUR QUI BAT
(A BEATING HEART)
(FRENCH)

A Pyramide release (MK2 Prods. USA in U.S.) of a Hachette Premiere et Cie-UGC-Avril SA-FR3 Films co-production with the participation of the CNC. Investimage 2, Investimage 3 and Canal Plus. Produced by René Cleitman. Written and directed by François Dupeyron. Camera (color), Yves Angelo; editor, Françoise Collin; music, Jean-Pierre Drouet; sound, Pierre Gamet; first assistant camera, Laurent Fleutot; production manager, Pierre d'Hoffelize; production supervisor, Christine Raspillere. Reviewed at MGM screening room (Paris), May 2, 1991. Running time: **100 MIN.**
Mado . . . . Dominique Faysse
Yves . . . . Thierry Fortineau
Jean . . . . Jean-Marie Winling
Luc . . . . Steve Kalfa
Hotel desk clerk . . . . . Daniel Laloux

This carefully composed love story makes good use of Paris locations to create a universe of its own. Sensitive performances and poetic yet grounded approach of "Un Coeur Qui Bat" lend arthouse appeal to this urban tale of 40-something adulterers.

In one of the swiftest overtures since "Betty Blue," man (Thierry Fortineau) follows woman (Dominique Faysse) off Paris metro train into cafe, sidles up to her at the bar and asks if there's a hotel nearby. They tryst, then part. She (Mado) is in no hurry to trade phone numbers, but accepts his (Yves') at his insistence. It's not long before she gets around to calling.

Pale and skittish with occasional moments of grace, red-haired Faysse looks like a cross between Stan Laurel and Venus on the Half-Shell (Botticelli's "Birth Of Venus").

She's an actress of sorts, married to an antique dealer (Jean-Marie Winling). They have a 17-

year-old son who's rarely at home, a beautifully appointed houseboat moored on the Seine. Mado still loves her husband, but she's not at all sure which way satisfaction lies. Her own tendency to vacillate troubles her.

Audience learns less about Yves except that he's also married and is seriously smitten with Mado. Story is all in the telling. Pic does a dandy job of examining a reverse courtship: *schtup* first, get acquainted later. Long takes and intelligent dialog build intimacy. Helmer's subtle sense of humor leavens tale of intermittently requited love.

Couple carry on the affair in hotels, leaving one such establishment in the red-light district at Pigalle only to take a brief stroll and spontaneously enter another. Hotel desk clerk composes for drumes, the instrument whose jungle-style thumping is used as punctuation throughout pic. Sonic device could have been trite in less skilled hands but percussionist Jean-Pierre Drouet works wonders in his first film score.

Entire film is lensed with taste and imagination. Touristy settings of Pigalle, Sacré-Coeur and flea markets area well-integrated into the narrative and could be a plus for foreign audiences. — *Ness.*

FOR DAGENE ER ONDE
(FOR THE DAYS ARE EVIL)
(NORWEGIAN)

A Norsk Film production. Produced by Hilde Berg. Executive producer, Odd Ween. Directed by Eldar Einarson. Screenplay, Einarson, based on Anne Karin Elstad's novel; camera (color), Björn Jegerstedt; editor, Yngve Refseth; music, Geir Böhren, Bent Aserud; sound, Sturla Einarson; production design, Harald Egede-Nissen; assistant director, Marianne Bjöorneboe. Reviewed at Saga Cinema, Oslo, March 1, 1991. Running time: **75 MIN.**
Hildegunn . . . . Anne Krigsvoll
Robert . . . . Pål Skjönberg
Tore . . . . Björn Sundquist

Making a picture out of Norway's best-selling novel of the 1980s wasn't a bad idea, but Eldar Einarson hasn't directed since the '70s and he's at sea from the beginning of the muddled narrative. Poorly written dialog hampers good actors, and bizarre events go unexplained.

Story deals with 70-year-old Robert returning from America and finding companionship in 35-year-old neighbor Hildegunn. She is married to a farmer, but starts seeing Robert regularly. Local fieldhands, relatives and even the clergy think it's a love affair and promptly begin harassing the couple, poisoning Robert's birch tree and drowning cats.

The measures seem harsh, true motives are not established and the pic ends with tragedy. The film has the material for an earthy village melodrama, but the characters lack character and their relationships, good or bad, lack specifics. Pluses are a good rainy opening scene and a few glimpses of Norwegian scenery, but here's one picture those majestic hills couldn't save. — *Olav.*

THERE'S NOTHING OUT THERE

A Valkhn Film & Video production. Produced by Victor Kanefsky. Executive producer, Alice Glenn. Written and directed by Rolfe Kanefsky. Camera (color), Ed Hershberger; editor, Victor Kanefsky; music, Christopher Thomas; sound, Natalie Budelis; associate producer, Michael Berlly; special effects supervisor, Scott Hart; creature design, Ken Quinn; casting, Bill Williams. Reviewed at Houston Intl. Film Festival, April 26, 1991. No MPAA Rating. Running time: **90 MIN.**
Mike . . . . Craig Peck
Doreen . . . . Wendy Bednarz
Jim . . . . Mark Collver
Stacy . . . . Bonnie Bowers
Nick . . . . John Carhart 3d
Janet . . . . Claudia Flores
David . . . . Jeff Dachis
Sally . . . . Lisa Grant

It's a bit late in the day for a spoof of "dead teen-ager movies" (Roger Ebert's description), but 21-year-old filmmaker Rolfe Kanefsky brings an amusingly satirical tone to the slasher melodrama of his "There's Nothing Out There." Pic should do well on what's left of the midnight-movie circuit, and even better on homevideo.

Actually, video is the perfect medium for this tongue-in-cheeky thriller, which takes dead aim at the clichés abounding in B and C list titles. Standard-issue plot has seven attractive teens on spring break driving to a secluded mountain cabin, where they are stalked by a killer.

The big difference is, one of the teens (Craig Peck) has "rented every horror film that's available on videotape." So he knows all the danger signals that indicate a mass slaughter in is store.

Naturally, the other six teens, three pairs of horny co-eds, are too busy planning romantic escapades when Mike offers dire warnings. Even after the killer, a recently crash-landed alien monster, starts gobbling up the guys and turning the girls into zombies, Mike has a difficult time prying the couples apart to run for their lives.

Much of the pic is played relatively straight, which actually sharpens its satirical edge. At one point, Kanefsky gets a big, goofy laugh by having a character escape the monster's clutches by grabbing hold of a conveniently low-hanging boom mike. Most of the time, though, pic stops well short of "Airplane!"-style surrealism as it pokes fun at genres.

Special effects are deliberately cheesy, but acting is slightly better than what's usually found in dead-serious slasher pics. A couple of the sexual interludes get surprisingly steamy, indicating Kanefsky wanted to satirize the genre's T&A action as well as its slice-and-dice mayhem. He lets things get out of hand, even by parody standards, but that, too, may help pic in the video rental market. — *Ley.*

L'AUTRE
(THE OTHER)
(FRENCH-ITALIAN)

A Pathe Europa release of a Carthago Films-Les Films de la Saga-Films A2-La Sept-Pathe Cinema (Paris)-Video Holdings (Rome) co-production. (Intl. sales: Pathe.) Executive producer, Mark Lombardo. Produced by Tarak Ben Ammar. Directed by Bernard Giraudeau. Screenplay, Giraudeau, from Andrée Chedid's book; camera (Eastmancolor), Giorgios Arvanitis; editor, Claude Frechede; music, S. Yiannatou; sound, Dominique Levert; production design, Jean-Pierre Clech; production manager, Michel Choquet; assistant director, Elie Adabachi. Reviewed at Unifrance screening room, Paris, May 2, 1991. Running time: **90 MIN.**
With: Francisco Rabal, Julian Negulesco, Smail Mekki, Wadeck Stanczak.

An unpretentious, beautifully shot and emotionally powerful film, "The Other" has the slightest of plots but considerable impact.

Set in a small Greek village near the sea, pic opens with an old man (Francisco Rabal) enjoying the landscape's serene beauty. He starts talking with a young male tourist he spies in the window of a small hotel. They're interrupted by a massive earthquake. The old man survives, but his new friend disappears.

The authorities believe no one could have survived the quake, but the old man stubbornly refuses to give up hope, and hangs around the disaster site determined that "the Other" must have been buried alive.

Eventually, his persistence pays off. Sounds are heard from underground, a skeptical rescue team is brought in and, after an agonizingly long wait, the missing man is rescued.

Writer-director Bernard Giraudeau takes this simple outline and fleshes it out with a poetic script, glorious images (photographed by Greek master Giorgios Arvanitis) and a noble performance from Spanish actor Rabal. Helmer is willing to take risks with the material so that the cathartic climax is handled with the camera focused unflinchingly on Rabal's face as he hears the rescue take place. Filmed on location in Cyprus, pic is a quietly impressive mood piece handled with distinction. — *Strat.*

DEEP BLUES
(DOCU)

A Radio Active Films-Oil Factory Ltd. production. Executive producer, David A. Stewart. Produced by Eileen Gregory, John Stewart. Directed by Robert Mugge. Camera (color), Erich Roland; editor, Mugge; music director-commentary-narration, Robert Palmer. Reviewed at Sydney Film Festival, June 11, 1991. Running time: **91 MIN.**
With: Big Jack Johnson, Roosevelt (Booba) Barnes, Junior Kimbrough, Jessie Mae Hemphill, R.L. Burnside, Booker T. Laury, Lonnie Pitchford, Jack Owens, Bud Spires, Jessie Mae's Fife and Drum Band, David A. Stewart, Robert Palmer.

World preemed at the Sydney film fest, Robert Mugge's music documentary examines the traditional blues musicians of the Mississippi Delta. With excellent sound recording and firstrate music, "Deep Blues" should find its target audience easily and be of lasting archival interest.

Saying "it's difficult to focus on the blues without being affected by them," Mugge proves blues music is still alive and well in the delta, though the musicians whose haunting work is captured on film are all getting on in years. Few, if any, young blues players are in evidence.

Most of the film records performances, not in a studio but rather on front porches and out in the open. Highlights include Jessie Mae Hemphill's rendition of "You Can Talk About Me," Booker T. Laury's "Memphis Blues" and Roosevelt (Booba) Barnes' "Heartbroken Man."

Exhilarating as "Deep Blues" is, the presentation of it is awkward. Mugge drags blues expert and the author of a book called "Deep Blues," Robert Palmer, plus the film's financial backer, David A. Stewart (of Eurythmics) on-camera to link the musical numbers and intro the artists. Neither Palmer nor Stewart seem comfortable in their roles, making for some amateurish moments.

But the music's the thing, and "Deep Blues" presents the rich delta traditions and musicians with love and enthusiasm.

— *Strat.*

MANE
(THE DWELLING)
(INDIAN)

A National Film Development Corp. of India production. Written and directed by Girish Kasaravalli. Camera (color), S. Ramachandra; editor, M.N. Swamy; sound, S.P. Ramanathan. Reviewed at Sydney Film Festival, June 15, 1991. Running time: **125 MIN.**
Rajanna . . . . Naseeruddin Shah
Geeta . . . . Deepti Naval
Also with: Mico Chandra, Rohini Hattangadi, B.S. Achar.

A highlight of this year's Indian Panorama in Madras, "The Dwelling" is an intriguing, if overlong, black comedy on the familiar theme of villagers coming to live in a big city. Further fest exposure is the likely route for this well-crafted picture.

Though the city is unnamed, the film was made in Bangalore. After a long search for suitable accommodation, Rajanna and Geeta rent an apartment in a compound and cheerfully set about redecorating it. They leave in place a large, ornate and slightly sinister double bed left behind by previous tenants.

All goes well until a tin shed in the backyard of the compound is taken over by some characters who work on something mysterious and noisy in the middle of the night. With their peace and quiet shattered, Rajanna and. Geeta

petition their neighbors to help them evict the shed people, but to no avail.

At this point, pic starts to take on Kafkaesque overtones, and writer-director Girish Kasaravalli proves himself adept at maintaining an unsettling mood of barely specified menace. Fine performances from Naseeruddin Shah and Deepti Naval as the beleaguered couple are an asset to this unusual and strikingly photographed pic.

With trimming, pic could stir up international interest because it's quite a change from the average Indian film, even though Indian customs and attitudes are an integral part of the story. Reaction at the Sydney fest, pic's first foreign exposure, was positive. — *Strat.*

TERMINATOR 2:
JUDGMENT DAY

A Tri-Star Pictures release, from Carolco, of a Mario Kassar presentation of a Pacific Western production in association with Lightstorm Entertainment. Produced and directed by James Cameron. Executive producers, Gale Anne Hurd, Kassar. Co-producers, B.J. Rack, Stephanie Austin. Screenplay, Cameron, William Wisher; camera (CFI color), Adam Greenberg; editor, Conrad Buff, Mark Goldblatt, Richard A. Harris; music, Brad Fiedel; sound (Dolby, Cinema Digital), Gloria S. Borders; production design, Joseph Nemec III; art direction, Joseph P. Lucky; set decoration, John M. Dwyer; costume design, Marlene Stewart; unit production manager, Dirk Petersmann; assistant directors, J. Michael Haynie, Terry Miller, Scott Laughlin, Frank Davis, Tony Perez, Dustin Bernard, James Lansbury, Xochi Blymyer; second unit director, Gary Davis; special makeup and Terminator effects, Stan Winston; ILM visual effects supervisor, Dennis Muren; special visual effects, Fantasy II Film Effects; special visual effects sequences, 4-Ward Prods., Robert Skotak, Elaine Edford; casting, Mali Finn. Reviewed at Cary Grant Theater, Culver City, Calif., June 23, 1991. MPAA Rating: R. Running time: **136 MIN.**
Terminator . . Arnold Schwarzenegger
Sarah Connor . . . . . Linda Hamilton
John Connor . . . . . Edward Furlong
T-1000 . . . . Robert Patrick
Dr. Silberman . . . . Earl Boen
Miles Dyson . . . . Joe Morton
Tarissa Dyson . . S. Epatha Merkerson
Enrique Salceda . . . . Castulo Guerra
Tim . . . . Danny Cooksey
Janelle Voight . . . . Jenette Goldstein
Todd Voight . . . . . Xander Berkeley

He's back all right, and with enough artillery to virtually ensure that this seven-year-removed sequel will blast through the competition and rank as one of the summer's highest-grossing films.

Whether the pic can ultimately justify a reported $100 million cost is for accountants to sort out, but Tri-Star and Carolco should see major boxoffice fireworks over the long Fourth of July weekend, and producer/director/co-writer James Cameron has succeeded in giving action and Arnold Schwarzenegger fans more than their money's worth.

As with "Aliens," Cameron has again taken a firstrate science fiction film and crafted a sequel that's in some ways more impressive — expanding on the original rather than merely remaking it.

This time he's managed the trick by bringing two cyborgs back from the future into the sort-of present (the math doesn't quite work out) to respectively menace and defend the juvenile John Connor (Edward Furlong) — leader of the human resistance against machines that rule

the war devastated world of 2029.

For some it will be too much of a good thing, and the film's relentless pace, length and decibel level no doubt will inspire more squeamish viewers to wish they could get off this ride somewhere before its anticlimactic finish.

And even the stunning effects become familiar through exposure, though hardly to the point where one loses appreciation of the remarkable technical wizardry.

For the most part, however, "Terminator 2's" aim is on target, and b.o. should benefit from Schwarzenegger's expanded star appeal in the intervening years, during which he's grown considerably as an actor even as he's slimmed down from his bodybuilding days.

For those reasons, Schwarzenegger is more comfortable and assured here than the first time around, reprising a role so perfectly suited to the voice and physique that have established him as a larger-than-life film persona.

The story finds John Connor living with foster parents, his mother Sarah (Linda Hamilton) having been captured and committed to an asylum for insisting on the veracity of events depicted in the first film. Thwarted in the earlier attempt to kill Sarah and prevent the boy's birth, the machines who rule the future dispatch a new cyborg to slay him while the human resistance sends its own reprogrammed Terminator back — this one bearing a remarkable resemblance to the evil one that appeared in 1984. (Apparently, any time you spread flesh over a cyborg chassis it comes out looking and sounding like an Austrian bodybuilder.)

The film's great innovation involves the second cyborg: an advanced model composed of a liquid metal alloy that can metamorphose into the shape of any person it contacts and sprout metal appendages to skewer its victims.

The effect actually takes a little-used element from Cameron's water-logged epic "The Abyss" and runs with it — giving rise to a creature that can be perforated and dismembered at will, only to keep coalescing back into its original form, played with stern-jawed menace by Robert Patrick.

Script by Cameron and William Wisher at times gets lost amid all the carnage, and the time-bending conundrum — how a visitor from the future can cause future events when he wouldn't have existed had those events not occurred — is as puzzling as it was the first time around, though it proves a minor distraction from the film's less intellectual pursuits.

Hamilton's heavy-handed narration also is at times unintentionally amusing, though through her Cameron again offers the sci-fi crowd a fiercely heroic female lead, albeit one who looks like she's been going to Madonna's physical trainer.

Cameron wisely has incorporated several catchphrases from the first pic into the dialog to provide a knowing wink to its fans, in the process relying on Schwarzenegger's inherent good humor to lighten the grim action and high casualty count.

Other human types generally hold their own against the plentiful pyrotechnics, among them Joe Morton as an ill-fated scientist and Furlong, an engaging enough if sometimes annoying young actor in his first bigscreen role.

Stan Winston and the horde of others involved in the Terminator/T-1000 effects merit Oscar consideration for their contributions, which include a major human-robot battle in the future and a dream sequence in which Los Angeles is vaporized. If the budget is a study in excess, at least a lot of it ended up on the screen.

Additional tech credits are uniformly superior, with sound at cannon-shot level and topnotch production design.

Editing is another matter, if only in that Cameron needs someone to rein him in with regard to length on this sort of action opus. Still, it hasn't prevented other pics from achieving blockbuster status, and "Terminator 2" just may end up as this summer's baddest buster on the block.
—*Bril.*

THE NAKED GUN 2½:
THE SMELL OF FEAR

A Paramount release of a Zucker/Abrahams/Zucker production. Produced by Robert K. Weiss. Executive producers, Jerry Zucker, Jim Abrahams, Gil Netter. Co-producer, John D. Schofield. Directed by David Zucker. Screenplay, David Zucker. Pat Proft; camera (Technicolor), Robert Stevens; editor, James Symons, Chris Greenbury; music, Ira Newborn; sound (Dolby), Richard Bryce

Goodman; production design, John J. Lloyd; set design, James Tocci; set decoration, Mickey S. Michaels; costume design, Taryn Dechellis; associate producers, Robert LoCash, Michael Ewing; assistant director, John T. Kretchmer; second unit director, Robert K. Weiss; casting, Mindy Marin. Reviewed at Paramount screening room, N.Y., June 20, 1991. MPAA Rating: PG-13. Running time: **85 MIN.**
Lt. Frank Drebin . . . . Leslie Nielsen
Jane Spencer . . . . . Priscilla Presley
Ed Hocken . . . . . . George Kennedy
Nordberg . . . . O.J. Simpson
Quentin Hapsburg . . . Robert Goulet
Dr. Meinheimer/
 Earl Hacker . . . . . Richard Griffiths
Commissioner
 Brumford . . . . . Jacqueline Brookes
Hector Savage . . . . . Anthony James
Baggett . . . . Lloyd Bochner
Fenzwick . . . . Tim O'Connor
Dunwell . . . . Peter Mark Richman
Ted Olsen . . . . Ed Williams
George Bush . . . . John Roarke
Barbara Bush . . . . . Margery Ross
John Sununu . . . . Peter Van Norden
Winnie Mandela . . . . . . Gail Neely
Blues singer . . . . Colleen Fitzpatrick

"The Naked Gun 2½" is at least two-and-a-half times less funny than its hilarious progenitor. But that still adds up to enough laughs (a large number of which are crammed into the trailer) to make this a lucrative bit of silliness for hot-weather audiences.

Original 1988 release, which was derived from the short-lived "Police Squad" tv series, gunned down $34.4 million in domestic rentals, and this one should roughly hit that target. First rule of successful sequels has been followed, as the four leading protagonists and same creative team have been retained for the followup. Even the tight running time is identical.

Only key players missing are two of the original four writers, longtime team members Jerry Zucker and Jim Abrahams, who have since moved on to their own directing careers and are credited here as exec producers. A couple of more gag minds would have been welcome here, as the level of insane invention and volume of jokes aren't up to those established in the first outing.

But even if the laugh machine isn't operating at top efficiency, it still cranks out a few choice bits of irreverent lunacy. Like the original, this one has an audaciously "political" opening, as Lt. Frank Drebin (the indelible Leslie Nielsen), now posted in Washington, D.C., instead of Los Angeles, makes a farce out of a White House dinner populated by the likes of President and Mrs. Bush, John Sununu, and even Nelson and Winnie Mandela.

Clothesline plot, designed to make the most of director David Zucker's environmental concerns, has bad guy Robert Goulet kidnaping the president's wheelchair-bound energy czar and replacing him with a lookalike who will endorse continued heavy reliance on oil, coal and nuclear power.

Case sees Drebin catching up with his erstwhile inamorata (Priscilla Presley) who, we learn, dumped him two years earlier. After an amusing rendezvous in a truly blue jazz boite, pair communes soulfully over a potter's wheel in a send-up of "Ghost," and Drebin doesn't seem threatened by a newspaper headline that announces, "Elvis Spotted Buying Condo In Aspen."

As before, basic approach has Drebin blithely bumbling through his responsibilities and repeatedly proving himself to be an ambulatory disaster area on the way to solving his case. To a great extent, comedy depends upon the character being blissfully oblivious to the chaos he churns up in his wake and here, Nielsen seems just a tad more self-aware than he was in the original.

But more crucially, too many gags just fall flat. Long stretches pass without serious laughs cropping up, while other jokes are belabored beyond the breaking point. Nothing here, finally, hits the high moments of hilarity reached repeatedly in the original or in the first Abrahams-Zucker-Zucker effort, "Airplane!"

Whereas O.J. Simpson, who reappears here as the hapless Nordberg, took the brunt of physical abuse in the first "Naked Gun," that honor in the sequel falls to Margery Ross, whose Barbara Bush hardly goes a minute without taking a nasty fall or hit. John Roarke's George Bush is just off-center enough to be weirdly right.

When the material is working, Nielsen is a total delight in his career-clinching role, while Presley and George Kennedy go along for the ride in the right spirit.

Connoisseurs of gag credits will have plenty of reason to stick around until the very end, for seldom in film history has the sound mixer been credited with a hearing aid, or the set dressers been assisted by cross dressers. Perhaps best of all, however, is the capper of the opening credits, as Zsa Zsa Gabor reenacts for posterity the act that has made her most recently famous.
—*Cart.*

AUX YEUX DU MONDE
(IN THE EYES OF THE WORLD)
(FRENCH)

A UGC release of a Les Prods. Lazennec-FR3 Films-SGGC-La Generale d'Images production, with the participation of Canal Plus. (Intl. sales: President Films, Paris.) Produced by Alain Rocca. Written and directed by Eric Rochant. Camera (Eastmancolor), Pierre Novion; editor, Catherine Quesemand; music, Gerard Torikian; sound, Jean-Jacques Ferran; production design, Thierry François; production manager, Xavier Amblard; assistant director, Jacques Royer; associate producer, Adeline Lecallier; casting, Pierre Amzallag. Reviewed at UGC Danton, Paris, May 5, 1991. Running time: **95 MIN.**
Bruno . . . . Yvan Attal
Schoolteacher . . Kristin Scott-Thomas
The driver . . . . Marc Berman
Juliette . . . . . Charlotte Gainsbourg
Bruno's mother . . . . Francine Olivier
Juliette's mother . . . Michele Foucher
Also with: Amelie Iazouguen, Benjamin Piton, Elinor Jagodnyk, Elisa Marie, Jonathan Ramos, Julie Autran, Maxence Camelin.

Eric Rochant's striking and widely acclaimed first feature, "A World Without Pity," won him a prize at the 1989 Venice fest as well as a César for best first feature. His second effort is further indication of an interesting talent, but is nonetheless a disappointment. Offshore business looks to be dubious.

Pic has a very simple premise. In a small village, Bruno is bored with life and the joshing of his friends. He's in love with a young hairdresser, Juliette, who lives in a neighboring village, and wants to impress her.

This he attempts to do by hijacking a school bus at gunpoint and taking children, a teacher and the bus driver hostage. He orders the driver to take the bus to Juliette's village. That's about all there is in the way of plot, with the teacher and driver trying to keep the children, and the deranged gunman, calm, and the police gradually closing in.

It might have worked with a more assured performance in the lead. But Yvan Attal, who was impressive in Rochant's earlier film (and won a César for best male newcomer) is encouraged to overplay this time; he has several scenes in which he rants and raves to tiresome effect.

More impressive are Marc Berman, as the stoical driver, and Kristin Scott-Thomas as the concerned teacher. "In The Eyes Of The World" isn't without merit, and there are a few scenes in which Rochant's obvious talents as a director shine through; as a screenwriter he has, on this occasion, provided material that's really too thin.

Technically, the film is fine, with sharp, fluid lensing by Pierre Novion especially noteworthy. — Strat.

DUTCH

A 20th Century Fox release. Produced by John Hughes and Richard Vane. Executive producer, Tarquin Gotch. Directed by Peter Faiman. Screenplay, Hughes; camera (color), Charles Minsky; editor, Paul Hirsch, Adam Bernardi; music, Alan Silvestri; sound, Stephan Von Hase; production design, Stan Jolley; art direction, Tracy Bousman; set decoration, Chris Burian-Mohr; set decoration, Jackie Carr; costume design, Jennifer Parsons; assistant director, Josh McLaglen; stunt coordinator, Buddy Joe Hooker; casting, Jane Jenkins. Reviewed at 20th Fox, L.A., June 26, 1991. MPAA Rating: PG-13. Running time: 105 MIN.
Dutch . . . . Ed O'Neill
Doyle . . . . Ethan Randall
Natalie . . . . JoBeth Williams
Reed . . . . . . Christopher McDonald
Brock . . . . Ari Meyers
Halley . . . . E.G. Daily
Homeless woman . . L. Scott Caldwell

Latest film to roll off the John Hughes production line is a sturdy and familiar model not destined for standout performance. Modest in intention and effect, this roadtrip comedy for 20th Century Fox resembles a beloved VW bug that will have to struggle to hold its piece of the road as the summer blockbusters thunder past.

In designing "Dutch," writer-producer Hughes lays in some oft-used parts, from the family holiday gathering to the travails of incompatible travelers.

In this case, the focus is on Ed O'Neill (tv's "Married . . . With Children") as Dutch, a salt-of-the-earth guy who's volunteered to pick up his girlfriend's snotty kid, Doyle (Ethan Randall), at an elite boarding school and bring him home for Thanksgiving. Little does Dutch know what he's in for.

Full of rage over his mother's divorce from his callous but absurdly wealthy dad (Christopher McDonald), Doyle wants nothing to do with either his doting mom (JoBeth Williams) or her new boyfriend, and he spews his towering contempt at working-class Dutch.

This being Hughes country, Dutch naturally has to teach the young reptile a thing or two about real values and good folks. It all depends on Dutch's ability to make good on his boast that he can make a friend of anybody —and O'Neill's ability to carry the picture, since audiences will definitely not be rooting for the stone-faced little Master of the Universe type.

The kid is so despicable that even Dutch soon loses his taste for the challenge. Therein lies the pic's weakness, as the boy's hateful behavior is so trying that this two-character journey — even with its attendant adventures with fireworks, hookers, tacky motels and homeless shelters — isn't all that enticing.

O'Neill is well cast as the tough and confident regular guy, but his comic gifts fall short of hilarious, and director Peter Faiman, helming his first project since "Crocodile Dundee," never really sets a rollicking groove.

Still, Hughes' script has its moments (asked "What'll it be?" by a truckstop waitress, Doyle replies icily, "Anything that won't make me vomit"), and the emotional scenes are truly affecting.

Young Randall is forced to keep his charisma under wraps for most of the pic, but he shows flashes of a winning style now and then and carries off his egghead dialog and superior stance with aplomb.

Filmed in Georgia, Tennesee, rural Illinois and on L.A. soundstages, film draws texture and comedy from locations and features some savory casting, including E.G. Daily and Ari Meyers as sly young hookers. Particularly effective is Alan Silvestri's deft score. — Daws.

SEUNG SING GUSI
(ALAN AND ERIC BETWEEN HELLO AND GOODBYE)
(HONG KONG)

An Impact Films production. Produced by Wallace Cheung. Executive producer, Eric Tsang, Chan Ho-sun. Directed by Chan. Screenplay, Barry Wong, Chi Li; camera (color), Jingle Ma; editor, Chan Ki-hap; music, Richard Lo. Reviewed at Metro 2, London, June 15, 1991. Running time: 98 MIN.
Alan . . . . Alan Tam
Eric . . . . Eric Tsang
Olive . . . . Maggie Cheung
Barry . . . . Barry Wong
(Cantonese dialog; Chinese and English subtitles)

Imagine an oriental "Jules et Jim" in H.K. and San Francisco, and you're halfway to meeting "Alan And Eric." Likable leads and smooth helming make this unusual Hong Kong item useful film-week balance between chopsocky and action fare.

Pic takes the real-life friendship between singer-actor Alan Tam and popular comic Eric Tsang and splices it into a fictional folderol with the loopy Olive (Maggie Cheung). Resulting yarn on love and friendship, narrated in flashback by the singer, has a fresher feel than much offshore Chinese product.

After an abstract intro sketching pair's boyhood dreams and Eric's spell Stateside with his father, pic settles down in Hong Kong in the early '80s. Alan is strumming for pennies in a trendy seaside bistro run by a grumpy boss (a neat cameo by co-scripter Barry Wong). When Eric rolls up one day the pair set up a chicken farm together.

Along comes Olive, in floppy hat and booties, and soon the three are into Truffaut territory. She takes a shine to fatty Eric but it's Alan who gets the t.l.c. Latter finally strikes it big as a rock star and former hits the slab in 'Frisco with diabetes.

The vignettish plot sometimes gets elbowed around by too many montage sequences, but amiable playing by the three leads (especially puppy-faced Tsang) keeps the emotional line intact and mostly free of mush. All tech credits are pro. Tam's songs could be trimmed for foreign dates, and the soppy handles on pic's title sawn off. The Chinese original literally means "A Tale Of Two Cities." — Del.

ASIAN AMERICAN

PALE BLOOD

A Noble Entertainment Group and Alpine Releasing Group presentation of a Leighton/Hilpert/Kaczmarczyk production. Executive producer, Max Hilpert. Producers, Omar Kaczmarczyk and Michael W. Leighton. Directed by V.V. Hsu. Screenplay, Takashi Matsuoka, Hsu; camera (Foto-Kem color), Gerry Lively; editor, Stewart Schill; music supervisor, George Cook; sound mixer, Steve Evans; production design, Shane Nelson; assistant director, Tony Brewster; casting, Aaron Griffith. Reviewed at 14th Asian American Intl. Film Festival, N.Y., June 21, 1991. MPAA Rating: R. Running time: 94 MIN.
Michael Fury . . . . . George Chakiris
Van . . . . Wings Hauser
Lori . . . . Pamela Ludwig
Jenny . . . . Diana Frank
Cherry . . . . Darcy DeMoss
Harker . . . . Earl Garnes
Frazer . . . . Frazer Smith
Lead singer . . Michael Anthony Palm
Lori's date . . . . . . Steven Bramble

Notable primarily for the unusual pairing of George Chakiris as a vampire and Wings Hauser as a vampire wannabe, "Pale Blood" is a bloodless updating of the Dracula legend. Utterly predictable from first bite to last, it ends up being more laughable than scary. Consider a theatrical run highly unlikely for this turkey.

Chakiris, who won an Academy Award for "West Side Story" 30 years ago, resurfaces as a vampire in search of a mate. To meet another eligible bloodsucker, he assigns a young researcher (Pamela Ludwig) to investigate a string of "vampire killings" in Los Angeles.

He soon encounters a photographer (Hauser) who wants to capture a real vampire on videotape. Hauser even has a vampire hunting sword. Doesn't everyone?

A montage of Los Angeles street scenes shows bikers, hustlers, shoppers and others innocently going about their business. The question is: Who will be the next victim? The other question is: Who cares?

Looking for the murderous vampire and potential mate, Chakiris checks out a trendy club. There he meets Jenny (Diana Frank), who returns with him to his stark apartment. Instead of killing her, Chakiris politely takes just enough blood to sustain himself.

The film offers some lame special effects, like Chakiris walking through windows and levitating out of his portable coffin. Visually, it resembles a tv movie, but most teleplays contain more plot twists than this cliché-ridden story.

As a result, the audience remains one step ahead of the movie at every turn. Even the bloody finale is drawn out too long, and the slow-motion confrontation packs little punch.

First-time director V.V. Hsu has the nerve to include footage from the silent classic "Nosferatu." But her unintentionally ridiculous retelling is actually closer to "Love At First Bite."

The best thing in the movie, other than Hauser's manic performance, is Agent Orange's song "Fire In The Rain." And Anthony Michael Palm, who stands in for the lead singer, is the only actor who even remotely resembles Bela Lugosi.

"Pale Blood" adds little to the vampire legend. Buffs may rent it as a joke, but they will be disappointed by the lack of gore.

Maybe "West Side Story" lovers will request it; after all, Chakiris may have to wait another 30 years for his next leading role. — *Stev.*

HIPPY PORN
(BLACK & WHITE)

An Apathy Prods. presentation. Produced and directed by Jon Moritsugu and Jacques Boyreau. Screenplay, Moritsugu; camera (black & white), Boyreau; editor, Moritsugu; sound recordist, Randi Brown; art director, Elizabeth Canning. Reviewed at 14th Asian American Intl. Film Festival, N.Y., June 21, 1991. No MPAA rating. Running time: **95 MIN.**
L. . . . . Victor E. of Aquitaine
M. . . . . Elizabeth Canning
Mick . . . . Marek Waldorf

This shoestring black & white production satirizes the pretensions of college esthetes, the kind who chain smoke, discuss art and suffer paralyzing ennui. Unfortunately, despite some amusing lines, "Hippy Porn" is itself pretentious and self-indulgent. Viewers will be as bored as the characters.

The fragmented, nearly plotless film revolves around three friends, played by Victor E. of Aquitaine, Elizabeth Canning and Marek Waldorf. In the opening scene, Canning runs over a dog on her way to school. That's about as action-packed as this picture gets. The remainder of the film consists of the three talking, listening to music and hanging out at a bohemian coffee house called Cafe Camus.

Eventually, Canning and Waldorf become more than just friends, although their idea of a fun date is hunting for rats in sewers. Later, Canning expresses her contempt for an art show by slashing the paintings.

The punk sensibility is continued in the soundtrack, being released by Matador Records. It will probably fare better than the film, which is slowed down by artsy visual touches.

The directors, Jon Moritsugu ("Der Elvis") and Jacques Boyreau, try too hard for a 1960s feeling. In one scene, they flash title cards with poetry and briefly turn the camera upside down. Such gimmicks get in the way of the innocuous dialog, which is often quite funny.

"All I do is write papers about rock bands," Waldorf moans. Later, a woman says, "There are those of us who can make a 15-year ordeal out of puberty."

Before putting on an appropriately silly act at the cafe with Aquitaine, Canning says, "The days move like molasses." That goes for the movie, too.

The directors do capture the group's apathy. And Aquitaine and Canning are convincingly blasé as the fashionable, do-nothing teenagers. With his mop of black hair, Waldorf looks the part of the bored punk, but he often seems to be reading his lines from a cue card.

Considering the tiny $15,000 budget, the directors achieved a surprisingly distinctive look.

With more action and fewer experimental effects, "Hippy Porn" might have been an enjoyable satire. As it is, audiences may agree with Aquitaine when he says, "I wish there was a way to fast forward to the good parts." — *Stev.*

FIRES WITHIN

A Pathe Entertainment-Metro Goldwyn Mayer release of a Nicita/Lloyd production. Produced by Wallis Nicita, Lauren Lloyd. Executive producer, Jim Bloom. Directed by Gillian Armstrong. Screenplay, Cynthia Cidre; camera (Panavision), David Gribble; supervising editor, Lou Lombardo; editor, John Scott; music, Maurice Jarre; production design, Robert Ziembicki; 1st assistant director, Marc Egerton; unit production manager, David Streit. Reviewed at Movies of Plantation, Fort Lauderdale, Fla., June 30, 1991. MPAA Rating: R. Running time: **86 MIN.**
Isabel . . . . Greta Scacchi
Nestor . . . . Jimmy Smits
Sam . . . . . Vincent Philip D'Onofrio

"Fires Within" moved into initial release in Miami, where it is set and where, presumably, its Cuban-American motif would get a strong kickoff from the film's most sympathetic audience. Hampered by a pensive approach, pic's crossover potential lies in the appeal of its romantic triangle more than its disavowal of Latin stereotype in order to hit dramatic chords.

Director Gillian Armstrong's handling of the politics-vs.-love theme is languid and emotionally indecisive, and thus unlikely to stir much enthusiasm. Director's penchant for extreme closeups and tight groupings will help the film's presumably quick transfer to the small screen, following a hard sell in metropolitan markets.

Despite a pair of steamy bedroom scenes that are simple inserts to assist marketing in theatrical release, the story floats on a plane somewhere between ideology and passion.

The timely, real-life situation involves an attractive emigre (Greta Scacchi) and her infant daughter (Brit Hathaway), among the "raft people" who continue to flee Cuba via open ocean on makeshift, floating deathtraps — hoping for landfall in the Florida Keys. They're rescued by a seaman (Vincent Philip D'Onofrio), with whom the woman forms a romantic relationship over the next eight years.

She left a husband behind in Cuba, Jimmy Smits as a writer imprisoned for criticizing the Castro regime. His sudden release and subsequent arrival in Miami as a hero creates a classic romantic triangle against the backdrop of Cuban emigre politics.

Director Armstrong's attempt to cover all the emotional and political ramifications of Cidre's thoughtful tale is, for the most part, dramatically respectable. But it is a cold narrative that never lingers on any situation long enough to generate either suspense or romance.

Scacchi's woman-in-the-middle role is confused at worst, detached at best. "Fires Within," at one time titled "Distant Shores," tells of, but does not show, the struggle for survival for herself and her daughter that supposedly colors her romantic involvements.

Smits, as the husband, garners the film's appeal. After much soul-searching regarding the ill effects of his political activities on his wife and daughter, he makes a belated (successful) effort to recapture the affections of both.

D'Onofrio, as Scacchi's rescuing seaman/lover, never has a chance as an actor or character. It appears as if the role was trimmed either in last-minute rewrites or the editing room, leaving D'Onofrio with the shell portrait of a sensitive redneck sucker who doesn't know when to quit. Reasons for his former, apparently intense relationship with the woman and the admiration of her child for him are unclear despite critical "why things are" dialog in the opening scene.

Motive for the seaman's cultural showdown on a dance floor in front of the woman's family and friends, which tips the romantic triangle's balance and sets up the denouement, is murky at best.

Cinematography is gritty. Appealing costumes and Maurice Jarre's score deliver more emotional impact than the lens' often-sepia portraiture. The effects can be incongruous, though. Smits is a clotheshorse from the moment he steps off the plane through the final credits: Where did a long-term political prisoner get such duds on the island, or get credit approval in Miami's Little Havana? — *Zink.*

THE POPE MUST DIE
(BRITISH)

A Palace Pictures release in U.K. (Miramax in U.S.) of a Palace-British Screen presentation in association with Film Four Intl.-Miramax-Michael White of a Palace/Stephen Woolley production. Produced by Stephen Woolley. Executive producers, Nik Powell, Michael White. Co-executive producers, Bob Weinstein, Harvey Weinstein. Directed by Peter Richardson. Screenplay, Richardson, Pete Richens; camera (Eastmancolor), Frank Gell; editor, Katherine Wenning; music, Anne Dudley, Jeff Beck; sound (Dolby), John Hayes, Campbell Askew, Hugh Strain; production design, John Ebden; art director, Sarah Horton (U.K.), Nened Pecur (Yugoslavia); costume design, Sandy Powell; associate director, Richens; assistant director, Glynn Purcell; co-producer, Elizabeth Karlsen; associate producer, Paul Cowan; casting, Hubbard Casting (U.K.), the Casting Co. (U.S.). Reviewed at Odeon West End, London, June 28, 1991. No MPAA Rating. Running time: **97 MIN.**
Father Dave Albinizi . Robbie Coltrane
Veronica Dante . . . Beverly D'Angelo
Vittorio Corelli . . . . . . Herbert Lom
Monsignor Fitchie . . . . . Paul Bartel
Paolo . . . . Salvatore Cascio
Joe Don Dante . . . . . Balthazar Getty
Cardinal Rocco . . . . Alex Rocco
Bish . . . . Peter Richardson
Father Rookie . . . . Adrian Edmondson
Also with: Robert Stephens, Khedjia Sassi, John Sessions, Steve O'Donnell.

Say no prayers for "The Pope Must Die," a barbed comedy about an honest goofball who boots the mob out of the Vatican when he's mistakenly made top banana. Cheeky script and mixed Anglo-Yank cast's playing should make this a lively performer in the right pulpits.

Pic has obvious ballyhoo angles for secular markets, starting with its provocative, sendup title. But official resistance in strongly Catholic territories looks likely. Even for the London preem run, the words "Must Die" were taken out of the subway ad campaign.

Scots comic Robbie Coltrane toplines as a priest who doubles as a car mechanic and rock musician in a rural Italian orphanage. When the pope kicks it in Rome, Father Dave Albinizi's name comes up thanks to a clerical error, and next thing he's riding around in the popemobile and dispensing blessings.

Mob boss Herbert Lom, who had his own candidate prepped for the post, is soon chewing the rug and putting out a contract on the portly pontiff. Meanwhile, Coltrane starts checking the books and finds the Vatican bank is being run as a money-laundering operation.

First to hit the cobblestones is the finance director (Alex Rocco), Lom's main inside man. But when Coltrane's ex-g.f. (Beverly D'Angelo) turns up and reveals they have a long-lost rock star son (Balthazar Getty), Rocco and his accomplice (Paul Bartel) inform the press.

Coltrane is soon singing on street corners, and Rocco is back in robes. Loony finale has Lom ventilating his henchmen and almost getting himself crowned pope before he's brained by a chunk of the Sistine Chapel.

Script has a much sharper edge than Coltrane's previous religious romp, "Nuns On The Run." That's mostly thanks to the writing team of Pete Richens and helmer Peter Richardson, founding members of the Brit tv satirical group the Comic Strip, specializing in genre sendups.

Loosely based (like "The Godfather Part III") on the Roberto Calvi banking scandal, yarn broadens out into a breezy satire of mob pictures and religious pics. Witty routines include Coltrane working out to a Vatican tv fitness video, munching holy wafers when he's hungry and doing a Jesus-and-the-moneychangers number in the bank. Plenitude of sight gags sometimes brings it close to a "Naked Bible 2½."

Coltrane is solid (and physically right) as the ingenuous lead, but pace slackens when he's left to make the running. Rest of the cast play it in the fast lane. Rocco well-nigh steals the pic as a fast-talking mobster, Bartel coasts ably as a campy monsignor and Lom mines the homicidal vein of his "Pink Panther" outings.

Second-billed D'Angelo, who doesn't show up until halfway through, has fun in a sassy part, and (re-voiced) Italo moppet Salvatore Cascio ("Cinema Paradiso") is cute in a bit as Coltrane's buddy. Helmer Richardson pops in and out as an unshaven Vatican security chief.

Apart from boxy sound in some scenes, tech credits are up to scratch, with convincing interiors by production designer John Ebden and eye-filling costumes by Sandy Powell.

Pic lensed last fall in Yugoslavia, with assist from Zagreb-based Jadran Film, under dummy title "Sleeping With The Fishes." End roller includes the blithe note: "Filmed entirely on location in Europe, not far from the Vatican." — *Del.*

PROBLEM CHILD 2

A Universal Pictures release of an Imagine Films Entertainment production. Produced by Robert Simonds. Directed by Brian Levant. Screenplay, Scott Alexander, Larry Karaszewski, based on characters created by Alexander, Karaszewski; camera (Deluxe color), Peter Smokler; editor, Lois Freeman-Fox; music, David Kitay; sound (Dolby), John M. Stacy; production design, Maria Caso; art direction, Allen Terry; set decoration, Damon Medlen; costume design, Robert Moore; associate producer-unit production manager, Kim Kurumada; assistant directors, Mitchell Bock, Polly Ann Mattson; casting, Valerie McCaffrey. Reviewed at Universal Studios screening room, L.A., July 3, 1991. MPAA Rating: PG-13. Running time: **91 MIN.**
Ben Healy . . . . John Ritter
Junior Healy . . . . . Michael Oliver
Big Ben Healy . . . . . . Jack Warden
LaWanda Dumore . . Laraine Newman
Annie Young . . . . Amy Yasbeck
Trixie Young . . . . . . Ivyann Schwan
Mr. Peabody . . . . . Gilbert Gottfried
Smith . . . . Paul Willson

After the inexplicable box-office success of "Problem Child" there's no telling how much cash this sequel can rake in since it's even worse than the first. Pic at least seems to understand its target audience by offering one excrement-inspired gag after another, until "gag" is the operative word.

At times this poor version of a sitcom seems written by 5-year-olds for 5-year-olds, so much so that one suspects its script was fingerpainted.

The plot has Ben (John Ritter) and Junior (Michael Oliver) moving to a new town of cloying divorcées, as Junior grapples with his fear of losing his adopted dad by reverting to various revolting if not terribly funny habits.

A second "problem child," a little girl (Ivyann Schwan, from "Parenthood"), eventually teams up with Junior to try to bring his lonely dad together with her sheepish mom (Amy Yasbeck).

The ultimate resolution would seem to provide the setup for "Problem Child 3," though it's hard to believe anyone would want to encourage the coupling of two people raising their children so abominably.

The most depressing aspect of the film stems from seeing Ritter and Laraine Newman, playing a rich femme fatale with her own designs on Ben, struggling against such fastidiously inane material. They both have been funny before, though at times during this ordeal it's hard to remember when.

Director Brian Levant, in his feature debut, manages to make the tv series he worked on (among them "The New Leave It To Beaver") look like "Citizen Kane." If there's a message about trust and teaching children to share the affection of their parents, it's lost.

Oliver remains an annoying child actor who mugs constantly. Pic uses voiceover narration (as well as a riff from the song "Bad To The Bone") to flesh out his two expressions: impish-cute and remorseful-cute.

Pic also suffers from a cheap look all the way around, including jokes using a stuffed dog that's supposed to be a real dog and an obviously styrofoam rock.

There's also a particularly lame sequence involving wholesale projectile vomiting that looks equally shabby, warranting a chuckle only in that it brings to mind similar, far funnier moments in "Stand By Me" and "Monty Python's The Meaning Of Life."

The film also presents numerous scenes that could lead to undesirable behavior among children if imitated. Then again, parents who take their kids to see this probably deserve whatever problems they get. — *Bril.*

WEDLOCK

An ITC Entertainment presentation of a Spectacor Films production. Produced by Branko Lustig. Executive producers, Frederick S. Pierce, Michael Jaffe. Directed by Lewis Teague. Screenplay, Broderick Miller; camera (CFI color), Dietrich Lohmann; editor, Carl Kress; music, Richard Gibbs; sound, Peter Bently; production design, Penny Hadfield; art direction, Virginia Hildreth; set design, Kris Miller; set decoration, Lauri Gaffin; costume design, Stephen M. Chudej; associate producers, Chris Sacani, Broderick Miller; assistant director, Branko Lustig; additional camera, Paul Ryan; 2nd unit director, George Bud Davis; 2nd unit camera, Michael Ferris; casting, Betsy Cohen. Reviewed at Cannes Film Festival (market), May 12, 1991. Running time: **100 MIN.**
Frank . . . . Rutger Hauer
Tracy . . . . Mimi Rogers
Noelle . . . . Joan Chen
Sam . . . . James Remar
George Holliday . Stephen Tobolowsky
Beverly Salinger . . . Sherri Paysinger
Teal . . . . Glenn Plummer
Sen. Travis . . . . . . Albert Stratton

Far from a study of married life, "Wedlock" is a derivative, throw-away actioner about convicts on the run. Semi-name leads won't be enough to catapult this out of the destined-for-video ranks and into major theatrical situations.

Opening sequence has burglars Rutger Hauer, his g.f. Joan Chen and James Remar pulling off a big diamond heist. In its aftermath, however, latter two betray Hauer, who is arrested and sent up the river to the latest in high security prisons. There are no walls; prisoners wear collars that blow up if they stray more than 100 yards away from a mate to whom each one is electronically connected.

Slammer also boasts such features as "floaters," a punishing form of sensory deprivation tanks, and "magic hour," during which time convicts may get it on in a sort of institutionalized red light district. Hauer spends more time in the former than in the latter, as he has become completely turned off women after the way Chen treated him.

After a couple of the bad dude prisoners get their heads blown off after a rough fight, Hauer manages to escape along with inmate Mimi Rogers, whose advances he has been resisting. From this point, Broderick Miller's screenplay borrows liberally from both the classic story "The Most Dangerous Game," as authorities chase the couple like wild animals, and Hitchcock's "The 39 Steps," in that the mostly antagonistic pair is forced to stick very close together.

Aside from eluding their pursuers, duo's main objectives through the home stretch are to safely disconnect their collars and to exact revenge on Chen and Remar. Suffice it to say that no major plot surprises are in order.

Undoubtedly recognizing the silliness of the enterprise, filmmakers have endeavored to play with the tone and moods a bit, but this just makes it all seem more facetious. Looking a little paunchier than usual, Hauer plays his hero as a dense fellow whose stubbornness just makes life more difficult for him. This hardly results in laughs.

Rogers is uncharacteristically abrasive and, of the others, only Stephen Tobolowsky, as the imperious prison owner, gets off some good moments.

Pic represents a step back into the semi-exploitation arena for director Lewis Teague. Technically, film is proficient, but it lands in a no man's land marketing-wise, as it is hard to imagine who the intended audience was meant to be. — *Cart.*

BAK SJU HAV
(BEYOND THE SEVEN SEAS)
(NORWEGIAN)

An Aprilfilm production in association with Norsk Filmstudio. Produced by Trond G. Lockertsen. Written and directed by Saeed Anjum and Espen Thorstenson. Camera (color), Halvor Naess; editor, Jan Toreg; sound, Peter Flateby, Gunnar Meidell, Toreg; sets, Ingeborg Kvamme; production manager, Inge Tenvik; costumes, Mona Sjüeng Hansen; makeup, Jennifer Jorfald. Reviewed at Saga Cinema, Oslo, Feb. 16, 1991. Running time: 88 MIN.
Aslam . . . . Sajid Hussain
Father . . . . Zafar Malik
Mother . . . . Rubina J. Rana
Grandfather . . . . Aziz Asri
Rashid . . . . Adeel J. Rana
Anders . . . . Hans Krúvel
Merete . . . . Pia K. Kristensen
Ase . . . . Marte L. Ness

"Beyond The Seven Seas," story of a Pakistani family's move from Lahore to Oslo told through a boy's eyes, contains warm moments and simple poetry, but the pace is sluggish and the narrative weak. It might still appeal to tv buyers looking for unpretentious presentation of the theme for audiences aged 5 to 10.

Film gives a balanced and sometimes humorous view of the boy's difficulties and provides alternatives to Norwegians' stereotypical views of Pakistanis. Similarly, pic pokes fun at myths about "arctic" Norway as conveyed by a Pakistani teacher.

Some of the problems encountered by Norway's immigrants — cultural gap, harsh climate, racism — are more hinted at than discussed, but the pic's perhaps better off without lectures.

Veteran cinematographer Halvor Naess effectively contrasts the warm, dusty colors of Pakistan with the grayness of Oslo in winter. The actors, most of them amateurs, look their parts, but performances are generally uneven. — *Olav.*

BIENVENUE A BORD!
(WELCOME ABOARD!)
(FRENCH)

A Blue Dahlia-Ciné 5-Pathe Cinema-Eurisma production. (Intl. sales: Pathe Cinema.) Executive producer, Michel Faure. Written and directed by Jean-Louis Leconte. Camera (Eastmancolor), Charlie van Damme; editor, Dominique Roy; music, Jean-Claude Vannier; sound, Philippe Lioret; production design, Dominique Andre; production manager, Henri Vart; assistant director, Michel Such. Reviewed at Unifrance screening room, Paris, May 3, 1991. Running time: 80 MIN.
The hitchhiker . . . . . Pierre Richard
Martin Placardi . . . . Martin Lamotte
Emilie . . . . Evelyne Bouix
Prostitute . . . . Catherine Frot
Varonsky . . . . Pavel Slaby
Inspector . . . . Christian Rauth

Pierre Richard forsakes his nerdy persona for a tough, slightly sinister type in this uneven pic. "Welcome Aboard!" is too slight a vehicle to make much of a mark.

Most of the film takes place at night in an immense traffic jam. Martin (Martin Lamotte), a salesman and would-be writer of pulp thrillers, is trying to get home after a business trip when a hitchhiker (Richard) suddenly gets into his car. Since the stranger seems to be a tough type, and news broadcasts have announced a wanted criminal is on the run, Martin soon suspects the worst, but is unable to get rid of his passenger.

To make matters worse, he calls his wife and hears a strange man answer the phone — or perhaps he dialed a wrong number. Eventually he abandons his car to Richard and gets a lift with an attractive woman (Evelyne Bouix) with whom he spends time in a motel. But the stranger catches up with him again, and the nightmare journey continues.

Pic ultimately suffers from a slim screenplay that hardly sustains even the relatively brief running time. While Richard is at times unnerving as the mysterious stranger, Lamotte gives an altogther too bland performance. Technically, the film is good, with the long traffic jam sequence effectively staged. — *Strat.*

MELBOURNE FEST

ISABELLE EBERHARDT
(FRENCH-AUSTRALIAN)

A Les Films Aramis-Flach Films (Paris)-Seon Films (Melbourne) co-production, with the participation of the Australian Film Finance Corp. Executive producer, Jacques Le Clere. Produced by Jean Petit, Daniel Scharf. Directed by Ian Pringle. Screenplay, Stephen Sewell; camera (Eastmancolor), Manuel Teran; editor, Ken Sallows; music, Paul Schutze; sound, Bernard Aubouy; production design, Bryce Perrin, Geoffroy Larcher; costume design, Mic Cheminal; production manager, Farid Carouche; assistant director, Phil Jones; co-producers, Jean-François Lepetit, Isabelle Fauvel; casting, Gerard Moulevrier. Reviewed at Melbourne Film Festival, June 8, 1991. Running time: 113 MIN.
Isabelle Eberhardt . . . Mathilda May
Slimene . . . . Tcheky Karyo
Major Lyautey . . . . . Peter O'Toole
Lt. Comte . . . . Richard Moir
Capt. Cauvet . . . . . Arthur Dignam
Victor Barracund . . . . Claude Villers
Brahim . . . . Nabil Massad
Hussein . . . . Ben Smail
Trophimowsky . . Wolfgang Harnisch

This ambitious French-Australian co-production is the biopic of a young woman of Russian-Swiss extraction who was a journalist in turn-of-the-century Algeria and sided with the Arabs against the French. Unfortunately, director, screenwriter and lead actress fail to bring this fascinating character to life, and as presented here, Isabelle Eberhardt remains an enigma. Boxoffice prospects don't look bright.

Part of the problem is the casting of Mathilda May, the attractive actress who made her mark in "La Passarelle" and Claude Chabrol's "Cry Of The Owl," and who was awarded a César as best newcomer of 1988. She gives a stolid performance with no hint of the fire and passion the real Eberhardt must have possessed. Too bad Isabelle Huppert, originally mooted for the role, didn't get to play the character.

Also at fault is Ian Pringle's remote approach to his character. This Aussie director ("Wrong World," "The Prisoner Of St. Petersburg") regularly places his alienated protagonists in dislocated settings, and this theme is present here, but the director treats his heroine with such reverence that she never comes alive.

At one point, Eberhardt reveals she's had many lovers in her life, which comes as a complete surprise to the viewer who has seen her only with Slimene (Tcheky Karyo), whom she eventually marries, partly to obtain a French passport to enable her to return to Algeria after she's been deported. Pic never makes clear that Slimene himself is an Arab, which would have added a major dimension to the love story.

The Stephen Sewell screenplay sees Eberhardt as a feminist, a radical and even a nihilist who scorns authority figures and who breaks all the rules. All of this suggests a vibrant character which simply isn't in the film.

Nor is the pic visually very interesting, despite a 10-week location stint in Tunisia. Manuel Teran's camerawork is so low-key as to be drab, and moments of beauty are few.

Fortunately, fine supporting performances offset the lackluster leads. Peter O'Toole returns to the desert to play a gentlemanly officer of the Foreign Legion secretly intent on annexing Morocco. He makes a late appearance in the film, and easily dominates every scene in which he appears in a beautifully modulated performance. Effective, too, is Aussie thesp Richard Moir as a brutal legion officer.

Made on a reported $7 million budget, "Isabelle Eberhardt" attests to the pitfalls of co-production between two such dissimilar countries. It might have worked with a more passionate and perhaps more operatic approach to the intriguing subject. — *Strat.*

MUNICH FEST

SLOMJENA MLADOST
(BROKEN YOUTH)
(YUGOSLAVIAN-ROMANIAN)

A Television Novi Sad-Romaniafilm-Profil production. (Intl. sales: Television Novi Sad.) Produced by Aleksander Petrovic. Directed by Marija Maric. Screenplay, Maric, Mihaia Avrameskua, based on novel by Mihai Auramesch; camera (color, 16m), Panta Cebzan; editor, Slobodan Jandric; music, Petru Popa; art direction, Aurel Dolinga; costumes, Tanja Korac. Reviewed at Munich Film Festival, June 23, 1991. Running time: **93 MIN.**
Zina . . . . Silvia Pincu
Siminica . . . . Carmen Trocan
Cola . . . . Dan Puric
Ilie . . . . Adrian Titieni
Vasile . . . . Radu Amzulescu
Cola's grandfather . . . . . Iova Dalea
Trifu . . . . Lavinel Dudic
Chia . . . . . . Ana-Niculina Ursulescu
(Romanian soundtrack)

Marija Maric's first feature, "Broken Youth," set in a Romanian community in Yugoslavia just before World War II, combines sociological insights with sensitive observation of human nature. Yugo village dramas have scored well at home in recent years, and this powerful one is likely to find fest slots, especially those with ethnic or feminine focus.

Meaning of the title is apparent from the first scene in which the biological initiation of a girl, Zina, into womanhood immediately sets off the family's search for a good husband. A real childhood is not permitted; instead, young people are thrust into hard work and marriage, becoming old before their time.

The harsh village regime bars input on decisions by women or young men. Zina's father and the grandfather of teen Cola meet

after a church service and make preliminary overtures toward matching up their offspring. The grandfather is attracted more by the vast landholdings of Zina's family than he is by her beauty, and he ignores his grandson's whimpers of protest. Zina is none too thrilled at the prospect of being hitched to sickly Cola. The slightly older girl openly mocks him after he comes calling in his Sunday best.

Colorful folkloric dances precede the wedding day. Once married, Cola is unable to consummate the marriage, and it isn't long before Zina is sneaking off with virile Vasile who had raped her shortly before her wedding day. Later, he brutally attacks her before abandoning her.

A parallel love story between Siminica, a lusty divorcée, and Ilie also is surreptitious because of Ilie's parents' disapproval. Their sensual trysts result in Siminica's pregnancy, and in a harrowing scene, a midwife rolls a bottle on her belly to induce an abortion. When Ilie finally bucks community pressure and brings Siminica home, their initial happiness is short-lived because she has been rendered sterile, and is therefore worthless as a wife.

Cola's military service, meanwhile, has apparently made him a man, as signified by his moustache, sour expression and penchant for beating his wife and drunken father. He also assumes his progenitive duties, and soon Zina is pregnant. Although the final scene calls for a speedy though implausible transformation of Cola's character, it brings an optimistic light to an otherwise depressing drama.

The women are standouts in this talented Romanian and Yugoslavian cast making their screen debuts, especially Silvia Pincu as Zina and Carmen Trocan as Siminica. Their supportive friendship provides a touching contrast to the overall impersonal interaction.

Helmer Maric's insistence on a free hand in casting, completed just before the Romanian revolution, paid off. She's now trying to get Romanian co-producers to release their nine 35m prints for further subtitling. Unavailability of an unsubtitled print made film ineligible for Cannes Directors Fortnight slot.

Lensing by Panta Cebzan in feature debut is noteworthy, and other tech standards are just fine. Color unification was off in

16m print unspooled at Munich fest but has been corrected in 35m version and five minutes trimmed off the 93-minute length. — *Sam.*

SUPERMARKET
(EGYPTIAN)

A Nagli Fathi Films (Try) production. (Intl. sales: Al-Anwar Cinema Distribution.). Produced by Nagla Fathi. Directed by Mohamed Khan. Screenplay, Assem Tawfik, based on story by Tawfik, Khan; camera (color), Kamel Abdelaziz; editor, Nadia Chukri; music, Kamal Bakir; sound, Magdy Kamel; production manager, Fathi Yussri. Reviewed at Munich Film Festival, June 24, 1991. Running time: **104 MIN.**
Amira . . . . Nagla Fathi
Dr. Azmy . . . . Adel Adham
Ramzy . . . . . Mamdouh Abdelalim
Mona . . . . Aida Riad
Khaled . . . . Nabil Halafawi
Nahed . . . . Maryiam Makhyoun
Rabab . . . . Mona Zakaria
Mahassen . . . . Zeinab Wahby
Mother . . . . Aida Abdelaziz
Grandfather . . . . Mohammed Tawfik

An entertaining, yet incisive view of the effects of Westernization on contemporary Egyptian family structure, "Supermarket" is worthy of film fest play and specialized distribution, although latter is limited to audiences willing to overlook technical limitations, which are more than offset by pic's content.

Ramzy (amiably played by Mamdouh Abdelalim) is the pianist at a deluxe Cairo hotel. Educated at a conservatory, he is sick of playing light standards for the likes of a wealthy and appropriately venal surgeon/playboy (Adel Adham). When Ramzy is told he'll be laid off soon, he agrees to teach the doctor how to sing and play piano, and doc will impart his secrets on becoming a millionaire.

After an argument with his crotchety sister-in-law and de facto landlord (Zeinab Wahby), Ramzy packs up and goes home to Mom (Aida Abdelaziz), who lives in an unfashionable Cairo neighborhood. Unemployed wife Mona (Aida Riad), a cute ballerina who pirouettes in mid-conversation, is nonplused, convinced he'll be home in short order.

Ramzy, however, rekindles a friendship with neighbor and childhood idol Amira (played by enormously appealing superstar Nagla Fathi). A divorcée, she works in the local supermarket to support her bright but demanding teen daughter Nahed (Maryiam Makhyoun) and aging

father (Mohammed Tawfik).

Then suddenly her long-lost ex-husband Khaled (Nabil Halafawi) pops up after a decade of work in Kuwait, returning with his pockets bulging with shekels and a snooty new wife (Mona Zakaria) who cannot have children. Khaled sets out to win daughter Nahed's love by showering her with expensive gifts and squiring her about upscale resorts. Amira is distraught at losing her daughter, but Nahed eventually gets homesick and returns to mom.

Unbeknownst to Ramzy, a thief chased by police tossed an attaché case crammed with money on the trailer carrying Ramzy's possessions. Police trace the case to the pianist when it's stolen a second time during his move back home. Cleared of the crime, he rues the bad luck that thwarted his dream of becoming rich but is cheered up by being rehired at the hotel piano bar.

Bittersweet finale, more realistic than sugar-coated, proves the surgeon's dictum that "Money tempts everybody." Tech credits are adequate, although color tones are occasionally off, cast is likable and commentary is at the forefront of Egypt's new wave, one combining social consciousness with commercial appeal.
— *Sam.*

DAS LACHEN DER MACA DARACS
(THE LAUGHTER OF MACA DARACS)
(AUSTRIAN-GERMAN)

A Fernsehfilmproduktion Dr. Heinz Scheiderbauer-ORF-ZDF production. (Intl. sales: Fernsehfilmproduktion.) Produced by Scheiderbauer. Directed by Dieter Berner. Screenplay, Peter Turrini, Berner; camera (Eastmancolor), Pascal Hoffman; editor, Ulli Schwarzenberger; music, Mathias Rüegg; sound, Karl Schlifelner; production design, Angela Hareiter; costume design, Heidi Melinc; makeup, Martina Angeletti. Reviewed at Munich Film Festival, June 24, 1991. Running time: **89 MIN.**
Maca Daracs . . . . Barbara Auer
Kurt Höllermoser . . . Nikolaus Paryla
Rudi Blaha . . . . Helmut Berger
Mäggy . . . . Andrea Klem
Hotel manager . . . . . Michael Gampe
Post commander . . . . Wolf Bachofner
Dr. Olschitzky . . . . David Olschitzky

Light-hearted comedy "The Laughter Of Maca Daracs" is a twist on "Green Card" in which an Hungarian gypsy desperately seeks a husband so she can work legally in Austria. Popularity of German actress **Barbara Auer should help pull in respectable b.o. in the two co-producers' territories, but outside home turf, prospects look best for tv and video.**

Maca Daracs (Auer) is a spunky Hungarian gypsy working in the kitchen of an Austrian ski resort. She sleeps on a cot in a tiny room and has to fend off the lecherous hotel manager (Michael Gampe), but life is better than the fate that awaits her back home. Her quest for a husband becomes more urgent after a cop spies her in the kitchen and orders her to produce her passport next day.

Her potential hubbies narrow down to two candidates. The first, Kurt (respected stage actor Nikolaus Paryla), is an eccentric paranoic who is found hiding in the kitchen. He was given indefinite leave from his work after being involved in an arms deal in Iran and narrowly escaped death.

He is convinced he is being trailed by Rudi Blaha (Austrian actor Helmut Berger), a prominent Socialist on a ski holiday with his precocious teen daughter Mäggy (Andrea Klem).

Maca proposed to the middle-aged oddball first, but he refuses because he has never married and doesn't intend to. Maca tantalizes the Socialist while delivering orders to his room and writhing seductively to his daughter's guitar music. He invites her to watch a video one evening and in the middle of his heavy groping, she pops the question to him. He admits hopping in the sack appeals to him, but a marriage of convenience for a man of his position is impossible.

Maca decides Kurt is a better prospect and accepts a date with him, borrowing Mäggy's knock-'em-dead red dress. They go to a cinema and within a short time are erotically entwined, but Kurt flees and leaves Maca stranded.

Maca leaves the resort with the immigration officer hot on her trail, and traces Kurt to a sanitarium. He proves his sanity by choosing Maca instead of the two matronly attendants in a "Let's Make A Deal" finale. Maca's finally got a groom.

Originally the fourth part of the tv series "Workers Saga," pic is an innocuous bit of fluff which got a good response in its theatrical preem at the Munich film fest. Auer plays the role for chuckles rather than sighs and conveys an indomitable good nature throughout her many trials. Tech credits are ordinary but okay. — *Sam.*

REGARDING HENRY

A Paramount Pictures presentation. Produced by Mike Nichols and Scott Rudin. Executive producer, Robert Greenhut. Directed by Nichols. Screenplay, Jeffrey Abrams; camera (Technicolor), Giuseppe Rotunno; editor, Sam O'Steen; music, Hans Zimmer; sound (Dolby), James Sabat, Gene Cantamessa; production design, Tony Walton; costume design, Ann Roth; art direction, Dan Davis, William Elliott; set decoration, Susan Bode, Amy Marshall, Cindy Carr; assistant director, Michael Haley; associate producer, Susan MacNair; co-producer, Abrams; casting, Juliet Taylor, Ellen Lewis. Reviewed at Beverly Connection Cinema, July 6, 1991. MPAA Rating: PG13. Running time: **107 MIN.**

Henry . . . . Harrison Ford
Sarah . . . . Annette Bening
Bradley . . . . Bill Nunn
Rachel . . . . Mikki Allen
Charlie . . . . Donald Moffat
Mrs. O'Brien . . . . . Nancy Marchand

A subtle emotional journey impeccably orchestrated by director Mike Nichols and acutely well acted, **"Regarding Henry" has a back-to-basics message that's bound to strike a responsive chord in the troubled aftermath of the '80s. It looks like the pic will win its case as an alternative to the summer's action lineup, bringing in solid longterm b.o.**

In a way, the pic is a variation on the old story of the husband who goes down to the corner for a pack of cigarettes and never comes back. The controlling, intolerant Henry Turner (Harrison Ford) who steps out of his Manhattan brownstone late one night for a pack of Merits, only to become the victim of mindless, hysterical violence, is certainly not the same man who has to be coaxed back home from the hospital after a lengthy rehabilitation.

Confused, hesitant and barely able to remember himself or his family, Henry has to start from scratch to regain such basic capacities as how to read, take a walk or make love to his wife.

But as the story develops and Henry is drawn back into the law firm where he was a prized player and where his return to form is anxiously awaited, it becomes more about what he has gained than what he has lost.

His innocence and daily struggle with disadvantage have brought him an ability to relate to the powerless that is completely foreign to the mindset of his peers. Pic begins to call into question just what the gifted members of society are choosing to do with their advantages.

Power of writer Jeffrey Abrams' blueprint and Nichols' direction is that the points are so gently made. Film doesn't exaggerate the villainy of Henry's colleagues. They are simply well-paid lawyers operating in a world where winning is valued more than justice, and they are sophisticated enough to have agreed not to question that.

Even in the excellent scene at a party where Henry and his wife (Annette Bening) are devastated when they overhear their friends discussing the couple's plight, the friends are not being unduly cruel. These are just the things people say.

Naturally, Henry changes. He no longer fits in. The grace of the script by 23-year-old Abrams — a work so pleasing in its rhythms and truths that it is bound to be the envy of many an older writer — is that it doesn't contrive a practical alternative for Henry. The change in his character is story enough.

On the other hand, there is the dimension contributed by Bening's intepretation of her role. She's an elegant society wife who bravely becomes Henry's truest friend when his former confidence deserts him. Without proclaiming itself as such, this film becomes quite possibly the love story of the year as Bening enacts this remarkable bond.

In a role as far removed as possible from her cunning Myra in "The Grifters," Bening sets a shining new standard of performance. The perfection with which she hits every note demanded of her is beyond expectation.

Ford operates with his usual firstrate precision, pushing the super-competent Henry slyly into the realm of humor, and suggesting the physical timidity and mental struggles of the debilitated Henry without overdoing it.

Among the film's charms is the close relationship he develops with his 12-year-old daughter, keenly portrayed by Mikki Allen in her film debut.

Director Nichols, in his most affecting picture since the gritty "Silkwood," has pulled off a complex contemporary message picture in which there is nary a false step. Exceptionally adept editing by longtime collaborator Sam O'Steen keeps the story brisk. Camerawork by Giuseppe Rotunno is fluid and engaging, and production design by Tony Walton is a rich, harmonious asset.

Among the circle of support-

ing players, Bill Nunn makes a major contribution as the high-spirited physical therapist Bradley, his lascivious energy carrying the picture for that portion while Henry is severely stricken. — *Daws.*

POINT BREAK

A 20th Century Fox release of a Largo Entertainment presentation of a Levy/Abrams/Guerin production. Produced by Peter Abrams and Robert L. Levy. Executive producer, James Cameron. Directed by Kathryn Bigelow. Screenplay, W. Peter Iliff, based on a story by Rick King, Iliff; camera (color), Donald Peterman; editor, Howard Smith; music, Mark Isham; production design, Peter Jamison; art direction, Pamela Marcotte; set design, Ann Harris; set decoration, Linda Spheeris; costumes, Colby P. Bart, Louis Infante; stunt coordinator, Glenn Wilder; assistant director, Herb Gains; co-producers, Michael Rauch, King; casting, Richard Pagano, Sharon Bialy. Reviewed at Odeon Cinema, L.A., July 10, 1991. MPAA Rating: R. Running time: **122 MIN.**

Bodhi . . . . Patrick Swayze
Johnny Utah . . . . . . Keanu Reeves
Pappas . . . . Gary Busey
Tyler . . . . Lori Petty
Beh Harp . . . . John McGinley
Roach . . . . .James LeGros
Nathanial . . . . John Philbin
Grommet . . . . . BoJesse Christopher

A hare-brained wild ride **through big surf and bad vibes, "Point Break" acts like a huge, nasty wave, picking up viewers for a few major thrills but ultimately grinding them into the sand via overkill and absurdity. No doubt there's an audience around somewhere for fare of this ilk, so pic might wash up some okay boxoffice through the summer.**

Offshore prospects look better for this first production from Largo Entertainment, since this ultra-stoked, ultra-noisy pic is the kind that might be improved by a bad translation.

Director Kathryn Bigelow ("Blue Steel") aims this hybrid tale of beach culture and bank robbery at adrenaline junkies, pumping it so full of fast action and extreme violence that one could never claim it lacks edge. What it lacks is subtlety, logic or any redeeming grace. "Too much testosterone here," says a femme surfer (Lori Petty), walking disdainfully away from a crude party. Comment fits.

Keanu Reeves plays a 25-year-old ex-footballer turned FBI agent who is assigned to penetrate the Southern California surf culture in search of some highly successful bank robbers. This gang of four wears rubber masks in the likenesses of Reagan,

Nixon, Carter and Ford and announces itself at each crime scene as "the ex-presidents."

Partnered with a cranky veteran fed (Gary Busey), who naturally doesn't like him, Reeves has to first learn to surf, then gain the trust of a radical dude named Bodhi (Patrick Swayze) who mixes mystical vibes with fearless thrill-seeking.

Bodhi turns out to be the bank job ringleader, and though the heavily seduced Reeves chases him to hell and back, he just can't seem to pull the trigger whenever he corners him.

Script by W. Peter Iliff (also credited on the forthcoming "Prayer Of The Rollerboys") tries to ride on the cockeyed relationship between these two rock-etheads, but since they spend most of the pic trying to throttle or maim each other, it's not very interesting. Even more bogus is the love story between Reeves and his surfing teacher Petty, which becomes a lame excuse for keeping Swayze alive after he takes her hostage.

To be sure, pic offers some awesome surf footage, white-knuckle chase scenes and breathtaking skydiving sequences, but the adrenaline rush is repeatedly wiped out by extreme violence and mental mayhem.

"Paddling out into the big surf is a total commitment," says a stoked-up dude in one scene, and it follows that filmmakers in a project of this scale better know what they're doing. Bigelow and company don't have the master moves that might have enabled a filmmaker like pic's exec producer, James Cameron, to stay on the board in waves like this.

Bigelow affects a hyperkinetic, agitated visual style that generates plenty of excitement, but hitches it to a story that repeatedly falls apart, often due to her tendency toward overkill. Actors, especially John McGinley as an FBI boss, behave as if injected with rocket fuel. One wonders if their heads had to be unscrewed from the ceiling after each take.

Tale rattles on long after audience lost interest in the fate of the murderous sun-bleached desperadoes, and reaches numerous crests of absurdity. At one point Swayze postulates that the people out there "crawling along the freeways in their tin coffins" are depending on him and his fellow robbers to prove people can still buck the system. Not likely, dude.

Admittedly, seeing the ex-presidents, a rubber-faced Mt. Rush-

more for this generation, pulling off bank jobs in their elegant attire is visually interesting. Iliff's script is not without hooks, just without logic.

Reeves holds the screen well as the stop-at-nothing young fed, and Swayze actually makes a fairly credible role out of the mystic with the faulty wiring.

Stunt coordinator Glenn Wilder certainly earned his paycheck, and the photography and editing are commendable. — *Daws.*

WHERE ANGELS FEAR TO TREAD
(BRITISH)

A Rank Film Distributors release (in U.K.) of a Stagescreen Prods. presentation of a Sovereign picture in association with LWT and Compact Television production. Produced by Derek Granger. Executive producers, Jeffrey Taylor, Kent Walwin, Nick Elliott. Directed by Charles Sturridge. Screenplay, Tim Sullivan, Granger, Sturridge, from novel by E.M. Forster; camera (Eastmancolor, Technicolor prints), Michael Coulter; editor, Peter Coulson; music, Rachel Portman; sound (Dolby), Peter Sutton, Hugh Strain, John Ireland; production design, Simon Holland; art director, Luigi Marchione (Italy), Marianne Ford (U.K.); costume design, Monica Howe; production manager, Walter Massi, Lil Stirling; assistant director, John Dodds (Italy), Cordelia Hardy (U.K.); associate producer, Olivia Stewart; co-producer, Giovanna Romagnoli; casting, Joyce Gallie, Rita Forzano. Reviewed at Odeon Haymarket, London, June 27, 1991. Running time: **112 MIN.**
Caroline Abbott . . . . Helena Bonham Carter
Harriet Herriton . . . . . . Judy Davis
Philip Herriton . . . . . Rupert Graves
Gino Carella . . . . . Giovanni Guidelli
Mrs. Herriton . . . . . Barbara Jefford
Lilia Herriton . . . . Helen Mirren
Mr. Kingcroft . . . . Thomas Wheatley
Irma . . . . Sophie Kullman
Mr. Abbott . . . . Vass Anderson
Mrs. Theobald . . . . . . Sylvia Barter

A turn-of-the-century costumer about cold-blooded Brits thawing out in sunny Italy, "Where Angels Fear To Tread" is a far more rewarding dip into the E.M. Forster tub than some of its predecessors. Slick mounting and strong playing should ensure solid biz with the literary crowd, but Forster fatigue and unfamiliar title could work against wider acclaim.

Based on the cult scribe's slim first novel (1905), yarn limns Forster's favorite theme of the liberating effects of warmer climes on the uptight, arrogant English. Paralleling the book's light, seriocomic tone, pic has none of the top-heaviness of David Lean's

"A Passage To India" or the starchiness of Merchant-Ivory's "A Room With A View."

Feisty widow Lilia (Helen Mirren) goes to Italy for some r&r with younger companion Caroline (Helena Bonham Carter) and tangles with Tuscan boytoy Gino (Giovanni Guidelli). When news reaches home, Lilia's bossy mother-in-law, Mrs. Herriton (Barbara Jefford), dispatches milquetoast son Philip (Rupert Graves) to buy off the hot-blooded Italo.

That idea goes down the tubes when the pair reveal they're already hitched. But their connubial bliss soon sours when Gino starts fooling around. Lilia gives Gino a son but dies in childbirth.

Back in England, Mrs. Herriton tries to keep the news hushed up. When that fails, she sends Philip and his elder sister Harriet (Judy Davis) on yet another expedition.

Pic's strength is the way in which characters come in and out of focus. Lilia, it turns out, is simply a catalyst: True love affair is a sexually blurred triangle of Philip, Caroline and Gino.

Helmer Charles Sturridge tweaks what could have been a talky telepic into proper theatrical product. Like his previous "A Handful Of Dust," pic plays well on the big screen, with tasty Italian vistas, sharp pacing and (apart from a few static interiors) sequences that really move.

Bonham Carter, who gives her strongest performance to date as the repressed Caroline, is ably supported by Graves. Duo's final scene, a "Brief Encounter"-like meet in a station, packs real emotional clout.

Mirren and Davis (the latter sporting an impeccable Anglo accent) both score in colorful roles, and Jefford makes the most of her too-brief scenes as the acid-tongued matron.

Rupert Everett lookalike Guidelli is sympathetic as the Mediterranean pretty boy, though he's basically sidelined once the Brits start tying themselves up in moral knots.

Tech credits are all dandy, with special praise for Michael Coulter's radiant lensing of the Italian landscape (on sites that originally inspired Forster) and Rachel Portman's buoyant orchestral score. Crisp editing by Peter Coulson is another asset. Occasional Italian dialog is well subtitled. — *Del.*

ÖNSKAS
(WANTED)
(SWEDISH)

A Sandrews release of a Sandrews-Swedish Film Institute-Metronome-Filmteknik-Nordisk Film & TV-SVT Kanal 1 production. Produced by Katinka Farago. Written and directed by Lars Johansson. Camera, Lasse Björne; editor, Michael Leszczylowski; music, Magnus Jarlbo; sound, Bengt Säll, Klas Dykhoff; production design, Sven Wichmann; costumes, Inger Pehrsson. Reviewed at the Olympia cinema, Stockholm, July 3, 1991. Running time: **77 MIN.**
With: Rolf Lassgard, Marie Richardson, Per Morberg, Mattias Holstensson, Gerd Hegnell, Halvar Björk, Camilla Asp, Martin Svalander.

A warm and low-key comedy akin to pics of Jiri Menzel and Milos Forman, "Önskas" should generate boxoffice in Sweden (it opened July 12) and could travel well on the international festival circuit.

Pic centers on Kring Bosse, an optimistic but not very successful guy in his early 40s who answers an ad for a maitre d' job at a boardinghouse far away in the north of Sweden. Bosse hopes this will enable him to impress his beautiful new g.f. Anita.

Things go wrong from the start. Bosse has to bring his son along, and Anita brings her two kids. The car repeatedly breaks down, and the boardinghouse turns out to be downtrodden and isolated; only steady income comes from post-funeral receptions.

Bosse, however, hears about plans for a new highway nearby, and sees visions of a glorious future. He goes about buying the place — whose owner secretly plans to get rid of it through arson when he's not making passes at the not-unwilling Anita.

Director Johansson's first feature is a well-crafted, well-told and amusing story, and Sandrews already has given him a new assignment. Most of the characters could be easy targets for laughter, but the sympathetic helmer stays away from that. The laughter he generates stems from every day situations, not loud voices and pratfalls, making the pic a rare Swedish film comedy and giving it more universal appeal.

Rolf Lassgard puts a lot of emotion in his overweight, down-on-his-luck but optimistic character. Marie Richardson, convincingly portraying the tough Anita, is understandably much in demand by Swedish film directors. She's got both looks and skill.

Acting overall (at least among the adults) and tech credits are fine. — *Gunn.*

NIGHT OF THE WARRIOR

A Trimark release of a Little Bear Films presentation of a Blueline/Ian Page production. Produced by Mike Erwin, Thomas Ian Griffith. Directed by Rafal Zielinski. Screenplay, Griffith; camera (color), Edward Pei; editor, Jonas Thaler; music, Ed Tomney; sound (Ultra-Stereo), Beau Franklin, Troy Wilcox; production design, Michael Helmy; costume design, Lynn Pickwell; assistant director, Matthew Clark; production manager, Craig Suttle; stunt coordinator-fight choreography, Rick Avery; choreography, Sarah Elgart; co-producers, Lorenzo Lamas, Max Kirishima, Mary Page Keller; casting, Marlyn-Turco. Reviewed on Vidmark videocassette, N.Y., July 9, 1991. MPAA Rating: R. Running time: **100 MIN.**

Miles Keane . . . . . . Lorenzo Lamas
Lynch . . . . Anthony Geary
Katherine Pierce . . Kathleen Kinmont
Oliver . . . . Ken Foree
Joy . . . . Felicity Waterman
Edie Keane . . . . Arlene Dahl
Chang . . . . Daniel Kamekona
Coco . . . . Bill Erwin
Ronnie . . . . Mary Ann Oedy
Chance . . . . Richard Redlin
Also with: Willie Dixon, Wilhelm von Hamburg, Sarah Elgart, Tita Omzee, Robin Antin, Naomi Newton.

Lorenzo Lamas turns into a believable martial arts star in "Night Of The Warrior," a family effort co-starring his mom and wife. Film was released theatrically in the midwest in June and will hit vidstores from Vidmark in September.

Dog-eared plot has Lamas (who also co-produced the feature) as a kickboxer who's paid off a loan from gangster Anthony Geary that financed his night club, co-owned by mom Arlene Dahl (Lamas' real-life mother).

Geary wants his meal ticket (Lamas) to keep fighting, but Lamas is determined to retire. The bad guy stops at nothing, killing a former girlfriend (Felicity Waterman) to blackmail Lamas, beating up Dahl and even kidnaping current g.f. Kathleen Kinmont (Mrs. Lamas) in his efforts to get him back kicking.

Final fight of Lamas against a Korean expert is exciting but pic takes too long to arrive at this point. Helmer Rafal Zielinski is better known for comedies ("Screwballs," "Ginger Ale Afternoon") than actioners.

Lamas is comfortable in the larger-than-life hero role, and film benefits from several flash dance interludes at his night club featuring choreographer Sarah Elgart and other dancers. It's nice to see Dahl again (her first feature film in 20 years) though her role as a faded star dreaming of her salad days is wafer-thin.

Extremely tall actress Kinmont is well-matched again opposite her husband, though she surprisingly went further in her romantic scenes opposite Wings Hauser in Hauser's recent "The Art Of Dying."

Soap opera star Geary hams it up as the self-pitying villain. Ken Foree, heretofore a good guy, handles a baddie role as Geary's henchman with panache. — *Lor.*

LA FEMME FARDEE
(FRENCH)

An ATC 3000-SGGC production. (Intl. sales: President Films, Paris.) Produced by Benjamin Simon. Directed by José Pinheiro. Screenplay, Pinheiro, Frederic Fajarde, Jacques Cortal, Jean-Jacques Bauvert, Lou Inglebert, from novel by Françoise Sagan; camera (Eastmancolor), Raoul Coutard; editor, Claire Pinheiro; music, Jean-Marie Servia; sound, Michel Laurent, Jean-Paul Loublier; production design, Theobald Meurisse; production manager, Leone Jaffin; assistant director, Olivier Peray. Reviewed at Unifrance screening room, Paris, May 3, 1991. Running time: **102 MIN.**

Doria . . . . Jeanne Moreau
Edna . . . . .Jacqueline Maillan
Julien Peyrat . . . . . André Dussollier
Clarisse Lethuillier . . Laura Morante
Eric Lethuillier . . . . Daniel Mesguich
Andreas Fayard . . . . Anthony Delon
Simon Bejard . . . Jean-Marc Thibault
Charley . . . . Philippe Khorsand
Olga . . . . Désirée Nosbusch

This adaptation of a Françoise Sagan novel is a standard "ship of fools" formula enlivened by an enjoyably ripe performance from Jeanne Moreau as a famous opera singer with a taste for young men. However, basically familiar fare will have trouble finding theatrical bookings in most territories.

The setting is a luxury cruise ship sailing across the Mediterranean to Mykonos. At night, guests are entertained by the warbling of aging diva Moreau, who's accompanied at the piano by an eccentric German.

The millionaire passengers include a plump film producer (Jean-Marc Thibault) who's accompanied by his latest "discovery," an attractive starlet (Désirée Nosbusch); a surly, leftwing jour-nalist (Daniel Mesguich); his beautiful but strange young wife (Laura Morante); an overbearing, blowsy woman (Jacqueline Maillan); her bored businessman husband (Yves Kerboul); and a handsome young gigolo (Anthony Delon).

What follows is mostly predictable, with the diva bedding down with the gigolo, the troubled wife finding solace in the arms of the charming art dealer (who, it transpires, is dealing in forgeries) and the swinish journalist seducing the starlet.

It's lovingly photographed by Raoul Coutard, but director and co-adaptor José Pinheiro can't make these essentially bland characters interesting or, indeed, relevant. The whole plot, though taking place in the present, smacks of another era.

Moreau is a delight as the diva, and Anthony Delon has all of his father's raffish charm as her ardent young lover. — *Strat.*

VAN GOGH'S EAR
(DUTCH)

An Intl. Art Film release (Theaterfilm Filmverleih in Germany) of a Pohle-Garcia Films-First Floor Features production. Produced by Herman Pohle. Directed by Tony Garcia. Screenplay, Sandra van Beek, Garcia; camera (color, 16m), Peter Grey; editor, Toni Lorraine Miller; music, Stan Haywood; sound, Pander Roscan; sound mix, Jan van Sandwijk; art direction, Ans Geurts. Reviewed at Cineco, Amsterdam, Feb. 12, 1991. Running time: **80 MIN.**

With: Chip Bray, Peter Faber, Leslie Hughes, Eva van Heijningen, Jake Kruyer, Frank Sheppard, Marc Hazewinkel, Rod Beddall, Stan Haywood.

(English soundtrack)

Actors and actresses from many countries enthusiastically romp through this slender, sympathetic debut film from young American Tony Garcia. "Van Gogh's Ear" is not a classic masterpiece, but pic's a nice way to pass time with nice, if dotty, characters.

The UCLA-educated filmmaker has been working for a number of years in Europe, mainly Amsterdam, as a legit director and a screenwriter. Garcia obviously likes the city and its people, as well as Americans, but he doesn't conceal a wicked grin when east and west of the Atlantic clash.

The working title, "No More Masterpieces," fits the pic better than "Van Gogh's Ear." There's no connection between title and pic, and it might be helpful for excursions abroad to cut off "Van Gogh's Ear."

Story is about the American Company (ACT), once among the world's top avant-garde troupes but now considered old-fashioned and out of breath. Their director, Joe Paine, thinks they might regain their leading position, if only they'd get the breaks.

He hustles a place for the group at a theater festival in Amsterdam. They are short of money, rich in theories and well stocked in grudges and love affairs. They lie constantly and with abandon.

The thesps are well directed, but small excursions into farce grate a bit. Most striking in the English-language film is the soundtrack in which dialog is unforced and music excellently selected and rendered.

Photography (by Australian Peter Grey) is very good. The rhythm of the pic is firm, fast and persistent. Producer Herman Pohle ("Max & Laura & Henk & Willie) manages to make a no-budget film look comfortably funded. — *Wall.*

MUNICH FEST

VERURTEILT: ANNA LESCHEK
(VERDICT AGAINST ANNA LESCHEK)
(GERMAN)

A Filmpool-ZDF production. Written and directed by Bernd Schadewald. Camera (color, 16m), Ingo Hamer; editor, Hedy Altschiller; music,Jurgen Knieper; costume design, Julia Strauss; production design, Norbert Sherer. Reviewed at Munich Film Festival, June 23, 1991. Running time: **98 MIN.**

Anna Leschek . . . . . . Ulrike Kriener
Rainer Buchka . . . . . Ulrich Pleitgen
Ines Leschek . . . . . . Sandy Schmitz
Ellen Buchka . . . . . . Donata Hoffer
Beata Hersfeld . . . . Angelika Bartsch
Olaf Rehm . . . . Walter Kreye

"Verdict Against Anna Leschek" is a well-intentioned drama about a lawyer on the skids who recovers when he defends an impoverished mother and daughter accused of robbing a bank. Its consciousness-raising often overwhelms the plot, which works best when it's not preachy. Technique and style are best suited for tv and video markets.

Just before Christmas in Cologne, police thwart an amateurish robbery attempt by two masked figures carrying toy pistols. They turn out to be Anna Leschek (Ulrike Kriener, best known for "Men") and her 13-year-old daughter (Sandy Schmitz).

Meanwhile, wealthy Olaf (Walter Kreye) bails out lawyer Rainer Buchka (Ulrich Pleitgen), hung over after being picked up again on a drunk and disorderly charge. Rainer's wife left him, and his clientele is dwindling due to his boozing. He seems aimless, and he halfheartedly takes mother and daughter's case.

Later, Rainer's g.f. (sensual Angelika Bartsch) breaks off their relationship because she's fed up with being with a loser. He goes berserk and tears up a bar.

The lawyer tries to win Anna's confidence in order to build her defense, but she's taciturn and suspicious. He begins to develop genuine interest in the case and becomes indignant with her continued incarceration, petitioning for her release on humanitarian grounds.

He wants to share his progress on the case with friend Olaf, but he discovers him in bed with the ex-g.f. His ex-wife (Renata Hoffer), a successful dentist who often lends him money, diagnoses his concern as twinges of the heart rather than conscience, but she teases him into forgetting his new amour for an evening so they can enjoy a frolic in bed.

Via sometimes confusing flashbacks, Anna's decline into poverty is traced from her struggles with a drunken husband killed in an auto accident. Left in debt, she is laid off from her sweatshop job and is unable to support her three kids but can't get a loan or government assistance.

Completely desperate, she takes a job as a stripper in a seedy nightclub. In a powerful scene, she moves out stage center, decked out in a garish feathered headdress and sequined halter and G-string. As she awkwardly tries to remove her long gloves, the audience begins booing and, humiliated, she bolts.

Rainer gets romantically interested in Anna, although it's uncertain whether this is prompted by true affection or a Pygmalion ego trip, while she envisions a whole new life with Rainer at her side.

She is given a two-year sentence she does not have to serve, but she loses custody of her children. Her inevitable disastrous end is forecast in melodramatic fashion while Rainer slides back into a dipsomaniacal fog.

Acting is good by the leads, especially Pleitgen as the lawyer, and technical credits are adequate. Plot, based on a newspaper account, is too unrelentingly bleak to appeal to a broad audience, but the pic could find a socially conscious middle class audience. — *Sam.*

JEAN GALMOT, AVENTURIER
(JEAN GALMOT, ADVENTURER)
(FRENCH)

A Partners Prod.-UGC-Hachette Première co-production. (Intl. sales: WMF.) Produced by Ariel Zeitoun. Directed by Alain Maline. Screenplay, Maline, Daniel Saint Hamont, Anne Théron, Santiago Amigoreno; camera (Cinemascope), Walter von den Ende; editor, Hugues Darmois; music, Romano Musumara; in Dolby Stereo; costumes, Florence Cadnot. Reviewed at Munich Film Festival, June 24, 1991. Running time: **135 MIN.**
Jean Galmot . . . Christophe Malavoy
Picard . . . . Roger Hanin
Jeanne Deshamps . . . Belinda Becker
Iqui . . . . Jean-Michel Martial
Leonie . . . . Anbre Thiaw
Charas . . . . Maxime Leroux
Marianne Galmot . . . . Désriée Nosbuch-Becker
Castallane . . . . . . Roger Planchon
Arlette . . . . Ute Lemper
Adianne Cernis . . . . . . Karine Silla
Stavinsky . . . . Benoît Régent

"**J**ean Galmot, Adventurer," focusing on a turn-of-the-century French writer and gold prospector, boasts lush, big-budget production values appealing to the eye but fairly dull and lacking in psychological depth. Biopic flopped at home, and there's no reason to expect appeal offshore.

Pic opens in 1926 in French Guiana as Galmot (Christophe Malavoy) muses over his experiences since moving there 20 years before. Back then, Guiana was a notorious French penal colony, and other residents included Creoles, half-castes and the aristocrats who exploited them.

The newcomer recruits workers to prospect for gold on land given to him by his father-in-law and promises a generous cut of the proceeds after three months. Huge, good-natured Guianan Iqui (credibly played by Jean-Michel Martial) shows Galmot the ropes, and Galmot makes him a partner.

Galmot makes bumbling overtures toward a stunning mulatto widow (Belinda Becker), who rebuffs him in the middle of an exuberant carnival dance. She tells the foreigner he doesn't understand their ways. (Although locals later highly regarded Galmot, there is no indication he

ever became integrated into their society.)

The boss wins his workers' trust when they strike gold, and, true to his word, he shares the wealth. The first of many run-ins with racists occurs when the lawyer Charas (Maxime Leroux) backs out of a partnership with Galmot when he finds out a black is involved.

The businessman continues to accumulate wealth, turning to making rum while fighting for rights for blacks and convicts. He becomes a folk hero to locals and is splashed over French newspapers, but establishment's animosity grows. He and the widow become lovers, a liaison that lasts until his death.

Galmot announces plans to build an opera house, but Parisian entrepreneurs balk at black casting. Galmot runs for office on a platform of racial equality and human rights. His rum plant is torched and the foreman killed.

The Frenchman is convicted of embezzlement and sent to prison. When released, he ignores warnings to stay clear of politics and becomes involved in the mayoral race. When the election is fixed, a bloodbath occurs as the enraged population kills the declared winner and destroys the establishment's property.

Considered a liability, Galmot is sentenced to death by a largely black-hooded peoples' court. In a hokey melodramatic finish, he is poisoned by one of his workers with his mulatto lover's knowledge, and he dies with her at his side.

Lensing of tropical landscapes is stunning, and the orchestral string score suitably sweeping with Wagner, Tchaikovsky and far too few syncopated tropical tunes thrown in. The extensively researched $18 million production utilized 2,000 extras, but it would have been more entertaining if more scenes of the Guianans were included and some of the tedious courtroom scenes in France were cut.

Malavoy is far too positive to be believable and shows little indication of the madness that must have characterized this Gallic Fitzcarraldo. Love scenes end short of the bedroom; visual appeal cannot compensate for missing passion. — *Sam.*

RYD
(RUST)
(ICELANDIC)

A Verstaedid-Connexion Film-Iceland Channel 2-Swedish Film Institute co-production. (Intl. sales: Manifesto Film, London.) Produced by Sigurjon Sighvatsson, Willi Bar. Directed by Larus Ymir Oskarsson. Screenplay, Olafur Haukur Oskarsson, based on his play "Baddes Garage"; camera (color), Goran Nilsson; editor, Monika Mertens; music, Wim Mertens, Egill Olafsson; sound, Hjortur Howser; production design, Karl Juliusson. Reviewed at Munich Film Festival, June 26, 1991. Running time: **99 MIN.**
Baddi . . . . Bessi Bjarnason
Sissa . . . . Christine Carr
Petur . . . . Egill Olafsson
Haffi . . . . Stefen Jonsson
Raggi . . . . . . Sigurdur Sigurjonsson
Magnus . . . . . Thorhallur Sigurdsson

One of the few all-Icelandic productions in recent years, "Rust" is a rugged psychological drama about an unsolved crime of passion and its violent aftermath when uncovered years later. The somber allegory set against a barren landscape should suit discerning arthouse and fest audiences.

Helmer Larus Ymir Oskarsson, noted for his road movie "The Second Dance" and other Swedish pics before making his first feature on native soil, has assembled a fine cast up to the challenge of conveying the raw passion that strikingly contrasts with the cold impassivity of their environment.

After being released from prison, Petur (Egill Olafsson) returns by bus to the scene of a crime he claims he didn't commit. His reappearance disturbs garage owner Baddi (Bessi Bjarnason) and stirs up unhappy memories of Petur's affair with his wife, although he allows him to work at the garage.

Petur disrupts the dictatorial order Baddi has established in the desolate community, almost completely deserted now. Petur develops a father-son relationship with Baddi's son (Stefen Jonsson), and shy daughter (Christine Carr) is drawn to him, subconsciously hoping for a key to the events she witnessed on the night of her mother's murder but can't recall.

Largely indifferent to her b.f. mechanic (Sigurdar Sigurjonsson), the daughter develops a sexual attraction to Petur and vice versa. The mechanic notices his g.f. and Petur's attachment, while Baddi begins to hit the bottle again and spies on Petur.

The barely repressed emotions finally explode in a violent finale after Petur and Baddi's daughter become lovers and she finally remembers how her mother was murdered. The title "Rust" refers to the corrosion in the defunct garage in the middle of nowhere, as well as the moral decay that occurs when people cut themselves off from the truth.

Oskarsson gets remarkable production values on a tiny budget of about $850,000, aided by use of a small cast and simple sets. Swede Goran Nilsson's striking cinematography is similar to that of Theo Angelopoulos' master lenser Arvanitis in its skill in capturing sparse, bleak landscapes under gray skies.

Veteran stage comic Bjarnason and pop singer/composer Olafsson as Petur prove their versatility while the younger Carr and Jonsson make impressive debuts. Minimalist composer Wim Mertens' music and Olafsson's catchy piano/accordion song add appeal, and true folk art is on display in the eye-catching garage paintings by prominent artist Magnus Kjartansson.

At home, "Rust" was a critical success but a lukewarm b.o. performer, probably because it's too close to reality for auds who prefer escapist entertainment. Still, it was an audience favorite at the Munich fest.

Script by prolific Olafur Haukur Oskarsson from his play contains enough substance for cinephiles to ponder. It's also well-paced and maintains suspense throughout. English subtitles contain literal translations of frequent profanities that may be offputting to some viewers.
— Sam.

BILETAS IKI TAJ MAHAL
(TICKET TO TAJ MAHAL)
(SOVIET)

A Film Cooperative Katarsis (Kasachstan) production. (Intl. sales: Vilfilm.) Directed by Algimantas Puipa. Screenplay, Rimantas Schawelis; camera (color, b&w), Rimantas Juodwalkis; music, Juosas Schirwinskas, A. Lomomosonas. Reviewed at Munich Film Festival, June 25, 1991. Running time: **93 MIN.**
Valeria . . . . Elena Balsyte
Fabiyonas . . . . Saulius Kysas
Also with: Kostas Smoriginas, Nijole Narmontaite, Vidas Petkevitschius.

A politically relevant and highly imaginative film with images of rare beauty, "Ticket To Taj Mahal" casts a magical spell that will delight film buffs and specialized audiences.

In post-World War II Lithuania shortly after its annexation by the Soviet Union, beautiful Valeria (Elena Balsyte) and husband Fabiyonas (Saulius Kysas) have survived German occupation only to be besieged by Stalinists who occupy their village house and make life miserable.

Privacy is minimal as Fabiyonas and his wife listen to a couple make love through paper-thin walls, arousing their lust, which can only be satisfied after Valeria puts a cloth over the face of their son, sleeping on a nearby cot.

Fabiyonas is losing touch with reality and often escapes by dreaming of visiting the Taj Mahal in the red light of sunrise. The delicate sepia tint of the film changes into full color during his reveries, and Indian sitar music by A. Lomomosonos creates a mystical atmosphere.

Meanwhile, the Russians force neighbor Tsigmas to serve his military service, but he's given a desk job and promised refuge if he agrees to marry the martinette investigator Dashka, who is to be sent to the Ukraine. Military corruption and in-fighting come to a head when Maj. Luzuhas is killed on a train.

Giving in to his quixotic passion, Fabiyonas gets on a train to India. Valeria is distraught when she finds him missing, but she never gives up hope over the long separation. She finds him in an asylum in Vilnius, and their reunion ends on a suitably ambiguous note.

"Ticket To Taj Mahal" is a rich cinematic work, with especially creative camerawork by Rimantas Juodwalkis. Timely pic by Lithuanian Film Studio director Algimantas Puipa (which had SRO screenings at the Munich fest) provides background on Lithuania's continuing struggle for independence. — Sam.

THANK YOU AND GOOD NIGHT
(DOCU)

An Aries Films release (in U.S.) of an American Playhouse Theatrical Film. A Red Wagon Films production. Produced by James Shamus, Katie Hersh. Written and directed by Jan Oxenberg. Camera (color, 16m), John Hazard; editor, Lucy Winer; music, Mark Suozzo; sound, Piero Mura; art direction, Pamela Woodbridge. Reviewed at Pesaro (Italy) Intl. Festival of New Cinema, June 16, 1991. Running time: **82 MIN.**

Like many selections in the Pesaro fest's program of U.S. indie pics, "Thank You And Good Night" melds documentary with fiction, and despite downbeat subject (death of filmmaker's grandmother), it's an insightful and often uplifting piece full of wry comic touches.

Pic should thrive on the festival circuit, and it's a good bet for arthouse engagements if given careful handling and time to let word of mouth work. American Playhouse/Channel 4 (U.K.) funding indicates subsequent tv dates are a sure thing.

Jan Oxenberg's docu-diary kicks off with a slow pan over a lineup of feet. The camera comes to rest on an infinitely sensible pair of granny shoes and pans up to reveal an unsmiling punkster. This quirky contradiction sets pic's uniquely off-the-wall observational tone.

While tracing the physical decline and eventual death of her grandmother, Oxenberg constructs a portrait of her through footage of family and friends, fictional recreations of key incidents, deadpan talking headshots (by turns eulogizing and kvetching), and a running commentary by a scowling cardboard cut-out of herself.

This cut-out dehumanizes the narrator to a point allowing her both intimacy and objectivity and serves to maintain the child's-eye-view inherent in pic's winning unpretentiousness.

Grandma Mae's homespun hints for Jan's happiness amount to "get married or get on a quiz show." Throughout the account of her illness, inventive snippets of gameshows, hospital soaps and witty kindergarten motifs appear to steer things away from becoming maudlin.

In one of pic's most affecting sequences, Jan rows out into the middle of a lake with a boatload of Gran-memorabilia for some exploratory rethinking of their relationship. The bond between the two is sketched in stylized vignettes from the author's childhood — a Saturday matinee outing to see "The Pajama Game"; a trip to Coney Island; a gastronomical reverie on Gran's home cooking — and the exchanges between them are funny without falling into cross-generational cutesiness.

When Mae dies, the normally agile camera (kudos to ace lenser John Hazard) becomes immobile and a series of fragmentary bedside still shots are presented. A similar series follows which clicks off images of the hospital-supplied carrier bag stamped "Patient's Clothing and Belongings." Emotionally heightened but totally unmanipulative moments like these give pic much of its resonance.

Mae's passing becomes a jumping-off point for more ruminations on life, death and the difficulty those left behind have in letting go. The final section is less focused but to Oxenberg's credit, she gives a wide berth to the traps of pictures like "All That Jazz," which explored similar themes in a more overblown way.

Apart from the occasional fuzziness on the soundtrack, tech credits are all good, especially Lucy Winer's spot-on cutting which weaves together material shot over a 12-year period in a tight rhythmic pace that doesn't flag for a second. — Rney.

BILL & TED'S BOGUS JOURNEY

An Orion Pictures release of an Interscope Communications production of a Nelson Entertainment Film. Produced by Scott Kroopf. Executive producers, Ted Field, Robert W. Cort, Barry Spikings, Rick Finkelstein. Co-executive producers, Connie Tavel, Stephen Deutsch. Directed by Peter Hewitt. Screenplay, Chris Matheson, Ed Solomon; camera (Deluxe color), Oliver Wood; editor, David Finfer; music, David Newman; sound (Dolby), Gene S. Cantamessa; production design, David L. Snyder; costume design, Marie France; art direction, Gregory Pickrell; set design, Gerald (Jay) Sigmon, Mark Poll, Carol Bentley; creature, makeup effects, Kevin Yagher; visual effects supervisors, Richard Yuricich, Gregory L. McMurry; assistant director, Barry Thomas; co-producers, Solomon, Matheson, Erwin Stoff, Paul Aaron; casting, Karen Rea. Reviewed at Mann's Chinese Theater, L.A., July 11, 1991. MPAA rating: PG. Running time: **98 MIN.**
Ted . . . . Keanu Reeves
Bill . . . . Alex Winter
Grim Reaper . . . . . . William Sadler

De Nomolos . . . . Joss Ackland
Ms. Wardrobe . . . . Pam Grier
Rufus . . . . George Carlin
Missy . . . . Amy Stock-Poynton
Sir James Martin . . . . . Jim Martin
Capt. Logan . . . . . . Hal Landon Jr.
Elizabeth . . . . Annette Azcuy
Col. Oats . . . . Chelcie Ross
Gatekeeper . . . . Taj Mahal
Bach . . . . Robert Noble

In aptly named "Bill & Ted's Bogus Journey," the characters of the dopey, sweet-spirited dudes from San Dimas, Calif., go undeveloped in a sequel that contrives another elaborate but non-excellent adventure. Despite pic's pre-stoked audience, take likely will fall well short of the $40 million raked in back in 1989, when the concept was fresh.

Same producing and writing team that designed "Bill & Ted's Excellent Adventure" pumps much effort into production design and special effects, creating a few triumphant moments, but not enough to sustain pic's running time.

This time, evil robot versions of Bill and Ted (Alex Winter and Keanu Reeves) have been sent from the future to kill the duo before their band, Wild Stallyns, can win a local talent contest and inspire a Bill and Ted following that changes the world.

The "evil us's," as B&T call them, throw the good dudes off a cliff, but before the Grim Reaper can claim them, they get to try to beat him in a contest, and since they pick the games (Battleship, Clue, Twister), they win. His Royal Deathness (played by William Sadler in a takeoff on Ingmar Bergman's "The Seventh Seal") is then at their service as they embark on an odyssey to try to overcome the evil robot dudes and win the battle of the bands.

Pic gets by for some time on the amusement of effects such as the techniques that have Bill and Ted confronting their doubles on screen, and a sterling bit in which a ghostly Ted (Reeves) inhabits the body of his uptight police chief dad (Hal Landon Jr.).

But while production resources appear lavish, ideas are less than brilliant, and pic bottoms out in third act with an unamusing trip to heaven, where B&T collect a pair of unappealing Martian "scientists" inexplicably named "Stations" who accompany them back to earth and fashion another set of robot Bill & Teds to defeat the metal miscreants from the future. Sequel grinds to the predictable big finish in the company of these most egregious creations.

Director Peter Hewitt (replacing Stephen Herek from the original) has a field day with the wide-open boundaries pic offers for cartoonish effects and surreal dream sequences, especially in hell, but performances of Winter and Reeves as Bill and Ted harden into complete caricatures under his guidance, and thus pic's essential appeal is dimmed.

These guileless airheads with the outrageous vocabulary are obviously a beloved creation, and filmmakers might have gotten more mileage if they'd rooted their adventure a bit more in reality. As is, pic zooms off into a wasteland of outlandishness, unlikely ever to return. — *Daws.*

RAMBLIN' GAL

An Aquarius release of a Ramblin' Gal production. Produced by Carl E. Person. Directed by Roberto Monticello, Lu Ann Horstman Person. Screenplay, Lu Ann Horstman Person; camera (color), Mik Cribben; editor, Jack Haigis, Jay Kessel, Richard Dama, Shu Lea; music, Augie Meyer, Tom Cerrone; songs, Lu Ann Horstman Person, sung by Shawn Colvin; sound, David Leitner; art direction, Tony Knoposki; assistant director, Stephanie Rogers; production managers, Kat Dillon, Roberta Posner, Michael Mayers. Reviewed on vidcassette, N.Y., June 29, 1991. No MPAA Rating. Running time: **106 MIN.**
Ruby . . . . Deborah Strang
Cyril Hammond . . . Andrew Krawetz
Will . . . . Kirk Condyles
Willy . . . . Douglas Cole

A perceptive feminist look at self-realization in the recording business, "Ramblin' Gal" is an entertaining little picture currently getting a theatrical tryout as a midnight movie. Made over a period of years, pic is worth a look-see for fans of U.S. indie fare.

Filmmaker Lu Ann Horstman Person has effectively integrated her own folk song compositions into this familiar tale of housewife and mother of four Ruby (Deborah Strang) who ups and leaves Kansas to head for the Big Apple and a songwriting career.

As in countless showbiz stories, she hits roadblocks and rejections, the difference being that her feminist lyrics turn off the male record label execs.

Ruby rooms in Greenwich Village with her weird uncle Cyril (Andrew Krawetz), a hypochondriac who's obsessed with completing the electrical experiments of Nikola Tesla. As a fish out of water Ruby is introduced to NYC folkways: Her motorcycle seat and gas tank are immediately stolen and she's arrested for prostitution when merely walking down 42nd Street.

Her first local gig is singing "Woman's Prison" at a gay rights rally in Central Park, and through mistaken identity she gets to sing in a night club. A slick record label yuppie tries to get her to soften her lyrics but Ruby sticks to her guns.

Though some scenes date back to 1982, the film remains topical and timely, as songs deal with the homeless and the pressures of commercialism.

Heroine Strang is a forceful presence, combining qualities of Sally Field and Jane Fonda to her populist role. Her singing is voiced-over by up-and-coming folk singer Shawn Colvin. As her uncle, Krawetz is endearing and lends a quirky '60s quality to the picture. — *Lor.*

BIKINI ISLAND

A Curb/Esquire Films presentation of a Rocky Point production in association with Wildcat Prods. Produced by Anthony Markes, Zachary Matz. Executive producers, Jim Jeknavorian, Richard Ardi. Directed by Markes. Screenplay, Emerson Bixby, from story by Markes, Diana Levitt; camera (color), Howard Wexler; editor, Ron Resnick; sound, Paul Coogan, Kraig Kishi; production design, Keith Downey; associate producer, Laura J. Lang, Dean Georgeopolous; assistant director, Rodney Smith; casting, Val DuBone. Reviewed at Skywalker Sound, L.A., July 10, 1991. MPAA Rating: R. Running time: **85 MIN.**
With: Holly Floria, Alicia Anne, Jackson Robinson, Sherry Johnson, Gaston LeGaf, Shannon Stiles, Kathleen McOsker, Terry Miller, Cyndi Pass.

Creators of "Bikini Island" have kept their ambitions and their budget low and pull off a campy, good-natured thriller populated by gorgeous girls on a swimsuit modeling shoot. Boxoffice in the limited theatrical run coordinated by the producers will likely be as scanty as the bathing suits, but a video payoff looks assured.

Director-producer Anthony Markes ("Invisible Maniac") has a good concept: bring the Sports Illustrated swimsuit issue to life for 85 minutes and throw in a light mystery/comedy plot to keep the picture moving.

Premise is staffers of Swimwear Illustrated must find a cover girl for their 15th anni issue. They round up five beautiful girls for a weeklong fashion shoot on a remote island. Once they're there, ensconced in a dreary hotel, the girls are picked off one by one by a mysterious killer who explains their absences with bogus goodbye notes.

Is it the aging former model (Sherry Johnson) who's jealous of the nightly sex play between the ad director (Jackson Robinson) and one or another of the girls? Is it the weird, wall-eyed hotel employe, Frab (barf spelled backward), played by Terry Miller?

Regardless, Markes achieves a harmless, tongue-in-cheek tone that gets maximum fun from a very thin setup and takes things amusingly over the edge in the final reel.

Fashion shoots on the rocky beaches of so-called St. Christopher Island (lensed in Malibu and Santa Barbara) occupy most of the screentime, and these are deftly staged, with the lithe, lively models, most of whom have top magazine credits, likely to more than satisfy the target audience.

Lensing and tech credits are fully competent. — *Daws.*

MONEY
(FRENCH-ITALIAN-CANADIAN)

A UIP (France) release of a Cinema-Telemax-Antenne-2 (Paris)-Pac Film (Rome)-Malofilm (Montreal) co-production. Executive producer, Claudio Mancini. Produced by André Djaoi. Directed by Steven H. Stern. Screenplay, Gordon Roback, Larry Pederson, from novel by Paul-Loup Sulitzer; camera (Eastmancolor), Franco Di Giacomo; editor, Yves Langlois; music, Ennio Morricone; production design, Jean-Michel Hulon; production manager, Irene Litinsky; assistant directors, Otta Hanus, Pascal Deaux. Reviewed at Pathé Concorde-Marignan, Paris, May 4, 1991. Running time: **95 MIN.**
Frank Cimballi . . . . Eric Stoltz
Sarah Watkins . . . . . Maryam D'Abo
Marc Lavater . . . . . . Bruno Cremer
Martin Yahl . . . Christopher Plummer
Will Scarlet . . . . F. Murray Abraham
The Turk . . . . Mario Adorf
Also with: Anna Kanallis, Bernard Fresson, Tomas Milian, Angelo Infanti.
(English soundtrack)

The international world of high finance depicted in this terminally lame thriller is dull indeed. "Money," based on a French book described as a "finance Western," crisscrosses the world in an effort to be sophisticated and modern, but it's about as exciting as waiting in line at the bank. Prospects are bearish.

Story shuttles from Paris to Nairobi to Hong Kong to Geneva to New York to Miami to Nassau and back again, with a stopover in the Canadian countryside. All this jet-setting is at the expense of plot and characters.

Eric Stoltz toplines as a raffish young man trying to take revenge on the man who robbed his father of millions of dollars. Stoltz enlists a French private eye (Bruno Cremer) and a wealthy Turk (Mario Adorf), but, like all the other characters, they're presented in strictly clichéd terms: The detective is world-weary and cynical, the Turk is a womanizer.

Christopher Plummer is the chief villain, and the audience is expected to believe he's old enough to have held a senior wartime position with the Nazis.

F. Murray Abraham has one big scene in which he's submerged under makeup that makes him look old and sick; this is a role for which actor anonymity might have been preferred.

Maryam D'Abo turns up in the Nairobi part (actually filmed in Zimbabwe) as a love interest for Stoltz, but she's abruptly dropped from the plot.

The choppy narrative is full of holes, and inept narration is used in vain to try to patch the gaps. A few action scenes, or at least a modicum of suspense, might have partly redeemed this lethargic picture.

It's unsurprising none of the actors is at his or her best. Franco Di Giacomo's camerawork is quite attractive, but Ennio Morricone's score is one of his weakest, and Yves Langlois' editing is choppy and disconnected. "Money" will have a tough time living up to its title. — Strat.

ISTEN HÁTRAFELÉ MEGY
(GOD WALKS BACKWARDS)
(HUNGARIAN)

A TPA-Filmex production. (Intl. sales: Cine Magyar, Budapest.) Produced by György Gát, Tibor Puszt. Directed by Miklós Jancsó. Screenplay, Gyula Hernádi; camera (Eastmancolor), János Kende, István Márton; editor, Zsuzsa Csákány, Eszter Kovács; music, László Dés, Vilmos Jánori; sound, Ottó Oláh; production design, Tamás Banovich. Reviewed at Hungarofilm screening room, Budapest, May 28, 1991. Running time: **90 MIN.**
With: Károly Eperjes, György Dorner, József Madaras, Lajos Balázsovits, András Kozák, Magdolna Rimán.

Despite being billed as the first pic in which he doesn't need to talk in metaphors, Miklós Jancsó's "God Walks

Backwards" is the same goulash of hypnotic camerawork, political babble and seductive symbols. It's also a moving testament by him and scripter Gyula Hernádi on a lifetime of working together. Pic could help to revive vet helmer's profile on the fest circuit.

Yarn, as usual, is paper thin. Two media bozos, a tv director (Károly Eperjes) and his sound man (György Dorner), stroll around a deserted police academy after the exit of the Soviets from Hungary. They come across Eperjes' turncoat uncle (József Madaras), another politico (András Kozák) and various warring factions. A naked French looker (Magdolna Rimán), the "flower of survival," sashays in and out of the rooms.

Meanwhile, per tv screens in the building, Mikhail Gorbachev is having trouble in Moscow. As the various Hungarian factions vie with each other; the Red Army returns off-screen and mows everyone down.

First twist then reveals the picture as a cast-and-crew screening. Jancsó himself addresses the gathering, summons up some booze and a stripper for entertainment, and in a long voiceover reminisces on lost friends and the ironies of history. A final switcheroo has Jancsó and Hernádi also gunned down by offscreen assassins.

Unlike "Jesus Christ's Horoscope" (1989), one doesn't need a Ph.D. in political history to decipher this one. It's a cynical, playful and pensive look at Hungarian perfidy and tendencies. The mix works thanks to some stunning staging and assured playing by regulars like Madaras and Kozák. Color lensing is tops. — Del.

REACH FOR THE SKY
(CANADIAN-ROMANIAN)

A Les Prods. La Fete and Romaniafilm co-production in association with Artexfilm. Produced by Rock Demers. Directed by Elisabeta Bostan. Screenplay, Vasilica Istrate, Elisabeta Bostan with the collaboration of Demers; camera (color), Ion Marinescu; editor, Helene Girard; music, Doru Caplescu; sound, Claude Langlois; art direction, Dumitru Georgescu; costume design, Carmen Mihaela Trifu; assistant director, Alexandra Foamete. Reviewed at Cannes Film Festival (market), May 16, 1991. Running time: **90 MIN.**
Corina . . . . Izabela Moldovan
Maria . . . . Alina Izvoranu
Lili . . . . Carmen Galin
Mitran . . . . Mircea Diaconu
Marian . . . . George Mihaita
Delia . . . . Diana Lupescu

Family-film producer Rock Demers once again has hit the mark with the 12th film in his "Tales For All" series. This thoughtful story about a pubescent Romanian gymnast who reaches for the sky and wins Olympic gold is sure to be a hit with young ambitious girls who will identify with heroine's struggle to be the world's best.

Film is not a biography but is dedicated to "those like" Olympic gold medalist Nadia Comaneci. It enlisted non-Olympic but superbly talented gymnasts, including Izabela Moldovan who plays the heroine.

The long, but ultimately rewarding, pic takes the spectator rung by rung through the emotional and physical triumphs and defeats of numerous young gymnasts in their grueling drive for perfection. Pic's morality dictates that the effort is as important as the reward.

Pic's tranquil pace — which will limit U.S. theatrical draw —is a result of helmer's attempt to present a realistic picture of the rigid training that leads to the top. After some 80 minutes of detailed but unsuspenseful training footage, pic predictably climaxes with the gold medal scene.

Romanian director Elisabeta Bostan quietly details the rigors of gymnastic training at the famous Deva School, winding into a spectacular finale.

Pic will give goosebumps to the attentive viewer. As with other "Tales For All," this one is likely to score well outside English-speaking North America and have a good tv and homevid life as well. —Suze.

RAGAZZI
(FRENCH)

An AAA Classics release of a Performance production. Executive producer, Corine Thomas-Le Brun. Produced by Mama Keita, Ivan Taieb. Directed by Keita. Screenplay, Taieb, Stephane Kelin; camera (Fujicolor), Thomas Cichawa; editor, Juliana Sanchez; music, Khalil Chahine; production design, Pierre du Boisberanger; assistant director, Valerie Le Goupil. Reviewed at Unifrance screening room, May 2, 1991. Running time: **95 MIN.**
Romain . . . . Ivan Taieb
Alexandre . . . . Ken Amrani
Lisa . . . . Sabrina Coile
Romane . . . . . . Romane Bohringer
Anne . . . . . Marie-France Gantzer
Also with: Richard Bohringer.

A disarming first feature, "Ragazzi" covers well-worn territory with freshness and

charm. Fests could seek this one out, and careful, limited theatrical release internationally isn't out of the question.

Mama Keita's pic, which has Bertrand Tavernier down as "artistic adviser," is about two young men and their search for the elusive "perfect woman." Pic opens at a wedding reception (absent bride and groom videotaped their speeches) where Alexandre sees lovely half-Italian Lisa. Only trouble is, she leaves with another man.

Alexandre and chum Romain follow the couple, and next day Romain goes to the girl's apartment to make a date for his pal. He gets a kiss by mistake. Later, Lisa agrees to meet the friends at a restaurant but brings her attractive mother with her.

"Ragazzi," a very French film depite the Italian title, coasts cheerfully along depicting the minor trials and tribulations of the two friends. It concludes that friendship is more important than sex, although Romain's attractive, affectionate young sister is obviously a factor in Alexandre's decision to abandon courtship of the remote Lisa.

All members of the young cast handle their chores with grace, especially Ivan Taieb (who also co-scripted) as the resourceful Romain. This is the kind of pic French filmmakers do well: a seemingly effortless light comedy with the ring of truth. It's a small-scale but most attractive debut. — Strat.

MEDITERRANEO
(MEDITERRANEAN)
(ITALIAN)

A Penta Film Distribuzione release of a Mario and Vittorio Cecchi Gori and Silvio Berlusconi Communications presentation of a Pentafilm and AMA Film production. Produced by Gianni Minervini, Mario and Vittorio Cecchi Gori. Directed by Gabriele Salvatores. Screenplay, Vincenzo Monteleone; camera (Telecolor), Italo Petriccione; editor, Nino Baragli; music, Giancarlo Bigazzi, Mario Falagiani; art direction, Thalia Istikopoulou; costumes, Francesco Panni. Reviewed at Labirinto Cinema, Rome, May 31, 1991. Running time: **105 MIN.**
Sgt. Lo Russo . . . Diego Abatantuono
Lt. Montini . . . . . . Claudio Bigagli
Farina . . . . . . Giuseppe Cederna
Novente . . . . Claudio Bisio
Strazzabosco . . . . . . Gigio Alberti
Colasanti . . . . Ugo Conti
Vassilissa . . . . Vanna Barba
Also with: Memo Dini, Vasco Mirandola, Luigi Montini, Irene Grazioli.

Final installment of Gabriele Salvatores' road pic trilogy,

"Mediterranean" has made a healthy showing at local boxoffices, and the comedy's seductive location and upbeat introspection should lead to brisk business on the art pic circuit beyond Italy.

Eight Italian soldiers are sent to garrison a remote, strategically unimportant Greek island during World War II. Their ship is blown up (a technical weak point as the explosions look like they were lifted from a video game) and their radio is broken, leaving them isolated and forgotten.

As they adapt to island life, the delicate comic moments stay just on the right side of schlocky: One soldier mourns his beloved donkey, a burly boy falls quietly in love with the sergeant, two brothers and a shepherdess have a sexily spiritual ménage à trois, and the group underdog and the local prostitute undergo a touching courtship.

Three years pass, making for a serious narrative flaw because the passage of time completely surprises the audience. An aviator arrives with the news that the enemy has become the allies. The soldiers wait out their return to a new Italy with fear, trepidation and wild expectations.

"Mediterranean" follows Salvatores' earlier "Marrakech Express" and "Turné" in its exploration of the dreams and disappointments and the eventual escape of the generation now pushing 40. The rabble rousing of 1968 becomes WWII, the heady idealism of the '70s becomes the Greek idyll, and the fizzled hopes of the '80s become the return to mamma Italia, at least for the central characters.

The film's conclusion slips unnecessarily into trite barbershop philosophizing as two of the soldiers, 40 years on, escape from their grand delusion by pulling up a chair to cop eggplants back at the island taverns. Written postscripts outlining each character's outcome would have done the job more tidily.

The pic is rich in affectionate new slants on old Italo emblems like soccer, sex and snappy dressing. The boys switch from snazzy soldier threads to the whitest underclothes this side of Calvin Klein showrooms to a bulging wardrobe of Greek chic.

Salvatores, like Mike Nichols, displays an assurance with actors that seems particular to filmmakers with a theater background. The ensemble quality of the work of the performers (led by Diego Abatantuono) and crew

(many of whom also worked on the trilogy's first two pics) give this pic much of its buoyancy. Like the earlier films, "Mediterranean" was shot with direct sound recording.

Technical credits are excellent, especially Italo Petriccione's crisp, unfussy lensing, which glides over the faint-making setting (the tucked-away island of Kastellórizo in the Dodecanese) without letting it become the star. Nino Baragli won a David di Donatello award for pic's editing. — *Rney.*

ANNABELLE PARTAGÉE
(FRENCH)

> A Ça Films production with the participation of Canal Plus. (Intl. sales: WMF.) Written and directed by Francesca Comencini. Camera (color), Michel Abramowicz; editor, Yves Deschamps; music, Etienne Daho, Les Valentins; sound, Philippe Combes; art direction, Valérie Grall. Reviewed at L'Empire screening room (Paris), May 3, 1991. (In Cannes Film Festival, Directors Fortnight.) Running time: **86 MIN.**
> Annabelle . . . . Delphine Zingg
> Richard . . . . . . François Marthouret
> Luca . . . . Jean-Claude Adelin

In "Annabelle Partagée," the 25-year-old title character must choose between her 50-year-old lover and a guy her own age. Despite explicit treatment of a potentially racy premise, pic is so tepid the audience doesn't care with whom she sleeps and is likely to be catching 40 winks by the time she makes up her mind.

In an introductory shot, Annabelle is framed as a headless body lounging in a bed. Richard, 50, is standing nearby, also cut off at the neck. "Headless" woman tells headless man she desires him. Erect penis in foreground shows the feeling is mutual. By the time their faces are seen and the age difference apparent, the power of their physical relationship is clear.

But something is missing. When Annabelle's roommate introduces her to Luca, just back from an extended trip to Africa, they click. Annabelle informs Richard that it's over between them.

Artsy lensing and pleasant use of Paris locations can't overcome a glacial, episodic script. Characters hold forth in quasi-poetic European movie talk ("To love someone is like dying a little." "Have you ever had sex on a train?").

Extensive use of closeups

doesn't bring us any closer to characters or their motivations. Earnest attempts to build a mood are consistently undercut by cardboard characters defined by their physical attributes and professions — and only Richard, an architect, actually has the latter.

Little is learned of the heroine except that she moved to Paris from elsewhere in France to rehearse ballet moves in a dance studio and ride her bicycle through picturesque city streets when not moping in other locations.

Pic's best moments nicely capture the heightened powers of observation Annabelle displays on rare occasions when she's feeling in tune with herself or the city. Songs, however, have a tacked-on feeling.

Hollow pic is a disappointment from Comencini (daughter of accomplished helmer Luigi Comencini), whose first film ("Piano Forte," 1984) showed real promise. — *Ness.*

ÁRNYÉK A HAVON
(SHADOW ON THE SNOW)
(HUNGARIAN)

> A Budapest Filmstudio production. Directed by Attila Janisch. Screenplay, András Forgách; camera (b&w, scope), Tamás Sás; editor, Anna Kornis; music, Steve Reich, et al.; sound (Dolby), István Sipos; production design, Attila Kovács. Reviewed at Hungarofilm screening room, May 29, 1991. Running time: **79 MIN.**
> With: Miroslaw Baka, Josef Kroner, Johanna Kreft-Baka, Zsófi Baji.

"Shadow On The Snow," an abstract thriller about a father and daughter on the run, is an intriguing feature bow by Magyar helmer Attila Janisch, 33. Pic's assured style, and tasty handling of b&w and scope, makes this a fest curio.

Mystifying plot opens with the man (Polish thesp Miroslaw Baka) and his 8-year-old daughter, Rebi, traveling on a bus across a desolate landscape. They take refuge in a deserted house, and it emerged he owes money to persons unknown.

Per flashback, he accidentally ended up with a sack of cash when a post office holdup by others went awry. His ex-wife is also giving him a hard time.

Meanwhile, he and Rebi move to the house of a priest friend (Josef Kroner) in the nearest village and, when the authorities come visiting, make a run for it across country. After ditching

his daughter, the man carries on alone, finally hiding out in an abandoned truck and chopping off his wounded leg with an ax. Curtain.

Jumbled narrative plays as if pic's reels are in the wrong order, and relationships are confused at best. But a strong sense of personal vision lies behind the lens, making the pic strangely watchable. Overall look recalls some of the best abstract Hungarian pics of the '60s and '70s, with no glitches on the technical front. All Janisch needs is a strong producer. — *Del.*

IL SENSO DEL VERTIGINE
(SENSE OF VERTIGO)
(ITALIAN)

> A Myskin Film production. Produced by Donatella Palermo. Written and directed by Paolo Bologna. Camera (color), Raffaele Mertes; editor, Mirco Garrone; music, Maurizio Giammarco; sound, Thomas Szabolcs; art direction-costumes, Alessandra Montagna. Reviewed at Mystfest, Cattolica, July 2, 1991. Running time: **85 MIN.**
> Giacomo . . . . Francisco Magaldi
> Sara . . . . Rosella Testa
> Renato . . . . Silvio Vannucci
> Giovanni . . . . Eros Pagni
> Engineer . . . . Duccio Camerini

Acting falls woefully short of the mark in this Italian version of "Body Heat," and a cheap, silly ending compromises a well-structured, well edited story.

"Sense Of Vertigo" is set in the provincial town of Viterbo, filling in for those small towns in American film noir where "nothing ever happens." An ex-soccer player (Francisco Magaldi) who works in a boat agency meets a wealthy young widow (Rosella Testa) suspected by the town of murdering her rich, older husband (Eros Pagni).

His attraction to her quickly turns to obsession, and he is drawn into a web of suspicion, deceit and blackmail. He commits murder and eventually goes mad, learning in the meantime she was innocent and her husband had been killed by land speculators who wanted his hotel (a nod to "Twin Peaks," complete with shots of owls).

Just when Magaldi is running for his life and losing his sanity, he suddenly wakes up: It's all been a dream inspired by the hard-boiled whodunit he was reading before dozing off.

In his second pic, director Paolo Bologna shows skill in building a narrative and creating a mood of ennui and danger. Editor Mirco Garrone's pacing and cutting are creditable. Dense sound effects and good jazz are weaved together well to enhance the mood.

Still, this is "Body Heat" without the heat. Zero sparks fly between the two main actors. Testa is appealing, but she doesn't have the voltage it traditionally takes to push leading men to murder. Magaldi is unappealing and scowls throughout the film. It's almost disappointing when it's learned he won't go to jail because it was just a dream.

The cop-out ending discredits the hard work director Bologna put into building his story and taunts audiences for having followed it. And the awkward voiceover is unintentionally comic at times, as when the fleeing Magaldi asks himself "I wonder what the Yugoslavian border is like right now." — *Vent.*

POUR SACHA
(FOR SACHA)
(FRENCH)

A UGC release of an Alexandre Films-SGGC-TF1 Films production. (Intl. sales: World Marketing Films, Paris.) Produced and directed by Alexandre Arcady. Screenplay, Arcady, Daniel Saint-Hamont; camera (Panavision, Agfacolor), Robert Alazraki; editor, Martine Barraqué; music, Philippe Sarde; sound, Jean-Louis Ughetto; production design, Tony Egry; production manager, Bernard Grenet; assistant director, Adi Shoval. Reviewed at UGC Biarritz, Paris, May 4, 1991. Running time: **117 MIN.**
Laura . . . . Sophie Marceau
Sacha . . . . Richard Berry
Paul . . . . Fabien Orcier
Simon . . . . Niels Dubost
Michel . . . . Frédéric Quiring
David . . . . Gerard Darman
Myriam's mother . Emmanuelle Riva

A romantic view of kibbutz life in the Golan Heights in the period leading to the 1967 Six Day War is presented in Alexandre Arcady's new film, which is handsomely produced but altogether too bland to make much international impact.

In 1967, when he was 20, Arcady spent time on a kibbutz, so his vision of a paradise peopled by pretty girls and hard-working youths comes from personal experience. "For Sacha" was shot on location in Israel last August and September, at about the time Iraq invaded Kuwait, lending an

authenticity to the production. But Arcady doesn't provide interesting narrative to flesh out his rose-colored vision.

Three young friends arrive at the kibbutz to help celebrate Laura's birthday. They knew her two years before in Paris, and all three are in love with her, though she's living with their friend Sacha. There's a dark element in their shared history: Another girlfriend killed herself when Sacha transferred his affections to Laura.

Even though Sacha has a fling with an Italian kibbutzer, Laura remains loyal to him and rejects the jealous advances of her friends. But Sacha doesn't survive the war, falling victim to an Arab bullet in front of the newly captured Wailing Wall in Jerusalem.

Sophie Marceau is lovely as the spirited Laura, and the rest of the cast gives her good support. Emmannuelle Riva (star of Alain Resnais' "Hiroshima, Mon Amour") is in for a bit part as the grieving mother of the girl who committed suicide.

Although the film is seen entirely from the perspective of the people living in the threatened kibbutz, Arcady carefully stresses, more than once, that friendly Arabs should be accommodated by the Israelis.

More could have been made of the war sequences, which are given perfunctory treatment. Overall, film would have benefited from a stronger and more committed screenplay. — *Strat.*

THE YEAR OF THE BLACK BUTTERFLIES
(GERMAN)

A Journal-Film Berlin and Bavarian Broadcasting Assn. co-production. Produced by Klaus Volkenborn. Directed by Alexandra von Grote. Screenplay, von Grote, from Franz Lutzius' novel "Abducted"; camera (b&w, Kodacolor), Heinz Pehlke, with Achim Poulheim; editor, Susann Lahaye; music, Andi Brauer; sound, Klaus Klingler; set design, Olaf Schiefner; costumes, Ingrid Zoré; assistant directors, Stefan Diepenbrock, Claudia Messemer; production manager, Michael Schwartz. Reviewed at the Graffiti, Berlin, April 11, 1991. Running time: **103 MIN.**
Robert . . . . Mark McGann
Luise . . . . Gabriele Osburg
Dr. Schaller . . . . . . Rüdiger Joswig
Schulte-Pelkim . . . . Ulrich Matschoss
Augusta . . . . Corny Collins
Chaplain Wolpers . . Matthew Burton
Dr. Hegemann . Hans-Peter Hallwachs
Irmgard . . . . Christel Merian
Peter . . . . Benny Gross
Margret . . . . . . Silke Pfeil-Klee
Maria . . . . Celine Geyer
(English soundtrack)

This earnest black & white drama about the Nazis' "final solution" for crippled, handicapped and Jewish children should have some film fest legs, but U.S. arthouse success will be limited by the small scale of "The Year Of The Black Butterflies."

In 1940 and '41, the German government legalized "euthanasia," and thousands of handicapped and mentally ill patients were taken away by Nazi doctors to be gassed or used in experiments. This film focuses on a Catholic home for crippled children that refused to give up their charges to SS officers.

Luise, a pediatrician at the home, is in love with Robert, the assistant director. When she is transferred to another hospital, she notices strange goings-on no one is willing to explain. Meanwhile, officers appear at the home with "transport lists" ordering the removal of 30 children to an unknown destination.

Robert appeals to both the judiciary and the clergy to stop their abduction, but to no avail. Luise sees that one of her former patients at the new hospital has been used as a human guinea pig for a horrifying experiment. She and Robert risk their lives to save him and the rest of the children.

Black & white photography is well used to evoke a contemporary feel for a somewhat slight drama saved by strong and inherently interesting subject matter. Sporadic color animation sequences representing the children's dreams of freedom are distracting and annoying, and they almost undermine the pic.

Helmer Alexandra von Grote seems uneasy defining her characters at the beginning of the pic, but picks up steam with both story and actors as the plot progresses. She's most effective when digressing from the plot, such as a chilling scene in which a Nazi doctor lectures students on the importance of eliminating "useless" lives. This small film deserves a look. — *Reli.*

SZTÁLIN MENYASSZONYA
(STALIN'S FIANCÉE)
(HUNGARIAN-GERMAN)

A Focusfilm-Factoryfilm production. Written and directed by Péter Bacsó.

Camera (Eastmancolor), Tamás Andor; editor, Éva Kármentő; music, Jörg Schoch; sound, in Dolby stereo. No other credits available. Reviewed at Hungarofilm screening room, May 29, 1991. Running time: **93 MIN.**
With: Juli Básti, György Cserhalmi, Nina Petri, Gyula Áts, János Bán.

A picaresque satire about a village idiot who turns the tables on her foes, "Stalin's Fiancée" lacks the puff to make its one-joke plot go the distance. Despite occasional bull's-eyes, pic lacks the wacky edge of Péter Bacsó's previous comedies, and his political targets seem soft in the current climate. Fest dates look iffy.

Story is set in a Ukrainian nowheresville during the first flush of Communist collectivization. Parana (Juli Básti) is the butt of villagers' jokes, and one day, after taking refuge against a poster of Uncle Joe, she gets the nickname "Stalin's fiancée."

Due to a misunderstanding, she's given the third degree by a district party honcho who reckons she's a foreign spy. On her return to the village, she unwittingly fingers most of her enemies when they trigger a reaction instilled during her interrogation. She's finally skewered by the local hunk (György Cserhalmi) after accusing his g.f. (Nina Petri) of being a spy.

As the sackcloth yo-yo, Básti (almost unrecognizable in blond mop, mouthful of teeth and radical de-glam job) is the pic's main strength, treading a precarious line between comedy and tragedy. Cserhalmi is okay in a thin role. Supports are all colorful.

Pic's other star is the realistic village set built in Hungary on which most of the sizable 75 million forint ($1 million) budget seems to have gone. (Film was first Magyar production to get Eurimage support.) All tech credits are of a high order. — *Del.*

ROMEO & JULIA

An Intercontinental Releasing Corp. presentation of a Kaufman Films production. Executive producer, Sandy Ratcliffe. Written and directed by Kevin Kaufman. Camera (color), Patrick Darrin; editor-associate director, Peter Hammer; music, Christian Hammer; sound, Chris Schwartz; costumes, Sunny Ralfini; art direction, Deborah Dawson; associate producer, Alan Jacobs; casting, Avy Kaufman. Reviewed at Houston Intl. Film Festival, April 21, 1991. No MPAA rating. Running time: **93 MIN.**
Romeo . . . . Bob Koherr
Julia . . . . Ivana Kane
Jake . . . . Patrick McGuinness
Tony . . . . Willard Morgan
Stella . . . . Karen Porter White
Dr. Neil/director . . . . Donovan Dietz

Kevin Kaufman's "Romeo & Julia" is a sweet-natured and indefatigably upbeat romantic comedy in highly questionable taste. Despite its relentless cheeriness, basic plot of two New Yorkers who think they have AIDS, but fall in love anyway, will repel many ticket buyers. Pic may find an appreciative audience on video and paycable, however.

Bob Koherr is Romeo, a compulsive practical joker whose put-upon co-workers decide to retaliate by hiring an actor to pose as a doctor with a bad-news diagnosis. Convinced he's dying of AIDS, Romeo heads for the Manhattan Bridge, planning to end it all. Instead, he strikes up a conversation with another would-be jumper, Julia (Ivana Kane), who's convinced that she, too, has the fatal disease.

Leaning on each other for support and humorous uplift, Romeo and Julia begin a spirited — but platonic — courtship. They decide to quit their stifling jobs, live for the moment and inspire other people around them to get out of their own ruts. Romeo's boss at a straight-laced advertising firm, Stella (Karen Porter White), decides to return to her first love, acting on stage.

It comes as no great surprise when it's revealed Julia doesn't really have AIDS, either. In fact, the most surprising (and, for some people, most offensive) aspect of the AIDS plot is just how timid Kaufman is about actually referring to the disease by name.

Even after Romeo and Julia discover they don't have "you know, it," each continues to think the other has "it." This leads to a finale where the lovers, now newlyweds, decide to throw caution to the wind and, consummate. Scene is meant to show how deep their love is, but it's likely to rattle viewers who take AIDS a great deal more seriously than Kaufman seems to.

Still, pic has moments of charm and wit and is graced with a winning romantic leads in Kane and Koherr. Production values are firstrate despite the obviously limited budget. Classical selections by Sergei Prokofiev (including, naturally, his "Romeo And Juliet" ballet score) are cleverly used to underscore key scenes. — *Ley.*

MOSCOW FEST

SUKINY DJETI
(SONS OF BITCHES)
(SOVIET)

A Fora Film Studio and Rym Studio of Mosfilm production. Produced by Andrei Razoumovsky, Yuri Romanenko, Yuri Kushnerev. Directed by Leonid Filatov. Screenplay, Filatov, Igor Shevtsov; camera (color), Pavel Lebeshev; music, Vladimir Komarov; production design, Leonid Pertsev. Reviewed at Moscow Film Festival, July 8, 1991. Running time: **100 MIN.**
With: Vladimir Ilyin, Leonid Filatov, Larisa Oudovichenko, Aleksander Abdoulov, Yevgeniy Yevtegneyev, Lia Akhedzhakova, Ludmilla Zaitseva, Maria Zoubareva, Larisa Poliakova, Tatyana Kravchenko, Yelena Tsiplakova.

Soviets fight the system — in this case, a Moscow theater company struggles for survival — in "Sons Of Bitches," a not terribly original examination of Soviet problems already familiar to Western audiences.

A popular Moscow theater group is threatened with termination by state authorities after its director defects during a tour abroad. One by one, members of the troupe visit the party official to try to convince him not to quash their company.

When reason doesn't work, the actors result to seduction and blackmail. Despite their efforts, the theater's death warrant is signed. The actors immediately forget their petty internal quarrels and unite in a hunger strike to save their art from callous and Philistine bureaucrats.

Some visual elements are baffling: Why are the actors in full period costumes and stage make-up all the time? Life, to them, seems to be a chronic dress rehearsal. Techwise, pic has a greenish tinge, due either to improper filters or low-quality film stock.

Based on a true story, pic lacks a strong enough storyline as well as the technical finesse to capture a Western aud's attention for the duration. While the theme of sacrificing all for art and ideology — and rising up in the face of the system — is noble, the handling of the material could have been more imaginative. — *Reli.*

H NICHTA TIS MYSTIKIS SYNANTISIS
(IMPOSSIBLE ENCOUNTER)
(GREEK)

A Panayiotis Antonopoulos-Greek Film Center-ET1 co-production. Written and directed by Takis Antonopoulos. Camera (Fujicolor), Andreas Sinanos; editor, Yannis Tsitsopoulos; music, Dimitris Marangopoulos; sound, Dinos Kittou; set design-costume design, Anthe Sofooleous. Reviewed at Athina Cinema, Athens, Feb. 1, 1991. (Also in Moscow Film Festival). Running time: **91 MIN.**
Dretos . . . . Cleon Georgiadis
Eleni . . . . Reni Pittaki
Dogi . . . . Christophorous Panoutsos
Combatant . . . . . Johnny Theodoridis
Photographer . . . . . Takis Margaritis
Little one . . . . . . Valeria Komninou
President . . . . . . Manolis Destounis

"Impossible Encounter" is an uninteresting search by a 40-something intellectual for her ex-lover that leads her to an unlikely fling with a disaffected youth. First flick by helmer Takis Antonopoulos failed to stir interest on the homefront and is unlikely to do so anywhere else.

A young biker (Cleon Georgiadis) is the implausible kingpin of a subculture of bored teenyboppers trying to look tough. Like a vampire, he emerges from his subterranean digs at night to participate in cycle drag races.

When the biker follows a photographer to find out why he has been snapping their pictures, he meets a middle-aged researcher (Reni Pittaki) who came to Athens from Paris to look for the man she lived with at the time of the military junta.

The biker trails her one night and takes her home from a bar when she's too tipsy to make it home on her own. He is taciturn and pouty; she is largely impassive except when talking about her ex. Both are immersed in their own obsessions so their interaction generates little chemistry, least of all in the sexual scenes.

In perhaps the pic's only realistic scene, the woman suddenly realizes the youth can't relate to her reminiscences of pre-junta days in 1966 because he wasn't even born then. He takes her comment as an insult and has a temper tantrum.

The actors mainly posture, the plot leads nowhere and editing is slapdash. Even the eye-catching nocturnal effects of talented lenser Andreas Sinanos don't maintain interest in the night-time rumbles. — *Sam.*

AL MOATEN AL MYSSRI
(WAR IN THE LAND OF EGYPT)
(EGYPTIAN)

Directed by Salah Abou Seif. Screenplay, Mohsen Zayid; camera, Tarik at-Telmissani; music, Yassir Abd Al-Rahman. Reviewed at Moscow Film Festival, July 9, 1991. Running time: **100 MIN.**
With: Omar Sharif, Izzat Al-Alayli, Safia Al-Umri, Abdallah Mahmoud.

Plotline of a father's betrayal of his son could have gone the noble tragedy route, but superficial handling and one-dimensional characters instead turn this drama of Egyptian haves and have-nots into a Dallas-on-the-Nile.

Even Omar Sharif can't salvage this Egyptian soap. His talents are wasted in the role of a wealthy landowner in Egypt in the mid-'70s whose fortunes increase when an agricultural reform bill is upset. Sharif recovers many acres of expropriated farmland, to the horror of local tenant farmers who have been eking out a living on the earth they must forfeit.

Sharif greedily revels in his increased wealth until he learns that his spoiled, good-for-nothing son is to be drafted. Taking advantage of a local peasant's insolvency, Sharif pays the man to send his son into the army in place of Tawfik. When the peasant's son is killed, his blood is on Sharif's hands.

Pic has little to offer aside from a rare and interesting glimpse into contemporary Egyptian village life. Characters are sketched as broadly as possible: Sharif's character is greedy, scheming and conniving. The peasants are relentlessly poor but noble.

When the peasant son is drafted, another film starts. Pic's second half forsakes village life and leaves the rest of the cast in the dust to follow his induction into army life. Since the peasant son's role in pic's beginning was minimal, film seems disjointed, never deciding which plotline or character it wants to stick to. Tech credits are adequate. — *Reli.*

THE DOCTOR

A Buena Vista release of a Touchstone Pictures presentation in association with Silver Screen Partners IV of a Laura Ziskin production. Produced by Ziskin. Executive producer, Edward S. Feldman. Directed by Randa Haines. Screenplay, Robert Caswell, based on Ed Rosenbaum's book "A Taste Of My Own Medicine"; camera (Technicolor, Eastman prints), John Seale; editor, Bruce Green, Lisa Fruchtman; music, Michael Convertino; sound (Dolby), Jim Tanenbaum; production design, Ken Adam; art direction, William J. Durrell Jr.; set decoration, Gary Fettis; costume design, Joe I. Tompkins; assistant director, Dennis Maguire; co-producer-unit production manager, Michael S. Glick; casting, Lynn Stalmaster. Reviewed at Avco Cinema Center, L.A., July 18, 1991. MPAA Rating: PG-13. Running time: **125 MIN.**

Dr. Jack MacKee . . . . . William Hurt
Anne Mackee . . . . . . Christine Lahti
June Ellis . . . . . . Elizabeth Perkins
Dr. Murray Caplan . . Mandy Patinkin
Dr. Eli Blumfield . . . . . Adam Arkin
Nicky MacKee . . . . . Charlie Korsmo
Dr. Leslie Abbott . . . Wendy Crewson
Dr. Al Cade . . . . Bill Macy
Also with: J.E. Freeman, William Marquez, Kyle Secor, Nicole Orth-Pallavicini, Ping Wu, Tony Fields, Brian Markinson, Maria Tirabassi.

"**T**he Doctor" grapples powerfully with themes seldom faced in today's escapist marketplace: mortality, compassion, social responsibility. William Hurt's perf as an emotionally constricted heart and lung surgeon faced with his own medical crisis is all the more moving for its rigor and restraint, even if the film intermittently fails to catch emotional fire.

Pic should defy conventional b.o. wisdom and succeed handsomely because of its sheer quality and guts.

The kind of doctor who relates better to people when they're unconscious, Hurt espouses a philosophy of emotional distance, claiming that empathy interferes with technical demands made on a surgeon. He carries over the approach into his sterile family life in affluent Marin County, keeping wife Christine Lahti and son Charlie Korsmo at arm's length.

Robert Caswell's spare and eloquent screenplay doesn't caricature Hurt but gives his medical arguments a seeming reasonableness before his life is thrown into turmoil when he is diagnosed with throat cancer.

Director Randa Haines, who previously guided Hurt in "Children Of A Lesser God," first cast Warren Beatty in "The Doctor" before they parted over differences of interpretation. She is fortunate, as it turns out, to have an icier actor such as Hurt in the role, because it's more of a stretch for him to evolve into a mensch.

The wrenching effect on Hurt when he learns he has cancer and his gradual acceptance of terror and uncertainty is conveyed mostly with an admirable absence of melodrama — except for the manipulative intrusion of Michael Convertino's syrupy music and the director's unsubtle use of rain effects to signal emotional release.

Haines' otherwise intelligent direction is methodical in the best sense of the word, using documentary-like storytelling techniques with lenser John Seale to take the viewer through the doctor's journey of self-discovery in Ken Adam's chilling silver-blue hospital set. The film is so intense it will make anyone share a visceral sense of imminent mortality — if not hypochondria.

Caswell and Haines also find a welcome leavening of humor in the story, all of it appropriate and incisive, from the gallows jokery and raucous pop music that keep the operating room staff alert to the petty humiliations the officious Hurt undergoes when reduced to the status of ordinary patient.

Accurately catching the strangely heightened mood that major illness induces, pic shows Hurt reacting with a newly critical awareness of the negligence of partner Mandy Patinkin and being repelled by the callousness of his doctor (Wendy Crewson) while at the same time finding fellowship with a colleague he previously mocked (Adam Arkin).

Hurt's initial self-pity begins to evaporate when he enters the incandescent presence of fellow patient Elizabeth Perkins. Though dying of a brain tumor and suffused with barely controlled rage over the inadequate treatment that failed to detect it, Perkins has a life-embracing candor and generosity of spirit that puts his lesser problems in perspective.

Their platonic but intimate relationship becomes the film's emotional crux as Perkins (in a wondrously good performance) teaches Hurt what he failed to learn in med school about unconquerable pain and acceptance of death.

Unfortunately, as Hurt becomes preoccupied with his illness and with Perkins, Lahti's character recedes into invisibility for long stretches and tends to become a thankless complaining-wife figure, despite the actress' forthright portrayal of anguish and frustration.

The scenes in the family's elegant but lifeless home suffer from the film's inability to cope three-dimensionally with Hurt's emotional neglect of his wife and son. Fine young actor Korsmo is barely in the film, much to its detriment as the child's inherited aloofness could have provided more of a window into the family's problems.

Haines seems so concerned with avoiding the melodramatic clichés of the disease-of-the-week genre that in some of the climactic moments when the film should cut loose with an emotional crescendo, it just sits there. Still, the film is full of more contained moments that convey Hurt's growth into a man of empathy. — *Mac.*

V.I. WARSHAWSKI

A Buena Vista release of a Hollywood Pictures presentation in association with Silver Screen Partners IV of a Jeffrey Lurie and Chestnut Hill production. Produced by Lurie. Executive producers, Penney Finkelman Cox, John P. Marsh. Co-executive producers, John Bard Manulis, Lauren C. Weissman. Directed by Jeff Kanew. Screenplay, Edward Taylor, David Aaron Cohen, Nick Thiel; screen story, Taylor, based on the V.I. Warshawski novels by Sara Paretsky; camera (Technicolor), Jan Kiesser; editor, C. Timothy O'Meara, Debra Neil; music, Randy Edelman; sound (Dolby), David Kelson; production design, Barbara Ling; art direction, Larry Fulton, William Arnold (Chicago); set design, Lauren Plizzi; set decoration, Anne H. Ahrens, Kathe Klopp (Chicago); costume design, Gloria Gresham; assistant director, Jack F. Sanders; 2nd unit director, Glenn Randall Jr.; co-producer, Doug Claybourne; casting, Glenn Daniels. Reviewed at Walt Disney Studios, Burbank, Calif., July 23, 1991. MPAA Rating: R. Running time: **89 MIN.**

V.I. Warshawski . . . Kathleen Turner
Murray . . . . Jay O. Sanders
Lt. Mallory . . . . . . Charles Durning
Kat Grafalk . . . . . . Angela Goethals
Paige Grafalk . . . . Nancy Paul
Horton Grafalk . . . . Frederick Coffin
Trumble Grafalk . Charles McCaughan
Boom-Boom . . . . . Stephen Meadows
Also with: Wayne Knight, Lynnie Godfrey, Anne Pitoniak, Stephen Root, Robert Clotworthy, Tom Allard, Michael G. Hagerty, Lee Arenberg.

You can't be much worse-offski then to sit through "V.I. Warshawski." Klutzy murder mystery was obviously intended to be the first in a hoped-for series about the eponymous femme detective impersonated by Kathleen Turner, but there will be about as many people clamoring for a follow-up as there were assorted producers and writers on this effort.

Audiences should be able to smell that this is just a low-grade tv meller with a star name and foul language, and stay away accordingly.

Somewhere behind the vast underachievement here, one can discern that there was screen promise in the blue collar female dick of Sara Paretsky's novels. The daughter of a cop and a habitue of sports bars on Chicago's North Side, this salty, sexy, streetwise straight-shooter clearly could have represented a refreshing new twist on the standard issue private investigator.

But a good concept is far from being everything, as this Hollywood Pictures potboiler painfully proves. Aside from four or five arguably amusing lines, film has nothing to offer — no thrills, no plausibility, no compelling characters and no production values aside from the always striking Windy City skyline.

The story has Warshawski, whose apartment affords a splendid view into right field of Wrigley Field, getting involved in dirty business among three warring brothers.

One brother, the good-looking Boom-Boom Grafalk, a former hockey player for whom V.I. has eyes, is killed in a suspicious dockside explosion. Field of suspects is immediately pretty much narrowed to the two other brothers, the elusive Horton and the menacing Trumble, who happens to be married to Boom-Boom's ex-wife.

Warshawski also is responsible for Boom-Boom's 13-year-old daughter Kat, for whom she was babysitting when the girl's father was sent into permanent slumber. More vulgar than her protector, Kat hates her mother as much as she loves making a scene, which helps the sleuth in her undercover work on at least a couple of occasions.

Warshawski gives as good as she gets, effectively manhandling men who dare take her on physically with some snappy martial arts moves. For action, scribes have concocted an implausible speedboat chase down the Chicago River that is capped by a one-liner that made the preview audiences groan in agony.

From a filmmaking point of view, it is all uninspired and perfunctory, utterly lacking in a sense of style that might have

made this punchy fun.

To pay off in any interesting ways and to aspire to serious levels it doesn't seem to have contemplated, film would have needed to paint a much stronger sociopolitical context. Ideally, it also would have displayed the same sort of irreverent, skeptical attitude toward men as is held by the leading character, an enlightened feminism informed by real life, not by books and academia.

Dialog is of the self-consciously hardboiled school, and is studded with the predictable running gags of people mispronouncing the detective's name, asking what the V.I. stands for, and getting rude answers in return.

Centerscreen throughout, Turner would seem to have been perfectly cast in such a sassy, confident part, but even she can't drive a totally rusty vehicle. Charles Durning is in briefly for a familiar big-city cop role; remainder of the cast is innocuous.

Clearly made on a budget, pic looks and sounds like lots of stuff that can be seen on any night of the week on television. V.I.W./R.I.P. — *Cart.*

MOBSTERS

A Universal Pictures release of a Steve Roth production. Produced by Roth. Executive producer, C.O. Erickson. Directed by Michael Karbelnikoff. Screenplay, Michael Mahern, Nicholas Kazan, from story by Mahern; camera (DeLuxe color), Lajos Koltai; editor, Scott Smith, Joe D'Augustine; music, Michael Small; sound (Dolby), Mike Dobie, Tim Dobie; production design, Richard Sylbert; art direction, Peter Lansdown Smith; set decoration, George R. Nelson; costume design, Ellen Mirojnick; assistant directors, Albert Shapiro, Albert Cho; casting, Bonnie Timmermann, Nancy Naylor. Reviewed at Avco Cinema Center, L.A., July 22, 1991. MPAA Rating: R. Running time: **104 MIN.**

Lucky Luciano	Christian Slater
Meyer Lansky	Patrick Dempsey
Bugsy Siegel	Richard Grieco
Frank Costello	Costas Mandylor
Arnold Rothstein	F. Murray Abraham
Mary Motes	Lara Flynn Boyle
Don Faranzano	Michael Gambon
Tommy Reina	Christopher Penn
Don Masseria	Anthony Quinn
Mad Dog Coll	Nicholas Sadler

Supposed cross between "Young Guns" and "Goodfellas" is more like "Lucky & Meyer's Bogus Journey" or "Mafia Lite" — less filling than the average gangster film, but with a third more gratuitous killings. Armed with teen appeal thanks to its leads, this hollow pic may mow down strong boxoffice early but will

start hemorrhaging quickly as mixed-to-poor word-of-mouth cuts off its legs.

"Mobsters" resembles a cart-before-the-horse case of putting marketing ahead of filmmaking, as the seemingly can't-miss premise of teen-heartthrob gangsters gets lost in self-important direction, a shoddy script and muddled storytelling.

The narrative is amazingly confused in light of its simplicity: Two Italian and two Jewish kids from the ghetto team up in the 1920s and get into organized crime, gradually finding themselves caught between two dons.

Story is based on the real-life exploits of mob boss Lucky Luciano (Christian Slater) and confederates Meyer Lansky (Patrick Dempsey), Bugsy Siegel (Richard Grieco) and Frank Costello (Costas Mandylor).

True highlights come from its longer-toothed characters, with Anthony Quinn's lusty portrayal of Don Masseria and F. Murray Abraham as the Yiddish-spouting no-goodnik Arnold Rothstein.

Luciano, through some sort of natural magnetic quality unapparent in Slater's performance, becomes leader of his 20-something group and proceeds to nettle the established dons, playing them against each other.

In terms of the look and period trappings, pic perhaps most closely resembles Sergio Leone's "Once Upon A Time In America," though any other resemblance between this film and that epic is purely coincidental.

Both films had plenty of bloodshed, but the violence in better gangster studies illuminated character and a certain lifestyle, while here it feels gratuitous.

None of the younger characters ever seem to connect, most notably Slater with Lara Flynn Boyle ("Twin Peaks") as a showgirl who falls too quickly and inexplicably into Luciano's life.

First-time director Michael Karbelnikoff occasionally betrays his roots in tv commercials, particularly with a ludicrous, gauzily shot love scene between Boyle and Slater that closely resembles a perfume ad.

An early sign that the story, which contains an occasional throwaway line worth keeping, is in trouble emerges when Karbelnikoff resorts to an action montage to advance it about 20 minutes into the film.

Slater still has his young Jack Nicholson act down pat, while Dempsey plays Lansky with an

unnatural and annoying vocal tic (supposedly to sound Brooklyn-Jewish). Grieco is strictly window dressing as ladies' man Siegel, who will appear in an older incarnation in Warren Beatty and Barry Levinson's "Bugsy." Mandylor is equally bland and ill-defined.

Other distinguished role belongs to a sadistic hitman (Nicholas Sadler), who actually carries off the part with enough cartoonish glee to entertain even if the tone is incongruous with the rest of the film.

Period trappings from meticulous costuming to cars, sets and cinematography are firstrate, though they can't cover up pic's structural deficiencies.

It's also noteworthy that no effort is made to age the characters through makeup, so it comes as a surprise near the end when 10 years have elapsed since the principal action began. Then again, for some, pic will feel like a life sentence. — *Bril.*

BULLSEYE!

A 21st Century Film presentation of a Menahem Golan production. Executive producers, Golan, Ami Artzi. Produced and directed by Michael Winner. Screenplay, Leslie Bricusse, Laurence Marcs, Maurice Gran, based on story by Winner, Bricusse, Nick Mead; camera (Rank color), Alan Jones; editor, "Arnold Crust" (Winner); music, John Du Prez; sound (Dolby), Paul Sharkey; production design, John Blezard; art direction, Alan Cassie; set dresser, Ian Whittaker; costume design, John Bloomfield; assistant director, Michael Murray; production managers, Bill Shephard, Clifton Brandon; stunt coordinator, Roy Alon; associate producer, Stephen Barker. Reviewed on RCA/Columbia vidcassette, N.Y., July 21, 1991. MPAA Rating: PG-13. Running time: **93 MIN.**

Lipton/Dr. Hicklar	Michael Caine
Gerald/Bevistock	Roger Moore
Willie	Sally Kirkland
Flo Fleming	Deborah Barrymore
Holden	Mark Burns
Hyde	Lee Patterson
Inspector Grosse	Derren Nesbitt

Also with: Deborah Leng, Christopher Adamson, John Cleese, Patsy Kensit, Alexandra Pigg, Jenny Seagrove.

Michael Winner's attempt at a rollicking caper comedy falls flat in "Bullseye!" Film opened in London last November but is just a direct-to-video title with big-name stars for domestic consumption.

Inspiration was evidently the smash "A Fish Called Wanda," whose star and creator John Cleese makes a cameo here. Unfortunately that film was probably a fluke since the caper format seems tired indeed this time. It's a pity, since Winner made one of the best '60s pics in the genre, "The Jokers."

Here, Michael Caine and Roger Moore front for a preposterous storyline. Both are criminals, whose exact lookalikes happen to be government scientists who've devised a nuclear fusion energy process that promises cheap electrical power.

With their old partner Sally Kirkland as instigator, they set about to steal the corrupt scientists' cache of diamonds (taken as bribes from foreign powers) from a safety deposit box.

This feat accomplished, second half of the film chases around Scotland as the criminals are supposedly working for U.K. and U.S. government agencies to get the scientists' formula and thwart the baddies attempt to sell it to the enemy.

Winner delivers his usual sprightly pace, but the frequent sight gags and dumb jokes aren't funny. Both Caine and Moore strain for laughs, former made up like W.C. Fields with false nose and latter bugging his eyes out in frequent astonishment. Moore's real-life daughter, pretty Deborah Barrymore, is cast as an unlikely 22-year-old CIA agent.

Kirkland, who wears gaudy outfits for no reason in the later reels like she did in "Cold Feet," is okay in a strictly functional role. In addition to Cleese, Jenny Seagrove and Patsy Kensit make pointless cameos.

Shot in 1989, pic has dated rapidly, especially a final gag involving a lookalike of then-prime minister Margaret Thatcher. John Du Prez, who scored "A Fish Called Wanda," punches up the film with catchy music, but his jaunty main theme is way too close to John Dankworth's classic "Morgan!" — Lor.

THE MAGIC RIDDLE
(AUSTRALIAN-ANIMATED)

A Greater Union Distributors (Australia) release of a Yoram Gross Film Studios production, made with the assistance of the Australian Film Finance Corp. (Intl. sales: Beyond Intl. Group.) Executive producer, Sandra Gross. Produced and directed by Yoram Gross. Screenplay, Leonard Lee, John Palmer, Gross; animation directors, Junko Aoyama, Sue Beak, Nobuko Burnfield, Nicholas Harding, Athol Henry; backgrounds, Richard Zaloudek; editor, Rod Hay; music, Guy Gross; animation supervisor, Paul McAdam; production manager, Jeanette Toms. Reviewed at Village Roadshow screening room, Sydney, June 28, 1991. Running time: **92 MIN.**
Voices: Robyn Moore (female voices), Keith Scott (male voices).

Latest animated feature from Sydney-based Yoram Gross playfully mixes together a half-dozen famous fairy tales for an amazing and at times delightful pic for small fry, though one unlikely to be revered by animation buffs. Commercial prospects, within its chosen market, are good.

Narrative is told by an old woman to her grandchildren, and she admits she gets things muddled up. So the story of Cinderella has the heroine dressing up as Little Red Riding Hood and meeting the Big Bad Wolf. She also disguises herself as Snow White to attend a ball, and meets the Seven Dwarfs (with different names from Disney's film), Pinocchio and the Three Little Pigs.

Visually, the film is good, with amusing character designs for the most part. Cinderella is a pert heroine who favors tight jeans and tank-top. The handsome hero, however, is Mr. Bland. The wicked stepmother, with her drooping breasts and cotton knickers, is a lively figure of fun. The backgrounds are attractive, but at times insufficiently animated.

Robyn Moore and Keith Scott essayed all the voices, and do an acceptable job (except Scott's routine voice portrayal of the hero). Various voices, including a few star names, would have helped.

Long credit crawl including Japanese, Chinese and Vietnamese names reflects the diversity of animation talents working in Australia. Pic ends with a plug for the next Gross animation feature, "Blinky Bill," to be released in 1992. — Strat.

BLOWBACK

A Northern Arts Entertainment release of a Blowback production. Written, produced and directed by Marc Levin. Camera (Duart color), Mark Benjamin; editor, Tim Squyres; music, Wendy Blackstone; sound, Mathew Price; production design, Kosmo Vinyl; costume design, Susan Lyall; assistant director, Ted Hope; co-producer, Paul Marcus; associate producer, Sue Crystal. Reviewed at Magno Review 2 screening room, N.Y., July 24, 1991. No MPAA Rating. Running time: **94 MIN.**
Owen Monroe . . . . . Bruce McCarty
Nancy Jones . . . . Jane Hamper
Emilio . . . . Eddie Figueroa
Dr. Crack . . . . Craig Smith
Dick Jones . . . . Don Cairns
Paul . . . . Matt Mitler
Counselor . . . . . . Leslie Levinson

Marc Levin's "Blowback" is a timely political satire about U.S. covert operations. Primi-

tive film technique will limit its exposure mainly to midnight and fringe situations, but subject matter could attract European interest.

Title refers to a mission that backfires, and that's exactly what happens to straight-arrow agent Bruce McCarty, a broad pastiche of Oliver North. He's in Miami speaking at a fundraiser for aid to Central American rebels while planning a communist-terrorist raid there that will be used as the excuse for repression.

Despite his sexual abstinence theories and other squareness, agent falls for a beautiful recovering addict (Jane Hamper) who coincidentally is the daughter of a retired general (Don Cairns) assisting in the fundraising.

Hero also is attempting to get a stolen "blowback file" back from another addict (Eddie Figueroa) enrolled in the g.f.'s rehab class. That file could blow the lid off of illegal CIA operations.

Film's strange, tongue-in-cheek incidents climax in the explosion of an "O-bomb," utilizing orgone energy that's been fabricated by a nutty scientist (Craig Smith). End credits are accompanied by a darkly amusing voiceover of the government's reactionary plans to round up drug abusers, HIV positives, pornographers and rap musicians.

Filmmaker Levin, debuting here after extensive docu work, succumbs to first film-itis in packing in too many stray plot threads and gimmicks. However, his shotgun approach often hits the target, notably in a wacked-out lecture by Figueroa covering Uncle Sam's connections with the drug trade, dating back to Lucky Luciano after WWII.

McCarty is a bit stiff in his Dudley Doright role opposite the uninhibited Hamper, who at times resembles Susan St. James. Craig Smith resembles Lou Castel playing Dr. Strangelove as he portrays the quietly nutty doctor. Scene stealer is Figueroa (who died last year), playing with the right intensity as most obvious "conscience" character.

Erratic sound mix and substandard production values are film's chief limitations. — Lor.

MELODRÁMA (SZABADSÁG ÉS SZERELEM) [MELODRAMA (LOVE AND FREEDOM)]
(HUNGARIAN)

A Hunnia Filmstudio production. Written and directed by Péter Gothár. Camera (Eastmancolor), Sándor Kardos; editor, Péter Timár; music, György Selmeczi; sound (Dolby), János Réti. Reviewed at Hungarofilm screening room, May 30, 1991. Running time: **96 MIN.**
With: István Gyuricza, Attila Magyar, József Szarvas, Andrea Söptei.

Onetime film fest favorite Peter Gothár bounces back with a screwy father-and-son comedy that never overreaches its limitations. Wordy script occasionally gets trapped on its own traffic circles, but pic's more restrained tone will appeal to those turned off by his extravagant "Just Like America" (1988).

Story opens at midnight on Aug. 20, 1968, with a Magyar tank division crossing into Czechoslovakia to "help" the government against "counter-revolutionaries." Feri enjoys a tumble with willing barmaid Jula and on the way home tries to take her and his tank to Vienna instead. That earns him 20 years in stir.

When he gets out, he finds his buddy Tomka has married Jula and the pair have a son, Lali. Tomka quickly defenestrates when Feri comes at him with a gun, and rest of pic is taken up with Feri and Lali wandering round Budapest in search of Tomka while the son plies his real father with questions about his past.

Rapid-fire dialog rarely palls thanks to Gothár's heightened direction, nimble camerawork and cutting, and varied playing by the four leads. The film is a clever twist on Hungarian cinema's hot theme of re-examining the recent past, and there's a welcome absence of easy answers and self-pity.

"Melodrama" started lensing last Aug. 20, exactly 22 years after the invasion referred to at the start. — Del.

MOSCOW FEST

OKHOTA NA SUTENERA
(HUNTING FOR A PIMP)
(SOVIET)

A Laterna Magika production. Directed by V. Derbenev. Screenplay, A. Shpeer. Reviewed at Moscow Film Festival (market), July 15, 1991. Running time: **85 MIN.**
With: Andrei Sokolov, Igor Volkov, Vera Sotnikova, Aristarkh Livanov.

Set in Moscow's underworld, this cops-and-robbers (and more robbers) drama is more accessible to Western auds than most Soviet fare. While Clint Eastwood may not be facing serious competition from Russia yet, "Hunting For A Pimp" entertains.

In this pic, there's no honor among thieves. Racketeers, prostitutes, black market traders, pimps and mobsters all conspire against each other to get greenbacks and all that they can buy. Plot follows the kidnaping of a pimp reputed to have a large stash of hard currency.

Packed with chase sequences, gritty street scenes with a docu feel, some sex and not-bad Soviet rock music, this is one USSR drama that incorporates the elements that play to foreign audiences. Tech credits are fine.
— *Reli.*

VOZDUSNIY POTZELUI
(BLOWN KISS)
(SOVIET)

An XXL Film Studios production. Produced by the Kazcomstroy Bank. Directed by Abai Karpikov. Screenplay, Karpikov, Igor Poberezhsky; camera (color), Georgy Gidt; music, Victor Vlazov; art director, Alexei Zolotukhim. Reviewed at Moscow Film Festival (market), July 12, 1991. Running time: **87 MIN.**
Nastja . . . . Katri Horma
Kolja . . . . Konstantin Podnyn
Musician . . . . Valentin Nikulin

"Blown Kiss," a simple tale of a young woman's sexual awakening, has little to recommend it for the Western market. Still, director Abai Karpikov manages to come up with more than occasional moments of compelling and astonishing weirdness.

Karpikov builds, but doesn't sustain, a dark and surrealistic edge, and his pic will probably never hit. Still, the helmer shows great promise as a member of the Soviet New Wave.

A young and pretty nurse (Katri Horma) is engaged to a surgeon at her clinic. Her good looks and sweet disposition make her the favorite of her colleagues and patients. Her perfect life begins to go awry when a handsome young racecar driver is brought to the clinic.

The nurse enters into a series of wordless erotic encounters with her new patient. When he is discharged from the clinic and disappears, she begins cracking up. She sinks into a "Repulsion"-esque depression and finds herself compelled to seduce or sexually use all the men in her life.

Pic's drawbacks include its dated look. Makeup and costumes are terminally rooted in the 1970s, prematurely dating the material for Western auds. The music is simply bad and distracting.

Again and again, however, little moments and sequences of quirky visual genius punctuate the film: the pretty nurse dispassionately eating an entire box of chocolates after being abandoned by her lover; a shocking attempted suicide by shotgun that can only be described as gynecological; a group of nurses in starched hats standing in a stiff, formal row singing a song.

Most of this pic looks like it was made for tv in '72, but lurking in the corners is heavyweight creative ability. — *Reli.*

DAS HEIMWEH DES WALERJAN WROBEL
(WALERJAN WROBEL'S HOMESICKNESS)
(GERMAN)

A Studio Hamburg and ZDF co-production. Produced by Hermann Kirchmann. Written and directed by Rolf Schübel. Camera (color), Rudolf Körösi; music, Detlaf Petersen. Reviewed at Moscow Film Festival, July 16, 1991. Running time: **94 MIN.**
Walerjan . . . . Artur Pontek
Michal . . . . Andrzej Mastalerz
Czeslaw . . . . . . Michal Straszczak
Lawyer . . . . Michael Gwisdek
Judge . . . . Peter Striebeck
Farmhand . . . . . . Ferdinand Dux
Farm wife . . . . Kyra Mladek

A competently done retelling of the true story of a naive 16-year-old Polish boy's nightmarish experience in Nazi Germany, "Walerjan Wrobel's Homesickness" has good European tv prospects, but theatrical outlook is fair to middling.

Walerjan Wrobel leads a contented life with his family in a small Polish village until the German occupation of 1941. Despite his tender age, he is sent to Germany to labor on a farm belonging to a war widow. Walerjan, who speaks not a word of German, tries his best to be dutiful and hardworking but pines for home and family. He sets a small fire in the barn, thinking he will be sent home for being a bad worker.

Artur Pontek delivers a strong, expressive performance in the role of the nearly mute, bewildered and uncomprehending boy who suddenly finds himself up against the German court system, accused of treason. As punishment for his deed, he is sent to a concentration camp. After surviving the camp, he learns his case is far from closed. Thinking he can finally return home, Walerjan is instead retried and sentenced to death by a judge invoking a litany of racist, Third Reich justice.

An interesting tale well told is hindered by weak casting in the supporting roles. Thesps cast as minor characters (mother, father, judge, prison guard) tend to be stiff and awkward, distracting from both the story and the period feel.

Overall, the pic is a respectable but unremarkable tale of the horrors of wartime Germany. Tech credits are fine. — *Reli.*

JERUSALEM FEST

G'MAR GIVIYA
(CUP FINAL)
(ISRAELI)

A Local Prods. film. Produced by Michael Sharfshtein. Directed by Eran Riklis. Screenplay, Eyal Halfon, from idea by Riklis; camera (color), Amnon Salomon; editor, Anat Lubarsky; music, Raviv Gazit. Reviewed at Jerusalem Film Festival, July 7, 1991. Running time: **110 MIN.**
With: Moshe Ivgi, Muhammed Bakri, Salim Dau, Bassam Zuamut, Yussef Abu Warda, Suheil Haddad, Sharon Alexander, Gassan Abbass.

"Cup Final's" antiwar plot might be overly familiar (soldiers on opposite sides come to recognize each other's humanity), but seeing it applied to the Israeli-Palestinian struggle is a novel idea. Pic's optimistic viewpoint of the Mideast conflict probably will be embraced more by audiences abroad than by Israeli viewers.

Fortunately, pic takes a largely comic view of a situation that could have turned overly preachy, a fatal weakness of many Israeli pics. Story focuses on a buffoonish middle-aged boutique owner called up for army reserve duty shortly after the start of the Lebanon War in 1982.

A rabid soccer fan, he doesn't get to use his tickets for the World Cup final in Spain, but his luck worsens when he's captured by Palestinian guerrillas. As the Palestinians and their hostage flee from the invading Israeli army toward the PLO's Beirut stronghold, the hostile relationship between prisoner and captors lightens up, particularly when both sides discover their mutual passion for soccer.

Pic's strong suit is the acting. As the hostage, Moshe Ivgi creates a funny but never exaggerated portrait of an Israeli nebbish who dredges up untapped reserves of courage and compassion. The Palestinians are played by a group of topnotch Israeli-Arab actors, the best known being the lean, charismatic Muhammed Bakri ("Hanna K").

Scripter Eyal Halfon's dialog is sharp and funny, and his portrayal of the diverse group of Palestinian guerrillas is thoughtful and balanced, if not always convincing.

Unfortunately, Riklis' direction, even in light of budget limitations, is rarely more than adequate. He depicts major characters being killed with barely a reaction from their comrades, and the climactic fire fight is handled almost perfunctorily.

Although most of "Cup Final" is as obvious as its overused war-sports metaphors, it's a likable, winning effort. Making films about the Israeli-Palestinian conflict is about as easy as solving it, and Riklis and company deserve credit for a decent attempt.
— *Cbd.*

SHUROO
(ISRAELI)

A Rosy Prods. film. Produced by Jonathan Aroch, Johanan Raviv. Directed by Savi Gavizon. Screenplay, Gavizon, Aroch, Raviv; camera (color), Yoav Kosh; editor, Tali Halter; music, Lior Tevet. Reviewed at Jerusalem Film Festival, July 11, 1991. Running time: **145 MIN.**
With: Moshe Ivgi, Sharon Brandon Hacohen, Sinai Peter, Karen Mor,

Shmuel Edelman, Ahuva Keren, Natan Zehavi, Ezra Kafri.

Israeli director Savi Gavizon has broken new ground with his witty, offbeat contemporary comedy which bypasses his country's overwhelming sociopolitical problems. Ironically, lack of a political dimension may make "Shuroo" a harder sell abroad than many far inferior Israeli pics.

Directorial debut by Gavison, recent grad of Tel Aviv U.'s film school, has already received several citations, including the Jerusalem Film Fest's Wolgin prize. Local critics hopefully refer to it as the starting point of a new wave in Israeli cinema.

Title is a nickname for the main character, a small-time Tel Aviv business hustler (amusingly played by Moshe Ivgi), whose latest scheme is promoting a "self-fulfillment" philosophy. After appearing on a talkshow, he gathers around him a tiny cult of emotionally and spiritually confused trendy Tel Avivians. After turning their lives upside-down, the conman's shady past catches up with him.

The film is atypical of Israeli cinema in acting, which is convincingly low-key rather than theatrically overblown; direction, visually sophisticated despite a low budget; script, with satire pointed but never obvious or mean; and characters, three-dimensional contempo Israelis who fall outside the usual categories of Holocaust survivors, Jewish-Arab lovers or morally tortured army officers.

Pic's weakness is a rambling story structure lacking in narrative tension. Gavizon has a laid-back storytelling style reminiscent of Scottish director Bill Forsyth. That, plus a welcome lack of big Mideast or Jewish issues may make the film a little too parochial for the world market.

Yet, if "Shuroo" is a small film with a small topic, it's also a big step forward for Israeli filmmaking. — Cbd.

DOC HOLLYWOOD

A Warner Bros. release. Produced by Susan Solt, Deborah D. Johnson. Executive producer, Marc Merson. Directed by Michael Caton-Jones. Screenplay, Jeffrey Price, Peter S. Seaman, Daniel Pyne, based on the book "What? ... Dead Again?" by Neil B. Shulman, adaptation by Laurian Leggett. Camera (Technicolor), Michael Chapman; editor, Priscilla Nedd-Friendly; music, Carter Burwell; sound (Dolby), Ken King; production disign, Lawrence Miller; art direction, Eva Anna Bohn, Dale Allen Pelton; set decoration, Cloudia Rebar; costume design, Richard Hornung; associate producer, Shulman; assistant director, J. Stephen Buck; casting, Marion Dougherty, Owens Hill. Reviewed at the Cineplex Odeon Showcase, L.A., July 27, 1991. MPAA Rating: PG-13. Running time: **103 MIN.**

Ben Stone	Michael J. Fox
Lou	Julie Warner
Dr. Hogue	Barnard Hughes
Hank	Woody Harrelson
Nick Nicholson	David Ogden Stiers
Lillian	Frances Sternhagen
Dr. Halberstrom	George Hamilton
Nancy Lee	Bridget Fonda
Melvin	Mel Winkler
Maddie	Helen Martin
Judge Evans	Roberts Blossom
Cotton	Tom Lacy
Aubrey Draper	Macon McCalman
Simon Tidwell	Raye Birk
Nurse Packer	Eyde Byrde

"Doc Hollywood" represents the latest attempt to rekindle the homespun humor and warmth of 1930s and '40s paeans to small-town American life. This heaping serving of recycled Capracorn has no real taste of its own, but, in its mildness and predictability, offers the reassurance of a fast-food or motel chain.

Amiable at times, this modest confection offers too little that's either fresh or funny to make a heavy score at the b.o.

Premise is so simple and old-fashioned that one can only wonder why the project spent years in development under many writers at Warner Bros. Arrogant young big-city doctor Ben Stone (Michael J. Fox) is, as he puts it, "waylaid in 'Hee-Haw' hell" on his way through the South to L.A. and prospective riches as a plastic surgeon.

Detained in Grady, S.C., the quaintest li'l ol' town you ever did see, the impatient Ben is forced to perform 32 hours of community service at the local clinic for destroying the judge's white picket fence with his Porsche.

Despite Fox' exasperation, it doesn't take long for those down-home virtues to take hold. Three delightful old biddies take Ben under their wings and make sure the little guy is well fed, while the mayor (David Ogden Stiers) and his good-ol'-boy city council try to make it worth his while to stay.

Treating the minor maladies of the charmingly eccentric locals, Ben can't help but become a bit hooked by town happenings and intrigue. But most of all he's taken with the unusually feisty and attractive ambulance driver Lou (Julie Warner), a young woman with a 4-year-old daughter. Lou is trying to keep fatuously cool customer Hank (Woody Harrelson) at arm's length.

Grady's need for a new medic becomes glaringly apparent when Ben is required to tend to grizzled Dr. Hogue (Barnard Hughes), who is so old that he presided over the births of virtually everyone in town.

When Ben delivers his first baby, he feels the pangs of attachment to the town. But even though he's danced real close with Lou at the Squash Festival social and kissed her under the stars, Ben finally heads off for Hollywood. One guess where he finally ends up.

Film's heart, synthetic as it may be, is in the right place, and the sweet mood created by the performers could convince one that everybody had a nice time during shooting. Script offers just enough in the way of roadblocks and romance to keep Ben put, and the portrait of small-town life is such a rosy fantasy that the viewer can only either sit back and enjoy the innocuous conventions for what they are or grouse at the utter unreality of it all.

But while the pic's message concerning homely virtues versus big-town ambition might be just as appealing as always, an old-hat story requires terrific imagination and new twists to justify retelling it, and those haven't been provided sufficiently here. Everything about this, from Michael Caton-Jones' confident staging to the sassy but sincere readings of the character actors, would have been entirely acceptable in a 1930s context. But nothing new has been added, except for a little nudity and profanity.

Fox' Ben remains brusque and self-centered for quite some time before entirely softening to the humanizing effects of the locals. Actor gives an energetic, agreeable performance. Newcomer Warner is also perfectly pleasant, if not too believable as a young lady from the deep South (her edginess is explained by her having studied in New York). Supporting cast is fine down the line, with George Hamilton putting in what amounts to a cameo as the head of a chic cosmetic surgery clinic.

As if almost embarrassed by the predictability of the ending, Caton-Jones wraps things up in a very hurried, perfunctory way, robbing the film of any emotional payoff and leaving the viewer rather let down. If one is to trade in artifice, it should be engaged thoroughly, not shied away from at the last minute.

Tech credits are good.
— *Todd McCarthy*

RETURN TO THE BLUE LAGOON

A Columbia release of a Price Entertainment/Randal Kleiser production. Produced and directed by William A. Graham. Executive producer, Randal Kleiser. Co-producer, Peter Bogart. Screenplay, Leslie Stevens, based on the novel "The Garden Of God" by Henry DeVere Stacpoole. Camera (Technicolor), Robert Steadman; editor, Ronald J. Fagan; music, Basil Poledouris; sound (Dolby), Paul Brincat; production design, Jon Dowding; art direction, Paul Ammitzboll; costume design, Aphrodite Kondos; assistant director, Bob Roe; underwater camera, Ron Taylor, Valerie Taylor; 2nd unit director, camera, Vincent Monton. Reviewed at Columbia Pictures, Culver City, July 29, 1991. MPAA Rating: PG-13. Running time: **100 MIN.**

Lilli	Milla Jovovich
Richard	Brian Krause
Sarah Hargrave	Lisa Pelikan
Young Lilli	Courtney Phillips
Young Richard	Garette Patrick Ratliff
Lilli (infant)	Emma James
Richard (infant)	Jackson Barton
Sylvia	Nana Coburn
Capt. Hilliard	Brian Blain
Quinlan	Peter Hehir

"Return To The Blue Lagoon" is a pointless spinoff of the 1980 hit, which was itself a remake of a 1949 British pic. It of course features beautiful young performers and scenic locations, but it will be a one-way ticket to dullsville for anyone much past puberty. This anemic entry will turn blue and expire quickly.

Rather than have Brooke Shields and Christopher Atkins turn up in cameos at the beginning to pass the teeny-bopper torch to the new generation, Leslie Stevens' script has the original's leading characters found dead in a tiny boat along with their young son, who has survived the journey in fine shape.

But the tyke is soon put out to

sea again to escape an outbreak of cholera on board the rescue ship and, along with straitlaced American Lisa Pelikan and her little daughter, washes up on the same tropical island his parents inhabited.

Major event of the next few years occurs when the devout Pelikan is forced to teach the kids about the birds and the bees. Her motherly duties now complete, she promptly kicks the bucket, leaving the budding beauties in paradisaic privacy to discover the rest for themselves.

And that they assuredly do. Once Lilli and Richard hit adolescence and assume the bodies of international model Milla Jovovich and tv hunk Brian Krause, they are disturbed to find that "nothing's the same."

The dawn of sexuality leads Lilli to declare that "everything's so confusing," and Richard's raging hormones send him off into the forbidden island mountains, where he encounters a band of cannibals.

But the couple soon realize that, if they're going to be stuck on the same little lump of sand together for the next 60 years, they may as well find a way to pass the time. For propriety's sake, they marry, then they splash about a lot as they begin what promises to be a very long honeymoon.

Only conflict crops up in the form of a visiting ship, which provides all sorts of trouble. Although the obliging captain offers to transport them to civilization in San Francisco, his scheming daughter arouses jealousy in Lilli by attempting to steal Richard away while a sailor ogles Lilli while she's bathing, robs her and tries to rape her.

There's scarcely a move in the film that isn't thoroughly predictable, and vet tv director William A. Graham is content to stick to pretty pictures rather than create a strong feeling for isolated life through the accretion of telling detail.

With original pic's director Randal Kleiser on board as exec producer, creative team decided to play it all safely, taking no chances and producing a film with no surprises at all.

Jovovich manages to project some good sense and resilience along with her cover girl beauty; the 15-year-old Soviet native makes a decent impression in her first bigscreen leading role. Krause looks like he's straight off the Southern California beaches but is sufficiently stalwart for the mostly physical demands placed on him here.

Lensed on Taveuni in the Fiji archipelago, film takes good advantage of inclement weather for the early island sequences. Robert Steadman's cinematography is unavoidably pretty, while Basil Poledouris' agreeable, ever-present score possesses echoes of Bernard Herrmann and John Barry, among others.

— *Todd McCarthy*

ANOTHER YOU

A Tri-Star release of a Ziggy Steinberg production. Written and produced by Steinberg. Executive producer, Ted Zachary. Directed by Maurice Phillips. Camera (Technicolor), Victor J. Kemper; editor, Dennis M. Hill; music, Charles Gross; sound (Dolby), Keith A. Wester; production design, Dennis Washington; art direction, John P. Bruce; set design, Richard McKenzie; set decoration, Robert R. Benton; costume design, Ruth Myers; stunt coordinator, Ernie Orsatti; associate producers, Robert Anderson, Louis D'Esposito, Allan Wertheim; assistant director, D'Esposito; casting, Mike Fenton, Allison Cowitt. Reviewed at United Artists Marketplace, Pasadena, Calif., July 27, 1991. MPAA Rating: R. Running time: **94 MIN.**
Eddie Dash . . . . . . Richard Pryor
George/Abe Fielding . . . Gene Wilder
Elaine/Mimi Kravitz . Mercedes Ruehl
Rupert Dibbs . . . . . . Stephen Lang
Gloria . . . . Vanessa Williams
Al . . . . Phil Rubenstein

Gene Wilder's frantic routines can't compensate for Richard Pryor's sadly depleted energy in "Another You," and producer Ziggy Steinberg's feeble script is given slapdash direction by the man who replaced Peter Bogdanovich on what is billed "a film by Maurice Phillips" (the best joke in the film). Pic should make a mercifully quick exit from theaters.

The setup isn't without promise, as the "mentally challenged" Wilder is released from a sanitarium into the dubious care of Hollywood street hustler Pryor, who's been ordered to do community service as a condition of his parole.

It does seem a bit odd, though, for Wilder to have been locked up for being a pathological liar —hardly a certifiable trait in contemporary American society.

Some amiable, if predictable, gags about Wilder's readjustment to the sleazy outside world give way all too quickly to tiresome plot mechanics as Stephen Lang and Mercedes Ruehl maneuver to use the gullible Wilder to impersonate a missing brewery heir.

Wilder's hysterical shtick is overly familiar, but he does offer a hilariously deranged outburst in a restaurant when Phil Rubenstein makes the mistake of insulting Pryor. After that, though, the character's smoothly mendacious streak takes over and he becomes boringly subdued.

Though Pryor shows flashes of his old comic brilliance and charm, it's painful to see how his health problems have affected him in this role.

He looks so gaunt that Wilder is forced to make the unfunny claim that he's ex-heavyweight champ Joe Frazier with a case of malaria.

Pryor's game struggle with the role makes his character's conman antics seem more desperate than funny.

The fact that Wilder is given much more screen time than top-billed Pryor underscores the difference between this film and their earlier, uproarious teamings.

The depressing mood of "Another You" is worsened by the murky color scheme of production designer Dennis Washington and lenser Victor J. Kemper, who somehow manage to make Wilder's BevHills manse look almost as unattractive as Hollywood Boulevard.

— *Joseph McBride*

DELIRIOUS

An MGM release of a Richard Donner production in association with Star Partners III Ltd. Produced by Lawrence J. Cohen, Fred Freeman, Doug Claybourne. Executive producer, Richard Donner. Directed by Tom Mankiewicz. Screenplay, Cohen, Freeman; camera (Deluxe color), Robert Stevens; editor, William Gordean, Tina Hirsch; music, Cliff Eidelman; sound (Dolby), David MacMillan, Les Lazarowitz (New York), Rick Alexander, Joel Fein, Jim Bolt; production design, Angelo Graham; art direction, James J. Murakami; set design, Richard Fernandez, Robert C. Goldstein, Peter J. Kelly, Lauren Polizzi, Diane I. Wager; costume design, Molly Maginnis; 2nd unit director-stunt coordinator, Terry J. Leonard; associate producers, Ann Ford Stevens, Jill Simpson; assistant director, John Kretchmer; 2nd unit assistant director, Scott Easton; 2nd unit camera, David Nowell; casting, David Rubin. Reviewed at Filmland screening room, L.A., July 16, 1991. MPAA Rating: PG. Running time: **96 MIN.**
Jack Gable . . . . John Candy
Louise/Janet
    Dubois . . . . . Mariel Hemingway
Laura/Rachel Hedison . Emma Samms
Carter Hedison . . . . . Raymond Burr
Blake Hedison . . . . . . Dylan Baker
Ty Hedison . . . . . . Charles Rocket
Dennis/Dr. Paul
    Kirkland . . . . . . David Rasche
Nurse Helen
    Caldwell . . . . . Andrea Thompson
Mickey . . . . Zach Grenier
Lou Sherwood . . . . . . Jerry Orbach
Arlene Sherwood . . . . Renee Taylor
Robert Wagner . . . . himself

"Delirious" is a witless comedy about soap operas in which the estimable John Candy mugs uncomfortably through a desperately unfunny script with a plot as tediously convoluted as those it spoofs. Given the tepid b.o. that greeted "Soapdish," which seems like "Citizen Kane" compared with this, prospects look grim.

Candy, as the head writer of a show called "Beyond Our Dreams," has an unrequited crush on the overripe star, Emma Samms, a clone of Joan Collins' Alexis character on "Dynasty." Mooning over Samms, who plays a treacherous and sluttish character both on and off the set, Candy naturally overlooks the true girl of his dreams, aspiring actress Mariel Hemingway.

A bump on the head sends Candy into a "Twilight Zone"-like reverie in which he finds himself trapped in the fictional small-town setting of his show and inhabiting the character of a Wall Street shark involved with both Samms and Hemingway.

Resemblances to the overly imitated "It's A Wonderful Life" abound in Ashford Falls, a combination of a studio backlot and Southern California locations that looks more like the setting for a primetime soap than a daytimer. Lighting, by Robert Stevens, is in the emptily glitzy style of a wine commercial.

Scripters Lawrence J. Cohen and Fred Freeman don't bother to establish some of the soap opera characters or story situations before they appear in Ashford Falls, making it even harder to relate to the clunky developments in the utterly unreal milieu.

Strained, overplayed pic leans heavily on Walter Mitty-isms in which the lovelorn Candy manipulates events with his typewriter, indulging in disjointed fantasies of heroism pilfered mostly from the Indiana Jones pics.

Reaching the screen after (though filmed before) his graceful seriocomic performance in "Only The Lonely," this film seems like a regression for Candy. There are glimmers of Candy's emerging offbeat romantic-leading-man style in his disenchanted dealings with Samms and his shyly earnest wooing of Hemingway, whose lovely girl-next-door quality is subverted by the regular pratfalls assigned her by the script.

Other perfs range from the amiably jokey (David Rasche, Charles Rocket, Dylan Baker, Robert Wagner) to the glumly wasted (Jerry Orbach, Raymond Burr) and the grossly offensive (Renee Taylor).

Tom Mankiewicz, who should know better, directed.

— *Joseph McBride*

HOT SHOTS

A 20th Century Fox release of a PAP production. Produced by Bill Badalato. Executive producer, Pat Proft. Directed by Jim Abrahams. Screenplay, Abrahams, Proft; camera (DeLuxe color), Bill Butler; editor, Jane Kurson, Eric Sears; music, Sylvester LeVay; sound design & supervision (Dolby), Sandy Berman, Randle Akerson; production design, William A. Elliott; art direction, Greg Papalia; set decoration, Jerie Kelter; costume design, Mary Malin; unit production manager, Stephen McEveety; associate producers, McEveety, Janet Graham, Greg Norberg; assistant directors, Tom Davies, Matthew Rowland; flying sequences director, Richard T. Stevens; casting, Mali Finn. Reviewed at the 20th Century Fox Little Theater, L.A., July 24, 1991. MPAA Rating: PG-13. Running time: **85 MIN.**
Topper Harley . . . . . . Charlie Sheen
Kent Gregory . . . . Cary Elwes
Ramada Thompson . . . Valeria Golino
Admiral Benson . . . . Lloyd Bridges
Lt. Commander Block . . . Kevin Dunn
Jim (Wash Out) Pfaffenbach . Jon Cryer
Pete (Dead Meat)
Thompson . . . . . . William O'Leary
Kowalski . . . . Kristy Swanson
Wilson . . . . Efrem Zimbalist Jr.

Jim Abrahams tries to tap the zany "Airplane!" vein with this "Top Gun" spoof but bats far too low a percentage with the usual rapid-fire assault of numbingly stupid gags. This bird never quite gets off the ground, although the few decent belly laughs and clever marketing could help the self-proclaimed "mother of all movies" nurture lukewarm b.o. returns.

Pic bogs down in motion picture in-jokes, drawing liberally on "Top Gun" and "An Officer And A Gentleman" while intercutting homages to scenes from "The Fabulous Baker Boys," "Nine 1/2 Weeks" and "Gone With The Wind."

The story is taken almost entirely from "Top Gun," and, in that sense, may be arriving a little late for many to appreciate all of the jokes. Charlie Sheen is the maverick pilot competing with self-obsessed Kent (Cary

Elwes). Even Sylvester LeVay's score sounds like a cross between the synthesized strains in "Gun" and the "Chariots Of Fire" theme.

One film spoof does provide the biggest belly laugh, quite literally, when Sheen begins erotically feeding Valeria Golino grapes and, in escalating passion, cooks breakfast on her sizzling stomach.

Abrahams and co-writer-exec producer Pat Proft relentlessly fire off the same sort of parodies, but in several instances (most notably a crashingly dull fantasy sequence in which Sheen and Golino reenact famous film love scenes) they push their idea far past its comic limits.

Some of the gags prove irresistibly stupid, but there are just too many duds in the bunch. And most characters are gratingly cartoonish, especially Lloyd Bridges' way over-the-top tin-headed admiral.

It was all fresh and spontaneous in the Zucker-Abrahms-Zucker pic "Airplane!" but twists like deadpanning stars and cooking instructions during the credits have lost their ability to surprise. Despite the recent megabuck opening for "The Naked Gun 2 1/2," the genre is starting to look creatively moribund.

Sheen has fun with his steely eyed pilot, almost a parody of his tough-guy roles in "Navy Seals" and "The Rookie." Golino is a good sport, if nothing else, but none of the other actors in the large ensemble cast really has enough to work with.

The filmmakers augment the comedic material with ace flying effects, and Mary Malin deserves kudos for the costumes. Too bad the pilots didn't have a flight plan to match that artillery.

— *Brian Lowry*

LA NOTE BLEUE
(BLUE NOTE)
(FRENCH-POLISH)

A UGC release (France) of a Oliane Prods.-Erato Films-G Films production. (Intl. sales: UGC.) Produced by Marie-Laure Reyre. Written and directed by Andrzej Zulawski. Camera (color), Andrzej Jaroszewicz; editor, Marie-Sophie Dubus; production design, Jean-Vincent Puzos. Reviewed at Cannes Film Festival (market), May 15, 1991. Running time: **102 MIN.**
George Sand . . . Marie-France Pisier
Frederic Chopin . . . Janusz Olejniczak
Solange . . . . Sophie Marceau
Eugene Delacroix . . . Feodor Atkine
Maurice . . . . Benoit Lepeca
Augustine . . . . . . Beatrice Buchholz
Fernand De Preaulx . . . Gilles Detroit

A passionate love triangle that includes Chopin, his lover and her daughter ought to be a hot number, but "Blue Note" strikes a flat chord.

Very French pic's occasional afternoon love scenes are dominated by political rhetoric, but for the rest of the world, pic's unfocused hedonist/feminist/artistic celebration will confuse.

Set at a country chateau in France during an eccentric picnic on the last day of Chopin's eight-year romance with the Baroness Dudevant (a.k.a. George Sand), pic is a squalor of decadence that hops semi-erotically from scenes of incest and indulgence to moving depictions of Chopin's fatal physical decay and inability to deal with the two women he loved.

Compared to the current Chopin and Sand love story, "Impromptu," or another composer-as-entertainer tale, "Amadeus," "Blue Note" is too European for Yanks and too meandering for Europeans; it never gets to the point.

Janusz Olejniczak portrays a dying man hopelessly incapable of deciding whom he truly loved (the mother? her daughter?). Chopin's general love of women is loosely depicted as a source of both confusion and inspiration for his music, but lack of tight script or editing allows pic to wallow in that confusion rather than enlighten the viewer as to what a man could feel in such an unusual predicament.

"Blue Note" is loosely about the famous Pole who was so verbally inadequate that he couldn't explain to either woman that his music took precedence over love. But it's also loosely about Sand's revolutionary/feminist sexual wanderlust, reminiscent of Sabina in Milan Kundera's "The Unbearable Lightness Of Being."

Sophie Marceau, who impudently plays the daughter, Solange, steals the show. Helmer Zulawski (a man reputed to break all rules to get a zealous performance) has evoked a heated performance from Marceau as a young woman hopelessly, genuinely, blatantly in love. She has captured the essence of adolescent abandon in her no-holding-back performance, but unfortunately she is subdued by a quagmire of confused and decadent characters.

There are so many characters and so much decadence that the viewer loses track of the all-important love triangle, which is never satisfactorily resolved. At

pic's Cannes preem, tradesters started wandering out 10 minutes before the anticlimax.

Actor-pianist Olejniczak's musical interpretation of Chopin is brilliant and provides a solid classical soundtrack for willing viewers. For Zulawski fans awaiting the next "Possession" (1980) or even "La Femme Publique" (1984), there's no revelation here.

— *Suzan Ayscough*

CSAPD LE CSACSI!
(SLAP-JACK)
(HUNGARIAN)

A Novofilm production. Produced by Pál Sándor. Written and directed by Péter Timár. Camera (Eastmancolor), Péter Szatmári; editor, Timár; sound, Tamás Márkus; production design, László Gárdonyi. Reviewed at Hungarofilm screening room, Budapest, May 30, 1991. Running time: **78 MIN.**
With: Vera Pap, Sándor Gáspár, Károly Eperjes, Enikö Eszenyi, Róbert Koltai, Mari Töröcsik, László Szacsvay.

A "War Of The Roses"-like farce with a political subtext, "Slap-Jack" is the sharpest of the current crop of Hungarian pics dealing with the country's recent changes. Inventive script and lively playing should make this a fest crowd-pleaser, with limited tube sales a possibility.

A young couple (Sándor Gáspár, Vera Pap) got along fine building their dream home in a comfy neighborhood, but problems start when wife gets a summons to get an anti-VD shot. She decides not to speak to hubby until he comes clean on who his mistress is.

She scissors his clothes; he burns her pantyhose. He brings home a prostie (Enikö Eszenyi); she nuzzles up to a cop friend. Meanwhile, as both sides go for broke, a nosy neighbor (Károly Eperjes) is secretly training Stalinist paramilitaries in an underground bomb shelter nearby.

Pic's theme, which reflects local popular opinion, is that the euphoria prior to the 1990 democratic elections has since gone sour as reality bites. Pre-election solidarity has turned into post-election bickering.

Pic ends with an earthquake wrecking the neighborhood, the VD misunderstanding cleared up and everyone happy again rebuilding their separate dreams.

Eperjes' commie Rambo, plus a neat cameo by vet Mari Töröcsik as Pap's mother who's seen it all before, are standouts in the strong ensemble playing. Helmer Péter Timár keeps the fizz coming, and technically the whole shebang is tops.

Hungarian title is the name of a crude card-game played by drunken males. — *Derek Elley*

TRIPLEX
(FRENCH)

A Gaumont release of a Gaumont-Gaumont Prods.-TF1 Films production. (Intl. sales: Gaumont.) Produced by Alain Poiré. Directed by Georges Lautner. Screenplay, Didier van Cauwelaert; camera (color), Yves Rodallec; editor, Georges Koltz; music, Raymond Alessandrini, production design, Jacques Dugied; costume design, Maika Guezel. Reviewed at Gaumont Convention, Paris, May 2, 1991. Running time: **90 MIN.**
Nicolas . . . . Patrick Chesnais
Nathalie . . . . Cécile Pallas
Frank . . . . . François-Eric Gendron
Also with: Jacques François, Sophie Carle, Jacques Jouanneau, Laurent Gamelon, Gilles Veber.

"**T**riplex" is a lightweight, laugh-worthy pic about an idealistic lawyer, her money-loving lawyer boyfriend and a wacky client. Story begins as a romantic comedy but quickly turns into a star vehicle for talented Patrick Chesnais. Though uneven, pic should be an easy sell as fluffy foreign vid programming, and it may appeal to arthouse crowds.

Plot depends on a delightfully inventive but mishandled love triangle. A lovely, low-paid lawyer (Cecile Pallas) happily defends the poor against her rich attorney beau (François-Eric Gendron). Trouble is, she's let her imprisoned client, a whiz programmer chiseled out of job, wife and favorite horse, into her private life. She dissuades the freed man from suicide and, after telling off her boyfriend, asks him to bed.

Chesnais, tall, intense and balding, is wonderfully morose as a man who's lost everything. Even when he obsesses on his dishy advocate and threatens suicide, he's touchingly funny. And when he arches one eyebrow, he turns into a wry observer of the dog-eat-dog business world.

Scripter Didier van Cauwelaert and director Georges Lautner walk Chesnais through well-worn comic paces, with mixed results. In a dusty yet still potent cinematic joke, depressed guy waits for death on a railroad track, only to hear train pass him by inches away. In the most up-to-date scene, he's a vengeful ex-

employee who installs a killer virus in the company computer.

Filmmakers waste pic's climax on a drawn-out sequence in which Chesnais tries to get arrested by insulting cops, mutilating the boyfriend's car and speeding like a wild man. Just as bad, the three-way comedy gets tangled up with material on male impotence. And the horse carefully introduced in pic's opening is all but forgotten by the last scene.

Lautner, who's made commercially successful pics, has a smooth touch, but he asks Pallas to shift too quickly from savvy professional to woman in crisis. Gendron's role as legal eagle is barely believable. He takes it on the chin too many times from his insulting rival.

Production details are sometimes sloppy. In a room knee-deep in water, Chesnais opens the hallway door but the water remains level. Other tech credits, however, are excellent, especially the opening shots of the hilly countryside.

— *Lee Lourdeaux*

VOJTECH RECENY SIROTEK
(VOJTECH, CALLED THE ORPHAN)
(CZECHOSLOVAKIAN)

A Barrandov Film Studios-FAMU production. Produced by Profile group. Director of production, Karel Czaban. Directed by Zdenek Tyc. Screenplay, Jiri Soukup, Jaromir Kacer, Tyc; camera (b&w), Kacer; music, Miloslav Kabelac, Martin Smolka; sound, Jiri Moudry; art direction, Oldric Bosak. Reviewed at Pesaro Intl. Festival of New Cinema, June 11, 1991. Running time: **83 MIN.**
Vojtech . . . . Peter Forman
Also with: Barbora Lukesova, Jana Dolanska, Vlastimil Zavrel, Bretislav Rychlik, Jiri Halek, Jaroslav Mares, Miroslav Zelenka.

Young Czech director Zdenek Tyc graduated from the FAMU film school in Prague with this promising but uneven allegorical fable. "Vojtech, Called The Orphan" has some affable moments, but it's technically raw and loaded with muddy symbolism. Pic will be indigestible to all but some film fest audiences.

Story takes place during the postwar euphoria of 1946. Released after an unjust prison term, Vojtech arrives in a South Bohemian village to make a fresh start. He quickly finds a job, shacks up with a local widow and throws himself into his work.

The villagers are immediately suspicious of the headstrong outsider, and he soon makes enemies. Antagonism escalates further still when they learn of his imprisonment, but he remains unperturbed. He pays no attention to friendly warnings, having fallen in love with a beautiful, genteel girl recovering from tuberculosis. Clashes with the villagers come to a head, and they drown him in the river.

Pic opens and closes well with some splendid shooting of Vojtech reborn in and ultimately reclaimed by the shimmering waters. Jaromir Kacer's black & white lensing makes the establishing shots of the Czech landscape look like Ansel Adams' California. But this strong visual scene-setting is something of a false start; pic too often gives way to clumsy framing and drab composition in underlit exteriors.

Attempts to invest the character of Vojtech with folk-heroic dimensions are underdeveloped, and with a team of three sharing the writer's credit, narrative problems may have been a case of too many cooks. Pic is episodic to the point of losing all fluidity. Characters and incidents often are confused or lost in storytelling rife with leaps and jumps that some cutting might have helped to smooth over.

— *David Rooney*

RIKTIGA MAN BAR ALLTID SLIPS
(REAL MEN ALWAYS WEAR TIES)
(SWEDISH)

A Sonet Films release of a Sonet-Swedish Film Institute/TV-4 production. Produced by Hans Iveberg. Executive producer, Peter Hald. Written and directed by Jonas Cornell. Screenplay, Cornell; camera (color), Erling Thurmann-Andersen; editor, Susanne Linnman; music, Jan Tolf; sound, Klas Engström; production design, Bengt Fröderberg; costume design, Gunnel Nilsson; assistant director, Peder Bjurman. Reviewed at Sonet screening room, Stockholm, July 1, 1991. Running time: **84 MIN.**
With: Philip Zandén, Marie Richardson, Rikard Wolff, Micke Dubois, Frej Lindqvist, Agneta Ekmanner.

Despite good acting and good ideas, this modern-day screwball comedy never gets going. Explicit nudity might be another obstacle to overseas success of "Real Men Always Wear Ties."

The film is based on an original script by director Jonas Cornell,

a veteran with a track record dating back to the '60s. Here he tells the story of the owner of a small nightclub in Stockholm. The main attraction is his beautiful girlfriend who works as a striptease dancer.

The club owner is high on anxieties, which, among other things, takes a toll on his sex life. Despite his g.f.'s understanding and attempts to help, he remains impotent. He convinces her she should take a lover, and reluctantly she chooses a hobo who moves in with them. But the impotent proprietor gets jealous and starts plotting murder.

Meanwhile, the owner is constantly hunted by a man who works for a loanshark who wants payment, and is trying to persuade a doctor to give him an operation he believes will cure his anxieties.

There's a lot crammed into the short running time, and the film bears signs of having been shortened prior to release (some of the jumps in the action are confusing). After a fairly amusing start, the film starts to seem longer than it is, and the humor wanes.

The leads are good, especially Philip Zandén (previously seen in "The Guardian Angel") and Marie Richardson, a very good actress and classic Swedish beauty who could have an international career waiting.

The title refers to a saying that men in power always wear ties, but the pic puts no emphasis on this. — *Gunnar Rehlin*

THE BIG SLICE
(CANADIAN)

A C/FP Distribution release (Canada) of an SC Entertainment Intl. production. Produced by Nicolas Stiliadis. Executive producer, Syd Cappe. Written and directed by John Bradshaw. Camera (color), Ludek Bogner; editor, Nick Rotundo; music, Mychael, Jeff Danna; sound, Kevin Ward, Trevor Ambrose; production design, Ian Brock. Reviewed at Uptown Backstage 2, Toronto, June 7, 1991. Running time: **85 MIN.**
Mike Sawyer . . . . . Casey Siemaszko
Jenny Colter . . . . Leslie Hope
Andy McCafferty . . . . . Justin Louis
Lieutenant Bernard . . Kenneth Welsh
Nick . . . . Nicholas Campbell
Rita . . . . Heather Locklear
Max Bernstein . . . . . Henry Ramer

Canadian comedy feature "The Big Slice" promises a lot but undercooks all ingredients, ensuring a quick trip to home-video. John Bradshaw's script is fresh with possibilities but gets mashed by his inept direction and sloppy editing and technical work.

Two young men want to get rich quick by writing a hot-selling novel but lack experience. So, one of them (Casey Siemaszko) ingratiates himself into a mobster's world and the other one (Justin Louis) becomes a volunteer cop, all to get firsthand research.

Their two roles collide when the cops chase the mobster (Nicholas Campbell) who flees after a failed drug deal. With two-timing girlfriends involved, the pals get trapped into a series of what should be amusing misadventures, including a brief stay in jail. They succeed in the end.

Key players, including Kenneth Welsh as a boozy cop and Henry Ramer briefly in as a publisher, are all handsome and deserve a better pic.

— *Sid Adilman*

THE COMMITMENTS

A 20th Century Fox release of a Beacon Communications presentation of a First Film Co.-Dirty Hands production. Produced by Roger Randall-Cutler, Lynda Myles. Executive producers, Armyan Bernstein, Tom Rosenberg, Souter Harris. Directed by Alan Parker. Screenplay, Dick Clement, Ian La Frenais, Roddy Doyle, based on Doyle's novel; camera, Gale Tattersall; editor, Gerry Hambling; music supervision, G. Mark Roswell; musical arrangements, Paul Bushnell; musical coordination, John Hughes; sound (Dolby), Clive Winter; production design, Brian Morris; costume design, Penny Rose; art direction, Mark Geraghty; Arden Gantly; set decoration, Karen Brookes; assistant director, Bill Westley; co-producers, Clement, La Frenais, Marc Abraham; casting, John & Ros Hubbard. Reviewed at 20th Century Fox, L.A., July 17, 1991. MPAA rating: R. Running time: **116 MIN.**

Jimmy Rabbitte . . . . . Robert Arkins
Steven Clifford . . . . Michael Aherne
Imelda Quirke . . . . . . Angeline Ball
Natalie Murphy . . . . . . Maria Doyle
Mickah Wallace . . . . Dave Finnegan
Bernie . . . . Bronagh Gallagher
Dean Fay . . . . Felim Gormley
Outspan Foster . . . . . Glen Hansard
Joey (The Lips)
    Fagan . . . . Johnny Murphy
Derek Scully . . . Kenneth McCluskey
Deco Cuffe . . . . Andrew Strong
Mr. Rabbitte . . . . . . Colm Meaney

At last a tough, authentic, behind-the-scenes film about how some of the truest music is born, lives and dies. Director Alan Parker's story of a band of hardscrabble young Dubliners playing American '60s soul isn't likely to overwhelm at the boxoffice, any more than a band like this one devoted to covering classics would get much mileage in the music industry.

Still, the pic is so fresh, well-executed and original that, properly handled, it should enjoy a long if modest run and inspire much hardcore devotion among music fans.

Set in the working-class north side of contemporary Dublin, where the music scene is rich and teeming, film, based on the novel by Roddy Doyle, tells the story of 21-year-old entrepreneur Jimmy Rabbitte (Robert Arkins), who envisions bringing soul music to Dublin. Recruited as manager of a dismal wedding band, he instead pieces together a 10-piece outfit with real musical potential from among his raw or semitalented contemporaries.

Dubbed the Commitments and billed as the Saviors of Soul, the band is instructed in the elements of the Dream by the resourceful Jimmy, a sharp thinker who often speaks in epigrams.

They're doubtful they can emulate James Brown videos, but Jimmy persuades them: "The Irish are the blacks of Europe; Dubliners are the blacks of Ireland, and on our side, we're the blacks of Dublin. So say it: I'm black and I'm proud!"

Diverse group includes a messianic 45-year-old trumpeter, Joey (Johnny Murphy) who claims to have toured with the American greats, a stout and vulgar lead singer (played by 16-year-old Andrew Strong) with a voice like a diesel engine, and three scrappy and fetching femme backup singers who blossom into singing leads. Constant friction among players means Jimmy spends much of his energy trying to hold the band together long enough to land at least one paying gig and pay off the rogue from whom he's more or less stolen the equipment.

Meanwhile, as band gains skill, exposure and a following, it pins their hopes on Joey's promise that Wilson Pickett, who's in town giving a concert, will join it onstage after his show.

Challenge most music films face is to avoid the rutted pathway of the by-the-numbers rise and fall story. Blessed with Doyle's richly authentic and unpredictable source material, pic succeeds where others have stumbled. Poetic outcome should be sweetly satisfying to those who've struggled with musical dreams.

Economic and creative climate from which much of the best music springs is admirably captured. Parker and the casting directors initially auditioned more than 3,000 Dublin hopefuls. They wound up casting mostly musicians with no acting experience. Ensemble cast, which underwent five weeks of rehearsal, handles itself extremely well, particularly Arkins as Rabbitte and Murphy as the trumpeter.

Script by veteran British writing team Dick Clement and Ian La Frenais is often very funny and chockablock with so many local vulgarisms that a glossary is being distribbed with promo materials. Mostly propelled by the spirit of Rabbitte's quest and the terrific live music segs, story sags somewhat once the band has been established, not really recovering until the impending Pickett visit is announced.

Nonetheless, the absence of the typical Hollywood story pattern is so welcome and the story's outcome so gracefully unfolded that the quibble is slight.

Lensed in 44 Dublin locations,

pic presents a gritty, inner-city tableau in which unemployed youths, many of them "on the dole," dwell in crowded homes with their large Catholic families. Amusingly, Jimmy's father (Colm Meaney), an around-the-bend Elvis fan, displays the Memphis icon's likeness on the wall above the Pope's. Camerawork is much like the music — raw, personal and stylish. Pictorially, the film is full of variety and unexpected pleasures, and the complex editing work by Gerry Hambling is marvelously accomplished.

Parker, a deft explorer of subcultures, exhibits an approach that's as fresh, upfront and energetic as the material requires. Film reps an outstanding debut for Beacon Communications.

Soundtrack, performed by the Commitments and loaded with tunes popularized by Pickett, Otis Redding, Aretha Franklin, Percy Sledge and their ilk, is bound to be a strong seller. — *Amy Dawes*

ROVER DANGERFIELD
(ANIMATED)

A Warner Bros. release of a Rodney Dangerfield production in association with Hyperion Pictures. Produced by Willard Carroll and Thomas L. Wilhite. Executive producer, Dangerfield. Directed by Jim George, Bob Seeley. Screenplay, Dangerfield; editor, Tony Mizgalski; music, David Newman; songs, Dangerfield, Billy Tragesser; production design, Fred Cline; sequence directors, Steve Moore, Matthew O'Callaghan, Bruce Smith, Dick Sebast, Frans Vischer, Skip Jones; associate producers, Sue Shakespeare, Maria C. Schaeffer; assistant director, Jonathan Levit; casting, Kevin Alber, Jon Robert Samsel. Reviewed at the Arden Fair, Sacramento, Calif., Aug. 6, 1991. MPAA Rating: G. Running time: **74 MIN.**

Rover . . . . Rodney Dangerfield
Daisy . . . . Susan Boyd
Eddie . . . . Ronnie Schell
Raffles . . . . Ned Luke
Connie . . . . Shawn Southwick
Danny . . . . Dana Hill
Rocky . . . . Sal Landi
With: Tom Williams, Chris Collins, Robert Bergen, Paxton Whitehead, Ron Taylor, Bert Kramer, Eddie Barth, Ralph Monaco, Tress MacNeille, Michael Sheehan, Lara Cody.

His fans may be attracted to Rodney Dangerfield as a dog in "Rover Dangerfield" . . . maybe that should be in a dog like "Rover Dangerfield" . . . well, either one will do.

Warner Bros. doesn't seem to be too fond of the picture, either, judging from its limited release. And the studio hasn't been reporting boxoffice figures.

Pic is definitely a Dangerfield

doing: He's exec producer, writer, story developer (with Harold Ramis) and songwriter (with Billy Tragesser). He gets credit for the story idea, and he provides the voice for Rover.

Fable starts with Rover as a wisecracking Las Vegas dog who lives the wild life as the pet of a chorus girl (Shawn Southwick). He gambles, he sings, he dances and gets into mischief with his pal (Ronnie Schell). While the chorine is on the road, however, her sleazy boyfriend (Sal Landi) dumps Rover over Hoover Dam.

Rescued by fishermen, Rover ends up on a farm, where he's expected to work for his keep. Work is a tough adjustment for Rover, but he is inspired by the love of Daisy (Susan Boyd), the collie next door.

(It's a sign of what you can get away with in a G-rated cartoon these days that the canine couple soon are sharing the same doggie bed without benefit of clergy.)

After various triumphs and misadventures, and lots of short songs of no particular merit, Rover returns to Vegas and his chorus girl just long enough to tell a few farm jokes and even the score with the boyfriend. Rover heads back to the farm to visit Daisy and gets a surprise. At least it may surprise people who never have been to a film before.

There's nothing terribly bad about any of this, but there's nothing terribly good about it either. The Las Vegas adventures seem a bit too fast and sophisticated for kids, but the farm follies may not be sophisticated enough.

The animation is not state of the art, but it's far above tv standards, reflecting the generally good work of animators and technicians in the U.S. and London. Cheap it wasn't, so Warner Bros. will have to hope "Rover" finds some revenue in homevid.

Oddly enough, there's not a cat among the major characters, so it's hard to account for the fact that the firstrun print had at least one, and sometimes two, big scratches running down the middle through the whole picture. — *Jim Harwood*

DEFENSELESS

A Seven Arts release through New Line Cinema of a New Visions Pictures presentation of a Bombyk/Missel production. Produced by Renee Missel, David Bombyk. Executive producers, Taylor Hackford, Stuart Benjamin. Directed by Martin Campbell. Screenplay, James Hicks, from a story by Hicks, Jeff Burkhart; camera (Deluxe color), Phil Meheux; supervising editor, Lou Lombardo; editor, Chris Wimble; music, Curt Sobel; sound (Dolby), Ed White; production design, Curtis A. Schnell; art direction, Colin D. Irwin; set decoration, Douglas A. Mowat; costume design, Mary Rose; associate producer, Whitney Green; assistant directors, Matia Karrell, Rip Murray; casting, Deborah Lucchesi, Elisabeth Leustig. Reviewed at the Carolco screening room, L.A., July 31, 1991. MPAA Rating: R. Running time: **104 MIN.**

T.K. Katwuller	Barbara Hershey
George Beutel	Sam Shepard
Ellie Seldes	Mary Beth Hurt
Steven Seldes	J.T. Walsh
Janna Seldes	Kellie Overbey
Bull Dozer	Jay O. Sanders
Jack Hammer	John Kapelos
Mrs. Bodeck	Sheree North
Monroe	Randy Brooks

A murder mystery with a fine cast and wild and woolly story, "Defenseless" almost continuously wobbles across the line between the deliberately ambiguous and the irritatingly murky. Modestly budgeted drama suffers from some highly implausible plotting strategies but gains strength as it moves along and leaves the viewer with a number of matters to chew on.

Shot more than two years ago and now being slipped out under the Seven Arts banner via New Line, pic doesn't figure to make much of a splash theatrically.

Barbara Hershey portrays T.K. Katwuller, a Los Angeles attorney who, for psychological reasons that remain unexplored, has managed to make a rather spectacular mess of her life.

Attractive and bright, she talks to herself and comes unglued all too easily for a big-city professional. A borderline hysteric, she seems to have no friends and has chosen for her lover a sleazy businessman involved in the porno underground.

She lives in a sparkling apartment building, but perhaps most emblematic of her confusion is her vehicle, a Karmann Ghia that looks like it survived World War II and has no top but does sport a car phone.

T.K. is drawn into a web of lies when she discovers that her lover and client, Steven Seldes (the reliably snaky J.T. Walsh), is married to her long-lost college roommate Ellie (Mary Beth Hurt).

T.K. denies her affair, stupidly goes for dinner at the Seldes' suburban home, where she meets the couple's sullen daughter, Janna (Kellie Overbey), and, again stupidly, goes to Steven's shadowy office on a dark and spooky night.

The couple have a bloody fight, from which T.K. escapes. But Steven is later found murdered, and the script asks the audience to swallow the idea that T.K., although she is a material witness to the crime, would become defense attorney for Steven's wife, who has been accused in the case.

Also hard to take is the notion that an ambitious young D.A. would choose this trial on which to rest his election hopes, as well as T.K.'s cover-up of her involvement with the Seldes family. But with all the absurdities, there are provocative delineations of character and behavior along the way, as well as a growing interest as the true depth of the lies, denial, betrayal and sordidness becomes apparent.

T.K. is an unusually troubled and conflicted heroine, and much of the intrigue stems from seeing if and when she will be called on her unpredictable, irrational decisions.

James Hicks' screenplay, from a story he wrote with Jeff Burkhart, at least gives the actors some strong, if sometimes goofy, emotions to play with, and they generally make the most of them.

Hershey throws herself into all aspects of her part, the strong-willed as well as the embarrassing, and tries to bulldoze past the unbelievable and unexplained sides. It's a full-blown performance, and ultimately effective.

Hurt is dead-on as an overly proper professional housewife whose stifled emotions and acute sociability mask her own brand of hysteria.

As a detective on the case, Sam Shepard quietly but intently gets across multiple motives — a dogged insistence on getting at the truth, a certain protectiveness toward T.K. and a fundamental mistrust of women, that, in this particular instance, serves his purposes. Supporting perfs are vivid throughout.

New Zealand-born, British-trained director Martin Campbell ("Criminal Law") pushes things a bit too hard at times but must be given credit for the consistent acting and teams with lenser Phil Meheux for an often fresh look. Curt Sobel's score underlines the obvious on all too many occasions.

Pic is dedicated to the late David Bombyk, who produced with Renee Missel.

— *Todd McCarthy*

BODY PARTS

A Paramount Pictures release of a Frank Mancuso Jr. production. Produced by Mancuso. Executive producer, Michael MacDonald. Directed by Eric Red. Screenplay, Red, Norman Snider; screen story, Patricia Herskovic, Joyce Taylor, based on novel "Choice Cuts" by Boileau-Narcejac; camera (Technicolor), Theo Van de Sande; editor, Anthony Redman; music, Loek Dikker; sound (Dolby), James M. Troutman; production design, Bill Brodie; art direction, Alicia Keywan; set decoration, Steven Shewchuk; costume design, Lynda Kemp; special makeup effects, Gordon J. Smith; assistant directors, Michael Zenon, Rocco Gismondi; co-producers, Jack E. Freedman, Herskovic; casting, Fern Champion, Casting Associates. Reviewed at Paramount Studio Theater, Hollywood, Aug. 2, 1991. MPAA Rating: R. Running time: **88 MIN.**

Bill Crushank	Jeff Fahey
Dr. Alice Webb	Lindsay Duncan
Karen Crushank	Kim Delaney
Remo Lacey	Brad Dourif
Detective Sawchuk	Zakes Mokae
Mark Draper	Peter Murnik
Ray Kolberg	Paul Benvictor
Charlie Fletcher	John Walsh
Bill Jr	Nathaniel Moreau
Samantha	Sarah Campbell

More than a little assembly would be required to fix "Body Parts," which is too absurd for widespread b.o. appeal and slow in getting to its gratuitous gore to please genre fans. What could have been a reasonably interesting thriller literally goes to pieces in its last third, until the brain seems the most salient part missing.

Film's most memorable facet likely will be the fuss over its release in Milwaukee because of revelations about serial killer Jeffrey Dahmer and Paramount's decision to pull advertising there.

Despite title, however, this isn't a conventional slasher opus, starting out as a potentially intriguing psychological tale about a man at war with his own arm — à la "The Beast With Five Fingers" — before crumbling as it races with inexplicable speed toward a bloody, inane conclusion.

The other key footnote is the source material, since the pic was inspired by a novel by French authors Thomas Narcejac and Pierre Boileau, who wrote the novel ("D'Entre Les Morts") that provided the basis for "Vertigo." Hitchcock and others, in fact, reportedly grappled with adapting this book, which makes its shoddy treatment here all the more puzzling.

Jeff Fahey plays a criminal psychologist who loses his arm in a car accident, only to have it replaced by a doctor (Lindsay Duncan) perfecting a new limb-grafting procedure.

The psychologist is told that the new limb belonged to a serial killer, prompting him to wonder if the murderer's arm might be invading his own soul.

The story moves gradually at first along those lines, as family man Fahey begins having nightmares and snapping at his kids. He even seeks out other donor recipients (Brad Dourif and Peter Murnik), who are initially unconcerned or unaware of any ill effects.

For a long while, director/co-writer Eric Red seems to buck the exploitative title and his own roots — having scripted such tense, bloody pics as "The Hitcher" and "Near Dark" — leaving mystery as to whether the evil stems from the killer's arm or the delirium of Fahey's mind.

An element of legitimate suspense resides in that uncertainty — the rift between madness or some physiological evil — with even Loek Dikker's brooding score apparently calculated to evoke memories of Bernard Herrmann's contributions to various Hitchcock classics.

Then, suddenly, the narrative hurriedly kicks into a slasher mode, replete with car chases, dismemberment and unintentional, if rather vulgar, hilarity.

Red has shown facility for scripting cinematic sadism, but the sudden change to that tone here lacks much-needed connective material that might have prevented it from feeling so tacked on and tacky. As is, the last 30 minutes come from nowhere and reflect indecision as to who the film was designed to reach.

Fahey is fine as the intense protagonist, while some of the other roles are small but showy — including Paul Benvictor as a tightly wound skid-row killer and Dourif's latest version of a thinking man's lunatic, providing the only laughs.

Tech credits are generally sound. Makeup effects occasionally look like a mannequin limb with an air bladder stuffed into it. Nothing else, except for the jarringly awkward storytelling, proves particularly disarming.

— *Brian Lowry*

FAST GETAWAY

A New Line Cinema release of a Cinetel Films production. Produced by Paul Hertzberg, Lisa M. Hansen. Executive producer, Harold Welb. Directed by Spiro Razatos. Screenplay, James Dixon; camera (Foto-Kem color), Jacques Haitkin; editor, David Kern; music, Bruce Rowland; additional music, Adam Rowland; sound (Dolby), Jon (Earl) Stein; production design, Chip Radaelli; assistant director, Benita Allen; production manager, Joan Weidman; stunt coordinator, Richard Butler; 2nd unit camera, Henning Schellerup; co-producer, Jefferson Richard; associate producers, Corey Haim, Catalaine Knell. Reviewed on RCA/Columbia Pictures vidcassette, N.Y., July 26, 1991. MPAA Rating: PG-13. Running time: **85 MIN.**
Nelson . . . . Corey Haim
Lily . . . . Cynthia Rothrock
Sam . . . . Leo Rossi
Tony . . . . Ken Lerner
Lorraine . . . . Marcia Strassman
Honey . . . . Shelli Lether

A pleasant, unpretentious action picture, "Fast Getaway" will appeal to video fans tired of overblown, hyped-up cinema. Typical of medium-range indie product today, pic had only brief regional test runs this spring before its ancillary release.

Drive-ins are the natural home for this amoral romp depicting the misadventures of an itinerant gang of bank robbers that includes Leo Rossi and his son Corey Haim.

Plot is set into motion when dissension splits up the quartet, leaving Cynthia Rothrock and Ken Lerner with a grudge against Rossi and fils. They fink to the cops, and Rossi is caught. Haim's real mother (Marcia Strassman) claims the youngster but poses as an old friend of his dad's rather than coming clean with her true identity.

Haim's reuniting with his dad (he breaks him out of jail) and gradual return to a nuclear family are the subplots to a pic heavy on chases and stunts.

Debuting feature director Spiro Razatos brings a background of stunt direction that pays off in several exciting sequences, notably a scene of our heroes hanging off a bridge far above a river.

Acting by the principals is fine, with Rossi and Haim a comfortable team and martial arts star Rothrock given a good showcase combining her high-kicking violent streak with sex appeal. Beautiful young actress Shelli Lether is a find as the neighbor who ends Haim's lingering virginity. — *Lawrence Cohn*

BÖRN NÁTTÚRUNNAR
(CHILDREN OF NATURE)
(ICELANDIC)

An Icelandic Film Corp. production in association with Max Film (Germany) and Metro Film (Norway). Produced by Fridrik Thór Fridriksson, Wolfgang Pfeiffer, Skule Hansen. Directed by Fridriksson. Screenplay, Einar Már Gudmundsson, Fridriksson; camera (color), Ari Kristinsson; editor, Hansen; music, Hilmar Örn Hilmarsson; sound (Dolby), Kjartan Kjartansson; art direction, Geir Ottarr Geirsson; costume design, Ragnheidur Olafsdóttir; makeup, Margret Benediktsdóttir; assistant director, Kristín Pálsdóttir. Reviewed at Stjörnubíó, July 31, 1991. Running time: **85 MIN.**
With: Gísli Halldórsson, Sigrídur Hagalín, Valgerdur Dan, Hallmar Sigurdsson, Rúrik Haraldsson, Baldvin Halldórsson, Egill Olafsson, Tinna Gunnlaugsdóttir, Magnús Olafsson, Gudbrandur Gíslason, Bruno Ganz.

"Children Of Nature" is an ambitious drama about the problems of old age. A masterly handling of landscapes and enthralling music paints a powerful picture that might have wide appeal. Setting is too big for television, but the story does not quite fill out a full-length feature.

Fridrik Thór Fridriksson, a filmmaker obsessed with Werner Herzog-like ideas, has not yet dragged a steamer across glaciers à la "Fitzcarraldo," but in his 1980 film "The Saga Of Burnt Njál," he burned a book containing the best loved Icelandic saga.

Fridriksson's style has matured a lot since then; still, he seems to be unable to move from bizarre ideas toward complex, full-blooded stories. Some of his ideas, however, are fine for tv pics, and his intensity seeps through.

The scenes at the old people's home and of a farmer shooting his "only trusted companion" (a dog) at pic's beginning are arresting. Dialog is sparse, but one senses the agony of people struggling to keep up appearances.

The farmer escapes from the old people's home in a stolen jeep. When the county police car is just a few meters away from the jeep, it disappears mysteriously.

One awaits a new and surrealistic world to open up, but the last minutes, in which the old man buries his love of youth and walks barefoot to a deserted army station, verge on melodrama. Still, audiences might shed a tear at this moment of catharsis.

Pic's latter half is a bit arty,

Sigrídur Hagalín portrays the sweetheart who raced with the old farmer to a desolate homestead. A sensitive actress but a bit too young for the part, Rúrik Haraldsson gives a randy inmate a memorable look. The rest of the acting also is quite good.

Even the representative of Eurimages fund (Gudbrandur Gíslason) is fine as the manager of the old people's home. But what is Bruno Ganz doing as an angel dressed in a heavy overcoat?

On the tech side, Hilmar Örn Hilmarsson's music deserves praise, Ari Kristinsson's cinematography is mostly impressive (but not always fluid) and sound is excellent, quite a feat for a $1 million budget. Unfortunately, few silver screens are to be found in old people's homes, so the landscapes end as miniatures.

—*Olafur M. Jóhannesson*

DARK CITY
(BRITISH-ZIMBABWEAN)

A Prima Film release of a Celestia Fox, CSL Films, BBC, Film Africa production. Directed by Chris Curling. Screenplay, David Lean; camera (color), Dick Pope; editor, David Mingay; music, David Dundas; sound, Robin Harris. Reviewed at Vues d'Afrique Film Festival, Montreal, April 28, 1991. Running time: **98 MIN.**
With: Sello Maake Ka-Kcube.

In the repetitive and amateur "Dark City," characters in the ongoing saga of violence between white government and black civilians in Africa are strictly one-dimensional. Uneven editing destroys pacing, dragging out an issue clearly meant to enrage, not bore, the viewer.

Confrontation arises when members of a massive, peaceful activist group dance and chant their way to the mayor's house for a chat. Barred from entry, the unarmed men and women hop the gate, but the terrified mayor shoots one man arbitrarily, creating panic. One pro-violence protester shoots a city council member in retaliation.

In the months that follow, protesters are forced to inform on each other, an informer is then killed by his own comrades, innocents are sentenced to death and unarmed protesters are shot by soldiers. Final scene sees the once-peaceful protest leader pick up a gun to join the armed resistance, his actions supposedly justified.

The makers of "Dark City" obviously had a noble intention

— explaining why peaceful protesters sometimes turn to violence. However, pic offers about as much insight as the evening news, without adding anything new. — *Suzan Ayscough*

JALOUSIE
(JEALOUSY)
(FRENCH)

A Bac Films release of a Paradis Films-Générale d'Images-Ciné Cinq (Paris)-Ellepi Films (Rome)-Center National de las Cinematographic-Canal Plus co-production. (Intl. sales: President Films.) Produced by Eric Heumann. Directed by Kathleen Fonmarty. Screenplay, Fonmarty, Magali Clement, Richard Andry; camera (color), Andry; editor, Jacques Comets; music, Philippe Sarde, Paolo Conte; sound, Dominique Levert; production design, Fred and Frédérique Lapierre; costumes, Christian Gasq. Reviewed at Munich Film Festival, June 26, 1991. Running time: **100 MIN.**
Camille . . . . Lio
Pierre . . . . Christian Vadim
Gisele . . . . Odette Laure
Claire . . . . Véronique Delbourg
Sabine . . . . Caroline Lecoyer
Abel . . . . Abel Jefri
Kevin . . . . Frederic Berthelot
Also with: Sulvia Losillet, Sophie Dalezio, Childrec Muller.

Kathleen Fonmarty's "Jealousy" harps on its theme of obsessive love, and, like a clinging lover, it becomes tiresome. Gallic audiences were unimpressed, and the usual crossover markets most likely will pass on this one.

A pretty photographer living in the south of France (Lio) meets a manipulative artist (Christian Vadim, son of Roger) who charms the pants off just about every woman he meets. The sweet photographer is a challenge, and he wildly pursues her.

Lio falls for the old ploy of posing nude and succumbs willingly to the artist's charms. Within short order, she moves into his flat in Aix-en-Province. The pic becomes a study in sado-masochism as she devotes her life to possessing the artist, and he gets his jollies by tormenting her with hints of infidelity.

The whining housefrau seems to do little other than vacuum when she is not going through demeaning antics such as opening her lover's mail or sniffing his clothes for perfume. The artist's friend (Frederic Berthelot) is attentive to Lio, but like every woman who loves too much, she is not interested in nice guys.

Scant attempts at humor, such as the encounter between Lio and her friend (Véronique Del-

bourg) and a mother and daughter on a train, fall flat.

When Vadim is hired as the artistic designer for an opera, he puts the moves on an attractive blond colleague. Tired of the cat-and-mouse game with pale and often hysterical Lio, he tells her to do her vacuuming elsewhere. Pic's finale, when Lio and Vadim meet some time later, suggests one partner in a love affair always loves more than the other.

Characters are too one-dimensional to arouse much interest, and the script is banal. Lio mostly looks neurotic, while Vadim rarely wipes a smirk off his face.

Mainly interior camerawork is okay but conventional. Original piano and horn score and strains of Mozart's "Don Juan" subtly accents visuals.

First feature of helmer and co-scripter Fonmarty, script girl for helmers Robert Altman and John Frankenheimer, among others, gives little indication that she picked up any of their skills in creating engaging films with memorable characters.
— *B. Samantha Stenzel*

LA DESENCHANTÉE
(THE DISENCHANTED)
(FRENCH)

A Pyramide release of a Cinea-La Sept production, with the participation of CNC, Sofica Sofinergie 2. (Intl. sales: Pyramide Intl.) Executive producer, Sylvie Blum. Produced by Philippe Carcassonne. Written and directed by Benoit Jacquot. Camera (Fujicolor), Caroline Champetier; editor, Dominique Auvray; music, Jorge Arriagada; sound, Michel Vionnet; production manager, Sylvie Barthet; assistant director, Laurent Argenson; casting, Marie-Christine Lafosse. Reviewed at Unifrance screening room, Paris, May 6, 1991. Running time: **79 MIN.**
Beth . . . . Judith Godrèche
Alphonse . . . . Marcel Bozonnet
The uncle . . . . Ivan Desny
Beth's mother . . . . . Thérèse Liotard
The Other . . . . . . Malcolm Conrath
Remi . . . . Thomas Salsman
Chang . . . . Hai Tuhong-tu
Also with: Francis Magé, Marion Perry, Stephane Auberghen.

The 17-year-old protagonist of "The Disenchanted," brightly played by newcomer Judith Godrèche, is old beyond her years. Benoit Jacquot's simple but effective film is a neat character study of a Parisian teen determined to escape her environment for a better life.

Pic, however, is too slight to make a commercial dent internationally, and Godrèche's sexual encounters are constantly played down. But if it makes the

fest circuit, the film should attract French cinema devotees.

A brilliant student, already something of an authority on the work of Rimbaud (who also was disenchanted with life), she lives with her sickly mother and kid brother in an apartment paid for by the mother's older lover, a doctor referred to as "uncle" by everyone. Uncle, played by vet Ivan Desny, makes it clear he would like to start sleeping with the daughter.

Beth has her own lover, a youth she calls "the Other," but she decides to end the affair when he suggests she prove her love for him by sleeping with someone else, preferably someone ugly.

Unfolding over a three-day period, pic explores Beth's relationships with the people in her life: her mother and brother; the Other, who turns nasty when she tells him they're through; Chang, a student who's her best friend; the lecherous "uncle"; Edouard, a clumsy rich boy she meets in a disco; and a mysterious man with an alarming knife collection.

The film exists mainly as a showcase for its central character, and Godrèche serves writer-director Jacquot well with a telling portrayal of a jaded, intelligent, fiercely independent young woman. — *David Stratton*

IMDAT ILE ZARIFE
(ZARIFE, THE DANCING BEAR)
(TURKISH)

A Yapim production. (Intl. sales: MTV Dunya Haklari.) Produced by Reha Arin. Directed by Nesli Çölgeçen. Screenplay, Çölgeçen, Hakan Aytekin, Irfan Eroglu; camera (color), Aytekin Çakmaçii, Turhan Yavuz; editor, Mevlut Koçak; music, Nadir Göktürk; art director, Annie G. Pertan. Reviewed at Istanbul Film Festival, March 28, 1991. Running time: **95 MIN.**
Imdat . . . . Sevket Altug
Menekse . . . . Selma Cetinal
Sufi . . . . Erkah Ozkurt
Zabite . . . . Can Kolukisa
Bahtigar . . . . Ustün Asutay
Zarife . . . . Ayse

"Zarife, The Dancing Bear" realistically looks into the life of Anatolian gypsies, focusing on Imdat and his trained bear. Pic is a well-done curio with limited commercial appeal, but it has potential for film fest slots and specialized theatrical and ethnic-themed tv programming.

Pastoral opening with the cub and her mother recalling Jean-Jacques Annaud's "The Bear"

(although helmer Nesli Çölgeçen says he conceived his script earlier) is followed by overlong graphic docu footage of the brutal training of a young bear after its mother has been killed. This is bound to provoke outcries, although animal welfare groups could use the pic as powerful testimony of cruel animal training methods.

Imdat relies on Zarife for his livelihood, and they travel with his family around Istanbul collecting change from tourists. Imdat becomes greedy and books Zarife into a nightclub, in which she is supposed to do a humorous belly dance. She doesn't take to the big time and turns on Imdat in the middle of the act.

The bear becomes ill-tempered, unreliable and dangerous. Imdat's superstitious father claims someone has put the evil eye on her, and it must be exorcized. The touching climax emerges as an allegory on freedom versus captivity.

The extraordinary bear is a personable performer. Imdat and his family are convincing, as are the real gypsies in the supporting cast, including the bear's real owner. Helmer's docu background is evident here as is his humanistic touch.
— *B. Samantha Stenzel*

ARCHIVE REVIEW

KUROTAKAGE
(BLACK LIZARD)
(JAPANESE)

A Cinevista release (in U.S.) of a Shochiku production. Directed by Kinji Fukasaku. Screenplay, Masashige Narusawa, based on novel by Rampo Edogawa as adapted for the stage by Yukio Mishima; camera (Grand Scope color), Hiroshi Dowaki; music, Isao Tomita; art direction, Kyohei Morita. Reviewed at Broadway Screening Room, N.Y., July 9, 1991. Running time: **86 MIN.**
Black Lizard . . . . Akihiro Maruyama
Detective Akechi . . . . . Isao Kimura
Jeweler . . . . Junya Usami
Sanaye . . . . Kikko Matsuoka
Hina . . . . Toshiko Kobayashi
Human statue . . . . . . Yukio Mishima
Akechi's friend . . . . . Tesuro Tanba

After almost a quarter-century, Japan's 1968 camp detective pic "Black Lizard" has been picked up for U.S. distribution and cultists may wonder if it was worth the wait. Although replete with laughs, the hackneyed plot, glaring genre treatment and egregious overacting often leave one wondering to what degree the camp is intentional.

Pic's main selling point is that it was based on Yukio Mishima's longrunning legit adaptation of Rampo Edogawa's eponymous novel. (Mishima also makes a brief appearance as a living samurai warrior statue.)

This facile entertainment is mainly a showcase for Mishima's former lover, Kabuki actor/female impersonator Akihiro Maruyama, who recreates his legit role as the femme fatale "Black Lizard," a notorious jewel thief who steals the show.

Never dull to watch, Maruyama is given ample opportunity to sport a wide array of outlandish costumes, utter outrageous clichéd lines of dialog and strike a variety of poses and postures. (Mishima fans may remember Maruyama from Michael MacIntyre's 1985 BBC docu "The Strange Case Of Yukio Mishima.")

Storyline is straight out of a comic book. The evil Black Lizard kidnaps a famous jeweler's daughter in order to ransom her for the famed "Star of Egypt" diamond. To protect himself, the jeweler hires Black Lizard's nemesis Akechi (Isao Kimura), Tokyo's top private eye.

The rest of the film offers various confrontations between the thief and detective as the Black Lizard tries to gain the upper hand against her worthy foe.

Art direction is strictly 1960s with atmospheric go-go clubs, mod suits and psychedelic miniskirts. Editing tends towards the terse and the zealous musical score is heavy on the horn section. — *Paul Lenti*

SEX, DRUGS, ROCK & ROLL

An Avenue Pictures presentation. Produced by Frederick Zollo. Executive producer, Cary Brokaw. Directed by John McNaughton. Screenplay, Eric Bogosian; camera (color, Crest prints), Ernest Dickerson; editor, Elena Maganini; sound design, Bernard Fox, Jan Nabozenko; sound mix, Frank Stettner; production design, John Arnone; lighting design, Jan Kroeze; assistant director, Randy Fletcher; associate producer, Paul Kurta; co-producers, Steven A. Jones, Llewellyn Wells. Reviewed at Raleigh Studios, L.A., Aug. 9, 1991. MPAA Rating: R. Running time: **96 MIN.**
With: Eric Bogosian.

Avenue Pictures can't go wrong with this straightforward presentation of Eric Bogosian's stage show. The New York monologist's dark gallery of self-destructive characters is both accessible and challenging. "Sex, Drugs, Rock & Roll" should do smart biz in limited urban bookings and enjoy a long video life.

Bogosian, whose stage creation for "Talk Radio" became the Oliver Stone film in which he also starred, is featured here in a one-man show, metamorphosing through 10 characters, from a N.Y. subway panhandler to a pot-smoking paranoid who tells us he's "stopped making art" because the world is too corrupt a place in which to be involved.

To an unusual degree, Bogosian's all-male creations share a darkness, a negativity expressed in various kinds of anger, aggression and delusionary means of escape, thus the "sex, drugs and rock & roll" of the title.

From the seething anger of a Dostoevskian urban outcast who

Original play

Frederick Zollo and Robert Cole, in association with 126 Second Ave. Corp. and Sine/D'Addario Ltd., presentation of a series of dramatic monologs in one act, written and performed by Eric Bogosian. Staged by Jo Bonney. Setting, John Arnone; lighting, Jan Kroeze; sound, Jan Nebozenko; stage manager, Pat Sosnow; associate producer, Ethel Bayer, William Suter; company manager, Marcia Goldberg; publicity, Philip Rinaldi. Opened Feb. 8, '90, at the Orpheum Theater, N.Y. $27.50 top weeknights, $29.50 weekends.
Cast: Eric Bogosian.

plots mass murder as revenge on those who've spurned him, to the revolting, but hilariously elaborate, environmental warning

sounded by an old man obsessed with the idea that the world is awash in a river of sewage, these are damaged characters without resilience. They're surviving, but from mangled positions.

Those on the "ups" (the bullying, lying, prosperous young entertainment lawyer; the working-class Italian-American dimwit on a nonstop party streak) are hilarious for their lack of self-awareness. Those on the "downs" (the nervous street scavenger railing about the price of a cup of coffee; the panhandler with his hard-luck spiel) are chilling for their lack of hope.

Show is laden with laughs, but he pulls no punches, either. His joint-toking philosopher theorizes that the homeless serve a useful function, keeping the rest of us in our cages "because we're afraid if we don't do what we're supposed to do, we'll end up one of them."

Beautifully crafted piece, which builds from lighter to progressively more impressive material, ultimately transcends its darkness by virtue of its poignance and humanity. Bogosian's theater craft gives us enough distance from his blustering or blathering characters to see their vulnerability. "No surrender" may be the war cry of his young Turks, lifted from a Bruce Springsteen song, but these guys already are prisoners.

First mounted at New York's 400-seat Orpheum Theater, the show made the transfer to cinema at a series of nine dates at Boston's 1,200-seat Wilbur Theater, geared specifically to the filming. Production designer John Arnone's set is a soaring construction of fence panels in a skyscraper configuration suggesting urban harshness and confinement.

Director John McNaughton ("Henry: Portait Of A Serial Killer") and cinematographer Ernest Dickerson ("Eddie Murphy Raw") mostly stay out of the way with an unobstrusive combination of effective angles and cuts, plus some mood-enhancing slow Steadicam floats during the stoned rap that ends the show.

Nonetheless, the picture suffers some oddly amateurish touches, such as the jokey use of repeated extreme closeups on a rock star's cigarette to contradict his half-hearted antidrug spiel. Also unfortunate is an abrupt cut at show's conclusion from the final monolog to an au-

dience applause seg.

Show is Bogosian's fifth stage creation, including "Talk Radio," and the first to be filmed in concert form for theatrical release. (His second, "Funhouse," became a homevideo and "Drinking In America" was an HBO special.) Stage show's producer Fred Zollo also handled the film.
— *Amy Dawes*

BINGO

A Tri-Star release of a Thomas Baer production. Produced by Baer. Executive producer, Warren Carr. Directed by Matthew Robbins. Screenplay, Jim Strain; camera (Technicolor), John McPherson; editor, Maryann Brandon; music, Richard Gibbs; sound (Dolby), Larry Sutton, Steve Maslow, Anthony D'Amico, Joe Citarella; production design, Mark Freeborn; art direction, David Willson; set decoration, Rose Marie McSherry, Annmarie Corbett; costume design, Larry S. Wells; animal trainers, Boone Narr, David J. McMillan, Mark Wiener, Paul Reynolds, Dawn Martin-Wiener, Kathy Anne Grant, Tracey Hunaus; stunt coordinator, Brent Woolsey; assistant director, David Rose; associate producer, Judith Craig Marlin; co-producer, John L. Jacobs; casting, Robin Lippin, Lynne Carrow. Reviewed at Edwards Alhambra Place, Alhambra, Calif., Aug. 10, 1991. MPAA Rating: PG. Running time: **87 MIN.**
Natalie Devlin . . . . . Cindy Williams
Hal Devlin . . . . David Rasche
Chuckie . . . . Robert J. Steinmiller Jr.
Chickie . . . . David French
Lennie . . . . Kurt Fuller
Eli . . . . Joe Guzaldo
Duke . . . . Glenn Shadix
Bingo . . . . Bingo/Maui/Max

Anyone beyond the moppet stage will find reruns of "Lassie" more diverting than "Bingo," a labored comedy about an anthropomorphic collie. Even with the dearth of non-Disney family entertainment out there, this flatulent "Benji" imitation had a poor opening weekend and seems headed for early impoundment in video stores.

Title character is an unbelievably resourceful pooch who runs away from mistreatment in a circus and straight into the heart of a Denver lad (Robert J. Steinmiller Jr.), son of a self-possessed jerk of a football player (David Rasche) and his ditzy wife (Cindy Williams).

When Rasche is traded to Green Bay, the parents refuse to let Bingo come along, so the intrepid dog sets out on a picaresque cross-country pursuit, menaced by assorted lowlifes including two sleazy crooks (Kurt Fuller, Joe Guzaldo) given far too much screen time.

Director Matthew Robbins and editor Maryann Brandon try to

keep the film moving, but Jim Strain's screenplay, with its witless pastiche of various film and tv genre clichés, generates little suspense or involvement.

Unlike in "Benji" pics, genuine animal stunts (dog riding uncertainly on a skateboard) are few in "Bingo," which relies heavily on sight gags abetted by editing (the kid tells Bingo to find food, he comes back with a fish in his mouth).

Still, the dog is much better than most of the hapless human actors trapped in a mangy script with a heart of brass. Only Steinmiller, in his film debut, manages to avoid irritating the audience.

Cindy Williams overdoes the mom's plastic personality, making this feature outing seem like a sitcom. Rasche plays a character so moronically buffoonish that when the barefooted placekicker is told by the baddies that they'll kill his son if he doesn't miss his field goals, he has trouble making up his mind and asks advice from his coach. Moments like that make the film something less than a laugh riot.

Evidently intending a pseudo-cynical update on heroic dog sagas, Strain and Robbins think it's clever to fill the screen with a pile of dog feces for the pompous Rasche to step in, or to indulge a stream of pee-pee jokes with the dog pursuing Steinmiller's scent along the highway.

Showing the dog coping with everyday human menace might have made for a more involving comedy, but the filmmakers' attempts at black humor come off as fancifully distasteful, such as showing Bingo saving mutts incarcerated by a mad butcher (Glenn Shadix) who chops up dogs and sells them as frankfurters at a roadside diner.

John McPherson's ugly lensing of picturesque Vancouver area locations compounds the feeling of depression that hangs smog-like over "Bingo."

— *Joseph McBride*

MYSTERY DATE

An Orion Pictures release. Produced by Cathleen Summers. Directed by Jonathan Wacks. Screenplay, Parker Bennett, Terry Runté; camera (Deluxe color), Oliver Wood; editor, Tina Hirsch; music, John DuPrez; sound (Dolby), Rob Young; production design, John Willett; costume design, Jori Woodman; art direction, Willie Heslup; set direction, Kim MacKenzie; associate producer, Susan Moore; assistant director, Dennis White; casting, Amanda Mackey, Cathy San-

drich, Stuart Aikins. Reviewed at Century City Cineplex Odeon, L.A., Aug. 8, 1991. MPAA rating: PG-13. Running time: **99 MIN.**

Tom McHugh	Ethan Hawke
Geena Matthews	Teri Polo
Craig McHugh	Brian McNamara
Dwight	Fisher Stevens
James Lew	B.D. Wong
Sharpie	Tony Rosato
Doheny	Don Davis

"Mystery Date" is indeed a surprise engagement as the outing proves not to be the sunny teen comedy of its marketing campaign but a dark, berserk comedy-whodunit about some grim goings-on and a case of mistaken identity. Younger crowd may be willing to go along for the ride for a couple of weekends, but the boxoffice relationship likely will be brief.

Genre-bending pic, given engaging verve by director Jonathan Wacks, is like a mildly diverting pinball game: Plot ricochets from one gaudy target to another, beaten back with bumpers, but eventually rolls down the hole with only a mediocre score.

Ethan Hawke, tongue-tied student from "Dead Poets Society," returns as another painfully shy youth who can't gather the nerve to ask out his beautiful neighbor (Teri Polo). When his brash older brother (Brian McNamara) blows in for the weekend, he grabs the phone and sets the couple up for more than they expected.

His confidence and resources bolstered by his brother's suit, car and credit card, nervous Hawke sets out on his dream date only to encounter a bewildering and perilous series of mishaps. The 1959 DeSoto may be a stylin' set of wheels but it's got problems — like two dead guys in the trunk. Continually mistaken for his brother, Hawke encounters a trail of acrimony that's surprisingly fresh, considering his brother supposedly lives far away at Stanford law school. Before long, Hawke's dodging the cops, the Chinese Mafia and an enraged flower delivery boy (Fisher Stevens), all the while struggling desperately to prevent his date from becoming a disaster.

Given the wide-open parameters, pic might have had more staying power if first-time scripters Parker Bennett and Terry Runté had set it up more cleverly, but plot mostly rides on haphazard coincidences and unlikely turns.

At one point Hawke's exas-

perated date lurches off into the night alone and on foot — after being pursued by killers, no less — and is of course immediately kidnaped, setting up the rest of the action. Even the pic's final minute betrays laziness, as Hawke proposes some wordplay between himself and the lady and then just skips it.

End result is a reasonably entertaining pic but too lame to generate word-of-mouth. Nonetheless, Wacks ("Powwow Highway") makes a smooth transition to mainstream fare, keeping things well-paced and visually appealing. Pic's stylish, high-gloss look is bound to appeal to teens.

Performances are generally fine but B.D. Wong (Broadway's "M. Butterfly") sweeps the others aside with his magnetic turn as a smiling Chinese Mafia prince. Wong's like a cat in man's clothing: sinuous, charismatic and slyly comedic, clearly enjoying himself in this first significant film role.

Meanwhile, another fine actor, Stevens, gets relegated to a Wile E. Coyote-type cartoon role as a character who keeps getting destroyed and then pops up again.

Lensed mostly at night in Vancouver, pic benefits from a lot of fresh and attractive locations and a smart production design.

— *Amy Dawes*

AMOGNST EQUALS
(AUSTRALIAN-DOCU)

A Jotz Prods.-Film Australia production. Executive producer, Paul Humphress. Written and directed by Tom Zubrycki. Camera (color), Joel Peterson; editor, Zubrycki; music, Paul Chartier; sound, Russ Hermann; production manager, Marie Delofski; narration, Graham Pitts. Reviewed at Mosman screening room, Sydney, July 20, 1991. Running time: **93 MIN.**

Talented Aussie docu filmmaker Tom Zubrycki ran into well-publicized trouble over his production of "Amongst Equals," a fascinating record of the Australian union movement. If he is ever able to finish the film, it should be sought-after fare at international film fests and could recoup some of the Aussie taxpayers' investment via tv and video sales.

Pic, funded by federal money and effectively banned by Australia's Council of Trade Unions, screened illegally at the recent

Melbourne Film Festival and at Sydney's AFI cinema. Actually, nothing in the docu is very provocative at all.

The ban seems extraordinary because Zubrycki's film is clearly what it was originally supposed to be: a historical appraisal of the turbulent role of trade unions in Australian life. In 1987, Zubrycki proposed the film for the country's 1988 Bi-Centenary, and received the support of the country's official docu film unit, Film Australia, as well as the Australian Bicentennial Authority.

The ABA, a federal unit, gave $A200,000 to the ACTU to make the film, and the council then contracted Film Australia to produce "Amongst Equals" with Zubrycki as writer-director. The contract specified that the film would be "a critical appraisal" of the trade union movement.

When the film was nearing completion in 1988, however, ACTU leadership clearly was critical of this "critical appraisal," and particularly objected to archive footage of historically well-documented union struggles. After months of discussion and five recuts, the ACTU slapped a ban on the film. Zubrycki, referring to the ABA coin, has accused the ACTU of misusing public money.

Docu covers the mass strikes during World War I, the battle for an eight-hour work day, ACTU formation in 1927 and the unions' first foray into foreign policy when they tried to prevent shipment of pig-iron to Japan in 1939. Zubrycki also explores the aftermath of World War II, with the election of a Labor government which sent the army in to break a crippling coal strike.

The filmmaker also explores union battles fought by women, migrants and aboriginal workers, especially the equal-pay-for-women campaigns. The so-called "green bans," invoked in the '70s by building unions to prevent demolition of historically important inner-city buildings, also are covered.

In addition to powerful archive footage, Zubrycki uses veterans of these old struggles to reminisce. The result is a vivid and impressive historical survey, and if the film seems sketchy on contemporary events, it's perhaps because the ACTU forced the helmer to remove (in an early cut) footage criticizing analysis of the current wages accord between government and unions.

— *David Stratton*

DOUBLE IMPACT

A Columbia Pictures release of a Stone Group Pictures presentation of an Ashok Amritraj-Jean-Claude Van Damme production. Produced by Amritraj, Van Damme. Executive producers, Moshe Diamant, Charles Layton. Directed by Sheldon Lettich. Screenplay, Lettich, Van Damme, from story by Lettich, Van Damme, Steve Meerson, Peter Krikes; camera (Deluxe color), Richard Kline; editor, Mark Conte; music, Arthur Kempel; sound (Dolby), Robert R. Rutledge; production design, John Jay Moore; art direction, Okowita; set decoration, Suzette Sheets; costume design, Joseph Porro; line producer, Evzen Kolar; supervising producer, Rick Nathanson; associate producer (Hong Kong), Charles Wang; assistant directors, Thomas J. Mack, David Kelly; 2nd unit directors, Vic Armstrong, Andy Armstrong; fight choreography, Van Damme; co-producers, Lettich, Terry Martin Carr; casting, James Tarzia. Reviewed at Columbia Pictures screening room, Culver City, Calif., Aug. 7, 1991. MPAA Rating: R. Running time: **108 MIN.**

Chad/Alex	Jean-Claude Van Damme
Frank Avery	Geoffrey Lewis
Nigel Griffith	Alan Scarfe
Danielle Wilde	Alonna Shaw
Zhang	Philip Chan Yan Kin
Kara	Cory Everson
Moon	Bolo Yeung

This double-dose of Jean-Claude Van Damme turns on a typically lame revenge plot while dragging out unimaginatively shot action sequences until no one will give a good Van Damme. Tedious storytelling should mute the pic's b.o. impact and lead to a quick leap to homevid, where it could do some high-stepping among the action star's hardcore fans.

The one-time karate champ nicknamed "muscles from Brussels" apparently wanted to stretch his acting hamstring in this dual role as twins separated at six months but only succeeds in proving that he can look okay with his hair greased back like Steven Seagal's.

A film like this can survive an inane story, but even the action sequences here lack punch, as director-co-writer-co-producer Sheldon Lettich continuously resorts to slow-motion shots that reduce the excitement factor to the level of lawn-bowling.

Pic starts off with the twins' parents being killed by an evil developer (Alan Scarfe). One grows up on the mean streets of Hong Kong, while the other was raised by a family friend (Geoffrey Lewis) and turns up 25 years later as a Los Angeles karate instructor.

Lewis' character discovers the other twin is alive and takes his charge back to Hong Kong, reuniting the mismatched pair to reclaim their inheritance. No one ever spells out exactly what that entails, but it provides a good excuse for indiscriminate killing of lots of Asian flunkies.

Van Damme uses two looks — glowering/nasty and friendly/bewildered — to differentiate the characters. For the most part, the filmmakers simply rely on hairstyling, wardrobe and idioms to draw the distinction: Chad wears Polo shirts and says things like "chill out," while Alex favors leather.

Script by Van Damme and Lettich proves humorless and bland when it isn't unintentionally amusing. It's also disturbing that not a single Asian character exhibits any redeeming features. (Few of the Caucasians do either, but it's not for lack of trying.)

Equal opportunities are provided in the evil henchmen ranks, however, where female bodybuilder Cory Everson joins so-called "Chinese Hercules" Bolo Yeung, a perennial martial arts bad guy who hasn't won a fight in one of these opuses dating back to "Enter The Dragon."

Lewis, a solid actor, looks a lot like G. Gordon Liddy with his shaved head but fares as poorly as the rest of the cast. Finale is noteworthy only in that it leaves, even the good guys thoroughly sliced up and bloodied.

Big innovation apparently is supposed to be the blue-screen and stand-in work used to show the twins together. While well-executed, technique is so familiar to filmgoers, it's hardly much of a draw, except perhaps to see producer-co-writer-star Van Damme (listed twice in the cast credits, as "Chad" and "Alex") give himself a well-deserved beating when the brothers feud over Alex' g.f. (Alonna Shaw).

Other tech credits are okay, though some of the night camerawork proves murky, which is at times a welcome relief.

— *Brian Lowry*

AGNES CECILIA
(SWEDISH)

A Svensk Filmindustri presentation of a Svensk Filmindustri-Kanal 1 Drama SVT-Swedish Film Institute production. Produced by Waldemar Bergendahl, Ingrid Dalunde. Directed by Anders Grönros. Screenplay, Grönros, based on Maria Gripe's novel; camera (color), Per Källberg; editor, Göran Carmback, Christer Furubrand; music, Johan Söderqvist; sound, Klas Dykhoff, Asa Lindgren-Dawidsson, Christjan Persson; production design, Niklas Ejve, Kristoffer Sjöström; assistant director, Anna Carlsten, Elisabeth Gillberg. Reviewed at Svensk Filmindustri screening room, Stockholm, Aug. 8, 1991. Running time: **133 MIN.**

With: Gloria Tapia, Ronn Elfors, Stina Ekblad, Allan Svensson, Vanna Rosenberg, Cecilia Milocco, Mimi Pollak, Meta Velander, Percy Brandt, Natasha Chiapponi-Grönos, Benjamin Elfors, Suzanne Reuter.

Thoughtful and moody, "Agnes Cecilia" combines a ghost story with a young girl's efforts to rid herself of childhood trauma. Pic should turn out a winner and travel well on the festival circuit.

Since his first feature in 1979, director Anders Grönros has worked mainly in television. Several of his works have dealt with death and near-death experiences, themes echoed in his second theatrical.

The story centers on Nora, whose parents were killed in a car accident when she was five. Told her parents moved far away, she's taken in by a couple with a son her age.

Ten years later, the family moves into an older apartment in their small city. Immediately sensing something strange, Nora hears footsteps when no one's there and sees mysterious lights. An old clock, deemed irreparable, starts to tick and its hands move backward. The family dog refuses to enter Nora's room, and someone — or something — seems intent on rescuing the young girl from accidents.

Through old photos and notes she finds hidden in the apartment, Nora attempts to unravel the increasingly intricate mystery involving Nora's family, her ancestors and a young girl who lived in the beginning of the century and with whom she has much in common. Eventually, Nora comes to terms with the death of her parents so she can put a stop to the loneliness and insecurity that has haunted her for 10 years.

Grönros has made a very good film, though somewhat overlong. He's good with actors and has a keen sense of visuals and sound. He creates a moody atmosphere amid everyday settings, and though nothing really scary happens, he manages to generate much suspense in the scenes where Nora begins sensing a supernatural presence.

Most of all, "Agnes Cecilia" (the title refers to two names important in solving the mystery) is a film about a troubled young girl's drive to come to terms with herself. Her story is told with earnest, low-keyed sincerity, with the help of thought-provoking symbols. Every occurrence isn't clearly explained, but the mystery provides fodder for discussion.

Acting overall is good, with special laurels to first-time screen actress Gloria Tapia. All tech credits are fine, especially cinematography by Per Källberg, who contributes much to pic's overall quality.

— *Gunnar Rehlin*

TE RUA
(THE STORE HOUSE)
(NEW ZEALAND)

A Pacific Films production in association with New Zealand Film Commission, Berlin Senate & Film Commission and Avalon. Executive producer, Renee Gundelach. Produced by John O'Shea. Written and directed by Barry Barclay. Camera (color), Rory O'Shea (Berlin), Warrick Attewell (N.Z.); editor, Simon Reece, Dell King; music, Dalvanius; sound, Kit Rollings, Mike Hopkins. Reviewed at Embassy Theater, Wellington, July 6, 1991. Running time: **96 MIN.**

Rewi Marangai	Wi Kuki Kaa
Peter Huata	Peter Kaa
Prof. Biederstedt	Gunter Meisner
Fiona Gilbert	Donna Akersten
Hamish MacMillan	Stuart Devenie
Hanna Lehmann	Maria Fitzi
Dr.Sattler	Walter Kreye
Helen Marangai	Vanessa Rare

"The Store House" might have been an involving high action drama with serious overtones, but it emerges as a film of fitful power and confused purpose. Theatrical exposure outside selected film fests is likely to be limited.

An old woman in a small Maori community in New Zealand keens for lost tribal carvings stolen many years earlier. The artifacts are now in the vaults of a Berlin museum. A Maori poet (Peter Kaa) touring the city senses the presence of his ancestors and is determined to return the art treasures to his homeland.

He persuades his uncle (Wi Kuki Kaa), a Maori businessman-diplomat based in Europe, to join the team that will spring the treasures. The uncle has his own plan to accomplish the mission.

Pic's disjointed and rambling narrative suggests shortcomings in film craft rather than premeditated creative intent.

What is essentially an action pic emerges surprisingly static and passive. Self-conscious rhetoric on white colonialism and patronage and Third World values too often chokes the flow. Camerawork is unimaginative. The performances give little indication of flesh-and-blood characters.

Barry Barclay is a fine docu filmmaker, but like his first feature, "Ngati" (1987 Cannes Critics Week item), "Te Rua" shows the helmer's inexperience with the acting process, a key to bringing features to life. The poorly handled actors in "Te Rua" are both professional and amateur thesps. — *Mike Nicolaidi*

DEAD AGAIN

A Paramount Pictures presentation of a Mirage production. Produced by Lindsay Doran, Charles H. Maguire. Executive producer, Sydney Pollack. Directed by Kenneth Branagh. Screenplay, Scott Frank; camera (color, black & white), Matthew F. Leonetti; editor, Peter E. Berger; music, Patrick Doyle; sound (Dolby), Gerald G. Jost; production design, Tim Harvey; art direction, Sidney Z. Litwack; set design, Henry Alberti, Joseph Hubbard, Eric Orbom; set decoration, Jerry Adams; costume design, Phyllis Dalton; assistant director, Steve Danton; co-producer, Dennis Feldman; casting, Gail Levin. Reviewed at Mann Plaza theater, L.A., Aug. 14, 1991. MPAA rating: R. Running time: **111 MIN.**
Mike Church/
  Roman Strauss . . Kenneth Branagh
Grace/Margaret
  Strauss . . . . . . Emma Thompson
Gary Baker . . . . Andy Garcia
Franklyn Madson . . . . . Derek Jacobi
Dr. Cozy Carlisle . . . . Robin Williams
Piccolo Pete . . . . . . Wayne Knight
Inga . . . . Hanna Schygulla
  Also with: Campbell Scott.

Director and star Kenneth Branagh brings the same zest and bravura style to this actors' romp of a mystery-thriller as he did to "Henry V," creating a film briskly entertaining enough to generate mostly positive word of mouth among mature audiences.

Paramount's ad campaign, however, seems to be aimed at youthful horror fans, whose numbers at the boxoffice will be limited by pic's baroque plot and tepid love story.

Supernatural tale of murder, hypnosis and reincarnation involves a woman (Emma Thompson) wandering around in an amnesiac daze, tormented by memories of someone else's life.

Taken into the care of a cavalier private detective (Branagh) who finds himself mysteriously drawn to her, she reveals to a hypnotist (Derek Jacobi) her shockingly vivid memories of a glamorous life as a 1940s concert pianist married to a celebrated composer who was sentenced to death after he allegedly murdered her with a pair of scissors.

Mystery is Thompson's true identity. Why does she have these nightmares? Is the detective really her ex-husband, come back to life to kill her again?

Branagh illustrates the 1940s segs in giddily stylized black & white, with a tongue-in-cheek Wellesian theatricality, while the present-day action takes place in a pungently humanistic L.A. rife with bizarre characters.

Engaging film style is buoyed by an infectious sense of fun and punctuated by wild and woolly character turns. Robin Williams plays a psychiatrist who's gone off the deep end, and Andy Garcia is a seedy journalist with an accent seemingly wafting in from various ports.

Branagh and real-life spouse Thompson — each of whom plays dual roles in past and present — are excellent thesps, but they don't make a very seductive screen couple. Film grinds to a halt whenever it focuses on their budding romance in the present.

Thompson, in the blank-slate role of Grace, doesn't get any help from wardrobe, which fits her in a mousy style better suited to selling pain reliever on tv, while Branagh, charismatic and glib in the role of the American private eye, doesn't draw much of a spark from her. Campbell Scott creates more of a stir when he dashes up in a cameo role claiming to be her fiancé.

Dense plot grows a bit musty as it dwells in the past, where the composer (Branagh) has become despondent over his dwindling fortune and suspects his wife (Thompson) of dallying with the newspaper scribe, but Branagh plays it for fun, giving the excellent cast free rein (perhaps too much in the case of Garcia's weird and wet-eyed performance).

Pic is pushed impishly over the top in a present-day scene in which the dying old newsman (Garcia in heavy makeup) demands a cigarette and smokes it through a respirator plugged into his throat. It's enough to make anyone quit. Or is it?

Thematic intersections of "Dead Again" with "Ghost" (also developed via Par exec Lindsay Doran) seem merely coincidental, and Branagh doesn't dwell on romantic sentimentality, choosing instead to build up suspense in pic's final reels. Final twists and turns of Scott Frank's mystery plot should prove quite satisfying to fans of the genre.

Oddly, Branagh and cinematographer Matthew F. Leonetti confine the adept and spirited camerawork to a tight frame throughout, and with nary a wide or establishing shot, pic suffers from lack of a clear sense of place and seems designed for the small screen.

Jacobi is a pure delight as the eccentric antiques dealer and hypnotist, alone worth the price of admission. — *Amy Dawes*

HARLEY DAVIDSON & THE MARLBORO MAN

An MGM presentation of a Krisjair/Laredo production. Produced by Jere Henshaw. Directed by Simon Wincer. Screenplay, Don Michael Paul; camera (color), David Eggby; editor, Corky Ehlers; music, Basil Poledouris; sound (Dolby), Don Johnson; production design, Paul Peters; costume design, Richard Shissler; art direction, Lisette Thomas; set decoration, Lynn Wolverton Parker; assistant director, Robert Rooy; associate producer, Missy Alpern; 2nd unit director-stunt coordinator, Billy Burton; co-producer, Paul; casting, Mike Fenton/Judy Taylor, Valerie Massalas. Reviewed at Pacific Theater, Hollywood, Aug. 17, 1991. MPAA Rating: R. Running time: **93 MIN.**
Harley Davidson . . . . Mickey Rourke
Marlboro . . . . Don Johnson
Virginia Slim . . . . Chelsea Field
Alexander . . . . Daniel Baldwin
Chance Wilder . . . . . . Tom Sizemore
Lulu Daniels . . . . . Vanessa Williams

Who are these brand-name guys? Not Butch Cassidy and the Sundance Kid, though this boneheaded biker Western makes a few lame swipes at imitation. Only a loser could love these action figures, and MGM-Pathe isn't likely to round up enough of 'em to keep this end-of-summer slot filler in theaters more than two weeks.

A dopey, almost poignantly bad actioner about two legends-in-their-own-minds, who bungle their way through a bank robbery on behalf of a friend, stands out only for big stars Mickey Rourke and Don Johnson. Why they signed up for it is a mystery too deep for contemplation here, though it's probably linked to childhood fantasies of dressing up in cowboy outfits and grimy leathers.

Also notable is the name of "Lonesome Dove" director Simon Wincer, though one would never guess from watching it that a talent of his caliber was aboard. Only the out-and-out spoof that Don Michael Paul's script begs to be could have wound up watchable, and though Wincer sends up some conventions here and there, the filmmakers apparently meant this outing to be taken to heart.

Set in the wild west of Burbank, Calif., in 1996, when gasoline has gone up to $3.50 a gallon and people are getting high on something called Crystal Drano — er, Crystal Dream — "Harley" has two rebellious drifters (Rourke and Johnson) blowing into town to check on an old friend who's in trouble because a bank wants to foreclose on his business, their old hangout, the Rock 'n' Roll Bar & Grill.

The big-hearted boys go into action to rob the bank, but their stunt eventually winds up getting all their buddies killed. It's partly because these guys are such relentless losers that "Harley" is a wipeout — they can't do anything right, and this is unfortunately not a comedy.

Paul's script has its share of inadvertent laughs ("If there's a God, I'd like to meet the dude," philosophizes Rourke), and a few intentional ones, but it basically wants to create a sense of romance around the image of these simple, free-wheelin' dudes. It might work if the audience were made up of 10-year-olds, but since the film is rated R apparently for language, violence and gratuitous female nudity, this could be a problem.

Pic scores mainly in the second unit and stunt department, with hotly staged bike chases and an abundance of breaking glass, falling bodies and shootouts, and the production design is an asset.

Johnson looks real good in rodeo garb and affects an easygoing tv cowboy drawl that bespeaks some weather-beaten wisdom.

Rourke seems to be wearing a new set of teeth that don't look real, and though he clearly relished the chance to play what could be his grubbiest, most obnoxious role yet — kind of a valentine to the real meatballs on bikes (not the Hollywood kind), perhaps — his work in "Harley" adds nothing to his oeuvre.

Well, they'll love it in France.
— *Amy Dawes*

TRUE IDENTITY

A Buena Vista release of a Touchstone Pictures presentation in association with Silver Screen Partners IV produced in association with Sandollar Prods. Produced by Carol Baum, Teri Schwartz. Executive producers, Sandy Gallin, Howard Rosenman. Directed by Charles Lane. Screenplay, Andy Breckman; camera (Technicolor), Tom Ackerman; editor, Kent Beyda; music, Marc Marder; sound (Dolby), Russell Williams, Tod A. Maitland (N.Y.); production design, John DeCuir Jr.; art direction, Geoff Hubbard; visual consultant, Ina Mayhew; set decoration, Karen A. O'Hara, Leslie Bloom (N.Y.); makeup design, John Caglione Jr., Doug Drexler; associate producer, Howard M. Brickner; assistant director, Ellen H. Schwartz; casting, Pat Golden. Reviewed at Avco Cinema, L.A., Aug. 20, 1991. MPAA Rating: R. Running time: **93 MIN.**
Miles Pope . . . . Lenny Henry
Carver . . . . Frank Langella
Duane . . . . Charles Lane
Houston . . . . J.T. Walsh
Kristi . . . . Anne-Marie Johnson
Anthony . . . . Andreas Katsulas
Harvey Cooper . . . . Michael McKean
Rita . . . . Peggy Lipton
Grunfeld . . . . Bill Raymond
Also with: James Earl Jones, Darnell Williams, Christopher Collins, Melvin Van Peebles, Ruth Brown.

The sterling talents of comic actor Lenny Henry shine through even in the feebly formulaic context of "True Identity." Just as Peter Sellers used to do, this master of impersonation cooks up a lot of laughs where they wouldn't otherwise exist, and pretty much singlehandedly makes the picture worth a look.

There's enough lowbrow humor here to please mainstream audiences, but Disney faces a formidable marketing challenge in getting this lightweight, black-oriented, no-name farce off the ground to begin with.

Director Charles Lane emerged on the scene two years ago with the ultra-low-budget, black & white silent comedy "Sidewalk Stories," and there were serious reasons to be concerned how such an individualistic, seemingly gentle talent would fare with the Touchstone combine.

Results are mixed, to say the least, as Lane's handcrafted approach has only incidental application to the essentially silly shenanigans devised by screenwriter Andy Breckman.

Tale plunges New York actor Miles Pope (Henry), whose great dream is to play Othello, into a whirlpool of jeopardy, as he has the misfortune of learning that a pillar of the community and arts patron (Frank Langella) is actually a gangster thought to have died several years earlier.

With a hitman hot on his trail, Miles places himself in the hands of his buddy Duane (played by the director), a makeup artist who decides to protect his friend by disguising Miles as a white man. Outraged at first, Miles soon gets into it, briefly assuming different peronalities and ultmately taking on the identity of the hitman himself after he kills him in a fight.

Farcical complications ensue with increasing predictability, as Miles desperately tries to interest the FBI in the case just as he prepares for his big break in —what else? — a production of "Othello," where the theater and life conveniently merge.

Conceit is so fabricated and slight that interest in the proceedings can never rise above the mild, yet Lenny Henry's comic dexterity keeps the humor bubbling much of the time. Long a favorite on British tv via "The Lenny Henry Show," which has been seen Stateside on the Bravo cable channel, Henry played a somewhat similar part in the 1989 Oscar-winning short, "Work Experience."

Mild-mannered and sporting an impeccable American accent as the aspiring thesp, Henry erupts into flashes of brilliance when mimicking various types, both black and white, and masterfully carries off the caricature of a lowlife thug when forced to pretend to be the man hired to kill him. Henry is obviously an important talent, unusual enough to warrant the careful design of roles and vehicles for him.

Otherwise, performances are on the broad side, and Lane directs the comedy in obvious, hard-to-miss fashion. Having gone the mainstream route with his second outing after such an idiosyncratic first feature, Lane will unavoidably indicate where he's headed with his next film, which one can only hope will be rather more personal and heartfelt than this one.

Melvin Van Peebles pops in briefly as a taxi driver, a likely homage by Lane to the director of "Watermelon Man," in which the late Godfrey Cambridge portrayed a white man turned black.

James Earl Jones puts in a welcome cameo as himself. Tech credits are routine except for the witty and accomplished makeup, costume and wig work.
— *Todd McCarthy*

ATLANTIS
(FRENCH)

A Gaumont-Cecchi Cori Group Tiger co-production. Produced by Claude Besson. Directed by Luc Besson. Camera (color), Luc Besson, Christian Pétron; music, Eric Serra; sound, William Flageolet; propertymaster, Marc Biehler; 2nd unit camera, Mathieu Schiffman, Vincent Jeannot; optical engineer, François Laurent; head diver, Jean-Marc Bour; scientific & technical advisor, Pierre Labout. Reviewed at Theatre Antique d'Orange, Orange, France, Aug. 16, 1991. Running time: **80 MIN.**

Three years in the making, Luc Besson's "Atlantis" is a labor of love consisting of nothing but underwater flora and fauna with music. Sans commentary, this 80-minute travelog speaks for itself, delivering a message that the seas abound in wondrous things. Pic should soak up Gallic viewers like a sponge and impress fans of superlative underwater lensing.

Carefully planned itinerary spanning 38 months enabled Besson, cinematographer Christian Pétron and three divers to anticipate weather conditions and the presence of desired subjects in the waters of the Galapagos Islands, New Caledonia, the Seychelles Islands, Australia's Great Barrier Reef, French Polynesia, British Columbia, Florida, the Bahamas, the North Pole and the tragically depleted Red Sea.

Armed with custom-built widescreen format camera gear, crew captured crisp, evenly lit and graceful footage. Completely fluid camerawork reflects the pace of marine life, speedy or serene.

Structured in segments devoted to various marine life forms, pic contains exquisite moments such as a manta ray gliding like a rubbery stealth bomber, its tubular eye protrusions made elegant by the accompaniment of a Maria Callas aria. In a contrasting episode, the camera takes an accelerated spin through seaweed to find a group of sleek sea mammals break-dancing.

In the penultimate segment, the camera journeys through a close-walled crevice toward the blue light of polar ice formations. No life is immediately apparent in this chilly domain filmed under extremely rigorous conditions, but the textures are impressive.

Eric Serra's perfectly integrated score, a blend of composer's own synthesizer work and live sessions recorded with London's Royal Philharmonic Orchestra, ranges from thunderously visceral to quasi-classical to playful pop. Score is sometimes on the obvious side but enjoyable.

"Atlantis" makes a seamless case for the silent world that has deteriorated to a frightening extent. It demands the breadth and height of the big screen.
— *Lisa Nesselson*

BOSTON FEST

LIEBESTRAUM

A Pathe Entertainment release of an MGM presentation. An Initial production. Produced by Eric Fellner. Written and directed by Mike Figgis. Camera (Eastmancolor), Juan Ruiz Anchia; editor, Mark Hunter; music, Figgis; sound, John Pritchett; production design, Waldemar Kalinowski; assistant director, Stephen Buck; co-producer, Michael Flynn; casting, Cary Frazier, Shani Ginzburg, Deborah Brown. Reviewed at Boston Film Festival, Aug. 16, 1991. MPAA Rating: R. Running time: **102 MIN.**
In Nick Kaminsky . . Kevin Anderson
Jane Kessler . . . . Pamela Gidley
Paul Kessler . . . . Bill Pullman
Lillian Anderssen . . . . . Kim Novak
Dr. Parker . . . . . . Thomas Kopache
Mary Parker . . . . . . Catherine Hicks
Sheriff Ricker . . . . . Graham Beckel
Barnard Ralston IV . . . Zach Grenier

Writer-director Mike Figgis returns to the territory of his earlier success, "Stormy Monday," with plenty of mood but not a lot of plot. Casting of Kim Novak may attract early curiosity for "Liebestraum," but lack of a payoff will hurt word of mouth.

Pic is set in a grimy town hoping for an economic turnaround via demolition of a defunct department store and the construction of a shopping mall. The town continues to have repercussions of a murder that took place 30 years before (and shown during the opening credits). Figgis gets good use of his Binghamton, N.Y., locations, including the old building that's the focus of much of the film.

The story proper begins with the arrival of architectural writer Kevin Anderson, summoned to the bedside of his dying mother (Kim Novak) whom he has never known. While in town he runs into old college buddy Bill Pullman, who's in charge of the demolition. He soon meets Pullman's wife (Pamela Gidley), who is suffering in a sexless marriage due to hubby's playing around, and they become involved.

Figgis' problem here is the confused script, which doesn't seem to have a point. It is suggested early on that the demolition work is being sabotaged, but that line is dropped without explanation or elaboration. After a party, Anderson accepts a ride with the town's sheriff, who turns a short trip into town into the Indy 500. Other than some momentary excitement, this diversion has no reason, and the sheriff — who relieves himself on camera for an extraordinarily long time — soon fades from view.

Biggest waste here is Novak, who spends virtually the entire film bedridden and moaning her few lines. When her role in the murder is revealed, it is hardly much of a revelation.

Rest of the thesping is professional, but unmemorable. Anderson fares best in the most demanding role, but with no character development, he doesn't have much room within which to move.

Title refers to the Franz Liszt composition, played during the opening murder and again at the end, but audiences may be forgiven if they are confused as to what it all means. (Writer-director Figgis is credited with the original music score.)

— *Daniel M. Kimmel*

NO TELLING

A Glass Eye Pix presentation of a Telltale Prods. film. Produced by Rachel Horovitz. Executive producer, Larry Fessenden. Directed by Fessenden. Screenplay, Fessenden, Beck Underwood; camera (color) David Shaw; editor, Maro Chermayeff; music, Tom Laverack; sound, Piero Mura; production design, Underwood; art director, Tina Klem; costumes, Azan Kung; assistant director, Christine Le Goff; casting, Amy Herzig, Laura Rosenthal. Reviewed at Boston Film Festival, Aug. 16, 1991. No MPAA rating. Running time: **117 MIN.**
Lillian Gaines . . . Miriam Healy-Louie
Geoffrey Gaines . . . Stephen Ramsey
Alex Vine . . . . . David Van Tieghem
Philip Brown . . . . Richard Topol
Frances Boyd . . . . Ashley Arcement
Chuck Boyd . . . . Robert Brady
Martha Boyd . . . . Susan Dee

An ecologically minded drama about a wife discovering the bizarre experiments performed by her husband, "No Telling" will play well for the animal rights crowd but seems polemical and overlong for nearly everyone else.

Miriam Healy-Louie and Stephen Ramsey play the couple renting a Catskills farmhouse for the summer to have a baby and work away from the city. She wants to paint and tend to the marriage, but he becomes increasingly obsessed with his medical experiments.

He is working on something called "chemo-electrical therapy" which will permit the transplantation of entire limbs. The husband is less interested in serving humanity than in being first in line for a patent.

Enter David Van Tieghem, who is trying to convince the locals to ditch their chemicals and switch to organic farming. For the wife, he also becomes an increasingly appealing alternative to her husband.

Film isn't dull, but has several things working against it, including a tendency toward long stretches that smack of lectures. First-time feature director Larry Fessenden (who co-wrote the script with Beck Underwood), engages in overkill when he attempts to overcome the talky script with tricky camera movements. At times he apes "Blood Simple," with dollies and zooms that have no reason except to show that the camera is moving.

Film also is overlong by at least 20 minutes, and could be easily tightened to press home the climactic scene in which the full amorality of the husband's experiments is revealed. Sluggish pace of pic's second half suggests a little judicious editing may be necessary for commercial release.

Fessenden manages to avoid turning the drama into melodrama, and the occasional shock scenes of animal experimentation (which the credits assure were faked) keeps the emphasis on the story rather than gore effects. That seriousness, however, forecloses this film as entry into the horror market.

Irish born stage actress Healy-Louie makes her film debut here with considerable presence. Tech credits are fine, with Fessenden establishing a nice foreboding mood early on by noting details like the boxes marked "rat guillotines" in the laboratory.

— *Daniel M. Kimmel*

MONTREAL FEST

RAMBLING ROSE

A Seven Arts release through New Line Cinema of a Midnight Sun Pictures production. Produced by Renny Harlin. Executive producers, Mario Kassar, Edgar Scherick. Directed by Martha Coolidge. Screenplay, Calder Willingham, based on his novel; camera (Duart & Deluxe color; Technicolor prints), Johnny Jensen; editor, Steven Cohen; music, Elmer Bernstein; sound (Dolby), Richard Van Dyke; production design, John Vallone; costume design, Jane Robinson; production manager, Mary E. Kane; assistant director, Randall Badger; casting, Aleta Chapelle. Reviewed at Magno Review 1 screening room, N.Y., July 29, 1991. (In Telluride, Boston, Montreal and Toronto film fests.) MPAA Rating: R. Running time: **113 MIN.**
Rose . . . . Laura Dern
Daddy . . . . Robert Duvall
Mother . . . . Diane Ladd
Buddy . . . . Lukas Haas
Willcox Hillyer . . . . John Heard
Dr. Martinson . . . . Kevin Conway
Dave Wilkie . . . . Robert Burke
Doll . . . . Lisa Jakub
Waski . . . . Evan Lockwood
Billy . . . . Matt Sutherland

Calder Willingham's memoir of the South "Rambling Rose" allows a talented ensemble to deliver the year's best screen acting so far. Funny and moving tale of an oversexed young woman will attract class auds after its film fest exposure and has the potential to cross over to mainstream hit status.

It is difficult to conjure up another actress to embody Rose better than Laura Dern, whose tall, angular figure and striking (rather than beautiful) face under a row of curls personifies the naive title character.

She's a girl from the wrong side of the tracks who starts her life over as maid to the family of Robert Duvall and Diane Ladd in a small Georgia town in 1935. Rose is under a cloud, and it turns out that rumors of her having been forced into prostitution at a tender age are true.

Both Duvall and his 13-year-old son Lukas Haas are immediately taken by Dern's raw sexuality, yet it is the boy who nearly has his first conquest with her when Dern innocently gets in bed with him one night in a funny and risqué scene.

Duvall is a proper gentleman, rejecting Dern's attempt at seduction and quickly adopting a fatherly concern for her. Family matriarch Ladd (Dern's real-life mom), is a Yankee educated at Columbia U. who also takes Dern under her wing and defends the girl under all circumstances.

Main source of conflict is Dern's promiscuous activities, which cause young men to loiter outside the house at all hours. This brings Duvall no end of grief in dealing with his uncontrollable charge.

Film climaxes in a classic scene involving Dern's future following her pregnancy scare that turns out to be an illness. Duvall and a stern Yankee doctor (terrifically played by Kevin Conway) come to a gentleman's agreement that a radical hysterectomy will end her loose ways. When Ladd stands up for the girl's rights, eliciting an apology and emotional turnaround from

Duvall, the film's main themes have been driven home with uncommon force and precision.

Pic is bookended by scenes of John Heard in 1971 portraying Haas grown to middle age, recalling the story and learning of Rose's fate from his aged father. Device is film's weakest link but does not detract from the power of the main footage.

Dern's naturalness in a very eccentric role confirms the promise of her earlier work and makes Rose one of the most memorable characters in recent cinema. Duvall and Ladd play off each other to perfection, with Duvall maximizing all the humor inherent in author Willingham's odd turns of phrase.

The wide-eyed innocence and curiosity Haas brings to his rites-of-passage assignment are remarkable and help avoid the potential tastelessness in Dern's "robbing the cradle" scene with him. As his younger siblings, Lisa Jakub and Evan Lockwood also are affecting.

Director Martha Coolidge and her technical crew have re-created the detail and texture of Southern life with great feeling, filming this Carolco-financed picture at Carolco's Wilmington, N.C., studio (formerly owned by defunct De Laurentiis Entertainment Group). Like "Driving Miss Daisy," this quaint setting allows moral issues to be developed with subtlety rather than the inevitable didactic approach of a modern story.

Elmer Bernstein's warm musical accompaniment is a key asset to the film, but Nat King Cole's '60s pop hit "Rambling Rose" is not used on the soundtrack.

Depending on the impact of the year-end releases, "Rambling Rose" stands a good chance of being remembered come awards time. Pic had its world premiere Aug. 22 as the opening night selection at the Montreal Film Fest. — *Lawrence Cohn*

LOCARNO FEST

OBLAKO-RAI
(CLOUD-PARADISE)
(SOVIET)

A Kinostudia 12-A production. (Intl. sales: Kinostudia 12-A, Moscow.) Directed by Nikolai Dostal. Screenplay, Georgi Nikolaev; camera (color), Yuri Nevski; editor, Maria Sergeyeva; music, Aleksandr Goldstein; song, Andrei Zhigalov; sound, Valentin Bobrovski; art director, Aleksei Aksenev; costume de-sign, Natalya Lichmanova. Reviewed at 44th Locarno Intl. Film Festival (competing), Aug. 12, 1991. Running time: **79 MIN.**
Kolya . . . . Andrei Zhigalov
Fyodr . . . . Sergei Batalov
Valya . . . . Irina Rozanova
Natalya . . . . Alla Klyuka
Tatyana . . . . . . Anna Ovsyannikova

An absurdist comedy about a smalltown nobody who becomes a somebody when he decides to head east, "Cloud-Paradise" is a refreshing antidote to some of the grim Soviet product doing the fest rounds. Slim vignette is good for some chuckles and never overstays its welcome.

An easygoing dummy (Andrei Zhigalov) drops in on a couple one day and, just to kill the boredom, suddenly announces he's leaving town — "all the way to the Pacific Ocean," he says. This immediately reaches the parts other conversation cannot reach, and from then on he becomes the toast of the community.

Babushkas who used to give him the brush-off now deign to talk to him. Friends gather for an instant party and start stripping his apartment. Even the frigid girl of his dreams (Alla Klyuka) melts a little. Meanwhile, the removal men start taking the furniture away.

Caught up in his own fiction, the simpleton has no choice but to go for broke. As the locals send him off with a musical parade through the streets, the bus arrives to transport him God knows where. Pic ends with the small community disappearing over the horizon and the traveler, alone in the bus, still bemused by his sudden popularity.

As a low-key satire on Russian provincialism, the film hits its mark with ease. Zhigalov, who also penned and sings the title song, plays Kolya with an Oliver Hardy-like easy charm, and he's supported by strong down-the-line playing, especially Sergei Batalov and Irina Rozanova as the bored couple.

Helmer Nikolai Dostal, in his fourth pic, gently exaggerates the townsfolk in close-up compositions without letting the comedy get out of hand. A long opening aerial track gives a nice idea of the small suburb's isolation, and several other sequences have an almost fairy tale, magical flavor. Tech credits are fine, with color processing acceptable.
— *Derek Elley*

HINTER VERSCHLOS-SENEN TÜREN
(BEHIND LOCKED DOORS)
(GERMAN-SWISS)

A Deutsche Film & Fernsehakademie Berlin-Mano Film production. (Intl. sales: DFFB, Berlin.) Directed by Anka Schmid. Screenplay, Schmid, Tania Stöcklin; camera (b&w, 16m), Ciro Cappellari; editor, Inge Schneider; music, Stefan Schiske, Klaus Wagner; sound, Sabine Hillmann, Jan Ralske; art director, Dea Hollman. Reviewed at 44th Locarno Intl. Film Festival (New Swiss Films section), Aug. 12, 1991. Running time: **78 MIN.**
With: Hans Madin, Walter Pfeil, Maria Fitzi, Susanne Fitzner, Jockel Tschiersch, Aline Krayewski.

A patchwork portrait of 17 occupants of an apartment block, "Behind Locked Doors" gets by on the strength of its perfs and sly sense of humor. Diploma work of Swiss-born Anka Schmid, 30, is perfect festival material.

Pic starts with long, atmospheric tracks through an unnamed German city, finally settling on the block in question. Characters are introed one by one, and gradually an overall picture emerges of the varied tenants.

There's precocious brat Paula, who sticks her chewing gum under the banisters; her edgy young mother and stepfather; a family with two pubescent daughters; wheelchair-bound Maria; an old couple with a spoiled pooch; wistful aunt Hannelore; black teacher Bona, who shares an apartment with a gay writer; and aging photog Kempinski who pores over photo albums.

It's Kempinski who finally gets everyone together to celebrate his 80th birthday, when he shows a film of old Berlin. Pic ends with him kicking the bucket.

There's an easy, relaxed pace to the film that gives the material a likable quality. Helmer Schmid looks ready for more ambitious feature assignments on the strength of this, and shows a good grasp of composition and pacing.

Occasional use of music is atmospheric, notably in a dreamlike montage based around the invalided Maria clicking some castanets in her wheelchair.
— *Derek Elley*

JACQUES & FRANÇOISE
(SWISS-FRENCH)

A Les Prods. JMH-Télévision Suisse Romande-Les Films du Phare production. (Intl. sales: JMH, Lausanne.) Produced by Jean-Marc Henchoz, Sylvette Frydman. Directed by Francis Reusser. Screenplay, Reusser, Emmanuelle de Riedmatten, based on the theatrical entertainment "Pauvre Jacques" by Carlo Boller (music), Fernand Ruffieux (book); camera (Kodak color), Joël David; editor, Sophie Cornu; music adaptation, Louis Crelier; sound (Dolby), François Musy, Marc Antoine Beldent; art director, Ivan Nicklass. Reviewed at 44th Locarno Intl. Film Festival (New Swiss Films section), Aug. 9, 1991. Running time: **81 MIN.**
With: François Florey, Geneviève Pasquier, Roland Amstutz, Michel Voïta.

"Jacques & Françoise" is a dirndl-and-breeches Swiss musical that won't ring many bells beyond the Alps. Period tale of a cowhand in love with a rich man's daughter is strictly for curio-seekers.

By-the-numbers story, set in 1788, has Jacques (François Florey) warbling in the meadows to Françoise (Geneviève Pasquier), whose father owns the local pasture. Dad gets Jacques carted off to milk the cows at the court of Versailles, thus clearing the way for a Swiss guard to marry his daughter. But when the Bastille falls, and the aristocrats flee, Jacques gets his freedom — and his girl.

Pic's ingenuous tone could have worked with a lighter touch, but most of it plays like Jacques Demy with a hangover. Former Swiss tv lenser Francis Reusser produces one decorative but unexciting visual after another, and Carlo Boller's score, pitched somewhere between Mozart and Michel Legrand, lacks harmonic and melodic character.

Variable color and obvious matte work cut the work off at the knees. A framing device of showing the piece shot as a movie is simply cute. Leads Florey and Pasquier (dubbed in the songs) are both pretty.

Pic is based on a *jeu scénique* produced in 1948, with a mixture of dialog and songs. Present version was shot in story's actual location of La Gruyère.
— *Derek Elley*

VISAGES SUISSES
(FACES OF SWITZERLAND)
(SWISS-DOCU)

A Vidéo Films production. (Intl. sales: Vidéo Films/Incoprom, Geneva.) Produced by Claude Richardet. Directed by Francis Reusser, Matteo Bellinelli, Simon Edelstein, Nicolas Gessner, Kurt Gloor, Claude Goretta, Thomas Koerfer, Pierre Koralnik, Urs Odermatt, François Reichenbach, Hans-Ulrich Schlumpf, Victor Tognola, Jacqueline Veuve. Screenplay, Richardet; camera (Kodak color), Bruno Lapostolle, Pio Corradi, Carlo Varini, Martin Fuhrer, Patrick Lindenmaier, Patrice Cologne; in Dolby. Reviewed at 44th Locarno Intl. Film Festival, Aug. 10, 1991. Running time: **98 MIN.**
(various languages; French subtitles)

A collection of 17 short segs that just escapes being a promo for the Swiss tourist board, "Faces Of Switzerland" casts an often quizzical eye over Europe's most self-absorbed and inward-looking country. Presence of w.k. helmers like Claude Goretta, François Reichenbach and Nicolas Gessner among the credits could stir mild foreign interest.

Linked by an overcute device of a moppet and her grandfather traveling by train through the country, the five-minute portraits each feature a local personality or figure.

Best are Kurt Gloor's send-up of a group of modern-day William Tells; Reichenbach's interview with a male dancer with some pointed remarks on the country; Goretta's hands-off look at Switzerland's first female mountain guide; Matteo Bellinelli's witty video diary of two Japanese girl tourists; and Simon Edelstein's sarcastic portrait of a Swiss businessman in Brazil.

Made to celebrate the 700th anni of the Swiss Confederation, docu looks and sounds good in 35m and Dolby Stereo. But beyond specialized outings, its true audience will be on the tube. Trimming by about 15 minutes would help. — *Derek Elley*

LATE FOR DINNER

A Columbia release of a Castle Rock Entertainment presentation in association with New Line Cinema of a Granite Pictures production. Produced by Dan Lupovitz, W.D. Richter. Directed by Richter. Screenplay, Mark Andrus; camera (Deluxe color; CFI prints), Peter Sova; editor, Richard Chew, Robert Leighton; music, David Mansfield; sound (Dolby), Art Rochester; production design, Lilly Kilvert; art direction, Scott Harris; set decoration, Rosemary Brandenburg; costume design, Aggie Guerard Rodgers; key makeup, Steve La-Porte; assistant director, Katterli Frauenfelder; co-producer, Gary Daigler; casting, Terry Liebling. Reviewed at Filmland screening room, Culver City, Calif., Aug. 23, 1991. (In Montreal Film Festival, noncompeting). MPAA Rating: PG. Running time: **92 MIN.**

Willie Husband	Brian Wimmer
Frank Lovegren	Peter Berg
Joy Husband	Marcia Gay Harden
Jessica Husband	Colleen Flynn
Leland Shakes	Kyle Secor
Dr. David Arrington	Michael Beach
Bob Freeman	Peter Gallagher
Little Jessica Husband	Cassy Friel
Little Donald Freeman	Ross Malinger
Dwane Gardener	Steven Schwartz-Hartley
Officer Tom Bostich	John Prosky
Dr. Dan Chilblains	Bo Brundin
Dr. Chris Underwood	Donald Hotton

Yet another tale about time travel and the transcendent power of love, "Late For Dinner" lays on the whimsicality with a trowel. After the initial promise of the early, quirky scenes, pic lapses into tiresome metaphysical vaudeville with a predictable emotional hook. Columbia release from Castle Rock is a marginal entry both critically and commercially.

Twist of this first produced screenplay by Mark Andrus — and W. D. Richter's first directorial outing since "The Adventures Of Buckaroo Banzai" seven years ago — lies in looking seriously at the emotional ramifications of jumping through time.

Unfortunately, the great majority of the modest running time is occupied by unfunny character comedy and silly digressions relating to cultural dislocation, so that when the dramatic hammer is lowered, the effect is artificial and uninvolving.

Offbeat prolog, which features the best timing and compositions in the picture, introduces Willie (Brian Wimmer), a solid, responsible young fellow, and his slow, earnest brother-in-law Frank (Peter Berg).

It is 1962, and the two are making their way through the desert from Sante Fe to Southern California after Willie has been shot in a ludicrous altercation stemming from a nasty real estate transaction and an alleged kidnaping.

Seeking treatment in Pomona, the pair instead get a heavy dose of cryonics from some local medics, which puts them in a deep freeze for 29 years. Upon thawing out, the buddies stumble into the audio blare and visual blight of downtown Los Angeles, 1991, take note of the high prices at a fast food restaurant and instantly long to return to the sleepy serenity of old Santa Fe.

Once back, however, the still-boyish Willie must confront the fact that his wife Joy (Marcia Gay Harden) is now in her 50s, and that their daughter Jessica (Colleen Flynn) has grown into womanhood not knowing him.

Jessica somehow manages to accept the notion of her long-lost father's return with reasonable composure, but Joy has a lot more trouble dealing with it. After giving up on Willie in the wake of his sudden disappearance, she married, then divorced someone else, and is now involved with another man.

Railing against the indecency of it all, Joy resists the man she's always loved for the longest time until the inevitable feelings take over.

Richter gives equal weight to both the fanciful and serious aspects of the script, but he can't push such flimsy material convincingly in either direction, resulting in a picture that's neither highly comic nor emotionally convulsive. Most scenes are flat two-character affairs, and the extended banter between Willie and his childlike companion grow increasingly tedious as matters progress.

With both Wimmer and Berg wearing out their welcome long before fadeout, and offering no star voltage in the bargain, interest falls naturally to the women in the film's final third. Looking good under 50ish make-up, Harden tries to make sense of a character that's supplied with no dramatic preparation for the climactic histrionics. Flynn comes off best as the grownup Jessica, the abandoned daughter who learned how to cope.

Film has a very small, sometimes threadbare feel, and ultimately plays into the story's, and the audience's, most sentimental instincts.

— *Todd McCarthy*

LIVIN' LARGE

A Samuel Goldwyn Co. presentation of a David V. Picker/WMG Pictures production. Produced by David V. Picker. Directed by Michael Schultz. Screenplay, William M. Payne; camera (Crest color), Peter Collister; editor, Christopher Holmes; music, Herbie Hancock; soundtrack coordinator, Faith Newman; sound (Dolby), Shirley Libby; costume design, John Dunn; art direction, Angie Riserbato; set decoration, Penny Barrett; line producer-unit production manager, Derek Kavanagh; assistant director, Victoria E. Rhodes. Reviewed at Samuel Goldwyn Pavilion theater, L.A., Aug. 22, 1991. MPAA rating: R. Running time: **96 MIN.**

Dexter	Terrence (T.C.) Carson
Toynelle Davis	Lisa Arrindell
Kate Penndragin	Blanche Baker
Baker Moon	Nathaniel (Afrika) Hall
Missy Carnes	Julia Campbell
Clifford Worthy	Bernie McInerney
Nadine Biggs	Loretta Devine
Martin	Dan Albright

Yo, man, here's a story about a brother on the way up who finds that livin' large in the white man's world means sellin' the only real thing you got — your soul. Goldwyn pickup is likely to do okay short-term biz based on fresh star appeal and engaging comic style.

Crossover potential, however, is slight as director Michael Schultz and writer William Mosley Payne's high-spirited comic fable about the wages of ambition winds up betraying its target audience via reverse racism and pandering.

T.C. Carson makes his film debut as young Atlanta homeboy Dexter Jackson, who ditches his job at a dry cleaner's for a career in tv news. He gets his break when he stumbles on a crime scene where a reporter has been shot, whereupon he picks up the fallen mike and resumes the report.

His energy and on-the-fly resourcefulness catch the eye of a crass, ratings-mad producer (Blanche Baker), who offers him a coveted slot on the news team and begins re-molding him for success. Clothes, car, tv exposure all seem like a dream come true until the pressure to succeed leads tv's new "Man About Town" to sell out himself and every friend he's got.

As a cautionary tale, pic is on the simplistic side, apparently aimed at an audience seg that wants to be reassured about the evils of ambition. Its negative stereotyping of whites as vacuous, power-hungry, sold-out careerists (who can't dance, to boot) serves no good purpose.

Also unsettling is its uneven take on the values that corrupt the tv news. White news execs are shown as ridiculously callous and self-serving, but Dexter's a hero when he steps over a corpse to further his own career. Pandering to a youthful audience for whom looks and celebrity are everything, pic seems to say that cute Dexter can rap with a mike, he's on tv, and that's where it's at. His vanity and callow self-centeredness are celebrated. Only when he starts to turn "white" is it a problem.

Pic's regressive themes separate it from the current wave of black films, as do poor and uneven lighting and film quality in the Atlanta-lensed production.

Still, pic has a loose, comfortable, infectious spirit that serves it well as a comedy vehicle. Nathaniel (Afrika) Hall, playing Dexter's main man Baker Moon, makes a likable tour guide of his friend's misadventures, and comic actress Loretta Devine as the newsman's feisty sister adds a lot of tang.

Carson makes an appealing debut as the newshound, playing both the polished pro and the scamming homeboy with aplomb. — Amy Dawes

TALENT FOR THE GAME

A Paramount Pictures release of a Martin Elfand production. Produced by Elfand. Executive producer, David Wisnievitz. Directed by Robert M. Young. Screenplay, David Himmelstein, Tom Donnelly, Larry Ferguson; camera (Technicolor), Curtis Clark; editor, Arthur Coburn; music, David Newman; sound (Dolby), Hank Garfield; production design, Jeffrey Howard; art direction, Keith Burns; costume design, Erica Edell Phillips; assistant director, Marty Eli Schwartz; production manager, Wisnievitz; casting, Mindy Marin. Reviewed on Paramount vidcassette, N.Y., Aug. 24, 1991. MPAA Rating: PG. Running time: **91 MIN.**
Virgil Sweet . . Edward James Olmos
Bobbie . . . . Lorraine Bracco
Tim Weaver . . . . . . Jamey Sheridan
Gil Lawrence . . . . Terry Kinney
Sammy Bodeen . . . . . . Jeff Corbett
Rev. Bodeen . . . . Tom Bower
Rachel Bodeen . . . . . . Janet Carroll
Fred . . . . Felton Perry
Paul . . . . Thomas Ryan

Paramount's baseball pic is an entertaining sports drama distrib tested in Florida last April with no further bookings. Pic will definitely please paycable and homevid fans.

Similar projects have long been in the works. From 1980 through 1983, 20th Century Fox developed "The Scout" for Peter Falk to star as the discoverer of a Fernando Valenzuela-type pitcher. By '89, that unrealized project had become a joint venture of Fox and Orion, to star Rodney Dangerfield and Sam Kinison, also never made.

This version takes a somewhat more serious tack, no surprise since filmmaker Robert M. Young and his frequent star Edward James Olmos favor pictures with something to say. Olmos is comfortably, nonethnically cast as a scout for the California Angels whose job is being eliminated.

New billionaire owner of the club (oily Terry Kinney) is doing away with the tradition of field scouts to save money. Olmos' last chance is to sign a phenom and earn a front office job.

When his car goes kaput during a drive with g.f. (and club exec) Lorraine Bracco, Olmos lucks into seeing a sandlot game in Idaho where 20-year-old Jeff Corbett is throwing amazing pitches. After a struggle with the boy's parents, Olmos takes him west to sign with the Angels.

Familiar story is as old as a Joe E. Brown baseball comedy or a boxing saga like "Kid Galahad," but Young invests the proceedings with infectious small-scale heroism. Evil Kinney forces the kid to immediately start in the majors as a publicity stunt. Olmos loses his cushy new job when he stands up for the boy's rights. Bracco quits in solidarity.

Film's climax is fanciful, but finale's clever irony sets it apart from more sentimental genre pics, such as the current indie release "Pastime." Olmos and Bracco do well with standard roles, as does tv star Jamey Sheridan as the equivocal buffer between them and the owner.

Corbett, who bears a striking resemblance to Paramount's recent wannabe karate star Jeff Speakman, is quite convincing as the fireballing pitcher. Tech credits are solid down the line. — Lawrence Cohn

ONE HAND DON'T CLAP
(DOCU)

A Rhapsody Films presentation of a Riverfilms production. Produced by Kavery Dutta, Bhupender Kaul. Directed by Dutta. Camera (Duart color), Don Lenzer, Alicia Weber; editor, Dutta; sound (Dolby), Nigel Noble, Peter Miller; production associate, Alicia Adams. Reviewed Aug. 21, 1991 at Magno Review 1, N.Y. Running time: **92 MIN.**
With: Lord Kitchener, Calypso Rose, Black Stalin, David Rudder, Mighty Duke, Natasha Wilson, Lord Pretender, Growling Tiger.

The calypso music in "One Hand Don't Clap" is engaging, but it can't compensate for this docu's routine concert footage. Producer/director/editor Kavery Dutta lets the performances and interviews run on too long. Item will appeal primarily to calypso fanatics.

Pic centers on prominent calypsonians Lord Kitchener and Calypso Rose. In one interview, Kitchener says, "I live for calypso." It shows. Singer, now in his 70s, still performs with tremendous energy and enthusiasm.

Calypso Rose is equally charismatic, whether singing and dancing during Carnival in Trinidad or posing for an album cover by the ocean. Two of the most interesting segments show her composing and recording a song called "Terrorism Gone Wild."

Made in 1988, docu also provides a taste of soca (soul calypso). Toward the end, the focus is shifted to three young singers in a climactic but uninvolving concert competition. As in the other concert scenes, the camerawork includes too many closeups and too few long shots, and the somewhat blurry images don't capture the show's excitement.

By contrast, the old clips of Kitchener in England during the '50s are crisp and clear. Both his and Calypso Rose's bios are high points. But for some reason, best footage and most exuberant music is saved for the credit sequence. Even though pic focuses on calypso, not Carnival, closing shots of the parade (where spectacular costumes are on display) are more vivid than anything else in the film. After the long, awkwardly filmed performances, viewers will wish they were attending a live show — or, better yet, Carnival in Trinidad. — William Stevenson

CHILD'S PLAY 3

A Universal Pictures release of a David Kirschner production. Executive producer, Kirschner. Produced by Robert Latham Brown. Directed by Jack Bender. Screenplay by Don Mancini, based on his characters; camera (Deluxe color), John R. Leonetti; supervising editor, Edward Warschilka; editor, Edward A. Warschilka Jr., Scott Wallace; music, Cory Lerios, John D'Andrea; sound (Dolby), David Ronne; production design, Richard Sawyer; costumes, Colby Bart; assistant director, Richard Peter Schroer; production manager, David Sosna; Chucky doll creator, Kirschner; Chucky design & engineering, Kevin Yagher; special makeup effects, Craig Reardon; optical effects, Apogee Prods.-supervisor, Roger Dorney; co-produc-

er, Laura Moskowitz; casting, Glenn Daniels. Reviewed at Universal screening room, N.Y., Aug. 27, 1991. MPAA Rating: R. Running time: **89 MIN.**
Andy Barclay . . . . . . Justin Whalin
De Silva . . . . Perrey Reeves
Tyler . . . . Jeremy Sylvers
Shelton . . . . Travis Fine
Whitehurst . . . . Dean Jacobson
Voice of Chucky . . . . . . Brad Dourif
Sullivan . . . . Peter Haskell
Col. Cochrane . . . . . Dakin Matthews
Sgt. Botnick . . . . . Andrew Robinson
Sgt. Clark . . . . Burke Byrnes

Foul-mouthed killer doll Chucky returns in this noisy, mindless sequel, well-positioned to scarf down strong attendance prior to the release of the latest "Nightmare On Elm Street" pic.

Universal, which inherited the profitable series from United Artists after wannabe studio owners Qintex nixed the first sequel two years ago, has got the genre goods in a period of few major horror releases.

Young protagonist Andy, previously played by Alex Vincent, is now a 16-year-old personified by handsome Justin Whalin. First reel prolog is devoted to venal businessman Peter Haskell starting up production on the Good Guy dolls eight years after the factory catastrophe limned in "Child's Play 2."

First doll off the assembly line is Chucky, possessed by the spirit of dead murderer Brad Dourif (who again ably voices the creature's wisecracks). Doll kills Haskell, setting the tone with his rhyming line "Don't ---- with the Chuck!"

Chucky tracks grown-up Whalin to a military school, has himself mailed there and then becomes obsessed with transferring his spirit to a pint-sized black cadet, Jeremy Sylvers. Other than his line "Chucky's gonna be a bro'," there's no logic to this ploy by scripter Don Mancini, whose main job this time out is to keep Chucky in the doll body for pic's duration.

A promising plotline stipulates the military academy be co-ed, with Perrey Reeves, a feisty young Jamie Lee Curtis type, bonding quickly with hero Whalin. Unfortunately, this device simply results in would-be pathos out of "Taps," as Chucky perversely reloads the cadets' guns with live ammunition for a war games segment.

Finale pointlessly takes place at a nearby amusement park, shifting "Child's Play 3" into a funhouse ride crassly aimed at potential spinoff into a U studio tour attraction. Expensive-looking production values here and in the main Missouri military school shoot give the fans their money's worth at least.

Fine doll effects and sporadic gore are par for the genre. Acting is good, with honors going to the original "Dirty Harry" nemesis, Andrew Robinson, amusing as the school's obsessive barber.

— *Lawrence Cohn*

SHOWDOWN IN LITTLE TOKYO

A Warner Bros. release of a Mark L. Lester/Martin E. Caan production. Produced by Lester, Caan. Directed by Lester. Screenplay, Stephen Glantz, Caliope Brattlestreet; camera (Technicolor), Mark Irwin; editor, Steven Kemper, Robert A. Ferretti; music, David Michael Frank; sound (Dolby), Mike LeMare; production design, Craig Stearns; art direction, Bill Rae; set decoration, Ellen Totleben; costume design, Robyn Smith; 2nd unit director-stunt coordinator, Terry J. Leonard; assistant directors, Joel Segal, Eric P. Jones; co-producer, John Broderick; casting, Michelle Guillerman. Reviewed at Mann Chinese Theater, Hollywood, Aug. 23, 1991. MPAA Rating: R. Running time: **76 MIN.**
Detective Kenner . . Dolph Lundgren
Johnny Murata . . . . . . Brandon Lee
Yoshida . . . . Carey-Hiroyuki Tagawa
Minako . . . . Tia Carrere
Sato . . . . Toshiro Obata

Dolph Lundgren continues to squander his potential as a major action star by appearing in shoddily produced vehicles. "Showdown In Little Tokyo's" subpar production values should limit the kickfest's appeal to martial arts enthusiasts and desperate-for-action homevid renters.

Thus, what could have spit some b.o. fire likely will go out like a wet blanket, even with distrib's marketing hook of pairing Lundgren with Bruce Lee's son, Brandon.

Story is all by-the-numbers revenge stuff, although screenplay skips a lot of numbers, the better to focus on nonstop and generally unimaginative action sequences. Once again, the Japanese mafia (or yakuza) provide the cardboard cutout villains for the good guys to knock over. Lundgren, whose parents top mobster Carey-Hiroyuki Tagawa sliced and diced during his boyhood, plays a raised-in-Japan supercop. Lee is his preppy, comic-relief Eurasian partner.

The towering Lundgren remains a striking presence visually, and the filmmakers seek to capitalize on it by showing him

shirtless, sleeveless and pantsless whenever possible.

Unfortunately, they undermine his stoic grit with at-times numbingly stupid scripting and direction, dressing him up like an oversized sushi chef (complete with matching headband) for the final confrontation.

Lundgren can hold his own with other action leads as an actor and could easily be Van Damme-marketable if only he'd devote as much attention to quality control as he does to pectoral development.

Several action sequences end up murkily shot in night settings, a sure sign of trying to hide budget and production deficiencies. Editing also proves choppy, with some seemingly out-of-sequence cuts and just plain silly ones, as the nubile femme lead (Tia Carrere) at one point shares a hot tub with Lundgren before demurely bedding him.

Lee, making his U.S. feature debut, has a gee-whiz delivery that seems plucked from another film. Still, there's some charisma here and a definite fighting flair waiting to be tapped by hands more able than those of director-producer Mark L. Lester and his screenwriters here.

Other tech credits are at best okay, with a solid synthesized score by David Michael Frank and the requisite crackling sound effects — the kind normally accompanied by high-pitched howls and out-of-synch dubbing.

— *Brian Lowry*

LOCARNO FEST

JOHNNY SUEDE

A Vega Films production in association with Balthazar Pictures, Arena Films, Starr Pictures. (Intl. sales: Mainstream, Paris.) Produced by Yoram Mandel, Ruth Waldburger. Executive producers, Waldburger, Steven Starr. Written and directed by Tom DiCillo; camera (color), Joe DeSalvo; editor, Geraldine Peroni; music, Jim Farmer; additional music, Link Wray; sound, Dominick Tavella; production design, Patricia Woodbrige; costumes, Jessica Haston; co-producers, Alain Klarer, Bruno Pesery, Janet Jacobson; casting, Marcia Shulman. Reviewed at 44th Locarno Intl. Film Festival, Aug. 17, 1991. (Also in Toronto and Deauville film festivals.) Running time: **95 MIN.**
Johnny . . . . Brad Pitt
Deke . . . . Calvin Levels
Darlette . . . . Alison Moir
Yvonne . . . . Catherine Keener
Mrs. Fontaine . . . . . . Tina Louise
Freak Storm . . . . Nick Cave

If Locarno's Golden Leop-

ard Award and the enthusiastic reception of the young audiences there is any indication, Tom DiCillo's easily likable first film augurs the presence of a new contender on New York's cult film scene.

Taking place in an imaginary slum that could be on the outskirts of any east coast metropolis (pic actually was shot in New York), DiCillo's gently ironic fantasy focuses on a dreamy young man who rejects reality and, after a pair of suede shoes is literally dropped on his head, adopts the name Johnny Suede and sets out to be a pop star, using the late Ricky Nelson as his model.

Sporting a ridiculous pompadour and flashy costumes, he is innocence incarnate, viewing life as the reflection of the soulful ballads his idol used to sing and which he tries his best to copy. With his friend Deke (Calvin Levels), he hopes to put together a band, but until that happens, they paint apartments.

In the best pop ballad tradition, Johnny starts a tentative affair with pretty young Alison Moir, who lives nearby with an older, abusive photographer. She's sweet, but Johnny is attracted to her also because her mother produces records for a big diskery. His dream fades once she decides she prefers rough treatment to Johnny's naive romancing.

On the rebound, he reluctantly picks up a tutor of retarded children (Catherine Keener), and under her guidance he starts on the journey that will land him with both feet on the ground. As the film ends, it's still not evident the journey has been completed, but with Johnny's pompadour ruffled and his clothes in disarray, it looks like his life is bound to change.

A modest but polished production, pic features Buñuelesque dream sequences, Godardian elliptical montage and a hero as detached from real life as Fellini's Gelsomina or Cabiria, with DiCillo cheerfully conceding the impact those classic filmmakers had on him.

One-time cameraman ("Stranger Than Paradise," "Variety"), DiCillo exploits pastel colors to advantage in order to flesh out Johnny's fantasy world, and the careful choice of locations offers, in contrast, desolate landscapes of decaying neighborhoods, crumbling buildings and rotting junkyards, which Johnny doesn't even seem to notice.

Brad Pitt, fresh from stealing scenes in "Thelma & Louise," gives Johnny the right kind of innocent appeal, and the rest of the cast surround him with loving care. Nick Cave, walking in and out of the picture as pop idol Freak Storm, is, if anything, the satirical image of Johnny's dream come true. The offbeat humor of DiCillo's script does not hinder his sympathy for the characters. Even if he doesn't take them seriously, it doesn't really matter. After all, this is a fantasy.

— *Dan Fainaru*

ANNA GOLDIN, LETZTE HEXE
(ANNA GOLDIN, THE LAST WITCH)
(SWISS-GERMAN-FRENCH)

A Columbus presentation of an Alpha Film (Munich), P&P Film (Solothurn) production, co-produced with Hexatel (Paris), TVE (Madrid), SRG (Zurich), Bayerische Rundfunk. Directed by Gertrude Pinkus. Screenplay, Pinkus, Evelin Hasler, Stephan Portmann, based on novel by Hasler; camera (color), Fritz Rath; music, Sine Nomine; sound, Gerard Rueff, Jurg von Allmen; art directors, Kathryn Brunner, Frank Geuer; costumes, Greti Klay; production manager, Reinhild Graber. Reviewed at 44th Locarno Intl. Film Festival, Aug. 14, 1991. Running time: **110 MIN.**
Anna Goldin . . . . . Cornelia Kempers
Dr. Tschudi . . . . . . Rudiger Vogler
Anne-Miggeli Tschudi . . . . Luca Kurt Kubli . . . . . . Dominique Horwitz
Steinmuller . . . . Dimitri
Jeanneret . . . . Roger Jaendly
Camerarius . . . . Pinkas Braun

Despite the best intentions, an academic and unimaginative piece such as "Anna Goldin, The Last Witch" has little chance to go much further than educational television, once it steps out of its own turf.

Depicting a w.k. episode in 18th century Swiss history, Gertrude Pinkus erroneously thinks she can dissimulate her hesitant approach behind Alpine sunrises and sunsets and spectacular mountain scenery.

Anna Goldin, a maid for Dr. Tschudi in the city of Glarus, was accused of feeding metal pins to the doctor's little daughter, and using her wiles to cripple the girl after being fired.

Chased and apprehended, she was brought back to Glarus, where she managed to heal the patient but to no avail. She was tortured and made to confess a number of imaginary sins. Brought to trial, she was condemned to death, but the sentence carefully avoided mentioning witchcraft, to spare the townspeople the scorn of other Swiss.

Proceeding ponderously, never really interesting but always correct, pic offers no insights into the characters or their motivation beyond the obvious, preferring to deal with facts only, and refraining from comments or interpretations.

Pic attempts to place the incident in a larger context by juxtaposing the witchcraft trial with the breakthrough of industry and commerce, an indication that Swiss were far more diligent in business than in ethics.

There are also hints that internal politics of the Swiss cantons might have had a hand in the court's final decision, and mention is made of the impending revolution about to erupt across the border in France. But in all these cases, the allusions are made in an obvious, heavy-handed manner.

Arbitrary editing prevents scenes from being fully explored, brusquely cutting away in order to move the plot from one piece of information to another. Direction of actors is clumsily stagy, all of them overacting.

Even a seasoned performer such as Rudiger Vogler, one of the best contemporary actors in German-lingo films, is unable to transcend the limits of caricature. — *Dan Fainaru*

IMMER & EWIG
(ALWAYS & FOREVER)
(SWISS)

A Dschoint Ventschr-Videoladen production. (Intl. sales: Megaherz/Videoladen, Zurich.) Directed by Samir. Screenplay, Samir, Martin Witz; camera (color), Samir, René Baumann; editor, Ronnie Wahli; music, the Young Gods; sound, Felix Singer; sound design, Peter Bräker; art director, Monika Schmid; Urs Beuter; costume design, Schmid; assistant director, Danielle Giuliani. Reviewed at 44th Locarno Intl. Film Festival (New Swiss Films section), Aug. 8, 1991. (Also in Toronto Film Festival.) Running time: **88 MIN.**
With: Oliver Broumis, Nicole Ansari, Stefan Stutzer, Heidi Züger.
(German dialog)

A modern version of the Orpheus and Eurydice myth for the MTV crowd, "Always & Forever" overstays its welcome by about an hour. Thin script doesn't match all the visual pranks.

Main twosome are urban anarchist (Oliver Broumis) and hairdresser (Nicole Ansari), who meet in the netherworld when a cop's bullet fells both in a market. They fall in love and are given 12 hours back on Earth to prove their feelings for each other. Meanwhile, the anarchist tries to warn his fellows that the police are on to their plan to blow up a Yank corporation's computer.

First half-hour is quite fun, with multiple collages and computer-generated effects, but pace slackens when the duo go head-on in a long dialog about politics and romance. After they hit the sack, pic turns into a routine Euro crime meller, with tragic results.

Bagdad-born, Zurich-based helmer Samir (a.k.a. Samir Jamal Aldin) can't be faulted for energy, and his young leads do the best with the material on hand. High-def video images are okay but flatly colored after transfer to film. — *Derek Elley*

NAZAR
(INDIAN)

An NFDC production. Directed by Mani Kaul. Screenplay, Kaul, Sharmistha Mohanty, based on Fyodor Dostoyevski's novel by camera (color), Piyush Shah; editor, Lalitha Krishna; music, Vikram Joglekar, D. Wood. Reviewed at 44th Locarno Intl. Film Festival (noncompeting), Aug. 8, 1991. Running time: **100 MIN.**
With: Sahambhavi Kaul, Shekhar Kapur, Surekha Sikri.
(Hindi dialog)

"Nazar" is an extended reverie by a middle-class Bombay husband on his young wife and their fragile marriage. Ambitious pic won't do much for the rep of Indian helmer Mani Kaul on the fest circuit. Most viewers will feel like jumping out the window long before the teenage bride.

Kaul came to fame with the stylized "Uski Roti" in 1969 and has since carved a career in the middle ground between naturalistic pics and more classical items. "Nazar" was made as a tv film in 1988, before "Siddeshwari," an abstract semidocu about a femme *thumri* singer that did the rounds two years ago.

Central character, an ex-soldier court-martialed for cowardice, runs an antique shop in Bombay, and lords it over his 17-year-old wife. He gradually falls apart as she asserts her individuality. Third member of cast is a middle-aged housekeeper.

Mostly set in the couple's high-rise apartment, action takes the form of Antonioni-esque exchanges and voiceovers. Color lensing is clear and sharp; postsynching is sloppy. — *Derek Elley*

SPRUNG AUS DEN WOLKEN
(FALLEN FROM THE SKY)
(GERMAN-SWISS-B&W-16M)

A Deutsche Film & Fernsehakademie Berlin-Neapel Film-Schweizer Fernsehen production. Directed by Stefan Schwietert. Screenplay, Schwietert, Nancy Rivas; camera (b&w, 16m), Arthur Ahrweiler; editor, Dagmar Pohl, Frank Belinke, Schwietert; music, Jan Schade; sound, Daniel Hermeling, Marc Ottiker; costume design, Ulrike Denk; paintings, Christoph Döring. Reviewed at 44th Locarno Intl. Film Festival (competing), Aug. 16, 1991. Running time: **75 MIN.**
Rosie . . . . May Buchgraber
Harry . . . . Rainer Winkelvoss
Micky . . . . Christian Spitzl
Art critic . . . . Oliver Held
Beauregard . . . Fortune Claude Leite

"Fallen From The Sky" is a likable triangle about three Berliners on the make shortly after the fall of the wall. Trim black-&-white low-budgeter should make friends bouncing around the fest circuit.

Pic opens in spring 1990 with arty couple Christian Spitzl and May Buchgraber making love. When he knocks East Berliner Rainer Winkelvoss off his bike one day, the couple adopts him professionally, and soon the g.f. is attracted by more than the newcomer's paintings. Film ends with Winkelvoss ditching her as he gets wise about Western ways.

In his first feature, director Stefan Schwietert shows a sure hand with the developing relationships, especially as the cocksure b.f. is gradually sidelined by the fast-learning artist. As the central femme, Buchgraber holds the loose story together with her characterful looks and easy style. Sequence of her and Winkelvoss making first base during a visit to her mom in West Germany is neatly paced and acted.

Technically, pic is fine, with tight cutting, quality 16m lensing and an atmospheric string quartet score by Jan Schade. Running time is just right.

— *Derek Elley*

A BRIGHTER SUMMER DAY
(TAIWANESE)

A Jane Balfour Films presentation of a Yang and His Gang Filmmakers production. Produced by Yu Weiyan. Executive producer, Zhan Hongzhi. Directed by Edward Yang. Screenplay, Yang, Yan Hongya, Yang Shunqing, Lai Mingtang; camera (Eastern color), Zhang Huigong, Li Longyu; editor, Chen Bowen; music supervisor, Zhang Hongda; sound, Du Duzhi; production design, Yu Weiyan, Yang; costumes, Chen Rofei, Wu Leqing, Zhu Meiyu; production manager, Wu Zhuang. Reviewed at 44th Locarno Intl. Film Festival. (Also in Toronto Film Festival.) Running time: **185 MIN.**
Father . . . . Zhang Guozhu
Mother . . . . Elaine Jin
Xiao S'ir . . . . Zhang Zhen
Older brother . . . . Zhang Han
Older sister . . . . Wang Juan
Ming . . . . Lissa Yang
Also with: Wang Qizan, Ke Yulun, Tan Zhigang, Tang Xiaocui.

It takes some time, but everything falls into place in "A Brighter Summer Day," giving this intimate saga a good chance of gaining many admirers. Some auds won't mind pic's running time or deliberate pace and may even agree with director Edward Yang, who's considering putting back a fourth hour cut for commercial reasons.

Based on Yang's adolescent memories, this elaborate, stylized and sensitive portrait of 1960 Taiwan evolves around a talented but self-centered student who refuses to compromise his moral standards with anyone — teachers, pals, parents or girlfriend.

Director observes the growing impact of U.S. culture on local traditions and life under military dictatorship. Yang deals with unemployment, immigration from Mainland China and Christianity and young people.

The strict school discipline disintegrates once students leave their overcrowded classes. They roam the streets and try to define their identity as they cope with macho inclinations, first romances, dreams of glory, pledges of friendship and the injustice of laws applied differently to the rich and to the poor.

Yang proceeds with a sure hand, exhibiting once again mature control. He never judges his characters and has sympathy and understanding even for the worst of them.

Every frame is accurately structured and if, at times, it's left empty for a brief second, it's only to achieve an effect using the viewer's imagination. The pace is never hurried, but an amazing amount of information is communicated, drawing a rich, incisive picture of a period in recent Taiwanese history that is rarely, if ever, tackled on screen.

Abundant music includes Elvis Presley's "Are You Lonesome Tonight," given a lot of exposure (the film's title is taken from the lyrics), as are several other American hits of the '50s, performed on stage by a group of students looking for a musical career.

One touching scene has the hero and girlfriend tentatively talking to each other in the school yard while the school band rehearses, not very successfully, a military march. But most scenes are played, effectively, only to natural sounds. Thus, an innocent kiss gains a lot from the absolute silence and the darkness surrounding it.

Darkness is a prominent feature here, justified in the screenplay's references to power shortages and splendidly exploited in one scene to enhance the violence to an almost unbearable point. However, moments of darkness are unnecessarily disturbing, and one would hope lighter prints than the one screened in Locarno will be provided in the future.

Natural, uninhibited but low-key performances by most of the populous cast fit in with Yang's respect for audience's intelligence. At home, this approach seems to have worked as the pic has almost recovered its cost in its first month of release.

Abroad, it may not be an instant hit, but carefully handled, it could easily become a favorite on the art circuits, and a surefire entry for film fests.
— *Dan Fainaru*

L'HOMME QUI A PERDU SON OMBRE
(THE MAN WHO LOST HIS SHADOW)
(SPANISH-SWISS-FRENCH)

A Tornasol Films-Filmograph-Gemini Films production. (Intl. sales: Metropolis Filmbetrieb, Zurich.) Produced by Gerardo Herrero, Alain Tanner, Paulo Branco. Written and directed by Tanner. Camera (Widescreen, color), José Luis Gómez Linares; editor, Monica Goux; music, Arié Dzierlatka; sound, Jean-Paul Mugel; art director-costume design, Ana Alvargonzález. Reviewed at 44th Locarno Intl. Film Festival (non-competing), Aug. 11, 1991. (Also in Montreal Film Festival.) Running time: **102 MIN.**

Antonio	Francisco Rabal
María	Angela Molina
Paul	Dominic Guard
Anne	Valeria Bruni-Tedeschi

(French and Spanish dialog)

Alain Tanner's latest pic looks set to divide audiences down the middle. A schematic roundelay between four characters in a dusty Spanish town, "The Man Who Lost His Shadow" will be tops for those who like their characters as icons and dullsville for those who prefer real conflict.

Swiss helmer's name will nudge pic along the fest circuit, but it won't cast a giant shadow at many wickets. World preem at Locarno fest triggered fierce debate after its packed screening in the open-air Piazza Grande. Pic is neither a dud nor a masterpiece.

Thin yarn has poe-faced Paris journalist Dominic Guard leaving pretty spouse Valeria Bruni-Tedeschi for some off-season meditation in Cabo de Gata, near Almería. Wife tracks him down through the help of ex-flame Angela Molina, a dance teacher, and the two femmes set off south to confront the self-centered dope.

Quartet is completed by the journalist's aged Franco-fighter pal Francisco Rabal, a gnarled restaurateur with whom he spends a lot of time philosophizing when he's not going off solo on his motorbike. The arrival of the two women at halftime strikes some sexual sparks that lead to Guard bedding both. When Rabal suddenly falls sick, the two femmes fly back to Paris and Guard returns to contemplating his navel.

Existential tone is nothing new in Tanner's work. Like most of his characters, the journalist is a dropout working out his pessimism in a foreign society. But it's difficult to understand the burr under his saddle — or what either of the two women see in him.

Tanner's script is not much help. The four leads go around in their own boxes and come out only for some quick sex or philosophizing. What starts as an intriguing variation on male/female emotional needs ends up as a formula jealousy drama, awkwardly capped by the old man dying. His final words to Molina: "Carry on the struggle against decaying flesh." Well, sure.

Everybody does their best with the material available. Vet

Spanish thesp Rabal is fine as the avuncular savant, and blond stunner Bruni-Tedeschi okay as the fey wife. Molina, largely stranded by the script once in Spain, is a suitably strong Latino firebrand opposite the more fragile Bruni-Tedeschi. Guard plays the French intellectual with a fixed middle-distance stare.

Widescreen lensing of the parched Andalusian landscape is firstrate, with no sense of strain when the camera shifts indoors. Arié Dzierlatka's chamber score intelligently underlines the toing and fro-ing onscreen. Editing is nimble, with frequent use of jump-cuts during long exchanges. — *Derek Elley*

L'ANNÉE DE L'EVEIL
(THE YEAR OF AWAKENING)
(FRENCH)

A Capricorn-FR3 Films-France K2-RTBF Belgium production in association with Sofica Création, Investimage 2&3, CNC, Canal Plus, S.A. Investico, ASLK-CGER Bank and Belgian French Community Executive. (Intl. sales: President Films.) Produced by Joelle Bellon. Directed by Gérard Corbiau. Screenplay, Corbiau, André Corbiau, Michel Fessler, based on Charles Juliet's novel; camera (color), François Catonne; editor, Denise Vindevogel; musical consultants, Roland Schoelink, David Miller; sound, Alain Lachassagne; art director, Gerard Viard; associate producers, Dominique Janne, Nadine Borreman; casting, Marie-Christine Lafosse. Reviewed at the 44th Locarno Intl. Film Festival, Aug. 13, 1991. (Also in Toronto Film Festival.) Running time: **102 MIN.**

François	Grégore Colin
Sargeant	Laurent Grevil
Lena	Chiara Caselli
Captain	Roger Planchon
Colonel	Christian Barbier

Also with: Martin Lamotte, Johan Rougeul, Claude Duneton, Vincent Grass.

Gérard Corbiau's second film isn't likely to go the way of his first one, "The Music Master," and grab another Oscar nomination. A predictable tale of growing up in a French military school, it piles miseries on its young hero to woo the audience to his side, parades every adolescent crisis in the book and leads to a melodramatic climax that wraps it all up in pink ribbons.

Dedicated to the memory of the late François Truffaut, who might have had a thing or two to say about it, story traces a year in the life of 14-year-old François. An orphan who never knew his parents, he is afraid to die in Indochina (the year is 1948 and

the French are still fighting there) when he graduates from school.

He stubbornly refuses to compromise his principals and bend to authority. He reflects on faith and is made to choose between brute force and intellect as his future weapons. Dreaming of becoming a prizefighter so he can teach the bullies in school a lesson they won't forget, the teen develops a crush on a handsome sergeant and ex-boxing champion. He sees a surrogate father figure in him, and he commits surrogate incest by discovering sex and romance with the sergeant's frustrated wife.

Meanwhile, François secretly hones his writing gifts into a fine art. A drunken tutor, teachers who discuss the Holocaust, and a general deception with the world of the adults, fill up the remaining space.

Vaguely reminiscent of every other coming-of-age film, including those by Truffaut, Corbiau's script fails to deliver anything better than cardboard characters, transparently manipulated to advance the plot. Heavy-handed direction leaves little to imagination. Music consists of several classical highlights, each representing a certain mood.

Softly focused images are supposed to induce a nostalgic atmosphere over the entire story and chauvinistic speeches evoke the spirit of the period. Performances are uninteresting even when well-intentioned, but technical credits are beyond reproach.
— *Dan Fainaru*

IL NODO ALLA CRAVATTA
(THE KNOT IN THE NECKTIE)
(ITALIAN)

An Excelsior Film-TV in collaboration with RAI Uno production. Executive producer, Marco Donati. Directed by Alessandro Di Robilant. Screenplay, Umberto Marino, Di Robilant, from a story by Di Robilant; camera (Eastmancolor), David Scott; editor, Mirco Garrone; music, Bruno Moretti; sound, Glauco Puletto, Gianni D'Amico; art director, Tommaso Bordone; costume design, Carolina Orgese; assistant director, Mauricio Sciarra. Reviewed at 44th Locarno Intl. Film Festival (competing), Aug. 11, 1991. Running time: **99 MIN.**
With: Patrick Bauchau, Delia Boccardo, Eleonora Danco, Fabio Ferrari, Sergio Orzesko.

A troubled teen item in which the elders are more interesting than the main character, "The Knot In The Necktie" is a pleasant but lightweight

Italo entry that should do equally pleasant biz and some fest dates.

Carlino, 13, is an antsy youth who's ignored by his stuffy father, thinks he is actually the product of his mother's former lover, and feels left alone when his elder sister marries. Dispatched to a Catholic school, he's soon picked on by the head teacher and runs away one night. His sister, whose marriage is already in trouble, takes him in; but when the newlyweds start bickering, Carlino feels that school is the easier option.

Film ends on a feel-good note. At a Christmas gathering, the sister announces she's divorcing her husband so each can go off with their lovers. Mother tells father that Carlino is really his son (her former lover was sterile). And Carlino starts getting come-on looks from the young daughter of some family friends.

Helmer Alessandro Di Robilant gets good performances from all the cast, especially Eleanora Danco as the sympathetic sister and vet Delia Boccardo as the kid's mother. But script has a once-over-lightly feel that runs the gamut from teen pranks to puberty blues without ever adding much that's new. Newcomer Sergio Orzesko is largely stolid as Carlino.

All tech credits are tops, with Bruno Moretti's propulsive-romantic score a real plus.

— *Derek Elley*

MONTREAL FEST

UNE ÉPOQUE FORMIDABLE
(WONDERFUL TIMES)
(FRENCH)

An AMLF release of an Arturo Prods.-Ciby 2000-TF1 Films-GPFI co-production with the participation of Canal Plus, Sofiarp, Soficas Investimages 2 & 3, Soficas Valor 1 & 2. (Intl. sales: Président Films.) Produced by Alain Depardieu. Directed by Gérard Jugnot. Screenplay, Jugnot, Philippe Lopes-Curval; camera (color), Gérard De Battista; editor, Catherine Kelber; music, Francis Cabrel; sound, Philippe Loiret, Gérard Lamps; costume design, Martine Rapin; makeup, Paul Le Marinel. Reviewed at Gaumont Convention, Paris, June 20, 1991. (In Montreal Film Festival.) Running time: **96 MIN.**
Berthier . . . . Gérard Jugnot
Toubib . . . . Richard Bohringer
Juliette . . . . Victoria Abril
Crayon . . . . Ticky Holgado
Mimosa . . . . Chick Ortega
Also with: Roland Blanche.

Full of humor and warmth despite its gritty setting, "Une Époque Formidable" is a tramp comedy about a family man who almost overnight becomes one of the Paris homeless.

Following an ex-executive and his three sidewalk buddies, story steers clear of sentimental portraits to deliver bittersweet laughs. A sure bet for arthouses and Euro tv, pic about one man's "incredible period" in life may also succeed in mainstream markets.

Director-star Gérard Jugnot is heavily into denial as a balding, newly fired exec who buys his wife and kids presents rather than tell them the bad news. Certain no one will love him without a job, he chooses to eke out a life on the streets.

Jugnot's misguided bum is easygoing and likable, the male equivalent of Giulietta Masina's wanderer: a sweet smile and a guileless heart. Even if he wields an ax to escape from the police, he returns seconds later to his old innocent self.

Richard Bohringer is equally topnotch as the charming rogue Toubib (slang for doctor). Part medic and part swindler, he helps his pals survive. He may doublecross Jugnot during a heist but eventually helps him rejoin his family.

Two small parts also stand out. Chick Ortega holds his own as a huge blond brute who turns aggressor at the drop of a dime, and Ticky Holgado completes the foursome as a big-hearted short guy with a bad leg.

Helmer Jugnot smoothly fills in the group dynamics without succumbing to big social statements. The few crowd scenes, such as a hundred homeless people bedding down in an underground metro station, speak for themselves. Helmer does, however, enjoy ridiculing media presentations of the poor.

Bright script by Jugnot and Philippe Lopes-Curval sparkles with oneliners. Still, pic's upbeat mood allows for serious moments, even a few cruel scenes.

In delicate scenes, such as the father's run-in with his skateboarding son, helmer shows a sensitive touch. Final number neatly sums up antihero's fear of rejection and hope for silent understanding, when he encounters his wife for the first time in months. Tech credits are first-rate. — *Lee Lourdeaux*

RUBIN AND ED

A Working Title production. Executive producer, Tim Bevan. Produced by Paul Webster. Written and directed by Trent Harris. Camera (Alphacine color), Bryan Duggan; editor, Brent Schoenfeld; music, Fredric Myrow; sound, Rick Waddell; production design, Clark Hunter; production manager, Elaine Dysinger; co-producer, David Stacey; casting, Betsy Fels. Reviewed at Montreal Film Festival (Cinema of Today & Tomorrow section), Aug. 24, 1991. (Also in Boston Film Festival.) Running time: **82 MIN.**
Rubin Farr . . . . Crispin Glover
Ed Tuttle . . . . . Howard Hesseman
Rula . . . . Karen Black
Mr. Busta . . . . Michael Greene
Poster girl . . . . . . Brittnew Lewis

A strange but amiable odd-couple pic lensed in Utah, "Rubin And Ed" is minor fare that could achieve cult status but otherwise looks doomed to marginal screenings.

This Yank effort on the part of Brit producer Tim Bevan's Working Title outfit has odd similiarities to another Yank-based British pic, Handmade Films' "Cold Dog Soup." That one didn't make it, and this one probably won't either, though it will have its supporters.

Howard Hesseman plays a none-too-competent real estate salesman who's ordered to find recruits for a sales seminar. He latches on to Crispin Glover, who, with his long hair, striped bell-bottom pants and bizarre platform shoes, looks akin to Aussie comic Yahoo Serious. The oddball lives in the hotel his mother manages; he has no friends, and mainly plays Mahler and keeps his dead cat in the freezer.

Glover agrees to come to Hesseman's seminar if the salesman will help him bury the pet. They set out into the desert to find a suitable place, and before long are lost and their auto breaks down. This gives the two opposites plenty of time to become friends and allies.

Pic is a rambling road/buddy oddity, in which Hesseman steals the show as the brightly clad, ever-optimistic salesman; Glover's introverted Rubin makes for a rather dull interpretation. Karen Black is in for a couple of scenes as Hesseman's nagging ex-wife.

First-time writer-director Trent Harris has a good feel for the desert locations, and has come up with an endearingly offbeat comedy which lacks the punch for anything other than limited release. Still, he shows talent,

and is worth watching in the future. Pic is technically good, with inventive lensing and brisk editing. — *David Stratton*

PAGE BLANCHE
(WHITE PAGE)
(CAMBODIAN-SWISS)

An MHK Films production. Written, produced and directed by Ho Quang Minh. Camera (color), Le Dinh An; editor, Bui Jim Hoang; music, Dam Linh; sound, Le Nghia. Reviewed at Montreal Film Festival (competing), Aug. 24, 1991. Running time: **99 MIN.**
Vixna . . . . Phuong Dung
Also with: Phay Phon, Bora, Hari, Lok Chan Nara, Van Thi, Ben Mari, On Pa Nha.

Vietnamese-born, Swiss-based filmmaker Ho Quang Minh, whose "Karma" premiered at Montreal six years ago, has come up with a remarkable inside look at the Cambodian killing fields of the late 1970s. Fact that this film was shot in Cambodia lends great power and authenticity to an extremely grim drama of horror and human survival.

Technically, the film is excellent, with fine camerawork and top-quality lab work. It should surface at several more film fests, and deserves a shot at the theatrical market.

Protagonist Phuong Dung and her two children are summoned from Paris by her husband, a Khmer Rouge official, to return to "liberated" Kampuchea in 1975. Immediately after she arrives, she knows something's wrong; her husband isn't there to meet her. She's taken into custody and separated from her kids.

Assigned to hard labor at a countryside commune, she's forced to undergo endless communist indoctrination from a group leader talking in meaningless slogans. She discovers her husband, who had "individualistic tendencies," was purged and later killed. Her children also perish, apparently poisoned. Skeletons and the dying are everywhere, although she is able to save a child abandoned in a pit of corpses.

Raped by the commune leader (whom she almost kills when he's sleeping), the woman survives until the country is "freed" by the arrival of Vietnamese troops in 1979. Pic ends with her trying to pick up the pieces of her life.

Ho Quang Minh tells this ultragrim tale very much from a

Vietnamese perspective, and tends to downplay the terrible saga's emotional aspects. Another director might have made the wife's plight unbearably moving, but this helmer keeps a certain distance.

Despite this offputting approach, pic still is a remarkable achievement. Use of actual locations lends an extraordinary power to the tragedy, and the recent downfall of communism in many parts of the world makes the Khmer Rouge rhetoric seem even more meaningless and inhuman. — *David Stratton*

THE BEGGAR'S OPERA
(CZECHOSLOVAKIAN)

A Czechoslovak Filmexport presentation of a Barrandov Film Studios production. Produced by Jiri Menzel, Jan Suster. Directed by Menzel. Screenplay, Menzel, from play by Vaclav Havel based on play by John Gay; camera (color), Jaromir Sofr; editor, Jiri Brozek; music, Jan Klusak; sound, Jiri Hora; art direction, Zbynek Hloch. Reviewed at Montreal Film Festival (competing), Aug. 25, 1991. Running time: **102 MIN.**
Macheath . . . . Josef Abrham
Lockit . . . . Rudolf Hrusinsky
Peachum . . . . Marian Labuda
Jenny . . . . Libuse Safrankova
Polly . . . . . . Barbora Leichnerova
Lucy . . . . Veronika Freimanova
Jim . . . . Oldrich Vizner
Jack . . . . Ondrej Vetchy
Harry Filch . . . . Jiri Zahajsky
Diana . . . . Katerina Frybova
Mrs. Peachum . . . . . Nina Diviskova
Mrs. Lockit . . . . Jana Brezkova
Harold . . . . Miroslav Stibich
John . . . . Rudolf Hrusinsky Jr.
Prisoner . . . . Jeremy Irons

It seems one doesn't mess with the president's words in Czechoslovakia: This verbally dense adaptation of Vaclav Havel's play "The Beggar's Opera" reads like a book and looks like theater.

While Havel's philosophizing on the underworld codes of morality is rich, director Jiri Menzel's screen version is little more than a stage production on film. As with Volker Schlöndorff's "Death Of A Salesman," "The Beggar's Opera" will be limited to arthouse venues and quality tv outlets.

Originally written by John Gay in 1728, this timeless piece depicts Mafia-like underworld gangs pitted against each other.

Josef Abrham steals the show with a delicious performance as the charming rogue Macheath. Acting on all fronts is outstanding, and considering the limited number of sets, the actors really are what carry the film.

Lighting is weak and other tech credits are average. Subtitles (per Menzel) are poorly translated, and wall-to-wall text requires speed reading. Length is also a bit exhausting.

But this politically poignant script is a treat. As with Milan Kundera's "The Unbearable Lightness Of Being," the multilayered dialog should attract connoisseurs and rogues alike.
— *Suzan Ayscough*

TENKAWA DENSETSU SATSUJIN JIKEN
(NOH MASK MURDERS)
(JAPANESE)

A Toei Co. release of a Haruki Kadokawa Films production. Produced by Kadokawa. Directed by Kon Ichikawa. Screenplay, Kuri-shitel, from Yasuo Uchida's novel; camera (color), Yukio Isohata; editor, Chizuko Osada; music, Fumio Miyashita; sound, Teiichi Saito; production design, Shinobu Muraki. Reviewed at Montreal Film Festival (noncompeting), Aug. 23, 1991. Running time: **110 MIN.**
With: Takaaki Enoki, Takeshi Kusaka, Keiko Kishi, Ittoku Kishibe, Rei Okamoto, Shuji Otaki, Tomoko Naraoka, Takeshi Kato, Kyoko Kishida, Shiro Ito, Koji Ishizaka.

Vet director Kon Ichikawa has come up with an entertaining, if sometimes complicated, whodunit which cunningly mixes contemporary and traditional Japanese concerns. Beautifully produced, "Noh Mask Murders" will appeal to Japanese culture aficionados.

Pic opens with a pre-credit sequence depicting three apparently unconnected events: In Tokyo, a businessman drops dead in the street. In mountaineous country near Nara, two lovers are disturbed by a falling branch, and, not far away, a young traveler has an unexpected encounter with an attractive, middle-aged woman.

Ichikawa creates a classical whodunit structured around members of a bickering family whose patriarch, a leading practitioner of Noh theater, has decided to retire. Plot hinges on who will succeed him, granddaughter or grandson.

The mysterious tale also involves a 600-year-old Noh mask depicting evil and used by the murderer to poison a second victim. Another character linked to the family also is iced.

The official investigation is led by two buffoonish Tokyo cops

who provide comic relief. Actual detection is done by the young traveler who turns out to be the brother of a famed investigator.

The plot is confusing at times, but all is clear by the end, and the identity of the killer is satisfyingly difficult to spot for much of the film. Ichikawa's habit of rapid crosscutting between parallel scenes adds to the film's visual excitement.

On a production level, pic is up with the best of contemporary Japanese films, with rich color photography and sumptuous production design. The sequences in which Noh plays are performed are particularly attractive.

All performances are pro.
— *David Stratton*

TELLURIDE FEST

PROSPERO'S BOOKS
(BRITISH-FRENCH)

A Miramax Films release (in U.S.) of an Allarts-Cinea-Camera One-Penta co-production in association with Elsevier Vendex Film-Film Four Intl.-VPRO TV-Canal Plus-NHK. Produced by Kees Kasander. Executive producers, Kasander, Denis Wigman. Directed by Peter Greenaway. Screenplay, Greenaway, adapted from William Shakespeare's "The Tempest"; camera (color), Sacha Vierny; editor, Marina Bodbyl; music, Michael Nyman; sound, Garth Marshall; production design, Ben Van Os, Jan Roelfs; associate producers, Masato Hara, Roland Wigman; assistant director, Gerrit Martijn; co-producers, Philippe Carcassonne, Michel Seydoux. Reviewed at Telluride (Colo.) Film Festival, Sept. 1, 1991. (Also in Toronto and competing at Venice film festivals.) Running time: **124 MIN.**
Prospero . . . . .John Gielgud
Caliban . . . . Michael Clark
Alonso . . . . Michel Blanc
Gonzalo . . . . Roland Josephson
Miranda . . . . Isabelle Pasco
Antonio . . . . Tom Bell
Sebastian . . . . . . Kenneth Cranham
Ferdinand . . . . Mark Rylance
Adrian . . . . Gerard Thoolen
Francisco . . . . Pierre Bokma
Trinculo . . . . . . Jim Van Der Woude
Stephano . . . . Michiel Romeyn
Ariel . . . . Orpheo, Paul Russell, James Thierree, Emil Wolk.

With more visual stimulation than a dozen normal films, Peter Greenaway's "Prospero's Books" is an intellectually and erotically rampaging meditation on the arrogance and value of the artistic process. The product of a feverish, overflowing imagination, this almost impossibly dense take on "The Tempest" displays both the director's audacious brilliance and lewd extravagance at full tilt, and it will polarize arthouse audiences worldwide.

John Gielgud's mesmerizing readings share center stage with what is most likely the greatest number of naked bodies ever assembled on a motion-picture stage. Erich von Stroheim would be green with envy.

Less compellingly melodramatic by nature than Greenaway's two most commercially successful outings, "The Draughtsman's Contract" and "The Cook, The Thief, His Wife & Her Lover," film will almost certainly have the additional liability domestically of an NC-17 rating.

In the first several minutes, many of Greenaway's familiar obsessions announce themselves: mechanical methods of perception, transforming reality into art, framing of objects with architecture, water imagery, human statues, numerical listing of topics and ideas, and massive amounts of full-frontal nudity, both male and female.

The playwright's tale is presented basically intact, but Greenaway's underlying gambit is to make Prospero the author of his own story. Through the use of exquisite calligraphy, the old man's writing is made vivid on the screen, and the device opens the way to Gielgud himself to supply the voices for many of the supporting characters, who are sometimes also voiced by Gielgud and another thesp simultaneously.

Overall, this minimizes the importance of the secondary roles to the point that they barely exist in their own right, but also serves to provide the pleasure of this great Shakespearean actor vocally performing "The Tempest" almost singlehandedly.

Although this can scarcely be "The Tempest" he dreamed of committing to film for so many years, Gielgud is very much the heart of the pic, if not its brain.

Still imperious, but with the smooth skin and clear eyes of a baby, the octogenarian is commanding, appealing and vocally a constant thrill. Dressed most of the time in duchal garb while those around him go undraped, he creates a rich career capper with Prospero (a role he has played onstage four times previously, the first in 1930, at 26), even if he goes on to make a dozen more films.

Shot entirely indoors in Amsterdam, the production is stunning from every physical point of view. Production designers Ben Van Os and Jan Roelfs have created a constantly changing environment within the recognizable confines of a rigidly architectural world, and Sacha Vierny's astounding cinematography is marked by numerous long lateral tracking shots that create moving tableaux. As always, Michael Nyman's vaulting, repetitive, lyrical score plays a major part in the effectiveness of a Greenaway film.

Always concerned with the way civilization records and catalogs information, Greenaway here ventures into new cinematic territory through the use of high-definition video (which accounts for the unusual 1.77:1 aspect ratio) and the Quantel Paintbox.

As a visual feast, "Prospero's Books" is so rich it provides vast pleasures as well as some burps, gas and indigestion. On a more serious level, the film also is too much. Greenaway strenuously applies heavy technique and much busy-ness to the story in making it his own. — *Todd McCarthy*

SCREAM OF STONE
(GERMAN-FRENCH-CANADIAN)

A Walter Saxer-Henry Lange-Richard Sadler presentation of a SERA Filmproduktions (Munich)/Molecule Films A-2 (Paris)/Les Films Stock Intl. (Montreal) production in association with ZDF-Canal Plus-Telefilm Canada-Lucky Red-RAI-2. (Intl. sales: Cine Intl.) Executive producer, Saxer. Directed by Werner Herzog. Screenplay, Hans-Ulrich Klenner, Saxer, based on an original idea by Reinhold Messner; camera (color), Rainer Klausmann; climbing photography, Herbert Raditschnig; editor, Suzanne Baron; music, Ingram Marshall, Alan Lamb, Sarah Hopkins, Atahualpa Yupanqui; sound (Dolby), Christopher Price; production design, Juan Santiago; set design, Kristine Steinhilber, Cornelius Siegel, Wolfgang Siegel; costumes, Ann Poppel; assistant director, Salvatore Basile; additional climbing photography, Fulvio Mariani, Gerhard Baur, Jorge Vignati, Claudius Kelterborn. Reviewed at Telluride (Colo.) Film Festival, Sept. 1, 1991. (Also competing at Venice Film Festival.) Running time: **105 MIN.**
Martin . . . . . . Vittorio Mezzogiorno
Katrina . . . . Mathilda May
Roger . . . . Stefan Glowacz
"Fingerless" . . . . Brad Dourif
Ivan . . . . Donald Sutherland
Also with: Al Waxman, Gunilla Karlzen, Chavela Vargas, Georg Marischka, Volker Prechtl.

Ever in search of new mad adventurers to catch his fancy, Werner Herzog has found them among mountain climbers for his latest South American epic, "Scream Of Stone." While it does feature some spectacular mountain photography in an area of the world few will ever see first-hand, the dramatic and psychological aspects remain so obscure as to become silly. Commercial outlook is strictly low altitude.

Struggling to find his way in the fictional arena since "Fitzcarraldo" in 1982, Herzog hasn't managed a successful comeback with this polyglot effort. When the unappealing characters finally shut up and climb the bloody mountain, things are okay. Unfortunately, there's more than an hour to get through before the ascent begins.

Clumsy prolog introduces two champion climbers. Martin (Vittorio Mezzogiorno) is a young hotshot who, for two years running, has won a televised indoor event by scaling an artificial cliff.

Roger (Stefan Glowacz), an older man and a quintessentially Herzogian figure, is the world-class climbing master who scoffs at Martin as a mere "acrobat."

A supreme egotist somewhat sympathetically revealed to be a maniac, Roger accepts a challenge to climb what he regards as the toughest mountain in the world, a needlelike peak in Patagonia that he has tried and failed to conquer twice before.

Accompanied by journalist Donald Sutherland, the rivals and their entourages assemble in Argentina and commence to wait around for ideal conditions for their climb.

Pic is poorly, sometimes laughably acted by an international cast playing uniquely dour, shallow, self-absorbed characters. No one offers any reasons for the often baffling things they do, and Glowacz doesn't answer when Sutherland asks him what he's been up to for a year.

But once the cameras get above ground level, Herzog offers quite a bit worth looking at. Clearly filmed under extremely hazardous conditions, the mountain climbing footage looks precarious, beautiful and thrilling, as the peak in question cuts like a stiletto into the brilliant sky, and changes in weather arrive with breathtaking suddenness.

Conclusion hits the same ironic, absurd note found in some of the director's previous pictures.

If nothing else, Herzog has once again opened the door on a part of the world few know about, but his best instincts remain those of a mystical documentarian, not a storyteller. — *Todd McCarthy*

MY OWN PRIVATE IDAHO

A Fine Line Features release of a New Line Cinema presentation. Produced by Laurie Parker. Executive producer, Gus Van Sant. Co-executive producer, Allan Mindel. Written and directed by Van Sant; camera (Alpha Cine color), Eric Alan Edwards, John Campbell; editor, Curtiss Clayton; sound (Ultra Stereo), Reinhard Stergar, Robert Marts (Seattle), Jan Cyr (Seattle), Jon Huck (Italy); production design, David Brisbin; art direction, Ken Hardy; set decoration, Melissa Stewart; costume design, Beatrix Aruna Pasztor; assistant director, Kris Krengel; line producer, Tony Brand. Reviewed at Sunset Tower screening room, L.A., Aug. 28, 1991. (Also in Toronto and competing at Ven-

ice film festivals.) MPAA Rating: R. Running time: **102 MIN.**
Mike Waters . . . . River Phoenix
Scott Favor . . . . Keanu Reeves
Richard Waters . . . . . James Russo
Bob Pigeon . . . . . . William Richert
Gary . . . . Rodney Harvey
Carmella . . . . Chiara Caselli
Digger . . . . Michael Parker
Denise . . . . Jessie Thomas
Budd . . . . Flea
Alena . . . . Grace Zabriskie

"My Own Private Idaho" gives the impression of a director so eager to make a highly personal masterpiece that he has almost indiscriminately thrown in nearly every cinematic idea he's had for the last 10 years. Rather less than the sum of its often striking parts, Gus Van Sant's appealingly idiosyncratic look at a pair of very different young street hustlers is one of those ambitious, overreaching disappointments that is more interesting than some more conservative successes.

Critical reaction will be divided, and the wide audience support generated by the director's "Drugstore Cowboy" won't be forthcoming this time.

Taking his title from a B-52s song, Van Sant begins his crooked yarn on a straight Idaho highway, where the scruffy outcast Mike (River Phoenix) succumbs to his affliction of narcolepsy and has visions of his lost home and mother.

In Seattle, Mike is a sex-for-hire boy, a sensitive but raw youth who will go both ways but has the unfortunate habit of passing out on the job.

Mike's cohort and soon-to-be best friend is Scott (Keanu Reeves). The wealthy son of Portland's mayor, Scott is clearly hanging with the boys as an act of rebellion against his family but warns early on that he will give up all his "bad behavior" when he turns 21.

After creating some intriguing hallucinatory effects to illustrate Mike's state of mind and drawing a nicely naturalistic picture of street life, aided by some seemingly unscripted head-on interviews with male prostitutes, Van Sant makes a sudden, fatal shift in tone and style.

The dialog begins sounding arch, the acting style becomes strangely theatrical and, for a while, the film becomes a modern, gay adaptation of Shakespeare's "Henry IV, Part 1." Section actually has the Falstaffian figure of Bob Pigeon (director William Richert) addressing such famous lines as, "The things that we have seen," and "We have heard the chimes at midnight," to a bunch of hustlers while seemingly eyeing them for his possible delectation.

Injection of such a screwy notion is so audacious that it must be considered seriously, but it just doesn't work, making the previously believable dramatic and psychological situation suddenly seem totally inauthentic.

Shakespearean side of the story falls short due to Reeves' very narrow range as an actor. Thesp does certain things well, but the demands of this part are beyond his grasp. By contrast, Phoenix cuts a believable, sometimes compelling figure of a young man urgently groping for definition in his life and a way of overcoming handicaps he can't ignore.

With all its drawbacks, the film offers a great deal to ponder and admire, as Van Sant experiments with many different ways of shooting scenes. Such diversity of effect within a single film is unusual, and clearly isn't always going to work. But it does keep things interesting.

For a story about two gay hustlers, film deals very little with sex. While the milieu may be enough to put off many viewers, others may complain that the two leads' predilections are not adequately clarified. Still others may be offended at the lack of mention of AIDS.

Pic offers many utterly memorable vignettes, notably those including a running character (Udo Kier) who keeps popping up in the boys' lives; Mike's visions of his old home on the range; the nouvelle vagueish confessions of hustlers in a cafe, and the stylish enthusiasm of one of Mike's johns (Mickey Cottrell).

Look of the film has been very carefully designed, and the soundtrack is particularly dense and sophisticated. After effectively working from literary sources and with other writers on "Mala Noche" and "Drugstore Cowboy," Van Sant wrote this one on his own, and the difference shows.
—*Todd McCarthy*

VENICE FEST

GIZLI YÜZ
(THE SECRET FACE)
(TURKISH)

An Alfa Film Ltd. production. Executive producer, Sadik Deveci. Directed by Ömer Kavur. Screenplay, Orhan Pamuk; camera (color), Erdal Kahraman; editor, Mevlut Koçak; music, Cahit Berkay; art director, Husper Akyürek. Reviewed at French Cultural Center, Istanbul, March 30, 1991. (Competing at Venice Film Festival.) Running time: **115 MIN.**
Woman . . . . Zuhal Olcay
Photographer . . . . . Fikret Kuskan
Clockmaker . . . . Savas Yurttas
   Also with: Sevda Ferdag, Arslan Kacar, Salih Kalyon, Rutkay Aziz.

Ömer Kavur's "The Secret Face," a fanciful tale in the Oriental tradition of "The Thousand And One Nights," is laden with atmosphere and hauntingly memorable images. Fests should welcome this outstanding example of Turkish art films. Distribution will be limited to arthouses.

A young photographer (earnest Fikret Kuskan) spins his tale of intrigue, a prolonged search through mystical locales to find an elusive woman (Zuhal Olcay) who has enchanted him. The photographer works at night in clubs and bars, and the next morning he takes the photos he has snapped to the woman, who examines them closely, looking for a particular face.

The woman's interest is aroused by the snapshot of a clockmaker (Savas Yurttas). Shortly afterward, she disappears and the photographer looks for the clockmaker, who has left as well. He begins his quest for them, traveling to the poetically named "City of Dead," "City of Sad" and then finally "City of Heart."

Exchanges are often cryptic and the clock symbolism pervasive. The photographer admits he loves the woman, and the message to "open your heart" may indicate all roads lead back to one's own soul. Becoming immersed in decoding, however, may defeat the simple pleasure derived from a story well told.

Erdal Kahraman's breathtaking lensing of picturesque Black Sea villages perfectly captures the mystical atmosphere. Cahit Berkay's score is fittingly moody, at times almost ominous, thereby heightening the suspense.

Tech credits are topnotch. Kuskan, establishing a niche for himself in contemporary films, is appealing as the photog, while well-regarded actress Olcay has the suitably exotic demeanor necessary to make his passion credible. — *B. Samantha Stenzel*

TORONTO FEST

BLACK ROBE
(CANADIAN-AUSTRALIAN)

A Samuel Goldwyn Co. release (Alliance in Canada, Hoyts in Australia) of an Alliance Communications (Montreal)-Samson Prods. (Sydney) co-production, with the participation of Telefilm Canada & Australian Film Finance Corp. Executive producers, Jake Eberts, Brian Moore, Denis Heroux. Produced by Robert Lantos, Stephane Reichel, Sue Milliken. Directed by Bruce Beresford. Screenplay, Brian Moore, based on his novel; camera (Eastmancolor), Peter James; editor, Tim Wellburn; music, Georges Delerue; sound, Gary Wilkins; production design, Herbert Pinter; costumes, Renee April, John Hay; production manager, Susan Murdoch; assistant director, Pedro Gandol; stunt coordinator, Minor (White Eagle) Mustain; Cree dialog consultant, Helen Bobbish Atkinson; casting, Claire Walker. Reviewed at Astral screening room, Montreal, Aug. 27, 1991. (In Toronto Film Festival.) Running time: **100 MIN.**
Father Laforgue . . . Lothaire Bluteau
Daniel . . . . Aden Young
Annuka . . . . Sandrine Holt
Chomina . . . . . August Schellenberg
Chomina's wife . . . . Tantoo Cardinal
Father Jerome . . . . . . Frank Wilson
Ougebemat . . . . . . Billy Two Rivers
Neehatin . . . . . . Lawrence Bayne
Awandoie . . . . Harrison Liu
Mestigoit . . . . Yvan Labelle

First official co-production between Canada and Australia is a magnificently staged combination of top talents delivering a gripping and tragic story about a 17th-century Jesuit priest's expedition through remote areas of "New France" (Quebec).

"Black Robe" should get a fine launch from its opening berth in the Toronto Festival of Festivals, and, depending on critical reaction, it should go on to good biz in select theaters worldwide. Comparisons are bound to be made with "Dances With Wolves," since "Black Robe" also deals with well-meaning but ultimately devastating attempts to befriend and convert native North Americans. Indian dialog is translated into English subtitles.

Saga begins in 1634 at Fort Champlain, where newly arrived French Jesuit priest (Lothaire Bluteau) is assigned to a difficult and dangerous journey 1,500 miles north to the mission outpost of Ihonatiria. He's accompanied by a handful of friendly Algonquin Indians, led by the chief (August Schellenberg), his wife (Tantoo Cardinal), daughter (Sandrine Holt) and young son.

Also joining the party is Aden Young as a young French carpenter who develops a passionate relationship with the Algonquin girl. Their lovemaking is observed by the disturbed and disapproving priest (whom the Indians call "Black Robe" because of his austere garb).

An encounter with violent Iroquois leaves the chief's wife and son dead, and the chief himself is seriously wounded. The travelers are captured, beaten and tortured; but the daughter uses her sexuality to help them escape (a scene which, with its brutal frankness, is most disturbing).

The priest arrives at his destination to find the priest in charge (Frank Wilson) dying and the local Indians decimated by a fever brought by the white men.

Director Bruce Beresford and writer Brian Moore have made this intriguing yarn a small epic of endurance. This is in no way light entertainment, and the theme may be too downbeat to attract a wide audience. Still, the production has an austere beauty and thoughtful approach to the courage and dedication of the churchmen.

Beresford, always a fine director of actors, has seamlessly meshed a cast that includes w.k. Canadian actors (Bluteau played the title role in "Jesus Of Montreal") and Native Americans as well as a couple of Australians. There's no hint of a clash of acting styles here, as sometimes occurs in co-productions.

Bluteau gives a moving performance in the central role, and Schellenberg is particularly notable as the friendly Chomina.

Beresford's fascination for stories that involve interaction between races ("The Fringe Dwellers," "Driving Miss Daisy," "Mister Johnson") confirms that he was an excellent choice to direct Moore's novel, and he has made what is probably his best film to date.

Peter James' cinematography of the majestic Quebec scenery is breathtaking. Georges Delerue provides a subtle and beautiful score. Tim Wellburn's tight editing keeps the film to a spare 100 minutes running time. And Herbert Pinter's production design looks authentic.

—David Stratton

NUIT ET JOUR
(NIGHT AND DAY)
(FRENCH-BELGIAN-SWISS)

A Pierre Grise release of Pierre Grise Prods. (Paris)-Paradise Films (Brussels)-George Reinhart Prods. (Zurich) co-production, with the participation of CNC, Canal Plus, Sofinergie 2, RTBF (Belgian television) & the Eurimages Fund of the Council of Europe. (Intl sales: Métropolis Film, Zurich.) Executive producer, Rosalie Lecan. Produced by Martine Marignac, Maurice Tinchant. Directed by Chantal Akerman. Screenplay, Akerman, Pascal Bonitzer, based on idea by Michel Vandestien; camera (color), Jean-Claude Neckelbrouck, Pierre Gordower, Bernard Delville, Olivier Dessalies; editor, Francine Sandberg, Camille Bordes Resnais; original music, Marc Hérouet; musical conception: Sonia Wieder-Atherton; sound, Alix Comte, Pierre Tucat; costume design, Brigitte Nierhaus, Michèle Blondeel; set design, Michel Vandestien, Dominique Douret; makeup, Nicole Mora; production managers, Pierre Wallon (France), Marilyn Watelet (Belgium). Reviewed at Club Publicis, Paris, Aug. 7, 1991. (In Toronto and Venice film festivals.) Running time: **90 MIN.**
Julie . . . . Guilaine Londez
Jack . . . . Thomas Langmann
Joseph . . . . François Negret

"Nuit Et Jour" is an engaging three-character drama more accessible and more humorous than usual for scripter/ helmer Chantal Akerman. Fine portrait of postadolescent lovers in thoughtfully lensed Paris should please international arthouse audiences, provided subtitles do justice to characters' straightforward reflections on love, happiness and fear.

Simple, elegant premise — one woman believes she can love two men equally and indefinitely — is shown with corresponding elegance and scored with just the right dose of violin music.

Film begins with taxi driver Thomas Langmann and Guilaine Londez stretched out in bed talking about love and sleep. They're enveloped in the former and forgoing the latter as it cuts down on their lovemaking time. Voiceover spoken by a omniscient femme narrator helps set the scene and move the story along.

New to Paris, the blissful couple live for the present, making nebulous plans to meet other people, make other friends and get a phone. When they go out their front door together, they're always bathed in radiant light.

Langmann introduces his g.f. to fellow cabbie François Negret. Londez is so secure in her love for Langmann that she sees no harm in acting on her attraction to Negret. In her carefully balanced time-sharing scheme, she loves both men equally but gives Langmann a slight edge because she knew him first.

Julie's neat straddling of two realms functions smoothly until the second cabbie begins to pressure her for greater commitment and the first cabbie begins sensing something's not right.

Pic takes place predominantly in the couple's apartment and on nighttime streets. Nice touches include an impromptu visit from Langmann's parents, who rapidly catch on that their son and g.f. would rather play footsie than make small talk.

Akerman directs seamless tracking shots and shots that caress naked bodies. She investigates what lovers say aloud and what they leave unsaid. Although the protagonists speak in a manner approaching pared down free verse, pic creates a convincing bubble of first love/true love and shows how it bursts.

Once awkwardness taints perfection, the mood is broken for the characters and, to some extent, for the viewer. Pic becomes more talky and less magical at about the three-quarters mark.

Theater-trained newcomer Londez seems freshly minted and yet instinctively self-assured. She is sensual, direct, uncomplicated. She beams when she's happy and dims her brights when she's troubled. Both men do a fine job, but it is Renoiresque Londez who steals the show.

— Lisa Nesselson

TINPIS RUN
(PAPUA NEW GUINEAN-
FRENCH-BELGIAN)

A JBA Prods.-Tinpis-La Sept-RTBF (Belgian tv)-Femmis-Skul Bilong Wokim Piksa co-production, in association with Channel 4. Executive producers, Jean-Pierre Mabille, Paul Frame, Philip Cridge. Produced by Jacques Bidou. Directed by Pengau Nengo. Screenplay, John Barre, Severn Blanchet, Martin Maden, Nengo; camera (color), Maden; editor, Andree Davanture, Murial Wolfers; music-consultant director, Blancet; sound, Eric Vaucher, Lahui Geita; set design, Thomas Gawi; production manager, Jacques Attia; assistant director-costumes, Maureen Mopio. Reviewed at Sydney Film Festival, June 10, 1991. (In Toronto Film Festival.) Running time: **94 MIN.**
Joanna . . . . Rhoda Selan
Papa . . . . Leo Konga
Naaki . . . . Oscar Wanu
Peter Subek . . . . . . Gerard Gabud
Also with: Stan Walker, Suzi Buri.

"Tinpis Run" is a cheerful road movie from Papua New Guinea, with dialog in the local variation on English. Supported by French and Belgian production entities and by Channel 4, pic is more a travelog of the island country than a wholly satisfying dramatic film.

This is the first feature made by the PNG director, however, and as such is a landmark in Pacific region cinema. Helmer Pengau Nengo produced it with the facilities of Skul Bilong Wokim Piksa, a film and television training center supported by the French government in the town of Goroka. The film, though thematically unambitious, is exciting in its depiction of the varied landscapes and cultures of the country.

The story centers on Papa, owner of a PMV (a private motor vehicle) which he operates as a taxi. After an accident caused by a drunken passenger, he's rescued by Naaki, and the two team up to buy a new PMV, which they acquired from an Australian who tries to swindle them. They're too clever for him, however, and the Aussie's the one who's swindled.

Rest of the film consists of the adventures of Papa and Naaki and the PMV they call "Tinpis" (which means "canned fish," a reference to the food favored by local village people rather than by city folk or Europeans). Their travels afford cinematographer Martin Maden (who co-scripted) the opportunity to capture the wild beauty of the young country, which was, until 1975, administered by Australia.

The two pick up an ambitious politician who uses "Tinpis" as a platform for his formula speeches to villages on an island off the coast. There's satire here at the expense of the pol, whose speeches are empty and whose audiences dwindle as the word spreads faster than he can travel.

Back on the mainland, Papa leaves Naaki to return to his village where a conflict has erupted with members of a rival village. These scenes are fascinating, since the battles are organized in a traditional way, with spears, arrows and dances. Peace negotiations, held on a dirt highway, are interrupted by the passing of trucks.

A slight romantic interest is added with Joanna, Papa's daughter, a "modern" woman who wants to choose her own husband and isn't certain she wants the womanizing Naaki. Rhoda Selan, who plays Joanna, as well as Leo Konga (Papa) and Oscar Wanu (Naaki) are nonprofessional actors, along with everyone else in the cast. They fill their roles with enthusiasm.

The only other native-language PNG feature film was "Wokabout Bilong Tonten," produced by Film Australia. "Tinpis Run" is a big advance on that 1974 item and should be a modest success on the fest circuit as well as a special event in quality small-screen programming.

— David Stratton

MONTREAL FEST

SALMONBERRIES
(GERMAN)

A Weltvertrieb presentation of a Pelemele Film production. Produced by Eleonore Adlon. Written and directed by Percy Adlon. Camera (color), Tom Sigel; editor, Conrad Gonzalez; music, Bob Telson, sung by K.D. Lang; sound, Jose Araujo; art direction, Amadeus Capra; costume design, Cynthia Flynt. Reviewed at Montreal Film Festival (competing), Aug. 31, 1991. Running time: **94 MIN.**
Kotzebue . . . . K.D. Lang
Roswitha . . . . Rosel Zech
Also with: Chuck Connors, Jane Lind, Oscar Kawagley, Wolfgang Steinberg.

This exquisitely shot love story is an unusual, emotionally demanding tale about a young untamed Eskimo woman and her unfulfilled lesbian desire for an eccentric ex-Berliner. "Salmonberries" divided critics at its preem at Montreal (where it garnered top honors), and cinephiles either loved it or hated it.

Despite a frustrating windup, pic could build on word-of-mouth and controversy with careful handling. It will definitely garner fans and will find a second life in specialized homevid outlets.

Lenser Tom Sigel uses the bleak and beautiful Alaskan landscape as a canvas where the silent, violent 19-year-old orphan (starkly played by Canadian country singer K.D. Lang) goes searching for her roots. She falls in love with a recluse (German thesp Rosel Zech) who fled from postwar East Berlin to the "edge of the world" after her daring escape (when her husband was gunned down by Berlin wall guards).

Their unlikely, yet carefully

nurtured, friendship peaks when they visit Berlin after the wall came down. Lang tries unsuccessfully to make love to Zech for the first time, but Zech says she's "not like that." Their relationship is never resolved, and their stifled physical love is one of pic's major problems.

Terrific title song "Barefoot" is a quiet, mournful tune showcasing the excellent range of Lang's crystal voice. Acting in her debut role, however, is extremely stiff, and she should stick to singing. Lang's perf pales beside that of Zech, who carries the film.

Zech shines as the recluse obsessed with picking and preserving salmonberries (salmon-colored arctic citrus berries) and covering her bedroom walls with hundreds of jars built into intricate patterns. She's a natural as a sexy but repressed and frightened emotional refugee who slowly blooms when loved.

Director Percy Adlon has once again developed characters as individual and eclectic as those in "Bagdad Cafe," but pic's homosexual subject will prove harder to market. "Salmonberries" contemplates a difficult, unresolved relationship in minute detail. — *Suzan Ayscough*

SENSO TO SEISHIN
(WAR AND YOUTH)
(JAPANESE)

A Shochiku release of a Kobushi production. Produced by Yutaka Osawa, Mitsuo Okamura. Directed by Tadashi Imai. Screenplay, Katsumoto Saotome, from his novel; camera (color), Kozo Okazaki; special camera, Jun Yanai; editor, Umeko Numazaki; music, Masaru Sato; sound, Tsutomu Honda; production design, Akira Haruki; costumes, Toshiharu Aida. Reviewed at Montreal Film Festival (competing), Aug. 31, 1991. Running time: **110 MIN.**
Yukari Hanabusa/Sakiko
as a girl . . . . Yuki Kudo
Kazuo Kazami . . . . . . Keisuke Sano
Yuta (father) . . . . Hisashi Igawa
Aunt Sakiko/
Lee Soon-ik . . . . Tomoko Naraoka
Teacher . . . . Kirin Kiki
Hayase (author) . Choichiro Kawarazaki
Uncle . . . . Tatsuo Matsumura
Kazuo's mother . . . Komaki Kurihara
Yukari's mother . . . . Yumiko Fujita

Veteran director Tadashi Imai, who made his first film in 1939 and has been in retirement for nine years, has done a fine job with a moving reflection on World War II for the new generation. "War And Youth" should have strong appeal on its home turf and could crack the international art-

house market.

Pic was funded in an unusual way. Producers put up $2.22 million of the $3.7 million budget; the rest was raised by people invited to invest $740 each to make up the budget shortfall. Public appeals for such investment met with a greater response than anticipated, allowing production to go ahead. The names of the 1,421 "citizen producers" are listed in pic's long end-credit roll.

Basically a sentimental romance about lovers parted, a child lost, madness, death and eventual reunion, the film does have an achingly sincere message about the horror of war. For non-Japanese audiences, however, the emphasis on the "murder" of Tokyo's civilian population in the massive U.S. air raid of 1945, will have to be accepted from the Japanese perspective. Mentioned, but not stressed, are wartime atrocities committed by the Japanese.

Pic's protagonist is a 17-year-old girl, Yukari (Yuki Kudo), who's diligent, wholesome, affectionate, fun-loving — and almost too good to be true. Her ignorance of recent history appears to be profound until a teacher assigns her class to write an essay on a family member's WWII experiences.

Yukari's aunt Sakiko was Yukari's age in '43, but is unable to help with the homework because she never talks and just sits silently on a park bench, staring at an old half-burnt telegraph pole which has somehow survived 45 years. Yukari's father, Yuta, Sakiko's younger brother, is reluctant to talk about the war but, under pressure from his daughter, finally reveals the family secret.

The aunt was in love with a young pacifist in 1943 who fled north to Hokkaido (where he was killed for trying to stop brutality against Koreans laborers). He left Sakiko pregnant, and on the night of the air raid that killed 100,000 people, Sakiko was separated from her baby daughter, and has pined for her ever since.

Soon after, the aunt dies after a car accident, and a scholar who helped Yukari turns up the fact that the missing baby had been found by a Korean couple and raised in that country. The film ends with Sakiko's daughter, blind and unable to speak Japanese, making her first visit to Tokyo with her own child.

It seems incredible such fami-

ly tragedy would not have been passed down, but the point of Katsumoto Saotome's screenplay is that the war has become almost a taboo subject. This traditionally made film is impressive in many ways, especially its sensitive performances. Kudo, playing both the teen and her aunt in flashback sequences, is quite touching, presenting a totally different image from her role in "Mystery Train."

Imai handles the dramatic scenes with a strong emotional touch, and restages the horrifying sequence of the notorious air raid with great skill.
— *David Stratton*

BOSTON FEST

SHAKES THE CLOWN

An IRS Releasing presentation. An IRS Media production. Executive producers, Miles A. Copeland III, Barry Krost, Harold Welb. Produced by Ann Luly, Paul Colichman. Written and directed by Bobcat Goldthwait. Camera (Foto-Kem color), Eliott Davis, Bobby Bukowski; editor, J. Kathleen Gibson; music, Tom Scott; sound (Dolby) Giovanni Di Simone; production design, Pamela Woodbridge; costume design, Stephen Chudej; makeup designer, Kathryn Kelly; assistant director, Matthew Clark; line producer, Michael Bennett; casting, Don Pemrick. Reviewed at Boston Film Festival, Aug. 28, 1991. No MPAA Rating. Running time: **83 MIN.**
Shakes the Clown . Bobcat Goldthwait
Judy . . . . Julie Brown
Binky . . . . Tom Kenny
Stenchy . . . . Blake Clark
Dink . . . . Adam Sandler
Lucy . . . . Kathy Griffin
Owen Cheese . . . . Paul Dooley
Jerry . . . . Robin Williams
Also with: Bruce Baum, Jack Gallagher, Florence Henderson, Paul Kozlowski, Jeremy S. Kramer, Lawanda Page, Dan Spencer, Greg Travis, Tom Villard, Martin Charles Warner.

Fans of comic Bobcat Goldthwait's bizarre sense of humor should get a kick out of "Shakes The Clown," a pedestrian story of an alcoholic hitting bottom but with a fresh twist: Virtually all the characters are clowns. Film is unlikely to have broad appeal, but it has the earmarks of a cult favorite.

Goldthwait (who wrote and directed) plays the title role, a "party clown" who entertains at children's birthday parties once out of his drunken stupor. Story gives him a delightfully ditzy g.f. (Julie Brown), loyal friends (Blake Clark, Adam Sandler) and a fatherly manager (Paul Dooley) all

urging him to quit the sauce and get his act together.

He hits bottom when his evil rival Binky (played to malicious effect by Tom Kenny) murders Dooley and sets up Goldthwait to take the fall. Story goes exactly where one might expect with few plot surprises.

Set in the town of Palukaville, pic focuses on the party clowns, who like to booze it up at a dive called the Twisted Balloon, and who enjoy beating up on mimes. Except for Goldthwait, the clowns remain in full makeup and costume for the entire film.

There's an overreliance on bodily-function jokes (Goldthwait is urinated on and then throws up before the opening credits). But the clown milieu is cleverly utilized (a bad guy takes cocaine by pouring it into his red clown nose).

One of the funniest bits is when Goldthwait, trying to avoid the police, attempts to pass himself off as a student at a mime school. Robin Williams has yet another unbilled role (after "The Adventures Of Baron Munchausen" and "Dead Again") as the school's instructor.

Tech credits are up to snuff, and credit should be given to colorful production design which uses the vivid costumes and makeup of the clown characters to play off against the ordinary settings. —*Daniel M. Kimmel*

THE BORROWER

A Cannon Pictures release of a Vision Pictures production. Executive producer, William H. Coleman. Produced by R. P. Sekon, Steven A. Jones. Directed by John McNaughton. Screenplay, Mason Nage, Richard Fire; camera (color), Julio Mercat, Robert New; editor, Elena Maganini; music, Robert McNaughton, Ken Hale, Jones; sound (Ultrastereo), Steven Halbert; production design, Robert Henderson; costume design, Theda Deramus; makeup, Kevin Yagher; assistant director, Elliot Rosenblatt, Larry Litton; casting, Jaki Brown. Reviewed at Boston Film Festival, Aug. 30, 1991. MPAA Rating: R. Running time: **88 MIN.**
Diana Pierce . . . . . Rae Dawn Chong
Charles Krieger . . . . . . Don Gordon
Julius . . . . Antonio Fargas
Bob Laney . . . . Tom Towles
Scully . . . . Neil Giuntoli
Connie . . . . Pam Gordon

John McNaughton, who burst on the scene with "Henry: Portrait Of A Serial Killer," shows that he can handle conventional sci-fi/horror with "The Borrower," a by-the-numbers production that should please genre fans and allow for

quick and profitable playoff.

Premise of the 1989 "Borrower" is a bloodier version of "The Hidden" (1987): An alien baddie banished to Earth is "genetically devolved" to fit among the lower species, i.e., humans.

Process has its drawbacks and the alien soon literally loses his head, and has to "borrow" one from a human to replace it. Along the way, he also absorbs the person's memories. Thus, alien is played by several people, including Tom Towles as a poacher and Antonia Fargas as a streetperson.

Hot on the trail of the decapitated corpses and the castoff heads are cops Don Gordon and Rae Dawn Chong, who has nightmares about a human killer (Neil Giuntoli), but subplot turns out to be something of a red herring.

Bloody effects do not approach the poetic grotesqueries of "Henry," sticking with more conventional bladder and stage blood effects. Shocks are mixed with leavening humor, and story ends with the setup for the inevitable sequel, assuming interest exists.

McNaughton and writers Mason Nage and Richard Fire manage several moments that are a cut above usual genre fare. However, the clear message of this as a follow-up to "Henry" is that McNaughton is no outlaw, and can work within the system as well. (McNaughton's third film, "Sex, Drugs, Rock & Roll," also is at the Boston fest.)
— *Daniel M. Kimmel*

THE BACHELOR

A Greycat Films release of a production of Edioscope Intl., Reteitalia and Media Park Budapest. Executive producer, Elda Ferri. Produced by Mario Orfini. Directed by Roberto Faenza. Screenplay, Ennio De Concini, Hugh Fleetwood, Faenza; camera (Technicolor), Giuseppe Rotunno; editor, Claudio Cutry; music, Ennio Morricone; production design, Giantito Burchiellaro; costumes, Milena Canonero; casting, Francesco Cinieri. Reviewed at Boston Film Festival, Aug. 23, 1991. No MPAA Rating. Running time: **105 MIN.**
Dr. Emil Grasler . . . Keith Carradine
Frederica/Widow . Miranda Richardson
Sabine . . . . . . Kristin Scott-Thomas
Katharina . . . . . Sarah-Jane Fenton
von Schleheim . . . . . Max von Sydow

"**T**he Bachelor" has the potential to be an arthouse success with strong possibilities for wider acclaim. Its mixture of romance, period costumes and picturesque settings should strongly appeal to audiences who loved "A Room With A View."

Based on novel by Arthur Schnitzler ("La Ronde"), pic focuses on a middle-aged physician (Keith Carradine) who leads a restrained life with his unmarried sister (Miranda Richardson). Shortly after the start of the story, set prior to World War I, the sister commits suicide and brother is left on his own.

He then meets the feisty daughter (Kristin Scott-Thomas) of an opera star (Max von Sydow, in little more than a cameo, but a delicious one), and finds himself falling in love. Unsure of himself, the bachelor hesitates to take the next step, and Scott-Thomas must be the provocateur. Carradine gets cold feet and — promising to be back — flees to his apartment in the city.

There he meets Sarah-Jane Fenton, and he is as forward with her as he is backward with Sabine. Whether he is overcompensating or sowing his wild oats isn't clear, but the doctor finds himself as unsure as ever as to what to do with his life.

Carradine also crosses paths with a young widow (Richardson again), who's as brash as his sister was gray. However, since his ultimate goal is to lead a life that is predictable and controlled, the ending — which might have been tragic — ends up a happy one, though richly ironic.

Pic is immensely aided by the production design, especially a scene set on an early 20th century subway seemingly all polished wood and brass. Film fully creates a world both more innocent and more repressed than today's. (Scant credits do not identify where the film was shot, but it looks to be an old European capital such as Budapest.)

Casting of Carradine (currently on Broadway in "The Will Rogers Review") is a plus. In previous films ("Pretty Baby," "The Moderns"), he has shown a facility with early 20th century characters instead of merely going through the paces in period drag. He makes the character sympathetic even as the doc stumbles through life.

Audiences will need to know that Richardson plays a dual role, adding the key fillip to the ending. Scott-Thomas and Fenton provide a fascinating contrast; between rural and city settings, and between intellectual and emotionally daring traits.

With the help of some favorable reviews in initial situations, Greycat has a winner here.
— *Daniel M. Kimmel*

COMPANY BUSINESS

A Metro-Goldwyn-Mayer release of a Steven-Charles Jaffe production. Produced by Jaffe. Written and directed by Nicholas Meyer. Camera (Technicolor), Gerry Fisher; editor, Ronald Roose; music, Michael Kamen; sound (Dolby), Martin Evans; production design, Ken Adam; art direction, Albrecht Konrad; costume design, Yvonne Blake; associate producer, Dirk Petersmann; 2nd unit director, Jaffe; assistant directors, Jim Maniolas, Tim Lonsdale (Washington, D.C.), Christopher Carreras, Marcia Gay, Eva-Maria Schonecker (Berlin), Pascal Salafa (Paris); casting, Jeremy Zimmerman, Howard Feuer. Reviewed at the Filmland Corporate Center, Culver City, Calif., Sept. 4, 1991. MPAA Rating: PG-13. Running time: **98 MIN.**
Sam Boyd . . . . Gene Hackman
Pyiotr Grushenko . Mikhail Baryshnikov
Elliot Jaffe . . . . . . Kurtwood Smith
Col. Grissom . . . . Terry O'Quinn
Mike Flinn . . . . . Daniel Von Bargen
Grigori Golitsin . . . . . . Oleg Rudnick
Natasha Grimaud . . Geraldine Danon
Faisal . . . . Nadim Sawalha

Even with marquee leads and quaint timing in terms of world events, this muddled comedic-thriller, which asks what spies do after the cold war, doesn't figure to have much company or do much business. Aside from a few amusing political references, the indecisive tone scuttles the film.

Pic's most interesting facet involves the pairing of Gene Hackman, who seems to have an innate drive to work, whatever the material, and Mikhail Baryshnikov, who does films with only slightly greater frequency than Soviet uprisings.

Hackman plays a former CIA agent wasting his talent in industrial espionage. He's drafted by "the company" to return a former Soviet mole (Baryshnikov) to the Soviets — along with $2 million in Colombian drug booty.

The swap goes bad, however, sending the two former spies racing around Europe, with their embarrassed and somewhat bumbling bosses from the CIA (Kurtwood Smith) and KGB (Oleg Rudnick) in lukewarm pursuit.

Writer-director Nicholas Meyer also is all over the map with his direction and script, which begins as a thriller (complete with portentously brooding music by Michael Kamen) then shifts to a sort of screwy comedy.

Some of the early gags have some timely zest, including a reference to Soviet leader Mikhail Gorbachev's shaky status and a wistful Arab arms dealer lamenting the advent of peace.

After the initial exchange goes bad, however, there's never any real sense of jeopardy for the protagonists but also not much that's truly funny. The government sort-of bad guys are a perfect example, not cartoonish enough to qualify as Keystone Kops or menacing enough to present much of a threat.

Hackman ambles through the proceedings with his usual efficiency, creating a likable figure in dangerous circumstances and mirroring his recent performances in "Narrow Margin" and "The Package." It's a character he can play with about the same ease as providing voiceovers for a major airline's advertising, although the latter probably requires more conviction.

Baryshnikov also is engaging but seems a little young to be playing a "dinosaur" whose spy games have become obsolete. Smith and Rudnick, meanwhile, are appropriately and characteristically smarmy as the two agents, while Geraldine Danon is mere window dressing as the woman who helps the fugitives in Paris.

Meyer also stumbles with the ending, which feels abrupt, but not unwelcome.

Gerry Fisher's camera provides a nifty travelog of Paris and Berlin, while other tech credits are also sharp. Still, with its theme, it's a pity "Company Business" isn't equal to current events in the Soviet Union. As is, its best moments wouldn't add up to a recent episode of "Nightline." — *Brian Lowry*

UNTIL THE END OF THE WORLD
(GERMAN-FRENCH-AUSTRALIAN)

A Warner Bros. release (U.S.) of an Anatole Dauman and Jonathan Taplin presentation of a Road Movies (Berlin)-Argos Films (Paris)-Village Roadshow (Sydney) production. Produced by Taplin, Dauman (Dauman credited as executive producer in U.S., Japan). Directed by Wim Wenders. Screenplay, Peter Carey, Wenders, based on an original idea by Wenders, Solveig Dommartin; camera (color), Robby Müller; editor, Peter Przygodda; music, Graeme Revell; sound (Dolby), Jean-Paul Mugel; production design-futuristic objects, Thierry Flamand; production design (Australia), Sally Campbell; costume design, Montserrat Casanova; sound editor-postproduction supervisor, Barbara von Weiterhausen; high-definition video design, Sean Naughton; line producer, Marc Monnet; associate producers, Masa Mikage, Julia Overton, Walter Donohue; assistant director, Marc Jeny. Reviewed at Skywalker Sound, Santa Monica, Calif., Sept. 6, 1991. Running time: **178 MIN.**
Trevor McPhee/
Sam Farber . . . . William Hurt
Claire Tourneur . . Solveig Dommartin
Eugene Fitzpatrick . . . . . Sam Neill
Henry Farber . . . . . Max von Sydow
Philip Winter . . . . . Rüdiger Vogler
Burt . . . . Ernie Dingo
Edith Farber . . . . . . Jeanne Moreau
Chico . . . . Chick Ortega
Krasikova . . . . . . Elena Smirnowa
Raymond . . . . Eddy Mitchell
Mr. Mori . . . . Ryu Chishu
Bernie . . . . Allen Garfield
Elsa . . . . Lois Chiles
David . . . . David Gulpilil
Also with: Justine Saunders, Charlie McMahon, Jimmy Little, Kylie Belling.

A dream project about allowing other people to see one's dreams, "Until The End Of The World" is a dream partly realized and partly still in the head of the director. Ambitious, personal sci-fi romance from arthouse favorite Wim Wenders, this international odyssey is too idiosyncratic, unconventional and undramatic to make the grade with a significant U.S. audience, but reception in Europe should be better.

Described by Wenders as "the ultimate road movie," the $23 million production was intended to shoot in 65m in 17 countries, but the format proved too unwieldy for all the location work, and budget limitations forced a cutback to nine nations.

Current three-hour version will go out internationally, but Wenders reportedly has a five-hour cut to show at fests and release on video.

Film conveys the feeling of an abridgment, as narration by Sam Neill wallpapers the gaps in the globetrotting of William Hurt, Solveig Dommartin and other characters. Set in 1999, vaguely futurized through the pervasive presence of video phones and tracking equipment, script by Wenders and Aussie writer Peter Carey presents a world threatened by a nuclear satellite careening toward Earth.

Party girl Claire Tourneur (Dommartin) is given stolen money by some bank robbers and, for kicks, she picks up a stranger, Trevor McPhee (Hurt), while transporting the loot to Paris.

Pursuing Trevor to Lisbon, Claire gets him into bed, but he takes off again. One step behind him to Berlin, Moscow, China and Japan, with the assistance of detective Philip Winter (Wenders regular Rüdiger Vogler), Claire finally wins Trevor's trust and learns his true agenda.

Detouring to San Francisco, pic comes to a rest after 78 minutes in Australia's outback. Tone and intent change radically here, as Hurt unveils the reason for his globehopping: He's recording images of the world with a special camera headset that can transmit pictures to the blind.

Hurt's mother (Jeanne Moreau) has been blind since childhood, and duration of the drama involves the emotional and physical effort involved in transferring pictures, as well characters' dreams, into images viewable by others. Much-feared end of the world also comes and goes as a new millennium dawns.

In the logistically taxing effort to get all this on screen, Wenders has sacrificed some of his customary poetry. His scenes of travel, so evocative in "Kings Of The Road," "The American Friend" and "The State Of Things," are surprisingly flat here.

And the grand emotion and obsession needed to carry the two lovers around the world isn't apparent in Hurt and Dommartin. Pair strike no sparks, and Hurt seems blank most of the time.

Hurt and Max von Sydow, who plays Hurt's scientist père, are believable as son and father, and their scenes together late in the film, along with some involving Moreau, are the strongest of the three hours.

Dommartin, who co-starred in Wenders' "Wings Of Desire," is alternately charming and perplexing, but she's not playing a character U.S. audiences, at least, are likely to warm to.

With Robby Müller's roving camerawork, the constant movement across the globe, the host of offbeat characters, the thematic adventurousness and the torrent of music from a variety of sources (from Neneh Cherry to U2), there is always a lot to engage interest here, even if Wenders' achievement hasn't quite matched his ambition.
— *Todd McCarthy*

UNDERTOW

A Capstone Films release of an Edmond D. Cruea and Capstone Films presentation of a Burtt Harris production. Produced by Harris, Thomas Mazziotti. Line producer, Christopher Quinn. Written and directed by Mazziotti, based on Neal Bell's play "Raw Youth"; camera (Technicolor), Kevin Lombard; editor, John Carter; music, Paata; sound (Dolby), Buzz Turner; production design, Michael Moran; costume design, Ticia Blackburn; assistant director, Marybeth Hagner; 2nd unit camera, Wayne Paul; casting, Joy Todd. Reviewed at Technicolor screening room, N.Y., June 5, 1991. Running time: **95 MIN.**
Sam . . . . Peter Dobson
Mel . . . . Burtt Harris
Nina . . . . Erica Gimpel
Marlene . . . . Anita Gillette
William Gary . . . . . Greg Mullavey
Hustler . . . . Tom Mazziotti

A lame little drama that cannot conceal its theatrical origins, "Undertow" trades in controversial matters in a marginal manner. Debut effort from writer-director Thomas Mazziotti gets into ambiguous and potentially intriguing gay and political issues, but muted result lacks dramatic fireworks and moral insight. Pic will quickly drown after surfacing for momentary theatrical release.

After a shock prolog in which a congressman commits suicide while delivering a speech, offbeat father-son story slips into the first of what becomes many two-character dialog scenes.

A beefy, middle-aged con man, Mel (Burtt Harris), has recently been released from prison. Exceedingly streetwise and persuasive, he manages to get his attractive son Sam (Peter Dobson), a former cop booted off the force for alleged corruption, to help him remain free by assisting him in a plan to entrap a purportedly gay congressman on behalf of the FBI.

While disgusted by the plan, Sam views it as a way to be reinstated and tries to allay the suspicions of his g.f. (Erica Gimpel), herself a cop, who imagines that his out-of-town mission has to do with another woman.

Second act largely focuses on the encounter between Sam and the intelligent congressman (Greg Mullavey). A tense, tentative affair at a ramshackle beach hotel surreptitiously taped by the FBI, rendezvous takes unpredictable twists and turns, but neither the tension nor the psychological revelations reach a genuinely rewarding level. Following a reunion between father and son, ending is patly cynical.

All too clearly based on a play, what with its abundant supply of long monologs, story wades into morally murky water. Notion of the FBI attempting to discredit or blackmail a politician via sexual means could be seen as business as usual, but having a father strongarm his son into sleeping with another man is a bit hard to take on at least a couple of levels.

Behavior of all the characters, including the victimized congressman, is duplicitous and hypocritical, which makes for less than edifying viewing when not framed by a strong artistic context.

Acting is solid without being sparkling. Harris, vet N.Y. producer of many Sidney Lumet films, exudes working-class horse sense and cleverness as Mel but basically hits the same gruff note throughout. Dobson is effectively agitated and impatient as the dissatisfied Sam, while Mullavey efficiently conveys the politico's neatly rationalized attitudes.

Shot in Connecticut on bleak coastal locations, low-budget indie production looks minimal but good, although repetitive, mostly synthesized music irritatingly throbs under many scenes.
— *Todd McCarthy*

DOGFIGHT

A Warner Bros. release of a Peter Newman production. Produced by Newman, Richard Guay. Executive producer, Cathleen Summers. Directed by Nancy Savoca. Screenplay, Bob Comfort; camera (Technicolor), Bobby Bukowski; editor, John Tintori; music, Mason Daring; sound (Dolby), John Sutton; production design, Lester W. Cohen; art direction, Daniel Talpers; set design, Sarah Stollman; set decoration, Jessica Lanier; costume design, Eugenie Bafaloukos; associate producer, Llewellyn Wells; assistant director, J. Miller Tobin; casting, Marion Dougherty. Reviewed at Telluride (Colo.) Film Festival, Aug. 30, 1991. MPAA Rating: R. Running time: **92 MIN.**
Eddie Birdlace . . . . . River Phoenix
Rose Fenney . . . . Lili Taylor
Berzin . . . . Richard Panebianco
Buele . . . . Anthony Clark
Benjamin . . . . . . Mitchell Whitfield
Rose Sr. . . . . Holly Near
Marcie . . . . E. G. Daily

An inherently repellent

subject has been given surprisingly benign treatment in "Dogfight." At its best, this second feature from "True Love" director Nancy Savoca illuminates how posturing and prescribed behavior inhibits true communication between the sexes, but too much of the action just drifts to generate much audience excitement. Pic probably reps an insurmountable marketing dilemma.

Title refers to the central event of ex-Marine Bob Comfort's intermittently intriguing screenplay — a party to which a bunch of young servicemen bring the ugliest women they can find.

Full of obnoxious military attitude and macho bravado, Eddie Birdlace and his three buddies hit the streets of San Francisco on the portentous eve of Nov. 21, 1963, and separately scout for a "dog" that might win the prize for most gruesome date. After a little trouble, Eddie (River Phoenix) manages to locate a candidate in young waitress Rose Fenney (Lili Taylor) and drags the unsuspecting young lady along to the nightclub.

The bringing together of a soldier headed for Vietnam and a future hippie on the night before President Kennedy's assassination represents a frightfully schematic screenwriting device. But Savoca underplays the character development to such an extent that the film has a muted, very modest impact.

Playing a tough, emotionally unawakened character, Phoenix makes something of a career departure here, but one that is only partially successful in that his Eddie remains opaque character throughout.

Rather, the picture belongs to Taylor's Rose. In her love for Dylan and Joan Baez and her blind idealism, Rose embodies portions of both the purest and most deluded aspects of the coming protest movement. Taylor brings engaging enthusiasm and vigor to the part.

Shot mostly in Seattle, the dark-looking film presents a strangely underpopulated San Francisco. Soundtrack makes good use of period tunes, particularly Dylan's "Don't Think Twice, It's Alright." The most provocative thing about "Dogfight" is that a woman chose to direct it. — *Todd McCarthy*

IN THE SHADOW OF THE STARS
(DOCU)

A First Run Features release. Produced, directed and edited by Irving Saraf, Allie Light. Camera (color), Michael Chin, (black & white) Charles Hilder; music, various; sound, Sara Chin, Michael Emery, Lauretta Molitor, Douglas Murray. Reviewed at Film Forum, N.Y., Aug. 14, 1991. Running time: **93 MIN.**

Promoted as a "A Chorus Line" of the opera world, "In The Shadow Of The Stars" looks at the lives of 11 San Francisco Opera choristers, interweaving interviews and backstage scenes with performance. Though not hitting the high notes of "Tosca's Kiss," docu has enough charm to make it a welcome attraction at specialty houses and in public tv slots.

While all the performers are engaging, few of them grip the viewer because screen time is diffused among so many individuals. Filmmakers Irving Saraf and Allie Light parse the range of personalities in the large group. In keeping with the anonymity of the chorus' role, participants are not identified onscreen unless incidentally revealed in the interviews.

Among the most appealing figures is a black baritone who recalls the emotional effects of racial prejudice and being teased about being fat. One of several chorus members longing to be a soloist, he notes the affinity he feels with Rigoletto.

Opera's romantic spirit also is affirmed in two married couples who met in the company. Another chorus man lives with a male partner who describes himself as "an opera widow."

Some choristers are caught between gratitude for their jobs and their yearning for solo stardom. Like many of their contemporaries, they are buoyed by dreams of the big time while debating if it's worth the hassle.

The choristers' feelings naturally are heightened by the transcendent power of opera to amplify the deepest longings.

Excerpted performances from the S.F. company, such as the appearance of the witches in Verdi's "Macbeth," should delight even non-opera fans.
— *Fred Lombardi*

TOTO LE HÉROS
(TOTO THE HERO)
(BELGIAN-FRENCH-GERMAN)

An Iblis Films-Prods. Philippe Dussart-Metropolis production. Produced by Pierre Drouot, Dany Geys. Executive producer, Jacqueline Louis. Directed by Jaco van Dormael. Screenplay, Van Dormael; camera (Eastmancolor), Walther van den Ende; editor, Susana Rossberg; music, Pierre van Dormael; song, Charles Trenet; sound, Dominique Warnier; art director, Hubert Pouille; costume design, An D'Huys, Anne van Brée; assistant director, Danilo Catti. Reviewed at 45th Edinburgh Intl. Film Festival (New Directors section), Aug. 24, 1991. (Also at New York, Montreal and Locarno film festivals.) Running time: **89 MIN.**
Thomas van
Hasebroeck . . . . Michael Bouquet
Thomas (as young man) . Jo De Backer
Thomas (as child) . . . . Thomas Godet
Evelyne . . . . Gisela Uhlen
Evelyne
  (as young woman) . . Mireille Perrier
Alice . . . . Sandrine Blancke
Alfred . . . . Peter Böhlke
Alfred (as young man) . Didier Ferney
Alfred
  (as child) . . Hugo Harrold Harrisson
Thomas' mother . . . Fabienne Loriaux
(French dialog)

"Toto Le Héros" is a winning blend of kid's fantasy and adult comedy that's as fresh as a hot croissant. Debut pic by Belgian helmer Jaco van Dormael is already a fest favorite, and looks set for offshore theatrical dates and tasty tube sales.

Multilayered plot kicks off in rollercoaster style with Thomas van Hasebroeck (Michel Bouquet) soliloquizing in a hospital bed about childhood buddy Alfred Kant "stealing his life." Jigsaw images include older Alfred seemingly murdered, baby Thomas in a flame-licked nursery and Thomas as a child introducing his mom and dad in a semi-musical montage.

As the smoke clears, it turns out that Thomas reckons he was given to the wrong family because of chaos during a hospital fire. The Kant family went on to become rich and famous, while Thomas was stuck with a workaway middle-class upbringing in a dull Belgian nabe.

Especially in its early stages, with kid Thomas' screwy view of life, pic often plays like a Euro version of "The World According To Garp." The tempo slows in the long central section dominated by the adult Thomas' affair with Evelyne (Mireille Perrier), who may or may not be his sister; but the pacey final reels, as he escapes from hospital and comes face to face with his wrinkled foe, rediscover the opening's élan and spring some neat twists in the bargain.

Former clown and children's theater director van Dormael unravels the complex skein with much assurance and shows a sharp talent for absurdist comedy. French vet Bouquet is in crusty form as the embittered Thomas, and both Perrier and Jo De Backer hit the right notes in lower-key parts. Thomas Godet is suitably wide-eyed as the moppet, with striking support from Sandrine Blancke (voiced by Perrier) as his nutty sis.

Technically it's fine all around, with perky use of the w.k. Charles Trenet song "Boum." Pic was a deserved winner of the Camera d'Or prize at this year's Cannes fest. — *Derek Elley*

ZOMBIE JA KUMMITUSJUNA
(ZOMBIE AND THE GHOST TRAIN)
(FINNISH)

A Marianna Films-Villaelfa production. Directed by Mika Kaurismäki. Screenplay, Kaurismäki, based on an idea by Kaurismäki, Pauli Pentti, Sakke Järvenpää; camera (color), Olli Varja; editor, Kaurismäki; music, Mauri Sumen. Reviewed at Andorra cinema, Helsinki, Aug. 22, 1991. (In San Sebastian and New York film festivals.) Running time: **88 MIN.**
Zombie/Antti Autiomaa . Silu Seppälä
Marjo . . . . Marjo Leinonen
Harri . . . . Matti Pellonpää
Mother . . . . Vieno Saaristo

After a stint making foreign-themed, big-budgeted pics, Mika Kaurismäki returns to Finland with "Zombie And The Ghost Train," a rock 'n' roll road movie about a loser drifting from Helsinki to Istanbul. Pic isn't a knockout, but it's a sensitive little film for those who care to listen.

Zombie, a self-destructive young man without a hold on his life, can't even commit suicide properly. He's offered promises for a better life when he meets a girl willing to share his attitudes. But soon he rejects the girl because he is afraid of responsibilities and restrictions. All he does is drift.

Stylistically, Kaurismäki's film has much in common with its protagonist (Silu Seppälä), a slender and delicate man with a melancholy look in his eyes. Pic's overall impression and tone is powerless melancholy. "Zombie" shows Finland at its ugliest: a freezing and colorless country with little comfort for strangers.

Kaurismäki describes the film as a "comic tragedy," but the comedy is hard to find. Either his sense of humor is very dry or it simply doesn't exist. "Zombie" lacks the witty wisecrack dialog one usually would expect from a Villealfa production.

As a matter of fact, the film is primarily a state of mind, more a mental landscape than a tale. For several reasons, "Zombie" resembles Kaurismäki's 1982 feature "The Worthless," especially in the laconic friendship between Zombie and his manager, a friendship confirmed in a beautiful final scene in spring-gray Istanbul.

Soundtrack's rock music is more like a decoration. Pic has some structural problems; every now and then it simply gets stuck. However, after a few disappointing comedies and the rather hollow "Amazon," "Zombie" is a step in the right direction.
— *Matti Apunen*

BOSTON FEST

LITTLE MAN TATE

An Orion release of a Scott Rudin-Peggy Rajski production. Produced by Rudin, Rajski. Executive producer, Randy Stone. Directed by Jodie Foster. Screenplay, Scott Frank; camera (Du Art color), Mike Southon; editor, Lynzee Klingman; music, Mark Isham; sound (THX), Douglas Axtell; production design, Jon Hutman; art direction, Adam Lustig; set decoration, Sam Schaffer; costume design, Susan Lyall; assistant director, Mike Tapoozian; 2nd unit director, Rajski; 2nd unit camera, Tony Janelli; casting, Avy Kaufman, Linda Todd. Reviewed at Telluride (Colo.) Film Festival, Aug. 31, 1991. (Also in Boston Film Festival.) MPAA Rating: PG. Running time: **99 MIN.**
Dede Tate . . . . Jodie Foster
Jane Grierson . . . . . . Dianne Wiest
Fred Tate . . . . . . Adam Hann-Byrd
Eddie . . . . Harry Connick Jr.
Garth . . . . David Pierce
Damon Wells . . . . P.J. Ochlan
Gina . . . . Debi Mazar
Winston F. Buckner . George Plimpton

Jodie Foster makes an appealing, if modest, directorial debut with "Little Man Tate." Her sensitive, emotionally straightforward approach to the heart-tugging story of rearing a child prodigy could well translate into solid public support.

Pic shows sympathy for out-siders and projects an intelligent attitude toward children. Its focus may be quite specific and insights unremarkable, but its effects are honestly earned.

Scott Frank, earning plaudits for his clever "Dead Again" script, penned this nicely observed tale of a year in the life of a 7-year-old genius. An accomplished painter, poet and pianist in addition to being a math wizard, Fred Tate (Adam Hann-Byrd) is being raised by his single mother, a mildly tough working-class woman whom he, along with the the the rest of the world, calls Dede (played with a vulgar accent by Foster).

The uneducated Dede has little idea how to accommodate her son's special needs, but she really is the only person in her son's life, as he is ostracized at school.

Before long, however, Fred comes to the attention of wealthy Jane Grierson (Dianne Wiest), a child psychologist and teacher of the gifted. First taken by Jane on an "odyssey of the mind" field trip, Fred moves in with her when he is invited to attend a summer college course, but she's at a loss to relate to him in any way but cerebrally.

Fred strikes up an engaging relationship with a somewhat older, titanically arrogant math genius named Damon (memorably impersonated by P.J. Ochlan), who takes him for a funny but unfortunate horseback ride, then manages a friendship of sorts with groovy college student Eddie (Harry Connick Jr.).

Most of the film's emotional power lies in the open, alert, eager-to-please face of Hann-Byrd, making his acting debut. He makes each moment and movement seem valid and authentic, drawing the viewer in.

Filled with small, telling moments rather than big events, film never really gets inside Fred's head, but it neatly sketches the external aspects of his predicament.

Although the story is not autobiographical, Foster's background makes her uniquely qualified to direct this film: She was raised by her mother, began her spectacular career at age 3 and has been in the limelight all her life.

The helplessness of all the characters to deal with the boy's exceptional status is well conveyed, although a couple of times Wiest, who cuts the right figure as a woman who was once a brainy child herself, is made to look ridiculous in her futile attempts to fill a mother's shoes.

Lenser Mike Southon helped Foster achieve a strong, bright look, and ace composer Mark Isham contributed a zippy, upbeat jazz score.

Foster has mostly succeeded in reaching the goals she sets for herself here and, as such, the film reps an auspicious debut.
— *Todd McCarthy*

BEHIND THE MASK
(IRISH-BRITISH-AUSTRALIAN-DOCU)

An Activision production. Produced and directed by Frank Martin. Screenplay, Danny Grilly, Nick Anning; camera (color) Deirdre Noonan; editor, Martin; music, Trevor Mathison; sound, Martin Culverwell. Reviewed at Boston Film Festival, Aug. 26, 1991. Running time: **75 MIN.**
Narrator: John Fitzpatrick.

A hard-hitting documentary about Northern Ireland, "Behind The Mask" combines news footage with original interviews of Irish Republican Army veterans. Some will call the pic propaganda, and others will call it a response to the Brits' side of the story. In any case, it has little chance for theatrical or even Stateside tv exposure because of its unrepentant pro-IRA stance.

Per pic's 20-year overview, the British soldiers are an army of "occupation" and the IRA is providing defense and counterattack forces for the put-upon and discriminated-against Catholic population.

The dozen or so interviews are with "former" IRA members, but no explanation is given of their status. All have been imprisoned or interned at one time or another and they may simply find it politic to disavow knowledge of the organization.

The filmmakers are immensely helped by their subjects' eloquence, particularly Brendan Hughes, who goes on for several minutes about his escape from prison and passage across the border to Ireland. (He subsequently went back to prison.)

Tech credits are shaky, even by video-to-film transfer standards. Color occasionally drops out of the picture. Distortions do not detract from the film but adds to its urgent cinema vérité quality. — *Daniel M. Kimmel*

LUNATICS: A LOVE STORY

A Renaissance Pictures presentation. A Sam Raimi-Robert Tapert production. Co-executive producers, Brian C. Manoogian, James A. Courtney. Produced by Bruce Campbell. Directed by Josh Becker. Screenplay, Becker; camera (color), Jeff Dougherty; editor, Kaye Davis; music, Joseph Lo Duca; production design, Peter Gurski; assistant director, John Cameron; co-producer, David Goodman. Reviewed at Boston Film Festival, Aug.27, 1991. No MPAA Rating. Running time: **87 MIN.**
Hank . . . . Theodore Raimi
Nancy . . . . Deborah Foreman
Ray . . . . Bruce Campbell
Comet . . . . George Aguilar
Presto . . . . Brian McCree

If one can imagine "David And Lisa" crossed with "Evil Dead II" by way of "Annie Hall," one has a good idea what "Lunatics: A Love Story" is like. Unlikely romantic comedy between two people unable to connect with reality will play to the hipper segment of audiences that flocked to the "Evil Dead" films, but not the gorehounds.

Taken on its own terms, pic's a touching love story between Theodore Raimi's delusional paranoid and Deborah Foreman's incredibly naive Iowa girl. Raimi has spent the last six months locked in his apartment, where his neighbors hear him yelling.

He's covered his walls with aluminum foil and believes spiders are running around his brain. Audience, taken into his delusions, sees them, too.

Pic works only if his dementia is taken as a comic metaphor for his alienation. Raimi plays him as a likable enough guy, but when he meets Foreman through an incredibly fortuitous wrong number, it becomes apparent how dangerous he could be.

Fortunately, she is in her own way as flaky as he, and they overcome various obstacles (including imaginary doctors and a real street gang) to find love before fadeout.

Acting is up to snuff, while special effects are a bit on the cheesy side. A climactic chase by a giant spider is obviously a process shot. But since pic won't take itself seriously, viewers are invited to gloss over things as well.
— *Daniel M. Kimmel*

SAMANTHA

A Planet Prods. presentation of a Donald P. Borchers production. Executive producers, Martin F. Gold, Alan Somers. Produced by Donald P. Borchers. Directed by Stephen La Rocque. Screenplay, John Golden, La Rocque; camera (CFI color), Joey Forsyte; editor, Lisa Churgin; music, Joel McNeely; sound (Ultra-Stereo), Steuart Pearce; production design, Dorian Vernacchio, Deborah Raymond; costume design, Stephen Chudej; assistant director, Kris Krengle; casting, Linda Francis. Reviewed at Boston Film Festival, Sept. 10, 1991. No MPAA Rating. Running time: **100 MIN.**
Samantha . . . . Martha Plimpton
Henry . . . . Dermot Mulroney
Walter . . . . Hector Elizondo
Marilyn . . . . Mary Kay Place
Elaine . . . . Ione Skye
Milos . . . . Marvin Silbersher
Also with: I. M. Hobson, Maryedith Burrell, Robert Picardo, Dody Goodman.

Comedy about young woman seeking her parents is too unfocused to stand much chance with general audiences. Solid thesping may attract some attention when film hits cable, where it is likely to play much better.

Martha Plimpton toplines as Samantha who, on her 21st birthday, is informed by her parents (Hector Elizondo and Mary Kay Place) that she was a foundling left on their doorstep. After a peculiar childhood (shown in flashbacks) this is the final straw, and she exits vowing to look for her "real" parents.

First third of film, poking fun at post-adolescent angst, works best, as parents, music teacher (Marvin Silbersher) and the boy next door (Dermot Mulroney) attempt to convince Plimpton to give up Rube Golberg-type suicide plan. Pic sags at midpoint as Plimpton engages in increasingly unfunny attempts to seek out her biological parents and as Mulroney takes up with Ione Skye (who sinks her teeth into bitchy "other woman" role).

Last third picks up some steam as the story shifts again, this time to the Plimpton-Mulroney-Skye triangle. Resolution of "parental" plotline is both quirky and unsatisfying.

The weakness here is in both the structure of the story and the illogical gaps in the narrative. At one point Plimpton takes a nasty fall down a flight of stairs, but it seems to have happened only to delay her for the arrival of another character. Likewise, Mulroney — ostensibly a student — lives in an elaborate loft with no source of income in evidence.

Plimpton proves a difficult choice for the lead role. A feisty, engaging presence, she at times overpowers the other performers to the extent that she loses audience sympathy. She needs someone strong to play off of, and amiable as Mulroney is, he seems like a puppy next to her. Elizondo and Place are reliably solid as the adoptive parents, and one wishes they could have been afforded more screentime.

— Daniel M. Kimmel

EDINBURGH FEST

LET HIM HAVE IT
(BRITISH)

A Fine Line Features release (U.S.) of a Le Studio Canal Plus-Film Trustees in association with British Screen presentation of a Vivid production. produced by Luc Roeg, Robert Warr. Executive producer, Jeremy Thomas. Directed by Peter Medak. Screenplay, Neal Purvis, Robert Wade; camera (Eastmancolor), Oliver Stapleton; editor, Ray Lovejoy; music, Michael Kamen; production design, Michael Pickwood; costume design, Pam Tait; assistant director, Henry Harris; associate producer, Jane Frazer; casting, Lucy Boulting. Reviewed at 45th Edinburgh Intl. Film Festival (New British Cinema section), Aug. 21, 1991. Running time: **115 MIN.**
Derek Bentley . . . . . Chris Eccleston
Chris Craig . . . . Paul Reynolds
William Bentley . . . . Tom Courtenay
Fairfax . . . . Tom Bell
Lilian Bentley . . . . . . Eileen Atkins
Iris Bentley . . . . Clare Holman
Niven Craig . . . . . . Mark McGann
Lord Goddard . . . . . . Michae Gough
Also with: Michael Elphick, Murray Melvin, Ronald Fraser, Clive Revill, James Villiers.

"Let Him Have It" takes one of the most controversial murder trials in postwar Brit history and comes up with a powerful mix of social conscience and solid entertainment. Excellent down-the-line playing, plus meaty perfs by two young leads, augers potentially tasty b.o. given careful handling in foreign markets.

Locally, the recent decision by the U.K. Home Secretary to re-evaluate the case after longtime lobbying by the deceased's family should provide extra ballyhoo angles among younger auds for whom affair is remote history.

Pic reconstructs the events leading to the 1952 rooftop shoot-out in south London between local cops and cocky, gun-crazy Chris Craig. At age 16, Craig was legally too young to be hanged so his 19-year-old partner, Derek Bentley, went to the gallows instead, despite public petitions and last-minute appeals.

Though innocent of any shooting, Bentley was heard to cry "Let him have it" to the rod-wielding Craig. The defense argued the words meant hand over the gun rather than shoot.

Craig, released in 1963 and living a reformed life, is the only person who knows what happened that night. But he played no part in the present production, though the filmmakers tried to contact him.

Pic studiously avoids a docu approach. The dramatic focus begins and ends on a tragic figure of Bentley (Chris Eccleston), an epileptic with the mental age of an 11-year-old and a distant relationship with his working-class father (Tom Courtenay) and reticent mother (Eileen Atkins). After a spell in an approved school, he's coaxed out of his shell by older sister (Clare Holman) and comes under the sway of swaggering Craig (Paul Reynolds) and Craig's crooked brother (Mark McGann).

Petty crime leads to an attempted break-in of a candy's firm's warehouse one night, and the nervy shootout when the cops arrive. Pic swiftly deals with the subsequent trial and then settles down into a powerful indictment of establishment obduracy and capital punishment as the days tick away. As in Krzysztof Kieslowski's "A Short Film About Killing," the execution process is shown in brief but shocking detail.

Neal Purvis and Robert Wade's script is sometimes overladen with exposition, especially in the family scenes and after-trial seg. But it succinctly captures the feel of suburban postwar Britain, with food coupons and cheap cafes, and its younger characters' search for thrills through Hollywood movies, flash cars and pop music. Michael Pickwood's detailed production design, with Liverpool standing in for the southeast London 'burb of Croydon, fits the action like a glove.

Peter Medak directs fluidly and with an eye for bigscreen values. Of the two juves, Reynolds is standout in the showier role of Craig, but Eccleston grows in stature as the quieter, introverted Bentley.

Latter has some fine intimate moments with Holman, excellent as his sympathetic sister, and in a lowkey but pivotal role Courtenay has rarely been better as the pair's tough but tender father. As the mother, Atkins is underemployed in an eye-rolling part; Tom Bell makes a brief mark as the lead rooftop cop. A host of w.k. Brit character actors pop up in solid bits.

All technical credits are topdrawer, with Michael Kamen's music blending contempo source music with atmospheric underscoring. Interiors (shot at Pinewood Studios) are well-matched.

— Derek Elley

THE GRASS ARENA
(BRITISH-16M)

A BBC production. Produced by Ruth Baumgarten. Executive producer, Mark Shivas. Directed by Gillies MacKinnon. Screenplay, Frank Deasy, from John Healy's autobiography; camera (16m, color), Rex Maidment; editor, Michael Parker; music, Philip Appleby; production design, Tony Burrough; costume design, Rosalind Ebbutt. Reviewed at 45th Edinburgh Intl. Film Festival (New British Cinema section), Aug. 20, 1991. Running time: **90 MIN.**
With: Mark Rylance, Pete Postlethwaite, Lynsey Baxter.

A grim tale of an ex-boxer's descent into alcoholism and emotional resurrection via chess, "The Grass Arena" is held together by convincing playing from newcomer Mark Rylance, but boxy direction limits this BBC item to the tube.

Film details in swift strokes young Brit John Healy's tough upbringing, bullying by an Irish father and schoolmates' joshing of him as a "Paddy." Flash forward to adulthood, and he's down and out in the local park hitting the sauce with vagrants and doing time in stir.

While in jail, Healy takes an interest in chess and soon develops the skill of playing games by memory. This gets him an intro, via cafes, into the snooty world of serious chess, where he trounces opposition but remains excluded from the high society that revolves around it. Pic ends on the hopeful note that Healy has finally found a forte in life.

As a study of an outsider scarred by a rough childhood and class barriers, pic moves with sullen, single-minded purpose. Frank Deasy's economical script omits connecting material to build a claustrophobic portrait of Healy and his demons, but Scottish helmer Gillies MacKinnon's direction lacks flair to bring the material alive.

As the short-fused, rebellious Healy, Rylance (also in "Prospero's Books") plays with intensity but on a single note. Pic livens up after the first hour as chess takes over his life, and there's a skillful performance from Lynsey Baxter as an upperclass looker who gives him the come-on but later slams the door. Other roles are well-cast.

Tech credits are okay, with atmospheric use of guitar music from Philip Appleby. Rex Maidment's 16m lensing is workmanlike. Pic won the Michael Powell Award for best new British film at the recent Edinburgh fest.

—*Derek Elley*

MEETING VENUS
(BRITISH)

A Warner Bros. release of an Enigma production. Produced by David Puttnam. Directed by István Szabó. Screenplay, Szabó, Michael Hirst; camera (Eastmancolor, Technicolor prints), Lajos Koltai; editor, Jim Clark; music, Richard Wagner (extracts from "Tannhäuser" conducted by Marek Janowski, played by the Philharmonic Orchestra, London); music consultant, Daisy Boschan; sound (Dolby), Simon Kaye; production design, Attila Kovács; assistant designer, Lorand Javor; costume design, Catherine Leterrier; production manager, Lajos Ovári; assistant director, György Ordódy; associate producer, Uberto Pasolini, Gabriella Prekop; casting, Patsy Pollock. Reviewed at 45th Edinburgh Intl. Film Festival, Aug. 23, 1991. (Also in San Sebastian and competing at Venice film fests.) MPAA rating: PG-13. Running time: **117 MIN.**
Karin Anderson . . . . . . Glenn Close
Zoltán Szántó . . . . . . Niels Arestrup
Jorge Picabia . . . . Erland Josephson
Jean Gabor . . . . Moscu Alcalay
Miss Malikoff . . . . Macha Méril
Monique Angelo . Johanna Ter Steege
Maria Krawiecki . . . . . Maite Nahyr
Stefano Del Sarto . . . . Victor Poletti
Von Schneider . . . . . Marian Labuda
Steve Taylor . . . . . . Jay O. Saunders
Von Binder . . . . Dieter Laser
Yvonne . . . . . . Maria de Medeiros
Jana . . . . Ildikó Bánsági
Edith . . . . Dorottya Udvaros

Glenn Close hits the high notes as a cool diva in "Meeting Venus," but lopsided pic won't get Warners many curtain calls beyond specialized situations. Romantic comedy set in a strife-torn Paris opera house is knocked on the head by a central love story that's dumb and uninvolving.

Film is the second out of David Puttnam's Enigma-Warners deal and an attempt by Magyar helmer István Szabó to go for lighter fare after the flopperoo of "Hanussen" three years ago.

Yarn opens in sprightly style with Budapest conductor (Niels Arestrup) flying in for a production of Wagner's "Tannhäuser" at the fictional Opera Europa. After being introduced to polyglot staff, he soon realizes that "here you can be misunderstood in six languages." The internal politics make old Eastern Europe look like a summer camp.

First off, the orchestra is always breaking for meetings. Next, the chorus leader turns out to be an autocrat. The conductor can't even collect the first half of his fee thanks to bureaucratic fumbling and, worse still, the players' union rep turns out to be an old lover (Ildikó Bánsági) from Hungary.

Nationalistic battles soon break out on all sides. Arestrup, brought up to believe that "art is order," is soon railing against Western democracy. He doesn't get any help from his lead soprano (Close), who initially dismisses him.

Meanwhile, production sponsor Eurogreen is being lambasted by the press for destroying the environment, and the conductor is being sidetracked by a singer (Johanna Ter Steege) who has the hots for him.

Plot grinds to a halt halfway when Close suddenly takes a liking to the humbled Arestrup, and they're soon exchanging confidences between the sheets. When he zips back to Budapest at the same time as her weekend concert there, his wife (Dorottya Udvaros) guesses what's up and boots him out. Film ends with the chaotic first night of "Tannhäuser" back in Paris and everyone briefly united by art.

What must have seemed on paper like a lighthearted satire on Euro-squabbling and the multilingual opera scene works okay in the opening rounds. Szabó and Michael Hirst's script takes neat potshots at "modern" productions, out-of-control egos and slick sponsors.

Szabó directed the same opera in Paris six years ago and makes no secret that the pic was inspired by his experiences. Playing by a large cast with mixed accents is also fine, with pic starting to recall Ernst Lubitsch ensemble comedies.

Things start to go wrong when the Close-Arestrup affair gets serious. Mostly limited to dull sack talks, their sessions lack that vital spark to make the relationship believable. Close looks

glowing and spends a lot of time saying she's in love; Arestrup looks confused. As the script never explains the story of the opera they're sweating over, plot parallels are left dim for general viewers.

That apart, it's still Close's pic. Her grandstanding entrance 25 minutes in gives the pic a real lift, and, with Arestrup playing by the numbers and most other parts reduced to bits, she's the motor that keeps "Meeting Venus" moving along the tracks. Swedish thesp Erland Josephson is solid as an administrator, Jay O. Saunders witty as gay singer Steve Taylor (an in-joke English translation of helmer István Szabo's name), and Victor Poletti fruity as a Pavarotti clone.

Moscu Alcalay, as Arestrup's embattled Magyar boss, handles some of the script's best throwaway lines (subtitled) with panache. French vet Macha Méril is wasted in a nothing part; ditto Maria de Medeiros ("Henry & June") as a ditzy young mooner.

Tech credits are snappy. Regular Szabó lenser Lajos Koltai gives a glow to the mainly Hungarian locations, and editing and design is trim. Actors' accents sometimes make dialog difficult to understand, but pic's main fault is the paucity of underscoring beyond the chunks of "Tannhäuser." Lipsynching is realistic, with Kiri Te Kanawa supplying Close's warbling and René Kollo standing in for Saunders.

— *Derek Elley*

TORONTO FEST

PARADISE

A Buena Vista release of a Touchstone Pictures presentation, in association with Touchwood Pacific Partners I, of a Jean-François Lepetit-Interscope Communications production. Produced by Scott Kroopf, Patrick Palmer. Executive producers, Lepetit, Ted Field, Robert W. Cort. Directed by Mary Agnes Donoghue. Screenplay, Donoghue, adapted from Jean-Loup Hubert's 1987 film "Le Grand Chemin"; camera (Technicolor prints), Jerzy Zielinski; editor, Eva Gardos, Debra McDermott; music, David Newman; sound (Dolby), Richard Lightstone; production design, Evelyn Sakash, Marcia Hinds; set decoration, Donna J. Hattin; costume design, Linda Palermo Donahue; assistant director, Fredric B. Blankfein, Paul Fonteyn; production manager, Tikki Goldberg; 2nd unit director, Palmer; casting, Johanna Ray. Reviewed at Loews Tower East theater, N.Y., Sept. 11, 1991. (In Toronto Film Festival.) MPAA Rating: PG-13. Running time: **110 MIN.**
Lily Reed . . . . . . Melanie Griffith
Ben Reed . . . . Don Johnson
Willard Young . . . . . . Elijah Wood
Billie Pike . . . . Thora Birch
Sally Pike . . . . . . Sheila McCarthy
Rosemary . . . . Eve Gordon
Catherine Reston Lee . Louise Latham
Earl McCoy . . . . Greg Travis
Darlene . . . . Sarah Trigger
Minister . . . . Richard K. Olsen

Pastoral drama "Paradise" is a comfortable romantic vehicle for the real-life team of Don Johnson and Melanie Griffith. Excellent ensemble acting and a feel-good payoff to this bittersweet tale could produce a sleeper hit for Disney.

Writer Mary Agnes Donoghue debuts as a film director with her careful adaptation of a 1987 French drama "Le Grand Chemin," which Miramax released domestically. Original's producer Jean-François Lepetit previously went the Disney remake route with the hit "Three Men And A Baby."

Story focuses on 10-year-old Elijah Wood, sent by his pregnant mom (Eve Gordon) to spend a school vacation in the sleepy town of Paradise. Griffith and husband Johnson, who are mysteriously cold to each other, take care of the boy. There's a third reel revelation that the death of their 3-year-old son in 1987 has driven a wedge between them.

The boy is befriended by 9-yearold Thora Birch, and film gently follows their pranks and adventures in an idyllic natural setting. Duo have in common the absence of a father; Wood's is supposedly away at sea while Birch's is a roller-skating instructor in a nearby town.

The new surroundings and supportive people allow Wood to mature and face his deepest fears (making for an exciting climax perched scarily atop a tall tower), while the boy's warmth succeeds in reconciling Johnson and Griffith.

Donoghue shows impressive self-assurance for a first-time helmer in not rushing the pace or overdoing the maudlin elements of this material. Instead there are many winning emotional moments, notably involving the precocious kids.

Birch is irresistible as the wise little girl, whose gestures and body language are a treat throughout the picture. Wood underplays and is very natural, boding well for "Radio Flyer," in which he landed the lead role.

Johnson and Griffith co-star for the first time with effective

Original film
LE GRAND CHEMIN
(THE BIG ROAD)
(FRENCH-COLOR)

An AAA release of a Flach Film/Séléna Audiovisuel (AAA)/TF-1 Films coproduction. Produced by Pascal Hommais, Jean-François Lepetit. Written and directed by Jean-Loup Hubert. Camera (Eastmancolor), Claude Lecomte; editor, Raymonde Guyot; music, Georges Granier; art director, Thierry Flamand; sound, Bernard Aubouy; assistant director, Olivier Horlait, Martine Durand; production manager, Farid Chaouche; casting, Marie-Christine Lafosse. Reviewed at Gaumont Ambassade cinema, Paris, April 1, 1987. (In Market at Cannes Film Festival.) Running time: **107 MIN.**

Marcelle	Anémone
Pello	Richard Bohringer
Louis	Antoine Hubert
Martine	Vanessa Guedj
Claire	Christine Pascal
Priest	Raoul Billery
Yvonne	Pascale Roberts
Solange	Marie Matheron
Simon	Daniel Rialet

overtones of a longstanding off-screen relationship (married twice). Both are deglamorized for their character roles and are convincing as a rustic, unsophisticated couple.

Donoghue mutes the film's overall impact (and avoids the "two-hanky pic" genre) by playing down the couple's most emotional scenes together compared to the children's stories. Shooting the duo's violent, raking-up-the-past confrontation in half-light diffuses its effect.

Supporting cast, headed by colorful Sheila McCarthy as Birch's flighty mom, is solid, and film's sexual frankness lifts it out of traditional Disney cuteness. David Newman's warm musical score is a key contribution as is lenser Jerzy Zielinski's evocation of the lovely South Carolina locations. — *Lawrence Cohn*

VENICE FEST

THE FISHER KING

A TriStar release of a Hill/Obst production. Produced by Debra Hill, Lynda Obst. Directed by Terry Gilliam. Screenplay, Richard LaGravenese; camera (Technicolor), Roger Pratt; editor, Lesley Walker; music, George Fenton; sound (Dolby), Thomas Causey, Dennis Maitland II (N.Y.); production design, Mel Bourne; art direction, P. Michael Johnston; set design, Jason R. Weil, Rick Heinrichs; set decoration, Cindy Carr; set decoration (N.Y.); Kevin McCarthy, Joseph L. Bird; costume design,

Beatrix Pasztor; associate producers, Stacey Sher, Anthony Mark; assistant directors, David McGiffert, Joe Napolitano; casting, Howard Feuer. Reviewed at TriStar screening room, Culver City, Calif., Sept. 8, 1991. (Competing in Venice Film Festival.) MPAA Rating: R. Running time: **137 MIN.**

Parry	Robin Williams
Jack Lucas	Jeff Bridges
Lydia	Amanda Plummer
Anne Napolitano	Mercedes Ruehl
Homeless cabaret singer	Michael Jeter

"The Fisher King" has all the ingredients of a major critical and commercial event: two actors at the top of their form, and a compelling, well-directed and well-produced story. This polished film about redemption has a hollow core, but the soft, heart-tugging ending almost certainly will lead to big boxoffice.

In his first outing as a director-for-hire, Terry Gilliam shows his strength at staging visually striking scenes and milking dramatic confrontations. Fans of "Brazil" and other Gilliam epics will be a bit let down by this rather schematic tale of dependence between two emotionally injured men.

First-time screenwriter Richard LaGravenese's lively, detailed original script deftly delineates the top and bottom rungs of human existence in Manhattan. Jack Lucas (Jeff Bridges) is a callous, egotistical radio shock-jock who falls apart when a caller he has blown off on the air proceeds to blow away seven yuppies in a trendy club.

Just as he is about to end it all, Jack is rescued by a goofy gang of derelicts led by a maniac named Parry (Robin Williams). While recovering from his suicidal state, Jack learns that Parry is obsessed with the Holy Grail, as well as with a gawky young lady Lydia (Amanda Plummer).

Jack's earnest attempts to return Parry to normal life and set him up with the elusive Lydia represent his chance at personal redemption.

Film's first two hours zip by quickly and are spiked with memorable scenes, such as a flight-of-fancy in which commuters waltz through Grand Central.

But the final 20 minutes unspool mechanically and interminably as Jack implausibly follows through on the mythological demands of the story by finding what Parry believes to be the Holy Grail and bringing his own emotional life to an unbelievable resolution.

Until then, however, outstanding work is displayed. Jeff Bridg-

es gives what is undoubtedly his strongest lead performance to date, hitting notes he's never tried before in conveying the turmoil inside an arrogant man.

It is impossible to imagine anyone but Williams in the Parry role. Endlessly inventive as usual, Williams shifts with ease from the lucidity of the insane to the emotional bashfulness of a teenager, and he plays an aggressive, emotionally needy character without ever getting on the nerves.

Plummer is terrific as the nerdy loner, and Mercedes Ruehl sizzles as Jack's upfront companion, Anne. Michael Jeter pulls out all the stops in a notable appearance as a homeless singer who helps out the main characters.

Employing Mel Bourne's elaborate production design to the utmost, Gilliam and ace lenser Roger Pratt stage many sequences in extreme deep focus, with the actors carrying on in the foreground while many details reveal themselves far in the distance. — *Todd McCarthy*

EDWARD II
(BRITISH)

A British Screen and BBC Films presentation of a Working Title production. (Intl. sales: The Sales Co.) Executive producer, Sarah Radclyffe, Simon Curtis. Produced by Steve Clark-Hall, Antony Root. Directed by Derek Jarman. Screenplay, Jarman, Stephen McBride, Ken Butler, based on Christopher Marlowe's play; camera (Eastmancolor), Ian Wilson; editor, George Akers; music, Simon Fisher Turner; sound, George Richards; production design, Christopher Hobbs; production manager, Sarah Swords; assistant director, Cilla Ware. Reviewed at Venice Film Festival (competing), Sept. 8, 1991. Running time: **90 MIN.**

King Edward II	Steven Waddington
Gaveston	Andrew Tiernan
Queen Isabella	Tilda Swinton
Mortimer	Nigel Terry
Lightborn	Kevin Collins
Kent	Jerome Flynn
Spencer	John Lynch
Bishop of Winchester	Dudley Sutton
Prince Edward	Jody Graber
Singer	Annie Lennox

Derek Jarman's provocative and challenging adaptation of Christopher Marlowe's "Edward II" likely will be the director's most commercial production to date. It's also likely to provoke lively debate that could help the pic in select arthouses.

Believed by some to be the first explicitly gay play written in English, "Edward II" is a lengthy (about four hours on-stage) bio of Britain's only ac-

knowledged gay monarch, whose preference for his lover over his queen sparked conflict with his barons and, eventually, civil war.

Cutting the play to the bone, Jarman fashions the 16th century drama into a radical attack on antigay prejudices in contempo Brit society. Drama is staged in modern dress, with contemporary police/military uniforms for the forces of repression.

Pic's attitude toward women is problematic. Queen Isabella, astringently played by Jarman regular Tilda Swinton, is cruelly treated in the film. Humiliated and rejected by her husband, she tries everything to win him back from his lover. The character finally turns into a raving monster who literally sucks the blood from her victims.

Jarman also fails to make the film accessible to heterosexual male audiences. Pic seems to be provoking straight viewers while celebrating the play's homosexual theme.

Throughout, Jarman attacks the church's antigay stance and lampoons the British establishment that presses the monarch to abandon his lover.

The film also contains several violent scenes, representing both the horrors of gay bashing as well as the king's terrible revenge on the men who kill his lover. Backed by the BBC, it remains to be seen if, as reported, pic can be shown on Brit tv without cuts. — *David Stratton*

ALLEMAGNE NEUF ZERO
(GERMANY NINE ZERO)
(FRENCH)

A Brainstorm-Antenne 2 production, in association with Gaumont, Peripheria. Produced by Nicole Ruelle. Written and directed by Jean-Luc Godard. Camera (color), Christophe Pollock, Andreas Erben, Stephan Brenda; editor, Godard; sound, François Musy, Pierre Alain Besse; production design, Romain Goupil. Reviewed at Venice Film Festival (competing), Sept. 11, 1991. Running time: **62 MIN.**

Lemmy Caution	Eddie Constantine
Count Zelten	Hanns Zischler
Delphine de Stael	Nathalie Kadem
Narrator	Andre Labarthe
Charlotte/Dora	Claudia Michelsen
Dox Quixote	Robert Wittmers
(French, German soundtrack)	

"Germany Nine Zero" is sort of a political thriller in which Jean-Luc Godard explores a reunified Germany with cynical eyes. The 62-minute film defies conventional commercial assessment, but it's more accessible than some of this cult director's recent work.

Godard brings back Lemmy Caution, as played with world-weary charm by Eddie Constantine. Caution was last seen in the director's 1965 "Alphaville."

While apparently searching for a missing girl, craggy-faced Caution meets up with several strange characters, including Don Quixote, in the shattered landscape of former East Germany.

References to Goethe, Pushkin, Kafka and Max Ophuls blend with such non sequiturs as "happiness can be found in the blank pages of history" and "between a German peace and a German war, there's not a difference of nature but of degree."

Voices overlap, titles proliferate, scenes from old movies are electronically altered. It's all a jumble, but a surprisingly entertaining one.

Pic looks good, with crisp 35m cinematography. It's also helped by Constantine's formidable presence. — *David Stratton*

L'AMORE NECESSARIO
(NECESSARY LOVE)
(ITALIAN-FRENCH)

A Titanus Distribuzione release (in Italy) of a Eidoscope Intl.-Cinemax co-production. Produced by Mario Orfini, Giovanna Romagnoli. Written and directed by Fabio Carpi. Camera (color), Fabio Cianchetti; editor, Alfredo Muschietti; sound, Georges Prat; production design, Amedeo Fago; costume design, Silvana Carpi. Reviewed at Venice Film Festival (competing), Sept. 6, 1991. Running time: **93 MIN.**
Ernesto . . . . Ben Kingsley
Valentina . . Marie-Christine Barrault
Diana . . . . Ann Gisel Glass
Giacomo . . . . Malcolm Conrath
Also with: Geoffrey Bayldon, Iris Marga, Silvia Mocci, Nestor Garay.

Elegantly shot but rather cold, "Necessary Love" is a Euro art film for people who like contemplative games. Director Fabio Carpi lovingly describes the diabolical seduction of a young couple by an older one. Pic's natural tv outlet is in danger, at least in Italy, because of its rating restricting viewers under 14.

Headlining Ben Kingsley and Marie-Christine Barrault, pic was lensed in two versions, English and French, with two negatives. It is being marketed worldwide in both languages.

In the English version screened at Venice, Kingsley turns in a strong performance as a suave architect who, like his wife (Barrault), claims to have reached "an age when one has only indecent thoughts." They have a long-standing pact that they are linked by "necessary love" but are free to enjoy the physical pleasure of "subordinate love" whenever they like.

Vacationing at a posh spa in the mountains, the pair set their sights on two sweet newlyweds (Ann Gisel Glass, Malcolm Conrath), who are exceedingly clean cut, innocent and very much in love. Kingsley and Barrault go about splitting them up with methodical cruelty. First they tempt Conrath to keep a tryst with a young hotel maid (Silvia Mocci) in film's most suspenseful scene.

Next Kingsley consoles a shocked Glass, while Barrault plants the seeds of desire in Conrath. All comes to pass as scheduled, with the twist that in the end the older couple gets burned as well as the younger. Everyone returns home unhappier than before.

Though nobody may be convinced that the balding, hypnotic-eyed Kingsley could orchestrate the newlyweds' feelings, the idea is entertaining enough.

Fabio Cianchetti's camera and Amedeo Fago's production design create a 19th century, Mitteleurope atmosphere just right for the decadent yarn. The spa setting is underlined by an upscale selection of classical scores and succinct dialog peppered with literary quotes and aphorisms.

Nudity is chaste, arty and infrequent. Quite the match of her husband, Barrault emanates a perverse fascination, while the younger thesps are nondescript and rather overwhelmed by their elders. — *Deborah Young*

LES EQUILIBRISTES
(WALKING A TIGHTROPE)
(FRENCH)

A Paris Classics-La Sept-FR-3-Chevereau-Caroline co-production. (Intl. sales: UGC Intl.) Produced by Humbert Balsan. Written and directed by Nico Papatakis. Camera (Eastmancolor), William Lubtchansky; editor, Delphine Desfons; music, Bruno Coulais; sound, Gerard Rousseau; production design, Gisele Cavali, Sylvie Deldon, Nikos Meletopoulos; costumes, Christian Gasc, Eva-Marie Arnault; associate producer, Simon Simsi. Reviewed at Venice Film Festival (competing), Sept. 6, 1991. Running time: **131 MIN.**
Marcel Spadice . . . . . Michel Piccoli
Franz-Ali Aoussine . . . . . Lilah Dadi
Helene Lagache . . . . . Polly Walker
Christa Paeffgen . . Doris Kunstmann
Freddy Babitchev . . . . Patrick Mille
Jacqueline Masset . . Juliette Degenne
The soldier . . . . Laurent Hennequin
Diekmann . . . . Olivier Pajot

Michel Piccoli portrays a famous but ruthless writer who craves the company of handsome and successful young men in this overlong but handsomely produced pic. Audience response to the fascinating material will vary, but with critical support, "Walking A Tightrope" could garner useful arthouse b.o. in major cities.

The Piccoli character is based on celebrated French playwright/author Jean Genet. Director Nico Papatakis produced the only film Genet directed ("Song Of Love," 1955) and based his own first feature, "Les Abysses" (1963) on the same source material as Genet's play, "The Maids." Papatakis says the incidents in his new film are factual.

Exuding casual charm with flashes of hot temper, Piccoli's writer uses his fame to get whatever he wants. A woman friend (Polly Walker) gets him introductions to young and talented men, but sometimes he heads for the train station to pick up a soldier for the night.

At pic's beginning, his eye has been caught by a handsome young man of German-Arab extraction (Lilah Dadi) who has a menial job in a Paris circus but yearns to be a tightrope walker. Through Walker, Piccoli meets the laborer and trains him in the art of tightrope walking. Accidents end the young man's chances, and Piccoli drops him for a new protégé. His callous act leads to the film's tragic conclusion.

Although stylishly made, pic overstays its welcome by about half an hour and takes itself too seriously without ending up very revealing. Writer-director is more interested in the fate of the aspiring tightrope walker than he is in the motivations of the writer, while Walker's role remains ambiguous to the end: Why would such an elegant woman allow herself to be used, even by a famous writer, to entrap guileless young men?

Despite these flaws, pic has considerable interest and is made with elegant precision. William Lubtchansky's camerawork is fine, and Bruno Coulais' score perfectly complements the narrative. — *David Stratton*

UNA STORIA SEMPLICE
(A SIMPLE STORY)
(ITALIAN)

A Columbia-TriStar release of a BBE Intl.-Claudio Bonivento production. Produced by Claudio Bonivento. Directed by Emidio Greco. Screenplay, Greco, Andrea Barbato, based on Leonardo Sciascia's novel; camera (color), Tonino Delli Colli; editor, Alfredo Muschietti; music, Luis Enrique Bacalov; art direction, Amedeo Fago. Reviewed at Venice Film Festival (competing), Sept. 3, 1991. Running time: **94 MIN.**
Prof. Franzò . . . . Gian Maria Volonté
Chief of police . . . Ennio Fantastichini
Brigadier Lepri . . . . Ricky Tognazzi
Superintendent . . Massimo Dapporto
Traveling salesman . . . Massimo Ghini
Carabinieri colonel . . . Paolo Graziosi
Public prosecutor . . . Gianluca Favilla
Roccella's son . . . Gianmarco Tognazzi
Father Cricco . . . . Omero Antonutti

No-frills shooting complements "A Simple Story," which first appears to be merely an intriguing detective yarn set in the Sicilian hinterland. But the richness and complexity of this tale emerge as film progresses, turning it into a class act that will appeal to arthouse auds.

This is the first of four Claudio Bonivento productions Columbia is releasing in Italy, giving the $4 million pic better domestic chances than usual.

Helmer Emidio Greco worked with Italy's famed tv commentator Andrea Barbato to bring the last novella of Sicilian writer and cultural hero Leonardo Sciascia to life. Without mentioning the Mafia or drugs, they paint a chilling portrait of a land where both are involved in a diplomat's death.

Diplomat, who appears in the film only as a corpse, went back to his abandoned villa outside a small Sicilian town to hunt for some letters Pirandello and Garibaldi wrote to his family. His call to the police triggers an investigation that gets more complicated as it goes along. Ending contains a painfully ironic twist.

Greco assembles a superb cast of old and new thesps, and Gian-Maria Volonté gives a grand performance as a wise, bitter prof.

Ennio Fantastichini makes a dapper police chief, and his showdown with his assistant (Ricky Tognazzi) is a memorable filmic duel behind office desks. Though earnest Tognazzi is one of the pic's weaker links, he provides viewers with a sympathetic figure with whom to identify.

Comic relief, with some tragic overtones, is offered by Massimo Ghini, a clean-cut salesman who inadvertently gets caught up in the bureaucratic net on his first trip to Sicily. Tonino Delli Colli's classic cinematography is an incitement to visit the locales.

— *Deborah Young*

NEW YORK FEST

NO LIFE KING
(JAPANESE)

A New Century Producers and Argoproject presentation, underwritten by Suntory Corp., Shicho-Sha and Nippon TV. Produced by Gakuto Niizu, Susumu Matsui, Takuo Murase. Executive producers, Yutaka Okada, Ryohichi Sato. Directed by Jun Ichikawa. Screenplay, Hiroaki Jinno, based on Seikou Ito's novel; camera (color), Osamu Maruike; editor, Shigeru Okuhara; music, Saeko Suzuki. Reviewed at New York Film Festival. Running time: **106 MIN.**
Makoto Ohsawa . . . . Ryo Takayama
Mamiko Ohsawa . . . . . Saeko Suzuki
Nobuhiko Mizuta . . . . . . Neko Saito
Salaried worker . . . . . Ogata Ittsusei

Jun Ichikawa's look at Japanese children's obsession with computers and videogames is stylish but ultimately boring. While kids may be obsessed with videogames, adult arthouse audiences probably couldn't care less about them.

"No Life King" opens on a long line of boys who've waited 5$^{1}/_{2}$ hours to buy the latest videogame, the Legend Of Life King IV. Eventually, Makoto (Ryo Takayama) and his friends become transfixed by the game.

A rumor goes around that the game is cursed and that anyone who plays it but does not finish will die. The school principal's sudden death — while delivering a speech about the dangers of videogames — only reinforces rumors of the curse.

As a result, children refuse to play the Life King game, and some even take to burning it. The rumors, in turn, engender other superstitions. Takayama's mother (Saeko Suzuki) becomes convinced that cakes are poisoned because the bakery site was formerly a graveyard.

At its best, pic makes knowing observations about the high-tech lives children lead. Plot quickly wears thin, however, and the characters lack individual personalities. Ironically, the videos are actually more vivid than the children's drab lives.

Suzuki, who makes a faint impression as the mother, contributed a suitably eerie, computerized score. Osamu Maruike's photography is striking, though the camera movements are at times jerky or painfully slow.

— *William Stevenson*

REBRO ADAMA
(ADAM'S RIB)
(RUSSIAN)

A Mosfilm (RITM Studio) production. Directed by Viatcheslav Krichtofovitch. Screenplay, Vladimir Kounine, based on Anatole Kourtchatkine's novel "House Of Women"; camera (color), Pavel Lebedev; editor, Inna Brozhovskaya; music, Vadim Khrapatchev; sound, Jan Potocki. Reviewed at Toronto Film Festival, Sept. 7, 1991. (Also in New York Film Festival.) Running time: **75 MIN.**
With: Inna Tchourikova, Sveltano Riabova, Macha Goloubkina, Elena Bogdanova.

This "Adam's Rib," whose only resemblance to the 1949 Hollywood pic is the title, is a lighthearted film that should please any audiences that don't mind subtitles.

Four women live together in a crowded Moscow apartment: A paralyzed grandmother, her twice-married and -divorced 50-year-old daughter and the latter's two daughters by different husbands.

Older daughter (Sveltano Riabova) carries on with a married lover who unexpectedly takes an office co-worker on the vacation planned with her. The Fifteen-year-old daughter (Macha Goloubkina) discovers she's pregnant by a punkish factory co-worker.

Their mother (Inna Tchourikova) has a new, wimpy man in her life. As they are about to have furtive sex in the apartment, the grandmother (Elena Bogdanova) breaks it up by ringing a bell by her bed, which is her only method of communication.

The mother later harangues the old lady, complaining she is domineering and responsible for breaking up her marriages because she feared being left alone. That's followed by an apology.

Pic culminates in a birthday party for ailing grandma, attended, at first awkwardly, by the former husbands and the new man. Party ends with everyone shouting at each other, but calmness reigns among the women, who find peace with the pregnancy.

The film concludes in a farcical manner, with the bell's clapper dropping on the grandma's head, leaving her able to speak and on her feet. Now the other women are speechless.

The four actresses are all lovely and excellent in roles giving each many individually funny and endearing moments. Interplay between the sisters is comic and realistic.

Viatcheslav Krichtofovitch directs Vladimir Kounine's charming script with élan. Tech values all contribute to the film's tone. English subtitles also are good.

— *Sid Adilman*

VENICE FEST

A DIVINA COMEDIA
(THE DIVINE COMEDY)
(PORTUGUESE-FRENCH)

A Madragoa Filmes (Lisbon)-Gemini Films (Paris) co-production. (Intl. sales: Metropolis Films, Zurich.) Produced by Paulo Branco. Written and directed by Manoel de Oliveira. Camera (color), Ivan Kozelka; editor, de Oliveira, Valerie Loiseleux; sound, Gita Cerveira; production design, Maria Jose Branco; production manager, Camilo Joao; assistant director, Manuel Joao Arguas. Reviewed at Venice Film Festival (competing), Sept. 8, 1991. Running time: **139 MIN.**
Sonya . . . . Maria de Medeiros
Raskolnikov . . . . . Miguel Guilherme
The prophet . . . . Luis Miguel Cintra
The philosopher . . . . . Mario Viegas
Eve . . . . Leonor Silveira
Ivan . . . . Diogo Doria
Jesus . . . . Paulo Matos
Adam . . . . Carlos Gomes
The director . . . . Ruy Furtado

Though Manoel de Oliveira's personal and demanding films are revered by film buffs in some parts of the world, especially France, the 82-year-old helmer has yet to make a dent in the English-speaking arthouse market. His original newie (not an adaptation of Dante's "Divine Comedy") won't change that.

Setting is a mental hospital where the inhabitants act out various roles. One young couple cavort nude in the garden as Adam and Eve; "Eve" later assumes the role of St. Teresa. One man thinks he's the murderer Raskolnikov, from Dostoyevsky's "Crime And Punishment," while another is Jesus Christ. There's a cynical philosopher who rejects all religion, and a devout prophet who carries a volume he claims is the Fifth Gospel, but which turns out to have blank pages.

Most of this very long film consists of debates and arguments between the characters, but the dialog, at least as translated from the Portuguese, isn't particularly sparkling, and the heavy seriousness about it all makes these lunatics, presumably representatives of the world at large, tiresome after a while.

Miguel Guilherme's Raskolnikov emerges as the most interesting character. Camerawork and sets are strictly functional, and the director seems content just to film his wordy screenplay in a straightforward manner.

In all, this respectable but unremarkable picture will find audiences wherever de Oliveira's reputation is established, but it will give the director no new converts. — *David Stratton*

MISSISSIPPI MASALA

A Samuel Goldwyn Co. release of a Cinecom Entertainment Group presentation in association with Odyssey/Cinecom Intl. of a Mirabi Films production in association with Movieworks. Produced by Michael Nozik, Mira Nair. Executive producer, Cherie Rodgers. Directed by Nair. Screenplay, Sooni Taraporevala; camera (color), Ed Lachman; editor, Roberto Silvi; music, L. Subramaniam; production design-co-producer, Mitch Epstein; associate producer, Lydia Dean Pilcher. Reviewed at Venice Film Festival (competing), Sept. 7, 1991. No MPAA rating. Running time: **118 MIN.**
Demetrius . . . . . Denzel Washington
Mina . . . . Sarita Choudhury
Jay . . . . Roshan Seth
Kinnu . . . . Sharmila Tagore
Tyrone . . . . Charles S. Dutton
Williben . . . . Joe Seneca
Anil . . . . Ranjit Chowdhry
Okelo . . . . Konga Moandu
Also with: Mohan Gokhale, Mohan Agashe, Tico Wells, Yvette Hawkins, Anjan Srivastava, Dipti Suthar.

Indian director Mira Nair's tragicomedy is less passionate and disturbing than many recent U.S. pics dealing with race relations. "Mississippi Masala" is handled with a light touch that will entertain and move audiences in many territories.

Shot largely in the Southern U.S., the Goldwyn release could reach out even farther than Nair's first film, "Salaam Bombay".

The dramatic opening, set in Uganda in 1972, shows a middle-class Indian family forced to leave when Idi Amin takes power. A liberal lawyer (Roshan Seth) who has defended blacks in court, his wife (Sharmila Tagore) and little daughter Mina catch the last plane out under an eerie, threatening state of siege.

Story jumps to present-day Mississippi, where the family has settled. Nair skillfully depicts an interracial small town where there's a minor traffic accident involving a white redneck, black youth Demetrius (Denzel Washington) and a pretty Indian girl, the grown-up Mina (Sarita

Choudhury.)

Mina and Demetrius are attracted to each other right away, and when fate throws them together again, they respond naturally to their feelings. On the surface, there is little opposition. Demetrius' family is poor but well bred. Mina hides the affair from her family until she and Demetrius are caught in bed. The consequences are dire, and racism looms.

Nair's outsider status gives her a rare objectivity in tackling U.S. racism. She is not self-conscious and has no political message to convey. The hierarchy of color is examined without the stridency of "Jungle Fever" — but also without its depth.

Washington is savvy and attractive as the enterprising carpet cleaner destined for a brighter future. Choudhury is a discovery as the Americanized Mina, who calls herself a kind of masala (mixed spices). Together, they carry the film smoothly and agreeably. Seth movingly conveys the sadness of his family's exile. Tagore, familiar from many Satyajit Ray pics, portrays the loyal wife as a strong woman.

Ed Lachman's versatile cinematography makes a witty comparison between the lush, otherworldly paradise of old Africa and the dusty pop architecture of modern Mississippi. Editor Roberto Silvi cuts the two continents together smoothly, letting them reflect on each other without confusion.

— *Deborah Young*

URGA
(FRENCH-RUSSIAN)

A Camera One-Hachette Premiere (Paris)-Studio Trite (Moscow) co-production. Produced by Michel Seydoux. Executive producer, Jean-Louis Peel. Directed by Nikita Mikhalkov. Screenplay, Mikhalkov, Roustam Ibraguimbekov; camera (color), Villenn Kaluta; editor, Joelle Hache; music, Eduard Artemiev; sound, Jean Umansky; production design, Alexei Levchenko; production manager, Leonid Vereschchaguine; associate producer, Rene Cleitman; assistant director, Anatoli Ermilov. Reviewed at Venice Film Festival (competing), Sept. 10, 1991. Running time: **120 MIN.**
Gombo . . . . Bayaertu
Pagma . . . . Badema
Sergei . . . . . . Vlodimir Gostukhin
Grandmother . . . . Babuskha
Also with: Bao Yongyan, Wurinile, Larissa Kuznetsova, Wang Zhiyong, Kinolai Vachtohiline, Baoynhexige.

Russian director Nikita Mikhalkov ("Slave Of Love," "Dark Eyes") has come up with a delightful and charming film made on location in Inner Mongolia. With its rare insight into Mongolian culture, entertaining structure and winning characters, "Urga" (Venice fest's Golden Lion winner) should make its mark in arthouses.

Inner Mongolia is a part of China, which poses a problem for a family of shepherds living in a primitive hut on the vast steppes. Gombo, the husband, is a passionate man but ignorant of birth control, and he and his wife, Pagma, already have two children (Chinese authorities' maximum.)

Sergei, a Russian truck driver who speaks a smattering of Mongolian, falls asleep at the wheel and careens off the road, eventually winding up half in a river. Gombo comes to the rescue and invites the Russian back to the hut for the night.

At first suspicious of the hospitality he's being offered, the driver gradually mellows under the influence of copious amounts of strong liquor. By the end of the night, the Russian and the Mongol are firm friends.

Title refers to a long pole with a lasso on the end, used by the shepherd to collar sheep but also placed in the ground to warn passers-by that lovemaking is taking place.

Clash of cultures — the ebullient, hard-drinking, foulmouthed but basically cheerful and friendly Russian versus his calm, serene, dignified hosts — is never condescending to either side.

Pic is a bit long, and a dream sequence in which Gombo imagines an encounter with his ancestor Genghis Khan is perhaps extraneous, but it's also fun.

Villenn Kaluta's photography of the steppes is top-notch, and the actors give natural, unforced performances, including the two delightful moppets. Technically, the film is flawless.

A majority-French production, pic is spoken in Mongolian and Russian, with some Chinese.

— *David Stratton*

ECRANS DE SABLE
(SAND SCREENS)
(FRENCH-ITALIAN-TUNISIAN)

An AMLF release (France) of a Carthago Films-Leil Prods.-La Sept Paris-Apec-Radio Television Tunisienne co-production in association with the French Ministry of Culture and French Foreign Ministry, Canal Plus, RAI-TV. Produced by Tarak Ben Ammar. Executive producer, Hassan Daldoul. Written and directed by Randa Chahal Sabbag. Camera (color), Yorgos Arvanitis; editor, Yves Des Champs; music, Michel Portal; sound, Fawzi Thabet, Gerard Rousseau; art direction, Sylvain Chauvelot; production managers, Michel Choquet, Mokhtar Labidi, Tao Guiga. Reviewed at Venice Film Festival (noncompeting), Sept. 8, 1991. Running time: **90 MIN.**
Sarah . . . . Maria Schneider
Mariame . . . . Laure Kiling
Dalal . . . . Sandrine Dumas
Talal . . . . Michel Albertini
Giorgio . . . . . . Tamim Kasdi Sahhal

Oppression of Arab women is the subject of the modern fable "Sand Screens," a first feature by Libyan-born Randa Chahal Sabbag. A very visual film with European sensibility and pace, the Tarak Ben Ammar production should find arthouse playoffs.

Maria Schneider is a main asset as a delightfully hard-boiled Arab lady in an unnamed sheikdom. Repudiated by her plenipotentate husband but kept under tight surveillance, she is a prisoner of luxury.

Pacing the empty halls of her Xanadu-like desert palace in the latest French couture, she rages against her boredom and lack of freedom. She tools around the desert in a black stretch limo, making obscene phone calls to strangers while knowing her chauffeur also is her captor.

Though as intensely sympathetic as a caged beast, the wife also has a perverse imagination heightened by years of solitude and frustration. Conceiving an escape plan, she buys the women's university "library" and hires a war-weary young Lebanese woman (Laure Kiling) to run it. Problem: There are no books, because it's dangerous to stock anything possibly anti-Islamic.

The new librarian is soon as frustrated as Schneider, and almost as isolated. Her only contact with people entails visits to Schneider and her deaf-mute cousin (Sandrine Dumas). But instead of feeling solidarity, the librarian is put off by the rich woman's caustic wit, cynicism and unfettered sex life (traits that make the villainous Schneider pic's runaway favorite).

Kiling and a computer man (Michel Albertini) have a pathetic tryst in an elevator. He whispers sad existentialist nothings to her, indicating their affair is doomed.

Schneider's scheme to slip out of the country using Kiling's passport fails. In a fit of pique, she turns Talal over to the club-wielding authorities. Mariame is left standing alone amid the shifting sand. Pic is shot with a handful of actors and lots of sand, giving it a pleasing elemental simplicity.

What's too pared down is the practically nonexistent story, and film winds down after an intriguing start full of atmosphere. After that, it only comes to life when Schneider stalks broodingly across the screen.

Yorgos Arvanitis' sweeping cinematography quickly establishes a "1,001 Nights" atmosphere that gives "Sand Screens" its aura of mystery, while Sylvain Chauvelot's minimalist white sets and Michel Portal's restrained modern score provide elegant backdrops. Kiling is attractive but remote as the woman jaded from the war in Lebanon. The men are hard to distinguish.

— *Deborah Young*

LE CIEL DE PARIS
(THE SKY ABOVE PARIS)
(FRENCH)

A Sara Films production, in collaboration with Canal Plus. (Intl. sales: World Marketing Film.) Produced by Alain Sarde. Executive producer, Christine Gozlan. Directed by Michel Bena. Screenplay, Bena, Isabelle Coudrier-Kleist, Cecile Vargaftig; camera (color), Jean-Marc Fabre; editor, Catherine Schwartz; music, Jorge Arriagada; sound, Jean-Pierre Duret; production design, Sylvia Laquerbe; costume design, Françoise Clavel; assistant director, Hubert Engammare; casting, Anne Isabelle Estrada. Reviewed at Venice Film Festival (noncompeting), Sept. 7, 1991. (Also in Toronto Film Festival.) Running time: **83 MIN.**
Suzanne . . . . Sandrine Bonnaire
Marc . . . . Marc Fourastier
Lucien . . . . Paul Blain
Clothilde . . . . Evelyne Bouix
Florist . . . . Tanya Lopert
Lucien's father . . . Armand Lecampe

"The Sky Above Paris," a first feature, is stylishly made and well acted but has nothing new to say. This tired story of a threesome won't make much of an impression.

Director Michel Bena shows talent in camera placement and movement and in creating tension among his actors, but this is just not enough to lift an unoriginal tale.

Marc Fourastier and the luminous Sandrine Bonnaire play roommates in a Paris apartment. They're fond of each other but occupy separate rooms. Neither of them has lovers; Fourastier prefers boys and Bonnaire has had an unhappy relationship. At a public swimming pool, they meet Paul Blain, who starts spending time with them. Inevitably, the gay roommate falls in love with him, but Blain prefers the woman.

There isn't much more to the story than that, and it isn't enough. The screenplay has no surprises. The characters talk a lot but say nothing interesting.

Bonnaire brings a lot more to the character of Suzanne than the script does, and her young co-stars are adequate. Too bad so much talent is wasted on such thin material.

— *David Stratton*

BOSTON FEST

THE MAN IN THE MOON

An MGM release of a Mark Rydell production. Executive producers, William S. Gilmore, Shari Rhodes. Produced by Mark Rydell. Directed by Robert Mulligan. Screenplay, Jenny Wingfield; camera (Eastmancolor), Freddie Francis; editor, Trudy Ship; music, James Newton Howard; sound (Dolby), Peter Bentley; production design, Gene Callahan; costume design, Peter Saldutti, Dawni Saldutti; associate producers, Bill Borden, Jerry Grandey; assistant director, Grandey; casting, Rhodes. Reviewed at Boston Film Festival, Sept. 5, 1991. MPAA Rating: PG-13. Running time: **99 mins.**
Matthew Trant . . . . . Sam Waterston
Abigail Trant . . . . Tess Harper
Marie Foster . . . . Gail Strickland
Dani Trant . . . . . Reese Witherspoon
Court Foster . . . . Jason London
Maureen Trant . . . . . Emily Warfield
Billy Sanders . . . . . Bentley Mitchum
Will Sanders . . . . Ernie Lively

Bucolic coming-of-age story will need some good reviews to kickstart it, but solid thesping overcomes problems of overly melodramatic third act and manages to put "The Man In The Moon" on a high road.

Pic is unlikely to catch fire at the boxoffice, but intimate drama of the first pangs of adolescent love seems destined for a strong ancillary life on cable and homevid.

Set in 1957 Louisiana, story follows Reese Witherspoon, the 14-year-old daughter of Sam Waterston and Tess Harper. She's envious of her college-bound sister (Emily Warfield) and moons over pictures of Elvis Presley. All that changes with the arrival of Jason London, 17-year-old son of a family that moves in next door.

London, the man of the house since his father's death, becomes friendly with Witherspoon against his better judgment. Her testing of the limits of how far either of them is prepared to go in their relationship provides much of the dramatic tension.

Inevitable conflict arises when London meets the old sister, and he quickly relegates Witherspoon to the status of kid sister. Unfortunately, vet director Robert Mulligan and tyro screenwriter Jenny Wingfield could not come up with a dramatic resolution to this triangle, and resort to a melodramatic device that at once brings the conflict between the two sisters to a head while removing the source of it. What has been a slowly paced but finely etched portrait of budding adolescence shifts to the level of soap opera.

The performances are all on the money, but two are outstanding and draw the viewer into the pic. Newcomer Witherspoon manages to strike exactly the right note as the tomboy on the verge of womanhood while Waterston works on several levels at once, showing a man who can act as a stern father while also being quietly amused to find himself in the role. Shot on location in Natchitoches, La., film is aided by cinematography of Freddie Francis, who catches the summer light and warmth important to the story.

— *Daniel M. Kimmel*

THE PUERTO RICAN MAMBO (NOT A MUSICAL)

A Cabriolet release of a Pinata Films presentation. Produced by Ben Model. Directed by Model. Screenplay, Luis Cabellero, adaptation by Model; camera (Duart color), Rosemary Tomosky-Franco, Vincent Manes, Paul Koestner; editor, Model; sound, Alina Avila. Reviewed at Boston Film Festival, Sept. 11, 1991. No MPAA Rating. Running time: **76 MIN.**
With: Luis Cabellero, Jeff Eyres, Susan Gaspar, Johnny Leggs, Sandy McFadden, Lucia Mendoza, Mike Robles, Carole M. Eckman, John Fulweiler, David Healy, Carolyn McDermott, Ben Model, Howard Arnesson, Mary Perez.

Give it an A for effort, but this showcase for Puerto Rican comedian Luis Cabellero is more a promise of things to come than anything else. Bookings in situations with Hispanic audiences seems like natural playoff for a pic in which sharp material compensates for

weak production values.

Framework is Cabellero doing his standup routine in front of plain background (similar to Woody Allen's opening of "Annie Hall") and then segueing into dramatizations of his material. One big problem is that Cabellero is very stiff on camera and (except when he appears in character in the sketches) appears extremely uncomfortable.

Moreover, the film has no real structure, merely flitting from one idea to another. It could use a strong narrative line from which to hang Cabellero's observations about life from a Puerto Rican perspective. This is obvious in the pic's best sequence where Cabellero and his "white friend" (producer-director-editor Ben Model) go to a party and fail to fit in, while a classy Puerto Rican Harvard grad (Johnny Leggs) keeps bragging about how he doesn't look Hispanic. This might have played better within a storyline.

Cabellero's observations are hit and miss, but many of them are right on target in pinpointing assumptions made about Puerto Ricans.

Tech credits are remarkable on a low-budget film reputed to have cost around $10,000, and blown up from Super 16m to 35m. However, the poor sound is a drawback. Everything is audible, but there is a "miked" sound to much of it, heightening the artificiality just when the audience should be getting drawn into Cabellero's routine.

Ultimately, the film may go nowhere, but the talent here is worth checking out.

— *Daniel M. Kimmel*

MONTREAL FEST

BEIJING NIZAO (GOOD MORNING BEIJING) (CHINESE)

A Beijing Film Studio-Youth Film Studio production. Directed by Zhang Nuanxin. Screenplay, Tang Danian; camera (color), Zhang Xigui, Hua Qing; music, Guo Wenjing; production design, Li Yongxin. Reviewed at Montreal Film Festival (Cinema of Today & Tomorrow section), Aug. 24, 1991. Running time: **104 MIN.**
With: Ma Xiaoqing, Wang Quanan, Jia Hongsheng, Jin Tiefing.

Aimed at China's youth audiences, "Good Morning Beijing" is a cautionary tale sug-

gesting that making a fast buck is no substitute for good honest toil. Pic has no commercial possibilities outside home market but could be of interest to fests and Chinese film events.

A Beijing bus driver, who's curious about the money to be made from working in joint venture companies, is in love with a ticket-taker, but she becomes pregnant by Singapore student.

Director Zhang Nuanxin seems to be wagging her finger at Chinese youth, but along the way she comes up with a fresh and attractive depiction of capital city life at the beginning of the '90s. No mention of the 1989 demonstrations, natch.

All members of the young cast perform well, and the location camerawork meets high tech standards. — *David Stratton*

RAMONA!

A CNI Cinemas production. Executive producer, L.M. Arnstein. Produced, written and directed by Jonathan Sarno. Camera (color), Russell Frazier; editor, Sarno; sound, Reinhart Sterger; production design, Evelyn Claude; costumes, Stanka Preberg; co-producers, Paul Wynne, Loredana Palivoda. Reviewed at Montreal Film Festival (Cinema of Today & Tomorrow section), Aug. 31, 1991. Running time: **89 MIN.**
Ramona . . . . Heidi von Palleske
Henry Sinclair . . . . Cain Devore
Paco . . . . Jason Scott
Also with: Shannon Bradley, Michael David Lally, Beata Pozniak, William Fichtner, Steffen Foster, Marilyn Adams, Bruno Bossio.

A promising theme and a couple of good performances don't survive scrappy treatment in this frustrating indie production. Good lensing and sound gives "Ramona!" a surface slickness, but theatrical bookings don't look promising for this too-tentative and unstructured effort.

Pic opens with footage shot in Tijuana as Mexicans flee into the U.S. by night. Writer-producer-director-editor Jonathan Sarno then takes up the story of a yuppie businessman (Cain Devore) who arrives in Tijuana and has a fling with attractive factory worker Ramona (Heidi von Palleske).

Back in the U.S., Devore discovers Ramona stowed away in the trunk of his car. After a few desultory scenes set in L.A., the couple, accompanied by a Latino friend of Ramona's, set out for Las Vegas, where Ramona is eventually nabbed by the authorities and deported.

Despite what appear to be large holes in the plot (and some choppy editing in the print caught), Sarno and talented Canadian thesp von Palleske manage to make the strong-willed Ramona an interesting character, though Devore is stuck with a wimpy role. Still, Ramona's ignorance of the U.S. seems at odds with her sophistication and all too often the character, like the film, seems adrift.

— *David Stratton*

SZAMUZOTTEK
(HOMELESS)
(HUNGARIAN-GERMAN-SOVIET)

A Satellit Film (Starnberg)-Europa 2000 KFT (Budapest)-Gruzia Film (Tbilisi)-WDR (Cologne) co-production, in association with MIT/MTV. Produced by Barna Kabay. Directed by Imre Gyöngyössy, Kabay. Screenplay, Gyöngyössy, Katalin Pentenyi, Erlom Achwlediani; camera (Eastmancolor), Peter Jankura; editor, Pentenyi; music, Zoltan Biro; production design, Naum Fuhrmann; costumes, Ija Kiknadze; co-producers, Rezo Tscheichedze, Gabor Banyai, Istvan Darday, Reka Gyöngyössy; production managers, Konstantin Kikabidze, Bence Gyöngyössy, Tibor Orosz. Reviewed at Montreal Film Festival (competing), Sept. 1, 1991. Running time: **104 MIN.**
With: Lidia Bock, Maria Reiss-Bock, Ananina Valentina Georgieevna, Berkun Vladimir Grigorjevits.
(German, Russian dialog)

Line between fiction and documentary is thoroughly blurred in this fascinating and deeply moving new film from the established Hungarian team of Imgre Gyöngyössy and Barna Kabay, though better structuring and tighter editing could have given "Homeless" wider international arthouse prospects.

Dealing with dispossessed people in the crumbling Soviet Union, timely pic centers on a small community of ethnic Germans who have lived in the Soviet Asian republic of Kazakhstan since 1941, when the Volga Germans were deported to Siberia and Kazakhstan on Stalin's orders in much the way Japanese Americans were confined during World War II.

Following drastic changes in the Soviet Union, an old German woman is determined to travel west to try to find her son, whom she lost in the chaotic period of relocation.

A dogged odyssey takes her to the notorious Moravia prison, where the man she seeks could either be the prison commandant or a prisoner in an isolation cell, both of whom were of German origin and were separated from their families. Other scenes depict the break-up of families as members of the younger generation seize the opportunity to emigrate, triggering tearful farewells. Another long sequence has an old woman and her granddaughter travel to the Volga region, where they're met with hostility and racism by local Russians who don't want Germans returning.

All this material, including the vivid picture of Soviet towns and villages in different parts of the vast and changing republics, is fascinating. Some scenes appear to be straight documentary; others are obviously staged for the camera, making this a hybrid film that gets its message across. Still, it raises questions about the validity of some scenes.

Pic is hard to follow, but this could still be corrected with editorial tightening and perhaps a few bridging titles to fill in obvious narrative gaps. It's not always clear how the characters are connected to each other.

Nonetheless, pic reps an achievement for its makers and should be in demand on the fest circuit with a chance for limited theatrical release as well.

—*David Stratton*

UN-MA NUN O GIANNUN DA
(SILVER STALLION)
(SOUTH KOREAN)

A Han Jin Enterprises production. (Intl. sales: Korean Motion Picutre Promotion Corp.) Produced by Han Kapchin. Directed by Chang Kil-soo. Screenplay, Chang, Cho Che-hung, based on Ahn Jung-hyo's book "White Badge"; camera (color), Lee Sokhi; editor, Cho Yong-sam; music, Kim Suchol; sound, Kim Pom-su; production design, Cho Yong-sam. Reviewed at Montreal Film Festival (competing), Aug. 27, 1991. Running time: **124 MIN.**
With: Lee Hyesuk, Kim Poyon, Chon Musong, Son Changmin, Pang Unhi, Lee Taero, Kim Hyongja.

"Silver Stallion," one of the more impressive Korean films to surface, is a powerful depiction of the havoc and distress brought to a small Korean village by U.S. soldiers during the Korean War. It could stand some pruning from its overlong running time but deserves further fest exposure.

Central character is a young widow who lives with her two small children in a village serving as a base for American troops with U.N. forces during the conflict. One night, a drunken Yank sergeant rapes her in front of her children.

Instead of giving her support, the village elder and others ostracize the woman for having been with an American. Unable to find work, she's forced into prostitution, and becomes one of a band of women hanging around the U.S. base.

Pic is an angry indictment of the exploitation of people by supposedly friendly soldiers and protectors. The story is given forthright treatment, with a good performance from Lee Hyesuk as the tragic widow.

Director Chang Kil-soo's item is hard-hitting and provocative, but tighter editing could have made the film more impressive. The deafening sound reproduction at the screening caught proved more of a liability than an asset. Lee Sokhi contributes some excellent cinematography, and all technical credits are tops.

— *David Stratton*

LA VIUDA DEL CAPITAN ESTRADA
(CAPTAIN ESTRADA'S WIDOW)
(SPANISH)

A Classic Films production. Produced by Eduardo Ducay. Written and directed by José Luis Cuerda, based on Pedro Garcia Montalvo's novel "A Madrid Story"; camera (Eastmancolor), Magin Torruella; editor, Juan Ignacio San Mateo; music, Salvador Bacarisse, Federico Moreno Torroba; sound, Enrique Molinero; production design, Rafael Palmero; production manager, Luis Diaz Gonzalez; assistant director, Raul de la Morena. Reviewed at Montreal Film Festival (competing), Aug. 23, 1991. Running time: **102 MIN.**
Luisa	Anna Galiena
Javier Zaldivar	Sergi Mateu
Baltasar	Nacho Martinez
Juan	Chema Mazo
Don Ignacio	Jose M. Escuer
Tomas	Gabino Diego
Mondejar	German Cobos

Anna Galiena's stylish performance in the title role graces this handsomely produced erotic melodrama, but the writer-director's inert handling fatally undermines "Captain Estrada's Widow."

Helmer José Luis Cuerda tackles a fascinating subject about conflicting loyalties and residual enmities in postwar Spain. The year is 1947, and the newly formed United Nations has voted on a blockade of fascist Spain, but little is made of this fascinating background.

His protagonist is a professional soldier (Sergi Mateu) who fought on Franco's side in the civil war and later with the German army against Russia. He returns from abroad to resume a liaison with a woman he always loved: a fellow officer's widow (Galiena), a complex woman with left-wing leanings. She is hiding a political refugee and occasionally visits a veteran leftist (also her lover).

Before long, she's involved in an affair with the mercenary, but when he discovers her secrets, his solution to his damaged personal and political pride is a violent one.

Galiena (notable in "The Hairdresser's Husband") is impressive as the sensual widow, but Mateu is wooden as her lover. The numerous lovemaking scenes in pic's second half fail to spark and even get ludicrous.

Despite the handsome production design, pic has a flat feel to it. Consequently, international arthouse bookings are unlikely, unless Galiena's growing rep proves to be a factor. Technically, the picture is flawless.

— *David Stratton*

FREUD FLYTTAR HEMIFRAN
(FREUD'S LEAVING HOME)
(SWEDISH)

An Omega Film & TV production. Produced by Peter Kropenin. Directed by Susanne Bier. Screenplay, Marianne Goldman; camera (color), Erik Zappon; editor, Pernille Christensen; music, Johan Söderqvist; sound, Ragnar Samuelsson; production design, Ulla Kassius; costume design, Nina Sandström. Reviewed at Montreal Film Festival (competing), Aug. 30, 1991. Running time: **103 MIN.**
Rosha Cohen	Ghita Norby
Angelique Cohen	Gunilla Röör
David Cohen	Philip Zanden
Deborah Cohen	Jessica Zanden
Ruben Cohen	Palle Granditsky
Adrian	Peter Andersson
Nurse	Stina Ekblad

A poignant family drama about a birthday reunion that turns into a wake, "Freud's Leaving Home" is an uneven but interesting first feature from Danish director Susanne Bier. Pic could find exposure at Jewish film events and modest release in selected large cities.

It's summer in Sweden, and Ghita Norby is about to celebrate her 60th birthday. She lives with her kindly antique-dealer husband (Palle Graditsky) and her younger daughter (Gunilla Röör), who's nicknamed "Freud" because of her fondness for psychoanalysis. The daughter wears braces on her teeth and should have left home long ago.

From abroad come Freud's two siblings (played by brother and sister actors). Her sister (Jessica Zanden) lives in Jerusalem and is very Orthodox; her brother (Philip Zanden) lives in Florida with a gay lover. Just as the birthday celebration is about to take place, the mother is taken ill, and she's diagnosed as having an inoperable brain tumor.

Freud reacts by picking up a biker in a disco and going to bed with him (he turns out to be surprisingly sympathetic), and then insisting her mother be brought home from the hospital. The birthday party eventually does take place, but Mom expires during the celebration.

Marianne Goldman's screenplay is a little contrived; every member of the family has some kind of problem. Still, Bier makes the potentially mawkish family saga of strained relationships constantly interesting and moving.

Norby is very good as the dying matriarch, while Röör is touching as the lively but insecure Freud. Her first love scene with the biker (Peter Andersson) is amusing.

Erik Zappon's camerawork, mostly confined to the interior of the family apartment, is subtle and attractive, and all other technical credits are high.

— *David Stratton*

TORONTO FEST

MARRIED TO IT

An Orion Pictures release of a Three Pair production. Produced by Thomas Baer. Executive producers, Peter V. Herald, John L. Jacobs. Directed by Arthur Hiller. Screenplay, Janet Kovalcik; camera (color), Victor Kemper; editor, Robert C. Jones; music, Henry Mancini; sound, Doug Ganton; production design, Robert Gundlach; art direction, Jeffrey Ginn (Toronto), Ann Cudworth (New York); set decoration, Gordon Sim (Toronto), George DeTitta (New York); costume design, Julie Weiss; assistant director, Tony Lucibello; casting, Howard Feuer, Stuart Aikins (Canada). Reviewed at Toronto Film Festi-

val, Sept. 11, 1991. MPAA rating: R. Running time: **110 MIN.**
John . . . . Beau Bridges
Iris . . . . Stockard Channing
Chuck . . . . . . Robert Sean Leonard
Nina . . . . . Mary Stuart Masterson
Claire . . . . Cybill Shepherd
Leo . . . . Ron Silver
Lucy . . . . Donna Vivino

There's nothing so bad about another adult ensemble comedy dealing with the ups and downs of marriage, but there's nothing so good about it either. Not when it's as unpersuasive and awkward as this one. "Married To It" can expect no happily ever after with this engagement, which has been put off from this month until next year.

Auds seeking the wit and polish of an Alan Alda or Neil Simon example of the form will do best to move on. This Arthur Hiller-directed version unfolds with an unaccountable clumsiness.

Story brings together three couples who gain perspective on their relationships through the course of their friendship. Problem here is one can never figure out why they're friends.

Mary Stuart Masterson and Robert Sean Leonard are the baby yuppies on the move. Born in 1966, these well-heeled "new traditionalists" actually have been a couple since they were 8 years old.

Stockard Channing and Beau Bridges also were born in the '60s — ideologically. Today he's still a welfare case worker, unhappily carrying the torch, and she's a homemaker for their teenage sons. They don't have much money or pizzazz in their lives.

Ron Silver and Cybill Shepherd are more of a crowd than a couple, given that his 13-year-old daughter and angry ex-wife are pretty much running their relationship — into the ground.

Shepherd's a mouthy, aggressive, Jaguar-driving financial whiz who makes far more money than her spouse. Strikingly rude and arrogant, she nonetheless ends up gal pals with the gracious Channing and sensitive Masterson after they rope her into serving on a school decorating committee.

Discriminating audiences, the only kind drawn to adult comedy, are bound to reject the flimsy premise that the couples are forced to interact in a round of dinner parties. Bonding of the two older men based on their hoary recollections of the '60s is unfunny and embarrassing. Much of the so-called comedy is on the

sitcom level.

Pic's most effective scenes are the knockdown fights about emotional issues, which finally give the actors something to get their teeth into. Message is that modern marital problems should be solved the old-fashioned way, with tenacity and faith. Nonetheless, pic loses out by ignoring the fact that some differences are sadly insurmountable.

Channing, Silver and Masterson give commendable performances, considering, but Shepherd is strikingly out of tune with the rest in a nervous, inept comic turn that would have fit in better in another film — say, "Moonlighting" colleague Bruce Willis' "Hudson Hawk."

Hiller's direction is often slapdash, particularly in the final reel. Use of Joni Mitchell's saccharine and obvious ditty "The Circle Game" as theme music has the desired saccharine and obvious effect.

Film was lensed in Toronto and New York, where former mayor Ed Koch pops up in a party scene cameo.

— *Amy Dawes*

ZONGHENG SIHAI
(ONCE A THIEF)
(HONG KONG)

A Milestone Pictures production. (Intl. sales, Milestone Pictures). Produced by Linda Kuk, Terence Chang. Directed by John Woo. Written by Woo, Clifton Ko, Janet Chun, camera (color), Poon Hang Seng; editor, David Wu; music, Violet Lam; art direction, James Leung. Reviewed at National Film Board screening room, Toronto, Aug. 30, 1991. (In Toronto Film Festival.) Running time: **108 MIN.**
With: Chow Yun-Fat, Leslie Cheung, Cherie Chung.

Ostensibly a romantic caper pic, "Once A Thief" is packed with so many hilarious, violent action sequences that it becomes silly, sophomoric fun. It's a natural for B-circuit theatrical play, though lumbered with terrible English subtitles.

In part an homage to Hitchcock's "To Catch A Thief," pic begins in France with three Hong Kong art thieves completing one last hair-raising theft. Cleverly dodging laser beams at a villa in Nice, they steal a painting only to discover that their Hong Kong boss, who trained them as orphan children to be thieves, double-crossed them.

Much later the thieves (two

men and a woman) seek revenge and steal the painting back. Director John Woo creates maximum suspense in the theft sequences. A prolonged dockside shoot-'em-up ends with one of the thieves smashing into a boat and apparently perishing.

Back in Hong Kong two years later, the surviving thieves fall in love and the one thought dead turns up in a wheelchair and quickly is enlisted for revenge.

Getting the painting back was easy compared to surviving the boss' henchmen, who turn up in hordes, one of them hurling deadly, razor-sharp playing cards.

Villains get their comeuppance, via such silliness as an exploding microwave oven that sends a flaming basketball into the chest of one of them. Plot initially makes sense, but Woo and crew display such a knack for zany fight scenes that story threads rip apart beyond repair.

Leads Chow Yun-Fat, Leslie Cheung and Cherie Chung make a snappy, attractive trio of thieves. — *Sid Adilman*

HEAR MY SONG
(BRITISH)

A Miramax release of a Film Four Intl., British Screen and Windmill Lane presentation of a Limelight production. Produced by Alison Owen. Executive producers, Simon Fields, Russ Russell, John Paul Chapple. Directed by Peter Chelsom. Screenplay, Chelsom, Adrian Dunbar; camera (Fujicolor), Sue Gibson; editor, Martin Walsh; music, John Altman; sound (Dolby), Peter Lindsay; production design, Caroline Hananna; art direction, Katharine Naylor; costume design, Lindy Hemming; assistant director, Crispin Reece; casting, Jane Frisby. Reviewed at Toronto Film Festival, Sept. 7, 1991. (Also in Boston Film Festival.) Running time: **113 MIN.**
Josef Locke . . . . Ned Beatty
Mickey O'Neill . . . . . Adrian Dunbar
Constable Abbott . . David McCallum
Nancy . . . . Tara Fitzgerald
Kathleen . . . . . . Shirley Anne Field
Mr. X . . . . William Hootkins
Fintan . . . . James Nesbitt

First feature from Peter-Chelsom goes straight for the heart with "Hear My Song," an unabashedly romantic fantasy likely to sweep along audiences like no imported film since "Cinema Paradiso." Critical fate is dubious, however, as the Brit director lays on the crowd-pleasing elements to the point of pandering.

Chelsom and co-writer Adrian Dunbar have spun a clever yarn about a concert promoter (Adrian Dunbar), a seat-of-his-pants operator who's this close to sealing a relationship with his beautiful g.f. (Tara Fitzgerald). The nightclub he's taken over in an Irish neighborhood of Britain is ever on the verge of collapse because of its unreliable bottom-rung bookings.

Desperate for a hit, the promoter books a Josef Locke look-alike (William Hootkins) who's quite mad but seems to fill the billing as "Mr. X — Is He Or Isn't He?" Legendary Irish tenor Locke fled from public view at the height of his popularity to avoid tax evasion charges.

Helmer Chelsom has a marvelous thing going, and it's unfortunate he didn't restrain himself a bit. No effect is left untried — from leprechaun-like characters to inserts of frogs croaking on fence posts against a red sky.

Ned Beatty does much to stem the tide of sentiment in a tough, grounded portrayal of the real Locke, a man of substance and self-awareness firmly entrenched in another life. But by the final reels, it's become too much.

Dunbar carries off the lead role in winning fashion, but the real discovery is likely to be Fitzgerald, whose gamine charm is perfectly introduced in this old-fashioned romance.

Pic's whimsical tone is aided amply by Sue Gibson's richly colorful lensing and the warm John Altman music.

— *Amy Dawes*

GRAND ISLE

A Kelly McGillis-Turner Pictures production. Produced by Kelly McGillis, Carolyn Pfeiffer. Directed by Mary Lambert. Screenplay, Hesper Anderson, based on Kate Chopin's novel "The Awakening"; camera (color), Toyomichi Kurita; editor, Tom Finan; music, Elliot Goldenthal; sound, Rudy Lara; production design, Michelle Minch; art direction, Marcus Kuhn; set decoration, Molly Flanegin; costume design, Martin Pakledinaz; assistant director, Michael Green; casting, Fern Champion. Reviewed at Toronto Film Festival, Sept. 8, 1991. No MPAA rating. Running time: **112 MIN.**
Edna Pontellier . . . . . Kelly McGillis
Leonce Pontellier . . . . . Jon DeVries
Robert LeBrun . . . . . Adrian Pasdar
Mademoiselle Reisz . . . Ellen Burstyn
Adele Ratignolle . . . . Glenne Headly
Alcee Arobin . . . . Julian Sands

Reputation of Kate Chopin's novel "The Awakening" will gain nothing from its screen adaptation. "Grand Isle" recreates the 1899 tale of a married woman's sexual and spiritual emancipation with a perplexing absence of drama, passion or skill.

Kelly McGillis stars in and co-produced this languorous Louisi-

ana period piece and, unfortunately, the lack of filmmaking experience at the top shows.

The McGillis character rebels against her comfortable married life after her bohemian instincts are awakened by an older artist friend (Ellen Burstyn) and the attentions of an idle young man (Adrian Pasdar) who helps her overcome her fear of swimming in the ocean.

Script, commissioned from writer Hesper Anderson ("Children Of A Lesser God"), offers prissy and unnatural dialog. Acting is obvious or wooden, and the Creole French accents are mismatched. Actors are lit and made up to poor effect, and camerawork, aside from a lyrical opening, is remarkably awkward.

Worst mistake is that the heroine is fatally unsympathetic. McGillis comes off as selfish, indulged and self-absorbed to the point of madness.

Edna's transformation is complete when she takes to the ocean, on her own and in the buff. While this is the one scene that McGillis fans may find worth catching, most will be dozing by then.

— *Amy Dawes*

U.S. RELEASES

DAMNED IN THE USA
(BRITISH-DOCU)

A Berwick Universal Pictures-Uptown Media Associates production for Channel 4. Produced and directed by Paul Yule. Camera (color), Mark Benjamin, Robert Achs, Luke Sacher; editor, John Street; sound, Barbara Zahm, Lawrence Loewinger, John Austin, Christen Johanesson, Mark Oliver, Donald Thomas, Alvin Jones; co-producer, Jonathan Stack. Reviewed at Margaret Mead Film Festival, Sept. 11, 1991. Running time: **68 MIN.**

This ambitious British documentary does an excellent job of covering the recent censorship controversy in America. By interviewing everyone from the Rev. Donald Wildmon to Christie Hefner, Paul Yule has produced a refreshingly evenhanded look at a highly contentious issue.

The opening shots are of Jesse Helms and Alphonse D'Amato denouncing from the Senate floor what they consider obscene art funded by the National Endowment for the Arts. As the credits roll, the camera pans the seedy Times Square area to the strains of Cole Porter's "Anything Goes."

The scene then shifts to a comedy club, where political comic Jimmy Tingle is performing. The first segment of his routine does not relate to censorship, and should have been cut. But in later scenes, Tingle effectively ridicules politicians for trying to shut down the NEA over a few works of art.

Andres Serrano's "Piss Christ" was the first controversial work targeted by Wildmon's American Family Assn. In addition to Serrano, Yule managed to interview Wildmon at his Tupelo, Miss., h.q. "I think it's sickness masquerading as art," says Wildmon, whose organization fights back through "economic persuasion."

The docu also discusses Robert Mapplethorpe's work, and shows many of his more provocative photographs. Ironically, these images may hurt the film's theatrical prospects and may have to be cut for U.S. tv. But **the director should be commended for including the much-discussed, little-seen art works.**

Excerpts from the trial of Dennis Barrie, who was charged on obscenity counts during the Mapplethorpe exhibition in Cincinnati, also are shown. More time should have been devoted to the actual trial, however, and less to the judge and his courtroom tour.

While Wildmon is given ample screen time, opposing voices are also heard. One of the most articulate is Christie Hefner of Playboy Enterprises. She thinks Wildmon and his followers "succeed by pretending they have more power in the marketplace than they actually do. They're a fringe group."

2 Live Crew's Luther Campbell gives another perspective on censorship, and his music is heard on the soundtrack. So is Madonna's "Like A Prayer," in a clip from her largely unseen Pepsi commercial.

Yule skillfully intercuts Congressional hearings, a NYC Halloween parade, the Mapplethorpe trial, videos, advertisements, interviews and the images themselves for a well-rounded look at the inflammatory national debate. The censorship controversy has since died down, but this docu should rekindle strong feelings on both sides of the issue.

— *William Stevenson*

FREDDY'S DEAD: THE FINAL NIGHTMARE
(PART 3-D)

A New Line Cinema release and production. Produced by Robert Shaye, Aron Warner. Executive producer, Michael DeLuca. Directed by Rachel Talalay. Screenplay, DeLuca, from Talalay's story, based on characters created by Wes Craven; camera (Deluxe color), Declan Quinn; editor, Janice Hampton; music, Brian May; music supervision, Bonnie Greenberg, Jill Meyres; sound (Dolby), Mark Weingarten; production design, C.J. Strawn; art direction, James R. Barrows; set decoration, Rebecca Carriaga; costume design, Nanrose Buchman; assistant director, Mike Topoozian; production manager, Patty Whitcher; Freddy Krueger's makeup created by David B. Miller; special makeup effects, Magical Media Industries; special visual effects, Dream Quest Images; 3-D supervision & special visual effects, the Chandler Group; 3-D miniatures, Steson Visual Services; mechanical effects design, Reel Efx; computer graphic special effects, Video Image; snake demon puppets, Jim Towler; dream demons animation, Pacific Data Images; house transformation created by True Vision Effects; 2nd unit director-associate producer, Michael Knue; 2nd unit camera, Phil Parmet; stunt coordinator, Dan Bradley; casting, Jane Jenkins, Janet Hirshenson, Roger Mussenden. Reviewed at Chelsea 7 theater, N.Y., Sept. 14, 1991. MPAA Rating: R. Running time: **90 MIN.**
Freddy Krueger . . . Robert Englund
Maggie . . . . Lisa Zane
John . . . . Shon Greenblatt
Tracy . . . . Lezlie Deane
Carlos . . . . Ricky Dean Logan
Spencer . . . . Breckin Meyer
Doc . . . . Yaphet Kotto
Orphanage woman . . Elinor Donahue
Also with: Roseanne Arnold, Tom Arnold, Alice Cooper, Johnny Depp.

Sixth and final edition in the "Nightmare On Elm Street" feature series delivers enough violence, black humor and even a final reel in 3-D to hit paydirt with horror-starved audiences.

Whether 24-year-old indie distrib New Line Cinema will decide to reverse the decision to bury Freddy Krueger for good is more a financial question than creative one.

Tired nature of the original Wes Craven concept initiated in 1984 is acknowledged by a new plotline for "Freddy's Dead." Exposition is awkwardly presented by debutante helmer Rachel Talalay, with vengeful, undead murderer Freddy Krueger (Robert Englund, again in fine form) supposedly having killed off all the local children and teens in a little Ohio town, now set 10 years in the future.

He's using a young amnesiac, John (Shon Greenblatt) to revitalize his powers and ultimately seeking his daughter (Lisa Zane), who works as a counselor in a teen rehab shelter, in an effort to spread his vengeance to Elm Streets worldwide. Freddy's power is attributed to dream demons, who appear in animated form during the 3-D finale.

This background is all largely irrelevant to the way the film unfolds, with Freddy blurring the lines between waking and dream states as he assaults the smaller than usual cast list.

Most imaginative sequence deals with hearing impaired teen Carlos (Ricky Dean Logan). Freddy tears out the kid's hearing aid and torments him silently. Then he affixes a monstrous growth on his ear that amplifies sound and proceeds to scratch a blackboard with his gloved knives. Effect in Dolby SR sound is impressive.

Less successful is the 15-minute 3-D capper. Projected using the old-fashioned anaglyphic (red & blue lenses) glasses, sequence's color is thereby distorted compared to the modern polarized lens efforts. There are a few pointy objects coming out of the screen but it's mainly 3-D for depth, crudely realized. Like the 1961 Canadian film "The Mask," at least the gimmick is only a brief annoyance rather than forcing one to wear the glasses and strain one's eyes for a full feature.

Beyond Englund's reliable turn, Zane is good casting as his evil-looking (but good-guy) daughter who could easily inherit the vengeance role after she blasts daddy to kingdom come. Lezlie Deane is fun as a tomboy who even bests Freddy in hand-to-hand combat using martial arts.

Guest stars Roseanne Arnold and hubbie Tom Arnold (cast as a childless couple of the future) and Alice Cooper (typecast as Freddy's abusive stepfather) add little to the stew while New Line's founder/major domo Robert Shaye has an in-joke cameo as an evil ticketseller. Johnny Depp, featured in Wes Craven's 1984 "Nightmare" original, pops up briefly as a teen on tv.

— *Lawrence Cohn*

BEASTMASTER 2: THROUGH THE PORTAL OF TIME

A New Line Cinema release of a Republic Pictures-Films 21 presentation. Executive producer, Stephan Strick. Produced and directed by Sylvio Tabet. Screenplay, R.J. Robertson, Jim Wynorski, Tabet, Ken Hauser, Doug Miles, from story by Wynorski & Robertson, based on characters created by Paul Pepperman & Don Coscarelli, adapted from Andre Norton's novel "The Beastmaster"; camera (CFI color), Ronn Schmidt; editor, Adam Bernardi; music, Robert Folk; sound (Dolby), Craig Felburg; production design, Allen Jones; art direction, Patrick Tatopoulos; set decoration, Ritch Kremer; costume design, Betty Madden; animal trainer, Brian McMillan; stunt coordinators, McMillan, Al Jones; visual effects supervisor, Frank H. Isaacs (MEL); assistant director, Thomas P. Smith; line producer, Jerrold W. Lambert; casting, Cathy Henderson. Reviewed at Raleigh Studios screening room, L.A., Aug. 7, 1991. MPAA rating: PG-13. Running time: **107 MIN.**
Dar . . . . Marc Singer
Jackie Trent . . . . Kari Wuhrer
Arklon . . . . Wings Hauser
Lyranna . . . . Sarah Douglas
Lead . . . . Charles Young

Despite this low-budget sequel's silly dialog and cheesy special effects, "Beastmaster 2: Through The Portal Of Time" is a mildly engaging tongue-in-cheek fantasy about mythical characters traveling through a time warp to battle it out in the mean streets of contempo L.A. Like its 1982 predecessor, pic should do well on homevid following a modest theatrical run.

Blond, lithely muscular Marc Singer returns in his loinclothed title role as a sort of violent St. Francis figure accompanied by a tiger, an eagle and two ferrets who help him out of scrapes with the evil rulers of his desert abode. Singer maintains a winning simplicity despite all the sword-and-sorcery hokum.

The dandy bad guy is laser-wielding Wings Hauser who turns out to be Singer's long-lost brother, and a half-human creature (John Fifer) gives Singer the unpleasant task of saving the land from destruction by committing fratricide.

This potentially heavy theme doesn't weigh down producer-director Sylvio Tabet and the film's numerous other writers, whose goofball script is rife with contemporary slang, even in the mythical kingdom. Hauser's voluptuous witch-companion (Sarah Douglas) has visited L.A. through the time warp.

Douglas, despite her awful lines, persuades Hauser to steal a nefarious weapon from a Southern California army base, a quest that provides glib running jibes at what Hauser calls the "brilliantly barbarous" mentality of the modern world.

Singer teams up with an airheaded L.A. rich girl (Kari Wuhrer) to track down and vanquish Hauser, in a plot recalling that of "Time After Time."

Ronn Schmidt's lensing is suitably noirish. — *Joseph McBride*

BLADE RUNNER (DIRECTOR'S VERSION)

Flaws and all, there's little doubt that Ridley Scott's "Blade Runner" was one of the two or three major sci-fi films of the 1980s. Whatever one might have said about script and narration problems, it was a truly original creation, and its stunning vision of a clogged, Asianized Los Angeles, as well as its languid pacing, have influenced both domestic and foreign films, and music videos.

Regardless of what one thought of it before, the director's original cut, which debuts in a two-week engagement at the Nuart in West L.A. beginning Sept. 27, proves a revelation. The film is immeasurably superior in this version on every possible level. All the problems are gone, and what was good before works even better now. The film is now all of a piece, with the moody, oppressive tone sustained without as much as a hiccup from beginning to end.

The tacked-on hardboiled narration by Harrison Ford — the most maligned aspect of the 1982 release version (reviewed in VARIETY, June 16, 1982) — is absent save one brief instance near the end, and it's not missed at all. Verbiage was reportedly added after preview audiences complained that the story, which involved a former cop in the next century tracking down mutinous replicants who have escaped to Earth from space, was too confusing.

Pic actually seems more coherent and straightforward in this definitive cut, perhaps because the lack of narration allows for more total absorption in the plot and mood.

Second huge improvement is the elimination of the silly ending in which Ford and Sean Young zoom off happily ever after. That could only have been the result of panic over marketing test results and/or preview cards.

Other changes are less monumental, but in every case the original prevails decisively over the release version. Some scenes, notably a long encounter between Ford and Young, play longer and more sensibly, while other material is tighter. There are no doubt at least dozens of small, but significant, editorial distinctions. Vangelis' score also is used differently, to awesome effect.

In short, what was once a significantly flawed major film now fully deserves to be called a classic of its kind. It is rare to see an alternative version of a film that would result in such a serious upgrading of its critical standing, but such is the case with "Blade Runner."

Based on the interest generated at two L.A. screenings of the 70m print of Scott's original cut, Warner Bros. had Technicolor make an interpositive from the 70m copy, since no negative exists, and struck one 35m print from that.

No further bookings have been made, pending commercial results of the Nuart engagement.

— *Todd McCarthy*

DECEIVED

A Buena Vista release of a Touchstone Pictures presentation in association with Silver Screen Partners IV of a Michael Finnell production. Produced by Michael Finnell, Wendy Dozoretz & Ellen Collett. Executive producers, Teri Schwartz, Anthea Sylbert. Directed by Damian Harris. Screenplay, Mary Agnes Donoghue, "Derek Saunders" (Bruce Joel Rubin) from Donoghue's story; camera (Medallion/PSA color, Technicolor), Jack N. Green; editor, Neil Travis; music, Thomas Newman; sound (Dolby), David Lee; production design, Andrew McAlpine; costume design, Linda Matheson; art direction, Gregory P. Keen, Christopher Nowak; set decoration, Gordon Sim; assistant director, Tony Lucibello; 2nd unit camera, Peter Norman; coproducer, Donoghue; casting, Deborah Aquila. Reviewed at Avco Cinema Center, L.A., Sept. 18, 1991. MPAA rating: PG-13. Running time: **103 MIN.**
Adrienne . . . . Goldie Hawn
Jack . . . . John Heard
Charlotte . . . . Robin Bartlett
Mary . . . . Ashley Peldon
Harvey . . . . Tom Irwin
Carol Gingold . . . . Maia Filar
Tomasz . . . . Jan Rubes
Ellen . . . . Anaïs Granofsky
Mrs. Peabody . . . Heidi Von Palleske
Detective Kinsella . Stanley Anderson

Thrills, chills and a convincing perf by Goldie Hawn should turn this stylishly absorbing thriller into a decent b.o. performer. Farfetched plot doesn't bear much scrutiny, but mesmerizing visual tone, macabre developments and sound entertainment value should sweep audiences along.

Hawn plays a New York art restoration expert who appears to be living a perfect life with her attractive career, cute kid (Ashley Peldon) and attentive, romantic husband (John Heard), who's also in the ancient art biz. But when a forgery's discovered

at the museum, fingers are pointed at Heard.

Hawn's trust is eroded as her husband's behavior begins turning up a trail of deceptions. Then he's killed in a car accident, and a Social Security worker informs Hawn her husband wasn't whom he said he was — the real guy died years ago.

Pic segues ably into thriller territory as the undead husband (corpse buried was actually a charred hitchhiker) begins haunting his former home to try to recover a stolen Egyptian necklace he left behind. Meanwhile, Hawn has turned sleuth and is closing in on the disheartening truth about the con she married.

Their inevitable encounter packs the requisite scream value, and pic heightens into a chilling game of cat and mouse, climaxed by a horrifically successful pursuit sequence.

Director Damien Harris appears in full control of the medium, weaving in some effective Hitchcockian allusions and a couple of intentional good laughs.

With cinematographer Jack Green, Harris creates a remarkably lush, moody visual tone that richly conveys the psychological textures of the piece, as well as helping cover up the flaws in the improbable scenario.

Also helpful is a solidly sympathetic turn by Hawn as a woman whose assumptions about her most intimate relationship are shattered. Heard is slyly convincing as the cold-blooded sham artist, and Robin Bartlett contributes vibrant support as Hawn's business partner.

Production design by Andrew McAlpine and costumes by Linda Matheson for the swank, comfortable east coast settings are particularly adept at sustaining the mood in this Toronto and New York-lensed feature.

— *Amy Dawes*

STEPPING OUT

A Paramount release (UIP in U.K.) of a Paramount production. Produced by Lewis Gilbert. Executive producer, Bill Kenwright. Directed by Gilbert. Screenplay, Richard Harris, based on his play; camera (Technicolor), Alan Hume; editor, Humphrey Dixon; music, Peter Matz; music arranger (dance), Peter Howard; sound (Dolby), Alan Bell, Bruce Carwardine, Gerry Humphreys; production design, Peter Mullins; art director, Alicia Keywan; set decorator, Steve Shewchuck; costume design, Candice Paterson; assistant director, Michael Cheyko; co-producer, John Dark; casting, Ross Clydesdale; choreographer, Danny Daniels. Reviewed at Empire

Theater, London, Sept. 21, 1991. Running time: **106 MIN.**
Mavis Turner . . . . . . Liza Minnelli
Mrs. Fraser . . . . . Shelley Winters
Geoffrey . . . . Bill Irwin
Maxine . . . . Ellen Greene
Vera . . . . Julie Walters
Sylvia . . . . Robyn Stevan
Lynne . . . . Jane Krakowski
Andy . . . . Sheila McCarthy
Dorothy . . . . Andrea Martin
Rose . . . . Carol Woods
    Also with: Luke Reilly, Nora Dunn, Eugene Robert Glazer.

It's Liza-as-you-love-her in "Stepping Out," a modest heartwarmer about a bunch of suburban left-feeters getting it together for a charity dance spot. Fragile ensemble item often creaks under the Minnelli glitz, but results are likable enough. Pleasant — not high-kicking —business looms.

Presence of Julie Walters should give the film extra clout at U.K. sites. British actress, who made her big-screen mark with director Lewis Gilbert's "Educating Rita," gets equal billing with Minnelli on British ads, despite her supporting role.

Adapted by Richard Harris from his award-winning play, action is switched from a London church hall to a Buffalo, N.Y., equivalent. Minnelli is a former pro hoofer who's now singing in bars with her domineering b.f. (Luke Reilly) and teaching amateur dance classes on the side.

Her current group includes a snooty Brit with a cleanliness fixation (Walters), a shy plain Jane with a bossy husband (Sheila McCarthy), a pretty, disillusioned young nurse (Jane Krakowski) and a working-class pants-chaser (Robyn Stevan).

Others in the octet are a sharp-tongued Brooklynite in the clothes biz (Ellen Greene), a bird-like librarian (Andrea Martin) and a buxom mother (Carol Woods). Token male is an uptight introvert (Bill Irwin).

Minnelli's problems start when her grumpy accompanist (Shelley Winters) threatens to walk out. She's then invited by a waspish acquaintance (Nora Dunn) at the Center for Performing Arts to put together an amateur tap routine for a charity show.

As the pressure builds, Minnelli finds she's pregnant and her man wants to move to L.A. Upbeat finale has the fumbling tappers scoring a hit and being invited back the following year.

Plot sounds on paper like a

Original play

Bill Kenwright presentation of a play in two acts by Richard Harris. Staged by Julia McKenzie. Set, Stuart Stanley; lighting, Jon Swain; choreography, Tudor Davies, Jenifer Mary Morgan. Opened Sept. 25, 1984, at the Duke of York's Theater, London. $11.70 top.
Cheryl . . . . Ann Gabrielle
Margaret . . . . . Sue Scott-Davison
Sue . . . . Eileen Dunwoodie
Mavis . . . . Barbara Ferris
Mrs. Fraser . . . . . Sheri Shepstone
Lynne . . . . Charlotte Barker
Dorothy . . . . . . Josephine Gordon
Maxine . . . . Barbara Young
Andy . . . . Gabrielle Lloyd
Geoffrey . . . . Ben Aris
Sylvia . . . . Diane Langton
Rose . . . . Peggy Phango

cross between "A Chorus Line" and any number of putting-on-a-show pics. But pic still plays more like a low-key Brit character piece rather than a backstage tears-and-smiles item.

That's where the Minnelli problem comes in. On one hand, she acts the has-been hoofer, but on the other, she drops knowing lines like: "I even auditioned for Bob Fosse once. I didn't get the job (pause) but I got to touch his sleeve."

Still, Minnelli's lost none of her pizzazz. Looking as fresh-faced and gamine as ever, and in good voice and shape, she provides the pic's emotional highs in a solo dance spot and the finale's John Kander-Fred Ebb title song, but as an actress, she's one-note perky.

Walters, culturally marooned by the shift of locale, still has a few moments with dry one-liners. McCarthy and Irwin mug through their shy romance. Krakowski plays it straight.

Vet British director Gilbert gives the whole thing a solid pro feel, with no tricks. Sole exception is a neat midway medley (to "Happy Feet") of the tappers rehearsing at home and work.

Technically, the Toronto-lensed pic is solid, with unfussy photography by Alan Hume and good editing by Humphrey Dixon. Candice Paterson's costumes are characterful, garbing Minnelli in black and Walters in eye-catching monstrosities. Peter Mullins' detailed church hall set has a proscenium-arch feel. Peter Matz' occasional underscoring is conventionally warm.

— *Derek Elley*

NECESSARY ROUGHNESS

A Paramount Pictures release of a Mace Neufeld & Robert Rehme production. Produced by Neufeld, Rehme. Executive producer, Howard W. Koch Jr. Directed by Stan Dragoti. Screenplay, Rick Natkin, David Fuller; camera (Technicolor), Peter Stein; editor, John Wright, Steve Mirkovich; music, Bill Conti; sound (Dolby), J. Paul Huntsman; production design, Paul Peters; costume design, Dan Moore; set decoration, Lynn Wolverton Parker; associate producer, Lis Kern; assistant directors, John Hockridge, Joseph J. Kontra; stunt coordinator, Allan Graf; casting, Mindy Marin. Reviewed at Mann National Theater, Westwood, Calif., Sept. 25, 1991. MPAA Rating: PG-13. Running time: **108 MIN.**

Paul Blake	Scott Bakula
Coach Gennero	Hector Elizondo
Coach Rig	Robert Loggia
Suzanne Carter	Harley Jane Kozak
Dean Elias	Larry Miller
Andre Krimm	Sinbad
Purcell	Fred Dalton Thompson
Chuck Neiderman	Rob Schneider

Also with: Jason Bateman, Andrew Bryniarski, Duane Davis, Michael Dolan, Peter Navy Tuiasosopo, Kathy Ireland.

This gridiron comedy piles up clichés the way Notre Dame racks up yardage, with an option-variety screenplay that promiscuously pitches the story in multiple directions. Still, "Necessary Roughness" is entertaining for the terminally undemanding and — with good timing before the first-string fall releases arrive — could grind out some modest boxoffice turf.

Essentially, this is a football version of the equally contrived and only slightly less hokey baseball comedy "Major League," also a Paramount release which slapped a b.o. double up the alley a few springs back.

Seemingly unable to settle on a single-wing hackneyed storyline, the filmmakers float at least three — a 34-year-old quarterback seeks to belatedly claim his college glory days, a female kicker joins a football team and a team of "real" students is assembled after a major college program is disbanded for recruiting violations — but basically settle on the former, with Scott Bakula carrying the ball.

Bakula plays a high-school star who never played college ball and is thus eligible to enroll as a freshman at Texas State U., which has brought in a squeaky clean coach (Hector Elizondo) to rebuild its program from the student body after being squashed by the NCAA infractions committee.

The hurdles Bakula faces include wooing his attractive journalism prof (Harley Jane Kozak) and outwitting the priggish dean (Larry Miller), who's intent on punting the football program off-campus once and for all.

The script is more predictable than the Oklahoma offense, with the team a group of wild eccentrics who endure a series of drubbings before they pull it together for a showdown with "the No. 1 team in Texas," apparently a new wrinkle on the Associated Press coaches poll.

Aside from the "Rocky" finish (all the way down to Bill Conti's score, full of hurricane-level bombast) other "Major League" elements include ongoing and occasionally amusing commentary from an announcer who unabashedly pulls for the home team ("Saturday Night Live's" lemur-like Rob Schneider).

Bakula is passable as the aging quarterback (based on the reaction, one would think no one over 18 has ever attended a college class), but the playbook keeps calling the number of supporting players, particularly Robert Loggia as Elizondo's snarling assistant, who delivers pregame and halftime speeches that would make Rockne proud.

Peter Navy Tuiasosopo also bears special mention as the massive Samoan center, enamored of the team's female kicker, played by supermodel Kathy Ireland, who fares much better when she's on film that doesn't move.

The most inspired moment has the squad scrimmaging with a team of convicts played by a parade of once and future NFL all-pros, including Dick Butkus, Ben Davidson and Jerry Rice. (Heavyweight boxer Evander Holyfield also is in the pack.)

Director Stan Dragoti, who doesn't take the material too seriously, draws several procedure penalties for the horribly corny finale, slow-motion shots during the closing football game and for letting the air out of the ball with some long lulls in the action.

Tech credits are solid, however, with a lot of oomph in the sound on all the teeth-rattling hits. The football choreography ranks somewhere between "The Best Of Times" and "North Dallas Forty," the latter a much more deserving Texas-set grid yarn. — *Brian Lowry*

McBAIN

A Shapiro Glickenhaus Entertainment release of a Boyce Harman production. Produced by J. Boyce Harman Jr. Executive producers, Leonard Shapiro, Alan Solomon. Written and directed by James Glickenhaus. Camera (TVC Precision color), Robert M. Baldwin Jr.; editor, Jeffrey Wolf; music, Christopher Franke; sound (Dolby), George Bossaers (Philippines), James Datri (N.Y.); production design, Charles C. Bennett; costume design, Shan Jensen; assistant director, Myron Hoffert, Ulysses Formanez (Philippines); production manager, Joey Romero (Philippines), Margaret Hilliard (N.Y.); special effects coordinator, Michael Wood; special visual effects, R/Greenberg Associates, supervisor-Joel Hynek; stunt coordinator, Jack Gill; Philippine co-producer, Lope V. Juban Jr.; associate producer, Gerrit van der Meer; casting, Donna De Seta, Ken Metcalf (Philippines). Reviewed at Cineplex Odeon Waverly 1 theater, N.Y., Sept. 21, 1991. MPAA Rating: R. Running time: **102 MIN.**

McBain	Christopher Walken
Christina	Maria Conchita Alonso
Frank Bruce	Michael Ironside
Eastland	Steve James
Dr. Dalton	Jay Patterson
Gill	T.G. Waites
El Presidente	Victor Argo
Simon Escobar	Hechter Ubarry
Pilot Daly	Russell Dennis Baker
Santos	Chick Vennera

Also with: Luis Guzman, Forrest Compton, Dick Boccelli, Nigel Redding.

Boasting excellent production values, "McBain" is a silly action film geared mainly toward overseas audiences. It reps a strong video title for the Shapiro Glickenhaus banner after its theatrical exposure.

James Glickenhaus, in his first writing-directing assignment since "Shakedown" three years earlier, has assembled the elements of an A-grade picture but failed to create an engrossing or believable narrative. Pic becomes a spoof of itself and the genre early on and never recovers.

Prolog has Chick Vennera and fellow soldiers rescuing POW Christopher Walken on the day the Vietnam War ended in 1973, so Walken owes him one. When Vennera is killed in an abortive coup of the Colombian government 18 years later, Walken agrees to help Vennera's sister, Maria Conchita Alonso, overthrow the drug cartel-run dictatorship there and let the common people come to power.

This timely theme of revolution is treated with a flippancy reminiscent of Sergio Leone's "Duck, You Sucker" and other Italian political Westerns, but Glickenhaus makes it far too easy for Walken and his group of Vietnam vets to reach their objective. Cartoonish action is amusing but never gripping.

Walken, no stranger to such roles ("The Deer Hunter," "The Dogs Of War") appears awkward and bored with a stiff-upper-lip assignment more suited to Glickenhaus' 1980 "Exterminator" leading man Robert Ginty. The extreme earnestness of Alonso as the freedom fighter is overdone. There is no romance in the pic and zero chemistry between the two leads, a glaring deficiency.

Supporting cast of reliable thesps such as Michael Ironside and Steve James mainly provides comic relief. Best acting is by Luis Guzman, who brings panache to his role as the philosophical major domo of a N.Y. crack den. Filming in the Philippines instead of South America results in Filipino extras who definitely don't look authentic.

Dominating the humans is top-notch special effects and stunt work that lift "McBain" above the norm in the action genre. This technical accomplishment is the pic's raison d'etre and will help it cross national and language barriers.
— *Lawrence Cohn*

GET BACK
(BRITISH-DOCU-COLOR/B&W)

An Entertainment release (U.K.) of an Allied Filmmakers-TDK presentation in association with MPL of a Front Page Films production. (Intl. sales: Majestic Films.) Produced by Philip Knatchbull, Henry Thomas. Executive producer, Jake Eberts. Directed by Richard Lester. Camera (Fuji & Eastmancolor, prints by Technicolor, b&w), Robert Paynter, Jordan Cronenweth; editor, John Victor Smith; sound (Dolby), Leslie Hodgson, Jeff Cohen; lighting design, Marc Brickman; 2nd unit camera, Aubrey Powell (35m), Charles Stewart (16m); visual consultant, Cronenweth; associate producer, Dusty Symonds. Reviewed at Cannon Panton St. Theater, London, Sept. 20, 1991. Running time: **90 MIN.**

A stagebound record of Paul McCartney's 1990 world tour, "Get Back" is heavy on nostalgia and light on visual zap. Low-tech item will score limited biz in specialized playoff before enjoying a long life on vidshelves, its true home.

Sans intro or background, pic kicks off on stage and stays there for 90 minutes. Filming took place in England, Holland, Brazil, Canada, Italy, Japan and the U.S., but individual locales are not identified. Audiences and songs blend into one big stage show.

Pic reunites the former Beatle with director Richard Lester, who helmed "A Hard Day's Night" and "Help!" There's none of those mid-'60s pics' ground-breaking élan here. By MTV standards, this is somewhere in a stone age.

Lester mostly lets the powerful songs (half Beatles classics) speak for themselves, crosscutting between fans mouthing the lyrics and Macca & Co. on stage. Occasionally, the Lester of old cheekily pops through: "Help!" features some bleary video extracts from the original film; footage of the Moscow McDonald's opening is cut into "Back In The USSR"; "Live And Let Die" is played over scenes of Arab-Israeli fighting and Tiananmen Square bloodletting.

Most elaborate number is "Good Day Sunshine" with split-screen effect showing fans in real-life pursuits. Biggest nostalgia trip is "Can't Buy Me Love," with black & white docu footage of the Beatles causing mass hysteria.

All concert footage was shot on 35m, apart from some Betacam vid material in Tokyo, which blends in okay apart from slight blurring in rapid motion. Audience material, shot on 16m, is often murky. Editing is on the ball. Dolby Spectral Recording sound has impressive spread but little perspective.

At screening caught, audience cheered and clapped along with each number. It's that kind of picture. — *Derek Elley*

NEW YORK FEST

DER ANDERE BLICK
(THE OTHER EYE)
(AUSTRIAN-U.S.-DOCU-COLOR/B&W)

An ORF production in association with Thalia Film and River Lights Pictures. Written and directed by Johanna Heer and Werner Schmiedel. Camera (color, b&w), Heer; editor, Heer, Schmiedel; sound, Schmiedel. Reviewed at New York Film Festival, Sept. 23, 1991. Running time: **125 MIN.**
With: Rudolph S. Joseph, Anne Friedberg, Harold Nebenzal, Francis Lederer, Heide Schlüpmann, Freddy Buache, Jean Oser, Jan-Christopher Horak, Henri Alekan, Micheline Presle, Michael Pabst, Hilde Krahl, Carl Szokoll, Aglaja Schmid, Herbert G. Luft, Ronny Loewy.

"The Other Eye" is a strangely elusive documentary on G.W. Pabst, the liberal filmmaker renowned for his works in the late 1920s and early

1930s. A good deal of fascinating material is caught between the crevices of this film's awkward structure. Originally shown on Austrian tv, the docu's exposure is likely to be limited to fest screenings and public tv.

Pabst left Germany after Hitler came to power but mysteriously returned in 1939 and wound up working for the Third Reich. Since the controversial portion of Pabst's career does not unfold until at least 90 minutes into the film, the filmmakers should have by then snared the viewer's interest in the man and his films.

Plunging into Pabst's directorial career with virtually no info on the director's background and upbringing, the documentary depends on the reminiscences of such surviving Pabst associates as Harold Nebenzal, the son of Pabst's early producer, and contemporary film scholars.

Unfortunately, the narrative takes something of a potshot approach with a number of observations not fully developed or of marginal value and few common threads about Pabst extended.

Another difficulty is the paucity of info on Pabst's life in the Third Reich during World War II. For direct testimony on this period, Heer and Schmiedel depend largely on actress Hilde Krahl, who had a limited association with the director, and Pabst's son, Michael, who was born in 1941. Michael refers to a diary his father decided to keep at this time (the diary of a lost filmmaker?), but it's not extensively quoted.

Pabst also worked briefly with Leni Riefenstahl on her film "Tiefland," but she was not interviewed (although passages are cited from her writings). The film cites differing opinions as to the propagandistic content of Pabst's films in this era, and clips excerpted are not definitive. The docu reasonably asserts, however, that any film work in Nazi Germany at the time could be considered an act of collaboration.

As in other post-"Shoah" docus, Heer and Schmiedel (who also narrate) largely eschew newsreel footage for lensing of narrative's locales as they exist today, but little is added or subtracted in the process. The most jarring sequence illustrates one of Pabst's 1930s visits to America with traveling shots around Rodeo Drive while a rock version of Kurt

Weill's "September Song" pounds on the soundtrack.

Among several pluses are interviews with such veteran thesps as Francis Lederer and Micheline Presle who appear in good shape. In fleeting contrasts, the film takes a critical look at Pabst's contemporary Fritz Lang who fled to the U.S.

Arthouse audiences may recall Lang attempting to direct a film version of "The Odyssey" in Godard's "Contempt," but this docu reminds us that this was Pabst's unrealized project and an apt metaphor for his career.

— *Fred Lombardi*

ROMANIAN FEST

UNDEVA IN EST
(SOMEWHERE IN THE EAST)
(ROMANIAN)

A Solaris Film production. Directed by Nicolae Margineanu. Screenplay, Augustin Bazura, Margineanu, based on Bazura's novel "Faces of Silence"; camera (color), Gabriel Kosuth; editor, Nita Chivulescu; music, Cornel Taranu; sound, Silviu Camil; sets, Magdelena Marasescu; costumes, Marin Peici. Reviewed at Romanian Film Festival, Costinesti, Romania, Sept. 9, 1991. Running time: **115 MIN.**
With: Remus Margineau, Valentin Voicila, Dorel Visan, Maria Ploae, Ion Fiscuteanu, Constantin Florescu.

While arthouse play is more than "Somewhere In The East" is equipped for, fest circuit prospects are strong. This well-scripted, handsome film is an eloquent and entertaining argument against communism that will be a big help in putting Romania on the film industry map.

In the '50s, a party functionary goes to rural Transylvania to collectivize village farms. A wealthy farmer resists relinquishing his wealth and doesn't want to be reduced to the level of those who never worked.

The concept of collectivization is summarized by an indignant villager who, obliged to work the land he no longer owns, grumbles to a party official, "You cut off my ----, put it in my hand and tell me, 'take it, it's still yours.' "

Margineau's three sons are forced to give up their academic studies as a result of their father's uncooperative attitude. Back home, two of them become outlaws, fighting alongside a wild-

eyed partisan who, Robin-Hood fashion, ambushes and humiliates Stalinist officers. In one of pic's funniest scenes, he forces them to strip and eat their party cards.

While the partisan and his band wait for U.S. forces to liberate the country, the wealthy farmer's third son, a philosophy student, is hidden in the cellar. Village officials arrest and torture the father to find his sons.

Fine acting and a wealth of richly developed minor characters and subplots give the pic strength. A strong plus is a coherent storyline that is straightforward and accessible, rare among central European pics.

Film's ending is problematic. Tighter editing could have helped wrap up many disparate plot points more neatly and concisely. But good tech credits, and Margineanu's competent combination of action, humor and humanity make this one worth attention. — *Rebecca Lieb*

TORONTO FEST

BLONDE FIST
(BRITISH)

A Blue Dolphin film in association with Film Four Intl. Produced by Joseph D'Morais, Christopher Figg. Written and directed by Frank Clarke. Camera (color, black & white), Bruce McGowan; editor, Brian Peachey; music, Alan Gill; sound, Ed Leatham; production design, Colin Pocock; costume design, Gill Horne; assistant director, Mike Gowans. Reviewed at Toronto Film Festival (Contemporary World Cinema section), Sept. 7, 1991. Running time: **100 MIN.**
Ronnie . . . . Margi Clarke
Lovelle . . . . Carroll Baker
Also with: Ken Hutchison, Sharon Power, Angela Clarke, Lewis Bester.

Margi Clarke packs a mean punch in "Blonde Fist" as a scrappy Liverpudlian and devoted mother who eventually wins in the boxing ring and at home. In a gritty "Thelma & Louise" meets "Rocky," Clarke is a knockout and pic is punchy, but the complex story drags.

After fleeing jail and ending up in New York, Clarke befriends a fun-loving, aging ex-stripper (superbly played by Carroll Baker) who becomes her ally and "manager" in the ring.

Fight scenes are dynamically choreographed, beautifully shot and provide pic's most engaging footage. But there are too many characters and scenarios for a tight film.

Clarke ("Letters To Brezhnev") is stunning as the tough-yet-tender '90s woman who doesn't take any guff. Pic is worthy of a carefully monitored theatrical release and is a natural for home-video — *Suzan Ayscough*

PICTURE THIS —
THE TIMES OF PETER BOGDANOVICH IN ARCHER CITY, TEXAS
(DOCU)

A Kino-Eye American production. Produced by Timothy Bottoms, Sam Bottoms. Executive producer, Barry Spikings. Written and directed by George Hickenlooper. Camera (color), Kevin Burget; editor, Howard Lavick; music, Stephen Bruton; sound, Paul Federbush. Reviewed at Toronto Film Festival, Sept. 12, 1991. No MPAA rating. Running time: **62 MIN.**

The craving for reunion and reassessment director Peter Bogdanovich sought to fill in making "Texasville," the sequel to "The Last Picture Show," has been better satisfied by documentarian George Hickenlooper in this remarkably skillful and revealing portrait.

Hickenlooper combines a flair for the telling visual image with the unearthing of some acutely private revelations from the creative personalities involved. Also in his favor is excellent use of archival materials, making this an item that should score high not only with cinephiles but with general audiences (beginning with Showtime cable airing).

Hickenlooper (co-director of "Hearts Of Darkness: A Filmmaker's Apocalypse") returns with the "Texasville" crew to Archer City, the town with one blinking stoplight, where his clever footage of the Southern Gothic denizens proves the scope of their minds to be about the same size as the burg.

Bogdanovich reveals he initially was disinterested in the Larry McMurtry "Picture Show" novel until the helmer's then-wife Polly Platt convinced him it could make a good film. Nor did actor Randy Quaid grasp how significant the film would be; he thought he was "making a softcore teen movie, something you'd see at the drive-in."

Docu explores the effect "Picture Show" has had on Archer City with an eye and ear for pungent detail. Of highest interest are the frank interviews about the emotional effect of Bogdanovich's on-set breakup with Platt to pursue an affair with ingenue Cybill Shepherd. All wounds appear to be remarkably fresh, 20 years later.

Shepherd says taking the role of Jacy meant "playing into everything people thought I might have been but I never was." Actor Timothy Bottoms, who insisted on producing the documentary as part of his contract to return to Archer City, reveals he fell in love with Shepherd on the set 20 years ago and has never gotten over it.

Given the prominence in film-lore of the multi-Oscar-winning "Picture Show," it seems a strange omission when docu doesn't comment that "Texasville" was a boxoffice and critical bust. Hickenlooper says the emotional thread he was following in the docu had little to do with the sequel's commercial fate.

Sensitive content of some interviews has led Bogdanovich to wrangle with the filmmaker for the past year over the final cut. Nonetheless, much that is remarkable remains in a fascinating glimpse of the emotional electricity that fueled the elegiac outcome of "The Last Picture Show." — *Amy Dawes*

VENICE FEST

LA PLAGE DES ENFANTS PERDUS
(THE BEACH OF LOST CHILDREN)
(MOROCCAN)

A Heracles production in association with the Ministry of Foreign Affairs, Ministry of Culture, Social Action Fund (France) and 2M Intl. (Morocco). Executive producer, Thierry Roland. Director of production, Mohamed Abderrahman Tazi. Written and directed by Jillali Ferhati. Camera (color), Gilberto Azevedo, Jacques Besse; editor, Natalie Perrey; music, Djamel Allam; art direction, Abdeldrim Akkelach. Reviewed at Venice Film Festival (competing), Sept. 3, 1991. Running time: **88 MIN.**

Mina . . . . Souad Ferhati
Salam . . . . Mohamed Timod
Zineb . . . . Fatima Loukili
  Also with: Larbi El Yacoubi.

"The Beach Of Lost Children" explores the delicate range of family feelings in an extreme situation. Its drama and spectacular pictorial views guarantee director Jillali Ferhati's third feature the small audience that Moroccan films have in Europe, plus further fest coverage.

Souad Ferhati, sister of the director and star of his "Poupées De Roseau," plays a retarded young woman with moving simplicity and intense humanity. She is seduced by an itinerant taxi driver, whom she accidentally kills and secretly buries on the beach under a mountain of salt used for preserving fish.

When her father (the dignified old Mohamed Timod) and youthful stepmother (Fatima Loukili) learn she's pregnant, they embark on a wild plan of deception. The woman is locked up and the sterile stepmother fakes pregnancy. When the baby is born, Loukili takes it as her own.

Ferhati has innate visual sense and good storytelling skills, keeping a lot of background action moving through the nine fateful months. The harsh life of the fishermen is brought out naturally and sans sentimentality.

Djamel Allam's score provides a strong and melodic musical commentary. Though many thesps (including the father and his wife) are nonprofessionals, the cast is perfectly convincing.

Technically, pic suffers from ill focus and dark, hard-to-read faces shot against the light. It also has a cavalier attitude toward details, like how the girl killed her wiry lover with a light tap on the head, or how she dragged the body to the beach to bury it.

The low-budget production received funding from several French government organizations and was presold to Morocco pay-tv network 2M.
—*Deborah Young*

THE PISTOL: THE BIRTH OF A LEGEND

A Premier Pictures release of an LA Prod. Group presentation, in association with LA Film Partners. (Intl. sales: Rich Intl.) Produced by Darrel Campbell. Executive producer, Frank C. Schroeder. Directed by Schroeder. Screenplay, Campbell, based on story by Campbell, Peter Maravich, Schroeder; camera (Allied + WBS color), Randy Walsh; editor, Schroeder; music, Brent Havens; music supervisor, Rick Jarrard; songs, Mirage; sound (Ultra-Stereo), Paul Ledford; production design, John Sperry Wade; costume design, Deanna Doran; assistant director, Craig Duncan; production manager, Christine A. Rylko; co-producers, Rodney Stone, Peter Andrews; associate producers, Rylko, L.E. Wallace. Reviewed on SVS videcassette. N.Y., Sept. 2, 1991. MPAA Rating: G. Running time: **100 MIN.**

Helen Maravich . . . . . Millie Perkins
Press Maravich . . . . . Nick Benedict
Pete Maravich . . . . Adam Guier
Coach Pendleton . . . . Boots Garland
Pete as adult . . . . Tom Lester
  Also with: Buddy Petrie, Darrel Campbell, Wendy LeBlanc, John Richardson, Rodney Stone, Eddie Hailey.

Quality throwback to family filmmaking, "The Pistol" is an entertaining and informative biopic of the late basketball star Pete Maravich. Pic has been playing regionally since January and will appeal to general tv and video auds.

Theatrical release was underwritten by a fast-food chain (Chick-Fil-A), a laudable effort to counter trends and back G-rated material.

Film wisely focuses on a single year in Maravich's life: 1959, when the 13-year-old basketball phenom got a break and made varsity at his Louisiana high school. Encouraged by his visionary college coach dad, little Pete's misadventures as odd man out among older teammates are well-directed by Frank Schroeder.

What gives the indie film oomph is casting of young Adam Guier as the hero. His precocious skill with a basketball is amply displayed in training and game footage, and the tyro actor gives a sympathetic performance. Film climaxes with his team finally pulling together and beating an all-black high school team in a non-sanctioned contest (during this segregated era).

Millie Perkins and Nick Benedict are solid as Pete's parents while Boots Garland (who also supervised the basketball scenes) avoids clichés in portraying the old-fashioned coach. He initially scoffs at Maravich's moves, saying "That's all right for the Globetrotters," but ultimately acquiesces while stressing fundamentals.

Pic is obviously a labor of love dedicated to the memory of Maravich, who died in 1988 with the record as all-time college scoring champ. Younger viewers will learn a lot about the early crossover of playing styles now taken for granted in both pro and amateur ranks.

— *Lawrence Cohn*

SHOUT

A Universal Pictures presentation. Produced by Robert Simonds. Executive producer, Lindsley Parsons Jr. Directed by Jeffrey Hornaday. Screenplay, Joe Gayton; camera (Deluxe color), Robert Brinkmann; editor, Seth Flaum; music supervisor, Karyn Rachtman; score, Randy Edelman; sound (Dolby), Willie D. Burton; production design, William F. Matthews; costume design, Eduardo Castro; art direction, P. Michael Johnston; set decoration, Jim Duffy; assistant director, Patrick H. Kehoe; production manager, Parson; casting, Nancy Nayor. Reviewed at Universal Studios, Oct. 2, 1991. MPAA rating: PG. Running time: **89 MIN.**
Jack Cabe	John Travolta
Jesse Tucker	James Walters
Sara Benedict	Heather Graham
Eugene Benedict	Richard Jordan
Molly	Linda Fiorentino
Bradley	Scott Coffey
Alan	Glenn Quinn
Toby	Frank Von Zerneck
Big Boy	Michael Bacall

Coming crop of film musicals better have more to sing about than "Shout," a 1950s rock 'n' roll fantasy that tries to have it all ways at once and winds up sorely out of tune. Even the target teen audience is likely to turn its back, as the young usually are quick to spot a phony.

Set in an isolated hamlet on the Texas plains, film purports to be about the liberating effect of the birth of rock 'n' roll, but as producers have not secured rights to any signature songs of that era, musical mix sounds wildly inauthentic.

Most prominent tunes on display are by Robbie Robertson and John Hiatt, circa late 1980s, and though these are lushly pleasing to the ear, they have nothing to do with telling the story.

Broadly etched tale is about a home for wayward and orphaned boys. Kid with the worst attitude (James Walters) clashes with the grim and heavy-handed headmaster (Richard Jordan), who espouses a regimen of hard labor and calisthenics.

Along comes a music teacher (John Travolta), a hepcat ahead of his time who indoctrinates the boys in the forbidden pleasures of rock 'n' roll. On the side, he's making time with the owner (Linda Fiorentino) of a dance club on the wrong side of the tracks and former flame of the town sheriff.

When the jealous lawman finds out the music teacher's a wanted man, Travolta goes into hiding, leaving rock 'n' roll dangling like a broken promise while the heartbroken orphan band slogs through John Phillip Sousa at the Fourth of July bash.

It's the kind of hokey scenario that would fly only if aided by a camp sense of humor or the promise of a good musical number about to break out, and neither of these are present. Music and dance elements are used naturalistically, as in "La Bamba," but rather sparingly, and without any top tunes to drive it, vehicle doesn't move.

Most annoying are the implausibilities. Story roots itself in the attitudes of a time and place but ignores history whenever convenient. The juke joint has contempo design features, interracial dancing and a clientele and rhythm & blues band that are way too hot for this Texas burg. In another scene, Travolta's dinky portable record player puts out a wall of wicked rock 'n' roll sound loud enough to lure the young 'uns in from the fields.

Meanwhile, kids wear longish hair and sideburns, Heather Graham plays a '50s girl in a '90s mode, career-bound and sexually forthright, and among the cast, only Travolta bothers to put on a Texas accent, and his thick, nuanced emoting clashes with the unadorned delivery of the others.

In all, ill-thunk scenario seem slung together by amateurs. The culprits are producer Robert Simonds (both "Problem Child" pics) and first-time director Jeffrey Hornaday ("Flashdance" choreographer), already collaborating with writer Joe Gayton on another pic.

On the plus side, pic, lensed on the Universal backlot and on a ranch outside Stockton, Calif., features gorgeous sun-drenched photography in a landscape of golds and browns and a mostly attractive cast, with a notably good perf by Scott Coffey among the boys in the band.

Still, when pic begins with Randy Edelman's sentimental score swelling around homespun visuals of the sedentary hamlet while a restless boy (Walters) rings the church bell and yells at the town to "Wake up! Wake up!" one can't help but think of a Kellogg's cereal commercial.

— *Amy Dawes*

UNDER SUSPICION
(BRITISH)

A Columbia (U.S.) and Rank Film Distributors release (U.K.) of a Columbia-Rank-LWT presentation of a Carnival Films production. Produced by Brian Eastman. Executive producers, Nick Elliott, Fred Turner, George Helyer. Written and directed by Simon Moore. Camera (Rank color, Panavision), Vernon Layton (U.K.), Ivan Strasburg (U.S.); editor, Tariq Anwar; music, Christopher Gunning; sound (Dolby), Christopher Ackland, Ian Fuller, Ken Weston, Stan Fiferman; production design, Tim Hutchinson; art direction, Tony Reading; set decoration, Stephenie McMillan (U.K.), Joel Washnetz (U.S.); costume design, Penny Rose; special effects supervisor, David Harris; special effects, Steve Hamilton; associate producer, Vincent Winter; assistant director, Terry Needham, Simon Hinkley; casting, Anne Henderson (U.K.), Mike Fenton (U.S.). Reviewed at Odeon Marble Arch Theater, London, Sept. 28, 1991. No MPAA rating. Running time: **99 MIN.**
Tony Aaron	Liam Neeson
Angeline	Laura San Giacomo
Frank	Kenneth Cranham
Selina	Alphonsia Emmanuel

Also with: Stephen Moore, Maggie O'Neill, Malcolm Storry, Alan Talbot, Martin Grace, Kevin Moore.

Writer-director Simon Moore makes a stylish bow with "Under Suspicion," an old-fashioned murder mystery flawed by wobbly playing from Irish actor Liam Neeson. British-set nostalgia item may need careful handling to hit its target in wider markets. Previously known under the titles "The Other Woman" and "Prime Suspect," suspenser is slated for February release in the U.S.

Pic is another big-screen outing by commercial web London Weekend Television, which has already scored theatrically with "A Handful Of Dust" and "Where Angels Fear To Tread." Sans those films' literary pedigrees, this one will have to get by on its curiosity value.

Tense prolog, set in Brighton, 1957, has a cop (Neeson) caught with his pants down with the wife (Maggie O'Neill) of a gangster he's trailing. Resulting shootout ends with a dead cop and Neeson kicked off the force.

Two years later, Neeson is a down-at-the-heels private investigator arranging phony divorce evidence. O'Neill, now his wife, poses as the other woman in hotel setups to get photographic court evidence. During one of these setups, she ends up with her brain splattered on the sheets next to an equally dead client.

Enter the hotel stiff's mysterious American mistress (Laura San Giacomo) who quickly heads the police list of suspects. She hires Neeson to investigate her lover's murder, but as the evidence builds, it points more toward the ex-cop having gotten rid of his wife. Despite Neeson's claim that San Giacomo is the murderer, he's put on trial and sentenced to hang.

Pic plays like a loving tribute to every film noir in the book. But despite vague parallels to Fritz Lang's "Beyond A Reasonable Doubt," it's more like a rainy-day Brit cross between "Jagged Edge" and "Body Heat."

Former tv scripter Moore, 32, keeps the dialog taut and the red herrings coming but he skimps on electricity between the two leads. Only occasionally does he stretch credibility to the breaking point.

San Giacomo looks good in lipstick and shades and plays the breathy femme fatale to the hilt. But Neeson has trouble balancing the several sides of his character and rarely holds the screen. Subtext of the Irish gumshoe and American mistress both being outsiders in the British coastal town never really gets out of the starting gate.

As Neeson's fatherly police pal, Kenneth Cranham is solid but mostly reactive. Alphonsia Emmanuel makes a brief mark as the dead man's vengeful widow, and there's a tasty bit of Stephen Moore as a gay lawyer.

Production design by Tim Hutchinson is polished, exactly catching the story's setting on the borderline of the more liberated '60s. Other credits are all neat, with Vernon Layton's Panavision lensing a real plus. A more thematic score by Christopher Gunning would have helped stoke the drama.

Pic was mostly shot in Brighton, with Portmeirion, north Wales, doubling for site of San Giacomo's out-of-town manse. Miami pops up briefly in the coda. — *Derek Elley*

ONE FALSE MOVE

An IRS Releasing presentation of an IRS Media production. Produced by Jesse Beaton, Ben Myron. Executive producers, Miles A. Copeland III, Paul Colichman, Harold Welb. Directed by Carl Franklin. Screenplay, Billy Bob Thornton, Tom Epperson; camera (color),

James L. Carter; editor, Carole Kravitz; music, Peter Haycock, Derek Holt; sound, Ken Segal; production design, Gary T. New; costume design, Ron Leamon; art direction, Dana Torrey; set decoration, Troy Myers; assistant director, Michael Grossman; casting, Don Pemrick. Reviewed at Raleigh Studios, L.A., Sept. 3, 1991. MPAA rating: R. Running time: **105 MIN.**

Dale (Hurricane) Dixon	Bill Paxton
Fantasia/Lila	Cynda Williams
Ray Malcolm	Billy Bob Thornton
Pluto	Michael Beach
Dud Cole	Jim Metzler
McFeely	Earl Billings
Cherylann	Natalie Canerday

Scenes of grimly realistic drug-related slayings set a nihilistic tone at the outset of "One False Move," which shocks but grows progressively more involving.

Offbeat scenario features an attractive young woman (Cynda Williams), who's escaped from rural Arkansas but fallen into very bad company in L.A. Her b.f. (Billy Bob Thornton) and his accomplice (Michael Beach), both vicious killers, are after a big cache of cash and cocaine.

They hit the road for Houston, where they plan to offload the drugs on a dealer. Also on the itinerary is a promised trip to small-town Arkansas to visit the baby Williams left behind.

Working for the most part in straightforward style, director Carl Franklin achieves considerable suspense by pitting the frailties of each party against the other.

Director, veteran of three Roger Corman films and a recent American Film Institute grad, pulls no punches in depicting violence or its consequences. But he allows the characters time to unfold in ways that considerably deepen story interest.

Unflinching realism is disturbing at pic's outset but serves it well later. Despite time and budget constraints in the approximately $2 million shoot, the pic in its finer passages has qualities many studio pics would covet.

Unorthodox structure of script by Thornton and Tom Epperson makes it difficult to establish focus, and it's a shame some of the implausibilities weren't shored up.

Williams (the aspiring singer in "Mo' Better Blues") slowly steals the show, and Bill Paxton provides strong support as an apparently simple man who's forced to own up to complex deeds. — *Amy Dawes*

IL MURO DI GOMMA
(THE INVISIBLE WALL)
(ITALIAN)

A Penta Distribuzione release of a Trio Cinema e Television-Penta Film production. Produced by Maurizio Tedesco, Mario & Vittori Cecchi Gori. Directed by Marco Risi. Screenplay, Sandro Petraglia, Andrea Purgatori, Stefano Rulli; camera (color), Mauro Marchetti; editor, Claudio Di Mauro; music, Francesco De Gregori; production design, Massimo Spano. Reviewed at Venice Film Festival (competition), Sept. 12, 1991. Running time: **120 MIN.**

Rocco	Corso Salani
Giannina	Angela Finocchiaro
Franco	Antonello Fassari
Corrà	Pietro Gislandi

Also with: Carla Benedetti, Mario Patane, Nicola Vigilante.

A passionately made film with strong emotional impact at home, "The Invisible Wall" has jumped to a top Italo boxoffice slot after its Venice fest premiere. Pic's thriller format offers a gripping albeit familiar hook, but the unsolved 1980 mystery of an Italian airliner downed by a missile makes too incomplete a story to bank on a automatic audience outside Italy.

This is director Marco Risi's third attempt at tackling topical social and political issues. Although "Wall" is based even more closely on reality than his streetkid tales "Forever Mary" or "Boys On The Outside," it lacks their universal punch.

Rocco, a newspaperman (played by tough-faced, soft-hearted newcomer Corso Salani), begins investigating what seems like a routine plane crash of an Itavia DC9 bound for Sicily and the death of all 81 passengers. But he stumbles across a much bigger mystery: The plane was hit by a missile of unknown origin. Worst of all, Rocco discovers a coverup apparently was orchestrated by the Italian air force, probably at the behest of another country.

Risi and his scriptwriters (one, Andrea Purgatori, is the real-life Rocco) skillfully build tension around the reporter's one-man investigation in a variety of original settings. He jogs around Rome with a rep from the U.S. embassy, trying to get info. He dines with an airplane manufacturer (played by music impresario David Zard), who denies the plane had structural defects. He flies to England to wring a few cryptic words from one of the scientists analyzing the plane's remains. Tense editorial meetings at Corriere della Sera, Rocco's paper, punctuate his research.

What keeps the film from making a wider impact is really its lack of a conclusion. The truth dribbles in over the course of years (time is marked by Rocco's otherwise useless fights with his girlfriend.)

Pic's ending, written at the beginning of this summer, suggests a North Atlantic Treaty Organization plane fired the missile, which may have been aimed at a Libyan aircraft with leader Muammar Qaddafi aboard. But since the black box was recovered only after pic was completed, the whole truth is unknown.

More than a whodunit, however, "Wall" is really a condemnation of arrogant Italian authorities who helped hide facts from the public. The coverup is the real scandal and threat to democracy, as the finale stresses. Risi makes a positive ending out of the reprimand given to the presumed culprits by a parliamentary investigating committee, but audiences may find it a little anticlimactic.

Scripters Stefano Rulli and Sandro Petraglia (who cameo as judges in the final scene) keep things unfolding at a steady pace despite the years the story covers. Technical work is fine.

Proof of film's local impact is that its title (literally, the rubber wall) has already entered colloquial Italian speech to refer to the many ways truth is deflected. — *Deborah Young*

BUICKEN
(THE BUICK)
(NORWEGIAN)

A Motlys production. Produced by Sigve Endresen. Written and directed by Hans Otto Nicolayssen. Camera (color), Kjell Vassdal; editor, Malte Wadman; music, Kenneth Sivertsen, Reidar Skår; sound, Øystein Boassen; production design, Anne Siri Bryhni; costumes, Laila Holm; production manager, Arve Figenschow. Reviewed at Norwegian Film Festival, Haugesund, Aug. 22, 1991. Running time: **87 MIN.**

With: Lasse Lindtner, Helge Jordal.

"The Buick" is a well-crafted picture, but it lacks substance and its conclusion is too lightweight for the tragedy depicted. Reception at the Haugesund film fest was polite, and its boxoffice potential appears marginal.

Two brothers grow up, and one moves with the times and becomes a hotshot financial adviser. The other becomes a blue collar worker and political agitator. They drift apart, but the adviser seeks out his brother when the latter, politically defeated, has isolated himself in a seaside cabin.

The blue collar brother, seen only in flashbacks, is a presence not strongly enough felt, though the part is well handled by lively, popular actor Helge Jordal. Lasse Lindtner plays the lead with restraint.

The fine editing job cannot disguise pic's essential thinness. — *Trond Olav Svendsen*

HARD PROMISES

A Columbia Pictures release of a Stone Group Pictures presentation and a High Horse Films production. Executive producers, Rick Bieber, Peter Mac-Alevey. Produced by Cindy Chvatal, William Petersen. Directed by Martin Davidson. Screenplay, Jule Selbo; camera (Deluxe color), Andrzej Bartkowiak; editor, Bonnie Koehler; music, Kenny Vance; production design, Dan Leigh; costume design, Susan Gammie; coproducer, Paul Kurta; assistant director, Joel Tuber; casting, Mary Colquhoun. Reviewed at Boston Film Festival, Sept. 5, 1991. MPAA Rating: PG. Running time: **95 MIN.**

Christine Coalter	Sissy Spacek
Joey Coalter	William Petersen
Walter Humphrey	Brian Kerwin
Dawn	Mare Winningham
Pinky	Jeff Perry
Beth Coalter	Olivia Burnette
Stuart Haggart	Peter MacNichol

Also with: Lois Smith, Ann Wedgeworth, Amy Wright.

Success of this slated fall release will pivot on audience expectations created by Columbia's ad campaign. Boston Film Fest bow touted pic as a romantic comedy toplining Sissy Spacek, which it's not. Whether there's an audience for what the film is — a quirky romantic drama centering on William Petersen — remains to be seen.

Petersen plays a footloose man who has largely absented himself from the lives of his wife (Spacek) and daughter (Olivia Burnette). He gets a wedding invitation to Spacek's marriage to Brian Kerwin, and hies back home to put a stop to it.

Early scenes make the film (shot in Austin, Texas) seem like a bucolic remake of "The Awful Truth." Best moment comes when Petersen and Spacek argue in front of the neighbors, who enjoy the street theater and provide their own refreshments. He soon learns from her lawyer (Peter MacNichol) that they have been divorced in absentia. Remainder of the film revolves around Petersen trying to win Spacek back and the refusal of the couple-to-be to relegate Kerwin to the Ralph Bellamy role.

Spacek is in fine form as the ex-cheerleader who married the football captain but now wants to regain control of her life. The only problem is that most of the drama in her character's story has *already* taken place before the start of the film. That goes for Kerwin, too, who offers no threat to the Petersen character's charisma, but who is obviously the better choice for Spacek.

Petersen (who also gets a producer credit) is the character in transition here, fighting for the status quo and wondering if it's too late for him to change in order to prevent losing Spacek. His closing scene with Burnette is especially touching.

The remaining characters are largely Greek chorus, although Mare Winningham and Jeff Perry manage to show that the life that Petersen was so eager to flee wasn't so bad after all. Some of the scenes, though, provide too much exposition, making the viewer wonder if the film might not have been better if it had started with Spacek's divorce rather than Petersen's discovery.

Tech credits are fine, with Andrezej Bartkowiak's cinematography helping to take the edge off of some scenes that might otherwise play too harshly. Kenny Vance's score should appeal to country & western fans but is unlikely to generate crossover interest.— *Daniel M. Kimmel*

GORUBAN
(THE SERGEANT)
(IRANIAN)

A Cadre Film production. Produced by Sirus Moquaddam. Written and directed by Masud Kimiyai. Camera (color), Mahmud Kalari; editor, Kimiyai; music, Giti Pasayi; sound, Fereydun Zurak; production design, costumes, Kimiyai. Reviewed at Venice Film Festival (noncompeting), Sept. 11, 1991. Running time: **86 MIN.**
The sergeant . . . . Ahmad Najafi
Golbakht . . . . . . Golcenre Sajjadiye
Bahman . . . . Sahed Ahmadlu

"The Sergeant" is a strident melodrama and one of the weaker Iranian pics to hit the fest circuit recently. Prospects outside its home turf are poor.

Pic starts promisingly with the homecoming of an army sergeant eight years after the Iran-Iraq

war's end. He had been thought killed, and he seems to be shell-shocked. His wife and son are pleased to welcome him home, but the wife decides to return with her mother to her birthplace in Azerbaijan, across the Soviet border.

Meanwhile, the sergeant wants a piece of woodland a property owner had promised him before he left, but the sneaky landowner demands far more than the original sum. When the single-minded veteran defies the landowner to work the land anyway, goons pummel him, and his life is saved by his small son's resourcefulness. He and a friend (an ex-cop) go to the landowner's home to demand justice and revenge.

The pic, which has some surprisingly violent scenes, at times seems like a remake of a Charles Bronson revenge opus. Picture remains one-dimensional, and the repetitive and tuneless music score is no asset. More successful is Mahmud Kalari's moody camerawork of the rain-swept countryside.

The climax takes place on the Iranian-Soviet border, providing an interesting backdrop to a sentimental conclusion to a basically clichéd picture. Best acting comes from young Sahed Ahmadlu as the sergeant's courageous son.
— *David Stratton*

SOCIAL SUICIDE

A Star Entertainment Group presentation of a Star Entertainment-Victoria Paige Meyerink production in association with Matovich Prods. and Pegasus Prods. Produced by Meyerink. Executive producer, Frank S. Rowe. Co-executive producer, Marlee Harrell Dailey. Directed by Lawrence D. Foldes. Screenplay, Elisa J. Charouhas, Foldes, from Charouhas' original story; additional screenplay material, Melanie Anne Phillips, Mark Buntzman, Adam Slater; camera (color), Stuart Kiehl; additional photography, Geza Sinkovics; editor, Phillips; music, Roger Bellon; sound (Dolby), Roberta Doheny; production design, Peter Kanter; art director, Elizabeth Simakis; set decorator, Nancy Arnold; costume design, Patte Dee; production supervisor, Slater; assistant director, Michael Engel; associate producer, Larry Chambers, Yelena Guzman; co-producer, Mitchel J. Matovich Jr., Aaron Speiser; special effects supervisor, Lisa Romanoff, Renee Teeter. Reviewed at Edinburgh Film Festival, Aug. 22, 1991. Running time: **111 MIN.**
Ava Sterling . . . . . . Bobbie Bresee
Kim Sterling . . . . . Shannon Sturges
Tom Garcia . . . Peter Anthony Elliott
Mildred Sterling . . . . Margaret Silbar
Bob Sterling . . . . . Dan Cashman
Constance . . . . Pamela S. Neill
Scott Robertson . . . . . Kenn Cooper
Sen. Robertson . . . . . . Jack Carter
Trini Lopez . . . . Himself
Also with: O.J. Bau, Kelly Nelson, Louis DeMangus, Leslie Horan.

At its best, "Social Suicide" plays like early John Hughes on speed. Anarchic romp through the California debutante scene may need careful handling to find its audience, but word-of-mouth could help it build a sizable cult following.

Plot recycles theme of pics like the Hughes-scripted "Some Kind Of Wonderful" and stirs in the loopiness of Paul Bartel's "Scenes From The Class Struggle In Beverly Hills." Spark that hits the social tinderbox is when a nice girl (Shannon Sturges) favors Chicano melon-packer (Peter Anthony Elliott) over preppie (Ken Cooper).

Girl's mom (Bobbie Bresee) first tries to buy off the handsome Latino only to find he lives in Bel Air, thank you very much. He's also shooting for a prestigious prize at Pacific Coast U. to raise the profile of fellow Hispanics; so preppie co-contender joins with Mom in the dirty tricks department.

Formula script springs few surprises, but pic is kept afloat by lively acting that hits most of the right notes. In-control direction by Foldes (who cameos as a delivery boy) pays dividends in the lengthy ball finale.

Horror queen Bresee, debuting in a comic role, is just right as the ghoulish mother; Margaret Silbar, as feisty Grandma, leaves one wanting more. Elliott plays it mostly straight as the hunky Chicano, and Sturges (granddaughter of director Preston) is a perky eyeful.

Slack editing often slows the tempo. All other tech credits are chipper, with special praise for Stuart Kiehl's high-sheen lensing and Roger Bellon's alert score of classical baubles.
— *Derek Elley*

DAHONG DENGLONG GAOGAO GUA
(RAISE THE RED LANTERN)
(CHINESE-HONG KONG-TAIWANESE)

An Orion Classics release (U.S.) of an Era Intl. (Hong Kong)-Salon Film (Hong Kong)-China Film co-production. Produced by Chiu Fu-sheng. Executive producers, Hou Hsiao-hsien, Zhang Wei. Directed by Zhang Yimou. Screenplay, Ni Zhen, based on Su Tong's novel "Wives And Concubines"; camera (color), Zhao Fei, Yang Lun; editor, Du Yuan; music, Zhao Jiping; art direction, Qao Jiuping, Dong Humiao. Reviewed at Telluride Film Festival, Aug. 30, 1991. (Also competed at Venice Film Festival) Running time: **126 MIN.**

With: Gong Li, Ma Jingwu, He Caifei, Qao Quifen, Jin Shuyan.

After scoring on the international art circuit with "Red Sorghum" and "Ju Dou," former cinematographer Zhang Yimou delivers again with "Raise The Red Lantern." An unusual co-production among China, Hong Kong and Taiwan, provocative film will perform solidly in appropriate offshore markets.

Something of a companion piece to "Ju Dou," new pic deals even more pointedly with the oppression of women in China. Set in the 1920s, before the communist revolution, film opens with a beautiful young woman tearfully agreeing to become a concubine for a wealthy master. "Isn't that woman's fate?" Songlian (Gong Li) asks.

In a lavish compound, Songlian takes her place as the youngest and most attractive of four wives. Insidious intrigue between the women immediately begins. With its slow accretion of insults, one-upmanship and diplomacy, film plays like a chess game. Pacing is deliberate, and absence of the overt melodrama and sexual heat of "Ju Dou" will make "Lantern" somewhat less of an audience pleaser.

But the story is still gripping and visual textures are extraordinary. Li's presence gives the film a constant erotic charge.

Settings, costumes and cinematography, featuring much use of long lenses, are dazzling, and film is exquisitely designed. Acting is firstrate. — *Todd McCarthy*

VINATOAREA DE LILIECI
(BAT HUNT)
(ROMANIAN)

A Star 22 production. Written and directed by Daniel Barbulescu. Camera (color), Alexandru Groza, Ion Dobre; editor, Mircea Ciociltei; music, Ileana Popovici; sound, Gheorge Ilarian; sets, Adriana Paun; costumes, Lucia Morariu. Reviewed at the Romanian Film Festival, Costinesti, Romania, Sept. 8, 1991. Running time: **95 MIN.**
With: Ion Haiduc, Florentin Duse, Florin Anton, Ion Chelaru, Jeanine Stavarache, Andrea Bradeanu.

This action pic about terrorists, Securitate officers and a stolen videocassette is bottom-of-the-barrel stuff. Amateurish to the extreme, "Bat Hunt" is an insult to the Yank B movies it tries to emulate. All prospects for this one are zip.

Plot is loosely hung on the December 1989 uprising in Romania, although it makes no apparent political statement. Pavel, a Securitate officer, enters a building occupied by revolutionaries. Finding a tv video cameraman dead in the building, Pavel takes his cassette tape, unaware that he is being observed by a colleague. Pavel becomes a hunted man when menacing agents try to get the tape back.

Plot details are as murky and haphazard as the cinematography and editing. Mainly, characters crisscross Romania in trenchcoats, intent on doing each other bodily harm. Whenever the director feels he's successfully pulled off an action shot (such as a character leaping across rooftops) he makes sure to insert it three or four times, hoping the audience isn't sharp enough to catch the repetition.

Title is never explained.
— *Rebecca Leib*

OY VI GUSI
(HEY, YOU WILD GEESE)
(SOVIET-B&W-COLOR)

A Lenfilm Studios production. Written and directed by Lydia Bobrova. Camera (black & white, color), S. Astakhov; editor, Z. Shorokhova; sound, O. Strugina; art director, G. Popov. Reviewed at 44th Locarno Intl. Film Festival, Aug. 14, 1991. Running time: **87 MIN.**
Mitka . . . . V. Sobolev
Petka . . . . Y. Bobrov
Sania . . . . V. Frolov
Raya . . . . G. Volkova
Dasha . . . . E. Usatova
Liubka . . . . S. Gaitman

A gloomy, uncompromising dark portrait of the Soviet Union, "Hey, You Wild Geese" may well help explain the events taking place there. Future programs on Soviet film of the '90s should definitely keep this one in mind.

Telling the story of the director's three brothers, pic's script stayed in a drawer for 10 years before it was allowed to film.

Pic takes place in a village and follows the daily routine of Mitka, an invalid refused work because of ill health; his wife Raya, an overworked seamstress with a bad heart; Mitka's brother Petka, a diminutive man married to Dasha, a majestic woman who works as a nurse in an old people's home, and finally Sanya, who returns after a long sen-

tence in the camps for murder. He picks up Liubka, a drunken tramp, on the way home.

Everyday misery, primitive living conditions, the meanness people are reduced to and the system's shortcomings are put in clear contrast with the colorful, costly ceremonies of the Moscow Olympics, which were supposed to rep a nonexistent dreamlike Soviet reality.

Most of the roles are entrusted to amateurs whom the director hired on location. They are only too familiar with the image she creates, and they envelop each character with love and understanding.

Pic was shot in unadorned, almost documentary fashion, but still it's tempting to refer to the pic as an allegory leading to clearly hopeless conclusions.
— *Dan Fainaru*

STEIN
(GERMAN)

A DEFA Studio Babelsberg-Gruppe Roter Kreis co-production. (Intl. sales: Progress Film.) Produced by Herbert Ehler. Directed by Egon Günther. Screenplay, Günther, Helga Schütz; camera (color), Erich Gusko; editor, Monika Schindler; music, Johannes Brahms, Henry Purcell, Karl Ernst Sasse; production design, Harald Horn. Reviewed at Munich Film Festival, June 28, 1991. Running time: **105 MIN.**
Ernest Stein . . . . Rolf Ludwig
Sara . . . . Franziska Herold
Laura . . . . Eveline Dahm
Josi . . . . Johanna Möhring
Also with: Margit Bendokat, Uwe Dag Berlin, Eckhard Doblies, Jörg Foth, Gerhard Händel, Alexander Hetterle.

East German Egon Günther's first pic on native soil in over 10 years, "Stein" is a quietly engaging tragicomic character study of an aging, withdrawn actor. Pic will have special appeal in united Germany and at film fests and could find audiences in some territories.

Pic opens on a slightly surrealistic note as Ernst Stein (Rolf Ludwig) carries on with his life despite gunshots, passing tanks and struggles with soldiers who attempt to break into his secluded country house. These distractions illustrate the struggle for freedom in East Germany before liberation.

Via flashbacks, Stein is seen as a prominent stage actor who became a legend after he protested the 1968 invasion of Czechoslovakia by exiting in the middle of "King Lear." He quit his career and became the center of a coterie of youths who hang out at his

house, providing him with an appreciative aud for his impromptu routines delivered anywhere from the living room to the loo.

Stein masks his loneliness and sensitivity with nonchalance and constant humorous jabs. He becomes vulnerable when he falls in love with a sweet-faced 20-year-old (Franziska Herold), a free spirit who relates to his youthful banter. A nymphet (Eveline Dahm) vies for his attention in scenes of amazing candor.

Ludwig gives a bravura performance as the quirky ailing actor, and his youthful supporting cast is terrific.

Much of the humor lies in quick retorts in a Berlin dialect impossible to convey through subtitles, although Ludwig's facial expressions and gestures transcend language barriers. Classical score adds dignity and depth to the character study, which might have benefited from trimming.

Marking Günther's welcome return to DEFA, "Stein" got a standing ovation at its Munich Film Fest preem, which took place over a decade since he emigrated to West Germany. Lensing in outdoor shots is crystal-clear and impressive, although interiors tend to be a bit murky.
— *B. Samantha Stenzel*

NEW YORK FEST

NIGHT ON EARTH

A JVC presentation, in association with Victor Corp. of Japan, Victor Musical Industries, Pyramide/Le Studio Canal Plus, Pandora Film and Channel 4, of a Locus Solus production. (Intl. sales: Saredi Films.) Executive producer, Jim Stark. Written, produced and directed by Jim Jarmusch. Camera (Duart color), Frederick Elmes; editor, Jay Rabinowitz; music, Tom Waits; songs, Waits, Kathleen Brennan; sound (Dolby), Drew Kunin; assistant director, Terence Edwards (L.A.), Howard McMaster (N.Y.), Jeanne Marie de la Fontaine (Paris), Joseph Rochlitz (Rome), Pauli Pentti (Helsinki); production manager, Susan Shapiro (L.A.), Kathie Hersh (N.Y.), Gilles Sacuto (Paris); Manuela Pineski-Berger (Rome); co-producer, Demetra J. MacBride; line producer, Rudd Simmons; co-executive producers, Masahiro Inbe, Noboru Takayama. Reviewed at New York Film Festival, Oct. 2, 1991. No MPAA Rating. Running time: **130 MIN.**
Corky . . . . Winona Ryder
Victoria Snelling . . . . . Gena Rowlands
YoYo . . . . Giancarlo Esposito
Helmut . . . . . . Armin Mueller-Stahl
Angela . . . . Rosie Perez
Paris driver . . . . . Isaach De Bankolé
Blind woman . . . . . . Béatrice Dalle
Rome driver . . . . . Roberto Benigni
Priest . . . . Paolo Bonacelli
Mika . . . . Matti Pellonpää

Jim Jarmusch's existential comedy "Night On Earth" is an easy-to-take followup to his last pic "Mystery Train." Episodic effort boasts name talent that will make it a leading attraction in Europe while playing to the same modest but loyal arthouse audience he's developed Stateside.

As his own producer with complete artistic control, even owning his film negatives, Jarmusch demonstrates an uncompromising approach. The material and message is generally transparent enough to lead one to an "is that all there is?" reaction, but Jarmusch's trademark quirky humor and a set of exuberant performances provides diverting entertainment.

Beginning with an outer-space shot gradually zeroing in on planet Earth, the director covers in five separate segments his favorite theme of lonely people interacting but ultimately facing the great void alone. Each takes place in a different city and is introed by a set of five clocks displaying the time zones, representing nearly simultaneous events occurring across the globe.

From this cosmic perspective he examines brief encounters between taxi drivers and their late-night fares. Opening L.A. segment is pic's weakest, as tomboyish cabbie Winona Ryder is matched against her patrician passenger Gena Rowlands. Predictable payoff has Rowlands the casting agent offering foul-mouthed Ryder the chance of a lifetime to become a movie star. Unlike previous Jarmusch thesps, Ryder *is* a movie star, and that fact takes the edge off the climax when she rejects the offer flat out, happy not to be in Rowlands' rat race.

Contrasting with this is a powerful finale, set in Helsinki with actors from the troupe of the Kaurismäki brothers (character names here are Mika and Aki as an in-joke to that pair of Finnish directors). Matti Pellonpää is genuinely moving as a cabbie pouring out his tragic story to a trio of drunken guys. It's a tale of faith and love unrewarded, ending almost "Bicycle Thief"-style with a just-fired guy crouched in the snow as morning breaks and workers start a new day.

En route to this somber finish, Jarmusch provides ebullient comedy in two winning routines: the hilarious and unlikely team (in matching floppy winter hats) of Giancarlo Esposito and Armin

Mueller-Stahl in New York as well as a goofy, all-stops-out monolog by Roberto Benigni as a Roman cabbie confessing to a back-seat priest about his sexual exploits with pumpkins and a sheep named Lola.

Parisian segment is an unsettling encounter between a bitter blind woman (Béatrice Dalle) and her Ivory Coast-transplanted driver Isaach De Bankolé. With her eyes rolled up to show whites-only, the "Betty Blue" star looks like a beautiful alien from outer space and is relentlessly nasty to De Bankolé in the episode that most cleverly demonstrates Jarmusch's mixture of the obvious and the cryptic.

Though used sparingly, Tom Waits' after-hours funky score is a perfect mood-setter. Tech credits are fine and cast delivers quality work in each segment. Filming in the languages of each city results in a feature about 60% English subtitled, a fact that will definitely impact at the boxoffice in the U.S., where "Night On Earth" is taking bids from prospective distributors.

— *Lawrence Cohn*

PICTURES FROM A REVOLUTION
(DOCU)

A GMR Film production. Produced and directed by Susan Meiselas, Richard P. Rogers, Alfred Guzzetti. Camera (color), Rogers; music, William Eldridge, Terry Riley; sound, Guzzetti; photo animation, Patricia Kelly; research, Abbie Fields. Reviewed at New York Film Festival, Oct. 3, 1991. Running time: **93 MIN.**

In "Pictures From A Revolution," photographer Susan Mieselas returns to Nicaragua a decade after the conflict she captured in her photos. Retracing her steps and seeking out the subjects of her stills on both sides, Mieselas and colleagues provide a portrait of a disillusioned nation and a meditation on the relation of truth to media images.

Resulting documentary Mieselas made with Richard Rogers and Alfred Guzzetti (team also responsible for the 1985 "Living At Risk: The Story of A Nicaraguan Family") should provide stimulating fare for specialty film situations.

The device of opening and closing the film with traveling shots of the Nicaraguan countryside and Mieselas' own off-screen com-

mentary suggest that, despite her interest in the country's fate, she has remained something of an accidental tourist. Encountering the beginning of the insurrection by chance in 1978, she spent some of the time of her subsequent visits braced for a U.S. invasion.

Nicaraguans interviewed from all social strata offer richly articulate accounts of their experiences and their disappointment with the revolution's aftermath. The filmmakers also pursued Nicaraguan exiles in Florida and Canada. A contra officer opines that his side was manipulated by the Americans just as the Sandinistas were by the Russians; his country was caught in superpower politics.

Depending on a montage of New York Times headlines to chronicle the Sandinistas' progress, the film makes no conclusions on what went wrong. A veteran of the Sandinista resistance argues that the revolution's wings were clipped from the beginning by the U.S. embargo and obstructions from the business class.

A Sandinista official proudly states that despite the economic problems, his government made strides helping the poor but none of the peasants interviewed found any economic change after the revolution. Clearly, the scope and intentions of the filmmakers were not up to a full-fledged inquiry on these issues, but a more detailed description of life under the Sandinistas would have been consistent with the film's aims.

Film also may be open to criticism from those who feel that the docu's view of the elusiveness of truth is a copout for media foibles. Docu, however, does make a strong case for the complexities involved and the difficulties in seeing the long view.

With echoes of "Blowup," Mieselas laments the limits of truth offered by photos and how documents of history wind up as symbols. (Her shot of a rebel throwing a Molotov cocktail was used in both Sandinista and contra posters.) Viewers also may be struck by the universal process of how quickly a revolution's stirring images become banal products. —*Fred Lombardi*

ALAS DE MARIPOSA
(BUTTERFLY WINGS)
(SPANISH)

A Gasteizko Zinema production. Executive producers, Juanma Bajo Ulloa, Joseba Nafarrate. Directed by Juanma Bajo Ulloa. Screenplay, Juanma & Eduardo Bajo Ulloa; camera (Eastmancolor), Aitor Mantxola, Enric Davi; editor, Pablo Blanco; sets, Satur Idaretta; music, Bingen Mendizabel; sound, Goldstein & Steinberg; associate producer, Fernando Trueba. Reviewed at San Sebastian Film Festival, Sept. 20, 1991. Running time: **110 MIN.**
Carmen . . . . Silvia Munt
Gabriel . . . . Fernando Valverde
Ami (child) . . . . Susana Garcia
Ami (adolescent) . . . . Laura Vaquero
Alejandro . . . . Txema Blasco
Corka . . . . Alberto Martin

The first part of "Butterfly Wings" by neophyte helmer Bajo Ulloa seems to be heading towards a watered-down Spanish version of "The Omen," but then in its second half veers off to become a conventional meller, with an almost ludicrous finale.

Yarn concerns a humble couple living in northern Spain, he a garbage collector, she a housewife with a 6-year-old girl. Mom's greatest ambition is to have a male heir for the family. The child, Ami, is fascinated with butterflies and seems to have a love-hate relationship with Mom, while Dad dotes upon her and urges her to turn to religion.

A few months after a new boy baby is born, Ami smothers it to death. Fast forward 13 years. Dad is still working with the garbage, mom spends the day washing dishes and complaining of headaches and Ami dreams only of escaping, but can't come up with the bread.

Packed into the final minutes of the overlong film are a clumsy rape scene, the father's turning into a vegetable and the unbelievable reconciliation of mother and daughter.

Good thesping and technical credits, okay direction and a notable performance by moppet Susan Garcia mark pic.

— *Peter Besas*

DEN STORE BADEDAG
(THE GREAT DAY ON THE BEACH)
(DANISH-SWEDISH)

An ASA Film-Nordisk Film-AB Svensk Filmindustrie co-production. Produced by Henrik Moller-Sorensen. Directed by Stellan Olsson. Screenplay, Olsson, Soren Skjaer, based on Palle Fischer's novel; camera (Eastmancolor), Skjaer; editor, Tomas Gislason, Grete Moldrup; music, Kasper Winding; sound, Leif Jensen; production design, Skjaer; costumes, Annelise Hauberg, Ole Glaesner; production maanger, Sanne Arnt Torp. Reviewed at San Sebastian Film Festival, Sept. 25, 1991. Running time: **96 MIN.**
Axel . . . . Erik Clausen
Svea . . . . Nina Gunke
Gustav . . Benjamin Rothenborg Vibe
Grandfather . . . . . Hasse Alfredsson
Emilie . . . . Liselotte Lohmann

"The Great Day On The Beach" is a little gem from Denmark that should charm discriminating arthouse audiences around the globe, and could be a bigger hit than "My Life As A Dog."

Though set in Copenhagen in 1936, political references remain mostly oblique. Limned with constant touches of humor, pic is a tender, but never maudlin, evocation of a key day in the life of a child when he discovers his father's claims of an adventurous past are mere bragadoccio.

Story, with initial and final off-screen narration by the boy grown to manhood, brings audience into the bosom of a working-class family: Overbearing, eccentric father who works as an ironsmith, a Swedish mom-housewife and their 6-year-old son.

Pic's string of vignettes about the boy's parents include the family's visit to the zoo and father's near arrest when he claims a llama is not the real thing because it doesn't spit back at him.

Touch is kept light throughout. Two Louis Armstrong songs played on a gramophone buoy family spirits. When the father takes the family to the beach for the first time — and invites along the neighbors whom he has never talked to — comical events culminate in son's discovery that dad's constant talk about what he supposedly did on the Pampas in his youth is fabrication.

A sterling performance by Erik Clausen, a fine supporting cast, excellent direction and a scintillating script make this a memorable film sure to become an arthouse crowd pleaser.

— *Peter Besas*

LOS PAPELES DE ASPERN
(THE ASPERN PAPERS)
(SPANISH)

A Virginia Films and Septimania Films production. Executive producer, Paco Poch. Directed by Jordi Cadena. Screenplay, Cadena, Manuel Valls, based on Henry James' novela; camera (Agfacolor), José G. Galisteo; editor, Laura Serra, Juana G. Saladie; sets, José María Espada; associate producers, Manuel Valls, Albert Sagalés. Reviewed at San Sebastian Film Festival, Sept. 23, 1991. Running time: **90 MIN.**
Tina Bordereau . . . . Silvia Munt
Pol . . . . Hermann Bonnin
Juliana Bordereau . Amparo Soler Leal
Madeleine . . . . Rosa Novell
Pasqual . . . . Marc Martinez
Assumpta . . . . Nuria Hosta
Cummor . . . . José Marí Pou

Henry James' famous novela, already taken to the screen on several occasions, is heated up again by the Catalans, who transpose the action of "The Aspern Papers" to Menorca in the Balearics, make the title character an American and ascribe his early death to a clue in the papers.

Pic, shot in reference sound and then dubbed into Catalan and Castilian, is a travesty upon James' subtle story, originally set in Venice. Instead of a Jeremy Irons in the lead, there's a bald Catalan. Instead of Venetian palazzos, there are low-budget facades and an old Mallorcan villa. Incredibly, during one closeup of a letter being written by the erudite Pol in English, there are two glaring spelling mistakes.

The purpose of venturing upon this remake, other than the subsidy coin, is hard to see. Presumably, pic will grind on local Catalan tv, but doesn't stand a chance theatrically. — *Peter Besas*

SHUTTLECOCK
(BRITISH-FRENCH)

A KM Films, Les Prods. Belles Rives production in association with Channel 4. Produced by Graham Leader. Executive producer, Christian Ardan. Directed by Andrew Piddington. Screenplay, Tim Rose Price based on Graham Swift's novel; camera (Eastmancolor), Denis Lenoir; editor, Jon Costelloe; music, Jan Garbarek; production design, Maurice Cain; costumes, Anne de Laugardiere. Reviewed at San Sebastian Film Festival, Sept. 20, 1991. Running time: **99 MIN.**
James Prentis . . . . Alan Bates
John Prentis . . . . . . Lambert Wilson
Dr. Quinn . . . . Kenneth Haigh
Marian Prentis . . . . Jill Meager
Martin Prentis . . . . Gregory Chisolm
Beatrice Carnot . . . Beatrice Bucholz

"Shuttlecock" is the code name of a British spy during World War II who decides to publish his memoirs 20 years later in Portugal, then still under the fascist Salazar government. But the title also fits pic's constant, confusing flashbacks, which make it nearly impossible to follow the story.

Tale is rendered in snippets with constant false leads: Alan Bates hobnobs with the fascist top brass in Lisbon at his villa. Escaping from the Nazis, he blows up a munitions dump in Occupied France, is threatened by a woman with a gun, who then is killed by a trolley car. His son flies down to Lisbon to find out about Bates, who, now in a trancelike state, lives in a clinic and is tended by an ominous doctor.

All the ingredients for an intriguing spy story are there, but they are put together so clumsily that most audiences will not be able to unravel the story. In addition, no effort seems to have been made to alter Bates' age for flashbacks. Nor is it clearly shown that the son works for Scotland Yard, nor what the character has been doing in Portugal for 20 years.

Though Bates and Wilson put in good performances, and first-time direction by Piddington is excellent, the diffuse story defeats their efforts. Theatrical prospects seem iffy, but pic should be okay for tv and homevid.
— *Peter Besas*

HIJO DEL RÍO
(SON OF THE RIVER)
(GERMAN-ARGENTINIAN)

A Trans-Film production in association with ZDF-Deutsche Film & Fernsehakademie Berlin-Mano Film. (Intl. sales: Trans-Film, Berlin.) Produced by Albert Kitzler. Executive producer, Ciro Cappellari. Directed by Cappellari. Screenplay, Cappellari, Jorge Luis Ubertalli; camera (color), Cappellari, Roger Heereman; editor, Tania Stöcklin; music, Dino Saluzzi; sound, Gabriel Coll, Marcelo Gareis; art director-costume design, Pepe Urúa; production manager, Ana Maria Malamud; assistant director, Anka Schmid. Reviewed at Latin American Film Festival, London, Sept. 15, 1991. (Also in San Sebastian and Trieste film festivals.) Running time: **96 MIN.**
With: Juan Ramón Lopez, Gabriel Mario Tureo, Norman Briski, Luisa Calcumil, Lorena Andrea Medina, Oscar Sepúlveda.

Familiar yarn of a kid from the sticks hitting the urban underbelly comes up fresh in "Son Of The River." Likable first feature by Berlin-based Argentinian helmer Ciro Cappellari will perfectly suit festivals and specialized tv webs.

Juan Ramón Lopez plays an 18-year-old Chorote Indian who's kicked off his reservation in northern Argentina and heads south with new buddy Frog (Gabriel Mario Tureo) to the bright lights of Buenos Aires. Ending up in a slum on the edge of town, they're given a room by Luisa Calcumil, who has connections with Lopez' home village. The newcomers soon fall into petty crime.

An uncle (Norman Briski) tries to keep the Indian on the straight and narrow, but when the gang he's fallen in with is wiped out, Lopez makes a getaway by sea. Ambivalent coda has him jumping ship at the last moment and swimming back to shore.

Cappellari, cameraman on the recent German pic "Behind Locked Doors" (by his partner Anka Schmid, who's also on board this one as a.d.), shows a watchful eye for character and lets the social messages speak for themselves. Occasional fantasy inserts of Juan's bandit hero jar with the naturalistic tone, but all other elements, including the kid's romance with the landlady's cute daughter (Lorena Andrea Medina), play easily.

Mixing of pro and semipro players pays dividends, with Lopez bringing an ingenuous, dreamy quality to the teen Indian and experienced thesp Calcumil standing out as the bruised, sympathetic landlady. Briski is solid as the moralizing uncle.

Tech credits are fine, with no hint of the $350,000 shoestring budget. — *Derek Elley*

LA NOCHE MÁS LARGA
(THE LONGEST NIGHT)
(SPANISH)

An Iberoamericana Films production, in association with IDEA and TV Española. Produced by Andrés Vicente Gómez. Directed by José Luis García Sánchez. Screenplay, García Sánchez, Manuel Gutiérrez Aragón, Carmen Rico-Godoy; camera (Eastmancolor), Fernando Arribas; editor, Pablo G. del Amo; music, Alejandro Masso; sound, Gilles Ortíon; set design, Pedro Moreno. Reviewed at San Sebastian Film Festival, Sept. 23, 1991. Running time: **93 MIN.**

Juan . . . . Juan Echanove
Gloria . . . . Carmen Conesa
Menéndez . . . . Juan Diego
Fito . . . . Gabino Diego
Antón . . . . Fernando Guillén
Also with: Alberto Alonso, Juan José Otegui, Paco Casares, Joaquin Climent.

Sixteen years later, José Luis García Sánchez presents a truncated version of the 1975 Burgos trial, when five terrorists were executed by the Franco regime. But the drama, tensions and mood of those tense days never comes across to audiences, nor is any attempt made to delve into the lives and motives of the accused.

Instead, script for "The Longest Night" focuses on the defense lawyer, a colorless, overweight mediocrity, and his ill-defined liaison with the sister of one of the terrorists.

Most of pic is told in long flashbacks after the prosecuting and defense attorneys meet on a train and rehash the events. The trial itself is glossed over, and it's not made clear which, in fact, is "the longest night." As a historical document, pic is feeble; as a dramatic reconstruction, it's little better.

Interest in this film to the new generation of Spaniards probably will be slight, and to those who lived through those days in Spain, the historical mistakes (no mention is made of the two Basque terrorists that formed part of the group) will prove irritating. In addition, not one single character in the film arouses sympathy or interest.
— *Peter Besas*

DUTCH FEST

FACE VALUE
(DUTCH-DOCU)

A Nederlands Filmmuseum-Intl. Art Film release of a Lucid Eye Film production. Produced by Johan van der Keuken, Noshka van der Lely. Written and directed by van der Keuken. Camera (color, 16m & 35m), van der Keuken; editor, Jan Dop, van der Keuken; sound, van der Lely, Jack Bol. Reviewed at Dutch Film Days, Utrecht, Sept. 25, 1991. Running time: **120 MIN.**

A documentary with neither story nor obvious message, "Face Value" moves freely from one European country to another, switching from language to language, without relaxing its fascinating hold over viewer attention. The film is a natural for the tube and, with intelligent marketing, a good bet for specialized screens.

Armed with co-financing from tv stations in the Netherlands, Belgium, France and Germany, helmer Johan van der Keuken filmed more than 80 portraits and situations last year. Lensing was followed by six months of editing in which footage was arranged into one idiosyncratic and beguiling whole.

Since making the first of his more than 40 films in 1957, van der Keuken has been recognized for his gift of "writing" with his camera, to give images a stature of their own. His most recent films give a more relaxed overview of a world in turmoil. His humanity governs his cinema.

In "Face Value," the men and women are not introduced; instead, they're merely focused out of a crowd in fleeting images. One still surmises their character and their life stories.

Noshka van der Lely's soundtrack, the virtuosity with which language and background noises are mixed to form an optimal accompaniment for van der Keuken's picture, is astonishing. Sound and music play a subordinate part, however, and words are generally dispensable, except in the few instances in which factual reporting is permitted a walk-on part.

Strangely, dialog begins to grate after a short time. Viewer is fixed to the screen and wants to see, not listen to, scenes such as a sheepish couple's wedding, a photographer and his wife talking quietly in a garden about what she should do after his imminent death, Franz Kafka's grave, a woman next to a coffin, another giving birth, her husband looking after her and feeling guilty and proud, all within a few seconds.

If one takes "Face Value" at face value, van der Keuken is approaching the stature of Joris Ivens, the important Dutch docu filmmaker. The closing pic at Dutch Film Days, "Face Value" received heavy applause, the critics' prize as best film and a Golden Calf for best documentary. It then preemed to SRO audiences in three theaters.

— *Gerry Waller*

DE PROVINCIE
(THE PROVINCE)
(DUTCH)

A Concorde Film release of a Horizon Film-NOS Televisie production. Produced by Frans Rasker. Directed by Jan Bosdriesz. Screenplay, Hugo Heinen, based on books by Jan Brokken; camera (color), Jules van den Steenhoven; editor, Hans Dunnewijk; music, Otto Ketting; sound, Erik Langhout, Annemiek Streng; art director, Harry Ammerlaan. Reviewed at Dutch Film Days, Utrecht, Sept. 18, 1991. Running time: **96 MIN.**
Frank . . . . Thom Hoffman
Peter . . . . Pierre Bokma
Koos . . . . . Gijs Scholten van Aschat
Lili . . . . Tamar van den Dop
Frank's father . . . . . Peter Oosthoek
Sartorius . . . . Gerard Thoolen

Feature debut by veteran editor and tv director Jan Bosdriesz, "The Province" is well thought out and imaginatively edited, but the pic is hindered by screenplay flaws and over-the-top performances. These factors, plus the considerable quantities of Dutch dialog, may restrict film's chances abroad.

On a tiny island not far from Rotterdam, a small, tightly knit community of strict churchgoers with a hotline to heaven has a few well-established wealthy families who are losing their influence and money but remain separate from the rest of the town.

Three boys and one girl, the latest generation of the first families, grow up together, and their friendship withstands even the perils of sex. Pic's main weakness is that it leaves the audience to figure out how the four friends, with their background, go from dreamily chewing blades of grass in the sun to wielding lethal blades.

Frank (Thom Hoffman), Peter (Pierre Bokma) and Koos (Gijs Sholten van Aschat) are first seen as adolescents. They know each other through and through, or at least think they do. Pretty and flighty Lili (Tamar van den Dop) excels in whatever she does, musically and romantically.

Frank breaks away, becomes a well-known reporter traveling the world, but, in a crunch, he returns to his friends and his father (Peter Oosthoek), the minister who's very much in charge of his congregation. Unexpectedly, people on the island crack, and a most gruesome murder is committed.

The film gets its strength from the acting. Newcomer van den Dop (20 years old and still in acting school) conveys the charm and shallowness of an intelligent but fatally impulsive girl.

The sex scenes, with nudity, are tastefully handled. Pic combines unforced humor and unforced tragedy in a brave first feature. — *Gerry Waller*

DE ZONDAGSJONGEN
(THE SUNDAY BOY)
(DUTCH)

A Meteor Film release of an Allarts-NOS co-production. Produced by Kees Kasander, Denis Wigman. Directed by Pieter Verhoeff. Screenplay, Jan Bosdriesz, Verhoeff, based on Cherry Duyn's novel; camera (color), Edwin Verstegen; editor, Ot Louw, Ewout Hendrikse; music, Jürgen Knieper; sound, Roberto van Eyden, Carla van de Meijs; art direction, Dorine de Vos; production managers, Karin van der Werff, Christoph Hanneiser. Reviewed at Dutch Film Days, Utrecht, Sept. 21, 1991. Running time: **90 MIN.**
With: Rik van Uffelen, Tom van Hezik, Magdalena Ritter, Toon Agterberg, Franz Braunshausen, Gerard Thoolen.

"The Sunday Boy" asks what happens to people who have no allegiance to any flag or tribe, no feeling of nationality because their roots are in more than one country. Pic's answers are not valid in all cases, as the complicated screenplay canters off in too many directions.

Pic's well made, but one senses that an exceptionally good film is trying to get out. Overseas chances are slim for this untranslatable Dutch-German story.

Anton, son of a Dutch magician and his German assistant, was born in Wuppertal, Germany, during World War II. After the war the family moved to Holland, but the father could not get work and the mother had to work as a cleaning woman. Marriage hits the skids, and mother and child go back to her parents.

Years later, the dad takes Anton back to the Netherlands for a few days' holiday, but later changes his tune: "I don't want you to become a Kraut," he tells Anton, who stays, covers up his German connection and becomes a tv director.

Some 30 years later, Anton's mom asks him to come to Wuppertal to see a dying uncle. After he revisits his past, he goes back to wife and son in Holland. He decides to admit his half-German

identity, but later, during a German-Dutch soccer championship game, his little boy on his shoulder, he taunts the Germans along with the crowd: Anton is loyal to the fence he straddles, and he can't be a traitor because he feels no nationality.

Cherry Duyns' semi-autobiographical novel about belonging nowhere is moving, but Pieter Verhoeff's film gets bogged down by flashbacks, historical political inserts and the desire to cover too much ground. Still, the petit-bourgeois surroundings in Germany, the cramped lifestyle in Holland, the excitement of the tv studio, the desolate German streets during and after the war all are well depicted.

Some performances are very good, some cameos are excellent, but in spite of all these efforts, the screenplay remains an insurmountable barrier to a broad audience. — *Gerry Waller*

DINGO
(AUSTRALIAN-FRENCH)

A Gevest Australia Prods. (Sydney)-AO Prods.-Dedra Films-Cine Cinq (Paris) co-production, with the participation of the Australian Film Finance Corp. Executive producers, Giorgio Draskovic, Marie Pascale Osterrieth. Produced by Rolf de Heer, Marc Rosenberg. Directed by De Heer. Screenplay, Rosenberg; camera (Panavision, Eastmancolor), Denis Lenoir; editor, Suresh Ayyar; music, Michel Legrand, Miles Davis; sound, Henri Morelle; production design, Judi Russell; production manager, Dixie Betts; assistant director, Christian Faure; costumes, Clarissa Patterson. Reviewed at Greater Union Pitt Center, Sydney, Oct 1, 1991. Running time: **109 MIN.**
John Anderson . . . . Colin Friels
Billy Cross . . . . Miles Davis
Jane Anderson . . . . . . Helen Buday
Peter . . . . Joe Petruzzi
Angie Cross . . . . Bernadette Lafont
Also with: Bernard Fresson, Brigitte Catillon, Steve Shaw, Helen Doig.

Presence of the late Miles Davis, in the only acting role of his career, gives an enormous boost to this simple tale of a friendship between two men from opposite sides of the world. With a splendid score and a few potent scenes of Davis playing trumpet, "Dingo" will hit with jazz lovers.

This Australian-French co-production, however, rarely soars to dramatic heights. Something went adrift in filming co-producer Marc Rosenberg's screenplay (winner of this year's Aussie Writers' Guild Award). Finished film's narrative is on the thin side, but jazz audiences won't care too much; they'll just want to see Davis.

Davis, playing a legendary (but fictional) Paris-based Yank jazzman, appears in a stunning sequence at the beginning and then dominates the last 40 minutes of the picture, participating in a couple of lively jam sessions.

Magical opening sequence, set in 1969, has the musician and his band make an unscheduled refueling stop in a remote western Australian township.

Young John Anderson and his pals, Jane and Peter, join the townspeople at the airstrip where Davis puts on an impromptu jam session. John is captivated and vows to become a trumpeter and to play with the famous jazzman.

Following sequences mark time as the adult John (well played by Colin Friels) is settled in a marriage to Jane (Helen Buday). He's jealous of Peter (Joe Petruzzi), who left home for success in the city, and he spends his time trapping dingos (wild dogs) and playing the trumpet.

Self-taught, John leads a small local band but yearns to go to Paris. Following an hour of fairly unenthralling footage, he finally makes it to the French capital, where, after a series of misadventures, he meets up with Davis and his wife (Bernadette Lafont). At this point, in a smoky Paris jazzclub, the film comes alive again as Davis cuts a great screen presence, with a raspy voice similar to that of the late Dexter Gordon.

His role as the musician is undemanding, but he makes the most of it and appears to have enjoyed himself. For once, this is a jazz film that's upbeat all the way. Friels holds his own, and his trumpet-playing appears convincing. Lafont is charming as Davis' French wife.

French cinematographer Denis Lenoir, lensing in anamorphic Panavision, makes the outback look spectacular and lights the Parisian scenes with flair. Other technical credits are topnotch, with the score by Michel Legrand and Davis (1991 Australian Film award winner for best music) particularly noteworthy.

Co-producer-director Rolf de Heer, however, seems strangely uninspired by the material, and he allows the film to drag on too long. Only in the opening sequence, in which young John hears music in the air before the Davis plane makes its unexpected landing, does de Heer show evidence of the inventive talent he brought to his previous pic, "Incident At Raven's Gate."

— *David Stratton*

SHATTERED

An MGM/Pathe release of a Bodo Scriba-Willi Baer-Capella Films production in association with Davis Entertainment Co. Produced by Wolfgang Petersen, John Davis, David Korda. Executive producers, Larry Sugar, Michel Roy. Directed by Petersen. Screenplay, Petersen, based on Richard Neely's novel "The Plastic Nightmare"; camera (Technicolor), Laszlo Kovacs; editor, Hannes Nikel, Glenn Farr; additional editing, Richard Byard; music, Alan Silvestri; sound (Dolby), Keith A. Wester; production design, Gregg Fonseca; art direction, Bruce Miller; set design, Gae Buckley, Lisette Thomas; set decoration, Dorree Cooper; costume design, Erica Edell Phillips; special effects supervisor, Roy Arbogast; assistant director, Peter Kohn; 2nd unit camera, Bobby Byrne; line producer, Neal Nordlinger; co-producers, Ortwin Freyermuth, Gail Katz, casting, Jane Jenkins, Janet Hirshenson. Reviewed at Directors Guild of America, L.A., Oct. 8, 1991. MPAA Rating: R. Running time: **98 MIN.**
Dan Merrick . . . . Tom Berenger
Gus Klein . . . . Bob Hoskins
Judith Merrick . . . . . . Greta Scacchi
Jenny Scott . . Joanne Whalley-Kilmer
Jeb Scott . . . . Corbin Bernsen
Dr. Berkus . . . . Theodore Bikel
Nancy Mercer . . . . Debi A. Monahan
Rudy Costa . . . . Bert Rosario
Sadie . . . . Jedda Jones
Jack Stanton . . . . Scott Getlin
Lydia . . . . Kellye Nakahara

"Shattered" goes to pieces almost instantly. A farfetched thriller about unlikable characters, Wolfgang Petersen's debut American feature aspires to Hitchcockian suspense and surprise, but the parade of hokey implausibilities puts the viewer off rather than drawing one in.

Not the first but, it's hoped, the last of the year's amnesia studies, MGM/Pathe release will be quickly forgotten at the b.o.

Petersen assembled an attractive cast to populate his adaptation of Richard Neely's novel "The Plastic Nightmare," a project he was contemplating even before his breakthrough success with "Das Boot" 10 years ago. Unfortunately, the roles the actors fill are nearly all unappetizing or uninteresting, leaving the audience with no emotional investment in their fates.

A devastating car wreck leaves an upscale Bay Area real estate developer (Tom Berenger) a disfigured mess, although his wife (Greta Scacchi) escapes virtually unscathed. Although plastic surgery restores his good looks, husband's memory is a blank, a deficiency his wife patiently spends countless hours to remedy.

Plagued by violent but vague memory flashes, Berenger eventually learns that he and his wife weren't getting along well before the accident and that she was having an affair with a certain Jack Stanton. Enter a private detective (Bob Hoskins), enlisted to help Berenger try to figure everything out.

Plot from this point offers a number of good twists, but it's already too late for them to make much difference. Not only do the characters lack depth and allure, but the fundamental implausibility of much of the action, which might not have mattered given craftier treatment, is underlined by an ultraserious, over-the-top style that encourages rejection and ridicule rather than rapt attention.

An upbeat element, the conclusion, in which one character thought to be dead miraculously turns up, proves especially hard to take.

If Petersen had hoped to bring the audience into the story from the afflicted man's p.o.v., as Hitchcock did repeatedly with James Stewart, for example, he picked the wrong actor in Berenger. Thesp manages character's outward anguish and bafflement but is not one who makes himself vulnerable enough to invite the viewer into his skin or mind. For most of the running time, the passive hero fails to stir the emotions.

The ever-gorgeous Scacchi has the meatiest role, that of a scheming liar accustomed to always getting her way, but full, Bette Davis-sized impact of the role is missed. If the picture had been properly realized, audiences would be cheering for her comeuppance by the end, but character's evil feels lightweight and by-the-numbers.

Hoskins enlivens things as a p.i. who works out of a pet shop. He, Scacchi and Joanne Whalley-Kilmer, the last-mentioned in a thankless victim role, all effectively conceal their natural British inflections with American accents. Corbin Bernsen hits a single overexuberent note as Whalley-Kilmer's husband and Berenger's successful partner.

As designed by Gregg Fonseca and shot by Laszlo Kovacs on Pacific Coast locations from Terminal Island to Oregon, production looks sleek enough, if not somewhat overmanicured. Very simple conversation scenes feature a surprising number of mismatched shot cuts. Alan Silvestri's score pounds home the dramatic moments in overbearing fashion. — *Todd McCarthy*

ERNEST SCARED STUPID

A Touchstone Pictures presentation in association with Touchwood Pacific Partners I. Produced by Stacy Williams. Executive producer, Martin Erlichman. Directed by John Cherry. Screenplay, Charlie Gale, Coke Sams, based on a story by Cherry, Sams; camera (Technicolor), Hanania Baer; editor, Craig Bassett; music, Bruce Arntson, Kirby Shelstad; sound (Dolby), Richard E. Schirmer; production design, Chris August; art direction, Mark Ragland; set decoration, Linda J. Vipond; costume design, Shawn Barry; associate producer, Mark Ragland; assistant director, Patrice Leung; casting, Ruth Lambert. Reviewed at Crest Theater, L.A., Oct. 9, 1991. MPAA rating: PG. Running time: **91 MIN.**

Ernest . . . . Jim Varney
Old Lady Hackmore . . . . Eartha Kitt
Kenny . . . . Austin Nagler
Elizabeth . . . . Shay Astar
Trantor . . . . Jonas Moscartolo
Tom Tulip . . . . . . John Cadenhead
Bobby Tulip . . . . Bill Byrge
Matt . . . . Richard Woolf
Mike . . . . Nick Victory
Joey . . . . Alec Klapper

Ernest saves the town as well as the picture in this grab-bag Halloween programmer that runs out of good ideas well before it ends. Low-brow comedy is crammed with tricks and gizmos, but it's Jim Varney, always a treat as rubber-faced redneck Ernest P. Worrell, who makes it watchable.

Disney opening three week-ends ahead of Halloween is confident, as "Ernest Scared Stupid" may be struggling by then, but smallfry demand should make vid biz profitable. Halloween gets off to a wacky start when Ernest ignores the warning of an old witch (Eartha Kitt) and accidentally unleashes an evil troll from its tomb in a grove of ancient trees. Troll terrorizes the forest and the town, turning kids into wooden voodoo dolls and bringing scores of other ghoulies to life.

Troll (Jonas Moscartolo) is a terrif creation, a hairy, grotesque Mr. Potato Head with mucky teeth, but he soon becomes too much of a good thing — he's harder to kill than the Terminator. Ernest's endless attempts to bash, smash and capture him drag things out about 20 minutes too long before kids hit on the secret weapon and ride out on bikes in Halloween costume, armed with squirt guns loaded to vanquish the troll army.

It's an inspired climax, peppered with nifty special effects, but when the smoke clears the No. 1 troll is still alive, left to face off against Ernest in yet another goofy round.

Ernest creator John Cherry achieves an entertaining mix of scary and silly in this fourth full-length feature based on the one-time tv pitchman, but pacing drags and focus is lost by midway through.

Script doesn't give Ernest anyone to connect with as magically as he did in "Ernest Saves Christmas" (though his truck-driving dog, Rimshot, should go over big), and Varney's trademark carnival of characters and voices are thrown in as distractions rather than worked into the story.

Nonetheless, creature effects and production design are a delight, and skillful lensing by Hanania Baer keeps the nighttime action out of the twilight zone. —*Amy Dawes*

29th STREET

A 20th Century Fox release of a David Permut production. Produced by Permut. Executive producer, Jerry A. Baerwitz. Directed by George Gallo. Screenplay, Gallo, from a story by Frank Pesce, James Franciscus; camera (Deluxe color), Steven Fierberg; editor, Kaja Fehr; music, William Olvis; sound, Steve Aaron; production design, Robert Ziembicki; costumes, Peggy Farrell; production manager, Jerry A. Baerwitz; assistant director, Carol Bonnefil; co-producer, Ellen Erwin; associate producers, Pesce, Franciscus; casting, Louis Di Giaimo. Reviewed at Montreal Film Festival (noncompeting), Sept. 2, 1991. Running time: **101 MIN.**
Frank Pesce Sr. . . . . . . Danny Aiello
Frank Pesce Jr. . . . Anthony LaPaglia
Mrs. Pesce . . . . Lainie Kazan
Vito Pesce . . . . Frank Pesce
Madeline Pesce . . . . Donna Magnani
Jimmy Vitello . . . . Rick Aiello
Also with: Vic Manni, Ron Karabatsos, Robert Forster, Pete Antico, Richard Olsen.

"29th Street" is an uneven but emotionally involving directorial debut for writer George Gallo (scripter of "Wise Guys" and "Midnight Run"). Based on the tragicomic true story of actor Frank Pesce, who won the first New York State Lottery in 1976, the film comes across as a lightweight "Goodfellas," sans violence.

This might not be compulsive b.o. fare, but richly comic performances by Danny Aiello and Anthony LaPaglia, plus appearance of the real Frank Pesce (playing his own brother) could generate audience interest.

The film opens on Christmas Eve at Madison Square Garden, where the lottery finalists have gathered for the big draw by Joe Franklin (playing himself). Pesce discovers that he's won over $6 million, yet he's not at all happy about it. Indeed, he's angrily throwing snowballs at a church when picked up by the police. In classic plot construction, his story unfolds in flashback.

This is where the film grinds to a halt for a while because Gallo is unable to make the lengthy family scenes more than marginally interesting, despite sterling work from all cast members.

Much time is spent on establishing Frank Jr.'s good fortune: He gets stabbed on a date, but the wound reveals a tumor that's removed before it becomes malignant.

Things pick up considerably in the final reels, and the post-flashback sequence packs an emotional wallop, thanks to Aiello and La Paglia's socko perfs.

Despite relentless use of four-letter words, "29th Street" is a surprisingly gentle picture. Technical credits are adequate on what appears to be a modestly budgeted effort. Audience reaction in Montreal was extremely positive. — *David Stratton*

TRUE CONVICTIONS

A Cabriolet Films presentation of an I Can I Will Pictures production. Produced by Donald Finnin. Written and directed by Robert Celestino. Camera (color), Walter Fricke; editor, Celestino; sound, Piero Mura, Neil Danager; art direction; Ingrid Vidas; assistant director, Tricia Hammann; casting, Sue Crystal. Reviewed at Boston Film Festival, Sept. 17, 1991. No MPAA Rating. Running time: **89 MIN.**
John Lagana . . . . . . Franke Hughes
Dom Lagana . . . . Clem Caserta
Ice Cream . . . Christopher Scotellaro
Brianna . . . . Tanya Soler

Low-budget homage to Martin Scorsese's "Mean Streets" and "Goodfellas" has a couple of interesting performances but suffers from needlessly arty effects. Commercial prospects appear slight.

Franke Hughes plays the son of a local mobster (Clem Caserta) in the Italian section of the Bronx, where the film was shot. Hughes lives in his father's shadow, collecting debts and wondering where he's heading. His father gives his life a vicious turn when he tells him his best friend (Christopher Scotellaro) is a rat and Hughes must kill him.

Romantic subplot entails Puerto Rican exotic dancer Tanya Soler becoming involved with Hughes. Best twist to the story is how the dancer becomes the key to getting Hughes to plug his friend.

While Hughes and Scotellaro are engaging, they are undercut by film school effects, from pointless lap dissolves to an annoying soundtrack ("designed" by Piero Mura) so busy with phone noises and radios that it distracts.

First-time filmmaker Robert Celestino, who takes a "by Celestino" credit under the opening title, also enjoys flashing forward and backward in time, but, again, it's to little effect.

What "True Convictions" needs is some gritty reality and a sense that Hughes is really suffering. The ideas are there, but execution falls short.

—*Daniel M. Kimmel*

PRIME TARGET

A Hero Films release. Written, produced and directed by David Heavener. Executive producer, Gerald Milton. Camera (color), Peter Wolf; supervising film editor, Christopher Roth; editor, Charles Coleman; music, Robert Garrett; original songs written, performed by Heavener; sound, Jeffrey Douglas; production design, Peter Gum; set decoration, Lauree Slattery; associate producer, Karen Kelly; 2nd unit director, John Stewart; 2nd unit camera, Michael Weaver; casting, Ruth Conforte. Reviewed at Egyptian Theater, L.A., Oct. 1, 1991. MPAA Rating: R. Running time: **84 MIN.**
John Bloodstone . . . David Heavener
Marrietta Coppella . . . . Tony Curtis
Capt. Thompkins . . . . . Isaac Hayes
Agent Harrington . . . . Robert Reed
Commissioner . . . . Andrew Robinson
Kathy Bloodstone . . Jenilee Harrison
Agent Robbins . . . . Michael Gregory
Manny . . . . Don Stroud

"Prime Target" can't hit the broad side of a barn. A would-be Clint Eastwood named David Heavener, who last year served up the instantly forgotten "Twisted Justice," takes shots here as producer, director, writer, star and even singer-songwriter but fires blanks in each category.

Theatrical release for this creatively parched actioner is a mere formality en route to the vid bin.

Would Eastwood ever be caught wearing a belt with "cowboy" spelled out on it? Heavener, playing a maverick small-town cop, turns up sporting one, and he wants to be like his hero so badly that he imitates the star's soft line readings, sarcastically says "Have a nice trip" when he blows people away, casts such former Eastwood nemeses as Andrew Robinson and Don Stroud in supporting parts, and lifts — er, pays homage to — the plots of "Dirty Harry" and "The Gauntlet."

Suspended from the force for barbecuing some bank robbers with a blow torch in the opening scene, hero is re-called to transport a big-time criminal (Tony Curtis) to a different prison.

Sure enough, it's all a setup, as corrupt FBI agents and local officials have no intention of letting the pair get through, for fear that Curtis will expose how naughty they've been.

Some good pics have gotten by on premises as simple as this, but this plays like a fourth-generation copy of its models, including "Midnight Run." Script is a product of the connect-the-dots school of screenwriting, and Heavener's inability to generate any excitement in his action scenes has nothing to do with budget limitations.

Given the star's monotonous screen presence, one looks to the secondary parts for relief. Curtis, as an old-style mafioso, is buoyantly game and amusing under severely constrained circumstances.

But the others, including a largely office-bound Isaac Hayes, one-note villains Robinson, Robert Reed and Michael Gregory, and patient wife Jenilee Harrison, don't offer much. A great deal of the dialog appears to have been postsynched.

Lensed in the Bakersfield, Calif., area, this is about as negligible as theatrical releases get these days. Heavener's recording of something called "I'm A Honkytonk Man" in rap style over the front and end credits is almost endearingly awful.

— *Todd McCarthy*

SUBURBAN COMMANDO

A New Line Cinema release of a New Line/Howard Gottfried production. Produced by Gottfried. Executive producers, Hulk Hogan, Kevin Moreton, Deborah Moore. Directed by Burt Kennedy. Screenplay, Frank Cappello; camera (Deluxe color), Bernd Heinl; editor, Terry Stokes; music, David Michael Frank; sound (Dolby), Walter Hoylman; production design, Ivo Cristante; costume design, Han Nguyen; assistant director, Ray Marsh; production manager, John H. Burrows; special visual effects, Perpetual Motion Pictures (producer, Jeff Okun; supervisors, Richard Malzahn, Robert Habros); mechanical effects, B&B Special Effects; creature effects & power suit, Steve Johnson's XFX; stunt coordinators, David Cass, Jack Crawford; casting, Fern Champion, Dori Zuckerman. Additional photography: directed by Gary Davis; camera, Ken Lambkin, Richard Clabaugh, Charlie Lieberman; production design, C.J. Strawn; special effects, Reel EFX. Reviewed at Loews 19th St. East 5 theater, N.Y., Oct. 5, 1991. MPAA Rating: PG. Running time: **90 MIN.**
Shep Ramsey . . . . Hulk Hogan
Charlie Wilcox . . . Christopher Lloyd
Jenny Wilcox . . . . . . Shelley Duvall
Adrian Beltz . . . . Larry Miller
Gen. Suitor . . . . William Ball
Margie Tanen . . . . . . JoAnn Dearing
Col. McHowell . . . . . . .Jack Elam
Zanuck . . . . Roy Dotrice
Also with: Christopher Neame, Michael Faustino, Tony Longo, Mark Calaway.

Some funny gags enliven the stupid sci-fi spoof "Suburban Commando." Lame vehicle for wrestler Hulk Hogan will appeal only to his diehard fans and marks a setback in his attempted shift from grappler to movie star.

The Hulkster scored a hit for New Line with his first starring effort, "No Holds Barred," which comfortably cast him as a wrestler. He's an executive producer on this one, but he selected poor material.

Screenplay by Frank Cappello (who also receives "gag guru" credit) is a bad "high-concept" effort marrying two elements. Hogan is an intergalactic warrior who travels to earth for some r&r, instantly becoming a fish out of water boarding at suburbanites Christopher Lloyd and Shelley Duvall's house. Lloyd is a Casper Milquetoast architect who briefly becomes the title character by donning Hogan's muscle-enhancing power suit.

Numerous "additional photography" credits, including a second director to enhance helmer Burt Kennedy's work, suggest filmmakers opted to sacrifice storyline for gags. This decision provides some moments of slapstick levity as Hogan wanders around town, notably a running gag at the expense of a mime. Hogan evidently wants to emulate such he-man film stars as Arnold Schwarzenegger and Sylvester Stallone in creating amusing vehicles lampooning the brawny image. Unfortunately, he's jumped the gun, as these leading men firmly established themselves in the superhero screen mold first.

Special effects are okay in copying and spoofing the "Star Wars" films, with good stunts as Hogan battles two intergalactic bounty hunters sent to kill him. His final battle with his evil nemesis (William Ball) is an underwhelming anticlimax.

Casting of top talent Lloyd and Duvall was a good idea, but both are underutilized. After his memorable work in the "Back To The Future" films, Lloyd seems constrained and restrained here. Duvall is wasted as his wife, though it's good to see her on the big screen again after many years as a tv producer.

Hogan relentlessly overdoes his character's stressed-out mock intensity, giving the film a one-note quality. This is leavened only by his inevitable sentimentality with little kids to perpetuate his wrestling career role

model.

Comic Larry Miller as Lloyd's mean boss delivers an embarrassingly similar performance to his more recent "Necessary Roughness" assignment.

— *Lawrence Cohn*

LUCKY LUKE
(ITALIAN)

A Tobis Filmkunst release (in Germany) of a Paloma Films-Reteitalia production. Directed by Terrence Hill. Screenplay, Lori Hill; camera (color), Carlo Tafani, Franco Transunto; editor, Eugenio Alabiso; music, Aaron Schröder. Reviewed at Sendlingertor Kino, Munich, June 21. 1991. Running time: **95 MIN.**
Lucky Luke . . . . .Terrence Hill
Lotta Legs . . . . Nancy Morgan
Joe Dalton . . . . Ron Carey
Averill Dalton . . . . . Fritz Sperberg
William Dalton . . . . . Dominic Barto
Jack Dalton . . . . Bo Cray

Actor/director Terrence Hill's latest clichéd comedy, "Lucky Luke" is a spaghetti Western lacking ingenuity and creativity, not to mention plot and character development.

Even the old gags — the gunfighter faster than his shadow —are poorly executed on a technical level. Pic fails as a parody, too, awkwardly using animated balloons or subtitles to explain flat gags.

Lucky for Daisy Town, where lawlessness and bawdiness prevail, Lucky Luke (Hill, sans screen comedy partner Bud Spencer) is on the way astride his superintelligent horse, Jolly Jumper. After establishing order in the town and reestablishing his relationship with the beautiful Lotta Legs (Nancy Morgan), he leaves town, disappointed by its people.

Meanwhile, his archenemies, the four Dalton brothers, have been robbing banks and trains. They persuade the peace-loving Indians to attack the settlers, but Lucky Luke comes to the rescue.

Pic is disappointing in terms of tech quality and sophistication with unimaginative camerawork (on Arizona locations) and minimal special effects.

— *Laurence H. Gross*

POVEST NEPO-GASHENNOY LUNY
(THE TALE OF THE UNEXTINGUISHED MOON)
(SOVIET)

A Mosfilm presentation of a Slovo Studios production. Produced by Vladimir Chudovski. Directed by Evgueni Tsymbal. Screenplay, Vitautas Zhalakyavichus, based on Boris Pilniak's short story; camera (color, b&w), Vadim Alisov, Alexandre Bondarenko; music, Vadim Khrapatchev. Reviewed at Montreal World Film Festival (competition), Aug. 26, 1991. Running time: **84 MIN.**
Defense minister . . . Vladimir Steklov
Party chief . . . . . . Victor Proskurin
Popov . . . . Sergei Artsybashev
Defense minister's
wife . . . . Natalia Danilova
Professor/doctor . . Vsevolod Larionov
Anesthetist . . . . . Vladimir Simonov

With remarkable timing on his side, Soviet helmer Evgueni Tsymbal premiered this powerful anti-communist drama the day President Mikhail Gorbachev declared the Russian communist party dead. Set in 1925, this story about Stalin's defense minister, who suddenly "resigns" because he's "sick," will appeal to scholars, film fests and specialized audiences due to its historical timeliness.

The characters in the dark, foreboding political tale have no names, but pic's defense minister is based on the late Mikhail Frunze. (Actor Victor Proskurin is a dead ringer for Stalin.)

The picture opens in post-Lenin years during Stalin's rise to power. His loyal defense minister also was gaining popularity at the time. Loyalty was Frunze's first mistake, one he realizes throughout the film, and it will cost him his life. Surprisingly, the official doesn't resist.

Frunze becomes ill and quickly realizes he's been poisoned. Party authorities force an old doctor to prescribe surgery for a supposed ulcer. As the film leads to the inevitable operation and death of Frunze (thanks to the anesthetist), black & white flashback sequences tell his tragic story. (However, some black & white scenes are not flashbacks, which is confusing.)

Frunze led soldiers to numerous military victories and ordered systematic slaughters of various enemy troops, scenes providing some disturbing footage. His unfailing loyalty to Stalin is meticulously established; still, the leader ordered his death.

Production values are average and dense political subject will deter commercial audiences. Film provides a fascinating insider's look at the corruption behind a defunct regime.

— *Suzan Ayscough*

VANCOUVER FEST

SHUANG-QI-ZHEN DAOKE
(THE SWORDSMAN IN DOUBLE-FLAG TOWN)
(CHINESE)

A China Film Export & Import Corp. presentation of a Xi'an Film Studio production. Produced by Zhao Wanmin. Directed by He Ping. Screenplay, Yang Zhengguang, He Ping; camera (color), Ma Delin; editor, Yuan Hong; music, Tao Long; sound, Wei Jia, Hong Yi; art direction, Qian Yunxuan. Reviewed at Vancouver Film Festival, Oct. 8, 1991. Running time: **95 MIN.**

Haige	Gao Wei
Haomei	Zhao Mana
Haoemei's father	Chang Jiang
One-Sword Knight	Sun Haiying
Wang Gang	Sand Flyer

There's never been a film quite like "The Swordsman In Double-Flag Town," China's first Western which crosses "The Long Riders" with "Chariots Of Fire." This terrific action/romance oater in which a young sword-slinger rises to single-handedly tame a wild bunch menacing residents of a desert town would make a welcome addition to any action homevid fan's collection.

Pic marks an impressive screen debut for martial artist Gao Wei who could teach Cuisinart a thing or two about twirling blades. He also has the range to play a child lover who defends his beautiful fiancée from rape.

In the process he accidentally kills a knight's brother, setting the stage for a showdown shot in graphic Peckinpah-esque closeup. Short takes are edited with lightning speed to effectively heighten the conflict.

A visual treat, pic is bathed in red hues that make the desert look inviting and the costumes vibrant. Tech credits meet Western standards.

—*Suzan Ayscough*

LONELY HEARTS

A Live Entertainment presentation of a Gibralter Entertainment production. Produced by Andrew Lane, Robert Kenner. Executive producers, Joel Levine, Richard N. Gladstein. Directed by Lane. Screenplay, Lane, R.E. Daniels, based on Daniels' story; camera (color), Paul Ryan; editor, Julian Semilian; music, David McHugh; sound, George Alch; production design, Pamela Woodbridge; costume design, Libbie Aroff Lane, Peggy Schnitzer; art direction, Carlos Barbosa; set decoration, Marty Huyette; assistant director, Greg Jacobs; associate producer, Gregory Small; casting, Michelle Guillermin. Reviewed at Toronto Film Festival, Sept. 13, 1991. (In Vancouver Film Festival.) No MPAA rating. Running time: **106 MIN.**

Alma	Beverly D'Angelo
Frank	Eric Roberts
Erin	Joanna Cassidy
Annie	Herta Ware

Filmmaker Andrew Lane's study of an obsessive-compulsive woman who enters into a dangerous liaison with a handsome con man is exceptionally well conceived and executed. Low-budget "Lonely Hearts," essentially made for video, is a strong example of the kind of fare that would thrive in a made-for-cable mode.

Beverly D'Angelo stars as Alma, who's recently emerged slim and attractive from a lifelong battle with overeating. Into her still-lonely life comes Frank (Eric Roberts), a too-good-to-be-true smoothie who lays it on thick for two exciting weeks and then suddenly disappears after she makes a small investment in one of his real estate deals.

Refusing to be put off, Alma tracks him down with the info that he's a professional con man. He congratulates her and tells her to get out while she can. She surprises him by not wanting to.

With no encouragement from Frank, Alma moves in and tries to mold their liaison into something she can live with. Posing as his sister, she aids his seduction of other women with a tale about how he straightened out her finances after her husband died. For a reward, she gets to watch him bed other women right under her nose, then strip them of their savings.

But women smart enough to have money are smart enough to stand up for themselves, and Frank's sins begin to catch up with him when a private detective (Joanna Cassidy) comes knock-

ing at his door. It's up to Alma to protect him or let go.

Lane fashions a taut, convincing meller that brings some painful issues into dramatic relief in a contemporary landscape. Women in particular should find this character-driven fare absorbing.

D'Angelo gives a fascinating and persuasive performance as the obsessive-compulsive who's willing to become a latter-day Myra Langtree to get her man, until the moral and emotional turbulence does her in. Roberts is back to top form in an equally demanding role.

Lane directs with nary a false move, save a highly unlikely murder scene halfway through the film, and production values are fully satisfying and beyond expectations for the budget range.

—*Amy Dawes*

BY THE SWORD

A Movie Group presentation in association with SVS-Triumph of a Foil-Film Horizon production. Produced by Peter E. Strauss, Marlon Staggs. Executive producers, Phillip Rose, Robert Straight, Frank Giustra. Directed by Jeremy Kagan. Screenplay, John McDonald, James Donadio; camera (color), Arthur Albert; editor, David Holden; music, Bill Conti; casting, Jay Todd. Reviewed at Vancouver Film Festival, Oct. 4, 1991. MPAA Rating: R. Running time: **91 MIN.**

Suba	F. Murray Abraham
Villard	Eric Roberts
Clavelli	Mia Sara
Trebor	Chris Rydell
Rachel	Elaine Kagan
Danny	Brett Cullen
Hobbs	Doug Wert

Little-explored world of competitive fencing is the setting for this dramatic crowd pleaser in which F. Murray Abraham delivers a riveting performance as a complex killer, ex-con, lover, janitor and swordsman. Engaging little film will need special handling to make it in the theatrical arena.

Oscar winner Abraham ("Amadeus") plays a disheveled ex-champion fencer fresh out of prison with a score to settle. Pic begins in flashback, where his surreal nightmares are haunted by the trainer he skewered 20 years earlier.

The dead man's son (Eric Roberts) is now an undefeated, coldhearted champ running a fencing academy, where most of the picture takes place.

Well-choreographed fencing scenes between Roberts' promis-

ing students are kept to a minimum and used as a backdrop for the mounting tension between Roberts and his dad's murderer.

The unassuming, out-of-shape Abraham accepts a job as a janitor at the academy, trains at night, jogs in Central Park, meets a lover and eventually teaches some of Roberts' students a thing or two about the importance of sportsmanship in battle.

The inevitable showdown between the duo unspools at the predictable last minute, but pic's well-structured pace, intermittent love stories and meticulous character development make for a triumphant finale.

Tech credits are good. Bill Conti's musical score fits the bill. Casting is superb.

— *Suzan Ayscough*

OTHER PEOPLE'S MONEY

A Warner Bros. release of a York-town production. Produced by Norman Jewison, Ric Kidney. Executive producers, Ellen Krass, Davina Belling. Directed by Jewison. Screenplay, Alvin Sargent, based on Jerry Sterner's play; camera (Technicolor), Haskell Wexler; editor, Lou Lombardo; music, David Newman; sound (Dolby), Jeff Wexler; production design, Philip Rosenberg; art direction, Robert Guerra, Nathan Haas; set decoration, Tom Roysden; costume design, Theoni V. Aldredge; associate producers, Kelley Baker, Sarah Miller Hayward; assistant directors, Ned Dowd, Marty Ewing; casting, Howard Feuer. Reviewed at Samuel Goldwyn Theater, Beverly Hills, Calif., Oct. 14, 1991. MPAA Rating: R. Running time: **101 MIN.**
Lawrence Garfield . . . Danny DeVito
Andrew Jorgenson . . . Gregory Peck
Kate Sullivan . . . Penelope Ann Miller
Bea Sullivan . . . . Piper Laurie
William J. Coles . . . . . . Dean Jones
Ozzie . . . . Tom Aldredge
Arthur . . . . R.D. Call
Harriet . . . . Mo Gaffney
Emma . . . . Bette Henritze
Marcia . . . . Leila Kenzle

Danny DeVito does a very entertaining star turn as a delicious personification of the greedy and heartless 1980s, but the softening of Jerry Sterner's biting theatrical success, problematic casting and a slightly dated quality relegate "Other People's Money" to middle-range boxoffice status.

First produced in 1987 and launched on a long run off-Broadway two years later with Kevin Conway and Mercedes Ruehl in the leads, acidly comic play effectively illustrated the vulnerability of old-fashioned virtues embodied in family-run, locally owned companies when preyed upon by takeover vultures looking for asset-rich firms.

Sterner also wrote some potent, erotically charged scenes between the relentless raider and the female attorney engaged to outfox him, interludes that will definitely be seen by auds over the next few weeks as particularly interesting from p.o.v. of mixing business and sex.

Bigtime Wall Street operator Lawrence Garfield (DeVito) sets his sights on a venerable old company run by folksy "Jorgy" Jorgenson (Gregory Peck), a major employer of working folk amid the beautiful turning leaves of Rhode Island.

Feeling secure in his ability to maintain control of the firm, Jorgy is inclined to ignore the threat but is convinced to call in Kate Sullivan (Penelope Ann Miller), a sharp young lawyer and daughter of his longtime assistant and companion (Piper Laurie).

Winning "the game" is the bottom line for the wily Larry, but he is also extremely taken with the foxy, deliberately provocative Kate, and the two perform a teasing tango in which he holds the upper hand in biz smarts, but she holds the sexual reins. Constant maneuvers and one-upsmanship ploys constitute good, peppery drama, and the strongly etched settings, both in Manhattan and New England, provide a vivid backdrop for this drama of capitalistic conflict.

Scenes and speeches that were strong in the play, such as Larry's tirade to his legal staff, his sexual bet with Kate and the climactic summaries of Jorgy and Larry espousing their business views still are powerful and sometimes explosively funny under Norman Jewison's pro direction.

But in Alvin Sargent's adaptation, the tension and complex web of relationships between the Jorgenson and Sullivan families has been entirely lost, which flattens out the scenes involving them and makes them into standard-bearers for a vanishing way of life rather than full-bodied individuals. Perfectly good performances by Peck and Laurie thus don't have the weight they might have had if the relationship between their characters, and between them and Kate, had been clarified and explored.

More crucially, Miller comes off about 10 years too young to play Kate. In an extremely juicy role, she struts her stuff in eye-catching manner, but she looks more like a law student than an experienced corporate attorney who could tangle with the likes of "Larry the Liquidator."

In his attempt to bed her, Larry tells Kate that they are, at bottom, the same in their avariciousness, but that doesn't ring true with this casting. Kathleen Turner or Mary Elizabeth Mastrantonio would have been more like it. Realistically cynical ending of the play also has been significantly softened for the film, which takes some of the teeth out of it (still, it's scary to imagine this cast enacting play's conclusion).

Nevertheless, it's DeVito's show to a great extent. Perfectly cast as the fascinatingly venal, fiercely self-justified profiteer, he acts up a storm, charging full steam ahead like the Wall Street bull he is and savoring every challenge as if he can never lose. The recessionary era may make Larry seem like an extinct creature, but he's still an undeniably riveting character.

From Haskell Wexler's lumi-

Original play

Jeffrey Ash and Susan Quint Gallin, in association with Dennis Grimaldi, presentation of the Hartford Stage Co. production of a drama in two acts by Jerry Sterner. Staged by Gloria Muzio. Setting, David Jenkins; costumes, Jess Goldstein; lighting, F. Mitchell Dana; sound, David Budries; stage manager, Steve Fleischer; casting, Judy Henderson; general manager, George Elmer; publicity, Shirley Herz Assocs. Opened Feb. 16, '89, at Minetta Lane Theater, N.Y. $25 top weeknights, $28 weekends.
William Coles . . . . . James Murtagh
Andrew Jorgenson . . . Arch Johnson
Lawrence Garfinkle . . Kevin Conway
Bea Sullivan . . . . Scotty Bloch
Kate Sullivan . . . . . Mercedes Ruehl

nous lensing and Philip Rosenberg's on-the-mark production design to Lou Lombardo's crisp editing and David Newman's lush music, pic is highly polished from head to foot. — *Todd McCarthy*

TACONES LEJANOS
(HIGH HEELS)
(SPANISH)

A Miramax release (U.S.) of an El Deseo and Ciby 2000 production. Executive producer, Agustín Almodóvar. Written and directed by Pedro Almodóvar. Camera (Eastmancolor), Alfredo Mayo; editor, José Salcedo; music, Ryuichi Sakamoto; songs, Luz Casal; sound, Jean Paul Mugel; set design, Pierre-Louis Thevenet; production manager, Esther García; costumes, José María Cossío; makeup, Gregorio Ros; associate producer, Enrique Posner. Reviewed at Cine Palacio de la Música, Madrid, Oct. 15, 1991. Running time: **112 MIN.**
Rebeca . . . . Victoria Abril
Becky Del Páramo . . . Marisa Paredes
Judge Domínguez . . . . . Miguel Bosé
Manuel . . . . Feodor Atkine
Alberto . . . . . Pedro Díez del Corral
Margarita . . . . Ana Lizarán
Rebeca (child) . . . . . . Rocío Muñoz
Also with: Mairata O'Wisiedo, Mariam Díaz Aroca, Cristina Marcos.

Much-awaited new Pedro Almodóvar film launches into its subject with helmer's usual irreverent, wacky style, but the droll story starts to run out of steam about halfway through.

Almodóvar presents a winsome amalgam of black humor, amusing bathos and tongue-in-cheek dialog, all set against Chanel/Armani gloss. But the melodramatics are not outrageous enough, and the story is treated too seriously instead of sticking to parody. Thus, pace slackens and the running time starts to weigh heavily.

Still, the look of the film, handling of the pastiche story and the occasional scenes when Almodóvar is charmingly outrageous should draw enough of his fans to make pic a hit at specialized wickets.

In the vein of familiar predecessors such as "Mommy Dearest," Almodóvar's at-first whimsical story concerns the relationship between a famous aging actress and her daughter. After a long absence, mother has returned to Madrid and as daughter waits for her at the airport, several flashbacks roll portraying the daughter as a pixielike imp who maliciously switches her stepfather's pills, causing his death.

She since has married one of her mother's many old flames, but the marriage is on the rocks. When the mother returns, she takes up with her former lover again, now her son-in-law.

Mixed into the yarn is an improbable, but initially pleasing, outlandish subplot about a judge (Miguel Bosé) who doubles as a tranvestite performer. When actress and daughter attend one of his nightclub shows, the transvestite sexually assaults the daughter in his dressing room, and she gives in. Later, the judge resurfaces in the story when he happens to be put on a case involving the murder of the daughter's husband.

But these potentially madcap situations are mostly played straight. Script dwells excessively on the daughter-mother conflict, which becomes tedious. Occasional touches of levity — inmates in the women's prison where the daughter is held suddenly break out into dance — don't work.

In one of pic's funniest sequence, the tv newscaster daughter confesses on the air to murdering her husband. Such touches of humor lighten the plot, but there aren't enough of them.

The inquiry into who killed the husband lacks suspense, and fails to advance the plot. The daughter's relation to the judge is left hanging, and pic ends on a soft note.

Acting all around is fine and technical credits are up to snuff, but set design is less spectacular than in earlier Almodóvar pics.
— *Peter Besas*

LES AMANTS DU PONT NEUF
(FRENCH)

A Gaumont release of a Films Christian Fechner-Films A2 co-production. Executive producers, Hervé Truffaut, Albert Prevost. Produced by Christian Fechner. Written and directed by Leos Carax. Camera (color), Jean-Yves Escoffier; editor, Nelly Quettier; set design, Michel Vandestien; sound, Henri Morelle; costume design, Robert Nardone; line producer, Bernard Artigues; production managers, Charles Ferron, Nicholas Daguet. Reviewed at Gaumont Ambassade, Paris, Oct. 1, 1991. (In Sarasota [Fla.] French Film Festival.) Running time: **125 MIN.**

Michèle . . . . Juliette Binoche
Alex . . . . Denis Lavant
Hans . . . . Klaus-Michael Grüber

Tedious in places and exhilarating in others, "Les Amants Du Pont Neuf" is scripter/helmer Leos Carax' labor of and about love which cost a mint to make. Grimy story of confirmed tramp's obsessive love for a well-born woman probably will have limited appeal for general audiences outside France. Pic has a certain cumulative charm despite flaws, but it's unlikely to recoup its costs.

Touch-and-go production spanned three years and as many producers. Much of the reported 160 million franc ($28 million) budget went into building a replica of Paris' oldest bridge and environs. Designer Michel Vandestien's astonishing decor, unfortunately, is more impressive than the uneven three-character melodrama played out on it.

It's clear from the outset this will be a grubby tale. Alex (Denis Lavant), his head shaved to banish lice, collapses in a drunken stupor one night and a passing taxi injures his leg. Michèle (Juliette Binoche), a disheveled young woman, sees Alex splayed unconscious in the road.

After a scene at a municipal facility (where docu-style footage catches the tattooed bodies and pickled faces of homeless alcoholics), Alex limps back home to the Pont Neuf where he finds Michèle sleeping in his spot. She has an eye patch (which moves briefly to the wrong eye in one continuity-confounding shot) and a portfolio of drawings (provided, like the film's oil paintings, by Binoche herself).

Suffering from a degenerative eye disease, she left her comfortable suburban home to sketch in the streets until she goes blind. Alex gets by as a fire-eater and is a decent enough gymnast when he's not plowed on cheap wine. (Athletic component of Lavant's role was considered so crucial that production shut down twice when he was injured.)

Alex and Michèle's courtship is made up of survival gestures tinged with mischief and sweetness. In one revel, they steal a powerboat and go night water-skiing on the Seine. With loot obtained by drugging cafe patrons, they escape to the seaside where, tastefully shot in silhouette against the surf, Binoche briskly leads Lavant down the beach by his erection.

Later, jealousy drives Alex to commit a deadly criminal act. He's arrested and sentenced to prison where, two years later, the cured Michèle visits him and promises to meet him on the bridge when he's released.

Footage shot during actual fetes for the 1989 Bicentennial of the French Revolution is rocky and scattered. Far better is the extensively restaged Bastille Day fireworks set to hard rock and Strauss waltzes as the duo dance in heady, sensate abandon.

Carax treated the theme of *l'amour fou* in his "Boy Meets Girl" and "Mauvais Sang." Earlier items were audacious and tightly controlled, but current effort suffers from trying to paint an intimate story on too broad a canvas. Lavant and Binoche are convincing, and theater director Klaus Michael Grüber makes a fine screen debut as a gruff but wiser older bum.

— *Lisa Nesselson*

MERCI LA VIE
(THANKS FOR LIFE)
(FRENCH)

An AMLF release of a Cine Valse-Film Par Film-Orly Film-D.D. Production-SEDIF-Films A2 production. (Intl. sales: Roissy Film.) Produced by Bernard Marescot. Written and directed by Bertrand Blier. Camera (Eastmancolor, black & white), Philippe Rousselot; editor, Claudine Merlin; sound, Pierre Gamet; production design, Theobald Meurisse; costumes, Jacqueline Bouchard; special effects, Raph Salis; production manager, Jacqueline Ben Loulou; assistant director, Luc Goldenberg; casting, Gerard Moulevrier. Reviewed at Greater Union screening room, Sydney, Oct 8, 1991. Running time: **119 MIN.**

Camille . . . . . Charlotte Gainsbourg
Joelle . . . . Anouk Grinberg
Dr. Worms . . . . . Gérard Depardieu
Father (young) . . . . . . Michel Blanc
Father (old) . . . . Jean Carmet
Mother (young) . . . . Catherine Jacob
Mother (old) . . . . . . Annie Girardot
SS officer . . . Jean-Louis Trintignant
François . . . . . . Thierry Fremont
1st film director . . . . François Perrot
2nd film director . . Didier Benureau
Dr. Worms' wife . . . . Christiane Jean

Bertrand Blier's latest, "Thanks For Life" is a bold, often exciting, sometimes frustrating but always challenging pic that already has sparked much discussion in France, where it opened in May.

A kind of feminist variation on the director's first hit, "Going Places," with asides on French war guilt, AIDS, wife-beating and filmmaking, pic is so filled with ideas and themes it may be too much for many viewers on one viewing, making it a less attractive arthouse bet than his last two efforts ("Too Beautiful For You," "Tenue De Soirée").

Pic opens in a seaside town where lonely young Camille (Charlotte Gainsbourg) encounters battered bride Joelle (Anouk Grinberg), who's just suffered a beating from a man who dumped her from a car ("Thanks, life," she mutters, providing pic's title.)

Pair team up and head off on a series of sexual exploits. They seduce a young house painter (Thierry Fremont) who'd been secretly ogling Camille, and destroy his car. Moving on "into danger," as Joelle puts it, they decide to take over an entire town.

The film, which alternates between color and black & white for no obvious reason, starts to mix flashbacks and fantasy sequences being shot for a fictitious pic, "Distress With Tears." Blier deliberately blurs the lines between these diverse elements, but a plot of sorts emerges.

Unscrupulous medico Dr. Worms (Gérard Depardieu) is using Joelle, who carries an unspecified sexual disease, to create an epidemic he then can treat.

Also involved are Camille's parents (Jean Carmet, Annie Girardot), but at this point the film enters yet another stage, taking the characters back (after Joelle has a mystical experience in the closet of Worms' bedroom) to a time before the girls were born, so that Camille can talk to her father (Michel Blanc) and mother (Catherine Jacob), who aren't getting along, and persuade them to get together so she can be conceived.

Frenetic pic then segues into another film-within-a-film, this time a 1943 Resistance effort titled "The Crucial Moment," with Jean-Louis Trintignant as an amorous SS officer, and the other characters, including Dr. Worms, involved. (Joelle quips, "I'm not in the Resistance — I never said no to anybody.")

Throughout, Blier calls attention to the filmmaking process. "Is this what they call a flashback?" asks Camille, as Blier goes into one. Later, during a b&w segment, she complains she wants to go "where movies are in color."

Filmmaking, sex and French politics also are mocked. Depardieu's self-serving character is seen to be a war hero but becomes "a right-wing louse" postwar.

Gainsbourg, who scored in "The Little Thief," brings her elfin qualities to a much tougher role than she usually plays, while Grinberg is a discovery as her uninhibited pal.

Supporting cast is unusually fine, and pic is technically superb, with some audacious special effects. Continuity, however, is not a concern; at one point, clothes worn by the young women abruptly change mid-scene.

Many will be puzzled as to Blier's message, and the film doesn't offer too many answers. But one thing's clear: It's never dull. —*David Stratton*

LA DOMENICA SPECIALMENTE
(ESPECIALLY ON SUNDAY)
(ITALIAN-FRENCH-BELGIUM)

A Titanus Distribuzione release of a Basic Cinematografica-Titanus (Italy)-Paradis Film-Intermedias (France)-Dusk Film (Brussels) co-production in association with RAI-2 and Eurimages. Produced by Giovanna Romagnoli, Amedeo Pagani, Mario Orfini. Directed by Giuseppe Tornatore, Marco Tullio Giordana, Giuseppe Bertolucci, Francesco Barilli. Screenplay, Tonino Guerra; music, Ennio Morricone. Reviewed at Titanus screening room, Rome, Oct. 8, 1991. Running time: **120 MIN.**

THE BLUE DOG
Directed by Tornatore. Camera (color), Tonino Delli Colli; art direction, Francesco Bronzi; production manager, Mario Cotone.
With: Philippe Noiret.

SNOW ON FIRE
Directed by Giordana. Camera (color), Franco Lecca; art direction, Gianni Silvestri; production manager, Tullio Lullo.
Caterina . . . Maria Maddalena Fellini
Bride . . . . Chiara Caselli
Priest . . . . Ivano Marescotti

ESPECIALLY ON SUNDAY
Directed by Bertolucci. Camera (color), Fabio Cianchetti; art direction, Nello Giorgetti; production manager, Attilio Viti.
Anna . . . . Ornella Muti
Vittorio . . . . Bruno Ganz
Marco . . . . Andrea Prodan
Girl . . . . Nicoletta Braschi
Motorcyclist . . Jean-Hughes Anglade

WOODEN CHURCHES
Directed by Barilli. Camera (color), Gianni Marras; art direction, Anna Fadda; production manager, Mario Cotone. With: Sergio Bini-Bustrik.

"Especially On Sunday" brings four of Italy's brightest new directing talents together for an entertaining quartet of short tales set on the Adriatic coast. Not all episodes are of equal quality, but overall effect is very watchable. Pic should be attractive as an Italian sampler for offshore arthouse fans.

The four stories are neatly sewn together by Fellini's scriptwriter Tonino Guerra and a Fellini-type score by Ennio Morricone. Script, locale and music combine to keep Fellini (who has nothing to do with the film) hovering over pic like an unenlisted guardian angel.

In "Snow On Fire," it's the director's 60-year-old sister Maria Maddalena Fellini who makes her film debut — and "Sunday's" outstanding performance. A warm mountain woman who habitually spies on her son and his wife while they make love, she brings a tenderly human note to the best story of the four. Marco Tullio Giordana, director who dropped out of sight after a few prizewinning pics (including "To Love The Damned"), helms.

Giuseppe Tornatore's "The Blue Dog" has Phillipe Noiret playing a dog-hating shoemaker/barber who is persecuted by the love of a cute mongrel. The story would be too schmaltzy, even for a kid pic, if it weren't for a heart-stopping closeup of the dog being shot in the stomach. Result is a bizarre sweet and sour mix that leaves a strong, unpleasant taste.

Giuseppe Bertolucci indulges his refined taste for bringing interesting casts together in surreal encounters, this one longer on atmosphere than logic. In "Especially On Sunday," Ornella Muti is attracted to a stranger in a convertible (Bruno Ganz), but her ambiguous companion (Andrea Prodan) keeps them from becoming intimate.

Most derivative of Fellini is the odd "Wooden Churches" by Francesco Barilli (best known as the lead in Bernardo Bertolucci's debut "Before The Revolution"). A wide-eyed "vitellone" character (Sergio Bini-Bustrik) knocks around gaudy, sex-obsessed Rimini ogling all the flesh. Suddenly everyone rushes to the beach as an extraordinary apparition appears: three floating wooden churches lit up like Christmas

trees in Las Vegas.

The difficulty people have in expressing love might serve to link the tales, all very distinct but made with feeling. High quality technical work gives pic a smooth surface.

— *Deborah Young*

AGANTUK
(THE STRANGER)
(INDIAN)

A National Film Development Corp. production. Written and directed by Satyajit Ray. Camera (color), Barun Raha; editor, Dulal Dutt; music, Ray; production design, Ashoke Bose; sound, Sujit Sarkar; costumes, Lalita Ray. Reviewed at Venice Film Festival (out of competition), Sept 13, 1991. Running time: **120 MIN.**
Sudhindra Bose . . . . . Deepankar De
Anila Bose . . . . . . Mamata Shankar
Satyaki . . . . . Bikram Bhattacharya
Manomohan Mitra . . . . . Utpal Dutt
Prithwish . . . . . Dhritiman Chatterji
Ranjan Rakshit . . . . Rabi Ghosh
Chhanda Rakshit . . Subrata Chatterji

Bengali director Satyajit Ray, 70 this year, has come up with his best film in several years with "The Stranger," which escapes his last two pics' static talkiness and tells a deceptively simple but affecting moral story. Arthouse chances in countries where Ray is known and admired are good.

Pic centers on a wealthy upper-class Calcutta couple who live a comfortable life with their bright 11-year-old son. Out of the blue, wife Anila receives a letter from her long-lost uncle, family's black sheep who went overseas in 1955 (the year Ray completed his first film, "Pather Panchali") and hasn't been heard from since.

Husband Sudhindra is instantly suspicious: What else could this wanderer want but money? Or maybe this isn't Uncle Manomohan, but an imposter. Suspicions aren't allayed once he arrives; he seems genuine but behaves in a strange and unworldly manner.

But as they get to know the old man, they discover he's an almost mystical character who left because he wanted to be a painter. Since then he's traveled to countries where tribal people survive, seeking inspiration from their knowledge and wisdom.

In a magical scene, the family follows him to a tribal village in the Bengali hinterlands, and, while watching the women performing a traditional dance, Anila, sophisticated, Westernized city

woman, is persuaded to join in.

Ray tells this story with calm serenity, and theme's charm and power only gradually creep up on the viewer, as indeed the charm of the uncle (beautifully played by Utpal Dutt) gradually imposes itself on the family. Mamata Shankar, too, excels as the wife who visibly mellows under uncle's influence.

There's still quite a lot of talk, but the static, theatrical feel of Ray's last two pics here gives way to a more graceful, cinematic style. Color was variable in the print unspooled in Venice, but the film is technically fine otherwise. Ray, per usual, provides a subtly attractive music score.

—*David Stratton*

CINEMA EUROPA

MISSISSIPPI ONE
(FRENCH-B&W)

A Take 5-Philippe Dussart-Le Nouvel Observateur co-production in association with Canal Plus. Produced by Philippe Dussart. Directed by Sarah Moon. Screenplay, Bénita Jordan, Moon; camera (b&w), Moon; editor, Roger Tkhlef; music, David Lowe; sound, Bernard Rochut; art direction, Aimé Deude, Daniel Maltret. Reviewed at Cinema Europa fest, Viareggio (competition), Oct. 2, 1991. Running time: 90 MIN.
Melodie Woolf . . . Alexandra Capuano
David Woolf . . . . David Lowe
Also with: Linda Macquet, Suzanne Moncur.

Crossing borders and liberally mixing languages, "Mississippi One" may well be the Euro art flick par excellence for 1992. This sweetly melancholy road movie should prove a favorite on the fest circuit and a strong contender for arthouse playoff.

In Paris, a young girl (Alexandra Capuano) is abducted by a lanky stranger (David Lowe). On the road, he forces her to phone her mother, and he cuts her hair to hinder identification. A closeup of his passport at the border indicates he shares the girl's last name, but whether he's her father remains a deliberate uncertainty.

As their journey continues, a fugitive bond forms and the girl's escape attempts are only half-hearted. He becomes more child-like and she more adult.

When the car breaks down, they are forced to interrupt their flight and check into a small hotel. When they stop, pic also loses

some of its momentum, though the break in pace gives the shocking ending more impact.

First-time helmer Sarah Moon, a former fashion photographer, lensed "Mississippi One" in handsome black & white. She balances narrative with experimentalism, but the story is coherent at all times.

Perfs by the two protagonists are extremely sympathetic, especially young Capuano, who is refreshingly natural and convincing in both English and French.

— *David Rooney*

L'AMICO ARABO
(THE ARAB FRIEND)
(ITALIAN)

An Aleph Film (Rome) production in association with Casanova Prods. (Milan). Produced by Michele Buono, Piero Riccardi. Written and directed by Carmine Fornari. Camera (color), Vincenzo Marano; editor, Silvio Baglivo, Cinzia Brezza; music, Antonio Aiazzi; sound, Pasquale Rotolo, Hechmi Joulak; art direction, Tajeb Jellouli; costumes, Roberto Guarducci. Reviewed at Cinema Europa fest, Viareggio, Oct. 4, 1991. Running time: 90 MIN.
Ernesto . . . . Luca Barbareschi
Amumen . . . . Hichem Rostom
Numa . . . . Johara
Numa's mother . . . . . Martine Gafsi

An independent Italo production lensed in Tunisia, "The Arab Friend" depicts an arrogant urbanite's spiritual awakening on primitive turf. Modest production values will limit pic's chances of a theatrical run, but its appealing unpretentiousness should attract healthy tube sales and some fest slots.

A disgruntled Italian (Luca Barbareschi) working at a Tunisian industrial plant heads home accompanied by a co-worker (Hichem Rostom). Their bus is attacked by desert bandits, and as they wait for help, Rostom tells a weird story:

At his wedding, he dueled with a tribal magician, and four of his bride's fingers were sliced off and carried away by desert winds. She died, and her mother sent him to find the fingers and bring her back to life.

When Rostom's character dies from wounds sustained during the raid, the Italian keeps the fingers that had been found. Action jumps forward to a much older Barbareschi, fully assimiliated into Arab way of life. He finds the last missing finger among an antique dealer's relics and takes it to the dead bride's mother, but in the end he says nothing.

Pic is at its best in midsection when memory overlaps with legend to lend it mystical proportions. Only serious flaw is that the absence of an onscreen passage of time makes Barbarelli's transformation from culturally superior European to placid guy in Arab duds hard to swallow.

Poor special effects in the storytelling sequence rob pic of some sophistication, but budget limitations may have quashed anything more lavish. (Film is one of few Italo efforts to reach the screen with neither RAI nor Fininvest coin.)

Other tech credits are good, including direct sound recording and Vincenso Marano's no-frills lensing, which effectively turns desert locations into harsh inhospitable expanses and avoids the travelog gloss of sand sagas like "The Sheltering Sky."

— David Rooney

I ALLI OPSI
(THE OTHER SIDE)
(GREEK)

A Greek Film Center production. Produced and directed by Tassos Psarras. Screenplay, Perikles Sfirides, Psarras; camera (color), Alexis Grivas; editor, Vangelis Goussias; music, Giorgos Boudouvis; sound, Yannis Haralambides; art direction-costumes, Ioulia Stavrides. Reviewed at Cinema Europa fest, Viareggio (competing), Sept. 30, 1991. (Also in Thessaloniki Film Festival.) Running time: **100 MIN.**
Marios . . . . Nikita Tsakiroglou
Margarita . . . . Anna Makravi
Myrto . . . . Dimitra Hatoupi
Katia . . . . Lydia Lenosi
Petros . . . . Minas Hatzisavvas

"The Other Side" is a curiously dispassionate and uninvolving drama with a style as bleakly dissatisfying as its conclusion. Pic has been picked up for theatrical release by a major Greek distrib, but prospects look grim, and a swift exit to the small screen seems likely.

A hotshot Athens lawyer (Nikitas Tsakiroglou) divides himself comfortably between a loveless marriage and a convenient longterm affair with a younger colleague (Dimitra Hatoupi, who won the Thessaloniki Greek fest's best actress award for this role). When a fellow lawyer collapses in court one day, the protagonist gives blood and soon after is informed that he is HIV positive.

Who to blame is his first major problem. Without confiding in his wife (Anna Makraki), he engineers a blood test for her, and it transpires she also is having an extramarital affair and may be HIV positive.

He asks for a divorce and decides his only hope is to marry his colleague. She refuses, saying that it's too late to change their situation, and reveals he may have caught the virus from her. (In film's one sequence displaying any wit, she makes him sit through a slide show of her holiday flings). Faced with no alternative, he heads back to the suffocation but safety of his marriage.

Pic almost exploitatively uses AIDS as a pretext to tell a slightly dated, uninteresting story. It's a talky, '80s-style pic, centering on soulless social climbers and careerists.

Rather than making the material more chilling, which seems to have been the desired effect, Psarras' detachment leaves it lifeless and unaffecting. Attempt to show AIDS as a phenomenon that could strike anyone misses its mark since unsympathetic characters disinvite identification.

Technically, film never goes much beyond adequacy. Constant slow camera pans, lowkey performances and visual flatness (endless scenes in drearily lit offices) have a monotonous, tv feel.

— David Rooney

VANCOUVER

STAN AND GEORGE'S NEW LIFE
(AUSTRALIAN)

A Lea Films production, in association with the Australian Film Commission. (Intl sales: Kim Lewis Marketing, L.A.). Produced by Margot McDonald. Directed by Brian McKenzie. Screenplay, McKenzie, Deborah Cox; camera (Fujicolor), Ray Argall; editor, Edward McQueen Mason; music, Michael Atkinson; sound, Lloyd Carrick; production design, Daryl Mills; costumes, Rose Chong; production manager, Lesley Parker; assistant director, Paul Healey; casting, Liz Mullinar, Greg Apps. Reviewed at AFI Cinema, Sydney, Aug. 14, 1991. (In Vancouver Film Festival.) Running time: **104 MIN.**
Stanley Harris . . . . Paul Chubb
George . . . . Julie Forsyth
Stan Sr. . . . . John Bluthal
Sheila Harris . . . . . Margaret Ford
Thomas Stearns . . . . . . Roy Baldwin
Geoffrey . . . . Bruce Alexander
Roma . . . . Iris Shand
Gordon . . . . Jack Perry
Gerald . . . . Robert Menzies

Documentary filmmaker Brian McKenzie's second dramatic film, "Stan And George's New Life" is a fitfully charming romance that gets hopelessly mired in disorganized plotting. Theatrical prospects are limited to fringe venues.

Pic starts promisingly as a "Marty"/"Only The Lonely" tale of a plump, 40-year-old bachelor hairdresser (Paul Chubb) who lives with Mum (Margaret Ford) and Dad (John Bluthal) and yearns for a better life. One day, he quits barbering and (somehow) manages to land a job at the local weather bureau.

At first his shyness and inability to relate to people makes for some bright, if slowly paced, comedy. Chubb, in his first starring role, proves he's a fine character actor. The ex-barber forms a tentative relationship with a coworker (newcomer Julie Forsyth), which leads to courtship and then to marriage.

McKenzie and co-scripter Deborah Cox, however, aren't content to chart the pitfalls of this awkward relationship, and the reactions of the in-laws involved. Instead, the film gets bogged down in an often incomprehensible plot about sabotage in the weather forecasting department, the discovery of which somehow leads to estrangement between the newlyweds.

As a docu director, McKenzie has often been unable to cut his material to the best advantage, bludgeoning his audience with overstatement. A much tighter and clearer script was needed in this item.

Thesping is fine down the line. McKenzie and cameraman Ray Argall fill the pic with delightful images, both in the overly bureaucratic office, where much of the film takes place, and in Chubb's cluttered home where his eccentric Mum fills the empty chairs at her dinner table with dummies.

Pic is technically good in all departments, though editing could have been tighter. An opportunity for a charming, offbeat comedy-romance has been missed here.

— David Stratton

THESSALONIKI

KLEISTI STROPHI
(U-TURN)
(GREEK)

A Panayotis Papachatzis production. Directed by Nikos Grammatikos. Screenplay, Grammatikos, Photini Siskopoulou, Prodromos Savidis; camera (color), Kostis Gikas; editor, George Mavropsarides; music, Kyriakos Sfetsas; sound, Antonis Samaras; set-costumes, Youla Zoiopoulou. Reviewed at Thessaloniki Film Festival (competition), Oct. 4, 1991. Running time: **85 MIN.**
Andreas . . . . . . Minas Hatzisavvas
Ismeni . . . Alexandra Sakellaropoulou
Hooker . . . . Stella Kazazi
Also with: George Ninios, George Morogianis, Nikos Dimitratos.

Nikos Grammatikos' "U-Turn," which shared the best first feature award at the Thessaloniki Greek film fest, furnishes a novel twist to a classic film noir. Pic, simply but capably rendered, sustains interest and could do well on the homefront if carefully placed. Offshore distribution, however, will center on the small screen.

A coarsely sexy car thief (Minas Hatzisavvas) has few friends other than a fisherman and a hooker (Stella Kazazi) whom he helps out with cash, though he's not one of her clients. After stealing a car in a great madcap scene, he picks up a comely motorist (Alexandra Sakellaropoulou) whose car has broken down. He tires of her evasions and leaves her stranded at a road stop.

Plot develops in "Body Heat" fashion with the opportunistic car thief pursued and manipulated by the conniving sexpot. The bedroom scenes are frank and sensual for a Greek pic. Thief's street smarts are eventually short-circuited by sheer lust, but fate enables him to escape the woman's carefully spun web.

Hatzisavvas gives an understated performance that won him the best actor award at Thessaloniki. Electronic score is fitting, and good camerawork incorporates some creative angles.

— B. Samantha Stenzel

PHANOUROPITTA
(ST. PHANOURIOS' PIE)
(GREEK)

A Greek Film Center-Dimitrios Yatzouzakis production. Written and directed by Dimitrios Yatzouzakis. Camera (color), Philipos Koutsaftis; editor, Georgios Triantafyllou; music, Nikos Mamagakis; sound, Nikos Papadimitriou; art director, Hero Zervaki; casting, Aristeidis Phatouros. Reviewed at Thessaloniki Film Festival (competition), Oct. 2, 1991. Running time: **62 MIN.**
Georgitsa . . . . Despina Bolla
Evanthia . . . . Ifigenia Makati
Papa Giannis . . . . . Lambros Tsagkas
Angelos . . . . Patis Koutsaftis
Phanouris . . . . Giorgos Liantos
Zacharias . . . . Arto Apartian
Also with: Nikos Papdimitriou, Dimitrios Yatzouzakis, Giannis Avramiotis.

"St. Phanourios' Pie" is a semi-docu about a custom linked with a religious celebration that runs amok when a woman decides to alter tradition. Pic is a wicked black comedy, unorthodox in many ways and, if marketed this way, it should have appeal beyond ethnic and academic screenings.

Evanthia (Ifigenia Makati) decides to be creative and embellish her St. Phanourios pie, a dish offered to the saint at a yearly church ritual in rural Greece. She departs from the recipe with the best intentions of treating the beggars who gather around the church during the service.

During the pie blessing, the priest looks askance at Evanthia's cream-filled concoction and voices his disapproval to her daughter (Despina Bolla). The beggars, a motley crew of cripples and half-wits, break into the chapel when the worshipers are outside and grab the tempting treat.

The ensuing melée rivaling Monty Python absurdity ends in an actual cliffhanger as the beggars cling to sheer rock and watch helplessly as a pack of dogs below tear apart the coveted sweet.

The audience at the pic's preem in Thessaloniki tittered nervously, visibly uncomfortable at laughing at a film with religion and handicapped people. (Auds in other territories will probably be less inhibited.)

Lensing is good, and soundtrack's pleasant folk music is a welcome contrast to a noisy electronic score in other segments. Casting, especially of the beggars, is inspired. Helmer Yatzouzakis shared the best direc-

tor (first film) award at the Thessaloniki fest.
— B. Samantha Stenzel

THE BUTCHER'S WIFE

A Paramount Pictures release of a Nicita/Lloyd production. Produced by Wallis Nicita, Lauren Lloyd. Executive producer, Arne Schmidt. Directed by Terry Hughes. Screenplay, Ezra Litwak, Marjorie Schwartz; camera (Technicolor), Frank Tidy; editor, Donn Cambern; music, Michael Gore; sound (Dolby), Beth Sterner, Cecelia Hall; production design, Charles Rosen; art direction, Diane Yates; set decoration, Donald J. Remacle; costume design, Theadora Van Runkle; assistant directors, Kenneth D. Collins, E. Carey Dietrich; casting, Gail Levin. Reviewed at Mann Regent Theater, L.A., Oct. 23, 1991. MPAA Rating: PG-13. Running time: **104 MIN.**
Marina . . . . Demi Moore
Alex . . . . Jeff Daniels
Leo . . . . George Dzundza
Stella . . . . Mary Steenburgen
Grace . . . . Frances McDormand
Also with: Margaret Colin, Max Perlich, Miriam Margolyes, Helen Hanft, Christopher Durang.

A gentle romantic comedy with a distinct 1940s flavor, "The Butcher's Wife" should slice off a choice cut of the boxoffice, with Demi Moore proving that her "Ghost"-ly part in getting moviegoers into theater seats was no fluke.

Blessed with a fine cast working from a storybook plot, the unpretentious and simple film has a "make 'em like they used to" quality. Its belief in modern-day magic (in a sense similar to "Moonstruck") softens an inherent predictability dictating that all loose ends be resolved to everyone's satisfaction in 100 minutes.

Moore plays a country clairvoyant whose visions of romance are answered in the surprising form of a New York butcher (George Dzundza) whom she marries immediately, returning with him to his neighborhood.

Her visions immediately start to touch all those who cross her path, in the process increasingly nettling the local psychologist (Jeff Daniels), whose patients seem to need him far less as they bathe in the comfort of Moore's future-gazing.

Those who encounter Moore include the shrink's girlfriend (Margaret Colin), a dowdy patient (Mary Steenburgen) with aspirations to sing the blues, and lesbian friend (Frances McDormand), who's told romance waits just around the corner.

Helmer Terry Hughes, a tv director ("The Golden Girls") whose only feature credit is "Monty Python Live At The Hollywood Bowl," and first-time screenwriters Ezra Litwak and

Marjorie Schwartz bring a fresh, uncynical eye to familiar terrain. Thus, pic unapologetically embraces its romantic elements and generally doesn't push the comedy, allowing the moments to grow from the characters.

Even the backdrop looks like nothing New Yorkers have seen lately. Magically lit skylines and shimmering moons put a sparkle on the Big Apple paralleling what "One From The Heart" sought to do for Las Vegas. Michael Gore helps that effort immeasurably with a sumptuous score loaded with lilting harp chords.

Those who remember Moore's famous Vanity Fair cover (photographed during her pregnancy) will admire her physique, shown off simply but effectively by Theadora Van Runkle's costumes.

While her golden locks and "Beverly Hillbillies" accent take some getting used to, Moore nonetheless turns in a luminous performance, slowly coming to realize that her vision may not be as clear in regard to her own future and feelings.

Daniels also has ample opportunity to display his gifts as a comic actor, providing the film's few belly laughs with some of his office outbursts as his carefully ordered world unravels.

Pic's only real revelation is Steenburgen, not for her considerable acting skills but for her fine voice in a trio of bluesy ballads.

Hughes and company give in to some sitcom elements in the form of peripheral characters, such as a pair of neighborhood busybodies and a peculiar patient (playwright Christopher Durang), but not to such an extent that it seriously detracts from the narrative.

Tech credits are firstrate, and though New Yorkers may snicker at the scrubbed and squeaky-clean streets, that setting properly mirrors the tidy nature of the storyline.
— Brian Lowry

CURLY SUE

A Warner Bros. release. Executive producer, Tarquin Gotch. Written, produced and directed by John Hughes. Camera (Technicolor), Jeffrey Kimball; editor, Peck Prior, Harvey Rosenstock; music, Georges Delerue; sound (Dolby), Charles Wilborn, John Reitz, Dave Campbell, Gregg Rudloff; production design, Doug Kraner; art direction, Steven Schwartz; set design, Gary Baugh, William Fosser, Masako Masuda; set decoration, Sam Schaffer, Marjorie Fritz-Birch; costume design, Michael Kaplan; production manager-associate producer, Lynn M. Morgan; assistant directors, James Giovannetti Jr., Jeanne Caliendo, Geoffrey Hansen; casting, Janet Hirshenson, Jane Jenkins. Reviewed at Mann Criterion Theater, Santa Monica, Calif., Oct. 19, 1991. MPAA Rating: PG. Running time: **101 MIN.**
Bill Dancer . . . . James Belushi
Grey Ellison . . . . Kelly Lynch
Curly Sue . . . . Alisan Porter
Walter McCormick . . . . . John Getz
Oxbar . . . . . Fred Dalton Thompson
Maitre d' . . . . Cameron Thor

Though marketed as a comedy, this predictable crowd-pleaser is at heart a two-hanky affair. With its mix of childish gags and shameless melodrama, "Curly Sue" could make off with a tidy boxoffice take.

John Hughes' latest outing clearly aspires to Capraesque sentimentality: A drifting con man (James Belushi) and his adopted 9-year-old daughter (Alisan Porter) scam a corporate attorney (Kelly Lynch) and gradually win her heart, much to the chagrin of her snotty boyfriend (John Getz).

Writer-helmer-producer Hughes strikes an uneasy balance between slapstick and sappiness, far too frequently relying on Porter's mugging and Georges Delerue's drippingly sentimental score.

Film also backs away from addressing the serious issues of poverty and homelessness other than using them to score easy points with the audience.

Lynch gives an impressive performance that proves to be the film's high point. Belushi is less convincing as the protective dad, while Porter is in the tear-evoking-tots tradition.

Tech credits are uniformly top of the line, and those who sit through the credits will be rewarded by Ringo Starr's lilting version of "You Never Know."
— *Brian Lowry*

AT THE MAX
(DOCU-IMAX)

A BCL Group presentation of an Imax Corp. production in association with Promotour U.S. Inc. Executive producers, Michael Cohl, Andre Picard. Creative consultant-location director, Julien Temple. Video director, Christine Strand. Concept, Cohl; camera (color), David Douglas, Andrew Kitzanuk; camera consultant, Haskell Wexler; editor, Daniel W. Blevins; additional editing, Toni Myers, Jim Gable, Lisa Regnier; Rolling Stones music producer, Chris Kimsey; Rolling Stones sound mixer, Michael Brauer; Imax sound mixer, Paul Massey; location sound supervisor, Peter Thillaye; postproduction sound, Bruce Nyznik; additional location directors, Roman Kroitor, David Douglas, Noel Archambault; line producer, Robbie Williams; co-producer, Martin Walters; associate producers, Nicholas J. Gray, Toni Myers. Reviewed at California Museum of Science & Industry Imax Theater, L.A., Oct. 16, 1991. No MPAA rating. Running time: **89 MIN.**
With: The Rolling Stones (Mick Jagger, Keith Richards, Charlie Watts, Ron Wood, Bill Wyman); Chuck Leavell, Matt Clifford (keyboards); Bobby Keys (saxophone); the Uptown Horns (Crispin Cioe, Arno Hecht, Hollywood Paul Litteral, Bob Funk); Bernard Fowler, Lorelei McBroom, Sophia Jones (vocals).

The future of concert films is here, and its name is Imax. The Rolling Stones' "At The Max" pairs the venerable rock band with director Julien Temple in the giant-screen format and makes 35m look like the visual equivalent of vinyl LPs.

How many fans will want to pay the stiff $15 a peep — nearly triple the typical Imax price — remains to be seen. But, with firstruns set to last between six months and a year, there should be ample time to recoup the $10 million production investment.

Shot during the European leg of the Rolling Stones' Steel Wheels/Urban Jungle tour in summer 1990, "At The Max" literally plunges the viewer into the concert experience.

Viewers who caught the Steel Wheels tour will find little new here, including the same awesome "Blade Runner"-inspired set and the same selection of songs, whittled down to 15 crowd-pleasers, including "Start Me Up," "Paint It Black" and "Honky Tonk Woman."

What's different is the point of view, augmented by the exhilarating sense of depth and space in the Imax frame and the pinpoint clarity of detail.

Pic also takes full advantage of the Imax sound capacity, a six-channel, four-way aural system that's so well-modulated, it never seems too loud.

Temple, a veteran of several features and countless musicvideos, including the Stones' controversial "Undercover," adapts to the unwieldy Imax cameras with admirable dexterity.

Stones fans will doubtless realize this is not the band at its peak as it was in "Gimme Shelter." The revelation here is the technology, which is sure to have other top acts clamoring to be next. — *Amy Dawes*

LIFE IS NICE
(16M-B&W)

An AFI USA Independent Showcase presentation of a Freakie Pig production. Written, produced and directed by Forest Wise. Camera (b&w, 16m), Eric J. Swanson; editor, Macieck Malish; music, Jesse Loya. Reviewed at American Film Institute, Sept. 27, 1991. No MPAA rating. Running time: **96 MIN.**
Josh . . . . Forest Wise
Silo . . . . Mike Dytry
Clara . . . . Kia Collins

"Life Is Nice" is an example of an indie filmmaker throwing out the rules, only to prove how much they're needed. Audience for this no-budgeter likely will be limited to the cast and crew.

Pic stars filmmaker Forest Wise and Mike Dytry as two do-nothing young postmodern guys who pass their days drinking, smoking and occasionally selling blood. Now and then they complain about their g.f. (Kia Collins), who pointlessly changes allegiance from one guy to the other mid-film.

As a study of ennui, pic definitely produces the equivalent effect. Its washout habitués are presented sans satirical viewpoint, though there's one moment of hilarity, intentional or not, in which a minor character does a performance piece around the phrase "---- off, I don't need you."

Audiences who've seen UCLA filmmaker Caveh Zahedi's "A Little Stiff," also in 16m black & white and starring two best friends and a girl, will pine for that picture's intelligence, wit, storyline and superior visual sense.

Photography and sound quality are poor, and offbeat camera angles are generally ineffective and annoying.
— *Amy Dawes*

CRACK
(ITALIAN)

A Columbia TriStar Films Italia release of a Numero Uno Intl. production, in collaboration with RAI-3 and the Ministry of Tourism and Entertainment. Produced by Claudio Bonivento. Directed by Giulio Base. Screenplay, Franco Bertini, Base; camera (color), Alessio Gelsini; editor, Claudio Di Mauro; music, Oscar Prudente; sound, Franco Borni; production design, Davide Bassan; costumes, Angela Taffani; production manager, Massimo Martino. Reviewed at Venice Film Festival, Sept. 6 1991. (Also in San Sebastian Film Festival.) Running time: **85 MIN.**
Wolfgango . . . . Giulio Base
Francesco . . . . . Gianmarco Tognazzi
Sascia . . . . Pietro Genuardi
Michele . . . . Giuseppe Pianviti
Rodolfo . . . . Franco Bertini
Roberta . . . . . . Antonella Ponziani
Coach . . . . Mario Brega
Gino . . . . Franco Pistoni

First-time helmer Giulio Base makes a strong debut with "Crack," an urban tragedy of violence, drugs and solitude that won the young director's prize at the San Sebastian fest. Pic should find fans among hip young Italo audiences and at international film fests.

Though action revolves around five young friends who hang out and box at the same gym, film is more about the psychological limits of living in a poor, no-way-out Roman neighborhood than about boxing.

Base's sharp and skillful direction brings out the emotional punch in what otherwise would be a fairly routine story.

Rodolfo (Franco Bertini) is torn between the demands of boxing and his studies. His g.f. (Antonella Ponziani) gives him an ultimatum (either give up boxing or her), but she's actually having an affair with an ex-pro (Giuseppe Pianviti), who's using her only to get his rival Rodolfo out of the ring.

When he's not in training, the ex-pro spends his time picking up girls and snorting coke supplied to him by Wolfgango (Giulio Base).

Rodolfo's seemingly sweet brother (Pietro Genuardi) overhears a conversation between the cokehead and the girl in the gym. Something in him snaps, and he rapes her in the locker room. Francesco (Gianmarco Tognazzi) and Rodolfo enter the gym looking for the girl and stumble upon the horrifying scene.

Rodolfo challenges the ex-pro to settle the issue in the ring, sending pic into a spiral of violence that moves the characters inevitably toward tragedy.

Acting by cast of young thesps is fine all around. Pic races along at video-clip speed without being superficial or overly stylized. Technically, film captures the dingy, urban sprawl of Rome tourists never see. — *Jennifer Clark*

HOUSE PARTY 2

A New Line Cinema release of a Jackson/McHenry production. Executive producer, Janet Grillo. Produced and directed by Doug McHenry and George Jackson. Screenplay, Rusty Cundieff, Daryl G. Nickens, based on characters created by Reginald Hudlin; camera (Deluxe color), Francis Kenny; editor, Joel Goodman; music, Vassal Benford; sound (Dolby), Steve Nelson; executive music supervision, Louil Silas Jr.; production design, Michelle Minch; art direction, Karen A. Steward; set design, Philip Madison; costume design, Ruth E. Carter; assistant director, Phillip Christon; co-producer, Suzanne Broderick; casting, Pat Golden, John McCabe. Reviewed at Sunset Towers screening room, L.A., Oct. 18, 1991. MPAA rating: R. Running time: **94 MIN.**
Kid . . . . Christopher Reid
Play . . . . Christopher Martin
Sidney . . . . Tisha Campbell
Sehila . . . . Iman
Bilal . . . . Martin Lawrence
Miles . . . . . . D. Christopher Judge
Prof. Sinclair . . Georg Stanford Brown
Zora . . . . Queen Latifah

The crowd's the same, but the atmosphere's different in this disappointing followup to New Line's 1990 low-budget hit "House Party." Absence of filmmakers Reggie and Warrington Hudlin, who've moved on to other things, is keenly felt in a film lacking the original's smarts and cinematic flair. B.o. partygoers may leave early.

Debut directors Doug McHenry and George Jackson ("New Jack City" producers) trace the continuing misadventures of rap team Kid 'N Play (Christopher Reid, Christopher Martin) as they tackle life after high school.

Kid has lost his father (the late Robin Harris) and plans on going to college, but Play is set on pursuing a record contract dangled by a shady promoter (fashion model Iman).

Unfortunately, pic relies heavily on vulgarities and no-brainer plot twists. Despite a well-intended emphasis on black studies and activism, the simplistic college scenario makes higher education look like a major waste of time. Stars Reid and Martin deliver pale reprisals of their original roles.

On the plus side, the solid soundtrack features Tony! Toni! Tone!, Ralph Tresvant and Keith Washington.

Harris is included in snippets from the first film, imaginatively framed in a bedside photo, and Whoopi Goldberg cameos as a nightmarish college disciplinarian in a dream scene.
— *Amy Dawes*

COOL AS ICE

A Universal Pictures release of a Koppelman/Bandier-Carnegie Pictures production in association with Alive Films. Produced by Carolyn Pfeiffer, Lionel Wigram. Executive producers, Charles Koppelman, Martin Bandier, Shep Gordon. Directed by David Kellogg. Screenplay, David Stenn; camera (Deluxe color), Janusz Kaminski; editor, Debra Goldfield; music, Stanley Clarke; sound (Dolby), Michael Hooser, Gary Macheel; production design, Nina Ruscio; art direction, Carey Meyer; set decoration, Sally Nicolaou; costume design, Ingrid Ferrin; assistant directors, Matthew Clark, Robert Lorenz, Clay Newbill; casting, Johanna Ray. Reviewed at AMC Century Theaters, L.A., Oct. 18, 1991. MPAA Rating: PG. Running time: **90 MIN.**
Johnny . . . . Vanilla Ice
Kathy . . . . Kristin Minter
Gordon Winslow . . . . . Michael Gross
Roscoe McCallister . . Sydney Lassick
Mae McCallister . . . . Dody Goodman
Singer . . . . Naomi Campbell
Grace Winslow . . . . . Candy Clark
Nick . . . . . . John Haymes Newton

Rap's white flavor-of-the-month proves 11 million record buyers *can* be wrong. While teenage girls may help turn a small profit with this extended musicvideo, Vanilla Ice's film act should round up a rather modest posse.

Johnny (Ice) and three motorcycling buddies ride into a small town, where the Vanilla One casts his eye on a straitlaced young woman (Kristin Minter).

The subplot, such as it is, involves the girl's parents, who have been located by two inept enemies after 20 years of safety under the Witness Protection Program.

None of the music-oriented sequences are particularly imaginative, while director David Kellogg's use of slow-motion and jarring editing only detract from any effort to tell a story between the videos.

Ice lacks the wit and the intensity of many rappers. Universal's hopes of springing another Elvis Presley on the screen are, at best, laughable.

Minter is a rather bland leading lady, while Michael Gross and Candy Clark play it way too straight as her parents.

Tech credits skate on the shoddy side, betraying the pic's modest budget and ambitions.
— *Brian Lowry*

ANTONIA AND JANE
(BRITISH)

A Miramax Film release of a Malofilm presentation and a BBC Films production. Produced by George Faber. Directed by Beeban Kidron. Screenplay, Marcy Kahan; camera (color), Rex Maidment; editor, Kate Evans; music, Rachel Portman; production design, John Asbridge; assistant director, Daphne Phipps; casting, Gail Stevens. Reviewed at Boston Film Festival, Aug. 22, 1991. (Also in Montreal Film Festival, noncompeting.) No MPAA Rating. Running time: **69 MIN.**
Antonia McGill . . . . . Saskia Reeves
Jane Hartman . . . . . Imelda Stauton
Howard Nash . . . . Bill Nighy
Steven Kalinsky . . . . Allan Corduner
Therapist . . . . Brenda Bruce

A BBC telefilm, "Antonia And Jane" has been picked up for Stateside distribution and, with careful promotion (and an appropriate short to fill out the program), it should attract arthouse audiences.

Pic starts out with Jane (Imelda Stauton) ruminating during a session with her therapist. She feels herself a failure since her b.f. gets aroused only when she reads aloud from Iris Murdoch.

Her schoolgirl chum Antonia (Saskia Reeves) is happily married to a photographer of body parts (Bill Nighy), who was once Jane's boyfriend.

The film alternates from Jane's story to Antonia's (told to the same therapist).

Marcy Kahan's script is full of invention both in incident and dialog.

Acting is on target, with the leads more than up to the challenge. Beeban Kidron's direction is crisp, and her compositions were obviously intended for the small screen.
— *Daniel M. Kimmel*

EXPOSURE
(HIGH ART)
(BRAZILIAN)

A Paulo Carlos de Brito production. Produced by Alberto Flaksman. Directed by Walter Salles Jr. Screenplay, Rubem Fonseca from his book; camera (color), Jose Roberto Eliezer; editor, Isabelle Rathery; music, Jurgen Kneiper, Todd Bekelheide; art direction, Nico Faria, Beto Cavalcanti; costume design, Mari Stockler. Reviewed at Viareggio Noir Festival, June 2, 1991. Running time: **100 MIN.**
Peter Mandrake . . . . . Peter Coyote
Knife master . . . . . . Tcheky Karyo
Marie . . . . Amanda Pays
(English soundtrack)

"Exposure" is a stylish, sophisticated manhunt film that goes off track. Director Walter Salles Jr.'s first feature gets off to a complex, well-shot start, but pic degenerates into a gory martial arts denouement that could put off audiences.

Peter Coyote toplines as a Yank photographer working in Rio. A young prostitute who has modeled for him asks for his help. She is being threatened by someone who left an important floppy disk in her apartment. When she's murdered, Coyote feels guilty and sets out to find her killer.

The photographer's questions take him into the seamy underworld of drugs and arm dealing. Believing Coyote may have the missing disk, thugs break into his apartment, stab him and rape his archaeologist g.f. (Amanda Pays).

Coyote decides to stop being a chump and goes to a master of the art of the knife, charismatically underplayed by Tcheky Karyo. It appears to take the photog about a week to learn all the knife moves, during which time Pays leaves him, distressed by the change in her sensitive boyfriend.

Well-crafted yarn, featuring crosses and doublecrosses and beautiful photography by Jose Roberto Eliezer, stops being a thriller halfway through and starts genre hopping.

The graphic showdown with the villain trades off suspense for shock value and literally goes for the jugular. When the Yank photog has spent his blood lust, pic changes track again, and he goes back to find his g.f.

Salles shows a sure hand at moving through various genres, but the result is a pastiche that could have been much more satisfying if he'd stuck to the genre he started with.
— *Catherine Ventura*

DEADLY CURRENTS
(CANADIAN-DOCU)

A Cineplex Odeon release (Canada) of an Associated Producers production. Produced by Simcha Jacobovici, Elliott Halpern, Ric Esther Bienstock. Executive producers, David Green, Jeff Sackman, Robert Topol. Directed by Simcha Jacobovici. Camera (16m color blown up to 35m), Mark Mackay; editor, Steve Weslak; music, Stephen Price; sound, Chaim Gilad; associate producer, Jane Logan. Reviewed at Bellevue Pathe screening room, Montreal, Oct. 18, 1991. Running time: **100 MIN.**

"Deadly Currents" is a remarkably balanced documentary about the Palestinian-Israeli crisis on the West Bank. Point/counterpoint structure simplifies conflict for beginners, yet thorough investigation also illuminates the complex deadlock. Pic should get some immediate theatrical mileage out of the upcoming Mideast peace talks.

Helmer Simcha Jacobovici realized this enlightening portrait without interviewing a single politician. He and ace cinematographer Mark Mackay took the camera to the streets, homes, war zones, stages and hospitals of Israeli soldiers, PLO rebels, academics, artists and journalists. Reps from both sides (which each claim the land) speak candidly and passionately about this latest chapter in a struggle that's raged for centuries.

Shot principally in the hot spot of Nablos where the Intifadah uprising began in December 1987, camera first travels with the Israeli Golani platoon, then the masked Palestinian Shabab youth activists, allowing each side an uncensored voice. Docu also travels through a refugee camp.

Interviews with veteran ABC, NBC and CNN journalists reveal that the presence of camera crews occasionally "creates" incidents. Editor Steve Weslak cunningly weaves opposing viewpoints to give both sides equal weight and simultaneously achieve a coherent picture. No easy task, and once both sides have had their say on a particular point, docu often cuts to political artists and dancers who mirror the tension.

The artists also provide comic relief and entertainment in an otherwise intense film. Unmanipulative docu allows viewers to draw their own conclusions.

Tech credits are surprisingly good given the rugged locations and often uncontrollable lighting situations. Predominate talking head format also is suited for tv.
— *Suzan Ayscough*

STINSEN BRINNER — FILMNEN, ALLTSA!
(THE STATIONMASTER IS ON FIRE — THE MOVIE, THAT IS!)
(SWEDISH)

A Svensk Filmindustri release of a Svensk Filmindustri-Kulturtuben-Claes Eriksson Produktion-Baldakinenrestaurangerna-RiFilm-Lefwander Kapitalförvaltning production. Produced by Waldemar Bergendahl, Anne Otto. Directed by Anders Eriksson, Claes Eriksson. Screenplay, Anders & Claes Eriksson, based on Claes Eriksson's original story; camera (color, b&w), Dan Myhrman; editor, Jan Persson; music, Claes Eriksson; sound, Lennert Forsen, Henrik Ohlin; production design, Rolt Allan Hakansson; costumes, Gunilla Henkler. Reviewed at Filmstaden cinema, Stockholm, Oct. 3, 1991. Running time: **100 MIN.**
With: Jan Rippe, Peter Rangmar, Kerstin Granlund, Knut Agnred, Claes Eriksson, Per Fritzell, Anders Eriksson.

This film version of a popular musical is understandably a hit in Sweden, but "The Stationmaster..." could well be stopped dead in its tracks if it tries to travel abroad.

Comedy team Galenskaparna/After Shave's second film in less than a year (previous pic "Macken" was last year's most popular Swedish film) is based on a musical the group successfully staged in Gothenburg and Stockholm.

Scriptwriting brothers Anders and Claes Eriksson have added several outdoor scenes to the film, but still it's basically filmed theater, and pic suffers from a claustrophobic feel.

Bureaucrats decide to close a small railway station in the Swedish countryside, but the stationmaster resists and keeps the depot open, tying up and gagging a government rep and pretending the trains are running late. The truth is disclosed sooner or later, but the ending is —surprise, surprise — a happy one.

As usual in Eriksson's works, song-and-dance-routines are liberally inserted. These are often the best parts, with catchy tunes, lunatic lyrics and inspired direction. Standout number is "Dad, I Want An Italian Guy," in which young girls express admiration for broad-shouldered, Italian pizzeria owners.

Dialog is often snappy and witty, but too many times it's based on misconceptions. Most of the Monty Python-style parts are played by the seven members of Galenskaparna/After Shave. They're all good, with special laurels going to Per Fritzell for his numerous softhearted jerks.

The humor is very Swedish, and the figures and situations this satire targets also are very Swedish. — *Gunnar Rehlin*

YEAR OF THE GUN

A Triumph release of an Edward R. Pressman production in association with Initial Films. Produced by Pressman. Executive producer, Eric Fellner. Directed by John Frankenheimer. Screenplay, David Ambrose, based on Michael Mewshaw's book; camera (color), Blasco Giuarto; editor, Lee Percy; music, Bill Conti; sound, Bernard Bats; production design, Aurelio Crugnola; art director, Luigi Quintili; set decoration, Franco Fumagalli; costume design, Ray Summers; assistant director, Tony Brandt; casting, Lou Digiamo. Reviewed at Toronto Film Festival, Sept. 10, 1991. MPAA rating: R. Running time: **111 MIN.**
David Raybourne . Andrew McCarthy
Lia Spinelli . . . . Valeria Golino
Alison King . . . . Sharon Stone
Italo Bianchi . . . . John Pankow
Giovanni . . . . Mattia Sbragia
Bernier . . . . George Murcell

A competent but routine thriller about a young American novelist in 1978 Rome who accidentally hits upon a terrorist kidnaping plot, "Year Of The Gun" is likely to come and go from U.S. theaters with little fanfare. Director John Frankenheimer still can make suspense scenes crackle, but in this case one has to wade through too many dull complexities to reach them.

Andrew McCarthy plays an expatriate U.S. journalist who's doing quite nicely in Rome with a rich Italian g.f. (Valeria Golino) and the insistent attentions of a beautiful and nervy American photojournalist (Sharon Stone).

Trouble is, Stone wants in on a book she believes he's writing about the Red Brigades terrorists, and McCarthy knows he can't pull the book off unless it stays a secret.

Indeed, Stone finds out and leaks it to a mutual friend (John Pankow), a university prof who leaks it to the Red Brigades, and suddenly the two Yanks are imperiled.

Terrorists get hold of the book and believe it's all true, and soon innocent people are dying because of the fictions in the journalist's "novel."

No one is who he seems in this deeply corrupt Italy, as McCarthy finds out when the bloody betrayals begin. Unfortunately, they don't begin, nor does the aforementioned plot, until deep into the film, after a laborious and uninvolving setup.

Stone adds some interest as the provocative photographer, though one never knows what makes her character such a maniacal careerist. McCarthy is merely serviceable in the lead.

Frankenheimer and cinematographer Blasco Giuarto do a standout job with the taut, hysterical action scenes, and naturalistic use of Rome backgrounds adds high visual interest, but photography is mostly too dark and somber and sound mix is often poor. — *Amy Dawes*

ISRAEL FEST

TIME FOR CHERRIES
(ISRAELI)

Produced by Abraham Guedalia, Huguette Elhadad-Azran. Executive producer, Riki Shelah. Written and directed by Haim Bouzaglo, Hirsh Goodman. Camera (color), Oren Schmukler; editor, Era Lapid; music, Adi Renert. Reviewed at Laemmle's Royal Theater, Oct. 11, 1991. (In Israel Film Festival, L.A.) No MPAA rating. Running time: **103 MIN.**
Miki . . . . Gil Frank
Joanna . . . . Idit Teperson
Choco . . . . Sasson Gabai

Israeli filmmaker Haim Bouzaglo scores a minor triumph with this poignant, seductive tale of a glib, good-looking copywriter who confronts his mortality when he's called up to fight in the Lebanese war. Gently humanistic piece, which U.S.-premiered in the eighth Israel Film Festival L.A., is a sure crowd pleaser in specialized settings and should whet appetites for more from all involved.

Dimpled, curly-haired Gil Frank embodies the spirit of the film as a callow, playful advertising man whose sensual exploits are interrupted when he's called up to the reserve to fight Shiite terrorists in Lebanon.

Pic's cheeky camera angles and sexy style give way to a brass-tacks look as the adman confronts the grim realities of wartime, most notably in an artful scene with a gravestone carver who points out the army's efficiency: Rows of empty graves already lie waiting.

The photogenic protagonist soon catches the eye of a U.S. journalist (Idit Teperson) who decides to make him the centerpiece of her war coverage. He deftly turns her pursuit of him into a sexual cat-and-mouse game, and the chemistry between the pouty Frank as the vain soldier and the stately, stormy Teperson as the journalist entrances.

Bouzaglo, whose style and sense of humor recall the gentle lunacy of Philippe de Broca's 1966 wartime saga "King Of Hearts," laces the film with elegiac touches, such as the enormous set of dove's wings mounted on the rear of the Jeep.

Events play out in a languid, funny style indicating ample improvisation by the actors as Bouzaglo creates a humanistic portrait of wartime travails that contrasts nighttime celebration and clowning with the grim deeds of the day.

Pic's simple, universal story, with its inevitable tragic punch, wouldn't work in the hard, contrived format of U.S. commercial films, but in this gentle, forgiving setting it's quite effective.

— Amy Dawes

UNKNOWN ISRAEL
(SOVIET-ISRAELI-DOCU)

A Fourth Dimension production of Centernauchfilm Studios (USSR), Soviet-American joint venture Co-Star & United Studios of Israel. Produced by Miriam Spielmann, Shlomo Paz, I. Kovalensky. Directed by Alexander Burimsky. Screenplay, Boris Scheinin; camera (color), Michael Komolikov, Pavel Tartakof; editor, M. Khorol; music, Igor Goloviev; assistant director, N. Sudman; narrator, Juri Jacoblev. Reviewed at Fine Arts theater, Beverly Hills, Calif., Oct. 21, 1991. (In Israel Film Festival, L.A.) Running time: **68 MIN.**

In a rapidly changing world, it's reassuring to see the Russians still crank out propaganda films, even if the subject is no longer their own country. Israel, of all places, is the focus of this utterly unrevealing panegyric, which would seem to have been aimed at Soviet Jews considering an exodus to the promised land. For informed Western audiences, "Unknown Israel" is an intelligence-insulting bore.

This first Soviet-Israeli coproduction resembles sociological travelogs Americans used to see in junior high school. Rolling right past the roots and current results of political and religious strife in the region, director Alexander Burimsky presents a postcard-deep portrait of the Jewish state.

Selecting aspects of life likely to set Russian auds drooling, he spends a lot of time on the beach, in produce-filled markets and on a kibbutz.

Simplistic narration relating statistics and banal facts drones on throughout, backed by incredibly dippy music, and almost total absence of live sound prevents the film from actually meeting anyone or airing anyone's opinions about anything, save for the mayor of Haifa, a city offered as an example of how Jews and Arabs can get along with few problems.

Archival footage of Golda Meir being presented as the first Israeli ambassador to the Soviet Union is of some interest in light of the two countries' recent restoration of full diplomatic relations. But even the title is a teasing misnomer, as there's virtually nothing in the film an average tourist couldn't photograph. — Todd McCarthy

NOUVEAU CINEMA

NUVEM
(CLOUDS)
(PORTUGUESE)

A Tropico Films production. Produced by Vitor Goncalves, Ana Luisa Guimaraes, Jose Bogatheiro. Directed by Guimaraes. Screenplay, Guimaraes, Goncalves, Joao Maria Mendes; camera (color), Octavio Espirito Santo; editor, Carla Bogalheiro; music, Andrew Poppy; sound, Francisco Veloso; production manager, Vitor Goncalo; assistant director, Ana Silva. Reviewed at Venice Film Festival, Sept. 6, 1991. (Also in Montreal Cinema Nouveau fest.) Running time: **99 MIN.**
Tomas . . . . Afonso de Melo
Laura . . . . Rosa Castro Andre
Raul . . . . Guilherme Filipe
Teresa . . . . São Jose Lapa
Julio . . . . Filipe Cochofel
Oscar . . . . Diogo Infante
Jaime . . . . Jose Wallenstein

Heavily indebted to Graham Green's "Brighton Rock," "Clouds" is a somber melodrama about an innocent young woman who foolishly becomes involved with a criminal. Though well handled, pic is too derivative and emotionally shallow to create much stir.

Walking home one night, a waitress (Rosa Castro Andre) is joined by a young man on the run from the gang he betrayed. When she leaves him, his pursuers catch up with him and he's killed.

The gang assigns Afonso de Melo to find out if Castro Andre saw them. He's convinced she knows nothing about the murder but starts dating her to be sure.

Once the youth's body is discovered, the gangster realizes that the waitress remembers his connection to the murder. Believing a wife cannot testify against her husband, de Melo persuades the girl to marry him.

Pic's other major character (and a frustratingly ill-defined one) is a suspended policeman (Guilherme Filipe) who's having an affair with Castro Andre's employer. He suspects the waitress' new husband from the start and sees his capture as a way of getting back into the police force (reasons for his suspension aren't spelled out).

Apart from the idea that marriage will silence a witness, first-time director Ana Luisa Guimaraes and her co-writers borrow another plot point from "Brighton Rock." In the original, the character of Pinky (played in the 1946 film by Richard Attenborough) is asked by the girl to record a love message to her. Unknown to her, what he says expresses his contempt for her, but this she doesn't discover until after his death. In "Clouds," de Melo makes a vidcassette declaration.

Castro Andre gives an unaffected performance, but the film is in no way remarkable, except for some moody location camerawork. Greene gets no acknowledgment in the credits.

— David Stratton

BILLY BATHGATE

A Buena Vista release of a Touchstone Pictures presentation in association with Touchwood Pacific Partners I. Produced by Arlene Donovan, Robert F. Colesberry. Directed by Robert Benton. Screenplay, Tom Stoppard, based E.L. Doctorow's book; camera (Duart color; Technicolor prints), Nestor Almendros; editor, Alan Heim, Robert Reitano, David Ray; music, Mark Isham; sound (Dolby), Danny Michael; production design, Patrizia von Brandenstein; art direction, Tim Galvin, Dennis Bradford, John Willett; set decoration, George DeTitta Sr., Hilton Rosemarin; costume design, Joseph G. Aulisi; choreographer, Pat Birch; assistant director, Brian Cook; casting, Howard Feuer. Reviewed at Walt Disney Studios, Burbank, Calif., Oct. 28, 1991. MPAA Rating: R. Running time: **106 MIN.**
Dutch Schultz . . . . . Dustin Hoffman
Drew Preston . . . . . . Nicole Kidman
Billy Bathgate . . . . Loren Dean
Bo Weinberg . . . . Bruce Willis
Otto Berman . . . . Steven Hill
Irving . . . . Steve Buscemi
Mickey . . . . Billy Jaye
Lulu . . . . John Costelloe
Dixie Davis . . . . Tim Jerome
Lucky Luciano . . . . . . Stanley Tucci
Julie Martin . . . . Mike Starr
Jack Kelly . . . . Robert L. Colesberry
Mr. Hines . . . . Stephen Joyce
Mary Behan . . . . . . Frances Conroy
Rebecca . . . . Moira Kelly
Arnold . . . . Kevin Corrigan

This refined, intelligent drama about thugs appeals considerably to the head but has little impact in the gut, which is not exactly how it should be with gangster films. Robert Benton's screen version of "Billy Bathgate," E.L. Doctorow's 1988 bestseller about the last act of Dutch Schultz' life, is beautifully realized and a pleasure to watch, but its center is hard to locate, making it absorbing but not compelling. Commercial prospects look moderate.

Returning to the 1930s criminal milieu for the first time since "Bonnie & Clyde," Benton has invested the picture with extensive class and storytelling smarts, and the $40 million-plus production bears no signs of the rumored troubles of its making. Nevertheless, there is a muted, remote quality to the story's emotional core.

Tom Stoppard's tight, neatly arcing screenplay kicks off powerfully with Schultz (Dustin Hoffman), arguably the king of the New York underworld in 1935, taking his once-trusted top enforcer (Bruce Willis) for a nocturnal tugboat ride, tying him up and planting his feet in cement.

Observing this showdown from close range is Billy (Loren Dean), a nervy kid who (as seen in an eventful 35-minute flashback) has worked his way up from the streets of the Bronx to become one of Dutch's valued flunkies. With Prohibition finished and Al Capone put away, Dutch still may be prospering, but the Feds are moving in mercilessly, pressing a case for income-tax evasion that the hoodlum can't buy his way out of.

All this is a backdrop to the personal drama that mainly concerns Billy earning a place in the gang and vowing to take care of the beautiful young Drew Preston (Nicole Kidman), the dead enforcer's former girlfriend. In many ways, she is the most interesting character. She uses her mysteriousness and sexual allure to navigate between her dead lover, apparently gay husband, gangster captor and Billy, her green but wily protector.

Unsurprisingly, she seduces Billy, which places him in treacherous water with his boss, who clearly fancies her but does strangely little about it. Indeed, the ambiguity of Dutch's intentions and feelings about Drew constitutes one of the film's most serious drawbacks.

Working for the first time from someone else's script, Benton lays out all the externals in handsome, impressive fashion, but the tale's beating heart remains elusive. Despite Dean's alert, open performance, Billy remains an opaque witness to events that are unfolding over his head.

Hoffman's performance also is problematic. As with his period outings in "Agatha" and in "Death Of A Salesman," there is a stiffness that sets these impersonations apart from his best contempo characterizations.

Kidman comes on strongly, showing both girlish frivolousness and steely resolve in her portrait of the opportunistic Drew. Steven Hill is outstanding as Dutch's rumpled adviser, Willis sparkles in an extended cameo as the doomed turncoat and Stanley Tucci registers heavily in a brief appearance as Lucky Luciano.

Production values are superlative, with lenser Nestor Almendros in top form. Quality of the light throughout is exquisite, and the dark tones of the urban first act are thrown into sharp relief by the warmer colors of the countryside.

Patrizia von Brandenstein's production design impeccably conjures up New York of a half-century ago, and Joseph G. Aulisi's costumes are as resplendent as they are numerous. Mark Isham's score gorgeously works

a different, more traditional vein than is usual for him, and a trio of film editors have brought snap to the storytelling.

— Todd McCarthy

HEAVEN IS A PLAYGROUND

A New Line release of a Heaven Corp. presentation in association with Aurora Prods. Produced by Keith Bank, Billy Higgins. Executive producers, William V. Stuart, Douglas S. Cook, Larry Edwards. Co-executive producers, William Eichengreen, Leonard Pomerantz. Directed by Randall Fried. Screenplay, Fried, based on Rick Telander's book; camera (color), Tom Richmond; editor, Lou Angelo; music, Patrick O'Hearn; sound, Hans Roland; production design, Gregory Wm. Bolton; costume design, Susan Kaufmann; assistant director, Matt Hinkley; co-producers, John Banta, Tony Kamin; associate producer, Bod Hudgins; casting, Jane Alderman, Susan Weider. Reviewed at American Film Market, L.A., Oct. 23, 1991. MPAA rating: R. Running time: **111 MIN.**
Zack . . . . D.B. Sweeney
Byron . . . . Michael Warren
Racine . . . . Richard Jordan
Truth . . . . Victor Love
Dalton . . . . Janet Julian
Matthew . . . . Bo Kimble
Casey . . . . Nigel Miguel

Pungent and punishing world of ghetto basketball is the focus of this engaging labor-of-love indie pic offering fine performances and a keenly felt appreciation of the sport and its players. Story's uncertain goals will prevent it from being a theatrical slam-dunk, but this admirable showcase for all talents involved has strong potential for ancillary markets.

Debuting feature filmmaker Randall Fried transplanted sportswriter Rick Telander's account from Flatbush, Brooklyn, to Chicago's Cabrini Green projects area, where a young, white, small-town lawyer (D.B. Sweeney) joins the all-black amateur hoopsters while idling away a transitional summer.

Rebuffed at first, he's soon taken under the wing of a self-styled coach/talent scout (Michael Warren), who controls the playground courts and takes a passionate, patriarchal interest in guiding ghetto ballplayers toward scholarships and pro deals.

Warren wants Sweeney's legal advice on a tricky contract for his major discovery, a raw but prodigiously talented college player (Victor Love). The lawyer joins the negotiations but falls prey to the machinations of a slick sports agent (Richard Jordan).

Meanwhile, the insecure hoopster is balking at the pressures of the pro spotlight and indulges in drugs and belligerence, even as Sweeney, who's begun coaching a team of playground misfits, tries to inspire the comeback of another neighborhood superstar (Bo Kimble) who long ago quit the game.

Episodic nature of the story, which has trouble choosing a character or plot to stay with, detracts from its momentum, though the rich texture of the material suggests strong possibilities for a tv series. Point of view toward the self-styled coach, the most compelling figure, is unclear. Helmer Fried paints a buoyant, affectionate portrait of him as neighborhood savior, but throws in half-hearted, unresolved allegations that he's a flesh peddler and profiteer.

Despite the difficulties inherent in fashioning a screen story from Telander's truthful sociological portrait, Fried makes a notable debut as a director of quality drama. Actors seem to be giving their utmost, with strong chemistry between Warren and Sweeney, and a memorable dramatic turn by the excellent Love as the tormented star player.

Nigel Miguel is also a standout in a minor role as a misfit ballplayer struggling to overcome his vices. Best of all are the court scenes: Lyrical, reverent slow-motion ballets keenly communicate the game's enduring pleasures.

Photography is firstrate, and the potent urban soundtrack makes a bracing contribution. The $2.6 million production, lensed in Chicago, where it opened this month, was brought to the screen via a 10-year-long effort on the part of the indie filmmakers. New Line acquired it for domestic and IRS Media for international distribution.

— Amy Dawes

THE HITMAN

A Cannon Pictures release of a Don Carmody production. Produced by Carmody. Executive producers, "Peter Welbeck" (Harry Alan Towers), André Link. Directed by Aaron Norris. Screenplay, Robert Geoffrion, Carmody; camera (Film House color), Joao Fernandes; editor, Jacqueline Carmody; music, Joel Derouin; sound (Ultra-Stereo), Martin Fossum; production design, Douglas Higgins; art direction, Eric Fraser; set decoration, Barry Brolly; costume design, Mary McLeod; assistant director, Don Hauer; production manager, Joyce Kozy King; dramatic supervisors, Richard & Leslie Brander; action coordinator, Dean Raphael Ferrandini; stunt coordinator, Bill Ferguson; casting, Stuart Aikens. Reviewed at 23rd St. West 1 theater, N.Y., Oct. 26, 1991. MPAA Rating: R. Running time: **95 MIN.**
Garret/Grogan . . . . . . Chuck Norris
Ronny Delaney . . . . . Michael Parks
Marco Luganni . . . . . . Al Waxman
Christine De Vera . . . Alberta Watson
Also with: Salim Grant, Ken Pogue, Marcel Sabourin, Bruno Gerussi, Frank Ferrucci.

Chuck Norris goes to Canada in this dreary, unconvincing action vehicle. His name will assure interest in ancillary markets, but pic has poor theatrical chances.

"The Hitman" is short on action and adopts a film noir visual style that masks its limited production values. For Norris, teamed again with his director brother Aaron, feature is a comedown from their last big-budget film "Delta Force 2."

Film should not be confused with a recent tv movie as well as a Forest Whitaker-starrer from Continental Film Group with similar titles.

Prolog has Norris and Michael Parks as cops on a stakeout, with Parks shooting Norris and leaving him for dead. Three years later Norris has a new identity and is in Seattle undercover as unsuspecting Italo gangster Al Waxman's No. 2 in command.

Working for agent Ken Pogue, Norris' assignment is to get the two rival mobs, Waxman's and Marcel Sabourin's French heavies in Vancouver, to unite so that both can be nabbed. Fly in the ointment is a group of Iranian thugs led by Frank Ferrucci.

There is momentary interest as Norris plays both ends against the middle, a ploy popularized by Clint Eastwood. Norris is okay as a pretend heavy, but a very poor script by Robert Geoffrion and producer Don Carmody violates many rules of the genre.

Norris kills bad guys in cold blood to impress his gangster partners, but, unlike James Bond, his ruthlessness seems out of line. Pogue criticizes his behavior, but the constraints that traditionally limit a hero's actions compared to his evil adversaries have been removed here in search of cheap thrills.

Best thing about "Hitman" is some good stuntwork. Picture is the first to credit "dramatic supervisors" (Richard and Leslie Brander), but despite their tutelage Norris walks through his role and is not helped by his unfunny one-liners after killing or beating somebody.

Waxman is a solid villain, while Parks, normally a good guy, seems bemused by his baddie assignment and appears only at pic's beginning and end. Canadian actress Alberta Watson is wasted as romantic interest for Norris as film builds up to a presumably torrid scene but cuts away before anything happens.
— *Lawrence Cohn*

BOKURA NO NANOKA-KAN SENSO
(SEVEN DAYS' WAR)
(JAPANESE)

A Triton Pictures (U.S.) release of a Kadokawa production. Produced by Katsuhiko Aoki. Executive producer, Haruki Kadokawa. Directed by Hiroshi Sugawara. Screenplay, Jyunnosuke Maeda, Sugawara, based on Osamu Souda's novel; camera (color), Satoshi Kawasaki. Reviewed at Japan Society, N.Y., Aug. 7, 1991. Running Time: **94 MIN.**
With: Rie Miyazawa, Kenichiro Kikuchi, Masaki Kudo, Motoi Tanaka, Masatake Kanehama, Ken Osawa, Hideaki Ishikawa.

"**S**even Days' War" is a slick, spirited satire of student revolt that retains its energy, if not its wit, in a facile climax.

Although solid production values and sprightly pacing could give it a crack at the U.S. market, its primary appeal should be to young auds, who have been xenophobic at the b.o.

Opening scenes of students live up to image of Japan as a disciplined and competitive society. Director Hiroshi Sugawara and co-scripter Jyunnosuke Maeda, however, convey instances of tough and repressive teaching methods with puckish humor.

Eight dissenting seventh grade boys take refuge in an abandoned factory. Joined by three girls, they construct a miniature society and develop skills stifled in the regimented school system. When the students are discovered missing, school officials deny the disappearances.

Sugawara deftly satirizes the situation with political and military metaphors. The balance shifts to more raucous humor as the teachers lay siege to the factory with military police.

The pic never aspires to the anarchic spirit of Jean Vigo's 1933 "Zero For Conduct" or even Lindsay Anderson's "If ... " The students' rebellion is a thoroughly middle-class appeal for reform.

A more delicate shading of the adult characters could have bol-

stered audience interest as well as storyline credibility. All the youngsters playing the recalcitrant juveniles acquit themselves well with Rie Miyazawa as the plucky heroine coming off best.
— *Fred Lombardi*

RIFLESSI IN UN CIELO SCURO
(REFLECTIONS IN A DARK SKY)
(ITALIAN)

A Starlet Film production in association with RAI-1, Cinecittà. Produced by Massimo Guizzi. Directed by Salvatore Maira. Screenplay, Maira, Massimo Franciosa, Luisa Montagnana; camera (color), Alfio Contini. Reviewed at Cinema Europa fest, Viareggio (competition), Oct. 4, 1991. Running time: **95 MIN.**
Valeria . . . . Françoise Fabian
Chim . . . . Anna Kanakis
Caterina . . . . Valerie Perrine
Also with: Peter Stormare, Maurizio Donadoni, Brigitte Christensen.

A harrowing two-hander, "Reflections In A Dark Sky" drags the viewer through the mire and offers few rewards in return. Pic has little chance of anything more than fleeting theatrical exposure and looks set for local tube consumption.

An alcoholic doctor (Françoise Fabian) quits career and family and settles into some serious solitary boozing. She invites a whoring heroin addict (Anna Kanakis) to stay, putting aside the bottle for some charitable work.

Kept prisoner in the doctor's cavernous apartment, the addict undergoes a grueling withdrawal as the women lock horns in a battle of wills. Cured of her addiction, Kanakis turns the tables on her keeper and, with equally obsessive force, steers her away from alcoholism.

Pic is hopelessly weighed down by heavy-handed theatricality and elements of Greek tragedy. Though written for the screen, the material has an oppressive staginess and a ton of leaden symbolism.

Core problem is ex-Miss Italy Kanakis' performance, all hair-tossing and nostril-flaring. She gives the pic some unintentional (but welcome) humor as she turns into a superwoman banshee and breaks the legs of the doctor's attackers.

French thesp Fabian fares better, giving a credible perf and often striking true chords. She's clumsily dubbed, however, and one wonders why helmer-co-scripter Salvatore Maira didn't just make the character French

or choose an Italo actress.

Tech credits are fine although Alfio Contini's unrelentingly dark lensing of the apartment seems superfluous in a pic already overloaded with blackness and gloom.
— *David Rooney*

THE ARC
(U.S.-BRITISH)

A Cinema Parallel production in association with Film Four Intl. Produced by J.K. Eareckson. Executive producer, Tom Garvin. Written, directed, photographed and edited by Rob Tregenza. In color. Reviewed at Toronto Film Festival, Sept. 14, 1991. Running time: **96 MIN.**
With: Marty Lodge, Katherine Kelley, Catherine Fogarty, Hugh Nees.

Director Rob Tregenza is back with another esoteric one-man show, "The Arc," an odd road movie for arthouses and film classes.

Manipulating pic's pace by using the length of shots as a metaphor for his protagonist's emotional state, Tregenza begins "The Arc" with a savage whirlwind of images as a welder's life falls apart. When he refuses to join a strike, he loses his job and his wife and hits the road with lightning speed.

During the trip through Baltimore, Georgia, Oklahoma, Texas and Montana, shots gradually grow longer and longer as the confused wanderer meets strange people somewhat frozen in time.

Gorgeous desert shots make the pic a visual treat, and trite script provides a few laughs.
— *Suzan Ayscough*

THE GIRL WHO CAME LATE
(AUSTRALIAN)

A Beyond Films release of a View Films production, in association with the Australian Film Finance Corp. Executive producer, John Cooper. Produced by Ben Gannon. Directed by Kathy Mueller. Screenplay, Saturday Rosenberg, with additional dialog by Michael Jenkins; camera (color), Andrew Lesnie; editor, Robert Gibson; music, Todd Hunter, Johanna Piggott. Reviewed at Beyond Films screening room, Sydney, Sept. 30, 1991. Running time: **86 MIN.**
Nell Tiscowitz . . . . . . Miranda Otto
Digby Olsen . . . . Martin Kemp
Wendy . . . . Gia Carides
Also with: Anne Looby, Bruce Venables, Katie Edwards, Kelly Walker.

Frisky as a colt and full of infectious good humor, "The

Girl Who Came Late" is a delightful and original Aussie comedy that could find audiences worldwide. Down Under, it should have good to very good b.o. success.

Produced as part of the Australian Film Finance Corp.'s 1990 Film Fund, the romantic comedy's talented new director, fresh new screenwriter and blossoming star Miranda Otto make an irresistible combination.

Pic's plot sounds unfunny at first: Nell (Otto) grew up on a farm and was regularly beaten by her father. She found comfort in the horses she adored. During her adolescence, she even acted like a horse, to the amazement of teachers, pupils and shrinks. Young Katie Edwards convincingly plays the horse-obsessed youngster in the pic, based on scripter Saturday Rosenberg's autobiographical experiences.

At 20, the aspiring actress still relates better to horses than to men. She drives around town in a beat-up Volkswagon filled with apples and parking tickets, and eventually collides with a Lamberghini owned by a theater producer/stud farm owner (Martin Kemp).

Plot is basically a latter-day "Bringing Up Baby": Life of the smooth, self-confident producer is hilariously disrupted by this unpredictable, but sweet, young woman.

Rosenberg and helmer Kathy Mueller employ basic slapstick routines, including a scene in which valuable horse sperm gets mixed up with ice cubes. Funny, too, are scenes in which Nell tries to eke out a living as a stand-up comic in a male strip club, where she must fend off a lecherous owner (Bruce Venables).

Mueller keeps the film cantering along with snappy pacing and a feel for comedy and romance. Turning in an accomplished comedy performance, Otto now looks like a good bet for international attention.

The supporting cast is all in fine form; the horses are magnificent. Technically flawless film incorporates a bright music score with hummable songs.
— *David Stratton*

THE IMPORTANCE OF BEING EARNEST

An Eclectic Concepts-Paco Global presentation. Produced by Nancy Carter Crow. Executive producer, Peter Andrews. Directed by Kurt Baker. Screenplay, Baker, Andrews, based on Oscar Wilde's play; camera (color), Mark Angell, Joseph Wilmond Calloway; editor, Tracey Alexander; music, Roger Hamilton Spotts; sound, Romeo Williams; art design, Lennie Barin; set design, Toni Singman; associate producers, Deani Wood, Jimmy Richardson. Reviewed at Harvard Film Archive, Cambridge, Mass., Oct. 25, 1991. No MPAA rating. Running time: **123 MIN.**
Algernon . . . . Wren T. Brown
Jack . . . . Daryl Roach
Gwendolyn . . . . Chris Calloway
Cecily . . . . Lanei Chapman
Lady Bracknell . . . . . . Ann Weldon
Dr. Chausible . . . . Brock Peters
Miss Prism . . . . C.C.H. Pounder
Lane . . . . Obba Babatunde
Merriman . . . . Barbara Isaacs

This new, all-black rendition of Oscar Wilde's epigrammatic comedy of manners recently premiered at Harvard's "Blacks In Black & White & Color" film symposium. Looking for a distrib, pic updates a few of Wilde's references but is otherwise true to source.

More likely to appeal to the audience for "A Room With A View" than for "New Jack City," "The Importance Of Being Earnest" will require special handling, but it should be able to attract crossover biz at specialty venues.

Wilde's play has been lensed before, most notably in 1952 by Anthony Asquith and starring Michael Redgrave. This version moves the story from the Victorian Era to present day England and is meant to showcase its talented African-American cast.

Plot involves two women who believe they can love only a man named Earnest and two men who each take on the name under false pretenses. Confusion reigns until delightfully absurd happy ending.

First-time director Kurt Baker, working with a $1-2 million budget, goes to some pains to open up the play. He is more successful in the second act, at Jack's country estate, where the action can naturally flow in and out of doors. In the London sequences (actually shot in Los Angeles), the overhead shots seem contrived.

Cast is more than up to the challenge of Wilde's florid dialog, although auds may need time to get used to listening to it. Ann Weldon is a standout as Lady Bracknell, especially in scenes where she grills Jack and Cecily to see if they are worthy of marrying into the family.

Brock Peters and C.C.H. Pounder offer able support, while the four leads are at their best in the second half as the plans of the characters come crashing down.

Tech credits are okay for a low-budget feature, with the exquisite costumes and settings making the film appear much glossier than might be expected.
— *Daniel M. Kimmel*

UN HOMME ET DEUX FEMMES
(A MAN AND TWO WOMEN)
(FRENCH)

An AAA release of a Films Alyne-Films A2-Selena Audiovisuel-SGGC-Canal Plus production. (Intl. sales: Gaumont.) Produced by Rene Feret. Directed by Valerie Stroh. Screenplay, Stroh, Feret, based on three stories by Doris Lessing; camera (color), Peter Suschitzky; editor, Charlotte Fauvel; music, Evelyne Stroh; sound, Michel Vionnet; production design, Georges Stoll. Reviewed at Greater Union Pitt Cinema 3, Sydney, Oct. 23, 1991. Running time: **84 MIN.**
Martha/Anne/
Freda/Judith . . . . . . Valerie Stroh
Dr. Paul Baudoin . . . Lambert Wilson
Isabelle . . . . Patricia Dinev
Pierre . . . . Yan Epstein
Fred . . . . Michael Vartan
Also with: Jean-Yves Berteloot, Julie Jezequel, Clotilde de Bayser.

Valerie Stroh, who made an impression two years ago in the lead role in Rene Feret's "Baptism," is even more impressive in her directorial debut, co-scripted with Feret. "A Man And Two Women," a thoughtful and multi-faceted look at the emotions and amours of four women (all played by Stroh), could well make a positive impression on the international art market.

Doris Lessing's tales of femme passion have been transposed to the provincial French city of Lille in 1960. Martha, a single mother, is undecided as to whether to join her doctor lover, Paul, in Paris, as he is urging, or to end their relationship. One sleepless night, she writes three self-contained dramas.

The first, "A Man And Two Women," revolves around Ann, who encourages husband Pierre and visiting friend Isabel to start an affair; her new baby apparently displacing her husband. Segment contains a fair amount of sexual tension, though the three-way relationship remains tantalizingly unresolved.

Next comes "One Another," a sensual piece in which the newly married Freda bids farewell to her husband and soon after welcomes her brother, Fred, to her bed. This forthright sequence, with its incest theme and uninhibited male-female nudity, could spark controversey.

Finally, "Our Friend Judith" revolves around an intellectual woman vacationing on the island of Elba. She has a liberating love affair with a handsome young hairdresser.

Stroh gives fine perfs as cool and dispassionate Martha, fiercely possessive yet provocative Ann, openly erotic Freda and remote yet sensual Judith. Thesp's sterling work, before and behind the camera, should considerably enhance her reputation.

Supporting cast members all are effective, but Stroh dominates. Pic is technically flawless, with Peter Suschitzky's attractive camerawork and Evelyne Stroh's flavorsome trumpet score, hauntingly played by Eric Le Lann. — *David Stratton*

LOLA ZIPPER
(FRENCH)

An AAA release (in France) of an Aria Films (Paris)-Ann Burke Prods. (Montreal)-Filmax (Paris)-Filmfutures-corp (New York) production. (Intl. sales: Motion Média, Paris.) Produced by Thierry Forte, Anne Burke. Written and directed by Ilan Duran Cohen. Camera (color), Philippe Lavalette. Reviewed at Pathe Montparnasse, Paris, June 8, 1991. Running time: **90 MIN.**
Lola Zipper . . . . Judith Reval
Gérard . . . . Jean-Paul Comart
Loretta . . . . Arielle Dombasle
Also with: François Perrot, Thibault de Montalembert, Tom Rack.

In "Lola Zipper," a distant but not-so-funny French cousin of "Pretty Woman," first-time helmer-scripter Ilan Duran Cohen fires off scenes of heroine's makeover but botches comic craft, with no help from his actors. Best chances for this fast-paced fizzless pic are in global tv markets.

Under pressure to find another star or lose his job, an agent (Jean-Paul Comart) bets his boss that he can turn a scruffy street woman into a star; namely, filthy, tough 18-year-old Lola (Judith Reval), whom he takes to his chic pad for a monthlong conversion.

Reval, in her film debut, is convincing as an obnoxious teen. Similar, milder behavior in ballet and acting classes, however, becomes tiresome. Comart's empty character, part spoiled yuppie and part drill sergeant, generates little sexual current with his ward until their abrupt first kiss at film's end.

Laugh lines are airless, and surefire setups, such as Lola demolishing the agent's bathroom, fall flat. Vet thesp Dombasle is a welcome face in her brief return to screen. Too bad she's full of silly advice for Lola.
— *Lee Lourdeaux*

ALAMBRADO
(FENCED IN)
(ITALIAN-ARGENTINE)

A Sacis presentation of an Aura Film (Italy), Oskar Kramer (Argentina) production, in association with RAI-3. Produced by Roberto Cicutto, Vincenzo de Leo. Executive producer, Diana Frey. Directed by Marco Bechis. Screenplay, Bechis, Lara Fremder; camera (color), Esteban Courtalon. Reviewed at Locarno Film Festival, Aug. 13, 1991. Running time: **90 MIN.**
With: Jacqueline Lustig, Martin Kalwill, Arturo Maly, Matthew Marsh.

Outlandish locations and their inhabitants are the main strengths of "Fenced In," in which powerful images and strong characters often compensate for a weak plot.

A stubborn Irish settler throws up the only obstacle to a British company's plans for a resort at the southernmost tip of South America. He won't give up his patch of land for an airport that's pivotal to the project.

The gruff settler builds a fence, bullying his teenage daughter and son to help. The fence is to keep strangers out but also to lock his family in.

Helmer Mario Bechis, who paints a remarkably lifelike image of the God-forsaken place near the Straits of Magellan, also focuses on the two teens' sexual awakening. Jacqueline Lustig attracts most of the attention, and her impertinent, adolescent sexuality may help win her a promising career. — *Dan Fainaru*

KASBA
(INDIAN)

An NFDC-Doordarsham production. (Intl. sales: NFDC, New Delhi.) Executive producer, Ravi Malik. Directed by Kumar Shahani. Screenplay, Bhishm Sahni, Gulzar, Fareeda Mehta, Shahani, based on Anton Chekhov's novella "In The Valley"; camera (color), K.K. Mahajan. Reviewed at Edinburgh Film Festival, Aug. 22, 1991. Running time: **114 MIN.** *(Hindi dialog)*
Tejo . . . . Mita Vashisht
Maniram . . . . Mandhar Singh
Dhani . . . . Shatrughan Sinha

Chekhov goes Indian in "Kasba," and both sides come away looking good. Involving Hindi drama is high-grade fest material with potential for specialized web sales.

Based on the Russian novella "In The Valley," pic is set in a small north Indian community that's also a smuggling route. Local honcho is Maniram, who's been cheating his customers for years and whose business affairs are largely run by low-caste, adopted daughter Tejo.

The dramatic screw tightens as eldest son Dhani is arrested for counterfeiting; his father, who has a bundle of the notes, panics. Tejo starts to make her play for what she sees as her due.

Episodic pic moves at a leisurely, but never boring, pace, thanks to topnotch acting by the entire cast and a strong script.

Kumar Shahani's helming is visually alert, with evocative use of the family's hillside manse, surrounding mountains and small-town locations. Playing, especially by the femmes, is understated but taut, with Mita Vashisht standout as the cool-headed Tejo.

Apart from unsubtle postsynching, tech credits are noteworthy. Color lensing is rich and tasty, and Vanraj Ghatia's Indo-Western score provides atmospheric interludes. Pic shows no signs of its rapid 26-day shoot on actual locations. Hindi title means "community" or "settlement."

— *Derek Elley*

ZAZAMBO
(THE FUNERAL)
(JAPANESE-B&W-COLOR)

A Shibata Organization presentation of a Nakagawa Yoshishisa-Shochiku production. Written, produced, directed, photographed and edited by Fumiki Watanabe. Reviewed at Locarno Film Festival, Aug. 15, 1991. Running time: **112 MIN.**
Fumiki Watanabe . . . . Himself
Tsugiko Watanabe . . . . Herself
Grandfather . . . . Arata Kokatsu
Grandmother . . . . Itsu Kokatsu
Mother . . . . Mayumi Morita

Confused narrative mars "The Funeral," an exciting and unconventional picture by Japanese enfant terrible Fumiki Watanabe.

Director, who has gained some notoriety from recent film fest showings of his work, leads family members both behind and in front of the camera to tell the true story of a boy who commit-

ted suicide years ago in one of Japan's southern provinces.

For Watanabe, the death is a symbol of the feudal system (never uprooted from the Japanese soul) and society's suppression of the individual.

Black & white flashbacks refer to the childhood of the teacher (Watanabe), while color flashbacks depict events in the story.

Helmer has had his share of arguments with co-producer Shochiku on this film, his first stab at cooperating with a Japanese major. He has deleted several shots the company deemed offensive. — *Dan Fainaru*

DANCE TO WIN
(U.S.-ITALIAN)

An MGM/UA release from MGM of a TPI-USA presentation, in association with Ascot Film. Executive producers, Guido De Angelis, Maurizio De Angelis, Giuseppe Giacchi. Produced by Aldo U. Passalacqua, Jefferson Richard. Directed by Ted Mather. Screenplay, Mather; camera (Telecolor), Dennis Peters; editor, Gianfranco Amicucci; music, Guido & Maurizio De Angelis; sound (Dolby), Dennis Carr; production design, Stephen Rice; costume design, Hollywood Raggs; choreography, Paula Abdul, Jerry Evans. Reviewed on Cinemax, Boca Raton, Fla., Aug. 6, 1991. MPAA Rating: R. Running time: **102 MIN.**
Slammer . . . . Carlos Gomez
Francis . . . . Daniel Quinn
Amanda . . . . Sally Stewart
Emma . . . . Christina Haack
Flash . . . . Sandor Black
Fingers . . . . Don Reed
Billy James . . . . Adrian Paul
Also with: Curtis Womack, Patricia Barry, Garrett Morris.

This okay youth-oriented musical was made by the same team that did "Dance Academy" with Julie Newmar. MGM pickup was briefly released in Philadelphia in late 1989.

Notable for choreography by Paula Abdul, "Dance To Win" is one of a half-dozen low-budgeters MGM acquired to fill its slate when the studio was stalled between owners in '89.

Familiar format has warring dance groups competing for a $100,000 prize for their L.A. dance school. Good guys are nominally the street gang led by Carlos Gomez, who have been court-ordered to paint the facade of mean Adrian Paul's dance academy after being caught applying graffiti. Their in-fighting and romantic travails involving pretty dancers like Christina Haack are as corny as the pic's antidrug message.

Dance numbers shine, however, including a musicvideo starring singer Sally Stewart.

Gomez, Haack and Stewart all bear potential, and Daniel Quinn effectively provides comic relief. Film is squeaky clean but earned an R rating for an outburst of foul language in the final reel.

— *Lawrence Cohn*

SESZELE
(SEYCHELLES)
(POLISH)

A Film Prodcers' Agency-Film Studio Zebra production. Produced by Andrzej Janowski. Directed by Boguslaw Linda. Screenplay, Cezary Harasimowicz; camera (color), Jaroslaw Szoda. Reviewed at Pesaro Intl. Festival of New Cinema, June 12, 1991. Running time: **103 MIN.**
Stefek . . . . . Zbgniew Zamachowski
Also with: Tadeusz Smymkow, Hanna Polk, Marek Walczewski.

Thesp-turned-helmer Boguslaw Linda's second outing as director is an often appealing bit of Kafkaesque fantasy, but "Seychelles' " anarchic structure probably will restrict it to the fest circuit.

Pic's opener comes on like "Lethal Weapon," with a well-shot car chase set to Wojciech Waglewski's pounding worldbeat soundtrack, but any resemblance to Hollywood product ends there.

A small-time racketeer (Zbgniew Zamachowski) evades mob bosses by passing himself off as a mentally unstable kleptomaniac and laying low in an asylum. The racketeer and his keenest devotee (Tadeusz Smymkow) escape from the hospital and find work at the opera (scene of some staggeringly bad lip-synching). Zamachowski becomes stage-doorman and soon discovers that the opera doubles as a brothel.

Director Linda has worked as an actor (for Krzysztof Kieslowski and Andrzej Wajda) and the experience has given him an obvious affection for backstage settings. He threads the action in and out of the wings and flies, and he draws likably understated performances.

Tech credits are fine, and pic has the odd well-judged moment, but despite its anti-structuralism, it often feels curiously flat. This very anarchy too often allows pic to lose itself and its audience.

— *David Rooney*

CHEROKEE
(FRENCH)

A Les Films de la Lune Vague release of a Quartet-Telema-Ciné 5 coproduction. Produced by Marie-Odile Meguerditchian. Directed by Pascal Ortega. Screenplay, Gérard Sterin, based on Jean Echenoz' novel; camera (color), Sterin; editor, Laurent Quaglio; music, Jeff Cohen; sound, Philippe Lioret. Reviewed at Ariane screening room, Paris, July 18, 1991. Running time: **85 MIN.**
Madame Benedetti . Bernadette Lafont
Bock . . . . Roland Blanche
Ripert . . . . Gérard Desarthe
Georges . . . . Alain Fromager
Fred . . . . Daniel Rialet
Jenny . . . . Carole Richert
Uncle Fernand . . Jean-Paul Roussillon

"Cherokee," a mildly rousing detective romp, is competently made but falls short of being special. The complicated, whimsical plot relies on the cast's collective charm.

Bernadette Lafont lends her abrasive voice and distinctive mannerisms to the role of a widow who runs a detective agency. An unsolved case concerns finding an heir to a rich estate.

At the request of a devoted publisher (Jean-Paul Roussillon), the gumshoe widow hired an affable loser (Alain Fromager) who has not seen his brother in 10 years. (They split up over their garage band's rendition of the Ray Noble standard "Cherokee.")

Back in town, the brother (Daniel Rialet) intends to pose as the heir to the valuable estate until he discovers his estranged brother works for the very detective agency he plans to rook.

Characters are ornery yet endearing. Careful setups in exterior sequences makes Paris seem like a city inhabited exclusively by the cast of this film. Title ditty is sung to good effect by gravel-voiced performer Arthur H. — *Lisa Nesselson*

A TÁVOLLÉT HERCEGE
(THE PRINCE OF ABSENCE)
(HUNGARIAN-B&W-COLOR)

A Dialog Film Studio production. Directed by Tamás Tolmár. Screenplay, Sándor Sultz, Hilda Hársing; camera (color, b&w), Gábor Halász. Reviewed at Munich Film Festival, June 26, 1991. Running time: **100 MIN.**
With: Péter Vallai, Juli Básti, Gézi Balkay, László Sinkó, Piroska Molnár.

"The Prince Of Absence" is so preoccupied with avant-garde visual technique that it completely abandons conventional narrative. General auds probably won't be patient or interested enough to unravel its metaphorical implications and may opt to be absent.

A 40-ish writer (Péter Vallai) working as a factory clerk uses vodka as a crutch to muster through his unsatisfying existence. A friend and his girlfriend move in with the writer when Vallai can't pay a debt. The Magyar versions of Kerouac and Ginsberg read rambling free-form verse on street corners to pick up extra cash.

Vallai lapses into hallucinogenic episodes. In one, he wanders around in a desert with bizarre Wagnerian-like settings populated by psychedelic frogs, Nubian priests and a blond Brunhilde figure, who join in a ritual surrounding the "prince of absence."

Changes from color to black & white become distracting, and the camera is so mobile and nervous, it's a wonder the actors manage to stay within frame.

In his second feature, Tomás Tolmár has enthusiastically joined the absurdist backlash against traditional Hungaro cinema. Pic shows influence of innovative director Peter Bacso, with whom he worked on "Banana Skin Waltz," but it lacks Bacso's understated wit and inner cohesion. — *B. Samantha Stenzel*

NARSKAR OXOTA
(A ROYAL HUNT)
(SOVIET-CZECHOSLOVAKIAN-ITALIAN)

A Ronin Films (Australia) release of a Lenfilm-Golos Studio (USSR)-Barrandov Studios (Prague)-Excelsior Film-Video Film (Rome) co-production. Directed by Vitali Melnikov. Screenplay, Leonid Zorin, based on his play; camera (color), Yuri Veksler. Reviewed at Walker Cinema, North Sydney, July 18, 1991. Running time: **134 MIN.**
Catherine
the Great . . . Svetlana Kryuchkova
Count Orlov . . . . Nikolai Yeremenko
Princess Elizabeth
Tarakanova . . . . Anna Samokhina
Also with: Mikhail Kononov, R. Ioseliani, S. Matyash.

"**A** Royal Hunt" is a lavishly produced, yet intimate, drama set during the 18th century reign of Catherine the Great. With a plot similar to the Elizabeth I/Mary Queen of Scots conflict, pic could attract audiences interested in its historical theme, though director Vitali Melnikov's low-key treatment detracts.

Those hoping for a spectacular old costume-drama will be disappointed as Melnikov's deliberate direction allows few dramatic highlights. Still, pic has a touching climax.

Svetlana Kryuchkova portrays the monarch as overweight, plain, sexually voracious and scheming. When she hears that Polish princess Elizabeth (Anna Samokhina) claims to be descended from a former Russian queen, she fears an attempt to overthrow her and dispatches one of her lovers, Count Orlov (Nikolai Yeremenko), to lure Elizabeth onto Russian territory.

Samokhina is convincing as the lonely young woman who falls for the charm of double-dealing Orlov. As the duplicitous Orlov, Yeremenko is properly hissable. The other actors are good, except those playing English and U.S. diplomats with thick Russian accents.

Visually, pic is handsome, with dazzling palaces used for both exteriors and interiors. The lovers' side trip to Pisa accounts for the Italian content in this three-way co-production.
— *David Stratton*

NOUVEAU CINEMA

J'ENTENDS PLUS LA GUITARE
(I CAN NO LONGER HEAR THE GUITAR)
(FRENCH)

A Les Films de l'Atlante production, with the participation of Centre National de la Cinematographie. Produced by Gerard Vaugeois. Written and directed by Philippe Garrel. Camera (color), Caroline Champetier. Reviewed at Venice Film Festival (competition), Sept. 11, 1991. (In Montreal Nouveau Cinema & Vancouver film festivals.) Running time: **100 MIN.**
Gerard . . . . Benoit Regent
Marianne . . . . . Johanna Ter Steege
Martin . . . . Yann Collette
Lola . . . . Mireille Perrier
Aline . . . . Brigitte Sly
Adrienne . . . . Anouk Grinberg

"**P**hilippe Garrel has been making films since the '60s, and has carved a cult niche for himself in France without making an international mark. It's doubtful his new effort, despite its qualities, will alter his status since "I Can No Longer Hear The Guitar" has nothing new to say about relationships.

Exploring a man's personal life over a number of years, Garrel focuses on Gerard, on holiday with his beautiful new g.f. Marianne and friends Martin and Lola. Gerard claims he will love Marianne to death — and beyond.

Time goes by and the couple experiment with drugs. Gerard also finds other women. Eventually, Marianne drops out of his life, though he sometimes sees her. He marries an earth mother type, Aline, and has a child with her, but he keeps having other affairs. One day he hears Marianne has died, and the news profoundly shocks him.

Garrel abruptly shifts forward in time without telling the viewer how long has passed since the last scene. The device is unduly frustrating and distancing.

With less confusing handling, Garrel might have made a moving tale of a man who never really knew what he had until he lost it. Many could have responded to this universal story, but the director's style precludes involvement with the characters.

Benoit Regent is wooden as Gerard, but the women all are good, especially Dutch thesp Johanna Ter Steege as the tragic Marianne and Brigitte Sly as Aline. Obviously shot on a modest budget, pic is technically fine.
— *David Stratton*

UNDERSTANDING BLISS
(CANADIAN)

A Films Transit release (in Canada) of an Unreal Prods. picture. Produced & co-edited by Terry Greenlaw. Executive producer, William D. MacGillivray. Directed & co-edited by MacGillivray. Screenplay, MacGillivray, Kathryn Cochran; camera (color), Steve Campanelli. Reviewed at Toronto Film Festival, Sept. 7, 1991. (In Montreal Nouveau Cinema fest.) Running time: **90 MIN.**
Elizabeth . . . . Catherine Grant
Peter . . . . Bryan Hennessey
The sister . . . . . . Rosemary House
The father . William E. MacGillivray Sr.

"**I**n the financially beleaguered climate of Canada's east coast, filmmaker William MacGillivray weaves a tale of superficiality, deceit and realization. Pacing problems make "Understanding Bliss" an unlikely product for conventional tv, since commercials would only heighten the time drag.

Via an affair between Elizabeth, a professor from Toronto, and Peter, a prof at the university in St. John's, Newfoundland, story intriguingly interprets the

---

effect of contrasting backgrounds on human interaction.

A trip to Peter's father's house exposes the differences between origin and status. She has come to the island to guest lecture at the university. Peter has arranged it so they can spend some time together after a four-month separation. Instead of a blissful reunion, the relationship falters when their priorities clash.

Katherine Mansfield, New Zealander whose short story "Bliss" this pic's plot parallels, holds little relevance in a place where the fall of the fishing industry has led to unemployment and economic hardship.

Unfortunately, a passionate script is bogged down by meandering passages in which characters slowly move through scenes. Long pauses between conversations and action with little or no link to the plot makes the film seem much longer.
— *Karen Murray*

DRIVE
(B&W)

A Megagiant Entertainment production. Produced by Jefery Levy, Gregory D. Levy. Directed by Jefery Levy. Screenplay, Colin MacLeod in collaboration with Jefery Levy; camera (b&w), Steven Wacks; editor, Lauren Zuckerman; music, Charles H. Bisharat, Dr. Lee; sound, George Lockwood; production design, J. Levy. Reviewed at Venice Film Festival (noncompeting), Sept. 11, 1991. (In Montreal Cinema Nouveau fest.) Running time: **86 MIN.**
The driver . . . . David Warner
The passenger . . . . . . Steve Antin
The girl . . . . Dedee Pfeiffer

"**D**rive," an ambitious black & white indie production, won't make much of a commercial mark but could spark cult interest.

Simple premise involves two men driving through L.A. in their 90-minute commute to work. The driver (David Warner) is a cynical, entertaining talker constantly rapping about everything under the sun. His younger passenger (Steve Antin), trying to recover from a broken love affair, mostly just listens.

Warner gives a fine reading of his role, and viewers will find him frequently funny if they can keep up with his nonstop rambling. Best scene is the one where Antin painfully relates the story of the one and only time he slept with the girl (Dedee Pfeiffer) he loves so much. Flashes of the rendezvous are shown, breaking up the drive's visual monotony.

Steven Wacks' fine monochrome photography makes the journey through L.A.'s endless suburban sprawl surprisingly arresting. Playing a few distancing games with the audience, first-time director Jefery Levy at one point allows Warner to flub his lines and do a second take, and, towards the end, he brings the filmmaking process into the trip.
— *David Stratton*

HIGHWAY 61
(CANADIAN-BRITISH)

A Cineplex Odeon Films release (in Canada) of a Shadow Shows production in association with Film Four Intl. (Intl. sales: Cinephile). Produced by Bruce McDonald, Colin Brunton. Executive producer, Daniel Salerno. Directed by Bruce McDonald. Screenplay, Don McKellar; camera (color), Miroslaw Baszak. Reviewed at National Film Board's John Spotton Theater, Toronto, Aug. 19, 1991. (In Montreal Nouveau Cinema, Toronto & San Sebastian film festivals). Running time: **110 MIN.**
Pokey Jones . . . . Don McKellar
Jackie Bangs . . . . . Valerie Buhagier
Mr. Skin . . . . Earl Pastko
Customs agent . . . . Jello Biafra
Peter Breck . . . . Mr. Watson

Despite many stop-and-go sequences, "Highway 61" is a hip, knowing road pic that will provide a fun trip of surprises for specialized auds.

A lonely small-town barber (Don McKellar) in northern Ontario plays the trumpet (badly) but dreams of hitting Highway 61 all the way south to New Orleans. He finds a dead man's body in his backyard and hits the front page of the town's newspaper.

The article attracts a female roadie (Valerie Buhagier) who pretends to be the deceased's sister. She hides stolen cocaine in the corpse's mouth and persuades the barber to drive the body to New Orleans for burial.

Trip is uneventful through Canada, but in the U.S. several wacko characters cross their path.

McKellar, also pic's inventive scripter, is terrific as the boyish, shy barber. Buhagier is dynamite as the roadie, and Earl Pastko makes a rollicking Satan.

Bruce McDonald directs with verve. Low-budget pic boasts good tech values, chiefly Miroslaw Baszak's camerawork and original hard-driving music by Toronto pop singer-writer Nash the Slash. But at 110 minutes, it's too long a trip. — *Sid Adilman*

PARIS S'EVEILLE
(PARIS AWAKENS)
(FRENCH)

An Arena Films (Paris)-Erre Prods. (Rome) co-production. Produced by Bruno Pesery. Written and directed by Olivier Assayas. Camera (color), Denis Lenoir; editor, Luc Barnier; music, John Cale. Reviewed at Cinema Europa fest, Viareggio (competition), Oct. 1, 1991. (In Montreal Nouveau Cinema fest.) Running time: **95 MIN.**
Louise . . . . Judith Godrèche
Clément . . . . . . Jean-Pierre Léaud
Adrien . . . . . . Thomas Langmann
Zablonsky . . . . . . Martin Lamotte
Agathe . . . . Ounie Lecomte
Victor . . . . Antoine Basler

"Paris Awakens" (provisional English title) is a smart urban drama delving into the difficulties of fitting into an often hostile society. Good scripting, tight direction and convincing, attractive leads should make this a good bet for international arthouse playdates.

Director Olivier Assayas throws the audience into the middle of his story. A 19-year-old (Thomas Langmann), on the run after driving the getaway bike from a crime scene, turns up at his father's house after a four-year absence. Dad (Jean-Pierre Léaud) lives with a wild girl (Judith Godrèche) who has an on-again, off-again drug habit. She is banking on Léaud's influence to kickstart a tv career.

Antagonism between the young 'uns turns to desire, and after a fight with Léaud, Godrèche runs off to live with Langmann in a derelict squat.

Assayas' script is both spare and poetic, and pic's visual style has nonstop electricity. Denis Lenoir's camera is particularly effective weaving through the father's labyrinthine apartment and swooping along Paris streets. Luc Barnier's rapid-fire editing works well with John Cale's music.

Perfs are uniformly excellent, and Assayas takes full advantage of his leads' good looks, frequently homing in for intense closeups. — *David Rooney*

CAPE FEAR

A Universal release of an Amblin Entertainment presentation in association with Cappa Films and Tribeca Prods. Produced by Barbara De Fina. Executive producers, Kathleen Kennedy, Frank Marshall. Directed by Martin Scorsese. Screenplay, Wesley Strick, based on James R. Webb's screenplay and John D. MacDonald's novel "The Executioners"; camera (Technicolor, Panavision), Freddie Francis; editor, Thelma Schoonmaker; music, Bernard Herrmann, adapted, arranged and conducted by Elmer Bernstein; sound (Dolby), Tod Maitland; production design, Henry Bumstead; art direction, Jack G. Taylor Jr.; set decoration, Alan Hicks; costume design, Rita Ryack; miniature special effects supervision, Derek Meddings; title sequence, Elaine & Saul Bass; assistant director, Joseph Reidy; casting, Ellen Lewis. Reviewed at Samuel Goldwyn Theater, Beverly Hills, Calif., Nov. 7, 1991. MPAA Rating: R. Running time: **128 MIN.**
Max Cady . . . . Robert De Niro
Sam Bowden . . . . Nick Nolte
Leigh Bowden . . . . . . Jessica Lange
Danielle Bowden . . . . Juliette Lewis
Claude Kersek . . . . . Joe Don Baker
Lieutenant Elgart . . Robert Mitchum
Lee Heller . . . . Gregory Peck
Judge . . . . Martin Balsam
Lori Davis . . . . Illeana Douglas
Tom Broadbent . Fred Dalton Thompson
Graciella . . . . Zully Montero

"Cape Fear" is a highly potent thriller that will strike fear into the hearts of a sizable public. This smart and stylish remake of the 1962 suspenser effectively delivers the chills that will put it over with general audiences, but it also sees Martin Scorsese taking conventionally plotted material and making it, in numerous dark and provocative ways, his own. B.o. outlook looms lusty.

As with "The Color of Money" five years ago, this clearly reps a case of Martin Scorsese taking on an obviously commercial project involving material outside his interests. "Cape Fear" is the most story-driven film he has ever made, as well as the one most rooted in genre. But, aside some over-the-top special effects shots and seemingly unavoidable horror film ploys, pic is thoroughly a Scorsese film.

Sharply written adaptation by Wesley Strick follows the basic plot of J. Lee Thompson's solid black & white Universal release, which featured Robert Mitchum as a white trash ex-con who returns from prison to torment the prosecuting attorney (Gregory Peck) who sent him up.

Strick and Scorsese's changes, however, enrich and blacken the material, making the characters squirm physically, morally and sexually. Instead of being a "normal," upstanding Southern family, the Bowdens (Nick Nolte, Jessica Lange and 15-year-old daughter Juliette Lewis) are troubled by father's history of infidelity and daughter's difficulties with both parents.

Enter Robert De Niro's Max Cady, a psychopath whose body is covered by a mural of threatening, religiously oriented tattoos, including the scales of "truth" and "justice" hanging off either side of a cross. Penned up for 14 years, Cady begins by just annoying the family, but soon launches his campaign of terror by killing the family dog and brutalizing a boozy young law clerk (Illeana Douglas) whom Nolte has been seeing.

This Sam Bowden had been Cady's defense attorney. Reluctant to take Cady on personally, Bowden hires private detective Kersek (Joe Don Baker) to handle things, but the crafty, demented Cady outfoxes both of them at every turn. After a bloody seige at the family home, the action shifts to a houseboat off Cape Fear, where Cady's terror reaches its violent climax.

In maximum souped-up style, Scorsese slams through the mandatory plot mechanics with powerful short scenes, dynamic in-your-face dollies and cranes and machine-gun editing. Instead of the lazy, sweaty, smalltown Old South of the original film, new pic offers the New South betokened by gleaming office buildings and antiseptic interiors.

Director and his collaborators really cut to the quick in the disturbing sexual component, mainly between Cady and the teen. Pic's most daring and mesmerizing scene, a very long one on a school theater stage in which all stylistic tricks are banished, has Cady manipulating the girl's awakening sexual interests and estrangement from her parents into a strange alliance between them.

Sporadically furious with her husband over his real and suspected dalliances, Leigh Bowden also develops a sexual connection with the maniac.

Quite distinct from Mitchum's more laconic villain, De Niro's Cady is a memorable nasty right up there with Travis Bickle and Jake La Motta. Cacklingly crazy at times, quietly purposeful and logical at others, Cady is a sickie utterly determined in his righteous cause, and De Niro plays him with tremendous relish and is extremely funny in several scenes.

Nolte copes admirably with a difficult role written as somewhat unsympathetic. Lange's role plays as rather subsidiary to the others, but the actress catches fire in her arguments with Nolte.

Lewis is excellent as the troubled, tempted teen, and tale begins and ends with brief narration from her p.o.v. Baker hits the bull's-eye as the investigator willing to employ any techniques to dispose of Cady, and Douglas has some standout scenes as the giddy woman who too easily makes herself available.

Mitchum, Peck and Martin Balsam, all of whom appeared in the '62 version, pop up here in astutely judged roles. Another adroit decision, which also bespeaks of the director's intense

Original film
CAPE FEAR

Universal Studios release of Melville-Talbot production, produced by Sy Bartlett. Stars Gregory Peck, Robert Mitchum, Polly Bergen; features Lori Martin, Jack Kruschen, Martin Balsam, Barrie Chase. Directed by J. Lee Thompson. Screenplay by James R. Webb, based on novel, "The Executioners," by John D. MacDonald; camera, Samuel Leavitt; music, Bernard Herrmann; editor, George Tomasini; asst. director, Ray Gosnel Jr. Reviewed at Universal homeoffice, March 1, '62. Running time: 105 MIN.

Sam Bowden	Gregory Peck
Max Cady	Robert Mitchum
Peggy Bowden	Polly Bergen
Nancy Bowden	Lori Martin
Mark Dutton	Martin Balsam
Dave Grafton	Jack Kruschen
Charles Sievers	Telly Savalas
Diane Taylor	Barrie Chase
Garner	Paul Comi
Officer Marconi	John McKee
Deputy Kersek	Page Slattery
Officer Brown	Ward Hamsey

film buffery, was the use of Bernard Herrmann's original score, adapted and rearranged by Elmer Bernstein.

Working for the first time in widescreen, Scorsese called upon veteran lenser Freddie Francis, and result looks terrific. Technical aspects are all first-rate, although the hand of Amblin is a bit too heavily apparent in the changing skies above the Bowden house and in the emphatic special effects of the climax.

—*Todd McCarthy*

BEAUTY AND THE BEAST
(ANIMATED)

A Buena Vista release of a Walt Disney Pictures production in association with Silver Screen Partners IV. Produced by Don Hahn. Executive producer, Howard Ashman. Directed by Gary Trousdale, Kirk Wise. Animation screenplay, Linda Woolverton, based on the classic French fairy tale; Technicolor prints; editor, John Carnochan; music, Alan Menken; songs, Ashman, Menken; sound (Dolby), Michael Farrow (songs), John Richards (score); art direction, Brian McEntee; story supervisor, Roger Allers; layout supervisor, Ed Ghertner; background supervisor, Lisa Keene; cleanup supervisor, Vera Lanpher; visual effects supervisor, Randy Fullmer; computer graphics images supervisor, Jim Hillin; supervising animators, James Baxter, Glen Keane, Andreas Deja, Nik Ranieri, Will Finn, Dave Pruiksma, Ruben A. Aquino, Chris Wahl, Russ Edmonds; supervising effects animators, Dave Bossert, Dorse Lanpher, Ted Kierscey, Mark Myer; associate producer, Sarah McArthur; casting, Albert Tavares. Reviewed at El Capitan theater, L.A., Nov. 5, 1991. MPAA Rating: G. Running time: **85 MIN.**
VOICES:

Belle	Paige O'Hara
Beast	Robby Benson
Lumiere	Jerry Orbach
Mrs. Potts	Angela Lansbury
Gaston	Richard White
Cogsworth/ Narrator	David Ogden Stiers
LeFou	Jesse Corti
Maurice	Rex Everhart
Chip	Bradley Michael Pierce
Wardrobe	Jo Anne Worley
Featherduster	Kimmy Robertson

A lovely film that ranks with the best of Disney's animated classics, "Beauty And The Beast" is sure to be a b.o. gold mine rivaling Disney's 1989 hit, "The Little Mermaid."

Despite the familiarity of previous versions, from Jean Cocteau's 1946 live-action "La Belle Et La Bete" to the recent TV series, tale is freshly retold. This is a timeless animated film with appeal for all.

Darker-hued than the usual animated feature, with a predominant brownish-gray color scheme balanced by Belle's blue dress and radiant features, "Beauty" engages the emotions with an unabashed sincerity that manages to avoid the pitfalls of triteness and corn.

The classical fairy tale of a bestial enchanted prince's love for a French maid not only carries a timely message of tolerance but also is effortlessly given a feminist slant that contemporary audiences will find uplifting, in contrast to the sexist undertones that marred the otherwise delightful "Little Mermaid."

The character of Belle, magnificently voiced by Paige O'Hara,

is a brainy young woman scorned as a bookworm by her townsfolk and kidnapped by the Beast. She finds her initial aversion overcome by a growing appreciation of his inner beauty and sensitivity.

While the usually soft-spoken Robby Benson might seem an odd choice for the voice of the Beast, his booming bass voice in the early sections and the increasingly boyish timbre of his voice in the later parts perfectly capture character's complexity.

Howard Ashman and Alan Menken's songs are witty, charming, richly orchestrated and smoothly integrated into the plot. There is not a standout number like "Under the Sea" in "Little Mermaid," but their songs and Menken's score for "Beauty" have a more consistent quality.

Debuting feature directors Gary Trousdale and Kirk Wise, art director Brian McEntee and the first-rate animation staff (James Baxter was supervising animator for Belle, Glen Keane for the Beast) bring a strikingly three-dimensional look to the film, augmented in some spots by Jim Hillin's state-of-the-art computer graphics images.

From the teeming village and alluring landscapes to the brooding interior of the Beast's castle, pic is a continual treat for the eye, with a sophisticated style that should dazzle auds accustomed to cut-rate animation.

In the best Disney tradition, supporting characters provide comic relief that keeps the sentiment from becoming sticky. Here it's the Beast's enchanted household, including the candelabra (Jerry Orbach), the matronly teapot (Angela Lansbury) and her teacup son (Bradley Michael Pierce), the fastidious mantel clock (David Ogden Stiers) and the feather-duster (Kimmy Robertson).

Lyricist/exec producer Ashman died of AIDS complications in March, and pic is dedicated to him.

— *Joseph McBride*

MONSTER IN A BOX
(BRITISH)

A Fine Line (U.S.)-ICA Cinema (U.K.) release of a Jon Blair Film Co. production. Produced by Jon Blair. Directed by Nick Broomfield. Screenplay, Spalding Gray, from his stage monolog; camera (Eastmancolor, Technicolor prints), Michael Coulter; editor, Graham Hutchings; sound, Sandy Macrae; production design, Ray Oxley; co-producer, Renee Shafransky; associate producer, Norman I. Cohen. Reviewed at ICA Cinema, London, Oct. 28, 1991. No MPAA rating. Running time: **88 MIN.**
With: Spalding Gray.

Spalding Gray struts his anecdotal stuff once again in "Monster In A Box," a frisky follow-up to "Swimming To Cambodia." Film rendition of the 1990 stage hit should scare up some biz in selected salons before settling down on video.

"Monster" may not match the cult status of 1987's "Swimming," which played as much on director Jonathan Demme's buff appeal as on Gray's verbal gymnastics. But Brit director Nick Broomfield scores equal points for his translation of Gray's stage act to celluloid.

Titular "Monster" is Gray's 1,800-page autobiography, "Impossible Vacation." Starting his peregrinations in 1987, Gray recounts how celeb status after "Swimming" gave him plenty of excuses to procrastinate.

The easy laughs come at the start: East Coaster Gray's barbed comments on Tinseltown, where execs invite him to "idea lunches" and CAA woos him in hyper meetings. Gray's search for "real" (non-movie) people in

Original play
MONSTER IN A BOX

Lincoln Center Theater presentation of a monolog in one act by Spalding Gray. Directed by Renee Shafransky. Lincoln Center Theater director, Gregory Mosher; executive producer, Bernard Gersten; general manager, Steven C. Callahan; production manager, Jeff Hamlin; publicity, Merle Debuskey. Opened Nov. 14, '90, at the Mitzi E. Newhouse Theater, $25.
With: Spalding Gray.

L.A. is the theme of his initial rondos.

Subsequent divertissements include Columbia Pictures' putting him on a U.S. fact-finding mission to Nicaragua (a comic horror show), AIDS hysteria in New York, a flying saucer project for HBO, taking "Swimming" to the

Moscow fest and Gotham critics' trashing of his perf in Gregory Mosher's Broadway production of "Our Town."

Just as "The Killing Fields" was the McGuffin in "Swimming," so the "monster" book is here. The difference that makes this pic funnier is that buffs won't be on tenterhooks for filmic revelations that never come, leaving one free to concentrate on Gray's machine-gun way with words.

Based on Gray mate Renee Shafransky's original stage production, pic was shot at London's Riverside Studios before a live aud (seen briefly at first and occasionally heard reacting). Setting is spare: Gray sits at a table before a changing backdrop with the "monster" at his elbow.

Editing and camerawork are nimble, and there's atmospheric use of lighting and sound effects. Laurie Anderson's synthesizer score is dramatically helpful if sometimes overinsistent.

— *Derek Elley*

JOHNNY STECCHINO
(ITALIAN)

A Penta Distribuzione release (Italy) of a C.G. Group Tiger Cinematografica-Penta Film production. Produced by Mario & Vittorio Cecchi Gori. Directed by Roberto Benigni. Screenplay, Vincenzo Cerami, Benigni; camera (color), Giuseppe Lanci; editor, Nino Baragli; music, Evan Lurie; art direction, Paolo Biagetti. Reviewed at Metropolitan Cinema, Rome, Nov. 1, 1991. Running time: **122 MIN.**
With: Roberto Benigni, Nicoletta Braschi, Paolo Bonacelli, Franco Volpi.

Italo comedy king Roberto Benigni takes on the mob in "Johnny Stecchino," a thoroughly enjoyable showcase for his anarchistic humor. The picture grossed $7 million in its first week of release onshore and shows every sign of breaking b.o. records.

Sold to all major territories, pic should have a strong run as the first Italo film in the five-nation Penta Europa slate in '92.

In this pure-blood Sicilian adventure, director/star/co-scripter Benigni (familiar to international auds for appearing in Jim Jarmusch films) limits his famous gabby monologs in favor of universal gags that have been around since silent comedy.

Pic's only slow part is its opening: Helmer Benigni takes his time establishing his character of nerdish school bus driver Dante. He has no luck with women and gets no respect from men; only the Down's syndrome schoolkids he merrily chauffeurs around love him.

The mysterious moll (Nicoletta Braschi) of mobster Johnny Stecchino, in hiding after turning state's evidence, cooks up a scheme to get the heat off her b.f. by setting up Dante to be bumped off in his place.

The classic mistaken identity plot unfolds with plenty of laughs as Benigni switches between the double role of simple Simon and hardened criminal. When he makes an ambiguous deal with a bigshot minister linked to the mob and receives a bag of cocaine as a gift, he imagines it is an American cure for diabetes.

The last scene — considered harmless in Italy — probably will be cut for offshore release, including the U.S. Back home, Dante offers coke to a diabetic teen, who sticks his head in the bag and takes off like a rocket. It should be noted, however, that pic's natural, uncondescending presentation of youngsters with Down's syndrome has been hailed.

Though not particularly original as a director, Benigni makes good use of full artistic control to let his comic inspiration run wild. The result is a genuinely funny update on the ancient comic art.

Braschi contributes a great deal as straight woman to the idiot savant Dante, managing to be seductive and impish at the same time. Peripheral cast is quite up to the mark, especially Paolo Bonacelli as a henchman.

Art director Paolo Biagetti creates a fairy-tale Palermo fitting right with the outlandish tale of cinematic mobsters. Evan Lurie's score and Giuseppe Lanci's cinematography are equally light-hearted. — *Deborah Young*

STRICTLY BUSINESS

A Warner Bros. release, in association with Island World, of an Andre Harrell production. Produced by Harrell, Pam Gibson. Executive producers, Mark Burg, Chris Zarpas. Directed by Kevin Hooks. Screenplay, Gibson, Nelson George; camera (Duart color; Technicolor prints), Zoltan David; editor, Richard Nord; music, Michel Colombier; sound (Dolby), Lawrence Hoff, Thomas Nelson; production design, Ruth Ammon; art direction, Rowena Rowling; set decoration, Sonja Roth; costume design, Beulah Jones-Black; assistant director, Gary Marcus; production manager, Victoria Westhead; 2nd unit director-co-producer, Dave Kappes; associate producer, George; casting, Julie Mossberg, Brian Chavanne; L.A. casting, Susan Dalla Betta. Reviewed at Criterion 3 theater, N.Y., Nov. 2, 1991. MPAA Rating: PG-13. Running time: **84 MIN.**

Bobby Johnson	Tommy Davidson
Waymon Tinsdale III	Joseph C. Phillips
Diedre	Anne Marie Johnson
David	David Marshall Grant
Natalie	Halle Berry
Drake	Jon Cypher
Monroe	Sam Jackson
Millicent	Kim Coles

"Strictly Business" is a feel-good comedy about young blacks moving up the social ladder that could do solid business if audiences respond to a kinder, gentler type of picture.

Film eschews the gritty approach of recent black-themed pics for a Pollyannaish tale in which even the top white execs are portrayed as reasonable and fair-minded. Crossing class and social barriers is the issue here, not race.

The two heroes, debuting on the big screen after TV experience, are handsome Joseph C. Phillips, intent on earning a partnership in a leading N.Y. real estate firm, and streetwise Tommy Davidson, his friend in the mailroom who dreams of making the management trainee program.

Key link between the two is beautiful restaurant hostess Halle Berry, with whom Phillips is immediately infatuated. Davidson knows her from the hood and agrees to fix them up in return for Phillips' help at work.

Comedy comes from Phillips having to learn how to relate to Berry and other blacks since his nerdish success-oriented behavior has turned him into an insular workaholic.

Except for the forced, strictly wish-fulfillment final reel, the film is kept evenly on track by a light touch from debuting director Kevin Hooks, also a TV recruit.

Phillips displays impressive comic timing in executing some hilarious physical shtick and is complemented by the verbal savvy of standup comic Davidson. Anne Marie Johnson as Phillips' bossy g.f. barks out orders during sex like a drill sergeant and earns some big laughs. Sam Jackson ("Jungle Fever") demonstrates his versatility as the mailroom boss.

Given a glamorous intro not unlike Bo Derek in "10" (complete with slow-mo torso photography), Berry is pic's revelation as a sexy and intelligent young woman. She's featured next in WB's Christmas pic "The Last Boy Scout."

Film benefits from an infectious score by Michel Colombier and several rap tunes by top artists like L.L. Cool J and Big Daddy Kane. — *Lawrence Cohn*

WHY HAVEL?
(CANADIAN-CZECHOSLOVAKIAN-DOCU-COLOR/B&W-16M)

A Cinema Plus release (Canada) of a Les Prods. Les Fete production. Produced by Rock Demers. Written and directed by Vojtech Jasny. Camera (color/b&w, 16m), Sylvain Brault; editor, Borek Sedivec. Reviewed at Montreal World Film Festival, Aug. 26, 1991. Running time: **100 MIN.**
Narrator: Milos Forman.

This fascinating docu on Czechoslovakia's playwright president dwells on ceremony and offers too few relevations of the man himself. When pic does slip behind the presidential show, however, Vaclav Havel confesses: "My act... is essentially a play." Pic will hit in eastern bloc countries where such freedom of speech is still a phenomenon.

Production values are not up to producer Rock Demers' usual standards, and docu looks like a homevideo. Still, it's ideal for quality TV outlets in the West.

Docu follows Havel from one reception or dinner to the next, and numerous pols and celebs pay tribute: Placido Domingo, Paul Newman, Arthur Miller, Dizzy Gillespie, George Bush, Paul Simon, Shirley Temple Black and Henry Kissinger.

Taste of Havel's humor: "I'm sorry I haven't prepared a speech, but today I didn't spend two hours in a prison," later adding, "President and prisoner are similar states of being."

Docu also surveys citizens on why they voted for Havel. One woman said: "He's suffered for his convictions so he merits our love." Capturing a slice of modern history in the making, pic portrays Havel as an every-man with a terrific sense of both humor and justice. — *Suzan Ayscough*

REVOLUTION!
(COLOR/B&W-16M)

A Dream Bird Prods. presentation. Produced by Travis Preston. Executive producer, Sidney Kahn. Written and directed by Jeff Kahn. Camera (Precision color, Duart b&w, 16m), Michael Stiller; editor, Chris Tellefson; music, Tom Judson; sound, Steve Robinson, Chris Tellefson, Tom Foligno; art direction, Kristen Ames; costumes, Eva Goodman; co-producer, John Friedman; assistant director, Tim Maner. Reviewed at Public Theater, July 1, 1991. No MPAA rating. Running time: **84 MIN.**

Suzy	Kimberly Flynn
Ollie	Christopher Renstrom
Steve	Johnny Kabalah
Billie	George Osterman
Kasha	Helen Schumaker
Prunievsky	Travis Preston

This low-budget romp about three aspiring revolutionaries living in New York is technically accomplished and features bright performances by unknown actors. Although frequently enjoyable, "Revolution!" ultimately suffers from an uneven tone.

Young director Jeff Kahn managed to make a polished film on a shoestring, but he wasn't sure whether he was making a romance, comedy or suspenser. Kahn's extended takes are self-indulgent and the pacing is lugubrious at times.

Pic opens with Russian revolution footage and segues to that hotbed of Marxism, the Lower East Side. The camera follows a roller-skating Kimberly Flynn to her dumpy apartment, which she shares with the handsome Christopher Renstrom, who spends most of his time sitting in the tub reading Karl Marx, and the depressed George Osterman.

In their Marxism class, Flynn and Renstrom pick up a fourth revolutionary (Johnny Kabalah). When they aren't hunting pigeons for lunch or rehearsing a nightclub act, the trio plots a half-baked revolution.

To finance it, they plan to rob Kabalah's wealthy aunt. Instead, the aspiring Communists make themselves at home and enjoy the bourgeois comforts. In the misguided final scene, the aunt returns with her b.f., the Marxism professor, and a long, poorly staged fight ensues. By the end, the tone has shifted too many times between farce and drama.

Even though pic is inconsistent, it amounts to a terrific audition piece for the actors, director and crew. Flynn, who makes a sultry nightclub performer, has a striking screen presence.

Kahn is a capable, if showy filmmaker who uses every film technique he knows. In one clever scene, black & white photography gives way to color as the revolutionaries leave the city for the country.

Mike Spiller's photography, Chris Tellefson's editing and Judson's music all deserve credit for making the film look and sound good. Even with its flaws, the $40,000 film has more life in it than many $40 million features.

— *William Stevenson*

THE PEOPLE UNDER THE STAIRS

A Universal Pictures release of an Alive Films presentation. Produced by Marianne Maddalena, Stuart M. Besser. Executive producers, Shep Gordon, Wes Craven. Written and directed by Craven. Camera (Deluxe color), Sandi Sissel; editor, James Coblentz; music, Don Peake; sound (Dolby), Paul Clay; production design, Bryan Jones; art direction, Steven Lloyd Shroyer; set decoration, Molly Flanegin; costume design, Ileane Meltzer; associate producer, Peter Foster; assistant directors, Nick Mastandrea, Rosemary C. Cremona; 2nd unit director-special effects supervisor, Peter Chesney; co-producer, Dixie J. Capp; casting, Eileen Knight. Reviewed at Beverly Center Cineplex, L.A., Nov. 1, 1991. MPAA Rating: R. Running time: **102 MIN.**

Fool	Brandon Adams
Man	Everett McGill
Woman	Wendy Robie
Alice	A.J. Langer
LeRoy	Ving Rhames
Roach	Sean Whalen
Grandpa Booker	Bill Cobbs
Ruby	Kelly Jo Minter

A pretense of social responsibility and most of the necessary tension get lost in a combination of excessive gore and over-the-top perfs in "The People Under the Stairs." While there's always an initial aud for horror, pic won't put many people in seats after the first weekend or two.

Writer-director Wes Craven sneaks in a post-Reagan era message about haves and have-nots by making his hero a 13-year-old ghetto kid. Pic's still an old-style haunted house film with spooky couple Everett McGill and Wendy Robie terrorizing their teen daughter (A.J. Langer) and keeping a horde of ashen youths locked in the basement.

Stumbling into the ample vulgarity within those walls is the aptly nicknamed Fool (Brandon Adams), brought along by his sister's b.f. to rob the place since the strange couple also are the boy's landlords on the verge of evicting the family.

Idea that the wisecracking boy establishes his identity and manhood through his ordeal simply doesn't pan out amid the absurdity of the narrative, featuring a handful of belly laughs, intended and unintended.

House of horrors includes cannibalism, McGill cavorting around in a leather suit and a blood-crazed Rottweiler. Cartoonish villains quickly thaw pic's initial chill, in the process trivializing the more serious issues (child abuse, poverty) that might

have been raised.

Craven conjures up a gothic atmosphere, employing tight camera shots as the characters careen through narrow passageways.

Call and Langer are attractive and gutsy young leads but can't navigate past numbing dialog, while Robie (making her feature debut) and McGill don't exactly stretch beyond their most recent TV roles ("Twin Peaks").

— *Brian Lowry*

LONDON FEST

ENCHANTED APRIL
(BRITISH-16M)

A Miramax (U.S.) and Curzon-Miramax (U.K.) release of a BBC Films production in association with Miramax Films & Greenpoint Films. Produced by Ann Scott. Executive producers, Mark Shivas, Simon Relph. Directed by Mike Newell. Screenplay, Peter Barnes, based on Elizabeth von Arnim's novel; camera (color, 16m), Rex Maidment; editor, Dick Allen; music, Richard Rodney Bennett; sound (Dolby), John Pritchard; production design, Malcolm Thornton; costume design, Sheena Napier. Reviewed at London Film Festival, Nov. 6, 1991. Running time: **101 MIN.**

Rose Arbuthnot	Miranda Richardson
Mrs. Fisher	Joan Plowright
Mellersh Wilkins	Alfred Molina
Lottie Wilkins	Josie Lawrence
Lady Caroline	Polly Walker
George Briggs	Michael Kitchen
Frederick Arbuthnot	Jim Broadbent

A slim comedy of manners about Brits discovering their emotions in sunny Italy, "Enchanted April" doesn't spring many surprises. Strong cast's reliable playing is undercut by a script that dawdles over well-trod territory. Period pic should drum up some biz from the lit-crit and connoisseur crowd but won't weave much of a spell on general auds.

Similar theme got more cinematic treatment in this year's E.M. Forster meller "Where Angels Fear to Tread." This one, a pickup by Miramax from BBC Films at script stage, too often betrays its small-screen origins in boxy closeups and less-than-ravishing 16m photography. Like the recent "Truly, Madly, Deeply" (a.k.a. "Cello"), pic derives from the British pubcaster's Screen Two series.

Story centers on four women who rent a medieval dwelling in San Salvatore, Italy. For two of them (Miranda Richardson, Josie Lawrence), it's an excuse to get

away from inattentive hubbies. Also on board are a waspish widow (Joan Plowright) and a society belle (Polly Walker).

The solo pleasures of the Italo landscape don't last long so Lawrence decides to invite her husband (Alfred Molina) over, and Richardson eventually fires off a letter to hers as well. Meanwhile, the house's British owner (Michael Kitchen), who'd already taken a shine to Richardson in Blighty, turns up one day.

Final piece in the jigsaw is Richardson's husband (Jim Broadbent), who has a pseudonymous rep on the London cocktail circuit as a writer of risque romances. Unaware that his wife has invited him down, he drops in with his sights on Walker.

All of this is a while coming, and for the first hour the pic idles pleasantly along in first gear with establishing material in rainy London and lazy afternoons in pasta land. Denouement is swift, with everyone except the widow pairing off happily.

Peter Barnes' dialog-heavy script is well turned but lacking in real conflict or development. All the actors give it their best shot, with Plowright spitting out bons mots with her usual aplomb and Molina brightening things up. Of the younger women, Walker is tops as the cool society vamp. Richardson and Lawrence are solid but get less to chew on.

Mike Newell's helming gets everything in the frame but rarely delivers more. Technically, pic is okay within its limitations. On the big screen, Rex Maidment's camerawork sometimes looks underlit in interiors and color-starved in the Italian scenes. More of Richard Rodney Bennett's Elgar-themed score would have been a bonus.

Pic was an okay but low-voltage opening attraction at the London film fest. — *Derek Elley*

TILL THERE WAS YOU
(AUSTRALIAN)

A Sovereign Pictures presentation of an Ayer Prods.-Five Arrow Films-Australian Film Finance Corp. production. Produced by Jim McElroy. Directed by John Seale. Screenplay, Michael Thomas; camera (color), Geoffrey Simpson; editor, Jill Bilcock; music, Graeme Revell; sound, Gary Wilkins; production design, George Liddle. Reviewed at AFI Cinema, Paddington, Aug 13, 1991. (In London Film Festival.) Running time: **93 MIN.**

Frank Flynn	Mark Harmon
Anna	Deborah Unger
Viv	Jeroen Krabbe
Rex	Shane Briant

By Australian standards, top cinematographer John Seale's first pic as a director is an expensive, high-concept affair aimed at the international, and especially the Yank, market. "Till There Was You" falls between several categories, however, and pic's a major disappointment.

Almost two years after principal photography was completed, pic has yet to obtain an Aussie distrib. Presumably, producer Jim McElroy and his backers conceived a large-scale romantic adventure à la "Romancing The Stone," but Michael Thomas' stolid and low-on-motivation screenplay was Seale's first hurdle.

The serviceable, if familiar, plot has Mark Harmon playing a New York sax player who wings off to a Pacific island on his brother's invitation. When he arrives he discovers his brother has been killed, and that he's not very welcome on the island.

Although Harmon does his best with his undemanding role, Canadian-born Aussie thesp Deborah Unger is miscast as the sultry wife of the dead brother's friend. Introed as "the most beautiful woman in the islands," the character is written as an ultra-glam Rita Hayworth type, but Unger is far too down to earth for the role.

Furthermore, there's no chemistry between her and Harmon though they're supposed to be having a passionate relationship. As her seemingly charming husband, Jeroen Krabbe brings a touch of menace to a conventional character until called upon to go way over the top in the film's awkward climax.

On the plus side, Geoffrey Simpson's camerawork on little-seen island locations is often spectacular. A plane crash in the jungle is superbly staged, and the local Vanuatans, mostly from Pentecost Island, prove to be natural actors.

Pic is unlikely to create much interest either critically or commercially. It's the kind of mid-Pacific pic Aussies are probably unwise to tackle, since on the whole U.S. producers and directors are far more adept at giving this kind of formula the slickness and story-telling elements that yield wide audience appeal.

— *David Stratton*

GLUCHY TELEFON
(CROSSED LINES)
(POLISH)

A Poltel Agency presentation of a Studio Tor-WFF-1 production. Directed by Piotr Mikucki. Screenplay, Barbara Fatyga, Piotr Mikucki; camera (color), Pawel Edelman. Reviewed at Montreal Nouveau Cinema fest, Oct. 25, 1991. Running time: **81 MIN.**
Katherine (wife) . . . . . Hanna Mikuc
Agatha . . . . . . Katarzyna Latawiec
Tomas (husband) . . . . . Maciej Orlos
Lucas . . . . Waldemar Kownacki

A Polish film with a happy ending is a phenomenon in itself, but "Crossed Lines" has universal appeal for patient viewers who relish philosophical and occasionally sordid details about troubled lovers.

An East Euro menage à trois with limited arthouse appeal, pic is a tangly, realistic tale of an intellectual couple whose stagnant marriage is put to the test.

The wife's audacious, sexy friend (Katarzyna Latawiec) unexpectedly arrives for an indefinite period. The husband (Maciej Orlos) initially detests the bold, seductive and uninvited stranger whose frank observations lead his wife to question their 11-year union.

Pic unfolds like chapters in a book on mid-life crisis with the hero in a state of transition and self-doubt. He's a taxi driver unmotivated to finish his masters in sociology: His marriage has degenerated into a sexless habit with minimal communication.

Predictably, the stranger's presence provokes change via conflict. Surprisingly, the husband and wife eventually rediscover their love for one another after brief affairs outside the marriage.

Pic's gentle pace lends itself well to meticulous treatment of an age-old subject. Tech credits are good. Ultimately optimistic tale should fare well in fests and east bloc countries.

— *Suzan Ayscough*

THE HOUSE BUILT ON SAND
(SOVIET)

A Sovexportfilm presentation of a Lenfilm Studios production. Directed by Niyole Adomenaite. Screenplay, Natalia Chepik; camera (color), Alexander Shumovich. Reviewed at Montreal Cinema Nouveau fest, Oct. 27, 1991. Running time: **84 MIN.**
With: Yelena Shachkova, Yelena Shiffers, Yuri Astafyev.

This hardliners' tale about nasty bourgeoise aristocrats who mistreat a poor trusting proletariat girl in 1930s Leningrad bears the mark of Soviet propaganda, making pic seem misplaced in a festival of new cinema.

Tale revolves around an innocent, tactless dressmaker (Yelena Shachkova) who tries to worm her way into a corrupt, adulterous bourgeoise crowd led by a high society manipulator (Yelena Shiffers).

When the dressmaker commits a faux pas, her friends send her a fake love letter. When the naive dressmaker responds, the joke becomes an ongoing correspondence ultimately ruining her life.

Pic won't generate much interest beyond the fest circuit. Cast and tech credits are fine.

— *Suzan Ayscough*

ALTA MAREA
(HIGH TIDE)
(ITALIAN-GERMAN)

A Roadmovies presentation of a DFFB-SFB-Centro Sperimentale di Cinematografia production. Directed by Lucian Segura. Screenplay, Segura, Sandro Caselli, Guisi Toninelli; camera (color), Frank Guido Blasberg. Reviewed at Montreal Nouveau Cinema fest, Oct. 26, 1991. Running time: **86 MIN.**
With: Marco Silverio, Giuseppina Toninelli, Luigi Marchetti, Maddalena Falzoni Gallerani, Stephane Herbert.

"High Tide" marks a respectable feature debut for helmer Lucian Seguro, but this circuitous road movie has few commercial prospects.

Five teens in serious party mode are driving around looking for a good time. Their frivolity comes to a screeching halt when one is beaten to death, for no apparent reason, by bouncers in a disco.

The panic-striken pals take the body and drive aimlessly in a night fog looking for a place to dump the corpse, which they discover isn't as easy as one may think. After several fruitless and comic attempts, the body is finally washed out to sea with the tide.

Amateur script focuses on teen angst and confusion when facing a tragic adventure. Other tech credits are fine. Pic will likely wind up on Italian TV.

— *Suzan Ayscough*

FOR THE BOYS

A Twentieth Century Fox presentation of an All Girl production. Produced by Bette Midler, Bonnie Bruckheimer, Margaret South. Executive producer, Mark Rydell. Co-producer, Ray Hartwick. Directed by Rydell. Screenplay, Marshall Brickman and Neal Jimenez & Lindy Laub, from a story by Jimenez & Laub; camera (Deluxe color), Stephen Goldblatt; editors, Jerry Greenberg, Jere Huggins; production design, Assheton Gorton; music, Dave Grusin; executive music producer, Joel Sill; sound, Jim Webb; choreography, Joe Layton; costume design, Wayne Finkelman; art direction, Dianne Wager, Don Woodruff; set decoration, Marvin March; key aging makeup artists, Jill Rockow, Michelle Burke; assistant director, Alan B. Curtiss; casting, Lynn Stalmaster. Reviewed at 20th Century Fox studios, Nov. 13, 1991. MPAA rating: R. Running time: **145 MIN.**
Dixie Leonard . . . . Bette Midler
Eddie Sparks . . . . James Caan
Art Silver . . . . George Segal
Shephard . . . . Patrick O'Neal
Danny . . . . Christopher Rydell
Danny (at 12) . . . . . . Brandon Call
Jeff Brooks . . . . Arye Gross

Fox's song-driven wartime showbiz meller "For the Boys" is a big, creaky balloon of a movie that lumbers along like a dirigible in a Thanksgiving parade, festooned with patriotic sentiment. The enthusiasm of Bette Midler fans, along with a smartly cut trailer, should mean lofty numbers when pic opens wide, but b.o. is likely to sag quickly.

Ambitious effort from director Mark Rydell, who collaborated with Midler and Fox 12 years ago on "The Rose," spans the 50-year relationship of two USO entertainers (Midler and James Caan) whose song, dance and innuendo carries them through three wars. Allegedly a "love story" between two difficult people who are each married to others, pic suffers from the couple's lack of electricity.

Midler steams through the outing with sass and charm, eking out laughs on her own merit whenever the script stumbles. But Caan, in a role that recalls his pallid backup to Barbra Streisand in "Funny Lady," seems pinioned by the script and generally uncomfortable.

Presented as a wildly popular comedian and legendary lady's man, he gives evidence of neither. Midler, as spunky singer Dixie Leonard, seems more like a gal enduring a tough job situation than a woman fighting an attraction to Caan's supposedly seductive Eddie Sparks.

Story begins in the present day, when a dapper production assistant (Arye Gross) arrives by limo to pick up Dixie for a major awards show. Midler makes a shocker of an entrance; pic then dissolves to 1942, when she was a bubbly young mother called up to join the famous Eddie Sparks in a London wartime revue. Sparks proves to be an abusive s.o.b., but Midler has the soldier boys eating out her hand, so a showbiz partnership is reluctantly formed.

Rydell directs at an exeedingly deliberate pace. First act alone is 50 minutes, and full song renditions take up plenty more screen time. The picture doesn't move, it regroups; from Europe to North Africa, then to Korea, through the bloodbath of McCarthyism and finally to Vietnam. The details of costume and design are convincing, but the main idea — that these two are so great together as to be America's sweethearts — isn't.

By the denouement, there is some sentimental pleasure in watching old duffers settle their grudges, but overall, "Boys" doesn't add up to anything like a great film.

On the plus side is the sparkling soundtrack, propelled by a previously unrecorded Hoagy Carmichael/Paul Francis Webster tune called "Billy A-Dick," great orchestration and Midler's fine performances.

Excellent support is provided by George Segal in a funny, fluid perf as Eddie's liberal Jewish headwriter; Christopher Rydell and Brandon Call are memorable as older and younger versions of Dixie's son Danny; and Dori Brenner stands out in brief exposure as a witty stage manager.

"Boys" handsomely re-creates the atmosphere and detail of its diverse times and places.
— *Amy Dawes*

THE ADDAMS FAMILY

A Paramount Pictures release of a Scott Rudin production. Produced by Rudin. Executive producer, Graham Place. Directed by Barry Sonnenfeld. Screenplay, Caroline Thompson, Larry Wilson. Based on the characters created by Charles Addams. Camera (DeLuxe color), Owen Roizman; editors, Dede Allen, Jim Miller; music, Marc Shaiman; sound (Dolby), Cecelia Hall; production design, Richard MacDonald; art direction, Marjorie Stone McShirley; set decoration, Cheryal Kearney; costume design, Ruth Myers; co-producer-unit production manager, Jack Cummins; associate producers, Bonnie Arnold, Paul Rosenberg; assistant directors, Joe Camp III, Ian Foster Woolf; visual effects supervisor, Alan Munro; stunt coordinator, David Ellis; makeup design, Fern Buchner; casting, David Rubin. Reviewed at the Paramount Studios screening room, Nov. 12, 1991. MPAA Rating: PG-13. Running time: **99 MIN.**
Morticia Addams . . . Anjelica Huston
Gomez Addams . . . . Raul Julia
Uncle Fester . . . . Christopher Lloyd
Tully Alford . . . . Dan Hedaya
Abigail Craven . . . . Elizabeth Wilson
Granny . . . . Judith Malina
Lurch . . . . Carel Struycken
Margaret Alford . . . . Dana Ivey
Judge Womack . . . . . Paul Benedict
Wednesday Addams . . Christina Ricci
Pugsley Addams . . . Jimmy Workman

Despite inspired casting and nifty visual trappings, the eagerly awaited "Addams Family" figures to be one of the season's major disappointments.

First-time director Barry Sonnenfeld never really gets past the skeletal plot, which plays like a collection of sitcom one-liners augmented by feature-film special effects — a combination that is stretched well beyond its limits as a 99-minute feature.

Caroline Thompson and Larry Wilson's script is one visual joke or pun after another based on the decidedly different family Charles Addams created in his New Yorker cartoons. The ABC tv series ran from 1964 to 1966.

The performers work gamely, but how many times are we expected to laugh at Morticia (Anjelica Huston) speaking wistfully about torture or Gomez (Raul Julia) imploring the disembodied digits Thing to "lend a hand?"

The disjointed plot turns on the long-missing Uncle Fester and an attempt by the family lawyer (Dan Hedaya) to cash in on Fester's absence — and gain access to Gomez's hidden fortune — by passing off the son of a loan-sharking client (Elizabeth Wilson) as Fester.

After becoming acclimated to the ooky-kooky-spooky clan, the son (Christopher Lloyd) grows increasingly fond of them, prompting his conspirators to engage in drastic tactics that provide added one-joke fodder but don't build toward a desperately needed narrative crescendo.

The filmmakers clearly waste a sequence, for example, in which the Addamses are forced to take real jobs after being evicted from their mansion. A manic dance number and party featuring the extended brood — including hairy Cousin It — falls equally flat.

Original TV series
THE ADDAMS FAMILY
ABC, Sept. 23, '64, 8:30 p.m.

Executive producer, David Levy. Producer, Nat Perrin. Directed by Arthur Hiller; writers, Ed James, Seaman Jacobs; music, Vic Mizzy. **30 MIN.** With: Carolyn James, John Astin, Jackie Coogan, Ken Weatherwax, Allyn Joslyn.

The only moment that lives up to the film's potential involves tots Wednesday (Christina Ricci) and Pugsley (Jimmy Workman) enacting a scene from "Hamlet" for the school talent show. They leave the assembled parents (with the exception of their own) agog and aghast. It's a taste of how the film might have lustily capitalized on the big-screen opportunity.

Huston is properly ethereal as Morticia, and Julia makes a swashbuckling Gomez, though neither can do much with the roles. Ricci is a perfect, somber Wednesday.

The special-effect highlight involves the wizardry that went into the creation of Thing, who never ventured out of his box during the TV show. Richard MacDonald's production design also creates gothic Addams abode (including a subterranean homage to "The Phantom of the Opera") that appears more true to Addams' original dark renderings.

Kudos as well to Marc Shaiman for the giddy score, which deftly incorporates snippets of the "Addams Family" theme. Too bad the film also leaves one listening repeatedly for another staple of the TV show — a much-needed laughtrack.
— *Brian Lowry*

CONFESION A LAURA
(CONFESSION TO LAURA)
(COLOMBIAN-CUBAN-SPANISH)

A Mélièse Producciones-Televisión Española (TVE)-Instituto Cubano del Arte e Industria Cinematográficos (ICAIC) production. Directed by Jaime Osorio Gómez. Screenplay, Alexandra Cardona Restrepo; camera (color), Adriano Moreno; editor, Nelson Rodríguez; music, Gonzalo Rubalcabar. Reviewed at Santafé de Bogotá Intl. Film Festival, Bogotá, Colombia, Oct. 15, 1991. Running time: **90 MIN.**
With: Vicky Hernández, Gustavo Londoño, María Cristina Galvez.

Colombian Jaime Osorio Gómez' first feature, "Confession to Laura," is a well-paced,

well-written drama that could find arthouse acceptance.

Action takes place during the turbulence of the "Bogotazo," when rioting erupted in Bogota following the assassination of presidential candidate Jorge Elíecer Gaitán on April 9, 1948.

The story concerns a cheerless middle-aged couple, Santiago and Josefina, who are virtual prisoners in their apartment because of the violence in the streets. The wife tries to block out reality by turning off the radio and baking a birthday cake for Laura, a spinster living across the street.

Santiago delivers the cake. But by now, snipers are on rooftops, shooting anyone below. It is impossible to return.

As the evening wears on, Santiago reveals the dissatisfied man inside. He confesses his frustrations to Laura: Rather than the ineffective government bureaucrat, he fancies himself an imposing figure, the potent man who sings and dances torrid tangos. Josefina watches their intimacy from across the way.

At times, the film is reminiscent of Ettore Scola's "A Special Day" as historical events intrude on individual intimacies, provoking catharses and change. The reality of the masses becomes the reality of the individual, developed through finely honed acting and a polished script that should attract international attention. — *Paul Lenti*

MONTRÉAL VU PAR ...
(MONTREAL SEXTET)
(CANADIAN)

A Cinéma Plus Distribution release (Canada) of a Cinémaginaire and Atlantis production in association with the National Film Board of Canada. Produced by Denise Robert (Cinémaginaire). Executive producers, Michel Houle, Peter Sussman (Atlantis). Directed by Denys Arcand, Michel Brault, Atom Egoyan, Jacques Leduc, Léa Pool, Patricia Rozema; editor, Michel Arcand; music, Claude Léveillé. Reviewed at Famous Players' Cinéma Imperial, Nov. 6, 1991. No MPAA Rating. Running time: **127 MIN.**

DESPERANTO
OR, LET SLEEPING GIRLS LIE

Written and directed by Patricia Rozema. Camera (color), Guy Dufaux; editor, Susan Shipton; music, Geneviéve Letarte, Diane Labrosse, Michel F. Coté; art direction, François Séguin.
With: Sheila McCarthy, Charlotte Laurier, Alexandre Hausvater, Robert Lepage, Denys Arcand, Genevieve Rioux.

LA TOILE DU TEMPS
(A CANVAS IN TIME)

Directed by Jacques Leduc. Screenplay, Marie-Carole de Beaumont, Leduc; camera (color), Pierre Letarte; editor, Pierre Bernier; music, Jean Derome; art direction, Louise Jobin.

With: Martin Drainville, Claude Blanchard, Michel Barrette, Pierrette Robitaille, Yves Jacques, Jean-Louis Millette, Normand Chouinard, Monique Mercure, Richard Fréchette, Suzanne Champagne.

LA DERNIERE PARTIE
(THE LAST PERIOD)

Directed by Michel Brault. Screenplay, Hélene Lebeau, Brault; camera (color), Jean Lépine; editor, Jacques Gagné; music, Osvaldo Montes; art direction, Anne Galéa.
With: Hélene Loiselle, Jean Mathieu.

EN PASSANT
(PASSING THROUGH)

Directed, written by Atom Egoyan. Camera (color and b&w), Eric Cayla; editor, Susan Shipton; music, Mychael Danna; art direction and costume design, Anne Pritchard.
With: Maury Chaykin, Arsinée Khanjian.

RISPONDETEMI

Directed, written by Léa Pool. Camera (color), Pierre Mignot; editor, Dominique Fortin; music, Jean Corriveau; art direction, Vianney Gauthier.
With: Anne Dorval, Sylvie Legault, Elyse Guilbault, Marcel Gauthier, Karine Mercier.

VUE D'AILLEURS
(SEEN FROM AFAR)

Directed by Denys Arcand. Screenplay, Paule Baillargeon; camera (color), Paul Sarossy; editor, Alain Baril; music, Yves Laferriere; art direction, Richard Paris, Linda del Rosario; assistant director, David Webb.
With: Domini Blythe, John Gilbert, Rémy Girard, Paule Baillargeon, Raoul Trujillo, Guylaine St-Onge.

In Montreal's version of "New York Stories," the whole is not necessarily greater than the sum of its parts. Five of the six vignettes are terrific, but the ensemble is too long and diverse to generate good b.o. beyond home turf, festivals or specialized venues.

"Montreal Sextet," a tribute to city's 350th anni in 1992, is an entertaining avant-garde travelogue helmed by the country's hottest directors. The shorts form a demanding compilation that changes gears every 15 or 20 minutes.

Patricia Rozema's engaging opener, "Desperanto, Or Let Sleeping Girls Lie," parodies an ordinary Toronto housewife desperately seeking *le joie de vivre* during a weekend fling.

Rozema ("I've Heard the Mermaids Singing") brilliantly uses subtitles to rescue the hopelessly unilingual housewife when she crashes a chic French party. In one scene, the housewife reads the subtitles herself to find out what's being said.

Feature bogs down in Jacques Leduc's historical short ("A Canvas in Time") before skating into Michel Brault's tragic love story, "The Last Period," shot during a hockey game at the Montreal Forum. Ace editing intercuts slap-

shots, goals and fights with a couple's own divorce game.

Cut to a generic tourist (played with cool curiosity by Maury Chakin) in "Passing Through," Atom Egoyan's chilling portrait of alienation in a foreign city. Communication occurs only through electronic devices: Chakin takes a walking tour of the city wearing a headset.

Pierre Mignot's roving camera provides the pic's most stunning footage of Montreal in Léa Pool's "Rispondetemi," about a woman who sees her life flash before her eyes after a car accident.

Denys Arcand follows tragedy with comedy in pic's most dynamic short, "Seen From Afar." Rémy Girard plays a bumbling consul-general who botches receiving-line introductions so thoroughly that viewers howl. The cocktail party parody gives way to drama as a guest recounts a sizzling, unforgettable encounter.

Pic will leave foreign viewers with the impression that Montreal is a city "where you can taste sensuality in the air" (per Egoyan's film); it's as full of sinful, tragic stories as any other metropolis. Pic achieves its goal.
— *Suzan Ayscough*

NORD
(NORTH)
(FRENCH)

A Bernard Verley presentation of a BVF/SGGC production. Produced by Bernard Verley. Directed by Xavier Beauvois. Screenplay, Beauvois, Arlette Langmann, Sophie Fillieres; camera (color), Fabio Conversi; editor, Agnes Guillemot; music, Philippe Chatiliez; sound, Rolly Belhassen; assistant director, Eric Sliman. Reviewed at Montreal World Film Festival, Aug. 24, 1991. Running time: **98 MIN.**
Madame Ferrand . . . . . . Bulle Ogier
The father . . . . Bernard Verley
Bertrand . . . . Xavier Beauvois
Fredo . . . . Jean-René Gossart

This static portrait of a man who destroys himself and his family through drinking marks the feature directorial debut of scripter Xavier Beauvois, who also plays the alcoholic's disturbed son. "Nord," an autobiographical tale, won the special jury prize and the international critics' award at the 1991 Montreal Fest.

Interminable establishing shot of a descending drawbridge sets the snail's pace. In a tiny town in France, a pharmacist by day is a

brute at night to his loving wife, distraught son and handicapped daughter.

Minimal dialogue and nonexistent soundtrack mark this dreary and realistic portrait of a booze hound. Pic wades through images of the splintered family staring at the tube and plodding silently through meals to avoid arguments.

After the father's drinking threatens his job, he reluctantly enters a detox center. Home life improves, but the mother and son, in the pic's only surprise scene, have an incestuous encounter. As with the pic's other crises, this relationship is never dealt with again.

Out of detox, the father hits the bottle again and unintentionally kills a child with the wrong prescription, leading him to commit suicide.

This sad tale provides little insight into a common sickness. But Beauvois' smooth performance lends credibility to the exercise. Lack of action and weak editing will cripple the pic in theatrical release.
— *Suzan Ayscough*

LA VIEILLE QUI MARCHAIT DANS LA MER
(THE OLD LADY WHO WADES IN THE SEA)
(FRENCH)

A C/FP release (Canada) of a President Films presentation of a Blue Dahlia/SFC Films/Antenne-2/J.M. Prods./Little Bear production. Executive producer, Gérard Jourd'Hui. Directed by Laurent Heynemann. Screenplay, Dominique Roulet, based on San-Antonio's book; camera (color), Robert Alazraki; sound, Michel Desrois; art direction, Valerie Grall. Reviewed at Toronto Film Festival, Sept. 9, 1991. Running time: **120 MIN.**
Lady M . . . . Jeanne Moreau
Pompilius . . . . Michel Serrault
Lambert . . . . Luc Thullier
Noémie . . . . Géraldine Danon

Jeanne Moreau gives the performance of a lifetime as an irresistible old rich bitch in "The Old Lady Who Wades in the Sea." Pic is a natural for French-lingo and Euro territories, but in the U.S. only serious arthouse audiences are ready for Moreau's challenging vision.

Lady M. is a selfish, vulgar con artist who mercilessly manipulates men and lives guiltlessly on the grift with her insipid partner

(Michel Serrault).

She becomes enthralled with a handsome beach boy (Luc Thullier) she meets while wading in the sea in Guadeloupe. Over her partner's mild protests, she invites the youth to their villa in the south of France, where she plans to make him her protégé.

The trio discovers the grift game has changed when they get caught heisting a princess' jewels. Lady M. degenerates into a pathetic old woman, jealous of her protégé's love for a beautiful young woman (Géraldine Danon) and oblivious to the devoted Serrault.

Helmer Laurent Heynemann tells a tough story to perfection. Acting is superb, and tech credits are excellent. Scenery is well used in both France and the Caribbean. Pic is a must-see for serious cinephiles.

— *Suzan Ayscough*

ALL I WANT FOR CHRISTMAS

A Paramount Pictures release. Produced by Marykay Powell. Executive producer, Stan Rogow. Directed by Robert Lieberman. Screenplay, Thom Eberhardt, Richard Kramer; camera (Technicolor), Robbie Greenberg; editors, Peter Berger, Dean Goodhill; music, Bruce Broughton; sound, Henry W. Garfield; production design, Herman Zimmerman; costume design, Nolan Miller; art direction, Randall McIlvain. Reviewed at Mann's National theater, Westwood, Nov. 2, 1991. MPAA rating: G. Running time: **92 MIN.**
Ethan . . . . Ethan Randall
Hallie . . . . Thora Birch
Catherine . . . . . Harley Jane Kozak
Michael . . . . Jamey Sheridan
Lillian . . . . Lillian Brooks

All any studio wants this Christmas is a hit, but Paramount will have to keep on wishing thanks to this package. Rushed through production by new studio topper Brandon Tartikoff, pic seems to have suffered most in the script development process, as story line comes close to desperation. Preseason release is wise, as this pic will get the heave-ho when the yuletide competition arrives.

Pic is about the fervent wish of 7-year-old Hallie (Thora Birch) and 13-year-old Ethan (Ethan Randall): They want their divorced parents reunited for Christmas. Hallie sojourns to Macy's to ask Santa Claus to grant the wish, and gangly, girl-crazy Ethan does his best to make the wish come true.

Seems Mom (Harley Jane Kozak) and Dad (Jamey Sheridan) are still in love, but the falling-out they had when Dad abandoned Wall Street to operate a diner seems insurmountable. Ethan figures if he can get his parents together on Christmas Eve, they'll reconcile.

Setup is touching, but this calculated fare is too timid to be convincing. It isn't much of a test for Kozak to choose between her dull fiance (Kevin Nealon) and the boyish, charismatic Sheridan. Nor is it much of a treat to watch the children ensnare their parents with an unlikely scheme and see how callously Nealon is brushed off.

Lauren Bacall gives a spirited portrayal as the children's grandmother, and Phil Leeds is slyly hilarious in a brief turn as a pet store owner. — *Amy Dawes*

SARASOTA FEST

BAR DES RAILS
(RAILWAY BAR)
(FRENCH)

A UGC release of a Titane-BC Films-UGC Image production in association with Canal Plus, Centre Nationale de la Cinematographie. Produced by Beatrice Caufman, Jean-Luc Ormieres. Directed, written by Cedric Kahn; camera (color), Antoine Roch. Reviewed at Venice Film Festival, Sept. 9, 1991. (In Sarasota [Fla.] French Film Festival.) Running time: **114 MIN.**
Marion . . . . Fabienne Babe
Richard . . . . Marc Vidal
Jeanne . . . . Brigitte Rouan
Alex . . . . Nicolas Ploux

A promising but overlong debut about a gloomy love affair between an inarticulate 16-year-old boy and a slightly older woman, "Railway Bar" could spark critical attention in France but seems unlikely to travel.

Director Cedric Kahn, one-time assistant film editor and co-screenwriter for Brigitte Rouan's "Overseas," has created a painful but truthful story of adolescent passion. Teen Marc Vidal lives in a housing project with his mother (Brigitte Rouan), a dressmaker. One of her clients is a woman of about 20 (Fabienne Babe) who lives nearby with her baby (no man in evidence).

The young mother falls hard for the surly teen, who can't return her love until it's too late.

Vidal is good as the clumsy, ardent and confused teen.

Tighter scripting and editing could have yielded a tough little film about the difficulties of teenage love, but the film runs out of steam long before the end.

Technical credits are fine, and Kahn may well emerge as an important director on the French scene if he tells his stories more succinctly.

— *David Stratton*

MON PÈRE CE HÉROS
(MY FATHER THE HERO)
(FRENCH)

An AMLF release of a Film Par Film/DD Prods./Orly Films/Paravision Intl./TF-1 Films Prod. co-production with the participation of Canal Plus. Produced by Jean-Louis Livi. Directed, written by Gérard Lauzier. Camera, Patrick Blossier; editor, Georges Klotz; music, François Bernheim; sound, Pierre Gamet; costume design, Gil Noir; set design, Christian Marti; production manager, Patrick Bordier; assistant director, Marc Jeny. Reviewed at Forum Horizon, Paris, Oct. 29, 1991 (in Sarasota [Fla.] French Film Festival). Running time: **103 MIN.**
André . . . . Gérard Depardieu
Véronique . . . . Marie Gillain
Benjamin . . . . Patrick Mille
Christelle . . . . . Catherine Jacob
Irina . . . . . . Charlotte de Turckheim

Gérard Lauzier's "Mon père ce héros," is a pleasant, lightweight comedy that makes the most of its one-joke premise.

After his g.f. leaves him, divorced Parisian dad André (Gérard Depardieu) picks up his 14-year-old daughter Véronique (newcomer Marie Gillian) for a Christmas jaunt to Mauritius. On the island, Véronique tries to impress a handsome windsurfer by telling him she's 18 and that Depardieu is her lover. Humor revolves around an innocent Depardieu behaving like a father while his fellow vacationers buy Véronique's story that he's really a dangerous gangster dying of a disease.

Once Véronique lets her dad in on the charade, he reluctantly does his best to appear menacing or at death's door, as required.

Gillain is right on the money as a teenager on the cusp of romance. Bulky Depardieu is agile in his athletically strenuous role, and Patrick Mille, as the object of Véronique's affections, is generally appealing.

Despite the beautiful setting, pic has a made-for-TV look.

— *Lisa Nesselson*

LONDON FEST

BREATHING UNDER WATER

A Periscope Prods. production in association with Australian Film Commission-Channel 4 (U.K.). Produced by Megan McMurchy. Directed, written by Susan Murphy Dermody. Camera (color), Erika Addis; editor, Diana Priest; music, Elizabeth Drake; sound (Dolby), John Dennison, Tony Vaccher; production design, Stephen Curtis; art direction, Michael Philips; costume design, Amanda Lovejoy; animation direction, Lee Whitmore; assistant director, Michael Faranda. Reviewed at London Film Festival, Nov. 9, 1991. Running time: **78 MIN.**
Beatrice . . . . . Anne Louise Lambert
Herman . . . . . . Kristoffer Greaves
Maeve . . . . Maeve Dermody
With: Pauline Chan, David Argue, Harry Gow, Elaine Gay, Gabriel Andrews.

"Breathing Under Water," the first feature by scripter and Sydney lecturer Susan Murphy Dermody, should prove a hit with card-carrying Greens and women's groups, but beyond that it's headed straight to tubesville.

Pic follows a young mother (Anne Louise Lambert) whose fears about the perilous state of the world lead her to a journey of the imagination into "Pluto's Republic." Accompanied by a mysterious cab driver (Kristoffer Greaves), she and her daughter (Maeve Dermody, the helmer's daughter) descend into Sydney's nether world.

Stops include a museum, a junkyard and a mortuary. At the pic's end, they stop at a sunny hill outside the city, where moppets romp in a consciously naive, optimistic finale.

Repeated theme is that for the world to survive, suppressed qualities like the feminine and the irrational must be unfettered.

There's no faulting the sincerity of Dermody's feelings, but she fails to develop her ideas.

Technically, pic is top-drawer, with neat 35m lensing by Erika Addis and well-integrated animation by Lee Whitmore. The mortuary scene, which shows a brain removed from a cadaver, provoked some shocked walkouts at the London fest world preem.

— *Derek Elley*

WHO NEEDS A HEART

A Black Audio Film Collective production in association with Channel 4 (U.K.) and ZDF (Germany). Produced by Lina Gopaul. Directed by John Akomfrah. Written by Akomfrah, Eddie George; camera (16m color), Nancy Schiesari; editor, Brand Thumim; production design, Paul Cheetham; sound, Trevor Mathison. Reviewed at British Film Institute, London, Oct. 25, 1991, at London Film Festival. Running time: **79 MIN.**
Faith . . . . Caroline Burghard
Sydney . . . . Treva Ettiene
Abigail . . . . Ruth Gemmell
Naomi . . . . . . Caroline Lee Johnson
Louis . . . . Kwabena Nanso
Millie . . . . Cassie MacFarlane
Jack . . . . Ian Reddington
Simmi . . . . Mo Sesay
Dominic . . . . Jay Villiers

A look at black consciousness in '60s London, "Who Needs a Heart" is a provocative blend of fact and fiction. Pic will be a nostalgia trip for some and an education for others. Theatrical prospects are limited, but film could pump some box office blood out of current high profile for black pics.

Complex structure begins in 1972 with British black power icon Michael X, a.k.a. Michael Abdul Malik. Film then flashes back to 1963, intercutting docu footage with a group of swingers whose lives are affected by the changing social fabric.

Sexual and political tensions eventually fracture the group. Pic ends with the news of Michael X's hanging.

Pic is confidently paced. Helmer John Akomfrah, who debuted in 1986 with the race-problem docu "Handsworth Songs," digs up some pointed footage.

Tech credits are smooth, with handsome 16m lensing by Nancy Schiesari and evocative use of colors by production designer Paul Cheetham for the main suburban location. Trevor Mathison's wild collage of sounds is another plus. — *Derek Elley*

THE REFRIGERATOR

An Avenue D Films production. Produced by Christopher Oldcorn. Written and directed by Nicholas Tony Jacobs. Camera (color), Paul Gibson; editor, P.J. Pesce, Suzanne Pillsbury, Oldcorn; music, Don Peterkofsy, Chris Burke, Adam Roth; sound, Thomas Szabolcs; art direction, Therese Deprez. Reviewed at Viareggio Noir Festival, June 24, 1991. (In London Film Festival.) Running time: **85 MIN.**
Eileen Bateman . . . . . . Julia Mueller
Steve Bateman . . . . . David Simonds
Juan the plumber . . . . . Angel Caban
Tanya . . . . Phyllis Sanz

A refrigerator door is the gateway to hell in first-time director Nicholas Tony Jacobs' smart, quirky horror spoof. Slick-looking production delivers its thrills with enough laughs to promise a cult following. Vid sales could be brisk.

Titular refrigerator is a classic '63 Norge. Newlyweds (and new New Yorkers) Julia Mueller and David Simonds move into a Lower East Side walkup where the fridge already has eaten the previous tenants.

Succumbing to the strange forces in the fridge, hubby tries to coerce his actress spouse into a traditional wife-and-motherhood role. Helped by the plumber (Angel Caban), a sensitive Bolivian flamenco dancer, wife sets out to destroy the appliance.

Acting is consistently good, and the tongue-in-cheek script is delivered with sincerity and brisk pacing. Caban deserves special mention as the caring plumber.

Screenplay cleverly sends up American values while developing the horror theme. The refrigerator is a witty metaphor for the evils of consumerism and greed, but the message is never heavy-handed.

Super-low budget film has a much pricier look. Jacobs shows a sure hand in setting up the suspenseful premise. Horror effects are kept to a minimum and are unrealistic enough not to spoil the fun for the squeamish.
— *Catherine Ventura*

DIPLOMATIC IMMUNITY
(CANADIAN)

An Astral Films (Canada) release of a Metropolis production, in association with Telefilm Canada, Ontario Film Development Corp., National Film Board and CBC. Executive producers, Michael Donovan, Lyn Goleby. Produced by Sturla Gunnarsson, Steve Lucas. Directed by Gunnarsson. Screenplay, Lucas; camera (Agfacolor), Harald Ortenburger; editor, Jeff Warren; music, Jonathan Goldsmith; sound, Jose Garcia. Reviewed at Montreal Film Festival, Aug. 28, 1991. (In London Film Festival.) Running time: **93 MIN.**
Kim Dades . . . . . . Wendel Meldrum
Les Oberfell . . . . . . Michael Riley
Sara Roldan . . . . . . Ofelia Medina
Jack Budyansky . . . . Michael Hogan

In this well-meaning but unconvincing melodrama, a Canadian diplomat gets involved with dispossessed peasants in El Salvador. Though "Diplomatic Immunity" has its mo-ments, Sturla Gunnarsson's first feature is merely routine.

Wendel Meldrum's character is presented as a dull, serious young career diplomat sent to El Salvador. She discovers that a Canadian housing project for the poor has been taken over by the military.

After taking time out to have an affair with ugly American Michael Riley, the diplomat befriends a church worker-commune leader Ofelia Medina. Pic's denouement is dramatically effective but extremely illogical.

Lensed in Mexico, the pic has neither the action to attract a mainstream audience nor the qualities to appeal to more serious patrons. Meldrum does her best with an inadequately scripted role, while Riley plays a strictly one-dimensional heavy.

Pic is technically okay, with convincing production design and solid camerawork.
— *David Stratton*

NOUVEAU FEST

ROUGH SKETCH OF A SPIRAL
(JAPANESE-DOCU-16M)

A Herald Ace presentation of a Bud Co. production. Produced by Kunio Takeshige. Executive producer, Nobusugu Tsubomi. Directed by Yasufumi Kojima. Camera (color, 16m), Hedeyuki Dobashi. Reviewed at Montreal Cinema Nouveau fest, Oct. 26, 1991. Running time: **104 MIN.**

Yasufumi Kojima's inquisitive feature debut is a socially taboo docu about a budding male homosexual community in Osaka. Naive point-and-shoot format gathers both candid confessions and group dynamics. Pic likely will resurface in gay film fests where it will be heralded for confronting stereotypes.

Kojima interviews various celibate, monogamous and polygamous gays, and an exceptionally androgynous transvestite.

Group's goal is to write, act and produce a play (called "Rough Sketch of a Spiral") which explains why they feel marginalized in a rigidly ordered society.

Cinema verité style documents the group's attempt to form a gay community that indirectly says as much about Japan as it does about the group itself.

Content ultimately triumphs over style. Amateur tech credits and roughly edited footage will unfortunately marginalize a docu which refreshingly presents three-dimensional homosexuals.
— *Suzan Ayscough*

LE CRI DU LÉZARD
(CRY OF THE LIZARD)
(FRENCH-SWISS)

A Vega Film presentation of a Vega Film production. Directed by Bertrand Theubet. Screenplay, Theubet, based on Alexandre Voisard's novel "L'Année Des Treize Lunes"; camera (color), Jean-Bernard Menoud. Reviewed at Montreal Nouveau Cinema fest, Oct. 26, 1991. Running time: **91 MIN.**
Clo . . . . Andréa Ferreol
Raton . . . . Yannis Schweri
Léonie . . . . Juliette Brac
Nadia . . . . Anouk Grinberg
Angelo . . . . Marc Citti
Jim . . . . Yves Aubry

Despite a warning that "disaster will strike in the year of the 13 moons," a gang of youths hit the road toward the Pyrenees in search of fictitious treasure. Their meeting with a young runaway (Yannis Schweri) and an older woman (Andréa Ferreol) does little to spike this dull road movie.

Pic's most interesting roles revolve around a 14-year-old boy's fascination with a mature woman. At first, she mothers the sexually curious teen, then succumbs to his advances and eventually reassumes the parental role, returning him safely to his suspicious family.

The thwarted treasure hunt disappoints the other youths, whose adventure ends when the car breaks down and their love affairs flounder.

Ferreol is terrific as the frustrated middle-aged woman. Tech credits are good, but this pointless adventure has little prospect outside French-lingo territories.
— *Suzan Ayscough*

PUERTO RICO

JERICO
(JERICHO)
(VENEZUELAN)

A Thalia Prods. and Foncine production. Directed, written by Luis Alberto Lamata. Camera (color), Andrés Agusti; editor and sound, Mario Nazoa; music, Federico Gaitorno; art director, Aureliano Alfonzo. Reviewed at Puerto Rico Intl. Film Festival, San Juan, Nov. 1, 1991. Running time: **90 MIN.**
With: Cosme Cortázar, Francis Nueda, Alexander Milic, Doris Diaz.

Luis Alberto Lamata makes an impressive debut with his first feature. "Jerico," coupled with next year's 500th anni of America's discovery, should generate international interest through its revisionist view of the Spanish conquest of the New World. As seen through the eyes of a Dominican friar, its sensitive pro-Indian stance finds a parallel in such recent world ventures as "Black Robe" and "Dances With Wolves."

The story chronicles the experiences of Friar Santiago (Cosme Cortázar), who accompanies a group of Spanish conquistadors to South America to bring God to the people. But he is the one who changes when confronted with the greed and cannibalism among the "civilized" Spaniards.

His faith is tried at every turn: His first attempt to say Mass, for example, finds the Indians at first curious before ignoring him completely. He is forcefully inducted into a cocaine ceremony, later shedding his habits and becoming a member of the tribe before he is eventually "rescued" by the Spaniards.

Pic is fascinating both as an anthropological study and in its comparison of the noble Indians with the brutal Spaniards.

Acting is strong all around. Technically, the film is also stunning, and Andrés Agusti's rich camerawork re-creates this lost world.
— *Paul Lenti*

AN AMERICAN TAIL: FIEVEL GOES WEST
(ANIMATED)

A Universal release of a Steven Spielberg/Amblin Entertainment (Amblimation Studios) presentation. Produced by Spielberg, Robert Watts. Executive producers, Frank Marshall, Kathleen Kennedy, David Kirschner. Directed by Phil Nibbelink, Simon Wells. Screenplay, Flint Dille, based on Charles Swenson's story & characters created by Kirschner; in color (Rank prints); supervising editor, Nick Fletcher; music, James Horner; songs, Horner, Will Jennings; art director, Neil Ross; layout supervisor, Mark Marren; supervising animators, Nancy Beiman, Kristof Serrand, Rob Stevenhagen; special effects supervisor, Scott Santoro; background supervisor, Shelley Page; sound (Dolby), Charlie Ajar Jr., Michael C. Casper, Daniel Heahy, Thomas Gerard; associate producer, Stephen Hickner; casting, Nancy Nayor, Valerie McCaffrey. Reviewed at Universal Studios, North Hollywood, Nov. 5, 1991. MPAA Rating: G. Running time: **74 MIN.**
VOICES:
Fievel Mousekewitz . . Phillip Glasser
Wylie Burp . . . . James Stewart
Mama Mousekewitz . . . . Erica Yohn
Tanya Mousekewitz . . Cathy Cavadini
Papa Mousekewitz . Nehemiah Persoff
Tiger . . . . Dom DeLuise
Miss Kitty . . . . Amy Irving
Cat R. Waul . . . . John Cleese
T.R. Chula . . . . Jon Lovitz

Complete with legendary James Stewart voicing broken-down lawdog Wylie Burp, "An American Tail: Fievel Goes West" is an amiable sequel to the 1986 animated smash featuring the Russian immigrant mouse. Box office should be good, but the Universal pic faces extremely tough competition from Disney's "Beauty and the Beast."

The story picks up the plucky Fievel and family living in grim, turn-of-the-century Bronx, menaced by omnipresent cats. Dark and gothic opening section is full of skewed angles and frenetic cutting capturing the nightmarish feeling of being a tiny creature in a metropolis.

The expansive shift to the Old West is welcome, as is the slowing of the pace to accommodate the relaxed, drawling and almost comatose personality of Fievel's hero/mentor Wylie Burp. Stewart's droll characterization is a further refinement of his Wyatt Earp caricature in John Ford's "Cheyenne Autumn" and his lazy Sheriff McCabe in Ford's "Two Rode Together."

"Fievel Goes West" cleverly draws on the oft-expressed thought that the mythic West was largely an immigrant's wide-eyed dream of what America should be, in opposition to hellish big-city reality and the old country left behind. And like all big-screen immigrant sagas, pic carries an emotional undercurrent of escape and discovery.

Phillip Glasser's sweet rendition of the mouse's voice is a major asset, as are the voice parts of Dom DeLuise, as Fievel's scene-stealing companion, a scaredy-cat who turns brave; John Cleese, as the unctuously villainous Cat R. Waul; Amy Irving, as the brassy saloon entertainer Miss Kitty; and Cathy Cavadini, Nehemiah Persoff and Erica Yohn as the rest of the Mousekewitz family.

There isn't much of a plot to speak of, however, and scripter Flint Dille doesn't quite explain why Cleese has to lure a colony of mice all the way west from N.Y. to entrap them. Nor is it entirely clear how the final confrontation with Cleese is resolved, and Fievel's family doesn't have enough to do in the story once it moves west.

But the Western riffs are irresistible as Wylie Burp teaches his old tricks to Tiger and Fievel, and the film's visual style is attractive and supple in the hands of directors Phil Nibbelink and Simon Wells and supervising animators Nancy Beiman, Kristof Serrand and Rob Stevenhagen.

None of the James Horner-Will Jennings songs measures up to the previous film's hit "Somewhere Out There," and the showpiece song, "Dreams to Dream," is given oddly perfunctory treatment. But Horner's score effectively employs Western themes, and the inclusion of the theme from the "Rawhide" vidseries is amusing.

And any film that ends with Stewart (even in voice only) imparting the meaning of life against a Western sunset is worth a glimpse by adult viewers as well as kids. Now if only Stewart could be lured in front of the camera again.
— *Joseph McBride*

OXEN
(THE OX)
(SWEDISH)

A Sandrews presentation of a Jean Doumanian, Sweetland Films production. Co-producers, Sandrews Filminstitutet-Sveriges Television, Kanal-1-Nordisk Film Production-Nordisk Film & TV Fund-Josephson & Nykvist. Produced by Doumanian. Executive producer, Jaqui Safra. Executive co-producer, Klas Olofsson. Directed by Sven Nykvist. Screenplay, Nykvist, Lasse Summanen; camera (color), Nykvist; editor, Summanen; production design, Peter Hoimark; costumes, Inger Pehrsson; sound, Bo Persson, Stefan Ljungberg, Jan Erik Lundberg. Reviewed at Sandrews screening room, Stockholm, Oct. 9, 1991. Running time: **91 MIN.**
With: Stellan Skarsgard, Ewa Froling, Lennart Hjulstrom, Max von Sydow, Liv Ullmann, Bjorn Granath, Erland Josephson, Rikard Wollf, Helge Jordal.

Cinematographer Sven Nykvist's first directorial effort since 1978 tells a simple story set in 1860s poverty-stricken Sweden. Starring Sweden's best-known actors, beautiful pic is a natural for arthouses and fests around the world. Film has been selected as Sweden's entry in the foreign-language film Oscar competition.

"The Ox" is based on a true story, told from generation to generation, which Nykvist has wanted to film since first hearing it as a child. This tale of the Swedes who stayed behind and faced famine when others emigrated to the U.S. was told from the emigrants' viewpoint in Jan Troell's 1970s epics "The Emigrants" and "The New Land," which starred Max von Sydow and Liv Ullmann, leads in "The Ox." They are part of a prestigious cast of actors, most of whom closely identified with Ingmar Bergman.

"The Ox" tells the simple and straightforward story of a poverty-stricken family in southern Sweden. Helge (Stellan Skarsgard) in desperation kills one of his employer's oxen and is sentenced to life in prison.

The priest (von Sydow) who turned him in is shocked by the harshness of the punishment and begins a campaign to get the sentence reduced. Meanwhile, Helge's wife (Ewa Froling) does anything she can to survive, including selling her body to a stranger offering food to her and her child.

Master cinematographer Nykvist has depicted the Swedish landscape during changing seasons in hauntingly beautiful images. At times they may be even too lyrical, diluting the harsh realities of poverty.

These sequences contrast effectively with the prison-bound scenes. When Helge is locked up, his growing desperation is conveyed in the darkening colors. The prison scenes are framed in order to maximize claustrophobia, and their surrealistic quality is reminiscent of Hieronymus Bosch paintings.

Acting is very good, with a special mention to von Sydow as the guilt-ridden priest. Tech credits are fine, but it's a pity Nykvist has chosen such a familiar piece of music, from Edvard Grieg's "Peer Gynt," to accompany the picture. What is heard during the final sequence almost parodies happy-ending music in U.S. films. — *Gunnar Rehlin*

DER VERDACHT
(THE SUSPICION)
(GERMAN)

A DEFA Studios Babelsberg film in cooperation with WDR (Cologne). Produced by Volkmar Leweck. Directed by Frank Beyer. Screenplay, Ulrich Plenzdorf, adapted from Volker Braun's story, "Unvollendete Geschichte"; camera (color), Peter Ziesche; music, Günther Fischer; sets, Alfred Hirschmeier, Lothar Kuhn. Reviewed at International cinema, Berlin, Oct. 10, 1991. Running time: **99 MIN.**
Karin . . . . Christiane Heinrich
Frank . . . . Nikolaus Gröbe
Also with: Michael Gwisdek, Christine Schorn, Marie-Anne Fliegel, Ulrike Krumbiegel.

Directed by vet DEFA helmer Frank Beyer, respectable tale of young love destroyed by the Communist Party may have better prospects east of Germany than west.

Pic is set in East Germany in the mid-'70s. Karin (Christiane Heinrich) is warned not to see her b.f. (Nikolaus Gröbe) anymore, but her obedient breakup doesn't last. Apprenticing at a newspaper, she is visited by party officials and threatened.

Eastern Europeans should be able to strongly identify with the tale, but despite a solid storyline and nice acting in supporting roles, topliner Heinrich lacks the magnetism needed to appear in every scene. Gröbe as the b.f. shows promise as a new young East German actor in his second major role this year.

Tech credits are good.
— *Rebecca Lieb*

AFRAID OF THE DARK
(BRITISH-FRENCH)

A Fine Line (U.S.) and Rank Film Distributors (U.K.) release of a Sovereign Pictures presentation of a Telescope Films (U.K.)-Films Ariane-Cine Cinq (France) production. Produced by Simon Bosanquet. Executive producers, Jean Nachbaur, Sylvaine Sainderichin. Directed, written by Mark Peploe. Camera (Technicolor), Bruno de Keyzer; editor, Scott Thomas; music, Richard Hartley; production design, Caroline Amies; art direction, Stephen Scott; costume design, Louise Stjernsward; sound (Dolby), Tony Jackson, Mark Auguste, Robin O'Donoghue; assistant director, Jonathan Benson; casting, Lucy Boulting. Reviewed at Century preview theater, London, Nov. 12, 1991. (In London Film Festival.) Running time: **91 MIN.**
Frank . . . . James Fox
Miriam . . . . Fanny Ardant
Tony Dalton . . . . . . Paul McGann
Rose . . . . Clare Holman
Dan Burns . . . . . Robert Stephens
Lucy Trent . . . . . Susan Wooldridge
Lucas . . . . Ben Keyworth

Bernardo Bertolucci scripter Mark Peploe makes an ambitious bow behind the lens with "Afraid of the Dark," a tricky mix of slasher movie and psychodrama that's strong on tease but weak on final delivery. Initial biz could be strong, but legs later may turn to jelly. Pic was the closing night attraction at the London Film Festival.

Double-headed plot centers on an 11-year-old (Ben Keyworth), whose dad (James Fox) is a cop and mother (Fanny Ardant) is blind. With a sicko terrorizing their west London nabe, kid is concerned for the safety of mom's blind friend (Clare Holman).

Worse, he reckons the razorman is someone he knows — the local window cleaner, locksmith or photog (Paul McGann), who has a sideline in nudie portraits.

At that exact halfway point, Peploe springs his main surprise, and rest of pic has trouble building up a matching head of steam. But for pure technique (and Hitchcock/Michael Powell homework), Peploe can't be faulted. One small pleasure is pic's patchwork portrait of an abstracted community, with fragments of lives half-glimpsed through windows and the kid's prying telescope.

As the scarily introverted boy, young Keyworth is on the money throughout. Holman, so good as the elder sister in "Let Him Have It," handles her key role with

style and shading, well matched by McGann. Fox is surprisingly flat as the moppet's dad, and Ardant (who only seems to be there because of French co-prod coin) makes a linguistically shaky British bow in a smallish part.

Peploe gets strong technical support from all departments, with handsome lensing by Bruno de Keyzer and a subtle sound mix by Robin O'Donoghue. Richard Hartley's score is mostly straight atmosphere.
— *Derek Elley*

LOSER

An LTM production. Produced by Steven Deshle. Executive producer, Mike O'Connor. Directed, written by Erik Burke. Camera (Technicolor, 16m), John Shepphird; editor, Burke; music, Joey Harrow, Matthew Fritz; production design, Ruth Ammon; art direction, Rowena Rowling; costume design, Julie Engelsman; sound, Diane Robinson; line producer, Douglas Katz. Reviewed at London Film Festival, Nov. 8, 1991. Running time: **83 MIN.**
Hank . . . . Brendan Kelly
Mike . . . . John Salemmo
Peggy . . . . Bernice DeLeo
Megan . . . . Nadine Miral
Dana . . . . Wendy Adams

An uneven comedy about a dude who wins a New York lottery, "Loser" won't win any ducats beyond fest outings. Low-budgeter has its moments, but they're fleeting.

Booted out by g.f. Bernice DeLeo, Brendan Kelly buys a lottery ticket on a whim. When he finds he's got a winning number worth $200 million, he paints the town with best pal John Salemmo, en route discovering DeLeo being wined and dined by a toffee-nosed Brit (Julian Stone).

The pals take up with party girls (Nadine Miral, Wendy Adams), and, as word of his lucky score spreads, friends and freeloaders flock to his Brooklyn apartment. Pic ends with an ironic, but not unexpected, twist.

Former slugger (and William Shatner look-alike) Kelly hits the right breezy notes as a king for a night. He's well supported by Salemmo as his ulcerous buddy and Miral as a good-time looker. Producer Steven Deshler puts in a neat cameo as a coke pusher.

Main problem is the stop-go script, which flunks as ironic comedy and isn't helped by some awkward delivery and choppy cutting. Joey Harrow and Matther Fritz's sassy musical score papers over some of the cracks and mostly keeps things moving. John Shepphird's 16m lensing is

workmanlike.

Erik Burke pic, first outing by Guerilla Films, was made as partial fulfillment of a master's degree at Columbia University.
— *Derek Elley*

LONDON KILLS ME
(BRITISH)

A Fine Line (U.S.) and Rank Film Distributors (U.K.) release of a Polygram-Working Title production, in association with Film Four Intl. (Intl. sales: Manifesto Film Sales.) Produced by Tim Bevan. Executive producer, Graham Bradstreet. Co-producer, Judy Hunt. Directed, written by Hanif Kureishi. Camera (color), Ed Lachman; editor, Jon Gregory; original music, Mark Springer, Sarah Sarhandi; music coordinator, Charlie Gillett; production design, Stuart Walker; costume design, Amy Roberts; sound (Dolby), Albert Bailey, Sue Baker; associate producer, David Gothard; assistant director, Benita Allen; casting, Joyce Nettles. Reviewed at London Film Festival, Nov. 19, 1991. Running time: **107 MIN.**
Clint . . . . Justin Chadwick
Muffdiver . . . . . Steven Mackintosh
Sylvie . . . . Emer McCourt
Dr. Bubba . . . . Roshan Seth
Headley . . . . Fiona Shaw
Hemingway . . . . Brad Dourif
Burns . . . . Tony Haygarth
Tom Tom . . . . Stevan Rimkus
Lily . . . . Eleanor David
Stone . . . . Alun Armstrong
Also with: Nick Dunning, Naveen Andrews, Garry Cooper.

Hanif Kureishi's "London Kills Me," a flabby slice of London street life among pushers and hustlers, drags itself across the screen for 107 minutes and collapses in a dramatic mess on the sidewalk. Biz looms bleak.

First directorial outing by the Anglo-Pakistani scripter of "My Beautiful Laundrette" and "Sammy and Rosie Get Laid" shows the same interest in London's culturally mixed sub-life, sans anti-Thatcherism subtext.

Main character is the Candide-like Clint (Justin Chadwick), who hangs out with a group led by small-time dealer Muffdiver (Steven Mackintosh). To raise the cash for a job in a swank local eatery, Clint joins in Muffdiver's plans to go big time and helps himself to latter's hidden stash. He's also got eyes for Muffdiver's heroin-hooked g.f. Sylvie (Emer McCourt).

Loose plot trawls in a host of other characters, including a sex-obsessed liberal (Fiona Shaw), an Indian (Roshan Seth) who runs a Sufi center and Clint's mom (Eleanor David), who lives in the country with a thuggish, middle-aged Elvis freak (Alun Armstrong).

What was obviously meant as an ironic look at lost souls in '90s London rapidly blurs into a string of undramatic incidents. Pic recalls free-living late '60s items, but without their buzz and color. Result, under Kureishi's unfocused helming, is drab.

Stronger leads might have rescued the project, but both Chadwick and Mackintosh lack the presence and delivery to bring Kureishi's self-consciously hip script to life.

The women score better. Irish thesp McCourt, excellent in "Riff-Raff," shows she has talent to spare but is mostly consigned to a giggling part. Shaw and David show what the film could have been with stronger down-the-line casting. Brad Dourif cameos strongly as the eatery boss.

Technically, pic is okay. Amy Roberts' costumes are characterful, and the lively musical soundtrack gives the opening reels some bounce. Locations in and around London's Notting Hill Gate and Portobello Road have a verismo feel. — *Derek Elley*

THE LOST LANGUAGE OF CRANES
(BRITISH-16m)

A BBC Television production in association with WNET New York. Produced by Ruth Caleb. Executive producers, Mark Shivas, Kimberly Myers (WNET). Directed by Nigel Finch. Screenplay, Sean Mathias, based on David Leavitt's novel; camera (color), Remi Adefarasin; editor, Sue Wyatt; music, Julian Walstall; sound, John Pritchard; production design, Bruce Macadie; costume design, James Keast. Reviewed at London Film Festival (British Cinema section), Nov. 14, 1991. Running time: **87 MIN.**

Owen Benjamin	Brian Cox
Rose Benjamin	Eileen Atkins
Philip Benjamin	Angus MacFadyen
Eliot Abrahams	Corey Parker
Geoffrey Lane	Rene Auberjonois
Derek Moulthorp	John Schlesinger
Jerene Parks	Cathy Tyson
Robin Bradley	Ben Daniells
Winston Penn	Nigel Whitmey

A knockout adaptation of David Leavitt's gay outing novel, "The Lost Language of Cranes" looks set to stir up controversy in whatever medium it's shown. High-quality production by pubcaster BBC (in its Screen Two series) will find a ready berth at fests but also could reach out to a somewhat broader audience.

A middle-aged academic (Brian Cox) is taken to haunting gay movie theaters, unbeknownst to his book editor wife (Eileen At-

kins). One day, their son (Angus MacFadyen) announces he's homosexual. Mother appears to take the news on the chin, but for dad it's the catalyst to his own slow but steady outing.

Pic shifts the original story's N.Y. Jewish setting to nondenominational, suburban London, to good effect. Sean Mathias' neatly paced, humor-flecked script takes the conventions of Brit living room drama and turns them on their head with the gay subject matter.

Also worked in — in grainy, dreamlike sequences — is the news story of a 3-year-old abandoned by his mother and who has developed a sign language of his own. Subtext of a parallel world of communication between gays is present but not labored.

Pic's other strength is the offhandedness of the male bonding sequences. Bedroom scenes are shot and played with the ease of hetero equivalents, and nudity is unblinking but natural in the context. (Producers have covered their bases with a "Jockey shorts" version for the U.S.)

Cox is tops as the middle-ager coming to terms with his sexuality. As the up-front son who's first bruised and then rebounds, MacFadyen comes over strongly. Atkins in many ways gives the strongest perf, maintaining an iron dignity.

Other players are solid, although Cathy Tyson ("Mona Lisa") is wasted in an underwritten part as one of MacFadyen's friends. John Schlesinger and Rene Auberjonois pop up in lively cameos.

Remi Adefarasin's 16m lensing shows its TV origins in too much tight framing but is sharp and clear. Other tech credits are fine.

Pic is skedded to take part in anuary's Sundance fest, and other bookings seem certain. Stateside tube exposure will be via PBS, as WNET New York came in at a late stage with finishing coin.

— *Derek Elley*

SCHACKO KLAK
(LUXEMBOURG)

A Samsa Film production. Produced by Paul Kieffer. Co-directed by Frank Hoffmann and Kieffer. Screenplay, Frank Feitler, Kieffer, based on Roger Manderscheid novel; camera (color), Jean-Louis Sonzogni, Jos Andries; editor, Nathalie Bosson; music, Marcel Wengler; art direction, Véronique Sacrez; sound, Thomas Gauder. Reviewed at Montreal World Film Festi-

val, Sept. 1, 1991. (In London, San Sebastian film fests.) Running time: **85 MIN.**

With: Michele Clees, Paul Greish, André Jung, Steve Karier, Josiane Peiffer, Claude Wagner, Shirin Fabeck.

First 35m feature out of Luxembourg is about a family's ordeal during Nazi occupation, told through youngster Christian Knapp. A relentless violin soundtrack overwhelms an otherwise charming film.

Christian and his young friends frolic in the countryside until nightmarish events begin, neighbors disappear and their world is on edge.

Tech credits are good. Intentions are noble. Luxembourg has produced a film that declares its innocence in World War II horrors with a personal vision.

— *Suzan Ayscough*

THE DARK WIND

A Seven Arts (U.S.) and Guild Film Distributors (U.K.) release of a Dark Wind Prods.-Northfork Motion Picture Co. production. Produced by Patrick Markey. Executive producers, Robert Redford, Bonni Lee. Co-producer, Richard Erdman. Directed by Errol Morris. Screenplay, Eric Bergren, Neal Jimenez, Mark Horowitz, based on Tony Hillerman's novel; camera (Technicolor; Duart prints), Stefan Czapsky; editor, Freeman Davies; music, Michel Colombier; production design, Ted Bafaloukos; art direction, John Reinhart; set decoration, Corey Kaplan; costume design, Eugenie Bafaloukos; sound (Dolby), David Brownlow; special sound effects, Randy Thom; associate producers, Allen Alsobrook, Steve Poley; assistant director, Peter Gries; stunt coordinator, Dan Bradley; 2nd unit director, Steve Perry; casting, Ellen Chenoweth. Reviewed at London Film Festival, Nov. 16, 1991. Running time: **109 MIN.**

Officer Jim

Chee	Lou Diamond Phillips
Lt. Joe Leaphorn	Fred Ward
Albert (Cowboy)	
Dashee	Gary Farmer
Jake West	John Karlen
Mr. Archer	Lance Baker
Larry	Gary Basaraba
Edna Nezzie	Arlene Bowman
Gail Pauling	Jane Loranger
Taylor	James Koots
Lomatewa	Neil Kayquoptewa

"The Dark Wind" is a good-looking version of Tony Hillerman's 1982 cult policier that goes for the same slow burn. Lou Diamond Phillips toplines strongly as the Navajo flatfoot, but moody pic will need extra-careful handling and plenty of word-of-mouth to succeed beyond specialized situations.

Corkscrew plot, set on an Arizona reservation divided between Navajo and Hopi, warms up grad-

ually with the discovery of a Navajo corpse with its palms and soles flayed. Then the cop, on tedious night watch by a disputed water-windmill, finds a crashed airplane with two dead coke smugglers on board.

Story fans out as the feds turn up. Phillips is warned off the case by his superior (Fred Ward), and the main smuggler's young widow (Jane Loranger) comes looking for justice. All the locals, including store owner John Karlen, act mighty suspicious.

Beneath the Native American background lurks a straightforward crime yarn. Although the screenplay ditches much of the novel's detail, pic's still a brave attempt at genre variation.

Despite the fact that most of the action is purely police procedure, the combination of Phillips' mystical voiceovers, Michel Colombier's atmospheric score and Stefan Czapsky's striking lensing of the ruddy mesa landscape keeps the mood taut.

Phillips gives an impressively contained performance, with a nice line of deadpan humor. He's surrounded by plenty of strong playing: Ward dependable as his knowing boss, Gary Farmer ulcerous as his Hopi colleague and Karlen menacingly friendly as the store owner.

Technically, pic is classy, with a subtle Dolby soundtrack by David Brownlow and Randy Thom. — *Derek Elley*

TURIN FEST

JUMPIN' AT THE BONEYARD

A 20th Century Fox release of a Kasdan Pictures presentation of a Boneyard production. Produced by Nina Sadowsky, Lloyd Goldfine. Executive producer, Lawrence Kasdan. Directed, written by Jeff Stanzler. Camera (color), Lloyd Steven Goldfine; editor, Christopher Tellefsen; music, Steve Postel; art direction, Caroline Wallner; sound, Catherine Benedek. Reviewed at Turin Intl. Young Cinema Festival competition, Nov. 9, 1991. Running time: **103 MIN.**

Manny	Tim Roth
Dan	Alexis Arquette
Jeanette	Danitra Vance
Mom	Kathleen Chalfant
Mr. Simpson	Samuel L. Jackson
Taxi driver	Luiz Guzman
Cathy	Elizabeth Bracco

A raw but promising debut feature, "Jumpin' at the Boneyard" makes a provocative play at taking auds down the blind alley of drug addiction without cushioning its blows. Indie project nurtured by Lawrence Kasdan ultimately falls short of its good intentions, so biz is unlikely to be jumpin', though strong cast of up-and-comers may spark interest. Fox release will receive U.S. debut at the Sundance fest in January.

On the emotional skids after a messy divorce, Tim Roth surprises crackhead brother Alexis Arquette and g.f. Danitra Vance as they're breaking into his apartment. After a violent initial reaction, Roth makes a personal crusade of his brother's salvation.

Arquette gets cleaned up and forced into a tearful con rontation with his mother en route to a detox clinic, but tragedy cuts the journey short and any glimmer of hope is left by the wayside.

Like Gus Van Sant's films, pic delves into urban sleaze and no-win lifestyles with an unflinchingly honest eye. But while Van Sant's strength lies in his knack for getting inside a lowlife realm without posturing or preaching, writer-director Jeff Stanzler's presence isn't always so unobtrusive. Dialog often doesn't ring true, and pic's midsection becomes a static two-handed theater piece that is too long-winded.

That said, script is brutally effective in exposing the financial and bureaucratic difficulties of getting into U.S. detox programs and strikes powerful chords in portraying crack addicts' awareness of their own doom.

Work by the talented group of thesps is solid all around, although British actor Roth's high-intensity turn suffers occasionally under the weight of a Yank accent.

Tech credits are fine given pic's lean budget (under $1 million), but undistinguished lensing has little visual impact. Wider use of Steve Postel's moody music might have contributed some much-needed tonality.

— *David Rooney*

UN NOS OLA LEUAD
(ONE FULL MOON)
(WELSH)

A Gaucho production for Ffilm Cymru. Produced by Pauline Williams. Directed by Endaf Emlyn. Screenplay, Emlyn, Gwenlyn Parry from Caradog Prichard's novel; camera (Metrocolor), Ashley Rowe; editor, Chris Lawrence; music, Mark Thomas; sound, Richard Dyer; art direction, Ray Price. Reviewed at Turin Intl. Young Cinema Festival (competition), Nov. 12, 1991. Running

time: **98 MIN.**
The man . . . . Dyfan Roberts
The boy . . . . Tudur Roberts
The mother . . . . Betsan Llwyd
Also with: Delyth Einir, Cian Ciaran.

A rural childhood reflection with dark overtones, "One Full Moon" gets a lift from the harsh beauty of the Welsh landscape and the seductive lilt of its language. Pic should be welcomed on the fest circuit and at arthouses, though tube slots appear a safer bet.

In a poor village in North Wales, a boy destined for the priesthood lives under the specter of sex, death and religion with his fragile mother. An incident with a maniacal relative sparks her mental downslide and subsequent betrayal by her son. Beside a vast lake, the boy commits an inexplicable crime for which he atones as a grown man.

Though pic's classy lensing and compositional richness tread the boderline of cold TV drama perfection, helmer Endaf Emlyn has a gentle touch that serves the material well and saves it from high-gloss lifelessness.

Lyrical yarn is buoyed by Tudur Roberts' dignified central performance as the son and given added depth by Emlyn's skill in making the locations a major character. First-rate sound mix balances music with natural elements to great effect.

— *David Rooney*

BRATAN
(BROTHER)
(SOVIET-B&W)

A Sojuztele Film-Tadzik Film production. Directed by Bachtjar Chudojnazarov. Screenplay, Leonid Machkamov, Chudojnazarov; camera (b&w), Georgij Dzalaev; editor, Tat'jana Mal'ceva; music, Achmad Bakaev; sound, Rustam Achadov; art direction, Negmat Juraev. Reviewed at Turin Intl. Young Cinema Festival, Nov. 10, 1991. Running time: **100 MIN.**
Farruch . . . . Firuz Sabzaliev
Poncik . . . . Timur Tursuniv

2 6-year-old debut helmer Bachtjar Chudojnazarov makes an impressive bow with "Brother," a poignant road movie shot in Central Asia. Pic took main prize at Turin Young Cinema meet and should find fans among festival and tube programmers interested in new Soviet cinema.

Two brothers leave town to join their doctor father, traveling cross-country through imposingly stark Tadzhikistan on a

ramshackle cargo train. Hopes of a better life with him fall through, and, turning back to each other, the brothers resume their journey.

Chudojnazarov's assurance in sketching an emotionally honest bond between the sibs furnishes minimal plotline's well-sustained momentum. Things veer a touch towards sentimentality, but the young actors' naturalness and director's unfaltering control over the material keep pic on track.

Editing and traveling music chug along in sync with the train's motion and the golden-hued black & white lensing is both simple and inventive. Film makes a pointed nod to Wim Wenders as an inspirational source.

— *David Rooney*

SARASOTA FEST

LA NEIGE ET LE FEU
(SNOW AND FIRE)
(FRENCH)

A Gaumont production in association with Marcel Dassault & TF1 Films, with the participation of the Ministere de la Defense. Produced by Alain Poire. Directed by Claude Pinoteau. Screenplay, Daniele Thompson, Pinoteau, based on an original idea by Claude & Jack Pinoteau; camera (color), Jean Tournier, editor, Marie-Josephe Yoyotte; music, Vladimir Cosma; sets, Jean-Claude Gallouin; costumes, Agnes Negre. Reviewed at Sarasota (Fla.) French Film Festival, Nov. 18, 1991. Running time: **125 MIN.**
Jacques . . . . Vincent Perez
Christiane . . . . . . Geraldine Pailhas
Michel . . . . Matthieu Roze
David . . . . Alexis Denisof

D espite some impressive production values and a strong lead performance by Vincent Perez, Claude Pinoteau's "Snow and Fire" is a ponderous and cliché-laden World War II romance. Pic likely will play best in TV markets.

Perez (Christian in Gérard Depardieu's "Cyrano de Bergerac") plays the cynical but brave rich kid who joins a ragtag band of freedom fighters during the German Occupation. After the liberation of Paris, he joins his old friend (Matthieu Roze), a concierge's son, in a French army regiment that sees action throughout the final months of the war.

The buddy loses his virginity to a beautiful nurse (Geraldine Pailhas) and is immediately smitten. But she falls for the broodingly handsome Perez, and remains enamored even after she

learns she is pregnant by the concierge's son.

Most of the movie is given over to familiar but generally well-staged battle scenes, interspersed with scenes back in Paris showing the nurse considering a marriage of convenience with a U.S. Army documentary filmmaker (Alexis Denisof). Time and again, audience is reminded that war is frequently fatal to boyish soldiers and, worse, greatly inconvenient to young lovers.

Pic's worst element is the anachronistic English dialog given to Denisof (who sounds like someone who inhaled helium) and other actors cast as U.S. soldiers. Perez has great screen presence, and he's given fine backup by Roze and Pailhas in filling out the romantic triangle. But neither they nor anyone else can do little about the script's tedious predictability.

Tech credits, especially Jean Tournier's lensing of the snow blanketed landscapes, are first-rate. — *Joe Leydon*

BOGOTÁ FEST

QUE VIVEN LOS CROTOS
(LONG LIVE THE HOBOS)
(ARGENTINE)

A Viada Prods. SRI production under auspices of the New Latin American Cinema Foundation. Co-produced with Televisión Española (TVE), in association with Channel Four-National Film Board of Canada-Instituto Nacional de Cinematografía de la Argentina. Executive producers, Eduardo Safigueroa, Ana Bas. Directed by Ana Poliak. Screenplay, Poliak, Willi Behnisch; camera (color), Behnisch; editor, Poliak, Luis Mutti; music, Gabriel Senanes. Reviewed at 8th Santafé de Bogotá (Colombia) Intl. Film Festival, Oct. 15, 1991. Running time: **75 MIN.**
With: José Américo (Bepo) Ghezzi, Filiberto Satti, Uda Conti, Mario Penone, Héctor Wollands, Pascual Vuotto, Pedro Yatauro, Hugo Nario, Pedro Loeb.

I n essence a documentary combined with fictional recreations, "Long Live the Hobos" is a nostalgic attempt to recapture Argentina's nomad past. Multi-national coprod, helmed by Ana Poliak, garnered best film laurels at the 1990 Havana Film Festival.

During the first half of the century, thousands of migrant workers and itinerant nomads roamed the pampas riding the trains and living hand-to-mouth more as a lifestyle than out of economic necessity.

Argentina's "crotos" (hobos) took their name from José Américo Ghezzi (Bepo), an unemployed anarchist quarryman, who felt the call of the road and — from 1930 to 1955 — lived this romantic lifestyle, searching for freedom and discussing philosophy with other nomads.

Now, 60 years later, Bepo is back in his hometown where he, his wife and friends discuss the different paths they chose. These informal testimonies alternate with scenes of hobos talking around a lone campfire, moving from place to place or riding the trains through the expansive Argentine landscape.

Beautifully photographed and briskly edited, pic maintains a rhythm as the testimony weaves in and out of the visual narrative. "Long Live the Hobos" is a stimulating national document.

— *Paul Lenti*

LAS TUMBAS
(THE TOMBS)
(ARGENTINE)

A La Maga Films-Pagina/12-Television Española (TVE)-Argentina Sono Film-Sociedad Estatal Quinto Centenario production. Directed by Javier Torre. Screenplay, Torre, based loosely on Enrique Medina's novel; camera (color), Javier Miquelez, Guillermo Benisch; editor, Juan Carlos Macías; music, José Luis Castiñeira de Dios; art direction, Aldo Guglielmone. Reviewed at 8th Santafé de Bogotá (Colombia) Intl. Film Festival (competition), Oct. 12, 1991. Running time: **87 MIN.**
María . . . . Norma Aleandro
Espiga . . . . Federico Luppi
El Pollo . . . . Eduardo Saucedo
La Gaita . . . . Jorge Mayor
Remolacha . . . . . Pompeyo Audivert
Gaucha . . . . Sara Benítez

Argentina's "The Tombs" offers an uninspiring look into the nightmarish world of corrective institutions for children, places seemingly headed by adults who sadistically abuse their power over helpless kids. Pic's monotonous, unrelenting theme, coupled with a go-nowhere storyline, should cause little stir.

Second feature by Javier Torre (son of w.k. Argentine filmmaker Leopoldo Torre Nilsson), film centers on El Pollo, played by child actor Eduardo Saucedo, who is thrown into clink for stealing.

Besides being made to feel sorry for him, viewer never is told much about his character or life before entering the institution.

Instead of presenting an insight into this world, as in Leonardo Favio's 1964 stark portrait of forsaken childhood "Crónica de un Niño Solo," the film's overall flatness of tone and continuous instances of degradation serve to alienate viewers and call attention to pic's major flaw: no plot.

Film is divided into three parts. The first section, set in a cathedral-like institution for boys, is straight out of Dante. Its atmospheric use of large spaces and mood lighting makes it appear as if Peter Greenaway were attempting a remake of "Pixote."

After a brief interlude of freedom when El Pollo escapes during a riot, story continues in a much more standard vein as the boy is recaptured and this time thrown into a church-run institution. While the first part showed the brutality of male guards, women are by no means shown abounding in maternal love. The second facility is run by some of the most sadistic women this side of "Caged Heat."

In the midst of this is actress Norma Aleandro who, albeit seems to befriend the boy, offers no real help nor any understanding of her role.

While tech credits are above par, script never comes together into a satisfying whole, and clichéd sadistic characterizations waste such notable acting talents as Aleandro and veteran thesp Federico Luppi.

—*Paul Lenti*

MY GIRL

A Columbia release of a Brian Grazer-Imagine Films Entertainment production. Produced by Grazer. Executive producers, Joseph M. Caracciolo, David T. Friendly. Directed by Howard Zieff. Screenplay, Laurice Elehwany. Camera (Consolidated Film Lab color; Technicolor prints), Paul Elliott; editor, Wendy Greene Bricmont; music, James Newton Howard; production design, Joseph T. Garrity; art direction, Pat Tagliaferro; costume design, Karen Patch; sound (Dolby), Steve C. Aaron; associate producer, Hannah Gold; assistant director, Robert V. Girolami; casting, Mary Colquhoun. Reviewed at Sony Studios screening room, Culver City, Calif., Nov. 22, 1991. MPAA Rating: PG. Running time: **102 MIN.**
Harry Sultenfuss . . . . . Dan Aykroyd
Shelly DeVoto . . . . Jamie Lee Curtis
Thomas J. Sennett . . Macaulay Culkin
Vada Sultenfuss . . . . Anna Chlumsky
Phil Sultenfuss . . . . . Richard Masur
Mr. Bixler . . . . Griffin Dunne
Gramoo Sultenfuss . . . . . Ann Nelson

As pleasant as a warm summer day and as ephemeral, "My Girl" skims discreetly over a mountain of emotionally traumatic material to emerge as agreeable Lite entertainment for the holiday season. Plenty of shrewd commercial calculation went into concocting the right sugar coating for this story of an 11-year-old girl's painful maturation, and chemistry seems right for this mild diversion to leg it out into a strong b.o. performance.

Enough quirky details and character traits lie scattered around first-time screenwriter Laurice Elehwany's script to suggest that some heartfelt personal elements motivated its creation. But potential weirdness and individual flavor of the life of a precocious young girl growing up in a small-town mortuary is slighted in favor of a pleasant but bland recapitulation of childhood memories designed to create a warm, nostalgic glow even when the recollections are tragic.

Set in an idealized Anytown, U.S.A., supposed to be in Pennsylvania but filmed in Florida, pic can afford to be relatively oblivious to events unfolding in 1972 because the man of the house (Dan Aykroyd) essentially stopped living a decade before.

Conducting his trade out of the basement of a lovely old house, the widower mortician takes barely a passing interest in the doings of his daughter Vada (Anna Chlumsky), an exceedingly bright girl who enrolls in an adult education poetry course because she has a crush on the

teacher (Griffin Dunne) and expresses her severe, Woody Allen-like hypochondria by regularly bursting in on a local doctor.

Things change around the funeral home when Dad hires a sexy hippie (Jamie Lee Curtis) to apply makeup to his cadavers. Living out of a charmingly old-fashioned motor home, she soon puts the make on her boss, easiest mark east of the Mississippi, and tries to befriend Vada, who's rather less cooperative.

Vada spends most of her time with an engaging neighbor (Macaulay Culkin), and although a bit young for a real romance, the two experience their first kiss together. Fate steps in and, as the grapevine has been reporting for weeks, Culkin is taken to the big playground in the sky. As if this weren't enough, Vada also has to contend with the upsetting news that her father is going to marry the interloping cosmetologist, and that her poetry teacher also is going to wed.

It's a rough summer for an 11-year-old, but director Howard Zieff paints it in the manner of a watercolor of a youthful idyll. Elehwany's script neatly handles a number of details — Curtis' aggressiveness and knowledge of how to make Aykroyd feel good about himself is just right, as is Vada's astonished, "My dad was funny?" upon being told this — but on larger matters falls into predictable patterns.

Performers are highly simpatico. Aykroyd's weight gain makes him almost all too believable as a schlumpy middle-American guy who has forgotten that women exist, but his vulnerability and slow reawakening are appealing. Curtis is snappy and smart as a woman with a past, but the resilience to bounce back, even if her taste in men is questionable. Culkin remains irresistible and unaffected, while a bit more subdued than in "Home Alone."

But pic belongs to Chlumsky. With dialog perhaps a shade too adult at times, she invests the lead role with an incredibly vibrant presence that will win over young and older viewers. Attractive but offbeat, she makes her neurotic character a thoroughgoing winner.

Production design, lensing and costumes combine to create a storybook image of small-town U.S.A., while James Newton Howard's score is supplemented by a soundtrack's worth of period pop tunes. — *Todd McCarthy*

K2
(BRITISH)

A Miramax (U.S.) and Entertainment (U.K.) release, in association with Majestic Films Intl., of a Trans Pacific Group production, in association with Screenscope (Washington) and Phanos Development (Tokyo). Produced by Jonathan Taplin, Marilyn Weiner, Tim Van Rellim. Executive producers, Melvyn J. Estrin, Hal Weiner. Directed by Franc Roddam. Screenplay, Patrick Meyers, Scott Roberts, from Meyers' play. Camera (Fujicolor; Technicolor prints), Gabriel Bernstain; editor, Sean Barton; music, Hans Zimmer; production design, Andrew Sanders; art direction, Richard Hudolin; set decoration, Ted Kuchera; costume design, Kathryn Morrison; sound (Dolby SR), David Stephenson, Martin Evans, Robin O'Donoghue; associate producer, Masa Mikage; assistant director, John Watson; 2nd unit camera, Peter Pilafian; casting, Victoria Thomas (London), Michelle Allen (Vancouver). Reviewed at Cannon Shaftesbury theater, London, Nov. 22, 1991. Running time: **111 MIN.**
Taylor . . . . Michael Biehn
Harold . . . . Matt Craven
Claiborne . . . . . . Raymond J. Barry
Takane . . . . Hiroshi Fujioka
Dallas . . . . Luca Bercovici
Jacki . . . . . . Patricia Charbonneau
Cindy . . . . Julia Nickson-Soul
Also with: Jamal Shah, Annie Grindlay, Elena Stiteler.

The buddy movie hits the Himalayas in Franc Roddam's "K2," an entertaining enough mountain-climbing saga that could do OK in fast playoff. Script's lack of oxygen is offset by pic's slick packaging plus good on-screen bonding between leads Michael Biehn and Matt Craven.

Co-scripted by Patrick Meyers and Scott Roberts from Meyers' Broadway play, story rapidly sets up two main characters: yuppie, womanizing Seattle lawyer Biehn and gentler, married-with-child professor Craven.

When a U.S. climbing group funded by millionaire Raymond J. Barry loses two of its members in an Alaskan training session, Biehn and Craven take their place for the big one — an attempt on K2, the world's second highest peak and a w.k. engorger of climbers.

By-the-numbers plot has most of the Pakistani porters heading for home halfway, Biehn and co-climber Luca Bercovici engaging in some macho face-offs, and Barry returning to base camp with health problems.

When Bercovici and Japanese partner Hiroshi Fujioka fail on the final run, Biehn and Craven go it alone. At this point the script, which has been coasting along in first gear for 90 minutes,

Original play
K-2

Mary K. Frank and Cynthia Wood, by arrangement with Saint-Subber, presentation of a drama in one act by Patrick Meyers. Staged by Terry Schreiber. Setting, Ming Cho Lee; costumes, Noel Borden; lighting, Allen Lee Hughes; audio composition, Herman Chessid; sound, David Schnirman; assistant director, William S. Morris; associate producers, Shaun Beary, Charles H. Duggan; general manager, Victor Samrock; company manager, Susan Bell; publicity, Joe Wolhandler Assoc.; stage manager, Arlene Grayson. Opened March 30, '83 at the Brooks Atkinson Theater, N.Y. $27.50 top weeknights, $30 weekend nights.
Taylor . . . . Jeffrey De Munn
Harold . . . . Jay Patterson

tries to get ambitious. But the denouement won't surprise anyone: Biehn and Craven discover the joys of male heterosexual love 28,000 feet up.

Both thesps perform far better than the script deserves, with Biehn cocksure but likable, and Craven serious but caring. Barry is solid as the aging sponsor and Bercovici ditto as Biehn's nemesis. Of the two women, Julia Nickson-Soul makes a stronger mark in her brief scenes as Craven's wife than Patricia Charbonneau, sidelined as the only femme in the expedition.

From the pop-video main titles onward, Roddam keeps up a frisky pace, with some truly breathtaking lensing of British Columbia and Kashmir locations that would have looked even better in Panavision.

There's no attempt at any mystical relationship between the characters and the mountain, nor any of the megalomania as in Werner Herzog's "Scream of Stone." Pic concentrates instead on sheer thrills and spills, with plenty of product placement.

Sean Barton's tight cutting and Hans Zimmer's crashing, electro-Mahlerian score both go for the jugular. Canada's Mt. Waddington doubled for the real K2, and producers impressively claim the whole shebang hasn't one studio shot or optical. — *Derek Elley*

CONVICTS

An MCEG release of a Jonathan D. Krane production, in association with Sterling Entertainment Co. Produced by Krane, Sterling VanWagenen. Directed by Peter Masterson. Screenplay, Horton Foote, based on his play. Camera (Duart color; Technicolor prints), Toyomichi Kurita; editor, Jill Savitt; music, Peter Melnick; production design, Dan Bishop; art direction, Dianna

Freas; costume design, Nile H. Samples; sound, Stephen Halbert; assistant director, David Womark; production manager, George Sweney; 2nd unit director, Jeff Jensen; line producer, Elliot Rosenblatt; associate produacers, David Anderson, Leah A. Palco; casting, Ed Johnston. Reviewed at Broadway screening room, N.Y., Nov. 19, 1991. No MPAA Rating. Running time: **92 MIN.**
Soll Gautier . . . . . . Robert Duvall
Horace Robedaux . . . . . Lukas Haas
Ben Johnson . . . . James Earl Jones
Jackson . . . . Mel Winkler
Leroy . . . . Calvin Levels
Martha Johnson . . . Starletta DuPois
Asa . . . . Carlin Glynn
Billy . . . . Gary Swanson

Robert Duvall adds another memorable character to his screen portfolio in Horton Foote's "Convicts," a static, uncinematic play to film adaptation. Despite good supporting turns, feature is strictly for Foote fetishists.

Given Duvall's stature and his quality work here it makes sense the 18 months-on-the-shelf pic is getting an Oscar qualifying run. Financial problems of its distrib MCEG account for tardy release.

Foote has provided Duvall with some of his best screen roles, including the Faulkner adaptation "Tomorrow" and "Tender Mercies." Simpatico "Convicts" team also includes director Peter Masterson, who acted in "Tomorrow" and directed Foote's "The Trip to Bountiful"; and producer Sterling VanWagenen, who made his directorial debut several months after this pic with "Convicts" co-star Lukas Haas starring in "Alan & Naomi." And Haas re-teamed a bit later with Duvall to great effect in "Rambling Rose."

Unfortunately "Convicts," the second play in a nine-play cycle Foote calls "The Orphan's Home," does not present the sort of material suitable for modern film auds. It might have worked best in the special-interest format of Ely Landau's "American Film Theater" adaptations of the early 1970s.

Set on Texas's Gulf Coast on Christmas Eve in 1902 (actually lensed on Louisiana locations), "Convicts" is told through the observations of 13-year-old Haas, working in a country store on Duvall's sugar cane plantation. Many years back, the land's tenant farmers were dismissed, and state convicts were contracted for low-cost labor replacements not unlike the original slavery system.

Civil War veteran Duvall runs the farm but is senile, his affliction allowing Foote to out-Pinter Harold Pinter in dialog repe-

tition. Duvall's interpretation is dead-on, as he continually asks Haas and anyone else in earshot the same inane questions to ultimately yield comic relief.

Presented without much continuity in elliptical vignettes, story does not have a cumulative, dramatic narrative. Instead various forms of cryptic behavior are observed via Haas' eyes. Haas is trying to earn enough money to buy a headstone for his late father's unmarked grave and Duvall, making accelerating promises of wealth to Haas, gradually takes the boy under his wing.

The convicts of the title die of overwork or are shot to death "escaping" almost randomly, with director Masterson emphasizing their symbolic function in the story by not explaining why. Duvall is so absent-minded he keeps asking if a specific convict is a Negro, and has to be reminded that they all are.

All the adult white people in the cast are constantly drunk, including Duvall's relatives Carlin Glynn and Gary Swanson who loll around the house aimlessly. Foote's portrait of a decadent society on its last legs will not please Southerners but is vividly realized in microcosm here.

Haas, as in "Rambling Rose," provides impressive naturalism to balance Duvall's barnstorming performance. Jones is also quite understated, and besides Winkler's convincing period portrayal there is a powerfully modern, almost militant turn by Calvin Levels as a convict in chains who tells his sad story to Haas.

Toyomichi Kurita's frequently backlit photography captures the atmosphere of the place but the location shooting fails to disguise the story's theatrical origins. — *Lawrence Cohn*

IL CONTE MAX
(COUNT MAX)
(ITALIAN-FRENCH)

An Artisti Associati Intl. release of a Produttori Associati-Reteitalia-Vittoria Cine (Italy)-President Film-Clea Prods. (France) co-production. Produced by Jacopo Capanna, Giuseppe Perugia. Directed by Christian De Sica. Screenplay, Gianfilippo Ascione, Adriano Incrocci, De Sica, from story by De Sica, Ascione; camera (Technicolor), Sergio Salvati; editor, Raimondo Crociani; music, Manuel De Sica; art direction, Giuseppe Mariani; costumes, Nicoletta Ercoli. Reviewed at Esperia Cinema, Rome, Nov. 1, 1991. Running time: **88 MIN.**
Alfredo/Max . . . . . Christian De Sica
Isabella . . . . Ornella Muti
Count Max . . . . Galeazzo Benti
Pierre's mother . . . . Maria Mercader

Pierre	Alain Flick
George	Bruno Corazzari
Marika	Anita Ekberg

Christian De Sica helms and headlines in second remake of "Count Max," a two-time comedy vehicle for his illustrious dad, Vittorio. Home-ground popularity of De Sica and co-star Ornella Muti should ensure steady Italo b.o., but plodding style and predictable plotting will attract few offshore fans.

Eager to escape from his humdrum daily grind, a Roman mechanic (De Sica) falls for a beautiful model (Muti) and, after a crash course in etiquette from fallen aristrocat Count Max (Galeazzo Benti), he follows her to Paris. Even on intended fairy-tale level,

Original film
IL SIGNOR MAX
(MR. MAX)
(ITALIAN)

Produced by Astra Film. Directed by Mario Camerini. Staged by Camerini and Mario Soldati; script, Amleto Palermi. Reviewed in Rome, Dec. 2, 1937.

Max	Vittoria De Sica
Society Woman	Ruby D'Alma
Her Sister	Adonella
Maid	Assia Norris

this provides pic's first credibility lapse. The minute the two get together, they're more like Laverne & Shirley than Romeo & Juliet.

De Sica passes himself off as the count and pools resources with Muti to take revenge on the millionaire (Alain Flick) who stripped the real Max of his fortune years earlier. Scheme takes them to Marrakesh, where they lose everything.

Flick's character turns out to be gay and smitten with De Sica. His doting mother (De Sica's real-life mother, Maria Mercader) orchestrates an Arab wedding for the two men, but here, as events become more madcap, pace peters out. Film lumbers to a ho-hum conclusion.

Pic heaps on the glitz with a faded glamor that recalls the early Bond films, and Sergio Salvati's lackluster lensing makes a lean meal of the exotic locations. De Sica's direction is strictly by the numbers and the cocktail-hour score by his brother Manuel is dated and irritating.

As an actor, De Sica also proves somewhat less than a chip off the old block, relentlessly imitating his father's inimitably styl-

ized speech. Muti looks gorgeous as always but acts like she's killing time, and rest of cast (especially Anita Ekberg in a cringingly miscalculated turn) play done-to-death caricatures.

— David Rooney

CAGE/CUNNINGHAM
(DOCU)

A Cunningham Dance Foundation presentation in association with La Sept. Produced by Cunningham Dance Foundation. Directed, photographed and edited by Elliot Caplan. Screenplay, David Vaughan; in color; music, John Cage; choreography, Merce Cunningham; sound, Caplan. Reviewed at Broadway Screening Room, N.Y., Nov. 26, 1991. Running time: **95 MIN.**

Spiced with interviews, videotapes and archival footage, "Cage/Cunningham" is a reverent homage to influential modernists John Cage and Merce Cunningham. Highbrow subject matter will limit pic's theatrical prospects, but it should find a home on public TV.

Although the dance and music excerpts are well chosen, the Cunningham Dance Foundation-produced documentary is a bit too flattering. Director Elliott Caplan is the company's filmmaker-in-residence, and screenwriter David Vaughan is the troupe's archivist. While they lack critical distance, they share (and show in the film) a passion for composer Cage and choreographer Cunningham's groundbreaking work.

Pair met in 1938 and first collaborated in 1942 and are still working together. The film shows how they work together, but it doesn't really explain how they have gotten along for so long.

Caplan talked to duo's one-time collaborators, such as Jasper Johns, Nam June Paik and Robert Rauschenberg, designer of sets and costumes for Cage and Cunningham who characterizes it as an excruciating but exciting combine because "nobody knew what anyone else was doing until it was too late."

Unfortunately, the dance excerpts are often too short and end rather abruptly. On the other hand, some of the interviews could have been edited further.

A valuable record of an enduring collaboration, pic lacks objective and critical POVs, but it succeeds as a glowing appreciation. *—William Stevenson*

BOGOTÁ FEST

SENSACIONES
(SENSATIONS)
(ECUADORAN)

A Vels Cordero Prods. production. Executive producer, Modesto Ponce. Directed, written by Juan Esteban Codero & Viviana Codero. Camera (color), Iván Acevedo; editor, the Coderos, Gonzalo Rivas; music, Juan Esteban Cordero; sound, Sebastián Cardemil, Santiago Luzuriaga. Reviewed at 8th Santafé de Bogotá (Columbia) Intl. Film Festival (competition), Oct. 13, 1991. Running time: **80 MIN.**

Zacarías	Juan Esteban Cordero
Isaías	Ricardo Contag
Ricardo	Luis Miguel Campos
Chiara	Viviana Cordero
Alfonsina	Adriana Uribe

Ecuador's first 35m feature, "Sensaciones" is a well-made, intelligent film that revolves around the interrelationships of fusion jazz musicians as they work together to create new material. If handled well, this valiant effort might strike the right chord on the international arthouse market.

Boasting a minimum of storyline, basic plot concerns a musician (Juan Esteban Cordero) who returns to Ecuador and joins with musician friends to make a new album fusing local folk music and jazz. Film also looks at contempo Ecuadoran youths trying to incorporate indigenous roots and culture into a current Western mode through music and modern technology.

Of pic's technical shortcomings, most of the shots are one-take with no corresponding alternative takes. But use of digital sound and rich camerawork, including the stunning Andean scenery, give the film a rich patina.

— Paul Lenti

UN SUEÑO EN
EL ABISMO
(A DREAM IN THE ABYSS)
(VENEZUELAN)

A Lucian Films-Bolívar Films production, under auspices of the Alcaldía de Caracas. Produced by Antonio Llerandi. Directed by Oscar Lucien. Screenplay, Lucien, Carlos Oteyza, Rodolfo Santana, based on Santana's play "Con los Fusiles Volados"; camera (color), Hernán Toro; editor; Serio Curiel; music, José Vinicio Adames; sound, Edgar Torres; art direction, Gerald Romer. Reviewed in competition at 8th Santafé de Bogotá (Colombia) Intl. Film Festival, Oct. 10, 1991. Running time: **98 MIN.**

With: Erich Wildpret, Frank Spano, Sonya Smith, Karl Hoffman, Dalila Colombo, Luis Fernández, Guillermo Feo, Anna Montefuego, Petunia Paredes.

"A Dream in the Abyss" is a surprisingly ambitious first feature by Venezuelan helmer Oscar Lucien about two youths who dream of scaling Mt. Everest. Lucien's well-rounded, fast-paced story line, combined with admirable tech credits, shows a filmmaker fully in control of his craft, and pic should attract a fair amount of interest.

The film is an indictment of bourgeois complacency and the country's indifference to those desiring to achieve more than is expected. Through admirable photography, brisk editing, imaginative sets and naturalistic acting, pic captures these urban teens' uphill struggle to draw national interest in their project.

They paint large signs, throw rallies, offer an aborted benefit rock concert and even perform media stunts such as a spectacular climb up a Caracas skyscraper. They are allowed to voice their dissatisfaction to the press before being hauled off by the police for reckless endangerment.

Pic paints a portrait of national frustrations mired in an age of pragmatism. It is set in contemporary Venezuela, a country grown cynical over an overwhelming foreign debt, a country that ceases to dream on a large scale. Rather than dreaming, the film reminds us that the country has been dozing and needs to wake up before it is too late.

Largely ensemble cast is always credible. *— Paul Lenti*

SARASOTA FEST

J'EMBRASSE PAS
(I DON'T KISS)
(FRENCH)

A BAC Films release (in France) of a President Films-BAC Films-Salome SA-Cine Cinq Roger-Andre Larrieu Gruppo Bema production, with the participation of Canal Plus and the Centre National de la Cinematographie. Executive producer, Alain Centonze. Produced by Maurice Bernart, Jacques-Eric Strauss, Jean Labadie. Directed by André Téchiné. Screenplay, Jacques Nolot, with adaptation and dialog by Téchiné, Nolot, Michel Grisolia; camera (color), Thierry Arbogast; editor, Claudine Merlin, Edith Vassard; music, Philippe Sarde. Reviewed at Sarasota (Fla.) French Film Festival, Nov. 15, 1991. Running time: **115 MIN.**

Romain	Philippe Noiret
Ingrid	Emmanuelle Béart

André Téchiné crosses "Candide" with "Midnight Cowboy" and comes up with a strong drama in "I Don't Kiss." Despite (or perhaps because of) its sordid subject matter, pic should get wide fest exposure and, with right handling, international arthouse playdates.

Manuel Blanc, an engaging Tom Hulce lookalike, is well cast as a naive youth from the provinces systematically disillusioned and hardened by big-city life. Starting out as a hospital orderly, he allows himself to be kept by a middle-aged nurse (Helene Vincent) as he muddles through acting classes. His talent is minimal, a fact he's made painfully aware of during a humiliating class exercise.

A gay TV interviewer (Philippe Noiret, generous with his immense talent in a small but key role) befriends the younger man and warns him about prostitution, but the neophyte street hustler comes to enjoy the easy money and the seedy allure.

Blanc makes a fascinating and emotionally persuasive transition from innocence to experience, remaining likable even as he becomes a street-smart hustler. Only when he makes the mistake of falling in love with a sultry hooker (Emmanuelle Béart) does he lose his professional detachment. He winds up beaten and forcibly sodomized by her pimp.

Téchiné renders all this nonjudgmentally but absorbingly. He gets exceptionally fine work from his actors, especially Blanc and Noiret. Cinematographer Thierry Arbogast provides suitably moody views of Paris after dark.
— *Joe Leydon*

LONDON FEST

CHIEDI LA LUNA
(ASK FOR THE MOON)
(ITALIAN)

An Eidoscope production for RAI-2, in association with European Co-production Assn. (Intl. sales: Titanus.) Produced by Cecilia Cope, Francesco Nardella, Nicola Orfini. Executive producer, Mario Orfini. Directed by Giuseppe Piccioni. Screenplay, Franco Bernini, Enzo Monteleone, Piccioni, from Bernini's screen story; camera (Eastmancolor), Roberto Meddi; editor, Angelo Nicolini; music, Antonio Di Pofi; art direction,

Massimo Corfevi; costume design, Marina Campanale; assistant director, Riccardo Cannone. Reviewed at London Film Festival (Italian Focus), Nov. 16, 1991. Running time: **85 MIN.**

Elena Bacchelli	Margherita Buy
Marco Salviati	Giulio Scarpati
Sergio	Roberto Citran
The hitchhiker	Sergio Rubini
Gianluca	Stefano Abbati
Daniela	Daniela Giordano
Poker player	Mauro Marino
Laura	Mary Sellers

"Ask for the Moon" is a neat blend of road movie and odd-couple romance that goes down a treat. Originally made as a TV film by Italo pubcaster RAI, pic is enjoying a theatrical release at home and could widen out to other arthouse markets.

Story is the old favorite about two opposites thrown together by a similar quest. Marco (Giulio Scarpati), searching for his errant brother, teams up with Elena (Margherita Buy), brother's ex-fiancée. Pair heads south from Verona on a shaggy-dog trek, meeting various oddball characters on the way.

Denouement is never really in doubt, with the straitlaced Marco thawing out under Elena's freewheeling tutelage. But topnotch performances by the radiant Buy (excellent in Sergio Rubini's "The Station") and Scarpati give the slim material plenty of charm and style.

Buy's real-life mate Rubini pops up in a witty cameo as a lovesick hitchhiker. Daniela Giordano is memorably waspish as the boss of an exclusive eaterie peopled by power-lunchers.

Helmer Giuseppe Piccioni, in his second feature, shows a good eye for composition and gives the characterful cast plenty of space to do their thing. Roberto Meddi's lensing of the Umbria landscape is sharp without turning the pic into a travelog, and Antonio Di Pofi's Ry Cooderlike guitar score is further offbeat delight. — *Derek Elley*

THE FAVOUR, THE WATCH AND THE VERY BIG FISH
(FRENCH-BRITISH)

A Rank Film Distributors (U.K.) release of a Films Ariane-Fildebroc (Paris)/Umbrella Films (London) production, in association with Sovereign Pictures. (Intl. sales: Sovereign, London.) Produced by Michelle de Broca. Executive producer, Antoine de Clermont-Tonnerre. Co-producer, Simon Perry. Directed by Ben Lewin. Screen-

play, Lewin, based on Marcel Ayme's short story "Rue Saint-Sulpice." Camera (color), Bernard Zitzermann; editor, John Grover; music, Vladimir Cosma; production design, Carlos Conti; costume design, Elizabeth Travernier; sound (Dolby), Edward Tise; special effects, Pierre Foury; assistant director, Eric Sliman. Reviewed at London Film Festival, Nov. 17, 1991. Running time: **87 MIN.**

Louis Aubinard	Bob Hoskins
Pianist	Jeff Goldblum
Sybil	Natasha Richardson
Norbert	Michel Blanc
Charles	Jacques Villeret
Elizabeth	Angela Pleasence
Zalman	Jean-Pierre Cassel
Grandfather	Samuel Chaimovitch
(English dialog)	

The only clumsy thing about "The Favour, the Watch, and the Very Big Fish" is its title. Surreal romantic farce about a Parisian photographer and a pianist who thinks he's Christ keeps the yocks coming and features tasty perfs from Bob Hoskins and Jeff Goldblum. Fast playoff could reap okay returns, though pic may need nurturing in the North American market.

Story has Hoskins as a bespectacled lenser specializing in biblical tableaux. His boss (Michel Blanc) thinks he's a wimp, and his sister tortures him with inedible food. One day, an actor friend (Jean-Pierre Cassel) asks him a favor — to take his place in a dubbing session.

Pic in question turns out to be a porno movie. Following a marathon orgasm with fellow dubber Natasha Richardson, the two become chums. Hoskins, who's secretly fallen for Richardson, agrees to meet ex-b.f. Goldblum when he gets out of jail. Several complications later, Goldblum saves Hoskins' job when he agrees to pose as Christ on the Cross for a photo shoot. Problems start when he gets really serious about the role and tries to perform miracles.

In his second feature (after the 1988 "Georgia"), Polish-born, Australian-raised helmer Ben Lewin shows a sharp eye for Euro-style loony-tune comedy. Though set in present-day Paris, pic has an almost fin de siècle feel, thanks to picturesque locations, clever costuming and heightened playing by all the principals.

Lewin's well-developed screenplay, which mixes pratfalls with meaty characterizations, is well served by the cast. Hoskins is in his element as the bemused lenser, Goldblum (looking like a cross between Rasputin and Jesus) has his best part since

"The Tall Guy" and Richardson clicks as the ditzy g.f. Anglo-French cast melds smoothly, with Cassel and Blanc joining in the fun.

Vladimir Cosma's operatic score is a neat fit to the on-screen action. All other tech credits are top-drawer, with special plaudits for Bernard Zitzermann's crisp photography and John Grover's antsy editing.
— *Derek Elley*

HOYAT GWAN TSOI LOI
(AU REVOIR, MON AMOUR)
(HONG KONG)

A Golden Harvest production. Produced by Leonard Ho. Executive producer, Chua Lam. Directed by Tony Au. Screenplay, Jerry Liu, Gordon Chan. Camera (color), Bill Wong, David Chung, Peter Bao, Peter Ngor; editor, Peter Cheung; music, Anthony Lun, Terry Chan; songs, James Wong (sung by Anita Mui); sound, Tsau Siu-lung, Chan Wai-yip, Adrian John Dorab; production design, Eddie Ma; art direction, Horace Ma; visual design, Ku Ka-lou; costume design, Peter Yao; assistant director, Chan Kwok; action director, Mang Hoi; associate producer, Chin Siu-wai; line producer, Lam Tsing; creative consultant Jerry Liu. Reviewed at London Film Festival (3 Continents: Asia section), Nov. 7, 1991. Running time: **126 MIN.**

Wu Mei-yi	Anita Mui
Liang Seng	Leung Kar-fai
Noguchi	Hidekazu Akai
Ping	Carrie Ng
Capt. Tieh	Tsui Siu-keung
Mei-yi's father	Kent Tseng
(In Cantonese; Chinese and English subtitles)	

A lush period meller set in wartime Shanghai, "Au Revoir, Mon Amour" should find a warm bed in Asian film weeks and fests. Fans of Hong Kong megastar Anita Mui ("Rouge") will need no further recommendation.

Mui plays a chantoosie at a nightclub owned by her father (Kent Tseng) who's arrested by the occupying Japanese. She's in love with a Nationalist Chinese (Leung Kar-fai) but, thinking him dead, marries Noguchi (Hidekazu Akai) to provide a father for her unborn child.

Two-hanky ending, set in Japan in 1946, has Leung finding Mui enjoying connubial bliss and even speaking the local lingo. In an impassioned speech, she defends her actions to the lovelorn Leung.

Director Tony Au gives the whole thing his visual polish (plus juicy spots for Mui to exercise her tonsils), without hitting the heights of his 1987 *chef d'oeuvre* "Profiles of Pleasure." Fault here is mainly the paper-thin script, which rarely knuckles down and gives Mui a chance to show what she's capable of.

Production design, recreating '40s Shanghai on Hong Kong backlots, is immensely detailed; pic did only minimal lensing in the actual city. Original Chinese title roughly means "One Day My Man Will Come Again," from film's catchy theme song.

— *Derek Elley*

I DREAMT I WOKE UP
(BRITISH-DOCU-16M)

A Merlin Films production for BBC Scotland. (Intl. sales: BBC Enterprises.) Produced by Sean Ryerson. Executive producer, John Archer. Directed, written by John Boorman. Camera (Technicolor, 16m), Seamus Deasey; editor, Ron Davis; music, Paddy Moloney; makeup, Maire O'Sullivan; prosthetic makeup, Fiona Connon; sound, Brendan Deasey; assistant director, David Keating. Reviewed at London Film Festival (British Cinema section), Nov. 16, 1991. Running time: **49 MIN.**
John Boorman . . . . Himself
Boorman's alter ego . . . . . John Hurt
Mysterious woman/Lady of the Lake/
Journalist . . . . Janet McTeer
The Green Man . . . Charley Boorman
Merlin . . . . Stan Gebnler-Davis
Turf Cutter 1 . . . . Philip Giles
Turf Cutter 2 . . . . Andy Byrne
Bog Man . . . . John Connon
Wood Sprite . . . . . . Alexander Hurt

John Boorman's "I Dreamt I Woke Up" is a whimsical journey through the director's imagination and his running obsession with landscape and myth. Semidocu, shot in and around his estate in County Wicklow, Ireland, is a fascinating career footnote for buffs but of limited appeal to general auds.

Pic is the second out of the gate in the BBC Scotland series "A Director's Place," following Nagisa Oshima's "Kyoto: My Mother's Place." Others commissioned so far include David Mamet, Susan Seidelman and Louis Malle.

Film begins with John Hurt, as Boorman's alter ego, waking up and finding himself entombed in his own living room. As the coffin lid closes, he sees a mysterious woman of his dreams (Janet McTeer) and by force of will snatches himself back from the nether world.

Pic segues into a loose series of episodes as Boorman/Hurt roams the area and meets colorful locals. Intercut are occasional refs to the director's career (with extracts from "Excalibur," shot nearby) and fantasy segs featuring helmer's son, Charley, as the

Green Man (spirit of the forest). Final section has Boorman being given a hard time by an aggressive femme journalist (McTeer again).

Sections showing Boorman chatting with locals are the best, revealing his love of the desolate Irish countryside, which made him settle there 22 years ago. Fantasy sections, with Hurt taking on director's persona, show the same mix of environmentalism and naivete found in the features "Where the Heart Is" and "The Emerald Forest."

Flashes of ironic humor, as in Boorman's meeting with a disinterred Bog Man or his scheme to build a mini-pagoda by a river, lighten the earnest tone.

Pic was shot in 10 days with a two-man crew. Hurt, who also lives in the area, enters convincingly into the spirit of things, and McTeer has fun as the hardnosed hack. Seamus Deasey's 16m photography is fine, and the limited effects make the most of the peanuts budget. — *Derek Elley*

BAROCCO
(ITALIAN)

A Globe Films-PFA Films production, in association with Istituto Luce Italnoleggio Cinematografica & RAI-1. (Intl. sales: Sacis.) Produced by Pietro Innocenzi, Pier Francesco Aiello. Directed by Claudio Sestieri. Screenplay, Sestieri, Antonella Barone. Camera (Eastmancolor), Raffaele Mertes; editor, Simona Paggi; music, Luigi Ceccarelli; art direction, Paolo Innocenzi; costume design, Vera Cozzolino; sound, Tommaso Quattrini; assistant director, Maria Teresa Elena. Reviewed at London Film Festival (Italian Focus), Nov. 20, 1991. Running time: **94 MIN.**
Valeria . . . . . . Cristina Marsillach
Attilio . . . . . . Massimo Venturiello
David . . . . Davide Bechini
Marco . . . . Matteo Gazzolo
Filippo . . . . Carlo Lizzani
Sandra . . . . Ottavia Piccolo
Also with: Agnese Nano, Eliana Miglio, Branca De Camargo, Matteo Bellina, voice of Luna Ward.

Glossy production values and an eye-catching perf by Cristina Marsillach can't hide that nothing much is happening in "Barocco." Semi-existential Italian drama about a foreign student trying to find herself will do better on the tube than with paying auds.

Marsillach is a young Spaniard studying art restoration in Rome. Cheesed off with her absent b.f., she moves in with a gay

couple, one of whom (Davide Bechini) she seduces. Befriended by her teacher (Ottavia Piccolo) and a famous novelist (Carlo Lizzani), she takes off for the countryside, where she meets a handsome former architect (Massimo Venturiello). But that doesn't work out either.

Pic has something to say about modern relationships conducted via technology, and also about Marsillach's growing isolation in a foreign, history-soaked capital. But script's avoidance of pinning down her problem makes the central character irritating rather than involving.

Marsillach is a stunner, and director Claudio Sestieri knows it. The rosy-afternoon sex scene between her and Bechini is a sizzler. Performances are okay, with Piccolo dependable as Marsillach's world-wise teach, and onetime Venice fest head Lizzani stealing his scenes as the w.k. scribe. Tech credits are all smooth. — *Derek Elley*

KEI WONG
(THE KING OF CHESS)
(HONG KONG)

A Golden Princess-Film Workshop production. (Intl. sales: Film Workshop.) Executive producer, Tsui Hark. Directed by Yim Ho. Screenplay, Yim, Leung Kar-fai, based on Zhong Acheng's short story & Chang Hsi-kuo's novel; camera (color), Poon Hang-seng, Yang Wei-han, Lo Wan-sing; editor, Mak Chi-sin; music, Lo Ta-yu; sound, Tang Siu-lam; art direction-costume design, David Chan, James Leung; postproduction supervisor, Mak; associate producer, Hou Hsiao-hsien; line producers, Chang Huakun, Chan Wai-Keung. Reviewed at British Film Institute preview theater, London, Oct. 25, 1991. (In London Film Festival, 3 Continents: Asia section.) Running time: **111 MIN.**
Wang Yisheng . . . . . Leung Kar-fai
Jade Ting . . . . Yang Lin
Ching Ling . . . . John Sham
Zhong Acheng . . . . Yim Ho
Whiz kid . . . . . . Wang Sheng-fang
Lanky . . . . Chin Shih-chieh
Prof. Liu . . . . . . Cheng Kuan-chung
(Cantonese soundtrack; Chinese and English subtitles)

Four years after it began shooting, Yim Ho's "King of Chess" makes it out of the cans with mixed results. Surreal drama of two chess wizards — one in '60s Maoist China, the other in modern Taiwan — scores high for political cheek but low for dramatic cohesion. Beyond fest circuit, it's likely to be b.o. checkmate.

Hong Kong-financed pic began lensing in Taiwan in late '87, but

Yim ankled the next year as budget escalated. Exec producer Tsui Hark took over, recast the female lead and patched together the final version.

Pic stitches together two independent originals with the same title, a short story by mainland Chinese scribe Zhong Acheng (who also wrote Chen Kaige's movie "King of the Children") and a 1978 fantasy novel by Taiwan's Chang Hsi-kuo. Former pokes wry fun at Cultural Revolution politics, latter at Taiwan's capitalist boom of the '70s.

Updated Taiwan seg has a visiting Hong Kong ad exec (John Sham) helping the career of a pert young emcee (Yang Lin) by training a moppet for her TV show "Whiz Kids World." This spurs the exec's memories of visiting his cousin in China in 1967, where he met a chess fanatic (Leung Kar-fai) on a train to a labor camp. Film crosscuts between both stories as the chess mavens go for the big finish.

Best bits are the Yim-directed Chinese scenes with their chaotic, rain-drenched portrayal of camp life and Maoist fervor. Flashier bits in modern Taiwan are less carefully lensed and flawed by stone-faced playing from Yang as the pretty emcee. Local songbird Yang, who played the lead in Hou Hsiao-hsien's "Daughter of the Nile," replaced actress Su Ming-ming.

Other roles are well cast, with co-scripter Leung good as the obsessive Mainland expert. Production design of gulag scenes (shot in Taiwan) is tops. Pic's bold subtext, which twins the dog-eat-dog worlds of Mainland communism and Taiwan capitalism, is spelled out in an opening and closing song.

Version caught was Cantonese-language one, which plays less authentically than the Mandarin print. Effect for buffs is like hearing an all-Brit cast speak with Brooklyn accents.

— *Derek Elley*

TURIN FEST

WUGE NUZI HE YIGEN SHENGZI
(FIVE GIRLS AND A ROPE)
(TAIWANESE)

A Thomson Films production. Produced by Tong Cun-lin. Directed by Yeh Hung-wei. Screenplay, Yeh, Lao

Chia-hua, Xiao Mao; camera (color), Yang Wei-han, Lee Yi-shih; editor, Yeh; music, Zhao Jiping; sound, Xiong Huachuan; art direction, Chiu Chung-chung. Reviewed at Turin Intl. Young Cinema Festival (competition), Nov. 15, 1991. Running time: **123 MIN.**

Mingtao . . . . Yang Chieh-mei
Guijuan . . . . Wang Hsiu-ling
Jinmei . . . . Wu Pei-yu
Aiyue . . . . Lu Yuan-chi
Hexiang . . . . Ai Jing
Also with: Chang Shih, Chang Ying.

With no metaphorical messing around, "Five Girls and a Rope" presents a majestic diatribe on oppression of women in rural China framed by knockout visuals and top-notch production values. Pic could lose a half-hour of its running time but is well-deserving of exposure in the art market, where prospects appear solid.

Pic has been banned both in Taiwan because of the casting of a Chinese thesp and in China to quash competition with a subsequently produced Chinese version of same story. Elsewhere, attention stemming from prizes at Tokyo and Turin fests could get pic noticed by specialized distribs.

Story follows five girls who grew up together and the series of injustices they suffer. Dreaming of a mythical garden paradise where women are treated humanely, the girls dress in ceremonial red robes (traditional color for Chinese brides) and go to a temple to hang themselves.

Film opens and closes with startling tableau of the suspended bodies. Director Yeh Hung-wei punctuates the action with similarly stirring operatic moments.

Perfs by the five leads (most of them newcomers) are tops all round, and Chang Shih has touching moments as a field worker.

Yeh's telling of each girl's story in separate strands without intercutting is unadventurous and detracts from film's overall flow, but direction is otherwise deft.

Tech credits are superlative, especially dazzling lensing of the spectacular location (pic was shot in northern China alongside Chen Keige's Cannes hit "Life on a String"). —*David Rooney*

JEWISH FEST

IZKOR: SLAVES OF MEMORY
(FRENCH-DOCU)

An IMA Prods.-Rhea Films-ZDF-Adam Prods. co-production. Produced by Reuben Kornfeld, Edgard Tannenbaum. Executive producers, Georges Benayoun, Paul Rozenberg. Directed by Eyal Sivan. Screenplay, Stefan Lavide. Camera (color), Rony Katzenelson; editor, Jacques Cometz; sound, Remy Atal. Reviewed at Boston Jewish Film Festival, Brookline, Mass., Nov. 11, 1991. Running time: **104 MIN.**

Eyal Sivan is a native-born Israeli working in France who has made a heartfelt docu criticizing and condemning the Israeli educational system. Unfortunately, the film neither proves his point nor is likely to generate much interest Stateside outside the circuit of Jewish film festivals.

Sivan's point is that the Israeli public schools emphasize Jewish victimhood to the exclusion of all else, and he focuses on a four-week period in 1990 that included the observances of Passover, Yom Hashoah (remembrance of the Holocaust) and Israeli Independence Day.

The film's title, "Izkor," is a reference to the Jewish memorial service. Chief spokesman for Sivan's view is Dr. Yeshayahau Leibovitz, an elderly scholar who thinks Jewish victimization is a subject for non-Jews to concern themselves with, not for Jews.

By largely limiting his on-camera voices to Leibovitz, students and teachers, Sivan fails to make his case beyond showing that he is more critical of the system that educated him than its present participants appear to be. He may have some valid points, but "Izkor" doesn't make them. — *Daniel M. Kimmel*

REAL TIME
(ISRAELI)

A Sunrise Films presentation. Executive producer, Uzi Guttshtadt. Produced by Doron Eran, Arnon Tzadok. Directed by Uri Barbash. Screenplay, Benny Barbash; camera (color) Amnon Salomon; editor, Tova Asher; music, Adi Rennert; associate producer, Arnon Tserak. Reviewed at Coolidge Corner Theater, Brookline, Mass., Nov. 16, 1991. (In Boston Jewish and Haifa film festivals). Running time: **106 MIN.**
With: Assi Dayan, Rivka Newman, NetaMoran, HanaMaron, ShlomoTarshish.

Director Uri Barbash, best known Stateside for his Oscar-nominated "Beyond the Walls" (1984), is back with "Real Time," a.k.a. "The War After," a fictional look at the aftermath of the Yom Kippur War. Pic should get some notice on the fest circuit, Jewish-themed and otherwise.

Downer story lacks the "sexy" topic of the Israeli/Palestinian conflict that propelled "Beyond the Walls" to international success. While tech credits on this one are okay, commercial prospects are questionable. Best shot seems to be for situations where film will have a built-in audience.

The story, which may draw readings as both allegory and psychological drama, focuses on a colonel (played by w.k. Israeli thesp Assi Dayan, son of Gen. Moshe Dayan) who finds himself in a jam after the 1973 war: He's blamed for the casualties of his armored division after opting not to remove them when reinforcements fail to arrive.

While there are occasional light spots, pic gradually draws viewer into the soldier's eventual breakdown as he realizes the toughest person he faces is himself. Dayan succeeds in making Hanegbi understandable without ever allowing viewer to forget that he is partly to blame for his plight.

In some ways, "Real Time" is almost like the post-Vietnam "Coming Home," told from the perspective of gung-ho officer Bruce Dern rather than good wife Jane Fonda.

Barbash noted at the Boston Jewish fest that the pic was not well-received in Israel earlier this year. It may be because he cuts too close to the bone.
—*Daniel M. Kimmel*

ARCHIVE REVIEW

DECEMBER 7TH: THE MOVIE
(DOCU-B&W)

A presentation of the War & Navy Dept. Produced by John Ford. Co-directed by Gregg Toland and John Ford. Screenplay, Toland; camera, Toland; editor, Robert Parrish; music, Alfred Newman; 2nd unit director, James C. Havens. Reviewed on vidcassette. Running time: **85 MIN.**
With: Walter Huston, Harry Davenport, Dana Andrews, Paul Hurst; George O'Brien, James K. McGuiness (narrators).

Timed for the 50th anni of the Pearl Harbor air raid, this video release by Kit Parker Films provides the first public glimpse of the original 85-minute version of "December 7th." Retrieved footage — chiefly, two long sequences — does little to enhance film aesthetically, but it should be of big interest to history and film buffs.

Released in 1943 after Navy criticism and military censorship led to extensive cutting, docu won an Oscar in its 34-minute form. "December 7th" is only nominally a docu since most of it has reconstructions or allegorical dramatizations.

For the government film, producer John Ford had assigned acclaimed cinematographer Gregg Toland to direct and gather newsreel material at Pearl Harbor. Dissatisfied with what was available, Toland shot his own version of the attack on 20th Century Fox's backlot and wrote a feature-length script.

Though reportedly somewhat offput by Toland's approach, Ford backed him and directed some sequences. Released version consisted largely of the reconstruction, which supposedly fooled most people as the real thing, followed by a profile of an aroused military preparing to strike back.

Originally excised sequence shows a complacent Uncle Sam (Walter Huston) being needled by an elderly materialization of his conscience, Mr. C (Harry Davenport), who chastises Sam for lack of military preparedness and points out the potential dangers of inhabitants of Japanese origin in Hawaii.

The other cut sequence has Dana Andrews personifying the American dead at Pearl Harbor and philosophizing with a cynical deceased veteran of World War I in a kind of military afterlife. The camera tracks behind them as they pass rows of graves from various wars.

Script has the characters talking in ill-advised baseball jargon: America didn't want to play in the "International League," Woodrow Wilson was left "at third base," but now that "Uncle Sam is in there pitching," everyone is working for a "World Series pennant called peace."
— *Fred Lombardi*

HOOK

A Tri-Star release of an Amblin Entertainment production. Produced by Kathleen Kennedy, Frank Marshall, Gerald R. Molen. Executive producers, Dodi Fayed, Jim V. Hart. Co-producers, Gary Adelson, Craig Baumgarten. Directed by Steven Spielberg. Screenplay, Hart, Malia Scotch Marmo, screen story by Hart, Nick Castle, based on J.M. Barrie's original stageplay and books. Camera (Deluxe color; Deluxe and Technicolor prints; Panavision widescreen), Dean Cundey; editor, Michael Kahn; music, John Williams; production design, Norman Garwood; visual consultant, John Napier; art direction, Andrew Precht, Thomas E. Sanders; set design, Henry Alberti, Thomas Betts, Joseph Hodges, Peter J. Kelly, Joseph G. Pacelli Jr., Jacques Valin; set decoration, Garrett Lewis; costume design, Anthony Powell; special visual effects, Industrial Light & Magic; visual effects supervisor, Eric Brevig; special effects supervisor, Michael Lantieri; stunt coordinator-action choreographer, Gary Hymes; choreographer, Vince Paterson; special makeup, Greg Cannom; associate producers, Bruce Cohen, Marmo; assistant director, Cohen; casting, Janet Hirshenson, Jane Jenkins, Michael Hirshenson. Reviewed at Avco Cinema, L.A., Dec. 4, 1991. MPAA Rating: PG. Running time: **144 MIN.**

Captain Hook . . . . . Dustin Hoffman
Peter Banning/
  Peter Pan . . . . Robin Williams
Tinkerbell . . . . Julia Roberts
Smee . . . . Bob Hoskins
Granny Wendy . . . . . Maggie Smith
Moira . . . . Caroline Goodall
Jack . . . . Charlie Korsmo
Maggie . . . . Amber Scott
Liza . . . . Laurel Cronin
Inspector Good . . . . . . Phil Collins
Tootles . . . . Arthur Malet
Pockets . . . . Isaiah Robinson
Ace . . . . Jasen Fisher
Rufio . . . . Dante Basco
Thud Butt . . . . . Raushan Hammond
Don't Ask . . . . James Madio
Too Small . . . . Thomas Tulak
Latchboy . . . . Alex Zuckerman
No Nap . . . . Ahmad Stoner

"Hook" feels as much like a massive amusement park ride as it does a film. Spirited, rambunctious, often messy and undisciplined, this determined attempt to recast the Peter Pan story in contempo terms splashes every bit of its megabudget (between $60 million and $80 million) onto the screen; commercial elements overflow in such abundance that major hit status seems guaranteed.

A shade sophisticated for small kids and too indulgent for more demanding adults, pic will find favor with mainstream audiences without, perhaps, being taken deeply to heart: The "E.T."-like magic doesn't click in, but it will certainly be one of the three or four biggest films of the year.

Often called a Peter Pan himself for his unparalleled ability to capture the innocent wonder of childhood in his films, Steven Spielberg has long wanted to put some version of the classic J.M. Barrie tale on the big screen. He found his way in with Jim V. Hart's screenplay, which, as amended by co-writer Malia Scotch Marmo, sends a modern, grown-up Peter, a man who has forgotten his youth, back to Neverland to rescue his children from the clutches of the ever-vengeful Captain Hook.

Material could scarcely be more pregnant with thematic possibilities for Spielberg, who has so often favored kids' p.o.v. over that of adults, and is now roughly the same age as the hero of the picture. His basic proposition is that to enter the state of mind where anything is possible, one must reawaken the child inside.

Setup is deftly done, sweeping the viewer right into world of the Banning family. Peter (Robin Williams) is a workaholic corporate attorney so busy he sends an underling to videotape his son's Little League games. But he manages to tear himself away to take his wife Moira (Caroline Goodall) and children Jack (Charlie Korsmo) and Maggie (Amber Scott) to London to visit Granny Wendy (Maggie Smith).

Back in Blighty, Jack and Maggie are spirited away, courtesy Captain James Hook. Mystified, Peter is visited by Tinkerbell (Julia Roberts) and, 36 minutes into the story, is transported to Neverland, where Hook (Dustin Hoffman) lords over a raucous Pirate Town from the deck of his enormous ship.

Humiliated by Hook, Peter is granted three days to prepare for his battle with the eager captain, who has been waiting ages for his rematch with the fellow responsible for his losing his hand to a crocodile. Woefully out of shape and still unaware of his previous identity, Peter is thrown in with the Lost Boys, Peter Pan's errant tribe of orphans who look askance at this pretender to their leadership.

Sweet and likable through the first half-hour, pic becomes dominated by a vaudeville tone and in-jokes during the pirate section (Glenn Close turns up in male disguise as a sailor victimized by Hook), and slides into environmental theme park hijinks once it reaches the boys' playground.

Devised by production designer Norman Garwood and visual consultant John Napier (and revealing the strong influence of the latter's stage designs for "Cats," "Les Miserables" and "Starlight Express") spectacular set is replete with tram tracks, vines, water holes, a treehouse and even a skateboard ramp, all of which are enthusiastically used by boys of all ethnic persuasions and tough attitudes, but which also emphasize the theatricality of the proceedings.

But a little of this stuff goes a long way, and pic's middle portion sags considerably as Peter's oafish efforts to recapture his former self are intercut with Hook's devilish and initially successful attempt to win the love of young Jack and convince him that Peter is a bad father.

Finally, after 97 minutes, Peter becomes "the Pan," taking wing in technically impeccable flying sequences and assuming definitive leadership of the Lost Boys. Despite the cascade of wondrous special effects, massive battles between the kids and pirates and face-offs between Pan and Hook, the film doesn't truly take flight, as it vigorously but mechanically works through several climaxes before settling back in London for the inevitable family reunion.

The sheer inventiveness and quantity of diverting elements make for a reasonable degree of entertainment value, but Spielberg lets it sprawl on for too long. Much of the action in the campground seems aimless and visually unfocused. Clearly engaged in working out the psychological, mythic and thematic aspects of the story, director loses his grip on concise storytelling and dramatic punch, sacrificing any suspense (which the original had) in the process.

Stature of the title character has also been reduced in this rendition, as jokiness gets the better of both Hoffman, who brandishes an erratic British accent and barely conceals the method in his badness, and Bob Hoskins, who plays the captain's loyal hand, Smee, with customary relish but little genuine humor.

Dialogue throughout has its share of snappy zingers, and elements from Barrie's original works are cleverly incorporated, but neither actor is furnished with sterling material that can quite match their abilities to put it across.

Williams was the most natural choice to play this resurgent Pan, and he inhabits the role splendidly. Properly uptight as the lawyer and absent father, he becomes an utterly convincing leader to his band of kids, and is a Peter Pan any viewer can believe in (although some with recent memories of "The Fisher King" will be amused at how he has shaved off his body hair for this role).

Playing scenes mostly alone or miniaturized opposite a looming Williams, Roberts makes a beguiling, leggy Tinkerbell, and Charlie Korsmo, remembered from "Dick Tracy," is fine as Peter's son who falls under Hook's spell.

But the standout supporting turns come from Smith, perfect as the aged Wendy, and Goodall, who transforms the potentially sticky role of Peter's wife into a beautiful miniature portrait of motherly love and devotion, with the best speech of the show.

Rockers Phil Collins and David Crosby pop up in bits, but there's no sign of Michael Jackson or Bruce Willis, both rumored during production to have been slipped into the cast.

Spielberg's theme of retaining youthful sense of wonder, playfulness and imagination carries plenty of resonance, and seems notably directed to materialists among his baby boomer generation. But it's so emphatically stated as to be less than entirely moving.

Pic is unquestionably one of the most stupendous productions ever mounted on soundstages. Surrounded by a cyclorama and lit from artificial sources, the Neverland sets provide constant distraction. The same goes for the costumes, makeup, stunts and special effects, all of which are as good as they get.

Dean Cundey's lensing glows in the opening and closing sections; Michael Kahn's editing is fluid and propulsive as always, while John Williams' ever-present score lays it on a bit thick this time.

Biggest laugh at the L.A. press screening came when Peter takes his family to London, and a stock airplane shot shows them traveling by Pan Am, which ceased operations the same day.

— *Todd McCarthy*

BUGSY

A TriStar release of a Mulholland Prods./Baltimore Pictures production. Produced by Mark Johnson, Barry Levinson, Warren Beatty. Co-producer, Charles Newirth. Directed by Levinson. Screenplay, James Toback. Camera (Technicolor), Allen Daviau; editor, Stu Linder; music, Ennio Morricone; production design, Dennis Gassner; art direction, Leslie McDonald; set design, Lawrence A. Hubbs; set decoration, Nancy

Haigh; costume design, Albert Wolsky; sound (Dolby), Willie D. Burton; sound design, Richard Beggs; special makeup effects, Rob Bottin; assistant director, Peter Giuliano; casting, Ellen Chenoweth. Reviewed at Sony Studios screening room, Culver City, Calif., Dec. 3, 1991. MPAA Rating: R. Running time: **135 MIN.**

Bugsy Siegel . . . . . . Warren Beatty
Virginia Hill . . . . . . Annette Bening
Mickey Cohen . . . . . Harvey Keitel
Meyer Lansky . . . . . . Ben Kingsley
Harry Greenberg . . . . . Elliott Gould
George Raft . . . . Joe Mantegna
Countess di Frasso . . Bebe Neuwirth
Esta Siegel . . . . . . Wendy Phillips
Jack Dragna . . . . . Richard Sarafian
Joey Adonis . . . . . Lewis Van Bergen
Charlie Luciano . . . . . . Bill Graham
Del Webb . . . . Andy Romano
Also with: Robert Beltran, Gian-Carlo Scandiuzzi, Stefanie Mason, Kimberly McCullough, Joseph Roman, James Toback.

A melancholy and intimate gangster saga about a romantic dreamer with fatal flaws, "Bugsy" emerges as a smooth, safe portrait of a volatile, dangerous character. An absorbing narrative flow and a parade of colorful underworld characters vie for screen time with an unsatisfactory central romance, and film is most interesting as a lively addition to Warren Beatty's gallery of idealistic losers.

Handsome pic about the inventor of Las Vegas lacks the fire and impact to make a b.o. killing, but TriStar's second-most expensive Christmas release (after "Hook") should do respectable biz.

A boyhood chum of both Meyer Lansky and George Raft, Benjamin Siegel was sent to L.A. to take over the West Coast rackets but stayed to become one of the legendary Hollywood characters of the 1940s.

A brash ladies' man and society figure who charmed and bullied people in equal measure, he aspired to levels of accomplishment and class beyond those imagined by his gangland cohorts.

As conjectured here, however, his romantic heart, carelessness and inescapably brutal nature did him in, and his adversaries were left to reap the benefits of his mad, visionary idea for a gambling oasis in the desert.

Siegel is a terrific subject for a film, but only part of the story comes across in this intelligently conceived drama. In James Toback's writing and Beatty's gutsy playing, Bugsy bursts out as a fully realized, psychologically complex character endowed with very human strengths and weaknesses.

Unfortunately, his great love and female counterpart, Virginia Hill (Annette Bening), remains a one-dimensional and annoying stick figure, throwing great sections of the film out of whack.

Firmly establishing that, whatever his other attributes, the title character is a ruthless killer, tale begins with Bugsy bumping off an underling for stealing. Repeatedly, just when it seems that Bugsy might be shaping up into a reasonable guy and actually believing his dictum that "Everybody deserves a fresh start," his maniacal side takes over, and anyone who crosses him better watch out.

Giving new meaning to the word "impulsive," Bugsy quickly acquires the BevHills mansion of an opera singer, a swank car and, as if in his spare time, intimidates the smallfry West Coast crime figures of the time into working for him. Shown around screenland by Raft, he also takes up with bit player Hill, the sometime g.f. of fellow mobster Joey Adonis.

A tart who's been around and admits that she's brought nothing but trouble to the men who have fallen for her, Virginia is as tough as Bugsy in the amorous trenches and gets an erotic kick out of his strong-arm tactics.

But why the cocksure Bugsy becomes a moonstruck, insanely jealous fool willing to divorce his wife over her remains a total mystery. As written by Toback, Virginia is a dime-a-dozen, standard-issue Hollywood hot number, her only vulnerable quality being her fear of flying.

Constantly threatening to walk out on her man or actually doing so, Virginia begins as merely uninteresting and progressively becomes a major drag, sending both the film and her b.f. into a tailspin whenever she's around. Bening, always impressive in her screen appearances until now, seems miscast and at a loss to bring any psychological insight to the role.

But the film manages to hold its own at other moments. Once installed as syndicate kingpin in L.A., Bugsy enjoys a palsy camaraderie with crime partner Mickey Cohen, plots the assassination of Mussolini, uses his connections downtown to beat a murder rap and convinces Lansky and Lucky Luciano to back his plan to build a resort hotel and casino, the Flamingo, in Vegas.

In what can be read as an analogy to the filmmaking process, Siegel proposes a $1 million budget for the project but ends up spending $6 million, telling his angered patrons, "If you're gonna do somethin,' do it right." But it's his blind faith in and unconditional love for Virginia that really does him in, leading to his w.k. rubout in BevHills.

Director Barry Levinson treats this punchy, emotionally eruptive story in fluid, almost dreamy fashion, rather like a sordid fairy tale. Using countless dissolves and sound overlaps, and backed by Ennio Morricone's quietly brooding score, Levinson tends toward visually recessive techniques at moments of highest drama, placing the action behind panels, glass or walls or simply moving it discreetly to the distance.

As effective as the film is at times, notably in the hauntingly weird mood of the nascent Las Vegas, it could be argued that the lyrical directorial style is precisely the opposite of the gritty, impassioned approach that might have most brought out the most in the material.

Although ethnically wrong and lacking a street-tough attitude, Beatty gives a dynamite performance, his most vital and surprising in a long time. The charm part seems easy, but the actor socks over scenes such as he has never before attempted.

Bugsy also follows in a memorable line of Beatty characters that notably includes John Mc-Cabe in "McCabe and Mrs. Miller" and John Reed in "Reds," quixotic romantics whose flawed nobility gets the better of them.

Despite boundless guts and aggressiveness, Bugsy has a little boy's eagerness to please and can't even bring himself to tell his wife he wants a divorce when the marriage is clearly over. This Bugsy may be a rose-colored variation on the real thing, but Beatty, Toback and Levinson's conception of his destiny has resonance.

Among the standouts in the impressive supporting cast are Harvey Keitel as a feisty, appealing Mickey Cohen; Ben Kingsley as the impeccably businesslike Lansky; and director Richard Sarafian as the pathetic Jack Dragna.

Elliott Gould effectively underplays the weak squealer Harry Greenberg, the late Bill Graham plays Luciano with authority, Wendy Phillips is Bugsy's eternally suffering wife and Joe Mantegna is oddly cast as Raft.

Lenser Allen Daviau suffuses the action in a rich, lustrous look, bringing out the outstanding and varied textures of Dennis Gassner's production design and Albert Wolsky's costumes.
— *Todd McCarthy*

THE PRINCE OF TIDES

A Columbia Pictures release of a Barwood/Longfellow production. Produced by Barbra Streisand, Andrew Karsch. Co-producer, Sheldon Schrager. Executive producers, Cis Corman, James Roe. Directed by Streisand. Screenplay, Pat Conroy, Becky Johnston, based on Conroy's novel. Camera (Technicolor), Stephen Goldblatt; editor, Don Zimmerman; music, James Newton Howard; production design, Paul Sylbert; art direction, W. Steven Graham; set design, Chris Shriver; set decoration, Caryl Heller, Arthur Howe Jr., Leslie Ann Pope; costume design, Ruth Morley; sound (Dolby), Dennis Maitland; assistant director, Thomas A. Reilly; casting, Bonnie Finnegan. Reviewed at Mann's Culver Plaza, Culver City, Calif., Nov. 26, 1991. MPAA Rating: R. Running time: **132 MIN.**

Tom Wingo . . . . Nick Nolte
Susan Lowenstein . . Barbra Streisand
Sallie Wingo . . . . . . Blythe Danner
Lila Wingo Newbury . . Kate Nelligan
Herbert Woodruff . . . Jeroen Krabbé
Savannah Wingo . . . . Melinda Dillon
Eddie Detreville . . . . . George Carlin
Bernard Woodruff . . . . . Jason Gould
Henry Wingo . . . . Brad Sullivan
Lucy Wingo . . . . . . Maggie Collier
Jennifer Wingo . . . . . Lindsay Wray
Chandler Wingo . . Brandlyn Whitaker
Also with: Justen Woods, Bobby Fain, Trey Yearwood, Tiffany Jean Davis, Nancy Atchison, Kiki Runyan, Grayson Fricke, Ryan Newman, Chris Stacy.

"The Prince of Tides" has a passion seldom found in contempo U.S. films and a quality not usually associated with Barbra Streisand — self-effacement. She hasn't been seen on screen in recent years, but there should be a big audience nonetheless for this lush romantic drama.

A deeply moving exploration of the tangled emotions of a dysfunctional Southern family, the lovingly crafted (though unevenly scripted) film of Pat Conroy's novel centers on Nick Nolte's performance of a lifetime.

Bringing her usual strengths of character to her role as Nolte's psychiatrist/lover, Streisand marks every frame with the intensity and care of a filmmaker committed to heartfelt, unashamed emotional involvement with her characters.

No doubt filmgoers seduced by the trendy glitz of most current pics will find Streisand's film old-fashioned and staid, but, to her credit, she doesn't feel the need to jazz up the compelling tale's telling, which covers a wide sweep of time with an artistically valid flashback structure and involves complex emotions.

Conroy and Becky Johnston's script picks up ex-teacher/coach Nolte in a midlife crisis unusually chaotic even for a Nolte character. He's jobless, drinking too much and struggling with a disintegrating marriage to Blythe Danner.

Nolte's disturbed sister Melinda Dillon, a N.Y. poet of some repute who has created an alternate literary persona as the child of Holocaust victims, has attempted suicide, and she lies catatonic in hospital restraints. Her brother is summoned north to help her psychiatrist (Streisand) piece together the splintered mirror of her past.

Making an uncharacteristically delayed entrance after a 12-minute intro about the South Carolina family, Streisand puts herself as director, star and character at Nolte's service, gradually drawing out his family secrets and long-suppressed anger and pain. In the process, this emotionally guarded doctor finds herself not only becoming Nolte's surrogate mother but also crossing the professional line to emotional and sexual involvement.

Again pairing her N.Y. Jewish character with a Gentile man, Streisand draws sparks and humor from the clash and then the melding of two disparate cultural viewpoints. Both characters prove to have repressions and passions that draw them together.

Though she spends most of her early scenes in the pic questioning Nolte and listening intently, Streisand does not neglect another side of her screen image that draws her fans — the narcissistic self-love of someone regarded as an ugly duckling but who knows that she's really "gorgeous," as she admitted in her first line in "Funny Girl."

In "The Prince of Tides," the director unabashedly shows off her shapely legs in repeated doting closeups. And lenser Stephen Goldblatt's handsomely burnished color scheme favors Streisand's silky-tan skin tones and makes the middle-aged star look glamorous.

Streisand's analytical probing into Nolte's past, triggering flashback episodes of strife caused by his abusive father (Brad Sullivan) and pathetically grandiose mother (Kate Nelligan), makes for a fascinating romantic detective story: Each revelation draws the initially aloof doctor closer in empathy and understanding to her reluctant patient.

Though the Streisand character's M.O. naturally is to bring suppressed feelings to the surface, script occasionally becomes too explicit in its verbalization of what should remain subtexts. Screenwriters Conroy and Johnston also underdevelop some characters (especially Dillon) while overdoing the boorishness of Streisand's musician husband (Jeroen Krabbé) and the "Golden Boy" subplot involving her violin-playing son (Jason Gould), who learns football from Nolte.

Pic's final third seems somewhat choppy and rushed, although James Newton Howard's surging score helps Streisand over the bumps.

It would have helped illuminate Nolte's conflicts to know more about his sister and mother, who remain fragmentary if tantalizingly well-played characters, and the film also somewhat neglects the superb Danner, though her scenes with Nolte are powerfully elliptical in their mostly unspoken emotions.

But the heart of the film is the relationship between Nolte and Streisand, a creative sparring match doomed to go nowhere but leaves an indelible imprint on each.

Nolte courageously leaves himself naked on screen, not only in his powerful emotional breakdown when Streisand probes his deepest secret, but also his display of utter weakness and vulnerability.

Once he and Streisand become physically involved, story lets up on tension. At first the film seemingly has nowhere to go once they've reached their meeting of minds, and they've gone beyond being doctor and patient. But the emotional force of the conclusion comes from the realization that Nolte's newfound maturity has drawn him back to his family and away from the woman who helped him come to terms with it.

It's a rare film that can make a male-female relationship so gripping on a nonsexual level, and that's one of the special pleasures of "The Prince of Tides," a film that, like Streisand's previous directorial effort, "Yentl," finds her a lover who's her intellectual equal. That's one of the advantages of having a woman director.

— *Joseph McBride*

KAFKA

A Miramax release of a Baltimore Pictures, Renn/Pricel S.A. production. Produced by Stuart Cornfeld, Harry Benn. Executive producers, Paul Rassam, Mark Johnson. Directed by Steven Soderbergh. Screenplay, Lem Dobbs. Camera (black & white, color; Duart prints), Walt Lloyd; editor, Soderbergh; music, Cliff Martinez; production design, Gavin Bocquet, Tony Woollard (additional shoot); art direction, Les Tomkins, Jiri Matolin, Philip Elton (special effects unit); set decoration, Joanne Woollard; costume design, Michael Jeffery; sound (Dolby), Paul Ledford; sound design, Mark Mangini; assistant directors, Guy Travers, Jiri Ostry, Steve Harding (additional shoot); casting, Susie Figgis. Reviewed at Sony Studios screening room, Culver City, Calif., Nov. 13, 1991. MPAA Rating: PG-13. Running time: **98 MIN.**
Kafka . . . . Jeremy Irons
Gabriela . . . . Theresa Russell
Burgel . . . . Joel Grey
Dr. Murnau . . . . Ian Holm
Bizzlebek . . . . Jeroen Krabbé
Grubach . . . . . Armin Mueller-Stahl
The Chief Clerk . . . . Alec Guinness
Castle Henchman . . . . . Brian Glover
Assistant Ludwig . . . . . Keith Allen
Assistant Oscar . . . Simon McBurney
Files Keeper . . . . . Robert Flemyng

The sophomore jinx has hit Steven Soderbergh just mildly with "Kafka." Defiantly not a biopic, helmer's first outing since he burst upon the scene with "Sex, Lies, and Videotape" nearly three years ago places the literary world's first modern alienated man in a sinister Prague, c. 1919, echoing author's fictional universe.

But the story ultimately feels too conventional, and the portrait of the artist is too shallow to stand as a compelling or convincing evocation of a complex mind. Opening for one-week runs to qualify for critics' and Oscar consideration, handsomely produced release looks to okay b.o. results on the specialized circuit.

Penned more than 10 years ago, Lem Dobbs' script tells of a mild-mannered insurance company clerk who, by night, writes strange stories for little-read magazines.

Although somewhat antisocial, Kafka (never Franz) lives a relatively routine, orderly life, and whatever troubles him deeply, or motivates his unique imagination, remains well concealed. In a black & white world of long shadows, furtive figures and unknown motives, mystery rears its head when a fellow worker turns up in the morgue.

Kafka (Jeremy Irons) is introduced to a group of anarchists by another co-worker (Theresa Russell), and although he rejects their overtures to him, Kafka is increasingly drawn into a maze of intrigue through an array of puzzling circumstances.

Oppressed at his vast, impersonal office by his snooping overseer (Joel Grey) and criticized as a "lone wolf" by his boss (Alec Guinness), he nonetheless is promoted and given two incompetent assistants who profess to be identical twins but look utterly unalike.

Soon the femme co-worker disappears, and Kafka finds himself with a briefcase bomb the late Eduard was carrying on a secret mission to the dreaded Castle. So to the Castle Kafka must ultimately go to try to penetrate the unknowable and to make sense of the unexplainable events that have come to dominate his life.

This sort of quandary, of course, is central to the work of Kafka the writer, although it was normally posited in terms at once more extreme and abstract. Soderbergh and Dobbs have created a crime melodrama with fairly explicit overtones, one that conjures up film worlds as readily as it does Kafka's literary oeuvre.

The villain of the piece is not named Dr. Murnau for nothing. The old-world setting and exaggerated visual style readily recall German Expressionism, which in turn helped spawn Hitchcock, the master of placing innocents amid extraordinary events.

The locations and occasional zither touches of Cliff Martinez's extremely effective and witty score call to mind "The Third Man," which raises the specter of Orson Welles, who himself filmed a powerful version of Kafka's "The Trial" 30 years ago. Even if "The Trial" was not entirely successful, it had in spades what "Kafka" lacks — a grand visual design that gave it artistic magnitude worthy of its subject.

Although shot on the virtually unchanged streets of Prague, and despite some strong staging of individual scenes, the new film is not sufficiently stylized or radical to convey the appalling insight of the man who inspired it. "Kafka" is, finally, too normal.

Decision to lense in black & white was apt but, unfortunately, cinematographer Walt Lloyd can't match the levels of the German and British masters his first time out of the box. Images look mostly gray, flat and washed out.

Ironically, Soderbergh scores his greatest visual coup when, 74 minutes in, he suddenly switches to color, à la "The Wizard of Oz," upon Kafka's penetration of the castle. This 14-minute section, superbly designed and shot, more successfully sustains a consistent tone of horror and surprise than any other portion of the picture.

Great actor that he is, tall, terrific-looking Irons can't quite convince as the retiring, bug-like paranoid who, in a timeless world, might have been played by Peter Lorre. Irons acts Kafka's bewilderment expertly but never truly seems like a pawn of society.

Nice one-dimensional character turns are put in by the distinguished men in the cast, but Russell, with her untempered U.S. accent and flat readings, sticks out like a sore thumb in this company.

Ultimately, plenty goes on here to hold interest, notably the production design of Gavin Bocquet and Tony Woollard. Soderbergh shows a new side to his talents in his skillful shooting and cutting of suspense sequences. But the story reduces Kafka to too mundane and melodramatic a level, a solver of crimes rather than an artistic visionary.

— Todd McCarthy

AT PLAY IN THE FIELDS OF THE LORD

A Universal Pictures release of a Saul Zaentz Co. presentation. Produced by Saul Zaentz. Executive producers, Francisco Ramalho Jr., David Nichols. Directed by Hector Babenco. Screenplay, Jean-Claude Carriere, Babenco, based on Peter Matthiessen's novel. Camera (color), Lauro Escorel; editor, William Anderson; music, Zbigniew Preisner; production design, Clovis Bueno; costume design, Rita Murtinho; art direction, Marlise Storchi, Antonio Vanzolini, Roberto Mainieri; supervising sound editor, Alan Splet; makeup-hair design, Jaque Monteiro; assistant director, Steve Andrews; associate producer, Paul Zaentz; 2nd unit director, Roberto Gervitz; aerial unit director, David Jones; casting (U.S.), Dianne Crittenden; casting (Brazil), Graca Motta, Jose Augusto de Souza. Reviewed at Universal Studios, L.A., Nov. 21, 1991. MPAA rating: R. Running time: **187 MIN.**

Lewis Moon . . . . Tom Berenger
Martin Quarrier . . . . . . Aidan Quinn
Hazel Quarrier . . . . Kathy Bates
Leslie Huben . . . . John Lithgow
Andy Huben . . . . Daryl Hannah
Wolf . . . . Tom Waits
Boronai . . . . Stenio Garcia
Father Xantes . . . . . . Nelson Xavier
Guzman . . . . Jose Dumont
Billy Quarrier . . . . . . Niilo Kivirinta
Aeore . . . . S. Yriwana Karaja
Tukanu . . . . Carlos Xavante

"At Play in the Fields of the Lord" is how half-breed Cheyenne mercenary Lewis Moon describes his location to missionaries before he para-

chutes into the Amazon jungle to seek his essence among a tribe called the Niaruna. Tale that follows — a challenging, cerebral and beautifully controlled take on Peter Matthiessen's revered novel — amounts to a cry of warning against outside interference with a delicate ecological and cultural balance.

"If you want to preserve something, stay away from it" is the essential message — not a notion most Americans will embrace. Unsentimental and unsparing, Saul Zaentz's $30 million-plus production could have a tough time breaking even, despite award-worthy achievements.

Central to this telling are two men: a callous, brooding jungle rat (Tom Berenger) and his nemesis (Aidan Quinn), a dedicated Evangelical worker. One is in the Brazilian jungle town of Mae de Deus to bring Christianity to the Indians; the other is there to bomb them out of their habitat so the Brazilian government can seize their land.

At fierce odds with each other and ill at ease with their respective tasks, each subverts his own mission, only to find that no matter how he purifies his intention, his presence among the natives can bring them only ill.

Matthiessen's story has inflamed the passions of many a filmmaker since its 1965 publication (John Huston, Bob Rafaelson, Paul Newman and Taylor Hackford all wanted to make it at various times), and producer Zaentz has pursued it over the course of 20 years.

It's easy to see why. Beyond its ecological warning, more acutely relevant today than ever, it's a richly involving adventure that pits modern man, with all his complications and internal damage, against the fierce and rude clarity of his primeval self.

Film has a bracing story told in an intimate and absorbing way, with a script by Babenco and Jean-Claude Carriere that hews remarkably close to the novel.

Action is a bit stiff and pedantic at first as it stakes out its philosophical turf but then softens and blooms. Diminished in scope without the magnificent voice of the author's prose, pic nonetheless gains something from the indelible perfs stamped out by a first-rate ensemble cast under Babenco.

Among them are Kathy Bates as Quinn's shrill, hysterically repressed wife; John Lithgow as a briskly buffoonish fellow mission-

ary; Daryl Hannah as Lithgow's sweetly blank and dogmatic wife; and Tom Waits in his best showcase ever as Moon's sidekick and soul of self-mocking depravity.

Berenger, who goes all but naked once he joins the Indians, projects a smoldering unpredictability and the charisma of a young, primitive Brando. Quinn is a revelation as he plays against type as the geeky, ineffectual but compassionate missionary struggling to stay in control amid overwhelming pressure.

A more challenging work than "Dances With Wolves," "At Play. . ." lacks that picture's romantic sweep but is just as respectful of the South American Indians, devoting abundant care and footage to their rituals and ways —sometimes to the detriment of dramatic flow.

A language for the fictional Niaruna has been created for the film, and subtitles are used sparingly. Shot over a harrowing six months in the remote jungle town of Belem, Brazil, pic boasts many technical achievements sure to be noticed at awards time.

Lauro Escorel's cinematography is spellbinding. Music by Zbigniew Preisner and the production, art and costume design elements are outstanding.

— Amy Dawes

DECEMBER

An IRS Media release of a Copeland/Colichman production. Produced by Richard C. Berman, Donald Paul Pemrick. Executive producers, Miles A. Copeland III, Paul Colichman, Harold Welb. Line producer, Kevin Reidy. Directed, written by Gabe Torres. Camera (Foto-Kem color), James Glennon; editor, Rick Hinson, Carole Kravetz; music, Deborah Holland; production design, Garreth Stover; art direction, Kenneth A. Hardy; set decoration, Margaret Goldsmith; costume design, Ron Leamon; sound (Dolby), Ken Segal; associate producers, Melissa Cobb, Toni Phillips, Steven Reich; assistant director, James B. Rogers; casting, Don Pemrick. Reviewed at Raleigh Studios, L.A., Dec. 4, 1991. MPAA Rating: PG. Running time: **91 MIN.**

Allister Gibbs . . . . . Balthazar Getty
Russell Littlejohn . . . . Jason London
Tim Mitchell . . . . Brian Krause
Kipp Gibbs . . . . Wil Wheaton
Stuart Brayton . . . . . . Chris Young
Headmaster Thurston . . Robert Miller
Mrs. Langley . . . . Ann Hartfield
Billy Wade . . . . Soren Bailey

More a school debate than motion picture, "December" is an earnest drama in which five young men face the question, "To serve or not to serve," in the wake of Pearl Harbor. Decidedly uncinematic material would probably have

been more at home onstage, and theatrical prospects are negligible.

The words of FDR fill the rooms of a tradition-filled eastern prep school as the president declares war on Japan. The news hits these seniors especially close to home, as they will be the first called up if they don't enlist.

Immediately packing his bags is the school's top athlete, Tim, an apparent bully who can't imagine why any red-blooded American wouldn't want to be on the front line wherever it is. Assuming his best buddy, Kipp, will join him at the recruiting office, Tim browbeats the sissified rich boy Stuart over his intention to work in his father's factory, while the immature Russell, refusing to deal with his fear, just curls up in bed with his "Captain America" comic books.

It soon transpires that Kipp has been expelled earlier in the day for writing a book report on "Johnny Got His Gun," Dalton Trumbo's pacifist novel, the library copy of which was thrown in the incinerator by the school's headmaster. Kipp's head has been turned around by the book, and remainder of the film focuses on his attempts to articulate the book's meanings to the others as they evolve their own decisions about serving their country.

Most of the action, such as it is, unfolds in dorm rooms, with brief excursions to an outdoor courtyard, dining hall and swimming pool to break the monotony.

Gabe Torres directs most of his dialogue at a fevered argument pitch, with the characters haranguing each other in emotional fashion on the subjects of patriotism, duty and responsibility. Result is more tiresome than edifying, as the same basic ideas are expressed repeatedly, and not all that articulately.

Young thesps are solid without really shining, although Brian Krause manages some nice shadings as Tim, and Balthazar Getty has a few strong moments as Kipp's brother who wants to enlist despite being underage.

Although pic suffers from its cramped quarters, tech credits are very good, especially James Glennon's burnished lensing, which brings a real warmth to the cozy rooms that offer a haven from the bitter world outside.

— Todd McCarthy

PIZZA MAN

A Megalomania production. Produced by Gary Goldstein. Directed, written by "J.D. Athens" (Jonathan Lawton). Camera (color), Fred Samia; editor, Athens; music, Daniel May; production design, Theodore Smudde; costumes, Debra Goold; sound, Clifford (Kip) Gynn; casting, Laura Lee Hoffman. Reviewed at Sunset Screening rooms, Nov. 27, 1991. No MPAA rating. Running time: **90 MIN.**

Elmo Bunn . . . . Bill Maher
The Dame . . . . . Annabelle Gurwitch
Vince . . . . David McKnight
Mayor Bradley . . . . . . Bob Delegall
Ronald Reagan . . . . . . Bryan Clark

Even for fans of underground movie madness, "Pizza Man" doesn't deliver. Stale attempt at madcap cultural parody is as cheesy as its title suggests. Writer-director J.D. Athens will get stiffed at the boxoffice on this order.

Athens is a pseudonym for "Pretty Woman" scripter Jonathan Lawton, who financed this $400,000 production himself and began a month-long four-wall stint Dec. 6 at the Vista Theater in L.A. and at the Village East in N.Y.

There's not enough flair in this outing to light up a freeway accident and not enough control to prevent one. Straight outta L.A. story is a listless semi-"Chinatown" parody involving a cynical pizza deliverer (Bill Maher) who gets dragged into a political conspiracy while trying to collect $15 for a large sausage and anchovy.

Instead of money, he gets guff from a gallery of '80s public figures — Reagan, Dukakis, Michael Milken, Geraldine Ferraro, Dan Quayle, Donald Trump, even Mayor Tom Bradley — all trying to work out their power plays while ignoring the pleas of working stiff Maher for the payment properly due him.

Intended as social comment on the '80s, it plays more like outtakes from a bizarre public access tv show. Occasionally funny, pic is more often perplexing, as in a pointless scene where the hero bludgeons a Marilyn Quayle lookalike black and blue.

"The '80s are over," runs its adline, a dated observation if ever there was one. Even pizza has to be delivered hot and fresh. Plagued by all manner of production glitches, pic will have a hard time finding paying customers.

—*Amy Dawes*

STAR TREK VI: THE UNDISCOVERED COUNTRY

A Paramount Pictures release. Produced by Ralph Winter, Steven-Charles Jaffe. Executive producer, Leonard Nimoy. Directed by Nicholas Meyer. Screenplay, Meyer, Denny Martin Flinn; story by Nimoy, Lawrence Konner, Mark Rosenthal. Based upon "Star Trek" created by Gene Roddenberry. Camera (Technicolor), Hiro Narita; editor, Ronald Roose; film editor, William Hoy; music, Cliff Eidelman; production design, Herman Zimmerman; art direction, Nilo Rodis-Jamero; set decoration, Mickey S. Michaels; costume design, Dodie Shepard; sound (Dolby SR), Gene S. Cantamessa; co-producer-unit production manager, Marty Hornstein; associate producer, Brooke Breton; assistant director, Douglas E. Wise; 2nd unit director, Jaffe; 2nd unit camera, John V. Fante; special visual effects, Industrial Light & Magic; visual effects supervisor, Scott Farrar; makeup supervisor, Michael J. Mills; special alien makeup, Edward French; casting, Mary Jo Slater. Reviewed at National Theater, L.A., Dec. 3, 1991. MPAA Rating: PG. Running time: **109 MIN.**

Kirk . . . . William Shatner
Spock . . . . Leonard Nimoy
McCoy . . . . DeForest Kelley
Scotty . . . . James Doohan
Chekov . . . . Walter Koenig
Uhuru . . . . Nichelle Nichols
Sulu . . . . George Takei
Lt. Valeris . . . . Kim Cattrall
Chancellor Gorkon . . . David Warner
Chang . . . . . Christopher Plummer
Sarek . . . . Mark Lenard

Also with: Grace Lee Whitney, Brock Peters, Leon Russom, Kurtwood Smith, Rosana DeSoto, John Schuck, Michael Dorn, Paul Rossilli, Christian Slater.

Lure of what's billed as the final voyage of the original Enterprise crew (with all its attendant sentiment heightened by the death of creator Gene Roddenberry) should help this sixth mission sail off with a sizable b.o. cargo, though probably short of the stratospheric numbers of "Star Trek IV." Weighed down by a midsection even flabbier than the long-in-the-tooth cast, director Nicholas Meyer still delivers enough of what "Trek" auds hunger for to justify the trek to the local multiplex.

Although the films haven't lived up to the TV series' best moments, they've come closest in the even-numbered entries, with the second film (also directed by Meyer) invigorating after the stately but ponderous opener.

This time, with Nimoy serving as exec producer and sharing in story credit, Par seeks to use the film as a bridge to the future represented in its syndicated TV series "Star Trek: The Next Generation," initiating a thaw in Federation-Klingon relations that's a not-at-all-veiled parable for the end of the Cold War.

Following a Chernobyl-like disaster, a Klingon leader (David Warner) seeks peace with the Federation, the Klingon economy and environment having been depleted by constant warring.

Kirk and Co. are sent, reluctantly, to escort the leader to peace talks on Earth, but conspirators seek to scuttle the detente by assassinating him and pinning the blame on the Enterprise.

Until then the film moves fairly well, highlighted by the smartly executed and conceived assassination sequence, as the killers travel through the crippled, gravity-less Klingon ship while globules of brightly colored blood float gently by them.

After that, however, the action grinds to a halt, with Kirk (William Shatner) and McCoy (DeForest Kelley) sentenced to a Klingon penal colony as Spock (Nimoy), who initiated the peace process, seeks to ferret out the murderers.

Unfortunately, the murder is a rather tepid mystery and the ice planet to which Kirk and McCoy travel feels like a pale imitation of the "Star Wars" films.

The Klingon makeup reps little more than bad prosthetics on parade. The starched white hair on the Federation president (Kurtwood Smith) makes him look a bit like Custer on amphetamines.

Pace and visual trappings pick up considerably in the final frames, when the Enterprise rides to the rescue of the peace talks, in the process dueling a Klingon vessel. Crew gets help from another Federation ship captained by former Enterprise helmsman Sulu (George Takei).

Film allows the Enterprise crew to age a bit more gracefully than in the past, and greying Shatner looks better and more natural than he has in years, even if his brief flirtation with a fellow captive (supermodel Iman, yet) is cause for an unintended chuckle.

Meyer and co-scripter Denny Martin Flinn also have loaded the film with sentimental touches. Spock's father Sarek (Mark Lenard), Yeoman Rand (Grace Lee Whitney) and Michael Dorn (a regular in the new "Star Trek) all appear. (Why Christian Slater turns up in an uncredited cameo is anybody's guess.)

Cliff Eidelman's terrific score manages to stand on its own yet still evoke earlier work associated with the pics and series. Dodie Shepard also has done a fine job designing the Klingon costumes, though production, set design and creature effects prove generally unimpressive and derivative, especially on the Klingon planet.

Sappy ending provides a fitting send-off (and ridiculously literal sign-off) to the groundbreaking series and its rabid fans, reinforcing its humanistic messages and fairy-tale trappings.

Though the portal has been left slightly ajar, Paramount should make good on its pledge and retire the cast before they need wheelchairs to navigate the bridge. No matter how well this voyage does, a "Star Trek VII" with the original crew would doubtless illustrate that one can boldly go where no man has gone once too often. — *Brian Lowry*

TALKIN' DIRTY AFTER DARK

A New Line Cinema release and production. Produced by Patricia A. Stallone. Executive producer, Kevin Moreton. Directed, written by Topper Carew. Camera (color), Misha Suslov; editor, Claudia Finkle; production design, Naomi Shohan; design consultant, Holger Gross; art direction, Daniel Whifler; costume design, Harold Evans; sound, Oliver Moss; associate producer, Cindy Hornickel; assistant director, Leslie Jackson; casting, Daniel Edwardo Espinosa. Reviewed at Coronet Theater, L.A., Nov. 27, 1991. MPAA rating: R. Running time: **86 MIN.**

Terry . . . . Martin Lawrence
Dukie . . . . John Witherspoon
Rubie Lin . . . . Jedda Jones
Bigg . . . . "Tiny" Lister Jr.
Aretha . . . . Phyllis Yvonne Stickney

Also with: Darryl Sivad, Renee Jones, Marvin Wright-Bey, Lance Crouther.

The people talkin' dirty will be those who fork over $7.50 or thereabouts for this amateur production. Already played off in portions of the country, this painfully cheap and crude-looking production is the visual equivalent of a bad party record and more than appropriate as a day-before-Thanksgiving release. This turkey will be gone before some people finish all their leftovers.

Five minutes at any comedy club on an off night still would yield more yocks than this mess, which attempts to depict the on- and off-stage shenanigans at a black L.A. club.

Comic routines deal almost exclusively with sex in raw but

sadly uninspired ways. Backstage, the owner comes on to one of the comediennes, the owner's wife pursues a hot young jokester, the emcee tries to win over his prim date while fending off the advances of two brassy babes.

This much mugging hasn't been seen since the NYPD took a day off, and tech credits are the cheesiest in memory: Sound seems to have been recorded in a phone booth and mixed underwater, and shots match about as often as snowflakes.

Not press-screened for obvious reasons, pic was attended at its first show at one L.A. theater, but unspooling was canceled when it was discovered that reels had been assembled upside down and backward. It might have been more interesting that way.
— *Todd McCarthy*

SECRET FRIENDS
(BRITISH)

A Whistling Gypsy production for Channel Four. (Intl. sales: Film Four Intl. North American sales: Geisler/ Roberdeau, N.Y.) Produced by Rosemarie Whitman. Executive producers, Robert Michael Geisler, John Roberdeau. Directed, written by Dennis Potter, suggested by his novel "Ticket to Ride." Camera (Metrocolor), Sue Gibson; editor, Clare Douglas; music, Nicholas Russell-Pavier; production design, Gary Williamson; art direction, Sarah Horton; costume design, Sharon Lewis; sound (Dolby), John Midgley; associate producer, Alison Barnett; assistant director, Edward Brett; casting, Kathleen Mackie. Reviewed at London Film Festival (British Cinema section), Nov. 17, 1991. Running time: **97 MIN.**
John . . . . Alan Bates
Helen . . . . Gina Bellman
Angela . . . . Frances Barber
Martin . . . . Tony Doyle
Also with: Joanna David, Colin Jeavons, Rowena Cooper, Ian McNeice.

Intellectual cute runs riot in "Secret Friends," about an illustrator who dreams of murdering his beautiful spouse. First feature by celebrated British scribe Dennis Potter will please his disciples but prove a snoozeroo for general viewers. Beyond fests or boutiques, pic is theatrical dead meat.

Many of the same themes got a good workout in Potter's 1989 four-part TV fantasy "Blackeyes." Current outing, for his own Whistling Gypsy Prods., was suggested by his novel "Ticket to Ride."

Film kicks off in virtuoso form with an eye-rolling Alan Bates threatening to dispose of his wife (Gina Bellman) and, on a train en route to London, becoming prey to a severe case of the flash-

backs. Viewers are led to believe the two met in a swank hotel when she was an escort girl; elaborate cutting suggests he murdered her with an ax and is suffering from amnesia.

Also stirred into the brew is the hotsy gal (Frances Barber) who may be a hooker or lover, two businessmen who seem fascinated by his exploits, and a realtor friend (Tony Doyle) who has his eye on Bellman. Other flashbacks limn Bates' repressive upbringing by Bible-bashing parents and his resort to fantasy, conjuring up secret friends.

Familiar Potter gambit of establishing a set of locations and cross-cutting to build up a dense fabric works OK for the first half. Thereafter, the flimsy structure starts taking water fast, with Potter resorting to O.T.T. imagery to keep the central idea afloat. Final explanation is pedestrian.

Bates keeps his finger on the hype button throughout, with an almost physical relish for Potter's sardonic wit. Bellman, the centerpiece looker of "Blackeyes," sizzles as the flashing-eyed dream woman but lacks the experience to bring over her character's other sides. Barber is excellent as the acid-tongued Angela.

Tech credits are sharp, with fine lensing by Sue Gibson and razor-edge cutting by Clare Douglas. Sharon Lewis comes up with some eye-popping costumes for Bellman.
— *Derek Elley*

IL CAPITANO
(SWEDISH)

A Sandrews presentation of a Pan Film production for Four Seasons Venture Capital-FilmTeknik-Bold Prods.- Svenska Filminstitutet in cooperation with Villealfa-Nordisk-Polyphon- Bayerischer Rundfunk, supported by Nordisk Film & TV Fund and Finlands Films. Produced by Göran Setterberg, Jan Troell. Directed by Troell. Screenplay, Per Olov Enquist, Troell, Setterberg. Camera (color), Troell; editor, Troell; music, Lars Ackerlund, Sebastian Oberg; production design, Stig Limer; costumes, Gunnel Blomberg; sound, Eddie Axberg; assistant director, Jimmy Karlsson. Reviewed at Film Teknik screening room, Stockholm, Oct. 24, 1991. Running time: **110 MIN.**
With: Maris Heiskanen, Antti Reini, Berto Marklund, Antti Vierikko, Harri Malenius, Marjut Dahlström, Eva Stellby, Matti Dahlberg.

Dark and threatening, this cinematic account of a real-life triple murder is forceful without indulging in violent excess

or gore. Arguably the best Swedish film of the year, Jan Troell's first feature in nine years will attract considerable international interest.

Troell's comeback picture deals with a crime that enraged all of Sweden in summer 1988 and packs all the strength and power of the director at his best.

Two youthful petty criminals from Finland brutally murdered a couple and their 15-year-old son at a cemetery in the north of Sweden. After a massive manhunt, the two were found in Denmark and sentenced to long prison terms.

Troell centers the storytelling on the femme killer, called Minna here. At the film's start, she is being questioned by police, the murders having already occurred.

A series of rhapsodic flashbacks show how she and Jari meet, start a relationship and go to Denmark. When Jari lands in jail for petty crimes, Minna tries to start a new life without him. But once he is released, he takes her along on a trip through Sweden, where they steal cars and commit burglaries.

Troell casts a shadow of impending doom and catastrophe over the couple's odyssey. Even Minna feels that their road leads to disaster, but she can't break free from her violence-prone and gun-worshiping b.f. The murders are treated with discreet realism. The shooting of the father and the boy is heard from a distance, and the slaying of the mother is shielded by a car door; yet, these sequences register as gripping and horrifying.

Troell's goal is to investigate what could lead to a tragedy of this kind, and he has succeeded. Without putting a message stamp on the film, he tells of two kids who always felt themselves to be outsiders.

Director accents their feelings of loneliness and isolation by depicting their travels through the vast forests of northern Sweden in long shots, where the couple's car is the only thing moving and no other human beings are in sight. He also treats the colors of the Swedish summer in a dark and moody manner.

Unknown actors are natural and authentic, and tech credits (Troell himself takes on cinematography and editing) are excellent.
— *Gunnar Rehlin*

GOSSEKIND
(STREETCHILD)
(GERMAN)

A Corazon Prods. presentation of a Corazon Filmproduktion production. Written, produced and directed by Peter Kern. Camera (color), Manfred Scheer; editor, Margit Bauer; music, Iwan Harlan, performed by Katrin Degenhardt; costume design, Ute Kercks; casting, Gerd Uhlenbrock. Reviewed at Vancouver Film Festival, Oct. 6, 1991. Running time: **89 MIN.**
Karl Brenner . . . . Winfried Glatzeder
Axel Glitter . . . . . . Max Kellermann
Jimmy . . . . Daniel Aminatey
Elisabeth Faber . . . . . Nicole Weber
Die "Katze" . . . . Daniel Berger
Hanna Brenner . . . Renate Krossner
Paul Brenner . . Philip van der Wingen
Axel's mother . . . . Manuela Alphons

Trying to turn the horrors of child abuse into entertainment, "Streetchild" serves up a menu of atrocities and then suddenly shifts focus to closet homosexuality.

It's never clear what this film is supposed to be about. In scenario one, writer/helmer Peter Kern focuses on Axel, a abused teenage prostitute for married men.

Pic quickly turns to closet homosexuality when Axel meets Karl, a husband and father who abruptly quits his job, empties his bank account and takes Axel to the fair.

The street kid theme is dismissed when Karl gives Axel his life savings, then discovers his wife with someone else and his young boy in a sexual encounter with the gardener (a scene abandoned for a horribly overdone take of Karl attempting suicide).

Pic wraps with the town whore delivering a Brechtian direct-to-the-camera speech about the night being "too short for happiness."

Acting is heavy-handed, but Winfried Glatzeder steals the show as the tortured gay.
— *Suzan Ayscough*

RUSH

A Metro-Goldwyn Mayer release of a Zanuck Co. production. Produced by Richard D. Zanuck. Directed by Lili Fini Zanuck. Screenplay, Pete Dexter, based on Kim Wozencraft's book. Camera (Deluxe color), Kenneth MacMillan; editor, Mark Warner; music, Eric Clapton; musical supervision, Becky Mancuso, Tim Sexton; production design, Paul Sylbert; set decoration, Phillip Leonard; costume design, Colleen Atwood; sound, Hank Garfield; assistant director, Katterli Frauenfelder; casting, Shari

Rhodes. Reviewed at MGM Filmland screening room, L.A., Dec. 3, 1991. MPAA rating: R. Running time: **120 MIN.**

Jim	Jason Patric
Kristen	Jennifer Jason Leigh
Dodd	Sam Elliott
Walker	Max Perlich
Gaines	Gregg Allman
Nettle	William Sadler

Moral ambiguity that has plagued America since the '60s is given a harrowing probe in this tale of undercover narcs who succumb to the temptation in their midst. Downbeat nature of this addiction saga may be too intense and draining for general audiences, but resounding implications of the subject are bound to touch a nerve. Superbly crafted pic is sure to generate much talk and slowly building box office.

Within the industry, buzz will likely center on the head-swiveling directorial debut of Lili Fini Zanuck, who lays out a tough, masculine scenario in a way that always emotionally riveting. She zeros in on the feel of each situation and puts it across with a keenness audiences won't soon forget.

A bearded Jason Patric stars as Jim, an earthy, direct, Texas narcotics cop who sees a spark in rookie Kristen (Jennifer Jason Leigh), a fresh-scrubbed comer who's serious about making a difference, and he chooses her for his partner.

Inducted by Jim into the dangerous game of buying drugs direct from frightening redneck drug dealers, Kristen soon finds Jim has a disturbing way of getting too involved with his work.

Though the two narcs are often forced to ingest cocaine, heroin and pills in the presence of dealers in order to establish trust, Jim is constantly consuming the evidence in off hours.

Kristen tries to draw the line, but she's already too emotionally involved both with Jim, who's become her lover, and the strange, secret and intoxicating rituals of drug buys and the underworld. Her new drug experiences have given her an illicit high she's not eager to give up.

Zanuck's explicit portrait of drug rituals and the narcotic intimacy they promote among the new lovers is weirdly seductive. Fortunately for pic's acceptance in this day and age, the director is unsparing in detailing ensuing depravity.

When narcs are in danger, they have only each other to rely on, Jim instructs Kristen at the out-

set, and as the moral ground beneath their feet crumbles the pair becomes more and more isolated from others in an unnerving portrait of true intimacy.

Set in the early '70s, when America was struggling to reinvent itself after the shattering events of the '60s, pic depicts a culture in which morality is one big gray area.

A powerful and unsparing film with more to think about than a kilo of others, "Rush" benefits from outstanding lead performances and an uncannily accurate picture of its time and place: the hard-ass, bare-bones world of long-haired working-class Southerners in the early '70s. Blues eminence Gregg Allman contributes an enigmatic turn as a cagey club owner, and choice musical cuts commissioned from guitar legend Eric Clapton blend with a keenly effective period soundtrack.

Patric dominates the screen in a way rarely seen and does it without gimmickry, playing an unsmiling loner who uses his masculinity to establish a hold over a woman and a situation, only to give way to weakness.

Jason Leigh rises to the challenge in her typically intriguing way, finding reserves of strength that seem to defy her petite, childlike person. Director Zanuck lays in a subtext of nascent feminism with sly TV snippets from "All in the Family" and "Saturday Night Live," to help define Kristen's journey.

Max Perlich, sniveling dealer in "Drugstore Cowboy," resurfaces as a sweet, dopey Southern pusher who becomes the picture's unlikely martyr in an impressive performance.

Much of the pic's clarity and narrative grace is owed to scripter Pete Dexter ("Paris Trout"), who adapted a work of fiction that former narcotics cop Kim Wozencraft based on her experiences.

Worth noting on the tech side are stand-out opticals vividly evoking the dizzy-sick blur of overindulgence in mind-altering substances and cinematography capturing the hazy, sensual sprawl of drug-pumped nights in a rough corner of the U.S.

Director Zanuck drops the pace and suffers some problems of clarity during a punishing passage of the third act, but for the most part hers is an amazingly sustained achievement.

— *Amy Dawes*

SKINLESS NIGHT
(JAPANESE)

An E-Staff presentation of an E-Staff Union production. Produced and directed by Rokuro Mochizuki. Screenplay, Mochizuki, Nobuyuki Saito; camera (color), Mashai Endo; editor, Junichi Kikuchi; music, Akira Kobayahsi; art direction, Hiseo Kato. Reviewed at Vancouver Film Festival, Oct. 7, 1991. Running time: **105 MIN.**
With: Kin Ishikawa, Tasuko Yagami, Aya Katsuragi, Masahiro Sato.

Like most pseudo-art pics about pornography, "Skinless Nights" has just enough titillation to satisfy softcore fans and also enough behind-the-scenes storylines that justify pic's presence at film festivals.

Like the Canadian docu, "Not A Love Story: A Film About Pornography," pic's real postfest audience is on New York's 42nd Street.

This semi-autobiographical item is about a frustrated Japanese porn director who wants to helm a skin flick with a theme. His producers snicker at him when he wants to squeeze in a love story about fate between fetish shots.

Predictably, the script he proposes to financiers becomes "Skinless Night," in which a married man has an affair before discovering he really loves his wife and child.

Touches of comedy occasionally perk up an otherwise flat tale. Pic should go straight to tape where VCR owners can fast forward to several creative erotic scenes. —*Suzan Ayscough*

SANS UN CRI
(FRENCH)

A Pyramide Intl. presentation of a French Production-Art Light Prods.-Jean Vigo Intl. (Italy)-Zenab (Belgium) production. Produced by Emmanuel Schlumberger. Directed, written by Jeanne Labrune. Camera (color), Andre Neau; editor, Guy Lecorne; music, Anne Marie Fijal. Reviewed at Sarasota (Fla.) French Film Festival, Nov. 16, 1991. Running time: **90 MIN.**

Anne	Lio
Pierre	Remi Martin
Nicolas	Nicolas Prive
Lola	Vittoria Scognamiglio

Jeanne Labrune's "Sans Un Cri" was hyped as "a bizarre menage à quatre" for its world preem at the Sarasota French film fest, but pic turns out to be less kinky and more commercially risky as a pre-

cisely detailed, carefully observed psychological drama about a dysfunctional family.

Spare storyline focuses on Pierre (Remi Martin), a truck driver, and Anne (Lio), his sexy wife. They share everything, even Pierre's long-distance road trips, until the birth of their son keeps her in their isolated home.

Over years, Anne gradually transfers all of her affections to the sickly son (Nicolas Prive) whom she smothers and spoils. Increasingly alienated from his family, Pierre in turn transfers his affections to his huge, often ferocious dog.

One wrong move, and pic could have turned silly. But Labrune skillfully sustains the suspense in a series of short, elliptical scenes. Pic becomes all the more unsettling as it drops vague hints of incestuous impulses in scenes with the sensually full-lipped mother and her vulnerable but crafty preadolescent son.

Still, Labrune prefers subtlety to overstatement. Nothing gets out of hand, not even during the bitterly ironic climax — the violence occurs off-screen.

Prive is a real find as the doe-eyed but possibly demonic youngster. Lio is effectively ambiguous as Anne, while Martin remains sympathetic even as he rages at his sickly son.

— *Joe Leydon*

JFK

A Warner Bros. release presented in association with Le Studio Canal Plus, Regency Enterprises & Alcor Films of an Ixtlan Corp. & A. Kitman Ho production. Produced by Ho, Oliver Stone. Executive producer, Arnon Milchan. Co-producer, Clayton Townsend. Directed by Stone. Screenplay, Stone, Zachary Sklar, based on the books "On the Trail Of The Assassins" by Jim Garrison and "Crossfire: The Plot That Killed Kennedy" by Jim Marrs. Camera (Duart color; Technicolor prints; Panavision widescreen), Robert Richardson; editors, Joe Hutshing, Pietro Scalia; additional editor, Hank Corwin; music, John Williams; production design, Victor Kempster; art direction, Derek R. Hill, Alan R. Tomkins; set design, Mary Finn; set decoration, Crispian Sallis; costume design, Marlene Stewart; sound (Dolby), Tod A. Maitland; associate producer-assistant director, Joseph Reidy; casting, Risa Bramon Garcia, Billy Hopkins, Heidi Levitt. Reviewed at Skywalker Sound, Santa Monica, Calif., Dec. 12, 1991. MPAA Rating: R. Running time: **189 MIN.**

Jim Garrison	Kevin Costner
Liz Garrison	Sissy Spacek
David Ferrie	Joe Pesci
Clay Shaw	Tommy Lee Jones
Lee Harvey Oswald	Gary Oldman
Lou Ivon	Jay O. Sanders
Bill Broussard	Michael Rooker
Susie Cox	Laurie Metcalf
Al Oser	Gary Grubbs
Dean Andrews	John Candy
Jack Martin	Jack Lemmon
Sen. Russell Long	Walter Matthau
Guy Bannister	Ed Asner
Colonel X	Donald Sutherland
Willie O'Keefe	Kevin Bacon
Jack Ruby	Brian Doyle-Murray
Rose Cheramie	Sally Kirkland
Marina Oswald	Beata Pozniak
Bill Newman	Vincent D'Onofrio
Carlos Bringuier	Tony Plana
Leopoldo	Tomas Milian
Earl Warren	Jim Garrison

A rebuke to official history and a challenge to continue investigating the crime of the century, Oliver Stone's "JFK" is electric muckraking filmmaking. This massive, never-boring political thriller, which most closely resembles Costa-Gavras' "Z" in style and impact, lays out just about every shred of evidence yet uncovered for the conspiracy theory surrounding the assassination of President John F. Kennedy. Pic's contentious P.O.V. and agitated manner will stimulate an enormous amount of thought and fresh debate, as well as printed opinion pro and con, assuring the release a high profile even beyond that guaranteed by the Stone and Kevin Costner names.

With a recent Gallup poll indicating that 73% of Americans believe Lee Harvey Oswald did not act alone in killing Kennedy, Stone is apparently playing to an already converted audience that should readily lap up his dramatically presented documentation. The Warren Report is treated as a cover-up, a myth against which the director, for lack of hard answers that never may be provided, is proposing a myth of his own.

Working in a complex, jumbled style that mixes widescreen, archival footage, tv clips, black & white, slow motion, docu-drama recreations, time jumps, repeated actions from various viewpoints, still photos, the Zapruder film and any other technique at hand, Stone uses the sum of conspiracy theory points made by New Orleans Dist. Atty. Jim Garrison and others since to suggest as strongly as possible that Oswald was, as he claimed before he was killed, "a patsy."

Film will be attacked by establishment mouthpieces and others for its lack of balance, and Stone's customary zeal, crushed idealism and sense of personal betrayal by the government undoubtedly get the better of him here and there. But even if he barks up the wrong tree at times, few films have the advantage of such a fascinating subject, or provoke so many potent questions.

Collaborating on the jam-packed script with journalist Zachary Sklar, Stone launches his epic with President Eisenhower's farewell warning about the dangers of the military industrial complex, then zips through a six-minute docu recap of the Kennedy era.

Arriving at Nov. 22, 1963, action cuts to New Orleans, where Stone introduces Southerners who had reasons to resent or hate the young, liberal president.

Suspicious about aspects of Oswald's former residency in New Orleans, D.A. Garrison (Costner) begins delving into a mysterious netherworld of right-wing, anti-Castro homosexuals populated by the bewigged David Ferrie (Joe Pesci), suave businessman Clay Shaw (Tommy Lee Jones) and unpredictable hustler Willie O'Keefe (Kevin Bacon).

With the spectre of Vietnam in the background and the Warren Report putting the official seal on the lone assassin theory, Garrison persists. Numerous witnesses to curious aspects of the killing have died, tremendous inconsistencies crop up, strange ties emerge, and Garrison begins to suspect that the U.S. government's military industrial complex initiated the killing.

This all sounds more like the stuff of documentaries, and "JFK" trades more freely in the techniques of nonfiction filmmaking than just about any feature this side of "The Battle of Algiers."

In fact, Stone's mixing of styles, designed to promote doubts and alternatives as well as to clarify, stands as an apt visual correlative to the confusion and mystery inherent in the material.

Where Stone takes this beyond documentary, however, is in the film's fabulously rich parade of personalities. With superior character actors and a handful of stars enacting key secondary figures, the picture is an amazing collection of types, from high government and military officials to criminals and lowlifes. Scene after scene is brought vividly to life by first-rate performances that sock over the script's many points.

Starting at the top, Stone uses Costner's Garrison as a sort of Capraesque Everyman, a determined, sometimes misguided, but essentially fair-minded fellow who just wants to get at the truth. Costner may not resemble the real Garrison much, and Stone no doubt slides over many of the attorney's flaws. But the actor, in a low-key but forceful performance, nicely conveys the requisite grit, curiosity and fearlessness.

Particularly noteworthy in the huge cast are Pesci as the volatile Ferrie, Jones as the superbly smooth Shaw, Laurie Metcalf as Garrison's assistant D.A., Gary Oldman as the creepy and off-balance Oswald, Donald Sutherland in a hypnotic turn as the investigator's Deep Throat, Bacon as a trick of Shaw's who squeals, Brian Doyle-Murray as the crude Jack Ruby, a surprising John Candy as a hip adversary of the D.A., Jack Lemmon as an informant, Ed Asner as a former FBI thug, and Michael Rooker and Jay O. Sanders as top assistants to Garrison.

Most conspicuous weakness comes in the depiction of Garrison's home life and in the idealization of Kennedy himself. As the investigator's wife, Sissy Spacek is stuck with almost nothing but nagging lines, complaining that his obsessive quest is driving them apart. Domestic scenes are conventionally portrayed and quickly forgotten once the political momentum picks up again.

It remains a matter of debate as to what Kennedy would have done about Southeast Asia had he lived, as well as how committed he was to civil rights and other liberal issues. The film insists that JFK had already decided to pull out of Vietnam if he won a second term, fully embraced the cause of blacks, wanted to backtrack on nuclear weapons and end the Cold War. Stone suggests these issues brought him to fatal odds with the entrenched powers in Washington, notably the Pentagon, CIA and J. Edgar Hoover, all of whom allegedly saw in LBJ someone they knew would play ball.

All these notions have been batted around for years, but what gives "JFK" so much impact is that they are collected here in one place and assembled so dramatically. Aspects of the case will undoubtedly be argued into eternity, and Stone enthusiastically stokes the fires of the debate.

Pic is filled with consummate technical achievements. Robert Richardson's cinematography further refines the docu-based style he and Stone initiated on "Salvador" and have pursued ever since, with exciting results. Editors Joe Hutshing and Pietro Scalia organized mountains of footage and information from many sources, and made it all work.

John Williams' score is atypical and properly troubling, while contributions of production designer Victor Kempster and his team, as well as costume designer Marlene Stewart, add to the time and place. Many of the actual locations in Dallas, including Dealey Plaza and the Texas School Book Depository, were used to tremendous effect.

—*Todd McCarthy*

THE LAST BOY SCOUT

A Warner Bros. release of a Geffen Pictures presentation of a Silver Pictures production. Produced by Joel Silver, Michael Levy. Executive producers, Shane Black, Barry Josephson. Directed by Tony Scott. Screenplay, Black; story by Black, Greg Hicks. Camera (Technicolor), Ward Russell; editor, Mark Goldblatt, Mark Helfrich; music, Michael Kamen; production design, Brian Morris; art direction, Christiaan Wagener; set design, Eric Orbom; set decoration, John Anderson; costume design, Marilyn Vance-Straker; sound (Dolby), Martin Raymond Bolger; assistant director, James W. Skotchdopole; stunt coordinator, Charles Picerni; special effects supervisor, Al Di Sarro; co-producer-unit production manager, Steve Perry; associate producer, Carmine Zozzora; casting, Marion Dougherty. Reviewed at Bruin Theater, L.A., Dec. 7, 1991. MPAA Rating: R. Running time: **105 MIN.**

Joe Hallenbeck	Bruce Willis
Jimmy Dix	Damon Wayans
Sarah Hallenbeck	Chelsea Field
Sheldon Marcone	Noble Willingham

Milo . . . . Taylor Negron
Darian Hallenbeck . . Danielle Harris
Cory . . . . Halle Berry
Mike Matthews . . . . . Bruce McGill

After a series of box office duds interrupted by the "Die Hard" pics, Bruce Willis looks primed to earn a much-needed B.O. merit badge via this entertaining if mindless shoot-'em-up. WB bills the film as "the only action in town," and while pic's tone isn't in the festive holiday tradition, it's well-positioned to cash in as a gritty alternative to the season's fantasy pics and dramas.

Despite the bidding war surrounding Shane Black's script (and its ultimate seven-figure purchase price), there's really nothing special about it other than an ample supply of amusing juvenile put-downs and elaborate action sequences.

Still, combine those elements under Tony Scott's direction, and they make "The Last Boy Scout" significantly better than the average recent buddy action movie.

Black should know the territory, having penned "Lethal Weapon" and the first draft of its sequel, and Scott manages to rub together the requisite elements and create some sparks, relying on loud noises and relentless pacing in what's by now a trademark of Silver productions.

Same could be said of the last Willis-Silver collaboration, "Hudson Hawk," which turned out to be a bird with feet of clay, but this latest effort benefits from a little more heart, flashes of wit and, perhaps most important, a more accessible and self-effacing character for Willis.

Equipped with a persona suited to his gifts: Willis limns a former Secret Service agent whose devotion to justice (accounting for pic's title) put him out on the street scrounging for work as a sleazy P.I.

Willis plays the part as a world-weary Bogart wannabe, grounded in domestic trappings by partial estrangement from his wife and daughter. That gives him a soft underbelly beneath his hard shell.

The plot, meanwhile, is a haze of barely connected story lines about political corruption, pro football, gambling, infidelity and blackmail —a sort of poor man's "The Big Sleep," but here all questions are answered by another car chase, smashing someone in the face or shooting someone in the forehead.

he finds enough charm in his

Hallenbeck gets yanked into the action when he's asked to protect a stripper (Halle Berry), g.f. of a former pro quarterback (Damon Wayans) banned from the game for gambling.

After her death and another elaborate rubout, the two inevitably team up to decipher what's going on, developing the usual grudging respect through the usual series of ordeals, with the usual opportunity for redemption and revenge against those who have wronged them.

There's not a lot of chemistry between Willis and Wayans, but both can be flat-out funny, and the script provides them plenty of opportunity to zing each other as well as the cartoonish bad guys.

Wayans, a brilliant comic (TV's "In Living Color"), might have been better served by a less demanding dramatic vehicle in his first major film role. Nonetheless, thinly drawn character to make the pairing an engaging one.

In other supporting roles, Noble Willingham is a properly smarmy bad guy as the rotund football owner, and Danielle Harris is likable as the spunky, foul-mouthed daughter.

Tech credits are top of the line, including a climactic helicopter stunt just gruesome enough to impress the film's target audience. In that regard, the Boy Scouts' "be prepared" motto could be taken as a warning to check one's brain at the door.

— *Brian Lowry*

FATHER OF THE BRIDE

A Buena Vista release of a Touchstone Pictures presentation in association with Touchwood Pacific Partners I of a Sandy Gallin production in association with Sandollar Prods. Produced by Nancy Meyers, Carol Baum, Howard Rosenman. Executive producers, Gallin, James Orr, Jim Cruickshank. Coproducer, Cindy Williams. Directed by Charles Shyer. Screenplay, Frances Goodrich, Albert Hackett, Meyers, Shyer, based on Edward Streeter's novel. Camera (Technicolor), John Lindley; editor, Richard Marks; music, Alan Silvestri; production design, Sandy Veneziano; art direction, Erin Cummins; set design, Martin (Geoff) Hubbard, Mark Poll, John Dexter; set decoration, Cynthia McCormac; costume design, Susan Becker; sound (Dolby), C. Darin Knight; assistant director, K.C. Colwell; associate producer, Bruce A. Block; casting, Donna Isaacson. Reviewed at Crest Theater, L.A., Dec. 7, 1991. MPAA Rating: PG. Running time: **105 MIN.**
George Banks . . . . . . Steve Martin
Nina Banks . . . . Diane Keaton
Annie Banks . . . . Kimberly Williams
Matty Banks . . . . Kieran Culkin
Bryan MacKenzie . . George Newbern
Franck Eggelhoffer . . . Martin Short
Howard Weinstein . . . . . B.D. Wong
John MacKenzie . Peter Michael Goetz
Joanna . . . . Kate McGregor Stewart

Winning antics of Steve Martin propel this sentimental domestic comedy past the pitfalls of a too-familiar subject and overlong treatment. Sunny, nondemanding family fare should go over nicely with the holiday shopping crowd and result in a modest box office bouquet.

Remake of the 1950 MGM pic with Spencer Tracy and Elizabeth Taylor bears little resemblance to the original. Modernized version shaped by filmmaking team Charles Shyer and Nancy Meyer ("Baby Boom," "Private Benjamin") gets by more on physical shtick than verbal sparkle.

Martin plays the scion of a comfortable San Marino, Calif., family that goes a little nuts when he learns his beloved 22-year-old daughter (Kimberly Williams) is engaged.

Beset by separation anxiety, he can't find anything right about her perfectly appealing fiancé (George Newbern) or the pricey wedding arrangements. He snoops around the home of the in-laws-to-be and watches "America's Most Wanted" in hopes of getting the goods on them.

Role was tailor-made for Martin after "Parenthood" and his emphasis on immature and neurotic aspects of the character supplys a contempo spin. Audiences who don't mind being spoon-fed (Martin's voiceover narration courts banality) should find all this very funny. Best stuff here comes straight from Martin, such as his frenzied antics at the in-laws' house or his ridiculous Tom Jones imitation in front of a mirror in a too-tight tuxedo.

A radiant Diane Keaton gives him first-rate support as the calm, sunny wife charged with the exhausting task of keeping up with him. The entire cast, including the head-over-heels young couple and little brother (Kieran Culkin) are on target in a generally smooth, well-executed piece of mainstream entertainment.

Main glitch is the running time: Pic runs on pointlessly and would have been more successful with a 10- or 15-minute trimming. Child-rearing viewers will reach for their hankies at the finale, but single folks might be left a little bored. — *Amy Dawes*

ELIAS
(DUTCH-BELGIAN)

A CinéTé Amsterdam-Antwerp production. Produced by Willem Thijssen, Hans Otten. Directed by Klaas Rusticus. Screenplay, Fernand Auwera, Rusticus, based on Maurice Gilliams' novella; camera (color), Jan van Caillie; editor, Peter Rump; music, Jan Brandts Buys; sound, Bert Koops, Jan van Sandwijk; art direction, Johan van Essche; production manager, Myrian de Boeck. Reviewed at Dutch Film Days, Utrecht, Sept. 24, 1991. Running time: **80 MIN.**
With: Brikke Smets, Jimmy de Koning, Lotte Pinoy, Bien de Moor.

Excellent photography, an astute screenplay and a fastidious style help shape "Elias," a very private and literary film. A small picture for a small audience, pic is suited for film fests.

In Maurice Gilliams' original novella, the writer describes autobiographical emotions and experiences of a 12-year-old surrounded by family in a grand manor house in a huge park. He takes stock of his life partly by thinking, mostly by feelings and sometimes by flashbacks.

The pictures are beautiful, and the putative menace of people and situations and the tentative seductions are implicitly described. — *Gerry Waller*

LOS DE LA KGB TAMBIEN SE ENAMORAN
(KGB AGENTS ALSO FALL IN LOVE)
(CHILEAN-SOVIET)

A Mosfilm Studio-Chile Films production. Produced by Andrés Albornos, Edward Volkov. Directed by Sebastián Alarcón. Screenplay, Alarcón, Alexander Adabashian, Alexander Borodianske; camera (color), Vadim Alisov; editor, Nero Ostrinskage; music, Horacio Salinas. Reviewed at V Americas Festival, AFI, Washington, D.C., Oct. 19, 1991. Running time: **84 MIN.**
With: Sergie Gazarov, Luz Croxato, Armen Djigarjanian, Gloria Munchmeyer.

Despite a humorous premise, Chilean director Sebastián Alarcón's "KGB Agents Also Fall In Love" is a muddled comedy that misses its possibilities and usually delivers a chuckle where a guffaw is in order. This ultimately light vehicle may do well domestically, but international appeal will be limited.

Dual story concerns a Chilean woman whose efforts to found a music school are financed by afternoons between the sheets; and a KGB employee who is transferred to Santiago after being caught with his pants down during an office tour. Through a forced script, the two cross paths and, after too many absurd plot complications, end up together.

Pic's strongest character is vivaciously played by Armen Djigarjanian, and its several humorous moments include a running joke about a Lenin statue. But overall, poorly developed script fails to tie up loose ends, and situations end up unsatisfactorily. Even the expectant romance between the two leads feels tacked on, without real preparation. — *Paul Lenti*

TED AND VENUS

A Double Helix release of a Krishna Shah/Randolf Turrow & William Talmadge presentation of a Gondola Films/ L.A. Dreams production. Produced by Turrow, Talmadge. Executive producer, Randall Kubota. Directed by Bud Cort. Screenplay, Paul Ciotti, Cort; story by Ciotti. Camera (CFI color), Dietrich Lohmann; editor, Katina Zinner; additional editing, Peter Zinner; music, David Robbins; music supervisor, Swamp Dogg; production design, Lynn Christopher; visual consultant, Susan Becker; art direction, Robert Stover; set decoration, Gene Serdena; costume design, Rosemarie Fall, Dana Weems; sound, Lee Orloff; associate producer, William Martens; assistant director, Tony Perez; 2nd unit camera, Gary Graver; casting, Rick Montgomery, Dan Parada. Reviewed at Raleigh Studios, L.A., Dec. 10, 1991. MPAA Rating: R. Running time: **100 MIN.**
Ted Whitley . . . . Bud Cort
Max Waters . . . . Jim Brolin
Linda Turner . . . . Kim Adams
Colette . . . . Carol Kane
Gloria . . . . Pamella D'Pella
Herb . . . . Brian Thompson
Poetry award
   presenter . . . . . Bettye Ackerman
Homeless
   Vietnam veteran . Woody Harrelson
   Also with: Dr. Timothy Leary, Andrea Martin, Martin Mull, Tracy Reiner, Vincent Schiavelli, Arleen Sorkin, Rhea Perlman, Gena Rowlands.

In his directorial debut, Bud Cort attempts to recapture some of the eccentric appeal of his 1972 starrer "Harold and Maude," but he's picked the wrong story and treated it far too seriously. A highly unpleasant yarn about a lovelorn sickie who endlessly torments a beautiful young woman, "Ted and Venus" could not come out at a time less receptive to such a tale of sexual harassment. Who would comprise the audience for this troubling indie production is hard to imagine.

Cort stars as Ted Whitley, a 35-year-old hippie on disability whose only distinction is a certain reputation as a poet among the Venice Beach literati. A virginal, pathetically earnest nerd, Ted has a vision of a gorgeous young lady emerging from the sea, and when she turns out to be Linda (Kim Adams), the community service worker helping him find an apartment, he feels compelled to pursue her.

Egged on by his buddy (Jim Brolin) and encouraged by her enthusiasm for his poetry and general friendliness, Ted begins a romantic campaign that quickly degenerates into obscene phone calls and other antisocial acts.

Although Ted compiles a record of multiple molestations, it takes the state quite some time to step in, and when it does, it still isn't enough, and Linda is ultimately forced to take the law into her own hands with a Dirty Harry-style solution.

The further Cort takes the story and his character down the road of maniacal, senseless behavior, the less clear it becomes what he expects the viewer to think or feel. Initially, Ted can be charitably viewed as a bumbling but probably harmless romantic, a dysfunctional fellow with a tragic poet's view of the world.

But when Ted is revealed as a dangerous mental case, what can one do but throw one's sympathies entirely with Linda and her efforts to get this guy put away? But Cort sticks with the poor schmuck through his increasingly demented and repellent behavior, while offering no edifying psychological or artistic p.o.v. to indicate how the situation is meant to be taken.

Aside from telling an actively offputting story, Cort the director hasn't done a bad job of putting it up on the screen. He has packed the cast with a lively assortment of actor friends, and newcomer Adams is a stunner with a winning personality.

But single stellar achievement is the evocation of time and place. Pic so impressively suggests the look and attitude of the time of the action (1974) that it almost could have been shot then. Clothes, beach apartment decorations, late hippie-era attitudes, casual sexual mores — all these are right on, and nicely backed up by background televised snatches of Nixon's spiral out of the presidency.

Pic is dedicated to the memo-

ries of Ruth Gordon, Hal Ashby and Colin Higgins, and the recognition that Cort's three principal collaborators on "Harold and Maude" are all gone is more poignant than anything in this film.
— *Todd McCarthy*

STALIN'S FUNERAL
(SOVIET-COLOR-B&W)

A Mosfilm production. Directed, written by Yevgeny Yevtushenko. Reviewed at Akademie der Künste, Berlin, Aug. 28, 1991. Running time: **101 MIN.**
With: Marina Kalinitschenko, Denis Konstantinov, Yevgeny Platochin, Vanessa Redgrave, Yevgeny Yevtushenko.

Both autobiographical and historical, Soviet poet Yevgeny Yevtushenko's latest film displays strong cinematographic talents. The film, which centers on the hysterical funeral of the Soviet despot, probably will do well on the fest circuit, but its stylization and abstraction makes it too esoteric for arthouse fare.

In 1952, Stalin, who caused thousands of deaths during his lifetime, caused still more after his death, as citizens were crushed to death in the rush to see his body. After reading the account in the poet's autobiography, John Steinbeck suggested Yevtushenko make a film.

The film unfolds in a dreamlike way, incidents sometimes connect, sometimes don't. Political atrocities, including torture and midnight arrests, are juxtaposed with surrealistic humor. Performances and cinematography are generally good, and Vanessa Redgrave turns up as a British photojournalist.
— *Rebecca Lieb*

THE GIVING

A Three Cats Inc. presentation in association with Jeremiah Pollock Associates. Produced by Cevin Cathell, Tim Disney, Eames Demetrios. Executive producer, Disney. Directed, written by Demetrios. Camera (B&W, Deluxe and Duart labs; Duart prints), Antonio Soriano; editor, Bruce Barrow, Nancy Richardson; music, Stephen James Taylor; production design, Diane Romine Clark, Lee Shane; sound (Dolby), Jerry Wolfe; assistant director, Donald L. Sparks; 2nd unit camera, Dino Parks, Kate Butler; casting, Laurel Smith. Reviewed at State Theater, L.A., Nov. 19, 1991. (In Cairo Film Festival.) Running time: **100 MIN.**
Jeremiah Pollock . . . . . Kevin Kildow
Gregor . . . . Lee Hampton
   Also with: Satya Cyprian, Kellie A. McKuen, Gail Green, Stephen Hornyak, Oliver Patterson, Paul Boesing, Russell Smith, Michael McGee, Southern Comfort, Eleanor Alpert, Joel (Wolf) Parker, Lois Yaroshefsky, Lionel Stoneham.

A low-budget picture about the homeless automatically creates expectations of a socially conscious, sentimentally liberal, uncontestably worthwhile endeavor doomed to the scrapheap of good intentions. "The Giving" has all of these attitudes, but this black & white indie production also surprises with its stylistic sophistication and arty approach to gritty material.

First feature by 29-year-old documentary and video maker Eames Demetrios, which recently premiered at the Cairo Film Festival, won't make much headway commercially but weighs in as a genuine curiosity.

A sort of serious, avant-garde counterpart to Mel Brooks' "Life Stinks," new pic charts the downward spiral and strange awakening of Jeremiah Pollock (Kevin Kildow), who in the opening scene pledges $10,000 to the homeless at a benefit dinner.

Afflicted with enlarged feelings of guilt and fear about society's have-nots, the slim blond L.A. bank exec buzzes downtown in his BMW and, shocked to witness squatters being hosed out of their makeshift encampment, signs on to serve food at a shelter.

Although severely mistrusted as a checkbook Samaritan by an imposing homeless leader (Lee Hampton), Jeremiah feels compelled to implicate himself more deeply in the lives of the dispossessed. He goes on a private hunger strike, sleeps in the open and rigs his bank's cash machines so street people can collect at will.

Once his superiors catch up with him, Jeremiah naturally finds himself out on the pavement as well, and Demetrios somewhat surprisingly takes his protagonist as far down his chosen path as he can go. Resolution has its sappy side but is still relatively bracing.

Biggest blank here is Jeremiah himself. Writer-director Demetrios has provided his main character with no history, no friends, no previous life that he leaves behind (save work) and no psychology other than guilt.

Demetrios goes for a style that edges toward the abstract and surreal, favoring for smooth lateral pans and dollies, straight-to-camera monologues and an assortment of techniques more frequently found in experimental films than commercial fare.

Despite film's total immersion in the life of the streets (it was lensed largely on Skid Row in downtown L.A.), it sheds little light on how society should deal with this major problem, other than to suggest that giving money alone is not the answer.

Pic doesn't satisfy, but it's fresh and unusual enough in its approach to warrant some notice.

— *Todd McCarthy*

DEUTSCHES MANN GEIL! DIE GESCHICHTE VON ILONA UND KURTI
(GERMAN GUY SEXY! THE STORY OF ILONA AND KURTI)
(AUSTRIAN)

An SK Film und Fernseh & WEGA Film production. Produced by Reinhard Schwabenitzky, Josef Korschier. Directed, written by Schwabenitzky. Camera (color), Frank Brühne; editor, Ingrid Koller; sound, Heinz Ebner; music, Ennio Morricone; sets, Fritz Hollergschwandtner; costumes, Heidi Melinc. Reviewed at Lupe 1 Cinema, Berlin, Nov. 18, 1991. Running time: **90 MIN.**
Ilona . . . . Elfi Eschke
Kurti . . . . Hanno Pöschl
Mama . . . . Louise Martini
Also with: Herbert Fux, Aviva Beresin, Milena Zupancic, Robert Hoffmann, Helma Gautier.

Highly successful at home in Austria, "German Guy Sexy!" should do some biz next door in Germany, and, with proper handling, this likable pic could play other Euro territories. Timely theme of European xenophobia is played with grace and humor.

Kurti and his mother are riding high after their landlady dies, as they've forged their way into her will. A rain-soaked Ilona, the landlady's long-lost daughter who grew up in the Balkans, shows up, swathed in frumpy clothes and speaking no German. She threatens their newfound wealth and could also land them in jail.

After a half-hearted attempt to bump Ilona off, mother and son realize she'd be more useful married to Kurti. He begins a comic courtship of the repressed and puritanical immigrant, and Ilona turns out to be not as ignorant as suspected, and is soon ruling the roost.

Clever writing and a fine cast help along a brisk, well-handled comic pace. Pic is consistently funny — often in terms of ribald, but never offensively handled, sexuality. Tech credits are good, especially the Ennio Morricone score. — *Rebecca Lieb*

TERRA NOVA
(NEW LAND)
(VENEZUELAN)

A Prods. Terra Nova-Cinelife SRL production. Directed by Calógero Salvo. Screenplay, Marisa Bafile, Riccardo Manao; camera (color), Giuseppe Tinelli; editor, Mauro Bonanni; music, José Vinicio Adames; sound, Carolos Bolivar; art direction, Tania Manela. Reviewed at 8th Santafé de Bogotá (Colombia) Intl. Film Festival (competition), Oct. 8, 1991. Running time: **100 MIN.**
With: Marisa Laurito, Antonio Banderas, Mini Lazo, Patrick Beauchau, Massimo Bonetti.

"Terra Nova" finds impetus in the friendship between the matriarch of a humble Italian immigrant family and an aristocratic local landowner. Script is weak, but this personal story achieves an intensity within its handling of change and self-acceptance themes.

Filmed in both Italian and Spanish, pic is set in a 1950s rural Venezuelan town. Haunted by the past, the immigrants are torn between returning to Italy and staying in the new world. Main characters find themselves at a turning point in their lives.

Actress Marisa Laurito's earthy portrayal is reminiscent of Anna Magnani, and her screen presence always dominates interest. Tech credits are average, and director Calógero Salvo keeps the focus where it belongs, firmly on the characters.

— *Paul Lenti*

SCORCHERS
(BRITISH)

A Nova release of a Goldcrest presentation. Produced by Morrie Eisenman, Richard Hellman. Executive producers, John Quested, Richard Becker, John La Violette. Directed, written by David Beaird. Camera (color), Peter Deming; editor, David Garfield; music, Carter Burwell; production design, Bill Eigenbrodt; costume design, Heidi Kaczenski; sound, Walt Martin; assistant director, Robin Oliver; casting, David Cohn. Reviewed at Toronto Film Festival, Sept. 7, 1991. (Also in San Sebastian, Vancouver film festivals.) Running time: **88 MIN.**

Splendid	Emily Lloyd
Talbot	Jennifer Tilly
Jumper	Leland Crooke
Thais	Faye Dunaway
Bear	James Earl Jones
Howler	Denholm Elliott
Dolan	James Wilder

Writer-director David Beaird's beguiling stage play about a bawdy, rollicking wedding night in the Louisiana bayou makes an uneven transfer to film. Despite some pungent performances, "Scorchers" is hampered by a nervous visual tone and inexplicable production flaws.

Difficulty in finding a marketing focus for this ephemeral ensemble piece will make it a tough theatrical sell.

Emily Lloyd plays a nervous 20-year-old virgin bride whose Cajun wedding night jitters are exacerbated by the community's lusty interest in the goings-on. Jennifer Tilly plays a preacher's daughter who can't get her husband to prefer her to the town whore (Faye Dunaway).

Film's flighty story eventually finds two successful places to roost — a bar and the bedroom in which Lloyd and her madly frustrated young husband (James Wilder) are counseled by Lloyd's father (Leland Crooke).

Film suffers from a murky sound mix obscuring initial dialog, which already is difficult to make out with the Cajun accents.

Working from the play he wrote and presented at his Whitefire Theater in Los Angeles, Beaird ("Pass the Ammo," "My Chauffeur") plunges the viewer into a world in which nothing comes easily, but the hard-won insights are eminently worthwhile. So too, are the pleasures of this rough-edged presentation.

— *Amy Dawes*

SOLO CON TU PAREJA
(LOVE IN THE TIME OF HYSTERIA)
(MEXICAN)

A Solo Peliculas presentation of a Solo Films-Imcine-Fondo de Fomento de la Calidad Cinematografica production. Executive producer, Rosalia Salazar. Directed by Alfonso Cuaron. Screenplay, Cuaron, Carlos Cuaron; camera ('Scope color), Emanuel Lubezki; editor, Alfonso Cuaron; sound, José Antonio Garcia; art direction, José Luis Aguilar; costume design, Mariestela Fernadez. Reviewed at Toronto Film Festival, Sept. 8, 1991. (In Vancouver Film

Festival.) Running time: **94 MIN.**

Tomas	Daniel Giménez Cacho
Clarisa	Claudia Ramirez
Mateo	Luis de Icaza
Teresa	Astrid Hadad
Sylvia	Dobrina Liubomirova
Tomas' boss	Isabel Benet

This bold Mexican version of a French sex farce is an amusing feature debut for Alfonso Cuaron, who's put a comical safe sex spin on the old Casanova story. Some repetitive scenes bog down an otherwise light, escapist love story.

In the long tone-setting scene, rogue Tomas has his nurse Sylvia in his apartment and his boss bedded down in a neighboring apartment. He tiptoes between boudoirs on a window ledge. En route, he spies on his new stewardess neighbor, Clarisa.

As soon as Clarisa is spotted, pic is predictable: Tomas will get caught by the rival women, and it becomes a question of time (the last scene) before he settles down.

Pic's twist on the Casanova-meets-his-match theme is the condom factor. Each conquest suggests protection, which Mr. Macho ignores. Thwarted nurse gets her revenge by falsely noting his HIV test as positive.

Pic is superbly shot.

— *Suzan Ayscough*

CHAINDANCE

A Festival Films presentation of an R&R production. Produced by Richard Davis. Executive producer, Michael Ironside. Directed by Allan A. Goldstein. Screenplay, Alan Aylward, Ironside; camera (color), Tobias Schliessler; editor, Allan Lee; music, Graeme Coleman. Reviewed at Vancouver Film Festival, Oct. 9, 1991. Running time: **108 MIN.**
J.T. Blake . . . . Michael Ironside
Eileen . . . . Rae Dawn Chong
Johnny Reynolds . . . . . Brad Dourif
Also with: Bruce Glover, Ken Pogue.

The premise of "Chaindance" oozes with earnest sentimentality. Absurd situation and witty script provide many comic moments in this heart-warming drama, but it's likely to fare better in homevid than theaters.

A hard-boiled prisoner (Michael Ironside) gets drafted into an experimental reform program and is handcuffed to the wheelchair of a cerebral palsy victim (Brad Dourif), whom he must then care for. Their instant hatred of each other predictably evolves into a strong friendship.

Ironside co-wrote himself a character that transcends his usual villain roles and makes the prisoner's own sense of justice believable. He initially wants nothing to do with the do-gooder welfare worker (Rae Dawn Chong) who coerces him into the program. He's cuffed to a miserable man who's a prisoner of his own body; Ironside and Dourif have to make the best of it.

Their superb perfs carry the film through the rocky debut of their unlikely but inevitable friendship, and Chong is energetic as the outspoken idealist. Tech credits are good. — *Suzan Ayscough*

ROBERT'S MOVIE
(TURKISH-FRENCH-GERMAN-BRITISH)

A Konsept Film (Turkey) co-production with Cinecam (Germany), Valprod (France), Michael White production (England). Produced by White, Valerie Seydoux, Horst Knechtel. Directed, written by Canan Gerede. Camera (color), Jurgen Jurges; editor, Albert Jurgenson; sound, Alain Curvelier; assistant directors, Ali Akdeniz, Bennu Gerede, Uli Hrobel. Reviewed at Montreal Film Festival, Aug. 29, 1991. Running time: **105 MIN.**
Robert . . . . Patrick Bauchau
Gogo . . . . Asli Altan
John . . . . John Kelly
Ali . . . . Sinan Cetin

Existential angst meets navel gazing in Istanbul when a 49-year-old war photographer seduces a Turkish pop singer half his age and wants to videotape their reality.

Robert's home movie is mainly bedroom voyeurism in which singer Gogo mildly protests before she falls hard for this self-centered brute.

Robert has supposedly taken war photos so politically volatile that his life is in danger and he's on the run. During a pitstop en route to Syria, he has an affair with Gogo, "who wasn't even born when he needed her." His old friends there don't like or trust him either. In the end, she shoots him (but there was no tango in Paris nor wanton lust in Istanbul).

Numerous sex scenes are carefully framed to avoid porn status, but weak script wraps little around the encounters. Characters never connect. Premise of mysterious photos never is resolved.

— *Suzan Ayscough*

NETCHAIEV EST DE RETOUR
(NETCHAIEV IS BACK)
(FRENCH-ITALIAN)

A BAC Films release of a Les Films de l'Ecluse-TFI Films (Paris)-Italmedia (Rome) co-production. (Intl. sales: President Films, Paris.) Produced by Yves Gasser. Directed by Jacques Deray. Screenplay, Deray, Don Franck, from Jorge Semprun's novel; camera (Fujicolor), Yves Angelo; editor, Henri Lanoe; music, Claude Bolling; production design, François de Lamothe; sound, Alain Sempe, Bernard Leroux; production manager, Lydia Setton; assistant director, Renaud Bertrand; casting, Siegfried Stula. Reviewed at Walker Cinema, Sydney, Oct. 15, 1991. Running time: **101 MIN.**
Pierre Marroux . . . . . Yves Montand
Daniel Laurencon/
Netchaiev . . . . . . Vincent Lindon
Brigitte . . . . Miou-Miou
Sonsoles . . . . Carolina Rosi
Leloy . . . . Patrick Chesnais
Also with: Maxime Leroux, Jean-Claude Dauphin, Phillipe Leroy-Beaulieu, Mireille Perrier.

A standard thriller boosted by Yves Montand playing a French security official and father of a notorious terrorist, pic generates a fair amount of suspense until the cop-out ending. International possibilities are modest.

Writer-helmer Jacques Deray and co-screenwriter Don Franck tackle potentially interesting themes, but they don't see them through. Early scenes' cynical tone gradually yields to standard cop fare, with the characters ultimately lacking depth.

It starts well, however. Netchaiev (Vincent Lindon), a terrorist thought to have been killed some years earlier in Gibraltar, returns secretly to Paris with other subversives to force release of an Arab prisoner by planting bombs in public places.

But Netchaiev has had enough of the terrorist life and tells a former colleague that he'll spill the beans on his cohorts in return for a clean slate for himself.

These former radicals from another era include Netchaiev's ex-g.f. (Miou-Miou), a couple of journalists and the g.f.'s ex-husband, a shady lawyer (Patrick Chesnais).

Tracking them down in order to locate Netchaiev before he's bumped off, security chief Montand is itching to locate the man everyone though was long dead, his son. He also discovers French government links with Netchaiev's former comrades-in-arms. Montand gives a solid perf

as the world-weary but determined cop, and Lindon (" 'Round Midnight") is compelling as the ambivalent son. Other cast members have little to do except behave suspiciously or violently.

Deray's use of Paris locations for all the mayhem is judicious, and he keeps the film humming along until the so-what finale.

— *David Stratton*

THE PLEASURE PRINCIPLE
(BRITISH)

A Palace Pictures (U.K.) release of a Psychology News production. (Intl. sales: Jane Balfour Films.) Produced, directed, written by David Cohen. Executive producers, Stephen Woolley, Robert Jones. Co-producers, Joe McAllister, Jan Euden, Alistair Fraser. Camera (Metrocolor), Andrew Spellar; editor, McAllister; music, Sonny Southon; production design, Cecelia Bretherton; costume design, Jackie Parry; sound, Albert Bailey; assistant director, Tracy Lane. Reviewed at London Film Festival (British Cinema section), Nov. 21, 1991. Running time: **98 MIN.**
Dick . . . . Colin Firth
Sammy . . . . Lynsey Baxter
Judith . . . . Haydn Gwynne
Charlotte . . . . Sara Mair-Thomas
Anne . . . . Sara Mair-Thomas
Malcolm . . . . Ian Hogg
Mrs. Malcolm . . . . . Francesca Folan

An amiable "Alfie" for the postfeminist '90s, "The Pleasure Principle" is a refreshing light comedy that simply asks its audience to lie back and enjoy. First feature of Haifa-born, British-based director David Cohen sports dapper ensemble playing that could enjoy a minor click in the right boudoirs.

In look and tone, pic also recalls swinging London items like "Here We Go 'Round the Mulberry Bush." There's no mention of safe sex, AIDS or any other modern paranoias; romantic pic is about the joys of sex and its emotional complications.

A womanizing journalist (Colin Firth) is divorced from a raving gay feminist (Sara Mair-Thomas), and his current mate is the unpredictable brain surgeon (Haydn Gwynne) who keeps an Alsatian dog in her bedroom and answers the phone in midorgasm.

Firth's sexual roundelay gathers steam when he also starts canoodling with a mousy divorcée (Lynsey Baxter) and beautiful yuppie lawyer (Lysette Anthony). Finally, the surgeon springs the trap and brings him to his senses.

Much of the action is of a superior bedroom farce type, with Firth desperately juggling his women and being given a hard time in return. Dialogue is sharp and candid and the sack scenes funny and natural.

Cohen gives the whole thing a bright, optimistic look, helped by fine lensing from Andrew Spellar, neat cutting by Joe McAllister and attractive use of London locations. Playing is fine all around, with Firth cutting an unwitting Casanova figure whose brains are half in his pants and TV thesp Gwynne a strong standout.

Indie pic was shot on a budget of £200,000 ($350,000) but looks solidly pro. Blowup from Super-16 is excellent. — *Derek Elley*

35 UP
(BRITISH-DOCU-COLOR/B&W)

A Samuel Goldwyn Co. release (in U.S.) of a Granada Television production. Produced by Michael Apted. Executive producer, Rod Caird. Directed, written by Apted. Camera (color, black & white), George Jesse Turner; editor, Claire Lewis, Kim Horton; sound, Nick Steer. Reviewed at Toronto Film Festival, Sept. 8, 1991. Running time: **128 MIN.**

Fifth installment of the remarkable British TV docu charting the growth of its subjects every seven years remains an intriguing social document with much to say about class, education and human potential. Previous chapters have found theatrical, cable and U.S. TV exposure, and there's no reason this one won't as well.

Still, the program is getting less newsy as its subjects settle into mostly conventional lives, and it's becoming rather too long as the record on each one grows. Some interviewees are dropping out, despite Apted's best efforts to persuade them to stay on, and the interest of viewers also may begin to taper off.

The ambitious series shows the uncanny ways in which the children have fulfilled or turned away from the traits they exhibited early on.

Nick, the farmer's son who wanted to know about the moon, has become a physicist; Tony, the scrappy East Ender who wanted to be a jockey, drives a cab and acts but gives riding lessons to his daughters; the bright and privileged prep school boys have become lawyers; the orphaned children have become laborers.

Among the new developments are the deaths of parents, quite movingly reported, and the status of relationships and kids.

Unfortunate is the sexist treatment of the women subjects, who are first approached with the question, "Do you have a boyfriend?" — which is never the first issue put to the men.

Some of the subjects say this periodic invasion of their privacy has been painful. A successful lawyer calls it "a poison pill." The only subject who entered show business (as a BBC TV producer) is ironically one of those who've dropped out of the docu.

Black & white footage of the 7-year-olds from the original 1963 show remains beguiling.

The Samuel Goldwyn Co. has acquired all North, South and Central American rights to the docu and plans a 1992 release.

— *Amy Dawes*

JESZCZE TYLKO TEN LAS
(STILL ONLY THIS FOREST)
(POLISH)

A Zespol Filmowy "Kadr" Unit production. Directed by Jan Lomnicki. Screenplay, Anna Stronska; camera (color), Artur Radzko; editor, Krystyna Gornicka; music, Piotr Hertel; sound, Piotr Knop; production design, Andrzej Waltenberger. Reviewed at Venice Film Festival (competition), Sept. 12, 1991. Running time: **90 MIN.**
Mrs. Kulgawcowa . . . Ryszarda Hanin
Rutka . . . . Joanna Friedman
Daughter . . Marta Klubowicz-Rozycka
Mother . . . . Marzena Trybala
Spy . . . . Marek Bargielowski

This traditional film from Poland, which looks and feels the same as films made a decade ago, is an earnest but predictable plea for racial tolerance. Despite good intentions, "Still Only This Forest" is too weak to register global impact.

Set in 1942, pic opens with an Aryan washerwoman's (Ryszarda Hanin) arrival at Warsaw's Jewish ghetto. The Jewish wife she worked for before the war hires her to take her young daughter to the countryside until the war is over. Realizing she has the upperhand, the maid is rude and overbearing with her former employer, allowing the desperate woman to shower her with gifts and money before she'll take the child away.

Later, they leave by train, but it's stopped, and old lady and child proceed on foot. By this time, the innocent youngster has begun to charm her crotchety companion, so that by the time they are stopped by a German patrol, the woman is prepared to risk her life for the child.

This story could have been made into an interesting and moving film, but director Jan Lomnicki doesn't seem to have his heart in it. Handling is perfunctory, and performances are routine.

Pic contains no surprises or tension, plodding along until the inevitable ending. Tech credits are average. — *David Stratton*

WAY UPSTREAM
(DUTCH)

A Cannon Tuschinski release of a Rolf Orthel-DNU production, in cooperation with Jan Rutger Achterberg. Produced by André Sjouerman. Directed by Sander Francken. Screenplay, Hugo Heinen, Francken, based on Alan Ayckbourn's play; camera (color), Tom Erisman; editor, Gust Vershueren; music, Paleis van Boem; sound, Peter Flamman, Jan van Sandwijk. Reviewed at Dutch Film Days, Utrecht, Sept. 19, 1991. Running time: **88 MIN.**
Jim . . . . Cees Linnebank
Wendy . . . . Geert de Jong
Joke . . . . Celia van den Boogert
Aldert-Jan . . . . . George van Houts
Kees . . . . Aus Greidanus

"Way Upstream" started life as a successful legit show, was later broadcast by BBC and now becomes a Dutch film, but the work remains theater.

Assertive and noisy Kees (Aus Greidanus) and understated Aldert-Jan (George van Houts) are partners in a medium-size company; their wives (Geert de Jong, Celia van den Boogert) are the non-executive directors. They rent a motor cruiser for a leisurely upriver trip during vacation.

After a near-accident, they take on their rescuer, the crafty, cunning tramp Jim (Cees Linnebank).

Dialogue and scenery are often enjoyable, but the greenery fails to open up the play. Pic does not grip the viewer, although acting is generally good. Editing is too close to stage effects, as is the direction by Sander Francken in his feature debut. His prizewinning shorts prove that he can do much better.

— *Gerry Waller*

A SMALL DANCE
(BRITISH-16m)

A Thames Television Intl. production. Produced, directed by Alan Horrox. Line producer, Julie Baines. Screenplay, Lucy Gannon. Camera (color), David Scott; editor, Olivia Hetreed; music, Richard Harvey; production design, Hayden Pearce; costume design, Sally Turner; sound, Mervyn Gerrard; associate producers, Cathy Elliott, Emma Wakefield; assistant director, Cilla Ware; casting, Joyce Nettles. Reviewed at London Film Festival (British Cinema section), Nov. 16, 1991. Running time: **94 MIN.**
Donna Matkin . . . . . . Kate Hardie
Brian Matkin . . . . James Hazeldine
Sandra Matkin . . . . . Linda Bassett
Nicola . . . . Suzanne Burden
Peggy . . . . Selina Cadell
Carmen . . . . . . Veronica Roberts
Rob . . . . Mark Aiken

Several notches above the average Brit telepic, "A Small Dance" is a moving, sensitively acted drama. This Prix Europa winner should display film fest appeal and minor art house potential before the tube swallows it up.

A 16-year-old farm girl (Kate Hardie) lives a sheltered life in east England's bleak fenlands. Dad (James Hazeldine) is a domineering type, and mom (Linda Bassett) is hooked on TV soaps. One day, the girl starts a secret liaison with a passing customer (Mark Aiken) at her roadside flower stall.

When the expected happens, she hides her pregnancy from parents and work mates, eventually giving birth one night in a nearby barn and abandoning the kid. Rest of pic limns her gradual attachment to the baby and chance for a fresh start in life.

Potentially downbeat material is given dramatic clout by Lucy Gannon's economical script and well-paced helming by Alan Horrox. Pic has shape and feel of a feature film rather than a slice-of-life semidocu.

Hardie is on the money as the lonely but inwardly tough teen, and Hazeldine and Bassett in tune as her conservative parents. Suzanne Burden makes a brief impression as a straight-talking nurse. Tech credits are fine, with David Scott's photography of the flat fenlands landscape and Richard Harvey's pastoral score adding plenty of atmosphere. — *Derek Elley*

SIMPLE MORTEL
(FRENCH)

An AAA release of a Cepac-Fildebroc-Ciné Cinq co-production with the participation of Soficas Investimage 2, Investimage & Canal Plus. (Intl. sales: Mainstream.) Produced by Michelle De Broca, Paul Claudon. Directed, written by Pierre Jolivet. Camera (color), Bertrand Chatry; editor, Jean-François Naudon; music, Serge Perathoner, Janick Top; costume design, Magali Bassenne; set design, Laurent Allaire; production manager, Ginette Mejinsky; make-up, Phuong Maittret; sound, Yves Osmu, Nadine Muse, Gerard Lamps; stunts, Roland Neureuther, Daniel Verite, Henry Villain. Reviewed at Club Gaumont, Paris, Aug. 6, 1991. Running time: **85 MIN.**
Stéphane . . . . Philippe Volter
Fabien . . . . . Christophe Bourseiller
Brigitte . . . . Nathalie Roussel
Insurance adjuster . . . Roland Giraud
Also with: Maaike Jansen, Marcel Marechal, Arlette Thomas, Daniel Schropfer.

From stylish opening credits to psychologically satisfying coda, "Simple Mortel" is real edge-of-the-seat widescreen entertainment. Writer/helmer Pierre Jolivet's fourth feature is an ultra-tight suspense thriller with hearty intellectual underpinning and tantalizing philosophical implications. Clever premise, action sequences and attractive lead should make the pic a simple sale in other markets.

Linguist (Philippe Volter) thinks he's cracking up when he receives — via radios, answering machines, Walkman, even an unplugged fax machine — maddeningly precise directives in an ancient language only he understands. The stakes in the messages are global (earthquake threat in Japan, for example), and the tasks he's told to perform escalate in their severity. Whenever Volter fails to do as he's told, the consequences are immediate and vicious.

Film demonstrates that, in the grand scheme of things, one man can make a difference and he needn't be a superhero or a cyborg to pull it off. As Volter wrestles with the responsibility that haunts him, viewer identifies with his outrageously unfair plight and applaud his courage.

Volter successfully carries the lion's share of screen time in an essentially three-character drama revolving around him, his colleague (Christophe Bourseiller) and g.f. (Nathalie Roussel of "My Father's Glory" and "My Mother's Castle").

Stunts and special effects are good. Editing is outstanding. Pic packs a visual and emotional wallop and features one late-arriving scene that will jolt the average viewer out of his seat.

Visually snappy with clever sound design to match, pic may lose impact if reviewers give away too much of the plot.

— Lisa Nesselson

NAKED LUNCH
(CANADIAN-BRITISH)

A 20th Century Fox release of a Jeremy Thomas production. Produced by Thomas. Co-producer, Gabriella Martinelli. Directed, written by David Cronenberg, based on William S. Burroughs' book. Camera (Film House color), Peter Suschitzky; editor, Ronald Sanders; music, Howard Shore; alto sax solos, Ornette Coleman; production design, Carol Spier; art direction, James McAteer; set decoration, Elinor Rose Galbraith; costume design, Denise Cronenberg; sound (Dolby), Bryan Day; special creatures & effects designed & created by Chris Walas Inc.; assistant director, John Board; casting, Deidre Bowen. Reviewed at 20th Century Fox screening room, L.A., Nov. 12, 1991. MPAA Rating: R. Running time: **115 MIN.**
William Lee . . . . Peter Weller
Joan Frost/Joan Lee . . . . Judy Davis
Tom Frost . . . . Ian Holm
Yves Cloquet . . . . . . Julian Sands
Dr. Benway . . . . Roy Scheider
Fadela . . . . Monique Mercure
Hank . . . . Nicholas Campbell
Martin . . . . Michael Zelniker
Hans . . . . Robert A. Silverman
Kiki . . . . Joseph Scorsiani

William S. Burroughs' notorious, and notoriously unfilmable, novel "Naked Lunch" has landed in the right hands. Stretching himself with each new work, David Cronenberg has come up with a fascinating, demanding, mordantly funny picture that echoes many of the book's chief concerns, but also stands as a distinctively personal creation in its own right.

This impressively rigorous and intellectual examination of addiction, bugs and the creative process will stir critics up but probably will appeal to no larger an audience than Fox's earlier compelling head-scratcher, "Barton Fink," to which it bears interesting comparison.

As Cronenberg has rightly remarked, "It's impossible to make a movie out of 'Naked Lunch.' A literal translation just wouldn't work. It would cost $400 million to make and would be banned in every country in the world." A cult novel since its publication in 1959 and a cause célèbre for its part in cracking censorship restrictions in the U.S., Burroughs' breakthrough non-narrative novel represented the literary equivalent of a Heironymous Bosch painting, a profane, outrageous explosion of riffs dominated by drugs, gay sex and a surreal evocation of society's control mechanisms.

Always drawn to alternate realities, Cronenberg had the key inspiration of turning his film into an imaginative analysis of Burroughs' own process of writing "Naked Lunch." It's a daring look at the unblocking of the creative mind, the liberation and transformation of the unconscious into art.

The film will be of principal interest to Burroughs buffs in particular and highbrow audiences in general. While there is a measure of patented Cronenberg weirdness here (anthropomorphized insects, aliens called Mugwumps that would have looked at home in the "Star Wars" cantina, talking anuses), the picture overall will almost certainly prove too obscure and rarified to cross over to more mainstream audiences.

At the center of this chilly emotional spiral is William Lee (Burroughs' alter ego and early pseudonym), an insect exterminator in New York City circa 1953. Telling two literary friends that he gave up writing at age 10 — "Too dangerous," he says — Lee (Peter Weller) lives in quiet squalor with his wife (Judy Davis) until, on a bug drug high, he accidentally shoots her while playing "William Tell."

Breaking into a hallucinatory state, Lee escapes to the realm of Interzone, an imaginatively demented rendition of Tangier heavily populated by artist addicts, homosexuals and secret agents where Lee is able to begin writing, even if what he is writing are "reports" over which he seems to have no actual control.

Who but Cronenberg would pull off the astonishing stroke of representing creative writing under a chemically induced state by turning typewriters into articulate insects, creatures that spew out pages, talk back to their owners through vividly realized orifices, act as agents to infiltrate enemy ideas into texts and function as an aphrodisiac for two literary geniuses?

Drawing audaciously on Burroughs' own life, the filmmaker throws Lee in with a decadent American couple (Ian Holm and, again, Judy Davis), as well as with an insidious German dealer (Robert A. Silverman), the sexually depraved wealthy Swiss (Julian Sands) and an attractive young local companion (Joseph Scorsiani).

In the most fundamental events of Cronenberg's startling, densely packed scenario, Lee struggles with his addiction while he continues to pile up pages without knowing where they came from, and attempts to get to the bottom of the control system in Interzone.

Among the pic's biographically inspired aspects are the Burroughs character's accidental shooting of his wife, the writing of "Naked Lunch" in Tangier in a drug-induced stupor and the author being visited by two friends from the States who help him organize his material. Some will complain that the gay orientation of the book has been diluted, but Lee is presented as being decidedly bisexual if not mostly gay, and film is clearly a personal interpretation by its writer-director, not remotely a representative rendition of the book.

Cloaked in long coats, hat and conservative clothes, and speaking in a monotone that manages to be both concealing and revealing, Weller is a superb Burroughs stand-in. Strongly holding centerscreen while not actually doing much, Weller has never been better on film.

Supporting cast is diverse and outstanding. Davis gives seductively world-weary shadings to her two roles, Holm personifies jaded sophistication, Sands oozes rarified depravity as a rich layabout, and Michael Zelniker and Nicholas Campbell score as Allen Ginsberg and Jack Kerouac-like writers. Roy Scheider, as Dr. Benway, and Monique Mercure lend relish to their roles as the powers behind the drug society.

Dissuaded from actually shooting in Tangier by the outbreak of the Gulf War, Cronenberg's team has memorably created an artificial world almost entirely on stages. Notable are the contributions of production designer Carol Spier, cinematographer Peter Suschitzky, special creature and effects designer Chris Walas and costume designer Denise Cronenberg.

Editor Ronald Sanders has helped the director achieve a very precise style, and dissonant jazz score by Howard Shore, with superior sax solos by Ornette Coleman, give the film a highly individual sound very much in keeping with its distinctive qualities.

— Todd McCarthy

GRAND CANYON

A 20th Century Fox release. Produced by Lawrence Kasdan, Charles Okun, Michael Grillo. Directed by Kasdan. Screenplay, Kasdan, Meg Kasdan. Camera (Panavision — Deluxe color), Owen Roizman; editor, Carol Littleton; music, James Newton Howard; production design, Bo Welch; art direction, Tom Duffield; set decoration, Cheryl Carasik; costume design, Aggie Guerard Rodgers; sound (Dolby), David MacMillan, Kevin O'Connell, Rick Kline; special visual effects, Dream Quest Images; associate producer, Meg Kasdan; assistant director, Grillo; casting, Jennifer Shull. Reviewed at 20th Century Fox screening room, L.A., Dec. 10, 1991. MPAA Rating: R. Running time: **134 MIN.**
Simon . . . . Danny Glover
Mack . . . . Kevin Kline
Davis . . . . Steve Martin
Claire . . . . Mary McDonnell
Dee . . . . Mary-Louise Parker
Jane . . . . Alfre Woodard
Roberto . . . . Jeremy Sisto
Deborah . . . . Tina Lifford
Otis . . . . Patrick Malone
Earvin (Magic) Johnson . . . . Himself

Life in L.A. is the pits, according to scripters Lawrence and Meg Kasdan in "Grand Canyon," their earnest, often moving but not totally successful new film. As a study of survival strategies in a disintegrating metropolis, pic brings a welcome seriousness and maturity to subject matter too often treated with flippancy and mindless romanticism.

Streaks of pretension and predictability, however, prevent this otherwise worthy item from achieving all its high artistic objectives. Strong reviews may help keep it from being lost in the commercial wilderness on its wide release in January.

Via its refreshing concentration on a black-white friendship (rare in non-action Hollywood pics), film explores contemporary racial tension and ambivalence.

Danny Glover (a tow-truck driver) and Kevin Kline (an immigration lawyer) come to a warm, if tentative, connection in their paradise-turned-hellhole, a city that still looks lustrous from the oddly smogless air but, up close, shows it's "gone to shit," as the film says of both L.A. and the country at large.

Theme of living on the edge of catastrophe, a staple of L.A. fiction, is spotlighted from the beginning by ample footage of Kline watching local hero Magic Johnson do his stuff with the L.A. Lakers. The brightly colored sequence is now emotionally shadowed by the recent revelation that the basketball star is HIV-positive.

Leaving the game, Kline takes a turnoff to avoid a traffic jam and his expensive car dies in a black neighborhood in Inglewood. He's menaced by some street punks before Glover, whom he later compares to an angel of deliverance, saves his life.

Glover is given a juicy role as the moral voice of a film mourning the loss of civility in a society torn apart by the widening chasm — the Grand Canyon — between rich and poor. Though his dialogue is sometimes improbably flowery, Glover speaks it with conviction and provides an anchor of sense and sensitivity.

Kline, also very good in his more understated way, conveys the edgy uncertainty of a white liberal struggling to cope with life in a city whose police routinely terrorize angry black inhabitants with low-flying helicopter surveillance and casual violence. The worst thing about such brutalization, as Kline's wife (Mary McDonnell) puts it, is that "we are getting used to it."

Kline's also living on the moral edge by carrying on a half-hearted affair with his secretary, fresh young Mary-Louise Parker, who's driven to distraction by his lack of emotional involvement. She's angered when he sets up Glover with one of her friends (Alfre Woodard) and that relationship quickly acquires a substance hers and Kline's will never have.

So far, so good, as the scripters deftly sketch in the characters' social milieus and avoid simplistic emotions in their depiction of believable people whose lives have a realistically gray moral tone.

The Steve Martin character, whose license plate reads "GRSS PTS" and who whines, "Nobody in this town will admit that a producer is an artist," is a wicked caricature of action pic maker Joel Silver. But the Kasdans' script vacillates uneasily between treating the character as a comic-relief spouter of buzz words and a voice of genuine wisdom.

Though it works beautifully as a mosaic of disparate lives in racially diverse L.A. — capturing through its elegant structure the accidental way in which people's lives all too tangentially intersect — pic sometimes seems as if it's piling on the horrors and disasters of a city whose ample downside needs no overstatement.

Though a husband-and-wife team wrote the script, the female characters, including muddled, vapid Parker and taciturn Woodard, never seem as intelligent or as richly developed as the Glover, Kline or Martin characters, a serious drawback of the film's pretensions of being a slice of L.A. life.

Another familiar theme in L.A. literature — that people come there hoping to find a miracle — is treated a bit too glibly and explicitly here, but the Kasdans' defiantly optimistic view of life ultimately carries emotional conviction.

Technically, "Grand Canyon" is first-rate. Owen Roizman's lensing is suitably somber, Bo Welch's production design knowingly conveys disparate locales, Carol Littleton's editing effectively bridges stark contrasts of lifestyles and James Newton Howard's music alternates edgy and buoyant moods. Helicopter pilot John Sarviss also deserves kudos for his work in the film's graceful aerial views. — *Joseph McBride*

THE INNER CIRCLE

A Columbia release of a Claudio Bonivento production. Produced by Bonivento. Directed by Andrei Konchalovsky. Screenplay, Konchalovsky, Anatoli Usov. Camera (Technicolor), Ennio Guarnieri; editor, Henry Richardson; music, Eduard Artemyev; production design, Ezio Frigerio; art direction, Gianni Giovagnoni, Vladimir Murzin; costume design, Nelli Fomina; sound (Dolby), Jean Claude Laureux; associate producer, Laura Balbi; assistant director, Felix Kleiman; casting, Robert Macdonald, Perry Bullington. Reviewed at Sony Pictures screening room, Culver City, Calif., Dec. 9, 1991. MPAA Rating: PG-13. Running time: **134 MIN.**
Ivan Sanshin . . . . Tom Hulce
Anastasia . . . . . Lolita Davidovich
Beria . . . . Bob Hoskins
Stalin . . . . Alexandre Zbruev
Prof. Bartnev . . . Feodor Chaliapin Jr.
Katya (16 years) . . . . . . Bess Meyer
Katya (10 years) . . . . Marla Baranova
Directress . . . . . . Irina Kuptchenko

A potentially fascinating subject has been only partly realized in "The Inner Circle," a dramatically messy, momentarily compelling look at Stalin's tyranny.

The first Western film to shoot within the Kremlin and KGB h.q., and Andrei Konchalovsky's first Soviet-based pic in 12 years, this idiosyncratic look at the life of Stalin's personal projectionist has numerous points of interest but is too muddled and misconceived to make much of a domestic b.o. impression. Foreign results should be better.

Set in Moscow beginning in 1939 and based on a true story, this odd tale focuses on Ivan Sanshin (Tom Hulce), a groveling, pathetic projectionist for the KGB who has a kind of greatness thrust upon him when he is summarily ordered to screen a film for the supreme leader.

Sweating out the showing, Ivan fortunately does not miss a changeover, and the young man is ready to die and go to workers' heaven when Stalin tells him, "You projected well, Sanshin."

At home on Slaughterhouse Street, Ivan and his bride (Lolita Davidovich) celebrate their honeymoon evening as a Jewish family is evicted from their building. Davidovich maintains an obsessive devotion to the family's orphan daughter, but Ivan forbids her over the years from having any contact with this offspring of purged enemies of the state.

The domestic scenes have a strangely unreal feeling, as they lack even passing moments of intimacy and almost always show the couple at odds. Ivan admits he loves Stalin more than his wife, and in having her give herself on a train one night to a notoriously brutal KGB head (Bob Hoskins), Konchalovsky literally makes his point that communist totalitarianism made citizens not only dupes and slaves, but also prostitutes.

Pic excels in glimpses of power at the top. Several scenes take place in Stalin's personal projection room, a salon of plush chairs and ample food and drink where the air is checked for possible poisoning. With the leader (played one-dimensionally but with imposing authority by Alexandre Zbruev) in the company of his aides, the atmosphere is thick with tension and intrigue, as all know their fates hang on the whim of this all-powerful man. In these sequences, Konchalovsky conveys a strong, creepy sense of the terror of absolute power.

Ultimately, however, the story proves unwieldy, with Konchalovsky and co-screenwriter Anatoli Usov unable to integrate the diverse sides of the tale and give it a proper dramatic arc.

Hulce's performance is typically enthusiastic, but the character is so thick-headed that one tires of him after more than two hours. Davidovich plays a frustrated soul and victim of society, but actress is stuck with wildly varied motivations that don't all hang together. Hoskins makes a sketchily conceived but utterly convincing thug, but mix of Anglo-American thesps with Russians speaking English creates an unmanagable alliance at times.

Location lensing provides its own extensive fascination, as does the imaginative peek into one corner of Stalin's life. But various elements don't coalesce into a fully convincing drama.

— *Todd McCarthy*

FRIED GREEN TOMATOES

A Universal Pictures release of a Universal & Act III Communications presentation in association with Electric Shadow Prods. of an Avnet/Kerner production. Produced by Jon Avnet, Jordan Kerner. Executive producers, Andrew Meyer, Anne Marie Gillen, Tom Taylor, Norman Lear. Co-producers, Martin Huberty, Lisa Lindstrom, Ric Rondell. Directed by Jon Avnet. Screenplay, Fanny Flagg, Avnet, based on Flagg's novel "Fried Green Tomatoes at the Whistle Stop Cafe." Camera (Deluxe color), Geoffrey Simpson; editor, Debra Neil; music, Thomas Newman; production design, Barbara Ling; art direction, Larry Fulton; set decoration, Deborah Schutt; costume design, Elizabeth McBride; sound, Mary Ellis; assistant director, Deborah Love; casting, David Rubin. Reviewed at Universal Studios screening room, Universal City, Calif., Dec. 9, 1991. MPAA rating: PG-13. Running time: **130 MIN.**

Evelyn . . . . Kathy Bates
Ninny . . . . Jessica Tandy
Idgie . . . . . . Mary Stuart Masterson
Ruth . . . . Mary-Louise Parker
Frank . . . . Nick Searcy
Ed . . . . Gailard Sartain
Big George . . . . Stan Shaw
Sipsey . . . . Cicely Tyson
Grady . . . . Gary Basarba
Smokey . . . . Tim Scott

Stories told by sweet old ladies are usually fond and sentimental, enhanced by the burnished glow of memory but marked by strange omissions, and "Fried Green Tomatoes" is no exception. Celebrating the crucial, sustaining friendships between two sets of modern-day and 1930s Southern femmes, pic emerges as absorbing and life-affirming quality fare, but still it lacks the edge to be more than a side dish on the Christmas menu. Box office outlook is fair to middling.

Kathy Bates plays a frumpy middle-aged Southern suburbanite, who's fighting a losing battle against weight gain and despair until she finds inspiration in the tales spun by a feisty nursing-home resident (Jessica Tandy).

Tandy's oldtime stories center on a gambling, brawling but good-hearted rural Alabama girl (Mary Stuart Masterson), and how she almost got fingered for murder. Seems the girl had developed a deep friendship with a demure, God-fearing young woman (Mary-Louise Parker) based on a bond that developed when the two witnessed a devastating tragedy — the accidental death of Masterson's adored older brother who was sweet on Parker.

Later on in life, Masterson became a fierce supporter of Parker's when she was having trouble with her abusive husband (Nick Searcy), and helped Parker find the courage to run off with the baby and come to work as the cook at her Whistle Stop Cafe.

But besides wearing pants and playing poker, Masterson has the peculiar habit of giving equal service to black folks at the cafe, and before long the Klan, including Searcy, comes around to scare some sense into her. When Searcy turns up missing and his truck is dragged out of the river, Masterson and her "colored man" (Stan Shaw) are arrested on suspicion of murder.

Actual trial is merely a peg for a story that's mostly about the stalwart friendship between the two young femmes, isolated in a world of ham-handed, bigoted menfolk who don't much understand 'em.

It's a welcome and moving subject, but since the Masterson character seems to have no use for able-bodied men and is clearly in love with Parker, it's annoying that pic skates over the question of her sexuality.

Meanwhile, developments in the modern-day parallel story, in which the much put-upon Bates starts to seek her feminine power in encounter groups, seem outdated, though amusing.

Still, Tandy is at her sparkling best as the endearing old storyteller. Bates is also terrif in a funny and sympathetic turn.

Director Jon Avnet, in his feature film debut, gets first-rate work from the featured performers and pulls off some vividly atmospheric and dramatic passages, but segs involving the Ku Klux Klan and the thuggish husband are heavy-handed and pierce the illusion.

Throughout, it is sometimes unclear which aspects of the tale are meant to be swallowed straight, and which taken with a grain of salt. For a story celebrating fearlessness, it's remarkably cautious, and lacks the edge and artistry of a bolder pic in the same vein, "Rambling Rose."

Cinematography is lovely, and designer Barbara Ling does a first-rate job in recreating the aging, tumbledown cafe, where fried green tomatoes are a menu staple. — *Amy Dawes*

LES ENFANTS DU VENT
(FRENCH)

A MC4 release of a MC4-Pathé Cinema-SGGC co-production with the participation of Pléograf & the CNC. Produced by Jean-Pierre Bailly, Jean-Bernard Fetoux. Directed by Krzysztof Rogulski. Screenplay, Agnès Poullin, Rogulski. Camera (color), Gilles Moison, Jacek Piusluski; editor, Agnès Poullin; music, Elisabeth Sikora; set design, Janusz, Ewa Rojek, Ewa Kowalska; costume design, Alzbieta Radke, Malgorzata Obloza. Reviewed at Club Publicis, Paris, Nov. 7, 1991. Running time: **100 MIN.**

With: Jacques Bonnafé, Thérèse Liotard, Marie Dubois, Pierre Vaneck, Brigitte Roüan, Jean-Claude Bouillon, Jerzy Rogulski.

Earnest but tedious account of six youngsters surviving in Nazi-occupied rural Poland, "Les Enfants du Vent" is shot with more of an eye for nature than compelling narrative. Because youngsters are the focus and the ending is happy, pic could find a place in children's film fests attended by patient children.

Story, based on actual events, concerns three city kids and three country kids who take it upon themselves to roam the mountains giving impromptu theatrical performances.

Individual sequences are often staged and lensed with skill, but the overall tone is arbitrary and without suspense, even though an adult guide is searching for the troupe, evil German patrols are on the prowl and the city kids have no idea if their Resistance-fighter parents are dead or alive.

Helmer details life in the country, makes good use of authentic Polish mountain dwellers and gets decent (dubbed) performances from the valiant children, but pic's most dramatic component remains the mountain vistas in the background.

— *Lisa Nesselson*

ZITTI E MOSCA
(THE PARTY IS OVER)
(ITALIAN)

A Penta Distribuzione release of a Mario & Vittorio Cecchi Gori & Silvio Berlusconi Communications presentation of a Pentafilm & Maura Intl. Film production. Produced by Bruno Altissimi, Claudio Saraceni, Mario & Vittorio Cecchi Gori. Directed by Allesandro Benvenuti. Screenplay, Ugo Chiti, Benvenuti. Camera (Telecolor), Cristiano Pogany; editor, Sergio Montanari; music, Patrizio Fariselli; art direction, Tommaso Bordone; costumes, Carolina Olcese; sound, Candido Raini. Reviewed at Farnese Cinema, Rome, Nov. 7, 1991. Running time: **95 MIN.**

Ivo . . . . Alessandro Benvenuti
Mara . . . . Athina Cenci
Massimo . . . . Massimo Ghini
Clara . . . . Alida Valli
Corpo . . . . Novello Novelli
Also with: Claudio Camiciottoli, Neri Pecchioli, Marco Pitera.

A bittersweet comedy taking jabs at recent changes in Italian leftist politics, "The Party Is Over" is doing brisk biz in Tuscany, where it's set, but is proving too regional to woo nationwide auds. Film's warm humor and energetic pace should find more partygoers on the fest circuit.

Basically "Nashville" in Chianti country, pic interweaves stories of some 50-odd characters at a political rally for the former Italian Communist Party, now the Democratic Left. Though lacking resonance, pic successfully uses a microcosmic community to explore larger themes.

Action takes in four generations: the old diehard party members disillusioned by change, a pair of 30-something old flames reunited by the rally, the young slackers who shrug off politics and the children who concoct a Red Menace monster yarn.

Most effective is the central strand, in which careerist politician Massimo Ghini returns to his birthplace and finds ex-g.f. Athina Cenci at bitter odds with the new party's dismissal of her late father's beliefs. The trio (completed by Alida Valli as Cenci's mother) work impeccably together, and in the large cast of accomplished ensemble players, Cenci's is the standout performance.

The biggest strength of Ugo Chiti and helmer Alessandro Benvenuti's script is its ability to quickly and convincingly sketch so many characters and race through countless comic vignettes without letting pic become episodic.

Benvenuti directs the ambitious piece with a sure hand, though his occasional lapses into stylized fussiness (most notably a frenzied sequence intercutting video game footage with some not-too-Steadycam work) seem overly mannered in context. Other tech credits are uniformly good.

— *David Rooney*

GET THEE OUT
(RUSSIAN)

A Lenfilm USSR production. Produced by Nevskaya Perspectiva. Directed by Dmitry Astrakhan. Screenplay, Astrakhan, O. Danila. Camera (color, black & white), J. Worontsov; music, Alexander Pantichin; production design, S. Kokovkin. Reviewed at Toronto Film Festival, Sept. 12, 1991. (Also in Telluride Film Festival.) Running time: **90 MIN.**
With: O. Mengvinetukutsesy.

This deeply affecting new Lenfilm production communicates the plight of Russian Jews who found themselves vulnerable to persecution in turn-of-the-century pogroms. Powerful chapters in Russian history come to cinematic light in "Get Thee Out," which signals a compelling talent in first-time director Dmitry Astrakhan.

Enterprising trader Motl Rabinovich (O. Mengvinetukutsesy) has brought his family comforts a step above those of his neighbors in his close-knit Ukraine village. He's a generous host to all, including long-staying relatives and a foolish, hard-drinking Gentile neighbor who's always bemoaning his sorrows. He's plagued by visions (expressed in striking black & white) of his family slain by outsiders, and when the cry to "beat up the Yids" goes out, sure enough, his drunken neighbor is the first to show up, ax in hand.

In a fascinating scene highlighting the macabre delicacy of village relations, the man realizes he's a posse of one, and he recovers and asks for a drink of Motl's vodka. Motl warily obliges. The violent tides of history eventually overtake the hamlet, and Motl and family are forced to flee. Later, he decides he will not be vanquished, and his Russian friends, including the young man who has just married his daughter, stand by him.

Director-co-writer Astrakhan memorably conveys the intimate texture of village life in which neighbors conspire to protect the Jews while pretending to the outside world they are dutifully oppressing and hounding them.

Working with great care and a gifted cast, Astrakhan creates a gently nuanced and cumulatively powerful film that brings to life a fearful stain on history that is still informing attitudes today.

Desultory pace and naturalistic style, perfectly suited to the material, will make it a hard sell other than to art house and ethnic specialty auds. — *Amy Dawes*

AMA
(BRITISH)

An Artificial Eye (U.K.) release of an Efiri Tete Films production for Channel 4 (Intl. sales: Jane Balfour Films.) Produced, directed by Kwesi Owusu, Kwate Nee-Owoo. Screenplay, Owusu. Camera (color), Jonathan Collinson, Roy Cornwall; editor, Justin Krish; music, Owusu, Vico Mensah, Nana Danso Abiam; art direction, Ruhi Chaudry, Nigel Ashby, Keith Khan; costume design, Farouk Abdillah; sound, John Anderton, Jason Russell; assistant director, Ingrid Lewis. Reviewed at London Film Festival (British Cinema section), Nov. 7, 1991. Running time: **100 MIN.**
Babs . . . . Thomas Baptiste
Corni . . . . Anima Misa
Ama . . . . Georgina Ackerman
Joe . . . . Roger Griffiths
Also with: Nii Oma Hunter, Joy Elias-Rilwan.

Intriguing culture-clash idea falls flat on its face in "Ama." Low-budgeter that tries to transplant African ritual to modern urban Britain is let down by a flabby script and lackluster acting. Theatrical prospects look bleak.

Title character is a 12-year-old of Ghanaian parents living in north London. Wandering in the countryside one day, she finds a gold-colored computer diskette among tribal artifacts containing warnings about her father and elder brother's health.

Despite her pleas (and those of her visiting uncle) for the father to return to Ghana, the old man has a fatal heart attack. The brother ends up hospitalized after a boxing match. Fantasy finale has her "re-meeting" dad in a street carnival parade.

Cute idea of mixing animistic beliefs with contempo urban values never gets far beyond unexplained hocus-pocus and beaucoup ethnic apparel. Sub-theme of blacks' search for identity in a foreign culture is left in the starting blocks.

In the title role, Georgina Ackerman doesn't convince as a mixed-up moppet. Apart from Roger Griffiths as Ama's boxing-obsessed brother, other players are routine. Tech credits are okay, with some notable lensing in Ghanaian inserts and a catchy score. — *Derek Elley*

DE LAATSTE SESSIE
(LAST DATE)
(DUTCH-DOCU-16m)

An IAF/NFM release of an Akka Volta/Nos TV production. Produced by Marian Brouwer. Directed by Hans Hyl-kema. Screenplay, Hylkema, with Thierry Bruneau. Camera (color, 16m), Deen van der Zaken; editor, Ot Louw; music, Eric Dolphy; sound, Piotr van Dijk, Lukas Boeke, Jan van Sandwijk. Reviewed at Intl. Documentary Film Festival, Amsterdam, Dec. 6, 1991. Running time: **90 MIN.**

Hans Hylkema, who has made 16 documentaries and fiction films in 16 years, displays a love for jazz in his latest docu about American composer-musician Eric Dolphy. An intriguing pic about the life, art and death of a virtuoso musician, "Last Date" could travel anywhere.

Dolphy's mastery of bass clarinet, alto sax and flute became jazz lore. The technical prowess of his compositions and his improvisations, both revolutionary and uncomfortably difficult to play, perplexed his colleagues. He dreamed of playing in a symphony orchestra, but he had no chance because, in his time (he died in 1964 at age 32), U.S. concert halls would not condone black sounds.

After a stint with Charlie Mingus' band, Dolphy stayed in Europe and played in Holland with Dutch musicians. More or less by accident, a concert and part of the rehearsal was taped, providing the material for Dolphy's best album, called "Last Date," and Hylkema's film.

From Holland, Dolphy went to Berlin, where he collapsed during a concert and died two days later. Medicos looked at his symptoms, his profession and his skin color and blamed drugs. But Dolphy never took drugs; his collapse was brought on by diabetes.

Hylkema's knack for interviewing (there's a good session with a woman in Los Angeles who was Dolphy's fiancée), excellent editing and imaginative structuring of the musician's life story make this docu a pleasure to watch and listen to. — *Gerry Waller*

DEN OFRIVILLIGE GOLFAREN
(THE ACCIDENTAL GOLFER)
(SWEDISH)

A Svensk Filmindustri presentation of a Viking Film production in co-operation with SF, Smart Egg Pictures and Cinema Art. Produced by Bo Jonsson. Directed by Lasse Aberg. Screenplay, Aberg with Jonsson. Camera (color), Rune Ericson; editor, Sylvia Ingemarsson; music, Stefan Nilsson; production design, Styrbjörn Engström; costumes, Inger Pehrsson; sound, Sven Fahlén; technical director, Peter Hald. Reviewed at Rigoletto cinema, Stockholm, Dec. 18, 1991. Running time: **100 MIN.**
With: Lasse Aberg, Jon Skolmen, Daniel Bergman, Hege Schoyen, Ulf Eklund, Marianne Scheja, Jimmy Logan, Margo Dunn, Lasse Haldenberg, Annalisa Ericson, Ingvar Kjellson.

Popular writer-actor-director-painter Lasse Aberg's new comedy "The Accidental Golfer" is his best pic to date and looks to be a surefire hit in Sweden, where his previous pics occupy four of the country's top five boxoffice slots.

Although some of the humor will be caught only by Swedish auds, this amusing look at amateur golfing may tee off in some territories where there's interest in the sport.

Here, Aberg's character is a shy introvert who makes a bet with the yuppie who caused him to lose his job: Can anyone be taught to play golf within a week? A golfer friend takes Aberg to Scotland where an old golf pro teaches him the basics, and he meets and falls in love with the pro's beautiful daughter.

Scotland scenes have a tenderness and warmth Aberg's previous films lacked, and here they effectively contrast with scenes of harsher and colder Sweden.

The humor is both visual and verbal, and this time out Aberg shows a sharpened eye for satire, with yuppies, land developers and upper-class golf fanatics as targets. Some scenes have an absurd, surrealistic quality.

Acting is good overall, with special mention owed Daniel Bergman (son of Ingmar) as the ruthless yuppie. Tech credits are good. — *Gunnar Rehlin*

AND YOU THOUGHT YOUR PARENTS WERE WEIRD

A Trimark Pictures release of a Panorama Film Intl. production. Produced by Just Betzer. Executive producer, Pernille Siesbye, Co-producers, Mark Slater, Bennie Korzen. Directed, written by Tony Cookson. Camera (color), Paul Elliott; editor, Michael Ornstein; production design, Alexander Kicenki; costume design, Sanja M. Hays; set decoration, Nancy Booth; sound, Thomas M. Cunliffe; robot design, Rick Lazzarini; assistant director, C.C. Barnes; associate producer, Joan Borsten. Reviewed at Raleigh Studios, Hollywood, Nov. 11, 1991. MPAA rating: PG. Running time: **92 MIN.**
Josh . . . . Joshua Miller
Max . . . . Edan Gross
Sarah . . . . Marcia Strassman
Matthew . . . . Alan Thicke
Alice . . . . Susan Gibney

Dad's spirit returns to inhabit a friendly domestic robot in this sentimental, lightly satisfying low-budgeter. Fourth domestic release from Trimark, theatrical arm of homevid company Vidmark, pic is likely to do most of its business on cassette, where its inventive blend of technology and "Ghost"-inspired magic should make pleasing family fare.

Story unspools like perfect recession-era entertainment, with earnest brothers Max, 10 (Edan Gross), and Josh, 15 (Joshua Miller), using their scientific smarts to help cash-strapped Mom (Marcia Strassman) hold on to their house.

Once they perfect and patent their stumpy little R2D2-like invention, they figure they'll sell it to save the family digs, endangered now that their investor dad is long gone, an apparent suicide. But after some voodoo hoodoo at a teen seance, the robot lights up with a witty, engaging new presence — Dad (voiced by Alan Thicke) — who proceeds to romance unwitting Mom and help the kids improve their invention.

With a cagey TV reporter (Susan Gibney) trying to get the scoop on the robot and rival inventors trying to steal it, there's plenty going on — maybe too much — as things get bogged down and overcomplicated in the final reels. Writer-director Tony Cookson lays on the sentiment with a spatula toward the end.

Still, story has plenty of heart, cast is enjoyable and Cookson has an instinct for the material that makes this humble outing uncalculated and even a bit soulful. No-frills production and unsually tight framing make this Trimark pickup look tailor-made for video. — *Amy Dawes*

ARCHIVE REVIEW

PLASTIC JESUS
(YUGOSLAVIAN)

A Centar Film-FRZ production. Directed, written by Lazar Stojanovic. Camera (color), Branko Perak; editor, Stojanovic; sound, Bata Pivnicki, Marko Rodic. Reviewed at Montreal Film Festival, Aug. 23, 1991. Running time: **76 MIN.**

With: Tomislav Golovac, Svetlana Gligorijevic, Vukica Djilas, Kristina Pribicenc, Zivojin Gligorijevic.

Made in 1971, "Plastic Jesus" was immediately banned by the Yugoslavian government, and its young writer-director Lazar Stojanovic was sentenced to three years in prison. Pic, which finally preemed in Belgrade last year, is a sure bet for fests but a long shot for theatrical bookings.

Very much a film of its time and clearly influenced by iconoclastic Yugo director Dusan Makavejev (whose controversial "W.R., Mysteries Of The Organism" was made the same year), "Plastic Jesus" cheerfully mixes a slim story line, newsreel footage, songs and political and sexual slogans. Stojanovic's bizarre but hilarious film is rougher than Makavejev's, however, since the story line is insubstantial.

Opening credits are sung by heavily bearded lead actor Tomislav Golovac, who plays an anarchist filmmaker with a Croatian-American g.f. constantly singing country & western standards (the song about "Plastic Jesus" gives the film its original English title). She leaves him, and he goes on to another woman and gets in trouble with the police. Eventually, he's bumped off by a jealous femme.

On this slight plot is strung a series of assaults on the Yugo-establishment. Then-President Tito makes a vacuous speech backed by a song previously heard backing a speech by Hitler.

A scene of the wedding of one of Tito's secret police officers was cut and destroyed when the film was banned and survives only as a still in the released pic.

Added to this is rare footage of the opening of the 1942 fascist Croatian parliament in Zagreb. Equally rare, and apparently never before seen, is footage of the 1968 student riots in Belgrade.

Pic isn't dated, however, since current upheaval in Yugoslavia is prophesied in Stojanovic's caustic film. — *David Stratton*

1992

THE HAND THAT ROCKS THE CRADLE

A Buena Vista release of a Hollywood Pictures presentation of an Interscope Communications production in association with Nomura Babcock & Brown. Produced by David Madden. Executive producers, Ted Field, Rick Jaffa, Robert W. Cort. Co-producer, Ira Halberstadt. Directed by Curtis Hanson. Screenplay, Amanda Silver. Camera (Alpha Cine color; Technicolor prints), Robert Elswit; editor, John F. Link; music, Graeme Revell; production design, Edward Pisoni; art direction, Mark Zuelzke; set design, Gilbert Wong; set decoration, Sandy Reynolds Wasco; visual consultant, Carol Fenelon; costume design, Jennifer von Mayrhauser; sound (Dolby), James Pilcher; assistant directors, Michael Daves, Ray Greenfield; casting, Junie Lowry-Johnson. Reviewed at Universal City Cinemas, Universal City, Calif., Dec. 31, 1991. MPAA Rating: R. Running time: **110 MIN.**
Claire Bartel . . . . Annabella Sciorra
Peyton Flanders . Rebecca De Mornay
Michael Bartel . . . . Matt McCoy
Solomon . . . . Ernie Hudson
Marlene . . . . Julianne Moore
Emma Bartel . . . . . Madeline Zima
Dr. Mott . . . . John de Lancie
Marty . . . . Kevin Skousen

"**T**he Hand That Rocks the Cradle" is a low-key thriller that will make baby boomers double-check the references of any prospective nanny. Diagramatic script channels the action in a predictable direction toward an inevitable climax, but fine performances and a refusal to pander to the audience's grossest instincts raise this a notch or two above the norm.

Disney is preceding the Jan. 10 launch with a massive national sneak preview blitz, which began on New Year's Eve and continued last weekend, in hopes of building word of mouth. B.O. prospects look decent in quick, wide playoff.

First screenplay by Amanda Silver, who is the granddaughter of the late, great screenwriter Sidney Buchman, trades in the same devil woman theme that anchored "Fatal Attraction," with the sanctity of the traditional family unit as the villain's target.

Scenario's schematic singlemindedness draws attention to the fact that story is basically a concoction designed to put characters, and audience, through the ringer, which it does adequately but without the blatant shocks expected of the genre.

Pleasant existence of pregnant Seattle housewife Claire Bartel (Annabella Sciorra) is disrupted when her new gynecologist crosses the proper boundaries during an exam. With the encouragement of her husband Michael (Matt McCoy), Claire files charges, upon which the doctor commits suicide; with his death, several other similarly abused women come forward.

Medic's demise sends his pregnant wife into hysterics, causing her to lose her baby. Cut to six months later, and this woman (Rebecca De Mornay), who now calls herself Peyton, turns up to offer her services as nanny to the Bartels. Impressed by her poise, demeanor and intelligence, they readily take her in, and the viewer knows the screw will soon begin turning.

Peyton employs assorted tactics to gradually undo the woman she blames for ruining her life, including turning her 5-year-old daughter against her, making her think the family handyman is molesting the child, encouraging her to imagine she has something going with her husband and wetnursing the new baby.

And this is just for starters, before the mortal battle between mother and her aspiring replacement really begins.

For the most part, yarn has been invested with enough emotional reality to sustain interest, but a couple of surprise reversals in Peyton's plans that she would have had to correct, as well as some malevolent humor, would have gone a long way to cranking up the excitement.

Director Curtis Hanson brings a tasteful level-headedness to the pic and refuses to insult the audience with vulgar shocks for their own sake. On the other hand, conditioned mainstream auds may be frustrated that they have to wait until the very end for any overt thrills.

Helmer has obtained taut, impressive performances, notably from cast women. A totally deglamorized Sciorra becomes unglued subtly and slowly, eliciting sympathy without begging for it. De Mornay, her Miss Congeniality exterior masking evil intent, is an ice queen viewers will enjoy watching get hers in the end.

Julianne Moore carries off a showy supporting part, that of Michael Bartel's ex-g.f., with terrific style, and Madeline Zima is a find as the little daughter.

Matt McCoy is okay as Claire's perfect, supportive husband, while Ernie Hudson manages to be quite moving despite the shameless sentimentality of his role as the retarded handyman who needs the love of the Bartel family.

Behind-the-scenes contributions are solid, although lack of any music for long periods contributes to a flat, arid feeling through long mid-section.
— *Todd McCarthy*

MATILDA
(ITALIAN)

An Angio Film production in association with So. Co. F. Imm. Produced, directed by Antonietta De Lillo, Giorgio Magliulo. Screenplay, Graziano Diana, Antonio Fiore, Stefano Masi. Camera (color), Magliulo; editor, Simona Paggi; music, Franco Piersanti; sound, Uberto Nijus; art direction, Paola Bizzari; costumes, Magda Bava. Reviewed at Grauco Cineclub, Rome, Dec. 12, 1991. Running time: **90 MIN.**
Torquato . . . . Silvio Orlando
Matilda . . . . Carla Benedetti
Also with: Luigi Petrucci, Gianni Agus, Milena Vukotic, Wanna Polverosi, Mario Santella, Tino Schirinzi.

A black comedy with a quirky thriller vein, "Matilda" is a rough-hewn diamond that should appeal to fest programmers looking for upbeat inserts. Italo indie's homeground biz has been marginal, but offshore prospects could be rosier.

Given the proliferation of Yank remakes of sophisticated Euro comedies, pic may also prove appetizing fodder Stateside for story scouts.

After the violent deaths of three consecutive soulmates, a well-heeled Neapolitan (Carla Benedetti) slips into an emotional slump. At the insistence of her oddball family, she picks up the pieces and takes out a lonely hearts ad. The matchmaking housekeeper of shy archivist Silvio Orlando fakes his reply and engineers the couple's first date.

Love blossoms and a future together looks set until the guy gets wind of the string of disasters in the woman's past, and he breaks with her. She steals his Sunday daubings and mounts a hit exhibition in a bid to win him back. Terrified of further mishaps, he reacts coolly, but the surprise denouement reveals the human origin of her bad luck with men.

Pic opens on a roller coaster and, aside from a brief dip when the pair split up, maintains this pace throughout. Though rooted in traditional Neapolitan comic concerns (love, superstition) it deftly bypasses schlock tendencies that have blighted the past decade of Italo comedies and slots into its own madcap sitcom sensibility.

Flawless casting places seasoned thesps alongside newcomers. Benedetti makes her character both irresistible and sinister enough to keep auds guessing and, as the overworked underdog, Orlando schleps through his run of accidents with Buster Keaton-style hilarity.

Pic avoids the clichéd quarters of Naples in favor of its rarely seen chic suburbia and is given visual zing by co-helmer Giorgio Magliulo's fluid camerawork. Sound recording often lacks polish, but tech credits are otherwise smooth. — *David Rooney*

A IDADE MAJOR
(ALEX)
(PORTUGUESE)

An Invicta Films production. Produced by João Pedro Bénard. Directed, written by Teresa Villaverde. Camera (color), Elfi Mikesch; editor, Manuela Viegas, Vasco Pimental; art direction, Miguel Nendes, Jeanne Waltz; sound, Pimental. Reviewed at Turin Intl. Young Cinema Festival (competition), Nov. 14, 1991. Running time: **120 MIN.**
Alex . . . . Ricardo Colares
Mario . . . . Vincent Gallo
Manuela . . . . Teresa Roby
Barbara . . . . . . Maria de Medeiros
Pedro . . . . Joaquim de Almeida

An intimate chronicle of a family's destruction, "Alex" kicks off well but runs out of steam. Result, overlong and flat, will have slim appeal outside local market, though presence of ZDF coin could lead to wider tube berths.

Tale is set during the early '70s in the waning days of Portuguese dictatorship. Young Alex (Ricardo Colares) waves his father (Joaquim de Almeida) off to war in Africa but stays close to him through letters. Things turn sour when son and his mother (Teresa Roby) lose contact with the soldier.

Via another returned soldier, Mom learns that her husband has been back for two months and forces him to come home. Peaceful reunion proves unworkable, and tragedy strikes.

Scripter/first-time helmer Teresa Villaverde's big mistake is setting up Alex as pic's pivotal character and then brushing him aside one third in. The intense young actor makes all his scenes count, but when focus shifts to his parents, pic stops moving. Decision to go for relentlessly low-key perfs from principals subtracts emotional highs and lows.

Technically, film is well-crafted though not well enough to compensate for monotone screenplay in which political parallels are too sketchily drawn to really work. — *David Rooney*

LES FLEURS DU MAL
(FRENCH)

A Sirius release of a Show-Off-Raan-Francis Drefus Music co-production with the participation of Canal Plus. Produced by Eliane Piliego, Gabrielle Cequiera. Directed, written by Jean-Pierre Rawson, based on writings of Charles Baudelaire. Camera (color), Elsa Roque; editor, Jacqueline Thiedot; music, Jean-Noel Chaleat; sound, Jean-Claude Reboul; artistic consultants, Pierre Duquesne, Maria Gonzaga. Reviewed at Club Publicis, Paris, Nov. 5, 1991. Running time: **85 MIN.**
Charles Baudelaire . . Antoine Dulery
Ernest Pinard . . Jean-Marie Lemaire
Jeanne Duval . . . Patrice Flora-Praxo
Mme. Sabatier . . Marianne Assouline
Boissard . . . Jean-Claude Bolle-Redat

Part courtroom drama, part interpretive anthology, Jean-Pierre Rawson's "Les Fleurs du Mal" is too risqué for the classroom (for which it was intended) and too stodgy for art houses. This lushly appointed account of poet Charles Baudelaire's trial for offending public decency could have used some Ken Russellesque excess, but pic lends itself to fests concerned with literature and censorship.

Film begins with poet's tumble down a staircase in 1866 and unfolds in flashbacks to his 1857 trial, intercut with illustrated recitations of the erotic poems successfully suppressed from the title volume.

Contrast between offending poems as spoken by the court bailiff vs. Baudelaire's own powerful recitation is well-handled, as is the intelligent animosity between accuser and accused. But love scenes are stilted, and entire pic is marred by sappy electronic music.

Helmer's stated objective was to make a film for 13- to 16-year-olds and to give the sound of the poems precedence over visual imagery. But when the poems are acted out, it comes across like second-rate perfume commercials. Possible exception is the vignette in which Baudelaire and a woman kiss passionately before launching into a spirited sword fight. Courtroom scenes are convincing and nicely lensed in an imposing decor.

Rawson seems to be suggesting the poet was a punk before his time, but this Baudelaire is not enough of an upstart to support the theory.

Stage actor Antoine Dulery bears a mild resemblance to the sensual, dandy poet. Patrice Flora-Praxo, as Baudelaire's Creole mistress, is spunkier in court than she is in bed, and Jean-Claude Bolle-Redat is amusingly spacey as a hashish den proprietor. Snappy rejoinders and the poems themselves would require outstanding subtitles.

Pic ends with the poet's work being rehabilitated by the literary establishment, along with shots of Baudelaire's grave at Montparnasse cemetery. To its credit, pic does leave one wanting to know more about the real Baudelaire. — *Lisa Nesselson*

MYEST
(REVENGE)
(KAZAKHSTANI)

A Studio Kazakhfilm production. Directed by Yermek Shinarbaev. Screenplay, Anatoly Kim. Camera (color), Sergei Kosmanev; editor, Polina Stein; music, Vladislav Shute; production design, Elena Eliseeva. Reviewed at Montreal Film Festival (Cinema of Today and Tomorrow section), Aug. 26, 1991. Running time: **97 MIN.**
With: Alexander Pan, Oleg Li, Kasim Dzhakibaev, Yuazas Budraitis, Zinaida Em, Valentin Te, Lubove Germanova, Rasim Jakibaev.

An unusual pic from Kazakhstan, "Revenge" tells a mystical story set in Korea and China. Fine camerawork and the director's poetic handling make for a strange and often beautiful picture that could get further fest exposure.

In ancient Korea, a powerful king orders his weakling son to be trained as a warrior; 20 years later, son is king and banishes a poet friend for criticizing him.

Pic skips forward to 1915 and a village school where a teacher inexplicably kills a young girl with an ax. Her father vows vengeance and pursues the killer into China, where he disappears. Ten years later, the father marries a deaf-mute woman. Their son is ordered by his dying father to continue the vendetta against the teacher.

Narrative is divided into chapters with title headings and episodes that stray from the main story, becoming more dreamlike as pic progresses. Director Yermek Shinarbaev favors high contrast, overlit shooting in some scenes, and misty lighting in others. Despite being set in Korea and China, pic seems steeped in Kazakh legends, though the Russian dubbing in the print caught reduces the authenticity.
— *David Stratton*

MUJER TRANSPARENTE
(TRANSPARENT WOMAN)
(CUBAN)

An Instituto Cubano del Arte e Industria Cinematográficos (ICAIC) production. Directed by Héctor Veitía, Mayra Segura, Mayra Valasí, Mario Crespo, Ana Rodríguez. Editor, Lina Baniela. Reviewed at 8th Santafé de Bogotá (Colombia) Intl. Film Festival (competition), Oct. 11, 1991. Running time: **100 MIN.**
ISABEL
Directed by Veitía. Screenplay, Veitía, Tina León. Camera (color), Julio Valdés; music, Mario Dalf.
Isabel . . . . Isabel Moreno
Husband . . . . Manuel Porto
ADRIANA
Directed, written by Segura. Camera (color), Raúl Pérez Ureta; music, Mario Dalf.
Adriana . . . . Verónica Lynn
JULIA
Directed, written by Vilasís. Camera (color), Julio Valdés; music, Lucía Huergo.
Julia . . . . Mirtha Ibarra
Lover . . . . Rolando Nuñez
ZOE
Directed by Crespo. Screenplay, Osvaldo Sánchez, Carlos Celdrán. Camera (color), Raúl Pérez Ureta; music, Alfredo Gómez.
Zoe . . . . Leonor Arocha
Student . . . . Leonardo Armas
LAURA
Directed by Rodríguez. Screenplay, Osvaldo Sánchez, Carlos Celdrán. Camera (color), Julio Valdés; music, Mario Dalf.
Laura . . . . Selma Sereghi

Cuba's first effort to incorporate new filmmakers, "Transparent Woman" offers five different visions of contemporary Cuban women. As with many anthology pics, overall film is uneven, depending on the strengths of its individual efforts. Pic should find some interest on the fest circuit.

Opening and closing tales are the strongest: Although the theme of the first story "Isabel," by Héctor Veitía, is not new, it has relevance in Cuba's macho society. Dominated by voiceover, pic concerns a wife and mother, who has denied her own life for nearly 20 years and has finally had enough.

On the other hand, "Laura," by Ana Rodríguez, deals with an important contempo topic: reconciliation between those who left Cuba and those who remain. Tale revolves around Laura, who goes to a Havana hotel to visit an old friend who had left the island 15 years earlier. While waiting in the lobby, Laura suffers indignities such as a bar that will not accept Cuban pesos or a desk clerk who ignores her in favor of foreigners. Sequence is well handled, incorporating archival images, and deals with a very real theme.

More marginal is Mayra Segura's "Adriana," a slight tale of a spinster who has billeted herself in her apartment following the revolution. She lives in her closed world until one day her solitude is broken by the visit of a telephone repairman.

"Julia," helmed by Mayra Vilasís, is the tale of a woman abandoned by her husband for another. Although Julia takes on a young lover and confronts life on her own terms, she still yearns for hubbie to return.

Weakest story is Mario Crespo's "Zoe," a rather pretentious portrait of an alienated, enigmatic art student who lures a conservative student into bed.

Due to the brief exposition time allotted, pic touts a surfeit of narrative voiceovers, present in almost all of the tales. Furthermore, tales' open endings come off more as incidents than complete stories. Tech credits and acting are up to par.
— *Paul Lenti*

MUNO NO HITO
(NOWHERE MAN)
(JAPANESE)

A KSS-Shochiku Dai-ichi Kogyo Co. production. (Intl. sales: Shochiku.) Executive producers, Toshiaki Nakazawa, Masaki Sekine. Produced by Kazuyoshi Okuyama, Shozo Ichiyama, Hirotsugo Yoshida. Directed by Naoto Takenaka. Screenplay, Toshiharu Maruchi, based on Yoshiharu Tsuge's comic strip. Camera (Fujicolor), Yasushi Sasakibara; editor, Yoshiyuki Okuhara; music, Gontiti; production design, Iwao Saitoh; sound, Mineharu Kitamura; production manager, Noriyuki Takahashi; assistant director, Yasuo Matsumoto. Reviewed at Venice Film Festival, Sept. 12, 1991. Running time: **107 MIN.**
Sukezo Sukegawa . . Naoto Takenaka
Momoko (wife) . . . . . . Jun Fubuki
Sansuke (son) . . . . . Kohtaro Santoh

A quirky, inventive comedy based on a popular comic strip, "Nowhere Man" is a sprightly mix of realism, humor and fantasy. Winner of the Fipresci international critics prize for noncompeting films at 1991's Venice fest, pic could garner an appreciative cult aud.

Central character is a cartoonist who couldn't keep up with the times and lost his job. Convinced that money is to be made from everyday objects, he briefly considers recycling hair from barbershop floors and then ends up erecting a stall by a river to sell stones he collects from the riverbed. His small son assists him, but, not surprisingly, customers are few.

From the bizarre premise of a man trying to sell something already free for the taking, screenwriter Toshiharu Maruchi has fashioned an endearingly odd film from Yoshiharu Tsuge's popular comic strip. A stone fan club is even organized (club prez' wife makes a half-hearted attempt to seduce the feckless hero).

Offbeat comedy (containing several bodily function jokes) also is a haunting fantasy, as the stone merchant frequently sees a large black bird turning into a man.

Performance of actor-director Naoto Takenaka in the lead role is enjoyable. In his first feature as a director, Takenaka displays a sure hand for comedy and pictorial style. Music, the first film score composed by the popular Japanese group Gontiti, is a major asset. — *David Stratton*

THE FEVER
(SOUTH AFRICAN-DOCU-16m)

A Distant Horizon production in association with Denonair Films (PTY) & the British Broadcasting Corp. Produced by David M. Thompson. Directed, written by Francis Gerard. Camera (color, 16m), Dewald Aukema; editor, Don Fairservice; music, Mbongeni Ngema; sound, Robin Harris. Reviewed at Montreal World Film Festival, Aug. 30, 1991. Running time: **78 MIN.**
Narrator: Ian Holm.

This powerful documentary is about a play that "caused controversy about the role of the arts in the new South Africa," per narrator Ian Holm. Footage of "Township Fever" at Johannesburg's Market Theater is crosscut with news footage of the 1985 township railway strike and interviews with artists and politicians. This charged docu is dynamite fare for quality TV stations.

Docu initially focuses on revolutionary theater director Mbongeni Ngema, whose "Sarafina!" played on Broadway for over a year. Ngema explains his casting of nonacting kids from the townships and his training program to make them superb actors who provide each play's authenticity.

"Township Fever" and "The Fever" are as much about fear and its resulting violence as it is about the strike that pitted black workers against apartheid.

Loaded with stats and interviews, pic also is informative. Theater play is shot cinematically (avoiding the point-and-shoot trap), and docu is tightly edited to simplify a complicated issue. — *Suzan Ayscough*

3-4X JUGATSU
(BOILING POINT)
(JAPANESE)

A Bandai-Shochiku-Fuji production. Produced by Hisao Nabeshima, Masayuki Mori, Takio Yoshida. Directed, written by Takeshi Kitano. Camera (color), Katsumi Yanagishima; editor, Toshio Taniguchi; art direction, Osamu Sasaki; sound, Senji Horiuchi. Reviewed at Turin Intl. Young Cinema Festival (competition), Nov. 13, 1991. Running time: **96 MIN.**
Masaki . . . . Masahiko Ono
Sayaka . . . . Yuriko Ishida
Takashi . . . . Takahito Iguchi
Kazuo . . . . Minoru Iizuka
   Also with: Hisashi Igawa, Bengal, Beat Takeshi.

A Japanese baseball/mobster comedy, "Boiling Point" is as far off center as its genre suggests. This goofy flipside to the neon-lit vice dens and ultra-cool killers of "Black Rain" and similar pics should score highly with festival auds and could tap into cult success on the art house fringe.

Luckless baseball player Masahiko Ono clashes with a local gangster at the gas station where he works and becomes a target for mob violence. He turns to Takahito Iguchi, a bar-owner with underworld connections. Iguchi sends him to Okinawa to get a gun from sadistic thug Beat Takeshi and his guileless henchman, and most of pic's action revolves around the errand's complications. Back home, Ono finds the mob wrecking havoc on his team and steals a fuel tanker for some explosive revenge.

Second directorial outing for popular Japanese TV comic Takeshi Kitano (the tough sergeant in "Merry Christmas Mr. Lawrence") has some teething troubles in the first reel and takes time to establish its off-the-wall tone. But once moving, it never stops.

Laughs are timed to perfection, especially by deadpan lead Ono and pic's helmer (acting as Beat Takeshi) as one of recent cinema's most likably loco bad guys.

Technically, film studiously avoids slickness using unconventional camera angles and a willfully funky editing style matching its comic strip attitude to sex and violence. Soundtrack carries barely a note of music, but pic has rhythm to burn. Original Japanese title refers to a baseball score. — *David Rooney*

OLD SCORES
(NEW ZEALAND-WELSH)

A South Pacific Pictures & HTV/Cymru production. Produced by Don Reynolds. Directed by Alan Clayton. Screenplay, Dean Parker, Greg McGee. Camera (color), Allen Guilford; editor, Jamie Selkirk, Mike Horton; music, Wayne Warlow. Reviewed at Downtown 6, Palmerston North, New Zealand, Sept. 23, 1991. Running time: **102 MIN.**
Evan Price . . . . Windsor Davies
Acid Aitken . . . . . Martyn Sanderson
Bleddyn Morgan . . . . . Robert Pugh
Barry Brown . . . . Tony Barry
Ewen Murray . . . . John Bach
   Also with: Roy Billing, Terence Cooper, John Francis, Alison Bruce.

"Old Scores" is a glamorless comedy of rugby passions destined to have little appeal outside its targeted audiences in New Zealand and Wales. Primarily made for tv, its theatrical life is marginal. Homevid sales to absolute rugger fans at home and in the U.K. may notch a small niche.

Story spins on a (fictional) controversial test match between New Zealand and Wales circa 1966. The deathbed confession of a sideline judge reveals that a Welsh player (Robert Pugh) should not have been awarded the winning try; he had stepped outside in his run to the goal.

To salvage respective glory, the rugby bosses propose a replay of the game with the original teams. Martyn Sanderson limns the coach of the now middle-aged, far-from fit, Kiwi pack, while Windsor Davies assembles an overweight Welsh team. Meanwhile, the man at the center of the controversy (Pugh) finds personal scores need to be settled off the field as well as on it.

Co-produced by South Pacific Pictures and HTV Wales, the comedy-drama rugby romance depends on some inside knowledge for its impact. For instance, who, outside New Zealand and Wales, will be able to identify the 17 "real" one-time players in the two teams?

Welsh director Alan Clayton delivers superficial treatment of a script more mundane than mean-

ingful. Overall production style is akin to B-grade Ealing Studios product of the late 1940s. Only Sanderson, in terrier-like form as the caustic Kiwi coach, is able to move things along.
— *Mike Nicolaidi.*

LA FRONTERA
(THE FRONTIER)
(CHILEAN-SPANISH)

Co-produced by Filmcentro Cine, Televisión Española, ION Prods., Cine XXI and Televisión Nacional de Chile. Produced by Eduardo Larrain. Directed by Ricardo Larrain. Screenplay, R. Larrain, Jorge Goldenberg. Camera, Héctor Ríos; editor, Claudio Martinez; music, Jaime de Aguirre; art direction, Juan Carlos Castillo. Reviewed at Cine Pedro de Valdivia, Santiago, Oct. 28, 1991. Running time: **115 MIN.**
Ramiro Orellana . . . Patricio Contreras
Maité . . . . Gloria Laso
Father Patricio . . . . Héctor Noguera
Delegate . . . . Alonso Venegas
Diver . . . . Aldo Bernales
Don Ignacio . . . . . Patricio Bunster
Hilda, the Machi . . . . Gricelda Nuñez
   Also with: Anîbel Reyna, Sergio Hernandez, Sergio Schmied, Elsa Poblete.

The best Chilean first feature in two decades, Ricardo Larrain's "The Frontier" is a promising local b.o. prospect and should get a fair amount of fest exposure in 1992. Foreign TV sales also are probable.

A math teacher (Patricio Contreras), condemned to internal exile by the military government, is taken to a village in the south of Chile where, uprooted from his urban milieu, he must adapt as best he can. The village had been destroyed 25 years earlier by a tidal wave, a memory that still tramatizes the locals.

The teacher is subjected to a village official's petty harassments, but he slowly finds his way in the simple life of this storm-swept region. In Santiago, the unhappy man had few emotional commitments and a basically skeptical attitude. Pic deals with his new relationships and his rediscovery of self.

The teacher and the spinsterish daughter (Gloria Laso) of a Spanish Republican mitigate each other's loneliness but, when faced with the choice, neither is willing to make sacrifices for the other's sake.

Other characters are a diver, a "machi" (native medicine woman) and a North American priest. Reinforced by Hector Rios' excellent photography, pic's really about a place where nature and the elements largely control human affairs.

Some of the characters tend to be one-dimensional, but Hector Noguera as the priest and Contreras and Laso are outstanding as complex and believable people. Individually or together, the leads are the center of several emotional climaxes.

Pic, adapted from a script that won the Havana Film Festival screenplay competition in 1990, is a drama enriched by opportune touches of humor. Technical credits are good.

— *Hans Ehrmann*

REVENGE OF BILLY THE KID
(BRITISH)

A Montage Films production. Produced by Tim Dennison. Executive producer, Dennison, Jim Groom, Richard Lake. Directed by Groom. Screenplay, Dennison, Groom, Richard Mathews; camera (Eastmancolor), David Read; editor, Groom; music, Tony Flynn; sound, Peter Kyle, Harry Barnes; special makeup-creature effects, Neill R. Gorton, Steven M. Painter; assistant director, John Abbott; production manager, Caroline Hodgson; stunt coordinator, Derek Ware; co-producer, Lake. Reviewed at Bijou preview theater, London, Nov. 1, 1991. Running time: **102 MIN.**
Gyles MacDonald . . . Michael Balfour
Ronnie MacDonald . Samantha Perkins
Gretta MacDonald . . . Jackie D. Broad
Ronald MacDonald . . . . Trevor Peake
Ronald MacDonald . . . Bryan Heeley
Billy T. Kid . . . . Julian Shaw
Mr. Allott . . . . Norman Mitchell
Lance Allott . . . . . Dean Williamson

Alusty low-budgeter about a half-human goat run amok, "Revenge of Billy the Kid" plays like a cross between "The Evil Dead" and a British "Li'l Abner." Gross-out local humor may not translate well in off-shore markets, but pro finish should ensure word-of-mouth biz on the gore circuit.

Loopy yarn, set on a fictional island, kicks off with a drunken farmer, Gyles (Michael Balfour), laying the family goat, resulting in a monster dubbed Billy that's cared for by Gyles' buxom daughter (Samantha Perkins).

This low-rent version of Tim Curry in "Legend" is soon sprouting horns and sharing the family dinner table. But one day the farmer, fearing his secret may get out, wraps it in a sack and chucks it in the local river. Beast survives, and soon he's chomping up the locals.

Veteran character actor Balfour keeps the pic on track in a scenery-chewing perf. Newcomer Perkins is fine as the goat-loving daughter, and Jackie D.

Broad scores as the appalling, pipe-smoking wife. Dean Williamson is passable as Perkins' sappy b.f. Lance. (Halfway through shoot, actor replaced Stephen Marzella, who can still be spotted in some scenes.)

Pic could benefit from trimming, but editor Jim Groom, debuting behind the camera, generally keeps the tempo lively. Tech credits are solid, with alert scoring by Tony Flynn. Creature effects, all sans opticals, are impressive, given budget. "Billy" was first feature to be shot on 16m high-grain Kodak EXR 7245 stock for 35m theatrical blowup.

— *Derek Elley*

BEERTJE SEBASTIAAN: DE GEHEIME OPDRACHT
(SEBASTIAN STAR BEAR: FIRST MISSION)
(DUTCH-ANIMATED)

A Corcorde Film release of a Frank Fehmers production. Produced, directed by Fehmers. Screenplay, Richard Felgate, Michael Jupo, Fabio Pacifico; in Cineco color; editor, Lorraine T. Miller; music, Henri Seroka; art direction, Pacifico; sound, Francis de Well, Ciel de Graaf; production supervisor, Ronnie Gerschtanowitz. Reviewed at Dutch Film Days, Utrecht, Sept. 24, 1991. Running time: **78 MIN.**
With voices of: Peter Banks, Thom Booker, Jana Goddard, Garrick Hagon, Jane Shelden, Shelly Tompson, Dick Vosburgh.

An animated pic for kids, "Sebastian Star Bear: First Mission" has gadgets galore, with old-fashioned but comfortable characters and animation. Pic in two versions (one English, one Dutch) should attract a wide audience.

Premise is that bears were deposed as masters of the animal kingdom. A dozen strong, wise bears escaped into the heavens, from where they protect their earthly cousins with 007-style bear agents.

On his first mission, Sebastian sets out to help a cub. Their quest leads them to China, and after various perils, things end triumphantly with a car chase in San Francisco.

A new studio in China did much of the animation work, including coloring by hand. Production money came from the Netherlands, both from public and private sources, without presales. In this case, the bear mar-

ket was quite optimistic, and probably with good reason.

— *Gerry Waller*

BILDER DER WELT UND INSCHRIFT DES KRIEGES
(IMAGES OF THE WORLD AND THE INSCRIPTION OF WAR)
(GERMAN-DOCU)

Directed, written by Haroun Farocki. Narrator, Cynthia Beatt. Reviewed at Film Forum, N.Y., Nov. 7, 1991. Running Time: **75 MIN.**

This occasionally provocative docu deals with two CIA employees' analysis of aerial photographs of the Auschwitz concentration camp during World War II and in the 1970s. Pic abounds in ironies as well as questionable assertions.

Director Haroun Farocki grinds out a Godardian deluge of information on the meaning of images, adding such diverse subjects as the development of metal pressing and photo scale measurements. His examination of the photos brings out the vagaries and limitations of perception as well as political and social mechanics.

For example, in an astute analysis of a picture taken of a woman prisoner at Auschwitz, he charts the strange interplay between the subject and the Nazi photographer.

Unfortunately, not all the elements coalesce, and the narration sometimes makes shaky assertions. Farocki's film also tries to make the obvious sound like personal discovery.

Discussing the camouflage of buildings during the war, the narrator proclaims that beside the real world a world of military fiction had been created. This should come as something less than a metaphysical breakthrough to even casual students of war, since distorting the reality of a situation to the enemy has always been a prime objective.

Farocki has made several other films before and after this 1988 effort. His erudition and fluidity in making associations may work better with them than in this flawed docu.

— *Fred Lombardi*

MARIA ANTONIA
(CUBAN)

An ICAIC production. Produced by Santiago Llapur. Executive producer, Camilo Vives. Directed by Sergio Giral. Screenplay, Armando Dorrego de Vegas, based on Eugenio Hernandez Espinoza's play. Camera (color), Angel Alderete; editor, Roberto Bravo, Marusha Hernandez; music, Sintesis; costume design, Heri Echeverria; sound, Herminal Hernandez; assistant director, Antonio Somoza. Reviewed at London Film Festival (3 Continents: Latin America section), Nov. 10, 1991. Running time: **102 MIN.**
Maria Antonia . . . . . Alina Rodriguez
Julian . . . . Alexis Valdez
Birds Hunter . . . . Roberto Perdomo
Babalao . . . . Jose A. Rodriguez
Nena Capitolio . . . . . Daysi Granados

Sergio Giral, Cuba's leading black helmer, comes up with a sweaty mix of Latino meller and Afro ritual in "Maria Antonio." This he-done-her-wrong yarn passes the time agreeably but won't earn much beyond Hispanic markets.

Story, set in the decadent mid-'50s (Fox's "Prince of Players" is showing downtown), concerns a gutsy prostie (Alina Rodriguez) who reclaims her man (Alexis Valdez) after a stint in stir. After a quick roll in the hay, Valdez gives her the heave-ho: He's got an upcoming boxing match and future glory at Madison Square Garden on his mind.

Meanwhile, to keep business going, Rodriguez beds a married man who's got the hots for her. Then she meets Mr. Nice, who cools her fires and with whom she dreams of "getting away." That doesn't last long: After poisoning Valdez one night, and torching his room, the married lover comes at her with a knife.

Despite a lot of Afro-Cuban mumbo-jumbo about the spirit world and Rodriguez's rejection of penitence, pic is essentially by-the-numbers melodrama. Giral conjures up a convincingly sleazy portrait of barrio life, pool halls and smoke-filled bars, with a cameo by w.k. Latin performer Daysi Granados for effect. Story's legit origins are well concealed.

Rodriguez is first-rate as the hotsy hooker, and Valdez okay as the muscular macho hunk. Tech credits are pro.

— *Derek Elley*

ZIMNIAYA VISHNIA
(WINTER CHERRIES)
(RUSSIAN)

A Lenfilm-Trinity Bridge Studio production. Directed by Igor Maslennikov. Screenplay, Vladimir Valutsky; camera (color), Vladimir Brylyakhova; editor, Zinaida Shorokhova; music, Vladimir Dashkevich. Reviewed at Montreal Film Festival (Cinema of Today and Tomorrow section), Aug. 26, 1991. Running time: **94 MIN.**
With: Vitaly Solomin, Elena Safonova, Irina Miroschnichenko, Irina Klimova.

Basically a road movie, "Winter Cherries" is a simple take of a businessman and his young girlfriend traveling across country to attend a birthday party at the family home.

Things go literally off the rails when the girl, driving too fast, propels the auto into a lake. They then have to take the train.

This romantic comedy is traditionally handled by director Igor Maslennikov, who takes a few swipes at people in high places whose liquor cabinets are filled with Western booze. Helmer generally is content to let the bickering lovers' characters carry what passes for a plot.

Camerawork is attractive, if overly freewheeling at times.

— *David Stratton*

HELLO HEMINGWAY
(CUBAN)

An Empresa Productora presentation of a ICAIC production. Produced by Ricardo Avila. Directed by Fernando Pérez. Screenplay, Mayda Royero; camera (color), Julio Valdés; editor, Jorge Abello; music, Edesio Alejandro; art direction, Onelio Larralde. Reviewed at Montreal World Film Festival (out of competition), Aug. 23, 1991. Running time: **90 MIN.**
Larita . . . . Laura de la Uz
Victor . . . . Raúl Paz
Josefa . . . . Herminia Sanchez
Tomás . . . . . José Antonio Rodriguez
Also with: Marta de Rio, Micheline Calvert.

"Hello Hemingway" is a thoughtful, lovely little film about a bright young neighbor of Ernest Hemingway's in pre-revolutionary Cuba who finds a metaphor for her own life in "The Old Man and the Sea." Aside from festivals, gentle pic's target market is Spanish-lingo territories.

Given the current anti-communist political wave, a film which hypes pro-socialist students (led by the young girl's b.f.) appears odd. However, main thrust of story, taking place circa 1956, is about her self-discovery while reading Hemingway's classic.

The youth (Laura de la Uz) is shocked that after all the old man's determination and effort to catch fish, he catches a fish bigger than his boat, only to lose it. In her personal life, the ace student has a chance to win a scholarship to study in the U.S., but she loses it because she's an orphan and her poor adopted family doesn't have the proper social status.

Pic wraps on a sad but realistic note with the girl, who never actually meets Hemingway, serving coffee to the woman who refused her scholarship.

Tech credits are good and many pastel shades create rosy visuals. Havana looks like a postcard.

— *Suzan Ayscough*

WILDFEUER
(WILDFIRE)
(GERMAN)

A Filmverlag der Autoren release of a Bavaria Film production. Produced by Reinhard Klooss. Directed by Jo Baier. Screenplay, Baier, Klooss. Camera (Fujicolor), Gernot Roll; editor, Elke Schmid; music, Norbert Schneider; production design, Jochen Schumacher; assistant director, Holger Barthel. Reviewed at Montreal Film Festival (out of competition), Aug. 29, 1991. Running time: **100 MIN.**
Emerenz Meier . . . . . . Anica Dobra
Gottfried . . . . Karl Tessler
Alfons Helmberger . Josef Bierbichler
Father . . . . Branko Samarovski
Mother . . . . Eva Horbiger

This first feature by Jo Baier is loosely based on the early life of poet Emerenz Meier. Centered on Anica Dobra's vibrant performance, "Wildfire" is well-directed but basically familiar material. Outside pic's home turf, an audience will be hard to find.

Emerenz, a pretty farm girl in turn-of-the-century Bavaria who has a writing knack, chafes at life in her village and sets off alone for the city of Passau. She meets a deaf-mute (Karl Tessler) who saves her from a lecherous landowner by felling the would-be rapist with a sickle. The deaf-mute becomes one of Emerenz's lovers.

The other lover is a rich innkeeper (Josef Bierbichler) who gives her a comfortable life and encourages her to write. But she's undecided which man she really loves, and, when the man who saved her dies after accidentally killing a prostitute, she leaves her rich protector and becomes a prostie herself before leaving for America.

Dobra is lively as the passionate, life-loving poet and easily carries the film. Another plus is the lovely camerawork that makes the Bavarian landscapes look achingly beautiful.

— *David Stratton*

TO BE NUMBER ONE
(HONG KONG)

A Johnny Mak presentation of a Golden Harvest Group-Johnny Mak Prods. Ltd. production. Produced by Shiu Yeuk Yuen. Executive producer, Johnny Mak. Directed by Poon Man Kit. Screenplay, Mak, Shiu Yeuk Yuen. Camera (color), Peter Pau; editor, Poon Hung; music, Chan Wing Leung; art direction, Lam Chak Tse; martial arts director, Leung Siu Hung. Reviewed at Toronto Film Festival (Asian Horizons section), Sept. 14, 1991. Running time: **149 MIN.**
With: Lui Leung Wai, Kent Cheng, Cecilia Yip, Amy Yip, Lee Chi Hung, Tsang Kong, Ng Kai Wah.

A must-see for fans of violent Hong Kong pics, this contempo gangster story spills gallons of blood as a mainlander becomes Hong Kong's No. 1 gang leader. Outside its native land, pic's target is homevid.

Hou (Lui Leung Wai) makes a deal with Boss Kun to operate his ring of sharks, hookers and drug dealers. As Hou rises through the ranks (and wins respect through fearless acts of violence), conflict arises between the two, and gory battles ensue, including a scene where one gang sets fire to another and axes them to bits. Overly long pic ends with Hou in prison.

Story is based on a real gangster (who's about to be released from jail) and aptly reflects Hong Kong's thriving war lord battles and police corruption.

Writer and exec producer Johnny Mak ("Long Arm Of The Law") paints a dark and exceptionally violent portrait of a society run amok. Mak makes "The Killer" helmer John Woo's vision look like Disneyland.

— *Suzan Ayscough*

YA NO HAY HOMBRES
(THERE ARE NO MEN LEFT)
(ARGENTINE)

An Argentina Sono Film production. Executive producers, Salvador D'Antonio, Carlo L. Mentasti. Directed by Alberto Fischerman. Screenplay, Fischerman, Elsa Osorio. Camera (color), Ticky García Estévez; editor, Darío Tedesco; music, Ulises Butrón; sound, Miguel Babuini. Reviewed at V Americas Festival, AFI, Washington, D.C., Oct. 23, 1991. Running time: **92 MIN.**
With: Giuliano Gemma, Georgina Barbarossa, Katja Alemann, Ricardo Bauleo, Roberto Carnaghi, Silvana Di Lorenzo.
(In Spanish, Italian, Portuguese)

"There Are No Men Left" treads an uneasy path between various genres: a contemporary woman's film, romantic comedy, farce, melodrama and poetic metaphor. Although pic boasts an interesting concept, uneven and unengaging handling lands it in limbo.

Story revolves around Ana (Georgina Barbarossa), a single mother and industrial engineer. Her son goes off on a trip early in the film, for the sole reason he doesn't intrude upon the story line. Ana socializes with her women friends at a local bar where they voice their dissatisfaction with men. Frustrated Ana creates a fantasy lover, one who takes on full dimensions for her, intruding upon her life.

When an Italian engineer arrives from Milan to study a merger of the two firms, lo and behold, it's the man of Ana's dreams, whom she at first mistakes for her imaginary lover intruding even further on her reality. The rest of the story follows along predictably with few surprises.

Overall film is stiff and talky, and, except for a few inspired moments, fantasy sequences lack believability. Tech credits and acting are okay. — *Paul Lenti*

SUSHI SUSHI
(FRENCH)

A UGC release of a Titane-Christian Bourgois Prods.-Films A2 co-production. Produced by Christian Bourgois & Jean-Luc Larguier. Directed by Laurent Perrin. Screenplay, Perrin, Michka Assayas in collaboration with Jacques Fieschi & Jerome Tonnere. Camera (color), Dominique Le Rigoleur; editor, Alice Lary; music, Jorge Arriagada; set decoration, Jacques Rouxel; costume design, Elisabeth Tavernier; sound, Daniel Olliver, Jean-Pierre Laforce; production manager, Joey Fare. Reviewed at UGC screening room, Paris, June 5, 1991. Running time: **90 MIN.**
Maurice . . . . André Dussollier
Richard . . . . Jean-François Stevenin
Claire . . . . Sandrine Dumas
Kiyoshi . . . . Kentaro Matsuo
Manu . . . . Frederic Deban
Helene . . . . Eva Darlan
Casier . . . . Michel Aumont

"Sushi Sushi," a lightweight comedy about capitalism, follows a formerly leftist art prof as he abandons teaching to launch a home delivery biz selling sushi. Saga is half-baked toward the end but has a certain charm thanks to pleasant cast and sharp observations about business in Paris.

The teacher, his younger g.f. and one of his students, a young Japanese man, join up with a working class buddy to start their business. Project genesis is peppy, funny.

Biz fails to take off, but a corporate baron comes to what seems the rescue, replacing one storefront outlet with dozens of sushi chefs, computerized ordering, a fleet of designer-clad delivery boys on sleek motorcycles, media coverage, etc.

As the revamped biz flourishes, personal loyalties are put to the test. The g.f. takes up with a young, ambitious employee, the corporation fires the working-class man, and the student resigns. The teacher is so ambivalent about his success that when the board offers to buy him out, his decision is far from obvious.

Entire cast is fine. Lensing throws an occasional wink at Japanese filmmaker Yasujiro Ozu. The catchy song "We Are Ninja," by group Franck Chicken, makes the abrupt ending more palatable. — *Lisa Nesselson*

NEHA
(TENDERNESS)
(CZECHOSLOVAKIAN)

A Slovenská Filmová Tvorba-Panorama Film production. Directed by Martin Sulík. Screenplay, Ondrej Salaj, Sulík. Camera (color), Martin Strba; music, Vladimír Godár; art direction, Frantisek Lipták; costume design, Anna Hrossová. Reviewed at London Film Festival (Intl. Frame), Nov. 7, 1991. Running time: **108 MIN.**
With: Mária Pakulnis, György Cserhalmi, Géza Benkö.

There's not much tenderness in this schematic drama of two men and a woman emotionally joined at the hip. First feature by Martin Sulík, 29, is high on looks but thin on script. Still, the Slovak theater/TV helmer can't be faulted for ambition.

A moody, introverted kid (Géza Benkö) from the country falls in with a bickering, childless couple in the city (György Cserhalmi, Mária Pakulnis). After spending the night at their apartment, he gets "adopted" into their game playing; and when the wife kicks

out her husband, they use him as an emotional shuttlecock.

The husband moves in with his pliant, deaf mistress, and the youth gradually falls for the wife. When she's revealed as a onetime Party prostie, the boy goes back home in a huff. Feel-good ending has the couple, now living apart but expecting a baby, dropping by for reconciliation.

Slovak screenwriter Ondrej Salaj's script leaves the cast plenty of time for existential emoting and pregnant pauses, but the sum effect is that viewer never really cares whether the screwed-up trio live or die. Pakulnis makes a striking object of beauty; well-known Hungarian thesp Cserhalmi goes through the motions, and Benkö is straight sullen. Tech credits are fine, with Martin Strba's noir-ish color lensing providing a sleek look.

— *Derek Elley*

TISHINA
(SILENCE)
(BULGARIAN)

A Boyana Studio-Debut Collective-64 Collective production. (Intl. sales: Bulgarian Cinematography, Sofia.) Directed, written by Dimiter Petkov. Camera (color), Hristo Bakalov; editor, Maria Dzhidrova; music, Ani Kulisheva; art direction, Vladimir Lekarski; costume design, A. Zaydner; sound, Mitko Moskov. Reviewed at London Film Festival (Intl. Frame), Nov. 8, 1991. Running time: **90 MIN.**
With: Hristo Gurbov, Zhoreta Nikolova, Petar Popyordanov, Andrei Andreyev, Ani Vulchanova.

Plenty of meaningful pauses mark "Silence," a Pinteresque political allegory from late-blooming Bulgaria. Stark tale has a slow-burning power, but not enough to carve a theatrical career offshore.

Set in spring '62, pic concerns an artist (Hristo Gurbov) whose avant garde style makes the Party goons uneasy. The local paper trashes the exhibition, which rapidly closes. The sculptor stores his artifacts away but they're later taken for scrap and melted down. Pic ends with the sculptor going down with his favorite piece (a winged figure of freedom) as the quarry he lives in is dynamited.

Slim story powerfully evokes Bulgaria's repressive past. Dialogue is spare and elliptical, and relationships between characters not entirely clear. Still, first-time helmer Dimiter Petkov draws strong perfs from his three

principals and seems to know exactly where he's going.

Film benefits markedly from Hristo Bakalov's striking chiaroscuro lensing and an inventive soundtrack. — *Derek Elley*

KUFFS

A Universal Pictures release of a Dino De Laurentiis presentation of an EvansGideon production. Produced by Raynold Gideon. Directed by Bruce A. Evans. Screenplay, Evans, Gideon. Camera (Technicolor), Thomas Del Ruth; editor, Stephen Semel; music, Harold Faltermeyer; production design, Victoria Paul, Armin Ganz; costume design, Mary E. Vogt; sound (Dolby), David Brownlow, Agamemnon Andrianos (S.F.); production manager-line producer, Mel Dellar; assistant director, Dennis Maguire; stunt coordinator-2nd unit director, David Ellis; 2nd unit camera, Paul Edwards; special effects coordinator, Dale Martin; associate producer, Lisa Fitzgerald; casting, Sally Dennison, Julie Selzer. Reviewed at Cineplex Odeon Worldwide 1 cinema, N.Y., Jan. 7, 1992. MPAA Rating: PG-13. Running time: **101 MIN.**
George Kuffs . . . . . Christian Slater
Ted Sukovsky . . . . . . Tony Goldwyn
Maya Carlton . . . . . . Milla Jovovich
Brad Kuffs . . . . . . Bruce Boxleitner
Capt. Morino . . . . Troy Evans
Sam Jones . . . . . . George de la Pena
Kane . . . . Leon Rippy
Also with: Joshua Cadman, Mary Ellen Trainor, Kim Robillard, Scott Williamson, Aki Aleong, Henry G. Sanders, Lu Leonard, Stephen Park.

Christian Slater's energy fails to carry "Kuffs," a mishmash cop comedy very reminiscent of several Eddie Murphy films. Pic from Dino De Laurentiis should be a fast fold at the box office.

Filmmakers Bruce Evans and Raynold Gideon, most famous for penning John Carpenter's "Starman," have failed to find the proper tone for yet another wacky cop picture. Film veers from ultra-violence to slapstick comedy in an arbitrary and irritating fashion. Hokey camera angles and flashy dissolves fail to pump up the action and seem better suited to a mystical film rather than a real world *policier*.

Slater is the fish out of water this time, inheriting his murdered brother's police protection business. Plot hook makes good use of the San Francisco setting, where neighborhoods have relied on these private Patrol Specials since the 1850s.

Gimmick allows ne'er-do-well high school dropout Slater to become an instant cop and prove his mettle under fire. Avenging brother Bruce Boxleitner's death is an utterly conventional quest, but the few laughs along the way are the film's raison d'être.

As Slater's unwilling partner, Tony Goldwyn ("Ghost") demonstrates solid comic talents and has a very funny physical routine after drinking a Mickey Finn Slater slipped in his coffee. Wearing a variety of goofy outfits, Leon Rippy makes a fun killer. Former ballet star George de la Pena (introduced as Herbert Ross's "Nijinsky") is utterly convincing as the slick villain.

Less fortunate is lovely Milla Jovovich, too young for the nothing part of Slater's g.f. Director Evans allows Slater too much ego-tripping in the form of extraneous dancing around, barechested scenes that even the star's fan club might deem excessive. A device, lifted from Michael Caine's "Alfie," of Slater frequently addressing the camera directly in conspiratorial fashion is muffed by unfunny writing of these monologues.

The feel and format of "Kuffs" often resembles Eddie Murphy's hits "Beverly Hills Cop" and "48 HRS.," not surprising given the spate of similar cop pics in recent years. However, musical score by Harold Faltermeyer features as its main theme a shamelessly similar tune to Faltermeyer's hit "Axel F" in a sort of Pavlovian attempt to elicit a similar audience response.

— *Lawrence Cohn*

MAYRIG
(MOTHER)
(FRENCH)

An AMLF release of a Carthargo Films-Quinta Communications-V Film-TF-1 & TF-1 Films-Les Prods. Artistes Associes co-production with the participation of CNC and (Soficas) Sofiarp-Cofimage 3-Investimage. Executive producer, Mark Lombardo. Produced by Tarak Ben Ammar. Directed, written by Henri Verneuil, based on his book. Camera (color), Edmond Richard; editor, Henri Lanoe; music, Jean-Claude Petit; costume design, Catherine Gorne; set design, Pierre Guffroy; sound, Alain Sempe; production manager, Michel Choquet; assistant director, Patrick Malakian. Reviewed at Pathe Marignan Concorde cinema, Paris, Dec. 23, 1991. Running time: **137 MIN.**
Araxi (Mayrig) . . . Claudia Cardinale
Hagop . . . . Omar Sharif
Anna . . . . Isabelle Sadoyan
Gayane . . . . Nathalie Roussel
Azad (age 7) . . . . Cédric Doucet
Azad (age 12) . . . . Tom Ponsin
Azad (age 20) . . . . . Stéphane Servais
Apkar . . . . Jacky Nercessian

Glowing with history and affection, scripter/helmer Henri Verneuil's autobiographical "Mayrig" is an old-fashioned, engagingly paced account of an Armenian immigrant family who settles in Marseille in 1921. Although less spectacular, this two-part saga (to be followed by "588 Rue Paradis") could attract the audience that enjoyed French dou-ble-headers "Jean de Florette"/ "Manon of the Spring" and "My Father's Glory"/"My Mother's Castle." Six-hour TV version should lend itself to quality tube sales.

Based on the 1985 book by the veteran helmer of some 35 features (since 1951), story isn't terribly original, but it's heartfelt and touching. Pic opens with docu-style shots of Armenian villages and builds sympathy by re-enacting the 1921 assassination of the Turkish minister responsible for the 1915 genocide of 1.5 million Armenians.

Six-year-old Verneuil surrogate Azad (whose thoughts are voiced by Richard Berry, who plays the grown Azad in part 2) docks in Marseille with his mayrig ("mother," in Armenian), his father (Omar Sharif) and his two devoted maternal aunts. Formerly well-to-do, their resources boil down to eight gold coins sewn into Mayrig's (Claudia Cardinale) dress.

Once the grown-ups get menial jobs, Azad is sent to the best school in town. Snubbed by classmates, he keeps to himself, excels in his studies and lies to his family, who believe he has immediately fit into Marseille society.

The momentous events of young Azad's life — a near-fatal illness and his first taste of cinema — are conveyed with humor and pathos. Story sidesteps smarminess to radiate a quiet dignity grounded in universal emotions. Thesping is first-rate, and international casting of the tight-knit family is utterly believable. (Still, it's awkward to hear the family speaking among themselves in perfect French straight off the boat.)

In the film where love and kindness pervade, vivid flashbacks to Turkish barbarity are highly effective. A family friend (Jacky Nercessian) is the lone survivor of a forced march during which a sizzling horseshoe was nailed to his foot.

Set designer Pierre Guffroy has lovingly recreated a quaint snippet of prewar Marseille, but certain exteriors still have an underbudgeted, make-do look. Process work on faked family snapshots is glaringly obvious.

Awash with tender observations and long-vanished courtly manners, pic is a loving tribute to the almost impossibly devoted souls that spurred a youngster to make his own way in the world. That way would point to filmmaking. — *Lisa Nesselson*

ALIAS 'LA GRINGA'
(PERUVIAN-SPANISH)

A Perfo Studio (Lima)-TV Española SA (Madrid) co-production, in association with Channel 4 (London). Produced by Andres Malatesta. Directed by Alberto Durant. Screenplay, Durant, Jose Watanabé, Jose Maria Salcedo. Camera (color), Mario Garcia Joya; editor, Gianfranco Annichini; music, Pochi Marambio; production design, Matanabé; sound, Guillermo Palacios; casting, Luis Peirano. Reviewed at Montreal Film Festival (Latin American Cinema section), Sept. 1, 1991. Running time: **100 MIN.**
La Gringa . . . . . . Germano Gonzales
Julia . . . . Elsa Oliveros
Also with: Orlando Sacha, Juan Manuel Ochoa, Ramon Garcia.

Far-fetched as its plot seems, "Alias 'La Gringa' " is handled with brash conviction, and Germano Gonzales gives a tough portrayal of the protagonist. Pic is basically action fare for undemanding Latino auds, but on its own terms it's efficiently and briskly handled.

This solid thriller is apparently based on the adventures of a real character, an outlaw known as "La Gringa" who's adept at escaping from prison. Pic begins with a prison escape and the "hero" returning to Lima and his girlfriend. Police break into their apartment and he's re-arrested. Sent to an island prison, La Gringa finds his life threatened by an old enemy who's egged on by the warden. His life is saved by an intellectual known as the Professor, who's in the cooler for terrorist activities.

La Gringa eventually manages to escape again, but he feels bad about leaving the Professor behind, so instead of fleeing with his girl to Ecuador, he returns to the prison in disguise only to find a riot is taking place.

Pic is Peru's submission for the foreign language film Academy Award. — *David Stratton*

LA BALLATA DI REN-HAM
(THE BALLAD OF REN-HAM)
(ITALIAN)

A Kineo presentation of an Il Volo del Gabbiani Co-op production. Director of production, Rosalba Di Bartolo Tonti. Directed by Maurizio Angeloni. Screenplay, Alberto Bennati, Angeloni. Camera (Telecolor), Giorgio Tonti; editor, Sergio Buzi; music, Carlo Siliotto; art direction-costumes, Itala Scandariato; sound, Gianni Sardo. Reviewed at Rialto Cinema, Rome, Dec. 8, 1991. Running time: **82 MIN.**
Roberto . . . . Andrea Cagliesi
Roberta . . . . Maria Tona
Ren-Ham . . . . Pino Misiti
Paolone . . . . Ferdinando Arena

"The Ballad of Ren-Ham" charts the effects of a "life lessons" seminar on young adults while attempting to weigh the validity of such programs. The pic is one of the lucky few from Italy's beleaguered indie circuit to find limited theatrical release, but it will be more tuneful to tube gazers than paying audiences.

Premise here is basically a throwback to '70s-style self-help principles and its appeal will depend on viewer sympathy (or tolerance) for actors in a liberation-through-improv process.

Signing up for a two-week "creativity-unharnessing" course with a visiting guru (Pino Misiti), students undergo seemingly fruitful changes, but the experience ultimately proves hollow.

Director Maurizio Angeloni's theater background gives him a sure hand in guiding the relatively inexperienced thesps. Students' talking head monologues are well-handled, with Ferdinando Arena's funny Pinocchio spiel a standout.

Characters are generally underwritten, however, and come across as interchangeably one-dimensional. An absurdly arcane naked rites-of-freedom romp only underlines script's dated feel and the limitations of its human nature angle.

Giorgio Tonti's able camerawork resists the cobbled charms of pic's Assisi locations, hugging close to the town's walls and letting the actors dominate. Other tech credits are fine apart from occasional shrillness on the sound mix. — *David Rooney*

NAKED MAKING LUNCH
(BRITISH-DOCU)

A Lucida production, in association with London Weekend Television. Produced, directed by Chris Rodley. Camera (Rank & Film House color, 16m), Jeff Victor; editor, Anne Sopel; music, David Cunningham; sound, John Thomson; associate producer, Claire Best. Reviewed at American Museum of the Moving Image, Astoria, N.Y., Jan. 8, 1992. Running time: **70 MIN.**

Chris Rodley's "Naked Making Lunch" sheds considerable light on one of the most offbeat films to come out of Hollywood in recent years,

David Cronenberg's "Naked Lunch." Via interviews and film clips, Rodley shows how Cronenberg managed to adapt William S. Burroughs' "unfilmable" novel.

Docu opens with Burroughs reading from his novel and shifts to a press conference with the author and Cronenberg. The director notes that if he had filmed the book literally, it would have cost $400-500 million and been banned in every country.

Instead, Cronenberg focused on Burroughs' drugged-out, bisexual life and filmed the process of writing the novel. "To convey the act of writing to someone who hasn't written, you have to be quite outrageous," Cronenberg notes. Indeed, he created typewriters that turn into bugs and speak through repulsive orifices.

"My first response was kind of one of horror," says actress Judy Davis, who plays two characters in the film. After one reading, she says she threw the script across the room. Producer Jeremy Thomas remembers wouldbe investors telling him, "You're completely mad."

"Naked Lunch" may outrage and disgust some audiences, but "Naked Making Lunch" makes sense of Cronenberg's take on the scandalous novel. The filmmaker discusses both his affinity for and differences from Burroughs. Cronenberg acknowledges that he approached the 1959 book (which includes explicit gay sex) from a heterosexual perspective, and adds that he has little experience with drugs.

Cronenberg also explains the use of grotesque Mugwump characters and other creatures as sexual metaphors. And the "talking asshole," per the Canadian director, is really Burroughs himself since it speaks basic, unmentionable truths.

For special effects buffs, the animation of the oversized insects is demonstrated; 13 different puppets were required to bring the talking typewriter bug to life.

Rodley touches on Cronenberg's other films and edits in footage from "Dead Ringers" and other pics. The British filmmaker is clearly a devotee, having profiled Cronenberg in his 1986 docu "Long Live the New Flesh." (The three-week Cronenberg retrospective at AMMI, which includes both documentaries, goes by the same creepy title).

The docu is not likely to appeal to a wide audience, but it should fascinate fans of Burroughs and Cronenberg. More than just a behind-the-scenes promo piece, Rodley's film is an illuminating look at idiosyncratic, remarkably inventive artists.

— William Stevenson

SO NO OTOKO, KYOBO NI TSUKI
(VIOLENT COP)
(JAPANESE)

A Bandai-Shochiku Fuji production. (Intl. sales: Shochiku Fuji.) Produced by Hisao Nabeshima, Takio Yoshida, Shozo Ichiyama. Executive producer, Kazuyoshi Okuyama. Directed by Takeshi Kitano. Screenplay, Hisashi Nozawa; camera (color), Yasushi Sakakibara; editor, Nobutake Kamiya; music, Daisake Kume; art direction, Masuteru Mochizuki; sound, Senji Horiuchi. Reviewed at London Film Festival (3 Continents: Asia section), Nov. 21, 1991. Running time: **103 MIN.**
Azuma . . . . Beat Takeshi
Kiyohiro . . . . Haku Ryu
Akari . . . . Maiko Kawakami
Yoshinari . . . . Shiro Sano
Iwaki . . . . Takeshi Hiraizumi
Iwaki's wife . . . . . . Mikiko Otonashi
Nindo . . . . Ittoku Kichibe

A weird Japanese take on "Dirty Harry," "Violent Cop" has an inevitable momentum like a truck running downhill. Slow tempo and arty look suits it for film festival dates, but pic lacks the slambang pyrotechnics that made Asian crimer "The Killer" a cult theatrical item in Western markets.

Film, which dates from 1989, was the first directorial item by local icon Takeshi Kitano, best known in the West for his role as the sergeant in Nagisa Oshima's "Merry Christmas, Mr. Lawrence." He also toplines as the eponymous cop under his popular moniker "Beat" Takeshi.

First half-hour is low-key: Kitano is hauled over the coals for kicking young punks around, and in his spare time he cares for his sick sister. When a vicesquad pal is implicated in a drug ring and ends up dead, Kitano, now busted from the force, takes on the big boss and his gay psycho assassin singlehandedly.

Kitano directs with much control, spinning a slow web of casual, sadistic violence in which he's a willing participant. Pic's final reels, with the cop's sister hooked on heroin and raped and the final shootouts with the nasties, have a formal power like a modern-day samarai pic.

Tech credits are fine, and Kitano himself is impressively monosyllabic as the shambling, dogged cop. Japanese title roughly means "This Man, He's Wild."

— Derek Elley

WONG FEI-HUNG
(ONCE UPON A TIME IN CHINA)
(HONG KONG)

A Golden Harvest presentation of a Film Workshop production. (Intl. sales: Singel Films, Amsterdam.) Produced by Raymond Chow. Executive producer, Tsui Hark. Directed by Tsui. Screenplay, Tsui, Yuen Kai-chi, Leung Yiuming, Tang Pik-yin; camera (color, 'Scope), David Chung, Bill Wong, Arthur Wong, Lam Kwok-wah, Chan Tung-chuen, Chan Pui-kai; editor, Mak Chi-sin; music, James Wong; production design, Lau Man-hung; art direction, Yee Chung-man; costume design, Yu Ka-on; action directors, Yuen Chongyan, Yuen Shun-yi, Lau Kar-wing; associate producer, David Lo. Reviewed at National Film Theater, London, Nov. 13, 1991. Running time: **133 MIN.**
Wong Fei-hung . . . . Jet Li
Leung Foon . . . . Yuen Biao
Buck Teeth Sol . . . . . Jacky Cheung
Aunt Yee . . . . . . Rosamund Kwan
Porky Lang . . . . Kent Cheng
(Mandarin soundtrack; Chinese & English subtitles)

A chopsocky epic with a modern message, "Once Upon a Time in China" is an overlong but dazzling slice of escapism that could find a limited Western audience with judicious trimming. Per its Anglo title, pic recalls Sergio Leone's oeuvre in several respects.

Chinese title is the name of the hero, a real-life turn-of-the-century kung fu artist who's already figured in some 98 Hong Kong quickies. Present item, set in Canton province, has him battling the tide of Western influence (including Yank soldiers) as well as Chinese, shipping gullible locals to a Stateside "mountain of gold" (San Francisco).

Compared with helmer Tsui Hark's other actioners ("Zu Warriors," "Swordsman"), this one is almost leisurely, with much detail of contemporary artifacts and a script that takes time to chew over issues like blind nationalism and emigration. It's also a gigantic farewell to a dying era.

Setpieces, such as the burning of Wong's clinic, an attempted hit during an opera show and a final fight on ladders inside the Yank stockade, are all tops. Rare for Hong Kong pics, James Wong's low-churning music cleverly plays against the action, letting the busy sets and 'Scope visuals speak for themselves.

Performances, by a host of w.k. locals, are reliable, with former Mainland action star Li Lianjie (now U.S. resident, under the name Jet Li) solid as Wong. Pic took a hotsy $HK28.5 million ($3.7 million) on local release this fall. London fest played the Mandarin, rather than more authentic Cantonese, version.

— Derek Elley

CUENTOS DE BORGES I
(BORGES TALES, PART I)
(SPANISH)

An Iberoamericano Film Intl.-TV-Española (TVE)-Sociedad Estatal Quinto Centenario production. Directed by Gerardo Vera, Héctor Olivera. Music, Alejandro Massó. Reviewed at Puerto Rico Intl. Film Festival, San Juan, Nov. 2, 1991. Running time: **106 MIN.**
LA OTRA HISTORIA ROSENDO JUAREZ (THE OTHER STORY OF ROSENDO JUAREZ)
Produced by Cristina Huete. Directed by Vera. Screenplay, Vera, Fernando Fernán Gómez. Camera (color), José Luis López Linares; editor, Pablo G. del Amo; art direction, Ana Alvargonzález; sound, Jorge Ruiz. Running time: **54 MIN.**
Rosendo Juárez . . . Antonio Banderas
Nicolás Paredes . . . Fernando Guillén
Manuela . . . . Pastora Vega
EL EVANGELIO SEGUN SAN MARCOS (THE GOSPEL ACCORDING TO ST. MARK)
. Executive producer, Andrés Vicente Gómez. Directed, written by Olivera. Camera (color), Féliz Monti; editor, Pablo G. del Amo, Eduardo López; art direction, María Julia Bertotto; sound, Abelardo Kuschnir, Alfonso Pino. Running time: **52 MIN.**
Baltasar Espinosa . . . . . . Hugo Soto
Gutre . . . . Miguel Dedovich
Emilia . . . . Mirna Suárez

Although Argentine writer Jorge Luis Borges wrote film reviews and dabbled in screenplays, most readers feel his dense, cerebral stories defy screen adaptation. This first package of projected works (six due in all) shows some truth in this, yet weight of Borges' name and the w.k. directors should draw international attention.

Most successful of the two tales is "The Gospel According to St. Mark," by Argentine helmer Héctor Olivera. Thesp Hugo Soto (the Martian in "Man Facing Southeast") plays a young man recently returned from studies abroad to his estate on the pampas. With newly acquired ideas of equality, he invites a family of farm laborers to his table, where he nightly reads them the Bible. Little does he know they take the scriptures literally, and in the end he is crucified.

Pic's tone depicts Borges' notions of internal and external action, and its complex microcosm. Location captures the writer's vision of Argentina.

On the other hand, Spanish director Gerardo Vega opts to relocate "The Other Story of Rosendo Juárez" in rural Spain of the 1930s. This change of location intrudes upon the narrative, while pic's impressionistic handling feels incomplete.

Pic stars Antonio Banderas in the title role of an idle young man who turns outlaw. After a fight that leaves his rival dead, the Civil Guard gives Rosendo a choice: go to prison or work as a hired gun for Don Nicolás Paredes. Rosendo chooses the latter.

Despite sumptuous and exciting photography, the fragmented tale is narrated in a series of unconnected scenes supposedly told in flashback or reverie.

— *Paul Lenti*

JUICE

A Paramount Pictures release of a Paramount presentation in association with Island World of a Moritz/Heyman production. Produced by David Heyman, Neal H. Moritz, Peter Frankfurt. Co-producer, Preston Holmes. Directed by Ernest R. Dickerson. Screenplay, Gerard Brown, Dickerson; story by Dickerson. Camera (TVC-Precision color), Larry Banks; editor, Sam Pollard, Brunilda Torres; music, Hank Shocklee & the Bomb Squad; music supervisor, Kathy Nelson; production design, Lester Cohen; set decoration, Alyssa Winter; costume design, Donna Berwick; sound (Dolby), Franklin D. Stettner; production manager, Brent Owens; associate producers, James Bigwood, Gerard Brown; assistant director, H.H. Cooper; casting, Jaki Brown. Reviewed at Paramount studio theater, Hollywood, Jan. 14, 1992. MPAA Rating: R. Running time: **96 MIN.**

Q . . . . Omar Epps
Bishop . . . . Tupac Shakur
Steel . . . . Jermaine Hopkins
Raheem . . . . Khalil Kain
Yolanda . . . . Cindy Herron
Radames . . . . . . Vincent Laresca
Trip . . . . Samuel L. Jackson

Apprehension over violence accompanying release of "Boyz N the Hood" and "New Jack City" last year will prompt many to overlook "Juice," Ernest Dickerson's technically superior, narratively flawed directorial debut. Controversy over its ad campaign will doubtless inhibit appeal to mainstream filmgoers but could spur curiosity within niche markets. Pic should deliver enough of its urban target audience for a modest box office bang.

Spike Lee cinematographer Dickerson starts off the pic promisingly, introducing a well-played quartet of ghetto youths and exploring their lives and frustrations in what could almost be viewed as an inner-city "Breaking Away."

After a sudden, tragic robbery attempt, the film takes a peculiar turn into the thriller realm, as one of the teens (Tupac Shakur) — high on the "juice" of having killed the grocery store clerk — begins menacing his one-time friends.

Dickerson obviously is trying to make a statement against guns, violence and crime as means of escape, while turning an eye on the hopelessness life in the ghetto creates.

Those points, however, likely will be lost on many of the people the film most wishes to reach. And those averse to such a message will find enough rap music, action, violence and vengeance to mistake "Juice" for more ex-ploitative fare and to come away with a less socially responsible message. Paramount has perhaps been unfairly criticized for its marketing campaign, a legitimate representation of the film's content and its audience. Any film that plays to such a volatile element within society carries with it certain risks, but who's supposed to go see this, the "Driving Miss Daisy" crowd?

Dickerson and co-writer Gerard Brown exhibit a sharp ear for dialogue and have some real finds in their largely unknown cast, particularly Omar Epps as Q, the most introspective and reasoned of the four friends. Shakur, of rap group Digital Underground, is also impressive, though the character suffers because the script lays little groundwork for his rapid descent into near-insanity.

There are several lurches in story logic, from the sudden agreement of the group's leader (Khalil Kain, giving a solid performance) to engage in the robbery, to Q's puzzling relationship with a somewhat older nurse (Cindy Herron).

Dickerson and his cinematographer, Larry Banks, provide a variety of looks in the film, deftly weaving through the gritty New York locales. Tech credits are topnotch, particularly in light of the modest budget.

"Juice" demonstrates the black community's untapped talent waiting for opportunities on both sides of the camera, but it also reflects the confined realm within which the filmmakers and performers are forced to operate, with elements outside the theater turning each effort into a *cause célèbre.*

From that perspective, "Juice" is an auspicious first feature but unworthy of the tumult with which it has unfortunately, if not entirely undeservingly, been shackled. — *Brian Lowry*

BLOODFIST III: FORCED TO FIGHT

A Concorde Pictures release. Produced by Roger Corman. Directed by Oley Sassone. Screenplay, Allison Burnett, Charles Mattera. Camera (Foto-Kem color), Rick Bota; editor, Eric L. Beason; music, Nigel Holton; production design, James Shumaker; sound (Ultra-Stereo), Bill Robbins; assistant director, Juan Mas; production manager, Jonathan Winfrey; stunt coordinator, Patrick Statham; martial arts choreography, Don (The Dragon) Wilson, Paul Maslak, Eric Lee; co-producer, Mike Elliott; associate producers, Catherine Cyran, Nancy Gechtman; casting, Steven Rabiner. Reviewed on New Horizons videcassette, N.Y. MPAA Rating: R. Running time: **88 MIN.**
Jimmy Boland
. . . . Don (The Dragon) Wilson
Samuel Stark . . . Richard Roundtree
Blue . . . . Gregory McKinney
Wheelhead . . . . Rick Dean
Goddard . . . . Richard Paul
Taylor . . . . Charles Boswell
Diddler . . . . John Cardone
Pisani . . . . Brad Blaisdell
Also with: Stan Longinidus, Tony DiBenedetto, Peter (Sugarfoot) Cunningham, Laura Stockman.

This prison story is the best screen vehicle to date for kickboxing champ Don (The Dragon) Wilson. Currently in regional theatrical release, "Bloodfist III" should prove a winner for fledgling homevid label New Horizons.

Action genre stars Sylvester Stallone, Tom Selleck and Jean-Claude Van Damme were in stir a couple years back, and the Big House also works well for Wilson. He's a wrongly convicted guy in a state pen who continually has to prove himself against bigger and feistier convicts.

Scripters Allison Burnett and Charles Mattera wisely resist the temptation to write in a round-robin competition or some other corny excuse to put Wilson and fellow champs Stan Longinidus and Peter Cunningham in the ring. Instead, all the pic's well-executed fights are part of the dramatic action.

Under director Oley Sassone (a.k.a. Francis Sassone), who previously co-scripted the radically dissimilar Disney family film "Wild Hearts Can't Be Broken," film is tightly constructed. Wilson befriends John Cardone, a nerdy prisoner shunned by the other inmates and is in turn taken under the wing of prison sage Richard Roundtree.

Racism is the key theme, as white and black cons are continually fighting, with "half-breed" (half-Japanese) Wilson caught in the middle. Per genre tradition, when the baddies attack Wilson's best friends, star whips into action and cleans up the place. In a character role, Roundtree is extremely sympathetic while laconic Wilson fits the bill as a no-nonsense hero. Cast is nearly all-male, except for a small role assigned Laura Stockman as a TV news reporter covering the prison beat.

— *Lawrence Cohn*

WORLD APARTMENT HORROR
(JAPANESE)

An Embodiment Films production (for Sony). Produced by Hiro Osaki, Yasuhisa Kazama. Directed by Katsuhiro Otomo. Screenplay, Otomo, Keiko Nobumoto. Camera (color), Noboru Shinoda. Reviewed at Vancouver Film Festival, Oct. 8, 1991. Running time: **97 MIN.**
With: Hiroki Tanaka, Yuji Nakamura, Weng Huarong, Kimiko Nakagawa.

Crossing gangster and horror genres, "World Apartment Horror" delivers plenty of laughs as it meanders between social comment, parody and schlock. Technical credits are good. Pic has potential as a homevid cult hit.

Katsuhiro Otomo's first live-action feature picks up the themes of his animated cult hit, "Akira." Behind the frenetic action and outrageous situations lies a subtle message of racial tolerance.

Hiroki Tanaka plays a cocky, aspiring gangster sent by his yakuza boss to evict an apartment full of Asian immigrants. His macho guise gradually disintegrates as first the tenants, and then a supernatural monster, rebuff his arrogant, ineffectual demands. Madness stalks the apartment and hallucinations abound as characters vie for control.

Otomo is playful in his critique of Japan's racial superiority complex. "Japanese are not Asian," Tanaka declares. "We are white!"
— *Suzan Ayscough*

BORN TO SKI
(DOCU)

A Warren Miller Entertainment release of a Nissan Pathfinder presentation. Produced by Kurt Miller, Peter Speek. Directed by Don Brolin. Screenplay-narration, Warren Miller. Camera (color), Bill Heath, Gary Nate, Brian Sisselman; editor, Katie Hedrick, Kim Schneider; music, Ronnie Montrose; associate producers, Max Bervy Jr., Bob Tunnell, Willi Vogl. Reviewed at Cinema Village 12th Street, Jan. 4, 1992. Running time: **101 MIN.**

Warren Miller's 42nd ski film packs in a slew of exciting action footage, which is a credit to his camera crew. "Born to Ski's" most interesting scenes show how the cameramen captured skiers jumping off cliffs, falling out of helicopters on snow-

boards and somersaulting 50 feet in the air.

While thrills (skiers dodging rocks on a nearly 90-degree slope) are plentiful, the "extreme" skiing (daredevils hurtling down a dirt cliff) eventually wears thin.

Pic could use more traditional skiing — a too brief segment shows Italo ski star Alberto Tomba's slalom technique —and fewer digressions to bungee jumping, sailboarding, in-line skating and parasailing.

Miller's trademark narration ranges from the witty to the banal. It also becomes repetitive, as pic's title pops up virtually every other sentence.

The most amusing sequence involves a situation most amateur skiers can relate to: falling after dismounting a chairlift. Non-skiers are likely to be nonplused by the whole film, which runs on too long at 101 minutes.
— *William Stevenson*

OOSTENDE
(FRENCH)

An AAA release of a Cine Feel-SGGC co-production with the participation of Canal Plus. Produced by Patricia & Pierre Novat. Directed by Eric Woreth. Screenplay, Alain Aidjes. Camera (color), Thierry Arbogast; editor, Pat Marcel, Anita Wandzel, Catherine Spanu, Virginie Barbay; costumes, Sophie Puig, Marie-Laure Lasson; set design, Philippe Maux; sound, Gérard Dacquay, Yvan Dacquay. Reviewed at Jacques Prévert cinema, Savigny-Le-Temple, Dec. 2, 1991. Running time: **80 MIN.**
Lyota . . . . Isabella Ferrari
Jim . . . . Jean-Claude Adelin
Jeannot . . . . Marc Andreoni

High-caliber lensing and sharp editing carry this atmospheric tale of two French buddies and the unusual foreign woman they meet in Oostende, Belgium. First feature from young helmer Eric Woreth could be a viable fest item.

The picture boasts the freewheeling sensibility of a road movie without covering much ground. Jean-Claude Adelin, as a sullen drifter, has the unfortunate burden of too closely resembling Mickey Rourke. Marc Andreoni is wildly energetic as the cheerful sidekick.

The duo pick up enigmatic Isabella Ferrari and share a few days of alternately spirited and morose adventures while Thierry Arbogast's camera makes the most of chilly seaside expanses and local architecture. Well-tempered design underscores the ac-

tion as tortured Adelin tries to lose himself in wild driving, excessive drinking and brutal sex.

The two pals are not above illegal dealings and gruff behavior, but no swear words are uttered. Andreoni's pithy lines are refreshing, coming from a character one could expect to often hear *merde*.

Pic was viciously dismissed by French critics and couldn't overcome the disadvantage of being released the same week Yves Montand's death dominated cultural news.

Natalia Negoda ("Little Vera") originally signed on for femme lead, but she was replaced by capable Italian thesp Ferrari. Pic plays in Italy in January.
— *Lisa Nesselson*

BLANC D'EBENE
(THE EBONY WHITE MAN)
(FRENCH-GUINEAN)

An Epithete-Ramses (Paris)-Onacig (Guinea) co-production. (Intl. sales: Métropolis Film.) Produced by Gilles Legrand. Directed by Cheik Doukouré. Screenplay, Doukouré, Guy Zilberstein. Camera (Eastmancolor), Patrick Blossier; editor, Luc Barnier; music, Marc Beacco; production design, Yan Arlaud; sound, Jeab-Marc Milan; production manager, Rodolphe Pelicier; assistant director, David Carayon; casting, Nian Diakite. Reviewed at Montreal Film Festival (competition), Aug. 29, 1991. Running time: **88 MIN.**
Cyprien . . . Bernard-Paul Donnadieu
Lanseye Kanté . . . . Maka Kotto
Marie-France . . . . . Marianne Basler
Also with: Paul Le Person, Tom Novembre, Mahmoud Zemmouri, Didier Flamand, Mariam Kaba, Sam Amidou.

Setting for this steamy tale of racism, madness and violence is a small village in French West Africa in 1943. Despite screenplay flaws, "The Ebony White Man" is strong enough, and certainly beautiful enough, to find outlets on European art house circuits.

A French warrant officer (Bernard-Paul Donnadieu) operates in a small village where he imposes taxes and recruits able-bodied men for the French army. He genuinely loves Africa and feels happy with his post, but he doesn't understand the people, nor they him.

Enter a villager (Maka Kotto) who's been away studying. The officer sees the new schoolteacher as a radical troublemaker. Conflict ends in violence, with the Frenchman killing an Arab storekeeper and framing the teacher.

Sketchy screenplay by first-time African director Cheik Dou-

kouré and Guy Zilberstein fails to establish clear reasons for the Frenchman's climactic madness. Nor is the character of his bored wife (Marianne Basler) more than a cypher; actress virtually has nothing to do.

Still, Doukouré shows talent as a director, presenting a vivid picture of the village and its people. He effectively stages the concluding action sequences, and he's helped by Patrick Blossier's stunning camerawork and his crew, who make the film visually sumptuous. Donnadieu gives a subtle portrayal of a dedicated but none-too-bright career officer steeped in French Army tradition, and Kotto is solid as his nemesis.

Though basically a familiar tale of colonialism and repression, pic is accessible festival fare exemplifying compelling African cinema. — *David Stratton.*

TALK 16
(CANADIAN-DOCU)

A Films Transit presentation of a Back Alley Film Prods. production. Produced, directed by Janis Lundman & Adrienne Mitchell. Camera (color), Deborah Parks; editor, Sally Paterson; music, Aaron Davis; sound, Peter Sawade. Reviewed at Toronto Film Festival (Perspective Canada section), Sept. 9, 1991. Running time: **110 MIN.**

Five radically different 16-year-old Canadian girls are questioned about premarital sex, school, parents, feminism, drugs, alcohol and the future. Emerging portrait is exceptionally candid and often hilarious. Docu might shock parents but could hit with teens, and it's a natural for homevid and TV.

First half of "Talk 16" is tightly edited to contrast the girls' differences. Punky Astra says, "I'm 15 years old, and I'm living the life of a 40-year-old junkie."

Anorexic overachiever and ace student Helen has strict Korean parents who impose a fine for not doing the dishes. Lina, a Russian immigrant, is obsessed with boys.

Rhonda, who opposes drug use, wants to be Canada's first "famous black actress." Wealthy Erin spends spring break in the Dominican Republic and can't believe "their houses are smaller than my summer cottage."

Patchy editing in pic's last 30 minutes slackens the pace, but the utter confidence the girls put in first-time feature helmers Janis Lundman and Adrienne Mitch-

ell makes this a remarkable docu.
— *Suzan Ayscough*

TICKETS FOR THE ZOO
(BRITISH-16m)

A Cormorant Films production for Channel Four. Produced by Christeen Winford. Directed by Brian Crumlish. Screenplay, Winford. Camera (color, 16m), Martin Singleton; editor, Fiona Macdonald; music, Wendy Weatherby; production design, Annette Gillies; costume design, Lynn Aitken; sound, Colin Nicolson. Reviewed at Edinburgh Intl. Film Festival (New British Cinema), Aug. 24, 1991. Running time: **93 MIN.**
Carol Forbes . . . . Alice Bree
Pogo . . . . Mickey MacPherson
George . . . . Tom Smith

Cloth-eared authorities get a bashing in "Tickets for the Zoo," angry, downbeat drama about homeless juves in economically depressed Edinburgh. Scottish cast's convincing perfs sock over pic's social message, but workaday direction limits playoff to the tube.

Central duo is a pert lass (Alice Bree) and her brother (Tom Smith), booted out of an orphanage when they turn 18. After finding a room, the sister works part-time as a secretary for their smoothie landlord (who's running a prostie agency on the side). After a row with him, the siblings are back on the streets.

Re-enter a local gangleader (Mickey MacPherson) and sometime friend of Bree who invites them into a communal squat. With jobs hard to find, tensions mount, and she runs off with a newfound b.f. After being dumped and now pregnant, she moves into a new place with her brother, and the gangleader becomes more concerned for her welfare.

Producer Christeen Winford's *vérité* script focuses more on personalities than social ills, and some shafts of dry humor lighten the way. As the dark-eyed, flinty lass, Bree shows the makings of a star player, and her scenes with MacPherson gain emotional clout as pic progresses. Other contributions are solid.

Wendy Weatherby's mournful sax score is helpful but repetitive. Lensing on Edinburgh locations in okay; sound is sometimes over-reverberant in interiors. Thick Scots accents make some of the dialogue tough to follow even for Brits south of the border, let alone North Americans. — *Derek Elley*

THE ROAD TO MECCA

A Distant Horizon & Videovision Enterprises presentation of a Local & Overseas Leisure Corp. Film. Produced by Roy Sargeant, Frederik Botha. Executive producer, Anant Singh. Directed by Athol Fugard, Peter Goldsmid. Screenplay, Goldsmid, based on Fugard's stage play. Camera (color), Andre Pienaar; editor, Ronelle Loots; music, Nik Pickard, Ferdi Brendgen; set decoration, Jeanne Henn; sound, Rudiger Payrhuber; assistant director, Martin Palmer. Reviewed at Palm Springs (Calif.) Intl. Film Festival, Jan. 12, 1991. Running time: **106 MIN.**
With: Kathy Bates, Yvonne Bryceland, Athol Fugard.

Athol Fugard's magnificent and moving stage play about spiritual courage and individuality gains little from this transfer to film except possibly a much wider audience, more likely to seek it out on video than on the wide screen.

Co-directed by the playwright and screenplay's writer Peter Goldsmid, "The Road to Mecca" stars Kathy Bates, who has played the role of Elsa on Broadway, and the late Yvonne Bryceland, who created the role of the aging Miss Helen on Broadway and also played her on the London stage. "Mecca" gets a rather straightforward rendering here, without the expanded parameters of mood, lighting and theme that a true film artist might have added.

Nonetheless, the cast, including Fugard himself as Rev. Marius, is ideal, and the performances are first-rate.

Bryceland plays the 65-year-old artist and widow who has created a whimsical sculpture garden of owls, peacocks, camels and pyramids, all pointing east to Mecca, a notion that bothers the devout Christians in her remote South African village.

Bates, playing the strongwilled Cape Town schoolteacher, visits her friend after receiving a letter containing a cry of

Original play

Yale Repertory Theater presentation of a drama in two acts by Athol Fugard. Staged by the author; setting, Elizabeth Doyle; costumes, Derek McLane; lighting, William B. Warfel. Opened May 4, '84, at the Yale Repertory Theater, New Haven, Conn.; $11 top weeknights, $17 weekend nights.

Helen . . . . Carmen Mathews
Elsa . . . . Marianne Owen
Marius . . . . Tom Aldredge

severe distress. But Helen puts on a cheerful front and is no longer willing to discuss what happened. With only one night left before she must leave, Elsa resorts to bullying the malleable Helen until she gets at the truth.

Play's courage theme is put across keenly and movingly. Fugard's skill as a dramatist is such that all points of view are so valiantly defended that one is at pains to sort out the truth.

There is less imagination in the filming, however. Footage of Elsa's trip to New Bethesda gives some sense of the vast loneliness of the South African plain, but most shots in the village seem superfluous. Camerawork is adequate but less than artful, even on pic's $4 million budget.

Bates, presenting herself as exceedingly plain with blunt-cut hair and baggy clothes, gives a fascinating, deeply moving perf in which she's as unsparing of herself as she is of Helen. Bryceland, with her large, sensitive

London play

National Theater of Britain presentation of a play in two acts by Athol Fugard. Staged by the author. Set, Douglas Heap; lighting, Rory Dempster. Opened Feb. 27, '85, at the Lyttleton Theater, London; $10.15 top.
Miss Helen . . . . . Yvonne Bryceland
Elsa Barlow . . . . Charlotte Cornwell
Marius Byleveld . . . . . . Bob Peck

eyes expressing terror as easily as childlike pleasure, often seems the younger of the two.

Filmed on location in New Bethesda near the birthplace of the celebrated South African playwright, production got the go-ahead from culture-boycott supervisors based on Fugard's exemplary anti-apartheid stance (in works like "Master Harold. . .and the Boys") and South African exec producer Anant Singh's credentials as producer of anti-apartheid pics ("Place of Weeping").
— *Amy Dawes*

COLD HEAVEN

A Hemdale Film Corp. production. Produced by Allan Scott, Jonathan D. Krane. Executive producer, Jack Schwartzman. Directed by Nicolas Roeg. Screenplay, Scott, based on Brian Moore's novel. Camera (Technicolor), Francis Kenny; editor, Tony Lawson;

production design, Steve Legler; art direction, Nina Ruscio; set decoration, Cliff Cunningham; costume design, Del Adey-Jones; sound, Jacob Goldstein; assistant director, Donald P.H. Eaton; casting, Joe D'Agosta. Reviewed at Palm Springs (Calif.) Intl. Film Festival, Jan. 10, 1992. Running time: **105 MIN.**
Marie . . . . Theresa Russell
Alex . . . . Mark Harmon
Daniel . . . . James Russo
Nun . . . . Talia Shire
Priest . . . . Will Patton

Infidelity has seldom offered as broad a canvas for torment and religious guilt as in Nicolas Roeg's "Cold Heaven," a tortured study of love on the rocks that comes off like a jumbled bad dream. Theatrical prospects for this Hemdale property, world-premiered at the Palm Springs Intl. Film Festival, are fleeting.

Theresa Russell stars as the restless wife of an unsuspecting surgeon (Mark Harmon). She gets involved with another doctor (James Russo) and plans to break things off with her husband during a Mexican business trip. Before she can do the deed, however, he's killed in a horrifying but oddly convenient boating accident. Or is he?

His body turns up missing from the hospital. Back home, the distraught wife gets a mysterious note requesting her presence in the cliffside hamlet of Carmel, at the same hotel where her infidelity began.

There she's forced not only to confront the consequences of her cheating but also to revisit the scene of a bizarre and troubling religious vision in which the Virgin Mary appeared to her in her first days of infidelity and beseeched her to "bring the priests, and rebuild the sanctuary."

Very much against her will, the agnostic Russell finds herself in a priest's office, angrily spilling out the tale, while back at the hotel her husband is hovering between life and death.

Intention of Brian Moore's novel on which "Cold Heaven" is based on was apparently to make the surgeon's pseudodeath a metaphor for the emotional effect of his wife's betrayal. Filmmaker Roeg found in the material another outlet for his obsession with life in a different plane of existence ("Don't Look Now," "Insignificance").

But the connection is all but buried in the film, a muddled and inadvertently ridiculous effort likely to leave viewers frustrated, lost and demanding a literal rather than metaphorical explanation for the husband's shadowy condition.

Pic begins on sure footing, with the boating accident handled in a skillful and visceral fashion that gets under the skin and sets an eerie tone, but many Stateside segs veer wide of the mark.

Russell, under husband Roeg's direction, does terrific work in her scene with the priest, but both she and Harmon have a tough and thankless task in playing out this tormenting psychodrama.

Much of the tale is told via quick-cut editing of a heavy patchwork of images, but technique fails to make the pic's psychological dimensions palatable.

— *Amy Dawes*

THE EVENTS LEADING UP TO MY DEATH
(CANADIAN)

A Flat Rock Films production. Produced, written, directed by Bill Robertson. Co-producer, Moira Holmes. Camera (color), Derek Underschultz; editor, David Ostry, Robertson; music, Mary Margaret O'Hara; additional scoring, Robertson; sound, Peter Clements. Reviewed at Palm Springs (Calif.) Intl. Film Festival, Jan. 10, 1991. Running time: **89 MIN.**
With: John Allore, Peter MacNeill, Rosemary Radcliffe, Linda Kash, Karen Hines, Maria Del Mar, Mary Margaret O'Hara.

Canadian filmmaker Bill Robertson emerges as a beguiling new talent in this amusingly twisted portrait of suburban family angst. Making its American premiere in Palm Springs, pic is likely too rough and rambling to interest U.S. distribs but displays plenty of wit and style.

Angus (John Allore) is the 21-year-old casualty of a dysfunctional family that traces all its maladies to Dad's inability to express his feelings — something he's trying to remedy by taking lessons from an attractive dance instructor (Mary Margaret O'Hara).

When Angus returns home for his birthday, Dad (Peter MacNeill) offers the rigid youth a present of a midnight lesson with the lady. Resulting silly self-expression sesh becomes a catalyst for the family to deal with emotional blocks, including long-buried suspicions involving a fraudulent watermelon and the death of their dog.

Robertson's script is talky and indulgent but clever, offering such characters as the sexually repressed sister (Linda Kash), an artist who bakes trayfuls of clay babies, plus a Mom (Rosemary Radcliffe) who's having a poignant affair with the doting milkman.

Pic's pithy dialogue yields sardonic pearls of wisdom, appealing cast does some fine comedic work and the quirky music, some of it sung by Robertson, gives the project a fresh, original stamp.

Shot in 21 days on a minimal budget from a script Robertson developed while he was at university, promising pic won a best screenplay award at the 1991 Vancouver Film Festival.

— *Amy Dawes*

I WAS ON MARS
(GERMAN)

A Luna Film production in association with Fama Film, Balthazar Pictures & Good Machine. Executive producers, Gudrun Ruzickova-Steiner, Rolf Schmid, Janet Jacobson. Directed by Dani Levy. Screenplay, Levy, Maria Schrader. Camera (color), Carl-F. Koschnick; editor, Susann Lahaye; music, Niki Reiser; production design, Dan Oullette; art direction, Monica Bretherton; costume design, Arndt Wiegering; sound, Chris Logan; assistant director, Tomi Streiff. Reviewed at Palm Springs (Calif.) Intl. Film Festival, Jan. 12, 1992. Running time: **86 MIN.**
Silva . . . . Maria Schrader
Alio . . . . Dani Levy
Nic . . . . Mario Giacalone
La Mama . . . . Antonia Rey
Waitress . . . . Penny Arcade

A morose young Polish woman comes to New York, has a lousy time, gets humiliated, revels in it, and then leaves in this minimalist tragicomedy by German filmmaker Dani Levy. Pic emulates "Stranger Than Paradise" but lacks the deadpan timing and snappy visuals.

Levy's monotonous preference for the drabbest and dingiest corners of NYC (to the point that the city is unrecognizable) and its most vile and pathetic characters, produces a comedy that will appeal to only a select few Statesiders.

Joke, apparently, is in the contrast between the Western luxury the young woman presumably imagined and the decaying sinkhole she actually encounters, but since Levy shows not a single glimpse of the city's storied glamour, the irony is lost.

Maria Schrader plays a prim and furtive creature who arrives in New York without a word of English and quickly loses her money to a con artist. Levy plays the creep, a kind of Robert De Niro-inspired greaseball with ski jump sideburns and a bad suit. The unhappy visitor trails him doggedly to get her money back, and soon is involved in a dispiriting sex triangle with him and his blobbish cousin (Mario Giacalone).

Pic gets off to a promising start with an immigrant's-eye view of a grungy New York, with its manically aggressive cabbies and assaulting urban music, and the comedy is goosed along by a whimsical accordion and xylophone score, but things soon slow to a crawl.

This kind of thing might be perceived as wacky fun by an Eastern Bloc survivor, but over here it's a pretty depressing trip.

— *Amy Dawes*

WHEN THE PARTY'S OVER

A WTPO production. Produced by James Holt, Ann Wycoff. Directed by Matthew Irmas. Screenplay, Wycoff, from a story by Irmas, Wycoff. Camera (color), Alicia Weber; editor, Dean Goodhill, Jerry Bixmai; music, Joe Romano; art direction, John Gary Steele; sound, Oliver Moss. Reviewed at Palm Springs (Calif.) Intl. Film Festival, Jan. 11, 1992. Running time: **115 MIN.**
Frankie . . . . Elizabeth Berridge
M.J. . . . . Rae Dawn Chong
Amanda . . . . Sandra Bullock
Alexander . . . . Fisher Stevens
Taylor . . . . Brian McNamara
Banks . . . . Kris Kamm

Debuting director Matthew Irmas and writer Ann Wykoff hold a mirror up to life without taking much of a position on it in this unfocused but occasionally adept portrait of young strivers in present-day L.A. Kind of a junior cousin to "Grand Canyon," this indie feature might snag distribution interest, but it falls somewhat short of looking like a theatrical contender.

Story centers on three femme friends: M.J. (Rae Dawn Chong), a fast-track financial broker with the morals of a cat in both sex and business; Frankie (Elizabeth Berridge), a sweet and sincere social worker who's directing a mural project in South-Central L.A.; and Amanda (Sandra Bullock), a voluptuous painter and free spirit who inspires the ardor of a fast-talking performance artist (Fisher Stevens).

Also involved are Frankie's b.f. Taylor (Brian McNamara), who's struggling toward maturity while nonetheless continuing an affair with her best friend, M.J., and a gay housemate and struggling actor (Kris Kamm).

Pic follows characters through their romantic and professional turbulence, culminating in a New Year's party at which conflicts come to a head, and the resulting blowout spells the end of life together as they knew it. On the plus side, writer Wykoff pulls off some engaging scenes, such as those involving Stevens' wackily romantic character. The actors all have their moments under Irmas' direction, and pics of this nature always gain a little from the impact of universal experience.

On the other hand, the writer doesn't seem to know how she wants the audience to feel about the pivotal Chong character, whose close friendship with the very different Berridge seems contrived indeed. Pic unfolds in a meandering pattern, without much in the way of metaphor to enliven its familiar turf.

Production values are adequate, reflecting pic's limited financing, with some rough edges still on view. — *Amy Dawes*

SUNDANCE FEST

A BRIEF HISTORY OF TIME
(BRITISH/U.S.-DOCU)

An Anglia TV-Gordon Freedman presentation produced in association with NBC-Tokyo Broadcasting System-Channel Four, U.K. Produced by David Hickman. Executive producer, Freedman. Executive producer (Anglia), Colin Ewing. Directed by Errol Morris. Based on the book by Stephen Hawking. Camera (Duart color, U.S.; Technicolor, U.K.), John Bailey, Stefan Czapsky; editor, Brad Fuller; music, Philip Glass; production design-matte drawings, Ted Bafaloukos; art direction, David Lee; motion control-visual effects photography, Balsmeyer & Everett; computer animation, Rhythm & Hues; sound design (Dolby), Randy Thom. Reviewed at Raleigh Studios, L.A., Jan. 7, 1992. (Competing in Sundance Film Festival). Running time: **84 MIN.**
With: Stephen Hawking, Isobel Hawking, Janet Humphrey, Mary Hawking, Basil King, Derek Powney, Norman Dix, Robert Berman, Gordon Berry, Roger Penrose, Dennis Sciama, John Wheeler.

Not, on the face of it, the most adaptable book for the screen, Stephen Hawking's "A Brief History of Time" has been turned into an absorbing, bracingly intelligent film by the iconoclastic documentary maker Errol Morris. **Destined for domestic showing by co-producer NBC, tight, exceptionally well-made pic is currently shopping for a theatrical distributor as it has its world preem at the Sundance Film Festival.**

Although not a mass audience item for theaters, venturesome docu will get a strong boost in all media thanks to the high profile of book and author, and it looks like an excellent bet as a major TV spec and video release.

The unlikely superstar of theoretical physics spent more than 100 weeks on the bestseller lists with his popularization of his findings on the birth and fate of the universe, making discussions of his specialties (black holes and the Big Bang theory of creation) at least somewhat comprehensible to the lay public.

Hawking has accomplished all this while confined to a wheelchair with ALS, which has caused his body to wither away. With the additional hurdle of being able to speak only through a special computer synthesizer, his condition serves as a relevant metaphor for humankind's humble place in the cosmos.

Faced with numerous imponderables regarding the material and the proper artistic approach to it, Morris paralleled the fascinating story of Hawking's life with an investigation of his work and theories. Comments of family, former classmates and scientific colleagues are supplemented by vivid and often unusual audiovisual aides. Along the way, the science becomes a little dense and not entirely understandable, but the same held true for the book, and it really doesn't impinge upon engagement with the film.

Born during the London blitz, Hawking grew up as an obviously brilliant student whose main fault was extreme laziness. But the onset of his disease, at 21, changed everything. His pleasingly blunt mother speculates that Hawking might never have accomplished so much had he not gotten sick, which she feels concentrated his energies.

The scientist is shown throughout sitting in his Cambridge office (which is dominated by a very sexy photo of Marilyn Monroe), working at his customized computer and narrating via passages from his book as well as more personal commentary.

Content is all very elusive to a commoner but unavoidably fascinating. Stressing, by sheer accumulation, the rarified world inhabited by the scientists who work in this conceptual field, Morris effectively illustrates that these people's minds really are terribly different from those of most people. These guys are way, way out there, and Hawking and Morris have done an admirable job in providing a glimpse of this.

This may be Morris' most traditional docu, more so than "Gates of Heaven" or "The Thin Blue Line," but it is still highly distinctive in almost every way.

Production designer Ted Bafaloukos built sets for all the interview subjects, and ace cinematographer John Bailey, with backup from Stefan Czapsky, shot them like a feature, resulting in a great looking picture.

Editor Brad Fuller comes up with unusual rhythms both austere and humorous, and while Philip Glass' contribution is more curtailed than it was on "Thin Blue Line," it still seductively invites the viewer into the world of the film.

Film was initially godfathered by Steven Spielberg as a project for Amblin Television, but there is no indication of this on the credits. — *Todd McCarthy*

FREEJACK

A Warner Bros. release of a James G. Robinson presentation of a Morgan Creek picture and Robinson/Ronald Shusett production. Produced by Shusett, Stuart Oken. Executive producers, Robinson, Gary Barber, David Nicksay. Directed by Geoff Murphy. Screenplay, Steven Pressfield, Shusett, Dan Gilroy; screen story by Pressfield, Shusett, based on Robert Sheckley's novel "Immortality, Inc." Camera (Technicolor), Amir Mokri; editor, Dennis Virkler; music, Trevor Jones; production design, Joe Alves; costume design, Lisa Jensen; sound (Dolby), Glenn E. Berkovitz; visual effects supervisor, Richard Hoover; associate producers, Alves, Linda Shusett, Anthony Jon Ridio; assistant directors, Jerry Ballew, Michael Haley; 2nd unit director-stunt coordinator, Mickey Gilbert; casting, Pam Dixon. Reviewed at Mann Village Theater, L.A., Jan. 17, 1992. MPAA Rating: R. Running time: **108 MIN.**

Alex Furlong	Emilio Estevez
Vacendak	Mick Jagger
Julie Redlund	Rene Russo
McCandless	Anthony Hopkins
Michelette	Jonathan Banks
Brad	David Johansen
Nun	Amanda Plummer
Boone	Grand L. Bush
Eagle Man	Frankie Faison
Morgan	John Shea
Ripper	Esai Morales

Chalk it up as one of life's little ironies that a pic about mind transfers would be so mindless. Employing a nightmarish vision of the year 2009 solely as a backdrop for a banal action yarn, "Freejack" has assembled a curious list of talent (Mick Jagger and Anthony Hopkins) that should prompt initial curiosity and minor box office fireworks before the film quickly dissipates.

The most aggravating aspect is that so much money and so little thought went into the production, as the filmmakers skip over exploring the roots of this grim futuristic society and instead focus on run-of-the-mill car chases and shootouts.

There's no shortage of talent. This is Jagger's first dramatic feature appearance since 1970's "Performance" and "Ned Kelly," and talented actors are cast in small, supporting roles. That, plus co-writer/producer Ron Shusett's credentials in high-tech mayhem, and pic looks all the more wan, misguided and wasteful.

The main problem may be that the story is distractingly set in a "Blade Runner"/"Soylent Green" future, with New York an armed, polluted camp of clearly divided haves and have-nots. Superhigh-tech cars run parallel to vintage autos from the present day, while billboards flash the word "suicide" as a not-too-subliminal message to the overcrowded masses.

An unexpected consequence of these trappings is that the primary plot — about a racecardriver (Emilio Estevez) who's plucked from a fiery death in 1991 to become a host body for the consciousness of a dying rich man —feels as superfluous as it is strained next to the other depressing evils on display.

Director Geoff Murphy, seen as an up-and-coming talent after his U.S. debut ("Young Guns II") and two productions in his native New Zealand ("Utu," "The Quiet Earth"), seems to have been either overwhelmed by the material or bored by it. Effect on the audience is a little of both.

With the circa '91 setup dispatched in less than 20 minutes, the film doesn't provide the hero enough personality for anyone to identify with him, other than the familiar Hitchcockian aspects of his plight.

The principal pursuers are equally one-dimensional, with Jagger as a body-snatching bounty hunter, and Jonathan Banks as the smarmy lieutenant of the business tycoon (Hopkins).

Energy lack is surprising in light of the talent involved. Hopkins' toothless cameo role comes as a particular letdown for those who have "The Silence of the Lambs" etched in their minds.

In addition to the oppressive production design, a number of minor points detract from the central action. Hero's g.f. (Rene Russo) and sleazy manager (David Johansen) appear not to have aged a day in the intervening 18 years. Cosmetic surgery may be heading into new areas, but couldn't someone at least have mentioned the how of it?

Estevez walks through his role with the same earnestly dopey expression he had in "Repo Man," which worked against such a darkly comic tapestry. Script and direction clearly fail him, since the character shows scant reaction to his new surroundings or the fact that he had "died" nearly two decades earlier.

Actually, the most notable performance is that of Amanda Plummer as an abusive, gun-toting nun, providing a rare comic highlight. It also ranks as the only element of the film that's unpredictable — as opposed to the payoff, which follows an impressive demonstration of mind-blowing animation à la "Tron."

Technically, the action and visual effects are well above average, but set and costume designs inconsistently depict the evolution of styles a decade into the next century. Trevor Jones' score also surpasses the action in terms of urgency, perhaps in pursuit of a better pic. — *Brian Lowry*

INTO THE SUN

A Trimark Pictures release of a Trimark/Hess-Kallberg production. Produced by Kevin M. Kallberg, Oliver G. Hess. Executive producer, Mark Amin. Directed by Fritz Kiersch. Screenplay, John Brancato, Michael Ferris. Camera (Foto-Kem color), Steve Grass; editor, Barry Zetlin; music, Randy Miller; production design, Gary T. New; art direction, Dana Torrey; set decoration, A. Rosalind Crew; sound, Ed White; assistant director, George Parra; production manager, Cristen M. Carr; visual effects supervisor, Richard Kerrigan; 2nd unit director-stunt coordinator, Ernie F. Orsatti; insert camera-aerial camera, Lee Redmond; additional editor, Marc Grossman; additional flying sequences, David Stipes Prods.; casting, Jack Jones. Reviewed at Broadway screening room, N.Y., Nov. 6, 1991. MPAA Rating: R. Running time: **100 MIN.**

Tom Slade	. . . . . . Anthony Michael Hall
Capt. Paul Watkins	. . . . Michael Paré
Maj. Goode	. . . Deborah Maria Moore
Mitchell Burton	. . . . . . Terry Kiser
Lt. DeCarlo	. . . . . . Brian Haley
Lt. Wolf	. . . . . . Michael St. Gerard
Dragon	. . . . Linden Ashby

"**T**op Gun" meets "The Hard Way" in the oddball comedy-adventure "Into the Sun." Film proves there's still life in flyboy pictures despite the genre spoofing of this summer's hit "Hot Shots!"

Premise inevitably recalls John Badham's "The Hard Way," a high concept b.o. disappointment with N.Y. cop James Woods reluctantly showing actor Michael J. Fox the ropes. This time U.S. pilot Michael Paré is assigned to show an action movie star (Anthony Michael Hall) how to portray the real thing.

Despite dialog too reminiscent of the prior film, the new version works better because Hall is *portraying* an egotistical, macho, method actor, rather than simply poking fun at himself the way Fox did. Paré is solid as the real McCoy and even gets to laugh and unbend a bit, compared to his usually stiff roles, as the twosome become friends.

Pic goes over the top when real-life skirmishes with unspecified Arab enemies in the Middle East break out, and Paré disobeys orders in taking the civilian into combat. Their derring-do, with Hall rising to the occasion, is fun if ridiculous. Pic is an important transition effort for Hall, who's comic timing is excellent.

Roger Moore's daughter Deborah (previously billed opposite Dad in "Bullseye!" as Deborah Barrymore due to a thesp with the same last name but here christened Deborah Maria Moore) is pert and attractive but overly reserved as the romantic interest of both heroes. Reliable comedian Terry Kiser earns some big laughs as a fast-talking agent.

Handsome Linden Ashby turns in a well-crafted but strange performance, not in tune with the rest of the picture, as an unctuous renegade Yank airman working for the Arabs.

Aerial dogfight scenes are okay, but lack the thrills of a previous straight drama from the same producers Kevin Kallberg and Oliver Hess, "Flight of Black Angel." —*Lawrence Cohn*

FINAL IMPACT

A PM Entertainment release. Produced by Richard Pepin, Joseph Merhi. Directed by Merhi, Stephen Smoke. Screenplay, Smoke; camera (Foto-Kem color), Pepin; editor, Geraint Bell, John Weidner; music, John Gonzalez; production design, Richard Dearborn; sound, Mike Hall; assistant director, Charla Driver; production manager, Jean Levine; fight choreography, Eric Lee. Reviewed on PM videcassette, N.Y. MPAA Rating: R. Running time: **102 MIN.**

Nick Taylor	. . . . . . Lorenzo Lamas
Maggie	. . . . Kathleen Kinmont
Danny	. . . . Michael Worth
Girl in bar	. . . . . . Kathrin Lautner
Jake	. . . . Jeff Langton
Joe	. . . . Mike Toney
Roxy	. . . . Mimi Lesseos

Actor Lorenzo Lamas continues to make inroads in the popular kickfighting genre with "Final Impact," a "Rocky V"-styled aging warrior picture.

After impressing in "Night of the Warrior, Lamas is cast as a cynical ex-champ who now manages fighters. Pushy young Michael Worth wants Lamas to pilot his career and Lamas agrees to do so, plotting to use Worth for his revenge against the current champ, Jeff Langton.

At times, pic has a more serious, even somber, tone than usual for the format, though directors Joseph Merhi and Stephen Smoke include exploitation angles such as sexy female oil wrestlers in the opening segment.

Though he's not a bona fide champ in real life, Lamas brings an animation to his role that's often lacking in belt holders. Worth is a promising newcomer, and Lamas's wife Kathleen Kinmont provides convincing support. There's also a nice bit by Kathrin Lautner as a Las Vegas hooker who reduces Lamas's self-esteem to zero.

The fights, choreographed by Eric Lee, are frequent and unexceptional. — *Lawrence Cohn*

BELTENEBROS
(SPANISH)

An Iberoamericana Films (Madrid)-Floradora Films (Warsaw) production in cooperation with Spanish TV (RTVE). Produced by Andrés Vicente Gómez. Directed by Pilar Miró. Screenplay, Miró, Mario Camus, Juan Antonio Porto, based on Antonio M. Molina's novel. Camera (color), Javier Aguirresarobe; editor, José Luis Matesanz; music, José Nieto; sets, Fernando Sáenz, Luis Valles; costumes, Pepe Rubio; sound (Dolby), Carlos Faruolo; production manager, José G. Jacoste. Reviewed at Cine Proyecciones, Madrid, Jan. 6, 1992. (Competing at Berlin Film Festival.) Running time: **110 MIN.**

Darman	. . . . . Terence Stamp
Rebeca	. . . . Patsy Kensit
Ugarte/Valdivia	. . . José Luis Gómez
Rebeca Osorio	. . . . . Geraldine James
Andrade	. . . . Simón Andreu

Also with: Alexander Bardini, John McEnery, Jorge de Juan.

(In Spanish; Spanish-dubbed)

Chalk up another entry in veteran Spanish helmers' ongoing fascination with the Franco era. This well-produced and directed political thriller pitting commies against fascists on a two-tier time level marks the return of femme helmer Pilar Miró.

"Beltenebros" (title meaning is never explained) delves into the inner conflicts of a reluctant Party hit man (Terence Stamp in a subdued performance) who's ordered to rub out a traitor in Madrid in 1962.

Pic unfolds in one long flashback, and then it flips back and forth between the Madrid of 1962 and 1946. Throughout, the killer remains almost unchanged in appearance.

Roster of characters includes an almost ludicrous fascist police commissioner, various intense underground Spanish Reds and a luscious dancer-hooker, ably played by Patsy Kensit.

The hit man is first seen in a British cottage surrounded by antiquarian books. Next he's in snowy Warsaw to receive orders to go to Madrid and kill the traitor. And finally he's cavorting in Spain amidst cops and Reds. However, 16 years earlier, he carried out a similar killing and has since been tormented by doubt about the victim's guilt.

The hit man never has to pull the trigger on his second victim; job is done by another communist. Finale is a histrionic shootout in an abandoned cinema.

As a political period drama, pic has done well in Spanish wickets. Camerawork is on the dark side, and Stamp could be more expressive. But item, though somewhat talky, holds interest and should garner some offshore sales. — *Peter Besas*

LA COMICHE 2
(THE COMICS 2)
(ITALIAN)

A Penta Distribuzione release of a Mario & Vittorio Cecchi Gori & Silvio Berlusconi Communications presentation of a C.G. Group Tiger Cinematografica & Penta Film production. Produced by Mario & Vittorio Cecchi Gori. Associate producers, Bruno Altissimi, Claudio Saraceni (Maura Intl. Film). Directed by Neri Parenti. Screenplay, Leo Benvenuti, Piero De Bernardi, Alessandro Bencivenni, Domenico Saverni, Parenti. Camera (Telecolor), Alessandro D'Eva; editor, Sergio Montanari; music, Bruno Zambrini; art direction, Maria Stilde Ambruzzi. Reviewed at Metropolitan Cinema, Rome, Jan. 17, 1992. Running time: **91 MIN.**

With: Paolo Villaggio, Renato Pozzetto. Roberto Della Casa.

Popular slapstick gagmeisters Paolo Villaggio and Renato Pozzetto reteam for "The Comics 2," a groansome dollop of buffoonery that delivers more yawns than yocks. Biz has been very brisk, and small screen future looks imminent.

Clever opening sequence has roly-poly duo coming to life from a billboard and fighting attempts to obscure them with a new poster. But inspiration ends there, and pic's relentless cartoon fatalities and crash-bang disasters wear thin fast.

Escapees' cavorting includes episodes as ambulence drivers wreaking havoc on a hospital and night watchmen investigating a department store break-in (with rampant brand name placement for Berlusconi's Standa store chain).

Gags are as old as Rome's seven hills, and a vague desperation lies beneath the madcap antics. Intended bigger-is-funnier premise falls flat since dirt-cheap sets are unconvincing, and camera sticks too close to action to show the extent of the large-scale destruction.

Pic's outmoded formula is matched by lame visual effects and hopelessly dated music which often drowns out dialog. Final shot announces "The Comics 3" for next Christmas.

—*David Rooney*

DRENGENE FRA SANKT PETRI
(THE BOYS FROM ST. PETRI)
(DANISH)

A Metronome co-production, with the Swedish Film Institute, Norwegian Film, Kinofinlandia & Kvikmyndasjódur (Iceland), the Danish Film Institute, DR/FI & the Nordic Film & TV Foundation. Produced by Mads Egmont Christensen. Executive producer, Bent Fabricius-Bjerre. Directed by Sören Kragh-Jacobsen. Screenplay, Kragh-Jacobsen, Bjarne Reuter. Camera (color), Dan Laustsen; editor, Leif Axel Kjeldsen; music, Jacob Groth; production design, Lars Nielsen; sound, Morten Degnböl. Reviewed at Dagmar Theater, Copenhagen, Oct. 11, 1991. Running time: **110 MIN.**
Gunnar . . . . Morten Buch Jörgensen
Lars . . . . Tomas Villum Jensen
Irene . . . . Xenia Lach-Nielsen
Jacob Rosenheim . . . . Philip Zandén
Otto . . . . Nikolaj Lie Kaas
    Also with: Bent Meiding, Solbjörg Höjfeldt, Helle Merete Sorensen.

This big-budget youth-oriented drama never quite grips or entertains, but it still has proved popular in homeland cinemas. With tech credits above par and a certain international feel to it, "The Boys from St. Petri" might be able to travel with some success.

Originally, pic was to tell the fact-based story of the Churchill Club, Resistance-fighting schoolboys from the large provincial city of Aalborg who spurred organized Danish resistance. However, helmer Sören Kragh-Jacobsen and screenwriter/novelist Bjarne Reuter liberated the pic from history and gave it a loose treatment dominated by youthful pranks and young love.

Brothers Gunnar (Morten Buch Jörgensen) and Lars (Tomas Villum Jensen) lead a gang of boys from posh public school St. Petri. Their Resistance fight begins as a series of elaborate practical jokes on the Nazis. A working class boy (Nikolaj Lie Kaas) who knows how to steal German weapons is enlisted, and the fight immediately becomes armed. The stakes get higher as the Gestapo probes the school.

Pic is bogged down by subplots of the brothers' ménage à trois with sweet Irene (Xenia Lach-Nielsen) and their friendship with a philosophical Swedish Jew (Philip Zandén).

Typical of screenwriter Bjarne Reuter ("Twist and Shout"), grownups are rendered in weak clichés: worried father who wants the boys to lay off the Nazis, and beautiful but poor mother who's despised for consorting with the Germans.

Kragh-Jacobsen ("Rubber Tarzan," "Emma's Shadow") knows how to handle young amateur actors. However, helmer's action sequences are often muddled and unsatisfying.

The good-looking pic (made on a budget of more than $4 million), has stylish photography and solid film music. In a reasonably convincing manner, Poland today stands in for '40s Denmark.

—*Peter Risby Hansen*

SUNDANCE FEST

IN THE SOUP

A Jim Stark presentation in association with Will Alliance Co. (Japan)-Pandora Film (Germany)-Why Not Prods. & Odessa Films (France)-Alta Films (Spain)-Mikado Film (Italy). Produced by Stark, Hank Blumenthal. Executive producer, Ryuichi Suzuki. Coexecutive producers, Chosei Funahara, Junichi Suzuki. Directed by Alexandre Rockwell. Screenplay, Rockwell, Tim Kissell. Camera (Duart b&w), Phil Parmet; editor, Dana Congdon; music, Mader; production design, Mark Friedberg; art direction, Ginger Tougas; costume design, Elizabeth Bracco; sound, Pavel Wdowczak; assistant director, Mary Beth Hagner; casting, Walken & Jaffe. Reviewed at Sundance Film Festival, Park City, Utah, Jan. 22, 1992. Running time: **93 MIN.**
Aldolpho Rollo . . . . . Steve Buscemi
Joe . . . . Seymour Cassel
Angelica . . . . Jennifer Beals
Dang . . . . Pat Moya
Skippy . . . . Will Patton
Old Man . . . . Sully Boyer
Louis Bafardi . . . . . Steven Randazzo
Frank Bafardi . . . . Francesco Messina
    Also with: Jim Jarmusch, Carol Kane, Stanley Tucci, Rockets Redglare, Elizabeth Bracco, Debi Mazar.

A sort of "Portrait of the Artist As a Young Stooge," "In the Soup" is a disarmingly offbeat shaggy-dog tale about an unlikely alliance. Prototypical, black & white New York indieprod isn't terribly substantial and at times feels self-conscious and calculated in its eccentricity, but winning performances and gentle, self-deprecating humor put this across as an audience pleaser for the specialized film crowd.

Fourth low-budget feature effort by Alexandre Rockwell bears autobiographical earmarks: He has given his protagonist, Aldolfo Rollo (Steve Buscemi), his own initials and the same aspirations. Unable to pay the rent on his shabby Lower East Side apartment, Aldolfo advertises for sale his 500-page screenplay, "Unconditional Surrender." Only taker is a fast-talking, fun-loving, physically expressive older fellow Joe (Seymour Cassel), who proposes himself as the epic's producer.

In what amount to goofy little blackout sketches, Joe, literally and figuratively, takes Aldolfo for a ride, using him as an innocent straight man in his numerous scams. A stolen Porsche sold for parts, Joe assures the directorial hopeful, will pay for all the raw stock they'll need.

And so it goes through a series of charming, light vignettes, as Joe's creepy, hemophiliac "brother" Skippy (a memorable Will Patton) drives Aldolfo to Jersey one night for no apparent reason, Joe induces Aldolfo's lowlife landlords (the indelible Steven Randazzo and Francesco Messina) to take no payments for awhile, and Joe eases the younger man into a quasi-romance with the spirited next-door neighbor (Jennifer Beals) Aldolfo has long been eyeing.

A crazy New Year's Eve romp around New York at first seems to promise the imminent production of Aldolfo's film, but winds up in inadvertent tragedy. Actual ending, with Aldolfo emerging as older but wiser and now really ready to direct a film, is weak and patly sentimental.

Buscemi is just right as the gullible patsy, an art-minded idealist who knows little of the real world. Cassel has the showier part and makes the most of it. Joe is a lusty kidder and terrific con man and the viewer just goes along with him, as does Aldolfo, because he's fun and unpredictable. Pic could give a real shot in the arm to this fine character actor at this stage in his career.

Having been seen in a handful of clinkers in recent years, Beals (Rockwell's wife) is radiant and utterly natural as a doubting woman with a complicated life. Jim Jarmusch and Carol Kane contribute amusing cameos as the crass producers of a nude public access cable talk show on which Aldolfo appears for money.

Rockwell's bright, on-its-toes shooting style is alert to the all the humor latent within the simple scenes and situations he wrote with Tim Kissell. Film's look is appealingly bargain basement. Pic was shot on color stock but printed, for theatrical release, in beautiful black & white; a color version will be available for vid, cable and tv, venues that essentially demand color for new films.

— *Todd McCarthy*

INNOCENTS ABROAD
(DOCU-16m)

A Dox Deluxe presentation from Flower Films, produced in association with BBC-Centre de l'Audio-Visuel à Bruxelles-La Sept, Paris-WNET New York-WDR-Miel Van Hoogenbemt. Produced by Vikram Jayanti. Directed by Les Blank. Camera (16m, Technicolor, U.K.; Monaco Film & Video color), Blank; editor-sound, Chris Simon; 2nd unit director, Van Hoogenbemt; 2nd unit camera, Louis Phillipe Capelle; 2nd unit sound, Phillipe Selier. Reviewed at Sundance Film Festival, Park City, Utah, Jan. 17, 1992. Running time: **84 MIN.**

Les Blank's lightly amusing "Innocents Abroad," an ambling documentary about Americans on a two-week European bus tour, is perhaps too amiable. Viewers may be better off watching the one-hour version, due Feb. 17 as "The Grand Tour" on PBS' "Travel."

Blank, a practiced chronicler of folk cultures and artists, and collaborators Vikram Jayanti and Chris Simon have essentially made a docu version of "If It's Tuesday, This Must Be Belgium."

Crew was allowed unfettered access to a typical tour conducted by Globus Gateway, the largest operator of group bus trips around the Continent, and proceeded to portray the experience from the perspective of the travelers, the guide and the Europeans they met.

Expected take on such material would be to skewer the asinine Yanks who would choose to experience Europe from behind moving plate-glass windows.

Blank gets in a few funny digs, with the active participation of his subjects, but his fundamentally sympathetic, humanistic approach rules out a mass lynching. He tries for something more honest, but his findings aren't all that surprising or culturally insightful.

The tour director, Brit Mark Tinney, is very professional and knows his history, while a French chef amusingly complains that Americans don't like to eat fish with bones.

From London to the Netherlands, Germany, Switzerland, Austria, Italy and France, the film grapples with the central dilemma of Europe's transformation into one vast museum, the populace of which is forced to kowtow to tourists for a buck.

Blank isn't the greatest photographer of architecture, but the lively and witty musical track is great fun. — *Todd McCarthy*

THE HOURS AND TIMES

An Antarctic Pictures production. Produced, written, directed and edited by Christopher Munch. Sound, Munch. Camera (black & white), Munch, Juan Carlos Valls. Reviewed at Sundance Film Festival, Park City, Utah, Jan. 21, 1992. Running time: **60 MIN.**
Brian Epstein . . . . . . David Angus
John Lennon . . . . Ian Hart
Marianne . . . . . . Stephanie Pack
Quinones . . . . Robin McDonald

Filmmaker Christopher Munch's fictitious speculation on what may have transpired on a 1963 vacation between Beatle John Lennon and his manager and friend Brian Epstein, who was gay, made a minor stir at the Sundance fest, both for its audacity and its nuanced investigation of challenging territory.

Financed entirely by Munch, an L.A.-based American filmmaker, and shot over just four days in Barcelona with a single camera assistant, spartan black & white production unspools in an unpolished cinéma vérité style that initially charms with its crude, nostalgic energy.

One-hour scenario has the worldly, refined Epstein (David Angus) and the coarse, impatient young Lennon (Ian Hart) leaving for a few days rest after a grueling tour that has positioned the Beatles on the verge of major importance. Both men are aware that Epstein would like their time together to be intensely personal, a thought which has John nervously casting about for female distraction in an especially nice stewardess (very smartly played by Stephanie Pack).

Once alone in Barcelona, talk gets abruptly to the point as John asks provocative questions about homosexual practices, trying to lead Epstein on and hold him off. He seems half inclined to give it a go, but not very happily, a situation putting both men in emotional turmoil. Munch's script perceptively expresses the ambiguity and tension of a situation in which the often rude and cutting Lennon apparently finds it difficult to know how to behave. But its sensibilities reside with the precise and rather mournful Epstein, who seems resigned to unfulfillment.

Interaction between the two famed figures is not much of a delight, since Epstein seems to bring out the worst in Lennon, and pic's mood is slow and arid.

British actors Angus and Hart provide flashes of uncanny resemblance, but bewigged Hart, having found a single dimension of Lennon to impersonate, sticks to it too firmly, propping himself up with furious gum-chewing and cigarette-smoking. More sophisticated in intent than execution, pic is nonetheless commendable. — *Amy Dawes*

RESERVOIR DOGS

A Live America presentation of a Lawrence Bender production in association with Monte Hellman & Richard N. Gladstein. Produced by Bender. Executive producers, Gladstein, Ronna B. Wallace, Hellman. Co-producer, Harvey Keitel. Directed, written by Quentin Tarantino. Camera (Foto-Kem color), Andrzej Sekula; editor, Sally Menke; music supervisor, Karyn Rachtman; production design, David Wasco; costume design, Betsy Heimann. Reviewed at Sundance Film Festival, Park City, Utah, Jan. 21, 1992. Running time: **105 MIN.**
Mr. White . . . . Harvey Keitel
Mr. Orange . . . . Tim Roth
Nice Guy Eddie . . . . . . Chris Penn
Mr. Pink . . . . Steve Buscemi
Joe Cabot . . . . . Lawrence Tierney
Mr. Blonde . . . . . . Michael Madsen
Mr. Brown . . . . . Quentin Tarantino
Mr. Blue . . . . Eddie Bunker
Also with: Kirk Baltz, Randy Brooks.

A show-off piece of filmmaking that will put debut writer-director Quentin Tarantino on the map, "Reservoir Dogs" is an intense, bloody, in-your-face crime drama about a botched robbery and its gruesome aftermath. Colorfully written in vulgar gangster vernacular and well played by a terrific cast, this piece of strong pulp will attract attention but looks like a modest b.o. performer.

Clearly influenced by Scorsese's "Mean Streets" and "Goodfellas" and Kubrick's "The Killing," Tarantino would love to be grouped in such company and employs many bravura effects in making his bid. Undeniably impressive pic grabs the viewer by the lapels and shakes hard, but it also is about nothing other than a bunch of macho guys and how big their guns are.

Strikingly shot and funny opening scene has eight criminals at breakfast arguing about the true meaning of Madonna's "Like a Virgin." This vulgar, unlikely discussion, coupled with subsequent shots of them emerging from the restaurant like the Wild Bunch, instantly demonstrates that a smart filmmaker is at work here.

Telling a story much like "The Killing" or "Odds Against Tomorrow," script fractures very cleverly into an intricate flashback structure that mixes the post-robbery mess with telling character and plot details from the planning stages.

To put it chronologically, crime kingpin Lawrence Tierney and son Chris Penn recruit six pros to whom they assign false, color-themed names, so that no one will know anything about the others. The diamond heist at an L.A. jewelry store goes awry, however, when it becomes apparent the cops have been tipped off. Two of the robbers and a couple of cops are killed, and the gang splits up.

Hotheaded Harvey Keitel takes his injured cohort, Tim Roth, to a hideout where they are soon joined by Steve Buscemi, who is obsessed with remaining "professional." As they ponder who the rat may have been, in comes the psychotic Michael Madsen with a hostage cop. The young officer is brutally tortured in a scene that drove numerous fest viewers from the unspooling here, and may make even the brave look away. The worst is left off-camera, but it's still a needlessly sadistic sequence that crosses the line of what audiences want to experience.

This launches the bloodbath for real, and when Tierney and Penn finally show up to identify the fink, Tarantino stages a rather amazing shoot-out that hilariously sends up the climaxes of Sergio Leone's "For a Few Dollars More" and especially "The Good, the Bad, and the Ugly."

Tarantino's complex plot construction works very well, relieving the warehouse setting's claustrophobia and providing lively background on robbery planning, the undercover cop's successful preparations and the gang's crude male bonding.

Dripping with the lowest sexist and racist colloquialisms, dialogue is snappy, imaginative and loaded with threats, and the director, presumably with the help of co-producer Keitel, has assembled a perfect cast. Seemingly relishing the opportunity to pull out all the stops, the actors could all be singled out for their outstanding work, but the same adjectives could be used to describe this terrific ensemble as they yell, confront, joke and strut powerfully and explosively.

With cinematographer Andrzej Sekula's considerable help, Tarantino has put strong visuals

on the screen, alternating from ominously moving cameras to recessive long shots to put the action in relief. Sally Menke's extremely impressive cutting keeps scenes tight and the time-jumping plot comprehensible.

As accomplished as all the individual elements are, however, pic feels like the director's audition piece, an occasion for a new filmmaker to flaunt his talents. Undeniably juicy, with its salty talk and gunplay, film is nihilistic but not resonantly so, giving it no meaning outside the immediate story and characters. Pic is impressive, but impossible to love. — *Todd McCarthy*

GAS, FOOD AND LODGING

An IRS release of a Cineville-Seth Willenson production. Produced by Daniel Hassid, Willenson, William Ewart. Executive producers, Carl-Jan Colpaert, Christoph Henkel. Directed, written by Allison Anders, based on Richard Peck's novel "Don't Look and It Won't Hurt." Camera (color), Dean Lent; editor, Tracy S. Granger; production design, Jane Ann Stewart; music, J. Mascis; art direction, Lisa Denker, Carla Weber; set decoration, Mary Meeks; sound, Clifford (Kip) Gynn; assistant director, Matthew J. Clark. Reviewed at Sundance Film Festival, Park City, Utah, Jan. 17, 1992. Running time: **100 MIN.**
Nora . . . . Brooke Adams
Trudi . . . . Ione Skye
Shade . . . . Fairuza Balk
John . . . . James Brolin
Dank . . . . Robert Knepper
Hamlet . . . . David Lansbury
Darius . . . . Donovan Leitch
Raymond . . . . Chris Mulkey

"Gas, Food and Lodging" is filled with the kind of personal, small-scale rewards indie filmmakers seem best at delivering. Premiering in dramatic competition at Sundance, Allison Anders' fresh and unfettered pic emerges distinctively as an example of a new cinema made by women and expressive of their lives.

Lensed on location in Deming, N.M., on a budget of about $1.3 million, pic faces the challenge of connecting with a potentially large working-class audience via the current theatrical distribution system, but it looks like a natural for cable exposure in its post-theatrical life.

Focus is on teenage Shade (Fairuza Balk) and her quest to find a man for her waitress mom, Nora (Brooke Adams) while sorting out her own romantic yearnings and dealing with her loose-living, surly-tempered older sister Trudi (Ione Skye).

Her imagination bigger than her dusty surroundings, Shade spends afternoons at the Mexican cinema watching impassioned star Elvia Rivera, while Trudi stays out late at night proffering real-life passions to disloyal and unappreciative locals.

Tensions run high between Trudi and Mom, who got pregnant too early and sees Trudi about to do the same, while Shade believes it's her mother's fault her father's not around.

Narrated from point of view of the naive but sensitive Shade (beautifully and distinctively evoked by Balk), pic deftly and instinctively conveys the women's attempts to understand their relation to the world, to men and to each other.

Shade's self-conscious but eager to reach out; Trudi's sexually wounded and haunted by the specter of male abandonment; while Nora's keeping men at a distance while trying to set an example for her daughters that they're too young to appreciate.

Anders works very much from a femme perspective, with the women's emotional and interior forces driving the story, while the actions of the men come and go in their lives, creating a unique and keenly appropriate pace and structure. Rich, multilevel work is full of rueful humor, fresh turns and small, elegant surprises, such as Shade's visit to the home of a Mexican boy she likes (Jacob Vargas) or her encounter with her dad (James Brolin).

Enhanced by cinematographer Dean Lent's sharp eye for the tumble-down essence of the working class West and by a down-to-earth jangly guitar score by J. Mascis, Anders' first solo directorial work (she co-directed "Border Radio," also lensed by Lent, with Kurt Voss), adds up to a unique but accessible work with a resonating authenticity.

— *Amy Dawes*

STAR TIME

Produced, directed, written by Alexander Cassini. Co-producer, Megan Barnett. Line producer, Reza Mizbani. Camera (Foto-Kem color), Fernando Arguelles; editor, Stan Salfas; music, Blake Leyh; production design, Carey Meyer, David Jensen; set design, Andrea Claire, James Abbott; set decoration, Iain Blodwell; costumes, Shawna Leavell; sound (Ultra Stereo), David Lerner; sound design, Donny Blank; associate producer, Salfas; assistant director, Gregory Everage; additional camera, Dean Hayasaka, Janusz Kaminski, David Makin; casting, Don Pemrick. Reviewed at Sundance Film Festival, Park City, Utah, Jan. 20, 1992. Running time: **85 MIN.**

Henry Pinkle . . . . Michael St. Gerard
Sam Bones . . . . John P. Ryan
Wendy . . . . Maureen Teefy

Some kind of critique of media and celebrity, "Star Time" is a technically superior but dramatically ghastly indie washout. Very few viewers outside of indulgent film festival-goers will sit still for this one.

First-time writer-director Alexander Cassini clearly has a number of things on his mind, mainly concerning the destructive influence of tv-generated images and the equality of celebrity and infamy in a media-dominated culture, but he's chosen off-putting and dramatically unreal means to express them.

Protagonist is a boring loser named Henry Pinkle who decides to commit suicide because his favorite tv show has been canceled. He is rescued from the L.A. rooftop by guardian angel Sam Bones, a slick operator who convinces Henry to join him in making a killing in showbiz.

Henry makes a killing, all right, but not the type he had in mind. A wealthy, seductive smooth-talker, "angel" turns Henry into the Baby Mask Killer, a mass murderer who commits his first crime while "It's A Wonderful Life" is playing on tv and ends up slaying 13 victims in a month.

The climactic victim of this rampage is meant to be a female social worker who has been trying to help Henry, and whom Sam deeply resents. Final reel is occupied with characters skulking from apartment to apartment and, inevitably, back up to the roof so that Henry can achieve his media bite of fame.

Story and characters are so repellent and one-dimensional that impatient squirming is the most natural reaction. However, an undeniable skill lies behind the visual and aural aspects of the film. Color schemes in the production design, lighting and lensing are all striking, and soundtrack is unusually complex, all of which at least provide some compensation for putting up with the murky storytelling.

Playing turn-off characters, thesps Michael St. Gerard, John P. Ryan and Maureen Teefy are uniformly overbearing. Fame will come to none of those involved through this effort.

— *Todd McCarthy*

STORYVILLE

A 20th Century Fox release of a Davis Entertainment Co. presentation of an Edward R. Pressman production in association with David Roe. Produced by Roe, Pressman. Executive producers, John Davis, John Flock. Co-executive producers, Les Lithgow, George Zecevic. Co-producer, Evzen Kolar. Directed by Mark Frost. Screenplay, Frost, Lee Reynolds, based on Frank Galbally & Robert Macklin's novel "Juryman." Camera (CFI color), Ron Garcia; editor, B.J. Sears; music, Carter Burwell; production design, Richard Hoover; art direction, Kathleen M. McKernin; set decoration, Brian Kasch; costume design, Louise Frogley; sound (Ultra Stereo), Stephen Halbert; associate producer, Chappy Hardy; assistant director, Deepak Nayar; casting, Johanna Ray. Reviewed at Sundance Film Festival, Park City, Utah, Jan. 22, 1992. Running time: **110 MIN.**
Cray Fowler . . . . James Spader
Natalie Tate . Joanne Whalley-Kilmer
Clifford Fowler . . . . . Jason Robards
Lee . . . . Charlotte Lewis
Nathan LeFleur . . . . Michael Warren
Michael Trevallian . . . Michael Parks
Pudge Herman . . . . . . Chuck McCann
Abe Choate . . . . Charlie Haid
Also with: Chino Fats Williams, Woody Strode, Jeff Perry, Galyn Gorg, Justine Arlin, Piper Laurie.

"Storyville" has a little trouble getting its story straight. A teeming cesspool of illicit sex, murder, suicide, family intrigue and political chicanery in exotic Louisiana, this would-be "Chinatown" is so overloaded with outrageous implausibilities that the temptation is very strong to consider it all a joke. But some of the weirdness pays off in the second hour, to the point where the film emerges with some interest. B.O. outlook appears limited.

In his first big-screen directorial outing, Mark Frost, a key force behind "Hill Street Blues" and David Lynch's partner on "Twin Peaks" for TV, has taken an Australian novel and relocated it in New Orleans, where just about anything goes.

What doesn't go, however, is pic's whole opening section. James Spader plays Cray Fowler, a callow, good-looking kid trying to carry his rich, corrupt family's tradition of political service into a third generation. His campaign for Congress is clouded by his father's suicide on the day he was to testify in an investigation of a shady mineral rights deal that brought the family its fortune. Encouraged by family patriarch Clifford Fowler (Jason Robards) in the old-boy-network school, Cray is divorcing his wife and seeking the support of black voters.

In the meantime, however, Cray is crazy enough to run off with the enticing Lee (Charlotte Lewis), a Vietnamese woman he's barely met, and unknowingly gets videotaped making whoopee with her in her jacuzzi. The next time he sees her, he is obliged to fight her maniacal father, who mysteriously winds up dead.

Bizarrely, Cray takes the lethal weapon, a knife, home with him, and when Lee is charged with the murder, Cray astoundingly offers his services as defense attorney. Opposing him will be a prosecutor (Joanne Whalley-Kilmer) who's his old flame.

If this sounds like enough jambalaya to induce a two-day bellyache, there's also a transvestite witness to the murder, Michael Parks' deranged Vietnam vet cop, Chino Fats Williams' gravel-voiced stripjoint hustler, Piper Laurie's Tennessee Williams-like faded Southern flower, and enough deceit and nastiness in the Fowler family to occupy a year's worth of "Dallas" episodes.

Given that he's a congressional candidate and presumably smart enough to earn a law degree, Cray does so many apparently stupid things, and the many jaw-dropping loopholes and long-shots in the first half make the film systematically unconvincing. It's dangerous to turn off an audience for so long before showing the good cards up one's sleeve.

But Cray smartens up when he takes Lee's case, and he gets the upper hand over those who would threaten or blackmail him. Story's craziness winds up a wild courtroom shootout, but if the context has been accepted by then, some goofy fun is to be had.

Enacting even the most ludicrous behavior with a straight face, Spader makes Cray seem so unserious about his life at the outset that he wouldn't seem to deserve to have anything go right for him. Still, his transformation ultimately results in a change of sympathies.

Whalley-Kilmer and Lewis are attractive in functional parts, and Robards serves up an old-school blowhard to a fare-thee-well. But the further one goes into the supporting cast, the tastier it gets, with Charlie Haid particularly stunning giving a definitive reading of a mean, crafty biker personality. Woody Strode also turns up as an aged witness to a long-ago political trick.

As always, New Orleans provides a colorful backdrop for dramatic action, one to which Frost, production designer Richard Hoover and lenser Ron Garcia are responsive. Carter Burwell's score is opulently Oriental in flavor. —*Todd McCarthy*

ZEBRAHEAD

An Oliver Stone presentation of an Ixtlan production. Produced by Jeff Dowd, Charles Mitchell, William F. Willett. Executive producers, Stone, Janet Yang. Co-executive producer, Peter Newman. Line producer, Stan Wlodkowski. Directed by Anthony Drazan. Camera (Duart color), Maryse Alberti; editor, Elizabeth Kling; music, Taj Mahal; music supervisor, M.C. Search; production design, Naomi Shohan; art direction, Dan Whifler; set decoration, Penny Barrett; costume design, Carol Oditz; sound (Dolby), Paul Cote; associate producer, Matthew Coppola; assistant director, Don Wilkerson; casting, Deborah Aquila. Reviewed at Sundance Film Festival, Park City, Utah, Jan. 18, 1992. Running time: **100 MIN.**

Zack Glass . . . . . . Michael Rapaport
Nikki . . . . N'Bushe Wright
Otis Wimms . . . . Paul Butler
Dee Wimms . . . . . DeShonn Castle
Marlene . . . . Candy Ann Brown
Mr. Modell . . . . Luke Reilly
Mr. Cimino . . . . Dan Ziskie
Dominic . . . . Kevin Corrigan
Saul . . . . Martin Priest
Nut . . . . Ron Johnson
Richard Glass . . . . . . Ray Sharkey
Diane . . . . Helen Shaver

"Zebrahead," a fresh reality-minded black-white teen romance set in racially polarized Detroit, teems with vivid details of youth culture. Highlighted by unusual relationships and scenes, indie effort from Oliver Stone's production company is less complex than it might have been and leans too far toward civics lessons, but it is entertaining and puts much new talent on display. The right distrib could market this low-budget effort to profitable returns.

First-time writer-director Anthony Drazan centers his story on Zack Glass (Michael Rapaport), a self-confident, blond Jewish kid who seems to have turned out pretty well despite having been raised by a slick hipster father (Ray Sharkey) whose only interests are sex and the vintage black music he sells in his record shop.

Zack idolizes black culture in the extreme, having absorbed his neighbors' and friends' vocal rhythms, gestures and attitudes to the extent that his black g.f. later tells him he's more homeboy than white boy.

To the consternation of more militant brothers, Zack's best pal is a sharp black fellow Dee (DeShonn Castle) whose hot cousin Nikki (N'Bushe Wright) transfers to the high school from New York — Romeo-and-Juliet time in the hood.

With integrationist ideals passé except in the romantic haze of young love, the blacks come down hard on the couple's budding relationship. Nikki's mother doesn't like it, the Islamic separatist types don't like it, and the school's baddest boy (Ron Johnson) razzes the couple whenever they go out and puts the make on Nikki when she has a falling-out with Zack.

Action is set in neighborhoods dominated by what look like former middle- and upper-class homes that are now ramshackle or bombed out, all backdropped by ghastly, pollution-spewing industrial complexes.

School is mostly black, with a sprinkling of whites, Hispanics and Asians. Detroit, quite unused as a film location until now, offers a potent tableau of metropolitan ills.

For all the characters' attitudinizing, this is essentially a sensitive youth story of the type common in the '50s, when films portrayed a society that just wouldn't let young lovers stay together to pursue their destinies.

Very straightforward script could have used more twists and turns and a subplot or two, and Drazan's directorial style is similarly straight-ahead.

A couple of scenes in which characters get to lecture on the state of race relations also bring the drama near the realm of "Afterschool Specials." But dialogue and performances are sharp and lively, and several elements are unusual enough to warrant special attention.

Zack's outright co-option of black traits and perceptions is portrayed sincerely and sympathetically, and makes for a continually interesting lead character. Michael Rapaport's emotional range seems limited here, but he effectively puts across the externals.

Further, never in memory has there been a father-son relationship quite like the one depicted here. Sharkey, funny and just right as the priapic Dad, always has some bimbo on his mind or in his bed, and he's concerned his son do as well as he does.

Wright is an alluring, mercurial Nikki, Castle brings a strong presence to Dee, and Johnson scores heavily as the dangerous-

ly unpredictable yet vulnerable Nut.

Soundtrack, by Taj Mahal with contributions from other artists, is a major plus.

— *Todd McCarthy*

THE TUNE
(ANIMATED)

A film by Bill Plympton. Screenplay, Plympton, Maureen McElheron, P.C. Vey. Camera (color), John Donnelly; editor, Merril Stern; music, McElheron; sound, Phil Lee; artistic supervisor, Jessica Wolf-Stanley. Reviewed at Sundance Film Festival, Park City, Utah, Jan. 17, 1992. Running time: **69 MIN.**

Voices: Daniel Neiden (Del), Maureen McElheron (Didi), Marty Nelson (Mayor, Mr. Mega, Mrs. Mega), Emily Bindiger (Dot), Chris Hoffman (Wiseone, Surfer, Tango Dancer, Note), Jimmy Ceribello (Cabbie), Ned Reynolds (Houndog), Jeff Knight (Bellhop), Jennifer Senko (Surfer, Note).

Hip, strikingly designed and mercilessly clever, Bill Plympton's first animated feature lives up to the promise of his acclaimed short work. Marketing this singular musical cartoon, and finding the target audience, will be challenging. Exclusive runs in specialized theaters would be indicated (brief running time is a handicap theatrically), followed perhaps by ballyhoo as a major event for a cable or TV network.

A favorite in such forums as the Intl. Tournee of Animation and MTV, Plympton has a distinctive style that keys into sophisticated adults more than kids. Charmingly warped and irreverent, Plympton kids around with pop culture in a playfully appealing manner and complements this with a drawing style that has a nice rough, offhanded edge.

Visually, pic belongs to no school other than its own, although conceptually its subversiveness and occasional sadism can be traced back to Tex Avery and beyond.

Story is a mere clothesline to which nearly a dozen musical vignettes have been attached. Del is a forlorn songwriter whose boss, the crass mogul Mr. Mega, gives him 47 minutes to compose a hit, or else.

Desperately searching for a chart-topper to make his name and hold on to his sweetheart Didi, who works for Mr. Mega, Del stumbles into a strange musical land presided over by a Tin Pan Alley-type crooner and a pompous old Wiseone.

In short order, Del encounters a parade of oddballs — a country & western waitress, a noseless cabbie who sings the blues, a hound dog of the Elvis variety, surfing beach partiers and tango dancers — who belt out winning tunes on demand.

Format makes the film feel rather like a succession of shorts strung together. At least a couple of the segments have been released previously to help fund and promote the bigger work.

Two sections stand out as notable for their hilarious ghoulishness. "The Lovesick Hotel" presents a demented panorama of the horrible deaths awaiting the lovelorn in their hotel rooms.

Another, an even more memorable nonmusical sequence, has businessmen out-slowburning Laurel and Hardy as each concocts ways to one-up the other in a startling escalation of mutilation and personal violence.

Plympton's rather spare style employs what look like pencil or charcoal drawings of caricatured figures making their ways across mostly empty pastel backgrounds. The principal figures move, throb and transform themselves stunningly in ways that can be both witty and beautiful. A quicksilver imagination is in evidence at every moment.

Unlike many more elaborate animated projects, "The Tune," in its visual aspect, feels very much like the work of a single artist who has personally drawn every frame (in fact, two assistants helped out to ink and paint Plympton's cels), and is all the more appealing for it.

Maureen McElheron's original songs are hugely important to the film's success. Drawing upon numerous musical idioms, songs are lively and lyrics affectionately satirize their sources.

— *Todd McCarthy*

THE WATERDANCE

A Samuel Goldwyn release of a JBW Prod. Produced by Gale Anne Hurd, Marie Cantin. Executive producer, Guy Riedel. Directed by Neal Jimenez & Michael Steinberg. Screenplay, Jimenez. Camera (color), Mark Plummer; editor, Jeff Freeman; music, Michael Convertino; music supervision, Sharon Boyle; production design, Bob Ziembicki. Reviewed at Sundance Film Festival, Park City, Utah, Jan. 21, 1992. Running time: **106 MIN.**

Joel . . . . Eric Stolz
Anna . . . . Helen Hunt
Bloss . . . . William Forsythe
Ray . . . . Wesley Snipes
Rosa . . . . Elizabeth Pena

Co-directing debut of writer Neal Jimenez ("River's Edge," "For the Boys") with Michael Steinberg is a smashing success if great performances and a deftly told, thoroughly absorbing tale mean anything. "The Waterdance," the writer's semi-autobiographical story of a young man's struggle to avoid despair after a crippling accident, emerged as an audience favorite at Sundance and appears destined to turn a handy profit in theaters as well.

Set in a hospital for paralyzed men where a young novelist (Eric Stolz) lands after a hiking accident, pic is about his coming to terms with the fate he shares with others in the ward; among them, a hostile white redneck biker (William Forsyth) and a restless, fast-talking black man (Wesley Snipes).

Hospital dramas depicting the tenacious human spirit are not new, but this pic dances just ahead of expectations. Not the usual egomaniacal dirge about a stricken prince who bullies and seduces those who serve him, pic has a protagonist who is as interested in observing others as in his own fate, and the ward comes very much alive.

Jimenez's script unfolds with a spirit and sparkle devoid of self-indulgence, and Stolz plays the lead with lightness, wit and balance, as well as a measure of despair and denial. Much of the pic concerns the anguish of these young men at losing sexual ability, and this aspect of paralysis is covered with a frankness heretofore unseen.

Also anchoring it is the complex relationship between the novelist and his married g.f. (Helen Hunt turns in an exceptional perf in the role particularly well-written by Jimenez), and the emerging friendship between the biker and the black guy (precisely and forcefully portrayed by scene-stealing Snipes).

Moving and occasionally hilarious, team-directed pic by Steinberg with Jimenez, who is confined to a wheelchair, had the audience in the palm of its hand within minutes. Financed by RCA/Col after Warner Bros., which originally developed the script, passed, and acquired for distribution this week by Goldwyn, pic looks to prove studio sages wrong. — *Amy Dawes*

SHINING THROUGH

A 20th Century Fox release presented in association with Peter V. Miller Investment Corp. and produced in association with Sandollar Prods. Executive producers, Sandy Gallin, David Seltzer. Produced by Howard Rosenman, Carol Baum. Co-producer, Nigel Wooll. Directed, written by Seltzer, based on Susan Isaacs' novel. Camera (Rank Film Laboratories color), Jan De Bont; editor, Craig McKay; music, Michael Kamen; production design, Anthony Pratt; art direction, Desmond Crowe, Kevin Phipps; set decoration, Peter Howitt; costume design, Marit Allen; sound (Dolby), Ivan Sharrock; special effects supervisor, Richard Conway; assistant director, Don French; 2nd unit director, Peter MacDonald; casting, Simone Reynolds, Mary Gail Artz, Barbara Cohen. Reviewed at Avco Cinema Center, L.A., Jan. 28, 1992. MPAA Rating: R. Running time: **132 MIN.**
Ed Leland . . . . Michael Douglas
Linda Voss . . . . . . Melanie Griffith
Franze-Otto Dietrich . . Liam Neeson
Margrete . . . . Joely Richardson
Sunflower . . . . John Gielgud
Andrew Berringer . . . Francis Guinan
Fishmonger . . . . Patrick Winczewski

An old-fashioned women's picture that could pass for a television movie except for its lavish trappings, this oddly titled melodrama turns out to be little more than a big, brassy Hallmark card with a World War II backdrop. Combining shameless romance with predictable spy intrigue, "Shining Through" could have pretty commercial prospects if it can tap into the audience that reads Sidney Sheldon novels and that made "Steel Magnolias" a hit.

Pic is very nearly undone by its major device: A middle-aged Linda Voss (Melanie Griffith) reminisces about her spy exploits for a BBC documentary. Her god-awful makeup job makes it impossible to discern how old she's supposed to be, and the heavy-handed voiceover narration is stiff and forced.

It is ironic this is supposed to be for a BBC special, since those who've seen any BBC docus would expect a lot more grit and bite than is in director David Seltzer's adaptation of Susan Isaacs' novel.

Griffith plays a half-Jewish, half-Irish woman, circa 1940, who goes to work for a mysterious attorney (Michael Douglas) who turns out to be a spy for the U.S. government. The two become lovers, and despite his reluctance, Linda, a lower-class girl hired because of her fluent German, is ultimately sent to Berlin as a spy, infiltrating the house of a German honcho (Liam Neeson).

Along the way, she hooks up with several Germans working undercover for the U.S., including the code-named Sunflower (John Gielgud) and a young woman of privilege (Joely Richardson).

Curiously, the cornball narration is used to skip showing pic's potential emotional crescendos: Audience is told that Ed (Douglas) and Linda have become lovers after the fact, without being shown the moment it happens.

Similarly, Seltzer sometimes fails to adequately connect scenes with potential wallop, such as the one in which Linda finally gets to go to the opera with her German keeper after missing the chance with Ed — a point that doubtless will be lost thanks to concurrent intrigue detracting from the scene.

There's also a fair degree of tension as the spy antics draw to a close, but the flashback structure diffuses some of it because it's the aged Linda, after all, who's recounting the tale.

To his credit, Seltzer does a good job establishing the period, from costumes and sets to newsreel footage giving way to black & white shots turning to color.

The dialogue, however, doesn't make any effort to capture that era, and Griffith's spunky secretary, despite appealing moments, seems more a '90s working girl than a '40s working-class girl.

Despite top billing for Douglas, it's really Griffith's show, and while she seems to be a little old for the role as written, she manages to produce a few worthwhile moments — particularly with her espionage knowledge gleaned entirely from a fascination with Hollywood spy pics.

Douglas has less to work with as the robotic soldier whose heart is turned to mush, as the hero's always is in the last few pages of romance novels. Neeson is similarly underemployed as the German officer, while Gielgud's performance amounts to a too-brief cameo. Aside from the two leads, only Richardson has a chance to do any real shining.

Cars and costumes enhance the film's opulent production values — underscored by massive crowd shots used in scenes at the opera, at train stations and during a Berlin bombing raid — though the sets at times look like spruced-up studio backlot shots.

Lensing took place at the Pinewood Studios in London and on location in Germany and Austria. — *Brian Lowry*

LOVE CRIMES

A Millimeter Films release of a Sovereign Pictures presentation, in association with Millimeter. Executive producer, Forrest Murray. Produced by Lizzie Borden, Randy Langlais. Directed by Borden. Screenplay, Allan Moyle, Laurie Frank, based on Moyle's story. Camera (Deluxe color), Jack N. Green; editor, Nicholas C. Smith, Mike Jackson; music, Graeme Revell, Roger Mason; production design, Armin Ganz; costume design, Irene Albright, Iris Lewis; sound (Ultra-Stereo), Brit Warner, Michael Haines (Dallas); assistant director, Lisa Zimble (Atlanta), Mike Dempsey (Dallas); production manager, Victoria Westhead (Atlanta), Dempsey (Dallas); stunt coordinator, Lonnie R. Smith Jr.; additional camera, Ben Butin, Phedon Papamichael (Dallas); additional editor, Christy Richmond; casting, Pat Golden, John McCabe, Carla Posey (Dallas). Reviewed at Loews 19th St. East 3 theater, N.Y., Jan. 24, 1992. MPAA Rating: R. Running time: **85 MIN.**
Dana Greenway . . . . . . Sean Young
David Hanover . . . . . Patrick Bergin
Maria Johnson . . . . . Arnetia Walker
Stanton Gray . . . . James Read
Det. Tully . . . . Ron Orbach
Also with: Fern Dorsey, Tina Hightower, Donna Biscoe.

"Love Crimes" is a poorly constructed thriller suffering from a bad lead performance by Sean Young.

Wide release through Miramax's Millimeter division should attract some curiosity seekers but will probably die quickly. Young toplines as a mannishly styled Atlanta assistant district attorney who disobeys her superior's orders and accompanies cops on their stakeouts and arrests.

She becomes obsessed with women's charges against a con man (Patrick Bergin) posing as a famous fashion photographer. He picks up plain-looking women, snaps semi-nude Polaroids, sexually dominates them and then robs them. Making like detective Nancy Drew, Young follows a lead and travels to Savannah to capture Bergin herself.

Screenplay by Allan Moyle and Laurie Frank (from Moyle's story based on a real-life '70s case involving a Richard Avedon impersonator) initially dangles an intriguing issue: Many of the women in retrospect seem to enjoy Bergin's treatment.

But director Lizzie Borden stacks the deck, showing Bergin mistreating the women but giving the actresses (other than Young) limited screen time in which to develop their characters. The complicated matter of victims identifying with their captors, treated controversially but directly by Liliana Cavani in "The

Night Porter," is sidestepped here. Instead pic proffers an obvious demonstration of the unequal power wielded by men in today's society, in this case a man with a camera.

Not helping the film's cause is casting of Bergin, who delivers a near-duplicate of his villainous role of a year ago in "Sleeping With the Enemy." Young is ice-cold as the assistant d.a. Once in his clutches, she attempts to trap Bergin by pouring on the sex appeal, yet plays the latter role as a zombie.

But Borden gets good performances from her supporting cast. Black femme cop Arnetia Walker, as Young's best friend, is sent to Savannah where she's befriended by local Jewish cop Ron Orbach. Their unusual teaming is pic's best thing.

Pic is awkwardly bookended by scenes of Walker telling the story (in flashback) to investigators. This sets up one of the worst endings imaginable, a closeup of Young burning evidence against herself, that had the paying audience in Manhattan booing loudly during the end credits.

Borden creates an effective film noir look with the aid of Clint Eastwood's regular cinematographer Jack N. Green. Film wastes tenor saxophone artist Wayne Shorter in a momentary cameo performing in a Savannah night club frequented by Bergin.
— *Lawrence Cohn*

BLAME IT ON THE BELLBOY
(BRITISH-U.S.)

A Buena Vista (U.S.)-Warner Bros. (U.K.) release of a Hollywood Pictures presentation, in association with Silver Screen Partners IV, of a Steve Abbott/Jennie Howarth production. Produced by Howarth, Abbott. Directed, written by Mark Herman. Camera (Technicolor), Andrew Dunn; editor, Michael Ellis; music, Trevor Jones; solo guitar, John Williams; production design, Gemma Jackson; art direction, Peter Russell; costume design, Lindy Hemming; sound (Dolby), Peter Glossop; casting, Irene Lamb. Reviewed at Cannon Oxford Street Theater, London, Jan. 28, 1992. Running time: **77 MIN.**
Melvyn Orton . . . . . . Dudley Moore
Mike Lawton/
　Charlton Black . . . . . Bryan Brown
Maurice Horton . . . Richard Griffiths
Bettino Scarpa . . . Andreas Katsoulis
Caroline Wright . . . . . Patsy Kensit
Rosemary Horton . . Alison Steadman
Patricia . . . . Penelope Wilton
Bellboy . . . . Bronson Pinchot
Mr. Marshall . . . . Lindsay Anderson

British farce meets the

ghost of the "Carry On" series in "Blame It on the Bellboy," a lightweight ensemble comedy that should check out fast from most hospices. Ingenious plotting is let down by weak dialog and stop-go direction that largely squanders the talent involved.

Plot gets off to a promising start with three similarly named characters — Orton, Lawton and Horton — checking into a Venice hotel. Thanks to a bellboy who can't speak English, their mail gets mixed up. Realtor Dudley Moore gets a letter for hit man Bryan Brown, who gets a letter for blind-dater Richard Griffiths, who gets a letter for Moore.

Moore is soon wired up to a generator by local mobster Andreas Katsoulis; Brown thinks his target is lonely blind-dater Penelope Wilton; and Griffiths schmoozes with sexy Patsy Kensit, who's into a real estate scam rather than a roll in the hay.

Half an hour of mistaken-identity shtick later, everyone realizes the truth. Meanwhile, Griffiths' wife (Alison Steadman) flies in on a surprise visit, and Katsoulis and his hoods run amok in the Lido with a suitcase bomb.

That's where the pic's problems start. First-time director-scripter Mark Herman couldn't decide to make a breakneck farce or goofy comedy.

The Brit actors mostly phone in their performaces. Griffiths rolls his eyes with every double entendre, Moore looks cute and helpless, and Steadman has some fun with a Huddersfield accent.

Kensit is decorative and Katsoulis a by-the-numbers gonzo mafioso. Best of the bunch is Brown, and vet helmer Lindsay Anderson turns in a witty voice cameo, forever harassing Moore over the phone from Blighty.

Tech credits are pro, with attractive lensing of Venice locations by Andrew Dunn and a bouncy Vivaldiesque score by Trevor Jones. Pic's molto brief 77 minutes include conspicuous padding of humorous end captions tracing the fortunes of the eight principals. — *Derek Elley*

ALAN & NAOMI

A Triton Pictures release of a Leucadia Film Corp. Maltese Cos. presentation. Executive producer, Jonathan Pillot. Produced by David Anderson, Mark Balsam. Directed by Sterling VanWagenen. Screenplay, Jordan Horowitz, based on Myron Levoy's novel. Camera (Allied & WBS color), Paul Ryan; editor, Cari Coughlin; music, Dick Hyman; production design, George Goodridge;

costume design, Alonzo V. Wilson; sound, Rick Waddell; assistant director, Rip Murray; production manager, David Blake Hartley; associate producers, Edward M. Grant, Horowitz; co-producer, Don Schain; casting, Walken-Jaffe, Fincannon & Associates (Wilmington). Reviewed at Broadway screening room, N.Y., Jan. 21, 1992. MPAA Rating: PG. Running time: **96 MIN.**
Alan Silverman . . . . . . Lukas Haas
Naomi Kirschenbaum . Vanessa Zaoui
Sol Silverman . . . . . Michael Gross
Ruth Silverman . . . . . Amy Aquino
Also with: Kevin Connolly, Zohra Lampert, Victoria Christian, Charlie Dow.

Good intentions aren't enough to put across "Alan & Naomi," a lifeless film about the rites of passage of two Jewish children in 1944 Brooklyn. Claustrophobic feature will play much better on TV following its theatrical run.

Lukas Haas, his voice literally breaking from scene to scene, does yeoman work here but is stuck in a do-gooder role as a 14-year-old forced by his parents to befriend a virtually catatonic neighbor girl Naomi (lovely French actress Vanessa Zaoui), who was traumatized when the Nazis killed her father.

Slow-paced opening reels show Haas patiently trying to break her out of her spell, though he would much rather be out playing stickball with chums like Irish kid Kevin Connolly.

With the aid of his ventriloquist's dummy, he gets through to her as Zaoui talks through her beloved doll. Film loses much of its built-up credibility when Naomi is suddenly "normal," after Haas gets her to talk directly to him rather than through the dolls.

In similar sensitive films about breaking through to someone, like the classics "Miracle Worker" and "David & Lisa," high drama and interesting detail usually bring the viewer inside. Unfortunately, scripter Jordan Horowitz and debuting director Sterling VanWagenen fail to come up with great moments, and the dialogue is stilted.

Climax in a boiler room where Zaoui is framed by a roaring furnace is an extremely heavy-handed allusion to the Holocaust which she's escaped from to America. Sad ending does not carry the intended emotional force.

Cast is overly theatrical, though Connolly's natural performance in support is faultless. Haas does well in his monologues but is consistently forced to rise above the material. Picture was shot just before his "Rambling Rose" assignment.

TV star Michael Gross and

Amy Aquino are affecting as Haas' parents, but kindly neighbor Zohra Lampert lays it on a bit thick with her heavy accent and mannerisms. Precocious Zaoui does a good job within the limits of her gimmick role and should have no trouble graduating to adult parts.

The former DEG studio in Wilmington, N.C., is too fresh-scrubbed looking to double for vintage Brooklyn, and film's technical credits are modest. Giving it a big boost is the flavorful big band score by Dick Hyman.
— *Lawrence Cohn*

THE PIANIST
(CANADIAN)

An Aska Film Distribution release (Canada) of an Aska Film production. Produced by Yuri Yoshimura-Gagnon, Claude Gagnon. Executive producer, Yuriko Matsubara. Directed, written by Gagnon, based on Ann Ireland's novel "A Certain Mr. Takahashi." Camera (color), Sylvain Brault; editor, André Corriveau; music, André Gagnon, played by Eric Trudel; production design, Gaudeline Sauriol; costume design, Nicoletta Massonne. Reviewed at Vancouver Intl. Film Festival, Oct. 13, 1991. Running time: **113 MIN.**
Jean . . . . Gail Travers
Colette . . . . Macha Grenon
Yoshi Takahashi . . . . . . Eiji Okuda
Samantha . . . . . Dorothée Berryman
Martin . . . . Ralph Allison
Cody . . . . Maury Chaykin

A neo-romantic drama about two Canadian sisters in love with a Japanese pianist strikes a flat chord as mid-20s actresses miserably attempt to play giggly preteens. Pic's last few reels (where adult sisters define their bond) capture the warm-hearted spirit scripter/helmer Claude Gagnon attempted throughout.

English-lingo pic from Quebec helmer Gagnon will undoubtedly garner negative reviews both at home and abroad, but the picture should draw modest TV viewership.

"The Pianist" opens with Gail Travers (as anorexic Jean) and Macha Grenon (as voluptuous Colette) in their early teens, outfitted in pinafores and braces. Thesps are too mature to carry it off, weakening pic's premise.

Both Canadian actresses struggle to portray immature girls who fall for a handsome Japanese pianist (Eiji Okuda) who moves into the house across the street. (Pic is shot in Vancouver and Montreal, though story's set in Toronto).

Once the tale has Travers and

Grenon playing adults dealing with the lifelong ramifications of their mutual first love, and reconciling their bond as sisters, melodrama strikes a kinship nerve for viewers willing to make the leap of logic. Pic's latter dialogue about sisterhood, men, marriage and love affairs rings true.

Pic's one modest love scene —with the three principals groping under the sheets — is well shot. Cinematographer Sylvain Brault delivers perfectly lit visuals. Version shown at Vancouver fest was slightly out of sync.

Choppy editing jumps between past and present create an ad hoc structure. André Gagnon's clever, but sparsely used piano score, provides welcome interludes. Thesp Maury Chaykin adds comic relief in a secondary role as a family friend.

— *Suzan Ayscough*

LIGHT SLEEPER

A Mario Kassar presentation from Seven Arts. Produced by Linda Reisman. Executive producer, Kassar. Co-executive producer, Ronna Wallace. Co-producer, G. Mac Brown. Directed, written by Paul Schrader. Camera (Duart color), Ed Lachman; editor, Kristina Boden; music, Michael Been; production design, Richard Hornung; art direction, Jim Feng; set design, Jessica Lanier; sound, Doug Michael; assistant director, Glen Trotiner; casting, Ellen Chenoweth. Reviewed at Sundance Film Festival, Park City, Utah, Jan. 24, 1992. Running time: **100 MIN.**
John LeTour . . . . Willem Dafoe
Ann . . . . Susan Sarandon
Marianne . . . . Dana Delany
Robert . . . . David Clennon
Teresa . . . . Mary Beth Hurt
Tis . . . . Victor Garber
Randy . . . . Jane Adams

With his appealing new film "Light Sleeper," Paul Schrader has created a pointed companion piece to his earlier portraits of lonely outcasts ("Taxi Driver," "American Gigolo"). Contemplative and violent by turns, this quasi-thriller about a long-time drug dealer leaving the business has a great deal to recommend it but could have been significantly better had Schrader done some fresh plotting and not relied on his standby gunplay to resolve issues. This product of Carolco's low-budget Seven Arts unit has moderate b.o. prospects.

Pic's basically an intellectualized, emotionally sympathetic consideration of a drug dealer's midlife crisis. A former heavy

user himself, Le Tour (Willem Dafoe) has long worked as a drug delivery boy for Ann (Susan Sarandon), who sees the handwriting on the wall and gives up the coke trade for cosmetics.

Like other Schrader protagonists, LeTour lives alone in an ascetic apartment and constantly pens (and narrates) pensive diary entries, one of which points him in the direction of personal transcendence, Schrader-style: "I can be a good person. What a strange thing to have happen h a l f w a y through your life." With four months to go before Ann packs it in, LeTour continues to drop off packets to characters who look like pathetic 1980s throwbacks. He runs into the love of his life, Marianne (Dana Delany), who has gone clean with difficulty and now wants nothing to do with him.

When Marianne slips off the wagon to an untimely demise, script becomes more melodramatic and enters highly familiar Schrader territory in which the hero must cleanse himself through a violent, purgative act.

Climactic scenes are tensely well done and satisfying enough, but the suspicion persists that, had he pushed harder and thought more deeply, the filmmaker might have been able to arrive at a different way for LeTour's spiritual catharsis than blowing people away. Once LeTour buys a gun (in a very interesting scene), it's clear Schrader is heading down the same path he's trod many times before.

Had LeTour willed his own change of career, instead of simply being put out of a job, his mental and emotional journey might have been more dramatic, challenging and meaningful.

Still, there's plenty to like. A more seasoned, mature attitude prevails here than in Schrader's previous films, and a coda, revealing the lead's transformation, is delicate and poignant.

A superb Dafoe contributes crucially to the degree of success the film achieves. Virtually never offscreen, he combines a mellow brooding quality with a surprising awkwardness and vulnerability. In two bracing and amusing scenes he goes to a psychic (Mary Beth Hurt) to try to see into the future. Sarandon's role is a bit archly written, but she's lively and quick-witted as usual. Delany is rather bland as the old flame. Better is Jane Adams as

her sympathetic sister.

Schrader uses the story to paint a portrait of the end of the '80s, which is augmented by Ed Lachman's shadowy, evocative, vaguely sinister lensing, suggesting the threat of the unknown. Richard Hornung's production design helps make the glitz of the past decade unappealing. Michael Been's song score provides a ruminative running commentary on the action. — *Todd McCarthy*

INCIDENT AT OGLALA
(DOCU)

A Miramax release of a Seven Arts/ Spanish Fork Motion Picture Co. presentation. Produced by Arthur Chobanian. Executive producer, Robert Redford. Directed by Michael Apted. Camera (color), Maryse Alberti; editor, Susanne Rostock; musical score producers, John Trudell, Jackson Browne; associate producer, Chip Selby. Narrated by Robert Redford. Reviewed at Sundance Film Festival, Park City, Utah, Jan. 19, 1992. Running time: **89 MIN.**

This account of the 1975 Pine Ridge Indian reservation clash that left two FBI agents dead is richly resourced and informative, with narration by exec producer Robert Redford, but the Michael Apted-directed docu takes a structural approach that somewhat limits its effectiveness. Pic looks like a high interest item for tv or cable, but theatrical future appears limited.

Alleged miscarriage of justice in the case of imprisoned Native American Sioux Leonard Peltier has long been a pet cause for various music and film biz figures. Via interviews and archival footage, filmmakers reconstruct the tensions on the vast but impoverished and stormy South Dakota Sioux reservation.

When two FBI agents illegally entered Sioux land, allegedly in pursuit of a petty thief, a firefight erupted and both were slain, launching the biggest FBI manhunt in history. In the end, Peltier was sentenced to two consecutive life terms and remains in Leavenworth despite his supporters' longstanding efforts to win him a new trial.

This impassioned exposé turns up damning disclosures and makes a strong case that the government really had no case against Peltier. Coups include a recent prison interview with Peltier himself and several of the U.S. attorneys involved (FBI declined to participate).

But pic's somewhat annoying

structure leaves dangling until the end the obvious question of what happened in a device that strings the viewer along and interferes with the ability to process the considerable amount of information that comes before it.

Ultimately, pic tries to make a courtroom case on film, and it inevitably comes down to a tedious splitting of hairs about the evidence. Filmmakers save for last their trump card: that a mysterious reservation dweller came forward and confessed to Peltier relatives, but not to authorities.

— *Amy Dawes*

BLACK AND WHITE
(U.S.-RUSSIAN)

An MN Prods., Elegant Logic, Trinity Bridge/Lenfilm & Sovexportfilm production. Produced by Cornelia Burnham, Evgeny Volkov, Boris Frumin. Directed, written by Frumin. Camera (color), Vladimir Ilyin; editor, Tamara Denisova; art direction, Mary Kate Willet; costume design, Helena Besfamilny; sound, Eduard Vanunts, Michael Carmine. Reviewed at Sundance Film Festival (competition), Park City, Utah, Jan. 20, 1992. Running time: **96 MIN.**
With: Elena Schevchenko, Gilbert Giles, Patrick Godfrey, Genia Delio.

Shot in New York but edited in Leningrad, this unpolished indie effort features a tentative romance between a young Soviet émigré and a black super. Story unfolds with scarcely a nod to attitudes on interracial relations, and that's the only virtue in this otherwise inexplicable selection for Sundance's dramatic competition.

Helmer Boris Frumin, a New York University film school instructor, seems fascinated with drab and monotonous environments and dispiriting human relations. In this context, Elena Schevchenko plays the émigré whose flight from a creep b.f. leads decent young super Gilbert Giles to offer her a flat in his Lower East Side building.

Predatory landlord Patrick Godfrey starts pursuing the girl, and most of the pic involves her unhappy efforts to find rent money. Her quest finally pairs her with the landlord as prostitute.

Pic bounces abrasively over the surface of its characters. Its human relationships, save the one between the super and his ailing dad, can best be described as pathetic. Performances are barely serviceable, dialogue is artless, and footage, including one outrageous continuity gaffe, is pointless. — *Amy Dawes*

ROCK SOUP
(DOCU-B&W-16m)

A Z Films presentation of a Rock Soup production. Produced, directed, edited by Lech Kowalski. Camera (black & white, 16m), Doron Schlair; music, Chico Freeman; associate producer, Gaetano Maida; line producer, Hilary White; sound, Joshua Landis. Reviewed at Toronto Film Festival, Sept. 12, 1991. (In Sundance Film Festival.) Running time: **81 MIN.**

In "Rock Soup," helmer Lech Kowalski took his camera to New York's Lower East Side in 1989 and captured American entrepreneurial spirit in homeless folk operating a soup kitchen. Revealing cinéma vérité-style docu is ideal for special events and the small screen.

The first in a series of four features dubbed "The Rock Soup Chronicles," pic takes its title from "an ancient tradition" of starting soup with a rock. Vagrants contribute a carrot or a potato until the nourishing broth is ready.

Up to 1,000 diners a day turned up, but ironically, the kitchen no longer exists as the city fenced off the corner lot site to build a home for the elderly (which never materialized). Docu deftly captures the confrontation between soup kitchen organizers, the elderly and the community leaders who closed it.

Kowalski's hand-held camera serves as a microphone giving America's homeless a voice. It statically records colorful opinions and voyeuristically surveys local arguments. His amateur techniques and black & white stock create a home movie effect.
— *Suzan Ayscough*

POISON IVY

A New Line Cinema release. Produced by Andy Ruben. Executive producers, Melissa Goddard, Peter Morgan. Line producer, Rick Nathanson. Directed by Katt Shea Ruben. Screenplay, Katt Shea Ruben, Andy Ruben. Camera (color), Phedon Papamichael; editor, Gina Mittleman; music, Aaron Davies; production design, Virginia Lee; art direction, Hayden Yates; set decoration, Michele Munoz; costume design, Ellen Gross; sound, Bill Robbins; associate producer, Jana Marx; assistant director, J.B. Rogers; casting, Jeffrey Passero. Reviewed at Sundance Film Festival, Park City, Utah, Jan. 21, 1992. Running time: **89 MIN.**
Ivy . . . . Drew Barrymore
Sylvie Cooper . . . . . . Sara Gilbert
Darryl Cooper . . . . . Tom Skerritt
Georgie Cooper . . . . . Cheryl Ladd

An inane "Teorema" for the '90s, "Poison Ivy" will make audiences itch to get out of the theater and into the open. This laughably bad meller about a sexy teen's disruptive influence on a dysfunctional rich family might be promoted into a couple of weeks' business, but it certainly has no place at a film festival.

Katt Shea Ruben's first film away from her Roger Corman training ground has Drew Barrymore as a tarty looking high schooler who befriends the bookish, withdrawn Sara Gilbert. Before long, she's living in Gilbert's opulent Hollywood Hills home with dad Tom Skerritt, a recovering alcoholic with a decided Humbert Humbert bent, and mom Cheryl Ladd, who is slowly expiring from emphysema.

Methodically, the blonde siren conquers not only all family members, but their pet dog as well. Parading around in bedridden Mom's fancy gowns, she gets Dad so worked up he takes to the bottle again, and the two appear to get it on while Mom is lying passed out in bed next to them.

Suicide, hints of lesbianism, murder, staged accidents and every other applicable melodramatic contrivance is dragged in, playing as just ludicrous and bad rather than tantalizing or exciting. No emotion in the script is believable, so it all comes across as hokey and contrived.

Unfortunate thesps take it all very seriously, while technical aspects are emptily polished.
— *Todd McCarthy*

TECHQUA IKACHI:
LAND — MY LIFE
(DOCU)

A Mano Prods. presentation. Executive producer, Rachel Schmid. Directed, written by James Danaqyumtewa, Agnes Barmettler, Anka Schmid. Camera (color), Anka Schmid, Jurg V. Walther; super-8 camera, Danaqyumtewa; editors, Anka Schmid, Inge Schneider; sound, Albert Gasser, Ciro Cappelari, Danaqyumtewa. Reviewed at Sundance Film Festival (competition), Park City, Utah, Jan. 21, 1992. Running time: **104 MIN.**
(Hopi language; English subtitles)

An astonishing record of Hopi history, thought and culture created by a 74-year-old Hopi tribesman, a Swiss artist and a young Swiss filmmaker, "Techqua Ikachi" is an invaluable resource for those seeking to include Native American themes in dramatic works.

Via present-day interviews, remarkable archival materials and super-8 footage of tribal history shot by Hopi James Danaqyumtewa, docu tells the dramatic story of the U.S. government's systematic crushing of the Hopi nation: a puppet tribal government was installed, children were packed off to boarding schools and parcels of "private property" (an alien concept to Hopi) were offered to tribesmen willing to abandon the old ways. The Hopi resisted and went on to endure eviction from their homeland, starvation, imprisonment and exile.

Told entirely in Hopi language (with English subtitles) and scored with traditional Hopi music and songs, pic deftly explores the Hopi ways, revealing a unique, and uniquely intelligent, way of life. Magical glimpses of traditional, disappearing ceremonies and desert landscapes of beauty and subtlety communicate a history of this land quite profoundly. — *Amy Dawes*

JO-JO AT THE GATE OF LIONS

A Nana Films production. Produced, directed, written &· edited by Britta Sjogren. Camera (black & white), Greg Watkins; music, Jonathan Sampson; art direction, Adam Braff; sound, Rory Kelly; assistant director, Caveh Zahedi. Reviewed at Sundance Film Festival, Park City, Utah, Jan. 23, 1992. Running time: **96 MIN.**
Jo-Jo . . . . Lorie Marino
Jon . . . . Chris Shearer
Luke . . . . David Schultz

Passivity, the driving force in "Jo-Jo at the Gate of Lions," is the only thing that will keep most people in their seats after the first hour. Dreamy, poetically charged meditation on a young woman haunted by a mystical voice, feature debut by L.A. filmmaker Britta Sjogren manages to weave a lightly captivating spell before it dissolves into tedious self-indulgence.

Short treatment might have been more successful, since even at feature length, pic is unlikely to see exhibition outside the festival and museum circuit.

Lorie Marino plays gamine Jo-Jo who, like a modern-day Joan of Arc, is guided toward spiritual sublimation by a gravelly E.T.-like voice prompting her to behave in contrary ways.

Jo-Jo's quirky passivity also makes her a magnet for boorish men, and before long she's being dominated by a creepy entrepreneur (David Shultz) who talks her into taking a phone sex job. He then falls for her and harasses the indifferent Jo-Jo to the point of tedium.

Events unfold without point of view so that one feels trapped in an arid and inactive world in which the protagonist struggles weakly, rather like a fly buzzing against a pane of glass.

Engagingly photographed by Greg Watkins in a black & white vérité style, pic suffers from poor sound quality in which street noise often muffles the dialogue.
— *Amy Dawes*

FATHERS & SONS

An Addis/Wechsler presentation. Produced by Jon Kilik. Executive producers, Nick Wechsler, Keith Addis. Directed, written by Paul Mones. Camera (color), Ron Fortunato; editor, Janice Keuhnelian; music, Mason Daring; production design, Eve Cauley; associate producer, David Pomier; casting, Marcia Shulman. Reviewed at Sundance Film Festival (competition), Park City, Utah, Jan. 18, 1992. Running time: **99 MIN.**
With: Jeff Goldblum, Rory Cochrane, Ellen Greene, Rosanna Arquette.

Struggle of modern fathers and sons to connect gets a strange twist in this beachtown melodrama: Mental telepathy literally saves the day, but pic is dampened by unauthentic, unconvincing elements and a somber tone.

Jeff Goldblum stars as a moody type who quit a demanding filmmaking job and runs a bookstore on the Jersey shore. Everything about son Rory Cochrane is at odds with his unlikely companions: thrill-seeking young lowbrows who lead him to drugs, crime and under-the-boardwalk sex.

Those pals, however, seem present mostly for contrast with Dad's educated but restless friends. Director Paul Mones cuts between scenes of dad and son's parallel lives, apparently to show the essential sameness despite the distance.

Problem is that he seems no more adept at navigating emotional territory than his protagonists, and pic operates on a forced, awkward and cerebral level. Too soft-focused to be a thriller, pic nonetheless brings in the lurking specter of a serial killer whose attack brings father and son together.

Mones overburdens the climax with an elaborate setup involving drugs, mental telepathy and a bizarre New Age book, to the point that it's hard to tell whether the breakthrough ESP connection is metaphor or reality. In any case, the journey toward openness isn't convincing.

Goldblum gives a complex, understated performance that more or less holds the film together. Rosanna Arquette makes a minor appearance in a daffy role as a flirtatious fortune-teller.

Cinematographer Ron Fortunato's work is excellent, and production values are solid in this indie effort that world premiered at Sundance. — *Amy Dawes*

WHERE ARE WE?
OUR TRIP THROUGH AMERICA
(DOCU)

A Telling Pictures production. Produced, directed by Jeffrey Friedman, Rob Epstein. Camera (color), Jean de Segonzac; editor, Ned Bastille; music, Daniel Licht; sound, Mark Roy; associate producers, Sharon Wood, Pam Moskow. Reviewed at Sundance Film Festival, Park City, Utah, Jan. 19, 1992. Running time: **73 MIN.**

Oscar-winning documentary filmmakers Jeffrey Friedman and Rob Epstein ("Common Threads") have turned out a sketchy, unfocused, unsatisfying effort trying to put their fingers on the pulse of America. Curiosity value makes "Where Are We?" a playable item for TV, but it feels like twice its 73-minute length.

Announcing upfront, "We're two gay men from San Francisco," Epstein (who also made Oscar-winning "The Times of Harvey Milk") and Friedman set out on an 18-day drive to the deep South shortly after the Gulf War's conclusion. They picked the South because it seemed so "foreign" to them, and yet deeply American.

To pointed questions such as "Are you happy? Do you have any regrets? What are you afraid of? What are your hopes for the future?", random citizens' answers are rather sad and scary, given the ignorance, limited world perspectives, lack of ambition and nonexistent curiosity beyond their immediate area of concern.

Pic careens from subject to subject so wildly that the combination of specifics remains just that and does not coalesce into an edifying broader picture.

Film is part "search for America," part unearthing of the grotesque (one man has built a mini-

ature Graceland for his Elvis-obsessed wife), part rumination by the filmmakers on their own lack of roots and part investigation into gay America.

In the latter context, camera visits a gay bar for servicemen near Camp Lejeune, as well as a home for AIDS patients in New Orleans. These sequences seem like part of a different film, perhaps the one Friedman and Epstein should have made.

Overall, film treats its subjects in very shallow fashion, and one is struck by the inability of the people depicted, as well as the filmmakers, to articulate their thoughts. — *Todd McCarthy*

FINAL ANALYSIS

A Warner Bros. release of a Witt/Thomas production in association with Roven-Cavallo Entertainment. Produced by Charles Roven, Paul Junger Witt, Tony Thomas. Executive producers, Richard Gere, Maggie Wilde. Co-producers, John Solomon, Ted Kurdyla. Directed by Phil Joanou. Screenplay, Wesley Strick; story by Robert Berger, Strick. Camera (Technicolor), Jordan Cronenweth; editor, Thom Noble; music, George Fenton; production design, Dean Tavoularis; art direction, Angelo Graham; set decoration, Bob Nelson; costume design, Aude Bronson-Howard; sound (Dolby), Lee Orloff; special visual effects, Dream Quest Images; visual effects supervisor, Hoyt Yeatman; associate producer, Kelley Smith; assistant director, Pat Kehoe; casting, David Rubin. Reviewed at Warner Bros. Studios, Burbank, Calif., Feb. 3, 1992. MPAA Rating: R. Running time: **124 MIN.**

Isaac Barr	Richard Gere
Heather Evans	Kim Basinger
Diana Baylor	Uma Thurman
Jimmy Evans	Eric Roberts
Mike O'Brien	Paul Guilfoyle
Detective Huggins	Keith David
Alan Lowenthal	Robert Harper
Pepe Carrero	Agustin Rodriguez
D.A. Brakhage	Harris Yulin

Succeeding much better than most attempts at reproducing old-fashioned Hollywood thrillers, "Final Analysis" is a crackling good psychological melodrama in which star power and slick surfaces are used to potent advantage. Despite improbable details, unusual tale is told convincingly enough to lure the viewer in, and tantalizing double-crosses mount right up to the eerie final scene. This is a Warner Bros. release even Jack Warner could love and looks like a solid late-winter performer.

From such major factors as plotting and casting to the more detailed matters of scoring, art direction and even the manipulation of real locations, pic embraces the old conventions with a bearhug and revives them in the process.

In the course of treating a patient, Uma Thurman, San Francisco psychiatrist Richard Gere takes the unusual step of meeting the young woman's older sister, who may know more about certain events in Thurman's past than the subject herself.

Sis turns out to be Kim Basinger, who gives Gere critical tidbits about her sister's troubled childhood and then has no trouble overcoming his tenuous sense of professional ethics about bedding a patient's sibling.

An aloof workaholic who complains that the downside of psy-

chiatry is hearing so many people's thoughts that "they stop surprising you," Gere becomes hopelessly ensnared in his secret affair with Basinger, who in turn promises to find a way out of her marriage.

Given the genre, and her husband's unstinting creepiness, the method she employs is not surprising, and sympathies ride with her in a murder trial in which Gere's best friend is the defense attorney, his closest colleague is an expert witness, he has slept with the accused and her sister is his patient.

But with the trial's conclusion, the vise tightens, and Basinger assumes the full dimensions of a Warner bad girl that Joan Crawford would have killed to play.

Screenwriter Wesley Strick, currently very hot after "Cape Fear" and with "Batman Returns" in the wings, sold this screenplay, his first, to WB years ago. It's a pastiche, with elements of numerous old films, including the S.F.-set "Maltese Falcon" and "Vertigo" stirred together, but still a strong example of its type, with plausibly attracted leads, colorful supporting parts and a number of juicy 180-degree plot turns.

Greatest hurdle for some viewers may be getting past the idea of Gere as a respected psychiatrist, and the intellectual side of his character is shortchanged. But the camera really goes for him somehow, and his unusual, passive, catlike masculinity, cloaked once again in Armani, plays very well here.

Similarly, Basinger is mostly surface effect, but it's considerable here, as she persuasively puts across her emotions as suffering wife, desirous lover, mental defective and lethal criminal. Befitting the film's high style, her wardrobe is stunning.

Difficult as it is to imagine Thurman playing anyone's plain sister, she is dressed down to successfully carry out that task, and to sketch a deeply neurotic woman. Giving his "Star '80" character a run for his money, bulked-up Roberts creates a memorable scumbag as the corrupt builder married to Basinger.

After the dismal "State of Grace," director Phil Joanou has rebounded splendidly, keeping the storytelling taut and creating several fine set pieces in the process, even if the running time comes in a bit too long.

Physical production is one of the film's major stars, as lenser Jordan Cronenweth and production designer Dean Tavoularis have conspired to create a darkly shadowed, outrageously attractive world that outdoes even San Francisco's natural beauties.

Not willing to leave well enough alone, and treading a bit heavily on Hitchcock territory, filmmakers have put a crucial lighthouse right under the Golden Gate Bridge, where there is no such thing. Achievements of special effects and matte artists in making this look believable are beyond reproach, but one can only imagine future tourists searching in vain for the nonexistent tower.

Putting the final melodramatic flourish on the proceedings is composer George Fenton, whose vigorous underscoring agreeably recalls nearly everything Bernard Herrmann and Miklos Rozsa ever did. — *Todd McCarthy*

MEDICINE MAN

A Buena Vista release of an Andrew G. Vajna presentation from Hollywood Pictures & Cinergi Prods. Produced by Vajna, Donna Dubrow. Executive producer, Sean Connery. Line producer, Beau Marks. Directed by John McTiernan. Screenplay, Tom Schulman, Sally Robinson, story by Schulman. Camera (Technicolor, Panavision widescreen), Donald McAlpine; editor, Michael R. Miller; music, Jerry Goldsmith; production design, John Krenz Reinhart Jr.; art direction, Don Diers, Jesus Buenrostro, Marlisi Storchi (Brazilian Indian crew); set decoration, Enrique Estevez; costume design, Marilyn Vance-Straker, Rita Murtimho (Brazilian Indian crew); sound (Dolby), Douglas B. Arnold; Brazilian Indian choreographer, Maria Fatima Toledo; special effects supervisors, John Thomas, Laurencio Cordero "Chovy"; assistant directors, Tom Mack, Sebastian Silva (Mexico); 2nd unit director, Fred Waugh; casting, Bonnie Timmermann. Reviewed at Avco Cinema, L.A., Feb. 5, 1992. MPAA Rating: PG-13. Running time: **106 MIN.**
Dr. Robert Campbell . . Sean Connery
Dr. Rae Crane . . . . . Lorraine Bracco
Dr. Miguel Ornega . . . . . Jose Wilker
Tanaki . . . . . . Rodolfo De Alexandre
Medicine Man . . Angelo Barra Moreira

This "Medicine Man" conjured up the wrong prescription. An indelicate attempt to create some "African Queen"-style magic while curing cancer and saving the rainforests in the bargain, this jumbo-budget two-character piece suffers from a very weak script and a lethal job of miscasting. Andrew Vajna's Cinergi Prods. stumbles in the starting blocks with its debut effort, which doesn't look to last long theatrically.

"Dead Poets Society" Oscar-winner Tom Schulman rode the crest of Hollywood's big-spending spree for original scripts when he sold what was then called

"The Stand" for about $3 million. An additional $1 million or so was spent on rewrites (by Sally Robinson and an uncredited Tom Stoppard) that were later deemed necessary.

Rarely has so much been laid out for so little. Tale is a frightfully predictable one about temperamental opposites who inevitably come to respect and, it seems, love one another through the course of tackling a tough piece of work. Rarely has one less wanted two romantic leads to end up together than in this concoction. For two scientists, Sean Connery and Lorraine Bracco have no chemistry at all.

Pony-tailed and bearded, Connery portrays a maverick biochemist who's been working in the Amazon for six years when his sponsoring company sends a researcher to his remote outpost to check up on him.

Pic's problems start right there, for the woman in question is played by Bracco, whose screeching New York accent is so pronounced that Connery immediately starts calling her "Bronx," and whose manner is so abrasive that it's a wonder Connery doesn't just toss her to the crocodiles.

While Connery tries to explain that he believes he's isolated a cure for cancer in a strain of wild flowers that only grows 100 feet up in the towering tropical trees, Bracco just brays, screams and argues with him. Allegedly a top scientist herself with degrees from three international universities, she would appear never to have crossed the Hudson, complaining and kvetching and carrying on so that one might imagine she was playing the lead in "Rhoda Goes to the Jungle."

In search of the rare blossoms, Connery takes Bracco on a major E-ticket ride up a series of counterbalanced rope riggings to the treetops, affording a breathtaking view of the jungle. Nonetheless, their personal story remains grounded by banality relieved only by a trek through the forest that sees Bracco indulging in some high-spirited substance abuse and getting stuck on a branch hundreds of feet above a gorge.

Climax brings the relentlessness of the rainforest's destruction to loggerheads with the urgent need preserve its many, and in some cases unknown, resources. In the process, it also points up the difficulty of making a film about this part of the world that makes something other than the obvious points

about greed and the recklessness of civilization in dismantling the wilderness.

The finger of blame can be pointed in many directions. Trying to show that he can do something other than action, which he does so well, helmer John McTiernan has not proved that he can. Also on board as exec producer, Connery remains watchable, as always, but these are not two of his better hours.

Bracco, very good up until now in New York-based pics, should presumably think twice in future about leaving town. Jerry Goldsmith's score is thunderingly overbearing. And Vajna had better read those scripts more carefully. — *Todd McCarthy*

TOUS LES MATINS DÙ MONDE
(EVERY MORNING OF THE WORLD)
(FRENCH)

A Bac Films release of a Film par Film-Divali Films-D.D. Prods.-Sedif-FR3 Films-Paravision Intl.-CNC-Canal Plus co-production. Produced by Jean-Louis Livi. Directed by Alain Corneau. Screenplay, Corneau, Pascal Quignard, based on Quignard's novel. Camera (color), Yves Angelo; editor, Marie-Joseph Yoyotte; music performed, directed by Jordi Savall; musical consultant-instructor, Jean-Louis Charbonnier; set design, Bernard Vezat; costumes, Corinne Jorry; sound, Gerard Lamps, Anne Le Campion; assistant director, Jerome Navarro. Reviewed at Max Linder Panorama, Paris, Dec. 31, 1991. Running time: **114 MIN.**
Saint Colombe . . Jean-Pierre Marielle
Marin Marais . . . . Gérard Depardieu
Madeleine . . . . Anne Brochet
Marais
  (young man) . . Guillaume Depardieu
Mme. de Saint Colombe . Caroline Sihol
Toinette . . . . Carole Richert
  Also with: Violaine Lacroix, Nadege Teron, Myriam Boyer, Yves Gasc, Jean-Claude Dreyfus, Yves Lambrecht.

A gorgeous, painterly meditation on the inspirations and aspirations of art, "Tous les Matins du Monde" is a feast for eyes and ears that's been doing steady local biz since its mid-December bow. Despite a leisurely pace, film's magnificent baroque score and standout performances could lure the more elite ranks of arthouse patrons worldwide. Casting of Gérard Depardieu and his son also will generate curiosity.

Director Alain Corneau's account of two real-life 17th-century French musicians brilliantly conveys his love for the *viola de gamba*, a stringed instrument that was all but obsolete before

its revival in the 1960s.

Film is bracketed by scenes of celebrated composer Marin Marais (a bewigged and powdered Depardieu) who, with the wisdom of old age, laments that his fame and accomplishments are nothing compared to the skill and devotion of Saint Colombe, his now dead teacher, a man who shunned the limelight and lived for music alone.

Permanently haunted by the loss of his wife, the gruff, uncompromising Saint Colombe (Jean-Pierre Marielle) builds a modest backyard shed in which he plays his instrument practically every waking hour.

When the youthful Marais (Guillaume Depardieu) asks to be taken on as a pupil, Saint Colombe does so only at the pleading of his two daughters; the elder (Anne Brochet) falls in love with the ambitious youth.

Their romance ends badly, and Marais pursues his dream of exalted social status at Versailles. Saint Colombe goes on playing in his shed where he appears to be visited by his dead wife, conjured from the tomb by the sincerity of his music and the inconsolable depth of his devotion.

Recorded *viola de gamba* performances by Jordi Savall, who helped revive the instrument, are captured with a moving blend of digital crispness, tempered by emotion.

Cinematographer Yves Angelo pays tribute to light and shadow in the manner of the paintings of Georges de La Tour. Versailles glamor during Louis XIV's reign is kept on the periphery, the better to play up Marais' simple country existence in harmony with nature.

Elder Depardieu delivers a resonant perf, and Guillaume, *fils*, makes an honorable debut. Brochet is exquisite in the flower of youth and convincing in her illness and decline.

But Marielle's towering performance steals the show. When, near death, the man who always refused to publish his compositions accepts a visit from his former pupil, all of the sacrifices that art demands seem concentrated in one modest wooden room. Pic is almost daunting in its carefully composed artfulness, but its rewards are undeniable.

Winner of the 1991 Louis Delluc Prize, pic has been nominated for 11 Césars.

— *Lisa Nesselson*

HA ETT UNDERBART LIV
(HAVE A WONDERFUL LIFE)
(SWEDISH)

A Sonet Film presentation of a Sonet-Svensk Filmindustri-Swedish Film Institute production. Executive producer, Hans Lönnerheden. Produced, written by Hans Iveberg. Directed by Ulf Malmros. Camera (color), Mats Olofsson; editor, Thomas Samuelsson; music, Studio 2; production design, Eric Johnson; sound, Mats Lindskog. Reviewed at Spegeln Cinema, Stockholm, Jan. 27, 1992. Running time: **94 MIN.**
With: Per Löfberg, Lina Perned, Kjell Bergqvist, Anneli Martini, Reuben Sallmander, Björn Holmden, Johan Humlesjö, Kare Mölder, Tova Magnusson, Kim Anderzon, Charlie Elvegard, Stig Ossian Ericson.

Charm and snappy direction compensate for a thin and illogical screenplay in this love story aimed at teenagers, an audience "Have a Wonderful Life" will probably reach, while adult auds will be elusive.

Peter and Hanna meet on the road from northern Sweden to Stockholm. He's been AWOL from the military since he discovered his g.f. in the city is cheating on him. Hanna is traveling with her father, with whom she recently was reunited.

In the course of this romantic road movie, the trio meet various characters and endure various disasters. Hanna and Peter fall in love (there's a lengthy lovemaking scene that could push an R rating towards an NC-17). They argue, but all is resolved in a happy ending in Stockholm.

The young lead actors are appealing. Helmer Malmros, who has made several music videos and commercials, knows how to move his film. Despite a thin story, gaps in logic and the cliché adult characters, pic has appeal enough. — *Gunnar Rehlin*

CONTE D'HIVER
(A WINTER'S TALE)
(FRENCH)

A Les Films du Losange release & production. Produced by Margaret Menegoz. Directed, written by Eric Rohmer. Camera (color), Luc Pages; editor, Mary Stephen; music, Sebastien Erms; costumes, Pierre-Jean Larroque; sound, Pascal Ribier. Reviewed at Sept Parnassiens, Paris, Jan. 30, 1992. Running time: **113 MIN.**
Felicie . . . . Charlotte Very
Charles . Frederic Van Den Driessche
Maxence . . . . Michel Voletti
Loic . . . . Herve Furic
Elise . . . . Ava Loraschi
La Mere . . . . Christiane
Also with: Rosette, Jean-Luc Revol, Haydee Caillot, Jean-Claude Biette.

"Conte d'Hiver" is an absorbing romantic melodrama about an ordinary beautician who, with 5-year-old daughter in tow, is obliged to sort out her feelings for three lovers. Eric Rohmer's second entry in a series on the seasons should generate strong b.o. in international art houses with its decisive heroine, surprise ending and no-nonsense talk on relationships.

Rohmer's well-known chat knack is intact. Small, uncluttered sets and tight lensing help focus on the naturalistic script, which occasionally takes a religious turn.

The 71-year-old helmer warms up his December story with a quick opening montage of summer snapshots: blonde Felicie blissfully happy with big-shouldered Charles on a Brittany beach.

Cut to Paris five years later in mid-December. Felicie is having an affair with Maxence, her beefy boss, while also living with Loic, a gentle librarian. To this love triangle Rohmer adds an original wrinkle: Felicie says she's never gotten over Charles, whom she hasn't seen since their chance beach encounter because of a simple mistake in address.

Rohmer starts laying out these love complications with a show stopper. In the beauty parlor one morning, Maxence tells Felicie he has finally left his wife and is moving his shop immediately to a small city. Will she and her daughter join him there?

Charlotte Very, as Felicie, is quietly outstanding as she hesitates over a life change, weighs her chances, and then embraces her boss/lover. Subsequent split with Loic is a modern classic in breakup scenes.

At work in the provinces, she's soon out of sorts as a beauty parlor manageress. With her daughter in front of a Christmas creche at a local cathedral, Felicie has a small-time epiphany: moving in with Maxence, who increasingly reveals his macho side, was a bad idea.

A blink of the eye and Felicie is back in Paris with the excruciatingly noble Loic, who is too intellectual by far for her. At this point the plot could fall apart, except for Rohmer's well-crafted storytelling. Now just friends, they attend Shakespeare's "A Winter's Tale," where Felicie is moved to tears when a statue of a loved one miraculously comes to life. Pic's joyful surprise ending is spellbinding.

Former Rohmer actresses Marie Riviere and Rosette appear in cameos. Excellent tech credits include a crystal-clear soundtrack. — *Lee Lourdeaux*

TIMEBOMB

An MGM/UA release from MGM of a Raffaella production. (Intl. sales, Dino De Laurentiis Communications). Produced by Raffaella De Laurentiis. Directed, written by Avi Nesher. Camera (color), Anthony B. Richmond; editor, Isaac Sehayek; music, Patrick Leonard; production design, Greg Pruss, Curtis A. Schnell; art direction, Robert E. Lee; costume design, Jill Ohanneson; visual consultant, William Elliott; sound (Dolby), Robert Anderson Jr.; assistant director, Artist W. Robinson; production manager, Joseph C. Cavalier; visual effects, Perpetual Motion Pictures, Richard Malzahn (supervisor); special make-up effects, Todd Masters; stunt coordinator, Paul Baxley; co-producer, Mike Petzold; line producer, Anthony G. La Marca; associate producer, Hester Hargett; casting, Craig Campobasso. Reviewed on MGM/UA vidcassette, N.Y. MPAA Rating: R. Running time: **96 MIN.**
Eddy Kay . . . . Michael Biehn
Dr. Anna Nolmar . . . . . Patsy Kensit
Blue . . . . Tracy Scoggins
Phillips . . . . Robert Culp
Col. Taylor . . . . Richard Jordan
Det. Sanchez . . Raymond St. Jacques
Also with: Billy Blanks, Jim Maniaci, Steven J. Oliver, Ray Mancini, Carlos Palomino, Harvey Fisher, Kate Mitchell.

Released regionally to theaters last November, "Timebomb" is a breathless sci-fi thriller that isn't original or large-scale enough to compete with the big pictures, but good action scenes and above-average cast should generate a favorable homevideo response.

Israeli director Avi Nesher, remaker of the classic "She" in '82 with Sandahl Bergman, concocts a paranoia plot line here. Similar to "Jacob's Ladder," a guy (Michael Biehn) who supposedly died in the Vietnam war is actually running around hallucinating.

It turns out he was part of a CIA experiment run by heavy Richard Jordan that used futuristic aversion therapy to create soulless operatives. Dated Cold War story material has Jordan trying to assassinate a pol who has vowed to sit on the CIA.

Biehn is working as a watchmaker and goes to customer Patsy Kensit for help after finding out she's a shrink. They're thrown together on the lam when Jordan's operatives are ordered to kill Biehn. Trail leads to the original research facility where Biehn relives the mind-altering experiment.

Nesher throws in snippets of story between vigorous action scenes, notable for quality stuntwork. Characters are pretty much one-dimensional, though Biehn engenders some sympathy, and Kensit is sexy as usual.

Casting Tracy Scoggins as a glamorous hit woman pays off, but ex-boxers Ray Mancini and Carlos Palomino are wasted (given zero lines to read) as two of her interchangable teammates.

Pic is the last of Raymond St. Jacques (as a dogged cop), who died in 1990. — *Lawrence Cohn*

QUANDO ERAVAMO REPRESSI
(WHEN WE WERE REPRESSED)
(ITALIAN)

A Columbia TriStar Films Italia release of a Numero Uno Intl. production. Produced by Claudio Bonivento. Directed, written by Pino Quartullo, based on his play. Camera (Technicolor), Roberto Meddi; editor, Antonio D'Onofrio; music, Stefano Reali, Sergio Cammariere, Massimo Nunzi; art direction, Mariangela Capuano; costumes, Ambra Danon; sound (Dolby), Gianni Zampagni. Reviewed at Quirinale Cinema, Rome, Jan. 30, 1992. Running time: **100 MIN.**
Isabella . . . . . . Francesca D'Aloja
Federico . . . . . Alessandro Gassman
Petra . . Lucrezia Lante Della Rovere
Massimiliano . . . . . . Pino Quartullo
The sexologist . . . . Vittorio Gassman

Coming in on a wave of successful stage-to-screen transfers, Pino Quartullo makes a solid feature bow with his hit play "When We Were Repressed." Pic would have benefited from further opening-out but zips along thanks to the fine cast of up-and-comers, all repeating their stage roles.

Seriously sexy comedy raised a ruckus when Italo censors (objecting more to subject than content) slapped a "no under-18s" tag on it. Subsequent appeal was won, and film has since gone out unrestricted, the uproar kick-starting lively Italo b.o. Pic should travel well with Euro playdates and fest slots elsewhere.

Action centers on two couples intent on banishing bedroom boredom. Uptight middle-classers Francesca D'Aloja and Alessandro Gassman have lost their sexual appetites so they consult a stuttering sexologist (a delightfully verbose cameo from papa Vittorio Gassman).

They then answer an ad for a weekend ménage à quatre with Quartullo and Lucrezia Lante Della Rovere, crass boutique owners whose store fronts as a meeting place for swinging couples.

Foursome rendezvous in adjoining rooms of a country hotel, and big class-distinction laughs are drawn out of the encounter between the seasoned sexual panthers and their prim prey. Ice is broken and, after some preliminary pairing off and much frank sex talk, all hit the sheets for a steamy sack scene.

Afterglow dims when Quartullo breaks out in an inexplicable rash. Accusations are made, skeletons come out of closets and the afternoon games suddenly look sordid. They split up and form same-sex pairs, opting for abstinence.

Pic goes slightly awry here as they replace sex with study, meditation, religion and obsessive order. Quartullo shows this with set pieces that flaunt their theatrical origins, looking contrived and unnatural in closeup. A moralistic tone creeps in and hangs around through pic's finale.

First-rate cast's energy and affection for the material shine through to gloss over pic's flaws. Quartullo handles events confidently and shows cinematic flair, especially in a sexy, well-choreographed shopping routine introing the boutique owners.

Sharply lensed, seamlessly edited pic has a snappy pace propelled by good use of Sergio Cammariere's songs. Sex scenes imply more than they show, and offshore censorship should pose no more problems than the average Almodóvar romp.

— David Rooney

SANGATSU NO RAION
(MARCH COMES IN LIKE A LION)
(JAPANESE)

A Yazaki Hitoshi Group production. (Intl. sales: Uplink, Tokyo.) Produced by Takashi Nishimura. Directed by Hitoshi Yazaki. Screenplay, Hiroshi Miyazaki, Sachio Ono, Yazaki; camera (color), Isao Ishii; editor, Ryuichi Takano, Yoshitaro Ogasawara; music, the Bolivian Rockers; art direction, Shuji Mizobe; sound, Akihiko Suzuki; assistant director, Shinichi Ishii. Reviewed at London Film Festival (3 Continents: Asia section), Nov. 8, 1991. Running time: **118 MIN.**
With: Yoshiko Yura, Cho Bang-ho, Koen Okumura, Shoko Saito, Kiyomi Ito.

Ten years after his "Afternoon Breezes," New Wave Japanese helmer Hitoshi Yazaki finally re-emerges with his second pic, "March Comes in Like a Lion." Quirky love story of sibling incest may win a following on alternative circuits, but non-buffs will be studying their watches after the first hour.

Sister and brother are Ice (Yoshiko Yura), who carries all her possessions in an icebox and sports an eye-catching line in mini-skirts, and Haruo (Cho Bangho), a painful introvert with designer sunglasses. One day she visits him in the hospital, where he's suffering from amnesia, and tells him she's his lover. They move into a building due for demolition, and tragedy unravels.

Rest of the pic is a free-form succession of small incidents: larking around the city streets, chats with an old couple about love and marriage and Ice's obsession with fairy tales. She earns some yen as a part-time hooker, he as a demolition worker.

Yazaki gives the tale a dreamy, fragile grace, mostly by playing the ditzy, childlike charms of the diminutive Yura off against the spaced-out, lanky Cho. The effect soon palls, however, as the script goes in circles, and Yazaki seems to forget the Japanese for "cut." Shafts of humor are rare.

Cinematographer Isao Ishii comes up with some striking compositions of modern, soulless Tokyo, lensed with almost classical balance. Blowup from 16m is okay. — Derek Elley

SCANNERS III: THE TAKEOVER
(CANADIAN)

A Malofilm Distribution release (Canada) & Republic Pictures release (U.S.) of a Malofilm Group production. Produced by Rene Malo. Executive producers, Pierre David, Renald Pare. Directed by Christian Duguay. Screenplay, B.J. Nelson, Julie Richard, David Preston, Malo (based on original characters created by David Cronenberg). Camera (color), Hughes De Haeck; editor, Yves Langlois; music, Marty Simon; production design, Michael Joy; art direction, Lynn Trout; set decoration, Andre Chamberland; costume design, Laurie Drew; special makeup, Mike Maddi; stunt coordinator, Peter Cox; sound, Gabor Vadnay; assistant director, Michael Williams. Reviewed at Cineplex Odeon cinema Dauphin, Montreal, Jan. 27, 1992. MPAA Rating: R. Running time: **101 MIN.**
Helena Monet . . Liliana Komorowska
Joyce Stone . . . . Valerie Valois
Alex Monet . . . . Steve Parrish
Dr. Elton Monet . . . . Collin Fox
Michael (the lawyer) . . . Daniel Pilon
Charlie . . . . Michel Perron
Dr. Baumann . . . . Harry Hill
Also with: Christopher Macabe, Michael Copeman, Claire Cellucci, Charles Landry, Chip Chuipka, Jean Frenette, Sith Sekae.

Schlock fans should be delighted with yet another brain-bursting sequel, "Scanners III: The Takeover," a rather comic chapter in the trilogy which will have a quick stint in theaters before its homevid destination.

Helmer Christian Duguay (who directed "Scanners II: The New Order") has once again squeezed a technically slick, relatively mindless thriller out of David Cronenberg's original characters who telekinetically scan minds to control or destroy bodies. Scanner trademark is to explode victims' heads with a big scan.

In this part, a mild-mannered scanner is transformed into a vicious, power-hungry vixen (played to the hilt by Polish-born thesp Liliana Komorowska) when she takes an untested drug to alleviate scanners' migraines.

Drug-crazed femme wreaks havoc on anyone who tries to thwart her takeover of her father's pharmaceutical empire. In perhaps a twisted metaphor for women clawing their way up the corporate ladder, she murders her father, his lawyer, a doctor, and she also enlists a band of renegade scanners to help her attain world dominance.

In a humorous subplot, Helena discovers she can scan and control normal citizens via TV. Hence, she buys a global sports network and attempts to brain-drain the viewers.

Enter the savior scanner: Her brother is forced to return from a Thai Buddhist monastery to save the day and effectively slay the monster.

Violence is less graphic and more creative than in the previous outing. Once again, all tech credits are excellent and thesps do as much as possible with roles of interminably good or hideously evil caricatures.

— Suzan Ayscough

LES CLÉS DU PARADIS
(THE KEYS TO PARADISE)
(FRENCH)

A UGC release of a Messine Prods.-TF1 Films co-production. Produced by Alain Terzian. Directed by Philippe De Broca. Screenplay, De Broca, with Alexandre Jardin. Camera (color), Jean-Yves Le Menier; editor, Hugues Darmois; music, Francis Lai; costume design, Sophie Marcou, Sylvie Marcou; set design, Tony Egry; sound, Jean-Charles Ruault; production manager, Philippe Lievre; assistant director, Paul Gueu. Reviewed at UGC Danton cinema, Paris, Dec. 3, 1991. Running time: **100 MIN.**

Paul . . . . Gérard Jugnot
Gaspard . . . . Pierre Arditi
Marie . . . . Philippine Leroy-Beaulieu
Isabelle . . . . Fanny Cottençon
Boileau . . . . François Perrot
Olga . . . . Micheline Dax

Only viewers awakened from 20-year comas will find Philippe De Broca's "Les Clés du Paradis" the least bit current in style or content. Heavy-handed whimsy about brothers' identity swap is passable tube fare.

A self-centered author (Pierre Arditi) running short on alimony and inspiration escapes from Paris to Brittany to visit his clumsy younger brother (Gérard Jugnot), a French teacher whose adored wife has been secretly sleeping with the author for years.

Fed up with their respective ruts, the literary celeb and the unassuming nebbish decide to trade lives — jobs, finances and womenfolk included. Sure enough, the suave brother becomes an instant klutz, and the meek brother not only wins over the author's gorgeous g.f. but lands a lucrative deal for his first novel. Running gags revolve around ghost writers, bird excrement and infidelity.

Arditi is practically breathless with forced enthusiasm, and Philippine Leroy-Beaulieu gamely plays a strange hybrid: a doormat with a mind of her own. De Broca even returns to his "King of Hearts" territory by putting Arditi in an insane asylum where he flourishes by faking amnesia.

Early fantasy sequences display satiric bite, but, as plot grows more contrived, pic sinks under its own gooey sentiment. Summer lensing in scenic Brittany is a plus. — Lisa Nesselson

THE LUNATIC

A Triton Pictures release of an Island Pictures presentation of a Paul Heller/John Pringle production. Produced by Heller, Pringle. Executive producers, Chris Blackwell, Dan Genetti. Directed by Lol Creme. Screenplay, Anthony C. Winkler, based on his novel. Camera (CFI color), Richard Greatrex; editor, Michael Connell; music, Wally Badarou; art direction, Giorgio Ferrari; costume design, Patricia Griffiths; sound (Dolby), Kim Ornitz; assistant director, Laura Groppe; co-producer, Matthew Binns; associate producers, Kathy Zebrowski, Marnée K. Bie. Reviewed at Broadway screening room, N.Y., Feb. 3, 1992. MPAA Rating: R. Running time: **93 MIN.**
Inga . . . . Julie T. Wallace
Aloysius . . . . Paul Campbell
Busha . . . . Reggie Carter
Service . . . . Carl Bradshaw

"**T**he Lunatic" is an annoyingly cute fable that seems to have popped from a time capsule dating back to the agressively life-affirming era of "King of Hearts" and "Harold and Maude." Jamaican-lensed feature's chances to win similar cult audiences are poor.

Novelist-scripter Anthony C. Winkler turns a colorful phrase but billboards all his themes unsubtly in this tale of an innocent black lad Aloysius (Paul Campbell in a winning interpretation) who talks to flora and fauna.

Everyone brands him a lunatic, but visiting German photographer Inga (British thesp Julie T. Wallace) makes him her love slave. Soon a menage à trois is set up when she takes a fancy to a butcher (Carl Bradshaw).

As one of many recent films with an interracial plot, pic defuses this controversial sexual theme by casting of the gargantuan actress Wallace. Best known in the title role of Philip Saville's '86 TV miniseries "Life and Loves of a She-Devil," grotesqueness and character's need to dominate men shifts the focus from titillation to satire.

Winkler pokes fun at race relations, reincarnation and respect for the Queen (a rude argument over whether the British monarch relieves herself like normal folk should rule out any royal performance for the pic).

Final reels turn unconvincingly melodramatic when Inga gets her two black friends to help rob the local bigshot landowner (Reggie Carter), ending in violence and an idiotic trial.

Debuting director Lol Creme, who has made many music vids with Kevin Godley, fails to keep a lid on pic's cuteness. Best efforts here are by Campbell as the naive hero and Carter as the oddly sympathetic major domo. Surprise is that the booming voice of Campbell's best friend, a tree, is provided by Carter as well.

Unlike similarly proportioned German thesp Marianne Sägebrecht of Percy Adlon pics (perhaps the only other well-known actress who could personify Inga), Wallace brings zero warmth to her role and quickly becomes a mere caricature.

Tech credits seem on the cheap side while a catchy reggae music score is *de rigeur* for Islands product. — *Lawrence Cohn*

LAPSE OF MEMORY
(MEMOIRE TRANQUÉE)
(CANADIAN-FRENCH)

A Jacques-Eric Strauss/President Films (Paris) release of a Max Films Prods.-Gérard Mital Prods. co-production. Produced by Roger Frappier, Gérard Mital. Directed by Patrick Dewolf. Screenplay, Dewolf, Philippe Leguay from Robert Cormier's book "I'm the Cheese." Camera (color), Eduardo Serra; music, Alexandre Desplats; editor, Fabienne Alvarez Giro; art direction, François Seguin; costumes, François Laplante. Reviewed at Viarregio Noir Fest, June 2, 1991. Running time: **90 MIN.**
Conrad Farmer . . . . John Hurt
Linda Farmer . . . . . Marthe Keller
Bruce Farmer . . . . Matthew Mackay
"Patrick" . . . . . Kathleen Robertson
Dr. Lauren Brint . . . Marion Peterson
(English soundtrack)

"**L**apse of Memory" takes a compelling look at a young boy caught in a web of deceit by parents who only meant to protect him. Patrick Dewolf makes an impressive directorial debut, aided by fine performances from John Hurt and Matthew Mackay. Lush lensing by Eduardo Serra heightens the irony of the disturbing theme.

Hurt plays a journalist who has learned too many secrets about the Mafia. After he testifies before Congress, the Witness Protection Program spirits him off to Canada. He, his wife and his 3-year-old son are given

1983 version
I AM THE CHEESE
(U.S.-COLOR)

An Almi Films release, of a Jack Schwartzman, Albert Schwartz and Michael S. Landes presentation, produced by David Lange. Directed by Robert Jiras. Screenplay, David Lange and Robert Jiras bvased on novel "I Am the Cheese" by Robert Cormier; camera (TVC color), David Quaid; editor, Nicholas Smith; music, Jonathan Tunick; assistant director, Jeff Silver; sound, Nat Boxer; production manager-assoc. producer, C. Mac Brown; (MPAA Rating, PG). Reviewed at Cine Victoria Eugenia (San Sebastian), Sept. 18, 1983. Running time: **95 MINS.**
Adam . . . . Robert Macnaughton
Betty Farmer . . . . Hope Lange
David Farmer . . . . Don Murray
Dr. Brint . . . . Robert Wagner
Amy . . . . Cynthia Nixon
Mr. Grey . . . . Lee Richardson
Arnold . . . . John Fiedler
Edna . . . . Sudie Bond
Young Adam . . . . . Frank McGurran

a new last name and Canadian passports.

Twelve years later, 15-year-old Bruce Farmer (Matthew Mac-

kay) finds his original U.S. passport with his real last name. His suspicions are further aroused by his parents' tense reactions to visits from a strange "friend" of the family. The teen grows frightened, wondering if the Farmers really are his parents and whether they intend to hurt him.

Son confronts Dad who is relieved to finally tell his son the truth. Mackay writes it all down in short-story form, using his father's real name as his pen name.

Unfortunately, the teen's girlfriend "Patrick" (appealingly played by Kathleen Robertson) secretly enters the story in a contest. When the story wins and gets published, the Farmers are forced to flee again, but the Mafia catches up with them this time and the parents are killed. Their son suffers from total amnesia as a result of the shock, pain and guilt.

Dewolf, scripter of such critical successes as "Monsieur Hire," lingers on the disturbing question of whether "protected witnesses" are the winners or losers. The film ends on an upbeat note, but audiences are left wondering how the kid will live with the memory of having inadvertently caused his parents' death.

Fine direction, acting and editing should add up to strong commercial potential for his English-language release. Unfortunately the quality effort is marred by a hazy flashback structure and a co-production snag: The French Canadian police inspector is amateurishly overdubbed in an unsuccessful attempt to hide his accent. — *Catherine Ventura*

IN THE HEAT OF PASSION

A Concorde Pictures release. Executive producer, Roger Corman. Produced, directed, written by Rodman Flender. Camera (Foto-Kem color), Wally Pfister; editor, Patrick Rand; music, Art Wood, Ken Rarick; sound (Ultra-Stereo), Chris Taylor, Cameron Hamza; production design, Hector Velez; costumes, Meta Marie Jardine; assistant director, Juan A. Mas; production manager, Jonathan Winfrey; 2nd unit director, Charles Philip Moore; 2nd unit camera, William Molina; co-producer, Mike Elliott; casting, Steven Rabiner. Reviewed on New Horizons vidcassette, N.Y. MPAA Rating: R. Running time: **85 MIN.**
Lee Adams . . . . Sally Kirkland
Charlie Bronson . . . . Nick Corri
Stan . . . . Jack Carter
Sanford Adams . . . . Michael Greene
Betty . . . . Gloria Le Roy
Det. Rooker . . . . . . Carl Franklin
Perez . . . . Carlos Carrasco

Sally Kirkland sizzles in the erotic thriller "In the Heat of Passion." With that genre currently popular in homevid, pic is a natural for couch potatoes following its current theatrical run.

Filmmaker Rodman Flender has fashioned a clever if farfetched plotline in which Nick Corri plays an itinerant actor who's cast as the Montclair Hills rapist on one of those reality TV shows, "Crimebusters."

Working by day as a mechanic, he strikes up a romance with married shrink Kirkland. When hubbie (Michael Greene) comes home and catches them in the act, Corri accidentally kills him in a struggle for a gun.

Duo make the killing look like the work of the rapist and seem to be fooling the police when, in true *film noir* tradition, both plotters lack trust. Final plot twists elegantly tie up various story threads as well as introing a surprise revelation at fade-out.

Sex scenes are hot, repping feature's main selling point. In addition to covering ground recently dominated by Tanya Roberts and Shannon Tweed vehicles, this casting also provides the older woman/younger man combo that has been a genre staple since "Private Lessons."

Fans lured by that come-on get a genuinely suspenseful picture to boot. — *Lawrence Cohn*

VACANZE DI NATALE '91
(CHRISTMAS VACATION '91)
(ITALIAN)

A Filmauro Distribuzione release of a Luigi & Aurelio De Laurentiis presentation of a Filmauro production. Produced by Luigi & Aurelio De Laurentiis. Directed by Enrico Oldoini. Screenplay, Oldoini, Alberto Sordi, Giovanni Veronesi, Rodolfo Sonego, Liliana Betti. Camera (Cinecittà color), Sergio Salvati; editor, Raimondo Crociani; music, Gianni Dell'Orso, Manuel De Sica; art direction, Osvaldo Desideri; costumes, Alessandra Oldoini. Reviewed at Reale Cineme, Rome, Jan. 16, 1992. Running time: **114 MIN.**
Nanni . . . . Massimo Boldi
Enzo . . . . Christian De Sica
Rino . . . . Nino Frassica
Leopoldo . . . . Ezio Greggio
Giuliana . . . . Ornella Muti
Mimmo . . . . Andrea Roncato
Sabino . . . . Alberto Sordi

Lowbrow tube item, "Christmas Vacation '91" is a laughless sex 'n' schlockfest that could have been made 20 years ago. Its predecessor was 1990's highest grossing Italo pic, while current offering is a big holiday hit,

chalking up $7.5 million.

Formulaic plotting follows stories of various St. Moritz vacationers: eccentric artist honeymooning with his second wife but haunted by the ghost of the first wife he supposedly murdered; an ambitious daughter and her humble hotel waiter father; a haughty Milanese couple forced to share a suite with loutish Romans, and a gay father juggling his son and his lover.

Male characters are all venal clutzes, women are sluts or harpies and gays are wrist-flapping sissies waiting to be "cured" by the right woman. Flatulence jokes abound in inept and numbingly familiar script in which conflicts arise out of nowhere and fizzle away just as clumsily.

Cast of tired TV comics is uniformly flat, and Italo superstars Alberto Sordi and Ornella Muti walk through their turns.

Proceedings are punctuated by lively ski footage and a seemingly arbitrary sprinkling of pop tunes (Bananarama over a funeral scene?!), but nothing can put life into pic's pedestrian direction and static lensing. Tech credits are all under par with dubbing often ludicrously out of sync.
— *David Rooney*

SUNDANCE FEST

SWOON

A Fine Line Features release of a Tom Kalin & Christine Vachon presentation of an Intolerance production produced in association with American Playhouse. Produced by Vachon. Executive producers, Lauren Zalaznick, James Schamus. Line producer, Zalaznick. Directed, written by Kalin. Collaborating writer, Hilton Als. Camera (Alpha Cine black & white), Ellen Kuras; editor, Kalin; music, James Bennett; production design, Therese Deprez; art direction, Stacey Jones; costume design, Jessica Haston; sound, Neil Danziger, Tom Paul; associate producer, Peter Wentworth; assistant director, Vachon; casting, Daniel Haughey. Reviewed at Sundance Film Festival, Park City, Utah, Jan. 23, 1992. Running time: **90 MIN.**
Richard Loeb . . . . Daniel Schlachet
Nathan Leopold Jr. . . . Craig Chester
State's Attorney Crowe . Ron Vawter
Det. Savage . . . . . . Michael Kirby
Dr. Bowman . . . . . Michael Stumm

A dramatization of the 1924 Leopold and Loeb murder case unlike any before it, "Swoon" is a studied, ultra-arty look at a notorious crime as seen through a thick filter of sexual politics. Evocatively shot in 14 days on an exceedingly low budget, brooding pic will **stir interest among sophisticated urban audiences inclined toward alternative subject matter and storytelling techniques.**

Sensational story revolves around Nathan Leopold Jr. and Richard Loeb, two wealthy, brilliant, Jewish teenage lovers whose crime spree culminated in the murder of a kidnapped boy in their native Chicago. Having left behind a trail of evidence, pair was quickly caught and later convicted in a massively publicized trial.

Tale has previously inspired Alfred Hitchcock's "Rope" and Richard Fleischer's "Compulsion," but Tom Kalin, in his first feature after making short films and videos, has taken another tack entirely, one specifically informed by gay politics.

In any conventional sense, "Swoon" is arid, lacking in narrative drive, blandly written and, given the passion the two characters feel for each other, sapped of life.

But the point of Kalin's approach lies elsewhere. The duo have always been characterized as feeling so smugly superior intellectually to those around them that they imagined they could get away with anything. Kalin extends this conception of apartness to their homosexuality, essentially equating gayness with outlaw status in a hostile society.

In this context, Leopold and Loeb commit the ultimate offense by murdering a child, surely the most fundamental symbol of the straight world. This reading of the case history makes the film provocative and an interesting addition to the canon of crime dramas.

Other notable aspect is the pic's look, and Ellen Kuras' cinematography in particular. Shot in black & white on regular 16m and blown up to 35m, and with New York State standing in for the Chi area, pic creates a rarefied world of privilege through its visual style that's part and parcel of its intellectual concerns. Few films of any budget or size are this carefully thought out pictorially.

On the downside, however, are meaningless sequences involving some gaudy "girls," voice-overs by both young men in which it is impossible to tell who is speaking and a major strategy switch in pic's latter third, when it becomes vastly more documentary-like and quite distant from the minute, highly detailed concerns of its early sections.

Kalin mixes in archival footage with his staged material and has used actual texts (diary entries, courtroom testimony and the like) for a substantial portion of the script.

Director's esoteric methods, much more than his subject matter, limit his intended audience to a very small group, but within it the film will find a degree of favor. — *Todd McCarthy*

INTIMATE STRANGER
(DOCU-COLOR/B&W)

Produced, directed, written, edited by Alan Berliner. Camera (Duart color, black & white), Berliner. Reviewed at Sundance Film Festival, Park City, Utah, Jan. 26, 1992. Running time: **60 MIN.**

A stunningly imaginative hand-made, one-man film, "Intimate Stranger" combines biography, personal inquiry, 20th-century history, a search for roots, family portraiture and cultural anthropology in a work of unusual resonance. This New York and Sundance festivals hit unfortunately will see its audience limited due to inevitable pigeonholing as a docu as well as its offbeat aesthetics.

A New York filmmaker who does it all himself, Alan Berliner has a unique style blithely unhampered by the strictures of either the fiction or documentary form. He tells the curious life story of his elusive, peripatetic maternal grandfather, Joseph Cassuto, a Palestinian Jew who spent the key part of his professional life as a trader in Japan while his family remained in Brooklyn.

Berliner has an unusually rich store of home movies and vintage photos to work with, using them at different speeds and in amusing ways.

Two factors give the film its special distinction. One is its dense, active editing style, which features the rat-a-tat-tat of typewriter keys to suggest Cassuto's actual writing of a strange third-person autobiography, as well as letter fragments, postmarks and stamps to indicate the extent of Cassuto's travels.

The other is the amazing running commentary of his surviving family and business associates. Children and grandchildren argue, dispute and speculate about the details of Cassuto's life, concurring only in the view that he treated his business associates much better than he did his family.

Postwar, Cassuto lived most of the year in Japan while his long-suffering wife raised the kids in New York. Berliner and the other family members try to make sense of this, as well as why Cassuto didn't amass a significant amount of money.

An early Zionist, fluent in seven languages, a man of influence, politically conservative, and "a professional advice machine," Cassuto may or may not have been a remarkable individual in his own way. But he has certainly received a remarkable "biography," one that is haunting in the manner it suggests the difference between knowable facts and knowledge of a man's true life.

Ironically, docu would speak more directly to the experiences of mainstream audiences than something like "The Last Boy Scout." — *Todd McCarthy*

BROTHER'S KEEPER
(DOCU)

An American Playhouse Theatrical Films presentation in association with Creative Thinking Intl. of a Hand-To-Mouth production. Produced, directed, edited by Joe Berlinger & Bruce Sinofsky. Executive producers, Lindsay Law, Berlinger. Camera (color), Douglas Cooper; original music, Jay Ungar, Molly Mason. Reviewed at Sundance Film Festival, Park City, Utah, Jan. 25, 1992. Running time: **120 MIN.**

Filmmakers Joe Berlinger and Bruce Sinofsky emerge as skilled and accessible documentarians in this fascinating account of a murder trial in a rural community. Winner of the audience-voted award as most popular docu at the recently wrapped Sundance fest, pic has been acquired for "American Playhouse" broadcast in 1994, but with strong promotion could do respectable big-screen biz during its theatrical window.

Faith-affirming, uniquely American tale shows how trial by jury can still be the truest route to justice. On June 6, 1990, a 60-year-old, barely literate, upstate New York dairy farmer was thrust into the public eye when his brother died in the bed they shared. Delbert Ward was accused of suffocating Bill, and with a signed confession, police characterized it as a mercy killing due to Bill's many ailments and threw Delbert in jail.

But neighbors were unwilling to believe the shy farmer could have killed his brother despite their mental feebleness and isolation in a filthy two-room cabin with no phone or plumbing. They rallied around a man they'd previously had little to do with, raising money for his legal defense at potlucks and dances and declaring Delbert's innocence in countless media interviews.

Filmmakers leave open the possibility that Delbert, whose IQ matches his age, may have suffocated Bill, but pic mainly shows how Delbert's plight transforms the town, prompting it to identify its unique rural values and stick up for one of its own.

Berlinger and Sinofsky, who financed this pic on credit cards and shot it on weekends away from their regular jobs, take advantage of the episode's courtroom drama to tell a nonfiction story in dramatic terms.

Running somewhat long in its festival version, particularly in courtroom scenes, pic will be trimmed 15 minutes for theatrical exhibition, per the filmmakers (who've worked for Maysles Films). — *Amy Dawes*

THE LIVING END

A Strand Releasing-Desperate Pictures production. Produced by Marcus Hu, Jon Gerrans. Executive producers, Evelyn Hu, Jon Jost, Henry Rosenthal, Mike Thomas. Co-producer, Jim Stark. Directed, written, edited by Gregg Araki. Camera (color), Araki; lighting, Chris Munch; music, Cole Coonce; sound, George Lockwood; associate producer, Andrea Sperling. Reviewed at Sundance Film Festival, Park City, Utah, Jan. 23, 1992. Running time: **92 MIN.**
Luke . . . . Mike Dytri
John . . . . Craig Gilmore
Darcy . . . . Darcy Marta
Peter . . . . Scot Goetz

Los Angeles underground filmmaker Gregg Araki ("The Long Weekend O'Despair") sets two doomed lovers on the road and then doesn't take them anywhere but down an edgy, irreverent but ultimately dead-end path that's all the more disappointing given its strong point of departure.

Intriguing premise has a malleable young gay writer (Craig Gilmore) taking up with a callow, volatile, hard-bodied drifter (Mike Dytri) shortly after both learn they are HIV positive. "Till death do us part" is their motto when they're forced to hit the road after the drifter shoots a cop.

Duo feels totally free with nothing to lose, but Araki can't think of anyplace interesting to take them, and their company gets pretty dull as locations change

but they don't. Meanwhile, they get it on more times than Sailor and Lula in "Wild at Heart" in explicit gay footage.

Tag-lined "an irresponsible movie by Gregg Araki," pic sets a cheeky, nihilistic tone at the outset and tools along smartly for several reels. Araki's dialogue can be wickedly clever within its underground parameters, and pic is occasionally fueled by a gleeful sick humor that owes something to Paul Bartel, who makes a cameo appearance.

Partly funded by an American Film Institute grant, Araki's first color, sync-sound pic puts remarkable value on screen for a budget given as $20,000.

Shot with economy and verve and deftly lit by filmmaker Chris Munch ("The Hours and Times," also at Sundance), pic is not without its sterling moments. At one point the pistol-packing trekker blows away a foe wearing a T-shirt that reads "Sex, Lies and Videotape," a scene that brought the house down at Sundance even as it raised the question of how much calculation can go into winning a slot in the fest competition. — *Amy Dawes*

THE INLAND SEA
(DOCU)

A Travelfilm Co. production in association with the Japan Foundation & the Hoso Bunka Foundation (Japan). Produced by Brian Cotnoir, Lucille Carra. Executive producer, Gerald Carrus. Directed, adapted by Carra. Written, narrated by Donald Richie, based on his book. Camera (Duart color), Hiro Narita; editor, Cotnoir; music, Toru Takemitsu; sound, Tom Hartig; associate producers, Larry Massett, Art Silverman. Reviewed at Sundance Film Festival, Park City, Utah, Jan. 21, 1992. Running time: **57 MIN.**

An "interior documentary" based on critic/historian Donald Richie's 30-year-old travel memoir, "The Inland Sea" captures the old Japan that is quickly and irreversibly being overrun by progress. Satisfyingly personal and idiosyncratic, this quietly observed, minor-key work is due to play at N.Y.'s Film Forum later this year. In the long run, however, TV and video will be the best bets.

Always intelligent but sometimes prickly even while being nostalgic, Richie intones that "one world is becoming a hideous possibility, and I wish to celebrate its differences as long as possible." Using this as a point of departure, filmmakers Lucille Car-

ra and Brian Cotnoir and lenser Hiro Narita retraced the journey Richie made decades ago to an area sometimes described as the Japanese Aegean Sea, a landlocked body of water surrounded by three of the nation's four major islands.

Director Carra and editor Cotnoir have matched travelogue-like footage of boat voyages, citizens at work and in repose, and tourists visiting temples and shrines with Richie's narration in sometimes offbeat, contrapuntal ways that keep a dialogue going.

Pic, best documentary award-winner at the recent Hawaii Intl. Film Festival, unfolds in leisurely fashion, and only eyebrow-raising interlude concerns the filmmakers' inadvertent landing on uncharted island that turns out to be a leprosarium.

The visual surface is picturesque and serene, leaving it to Richie, who finally appears on-screen at the end, to try to make inroads into Japan's impenetrability. — *Todd McCarthy*

IN SEARCH OF OUR FATHERS
(DOCU-16m)

A Conjure Films production. Produced, directed, written by Marco Williams. Camera (color, 16m), Nick Doob, Jean-Paul Mioto, Phil Abrahams, Williams; editor, Lisa Leeman; music, Billy Childs. Reviewed at Sundance Film Festival (competition), Park City, Utah, Jan. 24, 1992. Running time: **70 MIN.**

Fans of unblushingly personal, diary-style documentary might find sustenance in Marco Williams' search for his father, but those looking for a rich, enlightening exploration of the theme will likely find it limited and self-indulgent. Theatrical prospects are slight for this 16m docu.

Beginning with a phone call in which he makes his first-ever connection with the man he has learned is his father, Williams documents his seven-year quest for a personal meeting with the man, which takes him from Harlem to Boston, Paris, Philadelphia and Ohio as he interviews family members to learn about his absent father.

All this might have been rich if there had been a good story to uncover; as it turns out, his father had only the briefest relationship with his mother (who

barely remembers him) and didn't even know Marco existed until he was an adult.

By limiting his search to his own particular case, Williams has created a docu that says a lot less than it might have about the feelings of black men toward the children they father.

Williams' coda about the value of making a simple connection might be valid, but for an audience it's a weak payoff.

Financed by grants from such sources as the Rockefeller Foundation, the Intercultural Film/Video Fellowship, the National Endowment for the Arts and the American Film Institute, docu is presented with rough edges intact, though it's somewhat dressed up with location inserts and agreeable music.
— *Amy Dawes*

MY CRASY LIFE

An Allan/Marks production for BBC Television in association with FR3. Produced by Daniel Marks, Cameron Allan. Directed by Jean-Pierre Gorin. Screenplay, based on Marks' research; computer dialogue written by Gorin, Howard Rodman, spoken by Richard Masur. Camera (color), Babette Mangolte; editor, Brad Thumin; music, Joji Yuasa; sound, Ken King; associate producer, Nick Rothenberg. Reviewed at Sundance Film Festival, Park City, Utah, Jan. 21, 1992. Running time: **98 MIN.**

An ostensible documentary about a Samoan Crip gang in Long Beach, Calif., "My Crasy Life" is actually an 80%-scripted film that falls into a useless middleground between documentary and narrative. Dull and unenlightening, pic will appeal to few except for those searching for the exotic and certain critics who may be deluded into thinking this constitutes a new form rather than an inauthentic hybrid.

Director Jean-Pierre Gorin was Jean-Luc Godard's partner in the Dziga Vertov group during the late 1960s and early '70s, and has more recently taught and made films in San Diego. A gifted theoretician, Gorin was drawn to a subject that, on paper, sounds interesting: street gangs made up of immigrants from American Samoa.

To penetrate this culture at all reps an accomplishment of sorts, but it's a journey with no reward. After having spent time with the mostly burly young men, Gorin, working from research by his producer Daniel Marks, wrote most of their dialogue.

Many of his sequences, particularly those featuring police, involve obviously staged setups, while others record a lot of aimless hanging around intended to seem offhand and "real."

Surely Gorin meant to honor the truth of the gang's existence with his technique. But the scripting has disallowed the chance happening that can be vérité's greatest strength, while the faux-docu format deprives the film of a narrative's urgency and drive.

Result leaves the viewer suspecting Gorin didn't really want to make a documentary, took a step beyond that, but ultimately found himself ensnared by restrictions of the form.

Sociologically, film is less unusual than anticipated. With their Raiders and Kings caps, endless appetite for rap music, vocal and attitudinal mannerisms, devotion to the homeboy mentality and utter lack of interest in their own cultural background, these guys seem no different from other gang types. Nor do they reflect on their lifestyle with any insight.

Depicting nothing about these revenge-minded toughs in 98 minutes that couldn't have been conveyed in a half-hour, Gorin has ended up with an aggravatingly tedious docu-drama.

— *Todd McCarthy*

ARCHIVE REVIEW

DOMO ARIGATO
(THANK YOU VERY MUCH)
(3-D)

A Sherpix presentation of an Arch Oboler Prods. production. Produced, directed, written by Oboler. Executive producer, Louis K. Sher. Camera (Eastmancolor, Space-Vision 3-D), Donald Peterman; editor, Robert Angle; music, Sherry Mills (song sung by Bonnie Sher); sound, Mark Hopkins. Reviewed at London Film Festival, Nov. 13, 1991. Running time: **90 MIN.**
With: Jason Ledger, Bonnie Sher, Kyoko Masu, Jerry Kay.

Arch Oboler's final 3-D pic is a little-seen 1972 production that had no commercial release at the time, and it's easy to see why. Laborious trek along the Japan tourist trail with two dull Yanks has about as much going for it dramatically as "Cinerama Holiday."

Funded by Louis K. Sher, owner of exhib chain Art Theater Guild (which played art and porno pics), pic was the third of

Oboler's stereoscopic outings (after the 1952 "Bwana Devil" and 1966 "The Bubble") and the second in Space-Vision. Conceived by Armed Forces stereo photography expert Col. Robert V. Bernier, the single-projector process packs left- and right-eye information on one negative. Result, viewed through polarizer-film glasses, produces no eyestrain, unlike some 3-D efforts.

Loosely structured semi-docu is about a pushy G.I. (Jason Ledger) homebound from Vietnam and a 19-year-old Kansas girl (Bonnie Sher, daughter of producer). She starts by giving him the sexual runaround in Tokyo, and the duo then set out on a picture-postcard tour of Japan. Main plot point, revealed near the end, is that she's losing her sight.

Script is leaden ("Hey, the water looks great!"). Objects in the face include a crab, a samurai sword and a Japanese breakfast. Main excitement, 75 minutes in, is rescuing a Nipponese moppet who's fallen into a volcano.

Donald Peterman's widescreen photography is crisp and (apart from interiors) well lit. Sherry Mills' score is pleasant Muzak.

Oboler, who died in 1987, still had the rights to one more pic in Space-Vision after being forced to sell out to Capitol Records. His reputation is now kept alive by longtime assistant Jerry Kay, who cameos in the pic as a femme racing driver and who introed the London film fest retrospective of his 3-D works.

— *Derek Elley*

MIAMI FEST

THE MAMBO KINGS

A Warner Bros. release of a WB presentation in association with Le Studio Canal Plus, Regency Enterprises & Alcor Films of an Arnon Milchan production. Produced by Milchan, Arne Glimcher. Executive producer, Steven Reuther. Co-producer, Jack B. Bernstein. Directed by Glimcher. Screenplay, Cynthia Cidre, based on Oscar Hijuelos's novel "The Mambo Kings Play Songs of Love." Camera (Deluxe color, Technicolor prints), Michael Ballhaus; editor, Claire Simpson; executive music producer, Robert Kraft; original score, Kraft, Carlos Franzetti; mambo arrangements, Ray Santos; choreography, Michael Peters; production design, Stuart Wurtzel; art direction, Steve Saklad; set decoration, Kara Lindstrom; costumes, Ann Roth, Gary Jones, Bridget Kelly; sound (Dolby), Susumu Tokunow; associate producer, Anna Reinhardt; assistant director, Benjamin Rosenberg; casting, Billy Hopkins, Suzanne Smith. Reviewed at Miami Film Festival, Feb. 7, 1992. MPAA rating: R. Running time: **101 MIN.**
Cesar Castillo . . . . . Armand Assante
Nestor Castillo . . . Antonio Banderas
Lanna Lake . . . . . . Cathy Moriarty
Delores Fuentes . Maruschka Detmers
Desi Arnaz Sr. . . . . . . Desi Arnaz Jr.
Evalina Montoya . . . . Celia Cruz
Fernando Perez . . Roscoe Lee Browne
Miguel Montoya . . Vondie Curtis-Hall
Tito Puente . . . . Himself
Maria Rivera . . . . Talisa Soto
Carlo Ricci . . . . Joe Petruzzi
Ismelda Perez . . . . Anh Duong
Anna Maria . . . . . Cordelia Gonzales
Blanca . . . . . . Theodora Castellanos
Pablo . . . . Lazaro Perez
Mambo Kings Band: Pablo Calogero, Scott Cohen, Mario Grillo, Ralph Irizarry, Pete Macnamara, Jimmy Medina, Marcos Quintanilla, J.T. Taylor, William Thomas Jr., Yul Vazquez.

"The Mambo Kings" is an ambitious, old-fashioned Hollywood film that lovingly recreates the Latino ambience of its Pulitzer Prize-winning source material. With impeccable period sets and costumes and striking cinematography, pic beautifully evokes 1950s New York. while it may disappoint some fans of the Oscar Hijuelos novel, Arne Glimcher's condensed film version is bound to win converts to the intoxicating rhythms of Latino music. With a good critical reception, Warner Bros. could well have a hit in this moving musical drama.

Hijuelos' novel proved a challenge to adapt, and Glimcher and screenwriter Cynthia Cidre pared down the 407-page book to its essential story about the rise and fall of two Cuban immigrant musicians.

Glimcher takes full advantage of the book's cinematic opportunities, with its flashbacks to Cuba

and detailed nightclub scenes. Most striking sequences take place in smoky, crowded clubs, from the opening in Havana to the final image of Cesar Castillo (Armand Assante) singing in a New York club.

In between, Glimcher creates dynamic set pieces, filling the screen with exuberant singing and dancing to nonstop music. Authentic flavor is aided by Stuart Wurtzel's handsome production and the attractive costumes by Ann Roth, Gary Jones and Bridget Kelly.

Glimcher, an art galley owner and producer, makes a strong directing debut. In one amusing musical montage he shows the ups and downs of the brothers' career by cutting from a glittery nightclub to the meat packing plant where they work by day to a routine bar mitzvah, splicing the scenes together with a dancing couple.

Director also uses music to terrific effect, as in the wedding scene between Nestor Castillo (Antonio Banderas) and Dolores (Maruschka Detmers), in which salsa star Celia Cruz joyfully sings "Guantanamera."

Assante makes a likable skirt chaser and later conveys Cesar's downward spiral with great economy. But he occasionally slips into a New York accent and never sounds anything like brother Banderas, a Spanish actor in Pedro Almodóvar's films. As the tormented Nestor, Banderas gives a sensitive performance that may be a launching pad to more leading roles in American features.

Both are fine impersonating musicians. (Assante took voice lessons, while Banderas practiced the trumpet — and his English.)

As in the novel, film peaks with the brothers' appearance on the "I Love Lucy" show. With Desi Arnaz Jr. playing Desi Sr., Glimcher cleverly combines Lucille Ball in the real episode with matched footage of Assante, Banderas and Arnaz Jr.

Film then begins to stray from the book and is not always successful. Final scenes pass too quickly, with the sexual tension between Detmers and Assante left unexplored despite one steamy scene.

Dutch actress Detmers ("First Name: Carmen") is a touching Dolores. As Assante's lover Lanna Lane (Vanna Vane in the book), Cathy Moriarty makes the most of her best role since Vicki La Motta.

Casting of relative unknowns in major roles pays off, and Arnaz,

Cruz and Tito Puente also add to the film's authentic feel.

D.p. Michael Ballhaus deserves special mention for his deep-focus camerawork. Many scenes are shot in a muted golden-amber color scheme fitting for the period. — *William Stevenson*

HUNGARIAN FEST

THE LONG SHADOW
(U.S.-HUNGARIAN-ISRAELI)

A Prolitera Intl. production in association with Hungarian Television-The Fund for the Promotion of Israeli Quality Films. (World sales: Manley Prods. in association with Arianne U. Cipes.) Produced by János Edelényi, Paul Salamon. Executive producers Joe Gantz, William M. Zachman. Co-executive producers David Will, Richard Seale (U.S.), György Lendvai, Péter Somosi (Hungary). Directed by Vilmos Zsigmond. Screenplay, Salamon, Edelényi. Camera (Eastmancolor), Gábor Szabó; editor, Mari Miklós; music, György Selmeczi; production design, Avi Avivi, László Zsótér; costumes, Rakefet Levi, Zsófia Eórdögh; sound (Dolby), Moshe Yochay, István Sípos; associate producers, Pál Sándor, Zwi Spielmann; assistant directors, Csaba Kael, Avner Urshalimy; casting, Tova Tzipin. Reviewed at 23rd Hungarian Film Week, Budapest, Feb. 1, 1992. (Also in Berlin Film Festival, Panorama section.) Running time: **89 MIN.**
Gábor/
  Raphael Romóndy . . . Michael York
Katherine . . . . Liv Ullmann
Johann Graber . . . . Oded Teomi
Rachel . . . . Ava Haddad
Abu . . . . Babi Neeman
Rabbi Rosner . . . . Zoltan Gera
Theater director . . . . . Dezsö Garas
(English dialogue)

Lush lensing and some eye-filling Israeli locations can't rescue "The Long Shadow," a trite semi-meller sabotaged by the blah script and some dubious casting.

Michael York toplines weakly as a Hungarian Jew working out an Oedipus-Schmoedipus complex on a trip to the Holy Land. Directorial bow by Oscar-winning Magyar cinematographer Vilmos Zsigmond is strictly inflight fare. Pic could also draw some flak on release in Israel where the character of York's archaeologist father will draw comparisons with a w.k. real-life academic who's not even remotely Hungarian.

Yarn opens in modern-day Budapest where famous legit actor Gábor (York) gets a letter telling him his father has died in Israel. Though he hated his father for supposedly deserting him 40 years earlier, Gábor skips rehearsals for a production of "Hamlet"

and wings off to Jerusalem to visit Dad's grave. There he bumps into his father's second wife, Katherine (Liv Ullmann), a Christian German who's stayed on in her adopted country.

After some initial head-butting, the pair soon settle down into some heart-to-heart stuff at her mountainside retreat. When a German TV reporter friend of Katherine's (Oded Teomi) asks Gábor to impersonate his father in an unfinished docu, Gábor is forced to confront his longtime hangups and growing sense of Jewish identity.

Not much of this conflict gets in the script by Hungarian playwright Paul Salamon and TV lenser Janos Edelényi, which is often as confused as the main character. Lines such as, "Just like the Bible!" (York on first seeing his dad's archaeological dig), and the unlikely romance between York and Ullmann undercut the serious central theme of paternal love-hate and the mistakes of history. Parallels of "Hamlet" are left floating.

In the dual role of Gábor and his own father (seen in vid clips), York is seriously lightweight and even has trouble with a convincing Hungarian accent. Ullmann gives her best shot in an underwritten part, and Israeli thesp Teomi is solid as the journalist with the hots for her. U.S.-based actress Ava Haddad scores briefly as a pretty flight attendant who takes a shine to York.

Technically, pic looks much more expensive than its actual $5 million budget, mostly raised Stateside. Gábor Szabó's Eastmancolor lensing in the Israeli desert segs stands out, and György Selmeczi's melodious score papers over some of the cracks in the screenplay. Filming was interrupted for three months during to the Persian Gulf war, but finished product shows no hiccups.
—*Derek Elley*

BERLIN FEST

SHADOWS AND FOG
(B&W)

An Orion (through Columbia-TriStar foreign) release of a Jack Rollins & Charles H. Joffe production. Produced by Rollins, Joffe. Executive producer, Robert Greenhut. Co-producers, Helen Robin, Joseph Hartwick. Directed, written by Woody Allen. Camera (black & white, Deluxe prints), Carlo Di Palma; editor, Susan E. Morse; music, Kurt Weill; production design, Santo Loquas-

to; art direction, Speed Hopkins; set decoration, George DeTitta Jr.; Amy Marshall; costume design, Jeffrey Kurland; sound (Dolby), James Sabat; associate producer-assistant director, Thomas Reilly; casting, Juliet Taylor. Reviewed at MacMahon Cinema, Paris, Dec. 20, 1991. (In Berlin Film Festival, noncompeting.) MPAA Rating: PG-13. Running time: **86 MIN.**
Kleinman . . . . Woody Allen
Irmy . . . . Mia Farrow
Clown . . . . John Malkovich
Marie . . . . Madonna
Doctor . . . . Donald Pleasence
Prostitute . . . . Lily Tomlin
Prostitute . . . . Jodie Foster
Prostitute . . . . Kathy Bates
Student Jack . . . . John Cusack
Eva . . . . Kate Nelligan
Hacker's follower . . . . Fred Gwynne
Alma . . . . Julie Kavner
Magician . . . . Kenneth Mars
Hacker . . . . David Ogden Stiers
Mr. Paulsen . . . . Philip Bosco
Priest . . . . Josef Sommer
Vogel's follower . . . Kurtwood Smith
  Also with: Robert Joy, Wallace Shawn, Eszter Balint.

Exquisitely shot in black & white, Woody Allen's "Shadows and Fog" is a sweet homage to German expressionist filmmaking and a nod to the content of socially responsible tales since narrative film began. Allen's fans will regard this as a nice try that falls short. General audiences may be lured by the (extremely brief) presence of Madonna and left baffled by hit-or-miss philosophizing. Comic sparks are only intermittent, and box office prospects look foggy.

Already seen at gala private screenings in New York and Paris, pic began its world premiere engagement in Paris last week and unspooled out of competition at the Berlin Film Festival on Saturday. Domestic release, held up because of Orion's financial woes, is set for March 20.

Impeccable visuals can't entirely compensate for wobbly tone as pic probes the unfairness and serendipity of life, exploring other aspects of the territory so brilliantly handled in "Crimes and Misdemeanors."

Helmer throws in some Kafka (Allen's persecuted character is never sure what he's supposed to do), some evil (there's a killer on the loose, casting shadows in the fog), a spunky counterbalancing force (Mia Farrow) and a little magic.

Allen's one-note performance detracts and, in this outing, the feats of magic that were so smoothly incorporated into "Alice" smack too much of deus ex machina.

Film comes across like a technically superlative student film for which the director enlisted all the best talent from the drama

department, picked the right records for the soundtrack (Kurt Weill melodies from "The Threepenny Opera") and wrote jokes that are either about the stuff one hashes over in college (philosophy, religion, the meaning of life) or references to other films.

Farrow and boyfriend John Malkovich are part of a traveling circus that has pitched its tent near an unnamed European town where rival bands of vigilantes roam the nighttime streets in search of a marauding strangler.

Allen is awakened by neighbors and told to carry out his part in "the plan," without ever getting clear instructions. When Farrow catches Malkovich cheating on her with the strongman's wife (Madonna in a murky cameo), she walks out into the fog where she is befriended by streetwalker Lily Tomlin.

The stellar cast is in for a long night of murder and persecution, with a few personal epiphanies and a fair share of passing remarks about the power of evil and the essential role of illusion in the lives of men and women.

Farrow, who has much more to do than most of the characters, anchors the piece with a forthright approach. Allen's dialogue seems most forced when he delivers it himself.

In the great movie tradition of transgressing scientists, Donald Pleasence has an autopsy lab in which he is investigating territory best left to theologians. Pleasence, who starred in Roman Polanski's 1966 "Cul-de-Sac," is cornered on a, well, cul-de-sac.

Tomlin is good, and Julie Kavner also scores as a former Allen paramour. John Cusack hits all the right notes as a college student who cajoles Farrow into selling herself just once.

Several top thesps, including Jodie Foster and Kathy Bates, have been caught in surprisingly ordinary (and brief) perfs.

A freewheeling brothel confab about men and sex (not unlike the women's rap session in Spike Lee's "Jungle Fever") falls flat.

Pic does boast some classic one-liners (about prayer and ritual circumcision) and very funny moments. But despite Allen's gift for mining the humorous side of misfortune, the specter of random violence and the machinations of targeted persecution make laughter awkward.

That may well be part of Allen's intention, but pic's tone vacillates too much to be sure.

Although Kenneth Mars does his best as a circus magician who confronts the evil force, pic ends too abruptly to lend a satisfying sense of closure.

— *Lisa Nesselson*

EL LARGO INVIERNO
(THE LONG WINTER)
(SPANISH)

A Tibidabo Films co-production with Danon Audiovisuel (Paris), in collaboration with Televisió de Catalunya. Executive producer, Paco Camino. Produced, directed by Jaime Camino. Screenplay, Camino, Ramón Gubern, Juan Marsé, Nicolás Bernheim, Manuel Gutiérrez Aragón. Camera (color), Hans Burmann; editor, Teresa Alcocer; music, Albert Guinovart, performed by the Orquestra Ciutat de Barcelona conducted by Garcia Navarro; sets, Gil Parrondo, Eduardo Arranz Bravo; costumes, Gracia Bondia, Maria Teresa Alvarez, Juana Maria Julia; sound, Ricard Casals. Reviewed at Cine Capitol, Madrid, Jan. 31, 1992. (Competing at Berlin Film Festival.) Running time: **135 MIN.**

Claudio	Vittorio Gassman
Ramón Casals	Jacques Penot
Emma Stapleton	Elizabeth Hurley
Jordi Casals	Jean Rochefort
Casimiro Casals	Adolfo Marsillach
Assumpta de Casals	Asunción Balaguer
Lola de Casals	Teresa Gimpera

Also with: Ramón Madaula, Alex Casanovas, Judit Masco, Jordán Giralt, Yaiza Pérez, Sergei Mateu, J.L. López Vázquez, Silvia Munt, J.L. de Vilallonga.
(In Spanish, Spanish dubbed)

Jaime Camino's sequel to his memorable 1975 "Largas Vacaciones del 36" is an impressive, moving tribute to Catalans opposing the Fascists just before the 1939 fall of Barcelona. Handsome production values, topnotch thesping and a touching script make this one of Spain's top films of the year.

Republic's final months are seen through the eyes of a middle-class Catalan family, perhaps somewhat idealized but nonetheless convincing, despite use of French and British thesps. Happily, this is not the usual Europudding, but an intensely Spanish film, with good pacing and emotive punch.

Yarn is told in a long flashback as the grown son of a prestigious Republican surgeon, Ramón Casals, returns to his old mansion and encounters the only local survivor of the tumultous family drama: a butler, superbly played by Vittorio Gassman.

In over two hours, helmer Camino re-creates with sweeping touches the intrigues, violence, misery and passions of that winter, threading into the historical upheaval a love story between the idealistic surgeon and a U.S. freedom fighter. Mood of the times, fleeing of refugees, arrival of Franco's troops and the pitiless aftermath following the fall of Barcelona are superbly captured.

Pic has some flaws, such as the time frame (the returning son would be about 60, 20 years older than he looks on screen); nor is it explained why he didn't return earlier. But all in all, pic is a convincing and distinguished portrayal of the period with fine performances all around. Superb sets by Gil Parrondo, crisp, imaginative lensing by Hans Burmann and fine editing, music and other tech credits could draw audiences outside Cataluña and Spain.

— *Peter Besas*

NOWYJE SWEDENIJA O KONZE SWETA
(LATEST NEWS OF THE END OF THE WORLD)
(RUSSIAN-DOCU-COLOR/B&W)

A Sverdlovsk Studio Ural Film production. Directed by Boris Kustov. Screenplay, Vladimir Suvorov, Alexander Gromov. Camera (color, black & white), Kustov; music, S. Sidelnikov. Reviewed at Berlin Film Festival press previews, Jan. 27, 1992. (In Intl. Forum of Young Cinema.) Running time: **80 MIN.**

Uneven and bitingly sarcastic docu is often laugh-out-loud funny in its examination of the psychic/lunatic fringe of the former USSR. Pic will shine on the fest circuit, where it could gain some notoriety as Russia's first cult film.

Bracketed in its narration by a quartet of midgets dressed convincingly as Marx, Lenin, Brezhnev and Gorbachev, pic polls crackpot psychics, soothsayers, hypnotists, mystics, astrologists and Ouija-boarders about the future of Russia. The answers are as sincere as they are hysterical.

This pic couldn't have been made a year ago. "Hello, Vladimir Ilyevitch!" shouts a woman reading a Ouija board with a teacup as she finally connects with Lenin. "Is heaven boring?"

A large community of Russians, who say they are reincarnated American Indians, dress accordingly, live in teepees, rain dance, shoot bows and arrows and throw in their two kopecks worth of gloom 'n' doom predictions. Sequences are ably interspersed with scenes of equally hysterical and empty fervor from Stalin-era propaganda pics.

Better editing could have put a keener edge on the pic, which is bogged down by disjointed scenes. But the mean-spirited humor illustrating the spiritual vacuum in the ex-USSR is a refreshing perspective on a society desperately trying to get in touch with the rest of the world.

Ending, with a psychic earnestly offering to sell his prophesies for $100,000 deposited into a Swiss bank, is a gem.

— *Rebecca Lieb*

GHAMIS ZEKWA
(DANCE IN THE NIGHT)
(GEORGIAN)

A Filmstudio Armasi production. (Intl. sales: Ex Picturis, Berlin.) Directed, written by Aleko Tsabadse. Camera (color), Leri Machaidse; editor, Lali Kolkhidashvili; music, Avto Kolkhidashvili; sets, Gogi Tatishvili; sound, Madonna Tevzadse. Reviewed at Berlin Film Festival press previews, Jan. 29, 1992. (In Intl. Forum of Young Cinema.) Running Time: **128 MIN.**

Moshe	Zurab Begalishvili
Zhiba	Amiran Amiranshhvili

Also with: B. Intskirveli, B. Gabisonia, S. Uriadmkopeli T. Kuliyeva.

A slice of Georgian industrial town life focusing on two friends, "Dance in the Night" is long on running time but short on plot, action or coherent message.

Drifting in and out of the lives of steelworkers Moshe and Zhiba are two young prostitutes on holiday, a Moslem who has child after child, a pair of singing Vietnamese, local cops and Zhiba's relatives, who are trying to move into his house.

None of this leads anywhere until Zhiba commits a murder at the very end of the two-hour pic. Stupefying pic has almost all shots permeated with artificial light, and scenes frequently jump as if frames were missing. It is uncertain whether or not this is intentional.

Cinematography looks good overall, but there's nary a close-up. Instead, actors are shot in long or medium shot, making them downright unrecognizable and distancing auds from characters. — *Rebecca Lieb*

WAS SIE NIE ÜBER FRAUEN WISSEN WOLLTEN
(WHAT YOU NEVER WANTED TO KNOW ABOUT WOMEN)
(GERMAN-B&W-16m)

A Lothar Lambert production with NDR. Directed, written, edited by Lambert. Camera (black & white, 16m), Lambert, Albert Kittler. Reviewed at Berlin Film Festival press previews, Jan. 28, 1992. (In Panorama section.) Running time: **80 MIN.**

Nilgün	Nilgün Taifun
Dennis	Dennis Buczma
Doris	Doreen Heins
Renate	Renate Soleymany
Achmed	Baduri
Dr. Merkel	Lothar Lambert
Gerlinde	Dorothea Moritz
Masseur	Stefan Menche

Comic, anarchic drama about four women psychiatric patients sharing an apartment should do art house and TV biz locally, but 16m black & white format will not ease a move away from home.

The lunatics have taken over the asylum in Lothar Lambert's raucous comedy with a strong Berlin flavor. Three mild nut cases share a flat: Nilgün, Turkish and somewhat nymphomaniacal; dour, depressed lesbian Dennis; and Renate, an elderly, overweight motherly type who speaks only English. Doris, comparatively normal but an alcoholic, is told by her shrink (Lambert) that she should move in with the group.

Pic's strong docu feel is underlined by improv acting, handheld shots and the b&w photography. Thesps are good overall, and while there's not much plot, pic is engaging.

Sex scenes walk a fine line between hilarity and offensiveness (including incest and bondage). Pic suffers from an overwrought dream sequence at the end, and an Eartha Kitt disco song is repeated with overbearing frequency. — *Rebecca Lieb*

LA VOIX
(THE VOICE)
(FRENCH)

An AAA release of a Ciné Feel-FR3 Films-SGCC-Prodeveco-production with participation of Investimages 3. Produced by Patricia & Pierre Novat. Directed by Pierre Granier-Deferre. Screenplay, Christine Miller, with Granier-

Deferre, based on Pierre Drieu La Richelle's short story. Camera (color), Pascal Lebegue; editor, Marie Castro Brechignac; music, Philippe Sarde; set design, Jacques Saulnier; costume design, Brigitte Nierhaus; sound, Jean-Charles Rualt, Gerard Lamps; associate producer, Jean-Bernard Fetoux. Reviewed at Club Gaumont, Paris, Jan. 17, 1992. (In Berlin Film Festival, Panorama section.) Running time: **86 MIN.**

Lorraine . . . . Nathalie Baye
Gille . . . . Sami Frey
Laura . . . . Laura Morante
Maitre d' . . . . . Jean-Claude Dreyfus
Michele . . . . Georges Claisse

Within the deliberately theatrical constraint of two lovers having dinner in real time, "The Voice" makes the most of controlled artifice to examine the repercussions of a previous affair. Intelligently written and fancifully shot exercise in suspense and sophistication is well-suited to the tube, particularly as a highbrow rental item.

French couple Nathalie Baye and Sami Frey, on a romantic stay in Rome, are dining outdoors at a terrace restaurant when Frey recognizes a woman's voice coming from behind him, triggering vivid flashbacks to a wildly passionate affair he had.

But Frey refuses to turn around and see if the voice really belongs to Laura Morante, the beautiful married woman he hasn't seen in years. Instead, he recounts the affair to Baye, who suddenly feels threatened by the lingering power of his memories.

Set designer Jacques Saulnier's terrace cafe features a delightfully impossible view of Rome, squeezing together several monuments. As the intrigue advances, the studio decor becomes altogether believable. The convincing continuity of a personal crisis in a public place is bolstered by beautifully controlled dusk and nightfall effects.

His 'n' hers flashbacks, some shot on location in Paris and Rome, keep the scenes from becoming too dull or repetitive. Good thesping keeps intrigue aloft, despite slow patches.

Flashback in which Frey slyly intimidates Morante's husband on an elevator is quirky and original. Eatery scene in which Baye follows the presumed ex-lover into the ladies' room is amusing.

Despite sexy overtones and some daring maneuvers under the table, action is mostly chaste.
— *Lisa Nesselson*

SADY SKORPIONA
(GARDENS OF SCORPIONS)
(RUSSIAN-B&W-COLOR)

A Lenfilm-Experimental Studio-Cineclub Zerkala production. Directed, written by Oleg Kovalov. Editor, Subeava, A. Karelin; sound, Garri Velenki; special effects, L. Krasnova; production manager, V. Slik. Reviewed at Venice Film Festival, Sept. 13, 1991. (In Berlin Film Festival, Intl. Forum of Young Cinema section.) Running time: **100 MIN.**

In his first feature, Leningrad film critic Oleg Kovalov shows influence of early Dusan Makavejev. Just like Makavejev's "Innocence Unprotected," a reworking of a "good old movie," Kovalov uses as his basis for this collage film a bad old movie — the justly forgotten "The True Case of Sgt. Kotchetkom" (Alexander Razymnyi, 1955).

Plot of this cold war epic involves a fresh-faced blond Russian soldier who discovers that his fresh-faced blond g.f. and her dear old grandmother are spies for the West. "Sgt. Kotchetkom" looks like a terrible film, but, like many anti-U.S. cold war films of the '50s, it's unintentionally hilarious today.

Kovalov intercuts this tacky gem with other images of the Nikita Khrushchev era: scenes from a documentary about alcoholism in which patients are hypnotized to stem addiction and familiar but shocking footage of the 1956 Hungarian Revolution.

In footage apparently from the 1959 Moscow Film Festival, a moist-eyed Giulietta Masina acknowledges the acclaim of Russian crowds. Other feted visitors are Yves Montand and Simone Signoret, with the former singing a song (in French) for an adoring audience.

Even more amusing is color footage of Khrushchev's trip to the U.S., including his visit to the set of the Fox's "Can-Can." Maurice Chevalier looks faintly embarrassed as the Sov leader is greeted by Frank Sinatra and an ebullient Shirley MacLaine.

All this adds up to an irreverent, fun film for fests and special programming, though the underlying seriousness of that frosty era is always evident. Kovalov and his team have done a great job of editing the disparate material so that one sequence comments on the next. As a self-styled reflection on an era, pic is

full of interest.
— *David Stratton*

SUR LA TERRE COMME AU CIEL
(IN HEAVEN AS ON EARTH)
(BELGIAN)

A Man's Films production. Produced, directed by Marion Hänsel. Executive producer, Eric van Beuren. Screenplay, Hänsel, Paul Le with Jaco van Dormael, L. van Keerbergen. Camera (color), Josep M. Civit; editor, Susana Rossberg; music, Takashi Kako; sets, Thierry LeProust; costumes, Yan Tax; effects, Jacques Gastineau; sound, Henri Morelle; artistic advisor, Henri Colpi; production director, Michèle Troncon. Reviewed at Berlin Film Festival press previews Jan. 28, 1992. (In Panorama section.) Running time: **80 MIN.**

Maria Garcia . . . . . . Carmen Maura
Tom . . . . Didier Bezace
Jeremy . . . . Samuel Mussen
Editor . . . . Jean-Pierre Cassel
Professor . . . . André Delvaux
Hans . . . . Johan Leysen
Peter . . . . Serge-Henri Valcke
Jane . . . . Pascale Tison

File this one under sci-fi lite. Pic about fetuses deciding they don't want to be born into the terrible world starts off promisingly enough but descends into talkiness and loses credibility.

A hyper-successful TV journalist (Carmen Maura) zips around from her Brussels base to cover terrorist attacks, genetic engineering, the greenhouse effect and other modern issues. She turns down a plum assignment with the excuse that she's pregnant, although she won't name the father.

Pregnancy doesn't slow down this modern woman one whit. She continues to smoke, drink double espressos and wear high heels well into her third trimester. A colleague (Didier Bezace) courts her despite her disinterest and expanding girth.

Maura's due date comes and goes. The same is happening to her Lamaze classmates. Restless sitting at home waiting for contractions to begin, she accepts an assignment on overdue pregnancies. She discovers that the condition is epidemic, and, moreover, babies born under induced-labor conditions are dying. At this point, Maura's unborn baby starts talking to her at night, saying that the fetuses don't want to be born.

Helmer Marion Hänsel doesn't prepare auds for the way-too-discreet buildup of the script's sci-fi element. Despite a decent

performance by Maura, pic's credibility is slowly but surely undermined as her character starts to unhinge and tell medicos and the press what's happening.

She flees a hospital where a doc tries to induce labor and beats it to the coast, hoping the sound of wind, waves and gulls will give her child the will to be born. But by then audience sympathy is elsewhere. Tech credits are good. — *Rebecca Lieb*

KARLSVOGNEN
(THE BIG DIPPER)
(DANISH)

A Bent Fabricius-Bjerre, Metronome production, with the Swedish Film Institute, Sandrews, TV-1 Drama Stockholm og TV-2, subsidized by the Nordic Film & TV Foundation & the Danish Film Institute. Produced by Mads Egmont Christensen. Executive producer, Fabricius-Bjerre. Directed by Birger Larsen. Screenplay, Ulf Stark, Larsen, based on Stark's novel. Camera (color), Björn Blixt; editor, Birger Möller Jensen; music, Frans Bak; production design, Peter de Neergaard; sound, Henrik Langkilde. Reviewed at Dagmar Theater, Jan. 27, 1992. (In Berlin Film Festival, children's sidebar.) Running time: **90 MIN.**

Irma . . . . Sös Egelind
Tias . . . . Morten Schaffalitzky
Linda . . . . . Karen Molåbak Hansen
Tobbe . . . . Sam Gylling
Torsten . . . . Palle Granditsky
Also with: Anders Jönsson, Annika Nordenskjöld-Olsén, Tomas von Brömssen.

A young Danish boy moves into an old dark house in rural Sweden with his mother and kid sister and encounters love, adversity and mystery. Talented helmer Birger Larsen's touching and engaging family film should perform very well, especially in the Scandi marketplace.

Irma (Söos Egelind) is a drifter and single mother of two children, 15-year-old Tias (Morten Schaffelitzky) and 10-year-old Linda (Karen Molbäk Hansen). When Irma inherits an old derelict house in Sweden, she once again uproots her little family and, much to the kids' consternation, moves to Sweden.

In the rural Swedish town, kids befriend strange but charming Tobbe (Sam Gylling), a child prodigy who secretly plays the organ at the local church. Tia falls in love with Brittan (Annika Nordenskjöld-Olsén), the most beautiful girl in his class. She unfortunately dates the school bully (Anders Jönsson) and soon weird events start to haunt Tias and his family in the old house.

With this simple and entertaining fable, Larsen has extracted good performances from young amateurs. Headed by Schaffalitzky and Hansen, the youthful actors are uniformly excellent.

Among the adults, comedienne Egelind is convincing as the slightly reckless single mom, Tomas von Brömssen evokes sympathy from his nerdy school teacher and Swedish character actor Palle Graditsky is moving in the part of an old recluse mourning his long lost, unrequitted love.

Title refers to both the constellation and an old Ford Thunderbird that plays a mysterious part in the plot.

Like Larsen's first feature effort, 1990's "Dance of the Polar Bears" (also based on an Ulf Stark novel), "The Big Dipper" has entered the Kinderfilmfest in Berlin. Pic will later be released as a three-part miniseries which will provide it with an even bigger market.

— *Peter Risby Hansen*

LA VIE DE BOHÈME
(BOHEMIAN LIFE)
(FINNISH-FRENCH-B&W)

A Sputnik Oy-Pyramide Prods.-Films A2-Swedish Film Institute-Pandora Films production in cooperation with Canal Plus, de Sofinergie 2 Ministère de la Culture et de la Communication. (Intl. sales: Christa Saredi, Zurich.) Produced, directed, written by Aki Kaurismäki, adapted from Henri Murger's novel "Scènes de la vie de bohème." Executive producer, Klaus Heydemann. Co-producers, Paula Oinonen, Francis Boespflug, Willman Andersson. Camera (black & white), Timo Salminen; editor, Veikko Aaltonen; art direction, John Ebden; costumes, Simon Murray; sound, Jouko Lumme, Timo Linnasalo. assistant directors, Pauli Pentti, Nathalie Herr, Gilles Charmant. Reviewed at Berlin Film Festival press previews, Feb. 9, 1992. (In Intl. Forum of Young Cinema.) Running time: **100 MIN.**
Rodolfo . . . . Matti Pellonpää
Mimi . . . . Evelyne Didi
Marcel Marx . . . . André Wilms
Schaumard . . . . Kari Väänänen
Musette . . . . Christine Murillo
Blancheron . . . . . Jean-Pierre Léaud
Baudelaire . . . . Laika
Bartender . . . . Carlos Salgado
Henri Bernard . . . . . . Alexis Nitzer
Mme. Bernard . . Sylvie van den Elsen
Hugo . . . . Gilles Charmant
Gassot . . . . Samuel Fuller
Gentleman . . . . Louis Malle
With: Dominique Marcas, Jean-Paul Wenzel, André Penvern, Maximillian Regiani, Daniel Dublet, Philippe Dormoy, Louis Delamotte, Kenneth Colley.

Aki Kaurismäki's admirers have much to look forward to in this bittersweet, tragicomic melodrama. Finely crafted (especially in its creation of a timeless Paris) and deftly scripted and acted, pic shows the Finnish auteur is maturing as a director without losing his sardonic wit. Pic promises long legs on the fest and arthouse circuit.

Poet Marcel Marx (André Wilms) has been evicted from his squalid room in a shabby Paris neighborhood. A painter Rodolfo (Matti Pellonpää), an Albanian immigrant, invites the impoverished Marcel to share his supper in a small restaurant, and the two become instant friends. They return to Marcel's room to continue their discussion only to find Schaumard, an Irish composer who assumed occupancy following Marcel's eviction. The three become fast friends.

The cohorts are always one precarious step away from ruination — or success. Just as Marcel needs a decent suit to wear to a job interview, a rich industrialist (Jean-Pierre Léaud) appears at Rodolfo's studio to commission a portrait. As he sits for the painting, Marcel is able to borrow the suit just long enough to cinch the interview. The money from both coups buys a decent meal and a three-wheeled car for Schaumard. The cash is gone as quickly as it came.

Romance appears in the form of two not-so-young waifs from the provinces, Musette and Mimi. Musette is Marcel's co-worker on the highly unfashionable fashion magazine he edits for Gassot (Samuel Fuller). Rodolfo discovers Mimi on his doorstep, literally, only to lose her soon after.

Their love is thwarted repeatedly, and when he finally comes into enough money to secure their happiness, he winds up deported. Rodolfo manages to return to France some time later, and he wins Mimi again, only to lose her to illness.

Puccini's version of the famous story hardly comes to mind in this adaptation. Kaurismäki's characters communicate in elegant, scrupulously polite dialogue — a stark contrast and nice foil to the visual squalor. Despite the story's tragedy, the script's wit shines in scene after scene, underscored by great comic timing by actors and director.

Kaurismäki's best humor is visual, ranging from the surreal to pure kitsch. Music, ranging from silly rock songs to Tchaikovsky, is added with skill to simultaneously deepen the drama and lighten the mood.

Cast is strong. Pellonpää again shows strong talent for combining humor with dignity as the earnest Rodolfo, and Wilms, with his lived-in face, shines in pic's beginning. Léaud delivers a nice deadpan perf as the industrialist turned connoisseur. One wishes Christine Murillo as Musette and Kari Väänänen as Schaumard had been given more to do. Cameos by Sam Fuller and Louis Malle provide a wink to the cognoscenti. — *Rebecca Lieb*

U.S. RELEASES

THE RUNESTONE

A Hyperion Pictures-Signature Communications release & production. Produced by Harry E. Gould Jr., Thomas L. Wilhite. Executive producers, Peter E. Strauss, Frank Giustra. Line producer, David R. Cobb. Co-producer, Joe-Michael Terry. Directed, written by Willard Carroll, based on Mark E. Rogers' novella. Camera (Deluxe color), Misha Suslov; editor, Lynne Southerland; music, David Newman; production design, Jon Gary Steele; art direction, Stella Wang; costume design, Terry Dresbach; sound (Ultra-Stereo), Tony Smyles; special makeup effects, Lance Anderson; special visual effects, Max W. Anderson; associate producers, Maria C. Schaeffer, Greg Everage, Vicki Ellis; assistant director, Phil Robinson; casting, Kevin Alber, Jon Robert Samsel. Reviewed at Film Services screening room, L.A., Feb. 13, 1992. MPAA Rating: R. Running time: **101 MIN.**
Capt. Gregory Fanducci . Peter Riegert
Marla Stewart . . . . . Joan Severance
Lars Hagstrom . . . . . William Hickey
Sam Stewart . . . . Tim Ryan
Martin Almquist . . Mitchell Laurance
Chief Richardson . . Lawrence Tierney
Jacob . . . . Chris Young
Sigvaldson . . . . . Alexander Godunov

After the hundreds of low-budget shockers of the past 15 years or so, a horror film with a difference has become a real rarity, but that's what "The Runestone" is. Harking back to the principles of Val Lewton's 1940s horror cycle at RKO, first-time writer-director Willard Carroll has brought an unusual amount of wit and intelligence to the genre, and has enlisted a classy cast.

Despite the high body count and a few chilling moments, however, film's pleasures are relatively specialized, and this fact, along with odd title and adult, rather than teen, orientation, will no doubt prevent it from breaking out commercially.

Pic's premise is as hokey as that of any other scarefest that ever came down the pike. In a Western Pennsylvania mine is found a runestone, a large sixth century Norse rock engraved with inscrutable lettering and a carving of a monster.

Group of characters whose lives become entwined with the discovery include foundation head Mitchell Laurance; his ex-flame, artist Joan Severance; her b.f., archaeologist Tim Ryan; nutty Norse expert William Hickey; clockmaker Alexander Godunov; and a film revival house manager partial to a double bill of Dreyer's "Ordet" and "Gertrud."

Before long, Laurance, who keeps the runestone in his loft, begins behaving belligerently and then disappears altogether, to be replaced on the scene by a ghastly beast that stalks the streets of New York.

As the death count quickly mounts, sarcastic detective Peter Riegert takes on the case, but neither his cool logic, nor his men's bullets, are a match for the Viking monster come to life. "Every dogma must have its day," Hickey intones, as it takes a Norse solution to a Norse problem exported to distant shores centuries before Columbus.

Despite the plot's familiar contrivances, Carroll approaches its conventions without condescension and has the good sense to create characters who accept the menace on its own terms and don't defy or disbelieve it. By having mature adults who, while dealing with their own uncertainties and insecurities, take this bizarre evil seriously, writer-director encourages the viewer to take it seriously enough to lock onto his wavelength.

At the same time, script's sly humor gives the many obligatory genre scenes a nice twist, just as Riegert's sardonic nature takes the edge off any standard police heroics. Carroll stages two imaginatively satirical set pieces at snooty art galleries, has created a nice little montage intercutting some lovemaking with shots of the beast on the prowl, and controls the tone so well that he can have crusty police chief Lawrence Tierney remark of the monster, "It's a big guy in a bulletproof vest in a dog suit," and not see his picture descend into camp.

As usual, Riegert brings very welcome, self-conscious humor to the proceedings, and remainder of the cast is capable and agreeably grown-up.

Technically, low-budget production is highly accomplished. Lenser Misha Suslov has created a high-contrast, shadowy look that suits the material, and filmmakers have done an expert job making mostly L.A. locations convince as N.Y., with only a bit of Gotham second unit work.

David Newman's full-bodied score sounds as if it was composed in the '40s, which is meant as a high compliment, and Lance Anderson's monster makeup effects are dead-on.

— *Todd McCarthy*

THE RESTLESS CONSCIENCE
(DOCU-COLOR/B&W)

Produced, directed, written by Hava Kohav Beller. Camera (color, black & white), Volker Rodde, Martin Schaer, Gabor Bagyoni; editors, Tonicka Janek, Juliette Weber, David Rogow; music, Elliot Sokolov; consulting historian, Prof. Peter Hoffmann. Narrated by John Dildine. Reviewed at Walter Reade Theater, N.Y., Jan. 28, 1992. Running time: **113 MIN.**

"The Restless Conscience" is an engrossing documentary examining German resistance to Hitler's regime. Director Hava Kohav Beller's gimmick-free approach tells the story chronologically, utilizing newsreels and interviews. While the myriad of activities depicted and procession of talking heads takes a toll on viewers, this is essentially compelling material.

Coming on the heels of "The Nasty Girl" and the current flap over "Europa, Europa's" Oscar status, the docu serves as a contrasting reminder that there were genuine German heroes who resisted Hitler from the inception of the Nazi government to the aftermath of the failed assassination attempt on him July 20, 1944. While the film does not dispute that the movement was relatively small, it suggests a wider range of participation and activities than past histories have credited.

The tone of Beller's first docu feature is more elegiac than probing. Interviewees include only a scant number of surviving resistance fighters and a lengthy scrawl of names at the pic's end lists Germans executed by Nazis.

Docu might find its ideal venue with the Corp. for Public Broadcasting, provider of additional funding for the film.

—*Fred Lombardi*

WAYNE'S WORLD

A Paramount Pictures release of a Lorne Michaels production. Produced by Michaels. Executive producer, Howard W. Koch Jr. Directed by Penelope Spheeris. Screenplay, Mike Myers, Bonnie & Terry Turner, based on characters created by Myers. Camera (Technicolor), Theo Van de Sande; editor, Malcolm Campbell; music, J. Peter Robinson; production design, Gregg Fonseca; assistant director, John E. Hockridge; production manager, Tony Brown; sound (Dolby), Thomas Nelson; stunt coordinator-2nd unit director, Allan Graf; 2nd unit camera, Bobby Stevens; additional editor, Earl Ghaffari; associate producers, Dinah Minot, Barnaby Thompson; casting, Glenn Daniels. Reviewed at Loews Astor Plaza theater, N.Y., Feb. 6, 1992. MPAA Rating: PG-13. Running time: **95 MIN.**

Wayne Campbell	Mike Myers
Garth Algar	Dana Carvey
Benjamin Oliver	Rob Lowe
Cassandra	Tia Carrere
Noah Vanderhoff	Brian Doyle-Murray
Stacy	Lara Flynn Boyle
Russell	Kurt Fuller
Mrs. Vanderhoff	Colleen Camp

Also with: Alice Cooper, Donna Dixon, Michael DeLuise, Dan Bell, Lee Tergesen, Sean Gregory Sullivan, Frederick Coffin, Chris Farley, Meat Loaf, Ed O'Neill, Ione Skye, Robert Patrick.

"Wayne's World" weakly transfers the popular "Saturday Night Live" TV sketch to the big screen. Aggressively pitched at a young white male audience, feature is unlikely to appeal to mainstream moviegoers.

SNL regular Mike Myers created the characters of two overage heavy metal teens fronting a cable access TV show in Aurora, Ill. Like Weird Al Yankovic's flop Orion pic "UHF," the film satirizes various genres using TV as a starting point.

Playing an Art Garfunkel sidekick to Myers' Paul Simon, SNL mate Dana Carvey bounces back after his bland first film vehicle "Opportunity Knocks." Thin script by Myers and TV writing cronies Bonnie & Terry Turner is simply a skeleton for applying music and gags, all delivered in a knowing, winking-at-the-audience fashion (with frequent asides directly to the camera).

Ostensible plot has Rob Lowe as a slimy opportunist who buys the heroes' "Wayne's World" show and re-structures it to plug Brian Doyle-Murray's video arcade business. Wayne (Myers) falls in love with beautiful Hong Kong rock singer Tia Carrere and has to worry about womanizer Lowe stealing her away.

Director Penelope Spheeris, with her first major studio assignment (and eight-figure budget), delivers a colorful but uneventful picture. Far too much footage is devoted to Carrere's indifferent singing, the heroes' comical lip-synching or pointless filler like a visit to an Alice Cooper concert. Even for fans of the TV comics, the laugh-to-running-time ratio is extremely low.

Silliness includes a spoof of product plugs (that serves as an extended product plug) and typical cross-references to other Paramount properties like "Star Trek" and "Laverne & Shirley." As with Paramount's ill-fated "Clue" film, picture features three alternate endings, played back to back like the "Clue" video.

Myers, funny in small doses on the tube, overstays his welcome as the grinning, know-it-all Wayne while Carvey is childishly endearing as the nerdy Garth. Lowe smirks his way through a non-role, Carrere's beauty is featured in a variety of sexy outfits and Lara Flynn Boyle handles the slapstick.

Guest stars add almost nothing to the proceedings, including Dan Aykroyd's wife Donna Dixon as Carvey's beautiful dream girl, Ione Skye as Lowe's girlfriend, Meat Loaf as a bouncer and Ed O'Neill as a nutty donut shop manager. — *Lawrence Cohn*

BACK IN THE USSR

A 20th Century Fox release of a Largo Intl. N.V. production in association with JVC Entertainment. Produced by Lindsay Smith, Ilmar Taska. Executive producer, Louis A. Stroller. Co-producer, James Steele. Directed by Deran Sarafian. Screenplay, Smith, story by Taska, Smith. Camera (Deluxe color), Yuri Neyman; editor, Ian Crafford; music, Les Hooper; production design, Vladimir Philippov; set decoration, Nicolai Surovtsev, Yuri Osipenko; costumes, Cynthia Bergstrom; sound (Dolby), Gary Cunningham; associate producer, Anatoly Fradis; assistant director, Leo Zisman; casting, Jeremy Zimmerman. Reviewed at Cineplex Odeon Shirlington Seven, Arlington, Va., Feb. 7, 1992. MPAA Rating: R. Running time: **89 MIN.**

Archer	Frank Whaley
Lena	Natalya Negoda
Kurilov	Roman Polanski
Dimitri	Andrew Divof
Claudia	Dey Young
Georgi	Ravil Issyanov
Whittier	Harry Ditson
Chazov	Brian Blessed
Stanley	Constantine Gregory
Mikhail	Alexei Yevdokimov

"Back in the USSR" is an amateurish adventure about the Russian underworld shot entirely in Moscow. This attempt to capitalize on perestroika stumbles over a weak script, wooden acting and inferior tech credits. **A speedy demise is assured.**

Fox's launch of the Largo Entertainment item in a handful of markets over the weekend has all the earmarks of a contractual release agreement minimally fulfilled pre-video. Publicity was scant and screenings nil.

Distrib's apparent low confidence is justified. Among film's faults are pathetic dialogue and characters who cling to corny stereotypes. Inconsistent cinematography testifies to a rushed production schedule.

As with other joint U.S.-Russian artistic ventures, the final product betrays attempts at melding vastly different work standards, cultures and equipment. It was co-produced by screenwriter Lindsay Smith, founder of the American/Soviet Film Initiative and Russian producer Ilmar Taska.

Story involves vacationing young American Frank Whaley, whose amorous pursuits lead him into a cops-and-robbers escapade featuring a parade of loathsome characters. Russian actress Natalya Negoda is the love interest, and Roman Polanski plays the chief villain. In an obvious attempt at humor, nightclub owner Polanski is shown in one scene relishing nubile maidens on stage.

Script's chief ambition is to emphasize contemporary Moscow life over the familiar postcard perspective. Locales include shabby apartments, garish nightclubs, garages, back alleys and churches. GUM, the baroque shopping arcade opposite Red Square, is also employed in a rush-hour chase scene. Some loftier goals are desperately needed, such as building any relationship between the two leads.

— *Paul Harris*

EURO RELEASES

GLI ASSASSINI VANNO IN COPPIA
(KILLERS COME IN PAIRS)
(ITALIAN)

An Azione Cinematografica production. Produced, directed by Piero Natoli. Screenplay, Francesco Costa, Natoli. Camera (color), Carlo Cerchio; editor, Mimmo Varone; music, Carlo Crivelli; art direction-costumes, Paola Nazzaro; in Dolby. Reviewed at Politecnico Cinema, Rome, Jan. 21, 1992. Running time: **95 MIN.**

Roberto	Piero Natoli

Margherita	Paola Pitagora
Marco	Massimo Bonetti
Francesca	Manuela Gatti
Diana	Paola Nazzaro
Agostina	Claudia Poggiani
The father-in-law	Franco Interlenghi

Piero Natoli makes more impact as actor than helmer in "Killers Come in Pairs," an uneven hybrid love story/suspenser, fitfully envlivened by quirky comic touches. Competent but technically average pic owes more to TV cop shows than the Hitchcockian tradition it aspires to, and it would have fared better as telefilm fodder.

Disillusioned lawyer Natoli witnesses a murder in a sauna, but cops and kin don't swallow his story as no corpse is found and no other witnesses show. When the stiff turns up elsewhere, authorities label it suicide, and the unprotected lawyer is stalked by the killers.

Natoli makes the central character strong and sympathetic but is let down by an inconsistent supporting cast playing largely underwritten roles.

Helmer Natoli shows a sure hand in pic's lighter moments, but elsewhere he lacks the savvy to create suspense or passion, leaning heavily on overstated music or golden-huged flashbacks. — *David Rooney*

LA TOTALE!
(THE JACKPOT!)
(FRENCH)

An AMLF release of a Films 7-Film par Film-Paravision Intl.-MDG Prods.-RF1 Films Prod. co-production in conjunction with the Sofica Sofiarp. (Intl. sales: Roissy Films.) Produced, directed by Claude Zidi. Screenplay, Zidi, with Simon Michael, Didier Kaminke. Camera (color), Jean-Jacques Tarbes; editor, Nicole Saunier; music, Vladimir Cosma; set design, Françoise De Leu; costume design, Olga Pelletier; sound, Jean-Louis Ughetto. Reviewed at the Forum Horizon, Paris, Dec. 27, 1991. Running time: **103 MIN.**
François Voisin . . Thierry Lhermitte
Helene Voisin . . . . Miou-Miou
Albert "Einstein" . . . . Eddy Mitchell
Marcel/"Simon" . . . . Michel Boujenah
Sarris/Brenner . . . . . Jean Benguigui
Vanessa . . . . Claudy Wilde

Played to deadpan perfection by several of France's top comic actors, "La Totale!" is an energetic, cleverly constructed comedy of errors about a bored librarian whose humdrum existence is enlivened by the discovery that her husband is a topnotch undercover op-

erative. Silly, thoroughly enjoyable comedy by Claude Zidi is a medium-sized local hit that could possibly lend itself to a remake.

In Zidi's 20th film in as many years, Miou-Miou is fine as a mother of two who believes that her husband of 18 years (Thierry Lhermitte) is a pleasant but dull employee of the state-owned telephone company.

Lhermitte, in reality a career secret service agent, may know intimate details about foreign ambassadors, but he's oblivious to what's going on in his own family. His son is playing hooky, and his wife is contemplating an affair with a sleazy used-car dealer who scores with the chicks by convincing them that he's a secret agent constantly in danger.

Lhermitte becomes obsessed with his wife's secret life and mounts a phony sting operation to teach her a lesson. But a real caper involving illegal arms dealings intervenes, and compound mayhem ensues as Miou-Miou does her earnest, misguided best to help.

Lhermitte is a cool customer, a blue-eyed charmer who's fun to watch. Dry banter between him and gadget-concocting partner (Eddy Mitchell) is a plus.

Lensing is slick, and minor-league 007 stuff (such as a mini-VCR in a dog collar) is pulled off with zest. Lhermitte's job perks are amusingly deployed when fellow agents, including a helicopter crew, rally to track down the truant son.

— *Lisa Nesselson*

AOÛT
(AUGUST)
(FRENCH)

A MK2 release of a Les Prods. Lazannec-M6 Films-Hachette Première & Co.-UGC Images-SGGC Jean-Bernard Fetoux co-production. Produced by Adeline Lecallier, Alain Rocca. Directed, written by Henri Herré from Ödön von Horvath's "Casimir et Caroline." Camera (color), Luc Drion; editor, Anita Fernandez; music, Emmanuel de Gouvello; costume design, Gérard Barreaux; set design, Marc Anselmi; sound, Jean-Jacques Ferran; assistant director, Philippe Hagege. Reviewed at Club 13 screening room, Paris, Dec. 11, 1991. Running time: **90 MIN.**
Caroline . . . . Anouk Grinberg
Eugene Blouzette . . Dominique Pinon
Martin . . . . Jean-Claude Brialy
Lance . . . . .Jean-Louis Richard
Antoine . . . . Patrick Pineau
  Also with: Hélène Lapiower, Philippe Dormoy, Marianne Filali-Ansary.

Never boring but rarely

lucid, "August" follows a batch of memorable, though mostly unpleasant, characters as their destinies intersect over two days. Henri Herré's emotionally harsh, ultra-contemporary tale is a good bet for fests.

It's August, it's hot and a manned space capsule is about to land on Mars. Caroline (Anouk Grinberg) is excited about event's live TV coverage, but her gruff, suspicious b.f. Antoine (Patrick Pineau) is in a permanent bad mood.

When Caroline goes out to get an ice cream, she meets mild-mannered Eugene (Dominique Pinon, the slight, rubber-faced actor who has appeared in nearly 30 features since limning the terse punk in 1980's "Diva." With this pic and "Delicatessen," he's forging an unlikely leading man career).

An eminent career researcher (Jean-Claude Brialy) and his beefy boss (Jean-Louis Richard) attend a nearby medical conference. They try to show Caroline a good time while hot-tempered Antoine and his jailbird neighbor are up to no good. Comeuppances come up.

Carefully lensed in the sterile, hi-tech shadow of the new Grand Arch west of Paris, willfully stylish pic displays much of the romantic expediency that marks European art films, but convincing thesping makes the emotional trajectories seem a little less arbitrary than usual.

Every shot is carefully choreographed to good effect, although what exactly happens offscreen in an underground parking lot toward the end is anybody's guess. —*Lisa Nesselson*

ÄNGLAGÅRD
(ANGEL FARM)
(SWEDISH)

A Sonet Film presentation of a Memfis Film & TV production in cooperation with the Swedish Film Institute, Nordisk Film & TV Fund, NRK (Norway), DR (Denmark) & TV-2 Gothenburg. Produced by Lars Jönsson. Directed, written by Colin Nutley. Camera (color), Jens Fischer; editor, Perry Schaffer; music, Björn Isfält, Göran Martling; costumes, Sven Lundén, Britt-Marie Larsson; production design, Ulla Herdin; sound, Lasse Liljeholm, Eddie Axberg. Reviewed at Svensk Filmindustri screening room, Stockholm, Jan. 24, 1992. (In Gothenburg Film Festival.) Running time: **126 MIN.**
  With: Helena Bergström, Richard Wolff, Sven Wollter, Viveka Seldahl, Jacob Eklund, Gabriella Boris, Reine Brynolfsson, Ernst Gunther.

British helmer Colin Nutley's third feature is another moody, comic look at the Swedes and their moods. Pic's warmth, production values and acting should generate good box office results.

Nutley sets "Angelfarm" in the countryside and addresses the suspicions and bigotry that lead to racism and conflict — but it's all rendered humorously.

After a rich old man dies in an accident, his granddaughter, a girl no one else in the village knew existed, inherits his estate. Fanny, in her late 20s and a child of the city, is on the naive side, and she doesn't realize the effect of her flamboyance on the villagers. She becomes a catalyst for hidden conflicts within the community, and everything points to a violent solution.

Or would have, if the film had been, say, an American action pic. Here, no one is portrayed as totally evil, and the film ends on a hopeful note. Meanwhile, this amusing story provides insightful and tender character portraits and, through the lens of Jens Fischer, a beautiful depiction of Swedish summer.

Acting is good overall, especially Viveka Seldahl as the bigoted wife of the landowner who wants to buy Fanny's farm, and Ernst Gunther as a kind old man who becomes Fanny's most loyal supporter. — *Gunnar Rehlin*

EINAMAL ARIZONA
(ONCE ARIZONA)
(GERMAN)

A Tobis Filmkunst release of a Rialto Film production. Produced by Susan Nielebock. Directed, written by Hans-Günther Bücking. Camera (color), Bücking, Jürgen Podzkiewitz; editor, Helga Borsche; music, Nick Woodland; sets-lighting, Andreas Willim; sound, Rainer Wiehr; assistant director, Ilona Brennicke; assistant camera, Til Maier; director of production, Moritz Hänska. Reviewed at Zoo Palast Cinema, Berlin, Aug. 11, 1991. Running time: **90 MIN.**
  With: Nikolaus Gröbe, Helmut Berger.

(German & English soundtrack)

"Once Arizona" is another road movie about the U.S. southwest as only Germans can make 'em. Likable, simple pic could find a niche in urban U.S. art houses thanks to topnotch cinematography, humorous touches and Helmut Berger's unconventional perf.

First time helmer Hans-Günther Bücking shows promise as a

director, but his strongest point is cinematography. Lensing much of pic himself on budget of less than $600,000, his images of neon, diners, highway, desert, big sky and freight trains look like they cost much more.

Pic follows a young, motorcycle-obsessed East German (Nikolaus Gröbe) who America where he pursues his dream of visiting the annual biker meeting in Oatman, Ariz. Low on cash and lower still on English, he sets off on a chopper from LAX into Marlboro country.

En route he hooks up with Bruno, a disenfranchised Austrian (Berger) who prowls the desert with a video camera hoping to happen on a plane crash or similar disaster so he can "sell the footage to CNN for $100,000."

Other thesps are nonpro locals woven into the story for local color, not to bad effect. Dialogue is minimal; effective and often eloquent sight gags include the East German bewilderment upon encountering a Pepsi machine that produced a can of Coke.

Music, which often shifts gears abruptly between rock and country, is film's only jarring element. — *Rebecca Lieb*

LA DERNIÈRE SAISON
(THE LAST SEASON)
(FRENCH)

A Sirius release of a New Trust European production. Produced by Jean-Claude Dague, Lorène Russell, Jean Cherlian & Pierre Beccu. Directed by Pierre Beccu. Screenplay, Beccu, Jean-Louis Rapini, Jean-Claude Dague. Camera (color), Maurice Giraud; editor, Claude Guerin; music, Frederic Laperierre, Marc Aubert, Michel Martinier; costume design, Emmanuelle Salard; sound, Philippe Lecoeur. Reviewed at Club de l'Etoile, Paris, Dec. 23, 1991. Running time: **103 MIN.**
Jean Marsan . . . . Jean Davy
Laurent Ferrand . . Laurent Ferroud
Sophie . . . . Julia Monnerie
Suzanne . . . . Lorène Russell
Marthe . . . . Marie Dubois

Casually paced drama "La Dernière Saison" aims for total authenticity in evoking demanding cow-tending and cheese-making regimens in the French Alps. Portrait of two generations has its rewards for committed viewers.

Outstanding thesp Jean Davy plays a gruff codger whose family long ago thwarted both his scholastic promise and true love by sending him to tend cows.

Too old to handle all the chores, the lifelong mountain dweller mulls selling his rustic spread to a wheeler dealer who wants to build a vacation complex. For one last season, the old man reluctantly accepts the help of a local lad in his 20s who is thinking of seeking his fortune elsewhere. Nonprofessional Laurent Ferroud manages to hold his own in scenes with one-time Comedie Française member Davy. Their wary partnership rings true.

Young helmer Pierre Beccu, who apprenticed with Ermanno Olmi, economically tells a modest but nicely observed tale, set in the mountains where he himself grew up. Footage of artisanal cheese-making (mold-incrusted "Tomme de Savoie") is poignant in light of recent EEC legislation that likely will end centuries of sub-hygienic cheesecraft. — *Lisa Nesselson*

SISI UND DER KAISERKUSS
(SISI/LAST MINUTE)
(GERMAN-FRENCH)

A Dietrich Grönemeyer-Rainer Seibel presentation of a Calypso Film production in co-production with Maran Film, New Deal Films & G&S Produktionsgesellschaft. Directed, written by Christoph Boll. Camera (color), Rheinhard Köcher; editor, Helga Borsche; sets, Christian Bussmann; costumes, Bea Gossmann; sound, Andreas Mücke; production supervisor, Uwe Frank; director of production, Hans Christian Hess. Reviewed at Filmpalast Theatre, Berlin, Aug. 12, 1991. Running time: **95 MIN.**
Sisi . . . . Vanessa Wagner
Kaiser Franz-Joseph . . Nils Tavernier
Princess Helene . . Sonja Kirchberger
Sophie . . . . Kristina Walter Von
von Wrangel . . . . Bernadette Lafont
Duke Max . . . . Jean Poiret
Ludovika . . . . Cleo Kretschmer
Also with: Wichard von Röell, Joseph Ostendorf, Volker Prechtel.

Handsomely shot costume drama might find an audience in German-lingo territories, but those unfamiliar with the cult status of the Austrian empress will be hard to draw to "Sisi/Last Minute."

To young German girls, Sisi, the young Bavarian princess who married Austrian emperor Franz-Joseph, is a romantic confection somewhere between Barbie and Sleeping Beauty. She was immortalized in a string of sugar-sweet Romy Schneider-starrers.

This pic purports to tell the true story of 14-year-old Sisi, who becomes engaged to Franz-Joseph even though her sister, Princess Helene, has been preparing for the role all her life.

Thin and effete Franz-Joseph, meanwhile, languishes in his turret playroom directing toy soldiers on an enormous mock battlefield and avoiding the advances of numerous libidinous and predatory females.

Court ladies bare their breasts frequently at the emperor, and he looks away in chagrin. By film's end, when the emperor proposes to Sisi, the happily-ever-after seems to rest on the fact that Franz-Joseph is off the hook from having sex forever.

Tale is rich in costumes, handsome sets and good acting, but the machinations between the Bavarian and Austrian courts could have been more intriguing. Viewers are expected to have knowledge of, and interest in, the characters. — *Rebecca Lieb*

HOWARDS END
(BRITISH)

An Orion Classics release of a Merchant Ivory production, in association with Film Four Intl. Produced by Ismail Merchant. Executive producer, Paul Bradley. Directed by James Ivory. Screenplay, Ruth Prawer Jhabvala, based on E.M. Forster's novel. Camera (Super 35 Widescreen, Technicolor), Tony Pierce-Roberts; editor, Andrew Marcus; music, Richard Robbins; production design, Luciana Arrighi; art direction, John Ralph; set decoration, Ian Whittaker; costume design, Jenny Beavan, John Bright; sound (Dolby), Mike Shoring; assistant director, Chris Newman; production managers, John Downes, Caroline Hill; co-producer, Ann Wingate; casting, Celestia Fox. Reviewed at Magno Review 1 screening room, N.Y., Feb. 11, 1992. MPAA Rating: PG. Running time: **140 MIN.**
Henry Wilcox . . . . Anthony Hopkins
Ruth Wilcox . . . . Vanessa Redgrave
Helen Schlegel . Helena Bonham Carter
Margaret Schlegel . . Emma Thompson
Charles Wilcox . . . . . . James Wilby
Leonard Bast . . . . Sam West
Evie Wilcox . . . . . Jemma Redgrave
Jacky Bast . . . . Nicola Duffett
Aunt Juley . . . . Prunella Scales
Dolly Wilcox . . . . . Susan Lindeman
Tibby Schlegel . Adrian Ross Magenty
Miss Avery . . . . Barbara Hicks
Also with: Joseph Bennett, Jo Kendall, Mark Payton, Simon Callow.

E.M. Forster's "Howards End" makes a most compelling drama, perhaps the best film made during the 30-year partnership of Ismail Merchant and James Ivory. Orion Classics has a must-see picture for class audiences that could be as big a hit as "A Room With a View," which broke out for $25 million in domestic grosses.

Longtime Merchant Ivory collaborator Ruth Prawer Jhabvala (an Oscar-winner for "Room With a View") has distilled the 1910 novel into pungent, concise scenes that grab the viewer and maximize the impact of Forster's themes about class differences and the harm caused by repressing true feelings.

Aristocratic matriarch Ruth Wilcox (Vanessa Redgrave) on her deathbed scrawls a note bequeathing her beloved estate Howards End to a recent acquaintance, Margaret Schlegel (Emma Thompson). Schlegel and her siblings are about to lose their lease in London, and she's expressed a love for the countryside akin to Redgrave's own.

This sets into motion the strongest of all movie driving forces: the wronged individual. Redgrave's aristocratic husband Henry (Anthony Hopkins) and daughter Evie (real-life daughter Jemma Redgrave) hardly know Thompson and callously destroy the note to selfishly keep the estate in the family even though they don't live there anymore.

Forster's ironic scheme of fate and coincidence picks up momentum with further relationships between the two families leading improbably to Thompson's engagement to be married to the stuffy widower Hopkins.

A crucial, initially cryptic, subplot involves insurance company clerk Leonard Bast (Sam West) and his wife Jacky (Nicola Duffett). After chance encounters, Schlegel's high-spirited sister Helen (Helena Bonham Carter) begins to look out for West's welfare, resulting in an impromptu tryst and pregnancy. In a subplot of clear contemporary relevance, Hopkins' off-hand meddling eventually results in Bast losing his job and becoming terminally unemployed.

Hopkins' decade-ago relationship with Duffett comes to light, and film climaxes in unexpected violence, a scene vividly staged at Howards End. At fadeout, director James Ivory uses great subtlety in the almost throwaway manner by which Hopkins tells Thompson how he destroyed the inheritance note, asking her "I didn't do wrong, did I?"

Hopkins can certainly do no wrong in the acting department, portraying an uppercrust nasty with chilling understatement in his best screen role alongside "The Good Father" and "The Silence of the Lambs." In the film's largest role, Thompson is immensely sympathetic.

Bonham Carter, currently starring to strong effect in the other Forster release "Where Angels Fear to Tread," proves again that she's the best actress today at embodying the look and spirit of period roles. Vanessa Redgrave uses unusual phrasing to create an eerie presence in her successful casting against type as the matriarch in failing health.

Newcomers Sam West and Nicola Duffett make a distinctive impression as the doomed commoners whose fate gradually takes on tragic dimensions. Supporting parts are very well cast, including comedienne Prunella Scales (of TV's "Fawlty Towers") as Thompson's cute aunt and Barbara Hicks as the mysterious caretaker who has always lived at Howards End.

Producer Ismail Merchant's technical team contributes a top-notch setting for this film jewel, especially Tony Pierce-Roberts'

expansive visuals, the first wide-screen picture made by MIP (shot in the Super 35 process for blow-up to 70m in key engagements).

Also noteworthy are the contributions of Oscar-winning costume designers (for "A Room with a View") Jenny Beavan and John Bright and production designer Luciana Arrighi. MIP regular Richard Robbins leads the action with a suspenseful under score. — *Lawrence Cohn*

I DON'T BUY KISSES ANYMORE

A Skouras Pictures release of a Web-Marc Pictures production. Produced by Mitchel Matovich. Executive producer, Charles Weber. Line producer, Gary M. Bettman. Directed by Robert Marcarelli. Screenplay, Jonnie Lindsell. Camera (color), Michael Ferris; editor, Joanne D'Antonio; music, Cobb Bussinger; production design, Byrnadette di Santo; set decoration, Katherine Orrison; costume design, Patte Dee; sound, David Waelder; assistant directors, Gregory Everage, Lynn D'Angona; casting, Cathy Henderson. Reviewed at AMC Century 14 Cinemas, Feb. 17, 1992. MPAA rating: PG. Running time: **112 MIN.**
Bernie Fishbine . . . Jason Alexander
Theresa Garabaldi . . . . . Nia Peeples
Sarah Fishbine . . . . . . Lainie Kazan
Irving Fein . . . . Lou Jacobi
Frieda . . . . Eileen Brennan
Norman Fishbine . . . . . David Bowe
Connie Klinger . . . Michele Scarabelli
Ada Fishbine . . . . . . Hilary Shepard
Also with: Marlena Giovi, Ralph Monaco, Arleen Sorkin, Cassie Yates, Al Ruscio, Lela Ivey, Larry Storch.

A middle-brow romantic comedy steeped in Jewish and Italian stereotype, "I Don't Buy Kisses Anymore" has the odd distinction of crossover potential in the motivational video market, as its detailed portrait of a lifelong fatty who sweats and diets his way to a new life is really quite inspiring. Less convincing is its broad, clumsy love story. In limited release, this modestly budgeted heartwarmer has the potential to hold its own in theaters and weigh in solidly on video.

Jason Alexander plays Bernie, a lonely, chubby bachelor who slogs along under the thumb of his overbearing Jewish family and the shoestore he inherited from his dad.

Highlight of his routine life is stopping in at the corner candy store for a sack of chocolate kisses each night — until he meets peppy, ambitious aerobics nut Tress (Nia Peeples) at the bus stop and loses his heart. In no time he's joined her gym and is battering away at the extra 50 pounds on his stocky frame, while

trying unsuccessfully to date her.

Tress, pursuing a masters degree and singing in her uncle's Italian restaurant, keeps him at arm's length until she decides to make him the focus of her graduate thesis, a psychological study of an obese male.

Unsuspecting Bernie takes her interest to heart and has bought the engagement ring — as well as trimmed down, gained confidence, given up the candy and, unbeknownst to him, won Tress's heart — by the time he discovers the offending academic treatise. He storms off in a king-size tantrum while she's left to try to convince him she really cares.

Set in a blue-collar Philly suburb that has dodged the winds of change, pic explores the Jewish home where 30-year-old Bernie still lives with his overbearing mother (Lainie Kazan) and bombastic grandfather (Lou Jacobi), insightfully conveying the "food is love" mentality that has shaped Bernie's habits, as well as his frame.

Buoyed by a warm, engaging chemistry between Peeples and Alexander, pic tells a poignant story of a friendship and the changes it inspires but skimps on a convincing common ground between Bernie and Tress. Her full-somersault tumble for him remains unbelievable.

Director Robert Marcarelli finds plenty of sweet spots in the character comedy but lets the performances veer into mood-breaking melodramatic excess at several crucial turns.

Cast is uneven, with Eileen Brennan charming as the candy store owner and Kazan and Jacobi playing fully into unflattering ethnic stereotypes, to the detriment of an occasionally penetrating piece. — *Amy Dawes*

FALLING FROM GRACE

A Columbia Pictures release of a Little b Pictures production. Produced by Harry Sandler. Directed by John Mellencamp. Screenplay, Larry McMurtry. Camera (Technicolor), Victor Hammer; editor, Dennis Virkler; production design, George Corsillo; art direction, Todd Hatfield; set decoration, Sandi Cook; sound, Don Scales; assistant director, Michael Curtis; associate producer, Richard Mellencamp. Reviewed at Sony Studios, Culver City, Calif., Feb. 18, 1992. MPAA rating: PG-13. Running time: **100 MIN.**
Bud Parks . . . . . . John Mellencamp
P.J. Parks . . . . Kay Lenz
Alice Parks . . . . . Mariel Hemingway
Speck Parks . . . . Claude Akins
Ramey Parks . . . . Larry Crane
Sally Cutler . . . . . Dierdre O'Connell
Grandpa Parks . . . . . . Dub Taylor

Heartland rocker John Mellencamp, working from Larry McMurtry's fine script, turns his abiding interest in the heart of the common man into an absorbing, if occasionally murky, study of complex midwestern men and the women who put up with them. Rich in character and literary in tone, "Falling From Grace" looks headed for a quiet theatrical tour, but with targeted promotion, it should do solid video and ancillary biz.

Mellencamp, debuting as both film director and star, plays exuberant, easygoing Bud Parks, a country music star who returns home with his California wife (Mariel Hemingway) to help celebrate the 80th birthday of his grandpa (Dub Taylor)

The family farm in tiny, fictional Doak City, Ind., is enduring a crisis in which a disease is killing chickens by the thousands. But more disturbing to Bud is the relevation that his old high school g.f. P.J. (Kay Lenz) is having an affair with Bud's randy, uncontrollable father (Claude Akins). It hardly matters that she's long since married Bud's brother (Brent Huff) or that Speck, the mean-spirited dad, means not a whit to her. P.J.'s just keeping boredom at bay, a talent she's grown proud of.

Bud's odd reaction to the news is to take up with her himself, and before long he's spending afternoons in her bed while his restless wife stews and his relatives get mad at him.

Straight-talking P.J. defines their liaison as just a frolic, but Bud confuses it for the real thing and lets his marriage fall apart. What he's looking for is unclear even to him, but he may be running from the demands of a career he's losing interest in while trying to take back the refuge of his past. His wise, clear-eyed sister (Dierdre O'Connell) tells him he doesn't belong there anymore, but that's not enough to keep Bud from trying to ruin everything he's got.

Pic was shot in Mellencamp's hometown of Seymour, Ind., in the heart of the blighted farm belt, but it's very much McMurtry country, as the character-rich, bawdy and often penetrating script bears the hallmarks of the writer's best work, particularly in the creation of P.J., a sexually forthright, self-determining character who's carved out an original response to the cards life has dealt her.

Depressed farm situation is very much on the edge's of the character's minds, not surprising given Mellencamp's history as a founder of the Farm Aid music benefits, but film stays on track as a character study rather than a soapbox.

Very much in his element with this material, Mellencamp registers as a natural and likable screen presence, easily as appealing as musical colleague and occasional film actor Willie Nelson, and conveys Bud's surliness and moods as capably as his sunny, people-loving nature.

For the work of a rocker turned film director (Mellencamp has previously directed musicvid-), pic is admirably free of vanity or showboating, with same spareness, integrity and exuberance of his admirable body of music.

Best achievement is in the performances, with sharp work from the no-nonsense Lenz. Standout supporting players include O'Connell in an acutely on-target portrayal of the patient but worried former farm wife, musician Larry Crane as the half-brother Bud confides in, and Akins as the rotten apple patriarch. Hemingway rises to the occasion in some sharply written confrontations with Bud, and Taylor is a gem as the untamable grandpa.

Lensing is straight ahead and no-frills, a bit rudimentary at times but suited to the material. Unfortunately, pic has a serious flaw in the clumsy handling of a key scene involving a peculiar kick called "riding the cage."

Best not described here, to save a surprise for filmgoers, arcane sport functions as a metaphor for Bud's self-destructive desire to crawl back into the box of the small town and throw caution to the winds. But the night scene is so murkily lensed one can scarcely tell what's happening, let alone interpret it.

Soundtrack is a pleasing mix of classic country and newer stuff, with a strong new John Prine song ("All the Best") featured. Mellencamp doesn't perform in the film, save some casual strumming on the porch.
— *Amy Dawes*

RADIO FLYER

A Columbia Pictures release of a Stonebridge Entertainment production in association with Donner/Shuler-Donner Prods. Produced by Lauren Schuler-Donner. Co-producers, Jennie Lew Tugend, Jim Van Wyck, Dale R. de la Torre. Executive producers, Michael Douglas, Rick Bieber, David Mickey Evans. Co-executive producers, Richard Solomon, Peter McAlevey. Directed by Richard Donner. Screenplay, Evans. Camera (Panavision, Technicolor, black & white), Laszlo Kovacs; editor, Stuart Baird; music, Hans Zimmer; production design, J. Michael Riva; art direction, David Frederick Klassen; set decoration, Michael Taylor; costume design, April Ferry; sound (Dolby), Ronald Judkins; visual effects supervisor, Peter Donen; stunt coordinator, Mic Rodgers; Radio Flyer conceptualist, Michael Scheffe; associate producers, Sherry Lynn Fadely, Alexander Bernhardt Collett; assistant director, Van Wyck; 2nd unit director, Riva; 2nd unit camera, Bobby Byrne; casting, Mike Fenton, Judy Taylor, Valorie Massalas. Reviewed at Edwards Atlantic Palace 10, Alhambra, Calif., Feb. 15, 1992. MPAA rating: PG-13. Running time: **113 MIN.**

Mary	Lorraine Bracco
Daugherty	John Heard
The King	Adam Baldwin
Mike	Elijah Wood
Bobby	Joseph Mazzello
Geronimo Bill	Ben Johnson
Young Fisher	Sean Baca
Older Fisher	Robert Munic
Older Mike	Tom Hanks

"Radio Flyer" is a film one would like to like more. David Mickey Evans' underdeveloped screenplay about two boys' fantasy of escape from an abusive stepfather is sometimes moving but too often distant and literal-minded. Richard Donner's direction of a difficult subject is sensitive but lacks the delicacy François Truffaut brought to such material. Still, with proper nurturing by Columbia, this heartfelt pic could appeal to all audiences.

Given its troubled production history, "Radio Flyer" (made during the Frank Price regime at Col) might have been a disaster — or a masterpiece. Instead, its neither/nor quality seems built into its high-priced spec script.

Evans started the pic in June 1990 with Rosanna Arquette as the mother, but the first-time writer-director was soon fired. Production shut down before Donner moved the setting of the late '60s story from L.A. to rustic northern California. Pic was delayed twice from its original July '91 release.

Cast by Donner, Elijah Wood and Joseph Mazzello are extraordinarily good, and they hold the screen with intense sympathy. Wood, the older, has a believable mixture of strength and timidity in his attempts to protect Mazzello from the (mostly off-screen) beatings by their drunken stepfather (Adam Baldwin).

Film builds a quiet sense of dread as the boys, who feel they can't confide in their distracted mother (Lorraine Bracco), spend as little time as possible in a home that has become a purgatory. Mazzello, terrific as Baldwin's stoic victim, gives the film much of its intermittent emotional power.

Despite the many shortcomings of his script, Evans faces up to an important problem rarely dealt with in film. But as Truffaut once said, showing child abuse on screen is impossible; it can only be suggested, and Donner has handled the material with the necessary discretion.

Pic, however, has a feeling of distance reinforced by some major screenplay gaps and by heavy-handed narration read by unbilled Tom Hanks. As the grown-up Wood, Hanks bookends the film by telling his own sons what happened to their uncle.

But Hanks' crushingly literal voiceover undermines the children's point of view the film strives for, and it seems like a crutch for filmmakers all too aware of narrative problems in their film. When the boys hatch what they call their "big idea" of turning Mazzello's red wagon into a flying machine, Hanks not only tells us "the Radio Flyer was going to soar" but then explains, "It meant escape."

Meanwhile, the boys' POV shots of the villainous Baldwin (seen mostly in shadows or from the neck down) are frightening at first, but making the one-dimensional character more real would have been even scarier.

Bracco's character is seriously underwritten, perhaps because keeping her off-screen working double shifts as a waitress is the only way Baldwin gets away with his abuse.

Fantasy elements of the story are not always successful. A buffalo, first glimpsed by the boys in the seedy Wild West show of old coot Ben Johnson (wasted in the role), reappears at the boys' bedroom window one night to give some unmemorable advice to Wood. Narration anxiously oversimplifies the scene by labeling it a dream, undercutting magical overtones it might have had.

Only pic's last part, with the boys building and launching their flying machine, has a magical feeling. And beneath its superficial exhilaration, the ending carries an undercurrent of melancholia that lends the movie a degree of lasting resonance.

Hanks' presence finally pays off at the end, as his mournful expression suggests that his fantastic tale is his way of dealing with the unspeakable truth of what actually happened to his brother. If all of "Radio Flyer" had been as good as the last, it really could have soared.

Tech credits are fine, including the somber lensing by Laszlo Kovacs, the evocation of a blue-collar neighborhood by production designer J. Michael Riva and the buoyant score by Hans Zimmer. — *Joseph McBride*

LES ARCANDIERS
(FRENCH)

A Pan Européenne release of a Les Prods. Lazennec-FR3 Films-SGGC coproduction with the participation of Canal Plus & Cofimage. (Intl. sales: Président Films.) Produced by Alain Rocca. Directed, written by Manuel Sanchez. Camera (color, Scope), Sanchez; editor, Hélène Viard; music, Etienne Perruchon; costume design, Martine Harrar; set design, François Emmanuelli; sound, Luc Périni; production manager, Xavier Amblard; associate producer, Adeline Lecallier. Reviewed at Club de l'Etoile, Paris, Nov. 25, 1991. Running time: **95 MIN.**

Tonio	Simon de la Brosse
Bruno	Dominique Pinon
Hercule	Charles Schneider
Véronique	Géraldine Pailhas
The engineer	Yves Alfonso

"Les Arcandiers" features fine thesping and widescreen lensing. First feature from scripter/helmer Manuel Sanchez yields a poetic slice-of-life that could interest art house patrons who like morose fare leavened with humor.

"Arcandier" is regional slang for a small-time hustler who, despite valiant effort, never comes out ahead of the game. Too-pretty Simon de la Brosse is touching as the nominal brains of the outfit. Charles Schneider plays a dim-witted but affable oaf, and rubber-faced Dominique Pinon limns an occasional philosopher of the obvious.

Hoping to extort a ransom from a church in Nevers, the lovable losers kidnap the perfectly preserved body of St. Bernadette, only to discover that the church has other Bernadettes in stock.

Unable to fence the goods, they set her ornate display case adrift on the Loire. In pic's surreal gag, only the simpleminded lug notices that St. Bernadette is floating beside them every step of the way as he and his half-frozen buddies hug the contours of the river in their beat-up car.

An extremely accommodating hitchhiker (ghostly, forthright Géraldine Pailhas) and a wildly enthusiastic fan of French rock legend Johnny Hallyday (Yves Alfonso) enliven the route, as does the mocking, slightly mel-

ancholy original score. Pic has a chilled-to-the-bone look that suits its protagonists' black prospects.
— *Lisa Nesselson*

STOP! OR MY MOM WILL SHOOT

A Universal Pictures release of a Northern Lights production. Produced by Ivan Reitman, Joe Medjuck, Michael C. Gross. Executive producers, Joe Wizan, Todd Black. Directed by Roger Spottiswoode. Screenplay, Blake Snyder, William Osborne, William Davies. Camera (Deluxe color), Frank Tidy; editors, Mark Conte, Lois Freeman-Fox; music, Alan Silvestri; production design, Charles Rosen; art direction, Diane Yates; set design, Robert Maddy; set decoration, Don Remacle; costume design, Marie France; sound (Dolby), Thomas Causey; associate producers, Art Levinson, Tony Munafo; assistant director, Art Levinson; casting, Jackie Burch. Reviewed at Avco Cinema Center, L.A., Feb. 19, 1992. MPAA rating: PG. Running time: **87 MIN.**
Joe Bomowski . . . Sylvester Stallone
Tutti . . . . Estelle Getty
Gwen Harper . . . . . JoBeth Williams
Parnell . . . . Roger Rees
Paulie . . . . Martin Ferrero
Munroe . . . . Gailard Sartain
Mitchell . . . . Dennis Burkley
Ross . . . . J. Kenneth Campbell
Lou . . . . Al Fann
McCabe . . . . Ella Joyce

"Stop! Or my mom will shoot a sequel" would be an apt warning to the filmgoers who'll blithely encourage this kind of streamlined, cute 'n' dopey product by flocking to theaters to see it. Expertly produced in the mold of slick, juvenile action comedies like Ivan Reitman's "Kindergarten Cop," this buddy cop picture about a guy and his mom should roll into the hole as a mid-size hit for Universal and rack up an even higher score on video.

Producers couldn't have done better than to cast budding comic actor Sylvester Stallone ("Oscar") and proven laugh-getter Estelle Getty (TV's "Golden Girls") as a beleaguered L.A. lawman and his aggravating mother.

Visiting from the east coast, the hyper-meddlesome Getty, as New Jersey widow Tutti Bomowski, proves second to none in embarassing the pants off her Joey (Stallone). First she's telling humiliating stories to everyone on the plane, then she's showing baby pictures to the guys at the precinct, then she's commandeering his love life in her relentless quest to get him married.

Knowing that her visit will be brief is all that keeps Joey sane,

but then his mom becomes a key witness in a drive-by shooting, and the cops ask her to stay on indefinitely. Before long she's pushed her way even further into Joey's business as his pistol-packing partner in some perilous escapades. Mom may be obnoxious, but she's squarely on his side, and her spunky tenacity eventually wins the big boy's heart.

Always sidling past stupidity, plot just about does itself in in a painful early episode involving a kid on a ledge, but soon regains its footing and more or less clicks along at a cartoonish pace. To be sure, this is one-joke fare that persistently asks the question: How far will this woman go to drive a guy out of his skull? (Answer: even farther than that). But its very simplicity should be a bonus with the target audience.

Stallone, in a slim, articulate and disciplined incarnation, is the model of the amiable, put-upon comic hero, while the tiny Getty, her familiar technique and timing honed to a cutting edge, is worth triple her weight in ticket stubs. Mainstream audience should find her ability to make a sputtering baby out of tough-guy Stallone just adorable.

Director Roger Spottiswoode delivers purely pro product in his adept handling of both action and comedy scenes. JoBeth Williams is typically excellent in the light comic role of the precinct lieutenant who's also Joey's neglected flame, and all technical contributions are on-target for the genre. —*Amy Dawes*

BASKET CASE 3: THE PROGENY

A Shapiro Glickenhaus Entertainment release of an Ievins/Henenlotter production. Produced by Edgar Ievins. Executive producer, James Glickenhaus. Directed by Frank Henenlotter. Screenplay, Henenlotter, Robert Martin. Camera (TVC color), Bob Paone; editor, Greg Sheldon; music, Joe Renzetti; production design, William Barclay; art direction, Caty Maxey; costumes, Carleen Rosado; assistant director, Eric Mofford; production manager, Bob Baron; creatures & makeup effects, Gabe Bartalos, David Kindlon; sound, Palmer Norris; casting, Annette Stilwell. Reviewed at Waverly 1 theater, N.Y., Feb. 15, 1992. MPAA Rating: R. Running time: **90 MIN.**
Granny Ruth . . . . Annie Ross
Duane . . . . . Kevin Van Hentenryck
Uncle Hal . . . . Dan Biggers
Sheriff . . . . Gil Roper
Opal . . . . Tina Louise Hilbert
Little Hal . . . . James O'Doherty

Cult status of "Basket Case 3" is assured, but this idiosyncratic midnight horror comedy will find it difficult to obtain new recruits to helmer Frank Henenlotter's camp.

Pic opens with a lengthy dose of footage from "Basket Case 2," detailing sex between the two monsters Belial and Eve and the death of Eve's sister Susan. Part three begins with Eve's pregnancy.

Granny Ruth (jazz vocalist Annie Ross) takes Eve, papa-to-be Belial and a commune of unique individuals (i.e., monsters) to a small town in Georgia to stay with Uncle Hal (Dan Biggers), a doctor who will help with the mutant birth.

Ross is reunited there with her grotesque monstrosity of a son (stand-up comic James O'Doherty), while Belial's "normal" twin brother (series regular Kevin Van Hentenryck) gets a crush on the sheriff's pretty daughter (Tina Louise Hilbert).

This minimal plot line is mainly an excuse for eventual clashes between Southern crackers and the lovable monsters, with Eve's litter of a dozen babies stolen by the sheriff's deputies. Climax of Belial in a mechanical contraption battling the sheriff is an obvious homage to "Aliens."

Henenlotter's mix of wild overacting, cartoon color scheme and heavy-handed message regarding tolerance is tough to take for the uninitiated. His fans will enjoy seeing the growing menagerie of creatures, including the cute/grotesque progeny.

Though children might be the target audience for these weird-looking but sympathetic monsters, Henenlotter includes some extremely gory effects as well as a stimulating softcore sex scene when Belial dreams of dallying with two voluptuous twins (the impressive Carla and Carmen Morrell).

Van Hentenryck, identified with the "Basket Case" films for a decade, acts way over the top, while Ross literally dominates the film with her intensity and gets to lead the monsters in a sing-a-long of the golden oldie "Personality." Heroine Hilbert makes a good impression in a Jekyll & Hyde role.

Creature effects by Gabe Bartalos and David Kindlon are quite inventive. — *Lawrence Cohn*

LE BAL DES CASSE-PIEDS
(FRENCH)

A Gaumont Intl. release of a Gaumont-Prods. de la Gueville-TF1 Films co-production. Produced by Alain Poire. Directed by Yves Robert. Screenplay, Jean-Loup Dabadie, Robert. Camera (color), Robert Alazraki; editor, Pierre Gillette; music, Vladimir Cosma, Marie-Claude Herry; sound, Pierre Lenoir. Reviewed at Gaumont Convention, Paris, Feb. 12, 1992. Running time: **142 MIN.**
Henri Sauveur . . . . . Jean Rochefort
Louise Sherry . . . . Miou Miou
Mr. Vandubas . . . . Jean Carmet
Mrs. Vandubas . . . . . . Odette Laure
Marie Paule . . . . . . Helene Vincent
Desire . . . . Michel Piccoli
Also with: Jacques Villeret, Didier Gustin, Wojtek Pszoniak, Guy Bedos, Valerie Lemercier, Veronique Sanson, Claude Brasseur, Jean Yanne.

With a large cast of French comedians, "Le Bal des Casse-Pieds" is a light romantic comedy that starts out as quick sketches on life's little irritants for a well-to-do Paris veterinarian and ends with love. Despite the slow-down in the second half for the predictable romance with Miou Miou, pic stays afloat with nonstop skits that should generate solid b.o. for international art houses. U.S. remake seems likely.

Experienced comic helmer Yves Robert ("My Father's Glory," "My Mother's Castle") reworks concept from Noel-Noel's 1948 hit "Les Casse-Pieds." Title refers to anyone who's a pain-in-the-neck which, in Robert's cast of 70, includes vet's relatives, friends, clients, dinner host and Paris drivers.

Jean Rochefort's easygoing vet shrugs off each annoyance with Gallic charm. He turns almost blasé, at least before he begins his bumbling courtship of bemused, urbane Miou Miou. His most memorable shtick, in pic peppered with walk-on animal scenes, is his heart-to-heart talk with a female chimp.

Repeat star turns earn kudos for Helene Vincent as vet's motor-mouth sister, paunchy Jacques Villeret as his trouble-prone friend and Jean Carmet as a dog-crazy client. Standout cameos include Valerie Lemercier's awesomely boring dinner guest and singer Veronique Sanson, who explains the "casse-pieds" routine of bar womanizer Claude Brasseur.

Composer Vladimir Cosma's catchy theme helps pull scenes together. Tech credits are first-rate. — *Lee Lourdeaux*

THE LAWNMOWER MAN

A New Line Cinema presentation. An Allied Vision/Lane Pringle production in association with Fuji Eight Co. Produced by Gimel Everett. Executive producers, Edward Simons, Steve Lane, Robert Pringle, Clive Turner. Co-producer, Milton Subotski. Directed by Brett Leonard. Screenplay, Leonard, Everett, based on Stephen King's story. Camera (Deluxe color), Russell Carpenter; editor, Alan Baumgarten; music, Dan Wyman; production design, Alex McDowell; art director, Chris Farmer; costume design, Mary Jane Fort; sound, Russell Fager; associate producers, Peter McRae, Masao Takiyama; assistant director, Ian McVey. Reviewed at Coolidge Corner Theatre, Brookline, Mass., Feb. 16, 1992. MPAA Rating: R. Running time: **105 MIN.**

Jobe Smith	Jeff Fahey
Dr. Lawrence Angelo	Pierce Brosnan
Marnie Burke	Jenny Wright
Sebastian Timms	Mark Bringleson
Terry McKeen	Geoffrey Lewis
Father McKeen	Jeremy Slate
Director	Dean Norris

Dazzling computer animation and special effects overcome "The Lawnmower Man's" mundane story. Result should have auds agog at the visuals and the trade wondering how they can best be used next. Pic opens March 19 but was previewed in Boston over the President's holiday weekend at the 17th annual Science-Fiction Film Marathon, where reaction was overwhelmingly positive.

Loosely adapted from Stephen King, story has a mentally retarded gardener's assistant (Jeff Fahey) becoming a guinea pig for a scientist (Pierce Brosnan) experimenting with "virtual reality." The concept involves creating a computer simulation that seems real to nearly all the senses and in all directions. As Fahey's intelligence improves, he begins to rebel against those who have been abusing him, and eventually against the relatively benign Brosnan as well.

Tale has various literary influences from Daniel Keyes' "Flowers for Algernon" ("Charly") to Arthur C. Clarke's "Dial F for Frankenstein." The melodramatic elements are vintage King, and they are the pic's weakest parts. When Fahey's powers slip over into the extra-sensory, he wreaks revenge on his tormenters, and pic's dangerously close to "Carrie" territory.

The stunning visuals for the "virtual reality" sequences really put "The Lawnmower Man" over. The computer animation doesn't necessarily break new ground, but it marks the first time it has been so well integrated into a live-action story. Obvious comparison is with "Tron" —and the effects here amply demonstrate how far computer animation has come in 10 years.

The much ballyhooed animated sex sequence is imaginative and surreal, but all too brief, providing barely enough for a subplot. The issue is raised of what happens to people when computer simulation is more intense than reality, only to be dropped in favor of the more conventional story about Fahey and Brosnan's exploitation by the powerful corporation paying for the research.

The two actors are capable in the main roles, although Fahey is saddled with an unbelievable blond fright wig at the outset. Jenny Wright has a nice turn as the woman who becomes involved with him, but one senses there was more to her story line than appears in the finished film. Best supporting bit goes to Geoffrey Lewis as Fahey's amiable boss, who seems to be the reincarnation of actor Barry Fitzgerald in the role.

Virtual reality and computer simulation are hot topics in both the popular press and in written science-fiction, and this item taps into these concepts with ease. Until the actual virtual-reality hardware and software hits the marketplace, audiences should be fascinated by these cinematic substitutes. —*Daniel M. Kimmel*

MALEDETTO IL GIORNO CHE T'HO INCONTRATO
(DAMNED THE DAY I MET YOU)
(ITALIAN)

A Penta Distribuzione release of a Mario & Vittorio Cecchi Gori & Silvio Berlusconi Communications presentation of a C.G. Group Tiger Cinematografica & Penta Film production. Produced by Mario & Vittorio Cecchi Gori. Directed by Carlo Verdone. Screenplay, Verdone, Francesca Marciano. Camera (Cinecittà color), Danilo Desideri; editor, Antonio Siciliano; music, Fabio Liberatori; art direction, Francesco Bronzi; costumes, Tatiana Romanoff; sound, Benito Alchimede. Reviewed at Intl. Recording, Rome, Jan. 24, 1992. Running time: **115 MIN.**

Bernardo	Carlo Verdone
Camilla	Margherita Buy
Adriana	Elisabetta Pozzi
Attilio de Sorges	Giancarlo Dettori
Altieri	Alexis Meneloff

Roman comic Carlo Verdone is on form with "Damned the Day I Met You," a sprightly romantic comedy leaving behind his beloved home turf for Milan, London and Cornwall. Held back by Penta to avoid the overcrowded, fast-buck holiday frame, pic looks to be a sizable hit in Italy with crossover potential in some Euro markets.

Centerstage is a glowing comic turn from Margherita Buy, on the brink of full-blown Italo stardom since her art house credits ("The Station," "Ask for the Moon"). New pic should propel the actress into the local spotlight, with international attention a good bet to follow.

Rock music historian Verdone is reaching the crux of a Jimi Hendrix bio when his live-in g.f. (Elisabetta Pozzi) deserts him, bringing work and day-to-day functioning to a halt.

In analysis, he meets actress and fellow neurotic Buy (character's hilarious intro has her doing umpteen retakes of a jam commercial). Platonic friendship blooms as they exchange medication tips, and Verdone abets Buy's quest to woo their analyst (Alexis Meneloff). But jealousy creeps in, causing the pair to split bitterly.

Aside from an unsure start with what looks like the beginnings of an abandoned running gag, pic's first half is so full of giddily wonderful moments that when the action shifts to London, a slump hits hard.

On the trail of a scoop to crown his Hendrix bio, Verdone conducts a series of schtick interviews that belong in another film. He bumps into Buy, in London for an acting job, and they head to Cornwall to uncover mysteries surrounding the guitarist's death. The aching pleasure of the pair's stalled romance is dwarfed by magnificent scenery and gets buried under the unnecessarily elaborate contrivance of the Hendrix doings.

Though it never quite regains earlier heights, pic finds its feet with a pharmaceutical picnic scene that brings the duo back into focus and coasts along to a shamelessly romantic finale which should prove a big audience-pleaser.

Central relationship owes a gentle nod to "When Harry Met Sally" and Woody Allen's early serio-comedies. Verdone's good-natured self-mocker as the feeble neurotic has a hint of Allen with a Mediterranean twang, and Buy's worldly goofiness feels as much like Manhattan as Milan.

Smart script successfully marries a schlock sensibility with a comedy of words, and Verdone steers clear of the boyish vulgarity that marked some of his earlier pics. He shows a great knack for making Milan locations both peripheral and focal, and failure of this with U.K. locations may point to freshman's unease at working outside Italy.

Tech credits are smooth all round. Lensing is clean and uncomplicated, and Hendrix songs are used to good effect. Running time seems excessive for romantic comedy, and a 10-minute trim from the ailing London section might have tightened things up considerably. — *David Rooney*

BERLIN FEST

DIEN BIEN PHU
(FRENCH)

An AMLF release of a Mod Films-Antenne 2-Films A2-Flach Film-Production Marcel Dassault-GM Aviation Services-Seco Film co-production with the participation of the CNC & the Ministry of Defense & the assistance of the Hanoi Military Region, the Air Force of Vietnam & the National Orchestra of Hanoi. Produced by Jacques Kirsner. Directed, written, narrated by Pierre Schoendoerffer. Camera (color), Bernard Lutic; editor, Armand Psenny; music, Georges Delerue; art direction, Raoul Albert; costume design, Olga Pelletier; sound, Michel Laurent; special effects, Olivier Zeneski, Jean-Pierre Maricourt; assistant directors, Frédéric Schoendoerffer, Jean-Charles Smith, Madame Bach Diep. Reviewed at Max Linder Panorama, Paris, Feb. 10, 1992. (Also in Berlin Film Festival.) Running time: **140 MIN.**

Howard Simpson	Donald Pleasence
Capt. de Kervéguen	Patrick Catalifo
Béatrice Vergnes	Ludmila Mikael
French wire service reporter	Jean-François Balmer
Artillery lieutenant	Maxime Leroux
Capt. Morvan	Christopher Buchholz

Also With: François Negret, Luc Lavandier, Patrick Chauvel, Ludovic Schoendoerffer, Maïté Nahyr, Igor Hossein.

A rigorous and sober account of the 57-day battle that led to France's 1954 defeat in its colony of Vietnam, Pierre Schoendoerffer's "Dien Bien Phú" leaves the viewer with a vivid and draining impression of having been through the war.

Pic's title is as meaningful to France and Vietnam as Pearl Harbor is to the U.S. and Japan, but if the film is to achieve its full impact for foreign audiences, a written or spoken preface is needed to give background leading up to the film's crisp start on March 13, 1954, at 5 p.m.

Still, meticulous art direction and exceptionally fine lensing of life in the trenches and on the battlefields contribute to a well-orchestrated war film.

Action cuts back and forth between Hanoi and Dien Bien Phú, on the Laotian border in the north of Vietnam, not far from China. Helmer himself narrates, voicing dates and details throughout the siege as small groups of soldiers attack, take and abandon hills named for French women.

Pic begins with a gorgeous sunset that segues to the sounds of an orchestra gradually revealed to be made up of Vietnamese musicians beneath a huge, unmistakably French mural.

Without a word, Schoendoerffer has laid out his major themes with arresting subtlety: The sun is setting on the French presence in an age-old land; yet, whatever the sacrifices on either side, much of beauty remains.

An American war reporter (Donald Pleasence, speaking serviceable French) is being pedalled through the bustling streets of Hanoi, asking local newsmen, a Chinese bookie and a Eurasian opium den proprietress for tips on the imminent action that will cap nine years of French military effort against communist insurgents.

At a bar frequented by French Legionnaires, Pleasance meets an old friend from World War II, who introduces him to the group of soldiers whose fortunes the film will trace.

The scenes in Hanoi are competent and necessary, but the scenes depicting battle conditions are the strongest, dramatically and pictorially.

Shot at Tonkin in northern Vietnam, $27 million pic (with $5.6 million in services provided by Vietnam) occasioned restoration work on vehicles, weapons and aircraft, the building of an airstrip and the digging of an artificial river spanned by a vintage bridge.

Shoot marked first time in 37 years that French skydivers have jumped out over Vietnam. The start of the battle includes 480 explosions in one shot (out of 3,500 total detonations for the battle sequences).

Strikingly composed shots have grandeur and depth, and the bustle of actors and extras is choreographed with a natural touch by the director of "The Anderson Platoon" and "The Crab Drum."

Absorbing scenes include air-to-air shots of parachutes opening above fluffy clouds in a pale blue sky, matter-of-fact shots of dead bodies laid in open graves in the rain and down-to-the-wire suspense as air support bombs the approaching enemy before a French-held trench is overrun.

Smooth editing conveys the cosseted elegance of the Hotel Metropole in Hanoi versus the muck and mire of endless, pointless combat. Scenes in the situation room, marred by often wooden delivery, are pic's weakest moments.

On the evening of one particularly fierce battle, the performance in Hanoi of a haunting concerto for violin and orchestra (composed by Georges Delerue) provides the perfect excuse for grave melancholy music to underscore the fighting. Score is spare and moving.

Film illustrates but does not illuminate the pointlessness of the doomed campaign that marked the end of an era.

Officers in the field curse the brass who issue heartbreaking orders to abandon hard-won territory or to back off when a semblance of victory is in sight. Pic implies that the lunacy factor was part of the terrain long before U.S. advisors took up the relay.

According to Schoendoerffer, at the time of Dien Bien Phú, U.S. aid accounted for 80% of the cost of the war.

Although the open and hilly northern landscape looks far less menacing than the jungles of the American years, pic could interest American vets curious about their predecessors "in country."

Schoendoerffer, who was at Dien Bien Phú as an army cameraman and who was taken prisoner, is out to re-create a key moment in his life and the life of his nation, and to honor the memory of his fellow prisoners, three-fourths of whom did not survive.

Schoendoerffer did survive to tell the tale. It is hard to imagine anyone telling it with greater sensitivity. — *Lisa Nesselson*

MAHAPRITHIVI
(WORLD WITHIN, WORLD WITHOUT)
(INDIAN)

A GG Films production. Produced by Gautam Goswami. Directed, written by Mrinal Sen, from Anal Dutt's story. Camera (color), Shashi Anand; editor, Mrinmoy Chakraborty; music, B.V. Karanth, Chandan Roy Chowdhury; production design, Gautam Basu; sound, Sanjoy Mukherjee. Reviewed at Berlin Film Festival (Forum), Feb. 17, 1992. Running time: **103 MIN.**

Father	Soumitra Chatterjee
Mother	Gita Sen
Son	Victor Bannerjee
Son	Anjan Dutt
Daughter	Anasuya Majumdar
Daughter-in-law	Aparna Sen

Mrinal Sen, once one of the most active and impressive of Indian directors, has been quiet of late, and his new film is a disappointing rehash of themes he handled better in the past. "Mahaprithivi" isn't likely to find much support either at fests or on the art house circuit.

Calcutta-set pic opens with a family discovering that the grandmother has hanged herself, sparking a predictable round of recriminations and revelations.

It's the sort of thing Sen has done well before, but his heart doesn't seem to be in this one. Even the distinguished actors involved seem to be merely going through their paces, without much conviction. Direction is impersonal, and color processing frequently poor.

The action takes place at the time Germany was being reunified, but this point seems to be more a nod to Sen's German fans than representing anything more meaningful. — *David Stratton*

GUDRUN
(GERMAN)

A Geissendorfer production in association with Maran Film, B.A. Produktion. (Intl. sales: Filmverlag der Autoren.) Produced, directed by Hans W. Geissendorfer. Screenplay, Geissendorfer, Fitzgerald Kusz. Camera (color), Hans-Gunther Bucking; editor, Annette Dorn; music, Jurgen Knieper; production design, Thomas Riccabona; costumes, Ursula Welter; sound, Heiko Hinderks; assistant director, Stefan Diepenbrock; production manager, Andreas Habermaier; casting, Stefaan Schieder. Reviewed at Berlin Film Festival (competing), Feb. 14, 1992. Running time: **97 MIN.**

Gudrun	Kersten Gmelch
Grandmother	Barbara Thummet
Fritz	Roman Mitterer
Mother	Veronika Freimanova
Father	Bernd Tauber
Zagel	Michael Vogtman

A tale of innocence corrupted by war, "Gudrun" is a beautifully made but disappointingly uninvolving film. Outside its home turf, commercial prospects don't look bright.

Producer/director/co-screenwriter Hans Geissendorfer prefers to evoke the serene peace of the German countryside during a time of dreadful conflict. Pic is thus full of painterly images evocatively shot by Hans-Gunther Bucking but, despite a basically strong story line, lacks genuine emotion, suspense and drama.

In some aspects, pic is reminiscent of "Le Grand Chemin," recently remade as "Paradise." The mother of pubescent Gudrun is seeing a Nazi officer while her husband is away fighting on the Russian front. She offloads her sensitive daughter on the child's grandmother, who runs a cafe in a picturesque village.

The girl befriends Fritz, a boy her age with whom she shares a few mild adventures (such as learning to swim). Fritz yearns to be accepted into the Hitler Youth, but his father, the local priest, attacks the Nazis in his sermons until he's arrested.

Meanwhile, Gudrun's father deserts the army and hides out in grandmother's cellar. What follows is, unfortunately, entirely predictable. Geissendorfer seems unable to inject suspense into the material, even in a surefire scene as the father ventures up from the cellar just as the mother and her Nazi lover arrive.

Performances are on the whole unmemorable, although Kerstin Gmelch shows promise as the young heroine. Real star is the cinematography, but that's also the pic's downfall, as a much grittier approach was needed.
— *David Stratton*

THE LAST DAYS OF CHEZ NOUS
(AUSTRALIAN)

A Jan Chapman Prods.-Australian Film Finance Corp. production. (Intl. sales: Beyond Intl.) Produced by Chapman. Directed by Gillian Armstrong. Screenplay, Helen Garner. Camera (Eastmancolor), Geoffrey Simpson; editor, Nicholas Beauman; music, Paul Grabowsky; production design-costumes, Janet Patterson; sound, Ben Osmo; associate producer-assistant director, Mark Turnbull; casting, Liz Mullinar. Reviewed at Berlin Film Festival (competing), Feb. 14, 1992. Running time: **96 MIN.**

Beth	Lisa Harrow
J.P.	Bruno Ganz
Vicki	Kerry Fox
Annie	Miranda Otto
Tim	Kiri Paramore
Beth's father	Bill Hunter
Angelo	Lex Marinos
Sally	Mickey Camilleri
Beth's mother	Lynne Murphy

This post-feminist drama about two sisters involved with the same man is beautifully acted and crafted. Despite some script problems, "The Last Days of Chez Nous" seems likely to attract serious cinemagoers in many markets.

Director Gillian Armstrong, who alternates between U.S. projects ("Mrs. Soffel," "Fires Within") and pics produced in her native Australia ("My Brilliant Career," "High Tide"), again fares better on her home turf.

Helen Garner, who wrote the excellent script for Jane Campion's telepic "Two Friends," writes wonderful parts for women; in this case, three repping different age groups and sharing the same inner-city house with a couple of men. What happens to these femmes isn't exactly earth-shattering, but pic should connect emotionally with audiences, especially women.

Fortyish Beth (Lisa Harrow) works hard as a writer, bosses people around, lacks emotion and finds it difficult to "be part of a couple," which is hard on her French husband, J.P. (Bruno Ganz). Beth's daughter by her first marriage, Annie (Miranda Otto), is a gangly teen on the brink of her first love affair.

Despite tension in the household, which also includes a lodger (Kiri Paramore) who romances Annie, everyone gets along until the return from overseas of Vicki (Kerry Fox), Beth's younger sister who's sometimes mistaken for her daughter.

Secretly pregnant after an unhappy affair in Italy, Vicki is closer to her niece than to her older sister, and she starts a relaxed friendship with J.P. But this relationship gradually turns into love and, when Beth is away on a trip with her curmudgeonly father (Bill Hunter), Vicki and J.P. embark on an affair.

The plot line isn't very original, but the femme characters are observed and played with notable depth. Fox (from Campion's "An Angel at My Table") is every bit as good as Harrow, and, as the teen, Otto is sweet and lively (but not called upon to match her socko perf in "The Girl Who Came Late").

Given the rich femme characters, it's disappointing the men are so ill-defined. Nothing is known about Beth's first husband, and J.P. is frustratingly undeveloped, though Ganz makes up for the sketchy writing and succeeds triumphantly in creating a flesh-and-blood character. Hunter, as the stubborn, unlovable father, humanizes a basically ugly character.

The film is beautifully crafted, with subtle camerawork by Geoffrey Simpson, top-flight production design by Janet Patterson and a haunting, bluesy score by Paul Grabowski. Armstrong again demonstrates her strength with actors and subtle delineation of an emotional subject. —*David Stratton*

RAMINEREA
(FORGOTTEN BY GOD)
(ROMANIAN)

A Romaniafilm production. Directed, written by Laurentiu Damian. Camera (color), Anca Damian; editor, Christina Ionescu; music, Cornelia Tautu; production design, Daniel Raduta; sound, Anrei Papp; production manager, Lucian Gologan; assistant director, Lidia Slavu. Reviewed at Berlin Film Festival (Panorama), Feb. 18, 1992. Running time: **104 MIN.**
With: Mircea Albulescu, Monica Ghiuta, Maia Morgenstern, Dan Condurache, Valentin Uritescu, Luminita Gheorghiu.

Murky goings-on in a wild Romanian village are noisily exposed in "Forgotten by God," one of those films in which no one ever talks quietly. This first feature by young writer-director Laurentiu Damian is too familiar and too declamatory to make an impact.

Raminerea is the name of the village, and the story's told in flashback as a train traveler returns to his hometown (now almost abandoned) where his grandfather courted disaster by building a home atop a hill, higher than the church. The local priest, outraged at the insult, cursed the family, and six out of the seven children die young.

Surviving daughter grows into a lissome lass given to racing off into the bullrushes at night to canoodle with her beau. He, the cad (the word is actually used in the often wayward subtitles) refuses to marry her, however, so she turns up at his wedding with revenge on her mind, causing a fuss by killing a chicken and splattering the bride with blood.

And so it goes on, with people screaming at each other at top volume and the priest muttering in his beard. Subtle the film is not, and the villagers who are forever claiming that God has forgotten them, seem to have no one to blame but themselves.

Camerawork is mobile, editing choppy and performances strident. This is not a pic to win over audiences to Romanian cinema.
— *David Stratton*

EDES EMMA, DRAGA BÖBE — VAZLATOK, AKTOK
(SWEET EMMA, DEAR BÖBE — SKETCHES, NUDES)
(HUNGARIAN)

An Objektiv Filmstudio, with the cooperation of Manfred Durniok Filmproduktion. (Intl. sales: Cinemagyar, Budapest.) Directed, written by István Szbó, from an idea by Szabó, Andrea Veszits. Camera (Eastmancolor), Lajos Koltai; editor, Eszter Kovacs; music, Richard Schumann; production design, Attila Kovacs; costumes, Zsuzsa Stenger; sound, Gyorgy Kovacs; consultant, Gabriella Prekop. Reviewed at Hungarian Film Week, Budapest, Feb. 12, 1992. (Also competing at Berlin Film Festival.) Running time: **78 MIN.**
Emma . . . . Johanna Ter Steege
Böbe . . . . Eniko Börcsök
Headmaster . . . . Peter Andorai

The realities of day-to-day life in post-Communist Hungary are vividly brought to life in this compassionate, memorable film. Though the settings and narrative are understandably bleak, the treatment throbs with life and love, resulting in a most satisfying film that should make an impact in its Berlin launch.

István Szabó, who started his career in the '60s making personal low-budgeters about relationships and who moved on to impressive but expensive international co-productions in the '80s, returns to his Hungarian roots with this lissome yarn. The sorry state of his homeland obviously saddens and angers the director, but at the same time his humanity and compassion ensures that his film pulsates with life and love.

His eponymous protagonists are two young femme teachers who left the countryside for Budapest where life is supposedly richer. Unable to afford an apartment, they share a room in a rundown hostel near the airport. Emma (Johanna Ter Steege), the more sensitive, is having an unsatisfactory affair with the school's chauvinistic headmaster (Peter Andorai), a married father content to have a secret fling but insensitive to the impressionable Emma's.

The more self-reliant Böbe (Eniko Börcsök) picks up foreigners she meets in town in the hope that they'll at least buy her a good meal. Emma is forced to listen to sounds of her friend having sex at night.

Szabó's script is episodic but cumulatively depicts a femme friendship strongly reminiscent of the work of Irish writer Edna O'Brien. Szabó's women are richly drawn characters whose love of life surmounts their difficulties and disappointments.

Dutch actress Ter Steege (voiced by top Magyar thesp Ildiko Bansagi) is excellent as the vulnerable Emma who eventually finds the strength to try a new direction in her increasingly sterile life. Börcsök is almost as good as plump, silly Böbe, while Andorai makes the faithless headmaster suitably sleazy.

Apart from this two-character study, Szabó also is fascinated by changes in post-Communist Hungary. Emma once taught Russian, but there's no percentage in that anymore so now she's learning English. School staffers and teachers who used to be prominent Party members are frequently at loggerheads.

There are strong sensual elements to this tightly edited film, not only in the love scenes but also in Emma's recurring nightmare in which, naked, she finds herself falling down an endless slope. An amusing sequence reminiscent of early Milos Forman has the two friends audition nude with other women for extra roles in a film's harem sequence.

Szabó regular Lajos Koltai does his usual beautiful job behind the camera, and the classical music score is lovely and apt. This one of the best Hungarian films in quite a while.
— *David Stratton*

KALLE STROPP OCH GRODAN BOLL PA SVINDLANDE ÄVENTYR
(THE ADVENTURES OF KALLE STROPP AND THE FROG BALL)
(SWEDISH-ANIMATED)

A Sandrews presentation of a Cinemation production in cooperation with Sandrew Film & Teater, Filminstitutet & TV-3. Directed by Jan Gissberg. Screenplay, Thomas Funck. Music, Funck; design, Jan Gissberg; backgrounds, Peter Gissberg; animation, Jan Gissberg, Lars Emanuelsson, Flemming Jensden, Hans Hägerström, Jonas Dahlbeck, Jony Eriksson, Pernilla Hindsefelt; editor, Kerstin Hellgren. Reviewed at Filmstaden cinema, Stockholm, Jan. 14, 1992. (In Berlin Film Festival, children's pic section.) Running time: **84 MIN.**

Voices: Thomas Funck, Stig Grybe, Thorsten Flinck, Peter Dalle, Claes Månsson, Asa Bjerkerot, Eva Funck; Lasse Sarri, Inger Thunvall, Mikael B. Tretow, Yvonne Eliaesson, Jörgen Lantz, Jessica Laurén (songs).

This charming animated kidpic featuring the brain children of Thomas Funck should have a long, healthy commercial life, and exposure at the upcoming Berlin film fest could give it legs to travel abroad.

Cricket Kalle Stropp, his Frog Ball pal and other characters started in the 1940s and have been adapted to books, plays, radio shows, comic strips, records and a feature in the '50s.

New pic has captured most of the stories' charm and humor, at the same time taking them into the modern world. After a slow start, the heroes attempt to rescue the forest from greedy exploiters. Kids will find the ensuing exploits suspenseful, while adults will be amused by the sometimes grownup humor.

Animation, slightly cruder than Disney, feels very European. The voices, most of them by Funck, add to the characters' distinctive personalities.

"Kalle Stropp" is no "Beauty and the Beast," but it's entertaining in its own right, and could do well internationally in a dubbed version —even if this means losing Funck's voices.

— *Gunnar Rehlin*

DIE UNHEIMLICHEN FRAUEN
(THE FRIGHTENING WOMEN)
(GERMAN-DOCU-COLOR/B&W-16m)

Produced, directed, written by Birgit Hein. Camera (color, black & white, 16m), Hein; sound, Peter Dargel; production assistance, Claudia Gehrke, Nina Hein, Biddy Pastor, Maija-Lene Rettig, Claudia Schwartz, Claudia Schillinger, Ulrike Zimmerman. Reviewed at Berlin Film Festival press previews, Jan. 27, 1992. (In Intl. Forum of Young Cinema.) Running time: **100 MIN.**

Experimental feminist docu draws on shock tactics that will appall most audiences and leave the less faint-of-heart feeling they might qualify for a gynecology degree by pic's end, thanks to mucho lavish, explicit female nudity.

Feminism hasn't come this radical in a long time. Helmer Birgit Hein purports to destroy the myth of the ideal woman as "unaggressive, peaceful and asexual" by bombarding the viewer with an hour's worth of images of femmes run amok, mainly in the direction of violence, extreme sexual imagery or criminality.

Lengthy opening scene shows a woman cutting off her pubic and head hair and gluing it to the places where men usually have hair and women don't. An historical montage of bad/violent girls such as Medusa and Lucrezia Borgia segues into recollections of matricide as a pot of boiling milk symbolically fills the screen.

Narrator recounts sado-masochistic and scatological sexual fantasies, followed by archive footage of murderesses and femme soldiers.

Things start to get clinical with a long sequence on clitorechtomies, breast surgery and extreme closeups of female genitalia.

Film looks muddy, even for 16m, and soundtrack, laced with much tribal chanting, is muddier still. — *Rebecca Lieb*

HIKARIGOKE
(LUMINOUS MOSS)
(JAPANESE)

A Film Crescent-Neo-Life production. (Intl. sales: Herald Ace, Tokyo.) Produced by Taketoshi Naito, Tohru Aizawa. Directed by Kei Kumai. Screenplay, Taro Ikeda, Kumai, from Taijun Takeda's novel. Camera (color), Masao Tochizawa; editor, Osamu Inoue; music, Teizo Matsumura; production design, Takeo Kimura; sound, Kenichi Benitani. Reviewed at Berlin Film Festival (competing), Feb. 17, 1992. Running time: **118 MIN.**
Headmaster/Captain . Rentaro Mikuni
Nishikawa . . . . Eiji Okada
Hachizo . . . . Kunie Tanaka
Gosuke . . . . Tetsuta Sugimoto
Novelist . . . . Taketoshi Naito
Prosecutor . . . . Hisashi Igawa
Defense lawyer . . Masane Tsukayama
Judge . . . . Chishu Ryu

In "Luminous Moss," cannibalism is treated with seriousness but without much passion, resulting in an interesting, well produced, but cold-hearted film which will have difficulty finding audiences.

Theme of starving soldiers driven to cannibalism also was covered in Kon Ichikawa's 1965 "Nobi" (Fires on the Plain). That powerful pic dealing with Japanese soldiers in the Philippines at the end of the war was bursting with emotion and horror, while Kei Kumai's academic style in the new film is at odds with the horrific subject matter.

The picture is told in flashback and set in the north of Hokkaido, where winters are severe. The local headmaster is showing a famous novelist the sights, including caves where moss glows green in the dark. This triggers memories of a wartime incident in which a supply ship was wrecked off the coast and only the captain survived, to be greeted as a hero.

Further flashbacks reveal, however, that three members of the ship's crew made it to the caves, where lack of food and bitterly cold weather made conditions intolerable. When one dies, the others decide to eat the corpse (a scene handled in a very matter-of-fact way).

In the end, the captain is the only survivor as pic concludes with a stylized trial (vet Chishu Ryu plays the judge) where the captain defends his actions.

Rentaro Mikuni plays both headmaster and captain to good effect, but the film's consistently gloomy, downbeat theme and the awful subject matter are going to make "Luminous Moss" a very hard sell. Though Masao Tochizawa's photography is often beautiful, so much of the film takes place in cave gloom that the pic will have to be carefully graded for video and TV release.

Final impression is of a very strong subject handled with such discretion and lack of emotion that it seems to have been hardly worth the effort.

— *David Stratton*

UTZ
(BRITISH-ITALIAN-GERMAN)

A Viva Pictures-BBC Films (London)-Academy Pictures (Rome)-NDR (Hamburg) co-production. (Intl. sales: Cine Electra, London.) Produced by John Goldschmidt. Executive producer, William Sargent. Directed by George Sluizer. Screenplay, Hugh Whitemore, from Bruce Chatwin's novel. Camera (Eastmancolor), Gerard Vandenberg; editor, Lin Friedman; music, Nicola Piovani; production design, Karel Vacek; costumes, Marie Frankova; assistant director, Anouk Sluizer. Reviewed at Berlin Film Festival (competing), Feb. 18, 1992. Running time: **98 MIN.**
Von Utz . . . . . Armin Mueller-Stahl
Marta . . . . Brenda Fricker
Marius Fisher . . . . . Peter Riegert
Dr. Vaclav Orlik . . . . . Paul Scofield
Grandmother . . . . . Miriam Karlin
Utz (age 18) . . Christian Mueller-Stahl
Young Marta . . . . . Caroline Guthrie
Museum director . . . Pauline Melville

Dangers of pan-European production emerge in "Utz," disappointing new pic from Dutch director George Sluizer, whose "The Vanishing" was a deserved international art house hit. Despite Armin Mueller-er-Stahl's charming performance, the polyglot cast and crew can't provide a cohesive basis on which to pin a frustratingly fragmented screenplay. The ending is an audience turnoff, which will probably doom any chances of B.O. success.

The fine ideas in Bruce Chatwin's novel are mostly lost in Hugh Whitemore's muddled screenplay, with its wayward flashback inserts. At times the film's structure is so confusing, reels seem mixed up.

Basic story involves Mueller-Stahl as Baron von Utz, a charming Czech initially unfazed by the Communist regime's prescription of his movements. The self-professed "porcelain millionaire" has a Swiss bank account and visits Geneva regularly for "health reasons," but actually to buy new pieces for his porcelain collection.

On one trip he befriends an American art dealer (Peter Riegert in a second-string role) who visits Utz in Prague and meets his loyal housekeeper (Brenda Fricker) and his best friend, sardonic Dr. Orlik (Paul Scofield).

A good scene in a Prague eatery has all the trout allocated to Party members and the only fish available for others is carp, misspelt in the English menu as "crap." The art dealer also gets to see Utz's priceless haul of Meissen porcelain, which the old man's allowed to keep only on condition it goes to the state museum after he dies.

Meanwhile, flashbacks depict Utz's early life. He meets Marta, a country girl given to swimming nude in a lake with her pet goose (a bizarre scene which seems to belong to another film). Revelation about Utz's treatment of Marta will not endear the character to audiences.

But the real turn-off, apart from the mixed-up narrative, is pic's climax in which Utz, on his deathbed, orders Marta to destroy his porcelain rather than let it fall into the hands of the state. As a liberating moment, this fails desperately: The beautiful collection has been lovingly photographed throughout the film so the wanton vandalism comes across as pure philistinism. There goes any sympathy the viewer might have for Utz.

Technically, the film is fine,

with plenty of picture-postcard shots of Prague and Karlovy Vary (standing in for a Swiss resort). Nicola Piovani's music, typical of the composer, is attractive.

The principal performers, despite the wide variety of accents (Fricker's Irish brogue is at odds with the Czech countrywoman she's playing) are all good, with Scofield stealing the pic with some very dry comedy.

Sadly, it doesn't add up to anything, and box office chances look dim. — *David Stratton*

ROTTERDAM FEST

BOVEN DE BERGEN
(ABOVE THE MOUNTAINS)
(DUTCH)

An NFM/IAF release of a Studio Nieuwe Gronden production. Produced by René Scholten. Directed, written by Digna Sinke. Camera (Kodak color, black & white), Goert Giltaij; editor, Jan Wouter van Reijen; sound, Ad Roest. Reviewed at Rotterdam Film Festival, Jan. 27, 1992. (Also in Berlin Film Festival Panorama.) Running time: **107 MIN.**
Rina . . . . Catherine ten Bruggencate
Neeltje . . . . Roos Blaauboer
Vincent . . . . Johan Leysen
Stefan . . . . Esgo Heil
Jan Paul . . . . Eric Corton
Hélène . . . . Renée Fokker
Man from ferry . . Sacco van der Made

Well structured and meticulously thought out, "Above the Mountains" is less concerned with story and action than with characters. This pic about attitudes toward life was a most throught-provoking item at the Rotterdam fest and stands to provoke further discussion during Berlin.

Good-looking, humorous pic is about middle-aged, middle-class intellectuals who embark on a 300-mile hike from north to south of the Netherlands in search of mountains that reached awesome heights long ago.

Exercise, lack of comfort and haphazard eating loosen their tongues. Accepted values become dubious. The self-assured, arrogant leader turns out a deflated loser. A marriage full of venomous quarrels changes into a bond of loving sparring and elaborate, well-savored reconciliations.

Technical credits are excellent, but story and character are developed via dialog instead of pictures. The soundtrack dominates so much one could follow the pic on the radio. Sequences that *are* visual are too long and

too slow. Still, pic's creditable for originality, probing of human dilemmas and gentle treatment of human frailty. — *Gerry Waller*

ROY ROGERS, KING OF THE COWBOYS
(DUTCH-DOCU)

A Scorpio production, co-produced with NOS TV. Produced by Kees Ryninks. Directed, written by Thys Ockersen. Camera (color), Peter Brugman; editor, Stefan Kamp. Reviewed at Rotterdam Film Festival, Jan. 30, 1992. Running time: **80 MIN.**
With: Roy Rogers, Dale Evans, Roy Rogers Jr., William Witney, the Sons of the Pioneers, Trigger.

Thys Ockersen's enjoyable feature-length docu about his boyhood idols — Roy Rogers, Dale Evans and Trigger, world's smartest horse — starts with a scene of children noisily awaiting a new oater adventure during their weekly visit to a Dutch cinema.

Pic moves on to the Roy Rogers Festival and the Roy Rogers Museum in Portsmouth, Ohio, and an interview with Dale and Roy, now 79.

Trigger also is in the museum, but, alas, he's stuffed. Roy and Dale are not stuffy at all. They sing, and they even kiss, something they never did in the movies they began making a half-century ago. The docu is an engaging, unpretentious and well-made chapter of film history.
— *Gerry Waller*

ROOKSPOREN
(TRACES OF SMOKE)
(DUTCH-16m)

A NFM/IAS release of a Van de Staak production. Produced, directed, written by Frans van de Staak, based on Lidy van Marissing's play. Camera (color), Bernd Wouthuysen; editors, van de Staak, Habbeke Stark; music, Bernard Hunnekink; sound, Piotr van Dijk. Reviewed at Rotterdam Film Festival, Jan. 29, 1992. Running time: **105 MIN.**
With: Marlies Heuer, Peter Blok, Wim Meuwissen, Rein Bloem, Sacha Bulthuis, Ingrid Kuipers, Nanouk van der Meulen, Joop Armiraal, Thom Hoffman.

This film is the most recent product of Franz van de Staak's examination of cinematic space and language, light and movement. Based on a play by Lidy van Marissing, "Traces of Smoke" uses intelligent and precise dialog for the narration

of an imprecise story.

A woman under interrogation is accused of something, but viewer doesn't know what the crime is or whether she's guilty or innocent. Several witnesses are questioned in apartments, then later in a large room, sometimes individually, sometimes in groups.

Pic somehow avoids tedium; it's a fascinating work thanks to extraordinary acting, careful framing and use of colors, the propelling rhythm of the editing, and meticulous, imaginative direction.

As usual with Van de Staak's films, pic is an exercise for the spectator as well as for the filmmaker. — *Gerry Waller*

HAIMWEE NAAR DE DOOD
(NOSTALGIA FOR DEATH)
(DUTCH-DOCU-16m)

A NFM/IAF release of a Yuca Film production. Produced by Suzanne van Voorst, Floor Kooij. Directed, written by Ramòn Gieling. Camera (color), Goert Giltaij, Eugène van den Bosch; editor, Jan Dop; sound mix, Jan van Sandwijk. Reviewed at Rotterdam Film Festival, Jan. 27, 1992. Running time: **90 MIN.**
With: Olga Dondé, Melecio Vargas Mateos, Nicolás Ramirez.

In his docu described as a film essay, Ramòn Gieling attempts to elucidate Mexicans' feelings about death. This is primarily a pic for those willing to talk to death and to shake hands with her (here, death is female). Camerawork and editing are more than impressive; colors are beautifully used.

Death for a Mexican is "his favorite plaything, his durable love," per the docu, which uses passages from Octavio Paz's "The Labyrinthe of Solitude" and includes talks with a small-village priest, a painter from Mexico City and an 87-year-old man, who says, "Death is like love; both appropriate everything."
— *Gerry Waller*

HUNGARIAN FEST

FELALOM
(BRATS)
(HUNGARIAN)

An Objektiv Film Studio production. (Intl. sales, Cinemagyar; North American sales, TransCon Management).

Directed by Janos Rozsa. Screenplay, Istvan Kardos. Camera (Eastmancolor), Tibor Mathe; editor, Eva Szentandrasi; music, Gabor Presser; art direction, Csorsz Khell; costumes, Andrea Flesch; sound, Gyorgy Fek. Reviewed at Academy of Motion Picture Arts & Sciences Little Theater, Beverly Hills, Calif., Jan. 29, 1992. (In Hungarian Film Week.) Running time: **83 MIN.**
Rita . . . . Bernadett Visy
Zoli . . . . Csaba Ujvari
Attila . . . . Szabolcs Hajdu
Csoma . . . . Dani Szabo
Laci . . . . Zsolt Gazdag

The bleak outlook for Hungarian youth today is the focus of "Brats." Grim but not terribly analytical, Magyar entry in the foreign language film Oscar competition is well made and stands as a passably interesting expression of a difficult transitional time for the nation, but pic doesn't possess the high quality or trenchant insight necessary to put it on the international map in a major way.

Vet helmer Janos Rozsa has made several films about kids over the past 20 years, and this one looks at how a generation raised to expect the state to look after it must suddenly fend for itself, Western-style, but without any real preparation. "Brats" is being used as the English-language title, but actual, more poetic translation of the original is "Half-Asleep."

A loose-knit gang of four youths, ranging from 10 to 17, pulls off little crimes and scams, from petty larceny to washing car windows after rigging stoplights to stay red longer. Ragtag group consists of Zoli, the oldest; Attila, a true hoodlum in the making; Laci, a skinny, nerdy misfit; and Csoma, the youngest and most resourceful.

When Rita, a somewhat alluring girl from Romania, enters their midst, the guys all fall for her in their own ways. Unfortunately, this aspect of the pic fails to stir much interest since she hardly says anything and remains vague and uninspiring, rather than exotic and mysterious.

Almost as soon as Zoli gets something going with her, Rita is obliged to return home, and climactic scene in which the boys accompany her to the train station unravels into shocking, senseless tragedy.

By tackling the subject of wayward street kids in a hostile urban environment, Rozsa and screenwriter Istvan Kardos have invited comparison to such classics as "Los Olvidados" and "Pixote," among others, and by this standard come up far short. The adolescents here seem adrift in a suddenly unstructured society, and most compelling moments reveal how quickly a formerly communist nation has taken on some of the worst aspects of Western civilization.

Rozsa's direction is competent and professional, but rather overly slick and bright where a rougher, tougher approach would have been more appropriate. Overt references to the specific political situation are mostly avoided, which also makes the film less urgent and pointed than it might have been. Kids are all good, most notably Dani Szabo as the youngest, craftiest and, by implication, most likely to succeed.

—*Todd McCarthy*

KEK DUNA KERINGO
(BLUE DANUBE WALTZ)
(HUNGARIAN-FRENCH-U.S.)

An HR Prods.-NEF-Filmex co-production. Produced by Michael Fitzgerald, Robert Gardner. Co-producer, François Duplat. Directed by Miklos Jancso. Screenplay, Gyula Hernadi. Camera (Eastmancolor), Janos Kende; editor, Istvan Marton; line producer, Peter Miskolczi. Reviewed at Hungarian Film Week, Budapest, Feb. 11, 1992. Running time: **89 MIN.**
With: Gyorgy Cserhalmi, Dorottya Udvaros, Ildiko Bansagi, Andras Kozac, Jozsef Madaras, Lajos Balazsovits.

With U.S. and French coin, idiosyncratic Hungarian director Miklos Jancso has turned out another dazzling political thriller, this time blurring fantasy with reality as he satirizes post-Communist Hungary. Excitingly visual pic will delight and perplex film buffs, and it will be in demand at festivals. Commercial prospects, however, look almost as bleak for this one as previous Jancso efforts.

The concerns of the director and his regular screenwriter, Gyula Hernadi, are so specifically based in Hungary's current political scene that international audiences will be baffled by some of the references and characters. In some ways the director is harking back to his most famous films of the '60s ("The Round Up," "Silence and Cry") as he depicts the police investigation following the assassination of a political figure.

The murdered pol is none other than Hungary's new, nattily dressed prime minister (Jozsef Madaras), who's gunned down during a reception at a hotel overlooking the Danube. The in-

stigator appears to be a parliamentarian (Gyorgy Cserhalmi) and former friend of the slain leader, though the assassin was a woman (Dorottya Udvaros) close to both men.

As the security chief (Andras Kozac) mounts an investigation, Janos Kende's mobile camera sweeps giddily around the hotel, frequently picking up key action on the many video screens in the building.

But the film isn't always easy for non-Hungarians to decipher, and as the murders mount late in the film, the line between reality and fantasy becomes increasingly blurred. Jancso seems to be having a good time making ironic jokes about the post-Communist scene.

Performances are all flawless, and the film moves at a cracking pace. — *David Stratton*

A NYARALO
(THE SUMMER GUEST)
(HUNGARIAN)

A Hunnia Filmstudio-Objektiv Filmstudio production. (Intl. sales: Cinemagyar, Budapest.) Directed by Togay Can. Screenplay, Can, Edit Koszegi. Camera (Eastmancolor, black & white), Tamas Sas; editors, Agnes Ostoros, Maria Rigo; music, Janos Masik; production design, Gyula Pauer; sound, Gabor Erdelyi; Jozsef Bajusz; assistant director, Judit Biro. Reviewed at Hungarian Film Week, Budapest, Feb. 11, 1992. Running time: **80 MIN.**
With: Marta Klubowicz, Mari Töröcsik, Juli Basti, Geza Balkay, Jozsef Madaras.

An ethereal mood piece that deliberately avoids conventional plotting, "The Summer Guest" may entrance some viewers, but it seems more likely to empty theaters.

Helmer Togay Can avers that the film has no story but is "stalking" a narrative. The young director uses beautifully shot images of a peaceful village in summer as backdrop to characters and incidents.

A young man hitchhikes from the city to spend the summer with his mother. A beautiful young woman arrives in the village. The local barkeeper and his wife quarrel and make love; she is later found dead, but how or why is unknown. Children play erotic games. Can wants viewers to build a story around his clues, but his experiment comes across as overly precious and irritating.

A fine cast, including veteran Mari Töröcsik as the mother, can do little with their ill-defined

characters. The use of black & white African documentary footage, intercut seemingly to counterpoint the Hungarian scenes, remains obscure.

The result is a beautiful but totally sterile film, which will have a hard time finding paying customers. — *David Stratton*

A KORPIO MEGESZI AZ KREKET REGGELIRE
(SCORPIO EATS GEMINI FOR BREAKFAST)
(HUNGARIAN)

A Hunnia Filmstudio-Glob Film production. Produced by Pal Egri. Directed by Péter Gárdos. Screenplay, Gárdos, Zsuzsa Toth. Camera (Eastmancolor), Tibor Mathe; editor, Maria Rigo; music, Janos Novak; production design, Tamas Vayer; sound, Janos Reti; costumes, Emoke Csengey. Reviewed at Hungarofilm screening room, Budapest, Feb. 12, 1992. (In Hungarian Film Week.) Running time: **93 MIN.**
Tamas . . . . Peter Rudolf
Panni . . . . Enikö Eszenyi
Grandmother . . . . Mari Töröcsik
Dezso . . . . Dezsö Garas
Eva . . . . Erika Papai
Ella . . . . Hedi Temessy

A weak and ill-motivated screenplay is the downfall of this disappointing comedy from Péter Gárdos who, with "Whooping Cough" and other films, has been one of Hungary's most interesting filmmakers.

"Scorpio" starts with modest promise as music-loving Tamas celebrates the birth of a baby daughter with pretty wife Eva. Pic quickly turns nasty when, on the same day, the selfish, charmless hero meets an attractive blonde and starts an affair. She's apparently friends with one of his grandmother's pals, a violinmaker (Dezsö Garas). The affair has its ups and downs, and eventually Eva departs from Australia with her child, leaving the churlish Tamas behind to his fate.

Peter Rudolf tries hard to make Tamas appealing, but it's a losing battle; the guy's a creep. Enikö Eszenyi is quite pretty as the husband-chasing Panni, but it's essentially a thankless role. Best performance comes from Mari Töröcsik as Tamas' grandmother, who somehow cares for him despite his ugly behavior.

Gárdos attempts to keep this alleged comedy bubbling along, but to no avail. Technical credits are slick but no substitute for genuine wit and humor.

— *David Stratton*

VOROS VURSTLI
(RED FAIRGROUND)
(HUNGARIAN-B&W)

A FMS Studio-Novo Film production. (Intl. sales: Cinemagyar, Budapest.) Directed by Gyorgy Molnar. Screenplay, Molnar, Andras Nagy, Peter Sulyi, Geza Beremenyi. Camera (black & white), Gábor Szabó; editor, Eva Palotai; music, Ferenc Darvas; production design, Rita Devenyi; costumes, Judit Szekulesz; sound, Gyorgy Kovacs; assistant director, Szolnoki Balazs. Reviewed at Hungarian Film Week, Budapest, Feb. 9, 1992. Running time: **81 MIN.**
Blau . . . . Lorand Lohinszky
Ilona . . . . Eva Thuroczy
Oli . . . . Gergo Kaszas
Vilike . . . . Dani Javor

Visually elegant but dramatically thin pic deals with the stifling effect of Communism on free enterprise. Set in 1919, the year of a short-lived Communist takeover in Hungary, "Red Fairground" uses the microcosm of a Budapest fairground to make obvious points.

Like other enterprises, the fair is forced to accept the new realities of Communism, which robs the free-living sideshow folks of their freedoms. But director Gyorgy Molnar doesn't make his characters, including the fairground's supervisor and a young boy whose mother works as a "mermaid," terribly interesting.

Pic's big plus is its look, but that's also a liability. Gábor Szabó's beautiful black & white cinematography and the elegant sets and costumes make for a beautiful but empty pic, and regular use of mock newsreel footage becomes irritating after a while. Ferenc Darvas' music score vividly adds to the mood, but none of the members of the cast make much of an impression.

— *David Stratton*

A HAROM NOVER
(THREE SISTERS)
(HUNGARIAN)

A Hunnia Filmstudio production. (Intl. sales: Cinemagyar, Budapest.) Directed, written by Andor Lukats, based on Anton Chekhov's play. Camera (Fujicolor), Sandor Kardos; editor, Maria Rigo; music, Laszlo Des; production design, Zsolt Khell; costumes, Gyorgi Szakacs; sound, Istvan Sipos; assistant director, Aniko Pallagi. Reviewed at Hungarofilm screening room, Budapest, Feb. 11, 1992. (In Hungarian Film Week.) Running time: **120 MIN.**
Olga . . . . Eszter Csakanyi
Masa . . . . Ildiko Toth
Irina . . . . Eniko Börcsök
Natasha . . . . Anna Raczkevei

Anfisza . . . . Margit Lontay
Also with: Peter Andorai, Peter Blasko, Gabor Mathe, Dezsö Garas, Peter Gothar.

This ill-advised attempt to update Anton Chekhov's sublime play will not impress fans of the original. Director Andor Lukats' idea of setting the drama at a barracks for Russian soldiers based in Hungary between 1987 and 1991 (when Communism was collapsing) will not enhance commercial prospects.

Lukats, better known as an actor ("Je T'Aime," also in Hungarian Film Week) handles the material too literally to make it work. Though it's possible to see Chekhov's lonely, lovelorn characters as contemporary types, inclusion of incidents like a discussion of a duel are absurd in a modern context.

The cast is accomplished, and Lukats pulls off a few scenes with flair. But on the whole, his handling is static and uninspired, and the film is unlikely to introduce a new audience to Chekhov. — *David Stratton*

ERÖZIÖ
(EROSION)
(HUNGARIAN)

A Hétföi Mühely Studio Foundation-Hunnia Studio-Magic Media production. (Intl. sales: Cinemagyar, Budapest.) Directed by András Surányi. Screenplay, Gyula Illés, Edit Köszegi. Camera (Eastmancolor), Zsolt Haraszti; editors, Eszter Majoros, András Báthory; music, Károly Binder; sound, Péter Laczkovich; art direction, István Galambos; costume design, Ágnes Jodál; assistant director, Attila Herczeg. Reviewed at Hungarian Film Week, Budapest, Feb. 10, 1992. (Also in Berlin Film Festival Panorama.) Running time: **104 MIN.**
Joe Petunia . . . . . . Róbert Alföldi
Karola/Titánka . . . . . Tünde Murányi
Death . . . . Irén Psota
Mother . . . . Lili Monori
Father . . . . Miklós B. Székely
Claudius . . . . Lajos Kovács

An abstract, symbol-laden fantasy about a young man's withdrawal from adulthood, "Erosion" wears away the viewer's patience faster than a dripping tap. Pic may find some exposure at hardcore arty fests, but theatrical chances outside Hungary look like zip.

Magyar movie buffs will be reminded of earlier works by directors Péter Gothár or Pál Sándor in the film's allegorical, picaresque style. But "Erosion," based on the written experiences of a real-life mental patient,

keeps shooting itself in the foot with its relentless self-indulgence and lack of explanations.

Story centers on Joe Petunia (Róbert Alföldi), who starts work in a bare, waterlogged warehouse containing a variety of loopy characters. As death (in the form of a woman with a hearse) slowly claims his family, and sexy g.f. Karola drives him into the arms of the romantic Titánka, Joe decides the adult world sucks and withdraws, ending up in the loonybin.

Apart from suitably bleak playing by Alföldi, perfs are colorful throughout, with pert young newcomer Tünde Murányi tops in the dual roles of Titánka and Karola. Tech credits are all pro, and the adventurous music score by Károly Binder ransacks every genre in the book.
— *Derek Elley*

EUROPA KEMPING
(EUROPA CAMPING)
(HUNGARIAN)

A Hunnia Studio-Béla Balázs Studio production. (Intl. sales: CineMagyar, Budapest.) Produced by András Szöke, György Pálos, Mária Dobos. Directed by Szöke, Dobos, Göbor Ferenczi; camera (Eastmancolor), Pölos; editor, Andrea Szakács; music, Zoltán Polyák, Adam Dévényi; sound, György Kovács, Gábor Bányai; costume design, Dobos. Reviewed at Hungarian Film Week, Budapest, Feb. 8, 1992. Running time: **72 MIN.**
With: Sándor Badár, János Horváth, András Szöke, Gábor Harsay, Ágnes Kovács, Gábor Ferenczi, Péter Forgács.

A looney-tune comedy about a group of bozos in a southern Hungary summer camp, "Europa Camping" makes up in energy what it lacks in organization. Offbeat item recalls the early work of Richard Lester and could find a brief berth in late-night film fest slots.

Pic kicks off in fine style with railroad worker Sándor Badár and his equally loopy cyclist buddy János Horváth journeying to the idyllic riverside site Europa Kemping. Soon they're involved with a crazy Arab (wittily played by helmer András Szöke), Turkish women and a corkscrew subplot involving exploding melons.

Pic's main fault is that it never gets much beyond a series of one-off routines. Szöke and his co-filmers, who scored a local cult hit two years ago with the politically cheeky low-budgeter "Cotton Chicken," aren't short

of ideas but need to spend more time developing the longer line.

Still, there's much fun along the way, and for every gag that flops six more are just around the corner. Youngish ensemble playing is neat, and pic is technically okay, with antsy lensing by György Pálos and sharp editing by Andrea Szakács.
— *Derek Elley*

MEMOIRS OF AN INVISIBLE MAN

A Warner Bros. release & presentation in association with Le Studio Canal Plus, Regency Enterprises & Alcor Films of a Cornelius production. Produced by Bruce Bodner, Dan Kolsrud. Executive producer, Arnon Milchan. Directed by John Carpenter. Screenplay, Robert Collector, Dana Olsen, William Goldman, based on H.F. Saint's novel. Camera (Technicolor), William A. Fraker; editor, Marion Rothman; music, Shirley Walker; production design, Lawrence G. Paull; art direction, Bruce Crone; set design, Elizabeth Lapp, Lauren Polizzi, Gerald Sigmon; set decoration, Rick Simpson; sound (Dolby), Jim Alexander; assistant director, William M. Elvin; special visual effects, Industrial Light & Magic (supervisor, Bruce Nicholson); visual effects producer, Ned Gorman; digital effects supervisor, Stuart Robertson; computer graphics supervisor, Doug Smythe; casting, Sharon Howard-Field. Reviewed at Warner Bros. Hollywood Studio Theater, Hollywood, Feb. 21, 1992. MPAA Rating: PG-13. Running time: **99 MIN.**
Nick Halloway . . . . . . Chevy Chase
Alice Monroe . . . . . . Daryl Hannah
David Jenkins . . . . Sam Neill
George Talbot . . . . . Michael McKean
Singleton . . . . . Stephen Tobolowsky
Dr. Bernard Wachs . . . . . Jim Norton

Main problem with this mildly entertaining special effects showcase proves as transparent as its title character — namely that Chevy Chase, who can play only Chevy Chase, lacks leading-man qualities necessary to make this sort of Hitchcockian man-in-peril scenario work. Nifty visuals and a longtime cinematic fascination with invisibility could refract some initial green into Warner Bros.' spectrum, but long-term prospects suggest this "Invisible Man" will go largely unseen until it infiltrates homevideo.

Working from H.F. Saint's well-received novel, director John Carpenter and a trio of screenwriters go the espionage route with a comedy twist, but the film fails to fully satisfy on either level.

Chase is cast as detached stock analyst turned invisible by a freak accident, who then becomes the quarry of a ruthless government agent (Sam Neill) out to exploit his unique gift for the CIA.

The story plays as a cat-and-mouse game as Chase flees from his pursuers, in the process receiving help from a woman (Daryl Hannah) he met and became instantly enamored with just prior to the optical mishap.

Film departs from past explorations of the subject in two specific areas: The hero's clothes are rendered invisible as well, meaning he doesn't have to run about in the nude like cinematic predecessor Claude Rains; and anything he ingests stays visible within him, creating the rare opportunity at one point to see an invisible man upchuck.

The action is accompanied by a Faulkner-esque voiceover narration, and Carpenter tries halfheartedly to paint a portrait of "invisibility" in a broader sense — touching on Chase's failure to connect emotionally with people in his daily life and his newfound longing for contact now that he's been made an outcast.

Unfortunately, those efforts to invest pathos into the character don't work because Chase, who lacks the Cary Grant-type qualities required to put flesh and blood over the character's invisible bones, simply isn't engaging or believable enough to pull it off. Not surprisingly, the actor seems more comfortable with the fertile territory for one-liners or sight gags invisibility provides.

But in the film's structure, the comedy is at best a respite and at worst a distraction from the more serious central plot involving some of the same people-in-high-places paranoia found in previous Carpenter efforts ("They Live," "Starman") while lacking the same sense of conviction.

Those fractured story elements and Chase's deficiencies leave it to the wizards at Industrial Light & Magic to provide the real star power, and they deliver with an impressive display of visual effects based primarily on state-of-the-art computer animation.

The process allows Chase's character to interact with objects in the foreground as reflections of the same objects move freely in perfect sync. There's also a welcome homage to the original "Invisible Man" of 1933, as Chase dramatically sheds bandages to reveal his condition to the mystified Hannah.

Hannah is asked to do little but look beautiful, and she obliges admirably. Neill and Michael McKean are notably underemployed as the one-dimensional bad guy and Chase's best friend.

Other tech credits are solid, and cinematographer William A. Fraker makes the most of the picturesque San Francisco backdrop. Like the setting, pic has its own high points, but for the most part the lows are too numerous and its shortcomings crystal clear.

— *Brian Lowry*

WHITE TRASH

A Fred Baker Film & Video Co. production & release. Produced, directed by Baker. Screenplay, Mel Clay, based on his play. Camera (Hi-8 video color blowup to 35m), Baker; editor, Robert Simpson; music, Baker; art direction, Steve Nelson; costume design, Rikki Roberts; sound, Baker; assistant director, Niva Ruschell. Reviewed at Sunset Towers screening room, L.A., Feb. 11, 1992. Running time: **85 MIN.**
Casino . . . . John Hartman
John (Rio) . . . . . Sean Christiansen
Rotten Rita . . . . Periel Marr
Percy . . . . Wheaton James
CC's father . . . . Jack Betts
CC's sister . . . . . . Winnie Thexton
CC . . . . Brian Patrick

A believably gritty look at Hollywood street kids, indie filmmaker Fred Baker's "White Trash" is very rough-hewn filmmaking, but the style suits the subject. Remarkably, pic was made for a shoestring $46,000 with a handheld Hi-8 video camera and blown up to 35m with a fuzzy but playable result for the midnight screening circuit.

An astringent corrective to the fairy-tale view of Hollywood street life purveyed so profitably in "Pretty Woman," "White Trash" is a cautionary tale that should make any potential runaways who see it realize that Hollywood hookers don't end up like Julia Roberts. It's a timely indictment of U.S. society's throwaway attitude toward youngsters.

Using a semidocumentary style recalling John Cassavetes' landmark 1961 underground film "Shadows," Baker follows the characters like a sympathetic eavesdropper. He does not flinch from AIDS ("Everybody's dead," one character says) or from the casual brutality with which well-heeled male and female johns treat their youthful tricks.

Screenwriter Mel Clay, who based the script on his own play, writes authentic gutter dialogue and views his characters without condescension or glib moral judgments.

A major drawback, perhaps inherent in the material, is that the static, numbingly predictable nature of the hustlers' lifestyle makes the film drag somewhat once the situation is established.

Acting is on the semi-amateurish and mannered side, but effective nonetheless. Periel Marr, in the lead role of a pregnant hooker determined to keep her baby, tends to go over the top but earns her emotional response.

Manic Tom Cruise look-alike John Hartman and blond sadsack Sean Christiansen are on target as her male hustler roommates.

Veteran actor Jack Betts lends an air of professionalism to his fairly complex role as the guilt-ridden father of dead hustler Brian Patrick, an AIDS victim whose family rejected him when they learned he was gay.

Winnie Thexton, as Patrick's sister, has an interestingly seductive scene with Hartman that doesn't go anywhere. Wheaton James is strictly stereotypical as an evil drug dealer.

Baker's kinetic filming style and Robert Simpson's editing keep things moving briskly. The sound (largely postsynched) is uneven, but Baker's jazzy score and a "Trash Rap" by Blade provide suitably jangling musical accompaniment.

— *Joseph McBride*

AMAZON

A Cabriolet Films release of a Villealfa Film Prods. & Noema Pictures presentation in association with Sky Light Cinema Photo Arte Ltda./Brazil. Produced by Mika Kaurismäki, Pentti Kouri. Executive producers, Klaus Heydemann, Bruce Marchfelder. Co-producers, Diane Silver, Bruno Stroppiana, Paivi Suvilehto. Directed by Kaurismäki. Screenplay, Kaurismäki, Richard Reitinger. Camera (color, Cinemascope), Timo Salminen; editor, Michael Chandler; music, Nana Vasconcelos; art direction, Tony de Castro; sound (Dolby), Jouko Lumme; line producers (Brazil), Telmo Mais, Pauli Pentti; assistant director, Vicente Amorim; 2nd unit camera, Jacques Cheuviche. Reviewed at Raleigh Studios screening room, L.A., Jan. 8, 1992. No MPAA rating. Running time: **91 MIN.**
Kari . . . . Kari Väänänen
Dan . . . . Robert Davi
Paola . . . . Rae Dawn Chong
Nina . . . . Minna
Lea . . . . Aili Sovio
Julio Cesar . . . . Rui Polanah

Shot in Cinemascope with an international B movie cast playing foreigners at the ends of their ropes in the Brazilian jungle, "Amazon" plays like a dualer that might have been made in the 1960s by Samuel Fuller or Gordon Douglas starring Burt Reynolds or Stuart Whitman. This oddity from Finnish director Mika Kaurismäki has a few grace notes that can be appreciated by aficionados, but is neither bold nor weird enough to cut a swath on the art circuit, and grindhouses no longer exist.

Less widely known as a director than his prolific brother Aki, Mika Kaurismäki still has pro-

duced or directed 17 films in the last decade, and in English previously helmed "Helsinki Napoli All Night Long" (1988). Both brothers trade in a trendy, accident-prone ennui with varying degrees of humor, but if "Amazon" retains the accidents, its huge physical scope represents a departure, if nothing else.

Opening with the nearly surreal sight of a Finnish man and his two daughters attempting to travel on the hellish Trans-Amazonia Highway to the accompaniment of some noirish narration, pic briefly flashes back to explain that banker Kari Väänänen has fled Finland with the girls upon his wife's accidental death.

Arriving in Rio, his money is immediately stolen so the desperate man incredibly deposits his daughters in a favela while he takes a job driving a truck with suspiciously unknown cargo. When his partner is killed, Kari collects the girls and heads back for civilization by way of the jungle road.

But, lo and behold, they run out of gas, as does, in an amusing scene, their would-be savior, a bitter American bush pilot named Dan (Robert Davi). A mercenary and treasure hunter of the old school, Dan speaks of searching for gold using a debilitated bulldozer he's found, and eventually Kari joins him in his quest.

Meanwhile, however, Kari urgently needs to earn some cash, and a striking sequence of him toiling with thousands in an open pit mine calls to mind images of massive slave labor in "Land of the Pharaohs" and "Spartacus."

Happily for him, Kari can enjoy evenings with Rae Dawn Chong, who plays a teacher and environmentalist who begins to work on the man's mind about how what he and Dan intend to do constitutes ecological rape.

Visually, film is always stimulating, as Timo Salminen's widescreen compositions serve up a smorgasbord of movement, sweep and local color. Dialog by Kaurismäki and Richard Reitinger, latter the co-writer of "Wings of Desire," is frequently tart, and buffs may get a kick out of the hardboiled narration spoken by a dead man, à la "Sunset Boulevard."

But storytelling is wildly uneven, and Kaurismäki has an uncertain command of pic's tone. The daughters, who could easily have provided a good p.o.v. for the curious goings-on, are blanks who barely factor in the tale.

Chong's character seems mostly like a convenient mouthpiece for politically correct thinking, and the film never really delivers on the craziness initially implicit in the extreme situations or Dan's dangerous character.

Acting is okay: Davi makes for a believable sky cowboy who could be a brother to Tom Berenger's Lewis Moon in "At Play in the Fields of the Lord." Väänänen, a vet of many films by both Kaurismäki brothers, makes for a mildly engaging, unprepossessing hero.

For a film made with limited funds under clearly difficult conditions, pic looks and sounds very sharp. —*Todd McCarthy*

BEING AT HOME WITH CLAUDE
(CANADIAN-B&W/COLOR)

An Alliance Releasing release (Canada) of a Production du Cerf production in association with the National Film Board of Canada. Produced by Louise Gendron. Line producer, Nicole Hilareguy. Directed by Jean Beaudin. Screenplay adaptation, Beaudin, based on on Rene-Daniel Dubois' novel. Camera (black & white, color), Thomas Vamos; editor, Andre Corriveau; music, Richard Gregoire; art direction, François Seguin; costume design, Louise Jobin; sound (Dolby), Michel Charron; associate producer, Doris Girard; assistant director, Louis Bolduc; casting, Lucie Robitaille. Reviewed at Cineplex Odeon Berri theater, Feb. 17, 1992. Running time: **85 MIN.**
Yves . . . . Roy Dupuis
Inspector . . . . .Jacques Godin
Claude . . . . . Jean-François Pichette
Stenographer . . . . . Gaston Lepage
Policeman . . . . Hugo Dube

Unlike most murder mysteries, "Being at Home With Claude" defies precise classification. More of a "whydunnit" than a whodunnit, pic makes motive a mystery even to the murderer himself. If given proper fest exposure, pic is sure to grab some critical attention, but marketing this unique outing will be a challenge.

Pic avoids the pitfall of a flat social-psychological portrait of a killer (or victim) and tells the passionate tale of a gay hustler (Roy Dupuis) who murders his lover (Jean-François Pichette) and then turns himself in.

The gripping opening scene shot in black & white cinéma vérité style jump-cuts between the throbbing night life during the Montreal jazz fest, and two men making passionate love on a kitchen floor. This highly erotic scene reaches a tragic climax when the hustler slashes his lover's throat.

The rest of the film revolves around Dupuis' confession to a cop (Jacques Godin) in scenes shot in color in a single room. Black & white flashbacks about the love affair punctuate the accuser-accused dialogue and provide the film's best footage.

Veteran Quebec lenser Thomas Vamos puts an intensely stylized, avant-garde spin on flashbacks, effectively using odd angles, tight closeups and grainy stock. By contrast, he shoots color interrogation scenes in a straightforward point/counterpoint format. Editor Andre Corriveau marries the two effectively, but more flashbacks are needed.

On paper, this scenario might be tritely dismissed as a violent, marginal gay film, but Beaudin's even-handed treatment of Rene-Daniel Dubois' original novel defies such ghettoization, largely because there are crossover points to sustain a mixed audience.

Anchor for a mainstream aud is the "straight cop" (played superbly by Godin), although the investigation is merely a premise for helmer/scripter Beaudin to challenge stereotypical assumptions about both gay and heterosexual love.

Casting is right on the mark with Dupuis (Canadian TV's "Caleb's Daughters"), who ranges an emotional gamut from anger to compassion and eventually pity. Like Keenu Reeves in "My Own Private Idaho," Dupuis' androgynous good looks and toughboy charm generate interest for both sexes.

(Depuis' TV star status was an initial calling card for Quebeckers: Pic has played to full houses since it opened recently to rave reviews from local critics).

Beaudin also has cleverly situated the viewer in the position of a priest listening to a guilt-ridden confession (rather than as judge and jury). Art director François Seguin beautifully exploited the "confessional," using church-like stained glass windows as the interrogation room backdrop.

French-lingo pic (no apparent reason for the English title) has strong Quebec dialect that likely will be a barrier even in other French territories. But if this unique little pic is handled carefully, it could generate interest in art houses and should also do well in homevid, especially on French Canadian home turf.
—*Suzan Ayscough*

588 RUE PARADIS
(FRENCH)

An AMLF release of a Carthargo Films-Quinto Communications-V Film TF-1 & TF1 Films Production-Les Prods. Artistes Associes co-production with participation of CNC and (Soficas) Sofiarp/Cofimage 3/Investimage. Produced by Tarak Ben Ammar. Executive producer, Mark Lombardo. Directed, written by Henri Verneuil, based on his book "Mayrig." Camera (color), Edmond Richard; editor, Henri Lanoe; music, Jean-Claude Petit; set design, Pierre Guffroy; costume design, Catherine Gorne; sound, Jean-François Auge; assistant director, Patrick Malakian. Reviewed at George V Cinema, Paris, Feb. 4, 1992. Running time: **135 MIN.**
Pierre Zakar . . . . Richard Berry
Araxi (Mayrig) . . . Claudia Cardinale
Hagop . . . . Omar Sharif
Carole . . . . Diane Bellego
Astrig Setian . . . . Zabou
Alexandre . . . . Jacques Villeret
Gayané . . . . Nathalie Roussel
Apkar . . . . Jacky Nercessian

In "588 Rue Paradis," the freestanding second half of Henri Verneuil's autobiographical "Mayrig," young Azad Zakarian, the son of self-sacrificing Armenian immigrants, has grown up to be a successful playwright who traded Marseille for Paris and his real name for that of Pierre Zakar. Whereas first installment achieved a fine quotient of authenticity and sincerity, this episode's healthy tone of self-mockery is frequently eaten in by too much syrupy nostalgia.

Black & white opening credits summarize the first film. Action resumes four decades later with Verneuil surrogate Zakar (Richard Berry) coaching the cast of his latest play. Continuing the voiceover that narrated the first episode, Berry makes ironic observations about his career and his "perfect" wife and children. Berry, whose parents still run their tailoring shop in Marseille, has gone far in the theater but farther still from his Armenian roots.

His father (Omar Sharif) comes to Paris for the play's premiere. Sharif and Claudia Cardinale are a bit too spry of step and a bit top heavy on the latex wrinkles to make truly convincing oldsters, but the details of their fretting over their grown son have an Old World truth to them.

Sharif wants only to receive his son's hospitality at home, but Berry's wife has reserved an outrageously opulent suite for him at a five-star hotel instead. This gesture leads to a misunderstanding that prompts Berry to lash out at his father who, unfortunately, dies before Berry can apologize.

The son resolves to do more for his widowed mother and, after spending quality time with her, makes a childhood dream come true: Pic's title is the address of the last house on the street where the family settled when they arrived in France. Their first residence was a tiny flea-bitten dump; No. 588 is a mansion with formal gardens.

Berry is great fun to watch, but how the smart but submissive youngster of "Mayrig" turned into such a worldly fellow is not explained. His non-Armenian wife is a caricature of a frosty social climber, which makes a down-to-earth female acquaintance from Armenian stock (Zabou) much more appealing.

When not bogged down in sentiment, helmer can be wickedly observant about human nature. Berry's wry comments about the celebrities in the house on opening night are highly entertaining. Visit from a once-cruel bourgeois classmate (Jacques Villeret) who wants to get his son into show business, is a small gem of revenge eaten cold.

Tech credits are all okay, and thesping suits the sometimes cliché'd, sometimes touching material. — *Lisa Nesselson*

DONNE CON LE GONNE
(WOMEN IN SKIRTS)
(ITALIAN)

A Filmauro Distribuzione release of a Filmauro-Filmone-Piccioli Film production. Produced by Luigi & Aurelio De Laurentiis, Gianfranco Piccioli. Directed by Francesco Nuti. Screenplay, Giovanni Veronesi, Ugo Chiti, Nuti. Camera (Cinecittà color), Gianlorenzo Battaglia; editor, Sergio Montanari; music, Giovanni Nuti; art direction, Eugenio Liverani, Riccardo Marriotti; costumes, Maurizio Millenotti; sound (Dolby), Remo Ugolinelli. Reviewed at Barberini Cinema, Rome, Feb. 5, 1992. Running time: **115 MIN.**
Renzo . . . . Francesco Nuti
Margherita . . . . Carole Bouquet
Defense lawyer . . . . Gastone Moshin
Also with: Cinzia Leone, Didi Perego, Daniele Dublino, Antonio Petrocelli.

Florentine funnyman Francesco Nuti charts a mismatched couple's rocky history in "Women in Skirts," a lumpy, overlong comedy which comes on as informed social observation but comes off as empty-headed farce.

Targeted exclusively for the local market, pic has raked in a hefty $16 million since its yuletide release, making it the Italo season's second highest earner after "Johnny Stecchino."

Nuti is on trial for the abduction and imprisonment of his wife (Carole Bouquet), and his story unfolds in flashbacks during his lawyer's summation. After a frenzied Keystone Cops-style recap of his childhood, old-fashioned country boy Nuti meets worldly flower child Bouquet in the early '70s. They lose contact until years later when she's caught up in political terrorism and he saves her skin.

The duo marry and tackle their dwindling sexual desire with a botched attempt at partner-swapping. Bouquet's career skyrockets, leaving Nuti home alone. Faced with a divorce petition, he imprisons her in a remote farmhouse, using brute force to make her a dutiful wife.

Bouquet's unsympathetic (and ineptly dubbed) character is severely misjudged by scripters and thesp, broadly equating an intelligent, independent woman with a cold bitch. Generational parallels are strictly routine and script juggles familiar comic clichés with some blatant ideasnatching: dentistry gag from "Little Shop of Horrors," a major wreckage fight from "The War of the Roses" and the captive lover setup from "Tie Me Up! Tie Me Down!"

The skin-deep technical bravura in this high-gloss production is most obvious in the showy, hyper-agile Panavision camerawork, which often is distracting. — *David Rooney*

MA VIE EST UN ENFER
(MY LIFE IS HELL)
(FRENCH)

An AMLF release of a Ciby 2000-TF1 Films-Les Films Flam-GPFI co-production with the participation of Sofiarp & Investimages 3. (Intl. sales: Majestic Films Intl.) Produced by Jean-Claude Fleury. Directed by Josiane Balasko. Screenplay, Balasko, with Joel Houssin. Camera (color), Dominique Chapuis; editor, Catherine Kelber; music, Les Rita Mitsouko; costume design, Sophie Breton; set design, Hugues Tissandier; sound, Pierre Lenoir; production manager, Farid Chaouche; special makeup, Michel Deruelle; special effects supervisor, Daniel Riche; assistant director, Etienne Dhaene. Reviewed at Forum Horizon cinema, Paris, Dec. 9, 1991. Running time: **105 MIN.**
Léah . . . . Josiane Balasko
Abar . . . . Daniel Auteuil
Psychiatrist . . . . Richard Berry
Archangel Gabriel . . Michael Lonsdale
Flo . . . . Catherine Samie
Léah/Scarlett . . . . . . Jessica Forde
Chpii . . . . Jean Benguigui

In "My Life Is Hell," helmer/star/co-scripter Josiane Balasko pumps a little freshness into the deal-with-the-devil genre, but not enough to make a lasting impression. Pic is geared to vulgar slapstick-loving French auds. Other markets may find the premise tired and the pacing wearisome.

Balasko ("Too Beautiful for You") plays a dowdy single woman who accidentally conjures one of the Devil's sales force (Daniel Auteuil). Otherwise excellent thesp Auteuil ("Manon of the Spring") whoops it up as an immortal prankster, but his schtick soon wears thin.

The woman sells her soul in a fast-food joint and briefly enjoys a glamorous bod (Jessica Forde) before the Archangel Gabriel (deliciously understated Michael Lonsdale) vetoes the deal.

Jean Benguigui is suitably annoying as a swinging porn enthusiast neighbor, and Richard Berry is entertaining as a shrink who doesn't care one whit for his patients, but moments where everything clicks are rare.

Dim, somewhat muddy lensing is peppered with extreme camera angles. Score by trendy rock duo Rita Mitsouko is abrasive. Helmer obviously aimed high in sets and special effects, but in lieu of the pizzazz of "Damn Yankees" or the ineffable class of "The Witches of Eastwick," pic is histrionic, unsubtle and not very funny. — *Lisa Nesselson*

BERLIN FEST

REBECCA'S DAUGHTERS
(GERMAN-BRITISH)

An Astralma Erste Filmproduktion-Rebecca's Daughters Ltd.-Delta Film production, in association with BBC Wales & participation of British Screen. Produced by Chris Sievernich. Co-producer, Ruth Kenley-Letts. Executive producers, Ruth Caleb, Faramarz Ette-hadieh, Gert Oberdorfer. Directed by Karl Francis. Screenplay, Guy Jenkin, from Dylan Thomas' original screenplay-novel. Camera (Eastmancolor), Russ Walker; editor, Roy Sharman; music, Rachel Portman; production design, Ray Price; costume design, Mecheal Taylor; sound (Dolby), Jeffrey North; special effects, Martin Geeson, Dave Havard; assistant director, Dafydd Arwyn Jones; casting, Suzys Korel. Reviewed at Berlin Film Festival (Panorama), Feb. 16, 1992. Running time: **94 MIN.**

Lord Sarn	Peter O'Toole
Anthony Raine	Paul Rhys
Rhiannon	Joely Richardson
Davy	Keith Allen
Capt. Marsden	Simon Dormandy
Rhodri	Dafydd Hywel
Sarah Hughes	Sue Roderick
Mordecai Thomas	Huw Ceredig

Peter O'Toole goes way over the top and stays there in "Rebecca's Daughters," an irresistible period romp about Welsh peasants taking on the English tax men. Popular hit in the Berlin fest's Panorama section could turn a tidy groat or two in hardtop barns given a critical fair wind and careful marketing.

Script is based on a screenplay commissioned in 1948 from Dylan Thomas but never produced. Result, now out of print, was published in England in 1965. Present version uses some of Thomas' dialogue but tightens up the action. Original, per producers, would have made a four-hour movie.

Set in southern Wales in 1843, yarn opens with Anthony Raine (Paul Rhys) returning from service in India with thoughts of childhood sweetheart Rhiannon (Joely Richardson) uppermost on his mind. He soon gets wise, however, to the peasants' problems, including a tollgate tax levied by drunken lord of the manor (O'Toole).

With Rhiannon playing hard to get, he dresses up as a mysterious masked avenger, Rebecca (modeled on the Bible figure whose offspring rose up against their oppressors), to win her back and right local wrongs. He's soon leading a hit squad of yokels in drag who turn the tables on a snotty English captain (Simon Dormandy) in nocturnal raids.

Pic sends up the historical romance genre, complete with wave dissolves for Rhys' childhood memories of Richardson and plenty of down-in-the-mud jokes about the crafty Welsh. The aristos don't come out any better: O'Toole's character likes dressing up as Elizabeth I and spends his time insulting all and sundry.

Main surprise are the pic's rollicking tone, and O'Toole's scenery-chewing perf, recalling "My Favorite Year" and "The Ruling Class," doesn't hog the action. That's thanks more to Guy Jenkin's lively, balanced script rather than helming of Karl Francis, a Welsh-born director of TV dramas and docus who's okay with the basics but hasn't much of a clue how to stage action.

Editor Roy Sharman does a trim job with the material, and Rachel Portman's romantic-heroic score adds further shape and stature. Pic's climax of a masked ball finds the whole cast, and production designer Ray Price, working full tilt.

Richardson hits the right notes as the fey Rhiannon, Keith Allen is solid as a pig-loving Welsh meathead and Rhys is serviceable as the handsome hero. Main competition to O'Toole in the histrionics department is Dormandy, excellent as the crazed English captain.

Bulk of pic's $6 million budget was raised by producer Chris Sievernich from private German investors, with BBC Wales contributing a slice. In every other respect it's a British pic.
— *Derek Elley*

RUN OF THE HOUSE

A Zoo Prods. Ltd. production. Produced by Janice Holland. Directed, written by James M. Felter. Camera (color), Paul Ygelisias; editors, Felter, E. Rachel Sergi; music, Russell Young; production design, William Bordac, Scott Simms; sound, Pauly Laurito. Reviewed at Berlin Film Festival (Panorama), Feb. 23, 1992. Running time: **109 MIN.**
Sady . . . . Craig Alan Edwards
Tabby . . . . Lisa-Marie Felter
Issy Felchbaum . . . . Harry A. Winter
Barb Felchbaum . . . Susan Lynn Ross

Washington, D.C.-based James M. Felter's first feature seems to be aiming at the John Waters territory of exuberant tastelessness, but it falls short of the mark. This low-budget comedy may have a video life, but theatrical bookings loom limited unless a topnotch marketing campaign is devised. Right handling could secure marginal cult status for "Run of the House."

Felter sets up the Felchbaums as a middle-class white D.C. family with problems. Issy, a cab driver, is an insensitive slob; Barb has gay fantasies; their plain-Jane niece Tabby, with her glasses and elaborate orthodontia, yearns to look like Madonna.

Enter Sady, a black drag queen on the run after witnessing a murder. Issy gives her a ride in his cab and falls for her charms. This requires a great leap of faith since, as played by Craig Alan Edwards, Sady never looks or sounds like anything but a fairly muscular man in drag.

Besotted Issy hires Sady as a maid to help Barb cater a dinner for snobbish friends. Needless to say, Sady's influence on all the members of the household, including their cat, is profound.

Felter has some good basic comic ideas here, but he lacks either a light comic touch or a willingness to follow the Waters line into complete craziness. Film is weakly scripted and ploddingly directed (running time is way too long), and perfs, apart from Harry A. Winter's nerdish Issy, are arch and obvious.

Technically, pic is threadbare, but this wouldn't have mattered if a greater energy level had been up there on the screen.

— *David Stratton*

LA GUERRE SANS NOM
(THE UNDECLARED WAR)
(FRENCH-DOCU)

A Le Studio Canal Plus-GMT Prods.-Little Bear production. Produced by Jean-Pierre Guerin. Directed by Bertrand Tavernier. Screenplay, Tavernier, Patrick Rotman. Camera (Eastmancolor), Alain Choquart; editor, Luce Grunenwaldt, Laure Blancherie; sound, Michel Desrois; assistant director, Tristan Ganne. Reviewed at Berlin Film Festival (out of competition), Feb. 16, 1992. Running time: **246 MIN.**

Bertrand Tavernier's impressive, absorbing docu "The Undeclared War" is specific yet universal in its exploration of the Algerian War. The war's parallels to the Vietnam War make limited U.S. exposure for the film a possibility despite its four-hour length.

Tavernier takes a deliberately limited view of the war, which began in 1954 when Algerian nationalists rebelled against the French colonial rulers. Conservative politicians, declaring the North African country "part of France," sent in troops for what was expected to be a brief conflict. Thousands died on both sides during eight years of fighting.

The director focuses exclusively on veterans living in Grenoble, France. He uses no news footage, but he includes hundreds of photographs taken by soldiers.

The interviewees have diverse political beliefs, but their stories are similar. Most were reluctant to go to Algeria to participate in the no-win battle. Like Vietnam veterans, they returned to a homeland almost ashamed of them after the costly undeclared war failed to achieve its objectives.

That this is more than a talking-heads film is a tribute to Tavernier's skill. The interviews take place in a variety of locations —outdoors, and in a restaurant after a well-lubricated lunch. Several interviewees break down during painful recollections, and filming stops.

TV is probably the best outlet for this film, since theatrical prospects are limited by its length, the cost of English subtitles and the war's low international profile. BBC-TV is airing the film in April.

It is fascinating and moving to see these vets, many of whom haven't even discussed their war experiences with their families, almost poetically reveal their feelings. The film deserves to be widely seen, whatever the outlet. — *David Stratton*

MAMA
(MUM)
(CHINESE-B&W/COLOR)

A Xi'an Film Studio-Audio-Visual Publishing House of Peking Film Academy production. (Intl. sales: Fortissimo, Amsterdam.) Produced by Huang Xing, Zhang Yuan. Executive director, Zhang. Screenplay, Qin Yan. Camera (black & white, color), Zhang Jian; editor, Feng Shuangyuan; music, Wang Shi; art direction, Shu Gang; sound, Zhang Lei. Reviewed at Berlin Film Festival (market), Feb. 20, 1992. Running time: **83 MIN.**
Liang Dan . . . . Qin Yan
Dongdong . . . . Huang Haibo
Chi Li . . . . Pan Shaoquan
Lu Yang . . . . Ma Zheng
Xiao Zhang . . . . . . Yang Xiaodan
(Mandarin dialogue; English subtitles)

A stark but emotionally powerful drama about a mother and her mentally handicapped young son, "Mama" is an eye-opening item from China that should be snapped up by discerning fests. Semi-docu approach by young Peking Film Academy grad Zhang Yuan is a first-of-its-kind from the generally staid Mainland industry.

Pic has been little seen outside China, where it discomfited the authorities with its unblinking treatment of a social problem. Reportedly only two prints were struck for internal release. Tacked on is a statistic-packed end roller stressing government efforts to cope with the problem.

Central character is Liang Dan (played by scripter Qin Yan, who herself has a handicapped kid), deserted by her husband and caring for 13-year-old Dongdong, who suffered brain damage during an epileptic seizure at age 6. Pic follows her during everyday activities, talking with school authorities, working with colleagues at a library and meeting her ex.

These sections, beautifully lensed in black & white, form the bulk of the film. Extra clout is provided by color interviews with other women in the same situation. Switch effect is all the more powerful thanks to Qin's own low-key, deeply felt performance in the "fictional" segs, which ill-prepare the viewer for the emotional interviews.

— *Derek Elley*

THE PARTY:
NATURE MORTE
(GERMAN-B&W)

An Alert Film production. (Intl. sales: Alert Film, Berlin.) Produced by Alfred Hürmer. Directed, written by Cynthia Beatt. Camera (black & white), Elfi Mikesch; editor, Dörte Völz; sound, Peter Schmidt; art direction, Raimund Kummer. Reviewed at Berlin Film Festival (Forum), Feb. 14, 1992. Running time: **92 MIN.**
Queenie . . . . Tilda Swinton
Black . . . . Féodor Atkine
Burrs . . . . Lutz Weidlich
Also with: Leland Wheeler, Isabella Mamthis, Simon Turner.
(German & English dialogue)

"The Party" is a posey little flick to which most people will wish they weren't invited. Static item about a feuding couple and their pretentious pals will arouse curiosity from its casting of Derek Jarman icon Tilda Swinton but is most likely destined for fest sidebars.

Subtitle "Nature Morte" (Still Life) says it all. After a 10-minute prologue of Swinton rowing with mate Lutz Weidlich, she says, "I think it's time for a party." Enter a collection of pseuds and longhairs who take up positions in the couple's nouveau-warehouse-style flat and spend the next 80 minutes in minimalist conversation and poetic reveries.

Basic theme of Swinton looking for a bit of rapture in her life never gets further than whining she feels "like buried in sand up to your neck." Only real action is Swinton mildly flirting with the handsome Féodor Atkine, and two lesbians making it on a bed. Every now and then someone sings a song.

Elfi Mikesch's handsome black & white lensing makes the most of the single setting and tableau-like approach. Swinton is okay but capable of much more. Pic at least has the courage of its convictions, but most auds will decide the action's somewhere else in town. — *Derek Elley*

TA CHRONIA TIS MEGALIS ZESTIS
(THE YEARS OF THE BIG HEAT)
(GREEK)

A Greek Film Centre-Greek TV 1-Negative O.E. production. (Intl. sales: Greek Film Center, Athens.) Produced by Frieda Liappa, Kiriakos Angelakos. Directed by Liappa. Screenplay, Liappa, Maritina Passari. Camera (color), Yannis Smaragdis; editor, Takis Yannopoulos; music, Thanos Mikroutsikos; lyrics, Lina Nikolakopoulou; sound, Nikos Ahiadis, Nikos Papadimitriou; art direction-costume design, Maro Seirli; narrator, Nikos Savvatis. Reviewed at Berlin Film Festival (Panorama: Art & Essai section), Feb. 15, 1992. Running time: **93 MIN.**
With: Elektra Alexandropoulou, Periklis Moustakis, Sofia Seirli, Giorgos Constas, Thanos Grammenos, Mania Papadimitriou, Eleni Demertzi, Maritina Passari.

A promising idea gets buried by a mass of metaphysics in "The Years of the Big Heat," a preposterous Greek tragedy most auds will need footnotes to decipher. Strikingly lensed drama has attracted controversy at home, but pic won't raise much b.o. temperature beyond arty salons.

Helmer Frieda Liappa has a solid film fest rep for her metaphysical allegories ("Love Wanders in the Night," "A Quiet Death"). "Heat" has raised a stir in Greece for its bloody finale. Pic is reportedly banned there and the producers under threat of morality charges.

Wafer-thin story unfolds on an unnamed island (actually Milos) where a heat wave is driving everyone loony and a strange virus is destroying their memory. As the last guests linger on, the handsome Pavlos arrives and starts a robust affair with tavern operator Elektra, unlocking some dark secret from their past involving blood initiation.

Pic's opening is impressively taut, with elegant visuals, characters framed against the burnt landscape and a lean Bartók-like string score edging the drama along. Boredom quickly sets in as the characters continue to talk in riddles and aren't sufficiently defined to engage sympathy or attention.

Final half-hour lays on the shocks with a trowel, with full-frontal nudity (both sexes), crazed self-abuse and the final five-minute massacre, featuring a bawling baby in a cot who gets spattered with blood when a slasher interrupts a couple in flagrante. Scene won't make it past most censors' scissors.

Performances are solid as far as they go, but most thesps look as if they don't understand the script. Mania Papadimitriou has her moments as a mature teen who prays in caves.

— *Derek Elley*

IDENTIFIKATSIA ZHELANII
(IDENTIFICATION OF DESIRE)
(TAJIK)

A Tadjikfilm (Debut Group) production. Directed by Tolib Khamidov. Screenplay, Anvar Valiyev, based on themes from Abelardo Catilio's story "Ernesto's Mother." Camera (color), Aleksandr Myakota; editor, Nina Lapteva; music, Akhmed Bakayev; art direction, Manuchekhr Sobir; special effects, Nosir Rakhmanov; sound, Svetlana Kudratova; assistant director, Emma Krashanovskaya. Reviewed at Berlin Film Festival (Forum), Feb. 15, 1992. Running time: **61 MIN.**
Akbar . . . . Sharaf Khabinov
Sharof . . . . Djamol Dadadjanov
Odil . . . . Sandjar Khamidov
Latif . . . . Latif Sobirov
Mother . . . . Rosia Khaidarova
Uncle . . . . . Khabibullo Abdurasakov
Bordello owner . . . . Rajab Khuseinov
Blonde girl . . . . . . Marina Lemshi
(Russian dialogue)

A Central Asian shaggy dog story about youths who hire a friend's mother for a one-night stand, "Identification of Desire" is as trim and snappy as its title isn't. Surprise discovery in the Berlin fest's Forum is perfect for other film fests, with specialist tube sales likely thereafter.

Film starts strikingly with a long, overhead slo-mo shot of a half-naked teen turning in his sleep. After religious imagery and ambitious low-budget effects, pic segues into the more realistic story with intertitles ("The Son," "The Friends," "The Uncle," "Expectation") dividing the story into seven segs.

Plot is set in a dusty, heat-drenched corner of Tajikistan, where three young blades regularly lay a donkey for want of female company. They decide to do the real thing with a friend's mother, a dancer at weddings who occasionally moonlights at an uncle's bordello.

Rest of the film limns the lead-up to their close encounter, told in simple imagery and with a poker-faced, dry wit. Dialogue is sparse, but debuting Tajik director Tolib Khamidov gets characterful perfs from his young cast and doesn't push the flimsy material beyond breaking point.

Tech credits are acceptable in the circumstances, and the greeny, washed-out color adds to the surreal tone, heightened by tinting, overlapping dissolves and use of black & white. Original Russian dialogue matches the lips. — *Derek Elley*

LANA IN LOVE
(CANADIAN)

An Oneira Pictures Intl. production. Produced, directed by Bashar Shbib. Screenplay, Shbib, Daphna Kastner. Camera (color), Stephen Reizes; editor, Shbib, Meiyen Chan; music, Harry Mayronne Jr.; art direction, Janet Cunningham; sound, Clifford (Kip) Gynn. Reviewed at Montreal World Film Festival, Aug. 28, 1991. (In Berlin Film Festival, Panorama.) Running time: **85 MIN.**
With: Daphna Kastner, Clark Gregg, Susan Eyton-Jones, Ivan E. Roth, Michael Gillis, Cheryl Platt, Brian Swardstrom.

This love story has its comical moments but gets massacred midway by thesp Daphne Kastner overplaying the sexually repressed, emotionally hungry businesswoman, Lana.

"Lana in Love" begins as an amusing tale of mistaken identities but quickly falls apart as Kastner's shrill voice belittles love interest Marty, stifling both their budding romance and pic.

But legit thesp Clark Gregg makes an impressive screen debut as the plumber Marty who arrives at the wrong address. Lana is waiting for a podiatrist she found through the classified ads and assumes Marty is her mystery man.

A hilarious dinner scene works superbly as the two talk at cross purposes, but the pic's problems begin when Lana discovers the truth.

Kastner's fine as the bubbly, bumbling date but hopeless as an emotionally deprived, enraged woman. After the confrontation scene, Marty's pursuit of her is no longer believable. Tech credits are fine, but Kastner's shrieking scenes could have been edited considerably to make the package more palatable.

—*Suzan Ayscough*

DER BROCKEN
(RISING TO THE BAIT)
(GERMAN)

An Ecco Film production, with NDR (Hamburg), DFF (Berlin). (Intl. sales: Progress Film, Berlin.) Produced by Harald Reichebner. Directed by Vadim Glowna. Screenplay, Knut Boeser. Camera (Eastmancolor), Franz Ritschel; editor, Karola Mittelstadt; music, Nikolaus Glowna; production design, Gerhard Kulosa; sound, Harald Lambeck; assistant director, Andreas Drost. Reviewed at Berlin Film Festival (competition), Feb. 24, 1992. Running time: **103 MIN.**
Ada Fenske . . . . Elsa Grube-Deister
Zwirner . . . . Rolf Zacher
Svetlana . . . . . . Muriel Baumeister
Funke . . . . Ben Becker
Solters . . . . Gunter Körnas
Fiedler . . . . Franz Viehmann
Pastor Seidl . . . Hans-Joachim Röhrig
Geerke . . . . Roman Silberstein

"Rising to the Bait" is a cheerful, optimistic comedy about graft and corruption in contempo Germany as sharks from the West home in on the naive Easterners. It's romantic but topical and should be a hit in Germany. Offshore chances also are good.

The simple plot centers on old Ada Fenske (Elsa Grube-Deister), a widow whose farm is on an island near a Russian military base. While the lugubrious Russians are waiting to be sent home, the German Military Secret Service (MAD) has set its sights on Fenske's property.

The slimy Zwirner (Rolf Zacher) is dispatched to buy the place, but the old dame refuses to sell. So Zwirner locates a nephew (Ben Becker) she never knew she had and blackmails the mayor (by threatening to spread lies about his secret police background) into falsifying an application for a share of the property on behalf of the nephew.

Zwirner's plans go awry, thanks to Svetlana (Muriel Baumeister), the mayor's beautiful secretary, who spent some time in the West but now lives with Fenske. She figures out Zwirner's scheme and foils it.

Meanwhile, the old lady starts earning hard currency the way capitalists do, by selling cheap paintings and knitted sweaters for top prices.

Director Vadim Glowna extracts a good deal of fun from this situation, helped by a sprightly cast. Grube-Deister is formidable, while Baumeister shows promise with her charming perf. Zacher is suitably hissable.

Many of the gags, like the job switch of former a Communist Party big to filing clerk, will be appreciated more by German audiences than others, but much of the humor is international. Visually, the film is first rate,

— *David Stratton*

HAPPY BIRTHDAY, TURKE!
(HAPPY BIRTHDAY!)
(GERMAN)

A Senator Film release of a Cobra Filmproduktion, with ZDF. (Intl. sales: Cinepool, Munich.) Produced by Gerd Huber, Renate Seefeldt. Directed, written by Doris Dorrie, based on Jakob Arjouni's novel. Camera (color), Helge Weindler; editors, Raimund Barthelmes, Hana Muller; music, Peer Raben, Markus Lonardoni; production design, Claus Kottmann; sound, Michael Etz; assistant director, Ruth Stadler. Reviewed at Berlin Film Festival (New German Cinema), Feb. 20, 1992. Running time: **110 MIN.**
Kemal Kayankaya . . Hansa Czypionka
Ilter . . . . Ozay
Mrs. Futt . . . . . . Doris Kunstmann
Paul Futt . . . . Lambert Hamel
Yilmaz . . . . Omer Simsek
Eiler . . . . Ulrich Wesselmann
Hosch . . . . Christian Schneller
Hanna Hecht . . . . . . Meret Becker
Mother Ergun . Emine Sevgi Ozdamar
Susi . . . . Nina Petri

After a couple of disappointing pics, Doris Dorrie returns triumphantly with "Happy Birthday!" her best film since "Men." Only drawbacks here are slightly excessive length and the perception that genre pics don't perform well on the art house circuit. Still, pic should find international audiences.

This thoroughly entertaining private eye pic is faithful to the genre but full of originality. It's witty, suspenseful and technically fine, with great location photography.

The private eye in this case is a Turk who, orphaned and raised by German foster parents, can't speak Turkish. As played with wry charm by Hansa Czypionka, this great addition to the illustrious line of screen private eyes is a slob and a womanizer. He has a great sense of humor and a way of ferreting out the truth. He constantly fends off racial jibes because of his Turkish looks, but, ironically, Kemal speaks German better than many of the racists who mock him.

The case at first seems simple, as these things usually do. Kemal is hired by a Turkish woman (Ozay) to find her husband, who disappeared about the time her wealthy father was killed in a mysterious auto accident. Before long, the gumshoe finds drugs and prostitution in the case, but when he finally tracks down the missing man he has no time to talk to him before he's stabbed to death.

Although his client asks him to stop the investigation, the private eye unravels a web of police corruption and murder. A lot of nastiness is going on in the Frankfurt underworld, but Dorrie injects the film with a great deal of sardonic humor and fills the narrative with intriguing characters and suspects.

It's a tribute to "Happy Birthday!" (Kemal is celebrating his birthday at the beginning of the film) that a sequel would be welcome. — *David Stratton*

CILVEKA BERNS
(THE CHILD OF MAN)
(LATVIAN)

A Film Studio Tris production. (Intl. sales: Film Studio Tris, Riga.) Directed, written by Janis Streics, from Janis Klidzejs' novel. Camera (color), Harijs Kukels; editor, Maija Indersone. Reviewed at Berlin Film Festival (market), Feb. 15, 1992. Running time: **96 MIN.**
Bonifacijs Paulans . Andris Rudzinskis
Brigita (Bigi) . . . . . . Signe Dundure
Mother . . . . Akveline Livmane
Father . . . . Janis Paukstello
Grandfather . . . . . . Bolislavs Ruzs

Acute tale about a Latvian moppet who falls for the local looker, "The Child of Man" doesn't cut it as a theatrical item but could interest curio-seekers after product from the new Baltic Republics. Most likely destination is as a dubbed kidpic on the tube.

Set in an idealized district of pre-WWII Latvia, story is seen through the eyes of young Bonifacijs (Andris Rudzinskis), who dreams of medieval heroes and larks around in his picturesque village. Main conflict comes when the nubile Brigita (Signe Dundure) calls him "my little fiancé" and he takes her seriously.

Nothing much happens, but the telling is colorful and oozes ethnic detail. Pic ends with a big wedding bash for Brigita and the kid praying for her happiness.

Veteran Latvian helmer Janis Streics, who's been directing since the mid-'60s, knows where to put the camera but relies too much on zooms for effect. Color processing is fine; post-synching is loose and lacks perspective. Performances are adequate.
— *Derek Elley*

MIRACULI
(GERMAN)

A DEFA Studio Babelsberg (Berlin Group) production. (Intl. sales: DEFA, Potsdam.) Directed, written by Ulrich Weiss. Camera (color), Eberhard Geick, Johann Feindt; editor, Evelyn Carow; music, Peter Rabenalt; art direction, Solvejg Paschkowski; costume design, Werner Bergemann; sound, Edgar Nitzsche; assistant director, Roland Hella. Reviewed at Berlin Film Festival (out of competition), Feb. 18, 1992. Running time: **114 MIN.**
Sebastian . . . . Volker Ranisch
Fine . . . . Katrin Vogt
Head controller . . Hans-Peter Minetti
Controller . . . . . . Peter Dommisch
Mother . . . . Katrin Waligura
Father . . . . Klaus Manchen
Also with: Käthe Reichel, Thomas Lawincky, Eduard Burza, Sebastian Hartmann, Uwe Kockisch.

Baffling but clearly sincere pic by former East German helmer Ulrich Weiss, "Miraculi" will need a few miracles of its own to succeed with non-fest auds. Surreal yarn about East-West divisions in modern Germany never lowers its undercarriage after taking flight in the opening reel.

Based on a 1978 newspaper story about a lake that disappeared overnight in Mecklenburg, script was turned down by the (then) East German DEFA Studio for possible subversiveness. After being banned from filmmaking in 1983, Weiss got the chance to make the film after unification.

Pic opens with a group of six young punks roaming the night streets in a shabby area of town. Outside a movie theater called "Zur neuen Welt" (To the New World), they pick one of their number, the shy Sebastian (Volker Ranisch), to steal some cigarettes from a store. Thus begins his strange odyssey.

Sebastian's experiences include being hauled up in front of an ad hoc court and riding a tram full of obedient passengers (both symbolizing West Germany), and later training as a ticket collector back home. After adopting a Christ-like guise, he finally ends up (back in the West?) with a group of lakeside revelers. Pic ends with the lake suddenly going dry and everyone thrown into confusion.

Weiss seems to be drawing timely conclusions about the problems of uniting two disparate sections of the country, the one poor and lackadaisical, the other rich but regimented. Finale posits a bleak future in which both

sides lose. "It used to be so good," kvetches a rich reveler.

Ranisch is good in the main role as a sad, clown-like figure, and he's surrounded by a mass of colorful characters. But pic grinds to a fatal halt in the last third with a medico's long lecture about schizophrenia.

Pic is technically fine.
— *Derek Elley*

KYONGMACHANG KANUNGIL
(THE ROAD TO THE RACE TRACK)
(SOUTH KOREAN)

A Tae Hung Prods. Co. production. (Intl. sales: Tae Hung, Seoul.) Produced by Lee Tae-won. Directed by Chang Som-u. Screenplay, Ha Il-ji, from his novel. Camera (color), Yoo Young-gil; editor, Kim Hyun; music, Kim Soo-chul; art direction-costume design, Kim Yoo-jun; sound, Lee Young-gil; assistant director, Chung Byung-gak. Reviewed at Berlin Film Festival (Forum), Feb. 17, 1992. Running time: **135 MIN.**
J . . . . Kang Soo-yeon
R . . . . Moon Sung-gun
Wife . . . . Kim Bo-yeon
Father . . . . Yoon Il-joo
Mother . . . . Kwon Il-jong
Also with: Lee In-ok, Im Jong-mi, Kim Sun-kyung.

A wordy drama about an intellectual's obsession with a former lover, "The Road to the Race Track" will leave most festival auds guessing whether it's a black comedy or meaningful tract. This bout of South Korean navel-gazing won't make it past many exhibs' finish lines.

Hero is R (Moon Sung-gun), returning home after five years in France studying, three of them alongside J (Kang Soo-yeon). She meets him at Seoul airport and drives him south to his family in Taegu but is strangely evasive about any more intimacy. R's wife refuses to give him a divorce, so he spends his time traveling up the capital and trying to parlay his way back into J's bed.

She reveals she's marrying another man; the reason she stays in touch is that she got her literary reputation by publishing one of R's pieces under her own name. She finally gets over her prolonged headache, but their sessions together solve nothing.

Moon largely repeats his troubled intellectual from the recent "The Black Republic" (a.k.a. "They, Like Us"). Kang, memorable as the lead in Im Kwon-taek's 1986 costume drama "Surrogate Woman," is less convincing here. Kim Bo-yeon is good in

a small role as R's wife. Pic is technically up to scratch.
— *Derek Elley*

KRAPATCHOUK
(SPANISH-FRENCH-BELGIAN)

An Aries TV 92 (Madrid)-Alain Keytsman Prods. (Brussels)-Legend (Paris) production, in association with Antenne 3 & participation of Canal Plus. Produced by Jaime De Oriol, Keytsman. Co-producer, Jean-Bernhard Fetoux. Directed, written by Enrique Gabriel Lipschutz. Camera (Eastmancolor), Raul Perez Cubero; editor, Isabelle Dedieu; music, Viktor Kissine; production design, Victor Alarcón; costume design, Aida Trujillo; sound, Miguel Rejas; assistant director, Alain Monne. Reviewed at Berlin Film Festival (Panorama), Feb. 14, 1992. Running time: **96 MIN.**
Polni . . . . Guy Pion
Tchelovek . . . . . . Piotr Zaitchenko
Lisa . . . . Angela Molina
Lagachis . . . . Didier Flamand
Marceau . . . . . Jean-Pierre Sentier
Arthur . . . . Oscar Ladoire
Cornelia . . . . Mary Santpère
Ahmed . . . . Hadi El Gamal
Fuselier . . . . . . Serge-Henri Valcke
Philémon . . . . Serge Marquand
Minister . . . Jean-Christophe Bouvet
Alvarez . . . . Raul Fraire
(French dialogue)

A timely comedy about two East European hayseeds stranded in Paris when their country vanishes off the map, "Krapatchouk" fails to live up to the promise of its opening reels but whiles away the time pleasantly enough. Leisurely first pic by young Buenos Aires-born helmer Enrique Gabriel Lipschutz is unlikely to make the bound into foreign art houses.

Script, actually written seven years ago, has two farm laborers (Guy Pion, Piotr Zaitchenko) from the Slavic republic of Prajevitza changing trains in Paris to head home after a season's work abroad. Problem is, the ticket office's computer can't find their country any longer and soon afterward their luggage and passports are stolen.

Cops aren't much help, and a ministerial contact arranged by an eccentric French aristo leads to them being branded in the papers as Russian spies. Later they get adopted by a Spanish hatmaker (Angela Molina), with whom Zaitchenko slowly falls.

Pic's first half hour is right on the money, with delicious jokes about unknown republics, dumb officials and plenty of linguistic shtick between the meathead Zaitchenko and baby-faced Pion. But things slow down in the middle with duo's adoption by Paris' stateless expat community and the fairy-tale romance.

In between, Lipschutz tries to jump-start the script with knock-about humor involving harassed politicos who decide that, as Prajevitza no longer exists, the duo don't exist either. Final reel, with our heroes miraculously finding a way out of their quandary, belatedly recovers opening tone.

Lipschutz gets good perfs from his two leads, with Pion especially sharp as the diminutive Polni (Russian for "full"). Zaitchenko makes a good foil as the mustached Tchelovek ("person") but Molina, though beauteous, never seems to hit her stride as the foggily written Lisa.

Tech credits are fine. Meaning of pic's title is never explained.

— *Derek Elley*

HUNGARIAN FEST

AZ UTOLSO NYARON...
(THE LAST SUMMER)
(HUNGARIAN)

A Dialog Studio production. (Intl. sales: Cinemagyar.) Directed by Ferenc András. Screenplay, Dénes Csengey. Camera (color), János Kende; music, Görgy Kovács; assistant director, Judit Biró. Reviewed at Hungarian Film Week, Budapest, Feb. 10, 1992. Running time: **87 MIN.**
Imre . . . . György Cserhalmi
Rita . . . . Éva Igó
Also with: Tamás Jordán, Judit Halász, Virágh Csapó, Mai Kiss.

The chestnut about friends coming to terms with their lives during a weekend in the country looks a tad wrinkled in "The Last Summer." Strongly cast Hungarian production is torpedoed by a gabby script and lack of real drama. Offshore chances look wintry.

Director Ferenc András turned the spotlight on his own 40-something crowd much more sharply with the 1986 "Great Generation." This time it looks as if he's shooting a first-draft script with nothing new to add.

Story turns on 24 hours at the well-upholstered Lake Balaton country home of a w.k. '68 intellectual (György Cserhalmi) whose marriage is on the rocks. As various couples (all former radicals) pile down from the city, past and present problems surface. Mooning around in the background is a pretty blond neighbor's daughter (Éva Igó) whose heart pounds for the intellectual who's rapidly going to seed.

Midlife problems get a good airing as the sauce flows, but peripheral characters remain undeveloped and revelations are few. Main surprise is learning at the end why Igó is so brooding. Performances and tech credits are all solid. — *Derek Elley*

ZSÖTEM
(JE T'AIME)
(HUNGARIAN)

A Hunnia Studio-Hétföi Müuhely production. (Intl. sales: Cinemagyar, Budapest.) Directed, written by András Salamon. Camera (color), Sándor Kardos; editor, Ágnes Incze; music-songs, Peter Ogi; art direction, László Makai; costume design, János Breckl; sound, Tamás Márkus; assistant director, Gyöngyi Szabó. Reviewed at Hungarian Film Week, Budapest, Feb. 11, 1992. Running time: **90 MIN.**
Laci . . . . Andor Lukáts
Anita . . . . Enikö Börcsök
Sylvia . . . . Éva Kerekes
Anita's mother . . . . . Ildikó Bánsági
Also with: Antal Merkovits, Károly Somorjai, István Lugosi, Magdolna Márta, András Ozorai, László Makai.

A semi-road movie about three Magyars on the lam in Vienna, "Je t'aime" doesn't quite add up to the sum of its parts. But strong perfs and pic's canny mixture of T&A and emotional drama should ensure fest exposure and even some foreign tube sales.

Young women Anita (Enikö Börcsök) and Sylvia (Eva Kerekes), with the bright lights of the West in their eyes, take off to Austria with middle-aged operator Laci (Andor Lukáts), but they soon find out that work means stripping in peepshow joints with the ever-present fear of being thrown in the slammer for having no green cards.

Further souring their dream are emotional complications with the seriously unstable Laci. After an affair between Anita and Laci breaks up the women's friendship, Sylvia goes AWOL and Anita is left to sort out the mess.

Director András Salamon traveled some of this road in last year's Vienna-set "Voilà la liberté," which he wrote and co-directed with Péter Vajda. "Je t'aime" is a slicker, better organized production, with plenty of unselfconscious nudity and held together by a sensitive central performance from Börcsök, also standout in "Sweet Emma, Dear Böbe." Pic plays as a remembrance of things past through her eyes.

Lukáts goes at his part like a

demented Dennis Hopper. Kerekes is fine in the less charismatic role of brunette Sylvia.

— *Derek Elley*

GOLDBERG VARIÁCOK
(GOLDBERG VARIATIONS)
(HUNGARIAN)

An MIT production. (Intl. sales: Cinemagyar, Budapest.) Directed, written by Ferenc Grunwalsky. Camera (color), Grunwalsky, Zsolt Haraszti, Lajos Hegyaljai; editor, Klára Majoros; sound, András Vámosi; production manager, András Ozorai. Reviewed at 23rd Hungarian Film Week, Budapest, Feb. 12, 1992. Running time: **77 MIN.**
With: Sándor Gáspár, Erzi Cserhalmi, Károly Nemcsak, Ági Csere, Tibor Gáspár, Péter Andorai.

"Goldberg Variations" is a left-field but mesmerizing look at the effects of a 13-year-old boy's suicide on his parents. Potentially downbeat material emerges as an assured mood piece thanks to lenser-helmer Ferenc Grunwalsky's thought-out approach. Serious fests should pencil this one in for their avant-garde sidebars.

Director's own daughter committed suicide a couple of years ago, but pic is more than just a reworking of a personal experience. One of Hungary's most interesting experimenters, Grunwalsky has come up with a tight work that operates on several levels, not all of them clear on first viewing. It's his best work since the offbeat drama "One Whole Day" two years ago.

Pic opens "a day after the funeral," per opening caption. The mother is visited first by a grieving friend, then by a sinister cop and eventually by her son's girlfriend. The father goes on a guided tour of the crematorium and later realizes he hardly knew his dead offspring. Pic ends with the mother slicing his throat and drawing the shutters.

Interspersed throughout are shots of the kid during his final moments, plus fleeting hints (mostly via the soundtrack) of strange cosmic forces guiding the players' lives. Traces of black humor, as in the cop's questioning and the final bloodbath, lighten the tone. Pic could also be read as a dark metaphor for Hungary's current rudderless situation.

Tech credits are fine, and extracts from J.S. Bach's eponymous musical work add further style to the proceedings.

— *Derek Elley*

ARTICLE 99

An Orion release of a Gruskoff/Levy Co. production. Produced by Michael Gruskoff, Michael I. Levy. Directed by Howard Deutch. Screenplay, Ron Cutler. Camera (DuArt color; Deluxe prints), Richard Bowen; editor, Richard Halsey; music, Danny Elfman; production design, Virginia L. Randolph; art direction, Marc Fisichella; set design, Tom Stiller; set decoration, Sarah Stone; costume design, Rudy Dillon; sound (Dolby), C. Darin Knight; associate producers, Elena Spiotta, Roger Joseph Pugliese; assistant director, K.C. Colwell; 2nd unit camera, John Allen; casting, Karen Rea. Reviewed at the Directors Guild of America, West Hollywood, March 4, 1992. MPAA Rating: R. Running time: **100 MIN.**
Dr. Richard Sturgess . . . . Ray Liotta
Dr. Peter Morgan . . Kiefer Sutherland
Dr. Sid Handleman . . Forest Whitaker
Dr. Robin Van Dorn . . Lea Thompson
Dr. Rudy Bobrick . . John C. McGinley
Dr. Henry Dreyfoos . . John Mahoney
Luther Jerome . . . . Keith David
Dr. Diana Walton . . . . Kathy Baker
Sam Abrams . . . . Eli Wallach
Inspector General . Noble Willingham
Amelia Sturdeyvant . . . Julie Bovasso
Pat Travis . . . . Troy Evans
Nurse White . . . . . Lynne Thigpen
Dr. Leo Krutz . . . . Jeffrey Tambor
Shooter Polaski . . . . Leo Burmester

A timely and provocative topic is portrayed with broad strokes in "Article 99." With didactic intent behind a rabble-rousing story, filmmakers admirably draw attention to the scandalous condition of health care at the nation's Veterans' Administration hospitals while aiming for the seriocomic tone of "Mash," "Catch-22" and "The Hospital." Pic has enough going for it to make a certain b.o. impression but is ultimately more successful in awakening the viewer to a desperate social condition than in providing a good time.

Title refers to a fictional but apparently functioning regulation at the V.A. that withholds full medical benefits from vets if they can't prove their ailments are specifically related to military service. Through the characters of a Korean War vet in need of heart surgery and a novice medic, the audience is thrust into a nightmare world in constant emergency alert. Things only get done when a scam is pulled on the system.

Set almost entirely within a zoolike V.A. facility in Kansas City, Ron Cutler's screenplay presents a villainous bureaucracy ruled by hospital director John Mahoney. Opposing him are the irreverent but dedicated can-do doctors led by surgeon Ray Liotta, who has spent seven years mastering ways of to cut the red tape that keeps patients from receiving proper care.

Liotta and fellow medics Forest Whitaker, John C. McGinley and Lea Thompson naturally give newcomer Kiefer Sutherland a hard time, accusing him of having his sights set on a cushy private practice after a short stint in the trenches. Little by little, Sutherland's eyes are opened to the crazy methods his colleagues need to employ to do any good, and to the value of their work.

Under Howard Deutch's fever-pitch direction, which achieves no modulation since every moment is presented as an equal crisis, most of the film is devoted to laying out the insanity of everyday life in the hospital. Even if the action is somewhat exaggerated, the pic paints an appalling portrait and generates feelings of outrage and disbelief that things could ever have gotten so out of hand. In this sense, filmmakers have fashioned a call to action that may have a beneficial impact in the political arena.

After Mahoney finally manages to have Liotta dismissed for his subversive ways, story pushes toward an action climax in which the vets and doctors are essentially forced to declare war on the government they once served. Lack of respect generally accorded the vets is unmistakably conveyed, even if the physical confrontation between them and the Feds doesn't pay off in dramatic terms.

Overall, film's intent is seen more than felt, due in great measure to the unnuanced, machine-gun presentation. Deutch's direction is more cartoonlike than gritty, and the resolution tries to put a rosy spin on all the disturbing issues the film raises.

Liotta shows inexhaustible spirit and convincing leadership qualities as the crusading doctor, while Whitaker, McGinley and Thompson play their own variations of grace and humor under pressure. Sutherland is emotionally accessible but a bit too low-key as the freshman of the group who takes a special interest in ailing World War II vet Eli Wallach.

Kathy Baker enlivens every scene she's in as a warm-blooded shrink who gets right to the point when Liotta shows an interest in her, and Keith David sinks his teeth into the showy part of a patient who has turned his wheelchair into command central for the entire hospital. Mahoney's overlord is eminently hissable.

Lenser Richard Bowen has given the film a rough, vérité look, Richard Halsey's editing is relentless, and Danny Elfman's score edges toward the ennobling without going overboard.
— *Todd McCarthy*

GATE II

A Triumph release of a Vision p.d.g. presentation of an Alliance Entertainment/Andras Hamori production. Produced by Hamori. Executive producer, John Kemeny. Directed by Tibor Takacs. Screenplay, Michael Nankin; camera (Film House color), Brian England; editor, Ronald Sanders; music, George Blondheim; production design, William Beeton; costume design, Beth Pasternak; sound (Ultra-Stereo), Steve Joles; assistant director, Michael Zenon; production manager, Patti Meade; special visual effects and 2nd unit director, Randall William Cook; special makeup effects, Craig Reardon; special effects, Frank Carere; stunt coordinator, Ron Van Hart; line producer, Peter Gray; associate producer, Gordon Woodside; casting, John Buchan. Reviewed at Loews 19th St. East 5 theater, New York, Feb. 29, 1992. MPAA rating: R. Running time: **95 MIN.**

Terry	Louis Tripp
Moe	Simon Reynolds
Liz	Pamela Segall
John	James Villemaire
Art	Neil Munro
Mr. Coleson	James Kidnie
Minion	Andrea Ladanyi

After three years on the shelf, "Gate II" opens to reveal an idiotic horror film boasting good monster effects. Original, released in 1987, notably ran neck and neck at the box office with "Ishtar." Lame-duck sequel is better suited to video action.

Louis Tripp encores his role, now playing a nerdy teen (original was a PG-13 entry with young kids as protagonists). He chants ancient incantations in a spooky old house to summon demons and their minions from another dimension.

Michael Nankin, scripter of both "Gate" pics, takes (without-acknowledgement) as his launch point the lore of H.P. Lovecraft: There is a trinity of demons that has been confined behind a gate for billions of years, eager to reclaim Earth.

Nankin's storyline here is stupid, however. Student of demonology Tripp calls up this evil merely to be granted modest wishes, notably getting his alcoholic airplane pilot dad back on his feet. Tripp's teen buddies Simon Reynolds and James Villemaire misuse the cute little minion that Tripp calls up to get them money for a night on the town.

Gimmick is that wishes are granted only temporarily, with the booty and money literally turning into excrement. All three heroes are ultimately possessed by the trinity of demons, who plan to sacrifice Pamela Segall to bring about hell on earth. Film's trick ending is especially silly.

Saving grace is the monster work, including a mix of live action and puppetry to create the graceful, realistic movement of the tiny minion. Less successful is Randy Cook's creation of a 10-foot monster (the demon that possesses Villemaire), a reptilian creature that pays homage to the Venusian fashioned by Ray Harryhausen in 1957 for "20 Million Miles to Earth." Photography and design work are good.

Acting is uneven, with leads Tripp and Segall convincing, while Reynolds and Villemaire are ridiculous as stereotyped teens. Only sop to the film's north-of-the-border origins is Tripp amusingly donning hockey gear for protection to battle the minion. — *Lawrence Cohn*

GLADIATOR

A Columbia Pictures release of a Price Entertainment/Steve Roth production. Produced by Frank Price, Steve Roth. Directed by Rowdy Herrington. Screenplay, Lyle Kessler, Robert Mark Kamen, from a story by Djordje Milicevic, Kamen; camera (Technicolor), Tak Fujimoto; editors, Peter Zinner, Harry B. Miller III; music, Brad Fiedel; sound (Dolby), Glenn Williams; production design, Gregg Fonseca; costume design, Donfeld; assistant director, Christine Larson; production manager, Kenneth Utt; boxing coordinator, Jim Nickerson; casting, Amanda Mackey, Cathy Sandrich. Reviewed at 23rd St. West 2 theater, New York, Feb. 28, 1992. MPAA rating: R. Running time: **98 MIN.**

Lincoln	Cuba Gooding Jr.
Tommy Riley	James Marshall
Pappy Jack	Robert Loggia
Noah	Ossie Davis
Horn	Brian Dennehy
Dawn	Cara Buono
John Rile	John Heard
Romano	John Seda
Shortcut	Lance Slaughter
Leroy (Spits)	T.E. Russell
Miss Higgins	Francesca P. Roberts
Charlene	Debra Sandlund

"Gladiator" is an exercise in audience manipulation that probably will get a thumbs-down from the targeted younger audience. Interracial buddy pairing gives the calculated film some commercial potential, however.

To paraphrase the Coen brothers, it's as if producers Frank Price (two-time Columbia topper) and Steve Roth called in their writers and said, "Give us a boxing picture with some of that 'Barton Fink' feeling." Result is a formulaic attempt at an underdog saga that worked far better in the '30s and '40s.

Problem is that the filmmakers' bait-and-switch strategies are transparent. Cuba Gooding Jr. of Col's 1991 hit "Boyz N the Hood" receives top billing, but the film is relentlessly centered around his white pal, James Marshall ("Twin Peaks"). Early reels exploit the racial tensions in a Chicago high school en route to a predictable revelation that both sets of youngsters have a common enemy, the white businessman (Brian Dennehy) who stages their illegal boxing matches.

Marshall, cast as the new kid in school, is sullen and far too low key through much of the picture. His motivation to enter Dennehy's ring is poorly established; his down-and-out dad (busy thesp John Heard, popping in briefly in an underwritten role) has amassed gambling debts that Marshall feels bound to honor. Co-scripter Robert Mark Kamen did a much better job of cementing empathy with his transplant to a new school and environment in "The Karate Kid."

Nasty black students, led by Lance Slaughter and T.E. Russell, immediately get on Marshall's case. Slaughter is a dirty fighter who predictably puts Marshall's new Cuban pal John Seda in the hospital to provide further motivation for our hero.

Pic climaxes twice: Marshall is forced to fight ailing buddy Gooding, and after the twosome refuse to beat each other's brains out, a hokey finale is staged with Marshall fighting Dennehy for the bloodthirsty crowd. Film's previously plural title "Gladiators" would have better emphasized the Marshall/Gooding paring.

Though middle-aged Dennehy is presented as the ultimate ring-savvy dirty trickster, the sight of him squaring against the smaller but youthful Marshall, with his sculpted physique, is ridiculous.

Director Rowdy Herrington, who poured on the trash in "Road House," aims for a grittier feel this time, with dull results. Gooding is sympathetic and a convincing pugilist, but Marshall remains enigmatic.

Dennehy as a one-dimensional baddie and Robert Loggia as a cornball promoter are disappointing, while Ossie Davis brings some feeling to his clichéd corner-

man assignment.
— *Lawrence Cohn*

MY COUSIN VINNY

A 20th Century Fox presentation in association with Peter V. Miller Investment Corp. of a Dale Launer production. Produced by Dale Launer and Paul Schiff. Directed by Jonathan Lynn. Screenplay, Launer. Camera, Peter Deming; editor, Tony Lombardo; music, Randy Edelman; production design, Victoria Paul; costume design, Carol Wood; art direction, Randall Schmook; set decoration, Michael Seirton; sound, Robert Anderson Jr.; assistant director, Frank Capra III; casting, David Rubin. Reviewed at AMC Santa Monica 7 theater, Santa Monica, Feb. 27, 1992. MPAA rating: R. Running time: **119 MIN.**
Vinny . . . . .Joe Pesci
Bill Gambini . . . . . . .Ralph Macchio
Mona Lisa Vito . . . . . .Marisa Tomei
Stan Rothenstein . . Mitchell Whitfield
Judge Haller . . . . . . .Fred Gwynne
Jim Trotter . . . . .Lane Smith
John Gibbons . . . .Austin Pendleton

Lovable underdog turn by Joe Pesci as a hopelessly inept lawyer battling to prove himself in his first case could transform this dopey comedy into something of a sleeper for Fox. Critics will throw it out of court, but the pic may well win its case with mainstream audiences.

Tale, scripted by co-producer Dale Launer, has coarse Brooklynite Pesci called upon by family members to help his college-age cousin Bill (Ralph Macchio) out of a jam in the Deep South.

Seems Bill and his pal Stan (Mitchell Whitfield) were mistakenly nabbed for the murder of a store clerk. The lovable loser lawyer and his mouthy but beautiful girlfriend, Lisa (Marisa Tomei) must go to Alabama to extricate the pair.

Perfect example of pic's comedy is a scene in which Vinny arrives at the jail cell. Stan, who's never met Vinny, assumes he's a fellow prisoner come to have his way with him.

Their secret weapon, Bill promises the nervous Stan, will be Vinny's talent for argument, demonstrated for the audience in a latenight set-to with Tomei. But viewers have to wait 90 minutes for the first big payoff for this trait, and given the thinness of the setup, it's a long wait.

Pic's running joke is that Vinny can't stay awake in court; his narcolepsy is likely to be shared by those put off by the remedial plotting and pace. Launer ("Ruthless People," "Dirty Rotten Scoundrels") has done better.

In a complete turnaround from his despicable "Goodfellas" persona, the stumpy burglar from "Home Alone" carries the lead quite handily, coming across as a tenacious scrapper with a big heart and charming the audience with some inspired moments of physical shtick.

Tomei, sashaying through the proceedings as kind of a sexy hood ornament, has honed her ethnic-character comedy skills and created a buoyant chemistry with her combative b.f.

Macchio and Whitfield are stuck in poorly drawn roles, and Austin Pendleton's stuttering public defender won't be funny to people similarly afflicted.

Filmed mostly in Monticello, Ga., pic is somewhat disappointing in production aspects, with wan photography and drab, grungy production design that lacks any whimsy or verve.
— *Amy Dawes*

THE END OF THE GOLDEN WEATHER
(NEW ZEALAND)

A South Pacific Pictures production in association with New Zealand Film Commission, New Zealand on Air and Television New Zealand. Produced by Christina Milligan, Ian Mune. Directed by Mune. Screenplay, Mune, Bruce Mason. Camera (color), Alun Bollinger; editor, Michael Horton; music, Stephen McCurdy; sound, Greg Bell; production design, Ron Highfield. Reviewed at Embassy Theater, Wellington, Feb. 25, 1992. Running time: **102 MIN.**
Geoff . . . . .Stephen Fulford
Firpo . . . . .Stephen Papps
Dad . . . . .Paul Gittins
Mum . . . . . . .Gabrielle Hammond
Ted . . . . .David Taylor
Molly . . . . . . .Alexandra Marshall
Also with: Ray Henwood, Alice Fraser, Bill Johnson.

"The End of the Golden Weather" is an intimate and gentle coming-of-age comedy drama particular to its native New Zealand. While unlikely to attract significant theatrical interest offshore, the skills of helmer Ian Mune and reputation of South Pacific Pictures for high-quality adolescent fare should attract TV coin in most markets.

Pic also could have a healthy life on homevid.

Mune has sensibly opted for simplicity and subtlety in "Golden Weather," ased on a one-man show by the late dramatist and actor Bruce Mason that became part of Kiwi folklore during the 1950s and '60s. The film concen-

trates on the imaginative 12-year-old Geoff (Stephen Fulford), his friendship with the mentally out-of-kilter Firpo (Stephen Papps) and Geoff's family relationships.

Mune is at his best handling family dynamics. One sequence, involving an evening of home "theatricals" staged by Geoff and his much less enthusiastic younger siblings, is understated yet miraculously funny.

Less convincing is the helmer's treatment of the friendship between Geoff and Firpo. Papps is dramatically one-dimensional, and the music accompanying these scenes is often penetratingly obvious, as though acknowledging inherent dramatic shortcomings.

While more closeups might have been used to effect, Alun Bollinger's photography is always first rate, adding greatly to overall production values.
— *Mike Nicolaidi*

DE JOHNSONS
(THE JOHNSONS)
(DUTCH)

A Meteor Film release of a Movies Film production. Produced by Chris Brouwer, Haig Balian. Executive producer, Arnold Heslenfeld (B.V. Lenox Holding Amsterdam). Co-producer, Veronica Omroep Organisatie. Directed by Rudolf van den Berg. Screenplay, Leon de Winter, based on Rocco Simonelli's original script and Roy Frumkes' story. Camera (color), Theo Bierkens; editor, Wim Louwrier; music, Patrick Seymour; production design, Harry Ammerlaan; sound, Peter Flamman; sound mix, Marc Nolens, Paul Carr. Reviewed at Cinema Amsterdam, Feb. 3, 1992. Running time: **96 MIN.**
Victoria Lucas . . .Monique van de Ven
Emalee Lucas . Esmee de la Bretonière
Prof. Keller . . . . .Kenneth Herdigen
Also with: Rik van Uffelen, Olga Zuiderhoek, Nelly Frijda, Elise Hoomans, Johan Leysen, Carol van Herwijnen.

"The Johnsons" is awell-made horror pic with a good cast and shivers aplenty. Pic will be able to travel wherever horror buffs alight, but don't look for logic here.

Premise is that if Xangadix, the god of the Mahxitu Indians, can get seven brothers to inseminate their sister, she will give birth to a monster. Now, not so coincidentally, seven psychopaths are being held by a special army unit in a bunker in Holland. As children, they did not speak — they killed. As adults, they lust after their sister, although they don't know her. All exist because of a secret in vitro implantation 21 years earlier.

Meanwhile, sister Emalee

(Esmee de la Bretonière), a fine discovery by van den Berg) has terrifying nightmares about blood and rape. When Emalee and her mother stay in a tent near the bunker, things come to a head (and several people lose theirs, literally).

Pic comes to a strenuous but happy ending with maternal love conquering all.

Kenneth Herdigen, in his first lead role, valiantly keeps the story more or less together. Director of photography Theo Bierkens keeps ghosts and ghouls, ordinary people and special effects mixing smoothly on the screen.

Van den Berg did a great job treating this mumbo jumbo of a screenplay like a factual crime story rather than superstitious claptrap. — *Gerry Waller*

BERLIN FEST

RUAN LING-YU
(CENTER STAGE)
(HONG KONG-TAIWANESE)

A Golden Harvest release of a Golden Way-Paragon Films production. (Intl. sales: Singel Films, Amsterdam.) Produced by Leonard Ho, Jackie Chan. Executive producers, Willie Chan, Tsui Hsiu-ming. Directed by Stanley Kwan. Screenplay, Yau Tai On-ping, from Peggy Chiu's story. Camera (color), Poon Hang-seng; editors, Cheung Yan-chung, Keung Tsuen-tak, Cheung Kar-fei; music, Siu Chung; production design, Pat Lai; sound, Zhan Xin; special effects, Kwong Wai-hung; assistant director, Chow Wei-kwan. Reviewed at Berlin Film Festival (competition), Feb. 19, 1992. Running time: **154 MIN.**
Ruan Ling-yu . . . . .Maggie Cheung
Tsai Chu-sheng . . . . . .Tony Leung
Tang Chi-shan . . . . .Shin Hong
Also with: Carina Lau, Lawrence Ng, Waise Lee, Cheung Chung, Siu Sheung, Yip Sang.

A lengthy, lavishly filmed biopic of a great star of Chinese silent cinema who killed herself at age 25 during a scandal over her personal life, "Center Stage" has already been hailed in Hong Kong, where it won best actress prize for Maggie Cheung, who also bagged the best actress Silver Bear at the Berlin fest.

Ruan Ling-yu entered films when she was only 16 and played a number of impressive starring roles. Described as China's Garbo, she specialized in playing tragic women and achieved enormous popularity in the early '30s.

Stanley Kwan ("Rouge") has lovingly recreated the period when silent films were still the norm (sound films didn't come to China until 1935), and all the scenes depicting Ruan at work are of the greatest interest.

Not quite so satisfactory are scenes of her personal life. They lack the emotion that must have been present when Ruan's involvement with a married man led to a campaign of press vilification that triggered her suicide. Her last words were: "Gossip is a dreadful thing."

Kwan daringly inserts surviving film sequences featuring the real Ruan and also has his actors step out of character to discuss the roles they're playing and the mood of the period. There are also interviews about Ruan and her achievements.

All this makes for a lengthy pic. The version unspooled in Berlin was the director's cut and, at 154 minutes (fest catalogue claimed only 146), was over half an hour longer than the Hong Kong release version. Whether the 2-hour version would play better internationally than this 2½-hour version is something for the producers to decide.

Film is consistently fascinating, but there's an emotionless center which may prevent viewers from fully appreciating Ruan's plight. This is no reflection on Cheung; the actress (who replaced Anita Mui) is very fine in the role and painstakingly recreates celebrated sequences in which Ruan appeared.

The translation provided for the film was generally deemed inadequate; a new English subtitled version is being prepared.

Technically tops, pic will be of great interest to lovers of Chinese cinema, but it lacks the emotional wallop that might have made a significant impact in art house cinemas. Nonetheless, an impressive picture about a remarkable woman.
— *David Stratton*

OVER THE OCEAN
(ISRAELI)

A Marek Rozenbaum/Ron Ackerman production in association with Israel Broadcasting Authority & the Israeli Fund for Quality Films. Produced by Rozenbaum, Ackerman. Directed by Jacob Goldwasser. Screenplay, Haim Merin. Camera (color), David Gurfinkel; editor, Anat Lubarski; music, Shlomo Gronich; art direction, Emanuel Amrami; costume design, Rona Doron. Reviewed in L.A. (in Berlin Film Festival Panorama), Feb. 23, 1992. Running time: **88 MIN.**
Menachem Goldfarb . . . Arie Muskuna
Rosa Goldfarb . . . . . Daphna Rechter
Haim Goldfarb . . . . Uri Alter
Morris Greenspan . . . . . . Moti Giladi
Leizer . . . . Sinai Peter
Miri Goldfarb . . . . Mili Avital
Schultz . . . . Yair Lapid
Gabi . . . . Shai Idelson
Yhiel . . . . Oshik Levi
Rappaport . . . . Yosi Graber
(Hebrew soundtrack)

"Over The Ocean" has all the earmarks of a run-of-the-mill mainstream European family comedy but is given a little political and emotional weight by its setting in Israel during the country's formative years. Winner of nine local Academy Awards in its native country last year and the Israeli entry in the foreign-language film Oscar competition, easy-to-like pic makes its points in ways that are far too obvious for critics and the international art house crowd, so offshore chances appear limited.

Fundamentally a tale about spreading roots in new, sometimes difficult soil, third feature by Jacob Goldwasser ("Big Shots," "The Skipper") has the Goldfarb family at odds over whether to stick it out in Tel Aviv in 1962.

Menachem (Arie Muskuna) and Rosa (Daphna Rechter), survivors of the camps, are taking to life in their new home less easily than their 10-year-old son (Uri Alter) or Rosa's leftist-nationalist brother.

An amiable fellow, Menachem isn't content running a little shop, and when Morris, a prosperous fellow Holocaust survivor (Moti Giladi), arrives from Canada with tales of the unlimited opportunities that lie across the sea, Menachem can't wait to pack up the family and leave the land where war looms as a possibility each day.

Domestic troubles intervene: As the couple's sexy 20-year-old daughter takes up with a two-bit hoodlum and has to be sent on ahead to Toronto, fast operator Morris can't resist trying to revive his long-ago amour with Rosa, and the tax auditor dogs Menachem's every step.

For his part, the young son divides his time between plotting a secret trip across the border to Jordan and spying with high-powered binoculars on a heavily endowed young woman across the way.

Menachem, seeing only the drawbacks to the new society, takes the family to the brink of abandoning it; finale reinforces idea of Israel as a true home to the first generation who settled there.

Pic is far from subtle and is marked by hammy, shoulder-shrugging, vaudeville-style performances, particularly by musical comedy star Muskuna and stand-up comedian Giladi as the slick-talking businessman.

Rechter and Alter deliver solid, more sober characterizations.

With all the obviousness, however, comes an emotional tug that is hard to resist, and pic does a reasonable job of conjuring up the feeling of a specific time and place. Tech credits are okay. —*Todd McCarthy*

THE USUAL
(B&W-16m)

A Periferia production. (Intl. sales: Fortissimo, Amsterdam.) Produced by Emily Stevens, Sarah Auerswald, Eric Tretbar. Directed, written by Tretbar. Camera (16m, black & white), Jim Zabilla; set-costume stylist, Heather McElhatton; sound, Gerard Bonnette. Reviewed at Berlin Film Festival (Forum), Feb. 18, 1992. Running time: **80 MIN.**
Claire . . . . Lisa Todd
Aldo . . . . Steve Epp
Spike . . . . John Crozier
Also with: Eleanor St. Regis, Leonard Engman, Amy Aaland, Dominique Serrand.

An impressive first feature by Minneapolis-based Eric Tretbar, "The Usual" delivers much more than its title. Observant, gentle pic about a young woman's relationships with two guys announces a promising addition to the ranks of U.S. indie filmers. Despite its no-budget format, item should garner good word of mouth on the film festival circuit.

Central character is Claire (Lisa Todd), a Minnesota farm girl who moves to the big city, has a fling with Aldo (Steve Epp), and waitresses in a grill, where she takes up with fry-cook-cum-guitarist Spike (John Crozier). Problems start when Aldo returns from N.Y. to visit. That's about it on plot, but writer-helmer Tretbar, a strummer-turned-filmmaker, paces the material with considerable confidence and draws fine, understated perfs from main trio.

Stylistically, pic is non-tricksy, with a plain, easygoing feel that keeps the spotlight on the actors. As the unaggressive woman in the middle, Todd is just right, and Crozier is likable as the seemingly laid-back joker Spike. Expanded from Tretbar's 1989 Super-8 short "Shadow of the Spoon," film was partially

funded by a Film in the Cities regional film/video grant.
— *Derek Elley*

SHANGHAI JIAQI
(MY AMERICAN GRANDSON)
(TAIWANESE)

A Golden Film production. (Intl. sales: Anthex, Berlin.) Produced by Chou Hsüeh-yen. Executive producer, Tu Yuling. Directed by Ann Hui. Screenplay, Wu Nien-chen. Camera (color), Li P'ing-pin; editor, Liao Ch'ing-sung; music, Ch'en Yang. Reviewed at Berlin Film Festival (Forum), Feb. 18, 1992. Running time: **104 MIN.**
Ku Ta-te . . . . Wu Ma
Tommy Ku . . . . Huang K'un-hsüan
Jiao Li . . . . Carina Liu
Neighbor . . . . Wang Lai
(Mandarin dialogue; Chinese & English subtitles)

The Big Apple goes Shanghai in "My American Grandson," a feel-good culture-clash comedy about an old Mainlander saddled with a Stateside brat. Film lacks the personal edge of Hong Kong helmer Ann Hui's earlier "Song of the Exile," but likable pic is a respectable item for Asian film weeks and sidebars.

Ku (played with fine understatement by veteran Hong Kong actor Wu Ma) is a 60-ish retired musician who shares lodgings with the perky Jiao Li (Carina Liu), daughter of dead friends. The only bumps in the even tenor of his life are spats with a feisty neighbor (Wang Lai, also excellent in the Berlin Panorama item "Pushing Hands"). Then one day, gum-chewing, skate-boarding grandson Tommy (Huang K'un-hsüan) arrives for a vacation while his parents are in Europe.

Story follows the predictable line of communist school lessons, outside toilets, shared bedrooms and the rest. After absconding to the countryside, grandson finally returns and learns to like the place. Soon he's got the local kids playing basketball and working out with personal stereos.

Even during the final leave-takings, script stays just the right side of mushy. But the sharpest stuff is in the first hour, when "backward" mainland Chinese life-styles come in for a drubbing. Script is by prolific Taiwanese writer Wu Nien-chen, best known overseas for Hou Hsiao-hsien's "City of Sadness" and "Song of the Exile."

Hui took on the pic when it was already in preproduction, but she turns in a pro job. Perfs are fine all round, though Liu (an ex-Shanghainese herself) gets few chances in the underwritten role of the adopted daughter. Tech credits are okay; English subtitles are poor.

Complete version shown at Berlin included two funny sequences (at a public john and in a classroom) excised by the Taiwan producer under Mainland pressure when pic world bowed at the Hong Kong fest last year. Original Chinese title means "Shanghai Vacation."

— *Derek Elley*

GLI ULTIMI GIORNI
(THE LAST DAYS)
(ITALIAN)

A Ralaton Film production. Produced by Marco Risi, Monica Rametta. Directed by Corso Salani. Screenplay, Salani, Rametta. Camera (color), Riccardo Gambacciani, Marco Chairiotti; editor, Luigi dell'Elba; sound, Fabio Tosti; assistant director, Marina Zangirolami. Reviewed at Berlin Film Festival (Forum), Feb. 18, 1992. Running time: **85 MIN.**
Alberto . . . . Corso Salani
Marina . . . . Monica Rametta
Nicoletta . . . . Lorenza Indovina
Sara . . . . Lorenza Branzi
Gaetano . . . . Danilo Trotta
Giuseppe . . . . Fabio Sabbioni

"**T**he Last Days" is one of those small-scale Italian auteur films that manages to be fresh and appealing. Young director Corso Salani and co-producer Monica Rametta, who wrote the pic and play the lead roles, bring off a modest Rohmeresque charmer.

Salani plays a lovelorn Romeo who wants to marry Rametta, with whom he's enjoyed an off-on affair for some time. Given to talking to himself, he arrives by car to the island where his Juliet lives only to fine she's about to marry someone else. The poor guy finds himself staying in the flat being prepared for the newlyweds.

Deciding he can't take part in this wedding, he starts to leave, then decides to pull out all the stops to win the bride back, showering her with lovesick charm and affection and reminders of the good old days. What follows spans just a week, with the passing days indicated by titles.

It's not earth-shattering filmmaking, just a quietly amusing look at a determined young man trying to win back the girl he loves. Further fest exposure could help this charmer.

— *David Stratton*

SAM SUFFIT
(SAM'S ENOUGH)
(FRENCH)

A Les Prods. du 3me Etage production, in association with Paris Eiga-Tokyo-Cité Films-Paravision Intl.-Parafrance Communications. (Intl. sales: Motion Media, Paris.) Directed, written by Virginie Thévenet. Camera (Fujicolor), Jean-François Robin; editors, Catherine Renault, Luc Barnier; music, Keziah Jones; production design, Carlos Conti; art direction, Michka Assayas; costume design, Friquette Thévenet; sound, Jean-Claude Laureux; assistant director, Daniel Deleforgues. Reviewed at Berlin Film Festival (market), Feb. 17, 1992. Running time: **92 MIN.**
Eva . . . . Aure Attika
Peter . . . . Philip Bartlett
Chichi . . . . Rossi de Palma
M. Denis . . . . Claude Chabrol
M. Albert . . . . Jean-François Balmer
Lucie . . . . Bernadette Lafont

"**S**am Suffit" starts out like a "Betty Blue" clone but never falls into the trap of taking itself too seriously. Easygoing, colorful comedy about an ex-stripper trying to make something of her life is a trim item for offshore French film weeks, with presence of Claude Chabrol in the cast a hook for buffs. Local b.o. prospects look mild.

Newcomer Aure Attika is a willful young stripper in a Barcelona carnival who chucks her job, shacks up with a gay Yank painter (Philip Bartlett) and starts as a house cleaner for two aging queens (Chabrol, Jean-François Balmer). After a stint in a government department, she decides she wants a baby, and the Yank duly obliges with a one-night affair. Ending has her moving into the art world thanks to a chance encounter.

Wispy plot doesn't bear close inspection, but helmer Virginie Thévenet keeps the action moving along with plenty of neat comic touches, likable characters and bright, poster-color photography. Upfront attitude to a range of sexuality is in line with her previous works ("La Nuit Porte Jarretelles," "Jeux d'Artifices"). This one is her most confidently paced to date.

The offbeat Attika is a dead ringer for Béatrice Dalle ("Betty Blue") and with about the same range. Bartlett is pleasant enough as her friend but sounds uneasy in French. Chabrol and Balmer camp it up wildly, and the reliable Bernadette Lafont pops up at start and finish as Attika's ditzy mom.

Tech credits are pro, with Friquette Thévenet's mix-'n'-match

costumes a special plus. French title is some graffiti painted on Attika's beachfront hideaway.

— *Derek Elley*

RIEN QUE DES MENSONGES
(NOTHING BUT LIES)
(SWISS-FRENCH)

A Vega Film production, in association with Arena Films-SGGC-TV Suisse Romande. (Intl. sales: Mainstream, Paris.) Produced by Ruth Waldburger. Executive producer, Bruno Pesery. Associate producer, Jean-Bernard Fetoux. Directed by Paule Muret. Screenplay, Muret, Jean-François Goyet. Camera (Eastmancolor), Renato Berta; editor, Catherine Quesemand; music, Stéphane Delplace; art direction, Raul Gimenez; costume design, Marielle Robaut; sound, Louis Gimel, Jean-Pierre Laforce; assistant director, Richard Malbequi. Reviewed at Berlin Film Festival (competition), Feb. 15, 1992. Running time: **86 MIN.**
Muriel . . . . Fanny Ardant
Adrien . . . . Alain Bashung
Antoine . . . . Jacques Perrin
Basile . . . Stanislas Carré de Malberg
Jo . . . . Alexandra Kazan
Lise . . . . Christine Pascal
Alain . . . . Jean-Pierre Malo
Detective . . . . Dominique Besnehard
(French dialogue)

"**N**othing But Blah" would be a better title for this hollow slice of emotional Euro-kitsch. Fanny Ardant-starrer about a 30-something Parisian who's frustrated with her life weaves elaborate circles around a peanut-sized plot and ends up with zip. All but high-style fanatics should cotton on to the truth pretty quick.

The well-garbed Ardant is the well-garbed wife of a publisher (Jacques Perrin) who sleeps around and mother of a teenage son (Stanislas Carré de Malberg) who's growing up fast. She and her girlfriends (Christine Pascal, Alexandra Kazan) schmooze in cafes. Despite her respectable appearance, she also has a lover (Alain Bashung).

To get her life back into focus, she hires an investigator — but to photograph herself and her lover, not the errant hubby. When she finally shows the photos to the latter, nothing changes. "Just stay the way you are," he says. "I still feel a cheated woman," she says. Sure.

First-time Swiss director Paule Muret, who had a small role in Godard's "Sauve Qui Peut (La Vie)" before helming a couple of shorts, can't be faulted on sheer technique. Pic, though leisurely, has an inner tension that staves off boredom and an uncluttered

visual style that almost convinces more is going on below the surface than ever shows up in the script.

Ardant, who speaks and moves with a dreamy grace, is an elegant clotheshorse but not much more. Blues guitarist Bashung is a serviceable lover, and Perrin is pointed as the sketchily written husband. Pascal brings fleeting depth to her few scenes as Ardant's soulmate.

Technically, pic is smooth, with notable lensing of wintry Paris by Renato Berta (Muret's husband). Stéphane Delplace's churning, bass-laden score is a help in pinpointing key moments.

— *Derek Elley*

VACAS
(COWS)
(SPANISH)

A Sogetel production, with the collaboration of ICAA, the Spanish Ministry of Culture, the Culture Dept. of the Basque government. Executive producers, Jose Luis Olaizola, Fernando de Garcillan. Directed by Julio Medem. Screenplay, Medem, based on Midem's story. Camera (Eastmancolor), Carles Gusi; editor, Maria Elena Saiz de Rozas; music, Alberto Iglesias; production design, Rafale Palmero; sound, Julio Recuero. Reviewed at Berlin Film Fetival (Panorama), Feb. 20, 1992. Running time: **96 MIN.**
With: Emma Suarez, Carmelo Gomez, Ana Torrent, Manuel Blasco, Clara Badiola, Candido Uranga.

Strikingly unusual and visually impressive, "Cows" is an oddity that may make the fest circuit rounds on the strength of its original approach to the old family feud theme. Set in the Basque countryside, pic incorporates four stories set in four periods, spanning 1875 to 1936.

Pic begins during a brutal conflict in which two friends from neighboring farms find themselves fighting together in a trench; one is killed, the other daubs his face with his friend's blood and poses as dead, so escaping the ensuing massacre.

Years later, this character, now an old man on the verge of madness, sits around painting cows. His grandson is having a passionate affair with his former friend's granddaughter, charmingly played by Ana Torrent, who played the knowing little girl in Carlos Saura's "Cria."

Time goes on, and the illegitimate son of the love affair finds the going tough, with hints of incest entering the story. Final segment, set on the eve of the Spanish Civil War, surrenders to the ominous mood kept at bay in earlier segments.

"Cows" depicts a traditional community where passions run deep and where the local sport — an axman balances on the log he's furiously chopping — is a dangerous passion. With its themes of death and madness, it's an elemental tale in which the cows placidly observe the activities of the humans who tend them, becoming characters in the drama, too.

With lush cinematography, energetic performances and a strong sense of the mystery and terror to be found in the Great Outdoors, pic lingers in the memory as impressive and unusual.
— *David Stratton*

CÉLINE
(FRENCH)

A Gaumont release of a Gaumont-La Sorciere Rouge production. Directed, written by Jean-Claude Brisseau. Camera (color), Romain Winding; editor, Maria Luisa Garcia; music, Georges Delerue; sound, Jean Minondo. Reviewed at Berlin Film Festival (competition), Feb. 20, 1992. Running time: **86 MIN.**
Céline . . . . Isabelle Pasco
Genevieve . . . . Lisa Heredia
Mme. Giraud . . . . . Daniele Lebrun
Gerard . . . . Daniel Tarrare
Roland . . . . Damien Dutrait
Lucien . . . . Lucien Plazanet

Female bonding and mysticism combine uneasily in this limpid tale of a suicidal young woman who finds God. Attractive leads, lush images and a tuneful George Delerue score may not be enough to spark interest in this oddity.

As long as writer-director Jean-Claude Brisseau sticks to his theme of femme friendship, he's on solid ground, and the first two-thirds of the film is attractive, if lightweight.

Story is set in a small town where Genevieve (Lisa Heredia) works as a nurse. Her life is changed when she meets a suicidal young woman, Céline (Isabelle Pasco). Genevieve saves her from an o.d. and near-drowning, and discovers that Céline was an orphan adopted by a wealthy publisher who left her all his money.

Distraught at his death, and under pressure from her frosty stepmother, she rejected her inheritance, whereupon her boyfriend threw her over — hence the suicide attempt. Genevieve moves into Céline's lovely old house to care for the troubled woman and introduces Céline to yoga, and a firm friendship develops between the two.

Pasco ("Prospero's Books") is just right as the ethereal Céline, with Heredia bringing a necessary edge to Genevieve. With these two taking center stage, the supporting cast is reduced to walk-ons.

Catholic audiences may be better equipped than others to accept pic's ending, but Brisseau never adequately prepares the viewer for the abrupt change in direction from reality to religious mysticism, including a ghostly figure of death and bright lights.

Technically, the film is just about perfect in every department. —*David Stratton*

ZUPPA DI PESCE
(FISH SOUP)
(ITALIAN-FRENCH)

A Leader Cinematografica-RAI2 (Rome)-French Prods. (Paris) production. (Intl. sales: Sacis, Rome.) Produced by Raffaele Monteverde. Executive producers, Carlo Vacca, Graziella Civiletti. Co-producer, Emmanuel Schlummberger. Directed by Fiorella Infascelli. Screenplay, Infascelli, Patrizia Pistagnesi, from an idea by Infascelli. Camera (Eastmancolor; Technicolor prints), Acacio De Almeida; editor, Claudio Di Mauro; art direction, Gianni Silvestri; set decoration, Antonio Formica; costume design, Aldo Buti; sound, Bernard Bats; assistant director, Alessandro Valori; casting, Chiara Meloni. Reviewed at Berlin Film Festival (Panorama), Feb. 14, 1992. Running time: **107 MIN.**
Alberto . . . . Philippe Noiret
Caterina . . . . Macha Meril
Isabella . . . . Chiara Caselli
Isabella (child) . . . Francesca Martana
Anna . . Lucrezia Lante Della Rovere
Giulio . . . . Andrea Prodan
Lello . . . . Robert Patterson
Edoardo . . . . Meme Perlini
Also with: Renzo Montagnani, Nuccio Siano, Ivonne Scio, Valentina Lainati.
(Italian dialogue)

A slick mix of coming-of-age pic and father-daughter love story, "Fish Soup" is an enjoyable treat. Solid biz seems likely on the Continent, with possible exposure in Anglo territories, given the right marketing.

This semi-autobiographical work is expanded from the vid short "PA" Fiorella Infascelli made 10 years ago about her dad, '50s producer Carlo. Free-form story, set during summer stints at a family seaside villa in Tuscany, stretches from the '50s to the late '70s, with Isabella (Chiara Caselli) developing from a moody moppet to a self-assured young woman.

Apart from father (Philippe Noiret), Italo pic producer, family includes gentle mother (Macha Meril), half sister (Lucrezia Lante Della Rovere) and two half brothers (Andrea Prodan, Robert Patterson) who mostly give Isabella a hard time when they're not butting heads themselves.

Pic is essentially a series of small incidents separated by Noiret's up-and-down career. Caselli lolls around the house and beach, has men problems, sees her half sister marry and move away and experiences the death of a half brother.

Passage of time is marked by (unidentified) clips viewed by Caselli on her favorite toy, a moviola. These include sword-and-sandal epic "Sign of the Gladiator," Jacques Demy's "Umbrellas of Cherbourg" and Bernardo Bertolucci's "Partner." Quality of some of these is bleary.

As in her debut pic, "The Mask" (Helena Bonham Carter-starrer in Cannes' Un Certain Regard section four years ago), director Infascelli has no trouble conjuring up an endless series of feel-good sequences, accompanied here by lush lensing from Acacio De Almeida and a steady supply of existing movie music.

Pic's fragile structure is kept afloat by the charm of Noiret, adding another to his gallery of lovable eccentrics, and the ongoing thread of his edgy relationship with Caselli. Barbed refs to the Italo pic industry are general enough for non-buffs to grasp.

Caselli is okay in a challenging role, even if she has trouble with the aging process as pic progresses. French thesps Meril and Noiret (the latter dubbed by Paolo Ferrari) play off each other well, and Lante Della Rovere has some sizable moments as the half sis.

Pic is technically fine in all departments, though purists may quibble about the lack of period accuracy in the costumes.
— *Derek Elley*

INFINITAS
(RUSSIAN)

A Mosfilm (Rytm-Kamarad Studios)-Olimp 1 production. (Intl. sales: Mosfilm Intl.) Directed, written by Marlen Chuziev. Camera (color), Vadim Michailov, Andrei Jepischin; editor, Ludmilla Sviridenko; music, Nikolai Karentnikov; production design, Levan Shengalia; sound, Sergei Urusov. Reviewed at Berlin Film Festival (competition), Feb. 20, 1992. Running time: **207 MIN.**

Vladimir . . . . Vladislav Pilnikov
Volodia . . . . Alexei Zelinov
Also with: Marina Chazova, Anna Kudriavceva, Nina Pritulovskaya.

"**I**nfinitas," an emormously long, highly symbolic pic steeped in Russian culture and history, is a typically Russian film if there ever was one, but, at nearly 3 1/2 hours, it's a marathon that will find few takers outside Russia.

The idea itself is intriguing, and the film is filled with beautiful images. There's little story as such. A middle-aged Everyman wanders through the film encountering along the way a younger version of himself, as well as a young woman who may have been his lover.

Pic starts out in Moscow. A misunderstanding over a newspaper ad brings strangers to the man's apartment looking for buys. Wearily, he sells most of his belongings. The man takes a walk through crowded streets, then impulsively boards a train, gets off in the middle of nowhere and walks to a small town where people seem to know him.

Suddenly, summer changes to winter, and, as the man encounters various characters, from gravediggers to tragic children, he finds himself drifting into the past, to New Year's Eve 1899 and then to see Russian troops leave for the World War I front.

Director Marlen Chuziev qseems to be exploring Russia's past and linking it to a brighter future, but his message gets lost in the ponderous treatment. Every scene and shot is allowed to linger on much longer than it needs it; a point is neatly made, then made repeatedly. This indulgence results in a vastly over-long pic which, with drastic trimming, might have been powerfully symbolic and beautiful.

Gap between filmmaker's aims and achievements is enormous.
— *David Stratton*

ARCHIVE REVIEW

MNE DVADSTAT LET
(I AM TWENTY)
(RUSSIAN-B&W)

A Gorky Studio production. (Intl. sales: Sovexportfilm.) Directed by Marlen Chuziev. Screenplay, Chuziev, Gennadi Shpalikov. Camera (black & white), Margarita Pilikhina; music, N. Sidelnikov; art direction, I. Zakharova; costume design, K. Rusanovoy; sound, A.

Izbutsky. Reviewed at London Film Festival (Intl. Frame), Nov. 10, 1991. Running time: **175 MIN.**
Sergei Zhuravlyov . . . Valentin Popov
Nikolai Fokin . . . . Nikolay Gubenko
Slava Kostikov . . . Stanislav Lubshin
Anya . . . . . . Marianna Vertinskaya

Winner of the special jury prize at the 1964 Venice fest, Marlen Chuziev's "I Am Twenty" finally surfaces in its full version, some 90 minutes longer. Kaleidoscopic portrait of Soviet youth in the early '60s ranks as an outstanding achievement, with a freshness that belies its years and three-hour length.

Made over a period of two years, pic was condemned by Nikita Khrushchev when finished and heavily censored. Major scissored sequences include a long poetry reading featuring rising youth talents and a striking scene in which the central character meets his father's ghost.

Pic's most striking characteristic is its natural feel for the changing moods and everday life of the city. Chuziev takes his camera into the subway, onto buses, along the sidewalks and into the homes of its young people. Partying scenes (with late helmer Andrei Tarkovsky among the guests) lie side by side with more dramatic material showing Sergei and his pals slowly facing realities.

Perfs are all sharply etched among the males, and, of the women, Marianna Vertinskaya is just right as the secretive but assured Anya. Margarita Pilikhina's antsy camerawork shows an eye for composition throughout, and plenty of music makes the hours fly by. — *Derek Elley*

THE PLAYER

A Fine Line Features release of an Avenue Pictures presentation in association with Spelling Entertainment of a David Brown/Addis-Wechsler production. Produced by Brown, Michael Tolkin, Nick Wechsler. Executive producer, Cary Brokaw. Co-producer, Scott Bushnell. Co-executive producer, William S. Gilmore. Directed by Robert Altman. Screenplay, Tolkin, based on his novel. Camera (Deluxe color), Jean Lepine; editor, Geraldine Peroni; music, Thomas Newman; sound (Ultra-Stereo), John Pritchett; production design, Stephen Altman; art direction, Jerry Fleming; set decoration, Susan Emshwiller; costume design, Alexander Julian; associate producer, David Levy; assistant director, Allan Nichols. Reviewed at the Aidakoff screening room, L.A., March 9, 1992. MPAA Rating: R. Running time: **123 MIN.**
Griffin Mill . . . . Tim Robbins
June Gudmundsdottir . . Greta Scacchi
Walter Stuckel . . . . Fred Ward
Det. Avery . . . . . . Whoopi Goldberg
Larry Levy . . . . . . Peter Gallagher
Joel Levison . . . . Brion James
Bonnie Sherow . . . Cynthia Stevenson
David Kahane . . . . Vincent D'Onofrio
Andy Civella . . . . . . Dean Stockwell
Tom Oakley . . . . . . Richard E. Grant
Dick Mellen . . . . . . Sydney Pollack
Det. DeLongpre . . . . . . Lyle Lovett
Celia . . . . Dina Merrill
Jan . . . . Angela Hall
Sandy . . . . Leah Ayres
Jimmy Chase . . . . Paul Hewitt
Reg Goldman . . . . Randall Batinkoff
Steve Reeves . . . . . . Jeremy Piven
Whitney Gersh . . . . . . Gina Gershon
Frank Murphy . . . . . Frank Barhydt
Marty Grossman . . . . Mike E. Kaplan
Gar Girard . . . . Kevin Scannell
As themselves: Steve Allen, Richard Anderson, Rene Auberjonois, Harry Belafonte, Shari Belafonte, Karen Black, Michael Bowen, Gary Busey, Robert Carradine, Charles Champlin, Cher, James Coburn, Cathy Lee Crosby, John Cusack, Brad Davis, Paul Dooley, Thereza Ellis, Peter Falk, Felicia Farr, Kasia Figura, Louise Fletcher, Dennis Franz, Teri Garr, Leeza Gibbons, Scott Glenn, Jeff Goldblum, Elliott Gould, Joel Grey, David Alan Grier, Buck Henry, Anjelica Huston, Kathy Ireland, Steve James, Maxine John-James, Sally Kellerman, Sally Kirkland, Jack Lemmon, Marlee Matlin, Andie MacDowell, Malcolm McDowell, Jayne Meadows, Martin Mull, Jennifer Nash, Nick Nolte, Alexandra Powers, Bert Remsen, Guy Remsen, Patricia Resnick, Burt Reynolds, Jack Riley, Julia Roberts, Mimi Rogers, Annie Ross, Alan Rudolph, Jill St. John, Susan Sarandon, Adam Simon, Rod Steiger, Joan Tewkesbury, Brian Tochi, Lily Tomlin, Robert Wagner, Ray Walston, Bruce Willis, Marvin Young.

"The Player" is the deep dish on Hollywood, 1992. Mercilessly satiric yet good-natured, this enormously entertaining slam dunk represents a remarkable American comeback for eternal maverick Robert Altman. It quite possibly is the most resonant Hollywood saga since the days of "Sunset Boulevard" and "The Bad and the Beautiful."

A natural for sophisticated urban situations, this comic tale of murder and hypocrisy could, with luck and sharp marketing, cross over to a wider audience. Fabulous roster of cameo players will help.

Brilliantly scripted by Michael Tolkin ("The Rapture") from his own novel, "The Player" succeeds so well because of its precise dissection of a highly particular, not to mention peculiar, culture, and because the bitter pill is made to go down so enjoyably. Altman and Tolkin "get" Hollywood from the little details like car faxes and ludicrous pitch meetings to somewhat bigger matters, such as trivializing art, turning people into commodities and getting away with murder.

In a single take that self-consciously refers to the celebrated opening shot in "Touch of Evil," we are introduced to hotshot studio executive Griffin Mill (Tim Robbins) and his coterie of colleagues and subordinates, listen to Buck Henry pitch his idea for a sequel to "The Graduate," glimpse a group of Japanese inspecting the lot and see Alan Rudolph mistaken for Martin Scorsese. The result is a portrait of exceptional texture and vibrance.

Plot hinges on a series of threatening postcards received by Mill from an ignored screenwriter. The scribe unnerves the exec with anonymous messages such as, "In The Name of All Writers I'm Going to Kill You."

Mill tracks down the man he suspects of being the sender — the garrulous writer David Kahane (Vincent D'Onofrio) — at a revival screening of "The Bicycle Thief." Mill has a few drinks with the man and, in a fit of anger, accidentally kills him. The police identify Mill as the last person to have seen Kahane alive, but lack of solid evidence gets him off the hook, and Mill is able to continue his normal life of worrying about being edged out of the studio by the newly hired Larry Levy (Peter Gallagher).

The postcards keep coming, but once Mill finds he can live with having murdered an innocent man, he assumes the life of a hypocrite and is prepared for ascension to the upper echelons of power. He initiates a romance with his victim's sexy girlfriend, June (Greta Scacchi), then maneuvers brilliantly on a film project that provides "The Player" with its showstopping capper.

Altman frequently has been susceptible to charges of superiority and condescension to his characters, but there is no trace of this attitude here — which is remarkable, given his often contentious relationship with the powers-that-be in Tinseltown. He delivers a satirical group portrait that is true to life and telling.

Centerscreen throughout, Robbins is superb as Mill, his fundamental good nature making the morally loathsome character palatable.

Whoopi Goldberg brings cheerful vigor to her surprising role of a Pasadena police detective. Scacchi gives the untearful girlfriend a contemporary, ambiguous amorality, and Gallagher is the personification of the good-looking king of high concept who attends AA meetings "because that's where all the deals are being made."

Dean Stockwell and Richard E. Grant are a priceless team as, respectively, a manic agent and pretentious British auteur who manage to navigate in the New Hollywood. Sydney Pollack is dead-on as a wise industry attorney who advises Robbins that "rumors are always true, you know that." Cynthia Stevenson is the odd woman out as an overly sincere and virtuous young exec. D'Onofrio, Fred Ward and Brion James, the latter as the studio head, hit exactly the right notes in one-dimensional roles.

Glimpsed at restaurants, galas, parties, on the lot and just around, celebs from Cher, Nick Nolte, Anjelica Huston, Burt Reynolds, Susan Sarandon and Harry Belafonte to Jack Lemmon, Lily Tomlin, Elliott Gould, Rod Steiger and, hilariously, Julia Roberts and Bruce Willis, keep turning up. All contribute to the picture's aura of verisimilitude, just as the cameos by Buster Keaton and Cecil B. De Mille helped "Sunset Boulevard" so much.

Made independently on a modest $8 million, the picture looks like plenty more. Cinematographer Jean Lepine's images are overflowing with detail, thanks in part to Stephen Altman's resourceful production design (what other film ever has featured a poster for Losey's, not Lang's, "M"?). Thomas Newman's unusual, daring score is highly effective, and Geraldine Peroni's fluid editing makes the two-hour-plus running time seem not a minute too long. — *Todd McCarthy*

BASIC INSTINCT

A TriStar release of a Mario Kassar presentation of a Carolco/Le Studio Canal Plus production. Produced by Alan Marshall. Executive producer, Kassar. Directed by Paul Verhoeven. Screenplay, Joe Eszterhas. Camera (Technicolor, Panavision widescreen), Jan De Bont; editor, Frank J. Urioste; music, Jerry Goldsmith; sound (Dolby), Fred Runner; production design, Terence Marsh; art direction, Mark Billerman (S.F.); set design, Steve Berger, Barbara Mesney (S.F.); set decoration, Anne Kuljian; costume design, Ellen Mirojnick; special makeup effects designed, created by Rob Bottin; associate producers, William S. Beasley, Louis D'Esposito; assistant director, D'Esposito; 2nd unit director (S.F.), M. James Arnett; second unit camera, Michael Ferris; casting, Howard Feuer. Reviewed at Sony Studio, Culver City, March 11, 1992. MPAA Rating: R. Running time: **127 MIN.**

Det. Nick Curran . . . . Michael Douglas
Catherine Tramell . . . . Sharon Stone
Gus . . . . George Dzundza
Dr. Beth Garner . . Jeanne Tripplehorn
Lt. Walker . . . . Denis Arndt
Roxy . . . . Leilani Sarelle
Andrews . . . . Bruce A. Young
Capt. Talcott . . . . Chelcie Ross
Hazel Dobkins . . . . Dorothy Malone
John Correli . . . . . . Wayne Knight
Lt. Nilsen . . . . . Daniel von Bargen
Dr. Lamott . . . . Stephen Tobolowsky
Harrigan . . . . . . Benjamin Mouton

"**B**asic Instinct" is grade-A pulp fiction. Endlessly discussed prior to its release by people who hadn't seen it, this erotically charged thriller about the search for an ice-pick murderer in San Francisco rivets attention through its sleek style, attractive cast doing and thinking kinky things, and story, which is as weirdly implausible as it is intensely visceral. Men will no doubt respond more favorably than women, and while domestic b.o. looks big, results should be huge overseas, where a longer, more sexually explicit version will be distributed.

Prerelease gossip has centered on the alleged anti-gay content and the heat of the sex scenes. In the wake of promised gay protests timed to the March 20 opening and even attempts to dissuade people from seeing the film by naming the villain, debate will certainly persist on the first subject. View here is that pic is not anti-gay, and anyone who has seen all of Paul Verhoeven's previous work would know that he has shown more interest in and sympathy for his characters' distinctive and varied sexualities than 99% of all directors. At the same time, film is arguably misogynistic, but no more so than a thousand other films.

The sex scenes are very hot but, again, no more so than some in previous Verhoeven pics. Michael Douglas' description of Sharon Stone in the sack will no doubt become a byword for a while, and overseas travelers this summer may well want to check out the uncut version. Still, this is about as far as an R-rated film has ever gone, and it makes the NC-17 for "Henry & June" look ridiculously unwarranted.

Tale itself is a juicy, faintly trashy meller that gets off to a slambang start when, at the peak of mutual sexual excitement, an unidentifiable blonde ties up her lover's hands and does him in.

Back on the streets of San Francisco, detective Douglas and partner George Dzundza head up the coast to quiz the dead man's g.f., the fabulously wealthy and sexy Stone. A provocatively ungrieving survivor, Stone has published a novel in which an identical murder is depicted, so she is seen by the police as either the killer or the victim of a setup. The very tough and ice-cold Stone quickly begins tantalizing Douglas, who has recently gone cold turkey off cigarettes, booze, drugs and sex.

Stone bends Douglas so out of shape that, in the first torrid sex scene, he roughly assaults his former lover and police department shrink, Jeanne Tripplehorn.

Perhaps the most indigestible aspect of Joe Eszterhas' $3 million screenplay is how littered the story is with corpses. The main family members of all the leading characters have died violently or accidentally, and Douglas is nicknamed Shooter partly because innocent bystanders have come into his line of fire.

Stone remains the prime suspect all the way through the tale, which includes four more killings, one of which is a grisly ice-pick affair embellished with abundant gore by special effects ace Rob Bottin. Douglas himself becomes a suspect in one of them, and the extensively intertwined sexual histories of Douglas, Stone and Tripplehorn, not to mention Stone's jealous female lover Leilani Sarelle, throws suspicion all over the place.

Verhoeven has delivered a suspenseful, immaculately commercial thriller that delivers on its promises of tantalizing sex and violent action. Although the erotic encounters have plenty of impact, one can almost tell where the trims were made.

Douglas scores with a game and gamey portrayal of an iconoclastic cop not afraid to go over the line professionally or personally.

After a decade of marking time mostly in schlockers, Stone has a career-making role here as a beautiful, smart manipulator who is always several steps ahead of everyone else.

Newcomer Tripplehorn copes well with the complex role of Douglas' shrink and sometime lover, while Dzundza introduces some welcome levity as Douglas' regular guy partner.

Lenser and longtime Verhoeven collaborator Jan De Bont and production designer Terence Marsh have helped give the pic a lush, expensive look, and Frank J. Urioste's editing is as good as it gets. Top individual achievement, however, comes from composer Jerry Goldsmith, who has created an evocative, atmospheric score that instantly takes its place as one of his very best.

— *Todd McCarthy*

AMERICAN ME

A Universal release of a Y.O.Y. production in association with the Sean Daniel Co. Produced by Daniel, Robert M. Young, Edward James Olmos. Executive producers, Irwin Young, Floyd Mutrux, Lou Adler. Co-producer, Brian Frankish. Directed by Olmos. Screenplay, Mutrux, Desmond Nakano, story by Mutrux. Camera (Deluxe color), Reynaldo Villalobos; editor, Arthur R. Coburn, Richard Candib; music, Dennis Lambert, Claude Gaudette; sound (Dolby), Dennis Jones; production design, Joe Aubel; art direction, Richard Yanez; set design, Stephanie Gordon, Darrell Wight; set decoration, Martin C. Price; costume design, Sylvia Vega-Vasquez; associate producers, Randee Lynne Jensen, Antoinette Levine; assistant director, Richard Espinoza; casting, Bob Morones. Reviewed at Universal Studios, Universal City, March 5, 1992. MPAA Rating: R. Running time: **125 MIN.**

Santana . . . . . Edward James Olmos
JD . . . . William Forsythe
Mundo . . . . Pepe Serna
Puppet . . . . Danny De La Paz
Julie . . . . Evelina Fernandez
El Japo . . . . . Cary Hiroyuki Tagawa
Little Puppet . . . . . Daniel Villarreal
Pedro . . . . Sal Lopez
Huero . . . . Daniel A. Haro
Esperanza . . . . Vira Montes
Pieface . . . . Domingo Ambriz
Cheetah . . . . Vic Trevino
Dornan . . . . Tom Bower
Young Santana . . . . Panchito Gomez
Young JD . . . . Steve Wilcox
Young Mundo . . . . . . Richard Coca

The criminal life is portrayed with all the glamour of a mugshot in "American Me," a powerful indictment of the cycle of violence bred by the prisons and street culture. One of the grimmest films produced by a major studio recently, Edward James Olmos' searing directorial debut represents a massive downer by any conventional audience standards, and also runs the risk of attracting the type of crowd that will groove on the violence and ignore the message.

Having made such a daring picture, Universal should use care and patience to find an audience, which arguably exists across the spectrum of racial and socioeconomic brackets.

Project has been gestating since 1973, when Floyd Mutrux wrote the script. Al Pacino was once slated to star.

The story is much more than the saga of one gangster and his clique. More pointedly than any recent film, "American Me," which takes place across more than 30 years, charts the climate that has led to escalating urban mayhem and gang warfare.

It also delineates the hardened attitudes, the acceptance of violence as a part of daily life and the corrosive effect that drugs and criminality have had on the Latino community and the country at large.

In a punchy prologue, the central figure of Santana (played as an adult by Olmos) is shown to be, literally, a child of the Pachuco riots of 1943.

Pushed along by some incantatory, poetic narration, pic jumps to 1959, when the 16-year-old Santana forms a gang with his buddies Mundo and JD.

A skirmish with another gang leads to the inevitably tragic conclusion, and the three are already way down the path that will having them graduating from juvenile detention to the big house at age 18.

Long section detailing life at Folsom State Prison (where the company shot for three weeks) is as fascinating as it is disturbing.

Film sketches racial divisions within the pen, the rise of the so-called Mexican Mafia, how drugs are smuggled inside, the scams that can make life there safer and how men inside control things outside.

Santana, Mundo (Pepe Serna) and JD (William Forsythe) are widely respected within Folsom but can never let down their fearsome, steely resolve. Newcomers must commit brutal acts, preferably murder, to gain entrée into the group, which at any given moment comprises about eight members.

Eventually, JD and Santana

are released after 18 years of incarceration. Santana is as socially awkward as he is criminally expert, and he tentatively becomes involves with a woman in his old neighborhood.

Having lived only in a world of men, Santana has never been with a woman before. Resulting scene, in which Santana's rough preferences with Julie (Evelina Fernandez) are intercut with his minions' gang rape and eventual murder of an enemy in prison, will undoubtedly be too much for some viewers.

Despite this and other weird and brutal sequences, action slows in the latter stages as Santana comes to some understanding of his life.

Working with a confidence that inspires the viewer to accept that what's on screen is for real, Olmos and scripters Mutrux and Desmond Nakano have created a world that's just next door but as strange as the moon.

Olmos makes for a mesmerizing, implacable Santana, one of the least romanticized film gangsters since Paul Muni's Scarface. As a director, Olmos often opts for long Steadicam and crane shots, pulling the viewer along with the characters and action. It's not an artful debut but one that retains a resolutely unsentimental attitude about everything and everyone.

All members of the gargantuan, mostly Hispanic cast are believable. Gap-toothed and head shaved, Forsythe, who has a showier role in the upcoming "Waterdance," makes a vivid impression as JD. Serna creates a forceful Mundo.

Daniel Villarreal is a particular standout as Little Puppet, a young man who should not have become ensnared in gang life.

Tech credits, from Reynaldo Villalobos' gritty lensing and Joe Aubel's evocative production design to tense editing by Arthur R. Coburn and Richard Candib, are sharp.

Strong score by Dennis Lambert and Claude Gaudette is augmented by a vast number of pop tunes, with Kid Frost's despairing rendition of "No Sunshine" over the end credits pretty much summing things up.

— *Todd McCarthy*

ONCE UPON A CRIME

A Metro-Goldwyn-Mayer release of a Dino De Laurentiis presentation of a De Laurentiis Communications production. Produced by De Laurentiis. Executive producer, Martha De Laurentiis. Directed by Eugene Levy. Screenplay, Charles Shyer, Nancy Myers, Steve Kluger. Camera (Technicolor color), Giuseppe Rotunno; editor, Patrick Kennedy; music, Richard Gibbs; sound (Dolby), Ivan Sharrock; production design, Pier Luigi Basile; set decoration, Gianfranco Fumagalli; costume design, Molly Maginnis; line producer, Lucio Trentini; assistant director, Juan Carlos Rodero Lopez; casting, Francesco Cinieri. Reviewed at the Beverly Center Cineplex, Beverly Hills, March 6, 1992. MPAA rating: PG. Running time: **94 MIN.**
Augie Morosco . . . . John Candy
Neil Schwary . . . . . . James Belushi
Marilyn Schwary . . . Cybill Shepherd
Phoebe . . . . Sean Young
Julian Peters . . . . . . Richard Lewis
Elena Morosco . . . . Ornella Muti
Inspector Bonnard . Giancarlo Giannini
Alfonso de la Pena . . George Hamilton
Detective Toussaint . Roberto Sbaratto
Hercules Popodopoulos . Joss Ackland

Let's hope all those associated with this abysmal comedy enjoyed the European locales and cashed their checks, since the film won't be turning up on anybody's résumé. Clearly designed for overseas potential — with Italy's Giancarlo Giannini and Ornella Muti trapped aboard this bozo-laden bus — the film could spur some initial curiosity thanks to its high-profile cast before word of its cinematic misdemeanors leads to a quick sentencing to homevideo.

"SCTV" alum Eugene Levy makes his feature-film directing debut with a film that, ironically, would have provided ample fodder for a Second City spoof as a group of U.S. stars chews its way through Italy and France in search of a movie.

Levy plays the action at such a shrill pitch that the film seems little more than a six-way shouting match until comic Richard Lewis speaks for the audience by asking "When is this thing gonna end?"

The action is fittingly spurred along by a dog, as an out-of-work actor (Lewis) and just-jilted woman (Sean Young) find a stray dachshund and trek from Rome to Monte Carlo to collect the $5,000 reward for his return.

But the pair find the dog's owner murdered and, through a series of odd circumstances, get implicated in the crime, as do a compulsive gambler (John Candy), a too-ugly American (James Belushi) and his neglected wife (Cybill Shepherd).

George Hamilton also turns up playing his "Love at First Bite" riff as a suave gigolo, while Giannini walks in and out the least damaged as the detective investigating the case.

Giannini abruptly solves the case at the 90-minute mark, as if someone had realized enough time had elapsed, or the money was running out, or both.

Tech credits are significantly better than the action, with splashy costumes and sets as well as a jaunty score by Richard Gibbs.

Cinematographer Giuseppe Rotunno also provides some nifty travel footage, although flipping through a European guide book would be an equally helpful, less painful way to pass the time.

— *Brian Lowry*

THE WINTER IN LISBON
(SPANISH-FRENCH-PORTUGUESE)

A Castle Hill Prods. release of an Angel Amigo presentation of an Igeldo Zine/Impala/Jet Films/Sara Films/MGN Filmes e Espectaculos co-production. (Intl. sales, Manley Prods.) Executive producer, Tino Navarro. Directed by Jose Antonio Zorrilla. Screenplay, Zorrilla, Mason Funk, based on Antonio Muñoz Molina's novel; French dialogue adaptation, Pierre Fabre; camera (color), Jean Francis Gondre; editor, Pablo G. Del Amo, Ivan Aleso; music, Dizzy Gillespie; musical arrangements, Slide Hampton; additional music, Danilo Perez; sound, Ricardo Steinberg, Daniel Goldstein; art direction, Mario Alberto; costume design, Javier Artiñano; assistant director, Joseba Salegi; production manager, Jose Antonio Gomez. Reviewed at Quad 2 theater, N.Y., March 7, 1992. No MPAA Rating. Running time: **100 MIN.**
Jim Biralbo . . . . . . Christian Vadim
Lucrecia . . . . . . Hélène de St. Père
Bill Swann . . . . Dizzy Gillespie
Floro . . . . Eusebio Poncela
Malcolm . . . . Fernando Guillen
Morton . . . . Michel Duperial
Ramires . . . . . . Carlos Wallenstein
Daphne . . . . Aitzpea Goenaga
(French & English soundtrack)

Jazz fans and foreign film fans are both ill-served by "The Winter in Lisbon," a glum thriller guest-starring Dizzy Gillespie.

Spanish helmer Jose Antonio Zorrilla obviously likes movies (there are several nods to classic films included), but lacks the rudimentary skills for building a narrative or characterizations.

Stillborn story involves jazz pianist Christian Vadim falling in love with Hélène de St. Père when she visits the San Sebastian jazz club Lady Bird, where he's appearing with the Bill Swann quintet (led by Gillespie).

His not-so-torrid romance with her (there's nudity but strictly mechanical passion) unfolds like a musicvideo with Gillespie music on the soundtrack.

She disappears after a murder and turns out to be using Vadim as part of a complicated but uninteresting plot about arms trafficking, overthrowing the Portuguese government and a stolen Cezanne painting.

Zorrilla leaves most of the key action off-screen and gets zombie-like performances from his leads. Vadim, son of Catherine Deneuve and Roger Vadim, is a rising young star whose personality seems on hold in this vehicle.

Gillespie has one heartfelt scene lamenting the racism and drug use in the States which caused his character to flee for Europe. His score is effective, consistently dominating the listless visuals, with nice keyboard work by Danilo Perez. As the fictional Swann, Gillespie plays a straight horn, rather than his trademark bent bell trumpet.

— *Lawrence Cohn*

BERLIN FEST

TUI SHOU
(PUSHING HANDS)
(TAIWANESE)

A Central Motion Picture Corp. production, in association with Good Machine-Ang Lee Prods. (Intl. sales: Anthex, Berlin; North American sales: Good Machine, N.Y.) Produced by Emily Yiming Liu, Ted Hope, James Schamus, Ang Lee. Executive producer, Jiang Feng-chyi. Associate producer, Hsu Likong. Executive in charge of production, Cheng Shui-je. Directed, written by Ang Lee. Additional scenes written by Schamus. Camera (Technicolor), Jong Lin; editor, Tim Squyres; music, Xiaosong Qu; sound, Paul Thomas Christian; production design, Scott Bradley; art direction, Michael Shaw; costume design, Elizabeth Jenyon; assistant director, Linda Wilson; 2nd unit director, Liu; casting, Wendy Ettinger, Jeff Berman. Reviewed at Berlin Film Festival (Panorama), Feb. 17, 1992. Running time: **108 MIN.**
Mr. Chu . . . . Sihung Lung
Mrs. Chen . . . . Lai Wang
Alex Chu . . . . Bo Z. Wang
Martha Chu . . . . Deb Snyder
Jeremy Chu . . . . Haan Lee
Yi Cui . . . . Emily Liu
(Mandarin & English dialogue; English subtitles)

A gentle, well-observed comedy about a retired t'ai chi teacher from Peking who causes chaos for his son's Stateside family, "Pushing Hands" should garner good word-of-mouth on the fest circuit, with limited theatrical legs possible in art houses.

Feature bow by Taiwan-born NYU grad Ang Lee is a smooth addition to the ranks of works by other Chinese-American helmers.

Story is set in New York's Westchester County, where sprightly 70-year-old Chu (Sihung Lung) moves in with his son Alex (Bo Z. Wang), American daughter-in-law Martha (Deb Snyder) and their sprig, Jeremy (Haan Lee). The couple's marriage is rocky, and things aren't helped by Chu and Martha's communication troubles.

Chu takes a shine to widow Mrs. Chen (Lai Wang), who runs a cooking class at the local Chinese rec center. But Alex's plan to pair up the two goes awry, and Chu finally moves downtown to wash dishes in an eatery. A run-in with some Chinatown heavies brings all parties together by fadeout.

Cultural differences between Chinese and U.S. lifestyles is hardly fresh fodder, but Ang Lee finds some new wrinkles, thanks to generally strong casting and confident pacing. Pic's atmospheric 15-minute opening sets the tone for the whole pic, which only occasionally lapses into unnecessary histrionics.

Best scenes are between Lung and Lai Wang, who play very different Chinese (former direct from the Mainland, latter via prosperous Taiwan) bonded by their ancestry. Both thesps, actually from Taiwan, bring a rich glow to their segments, with Lai Wang giving one of her best perfs to date. Snyder handles a difficult role with skill, and Haan Lee (the director's son) is strong as the Americanized moppet.

Pic has a classy look, despite its 24-day shoot and minimal budget (less than $500,000) provided by Taiwan's state-funded Central Motion Picture Corp.

N.Y.'s Good Machine (James Schamus, Ted Hope), involved with "Poison" and Hal Hartley productions, came in for backend benefits. —*Derek Elley*

BULLETS FOR BREAKFAST

A Holly Fisher production. Produced, directed, written by Fisher. Camera (color, 16m), editor-sound, Fisher; sound mixer, Rick Dior. Reviewed at Berlin Film Festival (Forum), Feb. 17, 1992. Running time: **77 MIN.**
With: W. Ryerson Johnson, Nancy Nielson, Heide Schlüpmann, Betty Fitzsimmons, Roberta Hooper, Tiny Greene, workers of McCurdy Fish Co.

A self-styled scrapbook on "the seductive power of collective myths and stereotypes," Holly Fisher's "Bullets for Breakfast" blends Western pulp writers, Maine smokehouse workers and classic paintings into a mush of imagery.

Machine-gun style marks this strictly for avant-garde outing, with feminist crossovers a possibility.

Pic is a tribute to Fisher's skill with the optical printer, on which she combines Super 8 diary material with excerpts from John Ford's "My Darling Clementine." Theme of fiction vs. reality is interestingly expounded on by Western author W. Ryerson Johnson, who admits the American West was nothing like his pulp version.

Within its limitations, pic is technically okay.

— *Derek Elley*

GINEVRA (GUINEVERE) (GERMAN)

A Theuring-Engström Filmproduktion production. Directed, written by Ingemo Engström. Camera (Eastmancolor), Gérard Vandenberg; editor, Gerhard Theuring; sound, Arno Wilms; assistant director, Patrick Straumann. Reviewed at Berlin Film Festival (Panorama), Feb. 16, 1992. Running time: **157 MIN.**
Cecilia Linné Ginevra . Amanda Ooms
Luc/Lancelot . . . . . . Serge Maggiani
Nélida . . . . Michèle Addala
Manuel . . . . Diego Wallraff
Jan . . . . Zacharias Preen
Producer . . . . Christian Koch
Artus . . . . Gerhard Theuring
Also with: Eliane Tondut, Muriel Theuring, Sonia Saouchi.
(French & German dialogue)

"Ginevra" is a beautiful but boring German art film that thinks it's French. Overlong tale about an actress who goes AWOL to find herself could easily lose an hour before hitting the fest circuit. Commercial chances will center more on the frequent peeling by lead actress Amanda Ooms.

Helmer Ingemo Engström has been down this alienation road before ("Flight to Marseilles," "Flight to the North"). This time her main character heads south from Hamburg to the Pyrenees but, judging by the guffaws and walkouts at the Berlin fest world preem, she's going to lose many fellow travelers.

Ooms plays a w.k. screen actress first seen shooting a pretentious art pic. After collapsing in a bookshop and crashing her car in the French countryside, she throws away her belongings and gets taken in by a bar singer (Michèle Addala).

Rest of the pic is Ooms, who's adopted the name Ginevra (Guinevere), yo-yoing from her two boyfriends — Luc (Serge Maggiani) and Artus (co-producer Gerhard Theuring) — to the singer to the set of a pic called "Tears of an Angel." Frequent sex scenes break up the monotony, however.

Engström sees the picture as a modern take on the Camelot myth, but the whole Artus/Arthur and Luc/Lancelot subtext never gets beyond the printed synopsis. Dialogue is foggy, and material linking the various segs nonexistent.

Ooms (the shy one in Carl-Gustaf Nykvist's "The Women on the Roof") makes an elegant but vacuous heroine. Only player to impress as a real person is Addala.

Like Engström's previous work, pic has a classy look.

— *Derek Elley*

RCHEYLI (THE BELOVED) (GEORGIAN)

A Gruzia Filmstudio-Katharsis-Merani production. (Intl. sales: Gruzia Filmstudio, Tbilissi.) Directed by Mikhail Kalatosischvili. Screenplay, Kalatosischvili, David Achobadse, based on Prosper Mérimée's novella "Mateo Falcone." Camera (color), Artschil Achvlediani; editor, Dshulietta Besuaschvili; music, sound, Surab Nadaraja; production design, Tamara Pozchischvili; assistant director, L. Dschodshua. Reviewed at Berlin Film Festival (competition), Feb. 21, 1992. Running time: **99 MIN.**
With: Avtandil Macharadse, Nineli Tschankvetadse, Larisa Guzeyeva, Luka Chundadse, Maya Bagrationi, Gogi Margvelaschvili, Leo Antadse.

With the breakup of the Soviet Union, it was inevitable that the former republics would start to rewrite official history. In "The Beloved," a quietly grim film from Georgia set during the period following the 1917 Revolution, the Red Army is depicted as a group of sadistic bandits who slaughter and torture innocents.

A farmer and his beloved son live traditional, peaceful lives in the Georgian countryside. On his weekly visit to town, the father witnesses the slaughter of farmers by the Russians. It's gruesome stuff reminiscent of the Nazi Holocaust, which is obviously the intention.

The horror moves to the farm when, with his father away, the young son shelters a wounded partisan. When Russian soldiers arrive, the boy at first denies the man's existence. But the man's eventually captured and when the father returns, he feels compelled to mete out traditional punishment to his son.

The theme is certainly not cheerful, and the casual violence (including slaughter of a calf) will horrify some audiences. But the story is powerful and handled effectively by the director.

Mikhail Kalatosischvili is the grandson the Georgian director Mikhail Kalatozov ("The Cranes are Flying," an international art house success in the mid-'50s), and, like his grandfather, has a sure eye for striking visual compositions.

Pic is an excellent example of the new, independent Georgian cinema.

— *David Stratton*

PINEAPPLE TOURS (JAPANESE)

A Sukoboro Factor production. Produced by Haruhiko Daishima. Directed by Tsutomu Makiya, Yuji Nakae, Hayashi Toma. Screenplay, Makiya. Camera (color), Masafumi Ichinose; music, Rinken Teruya; production design, Fumio Wauke; sound, Osamu Takizawa. Reviewed at Berlin Film Festival (Forum), Feb. 21, 1992. Running time: **114 MIN.**
Rinsuke . . . . Rinsuke Teruya
Taru . . . . Koji Nakamoto
Reiko . . . . Reiko Kaneshima
Yukio . . . . Yukito Ara
Hideyoshi . . . . Go Riju
Hanuko . . . . Yuko Miyagi
Akira . . . . Shinichi Tsuha
Natsuko . . . . Aino Nakasone

Three short stories by three directors combine to provide a fitfully amusing comedy set on the lush Okinawan islands off Japan. The makers claim this is the first Okinawan film, and island locals treat Japanese characters as foreigners. Mood of the pic varies but is on the whole cheerfully laid back. "Pineapple Tours" could go the fest route, but theatrical chances are slim.

First episode, "Aunt Reiko," directed by pic's overall writer, Tsutomu Makiya, is the weakest. Apart from introing the cheerful types who appear in all three stories — musicians who ferry people to the islands from the mainland — this yarn is a rarely funny item about a former opera singer who's lost her voice and a stubborn, deaf old woman. It's not helped by Makiya's plodding treatment.

Things pick up with the second story, "Haruko and Hideyoshi," directed by Yuki Nakae. A Japanese postman courts a local girl, but when he finally makes love to her, her mother listens in the next room. This section is winningly acted and briskly helmed.

"Bomb Kids" (Hayashi Toma), about a couple of would-be punks and a reward offered for the discovery of an unexploded bomb left over from the Yank occupation, is also amusing.

Despite the flat first third, "Pineapple Tours" is a fresh and often invigorating, though very modest, pic, handsomely photographed on the lush island and energetically acted by an apparently inexperienced cast.
— *David Stratton*

ON MY OWN
(CANADIAN-ITALIAN-AUSTRALIAN)

An Alliance Communications Corp. (Montreal)-Ellepi Film SRL (Rome)-Rosa Colosimo Pty. Ltd. (Melbourne) co-production, with the participation of the Australian Film Finance Corp., Telefilm Canada, Ontario Film Development Corp., RAI Tre, Arbo Film and Maran Film (Munich). (Intl. sales: Alliance Film.) Produced by Leo Pescarolo, Elisa Resegotto. Executive producers, Lael McCall, Rosa Colosimo. Co-producers, Stavros C. Stavrides, Will Spencer. Directed by Antonio Tibaldi. Screenplay, Tibaldi, Gill Dennis, John Frizzell. Camera (color), Vic Sarin; editor, Edward McQueen-Mason; music, Franco Piersanti; sound, Allan Scarth; production design, Bill Fleming; costumes, Kathy Vieira; production manager, Suzanne Colvin; assistant director, Brian Dennis; casting, Allison Tribaldi. Reviewed at Berlin Film Festival (Market), Feb. 23, 1992. Running time: **99 MIN.**
Mother . . . . Judy Davis
Simon Henderson . Matthew Ferguson
John Henderson . . . David McIlwraith
The Colonel . . . . Jan Rubes
Shammas . . . . Michele Melega
Also with: Nicolas Van Burek, Colin Fox.

"On My Own," a gentle, rather sad film about a teenager who discovers that his mother is schizophrenic, is well made, but may not be substantial enough to make a mark theatrically. Major asset is yet another fine performance from Judy Davis, who plays the mother; she only has a few scenes, but she makes the most of them.

This Canadian-Italian-Australian co-prod was shot in Canada and Britain, with postproduction carried out mostly in Melbourne. Despite its disparate elements, the film succeeds in achieving a cohesive overall mood.

Fifteen-year-old Simon Henderson, played with sensitivity by Matthew Ferguson, is at a posh boarding school in the Ontario countryside. He looks forward to a Christmas reunion in Toronto with his divorced parents. His father now lives in Hong Kong with a girlfriend; his mother lives in the English countryside.

However, when he arrives in Toronto, he finds only his father (David McIlwraith in a strong perf); his mother is in the hospital.

Next term, the mother unexpectedly turns up and takes Simon to the nearby town for the night.

They have dinner and share the same hotel bed. The mother is naked, and a strange feeling of repressed sexual tension is well caught by director Antonio Tibaldi as she embraces her son, but the evening ends with a quarrel, and the mother hysterically smashing a window.

The slim story line, interspersed with Simon's dreams and nightmares, is given intelligent treatment, but stronger plotting would have helped.

Vic Sarin's camerawork is distinguished, and Franco Piersanti's music fits the mood perfectly.
— *David Stratton*

DEN HVITE VIKING
(THE WHITE VIKING)
(NORWEGIAN)

A Filmeffekt production. (Intl. sales: Filmeffekt, Oslo.) Produced by Dag Alveberg. Directed by Hrafn Gunnlaugsson. Screenplay, Gunnlaugsson, Jonathan Rumbold, from an original saga by Gunnlaugsson; camera (color), Tony Forsberg; editor, Sylvia Ingemarsson; music, Hans-Erik Philip, Oistein Boassen; sound (Dolby), Jan Lindvik; art direction, Ensio Suominen; costume design, Karl Júlfusson; special effects, Martin Gant, Jarle Blesvik; assistant director, Steven St. Peter; production manager, Jeanette Sundby; 2nd unit camera, Thomas Diseth. Reviewed at Berlin Film Festival (market), Feb. 16, 1992. Running time: **130 MIN.**
Askur . . . Gottskálkur D. Sigurdsson
Embla . . . . Maria Bonnevie
King Olav . . . . Egill Olafsson
Thangbrandur . . . . Tomas Norström
Thorgeir . . . . Helgi Skúlason
Ketill . . . . Jón Tryggvason
Thordur Fatguts . . . . . . Torgils Moe
(Icelandic dialogue)

Unsteadily paced but with a cumulative power, "The White Viking" is an authentic-looking, handsome Scandi epic. Feuding pagans and Christians won't cut much of a swath in theatrical markets but could notch up specialized web sales.

Pic also exists as a four-hour miniseries.

"Viking" comes trailing a rep as Norway's "Heaven's Gate" — it bombed locally last November after racking up a production tab of $7 million. Coin was assembled from several sources throughout the region, including the five Nordic TV companies; director is Icelandic, producer is Norwegian, editor and lenser are Swedish, composer is Danish and production designer is Finnish.

Helmer Hrafn Gunnlaugsson made a mark back in 1984 with the quirky saga "When the Raven Flies," a remodeling of Sergio Leone's "A Fistful of Dollars." Current item, third and most ambitious of his pics, is the best-looking, but it is flawed by a script that doesn't lay out its cards in a straight line.

Co-written by Gunnlaugsson and Brit Jonathan Rumbold, from "an original saga" by the former, story opens in late 10th century Norway, when Christianity was forcing out paganism. Askur (Gottskálkur D. Sigurdsson) falls for Embla (Maria Bonnevie), but is sent to convert the Icelanders across the sea. After much activity, Askur finally returns to rescue his bride.

Sets and costumes have a lived-in feel, and the action sequences an authentic lumbering quality. The largely Icelandic cast plays with neat touches of irony beneath the heroic posturing. Seventeen-year-olds Sigurdsson and Bonnevie are refreshingly youthful choices for the leads, but Egill Olafsson steals the show as Norway's crazy Christian king. Tech credits are uniformly tops, though pic would have benefited from wide-screen format rather than 1.66. — *Derek Elley*

OSTKREUZ
(GERMAN)

A Michael Klier Film production, in association with ZDF. (Intl. sales: World Sales Christa Saredi, Zürich.) Directed by Michael Klier. Screenplay, Klier, Karin Aström; camera (color), Sofia Maintigneux, Hervé Dieu; editor, Bettina Böhler, Birgit Berndt; music, Fred Frith; sound, Klaus Klinger, Peter Henrici; costume design, Detlev Pleschke, Nana Rebhahn; assistant director, Christian Hannoschöck; production manager, Elke Peters. Reviewed at 44th Locarno Intl. Film Festival, Aug. 8, 1991. (In Berlin Film Festival — New German Cinema.) Running time: **83 MIN.**
Elfie . . . . Laura Tonke
Darius . . . . Miroslav Baka
Edmund . . . . Stefan Cammann
Elfie's mother . . Suzanne von Borsody
Gustaw . . . . Gustaw Barwicki
Henry . . . . Henry Marankowski
Karla . . . . Beatrice Manowski

There aren't many laughs in "Ostkreuz," a gritty German low-budgeter about a fraulein from the East scrounging in West Berlin. Despite honest playing and good use of resources, pic is likely to make a quick crossing from fests to tube.

Elfie (Laura Tonke), 15, lives in West Berlin and falls in with streetwise crook Darius (Miroslav Baka), also from Eastern Europe.

Though Darius gives her a hard time, Elfie helps him in a shady deal. Finally she learns a few tricks of her own and has the ungrateful slob hauled off by the cops. Pic ends on a soppy note of Elfie buddying up with another street urchin.

Occasional shafts of black humor lighten the film's bleak tone, and Klier draws a sensitive performance from young Tonke. Borsody is solid as her glamorous mom, and Baka is okay as the not-so-slick Darius. Technically, pic is acceptable given its 16m origins, but color is dull throughout. — *Derek Elley*

BOBO
(THE BOGEYMAN)
(ARMENIAN)

An Aysor Filmstudio production. Produced by Vladimir Hairapetian. Directed, written by Narine Mkrtchian, Arsen Azatian. Camera (color), Albert Javurian; sound, Armen Saakjan. Reviewed at Berlin Film Festival (Panorama), Feb. 23, 1992. Running time: **67 MIN.**

This fascinating, but at times gruesome, documentary deals with the death of Armenian film director Sergei Paradjanov.

The artist (1924 to 1990) led a turbulent life and spent a number of years in a Soviet prison on charges of homosexuality and illegal dealing in antiques. He made a number of significant films, including "Shadows of Forgotten Ancestors," "Sayat Nova" and "Asik Kerib."

Video footage graphically shows him suffering a massive heart attack on a flight from Paris. Sparing little, the cameraman homes in on the dying man as doctors fight to save him. Later, the camera unflinchingly shows Paradjanov's face and head being fitted for a death mask.

There's also footage from his last, uncompleted, film, "Confession," with a voiceover interview with the director.

Footage from "Confession" indicates it would have been a typical Paradjanov pic, filled with gorgeous images steeped in Armenian history and culture.

"The Bogeyman" also contains footage of Paradjanov enjoying meals with friends, and attending a formal reception, where he appeared to have a great time.

But the scenes of the director on the brink of death and, later, lying dead are likely to make audiences who might have been interested in footage from his uncompleted final film squeamish.

— *David Stratton*

L'ANNONCE FAITE A MARIE
(THE ANNUNCIATION OF MARIE)
(FRENCH-CANADIAN)

A Desmichelle Prods.-La Sept-Sofica Lumière (France)-Pax Films Intl. (Canada). Produced by Hugues Deschimelle, Frederic Robbes, Jean-Marc Felilo, Mychel Arsenault. Directed, written by Alain Cuny, from Paul Claudel's play. Camera (color), Caroline Champetier de Ribes, Denis Clerval, Serge Dalmas; editor, Françoise Berger-Garnault; music, sound, François-Bernard Mache; production design, Herve Baley, Bernard Lavoie, Jacques Mizrahi; costumes, Anne Le Moal, Elaine Ethier. Reviewed at Berlin Film Festival (Forum), Feb. 14, 1992. Running time: **91 MIN.**
Pierre de Craon . . Roberto Benavente
Mara Vercors . . . . Christelle Challab
Vercors . . . . Alain Cuny
Violaine Vercors . . . . Ulrika Jonsson
Jacques Hury . . . . Jean des Ligneris
Elisabeth Vercors . . . . . Cecile Potot
Mayor . . . . Ken Mackenzie

At age 83, French actor Alain Cuny has directed his first film, a rigorously stylized pic based on a 1912 play by Paul Claudel (brother of sculptor Camille Claudel). Cuny, over the years, has been the most important interpreter of Claudel, and the playwright himself requested many years ago that the actor bring this particular play to the screen.

This is specialized fare, slow and deliberate, with artificial, theatrical perfs. It should be of enormous interest to students of French theater, and wider exposure is indicated on the originality of the treatment and the placid beauty of the material.

During the Crusades, beautiful Violaine (Ulrika Jonsson) is betrothed to Jacques (Jean de Ligneris) by her father (Cuny himself).

But Violaine is unable to marry Jacques because she's contracted leprosy, and instead the young man marries her sister, Mara (Christelle Challab). The child of this union dies soon after it's born, and Mara begs her sister to return from the isolated seclusion in which she's been living to restore the child to life.

Cuny seems the ideal interpreter for Claudel's intensely poetic and spiritual material. The actor stages the drama in a series of stunningly filmed tableaux. Location shooting in Quebec provides some glorious snowscapes against which several scenes unfold.

The film was awarded the Georges Sadoul Prize last year.

— *David Stratton*

ONOVA NESCHTO
(THAT THING)
(BULGARIAN)

A Studio Bojana, Production Group Chemus production. Directed by Georgi Stojanov. Screenplay, Christo Bojtshev. Camera (color), Andrei Tschertov, Krasimir Kostov; editor, Yevgenia Tasseva; sound, Ivan Venzislavov; production design, Georgi Guzev. Reviewed at Berlin Film Festival (Panorama), Feb. 24, 1992. Running time: **89 MIN**
Gospodin . . . . Velko Kanev
Verka . . . . Dobrinka Stankova
Teppa . . . . . Meglena Karalambova
Filip . . . . Naum Shopov
Prodan . . . . Pavel Poppandov
Shejno . . . . Petar Popjordanov

An odd, vaguely surreal comedy about an absent-minded professor and his pregnant wife who use a dilapidated factory to create a giant clock driven by steam, this symbol-filled film isn't funny enough, or lucid enough, to find an audience outside its home turf.

The prof is haunted by a "thing" that he hears on the roof of the factory at night. He and his friends spend hours trying to capture the mysterious creature but never even get to see it.

The allusions remain obscure, and the comedy is fitful and strained.

The players do their best, with Dobrinka Stankova charming as the prof's wife.

— *David Stratton*

BAI GANIU TREGNA PO EUROPA
(THE FUNNY ADVENTURES OF A BULGARIAN IN EUROPE)
(BULGARIAN)

A Bojana Filmstudio production. Directed by Ivan Nichev. Screenplay, Marko Stoychev. Camera (color), Ivan Velchev. Reviewed at Berlin Film Festival (market), Feb. 22, 1992. Running time: **96 MIN.**
Aleki Konstantinov . . . . . . Georgi Kaloianchev

One of the most popular locally produced pics ever made in Bulgaria, this comedy has been packing in audiences since its premiere in Sophia last October. It's by one of the country's best directors, Ivan Nichev, but it isn't one of his best. The single basic joke gets tiresome after a while.

A crass Bulgarian buffoon sets out by train for the West to make a fortune selling rose oil. He only makes it to Prague and Vienna, but causes dismay and chaos wherever he goes with his terrible manners, lack of scruples and lecherousness.

Georgi Kaloianchev gives a robust performance as the vulgar Bulgar and is surrounded by cast members who play it straight alongside his cheerful caricature. Nichev revels in the period settings, but this kind of comedy isn't his forte and the pace lapses at times. Pic could be of interest to programmers of comedy seasons, or on television where ethnic comedy of this nature is sought.

— *David Stratton*

RUN OF THE HOUSE

A Zoo Prods. Ltd. production. Produced by Janice Holland. Directed, written by James M. Felter. Camera (color), Paul Ygelisias; editor, Felter, E. Rachel Sergi; music, Russell Young; sound, Pauly Laurito; production design, William Bordac, Scott Simms. Reviewed at Berlin Film Festival (Panorama), Feb. 23, 1992. Running time: **109 MIN.**
Sady . . . . Craig Alan Edwards
Tabby . . . . Lisa-Marie Felter
Issy Felchbaum . . . . Harry A. Winter
Barb Felchbaum . . . Susan Lynn Ross

Washington, D.C.-based James M. Felter's first feature seems to be aiming at the John Waters territory of exuberant tastelessness, but it falls short of the mark. This low-budget comedy may have a video life, but that's about it.

Felt sets up the Felchbaums, Issy and Barb, and their niece Tabby, as a middle-class Washington family with problems. Issy, a cab driver, is an insensitive slob; Barb has gay fantasies; plain-Jane Tabby, with her glasses and elaborate teeth braces, yearns to look like Madonna. Enter Sady, a drag queen on the run after witnessing a killing.

Issy gives Sady a ride in his cab and falls for "her" charms. This requires a great leap of faith, since as played by Craig Alan Edwards, Sady never looks or sounds like anything but a fairly muscular man in a dress.

In any event, the besotted Issy hires Sady to help Barb cater a dinner for some snobbish friends. Needless to say, Sady's influence on all the members of the Felchbaum household, including their cat, is profound.

Felter has some good basic comic ideas here, but he lacks either a light touch or a willingness to follow into complete craziness. The film is weakly scripted and ploddingly directed (the 109-minute running time is way too long), and the performances, apart from Harry A. Winter's nerdish Issy, are arch and obvious.

Technically, the film is threadbare, but this wouldn't have mattered if a greater energy level had been up there on the screen.

— *David Stratton*

EL REY PASMADO
(THE DUMBFOUNDED KING)
(SPANISH-FRENCH-PORTUGUESE)

An Aiete Films (Madrid)-Ariane Films-Arion Prods. (Paris)-Infor Films (Lisbon) co-production. Produced by Imanol Uribe, Andres Santana. Directed by Uribe. Screenplay, Juan Potau, Gonzalo Torrente Malvido, from the novel "Chronicle of a Dumbfounded King," by Gonzalo Torrente Ballester; camera (Eastmancolor), Hans Burmann; editor, Teresa Font; music, Jose Nieto; sound, Gilles Ortion; production design, Felix Murcia; costumes, Javier Artinano; production manager, Ricardo Albarran; assistant director, Raul de la Morena. Reviewed at Berlin Film Festival (Panorama), Feb. 20, 1992. Running time: **110 MIN.**
The King . . . . Gabino Diego
Marfisa . . . . Laura del Sol
Father Almeida . Joaquim de Almeida
Lucrecia . . . . Maria Barranco
Father Villaescusa . . . . . Juan Diego
Grand Inquisitor . . . . . . Fernando Fernan Gomez
Dona Barbara . . . . . Alejandra Grepi
Valido . . . . Javier Gurruchaga
The Queen . . . . Anne Roussel

A comedy with a background of the Spanish Inquisition doesn't sound promising, but Imanol Uribe packs quite a few laughs into this lavishly staged romp. Spanish auds should appreciate the film, which was nominated for 14 Goya film awards. (Juan Diego won for supporting actor.)

It's 1620, and the young Spanish king (Gabino Diego) is kept sexually innocent by his religious counselors although he has a lovely young queen (Anne Roussel).

However, a friend introduces the king to Madrid's most elegant prostitute, Marfisa (Laura del Sol), and the naive monarch starts to see women in a new light. He demands publicly to be allowed to see the queen unclad, a demand that rocks the court and the Church.

The film's humor is derived not only from the king's innocence, but also from the hypocrisy of the Church establishment. The Grand Inquisitor, played by Fernando Fernan Gomez with his usual fruity good humor, happens to be a client of Marfisa himself; he tells one aide to have her arrested and orders another to make sure she goes into hiding.

Film gets a bit bogged down when a debate takes place as to whether the king committed adultery with Marfisa. But, for the most part, Uribe is content to have fun with the sexual and political court intrigues.

With its lavish sets and costumes, fine use of locations, attractive thesps (with plenty of nudity), the film provides undemanding but good-humored fare.

— *David Stratton*

NELJUBOV
(NON-LOVE)
(RUSSIAN)

A Mosfilm (Krug Group) production. Directed by Valeri Rubintshik. Screenplay, Renata Litvinova; camera (Fujicolor and b&w), Oleg Martinov; editor, Natalia Dobrunova; sound, Margarita Pasushina; production design, Irina Kalashnikova. Reviewed at Berlin Film Festival (Panorama), Feb. 21, 1992. Running time: **99 MIN.**
Rita . . . . Oksana Kachalina
The man . . . . Stanislav Ljubshin
Roma . . . . Dimitri Roschin

A freewheeling, downbeat romance that centers on a young woman with a Marilyn Monroe fixation, "Non-Love" is interesting enough to be picked up by festivals but is unlikely to cross over theatrically despite a perky performance from Oksana Kachalina as the waif-like heroine.

Rita has a boyfriend, Roma

(Dimitri Roschin), a student, and helps him look after his sickly mother. But she's restless and yearns for the kind of glamour epitomized by Monroe (a clip from "Gentleman Prefer Blondes" underlines what Rita thinks she's missing in life).

At a cinema, she meets a famous photographer (Stanislav Ljubshin) old enough to be her father. She dumps Roma to go off with this character, then spends the rest of the movie vacillating between the two men. There's plenty of nudity in the bed scenes, but director Valeri Rubintshik is mainly interested in establishing the character of a vulnerable, rather silly girl who finds that — as Monroe sang in "There's No Business Like Show Business — after she gets what she thought she wanted, she doesn't really want it after all.

The film switches from black & white to color and back for no apparent reason, but apart from this indulgence the handling is fresh and sympathetic.

— *David Stratton*

MIGRANTY
(MIGRANTS)
(RUSSIAN)

A Mosfilm Cineconcern-Talka Film production. Directed, written by Valeri Priomychov. Camera (color), Boris Broshovski; editor, Ludmilla Sviridenko; music, Boris Rytschkov; sound, A. Arzinovitch; production design, Svetlana Titova. Reviewed at Berlin Film Festival (Panorama), Feb. 17, 1992. Running time: **97 MIN.**
With: Oksana Arbuzova, Andrei Andreiev, Nina Ruslanova, Jekaterina Vasilieva, Irina Klimova.

One of those gritty, kitchen sink Russian films that depict a decaying society with vivid images, "Migrants" isn't likely to have theatrical success, but fests may be interested in this latest foray into the decline of the Russian civilization.

The migrants of the title are non-Russians who come to

Moscow and find low-level work. Many locals despise them and accuse them of taking away much-needed jobs from Muscovites.

Migrants Pavel and Pavlina are both ethnic Russians; he comes from a farm, she from one of the far-flung republics (now indie states).

Homeless Pavlina meets Pavel in a nightclub after a fight in which she becomes involved. They're picked up by the police, but freed, and she stays a night

in his cramped room.

Writer-director Valeri Priomychov is a former actor who gets fine, natural performances from his young leads. The Moscow he depicts is a sad, increasingly violent city that, according to the film, is turning its young people into criminals, with the overworked and unsympathetic police hardly able to cope.

— *David Stratton*

DUGUN [DIE HEIRAT]
(THE MARRIAGE)
(GERMAN)

A Wolfgang Krenz Filmproduktion production, in association with ZDF. Produced by Krenz. Directed, written by Ismet Elci. Camera (Eastmancolor), Martin Gressmann; editor, Doreen Heins; music, Nizamettin Aric; sound, Katharina Rosa; production design, Sadik Deveci; production manager, Sadik Deveci; assistant director, Ali Yayli; casting, Arslan Kalar. Reviewed at Berlin Film Festival (Panorama), Feb. 15, 1992. Running time: **91 MIN.**
Metin . . . . Oguz Tunc
Aygul . . . . Asli Altan
Ihsan . . . . Halil Ergun
Mother . . . . Gulsen Tuncer
Gulperi . . . . Ulku Ulker
Ercan . . . . Mustafa Suphi
Sait . . . . Kivilcim Noyan
Claudia . . . . Claudine Wilde
(Turkish soundtrack)

An indictment of age-old marriage customs that apparently flourish in rural areas of modern Turkey, "The Marriage" is a well-intentioned film with very limited international theatrical potential; TV airing is the way to go.

Writer-director Ismet Elci, who relocated from East Anatolia to Berlin in 1979, has made a passionate picture about a young man torn between two vastly different cultures. Metin (Oguz Tunc) lives in Berlin where he has a girlfriend he plans to marry. Summoned by his father, Metin reluctantly travels to his mountain village where he discovers to his horror that a wedding has been arranged between him and the daughter of his father's friend, a woman almost past marrying age.

At first, Metin is convinced he can argue his way out of the unwanted nuptials, but his deeply traditional father won't take no for an answer. The young man tries to escape, but is brought back to the village. The marriage is forced on him, but he ankles before it can be consummated, leaving behind his humiliated and suicidal bride.

There have been films on simi-

lar themes before, but it's always an eye-opener to see how deeply rooted archaic traditions are in some parts of the world. Elci tells his grim little story with barely restrained anger; the film is modest in every way (production values are minimal), but it packs a punch nonetheless.

— *David Stratton*

FAJR FEST

BADUK
(IRANIAN)

An Islamic Propagation Organization production. Directed by Majid Majidi. Screenplay, Seyed Mehdi Shojai, Majidi; camera (color), Mohammad Dormanesh; editor, Mohammad Reza Moini; art director, Mohammad Ghamshi; music, Mohammad Reza Aligholi; production manager, Ardashir Iran-Nezhad. Reviewed at the Fajr Film Festival (Tehran), Feb. 3, 1992. Running time: **90 MIN.**
Jafar . . . . Mehrolah Mazarzehi
Noredin . . . . Norahmad Barahoi
Abdollah . . . . . . Mohammad Kaesbi
Khalid . . . . Hossein Hajjar

The tragedy of exploited Iranian kids explodes in this shocking first film by Majid Majidi. Told from the point of view of a kidnapped 10-year-old boy, story has the excitement of a classic adventure tale (and occasionally allows itself to take some of the genre's improbable shortcuts). But this chilling tale of child slavery and abuse is no film for children.

After desert-dwelling Jafar (Mehrolah Mazarzehi) and his sister Jamal lose their parents, they head for the city. On the road they are caught by a slave trader who separates them and sells Jafar to a smuggler named Abdollah.

Abdollah houses a stable of young boys in the basement of his store. By day they are taken in trucks to the Pakistan border, where confederates on the other side pass cartons of cigarettes, cloth and drugs through the barbed-wire barrier. Under the blazing sun, hundreds of children and ragged adults — the "baduks" — run the smuggled goods back to town, dodging the border guards in a desperate race.

Soon Jafar learns that an equally terrible fate awaits his sister. She, along with dozens of other prepubescent girls, is being shipped to Saudi Arabia for princes. The sight of the tearful children, dolled up in silk dresses, ready to board a pirate ship, is nauseating.

Jafar escapes from Abdollah and, aided by a friendly Pakistani boy, risks his life to find Jamal.

Young Mazarzehi is resourceful and appealing, able to make direct contact with audiences. The adults are all depicted as lechers, murderers, tricksters or wretches, too real for comfort. Not one offers the children help.

Majidi (a former actor) is a skillful storyteller and director of his young cast. There are some disturbing over-the-top scenes at the end, when Jafar performs a few stunts that James Bond might have trouble pulling off. But most of the action rings true, thanks also to the exotic desert locale. — *Deborah Young*

ZENDEGI VA DIGAR HICH
(LIFE AND NOTHING MORE)
(IRANIAN)

An Institute for the Intellectual Development of Children and Young Adults production. Produced by Alireza Zarrin. Directed, written by Abbas Kiarostami. Camera (color), Homayun Pievar; editor, Changiz Sayad; sound, Hassan Zahedi, Sayad. Reviewed at the Fajr Film Festival (Tehran), Feb. 5, 1992. Running time: **108 MIN.**
Father . . . . Farhad Keradmand
Son . . . . Puya Pievar

Foreign auds who enjoyed Abbas Kiarostami's "Where Is My Friend's Home?" will find its semi-sequel, "Life and Nothing More," even more of a jewel.

After a major earthquake struck the poor villages where the first film was shot, Kiarostami took a camera crew back to learn the fate of his nonprofessional actors.

For all its simplicity, "Life" is no straightforward documentary. In the vein of Kiarostami's "Close-Up," it pushes the limits between docu and fiction in an intriguing way, first by casting actors to represent the filmmaker and his son; then by carefully scripting all the "improvised" dialogue and blocking out every apparently unplanned shot.

The viewer is constantly faced with the problem of how filming changes reality, even while the need to show reality is presented as an urgent matter. The filmmaker's journey to find his two young actors is real, but the

search is represented by other actors.

The children he meets along the way have really just been through an earthquake, but they have dressed up to appear in a fiction film. At one point, Kiarostami underlines his interference with the material by having an old man who appeared in the first film say, "They told me to say this was my house, but my real home was destroyed in the quake."

What is exalting about this simple film is how convincingly it shows human triumph over nature. The boys have survived the earthquake. The homeless people living a tent camp, who have lost their homes and families, get a TV set working to watch a big soccer match.

And the filmmaker character, in a splendid closing sequence that deserves its place in film history, gets his car over an incredibly steep mountain. His final victory makes for a euphoric climax, underlined by triumphant Western classical music.

Technical work is flawless.
— *Deborah Young*

NOISES OFF

A Buena Vista release of a Touchstone Pictures and Amblin Entertainment presentation in association with Touchwood Pacific Partners I. Produced by Frank Marshall. Executive producers, Kathleen Kennedy, Peter Bogdanovich. Co-producer, Steve Starkey. Directed by Bogdanovich. Screenplay, Marty Kaplan, based on the play by Michael Frayn. Camera (Technicolor), Tim Suhrstedt; editor, Lisa Day; music adaptations, Phil Marshall; production design, Norman Newberry; art direction, Daniel E. Maltese; set design, Richard F. McKenzie; set decoration, Jim Duffy; costume design, Betsy Cox; sound (Dolby), James E. Webb; associate producers, Joan Bradshaw, L.B. Straten; assistant director, Jery Ketcham; 2nd unit director, Marshall; 2nd unit camera, Don Burgess. Reviewed at the Avco Cinema, L.A., March 2, 1992. MPAA Rating: PG 13. Running time: **104 MIN.**
Dotty Otley
(& Mrs. Clackett) . . . Carol Burnett
Lloyd Fellowes . . . . . Michael Caine
Selsdon Mowbray
(& The Burglar) . . Denholm Elliott
Poppy Taylor . . . . Julie Hagerty
Belinda Blair
(& Flavia Brent) . . . Marilu Henner
Tim Allgood . . . . . Mark Linn-Baker
Frederick Dallas
(& Philip Brent) . Christopher Reeve
Garry Lejeune
(& Roger) . . . . John Ritter
Brooke Ashton
(& Vicki) . . . . . Nicollette Sheridan

Straight-out farce is one of the hardest things to pull off onscreen, and Peter Bogdanovich and company have done a very impressive job of it in "Noises Off."

Since Michael Frayn's ingenious stage comedy takes place entirely on and behind a theater stage, it has long stymied filmmakers who wanted to open it up for filming. Inevitably less immediate and uproarious than it was in its original medium, piece still serves up plenty of laughs, and in many ways it stands as a model transfer of a play to the screen.

Disney is launching the pic cautiously in modest platform release, and b.o. questions stem from the theatrical farce format and the largely middle-aged cast. With proper care, Disney might be able to propel this to the good grosses its yocks merit.

It is difficult to imagine anyone succeeding better than Bogdanovich has in choreographing this intricate comic ballet for the screen. This is broad, old-fashioned farce — with slamming doors, ludicrous disguises, crude pratfalls and groaner jokes — but done with panache, immaculate timing and good humor.

Frayn's play centered on a theatrical company bumbling

through the British provinces in a silly sex comedy, "Nothing On." With the first act taken up with a disastrous dress rehearsal, Frayn's *coup de théâtre* came in the second act, when the the the curtain came up on the behind-the-scenes shenanigans of a feuding cast. Third act was devoted to a presentation of the play so lax that most of the lines were ad libbed.

In Marty Kaplan's smart adaptation, the company is an American troupe working toward a New York opening. Action is framed — and the acts are divided — by director Michael Caine fretting outside a Broadway theater during the opening-night performance. Otherwise, Kaplan and Bogdanovich are faithful to their source.

Thesps include Carol Burnett as a slovenly housekeeper; John Ritter as a real estate agent planning to give sexy Nicollette eridan a personal tour of the

Original Play
NOISES OFF

Michael Codron presentation of a comedy in three acts by Michael Frayn. Staged by Michael Blakemore. Settings, Michael Annals; lighting, Spike Gaden. Opened March 31, 1982, at the Savoy Theater, London. $15.30 top.
Dotty Otley . . . . . Patricia Routledge
Lloyd Dallas . . . . . . Paul Eddington
Garry Lejeune . . . . . . Nicky Henson
Brooke Ashton . . . . Rowena Roberts
Poppy Norton-Taylor . . . . . Yveonne Antrobus
Frederick Fellowes . . Tony Mathews
Belinda Blair . . . . Jan Waters
Tim Allgood . . . . . Roger Lloyd Pack
Selsdon Mowbray . . Michael Aldridge
Electrician . . . . Ray Edwards

bedroom; Christopher Reeve and Marilu Henner as the owners of the home who slip back into Britain from their tax haven in Spain; and Denholm Elliott as an inept burglar.

Laughs start building through the "first act," as Ritter and Sheridan play musical doors trying to fulfill their assignation while avoiding Reeve and Henner.

As onstage, "Act 2" is the highlight. The performance almost never begins since some of the actors don't bother to show up, but once it does, the thesps are at each others' throats every moment. Bogdanovich and the actors have timed all this mayhem to produce numerous bellylaughs and almost constant amusement. The slight letdown of the "third act" comes almost as a relief after all the zaniness. The actors play fast and loose with the text, fulfilling their personal agendas with cutting asides.

Led by the droll, manipulative Caine, the entire cast delivers accomplished, satisfying comic turns. Ritter executes some of his patented pratfalls with aplomb and slyly sends up actors who can barely speak unless they have lines to say.

Burnett is the picture of the old pro making one more tour, while Elliott is convincingly one step beyond that. Reeve has no problem as the dunderheaded leading man whose trousers are often caught around his ankles. Henner is energetic, Hagerty charmingly seems permanently flummoxed and Sheridan is a saucy delight prancing around in her underwear.

Bogdanovich has judged his approach to the material astutely, resisting impulses toward comic overkill or transferring focus away from the stage. He covers the complicated stage action in long, roving takes that honor the work's theatrical origins. He takes his cue from the actors, and the camera is always in the right place.

Shot quickly on a low budget, pic features perfectly serviceable production values and a sprightly show-tunes-oriented score. — *Todd McCarthy*

THE LOVER
(L'AMANT)
(FRENCH-BRITISH)

An MGM (U.S.)/AMLF (France) release of a Claude Berri presentation from Renn Prods./Films A2/Burrill Prods. Produced by Berri. Directed by Jean-Jacques Annaud. Screenplay, Gerard Brach, Annaud, based on the novel by Marguerite Duras. Camera (color), Robert Fraisse; editor, Noelle Boisson; music, Gabriel Yared; art direction, Thanh At Hoang; costume design, Yvonne Sassinet de Nesle; sound, Laurent Quaglio; associate producers, Jacques Tronel, Josee Benabent-Loiseau. Reviewed at the Concorde Marignan Pathe Cinema, Paris, Feb. 6, 1992. Running time: **110 MIN.**
With: Jane March, Tony Leung, Frederique Meininger, Arnaud Giovaninetti, Melvil Poupaud, Lisa Faulkner, the voice of Jeanne Moreau.

"**T**he Lover," a sophisticated adaptation of Marguerite Duras' bestselling memoir about her love affair as a 15-year-old with a rich, older Chinese man, is a runaway success in France. Film lacks the distinctive voice and ambiance of the book, but the abundant sex — soft-core and tasteful — and the splendid sets make up for the film's banal style.

No expense has been spared — the film cost $22 million, a huge amount for a French production — in Jean-Jacques Annaud's evocation of the pungent atmosphere of the story's 1920s Vietnam setting.

However, in Annaud's capable but prosaic hands, "The Lover" becomes just another erotic film of sex with colonial overtones, a sort of upmarket "Emmanuelle."

Part of the fault lies with Jane March, a pretty 17-year-old English actress who plays the young Duras. She pouts to perfection but does not convey the jaded spirit of the girl.

This is supposed to be the story of a young girl's inability to experience her first love: She can only recognize the love she felt when she is on the boat going back to France.

Tony Leung is excellent as the shiftless scion whose love for the girl makes him emotionally naked and vulnerable.

In the film's well-handled subplot, Frederique Meininger is superb as the girl's exhausted schoolteacher mother. Most powerful scene deals with the mother's farewell to her son (Arnaud Giovaninetti), who is being sent back to France.

In its quiet, understated way, sequence works much better than the endless sex scenes, which testify to little else other than Annaud's abundant talent with chiaroscuro.

Curiously flat is Duras' narration, which works so well in the book. In a more sober film, the rich, gooey prose might have clicked, but Annaud's images are so explicit that the author's words, narrated in Jeanne Moreau's whiskey-and-cigarettes voice, amount to overkill.

The beautiful bodies, as well as the colorful shots of the Mekong Delta, are enough to guarantee box office success with aging yuppies of good taste the world over. — *Alexandra Tuttle*

THE POWER OF ONE

A Warner Bros. release of a Regency Enterprises/Le Studio Canal Plus/Alcor Films presentation with the participation of Village Roadshow Pictures. Produced by Arnon Milchan. Executive producers, Steven Reuther, Graham Burke, Greg Coote. Directed by John G. Avildsen. Screenplay, Robert Mark Kamen, based on the novel by Bryce Courtenay. Camera (Technicolor), Dean Semler; editor, Avildsen; music, Hans Zimmer, original songs and African music supervision, Johnny Clegg; production design, Roger Hall; art direction, Les Tomkins, set decoration, Karen Brookes; costume design, Tom Rand; sound (Dolby), Clive Winter; associate producer, Doug Seeling; assistant director, Clifford Coleman; casting, Caro Jones. Reviewed at General Cinema, Sherman Oaks, Calif., March 14, 1992. MPAA rating: PG-13. Running time: **111 MIN.**

P.K. at age 18	Stephen Dorff
Doc	Armin Mueller-Stahl
Geel Piet	Morgan Freeman
Headmaster St. John	John Gielgud
Fay Masterson	Maria Marais
P.K. at age 12	Simon Fenton
P.K. at age 7	Guy Witcher
Sgt. Jaape Botha	Daniel Craig
Gideon Duma	Alois Moyo
Hoppie Gruenwald	Ian Roberts
Daniel Marais	Marius Weyers

Bryce Courtenay's South African coming-of-age novel is brought to the screen with mixed success in this lushly mounted production from Warner Bros. and producer Arnon Milchan.

On the one hand a captivating and inspiring tale of a boy's journey to courage amid searing injustice, pic too often gives way to scenes of intense violence that are likely to bludgeon the very sensibilities it seeks to awaken.

Epic in scope and dense with plot developments, "The Power of One" might have been better realized as a miniseries.

In 1930s Zimbabwe, young white P.K. (played at age 7 by the beguiling Guy Witcher) is orphaned and sent to a boarding school. The only English boy among Afrikaaners, he is treated brutally, a victim of the bitter struggle among the two colonizing groups for control of South Africa.

Tale takes on mythological dimensions as the boy finds his teachers: kindly German composer and botanist Doc (Armin Mueller-Stahl), who educates his mind, and dignified black prisoner Geel Piet (Morgan Freeman), who teaches P.K. to defend himself in the boxing ring. Much of the story unfolds in a prison where Doc is interned by the British after Hitler comes to power.

Geel Piet molds P.K. (played at 12 by Simon Fenton) into a boxing champion and, recognizing the bright lad's unusual potential, spreads word among the hundreds of other black prisoners that hes the legendary Rainmaker, come to bring peace.

As P.K. grows up (played admirably at 18 by Californian Stephen Dorff), he decides to fulfill that destiny, defying the brutally racist regime and working with a charismatic black boxer

Gideon (Alois Moyo) to spread literacy among the African townships.

Beautifully produced and gorgeously shot on location in Zimbabwe by lenser Dean Semler, picture has depth, dimension and first-rate casting.

But director John Avildsen, after many impressive scenes, reverts in final reels to the kind of simplistic, string-pulling violence that fueled his greatest successes ("Rocky," "The Karate Kid"), to the detriment of a classy project. P.K.'s nemesis, a vicious Nazi (Daniel Craig), takes on a "Terminator"-like relentlessness.

Weakest scenes involve P.K.'s love interest (Fay Masterson), the pampered daughter of a rich racist (Marius Weyers), portrayed in clichéd fashion.

Power of Courtenay's novel — much of it preserved here in narration and pithy dialogue — is such that the rewards of the tale often transcend these flaws.

Fine performances abound, with Mueller-Stahl a standout as Doc. Soundtrack is excellent, with original songs by Johnny Clegg, who also compiled and supervised the stirring African tribal music. — *Amy Dawes*

THE CUTTING EDGE

A Metro-Goldwyn Mayer presentation of an Interscope Communications production. Produced by Ted Field, Karen Murphy, Robert W. Cort. Co-producers, Dean O'Brien, Cynthia Sherman. Directed by Paul M. Glaser. Screenplay, Tony Gilroy. Camera (Deluxe color), Elliot Davis; editor, Michael E. Polakow; music, Patrick Williams; music supervision, Ted Sexton, Becky Mancuso; production design, David Gropman; art direction, Dan Davis; set decoration, Steve Shewchuk; costume design, William Ivey Long; sound, David Lee; choreography, Robin Cousins; casting, Marci Liroff. Reviewed at Cineplex Odeon Century City, L.A., March 4, 1992. MPAA rating: PG. Running time: **101 MIN.**

Doug	D.B. Sweeney
Kate	Moira Kelly
Anton	Roy Dotrice
Jack	Terry O'Quinn
Hale	Dwier Brown

"**T**he Cutting Edge" it isn't, but this neatly formulaic romantic comedy from Interscope has a sharp enough combination of teen-oriented elements and style to slice out a sizable chunk of box office for distrib MGM. Set among figure skaters striving for Olympic gold, pic straggles onto the rink rather late, given that the real-life winter Olympians finished competing weeks ago.

Spun from an idea by producer Bob Cort about paired skaters who actually hate each other beneath the sport's romantic facade, pic pits frosty-tempered ice queen Kate Mosely (Moira Kelly) against brash, competitive Doug Dorsey (D.B. Sweeney), a former star of the U.S. Olympic hockey team who approaches figure skating with great misgivings.

His hockey career cut short by an injury that diminished his peripheral vision, Doug has a choice between small-town bartending and factory work or training for the winter Olympics as Moira's partner.

Doug's rough-hewn relatives view figure skating as a sport for sissies, plus he must contend with Moira's tendency to chew up and spit out would-be partners. He has a flinty first encounter with this spoiled, contemptuous rich girl.

But Doug rallies to the challenge, and the pic proceeds with this combustible young pair firing off verbal assaults at each other as they dig in to train, sweat and go for the gold.

Physical milieu and "Rocky"-esque setup are the kind that usually prove irresistible to young audiences. Sport's close physical contact provides some "Dirty Dancing"-style titillation, with interest heightened by the watchable actors.

Kelly ("Billy Bathgate") is definitely a comer, and even in this rather silly and exaggerated role her poise and intellectual edge contrast beguilingly with her pretty and youthful appearance. Sweeney ("Eight Men Out," "Memphis Belle") has a graceful, natural technique and a likability and physical charm.

Director Paul Michael Glaser opts for an impressionistic, adrenaline-pumped style in the sporting segs. Filmmakers use a skate-mounted Pogo Cam to get the point of view down where the blades meet the ice and the frost flies. Shooting and editing rhythms borrow video and commercial styles, but that's likely to be more of a help than a hindrance with the pic's target audience.

Problem is that leads Kelly and Sweeney are not champion skaters, so key skate scenes are of doubles. Glaser's impressionistic shooting style helps finesse the cheat, but pic suffers from lack of connection between the stars and the figures photographed.

Still, core is the love story, and that pays off sweetly.
— *Amy Dawes*

VICTOR'S BIG SCORE

A Mushikuki Prods. presentation. Produced, directed, written by Brian Anthony, based on the novel by John Hill. Executive producer, Carl Aaron Tandatnick. Line producer, Eric Korsh. Camera (color), Vilma Gregoropoulos; editor, Steven Gentile; music, Stephen Snyder; art director, Liz Barrows; sound, Stewart Adam; associate producers, John Curnock, Michael Bartell; assistant director, Joseph D'Angora. Reviewed at Coolidge Corner Theatre, Brookline, Mass., March 13, 1992. No MPAA Rating. Running time: **85 MIN.**
Victor . . . . Seth Barrish
Don . . . . Joe Biscone
Thelma . . . . Elaine Wood
Betty . . . . Eve Annenberg
Lucy . . . . Marci Rose

Locally financed and shot feature is a tremendous calling card for producer-director-writer Brian Anthony. Commercial possibilities are limited, with fest circuit and cable play seeming likeliest possibilities.

Comedy centers on Victor (Seth Barrish), a nebbish stuck in a dead-end job as a barber. His shady friend Don (Joe Biscone) suggests that if Victor can make a "big score," all his financial and romantic problems will be over.

Opportunity knocks when Victor rents a room from Thelma (Elaine Wood), an elderly woman with a quarter of a million dollars in the bank.

Most of the film consists of Victor first trying to get Thelma to change her will, then to marry him. None of this plays well with his new girlfriend, Betty (Eve Annenberg), or Thelma's niece Lucy (Marci Rose).

Thesping is acceptable, with Biscone weakest. However, Wood is a find.

Anthony compensates by filling his low-budget film with production values and gags that hearken back to the inventiveness of the early film comedians. It's easy to spot the slapstick roots of a restaurant scene in which the ketchup won't stay in the dispenser while Victor tries to romance Betty.

Tech credits are okay, with some intentionally funny special effects working well with a realistic live-action hurricane sequence. — *Daniel M. Kimmel*

SCHTONK
(GERMAN)

A Bavaria Film production. Produced by Günter Rohrbach, Helmut Dietl. Executive producer, Ulrich Limmer. Directed by Dietl. Screenplay, Dietl, Limmer; camera (Cinemascope, color), Xaver Schwarzenberger; editor, Tanja Schmidbauer; music, Konstantin Wecker; production design, Götz Weidner, Benedikt Herforth; costume design, Bernd Stockinger, Barbara Ehret; sound, Chris Price; casting, An Dorthe Braker. Reviewed at the Kurbel Cinema, Berlin, March 12, 1992. Running time: **110 MIN.**
Hermann Willié . . . . . . Götz George
Fritz Knobel . . . . Uwe Ochsenknecht
Freya von Hepp . Christiane Hörbiger
Karl Lentz . . . . Rolf Hoppe
Biggi . . . . Dagmar Manzel
Martha . . . . Veronica Ferres
Frau Lentz . . . . . Rosemarie Fendel
Prof. Strasser . . . . Karl Schönböck
Managing editor . . . . Harald Juhnke
Dr. Wieland . . . . Ulrich Mühe
Uwe Esser . . . . Martin Benrath
Kurt Glück . . . . . . Hermann Lause
Von Klantz . . . . . . Georg Marischka
SS officer . . . . Peter Roggisch
Knopp . . . . Andreas Lukoschik
Cornelius . . . . . . Thomas Holtzmann
Priest . . . . Hark Bohm

This satire, losely based on the 1970s scandal of the forged Hitler diaries, is going to be a big crowd pleaser at home. Its lavish look, prominent German cast and humor make it a standout in German cinema. Prospects offshore are less bright, as much of the humor is too local and satire focuses heavily on an insider's knowledge of German society. "Schtonk" is the first large-scale German pic to come down the pike in years; its $9 million budget shows, which could help change attitudes considerably about what German pics "look" like.

Story is complicated with a slapstick accent. Fritz (Uwe Ochsenknecht) has forged relics of the Third Reich since he was a small boy selling replicas of "Hitler's Sunday hat" as the real thing to American G.I.s. His current speciality is creating "original" Hitler portraits of Eva Braun.

He hooks up with Hermann (Götz George), a bumbling journalist for HH Magazine (a thinly veiled double for "Stern"), who is desperate to break onto the rag's cover. The two hatch the Hitler diary forgeries which, many plot machinations later, become a splendid *succès de scandale* before blowing up in their faces.

Pic is densely populated by characters and subplots encompassing a wide range of German types, making it a broad social satire about Germany's relationship with its past. Hermann's girlfriend, for example, is the very social Freya von Hepp, the proud niece of Hermann Göring. Fritz sells his paintings to the Lentz couple, the owners of a sewing machine factory and "connoisseurs" of Nazi art. While the characters, and the actors who play them, are recognizable to German auds, it's questionable whether they can travel with any success.

Title refers to a nonsense word used by Charlie Chaplin in "The Great Dictator" when he was pretending to speak German.
— *Rebecca Lieb*

OBECNA SKOLA
(THE ELEMENTARY SCHOOL)
(CZECH)

A Barrandov Film Studios, Creative Production Group Vydra and Dudova production. Produced by Jaromir Lukas. Directed by Jan Sverak. Screenplay, Zdenek Sverak, camera (color), F.A. Brabec; editor, Alois Fisarek; music, Jiri Svoboda; production design, Vladimir Labsky; costume design, Jan Kropacek; sound, Jiri Kriz. Reviewed at Museum of Modern Art, N.Y., March 10, 1992. Running time: **100 MIN.**
Igor Hnizdo . . . . Jan Triska
Soucek . . . . Zdenek Sverak
Mrs. Soucek . . . . Libuse Safrankova
Schoolmaster . . . . Rudolf Hrusinsky
Miss Maxova . . . . Daniela Kolarova
Eda . . . . Vaclav Jakoubek
Tonda . . . . Radoslav Budac
Tram driver's wife . . Irena Pavlaskova
Tram driver . . . . . . Oudrej Vetchy
Pliha . . . . Boleslav Polivka
Fakir . . . . Petr Cepek
Doctor . . . . Jiri Menzel
School inspector . . . . Karel Kachyna

Nominated for this year's foreign-language film Oscar, the Czech comedy "Elementary School" is a funny but thin exercise in nostalgia set in 1945 and '46. Despite making a few political points, it is a strong film.

Debuting director Jan Sverak shows competence in staging clever gags and re-creating an era with flamboyant crane shots, but the script by his dad (and pic co-star) Zdenek Sverak is not up to snuff.

The elder Sverak, who previously wrote Jiri Menzel's wonderful "My Sweet Little Village," portrays a power station worker nicknamed "Transformer." His 10-year-old son Eda (Vaclav Jakoubek) is in a class of bad boys who literally drive their teacher (Daniela Kolarova) nuts with their pranks.

Replacement teacher is a disciplinarian (Jan Triska, familiar from many Hollywood films) who claims to be an anti-Fascist war hero. Though he applies frequent corporal punishment the boys come to revere him.

Between the funny sight gags from the young cast, film's main subplot involves Triska's amorous adventures with nearly every pretty girl in sight, which almost cost him his job.

Script's sardonic jabs at the "model socialist state" being nurtured in Czechoslovakia after the war are old-hat, as is pic's overall theme about true heroism (Eda's dad) vs. celebrity (his teacher).

Attractive camerawork of the countryside, occasional musical nods and scenes involving Eda and his young friend Tonda (Radoslav Budac) pay homage to Bernardo Bertolucci's epic "1900." Film's light tone and sentimentality owe much to the work of directors Menzel and Karel Kachyna, both of whom pop up in cameo roles.

Acting by Triska, Sverak and supporting ensemble is uniformly good. — *Lawrence Cohn*

JESUS VENDER TILBAGE
(THE RETURN)
(DANISH)

A Constantin release of a Superfilm production in association with the Danish Film Institute. Produced, directed and written by Jens Jorgen Thorsen. Executive producer John Hilbard. Camera (color), Jesper Hom; editor, Jesper Osmund; music, Jimmy Dawkins and his Chicago Bluesmen, Richard Wagner, Maurice Ravel et al; production design, Thorsen, Hilbard, Soren Skjaer, Viggo Bentzon; sound, Hans Moller; assistant director, Anders Refn. Reviewed at the Palads Theater, Copenhagen, March 12, 1992. Running time: **102 MIN.**
Jesus . . . . Marco Di Stefano
Marianne . . . . Atlanta
The Pope . . . . Jed Curtis
Bum 1 . . . . . . Jean-Michel Dagory
Bum 2 . . . . Benny Hansen
Billy Graham . . . . . Jacob Haugaard
The Preacher . . . . . Johnny Melville
Also with: John Hahn-Petersen, Paul Hagen, Hans Henrik Baerentsen, Jim Russel, Hugo Oester Bendtsen, Pia Koch.

Two decades after its conception, this controversial second coming of Christ turns out to involve liberal amounts of sex, violence and rough satire aimed at the Catholic Church. Eccentric, uneven and often dated style makes it hard to imagine pic having anything like universal appeal, despite its English dialogue and international cast.

"The Return" is the result of 20 years of more-than-dogged persistence on the part of writer, director, painter Jens Jorgen Thorsen. Several times production was halted and funding revoked. Until a favorable high court ruling in 1990, the pic had been banned in Denmark.

Jesus (Italian thesp Marco Di Stefano) returns to Earth to save humanity from pollution. He quickly decides that he likes Paris better than Paradise. Trouble starts when he becomes entangled with a group of terrorists hijacking an airliner. Extremist Marianne (stunning Danish actress-model Atlanta), provides the savior with the steamy carnal knowledge for which he has been waiting 2,000 years.

Their happiness is short-lived, however, as the military wipes out the terrorists. Marianne escapes, but Jesus, mistaken for the leader, is condemned to death. The pope saves Christ from the firing squad on the condition that the Vatican will own the copyright on this religious phenomenon.

But Jesus escapes and takes to the road with two bums. In Copenhagen, he is reunited with the lusty Marianne, but the pope still has plans for him.

"The Return" treads an uneasy path through action, softcore porn, farce, satire and romance. Many of the initial action sequences are amateurish, and they're not helped along by sluggish editing.

Thorsen stabs vigorously at this old adversaries — the pope is depicted as a fat child molester by British actor Jed Curtis, and preacher Billy Graham is seen as a bewildered fool, personified by Jacob Haugaard.

Lensing was done all over Europe, with generally good-looking results. Many of the crowd scenes, involving hundreds of extras, belie pic's meagre $2.2 million budget.

In 1970, Thorsen had an international success with his Henry Miller adaptation "Quiet Days in Clichy." Had he been allowed to produce "The Return" in 1972, the sexual revolution and youth movement of the day might have been sympathetic toward the film. In the 1990s, it's doubtful that audiences will swallow this melange of peace, free love and anti-establishment posturing.
— *Peter Risby Hansen*

VOICES FROM THE FRONT
(DOCU)

A Frameline release. Produced, directed and edited by Robyn Hutt, Sandra Elgear, David Meieran. Camera (16m, color), various; co-producers, Hilery Joy Kipnis, Durwood Wiggins; associate producers, Carl Michael George, Marla Maggenti. Reviewed at Film Forum, New York, March 10, 1992. Running time: **88 MIN.**

Like Act Up and the other AIDS activist groups it features, "Voices From the Front" is a frontal assault on the government, health care industry and pharmaceutical companies. Using footage of protests, along with TV coverage of the AIDS crisis, the docu makes a strong argument that drug research is moving too slowly and medical care for AIDS patients is inadequate.

Unfortunately, the film's three directors seldom offer an opposing point of view. They take the side of the activists to such an extent that this is really a propaganda film. As such, it's quite effective. But it would be more credible as a documentary if the views of government officials and health care workers were presented, too.

Those who do speak, primarily activists and people with AIDS, eloquently convey the frustrations of dealing with unwieldy governmental and medical bureaucracies. Women and minorities wonder why they are not included in clinical trials for new drugs. And one man remembers a friend who was treated in a hospital hallway for nine days before dying two days later.

Their testimony, combined with alarming statistics of the accelerating number of AIDS deaths, is very moving. And the scenes of angry protestors storming the FDA, the NIH, the AMA and AIDS conferences convey the urgency of the activists' fight. With smoke bombs going off and police in riot gear, the NIH looks like a battlefield.

Much of the film is made up of video footage, transferred to 16mm. Instead of appearing blurry, this gives the demonstration scenes a cinema verité look.

In one entertaining clip, Dan Rather's usual composure is undone by a group of Act Up members who infiltrate the "CBS Evening News" set. There is no mention of the much-criticized St. Patrick's Cathedral demonstration, however.

Above all, the victims' testimony gives the film its power. At one point film historian Vito Russo says, "When it's over we're all going to be alive to make sure it doesn't happen again." But Russo did not live to fulfill his promise. In the docu's poignant closing moments there is a litany of all the activists shown in the film who have died of AIDS.
— *William Stevenson*

THE MAN WITHOUT A WORLD
(B&W)

A Milestone release of an Eleanor Antin production. Produced, directed, written by Antin. Camera (b&w) Richard Wargo; editor, Lynn Burnstan; music, Lee Erwin, Charles Morrow; art direction, Sabato Fiorella; costume design, Judy Ryerson; choreography, Melissa Cottle; assistant director, Marcia Goodman, David Antin; associate producer, Burnstan. Reviewed at National Film Theater (seventh Jewish Film Festival), London, Oct. 27, 1991. Running time: **98 MIN.**
Rukheleh . . . . Christine Berry
Sorreleh . . . . Anna Henriques
Zevi . . . . Pier Marton
Yisoel . . . . George Leonard
Gedaliah . . . . Don Sommese
Rukheleh's mother . . Marcia Goodman
Rukheleh's father . . . Sergun A. Tont
Zevi's mother . . . Luyba Talpalatsky
Also with: George Leonard, Don Sommerse, Lisa Welti, Bennet Berger, Ellen Zweig, Eleanor Antin, James Scott Kerwin, Nicolai Lennox, Sebato Fiorella.

Scholarship and silent movie shtick team up in the comic meller "The Man Without a World," but Mel Brooks it ain't. Affectionate tribute to the vanished worlds of Yiddish silents and Mittel European shtetl life looks set to become a cult item.

Opening crawl claims pic is the sole surviving copy of a silent masterpiece by controversial Soviet director Yevgeny Antinov, recently discovered, thanks to glasnost, in the Odessa Film Archive. In fact, it's the first feature-length movie by performance artiste Eleanor Antin, based at San Diego U.

Antin, a.k.a. Eleanora Antinova, has been down this road before: Her previous pic, "The Last Night of Rasputin" (1989), passed itself off as a Russian silent too.

Following a phony archive logo and Yiddish main title, film

segues into a loosely constructed meller, with English intertitles.

Plot, as such, concerns the romance between Yiddish poet Zevi (Pier Marton) and nice Jewish girl Rukheleh (Christine Berry). Her parents want her to marry the local butcher. So the lovers leave for a life of poverty in the Warsaw ghetto.

All that's just a hook on which to hang a patchwork portrait of Polish shtetl existence, all gone (per closing caption) by 1943, following the 1939 Nazi invasion.

Antin peoples her movie with funny-serious sterotypes: a fortune teller, a hotsy gypsy dancer (Antin herself), a local strongman, anarchists and socialists plotting in Moishe's Cafe and starving orphans.

For good measure, there's also the pesky dybbuk of a Talmudic scholar-turned-apostate ("a man without a world") that inhabits the body of a girl turned mute after a childhood rape. Exorcism of that demon is one of several extended sequences that detail Jewish rituals of the period.

Running parallel with the scholarly stuff is Antin's fond tribute to silent movies, from creaky F/X to loving iris shots.

What could have ended up as a one-yock movie is kept going by lively intertitles (often satirizing Jewish angst) and the plethora of characters. Some details may baffle gentile auds, but pic's appeal and nudging humor are broad-based enough.

Playing by the mixed amateur-pro cast is sharp, aping silent mannerisms without going over the top (pic was shot at 16 f.p.s. to give "authentic" jerky look).

Berry makes a notable heroine. Tech credits are fine, with Sabato Fiorella's art direction and Judy Ryerson's costumes both on the money. Pic shows no sign of its hasty 28-day shoot on sets built at San Diego U. Antin herself put up the $100,000 coin.

London screening was with an improvised piano accompaniment, in director's presence and with her consent. Other screenings will feature synchronized music track, played by theater organ whiz Lee Erwin.

— *Derek Elley*

COSIMAS LEXIKON
(COSIMA'S LEXICON)
(GERMAN)

A Tobis Filmkunst release of a Rialto Film production. Produced by Susan Nielebock. Directed, written by Peter Kahane. Camera (color), Andreas Köfer; editor, Angelika Siegmeier; music, Tamas Kahane; production design, Henry Nielebock, Christoph Schneider; costume design, Anne Hoffmann; sound, Rainer Wiehr; casting, Angela Marquis. Reviewed at the Kurbel Cinema, Berlin, March 16, 1992. Running time: **100 MIN.**

Cosima Richter . . . . . . Iris Berben
Klaus Borgmann . . . . . . Ralf Richter
Uschi Kowalski . . . . Karin Baal
Sven . . . . Sebastian Koch
Charlotte Steinhöfel . Tilly Lauenstein
Herr Storz . . Hans-Werner Bussinger
Frau Storz . . . . Regina Beyer
Herr Schulz . . . . . Thomas Putensen
Frau Schulz . . . . . Simone Thomalla
    Also with: Volkmar Kleinert, Heidemarie Schneider, Gerd Schönfeld, Daniel White, Dieter Landuris, Andreas Mannkopff, Steffi Spira, Hans Martin Stier, Jürgen Rothert, Constanze Herpen, Kristiane Kupfer, Helmut Strassburger.

Likable comedy about tenants in an East Berlin building trying to hold on to their apartments should do some biz in German-speaking territories. The East vs. West dimension may help bring it into the fest circuit.

A dozen residents of a crumbling building in East Berlin react in panic when architects show up to renovate the property — they fear renovations will up the rent and push them out. They elect Cosima (Iris Berben), a writer and therefore the most articulate of the group, to try to reason with the landlord. She discovers that the true owner of the building is Klaus (Richter), an alcoholic and bum, who unknowingly inherited the property from his father.

The tenants launch a campaign, spearheaded by Cosima, to clean and sober Klaus up so that he'll manage the building in their favor. After his transformation, Klaus and Cosima fall in love.

Script is often nicely witty, and leads are well played. Berben delivers an appealing perf as a strongly independent, sympathetic woman. Richter's bum act at the outset is over the top, but he mellows out and gives a strong showing as the reformed alcoholic.

Unfortunately, the neighbors — a group of highly diverse types — come and go as a bloc (no tenant organization has ever been this unified), and individual characters are not developed. If they had been, pic would have been much weightier.

Tech credits are good.

— *Rebecca Lieb*

HIGHWAY TO HELL

A Hemdale release of a John Daly, Derek Gibson presentation of a Goodman-Rosen/Josa/High Street Pictures production. Produced by Mary Ann Page, John Byers. Co-producers, Brian Helgeland, Daniel Rogosin. Line producer, Barry Rosen. Directed by Ate de Jong. Screenplay, Helgeland. Camera (CFI color), Robin Vidgeon; editor, Todd Ramsay; music, Hidden Faces; additional music, Tangerine Dream; production design, Philip Dean Foreman; costume design, Florence Kemper; sound (Dolby), Douglas Axtell; special makeup effects, Steve Johnson; special visual effects, Randall William Cook & Cinema Research Corp.; stunt coordinators, Christine Baur, Jack Gill; assistant director, Michael Waxman; second unit director, Gill; second unit camera, Philip Alan Waters; casting, Diane Dimeo, Darlene Wyatt (Arizona). Reviewed at Loews 19th St. East 6 theater, N.Y., March 13, 1992. MPAA Rating: R. Running time: **93 MIN.**

Beezle . . . . Patrick Bergin
Charlie Sykes . . . . Chad Lowe
Rachel Clark . . . . . Kristy Swanson
Royce . . . . Adam Storke
Clara . . . . Pamela Gidley
Sam . . . . Richard Farnsworth
Adam . . . . Jarrett Lennon
Sgt. Bedlam (Hellcop) . . . C.J. Graham
Hitchhiker . . . . Lita Ford
Hitler . . . . Gilbert Gottfried
Charon . . . . Kevin Peter Hall
    Also with: Anne Meara, Jerry Stiller, Amy Stiller, Ben Stiller.

"Highway to Hell" is a failed horror comedy in search of a bigger budget and far better script. Theatrical release, which debuted on Friday the 13th, has moderate prospects in the vid market.

Shot in 1989, film predates by more than a year the much larger-scale "Bill & Ted's Bogus Journey," which shares its plotline of teens going to hell.

Chad Lowe and Kristy Swanson are the kids who elope and find themselves on remote Black Canyon Road, where Last Chance gas station owner Richard Farnsworth warns them of dangers ahead.

A cop from hell (C.J. Graham, boasting excellent makeup effects on his bald dome) stops them, capturing Swanson. Farnsworth tells Lowe that 50 years ago he lost his lady love, Clara (Pamela Gidley), and says that, according to legend, Lowe has just 24 hours to rescue Swanson.

Lowe's subsequent adventures are silly, as Brian Helgeland's screenplay is long on puns and dumb gags but short on basic logic. Typical lame dialogue has Lowe asking sexy hitchhiker Lita Ford, "Do you know the fastest way to hell?" — a straight line with whiskers on it.

Most of this fantasy looks like an ordinary road movie as Lowe motors across attractive (but realistic) Arizona locations. In Hell City, cheesy sets and costumes betray a modest budget when fantastic flights of fancy were required.

There's some good stuntwork during the chase sequences and a strain of tastelessness that younger audiences might dig. For example, comic Gilbert Gottfried, portraying Adolf Hitler in hell, does his shouting routine with a Mittel European accent, and a table in hell has places reserved for personages ranging from Libyan leader Moammar Gadhafi to Jerry Lewis.

Lowe closely resembles his older brother Rob when he smiles but is colorless as the hero. Patrick Bergin is so typecast as a lecherous villain in U.S. films ("Sleeping With the Enemy," "Love Crimes") that he's transparently evil as the Devil in disguise.

— *Lawrence Cohn*

FEIYING GAIWAK
(ARMOR OF GOD II: OPERATION CONDOR)
HONG KONG

A Scenepalm (U.K.) release of a Golden Harvest presentation of a Golden Way production. Produced by Raymond Chow. Executive producer, Leonard K.C. Ho. Directed by Jackie Chan. Associate directors, Chen Chih-hua, Frankie Chan. Screenplay, Jackie Chan, Edward Tang, Ma Mei-ping. Camera (color, widescreen), Arthur Wong; editor, Peter Cheung; music, Peter Pau; art direction, Oliver Wong, Eddie Ma, Lou Ka-yiu; costume design, Thomas Chong, Ku Ka-lou; stunt coordinator, Jackie Chan Stunt Team; motor stunts, Remy Julienne's Group; associate producers, Willie Chan, Tang. Reviewed at Metro cinema, London, March 7, 1992. Running time: **103 MIN.**
Jackie . . . . Jackie Chan
Ada . . . . Carol (Dodo) Cheng
Elsa . . . . Eva Cobo de Garcia
Momoko . . . . Shoko Ikeda
    With: Aldo Sanchez, Kenn Goodman, Bruce Fontaine, Steven Tartaglia, Christian Perrochaud, Jonathan Isgar, Dan Mintz, Mark E. King, Bryan Baker.
(Cantonese dialogue; Chinese & English subtitles)

Hong Kong megastar Jackie Chan does the full Indiana Jones number in "Armor of God II: Operation Condor," a breezy actioner that's always watchable but doesn't rank with the best of his work. Pic was second biggest grosser in Hong Kong last year with a high-flying HK$39 million ($5 million), but non-Asian biz should be mostly limited to video.

Chan plays Jackie (a.k.a. "Condor"), a freewheeling adventurer first seen stealing a rock-size jewel from some spear-waving natives. Post-main titles, he's hired by a Spanish baron to find 240 tons of Nazi gold buried somewhere in the Sahara and bring it back safe for the United Nations.

Tagging along are the granddaughter (Eva Cobo de Garcia) of the German commander who'd been in charge of the gold, a feisty Chinese adviser (Carol Cheng) and a cute Japanese ethnologist (Shoko Ikeda). The first two get kidnapped by slave traders and are rescued by Chan; after wandering around the desert the quartet discovers the horde and does underground battle with the chief German nasty.

Chan comes up with the required number of set pieces, including an ingenious car chase in Spain (with the best bits reprised twice in slo-mo), a complex chase sequence in a Moroccan hotel and the final battle

But there's a by-the-numbers feel to much of the action.Chan gets no byplay with Hong Kong regulars and has trouble carrying the whole movie.

Talented comedienne Cheng goes through her usual double-take shtick but doesn't get much help from either Cobo de Garcia (pretty but wooden) or Ikeda (pretty). The villains are more like refugees from a Crosby & Hope "Road" movie than martial arts supremos.

Pic was two years in production, with the budget almost tripling to $HK115 million ($15 million), making it the most expensive Hong Kong production ever.

Saharan scenes are good looking, and were clearly arduous to shoot. Cutting, scoring and production design are all pro.

Beyond the name of Chan's character, pic has no connection with his 1987 "The Armor of God," on which he almost lost his life during shooting in Yugoslavia. Chinese title means "Project Eagle," the English title for its Japanese release last year.

—*Derek Elley*

THE ART OF MERRY-GO-ROUND
(DUTCH-DOCU-16m)

A Legestee production co-produced with NOS TV. Produced by Martin Legestee. Directed, written by Marijke Jongbloed. Camera (color, 16m), Paul Gibson; editor, Teun Pfeil; sound, J.T. Takagi. Reviewed at Rotterdam Film Festival, Jan. 28, 1992. Running time: **98 MIN.**

"**E**xploring the Labyrinth of the New York Art World" is the subtitle of Dutch helmer/interviewer Marijke Jongbloed's long docu, but it's not the definitive guide to Gotham's art world and circuitry; it's a casual introduction. Possible audiences: fests, art houses and art societies.

The American art market, seen from the outside, is baffling. Millions of dollars are spent for one painting, enormous reputations are built up one year and torn down the next. P.R., marketing, swagger, hype and kitsch all play their part alongside art, talent and genius.

Pic interviews important and well-informed subjects and displays some highly priced, rather horrible pictures, artsy-craftsy gallery hoppers, some genuine artists and some good art.

—*Gerry Waller*

NEW DIRECTORS

ADORABLE LIES
(CUBAN)

An Evilio Delgado production. Produced by Delgado. Directed by Gerardo Chijona; screenplay, Senel Paz, based on an original idea by Chijona. Camera (color), Julio Valdés; editor, Jorge Abello; music, Edesio Alejandro, Gerardo Garcia; sound, Carlos Fernández. Reviewed at New Directors Festival, March 13, 1992. Running time: **100 MIN.**
Sissy . . . . Isabel Santos
Jorge Luis . . . . . Luis Alberto Garcia
Nancy . . . . Mirtha Ibarra
Flora . . . . Thais Valdés

Gerardo Chijona's first feature combines comedy and melodrama with uneven results. At times it seems to be a tongue-in-cheek soap opera, but in other scenes its tone becomes too dark. While there are some funny moments, this Cuban sudser goes on too long and eventually grows tiring.

Script, developed at Sundance, involves a would-be screenwriter (Luis Alberto Garcia) who tries to woo a blonde (Isabel Santos) encountered at a screening. He pretends to be a film director and promises to test her for his film. She says she is an actress. Both give false names and conveniently neglect to mention that they are married.

There are enough twists in the story to keep things interesting. In one scene Santos seems to reveal to Garcia that she's married and was once involved in the black market. It turns out they are just practicing for her screen test.

Garcia's wife Flora (Thais Valdés) becomes jealous. Her worst fear is that Garcia is seeing a man, the director who wants to produce his script. Predictably, she walks in on Garcia when he is playfully imitating a woman, with a rose behind his ear, for his daughter's amusement.

At its best, "Adorable Lies" observes the up and downs of affairs — and the duplicity involved in sustaining them. The film also provides a frank look at life in Cuba, where fantasy can be more appealing than the reality of scarce food and cramped apartments.

But Nancy's (Mirtha Ibarra) frequent attempts to do away with herself come across as sad, not funny. Chijona seems to be aiming for Pedro Almodóvar's brand of black humor, but doesn't quite pull it off.

Even the look of the film suggests a TV show.

— *William Stevenson*

JUTAI
(TRAFFIC JAM)
(JAPANESE)

A Water Bearer Films release of a Mitsubishi Corp./Suntory Ltd./New Century Producers production. Produced by Yutaka Okada. Directed by Mitsuo Kurotsuchi. Screenplay, Kurotsuchi and Mineyo Sato; camera (color), Kenji Takama; editor, Akimasa Kawashima; music, Kenny G.; production design, Uji Maruyama. Reviewed at New Directors/New Films, Museum of Modern Art, March 9, 1992. Running time: **108 MIN.**
Father . . . . Kenichi Hagiwana
Mother . . . . Hitomi Kuroki
Son . . . . Eji Okada
Daughter . . . . Misa Shimizu

"**T**raffic Jam" satirizes the obsessive work ethic of Japan in a comedy of frustration with the emphasis on frustration. Likable characters and wistful moments help overcome the somewhat languid pacing and lack of more manic humor. Film may arouse some interest abroad as one of a number of current examples of Japanese self-criticism.

Story centers on a middle class family embarking on a four-day New Year's holiday to visit the father's parents, who live on an inland island. The dad, Fujimora (Kenichi Hagiwana), decides he can save money by making the journey by car, a trip he estimates should take eight hours.

However, all begins to go awry when the family car becomes trapped in traffic gridlock.

From the opening shots through the viewfinder of a video camera, director Mitsuo Kurotsuchi presents his protagonists as a sweet, gentle family. As tensions begin to mount, however, the mask of gentility dissipates and much of the first half of the film shows Fujimora bullying his wife and treating her as a scapegoat. In addition to the feminist subtext, Kurotsuchi also makes points about workaholic pressures, as when Fujimora blurts out to his wife, "You don't understand my job."

The couple are reconciled midway through the film in a tender stairway scene when Fujimora realizes the error of his ways. All kinds of other problems ensue, with the family finally having only one hour to spend on the island before they must head back home.

Ultimate "message" lines have characters wondering who's rich in industrial Japan, given all its modern pressures. Ferry ride to the island becomes an obvious journey back to the nation's past but still plays stirringly as traditional Japanese drumming pounds on the soundtrack.

Hitomi Kuroki as the wife registers sensitively and vividly as does Hagiwana, while Misa Shimizu and Eiji Okada are winning as their offspring. Kenji Takama's lensing effectively captures the changing moods and weather patterns of their odyssey.

— *Fred Lombardi*

MOTORAMA

A Two Moon Releasing release of a Planet Prods. presentation. Produced by Donald P. Borchers. Executive producers, Lauren Graybow, Steven Bratter, Barbara Ligeti, Barry Shils. Directed by Shils. Screenplay, Joseph Yacoe; editor, Peter Verity; music, Andy Summers; production design, Vincent Jefferds, Cathlyn Marshall; costume design, Dana Allyson; visual concepts, Fu-Ding Cheng; sound, Beau Franklin; associate producer, Rolf Braunels; casting, Linda Francis. Reviewed at Toronto Festival of Festivals, Sept. 11, 1991. (In New Directors/New Films series, N.Y.) MPAA Rating: R. Running time: **90 MIN.**
Gus . . . . Jordan Christopher Michael
Phil . . . . John Diehl
Kidnapping wife . . . . Mary Woronov
Andy . . . . Garrett Morris
Also with: Drew Barrymore, Meat Loaf, Flea, Michael J. Pollard, Susan Tyrrell.

Kind of a "Home Alone" for crime-prone juvies, "Motorama" is about a 10-year-old kid (Jordan Christopher Michael) who steals a car and sets out across a vast, fictional American landscape to enrich himself by playing a gas station card collector's game. Midnight movie and fringe video audiences should respond well to the fresh concept amusingly expressed, but pic's thin plotting and desultory pace will keep it from racking up exceptional mileage.

Michael plays young Gus as assertive, straightforward and a tad world-weary, but gives a two-dimensional rendering. Pic can't fly any higher than his performance.

Gus wants to win $500 million by spelling out M-O-T-O-R-A-M-A with the peel-off cards he collects at gas stops. Obsessive quest hurls him into a bizarre America full of people so self-involved they don't even notice he's underage, replete with all the ingredients of the lawless cult film world — grotesqueness, vulgarity, rock music and bad road food.

Visually, pic benefits from first-time feature director Barry Shils' vision of a surreal Southwestern landscape. Gus' encounter with other humans, such as a born-again gas station attendant (Johl Diehl), who sends messages up to God on a kite, have a kitschy appeal that provides some low-key laughs.

But overall, pic lacks the frenetic comic momentum that marked screenwriter Joseph Minion's "After Hours."

Cult-film favorites in the cast (Mary Woronov, Michael J. Pollard, Garrett Morris, Meat Loaf, Flea) are limited to unremarkable cameos. — *Amy Dawes*

FAJR FEST

RUZI, RUZAGARI, CINEMA
(ONCE UPON A TIME, THE MOVIES ...)
(IRANIAN)

Produced by Masud Jafari Jozani, Mohammad Mehdi Dadgu. Directed, written by Mohsen Makhmalbaf. Camera (color/sepia/b&w), Nemat Haghighi, Farajollah Heidari; editor, Davud Yusefian; sound, Ahmad Asgari; production design, Hassan Farsi. Reviewed at the Fajr Film Festival, Tehran (Feb. 8, 1992). Running time: **100 MIN.**
Cinematographer . . . Mehdi Hashemi
Shah, his son . . . Ezzatollah Entezami
Mali Jak . . . . Akbar Abdi
Servant . . Mohammad Ali Keshavarz
Golna . . . . . Fatemeh Motamed-Aria

Soboli . . . . Mahaya Petrosian
With: Dariush Arjomand, Parvaneh Masumi, Saeed Amir-Soleimani, Morteza Ahmadi, Jahangir Foruhar.

"Once Upon A Time, The Movies ..." is a love letter to the Iranian cinema. This lively picture, which runs from the silent days when censorship was born to the present, is rarely boring but often incomprehensible to those not intimately acquainted with the history of Iranian filmmaking.

There are hundreds of unfamiliar references to old movies. Pic is shot as a free-for-all, in which characters jump in and out of cameras, projectors and screens, time goes backward and forward in melancholy leaps and actors appear in multiple roles. Another element of confusion is pic's winking nudges at the current censorship code — like the taboo on showing women's hair — which will pass over the heads of most foreign viewers.

Director Mohsen Makhmalbaf has often borrowed from foreign film history (he refers to Italian neorealism and "Psycho" in "The Peddler"), but is famous for not liking Iranian cinema. In a turnaround, "The Movies" joyfully regales with intriguing snatches of Iran's filmic past. It cannibalizes film history, from its Charlie Chaplin-type hero, the Cinematographer, and to an exhilarating finale that strings together old film clips.

Admittedly, able subtitles (not available when film was reviewed) could clarify many points.

"The Movies" begins when the Cinematographer (Mehdi Hashemi in Chaplin makeup) takes the new invention to the old Shah (Ezzatollah Entezami). He earns favor as the court filmmaker and projector, especially with a damsel-in-distress series. Every time her rescuer lets the lady (very funny Fatemeh Motamed-Aria) drop off a cliff, she falls into the court and gets chased around the harem by the lovesick Shah until she hops back inside the camera/projector.

There isn't much narrative movement in "The Movies," but pic is so jammed with wacky, unexpected action it commands attention. Film's fantasy setting permits it to get away with some incredible scenes.

But the center of the film, the Cinematographer, is weak. Through all his makeup Hashemi never takes hold as a real charac-

ter or helps the viewer navigate.

Perhaps Makhmalbaf's own censorship woes (he shot and financed his last film in Turkey) inspired pic's sub-theme of the struggle between authority and artistic freedom. It also may account for some of the gratuitous chaos and symbolism — though these too have their lyrical moments, like the extended slow-motion scene of leaves and people being blown around by an irresistible gust of wind.
— *Deborah Young*

MOSAFERAN
(TRAVELERS)
(IRANIAN)

A Lisar Film Group production. Produced by Bahram Beizai, Abbas Sheikhzadeh, Majid Rudiani, Khosro Khosravi. Directed, written by Beizai. Camera (color), Mehrdad Fakhimi; editor, Beizai; music, Babk Bayat; art director, Iraj Raminfar; production manager, Mahvash Jazayeri. Reviewed at the Fajr Film Festival (Tehran), Feb. 7, 1992. Running time: **90 MIN.**
Bride . . . . Mozhdeh Shamsai
Mother . . . . Jamileh Sheikhi
Masfon . . . . Fatemeh Motemed-Aria
Mahou . . . . Majid Mozaffari
Brother . . . . . Jamshid Esmailkhani
With: Hamid Amjad, Homa Rusta, Mahbubeh Bayat, Farrokh-Lagha Hushmand, Atila Pasiyani, Enayat Bakhshi, Esmail Poor-Reza.

"Travelers," veteran Bahram Beizai's newest, is a mystical allegory completely unlike his naturalistic "Bashu, the Little Stranger." "Travelers" adopts sophisticated narrative techniques to describe a big middle-class wedding celebration that abruptly turns into a tragic funeral. It's much more distant than "Bashu," and will have less hold on foreign auds.

A carefree young girl (Mozhdeh Shamsai) is happily preparing for her marriage. But her sister, who lives in the country, turns to the camera and says she and her family will never reach Tehran — they are about to be killed in a car crash. And they are.

After this offbeat start, pic switches gears. As news of the tragedy reaches the bridal party, the white colors that dominate Mehrdad Fakhimi's cinematography and Iraj Raminfar's sets gradually turn to black mourning. Instead of a wedding, the family holds a big, tearful funeral. Guests who mistakenly turn up with wedding presents have to adjust to participating in a wake.

Only the the aged family ma-

triarch (Jamileh Sheikhi)is determined to see her granddaughter married on schedule. Mad with grief, the girl complies and changes into her white wedding clothes. As the ceremony is in progress, the dead sister appears, floating joyfully through the room with her husband and children, as though confirming the marriage is correct.

The ending does give audiences a chill, but shots of the happy ghosts go on so long and insistently they lose their shock value. Film's meaning is unclear.

A cast of top stage thesps underline the theatrical elements with expansive gestures and posturing. Like the lighting and sets, the perfs (which won multiple awards in Iran) are professional but distant. —*Deborah Young*

NARGESS
(IRANIAN)

An Arman Film production. Produced and directed by Rakhshan Bani-Etemad. Screenplay, Bani-Etemad, Freydun Jeirani; camera (color) Hossein Jafarian; editor, Shirin Vahidi; music, Mohammad Reza Aligholi; art direction, Amir Esbati; production manager, Jahangir Kosari. Reviewed at the Fajr Film Festival (Tehran), Feb. 9, 1992.
Adel . . . . Abolfazi Poorarab
Afagh . . . . Farimah Farjami
Nargess . . . . Atefeh Razavi
With: Reza Karamrezai, Vajiheh Loghmani, Mohammad Reza Khamseh, Majid Golpayegani, Mohammad Zarandi-Nia.

"Nargess" comes as a surprise mainly for its exceptionally honest look at characters who live outside strict Islamic law. Besides its sympathetic treatment of a shabby gang of thieves, it is a sensitive study of two completely different women.

Director Rakhshan Bani-Etemad, on her fourth feature film, uses the gangster genre to tell the tragic tale of a love triangle. Afagh (the appealing Farimah Farjami) is an aging thief who has lost her beauty and is in danger of losing her rakish young lover, Adel (Abolfazi Poorarab). When Adel meets Nargess, the angelic daughter of a poor family, he resolves to break with his old life and go straight. But finding an honest job proves too hard, and he goes back to the old gang for one last burglary, which ends in tragedy.

Bani-Etemad gives this hackneyed plot a number of twists

that completely turn it around. She also pushes the grim Iranian censorship code to the limit, managing to make her outsider characters believable and moving.

Nargess is a more complex character than she first appears. Her fragile exterior melts away as she goes through some very tough moments.

Poorarab (big box office and star of Iran's top-grossing film "The Bride") is a convincing object of contention, but the character is just an appealing rascal. This is really the women's film. Farjami is very touching.

Action is fairly swift-moving and technical credits are adequate. —*Deborah Young*

KHOMREH
(THE JAR)
(IRANIAN)

An Institute for the Intellectual Development of Children and Young Adults production. Producer, Alireza Zarrin. Directed, written by Ebrahim Foruzesh. Camera (color),Iraj Safavi; editor, Changiz Sayad; music, Mohammad Reza Aligholi. Reviewed at the Fajr Film Festival (Tehran), Feb. 7, 1992. Running time: 100 MIN.
With: Behzad Khodaveisi, Fatemeh Azrah, Alireza Haji-Ghasemi, Ramazan Molla-Abbasi, Hossein Balai, Abbas Khavaninzadeh.

A bare-bones story about a broken water jar in a desert schoolyard has the pleasing simplicity of a fable, marred only by excessive length. Pic should appeal to the same audiences who appreciated Abbas Kiarostami's "Where Is My Friend's Home?" and children's film fests.

Like "Home," "The Jar," second feature by Ebrahim Foruzesh, was produced by the Institute for the Intellectual Development of Children and Young Adults, which has become a de facto source of government funding for many Iranian films. Until recently, films that went through the Institute didn't have to submit their scripts to the censors, an added advantage.

"The Jar" reveals scenes of poverty and ignorance with powerful realism. It also points to a hopeful future in an upbeat ending.

There are no water fountains in this ancient, and highly photogenic, desert village — students drink from a huge old terracotta

jar in the school-yard. The alternative is taking a long hike to the dangerous river.

When the jar cracks, it's a major trauma. A local potter's repair work doesn't hold. After an accident at the river, one woman braves her neighbors' sarcasm to collect money for a new jar, and sends her son on a long trip to bring it back from the city.

Foruzesh establishes an extraordinary rapport with his tykes — all boys except for two veiled little girls — who emerge as real individuals. The adults are more symbolic incarnations of egoism, stubborness, determination. The schoolteacher remains distant and a little stupid in his ineffectual authoritarianism and over-sensitivity to gossip.

Foruzesh has a solid background in making short films and it shows in his ease of direction — but also in pic's overall lack of rhythm. Kiarostami worked on editing various sections of "The Jar," but pic needs general tightening and an overall vision to avoid seeming too long and repetitious.

— *Deborah Young*

THUNDERHEART

A Tri-Star Pictures release of a Tribeca/Waterhorse production. Produced by Robert De Niro, Jane Rosenthal, John Fusco. Executive producer, Michael Nozik. Directed by Michael Apted. Screenplay, Fusco. Camera (color, Duart), Roger Deakins; editor, Ian Crafford; music, James Horner; production design, Dan Bishop; costume design, Susan Lyall; art direction, Bill Ballou; set decoration, Dianna Freas; sound (Dolby), Chris Newman; assistant director, Chris Soldo; casting, Lisa Clarkson. Reviewed at Warner Bros. screening room, March 20, 1992. MPAA rating: R. Running time: **118 MIN.**
Ray Levoi . . . . Val Kilmer
Walter Crow Horse . . Graham Greene
Frank Coutelle . . . . . Sam Shepard
Maggie Eagle Bear . . . Sheila Tousey
Grandpa Sam Reaches
 . . . . Chief Ted Thin Elk
Jack Milton . . . . Fred Ward
Jimmy Looks Twice . . . . John Trudell
Dawes . . . . . Fred Dalton Thompson
Richard Yellow Hawk . . Julius Drum

"Dances With the Evidence" could be the title of this pic about a young, part-Indian FBI hotdog whose loyalties are tested when he discovers the power of his roots during a murder probe on a Sioux reservation. Reasonably engrossing as a mystery-thriller despite its overburdened plot, "Thunderheart" succeeds most in its captivating portrayal of mystical Native American ways.

Youth audience in particular might go for pic's beads 'n' feathers spirituality. In the current receptive climate for such fare, TriStar can look for fair to middling box office. Film is directed by Michael Apted, who covered similar territory, non-fiction style, in the forthcoming documentary "Incident at Oglala."

Val Kilmer stars as a sharp but surly and guarded young fed whose crewcut bristles when he learns he's expected to use his long-suppressed Indian heritage to help quell violence on a South Dakota reservation. Partnered with a crack FBI vet (Sam Shepard), he travels 'cross the lone prairie to "the Res," where the two city sharpies excel at shockingly insensitive behavior.

To the young FBI man, Indians are Third World refugees with drinking problems and too many junk cars in their yards, and militant Indians are enemies of the U.S. Natch, he soon finds out things aren't so black and white.

Befriended by a wary but compassionate Sioux sheriff (Graham Greene, in a standout portrayal), he's introduced to tribal spiritual elder (Chief Ted Thin Elk),

who points him toward his true self. Charged with the mission of ambushing a militant fugitive (John Trudell), Kilmer soon finds his loyalties so divided that he's torn between sides, literally within a single scene.

Pic takes a poignant, witty and often deeply moving journey into the Indian community to reveal the secrets of the Badlands landscapes, the messages carried by animals and the elements, and the magic of ancient beliefs and ceremonies, all against a tragic backdrop of historical oppression.

Set among the tinderbox tensions of the late '70s, when militant Indians waged bloody battles to take back their culture and lands, pic finds a lively platform for its essential view that the old ways were far wiser and better. Point is stressed in a damning environmental scheme at the murder mystery's core.

A great many revelations are crowded into the final reels of John Fusco's otherwise agile script, and Apted's attempt to lift the picture to mytho-poetic heights (including a "Thelma & Louise"-style false ending) doesn't quite fly.

Kilmer holds the screen strongly in an intense young Turk role, but when script calls for him to transform into a mythical Indian savior, he doesn't quite fill the moccasins.

Greene carves out a delightful new mold for the Western masculine hero as the sly, strong Native sheriff who's twice as perceptive as the feds and one step ahead of them, but willing to patiently show the obnoxious young agent the way toward growth.

Native American actress Sheila Tousey makes a striking screen debut as an Ivy League-educated activist whose dedication to her land captures Kilmer's attention, while Lakota chief Ted Thin Elk gives an endearing and surprising perf as the wily medicine man.

Shepard is effective in a role underscored with menace, while Fred Ward, as the cocky leader of a goonish band of tribal police, hasn't much to play.

The first film in which Robert De Niro has been involved solely as a producer, via his Tribeca Prods., "Thunderheart" was filmed on location at the Pine Ridge Reservation in South Dakota, the first feature production granted that access.
— *Amy Dawes*

RUBY

A Triumph Releasing Corp. release of a Polygram presentation of a Propaganda Films production. Produced by Sigurjon Sighvatsson, Steve Golin. Executive producer, Michael Kuhn. Coproducer, Jay Roewe. Directed by John Mackenzie. Screenplay, Stephen Davis, based on his play "Love Field." Camera (Deluxe color), Phil Meheux; editor, Richard Trevor; music, John Scott; production design, David Brisbin; art direction, Kenneth A. Hardy; set design, Annie Mei-Ling Tien; set decoration, Lauri Gaffin; costume design, Susie DeSanto; sound (Dolby), David Brownlow; associate producers, Richard Wright, Lynn Weimer; assistant director, Matthew Carlisle; casting, Johanna Ray. Reviewed at Sony Studios screening room, Culver City, Calif., March 20, 1992. MPAA Rating: R. Running time: **110 MIN.**
Jack Ruby . . . . Danny Aiello
Candy Cane . . . . . . Sherilynn Fenn
Maxwell . . . . Arliss Howard
David Ferrie . . . . Tobin Bell
Officer Tippit . . . . David Duchovny
Proby . . . . Richard Sarafian
Louie Vitali . . . . Joe Cortese
Santos Alicante . . . . Marc Lawrence
Lee Harvey Oswald . . . Willie Garson
Joseph Valachi . . . . Joe Viterelli
Sam Giancana . . . . . Carmine Caridi

Danny Aiello and Sherilynn Fenn's earnest, first-rate performances can't overcome strewed story elements of this otherwise well-put-together drama, which will inevitably be hurt by being the second JFK-related pic to hit theaters in a six-month span. Conspiracy theorists will find their share of shadowy intrigue, but "Ruby" has home video written all over it and doesn't figure to shine too brightly at the box office.

Highly fictionalized bio of the club owner and small-time hood who killed Lee Harvey Oswald traces the events leading up to that moment, again pointing a finger at organized crime and rogue elements within the CIA as the parties responsible for bringing Camelot to a crashing end.

The fiction stems in large part from Ruby's relationship with a stripper (Fenn) who, it's revealed at the end, is a composite of various characters. Ruby starts to be drawn in when he's sent to Cuba to kill an imprisoned Mafia don (Marc Lawrence) but instead turns on the con who sent him, in the process being drawn back into big-league mob activities.

Brit helmer John Mackenzie ("The Long Good Friday") knows his way around gangster yarns, but the problem with "Ruby" is that it plays too much like TV docudrama and, to paraphrase Winston Churchill, ends up a mystery wrapped in a riddle.

Writer Stephen Davis' central narrative device of structuring a story that's as confusing as the Warren Commission report may be good politics, but it's poor theater, despite the film's serious trappings and strong central performances.

Aiello is terrific as Ruby, a tough outsider who never quite was (and who comes to realize he never quite will be). Fenn turns in a performance hotter than a cup of "Twin Peaks" java as the power-seeking stripper, looking Monroe-like with her platinum blond locks and classic features. Considering the nature of the part, the sympathy and appeal she brings to the role are remarkable.

Also giving solid perfs are Arliss Howard as an oily government operative and Tobin Bell as David Ferrie, a much lower-keyed role here than in "JFK's" riveting rantings of Joe Pesci.

Pic slips toward dangerously silly territory in its final act when Ruby dresses up like a Blues Brother to carry out the Oswald hit in "Monday Night Football" slow-motion fashion.

Other than that, Mackenzie brings a fine visual flair to the production, and the period mood and settings, including the incorporation of '60s footage, are credible, even when compared to the technically magnificent work in that regard in "JFK."

Additional tech credits are also superior, especially John Scott's brooding score and Susie DeSanto's costumes. Still, when all's said and done, the best "Ruby" can hope to do is throw a few more sticks on the fire "JFK" started. — *Brian Lowry*

ROADSIDE PROPHETS

A Fine Line Features release. Produced by Peter McCarthy, David Swinson. Executive producer, Nancy Israel. Directed, written by Abbe Wool. Camera (CFI color), Tom Richmond; editor, Nancy Richardson; music, Pray For Rain; production design, J. Rae Fox; costume design, Prudence Moriaty; casting, Vickie Thomas. Reviewed at Sunset Tower screening room, West Hollywood, Feb. 13, 1992. MPAA Rating: R. Running time: **96 MIN.**
Joe Mosely . . . . John Doe
Sam . . . . Adam Horovitz
Othello . . . . David Carradine
Salvadore . . . . Timothy Leary
Harvey . . . . Arlo Guthrie
Sheriff Durango . . . . Barton Heyman
Labia Mirage . . . . Jennifer Balgobin
Casper . . . . John Cusack
Oscar . . . . Bill Cobbs
Celeste . . . . Lin Shaye

Abbe Wool wrote "Sid & Nancy" and will still use that as her calling card after a muddled directing debut that runs out of gas long before its abrupt, if welcome, end. Skidding along on an unleaded budget, "Roadside Prophets" has a self-indulgent, student-film feel that should limit even cult B.O. among alternative music fans that might have been naturally drawn to it.

Aside from the pairing of former X guitarist John Doe and the Beastie Boys' Adam Horovitz, pic is little more than an excuse to show off a lot of now-obscure counterculture figures (Arlo Guthrie, Timothy Leary) and slumming actors (John Cusack, David Carradine) in cameos, with little rhyme or reason to the practice.

Doe, playing a construction worker who takes off on his motorcycle from L.A. to Nevada in search of the El Dorado casino, is on a mission to scatter the ashes of a fellow biker electrocuted while playing a video game.

Tagging along after a stop or two is an odd young man (Horovitz) obsessed with staying at the equally mythical Motel 9 chain. While seeking El Dorado, the pair encounter a series of bizarre characters who launch into long, expository diatribes, repeatedly prompting Horovitz to observe, "He's insane, man." Yes, and boring, too.

Film's quirky approach is for the most part inoffensive, although its heavy-handed symbols (such the search for a mythical El Dorado) get a little tiresome.

The same goes for the cameos, and while hearing Leary expound on "transcendent reality" might amuse those who spent the '60s in a hallucinogenic haze, it won't mean much to younger viewers drawn to see Doe or Horovitz treading the highways.

Even writer Wool's message about chucking a humdrum life to pursue the open road has an anachronistic feel, and the oddball qualities lack the snap or originality that helped make producer Peter McCarthy's "Repo Man" (on which Wool was video coordinator) a cult favorite.

Doe lives up to his name as the laconic biker, while Horovitz proves appropriately boyish if too hyperactive, as if someone had hooked him intravenously to a coffee-maker.

Cusack, currently in another chatty cameo in Woody Allen's "Shadows and Fog," fares best among the walk-through visitors, appearing as an eye-patched loon who pontificates while consuming half the menu in a roadside diner.

Tech credits are okay considering the obvious limitations, and the soundtrack features tracks by Pray For Rain, the Pogues, Doe and former X mate Exene Cervenka. As it stands, though, "Roadside Prophets" is little more than a soundtrack, and an attitude, in search of a movie.
— *Brian Lowry*

THE QUARREL
(CANADIAN)

An Atlantis Films-Apple & Honey Prods. production. Produced by David Brandes, Kim Todd. Executive producer, Peter Sussman. Directed by Eli Cohen. Screenplay, David Brandes, based on Chaim Grade's story. Camera (color), John Berrie; editor, Havelock Gradidge; music, William Goldstein; art direction, Michael Joy; sound, Donald Cohen. Reviewed at Toronto Film Festival, Sept. 11, 1991. Running time: **88 MIN.**
Chaim Kovler . . . . . R.H. Thompson
Hersh Rasseyner . . . . . Saul Rubinek

Two estranged Jewish friends meet accidentally in Mount Royal park 15 years after the Holocaust and spend the day debating Judaism. Essentially a one-act play shot in one location, engaging dialogue makes "The Quarrel" perfect fare for quality TV outlets.

Canadian thesp R.H. Thompson is ideal as a Yiddish writer haunted by memories of family and friends lost during the Holocaust, a time when he lost his faith in God.

Hersh (Saul Rubinek) is more determined than ever to protect Judaism. His way of dealing with the Holocaust was to become an Orthodox Jew. Their debate addresses classic differences between the secular and religious worlds. Two of Canada's best known male thesps do justice to these extremely different roles.

Montreal's massive park provides an ideal location. Tech credits are good on the pic, slated for a spring release.
— *Suzan Ayscough*

TURTLE BEACH
(AUSTRALIAN)

A Warner Bros. release (Greater Union in Australia) of a Village Roadshow Pictures-Regency Intl. presentation of a Roadshow, Coote & Carroll production, with support of Australian Film Finance Corp. Produced by Matt Carroll. Executive producers, Graham Burke, Greg Coote. Line producer, Irene

Dobson. Directed by Stephen Wallace. Screenplay, Ann Turner, based on Blanche d'Alpuget's novel. Camera (color), Russell Boyd; supervising editor, William Russell; editors, Lee Smith, Louise Innes; music, Chris Neal; production design, Brian Thomson; costumes, Roger Kirk; sound, Ben Osmo; assistant director, Colin Fletcher; casting, Alison Barrett. Reviewed at Village Cinema City 1, Sydney, March 19, 1992. Running time: **85 MIN.**
Judith . . . . Greta Scacchi
Lady Minou Hobday . . . . Joan Chen
Ralph Hamilton . . . . Jack Thompson
Kanan . . . . Art Malik
Sir Adrian Hobday . . . Norman Kaye
Sancha Hamilton . . . Victoria Longley
Richard . . . . Martin Jacobs

"**T**urtle Beach," a lackluster adaptation of a popular book about an Aussie journalist covering the plight of Vietnamese boat people in Malaysia, was released in Oz sans advance review screenings. Apparent lack of distrib confidence isn't surprising since rarely has such an interesting story resulted in such drab fare. Warner will release it in the U.S. May 1 on 800 screens, but returns likely will be minimal.

Film may spark initial interest in Australia because of publicity on the Malaysian government's protests: In one scene, rampaging Malaysian villagers, labeled "disgusting" by one character, attack unarmed refugees with knives and machetes. The Aussie government has disassociated itself from the film, which was backed by the Film Finance Corp.

The Malaysians have a point. Pic, shot on location in Thailand, superficially treats the complex issue of longstanding differences between indigenous Malays and Chinese and Indians living in the country.

Pic centers on the relationship between an Aussie journalist (Greta Scacchi) and a former Saigon barmaid (Joan Chen) incongruously married to the Australian ambassador in Kuala Lumpur (Norman Kaye).

Scacchi wants a story about the terrible things the Malaysians are allegedly doing to refugees; Chen is obsessed with finding her three children who, she believes, are imminently arriving on a refugee boat. Hints of a lesbian relationship are established in the early scenes, but are quickly dropped.

The journalist, who covered Malaysian riots 10 years earlier (depicted in a somewhat grisly pre-credit sequence) packs her sons off to boarding school, leaves behind her estranged husband and goes to stay with friends (Victoria Longley, Jack Thompson). She resumes her friendship with Chen, and witnesses Malaysian villagers slaughter refugees on Turtle Beach.

Scacchi also embarks on a desultory affair with a charming Indian black marketeer (Art Malik), but this seems only an excuse for the obligatory Scacchi nude scene.

Though the basic story is promising film material (Peter Weir's "The Year of Living Dangerously" tackled similar material with success), "Turtle Beach" never begins to work.

Screenplay by Ann Turner seems a muddle, consisting of short, disconnected sequences written without flavor or distinction.

Russell Boyd's cinematography is drab, at least in the print caught. Supervising film editor William Anderson (who took over from pic's original editor, John Scott, during postproduction) has sheared the film to an ultra-lean 85 minutes, but there's no rhythm, no flow; just a series of choppy scenes.

Scacchi looks uncomfortable and is unflatteringly photographed, while Thompson doesn't even get an establishing scene. Malik makes the journalist's lover totally uncharismatic. Chen almost singlehandedly saves the film with a lively, sympathetic performance, and Kaye is also good as her kindly, elderly ambassador husband.

Direction is credited to Stephen Wallace, who has done solid work in the past ("Blood Oath"), but it's an open secret in the Aussie film industry that he was fired during postproduction, so it's possible a more cohesive, less disappointing film might have been produced under his guidance. —*David Stratton*

ROCK-A-DOODLE
(ANIMATED)

A Samuel Goldwyn release of a Goldcrest presentation of a Sullivan Bluth Studios Ireland Ltd. production. Produced by Don Bluth, Gary Goldman, John Pomeroy. Executive producers, John Quested, Morris F. Sullivan. Directed by Bluth. Screenplay, David N. Weiss. In color; music, Robert Folks; songs, T.J. Kuenster; co-directors, Gary Goldman, Dan Kuenster. Reviewed at Preview 9, N.Y., March 16, 1992. MPAA Rating: G. Running time: **77 MIN.**
Edmond. . . . . . Tony Scott Granger
Voices of:
Chanticleer . . . . Glen Campbell
Goldie . . . . Ellen Greene
Grand Duke . . . Christopher Plummer
Hunch . . . . . Charles Nelson Reilly
Snipes . . . . Eddie Deezen
Patou . . . . Phil Harris
Peepers . . . . Sandy Duncan
Pinky . . . . Sorrell Booke

Don Bluth's latest animated film, "Rock-A-Doodle," will entertain young children while underwhelming adults in search of the next "Beauty and the Beast." Some of the musical numbers are catchy, and two scenes expertly combine live action with animation. But theatrical prospects are likely to be modest, with any profits to come from video sales down the road.

Following a quick use of computer animation, the story opens with a barnyard scene establishing the animated characters led by a singing rooster, Chanticleer (voiced by Glen Campbell), who performs the peppy opening song, "Sun Do Shine." Unfortunately, narration interrupts the tune.

Plot initially focuses on the rooster, who one day forgets to crow. When the sun comes up anyway, he feels unnecessary and runs off to the city. After his departure, the Grand Duke (Christopher Plummer) whips up a storm that threatens the farm animals.

From the animated world, Bluth shifts to a live action scene in which a mother is reading the Chanticleer story to her son (Tony Scott Granger). The kid enters the animated world when Plummer's evil owl character appears in the boy's bedroom and turns him into a kitten.

Granger and the animals head for the city, via the sewer, in search of Chanticleer. It turns out he has become an Elvis Presley-like rock star called "The King," whose shows feature incredibly elaborate sets. Following a fast-paced chase, a predictable showdown ensues between the delightfully evil Plummer and the saccharine-sweet animals. Campbell finally gives up showbiz for the barnyard, and sunny weather returns.

The final production number, "Tyin' Your Shoes," is sure to alienate kids over five and is not likely to become a chartbuster. But the scene features a skillful mix of live action and animation as Granger, in human form, rejoins the animated characters.

This finale provides the technical highpoint, and there is solid animation throughout the film. Although Sullivan Bluth's work lacks the lush detail of the best Disney animation, it is vastly superior to most TV cartoons.

Pic's weak spot is the script, marked by ponderous narration and only a few laughs. Another flaw is the lack of leading female characters; Ellen Greene plays the rooster's ditzy blonde g.f. (a pheasant) and is given little chance to sing.

On the plus side, T.J. Kuenster's songs are quite lively, and they're given added punch by Campbell and the Jordanaires, Presley's original backup group. Between musical numbers, though, "Rock-A-Doodle" tends to lose its bounce.

— *William Stevenson*

FOREVER
(BRAZILIAN-ITALIAN)

A Scena Film-Reteitalia SPA-Cinearte production. Produced by Anibal Massaini Neto, Augusto Caminito. Directed by Walter Hugo Khouri. Screenplay, Khouri, Lauro César Muniz, Anthony Foutz. Camera (color), José Duarte de Aguiar; editor, Gino Bartolini, Eder Mazini; music, Carlo & Paolo Rustichelli; art direction, Duarte de Aguiar; sound, Roberto Petrozzi. Reviewed at V America Festival, AFI, Washington, D.C., Oct. 25, 1991. **96 MIN.**
Marcelo Rondi . . . . Ben Gazzara
Berenice Rondi . . . . . . Eva Grimaldi
Also with: Gióia Scola, Corinne Clery, Janet Agren, Cecil Thiré.
(*English language*)

Sao Paulo filmmaker Walter Hugo Khouri's latest effort is a pretentious psychological case study of an Electra complex. Pic seems to meander forever before getting to its point.

Set up as a quasi-mystery, "Forever" stars Ben Gazzara as a rich Sao Paulo businessman. When he's discovered dead of a heart attack, the police begin an investigation centering on an unknown woman, his final companion.

The businessman's brooding daughter (Eva Grimaldi) leads the quest, obsessively searching her father's clandestine love nest and discovering a slew of affairs. Through her eyes, pic becomes a tapestry of memories, flashbacks and incriminations as the identity of the end pal takes on the importance of a murder suspect.

The woman must come to grips with her father's sensuality, determining that she and her mother were not the only women in his life. But her search is also a circle, where memories bring her around to the beginning, only to discover that she herself was her father's final affair.

Unrelenting and strident tale quickly wears thin, and the endless shots of Grimaldi's listless face as she observes recreations of Dad's liaisons are numbing.

Tech credits are okay. Acting is uneven. Gazzara's performance is reduced to a series of poses, presenting few opportunities to show the complex character he is meant to portray. — *Paul Lenti*

SMALL KILL

A Rayfield Co. II production & release. Produced by Fred Carpenter, Tom Poster. Executive producers, Sid Farber, Alan Frankel, Leonard Weintraub. Directed by Rob Fresco. Gary Burghoff's scenes co-directed by Burghoff. Screenplay, Carpenter, James McTernan; camera (Technicolor), Gerard Hughes; editor, Suzanne Pillsbury; music, Mark Leggett; art direction, Jack Parente; sound (Dolby), Sandi Morrof, Jim Combs; assistant director, Krystie Lomax; special makeup effects, Bryant Holt; 2nd unit director, Phyllis Alia; 2nd unit camera, Norman Rafsol; line producer, Denise Conway; associate producers, McTernan, Christopher Cooke, Ruth Doering, Michael Nolan; casting, McTernan. Reviewed at Technicolor screening room, N.Y., Feb. 25, 1992. No MPAA Rating. Running time: **87 MIN.**
Fleck/Lady Esmerelda . Gary Burghoff
Mikie . . . . Jason Miller
Armand Conti . . . . . Fred Carpenter
Marty Bannon . . . . Donni Kehr
Dianna Conti . . . . . Rebecca Ferratti
Sharif . . . . Mark McKelvey
Capt. Jacobson . . . Christopher Cooke
Jonathan Barnes . . . . . . Tom Poster
Thomas Stanzak . . . . . Allan Popper
Jasmine . . . . Dona Monique

Gary Burghoff, likable "Radar" in TV's "Mash," becomes a heavy with excellent results in "Small Kill." Low-budget police thriller is debuting theatrically on its home turf on Long Island in April, with a Showtime cablecast to follow.

Burghoff toplines as a kidnapper of children who's working for a local drug lord (Mark Mc-Kelvey). He has an interesting m.o. using bank clerks to scout for families with the ability to pay before snatching their kids.

The diminutive actor underplays and uses a chilling vocal pattern to shake any image of his previous nice-guy roles. Script also paints the character as a pervert, with plenty of menace generated as to whether he will kill or abuse the children.

Young cops on the case Fred Carpenter (who also co-produced and co-scripted the feature) and Donni Kehr are new faces who make a comfortable team. Kehr is the self-destructive one, a recovering alcoholic, while Carpenter is the family man, replete with supportive wife Rebecca Ferratti (a former Playboy model).

Debuting director Rob Fresco keeps the suspense alive and handles action scenes well. Supporting cast is effective, with a nice turn by Jason Miller as a friendly

wino and sexy bit by Dona Monique as a stripper/prostitute almost as dangerous as Burghoff.

Film has an unusual end credit noting that Burghoff co-directed his scenes. Tech contributions including gory makeup effects are well done.

— *Lawrence Cohn*

LA BELLE HISTOIRE
(THE BEAUTIFUL STORY)
(FRENCH)

An AFMD release of a Les Films 13-TFI Films co-production. Produced, directed, written by Claude Lelouch. Camera (color), Jean-Yves Le Mener; editor, Helene de Luze; music, Francis Lai, Philippe Servain; costumes, Mimi Lempicka; sound, Harald Maury. Reviewed at Palais des Congres, Paris, March 18, 1992. Running time: **212 MIN.**
Jesus . . . . Gerard Lanvin
Odona . . . . Beatrice Dalle
Simon Choulel . . . . . Vincent Lindon
Marie . . . . Marie-Sophie L.
Pierre Lhermitte . . . Patrick Chesnais
Policeman . . . . Gerard Darmon

Claude Lelouch's "The Beautiful Story" is an epic romance that teases and entertains for 3 1/2 hours. Drawn-out yet mostly upbeat, pic has a mix of slowly converging contempo and flashback portraits making it too elusive for young audiences and too long-winded for adults. But with judicious cuts to speed up the destined romance between a gypsy chief and a sexy thief, pic's attractive cast and gypsy culture should generate solid B.O. at art houses.

Lelouch expands his past interest in life's coincidences to a full-blown theory of transmigrating souls, explained in voiceover. To make theory credible, he takes three hours to arrange the first meeting between a dark, handsome gypsy (Gerard Lanvin) and a spunky con woman (Beatrice Dalle).

Trouble is, director favors loosely intertwined plots padded with quasi-historical flashbacks: Lanvin performs a miracle by taming wild bees for a hillside leper community that's later slaughtered by Roman soldiers. Frequent inserts of the massacre, to reveal modern characters' prescience, come across as a labored message.

Pic's look shifts rapidly from careening pans of the Roman massacre to loving long shots of the gypsies' favorite circus ride. Extreme closeups and zooms complete pic's assertion of a turbu-

lent fate that pretty much knows what humans are up to. In the final reel's first meeting between the gypsy, played with casual grace by Lanvin, and Dalle's engaging, easygoing trickster, the conwoman, as in ancient times, is quickly lovestruck, though it takes a plane crash to bring them together and eliminate her lover (Patrick Chesnais) and Lanvin's true love —the gypsies' ethereal new schoolteacher (Marie-Sophie L.).

Too bad he didn't fret more about repeating his catchy theme song, Francis Lai and Philippe Servain's gypsy-like "La Belle Histoire." Tune drives home love's destiny at every juncture. Slightly more subtle is helmer's moralizing about Dalle bedding every man who can help her.

On the plus side, stagy scenes of gypsy dancing and torrid singing never fail to entertain, and the anecdotal thieving of Dalle and her blond pal also amuse.

Lelouche leans on heart-warming notes while offering excellent tech credits and sentimental classics by Jacques Brel and Charles Trenet. By the last obvious roll of fortune's wheel, the central lovers are finally together, and filmgoers can let out 'a big "ouf" — a French sigh of relief. — *Lee Lourdeaux*

BORDER LINE
(FRENCH-SWISS)

An Amorces Diffusion release of a Gemini Films (France)-SGCC (France)-Light Night (Switzerland) co-production with the participation of Canal Plus, the CN, L'Office Federale de la Culture (Berne) & TSR. Executive producer, Michel Mavros. Produced by Paolo Branco. Directed, written by Danièle Dubroux. Camera (color), Fabio Conversi; editor, Jean-François Naudon; music, Jean-Marie Senia; set design, Patrick Durand; costumes, Françoise Clavel; sound, Henri Maikoff, Jean-Paul Loublier; associate producer, Jean-Bernard Feteux; assistant director, Gilles Chevalier. Reviewed at MGM screening room, Paris, Feb. 11, 1992. Running time: **90 MIN.**
Hélène . . . . Danièle Dubroux
Julien . . . . David Leotard
Alexandre . . . . . . André Dussollier
Georges Birsky . . . . . Jacques Nolot
Irène . . . . Manuella Gourary
Also with: Marie-Christine Questerbert, Linda de Nazelle.

Quirky, suspenseful and very well acted, "Border Line" stars helmer/scripter Danièle Dubroux as a 40-something woman who impulsively leaves her husband for a 22-year-old man. Thoughtfully lensed tale, which defies expectations at most turns in its offbeat plot, could have modest international

al art house potential and would be a plus for any film fest interested in femme directors.

Hélène (Dubroux), who restores paintings, is married to Alexandre (André Dussollier), a heart specialist. Not having seen former flame Charles for over 20 years, Hélène goes to his Paris apartment only to be told by his son, Julien, that Charles was recently killed in an accident. Within days, Hélène and Julien are passionately involved. The intrigue revolves around Hélène's growing conviction that she and Julien are genetically linked.

Pic's title refers to the psychiatric designation "border line case." Dubroux (who bears a light resemblance to Charlotte Rampling) conveys budding and purposeful madness with perfect control. Dussollier is convincing as a cardiologist who can't fathom the workings of his own wife's heart. Manuella Gourary as an aging would-be starlet turned pedicurist is endearingly low-rent.

Helmer is fond of expressive closeups and telling visual details drawn from the Paris surroundings with literary finesse. Dialogue is often laugh-out-loud funny.

Suspense is carefully modulated from the start, aided by Jean-Marie Senia's intelligent score. Apart from a final, unnecessary flashback, helmer's third feature is self-assured and entertaining. — *Lisa Nesselson*

EN DAG I OKTOBER
(A DAY IN OCTOBER)
(DANISH)

A Egmont Film release of a Kenneth Madsen-Panorama Film Intl. production. Produced by Just Betzer, Philippe Rivier, Pernille Siesbye. Directed by Kenneth Madsen. Screenplay, Damian F. Slattery. Camera (color), Henning Kristiansen; art direction, Sven Wichmann; sound, Stig Sparre-Ulrich. Reviewed at Palads theater screening room, Sept. 5, 1991. Running time: **97 MIN.**
With: D.B. Sweeney, Kelly Wolf, Tovah Feldshuh, Daniel Benzali, Ole Lemmeke.
(*English language*)

First-time feature helmer Kenneth Madsen simply and suspensefully depicts the 1943 evacuation of Danish Jews to neutral Sweden. With Yank headliners and English-language, home B.O. has proved disappointing, but abroad, pic should have appeal on home-vid and TV.

Madsen, who has helmed blurbs and musicvids in the U.S.,

makes a sympathetic bow with this straightforward Resistance fight drama. Yank Damian Slattery also provides solid, no-nonsense craftsmanship in his screenplay based on the Danes' bold rescue of nearly all Danish Jews from German-occupied Denmark.

Plot centers around a Jewish family living comfortably in a Copenhagen suburb. The head of the family, a bookkeeper (Daniel Benzali), believes in minding his own business, even when the Nazis take over the radio factory he works at in order to produce rocket bomb parts.

The war nevertheless enters Benzali's backyard when Resistance fighters try to sabotage the bomb components. They miss the target, and all are killed except one (D.B. Sweeney). Seriously wounded, he is found by the bookkeeper's young daughter (Kelly Wolf), who, much to the horror of her mother (Tovah Feldshuh), brings him home.

Nursed back to health, Sweeney convinces the father to use his factory position to hide a time bomb. Shortly thereafter, Sweeney and comrades find out a major raid on Danish Jews is planned. A large-scale rescue is set afoot.

Sweeney is convincing and likable as the young Resistance fighter, and Wolf is a sweet, vulnerable love interest. Seasoned Broadway thesps Benzali and Feldshuh deliver fine perfs, and talented Danish actor Ole Lemmeke makes a scary heavy.

Tech credits are uniformly fine. Lensing by Henning Kristiansen is simple but suitably moody; art director Sven Wichmann evokes a convincing flashback to the occupied Denmark.

— *Peter Risby Hansen*

SANTA BARBARA

A MIDNIGHT CLEAR

An InterStar release of a Beacon Communications presentation of an A&M Films production. Produced by Dale Pollock, Bill Borden. Executive producers, Armyan Bernstein, Tom Rosenberg, Marc Abraham. Directed by Keith Gordon. Screenplay, Gordon, based on William Wharton's novel. Camera (Alpha Cine color; CFI prints), Tom Richmond; editor, Don Brochu; music, Mark Isham; production design, David Nichols; art direction, David Lubin; costume design, Barbara Tfank; sound (Dolby), John (Earl) Stein; assistant director, Scott Javine; production manager-associate producer, Margaret Hilliard; stunt coordinator, Steve Davison; casting, Gary Zuckerbrod. Reviewed at Planet Hollywood screening room, N.Y., March 17, 1992.

(In Santa Barbara Film Festival). MPAA Rating: R. Running time: **107 MIN.**
Will Knott . . . . Ethan Hawke
Bud Miller . . . . Peter Berg
Mel Avakian . . . . Kevin Dillon
Stan Shutzer . . . . Arye Gross
Vince (Mother) Wilkins . . Gary Sinise
Paul (Father) Mundy . . Frank Whaley
Major Griffin . . . . . John C. McGinley
Also with: Larry Joshua, David Jensen, Curt Lowens, Rachel Griffin.

A powerful evocation of the absurdity of war, "A Midnight Clear" benefits from solid ensemble acting. Good reviews could overcome the inevitable audience resistance to this uncommercial genre.

Keith Gordon, the actor who debuted as director with "The Chocolate War," has done an effective job adapting the novel by William Wharton ("Birdy"). Set in December, 1944, in the Ardennes Forest, tale concerns six young G.I.s sent on a hopeless mission by their martinet of a commander, perfectly cast John C. McGinley.

Ethan Hawke, maturing with each succeeding role, is the narrator and squad leader. The ringer amongst them is the eldest soldier whom they call Mother, Gary Sinise, shown at film's outset going crazy. The other soldiers cover for him, eventually causing pic's violent climax.

The squad occupies an abandoned mansion near a group of German soldiers who make cryptic contacts with the G.I.s. The Germans, led by Curt Lowens, agree to surrender if a fake skirmish is staged, but Sinise innocently botches that operation with fatal results. Hawke fabricates a cover story, then escapes with his men from a massive German offensive after McGinley predictably abandons his men. Ironic finale has Hawke ingeniously outwitting the enemy, only to find himself ordered back into combat.

Tightly directed by Gordon with a minimum of sentimentality, film harks back to numerous war pics of the late '60s that emphasized the futility of the situation ("Castle Keep," "The Long Day's Dying"). It's virtually an all-male cast, save for Rachel Griffin who's sympathetic in a silent role as the lonely woman who services the heroes on a weekend pass in flashback.

Hawke is consistently forceful and believable in the central role, well-teamed with Peter Berg and Kevin Dillon as dogfaces who luckily don't have his responsibilities. Arye Gross provides needed comic relief as a Jewish sol-

dier who ends up acting as interpreter with the friendly Germans, and Sinise is subtle as the unit's burnt-out case.

Park City, Utah, locations provide the proper atmosphere, and Tom Richmond's photography captures a nearly monochrome look in color against snowy backgrounds. Mark Isham's frankly anachronistic score (with modern instrumentation) provides an ethereal fantasy mood to the already abstract story.

— *Lawrence Cohn*

ALL-AMERICAN MURDER

A Prism Entertainment release of an Enchantment Pictures presentation, in association with Greenwich Films. Produced by Bill Novodor. Executive producers, Barry Barnholtz, Jonathan Stathakis. Directed by Anson Williams. Screenplay-co-producer, Barry Sandler. Camera (Allied-WBS color), Geoff Schaaf; editor, Jonas Thaler; music, Rod Slane; art direction, Jim French; production manager-line producer, Tom Held Jr.; sound (Ultra-Stereo), Walt Banfield; assistant director, Scott A. Clark; associate producer, Slane; casting, Penny Perry, Annette Benson, Beverly Grantham (Oklahoma). Reviewed on Prism vidcassette, N.Y. (In Santa Barbara Film Festival.) MPAA Rating: R. Running time: **93 MIN.**
P.J. Decker . . . . Christopher Walken
Artie Logan . . . . . Charlie Schlatter
Tally Fuller . . . . Josie Bissett
Lou Alonzo . . . . Richard Kind
Erica Darby . . . . . . Joanna Cassidy
Doug Sawyer . . . . Mitchell Anderson
Wendy . . . . Amy Davis
Also with: J.C. Quinn, Craig Stout, Woody Watson, Angie Brown.

Barry Sandler's quirky "All-American Murder" is an unusual film debunking the American Dream within the format of a murder mystery. Picture is being aimed directly at the video market, bypassing theatrical exposure.

Sandler's scripts for the gay-themed "Making Love" and Ken Russell's "Crimes of Passion" are solid preparation for this very strange tale. Russell was set to direct it for Vestron in 1989, but project was canceled when that distrib's financial woes hit home, with former TV actor Anson Williams getting the assignment two years later.

Young Charlie Schlatter stars as the new kid in school, immediately seduced by the dean's wife (Joanna Cassidy). After the conquest she tells him: "Last month alone I knocked off more undergraduates than Kent State," typical of Sandler's unrelenting black humor and fresh wit.

Schlatter gets a crush on beau-

tiful blonde coed Josie Bissett, and when she's burned to death in a fire, he gets blamed. It seems that Schlatter has a history of pyromania, making him an excellent fall guy.

With weird, tongue-in-cheek detective Christopher Walken assigned to the case, Schlatter is given a long leash to investigate himself. As a string of murders ensues Sandler injects effective red herrings (Schlatter's dad is a prominent judge, while Bissett's pop is a right-wing senator). Final twist is true to pic's anti-establishment theme and very surprising in its revelation about the true facts.

Schlatter is quite effective in a role reminiscent of Christian Slater's definitive turn in "Heathers." Film's chief drawback is that topbilled Walken is written out of most of the middle section, a shame since his flippant attitude is a key element to enjoying Sandler's off-kilter point-of-view.

Bissett makes a strong impression as the heroine hiding a secret life. Film's message and unclassifiable genre present a challenge to find an audience. Since direct-to-video releases are usually routine genre pics or leftover, would-be theatricals, its release experiment could prove interesting. — *Lawrence Cohn*

WHERE SLEEPING DOGS LIE

An August Entertainment release of a Sotela Pictures production. Produced by Mario Sotela. Executive producer, Paul Mason. Directed by Charles Finch. Screenplay, Yolande Turner, Finch. Camera (CFI color), Monty Rowan; editor, B.J. Sears, Gene M. Gemaine; music, Hans Zimmer, Mark Mancina; production design, Eve Cauley; art direction, Lisa Snyder; costume design, Lynn Pickwell; sound (Ultra-Stereo), Virgil Clemintine; assistant director, Bruce Franklin; stunt coordinator, Clay Boss; co-producer, Finch; casting, Kimba Hills. Reviewed at Broadway screening room, N.Y., Nov. 13, 1991. (In Santa Barbara Film Festival.) MPAA Rating: R. Running time: **89 MIN.**
Bruce Simmons . . Dylan McDermott
Eddie Hale . . . . Tom Sizemore
Serena Black . . . . Sharon Stone
Also with: Mary Woronov, David Combs, Shawne Rowe, Jillian McWhirter, Brett Cullen, Richard Zavaglia, Ron Karabatsos.

A clash of two dissimilar personalities is examined with mixed success in the thriller "Where Sleeping Dogs Lie." Restrained approach compared to recent films like "Cape Fear" spells modest box office.

Dylan McDermott portrays an

unsuccessful writer in Hollywood who's frustrated by the commercial need to write blood-and-guts stories. His agent Sharon Stone puts on the pressure, and he decides to write a detailed novel about a mass killer.

McDermott has just been evicted from his flat and moves into the creepy old mansion his day job real estate boss (Ron Karabatsos) has ordered him to sell. Gimmick is that he uses the house for inspiration, basing his novel on a notorious murder case that took place there.

Before the film can turn into a haunted house suspenser, Tom Sizemore shows up as a twitchy boarder. McDermott is mean to him, flaunting an air of superiority, but before long the tables are turned.

Director Charles Finch (son of the late actor Peter Finch) and his mother, co-scripter Yolande Turner, get good mileage from the insidious relationship that develops between the two protagonists, reminiscent of the Joseph Losey/Harold Pinter classic "The Servant."

Film requires a great deal of audience willingness to go along with several far-fetched plot twists, notably in McDermott's character. However, both leads' good acting makes it worth the effort, leading to an unsettling ending.

McDermott is properly macho and overbearing in an interesting departure from his previous straight-arrow roles ("The Blue Iguana," "Hardware"). Sizemore makes a strong impression as the unctuous worm who turns.

Stone ("Basic Instinct") is perfect in a small role as the bitchy agent. Rest of the cast has mere walk-ons in a film that reportedly was heavily trimmed to reach its current release version. Result is a vignette structure with little continuity between individual scenes.

Hans Zimmer and Mark Mancina's melodramatic score does a great job of setting and maintaining the creepy atmosphere.
— *Lawrence Cohn*

CARTAGENA FEST

O CORPO
(THE BODY)
(BRAZILIAN)

An Olympus Filme-Cine Arte Produces Cinematograficas-Embrafilme-

Distruidora de Filmes production & release. Directed by José Antonio García. Screenplay, Alfredo Oroz, based on Clarice Lispector's novel. Camera (color), Antonio Meliande, editors, Daniel Tadeu, Eder Mazini; music, Paulo Barnabé. Reviewed at 32nd Cartagena (Colombia) Intl. Film Festival, March 13, 1992. Running time: **85 MIN.**
Xavier . . . . Antonio Fagundes
Carmen . . . . Marieta Severo
Bia . . . . Claudia Gimenez
Policeman . . . . . . Sergio Mamberti
Monica . . . . Carla Camurati

An amusing black comedy, "The Body" is the picaresque tale of a philandering pharmacy owner who lives for love to the envy of all his male neighbors and friends. Picking up three awards at the Cartagena fest, including top pic, this commercial venture might find some crossover acceptance abroad.

Pic chronicles the sporting life of a dandy (Antonio Fagundes) who lives with two women while maintaining an affair with a cabaret singer on the side. When the two wives discover this infidelity, he is killed, and they move on to find a new mate.

The characters are aptly developed, especially the two wives who have formed a bond. Beautiful, cerebral Claudia Gimenez is decisive, while fleshy, concupiscent Marieta Severo is not so much bothered by her husband's infidelity than that the other woman might have cooked for him.

The ending is somewhat predictable, but other disquieting elements are on target, including the police investigator, who lets the women go free because he doesn't want their crime to interfere with his early retirement plans.

Tech credits are okay.
— *Paul Lenti*

DISPAREN A MATAR
(SHOOT TO KILL)
(VENEZUELAN)

A Foncine release of a Caralcine-Televisión Española (TVE)-Sociedad Estatal Quinto Centenario production. Executive producer, Donald Meyerson. Produced by Adolfo López Sojo. Directed by Carlos Azpurúa. Screenplay, David Suárez. Camera (color), Adriano Moreno; editor, Sergio Curiel; music, Waldemar D'Lima; art direction, Gilberto Pulido, Milton Crespo; sound, Carlos Bolívar. Reviewed at 32nd Cartagena (Colombia) Intl. Film Festival (competition), March 12, 1992. Running time: **90 MIN.**
Mercedes . . . . . . Amalia Pérez Díaz
Santiago . . . . . . Jeancarlo Simancas
Castro Gil . . . . . . Daniel Alvarado
Also with: Flor Núñez, Miguel Angel Landa, Héctor Meyerston, Víctor Cuica.

First fiction feature by veteran Venezuelan documaker Carlos Azpurúa, "Shoot to Kill" is a political thriller that has picked up a handful of international awards, including the top film prize at the 1991 Havana Film Festival and best first work at the Cartagena fest.

Although the script is well developed, Azpurúa gets caught up in the thesis and the resulting narrative tends to lack cinematic excitement. Yet, current political events in Venezuela make this ambitious pic particularly relevant.

Story begins as the police enact a sweep of a poor working-class neighborhood as a means to clean up crime. But things get out of hand and an innocent unnamed man is murdered while his mother looks on helplessly.

When the official version describes him as a desperate criminal, the mother (Amalia Pérez Díaz) goes to a reporter, whose work sparks an investigation. In an attempt to cover up the crime, the police kill a witness and intimidate the reporter and the woman's family. Although corruption wins out, the mother continues her fight.

Pacing is brisk, and Waldemar D'Lima's musical score is effective in maintaining tension. Thesping is also strong, especially Pérez Díaz in the role of Mercedes, while Daniel Alvarado's portrayal of the corrupt cop Castro Gil is villainy at its most evil.
— *Paul Lenti*

SHERLOCK HOLMES IN CARACAS
(VENEZUELAN)

A Foncine release of a Big Ben Prods., in association with Tiuna Films & Foncine. Produced by Franklin Whaite Jr., Juan Fresán. Directed, written by Fresán. Camera (color), Ricardo Younis; editor, Fresán, Carlos González; music, Miguel Noya. Reviewed at 32nd Cartagena (Colombia) Intl. Film Festival (Mecla market), March 13, 1992. Running time: **95 MIN.**
Sherlock Holmes
. . . . Jean Manuel Montesinos
Watson . . . . Gilbert Dacournan
Miss Parker . . . . . Carolina Luzardo
Ex-Miss Venezuela
. . . . María Eugenia Cruz
Also with: Giles Bickford, Richard Cumming, Chippili Ruthman.
(English language)

This curiosity owes more to the Firesign Theater's "Giant Rat of Sumatra" and Monty Python than to Arthur Conan

Doyle. Venezuelan filmmaker Juan E. Fresán's English-lingo venture "Sherlock Holmes in Caracas" is a self-conscious, low-budget, free-wheeling satirical mess that might possibly find homevideo interest.

Title is misleading since this deconstructed Holmes merely passes through Caracas on his way to Maracaibo to aid an old friend who is married to a former Miss Venezuela. Fantastic plot, which emerges late in the film, seems tacked on to give purpose to pic's constant mugging.

While weird dealings point to a pagan-worshiping governess, Holmes discovers that the ex-Miss Venezuela is really a vampire who threatens the lives of her children. In between, Holmes discusses his weak characterization, subtitles that draw attention to the sound effects, Watson shooting everything with his ubiquitous Betacam and lots of corny costumes and tropical sets.

Editing proceeds at a madcap pace, and the 20-gags-a-minute script actually pays off every once in a while. — *Paul Lenti*

NEWSIES

A Buena Vista release of a Walt Disney Pictures presentation, in association with Touchwood Pacific Partners I, of a Michael Finnell production. Produced by Finnell. Directed by Kenny Ortega. Screenplay, Bob Tzudiker, Noni White. Camera (Panavision, Technicolor), Andrew Laszlo; editor, William Reynolds; original songs, Jack Feldman, Alan Menken; songs orchestrated & conducted by Danny Troob; original underscore, J.A.C. Redford; production design, William Sandell; art direction, Nancy Patton; set design, Brad Ricker, Carl J. Stensel; set decoration, Robert Gould; costume design, May Routh; sound (Dolby), David Kelson; choreography, Ortega, Peggy Holmes; stunt coordinators, Michael M. Vendrell, Ceci Vendrell; special visual effects, Syd Dutton, Bill Taylor, Illusion Arts Inc.; associate producers, Ira Shuman, Marianne Sweeny; assistant director, Dennis M. White; casting, Elizabeth Leustig. Reviewed at El Capitan Theater, L.A., March 28, 1992. MPAA Rating: PG. Running time: **121 MIN.**

Jack Kelly/
  Francis Sullivan . . . Christian Bale
David Jacobs . . . . . . David Moscow
Les Jacobs . . . . Luke Edwards
Racetrack . . . . Max Casella
Crutchy . . . . Marty Belafsky
Boots . . . . Arvie Lowe
Mush . . . . Aaron Lohr
Bryan Denton . . . . . . Bill Pullman
Medda Larkson . . . . . Ann-Margret
Sarah Jacobs . . . . Ele Keats
Gov. Theodore
  Roosevelt . David James Alexander
Joseph Pulitzer . . . . . Robert Duvall
Weasel . . . . Michael Lerner
Snyder . . . . Kevin Tighe
Seitz . . . . Charles Cioffi
William Randolph Hearst . Ken Belsky

They should have filmed the pitch meeting for this project: "Hey, guys, I found a story I bet nobody's ever thought of making: How about a movie on the 1899 New York newsboys' strike? Robert Duvall's got a hole in his schedule; he could play Pulitzer." "Great! but let's get Ann-Margret and a lot of cute kids and make a musical!"

That Disney's "Newsies" is very well-crafted is almost incidental: Script seems cut out of whole cloth from an old Dead End Kids movie, and the number of people likely to get excited about the subject matter probably wouldn't fill a stadium.

A strange cross between "Oliver!" and Samuel Fuller's "Park Row," "Newsies" was made with care and affection by choreographer-turned-director Kenny Ortega. But writers Bob Tzudiker and Noni White have created cardboard cutouts instead of flesh-and-blood characters, and they've drawn the political issues in the broadest of strokes, without a trace of complexity or nuance.

Composer Alan Menken, whose music works hard at being rousing, badly misses lyricist Howard Ashman, his late partner: Jack Feldman's lyrics here are relentlessly banal and unmemorable, saddled with such Hell's Kitchen locutions as "Since when did you become me mud-dah?"

Cast has pleasant but ordinary voices, and it's only in the vigorous, "West Side Story"-style dancing, choreographed by Ortega and Peggy Holmes, that the film sporadically comes alive.

Making intelligent use of the wide Panavision frame with lenser Andrew Laszlo and editor William Reynolds, Ortega avoids the MTV fragmentation that's de rigueur in musicals today. Trained in the Gene Kelly school of movie tuners (Kelly receives a thank-you for his advice), Ortega keeps the dancers mostly in full frame and fills his space with graceful and visually striking movement. But the squeaky-clean look of what someone incongruously calls "these foul streets" works against pic's subject matter.

Christian Bale ("Empire of the Sun") plays the leader of the newsboys' walk-out against the penny-pinching Pulitzer (bearded Robert Duvall). Though Bale's "noivous" accent sounds like Huntz Hall, he's a charismatic figure, with a compelling blend of brashness and vulnerability.

Duvall is a cartoon figure of ranting hard-heartedness as publisher of the N.Y. World. He's colorless and lacks the wicked relish of a Thomas Nast caricature. Ann-Margret's Jenny Lind-like thrush, an improbable ally of the boys, is shoehorned into the film to provide s.a. in a male-dominated story. Only other female role of any substance is Ele Keats' bland tenement girl, who's around so Bale can serenade her and have someone to clinch at the end.

Bale's fellow newsies are lively and appealing, although the cast is a bit too heavy on white kids, and not all of them have that "touch of the gutter" Jimmy Cagney remembered from his childhood.

Audience can't help being 100% on the newsies' side when their commissions are cut by the ruthless Pulitzer, when "bulls" are sent by the corrupt city officials to break up the strike, and when justice triumphs in the end.

But the story's rougher edges are smoothed away, the social context is so broadly sketched and the black-and-white characterizations are so predictable that the story carries little emotional weight. Maybe "Newsies" shouldn't have been a musical.

If Warner Bros. had done the story back in the "Angels With Dirty Faces" era, it would have punched the audience in the gut with the newsboys' plight, making their story seem like something ripped from headlines rather than a distant, Disney-fied curiosity. — *Joseph McBride*

BEETHOVEN

A Universal Pictures release of an Ivan Reitman production. Produced by Joe Medjuck, Michael C. Gross. Executive producer, Reitman. Co-producer, Gordon Webb. Directed by Brian Levant. Screenplay, Edmond Dantes, Amy Holden Jones. Camera (DeLuxe color), Victor J. Kemper; editors, Sheldon Kahn, William D. Gordean; music, Randy Edelman; production design, Alex Tavoularis; art direction, Charles Breen; set design, Stan Tropp, Gary Diamond; set decoration, Gary Fettis; costume design, Gloria Gresham; sound (Dolby), Charles Wilborn; associate producer, Kahn; assistant director, Jerram A. Swartz; animal action coordinator, Karl Lewis Miller; casting, Steven Jacobs. Reviewed at Universal Studios screening room, Universal City, Calif., March 18, 1992. MPAA Rating: PG. Running time: **88 MIN.**

George Newton . . . . Charles Grodin
Alice Newton . . . . Bonnie Hunt
Dr. Varnick . . . . Dean Jones
Ryce . . . . Nicholle Tom
Ted . . . . Christopher Castile
Emily . . . . Sarah Rose Karr
Harvey . . . . Oliver Platt
Vernon . . . . Stanley Tucci
Brad . . . . David Duchovny
Brie . . . . ´. Patricia Heaton

Six-year-olds and animal rights activists should warm up to the titular big slobbering dog, his perfect family and the experimentation ring that brings them together, and the pic rallies at the end to prevent chaperoning adults from feeling their time was completely wasted. This could roll over into plenty of green.

The real star is a 185-pound St. Bernard. Stolen as a puppy, he stumbles into the Newton family's life. They are a demographically perfect group, with an uptight dad (Charles Grodin) who reluctantly agrees to adopt the beast.

Beethoven grows and, as only movie dogs can, manages to help the kids' lives in various creative ways, even as he mangles the house and antagonizes Dad. Ultimately, Grodin is forced into action when the dog becomes the victim of an animal-theft ring led by an oily vet (Dean Jones), leading to a resolution so predictable that even the youngest tots can feel smug in having guessed it.

Director Brian Levant cut his teeth directing sitcoms before turning to features with "Problem Child 2," and the influence shows, particularly in the cartoonish perfs he gets from villains.

Still, the largely mundane comic elements get a boost from the more dramatic finale, with the whole family riding to the rescue and giving the bad guys their comeuppance in a nice touch.

Grodin plays buttoned-up types better than anybody, but even he can't do much with Amy Holden Jones and Edmond Dantes' script. It does improve after initial bathroom humor.

Bonnie Hunt fares better as the understanding mom. Kids Nicholle Tom and Christopher Castile are agreeable, easier on the teeth than the average sitcom brood.

The film does warrant one caveat for its repeated habit of showing the big mutt being fed candy and other sweets, which, as any dog owner will tell you, are bad for dogs.

Tech credits are okay.
— *Brian Lowry*

MEMENTO MORI
(BRITISH-16m)

A BBC Television production, in association with WGBH/Boston & BBC Enterprises. Produced by Louis Marks. Executive producer, Mark Shivas. Directed by Jack Clayton. Screenplay, Alan Kelley, Jeanie Sims, Clayton, based on Muriel Spark's novel. Camera (color, 16m), Remi Adefarasin; editor, Mark Day; music, Georges Delerue; production design, Oliver Bayldon; costume design, Les Lansdown; sound, John Pritchard. Reviewed at Colour Film Services screening room, London, Mar. 27, 1992. Running time: **99 MIN.**

Dame Lettie Colston . . Stephanie Cole
Charmian Colston . . Renée Asherson
Godfrey Colston . . . Michael Hordern
Jean Taylor . . . . Thora Hird
Mabel Pettigrew . . . . . Maggie Smith
Guy Leet . . . . Maurice Denham
Percy Mannering . . . . . Cyril Cusack
Olive Mannering . . . Zoë Wanamaker
Henry Mortimer . . . . . . John Woo
  Also with: Elizabeth Bradley, Margery Withers, Barbara Hicks, Muriel Pavlow, Anna Cropper, Damaris Hayman, Paul Opacic.

Powerhouse casting and a peppy script almost make "Memento Mori" transcend its small-screen origins. Witty black comedy about a group of wrinklies thrown off-balance by threatening phone calls is a strong fest item on the strength of helmer Jack Clayton's name, even though it's unlikely to make the crossing to theatrical parlors.

Pic is the septuagenarian director's first feature since the Maggie Smith-Bob Hoskins starrer "The Lonely Passion of Judith Hearne" four years ago, as well as his first British TV movie. A pet project of Clayton's since the Muriel Spark novel was first published in 1959, the film airs April 19 as the closing item in the BBC's current Screen Two series, following a special director-attended screening at London's National Film Theater April 6.

Set in mid-'50s London, story centers on aging socialite Dame Lettie Colston (Stephanie Cole), her brother Godfrey (Michael Hordern) and his seemingly dotty wife Charmian (Renée Asherson), a former romantic novelist now enjoying a fresh rep. All of them receive anonymous calls in which a male voice announces, "Remember you must die."

Dame Lettie hires a former cop (John Wood) to investigate, but the calls keep coming to other members of the pensioners' circle. Meanwhile, the waspish Mabel Pettigrew (Maggie Smith), who's blackmailing Godfrey for a past indiscretion, takes over the job of Charmian's housekeeper/companion with her eyes on some disputed loot.

Despite its Agatha Christie-like premise, film is more a series of conversation pieces than a mystery-thriller. Clayton, his regular co-scripter Jeanie Sims and Alan Kelley preserve the essentials of Spark's novel while simplifying its tangled, character-strewn plot. Early problems in sorting out who's who quickly dissolve as the experienced thesps add their individual spins to the dialogue.

A-Z casting of Brit veterans put Smith in the meatiest role as the vengeful ladies' companion, spitting out her tart one-liners in familiar style. In the quieter but pivotal part of Charmian, Asherson grows as the pic progresses, handling the crucial final scene with warmth and mellow authority. Hordern as the lecherous Godfrey, Cole as the busybody sis, and Maurice Denham as a laid-back poet top playing that's strong down the line.

Despite the pic's often cramped look, Clayton keeps things moving with multiple setups that bespeak his feature experience, helped by Mark Day's tight cutting and mellifluous scoring by the late Georges Delerue. Remi Adafarasin's crisp lensing has a wintery, natural-light look. Period detail is fine.

— Derek Elley

ALLES LÜGE
(ALL LIES)
(GERMAN)

A Delta Filmverleih release of a Richard Claus production. Produced by Claus. Directed by Heiko Schier. Screenplay, Schier, Gerd Weiss. Camera (color), Jörg Jeshel; editor, Peter Adam; music, Piet Klocke; production design, Thomas Schappert; costumes, Maria Schicker; sound, Uwe Kersken. Reviewed at Kurbel cinema, Berlin, March 18, 1992. Running time: **87 MIN.**
Günter Kasulke . Dieter Hallervorden
Rudi Portmann . . . . Peter Fritz
Lizzy . . . . Billie Zöckler
Erich Honecker . . . . Himself
Rita . . . . Franziska Matthus
Hilde . . . . Petra Hinze
Also with: Corinna Kirchhoff, Florian Martens, Ottfried Fischer, Uli Anschütz.

Presence of cult comic Dieter Hallervorden should guarantee this pic a home audience, but foreign territories will be grateful their intelligence won't be insulted by this unimaginative, unfunny and occasionally offensive film.

Story revolves around an eastern German comedian's (Hallervorden) attempts to make it in reunified Berlin while locating his missing daughter. He hooks up with a rich and ditsy dame (Billie Zöckler) who tries to get into his pants, thinking he must be sex-starved after 40 years of socialism. Her husband (Peter Fritz) happens to be the comedian's ex-partner from the east who now runs a shady investment firm that bilks naive eastern Germans.

Comedy centers on sexual innuendo, airhead routines and slapstick. Gags are almost without exception not even remotely funny. Timing is off while the plot lumbers clumsily and aimlessly on. Towards pic's end, one scene is offensively homophobic.

Color is harsh and lurid, with a lighting mismatch at one point.

— Rebecca Lieb

BETTY
(FRENCH)

An MK2 release of an MK2 Prods.-CED Prods.-FR3 Films co-production with the participation of Canal Plus. (Intl. sales: MK2.) Produced by Marin Karmitz. Directed, written by Claude Chabrol, based on Georges Simenon's novel. Camera (color), Bernard Zitzermann; editor, Monique Fardoulis; music, Matthieu Chabrol; art direction, Jean-Pierre Lemoine, Pierre Galliard; set design, Franççoise Benoit-Fresco; costumes, Cristine Guegan; sound, Jean-Bernard Thomasson, Maurice Gilbert. Reviewed at Pathe Marignan Concorde, Paris, Feb. 7, 1992. Running time

100 MIN.
Betty . . . . Marie Trintignant
Laure . . . . Stéphane Audran
Mario . . . . . Jean-François Garreaud
Guy Etamble . . . . . Yves Lambrecht
Mme. Etamble . . Christiane Minazzoli
Also with: Pierre Vernier, Nathalie Kousnetzoff, Thomas Chabrol.

Claude Chabrol's recent heroines have gotten the guillotine ("Story of Women") and gobbled arsenic ("Madame Bovary"), but, as the title character in "Betty," Marie Trintignant makes a strong impression as a woman who chain-smokes, overdrinks, cheats on her husband and is basically rewarded for her behavior.

Adapted from a Georges Simenon novel, ferociously accurate portrait of two women who no longer fit the bourgeois mold could click as an art house item.

Well-dressed but disheveled Betty staggers out of a Paris bar with a peculiar man who drives her to an after-hours dive in Versailles. There she is befriended by stately and sympathetic Laure (Stéphane Audran), who takes the very drunk femme back to her posh hotel. Laure invites her to stay until she's feeling well again, which is convenient, since she has no place else to go.

Film alternates between hotel scenes and flashbacks. Betty, 28, caught in the act with an illicit suitor, was banished from home, husband and children in exchange for a generous allowance. Laure, a widow in her late 40s, was once happily married but has been living at the hotel and drinking at the dive for years. Her major source of joy seems to be trysts with the bar's proprietor.

Trintignant and Audran are compelling in their good manners (they never waver from the formal "vous," however intimate their confessions) and slightly twisted comportments. Under Chabrol's unforgiving glare, Trintignant's husband and in-laws are delectably pious. Mother-in-law announces that she saw a film about abortion that she didn't care for one bit — a self-mocking reference to Chabrol's "Story of Women."

Pic is a slightly deconstructed portrait of a free spirit boxed into the tedious, passionless confines of a bourgeois marriage. Story's tension springs from the fact that, as Laure extends greater kindness, Betty becomes more predatory.

Chronology juggling is engaging at first, but flashbacks and memory snippets eventually grow tiresome, despite convincing thesping. Literary sense of closure is marred as the last 15 minutes or so run out of visual steam, and helmer states the obvious in a wrapup voiceover.

— Lisa Nesselson

LADYBUGS

A Paramount release of a Ruddy & Morgan production. Produced by Albert S. Ruddy, Andre E. Morgan. Executive producer, Gray Frederickson. Co-executive producer, Lloyd Bloom. Directed by Sidney J. Furie. Screenplay, Curtis Burch. Camera (Deluxe color), Dan Burstall; editors, John W. Wheeler, Timothy N. Board; music, Richard Gibbs; production design, Robb Wilson King; set decoration, Penny Stames; costume design, Isis Mussenden; sound (Dolby), Jim Emerson; soccer technical advisor, Garry Moore; associate producer, Harry Basil; assistant directors, James Freitag, Newton Arnold; casting, Mike Fenton, Valorie Massalas. Reviewed at Mann Plaza Theater, West L.A., March 26, 1992. MPAA rating: PG-13. Running time: **90 MIN.**
Chester Lee . . . Rodney Dangerfield
Julie Benson . . . . Jackee
Matthew/Martha . . Jonathan Brandis
Bess . . . . Ilene Graff
Kimberly Mullen . . . . . Vinessa Shaw
Dave Mullen . . . . Tom Parks
Glynnis Mullen . . . . Jeanetta Arnett
Coach Annie . . . . . . Nancy Parsons
Coach Bull . . . . Blake Clark
Coach Cannoli . . . . . Tommy Lasorda

This picture doesn't deserve any respect. Sexist, homophobic and woefully unfunny to boot, Rodney Dangerfield's latest starring effort is a waste of comic talent. A klutzy would-be comedy about a girls' soccer team, "Ladybugs" will soon be booted off the screen.

Whatever happened to the Dangerfield who ate up the screen with bumptious glee in "Caddyshack" and "Back to School"? Either he has terrible taste in material or writers can't think up suitable settings for his sweaty, twitching middle-aged desperation.

In Curtis Burch's awful script, it seems Dangerfield is squirming not for comedy, but because he's trapped in an awful vehicle.

Paramount apparently thought it was ordering up another "Bad News Bears," but the garish "Ladybugs" has the look of a third-rate TV movie. Director Sidney J. Furie seems so bored with the material he doesn't even bother to stage his soccer scenes coherently.

As a salesman for a Colorado tycoon (Tom Parks), Dangerfield is put in charge of a soccer team. It's offensive enough that the pic mocks the girls' clumsiness (even stooping to fat jokes), but

"Coach" 's bright idea for turning them into winners is to have his fiancée's son join the team in drag.

Jonathan Brandis, saddled with a most embarrassing role, is the horny teen who makes minimal attempts to act like a girl but fools everyone anyway. Besides the notion girls are so inept they can't beat each other in sports without a boy's help, script peddles crude antigay and child-molestation jokes.

Pic's also inexplicably preoccupied with transvestism, which extends to a gratuitous scene of Dangerfield dressing up as Brandis' mother.

Most of the wisecracks the star gets here wouldn't go over with a drunken Vegas crowd. But mostly, the film turns Dangerfield into a dismayingly dull Mr. Nice Guy. "Have confidence in yourself," Brandis tells him. "You're a great guy, otherwise my mother wouldn't love you."

— *Joseph McBride*

BLOODLUST
(AUSTRALIAN)

A Windhover production. (Intl. sales: Kim Lewis Marketing.) Executive producers, Robert Ruggi, Mark Spratt. Produced, directed, written by Richard Wolstencroft, Jon Hewitt. Camera (color), Gary Ravenscroft; editors, Wolstencroft, Hewitt; production design, Nicolas Barclay; costumes, Anne Liedel; sound, Angie Black; music-sound effects, Ross Hazeldine. Reviewed at Barn Theater, Leura, Australia, March 29, 1992. Running time: **87 MIN.**
Lear . . . . Jane Stuart Wallace
Frank . . . . Kelly Chapman
Tad . . . . Robert James O'Neill
Brother Bem . . . . . . Phil Motherwell
Also with: Paul Moder, James Young, Max Crawdaddy, Ian Rilen, John Flaus, Colin Savage, Big Bad Ralph.

Striving for cult status, "Bloodlust" is a crudely made shlocker conceived along familiar lines. It contains enough sex, gore and drugs (as well as a punk rock score) to grab some bucks from the video market internationally, but theatrical possibilities are limited to fringe venues.

Pic, which never aims high but will probably hit its limited target, already opened in Melbourne at a small rep house, backed by an ad campaign noting that a print was recently seized by British customs, said to be a first for an Aussie film.

Yarn revolves around three hip, modern-day vampires roaming a city, leaving carnage in their wake. Opening sequences

intro Kelly Chapman as a voluptuous prostie who picks up a businessman in a hotel bar and feeds off him as she makes love; Jane Stuart Wallace as a svelte lesbian who slaughters a foot fetishist (John Flaus); and Robert James O'Neill as a long-haired punk who blows away a drug dealer.

On the trio's trail are a couple of dumb cops (with out-of-place phony Yank accents) and a religious cult, led by the murderous Phil Motherwell who believes a stake through the heart is the best form of conversion.

After a fair amount of bloody mayhem, coke-sniffing and raunchy sex, the vampires invade a drug den and walk off with $3 million. The dealer and his gang join in the chase, which climaxes in savage goings-on at a derelict country house.

Filmmakers Richard Wolstencroft and Jon Hewitt go for the jugular and don't worry about believable stunts or convincing makeup and effects. Entire film has a throwaway, cheesy look, with actors either overdoing it or delivering lines as if in a kindergarten play.

There's lashings of gore and a fair amount of softcore sex, all of which is presented in lieu of a coherent script or decent performances. The midnight crowd will accept anything, it seems to the filmmakers.

A prominent front-end credit is given to armorer John Fox who supplied extraordinary weaponry for the heavily armed ghouls, but this is pic's only original element. Revolting Cocks, Pailhead, Lead Into Gold and 1000 Homo DJs provided the music. — *David Stratton*

LES ENFANTS DU NAUFRAGEUR
(SHIPWRECKED CHILDREN)
(FRENCH)

A Gaumont release of a K'ien & Gaumont co-production. Produced by David Kodsi, Patrice Poiré. Directed by Jérôme Foulon. Screenplay, Foulon, François Cellier, Laurent Dusseaux. Camera (color), William Lubchansky; editor, Elisabeth Guido; music, François Staal; costumes, Brigitte Lauber; sound, Ricardo Castro. Reviewed at Pathe Montparnasse, Paris, Feb. 19, 1992. Running time: **138 MIN.**
Hélène . . . . Brigitte Fossey
Little Louis . . . . . . Jacques Dufilho
Paul . . . . Michel Robin
Old lame man . . . . Jean Marais
Captain . . . Pierre-Alexis Hollenbeck
Benoit . . . . Maxime Boidron
Also with: Amandine Dewasmes, Gary Ledoux, Elie Berder, Simon Poligne.

Suspenseful and sentimental, "Les Enfants du Naufrageur" is a children's murder mystery wrapped around the predictable story of a new schoolmarm in a small Brittany port. First feature by Jérôme Foulon should capture the market of French-speaking pre-teens.

Young helmer firmly anchors theme of "naufrageur" (anyone shipwrecked) with opening scenes of wild 10-year-olds stumbling on a reclusive old cripple, then flocking to port-side home of a beloved widowed teacher. Her sudden death and disappearance of her life savings trigger kiddy inquest and a homemade newspaper. Junior journalists pull pranks on uncooperative interviewees.

Imaginative, high-energy story line gives way to unsurprising scenes of Brigitte Fossey as the patient new teacher who must win over eight resentful pupils. Still, pic's slower midsection skillfully lays the groundwork for later tearful account of the old woman's death.

Lenser William Lubchansky's superb shots of Brittany coast add gritty energy to the port setting. Lensing also sets up naturalist scenes of claustrophobic village life in homes, church and pub, including convincing stereotypes of a tough bar owner, randy young laborer and ornery handyman. In this decidedly un-Disney port, none of the youngsters wants to grow up to be one of the "shipwrecked" locals.

Jean Marais limps on in a cameo as the old man who can't stay away from the old teacher's door. Tech credits are excellent.

— *Lee Lourdeaux*

STRAIGHT TALK

A Buena Vista release of a Hollywood Pictures presentation in association with Touchwood Pacific Partners I, produced in association with Sandollar Prods. Produced by Robert Chartoff, Fred Berner. Executive producers, Sandy Gallin, Carol Baum, Howard Rosenman. Directed by Barnet Kellman. Screenplay, Craig Bolotin, Patricia Resnick, from Bolotin's story. Camera (Technicolor), Peter Sova; editor, Michael Tronick; music, Brad Fiedel; original songs written & performed by Dolly Parton; production design, Jeffrey Townsend; art direction, Michael T. Perry; set design, Suzan Wexler; set decoration, Daniel L. May; costume design, Jodie Tillen; sound (Dolby), Glenn Williams; associate producer, Lynn Hendee; assistant director, John T. Kretchmer; 2nd unit directors, Townsend (Ill.), Victor Hammer (Ga.); 2nd unit camera (Ill.), Alan Thatcher; 2nd unit assistant director (Ill.), Tom Busch; casting, Mary Gail Artz, Barbara Cohen. Reviewed at GCC Avco Cinema, West L.A., April 1, 1992. MPAA Rating: PG. Running time: **91 MIN.**
Dr. Shirlee Kenyon . . . . Dolly Parton
Jack Russell . . . . James Woods
Alan Riegert . . . . . . Griffin Dunne
Steve Labell . . . . . Michael Madsen
Lily . . . . Deirdre O'Connell
Guy Girardi . . . . John Sayles
Janice . . . . Teri Hatcher
Dr. Erdman . . . . Spalding Gray
Milo Jacoby . . . . Jerry Orbach
Gene Perlman . . . . Philip Bosco
Tony . . . . Charles Fleischer
Gordon . . . . Keith MacKechnie
Zim Zimmerman . . . . . . Jay Thomas
Ann . . . . Amy Morton

Notion of Dolly Parton as a radio talk show personality might seem like hiding a big part of her appeal, but the infectious "Straight Talk" is perfectly tailored to her down-home charm. Glib but sunny romantic comedy, in which she's oddly but effectively paired with cynical Chi reporter James Woods, should be a B.O. winner.

Borrowing liberally from the classic "Mr. Deeds Goes to Town," with its story of a successful smalltown bumpkin conned by a big-city reporter feigning romantic interest to get material for an exposé, pic has Parton in the Gary Cooper role and Woods in Jean Arthur's. Major diff between the pics is "Straight Talk's" relative lack of interest in social issues. But Parton's winning personality shines in the amusing, if superficial, screenplay.

After leaving Flat River, Ark., to seek a better life, former dance teacher Parton is mistakenly hired as a radio psychologist and immediately captivates listeners with her folksy, blunt and empathetic approach to self-help.

She's a natural listener who likes people and has an endless supply of earthy aphorisms and advice. Her gift of gab, which she says she learned at "Screw U.," makes her believable as an overnight success in the big city, and the film has fun with her mildly outrageous interchanges with callers.

She meets-cute with Woods on the Irv Kupcinet Bridge after he spies her from a window in the Sun-Times office and mistakenly thinks she's committing suicide. Realizing something's amiss when this blue-collar country gal reappears as a radio "doctor of the heart," he starts digging into her past, prodded by his heartless "Front Page"-style editor, Jerry Orbach.

Although she initially resists the idea of masquerading as something she's not, Parton craves success (a pink Mercedes, a high-rise apartment) badly enough to go along with the deception engineered by hyperkinetic station program director Griffin Dunne, who's terrified she'll be unmasked, not realizing the audience wouldn't care if she's not a real doctor.

Woods isn't a conventional leading man, but that's an asset here, since he fits effortlessly into his role and is credible in his slippery behavior as he woos the guileless Parton for a story. Unlike in "Mr. Deeds," the reporter never prints the exposé, but quits his job instead after realizing that he's falling in love.

Parton's willingness to be corrupted is a telling commentary on the 1990s success ethic, but Woods' preemptive change of heart robs the film of sting. Pic also raises questions about the ethics of radio therapy that it too easily dismisses.

Parton's advice to one of her call-in guests — a recovering alcoholic whom she advises to dump his boozing wife — backfires when the woman (Amy Morton) angrily confronts her in person. Parton guiltily decides to quit the show, but the public and Woods persuade her to return.

Film seems to rush to a conclusion at this point (it runs only 91 minutes), leaving the feeling that a third act went unfilmed. A more probing exploration of the responsibility radio psychologists bear toward their public would have made for a comedy with more social resonance.

Barnet Kellman's TV-style direction is efficient but tends to be visually static, and doesn't loosen up enough to use the Chicago setting more than perfunctorily. Tech credits are OK, and Parton's song score is pleasant, though it sometimes gets in the way of the dialogue.

— *Joseph McBride*

CARTAGENA FEST

JOLIGUD
(HOLLYWOOD)
(VENEZUELAN)

A Foncine release of a Kromática Producciones Audiovisuales production. Produced by Yajaira Jaume Maya. Directed by Augusto César Pradelli Vaccariello. Screenplay, Pradelli Vaccariello, Consuelo González, based on Rutilio Ortega's book "Crónicas de El Saladillo." Camera (color)-editor, Ricardo Rubio; music, Daniel Castro, Claudio Ocando. Reviewed at 32d Cartagena (Colombia) Intl. Film Festival (Mecla market), March 13, 1992. Running time: **80 MIN.**

Sarita Estuche . . . . . . Marau Robelo
Vicentico Ferrebus . . Vidal Figueroa
Yeguita Papilunga . . . Fátima Colina
Also with: Gustavo Hidalgo, Héctor Peña, Juana Rivero.

"Joligud" is being touted as an example of Venezuela's regional filmmaking, but, besides the amusing phonetic title, short pic is a confused mess that loses its sense of purpose en route and ends up in cinematic limbo.

Concerning the Maracaibo working-class neighborhood of El Saladillo (torn down in '71 as part of a big renovation project), pic is based on Rutilio Ortega's popular slice-of-life book on the lives of the nabe's inhabitants.

Director Augusto César Pradelli Vaccariello loses control of the material early on and never decides what type of film he's making. Although pic brims with characters, mostly well played by nonpros, it centers on the ambitions of a local beauty (Marau Robelo) whom the neighbors groom for Hollywood fame. They send photos of her to "Metro Gordon Meyer, Joligud, U.S.," and wait for a studio rep who never arrives. Despite Robelo's dominance of the film, she speaks only one word — "nothing."

Somewhere in all this, film makes a point that the life of the neighborhood will supposedly continue to haunt the area. Unfortunately, Pradelli Vaccariello indulges in sensual fantasies, set to romantic ballads. When the wrecking ball finally arrives at pic's end, the audience is sufficiently indifferent to the neighborhood's fate.

Tech cedits are okay, and music by Daniel Castro and Claudio Ocando deserves wider notice.

— *Paul Lenti*

LUNA LLENA
(FULL MOON)
(VENEZUELAN-FRENCH)

A Foncine (Venezuela) release of a Tercer Cine-Foncine-Corpoindustria-French Cultural Ministry-French Foreign Relations Ministry-Altamira Prods. production. Produced by Adolfo López, Patricia Caressi, Marianella Ramos, Maagdalena Rossello (Venezuela), Fina Torres, Jerome Caraguel (France). Directed by Ana Cristina Henríquez. Screenplay, Henríquez, Johnny Gavlovski. Camera (color), Jimmy Nássar; editor, Armando Cordero; art direction, Gilberto Pulido; sound, Héctor Moreno, Carlos Bolívar, Orlando Anderson. Reviewed at 32d Cartagena (Colombia) Intl. Film Festival (competition), March 12, 1992. Running time: **90 MIN.**
Pedro . . . . Roberto Moll
Esperanza . . . . Beatriz Vásquez

Also with: Chela Atencio, Héctor Campobello, Dalila Colombo, Féliz Landaeta, Isabel Hungría, Saúl Arocha.

A love story between two Venezuelan mental patients, "Full Moon" is an effective, though not particularly exciting, directorial debut by USC film school grad Ana Cristina Henríquez.

Tale opens at a mental hospital where Roberto Moll is being held for violent behavior. He falls for a woman (Beatriz Vázquez) committed by her family for uncontrollable behavior, such as setting the house on fire. Although men and women are segregated, Moll finds ways to talk to his love, even at the risk of punishment. Vázquez initially rejects his attentions but slowly warms to him as she comes to relate to the world outside herself.

Pic delves into Venezuela's overburdened and underfunded medical system and touches on the theme of families incapable of dealing with mental illness at home.

Script could have used one more rewrite to incorporate loose elements. A crusading doctor, who fights out-of-date practices such as shock treatment, gets lost midway through the pic.

Acting is strong, especially Moll and Vázquez. Other thesps playing patients at the hospital also are well developed and never come off clichéd.

Filmed in super-16m and blown up to 35m in France, camerawork is functional, and other tech credits are okay. — *Paul Lenti*

MI QUERIDO TOM MIX
(MY DEAR TOM MIX)
(MEXICAN)

A Mexican Film Institute (Imcine) release of a Prods. Amaranta-Instituto Mexicano de Cinematografía-Fondo de Fomento a la Calidad Cinematografica (FFCC)-Government of Zacatecas production. Executive producer, Laura Imperiale. Produced by Jorge Sánchez. Directed by Carlos García Agraz. Screenplay, Consuelo Garrido. Camera (color), Rodrigo García Barcha; editor, Tlacatoetl Mata; music, Alberto Núñez Palacios; art direction, Tere Pecanins; sound, Nerio Barberis. Reviewed at 32d Cartagena (Colombia) Intl. Film Festival (competition), March 11, 1992. Running time: **120 MIN.**
Joaquina . . . . . Ana Ofelia Murguía
Cowboy drifter . . . . . Federico Luppi
Dr. Evaristo . . . . . . Manuel Ojeda
Felipe . . . . . Damián García Vázquez
Sr. Fong . . . . Zan Zhi Guo
Also with: Mercedes Olea, Jorge Fegan, Carlos Chávez, Eduardo Casab.

First feature by Mexican helmer Carlos García Agraz, "My Dear Tom Mix" is an uneven comedy adventure set in 1930s rural northern Mexico. A tribute to cinema, pic is making the fest circuit and may attract some limited interest.

Sporting a script developed at Gabriel García Márquez's screenplay workshop, film stars veteran actors Ana Ofelia Murguía and Argentine Federico Luppi.

Story concerns a sexagenarian (Murguía) who lives with her nephew (Manuel Ojeda) and his wife. The old lady has a habit of sneaking out to watch silent screen idol Tom Mix. She writes him fan letters and imagines him riding his white horse through town. When young Felipe (Damián García Vázquez) comes to visit, she draws him into her world, much to the family's consternation.

When the town is threatened by marauding bandits, she writes to Mix to save the day. Yet, when crisis arrives, she must help herself and revolve things.

Luppi plays a marginal, unnamed aging cowboy, who goes from town to town righting wrongs. He snaps into action only at the end.

Film includes some self-conscious anachronistic mugging: In one scene, Luppi practices his gunfighting technique in front of a mirror and says in English: "Are you talking to me? I said, 'are you talking to me?'" Pandering for laughs like this distances the audience.

At times, García Agraz loses control of the material. When the old lady is kidnapped by the bandits, ensuing unexciting chase scene is played out without interest.

Acting is good, especially Murguía and Ojeda as the kind-hearted small-town doctor who must often accept farm animals as payment for his services. Admirable camerawork is by Rodrigo García Barcha, son of García Márquez. — *Paul Lenti*

TIERNA ES LA NOCHE
(TENDER IS THE NIGHT)
(VENEZUELAN)

A Foncine release of a Prods. Post Meridan production. Produced by Donald Meyerson. Directed, written, edited by Leonardo Henríquez. Camera (color), Cezary Jaworski; music, José Vinicio

Adames; art direction, Carlos Castillo; sets, Nelson Varela, Eduardo Esconone; costumes, Titina Penziui; sound, Paco Ramos. Reviewed at 32d Cartagena (Colombia) Intl. Film Festival (Mecla market), March 10, 1992. Running time: **90 MIN.**

With: Constanza Giner, Diego Rísquez, Víctor Cuica, Mariangélica Ayála.

A monotonic self-indulgent exercise in non-narrative symbolism, "Tender Is the Night" appears destined for a grim future at national wickets. Outside fests and art houses, international interest also should prove pretty meager.

Latest effort by Venezuela's auteur filmmaker Leonardo Henríquez, pic is not based on Fitzgerald's novel or any of the other frequent literary allusions and conceits voiced within, including Kafka, Buñuel and Bolívar.

Dubious plot revolves around a woman who spends most of her time in a bar bathroom rhapsodizing about politics and the human condition, and a man who stands around downstairs looking at a fishbowl and listening to the bartender read aloud. Other persons appear, but not much else happens.

Boasting neither story line nor flesh-and-blood characters, pic's true stars are the topnotch photography, ambient lighting and post-modern art direction. Text tends towards pseudo-poetry. A 10-minute pic could have easily allowed the helmer to develop the same themes sans tedium.
— *Paul Lenti*

SANTA BARBARA

DIARY OF A HIT MAN

A Vision Intl. presentation of a Continental Film Group production. Produced by Amin Q. Chaudhri. Executive producer, Mark Damon. Directed by Roy London. Screenplay, Kenneth Pressman, based on his play "Insider's Price." Camera (color), Yuri Sokol; editor, Brian Smedley-Aston; music, Michel Colombier; production design, Stephen Hendrickson; costume design, Calista Hendrickson; art direction, Rusty Smith; sound, Steve Rogers; associate producers, Karen Montgomery, Robert Holof. Reviewed at Santa Barbara (Calif.) Film Festival, March 28, 1992. Running time: **91 MIN.**

Dekker . . . . Forest Whitaker
Jain . . . . Sherilyn Fenn
Kiki . . . . Sharon Stone
Koenig . . . . Seymour Cassel
Shandy . . . . James Belushi
Zidzyk . . . . Lewis Smith
Sheila . . . . Lois Chiles

An actors' piece invested with remarkable humanity by

debuting director Roy London and a gifted cast, the modest $2.5 million "Diary of a Hit Man" transcends an unlikely scenario to offer moments of cinema well worth savoring. Already in European release, it's destined for a low-key domestic outing via Epic.

A hired killer (Forest Whitaker) is losing his taste for his work, beset by doubts just when he needs to pull off one more job to come up with the down payment on his apartment.

He's hired to knock off the wife and child of a born-again commodities broker (Lewis Smith) who claims his wife's a drug addict and the infant is a crack baby and not his. The reluctant killer breaks professional-conduct rules by conversing with the victim (Sherilyn Fenn) — and discovers the broker lied.

Long scene that follows is the central conceit of the piece: that a killer and his intended victim could save each other. At times the going's dicey, but actors and director are working at such an engaging level that a viewer's doubts are willingly suspended.

Fenn is a revelation in the substance and texture she brings to the role. At times she recalls the late Sandy Dennis' controlled panic in "Who's Afraid of Virginia Woolf?"

Whitaker invests his beleaguered hitman with mesmerizing depth and unpolished reality, aided by abundant voiceovers elucidating his thoughts. More cuddly than menacing, bulky actor still makes the role all his.

Scripter Kenneth Pressman skillfully brings out the dimensions of the killer's everyday life.

London, a writer and acting coach whose pupils include Fenn and Sharon Stone (included in the cast as Fenn's tarty and obnoxious sister), demonstrates firm control of the medium and a knack for engaging flourishes.

Actors reportedly worked for scale, and it's easy to see what lured them. All are given premium handling, including Seymour Cassel in a pungent turn as Dekker's go-between and James Belushi as a playfully menacing cop.

Expanded by Pressman from his 45-minute play "Insider's Price" and shot mostly in Youngstown, Ohio, pic rates high on production values but has a sensible, economic feel that puts the focus where it should be — on the actors, who under London's direction turn the characters inside out. — *Amy Dawes*

NEW DIRECTORS

BLACK HARVEST
(AUSTRALIAN-DOCU)

Produced with assistance of the Australian Film Commission, in association with Broadcasting Commission, La Sept (France), Channel 4 (U.K.), Institute of Papua New Guinea Studies. Produced, directed by Robin Anderson, Bob Connolly. Associate producer, Chris Owen. Camera (color), Connolly; editors, Ray Thomas, Connolly, Anderson; sound, Anderson, Gethin Creagh; translators, Maggie Wilson, Ganiga Thomas Taim. Reviewed at New Directors/New Films, Museum of Modern Art, N.Y., March 23, 1992. Running time: **75 MIN.**

"Black Harvest" is a highly absorbing documentary chronicling the pitfalls of Third World entrepreneurial capitalism. Pic should do well in specialized situations and have a rich afterlife in various public TV and educational forums.

Story of the undoing of a partnership between a New Guinea tribe and a half-breed businessman exposes issues of racism, sexism and cultural regression. Events are told in a highly personal, dramatic way that underscores increasing similarity of docu to fictional forms.

Film may be viewed as a trilogy's last seg or part of a continuing saga recorded by filmmakers Robin Anderson and Bob Connolly. Their Oscar-nominated 1983 docu, "First Contact" showed how this highland region was affected by the white man, combining 1930s black & white footage taken by the first explorers with contemporary scenes of the indigenous population and recollections of the expedition's survivors.

Second film, 1989's "Joe Leahy's Neighbors," showed how the title character, born to a woman of the Ganiga tribe but fathered by an explorer, had become a businessman. After buying land from the Ganigas and making a tidy profit on it, Leahy agrees to team with them in using additional land for a coffee crop.

Since Leahy handles the business arrangements and supplies the coin, he insists on a 60-40 split. Ganigas are to be amply rewarded when profits start coming in, but instead a tumbling of the world coffee prices requires major belt-tightening.

The Ganigas suddenly appear armed, but instead of staging a revolt, they move to make war

on another tribe over some point of honor. Battlefield tableaus resembling outtakes from a Cy Endfield epic strike a tragically absurdist note, and, with ethnographic footage from "First Contact," provide a bitter contrast to the downtrodden Ganigas complaining to the camera of their economic plight.

As the man of two worlds in this drama of civilization and the jungle, Leahy feels deeply ambiguous. His bitterness at the forces that lead to his ruin are understandable, but despite some sympathy for the Ganigas, he seems insensitive to their needs.

Story's most tragic figure, however, is the Ganiga leader. Unable to stop the mad rush to war, he also feels used by Leahy. At pic's end, he's seriously wounded in battle, but epilogue notes he will survive.

Because of film's 75-minute length, exhibitors may want to use one of "Black Harvest's" prequels to fill out the program.
— *Fred Lombardi*

LAWS OF GRAVITY

Produced by Bob Gosse, Larry Meistrich. Executive producer, Meistrich. Directed, written by Nick Gomez. Camera (color), Jean de Segonzac; editor, Tom McArdle; production design, Monica Bretherton; sound, Jeff Pullman, Jean Gilliland; associate producer, Danny Silverman. Reviewed at New Directors/New Films, Museum of Modern Art, N.Y., March 10, 1992. Running time: **100 MIN.**

Jimmy . . . . Peter Greene
Denise . . . . Edie Falco
Jon . . . . Adam Trese
Celia . . . . Arabella Field
Frankie . . . . Paul Schulzie
Also with: Tony Fernandez, James McCauley, Anibal Lierras.

"Laws of Gravity" is a low-budget attempt to create the milieu of male bonding among young white hoods à la "Mean Streets," with the action transferred from Little Italy to Brooklyn. Unfortunately, the film is undermined by muddled craftsmanship and erratic scripting. Commercial prospects look marginal.

Pic's title is blithely ignored by hand-held camera movements that, early on, seem to careen all over the screen without conveying the impact of cinema verite techniques of Martin Scorsese and John Cassavetes.

Director Nick Gomez's attempts to charge a realistic atmosphere with sudden outbursts of violence often fail to ignite sparks. His pretentious tendency for screen blackouts while naturalistic sounds continue on track does not help matters.

After initial discomfort with helmer histrionics, film succeeds in evoking interest in its characters, chiefly Italian-Americans with some Hispanics. Wild card in the group is a baby-faced dynamo (Adam Trese) with a penchant for beating up his g.f. His instability is exacerbated by a gunrunner (Paul Schulzie).

Trese's best friend, a hood (Peter Greene) with streaks of decency, tries to humanize his cohort, but Greene's street smarts are dimmed by his allegiance to Trese. His well-intentioned effort to raise bail money for Trese leads to tragedy.

Greene, Trese, Edie Falco as the decent hood's wife and Arabella Field as the unfortunate g.f. all ring true but could have been better fleshed out by the script. — *Fred Lombardi*

AFURERU ATSUI NAMIDA
(SWIMMING WITH TEARS)
(JAPANESE)

A Cine Ballet production. Produced by Syujiro Kawakami. Directed, written by Hirotaka Tashiro. Camera (color), Koichi Sakuma; editor, Masahiro Matsumura; music, Hitoshi Hashimoto; sound, Toyohiko Kuribayashi. Reviewed at New Directors/New Films, Museum of Modern Art, N.Y., March 11, 1992. Running Time: **104 MIN.**
Ryoichi Kokubu . . . . Shiro Sano
Asami Agawa . . . . Jun Togawa
Fey Yokoyama . . . . . . Ruby Moreno
Shoichi Yokoyama . . Masayuki Suzuki

"**S**wimming With Tears" probes the plight of foreign workers in Japan via a Filipino mail-order bride (Ruby Moreno) who runs away from her Japanese farmer husband. Director-scenarist Hirotaka Tashiro dexterously ties in various plot strands until film is thrown off kilter by a bizarre subplot of star-crossed lovers that becomes more interesting than the woman's fate. Film could get a modest crack at the U.S. art house market.

After fleeing her husband and unable to afford passage home, the Filipino femme gets a job in Tokyo in a Chinese restaurant catering to foreigners. There she makes a friend (Jun Togawa) with a scholar b.f. (Shiro Sano).

Tashiro crosscuts to life back in the farmer's town where a meeting takes place to discuss the imported wife's disappearance. The Sturges-like elevation of family problems to council politics permits a few digs at foreigners used as mail-order brides in Japan and their treatment.

Meanwhile, the Filipino woman's predicament is compounded by her claim to be the daughter of a prominent Japanese businessman who refuses to acknowledge her. Plot kicker is that years before the businessman lost his wife and offspring to a kidnapper.

Convicted kidnapper/killer was then attacked by a young Japanese man outraged at his crime. The young avenger then took up with the murderer's contrite sister. They turn out to be Sano and Togawa. As they are now helping to care for the daughter he wants to forget, the businessman plots to expose them to the press.

These complications ultimately overwhelm the realistic portrayal of the Filipino's problems. Moreover, after all the moodily lit scenes of the tortured lovers and the businessman's Mabuse-like machinations, film's finale, with Moreno's husband suddenly turning up in the Philippines to bring her back home, is sweet but sappy. (Ending doesn't work as irony either.)

Talented director Tashiro may be heard from more favorably when he can better control his material. — *Fred Lombardi*

CITY OF JOY
(BRITISH-FRENCH)

A TriStar release of a Lightmotive production. Produced by Jake Eberts, Roland Joffé. Co-producer, Iain Smith. Directed by Joffé. Screenplay, Mark Medoff, based on Dominique Lapierre's book. Camera (Eclair Laboratories color), Peter Biziou; editor, Gerry Hambling; music, Ennio Morricone; production design, Roy Walker; supervising art director, John Fenner; art direction, Asoke Bose; set decoration, Rosalind Shingleton; costume design, Judy Moorcroft; sound (Dolby), Daniel Brisseau; cultural consultant, Sunil Gangopadhyay; assistant director, Bill Westley; casting, Priscilla John. Reviewed at Fine Arts Theater, Beverly Hills, Calif., April 3, 1992. MPAA Rating: PG-13. Running time: **134 MIN.**
Max Lowe . . . . Patrick Swayze
Joan Bethel . . . . Pauline Collins
Hasari Pal . . . . Om Puri
Kamla Pal . . . . Shabana Azmi
Ashoka . . . . Art Malik
Amrita Pal . . . . . . Ayesha Dharker
Shambu Pal . . . . . Santu Chowdhury
Manooj Pal . . . . Imran Badsah Khan
Anouar . . . . Nabil Shaban
Ram Chander . . . . . . Debtosh Ghosh
Ghatak, the
  Godfather . . . . Shyamanand Jalan

A picture divided against itself, "City of Joy" is half American-style gangster melodrama and half inspirational social consciousness. Impressively produced in Calcutta's teeming, poverty-ridden streets and slums, Roland Joffé's noble attempt to portray the tenacity and strength of the human spirit under the most trying conditions comes off as curiously ineffectual due to predictable plotting and character evolution. Commercial prospects are soft despite top-billed Patrick Swayze.

As he has with gradually decreasing effectiveness in his previous three films, Joffé combines the concerns of an adventurous cultural anthropologist with those of a self-serious history teacher hoping to convey universal truths through unusual stories of societal clashes. But while using a Western reporter plausibly provided a cinematic window on the Cambodian atrocities of "The Killing Fields," Swayze's burned-out M.D. is not nearly as convincingly a way into dense, mysterious India and some of its most deprived citizens.

Inspired by selected stories in Dominique Lapierre's 1985 international bestseller, "City of Joy" is, in playwright Mark Medoff's adaptation, a direct descendant of the "Casablanca" school, with a disenchanted, cynical Yank heading for exotic climes to both alleviate and exult in his ennui, and finally finding something in himself he thought had died or never existed.

Fleeing from the rigors of life as a surgeon in Houston, Swayze's Dr. Max Lowe arrives in Calcutta with the vague idea of seeking enlightenment. For the first 25 minutes, his initial experiences are intercut with the infinitely more rude awakenings of Hasari Pal, his wife and three children. Having lost their farm, latter have been forced to make their way in this labyrinthine city of 11 million; and Hasari, homeless and his money stolen, finally takes the only job he can get, pulling a rickshaw.

Assaulted and also robbed, Max is taken to the City of Joy Self-Help School and Dispensary, presided over by a beleaguered but selflessly saintly British woman (Pauline Collins). She tries to recruit Max for his medical expertise but, like any self-respecting Bogart character, Max is through trying to help anyone but himself. But an emergency childbirth presses him into service, and Max's predictable transformation is underway.

Max becomes a cheerleader for the dispossessed people of City of Joy in their battle against the local mafia. Poor neighborhood is presided over by a stern but approachable godfather (eminent theater actor-director Shyamanand Jalan, in a performance of Greenstreetian proportions). But as his health fails, control is wrested by his ill-tempered son (Art Malik, reminding somewhat of John Cazale in "The Godfather"), who foments a riot when lepers are treated and enjoys cutting people up with a double-edged razor.

Although distrusted as a Westerner and threatened by the mob, Max stays on to impart a good, old-fashioned, American "can do" attitude among his destitute friends at the clinic, and to inspire in them a rebelliousness that would have done Tom Paine proud. If the evil on earth were as easy to overcome as it is here, the world would indeed be as rosy as the skies in the climactic shot of the picture.

Nearly buried by all the melodrama and gangster intrigue is any notion of the viability of an operation such as the City of Joy. An almost automatic sense of worthiness comes across whenever Max successfully completes a procedure or Joan takes in more outcasts, but a full impression of what can and cannot be achieved by such a facility is missing. Furthermore, the characters and situations feel too contrived for a convincing dose of documentary realism to sink in.

Still, Joffé and company vividly conjure up sights and sounds of the overwhelmingly congested city streets, and scenes of a barefoot Hasari racing with his rickshaw through heavy traffic are almost enough to make the viewer perspire. Understandably unable to lense the central story in actual slums, production designer Roy Walker has overseen construction of a massive set, and result is one of seamless verisimilitude.

An admittedly chancy choice to play a jaded medic, Swayze gives it the old college try, but he doesn't have the depth to give gradations and nuance to the conventionally written aspects of his role. Appealing as always, Collins has nothing but routine buttons to push as she uses all her wiles to win the doc over to her cause. Om Puri comes off best as the earnest farmer struggling to enable his family to survive, and Shabana Azmi as his wife and the three child thesps also create favorable impressions.

Peter Biziou's protean cinematography is richly colorful, if perhaps too pretty at times, while Ennio Morricone's score is subdued and evocative.

— Todd McCarthy

FERNGULLY...
THE LAST RAINFOREST

A 20th Century Fox release of a FAI Films presentation in association with Youngheart Prods. of a Young & Faiman production. Produced by Wayne Young, Peter Faiman. Co-producers, Jim Cox, Brian Rosen, Richard Harper. Executive producers, Ted Field, Robert W. Cort. Co-executive producers, Jeff Dowd, William F. Willett. Line producer, Tom Klein. Directed by Bill Kroyer. Screenplay, Jim Cox, based on Diana Young's stories of "FernGully." Creative consultant, Matthew Perry; coordinating art director, Susan Kroyer; Deluxe color; original score, Alan Silvestri; music supervision, Tim Sexton, Becky Mancuso; editor, Gillian Hutshing; animation production consultant, Charles Leland Richardson; art direction-color stylist, Ralph Eggleston; art direction-layout design, Victoria Jenson; animation director, Tony Fucile; special effects animation director, Sari Gennis; Dolby sound; casting, Marci Liroff. Reviewed at 20th Century Fox screening room, L.A., March 31, 1992. MPAA rating: G. Running time: **76 MIN.**

Voices:
Hexxus . . . . Tim Curry
Crysta . . . . Samantha Mathis
Pips . . . . Christian Slater
Zak . . . . Jonathan Ward
Batty Koda . . . . . . Robin Williams

Magi Lune . . . . . . Grace Zabriskie
Ralph . . . . Geoffrey Blake
Tony . . . . Robert Pastorelli
Stump . . . . Cheech Marin
Root . . . . Tommy Chong
The Goanna . . . . Tone-Loc

"**F**ernGully . . . The Last Rainforest" is a colorful, lively, extremely "politically correct" animated feature pitting the elfin creatures of the wild against the rapacious monsters who would destroy their habitat. Knocked off in snappy style at a swift pace, pic will amply entertain tykes while feeding them an environmental lesson, and features enough amusing jokes and clever songs to make it palatable for adults.

Bolstered by word-of-mouth sneaks, and with appetite for a new animated musical perhaps growing as "Beauty and the Beast" finally begins to fade, B.O. results should be warm.

Drawn in brilliantly verdant colors immediately inviting the viewer into a special world, "FernGully" is certainly simple enough for any youngster to understand, yet is sufficiently hip around the edges to contain the sap.

Led by humanlike fairies who dart about like Tinkerbell, assorted daffy characters live a charmed existence in the dense, self-enclosed world of the forest. However, when the domain's pert young thing Crysta soars above the protective canopy of the treetops, she sees an ominous cloud of smoke rising not far away.

For years, the evil spirit that once destroyed the forest has been locked up, but it is suddenly unleashed by an enormous, omnivorous machine that gobbles up vegetation and leaves waste in its relentless path.

A workman on the machine, Zak, gets tossed into the jungle and is shrunk by Crysta down to her size, permitting a human to see things from the other POV, as well allowing for a meek romance. Main weakness of Jim Cox's script is the annoying banality of the central characters, essentially stock Ken and Barbie confections.

By refreshing contrast, supporting characters are full of vinegar and extremely well cast. Robin Williams asserts his unique personality and wacky humor amazingly well in an animated context as a crazed, brain-fried bat named Batty Koda, which will be the most popular character to emerge from the film. Without ever explicitly stating it, actor wittily sketches a longtime

acidhead who has become permanently deranged.

Cheech and Chong are reunited, at least vocally, as the raucous Beetle Boys; "Rocky Horror's" Tim Curry essays the villainous Hexxus, liberated to destroy the forest; and vocalist Tone-Loc oozes in to essay a threatening lizard. These performers, in addition to such singers as Johnny Clegg, Sheena Easton and Elton John delivering original numbers written by a host of w.k. songsmiths, bring considerable pizzazz and variety to the tightly conceived picture, and provide regular distraction from the more insipid leads.

Animation of the human-looking characters is relatively colorless, but the surroundings are gorgeously rendered. Many of the compositions executed under the direction of Bill Kroyer possess a strikingly three-dimensional quality, and entire enterprise — from the visual aspect and casting to the music and the message — has been approached and carried off with commendable care. *— Todd McCarthy*

A PLACE FOR JAZZ
(DOCU-16m)

A Cineresearch presentation of a Jazzhead Production. Produced by Richard Broadman, Jay Hoffman, Bob Pollak. Directed by Broadman. Camera (color), John Bishop; editor, Broadman; sound, Stephen Olech; associate director, Michael Haggerty. Reviewed at Brattle Theatre, Cambridge, Mass., April 7, 1992. No MPAA Rating. Running time: **68 MIN.**

In the mid-1980s, the 1369 Club was the place to jam in the Boston area. Documentary maker Richard Broadman uses the rise and fall of the hole-in-the-wall jazz club as a means to explore the contemporary jazz scene from the viewpoints of both performers and club operators. Result is a jazz aficionado's delight.

Pic presents many jazz artists performing at the club and talking about jazz and the musician's life. Bassist Larry Fishman notes philosophically that jazz is "just not the music of the United States." Archie Shepp remarks that he's a celeb in Europe but a virtual unknown on the local college campus where he teaches.

Musicians also discuss how they keep jazz alive and pass it on to the next generation, perhaps best exemplified by saxophonist Christopher Hollyday.

He recalls being invited to sit in on a jam session at the club when he was all of 12; he's now an international recording artist.

It's hard to see how those outside the jazz scene will relate to the film, and even one of the musicians notes how strange the music sounds to someone used to formulaic American pop tunes. However, this is one for anyone who's ever stood in line outside of a neighborhood dive to hear some jazz.

Tech credits are okay for a low-budget 16m docu, and pic's look and feel help recreate the atmosphere of the funky (and now defunct) club.

— Daniel M. Kimmel

DOUBLE TROUBLE

A Motion Picture Corp. of America release. Produced by Brad Krevoy, Steve Stabler. Co-producers, Chad Oman, Randy Pope, David Tausik. Directed by John Paragon. Screenplay, Jeffrey Kerns, Kurt Wimmer, Chuck Osborne, based on a story by Wimmer, Osborne. Camera (color), Richard Michalak; editor, Jonas Thaler; production design, Johan Letenoux, Gilbert Mercier; set decoration, Marisol Jimenez; sound, Jack Bornhoff; assistant director, Pope; casting, Jan McGill. Reviewed at Motion Picture Corp. of America screening room, Santa Monica, Calif., April 7, 1992. MPAA rating: R. Running time: **90 MIN.**

Peter . . . . Peter Paul
David . . . . David Paul
Chamberlin . . . . . . Roddy McDowall
Kent . . . . Steve Kanaly
O'Brien . . . . James Doohan
Danitra . . . . A.J. Johnson
Bob . . . . Bill Mumy
Leonard . . . . Troy Donahue

"**D**ouble Trouble" is what muscleman duo the Barbarian Bros. are in with an ill-conceived vehicle that's long on plot, short on fun. Distrib will have trouble lassoing even the target lowbrow audience for this perfunctory, bottom-rung actioner, which has already unspooled on Hawaiian screens and gets Stateside release later this month.

Pumped-up detective David (David Paul) gets a surprise when a wisecracking jewel thief turns out to be his long-lost twin brother, Peter (Peter Paul). The chief of police (James Doohan) pairs them up in exchange for info on a smuggling ring, and the feuding sibs are forced to work together to crack the ring.

It's less fun than it ought to be as the dry, rambling plot drags them through a dog-eared urban action scenario (set in L.A.) that fails to make much of their physical prowess, their presumed sex appeal or their potential for numbskull humor.

Scattered wisecracks in the team-written script are lame indeed, and action, under director John Paragon, seems to lag a few steps behind the speed of normal perception.

Not even the look-alike angle gets much play in this sunless scenario, and the boorish brothers, with their shaggy symmetrical haircuts and wildly inflated bodies, are no threat to the legitimate thesps. Roddy McDowall, to his credit, separates himself from the crowd in a precise, fey and ironic perf as the chief jewel smuggler.

Shoot, supervised by producer Brad Krevoy (a Roger Corman alum) and partner Steve Stabler, was an obvious quickie, with third-rate production values and a generic score that kicks in to signal an action seg. Call the bomb squad. — *Amy Dawes*

UNDER THE SUN
(BRITISH)

A Thames Television production. Produced by Alan Horrox. Directed by Michael Winterbottom. Screenplay, Susan Campbell, from a screen story by Campbell, Winterbottom. Camera (color, Super 16m), Daf Hobson; editor, Trevor Waite; music, Stella Maris; production design, uncredited; costume design, Rachael Fleming; sound, Simon Bishop; assistant director, Huw Jones; production manager, Valerie Farron. Reviewed at De Lane Lea Sound Centre screening room, London, March 25, 1992. Running time: **77 MIN.**
Ellie . . . . Kate Hardie
Linda . . . . Caroline Catz
Miguel . . . . Iker Ibañez
Tina . . . . Antonina Tramonti
Maria . . . . Stella Maris
Felipe . . . . Arturo Venegas
Pablo . . . . Pablo Duarte
Antonio . . . . Juan Manuel Cara Lara

A slick rites-of-passage yarn set on Spain's Costa del Sol, "Under the Sun" scores high for young cast's likable perfs and thoroughly cinematic helming. Second feature by director Michael Winterbottom ("Forget About Me") is a natural for fests looking for upbeat contempo Brit material. Theatrical chances rate slimmer.

Central character is bookworm Ellie (Kate Hardie), 19, who's set out from Manchester on a round-the-world trip. She gets stranded near Málaga, southern Spain, when her ditzy companion (Caroline Catz) goes off with a local loverboy.

After her belongings are stolen, Ellie falls in with a loopy German sax player (Antonina Tramonti), who gets her a job wait-

ing tables. Rest of pic limns Ellie's slow regeneration, ambivalent friendship with a young Spanish waiter (Iker Ibañez), and final decision whether or not to continue on to Africa.

Pic avoids any grand statements and settles for an engaging style that's mainstream European in its mix of character and emotions. Original script by Susan Campbell was reportedly embellished by the cast during actual shooting, but the finished result has a tight, improv-free feel, with a nice line in dry wacky humor.

Hardie ("A Small Dance") is fine as the sensitive Ellie, if a bit flat in her confessional voiceovers. Tramonti almost steals the pic as the German easy rider, and Catz (in at beginning and end) plays off well as Hardie's airheaded fellow Mancunian. Spanish thesps are solid and well cast.

Tech credits are bright, with sharp Super 16m lensing of locations around Málaga by Daf Hobson, and a bouncy pop-rock score providing extra lift at appropriate moments. — *Derek Elley*

THE RESURRECTED

A Scotti Bros. Pictures release of a Borde/Raich production. Produced by Mark Borde, Ken Raich. Executive producers, Tony Scotti, Tom Bradshaw. Directed by Dan O'Bannon. Screenplay, Brent V. Friedman, based on H.P. Lovecraft's novel "The Case of Charles Dexter Ward." Camera (Foto-Kem color), Irv Goodnoff; editor, Russell Livingstone; music, Richard Band; production design, Brent Thomas; art direction, Doug Byggdin; costume design, Marcella Robertson; sound (Dolby), Robert Vollum; assistant director, Anthony Atkins; production manager, Don McLean; special visual effects, Todd Masters; special physical effects coordinator, Gary Paller; stunt coordinator, Scott Ateah; 2nd unit director, Raich; 2nd unit camera, Kevin Flemming; co-producer, Shayne Sawyer; casting, Fiona Jackson, Penny Ellers. Reviewed on Live vidcassette, N.Y. MPAA Rating: R. Running time: **106 MIN.**
John March . . . . John Terry
Claire Ward . . . . Jane Sibbett
Charles Dexter Ward/
 Joseph Curwen . . . Chris Sarandon
Lonnie Peck . . . . . Richard Romanus
Holly Tender . . . . . Laurie Briscoe
Capt. Ben Szandor . . . Ken Cameroux
Raymond . . . . Patrick Pon
Dr. Waite . . . . . . Bernard Cuffling
Ezra Ward . . . . . . Charles Kristian
Eliza . . . . Megan Leitch
Main monster . . . . Deep Roy

"The Resurrected," originally titled "Shatterbrain," is an ambitious horror opus that genre fans will enjoy. It's scheduled for theatrical release in Germany and Japan but will be a video title Stateside.

Pic is the second filmization of

H.P. Lovecraft's classic tale "The Case of Charles Dexter Ward," first brought to screen in 1963 by Roger Corman as "The Haunted Palace" and marketed as an Edgar Allan Poe title. Since then Lovecraft, who died in 1937 but became popularized 30 years later with a folk-rock group even taking his name, has become a big name in horror films, second only to Stephen King.

John Terry toplines as an investigator in Providence, R.I., (Lovecraft's home town) who's hired by Jane Sibbett, the worried wife of the mysterious Charles Dexter Ward (Chris Sarandon). Terry discovers Ward is fixated on his 18th century ancestor, a sorcerer who experimented on bringing back the dead. Ward is an engineer for a cosmetics firm who's been accused of various crimes including graverobbing.

True to Lovecraft's storytelling methods, old manuscripts are found by Terry to advance the narrative. Exciting climax takes place in catacombs where Terry meets up with some of the results of those evil experiments.

Director Dan O'Bannon brings to the assignment a measured pace and obvious reverence for Lovecraft. Though final reel is chock full of monster effects, pic's flashbacks within flashbacks *within* flashbacks structure is a drawback to viewer involvement.

Sarandon's acting in a dual role and Todd Masters' convincing visual effects are the highlights. — *Lawrence Cohn*

MADRID FEST

LE VOLEUR D'ENFANTS
(THE CHILDREN THIEF)
(FRENCH-SPANISH-ITALIAN)

A Lotus Films Intl. (Madrid), GICA (Paris), Intl. Dean Film (Rome) & Starlet Film (Rome) co-production. Produced by Luis Méndez. Executive delegate producer, Sergio Gobbi. Executive producers, Yvon Crenn, Denise Breton. Directed by Christian de Chalonge. Screenplay, Dominique Garnier, de Chalonge, based on Jules Supervielle's book. Camera (color), Bernard Zitzermann; editor, Anita Fernández; music, Luis Llach; sets, Jaime Pérez Cubero; costumes, Cecile Balme; sound, Alix Comte. Reviewed at Multicines Ideal (Madrid), April 5, 1992. (Competing at Madrid Film Festival.) Running time: **112 MIN.**
Bigua . . . . . . Marcello Mastroianni
Desposoria . . . . Angela Molina
M. Armand . . . . Michel Piccoli
Roberto . . . . Daniel Martin
 Also with: Virginie Ledoyen, Loic Even, Nada Stran car, Caspar Salm-

on, Bejamin Doat, Nicolas Carre, Adrien Canivet.
(French, Spanish soundtrack)

Good period production values, fine direction and Marcello Mastroianni again doing his part as the bumbling Italo nebbish fail to rescue this rambling exercise of Europuff from ennui.

Utter linguistic melange has French, Spanish and Italo thesps speaking mostly heavily accented French, though the two protagonists are supposed to be Argentine (Molina's Spanish, of course, is pure Castilian). The story is as confusing as the accents; presumably, it's to be taken as a parable or a droll fairy tale.

A wealthy Argentine ex-colonel living in 1925 Paris lures children to his mansion, where he benignly shelters, feeds and dresses them as though they were his own family. By providing for the moppets, none of whom wants to run away or is sought by parents, the colonel finds a surrogate for children his own wife cannot bear him.

Touches of fantasy are added via a magician, elephants in the streets and clips from Eisenstein, which keep the rambling yarn off-balance. Plot thickens when the magician palms off his pretty daughter on the colonel, triggering a flow of libido from the boys in the menage and from the colonel himself.

Like so many Eurofilms, production values and thesping are fine, and some of the visual images are striking, but the strengths are undermined by loose script, excessive length and a story which never seems to make its point. — *Peter Besas*

SAN REMO FEST

DOGS BARK BLUE

A Falcon Arts & Entertainment presentation of a Joey Walker production. Produced by Joanne Watkins. Executive producers, Lisa Campbell, Mark Byers. Directed by Claudia Hoover. Screenplay, Hoover, David Urrutia, Christopher Steward. Camera (color), Stephen Sheridan; editor, Craig A. Colton; music, John Massari; art director, Stephen Cerbo; assistant director, Kristen Kenedy. Reviewed at San Remo (Italy) Intl. Film Festival (competition), March 29, 1992. Running time: **90 MIN.**
Martin Garrett Jr. . . . . . . Chris Cote
Claire Garrett . . . . Deborah Benson
Ruth . . . . Bridget Hoffman
Nick Garrett . . Gregory Paul Jackson
Martin Garrett Sr. . . . . . . Ron Colby

Director Claudia Hoover delivers deluxe results on a niggardly $50,000 budget in "Dogs Bark Blue," an ambitious talkfest in which thirtysomething friends re-examine their life choices. As a technician's calling card, pic scores highly, but as drama, it's barking up the wrong tree with an overly earnest script built on pop psychology dialogue and vanilla protagonists. Theatrical prospects look minimal.

Two brothers, a hotshot attorney (Chris Cote) and aspiring actor (Gregory Paul Jackson), are forced into some serious life reassessment after their dad's death. Old wounds inflicted by their fearsome father are reopened, and sibling rivalries restoked.

Jackson's struggling painter friend (Bridget Hoffman) also gnaws away at her psyche over her failure to make an inroad into the art market. The attorney son snaps under work pressure and his acutely strained personal ties. Tension between the brothers explodes and some bottled-up truths fly.

Though the fuzzy edges of this confrontation are clearly meant to reflect the ambiguities of life's lessons, the conflict is left up in the air. Hoffman's outcome is handled better as she hits the road in search of change.

Despite the premise born out of the family tragedy, pic centers mainly on Hoffman, and hers is the most sorely misjudged character. She's like a screwball figure trapped in a sea of angst, and thesp's gee-whiz delivery and forced eccentricity jar at every turn. Other perfs are more credible, though they struggle to hurdle artificial dialogue.

Technically, pic is smooth in all departments, and given the right script, Hoover (who directed the controversial docu on transsexuals, "Metamorphosis") has the earmarks of a shrewd filmmaker. John Massari's richly varied music score is a distinct plus.

— *David Rooney*

I LOVE VIENNA
(AUSTRIAN)

An EPO-Film production. (Intl. sales: Omnifilm, Paris.) Produced by Dieter Pochlatko. Directed by Houchang Allahyari. Screenplay, Reinhard Jud, Allahyari. Camera (color), Helmut Pirnat; editor, Charlotte Müllner; music, Tunament, Ismail Vasegi; art direction, Tommy Vögel; costumes, Martina List; sound, Mohsen Nassiri. Reviewed at San Remo (Italy) Intl. Film Festival (competition), March 29, 1992. Running time: **105 MIN.**

Ali Mohammed . . .	Frydun Farochzad
Marianne	
Swoboda	Dolores Schmidinger
Rudolf Swoboda	Hanno Pöschl
Mariam	Marjam Allahyari
Djamjid	Michael Niawarani
Karol	Artur Gawryluk
Selina	Marisa Mell

Middle East meets Mittel Europe in "I Love Vienna," a finely observed, freewheeling culture clash comedy about Iranians in the Austrian capital. A substantial hit in its eponymous hometown, pic serves up steady laughs at a breakneck pace and should inspire b.o. valentines in many offshore markets.

Arriving in Vienna en route to the U.S. with his sister and son, Iranian German teacher Frydun Farochzad is installed in a hotel for immigrants. Run by seen-it-all, done-it-all Hanno Pöschl and his flirtatious estranged wife (Dolores Schmidinger), and situated opposite a brothel, the hotel turns out to be a devout Moslem's worst nightmare.

The teacher slowly becomes unhinged watching his teen son led astray by hookers and his veiled sister flower under the attentions of a Polish suitor (Artur Gawryluk). Worn down by decadence, he gives in to temptation in a hilarious seduction scene. Playing the blushing virgin to Schmidinger's no-nonsense frau, he consents to a three-day marriage as a way around his strict religion.

Things fall apart when he learns that Schmidinger's divorce is not final. His sister breaks away to marry the Pole, and his son falls in with local pranksters and is arrested. When his U.S. visa comes through, Farochzad is forced to make some big decisions.

In his first nondramatic outing, helmer Houchang Allahyari shows a veteran's touch for comedy, maintaining comic equilibrium and never overplaying the cultural gap between his characters. As a Persian-born Austrian and a practicing psychiatrist, his observations on both Eastern and Western foibles are rich in affectionate truths, though the balance of his good-natured jibes swings heavily toward the Iranians, leaving the Austrians relatively unscathed.

Some auds may gripe that pic sanitizes and trivializes a dire problem with its squeaky-clean refugee accommodation and total absence of violent interracial conflict, but in playing it strictly for laughs, Allahyari makes an eloquent, nonpreachy bid for racial tolerance.

Performances are topnotch all round, especially w.k. Iranian entertainer Farochzad in his first film. Marjam Allahyari also is affecting as the sister who emerges from her cocoon. The oddball gallery of supporting characters is full of surprise jewels, notably Marisa Mell as a brassy Italo belly-dancer and helmer Allahyari as a fast-talking carpet salesman.

Technically, film looks and sounds terrific, and soundtrack's blend of Eastern and Western music works well.

— *David Rooney*

THE SECRETARY
(B&W-16m)

A Yes Yes production. Produced, directed by David Voda. Screenplay, Charles Anceney. Camera (b&w, 16m), Richard Putnam; editor, Phyllis K. Housen; music, Ellen Mandel; sound, Alessandro Cavadini. Reviewed at San Remo (Italy) Intl. Film Festival (competition), March 27, 1992. Running time: **93 MIN.**

Shelly Mackay	Susan Karlin
Chick Schwarz	Anna Lank
Dick Knight	Morrow Wilson
Dale Ryder	Douglas Gibson
Patrick	James Giffin

Also with: Mary Lou Phipps-Winfrey, Stephen Kasprzak, Beverly Braniff.

A punchy little critique of the work ethic, "The Secretary" uses a snappy sitcom style to deliver a pep talk to dissatisfied workers everywhere. Director David Voda won the best first feature prize at San Remo, where pic's upbeat message impressed the predominantly young audience. Tech shortcomings imposed by a meager $30,000 budget may rule out gainful employment in theaters, but temp engagements should open up fests and new director showcases.

Crushed under the thumb of a tyrannically workaholic boss (Morrow Wilson) and sapped after a grueling day, undervalued legal secretary Susan Karlin turns up late for a date with b.f. Douglas Gibson. He encourages her to toss in the no-win job and go back to college while he brings in the bucks, but she can't reconcile placing self-fulfillment over financial security.

The boss tracks them down in a diner and orders her back to the office to fix some crucial screwups. An altercation breaks out between boss and b.f., and Karlin finds herself questioning her dead-end situation. After learning that her raise has been forestalled, she makes a heroic, life-changing decision.

Sharp dialogue and director Voda's goofy sitcom feeling give this simplistic self-help yarn its breezy momentum and help pic succeed on its own refreshingly unambitious terms.

Performances slot deliberately into an unnaturalistic TV comedy mold well-suited to the material. Karlin and Gibson make appealing leads, and Anna Lank has fun with a showy wisecracking role that would have been played by Eve Arden. Only Wilson and Mary Lou Phipps-Winfrey as his wife stray too far into hamsville and threaten to upset pic's comic balance.

Tech credits are generally in line with pic's budget limits. Bleached-out black & white lensing lends a workaday bleakness (apt for subject), but Ellen Mandel's clanking music score never quite gets the mood right.

— *David Rooney*

SANTA BARBARA

NERVOUS TICKS

An IRS release of a Grandview Avenue Pictures presentation. Produced by Arthur Goldblatt. Executive producer, Harold Welb. Co-producer, John E. Jacobsen. Directed by Rocky Lang. Screenplay, David Frankel. Camera (color), Bill Dill; editor, Carri Coughlin; music, Jay Ferguson; production design, Naomi Shohan; art direction, Dan Whifler; set decoration, Amy Wells; sound, Tony Smyles; assistant director, Gary Sales; associate producer, John Robert Zaring. Reviewed at Santa Barbara Film Festival, April 4, 1992. MPAA rating: R. Running time: **93 MIN.**

York	Bill Pullman
Nancy	Julie Brown
Ron Rudman	Peter Boyle
Cole	Brent Jennings
Rusty	James Le Gros
Cheshire	Paxton Whitehead

Ninety nervous minutes in the life of a lovestruck luggage handler tick by in this frantic "real time" farce in which concept overrides all for a chaotic outcome. RCA/Columbia-financed item generates enough comic momentum to succeed on video, but theatrical outlook is scant.

Filmmaker Rocky Lang and scripter David Frankel set out to see how much chaos they could get out of the life of an ordinary putz (Bill Pullman) as he struggles to escape the country by plane with his married g.f. (Julie Brown). Plenty of mayhem ensues, most of it mindless.

Plot seems stitched together from stale scraps of 100 other capers as the luggage handler gets into trouble when a suitcase he finds for a frantic traveler (Brent Jennings) proves to be full of drug-related cash.

Railroaded into driving to the drug deal, the pushover bag man ends up a hostage to the dealer and a target of crazed gangsters. Things get worse when he arrives to pick up his nutso g.f. (Brown) and finds she's switched tracks and now wants him to kill her husband (Peter Boyle).

Sympathy for the couple's struggle dissolves, but focus is unwavering, as the harried Pullman fends off gun-toting ex-Marine Boyle, lesbian lovers who've taken over his apartment and other distractions blocking his path to the airport.

Action travels a shaky trail between out-and-out "Naked Gun"-style nonsense and the more grounded antics of an "After Hours." Logic is an early casualty, but helmer Lang ("Race for Glory") shows flair for the genre, and final sequences are winning.

Also worth the price of a video rental are some choice scenes between the menacing Boyle and the jittery Pullman as the latter lurks around the married couple's house posing as an electrician.

Much of pic's $3.5 million budget must have paid for stunts and explosions, as action gets progressively wilder.

Pullman does fine in a demanding turn as on-the-go centerpiece of this romp, but he doesn't register strongly enough to drive pic theatrically. Boyle and Brown are engaging and well-cast as the darkly bizarre spouses.

Production values, design and stunt action are strong, considering slim five-week shooting sked. Savvy scoring adds punch to some segs. IRS plans a fall theatrical release. Pic world-premiered at the San Barb fest. — *Amy Dawes*

CARTAGENA FEST

ROMPECORAZONES
(HEARTBREAKERS)
(ARGENTINE)

A Transborder Films release of a MTC Realizaciones-Cooperative El Aniceto production. Executive producer, Martín Larumbe. Produced by Claudia Soria. Directed, written by Jorge Stamadianos. Camera (color), Miguel Abad; editor, Oscar Gómez; music, Carmelo Saitta; art direction, Alfredo Iglesias; sound, Luis Corazza. Reviewed in competition at 32nd Cartagena (Colombia) Intl. Film Festival, March 11, 1992. Running time: **90 MIN.**
Mario . . . . Jorge Sasi
Viviana . . . . Teresa Constantini
Andrés . . . . David di Napoli
Also with: Jorge Diez, Grecia Levy, Margara Alonso, Willy Lemos.

In the who-is-sleeping-with-whom genre, "Heartbreakers" is a routine sex comedy capable only of breaking the hearts of its producers when confronted with pic's b.o. performance. That it figures among international festival offerings is surprising.

Plot focuses on the character of a professional woman who feels her biological clock's demands and wants to have children. But she works nightshift at a 24-hour dental clinic while her husband works days. Thus, when her car breaks down, she offers the tow truck driver and divorced father more than his usual fee.

When he falls in love with her, he is invited to live at the family home to the chagrin of her husband, who it turns out uses the house for his own amusement while his wife is treating teeth. Soon his girlfriend moves in and chaos reigns.

Plot is further complicated by several outlandish details not worth mentioning, but it all adds up to very few laughs and lotsa tedium. Situations and dialogue are forced throughout, and acting tends to be wooden. Tech credits are okay. — *Paul Lenti*

LA LENGUA DE LOS ZORROS
(THE LANGUAGE OF FOXES)
(PERUVIAN)

A Cinematográfica Kuntur-Grupo Chaski-Percy Velit-Instituto Cubano del Arte e Industria Cinematográficos (ICAIC) production. Produced by Pilar Roco Palacio. Directed by Federico García Hurtado. Screenplay, García Hurtado, Rafael Villalba. Camera (color), Danny Gavidia; editor, Justo Vega; sound, Máximo Santa Cruz. Reviewed at 32nd Cartagena (Colombia) Intl. Film Festival (competition), March 12, 1992. Running time: **85 MIN.**
Johnny . . . . Baldomero Cáceres
Soledad . . . . Lucía Melgar
Flute player . Federico García Hurtado
Also with: Zully Azurín, Ciro Umeres, Alfredo Verástegui.

"The Language of Foxes" is a disturbing and somewhat confusing portrait of domestic reality that might spark some international attention, but Peruvian director Federico García Hurtado's eighth pic may prove impenetrable with its local symbols and references.

Title refers to the lack of communication between Peru's coastal and mountainous communities: The foxes from above need a common language with the foxes from below.

When a young mountain climber (Baldomero Cáceres) arrives in a small Andean village, he becomes the focal point for recent terrorist violence plaguing the community. The villagers have explained away this violence by resorting to local myths, blaming the Pishtaco, a tall, light-skinned, blue-eyed monster who kills people to steal their fat. Thus, the visitor becomes immediately suspect.

Danny Gavidia's imaginative and expressive lensing borders on pretty travelogue footage. The Andes, usually depicted on film as majestic and beautiful, here are an avenger with raw force.

Using Andean mythology and symbolism, pic comes off hermetic and perplexing to those unfamiliar with Altiplano, a culture that, in the end, wins out and achieves poetic justice. Despite flaws, García Hurtado manages to maintain a disquieting tension throughout. — *Paul Lenti*

THE BABE

A Universal Pictures release of a Waterhorse/Finnegan-Pinchuk production. Written, produced by John Fusco. Co-producer, Jim Van Wyck. Executive producers, Bill Finnegan, Walter Coblenz. Directed by Arthur Hiller. Camera (Deluxe color), Haskell Wexler; editor, Robert C. Jones; music, Elmer Bernstein; production design, James D. Vance; art direction, Gary Baugh; set design, Michael Merritt, Karen Fletcher-Trujillo, Linda Buchanan, J. Christopher Phillips; set decoration, Les Bloom; costume design, April Ferry; sound (Dolby), Dennis Maitland; John Goodman's makeup-makeup supervisor, Kevin Haney; visual effects supervisor, Chuck Comisky; matte paintings, Illusion Arts Inc., Syd Dutton, Bill Taylor; stunt coordinator, Rick LeFevour; associate producer, Erica Hiller; assistant director, Van Wyck; casting, Nancy Nayor, Valerie McCaffrey, Jane Alderman (Chicago), Judy Welker (Indiana). Reviewed at Directors Guild of America theater, L.A., April 9, 1992. MPAA Rating: PG. Running time: **113 MIN.**
Babe Ruth . . . . John Goodman
Claire Hodgson Ruth . . Kelly McGillis
Helen Woodford Ruth . Trini Alvarado
Jumpin' Joe Dugan . Bruce Boxleitner
Harry Frazee . . . . Peter Donat
Brother Mathias . . . James Cromwell
Jack Dunn . . . . J.C. Quinn
Miller Huggins . . . . Joe Ragno
Col. Jacob Ruppert . . . Bernard Kates
Lou Gehrig . . . . Michael McGrady
Young George H. Ruth . . . Andy Voils
Johnny Sylvester (age 10) . Dylan Day
Johnny (age 30) . . . . Stephen Caffrey

With John Goodman's engaging and convincing performance, "The Babe" is better than might be expected, but producer John Fusco's uninspired script never gives the film a reason for being. Despite Haskell Wexler's alluring lensing, the thinly dramatized, overly episodic Babe Ruth biopic resembles a telepic that has lost its way to the big screen. Mild B.O. looms for pic falling between kiddie and adult fare.

In a redundant follow-up to last fall's WB TV/NBC "Babe Ruth" starring Stephen Lang, lovable TV star-erstwhile movie character actor Goodman plays one of America's most endearing folk heroes. Though heavier with a bigger torso and thicker legs than the Bambino's incongruously spindly pins, Goodman otherwise has been made up by Kevin Haney into a remarkable likeness of the real Babe.

Goodman has an exuberant, bumptious charm ideally suited to the overgrown child he's playing, a guileless "babe" of voracious appetites and seemingly effortless athletic skill. He also captured the graceful Ruthian swing and trademark home run trot.

Goodman hits a home run almost every time he swings the bat. Granted, the Babe was superhuman, but reducing this fine all-around athlete to a homer specialist is simplistic. Ruth's stellar pitching abilities are only glancingly acknowledged, and he's never shown in the outfield, which he covered with skill.

Director Arthur Hiller nevertheless approaches the subject with an abundant affection, and he's exceptionally well served by Wexler, production designer James D. Vance, costume designer April Ferry and visual effects supervisor Chuck Comisky in conjuring up the period (1902-1935) with luminous, nostalgic images.

Chicago's Wrigley Field plays itself, and an old stadium in Danville, Ill., effectively doubles for Boston's Fenway Park and Pittsburgh's Forbes Field. Superior matte work completes the illusion of old-time baseball settings, including Yankee Stadium (the remodeled "House That Ruth Built," seen in a prologue).

But what does Ruth mean to today's audiences? Though he's a figure who can't fail to intrigue even in the most perfunctory treatment, Ruth was a more complex man than Fusco makes him seem in this two-dimensional portrait, and pic barely suggests the importance of his role in U.S. life or the improbable extent of his celebrity.

Starting in his Dickensian childhood when he's abandoned into the care of boys school in Baltimore, pic touchingly shows how the fat, unloved boy (Andy Voils) blossoms into an athletic marvel under tutelage of a kindly Brother (James Cromwell).

But it skips too quickly over Ruth's turbulent adolescent years to show him leaving the school and becoming a pro ballplayer. The rage and feelings of neglect that fueled Ruth's ambition aren't explored adequately, although Goodman does his best to bring them out while trying to overcome the script's cartoonish bent.

With a nod to contemporary candor, pic does not neglect Ruth's uncouth eating, drinking and social habits, his sexual adventurism or his consorting with dubious characters.

But pic is so infatuated with the Babe, warts and all, that it fails to bring to life the feelings of his first wife (Trini Alvarado), who's understandably bothered to hear that he's had sex with four women at one time in a New Orleans brothel but still managing to come off like a whining nag complaining about it.

The pathos underlying Ruth's irresponsible antics emerges intermittently, but the script is more concerned with clocking off career highlights than exploring Ruth's unusual psyche.

His satisfying second marriage to a practical-minded showgirl (saucy Kelly McGillis) brings out a new strain of maturity in Ruth, but the heaviest dramatic conflict Fusco can find is Ruth's frustrated attempt to convince baseball hierarchy he's reformed enough to manage. Hardly big-league pic material.

Following an accurately ambiguous staging of his controversial "called shot" in the 1932 World Series, the film turns darker with Yankee owner Jacob Ruppert (Bernard Kates) coldly dismissing Ruth's managerial ambitions.

It's too bad the film didn't mention that Ruth himself had a brief shot at a movie career at the peak of his baseball fame in the 1920s. Reviewing First National's 1927 baseball romance "Babe Comes Home," in which Ruth starred with Anna Q. Nilsson, Abel Green wrote in VARIETY, "As a film star, Babe (George Herman) Ruth delivers almost as handily as on the diamond, which is saying much both ways for the King of Swat."

— *Joseph McBride*

LEAVING NORMAL

A Universal Pictures release of a Mirage production. Produced by Lindsay Doran. Executive producer, Sydney Pollack. Directed by Edward Zwick. Screenplay, Edward Solomon. Camera (Deluxe color), Ralf D. Bode; editor, Victor Du Bois; music, W.G. Snuffy Walden; production design-costume design, Patricia Norris; art direction, Sandy Cochrane; sound (Dolby), Rob Young; assistant director, Skip Cosper; special visual effects, Visual Concepts Engineering (supervisor, Peter Kuran); co-producer, Sarah Caplan; line producer, Fitch Cady; casting, Mary Colquhoun. Reviewed at Universal screening room, N.Y., April 1, 1992. MPAA Rating: R. Running time: **110 MIN.**
Darly . . . . Christine Lahti
Marianne . . . . Meg Tilly
66 . . . . Patrika Darbo
Harrison . . . . . . Lenny Von Dohlen
Leon . . . . Maury Chaykin
Emily . . . . Eve Gordon
Also with: James Eckhouse, Brett Cullen, James Gammon, Rutanya Alda.

Christine Lahti gives a powerhouse performance in the female buddy/road movie "Leaving Normal." Universal is following in the tiremarks of the similar "Thelma & Louise" and will have to work overtime to differentiate the two pics in the public's mind.

Edward Solomon's script uses the same launching point as Callie Khouri's Oscar-winning "Thelma" screenplay: Two women fed up with their lives hop into a convertible and motor down the highway.

Cocktail waitress Christine Lahti and battered housewife Meg Tilly meet in a parking lot, immediately bond and are soon headed from the small western town of Normal to Alaska where Lahti will claim her inherited home and land.

Their picaresque adventures differ from the Susan Sarandon-Geena Davis team, with no crime and little violence. First they stop off to visit Tilly's relatives in Portland and get an eyeful of the dreaded "perfect homemaker" existence (nicely caricatured by Eve Gordon as a sister).

After Lahti's GTO breaks down and is ransacked, they get a ride from friendly truckers Maury Chaykin and Lenny Von Dohlen. Lahti's distrust of all men after having been burned too often nips this relationship in the bud, but Tilly is determined to pursue Von Dohlen some day.

Solomon's episodic screenplay has the duo's route and key decisions left to chance. Director Edward Zwick, who previously piloted the quite dissimilar, nearly all-male war pic "Glory," uses optical effects, matte shots and other fantasy touches from the outset to avoid realism in depicting the women's fanciful saga.

Best segment memorably features scene-stealer Patrika Darbo as a chubby waitress with a funny way of speaking who briefly joins the troupe. She's comically written out of the film when Mr. Right appears and takes her away with him.

Not for all tastes, "Leaving Normal" has a serious undertone in its depiction of losers who keep struggling to assert themselves in an unfeeling and male-dominated world.

Though Lahti dominates much of the film as a brassy, tough-as-nails character, the waif-like Tilly gets to blossom in the final reel when she finally finds a home in Alaska and becomes the small town's cheerful mascot. A clever finale has the two women, still in a platonic, non-sexual relationship, settling down with a newly built home and ready-made family of two young Eskimo boys they've befriended.

Von Dohlen is very amusing as a modern-day Montgomery Clift type whose weeping while reading "The Grapes of Wrath" instantly wins over Tilly. James Gammon is excellent as a tough Alaskan who recognizes Lahti as a former topless dancer named Pillow Talk and hires her for $500 as a prostitute. Also impressive in a small role is Rutanya Alda as a nurse who is initially unsympathetic to Lahti's quest to find the daughter she abandoned 18 years ago.

Ralf Bode's photography of awesome Canadian vistas is atmospheric and occasionally upstaged by the mattework night skies and other opticals. Tech credits are fine. — *Lawrence Cohn*

DEEP COVER

A New Line Cinema release of a Pierre David/Henry Bean production. Produced by David, Bean. Executive producer, David Streit. Co-producer, Deborah Moore. Co-executive producer, Michael DeLuca. Directed by Bill Duke. Screenplay, Michael Tolkin, Bean, based on a story by Tolkin. Camera (Deluxe color; Film House prints), Bojan Bazelli; editor, John Carter; music, Michel Colombier; production design, Pam Warner; art direction, Daniel W. Bickel; set decoration, Donald Elmblad; sound (Dolby), Tony Smyles; assistant directors, Jerry Ziesmer, Hope Goodwin; 2nd unit director, Conrad Palmisano; 2nd unit camera, Frank Holgate; casting, Chemin Bernard. Reviewed at Sunset Tower screening room, L.A., April 2, 1992. MPAA Rating: R. Running time: **112 MIN.**
Russell Stevens Jr./
John Q. Hull . . . . Larry Fishburne
David Jason . . . . Jeff Goldblum
Betty McCutcheon . . Victoria Dillard
Jerry Carver . . Charles Martin Smith
Felix Barbosa . . . . . . Gregory Sierra
Ken Taft . . . . . Clarence Williams III
Hector Guzman . . . . Rene Assa
Molto . . . . Alex Colon
Eddie . . . . . Roger Guenveur Smith
Gopher . . . . Sydney Lassick
Also with: Kamala Lopez, Julio Oscar Mechoso, Glynn Turman, James T. Morris, Arthur Mendoza, Sandra Gould.

Convoluted and mostly unconvincing as a portrait of the drug underworld, "Deep Cover" still carries some resonance due to its vivid portrait of societal decay and a heavyweight performance by Larry Fishburne. Deeply cynical, almost despairing second feature from Bill Duke features enough promotable hard action, rough violence and bad attitude to make a small spring stash.

Eccentric screenplay by Michael Tolkin ("The Player," "The Rapture") and Henry Bean ("Internal Affairs") wobbles throughout between moments that are deeply felt and scenes of almost embarrassing illogic and expository baldness. What announces itself as a work of great integrity and probing acumen continually derails itself with screwy developments that repeatedly, and annoyingly, force the film to renew the viewer's faith in it.

Tough, straight-arrow cop Fishburne is recruited by government drug-enforcement chief Charles Martin Smith to infiltrate the cartel of dealer Arthur Mendoza, who controls 40% of the L.A. cocaine market on behalf of his uncle, a powerful Latin American politician the U.S. government would like to cut down to size.

Taking a grungy downtown room and hitting the streets, Fishburne begins working his way up as a small-time dealer, expanding his network until it includes suburban attorney dealer Jeff Goldblum, his supplier, vicious Gregory Sierra, and art importer-money launderer Victoria Dillard.

Goldblum is a peculiar guy, to say the least, wise-talking his way through most situations, expressing his concern for his family on the one hand while on the other promoting his scheme for manufacturing a synthetic — and legal — cocaine substitute.

Inevitably, Fishburne becomes increasingly caught up in his dangerous and extravagant new lifestyle. Enticed by Dillard, who likes her sex mixed with drugs, and forced by circumstances to kill, the seemingly unswerving Fishburne begins to waver, and finally goes over the edge into addiction and money mania.

Climax gives Fishburne the opportunity to choose which side of the law he wants to live on, as well as whether he'll be his own man or the pawn of a big organization, and ending has a nice zing that partially alleviates some of the previous bad mechanics and routine action stand-offs.

Fishburne delivers a commanding performance as a man who discovers the limits of his abormally great moral strength, but several of the scenes with big-cheese drug dealers smack of the same poses and dialogue exchanges that have been trotted out for years now, with little variation.

Still, a good sense of dark menace and foreboding in Duke's direction backdrops what intensity there is in the script. Pic's most potent point is its effective linking of the moral equivocation and spinelessness of government policy with the perception that the country is spinning down the toilet. Jerry Brown's constituency will dig it.

Performances are mostly of the intense, threatening and streetwise variety. Low-budget lensing ace Bojan Bazeli gives numerous sequences a sharp stylized look, but key behind-the-scenes contribution is Michel Colombier's superbly moody, dissonant jazz/rock score.

— *Todd McCarthy*

HÖFEBER
(HAYFEVER)
(DANISH)

A Pathe-Nordisk Film Distribution release of a Obel Film production in collaboration with Danish Film Institute. Produced by Michael Obel. Directed by Annelise Hovmand. Screenplay, Hovmand, Arne Forchhammer, based on Leif Panduro's novel. Camera (color), Claus Loof; editor, Jörgen Kastrup; music, Nanna Lüders Jensen; art direction, Sören Skjär; sound, Preben Mortensen. Reviewed at Palads Theater, Copenhagen, Dec. 12, 1991. Running time: **90 MIN.**
With: Frits Helmuth, Lisbet Dahl, Kirsten Lehfeldt, Peter Schröder, Axel Ströbye, Torben Jensen, Claus Ryskjaer, Peter Mörk, Ebbe Rode.

This uneven, bittersweet farce about the trials and tribulations of a reticent judge offers a few laughs and a host of popular actors. However, pic has had limited box office success locally and will have little appeal outside Denmark.

The quiet, well-organized life of a peace-loving judge (Frits Helmuth) crumbles when his frustrated wife (Kirsten Lehfeldt) desperately tries to make him jealous over her longtime infidelity with his best friend. This and other troubles, such as his son's drug arrest, give the poor judge a psychosomatic case of hay fever, leading to more exasperation.

At times, pic works as a lightweight black comedy. The script, based on a 1975 novel by satirist Leif Panduro, and the direction by veteran helmer Annelise Hovmand give the whole thing a dated feel. The seasoned character actors all do their thing, but the material fails to come alive. —*Peter Risby Hansen*

THE PLAYBOYS
(U.S.-IRISH)

A Samuel Goldwyn Co. release. Produced by William P. Cartlidge, Simon Perry. Directed by Gillies MacKinnon. Screenplay, Shane Connaughton, Kerry Crabbe. Camera (color), Jack Conroy; editor, Humphrey Dixon; music, Jean-Claude Petit; production design, Andy Harris; costume design, Consolata Boyle; sound (Dolby), Peter Lindsay; assistant director, Chris Carreras; casting, Pat Condron. Reviewed at Magno Preview 4 screening room, N.Y., March 19, 1992. MPAA Rating: PG-13. Running time: **110 MIN.**
Constable Hegarty . . . Albert Finney
Tom . . . . Aidan Quinn
Tara . . . . Robin Wright
Freddie . . . . Milo O'Shea
Malone . . . . Alan Devlin
Brigid . . . . Niamh Cusack
Cassidy . . . . Ian McElhinney
Also with: Stella McCusker, Niall Buggy, Anna Livia Ryan, Adrian Dunbar.

Excellent perfs enliven a story that's as old as the hills in "The Playboys." Latest in a spate of Irish-set films should attract a modest audience.

Pic started off with a hitch when originally cast star Annette Bening dropped out on the eve of production. Replacement Robin Wright (Mrs. Sean Penn) was a felicitous choice, in her best film acting to date.

Story by Shane Connaughton, who co-scripted "My Left Foot," concerns an Irish lass (Wright) in 1957 who's shamed by her fellow townsfolk for being an unwed mother. She refuses to name the father, and in an eventful opening reel, one of her suitors (Adrian Dunbar of "Hear My Song") commits suicide.

It turns out he wasn't the daddy, but a new love enters her life with the arrival of Milo O'Shea's troupe of traveling actors, "The Playboys." Newest thesp in the company (Aidan Quinn) immediately impresses Wright and eventually beds her. Fly in the ointment is the local constable (Albert Finney) who has always been in love with Wright and explodes into violence.

This familiar pattern of headstrong girl and passions brimming beneath the surface is well directed by first time Scottish helmer Gillies MacKinnon, though the pace slows in middle reels as plot gives way to the troupe's enjoyable stage performances. Subplots involving Wright as an amateur smuggler as well as troupe member Ian McElhinney's activities as an IRA terrorist are downpeddled.

Especially delicious is O'Shea's mummery, whether portraying "Othello" or staging an impromptu theatrical version of "Gone with the Wind" after watching the original at a local movie house.

Among the principals, American thesp Wright is vibrant and earthy. Heretofore used mainly as a decorative beauty ("The Princess Bride"), she gets to expand on the histrionics of her best previous assignment, the recently released 1987 feature "Denial" (a.k.a. "Loon").

Finney is a tower of strength as the repressed lover, and even gets to freak out in a violent scene reminiscent of Orson Welles as the elderly publisher busting up a room in "Citizen Kane." Quinn has the most ambiguous of the major roles but succeeds in keeping the audience guessing as to whether he's a good guy or not.

Jack Conroy, who previously lensed Jim Sheridan's features, captures the remote Irish countryside with miniaturist skill.
— *Lawrence Cohn*

LAST IMAGES OF WAR
(BRITISH-DOCU)

A Telesis Prods. Intl. production in association with the BBC & Dox Delux. Produced, directed, filmed, edited by Stephen Olsson, Scott Andrews. Screenplay, Olsson. Associate editor, Ken Schneider. Narrated by Ben Kingsley. Reviewed on videotape. (In Sundance Film Festival.) Running time: **80 MIN.**

Accomplished documentary filmers Stephen Olsson and Scott Andrews provide a compelling look at the 1979 to '88 Soviet-Afghan war in their moving portrait of four photojournalists who died there.

Film, which premiered in competition at the Sundance Film Festival, skimps on specifics about the history and purpose of the Soviet invasion — a frustrating omission, considering the interest the pic raises. Nonetheless, story's resulting universality could pay off in broader exhibition prospects.

American Jim Lindelof, Russian Sasha Secretaryov, British Andy Skripkowiak and Japanese Naoko Nanjo were drawn by divergent forces to record a David vs. Goliath conflict in which 1.5 million Afghans and at least 50,000 Soviets died, a devastating toll hidden from the world until news photos appeared.

Told via images recorded by the photojournalists plus additional footage, letters home and the accounts of companions and relatives, each of the four stories introduces a remarkable, heroic person whose loss underscores the waste of war. At the same time, filmers point out the psychological and spiritual needs such conflicts continue to serve.

One wishes that the filmmakers, who also covered the Afghan war as photojournalists and produced a separate docu, "Afghanistan: The Fight for a

Way of Life," had been more illuminating about the motives behind this war.

Narration by actor Ben Kingsley is excellent. Images and interviews are pieced together with depth and clarity. Self-financed by the filmmakers and finished with BBC funds, film debuted in February on the BBC docu series "Fine Cut" and is likely to air on PBS later this year.

—Amy Dawes

L'AFFÛT
(ON GUARD)
(FRENCH)

A Bac Films release of a Les Films de l'Equinoxe-Le Centre Européen Cinematographique Rhône-Alpes co-production with the participation of Canal Plus & Sofiarp. Produced by Les Films de l'Equinoxe (Yannick Bellon). Directed by Bellon. Screenplay, Bellon, Remi Waterhouse, in collaboration with Michel Fessler, Benjamin Legrand. Camera (color, widescreen), Pierre-William Glenn; editor, Michel Lewin; music, Antoine Duhamel; set design, Jacques Voizot, Patrick Weibel, Giuseppe Ponturo; sound, Jean-Marcel Milan, Thierry Delor. Reviewed at MGM screening room, Paris, Feb. 5, 1992. Running time: **103 MIN.**
With: Tcheky Karyo, Dominique Blanc, Patrick Bouchitey, Carlo Brandt, Pierre-Octave Arrighi, Michael Tisseur.

"L' Affût" earnestly examines the conflict between hunters in a rural French town and an interloping ornithologist who wants to turn the local marshes into a preserve. Director/co-scripter Yannick Bellon has her heart and her camera in the right places, but overall tone is too bland to sustain interest beyond the small screen, where impact of fine widescreen lensing will ebb.

Pic could be a useful tool for orienting community debates about land use and animal rights. Shot entirely in the Rhône-Alpes region, pic makes good use of changing seasons and is peppered with shots both pleasing and unnerving to animal lovers.

A single mom (Dominique Blanc) returns to her childhood village after 10 years with her 9-year-old son in tow. A local barkeep (Patrick Bouchitey), a widower also with a young son, still has a soft spot for Blanc, but she's abruptly drawn to the town's only other outsider (Tcheky Karyo).

Rugged but sensitive Karyo is a teacher and reformed alcoholic who can imitate duck calls to warn birds when hunters are coming. His students like his ec-

ological stance, but their parents, who consider hunting a birthright, don't appreciate him.

Thesping is fine all around, but the script — touching on the relationships of parent and child, sister and brother, friend and lover, citizen and community — fails to jell. Blanc/Karyo romance blossoms for no particular reason, unless it's because no women are in evidence apart from the town whore.

A falling out becomes inevitable when Karyo discovers that Blanc's brother has an illegal sideline in taxidermied endangered species, including a magnificent eagle nursed back to health after it was caught in a trap. Slo-mo of eagle in flight is quite lovely, in contrast with a kid's prank: A frog is forced to smoke a cigarette until the helpless amphibian explodes. Helmer employs queasy black humor in immediately cutting to dinner at the local vet's house: frog legs.

— Lisa Nesselson

SLEEPWALKERS

A Columbia Pictures release of an Ion Pictures/Victor & Grais production. Produced by Mark Victor, Mark Grais, Nabeel Zahid. Executive producers, Dimitri Logothetis, Joseph Medawar. Directed by Mick Garris. Screenplay, Stephen King. Camera (Technicolor), Rodney Charters; editor, O. Nicholas Brown; music, Nicholas Pike; production design, John DeCuir Jr.; sound (Dolby), Don H. Matthews; assistant director, Randall Badger; production manager-co-producer, Richard Stenta; special make-up effects, Alterian Studios; special visual effects, Apogee Prods. (supervisor, Jeffrey A. Okun); 2nd unit directors, Stenta, Rexford Metz; additional camera, Bert Dunk; casting, Wendy Kurtzman, Lisa Mionie. Reviewed at Village East 3 theater, N.Y., April 11, 1992. MPAA Rating: R. Running time: **91 MIN.**
Charles Brady . . . . . . Brian Krause
Tanya Robertson . . . Mädchen Amick
Mary Brady . . . . Alice Krige
Sheriff . . . . Jim Haynie
Mrs. Robertson . . . . . Cindy Pickett
Capt. Soames . . . . Ron Perlman
Don Robertson . . . . . . Lyman Ward
Andy Simpson . . . . Dan Martin
Also with: Glenn Shadix, Monty Bane, Stephen King, Joe Dante, John Landis, Clive Barker, Tobe Hooper.

Stephen King's "Sleepwalkers" is an idiotic horror potboiler which should achieve its goal of making a fast buck strictly by pouring on the gore.

King's new approach to the vampire legend is really a variation on that of Tri-Star's 1988 flop "The Kiss." Brian Krause and mom Alice Krige are incestuous monsters called Sleepwalkers who survive by draining the life force from virgin girls.

After a dumb prolog in Bodega Bay (site of Hitchcock's "The Birds"), film takes place in sleepy Travis, Ind., where Krause is the new kid in school claiming to be a transfer student.

In a wish fulfillment scene, he brutally murders his uppity teacher Glenn Shadix, who's figured out that Krause's transcripts and past are phony. He romances beautiful classmate Mädchen Amick, resulting in a pretentious date-rape scene in which Amick is saved from a fate worse than death *and* worse than rape.

King's screenplay has no internal logic and relies wholly on stupid gimmicks like the monsters' ability to become invisible and their vulnerability to cats. Unlike the recent TV movie "Strays," the hordes of pussycats on display here aren't scary even when they're dutifully attacking the monsters. Defying credibility, the lead cat turns out to be a trained pet that kindly deputy Dan Martin takes around with him in his police squad car instead of a dog. Script suggests some possibilities which are not followed up. The potential pathos of Krause and Krige as perhaps the last lonely members of their breed is undeveloped, and Krause's possible ambivalence at falling in love with Amick (though sexually satisfied by mama) is trashed in favor of him becoming a wisecracking sadist during Amick's date-rape scene.

Substituting for substance here are failed in-jokes. Many noted genre directors (Joe Dante, Tobe Hooper) as well as King himself have pointless cameo roles. Even Amick's name "Tanya Robertson" seems like a pun on sexy actress Tanya Roberts.

Mick Garris's crass direction uses shock effects like noise and sudden violence instead of suspense. He's in a rut, having treated the same mother/son incest theme in his last opus, the TV movie "Psycho IV."

Cast is physically appealing and could have generated some sympathy if permitted. Makeup and visual transformation effects for the monsters are okay but unspectacular. Backlot lensing shows up in a fake looking studio street.

— Lawrence Cohn

MEINE TOCHTER GEHÖRT MIR
(MY DAUGHTER BELONGS TO ME)
(GERMAN)

A Tobis-Filmkunst release of a Regina Ziegler production in cooperation with WDR. Produced by Ziegler. Directed by Vivian Naefe. Screenplay, Naefe, Walter Kärger; camera (color), Gernot Roll; editor, Susanne Schett; music, Hubert Bartholomae; production design, Detlef Fichtner; costumes, Ursula Welter; sound, Detlev Fichtner; casting, Risa Kes. Reviewed at Kurbel Cinema, Berlin, March 30, 1992. Running time: **100 MIN.**
With: Barbara Auer, Georges Corraface, Nadja Nebas, Nicholas Brieger, Aleka Paizi, Stefan Wolf-Schönburg.

Prospects outside of the small screen in Europe look dim for this unremarkable tale of an international child custody battle.

Nuts-and-bolts plot forges bravely ahead for pic's first half: A Greek father kidnaps his daughter from her busy career mom in Berlin and brings her home to live with his family.

In lots of back-and-forth action between the two countries, the mother is unable to get help from the authorities in bringing the daughter home (does the EC really have no guidelines on the issue?). She hires a professional kidnapper to nab the moppet.

Respectable story becomes disjointed as auds sits through the last half waiting for the inevitable resolution. To illustrate the situation's tension and hopelessness, the combative parents (both M.D.s) smoke a lot and finally sleep with each other, destroying much of the pic's credibility.

Since parents are hardly talking, minor characters give them a chance to say lines and vent feelings (the kid talks to a teddy bear). Story is not opened up with subplots or diversions. Tech credits are fine, although a distracting number of props are turquoise. *—Rebecca Lieb*

UOVA DI GAROFANO
(FAREWELL SWEET WAR)
(ITALIAN)

An 11 Marzo Cinematografica production in collaboration with RAI-2 and Ministry of Tourism & Entertainment. (Intl. sales: Sacis.) Directed, written by Silvano Agosti, based on his novel. Camera (color)-editor, Agosti; music, Daniele Iacono; art direction, costumes, Luigia Dal Re; sound (Dolby), Giuliana Zam-

ariola. Reviewed at Azzurro Scipioni Cinema, Rome, Feb. 27, 1992. Running time: **102 MIN.**
Silvano . . . . Federico Zanola
Elisa . . . . Elisa Murolo
Crimen . . . . Alain Cuny

Achildhood reminiscence of the waning days of World War II in Italy's crumbling Fascist state, "Farewell Sweet War" is a resourceful display of one-man, no-budget filmmaking saddled with an excess of poetic baggage. Lyrical memoir's fragmented narrative and acutely personalized approach will make it too obscure for all but the most persevering fest auds.

A man revisits his wartime home and, in a lofty dreamscape of storybook poppy fields and dramatic skies, is flooded by a confusing rush of memories.

From a child's-eye view, he retraces his bond with a reclusive old man ostracized by the villagers and witnesses an execution by firing squad. Observing his father's cowardice and fickle alliances first with Fascists and then with post-liberation occupying troops, the boy gradually awakens to the mendacity of the adult world.

Looming large over every frame is the burdensome shadow of Andrei Tarkovsky, and pic plays like a homage to his "Mirror." But where Tarkovsky used docu footage to anchor his autobiographical lyricism in reality, writer-director Silvano Agosti opts for a ponderous poet's POV all the way. Wartime events are sapped of impact grittier treatment might have given them.

Agosti's lensing is effective in conveying the otherworldliness of memory using only available light. Daniele Iacono's somber music works well.

Performances are generally fine given the script's often sketchy characterization. Federico Zanola's intensely expressive young face gives added depth to the central figure of the boy.
— *David Rooney*

AU NOM DE PÈRE ET DU FILS
(IN THE NAME OF THE FATHER AND THE SON)
(FRENCH)

An AAA Intl. release of a Tésta Rossa Films production with participation of CNC & Procirep. Executive producer, Nadine Perron. Produced, directed, written by Patrice Noia. Camera

(color), Armand Marco; editor, Marie-Pomme Carteret; music, Alexandre Desplat; costumes, Marie-France Allamel, Isabelle Ginet; sound, Frederic Ullman. Reviewed at Club 13 screening room, Paris, Feb. 18, 1992. Running time: **80 MIN.**
With: Judicaël Noia, Carolina Rosi, Pier Paolo Capponi, Patrice Noia.

In writing, producing, directing and acting in "Au Nom du Père et du Fils," sound technician turned director Patrice Noia has come up with an admirable but only mildly engaging film.

Helmer has drawn on an actual incident for inspiration: His father, who came to France from Italy, was murdered in his home near Bordeaux in 1978. Although the perpetrator was caught and sentenced, Noia was left with a gnawing sense of unfinished business overshadowing his life.

Realizing he barely knew his own father, Noia resolved to establish a closer relationship with his son. In this scripted film, he plays a father hitting the road from France to Italy in a Ferrari, with his 14-year-old son (Noia's real son Judicaël).

Visiting the murder site, Patrice reads from the police account of his father's death, annotating the official story in simple but striking language as he recalls seeing his father in the morgue and collecting his personal effects.

Father and son are sympathetic characters, although Patrice Noia is slightly stiff as an actor, and his son comes across as strong and sensitive. They shared the best-acting award in the 1991 La Baule Festival of European Films.

Well-lensed pic has technical polish but is often too naive in its presentation of complex concerns. Still, it addresses real human issues of filial love and scars of grief. Street life in Italian villages and cities, including Rome and Naples, is nicely conveyed. Score, which features accordion, violin and piano, is catchy.
— *Lisa Nesselson*

L'AMOREUSE
(FRENCH)

An AMLF release of a Les Films Alain Sarde-Films A-2 co-production with the participation of Canal Plus & CNC. (Intl. sales: WMF.) Executive producer, Christine Gozlan. Produced by Alain Sarde. Directed, written by Jacques Doillon. Camera (color), Christophe Pollock; editor, Catherine Quesemand; set design, Yan Arlaud; sound,

Jean-Claude Laureux; producers (Canadian segment), Claude Gagnon, Yuri Yoshimura-Gagnon. Reviewed at AMLF screening room, Paris, Feb. 13, 1992. Running time: **100 MIN.**
Marie . . . . . Charlotte Gainsbourg
Paul . . . . Ivan Attal
Antoine . . . . Thomas Langmann
Juliette . . . . Stéphanie Cotta
Also with: Thierry Maricot, Elsa Zylberstein, Paul Savoie, Hélene Fileire.

With good dialogue but too much random behavior, Jacques Doillon's "L'Amoureuse" is a talky, mildly engaging account of the push and pull in a ménage-à-trois. Pic should do reasonably well at Gallic wickets since the trio is played by three of France's best up-and-coming young thesps.

Contempo look at post-adolescent romance wants to evoke "Jules and Jim," yet begins from a premise so arbitrary that it upstages pic's charm until enough details accumulate to lend logic to the proceedings.

Lanky Marie (Charlotte Gainsbourg) lives with Antoine (Thomas Langmann). While he's away for a week, Marie meets Paul (Ivan Attal), a filmmaker visiting from Canada.

Paul is instantly smitten and promises he won't fuss if Marie marries him secretly. She puts him off by saying she and Antoine have decided to have a child. When Antoine returns, he becomes vividly jealous of his girlfriend's chaste encounter.

With much intervening chitchat and an array of verbal and physical confrontations, Marie has sex — separately — with both guys and soon believes she's pregnant. But by whom?

Although dialogue is pithy and frequently amusing, the characters are given no credible motivation and seem to live comfortably without visible means of support. Gainsbourg is a gifted performer, but nothing about her sketchy character or her tomboyish demeanor carries enough clout to convince viewers that two men would be irresistibly attracted to her.

Pic is carefully staged and agreeably lensed throughout, but rarely provides enough narrative heft to shore up any simple dilemma. A sex scene has Marie rushing to the sink after performing oral sex on Antoine, and he extrapolating that she's not cut out for motherhood.

All three leads imbue their roles with a mopey love-sick-

ness. Stéphanie Cotta is fine as Gainsbourg's flighty, frivolous sister. — *Lisa Nesselson*

WHITE SANDS

A Warner Bros. release of a James G. Robinson presentation of a Morgan Creek production. Produced by William Sackheim, Scott Rudin. Executive producers, Robinson, David Nicksay, Gary Barber. Directed by Roger Donaldson. Screenplay, Daniel Pyne. Camera (Eastmancolor; Panavision widescreen), Peter Menzies Jr.; editor, Nicholas Beauman; music, Patrick O'Hearn; production design, John Graysmark; art direction, Michael Rizzo; set decoration, Michael Seirton; costume design, Deborah Everton; sound (Dolby), Richard Goodman; associate producer, David Wisnievitz; assistant director, Joel Segal; casting, David Rubin. Reviewed at Warner Bros. screening room, Burbank, April 8, 1992. MPAA Rating: R. Running time: **101 MIN.**
Ray Dolezal . . . . Willem Dafoe
Lane Bodine
. . . . Mary Elizabeth Mastrantonio
Gorman Lennox . . . . Mickey Rourke
Greg Meeker . . . . Samuel L. Jackson
Bert Gibson . . . . . M. Emmet Walsh
Flynn . . . . James Rebhorn
Noreen . . . . Maura Tierney
Roz . . . . Beth Grant
Molly Dolezal . . . . Mimi Rogers
Also with: John P. Ryan, Fred Dalton Thompson.

The plot shifts as often as the desert dunes in "White Sands," an absorbing, tightly coiled thriller not always easy to follow. A fine cast, no-fat direction by Roger Donaldson, and nasties belonging to the all-purpose CIA-FBI consortium of evil vault this into the class of solidly commercial suspensers, even if viewers will be hard put to recount the plot afterwards.

Making a bid for wider appeal as a modern Western smalltown sheriff who may be the only honest man in the New Mexico territory, Willem Dafoe sets himself up for plenty of abuse when, after finding a dead Indian with $500,000 in cash in the middle of nowhere, he takes on the victim's identity in an effort to solve the case.

Making a contact in Taos, he is quickly beaten and robbed of the loot by two babes who look like they might have been friends of Mercedes McCambridge in "Touch of Evil." He is then abducted by the FBI, who are far from pleased that Dafoe has managed to lose the money they reveal was being used in a covert sting operation being headed by vet agent Samuel L. Jackson.

Latter demands that the stash be recovered and, to this end, Dafoe, in his identity as the dead courier, keeps an appointment in Santa Fe with mysterious Mickey Rourke. Magnetic and smoothly self-assured, this wily operator introduces him to another shadowy character, spoiled rich girl Mary Elizabeth Mastrantonio, who dabbles in international politics and dangerous men.

Pic builds tautly to a powerful first act peak, as Rourke takes Dafoe to White Sands for a meeting with two arms merchants. Tension mounts to a desert broil as the cowboy salesmen reneg on the original deal and demand a heftier sum for their heavy artillery, and the way Dafoe handles himself cements his standing as Rourke's partner, at least for the moment.

Intensity dwindles a bit, however, when Dafoe pairs off with Mastrantonio, to whom he appeals for the extra coin. Aware that Dafoe isn't who he pretends to be, and apparently turned on this fact, this wealthy society beauty comes on to him in almost ridiculously brazen fashion, only to be rebuffed.

Pair do share a literally steamy shower scene, but their would-be romance is mostly in her head, and archness of her character emerges as the most artificial element in a story that becomes increasingly farfetched as it unfolds.

Still, scenarist Daniel Pyne ("Pacific Heights") has quite a few more twists and turns in store, as Dafoe is buffetted between two black-and-white teams of FBI goons, Rourke shows his ruthless side, and several more people are killed before the inevitable return to the exquisitely barren white sands for a bizarre and rather original climactic shootout.

Some thrillers have gone down as classics through the years despite the lack of total narrative coherence, and while "White Sands" doesn't rate that high, its numerous stylistic and behavioral pleasures generally make one willing to forgive the confusion to see what lies ahead. Although director Donaldson has yet to match the incisive power of his early New Zealand effort "Smash Palace," this can hold its own with "No Way Out" as an audience-pleasing cliffhanger, and Pyne's dialogue offers a degree of wit along with its head-scratching elements.

Cool and laconic, yet with an internal rigor that compels attention, Dafoe makes a creditable claim to a little Gary Cooper turf and capably carries a picture suffused in corruption, cyni-

cism and a pervasive amorality. In what could be a smart career move after a string of starring stiffs, Rourke takes on a juicy character role with decidedly positive results. Although appealing as always, Mastrantonio gives the impression of an intelligent actress stuck in a role below her station.

Samuel L. Jackson, M. Emmet Walsh and a host of strong players in small parts give luster to a varied supporting cast. An uncredited Mimi Rogers appears briefly at the outset as Dafoe's wife.

Tech credits are first-rate. Peter Menzies Jr.'s widescreen lensing and John Graysmark's production design nicely capture the warmly rugged feeling of very well chosen New Mexico locations. Nicholas Beauman's to-the-bone editing keeps the suspense up and available moments to wonder at it all down, and Patrick O'Hearn's music enhances the dense atmospherics.

—Todd McCarthy

ZHOU ENLAI
(CHINESE)

A Yu Enterprises (Australia) release of a Guan Xi Film Studio production. Produced by Gao Honghu, Hu Juan. Directed by Ding Yinnan. Screenplay, Song Jialin, Liu Simin, Yinnan. Camera ('Scope, color), Yu Xiaoqun, Lei Jiaming; music, Cheng Dazhao; production design, Li Wenguang, Liu Sheng, Wang Dayu, Shu Gang; sound, Lin Guang, Huang Mingaung. Reviewed at Australian cinema, Sydney, March 12, 1992. Running time: **164 MIN.**
Zhou Enlai . . . . Wang Tiecheng
Deng Yingchao . . . . . Deng Xiaojuan
Mao Zedong . . . . Zhang Keyao
Liu Shaoqi . . . . Guo Feceng
Zhu De . . . . Liu Huaizheng
Deng Xiaoping . . . . Lu Qi

This lengthy, reverential pic about late Chinese premier Zhou Enlai will be heavy going for all except history buffs. Director Ding Yinnan's solemn, static treatment offsets a handsome, affectionate impersonation of the leader by Wang Tiecheng, who's played him before on screen.

The film has a feel of those Soviet tributes to Lenin in which a lookalike actor humanized the Communist leader. Zhou seems to have been genuinely loved and admired by the Chinese people, and comes across as more human and less didactic than his boss, Mao Zedong. This pic isn't a true biopic, however: It picks up on Zhou's story only at the mid-'60s, during the Cultural Rev-

olution which nearly toppled him.

Film concentrates on his espousal of better relations with the West, and an amusing meeting with Secretary of State Henry Kissinger is staged, prior to newsreel footage of President Nixon's historic arrival on Chinese soil.

Other themes include the defection and death (in a mysterious air crash) of senior Party man Lin Biao, and Zhou's continuing conflict with Jiang Qing, Mao's shrewish, radical wife who became leader of the notorious "Gang of Four."

Pic's set mainly in drab offices and conference halls, with the drama taking place during phone calls or meetings. Pic is a long slog, but Zhou's charisma and power comes through in Wang's faithful performance. The supporting cast also has an authentic veneer, but this static, talky item isn't likely to sell many tickets outside Chinese communities. — *David Stratton*

LA THUNE
(MONEY)
(FRENCH)

A Warner Bros. Transatlantic Inc. release of an Initial Groupe-Machinassou-SGGC co-production with the participation of Cofimage 2-Sofiarp & Canal Plus. Produced by Lila Cazes. Directed by Philippe Galand. Screenplay, Catherine Breillat, Galand. Camera (color), Hughes De Haeck; editor, Patricia Ardoun; music, Richard Horowitz, Stephane Vilar Bonga; costume design, Zelia Van Den Bulke; sound, Dominique Viellard; production manager, Vincent Bercholz; associate producer, Jean-Bernard Fetoux. Reviewed at Pathe Montparnasse cinema, Paris, Dec. 9, 1991. Running time: **90 MIN.**
With: Sami Bouajica, Sophie Aubry, Martin Lamotte, Meyriam Berrabah, Lea Drucker.

Charm and energy abound in "La Thune," a light, but not frivolous, pic addressing without violence or vulgarity the obstacles inherent in underclass initiative and cross-cultural romance. Savvy pic could interest young urban audiences in some markets.

Getting his hands on "la thune" (French slang for "money") is fast-talking optimist Kamel's (Sami Bouajica) daily concern. Since nobody will give him a job with a future, the French-born son of Algerian parents resolves to start his own company and soon discovers that his street smarts translate well to business.

Three-way juggling act ensues between Kamel's traditional Mus-

lim family, his essentially honest but unconventional business practices and the existential angst of his privileged g.f. (Sophie Aubry).

Alternating male and female voiceovers take viewers inside the characters' heads. The rich girl dates Kamel as much out of physical attraction as she does to irk her permissive bourgeois parents. Nicely handled is the 17-year-old g.f.'s reluctance to lose her virginity, even though her parents have given her their tacit approval by allowing Kamel to share her bed. Suspense as to how their relationship will turn out is sustained until the end.

Tech aspects are adequate and score is pleasant. Narrative is interspersed with cutaways of multi-ethnic life in Paris' low-rent projects. Camera grabs plenty of local color: street markets, break dancers, graffiti.

Kamel's dialogue is peppered with snappy maxims and his boundless self-confidence is presented as a priceless advantage most of his peers don't share.

Thesping is good all around, with special praise for charismatic Bouajica and for Martin Lamotte as the g.f.'s dad.
— *Lisa Nesselson*

MADRID FEST

THE RAILWAY STATION MAN
(BRITISH)

A Turner Pictures presentation of a BBC Films production in association with the First Film Co. & Sand Prods. Produced by Roger Randall-Cutler. Executive producers, Lauren Joy, Mark Shivas. Producer for BBC, Andree Molyneux. Directed by Michael Whyte. Screenplay, Shelagh Delaney based on Jennifer Johnston's novel. Camera (color), Bruno de Keyzer; editor, John Stothart; music, Richard Hartley; production design, Tony Burrough; associate producer (BBC), Simon Mills; co-producer, Amanda Marmot. Reviewed at Multicines Ideal, Madrid, April 10, 1992. (In Madrid Intl. Film Festival.) Running time: **94 MIN.**
Helen Cuffe . . . . Julie Christie
Roger Hawthorne . Donald Sutherland
Damian Sweeney . . . . . . John Lynch
Jack Cuffe . . . . . . Frank MacCusker
Manus Dempsey . . . . . Mark Tandy
Also with: Marie Hastings, Peadar Lamb, Ingrid Craigie, Niall Cusack.

Lacking poignancy and passion, "The Railway Station Man" is a bland love story between two aging adults set against a sketchy IRA background in Ireland. Neither the bumbling terrorists nor Julie

Christie and Donald Sutherland succeed in igniting any sparks. On-screen occurrences amount to tame European TV drama. Chances of theatrical release seem remote.

Story involves an Irish widow (Christie) who escapes to a small coastal village with her son after her husband is mistakently killed in a politically motivated ambush. The widow, who never has known real love, becomes a recluse and takes up painting.

Enter a quirky, maimed Yank (Sutherland), with a missing arm and a lame ear and leg. He's a train freak who decides to rebuild an old, unused railroad station. The outsider casts his spell on the widow, and she requites his advances, which culminate in a ludicrous sex scene aborted by the IRA-linked son.

Story fizzles out when the Yank accidentally crashes into a truck filled with IRA explosives, leaving the widow to return to her painting in the bucolic Irish hinterlands. — *Peter Besas*

PASSED AWAY

A Buena Vista release of a Hollywood Pictures presentation, in association with Touchwood Pacific Partners I, of a Morra/Brezner/Steinberg production. Produced by Larry Brezner, Timothy Marx. Directed, written by Charlie Peters. Camera (Duart color, Technicolor prints), Arthur Albert; editor, Harry Keramidas; music, Richard Gibbs; production design, Catherine Hardwicke; art direction, Gilbert Mercier; set decoration, Gene Serdena; costume design, Jennifer Von Mayrhauser; sound (Dolby), John Pritchett; assistant director, Matt Earl Beesley; casting, Gail Levin, Julie Mossberg/Rosalie Joseph (N.Y.), Nancy A. Mosser, Seddon C. Stolze (Pittsburgh). Reviewed at Avco Cinema Center, West L.A., April 20, 1992. MPAA rating: PG-13. Running time: **96 MIN.**
Johnny Scanlan . . . . . . Bob Hoskins
Jack Scanlan . . . . Jack Warden
Frank Scanlan . . . . William Petersen
Aunt Maureen . . . Helen Lloyd Breed
Mary Scanlan . . . Maureen Stapleton
Terry Scanlan . . . . . . Pamela Reed
Boyd Pinter . . . . Tim Curry
Peter Syracusa . . . . . Peter Riegert
Amy Scanlan . . . . Blair Brown
Father Hallahan . . . . Patrick Breen
Cassie Slocombe . . . . Nancy Travis
Rachel Scanlan . . . . Teri Polo
Nora Scanlan . . Frances McDormand

A rich ensemble cast of true-to-life eccentrics makes "Passed Away" a constant delight. Debuting director Charlie Peters' lively original script is full of unpredictable touches and droll humor, capturing the off-kilter behavior of a family gathered for the funeral of their paterfamilias (Jack Warden). Black comedy is a sure audience-pleaser, but its unusual subject will require careful handling to maximize its uncertain box office potential.

The film will evoke empathy from anyone who has lost a parent and experienced the tumultuous family reunion that accompanies a funeral. It's sort of the Irish equivalent of Sidney Lumet's underrated, caustically funny Jewish comedy about death, "Bye Bye Braverman" (1968), whose cast also included Warden.

Both films celebrate the joy of surviving and touch the heart without indulging in maudlin sentimentality. Pic's tone is set early on when star Bob Hoskins utters an Irish malapropism akin to Victor McLaglen lines in John Ford films: "We'll give Dad a wake he'll never forget."

Nothing very dramatic happens until a femme character abruptly goes into labor at the burial service. But even that surprise development is treated by filmmaker Peters in relaxed, unhurried fashion, as a celebration of life rescuing an otherwise de-

pressing occasion.

Peters' deceptively meandering but finely crafted script is served well enough by his utilitarian, unobtrusive direction. Script effortlessly draws odd moments of character revelation from its luxuriantly talkative characters, throwing them together in situations that evoke familiar experiences but still manage to avoid clichés.

Warden's habitual philandering, for example, never provokes the expected melodramatic upheaval. His widow (Maureen Stapleton) has reached some transcendent level of resignation (on the way to the cemetery she chats about the plot of a cowboy movie) and when a mysterious young woman (Nancy Travis) appears at the wake, she isn't the old man's mistress Hoskins at first thinks she is.

Quirky, oblique plot line leads Hoskins into a fervent declaration of love for Travis, who gently rebuffs him and sends him back to his wife (the underutilized Blair Brown). A restless gardener who calls himself an "arborist," Hoskins is having a midlife crisis that eventually leaves him more or less back where he started, but happier in his recognition of his newly substantial role as head of the family.

Ebullient, warm-hearted Hoskins is always a pleasure to watch, but it does take a considerable suspension of disbelief to accept him as the eldest son of a Yank clan. His bumptious British accent keeps popping through despite his best efforts at middle-American speech.

There's no problem believing Pamela Reed, a tart-tongued marvel as the sister stuck in a combative relationship with egomaniacal Broadway dancer Tim Curry. Despite her disdain for "this insipid little burg," she picks up again with easygoing hometown flame Peter Riegert, the embalmer who makes up Warden to look like Liberace. Reed's sardonic joie de vivre gives the film its true emotional core.

Travis also turns in a splendid performance, gradually revealing depths behind her illusory good-time-girl facade and playing against obvious emotional cues to express her own kind of subdued, nondemonstrative respect for Warden, a labor union leader who helped her over a difficult time of her life.

Rounding out the family ranks are Frances McDormand, amusingly tight-lipped and zealous as a nun and "liberation theologi-

an" working in El Salvador; William Petersen, on target but given too much screen time as a dull would-be pol who oozes "low-budget Kennedy charm"; and basilisk aunt Helen Lloyd Breed ("Nothing makes her happier than a funeral").

Pic frequently stops and turns the screen over to minor characters, such as callow young priest Patrick Breen, who gets bombed at the wake, stops singing liturgical songs and launches into an uproarious takeoff on Michael Feinstein singing Cole Porter's "You're the Top."

Most delightful and so unusual in today's marketplace is the joy the filmmaker takes in the incandescent glory of words. Hoskins, delivering the eulogy, comes out with a touching bit of off-hand poetry: "Heaven is a place where your father is a boy and your dog talks." — *Joseph McBride*

YEAR OF THE COMET

A Columbia Pictures release of a Castle Rock Entertainment presentation in association with New Line Cinema. Produced by Peter Yates, Nigel Wooll. Directed by Yates. Executive producers, Phil Kellogg, Alan Brown. Screenplay, William Goldman. Camera (Rank Film Laboratories color), Roger Pratt; editor, Ray Lovejoy; music, Hummie Mann; production design, Anthony Pratt; art direction, Desmond Crowe, Chris Seagers; set decoration, Stephenie McMillan; costume design, Marilyn Vance-Straker; sound (Dolby), Ken Weston; assistant director, Gerry Gavigan; casting, Noel Davis, Jeremy Zimmerman, Pam Dixon. Reviewed at Sony Studios screening room, Culver City, Calif., April 23, 1992. MPAA Rating: PG-13. Running time: **89 MIN.**
Margaret . . . . . Penelope Ann Miller
Oliver Plexico . . . . Tim Daly
Philippe . . . . Louis Jordan
Nico . . . . Art Malik
Sir Mason Harwood . . Ian Richardson
Ian . . . . Ian McNeice
Richard Harwood . . Timothy Bentinck
Landlady . . . . Julia McCarthy
Doctor Roget . . . . . Jacques Mathou

Harvested from the same field as "Romancing the Stone," this wine-soaked comedy-adventure never really ferments, in part due to a lack of chemistry between its romantic leads. Despite the auspices of Peter Yates and William Goldman, "Year of the Comet" should leave Columbia with sour grapes at the box office and make like its title, quickly streaking across the theatrical skies into the homevid orbit.

Billed as Goldman's first original script for the screen since "Butch Cassidy and the Sundance Kid" and his first collaboration with Yates since the 1972 release "The Hot Rock," the film's problems begin with its title, a reference to the once-mentioned vintage of an invaluable 150-year-old bottle of wine that sounds more like a sci-fi thriller.

That bottle brings together a wine auctioneer's daughter (Penelope Ann Miller), who discovers it, and a Texas millionaire's troubleshooter (Tim Daly) assigned to bring it back to his boss. Unfortunately, Miller has the bad luck of finding the bottle in a Scottish castle where a trio of researchers, led by Louis Jordan, are inconveniently torturing a scientist to obtain a secret formula, putting them in pursuit of the bottle.

Adding to the hijinks, another group joins the chase on behalf of a Greek magnate to whom Miller's snotty half-brother has promised the wine.

The wine-man's daughter is initially put off by Daly's character (he asks for Budweiser during their first encounter at a wine tasting), but she falls into step, and his bed, faster than a speeding comet, and without much regard to building sexual tension between the two.

In fact, what writer-producer Yates has created amounts to little more than a rather dull travelogue, with generally ineffective comic moments and Jordan oozing suave malice as the stock villain, seemingly reprising his bad guy from the two "Swamp Thing" pics.

As for the leads, Miller finds herself stranded by Goldman's screenplay, in which her character is a little bit of everything (spinster, repressed, ambitious), yet nothing in particular.

Daly doesn't fare a whole lot better as a dapper leading man, who proves full of surprises while unconvincingly going from boorish to sensitive as quickly as a writer can pull the strings.

Supporting players are all either too broadly comic to be menacing or too rotten to be funny, displaying the same indecisiveness as the principal players.

Technical credits are first-rate in a losing cause, from the stunning Scottish and French exteriors to Hummie Mann's intriguingly varied score, which fluctuates between genres much more comfortably than the film itself. — *Brian Lowry*

DESIRE & HELL AT SUNSET MOTEL

A Two Moon Releasing release of a Heron Communications & Image Organization presentation. Produced by Donald P. Borchers. Executive producers, Pierre David, Glenn Greene, David Bixler. Directed, written by Alien Castle. Camera (CFI color), Jamie Thompson; editor, James Gavin Bedford; music, Castle, Doug Walter; production design, Michael Clausen; set decoration, Jacquelyn Lemmon; costume design, Betty Pecha Madden; sound, Peter Devlin; associate producer, Linda Francis; assistant director, Kris Krengel. Reviewed at Raleigh Studios, L.A., April 16, 1992. MPAA rating: PG-13. Running time: **90 MIN.**
Bridey . . . . Sherilyn Fenn
Chester . . . . Whip Hubley
Deadpan . . . . David Hewlett
Auggie . . . . David Johansen
Manager . . . . Paul Bartel

The visuals are all that stand out in this low-budget sex comedy noir set against the stylish '50s motifs of the turquoise-and-sand Sunset Motel. Debuting writer-director Alien Castle, striving for a tongue-in-cheek blend of "Niagara" and "Union City," has produced a vague, immature scenario that's as glossy and empty as the L.A. it parodies. First pic from Two Moon Releasing will likely sink without a ripple.

Sherilyn Fenn stars as the knockout wife of a toy salesman (Whip Hubley) who checks them into the Sunset Motel in 1950s Anaheim for a sales meeting while she tries to get him to take her to Disneyland. Monkey business in no time, with Bridey toying with an amorous guy (David Johansen) who's got some anti-American goods on her husband; Chester hiring a beatnik criminal (David Hewlitt) to spy on his wife, and blackmail and mayhem ensuing in a badly jumbled plot that isn't worth sorting out.

Writer-director Castle has turned in a lazy, half-baked scenario, all the more regrettable for the cleverness and style in the visuals and the occasional flashes of fun in the loose, wordy, irreverent script.

Fenn, in a bombshell role and easily as photogenic as Madonna, finds a light sensual style pretty much her own, but Hubley generates no sparks as her husband. Stillness and dead space in general plague the pic, which wants to be a wicked parody but lacks the pacing and zing.

On the plus side, designer Michael Clausen aptly evokes a playground America suspended between sleaziness and innocence with his tropical and Old West motel room motifs. The abandoned Flamingo Motel in Santa Monica, which stood in for the Sunset, is a real find.

Lenser Jamie Thompson does excellent work throughout. Lighting and color considerably enhance pic's visual interest, and its imaginative approach to style includes a black & white-to-color shift at the outset.

Pic opened in L.A. April 24 and will play selected venues in other cities. — *Amy Dawes*

BAYANI
(HEROES)
(GERMAN-16m)

A Janetzko Film production, in association with ZDF. (Intl. sales: Janetzko, Berlin.) Produced by Christoph Janetzko. Directed, written by Raymond Red. Camera (color), Red, Yam Laranas; editors, Larry Manda, Red; music, Alan Hilario; production design, Cesar Hernando; art direction-costume design, Daniel Red, Wilfredo Calderon; assistant director, Melchor Bachani III. Reviewed at Berlin Film Festival (Forum section), Feb. 16, 1992. Running time: **83 MIN.**
Andres Bonifacio . . . . Julio Díaz
Emilio . . . . Raymond Alsona Artemio
Ricarte . . . . Crispin Medina
Gen. Noriel . . . . John Arcilla
(Tagalog dialogue)

Feature bow by Manila filmmaker Raymond Red is a wordy costume item handcuffed by its low budget and conventional visual style. Anti-colonial yarn will disappoint fans of Red's experimental shorts and confusing to those unacquainted with Philippine history. Limited fest exposure looms at best.

Set during the war of independence against the Spanish in the late 19th century, story centers on a peasant (Filipino star Julio Díaz) who finally falls victim to political infighting once the revolution gathers steam.

On that simple framework, Red builds a partly fictional interpretation of real events framed as a flashback narrative that becomes clear only at the close. Parallels with contempo Philippine headbutting are there for the taking, but pic's flat tempo and largely boxy look will prove a turn-off for most viewers.

Lensing in 16m by Red and Yam Laranas is sharp and well-lit, and production designer Cesar Hernando manages a handsome look on limited German coin. Editing is trim. Playing is downbeat. — *Derek Elley*

SPLIT SECOND
(BRITISH)

An InterStar Releasing release of a Muse Prods. & Chris Hanley presentation of a Challenge production. Produced by Laura Gregory. Executive producer, Keith Cavele. Directed by Tony Maylam. Subway train & additional sequences directed by Ian Sharp. Screenplay, Gary Scott Thompson. Camera (Metrocolor), Clive Tickner; editor, Dan Rae; music, Stephen Parsons, Francis Haines; production design, Chris Edwards; costume design, Antoinette Gregory; sound (Dolby), Peter Glossop; assistant director, Ray Corbett; 2nd unit action director-camera, Arthur Wooster; stunt coordinator, Colin Skeaping; creature effects, Stephen Norrington, Kate Murray, Ian Morce, Cliff Wallace; special effects supervisor, Alan Whibley, Ace Effects Ltd.; line producer, Laurie Borg; associate producer, Thompson; casting, John & Ros Hubbard (U.K.), Linda Francis (U.S.). Reviewed at Broadway screening room, N.Y., March 19, 1992. MPAA Rating: R. Running time: **91 MIN.**
Harley Stone . . . . Rutger Hauer
Michelle . . . . Kim Cattrall
Dick Durkin . . . . Neil Duncan
Rat catcher . . . . . Michael J. Pollard
Thrasher . . . . Alun Armstrong
Paulsen . . . . Pete Postlethwaite
Jay Jay . . . . Ian Dury
Robin . . . . Roberta Eaton
O'Donnell . . . . Tony Steedman

"Split Second" is an extremely stupid monster film, boasting enough violence and special effects to satisfy less discriminating vid fans.

Typecast Rutger Hauer plays a burnt-out cop tracking down a monstrous serial killer in this non-story set in London in the year 2008. Neil Duncan is the nerdish but ultimately resourceful partner he's saddled with by his taciturn police chief Alun Armstrong.

Opening crawl is more promising than the film proper, announcing a planet that's waterlogged due to global warming that suggests the premise of J.G. Ballard's sci-fi novel "The Drowned World." Unfortunately, low-budget pic emphasizes ugly, claustrophobic sets and a few puddles instead of large-scale imagery.

Gore is emphasized by director Tony Maylam as the barely glimpsed monster rips the hearts out of its victims in a ritual that Duncan deduces to be of satanic origin. Climax in the London Underground is well directed by Ian Sharp, but the man-in-a-rubber-suit monster is a poor imitation of "Alien" with lots of dripping K-Y jelly.

Hauer harumphs his way through a role that merely parodies his previous fantasy films while newcomer Duncan fares better in a multi-dimensional assignment. Kim Cattrall looks understandably uncomfortable as Hauer's romantic interest and is subjected to highly unflattering photography. Michael J. Pollard's final reel guest shot as a rat catcher is a complete waste.

The musical score annoyingly and cryptically includes several inappropriate plays of Justin Hayward's lovely Moody Blues song "Nights in White Satin."

— *Lawrence Cohn*

UNA MUJER BAJO LA LLUVIA
(A WOMAN IN THE RAIN)
(SPANISH)

An Atrium Prods.-Iberoamericana Films-Sogetel-Sogepaq co-production. Executive producer, Andrés Vicente Gómez. Directed by Geraldo Vera. Screenplay, Vera, Carmen Posadas, Manuel Hidalgo based on Edgar Neville's "La Vida en un Hilo." Camera (color), José Luis López Linares; editor, Pablo G. del Amo; music, Mariano Diaz; sets, Ana Alvargonzález; sound, Carlos Faruolo; production director, José Luis García Arrojo. Reviewed at Cine Azul, Madrid, April 17, 1992. Running time: **87 MIN.**
Mercedes . . . . Angela Molina
Miguel . . . . Antonio Banderas
Ramón . . . . Imanol Arias
Alicia . . . . Kitty Manver

Lacking the fireworks, wit and zany comedy it should have had, "A Woman in the Rain" fizzles out largely as silly ham acting with dud dialogs. In this particularly droll but mostly too restrained adaptation of an Edgar Neville story, all the social overtones of the original have fallen by the wayside.

On a rainy night in Madrid, a girl is offered the choice of getting a lift in the cars of either one of two strangers; a critical crossroads in her life since she'll wind up marrying one of them.

An on-screen narrator pulls back the curtain in a theater, and the camera moves in to depict both options. First scenario is her marriage to a wealthy fop (Imanuel Arias) who giggles idiotically, plays golf with inbred aristocrats and has a pastry chef's approach to sex.

Rewind to the girl in the rain and the second scenario: A real life artist (Antonio Banderas) with a rich patroness, is sexier, but the girl marries the fop, who conveniently has a heart attack, thus leaving the field open to the artist.

Thesps do what thay can with the fatuous script, but the cliché situations described (via interiors mostly) lack freshness. Though geared to the local market, pic might score some points in other markets with Banderas on the marquee. — *Peter Besas*

BRAIN DONORS

A Paramount Pictures release of a Zucker Bros. production. Produced by Gil Netter, James D. Brubaker. Executive producers, David Zucker, Jerry Zucker. Directed by Dennis Dugan. Screenplay, Pat Proft. Camera (Technicolor), David M. Walsh; editor, Malcolm Campbell; music, Ira Newborn; production design, William J. Cassidy; set design, Gary A. Lee, Robert Maddy, James J. Murakami; William J. Cassidy; set decoration, Jeannette M. Gunn; costume design, Robert Turturice; sound (Dolby), William B. Kaplan; assistant director, James S. Simons; choreographer, John Carrafa; casting, John Lyons, Donna Isaacson. Reviewed at GCC Beverly Connection Theaters, Beverly Hills, Calif., April 17, 1992. MPAA Rating: PG. Running time: **79 MIN.**
Roland T. Flakfizer . . . John Turturro
Jacques . . . . Bob Nelson
Rocco Melonchek . . . . . . Mel Smith
Lillian Oglethorpe . . Nancy Marchand
Lazlo . . . . John Savident
The Great Volare . George De La Pena
Lisa . . . . Juli Donald
Alan . . . . Spike Alexander
Blonde . . . . Teri Copley

The title "Brain Donors" sounds like a horror film and for those expecting a comedy, it is. The Zucker brothers must have inhaled some "Airplane!" glue before lending their names to this brainless tomfoolery, which Paramount quietly transplanted into 500 theaters April 17. Box office should be equally passive, with limited appeal among adolescents determined to escape the outdoors over spring break.

Patterned after "A Night at the Opera," "Brain Donors" (originally "Lame Ducks," inviting a separate barrage of well-deserved cheap shots) badly wants to be a latter-day Marx Bros. pic. "Badly" is the key word, but any other reference to the Marx Bros. should be limited to a written apology.

John Turturro, perhaps craving a lighter part after recent dramatic roles, ends up perched on a flat whoopie cushion as Roland T. Flakfizer — a Grouchoesque, ambulance-chasing (quite literally, like every other gag in the film) attorney out to fleece a well-heeled and well-fed widow (Nancy Marchand).

Bob Nelson and Mel Smith are his equally zany aides-de-camp, the former a clear Harpo derivative and the latter a British cab-

bie who at least never tries to play the piano.

Hoping to land a $500,000-a-year job heading the widow's ballet company, Flakfizer and his cohorts end up at odds with a snooty attorney (John Savident) and stuck-up dancer (George De La Pena) while championing the cause of two young lovers — staple Marx Bros. characters who, instead of singing sappy duets, perform tepid dance numbers.

Director Dennis Dugan's first feature, "Problem Child," was a curious box office success, and so he finds himself laboring on another broad farce, again with numbingly flat results.

Pat Proft, co-writer on "The Naked Gun" pics and "Hot Shots," gets sole credit here but follows the same formula, tossing in everything but the kitchen sink. But the hit-miss ratio skews so heavily toward "miss" that the duds pile up in the aisles, bringing to mind another household fixture, the one that flushes.

"Brain Donors" also gets a raspberry for its 79-minute running time: The end may be welcome, but that's not much of a reason for those shelling out their lunch money to see it.

Tech credits are undistinguished, except for clever Claymation opening credits fashioned by Will Vinton Prods., which provide pic's first and last moment of inspiration.

— *Brian Lowry*

OBIETTIVO INDISCRETO
(HIDDEN LENS)
(ITALIAN)

A Titanus Distribuzione release of a Casanova Entertainment presentation of a Reteitalia-Casanova production. Produced by Luca Barbareschi. Directed by Massimo Mazzucco. Screenplay, Sergio Altieri, Mazzucco. Camera (color), Vincenzo Marano; editor, Cecilia Zanuso; music, Andrea Centazzo; art direction, Enrico Luzzi; costumes, Silvia Bisconti; sound (Dolby), Amedeo Casati. Reviewed at Quirinale Cinema, Rome, April 14, 1992. Running time: **93 MIN.**
David . . . . Luca Barbareschi
Claire . . . . Sam Jenkins
Godard . . . . Marc De Jonge

In "Hidden Lens," an unorthodox photographer takes Paris by storm, concocting a dramatic campaign around the model he falls for. But "Funny Face" it isn't, and neat packaging can't dress up this half-baked treatise on reality vs. representation. Cloying combo of sexy sleaze and artsy intellectualizing may play on select-

ed Euro screens, but ultimately looks more fit for tube consumption.

Shock-mongering photojournalist Luca Barbareschi accepts a job for a Japanese company breaking into haute couture and cosmetics. He teams up with leggy looker Sam Jenkins, and an obsessive relationship develops. Using underhanded surprise tactics, he introduces the same violent element of truth that characterizes his reportage pics.

Barbareschi stages a last-minute switch of tame, traditional images for raw shock-shots, and his work becomes an unexpected hit. (That the multimillion-dollar promo gets to billboard stage without prior approval from his Japanese bosses is treated as a matter of course.) But success doesn't come on the photog's own terms, and his mind games may have cost him the girl.

Clearly inspired by Italo lensmeister Oliviero Toscani (who masterminded Benetton's controversial "United Colors" campaign), pic pussyfoots around some interesting angles on the fabrication of reality in art and advertising. Inconclusive ideas are clouded by frustratingly elliptical dialogue, and views on photography as a social document are put forward in lifeless didactic exchanges.

Produced by Barbareschi, who also had a hand in the story, pic plays like a vanity project for the popular thesp/TV presenter. It's an ill-conceived vehicle, however, and his mild-mannered Milanese smoothness seems at odds with his character's passionate artistic determination.

Massimo Mazzucco's able but anonymous direction lets pic hover about between romance, thriller and psychological drama without ever settling into a format that really fits, but tech work is strong, especially Vincenzo Marano's fluid camerawork.

— *David Rooney*

KNIGHT MOVES
(FACE TO FACE)
(U.S.-GERMAN)

A Columbia Pictures release of a Lamb Bear Entertainment & Ink Slinger presentation of an El Khoury/Defait production. Executive producers, Christopher Lambert, Brad Mirman. Produced by Ziad El Khoury, Jean Luc Defait. Co-producer, Dieter Geissler. Directed by Carl Schenkel. Screenplay, Mirman. Camera (color), Dietrich Lohmann; editor, Norbert Herzner; production design, Graeme Murray; costumes, Deborah Everton, Trish Keating. Reviewed at Hoyts screening room,

Sydney, April 8, 1992. Running time: **115 MIN.**
Sanderson . . . . Christopher Lambert
Kathy Sheppard . . . . . Diane Lane
Frank Sedman . . . . . . Tom Skerritt
Andy Wagner . . . . Daniel Baldwin
Willerman . . . . Charles Bailey-Gates
Yurilivich . . . . Arthur Brauss
Erica Sanderson . . . Katharine Isobel
Jeremy Edmonds . . Ferdinand Mayne

"**K**night Moves," a slick and occasionally suspenseful thriller in which a champion chess player becomes a chief murder suspect, already has played off in European territories and looks to do modest business elsewhere before a useful video career.

Reuniting some key members of the team that produced "Highlander II," including topliner Christopher Lambert and producers Ziad El Khoury and Jean Luc Defait, pic gets too convoluted at times, but it packs in enough suspense and tension to keep undemanding audiences happy.

Pic opens with a prologue set in 1972: Two boys compete in the Washington State Chess Tournament, and the winner is attacked by the hysterical loser. Twenty years later at the same tourney, winner from the opening scene (Lambert) faces a Russian challenger (Arthur Brauss).

On the first night of the contest, he beds a young woman in her hotel room. Soon after he leaves, she's murdered by an unseen assailant, her body's drained of blood, and the word "Remember" is scrawled in blood above her bed.

Local cops Tom Skerritt and Daniel Baldwin immediately suspect Lambert, who at first conceals his rendezvous with the dead woman. More young women are found killed under similar circumstances, but with a different word written each time; and there seem to be links with the chess moves Lambert makes in the tourney.

A young psychologist (Diane Lane) called in to help investigators gives Lambert a clean bill of health. She's soon having an affair with him as the killings continue and the clues keep pointing toward Lambert, despite other suspects and red herrings.

Swiss director Carl Schenkel, whose past work includes episodes of HBO's "The Hitchhiker" and the indie feature, "Out of Order," does a good, flashy job with the material, filling the wide screen with blinding lights and dizzy camera movements.

Lambert is solid as the suspect, Lane winning as the psych,

and Skerritt and Baldwin suitably frustrated as the mystified law officers. There isn't an awful lot of substance to "Knight Moves," but as thrillers go it's a lively effort. — *David Stratton*

TETSUO: THE IRON MAN
(JAPANESE-16m)

An Original Cinema release of a Kaijyu Theater production. Directed, written, edited by Shinya Tsukamoto. Camera (16m, black & white), Tsukamoto, Kei Fujiwara; music, Chu Ishikawa; sets, Tsukamoto; assistant director, Fujiwara. Reviewed at Film Forum, April 14, 1992. Running time: **67 MIN.**
Salaryman . . . . . . Tomoroh Taguchi
Girlfriend . . . . . . Kei Fujiwara
Woman in glasses . . . . Nobu Kanaoko
Metals fetishist . . . Shinya Tsukamoto
Doctor . . . . Naomasa Musaka
Tramp . . . . Renji Ishibashi

A gruesome parable about the mechanization of modern-day Japan, "Tetsuo: The Iron Man" features slick special effects, sharp black & white photography and fast-paced editing, but the graphic violence will turn off anyone who does not share the director's perverse sensibility.

Pic opens with the repellent sight of a "metals fetishist" (Shinya Tsukamoto) slashing his leg and inserting a metal tube in the gash. Surely this is taking an interest in metallurgy too far.

Between credits Tsukamoto (also director, screenwriter, editor, art director) is hit by a car. Soon after, car's driver, a "salaryman" (Tomoroh Taguchi), notices a piece of metal protruding from his cheek while shaving.

While Taguchi waits in the subway, a woman is attacked by a metal creature. Transformed into a hell-bent metal mama, she chases him through tunnels in a well-edited but disturbing sequence before Taguchi manages to kill her with much crunching of bones.

But the salaryman realizes that his body is becoming increasingly metallic. In fact, his penis turns into a giant metal drill beyond his control. His girlfriend's reaction is blasé: "Nothing much scares me." (What little dialogue there is in the film is often unintentionally funny).

The grotesque scene that follows gives a new, bloody twist to the term mechanical sex.

Deliberately repulsive pic also is derivative, combining thriller elements from "Frankenstein" to "Alien." "Tetsuo" also borrows from "Koyaanisqatsi" in its

extensive use of time lapse photography. Toward the end of the film, it is used in a climactic duel and then in the absurd finale, in which a glob-like fusion of men and metal glides through city streets.

The gore fest becomes even more laughable when one of the heads enmeshed in the metal behemoth proclaims, "We can mutate the whole world into metal."

Perhaps the very narrow target audience of "metals fetishists" will get a kick out of "Tetsuo," but for most viewers it will be the cinematic equivalent of being run over by a car and turning into a metal blob. It may last just over an hour, but "Tetsuo" feels excruciatingly long.
— *William Stevenson*

SAN REMO FEST

SENZURU K PAMJATI NE DOPUSKAJU
(CENSORSHIP HAS NO ACCESS TO MY MEMORY)
(RUSSIAN)

A Len-Interfilm Studio Rondina production. Directed, written by Aleksandr Porochovscikov. Camera (color, black & white), Aleksandr Ustinov; music, Evgeneij Gevorghjan; art direction, Yuri Pugach. Reviewed at San Remo (Italy) Intl. Film Festival (competition), March 28, 1992. Running time: **127 MIN.**
With: Aleksandr Porochovscikov, Elena Melnikova, Viktor Vassiliev.

A ctor-director Aleksandr Porochovscikov constructs an elaboratly personalized history of Stalinism in "Censorship Has No Access to My Memory." A script editor seemingly had no access either, and result is a powerhouse core of poignant semi-autobiographical drama struck between reels of numbing preamble and foggy conclusion.

Overlong pic should find berths on the fest circuit, but judicious cuts and a structural rethink could pave its way into art houses and tube outlets.

This appealingly and infuriatingly old-fashioned Russian film opens with a convoluted series of nonchronological events, including the death of Porochovscikov's mother. Close to an hour unspools with plot continually poised for takeoff but repeatedly stalled.

Action jumps back to Porochovscikov's World War II child-

hood and here, pic really soars. Switching to richly contrasting black & white, he retraces the experiences that scarred and hardened him. After his grandfather's arrest and his father's abandonment of the family, Aleksandr is raised by ma and grandma.

Ostracized by strangers and kin, he grows up as a solemn observer of injustice. Central section really hits home, skillfully showing life as a daily bout of humiliation and oppression. In one strong scene, a respected musician mistakenly anticipates his arrest and hurls himself from a window. Porochovscikov gives the suicide maximum impact by almost shrugging it off as a workaday fact of life.

Believing the girl he loves to be endangered by association with him, Porochovscikov abandons her. Film loses its hard-edged focus again as he plots to right the wrongs done to his grandfather and his people. But on learning he's a father, revenge plans are pushed aside. Closing dialogue hits a resonant note. Asked what's bothering him, Porochovscikov replies, "Nothing. Just that I'm Russian."

Based on personal experiences, the picture obliquely recounts a vast chunk of history and a grim vision of the future in an angry, uncompromising voice. Despite being cluttered with detail, approach to the overreaching plot is relatively simple. But the structure isn't, and action leaps in and out of so many time frames that events become hopelessly muddled.

A huge bear of a man, Porochovscikov's stern, dignified presence is the hook that keeps auds in their seats through an unrewarding first hour. The use of tight, unrelenting closeups in his scenes is effective. Other perfs from mainly nonpro cast are generally good, as are tech credits.
— *David Rooney*

GUADALAJARA

ANGEL DE FUEGO
(ANGEL OF FIRE)
(MEXICAN)

A Mexican Film Institute (Imcine) release of an Imcine-Prods. Metrópolis-Fondo de Fomento a la Calidad Cinematográfica-Otra Productora Más production. Produced by León Constantiner. Directed, co-produced by Dana Rotberg. Screenplay, Rotberg, Omar Alain Rodrigo. Camera (color), Toni Kuhn;

editor, Sigfrido Barjau, Rotberg; music, Ariel Guzik, Ana Ruiz; art direction, Ana Sánchez; sound, Nerio Barberis. Reviewed at 8th Muestra de Cine Mexicano, Guadalajara, March 28, 1992. Running time: **90 MIN.**

Alma . . . . Evangelina Sosa
Refugio . . . . Lilia Aragón
Sacramento . . . . Roberto Sosa
Noé . . . . Noé Montealegre
Renato . . . . Alejandro Parodi
Rito . . . . Salvador Sánchez
Also with: Mercedes Pascual, Gina Morett, Farnesio de Bernal.

Second feature by Mexican helmer Dana Rotberg, "Angel de Fuego" is a contemporary fable delving into society's underbelly and dealing with incest, fanatical religion, power and women's roles. Tightly controlled film should find major interest at international fests and the art house circuit.

With mystical trappings, pic focuses on Alma (Evangelina Sosa), a young trapeze artist who works as a fire-eater at the Fantasia Circus. Having been abandoned by her mother, the young woman carries on a love affair with her ailing clown father.

When he dies, leaving her pregnant, she departs from the scorn of her fellow carnies, first working in the streets as a fire-eater, and eventually winding up with an itinerant marionette theater, run by the domineering Refugio, zealously played by Lilia Aragón. The puppets are made and manipulated by her son, Sacramento, played by Sosa's real-life brother, Roberto Sosa.

Troupe travels to poor neighborhoods presenting harsh Old Testament tales, basically offering multi-leveled stories within pic's overall story. Under Refugio's rule, Alma must undergo a rigorous purification ritual for her blasphemy, placing her will and unborn babe in Refugio's hands. With wonderful attention to art direction and lean use of the camera, Rotberg guides viewers through this slim allegory offering a closed world within worlds, exploring marginal characters living on the outskirts of the city and the edge of society. Characters' names are also important on a symbolic level: Alma (soul), Refugio (refuge), Sacramento (sacrament), Noé (Noah).

Displaying talent and firm control of her material, Rotberg is one of Mexico's most exciting new filmmakers to emerge in the past decade. — *Paul Lenti*

COMO AGUA PARA CHOCOLATE
(LIKE WATER FOR CHOCOLATE)
(MEXICAN)

A Cinevista release of an Arau Films Intl.-Mexican Film Institute (Imcine)-Fonatur-Cinevista-State of Coahuila production. Produced, directed by Alfonso Arau. Screenplay, Laura Esquivel, based on her novel. Camera (color), Emmanuel Lubezki, Steve Bernstein; editor, Carlos Bolado; music, Leo Brower; art direction, Denise Pizzini, Marco Antonio Arteaga, Leo Brown; sound, Juan Carlos Prieto. Reviewed at 8th Muestra de Cine Mexicano, Guadalajara, April 1, 1992. Running time: **144 MIN.**

Tita de la Garza . . . . . Lumi Cavazos
Pedro Muzquiz . . . . . Marco Leonardi
Mother Elena . Regina Torné John Brown . . . . Mario Iván Martínez
Nacha . . . . Ada Carrasco
Also with: Claudette Maille, Yareli Arizmendi, Pilar Aranda, Rodolfo Arias.

Strong material has been wasted by inept filmmaking in "Como Agua Para Chocolate." Still, this epic two-hour-plus film is bound for local blockbuster status on story strength alone, which somewhat manages to override pic's tremendous directorial flaws. International interest will be limited, although a remake is worth considering.

Sixth feature by Mexican actor-director Alfonso Arau (known to world audiences for roles in "The Wild Bunch" and "Romancing the Stone") suffers from an in-your-face approach to direction, with the entire story told mostly in closeup. The film screams to be opened up to northern Mexico's sweeping landscape and the broader notions of the story line.

Title can more aptly be translated as "boiling mad," since it refers to anger at the boiling point like water for hot chocolate. Screenplay was penned by Arau's wife, Laura Esquivel, based on her delightful bestseller combining "magic realism" romance and recipe book.

Historical pic opens in the early 1900s on a large estate near the Texas border with the birth of the youngest of three sisters. Unfortunately, Tita (Lumi Cavazos) is part of a family tradition where the youngest daughter is denied matrimony in order to care for her mother in her old age. When Pedro Muzquiz ("Cinema Paradiso's" Marco Leonardi) comes to ask for Tita's hand, he's told by her domineering mother (admirably played by Regina Torné) that the marriage is impossible. Instead, he's offered Tita's elder sister Rosaura, and he accepts so he can be close to Tita, who is the cook at the hacienda.

The film chronicles this sweeping, lifelong romance between an impossible love consummated only through the meals Tita prepares. She pours so much love into her quail-with-rose-petal dish that everyone at the table has an orgasm, and one of her sisters even catches on fire.

Art direction by Denise Pizzini, Marco Antonio Arteaga and Leo Brown is beautiful, although denied scope, while Emmanuel Lubezki and Steve Bernstein's rich cinematography is misused throughout.

This classic love story bridging generations is so compelling and splendidly expressed in the script that the frustrated filmgoer can only shake his head at the incompetent handling. Recutting is rumored, but shots to improve this work and open it up just aren't there. — *Paul Lenti*

MODELO ATIGUO
(OLDER MODEL)
(MEXICAN)

A Mexican Film Institute (Imcine) release of a Aries Films-Imcine-Fondo de Fomento a la Calidad Cinematográfica production. Executive producer, Fernando Sariñana. Produced by Alejandro Pelayo, Miguel Necoechea. Directed by Raúl Araiza. Screenplay, Luis Eduardo Reyes, Consuelo Garrido, Pelayo, Erick Krohnengold, Walter de la Gala. Camera (color), Rosalío Solano; editor, Enrique Puente P.; music, Osni Cassab; art direction, Gloria Carrasco; sound, Rogelio Pichardo. Reviewed at 8th Muestra de Cine Mexicano, Guadalajara, Mexico, March 27, 1992. Running time: **95 MIN.**

Carmen . . . . Silvia Pinal
Juan . . . . Alonso Echánove
Gabriel . . . . Raúl Araiza Jr.
Young Carmen . . . . Stephanie Salas
Laura . . . . Daniela Duran

A three-hankie melodrama of the type not seen in recent years, "Older Model" is little more than a vehicle for star Silvia Pinal (Luis Buñuel's "Viridiana"). Nostalgic and artificial story may find a soap-opera loving public who doesn't mind slurping syrup at the expense of its unabashedly sappy dialog's unintentional humor.

This basic lady-and-the-tramp tale pairs dying older-woman radio announcer Carmen (Pinal) with lowly cabby Juan (Alonso Echánove in his characteristic "macho sabroso" role). Though the title refers to Pinal's classic car, it also brings to mind Pinal herself and expands further to include the shopworn melodrama form.

When Carmen discovers she has little over a month to live, she decides to come to grips with her unresolved life. Memories surface in a fit of flashbacks, chronicling her once forbidden love to her brother that, when discovered, ended in multiple family suicides. Since then, she had renounced love while living on remnants of the family fortune.

Meanwhile, the cabby finds himself attracted to this aging beauty. He abandons his feisty g.f. (Daniela Duran) — surely the best character in the film — for Pinal, who shares with him her world of art museums and fancy restaurants, while he takes her on tours of Mexico City's demi-monde of late-night salsa clubs. The two drive around the city together in her classic antique Cadillac until a melodramatic ending recalling such classic weepers as "Back Street" but seemingly artificial and tacked on.

Glossy tech credits are first-rate and sappy script should find a nitch among viewers weaned on sentimental soaps and those who follow Pinal's weekly Mex TV series: "Woman: Real Life Stories." — *Paul Lenti*

EL BULTO
(EXCESS BAGGAGE)
(MEXICAN)

A Río Mixcoac SCL-Conexión-Fondo de Fomento a la Calidad Cinematográfica production. Executive producer, Gonzalo Lara. Produced, directed by Gabriel Retes. Screenplay, Retes, Gabriela Retes, María del Pozo. Camera (color), Chuy; editor, Saúl Aupart; music, Pedro Plascencia Salinas; art direction, Tomás Guevara, Francesca Apentzeller; sound, Antonio Diego. Reviewed at 8th Muestra de Cine Mexicano, Guadalajara, March 28, 1992. Running time: **114 MIN.**

Lauro . . . . Gabriel Retes
Alberto . . . . Héctor Bonilla
Adela . . . . Lourdes Elizárraras
Toño . . . . José Alonso
Alba . . . . Delia Casanova
Also with: Cecilia Camacho, Lucila Balzaretti, Luis Felipe Tovar.

Reminiscent of "Awakenings" and "Regarding Henry," Mexican helmer Gabriel Retes' latest pic is a well-made commercial venture that presses all the right buttons while narrating a riveting tale of a modern Rip Van Winkle's efforts to integrate himself into contempo society. Well-paced and well-shot pic should wake up a degree of international interest.

Co-written, directed and starring Retes, pic is a family affair:

Retes plays the lead, and his mother, two children and mate play their corresponding real-life roles in the film, and to good effect.

"El Bulto" follows on the heels of the 1989 pic "Rojo Amanecer," which first broke Mexico's long censorship of the army's violent repression of student riots in the 1960s. Tale concerns leftist journalist Lauro (Retes), clubbed on the head during student riots in 1971 and suddenly awakening from a 20-year coma. His wife has since taken up with another man, his children are grown and his former leftist friends work for the government.

"El bulto" (the baggage) is an ironic term the children had used to refer to comatose Dad, excess baggage that could have been easily discarded by simply pulling the plug. For two decades, they visited him at the hospital, exercising his muscles, bathing him and clipping his nails.

Rather than an overnight awakening, Lauro endures a slow, painful physical recovery and the even slower pace of coming to grips with a new world that everyone tells him is better than the one he left behind. His former ideals are seen as old-fashioned in a world where even the Soviet Union no longer exists.

The ex-leftist finds himself filled with intransigent reactionary notions concerning his wife's decision to live with another man and his daughter's relationship with her b.f. The children suddenly find a father they had never known and are demanded to respect and obey him.

While the decidedly schematic script could have fallen into easy traps (such as playing for laughs or making facile political statements), Retes tows a delicate line opting for the human story of the anachronistic man who must come to grips with himself and others around him.

Although the film can be accused of totally discrediting '60s ideals in favor of selling out to today's new free-market world order, overt politics are played down in favor of Lauro's personal growth. Script tends toward talky, while tech credits are all first-rate.

— *Paul Lenti*

ANOCHE SOÑE CONTIGO
(DREAMING ABOUT YOU)
(MEXICAN)

A Clasa Films Mundiales-Prods. Tragaluz production. Executive producer, Carlos García Aguilar. Produced by Pablo Barbachano, Francisco Barbachano. Directed by Marysa Sistach. Screenplay, José Buil. Camera (color), Alex Phillips; editor, Sigfrido García Jr.; music, Alberto Delgado; sound, Fernando Cámara. Reviewed at 8th Muestra de Cine Mexicano, Guadalajara, March 29, 1992. Running time: **90 MIN.**
Azucena . . . . Leticia Perdigón
Toto . . . . Martín Altomaro
Mother . . . . Socorro Bonilla
Chabela . . . . Patricia Aguirre
Quique . . . . Moisés Iván Mora

"**D**reaming About You," yet another rites-of-passage pic about a young boy and his first sexual awakenings, comes from woman director Marysa Sistach, but the results are surprisingly male-oriented and mediocre. Material gets neither female insights nor anything else to distinguish it from such well-explored film territory.

The upbeat music, juvenile humor, young characters and sexual theme will doubtless give the film some commercial life in its target market of local youth, but wider distrib possibilities are doubtful.

While her first feature "Los Pasos de Ana" dealt with the complexities of a contemporary woman, the marked male P.O.V. is handled here with indifference, as if the filmmaker can't relate to the script's dictates of the boy's fantasies and behavior.

Toto (Martín Altomaro) falls for his visiting cousin (Leticia Perdigón), in town to get over a broken romance. That they will end up in the sack is apparent from the beginning; the question (if anyone cares to ask) is when?

While tech credits are above par, overall effect is fairly numbing with nothing new beyond clichés played for cheap laughs such as shots of women's derrieres as they bend over.

— *Paul Lenti*

PLAYA AZUL
(BLUE BEACH)
(MEXICAN)

A Mexican Film Institute (Imcine) release of a Noos Films-Imcine-Fondo de Fomento a la Calidad Cinematografica production. Executive producer, Gerardo Moscoso. Directed by Alfredo Joskowicz. Screenplay, Víctor Hugo Rascón Banda, Joskowicz, Teresa Velo, based on Rascón Banda's play. Camera (color), Rodolfo Sánchez; editor, Francisco Chiu; music, Amparo Rubín; sound, Miguel Sandoval. Reviewed at 8th Muestra de Cine Mexicano, Guadalajara, March 27, 1992. Running time: **93 MIN.**
Thé engineer . . . . Sergio Bustamante
His wife . . . . Pilar Pellicer
Silvia . . . . Mercedes Olea
Don Matias . . . . Ignacio Retes
Sergio . . . . Mel Herrera
Teresa . . . . Lourdes Villareal

Although thematically important on a national level, Alfredo Joskowicz's latest pic "Playa Azul" suffers from being too close to its source material and is reduced to a talky polemic bordering on tedium.

Based on the stage play by Víctor Hugo Rascón Banda, film's basic structure is to present a crisis that brings together people with lots of past sins, and then sit back and watch the sparks fly as allegiances shift back and forth, and all the dirt is eventually shaken from the carpet. This may work on stage.

Story concerns a medium-level politician caught up in the changeover of government administrations. In Mexico, sacrificial lambs usually are chosen to accept blame for past failures and must simply lie low for a couple of years before re-emerging into political life.

In this case, a corrupt engineer (Sergio Bustamante) really believes he's innocent and immune to prosecution. He gathers his family together to fight impending charges, but soon realizes he can no longer count on anyone. There is too much water under the bridge, and one by one everyone fails him, leaving him impotent and alone and guilty as charged.

From the beginning, when the engineer rejects a suggestion to flee the country, the die is cast and the succeeding tragedy is obvious. By deluding himself with the notion he still welds power, he has opted for self-destruction.

Legit structure gives each character a major scene and speech where thesps have a chance to overact to the point of hysteria.

Technically, the film also barely manages. — *Paul Lenti*

VILLE A VENDRE
(CITY FOR SALE)
(FRENCH)

An AFMD release of an Alain Sarde-TF1 Films co-production. Produced by Alain Sarde. Directed by Jean-Pierre Mocky. Screenplay, Mocky, André Ruellan. Camera (color), Jean Badal; editor, Mocky, Annie-Claire Mittelberger; music, Vladimir Cosma; costumes, Martine Rapin; sound, Adrien Nataf. Reviewed at Gaumont Convention, Paris, Feb. 26, 1992. Running time: **102 MIN.**
Orphée . . . . Tom Novembre
Elvire . . . . Valérie Mairesse
Rousselot . . . . . . Michel Serrault
Monnerie . . . . . . Richard Bohringer
Boulard . . . . Philippe Léotard
Capt. Montier . . . . . Daniel Prévost
Also with: Bernadette Lafont, Darry Cowl, Feodor Atkine.

With French unemployment at 9.8%, "Ville à Vendre" is a timely murder mystery about a hitchhiker who wanders into a dying industrial town. Witty screenplay and offbeat acting turn a string of murders into entertaining satirical farce. Peppered with sexual innuendo, pic should generate strong b.o. at art houses and secure a niche as cult video.

Vet helmer Jean-Pierre Mocky, who's been scripting nonconformist pics almost annually since 1960 ("A Mort l'Arbitre"), here favors single head shots, darkish sets and distorting makeup, which together create just the right mood for the wacky unemployed town. Snappy editing and creepy murders ensure a fun ride up to the sarcastic surprise ending.

Pic opens in a decaying town near France's eastern border where a lanky hitchhiker (singer Tom Novembre) discovers locals, with comfy unemployment checks, on their way to a masquerade fest. Witnessing the apparent murder of a woman pharmacist, he teams up with the victim's vulgar female assistant (Valérie Mairesse), only to discover he's the chief suspect in a blatant coverup by everyone connected with the town's medical supplies.

As the body count rises, helmer strings out amusing, weird shticks such as a dog-like man (Darry Cowl), phone calls from the dead and a doped-up, randy police chief (Daniel Prévost). Michel Serrault stands out as a greedy mayor, while smooth Richard Bohringer is less visibly on the take as the scheming M.D. who knows what's really happening.

Easygoing Novembre shows fine comic talent, even if he's

later upstaged by Bernadette Lafont's crusty, out-of-town investigator. Helmer pulls out the stops in his comic cameo as a discreet big investor standing beside a model of the Empire State Building while speechifying in a thick Luxembourg accent, an homage to Peter Sellers' general in "Dr. Strangelove."

The ideological points add sting to the fast-paced wrap-up, and all technical credits are on target. — *Lee Lourdeaux*

TIME WILL TELL
(BRITISH-DOCU-COLOR-B&W)

A Theatrical Experience (U.K.) release of an Island Visual Arts-Polygram Video Intl. presentation of an Initial Film & TV production. Produced by Rocky Oldham. Executive producers, Neville Garrick, Malcolm Gerrie. Directed by Declan Lowney. In color; editors, Peter Bensimon, Tim Thornton-Allen; animation, Sue Young; associate producer, Chris Phipps. Reviewed at Prince Charles Theater, London, April 27, 1992. Running time: **89 MIN.**

Hardcore fans of late reggae superstar Bob Marley will groove over "Time Will Tell," a cut-and-paste docu on the Rastafarian's life and music. Vid-to-film production by Island, the Jamaican-born singer's diskery, doesn't offer many insights for general audiences.

Bulk of the footage is of the dreadlocked Marley and the Wailers performing in concert, from London to California to a 1980 independence day gig in Zimbabwe. The dozen or so numbers take in all the classics, plus some homevideo of the man himself jamming privately.

Aside from dated captions for each song, pic has few signposts for the uninitiated. Narration is limited to Marley's own words from interviews, but only trained ears will catch more than half of what he's mumbling in heavy patois.

Most interesting segs for the non-fan are in the opening sketching Marley's upbringing in the poor Trenchtown quarter of Kingston, and the moving footage of his public funeral in Jamaica after his death of lymphatic cancer in Miami on May 11, 1981, at age 36.

Editing is smooth and mobile without resorting to MTV-style hype. Vid transfer to 35m is okay but limited by the variable quality of the original material.
— *Derek Elley*

WILD ORCHID II: TWO SHADES OF BLUE

A Triumph Films release of a Vision Intl. presentation of a Saunders/King production. Produced by David Saunders, Rafael Eisenman. Executive producer, Mark Damon. Directed, written by Zalman King. Camera (Foto-Kem color), Mark Reshovsky; editor, Marc Grossman, James Gavin; music, George S. Clinton; production design, Richard Amend; sound (Ultra-Stereo), Stephen Halbert; assistant director, Roger La Page; additional camera, David Rudd, Peter Lyons Collister; associate producer, Steve Kaminsky; casting, Ferne Cassel. Reviewed at Sony screening room, N.Y., April 16, 1992. MPAA Rating: R. Running time: **107 MIN.**

Blue	Nina Siemaszko
Elle	Wendy Hughes
Ham	Tom Skerritt
Sully	Robert Davi
Josh	Brent Fraser
Dixon	Christopher McDonald
Mona	Liane Curtis
Jules	Joe Dallesandro
Col. Winslow	Stafford Morgan

A sequel in name only to the Mickey Rourke-starrer "Wild Orchid," Zalman King's pretentious exercise in softcore erotica is hot stuff only for pay-cable and homevid markets.

Filmed as "Blue Movie Blue" and on the shelf since last fall, pic has already been followed by a third "Wild Orchid" feature "Red Shoe Diaries," which debuts on Showtime almost simultaneously with "Blue" theatrical release.

All three films have in common the focus on a beautiful young woman's rites of passage. Here petite Nina Siemaszko portrays Blue, a California teen who's orphaned in 1958 when her heroin-addicted jazz trumpeter dad (Tom Skerritt) dies in a freak car accident.

She's taken under the wing of brothel madam Wendy Hughes and introduced to a life of prostitution. Her sexual deflowering has already occurred at the hands of sleazy jazz club owner Joe Dallesandro.

There's a certain amount of interest generated in Blue's fate as King's slowly paced melodrama unfolds, but Siemaszko's zombie-like performance denies the put-upon character much sympathy. Artsy photography is very distracting, as are several music video-styled interludes.

The picture's original title stems from a key plot point: Siemaszko is coerced into appearing in an unfinished stag film, or blue movie. Extremely disappointing finale has not one but two white knights appearing to save her: a platonic lover

Robert Davi and all-American boy Brent Fraser. King evidently intends this as a storybook fantasy but destroys all credibility with such lame devices.

Siemaszko's extremely alluring figure (which she bares) counts more than her acting ability this time out. She's briefly upstaged by Canadian thesp Lydie Denier as the loveliest brothel girl. Aussie actress Hughes adopts a neutral accent and severe manner in the villainess assignment. One can infer she's a lesbian doting on Blue, but King plays down numerous opportunities to make this subplot explicit.

Rest of cast is stuck with stereotyped roles, resulting in over-playing by Davi as the brooding Hughes henchman who turns over a new leaf, Dallesandro as the lech and Christopher McDonald as an evil senator. Fraser is forced to gush unconvincingly as the handsome rich kid who has his first sexual experience with Blue at the cathouse but doesn't recognize her before or after without her Louise Brooks-styled wig.

Pic is technically well-made. As with King's Sherilyn Fenn-starrer "Two Moon Junction," there is plenty of camp potential here (e.g, prostitute Blue going back to school as just another bobby-soxer), but it remains still-born under King's ponderous, self-important direction.
— *Lawrence Cohn*

ASSOLTO PER AVER COMMESSO IL FATTO
(ACQUITTED FOR HAVING COMMITTED THE DEED)
(ITALIAN)

A Filmauro Distribuzione release of a Luigi & Aurelio De Laurentiis presentaton of a Mito Film production in association with RAI-1. Produced by Ferdinando & Flavia Villevieille Bideri. Directed by Alberto Sordi. Screenplay, Rodolfo Sonego, Sordi. Camera (Telecolor), Armando Nannuzzi; editor, Tatiana Casini Morigi; music, Piero Piccioni; art direction, Marco Dentici; costumes, Paola Marchesin. Reviewed at Barberini Cinema, Rome, April 24, 1992. Running time: **118 MIN.**

Emilio Garrone	Alberto Sordi
Mariuccia	Angela Finocchiaro
Enzo	Enzo Monteduro
Nex	Marco Predolin

Italo king of comedy Alberto Sordi wears a tarnished crown in "Acquitted for Having Committed the Deed," a lackluster comedy that meekly satirizes Mediterranean media

moguls in the Silvio Berlusconi/ Giancarlo Parretti league. Sordi's popularity should ensure at least minor b.o. at home, but even diehard fans will quickly toss this one out of court.

Sordi, as a retired rights society official Emilio Garrone, fraudulently acquires the majority of Italy's private radio and TV stations by hitting them up for unpaid rights. A parliamentary bill blocking new private broadcasters is passed, and media baron Serra (Roberto Sbaratto, a dead ringer for Berlusconi) is cornered into a deal with the trickster.

After setting up a lucrative web in Africa, Garrone absconds during a revolt, then moves in on monster U.S. network BCB. Aided by Japanese waiters posing as rival execs (for Soky Corp.), and using the nonexistent African funds as leverage, he pulls off the ultimate coup without spending a cent.

Any potential for serious satire is tossed away in favor of lame farce. Garrone's adversaries are too inept to be real, especially the cartoonish U.S. honchos (top-rung execs in decidedly downmarket L.A. offices, speaking goofy Yank-accented Italian). Only the Berlusconi clone remains slickly dignified even as he's being outmaneuvered.

Pic's sugary revelation makes its bite even weaker: The cunning upstart's rampant asset accumulation is driven not by lust for money or power, but by love for his cutesy granddaughter.

Directing and headlining, Sordi does his standard shtick. Pic's scanty laughs come instead from rising comic Angela Finocchiaro as his unflappable secretary.

Technically shoddy effort makes poor use of Italian and U.S. locations, and dull lensing does nothing to disguise glaringly fake stand-ins for Africa and the Bahamas. Sound is way below par. —*David Rooney*

HURRICANE SMITH
(AUSTRALIAN)

A Warner Bros. release (Greater Union of Australia) of a Village Roadshow Films production. Executive producers, Graham Burke, Greg Coote, John Tarnoff. Produced by Daniel & Stanley O'Toole. Co-produced by Kevin Dobson, Sara Altsheil. Directed by Colin Budd. Screenplay, Peter Kinloch, from an idea by Dobson, Kinloch. Camera (color), John Stokes; editor, Pippa Anderson; music, Brian May; production design, Martin Hitchcock; sound, Ian Grant; assistant director, Charles Rotherham; 2nd unit director-stunt coordinator, Guy Norris. Reviewed at Village Cinema City 4, Sidney, April 9, 1992. Running time: **84 MIN.**
Billy Smith . . . . Carl Weathers
Charlie Dowd . . . . Jürgen Prochnow
Julie . . . . Cassandra Delaney
Howard Fenton . . . . . . Tony Bonner
Shanks . . . . David Argue

Already released regionally in the U.S., "Hurricane Smith," a 1990 production, quietly limped into a token major city release in Australia prior to its natural home on video shelves. No relation to the 1952 Jerry Hopper actioner, pic toplines Carl Weathers in a routine yarn about a Yank searching for his missing sister on Australia's seemingly violent Gold Coast.

Too bad writer Peter Kinloch didn't come up with a more original screenplay, as director Colin Budd and especially second unit director-stunt coordinator Guy Norris provide good action scenes in the final reel. The excitement, including dangerous-looking stunts with an exploding speedboat and a hijacked cop copter, comes too late to save a tired, predictable potboiler.

As the stranger in town, Weathers sleepwalks through his undemanding role, while Jürgen Prochnow glowers unconvincingly as the villain. It takes an age for Weathers to figure out Prochnow, hitman for brothel owner Tony Bonner, murdered his sister, something obvious to the audience since scene one.

Pic's Aussie actors fare rather better than the leads. David Argue, whose specialty is off-the-wall characters, has fun playing a scruffy type devoted to heroine Cassandra Delaney, in a standard prostitute-with-a-heart-of-gold role. And veteran John Ewart is a delight as Delaney's crusty old grandfather, whose dislike of Americans harks back to World War II, but who proves, in a pinch, to be a brave ally for Weathers.

Technically robust pic's deficiencies are all in the concept —in the script and the principal casting. — *David Stratton*

PROMENADES D'ÉTÉ
(SUMMER STROLLS)
(FRENCH)

A Gaumont release of a Films Alyne-Films du Roseau-Gaumont co-production. (Intl. sales: Gaumont.) Produced by Christian Caillo. Directed, written by René Féret. Camera (color), Pierre Lhomme; editor, Charlotte Fauvel; costumes, William MacPhail; sound, Michel Vionnet. Reviewed at Club Publicis, Paris, March 5, 1992. Running time: **91 MIN.**
Caroline . . . . Valérie Stroh
Thomas . . . . Michael Varton
François . . . . . . José-Maria Flotats
Magali . . . . Marie Guillard
Stéphane . . . . . Jean-Yves Berteloot

Tale of an amateur acting camp starts out promisingly as a spirited group comedy, only to shrink down to leading man's emotional coming of age. Underdeveloped screenplay and soap ending nix commercial prospects, except as middling adult homevideo of good-looking youths in lush countryside.

As a student troupe arrives in bucolic Dordogne to do a French version of "As You Like It," no fewer than four romances are in the offing, but helmer-scripter René Féret passes this over to focus on 20-year-old leading man who has eyes for scene decorator's 30ish wife. Funny fellow students, such as a self-styled opera singer and a hopelessly amorous Spaniard, thus end up as puppets dropped hurriedly into scenes.

Féret's first comedy has the right light tone and tempo but botches character development. First-rate Valérie Stroh, in her fifth Féret film, limns the seductive older woman who turns weepy in pic's final third and says she loves two men, in effect reneging on her role. Solid comic material turns into mish-mash meller.

At least Michael Vartan shines as talented top student, finely modulating boyish innocence to allow for pained confusion about love's complications. Tech credits, especially Pierre Lhomme's lensing of green fields and stream-side love-sex, are excellent. — *Lee Lourdeaux*

CARAVANA
(CONVOY)
(CUBAN-ANGOLAN)

An Instituto Cubano del Arte e Industria Cinematográficos (ICAIC)-Estudios Grama-Laboratorio de Cine Angolano production. Produced by Lupercio López. Directed by Julio César Rodríguez, Rogelio Paris. Screenplay, Raúl Macías. Camera (color), César Rodríguez; editor, Nelson Avila; music, Edesio Alejandro; sound, José León. Reviewed at 8th Santafé de Bogotá (Colombia) Intl. Film Festival, Oct. 11, 1991. Running time: **100 MIN.**
With: Manuel Porto, Omar Moynello, Patricio Wood, Samuel Claxton, Saturnino de Nascimiento, Joel Núñez, Salvador Wood, Enrique Molina, Nancy González.

Although it tries vainly not to imitate previous war films glorifying uncommon valor, "Convoy" is reminiscent of the spate of post-World War II films. Cuba's first feature to deal with its 16-year involvement in the Angolan civil war should do well in the home market.

Rather than follow a John Wayne-style hero, pic tracks a troop of soldiers, concentrating on collective effort over that of the individual — but to much the same effect.

Shot entirely in Angola and co-produced by the Cuban Army, pic documents the movements of a Cuban convoy sent to deliver food and medical supplies to the interior of the country. South Africa-backed Unita troops try at various times to stop them.

The film is not without its social criticism (a Cuban soldier is reprimanded for trying to barter supplies for unwilling female companionship), but overall, the soldiers are shown as valiant boys next door far from home engaged in a just battle for freedom.

Well-handled battle scenes come off more realistically than the massive fireworks in similar Yank ventures, centering more on soldiers' efforts than high artillery.

While tech credits are adequate and acting is okay, pic ultimately seems destined for the home market where the pic offers a national catharsis for a war that affected 50,000 Cuban troops and technicians. (After an estimated 8,000 casualties, Cuba withdrew from Angola as result of the May 31, 1991, peace accord.) — *Paul Lenti*

MAD BOMBER IN LOVE
(AUSTRALIAN)

A Pinchgut production. Produced by George Mannix. Directed by James Bogle. Screenplay, Bogle, Mannix, Peter Rasmussen, Martin Brown, Leon Marvell. Camera (video, color), John Brock; editor, Laura Zusters; music, Michael Roberts, Phil Rigger; production design, Brown; sound, Nigel Brooks; associate producer, John Swindells; assistant director, Geoffrey Giuffre. Reviewed at Barn Theater, Leura, Australia, April 3, 1992. Running time: **85 MIN.**
Bernard . . . . Craig Pearce
Julia . . . . Rachel Szalay
Kevin . . . . Alan Lovell
Bill . . . . Zachery McKay
Gunther . . . . Alex Morcos
Mary Lou . . . . . . Laura Keneally
Alistair . . . . Anthony Ackroyd
Also with: Max Cullen, Craig McLachlan, Paul Chubb, Zoe Carides, Helen Jones, Marcus Graham, Sandie Lillingston, James Bogle.

Shot on video, on a self-proclaimed "zero budget," "Mad Bomber in Love" is funny enough as a spoof thriller to merit exposure on the cult cinema circuit. Well scripted and acted, the pic overcomes its impoverished production values with a raffish charm.

Director James Bogle and his collaborators have taken a suspense story about a maniac holding innocent people captive in their house into a witty post-feminist comedy. Good casting, with personable young players in the leads, and several w.k. Aussie film and TV names in cameo roles, is a major asset.

Sydney is a-buzz with news of a "mad bomber" who targets official buildings. Julia, a liberated young woman, shares an inner-city house with Gunther, Bill and Mary Lou. They have room for another tenant.

Enter well-dressed, charming Bernard, who romances Julia and moves into the house, upsetting the other tenants with his mania for law and order. Julia soon latches on that Bernard is the Mad Bomber, but it's too late: He traps Julia and the others in the house, and, after Bernard kills Gunther and the other two in an escape attempt, in the end it's left to the resourceful Julia to overcome the Mad Bomber.

The material may not sound promising, but it's handled with a light touch, and the talented young cast brings style to the amusing screenplay. Editing ellipses utilize video techniques with imagination.

A lengthy end credit crawl prominently acknowledges the

support of Sony in the production of this extremely modest effort, which was made without official Aussie government support. —*David Stratton*

TEQUILA
(MEXICAN)

A Manley Prods. release of a Clasa Films Mundiales production. Executive producer, Myrna Ojeda. Produced by Manuel Barbachano Ponce. Directed, written by Rubén Gámez. Camera (color), Gámez; editor, Rafael Castanedo; sound, Ernesto Estrada, Fernando Cámara; choreography, Pilar Urreta. Reviewed at 8th Muestra de Cine Mexicano, Guadalajara, March 26, 1992. Running time: **85 MIN.**
With: Hugo Stiglitz, Yihra Aparicio, María Rojo.

After almost 30 years since making his awarding-winning short "Formula Secreta," Rubén Gámez's latest effort is a cinematographer's sketchbook of impressions of modern Mexico that may provoke interest via art house or cultural TV outlets.

In a way, "Tequila" appears to be a cinematic extension of Mexico's muralist tradition, a contemporary equivalent of the works of Diego Rivera or David Alfaro Siqueiros with vignettes, quick ideas, visual puns and cartoons, political statements, etc.

Boasting a minimum of text or scripted sequences, film never bogs down or gets boring through its visual and audio power, much like Godfrey Reggio's "Koyaanisqatsi."

Not all sequences work, but some images are surprisingly arresting, such as the night-time aerial views of Mexico City, which are truly impressive. A re-edited 60-minute version could tighten the overall effort and weed out the weaker sections.
— *Paul Lenti*

MAU MAU
(GERMAN)

A Pandora Film release of an Uwe Schrader production. (Intl. sales: Brussels Avenue.) Directed by Uwe Schrader. Screenplay, Schrader, Daniel Dubbe. Camera (color), Peter Gauhe; editor, Klaus Müller-Laue; music, Uli Goldhahn; production design, Jerome Latour-Burckhardt; costumes, Brigit Gruse; sound, Günter Knon. Reviewed at Filmkunst 66 cinema, Berlin, April 29, 1992. Running time: **92 MIN.**
With: Emanuel Bettencourt, Henryk Bista, Catrin Striebeck, Marlen Diekhoff, Peter Franke, Peter Gavadja, Myriam Mezieres, Rosemarie Nöthel.

A low-on-narrative pic about a busy bar and its nocturnal denizens, "Mau Mau" is missing the technique or experimentation that would compensate for the lack of a story line and make the film ultimately satisfying. Still, some fest play is possible.

Film's characters, some of whom are more developed than others, include bar owner Inge, who spends her time standing behind the bar, slowly tippling whiskey and observing her B-girl and petty criminal clientele.

Best perfs are given by Catrin Striebeck as a pretty, sassy young woman destined for a better life than the bar and her jealous Arab b.f., and Myriam Mezieres as the best friend stripper.

Film weaves in and out of bar, bedrooms and parlors of its clientele, who drift in and out of involvement with each other. An episode in which a character goes into a state of frenzy in his living room before a flashing neon crucifix is a brazen rip-off of the John McGiver scene in John Schlesinger's "Midnight Cowboy."

Seeing "Mau Mau" is like hanging out in a bar for a couple of hours: When it's over, nothing's changed. What pic ultimately lacks is a message. No conclusions can be drawn at the end about the characters, and while the filmmaking is competent, little attempt is made at innovation. Music tracks concentrate on 1970s disco hits, often in German versions. — *Rebecca Lieb*

AU SUD DU SUD
(FROM SOUTH TO SOUTH)
(FRENCH-DOCU)

A Noêdis-Prestations release of a Les Films d'Ici-Antenne 2-Films A2-Radio TV Suisse Romande-Transantarctica Expedition co-production. Produced by Yves Jeanneau. Directed by Laurent Chevallier. Camera (color), Chevallier; editor, Ange-Marie Revel; music, Michel Portal; sound, Marie-Hélène Quinton. Reviewed at George V Cinema, Paris, March 4, 1992. Running time: **103 MIN.**
With: Jean-Louis Etinne (France), Will Steger (USA), Victor Boyarsky (Russia), Geoff Somers (Great Britain), Keizo Funatsu (Japan), Dahe Qin (China).

Snappy editing and lotsa personal moments mark "Au Sud du Sud," a winning documentary about the first sled trek across Antarctica. Attractively lensed docu should generate strong b.o. at family-oriented sites, with success sure to follow as an expedition video.

Capturing subtle team spirit among six men from six different countries who live and work together (with 32 huskies) for seven months in a life-threatening environment, docu conveys the theme of "living in peace under the most extreme conditions."

Along the 4,000-mile trek from July 1989 to March 1990, pic gradually introduces a droll French sports doctor, a restless Brit, an extroverted Russian, a quiet Chinese engineer, a chipper young Japanese and an American dog trainer. Except for one brief dispute, the group functions smoothly since each man swallows his anger rather than complicate life.

In fluid montage, helmer-lenser Laurent Chevallier notes mood shifts from the engineer's comical first attempt on skis to the team's siege mentality in a howling storm. Nature comes into focus in the occasional far shot of an ice-blue mountain or the rare zoom on an immense crevasse. Frequent closeups of dogs straining in harnesses or sleeping outdoors in blizzards make them the unsung heroes.

Rounding out this warm, snowbound docu are the helmer's judicious flashbacks to meetings, medical tests and dog training. The modest beginnings point up the power of a few determined individuals, though the real focus is on the group dynamics of survival, climaxing in an anxious night search for a lost man.

All technical credits are excellent. — *Lee Lourdeaux*

HUSBANDS AND LOVERS
(ITALIAN)

A Columbia TriStar Home Video release (U.S.) of a Vision Intl. presentation of a PAC, Metrofilm production. Produced by Galliano Juso. Directed by Mauro Bolognini. Screenplay, Sergio Bazzini, based on Alberto Moravia's novel "The Friday Villa." Camera (Fotocinema color), Giuseppe Lanci; editor, Sergio Montanari; music, Ennio Morricone; sound, Carlo Palmieri, Piero Fondi; production design, Claudio Cinini; costume design, Alberto Spiazzi, Giorgio Armani; assistant director, Andrea Bolognini. Reviewed on Col TriStar vidcassette, N.Y., April 19, 1992. No MPAA Rating; also available in R-rated version. Running time: **94 MIN.**
Stefan . . . . Julian Sands
Alina . . . . Joanna Pacula
Paolo . . . . Tcheky Karyo
Louisa . . . . Lara Wendel
(English-language soundtrack)

Erotic drama "Husbands and Lovers" is a well-mounted adaptation of the late Alberto Moravia's novel "The Friday Villa." Pic flopped in Italy last season but should be arousing for Stateside vid voyeurs.

Vet director Mauro Bolognini, whose best work includes classic '50s collaborations with Pier Paolo Pasolini like "From a Roman Balcony," made an all-star miniseries for Italian TV from Moravia's "Time of Indifference" in 1987. Working in English this time, he emphasizes the material's sexual nature, featuring an overabundance of nude scenes with the two principal players.

Married couple Julian Sands and Joanna Pacula fancy themselves modern and free-thinking enough to have affairs and not feel guilty. He works as a screenwriter, and they rent a lavish villa for weekends (hence pic's original "The Friday Villa" moniker), but Pacula spends every Saturday and Sunday with her lover (Tcheky Karyo).

Supposedly Sands doesn't care, but despite Pacula's obvious allure (she spends most of the film in the buff though occasionally donning Giorgio Armani costumes), he obsessively picks up prostitutes to meet his sexual needs. Matters come to a head when Sands discovers that Karyo is abusing Pacula, beating her and involving her in kinky sadomasochistic rites. Punch line is that she likes it.

True to Moravia's thematics, film ironically stresses that husband Sands is still deeply in love with his wife but has lost his desire for her. Instead of the expected violent climax (at one point Sands is poised to shoot Pacula), film ends on a tentative note of reconciliation.

Imported cast adds class to what might have appeared a mere sex film in other hands. Topnotch technical support likewise differentiates this item from a horde of recent unrated sexploitation pics. — *Lawrence Cohn*

L'ANGELO CON LA PISTOLA
(ANGEL OF DEATH)
(ITALIAN)

A Penta Distribuzione release of a Mario & Vittorio Cecchi Gori & Silvio Berlusconi Communications presentation of a C.G. Group Tiger Cinematografica & Penta Film production. Produced by Mario & Vittorio Cecchi Gori. Executive producer, Luciano Luna. Directed by Damiano Damiani. Screenplay, Damiani, Dardano Sacchetti, Carla Giulia Casalini; story, Mario Cecchi Gori, Damiani. Camera (color, black & white), Sebastiano Celeste; editor, Antonio Siciliano; music, Riz Ortolani; art direction, Umberto Turco; costumes, Roberta Guidi di Bagno. Reviewed at Academy Hall Cinema, Rome, April 8, 1992. Running time: **100 MIN.**
Lisa . . . . Tahnee Welch
Police commissioner . . . Remo Girone
Teresa . . . . Eva Grimaldi

Attempting to make an earnest moral statement instead of going for irresponsible, violent pyrotechnics, "Angel of Death" is a no-frills, no-thrills vigilante pic that never takes wing. Pic should fly higher as video and tube fare.

Fed up with watching Genoa's crime lords go unpunished, the top cop (Remo Girone) is ready to quit. The murder of a mob lawyer dissuades him. Rather too simply, he links the killing to Lisa (Tahnee Welch), a waitress who (revealed in handsome black & white flashback) saw her family mowed down for unwittingly witnessing a mob slaying.

She promptly confesses to Girone, then proposes that they join forces to rid the city of scum. Lack of psychological background and any convincing attraction between the characters makes this hard to swallow, but Girone's character buys it. After a morning of target practice, Lisa is as handy with 007-style weaponry as she is with breakfast orders.

Mob honchos start dropping, leaving cops and mobsters mystified. A hooker (Eva Grimaldi) sees Lisa in action and reluctantly leads the thugs to her. Lisa narrowly escapes, but the police commissioner doesn't. Still thirsty for revenge, the waitress and the hooker team up and go after the mob's numero uno.

Helmer Damiano Damiani, who made a splash with Italy's widely exported Mafia miniseries "The Octopus," falls back on the teledrama approach to this tired amalgam of "Angel of Vengeance," "Death Wish" and just about every other edge-of-justice pic.

Despite the improbable plot and poor characterization, perfs by the three leads are fine. The bad guys are exclusively one-dimensional.

Tech work is functional, though dialogue is sloppily postsynched and Sebastiano Celeste's lensing confuses neorealistic grittiness with underlit drabness. — *David Rooney*

CANNES FEST

BAD LIEUTENANT

An Odyssey Distributors release (intl.) of an Edward R. Pressman production. Domestic distribution rights, Live Entertainment. Produced by Pressman, Mary Kane. Co-producer, Randy Sabusawa. Executive producers, Patrick Wachsberger, Ronna B. Wallace. Directed by Abel Ferrara. Screenplay, Zoe Lund, Ferrara. Camera (Foto-Kem color), Ken Kelsch; editor, Anthony Redman; music, Joe Delia; production design, Charlie Lagola; costume design, David Sawaryn; sound, Michael Barosky; assistant director, Drew Rosenberg; production manager-line producer, Diana Phillips; casting, Meredith Jacobson (N.Y.), Kimba Hills (L.A.). Reviewed at Broadway Screening Room, N.Y., April 10, 1992. (In Cannes Film Festival, Un Certain Regard.) MPAA Rating: NC-17. Running time: **96 MIN.**
LT . . . . Harvey Keitel
Nun . . . . Frankie Thorn
Zoe . . . . Zoe Lund
Lite . . . . Anthony Ruggiero
Jersey girl (driver) . . . Eddie Daniels
Jersey girl (passenger) . Bianca Bakija
Bowtay . . . . Victoria Bastel
Ariane . . . . Robin Burrows
Bet cop . . . . Victor Argo
Jesus . . . . Paul Hipp
Julio . . . . Fernando Velez
Also with: Joseph Michael Cruz, Paul Calderone, Leonard Thomas, Bo Dietl, Vincent Laresca, Minnie Gentry, Iraida Polanco, Frank Adonis.

Abel Ferrara's uncompromising "Bad Lieutenant" is a harrowing journey observing a corrupt N.Y. cop sink into the depths. Film's frank treatment of drug addiction, obsessive sexuality and loss of religious faith spells instant controversy. Its world preem in a Cannes sidebar slot may overshadow the competing entries, especially in light of Harvey Keitel's extraordinary and uninhibited perf in the title role.

Beyond the critical debate pic will engender, presenting a challenge for some adventurous domestic distributor yet to be signed, "Bad" reps first true test of the 2-year-old NC-17 rating since Universal's 1990 release of "Henry and June." Beyond individual scenes like a nun being gang-raped in church, the film as a whole is serious material aimed at adults only and could give impetus to committed filmmakers to make use of the heretofore dreaded tag.

Zoe Lund's screenplay ambitiously takes on taboo issues in looking at a degraded subculture in an era of faithlessness and despair. Not since Ingmar Bergman's "The Silence" (which also confronted censorship back in 1963) has a film tackled the subject of God's absence from people's lives in such a sexually explicit and morbid context.

Foul-mouthed cop Keitel's almost constantly sniffing, smoking or injecting drugs he's stolen from police busts while also indulging in alcohol and time-outs for sex. Cumulative effect is a far stronger antidrug message than any lecture on screen could be.

In his stupor, Keitel is investigating random murders, but his mind is on the Mets vs. Dodgers baseball playoffs. By film's end he owes an unfriendly bookie $120,000 in a betting motif reminiscent of James Toback's 1974 script "The Gambler." Device serves to knit together the film's otherwise loosely connected series of vignettes.

Turning point for Keitel is being assigned to the case of the raped nun. He's a lapsed Catholic who makes light of the event, but when nun Frankie Thorn (in an unadorned, affecting performance) not only forgives her assailants but expresses great sympathy for them, Keitel faces a religious crisis of conscience. His attempts at self-redemption are moving but come too late.

Lund, who made her screen debut billed as Zoe Tamerlis in the title role of Ferrara's 1980 pic "Ms. 45," not only is scripter but an impressive natural actress. Her sequence shooting up drugs and then injecting Keitel on camera is intense and riveting.

Even more impressive is a lengthy scene that could become a staple for acting classes in years to come, akin to the Brando-Steiger backseat "Palookaville" conversation in "On the Waterfront." Keitel stops two young sisters (Eddie Daniels, Bianca Bakija) from Jersey driving in the rain and harasses them while standing outside their car window. His tour de force, seemingly improvised method acting is matched against their unaffected, nervous naturalism. Sexual content of this scene is suggested rather than explicit but proves quite startling.

Elsewhere, Keitel lets it all hang out in a nude Christ-like pose, and spends the final reel in howls of despair as he hallucinates the presence of Christ (played by Paul Hipp, who with specs portrayed Buddy Holly on Broadway) in a church. His risk-taking here ups the ante on what stars can dare on screen, much the way Brando pushed the envelope 20 years ago in "Last Tango in Paris."

Wide-angle photography by Ken Kelsch (who photographed Ferrara's first feature "Driller Killer" 13 years ago) is used by the director to clinically observe Keitel's wayward activity in the manner Stanley Kubrick depicted Malcolm McDowell's antihero in "A Clockwork Orange." Real Manhattan locations from Limelight night club to the Port Authority Bus Terminal add to the verisimilitude.

Ferrara, who recently completed a remake of "Invasion of the Body Snatchers," plans to do a biopic on the last days of slain director Pier Paolo Pasolini. With "Bad Lieutenant," he establishes himself as the new standard bearer for Pasolini's poetic realism on screen.

— *Lawrence Cohn*

SOLDIER'S FORTUNE

A Republic Pictures Home Video release of a Biber-Hogue production. Produced by Michael Biber, Jeffrey C. Hogue. Executive producers, Hogue, Gerald J. Rappoport. Directed by Arthur N. Mele. Screenplay, Charles Douglas Lemay, Hogue, based on story by Hogue, Fred Olen Ray. Camera (Filmservice color), William Hayes; editor, Chris Roth; music, Chuck Cirino; sound (Ultra-Stereo), Alexander (Sasha) Welles. Reviewed on Republic vidcassette, N.Y. (In Cannes Film Festival market.) MPAA Rating: R. Running time: **95 MIN.**
Robert E. Lee Jones . . . . Gil Gerard
Hollis Bodine . . . . . . Dan Haggerty
Col. Blair . . . . Charles Napier
Debra . . . . P.J. Soles
Susan Alexander . . Barbara Bingham
Link . . . . Grainger Hines
Alex Prichard . . . . Janus Blythe
Jennifer . . . . Cynthia Guyer
Fresno Bob Bodine . . . Wild Bill Mock
T. Max . . . . . . George (Buck) Flower
Big Sam . . . . Randy Harris
Low Eddie . . . . Juan Garcia

Former TV star Gil Gerard goes homevid as the strong silent hero of the actioner "Soldier's Fortune." Lack of pizzazz or novelty puts a lid on this title's chances.

Gerard is called in when his ex-wife's daughter is kidnapped in suspicious circumstances. He's literally a soldier of fortune, called away from a guerrilla war in Central America.

Corny plot revelation is that the missing girl (Barbara Bingham) is really the daughter Gerard never knew he had. He sets about recruiting a rescue team of old cronies, notable only for a feisty woman (Janus Blythe) who insists on coming along because her sister was also a kidnappee.

Film lags after the kidnapping and lacks suspense. Final showdown between Gerard and his old nemesis Charles Napier is an anti-climax. — *Lawrence Cohn*

SECRETS
(AUSTRALIAN-NEW ZEALAND)

A Beyond Films presentation of a Victorian Intl. Pictures (Australia) & Avalon/NFU Studios (New Zealand) co-production, with participation of Australian Film Finance Corp. & Film Victoria. (Intl. sales: Beyond Films.) Executive producers, David Arnell, Michael Caulfield, William Marshall. Produced, directed by Michael Pattinson. Screenplay, Jan Sardi. Camera (color), David Connell; editor, Peter Carrodus; music, Dave Dobbyn; production design, Kevin Leonard-Jones; sound, Ken Saville; line producer, Lynda House; assistant director, Dave Norris; casting, Liz Mullinar. Reviewed at Beyond Films screening room, Sydney, March 17, 1992. (In Cannes Film Festival market.) Running time: **91 MIN.**
Emily . . . . Beth Champion
Danny . . . . Malcolm Kennard
Didi . . . . Dannii Minogue
Vicki . . . . Willa O'Neill
Randolph . . . . Noah Taylor

Focusing on a clutch of eager Beatlemaniacal teens, "Secrets" has a lot in common with Robert Zemeckis' "I Wanna Hold Your Hand." Good natured and very well-acted new film, however, suffers from a claustrophobic setting. Still, engaging characters and lively soundtrack should provide modest success on home turf; offshore possibilities also are indicated.

The Beatles' 1964 visit to Australia caused the same near-riots their U.S. tour provoked. Simple premise of Jan Sardi's somewhat wordy screenplay is to bring together four Fab Four fans and one anti-Beatle Elvis supporter. The five find themselves locked in the basement of the Melbourne hotel where the band is staying.

Early scenes introduce Emily (Beth Champion), a farm girl seemingly the least sophisticated of the bunch; Didi (Dannii Minogue), a 13-year-old Catholic schoolgirl who looks way older; Vicki (Willa O'Neill), a blowsy hairdresser's assistant; and Randolph (Noah Taylor) who adopts a Liverpool accent and claims to be George Harrison's cousin. Elvis fan Danny (Malcolm Kennard), the most assured and arrogant, is soon canoodling with Didi while charming the impressionable Emily.

Having established (via original newsreel material and some restaged scenes) the overwhelming throngs of fans and placed the five main characters in the hotel basement, Sardi's script really has nowhere to go. Later scenes gradually reveal more about all five: Emily isn't the innocent girl she appears to be; Didi isn't the brazen girl *she* appears to be; Vicki's pregnant and can't identify the father; Randolph is painfully shy and inexperienced; and Danny is scarred with painful childhood memories.

Champion radiates warmth as Emily, while Dannii Minogue's screen debut is more auspicious than that of her older sister (Kylie Minogue in "The Delinquents"). Taylor proves again that he's a fine young comedian, O'Neill is touching as Vicki and Kennard displays potential star quality.

Mostly beguiling Aussie-Kiwi co-prod, shot in film studios in New Zealand, is well produced, with fine camerawork and production design. Four Beatles originals are used, with numerous other Beatle compositions rearranged for the film by Dave Dobbyn. Result, despite limitations, is pleasurable low-key entertainment.

Though the dialogue is bright, the young cast enthusiastic and the Beatles music flooding the soundtrack invigorating, pic's restricted scope will limit its appeal. This will make it better suited for small screen exposure in many territories.
— *David Stratton*

WARSZAWA
(WARSAW — YEAR 5703)
(FRENCH-GERMAN)

A Molécule (Paris)-CCC Filmkunst (Berlin) co-production in association with Zodiac (Warsaw). (Intl. sales: George Pilzer.) Produced by Henry Lange, Artur Brauner. Directed by Janusz Kijowski. Screenplay, Kijowski, Jerzy Janiki. Camera (color), Przemyslaw Skwirczynski; editor, Wanda Zeman; music, Jan-Kanty Pawlvskiewicz; set design, Andrzej Przedworski; sound, Frederic Ullman, Bernard Borel. Reviewed at Club de l'Etoile, Paris, April 28, 1992. (In Cannes Film Festival Directors Fortnight.) Running time: **110 MIN.**
Alek . . . . Lambert Wilson
Fryda . . . . Julie Delpy
Stephania . . . . . . Hanna Schygulla

Three top Euro-thesps are put through their paces with mixed results in "Warszawa," a downbeat French-lingo drama set in 1943. Polish-born helmer Janusz Kijowski's sixth feature is suitable for festivals and TV, but, due to its claustrophobic, somewhat stagey approach, is unlikely to tap into more than a tiny segment of the audience that embraced "Europa, Europa."

In the winter of 1943 two young Jews (Lambert Wilson and Julie Delpy) escape, via sewer tunnels, from the atrocities underway in the Warsaw ghetto. Wilson, entrusted with undeveloped photos of the horrors within, makes his way to a supposedly safe apartment only to find it occupied by Germans.

Another tenant, an Aryan Pole (Hanna Schygulla), abruptly offers to shelter him in her large, comfortable apartment. The enigmatic Schygulla comforts the jittery young man and they make love that very night.

Schygulla is uncommonly generous and willing to jeopardize her own safety by harboring a Jew. When Wilson brings up the fact that he left his "little sister" at a nearby church, Schygulla herself rescues Delpy and welcomes her into her home. But Delpy is ungrateful and proceeds to sabotage the trio's safety in insidious ways.

Apart from opening scenes, set in a cold blue ghetto overrun by brutal Nazis, three-character drama transpires almost entirely in Schygulla's apartment. Effective art direction and appropriate camerawork convey a definite sense of place. Issues of allegiance, risk and survival are explored, but the spark of inspired direction that would make the characters' interdependent plight truly harrowing is missing. Viewers may or may not guess Delpy's motivation before it is revealed.

Although Wilson has sharp, sunken features, both he and Delpy seem too robust to have been ghetto inmates. Only later, when the food supply runs out, are they made to look famished and unsteady on their feet.

Delpy, who played a perfect pro-Hitler German youth in "Europa, Europa," brings defiance to her role as a Polish Jewess but doesn't inspire much sympathy.

With her long loose hair, broad open face and trademark "Maria Braun" legs, Schygulla's "older woman" appeal is evident.
— *Lisa Nesselson*

ARCHIPEL
(ARCHIPELAGO)
(FRENCH-BELGIAN)

A Locus Solus Prods.-Les Films Dancourt-What's On-Ciné Cinq co-production with participation of Canal Plus. Produced by Norbert Saada, Jean-Marie Duprez. Executive producer, Roger André Larrieu. Directed by Pierre Granier-Deferre. Screenplay, Granier-Deferre, Jacques Fieschi, based on Michel Rio's book "Archipel." Camera (color), Charly Vandamme; editor, Anne-Marie L'Hote; set design, Jacques Saulnier; sound, Frank Struys, Bernard Leroux. Reviewed at CNC screening room, Paris, April 27, 1992. (In Cannes Film Festival Cinemas en France.) Running time: **103 MIN.**
Leonard Wilde . . . . . Michel Piccoli
Alexandra Hamilton . . Claire Nebout
Michel . . . . Melvil Poupaud
Miss Elliott . . . . . Ludmila Mikaël
Also with: Samuel West, Anaïs Jeanneret, Michel Aumont.

"Archipel," is a tasteful, mildly titillating art film in which the romantic inclinations of a teenage boy, two adult women and a frustrated older man become perversely interconnected. Formal, somewhat old-fashioned approach and slow pacing suggest tube and video sales rather than serious theatrical prospects.

Soon to turn 17, Michel (Melvil Poupaud) is a scholarship student at the exclusive Hamilton boarding school, a bilingual academy where staff and students speak French, situated on an island off the southern coast of England. There are over 300 boys and only three women on the remote estate: the lovely and aloof owner, Alexandra Hamilton (Claire Nebout), her attractive and businesslike housekeeper (Ludmila Mikaël) and the school nurse. When the other students leave on a holiday break, Miss Hamilton invites Michel to live in her house.

Although the nearly deserted island setting lends itself to a mysterious semi-erotic tale of closed ranks, insinuation and long-standing rituals, pic exudes a tone so reserved as to be uninvolving. Warm-weather lensing is adequate.

Poupaud is convincing as the sensitive young man on the cusp of sexual experience. He holds his own in a drunken scene where he begins to suspect that he is a pawn being used to spice up the sex lives of his elders.

Nebout is a bit stilted as the mistress of the estate, who always makes a point of standing in front of an open window when undressing and bathing. Mikaël is okay as her no-nonsense housekeeper. As the curmudgeonly and hunchbacked school librarian, Michel Piccoli manages to inject a note of tenderness into his role as an emotionally stunted voyeur.

A scene set in a small boat during a storm borders on the ridiculous — only in a book or a not-altogether-plausible movie would two characters split philosophical hairs while one is in imminent danger of drowning. Third act, in which motives click, has a few strong confrontations, but remains wobbly in places.

— *Lisa Nesselson*

SAN FRANCISCO

A JUST WAR?
(SWEDISH-DOCU)

A Rotunda Film-Produktionsgruppen production with support of the Swedish Filminstitute Shortfilm Fund. Produced by Staffan Hedqvist. Directed by Maj Wechselmann. Camera (color), Michael Rosengren; music, Anders Koppel; sound, Joachim Hallman. Reviewed at San Francisco Film Festival, April 24, 1992. Running time: **60 MIN.**

Despite its title, "A Just War?" does little to question U.S. involvement in the Persian Gulf war. Focus of this short but harrowing Swedish docu instead falls on the conflict's catastrophic consequences for Iraq's civilians.

Since extent of damage was largely kept out of mainstream U.S. media, this film could be a hot film fest item. A short but busy specialty gig/TV career also seems likely.

Docu points up war's agricultural and health consequences. Over half the country's sheep and other livestock died in the last year, sending food prices through the roof. Infant mortality is up 350%. U.N. sanctions against importing medical supplies have left people to die of such routine illnesses as asthma and hypertension.

Film also explores gruesome military tactics (soldiers on both sides were blinded by U.S. laser range-finders) and contains a short history of the 40-years' lead-in to the war.

Action is often hard to watch, but Brit narrator's cool BBC tone helps avert any sense of overt agitprop. He sums up the film's essential point early on: "How hard must a people be punished for being ruled by a despot?"

— *Dennis Harvey*

SWORDSMAN II
(HONG KONG)

A Film Workshop Co. Ltd. release. Produced by Tsui Hark. Line producer, Cho King Man. Directed by Ching Siu Tung. Screenplay, Hark, Hanson Chan, Tang Pik Yin; story by Louis Cha. Camera (color), Lau Moon Tong; editor, Mak Chi Sin; music, Richard Yuen; costume design, William Chang, Yu Ka On; special effects, Cinefex Workshop. Reviewed at San Francisco Film Festival, April 23, 1992. Running time: **110 MIN.**
With: Jet Li, Brigitte Ching-Hsia Lin, Michelle Li, Rosamund Kwan, Fannie Yuen, Yan Yee Kwan, Lau Shun, Waise Lee, Candice Yu, Chin Ka-Lok, Cheung Kwok-Leung.

A dizzying pileup of hyper-adrenalized action, "Swordsman II" will please ethnic auds and fans of Hong Kong cinema's brand of spectacle. But narrative incoherency and a bleak undercurrent to the surface frenzy make this period fantasy an unlikely candidate for crossover success.

Overloaded plot has young swordsman Ling traveling with comically spacy sis Kiddo in search of monastic seclusion with the Sun Moon sect. But sect's master has been imprisoned by flunky Fong the Invincible, whose possession of the Sacred Scrolls has allowed his magical mutation into the body of a woman. Meanwhile, Japanese troops threaten mainland Chinese takeover. Confusing but kinetic battles between various factions dominate the pic.

Fantastic elements bring this saga close to the realm of the "Chinese Ghost Story" pics, as nearly all protagonists possess supernaturally heightened martial art powers.

There's no denying the energy and panache with which all this action is executed. But the script lacks the redeeming narrow focus of Hong Kong pics like "The Killer," and its convolutions rob the film of narrative build.

"Wherever there are people, there is inevitable conflict," says one character, but this tragic theme mixes awkwardly with the comic-book tone and pace. The mix is exhausting in ways presumably not intended. Tech credits are expectedly high-grade.

— *Dennis Harvey*

A QUESTION OF ATTRIBUTION
(BRITISH)

A BBC production. Produced by Innes Lloyd. Executive producer, Richard Broke. Directed by John Schlesinger. Screenplay by Alan Bennett, based on his stage play. Camera (color), John Hooper; editor, Mark Day; music, Gerald Gouriet; production design, Barbara Gosnold. Reviewed at San Francisco Film Festival, April 23, 1992. Running time: **70 MIN.**

Sir Anthony Blunt	James Fox
Radiologist	Gregory Floy
Donleavy	Geoffrey Palmer
Chubb	David Calder
Collins	Edward De Souza
Colin	Jason Flemyng
Restorer (Robertson)	John Cater
Consultant	Richard Bebb
Mrs. Chubb	Ann Beach
Receptionist	Julia St. John
Phillips	Mark Payton
Miss Bracewell	Anne Jameson
County Lady	Barbara Hicks
H.M.Q.	Prunella Scales

Dry, brittle "Question of Attribution" reunites writer Alan Bennett and director John Schlesinger in a sequel of sorts to their Atlantic-crossover BBC hit "An Englishman Abroad."

While the short running time and visible (though expertly employed) TV roots will limit Stateside theatrical action, specialty gigs and a long life on public television seem certain.

In "Englishman," Bennett adapted his own stage play about the notorious Brit aristocrat Guy Burgess, who was eventually found out to be a Soviet spy. Here the focus goes to Burgess' partner in espionage, Sir Anthony Blunt (James Fox), on the eve of his own public embarrassment.

Arch and arrogant in Fox's razor-sharp characterization, Blunt has hidden behind his legacy of privilege — he been "survey-or of pictures" to the queen, a sort of royal art historian — for years. But when new government interrogator Chubb (David Calder) is assigned to the case, the cat-and-mouse game between the two begins to crumble Blunt's facade.

Despite his gruff exterior, Chubb is a sly one, and his prey begins to feel the heat of inevitable exposure. (Blunt confessed in 1964 — when this scenario takes place — and was publically named by Prime Minister Margaret Thatcher in 1979.)

Prunella Scales takes the pic into a sphere of delicious drollery with her bizarre yet respectful portrait of Elizabeth II, British TV's first fictive sketch of the queen.

Couching its drama in clever recurring threads of art and philosophy (Blunt is investigating the mystery of faces hidden beneath the surface of a Titian portrait), the film should prove a major hit with its targeted Anglophile audience.

Tech values are fine if recognizably on the level of televid production. — *Dennis Harvey*

VIRGINA
(YUGOSLAVIAN-FRENCH)

A Maestro Film (Zagreb)-Centar Film (Belgrade)-Constellation Prods. (Paris) production. Produced by Rajko Grlic, Mladen Koceic, Djordje Milojevic, Laudie Ossard, Cedomir Kolar. Directed, written by Srdjan Karanovic. Camera (color), Slobodan Trninic; editor, Branka Ceperac; music, Zoran Simjanovic; set design, Nikola Pajic; costumes, Maja Galasso. Reviewed at San Francisco Film Festival, April 27, 1992. Running time: **100 MIN.**

Timotije	Miodrag Krivokapic
Stevan	Marta Keler
Dostana	Ina Gogalova
Mijat	Igor Bjelan
Paun	Slobodan Milovanovic

Also with: Matija Praskalo, Mirko Vlahovic, Sladjana Bebic, Vjenceslav Kapural, Nada Gacesic Livakovic, Natalija Karna, Lana Djurkin, Andrijana Videnovic, Miodrag Macura, Petar Popovic, Darko Kralj, Milan Bradas, Ante Ivkovic, Radovan Veslinovic.

Srdjan Karanovic's "Virgina" creates an engrossing fictive narrative out of an odd secret tradition. Pic's prospects outside Europe are iffy, but emphasis on the fascination of its bizarre subject could coax modest art house biz.

Until fairly recently in parts of Yugoslavia, families without male children were considered cursed by the gods. In desperation, they'd occasionally cast a female offspring as a "virgina" — raising and passing her off to the community as a boy. Already saddled with three young girls, farmer Timotije and wife Dostana live in the extreme poverty of late 19th century rural Serbia. Fellow villagers even blame the family's "misfortune" for a punishing drought.

When Dostant gives birth to yet another girl, Timotije comes close to killing the infant but instead opts to re-make the child as male "Stevan." Neighbors rejoice at the lie, and miraculously rains soon fall.

Most of "Virgina" takes place years later, as Stevan grows into confused adolescence. After being kept a virtual prisoner for years, the girl-boy must constantly avoid being "found out" by the community.

The unrelievedly harsh, centuries-old ways of this culture are well-detailed, as is its overbearing misogyny — both wrapped in a heavy shroud of religious-superstitious masochism. But Karanovic manages to wring surprising dry humor from this strange coming-of-age story.

Meanwhile, pic's gender-blurring comedy is quite engaging as Stevan simultaneously protects and chafes against the family secret.

Acting is very good, as are technical credits. The washed-out photography conveys the bleakness of the landscape while allowing a mini-epic feel.

— *Dennis Harvey*

HOUSTON FEST

CENTER OF THE WEB

A Pyramid Distribution release of a Winters Group production in association with Sovereign Investment Group. Produced by Ruta K. Aras. Executive producers, David Winters, Marc Winters. Directed, written by David A. Prior. Camera (color), Andrew Parke; editor, Tony Malanowski; music, Greg Turner; art direction, Linda Lewis. Reviewed at WorldFest/Houston, April 25, 1992. No MPAA rating. Running time: **91 MIN.**
Richard Morgan . . . . . . Robert Davi
Kathryn Lockwood . . Charlene Tilton
John Phillips . . . . Ted Prior
Frank Allesendro . . . . . Bo Hopkins
Tony . . . . William Zipp
Stephen Moore . . . . Tony Curtis
Also with: Charles Napier.

"**C**enter of the Web" is a lively but overplotted thriller best suited for the international action market. Good cast, including top-billed Robert Davi in an atypical good-guy role, also may attract some respectable video rental coin.

Filmed on location in Mobile, Ala., pic begins with drama teacher Ted Prior being mistaken for a notorious hit man and forced into a car by two thugs. After drive-by gunmen spray the car with bullets, one thug is dead, another flees and Prior is left to explain things to the cops.

Fortunately, Prior's g.f. (Charlene Tilton) is an assistant D.A. and gets him sprung from jail. Unfortunately, a mysterious Justice Dept. official (Robert Davi) threatens to put Prior back behind bars unless he continues to pose as the hit man, who's been hired to assassinate a visiting governor.

This sets up pic's best line, from Prior: "You need Al Pacino

for this, not me! If I were that good an actor, I wouldn't be teaching!"

Naturally, nothing is what it seems, and nobody can be taken at face value. Prior turns out to be a deep cover fed agent, but that doesn't help much when he learns that the hit man has been set up as a fall guy by assassination conspirators. Tilton seeks help from an old family friend, a retired CIA operative (Tony Curtis). But neither Tilton nor Curtis can be trusted completely. And D.A. Bo Hopkins can't be trusted at all.

Writer-director David A. Prior's screenplay contains even more double- and triple-crossing than "White Sands." Some of the plot explanations must be delivered in the kind of rapid-fire dialogue that generates convulsive giggles more than sweaty-palmed suspense. Even so, Prior keeps "Center of the Web" racing along just fast enough to make it diverting B-movie fun.

Davi is a standout with his imposing underplaying. Other members of the cast deliver the goods, with Tilton managing to maintain her dignity during a totally gratuitous nude scene. Prior — the actor, not the filmmaker — handles the action-hero stuff more than adequately.

Tech credits are fine, with particularly strong work from the special effects and stunt crews during a chase that has Prior's car repeatedly rammed by a bad guy in a commandeered school bus. The bad guy, incidentally, is played by William Zipp with a hairdo best described as ersatz Lyle Lovett. — *Joe Leydon*

KNOWING LISA

An Imagining Things Enterprises production. Produced by Bruce Campbell. Executive producer, Sharon Linnea. Directed, written by Robert Owens Scott. Camera (color), Lukasz Jogalla; music, Stephen Webber. Reviewed at WorldFest/Houston, April 25, 1992. Running time: **85 MIN.**
Bennett . . . . Bruce Kuhn
Lisa . . . . Karin Levitas
Peter . . . . Johnny Kline
Franco . . . . Francis Henry
Francie . . . . Navida Stein
Annie . . . . Cathi Hanauer

"**K**nowing Lisa" is the sort of amateurish, charmless and blatantly self-indulgent effort that can give low-budget labors of love a bad name. Theatrical and vid prospects are nonexistent.

Writer-director Robert Owens

Scott, an Off Off Broadway veteran, tries to blend mild comedy and subjective fantasy in his story about a straight-laced high school teacher (Bruce Kuhn) who has second thoughts about his seemingly demure fiancée (Karin Levitas).

The teacher's suspicions are aroused when a roommate shows him a nude drawing of his girlfriend on display in a seedy bar. Things only get worse when Kuhn learns another roommate, a handsome artist, has been using his fiancée as a nude model.

Rest of pic jerks back and forth, arbitrarily and confusingly, between fantasy and reality. Scott tries to play it for laughs, but the pic too often comes across as creepily perverse. Indeed, the upbeat ending isn't really all that upbeat, since the teacher shows every sign of being a borderline psychotic.

Performances range from barely adequate to embarrassing. Tech credits are poor. Locations in and around Montague, N.J., are generally attractive.

— *Joe Leydon*

CANNES FEST

FAR AND AWAY

A Universal release of an Imagine Films Entertainment presentation of a Brian Grazer production. Produced by Grazer, Ron Howard. Executive producer, Todd Hallowell. Co-producers, Bob Dolman, Larry DeWaay. Directed by Howard. Screenplay, Dolman, story by Dolman, Howard. Camera (Deluxe color, Panavision Super 70m), Mikael Salomon; editors, Michael Hill, Daniel Hanley; music, John Williams; production design, Jack T. Collis (Montana), Allan Cameron (Ireland); art direction, Jack Senter; art direction (Ireland), Steve Spence, Tony Reading; set design, Joseph Hubbard, Robert M. Beall; set decoration, Richard Goddard; costume design, Joanna Johnston; sound (Dolby), Ivan Sharrock; associate producer, Louisa Velis; assistant director, Aldric La'auli Porter; 2nd unit director, Hallowell; casting, Karen Rea, Ros Hubbard, John Hubbard. Reviewed at Coronet Theater, N.Y. (In Cannes Festival — closing night), May 1, 1992. MPAA rating: PG-13. Running time: **140 MIN.**
Joseph Donelly . . . . Tom Cruise
Shannon Christie . . . . Nicole Kidman
Stephen . . . . Thomas Gibson
Daniel Christie . . . . . Robert Prosky
Nora Christie . . . . Barbara Babcock
Kelly . . . . Colm Meaney
Molly Kay . . . . Eileen Pollock
Grace . . . . Michelle Johnson
Also with: Douglas Gillison, Wayne Grace, Barry McGovern, Niall Toibin, Rance Howard, Clint Howard.

Old-fashioned is the word for "Far and Away," a time-worn tale of 19th century immigrants making their way in the New World. Handsomely mounted and amiably performed, but leisurely and without much dramatic urgency, Ron Howard's robust epic stars Tom Cruise and Nicole Kidman as class-crossed lovers who take nearly the entire picture to get together. Cruise's name and Howard's commercial rep point to a healthy but probably not boffo b.o. life.

Set as the closing night attraction at Cannes, pic is notable as the first narrative, non-effects-oriented Hollywood feature in more than two decades to have been shot on 65m stock (with Panavision's new Super 70 equipment), and released in 70m. As created by Mikael Salomon, images have a wonderful crispness and luminosity that make the effort worthwhile.

Buffs will note that the new process, at least as used here, boasts a normal Panavision aspect ratio, one not as wide as the similarly named Super Panavision 70 process of the 1960s.

Long-in-gestation story by screenwriter Bob Dolman and

Howard is a standard-issue tale of a lower-class lad who gets involved with the feisty daughter of a wealthy landowner. Dozens of fights, confrontations and misunderstandings, thousands of miles and nearly 2½ hours later, the two headstrong youngsters give in to the inevitable physical impulses obvious to everyone else from the beginning.

This script would have perfectly suited Tyrone Power or Errol Flynn in the 1930s. With just a few mildly salacious adjustments to suit modern sensibilities, Cruise ably picks up the reins as a tenant farmer in Western Ireland, circa 1892, who wants to kill his absentee landlord for torching the family home and, in effect, murdering his father.

Exemplifying script's notions of both manifest and spiritual destiny, Pa gives son Joseph (Cruise) an inspirational deathbed speech about the connection of one's soul to one's land, and how Joseph ought to go to America. First, however, son means to do in the landlord (Robert Prosky), who, when met, turns out to be a nice chap who feels as victimized, in his way, as Joseph.

In fact, just about every character here insists they are oppressed. Prosky's pampered, spirited daughter Shannon (Nicole Kidman) is kept on the tightest of leashes by her mother (Barbara Babcock), and is constantly badgered by her darkly handsome suitor (Thomas Gibson). Latter challenges the uppity Joseph to a duel but, saved by the fog at dawn, Joseph makes off with Shannon for the States, disagreeably consenting to work as her servant shipboard.

Arriving in Boston (actually streets of Dublin nicely redressed) at the 45-minute point, the couple is instantly thrown in with the hordes of immigrant riffraff when Shannon's silver is stolen. Sharing a room at a brothel, the two must fend for themselves While Shannon toils plucking chickens, Joseph, in pic's most engaging scenes, makes a name for himself as a scrappy bare-knuckles boxer.

However, the land still beckons, and by the next year all the characters (the Christies, as well as Joseph, have also come to America) find themselves in the epochal Oklahoma land rush.

All chords struck by Howard and Dolman are the familiar homespun variety. While fine and dandy for mainstream audiences seeking a comforting good time,

it also makes for a picture with no edge. A little irreverence and some revisionist strokes would have lent some welcome spice to this bland meat-and-potatoes serving of U.S. history.

Some of the detail results in needless dawdling. Joseph's sentimental dreaming of Shannon and the couple's let's-pretend-we're-rich interlude in a Boston mansion are embarrassing, and the lull before the big land rush is just padding.

Most of the film's pleasures are purely physical. Seeing Western Ireland, especially on the big screen, is always inspiring (ironically, one of the last true 70m productions was the similarly set "Ryan's Daughter"), and Montana, standing in for Oklahoma, is also pretty easy on the eyes. Irish production designer Allan Cameron has created a vivid, instantly interesting portrait of late 19th century Boston slums, and Joanna Johnston's costume designs are also notable.

Cruise's physicality is forcibly in evidence, which will not be unwelcome to his many fans. Stripped down frequently, he is genuinely impressive in the fisticuff action of pic's midsection. His horseback riding (it's obviously him) is also thrilling in the monumentally staged land race, the likes of which hasn't been seen on screen for some time. Cruise's Irish accent is quite acceptable, to the point where one stops really noticing it.

Heavily garbed, unlike her husband and co-star, Kidman has the requisite grit and defiant spirit in her eyes. As the one-dimensional villain, Gibson dashingly reminds of Timothy Dalton, while Prosky is a kick as the resilient landowner. Michelle Johnson has a few nice moments as a busty dancer who takes a shine to Joseph at the height of his boxing fame.

In a dream job for a cinematographer, Salomon fashions a world of great color, loveliness and physical grandeur, although his favoring of soft backgrounds indicates that the full sharpness of the new 70m equipment has yet to be displayed. Also effective is John Williams' fully supportive, but not at all overwhelming score. — *Todd McCarthy*

IL LADRO DI BAMBINI
(THE STOLEN CHILDREN)
(ITALIAN-FRENCH)

A Darc release of an Erre Produz-

ioni (Rome)/Alia Film (Rome)/Arena Films (Paris) co-production, in association with RAI-TV Channel 2 (Rome) & Vega Film (Zurich). (Intl. sales: Sacis.) Produced by Angelo Rizzoli. Executive producer, Enzo Porcelli. RAI-2 producer, Stefano Munaf(sc203). Directed by Gianni Amelio. Screenplay, Amelio, Sandro Petraglia, Stefano Rulli. Camera (color), Tonino Nardi, Renato Tafuri; editor, Simona Paggi; art direction, Andrea Crisanti; music, Franco Piersanti; sound, Alessandro Zanon. Reviewed at Nuovo Sacher Cinema, Rome, May 3, 1992. (Competing at Cannes Film Festival.) Running time: **112 MIN.**

Antonio	Enrico Lo Verso
Rosetta	Valentina Scalici
Luciano	Giuseppe Ieracitano
Martine	Florence Darel
Nathalie	Marina Golovine

Also with: Fabio Alessandrini, Agostino Zumbo, Vincenzo Peluso, Santo Santonocito, Vitalba Andrea, Massimo De Lorenzo, Celeste Brancato.

"**T**he Stolen Children," Gianni Amelio's "Viaggio in Italia" for the '90s, is a powerful portrait of people and places likely to earn a special niche in Italian film history. This small gem of a picture has a capacity to communicate profoundly, without clichés, to selected audiences — perhaps even better abroad than locally.

In Italy, producer Angelo Rizzoli's Darc has opened the film in a single theater in Rome, where it has attracted steady interest.

Two innocent kids, accompanied by an honest young carabiniere, travel from Milan to Palermo in a powerful vision of a humanly rich but socially impoverished country. The family drama is sketched in a quick, chilling opener seen through the morose eyes of 9-year-old Luciano.

He knows his mother, a Sicilian-born slum-dweller in Milan, has been quietly prostituting his 11-year-old sister Rosetta for years. When the police turn up, the silent little boy clearly was expecting them — he's the informer. Cop cars zoom everyone away.

Without wasting time on the obvious, Amelio next introduces young carabiniere Enrico Lo Verso, the most stalwart, moral hero seen in an Italian film in decades. Dumped by his partner, Lo Verso is strapped with the thankless task of transporting the two kids to an orphanage in Bologna. The girl is tauntingly rebellious, a potential runaway; the boy is asthmatic and locked in mute melancholy. Lo Verso concentrates on discharging his duty as quickly as possible.

But when the orphanage refuses to take Rosetta, he's forced to embark on a journey that ultimately leads all three characters, along with the audience,

into a bittersweet friendship and a clash of well-intentioned people against callous institutions.

Amelio makes ferocious use of understatement, simplicity and significant detail to bring home his point without belaboring the self-evident. The horrible truth about Rosetta's visitor in a business suit dawns in a closeup of two hands.

"Il Ladro di Bambini" returns to devices used in postwar neorealism (nonpro actors, heavy location work) to make scenes ring desolately true. As the title suggests, Vittorio De Sica's neorealist classic "Il Ladro di Biciclette" (Bicycle Thief), which also showed an adult's humiliation through a child's eyes, is not far away. But Amelio's aversion to easy emotion and the care for detail and closeup with which he constructs unposed images links him more to the supreme cinematic simplicity of Roberto Rossellini.

The story (which Amelio co-wrote with Stefano Rulli and Sandro Petraglia, young writing duo known for their treatment of social themes) is nothing more than a burgeoning friendship on the road, leading from Milan and Bologna to Rome and the Calabrian hinterlands, and finally across the straits into Sicily.

As the ice slowly melts between officer and kids and a deep rapport develops, Amelio is careful to avoid Hollywood-style heart-tugging. The payoff is much larger (though the audience may be much smaller).

Instead of milking the latent sentimentality of straight human relations, pic keeps veering off to take a deeper look into Italy's hidden social malaise. Film peaks when private and public ills complement each other.

Child actors Valentina Scalici and Giuseppe Ieracitano produce extraordinarily convincing perfs. Neither had any previous brush with show business, nor were they allowed to read the film's script before (or after) shooting. Yet their gentle, half-knowing expressions are as effective as Garbo's blankness at the end of "Queen Christina" —the meaning is for the viewer to supply.

Same naturalness and spontaneity spark professional actor Lo Verso's slow-burning fire as the public servant undone by his old-fashioned, naive idealism. Under Amelio's iron-hand direction, the three make a memorable, moving ensemble.

Two of Italy's major cinematographers (Renato Tafuri, Tonino Nardi) plumb the characters' depths in color images so rigorous but unpretentious they leave a retroactive impression of being black & white. Production designer Andrea Crisanti describes a series of icy corridors, from police stations to orphanages and train stations, that visually sum up pic's condemnation of institutional cruelty.

Music is an eclectic mood mix usually hitting the target (like Franco Piersanti's vaguely Arab-sounding theme) but occasionally stepping a little too far forward with familiar songs.

— *Deborah Young*

STRICTLY BALLROOM
(AUSTRALIAN)

A Ronin Films (Australia) release of an M&A Film Corp. production, with participation of the Australian Film Finance Corp. (Intl. sales: Beyond Films.) Produced by Tristram Miall, Ted Albert. Executive producer, Popsy Albert. Line producer, Jane Scott. Directed by Baz Luhrmann. Screenplay, Luhrmann, Craig Pearce. Camera (Eastmancolor), Steve Mason; editor, Jill Bilcock; music, David Hirshfelder; production design, Catherine Martin; costumes, Angus Strathie; assistant director, Keith Heydate. Reviewed at Valhalla cinema, Sydney. (In Cannes Film Festival, non-competing), March 11, 1992. Running time: **92 MIN.**
Scott Hastings . . . . . . Paul Mercurio
Fran . . . . Tara Morice
Barry Fife . . . . Bill Hunter
Doug Hastings . . . . Barry Otto
Shirley Hastings . . . . Pat Thompson
Liz Holt . . . . Gia Carides
Les Kendall . . . . Peter Whitford
Ken Railings . . . . John Hannan
Tina Sparkle . . . Sonia Kruger-Taylor
Wayne Burns . . . . Pip Mushin

This bright, breezy and immensely likable musical-comedy, a remarkably confident film debut for co-writer/director Baz Luhrmann, looks set to waltz away with a sizable box office return when it opens Down Under. Internationally, this modestly budgeted charmer should also make its mark, with festival slots definitely indicated. (Pic world preems at Cannes in a noncompeting slot).

A behind-the-scenes look at a contest for ballroom dancers, pic unfolds a classical tale of a young dance star who wants to break the rules and the opposition he faces from the establishment. Within the confines of this tried-and-true formula, Luhrmann has concocted a feel-good entertainment which is lively, original (in an old-fashioned sort of way) and charming.

A couple of talented newcomers play the leading roles. Paul Mercurio, son of vet character actor Gus Mercurio) is a real find, a handsome leading man who, in addition, is obviously a top-flight dancer. Opposite him, Tara Morice shines as a plain Jane who turns from ugly duckling to swan when she's on the dance floor.

Scott (Mercurio) has been preparing for the Australian Ballroom Dance Federation Championships since he was 6. His shrewish mother (Pat Thomson) teaches classical dance at Kendall's Dance Academy; Kendall himself (Peter Whitford) is her ex-dance partner.

Meanwhile, Scott's henpecked father (a touching Barry Otto) stays home and sometimes, when no one's looking, tries out a few dance steps himself.

Scott, partnered with the lovely but waspish Liz (Gia Carides) blows the semifinals when he breaks federation rules by improvising on the floor. Liz segues to a new partner (John Hannan, a standout) and Scott gets a dressing down from the federation prez (a suitably pompous Bill Hunter).

Enter Fran (Morice), a shy Spanish girl with bad skin and glasses. Only a beginner, she shares Scott's ideas about trying new steps and manages to persuade him to take her on as his new partner. With help from her father and grandmother, they work on a flamenco routine they know will be anathema to the federation honchos, but, this being a wish-fulfillment pic, everything turns out fine at fadeout.

Except for the very cynical, audiences are likely to respond to the positive values and appealing love story, and also to the rich vein of humor Luhrmann uncovers in the refined world of formal dancing.

The unraveling of the plot (and a secret in the Hastings' family's past) could have been handled with a lighter touch in the closing reel, and gay stereotyping isn't entirely avoided, but otherwise, "Strictly Ballroom" is strictly entertainment and a credit to all concerned. — *David Stratton*

KRISTALLINES NICHTES
(CRYSTAL NIGHTS)
(GREEK)

A Greek Film Center production. (Intl. sales: Centre du Film Grec.) A Kentavros Ltd./ET-1 (Greece)/Sofracima (France)/Slotint (Switzerland) co-production. Directed by Tonia Marketaki. Screenplay, Marketaki, Malvina Korali. Camera (color), Stavros Hassapis; editor, Michel Lewin; music, Giorgos Papadakis. Reviewed at CNC screening room, Paris, April 23, 1992. (In Cannes Film Festival, Un Certain Regard.) Running time: **138 MIN.**
With: François Delaive, Michèle Valley, Tania Tripi.
(In Greek, German, Hebrew; French subtitles)

"Crystal Nights" is a heavy-handed amalgam of history, sorcery and reincarnation theory following two infernal lovers as they play out a recurring pattern of sex, betrayal, death and rebirth over the course of several decades in Greece. Despite attractive leads, supernatural-tinged saga seems to last a lifetime on screen. Muddled fare might go over as a horror video, although it unsuccessfully aims higher than that.

While being intiated into a psychic-satanic cult, Isabelle, a young German woman, is told that her ideal male counterpart will be born on her wedding day. The year 1936 finds Isabelle, 40, married to a Greek military officer and living with her two daughters in Greece. War is brewing and anti-Semitic conversation flourishes. When Isabelle first lays eyes on Alberto, an 18-year-old Greek Jew, she concludes he's the perfect lover her god had promised.

The two protagonists can literally read each other's minds and, in a prolonged artsy segment, make passionate love while musing on their linked destinies. After their bout of terrific sex, however, Alberto objects to their age difference. He marries a woman his own age, whereupon Isabelle kills herself and manages to be reborn as a child, Anna, who returns to protect Alberto from the Germans during the war.

When Anna grows up, she sets her sights on the now older and divorced Alberto, who repeats the mistake of marrying a woman his own age despite Anna's irresistible carnal lure. Alberto and Isabelle/Anna are irrevocably bound to each other through time, doomed to repeat the same damnable ritual.

Lead actor, whose blue eyes are likened to those in a portrait of the devil, has an interesting, delicate face worth watching. Both female leads have dark good looks befitting a sorceress bent on revenge.

Hazy symbolism is all over pic's script (developed with assistance of the European Script Fund and made with financial support from the Eurimages Fund of the Council of Europe). The swastika is evoked as an ancient symbol of reincarnation and perhaps, on paper, this sounded like a potentially interesting twist on the oft-used theme of love and hate between German and Jew during World War II.

Alternating between sepia tones and color, pic uses Alberto's Judaism and the WWII time frame to throw in Nazi propaganda newsreels and chilling death camp imagery. These visuals lend specious heft to a jumbled horror film-cum-love-story that grows dreary and repetitive.

Reincarnation theme is capped in a voiceover coda set in 1903. Production values are fairly high throughout.

— *Lisa Nesselson*

EL SOL DEL MEMBRILLO
(THE QUINCE TREE SUN)
(SPANISH-DOCU)

A Maria Moreno production, with Euskal Media & Igeldo Zine Produkzioak. Executive producer, Maria Moreno. Directed by Victor Erice, from an idea from Erice, Antonio López. Camera (color), Javier Aguirresarobe, Angel Luis Fernández; editor, Juan Ignacio San Mateo; music, Pascal Gaigne; sound, Ricardo Steinberg, Daniel Goldstein; associate producer, Angel Amigo. Reviewed at Cine Dore, Madrid, May 5, 1992. (Competing at Cannes Film Festival.) Running time: **139 MIN.**
With: Antonio López, Maria Moreno, Enrique Gran, José Carrtero, Maria López, Carmen López, Elisa Ruiz.

Victor Erice ("The Spirit of the Beehive," "The South") here tackles the inner and outward workings of the creative process, using one of Spain's foremost realistic painters, Antonio López, as his subject. What might have proven a poignant statement on life and art unfortunately runs so long impact is diluted.

Nonetheless, the 2¼-hour study of how López spent over a year painting a quince tree in his backyard is a fascinating filmic document. Erice minutely chronicles each preparatory detail as Lopez prepares for the painting, intercutting shots of Madrid as though Erice were providing his own painted filmic canvas of the world beyond the yard as a parallel effort.

Erice also introduces a group

of Polish masons who speak no Spanish and are rebuilding an adjacent house. They serve as counterpoint, as they occasionally traipse into the painter's yard, making pedestrian comments about the canvas and the tree, and ultimately eating one of the quinces which they find bland and uninteresting.

Those given to symbolic interpretations will find ample material here, from the news of the Gulf War on the radio, to various conversations between López and visitors while he paints, at times in the pouring rain under a large plastic canopy.

Pic is slow and moody, even by PBS standards, and much too long. It will probably be relegated to an honored place in art museums and cultural archives.

— *Peter Besas*

AVERILLS ANKOMMEN
(THE ARRIVAL OF AVERILL)
(AUSTRIAN)

A Neue Studio Film production. Directed by Michael Schottenberg. Screenplay, Schottenberg, Micheal Juncker. Camera (color), Michi Krausz; editor, Ortrun Bauer; music, Mischa Krausz; costume design, Erika Navas. Reviewed at CNC screening room, Paris, April 24, 1992. (In Cannes Film Festival, Un Certain Regard.) Running time: **95 MIN.** With: Andras Jones, Maria Bill, Umberto Conte.

Viewers who aren't demanding about narrative coherence might tolerate this visually polished pic that's utterly askew in the storytelling department. It's unlikely "The Arrival of Averill" will be going places.

First 20 minutes or so hold enormous promise, only to devolve into slick but completely unsatisfying nonsense. Unless pic's French subtitles are somehow faulty, this exercise in depositing an attractive protagonist in an existential outpost among cartoon-like characters remains willfully opaque.

En route to visit his father, handsome Averill arrives at the train station of a heavily atmospheric city, only to learn he's stranded due to an all-encompassing strike. Terrific set design and fine camerawork accentuate the dank, unwelcoming, postindustrial surroundings. Place and time at first appear to be somewhere in Europe during World War II, but the presence of television sets and video equip-

ment later suggests either the present or the near future. Modern industrial music is also a tip-off.

Averill checks into a peculiar hotel whose other guests seem to have come out of a George Grosz painting reworked by a rock video aesthetic. Refugee-like people with odd faces or unusually shaped heads of bodies move through garishly lit subterranean tunnels and pass the time in a café with all the charm of a fallout shelter.

While exploring a once-elegant apartment building, Averill gets caged up in a high-ceilinged room sectioned off by a chain link fence. Much naked flesh will be pressed against the fence as Averill jealously pursues a carnal relationwhip with a TV newswoman twice his age.

The strike drags on, as does what passes for a plot. Averill may or may not have found one relative and killed another. Co-scripter/helmer's terse and vividly hued 1989 feature "Caracas" had both a setup and a punch-line. This ultimately tedious pic is all flash and no payoff.

— *Lisa Nesselson*

THE LONG DAY CLOSES
(BRITISH)

A Mayfair Palace (U.K.) release of a British Film Institute & Film Four Intl. presentation of a British Film Institute production. (Intl. sales: FFI, London.) Produced by Olivia Stewart. Executive producers, Ben Gibson, Colin MacCabe. Executive in charge of production, Angela Topping. Directed, written by Terence Davies. Camera (Eastmancolor, Metrocolor prints), Michael Coulter; editor, William Diver; music, Bob Last, Robert Lockhart; production design, Christopher Hobbs; art direction, Kate Naylor; costumes, Monica Howe; sound (Dolby), Moya Burns; associate producer, Maureen McCue; assistant director, Gus Maclean. Previewed at Curzon West End theater, London, April 29, 1992. (Competing at Cannes Film Festival.) Running time: **83 MIN.**
Mother . . . . Marjorie Yates
Bud . . . . Leigh McCormack
Kevin . . . . Anthony Watson
John . . . . Nicholas Lamont
Helen . . . . Ayse Owens
Edna . . . . Tina Malone
Curly . . . . Jimmy Wilde
Also with: Robin Polley, Peter Ivatts, Joy Blackman, Denise Thomas, Patricia Morrison, Gavin Mawdsley.

Terence Davies' "The Long Day Closes" is a technically elaborate, dryly witty mood-piece centered on a shy young daydreamer in mid-'50s working-class Liverpool. Pic will delight the British helmer's sizable following, win over some doubters and see plenty of day-

light at specialized wickets.

Pic builds on the basic elements of Davies' 1988 Cannes Critics' Award winner, "Distant Voices, Still Lives," but takes its emotional cue from that work's gut-churning setpiece: the rising crane shot outside a rain-drenched movie theater to the lush strains of "Love Is a Many-Splendored Thing." After a still-life main title to a Boccherini minuet, "Long Day" lets rip with the 20th Century Fox fanfare (plus CinemaScope extension) and segues into a free-form ride down the helmer's memory lane of family, friends, Catholicism and cinema.

Central character is Bud (movingly limned by 13-year-old newcomer Leigh McCormack), a shy loner who's given a hard time at school, idolizes his mom (Marjorie Yates) and elder sister (Ayse Owens), and finds escape from the grayness of '50s Britain in movie theaters.

Story centers on his coming to terms with school life and the various forces shaping the community. But there's little resolution in conventional terms: Davies simply builds a kaleidoscope out of memory fragments and shakes it every which way in a series of visual vignettes.

Davies' self-confessed interest in "poetry of the commonplace" gets a thorough workout: neighbors chatting, young women dressing up for a Saturday night out, Mom serenading herself with w.k. ditties, family get-togethers in cramped rooms or on street doorsteps. At other times, Davies brakes his mobile camera, strikes a still-life tableau (Bud sitting on the stairs; a shot of a patterned carpet), and lets the lighting and busy soundtrack do the work.

As in "Distant Voices," pic celebrates community spirit rather than individuals. Characters are barely introduced, there's only one specific reference to period (1955 to '56) and dialog comes in brief, intermittent bursts. In its play with legit-like scene changes and heightened reality, pic often plays like a Brit take on Francis Coppola's "One From the Heart." And with its antsy camerawork and musical construction, pic even recalls the celebratory exercises of Magyar helmer Miklós Jancsó, swapping open plains for the confined urban dreariness of northern England.

Pic's major weakness is its stop-go tempo. Individual segs are stunningly mounted (an overhead, four-part lateral track to

the strains of "Tammy"; Bud dreaming of a mighty galleon) but a longer dramatic line, a reluctance to go with the flow. Davies is still a miniaturist working in a feature-length format.

Nonbuffs could be flummoxed by the soundtrack, a knowing mix of popular melodies, snatches of movie dialogue ("The Magnificent Ambersons," "The Ladykillers," "Private's Progress") and MGM baubles. Refs to minutiae of postwar Brit life, as well as the kids' thick Liverpudlian accents, also may puzzle North American audiences.

Strength of Davies' vision is the crux, and it holds the line to the final, confident fadeout. Perfs by the no-name cast are all on the money, with Yates excellent as the loving, understanding mom and Tina Malone bringing welcome shafts of humor as a sharp-tongued neighbor.

Michael Coulter's grainy, desaturated lensing (partly achieved by eliminating the last wash in printing) bathes the film in a warm, nostalgic glow. Christopher Hobbs' recreation of Davies' remembered streets (built at the London studio of Sands Films, producers of "Little Dorrit" and "The Fool") squeezes the most out of the slim £1.7 million ($3 million) budget. Monica Howe's costumes have a natural, lived-in feel. Trim 83-minute running time is not a frame too long. — *Derek Elley*

THE GROCER'S WIFE
(CANADIAN-16m-B&W)

A Cinema Libre presentation (Quebec) of a Medusa Film production. Executive producer, Gregory E. Lavier. Directed, written by John Pozer. Camera (16m, black & white), Peter Wunstorf; editor, Reginald Dean Harkema, John Pozer; music, Mark Korven; production design, Lynne Stopkewich; sound, Ross Weber; assistant directors, Marlene Lynch, Mina Shum. Reviewed on video-cassette in Montreal. (In Cannes Film Festival, Un Certain Regard.) Running time: **103 MIN.**
Mildred Midley . . . . . Andrea Rankin
Tim Midley . . . . Simon Webb
Mrs. Friendly . . . . Nicola Cavendish
Mr. Friendly . . . . . . Leroy Schultz
Barber . . . . Jay Brazeau
Anita Newlove . . . . Susinn McFarlen
Minister . . . . Walter Mills
Herman . . . . Alec Burden

"The Grocer's Wife" is more than just a film: It's a little miracle. Debutant director John Pozer turned a mere $C150,000 into a slick, studied film noir which should earn him critical raves and enthuse art film aficionados worldwide.

In stark contrast to the typical sun-drenched image of Canada's glorious mountains and lakes, Pozer has shot a black & white tale about an emotionally stifled smog-level inspector (Simon Webb) in a grimy town in British Columbia.

From the opening shot of a towering smokestack belching out smog, Pozer's dingy stage is set. Billowing clouds of pollution shroud a town whose inhabitants all smoke like chimneys themselves. Filthy alienation blurs not only their visions but their relationships as well.

The inspector is a heroic wimp dominated by a monstrous mother (Andrea Rankin) who accidentally leaves her window open overnight and winds up intoxicated in the hospital (where she later dies).

Poor son is barely rid of her when control of his pathetic life is usurped by a transient stripper (Susinn McFarlen) who unabashedly moves into his mother's room and adopts both her wigs and domineering ways, despite his feeble pleas.

This spineless male's attempt to murder the stripper (by secretly leaving her bedroom window open one night) fails miserably. He finds his freedom only when a mysterious pen pal lover (Alec Burden) shows up and falls in love with her in a case of mistaken identity, thinking the stripper is the mother.

Even the grocer's wife (Nicola Cavendish), who loves the inspector despite his inability to respond, provides little more than a glimmer of hope.

Pic is as grim and difficult to market as it sounds. But pic's remarkable for Pozer's even-handed control of a minimalist script and carefully controlled, calculated shots. Lighting in this drab world is stunning.

Understated acting (from a cast of virtual unknowns with theater backgrounds) effectively adds to the atmosphere of human drudgery and industrial manipulation.

Pozer's style begets comparison with Finland's renowned helmer Aki Kaurismäki in "The Match-Factory Girl" or Fritz Lang's visual technique in "Metropolis." Like that of his colleagues, Pozer's bleak vision is of mankind as a cog in the industrial machine.

Pozer may find himself under attack as a misogynist for his portrayals of imperious women. However, it could easily be argued they are products of that overbearing town itself.

Pic ultimately will be seriously appreciated by a select few and undoubtedly launch a brilliant directorial career for Pozer.
— *Suzan Ayscough*

OVER THE HILL
(AUSTRALIAN)

A Greater Union Distributors (Australia) release of a Village Roadshow Pictures presentation of a Glasshouse Pictures production, in association with the Rank Organisation and Australian Film Finance Corp. Executive producers, Gregory Coote, Graham Burke. Produced by Robert Caswell, Bernard Terry. Directed by George Miller. Screenplay, Caswell, based on Gladys Taylor's book "Alone in the Australian Wilderness." Camera (Panavision, color), David Connell; editor, Henry Dangar; music, David McHugh; production design, Graham (Grace) Walker; sound, Gary Wilkins; line producer, Ross Matthews; associate producer, Liz Strout; assistant director, Chris Webb; casting, Liz Mullinar. Reviewed at Village Cinema City 2, Sydney, April 30, 1992. (In Cannes Film Festival market.) Running time: **99 MIN.**

Alma Harris . . . . . Olympia Dukakis
Elizabeth . . . . Sigrid Thornton
Dutch . . . . Derek Fowlds
Maurio . . . . Bill Kerr
Benedict . . . . Steve Bisley
Jan . . . . Andrea Moor
Margaret . . . . . . Pippa Grandison
Forbes . . . . Martin Jacobs
Nick . . . . Aden Young
Hank . . . . Gerry Connolly
Hank's wife . . . . . . Jenny Williams
TV reporter . . . . Anne Looby

Olympia Dukakis gives a game performance as a 60-year-old widow from Bar Harbor, Maine, who discovers a new life in the Australian outback, but the film in which she toplines doesn't deliver the goods. Spectacular photography of varied Australian landscapes is wasted on a thin, unconvincing vehicle.

Screenplay of "Over the Hill" was suggested by a book by Canadian Gladys Taylor. The original concept promised a more feminist slant than the pic delivers: Prominent Oz screenwriter Eleanor Witcombe ("My Brilliant Career") penned an early draft, and Nadia Tass ("Malcolm," "Pure Luck") originally was announced as the pic's director. The screenplay on the completed film is solely credited to Robert Caswell, but it's difficult to reconcile his undistinguished work here with his other work ("A Cry in the Dark," "The Doctor").

George Miller (the "Neverending Story 2" helmer, not the "Mad Max" George Miller) does a routine job with the material.

Pic opens in wintry Bar Harbor, where Alma (Dukakis) lives with her policeman son and his family. On a whim, she visits her daughter in Sydney in summer to discover the daughter (Aussie thesp Sigrid Thornton with a Yank accent) is one of Australia's "best dressed women" and is married to a politico in the middle of an election campaign. Feeling unwanted, Alma borrows a brightly colored 1959 Chevrolet Bel Air from her granddaughter's boyfriend and sets off for Melbourne.

She never gets there, instead experiencing various outback adventures. She befriends an easy-going married couple (Steve Bisley, Andrea Moor), who turn out to be con artists, and gets a job at a remote desert store where the lonely owner (Bill Kerr) takes a shine to her.

Dukakis also joins in an aboriginal ceremony in which she goes topless to allow the aborigines to paint her breast, and she finds romance with a 60-ish retired dentist (Derek Fowlds) driving around the country in a well-equipped camper.

Though Dukakis gives the Alma character her best shot, she can't overcome the thin concept. Crucially, there's little on-screen empathy for the character. As her ungrateful daughter, Thornton (who worked well with director Miller on "Snowy River") looks lovely but is stuck with a shrill, shrewish character.

Fowlds, from the British TV series "Yes Minister," seems a bit bemused by it all in his early scenes but settles into the role eventually. Aussie thesps in support roles fare rather better, especially Kerr, touching as a lonely storekeeper, and Bisley as a likeable rogue. Aden Young has a nothing role here as the granddaughter's b.f.

The picture's real star is the Aussie countryside, lovingly shot in lush wide-screen images by David Connell.

Problems in Caswell's screenplay are the reliance on coincidence in the setting up of several key encounter scenes and dialogue lacks sharpness and wit. In the end, Alma's journey of liberation doesn't communicate to the audience the good vibes that it should. Chalk this pic down as a disappointment, albeit a beautiful one. — *David Stratton*

CHARLIE'S EAR

A Walnut Street Prods. presentation. Produced by Chuck McCrory, Gary Chason. Executive producers, Chuck McCrory, Betty Lee. Directed, written by Gary Chason. Camera (black & white, color), Claudia Raschke; editor, Bill Moore; music, Arthur Gottschalk; art direction, Tom Dornbusch; sound, Scott Szabo; line producer, Susan Elkins; casting, Caryn Gorme. Reviewed at World-Fest/Houston, April 28, 1992. No MPAA rating. Running time: **100 MIN.**
With: Austin Pendleton, Catherine Hyland, Sebastian Massa, Tony Fields.

Casting director turned filmmaker Gary Chason claims "Charlie's Ear" is based on a legit play he premiered 15 years ago. But this badly dated, drearily predictable piece of canned theatrical absurdism seems much older. Box office prospects are dim to nonexistent.

Houston-produced indie pic invites comparisons to early works by Harold Pinter (especially "The Birthday Party") and Eugene Ionesco, and suffers accordingly. With its sharp black & white lensing by Claudia Raschke, and Austin Pendleton looking so much like Woody Allen in the lead role, "Charlie's Ear" also bears an unfortunate resemblance to "Shadows and Fog," Allen's equally ill-conceived attempt at visualizing Kafkaesque menace on film.

Nebbishy office worker Pendleton shares a dreary apartment with his braying, chain-smoking wife (Catherine Hyland), whom he despises and daydreams of killing. One day, he returns home from work and finds two cryptic, intimidating strangers in his living room. He claims not to know them, but they say he hired them — to murder his wife.

The wife returns home unexpectedly early, cuing an interminable drinking-and-dialogue sequence that Pinter might have written as a schoolboy (and then, after reading it, tossed into the trashcan). Chason struggles to create and sustain a mood of dark, sweaty-palmed dread, but only succeeds at making his audience squirm impatiently.

Eventually, the strangers kill Hyland, gangsters kill the strangers and police arrest Pendleton. Only it all turns out to be an elaborate hoax, to distract Pendleton from Hyland's preparations for his surprise birthday party. But then the party, along with everything before it, turns out to be a bad dream. Only maybe it isn't really a dream after all.

Only cast member to come off well is Tony Fields, who, as the more sedate homicidal stranger, demonstrates a smooth, self-confident presence that should mark him for better projects.

Technical credits, including Tom Dornbusch's claustrophobic art direction and Raschke's evocative cinematography, are better than the pic deserves.

— *Joe Leydon*

NICKEL & DIME

An August Entertainment release of a Five & Ten Prods. production. Produced by Ben Moses, Lynn Danielson. Executive producer, Paul Mason. Directed by Ben Moses. Screenplay, Seth Front, Eddie Polon. Camera (color), Henry M. Leba; editor, Joan E. Chapman; music, Stephen Bedell; sound, Trevor Black; associate producer, Fred Wardell. Reviewed at WorldFest/Houston, May 3, 1992. No MPAA rating. Running time: **95 MIN.**

Jack Stone	C. Thomas Howell
Everett Willits	Wallace Shawn
Cathleen Markson	Lise Cutter
Sammy Thornton	Roy Brocksmith

Homevideo and cable it is for "Nickel & Dime," fitfully amusing mediocrity that looks and sounds like an unsold TV pilot.

C. Thomas Howell toplines as a cheerfully seedy heir hunter who owes a bundle in back taxes, and even more to his senile father's nursing home. Desperate to make a huge finder's fee, he sets out in search of the lost-lost daughter of a dead businessman.

Things get complicated when the daughter turns out to be assistant D.A. Lise Cutter, whom Howell left standing at the altar years earlier. More complications emerge as hired thugs, searching for gems hidden by the deceased, and a rival heir hunter (Roy Brocksmith) arrive.

Howell is game and engaging, Cutter is perky, and Wallace Shawn has a few funny moments as a button-down, by-the-book tax accountant who reluctantly becomes Howell's investigative partner.

Director Ben Moses relies more on the charm of his players than the by-the-numbers script to keep things light and bright. Tech credits are okay. — *Joe Leydon*

MINDWARP

A Fangoria Films presentation. Produced by Christopher Webster. Executive producers, Steve Jacobs, Norman Jacobs. Directed by Steve Barnett. Screenplay, Henry Dominic. Camera (color), Peter Fernberger; editor, Adam Wolfe; music, Mark Governor; production design, Kim Hix; sound (Ultra Stereo), Hans Roland; stunt coordinator, Gary Paul; special makeup effects, KNB Effects Group; assistant director, J.B. Rogers; co-producer, Damon Santostefano; line producer, Alexandra Reed; casting, Kent DeMarche (L.A.), Jeff Segal (Chicago). Reviewed at WorldFest/Houston, April 26, 1992. No MPAA rating. Running time: **96 MIN.**

With: Bruce Campbell, Angus Scrimm, Marta Alicia, Elizabeth Kent, Mary Becker.

Fangoria, the movie buff magazine least likely to feature Julia Roberts on its cover, launches its feature production arm with "Mindwarp," a modest but competent sci-fi horror opus best suited for the video trade.

Helmer Steve Barnett does yeoman duty on an obviously limited budget, with help from the makeup/special effects team from KNB Effects Group. Some gory moments likely will limit pic's appeal to Fangoria readers and like-minded fun-seekers.

Henry Dominic's derivative but serviceable script imagines yet another post-apocalyptic society. The lucky folks live in In-World (resembling an austere high-tech hotel), where inhabitants spend most of their times hooked up to a dream-weaving network called Infinisynth. Angry young woman Marta Alicia rebels against the nonstop mind control, and is banished to the OutWorld, where surviving humans are hunted by hideous, flesh-eating mutants.

It's even worse below the ground where a religious sect of mutants, led by a hooded human, digs through the debris of pre-apocalyptic society. The Seer (Angus Scrimm) keeps his flock in line with sporadic mutant (and human) sacrifices. He slices and dices his victims in a Rube Goldberg-type of machine that, oddly enough, recalls a similar device in Dan Aykroyd's "Nothing but Trouble."

Bruce Campbell has some heroic moments as a mutant-battler who joins Alicia underground, and Scrimm's nicely over-the-top Seer reveals himself as the heroine's long-lost father. Alicia begins uncertainly, but gains confidence as the story continues, indicating pic may have been shot in continuity.

The violence is wet, messy and mercifully infrequent. Most of the victims are the mutants, all of whom would be right at home on the cover of Fangoria. Except for the monster makeup, the tech credits are largely undistinguished. — *Joe Leydon*

U.S. RELEASES

INDOCHINE
(INDOCHINA)
(FRENCH)

A Sony Pictures Classics (U.S.)/ BAC Films (France) release of a Paradis Films/La Generale d'Images/BAC Films/Orly Film/Cine Cinq co-production. Produced by Eric Heumann. Directed by Régis Wargnier. Screenplay, Erik Orsenna, Louis Gardeal, Catherine Cohen, Wargnier. Camera (color), François Catonne; editor, Genevieve Winding; music, Patrick Doyle; costumes, Gabriella Pescucci; sound, Guillaume Sciama. Reviewed at Pathe Montparnasse, Paris, April 25, 1992. Running time: **158 MIN.**

Eliane	Catherine Deneuve
Jean-Baptiste	Vincent Perez
Camille	Linh Dan Pham
Guy	Jean Yanne
Yvette	Dominique Blanc
Emile	Henri Marteau
Shen	Mai Chau
Mrs. Minh Tam	
	Thi Hoe Tranh Huu Trieu

Also with: Carlo Brandt, Gerard Lartigau, Hubert Saint-Macary, Andrzej Seweryn, Alain Fromager, Chu Hung.

Set during rising communist protests in the 1930s, "Indochine" is a riveting romantic saga. Once non-French auds make small adjustments for historical context, Régis Wargnier's pic will have long legs in art houses and solid B.O. in mainstream theaters, thanks to Catherine Deneuve's classy performance, a sizzling story line and eye-catching locales in Vietnam.

Pic sticks close to its three main characters: a Frenchwoman who runs one of the country's biggest rubber plantations, her adopted Indochinese daughter and the dashing French navy officer who loves each woman in quick succession.

Pic opens strong and never lets up. Deneuve's Eliane is cool if courteous when she meets handsome naval newcomer (Vincent Perez), but she falls for him despite herself.

Since teenage daughter Camille knows nothing of mom's passionate affair, she falls instantly in love when the same officer saves her from a terrorist. Mother chooses daughter's happiness, and frustrated beau asks for a faraway post in the north.

But stubborn daughter takes off after him on foot, discovering along the way her country's miseries. She's rounded up for peasant labor, kills a French slave auctioneer and flees with her stunned officer.

After the couple hides together for months, she watches him get arrested with their baby, whom Eliane then raises like her own son.

Halfway into pic, its intriguing frame becomes clear: In Geneva, at the close of the Indochinese war, Eliane is telling her grown ward his parents' history, since he's about to meet his mother, a Communist Vietnamese representative, for the first time.

Deneuve delivers a stunning portrait of a complex woman. She's a stern taskmaster who whips runaway workers, but with family and peers she's sensitive, cultivated, gracious, affectionate. In short, Deneuve's impeccable performance brings to life the best and the worst of French colonialism.

Perez, first an uncommitted lover and then a feisty Frenchman on the run, handles his fast-changing role with great sensitivity. Newcomer Linh Dan Pham shines as sheltered daughter and hardened revolutionary.

Secondary roles harbor several jewels, such as Jean Yanne, corpulent security chief who's crafty, dangerous yet visibly amorous in Eliane's presence. His lover (Dominique Blanc) is a wonderfully ill-humored tease and sings a catchy cabaret number.

With terse script in hand, helmer Wargnier smoothly advances his long story line, avoiding pulp romance and an overload of historic detail. He has a keen eye for mixing fields of vision, and a sure hand with visual spectacles such as the opening river funeral, an upper-class wedding and a boat race.

Kudos are deserved all round for technical production, though especially for the French and Indochinese costumes and François Catonne's lensing of misty mountain lakes.

— *Lee Lourdeaux*

MISTRESS

A J&M Entertainment presentation of a Tribeca Prods.-Meir Toper production. Executive producer, Ruth Charny. Produced by Teper, Robert DeNiro. Co-producer, Bertil Ohlsson. Directed by Barry Primus. Screenplay, Primus, J.F. Lawton, from Primus' story. Camera (CFI color), Sven Kirsten; editor, Steven Weisberg; music, Galt MacDermott; production design, Phil Peters; costumes, Susan Nininger; sound, Jacob Goldstein; casting, Gail Levin; assistant director, Bruce Franklin. Reviewed at Gaumont Champs Elysees, Paris, May

3, 1992. Running time: **108 MIN.**
Marvin Landisman . . . . Robert Wuhl
Jack Roth . . . . Martin Landau
Evan Wright . . . . . . Robert DeNiro
Carmine Rasso . . . . . . Danny Aiello
George Lieberhof . . . . . Eli Wallach
Stuart Stratland Jr. . . Jace Alexander
Peggy . . . . Tuesday Knight
Beverly . . . . Sheryl Lee Ralph
Warren Zell . . . . Christopher Walken
Ernest Borgnine . . . . Himself
Also with: Laurie Metcalf, Jean Smart.

Actor Barry Primus tries his hand at direction with this insipid insider's look at Hollywood. "Mistress," in release in France ahead of U.S. unveiling, can't seem to decide if it's supposed to be a comedy about Hollywood small-timers trying to get an indie pic off the ground, or a somber drama in which greed and lust overwhelm art.

Pic, co-produced by Robert DeNiro's Tribeca outfit, looks to fade fast. "The Player" it's not.

Part of the problem is the casting of Robert Wuhl in the central role of a 40-ish washed-up director who showed early promise years before until the suicide of an actor (a cameo for Christopher Walken) on his set ended his career. Wuhl gives a monotonous reading of the character, and it's hard to root for such a dull and self-righteous type.

Far more effective is Martin Landau as an ex-Universal exec desperate to get an indie feature up and running. He discovers an old script ("The Darkness and the Light") penned by the has-been helmer and, despite the fact that it deals with an artist who suicides, claims to see potential in it.

Without consulting the writer-director, Landau brings on board the son (Jace Alexander) of a famous, Academy Award-winning scripter who, as he keeps telling everyone, had the same film school profs as Steven Spielberg.

At first, Wuhl is adamant that one word of his script will be changed, but gradually he starts to compromise. Trouble is, every money man Landau brings onto the project wants a role for his latest mistress, an old Hollywood gag which ultimately assumes center stage in Primus' film. Two of the financiers (an urbane Robert DeNiro and a flustered Danny Aiello) are actually sharing the same mistress (Sheryl Lee Ralph), while Stratland starts secretly bedding Peggy (Tuesday Knight), the blonde g.f. of Eli Wallach.

Primus never makes the most of promising ideas, and the jokes (like having business conferences at L.A.'s least fashionable eateries) quickly become tiresome. Nor is the film technically interesting, with flat, rushed-looking lensing by Sven Kirsten and indulgent editing by Steven Weisberg. Galt McDermott's sparse score is no help.

Presence of the infinitely superior Robert Altman pic this summer will render "Mistress" even less marketable than it might otherwise have been. It'll have to rely on the names involved to make any kind of impression, and a quick segue to video is indicated.

— *David Stratton*

THE LINGUINI INCIDENT

An Academy Entertainment release of a Rank Film Distributors, Isolar Enterprises presentation of an Orgolini/Gagnon production. Produced by Arnold Orgolini. Executive producer, Richard Gagnon. Directed by Richard Shepard. Screenplay, Shepard, Tamar Brott. Camera (CFI color), Robert Yeoman; editor, Sonya Polonsky; music, Thomas Newman; additional music, Mark Lundquist; production design, Marcia Hinds-Johnson; art direction, Bo Johnson; costumes, Richard von Ernst; sound (Ultra-Stereo), Vic Carpenter, David Chornow; assistant director, Phillip Christon; additional camera, David Sperling; additional editor, Susan R. Crutcher; co-producer, Sarah Jackson; line producer, Patricia Foulkrod; associate producer, Susan Hopper; casting, Danielle Eskanazi. Reviewed at Loews Village 2 theater, N.Y., May 2, 1992. MPAA Rating: R. Running time: **98 MIN.**
Lucy . . . . Rosanna Arquette
Monte . . . . David Bowie
Vivian . . . . Eszter Balint
Dante . . . . André Gregory
Cecil . . . . Buck Henry
Miracle . . . . Viveca Lindfors
Jeannette . . . . Marlee Matlin
Also with: Eloy Casados, Michael Bonnabel, Maura Tierney, Lewis Arquette, Iman, Julian Lennon.

Energetic actors can't overcome the uninspired, poverty-row production values in "The Linguini Incident," being briefly released to theaters by its video distrib to set up ancillary values.

On the shelf for a year, stillborn comedy lacks interesting characters and situations. Instead it's a lame attempt to recapture some of that "Desperately Seeking Susan" quirkiness that Rosanna Arquette delivered so well seven years ago.

She's cast as a waitress in a trendy New York restaurant who dreams of launching a magic act. Arquette's obsessed with Harry Houdini and decides to rob the restaurant to raise the $5,000 needed to purchase from antique shop owner Viveca Lindfors a wedding ring once belonging to Mrs. Houdini.

Also out to rob the establishment is its new British bartender David Bowie, ostensibly to get $10,000 so that cashier Marlee Matlin will marry him to get him a green card. It turns out that Bowie is actually trying to win a million-dollar bet with proprietors Buck Henry and André Gregory that he can marry one of their waitresses (or cashiers?, a fine point the script doesn't clarify) within a week.

With the aid of Arquette's best friend, goofy undergarments designer Eszter Balint, the trio pull off their crime caper and of course Bowie decides to marry Arquette. Unconvincing complications lead to a further bet that requires Arquette to perform a Houdini-esque escape trick underwater at film's climax.

Garbed in retro costumes leaning toward the Roaring '20s, Arquette is attractive and perky in a performance that consistently transcends the rest of the film.

Bowie, who has been desperately seeking screen stardom for nearly 25 years, is completely miscast. He looks too old and more like a toothy alien (à la his best assignment to date, "The Man Who Fell to Earth") than a romantic lead. There's no sexual attraction at all between him and Arquette despite the script's requirements of same.

Balint and Matlin are amusing, but the film's main laughs go to Gregory in a barnstorming performance as the flamboyant boss you love to hate.

Two cast casualties: Kelly Lynch was announced as co-star during pre-production in the role that went to Balint; while Shelley Winters was listed in the VARIETY production chart when the film was shooting; presumably Lindfors inherited her assignment. In the final print are pointless brief cameos by Julian Lennon (understandably yawning) and Iman. A thank you credit to actor Julian Sands is cryptic (he doesn't show up), though he could have handled Bowie's role with ease.

Production looks threadbare whenever it strays from the gaudy main restaurant set to seedy downtown locations. Director Richard Shepard fails to provide adequate transitions between scenes and has an aloof camera style that works against the comedy. — *Lawrence Cohn*

FOLKS!

A 20th Century Fox release of a Mario & Vittorio Cecchi Gori & Silvio Berlusconi presentation of a Penta Pictures & Victor Drai production. Produced by Drai, Malcolm R. Harding. Executive producers, Mario & Vittorio Cecchi Gori. Directed by Ted Kotcheff. Screenplay, Robert Klane. Camera (Technicolor; Deluxe prints), Larry Pizer; editor, Joan E. Chapman; music, Michel Colombier; production design, William J. Creber; costumes, Jay Hurley; sound (Dolby), Scott D. Smith; assistant director, Howard Ellis; 2nd unit director-stunt coordinator, Conrad E. Palmisano; associate producer, Burton Elias; casting, Lynn Stalmaster, Jane Alderman & Susan Wielder (Chicago). Reviewed at Cineplex Odeon Chelsea 1 theater, N.Y., May 1, 1992. MPAA Rating: PG-13. Running time: **106 MIN.**
Jon Aldrich . . . . Tom Selleck
Harry Aldrich . . . . . . Don Ameche
Mildred Aldrich . . . . . Anne Jackson
Arlene Aldrich . . . Christine Ebersole
Audrey Aldrich . . . . Wendy Crewson
Fred . . . . Robert Pastorelli
Ed . . . . Michael Murphy

Tom Selleck flounders in the ill-fitting comedy vehicle "Folks!" Made by the team behind low-brow hit "Weekend at Bernie's," feature proves bad taste isn't enough.

"Folks!" marks an inauspicious first release (via Fox) of the Italian-backed production outfit Penta Pictures. Two more star vehicles, toplining Jack Nicholson and Kathleen Turner, are due out soon.

Scripter Robert Klane, having scored with the stiff comedy of "Bernie's," attempts to mine black humor from other taboo areas here. The embarrassment of watching Don Ameche grotesquely essay a senile old man is exceeded only by Klane's idiotic spoofing of euthanasia.

Rickety plot devices begin with Chicago mercantile exchange trader Selleck called to Florida to sign consent forms for mom Anne Jackson's operation. While he's gone, co-worker Michael Murphy proves to be an FBI man pulling a sting operation at Selleck's firm. Under suspicion for leaving so abruptly, Selleck's funds are frozen.

Jackson recovers, but Selleck's senile old man (Ameche) burns down his Florida home and wreaks havoc with reckless driving in his vintage Cadillac. (Why all the problems start only when Selleck arrives is unexplained.) When hard-hearted Floridian sister Christine Ebersole won't take the old folks in, Selleck drives them back to Chicago to live with his wife and kids.

Main running gags involve

Ameche's senility (every reel he has the same revelation that Selleck is his long-gone son) and Selleck's accident-prone behavior. The virile star is put through the ringer doing unfunny pratfalls resulting in endless injuries and supposed laff riot involving testicle amputation.

Second half of the film makes no sense at all, as the FBI suddenly decides Selleck is clean, but he's served a 30-day eviction notice, just enough time for his wife to leave him and Ebersole move in with her two brats. In despair Ma Jackson asks Selleck and Ebersole to kill her and Ameche for the insurance money, setting into motion ridiculous murder attempts.

One of many low points is a brief scene where Ameche gains full lucidity merely to deliver necessary exposition. To take the edge off the euthanasia subplot, battered Selleck becomes senile himself for a reel or two, and doesn't seem much brighter during a telegraphed, convenient happy ending.

Marking severe career setbacks for Ameche and Selleck, "Folks!" obviously miscalculates the low intelligence of the mass audience. Though picture is technically well put together, especially the frequent stuntwork directed by Conrad Palmisano, its gags don't work.

Best characterization is the hateful sister portrayed with consistency by Ebersole. Selleck's mom Jackson and wife Wendy Crewson are just along for the ride.

— *Lawrence Cohn*

U.S. RELEASES

LETHAL WEAPON 3

A Warner Bros. release of a Silver Pictures production. Produced by Joel Silver, Richard Donner. Co-producers, Steve Perry, Jennie Lew Tugend. Directed by Donner. Screenplay, Jeffrey Boam, Robert Mark Kamen; story by Boam. Based on characters created by Shane Black. Camera (Technicolor color), Jan De Bont; editors, Robert Brown, Battle Davis; music, Michael Kamen, Eric Clapton, David Sanborn; production design, James Spencer; art direction, Greg Papalia; set decoration, Richard Goddard; costume supervisor, Nick Scarano; sound (Dolby), Thomas Causey; associate producers, Alexander B. Collett, Michael E. Klastorin; assistant director, Michael Alan Kahn; stunt coordinators, Charlie Picerni, Mic Rogers; special effects supervisor, Matt Sweeney; casting, Marion Dougherty. Reviewed at Mann Village Theater, L.A., May 12, 1992. MPAA Rating: R. Running time: **118 MIN.**

Martin Riggs	Mel Gibson
Roger Murtaugh	Danny Glover
Leo Getz	Joe Pesci
Lorna Cole	Rene Russo
Jack Travis	Stuart Wilson
Captain Murphy	Steve Kahan
Trish Murtaugh	Darlene Love
Rianne Murtaugh	Traci Wolfe
Nick Murtaugh	Damon Hines
Carrie Murtaugh	Ebonie Smith

The first sequel in this series became a blockbuster by adding ample comedy to the original's core of vengeance and violence, and the recipe again works here, producing a pic that's really more about moments — comic or thrilling — than any sort of cohesive whole. Even with some flat mid-stretches, the third "Weapon" has plenty of ammunition and figures to blast its way into this summer's elite $100-mil club.

With Joe Pesci back as the hyperkinetic Leo Getz, the Abbott & Costello-type comedy may be played even broader than in "Weapon 2," and the addition of Rene Russo as a tough internal affairs cop allows women to join the butt-kicking boys club.

The plot, meanwhile, hinges on a wispy premise about an ex-cop (Stuart Wilson) providing confiscated guns to gangs, and while the bad guys aren't as menacing as in earlier installments, they make serviceable straw men to be loudly knocked down.

Producer-director Richard Donner has the mayhem down to a science by now, and it helps having actors the caliber of Mel Gibson and Danny Glover to bring a little weight to what otherwise would be a typical Joel Silver tribute to destroying property

and the wonders of Dolby stereo.

This time, the emotional focus is on Glover's Roger Murtaugh, who counts down the days to his retirement even as he grapples with whether hanging up his gun will make him an old man.

Murtaugh and gonzo partner Martin Riggs (Gibson) stumble onto the gun racket, bringing them into contact with high-kicking investigator Lorna Cole (Russo), a woman who wins Riggs' heart by demonstrating that she can inflict as much damage as he can.

For the most part, however, this pic is all about chases and comedy schtick, and in this case the sum of the parts really adds up to more than the whole.

Thus, film's entertainment factor comes down to individual scenes, and writer Jeffrey Boam (who wrote "Weapon 2" and shares credit here with Robert Mark Kamen) borrows from the best — from a terrific wrong-way freeway chase reminiscent of "To Live and Die in L.A." to a comparison of scars straight out of "Jaws," although in this case it functions as foreplay for Riggs and tomboyish Cole.

Pesci also shows off his unique ability to go absolutely ballistic in rat-a-tat fashion, and Gibson's comic high points include dropping on all fours to win over a ferocious-looking guard dog.

Not all of the moments work as well, including an early chase involving armored cars and an action sequence set around an L.A. Kings game. (What's so exciting, after all, about a fight breaking out at a hockey game?)

There are also coincidences too numerous to mention, and Riggs' own brand of police brutality, which includes punching out a handcuffed suspect, will doubtless cause some squirming among those for whom the L.A. riots are still a vivid memory.

Still, the pic manages to be highly entertaining and sanctions all its violence by making the bad guys so despicable that death seems to be the only solution. The broad scope of the action also brings a requisite make-believe quality to the narrative, even if some of the transitions from kooky comedy to more dire situations prove a bit jarring.

Jarring is also the word for the film's tour-de-force technical credits, which feature top-flight stunts, spectacular explosions and sound effects played at a decibel level that occasionally threatens the dialogue.

Michael Kamen, Eric Clapton and David Sanborn turn in an admirable score, and Sting's song during the opening credits should help woo the MTV crowd.

Gibson and Glover appear to have the luxury of using the "Lethal Weapon" series to finance more prestigious projects, from Gibson's "Hamlet" to Glover's "To Sleep with Anger." With that in mind, it's doubtful Murtaugh will be able to embrace retirement anytime soon.

— *Brian Lowry*

CRISS CROSS

An MGM release of a Hawn/Sylbert Movie Co. production. Produced by Anthea Sylbert. Executive producer, Bill Finnegan. Co-producer, Robin Forman. Directed by Chris Menges. Screenplay, Scott Sommer, based on his novella. Camera (Continental Film Laboratories color), Ivan Strasburg; editor, Tony Lawson; music, Trevor Jones; production design, Crispian Sallis; art direction, Dayna Lee; set decoration, Leslie Morales; costume design, Lisa Jensen; sound (Dolby), Edward Tise; assistant director, George Parra; casting, David Rubin. Reviewed at GCC Beverly Connection Theater, Beverly Hills, Calif., May 8, 1992. MPAA Rating: R. Running time: **100 MIN.**

Tracy Cross	Goldie Hawn
Joe	Arliss Howard
Emmett	James Gammon
Chris Cross	David Arnott
John Cross	Keith Carradine
Jetty	J.C. Quinn
Louis	Steve Buscemi
Blacky	Paul Calderon

Told from the perspective of a 12-year-old boy, this earnest, languid drama might have worked if it weren't so painfully obvious and slow. Add to that its close proximity to another Goldie Hawn release (the more marketable "Housesitter," a Universal comedy with Steve Martin) and the film figures to have its box office wires crossed with barely a spark to show for it.

Set at the time of the 1969 moon landing, "Criss Cross" deals with a boy, Chris (David Arnott), who's lost his moral compass, living with his mom (Hawn) in a run-down Key West hotel.

Hawn's a waitress who turns stripper to pay the rent, while Dad (Keith Carradine, in a brief cameo) split three years earlier, to join a monastery (no kidding) after dropping bombs on a village of innocents in Vietnam.

Almost an hour in, the story finally stumbles into a plot as Chris discovers he's been transporting hidden cocaine from a fisherman to one of the locals. He decides to try and score some cash on his own to help his mother find a respectable job.

Such is the cliché-ridden nature of Scott Sommer's screenplay, which suffers from an equally ham-handed narration by Arnott, an attractive, natural young performer who unfortunately mumbles his dialogue.

Cinematographer-turned-director Chris Menges, who made his directing debut with the '88 release "A World Apart," has a good eye for trappings of the Key West lifestyle but doesn't bring any life to the story or characters.

Chris' hero-worship of his pilot dad gets shot down early on, leaving little drama until the drug plot washes up, a rather forced device to resolve the rift with his mom, which is neither compelling nor convincing.

Hawn's company understandably sought a grittier showcase than the silly comedies she's done, but this pic doesn't display much except off-screen sessions with a physical trainer, evident thanks to the skimpy Key West attire and a striptease number.

The rest of the cast has little to do but work on their impressive tans, including Arliss Howard and James Gammon, strong character actors stuck with bland, poorly defined roles.

Tech credits are adequate, though Trevor Jones' maudlin score would probably be better suited to a Hallmark commercial. Then again, some of those 30-second ads provide more emotional resonance than "Criss Cross" scratches out.

— *Brian Lowry*

SEVERED TIES

A Fangoria Films release. Produced by Christopher Webster. Executive producers, Norman Jacobs, Steven Jacobs. Directed by Damon Santostefano. Screenplay, John Nystrom, Henry Dominic, based on story by Santostefano, David A. Casci; additional material written, directed by Richard Roberts. Camera (Foto-Kem color), Geza Sinkovics; editor, Roberts; music, Daniel Licht; production design, Don Day; costume design, Susan Bertram; special makeup & creature effects, KNB EFX Group; 2nd unit director, Gregory Nicotero; 2nd unit camera, Mark Melville; sound, Jack Lindauer; line producer, Rex Piano. Reviewed at Magno Review 1 screening room, N.Y., Sept. 25, 1991. MPAA Rating: R. Running time: **96 MIN.**
Dr. Hans Vaughan . . . . . Oliver Reed
Helena Harrison . . . . . Elke Sommer
Stripes . . . . Garrett Morris
Harrison Harrison
. . . . Billy Morrissette
Preacher . . . . Johnny Legend
Eve . . . . Denise Wallace
Lorenz . . . . Roger Perkovich
Uta . . . . Bekki Vallin
Dr. Harrison . . . . Gerald Shidell

Lip-smacking performances by Oliver Reed and Elke Sommer lift the horror film "Severed Ties" above the pack of low-budget shockers. Col TriStar Home Video should have good results with this third entry from Fangoria's film unit.

Tongue-in-cheek effort has Sommer as an extremely possessive mother who has her son Billy Morrissette imprisoned to work on perfecting the gene-bonding regeneration experiments left unfinished by her late husband.

Morrissette comes up with the solution, but it's imperfect, resulting in a severed arm that becomes a lizard-like creature with a life of its own.

Film fits into the grotesque horror genre dominated by Frank Henenlotter ("Basket Case"). Combo of grotesque gore effects and over-the-top acting is a winning one.

Oliver Reed as Sommers' partner in evil, planning to exploit the son's formula, is a superior villain and Morrissette delivers as the young antihero.

— *Lawrence Cohn*

THE TERROR WITHIN II

A Concorde Pictures release. Executive producer, Roger Corman. Produced by Mike Elliott. Directed by Andrew Stevens. Screenplay, Stevens, based on characters created by Thomas M. Cleaver; creative consultant, Lee Lankford. Camera (Foto-Kem color), Janusz Kaminski; editor, Brent Schoenfeld; music, Terry Plumeri; production design, Johan Le Teneux; costume design, Greg Lavoi; assistant director, Tom Koranda; special makeup effects, Dean & Starr Jones; additional camera, Jim Mathers; stunt coordinator, Patrick Statham; sound (Ultra-Stereo), Cameron Hamza, Bill Robbins, Chris Taylor; associate producer, Jonathan Winfrey; casting, Steve Rabiner. Reviewed on Vestron Video vidcassette, N.Y. MPAA Rating: R. Running time: **84 MIN.**
David Cunningham . Andrew Stevens
Kara . . . . Stella Stevens
Kyle . . . . Chick Vennera
Von Demming . . . . . . R. Lee Ermey
DeWitt Thompson
. . . . Burton (Bubba) Gilliam
Ariel . . . . Clare Hoak

Andrew Stevens makes a creditable feature helming debut with this followup to the sci-fier he starred in. Released theatrically last year, pic's currently in video stores.

Pic notably has Stevens directing his mother, Stella Stevens, who made her own directing debut in 1989 with "The Ranch" starring Andrew.

Well-plotted, with a script by Stevens and Lee Lankford, "Ter-

---

ror Within II" limns Stevens' adventures following a biological war that has wiped out nearly all of humanity. He's en route to the underground Rocky Mountain lab manned by R. Lee Ermey and a co-ed crew.

Accompanied by his trusty dog, he fights off mutants and other foes, and rescues lovely damsel Clare Hoak. Back at the lab, Ermey and medical officer Stella Stevens have to deal with a monster on the loose.

Subplots include a mutant raping Hoak, giving rise to a monster baby, and a mutant's severed finger growing in the lab into a grotesque blob-style monster. Stevens' direction keeps the pic chugging along well.

Cast is fine, with maximum pulchritude provided by Hoak and Barbara Alyn Woods. Monster makeup and gore is low-budget but effective.

— *Lawrence Cohn*

CHILDREN OF THE NIGHT

A Fangoria Films release. Produced by Christopher Webster. Executive producers, Norman Jacobs, Steven Jacobs. Directed by Tony Randel. Screenplay, Nicolas Falacci, based on original screenplay by William Hopkins, story by Falacci, Webster. Camera (Foto-Kem color), Richard Michalak; editor, Rick Roberts; music, Daniel Licht; production design, Kim Hix; assistant director, Alexandra J. Reed; production manager-line producer, Sandy Nelson; special makeup effects, KNB EFX Group; stunt coordinator, Gary Paul; 2nd unit director, Webster; 2nd unit camera, Marcus Hahn; sound (Ultra-Stereo), Hans Roland; co-producers, Howard Nash, Damon Santostefano; casting, Robin Monroe. Reviewed at Bruno Walter Auditorium, N.Y., April 18, 1991. MPAA Rating: R. Running time: **90 MIN.**
Karen Thompson . . . . . Karen Black
Mark Gardener . . . . . Peter DeLuise
Lucy Barrett . . . . Ami Dolenz
Cindy Thompson . . Maya McLaughlin
Frank Aldin . . . . . Evan MacKenzie
Matty . . . . Garrett Morris
Czakyr . . . . David Sawyer
Officer Gates . . . . . Josette DiCarlo

Continuity and credibility problems plague Fangoria's "Children of the Night," an otherwise okay horror entry (second following "Mindwarp" in the magazine's entree into film production). Name cast will help its video future, to be released by Columbia TriStar Home Video.

Karen Black toplines as a vampire who with her daughter Maya McLaughlin is about to carry on the family's tradition dating back to 1568. An evil priest, who is McLaughlin's uncle, has the

---

women under his control. Visiting teacher Peter DeLuise is sent to free them along with his endangered g.f. Ami Dolenz.

Poorly constructed film confuses the time sequence and presentation of events in two small-town locations. Director Tony Randel, of "Hellraiser II" and Playboy at Night's "Inside Out" TV series, does better with the action set pieces than the dramatic or exposition material.

Lensed in Wisconsin and Michigan, film boasts an atmospheric setting of an underground crypt beneath the smalltown church in which Dolenz has to swim as a rite of passage. Town's children are kept underwater in suspended animation to be fed upon by the master vampire (David Sawyer).

Dolenz and McLaughlin are attractive young heroines and Black gets to camp it up again under grotesque makeup. Josette DiCarlo as a nutty femme cop provides welcome comic relief.

— *Lawrence Cohn*

BIG GIRLS DON'T CRY ...THEY GET EVEN

A New Line Cinema release of a New Line production in association with Perlman Prods. & MG Entertainment. Produced by Laurie Perlman, Gerald T. Olson. Directed by Joan Micklin Silver. Executive producers, Peter Morgan, Melissa Goddard. Screenplay, Frank Mugavero. Camera (CFI Color), Theo Van de Sande; editor, Janice Hampton; music, Patrick Williams; production design, Victoria Paul; art direction, Brad Ricker; set decoration, Joyce Anne Gilstrap; set design, Maya Shimoguchi; costume design, Jane Ruhm; sound (Dolby), Susumu Tokumow; assistant director, David Sardi; casting, Linda Lowy. Reviewed at Sunset Towers screening room, L.A., April 20, 1992. MPAA Rating: PG. Running time: **102 MIN.**
Laura . . . . Hillary Wolf
Keith . . . . David Strathairn
Melinda . . . . Margaret Whitton
David . . . . Griffin Dunne
Barbara . . . . Patricia Kalember
Stephanie . . . . Adrienne Shelly
Josh . . . . Dan Futterman

This tale of a teenage girl overlooked by her parents never escapes its sitcom premise and finally gives in to an ending so hackneyed it practically defines the term. There are a few worthwhile moments in between, but not enough to keep "Big Girls" from looking small and frail at the box office.

Even with the reasonably deft guidance of director Joan Micklin Silver, the film struggles under its heavy-handed screenplay, featuring a stilted narration by teen protagonist Hillary Wolf that's a mix of bad one-liners and romance-novel angst.

Wolf resides with her uncaring mother (Margaret Whitton), rich stepfather (David Strathairn) and three step-siblings, while her biological father (Griffin Dunne) is estranged from his kind second wife (Patricia Kalember) and shacked up with his pregnant, much-younger New Age g.f. (Adrienne Shelly).

Muddle gets worse when Wolf flees to the woods with her stepbrother (Dan Futterman) to escape a family trip to Hawaii, with rest of her extended family in hot pursuit. Unwittingly, the flight provides the vehicle by which the rest of the brood, uncomfortably assembled in a rustic setting, work out respective problems.

Silver has directed some fine films ("Chilly Scenes of Winter" also employed wry direct-to-camera narration by its protagonist) but labors to make sense of Frank Mugavero's script.

Most of the kids prove annoyingly precocious, and even the generally appealing Wolf gets stuck with dialogue that clearly sounds written for her by a third party and not like the ruminations of a teenage girl.

Strongest asset is its well-assembled song score, which instills in the pic a certain vitality even during moments when the action fails to provide it. Other tech credits are adequate but, like the picture, nothing either to shout or cry about.

— *Brian Lowry*

CANNES FEST

BOB ROBERTS

A Paramount/Miramax release (U.S.) of a Polygram & Working Title production in association with Barry Levinson, Mark Johnson, Live Entertainment. (Intl. sales: Manifesto.) Produced by Forrest Murray. Executive producers, Ronna Wallace, Paul Webster, Tim Bevan. Directed, written by Tim Robbins. Camera (Technicolor), Jean Lepine; editor, Lisa Churgin; music, David Robbins; songs, David Robbins, Tim Robbins; production design, Richard Hoover; art direction, Gary Kosko; set decoration, Brian Kasch; costume design, Bridget Kelly; sound (Dolby), Stephen Halbert; associate producers, James Bigwood, Allan Nicholls; casting, Douglas Aibel, April Webster (L.A.). Reviewed at Cannes Film Festival (Directors Fortnight), May 12, 1992. Running time: **105 MIN.**
Bob Roberts . . . . Tim Robbins
Bugs Raplin . . . . Giancarlo Esposito
Chet MacGregor . . . . Ray Wise
Terry Manchester . . . . Brian Murray
Sen. Brickley Paiste . . . . Gore Vidal
Delores Perrigrew . . Rebecca Jenkins
Franklin Dockett . . . Harry J. Lennix
Clark Anderson . . . . . John Ottavino
Bart Macklerooney . . Robert Stanton
Clarissa Flan . . . . Kelly Willis
Also with: John Cusack, Peter Gallagher, Pamela Reed, Alan Rickman, Susan Sarandon, James Spader, David Strathairn, Fred Ward, Bob Balaban, Helen Hunt, Fisher Stevens.

A sort of political "This Is Spinal Tap," "Bob Roberts" is both a stimulating social satire and a depressing commentary on the devolution of the U.S. political system. Caustic docudrama about a wealthy cryptofascist folk singer who runs for U.S. Senate showcases the impressive multiple talents of Tim Robbins as director, writer, actor, singer and songwriter.

Unusual Paramount/Miramax distribution collaboration guarantees plenty of muscle behind domestic release, and the timing with the presidential election campaign this fall is another plus. But film's form and content assure nothing more than moderate b.o.

Despite its fresh observations, pic has plenty of antecedents — from "A Face in the Crowd" and "Privilege" to "The Candidate" and "Tanner '88." But Robbins is relentless in pursuit of his ideas about the depths of cynicism, corruption and deceit in public life today.

Roberts (Robbins) is a self-assured, highly successful singer who attempts to ride his popularity into public office. Castigated as yuppie scum by his detractors, he has secured his niche as an anti-1960s folk artist who blames the country's ills on liberals and the social programs of the Great Society.

Roberts' aim is to unseat longtime Pennsylvania Sen. Brickley Paiste. In a brilliant bit of casting, this man of refined sensibility and reason is portrayed by Gore Vidal.

Entire film is framed as a British TV documentary being prepared on Roberts' campaign. Docu team not only charts Roberts' progress in the weeks leading up to the 1990 election, set against the backdrop of the Desert Shield buildup, but also depicts the inane TV coverage of the race — including sexual slander of Sen. Paiste and charges brought against Roberts' campaign adviser and former CIA operative (the always incisive Alan Rickman).

Dogging Roberts' heels on the campaign trail is one Bugs Raplin (Giancarlo Esposito), a black journalist for an underground rag called "Troubled Times." Bugs is the kind of disheveled kook the establishment can easily dismiss, but he ultimately becomes involved in Roberts' political and personal fate in a surprising and tragic way.

Many of the absurd trappings of the campaign process are here — the sound bites, appearances at beauty pageants, empty slogans, twisted ideological meanings, mad schedules, technological overload, officious managers — as well as the unusual element of Roberts' singing gigs. Tunes penned by David Robbins and Tim Robbins effectively convey the candidate's reactionary attitudes, and latter performs them with ease and authority.

Some viewers may find it difficult spending all this time with as loathsome a character as Roberts, who is presented as a representative of unsavory politics. That the film so successfully states many truths about current conditions makes it a sorrowful spectacle indeed.

Another drawback is that the docu format exposes only public moments resulting in a relatively one-dimensional experience. While all the points are legitimate and sharply scored, most of them are relatively familiar. The element of preachiness should make pic a favorite of liberals and a turn-off to others.

Still, political filmmaking in America is rare enough, so Robbins' work is a very welcome addition to the landscape of a crazy, unpredictable election year. Although "Roberts" is not based on a recognizable politician, there are eerie reverberations of H. Ross Perot in multimillionaire Roberts' self-financed campaign and self-characterization as a rebel outsider intent on shaking up Washington.

Robbins is spookily dead-on projecting the candidate's bland confidence and homogenized middle-American personality. Since the performers aren't playing full-blooded characters, they must quickly assert impressions, and most successfully do so.

Perhaps taking a cue from "The Player," Robbins has cast a healthy number of w.k. thesps to enact cameos, mostly as cute, superficial and dumb TV newscasters. Largest of these roles goes to Rickman, ferociously good in a part that mainly has him heatedly denying major misdeeds.

Technical team has created a kind of elevated TV look that doesn't precisely match TV docus but creates a good enough impression. — *Todd McCarthy*

TWIN PEAKS: FIRE WALK WITH ME

A New Line Cinema release of a Francis Bouygues presentation of a Lynch/Frost-CIBY Pictures production. Produced by Gregg Fienberg. Executive producers, Mark Frost, David Lynch. Co-producer, John Wentworth. Directed by Lynch. Screenplay, Lynch, Robert Engels. Camera (CFI color), Ron Garcia; editor, Mary Sweeney; music, Angelo Badalamenti; production-costume design, Patricia Norris; set decoration, Leslie Morales; sound (Dolby), Jon Huck; sound design, Lynch; associate producers, Johanna Ray, Tim Harbert; assistant director, Deepak Nayar; casting, Ray. Reviewed at Carolco screening room, L.A., April 27, 1992. (Competing at Cannes Film Festival.) MPAA Rating: R. Running time: **135 MIN.**
Laura Palmer . . . . Sheryl Lee
Donna Hayward . . . . . . Moira Kelly
Phillip Jeffries . . . . David Bowie
Chester Desmond . . . . . Chris Isaak
Carl Rodd . . . . . Harry Dean Stanton
Leland Palmer . . . . Ray Wise
Special agent Dale Cooper
. . . . Kyle MacLachlan
Bobby Briggs . . . . . Dana Ashbrook
Sam Stanley . . . . . Kiefer Sutherland
Norma Jennings . . . . . Peggy Lipton
James Hurley . . . . . James Marshall
Sarah Palmer . . . . . Grace Zabriskie
Teresa Banks . . . . . . Pamela Gidley
Gordon Cole . . . . David Lynch
Shelly Johnson . . . . Madchen Amick
Albert Rosenfeld . . . . Miguel Ferrer
Annie Blackburn . . . Heather Graham
Woodsman . . . . . . Jurgen Prochnow
Sheriff Cable . . . . Gary Bullock

A feature prequel to the celebrated but short-lived TV series, "Twin Peaks: Fire Walk With Me" is like an R-rated episode embodying both the pros and cons of the intriguingly offbeat program. A detailing of the final week in the life of the quasi-legendary Laura Palmer, with plenty of digressions and artistic doodlings, as well as the occasional striking sequence, pic will inevitably attract die-hard fans but is too weird and not very meaningful for general audiences. Ultimately, this feels like David Lynch treading water before moving on to new terrain.

Anyone with a passing interest in American culture of the last couple of years knows the phrase, "Who killed Laura Palmer?" — a question promulgated by the discovery of her body in the superb two-hour pilot telefilm, and the answer to which was sidestepped for far too long, to the detriment of the series.

Almost equally familiar is the knowledge that Dad did it. Despite an abundance of fishy activity by the teenagers and powers-that-be in the small Washington State community, and a lot of pseudo-psychic hocus-pocus involving Kyle MacLachlan's special agent Dale Cooper, the root of Laura's problems were to be found at home.

After a strikingly amusing opening image involving destruction of a TV set, pic launches into what is essentially a 33-minute prologue detailing the FBI's investigation of the Portland murder of a woman named Teresa Banks.

Bureau's look-see is orchestrated by a shouting, hard-of-hearing supervisor played by the director himself, and section is filled with many series trademarks — insolent small-town police, a tiny piece of paper under a fingernail, an intense interest in coffee, difficult-to-understand dwarfs — as well as odd and extremely brief cameo turns by the likes of David Bowie, as a weird apparition, and Harry Dean Stanton, as a trailer park denizen, and a prediction by Cooper that the killer will strike again.

Cued by the first strains of Angelo Badalamenti's famous, mood-setting theme music, action then cuts to one year later in Twin Peaks, where Laura (Sheryl Lee) prepares for class by snorting some coke. Events that follow, in the expected dream-like, sometimes captivating, occasionally enervating Lynchian style, largely center on Laura's downward spiral of drug use, promiscuity and crime, up to the moment of her killing, which leaves things off where they all started on TV.

Suspense is clearly lacking in this story with a preordained outcome. Another significant drawback is that Laura, after all the talk about her, is not a very interesting or compelling character, and long before the climax has become a tiresome teen. Almost everything she does is misguided and self-destructive, and she scarcely knows what to do with her odd moments of telepathic insight or desire that her best friend Donna (Moira Kelly) not share her dismal fate.

Because no crime has yet been committed in the community, no police or FBI investigation is going on here, and hence no opportunities for interaction between the authorities and the many diverse characters offered in the series, or development of relationships that came later.

Many of the show's familiar performers (Lara Flynn Boyle, Sherilyn Fenn, Richard Beymer and Joan Chen just for starters) aren't on view here, while others, including Peggy Lipton and Madchen Amick, materialize so briefly as to be pointless. Singer Julee Cruise turns up briefly for one musical interlude.

Still, the film has its share of unique conceptual sequences. The first, in the prologue, involves a demonstration of the acute powers of observation that a Lynchian federal investigator is expected to possess. Others most pointedly include two very debauched visits to a club across the Canadian border that feature raunch rivaling "Blue Velvet" and "Wild at Heart" and activities unthinkable on network TV.

Performances are solid but unremarkable across the board, and craft contributions are very attractively similar to what was accomplished on the small screen. Film remains engagingly intriguing throughout most of its slightly overlong running time, and perhaps the strangely mesmerizing mood Lynch has orchestrated for the entire "Twin Peaks" undertaking should not be underestimated.

But the feeling persists that, to a considerable degree, Lynch is marking time with this project, creating new riffs and variations on themes he had already largely worked out.
— *Todd McCarthy*

CAREFUL
(CANADIAN)

A Cinephile release of a Greg Klymkiw production with participation of Telefilm Canada & CIDO (Canada-Manitoba Cultural Industries Development Office). Executive producer, Andre Bennett. Produced by Klymkiw, Tracy Traeger. Directed by Guy Maddin. Screenplay, Maddin, George Toles, from Toles' story. Camera (color), Maddin; editor, Maddin; music, John McCulloch; production design, Maddin; art director, Jeff Solylo; costumes, Donna Szoke; sound, Russ Dyck; assistant director, Liz Jarvis; casting, Klymkiw. Reviewed at Cannes Film Festival market, May 10, 1992. Running time: **96 MIN.**
Grigorss . . . . Kyle McCulloch
Zenaida . . . . Gosia Dobrowolska
Klara . . . . Sarah Neville
Johann . . . . Brent Neale
Count Knotgers . . . . Paul Cox
Herr Trotta . . . . Victor Cowie
Blind Ghost . . . . . Michael O'Sullivan
Franz . . . . Vince Rimmer
Sigleinde . . . . Katya Gardner
Frau Teacher . . . . Jackie Burroughs

Winnipeg-based Guy Maddin's third feature is every bit

as wayward and intriguing as his earlier films ("Tales from the Gimli Hospital," "Archangel"). Though certainly not to everyone's taste, his inventive, original film should make its mark with cult audiences worldwide and add to his growing reputation.

Maddin is obsessed with the style and emotional range of vintage cinema. His earlier films recall the silents, but "Careful" plays like an early talkie, circa 1928, with intertitles bridging scenes and a deliberately scratchy soundtrack evoking pioneering Vitaphone.

He also films entirely on studio sets, even exteriors, and uses other visual devices to recreate the mood and style of long-gone filmmaking; here, bright, vivid colors reminiscent of early two-strip Technicolor.

The story is inspired by German mountain films of the '20s. The villagers of Tolzbad constantly fear of avalanches, and so must speak quietly and avoid loud noises.

In this refined atmosphere, passions run riot. The widow Zenaida (Aussie thesp Gosia Dobrowolska) lives with her sons: the oldest, Franz (Vince Rimmer), lurks in a cobwebbed attic, while handsome Grigorss (Kyle McCulloch) and Johann (Brent Neale) attend Jackie Burroughs' butler school.

Johann loves Klara (Sarah Neville), the feisty daughter of Herr Trotta (Victor Cowie), but he has disturbingly erotic dreams about his mother. One night he spies on his mother as she takes a bath, and later drugs her and makes love to her. Later overcome with shame, he cuts off his fingers and throws himself from the mountain top.

Zenaida, unaware that her son has ravished her, soon becomes engaged to marry Count Knotgers, the reclusive, pipe-smoking nobleman for whom Grigorss works. Egged on by Klara, who's also been having an incestuous relationship (with her father), Grigorss challenges the count to a duel.

Maddin's playful sense of humor starts with the casting. Australian director Paul Cox, who has made three films now with Dobrowolska, plays the count with stiff elegance; the duel scene is extremely funny. Dobrowolska is obviously far too young to have sired three such strapping sons, and her costumes are as wonderfully weird as the pastel-colored house in which she and her sons live.

There's plenty to chuckle at in "Careful," but Maddin's rigorous recreation of cinema of over 60 years ago is also beautiful and inventive. A natural for ambitious fest programming, pic should recoup its presumably modest production costs.
— *David Stratton*

VAGABOND
(FRENCH)

An MC Films/M-6 Films/Ellipse Groupe Gamma/BMF/Groupe TSF co-production with partcipation of Canal Plus. Directed by Ann Le Monnier. Screenplay, Le Monnier, Philippe Cosson, Anny Dranché, based on Bernard Pouchèle's novel "L'Etoile et le Vagabond." Camera (color), Pierre Novion; editor, Anny Danché; music, Jean-Louis Valéro; set design, Dominique Piolé; sound, Gérard Lecas. Reviewed at CNC screening room, Paris, April 27, 1992. (In Cannes Film Festival, Cinemas En France.) Running time: **89 MIN.**
Quentin . . . . Gérard Darmon
Marie . . . . Ludmila Mikaël
Also with: Jean-Jacques Moreau, Thierry Rey, Jacques Canselier.

"Vagabond," nicely observed study of a heartsick itinerant, is a casually paced but engaging first feature that bodes well for director Ann Le Monnier's future.

Gérard Darmon turns in a fine perf as a sensitive 40ish drifter whom people take an immediate liking to, but he makes a point of moving on. Darmon's laid-back charisma lends depth and authenticity to what could have been a slight, clichéd exercise.

The seemingly self-sufficient drifter is haunted by vivid flashback dreams of the young teacher he loved to distraction. When he meets an attractive social worker and single mother (Ludmila Mikaël), he's wary of intimacy but increasingly attracted to the idea of settling down. He drops his emotional armor with bittersweet results.

Down-to-earth tale of human longings and dashed expectations is well served by a melancholy score and evocatively lensed, if somewhat dreary, landscapes.
— *Lisa Nesselson*

LE RETOUR DE CASANOVA
(CASANOVA'S RETURN)
(FRENCH)

A Les Films Alain Sarde/Films A2 production in association with Centre National de la Cinématographie/Canal Plus/Région Languedoc Roussillon. Produced by Alain Sarde. Executive producers, Alain Delon, Christine Gozlan. Directed by Edouard Niermans. Screenplay, Jean-Claude Carrière, Niermans, based on Arthur Schnitzler's novella "Casanovas Heimfahrt." Camera (color), Jean Penzer; editor, Yves Deschamps; music, Bruno Coulais, Michel Portal; art direction, Carlos Conti; costume design, Yvonne Sassinot de Nesle; sound, Paul Lainé, Paul Bertault. Reviewed at Cannes Film Festival (competing), May 8, 1992. Running time: **96 MIN.**

Casanova	Alain Delon
Camille	Fabrice Luchini
Marcolina	Elsa
Lorenzi	Wadeck Stanczak
Amélie	Delia Boccardo
Olivo	Gilles Arbona
Marquise	Violetta Sanchez
Abbé	Jacques Boudet
Emissary	Philippe Leroy Beaulieu
Marquis	Alain Cuny

Alain Delon fills the 18th-century lover's britches to ho-hum effect in "Casanova's Return," an entertaining costumer flawed by a foggy script and routine direction. Handsome pic could score okay Euro biz on the strength of its mixed-nationality cast, but it isn't likely to travel far overseas.

Based on Austrian scribe Arthur Schnitzler's 1918 novella, yarn follows the w.k. Italo libertine on his return to Venice after a long exile, transposing the action from the original's northern Italy to southern France. Aging (now in his early 50s), penniless and on the run from the law, Casanova lodges with a grateful friend, Olivo (Gilles Arbona), and promptly sets about trying to bed his savvy 20-year-old niece Marcolina (Elsa).

Flies in the sexual ointment include Olivo's wife (Delia Boccardo), a prior conquest who's been kneeling on broken glass for 13 years in hopes of his return; a cocky young soldier (Wadeck Stanczak) who's out to trash Casanova's rep; and Marcolina's steadfast rebuffs of the Latin lover's advances. Story climaxes in an all-night card game in which the soldier meets his Waterloo and Marcolina is bedded by Casanova.

Pic draws a Casanova very different from previous screen incarnations, including Donald Sutherland's cynical lover in Fed-erico Fellini's 1976 extravaganza and Marcello Mastroianni's exhausted portrait in Ettore Scola's 1982 "La Nuit de Varennes." But there's a lack of focus in Delon's role that's partly the fault of Jean-Claude Carrière's script and partly of the thesp himself.

Pic implicitly criticizes Casanova for his dissolute past and knee-jerk profiteering but comes down finally on the side of experience over youth (latter unappealingly personified by the arrogant soldier and prissy niece). Delon, wearing mostly a weary expression, doesn't provide many answers.

With this neutral center, pic basically keeps going on the strength of its supporting cast. As the cuckolded marquis, Alain Cuny steals all his scenes with gravel-voiced aplomb. Fabrice Luchini, as Delon's sparky valet (invented for the movie), gets the best of the rest, rolling his eyes and spewing out priapic jokes like a Renaissance theatrical fool.

Other perfs are okay, from Stanczak's self-assured younger version of Delon to Boccardo's goo-goo-eyed mature lover. Gallic looker Elsa's hard-soft Marcolina hits the right notes.

Helming by Edouard Niermans ("Poussière d'ange") doesn't add much atmosphere this time round. Technically, pic has a verismo look, with lived-in but colorful costumes by Yvonne Sassinot de Nesle and smart use of actual locations in southern France by production designer Carlos Conti. Jean Penzer's lensing is okay but often flatly lit.

— *Derek Elley*

SIMPLE MEN

A Fine Line Features release of a Zenith & American Playhouse Theatrical Films presentation in association with Fine Line Features/Film Four Intl./BIM Distribution of a True Fiction production. Produced by Ted Hope, Hal Hartley. Executive producers, Jerome Brownstein, Bruce Weiss. Directed, written by Hartley. Camera (Technicolor), Michael Spiller; editor, Steve Hamilton; music, Ned Rifle; production design, Dan Ouellette; art direction, Theresa DePrez; set decoration, Jeff Hartmann; costume design, Alexandra Welker; sound (Dolby), Jeff Pullman; assistant director, Greg Jacobs; casting, Liz Kiegley. Reviewed at Cannes Film Festival (competing), May 11, 1992. Running time: **106 MIN.**

Bill McCabe	Robert Burke
Dennis McCabe	William Sage
Kate	Karen Sillas
Elina	Elina Lowensohn
Martin	Martin Donovan
Mike	Mark Chandler Bailey

Both at one with his prior work and a significant step beyond it, Hal Hartley's "Simple Men" is a beautifully realized American art film. Tale of two brothers' search for their renegade father, and the major life change one of them experiences, possesses exceptional literary and cinematic qualities, as well as an emotional resonance new for the director. Pic is too rarefied to break out commercially but is a natural for fests and specialized venues.

Hartley's trademark arch dialogue, oddball philosophical aphorisms, laid-back silences, fractured family relationships and boldly colored visuals are all abundant. But the structuring of this restrained yet ultimately powerful piece has the deceptive simplicity of a classic novella, with even the smallest details selected with judicious care.

Startling opening sequence has small-time criminal Bill McCabe (Robert Burke) doubly betrayed by his g.f., who runs off with their mutual partner and stiffs him of his loot.

Meanwhile, Bill's father, a former Brooklyn Dodgers shortstop-turned-radical anarchist on the run for a deadly bombing of the Pentagon, has apparently escaped somewhere on Long Island. Bill's younger brother, a college student named Dennis (William Sage), is anxious to track the old man down and shanghais Bill to join him in the quest.

Deeply burned by his lover, Bill, in an extraordinary scene, announces to his brother how he plans to behave with the next woman he meets. He will calculatedly remain aloof, not fall in love, use her and get out when he's done. Stunning nuggets like this are dropped like depth charges amid a string of scenes featuring weird provincial characters spouting facetiously humorous remarks. Some of these serve to give the film a hipper-than-thou edge that would be off-putting if indulged in at greater length.

But the drama takes on a significant new dimension when the fellows meet Kate (Karen Sillas), a lovely, divorced earth mother type who runs a homey rural inn. Despite his bitter proclamations of the previous day, Bill instantly falls for Kate so hard that he knows he wants to spend the rest of his life with her. Scenes between the two are written and played with Hemingwayesque obliqueness and understatement.

At the same time, taciturn Dennis encounters a sexy young Romanian woman named Elina (Elina Lowensohn) who turns out to be his father's lover. Attracted to her himself, Dennis can't use Elina to get to his father as easily as he hopes, but the longer the two brothers extend their stay at Kate's idyllic retreat, the more the real world seems to loom ominously over their dreams.

Even more than on their earlier efforts, Hartley and lenser Michael Spiller have framed the yarn in vivid images notable for their organized color schemes. Editing rhythms are also utterly precise.

Thesps are similarly a constant pleasure to watch. Burke, who starred in Hartley's first pic, "The Unbelievable Truth," cuts a very appealing figure as Bill and increasingly resembles a slighter Clint Eastwood facially and in his low-key line readings.

Sage's screen-idol good looks and laconic manner mark him as a young actor to watch. Sillas and Lowensohn bring intriguingly offbeat personalities to the main female roles, and remainder of supporting cast is best described as quirky.

No matter how arbitrary or bizarre some of Hartley's ploys may seem at first, pic is so carefully constructed that they all resurface to pay off in the end. Director is still working in a minor key that plays principally to sophisticated viewers, but his stylistic confidence and thematic complexity have decidedly reached new levels here.

— *Todd McCarthy*

A STRANGER AMONG US

A Buena Vista release of a Hollywood Pictures presentation in association with Touchwood Pacific Partners II of a Propaganda Films production in association with Sandollar. Produced by Steve Golin, Sigurjon Sighvatsson, Howard Rosenman. (Intl. sales: Manifesto.) Executive producers, Sandy Gallin, Carol Baum. Co-producers, Susan Tarr, Robert J. Averech. Line producer, Burtt Harris. Directed by Sidney Lumet. Screenplay, Averech. Camera (color), Andrzej Bartkowiak; editor, Andrew Mondshein; music, Jerry Bock; production design, Philip Rosenberg; costume design, Gary Jones, Ann Roth; associate producer, Lilith Jacobs; assistant director, Harris; casting, Joy Todd. Reviewed at Cannes Film Festival (competing), May 14, 1992. No MPAA rating. Running time: **111 MIN.**

Emily Eden	Melanie Griffith
Ariel	Eric Thal
Levine	John Pankow
Mara	Tracey Pollan
Rebbe	Lee Richardson

Leah	Mia Sara
Nick	Jamey Sheridan
Yaakov	Jake Weber

Likely to be known in the trade as "Vitness," Sidney Lumet's fish-out-of-water mystery about a case-hardened Wasp female cop investigating a murder in New York's cloistered Hasidic community tries to make up in local color what it lacks in dramatic plausibility. Probe into this unusual, little-known religious culture has numerous points of sympathetic interest, but extreme predictability and relaxed pacing cause "A Stranger Among Us" to fall well short of its intended impact. Commercial prospects look limited.

Entitled "Close to Eden" until recently, Robert J. Averech's first produced screenplay since "Body Double," which also starred Melanie Griffith, tries to introduce general audiences to some of the mysteries of the Hasidim.

Griffith stars as a seen-it-all cop who, after having killed a thug who stabbed her lover-partner, is assigned to the low-pressure case of a vanished Hasidic jewelry dealer. When this fellow turns up dead in his office with $720,000 in diamonds missing, Griffith's mission assumes greater proportions, prompting her to move in with the Brooklyn group's Rebbe (Lee Richardson) and his adopted children Eric Thal — the next Rebbe designate — and Mia Sara in order to penetrate the community in search for the killer.

A tough-talking, short-skirted, cigarette-smoking babe at the outset, Griffith is induced to tone down her act by the strict rules of the Hasidim. Much is made of their many curious regulations, and lots of talk is given over to Griffith querying Thal. This is all very interesting from a theological and sociological p.o.v. but is scarcely adequate as dramatically propulsive dialogue.

Other angle being played here is the forbidden romance between the utterly devout Thal, for whom premarital sex is unthinkable, and the obviously experienced Griffith, whose recovering b.f. begins pressuring her for a serious commitment. Under the circumstances, script has Griffith getting too upset that Thal won't just jump in the sack with her — as all other men want to do — and erotic tension between them is minimal.

Plot is overloaded with hard-to-take factors, while the revelation of the killer is far from surprising.

More importantly, the nature of the Hasidic community effectively prevents Griffith from conducting any kind of penetrating investigation. Very little time is actually spent tracking down clues, questioning people or developing hunches, whereas Griffith hangs out with Thal as much as possible.

It could be argued that the emphasis is more on her character growth than on crime. The best moments are those that display the outsider's growing appreciation of the richness and supportiveness of the Hasidic lifestyle (the rigidly traditional role for women in the culture is tacitly noted and accepted, but not discussed in any depth).

Griffith's unspiritual, career-oriented, hardening life, including a retired cop father to whom she cannot communicate, is effectively contrasted to the warmth of this Jewish group and its traditions, some of which are depicted at interesting and vaguely exotic length by Lumet, who as much as any director has concentrated upon the myriad facets of New York life during the course of his career.

Griffith is at her best in the role's moments of awakening, when she realizes she is no longer satisfied with the prosaic interests of her cop b.f. and that she may have a spiritual side that has never been acknowledged. Newcomer Thal is okay, but if he has exceptional talents they remain largely hidden behind his beard and payess. Mia Sara is exceedingly lovely and sympathetic as Thal's friendly sister, and longtime Lumet producer Burtt Harris has a powerful scene as Griffith's gruff dad.

Tech contributions are pro, although Jerry Bock's score lays the ethnic lyricism on a bit thick.
— *Todd McCarthy*

THE MEDIUM
(MEDIUM RARE)

A Krishna Shah/Double Helix Films presentation of a Derrol Stepenny production. Executive producer, Errol Pang. Produced by Graham Moore. Directed by Arthur Smith. Screenplay, Margaret Chan, Rani Moorthy. Camera (color), Smith. Reviewed at Cannes Film Festival market, May 10, 1992. Running time: **91 MIN.**
With: Dore Kraus, Margaret Chan, Jamie Marshall.
(Chinese subtitles)

"The Medium" takes an intriguing, apparently true, story and does very little with it. Set in Singapore, this somnolent thriller about a Western woman who falls under the spell of a Chinese medium is bland fare for video shelves.

Adrian Lim, a medium, actually was executed in Singapore some time ago for the murder of his wife and her sister. With that starting point, writers Margaret Chan and Rani Moorthy unfold a yarn about an attractive Aussie photojournalist who sees Lim go into a trance during a public display of his powers, and decides to do a story on him. But when she confronts him, she discovers his powers are greater than she thought, and since he seems to have sex on his mind, she's in trouble.

Singapore locations provide a few attractive settings for the murky goings-on, but the pic is indifferently acted and sluggishly paced, and it doesn't really deliver the promised exotic mayhem.

Technically pic is fine, though it's too protracted.
— *David Stratton*

LYUBOV
(LOVE)
(RUSSIAN)

A TTL Films/Zodiak Studio/Gorki Studio production. Executive producer, Yosif Sosland. Directed, written by Valeri Todorovsky. Camera (color), Ilya Dyomin; editor, A. Strelnikova; music, Vyacheslav Nazarov; sound, Gleb Kravetsky; art direction, Viktor Safronov. Reviewed at Cannes Film Festival (Directors' Fortnight), May 9, 1992. Running time: **109 MIN.**
With: Yevgeni Mironov, Natalya Petrova, Dmitri Marianov, Tatyana Skorokhodova.

A rites of passage double-header set in contempo Moscow, "Love" makes up in charm what it lacks in originality. Likable perfs by the two lead pairs and an episodic style recalling '60s New Wave pics make a refreshing change from Russian product focusing on social ills. Careful handling and good word-of-mouth could give pic a minor leg-up beyond the fest circuit.

Paper-thin story centers on easygoing teens Sasha (Yevgeni Mironov) and Vadim (Dmitri Marianov), the first a boyish charmer, the second a practiced roué. At a party to find love, Vadim hooks up with the passionate Marina (Tatyana Skorokhodova) and is soon between the sheets. Sasha goes for the more serious Masha (Natalya Petrova) and has a harder time getting to first base, even when he invites her to his family's rundown dacha.

Masha's family wants her to marry only a Jew and the household is about to emigrate to Israel due to a stream of anti-Semitic phone threats. Sasha still hangs in, convinced that love will conquer all; to prove his commitment he even tries to unmask the anonymous caller.

First-time helmer Valeri Todorovsky makes no bones of his admiration for the early works of directors like François Truffaut, and there's the same mix of romantic realism and bittersweet light comedy. Story's anti-Semitism thread isn't allowed to snag the main action, which always centers on the characters' emotions.

On that level, "Love" works fine, even if it doesn't have much new to say. As the male duo, Mironov and Marianov make well-matched buddies, though the more colorful Marianov unfortunately gets sidelined once Mironov's relationship picks up speed. As the two femmes, Petrova and Skorokhodova are okay within the limits of the male-oriented story line, with able support from elder players as family members.

Technically, pic looks fine on its 2 million rouble budget, with classical music excerpts adding plenty of fizz. —*Derek Elley*

MAD DOG COLL
(U.S.-RUSSIAN)

A 21st Century Film Corp. presentation of a Power Pictures-Start Corp. production. (Intl. sales: 21st Century, L.A.) Produced by Menahem Golan. Executive producers, Ami Artzi, Ivan Mendzheritsky. Directed by Greydon Clark, Ken Stein. Screenplay, Neil Ruttenberg, Stein. Camera (Deluxe color), Janusz Kaminski; editor, Patrick Rand; music, Terry Plumeri; production design, Clark Hunter; associate producer, Galina Tuchinsky; line producer, Mark Slater; casting, Abigail R. McGrath. Reviewed at Cannes Film Festival market, May 10, 1992. Running time: **98 MIN.**
With: Christopher Bradley, Bruce Nozick, Rachel York, Jeff Griggs.

A low-rent gloss on the mobster genre, "Mad Dog Coll" plays like a solid '50s programmer in color. Quick playoff in undiscriminating markets will be followed by an equally quick trip to vid shelves.

Central characters this time round are the Coll brothers, "Mad Dog" Vincent (Christopher Bradley) and Peter (Jeff Griggs). Starting out as muscle for N.Y.'s Irish gangs, the teen siblings soon switch allegiances to old pal Dutch Schultz (Bruce Novick), running liquor during Prohibition. When Dutch won't let them start their own operation, the Colls take him head-on.

The script doesn't get much farther than lines like "Bring on the cement." But the action clips along at a merry pace that should keep genre fans amused, and Gothamites will have fun seeing Russian locations doubling for late '20s N.Y. Almost all of the pic's exteriors are nocturnal; interior sets are cheesy. Violence and language are restrained by current standards.

Bradley makes a fair stab at the title role, but he's wiped off the screen by Novick as the bumptious Schultz. Other perfs are standard, and Rachel York has her moments as Bradley's chantoosie wife. A final voiceover stresses the youthfulness of the period's mobsters, and in that respect at least the pic is accurate. Tech credits are okay, with a helpful symphonic score by Terry Plumeri. —*Derek Elley*

DEN GODA VILJAN
(THE BEST INTENTIONS)
(SWEDISH)

An SVT1 Drama production in association with ZDF/Channel Four/RAI-2/La Sept/DR/YLE 2/NRK/RUV. (Intl. sales: Film Four Intl., London.) Produced by Lars Bjälkeskog. Executive producer, Ingrid Dahlberg. Directed by Bille August. Screenplay, Ingmar Bergman. Camera (color), Jörgen Persson; editor, Janus Billeskov Jansen; music, Stefan Nilsson (conducted by Esa-Pekka Salonen); sound, Lennart Gentzel, Johnny Ljungberg; production design, Anna Asp; costume design, Ann-Mari Anttila; assistant director, Stefan Baron. Reviewed at Cannes Film Festival (competing), May 13, 1992. Running time: **180 MIN.**
Henrik Bergman . . . . Samuel Fröler
Anna Bergman . . . . Pernilla August
Johan Åkerblom . . . . Max von Sydow
Karin Åkerblom . . . . . . Ghita Nørby
Nordenson . . . . . Lennart Hjulström
Alma Bergman . . . . Mona Malm
Frida Strandberg . . . . . Lena Endre
Fredrik Bergman . . . . . Keve Hjelm
Ernst Åkerblom . . . . Björn Kjellman
Carl Åkerblom . . . . . Börje Ahlstedt
Rev. Gransjö . . . . . . Hans Alfredson
Queen Viktoria . . . . . . Anita Björn

An epic story of mismatched love shaped in the most intimate terms, the Ingmar Bergman-scripted "The Best Intentions" packs a sustained emotional wallop that lightens its three-hour span. Pic should attract solid art house biz on the back of the filmmakers' reps and critical support.

Focusing on the early years of the Swedish helmer's strong-willed parents, it's a powerful confirmation of the talents of Danish-born director Bille August, who hit three years ago with the Oscar-winning "Pelle the Conqueror."

Bergman first had the idea when writing his reminiscences "The Magic Lantern" and, after finishing the script in 1989, sent it to August. Exec producer Ingrid Dahlberg, head of Swedish web SVT1's drama department, assembled the 67 million kronor ($11 million) budget from a slew of European broadcasters. Pic's eight-month shoot started in July 1990, with separate scripts for a six-hour TV version (aired last December in Scandinavia) and the present three-hour theatrical release.

Story spans 10 crucial years in the relationship of Henrik Bergman (Samuel Fröler) and Anna Åkerblom (Pernilla August), from their first meeting in 1909 to the early summer of 1918. (Real names of Bergman's parents were Erik and Karin; other characters' names are unchanged.) He's a financially strapped theology student in the university town of Uppsala, and she's the strong-minded daughter of rich, doting parents (Ghita Nørby, Max von Sydow).

Henrik has been seeing another woman, Frida (Lena Endre). Despite that, Anna hangs in and they make love, but Henrik is forced to withdraw when Anna's mother puts her foot down. Only when Anna's father dies — while she and mom are vacationing in Italy — are the two finally allowed to meet again, in a moving scene some 80 minutes in that effectively wraps the story's exposition.

Pic's remainder follows the couple to the northern village of Forsboda, where Henrik's been posted as a pastor. Rifts between the now-married couple deepen when they take in a withdrawn kid, Petrus (Elias Ringquist). The strain proves too much for Anna and when Petrus tries to drown their young baby, she finally starts to rebel against her husband's obsessive samaritanism.

Henrik becomes more solitary, and Anna is angered that he's rejected a comfortable royal posting in Stockholm. She finally packs her bags and moves back in with mother. Pic ends with a shamed Henrik asking for a second chance as Anna is already swollen with the future Ingmar.

Unlike Bergman's own "Fanny and Alexander," with which the film shares some themes, "Best Intentions" eschews a busy canvas of characters in favor of a simple story about two lovers separated by their ideals. Bergman's script succinctly weaves in refs to themes explored in his own earlier films, notably the destructive force of worship when used as a crutch for human weaknesses.

The emotional core remains firmly in female hands. Despite an opening sequence that stresses the stubbornness behind Henrik's boyish exterior, the real running is made by Anna, especially when she finds herself gradually sidelined by the demands of her husband's work in the simple northern community. The couple's angry head-to-head after their move north, in which their different social backgrounds become an issue for the first time, is all the more powerful for the pic's emotional restraint during the first half, in which both were united by the common enemy of her parents' opposition.

No dates are ever provided and socio-historical background is lacking. Present version includes brief refs to striking workers and exploitative bosses, and a couple of crowd sequences, but that's it. At every stage, the focus is kept tight on the couple's emotional ups and downs.

As the tunnel-visioned Henrik, Fröler sometimes seems a shade lightweight but packs quite a punch (literally as well as dramatically) in his sudden outbursts of rage. It is August, however, who carries the pic's heart and soul in a performance that is sure to garner awards: Although a mite old-looking in the early scenes, the Swedish thesp (wife of the director and, as Pernilla Ostergren, the maid in "Fanny and Alexander") holds the screen in a series of throat-catching sequences.

Supporting players are all on the money, with Danish actress Nørby working wonders with the two-faced role of Anna's mother, and Von Sydow turning in a fine extended cameo as her caring but ultimately weak father.

Other roles are virtually bits but both Endre, as Henrik's other woman, and Lennart Hjulstrúm, as a proud local big shot, deliver the goods. Vet actress Anita Björk squeezes a lot into a brief spot as Queen Viktoria.

Jörgen Persson's crystalline lensing of the Swedish exteriors (with some lustrous sidebars in sun-drenched Italy and Switzerland) is matched by pic's precision-tool editing and director August's immaculate compositions. Stefan Nilsson's underscoring, more frequent than in many Scandi pics, effectively juxtaposes a bare piano melody with a warmer string theme but is short on real development. Costuming and production design are both richly detailed. — *Derek Elley*

AM ENDE DER NACHT
(AT THE END OF THE NIGHT)
(SWISS)

A Dschoint Ventschr./Christoph production, with Swiss TV & Teleclub. (Intl. sales: Filmverlag der Autoren, Munich.) Produced by Susanna Rüdlinger. Directed by Christoph Schaub. Screenplay, Martin Witz, from an idea by Schaub. Camera (color), Ciro Cappellari; editor, Fee Liechti; music, Thomas Bächli; production design, Karin Tissi; sound, Florian Eidenbenz; assistant director, Anna Schmid. Reviewed at Cannes Film Festival (Directors' Fortnight), May 9, 1992. Running time: **88 MIN.**
Robert Tanner . Peter von Strombeck
Edith Tanner . . . . Jessica Früh
Maria Klever . . . . Eva Scheurer
Werner . . . . Peter Bollag
Keller . . . . Rene Schönenberger
Kurt . . . . Peter Steiner
Lucca . . . . Manuel Heurer
Beni . . . . Ivan Schauwecker

In "At the End of the Night," Swiss helmer Christoph Schaub unfolds a grim little tale of a seemingly normal husband driven to madness and murder. Despite a strong performance from Peter von Strombeck, pic essentially treads no new ground. Commercial prospects are dull.

Von Strombeck plays a suburban supermarket manager who seems happily married with a cute son. But all isn't as secure as it seems: He's in debt and must sell his car and borrow from the store. Tensions with family and friends mount.

One night, he simply smothers his wife and son as they sleep, and next day sets out by train as if on vacation. He meets up with an attractive woman, but although she seems willing, he doesn't pursue her. When he sees a story about the murders in a paper, he makes a rendezvous with a journalist, who alerts the police.

Schaub builds up tiny details in the domestic scenes to prepare for the man's ultimate, insane act and then lets the film slip into a strange anticlimax as the murderer simply takes off

into the countryside. This mildly intriguing film is not sufficiently robust to create much interest outside its home turf. Technical credits are all pro.
— *David Stratton*

SAMOSTOIATELNAIA JIZN
(AN INDEPENDENT LIFE)
(RUSSIAN-FRENCH)

A DAR (St. Petersburg)/PXP Prods./ PCC/La Sept (Paris) co-production with participation of Canal Plus, French Ministry of Culture & Ministry of Foreign Affairs. Executive producer, Françoise Galfre. Produced by Patrick Godeau, Vitali Kanévski. Directed, written by Kanévski. Camera (Eastmancolor), Vladimir Bryliakov; editor, Helene Gagarine; music, Boris Rytchkov; sound, Kirill Kouzmine. Reviewed at Cannes Film Festival (competing), May 7, 1992. Running time: **99 MIN.**
Valerka . . . . Pavel Nazarov
Valka . . . . Dinara Droukarova
Yamamoto . . . . Toshihiro Watanabe
Mother . . . . Elena Popova
Sofia Arkadievna . . . . . Liana Jvania

This sequel to writer-director Vitali Kanévski's remarkable debut, "Freeze—Die—Come to Life" (Un Certain Regard item awarded the Camera d'Or for best first feature two years ago at Cannes) is even grimmer than its predecessor. Though working this time in color, the director makes no allowances for audience sensitivities in continuing his bleak personal story, set in Eastern Russia following World War II.

Kanévski takes up the story of young Valerka (again played by Pavel Nazarov), who, after the brutal death of his friend Galia at the end of the earlier film, is back living with his mother. Galia's sister, Valka (Dinara Droukarova, Galia in the prior pic) is Valerka's only friend.

The youth is expelled from school after the unscrupulous headmaster accuses him of participating in the gang rape of a girl, although he was innocent. After quarreling with his mother, Valerka leaves on a trek north in search of relatives he's never met, only to discover a world of casual violence, drunkenness, loveless sex and near starvation wherever he goes.

Kanévski's vision is uncompromising. His narrative proceeds in fits and starts, and many scenes are so gloomy as to be almost indecipherable. Scenes of sex and violence, far from being cathartic, only add to the chilly,

depressing mood. A hospital scene in which Valerka's mother undergoes a brutal abortion is just one of many rugged scenes.

Valerka's tentative friendship with a Japanese soldier (Toshihiro Watanabe) left behind at war's end goes unresolved.

"An Independent Life," the second part of a proposed autobiographical trilogy, is an impressive, personal pic with little optimism. Actors give extremely natural, unaffected performances, and the varied settings, almost all of them ugly and rundown, appear wholly authentic.

Pic's last-minute withdrawal from the Berlin Film Festival competition in favor of its Cannes slot caused some fuss earlier this year. — *David Stratton*

AU PAYS DES JULIETS
(IN THE COUNTRY OF JULIETS)
(FRENCH)

An Erato Films/CEC Rhône Alpes/ FR3 Films production, in association with Investimage 3/CNC/Canal Plus/ Région Rhône Alpes. (Intl. sales: Mercure, Paris.) Produced by Daniel Toscan du Plantier. Executive producers, Jérôme Paillard, Claude Barnault. Directed, written by Mehdi Charef. Camera (Fujicolor), Gérard de Battista; editor, Christian Dior; music, Penguin Cafe Orchestra; art direction, Alain Poirot; costume design, Catherine Taisson; sound, Pierre Gamet, Bernard Chaumeil; assistant director, Marianne Chouchan; casting, Claude Martin. Reviewed at Cannes Film Festival (competing), May 9, 1992. Running time: **96 MIN.**
Thérèse . . . . Laure Duthilleul
Henriette . . . . Claire Nebout
Raïssa . . . . Maria Schneider

Self-styled "story of three babes on parole for 24 hours," Mehdi Charef's "In the Country of Juliets" ends up handcuffed by its over-schematic script. Despite some fine early moments and a well-sustained perf by Claire Nebout, pic doesn't pack much emotional clout in its transition from page to screen. Commercial prospects look iffy.

The femme cons are Laure Duthilleul, as a political terrorist; tomboyish Nebout, who accidentally caused the death of her child; and uptight Maria Schneider, in for killing her spouse. Thrown together because of a strike at the local railroad station, the three end up roaming nearby Lyon, where they buddy up, spat, get separated and finally come to a mutual understanding by the time they return next morning.

Pic falls neatly into three parts. After much female bonding in the opening half-hour, tone hardens as they suddenly turn on each other in a public park and split up. Schneider tries to reach her family by phone, Nebout's friends are all away or not answering the door and Duthilleul gets progressively lonelier.

Final section at night, as the three reunite by chance, is more stylized. After settling their differences, they mellow out in a bar and pick up some men. Extended coda next morning finds the strung-out Schneider unsure whether to return to stir.

On paper, and with such a handpicked cast, pic sounds promising, if hardly original, with Charef gradually easing the viewer into the streets and winding alleys of Lyon. Problems begin in the middle section where Nebout's character continues to grow but Schneider and Duthilleul's stall. Emotional setpieces by the last pair (Duthilleul in the rain, and Schneider over the phone) fail to register because their characters are so murkily drawn.

Algerian-born Charef, whose pics have shown extremes of personality, works here on a much broader emotional palette, and seems unsure of how to mesh the characters into something more than the sum of their parts. Film-buffy refs in the form of clips from "Breathless" and "La Strada" (Nebout is a failed actress who once worked in a cinema) simply look like showing off.

Duthilleul is a fine thesp starved of a real role, and scarcely believable as a bomb-chucking terrorist. Schneider achieves a startling transformation as a middle-aged mother (all cropped hair and smart suit) but spends almost the whole pic looking as if she's forgotten to turn off the gas at home. It's left to Nebout, in thick specs and boyish jeans, to provide real emotional depth.

On the technical side, pic is always easy on the eyes, with Gérard de Battista's sharp, clear lensing of Lyon and the surrounding countryside. On that level, pic is Charef's slickest of his four to date. — *Derek Elley*

FOREVER

A Triax Entertainment Group/DDM Film presentation of a Jackelyn Giroux production. Produced by Giroux. Executive producers, Olive McQueen, Mel Pearl, Don Levin. Directed by Thomas Palmer Jr. Screenplay, Giroux, Palmer. Camera (Film Services color), Gary Grav-

er; editor, Jeffrey Fallick; supervising editor, Palmer; music, the RH Factor; set decoration, Stacie Burton; costume design, Linda Susan Howell; sound (Ultra-Stereo), Leslie Chew; dimensional laser imagery, Laser Images; assistant director, Paul LeClair. Reviewed at Cannes Film Festival market, May 9, 1992. Running time: **87 MIN.**
Angelica . . . . Sally Kirkland
Mary Miles Minter . . . . . Sean Young
Ted Dickson . . . . Keith Coogan
Mabel Normand . . . . . . Diane Ladd
Wallace Reid . . . . Terence Knox
Billy Baldwin . . . . . . Nicholas Guest
Charlotte . . . . Renee Taylor
William Desmond Taylor
. . . . Steve Railsback
Mary Pickford . . . . . . Ashley Hester

Bemoaning how the quality of modern films has slipped, a character here remarks, "I think somehow the magic has gotten lost." Seldom has this notion been more conclusively validated than in "Forever," a sweetly intended Hollywood saga of embarrassing awkwardness. An unappetizingly incongruous mishmash of the supernatural, rock videos, Hollywood history and soft-core porn, indie production is headed straight for the video bin.

The ghosts of some of the silent cinema's legendary stars are literally summoned up for this low-budgeter. Callow young music video whiz Keith Coogan moves into the Hollywood villa where, 70 years before, film director William Desmond Taylor was murdered.

When Coogan begins looking at film he finds spooled on an ancient Movieola, the personalities included therein — Mary Pickford, Wallace Reid, Billy Baldwin, Fatty Arbuckle, Mabel Normand and, most important, Mary Miles Minter — spin into his life and distract him from his video assignments, much to the consternation of his crass agent and sometime lover, Sally Kirkland.

Story's core has Coogan falling in love with Minter, but instead of exploring the metaphysical romance, klutzy script by producer Jackelyn Giroux and director Thomas Palmer Jr. has Minter exclaiming about the wonders of movies on cable TV and complaining about the inferiority of wine coolers to champagne.

Shot mostly in the house location, pic is notable for the exceptional stiffness of its numerous sex scenes. Coogan looks about half as tall as both Kirkland, who does her raunchy thing once again, and Sean Young, a most implausible Minter, and none of them looks happy to be there. No better are Steve Railsback and Diane Ladd.

Film buffs who've heard of these characters will be appalled, while general auds could scarcely care less. — *Todd McCarthy*

MY NEW GUN

A New Gun production. (Intl. sales: IRS Media Intl.). Produced by Michael Flynn. Co-producer, Lydia Dean Pilcher. Executive producers, Miles A. Copeland III, Paul Colichman, Harold Welb. Directed, written by Stacy Cochran. Camera (Duart color; Fotokem prints), Ed Lachman; editor, Camilla Toniolo; music, Pat Irwin; production design, Toby Corbett; costume design, Eugenie Bafaloukos. Reviewed at Cannes Film Festival (Directors Fortnight), May 10, 1992. Running time: **99 MIN.**
With: Diane Lane, James LeGros, Stephen Collins, Tess Harper, Bill Raymond, Bruce Altman, Maddie Corman.

First-time writer-director Stacy Cochran achieves an original, offbeat tone in "My New Gun," but it's a note that proves difficult to sustain over feature length. Wry investigation of contempo American foibles, obsessions and presumption rides on a distinctive style that will generate enough support in critical quarters to spark interest on the specialized circuit.

Provocative premise has the suburban lives of married couple Diane Lane and Stephen Collins thoroughly derailed by a gun which the husband insists on giving his reluctant wife as a gift. The unwanted object doesn't last long in the household, however, as local weirdo James LeGros manages to steal it for his own mysterious purposes.

Recovering the weapon, Collins immediately manages to shoot himself in the foot, which lands him in the hospital and opens the door for LeGros to insinuate himself into Lane's life. The deliberately mysterious character, who lives with his mother (Tess Harper), makes many strange requests of his sexy neighbor, which curiously, she tends to grant.

Lane's unanalyzed passivity begins to be irritating as one waits for her to stop exploiting herself and take the situation in hand. Paradoxically, however, Lane's coolly magnetic performance, surely her best to date, ends up giving the film the gravity it needs to balance Cochran's persistent whimsicality in plotting.

Quietly observing the off-kilter behavior of all those around her, Lane conveys an understandable skepticism in the face of the pervasive irrationality of the events that uncoil around her, including having allowed the gun into her life in the first place.

Cochran is interested in a very particular brand of black humor that is neither mordantly funny nor bleakly pessimistic but is cognizant of the fact that people do things for the weirdest reasons. Everything that happens has been lurking behind the banal surfaces waiting for a trigger to set it off, and Cochran relates it in a confidently individualistic style that keeps the viewer interested.

Still, much of what transpires feels rather arbitrary, and some of the goofball goings-on — especially toward the end — are a bit much.

LeGros underplays to the max while still managing to invest his creepily seductive character with a strong edge, while Collins punches up the comedy as the selfish hubby. Supporting perfs are on the broad side. Helping create a very polished work on a restricted budget, lenser Ed Lachman and production designer Toby Corbett have conspired for a look of heightened reality without pushing into distortion or caricature. Pat Irwin's score helps point the film in the direction of mirth.

— *Todd McCarthy*

SARAFINA!
(SOUTH AFRICAN)

A Miramax release (U.S.) of an Anant Singh presentation of a Distant Horizon & Ideal Films production in association with Videovision Enterprises/Les Films Ariane/VPI/BBC. Produced by Singh. Producer for BBC, David M. Thompson. Executive producers, Kirk D'Amico, Sudhir Pragjee. Directed by Darrell James Roodt. Screenplay, William Nicholson, Mbongeni Ngema. Camera (color), Mark Vicente; editors, Peter Hollywood, Sarah Thomas; music-lyrics, Ngema; additional songs, Hugh Masekela; music score, Stanley Myers; production design, David Barkham; choreography, Michael Peters, Ngema; Dolby sound; associate producers, Helena Spring, Sanjeev Singh. Reviewed at Cannes Film Festival (non-competing), May 11, 1992. Running time: **115 MIN.**
With: Leleti Khumalo, Whoopi Goldberg, Miriam Makeba, John Kani, Mbongeni Ngema.

Opening up "Sarafina!" for the screen has given the popular musical a dimension it never had onstage. Powerfully lensed on location in Soweto, emotionally and politically impassioned piece effectively registers the antiapartheid movement's anger and hope in an infectious musical context, and has been imaginatively reconceived for film. With in-depth promo targeting all potential audience segments, b.o. picture could be bright.

Mbongeni Ngema's theatrical production, a Broadway hit in 1988 and still on international tour, was set principally at the township high school. Institution still serves as the symbolic center of the action, but, along the lines of "West Side Story," liberating the show from a restricted environment has created innumerable opportunities for expanding the story's impact.

In theory, idea of having dozens of teens romping in rambunctious choreography through dusty, impoverished neighborhoods under the threatening surveillance of armed police stood a good chance of not working — placing such stylized activity in grimly realistic setting has misfired in the past.

After a somewhat dubious opening in which Soweto literally goes Hollywood, complete with a gigantic "Soweto," sign and mock Oscar, pic clicks in as students try to pursue such normal activities as getting an education and putting on a show under the strictures of emergency rule.

Inspiring teacher Whoopi Goldberg gives an amusingly apt history lesson, but casting a pall over everything is a firebombing of the school. Clearly, an element among the students sees violence as the only solution, something the authorities are only too happy to repay in kind.

The beautiful Sarafina provides a window for a compressed history of South Africa from the mid-'70s through the mid-'80s. Living in the township while her mother works as a domestic in an affluent white suburb, Sarafina, who idolizes Nelson Mandela, sees a fellow student she may fancy shot dead by police, participates in the rioting following the shooting of more blacks, takes part in the torching of a black officer who works for the whites, and is tortured in prison during a time when as many as 8,000 children were incarcerated.

The violence is presented in fully realistic detail, and all of it, especially the mob killing of the cop, carries a tremendous impact. So do scenes between Sarafina and her mother, where two generations come to terms with the different ways they have fought the same struggle.

Terrific songs by Ngema and Hugh Masekela propel the work at a fine clip and are exceedingly well performed and staged. Technical side of the film matches anything Hollywood could have done with much more money.

Tony-nominated for her performance in the role on Broadway, Leleti Khumalo is a sensational Sarafina. Goldberg socks over her sizable supporting role as an irreverent, politically aware teacher, and Miriam Makeba virtually defines dignity and compassion as Sarafina's mother. Performances down the line by the huge cast are strong.

Young South African director Darrell James Roodt ("Place of Weeping," "The Stick" and "Jobman") has done an impressive job of reconceiving a well-loved piece in cinematic terms. Only letdown is the climactic production number imagining the day of Mandela's release, which is rather sketchily realized and abbreviated. — *Todd McCarthy*

SISTER ACT

A Buena Vista Pictures release of a Touchstone Pictures presentation in association with Touchwood Pacific Partners I of a Scott Rudin production. Produced by Teri Schwartz. Executive producer, Rudin. Co-producer, Mario Iscovich. Directed by Emile Ardolino. Screenplay, Joseph Howard. Camera (Technicolor color), Adam Greenberg; editor, Richard Halsey; music, Marc Shaiman; production design, Jackson DeGovia; assistant art director, Eve Cauley; set decoration, Thomas L. Roysden; set design, Robert M. Beall, Ann Harris; costume design, Molly Maginnis; sound (Dolby), Darin Knight; associate producer, Cindy Gilmore; assistant director, Joe Camp III; musical numbers staged by Lester Wilson; casting, Judy Taylor, Lynda Gordon, Johnson-Liff & Zerman. Reviewed at AMC Century 14 Theater, L.A., May 16, 1992. MPAA Rating: PG. Running time: **100 MIN.**

Deloris . . . . Whoopi Goldberg
Mother Superior . . . . . Maggie Smith
Mary Patrick . . . . . . Kathy Najimy
Mary Robert . . . . . Wendy Makkena
Mary Lazarus . . . . . . Mary Wickes
Vince LaRocca . . . . . Harvey Keitel
Eddie Souther . . . . Bill Nunn
Joey . . . . Robert Miranda
Willy . . . . Richard Portnow
Also with: Ellen Albertini Dow, Carmen Zapata, Pat Crawford Brown, Prudence Wright Holmes, Georgia Creighton, Susan Johnson, Ruth Kobart, Susan Browning, Darlene Koldenhoven, Sheri Izzard, Edith Diaz, Beth Fowler.

Amid summer blockbusters, there's usually room for one sleeper comedy hit, and this could be it. Blessed with the from-on-high concept of Whoopi Goldberg bringing rock 'n' roll to a nuns' chorus, this infectious little throwaway should strike a responsive chord with sequel-weary audiences and very well prove habit-forming.

All the more wonder that Goldberg reportedly has opted not to promote the film, originally seen as a vehicle for Bette Midler, which should provide her with a successful solo follow-up to "Ghost." While far from perfect, audiences will likely overlook this act's numerous shortcomings due to the warm-hearted story and engaging premise.

Goldberg plays Deloris, a Reno lounge singer who witnesses a murder by her mobster b.f. Vince (Harvey Keitel) and ends up on the lam. The detective trying to bust Vince, played by Bill Nunn, pops Deloris into a San Francisco convent for safekeeping, where the one-time Catholic school girl promptly outrages the mother superior (Maggie Smith).

Deloris and the movie find their respective callings about halfway in when she's asked to take over the convent's dreadful choir, introducing '60s rock to the nuns through adapted renditions of "My Guy" (becoming "My God") and songs like "I Will Follow Him," which takes on a new and hilarious meaning.

It's a divine concept, and after a weak start director Emile Ardolino ("Dirty Dancing," "Three Men and a Little Lady") milks it for all the laughs it's worth, while deriving requisite warmth from Goldberg and Smith's solid performances.

The comic element gets a major boost, meanwhile, from supporting players, particularly Kathy Najimy's ebullient Sister Mary Patrick and dour Mary Wickes as the former choir-master.

Ardolino does fall into certain traps of the genre, among them the annoying habit of telling big chunks of story through long musical montages, and Keitel and his henchmen are too cartoonish to be truly menacing.

In a more provocative sense, the film touches on, but basically steers away from, addressing how the Church can be more relevant in modern society, as well as its inner conflict over adapting to face current realities, a point made subtly by Deloris' grappling with the mother superior over styles of music.

Still, few summer filmgoers will be bothered by those flat notes, and as a PG-rated comedy, Goldberg's cleaned-up act should pick up additional coin as one to which parents can bring their kids.

Technical credits are highlighted by Lester Wilson's staging on the numbers and Marc Shaiman's clever musical adaptations. Production designer Jackson DeGovia also does a fine job of turning the dreary church into a glitzy main room as the chorus starts filling up benches.

"Sister Act" may be a benchmark for Goldberg, as well, and for other summer comedies, a tough act to follow.

— *Brian Lowry*

ALIEN 3

A 20th Century Fox release of a Brandywine production. Produced by Gordon Carroll, David Giler, Walter Hill. Executive producer, Ezra Swerdlow. Co-producer, Sigourney Weaver. Directed by David Fincher. Screenplay, Giler, Hill, Larry Ferguson; story by Vincent Ward. Based on characters created by Dan O'Bannon, Ronald Shusett. Camera (Rank Laboratories color), Alex Thomson; editor, Terry Rawlings; music, Elliot Goldenthal; production design, Norman Reynolds; art direction, Fred Hole, James Morahan; set decoration, Belinda Edwards; costume design, Bob Ringwood, David Perry; sound (Dolby), Tony Dawe; special effects supervisor, George Gibbs; visual effects produced by Richard Edlund; alien effects, Alec Gillis, Tom Woodruff Jr.; original alien design, H.R. Giger; stunt coordinator, Marc Boyle; assistant director, Chris Carreras; 2nd unit director, Martin Brierley; casting, Priscilla John (U.K.), Billy Hopkins (U.S.). Reviewed at Avco Center Cinema, L.A., May 18, 1992. MPAA Rating: R. Running time: **115 MIN.**

Ripley . . . . Sigourney Weaver
Dillon . . . . Charles S. Dutton
Clemens . . . . Charles Dance
Golic . . . . Paul McGann
Andrews . . . . Brian Glover
Aaron . . . . Ralph Brown
Morse . . . . Danny Webb
Rains . . . . . Christopher John Fields
Junior . . . . Holt McCallany
Bishop II . . . . . . Lance Henriksen

The shape-shifting "Alien" trilogy reverts back to the form of the first film in this third close encounter, a muddled effort offering little more than visual splendor to recommend it. Although certain to open strong thanks to the must-see faithful, look for a quick fade beyond the first couple of box office orbits as word-of-mouth and the dour tone pull "Alien 3" down to earth, making it a likely also-ran among this summer's blockbusters.

In interviews, star/co-producer Sigourney Weaver has spoken of the producers' conflict with Fox over crafting a more cerebral film rather than an outright thriller, and that indecisiveness shows. More pointedly, "Alien 3" may have been done in from the start by "Aliens," James Cameron's tremendous first sequel, which took the original — essentially a haunted house movie with space as a foreboding means of preventing escape — and moved it in a thrilling new direction by staging full-blown combat with an alien horde.

Taking a more intimate approach, the latest sequel goes back to square one and proves inferior to both its predecessors. The action picks up in the opening credits where "Aliens" left off, as Ripley's hybernation pod crash-lands on a grim, all-male penal colony planet. It seems an alien egg was still on the shuttle (how is anybody's guess), and the rapid dispatch of survivors from "Aliens" will doubtless feel like an emotional rip-off.

In any event, Ripley (Weaver) finds herself stranded on a planet with a bunch of converted convicts who've embraced religion, led by Charles S. Dutton of TV's "Roc." The colony's kindly doctor (Charles Dance), with whom Ripley shares another kind of close encounter, suspects something is wrong, but throughout the early part of the story Ripley won't share her suspicions with him that an alien has landed on the planet.

That reticence is only one of numerous inexplicable aspects of "Alien 3," which again relies on the same faceless "company" as an unseen heavy while toying furtively with the sexual politics of a lone woman trapped on a planet of murderers, rapists and miscreants.

A significant problem stems from the fact that aside from Ripley and perhaps Dutton and Dance, none of these characters has a defined persona, making the bald convicts all virtually indistinguishable alien-bait.

That shortcoming is never more evident than in an extended sequence in which the survivors seek to trap the monster, though no one watching will have any way of discerning whether they're coming close to achieving that goal.

Musicvideo director David Fincher doesn't reveal much finesse with actors in his big-screen debut, and the screenplay (by producers Walter Hill and David Giler, plus Larry Ferguson) proves fraught with lapses in reason, motivation and logic.

That leaves Weaver to carry the load, but her character is so encumbered with baggage that she can't really showcase the qualities (particularly evident in the second film) that made the audience empathize with her.

As for the much-discussed reshoot of the movie's ending, one can only judge what's on screen, which demonstrates that the screams of heavy-handed religious symbolism can be heard even in space.

The alien itself remains a technical marvel in its three repugnant forms, more a tribute to H.R. Giger's original design than anything else. Fincher, turning to music-video editing techniques, resorts to rapid-fire glimpses of the beast.

Other technical aspects are also top of the line, although the production design proves so relentlessly bleak that there's no relief from the film's oppressiveness, even when there are lapses in the tension. While the look is an accomplishment, this isn't the sort of environment that tag-along filmgoers — or even those who bring them — will relish visiting.

— *Brian Lowry*

ENCINO MAN

A Buena Vista release of a Hollywood Pictures presentation, in association with Touchwood Pacific Partners I. Produced by George Zaloom. Executive producer, Hilton Green. Co-executive producer, Michael Rotenberg. Directed by Les Mayfield. Screenplay, Shawn Schepps, from story by Zaloom, Schepps. Camera (Technicolor), Robert Brinkmann; editor, Eric Sears; additional editor, Jonathan Siegel; music, J. Peter Robinson; sound (Dolby), Robert Allan Wald; production design, James Allen; costume design, Marie France; choreography, Peggy Holmes; assistant director, Jerry Ketcham; casting, Kathleen Letterie. Reviewed at Loews Tower East, N.Y., May 18, 1992. MPAA Rating: PG. Running time: **89 MIN.**

Dave Morgan . . . . Sean Astin
Link . . . . Brendan Fraser
Stoney Brown . . . . . . Pauly Shore
Robyn . . . . Megan Ward
Ella . . . . Robin Tunney
Matt . . . . Michael DeLuise
Phil . . . . Patrick Van Horn
Mrs. Morgan . . . . . Mariette Hartley
Mr. Morgan . . . . . . Richard Masur

"Encino Man" kicks off the silly summer season with mindless would-be comedy aimed at the younger set. Low-budget quickie (lensed five months ago) is insulting even within its own no-effort parameters.

Shawn Schepps' incompetent screenplay dawdles over the introductions, with well over a reel elapsing before Cro Magnon man Brendan Fraser unfreezes after turning up in a block of ice uncovered by Encino teen Sean Astin while digging a backyard swimming pool.

Fraser covered in mud looks a lot like Christophe Lambert in the latest Tarzan opus "Greystoke." Filmmakers stoop to ripping off earlier incarnations of the Burroughs' epic in a lengthy scene of Astin naming the boy Link, played in "me Tarzan, you Jane" fashion.

Film proceeds to duplicate intact its trailer's sequence of Astin and buddy Pauly Shore bathing and styling the caveman while Right Said Fred's catchy "I'm Too Sexy" song plays on the soundtrack.

Pic's sci-fi pretense is immediately abandoned in favor of lame regurgitation of mid-'80s teen comedies like Orion's "The Heavenly Kid." Astin and Shore contrive to pass off Fraser as a transfer student to Encino High and hope that his coolness will bring them popularity as his pals.

Of course Fraser is an instant hit with the other students. Only tension is that he wins the hearts of femmes, including Astin's dream girl Megan Ward. Schepps' script sidesteps the buddies' ultimate confrontation in favor of a handy earth tremor spitting out a cavegirl (who looks like a Valley Girl) for Fraser as a finale.

Debuting feature director Les Mayfield exhibits low aptitude for comedy, resorting to pratfalls and food sloppiness for laughs. Film is nominally a vehicle for MTV comic Pauly Shore, who flunks out on screen with his tediously unfunny patter and smaller-than-life personality.

Topbilled Astin has little to do except tag along with Fraser, who's winsome as the highly physical, imitative caveman. Pretty heroine Ward is boring, consistently upstaged by her feistier, sexier friend Robin Tunney. Mariette Hartley and Richard Masur look bewildered as Astin's parents.

Michael DeLuise, who recently directed the Tanya Roberts sex comedy "Almost Pregnant," overplays embarrassingly as the school bully who gets his comeuppance at the prom in an anti-climactic final reel.

Best technical credit is Marie France's costumes, which colorfully capture the Valley life style.

— *Lawrence Cohn*

CANNES FEST

OF MICE AND MEN

An MGM release of a Russ Smith/ Gary Sinise production. Produced by Smith, Sinise. Executive producer, Alan C. Blomquist. Directed by Sinise. Screenplay, Horton Foote, based on John Steinbeck's novel. Camera (Deluxe color), Kenneth MacMillan; editor, Robert L. Sinise; music, Mark Isham; production design, David Gropman; art direction, Dan Davis; set design, Cheryl T. Smith; set decoration, Karen Schulz, Joyce Anne Gilstrap; costume design, Shay Cunliffe; sound (Dolby), David Brownlow; assistant director, Cara Giallanza; 2nd unit camera, Alan Caso; casting, Amanda Mackey, Cathy Sandrich. Reviewed at Cannes Film Festival (competition), May 17, 1992. Running time: **110 MIN.**

Lennie . . . . John Malkovich
George . . . . Gary Sinise
Candy . . . . Ray Walston
Curley . . . . Casey Siemaszko
Curley's Wife . . . . . Sherilyn Fenn
Slim . . . . John Terry
Carlson . . . . Richard Riehle
Whitt . . . . Alexis Arquette
Crooks . . . . Joe Morton
The Boss . . . . . . Noble Willingham

Well-mounted and very traditional, "Of Mice and Men" honorably serves John Steinbeck's classic story of two Depression-era drifters without bringing anything new to it. Fine performances down the line and sensitive handling justify this attempt to introduce a new generation to the small tragedy of George and Lennie, although lack of any edge or fresh motivation to tell the tale will keep enthusiasm, and B.O. results, at a moderate level.

First published in 1937, the novel has had continued life as a Broadway play, a Hollywood film starring Lon Chaney and Burgess Meredith, and a 1980 stage piece at Chicago's Steppenwolf Theater that featured John Malkovich and Gary Sinise, who repeat their roles here.

Set in a lonely world of itinerant men in 1930, drama has a simplicity and a gruff sentimentality that makes for almost surefire pathos if done properly. It's a story of vulnerable creatures — human and animal — and how a rough world makes life very tenuous for those without a proper set of defenses.

Horton Foote's intelligent adaptation begins with George and Lennie fleeing a posse of dogs and armed men across the sun-baked California countryside. However, they are not at loose ends for long, as they have jobs lined up at a farm near Soledad, where acres of wheat need harvesting.

George (Sinise) is a quick-witted man of few but well-chosen words with no family or money to his name. His only charge is Lennie (Malkovich), a lumbering simpleton who has the mind of a child but the strength of an ox. People can't quite understand why George has saddled himself with Lennie, and George spews out his resentment of his companion in one early scene, but they've gone as far as choosing a small spread they hope to buy if they can earn enough money.

Dramatic gears start turning when belligerent farm boss son Curley (Casey Siemaszko) starts picking on Lennie. Before long, son's lovely, lonely wife (Sherilyn Fenn) begins hanging around the bunkhouse and barn, seemingly with an eye for George.

Story's subsequent small events have a withering old farm-hand (Ray Walston) coming apart when his old dog is taken out to be shot, after which he proposes to join with the new arrivals in buying a place, and Lennie crushing Curley's hand after the latter provokes a fistfight.

Lennie, not knowing his own strength, accidentally kills the puppy he's adopted, then manages to tragically do the same to Curley's wife, who made the mistake of offering him some tenderness and intimacy. Both George and audience must come to terms with the sad inevitability of the situation's resolution.

Captured in lovely, burnished hues by lenser Kenneth MacMillan and evocatively realized by production designer David Gropman, the working world of the men is a hot, dusty place devoid of emotional outlets and career possibilities, and could not look more different from the studio-bound Lewis Milestone rendition of more than 50 years ago.

Other alterations engineered by Foote and Sinise include rounding out the wife's character (never given a name by Steinbeck) to emphasize her need for human interaction; building up the role of a black animal hand (Joe Morton) who has a meaningful exchange with Lennie, the farm's other total outcast; and changing the nature of Lennie's death.

Performances are sterling. Malkovich's odd looks, slightly crossed eyes and slurred speech are perfect tools with which to build a convincing Lennie. Even if the actor is not the giant described, he conveys the requisite gentleness and strength, as well as the sense of not being able to help himself when enraged.

Sinise is surprisingly effective, bringing to his role a reedy quality that contains both bitterness and qualified hope for better times ahead. His reticence makes believable his admission that he's never had a sweetheart, and the harshness of the life he's led shows through his good looks.

Outstanding supporting turn is delivered by Walston, who has rarely had the opportunity to shine on-screen. Fenn hits a good combination of flirtatiousness and need as the ill-fated wife, and John Terry is quietly notable as the evenhanded foreman. Solid in more one-note performances are Siemaszko and Morton.

Returning to the screen after his failed first feature ("Miles From Home") and his stage success with "The Grapes of Wrath," Sinise demonstrates that he knows how to deliver the dramatic goods on film, even if his interpretation of the work is very straightforward. While not especially exciting, this adaptation still proves emotionally engaging and somewhat moving.

Action is underlined with subtle effectiveness by Mark Isham's fine score. — *Todd McCarthy*

HAY QUE ZURRAR A LOS POBRES
(LET'S TRASH THE POOR)
(SPANISH)

An Altair Producciones Filmograficas/ Moria Films production. Executive producers, Miguel Angel Perez Campos, Santiago San Miguel. Directed, written by San Miguel. Camera (color), Jose Luis Alcaine; editor, Luis Villar; production design, Isabel Dorante, Jaime Llorente; sound, Jose Antonio Arigita. Reviewed at Cannes Film Festival (Directors Fortnight), May 15, 1992. Running time: **90 MIN.**
With: Juan Ribo, Francisco Merino, Mireia Ros, Francisco Casares, Perla Vonasek, Sandra Toral, Mulie Jarju, Ana Leza, Juan Jesus Valverde, Agustin Gonzales.

The poor trashed in this modestly budgeted romp are hardly destitute, but perhaps they're impoverished in other ways. Writer/director Santiago San Miguel's pic is an uninhibited item set in a crowded boardinghouse, perhaps intended as a microcosm of contemporary Spain.

The place is managed by a bedridden, bad-tempered tyrant who expires early on. With his death, the discipline that bound the residents vanishes, and mayhem takes over. An artist hires a precocious young woman to pose nude for him (though his painting is simply of a seascape), and she starts the tenants' sexual juices flowing in a big way. Also involved is a Mauritanian determined to assert himself alongside the whites in the building.

San Miguel directs with plenty of energy in the restricted confines, but he basically has nothing much new to say about his "poor" people, and pic's denouement is quite predictable.

Fleetingly enjoyable pic is well acted and technically good, but it looks to have little impact outside Spanish-lingo territories.

—David Stratton

L'OEIL QUI MENT
(DARK AT NOON, OR EYES AND LIES)
(FRENCH-PORTUGUESE)

A Sideral (Paris)/Animatografo (Lisbon) co-production with Canal Plus. Produced by Leonardo de la Fuenta. Line producer, Antonio da Cunha Telles. Directed by Raul Ruiz. Screenplay, Ruiz, Paul Fontaine-Salas. Camera (color), Ramon Suarez; editor, Helene Weiss-Muller; music, Jorge Arriagada; production design, Luis Monteiro; special effects, Alain Le Roy. Reviewed at Cannes Film Festival (competition), May 15, 1992. Running time: **102 MIN.**
Anthony/the Marquis . . . . John Hurt
Felicien . . . . Didier Bourdon
Ines . . . . Lorraine Evanoff
Ellic . . . . David Warner
Priest . . . . Daniel Prevost
(In English)

Prolific Raul Ruiz comes up with one of his best and most accessible pics in "Dark at Noon," a funny, quirky period piece sumptuously produced on Portuguese locations. Mostly English soundtrack and John Hurt and David Warner's robust performances should help the pic find adventurous audiences in all markets.

In 1918, very correct Frenchman Felicien (Didier Bourdon) travels from Paris to a Portuguese village where his late father invested money in a factory. As he approaches the village, his coachman refuses to take him any further, and the landscape is littered with crutches.

Once in the village, he finds dogs eating corpses and the man he came to look for, Anthony (John Hurt), a seemingly normal character with a lovely fiancée (Lorraine Evanoff) with a dry wit. Also present is a strange artist (David Warner) and a priest (Daniel Prevost) who says he's fed up with miracles.

That's not surprising, because miracles seem to be taking place all the time. Visions of various Madonnas hover in the sky, and the "Finger of God" literally descends into Felicien's bedroom.

Pic contains some of the most peculiar sequences seen in quite awhile. There are references to Luis Buñuel, who liked to tweak the noses of the Church and the aristocracy, but Ruiz is his own auteur, and the lush, weird beauty of the film is all his own.

Camerawork, production design and special effects are all first class, and Jorge Arriagada's music score is rich and impressive. The actors seem completely at home with their bizarre characters and give beautifully modulated performances, even managing to keep straight faces during some of the director's more outrageous flights of fancy.

"Dark at Noon" won't be easy to market in territories where Ruiz's work is unknown, but this could be his breakthrough film because of its zany humor, imagination and visual brilliance. Further fest exposure would help spread the word.

—David Stratton

EL VIAJE
(THE JOURNEY)
(ARGENTINE-FRENCH)

A Cinesur (Argentina)/Les Films du Sud (France) co-production in association with Films A-2, Television Española, Sociadad Estatal Quinto Centenario, Channel 4, Imcine, Ministry of French Culture, with participation of Canal Plus, Antenne 2, Telemünchen, BIM Distribuzione, Herald Ace, Malo Films, Instituto Nacional de Cinematografica. Executive producers, Djamila Olivesi, Assuncao Hernandes, Luis Figueroa. Produced by Envar El Kadri. Directed, written by Fernando E. Solanas. Camera (color), Felix Monti; editors, Alberto Borello, Jacqueline Meppiel; music, Egberto Gismonti, Astor Piazzolia, Solanas; production design, Solanas; sound, Anibel Libenson; assistant director, Horacio Guisado. Reviewed at Cannes Film Festival (competition), May 11, 1992. Running time: **146 MIN.**
Martin . . . . Walter Quiroz
Vidala . . . . Soledad Alfaro
Celador Salas . . . . . Ricardo Bartis
Violeta . . . . Cristina Becerra
Helena . . . . Dominique Sanda
Nicolas . . . . Marc Berman
Paizinho . . . . . . Chiquinho Brandao
Tito the Hopegiver . . . Carlos Carella

Aptly titled "The Journey" is a marathon film covering almost as much territory as Wim Wenders' "Until the End of the World." Saga of a young Argentine's search for his father was hot in five Latin American countries, from snowy southern Argentina to tropical Mexico, but it's a long slog, and helmer Fernando Solanas doesn't maintain interest.

Pic opens in Ushuaia, world's southernmost city, where Martin (Walter Quiroz) lives with his mother (Dominique Sanda) and stepfather. He longs to see his father, last heard working as an anthropologist in Brazil. So Martin sets out, incongruously, on a bicycle on the long journey north.

Solanas, whose films ("Hour of the Furnaces," "South," "Tangos") have always been radical, uses the journey to underpin an overview of Latin America in the early '90s, and the uneven film contains sections of savage satire mixed with semi-docu segs on the plight of Indian peoples.

Director takes a pungent swipe at U.S. involvement in Latin America, with the visit of a George Bush lookalike who's greeted by his Latin hosts from a kneeling position. The president of a Latin country is called Rana ("frog") and dons flippers to address the public when floods ravage his capital city.

Solanas includes visually striking sequences, like a repeated shot of old buildings being razed. On the whole, however, this is a long trek indeed, and the director's concerns about ecology and aboriginal people could have been better expressed in a tighter format. Fine camerawork and lively music can't sustain the spotty satire and banal romanticism.

In territories where Solanas has a reputation, such as France, pic may perform modestly well, but without drastic pruning, it's unlikely to find favor elsewhere.

— David Stratton

LUNA PARK
(RUSSIAN-FRENCH)

A UGC release (in France) of an Ima Prods./Ciby 2000 (France)/L Prods. (Moscow) co-production in association with Canal Plus, Blues Films, CNC. Producer, Georges Benayoun. Line producers, Angelo Pastore, Vladimir Repnikov. Directed, written by Pavel Lounguine. Camera (color), Denis Evstigneev; editor, Lounguine; music, Isaac Schwartz; art direction, Pavel Kaplevitch; sets, Vladimir Pasternak. Reviewed at Cannes Film Festival (competition), May 8, 1992. Running time: **112 MIN.**
Andrei . . . . Andrei Goutine
Naoum Kheifitz . . . . . Oleg Borisov
Aliona . . . . Natalia Egorova
Also with: Nonna Mordioukova, Michael Goloubovich, Alexandre Feklistov, Tatiane Lebedkova, Alexandre Savin, Igor Zolotovitski, Rita Gladounko, Inge Ilm.

A neo-Nazi Russian skinhead discovers his father is an adorable old Jewish composer in "Luna Park," a film veering recklessly between surrealism, horror and black humor. Thanks to some spectacularly violent scenes and flashy lensing, this is one of the few Russian films that stands a chance of making it.

A large part of the $3 million budget was put together by French producer Georges Benayoun, and pic has been presold to major Euro territories. Its subject should fascinate Western art house auds, especially the ones who liked helmer Pavel Lounguine's debut, "Taxi Blues."

Even if its over-the-top narrative and technical pizzazz lack the power to penetrate very far beneath the surface, film uses raw energy to paint a memorable portrait of a disintegrating, lawless society, filmed just after the abortive coup last August.

A musclebound 20-year-old (Andrei Goutine) who admires Arnold Schwarzenegger leads a ferocious neo-fascist gang. "The Cleaners" aim to clean up Russia by eliminating impure elements — Jews, foreigners, homosexuals and anybody into Western lifestyles. In a shocking, fast-paced opener setting pic's futuristic/nightmare tone, Lounguine stages a murderous clash between skinheads and a Hells Angels-style gang. The guiding spirit behind the youth's gang is his incestuous mother (Natalia Egorova), a fleshy blonde ex-gymnast who has wound up singing in restaurants and selling tickets at Luna Park, a tawdry local fairgrounds. A completely evil character, the mother is shown in multiple guises, like a devil that changes shape. She nourishes a burning hatred for everything "non-Russian," which she delights in communicating to her son between caresses.

Trouble starts when Mama gets drunk and reveals that the youth's real father is not a dead war hero, but well-known Jewish composer Naoum Kheifitz (Oleg Borisov). After seducing her as a girl, he blackballed her for an important singing role, and, after 20 years of brooding, she wants his head.

Blinded by a raging identity crisis, the gang leader tracks Papa down to a genteel old Moscow apartment. Retired and ailing, he rents his once-elegant digs out to anybody willing to pay — from ladies' clubs to whores.

The head "Cleaner" periodically goes on rampages, but he barely makes a dent in the general chaos in the house. His father appears blissfully unaware of his fascist nature, shrugging off his anti-Semitic tirades and proudly introducing him around.

In the end, the doltish young Hercules succumbs to the old goat's charm. Switching sides, he runs afoul of mother and gang, but in a heroic finale, he saves his newfound father and they escape on a train.

Lounguine bridges the gap between a violent gang pic and a wacky absurdist comedy with

intuitive ease that keeps tension high. Pic is consistently amusing when not terrifying. Actual young fascists were recruited for the cast, and their obtuse conviction is evident. Unlike Goutine, a confused junior Terminator with enough heart to turn his life around, most of his nationalist comrades, sadly, seem unlikely to change their ways.

Egorova courageously takes on the lurid role of the evil mother with no redeeming virtues. Counterweight is provided by Borisov, a winning entertainer able to communicate instantly with audiences.

Denis Evstigneev's pro camerawork is full of bravura handheld work, which Lounguine edits to a nervous, contempo rhythm. Pavel Kaplevitch has fun with the decor; the composer's apartment and a bootlegger's sordid kitchen on their own provoke laughs. -- *Deborah Young*

COUSIN BOBBY
(U.S.-DOCU)

A Cinevista (U.S.) release of a Tesauro presentation. Produced by Edward Saxon. Directed by Jonathan Demme. Camera (color), Ernest Dickerson, Craig Haagensen, Tony Jannelli, Jacek Laskus, Declan Quinn; editor, David Greenwald; music, Anton Sanko; sound, Judy Karp, J.T. Takagi, Pam Yates; associate producers, Valerie Thomas, Lucas Platt. Reviewed at CNC screening room, Paris, April 24, 1992. (In Cannes Film Festival Un Certain Regard.) Running time: **70 MIN.**

"**C**ousin Bobby," a low-key, occasionally touching documentary, is essentially a home movie, but one with broad appeal. "The Silence of the Lambs" director Jonathan Demme looked up the Rev. Robert Castle, an older cousin whom he hadn't seen for over 30 years, and followed his crusading kin around at intervals spanning a year and a half.

A natural for public TV broadcast, this portrait of a confirmed activist who literally practices what he preaches should have a useful second life among grassroots organizers and in American studies resource libraries.

Spiritual leader at St. Mary's Episcopal Church in Harlem, N.Y., Rev. Castle, who is white, is clearly a respected and valuable presence in the predominantly African-American and Hispanic community he serves.

Bobby is seen at work in Harlem: demanding that a traffic

light be installed at a dangerous intersection, marshalling public support to keep local hospital facilities for childbirth open and campaigning for more drug rehab.

Utterly laid-back helmer Demme, heard in voiceovers and seen on camera in casual garb, interviews his cousin's parishioners and family and walks the city streets where Bobby grew up. Helmer comes across as curious about his cousin's life but, somewhat endearingly, has trouble keeping track of the family tree.

In the 1960s, as a young clergyman with a family, Bobby's encounter with a local Black Panther gave his work a controversial spin. The reverend's ex-wife jokes about how their children began to take it for granted that their dad was in jail somewhere in connection with his militant pro-civil rights stance.

Demme's father and Bobby, 60, are reunited on camera for the first time in decades. Bobby, a born orator, speaks movingly of the drowning death of one of his sons. Archival footage of race riots past is bound to strike a chord with viewers who witnessed recent violence in L.A.

Not every home movie has the likes of Ernest Dickerson behind the camera or so thoughtful a score of contemporary multi-cultural sounds. Despite these big-league touches, pic remains loosely structured and intimate, most noteworthy for its heart.

-- *Lisa Nesselson*

HYENES
(HYENAS)
(SWISS-FRENCH)

A Thelma Film (Zurich)/ADR Prods. (Paris) co-production in association with Maag Daan (Dakar), George Reinhart Prods., Television Suisse DRS (Zurich), Channel 4 (London), Filmcompany (Amsterdam). Produced by Pierre-Alain Meier, Alain Rozanes. Directed, written by Djibril Diop Mambety, based on Friedrich Durrenmatt's novel. Camera (color), Matthias Kalin; editor, Loredana Cristelli; music, Wasis Diop; costumes, Oumou Sy. Reviewed at Cannes Film Festival (competition), May 13, 1992. Running time: **110 MIN.**
Draman Drameh . . . . Mansour Diouf
Linguere Ramatou . . . Ami Diakhate
Mayor . . . . Mahouredia Gueye
Professor . . . . Issa Ramagelissa Samb
Mrs. Drameh . . . . Faly Gueye
Also with: Kaoru Egushi, Djibril Diop Mambety, Mbaba Diop, Omar Ba.

A poor African village is destroyed by greed in Djibril Diop Mambety's second feature, "Hyenas." European coin, which made the $1.8 million

pic possible, also kickstarts TV sales. Film's quality and uniqueness should take it into fests and some specialized playoffs.

Film adapts Friedrich Durrenmatt's famed "The Visit" to the Senegalese countryside with amazing naturalness, making this parable on hypocrisy and avarice seem like a reworked native myth. The strong story line, reinforced by fine ensemble acting, provide a much faster, more easily assimilated rhythm than many African pics.

Mambety intros the village of Colobane via Draman (Mansour Diouf), the chipper old grocer/barkeep, and Linguere Ramatou (superbly played by the proud and crusty Ami Diakhate), who returns and overturns the town's social fabric from inside out.

Abandoned by Draman when she was a pregnant 16-year-old so he could marry a richer girl, Linguere left the village and became a prostitute. Upon her return, the fabulously wealthy old lady promises the starving townsfolk she will donate a fortune to them all -- on the condition her former lover is executed.

At first horrified and indignant, villagers soon change their tune and begin buying on credit; first necessities, then luxuries. Mambety playfully jumps back and forth in time, using 19th century costumes and carriages in one shot; sunglasses and electric appliances in the next. Point is, this is a timeless story, ending sometime in the present, with the razing of the village and the construction of a modern city.

Diouf lends Draman the right measure of flawed humanity to make the old grocer a sympathetic hero, even though story's fable-like quality cuts down emotion. His initial self-interest and fear for his life turns to resignation and, finally, a noble disdain for fellow villagers willing to ignore their consciences and kill him for personal riches. The emphasis on consumer goods attacks the superfluity of their gain and gives the film a wider significance.

As Ramatou, Diakhate stresses the homicidal cynicism of a woman who has gone through the school of hard knocks and came out a cutthroat. Her artificial limbs and her train of bejeweled servants (including a smartly dressed Japanese policewoman/bodyguard) get a laugh.

Mambety lightens the tragic German tale with all kinds of humorous touches, handled as un-self-consciously as the sporadic appearance of hyenas and elephants on the screen.

Matthias Kalin's cinematography is high quality, capturing both village color and the golden African desert in sharp images. Wasis Diop's original score is various and interesting listening. — *Deborah Young*

INGALO
(ICELANDIC)

A Gjóla production, in association with Trans-Film-Filminor-Nordic Film & Television Fund. (Intl. sales: Seawell Films, Paris.) Produced by Martin Schlüter, Albert Kitzler. Directed, written by Ásdís Thoroddsen. Camera (color), Tahvo Hirvonen; editor, Valdís óskarsdóttir; music, Christoph Oertel; sound, Martin Steyer, Thorbjörn Á. Erlingsson; production design, Anna Th. Rögnvaldsdóttir; costume design, Geir óttarr. Reviewed at Cannes Film Festival (Critics Week), May 11, 1992. Running time: **100 MIN.**
Ingaló . . . . Sólveig Arnarsdóttir
Sveinn . . . . . Haraldur Hallgrímsson
Skúli . . . . Ingvar Sigurdsson
Vilhjálmur . . . Thorlákur Kristinsson

Slim but affecting, "Ingaló" reps an impressive feature debut by young Icelandic director Ásdís Thoroddsen. Moody, hard-edged portrait of smalltown Icelandic life and tensions recalls the earlier works of Brit Ken Loach in its mix of social realism and fiction. Fest dates and specialized tube sales look likely.

After a fight at a dance hall, fisherman's daughter Ingaló (Sólveig Arnarsdóttir) and younger brother Sveinn spend time in Reykjavik where she's been sent for a character assessment by the authorities. She has a one-night stand with a guy, and Sveinn finds work on a fishing boat, taking sister on as a cook.

When the boat docks after a poor catch, the crew are lodged in run-down quarters where Sveinn is humiliated by co-workers and Ingaló falls for luggish chief engineer Skúli. Things come to a head as Skúli leads a strike, and after some wild partying they set sail on a fateful voyage.

Thoroddsen, 33, a Berlin film school grad, draws a broad portrait of smalltown fishing life rather than a tightly focused study of the young girl. Pic is sometimes difficult to follow due to the lack of connecting sequences and diffuse cast, and pic tends to assume too much for non-locals.

Still, the general thrust is always clear, with the girl more spectator than prime mover and

shaker. As Ingaló, blonde Arnarsdóttir looks the part but doesn't give much of a clue as to what she's thinking beyond a general boredom.

Other roles are more clearly drawn but equally low-key. A sly strain of Nordic humor surfaces in several sequences, such as Arnarsdóttir mistaking a finger-dip for the soup course and a loony-tune islander who wanders around with a steering-wheel in his hands.

Visually, pic shows its 16m origins but is otherwise fine in all departments, particularly lensing of the bleakly beautiful Icelandic landscape. — *Derek Elley·*

LIEBE AUF DEN ERSTEN BLICK
(LOVE AT FIRST SIGHT)
(GERMAN)

A Futura Filmverlag release of a Moana Film production. (Intl. sales, Filmverlag der Autoren.) Directed, written by Rudolf Thome. Camera (color), Sophie Maintigneux; editor, Dörte Völz; music, Chico Hamilton; sound, Gunther Kortwich; sets, Jan-Christian Stoehr; art direction, Martina Faust. Reviewed at Cannes Film Festival (Director's Fortnight), May 16, 1992. Running time: **103 MIN.**
Elsa Süsseisen . . . . . Geno Lechner
Zenon Bloch . . . . . . Julian Benedikt
Also with: Margarita Broich, Kyana Kretzschmar, Nicolai Wolf Thome, Joya Thome, Sophie Grüber.

Audiences aren't going to love this slow mover at first sight, and they'll like it even less as it drags on. "Love at First Sight" is likely to remain out of sight.

It's hard to think of a film with less on-screen chemistry between the leads than this one. When West Berliner Elsa comes on to Zenon in a playground, where the two single parents have taken their children, auds will wonder why she even struck up a conversation with the nondescript nobody. Even more baffling is why they even bother to stay in touch after their first, nearly wordless date over coffee.

Thome's script does its best to emphasize the differences between the couple in a heavy-handed way: She's a West German and he's from the East; she's a futurologist and he's an archaeologist. Little transpires between the two even after they've decided they're in love.

Much of the pic is dedicated to

tedious real-time portrayals of the two caring for their collective brood of three little kids. They scarcely kiss or even touch, outside of the requisite bedroom scene, which bad dialogue turns into a real wincer.

Script has almost no conflict, nor does it provide any reason for the viewer to have any more interest in the lackluster duo than they seem to have for each other. Tech credits are fine, but pic's look is uninspired. Score sounds unoriginal, jarring and inappropriate. — *Rebecca Lieb*

BRAINDEAD
(NEW ZEALAND)

A WingNut Films production in association with the N.Z. Film Commission & Avalon/NFU Studios. (Intl. Sales: Perfect Features, London.) Produced by Jim Booth. Directed by Peter Jackson. Screenplay, Jackson, Stephen Sinclair, Frances Walsh. Camera (color), Murray Milne; editor, Jamie Selkirk; music, Peter Dasent; production design, Kenneth Leonard-Jones; sound, Mike Hedges, Sam Negri; creature-gore effects, Richard Taylor; prosthetics design, Bob McCarron; associate producer, Selkirk; assistant director, Chris Short; casting, Frances Walsh. Reviewed at Cannes Film Festival market, May 13, 1992. Running time: **101 MIN.**
Lionel . . . . Timothy Balme
Paquita . . . . Diana Penalver
Mum . . . . Elizabeth Moody
Uncle Les . . . . Ian Watkin
Nurse McTavish . . . . Brenda Kendall
Father McGruder . . . Stuart Devenie
Void . . . . Jed Brophy
Zombie Mum . Elizabeth Brimilcombe
Zombie McGruder . . . Stuart Devenie
Scroat . . . . Murray Keane
Mrs. Matheson . . . . Glenis Levestam
Mr. Matheson . . . . . . Lewis Rowe
Rita . . . . Elizabeth Mullane
Grandmother . . . Davina Whitehouse

This is one of the bloodiest horror comedies ever made, and that will be enough to ensure cult success in cinemas and especially on video. Kiwi gore specialist Peter Jackson goes for broke with an orgy of bad taste and splatter humor. Some will recoil, but "Braindead" wasn't made for them.

Set in 1957, the standard zombie plot is played for laughs with a nerdy hero (Timothy Balme) whose domineering Mum (Elizabeth Moody) is bitten by a rare carnivorous monkey while spying on her son and his Spanish g.f. (Diana Penalver) at the Wellington Zoo.

Mum goes rabid fast and attacks a nurse, who also becomes a zombie. The poor son locks the creatures in the cellar and tries to pacify them with liberal doses of a tranquilizer administered

via a giant hypo.

But at Mum's funeral, the body runs amok and the minister becomes another zombie. He couples with the nurse, instantly resulting in a zombie baby. The plague continues as hero's house fills up with rampaging monsters until an incredibly bloody climax in which Balme attacks the creatures with a lawnmower.

Dismemberment, disemboweling, beheading and the like are all handled with bloody conviction and great good humor. Comic highlights include Balme trying to pacify the zombie baby in a public park (horrified moms look on as he beats the creature into submission), and Balme literally re-entering his mother's womb in the gore-spattered end.

Technically, this is Jackson's best pic to date, with state-of-the-art creature and gore effects by Richard Taylor and prosthetics design by Bob McCarron. Pic's perhaps a shade too long, but the aficionados won't mind.

Performances hit just the right notes, with lanky Balme very funny as the hero, and Panalver lovely as his determined g.f. Helmer turns up in a cameo as an undertaker's assistant, while producer Jim Booth is seen in a bedside photo of the hero's long-dead dad. —*David Stratton*

ISIMERIA
(EQUINOX)
(GREEK)

A Nikos Cornilios/Greek Film Center/ Greek Television RT1/Trois Lumieres Prods./Antea/Eurimages production. Directed, written by Cornilios. Camera (color), Andreas Sinanos; editor, Takis Yannopoulos; music, Cornilios; sets, Antonis Daglidis; costumes, Ariadne Papatheotanous; sound, Marinos Athanassopoulos. Reviewed at Thessaloniki Film Festival, Oct. 3, 1991. (In Cannes Film Festival market.) Running time: **105 MIN.**
French archaeologist . . Andre Wilms
Assistant . . . . . . Antigone Amanitou
Teacher . . . . Vassilis Daimantopoulos
Daughter . . . . Vicky Vollioti
Journalist . . . . Vanni Corbellini
Astronomer . . . . Nikitas Tsakiroglou
Bartender . . . . . Giorgios Ninios
Trumpet player . . . . . Arto Apartian
(In Greek and French)

"Equinox," an ambitious bow for composer and theatrical director Nikos Cornilios, is a stunningly lensed psychological drama with a top cast.

Summer night setting bears intriguing traces of Shakespeare and classical Greek drama, but the various elements don't always mesh. Some auds might not have patience for pic's minimalist style. Most likely crossover market will be France.

A neurotic French archaeologist (Andre Wilms) and his Greek assistant (Antigone Amanitou) work on a dig on a Greek island. The archaeologist's daughter (Vicky Vollioti) arrives and soon gets involved with a Machiavellian Italo journalist (Vanni Corbellini), later suspected of antiquities smuggling. Always lurking in the shadows is the dying philosopher (Vassilis Diamantopoulos) whose poetic recitations of "Agamemnon," often in the ancient theater, provide a solo equivalent of a Greek chorus.

Pacing is uneven, with a flurry of action and agitated conversation followed by long sequences with almost no dialog. Lack of necessary buildup for some scenes disrupts continuity.

Cast femmes are most sympathetic, with established thesp Amanitou distinguishing her part as the assistant. Vollioti, a fresh young newcomer with a compelling screen presence, is a real find. Giorgios Ninios, in a cameo as a sexy bartender who takes the daughter on a motorcycle ride she'll never forget, has one of the most viable screen presences among Greek actors.

Flawless photography of the rugged island terrain is by accomplished Greek lenser Andreas Sinanos. — *B. Samantha Stenzel*

EL PATRULLERO
(HIGHWAY PATROLMAN)
(MEXICAN)

A Cable Hogue-Marubeni presentation of a Together Bros.-Ultra Films production. (Intl. sales: Overseas Film Group.) Executive producers, Sammy Masada, Kuniaki Negishi. Produced by Lorenzo O'Brien. Co-producer, Jean Michel Lacor. Directed by Alex Cox. Screenplay, O'Brien. Camera (color), Miguel Garzon; editor, Carlos Puente; music, Zander Schloss; production design, Cecilia Montiel; casting, Miguel Sandoval, Claudia Becker. Reviewed at Cannes Film Festival market, May 11, 1992. Running time: **91 MIN.**
Pedro Rojas . . . . Robert Sosa
Anibal . . . . Bruno Bichir
Maribel . . . . Vanessa Bauche
Griselda . . . . . Zaide Silvia Gutierrez
Also with: Pedro Armendariz Jr., Jorge Russek, Ernesto Gomez Cruz, Eduardo Lopez Rojas.

British director Alex Cox crops up in Mexico with this gritty pic about the problems faced by a naive young highway patrolman. Lacking action scenes that would give it appeal in urban situations and on

video, but not quite right for the art house circuit, the film will have to find its niche elsewhere. Latin territories are the best bet.

Cox and screenwriter Lorenzo O'Brien (also producer) present a bleak vision of everyday pressures and corruption ensnaring basically honest cops.

Pedro Rojas (Roberto Sosa) graduates from a national police academy and is assigned to patrol sparsely populated territory (Matimi, in Durango) where drug-running is rife. All too soon he woos and weds a local girl, who, once married and pregnant, starts complaining Pedro's wages are too low. For awhile, Pedro drowns his sorrows during off-duty hours with beer and tequila, and then takes up with a pretty hooker addicted to coke.

He starts taking the bribes he originally rejected and gets caught in a downward spiral. When his best friend is killed by drug-runners, Pedro decides to take revenge.

Pic isn't so much an action film as a serious exploration of a social problem. It's handled with some flair and consistently inventive camerawork by Miguel Garzon, but stronger plotting could have given the pic more of a chance on the world market.
— *David Stratton*

PEN PALS
(U.S.-JAPANESE)

A Cinemabeam presentation of an Affinity Films/Orenda Films production. (Intl. sales: Ucore, Paris.) Produced by Lisa Bruce, Robert Nickson. Directed, written by Mary Rosanne Katzke. Camera (Agfacolor), Edmund Talavera; editor, Mark Juergens; music, Michael Bacon; production design, Susan Bolles; art direction, Stacey Jones; costume design, Clyde Ray Brual; sound, Felix Andrew; assistant director, Risa Koren; casting, Marcia Shulman. Reviewed at Cannes Film Festival market, May 9, 1992. Running time: **86 MIN.**
Stanley . . . . Richard Lemerise
Helen . . . . Barbara Summerville
Fantasy Olivia . . . . . Cheryl Foster
Olivia . . . . Laurel Thornby

New York University film alum Mary Katzke makes a smooth bow with "Pen Pals," a high-sheen low-budgeter about a Big Apple exec with a 24-year itch. Shaggy-dog story sometimes feels like a half-hour short stretched to feature length but could pull in a few friends in undemanding markets before crossing over to the tube.

Stanley (Richard Lemerise) is

a wealthy, middle-aged exec with a snazzy limo and a marriage in which "nothing's happening." In a bid for some vicarious excitement, he turns to the lonely hearts columns, eventually hitting paydirt with the sultry "Olivia." The catch is that she'll only correspond with him: One after another liaison is canceled, and Stanley's erotic fantasies about his dream woman become wilder with each letter. In desperation he hires a p.i. to track her down.

Pic's first half-hour, with the exec's cage gradually being rattled by the femme's passionate missives, promises more than is ever delivered, especially when it becomes clear Olivia isn't going to make her entrance until the final reel. Still, Katzke stokes up the temperature with witty, soft-core fantasy sequences and gets considerable mileage out of the florid written exchanges, heard in voiceovers. Final payoff, mildly preachy on male-female relationships, could be sharper.

Cast of unknowns acquit themselves well, with Lemerise keeping his Walter Mitty character the right side of frantic. Tech credits are all tops, with standout lensing (especially in the fantasy segs), smooth cutting and resourceful use of N.Y. locations.

Pic, made in association with NYU's graduate film program, was entirely financed by Japan's Cinemabeam, a consortium led by Tokuma Japan Communications devoted to first features worldwide. —*Derek Elley*

EIGHT BALL
(AUSTRALIAN)

A Meridian Films production in association with Australian Broadcasting Corp. & Australian Film Finance Corp. (Intl. sales: Kim Lewis Marketing.) Executive producers, Jill Robb, Bryce Menzies. Produced by Timothy White. Directed by Ray Argall. Screenplay, Argall, Harry Kirchner. Camera (color), Mandy Walker; editor, Ken Sallows; music, Philip Judd; production design, Kerith Holmes; sound, Ian Cregan; assistant director, Evan Keddie; associate producer, Denise Patience; casting, Diana Mann, Alison Barrett. Reviewed at Cannes Film Festival market, May 8, 1992. Running time: **87 MIN.**
Charlie . . . . Matthew Fargher
Russell Porter . . . . Paul Stevn
Jacqui Porter . . . . . . Lucy Sheehan
Julie . . . . Angie Milliken
Douggie Porter . . . . Matthew Krok
Mal . . . . Frankie J. Holden
Eric Biggs . . . . Ollie Hall

"Eight Ball" is a disappointing, soft-centered follow-up to former cinematographer

Ray Argall's outstanding first feature, "Return Home." A tale of friendship between two men of dissimiliar backgrounds, pic suffers from a very thin screenplay and lethargic pacing. It may play better on the small screen, but it looks like a dubious bet for cinema release.

Matthew Fargher plays a Melbourne designer whose g.f. (Angie Milliken) is a TV news reporter promoted to a job in Canberra. He's uncertain whether to join her there or risk the end of a happy relationship. He and his colleague (Frankie J. Holden) are working on the design of a giant fish to be built at a tourist site in the Victorian hinterland.

An ex-con (Paul Stevn) jailed for car theft is trying to get close to his feisty 8-year-old son (Matthew Krok) who was living with his aunt (Lucy Sheehan) while Dad was in the clink. Unable to find work in the city, the ex-con gets a job on the designer's troubled fish project, and the two men spark up a tentative friendship.

Trouble is, little happens in the film, and dialogue is nowhere near sharp enough to offset the lack of narrative. Nor are the principal actors able to flesh out their admittedly thin roles, although young Krok steals every moment he's on screen.

Visually, pic is expectedly attractive, but not overly so. A major rewrite could have boosted the vapid level of dialogue. In his first film, Argall proved adept at catching nuances of relationships, but here he seems way out of his depth. — *David Stratton*

COUPABLE D'INNOCENCE
(GUILTY OF INNOCENCE)
(FRENCH-POLISH)

An Atria Films/La Sept Cinema (Paris)/MS Film Prods./Telewizja Polska (Warsaw) co-production with participation of Canal Plus, CNC & Ministry of Foreign Affairs. (Intl. sales: Mercure Films.) Produced by Michael Szczerbic, Claire Davanture. Directed by Marcin Ziebinski. Screenplay, Andrzej Rychcik. Camera (color), Dariusz Kuc; editor, Grazyna Jasinska-Wisniarowska; music, Jean-Claude Petit; set design, Ewa Braun, Marek Burgemajster, Grzegorz Piatkowski; sound, Yves Osmu. Reviewed at Club de l'Etoile, Paris, April 29, 1992. (In Cannes Film Festival, Cinemas En France.) Running time: **110 MIN.**
With: Jonathan Zaccai, Philippine Leroy-Beaulieu, Ute Lemper, Wojtek Pszoniak, André Wilms, Janusz Gajos, Jan Peszek.

Twenty-five-year-old director Marcin Ziebinski's "Coupable d'Innocence" is very accomplished for a feature debut. Lushly appointed period drama about a young craftsman cruelly manipulated by decadent aristocrats is bound to be compared to Peter Greenaway's "The Draughtsman's Contract." Helmer breaks no new ground but will be noticed for his aggressive visual style applied to an ambitious, intricate tale.

In 1791, inventor Alexandre Plant invites Max Bardo, a Viennese master clockmaker just 18 years old, to repair the clocks at his chateau. When the youth arrives, he learns that his host has died suddenly. Conniving aristocrats of both sexes are on hand to lay claim to Plant's estate, which may or may not include his secret plans for a highly coveted machine. Bardo stays on to fix clocks and soon finds himself in a duel against a prime contender for the inheritance.

Although Bardo deliberately aims well away from his target, the gent ends up dead from a bullet smack in the throat. Bardo and most of the guests know he's innocent, but the dead man's fiancée summons a slimy associate to orchestrate revenge. More deaths and machinations occur before the authorities step in.

Jonathan Zaccai, as Bardo, has a winning smile and boyish charm. He is convincing as a pawn in an elaborate game whose unspoken rules escape him. The performances of Philippine Leroy-Beaulieu and Ute Lemper seem a little too contemporary, but the men in the cast seem to embody the European upperclass of two centuries ago.

Staging, lighting and camerawork are thoughtful throughout, but pic's pace slows a bit in the middle and the intrigue is dragged out a touch too long. If Ziebinski can also apply his talents to contemporary stories, he may become a familiar name on the European film scene.

— *Lisa Nesselson*

EQUINOX

A Nicolas Stiliadis & Syd Cappe presentation for SC Entertainment Intl. of a David Blocker production. Produced by Blocker. Executive producers, Stiliadis, Cappe, Sandy Stern. Directed, written by Alan Rudolph. Camera (Alpha Cine color), Elliot Davis; editor, Michael Ruscio; production design, Steven Leg-ler; art direction, Randy Eriksen; set decoration, Cliff Cunningham; costume design, Sharen Davis; sound (Dolby), Susumu Tokunow; associate producers, Claude Castravelli, William Fay, Michael Scording, Gary Whalen; assistant director, Dwight Williams; casting, Pam Dixon. Reviewed at Cannes Film Festival market, May 12, 1992. Running time: **115 MIN.**
Henry/Freddy . . . . Matthew Modine
Beverly . . . . Lara Flynn Boyle
Sonya Kirk . . . . Tyra Ferrell
Rosie . . . . Marisa Tomei
Richie Nudd . . . . Tate Donovan
Russell Frankel . . . Kevin J. O'Connor
Sharon Ace . . . . Lori Singer
Dandridge . . . . Gailard Sartain
Pete Petosa . . . . . . M. Emmet Walsh
Paris . . . . Fred Ward

"Equinox" is one of Alan Rudolph's patently personal ensemble pieces about criss-crossing destinies. More deeply mysterious than many of his pics, and more socially minded in its depiction of a decaying society some of the characters yearn to escape, film is full of ideas and evocative scenes. But its low-key, subtle aesthetic and plot line that deliberately takes most of the running time to reveal itself will keep b.o. potential modest.

Matthew Modine toplines in a double role. Henry is an awkward, nerdy chap who remarks, "My whole life seems to be taking place without me in it," while being induced to reignite a tentative romance with the lovely, painfully shy Beverly (Lara Flynn Boyle).

Modine also appears as Freddy, a swaggering smalltime hood who is married to Sharon (Lori Singer) and works his way up in a gang controlled by Paris (Fred Ward).

At least the first half of the film is taken up with Rudolph laying down lots of dots but not connecting any of them: A homeless woman dies, leaving a mysterious envelope found by a morgue worker and aspiring writer (Tyra Ferrell). Mobsters unpleasantly move in on an Italian family restaurant, which serves as one of Rudolph's trademark public places where his characters can ultimately converge, and an unignorable number of street people crowd around the fringes of the action, creating a backdrop of urban malaise that places everyone's personal struggles into relief.

So impressionistic and intentionally obsfucating is Rudolph's technique that it remains unclear for a long time whether one of Modine's characters is supposed to be a dream, a fictional creation of the other, an alter ego, a twin or something else.

For some, this will make the story all the more intriguing, but most audiences will no doubt feel unduly teased or frustrated that it takes so long to get a handle on the story.

But for those with a taste for the director's methods, "Equinox" is full of lovely scenes and many artistic and emotional pleasures. Using his characteristically soft but colorful palette, Rudolph, with lenser Elliot Davis, creates a warmly textured interior world that provides a buffer to the harsh realities of the streets (pic was shot on seldom-seen Minneapolis locations), and sketches in a charmingly eccentric group of characters.

At the film's heart is a touching little-people romance between Henry and Beverly. Few opportunities have entered the lives of these apartment dwellers, and the difficult time they have breaking through their mutual reticence and fear of love allows Rudolph to strongly broach the theme of seizing any chances for happiness in life that come along.

Modine and Boyle, both very attractive performers, are effectively dressed down for these roles, and Boyle, in particular, strongly registers the effort it takes for such a thin-skinned character to leap off the deep end into the emotional whirlpool.

Although her part is very tenuously connected to the other action, Ferrell shines as a bright, ambitious young woman pursuing the mystery of the Modine characters' legacy, and Ward has fun as a gangster who likes to have a naked woman in proximity whenever possible. Every performance in the attractive ensemble is injected with life and a dash of extra spice, a tribute to Rudolph's way with actors.

After building up to a tense, entrancing climax which has Modine's two characters finally meeting in a scene capped with a surprising spasm of violence, pic concludes on an open, genuinely puzzling note that offers no sense of closure. Title's meaning becomes clear enough, but import of the ending remains elusive.

Shot on modest means, pic is loaded with old tunes that amplify that emotional resonance of the characters' relationships. All behind-the-scenes craftspeople have helped create a richly appealing look. — *Todd McCarthy*

MAC

A Tenenbaum/Goodman presentation of a Macfilms production (Intl. sales: World Films). Produced by Nancy Tenenbaum, Brenda Goodman. Directed by John Turturro. Screenplay, Turturro, Brandon Cole. Camera (Technicolor), Ron Fortunato; editor, Michael Berenbaum; music, Richard Termini, Vin Tese; production design, Robin Standefer; art direction, John Magoun; costume design, Donna Zakowska; sound (Dolby), Billy Sarokin; casting, Todd Thaler. Reviewed at Cannes Film Festival (Directors' Fortnight), May 17, 1992. Running time: **117 MIN.**
Niccolo (Mac) Vitelli . . John Turturro
Vico Vitelli . . . . . Michael Badalucco
Bruno Vitelli . . . . . . Carl Capotorto
Alice Vitelli . . . . Katherine Borowitz
Oona . . . . Ellen Barkin
Nat . . . . John Amos
Gus . . . . Steven Randazzo

John Turturro's intense, offbeat personality as an actor comes through equally clearly in his directorial debut, "Mac." A tribute to the notion of craftsmen loving their work, as well as an expression of quirky humor among three Italian-American brothers, pic is appealing in an idiosyncratic way and has some limited potential on the fest and specialized theatrical circuits.

Dedicated to Turturro's father, and inspired by his career as a carpenter, film is fired by the urge to get ahead in suburban America of the 1950s, pride in building something of value, and irrepressible ethnic emotionalism, blood ties and mirth. Structuring and storytelling has its ragged, unmodulated side, and pic is at its best in specific individual scenes that burst with fresh, unexpected attitudes and dialogue.

Story is centered on the title character, the oldest of three brothers who live in Queens. In the wake of their father's death, the temperamental Mac leaves his construction job to start his own business, determined that he can build better houses and run a crew better than his cheap Polish boss.

Various obstacles present themselves: The Pole deliberately bids on property Mac wants in order to drive the price way up, workers leave random items buried in drying foundation cement, the former cattle pasture upon which Mac builds his houses leaves a residue smell of manure. And a final fracture in the tight-knit clan concludes matters on a surprisingly downbeat note.

But several scenes exude a vitality and original outlook that bespeak of unmistakable raw talent and a genuine feeling for working class individuals. In its eccentric character humor and passionate eruptions of emotion, "Mac" follows in the vein of American cinema arguably started by John Cassavetes and taken up, most prominently, by Martin Scorsese.

Michael Badalucco, who plays the hefty middle brother, does a wonderful riff on the relative importance of a man's magnetism and physical weight where women are concerned, and who ever thought they'd see Ellen Barkin, playing a suburban beatnik lying naked on a bed covered by what look to be hundreds of pieces of Wonder bread.

Performances are sharp, led by Turturro's own as the headstrong leader of the clan. Badalucco and Carl Capotorto are both distinctive and entirely complimentary as the brothers, and Katherine Borowitz, as Turturro's wife, and Barkin are vibrant as the main women on hand.

Pic is shot in an entirely modern, low-budget manner, with no stylistic concessions being made for the mid-1950s setting. Even if Turturro isn't yet a smooth storyteller or master of technique, his grit and ability to evoke the complexity of family relationships bode well for future outings.

— *Todd McCarthy*

FROZEN ASSETS

A Frozen Assets Prods. production. Produced by Don Klein. Associate producers, Lee Imperial, Howard Lam. Directed by George Miller. Screenplay, Klein, Tom Kartozian. Camera (Eastmancolor), Ron Latoure, Geza Sinkovics; editor, Larry Bock; music, Michael Tavera; production design, Dorian Vernacchio, Deborah Raymond; costumes, Sandi Culotta; sound, Reinhard Sterger; assistant director, George Parra; casting, Meryl O'Loughlin. Reviewed at Cannes Film Festival market, May 9, 1992. Running time: **93 MIN.**
With: Shelley Long, Corbin Bernsen, Larry Miller, Dody Goodman, Matt Clark, Gloria Comden, Gerrit Graham, Jeanne Cooper, Paul Sand.

A thin comedy about a corporate exec who mistakenly thinks he's been offered the presidency of a small-town bank only to discover it's a sperm bank, "Frozen Assets" is yet another waste of the talents of Shelley Long, but she's the film's one real asset. Theatrical release. if any. should be

brief.

Corbin Bernsen limns the exec who winds up in Hobart, Ore., appalled to discover he's in charge of sperm not dollars. Determined to make a successful commercial venture, he dreams up a stud-of-the-year contest, the winner to receive $100,000 for the quality of his sperm count.

Along the way, Bernsen finds time to romance Long, the M.D. who previously ran the sperm bank, and to befriend an eccentric millionaire (Larry Miller).

Starting from a very thin premise, screenplay by Tom Kartozian and producer Don Klein, needed a lot more work before the cameras turned. Aussie director George Miller ("Man From Snowy River," not "Mad Max") tries to beef things up by encouraging the actors to play to the hilt. It only makes things worse.

Technically adequate pic may have a life on video, if well packaged. — *David Stratton*

EUX
(THEM)
(GEORGIAN)

A Banque Atlanta production (Tbilisi). Directed by Levan Zakaretchvili. Screenplay, Zakaretchvili, Ghia Badridze. Camera (color), Oleg Bachnine; editor, Lali Kolkhidachvili; music, Tamaz Kourachvili; art direction, Tamara Potskhichvili, Ghia Laperadze. Reviewed at Cannes Film Festival (Directors Fortnight), May 10, 1992. Running time: **160 MIN.**
With: Zaza Kolelichvili, Mindia Lordkipanidze, Keti Pantskhava, Matliouba Alimova, Beka Djgoubouria.

Recent political upheavals in Georgia blocked the shooting of Levan Zakaretchvili's fine (but overlong) "Them." The total honesty of approach toward a young loafer who turns to crime against his will may be one reason it so upset the authorities. The 160-minute epic could have strong art house appeal if it were significantly shortened by a pro editing job.

In his first theatrical, Zakaretchvili takes more than an hour of screen time to establish young Ghia's basic innocence before the film gets going. As a 20-year-old in the Leonid Brezhnev years, Ghia hangs out with his buddies, Tbilisi "vitelloni" who pass the long, hot summer smoking grass, going to the river, hunting down seaside relatives. Somewhere in the middle, without particular

emphasis, they bust in on some mean pushers and swipe some dope for quick resale.

"To be born only once, and in the land of the Soviets!" muses one of the bored boys in disgust. To do something new, Ghia and pal drive outside Georgia and shoot heroin. The friend goes into convulsions and dies on the spot. That gets the pic started.

When he needs to, Zakaretchvili can be dramatically concise. Next scene shows Ghia doing time in an icy gulag. He gets beaten up by the pushers he robbed, and in a moment of rage stabs one to death. On to Siberia.

Next gulag is so bad, pic switches actors, abandoning the wholesome-looking young Ghia for a scar-faced man with haunted eyes. He saves an Uzbek convict's life, making a friend. He learns his mother has died, and tries to commit suicide. Finally he gets out.

Third part of "Them" is the most interesting for Western auds, showing Ghia's life in Tashkent, Uzbekistan. He has fallen in with a drug ring run by his Uzbek pal, a potent local crime lord, and starts living with a sad-eyed prostitute.

Oleg Bachnine's camerawork is a treat, concentrating on bringing out a few essentials in each shot. Willfully depressing soundtrack quotes old Western hits and Uzbek tunes, almost always blaring from a scratchy radio. Cast is finely directed, and the two thesps who play the hero are faces to remember.

— *Deborah Young*

ROMPER STOMPER
(AUSTRALIAN)

A Seon Films production, in association with the Australian Film Commission, Film Victoria. Produced by Daniel Scharf, Ian Pringle. Directed, written by Geoffrey Wright. Camera (Eastmancolor), Ron Hagen; editor, Bill Murphy; music, John Clifford White; producton design, Steven Jones-Evans; sound, Frank Lipson; costumes, Anna Borghesi; assistant director, Chris Odgers; associate producer, Phil Jones. Reviewed at Cannes Film Festival market, May 8, 1992. Running time: **92 MIN.**
Hando . . . . Russell Crowe
Davey . . . . Daniel Pollock
Gabe . . . . . . Jacqueline McKenzie
Martin . . . . Alex Scott
Sonny Jim . . . . Leigh Russell
Also with: Daniel Wyllie, James McKenna, Eric Mueck, Frank Magree, Christopher McLean.

"Romper Stomper" is "A Clockwork Orange" without the intellect. In many ways genu-

inely appalling, pic centers on a gang of moronic neo-Nazi skinheads who regularly do battle with Melbourne's Vietnamese community. It may well make a lot of money, especially in video.

Writer-director Geoffrey Wright opts simply to depict young monsters without actually condemning them, and because the audience is given no positive characters to root for, misgivings about pic's effect on impressionable audiences seem justified. Possible ensuing controversy may abet commercial success.

Russell Crowe ("Proof") gives a powerful performance as skinhead leader Hando, a brute with a veneer of charm whose bible is "Mein Kampf." The late Daniel Pollock is also impressive as Davey, his friend and lieutenant, portrayed as being marginally more sensitive (and of German extraction). The rest of the headshaven, tattooed gang go along with their leaders. One of them (James McKenna) is only a boy.

Gang is joined by Gabe (Jacqueline McKenzie), a spaced-out drug addict whose father (Alex Scott) has abused her in an incestuous relationship. She becomes Hando's girl for a short time, though their lovemaking is functional rather than passionate.

When the gang attacks Vietnamese in the process of purchasing the skinheads' favorite bar, the "gooks" (as they're called) counterattack with a large force, driving the skinheads from their warehouse base. This long, brutally violent battle sequence, accompanied by rousing punk music, is staged in such a way that significant numbers of unthinking white viewers may identify with the nauseating Nazis. It's sadly typical of the film's rascist attitude.

Gabe leaves Hando for Davey (cue for a sex scene of almost "Basic Instinct" intensity) and betrays the gang to the law. Climax on a windswept beach asks the audience to choose between a bad Nazi and a less bad Nazi —not much of a choice. A final point about Asians in Australia (Japanese tourists taking photos of the skinheads on the beach) badly misfires, and once again smacks of racism.

Art house patrons are likely to be turned off by the brutally depicted violence and dominant antisocial behavior. Young urban audiences may be turned on by it all, but the underlying message is truly frightening.

Pic is well acted and directed

with a certain slickness, but rarely has there been such a disturbing, essentially misconceived pic.
— *David Stratton*

LA SENTINELLE
(THE SENTINEL)
(FRENCH)

A Pan Européenne release of a Why Not Prods./2001 Audiovisuel/La Sept Cinema/Films A2 production. (Intl. sales: Odyssey Distributors.) Produced, directed, written by Arnaud Desplechin. Camera (color), Caroline Champetier; editor, François Gedigier; music, Marc Sommer; production design, Antoine Platteau; sound, Laurent Poirier. Reviewed at Cannes Film Festival (competition), May 13, 1992. Running time: **145 MIN.**
With: Emmanuel Salinger, Thibault de Montalembert, Jean-Louis Richard, Valerie Dreville, Marianne Denicourt, Jean-Luc Boutte, Bruno Todeschini, Philippe Duclos, Fabrice Desplechin, Emmanuelle Devos, Philippe Laudenbach.

Way too long and needlessly obscure, this first feature has an interesting idea and occasional flashes of originality, but audiences are likely to be more frustrated than intrigued. "The Sentinel" is a non-event.

Writer-director Arnaud Desplechin takes nearly 2½ hours to tell a story that could easily have unfolded in 90 minutes, frittering away any suspense the basically intriguing yarn might have contained.

A French diplomat's son (Emmanuel Salinger) decides to leave Germany by train to continue his medical studies in Paris. At the border, he's treated like a criminal by a plainclothes official, and when he gets to Paris, he finds a mummified head in his baggage and figures the customs man must have put it there.

At first repelled then intrigued, the medical student opts not to report the head and sets about dissecting and analyzing it, eventually coming up with a theory involving a Russian who met his fate in Asia.

Meanwhile, the French youth starts to romance a young art student and hangs out with friends and his sister. "Get to the point," one of the characters tells him, and that's something the filmmaker never seems to do. Pic moves in fits and starts, with long scenes eventually proving to be marginally important to the narrative.

With all its post-Cold War concerns, pic remains a mystery, and sterile, obscure and profoundly dull. — *David Stratton*

THE NAKED TARGET
(SPANISH)

A Jose Frade production. (Intl. sales: Overseas Filmgroup.) Produced by Frade. Directed by Javier Elorrieta. Screenplay, Santiago Moncada. Camera (Eastmancolor), Angel Luis Fernandez; editor, Jose Rojo; music, Udi Haspar; production design, Tony Cortes; sound, Gilles Ortion; assistant director, Richard Walker; casting, Nina Axelrod. Reviewed at Cannes Film Festival market, May 9, 1992. Running time: **97 MIN.**
Adam Kent . . . . . . Clayton Rohner
Maria . . . . Cristina Piaget
Ernest Peabody . . . Roddy McDowall
Mechanical Man . . . Anthony Perkins
Brigadier . . Jose Luis Lopez Vasquez
Reverend . . . . Aramis Ney
(English & Spanish soundtrack; English subtitles)

Wildly improbable as it is, this fast-paced comedy-thriller is surprisingly enjoyable. "The Naked Target" certainly should have a life in video.

The Hitchcockian plot begins with a mild-mannered, bespectacled New York exec, Adam Kent (Clayton Rohner) assigned by his boss to take a valuable briefcase, to which he's handcuffed, to Madrid. His contact there, he's told, will have the key, but if anyone else tries to detach the case, it will explode.

When the contact at Madrid Airport is gunned down by Arabs, the chase is on. The bewildered courier is befriended by the U.S. Embassy's urbane Peabody (Roddy McDowall) and lissome Maria (Cristina Piaget), who hides him in her apartment.

When the Arabs attack again, they catch him, literally, without his clothes on. For a long section of the pic, the unfortunate Adam, still attached to the pesky case, is running all over Madrid stark naked. He even winds up in the apartment of a gung-ho army officer (very amusingly played by top Spanish thesp Jose Luis Lopez Vasquez), who suspects his wife has a lover.

Later on, dressed as a prostitute, Adam meets the Mechanical Man, surely the weirdest role in Anthony Perkins' career thus far. He plays a one-eyed, one-armed motorist who boasts of all the crashes he's had, hence his battered state.

Director Javier Elorrieta keeps the action and the laughs boiling cheerfully for most of this caper, though the tension slackens toward the end in a longish sequence set in a club where women ogle male strippers. By this time, Adam is disguised as a nun and is being pursued by a killer dressed as a priest.

Rohner makes an amiable hero, and Piaget, though she has little to do, is an attractive heroine. McDowall seems to be having fun. Stuntwork is good, and the Spanish crew have done their usual fine work.

The plot makes no sense in retrospect, but it's all just an excuse for the amusing, sometimes hair-raising, misadventures of the intrepid hero.
— *David Stratton*

LA POSTIÈRE
(THE POSTMISTRESS)
(CANADIAN)

An Aska Film Distribution release of an Aska Film production. Produced by Yuri Yoshimura-Gagnon, Claude Gagnon. Line producers, Alain Gagnon, Luc Vandal. Directed by Gilles Carles. Screenplay, Carles, with Jean-Marie Esteve. Camera (color), René Verzier; editor, Christian Marcotte; music, Philippe McKenzie; production design, Jocelyn Joly; art direction, Ronald Fauteux; costume design, Denis Sperdouklis; sound, Serge Beauchemin. Reviewed at Cineplex Odeon Cinema Berri, April 26, 1992. (In Cannes Film Festival market.) Running time: **93 MIN.**
Rachel Plamondon . Chloé Sainte-Marie
Mayor's mistress . . . Michèle Richard
Mayor's wife . . . . . Louise Forestier
Cora . . . . Marzia Bartolucci
Fernand . . . . Nicolas François Rives
Amédée . . . . Steve Gendron
Mayor . . . . Roger Giguère
Tim . . . . Michel Barrette
Tonio . . . . . . Alain Olivier Lapointe

Depending on one's progressiveness, "The Postmistress" is either a harmless sex farce or an insulting sexist comedy. Cast of familiar Quebec actors will be a drawing card for local b.o. and homevid but of no use to foreign distribs.

Moreover, pic isn't an impressive comeback for helmer Gilles Carles, whose heyday films from "La Vraie Nature de Bernadette" (1972) to "Les Plouffe" (1981) were regular fare in official competition at Cannes.

As Carles did with his previous partner (Carole Laure), he has cast his real-life love interest Chloé Sainte-Marie in the title role of the postmistress and general store manager in prewar rural Quebec. (Sainte-Marie also starred in Carles' last feature in '86, "La Guepe," considered a commercial and critical flop.)

Sainte-Marie adds little depth to Rachel, a lascivious storekeeper with her eyes on the handsome new engineer in town, Fernand. Newcomer thesp Nicolas François Rives is equally shallow as a playboy who prefers one-night stands because he's not obliged to talk to the woman. From the first reel, their unimaginative sexual escapades are predictable.

Supporting cast isn't much better and the roles are strictly caricature. Michèle Richard (TV icon known as "Quebec's Liz Taylor") plays the mayor's mistress, who unabashedly dons any kinky costume to satisfy his fantasies.

In one particularly jolting scene, Richard is scantily clad in a doe-like outfit, crawling through a forest while the mayor "hunts" her with a loaded shotgun.

A subplot involves the town prostitute (Marzia Bartolucci) and her dull lover (Alain Olivier Lapointe). The three women essentially play variations on the western genre's hooker with a heart of gold, whose sole purpose is to seduce and satisfy her man before moving on to the next.

Pic is scripted and shot coyly enough. However, love scenes (and costumes) could have been conjured up by the editor of a Frederick's of Hollywood lingerie catalogue. Such a colloquial sex farce would be lost on an even slightly sophisticated audience. — *Suzan Ayscough*

CRUSH
(NEW ZEALAND)

A Hibiscus Films production in association with N.Z. Film Commission, Avalon/NFU Studios & NZ On Air. (Intl. sales: The Sales Co., London.) Produced by Bridget Ikin. Directed by Alison Maclean. Screenplay, Maclean, Anne Kennedy. Camera (color), Dion Beebe; editor, John Gilbert; music, JPS Experience; production design, Meryl Cronin; costumes, Ngila Dickson; sound, Robert Allen; associate producer, Trevor Haysom; assistant director, George Lyle; casting, Diana Rowan, Deborah Aquila (U.S.), Faith Martin (Australia). Reviewed at Cannes Film Festival (competition), May 12, 1992. Running time: **96 MIN.**
Lane . . . . Marcia Gay Harden
Christina . . . . Donogh Rees
Angela . . . . Caitlin Bossley
Horse . . . . Pete Smith

"Crush" is a dark, brooding and at times ugly drama about the relationship between three women and a man set against the striking background of the New Zealand hot springs city of Rotorua. However, Alison Maclean, in her first feature after some exciting short films, fails to come up with the right mix of tangled relationships, lust and revenge for which she seems to have been aiming. Returns are likely to be spotty.

Joseph Losey-Harold Pinter films are evoked in the screenplay Maclean penned with Anne Kennedy. "Crush" opens well and provides a genuinely chilling final reel, but in between Maclean lets the tension level drop. Indifferent casting and characters that are hard to identify with add to the film's problems.

Pic starts out with an intriguing relationship between a N.Z. journalist, Christine (Donogh Rees), an outspoken American woman, Lane (Marcia Gay Harden). Christine is traveling by car with Lane to Rotorua to interview a writer, but when Lane takes over the driving she causes a near-fatal crash and leaves her friend for dead.

Unfortunately, Maclean and Kennedy never bother to reveal who the enigmatic Lane is, what she's doing in N.Z. or how she befriended Christine.

While Christine languishes in the hospital, Lane introduces herself to the writer, Colin (William Zappa), and his shy teenage daughter, Angela (Caitlan Bossley). Lane and Colin start an affair, leaving Angela and Christine (whose legs and vocal chords have been badly injured) to form an alliance.

Part of the film's problems lie in the script, which was developed over a long period (including a time at the Sundance Institute), but fails to give its characters motivation. Problematic casting makes Harden seem out of place as the mysterious Lane, and Zappa makes the writer an uninteresting character so the passions swirling around him remain incomprehensible. Audience identification is absent here.

Still, Maclean creates an often eerie mood of sexual tension, and the climax, when it comes, is a knockout. Chalk "Crush" down as an intriguing failure from a director who may deliver the goods the second time around.

— *David Stratton*

DON QUIJOTE DE ORSON WELLES
(DON QUIXOTE OF ORSON WELLES)
(SPANISH-B&W)

An El Silencio production. Produced by Patxi Irigoyen. Editor-head of post-production, Jess Franco. General supervisor, Oja Kodar. Dialogue adaptation, Javier Mina, Franco; editing, Rosa Maria Almirall, Fatima Michalczik; music, Daniel J. White; associate producer, Juan A. Pedrosa; with the participation of Fernando Rey.
Original shoot: Produced by Oscar Dazingers, Alessandro Tasca, Francisco Lara. Directed, written by Orson Welles. Camera (black & white), Jose Garcia Galisteo, Juan Manuel de la Chica, Edmond Richard, Jack Draper, Ricardo Navarrete, Manuel Mateos, Giorgio Tonti; editors, Maurizio Lucidi, Renzo Lucidi, Peter Pareshelles, Ira Wohl, Alberto Valenzuela. Reviewed at Cannes Film Festival (Directors Fortnight), May 16, 1992. Running time: **118 min.**
With: Francisco Reiguera (voice of Jose Mediavilla), Akim Tamiroff (voice of Juan Carlos Ordonez), Orson Welles (voice of Constantino Romero).

Orson Welles' "Don Quixote" has been among the most eagerly anticipated films among cinephiles for more than 30 years, but "Don Quixote of Orson Welles" is not what they have been waiting to see. An unquestionably earnest effort to approximate the film Welles might have created had he ever finished editing his highly personal, near-mythic adaptation of Cervantes' masterpiece, this Spanish venture is perhaps best described as a documentary about other people's ideas concerning Welles' intentions. In any event, result is a travesty that will please no one, least of all Welles enthusiasts.

Entire history of Welles' "Don Quixote" is too complicated and lengthy to recount here. But using his own money, the director began shooting it around 1955 and, between his many other activities, continued lensing in bits and pieces for some years thereafter. He reportedly edited numerous sequences, and possibly multiple potential versions, but never completed final editing or postproduction on a cut he considered definitive.

Several years ago, the Cannes Film Festival presented 40 minutes of material from the picture that had been put together by Costa-Gavras under the auspices of the Cinematheque Française, and last year L.A.'s American Cinematheque held a private showing of somewhat different footage.

In 1990, a Spanish team led by producer Patxi Irigoyen and director Jess Franco (second unit director on Welles' "Chimes at Midnight" and the unfinished "Treasure Island") acquired the rights to all the known "Don Quixote" footage from Oja Kodar, Welles' longtime companion who controls the rights to his unfinished works, and Suzanne Cloutier, who held much of the footage. Sole holdout was film editor Mauro Bonanni, who withheld, at least, an edited sequence featuring Don Quixote jousting with a cinema screen.

Result, then, purports to present all the pertinent footage shot by Welles in something resembling proper order. Working from Welles' notes, indications on his 62-minute soundtrack of narration and dialogue, Kodar's advice and other sources, and gathering footage shot in 35m and 16m, Franco and company put together a semblance of a film.

Given the uniqueness of Welles' editing style, especially in his later period, it is highly questionable that anyone else could ever fairly complete one of his unfinished works in satisfactorily representative fashion. But even putting aside that concern, the reconstructionists have placed the work they love in a highly unfavorable light on two major counts.

First, the visual quality of the copy unspooled in Cannes is appalling. At the earlier screenings of footage in Cannes and L.A., "Don Quixote" had a brilliant, high-contrast black & white look that was unmistakably Wellesian and satisfied viewers even in a very rough assembly.

Here, the material appears, for the most part, like third-generation dupes. Many of the images are very fuzzy, and there is an annoying preponderance of seemingly lab-generated effects, including freeze-frames, animation and artificial zooms. Very little of the footage has the breathtaking clarity of the scenes or stills seen previously.

Second, the dialogue and commentary has been dubbed into Spanish by new actors. Original soundtrack featured Welles himself speaking the lines of the two main characters, as well as delivering the narration. The loss in this regard is incalculable, on top of the fact that anything resembling lip synch has been thrown to the wind.

Combination of murky images and wrong-headed soundtrack makes for a trying two hours, even for someone who has long awaited the chance to see this legendary work. The impulse to evaluate Welles' own accomplishments through the thick veil draped around it should be resisted, since all critical intuition leads to the conclusion that this document badly represents Welles' intentions.

For the record, however, "Don Quixote of Orson Welles" begins with documentary-like footage of Welles, camera in hand, being driven around Spain. Following an introduction to Spanish cities and Cervantes' work, Don Quixote and Sancho Panza, aboard thin white horse and diminutive mule, respectively, ride onto the contemporary Spanish landscape, bantering as they go and becoming involved in numerous semi-humorous incidents.

The two are swept up in a modern religious procession, the knight errant tilts briefly at windmills and fights some hooded warriors, and Sancho becomes separated from Quixote for quite some time, only to find the destitute knight in a modern city, whereupon the two consider going to the moon.

Only two sequences that come across with any sense of exhileration is a stunning running of the bulls, which reveals dozens of men getting trampled and tossed about, and a charming village interlude in which Sancho dances for a group of children. Despite the handicaps of the presentation, one has the sense of Akim Tamiroff as the perfect Sancho Panza.

At a few points, notably during the bullfight, Welles himself appears onscreen, implicitly as the man who Sancho notes will make Quixote and him famous by putting them in a film. Final bit of Wellesian narration states, "This film was directed, written and produced by a man whose ashes were scattered over Spain. His name was Orson Welles."

At the Cannes screening, producer Irigoyen claimed that a better print of "Don Quixote of Orson Welles" would be available in a few weeks, and that an English-language version is in the works. Perhaps these developments will represent substantial enough improvements to warrant a reevaluation. But why an unsatisfactory version should have been rushed before the public in Cannes is unfathomable.

— *Todd McCarthy*

HOSTAGE
(BRITISH)

A Pinnacle Pictures presentation of a Portman Entertainment/Jempsa Medios & Entretenimiento/Independent Image production in association with Tyne Tees Television. (Intl. sales: Pinnacle, U.K.) Produced by Tom Kinninmont. Executive producers, Ian Warren, Adrian Metcalfe. Directed by Robert Young. Screenplay, Arthur Hopcraft, based on Ted Allbeury's novel "No Place to Hide." Camera (Eastmancolor), Alex Phillips; editor, Tariq Anwar; music, Richard Harvey; art direction, Eduardo Capilla; assistant director, Claudio Reiter; associate producer, Andrew Warren. Reviewed at Cannes Film Festival market, May 14, 1992. Running time: **98 MIN.**

John Rennie . . . . Sam Neill
Joanna . . . . Talisa Soto
Hugo Paynter . . . . James Fox
Kalim Said . . . . Art Malik
Gabriella . . . . . . Cristina Higueras
Fredericks . . . . . . Michael Kitchen
Also with: Jean Pierre Reguerraz.

There's a curiously old-fashioned feel to "Hostage," a straight-arrow Brit spy-on-the-run number that could almost have been made in the '60s. Pic could hijack some loose change in undemanding territories, but not many mainstream auds will cough up coin for such routine fare.

Sam Neill is an MI-6 op who, in the words of his ex-wife, has done "one dirty job too many" and wants out. Jetting back to Buenos Aires, site of his last assignment, Neill holes up in a seedy hotel and recites his grievances into a tape recorder.

Flashbacks limn his attempts to rescue a fellow operative tortured by terrorists and about to spill the beans. Neill follows a hunch and gets to know a rich local businessman (Art Malik), a Turkish Kurd, and parlays his way into the bed of Malik's sexy sister-in-law (Talisa Soto). Neill starts to get crises of conscience when he falls for Soto while setting up a kidnapping of Malik's daughters to force his hand.

Hardly enough dirt goes on to make a killing machine like Neill suddenly have thoughts of quitting. There's also a noticeable lack of electricity between him and Soto, due partly to the dull script and partly to the latter's mannequin performance.

Neill works hard to keep the drama afloat but doesn't get much help from the rest of the cast. James Fox, as a public school MI-6 type, looks as if he's working off a contract obligation; Malik is uncharismatic as the terrorist sympathizer.

Richard Hartley's well-placed score adds some dramatic color, as does Yank lenser Alex Phillips' photography of the Argentinian capital. — *Derek Elley*

C'EST ARRIVÉ PRÈS DE CHEZ VOUS
(MAN BITES DOG)
(BELGIAN-B&W)

A Les Artistes Anonymes production. (Intl. sales: French Community of Belgium.) Produced by Rémy Belvaux, André Bonzel, Benoit Poelvoorde. Directed by Belvaux. Screenplay, Belvaus, Bonzel, Poelvoorde, Vincent Tavier. Camera (black & white), Bonzel; editors, Eric Dardill, Belvaux; music, Jean-Marc Chenut; sound, Alain Oppezzi, Vincent Tavier; special effects, Olivier de Lavelaye; assistant director-production manager, Tavier. Reviewed at CNC screening room, Paris, April 21, 1992. (In Cannes Film Festival Critics Week.) Running time: **95 MIN.**

Ben . . . . Benoit Poelvoorde
Reporter . . . . Rémy Belvaux
Cameraman . . . . . . André Bonzel
Also with: Jean-Marc Chenut, Alain Oppezzi, Vincent Tavier.

Reality programming meets "Henry: Portrait of a Serial Killer" in "Man Bites Dog," an offbeat, darkly hilarious portrait of a freelance hit man whose every move is recorded by a documentary film crew. Pic will be most resonant in markets where reality programming has made major inroads.

Well served by black & white verité-style lensing, mordant send-up of questionable newsgathering practices was written, produced, directed by and stars a Franco-Belgian trio whose first feature provides clever patter with its splatter. Violent yet trenchant, potential sleeper should attract a cult following and will look just right on video.

A youthful hit man (Benoit Poelvoorde) is both a philosopher and a man of action. When he's not killing people (two dozen graphic murders are committed during the film), he plays chamber music and recites poetry.

A font of both practical and esoteric knowledge, the opinionated and urbane hit man scares an old woman into cardiac arrest in order to save on bullets, then strips the house of hidden cash. In one great bit, he slaughters a rival team of reporters simply because they're using videotape instead of film stock.

Filmmakers cook up situations to yield a well-balanced report on an unbalanced character. With evolving irony, camera crew is not immune to danger or from the seductive lure of the hit man lifestyle. At first reluctant even to dine with their immoral subject, crew graduates to joining in on the gang rape and disembowelment of a woman in her own home. Not for the righteous or the squeamish, irreverent film follows through to its logical conclusion.

Apart from an amusingly tasteless segment in which a mixed drink recipe refers to a sensational French child murder case in the '80s, French-lingo pic is accessible to hip audiences, provided subtitles accurately capture the jaunty tone of the hit man's running commentary.

—*Lisa Nesselson*

HOUSTON FEST

VALHALLA

An Arclight Film presentation. Produced, directed, written by Jonathan D. Gift. Executive producer, Jan S. Utstein. Camera (Panavision Cinemascope, Deluxe color), Bryan England; editor, Michael B. Hoggan; music, David M. Matthews; costumes, Mona May; production design, Cat Dragon; sound, Paul Coogan. Reviewed at WorldFest/Houston, May 2, 1992. No MPAA rating. Running time: **87 MIN.**

Paul . . . . Christopher Thornton
Mark . . . . Frank C. Gallagher
James . . . . Kevin Symons
Dad . . . . Charles Carmine
J.D. . . . . Suzanne Averitt
Billy Boy . . . . George Parker
Snowflake . . . . Lisa LeCover
Siegfried . . . . Deron McBee

"Valhalla" is a bright showcase for fresh talent and affectionately goofy humor. Indie pic might require imaginative marketing (tie-in premieres with local opera and symphony companies would be naturals), but extra effort could pay off with respectable coin in urban markets.

There's definite sleeper potential in this oddball yet heartfelt comedy, which makes the most of a seemingly limited premise.

First-time filmmaker Jonathan D. Gift tells his story as the extended flashback of a dutiful son. Paul (Christopher Thornton) returns to his old family home and recalls four evenings in 1984 when he and his brothers staged a scaled-down, lip-synched production of Richard Wagner's "Ring" cycle for his ailing opera buff father (Charles Carmine).

It helps that Paul works as a movie effects designer and can utilize his abilities to stage the Wagner marathon in a cramped space — his father's living room.

A more determinedly commercial pic might have played the situation for broader across-the-board yocks and backstage flubs. But the film is after gentler, subtler humor. With actors so caught up in the roles that their private lives are affected, pic resembles "Jesus of Montreal," but here, the result is less profound and more playful.

The show is aided by Billy Boy (George Parker), a biker who knows all about Wagner but admits he's "sort of partial to Puccini." Snowflake (Lisa LeCover), a striking biker chick playing Brunnhilde, begins to understand the opera when someone suggests she think of it as the musical version of "Conan the Barbarian."

Pic works surprisingly well on different levels. As narrator, Thornton offers a respectful yet tongue-in-cheek guide through the complicated "Ring" plot. Despite a few naughty words, pic might actually work as an instructional tool in high school and college music classes.

The actual opera productions resemble low-budget, high-energy efforts by storefront legit theaters. The stagings get increasingly more complex and detailed as the cycle continues, and the amateur actors immerse themselves in their parts.

Still, the film never allows anything to get so elaborate that it cannot be persuasively contained within a large living room. That, too, is part of the pic's charm.

Performances are spirited and on target. Thornton and Parker make particularly strong impressions. Deron McBee, an "American Gladiators" alum, is amusingly well cast as a muscular Malibu surfer who really enjoys playing Siegfried.

Pic ends on an ironic note that's no less emotionally effective for being predictable. A silly subplot involving nosy neighbors could be left on the cutting room floor without being missed.

Tech credits, especially Bryan England's resourceful lensing and Cat Dragon's witty production design, are first-rate. More than just a promising debut, "Valhalla" is a good pic by any standard. — *Joe Leydon*

SKETCH ARTIST

A Motion Picture Corp. of America production. Produced by Brad Krevoy, Steve Stabler. Co-producer, Chad Oman. Directed by Phedon Papamichael. Screenplay, Michael Angeli. Camera (color), Wally Pfister; editor, Carole Kravetz; music, Mark Isham; production design, Phedon Papamichael Sr.; art direction, Virginia Lee; sound, Peter V. Meiselmann; associate producer, Raimond Reynolds; assistant director, J. B. Rogers; casting, Robyn Ray, Ed Mitchell. Reviewed at WorldFest/Houston, April 26, 1992. No MPAA rating. Running time: **88 MIN.**

Jack	Jeff Fahey
Rayanne	Sean Young
Daisy	Drew Barrymore
Milon	Frank McRae
Paul Corbeil	Tcheky Karyo
Tonelli	James Tolkan

Also with: Charlotte Lewis, Ric Young, Stacey Haiduk, Mark Boone Jr.

Cinematographer Phedon Papamichael ("Love Crimes") makes a solid directorial debut with "Sketch Artist," a well-crafted mystery that boasts a smart script by journalist Michael Angeli. The picture, set for a June debut on the Showtime cable network, should perform respectably in Canadian and European feature markets and enjoy a long shelf life on homevideo.

Jeff Fahey hits the right notes of nervous intensity and mounting dread in the title role, essaying a scruffy artist newly hired by L.A. police to sketch pictures of suspects based on eyewitness recollections.

After a high-profile fashion designer is slain, Fahey goes to work with a courier (Drew Barrymore) who saw a woman leaving the scene of the crime. Barrymore describes a face that looks an awful lot like that of Fahey's wife (Sean Young), an upwardly mobile interior designer. Shocked and eager to protect his wife, Fahey scraps the sketch and draws a different face.

Things get complicated when a photog (Belle Avery) who looks just like the altered sketch is picked up for questioning, and Barrymore is found dead shortly after a neighbor saw Fahey trying to enter her apartment.

Script gives a nod to the Hitchcock tradition as Fahey becomes the subject of a police dragnet as he tries to find the real killer(s). But the pic really is more interested in developing a film noir mood, even though Papamichael wisely resists the temptation to go for obvious noir visuals. Considerable suspense is generated as Papamichael dangles the pos-

sibility that the frantic artist may have killed the courier to protect his wife — even though his wife might very well be guilty of murder.

Red herrings include French thesp Tcheky Karyo as the fashion designer's partner, Stacey Haiduk as a not-so-grieving widow, and Charlotte Lewis as a high-priced call girl who knows a lot about the designer's business dealings. But pic plays fair and keeps the coincidence rate to a minimum.

In probably his best film work to date, Fahey offers an excellent modern-day variation of the classic film noir flawed hero: a hard-drinking, chain-smoking malcontent who can redeem himself only by getting in way over his head.

Young is aptly ambiguous as the wife, while Frank McRae is amiably bearish as Fahey's best friend on the police force. Barrymore, recently photographed by Papamichael in Katt Shea's "Poison Ivy," makes the most of a small but key role. Other supporting players are first-rate.

Tech credits are fine. Special credit goes to Mark Isham for an evocative musical score that greatly enhances the mood of steadily escalating uneasiness.

— *Joe Leydon*

PAST MIDNIGHT

A Cinetel Films release. Produced by Lisa M. Hansen. Executive producer, Paul Hertzberg. Directed by Jan Eliasberg. Screenplay, Frank Norwood. Camera (FotoKem color), Robert Yeoman; editor, Christopher Rouse; music, Steve Bartek; art direction, Daniel Self; sound (Dolby), Robert Marts; assistant director, Mary Ellen Woods; casting (Seattle), Alison Roth Casting. Reviewed at WorldFest/Houston, May 3, 1992. MPAA rating: R. Running time: **100 MIN.**

Ben Jordan	Rutger Hauer
Laura Mathews	Natasha Richardson
Steve Lundy	Clancy Brown
Dorothy Coleman	Kibibi Monie
Lee Samuels	Tom Wright

Also with: Dana Eskelson, Ted D'Arms, Paul Giamatti, Guy Boyd.

Rutger Hauer's arrestingly ambiguous portrayal of a convicted killer who may be innocent after all isn't quite enough to fire this would-be erotic thriller, strictly low voltage in all regards. Look for "Past Midnight" to spend little time in theaters before it winds up on video.

As a parolee released after 15 years in prison for the stabbing murder of his pregnant wife,

Hauer is relocated to a neighboring small town in Washington state. His smart and sexy social worker (Natasha Richardson) is repulsed by details of his crime but later intrigued when she starts uncovering inconsistencies in the police records.

Unfortunately, after she falls in love with the guy, she begins to uncover inconsistencies in the inconsistencies. That's when she starts to worry that, hey, maybe the jury was right in the first place.

Screenwriter Frank Norwood (who worked 15 years as a social worker) has some mildly clever ideas, but does little with them. Climax openly defies plausibility. "Past Midnight" may be the first pic ever to list in its closing credits its actresses cast as "Super-8 Film Victims."

TV vet Jan Eliasberg makes an inauspicious feature directing debut, developing the mystery plot in a flat, by-the-numbers fashion. She doesn't even generate much heat in the lovemaking scenes in which Richardson and Hauer bare (almost) all.

Hauer does more for pic than it does for him. He's especially fine in the early scenes in which he angrily discourages Richardson from trying to clear his name, claiming that, after 15 years in prison, all he wants to do is forget what little he remembers. (He was drunk on the night of the killing.) Of course, she doesn't listen to him.

Richardson is as good as she can be in a role that calls for the supposedly smart social worker to do some incredibly dopey things. There's fine support from Clancy Brown as Richardson's protective co-worker and former lover, Guy Boyd as Jordan's last best friend and, briefly, Tom Wright as a cop who has no doubts about Jordan's guilt.

Robert Yeoman's moody cinematography of the small-town and rural Washington locations is a plus. Other tech credits are pro. — *Joe Leydon*

L'HOMME DE MA VIE
(THE MAN OF MY LIFE)
(FRENCH-CANADIAN)

A Sirius release of an Optima Prods./ Ciné Cinq/Prodeve/Cinéroux Films co-production in association with Sofica Valor 2 with participation of Canal Plus, CNC & Telefilm Canada. Produced by Gabriel Boustani. Directed, written by Jean-Charles Tacchella. Camera (color), Dominique Le Rigoleur; music, Raymond Alessandrini; costume design, Sylvie de Segonzac; set design, Serge Douy; sound, Henri Blondeau. Reviewed at Club de l'Etoile theater, Paris, April 28, 1992. Running time: **104 MIN.**

Aimée	Maria de Madeiros
Maurice	Thierry Fortineau
Malcolm	Jean-Pierre Bacri
Catherine	Anne Letourneau
Arlette	Ginette Garcin

Inventive and with charm to spare, Jean-Charles Tacchella's "L'Homme de Ma Vie" is a first-rate comedy of manners about a woman who has decided to land a husband without further ado. Splendid dialogue, an outstanding score and a likable cast point to a promising career in art houses worldwide.

Maria de Madeiros, Portuguese-born French actress (Anaïs Nin in "Henry and June") is irresistible as Aimée, a 28-year-old who figures marriage must be a better economic bargain than being laid off from one job after another. She puts on her red dress, hops in her sports car and sets her sights on nearby bachelors who meet her criteria.

A local bookseller (Thierry Fortineau) would do if he weren't a penniless "epicurean misanthrope." Craving material comfort, she marries a famous restaurant critic (Jean-Pierre Bacri) who takes his tastebuds so seriously he comes to blows with the chef at his own wedding feed.

The flagrant delicto episode Aimée stages in order to secure a divorce is a small gem in the annals of screen adultery. Although Aimée would appear to have an old-fashioned goal, her determination makes her both modern and appealing. She holds a brown belt in judo and employs Hindu concentration methods to resist the bookseller's exploratory advances. There is condom talk prior to the love scene — still a rarity in French films.

Bright airy lensing around Versailles serves the story. Tour de force score written and directed by Raymond Alessandrini is truly special. Tacchella creates offbeat characters who know how to flirt and who can sustain a bout of verbal sparring. These are roles Katharine Hepburn and Jimmy Stewart or Audrey Hepburn and Gregory Peck could have played. The pace never flags, and one is sorry to bid the lovers goodbye. — *Lisa Nesselson*

NOVEMBER DAYS
(BRITISH-DOCU)

A BBC-TV production in association with Regina Ziegler & Arthur Cohn. Executive producer, Paul Hamann. Produced, directed by Marcel Ophuls. Camera (video, color), Peter Boultwood, Pierre Boffety, Anette Metzger; editors, Sophie Brunet, Albert Jurgenson, Catherine Zins; sound, Michael Busch; research, Dieter Reifarth, Matias Remmert, Elisabeth Publig-Schuder; assistant producer, Sara Fletcher. Reviewed at Human Rights Watch Film Festival, Loews Village Theater VII, N.Y., May 8, 1992. Running time: **129 MIN.**

Probing the reunification of Germany, director Marcel Ophuls' latest offering centers on the 1989 period when free travel between East and West Berlin was resumed. Result is a provocative, contemplative film marred occasionally by the director's recent penchant for supercilious commentary.

A more unfortunate drawback is the appalling unwillingness of the producers of this project, originally a BBC docu, to finance showings on film, necessitating screenings with an awkward video print. Conversion to film for meaningful distribution would seem a technical necessity.

Although aesthetically acceptable in its present length (129 minutes, skimpy by Ophulsian standards), the political complexities and Ophuls' track record with long films suggests docu would likely benefit from director's desire to add footage.

Pic opens in London with BBC news reports on easing of restrictions and moves to the scene in Berlin. Ophuls is seen interviewing participants some time later and trying to gauge how events got out of East German control. Apparent implication that events were being orchestrated from Moscow is smartly but briefly introduced given pic's limited resources for investigating the Russian side.

Even with the bizarrely happy turn of events, Ophuls' appearances on camera often seem unduly effusive, with the filmmaker sometimes caustically breaking into song. When conductor Kurt Masur refuses to answer one of Ophuls' queries and attacks the

director's mode of questioning, the feeling is less of sympathy for Masur than relief that someone has at last talked back.

It is to Ophuls' credit that this scene is included, and given the procession of liars and fools among the East German leadership and intelligentsia interviewed, he is entitled to some sympathy of his own. However, more incisive questioning rather than prosecutorial needling might have been more appropriate.

Ophuls' use of associative editing to hammer home points also seems excessive. But his presence and personal experience also enhance the film, as when he reminisces with Barbara Brecht-Schall, Bertolt Brecht's daughter, when their families were refugees in Hollywood. On a deeper level the film works as a cosmic comedy with all the evasions of logic and responsibility of Ophuls' anti-Nazi docus being repeated with somewhat less horrific results.

It is also a cautionary tale of the dangers of economic instability in the new Germany. Ophuls vocally downplays this threat, but his scenes of flourishing neo-Nazi groups waiting in the wings for an econo-disaster provide unappetizing food for thought.
— *Fred Lombardi*

DIRTY AFFAIR
(GUMAPANG KA SA LUSAK)
(FILIPINO)

A Viva Films production. Produced by Vic del Rosario. Directed by Lino Brocka. Screenplay, Ricky Lee. Camera (color), Pedro Manding, Jr.; editor, George Jar Leer; associate director, Jun L. Ching. Reviewed at San Francisco Film Festival, April 28, 1992. Running time: **120 MIN.**
With: Christopher de Leon, Dina Bonnevie, Bembol Roco, Eddie Garcia, Charo Santos, Allan Paule.

Late Filipino helmer Lino Brocka's last significant pic, "Dirty Affair," mixes spiraling melodrama with a scorching view of official corruption in his homeland.

Political content and high-impact presentation score, but the lurid surface places pic in a netherland between commercial and art house appeal. Exposure probably will be limited.

Complicated plot centers on a beautiful ex-movie star whose legit career ended when her illegit one began — as mistress to the mayor, who built her a house and sustained her working-class

family via pilfering of public funds while jealously keeping hired goons trained on her every move.

But the mayor's wife (a wicked Imelda Marcos parody) has her own political interests in mind. Though aware of her husband's past liaisons, she's not about to let the imminent scandal of his long-term association with the actress get in the way of a heated upcoming election.

Conventionally glamorous early scenes on a film set and at a disco soon fade into effectively brutal violence demonstrating the lengths to which the politician and wife will go to stay in power. Still, there's ample humor — notably in the richly satirical scenes where the hypocritical pair strike connubial-bliss postures on the campaign trail.

Though long, the screenplay fills every moment with exciting and generally credible plot twists. Performances are appropriately heated, and tech credits decent down the line.

Brocka, the Philippines' most popular and esteemed director, died in a car accident last spring. His subsequent work was more overtly commercial, in keeping with his career strategy of turning out potboilers in order to fund the more trenchant pic like this item. — *Dennis Harvey*

AMERICAN HEART

An Avenue Pictures presentation in association with World Films of an Asis/Heller production. Produced by Rosilyn Heller, Jeff Bridges. Executive producer, Cary Brokaw. Co-producer, Neil Koenigsberg. Directed by Martin Bell. Screenplay, Peter Silverman, from story by Bell, Mary Ellen Mark, Silverman. Camera (color), James Bagdonas; editor, Nancy Baker; music, James Newton Howard; production design, Joel Schiller. Reviewed at Cannes Film Festival market, May 11, 1992. Running time: **113 MIN.**
Jack Keely . . . . Jeff Bridges
Nick Keely . . . . . . Edward Furlong
Charlotte . . . . Lucinda Jenney
Also with: Don Harvey, Tracey Kapinsky, Maggie Welsh.

The determination to rebuild messed-up lives lies at the heart of "American Heart," a gritty, well-meaning drama about a father and son on the fringes of society. First fictional feature from Martin Bell, director of the powerful 1984 docu "Streetwise," has plenty of passion and commitment but is rather too straightforward

and disappointingly resolved to qualify as a total success.

The toplined names of Jeff Bridges and Edward Furlong, as well as a likely fair share of critical kudos, should give a domestic distrib enough to work with for decent returns on the specialized circuit.

A long-in-the-works labor of love for all concerned, pic is rooted in an elemental story about an irresponsible, ex-con father and his teenage son, who is so ignored he must fend for himself on the streets.

Around the edges are a host of observations about the sorry state of urban America, and grafted on is a bit of crime melodrama that provides some conventional chase and shoot-'em-up action.

Released from prison on a work furlough program, Jack Keely (Bridges) reunites in Seattle with his 14-year-old son Nick (Furlong), who has been staying with his aunt in the country. Installed in a cheap boardinghouse, Jack resists an ex-partner's entreaties to return to robbery and manages to find a job washing windows downtown.

Bright, resourceful Nick is discouraged from signing up at school and, given the abuse he sometimes gets from his dad, increasingly hangs around with other dispossessed kids on the block.

As hard as he tries, Jack has trouble assuming the responsibilities of fatherhood, preferring to spend time with his g.f. (Lucinda Jenney), and life for both father and son is a tough, day-to-day proposition.

When Jack begins dreaming aloud of moving up to Alaska as a way of starting over, he doesn't even include his son in his plans. But in time this becomes a joint project, with both saving for imminent departure.

But fate deals these down-and-outers a rotten hand. Jack loses his job, and Nick, to please a cute girl he's begun to fancy, is drawn into petty crime. But once again, bullets fly, as it all ends in a flurry of gunplay lending a deflatingly Hollywood-style ending to what has otherwise been an unformulaic work of obvious integrity.

Peter Silverman's screenplay (based on a story by himself, director Bell and associate producer Mary Ellen Mark, a photographer who also is Bell's wife) offers many honest, reality-grappling scenes, but it could have used a dash of reality-heightening poetry to lift the pic out of the ordinary. Similarly, Bell's straight-ahead handling of scenes tackles issues directly, without particular subtlety or nuance.

Still, the film packs considerable power, thanks largely to the lead performances. Looking as working-class as can be in ponytail and moustache, Bridges pours all his raw energy into this portrait of a limited man who tries to curb his mistakes, but still can't help letting his unconsidered emotions get the better of him. One can feel the actor/co-producer's commitment to the concerns of story in every scene.

Young Furlong ("Terminator 2: Judgment Day") continues to amaze here. An actor to whom the camera and viewer are naturally drawn, he projects intelligence, sensibility and charisma.

With heavy dramatic demands placed on him here, he always seems real, never awkward, and effortlessly holds his own with the vet Bridges.

In the end, pic is a shade too prosaic and laborious to excite major enthusiasm but is also meaty and very respectable as a first film.

Tech credits are solid, if unexceptional. — *Todd McCarthy*

SHISHENG HUAMEI
(THE SILENT THRUSH)
(TAIWANESE)

A San Pen Enterprises Stock Co.-Yüan Tai Film Co. production. (Intl. sales: Anthex, Berlin.) Produced by Wang Ying-hsiang, Li K'ang-nien. Executive producers, Yü Shu, Yü Chi-wei. Directed by Cheng Sheng-fu. Screenplay, Yü Chi-wei, Li, Cheng, from Ling Yen's novel. Camera (color), Ch'en Jung-shu; editor, Ch'en Po-wen; music, Wu Wen-tung; art direction, Huang Tse-ch'ing; sound, Huang Mao-shan; assistant directors, Huang Tse-ch'ing, Li Chih-wei; associate producers, Ni Ya-ting, Hsiao Feng. Reviewed at Cannes Film Festival market, May 10, 1992. Running time: **88 MIN.**
Ah-yün . . . . Li Yü-shan
Chia-feng . . . . Lu Yi-ch'an
Ai-ch'ing . . . . Chang Ying-chen
Tou-yu . . . . Yüan Chia-p'ei
  Also with: Chang Pai-tan, Yüeh Hung, Hsiao Feng, Chu P'ing-yüan, Wang Mei-ching, Chiang Ch'ing-hsia, Wang Pai-ch'ing.
(Hokkien & Mandarin dialogue; English & Chinese subtitles)

A complex portrait of conflicting passions in a Taiwanese opera troupe, "The Silent Thrush" is a solid festival item that could score wider attention via its lesbian-themed storyline. Occasional soft center

doesn't mar a generally well-intentioned effort.

Pic, which bombed on local release in April (often a good sign for quality product), reps a strong comeback for Cheng Sheng-fu, 50, who directed and acted in local-dialect films and TV as Chiang Lang. Current pic is based on Ling Yen's prizewinning novel.

Cyan-tinted opening, set in 1974, limns main character Ah-yün's infatuation with local Taiwanese opera. Main story opens in 1986 with Ah-yün, now a young woman graduated from senior high, deciding to join a troupe and work her way up.

It soon becomes clear that the life isn't easy. The troupe boss is forced to insert girlie numbers to make ends meet; the troupe members (almost all women) are a foul-mouthed, quarrelsome lot; and she eventually falls prey to the sexual attentions of one of her childhood heroines, star performer Chia-feng. This excites the jealousy of Chia-feng's stage and bed partner, Ai-ch'ing.

Emerging gradually from the web of relationships laid out in the opening half-hour, pic's gay strands aren't allowed to overwhelm the film. Poor English subtitles and troupe members' heavy opera makeup don't help in initially sorting out the characters.

Still, performances are all vivid, and the thespians' day-to-day existence as they move through small villages is drawn with considerable care and affection.

Occasional sex scenes, though strong in local terms, are visually discreet and presented with Asian delicacy. Li Yü-shan, as Ah-yün, never gets beyond winsome. Lu Yi-ch'an, who made her name in a series of '80s femme avenger pics, is well-cast as the predatory lesbian; fine local actress Chang Ying-chen is underused as her spurned lover. Strongest female perf comes from Yüan Chia-p'ei, as the butch business manager who movingly reminisces about the good old days.

Visually, pic is quite a treat, with fine cinematography by Ch'en Jung-shu. Postsynching is unsubtle but acceptable.
— *Derek Elley*

MAP OF THE HUMAN HEART
(BRITISH-AUSTRALIAN-FRENCH-CANADIAN)

A Miramax release (U.S.) of a Polygram presentation of a Working Title (U.K.)-Vincent Ward Prods. (Australia)-Les Films Ariane (France)-Sunrise Films (Canada) co-production in association with Australian Film Finance Corp., Nippon Herald, Channel 4 & Telefilm Canada, (Intl. sales: Manifesto Film.) Executive producers, Graham Broadstreet, Harvey Weinstein, Bob Weinstein. Produced by Tim Bevan. Co-producers, Timothy White, Vincent Ward. French co-producer, Sylvaine Sainderichin. Canadian co-producers, Linda Beath, Paul Saltzman. Directed by Ward. Screenplay, Louis Nowra, from Ward's story. Camera (color), Eduardo Serra; editor, John Scott; music, Gabriel Yared; production design, John Beard; costumes, Renée April; sound, Andrew Plain; special effects, Richard Conway; assistant director, Pedro Gandol; associate producer, Redmond Morris; casting, Lucie Robitaille, Kate Dowd, Johanna Ray, Donna Jacobsen. Reviewed at Cannes Film Festival (out of competition), May 11, 1992. Running time: **126 MIN.**
Avik . . . . Jason Scott Lee
Young Avik . . . . . . Robert Joamie
Albertine . . . . Anne Parillaud
Young Albertine . . . . Annie Galipeau
Walter Russell . . . . . Patrick Bergin
  Also with: John Cusack, Jeanne Moreau, Ben Mendelson, Clotilde Courau, Jerry Snell, Jayko Pitseolak.

Shown as a work in progress in a noncompeting slot at Cannes, New Zealander Vincent Ward's third film is an immensely ambitious and audacious love story spanning 30 years and two continents.

Filled with magnificent scenes, pic in this version is marred by an awkward ending that could be modified for far greater impact. Prelim reactions, however, were positive.

Although there are elements here of Ward's previous work, "Map" unfolds on a far broader canvas than either "Vigil" or "The Navigator." Much of it is set and filmed above the Arctic Circle in northern Canada, providing breathtaking icescapes for Eduardo Serra's camera. French influence is noticeable; at times pic's large cast and romantic story line recall the work of Claude Lelouch.

The story unfolds in flashback, starting in 1965 as an old Inuit Eskimo tells a Yank mapmaker (a small role for John Cusack) his life story. Back in 1931, a vintage aircraft lands on the ice near the Inuit village, bringing with it a dashing Brit, Walter Russell (Patrick Bergin), who intends to chart the area.

He befriends Avik (Robert

Joamie) a cheerful young Inuit, and is saddened to discover that he, like many Eskimo boys, suffers from TB. When Russell leaves, he takes Avik with him to Montreal and places him in a hospital. Here the lonely and disgruntled boy forms a close relationship with a half-French Canadian, half-Indian girl, Albertine (Annie Galipeau), who is also a patient, launching pic's central love story.

Ten years later, in 1941, Russell returns to the Arctic on a mission to track down a German U-boat and meets Avik (Jason Scott Lee) again. Hearing that Albertine is in Europe, Avik enlists in the Canadian air force, but by the time the two meet, in England, Albertine and Russell have become involved. Still, the two Canadians finally make love in a striking, wonderfully strange scene atop a barrage balloon being raised above an ancient British landmark, the White Horse at Uffington.

Subsequently, Avik takes part in the notorious bombing of Dresden, where he is forced to parachute from his plane and witness the destruction of the city from ground level. Pic's last act, set in the '60s, records Avik's encounter with the daughter he never knew he had, who has come searching for her Inuit father.

Ward and celebrated Australian playwright Louis Nowra, who penned the screenplay, evidently aimed to create one of those sweeping romantic sagas that are from time to time popular screen fare. They almost succeed, but more romantic passion would have helped. Crucially, Avik and Albertine don't have enough scenes together as adults to establish their long-term love story. The ending (or, rather, endings) fail to tie up the threads of the epic story. Many of these problems can probably be solved via further postproduction tinkering.

On the plus side, "Map" is filled with spectacular sequences. The early Arctic scenes are stunningly handled, the balloon love scene is odd but beautiful, and the segment on the Dresden bombing is an astonishing amalgam of special effects and cinema artistry.

The various casting agencies have done a fine job, with moppets Joamie and Galipeau convincingly growing up into Lee and Annie Parillaud ("La Femme Nikita.") Needed humor is supplied by Jeanne Moreau, as a hospital nun who hates Protestants, and Aussie thesp Ben Mendelson as an airman.

Technically, "Map" is superb and there's a top score by French composer Gabriel Yared. However, it remains to be seen if further fine tuning will enhance the picture's international b.o. potential. — *David Stratton*

LÉOLO
(CANADIAN-FRENCH)

An Alliance Films release of a Les Prods. de Verseau-Flach Films co-production with participation of National Film Board of Canada, Telefilm Canada, French Ministry of Culture. (Intl. sales: Alliance Films.) Executive producers, Aimée Danis, Claudette Viau. Produced by Lyse Lafontaine, Danis. Co-producers, Isabelle Fauvel, Jean-François Lepetit. Directed, written by Jean-Claude Lauzon. Camera (color), Guy Dufaux; editor, Michel Arcand; production design, François Seguin; costumes, François Barbeau; sound, Yvon Benoit; sound design, Marcel Pothier; assistant director, Jacques W. Benoit; casting, Lucie Robitaille. Reviewed at Cannes Film Festival (competition), May 16, 1992. Running time: **107 MIN.**
Léolo . . . . Maxime Collin
Mother . . . . Ginette Reno
Father . . . . Roland Blouin
Grandfather . . . . . . .Julien Guiomar
Word tamer . . . . . Pierre Bourgault
Bianca . . . . Giuditta del Vecchio
Psychiatrist . . . . Andree Lachapelle
Career counselor . . . . Denys Arcand
Teacher . . . . Germaine Houde
Fernand . . . . . . Yves Montmarquette
Fernand's enemy . . . . Lorne Brass
Narrator . . . . Gilbert Sicotte

Although Jean-Claude Lauzon's second feature, "Léolo," covers familiar territory — the life and dreams of a young boy on the threshold of manhood — it does so with such audacity, originality and dark humor that it seems certain of making an international art house impact. It got a fine launch in the Cannes competition.

Lauzon (whose previous film was the brooding, fascinating "Night Zoo") has come up with a florid tale about an imaginative youngster and his strange family living in working-class East Montreal. His name is really Leo, but, as the somnolent narrator of his memories repeatedly notes, he's a dreamer and imagines that his real father is an Italian peasant whose sperm came to Canada via a consignment of tomatoes. Leo's mother accidentally fell on the tomatoes, impregnating her. Because of this hilarious premise, he demands to be called "Léolo."

Apart from Léolo, the only comforting person in his house is his rotund mother (beautifully played, in her first film role, by singer Ginette Reno). His father seems interested in nothing but the bodily functions of his family. His older brother, Fernand, is a frightened wimp who takes a body-building course and becomes a frightened muscle-man. His sisters spend much of their time in mental homes. Léolo blames his grandfather (French thesp Julien Guiomar) for his family's ills; a hilarious attempt to hang Grandpa while he sits in his bath ends with Léolo nearly killing himself.

A solitary child who likes to read (but the only book in the house is used to prop up a table), Léolo is also fascinated with his neighbor, the lovely Bianca, an Italian girl a little older than he. He spies on her, and discovers that his grandfather pays her to strip for him and bathe him.

Lauzon handles the scenes of Léolo's reality contrasted with his dream world with freshness and imagination. But a miscalculated scene in which a gang of boys abuse a cat could easily be dropped to the film's overall benefit. Also, Lauzon doesn't seem to know quite when to end pic.

Nevertheless, this unquestionably exciting film should do well in Quebec and, via further fest exposure, find its way into art houses in other territories. It is technically superb, with imaginative lensing by Guy Dufaux and a rich soundtrack.

— *David Stratton*

VISIONS OF LIGHT:
THE ART OF CINEMATOGRAPHY
(U.S.-JAPANESE-DOCU-COLOR/B&W)

An American Film Institue-NHK/ Japan Broadcasting co-production. Produced by Stuart Samuels. Executive producers, Terry Lawler, Yoshiki Nishimura. Co-producer, Arnold Glassman. Directed by Glassman, Todd McCarthy, Samuels. Screenplay, McCarthy. Camera (color, black & white, high definition TV), Nancy Schreiber; editor, Glassman; associate executive producer, Mariko Jane Hirai. Reviewed at Cannes Film Festival (out of competition), May 14, 1992. Running time: **90 MIN.**
With: Nestor Almendros, John Alonzo, John Bailey, Michael Ballhaus, Stephen Burum, Bill Butler, Michael Chapman, Allan Daviau, Caleb Deschanel, Ernest Dickerson, Frederick Elmes, William Fraker, Conrad Hall, James Wong Howe, Victor Kemper, Lazslo Kovacs, Charles Lang, Sven Nykvist, Lisa Rinzler, Owen Roizman, Charles Rosher Jr., Sandi Sissel, Vittorio Storaro, Haskell Wexler, Robert Wise, Gordon Willis, Vilmos Zsigmond.

Cleverly structured and compiled, **this fascinating documentary brings audiences face-to-face with 26 leading cinematographers talking about their work and that of others, combined with well-chosen excerpts from famous films. Shown at Cannes on HDTV, "Visions of Light" will be released as a 35m print for specialized exhibition.**

At a time of expanded interest in the way films are made — witness the number of TV docus on "The Making of . . . " — this revealing study of the cinematographer's job of putting images on film is constantly absorbing and frequently exciting. The camera people herein all have pertinent observations to make about how and why they photographed certain films the way they did, and how past cinematographers' works have influenced them.

The 125 or so film excerpts encompass a visual history of mostly U.S. films, from Billy Bitzer's "Birth of a Nation" to Gregg Toland's "Citizen Kane," through to "The Godfather, Part III," shot by Gordon Willis (called "the Prince of Darkness" by Conrad Hall). From beautiful closeups to sweeping crane shots, it provides a new appreciation of that overworked phrase: "the magic of the movies."

The naturally set, carefully lit and comfortably relaxed interviews were shot on HDTV and are never too long between excerpts. The clips are from 35m prints, most in perfect condition and respectful of differing aspect ratios.

From the many conclusions to be drawn from the cinematographers' achievements and experiences, it becomes clear from their ideas and those of their predecessors that their camerawork was always ahead of technology. Their improvisations became models. Tribute is paid to Robert Surtees who, at 65, was still experimenting while shooting "The Graduate."

With the American Film Institute as co-producer, this documentary confines itself largely to American cinematographers and European camera people who have worked on Yank films. As always with such compilations, some favorites are missing, perhaps because of unavailable cinematographers and elusive clip rights.

Memorable segments: Allen Daviau's ("E.T.," "Empire of the Sun") enthusiastic and informed recollections, William Fraker's funny anecdote about shooting "Rosemary's Baby," discussion of a "New York" style of cinematography and Conrad Hall's comments on how he and his contemporaries helped make "mistakes" (such as camera flair) acceptable to studio heads.

Apart from the docu's appeal to buffs and general audiences, this is a work with a long life ahead of it in film instruction everywhere. Arnold Glassman, Stuart Samuels, Todd McCarthy and their colleagues have produced an elegant and insightful chronicle proving once again that American film at its best is truly an art. — *Gerald Pratley*

MAD AT THE MOON
(COLOR/B&W)

A Michael Jaffe Films-Spectacor Films presentation of a Cassian Elwes/ Kastenbaum Films production. (Intl. sales: IRS Media Intl.) Produced by Michael Kastenbaum, Elwes, Matt Devlen. Executive producer, Michael Jaffe. Co-producers, Seth Kastenbaum, Daniel Jakub Sladek. Directed by Martin Donovan. Screenplay, Donovan, Richard Pelusi. Camera (Deluxe b&w, Pacific Film Labs color), Ronn Schmidt; editor, Penelope Shaw; music, Gerald Gouriet; sound, Cameron Frankley, Clifford Gynn; production design, Stephen Greenberg; costumes, Grania Preston. Reviewed at Cannes Film Festival market, May 11, 1992. (Also in Seattle Film Festival.) Running time: **97 MIN.**
With: Mary Stuart Masterson, Hart Bochner, Fionnula Flanagan, Cec Verrell, Stephen Blake, Daphne Zuniga.

Miscasting and klutzy plot development take the shine out of "Mad at the Moon," a Wild West amour fou movie that sprouts hairs halfway and turns into a werewolf pic. Slimly plotted item may attract the midnight crowd at specialized outings but is unlikely to raise much of a howl with mainstream auds.

The second picture by Argentinian-born Martin Donovan (a.k.a. Carlos Enrique Varela y Peralta-Ramos), who staked a cult film claim with the quirky "Apartment Zero," shows the same glee in blending genres and going for broke. The main problems here are accepting topliner Mary Stuart Masterson as a 25-year-old virgin and figuring out a story line that takes a left turn 50 minutes in.

Setting, per production notes, is "somewhere in America, 1892." Confident intro straightaway sets up an operatic tone with a troupe of singers performing in an open plain at night and unexplained black & white flashbacks of two young tykes and a mysterious stranger (Hart Bochner).

Mood is sustained for a while as pretty but repressed Jenny (Masterson) has a backstreets rendezvous with charismatic bum Miller Brown (Bochner), whom she's had the hots for since childhood. Despite her secret desires, she bows to the wishes of her mom (Fionnula Flanagan) and marries local milquetoast James Miller (Stephen Blake), the bum's half-brother.

Things start to go awry (with the pic, too) as soon as the couple settle in James' remote farmhouse. The marriage is unconsummated, Miller haunts the plains outside and Jenny experiences hubby's "moonsickness," during which he starts howling and turns partly vulpine.

On paper the idea sounds promising, if a trifle outré. Donovan skillfully sets up the board but seems less sure of how to make the game play. The half-brothers' crucial bond is mistily drawn, and the moonsickness stuff dominating pic's second half is never developed beyond a horror sidebar that doesn't deliver for genre fans.

Equally damaging is the lack of depth in the relationship between the two leads. Masterson, so good at portraying hidden passions in the more naturalistic "Fried Green Tomatoes" and "Some Kind of Wonderful," never seems to get a handle on her part and simply looks too knowing for a naive virgin. Bochner, okay in "Apartment Zero," mostly gets by with lingering looks and unshaven-hunk appeal.

Still, Donovan shows he has talent to spare as a pure technician. Pic has a confident feel which suggests the helmer himself knows where he's going, even if he sometimes forgets to check the rear-view mirror for fellow passengers. Pic works best when no one's talking and Donovan can stoke up the atmosphere via sound, music and images alone. Masterson's solo reveries and a later dinner scene are fine in this respect.

Of the supports, Flanagan fares best as the canny Irish mom, with few but characterful scenes. Blake doesn't get many chances as the weak husband. Daphne Zuniga pops up briefly in the flashbacks as the young Flanagan.

Technical credits are all top drawer. Sound design by Cameron Frankley is consistently subtle and evocative, complementing Ronn Schmidt's light-play lensing and the Sergio Leone-flavored production design and costuming by Stephen Greenberg and Grania Preston. Gerald Gouriet's big-number orchestral score, including the fake Italian opera segment at the start, is a further hokey delight.

— Derek Elley

GUNCRAZY

A Zeta Entertainment presentation in association with First Look Pictures. (Intl. sales: Overseas Filmgroup.) Produced by Zane W. Levitt, Diane Firestone. Co-producer, Mark Yellen. Directed by Tamra Davis. Screenplay, Matthew Bright. Camera (Foto-Kem color), Lisa Rinzler; editor, Kevin Tent; music, Ed Tomney; art direction, Kevin Constant; costume design, Merrie Lawson; sound (Ultra-Stereo), Daniel D. Monahan; associate producer, Alison Stone; assistant director, Rod Smith; casting, Partners In Crime. Reviewed at Cannes Film Festival market, May 14, 1992. Running time: **93 MIN.**
Anita Minteer . . . . Drew Barrymore
Howard Hickock . . . . James LeGros
Hank Fulton . . . . Billy Drago
Tom . . . . Rodney Harvey
Rooney . . . . Joe Dallesandro
Mr. Kincaid . . . . . Michael Ironside
Joy . . . . Ione Skye

A shoot-'em-up exploitationer with a few interesting ideas, "Guncrazy" lacks the exhilaration of a first-class lovers-on-the-run crime drama. After a promising beginning, competently made indie effort settles into a surprisingly somber mood that suppresses the possibilities latent in the story and actors. A flashy campaign built around Drew Barrymore as bad girl could generate some quick coin on the action circuit, with better results on video.

Matthew Bright's original screenplay contains echoes of Joseph H. Lewis' B classic, "Gun Crazy," among other similarly plotted tales of youth gone wild. But script is not explicitly based on any recognizable antecedents, as characters and situations are thoroughly modern.

Barrymore plays Anita, a ripe, lower-class 16-year-old whose lack of possibilities and parental guidance make her ready for the first interesting opportunity that comes along. She's presented matter-of-factly as the class slut, a girl who will willingly have sex with different boys because it's the only way she can feel liked. She also lets herself be bedded by her absent mother's b.f. (Joe Dallesandro), with whom she shares a miserable trailer.

For a class pen pal project, Anita starts corresponding with an imprisoned man whose direct emotionalism touches her so much they begin to conduct a love affair by mail. When the convict, Howard (James LeGros), writes, "I always dreamed of a girl who likes guns," Anita learns to shoot, which results in her killing her mom's beau as she tries to call off their special relationship.

Helping spring Howard early by finding him a job, Anita welcomes him with feverish anticipation but, in a nod to "Bonnie and Clyde," understands when he says he's not really ready for sex. Instead, to demonstrate his willingness to reform, he becomes a born-again Christian and they try to live the straight life.

But gun lust begins to get the better of them and, almost by accident, they begin killing. Howard's first reaction is fury at being pulled back down to his former level, but he finally accepts his destiny, telling Anita on the run, "Our lives are over now."

Aside from Anita's character, which Barrymore pulls off impressively, main points of interest lie in the dismal portrait of a society that can scarcely help but breed criminal-minded kids. Stuck in an ugly rural California town, with dumb, horny rednecks on one side, righteous squares on the other and Jesus freaks around the fringe, Anita can hardly be blamed for her impulses.

Unfortunately, eliminating the sexual element from the pair's relationship saps the story of the thrill it might have had. Furthermore, filmmakers don't follow up on their initial sociological observations with any broader points about contemporary society, the gun culture or the lack of sustenance in young people's lives. Ed Tomney's somber, plaintive score also serves to dampen the proceedings.

Still, music video director Tamra Davis applies some thought to low-budget genre filmmaking and makes a creditable debut in territory mined many times over. LeGros, saddled with miniscule character background and motivation, makes less of an impression here than he does in "My New Gun," also shown in Cannes. Other performances and tech credits are okay.

— Todd McCarthy

TCHEKISTE
(THE CHEKIST)
(RUSSIAN-FRENCH)

A Trinity Bridge (St. Petersberg)/Sodaperaga (Paris) co-production. Directed by Alexander Rogozhkin. Screenplay, Jacques Baynac, Andre Milbet. Camera (color), Valeri Mulgaout; editor, Tamara Denissova; music, Dimitri Pavlov; production design, Grigori Obraztsov. Reviewed at Cannes Film Festival (Un Certain Regard), May 17, 1992. Running time: **89 MIN.**
With: Igor Sergeyev, Alexei Polouyan, Mikhail Vasserbaoum, Nina Oussatova, Alexander Kharahkevitch, Sergei Issavnine.

"The Chekist," a relentlessly grim picture about the bloody aftermath to the Bolshevik Revolution in Russia, is of fest interest, but commercially it will be a very tough sell.

Director Alexander Rogozhkin (who made "The Guard," an anti-KGB film that made its mark in Berlin two years ago) provides a chilling depiction of institutionalized murder, and touches of grim humor make the terrible subject even more disturbing.

Title character is Sroubov (Igor Sergeyev), a bland functionary in charge of executing "enemies" of the new Communist state — priests, old nobility, anti-Communist union leaders, intellectuals and ordinary citizens run afoul of the regime.

There are no trials; names are read and instant death sentences handed out. Male and female victims are photographed and then taken to a cellar where they're forced to strip naked and are then shot; bodies are winched up to ground level, where they're placed in carts to be carried off for mass burial.

The director depicts this ritual over and over again, until the horror becomes numbing. The appalling work takes its toll, and Sroubov is driven mad.

Film had a mostly hostile reception at its official Cannes unspooling, but there's no doubting the power of Rogozhkin's implacable images and the anger against the Communists who, per pic, so single-mindedly set out to destroy their opposition.

Technical credits are all fine, but audiences for this ultra-grim pic will be hard to find.

— David Stratton

SHAONIAN YE, AN LA!
(DUST OF ANGELS)
(TAIWANESE)

A City Films production. (Intl. sales: Cine Electra, London.) Produced by Chiang Wen-hsiung, Chang Hua-k'un. Executive producer, Hou Hsiao-hsien. Directed, written by Hsü Hsiao-ming. Camera (color), Chang Hui-kung; editor, Liao Ch'ing-sung; music, Baboo Lim Giong, Wu Chün-lin; art direction, Chang Hung, Tu Chih-ching; costume design, Kaba Chang; sound (Dolby), Tu Tu-chih, Yang Ching-an; assistant director, Ch'en Huai-en; associate producers, Chan Hung-chih, Ch'en Kuo-fu. Reviewed at Cannes Film Festival (Directors' Fortnight), May 16, 1992. Running time: **105 MIN.**

Hsiao Kao	Jack Kao
Mei-mei	Vicky Wei
A-kuo	Yen Cheng-kuo
A-tou	T'an Chi-kang
Chi-chi	Chang Yi-han
Uncle Yung	Ch'en Sung-yung
The killer	Chang Shih

(Hokkien & Mandarin dialog)

A bleak and bloody study of nihilistic youth in modern Taiwan, "Dust of Angels" is a powerful bow by Taiwan's Hsü Hsiao-ming, previously assistant director to some of the island's leading talents. Slow-brewer will create a flutter on the fest circuit and in Asian sidebars, but arty pacing and oblique story line make it a tougher sell to wider auds.

Closing item at Cannes' Directors' Fortnight was very much hung on the coattails of w.k. Taiwan director Hou Hsiao-hsien, who exec produced through his City Films and with whose works the film bears several stylistic parallels. But Hsü's own imprint goes beyond simple copycatting.

First 70 minutes take place in the small harbor town of Pei-kang, in west central Taiwan. After an atmospheric intro in which a local hood is wasted in a restaurant, impressionable teens A-kuo and A-tou (Yen Cheng-kuo, T'an Chi-kang) join up with tattoed mobster Hsiao Kao (Jack Kao) to take revenge.

Kao is wounded in a subsequent gunfight and goes into hiding with g.f. Mei-mei (Vicky Wei). A-tou plans to go to the U.S. (giving his father a heart attack when he hears) and A-kuo stays with his uncle (Ch'en Sung-yung) until the heat's off.

The two kids head north to Taipei, hoping to track down their idol Kao through one of his girls, Chi-chi (Chang Yi-han). Final half-hour is an all-night tour through the underbelly of the capital, with a "Taxi Driver"-like descent into personal hell.

Pic has a real feel for Taiwanese street life and precisely catches the escalating problem of casual violence and aimless youth there. A simmering menace is found in many scenes in which boredom can quickly turn to anger, and friendship to enmity.

Most of the dialog (90% in the earthy Hokkien dialect rather than more formal Mandarin Chinese) is of the four-letter kind, with a semi-improvised feel. Pic's shape and power come more from Hsü's stylized compositions, strong on long takes and fixed setups, which are in direct contrast to his characters' undisciplined lives.

But as in Hou's own films, such as "A City of Sadness" and the earlier "Boys From Feng-kuei" (to which "Angels" is a darker twin), there's a reluctance to spell out basic details and relationships that makes the pic a confusing ride for nonlocals. Some Western viewers may spend the first hour simply trying to sort out who's who.

Still, the performances are etched sharply enough to hold the interest. Kao makes a charismatic mobster in designer shades and black suit, and former child star Yen (whose own experiences pic partly evokes) makes a genuinely frightening A-kuo, a swaggering young punk with a ready pump gun.

Tech credits are strong, benefiting from postproduction work in Japan and a Dolby soundtrack. Original Chinese title roughly means "Hey, kids, cool it!"
— *Derek Elley*

MALIZIA 2MILA
(MALIZIA 2000)
(ITALIAN)

A Warner Bros. Italia release of a Clesi Cinematografica production. (Intl. sales: Adriana Chiesa Enterprises.) Produced by Silvio Clementelli, Annamaria Clementelli. Directed by Salvatore Samperi. Screenplay, Ottavio Jemma, Samperi. Camera (Eastmancolor, Technicolor prints), Paolo Carnera; editor, Sergio Montanari; music, Fred Bongusto; production design, Ezio Altieri; sound, Danilo Moroni; assistant director, Marina Mattoli. Reviewed at Cannes Film Festival market, May 12, 1992. Running time: **103 MIN.**

Angela	Laura Antonelli
Ignazio La Brocca	Turi Ferro
Lance	Roberto Alpi
Jimmy	Luca Ceccarelli

There's not much of the original's magic second time around in "Malizia 2mila." Those with cherished memories of the 1973 Italo mini-classic will enjoy re-acquainting themselves with still-beauteous Laura Antonelli, but first-timers may wonder at the fuss. Light comic yarn about a youngster obsessed with an older woman is average fare.

Pic reunites many of the original's makers. Aside from Antonelli, Turi Ferro reprises his role as the paterfamilias (now aging husband of Antonelli); scripter Ottavio Jemma reteams with director Salvatore Samperi; and editing, production design and music are in the same hands. Clesi Cinematografica again produces, with Warners (which handled the original in many foreign territories) distribbing locally.

"Malizia" was a highly atmospheric mix of simmering eroticism and young males' pranks in a Sicilian household, where country girl Antonelli played servant and surrogate mother to Ferro's three sons. Darker edge came from the middle son's infatuation with Antonelli and his "malicious" sexual games.

Present item reprises the rites of passage theme with a new generation (time is 2000, though it could be now). Antonelli and Ferro — the sons have flown the coop — invite a handsome archaeologist (Roberto Alpi) and his pubescent son (Luca Ceccarelli) to stay while excavating below their villa.

Antonelli soon nixes the teen's passions ("I'm out of practice," she says), but he carries on sending her red roses and notes. Soon she doesn't know who's winding her up, and even suspects the boy's father and her own husband. Finale unites all the various strands into a night of farce and passion.

Pic sensibly doesn't try to shock '90s viewers by simply reworking material that was hot two decades ago; it's more a light comedy of manners with refs to the earlier film thrown in.

Ferro steals all his scenes with a hammy performance as a past-it roué, and further schtick is provided by the couple's klutzy, gum-chewing Filipino maid. Antonelli, often bathed in soft focus, exudes plenty of sex appeal tinged with a maternal edge. Her uneven performance is more problematic: Sometimes she looks and sounds tired, and she doesn't project her part with enough force. There's no nudity to write home about.

Technically smooth pic includes Fred Bongusto's breezy score. Paolo Carnera's photography is attractive without giving original pic's lenser Vittorio Storaro (whose career has since gone into separate orbit these past 20 years) any cause to look over his shoulder. — *Derek Elley*

ANMONAITO NO SASAYAKI WO KIITA
(I'VE HEARD THE AMMONITE MURMUR)
(JAPANESE)

A Euro Space production. (Intl. sales: Euro Space, Tokyo.) Produced by Kenzo Horikoshi. Directed, written by Isao Yamada. Camera (color), Tomohiro Asoh; editor, Keiichi Uraoka; music, Simon Fisher Turner; production design, Hideaki Sasaki; sound, Tsutomu Honda; line producer, Yohichi Yamazaki. Reviewed at Cannes Film Festival (Critics' week), May 14, 1992. Running time: **69 MIN.**

Brother	Kenzo Saeki
Sister	Hiroko Ishimaru
Brother (child)	Tetsuya Fujita
Sister (child)	Reina Oshibe

Also with: Arinori Ichihara, Takeo Kimura, Ichiko Hashimoto, Reo Oshibe.

Abstract to the point of disappearing in its own metaphors, "I've Heard the Ammonite Murmur" plays like a mind game without the manual. Visually teasing journey through a young man's memories could rack up some mileage on the fest circuit but is too inaccessible even for much art house playoff.

Pic is the first feature of Sapporo-based Isao Yamada, production designer on pics of the late Shuji Terayama. Yamada's picked up plenty of his sensei's visual tricks but needs to broaden his palette if he's to carve his own rep.

Free-form structure starts with a mineralogist (Kenzo Saeki) travelling to visit his sick sister (Hiroko Ishimaru), en route reading a mysterious letter she wrote. Memories flood back to their times together, their elegant mother and his countryside hikes observing nature's mineral wonders.

Despite the density of the imagery, Yamada fails to make the necessary connections for the cocktail to work, especially in the relationship between the kid's mineral fixation and his sibling love. Still, he comes up with striking imagery of Hokkaido locations and some one-off abstract settings owing a lot to his background as a conceptual artist.

Rhapsodic scoring by Derek Jarman collab Simon Fisher Turner does the best it can in glueing the parts together. Blowup from 16m original is generally okay.

— *Derek Elley*

HIT THE DUTCHMAN
(U.S.-RUSSIAN)

A 21st Century Film presentation of a Power Pictures-Start Corp. production. (Intl. sales: 21st Century) Produced, directed by Menahem Golan. Executive producers, Ami Artzi, Ivan Mendzheritsky. Screenplay, Joseph Goldman, from a story by Alex Simon. Camera (Deluxe color), Nicholas Von Sternberg; editor, Bob Ducsay; music, Terry Plumeri; production design, Clark Hunter; costume design, Natasha Landau; sound (Ultra-Stereo), Alexander Gruzdev; assistant director, Alexander Yurchikov; associate producer, Galina Tuchinsky; line producer, Mark Slater; casting, Abigail R. McGrath. Reviewed at Cannes Film Festival market, May 15, 1992. Running time: **118 MIN.**

Dutch Schultz	Bruce Nozick
Joey Noey	Eddie Bowz
Legs Diamond	Will Kempe
Emma	Sally Kirkland
Bo Weinberg	Matt Servitto
Vincent Coll	Christopher Bradley
Peter Coll	Jeff Griggs
Frances Ireland	Jennifer Miller
Frances	Abigail Lenz
Thomas E. Dewey	Jack Conley

Also with: Jennifer Pusheck, Leonard Donato, Rick Giolito, Menahem Golan.

"**H**it the Dutchman" should make a quick killing in easy markets and see plenty of action beyond theatrical. Fast-moving, splendidly trashy mobster yarn reps a strong behind-the-lens comeback by 21st Century topper Menahem Golan, who dishes up the genre goods with grindhouse glee.

Pic is the top-ruble half of two back-to-backers lensed in Russia, with similar casts and crews and overlapping plots. "Dutchman" — with bigger production values, stronger violence, sex and language and a larger story reach — will need to give its sibling "Mad Dog Coll" a head start to prevent swallowing up the latter theatrically.

Golan first touted "Dutchman" at Cannes in 1974 with George Segal as the Prohibition hood. Here Bruce Nozick toplines as Arthur Fleggenheimer, a cocky 24-year-old Jewish con who's freed from West Hampton pen and straightaway slips off the straight and narrow.

After literally biting the nose off Vincent Coll (Christopher Bradley), he's introed to Legs Diamond (Will Kempe) by best friend Joey (Eddie Bowz) and soon starts sniffing around Legs' warbler g.f. Frances Ireland (Jennifer Miller). He also adopts the name Dutch Schultz.

Joey converts to Judaism to marry Dutch's baby sister (Jennifer Pusheck) and the pair quit Legs' organization. After being ditched by Frances and seeing Joey shot, Dutch sets out after Legs and his territory. Rest of the pic limns his growing arrogance and eventual death in late 1935, with ex-West Hampton governor Thomas E. Dewey (Jack Conley) his tireless nemesis.

Unlike "Coll," pic isn't constrained by endless interiors and night scenes. Look is considerably bigger budget (though not enough to forge a convincing New York) and the wealth of characters and incidents easily fill up the running time. Cutting (using the EditDroid system) is zippy, and the large cast plays the dime-novel script at full tilt.

Nozick, a bundle of energy in "Coll," grabs the role here like a dog with a bone, butting heads with all and sundry. Playing is strong down the line, with Sally Kirkland lightening the tone with funny Jewish mother schtick, and Leonard Donato making a strong late play as Lucky Luciano, responsible for Dutch's downfall. Golan himself cameos as mobster Hymie Weinstock.

Pic's strong Jewish flavor is underlined by Terry Plumeri's churning Hebraic score. Period detail is B-picture authentic.

— *Derek Elley*

BENNY'S VIDEO
(AUSTRIAN-SWISS)

A Wega Film Prods. (Vienna)/Bernard Lang AG (Zurich) co-production. Produced by Veit Heiduschka, Bernard Lang. Directed, written by Michael Haneke. Camera (color), Christian Berger; editor, Marie Homolkova; sound, Karl Schlifelner; costumes, Erika Navas; production design, Christoph Kanter. Reviewed at Cannes Film Festival (Directors' Fortnight), May 13, 1992. Running time: **105 MIN.**

With: Arno Frisch, Angela Winkler, Ulrich Mühe, Ingrid Stassner.

A chilling portrait of a morally bankrupt adolescent, "Benny's Video" neatly states its case against the anesthetizing properties of too much violent imagery too soon. Urban terror story plays like an icy thriller, but the message runs deeper, lending an intellectual edge.

Video has such a hold on 14-year-old Benny (Arno Frisch) that he keeps his bedroom shades drawn and watches the view out his window on a video monitor. Since Benny's well-to-do parents (Angela Winkler, Ulrich Mühe) leave him pretty much on his own, his values are formed almost entirely by the video fare he uncritically absorbs.

Benny invites a young girl to his house where, with his camcorder running, he ends up murdering her. After stashing the body in a closet and attending a party, the remorseless teen breaks the bad news to his folks by running the tape for them.

Stripped down video-inflected visuals give the story matter-of-fact authority, and the murder sequence is handled mostly through potent off-screen suggestion. Low-key thesping is convincing throughout, particularly when Benny's parents calmly consider their unsavory options.

"Benny's Video" follows "The Seventh Continent" as the second item in a planned trilogy on growing alienation in Austria which, per helmer, "is intended as a polemic statement about the American sensational cinema and its power to rob viewers of their ability to form their own opinions." Pic's creepy denouement will not leave viewers indifferent. — *Lisa Nesselson*

WHO DO I GOTTA KILL?

An RSVP Prods. presentation of a Writers Ltd. Partnership production. (Intl. sales: RSVP, N.Y.) Produced, directed by Frank Rainone. Executive producer, Nicholas Spina. Co-producer, Vincent Viola. Screenplay, Rocco Simonelli, James Lorinz, Rainone. Camera (Technicolor), Adam Kimmel; editor, Michelle Gorchow; music, Doug Katsaros; music producer, Phil Ramone; production design, Susan Bolles; art direction, Rachael Weinzimer; costume design, Barbara Kramer, Kim Druce; sound, Peter Waggoner; assistant director, J. Miller Tobin; line producers, Christina Rosati, Lemore Syvan; casting, Todd Thaler, Caroline Sinclair. Reviewed at Cannes Film Festival market, May 16, 1992. Running time: **86 MIN.**

Jimmy Corona	James Lorinz
Tony Bando	Tony Darrow
Bink-Bink Borelli	John Costelloe
Fixer Giachetti	Frank Gio
Birdman Badamo	Vinny Pastore
Angie Giachetti	Gemma Nanni
Lori	Sandra Bullock
Bobby Blitzer	Stephen Lee

Also with: Anthony Michael Hall.

Dumb fellas meet writer's block in "Who Do I Gotta Kill?", a slim but good-looking comic low-budgeter. Rapid-fire dialog and black humor are only partly on target, but likable indie item could notch up an initial rep on the fest circuit.

Opening scenes, which could be tightened, have author Jimmy (James Lorinz) hassled by his agent (Stephen Lee) to come up with "some nitty-gritty street stuff" instead of another JFK conspiracy tome. After several botched suicide attempts, Jimmy gets the idea from a headline to do an inside story on the mob.

Pic finds its feet after Jimmy's wise-guy uncle (Tony Darrow) takes him on board, assigning hit man (John Costelloe) to teach him the ropes. After bungling several jobs, Jimmy is pressured by some cops to get the goods on his uncle's capo (Frank Gio). But Jimmy's hidden transmitter starts broadcasting the local ball game during a mob meet.

Mix of over-the-top Italos and Lorinz's hard-boiled narration often brings pic close to a colorized "Broadway Danny Rose" with bits of "Play It Again, Sam" stirred in. But first-time helmer Frank Rainone, from a background in commercials and trailers, devises enough plot twists in the final half to make time pass easily.

Darrow, an accomplished hand at Brooklynite mob parts ("Goodfellas," "Street Trash"), is the pic's engine, with fine backup from Costelloe and Gio. Only weak link is co-scripter Lorinz in the central role, who's good at the gangster schtick but can't hold the screen when the older players start in. Of the few femmes in the cast, Sandra Bullock scores a raunchy cameo as Jimmy's girlfriend.

Technically slick, $1 million pic is the initial production of N.Y.-based indie RSVP Prods., teaming Rainone with two Wall Street financiers. Phil Ramone contributes smooth music production. — *Derek Elley*

RAGE AND HONOR

An IRS Media presentation of a Copeland/Colichman production. Executive producers, Miles A. Copeland III, Paul Colichman, Harold Welb. Produced by Donald Paul Pemrick, Kevin Reidy. Directed, written by Terry H. Winkless. Camera (Foto-Kem color), Thomas A. Callaway; editor, David B. Lloyd; music, Darryl Way; production design, Billy Jett; associate producers, Melissa Cobb, Cynthia Rothrock, Richard Norton; line producer-production manager, John Schouweiler; assistant director, Chris Edmunds; casting, Shelly Boies, Don Pemrick. Reviewed at Cannes Film Festival market, May 13, 1992. Running time: **90 MIN.**

Kris Fairchild	Cynthia Rothrock
Preston Michaels	Richard Norton

Also with: Terri Treas, Brian Thompson, Catherine Bach, Alex Datcher.

This very routine martial arts pic has little theatrical potential, but it will have a video life for fans of this particular subgenre of action flicks.

By-the-numbers plot has an inner-city high school teacher and martial arts expert (Cynthia Rothrock) team up with Aussie undercover cop Richard Norton to get the city's drug lords and corrupt policemen.

Dialogue is minimal, with the laconic Aussie hero regularly spouting such clichés before kicking into action. Pic is just an excuse for endless and familiar martial arts scenes, many of them involving femmes, all of them routinely handled and strictly for indulgent fans.

Technical credits are passable.

— *David Stratton*

LE PETIT PRINCE A DIT
(AND THE LITTLE PRINCE SAID)
(FRENCH-SWISS)

A Ciné Manufacture SA (Lausanne)-French Prods. (Paris) production. Produced by Robert Boner. Directed by Christine Pascal. Screenplay, Pascal, Boner. Camera (color), Pascal Marti; editor, Jacques Comets; music, Bruno Coulais; costume design, Catherine Meurisse; sound, Dominique Vieillard, Jean-Pierre Laforce; assistant director, Manuel Flèche; associate producer, Emmanuel Schlumberger. Reviewed at Cannes Film Festival (Cinemas en France section), May 9, 1992. Running time: **105 MIN.**
Adam Leibovich . . . . Richard Berry
Mélanie . . . . Anémone
Violette . . . . Marie Kleiber
Also with: Lucie Phan, Mista Préchac, Claude Muret, Jean Cuenoud.

In "Le Petit Prince a Dit," helmer/co-scripter Christine Pascal creates a genuinely moving portrait of a terminally ill 10-year-old girl and her divorced parents. Excellent thesping, sensitive dialogue and fine lensing boost a potentially morbid tale, which could certainly double as a counseling tool after an art house run.

Balancing humor and raw emotions, pic avoids melodramic pitfalls while exploring a child's acceptance of death and her impending death's impact on the adults around her.

A man of science accustomed to having complete control over his fast-paced life, Adam (Richard Berry) is thrown for a loop when his only child, bright and chubby Violet (Marie Kleiber), is diagnosed with a brain tumor. Rational behavior goes straight out the window as Berry snatches his daughter and embarks on an impromptu road trip through Switzerland, Italy and France.

Berry excels as a man determined to both seize the moment and quantify his feelings. Anémone is touching as Violet's mom, a boozy actress whose emotions hug the surface. Kleiber is utterly convincing as the child who takes her fate in stride and wants only to reunite her parents.

In one well-handled sequence, the girl explains her illness from her own serene POV only to have her father counter with a clinical account of cell mutation. The unfairness of a mother outliving her daughter is gently underscored in an episode in which actress mom rehearses a scene before and after a phone call confirming her worst fears.

Score borders on syrupy, but that's the only minor departure from an unforced tone.

— *Lisa Nesselson*

GALAXIES ARE COLLIDING
(U.S.-CANADIAN)

An SC Entertainment Intl. presentation of a Covert Prods. production in association with Film Horizon. (Intl. sales: SC Entertainment, Toronto.) Produced by Stanley Wilson, John Ryman. Executive producers, Rob Straight, Syd Cappe, Nicolas Stiliadis. Directed, written by Ryman. Camera (Deluxe color), Philip Lee; editor, Ivan Ladizinsky; music, Stephen Barber; songs, Jim Lauderdale; art direction, Ted Sharps, Johannes Spalt sound (Ultra-Stereo), Margaret Duke; assistant directors, Steve Ray, Mark West. Reviewed at Cannes Film Festival market, May 12, 1992. (Also in Seattle Film Festival.) Running time: **93 MIN.**
Adam . . . . Dwier Brown
Beth . . . . Susan Walters
Margo . . . . Karen Medak
Psycho . . . . James K. Ward
Also with: Kelsey Grammer, Rick Overton.

"Galaxies Are Colliding" is a strung-out short that just about makes it over the 90-minute finish line through sheer technique. Offbeat satire about a West Coaster flipping his lid in the Mojave Desert could score a hit with festival audiences but won't make much of a dent theatrically.

First feature by John Ryman opens with Adam (Dwier Brown) in tux and shades walking zombie-like through sun-blasted scrubland. Face-to-camera interviews with kin tell how he deserted fiancée Beth (Susan Walters) on their wedding day and was supposedly zapped by the Air Force after driving into a practice zone.

While everyone in L.A. thinks

he's dead, Adam comes across a collection of weirdoes who use him as a sounding board. First up is a loony impressionist; then in a roadside diner he meets Margo (Karen Medak), an East European babe sleeping her way to Hollywood. She's the one who finally makes him reconnect with reality.

Ryman's script vaults over the problem of having a largely silent central character by including flashbacks to the roots of his withdrawal. Comedy here is decidedly off-the-wall: While Beth is choosing color schemes for their future abode, Adam is dreaming about soil erosion in Africa and the coming apocalypse.

On that basis, pic's simply a farther-out take on late 20th-century Yank obsessions — sex, "relationships," the "death" of U.S. culture and the generally screwed-up planet. But like the central character, the script keeps going around in ever-decreasing circles leading no place special.

Still, Ryman's neat and balanced compositions, with sharp lensing on real locations and unfussy editing, impose a sense of order that almost convinces the film is more significant than it is. A busy soundtrack of country & western, radio broadcasts sendups, plus classical lollipops (notably Dvorák's "From the New World" symphony) further engages attention. Performances are fine within material's confines, with Medak's tour de force as the ditzy Margo livening up the second half. — *Derek Elley*

A WOMAN, HER MEN, AND HER FUTON

An Interpersonal Film presentation in association with First Look Pictures. Produced by Dale Rosenbloom, Mussef Sibay. Executive producer, Roy McAree. Directed, written by Sibay. Camera (CFI color), Michael Davis; editor, Howard Heard; music, Joel Goldsmith; production design, Peter Paul Raubertas; costumes, Lothar Delgado; visual consultant, Alexander Graves; art direction, Florina Roberts; sound (Surround Stereo), Austin H. McKinney, Marty Kasparian; assistant director, Louie Lawless; casting, Andrea Stone Guttfreund, Laurel Smith. Reviewed at WorldFest/Houston, May 2, 1992. (In Cannes Film Festival market.) MPAA rating: R. Running time: **90 min.**
Helen . . . . Jennifer Rubin
Donald . . . . Lance Edwards
Randy . . . . Grant Show
Paul . . . . Michael Cerveris
Max . . . . Robert Lipton
Gail . . . . Delaune Michel
Jimmy . . . . Richard Gordon

Provocative title and a few

steamy scenes are the only conceivable selling points for Mussef Sibay's "A Woman, Her Men, and Her Futon." Small-budget pic is by turns laughably stilted and sophomorically self-referential as a drama about L.A. wannabe screenwriters, their sexual hang-ups and their mind games.

Jennifer Rubin (of cult fave "Delusion") plays a recently divorced, sexually active young woman searching for her true identity while writing a screenplay about a recently divorced, sexually active young woman searching for her true identity.

While working at a video company, she is friendly with, but refuses to be the lover of, a well-to-do budding filmmaker (Lance Edwards) who's plotting a movie about a poor fellow who pretends to be well-to-do so he can impress the woman he loves.

It doesn't take long before writer-director Sibay tips his one clever idea: Both Rubin and Edwards, whether consciously or otherwise, are mining their relationship for nuggets to use in their screenwriting.

Rubin's character, evidently intended as some sort of stereotype-breaking portrait of a modern woman, comes off as an ambiguous muddle. All too often, it's easy to share Edwards' suspicion that she is merely a manipulative bitch with serious psychosexual problems.

Edwards might gain a lot more sympathy for his lovesick plight if his character didn't come off as such a thick-witted wimp. As it stands, when Rubin finally rolls up her futon mattress and moves out, the only reaction the audience can summon is one of relief.

Pic repeatedly calls attention to its own alleged cleverness by reminding the audience they're watching the kind of no-frills, straight-from-the-heart independent pic that the characters constantly talk about.

Performances throughout are doggedly sincere and strenuously emphatic, as though the actors were trying to convey information to a classroom of slow learners. It's hard to tell who's more to blame: the people speaking the unspeakable lines or the person who wrote them.

Tech credits are as competent as the budget allows.

— *Joe Leydon*

O TZONIS KELN KYRIA MOU
(JOHNNY KELN, MADAM)
(GREEK)

A Greek Film Center/Giorgos Tsiokos/ Greek Film Television ET1 production. Directed, written by Thanassis Scroubelos. Camera (color), Giorgos Tsiokos; editor, Christos Santatzoglou; music, Giorgos Katsaros; set design, Sakis Koutroumbis, Aris Georgakopoulos; sound, Marinos Athanassopoulos. Reviewed at Thessaloniki Film Festival, Oct. 4, 1991. (In Cannes Film Festival market.) Running time: **108 MIN.**

Johnny Keln . . . . . Christos Tsangas
Mitsi . . . . Tatiana Ligari
Sonia . . . . Maria Baketea
Madam . . . . Despo Diamantidou
Mother . . . . Gisela May

"**J**ohnny Keln Madam," a rough-hewn character study of a paradoxical pimp and murderer, is a Hellenized "Blue Velvet" exposing the underbelly of Athens. Pic's crude appeal overrides an uneven and sometimes uncomfortable mixture of genres. Offshore markets loom larger at fests than commercial venues.

Johnny Keln (Christos Tsangas) oozes sleaze from his first scenes when he coldheartedly bumps off his dolly bird companion and callously takes her valuables for good measure. Before long, he latches on to another meal ticket (Tatiana Ligari), a boozy tart whose sweet daughter (Maria Barketea) stirs some long-buried sentimental responses. Plot hinges on Johnny's dilemma as he eludes other dangerous thugs and struggles with unfamiliar altruistic impulses.

Helmer/scripter Thannasis Scroubelos in his first feature successfully fleshes out his characters, but he runs into trouble with his plot, which goes in too many directions. References to classic German films such as "Blue Angel" (in flashbacks to his mother, born in Cologne) are interspersed with nods to contemporary U.S. pics, most notably "Blue Velvet" in the Kolonos (Athenian neighborhood) segues.

Still, pic has a raw strength suggesting Scroubelos' talent may come to fruition in his next project. Tech credits are okay for a very low-budget pic, although some of the color separation and editing is a bit rough.

Cast is good with a tight perf by Tsangas and a memorable guest turn as the madam by Despo Diamantidou (Woody Allen's mother in "Love and Death").
— *B. Samantha Stenzel*

SEATTLE FEST

WHO KILLED THE BABY JESUS

A Douglas Borghi production. Produced by Mark Wolf. Co-producer, Rodney Byron Ellis. Directed, written by Borghi. Camera (Agfa color), Alex Leyton; editor, Stewart Schill; music, John Clifforth; production design, Kathleen B. Cooper; assistant director, Carole Lynn; casting, Dori Zuckerman. Reviewed at Seattle Intl. Film Festival, May 25, 1992. Running time: **92 MIN.**

Eve Cody . . . . Tuesday Knight
Travis Adams . . . . Billy Wirth
Kirk Vaughn . . . . Sandy Ward
Lee Holden . . . . Hubert Kelly
Gordon Vaughn . . . . . . Tony Maggio
Roger Cutter . . . . Alan Toy
Dee Cody . . . . . Rende Rae Norman

Fast-paced, tightly written and strongly acted, "Who Killed the Baby Jesus" is a promising start for first-time director Douglas Borghi, but the predictable pic fails to induce stomach-tightening tension usually associated with violent crime dramas. It should appeal to audiences who relish profiles of psychopaths.

Set in a desert in the Southwest, the story centers on a tough, beautiful and very evil mother (Rende Rae Norman) and her stormy relationship with her equally beautiful and thoroughly manipulated daughter (Tuesday Knight) as they plan to pull off a heist that will put them on easy street. They enlist a handsome young hit man (Billy Wirth) whose knowledge of the heist's details unfolds slowly with surprising turns.

Norman delivers a strong performance as an amoral individual who trusts no one and offers plenty of reasons for her social alienation. Naturally, Mom imbues the same sociopathic traits in her daughter, with whom she has a love-hate relationship.

While Borghi, who also wrote the screenplay, may have created a brutally realistic world, he unfortunately also created a fairly predictable one, thus weakening the dramatic tension. Mother's actions lack mystery, and the daughter predictably flees Mom in the final scenes because she doesn't trust her.

But this isn't a fatal flaw, and the pic does provide an interesting character study with enough twists and turns to sustain interest. Performances are sharp, superbly led by Norman. Knight is impressive as the daughter struggling to break free of her mother's grip, and Wirth delivers a very credible performance of a heartless hit man longing for love. Pic's tech credits are okay.
— *Maggie Brown*

DO SVIDANIYE, MALCHIKI
(GOODBYE, BOYS)
(RUSSIAN-B&W)

A Mosfilm production. Directed by Mikhail Kalik. Screenplay, Boris Balter, Kalik, from Ye Bauer's story. Camera (black & white), Levan Paatashvili; editor, L. Kuznetsovoy; music, M. Tariverdiev; art direction, T. Antonova; sound, V. Zorin. Reviewed at British Film Institute preview theater, London, Oct. 30, 1991. (In Seattle Intl. Film Festival.) Running time: **80 MIN.**

With: Yevgeni Steblov, Mikhail Kononov, Nikolai Dostal, Natalya Bogonova, Viktoria Fyodorova.

A lyrical evocation of three Soviet kids' final days before World War II service, Mikhail Kalik's "Goodbye, Boys" is a major find from the dusty vaults of Soviet cinema. On the strength of this and the just-restored "To Love . . .," Kalik's rep is due for a major overhaul.

Russo-Jewish helmer, who emigrated to Jerusalem in 1971 after 20 years of official hassles, was hailed in the '60s as the peer of Andrei Tarkovsky and Sergio Paradjanov. This pic was made in '64 and given only limited release two years later. Attacked for its alleged pessimism, it was deep-sixed.

Loose tale centers on a Communist Youth Party trio in the seaside town of Odessa. Story unfolds as a reminiscence by one, Volodya (Yevgeni Steblov), who's trying his luck with shy g.f. Inka. His pals are the Jewish Sasha (Nikolai Dostal) and lanky Vitya (Mikhail Kononov), son of a champion worker.

Volodya and Vitya get drafted into the army and Sasha into a military medical school. Before they leave on the train to Leningrad, audience is casually told that Vitya got killed in 1941 and Sasha's name was posthumously "rehabilitated" after the war.

Most of the action is everyday stuff — first kiss, first shave, lots of larking around in boats and by the shore. Pic's lazy-day feel is accentuated by a dreamy score and Kalik's free-form structure.

Performances are all tip-top, with the three kids neatly balancing the wistful and humorous script. Black & white lensing of the Odessa locations has a Nouvelle Vague-ish feel. And to often striking effect, Kalik cuts in docu footage of the Nazi threat.

For buffs there's the extra treat of spotting beautiful Russian thesp Viktoria Fyodorova (from Mikhail Bogin's famed 1965 diploma work "The Two") as Vitya's g.f. and Dostal, director of the recent Locarno fest prizewinner "Cloud-Paradise," as Sasha.
— *Derek Elley*

PATRIOT GAMES

A Paramount release of a Mace Neufeld & Robert Rehme production. Produced by Neufeld, Rehme. Executive producer, Charles H. Maguire. Directed by Philip Noyce. Screenplay, W. Peter Iliff, Donald Stewart, based on Tom Clancy's novel. Camera (Technicolor, Panavision), Donald M. McAlpine; U.K. camera, Stephen Smith, James Devis; editors, Neil Travis, William Hoy; music, James Horner; production design, Joseph Nemec III; art direction, Joseph P. Lucky, Alan Cassie (U.K.); set design, Walter P. Martishius; set decoration, John M. Dwyer; costume design, Norma Moriceau; sound (Dolby), Jack Solomon, Ivan Sharrock (U.K.); stunt coordinators, David R. Ellis, Steve Boyum, Martin Grace (U.K.); special effects coordinator, Dale L. Martin; visual effects-video displays, Video Image; associate producer, Lis Kern; assistant director, Dennis Maguire; 2nd unit director, David R. Ellis; 2nd unit camera, Michael A. Benson; 2nd unit assistant director, Christopher T. Gerrity; casting, Amanda Mackey, Cathy Sandrich; U.K., Ireland casting, John Hubbard, Ros Hubbard. Reviewed at Mann National Theater, West L.A., June 1, 1992. MPAA Rating: R. Running time: **116 MIN.**

Jack Ryan	Harrison Ford
Cathy Ryan	Anne Archer
Kevin O'Donnell	Patrick Bergin
Sean Miller	Sean Bean
Sally Ryan	Thora Birch
Lord Holmes	James Fox
Robby	Samuel L. Jackson
Annette	Polly Walker
Marty Cantor	J.E. Freeman
Adm. Greer	James Earl Jones
Paddy O'Neil	Richard Harris
Dennis Cooley	Alex Norton
Watkins	Hugh Fraser

Tom Clancy was right the first time. Paramount's "Patriot Games" is an expensive stiff. Mindless, morally repugnant and ineptly directed to boot, it's a shoddy follow-up to Par's 1990 hit "The Hunt for Red October." Also based on a bestselling Clancy novel about intrepid CIA analyst Jack Ryan, the ultra-violent, fascistic, blatantly anti-Irish "Patriot Games" stars a dour Harrison Ford, whose box office allure should ensure a big opening before downbeat word-of-mouth spreads like wildfire.

The "Patriot Games" novel is a right-wing cartoon of the British-Irish political situation, full of implausibilities and tending toward overblown action setpieces, but it has an inescapable gut-wrenching emotional power lacking in this adaptation by W. Peter Iliff and Donald Stewart.

Director Philip Noyce, whose major previous credit was the low-budget Aussie pic "Dead Calm," is way out of his depth here, relying on tight closeups that eliminate visual and social context and incoherently handling action sequences in the would-be spectacular climax.

Ford's Ryan, at the onset, has left the CIA to teach naval history at Annapolis. A visit to London with his family places him in the middle of an attack on a high British official (James Fox) by what Ford later identifies as "some ultra-violent faction of the IRA." His rescue of Fox and killing of one attacker makes him the quarry of a revengeful, ice-blooded IRA man (Sean Bean).

The novel's pontifications on the political context are shallow and biased toward the British, but the book does take the time to address the subject. That's more than can be said for the film, which takes about 20 seconds to do so in a TV sound bite of a Sinn Fein political rep (Richard Harris), whose comments can barely be heard above the Ford family's chatter.

Harris makes a point that should have been allowed to play much more loudly: that when Americans talk of their own uprising against their British colonial rulers, they call the revolutionaries "patriots," not "terrorists." This film has little time for such distinctions or for the nuances of the Irish cause.

The case is sentimentally loaded by painting the IRA faction as monsters who don't hesitate to attack Ford's wife (Anne Archer) and daughter (Thora Birch) as part of Bean's vendetta.

Prince Charles and his family are the targets in the book — an angle that no doubt would have presented insuperable problems on screen — and while making the minister of state for Northern Ireland the target would seem to make more sense politically, Fox also is a royal (a distant cousin of the queen), which makes his attackers seem as foolishly reckless as those in the book.

A major implausibility in both versions is that the radical cell would allow and help a grieving member (Bean) to put political realities aside to hunt down a CIA man on his home turf. Mad dog Bean and his brighter superior (Kevin O'Donnell) argue about this, but Bean prevails.

Nor does it make sense that the cell would be able to operate so easily and with such massive firepower on American soil, or that Fox would be so poorly protected when visiting Ford's home as he is in the film. Even a master action director would have trouble making the audience swallow those points, and Noyce's staging of the elaborate finale (much of it in semi-darkness) is laughable.

While Ford is a solid blend of thought and action in his James Bondish role, and his need to protect his family gives the film some gripping moments, the film's moral viewpoint is strictly neanderthal. Archer, who's playing a supposedly sensitive eye surgeon, defines the moral tone by telling Ford about Bean, "You get him, Jack. I don't care what you have to do — just get him."

Technically, the film doesn't look or sound good, aside from some fascinating simulations by the Video Image process of CIA satellite surveillance.

"Hunt for Red October" star Alec Baldwin's decision to forego this project for the Broadway revival of "A Streetcar Named Desire" was greeted with smug head-shaking in Hollywood at the time, but now seems like a wise career move. If producers Mace Neufeld and Robert Rehme don't raise their standards next time out (Ford is pacted for two more Clancy films), Par's Jack Ryan tentpole may collapse prematurely. — *Joseph McBride*

ACES: IRON EAGLE III

A New Line Cinema release of a Ron Samuels production. (Intl. release, Carolco Pictures.) Produced by Samuels. Directed by John Glen. Screenplay, Kevin Elders, based on characters created by Elders, Sidney J. Furie. Camera (CFI color; Technicolor prints), Alec Mills; editor, Bernard Gribble; music, Harry Manfredini; production design, Robb Wilson King; costume design, Lesley Nicholson; sound (Dolby), Susumu Tokunow; production manager-co-producer, Stan Neufeld; assistant director, James M. Freitag; model & special effects, John Richardson; stunt coordinator, Bob Minor; aerial unit director, David Nowell; associate producer, Michael R. Casey; casting, Vicki Huff. Reviewed at Broadway screening room, N.Y., Nov. 14, 1991. MPAA Rating: R. Running time: **98 MIN.**

Chappy	Louis Gossett Jr.
Anna	Rachel McLish
Kleiss	Paul Freeman
Leichman	Horst Buchholz
Palmer	Christopher Cazenove
Horikoshi	Sonny Chiba
Stockman	Fred Dalton Thompson
Simms	Mitchell Ryan
Tee Vee	Phill Lewis

Also with: Rob Estes, J.E. Freeman, Tom Bower, Juan Fernandez, Ray Mancini, Inez Perez, Branscombe Richmond.

New Line should do fine business with "Aces," an action-packed, campy entry in Lou Gossett's "Iron Eagle" series. Pic was originally slated as an off-season January 1992 release by since defunct distrib 7 Arts, but now receives a prime summer slot.

Best in its cartoonish moments, this followup helmed by James Bond director John Glen notably introduces the beautiful bodybuilder Rachel McLish. Though she has to strive mightily to get out her lines of dialogue, the fledgling actress is perfectly cast and could well become an important action heroine.

Producer Ron Samuels shifts here from the youth-oriented storyline of the first two "Eagle" pics (both helmed by Sidney J. Furie) to an over-the-hill gang premise reminiscent of the British "Wild Geese" pics.

Air Force pilot Gossett rounds up a group of fellow veteran fighter aces to fly to Peru and blow up a cocaine factory.

The U.S. government won't support this mission so the guys use vintage World War II era planes they've been flying in air shows.

Gossett fights the drug lords because a friend was killed by them and his sister (McLish) captured and tortured. He frees McLish, who turns out to be more than the equal of any of the male combatants.

Scripter Kevin Elders, who has worked on all three "Eagle" films, throws in a streetwise ghetto kid (Phill Lewis) who stows away on the mission and offers a combination of comic relief and heroism.

Film's camp value derives from the mocking use of the fighter aces, including Christopher Cazenove in the Roger Moore role, vet action star Sonny Chiba as the Japanese kamikaze pilot and a very fit looking Horst Buchholz as the German wiz.

When not making corny patriotic speeches Gossett is a steadying force here.

McLish is terrific in action scenes and merely needs intensive coaching on her acting to supercede Sigourney Weaver and Linda Hamilton in genre roles.

Paul Freeman reprises his stock Nazi from "Raiders of the Lost Ark" as the nominal heavy.

Dogfights in the air and pyrotechnics on ground are up to the high standards of Glen's 007 credits. — *Lawrence Cohn*

HOUSESITTER

A Universal release of an Imagine Films Entertainment production. Produced by Brian Grazer. Executive producer, Bernie Williams. Directed by Frank Oz. Screenplay, Mark Stein, from a story by Stein, Grazer. Camera (Deluxe color), John A. Alonzo; editor, John Jympson; music, Miles Goodman; production design, Ida Random; art direction, Jack Blackman, Jeff Sage; set design, Philip Messina; set decoration, Tracey A. Doyle; costume design, Betsy Cox; sound (Dolby), Martin Raymond Bolger, Lee Dichter; house design, Trumbull Architects (N.Y.); associate producers, Karen Kehela, Michelle Wright; assistant director, James W. Skotchdopole; casting, John Lyons. Reviewed at Universal screening room, North Hollywood, May 7, 1992. MPAA Rating: PG. Running time: **100 MIN.**

Davis	Steve Martin
Gwen	Goldie Hawn
Becky	Dana Delany
Edna Davis	Julie Harris
George Davis	Donald Moffat
Marty	Peter MacNicol
Ralph	Richard B. Shull
Mary	Laurel Cronin
Moseby	Roy Cooper
Rev. Lipton	Christopher Durang
Travis	Heywood Hale Broun
Patty	Cherry Jones
Karol	Vasek Simek
Moseby's secretary	Suzanne Whang
Lorraine	Mary Klug
Hazel	Alice Duffy
Harv	Ken Cheeseman

"Housesitter," a tediously unfunny screwball comedy, is a career misstep for both Steve Martin and Goldie Hawn. Hawn is grating as the kind of giggly flake she played two decades ago on "Laugh-In," and Martin is more obnoxious than endearing as the architect whose life she invades. This looks like a B.O. dud.

Martin's in love with wholesome Dana Delany, who lives in the quaint New England village of Dobbs Mill, but she deals him an emotional blow by refusing to marry him and move into the new architectural showcase he's built out in the countryside.

Enter Hawn. After they meet while she's working as a waitress and putting on a Hungarian accent, they have a one-night stand. He leaves without saying anything the next morning, so she tracks him to the empty house. She moves in, telling everyone in town that she's his new wife, and they believe her.

The setup isn't very amusing, but the plot machinations once Hawn hits the small town are languidly paced and excruciatingly obvious. The only suspense is whether Delany will change her mind about Martin, due to her growing jealousy over Hawn, which he encourages. It isn't enough to sustain interest.

Although Hawn has audience sympathy initially because of Martin's callous snobbery after their sexual encounter, her supposedly zany antics quickly become wearying. Though she looks terrif, it's unbecoming for a middle-aged woman to be playing the kind of goofball she played in her youth.

The mendacious character comes off as mentally unbalanced, not charming, and her intrusion into Martin's life seems faintly sinister, like that of a deranged fan stalking a celebrity. Her conning of Martin's estranged parents (Donald Moffat, Julie Harris), who are delighted that their flighty son is settling down, comes off as a cruel toying with their emotions.

Despite her declaration that she "didn't want to marry a dreamer — I'm not that brave," the forthright Delany seems far more appealing than Hawn, but that makes her hesitation all the more exasperating, both for Martin and for the viewer.

Martin has patented wild-and-crazy moments here and there (including a wonderful pratfall), but appears uncomfortable for much of the pic, never more so than when he has to sing an Irish lullaby to his father at a party. The rendition starts out as tongue-in-cheek droll, but winds up making the audience squirm.

Frank Oz proves no wizard with his direction of this nonsense. John A. Alonzo's crisp, sunny lensing is about all that keeps the pic bearable to watch.

— *Joseph McBride*

PAINTING THE TOWN

A Padded Cell release of a Behar & Sackner production. Produced by Sara Sackner. Directed by Andrew Behar. Screenplay, Richard Osterweil. Camera (Duart color), Hamid Shams; editor, Sackner, Behar; music, Peter Fish; production design, Sackner; sound, Edward Campbell, Fish, Chazz Menendez; 2nd unit director, Ron Honsa; associate producer, Sheila Szczepaniak. Reviewed at Walter Reade theater, N.Y., May 30, 1992. No MPAA Rating. Running time: **78 MIN.**
With: Richard Osterweil.

Party crasher/painter Richard Osterweil's monologue provides offbeat entertainment in the autobiographical portrait film "Painting the Town." Specialized audiences will get a kick out of this droll character's curious lifestyle.

With receding hairline and soft, ingratiating voice, 39-year-old Osterweil resembles a non-singing Art Garfunkel, calmly relating his 15 years of sneaking into celeb funerals, parties and preems.

He states that the reason he came to New York was to see celebrities. Result is closeup encounters with celebs like Katharine Hepburn and Princess Grace. Osterweil supports himself as a cab driver and in odd jobs like coat checker at a restaurant (he tries on all the celebrity coats), while painting hundreds of canvases, mainly pastiche.

Reciting the numerous big-name funerals he's attended, from Andy Warhol to William Paley, Osterweil claims his is not morbid interest but rather an attempt to become part of history. Actually, he resembles Warhol in the need to be always on the scene, though his paintings are not innovative and hardly set to propel him to Warhol status.

Using "Gone With the Wind" as his model for behavior, Osterweil's vicarious existence comes through identifying with women, haunted by their glamor and even trying on their garments. He almost takes on the pathos of the gay black models in Jennie Livingston's docu "Paris is Burning," a life lived second-hand pressing up to thrill of standing next to the rich and famous.

Filmmakers Andrew Behar and Sara Sackner keep things simple by merely photographing Osterweil's spiel, though picture would have been improved by testimony from his friends, adversaries or hard-won socialite friends, such as Mrs. Samuel Peabody, the subject of many of his paintings.

A cop-out end credit notes that Osterweil's remarks are "loosely based on the life and fantasies of Richard Osterweil," and evidence of his embroidering on the facts is ample.

In sum, he emerges as sort of an unpaid journalist, forging or sneaking his way into events and then writing them up in his diary rather than a gossip or society column. Like many in the media, he grades the soirées according to the quality of food served (or lack thereof) but his gee-whiz anecdotes fail to impart the dreariness of many of the events cited. Presumably the danger of crossing class barriers and crashing society makes it all worthwhile.

— *Lawrence Cohn*

MUNCHIE

A Concorde Pictures release. Produced by Mike Elliott. Executive producer, Roger Corman. Directed by Jim Wynorski. Screenplay, R.J. Robertson, Wynorski; additional Munchie dialogue, Vin DiStefano. Camera (Foto-Kem color), Don E. Fauntleroy; editor, Rick Gentner; music, Chuck Cirino; production design, Stuart Blatt; art direction, Carey Meyer; costume design, Lisa Cacavas; sound (Ultra-Stereo), Christopher Taylor; Munchie creators, Gabe Bartalos, Dave Kindlon; assistant director, Larry Kent Linton; 2nd unit director, Steve Mitchell; stunt coordinator, Patrick Statham; co-producer, Michele Weisler; casting, Andrew Hertz. Reviewed on New Horizons vidcassette, N.Y., June 1, 1992. MPAA Rating: PG. Running time: **80 MIN.**

Cathy	Loni Anderson
Voice of Munchie	Dom DeLuise
Elliott	Andrew Stevens
Gage Dobson	Jaime McEnnan
Prof. Cruikshank	Arte Johnson
Andrea	Love Hewitt
Ashton	Scott Ferguson
Leon	Mike Simmrin
Mrs. Blaylok	Toni Naples
Miss Laurel	Monique Gabrielle
Principal Thornton	Ace Mask
Mr. Kurtz	Jay Richardson

Also with: Angus Scrimm, George (Buck) Flower, Fred Olen Ray, Becky LeBeau, Brinke Stevens, Linda Shayne, Paul Hertzberg, Chuck Cirino, R.J. Robertson.

T&A director Jim Wynorski tries on the family film with good results in "Munchie." Picture opened in May in Nashville but is mainly of interest to vid fans.

Title is a bit confusing, since the singular "Munchie" is a sequel to Bettina Hirsch's 1987 film "Munchies." That kind of moniker reversal is rare, though Universal remade the 1939 classic "Destry Rides Again" in 1954 as simply "Destry." (Adding confusion, U's original 1932 version was also called "Destry Rides Again").

This time, the one critter, an oversize smiling puppet voiced in wisecracking style by Dom DeLuise, is discovered in a mine shaft by young Jaime McEnnan and becomes his pal, helping him with bullies at school and magically granting other wishes.

Film lacks the frenetic nature of its models, such as "Gremlins" and other imitations like the "Critters" and "Ghoulies" series. However, Wynorski's pacy direction and frequent sight gags keep things moving and entertaining.

McEnnan is an ingratiating young hero, and Loni Anderson makes for a most glamorous single parent. Arte Johnson has little to do as a neighboring archaeologist (filling the role of Harvey Korman from the original), while Andrew Stevens overplays his nominal heavy as the hero's future stepdad.

Effects, such as a flying pizza, are minor, with the accent on comedy. Wynorski's trademark of buxom women in the cast is amply delivered not only by Anderson but Toni Naples as McEnnan's math teacher and Monique Gabrielle as a sexy secretary to the principal. — *Lawrence Cohn*

LA MONJA ALFEREZ
(THE LIEUTENANT NUN)
(SPANISH)

A Goya Films & Actual Films production. Directed, written by Javier Aguirre, based on Catalina de Erauso's "Memorias" & Thomas De Qunicey's "The Spanish Military Nun." Camera (Eastmancolor), Domingo Solano; editor, Guillermo Maldonado; music, Antton Larrauri; sound, Ignacio Ros Urbieta. Reviewed at Public Theater, N.Y., May 20, 1992. (In Intl. Festival of Lesbian and Gay Film, N.Y.) Running time: **115 MIN.**
With: Esperanza Roy, Blanca Maarsillach, Conrado San Martin, Isabel Luque, Luis Iriondo.

Telling the incredible true story of a woman who fled a convent and lived most of her life disguised as a man, "La Monja Alferez" is an absorbing historical film. Handsome photography and period detail complement the solid script and acting. Unfortunately, the hard-to-believe plot may be a hard sell.

Catalina de Erauso, known as *la Monja Alferez*, was born to a noble Spanish family in 1592. Her choices were to marry or become a nun, and she reluctantly decided on the latter. But she was not cut out for the convent and rebelled against her superiors.

She fell in love with another nun, Inez, who soon became sick and died. After pleading with her father to release her — "I don't want a husband! I want my freedom!" — she escaped the convent dressed as a man.

Eventually, de Erauso sailed to the New World. Passing as a man, she signed up with the Spanish Army, dueled with rivals, nearly froze to death crossing the Andes and fought off the advances of admiring women.

Once revealed as a woman, she returned to Spain to meet with the King. Amazingly enough, he granted her a pension, made her a lieutenant and allowed her to dress as a man.

Under Javier Aguirre's direction, the fascinating story never lags despite the nearly two-hour running time. Aguirre's script manages to trace a number of dramatic events, though it's too dependent on narration.

Of the two strong actresses playing De Erauso, Esperanza Roy takes over when she becomes a man and pulls off the difficult task of playing a rather masculine woman without overdoing it.

Technical credits, including lush 35m photography and immaculate costumes, make "La Monja Alferez" a polished historical production. The only jarring element is the very un-17th century synthesizer music.

Otherwise, it is a compelling drama of a remarkable woman. Made in 1987, the drama may have trouble finding a distributor despite its merits. Perhaps it could be sold as a Spanish, period version of "Sister Act."
— *William Stevenson*

THE HUMAN SHIELD

A Cannon Pictures release & production. Produced by Christopher Pearce, Elie Cohn. Directed by Ted Post. Screenplay, Mann Rubin; story by Rubin, Mike Werb. Camera (Deluxe color), Yossi Wein; editors, Daniel Cahn, Matthew Booth; music, Robbie Patton; production design, Itzik Albalak; art direction, Yehuda Ako; costume design, Rakefet Levy; sound, Eli Yarkoni; special effects, Yoram Pollack; stunt coordinator, Guy Norris; assistant director, Eli Cohn; 2nd unit camera, Danny Schneor; casting, Dalia Hovers. Reviewed at Cineplex Odeon Fairfax, L.A., May 30, 1992. MPAA Rating: R. Running time: **90 MIN.**
Doug Matthews . . . Michael Dudikoff
Ben Matthews . . . . . Tommy Hinkley
Lila Haddilh . . Hana Azoulay-Hasfari
Ali Dallal . . . . Steve Inwood
Also with: Uri Gavriel, Avi Keidar, Geula Levy, Gil Dagon, Michael Shillo.

Reportedly the first fiction feature to deal directly with the Persian Gulf conflict, "The Human Shield" is a lame, small-budget actioner that exploits its political context without delivering the expected thrills of the genre. Short on big-scale set-pieces and saddled with a preposterous plot, pic will quickly die at the B.O. and head straight for video.

Following a short prologue depicting a brutal massacre of innocent villagers by Iraqi soldiers in 1985, story switches to August 1990, right after the invasion of Kuwait. Hero Michael Dudikoff, playing a former U.S. Marine instructor with the CIA who trained Iraqi soldiers to fight Iran, goes back to Iraq when his diabetic brother Tommy Hinkley is taken hostage by a ruthless, power-mad Iraqi general who, as essayed by Steve Inwood, looks and acts like Iraqi leader Saddam Hussein.

Formulaic pic borrows heavily from "Rambo" and assorted Cannon actioners such as "Missing in Action," relying on the overly familiar sequencing of imprisonment, rescue and escape, peppered with the obligatory chases and explosions.

Mann Rubin's screenplay, based on a story by him and Mike Werb, is embarrassingly predictable and simplistic. Helmer Ted Post, a proficient craftsman ("Hang 'Em High," "Go Tell the Spartans"), commits the fatal mistake of unfolding his narrative at a slow pace, which allows the viewer to remain ahead of the story. Climactic showdown between Dudikoff and the general at a chemical weapons plant is poorly executed.

Film was shot entirely in Israel, doubling convincingly as Iraq and Jordan. Cast consists of many Israeli actors attempting, none too effectively, Iraqi accents. Production values are unimpressive.

With the exception of the handsome Dudikoff, who carries his duties with the required assurance, acting is downright weak. Inwood plays the Iraqi officer in a manner that puts to shame the most outrageous German and Japanese villains in World War II pictures.

Pic may be most noteworthy for featuring a CIA officer as its hero, a rarity in recent U.S. films. Post claims in the press notes that he wanted to show the differences between the Iraqi and U.S. cultures because "ignorance and misperception are the enemy of effective communication." However, judging by what's on the screen, his film might perpetuate stereotypes Americans have about Iraq. — *Emanuel Levy*

VIA APPIA
(GERMAN-16m)

A Strand Releasing presentation. Produced by Norbert Friedlander. Directed, written by Jochen Hick. Camera (color, 16m), Peter Christian Neumann; editor, Claudia Vogeler; music, Charly Schoppner; sound, Marc van der Willigen. Reviewed at Public Theater, N.Y., May 19, 1992. (In Intl. Festival of Lesbian and Gay Film, N.Y.) Running time: **90 MIN.**
Frank . . . . Peter Senner
Jose . . . . Guilherme de Padua
The director . . . . Yves Jansen
Lucia . . . . Margarita Schmidt
Sergio . . . . . . Jose Carlos Berenguer
Ulieno . . . . Gustavo Motta
Mario . . . . Luiz Kleber

"Via Appia," billed as an "enacted documentary," is a film within a film about a German who returns to Rio de Janeiro to make some sense out of why he has AIDS, taking along a film crew to document his search for the man who gave him the virus. While the premise is interesting, something got lost in the execution.

Frank (Peter Senner), a former flight attendant now stricken, and the film director (Yves Jansen) tour the city's gay bathhouses, hotels, discos and parks. Their guide is Jose (Guilherme de Padua), who promises to deliver Mario, the man who scrawled "Welcome to the AIDS Club" after spending the night with Senner. Incredibly enough, the pic manages to make Rio —locale of a street populated by hustlers that provides pic's title — boring.

Senner's only record of Mario is a photograph, one of many nude photos he has taken of hustlers. The plot device is an excuse for writer/director Jochen Hick to include plenty of male nudity, beginning with the opening titles.

With more on his mind than gratuitous nudity, however, Hick also wants to show a man dealing with AIDS by searching for the cause of it and creating art at the same time. In Hick's creditable approach to AIDS, Senner is resigned and sometimes depressed, but he doesn't give up hope.

At the picture's finale, Senner, dressed in his flight attendant uniform, walks into the ocean. A moment later he's back on the beach, telling the camera he doesn't know what he'll do next. The cameraman says there's no more film, and the pic ends.

"Via Appia" has good intentions, but they don't amount to a satisfying film. Plot of this intriguing piece of self-reflexive filmmaking is minimal, and the pacing is glacially slow. Acting is low-key, like the rest of the film. If anything, "Via Appia" is too understated.

Made for just $300,000, it is visually rough. The hand-held camerawork and natural lighting give it a cinéma vérité look, but at times the darkness makes it a challenge to follow the action — or lack thereof.
— *William Stevenson*

MUTANDE PAZZE
(CRAZY UNDERWEAR)
(ITALIAN)

A Penta Distribuzione release of a Penta Film/Officina Cinematografica production. Director of production, Angelo Zemelio. Executive producer, Luciano Luna. Directed by Roberto D'Agostino. Screenplay, D'Agostino, Fiorenzo Senese. Camera (Cinecittà color), Alfio Contini; editor, Antonio Siciliano; music, Gianni Mazza; art direction, Leonardo Conte, Emita Frigato; costumes, Camilla Righi; sound, Benito Alchimede. Reviewed at Metropolitan Cinema, Rome, March 12, 1992. Running time: **97 MIN.**
Amalia . . . . Monica Guerritore
Stefania . . . . Eva Grimaldi
Alessia's aunt . . . . . Marisa Merlini
Alessia . . . . Deborah Cali
Beatrice . . . . Barbara Kero
Game show host . . . . Sergio Vastano

Maverick Italo media commentator Roberto D'Agostino makes a bundled bow as helmer-scripter with "Crazy Underwear," a stale comedy about small screen divas sleeping their way to stardom. The promise of T&A aplenty and a lively round of who's really who among a thinly veiled gallery of local celebs might create a brief b.o. flurry, but word of mouth should dig pic an early grave. Offshore outlook looks like zip.

Yawnsome yarn follows four femmes: daytime star Monica Guerritore attempting to jump to primetime via the CEO's bed; soft-porn star Eva Grimaldi angling for the lead in a Tinto Brass-style pic (helmer here is named Crass); her seemingly innocent pal Barbara Kero with designs of her own, and ambitious soubrette Deborah Cali, served up as a producer's plaything by her monstrous mother and aunt (Irma Capece Minutolo and Marisa Merlini, as subtle as pantomime dames).

Known for his stylishly acute observations on the inanities of Italo tubedom, D'Agostino limits himself here to pedestrian jibes about intellectually bereft game shows and glitzy current affairs coverage. Desperately wacky set-pieces seem tossed in for easy laughs, paying no heed to logic or threadbare plot.

Lest the whole shebang be misread as another trifling sex comedy, D'Agostino gives each main character a talking head shot to remind auds that it's intended as stinging satire. The girls get to justify their venal behavior with airhead philosophizing and some abstract slants on post-feminism.

Perfs are mostly strident and arch, with simian sex queen Grimaldi downright embarrassing. Legit thesp Guerritore rises momentarily above the mire as pic's only character given a glimmer of self-doubt and potential redemption. Like the script, garish art direction and costumes strain for stylized Almodóvarian outrageousness but fall way short as grotesque shopworn kitsch. D'Agostino's lack of control over the medium is brought glaringly to light in a sloppily orchestrated, all-out brawl that serves as pic's abrupt, inconclusive finale.

— *David Rooney*

BUFFALO JUMP

A Machipongo Inlet Films production. Produced by James Flack. Directed, written by Chris Johnstone. Camera (Fuji color), Thomas Lappin; editors, Amanda Vogel, Jennifer Fleming; sound, Bernard Hajdenberg; music, Nicholas Smiley; assistant producers, Jennifer Clement, Sarah Pollinger. Reviewed at WorldFest/Houston, April 26, 1992. Running time: **76 MIN.**
Nick Devane . . . . Nicholas Backlund
Leigh Morgan . . . Catherine Fogarty
Maryland . . . . Mary Elizabeth Keller
Trevor . . . . Tobias Baker
Carly . . . . Pamela Stewart
Duke . . . . Wayne Haycox

Novice writer-director Chris Johnstone makes a small but commendable splash with "Buffalo Jump," a witty and well-observed indie effort that should play well on the fest circuit and in specialized urban markets. Pic recalls the low-key humor and insight of another no-frills debut, John Sayles' "Return of the Secaucus Seven."

Plot deals with two 30ish wanderers, Nick (Nicholas Backlund) and Leigh (Catherine Fogarty), who co-starred as teens on a '70s sitcom, "Heaven Help Poppa." Fleeing when reruns of their show appear on cable TV, they aimlessly drive from town to town with their self-appointed travelling companion, Maryland (Mary Elizabeth Keller), who has become Leigh's lover.

Nick, who was romantically attached to Leigh during the run of their series, is the outspoken smart-aleck of the trio, but when the wanderers stop in a small Virginia fishing village, it is Nick who decides he wants to settle down and live off his residuals. He also finds a lover in a free-spirited, crab-shooting eccentric (Pamela Stewart).

Old wounds are opened up when the trio learns of another sitcom co-star's death, cueing pic's most technically and dramatically impressive scene.

"Buffalo Jump's" quirky humor and engaging bit-player riffs are held together by a thin wisp of a plot. But that's no problem since there's more mood (skillfully, playfully developed) than matter here.

Lead performances, especially Backlund and Stewart's, are first-rate. Also worth noting is Tobias Baker as an improbably transplanted Englishman who happens to be a big "Heaven Help Poppa" fan.

Perhaps because of financial limitations, pic doesn't have clips from the fictional sitcom that might have helped illuminate the characters' bitterness about the show. (A minor, eminently disposable subplot involves a proposed TV reunion special.) Otherwise, pic makes the most of a small budget. Blow-up to 35m from Super 16m is very good.

— *Joe Leydon*

SEATTLE FEST

HOLD ME, THRILL ME, KISS ME

Produced by Travis Swords. Directed, written by Joel Hirshman. Camera (Foto Kem color), Kent Wakeford; editor, Kathryn Himoff; music, Gerald Gouriet. Reviewed at Seattle Intl. Film Festival, May 28, 1992. Running time: **92 MIN.**
Dannie . . . . Adrienne Shelly
Eli/Bud/Fritz . . . . Max Parrish
Twinkle . . . . Sean Young
Lucille . . . . Diane Ladd
Sabra . . . . Andrea Naschak
Laszlo . . . . Bela Lehoczky
Olga . . . . Ania Suli
Mr. Jones . . . . Timothy Leary
Also with: Joseph Anthony Richards, Vic Trevino, Mary Lanier.

Imagine Pedro Almodóvar and John Waters getting together to make a love story for the '90s, and the result could be this pic about Americana at its worst. "Hold Me, Thrill Me, Kiss Me," an eccentric comedy peopled by assorted vividly drawn, oddball characters, will not be to everyone's taste, but this original creation should make its mark with cult audiences via good word-of-mouth.

Lensed on a shoestring budget in 18 days in El Monte, Calif., pic also bodes well for first-time helmer Joel Hirshman and provides an excellent feature debut for thesp Max Parrish.

Parrish plays a burglar who accidentally shoots his fiancé (Sean Young) during a forced-gun wedding. He flees with her $200,000 and hides out in an El Monte trailer park until he can obtain false ID to get himself out of the country. His contact is a con artist (Timothy Leary).

What follows could have become a typical love story, except for the characters who live at the trailer park: a sadistic porno star (wonderfully portrayed by Andrea Naschak) who collects Barbie dolls; her virginal younger sister (Adrienne Shelly); a washed-up Hungarian opera singer (Ania Suli); her foul-mouthed son (Bela Lahoczky), and two down-on-their-luck aging Southern belles (Diane Ladd and her real life mother Mary Lanier), who lust after Parrish.

Characters pursue their desires in a series of truly hilarious scenes, with each part played to the max for optimum effect. Lenser Kent Wakeford creates a polished work on a restricted budget, and Gerald Gouriet's musical score adds both the perfect raunchy accompaniment, and, at the moment of Shelly's loss of virginity, the perfect touch with the playing of the vintage hit from which the pic earns its name.

— *Maggie Brown*

THE ENQUIRERS

Produced, directed, written, edited by Rick Barnes. Camera (color), James Sander; music, Marc Barreca. Reviewed at Seattle Intl. Film Festival, June 1, 1992. Running time: **100 MIN.**
Ramona . . . . Toni Cross
Eudie . . . . Brian Finney
Vince . . . . August Kelley
Bussy . . . . Stephen Lohrentz
Marlin . . . . Rick Barnes

Newcomer Rick Barnes directed, produced, wrote and edited "The Enquirers," presenting a potentially humorous plot in the process, but execution falls short of promise, and pic's a dubious bet for theatrical release.

Basic premise: What if all those Elvis sightings reported in the likes of the National Enquirer are real? What if Elvis really is alive and has just returned from another galaxy where he entertained for the last several years until his contract ran out, and he decided to escape back to earth?

Story centers on an alien entrepreneur (Brian Finney) in Seattle not only searching for his errant client, Elvis, but also doing a little interplanetary talent scouting. He discovers a struggling comic (Stephen Lohrentz) and offers him a chance at the really big time — light years away from Earth.

He also discovers a droll Elvis impersonator (Rick Barnes), whose likewise offered a contract in hopes that such impersonators will become popular on his planet now that "The King" is gone. Also entering the picture is a barfly (Toni Cross), who delivers an incredible, out-of-nowhere harangue against television. Throughout the pic, one wonders why this character is even included, but at the end, it's strongly suggested she's really Elvis, who was tired of his gig and did a body swap.

Pic's inability to deliver any comedic punch —the jokes aren't funny, monologues become boring speeches — and lack of action underscores its lethargic pacing. Shot on extremely modest means, tech credits are adequate at best.
— *Maggie Brown*

DUGUN — DIE DEIRAT
(THE WEDDING)
(GERMAN)

A Wolfgang Krenz Film production. Produced by Wolfgang Krenz. Directed, written by Ismet Elci. Camera (Eastmancolor), Martin Gressman; editor, Doreen Heins; music, Nizamettin Aric; sets, Erdal Sumer; sound, Katharina Rosa. Reviewed at Seattle Intl. Film Festival, May 28, 1992. Running time: **91 MIN.**
With: Oguz Tunc, Asli Altan, Halil Ergun, Gulsen Tuncer.

"**T**he Wedding" is a poignant examination of a Turkish man caught between two different cultures and his painful struggle to shape his own identity. Pic deserves to attract art house attention, especially in the U.S. where these Eastern European cultural clashes are a mystery to most.

Newcomer director-writer Ismet Elci, aimed by lenser Martin Gressman, effectively uses the harsh, yet stunning landscape of eastern Turkey to help convey his story with distinct, plain images and without too many words. The result is a powerful and interesting snapshot of Islamic Turkish life in a small village, still centuries away from the "modern world."

Story focuses on Metin, a Turk in his mid-20s, who moved to Germany (as many Turks before him) in search of a better life. When his mother is dying, he returns to his East Anatolian village for the first time in 10 years. He arrives full of dread, only to find his mother in good health and the entire village in the midst of preparations for his wedding.

Perhaps humorous at first to the uneducated, this is not a laughing matter because the village men — including his father — will kill Metin if he fails to marry the woman to whom he was promised as a child, despite the fact they do not know each other and Metin already is engaged to a German woman. The wedding must and does take place, but so does a funeral. Predictable ending underscores, rather than dampens, the story's effect.

Oguz Tunc delivers a fine performance as the sensitive yet rebellious Metin. Asli Altan is impressive as the tormented fiancé, Aygul, who desperately wants to marry Metin so the villagers will stop calling her an old maid. Halil Ergun is sharp as Metin's forceful father, as is Gulsen Tuncer as Metin's loving yet equally inflexible mother.

Tech credits, including well-done subtitling and haunting musical score, are fine in this low-budgeter. — *Maggie Brown*

CANNES FEST

BEZNESS
(FRENCH-TUNISIAN)

A Cinétéléfilms/ERTT (Tunisia)/Flach Films/Transméditerranée/Studio Canal Plus (France) co-production with participation of Channel 4 (England)/Sundwestfunk-Akged (Germany)/French Ministry of Culture & Communications, French Ministry of Foreign Affairs, Federal Bureau of Foreign Affairs (Switzerland). Produced by Ahmed Baha Eddine Attia, Jean-François Lepetit. Executive producers, Mokhtar Lahidi, Isabelle Fauvel. Directed, written by Nouri Bouzid. Camera (color), Alain Levent; editor, Kahena Attia; music, Anouar Braham; costume design, Naama Jazy, Pierre-Yves Gayraud; set design, Khaled Joulak; sound, Hachemi Joulak. Reviewed at Cannes Film Festival (Directors Fortnight), May 14, 1992. Running time: **100 MIN.**
Roufa . . . . Abdel Kechiche
Fred . . . . Jacques Penot
Khomsa . . . . Ghalia Lacroix
Navette . . . . Ahmed Ragoubi
Also with: Manfred Andrae, Mustapha Adouani, Adel Boukadida.
(In French & Arabic)

"**B**ezness," the story of a Tunisian gigolo torn between **tradition and the promise of a better life in Europe, benefits from convincing characterization and plenty of local color.** Scripter/helmer Nouri Bouzid's catchy approach to multicultural conflict has enough sex appeal and dramatic tension to make for a fine film fest item and one that could score in art houses beyond the French-lingo circuit.

"Bezness," originally taken from the English word "business," is the local term for young gigolos who sell their charms to tourists of every age and both sexes. Hunky Roufa (Abdel Kechiche) is kept busy during tourist season in the coastal resort of Sousse by servicing visiting women, maintaining a steady German male client who wants to take him to Europe and laying down the law for his chaste g.f. Khomsa.

Beautiful Khomsa yearns for greater freedom and objects to Roufa's womanizing while she's expected to stay home. Fred, a French photographer snapping a forbidden photo essay on local women, finds himself increasingly drawn to Khomsa.

Photog's shot of two women emerging from the surf — one a topless European and one a Muslim Arab woman with covered head and body — nicely sums up the double standard between Islamic tradition and Western permissiveness permeating life in the Tunisian tourist resort.

Much of the story is told with glances and body language. Tunisian hustlers speak Arabic among themselves, French to foreigners. Techniques for picking up women are both educational and amusing. The French photog subplot is less successful.

Although she has little experience and no street smarts, Khomsa makes out better in the end than any of the male characters.

Tragic conclusion is a little long in coming but leaves a lingering impression. — *Lisa Nesselson*

MODERN CRIMES
(DUTCH)

An Allarts production. (Intl. sales: The Sales Co., London.) Produced by Kees Kasander. Executive producer, Denis Wigman. Directed, written by Alejandro Agresti. Camera (color), Nestor Sanz; editor, Stefan Kamp; music, Paul M. van Brugge; art direction, Wilbert van Dorp; sound, Hugo Helmond; assistant director, Gerrit Martijn. Reviewed at Cannes Film Festival (Un Certain Regard), May 13, 1992. Running time: **82 MIN.**

Tim van Sandwijk . . . . . . Roy Ward
Man in train . . . . Adrian Brine
Alex . . . . Alejandro Agresti
Sara . . . . Helen Limon
Witness . . . . Frank Sheppard
Also with: Bonnie Williams, Jake Kruyer.
(English soundtrack)

"**M**odern Crimes" is a posey little art movie that has something important to say but can't spit it out. Shot in English, this intellectual thriller about a Dutch radio ham disturbed by his best friend's suicide may have worked better with a more experienced cast. But uncharismatic thesping and a script that will only fool subtitled auds won't earn "Crimes" much furlough beyond the fest circuit.

Pic continues the political themes of writer-director Alejandro Agresti, an Argentinian based in the Netherlands since 1986 and frequent collaborator with Peter Greenaway producer Kees Kasander. Like Agresti's previous "Secret Wedding" and "Luba," the thrust is modern society's destruction of people's spirit.

Tim (Roy Ward), a 29-year-old TV repairman, is a classic existentialist case who's building a radio in his spare time "to talk to someone." On the train one day he meets a street-philosopher type (Adrian Brine) who tells him "people don't die, they get killed." While Tim mulls over this thought, he gets a phone call that his pal Alex (well played by Agresti himself) has seemingly done himself in.

Rest of the movie follows Tim's rapidly confused state of mind as he recalls his last meeting with the intense Alex, has more chats with the train solon and learns from Alex's g.f. (Helen Limon) that Alex had begun to paint his apartment black.

Agresti turns in a handsome looking product on a slim $300,000 budget and less than three weeks' shoot. Nestor Sanz's immaculate visuals in and around Amsterdam paint a sterile, consumerist society with the spirit sucked out of it.

Unfortunately, the same goes for most of the performances and the woolly script. A sequence in which Ward talks to a fellow radio ham in Argentina shoehorns a directly political element into the pic that seems out of place in the otherwise abstract goings-on. — *Derek Elley*

APFELBAUME
(APPLE TREES)
(GERMAN)

An Alert Film production. (Intl. sales: Filmverlag der Autoren.) Produced by Alfred Hürmer. Directed, written by Helma Sanders-Brahms. Camera (color), Jurgen Lenz; editor, Monika Schindler; music, Marc Beacco; production design, Marlene Willmann; sound, Bernd-Dieter Hennig; assistant director, Barbara Heck. Reviewed at Cannes Film Festival (Un Certain Regard), May 15, 1992. Running time: **111 MIN.**
Lena . . . . Johanna Schall
Heinz . . . . Thomas Rüchel
Sienke . . . . Udo Kroschwald
Lena as a girl . . . . . . Anna Sanders
Grandmother . . . . Steffi Spira
Sienke's wife . . . . . Andrea Meissner
Party secretary . . . . . . Peter Pauli

Reunification's effect on former East Germany is provocatively depicted in Helma Sanders-Brahms' touching, beautifully made film. Via a deceptively simple story about a family destroyed by political events, filmmaker poses questions that remain unanswered in Germany today.

Pic's setting is an apple-growing region in East Germany. Lena (Johanna Schall) marries Heinz (Thomas Büchel), a young laborer, and they settle down to work under Communism in their village. Sienke (Udo Kroschwald), the leader of the local co-op, has the hots for Lena, who helps look after his sickly wife. One night, at a social function, the jealous Heinz attacks Sienke and, as a result, is imprisoned.

In jail, he's contacted by members of Stasi (East German secret police) who offer him freedom if he'll help trap Sienke, who they suspect (rightly) is planning to defect to the West. But the trap misfires, and Lena, who was accompanying her husband, is arrested.

With their marriage at an end and Lena giving birth to a son in prison, the Wall starts tumbling down. She goes west to seek Sienke's help, but he's more concerned with claiming his land in the East. The local apples traditionally don't come up to European Community standards, so Sienke has the orchards destroyed to make way for an amusement park.

That makes a potent metaphor for the destruction of many positive things in the former East Germany in the blind rush for progress. Sanders-Brahms makes the point eloquently and shows how easy it was for people to become Stasi informers, and to be branded as such in the post-unification era.

The film takes a little while to get started (slight pruning would help), but it's beautifully made and well acted down the line. The director's daughter appears in an early scene as young Lena.

With its deeply felt criticisms of present-day Germany, Sanders-Brahms has followed up her earlier success, "Germany Pale Mother," with another fine film which deserves fest exposure and art house play. — *David Stratton*

HOCHZÄITSNUECHT
(WEDDING NIGHT —
END OF THE SONG)
(LUXEMBOURG)

A Videofin production. (Intl. sales: Videopress) Produced, directed by Pol Cruchten. Screenplay, Cruchten, Marc Giraud, from Ernst M. Binder's stage play "Hochzeitsnacht." Camera (Eastmancolor), Daniel Barrau; editor, Marie Robert; music, André Mergenthaler; production design, Jeanny Kratochwil; art direction, Patrice Renault; costume design, Jacqui Mandy; sound, Jean Umansky, Jean-Bernard Thomasson; assistant directors, Emmanuel Frideritzi, Didier Borgnis; associate producer, Jeannot Theis. Reviewed at Cannes Film Festival (Un Certain Regard), May 15, 1992. Running time: **107 MIN.**
Catherine . . . . Myriam Müller
Christian . . . . Thierry van Werveke
Tony . . . . Ender Frings
Catherine's father . . . . Paul Scheuer
Catherine's mother
. . . . Marja-Leena Junker
Christian's mother
. . . . . . Marie-Paule von Roesgen
Catherine's friend . . Danièle Gaspard
(Luxembourgish dialog)

Despite a seriously nasty undercurrent that will prove more of a turn-off to more viewers than a turn-on, "Wedding Night" is a stylized, David Lynch-like study of two druggies locked in chemical hell repping a startling feature bow by Luxembourg's Pol Cruchten. Pic could score limited openings beyond festivals, local censors permitting.

Unlikable couple are Catherine (Myriam Müller), spoiled daughter of a rich industrialist, and Christian (Thierry van Werveke), a weak, impoverished slob. Halfway through their starchy wedding dinner, she nags him to score some smack.

Christian traipses round town and finally connects with pusher Tony (Ender Frings) who says he'll call them back at 3 a.m. After another kvetching session with her husband, Catherine goes to meet Tony in a deserted facto-ry, and from then on the newlyweds' lives spiral relentlessly downwards.

Cruchten touts the pic as "a Shakespearean rock 'n' roll fable of the '90s." In fact, it's a highly formal art film that has more in common with moodpieces of directors such as Chantal Akerman, though with a much darker edge. Matte colors, long takes, and trash-déco production design conjure up a self-contained, claustrophobic universe.

Unfortunately, there's not too much going on beneath all the style. Pic drags in the middle section, which could easily lose 15 minutes, and only gets its second wind during the final descent into hell. Performances by the wan-faced principals are okay. — *Derek Elley*

HOME FIRES BURNING

A William B. O'Boyle presentation of a White Deer/L.A. Puopolo production. (Intl. sales: Overseas Film Group.) Produced, directed by Puopolo. Co-producer, O'Boyle. Screenplay, Puopolo, Chris Ceraso, based on Ceraso's play. Camera (color), J. Michael McClary; editor, Lesley Topping; music, Herb Pilhofer; production design, Mike Moran; sound, Mike Tromer; line producer, Chris Ann Verges; associate producer-production manager-assistant director, Matthew Carlisle; casting, Deborah Brown. Reviewed at Cannes Film Festival market, May 12, 1992. Running time: **103 MIN.**
Glory . . . . Karen Allen
Mark Harnish . . . . Raymond J. Barry
Clifford Harnish . . . . . Michael Dolan
Martha Harnish . . . . . . Tess Harper
April Cavanaugh . . . Gillian Anderson

This adaptation of Chris Ceraso's play, though shot on location in Pocahontas, Va., still smacks of the theater. Though it packs an undeniable emotional punch, pic comes across as overwritten and contrived as a cinema experience.

The theme is an important one: Resurgence of grassroots fascism as a worldwide phenomenon. Ceraso and adaptor/director L.A. Puopolo depict the disturbing trend in forceful terms.

A 22-year-old (Michael Dolan) returns home after a long time away and discovers that his lonely and frustrated mother (Tess Harper) has taken to the bottle, and that his father (Raymond J. Barry) has taken up with another woman (Karen Allen).

Pausing to dally with his childhood sweetheart (Gillian Anderson in an attractive debut), the deeply right-wing youth, who has been involved in both Klan and Nazi organizations during his time away, comes on to Allen in her home and threatens her with violence unless she ends the relationship with his father.

Dolan makes the good-looking, all-American boy a genuinely scary character, and the rest of the cast deliver also strong performances.

Pic's resolution comes as an anticlimax, since the audience has been led to anticipate an act of cathartic violence that never occurs. This will limit the pic's appeal somewhat, though it will make absorbing home-screen viewing.

Film is technically fine except for the obvious intrusion of a sound boom visible in a couple of shots. — *David Stratton*

QUELQUE PART VERS CONAKRY
(SOMEWHERE NEAR CONAKRY)
(FRENCH)

A Les Films de l'Ecluse production with participation of Canal Plus, CNC, Procirep & the Société Financière de Participation Cinématographique (Geneva) in conjunction with ONACIG (Guinea). Produced by Yves Gasser, Christine Lipinska, Serge Khayat. Directed, written by Françoise Ebrard. Camera (color), Dominique Gentil; editor, Sophie Schmit, Hugues Darmois; music, Serge Franklin; production design, Pierre-Yves Prieur, Stephane Dwernicki; sound, Jerome Thiault; technical advisor, Alain Maline. Reviewed at Cannes Film Festival (Cinemas en France), May 14, 1992. Running time: **86 MIN.**
Jacques . . . . . . Damien MacDonald
Madiou . . . . Ibrahim Oury Bah
Madiou's uncle . . . . . Pascal N'Zonzi
Madiou's mother . . . . Delphine Rich
Jacques' father . . . . Philippe Jutteau
Also with: Iona Craciunescu, Abdoulaye Diallo, Madame Kake, Pierre Bouchet.

Story of an African boy and a French boy's friendship "somewhere near Conakry" (capital of Guinea, west-central Africa) is set in 1971, the year a wave of terror endorsed by reigning despot Ahmed Sékou Touré swept the country. Political specifics will probably limit this item to festivals and Gallic wickets, although it should strike a chord with anyone interested in the legacy of colonization.

First film by French-born scripter/helmer Françoise Ebrard, who grew up in Guinea but was abruptly forced at age 11 to trade the African brush for the regimented playgrounds of France, is told from youngsters' point of view.

Young leads are appealing and their friendship rings true. Their mutual loyalty despite pressures from their parents and the outside world has universal appeal, unlike the pontificating of the local party boss and the somewhat foggy details of insurrection, revolution and counter-revolution in the strife-torn early 1970s.

Evocatively lensed pic is full of the young boys' raw athletic energy. The tension of a locale where revolution brews is well-conveyed, as is dismay of foreigners who have invested years of their lives in a place they will soon be forced to leave.

— *Lisa Nesselson*

ME MYSELF AND I

An IRS Media production. (Intl. sales: IRS Media Intl.) Produced, directed by Pablo Ferro. Screenplay, Julian Barry. Camera (Foto-Kem color), James Glennon; editor, Allen Ferro; music, Odette Springer, Harry Nilsson; production design, Carlos Barbosa; art direction, Richard Brunton; costume design, Gregory Poe; sound (Dolby), Lew Goldstein; assistant director, Michael Grossman. Reviewed at Cannes Film Festival market, May 16, 1992. Running time: **94 MIN.**
Diane . . . . .JoBeth Williams
Buddy Arnett . . . . . . .George Segal
Irving . . . . Don Calfa
Jennifer . . . . Shelley Hack
Jailbait . . . . Betsy Lynn George
Sydney . . . . Bill Macy

"**H**ow did I get into this?" screams George Segal way too late in "Me Myself and I." Not many people will be around to give him an answer. Desperately unfunny N.Y. apartment pic thrashes around on the mat after being cut off at the knees by its jumbled, lackluster opening reels.

Segal is a blocked Hollywood writer separated from West Coast lesbian wife Shelley Hack and trying to work in a colorful Gotham apartment block. He's going slowly bananas harrassed by nosy neighbor JoBeth Williams who suffers, in her own words, from a "multiple personality disorder."

Segal is more interested in a 14-year-old upstairs (Betsy Lynn George) but eventually makes up with Williams between the sheets and hires her as his secretary. That doesn't work out, either: She gets in his way on a shoot of one of his works (a Vietnam novel transposed to Iraq and shot in Spain) and becomes jealous when Hack, back in the heterosexual camp, pops by for a quickie.

Pic plays like a tired rerun of the mismatch comedies Segal starred in 20 years ago, sans smart pacing and starpower performances. Clumsy editing, and an interior-bound script laid out like a three-act play, grounds the whole operation before it begins. Only sequences that work are the more intimate moments between Segal and Williams; when it tries for loony comedy, pic falls apart completely.

Helmer Pablo Ferro isn't entirely to blame for the mess. Fatal flaw is the miscasting of Williams, okay as the sane half of her personality, but can't handle the crazy stuff. Hack shines in a small part and George is right as the precocious jailbait.

Other credits are standard.

— *Derek Elley*

GREENKEEPING
(AUSTRALIAN)

A Central Park Films production in association with the Australian Film Commission. Produced by Glenys Rowe. Directed, written by Davis Caesar. Camera (Eastmancolor), Simon Smith; editor, Mark Perry; music, David Bridie, John Phillips; production design, Kerith Holmes; costumes, Tess Schofield; sound, Liam Egan; assistant director, Vicki Sugars; casting, Liz Mullinan. Reviewed at Cannes Film Festival market, May 15, 1992. Running time: **86 MIN.**
Lenny . . . . Mark Little
Sue . . . . Lisa Hensley
Tom . . . . Max Cullen
Doreen . . . . Jan Adele
Gina . . . . Gia Carides
Milton . . . . Syd Conabere
Also with: Robyn Nevin, Frank Whitten, David Wenham, Kristoffer Greave, Kazuhiro Muroyama, Scott Higgins.

First-time feature director David Caesar, maker of some intriguing docus, shows promise as a helmer but needs help as a screenwriter. "Greenkeeping" is a visually witty and attractive film with a personable cast and a very laconic, very Australian sense of humor. But the narrative is painfully thin, and many will find watching the film about as exciting as watching a game of lawn bowls.

Amiable Lenny, fresh out of prison, works as a greenkeeper for a suburban Sydney bowling club, but he isn't very good at it, though he's energetic and hardworking. He's married to the lovely Sue (Lisa Hensley), who doesn't work but spends a fortune on pot; they owe a drug dealer $3,000.

Around this slim premise, Caesar has structured a film attempting to show Australia in transition. Japanese influence is depicted via incongruous young Japanese presence at the bowling club, mostly populated by elderly Aussies (for whom this ultra-slow sport is exciting enough). And the point is made that the recession has made paupers of the former middle-class.

All fair enough material for a comedy, and with the fine cast assembled, Caesar might have come up with something genuinely funny and pertinent if his screenplay had been pumped up.

Despite its many qualities, pic faces an uphill battle in the international marketplace. In Australia, it might have a chance if well marketed and indulgently treated by critics.

Technically, the modestly budgeted effort is first-rate and a credit to producer Glenys Rowe, although the repetitive music score is irritating.

— *David Stratton*

GARBO
(AUSTRALIAN)

An Electic Films production in association with Australian Film Finance corp. (Intl. sales: Beyond Films.) Produced by Hugh Rule. Directed by Ron Cobb. Screenplay, Patrick Cook, Neill Gladwin, Stephen Kearney, from a story by Rule, Gladwin, Kearney. Camera (Fujicolor), Geoff Burton; editor, Neil Thumpston; music, Allan Zavod; production design, Richard Bell; sound, John Phillips; line producer, Margot McDonald; associate producers, Gladwin, Kearney; casting, Richard Kent. Reviewed at Cannes Film Festival market, May 12, 1992. Running time: **103 MIN.**
Steve . . . . Stephen Kearney
Neill . . . . Neill Gladwin
Wal . . . . Max Cullen
Detective . . . . Simon Chilvers
Trevor . . . . Gerard Kennedy

Big-screen breakthrough for cult stand-up comics Stephen Kearney and Neill Gladwin is a fizzer completely failing to capture their comic style. Dull returns may be expected in Australia, with overseas prospects even dimmer.

Kearney and Gladwin make a personable duo, but in this film their comedy is curiously undefined. Closest resemblance is to early Martin and Lewis, with Kearney talking funny and playing the myopic nerd with Gladwin his wimpy pal.

Routines that may have worked with a live audience remain stillborn in a film burdened with a clumsily told, often incomprehensible story line about corruption in inner-city local government, with the pair playing garbagemen ("garbos" in Aussie vernacular).

Unfunny script is wafer-thin, and the comics themselves are self-conscious and awkward. Matters are hardly helped by the choice of American Ron Cobb as director of this quintessentially Aussie material.

Geoff Burton does his usual professional job behind the camera but can't save a chronically misconceived production. All tech credits are good, but it's all too tempting to label the film a load of garbage. — *David Stratton*

PRAGUE
(FRENCH-BRITISH)

A Christopher Young/Constellation/UGC/Hachette Premiere co-production. (Intl. sales: The Sales Co.) Produced by Christopher Young. Co-producer, Claudie Ossard. Directed, written by Ian Sellar. Camera (color), Darius Khondji; editor, John Bloom; music, Jonathan Dove; production design, Jiri Matolin; associate producer, David Brown. Reviewed at CNC screening room, Paris, April 23, 1992. (In Cannes Film Festival, Un Certain Regard.) Running time: **88 MIN.**
Alexander . . . . Alan Cumming
Elena . . . . Sandrine Bonnaire
Josef . . . . Bruno Ganz
(English soundtrack)

This leisurely paced lightweight effort for scripter/helmer Ian Sellar comes across like a collection of ideas for a Euro co-production to be lensed in a photogenic city rather than an accomplished and vital picture. Semi-whimsical with a sad event at its core, pic has most of the ingredients for a charming film but not enough narrative backbone to coalesce. Art house patrons will find "Prague" competent but unexceptional.

On his maiden journey to Prague, young Alexander (Alain Cumming) arrives from the U.K. in search of newsreel film supposedly stored at Czech film archives. Alex knows exactly what he's looking for but has not anticipated the sluggish serendipity of the archive and its two key employees, Elena (Sandrine Bonnaire) and Josef (Bruno Ganz).

Alex, whose Czechoslovakian-born mother survived the war thanks to a bold family gesture, is looking for visual clues to his past. Elena, romantically linked to Josef, is looking for a key ingredient in her future.

Individual characters have endearing quirks, but no one is strong enough to carry the film; Cumming is too doughy and nebulous to be completely engaging. In better-than-average casting for an English-language Eurocoprod, Bonnaire and Ganz are convincing as Czechs, but much of what they do and say is either two arbitrary or too obvious.

As with helmer's earlier "Venus Peter," visuals (shot on location in Prague) are pleasing and evocative. Musical score is also very nice.

Film's central incident is telegraphed way in advance but is still likely to touch anyone with a soft spot for original nitrate footage. — *Lisa Nesselson*

THE SILENCER

A Crown Intl. Pictures release of a Marimark production. Produced by Brian J. Smith. Executive producer, Marilyn Jacobs Tenser. Directed by Amy Goldstein. Screenplay, Scott Kraft, Goldstein. Camera (Eastman & Fujicolor, Foto-Kem prints), Daniel Berkowitz; editor, Rick Blue; music-songs, Carole Pope; additional music, Ron Sures; sound design, Tony Cannella; production design, John Myhre; costume design, Pilar Limosner; assistant director, Rod Smith; stunt coordinator, Cole McKay; casting, Carol Lefko. Reviewed at Cannes Film Festival market, May 9, 1992. Running time: **84 MIN.**

Angelica	Lynette Walden
George	Chris Mulkey
Tony	Paul Ganus
Didi	Brook Parker

As slick as an ad for designer biker wear, "The Silencer" presses all the right buttons. Knowing mix of softcore tease and style-trash visuals wrapped around a "Nikita" rip-off plot should be a strong performer in its target markets, with plenty of action in video.

Lynette Walden is a professional hit woman lured out of retirement by former employer (the Agency) to waste five sleazebags behind an L.A. child-slave ring. Hot on her trail is former lover Chris Mulkey, who follows her exploits on an arcade vidgame called "The Silencer." He's more interested in getting her back into "the game" rather than the sack.

Pic quickly settles down into a series of set-pieces, with Walden changing her wardrobe for each hit and working off her frustrations between times with bemused b.f. Paul Ganus. Aside from Mulkey's gravel-voiced commentary on her performance, the computer-generated script's only other subplot is Walden's female solidarity with a black street girl

(Brook Parker).

Debuting director Amy Goldstein delivers the goods on every level, with occasional upfront humor adding to the knowing tone. In her first leading role, Walden, tops as a supporting player, maintains her femininity in the action sequences, cut and framed to show her "Madonna with a pistol" to best effect. Mulkey ("Twin Peaks") is serviceable as her leather-clad nemesis.

Largely shot in L.A. back streets and alleys, pic is technically top drawer, with a pumping rock soundtrack and eye-popping costumes. Nudity and violence are relatively restrained. — *Derek Elley*

HOMEVIDEO

EYE OF THE STORM
(GERMAN-U.S.)

A New Line Home Video release of a Hanno Huth, Michael Krohne presentation of a Eurofilm production. Executive producers, Roland Emmerich, Huth. Produced by Carsten H.W. Lorenz, Oliver Eberle. Directed by Yuri Zeltser. Screenplay, Zeltser, Michael Stewart. Camera (Foto-Kem color), Karl Walter Lindenlaub; editor, Michael J. Duthie; music, Christopher Franke; art direction, Michael Manson; costume design, Laurie Henriksen; sound (Dolby), Preston Oliver II, Neal Lampert; assistant director, Steve Love; associate producer, Ute Emmerich; casting, Carol Lewis. Reviewed on New Line vidcassette, N.Y. MPAA Rating: R. Running time: **93 MIN.**

Ray	Craig Sheffer
Steven	Bradley Gregg
Sandra Gladstone	Lara Flynn Boyle
Martin Gladstone	Dennis Hopper
Sheriff	Leon Rippy

New Line has a sleeper in this thriller, made in America by German producers. Direct-to-video release could also score in the pay-cable market.

Interesting premise by director Yuri Zeltser and co-scripter Michael Stewart traces the fate of two young brothers living at a highway gas station/motel/diner who witness their parents' brutal murder by a robber couple.

Ten years later, older brother Craig Sheffer is taking care of youngster Bradley Gregg, who was blinded in the violent incident. They're sympathetic characters, but the script keeps one guessing as to whether one (or both) of them has become a Norman Bates-esque psychotic.

Matters come to a head when Dennis Hopper's car breaks down and he stays at the boys' gas

station with his sexy young wife Lara Flynn Boyle. As in "Paris Trout," Hopper makes a perfect boorish heavy, and under Zeltser's direction, the viewer's sympathy is frequently inverted regarding who to root for.

Film climaxes violently and satisfyingly during a thunderstorm in which emotions flare according to the barometer.

Boyle, post-"Twin Peaks," continues to be one of the sexier young actresses on screen and entire ensemble cast is good. Tech credits are modest.

— *Lawrence Cohn*

CAPTAIN AMERICA

A Columbia TriStar Home Video release of a 21st Century presentation, in association with Marvel Entertainment Group, of a Menahem Golan production. Produced by Golan. Executive producer, Stan Lee. Directed by Albert Pyun. Screenplay, Stephen Tolkin, based on story by Lawrence J. Block, Tolkin, from characters created by Joe Simon, Jack Kirby. Camera (Rank color), Philip Alan Waters; editor, Jon Poll; music, Barry Goldberg; production design, Douglas Leonard; costume design, Heidi Kaczenski; sound (Dolby), Ian Brown; assistant director, Michael Katleman; stunt coordinator-2nd unit director, Tom Elliott; special visual effects, Fantasy II Film Effects; special makeup effects, Greg Cannom; line producer, Tom Karnowski; associate producer, Tolkin; casting, Ann Bell, Teri Blythe, Anna Dwan. MPAA Rating: PG-13. Running time: **97 MIN.**

Steve Rogers	Matt Salinger
Pres. Tom Kimball	Ronny Cox
Kolawetz	Ned Beatty
Gen. Fleming	Darren McGavin
Col. Lords	Michael Nouri
Mrs. Rogers	Melinda Dillon
Valentina DeSantis	Francesca Neri
Bernice/Sharon	Kim Gillingham
Red Skull	Scott Paulin
Dr. Vaselli	Carla Cassula

Shelved for over two years, "Captain America" is released direct-to-video as a strictly routine superhero outing.

Menahem Golan produced the picture in Yugoslavia in 1989 and sold it to Columbia the following year. Posters for its theatrical release went up in Manhattan, but the film never showed up, though it would have made passable Saturday matinee fodder.

Following a 1944 serial, Reb Brown toplined in two TV movies of the comic strip hero a decade ago, and Matt Salinger ably embodies his all-American spirit here. Film opens in 1936 where experiments by Italian scientists result in a boy with superhuman strength, named Red Skull.

Seven years later the Allies are working with emigrée Ital-

ian scientist Carla Cassula to develop a regiment of U.S. superheroes. Only one test subject emerges, Salinger, who's christened Captain America. He loses a battle with Red Skull (in which CA's shield is thrown like a Frisbee) and is launched by rocket to destroy the White House.

Salinger is able to veer off course and lands in Alaska where he remains frozen in ice until the present day. Unthawed, he whips into action to prevent an evil U.S. general (Darren McGavin) plotting with Red Skull to control the U.S. prexy (Ronny Cox) with a brain implant device.

Salinger has some good moments dealing with the cultural shock of his Rip Van Winkle reawakening, but film never takes flight under Albert Pyun's leaden direction. (Pyun was earlier set to direct a film of Marvel's popular "Spiderman" character, but that has yet to be realized.)

Under heavy makeup, Scott Paulin makes little impression as pic's villain Red Skull. Pretty heroine Kim Gillingham and Italian femme fatale Francesca Neri (as Red Skull's daughter) provide decorative touches.

Pic is already quite dated, as McGavin and Paulin plan to blame everything on the nasty Soviets. Photogenic locations and cheap chase and action sequences do not hide the fact that this fantasy adventure is missing the large-scale setpieces to which action fans in the age of Schwarzenegger have become accustomed.

— *Lawrence Cohn*

DEADLY BET

A PM Home Video release. Produced by Richard Pepin, Joseph Merhi. Executive producer, Raymon Khoury. Directed by Richard W. Munchkin. Screenplay, Merhi, Robert Tiffe. Camera (Foto-Kem color), Pepin; editor, John Weidner, Geraint Bell; music, Louis Febré; production design, Greg Martin; sound, Mike Hall; assistant director, Peter Jackson; fight choreography, Eric Lee; associate producer, Jean Levine; casting, Nancy Borgnine. Reviewed on PM vidcassette, N.Y. MPAA Rating: R. Running time: **91 MIN.**

Angelo	Jeff Wincott
Rico	Steven Vincent Leigh
Isabella	Charlene Tilton
Frank	Jerry Tiffe
Johnny	Mike Toney
Greek	Michael Delano
Doris	Sherrie Rose
Charlie	Ray Mancini
Xmas	Patty Toy

"Deadly Bet" presents an interesting variation on the kickboxing genre. Las Vegas-set action drama is an okay video title.

Curiously, film uses the same premise as the upcoming summer release starring Nicolas Cage, "Honeymoon in Vegas." Hero Jeff Wincott bets his g.f. Charlene Tilton on a kickboxing match and loses, so she must go with the victor, charming villain Steven Vincent Leigh.

Pic then follows a familiar "Rocky" story line, as deep-in-debt Wincott finally gets his act together, gives up drinking and gambling and wins back his reputation and girl. Least convincing plot element is a big gambler/gangster forcing Wincott to *win* the big tournament match at all costs. (In the boxing genre one has to *throw* a fight, not win it in the case of a fix.)

The fight scenes, both in the ring and outside, are well-choreographed by Eric Lee and executed with skill by leads Wincott and Leigh. Supporting cast led by romantic interest Tilton are fine, including former boxing champ Ray Mancini as a minor henchman. — *Lawrence Cohn*

BATMAN RETURNS

A Warner Bros. release. Produced by Denise Di Novi, Tim Burton. Executive producers, Jon Peters, Peter Guber, Benjamin Melniker, Michael Uslan. Co-producer, Larry Franco. Directed by Burton. Screenplay, Daniel Waters, story by Waters, Sam Hamm. Based on characters created by Bob Kane & published by DC Comics. Camera (Technicolor), Stefan Czapsky; editor, Chris Lebenzon; music, Danny Elfman; production design, Bo Welch; supervising art director, Tom Duffield; art direction, Rick Heinrichs; set design, Nick Navarro, Sally Thornton; set decoration, Cheryl Carasik; costume design, Bob Ringwood, Mary Vogt; sound (Dolby), Petur Hliddal; visual effects supervisor, Michael Fink; special effects supervisor, Chuck Gaspar; special Penguin makeup & effects produced by, Stan Winston; key makeup, Ve Neill; assistant director, David McGiffert; associate producer, Ian Bryce; 2nd unit directors, Billy Weber, Max Kleven; 2nd unit camera, Don Burgess; additional 2nd unit camera, Paul Ryan; casting, Marion Dougherty. Reviewed at Raleigh Studios, L.A., June 9, 1992. MPAA Rating: PG-13. Running time: **126 MIN.**
Batman/
    Bruce Wayne . . . . Michael Keaton
Penguin/
    Oscar Cobblepot . . . Danny DeVito
Catwoman/
    Selina Kyle . . . . . Michelle Pfeiffer
Max Shreck . . . . Christopher Walken
Alfred . . . . Michael Gough
Mayor . . . . Michael Murphy
Ice Princess . . . . . . Cristi Conaway
Chip Shreck . . . . Andrew Bryniarski
Commissioner Gordon . . . Pat Hingle
Organ Grinder . . . Vincent Schiavelli
Josh . . . . Steve Witting
Jen . . . . Jan Hooks

On all counts, "Batman Returns" is a monster. Follow-up to the sixth-highest grossing film of all time has the same dark allure that drew in audiences three years ago, but many non-fans of "Batman" will find this sequel superior in several respects. Tim Burton's latest exercise in fabulist dementia should receive even stronger across-the-board acceptance than the original. Warner Bros.' reported $80 million-plus investment will be an afterthought in the wake of the b. o. cascade, which should approach the $250 million neighborhood of the first pic domestically.

Batman's new foes, Penguin and Catwoman, are both fascinating creations, wonderfully played. Much of the film is massively inventive and spiked with fresh, perverse humor. Burton has once again managed to pursue his quirky personal concerns in the context of commercial entertainment, although it shows that the villains' idiosyncracies interest him far more than the Batman's programmable heroics and related mandatory action sequences.

Like its predecessor, "Batman Returns" is one big glob story-wise: No strong dramatic arc and weak narrative muscles. Fortunately, however, screenplay by Daniel Waters offers up a succession of scenes ranging from the mildly intriguing to the genuinely inspired, and dialogue has an irreverent weirdness that often provokes mental double takes and unexpected laughs.

Interest gets cranked up high immediately by a prologue that illustrates the creation of the Penguin. Playing the infant's parents, Diane Salinger and a virtually unrecognizable Paul (Pee-wee Herman) Reubens dump the cradled tot into a freezing stream in a park. Like Moses, he survives, although the flock he gathers under the streets of Gotham City is of an entirely different sort, comprised of crazed circus rejects and actual penguins.

Disrupting a civic Christmas celebration in a striking, architecturally fascistic reimagining of Rockefeller Center Plaza, Penguin (Danny DeVito) announces that he wants some respect.

Forming an alliance with tycoon Max Shreck (Christopher Walken), a specialist in industrial waste and leeching off the city, Penguin decides to run for mayor — an interesting coincidental twist in this year of the independent candidate — while simultaneously hastening the community's ruin with his maniacal terrorist attacks.

Equally intriguing character of Catwoman evolves out of the demeaning treatment dished out by Shreck to his lovely, somewhat disheveled secretary Selina Kyle. Rather comically continuing her "Frankie and Johnny" routine as a forlorn single woman barely getting by in a shabby, big-city apartment, Michelle Pfeiffer becomes a kitten with a whip who can very much hold her own with Batman.

Oh yes, Batman has to fit in here somewhere. Unfortunately for the twisted imaginations of Burton and Waters, the winged one must remain relatively straight and upstanding, and therefore of limited interest to them. Hero comes to the perfunctory rescue of numerous anonymous individuals, but actually spends much of his time being humbled and humiliated by his highly imaginative opponents.

In fact, edgy relationship between Bruce/Batman and Selina/Catwoman develops through some tantalizing scenes. In one, Batman gets a literal licking from her, and in another at a masquerade ball where, very wittily, they are the only people to arrive without masks.

It is an unmistakable Burton touch to have emphasized the extreme isolation in which all three of his major characters live, and pic's real accomplishment lies in the the amazing physical realization of imagination. Where Burton's ideas end and those of his collaborators begin is impossible to know, but result is a seamless, utterly consistent universe full of nasty notions about societal deterioration, greed and other base impulses.

Lensed seemingly entirely indoors or on covered sets, pic is a magnificently atmospheric elaboration on German Expressionist design principles. As freshly imagined by production designer Bo Welch based on the Oscar-winning concepts of the late Anton Furst in the first installment, Gotham City looms ominously over all individuals, and every set — from Penguin's aquarium-like lair to Bruce Wayne's vaguely "Kane"-like mansion and simple back alleys — is brilliantly executed to maximum evocative effect.

Similarly, costumes by Bob Ringwood, carrying on from the initial outing, and Mary Vogt evince imagination pushed to an advanced level. Batman's outfit has been altered to a sharper, more armored look. Catwoman's form-fitting black leather look has been given an extra dimension by the homemade stitching that gradually comes apart. And Penguin's amorphous shape is often clothed in oddly Victorian garb emphasizing his otherness. All the way down the line, behind-the-scenesters can take deep bows, notably including lenser Stefan Czapsky (taking over on camera from Roger Pratt), Penguin makeup-effects producer Stan Winston, key makeup artist Ve Neill, visual effects supervisor Michael Fink, special effects supervisor Chuck Gaspar, composer Danny Elfman and the almost endless lineup of craftspeople, artisans and technicians.

On the performance side, the deck is stacked entirely in favor of the villains. Briskly waddling, cawing his rude remarks and conveying decades' worth of resentment and bitterness, DeVito makes Penguin very much his own in a unique and far from endearing performance that's al-

June 15, 1992 (Cont.)

ways fascinating to watch.

Although some doubted that she was the ideal choice after she replaced the pregnant Annette Bening in the role, Pfeiffer proves to be a very tasty Cat-woman indeed. Endearingly klutzy initially as Selina, she looks amazing in her skintight, S&M-like leather skin, wins the viewer over to her new incarnation with her intimidating display of whip mastery in a department store, then dazzles as she cart-wheels through Gotham City on her enigmatic mission vis-à-vis the grand power struggle.

Wild-maned Walken has the right comic understatement and sang froid as the metropolis' leading businessman Max Shreck, a character named, as an in-joke, after the German actor Max Schreck (1922's "Nosferatu").

As in the first film, Michael Keaton is encased in a role as constricting as his superhero costume, and while the actor's instincts seem right, the range he is allowed is distinctly limited. Given the psychological dimension provided to the other lead characters, the vacuum at the center stands as the most prominent shortcoming of the "Bat-man" features to date.

It's also clear that Burton is not, at heart, an action director. In big scenes of mass mayhem, gigantic explosions and crowd movement, the film becomes flat and uninvolving. At 126 minutes, pic runs exactly as long as the original, but trimming by 10 or 15 minutes, mainly from the final section, would have vastly enhanced pace and impact.

— Todd McCarthy

IP5: L'ILE AUX PACHYDERMES
(IP5: THE ISLAND OF PACHYDERMS)
(FRENCH)

A Gaumont release of a Cargo Films/Gaumont co-production. Directed by Jean-Jacques Beineix. Screenplay, Jacques Forgeas, Beineix. Camera (color-widescreen), Jean-François Robin; editor, Joëlle Hache; music, Gabriel Yared; set design, Dan Weil; costume design, Emmanuelle Steunou; sound, Pierre Befve, Dominique Hennequin, Jean Gargonne. Reviewed at Gaumont screening room, Neuilly, June 9, 1992. (In Seattle Film Festival.) Running time: **119 MIN.**
Léon Marcel . . . . Yves Montand
Tony . . . . Olivier Martinez
Jockey . . . . Sekkou Sall
Gloria . . . . Géraldine Pailhas
Clarisse/Monique . . . Colette Renard

Jean-Jacques Beineix's fifth film and Yves Montand's last, "IP5" mixes trendy elements with old-fashioned sentiment. Beautifully shot but conceptually uneven road movie about three men in search of love seems certain to appeal to young moviegoers. Pic is also likely to attract fans of all ages curious about Montand's final touching performance as a man whose days are numbered. World preem took place last weekend at the Seattle Film Festival in advance of French launch this week.

Traces of rap music (including a clever Beineix composition), graffiti art, a few well-placed references to ecology and a devil-may-care approach to expedient theft are grafted on to the trusty, if mundane, theme that a life without love is incomplete.

With his resilient young buddy Jockey (Sekkou Sall) in tow, self-satisfied but emotionally hollow graffiti artist Tony (Olivier Martinez) sets off from the Paris suburbs on a mission to Grenoble forced upon him by local toughs. Tony abruptly decides to abandon his tack and detours to Toulouse in search of a beautiful young nurse he hardly knows but has fallen in love with.

The protagonists are skillfully established as likable urbanites. But 20 minutes into the story, the pair becomes substantially less likable when Tony viciously assaults a man in order to get his car keys. The duo repeatedly steal cars with impunity and even a severe crash has no lasting consequences. These lapses in conduct are redeemed by the two youths' eventual befriending of the elderly Montand, a passenger in one of the stolen vehicles.

Montand projects charm and dignity as a man keenly in touch with nature and determined to relocate to "the island of pachyderms" (site of a memorable episode in his youth) before succumbing to a chronic heart condition. Montand can literally walk on water, a mystical touch offered without explanation. The late entertainer is never ridiculous — though his character strips to his underwear and embraces trees.

Despite characters' sometimes vague motivations, helmer secures fine performances all around. Sad scene between Montand and a woman from his past is movingly handled as is a hospi-

tal scene in which always bubbly Jockey breaks down and reveals his fears and troubles to ailing Montand. Pic's major revelation is adorable 11-year-old Sall, a scrawny, wide-eyed imp of Senegalese descent with promising range.

Friendship between the black youngster and slightly older white artist is utterly believable, but their relationship with Montand makes far less sense. Tony gives Montand a ferocious whack on the forehead, but this doesn't leave a dent in their budding interdependence.

Widescreen lensing lavishes special attention on the colors of nature, and pic is peppered with striking visuals.

"IP5" has practically none of the slam-bang action of "Diva," foregoes the surreal excess of "The Moon in the Gutter" and its love story between Tony and the nurse is a nursery rhyme compared to the carnal couple in "Betty Blue." Theme of doggedly pursuing one's dreams, which fell flat in "Roselyne and the Lions," works better here.

"IP" in title is apparently an abbreviation for "Island of Pachyderms" and "5" indicates Beineix's fifth opus.

— Lisa Nesselson

LOST PROPHET
(B&W-16m)

A Rockville Pictures release of a J-5-1 production. Executive producers, Ann de Avila, Rolando de Avila, Rose Stewart, Diana Neeley, Anne Maria Cronin, Pilar Pinsley, Howard Pinsley. Produced, directed by Michael de Avila. Screenplay, Michael de Avila, Drew Morone, Larry O'Neil, Shannon Goldman. Camera (Duart b&w, 16m)-editor, Michael de Avila; music, TRF Music Libraries; sound, Chris Cliadakis, Marissa Bennideto; assistant director, Goldman. Reviewed on vidcassette, N.Y. No MPAA Rating. Running time: **72 MIN.**
Jim . . . . James Burton
Kym . . . . Zandra Huston
Real estate agent/
 Mick Prophet . . . . . Drew Morone
Kid . . . . James Tucker
Also with: Steven Tucker, Shannon Goldman, Larry O'Neil, Christian Urich, Sophia Ramos.

The experimental feature "Lost Prophet" contains some arresting visual imagery but lacks the narrative to sustain audience interest. It's booked for a one-week stand at Gotham's Le Cinematographe.

James Burton, who looks a bit like Tom Hulce, is featured as a lonely wanderer shown in Jack London-esque survival situations in an opening reel in forests and

paddling across a lake in a canoe.

Debuting director Michael de Avila uses an annoying technique of blackouts between sequences in which Burton's voiceover is unintelligible mumbling about a prophet. Hero meets a strange young woman (Zandra Huston) who spouts mystical mumbo jumbo and reads from a book entitled "Mick Prophet."

Burton's wanderings in a strange mansion are relatively uneventful, and random incidents involving a foul-mouthed young kid (James Tucker) and real estate agent (Drew Monroe) don't add up to much. Monroe also appears as the shaggy-haired Mick Prophet, with Burton or his alter ego donning a wig in the Prophet role as well.

Lack of continuity or explanation of the author's various symbols is a serious drawback which denies "Lost Prophet" any commercial future. Acting by the ensemble is unimpressive.

— Lawrence Cohn

PATRICK DEWAERE
(FRENCH-DOCU)

A Pan Européenne release of a PXP Prods./Les Films de la Colline/PCC Prods./Cinévalse/Summertime/INA Enterprise co-production with participation of Canal Plus, Investimage 4, Sofiarp, CNC, LTC & Group VDM. Produced by Christiane Graziani Traube, Jean-Marie Bénard. Executive producer, Baudoin Capet. Directed by Marc Esposito. Camera (color), Eric Weber; editor, Claudine Merlin; music, Patrick Dewaere (songs), Murray Head (opening credits song); sound, Jean Mallet, Jean Minondo. Reviewed at Saint-André-des-Arts theater, Paris, June 3, 1992. (In Cannes Film Festival, noncompeting.) Running time: **85 MIN.**
 With: Angèle, Bertrand Blier, Alain Corneau, Serge Rosseau, Miou-Miou, Claude Sautet, Sotha, Maurice Dogowson, Elsa Dewaere.

"Patrick Dewaere," a documentary reconsideration of the French actor 10 years after his death, is a sad, reverent tribute to a sensitive and gifted performer. Marc Esposito's first film is a competent compendium of film clips intercut with recent interviews with Dewaere's colleagues and kin. Labor of love is very much a Gallic item that would complement any retrospective of the prolific thesp's screen work.

Shown out of competition in the Official Selection at Cannes, pic was broadcast same day on pay-TV channel Canal Plus prior to commercial release on one Paris screen.

Esposito, editor of the film

monthly "Studio," takes a straight-forward, mostly chronological approach that skimps on info about thesp's upbringing and education but allows excerpts from Dewaere's many and varied screen performances to speak for themselves. Even out of context, many of the clips of the handsome actor, who excelled at playing troubled losers, are riveting.

Irony is on helmer's side in an excerpt from Bertrand Blier's Oscar-winning "Get Out Your Handkerchiefs," in which Dewaere complains to Gérard Depardieu that Mozart's death at age 35 was a lamentably premature waste of talent, a major loss that took place in an era of imbeciles. On July 16, 1982, Dewaere, himself 35, fired a fatal shot into his mouth, ending a 30-year career.

Starting at age 4, Dewaere appeared in 34 features, starred in successful TV series, composed and performed original songs and co-founded the Café de la Gare, a Second City-style performance space that helped launch many leading French talents.

But it was Blier's 1973 "Going Places" that really started the ball rolling for its starring trio: Dewaere, Depardieu and Miou-Miou.

Blier remarks that Depardieu and Dewaere, acknowledged to be the two best actors of their generation, took turns in being perceived as top man on the A-list. By all accounts a friend as well as a colleague, Depardieu is conspicuously absent from the record of those interviewed on screen.

Most touching are the segments with actress Miou-Miou and those with her daughter by Dewaere, Angèle, now 17. Dewaere's first wife, actress/playwright/lyricist Sotha, and Elsa, his wife at the time of his death, lend insight to his break-out performances as a young man and to his state of mind toward the end.

Promotional photos taken the day before his death show a fit and happy man in training to play the boxer Marcel Cerdan in Claude Lelouch's "Edith and Marcel." Blier describes his encounter with Dewaere the night before the actor's suicide, obviously regretting that subtle signs of distress became clear only in retrospect. No one who knew him offers a satisfactory explanation for Dewaere's fatal gesture.

A possible factor: After Dewaere punched a journalist who

had printed confidential information about his personal life, much of the press corps closed ranks and slighted or ignored the actor's subsequent work.

A particularly damning sequence begins with Dewaere's interview at Cannes in 1979 in connection with his tour de force performance in Alain Corneau's bleak "Série Noire" (based on Jim Thompson's "A Hell of a Woman"). Dewaere remarks that he has never been nominated for an acting prize. Clips from Cesar Awards ceremonies follow, clearly demonstrating he was nominated for best actor five times (1977, '78, '80, '81 and '82) only to be passed over every time.

Dewaere never received the official recognition of his peers, but, a decade after his death, he clearly created a lasting body of work in French cinema.

— Lisa Nesselson

BLACK TO THE PROMISED LAND
(ISRAELI-DOCU-16m)

A Blues Prods. presentation of a Renen Schorr-Schlomo Roglin production. Produced by Madeleine Ali, Schorr, Rogalin. Directed by Ali. Camera (color, 16m), Manu Kadosh; editor, Victor Nord; music, Branford Marsalis; graphic design, Shai Zauderer; sound, Yossi Vanon, Amir Boverman, Danny Natovich. Reviewed at AMC Kabuki 8 Cinemas, San Francisco, May 1, 1992. Running time: 75 MIN.

A 1989 visit by 11 black students from Brooklyn to an Israeli kibbutz is the unlikely but irresistible subject of "Black to the Promised Land," a terrific feature bow for director Madeleine Ali. With its humorous cross-cultural slant and touching commentary on frustrations in the U.S. black community, upbeat documentary deserves a wide audience and could turn a tidy theatrical profit if properly marketed. It should certainly find eager viewers via TV sale.

The six boys and five girls, aged 15 through 18, attend the Bedford-Stuyvesant Street Academy, an alternative school for those with a history of trouble in public schools. Hailing from one of Brooklyn's most troubled neighborhoods, these kids impress the audience right off with their candor and humor.

Teacher Stewart Bailer man-

aged to raise funds for the group's travel and 10-week stay in a 1,500-acre kibbutz near the northern Syria and Lebanon borders. Focus stays on the kids, from their pre-journey excitement (and amusingly sketched attendant local media blitz) onward.

Stereotypical expectations abound on both sides: The Yank teens anticipate some sort of pious/close-minded desert wasteland. One kibbutz dweller fears that "stealing, selling drugs [is] their everyday life."

Expected to conform to the kibbutz's all-for-one work ethic, U.S. kids initially chafe at days starting at 6 a.m., with long hours of agricultural or assembly-line toil. "I feel like Sissy Spacek in 'Coal Miner's Daughter,'" sighs one girl.

But by the end, a wonderful mutual bonding has taken place. The teens have come to enjoy their work and the value placed on it; the kibbutz has wholeheartedly accepted them into its extended family.

The postscript realities back in Brooklyn are sad: One of the kids gets a street beating within days of his return. Most long to return to the now seemingly idyllic kibbutz, but there's no money for that, or even for college.

Beyond the odd visible mike or other glitch, tech values are fine, especially the zippy editing. Branford Marsalis' jazz-combo score (plus hip-hop tunes for the U.S. framing segments) keeps the mood on the upswing.

Explicit discussion of Israeli-Arab relations and the generally perceived anti-black and anti-Semitic sentiments, is omitted here. That's wholly appropriate, as the message is that given half a chance, anyone, especially young people, can overcome prejudices. — Dennis Harvey

CLASS ACT

A Warner Bros. release of a Wizan Black/Gordy de Passe production. Produced by Todd Black, Maynell Thomas. Executive producers, Joe Wizan, Suzanne de Passe. Co-producer, Jean Higgins. Directed by Randall Miller. Screenplay, John Semper, Cynthia Friedlob; story by Michael Swerdlick, Wayne Rice, Richard Brenne. Camera (Technicolor), Francis Kenny; editor, John F. Burnett; music, Vassal Benford; production design, David L. Snyder; assistant art director, Sarah Knowles; set decoration, Robin Peyton; costume design, Violette Jones-Faison; sound (Dolby), Will Yarbrough; assistant director, Barry K. Thomas; casting, Jaki Brown. Reviewed at Mann Plaza Theater, L.A., June 3,

1992. MPAA rating: PG-13. Running time: 98 MIN.
Duncan . . . . . Christopher (Kid) Reid
Blade . . . . Christopher (Play) Martin
Ellen . . . . Karyn Parsons
Damita . . . . Alysia Rogers
John Pinderhughes . . Meshach Taylor
Popsickle . . . . Doug E. Doug
Reichert . . . . Rick Ducommun
Principal Kratz . . . . Raye Birk
Wedge . . . . Lamont Johnson
Julian Thomas . . . . . . Pauly Shore
Duncan's mom . . . . . Mariann Aalda
Blade's Mom . . . . . Loretta Devine
Jail guard . . . . Andre Rosey Brown
Miss Simpson . . . . . Rhea Perlman

Mixing elements of "Trading Places" with a Three Stooges short, this latest test for rap duo Kid 'N Play scores low on the SAT spectrum. "Class Act" will be dismissed from theaters after a couple of weekends.

Infused with some of the energy but not the smarts of pair's debut "House Party," pic actually has a reasonably engaging premise that gets lost amid the too-broad cartoon elements and emphasis on teen T&A.

Two newcomers to a high school — one a certified genius, the other a paroled felon with a nasty reputation — swap identities, giving the nerd the tough guy's rep while placing his counterpart among the snooty elite. Each is later willing to give up the ruse, except they've both met girls (Alysia Rogers, Karyn Parsons; both very appealing in rather thankless roles) within their new worlds and are reluctant to endanger those relationships by revealing the deception.

The concept provides fodder for comedy but also could have illustrated a more subtle point about how schools and others prejudge on the basis of reputation, with expectations dictating perceptions.

Subtlety, however, is a four-letter word to director Randall Miller, a first-time movie helmsman whose TV credits include the series "Parker Lewis Can't Lose."

Action comes to a dead stop near the end so Kid 'n Play can deliver an anti-drug rap number, but scene feels so tacked on and gratuitous one suspects no one's heart was really in it.

Some amusing moments do emerge, thanks largely to the attractive young cast. Kid (Christopher Reid) and Play (Christopher Martin) also reinforce their ability to provide engaging surrogates for the teen set. Comic Pauly Shore also turns up in an insignificant cameo.

Tech credits get a B-plus on the modest production, with extra credit to costume designer Violette Jones-Faison, production designer David L. Snyder and cinematographer Francis Kenny.

— *Brian Lowry*

TWOGETHER

A Twogether L.P. production. (Intl. sales: GEL Distribution, L.A.) Produced by Emmett Alston, Andrew Chiaramonte. Co-producer, Todd Fisher. Directed, written by Chiaramonte. Camera (Agfacolor, Deluxe prints), Eugene Shlugleit; editors, Fisher, Chiaramonte; music, Nigel Holton; production design, Philip M. Brandes; art direction, Phil Zarling; costume design, Jacqueline Johnson; casting, Lori Cobe. Reviewed at Cannes Film Festival market, May 11, 1992. Running time: **108 MIN.**
John Madler . . . . . . Nick Cassavetes
Allison McKenzie . . . . Brenda Bakke
Arnie . . . . Jeremy Piven
Oscar . . . . Jim Beaver
Paul . . . . Tom Dugan
   Also with: Damian London, William Bumiller.

"**T**wogether" is the kind of pic that could do serious damage to careers if let loose. Napkin-thin pic about two West Coast airheads starts falling apart in the first reel and just keeps on going. Audience should be limited to the filmers' friends and family.

Nick Cassavetes (son of late helmer John) and Brenda Bakke topline as a struggling Venice, Calif., artist and rich girl with parent problems. After meeting at a gallery benefit and leaping into the sack, they impulsively marry, only to change their minds pronto and split up. When Bakke delivers the divorce papers six months later, more sack action gets her pregnant.

Pic's second half limns their life with baby, more spats and Cassavetes' artistic crises as he becomes famous. Main excitement is Bakke finally discovering what he keeps in a locked chest (answer: nudie Polaroids).

Pic briefly promises to be a witty take on the California "relationships" genre, but the slack script and seriously shallow people soon sink that idea. It's a long haul through a pic that can't seem to decide whether it's drama or comedy.

Cassavetes and Michelle Pfeiffer-lookalike Bakke are at their best in the tart opening scenes, but thereafter it's downhill all the way. Only person to emerge with any credit is cinematographer Eugene Shlugleit, who makes the beautiful couple look far better than they deserve. A

full-frontal closeup of the birth of Bakke's baby seems simply gratuitous. — *Derek Elley*

AMERICAN ORPHEUS

A L.L. production. Produced, directed, written, edited by Rick Schmidt. Camera (color/b&w), Kyle Bergerson; sound, Neelon Crawford. Reviewed at Seattle Intl. Film Festival, June 1, 1992. Running time: **93 MIN.**
   With: Jody Esther, Karen Rodriguez, Deborah Daubner, Jasmine Carver, Aaron Carver, Willie Boy Walker, Curtis Imrie.

A resolutely independent filmmaker, Rick Schmidt has made low-budget movies for 19 years, working with non-professional actors and people who play themselves. Perhaps this lack of acting experience drags down "American Orpheus," an interesting idea that falls curiously flat when it should be emotionally charged. It has some limited potential on the fest and specialized theatrical circuits.

Intended as a tribute to Jean Cocteau's classic, "Orphée," Schmidt gives the Orpheus legend a contemporary twist. Here the central bond — the love which extends beyond the grave — is between a single mother, Fay (Jody Esther), and her young daughter (Jasmine Carver).

They live in a small coastal Washington town, but Fay fears that her ex-husband (Willie Boy Walker) will find her. Yet, from the pic's depiction of husband, it's hard to understand why Fay should fear her ex. And, in the end, they indeed appear to reconcile as a happy family unit.

The film is infused with a spiritual approach to life and death; a sort of mix between New Age, astrology and Herman Hesse's "fate rules" philosophy. It could be interesting, but the film fails to deliver any kind of emotional punch. Even when the young child dies and Fay is comforted by a friend, the tone is more like a speech than an heart-rending sharing of experiences.

Staging, lighting and camera are thoughtful throughout, and despite low-budget, the tech credits are definitely better than the theatrical. — *Maggie Brown*

ALMOST BLUE

A Curb/Esquire Films release of a First Films presentation of a Postcard Pictures production. (Intl. sales: Curb/Esquire.) Produced by Anthony Park-

er, Doug Olson. Executive producer, A. B. Goldberg. Directed, written by Keoni Waxman. Camera (Technicolor, b&w), Steven Finestone; editor, John Venzon; music, Nelson G. Hinds; production design, Charles Armstrong; art direction, Todd Cole; costume design, Mari-An Ceo; sound (Ultra-Stereo), Phillip Lloyd Hegel; assistant director, Molly Mayeux; associate producer, Michael Thompson; casting, Linda Francis. Reviewed at Cannes Film Festival market, May 15, 1992. Running time: **99 MIN.**
Morris Poole . . . . . Michael Madsen
Jasmine . . . . Lynette Walden
Charles . . . . Garrett Morris
Darcy . . . . Gale Mayron
Terry . . . . Yaphet Kotto
Icarus . . . . Ed Battle

There are moments in "Almost Blue" that seem to be a cut-price jazz take on "Barton Fink." Sassy, self-conscious low-budgeter about a tenor sax player whose muse has gone AWOL is slim but curiously watchable stuff, thanks to attractive playing and lack of overseriousness. Rushed to the Cannes market, this first feature by Keoni Waxman would benefit from further tightening and more work on the soundtrack before hitting limited cellars.

Michael Madsen ("Thelma & Louise," "Reservoir Dogs") toplines as Morris Poole, a former horn star who's gone to seed since his g.f. fell out the window five years ago. His black agent Charles (Garrett Morris) can't get him composing again, but sexy blonde dancer Jasmine (Lynette Walden) does the trick one sweaty summer day, eventually becoming a permanent fixture.

All goes well until Morris feels she's cramping his style. He starts to crack up again, paranoid about one of his missing tapes. An over-neat finale, which replays the opening with a twist, wraps up the episode in his life.

The script doesn't add up to a heap of beans, but small cast's performances are colorful and easy, and the self-consciously '50s-manqué flavor, almost all achieved through interiors, is held straight down the line. Only false notes are the over-arty black & white flashbacks for Madsen's earlier days.

Madsen is convincing as the screwed-up musician, if a bit over-reliant on beefcake looks. Sinuous Walden, hot in "The Silencer," strikes major sparks here as the loose-limbed Jasmine, curling her lips round dialog torn straight from a noir vamp's kisser.

Other perfs are sparky, with Gale Mayron getting too little screen time as Walden's tough-talking friend, Yaphet Kotto su-

percool as a jazz dude, and Morris wild in his bits as Madsen's agent. Shot in Denver, pic looks fine on its clearly limited budget, with Nelson Hinds' original score a further mood asset.

— *Derek Elley*

GOODBYE, PARADISE

A Latitude 20 Pictures presentation of a Mixed Media production. Produced, directed by Dennis Christianson, Tim Savage. Screenplay, Christianson, Susan Killeen. Camera (color), Graham Driscoll; editors, Jay K. Evans, Leo Nickel; music, Stan Wentzel; art director, Lynn Fujioka; costumes, Kathe James; make-up, Bryan Furer, Laura Van Wagner; sound (Ultra-Stereo), Mike Michaels; assistant director, Emmett J. Dennis III; line producer, Renee Confair; associate producer, Irish Barber; casting, Anna Fishburn. Reviewed at WorldFest/Houston, April 29, 1992. Running time: **105 MIN.**
Joe Martin . . . . Joe Moore
Billie . . . . Elissa Dulce
Cook . . . . James Hong
Tiny . . . . Richard Vales
Big Sharon . . . . Veroa Tiki
Little Sharon . . . . Megan Ward
Lt. Nomura . . . . . Danny Kamekona
Ben . . . . Pat Morita

No source material is listed in the credits, but Dennis Christianson and Tim Savage's "Goodbye, Paradise" plays like some obscure Off Broadway comedy-drama opened up only slightly for the screen. Leisurely paced indie effort is easy to take but not quite compelling enough to generate necessary word of mouth. With Pat Morita (in a relatively small role) the only name in the largely unknown cast, box office prospects appear limited.

Most of the action takes place inside the Paradise Inn, a seedy bar and grill about to be turned into an upscale restaurant in Honolulu's gentrifying Chinatown district. Entire pic takes place on closing night as the manager (Joe Moore) gamely greets the regulars and curiosity seekers one last time.

Moore is anxious about his and his staff's new role and even more worried about the elderly residents of the building's upstairs apartments and a near-senile derelict (Morita) who lives on handouts from the Paradise kitchen. The manager's worst expectations are realized when the new owner (Dennis Chun) demands upstairs evictions and appoints his wife (Eileen Fairbanks) as the new manager.

Susan Killeen and Christianson's rambling screenplay allows just about everyone to have the dramatic equivalent of an aria, showcasing his or her quirks.

Pic's best moments are those that focus on newcomer Elissa Dulce as a tart-tongued, warmhearted bartender who's sweet on Moore. Tech credits are good. Graham Driscoll's lensing vividly conveys both the seediness and the hominess of the bar.

— *Joe Leydon*

SEEING RED
(AUSTRALIAN)

A Goosey Ltd. production. Executive producer, William T. Marshall. Produced by Virginia Rouse, Tony Llewellyn-Jones. Directed by Rouse. Screenplay, Roger Pulvers. Camera (color), Ian Jones; editor, Mark Atkin; music, Andrew Yencken; sound, Jock Healy. Reviewed at Cannes Film Festival market, May 12, 1992. Running time: **87 MIN.**

Duncan Banks	Tony Llewellyn-Jones
Hugh Banks	Hugh Llewellyn-Jones
Amanda	Anne Louise Lambert
Vivian	Peta Toppano
Red Sessions	Zoe Carides
Mark	George Spartels
Nyguen	Anthony Wong
Louie Leeds	Henri Szeps
Gorman	Peter Sumner
McPherson	Bruce Venebles

This modestly budgeted, independently financed pic has an intriguing story and topflight cast, but an uncertain tone and tentative treatment limit theatrical possibilities. Still, "Seeing Red" should perform adequately on vid and TV.

Despite some good ideas, Roger Pulvers' screenplay contains too many coincidences and contrivances. Virginia Rouse, in her second pic after "To Market to Market," directs with an indecisive blend of comedy and suspense that fails to produce the comedythriller she seemed to be striving for.

Tony Llewellyn-Jones plays Duncan, the single father of a sprightly 3-year-old, Hugh (moppet son of the director and lead actor). Dad's a writer whose book about corporate corruption is about to be published; a shady entrepreneur and a government minister conspire to prevent that.

The women in Duncan's life are Vivian (Peta Toppano), a sexy gallery owner, and Amanda (Anne Louise Lambert), an adoring earth mother who likes caring for the boy. Also interested in Duncan is Red (Zoe Carides), a photographer with an exhibition at Vivian's gallery.

The businessman sends thugs to spy on Duncan and Hugh. Wrongly believing Amanda is Duncan's g.f., they kidnap her, though they make no demands.

Meanwhile, Hugh disappears while at a shopping mall with his father. Later, while in the gallery owner's company, the child is apparently kidnapped, but not, as Duncan (still unaware of Amanda's disappearance) assumes, by order of the businessman.

Pic's mood veers from drama (distraught father searches for son) to bathos as Amanda and a Vietnamese youth kidnapped with her easily escape their inept snatchers. A final revelation explains the motive for Hugh's kidnapping and the fate of Duncan's wife, ending the film on a poignant note.

The cast is excellent, especially the three actresses, who give sympathetic, touching performances. Technically, the film belies its small budget, with good photography (Ian Jones) mostly on Sydney locations. Editing (Mark Atkin) is a bit ragged, and the film doesn't always flow smoothly. — *David Stratton*

NAUFRAGHI SOTTO COSTA
(SHIPWRECKS)
(ITALIAN)

An Orango Film production. Produced by Alessandro Verdecchi. Directed by Marco Colli. Screenplay, Colli, Giovanni Di Gregorio, Claudio Spadaro. Camera (color), Antonio Farina; editor, Roberto Schiavone; music, Lamberto Macchi; art direction, Giancarlo Aymerich; costumes, Antonella Romagnoli; sound, Piero Parisi. Reviewed at Politecnico Cinema, Rome, June 5, 1992. Running time: **81 MIN.**

Iole	Sabrina Ferilli
Ioiò	Tony Palazzo
Manfredi	Claudio Spadaro
Iano	Giorgio Trestini
Antonio	David Brandon

Five characters' destinies hinge on an ancient Greek statue, and Greek tragedy is the underlying tone as this slowburning drama rises to a desolate crescendo. Curious throwback to traditional dramatic concerns could land some film fest exposure, but "Shipwrecks" seems most likely to wash up as a Euro tube item.

Action unfolds on the tiny Sicilian island of Mozia, where the terse custodian (Giorgio Trestini) of a museum of Phoenician relics lives alone with his surly, sultry daughter (Sabrina Ferilli). Aside from a daily tourist boat, lone visitor is mainlander Tony Palazzo who loves Ferilli behind Pa's back. He sneaks over at night to scrounge trinkets from

the unexplored ruins, which he sells to a shady aristocrat (co-scripter Claudio Spadaro).

A wounded prison escapee (David Brandon) also turns up, and the father and daughter take him in. Anxious for a large haul to pay off his gambling debts, the aristocrat engineers the theft of the museum's plum piece, a marble statue fished out of local waters. Cottoning on to the escapee's identity, Spadaro ropes him in as an accomplice.

A neat round of betrayal and retribution follows, which culminates with Trestino offering the statue back to the sea and paying with his life.

Marco Colli's direction is skillful, if a little straightforward apart from a stylish sequence in which Ferilli takes a moonlight dip. Walking on a half-submerged road left over from another civilization, she appears to be walking on the shimmering water.

History and the weight of past civilizations are a strong presence lurking beneath the pic, but the sense of remoteness that would have upped the tragedy's voltage never really registers. Antonio Farina's fluid but stingily lit camerawork sticks too close to the actors to make the great expanse of water surrounding them effective. But lensing on mainland Sicily has a suitably hardened quality, making it look more like African than Italo turf.

Perfs are fine all round but occasionally overstaged. Lamberto Macchi's richly varied music is well-used to sustain pic's quietly brooding atmosphere.

— *David Rooney*

ROTE OHREN SETZEN DURCH AFCHE
(FLAMING EARS)
(AUSTRIAN-16m)

A Woman Make Movies release. Produced, directed, written by Angela Hans Scheirl, Dietmar Schipek, Ursula Puerrer. Associate producer, Ulrike Zimmerman. Camera (color), Margarete Neumann, Curd Duca, Hermann Lewetz, Manfred Neuwirth; music, Schipek; models-special effects, Anthony Escott, Andrea Witzmann. Reviewed at Public Theater, N.Y., May 22, 1992. (In Intl. Festival of Lesbian and Gay Films.) Running Time: **83 MIN.**

Spy	Susanna Heilmayr
Volley	Ursula Puerrer
Nun	Angela Hans Scheirl
M (chauffeur)	Margarete Neumann
Blood	Gabriele Szekatsch
Man with cactus	Anthony Escott
Little girl	Luise Kubelka
Undertaker	Dietmar Schipek

Opening entry in New York's Intl. Festival of Gay and Lesbian Films, "Flaming Ears" is a futuristic lesbian movie unlikely to attract more than a fringe audience. However, pic's rich and moody atmospherics could muster some interest at special locales designed to attract a core constituency. Film is set to bow in the U.S. with midnight screenings at N.Y.'s Angelika Theater.

Story is set in the year 2700 in the burnt-out city of Asche. Most of the visible populace appear to be women; a few men turn up to perform minor duties. The film first focuses on Spy (Susanna Heilmayr), a comic strip artist who sets out into the streets after she learns her printing office has been burned.

In her odyssey, she will encounter the film's allegorical denizens: pyromaniac Volley (Ursula Puerrer) and Nun (Angela Hans Scheirl), a terminator-like creature dressed in red plastic. The characters are engaged in anarchic pursuits of power, pleasure and love, and spout delicious lines like "I want you to cut down on your perverted obsessions."

While the film draws on imagery from pop sci-fi and art films such as "Metropolis," "Last Year at Marienbad" and even "Rollerblade," its narrative follows many of avant-garde cinema's non-linear rituals, such as scenes of death and rebirth (the latter courtesy of a resuscitating vampire). Working with threadbare resources, the directors (who also star in the film) make adroit use of hand-held shots, stopaction animation and stylized miniatures to yield a suitable and alluring ambience.

This is the first feature for the trio of filmmakers who heretofore have done Super-8 shorts.

— *Fred Lombardi*

SHUANG CHO
(TWIN BRACELETS)
(TAIWANESE/HONG KONG/CHINESE-16m)

Produced by Liu Tien Chi. Directed by Huang Yu Shan. Screenplay, Liang Shu Hua, from Lu Chao Wan's story. Camera (color), Bob Thompson; editor, Chiang Kuo Chuan; music, Lo Ta Yu; artistic design, Li Kuo Kuang; sound, Lo Ta Yu. Reviewed at Public Theater, N.Y., May 20, 1992. (In Intl. Festival of Lesbian and Gay Films.) Running Time: 100 MIN.
Hui Hua . . . . Chen Te Jung
Hsui . . . . Liu Hsiao Hui
Kuang . . . . Kuo Chun An
Hui Hua's mother . . . . Lily Liao
Hui Hua's brother . . . . . Tao Ta Yu
Ta Hsiung . . . . Tsung Yang
Jane's husband . . . . . . Chou Tien Te
Jane . . . . Tsai Chia Li
(In Cantonese; Mandarin-dubbed)

Said to be the first lesbian film shot in mainland China, "Twin Bracelets" is a sensitive coming-of-age tale set in an island village wracked by cruel patriarchal traditions. Despite some overemphasis on sentimentality, pic should be good fare for specialized fests and markets.

Film opens with adolescent Hui Hua (Chen Te Jung) observing the wedding of her chauvinistic brother. Via her sister-in-law's tribulations, Hui Hua soon learns the plight of the village's married women. Among the Spartan customs, a wife is permitted to see her husband only three times a year until a son is born.

Depicting a situation in which lesbians are made and not born, Hui Hua forms an intense friendship with Hsiu (Liu Hsiao Hui). What might have been the usual bonding between two young women growing up develops into a ritualized sanctuary against marital oppression. The two vow to be faithful to each other as if married. Hsiu is pushed into an arranged marriage, and her husband turns out to be a decent, self-deprecating man who genuinely cares for her welfare. Hui Hua becomes convinced that Hsiu has broken her vow and plots a murder/suicide. She relents when she learns that Hsiu is pregnant and plans to leave the island for good with her husband. Unable to adopt to her own convoluted family situation, Hui Hua commits suicide.

As Hui Hua, Chen Te Jung is given to some mugging in the early scenes, but her performance develops fittingly with her character. Liu Hsiao Hui is quietly compelling as her compan-

ion. Taiwanese director Huang Yu Shan (whose family hails from the Mainland) advances her story with delicate and restrained imagery. Tech credits are good.
— *Fred Lombardi*

NOTTE DI STELLE
(STARRY NIGHT)
(ITALIAN)

A Mikado Film release of an MP production with participation of Ministry of Tourism & Entertainment. (Intl. sales: Sacis.) Produced by Marina Piperno. Directed, written by Luigi Faccini. Camera (Telecolor), Faccini; editor, Lorenza Franco; music, Luis Bacalov; art direction, Alfonso Rastelli; costumes, Innocenza Coiro; sound, Glauco Puletti. Reviewed at Augustus Cinema, Rome, May 20, 1992. Running time: 89 MIN.
Lucio . . . . Fabio Bussotti
Luana . . . . . . Antonella Taccarelli
Carlo . . . . Tiziano Giuffrida
Luana's mother . . . . Norma Martelli
Luana's father . . . . Claudio Angelini
Carlo's father . . . . . Ivano Marescotti

A disparate, desperate young trio cross paths for one fleetingly hopeful moment in "Starry Night," a sobering tour of Rome's stark, suburban no-man's land. As a window on life in another 'hood, pic packs no small amount of punches, but the core drama is unevenly played and lacking in conventional payoff, making it tough to place commercially.

A social worker (Fabio Bussotti) hooks up with a small-time singer (Antonella Taccarelli) and a graffiti artist (Tiziano Giuffrida) fresh out of prison with a drug habit behind him. Involving them in a homespun film project, Bussotti brings a brief sense of direction and camaraderie into their lives.

Complications arise when his relationship with the singer gets serious, shutting out the ex-con, who turns back to the needle. All three come up against their own brick walls: Bussotti with the inflexibility of the kids whose lives he's trying to change; Taccarelli with her frustrated ambitions; and Giuffrida with a growing sense of alienation that leads him to tragedy.

Writer-director Luigi Faccini gives the uncompromising yarn an appropriately rough texture with extensive use of grainy video footage. Shrewdly introduced (and seemingly unscripted) docudrama touches, such as local kids being interviewed on their family life and future plans, add to pic's overall sincerity and help compensate for the weaknesses

of its central thrust.

Though script's standpoint is rigorously honest, large snatches of dialogue are overwritten and enigmatic where austere plain talk would have been more on-target.

Use of nonpro actors pays off with Giuffrida, who has high-impact moments as the doomed junkie. But the ploy goes badly wrong with Taccerelli as the character on whom everything hinges. Looking uncomfortable throughout, she adopts a forced hipness and is rarely convincing. Bussotti (the only professional thesp of the three) is fine but seems miscast as the ultra-earnest do-gooder.

Tech work is on the money given pic's slim budget. Faccini's agile camerawork has a hard, edgy quality that's nicely complemented by Lorenza Franco's smooth intercutting of vid sequences. — *David Rooney*

UNLAWFUL ENTRY

A 20th Century Fox release of a Largo Entertainment presentation in association with JVC Entertainment of a Charles Gordon production. Produced by Gordon. Line producer, Gene Levy. Directed by Jonathan Kaplan. Screenplay, Lewis Colick, story by George D. Putnam, John Katchmer, Colick. Camera (Deluxe color), Jamie Anderson; editor, Curtiss Clayton; music, James Horner; production design, Lawrence G. Paull; art direction, Bruce Crone; set design, Dawn Snyder; set decoration, Rick Simpson; costume design, April Ferry; sound (Dolby), Glenn Anderson; associate producer, Sulla Hamer; assistant director, D. Scott Easton; casting, Jackie Burch. Reviewed at 20th Century Fox Studios, L.A., June 18, 1992. MPAA Rating: R. Running time: 111 MIN.
Michael Carr . . . . . . Kurt Russell
Officer Pete Davis . . . . . Ray Liotta
Karen Carr . . . . Madeleine Stowe
Officer Roy Cole . . Roger E. Mosley
Roger Graham . . . . . . Ken Lerner
Penny . . . . Deborah Offner
Jerome Lurie . . . Carmen Argenziano
Captain Hayes . . . . . . Andy Romano
Ernie Pike . . . . Johnny Ray McGhee
Leon . . . . Dino Anello

Although it exists primarily to send an audience into a bloodthirsty frenzy, and has major credibility problems in the bargain, "Unlawful Entry" still works as an effective victimization thriller. Following the "Fatal Attraction" pattern to the point of having a very similar climax, well-crafted concoction trades in the sort of elemental concerns and fears that get people mightily worked up. This, combined with controversy pic may engender based on its prominent plot element of excessive police violence, gives it potential to become a summer sleeper hit.

As he usually does, director Jonathan Kaplan pushes his material toward interesting areas of social and class-structure observations, notably suggesting that cops exist on a plane of society all their own that sets them apart from normal citizens in negative ways. At the same time, this is one more story about a sicko that the viewer, but not most of the characters, can spot a mile away, resulting in a plausibility line that gets crossed repeatedly.

Tense opening scene has a black intruder breaking into the lovely L.A. home of attractive married couple Kurt Russell and Madeleine Stowe. The man escapes after a scuffle with Russell and holding a knife to Stowe's throat, and the policemen (Ray Liotta and Roger E. Mosley) are the picture of helpfulness and encouragement.

Problem is that Liotta becomes excessively solicitous, arranging for the installation of a topnotch security system in the couple's home, eagerly accepting an invitation to dinner, and inviting Russell on a nocturnal "ride-along" in his police car. Obligingly, Liotta nabs the guy who broke into Russell's house and, when the latter refuses the cop's invitation to use his baton to take physical revenge on the cowering criminal, Liotta beats the hell out of the guy himself.

This turns Russell against Liotta forever, but Stowe prefers to think of him as a good man whose job-related proximity to violence just gives him a somewhat different way of seeing things. After speaking nicely to a class at the elementary school where Stowe and her friend Deborah Offner teach, Liotta comes on to Stowe in a quiet but insidious way, and from this point will stop at nothing to get Russell out of the way and have Stowe for himself.

Main problem from the outset is that it is perfectly apparent to everyone except Stowe that Liotta is a creep to be avoided at all costs. Mosley moans audibly when he realizes in their opening scene that Liotta is interested in the lady of the house, but Stowe gives the man every opening, while seeming to remain naïve about his true intentions.

Conversely, for the sexual tension of the climax to pay off properly, Stowe should be shown to have been erotically intrigued by danger and edginess represented by Liotta. Latter repeatedly suggests that Russell is not man enough to take care of her, that only he, as a smart cop, can keep her safe. But any deep or even repressed feelings Stowe may have for this man of action remain so unexplored as to possibly not even be present, which makes her behavior towards the end impossible to read.

With his inside knowledge and tricks, Liotta manages to get Russell put behind bars, and last section of the picture becomes a race between the wronged husband to spring himself from jail and the maniac cop's effort to have his way with the woman.

Conclusive showdown between the two men feeds on basic instincts that go back to animals and their caves, and therefore will have audiences hooting and hollering in vengeful anticipation of payback and comeuppance.

Kaplan stages the mayhem very well and manages to throw in a couple of nice diversions and surprises, even if it's all been done before and arouses some of people's crasser tendencies.

Had the Liotta character been presented as an essentially decent cop gone wrong, story might have achieved genuinely chilling dimensions. Instead, fact that he's clearly off-base and demented from the beginning gets everyone off the hook.

Scenes of Liotta's brutality are disturbing despite the fact that he's a nut, and will certainly be widely commented upon in light of the Rodney King case.

Liotta effectively conveys both the nice and nasty sides of his character but, as indicated, the true sexual tension between him and Stowe is absent, and he tips his hand too early regarding the man's instability. Russell is solid as the husband, while Stowe is opaque as the wife. Mosley and, as Russell's lawyer, Ken Lerner register very well.

Tech contributions are strong, notably Jamie Anderson's broodingly atmospheric lensing, Curtiss Clayton's alert editing and James Horner's suspenseful score. — *Todd McCarthy*

LA CHÊNE
(THE OAK)
(FRENCH-ROMANIAN)

An MKL release (in France) of a Parnasse Prods./Scarabee Films/MK2 Prods./La Sept Cinema co-production in association with Le Centre National de la Cinematographie, Canal Plus, Studio of Cinematographic Creation of Romanian Ministry of Culture. Executive producer, Constantin Popescu. Produced by Eliane Stutterheim, Sylvain Bursztejn, Lucian Pintilie. Directed, written by Pintilie, based on Ion Biaesu's novel. Camera (color), Doru Mitran; editor, Victorita Nae; art direction, Calin Papura. Reviewed at Cannes Film Festival (official selection, noncompeting), May 17, 1992. Running time: **105 MIN.**
Nela . . . . Maia Morgenstern
Mitica . . . . Razvan Vasilescu
Mayor . . . . Victor Rebengiuc
Country priest . . . . . . Dorel Visan

The major Romanian film of the post-Ceausescu period is "The Oak" by veteran Lucien Pintilie, lensed with French money and moral support. Its tense, disjunctive story conveys the frightening reality of life during the last days of the dictatorship better than any documentary. Pic's necessary viewing for anyone hoping to get a fix on this tragic nation.

Shot on a good-sized $3.7 million budget with imported film stock and equipment, pic strangely partakes of the poverty it shows on screen. Rejecting lush photography and a sweeping score, Pintilie's spartan lensing style seems to mimic the brusque, no-nonsense quality of his heroine Maia Morgenstern.

Shrugging off her wealthy, privileged background and stubbornly ignoring the repressive political climate, Morgenstern sets off for a teaching post in the provinces. The train ride is a nightmare, and when she finally arrives, she is gang-raped outside the station. This is how she meets Razvan Vasilescu, a like-minded, free-spirited doctor at the run-down hospital.

Pic often resorts to black humor to recount some of the unbelievable incidents in and out of the hospital. Patients die from bureaucracy, the secret police raid the morgue in search of a dead man's notebook, Vasilescu keeps nurses and co-workers in line by slugging them. The characters' shocking brutality is presented as a natural fact, practically a survival instinct.

Morgenstern, who lets a pet mouse romp through her hair, counts as one of the toughest film heroines. To get her man Vasilescu out of jail, she seduces the state prosecutor and threatens to send photos of him naked to his wife. The natural rebel couple seem able to laugh off everything until they witness a casual massacre in which baby-faced soldiers machine-gun a school bus.

The film makes the audience so inured to horror, injustice and brutality that the sickening finale — staged without much drama — loses shock value, which is perhaps Pintilie's point. The acting conventions also look a little over the top at the beginning, but by pic's end Morgenstern, Vasilescu and the fine supporting cast appear controlled and professional.

The helmer has lived in self-exile in France for the last 20 years, working steadily in theater and returning to Romania only after Ceausescu's fall in 1990. "The Oak" depicts the grief of an exile back in his devastated country (where Pintilie, now head of cinematography at the Ministry of Culture, is attempting to build up the Romanian film industry). — *Deborah Young*

MUSIC FOR THE MOVIES:
BERNARD HERRMANN
(DOCU-COLOR/B&W)

An Alternate Current/Les Films d'Ici/La Sept/Channel Four presentation. Produced by Margaret Smilow, Roma Baran. Executive producers, Richard Copans, Yves Jeanneau, Smilow. Directed, edited by Joshua Waletzky. Camera (color/b&w), Mark Daniels, Jerry Feldman; associate producers, Christine LeGoff, Judith Aley; narrator, Philip Bosco. Reviewed in L.A., June 7, 1992. (In AFI/L.A. FilmFest.) Running time: **60 MIN.**
With: Bernard Herrmann, Lucille Fletcher, James G. Stewart, Louis Kaufman, Don Cristlieb, David Raskin, Elmer Bernstein, Paul Hirsch, Christopher Palmer, Royal S. Brown, Norman Corwin, Claude Chabrol, Virginia Majewski, Alan Robinson, Claudine Bouche, Martin Scorsese.

Everybody's favorite Hollywood film composer, Bernard Herrmann, receives exceptionally intelligent treatment in this first-class analytical docu. Film scholar and casual fan alike will learn a great deal from this look at a man who professed disgruntlement with his work but turned out an inordinate number of great motion picture scores. At 60 minutes, pic is obviously designed for TV broadcast, but it would also be welcome at fests or other venues receptive to film-oriented documentaries.

Adeptly weaving vastly entertaining clips with perceptive interviews and a healthy share of rare footage of the late composer himself, filmmaker Joshua Waletzky ("Image Before My Eyes," "Partisans of Vilna," "Heavy Petting") vividly illustrates how Herrmann revolutionized film scoring with his emotional power, nonlinear approach and belief that the picture should dictate musical structure.

Kicking off with the stunning title sequence to "North by Northwest" and continuing on through the likes of "Citizen Kane," "The Ghost and Mrs. Muir," "On Dangerous Ground," "The Man Who Knew Too Much," "Sisters" and "Taxi Driver," Waletzky, who studied music formally, has no trouble exciting the viewer about his subject's talent.

Significantly, however, he has found admirers who can lucidly explicate Herrmann's accomplishments for the layman. Elmer Bernstein, who recently adapted Herrmann's "Cape Fear" score for Martin Scorsese's remake, sits at a piano explaining the simplicity of his predecessor's art. Also at the keyboard, Prof. Royal S. Brown superbly illustrates Herrmann's use of thirds in parallels, his repetitions and his refusal to resolve a musical phrase in order to achieve greater suspense. As one observer puts it, his music never "calms down."

Pic traces Herrmann's early experience as a CBS Radio orchestra conductor beginning in 1934, his involvement in Aaron Copland's circle, his move to Hollywood at the behest of Orson Welles for "Kane," his stated hatred for Hollywood and his paradoxical inability to cope after the collapse of the old studio system, which hastened his move to the U.K. in the 1960s.

Home movies and interviews in Paris and London help put the man himself into the picture, and some of his colleagues don't hesitate to describe Herrmann's contrariness. One dubs him "a 19th century manic depressive," and another states that he was a major egotist who was nasty to people, concluding, "He was not a rational man."

Although he had composed a symphony and an opera by the time he was 40, Herrmann, in an archival interview, admits frustration at "my own lack of achievement," and complains that, "I never had time for my own reflection and work." His ex-wife allows that he probably would have been happiest as a classical symphony conductor.

Highlight of Herrmann's career was his eight-film, 11-year collaboration with Alfred Hitchcock. Waletzky strikingly demonstrates Herrmann's contribution to the director's work by showing the "Psycho" sequence in which Janet Leigh drives through the rain with and without music. Sans score, the images are remarkably plain, drab and without tension; once the music is added, scene overflows with anxiety and brewing panic. Saul Bass' storyboards for the shower sequence are also edited together and presented with Herrmann's shrieking violins.

Of greatest interest to buffs will be an excerpt from Hitchcock's "Torn Curtain" shown, for the first time, with Herrmann's score. Colleague Norman Corwin observes that Herrmann "was gravely wounded" when Hitchcock rejected the composer's work for the film and abruptly ended their relationship. Immediately thereafter, however, Herrmann was hired by Hitchcock fan François Truffaut, and

some fascinating docu footage features the composer-conductor with the French director at a scoring session for "The Bride Wore Black."

In a very tight hour, this film convincingly demonstrates why its subject was important, and reveals how an outstanding score can add immeasurably to the emotional and psychological impact of a picture. At very least, this is a documentary with a lot of great music in it. — *Todd McCarthy*

LIFE ON THE EDGE

A Festival Entertainment release of a Movers & Shakers production. Produced by Eric Lewald, Andrew Yates. Executive producer, Bill Yates. Directed by Andrew Yates. Screenplay, Mark Edens. Camera (Foto-Kem color), Tom Fraser, Nicholas von Sternberg; editor, Armen Minasian; music, Mike Garson; production design, Amy Van Tries; art direction, Greg P. Oehler; sound (Ultra-Stereo), Clifford (Kip) Gynn; assistant director, Randy Pope, Keith Carpenter; special visual effects supervisor, Barry A. Nolan; co-producer, Miriam Preissel; associate producer, Jesse Long; casting, Jean Sarah Frost. Reviewed at Magno Preview 4 screening room, N.Y., June 16, 1992. No MPAA Rating. Running time: **78 MIN.**
Ray Nelson . . . . Jeff Perry
Karen Nelson . . . . . Jennifer Holmes
Joanie Hardy . . . . . Greta Blackburn
Roger Hardy . . . . . . Andrew Prine
Also with: Thalmus Rasulala, Martine Beswicke, Jennifer Edwards, Denny Dillon, Susan Powell, Kat Sawyer-Young, Tom Henschel, Liz Sagal, Ralph Bruneau, Ken Stoddard, Michael Tulin, Jessie Scott.

The wafer-thin comedy "Life on the Edge" mildly mocks trendy West Coast types into New Age this and mystical that. Vanity production has few laughs and its theatrical release is not going to draw flies. Pic's faults (harshly lighted pic was lensed at New World's television studios in 1989) show up unflatteringly on the big screen. Video and TV syndication are its best bets.

Debuting feature filmmaking team of Andrew Yates (director) and Mark Edens (writer) has concocted a sophomoric film trapping viewers at an endless party populated by bores. Occasional bon mots and stupid double entendres do not make the very long 78 minutes pass any faster.

Nebbish hero Jeff Perry is under the gun from the outset, with a day to come up with $100,000 to pay loan sharks from Las Vegas. His money is sunk in a doomed condo project Point Andreas. Attending a party at his neighbors' home in the canyon with depressed wife Jennif-

er Holmes, he's trapped there with the other guests following an earthquake (film's shooting title was "The Big One").

The quake destroys Perry's home and Point Andreas sinks into the Pacific. Situation comedy ensues, limning zoftig party hostess Greta Blackburn's successful seductions of Perry and other guests; an impromptu lesbian love affair between performance artist Liz Sagal and newscaster Kat Sawyer-Young; and born-again Michael Tulin literally coming out of the closet in film's only surefire gag.

Jennifer Edwards gives a cute Julie Hagerty-esque performance as a New Age faddist into mystical pursuits like calling on Mothra (no, not the monster called to action by young native princesses in Japanese horror flicks) for spiritual guidance. Film is most similar in format to her dad Blake Edwards' 1968 Peter Sellers vehicle "The Party," but lacks that film's fluid camerawork and physical shtick.

Last half of the film lamely stresses Perry's misadventures trying to find host Andrew Prine's hidden treasure trove of gold coins. Hokey finale, reminiscent of Steve DeJarnatt's "Miracle Mile," paints the lead characters into a corner and leaves them hanging.

Perry, who resembles a chunky U.S. version of Kenneth Branagh, isn't funny with his one stupified expression and poorly staged pratfalls. Rest of the cast overacts, including the late Thalmus Rasulala as a survivalist type.

Pic is unrated but would probably garner an R thanks to brief topless scenes featuring Sawyer-Young and Blackburn.
— *Lawrence Cohn*

DEAD BOYZ CAN'T FLY

A Stonecastle/Command production. Executive producers, Bradley Winters, Michael Adam Winters. Produced, directed by Howard Winters. Screenplay-co-producer, Anne Wolfe. Camera (color), Feliks Parnell; editors, Dow McKeever, Richard Dama, John Donaldson; music, Rich Sanders; production design, Sarah Knowles; costumes, Karen M. Sotiriou, Prudence Frinzi; sound, Bernie Hajdenberg; associate producer, Allison Winters; casting, Erica Goodman, Dorothy Palmer. Reviewed at WorldFest/Houston, April 26, 1992. Running time: **104 MIN.**
With: David John, Brad Friedman, Ruth Collins, Jason Stein, Daniel J. Johnson, Sheila Kennedy, Judith Cummings.

"Dead Boyz Can't Fly" is

a stupid and repulsively violent drama, suitable only for the least discriminating video audiences.

Thin plot has three vicious punks (including a mother-fixated, drag-queenly Brad Friedman) invading a quiet Manhattan office building during a holiday weekend and terrorizing the unlucky folks inside. The office-by-office assault begins as revenge for a businessman's slight to one of the punks, who warms up for the bloody spree by killing a beautiful blonde on an elevator.

Opening scenes are played at a stylized, almost cartoonish pitch, with a sight-gag nod to Marilyn Monroe in "The Seven Year Itch." Intended comedy's mood changes drastically with the first killing, and things go steadily downhill, then below ground, after that.

Even by contempo standards of exploitation movie mayhem, pic is inexcusably horrific. Producer-director Howard Winters never misses an opportunity to photograph women being punched and stabbed, usually in lip-smacking closeup.

The pic's most mean-spirited sadism is reserved for female characters. In the unlikely event this item gets theatrical distribution, pic will elicit protest from women's groups of all political persuasions. Filmmakers demonstrate a colossal amount of nerve in the closing credits, reminding the audience about the rising U.S. murder rate and making a plea for victims' rights.

Tech credits are no better than they absolutely have to be, and the performances are worse.
— *Joe Leydon*

ALL MY HUSBANDS
(FRENCH)

A Cinéflor production in association with Canal Plus/La Cinq/French Ministry of Culture. (Intl. sales: Sacis, Rome.) Produced, directed by André Farwagi. Screenplay, Russell Manzatt, from a story by Lucient Lambert; adaptation & dialogue, Farwagi, Lambert, Jean Cosmos. Camera (color), Jacques Renoir; editor, Jacques Witta; music, Johnny Caruso; production design, François de Lamothe; sound, Philippe Schilovitz; assistant director, Yann Gilbert. Reviewed at Cannes Film Festival market, May 8, 1992. Running time: **85 MIN.**
Emily Simonin . . . . Cecilia Peck
Philippe Simonin . . . Patrick Chesnais
Steve Anderson . . . . . . Mark Lazard
Charlotte . . . . Céline Samie
Also with: Adriana Russo, Ambre Siali, Bernard Crombey.
(French & English dialogue)

A goofball comedy about a French-Yank couple suffering with marriage lag, "All My Husbands" won't travel far from mainland Europe despite an energetic performance by Gregory Peck's daughter, Cecilia. Mixed-nationality cast and spy-antics plot has an unmistakable '60s flavor.

Peck is the wife of architect Patrick Chesnais and still has romantic dreams seven years into their dull marriage. When Chesnais' employer is exposed by CIA operative Mark Lazard as a front for an industrial espionage network, the couple separately exploit the situation to bring excitement into their lives.

Gallic thesp Chesnais has some fun dressing up like Dick Tracy (yellow coat and hat), on the run from the authorities. Peck, cute in a mini-jupe and handling her French dialogue with ease, squeezes the maximum out of her part as his feisty wife. Lazard is okay as a clichéd Yank in Europe.

Pic is a swift mover, which is just as well. Tech credits are standard. — *Derek Elley*

EMMA AND ELVIS

A Northern Arts Entertainment release. (Intl. sales: Jane Balfour Films.) Produced by Brenda Goodman, Julia Reichert. Directed by Reichert. Screenplay, Steven Bognar, Reichert, Martin M. Goldstein; story by Bognar, Reichert. Camera (color), Larry L. Banks; editor, Pamela Scott Arnold; music, Wendy Blackstone; production design, David Potts; art direction, John McFarlane; sound, Melanie Johnson; associate producers, Sallie Collins, Bognar, Stanley Plotnick; assistant director, J. Miller Tobin; casting, Deborah Brown. Reviewed at Cannes Film Festival market, May 16, 1992. Running time: **105 MIN.**
Alice Winchek . . . . . Kathryn Walker
Ben Winchek . . . . Mark Blum
Eddie . . . . Jason Duchin
Findley . . . . Mike Hodge
Jenny . . . . Margo Martindale
Larry . . . . Jody O'Neil
Croswell . . . . William Cain
Harris . . . . Mark Mocahbee

Residual 1960s activism gets a workout in "Emma and Elvis," first narrative feature by Julia Reichert, co-director of the acclaimed leftist docus "Seeing Red" and "Union Maids." With a few fest dates and limited theatrical runs in Ohio behind it, pic is a decent bet for market-by-market nurturing in college towns and communities open to alternative programming.

Alice is a middle-aged, coun-tercultural documentary film-maker in Dayton, Ohio, who has been working on a docu about the 1960s for so long that it's become a joke, especially to her husband Ben. No one can figure out why she doesn't get the '60s out of her system already, but Alice is clearly obsessed, and troubled by 1989 events, notably Tiananmen Square and the suicide of Abbie Hoffman.

Yanking her out of her cloistered mental world is Eddie, a 24-year-old videomaker for a local public access cable outlet. Angry and arrogant upon meeting her, he is initially highly derisive of Alice and her generation for having copped out and given him such a lousy world to live in, snapping, "You guys were supposed to be making a revolution, right? Well, why did you quit?"

Nevertheless, these two misfits' mutual discontent draws them together in a strange way, and Alice begins hanging around the cable TV station, where she finds political activists whose passion reminds her a lot of her radical days. The issues have changed, with AIDS now the leading concern, but Alice finds in these kids a stimulating embodiment of the attitude, "think globally, act locally."

While engaging herself in the station's effort to fight off the prudish regulators who would censor its programs' content, Alice also enters into a very tentative romance with Eddie. This development borders on the dramatically unbelievable, but fortunately it isn't pushed very far, and the whole experience at least helps her finish her docu.

In an earnest, righteous, basically likable way, pic draws a connection and distinction between the relative brands of political activism of the '60s and today. With humor no doubt somewhat self-directed, Reichert also draws a wry contrast between the self-absorbed docu filmmaker who labors over a project for years, and the shoot-from-the-hip video generation whose efforts are viewable instantaneously for immediate impact.

At the same time, Reichert shows her nonfiction, polemical roots in the way she hits her subject directly on the head, without nuance or subtlety. As a storyteller, she has yet to be introduced to such essential devices as subtext, oblique dialogue, dramatic weaving and counterpoint. But in this instance, she is so clearly working out many of the same problems faced by Alice that her good intentions count for a good deal, inspiring a generous reaction to her endeavor.

Acting is okay, and same can be said for the plain, straightforward production values. Title refers to the leads' mutual heroes, with Alice calling herself Emma Goldman and Eddie adopting the monicker Elvis Costello.
— *Todd McCarthy*

DARK HORSE

A Republic Pictures Intl. production. (Intl. sales: Republic.) Produced by Alan Glaser. Executive producers, Larry Sugar, Peter McIntosh, Richard Gladstein. Co-producer, Bonnie Sugar. Directed by David Hemmings. Screenplay, J.E. Maslin, from story by Tab Hunter. Camera (color), Steve Yaconelli; editor, Marjorie O'Connell; music, Roger Bellon; art direction, Prudence Hemmings, Bernard Hyde; costume design, Dona Granata; sound (Ultra-Stereo), Mary Jo Devenney; assistant director, Tony Adler; associate producer, Michael Alden. Reviewed at Cannes Film Festival market, May 11, 1992. Running time: **90 MIN.**
Jack Mills . . . . Ed Begley Jr.
Dr. Susan Hadley . . . . . Mimi Rogers
Curtis . . . . Samantha Eggar
Allison Mills . . . . Ari Meyers
Perkins . . . . Tab Hunter
Also with: Donovan Leitch, Bojesse Christopher.

Natural performances by Mimi Rogers and Ari Meyers aren't enough to coax "Dark Horse" very far into the commercial paddock. Home-on-the-range number about a cynical L.A. kid who learns true values in the sticks is too MOW-ish to score major points beyond the tube. Idaho-lensed pic will need careful selling to reach its target family audience.

Meyers plays the 14-year-old daughter of Ed Begley Jr., a hot-shot architect who moved to the small town of Cheltenham after his wife's death. Meyers starts partying with local boys even though she reckons they're all "geeks." Her uncurricular activities land her a 10-weekend work stint at a ranch where disabled kids learn to ride horses.

Ranch owner Rogers, herself under financial pressures, gets the city tyke to knuckle down, and Meyers eventually gets to like the place. So does Begley, who pops around for afternoon rides with Rogers. When Meyers and her favorite horse are both crippled in an auto accident, the stage is set for a dose of spiritual regeneration.

Director David Hemmings has a good track record of working with kids, and, reining back on unnecessary goo, he draws easy, likable playing from Meyers and the rest. Rogers, out of designer gear for a change, is refreshingly good as the strong-willed veterinarian, meshing easily with the cast. Samantha Eggar is in for a small bit as Meyers' teacher.

Editing is tight, matching the economical script. Roger Bellon's piano-and-strings score wallpapers the action in homey style.
— *Derek Elley*

NOUS DEUX
(THE TWO OF US)
(FRENCH)

An IMLF release of a Renn/A2/Aura co-production. Produced by Claude Berri. Directed by Henri Graziani. Screenplay, Anne Maurel. Camera (color), Patrick Blossier; editor, Denise de Casabianca; music, Michel Raffelli; costumes, Christine Guegan; sound, Antoine Bonfanti. Reviewed at Gaumont Convention, Paris, April 26, 1992. Running time: **94 MIN.**
Toussaint . . . . Philippe Noiret
Madeleine . . . . . Monique Chaumette
Napoleon . . . . Serge Merlin
Martin . . . . Patrick Fierry

"Nous Deux" is a soporific little film about a 60ish Paris couple who retire to their childhood village in Corsica. Full of elderly ambience, pic is a star vehicle that wastes top talents in meandering scenes where nostalgia, bickering and beaches barely fill the days.

Pic is targeted for Parisians fed up with big-city hassles and eager for their annual month in the country. But the best audience for this long-winded non-actioner probably has retired to the hereafter.

Opening holds out tepid promise when Philippe Noiret retires after 30 years of service in the Paris Metro, and he and his wife (Monique Chaumette) head for a rural town where they will rediscover their roots and grow most of their own food. But they find a town in which not much happens.

Pic's polished leads (spouses in real life) each get a brief tour de force, but their talent is misspent here. Too bad, since the ensemble acting is finely understated and always in sync.

Long after this distraction grows tiresome, an influx of summer homeowners briefly injects life into pic's second half, including son's visit and off-screen romance with dark-haired letter carrier. The immediate family issue is whether doctor son will abandon his city practice to marry unmovable local sweetheart.

But pic's underwhelming, long-range concern is which parent will die first. Noiret feels confident his wife will outlive him, and the mistaken assumption paves the way for a dreary ending. Helmer Henri Graziani could have interjected at least a few flashbacks to flesh out his characters. Tech credits are fine across the board. — *Lee Lourdeaux*

MEATBALLS 4

A Moviestore Entertainment release & production. Produced by Donald P. Borchers. Executive producer, Ken Halloway. Directed by Bob Logan. Screenplay, Logan. Camera (Film House color), Vance Burberry; editor, Peter H. Verity; music, Steve Hunter; production design, Dorian Vernacchio, Deborah Raymond; costume design, Angela Calin; sound (Ultra-Stereo), Beau Franklin; assistant director-associate producer, Kris Krengel; water ski coordinator, P.J. Marks; stunt coordinator, Kurt Bryant. Reviewed on HBO vidcassette, N.Y., June 9, 1992. MPAA Rating: R. Running time: **87 MIN.**

Ricky Wade	Corey Feldman
Neil Peterson	Jack Nance
Monica	Sarah Douglas
Wes	Bojesse Christopher
Victor	Johnny Cocktails
Howie	J. Trevor Edmond
Jennifer	Paige French
Dick	John Mendoza
Kyle	Bentley Mitchum
Hillary	Christy Thom
Kelly	Deborah Tucker

Wise-cracking Corey Feldman highlights this summer comedy, which should do just fine for HBO Video in the rental market. Film received a modest theatrical run in March in Cincinnati and various Southern cities.

Series dates back 13 years to the Ivan Reitman-helmed Canadian comedy "Meatballs," which launched Bill Murray as a major movie star. Subsequent entries have strayed from the young campers format; the fourth more closely resembles "Hot Dog ... The Movie" on water skis.

Feldman portrays a ne'er-do-well water skier hired by owner Jack Nance to serve as recreation director of Lakeside Water Ski Camp. Their enemy is Sarah Douglas of nearby Twin Oaks camp who wants to buy Nance out and use his site for real estate development.

Two camps are competing in an annual ski meet and Douglas' henchmen contrive to sabotage Feldman's efforts. Lakeside wins anyway and film climaxes in a corny, winner-take-all rematch.

Lame plotting is just an excuse for some okay water skiing

stunts. Filmmaker Bob Logan takes care to include t&a jiggle scenes of his scantily clad female cast (such as a game of strip charades), which should gain high marks among adolescent video renters.

Feldman's act is obnoxious, but that's what the script calls for. He even includes some self-deprecating humor at fadeout, when he turns to the camera to protest that he's a movie star: "I was in 'Goonies'!"

Nance, prematurely aged-looking since starring in David Lynch's "Eraserhead," is amusing, as is the colorfully monikered chubby comedian Johnny Cocktails. Distaff cast is pretty but not given much to do acting-wise. — *Lawrence Cohn*

LE AMICHE DEL CUORE
(CLOSE FRIENDS)
(ITALIAN)

A CDI release (in Italy) of a Pladi Audiovisivi production in association with Clemi Cinematografica & RAI-2. Produced by Giovanni Di Clemente. Directed by Michele Placido. Screenplay, Angelo Pasquini, Placido, Roberto Nobile. Camera (color), Giuseppe Lanci; editor, Ruggero Mastrioanni; music, Nicola Piovani; production design, Francesco Frigeri. Reviewed at Cannes Film Festival (Directors Fortnight), May 13, 1992. Running time: **106 MIN.**

Sabrina	Asia Argento
Father	Michele Placido
Lucio	Enrico Lo Verso
Morena	Carlotta Natoli
Claudia	Claudia Pandolfi
Also with: Simonetta Stefanelli, Laura Trotter, Orchidea De Santis.	

"Close Friends" takes a grave look at incest between a middle-class Roman father and daughter. Director/thesp Michele Placido tackles the theme with enough seriousness and delicacy to ensure a TV pickup despite the film's early (and subsequently overturned) ban at RAI-TV, associate producer.

Banking on his immense popularity in Italy, where he starred in the popular anti-Mafia TV series "The Octopus," Placido casts himself in the thankless role of a mild-mannered but secretly diabolical father. His 15-year-old daughter (Asia Argento) has lived with him since he split with her mother. Though at first her stand-offishness towards Dad seems like just a phase, a sense of something unhealthy gradually surfaces.

Argento's best friends, the outgoing Carlotta Natoli and Claudia Pandolfi, enjoy dating, but when they set her up on a date,

she becomes violently ill when the boy tries to kiss her. Later, she is strangely tense when her father wants to sit close to her on the sofa. The film has no explicitly erotic scenes, nor any uncomfortable scenes of Placido and Argento kissing. Yet the unwholesomeness comes across clearly.

Everything takes a turn for the better when Argento, who has dropped out of high school, get a job in a jeans shop and falls for salesman Enrico Lo Verso. Their touching love affair seems destined to pull her life together, but instead it becomes the prelude to tragedy when her father gets jealous. In a sea of standard acting, young thesps Argento and Lo Verso (hailed in Italy for his role in "The Stolen Children") stand out, making their hearts-and-flowers romance seem like the real thing. Called upon to run the gamut from youthful joy to depression, Argento carries off her final melodramatic scene with subdued understatement.

Placido is less persuasive as a guilt-ridden padre padrone, but he does succeed in giving the creepy father a human side.

Natoli and Pandolfi supply plenty of verve in stereotypical supporting roles designed to show minors' subtle exploitation by supposedly responsible adults. Natoli, a student nurse, is forced to bring heavy tranquilizers home to her doped-up mother. Pandolfi, who wants to become a model, moves in with her lesbian agent to get her career going.

As a director, Placido has a strong, if conventional, sense of storytelling and character, and of course he gives the actors lots of space. Cinematographer Giuseppe Lanci gets to open the film with a knockout aerial tracking shot pinpointing the neighborhood in relation to the Rome that tourists know. Several abruptly truncated scenes are deftly smoothed over by Ruggero Mastroianni's pro editing job.
— *Deborah Young*

OCTOBER 32ND
(BRITISH)

A United Film Mākers Inc.-Shining Armour Communications presentation of a Shining Armour Communications production in association with Slovakoturist. (Intl. sales: SAC, France.) Produced by Peter Collins, Paul Hunt. Executive producers, Cristina Collins, Peter Collins. Directed by Hunt. Screenplay, Nick McCarty, from a story by Hunt, McCarty. Camera (color), Gary Graver; editor, Phil Sanderson; music, William Campbell Jr., Michael O'Donnell; production design, Chris Tulloch; costume design,

Zdenek Sansky; stunt coordinators, John Stewart, Jaroslav Tomsa; sound (Dolby), Paul Le Mare, Peter Best; additional direction, Graver; action sequences direction, Stewart; associate producer, Natalia Tomasovicova. Reviewed at Cannes Film Festival market, May 17, 1992. Running time: **129 MIN.**

John Pope	Peter Phelps
Pendragon	Richard Lynch
Loong Tao	James Hong
Christy Lake	Nadia Cameron
Merlin	Rodney Wood
Dr. Mycroft	Desmond Llewelyn
Also with: Ted Markland, Robert Padilla, Pamela Mandell, John Stone.	

"October 32nd" is a lame sword-and-sorcery pic that'll fast-forward straight to the vidbins. British-funded, mixed-accent item, shot in Czechoslovakia repping Californian locations, would do well to lose a good 40 minutes on the way to the copying plant.

Mishmash of "Excalibur" and '60s Mario Bava pics starts in the Dark Ages with knight John Pope (Peter Phelps) winning from the evil Pendragon (Richard Lynch) the Sword of Power to guard Merlin's daughter, Crystal of the Lake (Nadia Cameron). Post-main title, in October 1892, a scientist (Desmond Llewelyn) warns his student (Phelps again) that October 32 is drawing nigh, "the day when time stands still" and chaos reigns.

Segue to the present day and pretty young San Francisco reporter Christy Lake (Cameron again) arriving in the sleepy town of Landsdown to investigate a mining story. Local bigshot is the head of Pendragon Holding Enterprises (Lynch again); local hero is handsome geologist John Pope (Phelps, third time around).

Pic's most surprising aspect is that it just keeps on going. Laughable script ("I want the girl alive") and wobbly Yank accents by the uncharismatic Phelps and Cameron are matched by low-tech effects and workaday direction and lensing. Chief nasty Lynch is the only one who plays it broad enough. A thunderous, pounding synthesizer score does its damnedest to inject some excitement. — *Derek Elley*

KINDER DER LANDSTRASSE
(CHILD OF THE OPEN ROAD)
(SWISS-GERMAN-AUSTRIAN)

A Rialto Film (Zurich) release of a Panorama Films (Zurich)-Lichtblick Filmproduktion (Hamburg)-Wega Film (Vienna) co-production. (Intl. sales: Metropolis, Zurich.) Produced by Johannes Bösiger, Peter Spoerri. Directed by Urs

Egger. Screenplay, Bösiger. Camera (color), Lukas Strebel; editor, Barbara Hennings; music, Detlef Petersen; art direction, Kathrin Brunner; costume design, Sabina Haag; sound, Thomas Szabolcs. Previewed at Le Paris Cinema, Zurich, April 30, 1992. Running time: **117 MIN.**

Jana Kessel	Jasmin Tabatabai
Jana (5 years)	Martina Straessler
Jana (9 years)	Jara Weiss
Theresa Kessel	Andrea Eckert
Paul Kessel	Herbert Leiser
Dr. Schönefeld	Hans Peter Korff
Fräulein Roth	Nina Petri
Roger Kessel	Mathias Gnädinger
Andrina Kessel	Noemi Steuer
Anton Kessel	Otto Dornbierer
Django	Andreas Schindelholz
Marina Simowitsch	Sigi Pawellek
Latscha Simowitsch	Georg Trenkwitz
Hans Simowitsch	Marcel Ruckstuhl
Franz	Georg Friedrich
Franz (10 years)	Maurice Suhr
Hildi Mauerhofer	Charlotte Joss
Kurt Mauerhofer	Urs Bihler
Mother Superior	Sibylle Brunner
Claudine	Beatrice Kuemin
Eva Hottinger	Dagmar Schwarz
Heinrich Hottinger	Wolf Dietrich Berg

"**C**hild of the Open Road" is based on true events that shocked the Swiss public 20 years ago. Creative team's personal engagement and heartfelt belief in the material emanates from the screen at all times and adds to the film's emotional impact. Made on a budget of just over $3 million, pic is a respectable achievement and may well have legs when word-of-mouth spreads.

In 1926, prominent Swiss youth aid foundation Pro Juventute, with Swiss government okay, founded an organization aimed at "saving" children of gypsy families from life on the road and integrate them to a "normal" life in foster homes, orphanages, convent schools and sometimes prisons or psychiatric wards.

Over 700 children were separated from their parents by force. When the tragedy was uncovered in 1972, it created a scandal, and the organization was soon dissolved. Rehabilitation and government funding for the victims have been slow in coming.

In director Urs Egger and co-producer/scriptwriter Johannes Bösiger's fictitious but fact-inspired story line, 5-year-old Jana is removed from her gypsy parents and placed in various foster homes and institutions. Her escape attempts end in disaster, and she is invariably reminded she's "only a child of the open road."

She falls in love, gets pregnant, but when the child is born, the organization takes it under custody. Meanwhile, her fiancé, desperate for money to get out of the country, attempts a burglary and gets locked up. Jana kidnaps her own child and flees toward the border to await her fiancé's release.

The film's impact lies in its simple, direct storytelling which avoids maudlin sentimentality. The no-name cast is handpicked down to the last bit part (60 speaking parts in all). With an expressive face and a good screen presence, Jasmin Tabatabai as 16-year-old Jana is especially impressive. Among the many smaller parts, massive Swiss actor Mathias Gnädinger stands out as one of the gypsies.

Tech credits are all above par, especially Lukas Strebel's beautifully atmospheric lensing and Barbara Hennings' sharp editing. Another asset is Detlef Petersen's accordion music, alternately moody and melancholy or gay and lilting to fit to story's various moods. — *George Mezöfi*

HAK MAU
(BLACK CAT)
(HONG KONG)

A D&B Films Co. production. Produced by Dickson Poon. Executive producer, Stephen Shin. Directed by Shin. Screenplay, Lam Wai-lun, Chan Boshun, Lam Tan-ping. Camera (color), Lee Kin-keung; editors, Wong Wing-ming, Kwok Ting-hung, Wong Chau-on; music, Danny Chung; art direction, Fu Tsi-tsung; costume design, Lau Bo-lam; special effects, Gary Paller; special effects makeup, Tibor Farkas; sound, Leung Lik-tsi; assistant directors, Irene Lee (Canada), Lam Wai-lun, Ng Kwan-yuk; line director, Tseng Siu-keung; action directors, Kong Tao-hoi, Poon Kin-kwan; stunt coordinator, Owen Wai-strom; 2nd unit camera, Tseng Siu-keung; associate producers, Sunny Chan (Japan), Shan Tam (U.S. & Canada); line producers, Fermand Ngan (Hong Kong), Michael Parker (Canada), Nancy Tong (U.S.), Wong Hon-kwong (Japan). Reviewed June 10, 1992, in London. Running time: **99 MIN.**

Catherine	Jade Leung
Brian	Simon Yam
Allen Yeung	Thomas Lam

(Cantonese & English dialogue; Chinese & English subtitles)

Hong Kong actioner fans should come away purring from "Black Cat," a sexy spin on the genre coming within a whisker of being a straight ripoff of "La Femme Nikita." Pic has already developed a minor cult following among Western buffs and could go wider as a dubbed vid with the right marketing.

Helmer Stephen Shin, who made his rep with a string of Hong Kong yuppie comedies during the '80s, originally intended a straight remake of the Gallic original but changed course when he found the rights had been snapped up Stateside. Result, which poses no commercial threat to the skedded U.S. remake, still has clear parallels with the Luc Besson pic (mostly during the early training scenes) but is also simply a further variant on Hong Kong's long-established femme actioner genre.

Central character is hardboiled loner Catherine (newcomer Jade Leung), who's arrested for killing a horny truck driver at a roadside diner. After shooting her way out of a Gotham courthouse, she's kidnapped by the CIA, implanted with a microchip called "Black Cat" and put through a gruelling program by an agent (Simon Yam) to train her as an obedient assassin.

She's sent to Hong Kong where, in between hits on the prez of the World Wildlife Fund and a local businessman, she falls for a photog (Thomas Lam) who's ignorant of her trade. Pic climaxes in Japan as she and her b.f. go on the run after she's sliced a Nipponese big shot.

Underlying theme is meant to be Leung's inner conflict between obedience and personal freedom, but that doesn't get much further than an obvious scene in which she frees a caged bird. After a gritty first half of her being worn down into submission, rest of the thinly scripted pic is mostly a series of well-staged action sequences separated by mushy, mildly softcore moments with Lam.

Former model Leung is excellent in the bruising opening reels, and her crop-haired, statuesque looks add an edge to the designer violence later on. Local name Yam is well-cast as her cool CIA nemesis.

Tech credits are all pro for the genre, with zippy editing, a pacy synth score and occasional arty visuals by Shin. Locations in and around Vancouver substitute for most of the Stateside sequences. Pic took a middling HK$10.9 million ($1.5 million) on local release last August. Plans for a series have so far come to naught.
— *Derek Elley*

DOLLY DEAREST

A Trimark release of a Patriot Pictures production in association with Channeler Enterprises. Executive producer, Pierre David. Produced by Daniel Cady. Directed by Maria Lease. Screenplay, Lease, from story by Lease, Peter Sutcliffe, Rod Nave. Camera (CFI color), Eric D. Andersen; editor, Geoffrey Rowladn; music, Mark Snow; production design, W. Brooke Wheeler; costume design, Scott Tomlinson; sound (Ultra-Stereo), Paul Coogan; assistant director, Larry Litton; Dolly & special makeup effects, Michael Burnett Prods.; special visual effects supervisor, Alan G. Markowitz; special Dolly visual effects, Prime Filmworks Inc.; stunt coordinator, Cole McKay; associate producers, Channon Scott, Nave, Paul Aguilar; casting, Billy Da Mota. Reviewed on Vidmark videcassette. MPAA Rating: R. Running time: **93 MIN.**

Marilyn Reed	Denise Crosby
Eliot Reed	Sam Bottoms
Jimmy Reed	Chris Demetral
Jessica Reed	Candy Hutson
Camilla	Lupe Ontirveros
Luis	Will Gotay
Alva	Alma Martinez
Estrella	Enrique Renaldo
Dr. Karl Resnick	Rip Torn
Dolly double	Ed Gale

A low-budget variant on "Child's Play," "Dolly Dearest" is a scary horror film about a devil doll. Pic received theatrical exposure in the Midwest in January ahead of its video release.

Denise Crosby and Sam Bottoms move with their two young children to Mexico set up a doll factory, little suspecting that the decrepit facility is near an archaeological dig that's recently set forth supernatural forces.

The dolls are animated by spirits dating back to a tribe that lived many centuries ago in the region. Crosby's housekeeper Lupe Ontirveros senses the danger but is murdered by daughter Candy Hutson's cute little Dolly.

Aided by Mark Snow's spooky and suspenseful music, film builds to a well-staged climax. Unlike the big-budget Chucky of the "Child's Play" films, Dolly's movements are suggested rather than shown, with quick shots of a live action double (Ed Gale). Even so, the effect is convincing enough. As the young heroine who comes under her Dolly's spell, Hutson is an impressively precocious adorable/hateful character. Rest of the cast, including Rip Torn as a local prof, has less interesting assignments.

Clutzy dialogue is pic's chief drawback. Serious mood is also undercut by corny reversion to the genre cliché (as in the Chucky and Freddy Krueger films) of having the Dollys shout dumb one-liners during the final reel.

— *Lawrence Cohn*

DESERT HAWK

A 21st Century Film Corp. presentation of a Wells Co. production. (Intl. sales: 21st Century.) Produced by William G. Dunn Jr. Executive producers, Menahem Golan, Ami Artzi. Co-producer, Jim Lotfi. Directed by Isaac Florentine. Screenplay, Florentine, Lotfi, from Florentine's story. Camera (Deluxe color), David (Dudy) Namir; editor, Karen Horn; music, Roy J. Ravio; sound design (Ultra-Stereo), Jan Lucas; sound, Thomas Varga; production design, Heather Lynne Ross; costume design, Sashanna Kaplan; fight choreography, Florentine; assistant director, Jennifer Marchese. Reviewed at Cannes Film Festival market, May 16, 1992. Running time: **85 MIN.**

Joe Highhawk (Hawk)
. . . . John Haymes Newton
Claudia Valente . . . . . Judie Aronson
Anthony Valente . . Sam DeFrancisco
Santos . . . . Paul L. Smith
Bruno . . . . Michael M. Foley
Also with: Robert O'Reilly, Biff Maynard.

A dumb actioner about a part-Indian kickboxer taking on coke smugglers in Arizona, "Desert Hawk" doesn't deliver on any level except tedium. Low fighting quotient won't cut the mustard with martial arts buffs, and former "Superboy" lead John Haymes Newton mostly looks as if he's lost his way to the beach.

Newton is Joe Highhawk, a former S.F. cop and champion martial artist, who's getting bored helping the Arizona police hunt down two-bit pot runners. When he comes across a beautiful accountant (Judie Aronson) and her retarded brother (Sam DeFrancisco) on the run from coke king Santos (Paul L. Smith), he has to decide whether to break his vow never to kill again.

The no-nonsense script goes through the motions of trying to build a character out of the lead. But sequences like Newton retraining in the desert after he's almost been killed by Smith's heavies are embarrassingly unmythic, despite Roy J. Ravio's heroic score.

Rest of the pic plays like 25-year-old TV fodder. Perfs are all routine, as are tech credits. Bargain basement effects extend to clearly visible guidewire on an arrow in a bad guy's chest.

Fight choreography, by helmer Isaac Florentine, is low-voltage, mostly relying on lotsa slomo. Only true martial artist in the pic is Michael M. Foley, who briefly shows his stuff in the final reel before a rapido finish.

— *Derek Elley*

BOOMERANG

A Paramount Pictures release of an Eddie Murphy production, in association with Brian Grazer/Imagine Films Entertainment. Produced by Grazer, Warrington Hudlin. Executive producer, Mark Lipsky. Directed by Reginald Hudlin. Screenplay, Barry W. Blaustein, David Sheffield, based on Murphy's story. Camera (Deluxe color), Woody Omens; editor, Earl Watson, John Carter, Michael Jablow; music, Marcus Miller; production design, Jane Musky; art direction, William Barclay; set decoration, Alan Hicks; costume design, Francine Jamison-Tanchuck; sound (Dolby), Russell Williams II; assistant director, Joseph Ray; stunt coordinator, Jery Hewitt; additional camera, Peter Deming, Richard Quinlan; co-producers, Blaustein, Sheffield; associate producer, Ray Murphy Jr.; casting, Aleta Chappelle. Reviewed at Loews Astor Plaza, N.Y., June 25, 1992. MPAA Rating: R. Running time: **118 MIN.**

Marcus . . . . Eddie Murphy
Angela . . . . Halle Berry
Jacqueline . . . . Robin Givens
Gerard Jackson . . . David Alan Grier
Tyler . . . . Martin Lawrence
Strangé . . . . Grace Jones
Nelson . . . . Geoffrey Holder
Lady Eloise . . . . Eartha Kitt
Bony T . . . . Chris Rock
Yvonne . . . . Tisha Campbell
Christie . . . . Lela Rochon
Mr. Jackson . . . . John Witherspoon
Mrs. Jackson . . . Bebe Drake-Massey
Todd . . . . John Canada Terrell
Chemist . . . . Leonard Jackson
Lady Eloise's butler . Jonathan P. Hicks
Box office clerk . . . . . . Irv Dotten
Salesman . . . . . . Tom Mardirosian
Editor . . . . . . Melvin Van Peebles
Waitress . . . . Rhonda Jensen
Noreen . . . . Alyce Webb
Woman from Holland . . Louise Vyent
Also with: Frank Rivers, Angela Logan, Chuck Pfeifer, Raye Dowell, Reginald Hudlin, Warrington Hudlin.

In "Boomerang" Eddie Murphy straitjackets himself in an ill-fitting comedy vehicle that's desperately in need of a reality check. With several very funny scenes, film should do well enough in the summer comedy box office sweepstakes but is unlikely to rank with the star's big hits.

For his 11th feature film, Murphy's credited with the high-concept story, developed by scripters Barry Blaustein and David Sheffield as a cornball tale of comeuppance.

He's a marketing exec at a New York cosmetics firm that women find irresistible (all six female leads want to seduce him). After a merger with a French firm, his new departmental boss, Robin Givens, turns the tables on Murphy and treats him the way he's been treating women all his adult life.

Film works best when Murphy plays up his strong suits, including a childlike innocence, flair for mimicry and self-depre-

cating humor. Unfortunately, his character's fat ego keeps hogging center stage. The fact that he's dominated during the middle reels by aggressive Givens doesn't make up for the blatant sexism of the script.

Only naturalistic character in a cast of caricatures is cute subordinate Halle Berry during the film's first half. Continuing her persona from her previous film, a similar comedy about upwardly mobile blacks, "Strictly Business," Berry suddenly becomes aggressive and as one-note as Givens in the schematic later reels.

Director Reginald Hudlin, along with his producer brother Warrington Hudlin making the big jump here from low-budget "House Party" to major studio filmmaking, handles individual scenes well but misses the big picture.

"Boomerang" never questions its characters' values, seemingly torn from a glossy magazine: sex, glamor and moving up the corporate ladder. Creativity is either mocked, as in the grotesque TV commercials directed by Murphy's associate Geoffrey Holder, or co-opted, as when artist Berry uses her drawings for marketing campaigns to become Murphy's equal at a rival cosmetics firm.

The film might have worked if the thoroughly selfish characters were striving after *something*, like the mythic protagonists in Ayn Rand's "Atlas Shrugged" or "The Fountainhead." Settling down in "meaningful relationships" or marriage is a pretty lame script device to resolve their infantile conflicts.

Though set in contemporary Manhattan, the picture's iconography is a fantasy world almost on the level of Philip Wylie's "The Disappearance." Redressing the traditional Hollywood formula, the white characters (instead of the blacks) are in menial positions for comic relief, e.g., a silly waitress, a bigoted clothing store clerk and muscular slaves pulling supermodel Grace Jones' chariot.

Whites appear briefly in positions of power, in high-level executive meetings or as the comical French owners of Murphy's firm, but they're strictly absentee landlords. As film's subtext, this structure presents a fashionably separatist theme: Whites are not the enemy but are irrelevant. Such a scheme is self-defeating, as other minorities like Hispanics and Asians are com-

pletely absent from this New York.

Murphy's funny scenes, notably simulating an orgasm in bed with Givens, can't mask his smug, taking-it-easy performance in one of those roles where one's hair is never mussed.

Supporting cast is strong: Givens is very convincing in the Rosalind Russell role; Berry is alluring throughout. Murphy's inevitable sexist buddies David Alan Grier (the nerd) and Martin Lawrence (the stereotyped militant) are very funny sidekicks.

Scene stealers include the arch aide-de-camp Holder; John Witherspoon, hilarious as Grier's embarrassingly coarse dad; Grace Jones, perfectly vulgar as the fragrance model; and a game Eartha Kitt as the company figurehead who takes Murphy to bed. Wisecracking Tisha Campbell gets in her licks as the star's ex-girlfriend who lives next door.

Costume designer Francine Jamison-Tanchuck and the rest of the crew have fashioned a wish-fulfillment context of glamor that is escapist par excellence. Editing is inconsistent, with early scenes running too long and many truncated ones in the last half. At 118 minutes, the episodic film might profitably have dropped a full reel. — *Lawrence Cohn*

A LEAGUE OF THEIR OWN

A Columbia release of a Parkway production. Produced by Robert Greenhut, Elliot Abbott. Executive producer, Penny Marshall. Co-producers, William Pace, Ronnie Clemmer, Joseph Hartwick. Directed by Marshall. Screenplay, Lowell Ganz, Babaloo Mandel, based on a story by Kim Wilson, Kelly Candaele. Camera (Technicolor, Panavision widescreen), Miroslav Ondricek; editor, George Bowers; film editor, Adam Bernardi; music, Hans Zimmer; production design, Bill Groom; art direction, Tim Galvin; set decoration, George DeTitta Jr.; costume design, Cynthia Flynt; sound (Dolby), Les Lazarowitz; associate producer, Amy Lemisch; assistant director, Michael Haley; additional camera, Thomas Priestley; casting, Ellen Lewis. Reviewed at Sony Studios, Culver City, Calif., June 24, 1992. MPAA Rating: PG. Running time: **128 MIN.**

Jimmy Dugan . . . . Tom Hanks
Dottie Hinson . . . . . . Geena Davis
Mae Mordabito . . . . Madonna
Kit Keller . . . . Lori Petty
Ernie Capadino . . . . Jon Lovitz
Ira Lowenstein . . . . David Strathairn
Walter Harvey . . . . Garry Marshall
Marla Hooch . . . . . Megan Cavanagh
Doris Murphy . . . . . Rosie O'Donnell
Alice Gaspers . . . . . Renee Coleman
Shirley Baker . . . . Ann Cusack
Helen Haley . Anne Elizabeth Ramsay
Betty Horn . . . . Tracy Reiner
Evelyn Gardner . . . . . Bitty Schram
Ellen Sue Gotlander . Freddie Simpson

Awash in sentimentality and manic energy but only occasionally bubbling over with high humor, "A League of Their Own" hits about .250 with a few RBI but more than its share of strikeouts.

A comic look at the first season of the women's baseball league in 1943, Penny Marshall's gangly fourth film benefits from a fresh, unusual subject, the joy of baseball being played by women having the time of their lives and a wonderful central performance by Geena Davis. Downside includes contrived plotting, obvious comedy and heart-tugging, some hammy thesping and a general hokiness.

Pic is amiable enough to please mainstream summertime audiences, but the reported $50 million budget doesn't show on screen, and assorted story elements (baseball, women's subject, period setting) represent a mixed bag of commercial assets and liabilities that makes for an uphill marketing struggle.

The All American Girls Professional Baseball League, formed at the height of World War II when the dearth of male athletes threatened the continued existence of the major leagues, called on talented femmes from all over North America to play a sport professionally where no such expectations or possibilities had previously existed.

With his hilarious gruffness and urban airs, Jon Lovitz gets things off to a promising start as a scout for the nascent league who tracks down softball star Geena Davis in rural Oregon. Married to an overseas soldier and with no real ambition, Davis agrees to train to Chicago for tryouts as long as her sister, pitcher Lori Petty, can come too.

After picking up a female Babe Ruth, Megan Cavanagh, in Colorado, group arrives at Harvey Field, where more than 1,000 women compete for the 64 slots available on four teams. Workouts were actually shot at venerable Wrigley Field, appropriate in that Cubs owner Phillip K. Wrigley actually spearheaded formation of the Girls League.

Once the teams are picked, only so many plotting possibilities are open to the commercially reliable team of Lowell Ganz and Babaloo Mandel, and most of the

obvious ones pop up: the attempts of the women to skirt the strict behavior code, the marriage and departure of one of them, the death of another's husband at war, the gradual improvement of their play and resulting growth of popularity and respect, and the inevitable, cornball showdown between rival sisters.

Adding a little testosterone to the recipe is Tom Hanks, a former big-league star who sees life from so deep in the bottle that he virtually sleeps through practice and the initial games. Slowly, the bloated, grizzled manager comes alive to the potential and excitement of the women's play, but his early comic contributions consist mainly of spitting and taking the screen's longest recorded leak.

Anchoring the proceedings, and preventing them from flying off in too many frivolous directions, is the splendidly serious Davis. The catcher and team ace, the imposing Davis rises to every occasion and reacts with the graceful equanimity of a born winner to triumph as well as adversity. Totally convincing as a pro athlete, Davis remains classy even when the film sputters.

The spectacle of the women playing good baseball provides a nice kick, and the well-trained actresses seem pretty capable despite coverage that favors cheatable closeups and editing that breaks up what should be continuous action into separate bites of play.

The women's baseball careers will forever stand as the high point in their lives. Like the women who went to work when the boys went overseas, they will largely return to the conventional wifely roles prescribed for them at war's end, and this adamantly politically correct picture trades heavily on the nostalgia contained in this one, brief shining moment.

Sentimental quotient is indulged to the max in the framing device of the women, now in their 60s and 70s, journeying to Cooperstown for a reunion and induction of the women's league into the Baseball Hall of Fame. Actual former league players go through their paces in an exhibition game re-created for end credits sequence.

Despite the lavish budget, period feel isn't fully realized, as locations are pretty much restricted to ballparks and boardinghouses, and song selection and Hans Zimmer's score lend a more modern than vintage feel.

Of the large cast, Rosie O'Donnell stands out as the brash, smooth-fielding third basewoman, and Cavanagh makes an impression as the dumpy slugger who finds unexpected romance on the road. A brunette Madonna plays a predictably sassy and irreverent type who shows her underwear whenever she can, and Petty is irritatingly petulant as Davis' cry-baby little sister.

An extraordinary effect is created by the appearance of Davis' character as an older woman at the beginning and end. Is it a great makeup job, or an older actress uncannily representing Davis' looks 40 years hence? Answer is the latter, although Davis reportedly dubbed the line readings. — *Todd McCarthy*

THE MUSIC TELLS YOU
(DOCU)

A Pennebaker Associates release of a Columbia Records & Pennebaker Associates presentation. Produced by Frazer Pennebaker. Executive producers, Steve Bekowitz, Ann Marie Wilkins. Directed by Chris Hegedus, D.A. Pennebaker. Camera (color), Nick Doob, Ronald Gray, Crystal Griffiths, Hegedus, D.A. Pennebaker; editor, Hegedus, D.A. Pennebaker, Erez Laufer; music, Branford Marsalis; sound (Dolby), Patrick Smith. Reviewed on vidcassette, N.Y., June 24, 1992. No MPAA Rating. Running time: **60 MIN.**
With: Branford Marsalis, Robert Hurst, Jeff (Tain) Watts, Sting, Jerry Garcia, Bruce Hornsby, Prof. David Baker.

Portrait film of jazz saxophonist Branford Marsalis is an ephemeral look at a popular figure, its release well-timed to exploit his current high visibility as musical director on "The Tonight Show with Jay Leno." Though made by the renowned documentarist Donn A. Pennebaker and his frequent collaborator Chris Hegedus, this Columbia Records-funded effort lacks insight and presents unmemorable music.

Marsalis' sense of humor comes out in backstage and tour-bus camaraderie with pals and fellow musicians, bass player Robert Hurst and drummer Jeff Watts. Unfortunately, his extreme pretensions are also present, as Marsalis frequently makes pithy pronouncements on his philosophy of jazz, its history and racism that his own silver-spoon status and lack of proper dues-paying can't justify.

His stress on touring as fundamental to a jazz man's life and career is immediately contradicted by his taking the bread job in the shadow of Doc Severinsen. The rigors of a tour is unconvincingly exemplified here by a concert at Indiana University, with the trio filmed in sterile fashion lacking the atmosphere of a night club setting.

Film's title comes from an interview in which Marsalis properly states that the popular notion of jazz equals freedom is not so. In fact the dictates of the musical setting determine the parameters of what a soloist plays. Unfortunately the group's performances of various originals, with Marsalis mainly on soprano rather than tenor sax, are uninspired and hardly worth preserving on film.

Pennebaker and Hegedus would have done better to record a special event or extraordinary performance. Their work is briefly upstaged by a clip from Michael Apted's superior 1985 documentary "Bring on the Night" showing Marsalis performing with Sting.

Elsewhere the sax star plays the national anthem with pianist Bruce Hornsby at the 1991 NBA All-Star game; chatting with Jerry Garcia before an unseen Madison Square Garden guest gig with the Grateful Dead; speaking to students at Prof. David Baker's Indiana U. class; and in a studio recording the soundtrack for what looks like a TV documentary about Spike Lee's "Mo' Better Blues."

Marsalis is undoubtedly talented, but his place in jazz history remains to be seen.
— *Lawrence Cohn*

BLAST 'EM
(CANADIAN-DOCU)

A Silent Fiction Films & Cinema Esperanza Intl. presentation. Produced by Anders Palm. Executive producers, Palm, Lars Ake Johansson, Johan Sanden. Directed, written by Joseph Blasioli. Camera (color), Robert Garrard; editors, Blasioli, Egidio Coccimiglio; music, Yuri Gorbachow; sound, Antonio Arroyo, Ivan, Marty Casparian; co-director, Coccimiglio. Reviewed at Film Forum, N.Y., June 23, 1992. Running time: **100 MIN.**
With: Victor Malafronte, Nick Elgar, Rick Maiman, Gerardo Somosa, Steve Sands, Albert Ferreira, Eugene Upshaw, Virginia Lohle, David Whitehead, Sally Kirkland, Felice Quinto, Randy Bauer, Queerdonna, John Barrett, David McGough, Ron Galella.

Its title sounds militaristic, but "Blast 'Em" is an entertaining documentary about the frenzied competition among paparazzi for celebrity photos. Funny and illuminating pic should appeal to anyone interested in star worship and its consequences. Two-week booking at N.Y.'s Film Forum may muster enough interest to justify a longer commercial run.

Docu focuses on Victor Malafronte, a young photographer who aggressively pursues his celeb prey. When he's not crashing galas, he stakes out John Kennedy Jr.'s office and Michael J. Fox's apartment building. His triumphs include capturing Kennedy on roller blades and snagging the first shot of Fox with his wife *and* baby.

Like most celeb photogs, Malafronte has little concern for his subjects' privacy. "I don't have any sympathy for a guy who makes 20 or 30 million," he says. And, as someone else points out, "A picture of a celebrity is like hard currency."

Other, but seldom identified, photographers are interviewed as well. In one amusing segment, a flashback to the origins of the term "paparazzi," an Italian photographer recalls Anita Ekberg shooting him with a bow and arrow and kicking him in the groin.

By comparison, most of the celebs seen in "Blast 'Em" are quite tolerant of "assault photographers." Even Sean Penn flashes a smile for Malafronte. Familiar faces also include Robert De Niro, Matt Dillon, Madonna, Marla Maples, Jack Nicholson and Sigourney Weaver.

Not surprisingly, the cameramen often had trouble keeping up with the persistent, tireless shootist. But the occasionally wavering camerawork captures the guerilla-like aspect of ambush photography.

Other technical credits are fine, though the music gets too heavy when Malafronte fails to get a photo. Writer-director Joseph Blasioli also occasionally takes his subject too seriously.

But most of the time, docu has a suitably light, amused tone. An Italo photographer brags about capturing starlets' exposed breasts. Sally Kirkland prepares for the Oscars as she would prepare for battle. And Malafronte waits and waits and waits for pint-sized Fox to emerge from his Central Park West home.

The director might have interviewed a few stars — besides spotlight-seeking Kirkland — to hear their side of the story. But he does show the absurdity of trying to satisfy Americans' obsession with celebrity. That obsession is, after all, the reason why paparazzi exist.

—*William Stevenson*

AFFENGEIL
(LIFE IS LIKE A CUCUMBER)
(WEST GERMAN-DOCU)

A Rosa von Praunheim presentation. Produced, directed, written by von Praunheim. Executive producer, Elke Peters. Camera (color), Mike Kuchar, Klaus Janschewski; editor, Mike Shephard; music, Maran Gosov, Thomas Marquard; art direction, Volker Marz. Reviewed in San Francisco, June 2, 1992. (In S.F. Intl. Lesbian/Gay Film Festival.) Running time: **87 MIN.**
With: Lotti Huber, Rosa von Praunheim, Helga Sloop, Gertrud Mischwitzky, Thomas Woischnig, Hans Peter Schwade, Frank Schafer.

Semi-notorious West German gay filmmaker Rosa von Praunheim has created perhaps his best feature to date with the ostensible documentary "Affengeil," about his friendship with aging German actress Lotti Huber. International prospects for the 1990 feature are modest at best, but emphasis on its campy/eccentric sides could locate a cult audience.

Huber is a colorful character, a 76-year-old imp not above milking her age for comic or plaintive riffs. In 1937, the "little dark whirlwind" eloped with the son of the mayor of a small German town. She was a Jewess, he was "pure Aryan," and her lover was soon killed in prison for "breaking race laws," while she was sent to a concentration camp.

She fled to Jerusalem, where she continued to study dance and art with other escapees. Becoming a bawdy nightclub dancer to survive in hard times, she discovered her own comic style.

Much later back in Germany, her last husband's death left Huber impoverished. She succeeded in selling her outrageous personality via TV commercials, along the way becoming a sort of dotty mascot for the West German lesbian/gay community.

At the start of "Affengeil," the slightly daft grande dame allegedly shoplifts a camcorder so von Praunheim can "film my life, as I am." But they bicker throughout the film — quite amusingly, though these scenes are often questionably spontaneous.

The director, who's rarely off-screen, comes across as a handsome narcissist (at one gratuitous point shown cavorting semi-nude with two younger buddies in bed), displaying his self-conscious angst on equal terms with the subject's suffering postures.

This stalemate of unwieldy egos is, thankfully, entertaining. Huber alternately accuses her director of tastelessness and revels in risque behavior herself. She sings songs, enacts bizarre little fantasy scenes (largely clips from her appearances in the director's prior efforts) and appears on a balcony to cheers by Gay Pride marchers below. But she also seethes with indignation at anti-Semitism.

It's impossible to know if this calculatedly flamboyant woman is ever telling the full truth about her life, but the blur between reality and self-willed fancy is von Praunheim's point here.

Tech values are okay, with lensing (16m blown up to 35m) tending toward director's trademark kitschy bright coloration. Silly, affectionate, quarrelsome and sad, pic is a fitting tribute to its larger-than-life heroine.

— *Dennis Harvey*

WONG FEI-HUNG II
(ONCE UPON A TIME IN CHINA II)
(HONG KONG)

A Golden Harvest presentation of a Film Workshop production. Produced by Tsui Hark, Ng See Yuen. Executive producer, Raymond Chow. Line producer, Cho King Man. Directed by Tsui. Screenplay, Tsui, Hanson Chan, Cheung Tan. Camera (color), Arthur Wong; editor, Mak Chi Sin; music, Richard Yuan, Johnny Njo; art direction, Ma Poon Chiu; costume design, Chiu Kwok Shun; martial arts direction, Yuen Woo Ping; special effects, Cinefax Worshop. Reviewed at Sun Sing Theater, N.Y., June 9, 1992. (In Asian American Intl. Film Festival.) Running time: **106 MIN.**

Wong Fey Hong	Jet Li
Aunt Yee	Rosamund Kwan
Lan	Yen Chi Tan
Luke	David Chiang
Fu	Mok Siu Chung
Kung	Xiong Xin Xin
Sun Yat Sen	Zhang Tie Lin
Ambassador	Paul Fonoroff
Chung	Yan Yee Kwan

(In Cantonese)

"Once Upon a Time in China II" continues Tsui Hark's attempt at a kung-fu fin de siècle epic à la Sergio Leone with better results than the first film. From the opening sequence of white-robed xenophobes cavorting in a lantern-lit Taoist temple, Tsui's visual mastery is reconfirmed. To an even greater extent than "Once I," pic manages to offer spectacular martial arts mayhem while devoting generous time to story line and historical details.

Unfortunately, the narrative remains at the juvenile adventure level, and when an historical figure like Sun Yat-Sen appears, he's treated with greater reverence than even the subjects of old Warner Bros. biopics. Tsui would be able to bolster his b.o. by adding more edge to the plot line in a future sequel.

Tsui already has shown a flair for varying the conventions of kung fu actioners and other genres. This film's predecessor reversed the protagonists of countless Western adventure films (dating from the silents to Hammer's "Terror of the Tongs") in which Orientals were cast as menacing white slavers and Caucasians as heroes. While Westerners are now depicted as the exploiters of Chinese womanhood, the first "Once" also affirmed the benefits of Western modernization.

Current opus, even more rife with political references, is set in Canton in 1895. Soundtrack early on refers to Japan's growing power, which nabbed Taiwan from China. The White Lotus fanatics who want to exterminate foreign influence are depicted as frauds and villains. Crying "free the poor" and burning a British flag, they are likely reminders of another potential danger at Hong Kong's threshold.

Though portrayed more sympathetically, the English here are more bumbling than benign and prove hapless victims when not supported by Jet Li's Chinese hero. One of the set-pieces that should resonate with Western viewers is the siege of the British embassy by the White Lotus sect and the government's witdrawal of protection to the Westerners.

Jet Li and Rosamund Kwan reprise their respective roles as the stalwart Wong Fey Hong and his young Westernized Aunt Yee. Mok Siu Chung doesn't elicit many laughs as the comic relief Fu, but Yen Chi Tan is a strong villain as Commander Lan.

Visuals remain exciting although the first film's 'Scope format was shunned and nothing here matches the "ladder duel" of the first film. Richard Yuan and Johnny Njo's score also lends dignity to the proceedings.

— *Fred Lombardi*

STCHASTLIVYE DNI
(HAPPY DAYS)
(RUSSIAN-B&W)

A First Film & Experimental Film Studio (Lenfilm) production. Produced by Alexei Gherman. Directed, written by Alexei Balabanov. Camera (b&w), Sergei Astakhov. Reviewed at Cannes Film Festival (Un Certain Regard), May 16, 1992. Running time: **80 MIN.**
With: Viktor Sukhorukov, Lika Nevolina.

Something about life in the Confederation of Independent States (ex-USSR) must lend itself to black humor: Alexei Balabanov's wacky "Happy Days" more successfully captures the sickening sense of things being hopelessly, irreparably askew than most of the new realist, socially concerned films.

Produced by Alexei Gherman's First Film and Experimental Film Studio (which recently broke off from parent Lenfilm), this bona fide avant-garde work shot in seductive black & white will reward the patience of the few hardy viewers willing to go along with its nuttiness. Abroad, art house programmers will be tempted but may pass.

In an atmosphere that might have appealed to David Lynch while shooting "Eraserhead," Balabanov introduces his nameless young hero, played like a shell-shocked zombie by Viktor Sukhorukov. Released from the hospital while his head is still bandaged, he wanders the empty streets of St. Petersburg hunting for a room to live in like any self-respecting Dostoevsky antihero. His first lodging is a barren room in a huge apartment whose enticing landlady puts everything off bounds but herself.

Kicked out by the lady's burly lover, Sukhorukov makes several comic forays into the world of rented rooms, but he ends up sleeping in a cemetery. There his peace is disturbed by a waiflike blonde (Lika Nevolina) who has a soft spot for the tattered misanthrope Sukhorukov has become. She virtually forces him to move into her place.

Despite her extreme delicacy, the girl scrapes by prostituting herself to noisy clients in the next room. Sukhorukov sleeps with his face to the wall, stubbornly refusing contact until she announces "they" are having a baby. He is briefly aroused to life, but when the baby is born,

he finds himself unceremoniously kicked out on the street again.

Balabanov has an elfish sense of malice that projects itself onto people, places and objects. Film contains so few of all three, he can afford to energize anything that actually gets in front of the lens. Pic has a theatrical sense of timing, and its uncinematic rhythm can risk putting some viewers to sleep.

Pic's strange creatures seem perfectly normal outgrowths of the times, maybe a little less sordid than the denizens of some other angry Russian films. Sergei Astakov's cinematography is a magnificent parade of black & white images. Soundtrack favors Richard Wagner over the very sparse dialogue.

— *Deborah Young*

WUNDERJAHRE
(WONDER YEARS)
(GERMAN)

An Objectiv Film-DEFA Studio Babelsberg production. (Intl. sales: Exportfilm Bischoff, Munich; Excelsior Films, Antwerp.) Produced by Jutta Lieck. Directed, written by Arend Agthe. Camera (color), Michael Wiesweg; editor, Ursula West; music, Matthias Raue; production design, Jürgen Kiefer; costume design, Stephanie Polo; sound, Jürgen Matuschek; assistant director, Claudia Gläser. Reviewed at Cannes Film Festival market, May 15, 1992. Running time: **98 MIN.**
Hannelore . . . . . Gudrun Landgrebe
Hanna Hoffmann . . . . . . Silvia Lang
Friedrich . . . . Jens Weisser
Bernhard . . . . Christian Müller-Stahl
Clemens . . . . Kirill Falkow
Wonny . . . . Nicole Motzek
Susi . . . . Elizabeth Romano

A solidly crafted study of growing up in postwar Germany, "Wonder Years" lacks a strong enough tone to make it on the art house circuit but could attract festival booking and tube sales. Work also exists in a TV miniseries version but stands on its own in present theatrical cut.

Young Hanna (Silvia Lang) is taken in by a family in Mittelstadt and soon finds the mother (Gudrun Landgrebe) still carries a torch for her long-lost son, Clemens (Kirill Falkow). One day, Hanna finds Clemens' ID card in a quarry and the introverted kid, who's been living rough since escaping from a war orphans' camp, is finally returned to his parents.

Second half shows the family slowly hit by social and political

tensions. Clemens, who was cared for by a Russian woman, has to learn to be German again; eldest son Bernhard, expelled from school for exposing a teacher as an ex-Nazi, becomes a journalist. Pic ends with Hanna officially adopted into the family as she stands on the brink of womanhood.

The drama never goes very deep, but all characters are well drawn, reflecting late 1950s Germany. What could easily have become a simple rites-of-passage retro item is held on course by solid performances and direction, with period detail economically drawn (youngsters worship Yank music). Final montage, with an exhilarating score by Matthias Raue, wraps proceedings with some style.

Landgrebe ("A Woman in Flames") is restrained in a smallish part. Lang is more an observer of events than a true participant. Tech credits are all fine.

— *Derek Elley*

AFI/L.A. FEST

THE GOOD FASCIST
(SOUTH AFRICAN)

A Living Pictures presentation. Produced, directed, written by Helen Nogueira. Camera (Irene Labs color), Alwyn Kumst, Chris Schutte; editor, Ronelle Loots; music, Ian Solomon; production design, Jeanne Henn; costume design, Sue Steele, Lisa; sound, Kevin Montenari; additional camera, Peter Palmer. Reviewed at Monica 4-Plex, Santa Monica, Calif., June 22, 1992. (In AFI/L.A. FilmFest.) Running time: **107 MIN.**
Suzannah Leal . . . . . . Jana Cilliers
Filipe Leal . . . . . Tertius Meintjies
Tsepo . . . . . Sello Maake Ka-Nkube
Gisela . . . . Grethe Fox

"The Good Fascist" attempts, with mixed results, to elucidate the tragic human factor in recent South African history under cover of a political thriller-cum-courtroom drama. Inflammatory material and succession of incredible events certainly hold the interest, but director-writer Helen Nogueira has not dramatized the emotional, intimate side of the story sufficiently to fully realize its potential power, and structure and some plot developments are a bit confusing, at least for Yank audiences.

Due for wide release in its native country in October, the picture would be limited to polit-

ical and foreign film forums in North America.

Around the central figure of a guilt-ridden white liberal teacher, Nogueira presents the extremes of the white supremacist movement and black activists. Filmmaker is so busy getting all her info and incidents up on the screen that a strong p.o.v. never takes hold, leaving the viewer uncertain what to make of it all, except to register the usual outrage over apartheid and the far right's nasty shenanigans.

Suzannah teaches at a racially mixed school and takes an interest in the frustrations of a passionately political black student named Tsepo. Meanwhile, her husband Filipe is an easy mark for blonde Nazi Gisela, who recruits him to the cause with a little below-the-belt convincing.

A rash of right-wing bombings breaks out, and Filipe, who now seems like a zombie, leaves home without a word. He and Gisela are soon arrested for terrorism, and after about 40 minutes, pic enters its trial phase, which allows a look at the curious South African justice and journalism systems in action (although how accurately it's hard to know).

Legal proceedings are conducted privately, without press or public present, before three judges who look like they were born under Queen Victoria. Prosecution seems to have an airtight case, given the cache of weapons found at the arrest site, and state seems anxious to prove that it can even-handedly mete out punishment to the right.

But charges against the devil-woman Gisela, who is clearly an Aryan ringleader, are suddenly and mysteriously dropped, leaving the dupe Filipe to meet his destiny in prison alongside Tsepo, who has also been flushed into the pen. Whomever the state has no use for can easily be made to disappear.

Jana Cilliers is an appealing, warm actress, but her character's reactions, as written, are difficult to fathom. Suzannah more or less takes it in stride when he is revealed on TV to be a terrorist and adulterer and has vague intentions when it comes to Tsepo.

Legal system vagaries lead to further head-scratching so that Nogueira's admirable effort to illuminate the gray areas of the South African dilemma are significantly mitigated by an uncertain handling of the narrative that often omits the scenes one most wants to see. Lumpen structure also provides no clue as to the time frame of the protracted succession of events.

Still, grim tale, based on a true story, has a fair degree of gut-level impact, and it remains interesting to hear the diverse characters air often misguided assumptions.

Sello Maake Ka-Nkube makes a favorable impression as the angry student who rejects even the most unassailable achievements of white culture worldwide, and pic makes notable use of numerous contrasting Johannesburg locations.

— *Todd McCarthy*

STREET WARS

A Jamaa Fanaka Production. Executive producers, Cordell & Clarine MacDonald. Produced by Fanaka, Bryan O'Dell, Ben Caldwell. Directed, written by Fanaka. Camera (color), John Demps; editors, Alain Jacubowicz, Taesung Yim; music, Michael Dunlap, Yves Chicha. Reviewed at Monica 4-Plex, Santa Monica, Calif., June 20, 1992. (In AFI/L.A. FilmFest.) Running time: **94 MIN.**
Sugarpop . . . . . . Alan Joseph Howe
Frank . . . . Bryan O'Dell
Humunus . . . . Cliff Shegog
Also with: Jean Pace, Brigid Coulter.

Jamaa Fanaka's indie "Street Wars" is a provocative crime pic with a twist, an offbeat gangster drama that also provides commentary on the genre. In the wake of L.A.'s recent civil unrest, film's timely concerns, original structure and bold visual conception should appeal to young black auds, but lack of traditional narrative and moral weight might limit crossover appeal.

Tale's tone and message are established in the pre-credits sequence in which L.A. drug lord Frank (Bryan O'Dell) instructs his younger brother Sugarpop (Alan Joseph Howe), a "top gun" aviation cadet at an elitist academy, that there's no right and wrong, just power, but there's no power without money. Frank has made the money; now he expects Sugarpop to gain legitimacy and respect.

In pic's rather routine first half, Frank is viciously assassinated in a restaurant. Avenging younger sib takes charge of the operation, vowing to make it legit in two years. Trained in ultralight aircraft, Sugarpop turns his men into a lethal ghetto air force.

Pic takes a satirical view of its vividly drawn, oddball characters, and no element, black or white, remains unscathed by Fa-

naka's criticism. The police chief is a caricature who labels the gangsters a bunch of animals and lowlifes. Cliché-spouting TV reporters embellish their stories to boost ratings. Community residents are depicted as selfish and indifferent.

Unlike "Do the Right Thing," in which mainstream society values are challenged, Fanaka accepts dominant white culture — he just wants a more active share of it. Fanaka's militant pic goes one step beyond Spike Lee and John Singleton, chroniclers of frustrated and angry ghetto youth. Here, rage is channeled into action: Fanaka's young men are not morally confused — they know what needs to be done.

Violence is excessive and, when shot in slow-motion, gratuitous. Most shootouts erupt randomly and suddenly without much context. But fanciful pic is highly stylized and surprisingly upbeat. Frank's grand funeral is celebrated with a disco music.

Decidedly unsentimental and nonjudgmental, pic is not a narrative in which viewers are asked to sympathize with the characters. Defying easy categorization, modernist pic switches gears from family melodrama to sex farce to crime-gangster yarn.

Endowed with stunning looks and great screen presence, Howe plays the lead without much depth. Rest of cast is uneven, but fortunately pic's impact doesn't depend on acting. Visuals are strong: John Demps' lensing is imaginative, the sets and costumes deliberately ostentatious. — *Emanuel Levy*

SYDNEY FEST

MODERN TIMES
(AUSTRALIAN-DOCU)

A Mayfan production. (Intl. sales: Film Australia.) Produced by Graeme Isaac. Directed, edited by Graham Chase. Camera (color), Andy Fraser; sound, Chase. Reviewed at Sydney Film Festival, June 7, 1992. Running time: **90 MIN.**

Documaker Graham Chase returned to his South Australian hometown, the small industrial city of Port Pirie, to make this quirky, laconic docu about an ordinary Australian's struggle with the recession. Viewers will find his portrait of the community soft-centered but appealing.

Port Pirie has the largest lead smelter and refiner in the world, and the pollution has brought the city bad publicity in recent years. Chase's father and grandfather both died of lead poisoning. But the locals fiercely defend their city and the smelter, which has been laying off workers at an alarming rate.

Rather than take the obvious route of observing the city and its people through his own eyes, Chase (who hadn't been home in 30 years) uses the p.o.v. of the teenage daughter of his former best friend. An aspiring radio journalist, she is working on a radio docu about unemployment in the city.

Result is an okay portrait of a provincial Australian city enduring crisis with good humor and optimism. — *David Stratton*

THE FOOTSTEP MAN
(NEW ZEALAND)

A John Maynard Prods. Ltd. production in association with New Zealand Film Commission, Avalon/NFU Studios & N.Z. on Air. (Intl. sales: The Sales Co., London.) Produced by Maynard. Directed by Leon Narbey. Screenplay, Narbey, Martin Edmond. Camera (color), Allen Guilford; editor, David Coulson; music, Jan Preston; production design, Kai Hawkins; costumes, Barbara Darragh; sound, Kit Rollins; assistant director, Greg Stitt; casting, Norelle Scott. Reviewed at Sydney Film Festival, June 14, 1992. Running time: **87 MIN.**
Sam Jolley . . . . Steven Grives
Vida . . . . Rosey Jones
Mireille . . . . Jennifer Ward-Lealand
Toulouse-Lautrec/
  Barman . . . . Michael Hurst
Marcelle . . . . Sarah Smuts-Kennedy
Ricardo . . . . Jorge Quevedo
Jake . . . . Peter Dennett

"The Footstep Man" is an intriguing variation on the "Purple Rose of Cairo" notion of a film character coming to life. Modest returns can be expected, particularly from industry and buff audiences.

Sam Jolley (Steven Grives) is an Auckland Foley artist (called a "footstep man" Down Under) whose work pressures led to his wife and daughter leaving him and moving to Ireland. He's working on a picture about Toulouse-Lautrec and two prostitute/models, Mireille and Marcelle. Film's director Vida (Rosey Jones) quickly takes exception to the negative attitudes expressed by Sam's assistant, Jake (Peter Dennett); she insists that Jake be fired.

Sam becomes obsessed with the character of Mireille (Jennifer Ward-Leland) who, in the film he's working on, contracts syphi-

lis and drowns herself in the Seine. Sam imagines she "talks" to him from the screen. To keep Mireille from suicide, Sam sets about persuading the director to change the ending. In the process, he starts an affair with her.

All this is fine, as far as it goes, and scenes of the Foley artist at work, dubbing not only footsteps but other soundtrack effects, are fascinating. The trouble is that the film-within-the-film is so banal, Jake's violent criticisms of it seem entirely justified.

This, in turn, prevents audience identification with Vida, since she's clearly making a lousy film. On top of that, she's too easily swayed by Sam to make crucial structural changes to it.

Thesping is adequate, but the film could have used a little more humor. Buffs should enjoy this inside look at the postproduction process, but for wider audiences, the themes and situations may appear remote.

Technical credits are fine.
— *David Stratton*

GENTLE 12
(JAPANESE)

An Argo Project/Suntory/NCP production. Directed by Shun Nakahara. Screenplay, Koki Mitani. Camera (color), Kenji Takama. Reviewed at Sydney Film Festival, June 11, 1992. Running time: **115 MIN.**
With: Kazuyuki Aijima, Katsumi Muramatsu.

Shun Nakahara's "Gentle 12" is an unambitious, predictable comedy inspired by Sidney Lumet's classic "12 Angry Men."

Setup is the exact reverse of the Lumet film: At the outset, 11 of the jurors are convinced that a woman accused of murdering her husband is innocent. A studious type wants a guilty verdict.

From this point on, there are few surprises. The jury members, all standard types, get a share of screen time for a dramatic, or comic, declamation.

Result is a curiosity of limited international appeal.
— *David Stratton*

YOJARANUN IYUMANURO
(BECAUSE YOU ARE A WOMAN)
(SOUTH KOREAN)

A Ye Film Co. Ltd. production. Produced by Go Gyu-Sup. Directed by Kim

Yu-Jin. Screenplay, Lee Yun-Taek, Lee Seong-Su, Nah Hyo-Jeong. Camera (color), Yu Young-Il; editor, Kim Hyun. Reviewed at Sydney Film Festival, June 13, 1992. Running time: **104 MIN.**
With: Won Mi-Kyung, Lee Young-Ha, Shon Sook, Lee Kyung-Young, Chin Hee-Jin, Kim Min-Jong.

Based on a 1989 incident, "Because You Are a Woman" is an impassioned indictment of the treatment of Korean rape victims. This well-acted, well-staged film overcomes some directorial excesses, unimaginative use of music and (in the version caught) appallingly crude English subtitles.

Helmer Kim Yu-Jin deals with the case of Chung-Hee (Won Mi-Kyung), who runs a restaurant with her husband. One evening, Chung-Hee's sister-in-law stops by to complain that her husband has beaten her. Chung-Hee agrees to walk the battered wife home, and along the way reluctantly stops at a bar.

The sister-in-law is picked up by a man, and Chung-Hee is left alone. She's then attacked by two students who attempt to rape her. Defending herself, she bites off the tongue of one student, who later accuses her of assault. She's arrested and tried.

A major part of the film involves two court appearances in which Chung-Hee seeks justice. Handling of these hearings is foreign to Western audiences, to put it mildly. Even the judges act as if women invite rape and should submit to it.

This is a strong item for Korea, but wider Western exposure will depend on decently translated, spelled and printed English subtitles. Won gives a stellar performance, and the supporting players acquit themselves well. Pic is technically adequate.
— *David Stratton*

PESARO FEST

KAE BYOK
(FLY HIGH RUN FAR —
KAE BYOK)
(SOUTH KOREAN)

A Chun Woo Film Co. production. Produced by Han Yong-su. Directed by Im Kwon-taek. Screenplay, Kim Yong-ok. Camera (color), Jung Il-sung; editor, Park Soon-duk; music, Shin Byung-ha. Reviewed at 28th Intl. Festival of New Cinema, Pesaro (Italy), June 15, 1992. Running time: **130 MIN.**
With: Lee Duk-hwa, Lee Hye-young, Kim Myong-kon.

An impassioned chronicle of the life of a 19th century religious leader, "Fly High Run Far — Kae Byok" is a massive, full-tilt epic given magisterial handling by South Korea's top director Im Kwon-taek. Pic was a commercial flop at home, and its density of historical data will make it unpalatable to wide audiences. Consummate craftsmanship and lofty production values, however, should secure offshore fest dates and art house slots where quality Asian cinema has a niche.

Focus is the Dong-Hak doctrine of Korea, and Hae-Wol, who became the sect's leader after its founder was executed (pic's opening scene). Based on the principle that God is everyone and everything, the movement strived for Kae Byok (creation and transformation of a new world) until its rise was truncated by Japanese intervention in an 1894 uprising.

Im and scripter Kim Yong-ok stick rigorously to established historical fact, but they underplay the story's bloodier elements (insurrection, torture, constant oppression) to concentrate on the teachings of their nonviolent, humanitarian hero. Pic is obviously a labor of love, and part of its quiet, inspirational power lies in the filmmaker's success in bringing an intensely personal p.o.v. to the huge, sprawling saga.

Background info is supplied through frequent subtitles, and by necessity, Im sometimes adopts a slightly didactic approach to wade through historical complexities. The philosophy's teachings, for example, are spelled out in an instructional family scene where Hae-Wol strolls in a dreamily lit field spouting wisdom to his family. Scene borders on sitcom sweetness, but Im's unfaltering authority as a director makes it work.

Only fictional detour is an effective subplot following the son of a military officer killed after a Dong-Hak skirmish. He vows revenge against Hae-Wol but eventually is won over by the man's compassion.

Despite its length (director trimmed the print unspooled at Pesaro from 146 minutes to 130), pic unfolds with rigid economy in short, loaded scenes woven together in silky-smooth editing.

The $1.2 million production is visually superlative, thanks to Jung Il-sung's glowing lensing. Recurring shots of Hae-Wol's lone figure in a vast landscape use warm, muted colors to magically capture the Korean countryside in all four seasons.
— *David Rooney*

URIBANUL
CHASUBNIDA
(SEARCHING FOR OUR CLASS)
(SOUTH KOREAN)

A Mul Kyol production. Produced, directed, written by Hwang Gyu-deok. Camera (color), Cheong Il-seong; editor, Kim Hui-soo; music, Park Soo-jin. Reviewed at 28th Intl. Festival of New Cinema, Pesaro (Italy), June 16, 1992. Running time: **103 MIN.**
With: Lee Soo-il, Yu Kyang-ah, Moon Seong-gun.

Democracy may have replaced military dictatorship in South Korea, but the school system still runs on another kind of regime steam per "Searching for Our Class." Repping a sure-footed feature debut for producer-director-writer Hwang Gyu-deok, this immensely likable teen pic is ideal for young cinema meets and class-act tube programming.

Hwang worked as assistant director to veteran Im Kwon-taek and prominent newcomer Park Kwang-su, but his style owes much to Western pop culture. Edited down to the bone at music video speed, the film makes visually snappy use of advertising, video games and other teen-scene paraphernalia to talk directly to kids sans pandering.

Pic works best as an exposé of an antiquated educational system. Students in a fictional Southern Seoul high school are required to channel all their energy, both in class and out, into preparing for a university entrance exam only 25% of them will pass.

Diversions from academic drilling are punished using infantile humiliation tactics, and even hair length is regimented with military strictness. Hwang is a sure hand at instilling instant audience sympathy for the irrepressible kids as they goof off against all odds. In a wry sideswipe, he shows teachers behaving similarly at a staff meeting.

Personal problems and fears of individual class members are touched on, but the main strand follows the class prez and his music student g.f. Less successful with this sugary, romantic track than with his overall aim, Hwang nevertheless makes a strong case against parents' ambitions overriding their kids'. Denied the chance to study literature and forced to continue grueling music studies, the girl breaks down.

Technical contributions are first-rate, and acting by the 60 or so school kids (most of them presumably nonpro) is appealingly natural. A neat end titles sequence throws together vid footage of the students really cutting loose. — *David Rooney*

CHEONGSONGURO
GANUNKIL
(THE WAY TO CHEONG SONG)
(SOUTH KOREAN)

A Doo Sung Cinema Corp. production. Produced, directed by Lee Doo-yong. Screenplay, Ko Yong-sok. Camera (color), Lee Seong-choon; editor, Lee Kyung-ja; music, Choi Chang-kwon; art direction, Toh Yong-woo. Reviewed at 28th Intl. Festival of New Cinema, Pesaro (Italy), June 11, 1992. Running time: **100 MIN.**
With: Joong Kwang, Cho Hyung-ki.

Both a hymn to human spirit and a plea for across-the-board tolerance, "The Way to Cheong Song" traces the last downward spiral of a broken but dignified everyman. Sometimes syrupy but often genuinely moving, pic should make a minor showing at Asian cinema meets, but it would do better losing 15 minutes of flabby midsection.

Director Lee Doo-yong's 1985 pic "Jangman" (First Son) dealt with modern Korean families shirking responsibility for their elders. This time he shows how adverse circumstances can push honest folks to crime.

Schlepping through Seoul, Joong Kwang meets a wall of indifference as he looks for work, even being rejected as a blood donor. He snatches an untended goat, muttering that if he's caught, he'll at least be fed in jail. But being a repeat offender, he's automatically sentenced to a prison for habitual criminals.

Most of pic's action takes place in the interim between Hojuki's arrest and his transfer to prison. A spate of observational scenes convincingly evoke cellmate camaraderie and the inmates' love-hate relationship with the oddball hero.

Varying in tone from brutal to comic, this central section wavers from lack of a coherent mood. But the mishmash keeps moving, and the stories Hojuki tells from his past gradually reveal a simple man with intrinsic goodness. Joong's central performance is a marvelous mix of awkward underdog and silently suffering tragedian, and support thesping is fine. Technical aspects are well-handled, with effective backbone to the film's emotional pull provided by Choi Changkwon's melancholy music.

—David Rooney

PRELUDE TO A KISS

A 20th Century Fox release of a Gruskoff/Levy production. Produced by Michael Gruskoff, Michael I. Levy. Executive producer, Jennifer Ogden. Co-producers, Craig Lucas, Norman Rene. Directed by Rene. Screenplay, Lucas, based on his play. Camera (Duart color), Stefan Czapsky; editor, Stephen A. Rotter; music, Howard Shore; production design, Andrew Jackness; art direction, W. Steven Graham, Maxine Walters (Jamaica), Ray Kluga (N.Y.); set design, Karen Fletcher; set decoration, Cindy Carr, Sue Raney (N.Y.); costume design, Walker Hicklin; sound (Dolby), Les Lazarowitz, James Sabat (Jamaica); associate producer, Deborah Schindler; assistant directors, Michael Steele, Tony Adler (N.Y.); casting, Jason LaPadura, Natalie Hart. Reviewed at Avco Cinema, L.A., July 6, 1992. MPAA Rating: PG-13. Running time: **106 MIN.**

Peter Hoskins	Alec Baldwin
Rita Boyle	Meg Ryan
Leah Blier	Kathy Bates
Dr. Boyle	Ned Beatty
Mrs. Boyle	Patty Duke
Old Man	Sydney Walker
Jerry Blier	Richard Riehle
Taylor	Stanley Tucci
Tom	Rocky Carroll

Thanks to a magnetic cast and intelligent adaptation, "Prelude to a Kiss" has made a solid transfer from stage to screen. Back in the 1930s or '40s, this sort of sophisticated, literary-oriented treatment of a simple romantic idea would have been the norm. Today's general audiences, however, may be put off by the quick-witted talk and mildly confused by the central device, despite its resemblance to "Ghost."

Very appealing leads constitute a b.o. plus, and an audience for this engaging, small-scale fantasy could conceivably be cultivated, particularly among women and urban couples, but it would be an uphill struggle.

Craig Lucas' 1988 fairytale play about commitment and transcendent romantic love enjoyed a nice run on Broadway in 1990 after a limited off-Broadway engagement with Alec Baldwin toplined. In their second motion picture outing, after "Longtime Companion," Lucas and his longtime legit director Norman Rene have treated their baby with care and tact, even if the emotional resonance of the piece has been somewhat slighted.

Zippy opening reel nicely conveys the headiness of love's first stage. Peter (Baldwin) and Rita (Meg Ryan) meet sexily at a party and combust so quickly that they're in bed before they've even had a proper date. Fast talkers who totally connect mentally, emotionally and physically, the two exult in the joy two people can share relishing the realization they are meant for each other.

Although Peter must counter Rita's spirited brand of fatalism, and jokey apprehensions about marriage occasionally cloud the air, they soon tie the knot at a lovely lakeside ceremony that turns curious with the arrival of a mysterious old man who asks to kiss the bride. Strangely drawn to the oldster, Rita agrees, then scarcely knows what hit her.

Neither does Peter. During their Jamaica honeymoon, Rita doesn't seem at all like her old self. Naturally, it takes Peter awhile to figure out what happened, and when he does, Rita flees back to her parents, leaving Peter to track down the old man whose ailing body now contains his wife's personality, and then to effect a retransference.

Lucas' overarching theme has to do with the spiritual prevailing over the physical, of the primacy of true love no matter what the temporal obstacles. This profound, oft-expressed notion goes down easily and appealingly in this relatively lightweight context, although its full weight is not felt due to a certain fuzziness, even faintheartedness, in a climactic section.

Peter's emotional breakthrough comes after having spent nearly a week with the old man. Peter affirms his complete acceptance of Rita in a different shell by kissing him/her. Whether or not this key scene has been muted in reaction to reported disapproval by young test audiences, Peter's full, but quite unsexual, kiss of the geezer is shown skittishly, and cut away from immediately. This perhaps reduces the potential for risible reactions among some viewers, but more crucially dilutes the intended emotional catharsis. Last section of the film goes cold as a result.

This is too bad, since Baldwin and Ryan make such a winning pair. Looking great and playing a normal guy whose optimism has prevailed over his troubled past, Baldwin is a romantic lead both men and women can enjoy watching. Cuter-than-cute Ryan rambunctiously embodies the life force even when playing a basically aimless young woman, and pic suffers during her prolonged absence in the later stages.

Vet stage actor Sydney Walker, who played the part onstage in the Bay Area, hits all the right notes of quizzicality and resignation as the strange old-timer, although it's anybody's guess if the screen savvy of Alec Guinness, who was originally intended for the role, would have brought an additional quality to it. Ned Beatty and Patty Duke wring every possible bit of humor and sentiment out of their cutesy assignments as Rita's parents, while Kathy Bates basically has just one big scene as Walker's preoccupied daughter. Stanley Tucci and Rocky Carroll score nicely in support roles.

Gothic character of Rita's residential block astutely suggests the mood of a dark fairytale, and Stefan Czapsky's suggestive lensing provides sufficient shadows in Andrew Jackness' smart production design for portents to inhabit.

Of particular note is the splendid score. Pic's title is derived from the Duke Ellington standard, and Howard Shore's original compositions have been combined with more than a dozen tunes of varied vintage to outstanding effect.

— Todd McCarthy

COOL WORLD

A Paramount Pictures release of a Frank Mancuso Jr. production. Produced by Mancuso. Directed by Ralph Bakshi. Screenplay, Michael Grais, Mark Victor. Camera (Technicolor), John A. Alonzo; editors, Steve Mirkovich, Annamaria Szanto; music, Mark Isham; production design, Michael Corenblith; art direction, David James Bomba; set decoration, Merideth Boswell; set design, Lori Rowbotham, Mitchell Lee Simmons; costume design, Malissa Daniel; sound (Dolby), James Thornton; associate producer, Vikki Williams; assistant director, Marty Eli Schwartz; conceptual design, Barry Jackson; animation supervisor, Bruce Woodside; character layout-design, Louise Zingarelli; design, layout & animation, Thomas McGrath, Evan Gwynne; layout-animation, Greg Hill, David Wasson; animation production coordinator, Gina Shay; Cool World background characters, Milton Knight, Mark S. O'Hare; casting, Carrie Frazier, Shani Ginsberg. Reviewed at Plaza Theater, L.A., July 9, 1992. MPAA Rating: PG-13. Running time: **102 MIN.**

Holli Would	Kim Basinger
Jack Deebs	Gabriel Byrne
Frank Harris	Brad Pitt
Jennifer Malley	Michele Abrams
Isabelle Malley	Deidre O'Connell
Comic bookstore cashier	Carrie Hamilton
Frank Sinatra Jr.	Himself

Voices of:

Nails	Charles Adler
Doc Whiskers/Mash	Maurice LaMarche
Lonette/Bob	Candi Milo
Sparks	Michael David Lally
Slash/Holli's Door	Joey Camen
Bash	Gregory Snegoff

Style has seldom pummeled substance as severely as in "Cool World," a combination funhouse ride/acid trip that will prove an ordeal for most visitors in the form of trial by animation. Visually dazzling but utterly soulless, this film-as-extended-music-video/trailer is perfectly geared to a savvy marketing campaign. Paramount has no doubt generated ample curiosity, but solid early boxoffice returns will be short-lived as word-of-mouth makes this a small "World," after all.

Director Ralph Bakshi has let his imagination run wild with almost brutal vigor, resulting in a guerrilla-like sensual assault virtually unchecked by any traditional rules of storytelling.

The result is heady to the point of needing to pop a couple of aspirin, as the director takes a fertile concept that might have made for an intriguing animated short and stretches it into a feature-length series of cels from which there's no escape.

Although comparisons have been made to "Who Framed Roger Rabbit" because of the live-action/animation mix, this really more closely resembles Joe Dante's "Gremlins" in its reliance on exploding the conventions of Warner Bros. cartoons, blended with the most primal adolescent sexual fantasies about seduction by cooing cartoon characters with hourglass figures.

The comic-book premise hinges on parallel worlds — the real world and a sphere of animated characters, known as Cool World, which exists independently but has also been captured in the "noid" (as in human, not Domino's Pizza sloganeer) plane by cartoonist Jack Deebs (Gabriel Byrne).

Pulling Deebs into the Cool World is curvaceous fantasy girl Holli Would, a "doodle" (i.e. cartoon) who dreams of becoming human. That wish can only be fulfilled by coupling with a flesh-and-blood male — a forbidden union with the potential, however vague, of bringing about the destruction of both universes.

The odd-character-out in the story is Frank Harris (Brad Pitt), a human yanked into Cool World in the '40s. Harris has settled into life there as top cop, despite the limitations the no-sex rule places on him and his doodle g.f. Lonette.

Kim Basinger, who doesn't appear in the flesh until nearly an hour into the film, is one of the few actresses who could convincingly breathe life into Holli, a 36-18-36 bombshell in animated form seemingly pulled straight from the paintings of Frank Frazetta, whose art inspired Bakshi's little-seen fantasy feature "Fire and Ice."

As a living cartoon, she's also the only character not encumbered by Michael Grais and Mark Victor's two-dimensional script, which drops plot points as often as safes and other objects plummet from the sky onto unsuspecting doodles.

Because the characters are so undeveloped — from Deebs' unexplored imprisonment for murdering his wife's lover to the not-so-nosy neighbors — "Cool World" is a realm with precious little humor and zero pathos, to be admired only for its brilliant synthesis of live-action and animation, as well as the staggering creation of credible comic book sets around human actors.

The beating Bakshi gives the eyes is exacerbated by a corresponding aural attack, with a relentless parade of cartoon sound effects over a droning and repetitive score. Only respite comes too late, over closing credits, with a terrific title song by David Bowie.

Even the good lines of dialogue, such as a bunny gravely paraphrasing the "Bambi" line by saying "Man is in the bedroom," are so few and far between that it takes a beat to respond to them.

Bakshi has been an innovator in the field of adult animation (or rather, in demonstrating that animation can be used for more than just lyrical Disney fairy tales), and he proves here that given the tools he can produce work of tremendous quality. Character and set designs in Cool World, led by conceptual designer Barry Jackson, are eclectic and fascinating, and the animation is both marvelously fluid and nicely choreographed.

Basinger's slinky costumes add to the feeling of a doodle come to life, and John A. Alonzo's cinematography seamlessly leaps back and forth between worlds. That wizardry can't overcome the other pitfalls, however, and might be better appreciated on homevid, where viewers can take a break from the picture's concussive force.

Despite the long lag since "Roger Rabbit," this exercise (and it amounts to little more than that) should reinforce the genre's potential creatively, if not commercially. "Cool World" could have scored in that respect as well had it delivered the goods. To paraphrase the marquee line, it could if it did . . . but it doesn't.
— *Brian Lowry*

MÖV OG FUNDER
(THE HIDEAWAY)
(DANISH)

A Egmont Film release of a Per Holst production with support of the Danish Film Institute & SFC. Produced by Holst. Directed by Niels Graaböl. Screenplay, Graaböl, Per Daumiller. Camera (color), Jacob Banke Olesen; editor, Ghita Beckendorff; music, Fuzzy, M.C. Einar. Reviewed on videocassette, Copenhagen. Running time: **70 MIN.**
Möv (Martin) . . . . . Kasper Andersen
Funder . . . . Allan Winther
Mother . . . . Ditte Knudsen
Also with: Niels Skousen, Master Fatman, Kristine Horn.

This slight, lightly entertaining drama depicting the friendship between a lonely boy and a wounded juvenile delinquent has a telefilm look but has been doing okay in children's film festivals.

Twelve-year-old Möv has been abandoned for the weekend by his divorced parents. In the cellar of his apartment building, he finds Funder, who has been wounded in a barroom brawl. Möv hides the small-time desperado, who becomes a rather dubious role model for the lonely boy. The police, however, are hot on the heels of the young punk (in an unlikely effort).

First-time helmer Niels Graaböl shows promise as he constantly tries to fill this straightforward, amusing children's drama with suspense and professional touches. Although the friendship is conveyed with conviction, it's also questionable and clichéd. — *Peter Risby Hansen*

UNIVERSAL SOLDIER

A TriStar release from Carolco of a Mario Kassar presentation of an IndieProd production in association with Centropolis Film Prods. Produced by Allen Shapiro, Craig Baumgarten, Joel B. Michaels. Executive producer, Kassar. Co-producer, Oliver Eberle. Directed by Roland Emmerich. Screenplay, Richard Rothstein, Christopher Leitch, Dean Devlin. Camera (Technicolor), Karl Walter Lindenlaub; editor, Michael J. Duthie; music, Christopher Franke; production design, Holger Gross; art direction, Nelson Coates; set decoration, Alex Carle; sound (Dolby), David Chornow; assistant director, Steve Love; 2nd unit director-stunt coordinator, Vic Armstrong; special effects supervisor-designer, Kit West; special makeup effects, Larry R. Hamlin, Michael Burnett; casting, Penny Perry, Annette Benson. Reviewed at Cineplex Odeon Century Plaza Cinemas, L.A., June 26, 1992. MPAA Rating: R. Running time: **104 MIN.**
Luc . . . . . . Jean-Claude Van Damme
Scott . . . . Dolph Lundgren
Veronica . . . . Ally Walker
Col. Perry . . . . Ed O'Ross
Dr. Gregor . . . . Jerry Orbach
Woodward . . . . Leon Rippy
Garth . . . . Tico Wells
GR76 . . . . Ralph Moeller
Motel owner . . . . Robert Trebor

The combination of martial arts studs Jean-Claude Van Damme and Dolph Lundgren on one marquee — plus a complete disregard for life and property — should help this summer warrior bayonet strong early box office returns, overcoming a terrible premise and script. Appeal will be less universal than it might have been, however, had a brain powered those chiseled bodies.

Despite its not-insignificant production values, the story feels like a late-night sci-fi movie patched together with a mix of elements from "Robocop" and "The Terminator," with a dash of Captain America comic books. The result is almost as many derisive laughs as dead bodies.

During the introduction, for instance, a crazed Vietnam platoon leader (Lundgren) refers to his thickly accented subordinate (Van Damme) as "farmboy," a confusing allusion not explained until nearly 90 minutes later.

The two soldiers waste each other prior to the opening credits during a 1969 Mai Lai-type massacre, only to pop up 23 years later as re-animated corpses, brought back by the Defense Dept. to act as an elite terrorism-fighting unit.

Something goes wrong, however, and Luc (Van Damme) begins to recover his memory, taking off accompanied by a pretty young reporter (Ally Walker), with Lundgren, his mind still addled with 'Nam hysteria, and other brigade members in hot pursuit.

Thanks to the premise, the film is on the wrong foot from the get-go, since it's difficult to have much empathy for walking corpses with superhuman strength whose flesh regenerates when punctured.

The central story also brings governmental paranoia to heights that might alarm even Oliver Stone, although it's so obviously a plot device (and a bad one at that) that there seems not a shred of conviction behind it.

In an equally damning commentary on the acting and Roland Emmerich's direction, Lundgren and Van Damme are both more convincing as stoic cadavers than they are once their memories start to return.

Although both have proven convincing action stars in the past, neither fares particularly well here, and their climactic encounter is shot so murkily that it's often difficult to tell who's clobbering whom.

After his rendition of twin brothers in "Double Impact," Van Damme offers nothing new here other than baring a little more of his physique than had been his norm.

Lundgren remains an imposing presence who hasn't been properly used since "Rocky IV," though he'll probably score points with some moviegoers thanks to his character's morbid penchant for collecting victims' ears. In this regard, "Soldier" proves notably repulsive in places, even by genre standards.

As the reporter, Walker is the modern damsel-in-distress blend of tomboy tough and conveniently available, with a few Fay Wray shrieks thrown in. Most of the other roles fall into the category of either nonverbal behemoths or cannon fodder. Jerry Orbach is in an extremely brief cameo as the project's mastermind.

Tech credits are generally okay, although some edits prove confusing, and there's the final sequence's darkness. Considering the scope of the production, it also sorely lacks memorable action sequences — except a scene in which Van Damme eludes pursuers by crashing through a series of flimsy motel walls.

The urge to escape from "Universal Soldier" isn't quite that strong, but it comes close.

— *Brian Lowry*

GOLPE DE SUERTE
(LUCKY BREAK)
(MEXICAN)

A Mexican Film Institute (Imcine) release of a Ryat Asociados-Fondo de Fomento a la Calidad Cinematográfica production. Executive producer, Fernando Hidalgo. Produced by Hidalgo, Fernando Flores, Fernando Tostado. Directed by Marcela Fernández Violante. Screenplay, Fernández Violante, Luis Eduardo Reyes. Camera (color), Alex Phillips; editor, Saúl Aupart; music, Roberto Félix, Gerardo Cortina. Reviewed at Imcine, Mexico City, April 6, 1992. Running time: **100 MIN.**
Gerónimo. Sergio (El Comanche) Ramos
Patricia . . . . Lucha Villa

Vicente . . . . Bruno Bichir
Luis . . . . Odiseo Bichir
Don Amador . . . . . Miguel Manzano
Fortune-teller
. . . . Patricia Reyes Spíndola

"Golpe de Suerte," sixth feature by Mexican femme filmmaker Marcela Fernández Violante, is a Chekhovian tragicomedy centering on the foibles of a petty government official who becomes a casualty of consolidation. Although the tale tends to meander, this quirky film should generate some interest on the fest and art house circuit.

Functionary Gerónimo (Sergio Ramos) has everything going for him: He is awarded a silver medal for his tireless years as a bureaucrat, his petition for a state-financed home has been okayed and youngest son Vicente is following in his footsteps into government service.

While his father Don Amador (Miguel Manzano) had worked all his life and ended up with only their crowded apartment, Gerónimo is now a homeowner and will pass the apartment on to Vicente when he marries.

Gerónimo truly believes ceaseless dedication has rewarded him for his efforts — until he hears his department is being phased out. He's pink-slipped and suddenly, his dreams come to a grinding halt. He goes to the main square to protest the action but shows up with a "Down With . . . !" placard on the day designated for the "Up With . . . !" marchers.

Solid cast of characters include veteran singer-actress Lucha Villa as wife Patricia. Dilettante older son Luis (Odiseo Bichir) runs a garage sale to raise money to save the house, while the grandfather has a plan to rob the bank downstairs by breaking through the ceiling.

Alex Phillips' characteristic cinematography is topnotch, and Fernández Violante manages to maintain an ironic tone over the proceedings. Also, many w.k. Mexican artists and intellectuals appear in the film in walk-on roles.

— *Paul Lenti*

CHANGING OUR MINDS:
THE STORY OF DR. EVELYN HOOKER
(DOCU-COLOR/B&W)

An Intrepid Prods. presentation. Produced by David Haugland. Executive producer, James Harrison. Co-produced, directed by Richard Schmiechen. Written by Schmiechen, Harrison. Camera (color/B&W), Joan Churchill, William Megalos, Cathy Zheutlin; music, Absolute Music; sound, Flora Moon, Michael Moore, John Hagen; associate producers, Flora Moon, Catherine Valeriote, Nancy Langer. Reviewed in San Francisco, June 1, 1992. (In S.F. Intl. Lesbian/Gay Film Festival.) Running time: **75 MIN.**

Though the ostensibly clinical subject matter might prove a hard sell for theatrical, "Changing Times" is a thoroughly engrossing docu that's a sure bet for recurring major TV exposure. Careful marketing focusing on the urban gay market could plumb modest art house business.

Director Richard Schmiechen (co-creator of "The Times of Harvey Milk") casts a wide net in telling the story of Dr. Evelyn Hooker, whose trailblazing research eventually led to the dropping of "homosexuality" from the American Psychiatric Assn. list of mental illnesses.

Startling archival footage offers glimpses of gays undergoing primitive "treatments" for their alleged illness: electroshock, lobotomy, estrogen/testosterone injections, hysterectomies and castrations. Docu's major flaw is failing to mark the time and place of these shocking segments. The treatments dated at least back to the 1930s, but the clips seem to date to the '50s and early '60s.

Dr. Hooker, still feisty at 85, is a delightful interviewee. She tells her own colorful (heterosexual) history as a gangly, Midwest-bred student who studied briefly in prewar Nazi Germany (her horror at mass indoctrination led to a quick departure), later settling down in Southern California as an academic.

Hooker became friendly with a postwar homosexual elite. Home-movie footage shows her entertaining author Christopher Isherwood at a backyard party. Social life spilled into the professional sphere when a gay student urged her to "study people like us" as "your scientific duty."

Her meticulously researched findings indicated gays scored little differently on intelligence and sanity tests from heterosexuals. Ergo, gays weren't insane, just "different" from status quo.

Still a strong community advocate, Hooker is frail but active in the Santa Monica home where she's lived since the death of her writer husband many years ago. A terrifically engaging and inspirational paragon of coolly reasoned thought, she has no patience for witch-hunting conservative mindsets, whether in the McCarthy era or in the 1990s. Docu's polished but rather hurried in condensing Hooker's own story — plus gay history and the psychology field's shift on homosexuality; film could have easily been stretched out.

But the compassionate, balanced viewpoint of both subject and filmmakers is winning. Pic is calmly conventional in approach, but the topic and Dr. Hooker herself provide exciting and enjoyable documentary education.

— *Dennis Harvey*

AFI/L.A. FEST

VENICE/VENICE

A Rainbow release of an Intl. Rainbow Picture. Produced by Judith Wolinsky. Directed, written, edited by Henry Jaglom. Camera (Deluxe color), Hanania Baer; sound, Sunny Meyer (L.A.), Vito Catenia (Italy). Reviewed at Monica 4-Plex, Santa Monica, Calif., July 2, 1992. (In AFI/L.A. FilmFest.) Running time: **92 MIN.**
Jeanne . . . . Nelly Alard
Dean . . . . Henry Jaglom
Peggy . . . . Melissa Leo
Carlotta . . . . Suzanne Bertish
Eve . . . . Daphna Kastner
Dylan . . . . David Duchovny

"Venice/Venice" represents the definition of a vanity production. Sliding way over the line between personal cinema and egotism, Henry Jaglom's ninth feature lacks either the colorful characters or innately interesting subject matter of his better films, telling essentially a non-story in slight, schematic fashion. This will hardly match the success of Jaglom's last effort, "Eating," on the domestic specialized circuit.

Many directors make at least one picture about the filmmaking process or the world of cinema. Some are caustic critiques ("Sunset Boulevard," "The Player"), others emerge as meditations on romantic love ("A Star Is Born," "Contempt"), a few analyze the artistic process ("8½") or weigh the wages of celebrity ("Stardust Memories"), and at least one is disguised as something else ("Hatari!").

Even when a filmmaker as eminent as François Truffaut made "Day for Night," he played a workaday director less talented than himself, and when Jaglom hero Orson Welles made his unfinished "The Other Side of the Wind," he cast John Huston, rather than himself, as a veteran director.

Jaglom takes a rather different approach. Portraying the director of the only American film in competition at the Venice Film Festival, Jaglom announces at the outset that he is a maverick: "I am the representative of the anti-establishment."

His own self-image thus established, Jaglom builds a fragile little story about his curious relationship with attractive French journalist Nelly Alard, who is obsessed with his work. Jaglom gives her a sort-of-interview that allows him to expound upon his own talents, pursue her a bit at lunch and around the pool and finally make out with her during a scenic gondola ride.

But Jaglom's true intentions with her never become clear (he doesn't suggest that they sleep together), and Alard comes to seem annoying and naive when she petulantly complains that Jaglom isn't spending all his time taking care of her. As a working journalist, doesn't she have films to see, reviews to write, people to interview? This relationship doesn't feel right from the beginning, which alone would be enough to sink the picture.

After an hour, setting shifts to Venice, Calif., as Alard wanders in on a party Jaglom is throwing. Nothing much happens here except for some auditions in which Jaglom is looking for a woman to play his wife in an upcoming film, "Happy Endings." Director veers vaguely into Truffaut territory with his deliberations on the relative importance of movies and life, with inconclusive results.

Stylistically, pic could serve to illustrate Hitchcock's pet peeve, "photographs of people talking." Staging consists mostly of placing people in chairs and plunking the camera down right across from them. Utterly elementary coverage is reduced even further by cutaways to unrelated objects or nearby people that function merely as a way of jump-ing to another point in the ongoing conversation.

Except for a couple of sequences, Venice, Italy, seems so depopulated that it's hard to know if there's even a film festival going on. Setups are generally kept so tight that almost no location atmosphere is created, a shame given the existing opportunity to draw an interesting visual comparison between the two unique cities.

Threaded through the picture is a chorus of straight-on interviews-to-camera in which a variety of women complain that their childhood experiences at the movies misled them about real life. Familiar notion isn't developed in any provocative way, rendering the device redundant and quickly tiresome.

A few showbiz figures, such as director John Landis, production stalwart Pierre Cottrell, actress Diane Salinger, journalist Edna Fainaru and the late producer Klaus Hellwig, to whom the film is dedicated, turn up, but not nearly in the abundance necessary to provide enough authentic texture.

Seemingly given their heads in the dialogue department, thesps seem at a loss where to take the scenes. As with all of Jaglom's films, a certain amount of charm and goodwill is generated by the homemade quality of the enterprise, but this fuzzy effort suffers from a feeling of not having been focused sufficiently in advance.

— *Todd McCarthy*

MUSUKO
(MY SONS)
(JAPANESE)

A Shochiku Films production. Executive producers, Nobuyoshi Otani. Produced by Shigehiro Nakagawa, Hiroshi Fukazawa. Directed by Yoji Yamada. Screenplay, Yamada, Yoshitaka Asama, based on Makoto Shiina's novel. Camera ('Scope, color), Tetsuo Takaba; editor, Iwao Ishii; music, Teizo Matsumura; art direction, Mitsuo Degawa; sound (Dolby), Takashi Matsumato. Reviewed at Monica 4-Plex, Santa Monica, Calif., June 19, 1992. (In Sydney, Munich, AFI/L.A. film festivals). Running time: **120 MIN.**
Akio Asano . . . . . . Rentaro Mikuni
Tetsuo . . . . Masatoshi Nagase
Seiko Kawashima . . . . . Emi Wakui
Tadashi . . . . Ryuzo Tanaka
Toshiko . . . . Miyoko Asada
Reiko . . . . Mieko Harada

Yoji Yamada's "My Sons," contempo melodrama about the generation gap in ever-changing Japan, belongs to the same tradition as Ozu's 1953 classic "Tokyo Story," thematically if not stylistically. Pic's universal concerns and mild humor, plus Masatoshi Nagase's charisma, should help it in fests and in big cities with a built-in interest in Japanese cinema.

Rentaro Mikuni gives a stellar performance as Akio Asano, a patriarchal widower who lives alone in the country. Immensely proud of his rural roots, the aging man sees the move of his two sons to Tokyo as betrayal. The otherwise very different sons share a common desire for independence from their strong-headed father.

Tale begins in Akio's village with a big family gathering commemorating the first anniversary of his wife's death. Tetsuo (Nagase, featured in Jim Jarmusch's "Mystery Train"), the youngest and a "problem" child, upsets his father when he arrives at the temple late wearing a dirty shirt. Worried about Dad's solitary life and deteriorating health, the children suggest he move to Tokyo and live with his eldest son (Ryuzo Tanaka), who works in a big firm. But the stubborn man insists he can still fend for himself.

Most of the narrative deals with the Tetsuo's adventures in Tokyo. Determined to prove himself, he takes a physical job at a steel factory. Tetsuo also meets a girl (Emi Wakui) who seems to be too shy — until her hearing impairment is revealed. The dignified manner in which she is presented and the courtship between the youngsters are two of pic's most charming highlights.

Pic's second half traces the father's visit to Tokyo for a World War II army reunion. In an interesting contrast to U.S. youth pics taking the children's point of view, "My Sons" sides with the father, preaching for a reconciliation between the generations. In pic's most amusing scene, the father literally comes to life — drinking beer and singing in the middle of night — after he meets Tetsuo's fiancée. Yamada, best-known for the long-running "Tora-san" films (44 features to date), directs with a remarkably firm but unostentatious hand, treating the material functionally and matter-of-factly.

He sometimes shoots the family scenes Ozu-like; with a stationary camera from a low angle. Leisurely paced and restrained pic lacks the high voltage and melodramatics of similarly themed Yank films. Though preaching for old family values, pic is decidedly unsentimental.

Lenser Tetsuo Takaba contributes handsome visuals. Visual contrast between city and country is aided by Teizo Matsumura's soft evocative music, particularly effective in the transition of scenes.

At the end, when Asano returns to his beloved country home, he carries with him one important present — a fax machine. In this ironic turn, pic suggests modern technology's inevitable penetration into the smallest and most remote village.

— *Emanuel Levy*

FRIDA — MED HJERTET I HANDEN
(FRIDA — STRAIGHT FROM THE HEART)
(NORWEGIAN)

A Teamfield/NRK production. Produced by Mattis L.R. Mathiesen. Directed by Berit Nesheim. Screenplay, Torun Lian. Camera (color), Herald Paalgard; editor, Lillian Fjellvaer; music, Geir Bohren, Bent Aserud. Reviewed at Monica 4-Plex, Santa Monica, Calif., June 27, 1992. (In AFI/L.A. FilmFest.) Running time: **114 MIN.**
Frida . . . . Maria Kvalheim
Bente . . . . Ellen Horn
Karl . . . . Helge Jordal

Abundant charm, fresh observations about love and family and Maria Kvalheim's exuberant performance could ingratiate "Frida — Straight From the Heart" to diverse audiences beyond the fest circuit. With tighter editing and a shorter running time, film has the potential to become an international hit akin to the Swedish smash "My Life As a Dog."

Almost every national cinema makes films about children, and once in a while a classic emerges. The winning, poetic "Frida" is Norway's latest contribution to the perennial coming-of-age genre. Yarn's point of departure is Erich Fromm's book "The Art of Loving," which Frida (Kvalheim) uses as her guide for relationships.

At 13, Frida is too bright and inquisitive for her own good. Pic astutely records her romantic tribulations and meddling with the love affairs of her mother, sister, neighbor and just about everyone she encounters. Upset with her father, who took up with a black woman in the States, she hangs up on him when he telephones. The pragmatic teen regularly updates the chart on her wall listing her boyfriends' names and scores.

Pic captures the symbolic end to Frida's childhood and the sudden realization that she's not a girl anymore, showing Frida's vulnerability and unexpected toughness in the process.

Fresh, light and devoid of formulaic material, Torun Lian's script is rich in one-liners. The scenario is not a random collection of loosely related sketches, and Lian shuns easy laughs and doesn't glamorize Frida at the expense of the adults around her.

Herlad Paalgard's mobile camera stays close to Frida. Dominating every frame, Kvalheim sparkles, projects verve and boundless energy and carries the film with a pro's self-assurance. Under Berit Nesheim's generous guidance, rest of the cast rises to the occasion.

— *Emanuel Levy*

DUKE ELLINGTON:
REMINISCING IN TEMPO
(DOCU)

> A Robert S. Levi Films production. Produced, directed by Levi. Written by Geoffrey C. Ward, Levi. Camera (color), Levi; editor, Ken Eluto; music, Duke Ellington. Reviewed at American Film Institute, L.A., June 5, 1992. (In AFI/L.A. FilmFest.) Running time: **87 MIN.** Narrator: Julian Bond.

Robert S. Levi's "Duke Ellington: Reminiscing in Tempo" is a loving, uncritical documentary of the great American musician who for 50 years led big bands around the world and created more than 1,500 compositions. Ellington's reputation will carry the pic through film fest, cable, public TV and video showings.

Narrated by Julian Bond, docu chronicles the highs and lows of Ellington's intriguing career: his reign at Harlem's Cotton Club, his leadership of renowned bands, his declining popularity with the rise of bebop and his comeback at the 1956 Newport Jazz Festival.

Ellington is celebrated as the ultimate pro who never missed a performance, continuing to work up to his 1974 death despite incurable cancer.

Levi paints a portrait of a genius who wouldn't be stopped by stereotypes, racial or musical. His eclectic work, untempered by formal training, extending the

form of jazz and changed the course of American music.

The film's strong points include illuminating, never-before-seen interviews with Ellington, rare performance footage of his famous orchestra, a discussion of Ellington's 28-year association with composer-arranger Billy Strayhorn and a memorable recreation of Ellington's first meeting with Martin Luther King.

Helmer-lenser Levi, who co-scripted with Geoffrey C. Ward, provides a chronology of Ellington's life and art, but docu lacks insight into the difficulties of being a celebrity in a segregated society, one whose music crossed over to white audiences.

Criticized by civil rights activists for not putting himself on the line, Ellington was no crusader, but his philosophy of universality ("I am interested in the people, not my people") remains obscurely articulated.

Still, Ellington's exuberant personality and music, placed in a changing political backdrop, make up for the docu's flaws. Composer's creations ("Sophisticated Ladies," "Prelude to a Kiss") are well integrated into this portrait, whose tech credits are top-drawer, especially Ken Eluto's editing. — *Emanuel Levy*

LOVE IS LIKE THAT

> A Boomerang production. Produced by Jonathan Reiss, Matt Devlen. Directed by Jill Goldman. Screenplay, George Gary. Camera (Foto-Kem color), Gary Tieche; editor, Esther Russell; art direction, John Guedon; sound (Ultra-Stereo), Craig Felburg; assistant director, Harry Jarvis; 2nd unit director, Malcolm Abbey. Reviewed at Monica 4-Plex, Santa Monica, Calif., June 25, 1992. (In AFI/L.A. FilmFest.) Running time: **92 MIN.**
> Lenny . . . . Tom Sizemore
> Eloise . . . . Pamela Gidley
> Boss . . . . Joe Dellasandro
> Ms. Alman . . . . Jennifer O'Neill
> Uncle Bud . . . . Seymour Cassel
> Bubba . . . . Rick Edelman
> Cashier . . . . . Margaux Hemingway

A story of full-time losers, "Love Is Like That" is first-time director Jill Goldman's tale of amour fou set in L.A.'s grubby nether regions. Pic offers no artistic or psychological reward to the audience for tolerating the protagonist's endless succession of wrong moves and idiotic decisions. Commercial prospects for this indie effort are marginal.

Goldman takes an aesthetically gritty approach to scenarist George Gary's fringe-dwelling characters, but their personali-

ties and the words put in their mouths are too mild and banal to provoke much interest.

In a low-life meet-cute, hapless gas station attendant Lenny (Tom Sizemore) walks away from his job to chauffeur a stranded foxy lady, Eloise (Pamela Gidley), to a job interview. Back at her place, they get it on immediately, beginning a relationship soon bearing the sweet earmarks of true love and providing the comfort of a protective cocoon from the harsh outside world.

Trouble is, Lenny is a thoroughgoing jerk who sabotages any good thing he stumbles onto. His uncle (Seymour Cassel) keeps setting him up in jobs he invariably botches. Lenny also flies into unprovoked hysterics over Eloise's former relationships, even asking her which guys were responsible for which stains on the mattress.

While Lenny is blowing one job after another (a porno shoot he works on even gets raided), Eloise becomes assistant to a wealthy movie star (Jennifer O'Neill). Lenny and Eloise break up and get back together, but when he brings home a new mattress, it isn't long until it's repossessed.

Soon, they're evicted from her apartment. They sleep on the beach for awhile, their love seemingly intact, but in an attempt at one big score, Lenny commits a crime so appalling as to confirm that he's an even bigger moron than one has suspected from the beginning.

The violent climax, vaguely anarchic attitude and Gidley's Jean Seberg haircut prompt the idea that Goldman and Gary might have been aspiring to a 1990s "Breathless."

A few of the more tender moments have a certain appeal, and some good humor emerges on the porno set when the director yells instructions the lead actor is physically unable to follow.

But there is scant insight into why people get involved in such hopeless, self-destructive relationships, and evocation of society's margins isn't achieved with much specificity or relevance.

Okay thesping by Sizemore and Gidley can't overcome the characters' inertia and wrongheaded decisions. Tech credits are on the raw side.

— *Todd McCarthy*

SOLITAIRE
(CANADIAN)

> A Highway One Motion Pictures production. Produced by Lars Lehmann. Executive producer, Lorne W. MacPherson. Co-producer, Francis Damberger. Directed, written by Damberger. Camera (color), Peter Wunstorf; editor, Lenka Svab; music, Michael Becker; production design, John Blackie; costumes, Jill Blackie; assistant director, Jim Long. Reviewed at Monica 4-Plex, Santa Monica, Calif., June 26, 1992. (In AFI/L.A. FilmFest.) Running time: **105 MIN.**
> Burt . . . . Paul Coeur
> Maggie . . . . Val Pearson
> Al . . . . Mike Hogan

"Solitaire" would have made a creditable Off-Broadway play or live TV drama — in the 1950s. An examination of the fears, vulnerabilities and delusions of three "little people," Francis Damberger's low-budgeter is extremely well constructed, acted and shot. But its one-set location is constricting, calling to mind filmed theater, and same themes have been rehashed so many times that yawning familiarity outweighs pic's qualities. Domestic B.O. possibilities are nil.

Damberger has fulfilled all the classical requirements of gradual character revelation, the withholding of secrets and eventual growth and catharsis in telling this story of three losers stuck in an isolated Western Canadian cafe on Christmas Eve.

Slowly and with considerable care, the dramatist introduces Maggie, the eatery's eternal proprietress, a lonely woman who plays the eponymous card game when there's no business, and Burt, a shy, nerdy bachelor and a regular at Maggie's joint.

On this slowest of all evenings (one wonders why the place is even open), Burt announces that Al, their old high school friend, is returning that night for the first time in 25 years. This makes Maggie all aflutter, as it appears that Al was Mr. Popularity as a teen, the best athlete and singer before setting out to conquer the world. When Al makes his grand entrance, he turns out to be a high-spirited middle-aged cowboy who brings the glazed Maggie and Burt back to life and seems like he might be everything he's cracked up to be.

Unsurprisingly, Maggie, one of Al's "good-time girls" back in school, has been in love with Al all this time, while Burt was just a flunky who always looked up to his glamorous hero. Over the course of the evening, the shine comes off of Al's glittering image (also hardly surprising), and Maggie and Burt can finally emerge from his shadow and move on with their lives.

Damberger paints his character portraits methodically and fully, giving the viewer well-rounded, recognizable human beings with vivid pasts and convincing psychological profiles. More than that, he knows how to frame and edit his images, and keeps things moving visually through the pages and pages of dialogue.

But the writer's method is just too familiar, and the eventual revelations too predictable, to excite audience interest.

The three characters here are totally caught up in their mutual pasts, and can only wax nostalgically for their days of dubious glory in high school, when things at least mattered. Thesps Paul Coeur, Val Pearson and Mike Hogan are first-rate, and tech contributions are spare but pro.
— *Todd McCarthy*

KAMIN OUNAYNOUTIAN
(THE WIND OF EMPTINESS)
(ARMENIAN)

An Armenfilm Studios production. Directed by Haroutiun Katchatrian. Screenplay, Mikayel Stamboltsian, Katchatrian. Camera (color), Vrej Petrossian; music, Avet Terterian. Reviewed at American Film Institute, L.A., June 2, 1992. (In AFI/LA FilmFest.) Running time: **99 MIN.**
Ruben of Yerevan . . Ruben Hakhvertian
Plush . . . . Gevorg Aghegian
Stage director . . . . Haig Katchadrian

"The Wind of Emptiness" is Haroutiun Katchatrian's excellent exploration of alienation and rootlessness among Armenian exiles. Weaving real and fictional material in cinéma vérité style, pic should find international film fest auds.

Film opens with docu video footage of a massive 1988 freedom rally in Yerevan's Opera Square. An Armenian pop singer (Ruben Hakhvertian) entertains the crowd with songs celebrating freedom and condemning totalitarianism.

Narrative then follows Ruben and his terminally ill friend Plush (Gevorg Aghegian) as they travel across the former Soviet Union, interviewing Armenians living in self- or imposed exile. Pic raises existential questions about national identity and meaning of

home, literally and figuratively.

A Moscow with an aura of doom and despair is the first of three stops. Most interesting sequence, in Estonia's Tallin Square, consists of a long, sad interview with a painter who doesn't differ between the Russian and previous Turkish domination. Final seg, set in a remote Siberian fishing village, has a theater director throwing himself with gusto into his work.

Visuals are strong, particularly long shots of Siberia's desolate winter landscape. Symbolism is extensive, at times heavy-handed: A languid closeup of a fish out of water is meant to signal the doomed Plush's state of mind.

The last powerful images, a succession of shots of earthquake-devastated Armenia, render broader context to both Plush's death and a country wrought by disasters, natural and military.

Despite its specific time and place, pic also brings out the universal values of survival while providing a painful demonstration of personal and political alienation among exiles desperate to find meaning in their daily existence. — *Emanuel Levy*

NOIR FEST

TOUTES PEINES CONFONDUES
(SWEETHEART)
(FRENCH)

An AMLF release (in France) of an Eléfilm CEC Rhône-Alpes FR3 Films-Générale d'Images co-production with participation of Canal Plus, Soficas Sofiarp, Investimage 3. (Intl. sales: Hugo Intl.) Produced by Rosalinde Deville. Directed by Michel Deville. Screenplay, Rosalinde Deville, based on Andrew Coburn's novel. Camera (color), Bernard Lutic; editor, Raymonde Guyot; art direction, Thierry Leproust; costumes, Cécile Balme; sound (Dolby), Guillaume Sciama, François Groult. Reviewed at Noir Fest (competition), Viareggio (Italy), June 24, 1992. Running time: **107 MIN.**
Gardella . . . . Jacques Dutronc
Vade . . . . Patrick Bruel
Jeanne Gardella . . . . . Mathilda May
Scandurat . . . . Bruce Myers
Roselli . . . . Eric Da Silva
Laura . . . . Sophie Broustal
Thomas . . . . Benoit Magimel
Kimbler . . . . Jurgen Zwingel
Scatamacchia . . . . Hans-Heinz Moser
Deckler . . . . Jean Dautremay
Thurston . . . . . . Vernon Dobtcheff

Weaving his trademark web of psychological intrigue to convoluted new heights, Michel Deville orchestrates a tantalizing round of mind games in "Sweetheart." Pic is too frequently indecipherable to make the same splash the Gallic stylist's "La Lectrice" did, but its chilly allure is as magnetic as it is confusing, and pic should find fringe favor with sophisticated art house auds.

Story pits devious Interpol chief Vernon Dobtcheff against icy businessman Jacques Dutronc, kicking off with mob mischief as Dutronc's parents are killed in a fire. Using the crime as a means to move in on the dubious shark, Dobtcheff dispatches his upstart underling (Patrick Bruel) to investigate.

Deville teases and toys with his audience, introducing an exhausting string of complex characters (not one of them totally sympathetic) and giving away the narrative only in measured hints and perplexing exchanges of skewed dialogue. Attraction to the dark side exerts a powerful pull on all the characters, with loyalties and emotional bonds continually tested.

Bruel is soon wooing Dutronc's wife (Mathilda May), while a fascination bordering on attraction springs up between the two men. The upper hand switches from one to the other, and Deville stirs in a spicy subplot involving a clumsy cop on the take and a beautiful woman (Sophie Broustal) enlisted by Dutronc for some high-class whoring.

Deville sets the Dobtcheff and Dutronc camps on either side of the French-Swiss border, but he effortlessly establishes the wafer-thin line dividing honesty from dishonesty. The duplicity is compellingly played right down the line by a topnotch cast.

Pic is a precision instrument on every level. The handsome but orderly landscape and deceptively placid lakeside setting are as carefully considered as the punchy editing and lean, uncluttered lensing. Some auds may find the rigorously compositional look too mannered, but pic's elegant color schemes and unrelenting technical dazzle can't fail to impress. Nervous energy level is kept aloft by feverish use of Dmitry Shostakovich music.
— *David Rooney*

THE JFK ASSASSINATION:
THE JIM GARRISON TAPES
(DOCU-COLOR/B&W)

A Blue Ridge/Filmtrust presentation of a Fred Weintraub production. Produced by Weintraub. Executive producer, Tom Kuhn. Co-executive producer, Lamar Card. Co-producer, Sarita Barbour. Directed, written by John Barbour. Camera (color/b&w), Greg Bader, Dennis P. Boni, Steve Elkins, Robert Perrin; editor, Ronald D. Burdett; music, David Wheatly; sound, Michael Weatherwax; associate producer, Christopher Barbour. Reviewed at Noir Fest, Viareggio (Italy), June 23, 1992. Running time: **92 MIN.**

Presenting the nuts-and-bolts version of evidence served up in "JFK," "The JFK Assassination" pitches another potent case against the one-man/one-gun theory. Audiences who didn't respond to Oliver Stone's artfully exhaustive bombardment of facts and theories may well be swayed by this level-headed summation. Well-handled docu should make a briskly saleable tube item in many territories.

TV journalist John Barbour assembles the case against the Warren Commission's findings around direct testimony from former New Orleans district attorney Jim Garrison. Starting with background info on Garrison and a political rundown of the John Kennedy years, pic painstakingly recaps events in Dealy Plaza using archive clips (including the Zapruder film and a second home movie) and reports from eyewitnesses and experts.

Though not entirely new, evidence underlining the implausibility of Lee Harvey Oswald's guilt is presented with illuminating clarity. The famous Life magazine photo of Oswald holding the rifle he supposedly used to kill Kennedy is scrutinized to show mismatched shadows. Seemingly reliable testimony places him at street level during the shooting, not upstairs in the book depository.

Docu's real strength, however, lies in its surefooted detailing of cover-up measures. Interviews with ex CIA-Pentagon liaison Fletcher Prouty (purported basis for Donald Sutherland's Col. X in "JFK") show evidence of high-level premeditation. A strong case to support a large-scale conspiracy theory is put together, without the overt anti-establishment stance that led some to dismiss Stone's film as unbalanced.

Barbour stacks pointed facts with unequivocal certainty: the FBI's labeling of the Zapruder film as "of no evidentiary value," failure to arrest a right-wing extremist identified at the scene who was known to have previously discussed assassination plans and coercion of key witnesses to stick to an official version of events.

The gay underworld slant linked to Clay Shaw and his cohorts in Stone's film is underplayed here, as is the personal ramifications of the investigation on Garrison.

Pic's epilogue notes Garrison's partial vindication with credence from certain sectors in Washington and an upsurge of support since "JFK's" release. Final comment brings home the bitter irony that the last surviving witness who saw two men running from the scene with a rifle can't hear or speak.

New and existing footage is efficiently strung together in straightforward journalistic style, sans editing tricks. Quality of archival footage varies, but pic is technically competent in all quarters. Docu also testifies to the remarkable casting in Stone's film: Actors John Candy and Joe Pesci especially are dead ringers for the real-lifers.

— *David Rooney*

BRANDNACHT
(NIGHT ON FIRE)
(SWISS-GERMAN)

A Cine Intl. World Distribution release of a Boa Filmproduktion (Zurich)/Kick Film (Munich) co-production in association with ZDF, SRG. Produced by Jörg Bundschuh. Directed by Markus Fischer. Screenplay, Rosemarie Fendel, Fischer, based on Sam Juan's novel. Camera (color), Jörg Schmidt-Reitwein; editor, Fischer; music, Markus Fritzsche; art direction, Hans Gloor; costumes, Monika Hinz; sound, Jürg von Allmen. Reviewed at Noir Fest (competition), Viareggio (Italy), June 24, 1992. Running time: 108 MIN.
Peter Keller . . . . Bruno Ganz
Uta Schwengeler . . . . Barbara Auer
Tobler . . . . Rolf Hoppe
Josef Zing . . . . Ueli Jäggi
Also with: Suzanne V. Borsody, Markus Signer, Dietmar Schönherr.

Swiss director Markus Fischer's "Night on Fire" starts out with a tight hold on the murder mystery genre but loses its grip midway. Easy-on-the-eye visuals and the compelling presence of Bruno Ganz playing an unflappable Eurodude should help pic into festival slots, but commercial life looks set to flicker, not ignite.

Accusations of murder against an old army buddy summon Ganz from his faraway niche in Berlin to his native village in rural Switzerland. The idyllic Emmental valley setting covers for a cesspool of shifty locals, all of whom seem to have something to hide.

As Ganz pries into village infighting and the doings of a local religious sect, he meets with suspicion and sometimes outright hostility. Help comes from another outsider, free thinker Barbara Auer, who lives in a commune seen as a thorn in the villagers' side.

Ganz uncovers a plot to usurp land rights from the religious group and eventually pins down the murder culprit, but the villagers' needs dictate that guilt be attributed elsewhere.

Script by Fischer and Rosemarie Fendel allows for too much foot-dragging before coming to any kind of climax, and it piles on exacting literary detail that produces ploddingly cerebral mystery fodder. Some heating up of Ganz and Auer's low-voltage romance might have added the thrust lacking in later reels.

Lead perfs are strong, though the shadowy supporting characters, played as a pallid and unremarkable band, fail to create much tension. Tech work is unerringly pro, with Jörg Schmidt-Reitwein's crisp lensing doing justice to the Swiss countryside without being overly enamored of its chocolate-box charms.

— *David Rooney*

WAXWORK II:
LOST IN TIME

A Live/Seven Arts release of an Electric Pictures production. Produced by Nancy Paloian. Executive producer, Mario Sotela. Directed, written by Anthony Hickox. Camera (color/b&w), Gerry Lively; editor, Christopher Cibelli; music, Steve Schiff; production design, Steve Hardie; costumes, Mark Bridges; special makeup-effects, Bob Keen. Reviewed at Noir Fest, Viareggio (Italy), June 23, 1992. MPAA rating: R. Running time: 104 MIN.
Mark Loftmore . . . . Zach Galligan
Eleanore Pratt . . . . . . Sophie Ward
The master . . . . Alexander Godunov
John Wright . . . . . . Bruce Campbell
Sir Wilfred . . . . Patrick Macnee
Baron Frankenstein . . . Martin Kemp
Sarah . . . . Monica Schnarre
Beggar . . . . David Carradine
Gloria . . . . Mirina Sirtis

A loopy gags-and-gore fest striving a mite too self-consciously for cult status, "Waxwork II: Lost in Time" fails to find secure footing as either comedy or horror. This patchy time-travel yarn landed on video shelves last month.

Picking up where its 1988 predecessor left off, pic opens with leads Zach Galligan and Monica Schnarre fleeing from the burning wax museum where waxworks have come to life and killed 200 people. The only other escapee is a malevolent version of "The Addams Family" Thing, which follows Schnarre home and promptly mangles her stepfather.

Setting out to prove that dead flesh did the deed, Schnarre and Galligan stumble on a time-travel locket, and pic switches gears, seemingly dumping its central plot premise along with any pretense of being a sequel.

Zipping through time zones, duo lands in a goofball Frankenstein riff, a hokey black & white haunted-house story and a straight-faced retake on the "Alien" pics. While it's all affable and jokey enough, writer-director Anthony Hickox seems to toss in every trick he knows with nothing more purposeful in mind than filling out feature length.

Action dawdles longest in the least imaginative era, 18th century England, in a castle ruled over by evil warlord Alexander Godunov. Entering into "God's Nintendo game," an eternal battle between good and evil, Galligan lops off a bad guy's hand and steers Schnarre back to the 20th century with still-moving mitt.

Upscale actors are better than the material. Countless junk movie references will please buffs, as will the string of sometimes funny, sometimes pointless cameos (Maxwell Caulfield, Juliet Mills, Drew Barrymore).

Pic is technically smooth in all departments. Bob Keen's effects are consistently inventive, but hardcore genre fans may find the gore quota a little low.

— *David Rooney*

HONEY, I BLEW UP THE KID

A Buena Vista release of a Walt Disney Pictures presentation in association with Touchwood Pacific Partners I. Produced by Dawn Steel, Edward S. Feldman. Co-producer, Dennis E. Jones. Executive producers, Albert Band, Stuart Gordon. Co-exec producer, Deborah Brock. Directed by Randal Kleiser. Screenplay, Thom Eberhardt, Peter Elbling, Garry Goodrow, from Goodrow's story, based on characters created by Stuart Gordon, Brian Yuzna & Ed Naha. Camera (Technicolor), John Hora; editors, Michael A. Stevenson, Harry Hitner; additional editing, Tina Hirsch; music, Bruce Broughton; production design, Leslie Dilley; art direction, Ed Verreaux; lead set design, Antoinette J. Gordon; set design, John Berger, Gina B. Cranham; set decoration, Dorree Cooper; costume design, Tom Bronson; sound (Dolby), Roger Pietschmann; visual effects producer-unit director, Thomas G. Smith; visual effects coordinator, Michael Muscal; visual effects camera, John V. Fante; visual effects unit assistant director, Benita Allen; Buena Vista Visual Effects supervisor, Harrison Ellenshaw; BV Visual Effects producer, Carolyn Soper; BV Visual Effects co-supervisors, Mark Dornfeld, Kevin Koneval; Baby Adam special makeup effects, Kevin Yagher; stunt coordinator, Bobby J. Foxworth; assistant directors, Frank Capra III, Douglas C. Metzger; 2nd unit director, Dilley; 2nd unit assistant director, Jeffrey Wetzel; 2nd unit camera, Allen Easton; casting, Renee Rousselot. Reviewed at GCC Avco Cinema, West L.A., July 13, 1992. MPAA Rating: PG. Running time: 89 MIN.
Wayne Szalinski . . . . . Rick Moranis
Diane Szalinski . . . Marcia Strassman
Nick Szalinski . . . . . . Robert Oliveri
Adam Szalinski . . . . Daniel Shalikar,
Joshua Shalikar
Clifford Sterling . . . . . Lloyd Bridges
Charles Hendrickson . . . . John Shea
Mandy Park . . . . Keri Russell
Marshal Brooks . . . . . Ron Canada
Amy Szalinski . . . . . . Amy O'Neill
Smitty . . . . Ken Tobey

Honey, I Blew Up the Kid" is a diverting, well-crafted sequel to Disney's '89 hit "Honey, I Shrunk the Kids." Taking its cue from 1950s sci-fi pics and inverting the shrinking gags from the original "Honey," the sequel has wacky inventor Rick Moranis accidentally blowing up his 2-year-old to huge proportions. This lighthearted summer entertainment will give kids a vicarious kick while the elaborate visual effects help keep parents intrigued. Disney should make merry again at the boxoffice.

Rampaging baby Adam, engagingly played by identical twins Daniel and Joshua Shalikar, is a monstrous exaggeration of the "terrible twos." Every parent will recognize the tyke's tirades with a wry smile, and kids will see him as an embodiment of their wildest fantasies.

There's nothing genuinely menacing about the baby, though, and even his cartoonish would-be captor John Shea, who wants to make him a guinea pig for government experiments, doesn't unduly darken the mood of this tongue-in-cheek yarn, smartly scripted by Thom Eberhardt, Peter Elbling and Garry Goodrow from a story by Goodrow.

Nor does "Kid" have the creepy feeling of the original, in which the kids struggled to escape from the backyard grass after Moranis' invention accidentally shrank them to mite size. That's an observation that cuts both ways because, while the sequel is more jovial, it lacks the original's tension and adventure.

But "Kid" is a romp, escapism at its breeziest, smoothly engineered by director Randal Kleiser and a top-flight tech staff. Editors Michael A. Stevenson, Harry Hitner and Tina Hirsch keep the pace zipping right along most of the time, seldom allowing the effects shots to linger too long or the gags to get tiresome.

The filmmakers were faced with overcoming the built-in handicap of a one-joke plot, and despite some repetitiveness they've largely succeeded by steadily varying the size of the baby and the scale of the sight gags.

Initially growing into a 7-foot housewrecker, Adam soon passes the 50-foot mark and eventually balloons into a blithe 112-foot behemoth stomping down the Las Vegas Strip like "The Amazing Colossal Man."

The sequel picks up Moranis and family living in slightly more upscale digs in a Vegas suburb jokingly named Vista del Mar. A lousy businessman, Moranis has made the mistake of selling his invention to a sinister company headed by Lloyd Bridges, whose huge warehouse includes such items as the Rosebud sled.

Moranis and Shea are supposed to be co-directors of the project to develop a new version of his ray machine to enlarge objects for government use, but Moranis has been frozen out and is spending most of his time around the house tinkering with new ideas while wearing a helmet festooned with electronic gizmos.

The "Honey" franchise is Disney's contemporary equivalent of its successful 1960s special effects comedies featuring Fred MacMurray's absent-minded professor. Moranis has an endearingly childlike quality as the goofball scientist whose family can't help finding him lovable

even when his work keeps backfiring on them.

Besides Adam, his brood includes his look-alike son (Robert Oliveri), now a teen who worries that he's inherited his dad's nerdiness, and daughter (Amy O'Neill), who gets shipped off to college early in the pic. Joining Moranis' quest to rescue Adam and bring him back to normal is the kid's babysitter (Keri Russell).

Moranis' extremely tolerant wife (Marcia Strassman) faints again on cue when she hears what's happened to her offspring but otherwise avoids sexist clichées with her winning determination and a bright idea that enables her to save the baby from Shea's clutches.

Bridges has fun with his sympathetic tycoon role by playing it totally straight, aside from a droll gag in the finale that alludes to his role in "Airplane!" In another of the film's homages, '50s sci-fi stalwart Ken Tobey pops up as the guard at Shea's lab.

The giant baby effects are a fascinating and mostly seamless blend of composites, miniatures, puppetry and other gimmicks, expertly overseen by visual effects producer and unit director Thomas G. Smith, working with Buena Vista Visual Effects supervisor Harrison Ellenshaw.

The work of production designer Leslie Dilley and lenser John Hora gives "Kid" a more subdued and attractive color scheme than that of the previous "Honey" pic. Bruce Broughton's music is appropriately bouncy.
— *Joseph McBride*

MAN TROUBLE

A 20th Century Fox release of a Mario & Vittorio Cecchi Gori & Silvio Berlusconi presentation of a Penta Pictures, American Filmworks/Budding Grove production. Produced by Bruce Gilbert, Carole Eastman. Executive producer, Vittorio Cecchi Gori. Co-executive producer, Gianni Nunnari. Directed by Bob Rafelson. Screenplay, Eastman. Camera (Technicolor; Deluxe prints), Stephen H. Burum; editor, William Steinkamp; music, Georges Delerue; production design, Mel Bourne; set decoration, Samara Schaffer; costume design, Judy Ruskin; sound (Dolby), David Ronne; assistant director, Marty Ewing; stunt coordinator, Loren Janes; associate producer, Michael Silverblatt; casting, Terry Liebling. Reviewed at Chelsea 3 theater, N.Y., July 17, 1992. MPAA Rating: PG-13. Running time: **100 MIN.**

Harry Bliss	Jack Nicholson
Joan Spruance	Ellen Barkin
Redmond Layls	Harry Dean Stanton
Andy Ellerman	Beverly D'Angelo
Eddy Revere	Michael McKean
Laurence Moncrief	Saul Rubinek
June Huff	Viveka Davis
Helen Dextra	Veronica Cartwright
Lewie Duart	David Clennon
Det. Melvenos	John Kapelos
Adele Bliss	Lauren Tom
Lee MacGreevy	Paul Mazursky
Butch Gable	Gary Graham
Socorro	Betty Carvalho
Hospital administrator	
	Rebecca Broussard
Nurse Sonya	Mary-Robin Redd

Jack Nicholson fans should feel cheated by "Man Trouble," an insultingly trivial star vehicle. After some initial business attracted by his name on the marquee, film is fated for pay-cable use.

Pic reunites Nicholson with the creative team of director Bob Rafelson and scripter Carole Eastman, who in 1970 propelled him to stardom with "Five Easy Pieces." This belated followup is strike two for Italian-funded Penta Pictures, after its recent Tom Selleck flop "Folks!"

In a role that's way too comfortable for him, Nicholson portrays a dog trainer who meets opera singer Ellen Barkin when she needs a guard dog after a break-in and other harassment. Film appears initially promising, with Nicholson and Barkin speaking in German to the German Shepherd called Duke.

In a screenplay resembling stage farce rather than a movie, Eastman drags in several pointless subplots. Main one concerns Barkin's sister Beverly D'Angelo, who's penned a tell-all book about her relationship with reclusive billionaire Harry Dean Stanton. Barkin is getting divorced from her conductor/husband David Clennon and has been threatened by some homicidal thug who may be the notorious local slasher.

None of this adds up to entertainment or even momentarily involving escapism, as the romantic comedy/thriller genre typified by "Charade" or "Foul Play" seems beyond the filmmakers' combined grasp. Instead there's strenuously overacted comic setpieces, most of which fail.

Nicholson's patented ne'er-do-well persona seems on automatic pilot, though Lauren Thom as his Japanese wife is amusing in her pidgin-English Bickersons routine with him in front of a marriage counselor. Barkin is saddled with completely unnatural dialogue as well as some overdone physical shtick that seems left over from her last comedy, "Switch."

D'Angelo steals a couple of scenes as Barkin's sister, enough to indicate the film would have improved considerably if she and

Barkin had swapped roles. As it is, the Nicholson-Barkin chemistry never percolates.

A talented supporting cast is wasted, including director Paul Mazursky in a nothing role. Film buffs should look for Mary-Robin Redd as a nurse; this co-star 26 years ago in Sidney Lumet's "The Group" hasn't been on the big screen of late.

Tech credits, from Stephen H. Burum's lensing to the late Georges Delerue's minor musical score, are slick.

Final insult is the arbitrary overlay of the end credits smack dab in the middle of the final scene for no apparent reason other than to chase what's left of the audience. — *Lawrence Cohn*

FERDINANDO UOMO D'AMORE
(FERDINANDO, MAN OF LOVE)
(ITALIAN)

An Angelo Rizzoli & Enzo Porcelli presentation of an Antea Co-op production in association with Erre Produzioni & RAI-3. Produced by Porcelli. Directed by Memè Perlini. Screenplay, Nico Garrone, Perlini, based on Annibale Ruccello's play, "Ferdinando." Camera (Fotocinema color), Romano Albani; editor, Fernanda Indoni; music, Carlo De Nonno; art direction, costumes, Antonello Aglioti; sound, Fulgenzio Ceccon. Reviewed at Politecnico Cinema, Rome, May 2, 1992. Running time: **100 MIN.**

Donna Clotilde	Ida Di Benedetto
Ferdinando	Marco Leonardi
Don Catellino	Memè Perlini
Gesualda	Alessandra Acciai

A lean and lusty four-character costumer, "Ferdinando, Man of Love" is a potent brew of sex, enslavement, hypocrisy and betrayal given extra kick by Neapolitan actress Ida Di Benedetto's magnificent star turn. Pic's stage parameters are too intact for wide art house exposure, but its strong source material and shrewd playing will attract Italian theater aficionados and specialized viewers.

Set late last century in the wake of Italy's unification under a single monarchy, pic revolves around an acid-tongued Bourbon baroness (Di Benedetto) stricken by the turn of Italo politics. She withdraws to a remote, ramshackle property and feigns illness, tended by a poor cousin (Alessandra Acciai). A slippery curate (Memè Perlini) follows his formal bedside visits with not-so-formal romps in the stables with Acciai.

Enter smooth-skinned talker Ferdinando (Marco Leonardi), who passes himself off as kin and seduces each member of the melancholy trio. Plotting to make off with the baroness' fortune, the imposter soon has them pitted against each other, and the women conspire to kill the lovestruck priest.

A leading light of Italo avantgarde theater, actor-director Perlini here sticks mainly to an orderly, no-frills approach which lets the sharply penned text (most of it in rich Neapolitan dialect) speak for itself.

Di Benedetto's bravura fireworks are given strong support by Acciai as her vengeful, longsuffering companion, and Perlini, who effortlessly morphs the opportunist priest into a tragic, doomed pawn. Leonardi (the teenage Salvatore in "Cinema Paradiso") looks the part but appears tense and slightly wooden beside the more seasoned thesps.

Modestly budgeted picture's technical credits are average, and period reconstruction is thrifty but effective. — *David Rooney*

PRIMARY MOTIVE

A Fox Video release of a Blossom Pictures production. Produced by Thomas Gruenberg, Don Carmody, Richard Rosenberg. Directed by Daniel Adams. Screenplay, William Snowden, Adams. Camera (Rank color), John Drake; editor, Jaqueline Carmody; music, John Cale; production design, Dan Yarhi; costume design, Julie Engelsman; makeup, Bill Miller-Jones; sound, R. Trevor Black; assistant director, Alan Goluboff; casting, Lynn Kressel. Reviewed at United Artists Eastside Cinema, N.Y., June 9, 1992. MPAA Rating: R. Running time: **93 MIN.**
Andrew Blumenthal . . . Judd Nelson
Darcy Link . . . . . . Justine Bateman
Chris Poulas . . . . . . Richard Jordan
Wallace Roberts . . . . . . John Savage
Ken Blumenthal . . . . Malachi Throne
Paul Melton . . . . Joe Grifasi
John Eastham . . . . . Frank Converse
Stephanie Poulas . . . Jennifer Youngs
Helen Poulas . . . . . . Sally Kirkland

This Judd Nelson vehicle about political intrigue and naive trust wants desperately to be taken seriously as a timely part of the election year debate. But slipshod dialogue and the cursory look of its lighting, sound and staging reduce it to parody. "Primary Motive" is headed for the video shelf after brief regional theatrical release.

The Boston-based drama follows a Kennedy School grad (Nelson) into the halls of political power, where his retired congressman dad (Malachi Throne) gets him a press secretary job with straitlaced gubernatorial candidate Frank Converse.

His opponent is a con man (Richard Jordan) with a falsified record and a checkered family life. Nelson's girlfriend (Justine Bateman) goes undercover as a volunteer in the Jordan camp to dig up dirt. Nelson leaks several lies to seedy reporter John Savage, who quickly puts the candidate on the defensive.

The corrupt politician successfully makes it all look like a press smear, however, and Bateman gets sucked in by his slippery charm. She has the trusting Nelson leak a falsified letter saying Jordan's daughter (Jennifer Youngs) was committed to a mental hospital against mom Sally Kirkland's wishes. But Jordan just surges ahead, buoyed by clever handlers and his daughter's timely suicide.

The actors are in trouble with ham-fisted dialogue that keeps director Daniel Adams' good intentions from becoming more than caricature. Particularly weak is a seduction scene where Bateman croons to Jordan, "Come here, lover boy" and slips onto the couch in an inviting pose. Earnestly played scenes are only slightly more convincing.

Nelson reprises his portrayal as intense, charming rogue, but he fails to make it work here. The hard-working Jordan turns in a manic performance, while Kirkland, whose role is no more than a foil for her husband's evil rantings, looks uncomfortable with nothing to do but break down. Savage's rumpled reporter is cartoonish, but real comic relief is supplied by a tough Joe Grifasi as Nelson's dirty tricks mentor.

On the tech side, the project looks hurried, with flat, tinny sound and lighting that often looks like an afterthought. The Boston and Luxembourg sets are varied enough, but their strictly low-budget look takes away from the grandeur that seems to be Adams' goal. Costumes and makeup were not a priority here, giving an uneven impression that distracts from the story. A brooding score creeps in whenever the shady candidate delivers a threatening monologue.
— *Christian Moerk*

OFF AND RUNNING

A Rank Film Distributors (U.K.) release of a Rank Organisation & Aaron Russo Entertainment presentation of an Aaron Russo Films production. Produced by Russo, William C. Carraro. Directed by Edward Bianchi. Screenplay, Mitch Glazer. Camera (color), Andrzej Bartkowiak; editor, Rick Shaine; music, Mason Daring; production design, Maher Ahmad, Nina Ramsay; costume design, Bobbie Read; sound (Dolby), Michael R. Tromer; assistant director, Ken Ornstein; casting, Julie Hughes, Barry Moss, Ellen Jacoby. Reviewed at Odeon Mezzanine, London, June 12, 1992. Running time: **90 MIN.**
Cyd . . . . Cyndi Lauper
Jack . . . . David Keith
Pompey . . . . Johnny Pinto
J.W. (Woody) Vilela . . . . . Jose Perez
Reese . . . . David Thornton
Florence . . . . Anita Morris

A lame meld of comedy, thriller and romance, "Off and Running" doesn't make it far off the starting block. Second screen appearance by Cyndi Lauper (after 1988's "Vibes") will appeal only to the petite popster's hardened devotees.

Made in 1990 and already shown on the inflight circuit, pic has been sneaked out, sans press previews, to a handful of U.K. sites by local distrib Rank.

With her distinctive voice and offbeat looks, Lauper still could be a passable screwball thesp given a decent script and director, but she gets neither here.

Limning a tacky would-be actress marking time as a mermaid in a Florida hotel bar pool, Lauper is proposed to by stud-farm owner Jose Perez. She flees north when he's killed by a greedy business associate closely pursued by a martial artist heavy with an Elvis hairdo (David Thornton, since become Lauper's husband). En route she meets up with nice-guy golf pro David Keith, and street-smart Latino kid Johnny Pinto who swallows a key Thornton is after. Weak finale, back on Perez's farm, reveals the key unlocks a canister containing the frozen sperm of a megabuck racehorse.

Pop-colorful main title crawl and Lauper's early voiceover promise a loopy kind of comedy à la Susan Seidelman, and Lauper's tart one-liners make for occasional auspicious moments. But pic's labored pace and Edward Bianchi's relentlessly flat direction sinks the enterprise early on.

Keith works hard and is okay under the circumstances, but the only real sparks fly from Anita Moore's cameo as Lauper's mom.

Technically, pic is only average, with some poor sound balancing and lackluster color. Lauper warbles segments of three songs: "Blue Moon," "Big Spender" and "Unabbreviated Love."
— *Derek Elley*

FATAL BOND
(AUSTRALIAN)

A REB release of an Avalon Films production in association with Australian Film Finance Corp. (Intl. sales: Beyond Intl.) Produced by Phil Avalon. Directed by Vince Monton. Screenplay, Avalon. Camera (Agfacolor), Ray Henman; editor, Ted Otten; music, Art Phillips; production design, Keith Holloway; sound, Bob Clayton; associate producer, Gary Hamilton; assistant director, Robin Newell; casting, Shirley Pearce. Reviewed at Hoyts Warringah Mall 6, Sydney, May 27, 1992. Running time: **90 MIN.**
Leonie Stevens . . . . Linda Blair
Joe T. Martinez . . . . . Jerome Ehlers
Anthony Boon . . . . . Stephen Leeder
Rocky . . . . Donal Gibson
Det. Sgt. Shenker . . . . Caz Lederman
Shamus Miller . . . . Joe Bugner

"Fatal Bond," which crept into Sydney suburban theaters sans press screenings or downtown exposure, is a lame thriller smacking of the hoary classic "Love From a Stranger" with a bit of "Cape Fear" thrown in. With a script by producer Phil Avalon that makes absolutely no sense, the only mystery here is why the Australian Film Finance Corp. ever backed such a commercially dubious project.

The story, supposedly based on a real incident, has the core of a good idea: A young woman suspects that the handsome, charming stranger she's seeing may be guilty of murdering teenage girls. But Avalon burdens his script with scenes and subsidiary characters detracting from, rather than adding to, the suspense.

Linda Blair is incongruously cast as the femme who gets the hots for Jerome Ehlers at first sight. She drops everything, lends him a lot of money and heads north with him even though he's wanted by the police (for unpaid parking fines, he says).

Along the way, the couple stop at a beachside resort, and the stranger abruptly leaves Blair pining in her motel room while he makes a conquest of a precocious surfer girl. Next day, she's found murdered, and her ultrareligious father (Stephen Leeder) swears vengeance.

As femme cop Caz Lederman investigates, Blair and Ehlers continue their trek north (although Sydneysiders will sense they're traveling in circles around the city's northern beaches) with Leeder in hot pursuit.

Director Vince Monton, ex-cinematographer whose first helming job was the sexy Nicole Kidman-starrer "Windrider," does a better job than could have been expected with the unpromising material. He and cinematographer Ray Henman do their best to make the pic visually interesting. Still, technically adequate pic gets more absurd as it goes on. — *David Stratton*

ARCHIPIELAGO
(ARCHIPELAGO)
(CHILEAN-SPANISH-FRENCH-BRITISH)

A Pablo Perelman/IMA Prods./ RTVE/Channel 4 co-production. Produced by Edgar Tenembaum, Pablo Perelman. Directed, written by Perelman. Camera (color), Gaston Roca; editor, Fernando Valenzuela; art direction, Juan Carlos Castillo; music, Jaime de Aguirre. Reviewed at Cannes Film Festival (Critics Week), May 14, 1992. Running time: **85 MIN.**
Architect . . . . Hector Noguera
Also with: Toto Bustamante, Ximena Rodriguez, Alicia Fuentes, Sergio Schmied, Amparo Noguerra.

Cleverly cutting back and forth between past, present and nightmare, director Pablo Perelman injects narrative tension into an otherwise conventional story about secret police pursuing a political dissident. "Archipielago" gains force and credibility via its complicated structure, but pic will lose action-oriented audiences looking for a thriller. It could do well on specialized circuits, however.

Police raid an anti-government student meeting in Santiago and brutally slay the young people, inexplicably letting an aging architecture prof (Hector Noguera) slip through their net. Dazed and scared, he flees to an island where he's been asked to restore an historic mission church.

Noguera starts having surrealistic flashbacks to the days when native Chonos Indians inhabited the island. In his mind, he casts himself as a missionary who has come to save their souls and their skins against conquistadors.

This recurring vision has the same weight as the other two interwoven stories: the horrifying police roundup and the architect's reconstruction of the mission church with Japanese money. All three of the prof's "lives" seem equally real and relative.

Back-and-forth structure, however, threatens to be repetitive, and when the paranoid prof asks for the 20th time, "Why don't they take me?", audience cannot

be counted on for a sympathetic response. Trick ending unites the threads and solves the riddle.

Gaston Roca's excellent cinematography creates a magical atmosphere in which time shifts fluidly from shot to shot. Film uses almost no music, the better to hear the rainforest's pregnant silence or screams of dying students. Acting takes a backseat to the various characters Perelman presents, ranging from naked Indians to sophisticated Japanese. — *Deborah Young*

TEXAS TENOR:
THE ILLINOIS JACQUET STORY
(DOCU-B&W)

An Arthur Elgort Ltd. production. Produced by Ronit Avneri. Executive producer, Elgort. Directed by Elgort. Camera (b&w), Morten Sandtroen; editor, Paula Heredia; sound, Anveri; associate producer, Sandtroen. Reviewed at JVC Jazz Film Festival, Film Forum, N.Y., June 20, 1992. No MPAA Rating. Running time: **81 MIN.**

An entertaining but misleading jazz documentary, "Texas Tenor" is for mid-level and advanced fans of the music. Neophytes will learn precious little about Illinois Jacquet and his secure but minor place in jazz history.

Director Arthur Elgort strongly captures Jacquet in performance at New York's Blue Note club in 1988 and on tour in Europe in 1990. Jacquet's energetic soloing, in the so-called Texas school he pioneered with Herschel Evans, Arnett Cobb and Buddy Tate, speaks for itself in presenting an unreconstructed form of swing music popular in the '40s.

Where Elgort lets the viewer down is in sketchy research and mis-emphasis. Jazz giants such as Lionel Hampton (who had Jacquet switch from alto to tenor and made him a star in 1942), Dizzy Gillespie and Sonny Rollins make unenlightening comments about Jacquet and the lasting importance of his popular solo on Hampton's hit "Flying Home."

What emerges is a popular showman who had hit records 40 to 50 years ago and re-established himself over the last decade as a big band leader in the tradition of his former employer Count Basie.

Morten Sandtroen's closeup black & white photography atmospherically captures the club and European locations as well

as Jacquet's passion while playing. The Louisiana-born tenor man's colleagues and pals (Tate, Milt Hinton, Cecil Payne) are friendly enough to win over any viewer's sympathy.

Several key omissions dilute pic's impact. Hovering in the background is the star's manager, Carol Scherick, an elderly woman who never gets to put her two cents in. She remains too enigmatic, especially in light of other, rather pointless, interviews here.

Docu never mentions, let alone shows, Jacquet playing the bassoon; he's virtually the only jazz soloist on that difficult instrument.

Pic is first in a planned series by Elgort profiling "American Heroes," including pianist Dorothy Donegan (who appears briefly here) and rodeo star Bruce Ford. — *Lawrence Cohn*

HIMMEL ODER HOLLE
(HEAVEN OR HELL)
(AUSTRIAN-B&W/COLOR-16m)

A Wolfgang Murnberger & the National Film School of Vienna production. Directed, written by Murnberger. Camera (b&w, color, 16m), Fabian Eder; editor, Murnberger; music, Robert Stiegler, Kurt Hintermayr; sound, Helmut Wimmer, Maria Scharf. Reviewed at Walter Reade Theater, N.Y., June 22, 1992. Running Time: **75 MIN.**
Wolfgang at 10 . . . . Adi Murnberger
Wolfgang at 5 . . . . Fabian Weidinger
Mother . . . . Maria Murnberger
Father . . . . Ernst Murnberger
Also with: Johannes Habeler, Lukas Habeler, Ines Ledwinka, Simon Scharf.

For those who found "Cinema Paradiso" too sentimentally gooey, this other Dantean title provides an alternate tale of a young boy growing up in a projectionist booth (his dad's). "Heaven or Hell," unfortunately, will be viewed as too morbidly dreary by all but the most diehard members of the art house aud. Film's largely nonnarrative form and occasionally striking imagery at best render it an interesting curiosity.

Made by helmer Wolfgang Murnberger as his thesis for the National Film School of Vienna, pic has the earmarks of a work of some talent but basically hermetic concerns. Set in the early '70s, the film flaunts its autobiographical links both by its protagonist's first name and his standing alongside a family plot with the Murnberger name.

Young Wolfi's concern with death and sex (mostly death) emanates not only from sojourns

at his father's theater but also from the iconography of his Catholic faith. Additionally observing Wolfi at his part-time job at his uncle's slaughterhouse, Murnberger's morbidity becomes increasingly banal.

One of the better scenes with metaphysical overtones has Wolfi, fresh from a viewing of Dario Argento's "Four Flies on Grey Velvet," hacking apart the eye of one of his uncle's dead animals in quest of the beast's final image of life.

An early scene of Wolfi holding up a film frame to the sky suggests his vision of life as a movie. Murnberger's visual strategy even has shots of Wolfi's activities in black & white while most of what he sees appears in color. Since very little of the film shows the kind of person Wolfi is becoming, there's no way of gauging the effects of his thanatological curiosity. Unless Murnberger arouses interest in his upbringing by making some really fine films, current effort must be viewed as a literal dead end. — *Fred Lombardi*

MUNICH FEST

DIE DISTEL
(THE THISTLE)
(GERMAN)

An Avista Film & Television production. (Intl. sales: Beta Film.) Produced by Alena & Herbert Rimbach. Directed by Gernot Krää. Screenplay, Krää, M. Evert. Camera (color), Frank Brühne; editor, Helga Borsche; music, Klopprogge/Wildermuth; art direction, Josef Sanktjohanser; costumes, Friederike May; sound, Günter Knon. Reviewed at Munich Film Festival (Children's Filmfest), July 1, 1992. Running time: **95 MIN.**
Trudi . . . . Leni Tanzer
Rollo . . . . David Cesmeci
Tom . . . . Fabian Kübler

A vigorous amateur detective yarn for kids, "The Thistle" combines the best tradition in children's crime flicks with a distinctly contempo flavor and a healthy helping of socially responsible realism. Theatrical exposure looks set for German screens, and pic should work elsewhere as dubbed TV fare.

A Sherlock Holmes-obsessed 11-year-old girl takes a stab at sleuthing when a local Turkish fast food bar gets trashed. She enlists help from a computer whiz classmate and a street-smart boy whose shady connections prove useful. The threesome (who call themselves the Thistle — nice to look at, but prickly) uncover an extortion racket and oust a slimy landlord.

Debuting feature director Gernot Krää has fun with the plot's close shaves and obligatory chase scenes and freshens up the formula with a sense of humor that's both sophisticated and accessible to kids.

Where children's drama often glosses over society's imperfections, this pic acknowledges a whole spate of them (racist violence, dysfunctional families, prostitution and even neo-Nazism) in a naturalistic way that ostensibly presents them without comment. Tech credits are fine across the board, and acting by the young trio is bright and unforced.

— *David Rooney*

LA CRUZ DEL SUR
(THE SOUTHERN CROSS)
(SPANISH-DOCU)

A TVE presentation of a Quasar Films production. (Intl. sales: Televisión Española.) Executive producer, Alicia Crespo. Director of production, Rafael García. Directed, written by Patricio Guzmán. Camera (color), Antonio Rios; editor, Marcello Navarro F.; music, José Antonio Quintano; sound, Walter Goulart. Reviewed at Munich Film Festival (Intl. Program), June 29, 1992. Running time: **80 MIN.**
Narrator: Fernando Ulloa.

Chilean-born documaker Patricio Guzmán ("The Battle of Chile") blends impressionistic historical scenes with interviews and documentary footage to examine conflicts between ancestral Latin American religions and Christianity in "The Southern Cross." Spiritually charged, humorous and passionately probing picture should make a prime item for festivals and arts institute circuits. A three-part TV version also exists.

Eschewing over-explanatory narration and operating with a cool sense of irony, Guzmán builds a mosaic-style pic amassing glimpses of various countries, cultures and religions, and the changes they've undergone since the arrival of European settlers.

Opening with the first historic contact between invaders and Latin American natives, helmer then cuts to military drills in present-day Guatemala. Analytical in a free-flowing, reflective way, the film juxtaposes ancient religious traditions and humanistic concerns with unbending Church politics and ongoing military occupation.

Guzmán tosses a stream of theological and ideological questions in the air, and never pretends to know all the answers. His point is that individual beliefs and religious practices survive despite the onslaught of Catholicism, which attempted to suppress, or at least homogenize them.

Edited with the same unbound, nonlinear vitality with which Guzmán approaches his subject, the film sometimes sacrifices clarity by not readily indentifying countries and faiths in conventional docu terms. But its fully realized aim seems to be for the soul first and the head second.

Technically polished pic's impressive sound recording is enhanced by the quiet, atmospheric rhythms of José Antonio Quintano's music. Antonio Rios' graceful, deliberate camerawork gives real power to the lush jungle landscapes and reverential detail to the intricacies of religious ritual. — *David Rooney*

KLEINE HAIE
(LITTLE SHARKS)
(GERMAN)

A Scotia Film presentation of an Olga production. (Intl. sales: Scotia.) Produced by Harry Kügler, Molly Von Fürstenberg. Executive producer, Peter Genee. Directed by Sönke Wortmann. Screenplay, Jürgen Egger, Wortmann. Camera (color), Gernot Roll; editor, Ueli Christen; music, Torsten Breuer; art direction, Dieter Bächle; costumes, Katharina Von Martius; sound, Simon Happ. Reviewed at Munich Film Festival (New German-language Films), June 30, 1992. Running time: **92 MIN.**
Ingo . . . . Jürgen Vogel
Johannes . . . . Kai Wiesinger
Ali . . . . Gedeon Burkhard
Herta . . . . Meret Becker
Bierchen . . . . Armin Rohde

An energetic comedy about a twentysomething trio angling to get into acting school, "Little Sharks" is a slick, if slightly empty vehicle given considerable speed by the breezy charms of its young leads. An audience favorite at Munich's New German Cinema lineup, pic looks like medium-sized hit material for German-speaking territories, with small screen potential further afield.

Funny opening has Essen busboy Jürgen Vogel stuck on an errand at a performing arts school, where he's mistaken for an auditioning acting student. He's forced to wait hours before the selection panel sees him. Still unwise to the mix-up, Vogel loses his cool and the panel takes his fireworks to be an inspired improv piece.

He meets Kai Wiesinger, who bombed at the audition, and the pair travel to Munich to try another school. En route they pick up rich ladykiller Gedeon Burkhard who's headed for the same tryouts. Love interest comes in with a local busker.

Their trials, tribulations and burgeoning self-discovery as they prepare to audition are well-paced and affably played, skating over a nagging lack of script depth. Vogel and Wiesinger are especially good, their characters operating with head and heart, respectively. Burkhard, whose pretty-boy role centers a little lower down, has less to do.

First-feature director Sönke Wortmann (his previous made-for-TV film had a successful theatrical run after attention at the 1991 Munich meet) handles events confidently, hitting the right notes with the disappointment and compromise of the auditions, and following with a feel-good postscript. Where he falters is in relying too often on predictable teen jokes which eat away at pic's overall freshness.

Dieter Bächle's snappy production design and Gernot Roll's agile lensing give the picture a crisp, efficient look, and Torsten Breuer's upbeat music wraps up the smooth package.
— *David Rooney*

WIPING THE TEARS OF SEVEN GENERATIONS
(DOCU)

A Kifaru production in association with Eagle Heart Prods. Produced by Gary Rhine. Directed by Rhine, Fidel Moreno. Written by Rhine, Phil Cousineau. Camera (color, video), Rhine, Moreno; editor, Laurie Schmidt; music supervisor, Robert La Bratte; associate producer, Moreno. Reviewed at Munich Film Festival (Independent Program), July 4, 1992. Running time: **60 MIN.**
Narrator: Hanna Left Hand Bull Sixico.

Documenting a memorial ride by Lakota horseback riders to the site of the 1890 Wounded Knee massacre, "Wiping the Tears of Seven Generations" is both a stirring record of a spiritual ceremony to end a century of mourning and an authoritative insight into Native American history and culture. Shot on video, this passionately made docu is being transferred to 16m for wider exposure, and it should score highly at specialist venues and on public TV and cable.

Retelling history from the Lakota perspective, pic traces the nation's first encounters with Europeans and the methodical campaign to seize their land. Using historical documents and stills, filmmakers Gary Rhine and Yaqui/Huichol Indian Fidel Moreno recap the extermination of 50 million Indians by war, starvation and European disease.

Indians' refusal to give up their land and traditions spurred years of bloody suppression by armed forces, culminating in a ruthless wipe-out raid on Wounded Knee in which over 300 unarmed Lakota were slaughtered.

The 250-mile memorial ride took place each December from 1986 to '90. Footage used here is of the final ride, undertaken in conditions of spiritual and physical hardship.

Present-day older tribes-people give moving acounts of horrific past injustices, and young Lakota voice future hopes. The cleansing ceremony is intended to herald Lakota nation rebirth, the rediscovery of their culture, language and traditional ways, and the return of their land in the Black Hills of South Dakota.

The powerful imagery of the 300 memorial riders is matched by the portrait of the Lakota people's unity, dignity and astonishing will to forgive. Never-preachy docu makes a plain statement of facts without being overtly accusatory, wielding the impact to strike a rich vein of informed guilt and inform the uninformed.

Made for a modest $100,000, the pic is a credit to all concerned. Much of the historical retelling relies on still photos and paintings, but Rhine and Moreno have avoided a static visual feel by inventively rephotographing their material and rhythmically interweaving live footage.

— *David Rooney*

DZAYN BARBORAH
(THE VOICE IN THE WILDERNESS)
(ARMENIAN)

An Armenfilm/Goyac Film Studios production. Produced by Agasi Aivazian, Vigen Chaldranian. Directed by Chaldranian. Screenplay, Aivazian, Chaldranian, Ara Stepanian. Camera (color), Vrej Petrosian, Arto Melkoumian; music, Ardashes Kartalian; art direction, Yevgenia Sarkissia. Reviewed at Monica 4-Plex, Santa Monica, Calif., June 22, 1992. (In AFI/L.A. FilmFest.) Running time: **122 MIN.**
Martiros . . . . . . Vigen Chaldranian

"**T**he Voice in the Wilderness," the second part in Vigen Chaldranian's planned trilogy in tribute to the Armenian people, is an ambitious religious epic set in medieval Armenia. Heavy symbolism, religious text and disjointed structure will restrict its appeal to the international fest circuit.

Historical pic bears the unmistakable signature of Chaldranian, who helmed, co-produced, co-scripted and stars. It follows a monk (Chaldranian) from the island of Yerzenga on his worldwide search for truth and "a place where there's no oppression."

Through torture, sacrifice and pain, he learns again to appreciate friendship and love. Moralistic parable uses a series of dichotomies to accentuate its lessons, contrasting military with spiritual power, carnal with romantic love, materialism with idealism, theater with reality.

Chaldranian, assisted by lensers Vrej Petrosian and Arto Melkoumian, strives for spectacle, and for the most part succeeds. Costumes are resplendent. But the director seems more interested in capturing the spirit of medieval times than in re-creating them, and the pic's overall quality is uneven.

Because of its extensive symbolism, narrative is sometimes obscure. And the transition from poetic dialogue to ordinary speech makes it hard to get involved.
— *Emanuel Levy*

MOONDANCE

A Mozumdar production. Produced, directed, written, edited by Martin L. Aguilar. Camera (color), Gregory Von Berblinger; music, Michael R. Smith. Reviewed at Monica 4-Plex, Santa Monica, Calif., June 29, 1992. (In AFI/L.A. FilmFest.) Running time: **83 MIN.**
Francis . . . . Lisa Moncure
Eric . . . . Joris Stuyck
Amy . . . . Patti Tippo
Willie . . . . Steve Ruggles

"**M**oondance" is a small, commendable seriocomedy about modern marriages. Despite a weak center, film's witty dialogue, assured direction and inspired performances may help get the pic beyond film fest and art house audiences.

Story contrasts the relationships of two white upper-middle class couples reunited at a secluded mountain cabin. For a while, the film seems to head toward "The Big Chill" or "Return of the Secaucus 7" territory, but filmmaker Martin L. Aguilar deftly steers his narrative in another direction.

Eric (Joris Stuyck) is an angry young man tormented by financial problems and a frustrating relationship with his dying father. His sensitive wife (Patti Tippo) makes every effort to understand him but invariably ends up humiliated. On the opposite end of the spectrum are fun-loving, free-spirited Francis and Willie (Lisa Moncure, Steve Ruggles). Of course, the relationships are not what they appear to be.

Avoiding melodramatic clichés of reunion-themed movies, Aguilar combines novelistic detail with insightful observations about friendship and marriage. Script is thoughtfully constructed with neatly placed shards of humor and irony. Gleeful dialogue is always fluent.

After a stretch of realism, however, helmer regrettably shifts to a fantasy sequence in which characters express secret desires, rekindle old passions and confront risky issues. Though never boring, this overly long section falters. Scheme's conceits are not ingenious or funny enough.

Entire cast is strong, but Moncure gives a standout perf as the mischievous and cynical Francis.

As scripter and director, Aguilar avoids both condescension and idealization of his characters, shaping each personality vividly and with a merciless satirical edge.

Technically, the pic is first-rate, particularly Gregory Von

Berblinger's crisp lensing and Michael R. Smith's soft and moody music. — *Emanuel Levy*

RETURN TRIPS
(DOCU-COLOR/B&W)

A Rosenbush/Siegal production. Produced by Mimi Rosenbush, Beverly Siegel. Directed by Rosenbush. Written by Siegel. Editors, Rosenbush, Sharon Kerp; music, Elliot Delman. Reviewed at American Film Institute, L.A., June 26, 1992. (In AFI/L.A. FilmFest.) Running time: **60 MIN.**

"**R**eturn Trips," a chronicle of religious revival among young American Jews, places the subject in the broader context of modern Jewish history. Unexamined topic might help the film earn berths on festival skeds, public TV and conferences on ethnic studies.

Using narrated footage and still photos, director Mimi Rosenbush stresses that, for decades, American Jews were "illiterate in Judaism but expert in everything else." Acculturation was based on the belief that one could be "too Jewish." Hollywood is used as an example of assimilation; most moguls were self-effacing Jews, and Jewish actors (Paul Muni, Paulette Goddard, Edward G. Robinson) anglicized their names.

Suburbanism in the 1950s resulted in increased synagogue membership, but typical Jewish lifestyle consisted of Hebrew school, bar mitzvah and three annual visits to synagogue.

The turning point in the history of American Jewry was Israel's Six Day War in 1967. After that, more funds were allocated to Israel, emphasis was placed on education rather than social services and a younger generation began to reexamine its roots.

Docu's last 10 minutes, which focus on Rosenbush's personal story, are the most interesting. Helmer and her husband talk candidly about the strain religion has put on their marriage: Rosenbush teaching her children how to kosher silverware as her father wonders if his daughter is really a "religious fanatic."

Unfortunately, docu tries to cover too many issues in an hour. As a result, it doesn't delve deeply enough into Rosenbush's personal experience. Also missing is contrast with the religious revival among Israel's younger generation, which took place at the same time. — *Emanuel Levy*

DI CERIA DELL'UNTORE
(THE PLAGUE SOWER)
(ITALIAN)

A Movie Machine production with Instito Luce. Produced by Massimo Vigliar, Franco Nero. Directed by Beppe Cino. Screenplay, Cino, Gesualdo Bufalino, based on Bufalino's novel. Camera (color), Franco Delli Colli; music, Carlo Siliotto, Alberto Alessi. Reviewed at Monica 4-Plex, Santa Monica, Calif., June 25, 1992. (In AFI/L.A. FilmFest.) Running time: **96 MIN.**
Gesualdo . . . . Franco Nero
Doctor . . . . Fernando Rey
Sister Crucifix . . . Vanessa Redgrave
Marta . . . . Lucrezia Rovere
Adelmo . . . . Salvatore (Toto) Cascio

Set in Italy in 1946, "The Plague Sower" is a moody, sentimental melodrama about the survival instincts of a group of terminally ill patients. International cast might help pic in theatrical markets overseas, but timid direction and maudlin treatment of a downbeat story will restrict appeal.

Pic aspires to be a psychological study of six diverse characters in an isolated sanitarium following Italy's defeat in World War II. This cross-section includes a cynical and eccentric doctor who is himself dying; a couple of soldiers from different social classes; a beautiful former ballerina; and a professor who survived the war but contracted tuberculosis. Rounding out the group is a sensitive, frustrated nun who nurses the patients.

Narrative depicts the passionate love that evolves between the prof (Franco Nero) and ballerina (Lucrezia Rovere), a troubled woman who witnessed the killing of her lover, an SS officer. Her wild spirit and playful nature are the only upbeat elements in this grim tale.

The amorphous script is episodic rather than dramatic, going from one poignant situation to another.

Audience feels the war's damaging effects on Italy's psyche and spirit, but the uneven script doesn't reveal more in the characters than the plot requires.

The aging but still handsome Nero holds things together with his intelligent and restrained performance. Regrettably, the nun, played by Nero's long-ago mate Vanessa Redgrave, is less a character than a plot function. Casting of Redgrave and Fernando Rey (as the M.D.) smack of marketing ploys. The two formidable actors, whose voices are dubbed, are wasted.

Tech credits, especially Franco Delli Colli's lensing, are solid. But the rousing music is too obvious. — *Emanuel Levy*

MALA
(THE LITTLE ONE)
(YUGOSLAVIAN)

A Beograd Film production. Produced by Valdan Sobajic. Directed by Predrag (Gaga) Antonijevic. Screenplay, Radoslav Pavlovic. Camera (color), Pavlovic; editor, Lana Vukobratovic; music, Goran Bregovic. Reviewed at American Film Institute, L.A., June 29, 1992. (In AFI/L.A. FilmFest.) Running time: **92 MIN.**
Militza . . . . Mirgana Jokovic
Bozidarka . . . . . Mirjana Karanovic
(In Serbian; English subtitles)

Though set in 1963, this Yugoslavian political drama is a timely allegory about the all-destructive power of a Party-controlled state. Ploddingly directed film's emotional impact is based on its harrowing story focusing on the intrusions of Communist politics into personal lives. But engaging plot and stirring ideas barely overcome artistic flaws, relegating film to the fest circuit and retrospectives of Eastern European cinema.

Like the award-winning "When Father Was Away on Business," "The Little One" tells of a family break-up after the father's sentencing to a labor camp for alleged crimes against the state. Another link is Mirjana Karanovic, who played the long-suffering mother in the 1985 pic and appears here as Bozidarka, a woman who has chosen to testify against her husband rather than lose her young child Militza (the little one).

Story begins when husband Kosta is released from prison and begins searching for his child. It's been 14 years since his arrest, and Bozidarka persistently tells Militza that her father died.

Pic's best facet is its thick melodramatic plot detailing police state's devastating effects on half a dozen characters. Film forcefully documents pervasive fear and paranoia and shows how average people lose their humanity and dignity as a direct result of Party's abuses.

However, the film lacks a consistent point of view and has no visual style. Lenser Radoslav Pavlovic, also scripter, seems to be more concerned with straightforward storytelling than in creating a visually satisfying film.

Predrag Antonijevic's undistinguished direction wastes the efforts of his talented cast. Even potentially powerful scenes lack the acute poignancy they could have had.

In pic's last half-hour, the melodrama comes fast and furious: Proceeding from one harrowing episode of rape, murder and suicide to another, story rushes toward the desired father/daughter reunion, which appropriately ends the nightmarish tale.

Still, in the context of Yugoslavia's current upheaval, helmer's sense of urgency in unraveling the story, though neglecting production values, may be justified. — *Emanuel Levy*

DEATH BECOMES HER

A Universal release. Produced by Robert Zemeckis, Steve Starkey. Co-producer, Joan Bradshaw. Directed by Zemeckis. Screenplay, Martin Donovan, David Koepp. Camera (Deluxe color), Dean Cundey; editor, Arthur Schmidt; music, Alan Silvestri; production design, Rick Carter; art direction, Jim Teegarden; set design, Lauren Polizzi, Elizabeth Lapp, Masako Masuda, John Berger; set decoration, Jackie Carr; costume design, Joanna Johnston; sound (Dolby), William B. Kaplan; visual effects supervisor, Ken Ralston; special visual effects, Industrial Light & Magic; makeup design, Dick Smith; prosthetics makeup supervisor, Kevin Haney; special body effects design, creation, Tom Woodruff Jr., Alec Gillis; assistant director, Marty Ewing; 2nd unit directors, Max Kleven, Ralston; 2nd unit camera, Don Burgess; casting, Karen Rea. Reviewed at Avco Cinema, L.A., July 23, 1992. MPAA Rating: PG-13. Running time: **103 MIN.**
Madeline Ashton . . . . . Meryl Streep
Ernest Menville . . . . . . Bruce Willis
Helen Sharp . . . . Goldie Hawn
Lisle . . . . Isabella Rossellini
Chagall . . . . Ian Ogilvy
Dakota . . . . Adam Storke
Also with: Nancy Fish, Alaina Reed Hall, Michelle Johnson, Mary Ellen Trainor, William Frankfather, John Ingle.

Mordant, daring and way, way out there, "Death Becomes Her" is a very dark comedy yielding far more strange fascination than outright laughs. Robert Zemeckis' latest stretch of state-of-the-art special effects within a character-oriented context is a treat for somewhat specialized tastes. Pic must be marketed to the widest possible public due to its clearly big-time budget (estimated at $40 million), but general audiences are very unlikely to warm to this wickedly cold-hearted tale despite the abundance of eye-popping effects. Universal can be commended for backing such an unusual and risky project, but that's not what it needs right now.

In tone, pic somewhat resembles Billy Wilder's work. Martin Donovan and David Koepp's luridly imaginative screenplay has a comic precision further sharpened by the stops-out performances of Meryl Streep and Goldie Hawn. Some may complain of misogyny, others will find the concerns silly, and there is no doubt that the cultivated archness of style creates a distance that produces admiration more than enthusiasm.

Long-arc script describes the epic competition between vain actress Streep and troubled author Hawn, initially for the love of superstar plastic surgeon Bruce Willis, but, more important, for the secret to eternal life and youth. After an amusing prologue pithily sketching how Streep steals Willis away from Hawn, Zemeckis serves up his first amazing scene with the introduction, seven years later, of Hawn as an embittered fat slob.

Audiences will gasp and gape at Hawn, convincingly made up and prostheticized to look twice her normal weight. As everywhere else here, effects work is seamless and first-rate.

Another seven years pass, and Streep, now a washed-up mess, is living in sterile BevHills splendor with Willis, whose alcoholic unhappiness has contributed to his professional demotion to mortician to the stars. In order to gloat over her old rival's obesity, Streep insists on attending a chic book party for Hawn, but is horrified to discover the 50-year-old writer looks like a health club ad.

Frantic to outdo her bitter enemy, Streep ends up at the fabulous mansion of Isabella Rossellini, a kinky beauty who turns out to be a high priestess of eternal life. Good cheap laughs are had as the priestess' potion makes Streep's rear end tighten and breasts move up and in. Later, Hawn gets her turn at F/X immortality when she begins parading around with an enormous bullet hole where her belly used to be. See-through effect is clever and beautifully executed.

While all manner of viewers will appreciate these scenes, the humor is more rarified and sophisticated. Despite mainstream trappings, pic's subjects of concern and targets of satire remain more narrowly defined and probably of slight interest to younger audiences.

Streep does an acid sendup of aging beauty queens that will be relished by devotees of showbiz and its icons. Her commanding shrillness reminds at times of Elizabeth Taylor, and her comic timing is highly tuned. Hawn plays very well with her co-star but is mostly limited to rabid vengeance. Except for her fat incarnation, the laughs are not hers to grab. Looking determinedly middle-aged as the rattled former surgeon, Willis is okay, but lacks the daft quality of Kevin Kline, original choice for the role.

Rossellini brings the right exoticism to the part of the witch-like dispenser of the ultimate Hollywood libation, while an uncredited Sydney Pollack is great fun as a BevHills doctor.

Action slows during a mid-section overly devoted to Hawn's abrasive demands that Willis knock off his wife, but Zemeckis' direction is ultra-professional. He maintains a consistently dark tone amid all the technical wizardry. Rick Carter's production design and Joanna Johnston's costumes are vastly resourceful, and Alan Silvestri's active score astutely conjures up the feeling of 1940s melodrama.

But major bows will be taken by the many artists who contributed to the assorted effects. All of them have come up with things here that have never been seen before, and have pulled them off superbly. — *Todd McCarthy*

MO' MONEY

A Columbia Pictures release of a Wife N' Kids production. Produced by Michael Rachmil. Executive producers, Damon Wayans, Eric L. Gold. Directed by Peter Macdonald. Screenplay, Wayans. Camera (color), Don Burgess; editor, Hubert C. de la Bouillerie; music, Jay Gruska; songs, Jimmy Jam & Terry Lewis, others; production design, William Arnold; costume design, Michelle Cole; sound (Dolby), Russell Williams II; assistant director, Tyrone L. Mason; co-producer, Carl Craig; casting, Aleta Chappelle. Reviewed at Loews 34th St. Showplace 2 theater, N.Y., July 24, 1992. MPAA Rating: R. Running time: **89 MIN.**
Johnny Stewart . . . . Damon Wayans
Seymour Stewart . . . Marlon Wayans
Amber Evans . . . . . . Stacey Dash
Lt. Raymond Walsh . . . . .Joe Santos
Keith Heading . . . . .John Diehl
Tom Dilton . . . . . . Harry J. Lennix
Chris Fields . . . . . Mark Beltzman
Charlotte . . . . .Almayvonne

Damon Wayans and his younger brother Marlon Wayans make a terrific comedy team in "Mo' Money." Loosely structured film has trouble meshing its very funny gag scenes with rough action footage, but it should earn mucho change from escapist fans.

Following up his solid turn co-starring opposite Bruce Willis in "The Last Boy Scout," Damon Wayans exhibits plenty of irreverent comic invention as star, writer and exec producer here. He needs a stronger hand than action helmer Peter Macdonald ("Rambo III") to fully realize a satisfying feature film beyond a mere collection of funny sketches.

He casts himself as a ne'er-do-well street punk who sets a poor role model for younger brother (played by Marlon Wayans). Their father was a cop who died in the line of duty, with his part-ner Joe Santos trying in vain to set the Wayans brothers on the right track.

To pursue a lovely romantic interest (Stacey Dash), Damon gets a job in the mailroom for her credit card company. Soon the Wayanses have cooked up a scam using uncanceled credit cards to finance a shopping spree.

Coincidentally (and this is where Wayans' script starts to fall apart), cop Santos is investigating a murder that's linked to a much larger credit card scam at the same company. Evil exec John Diehl is the ruthless mastermind who soon blackmails Damon into becoming his reluctant henchman.

Finale of Damon using his street smarts to act like his late father and collar the criminal is telegraphed many reels ahead but well staged in a showy, violent finale.

Between the killings and heavy-duty action setpieces, "Mo' Money" comes to life as expertly conceived and executed burlesque bits. Damon and rubber-faced Marlon work very comfortably together and even pull off such difficult routines as posing as gay lovers to humiliate (and scam) a white jewelry store clerk.

Damon has written many colorful characters, both black and white, including a tall, aggressive co-worker (delightfully played by Almayvonne) who sets her sights romantically on each of the brothers. He's persuasive as an action hero, too, but the action here is not convincingly dovetailed with the comedy.

Marlon shows athletic grace and is perfect as a sidekick, adding fuel to his rumored casting as Robin in an upcoming film of the "Batman" saga. Green-eyed Stacey Dash is a dreamy love interest, and Diehl is perfect as a smiling villain.

Film is well-made, though fancy wipes and transitions don't mask the absence of a strong narrative line. Song score by Jimmy Jam & Terry Lewis, featuring such top performers as Janet Jackson, Luther Vandross and Public Enemy, is an important element in the concoction. — *Lawrence Cohn*

MOM AND DAD SAVE THE WORLD

A Warner Bros. release of an HBO presentation in association with Cinema Plus L.P. & Mercury/Douglas Films of a Michael Phillips production. Produced by Phillips. Line producer, Daryl Kass. Co-producers, Michael Irwin, Max Kirishima. Directed by Greg Beeman. Screenplay, Chris Matheson, Ed Solomon. Camera (Foto-Kem color), Jacques Haitkin; editor, W.O. Garret; additional editing, Michael Jablow; music, Jerry Goldsmith; production design, Craig Stearns; art direction, Randy Moore; set design, Bill Rea; set decoration, Dorree Cooper; costume design, Robyn Reichek; sound (Dolby), James Thornton; creature effects, Alterian Studios; creatures created by Tony Gardner; special visual effects, Perpetual Motion Pictures; visual effects coordinator, Michael Muscal; stunt coordinator, Dennis (Danger) Madalone; associate producer, Deirdre Kelly Sullivan; assistant director, Richard W. Abramitis; casting, Lisa Beach. Reviewed at Warner Bros. screening room, Burbank, Calif., July 15, 1992. MPAA Rating: PG. Running time: **88 MIN.**
Marge Nelson . . . . .Teri Garr
Dick Nelson . . . . .Jeffrey Jones
Emperor Tod Spengo . . . .Jon Lovitz
Afir . . . . .Thalmus Rasulala
Sibor . . . . .Wallace Shawn
King Raff . . . . .Eric Idle
Sirk . . . . .Dwier Brown
Semage . . . . .Kathy Ireland

Little kids will find some infantile laughs in "Mom and Dad Save the World," but adults will be looking at their watches during this silly sci-fi comedy. Teri Garr and Jeffrey Jones gamely struggle with inane dialogue as a California couple transported to a tacky-looking "planet of idiots." It's a minor summer gap-filler for exhibs.

With garish color, goofy-looking creatures in rubbery costumes and sets parodying old Flash Gordon serials, pic flaunts its modest budget with engaging candor. Production designer Craig Stearns, visual effects coordinator Michael Muscal and creature creator Tony Gardner carry off the intentionally ridiculous assignment with panache and imagination.

Basic trouble is with the script by "Bill & Ted" writers Chris Matheson and Ed Solomon, whose dumbness jokes, in the absence of any other kind of humor, are stretched too far.

Pic's obvious fun-poking at San Fernando Valley suburbanites wears thin, but not as quickly as the smarmy antics of a half-witted emperor (Jon Lovitz). The adept comic actor (terrif in "A League of Their Own") chews the scenery here in an overextended part as the sadistic lout who's taken over the planet from Eric Idle's imprisoned king.

Conceiving a mad passion for Garr's ditzy Earthling after spying her through his telescope, Lovitz has her transported to the planet with Jones in their station wagon by electromagnetic beam.

Although the kiddies will enjoy watching the outlandish creatures, there aren't any juve characters along for the ride. How much time do kids want to spend watching Mom and Dad act like idiots?

Garr's blithe lack of alarm over her predicament helps her survive the pic with minimal damage. Jones is saddled with the part of a draggy couch potato but tries hard to strike some sparks when he leads a rebel band to reclaim the planet for Idle. He's aided by Dwier Brown and Kathy Ireland, playing characters whose chest measurements exceed their IQs.

Smoothies Wallace Shawn and the late Thalmus Rasulala bring a welcome stylishness to roles as Lovitz's disloyal henchmen.

Director Greg Beeman's overly broad approach makes this comedy seem like a Three Stooges short stretched to 88 minutes. — *Joseph McBride*

JUST OFF THE COAST
(B&W/COLOR)

A Wing & Wing production. Produced, written by Charles Bugbee. Directed by Bugbee, Christopher Markle. Camera (b&w, color), Richard Van Kaenel; editor, Gary Sharfin; music, Chuck Hammer, Michael Hinton, Clay Ruede; sound, Paul Soucek, John Sullivan, Mimi Wlodarczyk. Reviewed at Utopia République Cinema, Avignon, France, July 2, 1992. (In French-American Film Workshop competition.) Running time: **101 MIN.**
Wendy Burroughs . . Mary O'Sullivan
Daniel Claymore
. . . . . . William Converse-Roberts
Anne Claymore. .Charlotte d'Amboise
Edward Burroughs
. . . . William Duff-Griffin
Also with: Randy Rollison, Tim White, Brian Keene, Christopher Markle.

"Just Off the Coast," indie filmmaker Charles Bugbee's feature debut, is a better example of determination and persistence than polished filmmaking, but pic shows hints of a baroque vision which, with some narrative fine tuning, could work on TV and video. Visually ambitious but leisurely paced drama might also land a few fest berths.

Shot over a three-year period, pic kicked off the American Independents Showcase at the Cannes film market and was presented in competition at the French-American Film Workshop, Avignon. Bugbee took over helming duties and oversaw post-production when co-director Christopher Markle, who shot about a third of the footage, dropped out due to scheduling conflicts.

Daniel (William Converse-Roberts), a painter, has left his status-seeking lawyer wife (Charlotte d'Amboise) and fled to an island off the New England coast where he rents a room in an inn tended by William Duff-Griffin and his tomboyish, eerily blunt granddaughter (Mary O'Sullivan). As Daniel rethinks his priorities, the girl sets her sites on the emotionally vulnerable painter.

Making the most of expansive dunes and surf, lenser Richard Von Kaenel has captured the off-season feel of an island retreat. In director's lone answer print (printed on color stock to accommodate dream interludes shot in color), timing of black & white sequences varies from moody amber and sepia to various points on the gray scale. Patchwork of tones is interesting, if unintended.

Several dream sequences convey sly logic, subconscious fears and wishful thinking, while other inserts, including couple's argument in flashback, are too reminiscent of video-clip illustration.

Story-within-story — a mermaid fable O'Sullivan reads to gramps at bedtime — is a somewhat stilted touch that might have lent the desired layer of resonance if more skillfully directed.

D'Amboise appears to be acting more for the stage than the screen, but O'Sullivan and Converse-Roberts are convincing and maintain good character continuity despite spread-out shooting schedule. Music, at first aptly ominous is less striking later on.

Made on a deferred-payments budget in which raw stock and processing were the major expenses, pic would certainly have benefited from retakes in some scenes, but Bugbee, a sound mixer on Broadway, has proven he can hold a feature together.

— *Lisa Nesselson*

INSIDE MONKEY ZETTERLAND

A Coast Entertainment production. Produced by Chuck Grieve, Tani Cohen. Executive producers, Lewis Jay Pearlman, Jefery Levy. Directed by Levy. Co-produced, written by Steven Antin. Additional voiceover & dialogue, John Boskovich. Camera (color), Christopher Taylor; editor, Lauren Zuckerman; music, Rick Cox, Jeff Elmassian; production design, Jane Stewart; costume design, Steven Earbino, Hayley Marcus. Reviewed at Directors Guild of America, West Hollywood, July 18, 1992. (In L.A. Intl. Gay & Lesbian Film & Video Festival.) Running time: **92 MIN.**

Monkey Zetterland	Steven Antin
Honor Zetterland	Katherine Helmond
Grace Zetterland	Patricia Arquette
Brent Zetterland	Tate Donovan
Mike Zetterland	Bo Hopkins
Imogene	Sandra Bernhard
Sophie	Martha Plimpton
Sasha	Rupert Everett
Cindy	Sofia Coppola
Bella	Rikki Lake
Daphne	Debi Mazar
Psychiatrist	Lance Loud
Grandma	Francis Bay
Boot guy	Luca Bercovici

A charming comedy about contempo L.A. life, "Inside Monkey Zetterland" is infused with a sophisticated gay sensibility. Although pic is populated by gay and lesbian characters, its broad canvas, humanistic vision, magnetic cast and inspired writing extend its appeal to all young, educated urban audiences. Prospects for theatrical release are excellent.

In his stunning debut as a scripter, Steven Antin demonstrates a rare appreciation for the eccentric details of today's edgy, violent existence. At the heart of Antin's poetic, loosely autobiographical comedy is the complex, Oedipal relationship between aspiring writer Monkey Zetterland (Antin) and his domineering Jewish mother (Katherine Helmond), a TV soap star.

Dad Mike (Bo Hopkins) is not around much, but Monkey is close to his brother (Tate Donovan), a handsome hairdresser, and even closer to his lesbian sister (Patricia Arquette), who moves into his house during a strain in her relationship with her lover (Sofia Coppola).

Monkey's rich world also contains a large network of friends, neighbors and strangers. Pic's best sequences depict collective gatherings (Thanksgiving dinner, evenings in front of the TV) in which Monkey's friends behave like one big, extended family, expanding the conventional meaning of family life.

Dealing with convoluted lives and romantic entanglements of a dozen characters, pic provides astute meditation on love, loneliness and violence in L.A. Like "L.A. Story," the film is basically a love song to the laid-back, nutty city. Antin's characters are just as charming as those in the Steve Martin pic, only younger and quirkier.

In tone, the pic resembles Alan Rudolph's best pics ("Welcome To L.A.," "Choose Me") and its ironic view and whimsical absurdity contain light and dark humor in equal measure. Nonjudgmental comedy refuses to

distinguish between normal and abnormal, healthy and perverse, and shows love and empathy for each character.

Fusing hipness and lyricism, Antin's distinct comic vision perceives the world as both funny and odd, evincing a sense of wonder in the most mundane situations. Though dealing with somber events (random violence, tragic death), film is ultimately ennobling because of its emphasis on the will to survive.

Jefery Levy's fluid, unforced direction avoids obvious jokes, and he achieves ironic laughs without overworking them, building humor through a leisurely accumulation of many small, telling details.

Unfortunately, the film's last half-hour becomes too cute and TV-like in its artificial tempo. Pic also errs in deliberating on its least convincing subplot involving a terrorist act against a homophobic insurance company. A pat, fairy-tale ending is also incongruent with pic's dominant texture.

But the performers are terrifically charismatic, and helmer Levy handles his large cast with apparent ease, giving each thesp the chance to show off his/her special qualities. In the central role, Helmond provides the big, irritating personality on which much of the humor is dependent. Helmond and Antin display great chemistry in scenes that often crackle.

Martha Plimpton almost steals the show as a bulimic, foul-mouthed activist, and Coppola gives a stand-out, shaded perf as a lesbian impregnated by a man she met at a Women Against Pornography rally. Sandra Bernhard mixes a devious edge with light self-mockery. Arquette carries off the sensitive sister with physical grace and verbal delicacy. Debi Mazar has an original fierceness about her as Antin's g.f., and Rikki Lake provides another strong presence as a TV fanatic.

Small-budget project's production values are superlative. Christopher Taylor's exquisite lensing has a snazzy verve, luminous yet informal. Lauren Zuckerman's sharp editing brings a snap to the storytelling.

Funny, sharp-tongued and devious, but never wicked or nasty, pic has a resonant comedy so attuned to the L.A. zeitgeist that any urban dweller will find something relevant in it.

— *Emanuel Levy*

TRIBULATION 99: ALIEN ANOMALIES UNDER AMERICA
(DOCU-16m)

An Other Cinema production. Directed, written, edited by Craig Baldwin. Camera (color, 16m), Bill Daniel; music, Dana Hoover; narrator, Sean Kilcoyne. Reviewed at AMC Kabuki 8 Cinemas, San Francisco, May 1, 1992. Running time: **49 MIN.**

A hilarious and bizarrely absorbing collage of pre-existing footage, Craig Baldwin's "Tribulation 99" posits 20th-century global history as one unending conspiracy theory running straight toward apocalypse.

While sub-feature length is an obvious limitation, film's unique take on myriad current political issues could have crossover potential under specialized circumstances. Pic grabbed the top "New Visions" prize in the San Francisco film fest's Golden Gate Awards.

Baldwin compiles myriad visual sources — Biblical and James Bond flicks, nature/science docus, news footage, cartoons, commercials, monster movies, et al. — into a fantasy narrative in which aliens fleeing planet Quetzalcoatl are revealed to have manipulated Earth politics for decades.

Global warming, the Cold War, Watergate, Latin American turmoil and natural disasters all emerge as consequences of this self-proclaimed "pseudo-pseudo-documentary." In the current climate of escalating local and international disasters, the effect is at once hilarious — and almost credible.

Witty sound and visual editing keeps stimulus at a max, although it's coherent enough to avoid strictly experimental appeal. — *Dennis Harvey*

DAS FACHERS SCHNEIDE
(THE KNIFE BEHIND THE FAN)
(GERMAN-DOCU)

A BrigiGenshyu'stte Krause production. Directed, written, edited by Brigitte Krause. Camera (color), Michael Sombetzki; music, Kyosuka Suzuki, Richard Hartwell. Reviewed at Monica 4-Plex, Santa Monica, Calif., June 27, 1992. (In AFI/L.A. FilmFest.) Running time: **87 MIN.**

With: Genshyu Hanayagi, Genjuro Abe, Torai Shida.
(In Japanese; English subtitles)

Brigitte Krause's "The Knife Behind the Fan" is a fascinating docu about artist Genshyu Hanayagi, Japan's enfant terrible. Genshyu's eccentric personality, great performance pieces, wry humor and feminist commentary on her country's social mores might broaden pic's appeal beyond festival and art house auds.

"Fighting women get way with a knife," says Genshyu in one of the film's more illuminating interviews. She isn't kidding. In 1980, she stabbed the headmistress of a famous dance school, then spent eight months in prison. Though superficial, the wound was a symbolic protest against the Lemoto, a rigid system under which a few families dominate traditional art forms.

In an effort to topple that domination, Genshyu established a theater in a town far from Tokyo. Her dream is to establish folk theaters in many regions.

The artist challenges just about every aspect of Japanese society, from imperial rule to dress codes for women, which forbid accentuation of the breasts and waist.

Krause does not impose a chronological structure on her material but lets her subject talk freely. A child of traveling performers, the lowest rank of artists, Genshyu vowed early on "to battle to compensate all disgraces of childhood." She channeled her frustrations into her work, forging new art forms and reinterpreting classic plays.

Docu celebrates a woman who lives by her own code of ethics. Integrated with the interviews are two exquisite performance pieces, both with strong ideological subtexts.

Docu's production values are accomplished, especially lensing and evocative music by Japanese and English composers. Here is an 87-minute docu that for once feels too short to encompass its artist's complex personality. — *Emanuel Levy*

STICKIN' TOGETHER

An August Entertainment presentation of Bellrock Entertainment production. Produced by David Frost. Directed by Herb Freed. Screenplay, Marion Segal, Freed. Camera (color), Mackenzie Waggaman; editor, Segal; music, Glynn Turman. Reviewed at WorldFest/Houston, April 30, 1992. Running time: **109 MIN.**
Samson . . . . Steve Lieberman
Terrine . . . . Francine La Pencee
Shebez . . . . David Winston
Dumonde . . . . . . Barrett Grayson
Fleetfoot . . . . . Lucas La Fontaine
Dabdu . . . . Robert Restaino
Jorell . . . . Gregory Battle
Sweet Tooth . . . . Aromuz

This sincere but hopelessly simplistic drama playing like a foul-mouthed, slightly sexed-up "Afterschool Special" might arouse mild curiosity in urban markets with an ad campaign emphasizing the plot line about boys in the 'hood turning to crime. It's more likely "Stickin' Together" will get stuck in homevid and on pay-TV.

Director/co-scripter Herb Freed and co-scripter Marion Segal focus on Samson (Steve Lieberman), a troubled teen who lands in a juvenile detention center after a petty crime spree. Once he's inside, audience learns he is the son of a drug addict mother whose other children, by various fathers, constitute a virtual rainbow coalition.

It appears there's hope for Samson when a dedicated teacher gets the boy interested in classics such as Charles Dickens' "A Tale of Two Cities." But it quickly becomes the worst of times when Samson breaks out.

Quick-tempered pal Shebez (David Winston) has a brother, Jorell (Gregory Battle), a mid-level crime boss who hires the youths but insists they refrain from actually killing anybody. It doesn't take long for Shebez to break this rule, and it takes even less time for Jorell to make his grave displeasure known.

In the end, Samson kills Jorell and another drug dealer in self-defense. (It may upset some moviegoers that Samson, who is white, kills two black bad guys.) Then he and Terrine hitchhike off into the sunset, presumably to settle down someplace where Samson can read more Dickens.

The performances lack conviction, the direction lacks subtlety and the script abounds in artifice and clichés. Tech values are about what would be expected from the reported $3 million budget.
— *Joe Leydon*

LOS AÑOS DE GRETA
(GRETA'S YEARS)
(MEXICAN)

A Mexican Film Institute (Imcine) release of an Almavisión Prods./Imcine/Fondo de Fomento a la Calidad Cinematográfica production. Executive producer, Norma Hilda Castañares. Produced, directed by Alberto Bojórquez. Screenplay, María Diego Hernández, Bojórquez. Camera (color), José Ortiz Ramos; editor, Sigfrido G. Case; sound, Roberto Camacho; art direction, Fernando Solorio. Reviewed at Imcine, Mexico City, April 6, 1992. Running time: **105 MIN.**
Greta . . . . Beatriz Aguirre
Gustavo . . . . . Pedro Armendáriz
Nora . . . . . . : . . . . Helena Rojo
Pascual . . . . Luis Aguilar
Gloria . . . . Meche Barba
Norita . . . . Evangelina Sosa
Piloncito . . . . Alejandro Cedillo

Eighth feature by Mexican director Alberto Bojórquez, "Los Años de Greta" deals with the complex question of what to do with the elderly. Although a serious attempt to deal with a serious theme, the sometimes painful subject matter, along with uneven and didactic handling, could alienate filmgoers. The small screen may be more appropriate.

Veteran actress Beatriz Aguirre offers a palpable performance in the title role of a 72-year-old woman who lives off the grace of her nephew (Pedro Armendáriz). She shares a room with his kids, although her erratic hours disturb their sleeping. Though she means to be helpful, she forgets messages and breaks dishes.

The well-meaning but bewildered family moves her into the maid's room on the roof. When she breaks a leg running for a bus, she becomes bedridden and needs constant attention.

Enter Greta's vivacious friend Gloria (Meche Barba), who offers to take Greta in for company. Showing that being old doesn't exclude fun and romance, Gloria carries on with picaresque Luis Aguilar.

At times the film's didactic tone takes over, with the wholesale insertion of mini-messages aimed at society about the problems of seniors.

Technically, the low-budget film is passable, although not exciting. Many of Mexico's w.k. older actors appear in walk-on roles.
— *Paul Lenti*

TOWARD JERUSALEM
(AUSTRIAN-DOCU-16m)

A Filmladen production. Produced by Josef Aicholzer, Ruti Singer. Directed, written by Ruth Beckermann. Camera (Kodak color, 16m), Nurith Aviv, Claire Bailly du Bois; editor, Gertraud Luschützky; music, Edek Bartz, Meredith Monk; production design, Ruth Beckermann; sound, Jochai Mosche, Othmar Schmiederer; narrator: Niki Kunz. Reviewed at Walter Reade Theater, N.Y., July 8, 1992. Running time: **87 MIN.**

Billed as "a documentary road movie," this intimate look at Israel meanders from Tel Aviv through a host of characters to Jerusalem, occasionally focusing sharply on some of them. But this piece, for aficionados only, lingers too long on insignificant detail and often skips over people viewers are just beginning to care about. Except as an alternative companion to otherwise bland TV reportage from the Middle East, Ruth Beckermann's trek has limited possibilities.

The Austrian director/interviewer let her 16m camera do most of the talking as she captured the cheap neon facade of nighttime Tel Aviv, met Jewish immigrants from Russia and got just below the surface of the Intifadah in a few telling moments. But the handful of sharply drawn contrasts audience is allowed to glimpse are drowned out by a cacophony of disjointed images and noise.

A short narration in the beginning sets the mood as it asks, plaintively and a bit pathetically, why the Jews sought a homeland. The film then seeks to answer, giving many reasons that eventually point in as many directions as there are faces on the reel.

Technically, the format is invariably low-tech, with the bumpy, "you-are-there" quality of frontline photography, and a muffled sound to match. But the editing is done gingerly, as Beckermann indulges in long sweeps of barren wasteland and low-rent architecture to make her point, rather than train the lens on the few truly compelling characters she encounters. The score is incidental, and the same piece of music lingers only briefly each time it's introduced.

Had this pic had a map or a script, the bright moments would have been elevated the format to a higher level. As is, it needs lots

of audience patience to make it.
— *Christian Moerk*

TO LIV(E)

> A Riverdrive Prods. production. Produced by Willy Tsao. Executive producer, Mira Macbeth. Directed, written by Evans Chan. Camera (color), Wong Ping Hung; editor, Sammy Chow; music, Somei Satoh; art direction, Chin Yiu Hang; sound, Jim Shumi; assistant director, Lam Yuet Man. Reviewed at American Film Institute, L.A., June 4, 1992. (In AFI/L.A. FilmFest.) Running time: **108 MIN.**
> Rubie . . . . Lindzay Chan
> Teresa . . . . Josephine Ku
> Tony . . . . Wong Yiu Ming
> John . . . . Fung Kin Chung
> Mom . . . . Ha Ping
> Pa . . . . Ma Pa Nu
> Michelle . . . . Carmen Ling
> Trini . . . . Margaret Lee
> Nuclear Goddess . . . Suen Ming Chui
> *(In English, Cantonese with English subtitles)*

Evans Chan's first feature, appropriately titled "To Liv(e)," was prompted by actress Liv Ullmann's 1990 public condemnation of Hong Kong for deporting 51 Vietnamese refugees. Focusing on the anxiety and uncertainty of Hong Kong in the aftermath of Tiananmen Square massacre, this engaging family melodrama is interspersed with imaginary letters to the actress. Pic's distinctive quality should take it into fests and some specialized playoffs.

Focus is on a young magazine editor (Lindzay Chan) and her relationships with her parents, brother and boyfriend. Her strained interactions form the backdrop of a story that combines real and imaginary characters to examine the peculiar status of Hong Kong, which will revert to Chinese rule in 1997. Some plan to leave; others, like the British poetess Elsi (who is interviewed), expect to stay and "have a date with history."

The editor's spiritual-political journey, punctuated by personal crises, offers meditation on exile, identity, East/West culture clash and, above all, the fate of Hong Kong as an "entrapped corner of global politics." Excellent lensing of the city's modern, Western look stresses its lack of character — it was "planted there at random," as Chan says.

"To Liv(e)" recalls Ingmar Bergman's existential angst in such classics as "Shame" (1968), with Ullmann and Max von Sydow as musicians morally challenged by a civil war. But this pic's narrative strategy attempts a Godardian style. It's too bad the editor's writing lacks the wit and sophistication of Jean-Luc Godard's 1972 "Letter to Jane," in which he engaged in political discourse with Jane Fonda about her notorious Hanoi stint. The letters here are too literal.

Still, the missives manage to add the necessary tension between pic's personal and political dimensions.

Low-budget ($150,000) indie boasts accomplished lensing and editing. Chan, who won an acting award at the Portugal Sinatra Festival, heads a uniformly good cast.

George Bernard Shaw's words, "China, help thyself," written after his unpublicized 1933 visit to Hong Kong, highlight the subtext, proving timelier than ever.

— *Emanuel Levy*

KARLOVY VARY

CERNI BARONI
(THE BLACK BARONS)
(CZECHOSLOVAKIAN)

> A Space production. Directed by Zdenek Sirovy. Screenplay, Miloslav Svandrlik, Sirovy, based on Svandrlik's novel. Camera (color), Jiri Machane; editor, Ivana Kacirkova; music, Lubos Fiser; sound, Vladimir Skall. Reviewed at Karlovy Vary Film Festival, July 12, 1992. Running time: **100 MIN.**
> With: Pavel Landovsky, Bronislav Poloczek, Alois Svehlik, Rudolf Hrusinsky, Jiri Schmitzer, Miroslav Donutil, Josef Dvorak, Ondrej Vetchy, Vladimir Javorsky, Milan Simacek, Boris Rosner.

Strong script, fine acting and good production values elevate this fine comedy well above the level of most recent Czech productions. With the right handling, "The Black Barons" could perform in European art houses and travel still further on the film fest circuit.

Based on a bestselling novel, pic is a lighthearted comedy about a post-World War II Czech regiment. Newsreel footage of pompous bureaucrats opens the action and sets the tone for a consistently clever, if not deep or analytical, story.

The Black Barons never saw action but instead were assigned to work in a quarry. Basically a series of you're-in-the-army now sketches, unfit and unmotivated recruits do their best to cope with, or avoid, military service. People's Army officers are objects of ridicule rather than scorn. In one of the picture's funniest scenes, the brass is found to be utterly uneducated in the fundamentals of communist ideology. "The American imperialists would be thrilled to hear this," comments a general morosely.

Fine comic timing and editing underscore pic's comedy.

— *Rebecca Lieb*

IR TEN KRANTAI SMELETI
(THERE ARE SANDY BEACHES TOO)
(LITHUANIAN)

> A Katarsis Film Cooperative production. (Intl. sales: Vilfilm, Vilnius.) Directed, written by Algimantas Puipa. Camera (color), Rimantas Suzrila. Reviewed at Karlovy Vary Film Festival, July 11, 1992. Running time: **88 MIN.**

This muddy, impenetrable and directionless pic is a case study of everything that can go wrong in filmmaking in the former Soviet bloc. Film almost entirely lacks a screenplay, and the narrative is almost incomprehensible.

Somewhere in rural Lithuania, an unnamed doctor encounters the villagers with whom he has professional and personal relationships. When events do occur, they are discussed rather than shown on screen. There is no cohesive plot or story flow, nor the sandy beaches of the title.

The doctor does have on his desk one of those gadgets in which sand falls slowly through a dense liquid, but the symbolic content of the image is impossible to fathom. — *Rebecca Lieb*

STILLES LAND
(SILENT COUNTRY)
(GERMAN)

> A Max Film, Wolfgang Pfeiffer production, co-produced with Hochschule fur Film & Fernsehen, MDR & SWF. (Intl. sales: Ex Picturis, Berlin.) Directed by Andreas Dresen. Screenplay, Dresen, Laila Stieler. Camera (color), Andreas Hofer; editor, Rita Reinhardt; music, Tobias Morgenstern; art direction, Joachim Otto; sound, Karl-Heinz Sass. Reviewed at Karlovy Vary Film Festival, July 13, 1992. Running time: **98 MIN.**
> Kai . . . . Thorsten Merten
> Claudia . . . . Jeanette Arndt
> Walz . . . . Kurt Bowe
> Thomas . . . . Burkhard Heyl
> Uschi . . . . Petra Kelling
> Also with: Horst Westphal, Katrin Martin, Asad Schwarz, Mathais Noack, Hans-Uwe Bauer, Wolf-Dieter Lingk, Hans-Jochen Rührig, Roman Silberstein.

Pleasing but undistinguished drama set against events leading to the fall of the Berlin Wall could garner interest at home and at festivals for its historical dimension, but script and characters lose depth, ending the picture on a weak note.

Kai (Thorsten Merten), a 26-year-old director, arrives full of enthusiasm and ideas in a remote and depressing East German town to work in the local theater. His spirits hardly flag when he learns his cozy co-workers are as hostile to his intrusion as the locals who beat him up for ordering tea in a bar. Only one with something in common with Kai is pretty young Claudia (Jeanette Arndt), who feels stranded in the grey, industrial town.

As Kai begins to mount an experimental production of "Waiting for Godot," the troupe begins to hear rumblings of the unrest in faraway Berlin, and of East Germans escaping over the Hungarian border. As the half-heard snippets of news become undeniable, the new spirit of a popular uprising coalesces the group, informing both their work and their relationships.

After initially gaining creative strength from the political events, Kai suddenly and inexplicably runs out of gas, becoming pale, wan and impotent. A brief affair with Claudia fizzles, and she returns from a trip to observe the fall of the Wall suddenly in love with a West German actor. The actor rolls up his sleeves and tries to jumpstart the small theater, but his deus ex machina appearance is jarring, as he begins to inform the bewildered troupe about concepts like publicity.

First-time helmer Andreas Dresen shows promise as a director. He's especially strong developing the roles of minor characters to support the story line: A young actor is arrested for bringing an antenna back to town to try to pick up West German TV broadcasts.

Tech credits are good, but Dresen would have done well to have added some East German landscape shots for viewers unfamiliar with the bleakness of the country. — *Rebecca Lieb*

LOCH POBEDITEL VODY
(DUDE WATER WINNER)
(RUSSIAN)

A Trinity Bridge production. (Intl. sales: Ex Picturis, Berlin.) Directed, written by Arkadij Tegaj. Camera (color), Yuri Veksler; costumes, N. Jaskun. Reviewed at Karlovy Vary Film Festival, July 11, 1992. Running time: **87 MIN.** With: Sergei Kurechin, Larissa Borodina.

Although it suffers from a plot that eventually disintegrates, "Dude Water Winner" is set to carve a niche as one of the best examples of new Russian cinema, making it a natural for fests and post-communist cinema retrospectives. Tale of a young man's quest to avenge his friend's death at the hands of gangsters has a gritty, street-smart edge.

A Moscow gang destroys the computer store Gorelikov runs with his friend Kostja, who is killed. Bent on revenge, Gorelikov taps into his technological knowledge to become a low-rent James Bond. Through a desperate, chaotic Moscow, he stalks the toughs with a wide arsenal of homemade surveillance devices and encounters characters unusual in Russian cinema, including a transvestite.

In a tragicomic detective story with noir overtones, Sergei Kurechin is fine as the computer nerd turned superhero, and Western audiences will no doubt see more of him. Film's flaw is that the narrative falls apart towards the end of the story, causing a carefully constructed atmosphere to go down with it. But helmer Arkadij Tegaj's first feature is nevertheless full of promise.

— *Rebecca Lieb*

BERLIN REPORT
(SOUTH KOREAN)

A Morgard Korea Ltd. production. Executive producer, Chul Shin. Produced by Byung-gi Suh. Directed, written by Kwang-su Park. Camera (color), Kwang-suk Chung, Bee-joo Park; editor, Hyun Kim; music, Soo-chul Kim; production design, Kwang-hyun Shim; makeup, Seng-hee Kim; assistant director, Hyun-sung Lee. Reviewed at Karlovy Vary Film Festival, July 15, 1992. Running time: **100 MIN.**
Sung-min . . . . Sung-ki Ahn
Marie Hélene . . . . . . Soo-yeon Kang
Young-chul . . . . Sung-gun Moon
Detective . . . . Jean-Marie Fon Bonne
Chantale . . . . Marianne Loyen
Also with: Jacques Seiler, Fuan Pires Ramos, Jae-young Lee, Kyun-dong Yuh, Nina Yoonja Freund.

A muddled metaphor for the plight of a divided Korea set against the backdrop of German reunification, "Berlin Report" is too clumsily constructed to play anywhere but home.

Despite its title, most of pic takes place in Paris. Sung-min, a Korean journalist, becomes interested in the case of a woman of Korean descent accused of murdering her French stepfather. Marie-Hélene has been rendered mute somehow by the event. Sung-min goes to Berlin in search of Marie-Hélene's brother. The siblings are supposed to represent the division of North and South Korea.

The plot bumbles along from one pointless encounter to another. Sung-min spends much of his time at graffiti-besmirched buildings asking the whereabouts of various people. Minor characters seem to serve no role, including Sung-min's French g.f.

Events end as abruptly as they begin, without serving the story. A scene in which Sung-min arrives to interview an official and cuts to him leaving the meeting only baffles the audience.

Director Park seems interested in viewing two European capitals on film but has little to say. Unimaginative camerawork and clumsy editing, not to mention a score that sounds sentimental and dated, don't help.

— *Rebecca Lieb*

MUNICH FEST

WARRIOR:
THE LIFE OF LEONARD PELTIER
(DOCU-16m)

A Good Machine production. (Intl. sales: Stutz Co., Berkeley, Calif.) Produced, directed by Suzie Baer. Executive producer, James Schamus. Co-producer, Ramin Niami. Written by Owen Ranta, John Mullen. Camera (Duart color, 16m), Evan Estern; editor, John Mullen; music, Lanny Meyers; sound, Robert Kitson, Todd Morgan, Amanda Vogel, Pamela Yates, Ronald Grey; associate producers, Ingrid Washinawatok, Ranta, Robert Kitson. Reviewed at Munich Film Festival (Independent Program), June 30, 1992. Running time: **85 MIN.**

A cool-headed, persuasive piece of investigative journalism, "Warrior: The Life of Leonard Peltier" builds an utterly convincing case against the subject's conviction for "aiding and abetting" the killing of two FBI agents on the Pine Ridge Indian reservation in 1975. Well-crafted, deeply committed docu should draw attention via quality TV and cable outlets.

Made with support from Peltier's defense committee and author Peter Matthiessen (who appears in interviews, and whose book "In the Spirit of Crazy Horse" was filmmaker Suzie Baer's starting point), pic risks being unjustly overshadowed by Michael Apted's "Incident at Oglala." Working with a fraction of that pic's budget, Baer (whose project kicked off over a year earlier) covers similar ground but gives a wider view of the issues.

Baer outlines how corrupt, U.S. government-aligned tribal councils gave away one-third of the Oglala nation to multinational corporations, presumably for hefty kickbacks. The deal's economic magnitude ($3.5 billion in mining revenues over a decade from only a small slice of available land) explains Pentagon interest in the area and hostility against a small but threatening group of people.

Well-researched archive material and interviews document a stepped-up campaign to divide Indian communities. Paramilitary operations were stealthily introduced into Native American lands just prior to the Pine Ridge incident. A fearsome goon squad established a climate of fear and tension and opposed American Indian Movement activists. Many believe the FBI deaths were an unforeseen side effect of an organized skirmish to distract national media from land issues.

Interviewed in Leavenworth where he's serving two consecutive life sentences, Peltier is shown as less a warrior than a quietly determined man still committed to his people after more than 13 years in prison. Baer mercilessly parallels this portrait with clips of a Fed's gung-ho vows to stamp out evil and have fun doing it.

What really happened remains only partially clear, but Baer neatly assembles formidable evidence detailing falsified affidavits, hidden ballistics reports and perjured testimony before a judge known to be highly prejudiced. Only evidence directly linking Peltier to the deaths was acknowledged to be fraudulent, but requests for a retrial continue to be refused. — *David Rooney*

KINDERSPIELE
(CHILD'S PLAY)
(GERMAN-16m)

An FFG production. (Intl. sales: ZDF.) Directed by Wolfgang Becker. Screenplay, Horst J. Sczerba, Becker. Camera (color, 16m), Martin Kukula; editor, Becker; music, Christian Steyer; art direction, Peter Bausch. Reviewed at Munich Film Festival (New German-language Films), July 2, 1992. (Also in Locarno Film Festival, noncompeting.) Running time: **107 MIN.**
Micha . . . . Jonas Kipp
Kalli . . . . Oliver Bröker
Father . . . . Burghart Klaussner
Mother . . . . Angelika Bartsch

Kids' games mirror the adult world's cruelty in "Kinderspiele," a story of a fractured family that cuts a devastating path to tragedy. Winner of the young director prize in the Munich fest's new German-language lineup, pic is a cinch for critical kudos both locally and at international fests (starting at Locarno next month), but its brutal honesty may prove too downbeat for commercial breakout.

Story centers on a pre-teen boy Micha (Jonas Kipp, perfectly balancing sinister and sympathetic sides) and his dictatorial father, indifferent mother, physically handicapped grandmother and spiteful moppet brother.

Viciously beaten by his father for minor infringements of household rules and getting scant support from other family members, Micha wages a personal war against them, fueling conflicts between his parents and strife for his brother.

Director Wolfgang Becker grimly depicts a state of absolute emotional squalor, and the harshness at home extends to Micha's interaction with other kids. Unflinching scenes with his ruffian best friend show them engaged in morbid power games.

Becker builds events to a shattering, unexpected climax, detouring into lighter territory only with a barbed double edge. One strong scene has Micha and pal staging a mock trial of the friend's senile grandmother at which they renege on the death sentence only after thoroughly scaring her.

Martin Kukula's unembellished lensing is as stark and harshly focused as pic's depiction of family disintegration. Brief flights of fancy are admitted only when Micha escapes into a dream world.

Technical work is all first-rate, as are performances.

— *David Rooney*

L'ENVERS DU DECOR
PORTRAIT DE PIERRE GUFFROY
(BEHIND THE SCENES: A
PORTRAIT OF PIERRE GUFFROY)
(FRENCH-DOCU)

An Eden Films/FR-3 Oceaniques/ Robert & Isidore Salis presentation of an Eden Films production with participation of Centre National de la Cinematographie & Procirep. Produced, directed by Robert Salis. Camera (color), François About, Dominique Le Rigoleur; editors, Josie Miljevic, Marie Salis; music, Philippe Sarde, Ennio Morricone; sound, Claude Hivernon, Vincent Arnardi, Michel Klochendler, Agnes Burrus. Reviewed at Munich Film Festival (Special Screenings), June 28, 1992. Running time: **132 MIN.**
With: Nastassja Kinski, Harrison Ford, Roman Polanski, Milos Forman, Nagisa Oshima, Tarak Ben Ammar, Martina Skala, Rene Loubet.

A lovingly detailed tribute to French production designer Pierre Guffroy, "Behind the Scenes" is a fascinating trip for anyone with a passion for the moviemaking process, and it should make a useful instructional tool for set design students. Exhaustive, exhausting pic is too long to make a showing beyond the fest circuit, but a ruthless editing hand could prune it down into a top tube vehicle.

Guffroy's services have been tapped by Jean Cocteau, Luis Buñuel, François Truffaut, Robert Bresson and Nagisa Oshima. He won an Oscar in 1981 for his work on Roman Polanski's "Tess."

Shot between 1986 and '90, docu delves mainly into recent achievements, including reconstructions of Prague (in Lyon) for Philip Kaufman's "The Unbearable Lightness of Being," 18th century France for Milos Forman's "Valmont" and Paris rooftops for Polanski's "Frantic."

Guffroy continually underplays his role in the filmmaking process and humbly confesses the uncertainty of how things will look until the dailies are seen. A patient perfectionist, he details the importance of facilitating shooting and sound concerns in his designs, and not forcing technicians to accommodate impossible spaces. His illuminating comments on set design see it not as pure artifice, but as a means for putting an original, deliberate slant on reality.

Countering Guffroy's modesty are warm testimonials from directors, actors and producers. Forman's a good-humored standout among them.

Filmmaker Robert Salis spends a little too much time examining Polanski's films, somewhat blurring docu's focus, and he seems overly enamored of Nastassja Kinski, allowing her to gush at length without saying anything concrete.

One point that resurfaces repeatedly is resentment that the creative process can be reduced to rubble by critical dismissal. Sore point seems clearly to be the unequivocal keel-hauling given to Polanski's "Pirates."

Film clips are well-chosen and highly illustrative of the designer's contributions. Buffs will especially enjoy close looks at sets for Buñuel pics and Polanski's "The Tenant." Salis sticks to a straightforward docu format apart from a poetically outré device used to open and close pic: Guffroy on trial for entering a world of dreams and imagination. — *David Rooney*

UNFORGIVEN

A Warner Bros. release of a Malpaso production. Produced, directed by Clint Eastwood. Executive producer, David Valdes. Screenplay, David Webb Peoples. Camera (Technicolor, Panavision widescreen), Jack N. Green; editor, Joel Cox; music, Lennie Niehaus; production design, Henry Bumstead; art direction, Rick Roberts, Adrian Gorton; set design, James J. Murakami; set decoration, Janice Blackie-Goodine; sound (Dolby), Rob Young; associate producer, Julian Ludwig; assistant director, Scott Maitland; casting, Phyllis Huffman, Stuart Aikins (Canada). Reviewed at Warner Bros. studios, Burbank, Calif., June 24, 1992. MPAA Rating: R. Running time: **130 MIN.**
Bill Munny . . . . Clint Eastwood
Little Bill Daggett . . . Gene Hackman
Ned Logan . . . . . . Morgan Freeman
English Bob . . . . Richard Harris
The "Schofield Kid" . . Jaimz Woolvett
W.W. Beauchamp . . . . Saul Rubinek
Strawberry Alice . . . Frances Fisher
Delilah Fitzgerald . . . Anna Thomson
Quick Mike . . . . David Mucci
Davey Bunting . . . . . Rob Campbell
Skinny Dubois . . . . . Anthony James

"Unforgiven" is a classic Western for the ages. In his 10th excursion into the genre that made him a star more than 25 years ago, Clint Eastwood has crafted a tense, hard-edged, superbly dramatic yarn that is also an exceedingly intelligent meditation on the West, its myths and its heroes. With its grizzled cast of outstanding actors playing outlaws who have survived their primes, this is unapologetically a mature, contemplative film, with all that implies for b.o. prospects.

Buffs, longtime Eastwood fans and connoisseurs of the form should love it, resulting in good word-of-mouth and sustained business through Labor Day and possibly beyond.

Eastwood has dedicated the film "to Sergio and Don," references to Sergio Leone and Don Siegel. Not only a tip of the hat to his most important mentors, the salute signals Eastwood's intention to reflect upon the sort of terse, tough, hard-bitten characters he became famous for in their pictures, a man described here as being "as cold as the snow."

Eastwood's Bill Munny can be seen as a hypothetical portrait of the Man With No Name in his sunset years. A widower with two kids, Munny has nothing to show for wayward youth except a decrepit pig farm. When a hotshot named the "Schofield Kid" (Jaimz Woolvett) turns up offering to split a $1,000 reward being offered for the hides of two men

who gruesomely sliced up a prostitute, Munny reluctantly straps on his holster for the first time in more than a decade.

To the Kid's annoyance, Munny insists upon bringing along his former partner in crime (Morgan Freeman). Beating this group to their destination of Big Whiskey is railroad gunman English Bob (Richard Harris), an arrogant mythomaniac traveling with a biographer (Saul Rubinek) who memorializes his bloody accomplishments in dime novels.

Outlaws and bounty hunters around Big Whiskey face a problem by the name of Sheriff Little Bill Daggett (Gene Hackman), a brutal ex-badman who allows no one to carry guns in town.

Resolution to the leisurely but tightly wound drama comes not in an expected, standard showdown, but much more complexly, in a series of alternately tragic and touching confrontations.

Final shots — as the survivor of the climactic bloodbath rides off, not into the sunset, but into a nocturnal downpour — constitute a hauntingly poetic variation on the Western fadeout.

Eastwood's telling of this grim, compelling tale is at least as impressive as in his best prior outings as a director ("The Outlaw Josey Wales," "Bird," "White Hunter, Black Heart"). But the acting ensemble is stronger than in any previous Eastwood pic, and David Webb Peoples' resonant screenplay has inspired the filmmaker to fully develop several recurring themes in his work, which is what finally puts "Unforgiven" on such a high level in its genre.

The dilemma of the outlaw whose infamous past makes it hard for him to put down his guns has cropped up in many films, most notably "The Gunfighter," but Eastwood and Peoples' approach is bracingly antimythic and antiheroic.

As he comes ever closer to his rendezvous with the sheriff and his former self, he becomes increasingly physically ill until facing up to what he has to do. Along the way, Munny teaches the Kid a few things about what it means to shoot someone. After the countless people Eastwood characters have gunned down over the years, the pain and difficulty invested in each killing here lends them an extraordinary and profound weight.

Recurring Eastwood themes involving humiliation and physical pain are present, and a strong feminist streak runs through the center of the story. A close-knit group of hookers defy Sheriff Daggett in the first place and put up the reward money for their mutilated co-worker.

Playing a stubbly, worn-out, has-been outlaw who can barely mount his horse at first, Eastwood, unafraid to show his age, is outstanding in his best clipped, understated manner.

Hackman deliciously realizes the two sides of the sheriff's quicksilver personality, the folksy raconteur and the vicious sadist.

Freeman, whose race is never remarked upon by the other characters even though the Kid clearly resents him, poignantly portrays a man whose loyalty to his old partner wars with his common sense. Harris has a high old time looking mean and menacing.

Technically, film is also superior. Vet production designer Henry Bumstead has designed a distinctive old Western town, and lenser Jack Green's widescreen images have a natural, unforced beauty that imaginatively make use of the mostly flat expanses of the Alberta locations. Lennie Niehaus' lovely score is mournful and melodious.

Storytelling pace may seem a bit deliberate for short-attention-span youngsters, but the richness of the material fully merits the extended, expert treatment. Anyone with a taste for Western films and the myths born on the frontier will have a feast.

— *Todd McCarthy*

DIGGSTOWN

A Metro-Goldwyn-Mayer release of a Schaffel/Eclectic Films production. Produced by Robert Schaffel. Co-producer, Youssef Vahabzadeh. Line producer, Art Schaefer. Directed by Michael Ritchie. Screenplay, Steven McKay, based on Leonard Wise's novel "The Diggstown Rangers." Camera (DeLuxe color), Gerry Fisher; editor, Don Zimmerman; music, James Newton Howard; production design, Steve Hendrickson; art direction, Okowita; set design, Gregory Van Horn, Michael Devine; set decoration, Barbara Drake; costume design, Wayne A. Finkelman; sound (Dolby), Kim Harris Ornitz; associate producers, Sharon Roesler, McKay; assistant director, Tom Mack; fight coordinators, James Nickerson, Bobby Bass; casting, Rick Pagano, Sharon Bialy, Debi Manwiller. Reviewed at UA Coronet Theater, L.A., July 22, 1992. MPAA Rating: R. Running time: **97 MIN.**
Gabriel Caine . . . . . . .James Woods
"Honey" Roy Palmer . Louis Gossett Jr.
John Gillon . . . . Bruce Dern
Fitz . . . . Oliver Platt
Emily Forrester . . . Heather Graham
Wolf Forrester . . Randall (Tex) Cobb
Robby Gillon . . Thomas Wilson Brown
Hambone Busby . . . . . Duane Davis
Hammerhead Hagan . . . Willie Green
Victor Corsini . . . . Orestes Matacena

Blending elements of "Rocky" and "The Sting," this crowd-pleaser mixes it up with boxing, revenge and salty one-liners that should satisfy audiences, assuming MGM can convince anyone to see it. The unappealing title and ad campaign certainly aren't much incentive, so it's up to star appeal and positive word-of-mouth to fill arenas and save this well-oiled middleweight from a trip to Palookaville.

Story offers a simple premise and only slightly more elaborate scam, dropping or neglecting several plot points as it seeks to finish its roadwork in 97 minutes.

Few will mind, however, as the film recovers from sluggish early rounds with plenty of action in the second half, Steven McKay's screenplay jabbing away with jokes that connect frequently enough to carry through several dour sequences to a big and clever payoff.

James Woods demonstrates his trademark intensity along with a comic flair (a balance he tried less successfully in "The Hard Way") as a just-paroled hustler who sets up a big-money boxing match pitting his ringer "Honey" Roy Palmer (Louis Gossett Jr.) against any 10 men from the burg of Diggstown.

Like "The Sting," the target is truly despicable, and few can fit that description more capably than Bruce Dern, whose character stole the town from its citizens and rubs out anyone who crosses him.

All the trademark flourishes are there, including a couple of murders for motivation, a beautiful woman (Heather Graham) of little narrative consequence, a tenuous relationship between Dern and his son (a suddenly quite grown-up Thomas Wilson Brown), and Woods and Gossett's scam-gone-wrong history, leading to ample good-natured bickering.

Despite thinness of the material, director Michael Ritchie (whose sports-related pics include "Downhill Racer," "The Bad News Bears," "Semi-Tough" and "Wildcats") has done a solid job in building audience interest, getting amiable perfs out of his leads and colorful moments from supporting players.

The material is so familiar, in fact, that the filmmakers can drop or pick up story threads (the lack of relationship between Woods and Graham or late-arriving fa-

ther-son conflict) without it being obvious that the ideas haven't been developed.

Fight coordinators James Nickerson and Bobby Bass haven't broken any new ground, but the boxing sequences are compelling, and Gossett convincingly comes across as an aging brawler with a potent right cross.

With the exception of the narrative gaps, tech credits also go the distance, from Woods' garish wardrobe to James Newton Howard's brassy score. The question nevertheless remains whether MGM can sound its trumpets loud enough to put "Diggstown" on the map. — *Brian Lowry*

RAISING CAIN

A Universal Pictures release of a Pacific Western production. Produced by Gale Anne Hurd. Directed, written by Brian DePalma. Camera (Deluxe color), Stephen H. Burum; editors, Paul Hirsch, Bonnie Koehler, Robert Dalva; music, Pino Donaggio; production design, Doug Kraner; costume design, Bobbie Read; sound (Dolby), Nelson Stoll; assistant director, James Dyer; co-producer, Michael R. Joyce; casting, Pam Dixon. Reviewed at Worldwide 1 theater, N.Y., July 21, 1992. MPAA Rating: R. Running time: **95 MIN.**
Carter/Cain/Dr. Nix/
Josh/Margo . . . . . . John Lithgow
Jenny . . . . Lolita Davidovich
Jack . . . . Steven Bauer
Dr. Waldheim . . . Frances Sternhagen
Lt. Terri . . . . Gregg Henry
Sgt. Cally . . . . Tom Bower
Sarah . . . . Mel Harris
Also with: Teri Austin, Gabrielle Carteris, Barton Heyman, Amanda Pombo, Kathleen Callan.

Brian DePalma's thriller "Raising Cain" is a superficial, often risible, exercise in pure aesthetics that's likely to turn off mainstream audiences, spelling a fast flop. As a showcase for John Lithgow's acting talents and a visual tour de force, the film may delight the director's most camp followers.

As he succeeded the big-budget "Scarface" with 1984's scaled-back "Body Double," DePalma shifts gears from the notoriously overstuffed "The Bonfire of the Vanities" to make a modest-budget ($11 million) shocker.

With new wife and highly successful producer Gale Anne Hurd partnered, the film could reasonably be expected to be more commercial. Instead DePalma the writer is so self-indulgent with cute homages and in-jokes that the bravura stagings by DePalma the director are merely ends in themselves. It's a fatal case of playing to the buffs.

Though there are plenty of

nods to Alfred Hitchcock's 1960 "Psycho" here, DePalma's point of departure is Michael Powell's classic "Peeping Tom" (also released in 1960), in which a scientist experimented on his young son, causing him to grow up as a psychotic killer.

Lithgow portrays both scientist and son, among several other contrasting roles, in an impressive display of surface acting skills. Like the rest of the cast, there's no depth to his showy turns.

Lithgow's central role is Carter, a milquetoast of a child psychologist who dotes on his young daughter Amy, even rigging a closed-circuit TV surveilliance system at home to keep tabs on her. Film begins promisingly with daylit horror, as the meek Carter turns suddenly sinister, attacking a family friend (Teri Austin) to kidnap her young son. He's almost apprehended with her unconscious behind the wheel of her car when out of nowhere his alter ego, twin brother Cain, pops up to save the day and take over Carter's identity.

It seems that 20 years ago their father, Dr. Nix (also played by Lithgow with convincing make-up job) was performing experiments in child development that required a control group of five kids. The doc fled the country after being arrested for attempted child buying.

Now Carter and Cain are rounding up five kids, including Carter's daughter, for their dad who's returned to America to complete his experiments. Instead of buying kids, they're ruthlessly killing whoever's minding each child.

That's the stuff of scary melodrama, especially with children in jeopardy. Unfortunately, DePalma fails to deliver real fright or titillation to his target audience, instead opting for satire; hence, the desperate ad campaign lamely declaring "De Mented, De Ranged, De Ceptive, De Palma."

Pic loses its footing midway through with the introduction of a spoofed romantic subplot involving Carter's wife Lolita Davidovich and her old flame, Steven Bauer. Using awkwardly inserted (on purpose) and very showy flashbacks, DePalma deconstructs his narrative and has trouble regaining momentum.

Lithgow elaborately frames Bauer for his murders of mothers and babysitters in the film's cleverest plotting. Davidovich's many nightmare wakeup scenes serve to involve the viewer in a game of deciding which obviously bizarre footage is real and which is a dream, somewhat like John Landis' "An American Werewolf in London." However, when Davidovich keeps coming back after Lithgow has apparently killed her (recalling the famous ending of DePalma's "Carrie"), "Raising Cain" lapses into farce.

En route to a couple of audience-groaning anticlimaxes, film is sustained by Lithgow's multiple personalities, allowing him to portray a nutty Norwegian father; a 7-year-old (Josh); a sinister woman (Margo) and the two contrasting twins.

DePalma's trademark mobile camera, executed colorfully by cinematographer Stephen H. Burum and two Steadicam operators, is used for lengthy takes, including an "in and out of an elevator" homage to Orson Welles' "Touch of Evil." At one point, nutty scientist Frances Sternhagen (in terrific comic form) is rattling off ridiculous exposition to cop Gregg Henry in an endless walk and talk scene and Henry catches himself before breaking out laughing, typical of pic's nod-and-wink approach.

With a romantic and suspenseful score by Pino Donaggio, it's a shame the director didn't make the emotional investment to play straight the Davidovich/Bauer coupling or Lithgow's predicaments. In Paul Schrader-scripted "Obsession" (also featuring Lithgow), DePalma proved he could handle honest sentiment without sending it up. Here he tips the balance towards self-satire. — *Lawrence Cohn*

WHISPERS IN THE DARK

A Paramount release of a Martin Bregman production. Produced by Bregman, Michael S. Bregman. Executive producers, Eric Freiser, Richard Gitelson, William Link, Andrew Deane. Co-producer, Stephen F. Kesten. Directed, written by Christopher Crowe. Camera (Duart color; Deluxe prints), Michael Chapman; editor, Bill Pankow; music, Thomas Newman; production design, John Jay Moore; set decoration, Justin Scoppa Jr.; costume design, John Dunn; sound (Dolby), Allan Byer; assistant director, Anthony H. Gittelson; 2nd unit director, David Ellis; additional camera, Richard J. Quinlan; 2nd unit camera, Michael Benson; casting, Mary Colquhoun. Reviewed at Paramount Studios, L.A., July 30, 1992. MPAA rating: R. Running time: **102 MIN.**
Ann Hecker . . . . . Annabella Sciorra
Doug McDowell . . . . Jamey Sheridan
Morgenstern . . . . Anthony LaPaglia
Sarah Green . . . . Jill Clayburgh
Johnny C. . . . . John Leguizamo
Eve Abergray . . . . . Deborah Unger
Leo Green . . . . Alan Alda

Paul . . . . Anthony Heald
Mrs. McDowell . . Jacqueline Brookes
Billy O'Meara . . . . . . Gene Canfield

A turn-off psycho-sexual thriller, "Whispers in the Dark" grows steadily more absurd by the reel until literally stumbling into the ocean at its climax. Sneak-previewed Aug. 1 in advance of this weekend's opening, this one seems a dubious bet for good word-of-mouth, although presence of Annabella Sciorra in a follow-up suspenser to her "The Hand That Rocks the Cradle" hit might be promotable in the short run.

Looking pale and vulnerable, Sciorra this time essays a meek Gotham shrink who begins getting turned on by the tales of bondage and great sex confided to her by patient Deborah Unger, a disturbing development she confesses to her professional mentor, Alan Alda.

Ending a relationship with b.f. Anthony Heald, Sciorra begins falling for straight-arrow pilot Jamey Sheridan, but then, in a major coincidence, discovers that Sheridan is the sex partner Unger so deliciously describes in her session. In a tiff, Unger makes off with some of Sciorra's private files and tapes but, before you can say ropes and handcuffs, Sciorra finds Unger murdered in her gallery.

As it happens, Sciorra is also treating disturbed Latino artist John Leguizamo, whose penchant for painting angels he then desecrates may carry over into his personal treatment of women.

Detective Anthony LaPaglia develops a thing for Sciorra while investigating the case, and it all devolves into a guessing game over which of these men killed Unger and may or may not be threatening Sciorra.

Some initial interest is generated by the intensely erotic performance of Unger, who during one office visit feels compelled to strip and masturbate in front of her shrink as a physical correlative to her emotional nakedness, and by the unavoidable voyeuristic appeal of the numerous private sexual revelations.

But a succession of psychiatric sessions do not a plot make, and writer-director Christopher Crowe nudges the picture along a very narrow track without coupling the viewer to the train. One is supposed to be in Sciorra's corner all the way, but her character is so wimpy and unassertive that she doesn't engage one's enthusiasm, and her lethar-

gy in the face of so much jeopardy becomes a cloud of negative energy. Pages of dialogue devoted to issue of doctor-patient confidentiality also feel like excess baggage.

Although Michael Chapman's prowling, sinuous camera moves create some initial mood and mystery, Crowe ultimately exhibits a draggy, unmodulated style that is cold and allows the climactic confrontation between Sciorra and her predator to seem risible. Script and performances don't allow even a glint of humor anywhere.

With the exception of Unger, thesping is no more than okay. Alda makes a rare straight dramatic appearance in a supporting role as a psychiatric honcho, with Jill Clayburgh on board as his concerned wife. Tech contributions are modest.
— *Todd McCarthy*

BEBE'S KIDS
(ANIMATED)

A Paramount release of a Hudlin Bros./Hyperion Studio production. Produced by Willard Carroll, Thomas L. Wilhite. Co-producer, David R. Cobb. Executive producers, Reginald Hudlin, Warrington Hudlin. Directed by Bruce Smith. Animation directors, Lennie Graves, Chris Buck, Frans Vischer. Screenplay, Reginald Hudlin, based on characters created by Robin Harris. Deluxe color; editor, Lynne Southerland; music, John Barnes; production design, Fred Cline; art direction, Doug Walker; sound (Dolby), Robert L. Harman, Jerry Clemans, Dan Hiland; associate producer, Southerland; assistant director, Michael Serrian; casting, Eileen Knight. Reviewed at Plaza Theater, West L.A., July 30, 1992. MPAA Rating: PG-13. Running time: **73 MIN.**
Voices of:
Robin Harris . . . . Faizon Love
Jamika . . . . . Vanessa Bell Calloway
Leon . . . . Wayne Collins
LaShawn . . . . Jonell Green
Kahlil . . . . Marques Houston
Pee Wee . . . . Tone Loc
Dorothea . . . . Myra J.
Vivian . . . . Nell Carter

Based on a comedy routine by the late Robin Harris about his encounters with some "bad-ass kids" from the inner city, "Bebe's Kids" is a sassy, good-looking animated pic aimed effectively at the African-American family audience. Blended with broad sight gags is a pointed message about the resentment of latchkey kids who, echoing Aretha Franklin, proclaim that they don't get any "R-E-S-P-E-C-T."

Harris' nightclub and record routine was being developed as a live-action pic by the Hudlin Bros. before Harris' death in 1990.

Filmed bits of the routine under the credits lead into a Reginald Hudlin-scripted cartoon version of the roly-poly Harris, a smooth-talking, endearing character whose cynical exterior conceals a genuine affection for children.

Influenced by Kenyan art and the paintings of Harlem Renaissance artists, director Bruce Smith's pic for Hudlin/Hyperion evocatively captures the subdued, menacing urban landscapes and the flamboyant shapes of the amusement park visited by Harris with his saucy lady friend Jamika and four kids, three of them belonging to her absent friend Bebe.

Though Bebe's kids are terrors, cutting a destructive swath through the park, the viewer gradually comes to recognize the reasons they have such massive chips on their shoulders. Their rebellion against the regimentation of the Disneyland-like amusement park and the menacing white security force also engenders growing sympathy, mixed with exasperation, in both Harris and the audience.

Playing with "Bebe's Kids" is director Matthew O'Callaghan's Hyperion short "The Itsy Bitsy Spider," a frenetic example of cartoon overkill about an exterminator's calamitous attempts to do away with a pesky household arachnid. — *Joseph McBride*

BUFFY THE VAMPIRE SLAYER

A 20th Century Fox release of a Sandollar/Kuzui Enterprises production. Produced by Kaz Kuzui, Howard Rosenman. Executive producers, Sandy Gallin, Carol Baum, Fran Rubel Kuzui. Co-producer, Dennis Stuart Murphy. Directed by Fran Rubel Kuzui. Screenplay, Joss Whedon. Camera (Deluxe color), James Hayman; editors, Camilla Toniolo, Jill Savitt; music, Carter Burwell; production design, Lawrence Miller; art direction, James Barrows, Randy Moore; set decoration, Claire Bowin; costume design, Marie France; sound (Dolby), Steve Aaron; associate producer, Alex Butler; assistant director, Josh King; stunt coordinator-2nd unit director, Terry J. Leonard; additional camera, Tim Surhstedt; casting, Johanna Ray. Reviewed at Avco Cinema, L.A., July 29, 1992. MPAA Rating: PG-13. Running time: **86 MIN.**
Buffy . . . . Kristy Swanson
Merrick . . . . . . Donald Sutherland
Amilyn . . . . Paul Reubens
Lothos . . . . Rutger Hauer
Pike . . . . Luke Perry
Jennifer . . . . Michele Abrams
Kimberly . . . . Hilary Swank
Nicole . . . . Paris Vaughan
Benny . . . . David Arquette
Jeffrey . . . . Randall Batinkoff
Buffy's Mom . . . . Candy Clark
Also with: Andrew Lowery, Sasha Jenson, Stephen Root, Natasha Gregson Wagner, Mark DeCarlo.

"Buffy the Vampire Slayer" is a bloodless comic resurrection of the undead that goes serious just when it should get wild and woolly. The marginal buoyancy of the opening reels quickly disappears from this threadbare (reportedly only $7 million) production, more effective as a sendup of Valley girls than as a clever take on bloodsuckers. Still, attractive young cast with plenty of teen appeal and a smart, vigorous ad campaign look to rouse some perky numbers before the next full moon hits in a couple of weeks.

Vampire hunting is not exactly the sport of choice at Hemery High in the San Fernando Valley, where blonde, bouncy Buffy (Kristy Swanson) is lead cheerleader and Miss Popular in the senior class. Early scenes of Buffy and her vacuous girlfriends making the rounds at the mall and issuing putdowns in Valleyspeak possess a certain amusement value and will stand as points of identification for much of the intended audience.

But just as vampires live through the ages, so, apparently, do female vampire slayers. A dirty old man in a long overcoat (Donald Sutherland) turns up to inform Buffy that she is one of this breed and requests that she accompany him to a graveyard, where she passes her trial by fire with flying colors when she subdues two marauding cretins.

For awhile, dates with her slay trainer have to compete for her time with cheerleading practice, but when it becomes apparent that L.A. is under threat of a serious vampire invasion led by king Rutger Hauer and cackling henchman Paul Reubens, Buffy dives into an Olympian workout regimen to sharpen her skills with a stake.

Unfortunately, what meager humorous elements can be found in first-timer Joss Whedon's screenplay vanish at this point, so that even those who go in primed to enjoy this disposable diversion will feel deflated by the end. After biting a few teens and menacing Buffy and her would-be b.f. (Luke Perry), the vampires crash a high school dance in a limp rehash of the big set-piece in "Carrie." Vampires are vanquished but will surely return to molest Buffy in college if grosses warrant a sequel.

Swanson has a robust, athletic sexiness that will keep boy viewers happy, while the amiable Per-

ry, in his first screen appearance since hitting with "Beverly Hills, 90210," will make this a must-see for many adolescent girls. The convoluted language of Buffy's air-headed clique constitutes the main source of laughs regardless of gender or age.

Hired to replace Joan Chen in the role of the No. 2 vampire, a manic, bearded, shaggy Reubens mainly gets to bare his fangs and snarl a lot but does enact some amusingly protracted death throes. Sutherland walks through this one, while the usually reliable Hauer is colorless.

Technically, this is bargain basement stuff for a major studio feature. Director Fran Rubel Kuzui, whose previous credit was the so-so indie "Tokyo Pop," keeps her camera subjects very close to the lens and aims to accomplish no more than one piece of action per shot. Pic's style is rudimentary, while tone goes flat when it should expand into greater dementia and comedic terror. — *Todd McCarthy*

CRISIS IN THE KREMLIN

A Concorde Pictures release. Executive producer, Roger Corman. Produced by Steven Rabiner. Directed by Jonathan Winfrey. Screenplay, Jonathan Fernandez, Daryl Haney, Catherine Cyran, based on Matt Leipzig's story. Camera (Foto-Kem color), Krassimir Kostov, Mike Wojokowski (L.A.); editor, Nina Gilberti; music, Stephan Dimitrov; sound, Vladimir Sivriev, Chris Taylor (L.A.); production design, Maria Ivanova, Aaron Osborne (L.A.); costume design, Leesa Evans; 2nd unit director, Brian Rudnick; stunt coordinator, Svetolsav Ivanov; casting, Rabiner. Reviewed on New Horizons videocassette, N.Y., July 19, 1992. MPAA Rating: R. Running time: **85 MIN.**

Jack Reilly . . . . Robert Rusler
Leo . . . . Theodore Bikel
Yanina . . . . Denise Bixler
Vlad . . . . Doug Wert
Ambrazis . . . . Stephan Danailov
Gen. Chernov . . . . . Borris Loukanov
Boris . . . . Jocko Rositch
Vytas . . . . George Novakov
Father Andris . . . . Stoycho Mazgalov

The attempted coup last year in the former Soviet Union is fodder for an okay low-budget actioner "Crisis in the Kremlin." Originally titled "Red Target," pic benefits from atmospheric location filming.

Robert Rusler toplines as a young CIA agent who's sent from Moscow to Vilnius to foil a supposed plot by Lithuanian freedom fighters to kill Gorbachev. Quickly it's learned that evil Soviet Gen. Chernov (Borris Loukanov) is behind the plot, with

an honest Lithuanian boy Vlad (Doug Wert) chosen as the hitman.

Amidst some exciting chase scenes shot in Bulgaria, Russia and Germany, Rusler teams up with Vlad's sister-in-law Yanina (Denise Bixler) to head off the killer. Theodore Bikel guest stars as a former KGB operative.

Vlad's escapes are unbelievable, mainly inserted to keep the pot boiling. A happy ending is contrived that reflects the increasing difficulty of finding suitable bad guys in post-Cold War thrillers.

Jonathan Winfrey, who's worked his way up in Roger Corman's Concorde school of filmmaking, directs competently and humorlessly. Cast is adequate though several supporting players are crudely dubbed.
— *Lawrence Cohn*

UN LUGAR EN EL MUNDO
(A PLACE IN THE WORLD)
(ARGENTINIAN)

A Transmundo presentation of a Cooperative production. Produced, directed by Adolfo Aristarain. Screenplay, Aristarain, Alberto Lecchi, from story by Aristarain, Kathy Saavedra. Camera (color), Ricardo De Angelis; music, Patricio Kauderer; art director, Abel Facello. Reviewed at Ambassador theater, Buenos Aires, April 9, 1992. Running time: **95 MIN.**

With: José Sacristán, Federico Luppi, Cecilia Roth, Leonor Benedetto, Gastón Batyi, Rodolfo Ranni, Hugo Arana.

Adolfo Aristarain's latest opus, the best Argentine film in many moons, looks at people who, having fought for a better world, are in the aftermath of defeat. Whatever political meaning pic might have had is secondary to a highly entertaining story briskly told in touching human terms.

Federico Luppi plays a teacher who is back from a long exile he shared with his doctor wife Cecilia Roth. Both are living with teen son Gastón Batyi in a San Luis valley 700 miles away from Buenos Aires. While baking bread for his poor pupils, Luppi inspires and leads a community effort aimed at getting fair prices for the farmers' output, sidestepping ruthless landowner Rodolfo Ranni.

Roth, meanwhile, devotes herself to her neighbors' health, aided by Leonor Benedetto, a strong-willed nun always dressed in civilian clothes, and José Sacristán,

a Spanish geologist whose cynicism thaws as he understands the ethics of his new friends.

The characters and conflicts that keep the story moving fluently are reminisced in flashback by Batyi. The son also recalls his first romance with Lorena De Río, a coming of age troubled by the jealousy of her father Hugo Arana, Ranni's fiery foreman. Pic has some suspenseful and funny action parts.

Aristarain assembled an outstanding cast to convey the characters' inner stength, down-to-earth behavior and sharp dialogue. The countryside's autumnal visuals match the mood of the music played by the renowned Camerata Bariloche and, together with the tight editing, add key pieces to a seamless picture.
— *Domingo Di Nubila*

UDJU AZUL DI YONTA
(YONTA'S BLUE EYES)
(GUINEA BISSAU)

A Vermedia production (Lisbon). Produced by Paul De Sousa. Directed by Flora Gomes. Screenplay, Gomes, Ina Cesar, David Lang, Manuel Rambout Barcelos. Camera (color), Dominique Gentil; editor, Dominique Paris; music, Adriano Ferreira. Reviewed at Cannes Film Festival (Un Certain Regard), May 17, 1992. Running time: **95 MIN.**
Yonta . . . . Maysa Marta
Vicente . . . . . Antonio Simao Mendes
Ze . . . . Pedro Dias
Also with: Bia Gomes, Dina Vaz, Mohamed Seidi.

In "Yonta's Blue Eyes," an offbeat, lilting film with a dreamy, quasi-Caribbean rhythm, Guinea Bissau director Flora Gomes uses a simple tale about a smart and pretty girl to assess the progress his country has made on its long march to independence. The story is clear enough to allow offshore audience appreciation.

The captivating Yonta (Maysa Marta) is in love with an older man who ignores her, while she overlooks a worthy youth who cares. The man she's after is Vicente, the politically preoccupied manager of a local fish wholesaler more interested in locating a missing comrade-in-arms than romance.

The boy Ze has come from the countryside to study and becomes Vicente's chauffeur to support himself. Yonta is enthralled by a poetic love letter he sends her anonymously, and she sets out to find the sender. In the end, both Yonta and Vicente find the people they want, but their discoveries are anticlimactic and disappointing.

Gomes has no problem showing the hedonistic, laughing side of the city, where people walk down the street seemingly in time with the excellent score, and the women's costumes are entertainment in themselves. Yonta's joie de vivre (and that of her Bart-like little brother) keep story light and rolling.

Moreover, Gomes succeeds in smoothly melding youthful fun with somber events, such as an old lady's eviction and Vicente's tormented memories of the independence struggle against the Portuguese. In her natural wisdom, Yonta's able to bridge these two poles effortlessly; laugh and enjoy life while being part of a struggling new society.

Pic, third feature film ever made in Guinea Bissau, is rife with clever devices to recall the nation's history. Pic opens with a slew of 6-year-olds rolling tires with years painted on them, a gag showing that 18 years have rolled by since the country's independence. — *Deborah Young*

BECOMING COLETTE
(U.S.-GERMAN)

An Intercontinental Releasing Corp. presentation of a Bibo Film Prods./BC Prods./Les Films Ariane S.A. production. Produced by Heinz J. Bibo, Peer J. Oppenheimer. Executive producers, Todd Black, Kathryn Galan, Joe Wizan. Supervising producer, Konstantin Thoeren. Directed by Danny Huston. Screenplay, Ruth Graham; screenplay revision, Burt Weinshanker. Camera (Technicolor), Wolfgang Treu; editors, Peter Taylor, Roberto Silvi; music, John Scott; production design, Jan Schlubach, Serge Douy; costumes, Barbara Baum; sound (THX Dolby), Axel Arft; choreographer, Andy Lucas; assistant directors, Eva-Maria Schoenecker, Simon Moseley. Reviewed at WorldFest/Houston, May 3, 1992. Running time: **97 MIN.**
Henri Gauthier-Villars
. . . . Klaus Maria Brandauer
Sidonie Gabrielle Colette
. . . . Mathilda May
Polaire . . . . Virginia Madsen
Chapo . . . . Paul Rhys
Albert . . . . John van Dreelen
Captain . . . . . . Jean Pierre Aumont
Sido . . . . Lucienne Hamon
Creditor . . . . Georg Tryphon

Not even Klaus Maria Brandauer's twinkly eyed, scenestealing turn is enough to enliven "Becoming Colette," a lumbering period drama based on the early life of novelist Sidonie Gabrielle Colette. Danny Huston's sophomore feature (after "Mr. North") is lovely to look at but dramatically inert. International TV market may be its most fitting venue.

Episodic script is structured as an extended flashback, with Colette (Mathilda May) recalling her salad days after spotting her ex-husband (Brandauer) in the audience during one of her avantgarde theater performances.

Back in a small French town in the early 1890s, her financially pressed father allowed her marriage to Henri Gauthier-Villars, better known as Willy, a rakish publisher who swept her away to Paris. Until she split from Willy in 1904, he kept her in virtual literary bondage, forcing her to write erotic novels that were published under his pseudonym. (He rationalized that Paris readers would never accept such stuff from a woman author.) She began writing as Colette in 1916.

Playing like a truncated feature version of an epic miniseries, pic sporadically spices up its rote recapitulation of facts with the sort of high-gloss, softcore steaminess that used to be Radley Metzger's stock-in-trade. A nude love scene with Colette and a music-hall performer (Virginia Madsen, the director's wife) suddenly becomes three-part harmony when Willy joins in.

With scenes like that, the pic might have been campy fun if Huston and company had dropped the literary pretense. Pic struggles to make some sort of feminist statement about Colette's determination to publish her stories under her own name and gain the literary recognition she deserves.

May's performance simply isn't compelling enough to generate empathy or admiration. Madsen is much livelier and more engaging in a smaller role. Brandauer is hugely enjoyable in a perf that could be labeled Swift's Premium and sold by the pound.

Paul Rhys, Jean Pierre Aumont and John van Dreelen are among the notables briefly glimpsed in the margins. Everybody — stars, supporting actors, bit players, walk-ons — seems to have a different accent.

Pic was handsomely lensed by Wolfgang Treu in Berlin (mostly interiors at CCC Studios) and Bordeaux. Unfortunately, the scenes set in the famed Moulin Rouge only serve to remind audiences of a much better pic by the director's father. Other tech credits, especially Barbara Baum's costumes, are first-rate.
— *Joe Leydon*

LE ZÈBRE
(THE ODDBALL)
(FRENCH)

A Bac Films release of a Lambart Prods./TF-1 Films co-production. Produced by Thierry de Ganay. Executive producer, Monique Guerrier. Directed by Jean Poiret. Screenplay, Poiret, in collaboration with Martin Lamotte, based on Alexandre Jardin's novel. Camera (color, Panavision), Eduardo Serra; editor, Catherine Kelber; music, Jean-Claude Petit; costumes, Caroline de Vivaize, Florence Desouches; sound, Alain Lachassagnes. Reviewed at Forum Horizon, Paris, June 28, 1992. Running time: **94 MIN.**
Hippolyte . . . . . . Thierry Lhermitte
Camille . . . . Caroline Cellier
Grégoire . . . . Christian Pereira
Nathalie . . . . Carine Lemaire
Laurent . . . . Walter Allouch

In "Le Zèbre," a successful notary's aggressive unpredictability keeps his 15-year marriage fresh. Only film directed by accomplished actor/playwright Jean Poiret, who died in March, is an offbeat love story played with charm and enthusiasm by attractive leads. Effortless comic timing leading to a bittersweet twist suggests possible art house exposure beyond France.

Thierry Lhermitte is solidly entertaining as an inventive fellow determined to be urbanely wacky in everything. In handling premarital pacts and divorces, he's seen first-hand the end of the spark in even the most promising romances, and so he's made it his mission to sustain courtship-intensity passion with his wife.

In the name of constant excitement, Lhermitte puts his marriage in jeopardy with elaborate pranks, including threatening to leave his wife (Caroline Cellier) to see if she'll be upset, and recklessly driving their car into a lake to see if she's "willing to die" for him.

Cellier (helmer Poiret's wife of 22 years) is never bored by hubby's antics but would gladly settle for less originality and more peace and quiet. Plot thickens when she starts to receive anonymous love letters and considers a tryst with her secret admirer.

Perfectly matched as the bright and loving spouses, Lhermitte and Cellier never hit a false note as they cover emotional territory ranging from glee to despair, good-natured exasperation to grief.

Poiret, "La Cage aux Folles" playwright and long-time co-star

with Michel Serrault, obviously understood actors and displayed fine control over the shifting material. Film can also be looked at as a parting gift to Cellier, an excellent stage and screen actress who has been underutilized in films. — *Lisa Nesselson*

WADECK'S MOTHER'S FRIEND'S SON
(B&W-16m)

An Accordion Films presentation. (Intl. sales: Claude Rae.) Produced by Andrew Fierberg. Co-producer (France), Michel Mauros. Directed, written by Arnold Barkus. Camera (Duart b &w; Bucks Motion Picture Labs prints), Mike Spiller; additional camera, Greg Watkins, Laetitia Merson; editor, Cedric Kahn; music, Jonathan Sampson; decor-costumes, Brigitte Corbiar; sound, Olivier Do Huu. Reviewed at Monica 4-Plex, Santa Monica, Calif., June 27, 1992. (In AFI/L.A. FilmFest.) Running time: **87 MIN.**
Anton . . . . Arnold Barkus
Wadeck/Alex . . . . . . Ranko Chepin
Barbara . . . . Zazie Dinev
Guy . . . . Dominic Gould

"Wadeck's Mother's Friend's Son" neatly crosses downtown New York hipsterism with a vaguely absurdist Eastern European sensibility, giving rise to a genially offbeat romantic comedy of societal displacement. Despite obvious low budget and technical limitations, a venturesome distrib could probably get a little mileage out of this with shrewd handling in top urban markets and university towns.

Writer-director Arnold Barkus toplines as Anton, a naive, obnoxious Polish sailor who invades the lives of two other foreigners: comely Parisienne Barbara and her antic, overbearing Polish roommate, Wadeck.

Barbara's Lower East Side apartment is too small for all of them, so crazed Wadeck soon departs. Unwanted and without prospects in the U.S., nutty Anton conveniently manages to miss his boat back to Poland.

When Barbara faces a visa crisis that will soon mean her expulsion from the U.S., Anton swings into action, towing her around and asking every guy on the street if he'll marry her.

Somewhat surprisingly, this approach works, after a fashion, and the three immigrants — along with Barbara's rich and strange new husband — eventually find themselves, in a melancholy but hopeful mood, on the lush but rather inhospitable terrain of California.

The specter of Jim Jarmusch, and particularly "Stranger Than Paradise," looms unavoidably: low-rent but carefully composed black & white images, cuts timed for their offbeat comic rhythms, foreign characters and below-Houston Street settings. And "Wadeck" also started life as a half-hour short and became a feature only after Barkus had raised more coin over a couple of years.

Setting the film apart are spritely performances by Barkus, initially irritating but ultimately winning as the bell-bottomed, goateed, irrepressible Anton, and the sweet-faced Zazie Dinev as the game, lively Barbara.

Of particular note is the outstanding soundtrack — and not just Jonathan Sampson's distinctive score. Subtle city sounds and noises have intelligently and humorously been laid over certain scenes, considerably enriching pic's texture.

Story turn involving Barbara's marriage makes little sense from the man's p.o.v., and many scenes exist entirely for their modestly whimsical import. But Barkus displays a definite knack for writing, directing and performing off-kilter comedy, and he should be heard from again.
— Todd McCarthy

SATURDAY NIGHT, SUNDAY MORNING:
THE TRAVELS OF GATEMOUTH MOORE
(DOCU-COLOR/B&W)

A Co-Media production. Produced, directed by Louis Guida. Camera (color/b&w), Richard Gordon; editor, David Carnochan; sound-lighting, Tim Callahan. Reviewed at American Film Institute, L.A., June 3, 1992. (In AFI/L.A. FilmFest.) Running time: **65 MIN.**
With: The Rev. A.D. (Gatemouth) Moore, B.B. King, Al Green, Rufus Thomas, Benjamin Hooks.

A gently reverential commemoration of an almost-forgotten life, Louis Guida's "Saturday Night, Sunday Morning" offers a look at the remarkable story of blues singer-turned-minister A.D. (Gatemouth) Moore. Low-key but original docu has some limited potential on the film festival circuit and public TV.

Moore was a nationally prominent band singer when he experienced religious conversion in a Chicago night club in 1949 and quit his career. Heading back to the Mississippi River Delta, he forged a new life as an evangelical preacher.

Composed of a series of engaging recollections, docu is held together by a lengthy interview with Moore as he drives across the Deep South. He has devoted most of his life to traveling (always in a Cadillac), first as singer, than as a revival leader and gospel minister.

At 16, Moore ran away from small-town Kansas and began to perform. In 1934, he hit Beale Street, Memphis' black culture center, soon learning the meaning of TBA (tough on black artists). In the next decade, he penned such hits as "Did You Ever Love a Woman," written for his beloved first wife, and "I Ain't Mad at You, Pretty Baby."

B.B. King describes Moore as "the greatest blues singer ever." NAACP director and Memphis minister Benjamin Hooks believes Moore would have become a national sensation if his showbiz career had started later.

Aptly titled pic explores the interplay between the secular (Saturday night) and spiritual (Sunday morning), two symbols that capture the essence of Moore's life as well as the vitality and tension of African-American culture in the South. Scenes alternate between present and past, the sacred and profane, underscoring the two irreconcilable chapters in Moore's life.

Modest-looking film doesn't really delve into the context of Moore's religious conversion, but it impressively imparts the transformation of a man who has found a new mission and peace of mind.
— Emanuel Levy

LABYRINTH
(GERMAN)

An Art Oko Filmproduction/Karel Dirka/David Braun Prods. presentation. (Intl. sales: Newberger Entertainment Group.) Produced by Dirka, Braun. Directed by Jaromil Jires. Screenplay, Jires, Alex Koenigsmark, Hans-Jorg Weyhmuller. Camera (color), Ivan Vojnar; editor, Alois Fisarek; music, Lubos Fiser; production design, Boris Halmi; art direction, Jiri Bartu; costumes, Jan Kropacek, Petra Barochova; sound, Antonin Kravka; assistant director, Helena Brown; casting, Stephanie Hanau. Reviewed in L.A., June 17, 1992. (In AFI/L.A. FilmFest.) Running time: **90 MIN.**
Maximilian Schell . . . . Himself
Franz Kafka . . . Christopher Chaplin
Also with: Christian Thuri, Milos Kopecky, Vlastimil Brodsky, Antonie Miklikova, Daniel Margolius.
(In German; English subtitles)

"Labyrinth" is a very specialized, intellectually bracing investigation of the connection between the fictional world of Franz Kafka and the historical persecution of the Jews culminating in the Holocaust. Rarefied subject and structural format recalling a one-man theater piece will prevent this from going very far on the global art house circuit, but fests and venues favoring Jewish themes should take note.

Framing his intense drama with recitations of the human rights denied to Jews under the Third Reich, vet Czech helmer Jaromil Jires creates the alter ego of Maximilian Schell as director moving to Prague to prep a film about Kafka.

Living in a small apartment overlooking a labyrinthine cemetery, Schell announces he's looking for Kafka's "Rosebud" and feels compelled to conduct abundant research since he is not Jewish. This takes him back, via re-creations and, eventually, archival footage, through the mistreatment and persecution of the Jews dating from the 13th century, then on to a succession of Jewish rituals as represented by incidents in the life of Kafka's family.

Pic moves into more surreal and gripping territory as Schell/Jires tries to link the origins of the writer's feelings of persecution with his artistically unique expression of them. Staging scenes of Nazi inquisition and torture evoking famous passages in Kafka's fiction, Jires posits Kafka as a prophet of — or sort of pre-witness to — the Holocaust.

For audiences interested in Kafka and Jewish history, pic provides food for thought and a reasonably stimulating p.o.v. But its narrow focus borders on the academic and obscure, and absence of characters in the normal sense gives the viewer only Schell's inquiring mind to latch onto. This is fine for some, but will leave others out in the cold.

Film is quite beautifully made, and Schell outstandingly varies his moods and readings to sustain interest in what amounts to a solo performance. Christopher Chaplin, a son of Charlie, stands in effectively in the largely symbolic role of Kafka.
— Todd McCarthy

VAMPIRE HUNTER D
(JAPANESE-ANIMATED)

A Streamline Pictures release from Epic/Sony, Movie Inc. & CBS Sony Group of an Ashi production. Produced by Hiroshi Kato, Mitsuhisa Koeda, Yukio Nagasaki. Executive producers, Shigeo Maruyama, Yutaka Takahashi. Directed by Toyoo Ashida. English-language version produced, directed by Carl Macek. Screenplay, Yasushi Hirano; adaptation, Macek; English dialogue, Tom Wyner; music director, Noriyoshi Matsuura; art direction, Ashida; character design, Yoshitaka Amano; sound, Deb Adair. Reviewed on Streamline vidcassette, N.Y., June 13, 1992. Running time: **76 MIN.**
Voices of: Michael McConnohie, Barbara Goodson, Jeff Winkless, Edie Mirman, Kerrigan Mahan, Steve Kramer, Steve Bulen, Joyce Kurtz, Lara Cody, Tom Syner, Kirk Thornton.
(English-dubbed; also available in Japanese with English subtitles)

This imaginative Japanese cartoon for adults is an atmospheric title for horror fans, imported in subtitled form for specialized bookings and a well-dubbed video version.

Set in the distant future, feudal tale has the stoic hero D turning out to be a "vampyr," a human/vampire composite hunting the race of evil vampires led by Count Magnus Lee and his beautiful daughter Anneka, descendants of Count Dracula.

D's gory adventures are animated with gusto by Toyoo Ashida, who also includes brief nude scenes that definitely brand this as non-kiddie fare.

Apocalyptic climax has Anneka stressing her nobility, choosing to end her family's line rather than tolerate the count's mating with commoners.

Story is told from the point-of-view of wholesome youngsters Doris and her brother Dan, leading to a rather silly "Shane"-emulating ending. Impressive backdrops and action scenes mark the way.

The English dialog is a bit glib, but otherwise Carl Macek and Tom Wyner's American adaptation is serviceable. Film was originally produced and released in Japan in 1985.
— Lawrence Cohn

THE FLYING SNEAKER
(CZECHOSLOVAKIAN-CANADIAN)

A Kratky Film Praha/Les Prods. La Fete co-production. Produced by Rock Demers, Bedrich Strand, Zdenek Polak. Directed by Bretislav Pojar. Screenplay, Pojar, Jiri Fried. Camera (color), Ervin Sanders, Vladimir Malik; editor,

Alois Fisarek; music, Petr Skoumal; art direction, Vladimir Labsky, Tomas Moravec; costumes, Jitka Moravcoca-Polednova; special effects, Zdenek Pospisil; puppet creator-head animator, Pojar; puppet animation, Jan Klos, Vlasta Pospisilova; cartoonist, Paval Koutsky; sound, Ivo Spal, Lumir Turek. Reviewed at Cannes Film Festival market, May 15, 1991. Running time: **90 MIN.**

Alec . . . . Ludek Navratil
Lucy . . . . Katka Pokorna
Alec's mother . . Katerina Machackova
Alec's father . . . . . Jaromir Hanzlik
Alec's grandfather . . . . Lubor Tokos
Dr. Renc . . . . . . Vlastimil Brodsky
Teacher . . . Jaroslava Kretschmerova
Principal . . . . Jirina Jiraskova
Lucy's mother . . . . Lenka Skopalova
Lucy's father . . . . . . Jan Hrvsinsky

Vet Czech animator Bretislav Pojar makes a welcome return to North American screens with the 14th of Rock Demers' "Tales for All." This delightful mix of live action and animation should find a receptive audience in markets where animated pics click.

Simple, nonviolent story focuses on 11-year-old Alec, whose father, a ship's captain, is away for long periods of time. The boy doesn't mix with other kids and daydreams of the faraway places he sees on his father's postcards.

Alec gets a strange collection of cocoons from Dad and the next morning awakens to find his room filled with wonderful butterflies, among them a beautiful fairy whom Alec eventually befriends. When they play together, the screen lights up with a clever and charming combination of puppets and animation.

Through the fairy butterfly's magic, Alec impresses at school with tricks including making his sneaker fly. But he derives no real satisfaction from this because they are not of his own making. Eventually his father returns, the fairy flies home to the moon and Alec has learned that solitary days of fantasy are not the way to live.

Technically, pic is an imaginative marvel, and it should do well on children's video shelves after its cinematic release. Originally filmed in Czech, the English version has been carefully dubbed.
— *Gerald Pratley*

SINGLE WHITE FEMALE

A Columbia release. Produced, directed by Barbet Schroeder. Executive producer, Jack Baran. Co-producer, Roger Joseph Pugliese. Screenplay, Don Roos, based on John Lutz's novel "SWF Seeks Same." Camera (Technicolor), Luciano Tovoli; editor, Lee Percy; music, Howard Shore; production design, Milena Canonero; art direction, P. Michael Johnston; set decoration, Anne H. Ahrens; sound (Dolby), Petur Hliddal; sound design, Gary Rydstrom; associate producer, Susan Hoffman; assistant director, Jack Baran. Reviewed at Sony Studios, Culver City, Calif., June 26, 1992. MPAA Rating: R. Running time: **107 MIN.**

Allison Jones . . . . . . Bridget Fonda
Hedra Carlson . . Jennifer Jason Leigh
Sam Rawson . . . . Steven Weber
Graham Knox . . . . . Peter Friedman
Myerson . . . . . Stephen Tobolowsky

Fresh off his sterling work on "Reversal of Fortune," director Barbet Schroeder has made a calculated attempt to cross an acutely observed character study with a slasher pic. But despite excellent lead performances and numerous memorable scenes, "Single White Female" feels like two different movies in one.

Commercial prospects for this curiously schizophrenic film look good, as the "roommate-from-hell" premise puts this one in the same camp as "Fatal Attraction" and "The Hand That Rocks the Cradle," a concept that hasn't failed yet but inevitably will someday.

Pleasingly suggesting the director's European roots, opening reels conjure up the weird, unsettling mood of Roman Polanski's apartment films ("Rosemary's Baby," "The Tenant"), while promising a story of psychological blurring à la Ingmar Bergman's "Persona."

Giving her unfaithful b.f. the heave, smart, upwardly mobile designer/software expert Bridget Fonda takes waify Jennifer Jason Leigh in to share her attractive Upper West Side flat. They become instant best friends, and the needy Leigh seems reassured by Fonda's vow she'll never take her cheating man back.

Light, airy and underlined with only the slightest hint of menace, these early scenes charting the women's burgeoning friendship are characterized by a naturalness and many lovely details. Even after Fonda returns to her errant lover (Steven Weber) and becomes engaged, the ways in which Leigh tries to nicely insin-

uate herself into the "family" remain beautifully observed and psychologically true.

But pic gradually tilts in the direction of a production line thriller, until finally assuming the full personality of a Hollywood killing machine. Turning point arrives when Leigh, after assuming many of Fonda's characteristics and buying similar clothes, gets her hair cut and dyed just like Fonda's pert carrot-top.

From here on, it's a race between Fonda's efforts to get Leigh out of her life and Leigh's brutal butchering of the cast. Inevitably, it all ends in a violent struggle between the two women which is agonizingly protracted in standard Hollywood manner.

Most of pic's virtues are subtle, while the flaws are blatant. Under Schroeder's careful guidance, both Fonda and Leigh play with an ease and unselfconsciousness that are bracingly refreshing. Some of their scenes together feature a casual intimacy rare in U.S. films.

At the same time, Schroeder and scripter Don Roos have come up with some sexual sequences unlike anything in recent memory. A haunting moment shows Fonda, having taken her b.f. back, listening to Leigh masturbating in her bedroom. Later on, more startlingly and disturbingly, Leigh sneaks in on Weber while he sleeps and begins molesting him sexually.

Thriller aspects of the story, and suspense leading up to the climactic showdown, are handled expertly enough to get audiences lathered up. Still, it's only a question of time until the conventions of this predator-from-hell subgenre are rejected by the mass audience that has so avidly embraced them. Formula basically works here, although it's beginning to wear a bit thin.

Pic looks terrific, with major credit going to the initial decision to place Fonda's apartment in the fading grande dame of NYC dwellings, the Ansonia. The nearly century-old venue, with its endless hallways, wild design and eavesdropping-friendly heating ducts, bestows the film with a unique, creepy grandeur, superbly augmented by production designer Milena Canonero.

Color schemes, fabrics and details of decor all play telling roles here, indicating a promising new direction for Canonero, who heretofore has been a top costume designer. (Although she also handled costuming and hair chores here, her contract restricted her

to production design credit.)

Working in perfect tandem is lenser Luciano Tovoli, who gives the mostly studio-shot interiors the glowing feel of natural light. Other tech contributions are of an equally high level.
— *Todd McCarthy*

THE PANAMA DECEPTION
(DOCU)

An Empowerment Project production in association with Channel 4. Produced by Barbara Trent, Joanne Doroshow, Nico Panigutti, David Kasper. Directed by Trent. Written, edited by Kasper. Camera (video, color), Michael Dobo, Manuel Becker; music, Chuck Wild. Reviewed at Directors Guild of America, West Hollywood, July 30, 1992. Running time: **91 MIN.**
Narrator: Elizabeth Montgomery.

"The Panama Deception" is a forceful, straightforward condemnation of Reagan-Bush policies in Panama, particularly the 1989 U.S. invasion. Despite pic's modest production values, timely election-year release will increase its visibility in major theatrical markets, cable TV and video.

Shot and initially presented on video but to be distributed in a 35m transfer, Barbara Trent's new docu places the invasion in a broad historical perspective, chronicling U.S. involvement in the region since 1903, when the U.S. gained control of Panama from the French.

Docu examines the rise of Manuel Noriega to power and how Ronald Reagan and George Bush first supported him (Bush boosted his income when he was on the CIA payroll), then turned him into a "mythic" villain by labeling him "a vicious drug-lord dictator." According to the docu, Bush also had a personal agenda in Panama, wishing to wipe out his wimp image.

Pic claims that protection of U.S. citizens, Noriega's drug trafficking and a Marine's death were excuses for implementing a long-planned policy to challenge and renegotiate the 1977 Carter-Torrijos canal treaties. The disastrous effects of the U.S. invasion are on display: massive carnage, brutality against innocent citizens, refugees living in poverty.

But pic's most potent aspect is its merciless indictment of the news media (print and TV) as puppets manipulated by the White House. Interviewing scholars, officials and journalists, docu holds that the news media is part of the military-industrial complex and lacks the independence to criticize the power elite.

Film juxtaposes official statements with actual footage of the invasion's atrocities and life in a military-controlled country. Official estimates of casualties vastly differ: 500 according to Gen. Maxwell Thurman, 3,000 to 4,000 according to U.N. and Panamanian human rights groups.

But "The Panama Deception" is not as powerful as Trent's acclaimed 1988 "Cover Up: Behind the Iran Contra Affair." There is little truly new info, and Elizabeth Montgomery's functional narration lacks emotional impact. (Sting, Jorge Strunz, Jackson Browne and Ismael Rivera contribute to the music.)

A major deficiency is the English-dubbed testimony of Panamanian refugees; their evidence would have been more authentic and wrenching if it had been subtitled. Considering the censorship and restrictive control of the media during and after the invasion, however, it's amazing Trent obtained this footage at all. — *Emanuel Levy*

3 NINJAS

A Buena Vista release of a Touchstone Pictures presentation of a Global Venture Hollywood production. Produced by Martha Chang. Line producer, Susan Stremple. Co-producers, Hiroshi Kusu, Akio Shimizu. Executive producer, Shunji Hirano. Co-exec producer, James Kang. Directed by Jon Turtletaub. Screenplay, Edward Emanuel, from Kenny Kim's story. Camera (Technicolor prints), Richard Michalak; additional camera, Chris Faloona; editor, David Rennie; music, Rick Marvin; production design, Kirk Petruccelli; art direction, Ken Kirchener, Greg Grande; set decoration, Carol Pressman; costume design, Mona May; sound (Dolby), Bill Robbins; stunt coordinator, Rick Avery; associate producer, Richard Park; assistant directors, J.B. Rogers, Scott Harris; 2nd unit director, Charlie Kao; casting, Kim Williams. Reviewed at El Capitan Theater, L.A., Aug. 1, 1992. MPAA Rating: PG. Running time: **84 MIN.**
Grandpa . . . . Victor Wong
Rocky . . . . Michael Treanor
Colt . . . . Max Elliott Slade
Tum Tum . . . . Chad Power
Hugo Snyder . . . . . Rand Kingsley
Sam Douglas . . . . Alan McRae
Jessica Douglas . . . Margarita Franco
Rushmore . . . . Toru Tanaka

Touchstone Pictures may have a sleeper in "3 Ninjas," judging from surprisingly strong reaction to national previews Aug 1. Though there aren't any name actors in the chopsocky comedy and the plot is thin and formulaic, the grace-

fully choreographed spectacle of three little boys outfighting hordes of evil adult ninjas is a surefire juve crowd-pleaser.

Borrowing liberally from "The Karate Kid" and "Home Alone," the filmmakers tap knowingly into kids' fantasies by showing little guys Michael Treanor, Max Elliott Slade and Chad Power hurling baddies through the air and flattening the massive, seemingly invincible Toru Tanaka.

Director Jon Turtletaub and editor David Rennie keep things zipping along, wisely not wasting much time with the ninjas' arms dealer boss, sneering Steven Seagal clone Rand Kingsley, or with his antagonist, the boys' blandly inattentive FBI agent father (Alan McRae).

When taken hostage, the Southern California boys have to rely on the martial arts lessons learned from their grandfather (the charming Victor Wong), who has shadowy past connections with Kingsley but takes their side in the battle royal.

While some parents may become temporarily queasy with Grandpa training the boys to disable an attacker by going for the groin and the jugular, the fight scenes are innocuously cartoonlike in this slickly produced first pic from South Korean filmmaker Sang Okk Sheen's Global Venture Hollywood.
— *Joseph McBride*

ORQUESTA CLUB VIRGINIA
(CLUB VIRGINIA ORCHESTRA)
(SPANISH)

A Warner Bros. Española release in Spain of an El Catalejo & Fernando Colomo production. Executive producer, Ana Huete. Directed by Manuel Iborra. Screenplay, Iborra, Joaquin Oristrell, based on life of Santi Arisa. Camera (Eastmancolor, Panavision), Javier Salmones; editor, Miguel Angel Santamaría; music, Santi Arisa; sets, Miguel Chicharro; costumes, Helena Sanchís; sound (Dolby), Julio Recuero, Gilles Ortión; associate producer, Fernando Colomo. Reviewed at Cinearte, Madrid, July 23, 1992. Running time: **85 MIN.**
Tony . . . . Jorge Sanz
Sr. Domenech . . . . . Antonio Resines
Negro . . . . Santiago Ramos
Curt . . . . . . Enrique San Francisco
Mano . . . . Juan Echanove
Soliman . . . . Pau Riba
Also with: Emma Suárez, Natasha Hovey, Torrebruno.

Set in 1967 and shot in Morocco (doubling for Egypt), this "The Mambo Kings"-like pic about six Spanish musi-

cians on tour has good thesping, some catchy music and touches of raw humor, but the linear script never sufficiently delves into the characters or exploits potentially dramatic moments.

Throughout, the story is tiresomely narrated by the adolescent Tony (thesp Jorge Sanz is 22), based on an experience of the young Santi Arisa who started his own rock 'n' roll band when he was only 13. The group sets sail from Valencia on the way to Beirut, where it supposedly has a contract to play in the Hilton. But the musicos never get beyond Cairo and Amman, where they wind up playing for peanuts in cheap clubs.

The Spaniards while away the time whoring, drinking, cussing and playing their repertoire of mambo and pop classics. Tempers sometimes flare as Iborra limns the relationship between Tony and his father, who heads the band and is unconvincingly played by Antonio Resines (himself only 38).

Stealing the show is thesp Santiago Ramos as the dissipated trumpet player whom the young Tony warms up to, and who finally walks out on the fleabag band.

There is no social comment here, no allusion to the Franco Spain the band comes from and really little character insight. Perhaps what's most lacking is a touch of Almodóvarian zaniness, or, in lieu of that, a script that brings some poignancy into what here are only the pointless shenanigans of a third-rate band.
— *Peter Besas*

SUP DE FRIC
(CASH ACADEMY)
(FRENCH)

An AMLF release of a Lapaca Prods./TF-1 Films Prod./M6 Films/Prodeve co-production. Produced, directed, written by Christian Gion. Camera (color), Bernard Joliot, Michel Thiriet; editor, Héléne Plemiannikov; music, Graham de Wilde, Richard Harvey; costumes, Olga Pelletier; set design, Marc Marmier; sound, Bernard Rochut. Reviewed at Club Gaumont screening room, Paris, July 16, 1992. Running time: **90 MIN.**
Cyril Dujardin . . . . . . Jean Poiret
François Cardeau . . . Anthony Delon
Victor Dargelas . . . . . Cris Campion
Jimmy Leroy . . . . . . Roland Giraud
Also with: Valérie Mairesse.

Strictly run-of-the-mill execution undermines "Sup de Fric," a comedy about two

young losers who get the last laugh by turning classroom theories into a business world coup. Low-budget look and ready-for-commercial-breaks pacing point to TV.

Rich kid Anthony Delon and commoner Cris Campion room together at a pricey private school that teaches management techniques to well-to-do young men who were turned down by France's elite universities. Computer hacker Campion has been offered a full scholarship in return for removing a virus from the school's computers. But the school's slick, unscrupulous director Jean Poiret is embezzling from the school and plans to frame Campion.

Pic's premise — that the roomies will use Poiret's teachings to secretly purchase their own school in a leveraged buyout — presents many sharp possibilities for humor and suspense, nearly all of which are flattened out by writer/helmer Gion.

Usually handsome lads Delon and Campion are lensed to look weatherbeaten and ghoulish. Roland Giraud is entertaining as a leading businessman who agrees to advise the junior raiders. Renée Saint-Cyr also scores as a financially savvy baroness.

Title is a pun on the most eminent French school for business and management students. Pic is dedicated to Poiret, who died in March. — *Lisa Nesselson*

DETOUR

Produced, directed by Wade Williams. Screenplay, Roger Hull, Williams, based on Martin Goldsmith's story. Camera (Deluxe color), Jeff Richardson; editor, Herbert L. Strock; music, Bill Crain; associate producers, Ben Mossman, Brian Mossman. Reviewed at Film Forum, N.Y., July 31, 1992. Running time: **89 MIN.**
Al Roberts . . . . Tom Neal Jr.
Vera . . . . Lea Lavish
Sue Harvey . . . . Erin McGrane
Charles Haskell . . . . . Duke Howze
Evvy . . . . Susanna Foster
Cowboy . . . . Brad Bittiker
Truck driver . . . . . . Patrick Waters

Fans of Edgar G. Ulmer's noir classic, "Detour," are in for a disappointment: Wade Williams' low-budget remake features both laughable dialogue and inept acting. And despite vintage cars and flashing neon, the attempt to create a period look is only intermittently successful. Williams should shelve the remake and reissue

Ulmer's superb version (he holds those rights).

The plot, and even some of the dialogue, is straight out of the hard-boiled original. Like the 1945 film, the remake centers on the incredibly bad fortune of Al Roberts (Tom Neal Jr., whose father played the same part in the first "Detour").

Sitting in a lonely highway diner and looking despondent, Roberts recalls how he ended up in his present jam. The film flashes back to a New York club, where he accompanies the singer Sue Harvey (Erin McGrane). Roberts falls in love with her, but she leaves him behind to try her luck in Los Angeles.

Roberts eventually quits his job and hitchhikes cross country, aiming to marry Sue. He bums a ride with Charles Haskell (Duke Howze) and notices claw marks on his hand. Haskell suddenly drops dead en route, and Roberts leaves the body while taking Haskell's car and money. In a bizarre twist of fate, Roberts picks up a tough broad named Vera (Lea Lavish), who turns out to be the same woman who scratched Haskell. She recognizes the car and threatens to turn in Roberts if he doesn't give her the bulk of the loot.

The remake's only significant departure from the original is in devoting more time to the singer's character in L.A. Unfortunately, her scenes are among the film's weakest.

Nearly all the performances are strictly third rate. While the original came alive with the appearance of Vera (played by the fiery Ann Savage), Lavish's Vera is merely annoying. As her ill-fated traveling companion, Neal gives a comparatively believable, low-key performance. His close resemblance to his father only brings to mind the original's superiority.

Although Williams inserts some good period touches, as well as terrific period footage of 1940s New York and L.A., his direction is generally awkward. Even the climactic death scene by phone cord is filmed clumsily.

But it is the ridiculously over-the-top acting that makes the remake nearly unwatchable. If Ann Savage was memorably evil, Lavish's bulging eyeballs and snippy delivery come across as silly. And the histrionic acting only calls to attention to the often ludicrous dialogue.

Instead of illuminating the mysterious workings of fate, this "Detour" provides a textbook lesson in how *not* to remake a memorable B-movie.

— *William Stevenson*

UNBECOMING AGE

A Ringelvision production. Produced, directed by Alfredo Ringel, Deborah Ringel. Line producer, Charla Driver. Screenplay, Meridith Baer, Geoff Prysirr. Camera (CFI color), Harry Mathias; editor, Alan Geik; music, Jeff Lass; production design, Phil Dagort; costumes, Katheryn Shemanek; sound (Ultra-Stereo), Michael Evje; assistant director/2nd unit director, Craig Respol; casting, Betsy Fels. Reviewed at Monica 4-Plex, Santa Monica, Calif., July 1, 1992. (In AFI/L.A. FilmFest). Running time: **90 MIN.**
Julia . . . . Diane Salinger
Charles . . . . John Calvin
Grandma . . . . Priscilla Pointer
Mac . . . . George Clooney
Deborah . . . . Colleen Camp
Dr. Block . . . . Wallace Shawn
Letty . . . . Shera Danese
Dooley . . . . Nicholas Guest
Jake . . . . Anthony Peck
Alfredo . . . . Don Diamont
Also with: Michael Greene, Dayle Haddon, Lyndsay Riddell, Michael Boatman, Adam Ryen, Betsy Lynn George.

The spirit is winning but the inspiration is missing in "Unbecoming Age," an unbecoming comedy about a woman who would rather act like a child than mature gracefully. This one-joke bit of yuppie hokum would be more appropriate on TV than on theater screens, where it stands scant chance of drawing an audience.

First feature by the husband-and-wife team of Alfredo and Deborah Ringel takes its central device from Howard Hawks' 1962 farce "Monkey Business," in which Cary Grant and company started behaving like teens after ingesting rejuvenation serum.

Here, suburban housewife Diane Salinger finds herself notably depressed on her 40th birthday. Some magic bubbles keep her the same physically but cause her to transform into an 8-year-old mentally. Outwardly, she expresses her unbridled new personality by bouncing around on her bed, playing bunny rabbit with her daughter and sulking when hubby John Calvin doesn't show an inclination to match her boundless energy.

Instead, he sends her to shrink Wallace Shawn, but Salinger continues to rebel by indulging in a heavy flirtation with young hipster George Clooney and carting Calvin's ailing mother, Priscilla Pointer, off to Las Vegas, where she promptly dies at the blackjack table.

Salinger protests that Pointer died happy, that people should be allowed to follow their hearts and do what they want, until Calvin finally objects, "I'm fed up with this stupid act of yours," a sentiment with which most viewers are likely to concur.

Basic conceptual problem is that the fantasy element, relating to what a middle-aged woman would do with newfound youth, is exasperatingly tame. Given totally recharged energy and a fresh outlook, would one just jump up and down in the bedroom and stay out late at a fast food restaurant? Screenwriters Meridith Baer and Geoff Prysirr have kept their imaginations too inhibited and domesticated where greater flights of fancy would have been welcome.

One's sympathy goes out to Salinger, who has been asked to do all sorts of ungainly, infantile things and goes all out in compliance. Actress manages to remain somewhat likable no matter how unbridled her behavior becomes, which helps get one through the picture, but many of her antics border on the embarrassing.

Comic approach throughout leans toward the brash and garish, with subtlety nowhere to be found. A number of talented thesps brighten up the supporting cast, but few will count this among their more stellar credits.

— *Todd McCarthy*

LIFE IN THE FOOD CHAIN
(AGE ISN'T EVERYTHING)

A Katzfilms production. Produced by Joan Fishman. Directed, written by Douglas Katz. Camera (color), Mike Spillar; editor, Dorian Harris; music, Glen Roven; casting, Deborah Brown. Reviewed at American Film Institute, L.A., June 24, 1992. (In AFI/L.A. FilmFest.) Running time: **89 MIN.**
Seymour . . . . . . Jonathan Silverman
Max . . . . Paul Sorvino
Rita . . . . Rita Moreno
Grandpa Irving . . . . . Robert Prosky

Douglas Katz's feature directorial debut, the indie "Life in the Food Chain," is a satire about a young Wall Street exec who suddenly turns into an old man. Formulaic narrative, Jonathan Silverman's monotonous performance and lack of comic vitality restricts theatrical potential. Indeed, pic was retitled "Age Isn't Everything" and released as a homevideo last November via Live Entertainment.

Born into a materialistic suburban Jewish family, Seymour abandons a childhood fantasy to become an astronaut, instead going to Harvard and getting a good job. He's stricken with a mysterious aging disorder, and before long he behaves like an 83-year-old. An intermittently amusing concoction of encounters with his family, friends, doctors and rabbi ensues.

Pic contains potentially hilarious situations, but they don't gel. Narrative is predictable, and once the premise is spelled out, plot machinations get obvious.

Problematic structure alternates dialogue scenes with voiceover narration and interviews addressed to the camera. Acting of entire cast of pros is inexplicably mediocre. Rita Moreno as the mother, Robert Prosky as grandfather and Paul Sorvino as father all try hard to pump some life into their roles, but to no avail.

Worse yet is Silverman's pedestrian, charmless performance in an admittedly demanding role. He takes a heavy-handed approach, beginning with an overblown Yiddish accent.

Director Katz exhibits low aptitude for satire, particularly pacing, loading on exposition and belaboring comic setups. Tech credits and behind-the-scenes contributions are modest.

— *Emanuel Levy*

A TRIP TO SERENDIPITY
(CANADIAN-16m)

A Marano Prods. presentation. Produced, directed, written by Nancy Marano. Camera (color), Jim Stacey; editors, Peter Svab, Shannon Mitchell; music, Bruce Leitl; art direction, Anne Rickhi; costumes, Nancy Boswell; sound, Chris MacIntosh; casting, Jaci Majer, Therese Reinsch. Reviewed at WorldFest/Houston, April 25, 1992. Running time: **81 MIN.**
Luna . . . . Donna Larson
Bum . . . . James Bell
Henry . . . . David Brindle
Luna (at 12) . . . . Edana Fedje
Mime . . . . Don Spino
Shoe doctor . . . . Patrick Brown
Charlie . . . . James Bell

Just about the only thing worse than strained whimsy is graceless fantasy, and Nancy Marano's "A Trip to Serendipity" has both in abundance. Indie effort produced in Calgary faces an uphill climb to find an audience.

Pic is yet another anti-yuppie fable. Donna Larson stars as an upwardly mobile exec who trips and injures her leg while rushing to a meeting. She is helped to her feet by an aggressively cheerful bum (James Bell) who insists on their taking a detour through a nearby park.

During their stroll, they argue about life values, cuing flashbacks to exec's idealistic youth. She wanted to be a ballerina, but switched over to business school to gain her parents' attention.

Various figures (hot-dog vendor, also played by Bell; a mime, a shoe salesman) appear from behind trees or bushes to offer advice. Eventually, Larson gets the point, decides to rekindle her artistic ambitions and chucks her business papers into a trashcan.

Pic, hopelessly amateurish on both dramatic and technical levels, is so insistent on sharing what the filmmaker obviously feels are novel insights that it's difficult to view the ultra-low-budget pic as anything but a misguidedly didactic vanity production.

Worse, there's something slightly offensive about a pic in which a successful woman is forced to listen to a group of patronizing men tell her everything that's wrong with her life and encourage her to start acting like a child again. The absolute nadir is reached when the hot-dog vendor refuses to give the exec anything to eat unless she sings a song, or dances. — *Joe Leydon*

THE CLEAN MACHINE
(CANADIAN)

A Les Prods. La Fete production and release. Produced by Rock Demers. Line producer, Lorraine du Hamel. Co-producer, Kevin Tierney. Directed by Jean Beaudry. Screenplay, Jacques A. Desjardins in collaboration with Beaudry. Camera (Eastman Kodak color), Eric Cayla; editor, Helene Girard; music, Robert M. Lepage; art direction, Vianney Gauthier; costumes, Gaetanne Levesque. Reviewed at Cannes Film Festival market, May 12, 1992. Running time: **90 MIN.**
Ben . . . . Vincent Bolduc
Charles . . . . Pierre-Luc Brillant
Maggie . . . . Delphine Piperni
Chloe . . . . Alexandra Laverdiere
Julian . . . . Mathieu Lachapelle
Chris . . . . Maxime Collin
Louis . . . . Pierre-Paul Daunais
Also with: Denis Bouchard, Dorothee Berryman, Normand Chouinard.

Films teaching kids business management and ethics in a natural and easygoing way are rare, but "The Clean Machine," No. 13 in Rock Demers' "Tales for All," succeeds effectively. This deceptively sim-

ple story of youths learning responsibility and dealing with the complications of starting their own business should please both children and parents.

Led by spoiled 12-year-old Charles, an enterprising group of children sets up a house and yard cleaning company to make money during the summer. Another kid, Maggie, is a budding filmmaker who's making a video commercial of their activities. Unfortunately, the young entrepreneurs each have their own reasons for participating, and the "company" soon finds itself in trouble.

Jacques Desjardins' thoughtful screenplay deftly weaves a series of underlying moral principles revealed in the various reasons each child wants to make money, and why each unthinkingly misbehaves.

Director Jean Beaudry brings out the main characters' contrasting attitudes and shifting relationships. All credits in this entertaining and appealing pic are satisfactory, and the children are at home in their roles.

Filmed in French under the title "Tirelire Combines & Cie.", this English version is expertly dubbed so far as its intended audience is concerned.
— *Gerald Pratley*

VEGAS IN SPACE

A Phillip R. Ford presentation from Fish/Ford Film. Executive producer, Doris Fish. Produced, directed by Ford. Screenplay, Fish, Miss X, Ford. Camera (color/b&w), Robin Clark; editors, Ed Jones, Ford; music, Bob Davis; production design, Fish; sound, Todd Ritchie; associate producers, Dalton Bradley Chandler III, Laura Milligan. Reviewed at ICA Theater, Boston, July 12, 1992. (In Boston Gay/Lesbian Film/Video Festival.) R. Running time: **85 MIN.**
Dan Tracy/Tracy Daniels . . Doris Fish
Vel Croford/Queen Veneer . . . Miss X
Empress Nueva Gabor . Ginger Quest
Mike/Sheila . . . . . . Ramona Fischer
Steve/Debbie . . . . . . Lori Naslund
Lt. Dick Hunter . . . . Timmy Spence
Princess Angel . . . . Tippi

Futuristic no-budgeter is showcase for drag sensibilities of the late Doris Fish. Shot on a veritable shoestring in the mid-1980s, film premiered late last year in a San Francisco midnight showcase and has since been rounding various fests. Success of bookings will depend on the depth of a local public interested in supporting witless film that coasts on outlandish makeup and outfits and cheesy special effects, all designed by Fish.

Crew of the USS Intercourse is sent to the planet Clitoris to solve a jewel heist. If rare gems are not recovered, the pleasure planet — where men are forbidden — will be destroyed. The crew (played by both men and women) is all male and undergoes a sex change to fit in on the planet as a touring lounge act.

Plot is merely an excuse for mostly male cast to get decked out in the most outrageous collection of fashions and colors since the heyday of the Freed musical unit at MGM. Acting is amateurish, but they give it their all.

Story of pic's production is much more interesting. It was shot between 1983 and 1985 in starts and stops, in black & white and in color, with the script evolving as new money became available. Total budget for the entire film is reported at $65,000.

Director Phillip R. Ford manages to somehow keep it coherent and not a collection of random bits, and Robin Clark's cinematography brings out full value of the garish sets and costumes. Only the sound betrays the low-budget nature of tech credits.

While this will probably never reach widespread cult status, it pleases its intended audience. Many more expensive productions can't even boast that.
— *Daniel M. Kimmel*

CORPUS DELICTI
(CZECHOSLOVAKIAN)

A Barrandov Studios Creative Team Vydra-Dudová production. (Intl. sales: Filmexport Praha.) Directed by Irena Pavlásková. Screenplay, Pavlásková, Nelly Pavlásková. Camera (color), F.A. Brabec; editor, Jan Svoboda; music, Jirí Chlumecky, Jirí Vesely; production design, Libuse Jahodová, Karel Lier; costumes, Simona Rybáková; sound, Jaroslav Novák. Reviewed at Karlovy Vary Film Festival, July 10, 1992. Running time: **110 MIN.**
Jana . . . . Lenka Korínková
Tomás . . . . Simon Pánek
Viktorie . . . . Jirina Bohdalová
Jaromír . . . . Karel Roden
Pulice . . . . Jitka Asterová
Dr. Chlad . . . . Michal Docolomansky
Marta . . . . Magda Cermáková
Gojko . . . . Daniel Malaniuk
Admirerer . . . . Jan Nemec

Lusty, exuberant performances distinguish this tale of three couples whose lives intertwine in Prague just before the fall of the Communist regime. Helmer/screenwriter Irena Pavlásková shows a sure touch in making one of Czechoslovakia's strongest contemporary pics.

Well-defined characters are the

film's strong point. Jaromír is a big-talking, hard-drinking, self-proclaimed artist who produces nothing and possesses no talent. He preys on the young, dependent, doe-eyed Pulice, who fears being alone and is willing to tolerate any amount of abuse from Jaromír.

In a tragicomic scene, as she attempts to engage him in love-making by crawling on his prone body, he complains, "Can't you find anywhere else to sit?"

Jana and Tomás are members of Prague's intelligentsia but cannot find a place for themselves in society. They feel trapped by communist ideology, but they don't wish to fall prey to consumerism.

The couple acting as catalyst for the sextet is Viktorie and her nearly estranged doctor husband Karel. Played with operatic lust by Jirina Bohdalová in a walloping performance, Viktorie is the film's biggest treat. This eccentric and powerful woman's advancing age has in no way diminished her passion for life. She drinks, rants, sings and takes a young, dreadlocked punk for a lover.

Pic deftly moves between the touching and the comic, examining political and social themes along the way. Tech credits are fine. A somewhat weak ending mars an otherwise respectable film. — *Rebecca Lieb*

YMA SUMAC:
HOLLYWOOD'S INCA PRINCESS
(GERMAN-DOCU-16m)

A Rubicon Film production. Directed by Gunther Czernetsky. Screenplay, Czernetsky, from an idea by Alon D'Armand. Camera (color), Paco Joan, Toni Sulzbeck, Peter Gold, Radu Simionescu, Vlad Ilnitsky; editor, Beate Koster; music, Moises Vivanco, Yma Sumac, Antonio Pantoja, Les Baxter, Billy May, Georges Brun; sound, Richard Altman; narrators, Sabine Kastius, Stephan Rehm, Wolfgang Kuck. Reviewed at Roxie Cinema, San Francisco, June 24, 1992. (In S.F. Lesbian/Gay Intl. Film Festival.) Running time: **90 MIN.**
(In English, German, Spanish)

Made for German television, the feature documentary "Yma Sumac: Hollywood's Inca Princess" maps the career of the Peruvian warbler whose $4^1/_2$-octave range earned her international fame in the 1940s and '50s. Exotic silliness of her Capitol Records discs and her image from that period have long since made her a nostalgic camp icon, though her vocal gifts remain striking. Best bets for this okay, but far-from-definitive docu lie in targeting cult audiences less interested in musicology than in another era's kitschy glamor.

Sumac's history remains shrouded in mystery. She evidently rose to prominence in Peru from a poor background there before traveling to the U.S. with husband-composer Moises Vivanco in the early '40s. Once signed, her remarkable, almost avantgarde vocal effects — capable of imitating twittering birds and grunting beasts — became an unlikely rage when set amid lavish orchestral spins of traditional Peruvian folk tunes.

Capitol fanned the flames by devising a phony bio telling of a village lass descended from Inca royalty who'd been kidnapped by urban talent scouts. The cynical backlash (accusations flew that she was actually anagrammatic "Amy Camus," a Brooklyn voice student) probably did more to harm her career in the long run. While she appeared in one flop Broadway musical ("Flahooey") and a middling-success Hollywood actioner ("Secret of the Incas," with Charlton Heston), Sumac was passé by the end of the '50s. Her cult rep flourished, however, with a late-'80s comeback tour.

Major drawback: Sumac declined to participate in the docu, though TV news footage of her '80s club shows is glimpsed. Interviewees include her early Peruvian showbiz comrades, Capitol tradesters, international fans and a music expert who uses computer technology to examine her remarkable range.

Pic's a fascinating footnote-to-music-history saga, but it lurches unevenly from straightforward bio material to a more campily appreciative mode. Item's entertaining, but maybe another filmmaker will be able to persuade Sumac to be an on-camera commentator for a more complete view of her unique career.
— *Dennis Harvey*

CHUNUK BAIR
(NEW ZEALAND)

A Daybreak Pictures & Avalon Television Center/National Film Unit production. Produced by L. Grant Bradley. Directed by Dale G. Bradley. Screenplay, Grant Hinden Miller, based on Maurice Shadbolt's play. Camera (color), Warrick Attewell; editor, Paul Sutorius; music, Stephen Bell-Booth; production design, Kevin Leonard-Jones; sound, Don Paulin. Reviewed at Downtown 6, Palmerston North, New Zealand, April 24, 1992. Running time: **106 MIN.**
Sgt. Maj. Frank South . Robert Powell
Col. Connelly . . . . . Kevin J. Wilson
Pvt. Fred South . . . . . . Jed Brophy
Porky . . . . John Leigh
Smiler . . . . Murray Keane
Signals . . . . Danny Mulheron
Lt. Harkness . . . . . Richard Hanna
Gen. Fairweather . . . . Lewis Rowe
Also with: Stephen Ure, Peter Kaa, Darryl Beattie, John Wraight, Tim Bray.

"Chunuk Bair" is a dramatic reprise of the disastrous Gallipoli campaign in Turkey during World War I in which the colonial boys from Down Under were willingly used as cannon fodder by Mother England. Kiwi account is smaller scale than the Aussies' "Gallipoli" and has its affecting moments, but low-budget stringencies and considerably less-than-incisive script and direction will make it a difficult sell offshore outside TV and video.

Chunuk Bair is a hill on the coast of Turkey which the Wellington Regiment is ordered to hold to the last man while its British commanding officer, Gen. Fairweather (Lewis Rowe), shelters cozily in his trench far below.

Col. Connelly (Kevin J. Wilson) leads his men to the greater glory of "ourselves" rather than the British Empire. He is aided by Sgt.-Maj. South (Robert Powell), whose primary concern is to protect the life of his younger brother (Jed Brophy), also in the ill-fated corps.

Working against all expectations arising from rookie feature director, no stars and tiny budget (well below seven figures), the entwining war themes of human loss and individual salvation do emerge.

However, script's legit origins lock the film into staginess, and helmer Dale Bradley's inexperience in weaving action and human drama often shows. Overall, opus does not have the textural depth of sound, locations and technical effects the subject demands.

The bonuses come from the performances. Wilson is always compelling, when given the chance, as the independently spirited Connelly. Pic evidences the depth of talent among young male Kiwi thesps. — *Mike Nicolaidi*

NOTTATACCIA
(WHAT A NIGHT!)
(ITALIAN)

A Penta Distribuzione release of a Mario & Vittorio Cecchi Gori & Silvio Berlusconi Communications presentation of an Esterno Mediterraneo Film production in association with Penta Film. Produced by Gaetano Daniele. Directed by Duccio Camerini. Screenplay, Camerini, Stefano Amatucci, based on Camerini's play. Camera (color), Maurizio Dell'Orco; editor, Angelo Nicolini; music, Antonio Di Pofi; art direction, Francesco Frigeri; costumes, Cristiana Lafayette; sound, Tommaso Quattrini. Reviewed at Alcazar Cinema, Rome, May 7, 1992. Running time: **90 MIN.**
Susanna . . . . Stefania Sandrelli
Andrea . . . . . . Massimo Wertmüller
Gino . . . . Massimo Bellinzoni
Also with: Massimo Bonetti, Giorgio Gobbi, Maurizio Mattioli.

Three malcontents square off in a stormy scramble for love in "What a Night!" Pic's appealing, high-energy cast makes a valiant bid to inject some bounce into the proceedings, but the broad stage farce gets irremediably stalled as a screen vehicle. Commercial prospects look tepid.

When maintenance men knock a hole in his apartment wall, an emotionally stifled schoolteacher (Massimo Wertmüller) grabs a video camera and starts secretly filming his lovelorn psychiatrist neighbor (Stefania Sandrelli). In a well-played, bittersweet sequence, he shares a lonely meal with her small screen incarnation, and his dormant heart jumps into action.

One of the shrink's patients (Massimo Bellinzoni), a low-rent transvestite hooker who insists on old-fashioned courtship from his otherwise-inclined johns, lands on doc's doorstep, hiding out from an angry pimp. A mistaken identity scenario follows, with the teacher falling for his neighbor's body but her patient's voice. Outcome is a chaste solution à trois.

Adapting his own play, first-time director Duccio Camerini gives the potentially offbeat yarn frustratingly outmoded comic treatment. Dialogue is flat and rarely funny, and though the three leads outshine their material, they seem to be playing rusty plot mechanisms rather than real people. Sandrelli, especially, has no character to play.

Technically, pic looks and sounds good, but the dated feel isn't helped by the '70s taint in sets and costumes and Antonio Di Pofi's obtrusive, inappropriate music.

— *David Rooney*

HOLOD 33
(FAMINE '33)
(UKRAINIAN-COLOR/B&W)

A Dovzhenko Feature Film Studios production. Produced by Oleksij Chernishov. Directed by Oles Yanchuk. Screenplay by Serhij Diachenko, Les Taniuk. Camera (color/b&w), Vasyl Borodin, Mykhajlo Kretov; editor, Natalia Akajomova; music, Mykola Kolandjonak, Victor Pacukevych. Reviewed at Monica 4-Plex, Santa Monica, Calif., June 26, 1992. (In AFI/L.A. FilmFest.) Running time: **95 MIN.**
Kateryna . . . . Halayna Sulyma
Katrannyk . . . . Goergi Moroziuk

It took 57 years for Ukrainian Communist Party heads to admit that the 1933 famine, which killed more than 7 million people, was instigated by Josef Stalin. "Famine 33," Oles Yanchuk's feature film debut, investigates this historical disaster. Pic's astonishing physical spectacle and emotional power should make it welcome at international fests.

Loosely based on "The Yellow Prince," a novel about the famine, co-scripters Serhij Diachenko and Les Taniuk have fashioned a story that focuses on one family's struggle and demise.

Frustrated by the slow progress of the revolution, Stalin began a forced collectivization of agriculture in 1933. Innocent farmers were suddenly labeled "enemies of the people." Story is told through Katrannyk (Goergi Moroziuk), his wife (Halayna Sulyma) and their three children.

Pic shows the devastation caused when the state seized the crops. It chronicles the brutality of the army's raids on fields and torture of farmers. Even more stirring are sequences depicting betrayals by friends, stealing of children, and cannibalism.

Once in a while, the helmer gets carried away with visual documentation. Pic's longest sequence describes a nasty massacre in which trainloads of farmers, some still alive, are dumped into a burial site.

With its long takes and lyrical style, pic may remind viewers of Andrei Tarkovsky. It contains many expressive tableaux, like one depicting the entire family eating out of a single soup bowl.

The pic is filled with visual pleasures. Vasyl Borodin and Mykhajlo Kretov's camera takes on an aggressive personality of its own, panning across the landscapes, showing characters in impressive long shots, then scrutinizing their faces in intimate closeups. Evocative lensing is aided by editing that smoothly integrates flashbacks into story.

One point that may stir controversy is pic's claim that Walter Duranty, a New York Times reporter who visited the Soviet Union in the '30s, knew about the famine but assisted in a coverup. — *Emanuel Levy*

YANZHI
(THE STORY OF TAIPEI WOMEN)
(TAIWANESE)

A Central Motion Picture Corp./ Wan Jen Film Co. production. (Intl. sales: Anthex, Berlin.) Produced by Chiang Feng-ch'i, Wan Jen. Executive producer, Cheng Shui-chih. Directed, written by Wan, from Yi Shu's novel. Camera (color), Yang Wei-han; editor, Liao Ch'ing-sung; music, Peter Chang; art direction, Li Fu-hsiung; costumes, P'an Mei-li; sound, Hsin Chiang-sheng, Tu Tu-chih, Hu Ting-yi; assistant director, Wang P'in; associate producer, Hsü Li-kung; line producer, Hou Chien-wen. Reviewed at Cannes Film Festival market, May 12, 1992. Running time: **108 MIN.**
Yang Chih-chün . . . . . Su Ming-ming
Mother . . . . Jeanette Lin Tsui
T'ao-t'ao . . . . Wu P'ei-yü
Uncle Yeh . . . . Kent Tseng
Son . . . . Ch'en Chün-sheng
Also with: Lei Ming, Ch'iu Hsiu-ying.
(Mandarin & Shanghainese dialogue)

"The Story of Taipei Women" is a brave stab at Asian genre-bending that could find slots in specialized film weeks. More general audiences are likely to be baffled by the juxtaposition of cool style and soapy content.

Director Wan Jen, known on the fest circuit for "Ah Fei" and "Farewell to the Channel," takes a commercial subject (a novel by popular Hong Kong authoress Yi Shu) and gives it his usual polished treatment. Wistful, rondo-like result adds up to a light gloss on generational problems, Taiwan-style.

Story, transposed from the original's Hong Kong setting, centers on three women: mid-30s interior designer Yang (Su Mingming), and her Shanghainese mother (Jeanette Lin Tsui) and teenage daughter (newcomer Wu P'ei-yü). Yang is overprotective of her daughter, whom she's raised on her own; relations with her own mom, a hard-nosed former socialite, are also strained.

Enter Yeh (Kent Tseng), a former b.f. of Yang's mom, and his handsome son (Ch'en Chünsheng). When the latter tries to romance Yang, relations between the three women are tested.

Wan neatly irons the discursive novel into a tidy script, but there's still no disguising its soap-opera content. Pic's special flavor (like that of another recent Taiwanese film, "Autumn Moon") comes from taking material that's fuelled hundreds of local mellers and pouring it into an art movie mold.

Su is fine in a highly contained perf as Yang and even convinces in the tinted flashbacks to her own troubled teen years. Veteran actress Lin ("Iron and Silk") is stiff as her mother but otherwise fits the part.

Tech credits are excellent, with standout color work by one of Taiwan's top lensers, Yang Weihan, and precision editing. Plentiful use of a waltz-like theme (and a group of serenading musicians recalling Billy Wilder's "Love in the Afternoon") results in a lovely final sequence that neatly wraps up the whole confection. Chinese title literally means "Rouge." — *Derek Elley*

OTRAZHENIIE
V ZERKALE
(REFLECTIONS IN A MIRROR)
(RUSSIAN)

A Lenfilm Studios/Kanar Ltd. co-production. Directed by Svetlana Proskurina. Screenplay, Andrei Chernikh. Camera (color), Dmitri Mass; art direction, Yuri Pachegorev; editor, Leda Semionova; music, Viacheslav Gaivoronski. Reviewed at Cannes Film Festival (Directors Fortnight), May 17, 1992. Running time: **78 MIN.**
Viktor . . . . Viktor Proskurine
Also with: Natalia Pavlova, Evgenia Dobrovolskaya, Inna Pivars.

A humorless, overly abstract core makes "Reflections in a Mirror" a hard film to warm up to. Little in this tale of a popular stage actor's midlife crisis is specifically Russian, except its frequent murkiness. Prospects for contact with offshore audiences look limited.

Director Svetlana Proskurina ("Accidental Waltz") traces the malaise of well-to-do actor Viktor Proskurine in a series of symbolic tableaux involving the women in his life.

Much of the pic seems to be adapted from a stage play; there is little movement and the emphasis is on acting and dialogue. Proskurine, the successful 40ish thesp, jumps into bed with a teenage fan. Relations with his beautiful, high-strung wife are strained.

A third woman, whom Proskurine is courting for unknown reasons, is plain and has been made ferociously morose by a handicap that requires her to use crutches. The more she glowers at him and taunts him for his affection, the more he throws himself into the role of suppliant lover.

In the end, he realizes all his tormented relationships are merely parts he's acting out, which drives him mad. He can do nothing but watch himself in their mirror, reflecting an image that isn't really him.

Pic is as elusive as a reflection. The anxieties of the St. Petersburg intelligentsia are so abstract they are almost impossible to understand, much less identify with. An excellent professional cast can do little to raise the energy level, which is very close to zero. — *Deborah Young*

AMAR Y VIVIR
(TO LOVE AND LIVE)
(COLOMBIAN)

A RTI Colombia, Cine Colombia & Colombiana de Televisión production. Executive producer, Catalina Brigde. Directed by Carlos Duplat Sanjuan. Screenplay, Sanjuan, Luz Mariela Santofimio. Camera (color), Julio Luzardo; editor, Luis Alberto Restrepo; music, Harold Orozco; art direction, José Vicente Chávez; sound, Heriberto García. Reviewed at V Americas Festival, American Film Institute, Washington, D.C., Oct. 23, 1991. **110 MIN.**
Irene . . . . María Fernando Martínez
Joaquín . . . . . . Luis Eduardo Motoa
Cuellar . . . . Waldo Urrego
Otilia . . . . Patricia Grisales
El Chacho . . . . Horacio Tavera

A commercial melodrama, "To Love and Live" was adapted from the long-running Colombian soap of the same name and stars María Fernando Martínez and Luis Eduardo Motoa. While pic is the highest-grossing national film in Colombian history, its faithfulness to source material may limit international interest.

Meandering story — rife with issues of violence, crime, rural population's exodus to the cities, music and popular local characters — begins in the small town of Bellavista. Young Joaquín (Motoa), forced to leave by a local boss, arrives in the capital and finds a job at an auto shop. He falls into crime and begins courting a humble vender and part-time singer (Martínez).

Tech work is polished and lo-cation work is extensive, but pic suffers mostly from trying to be too faithful to the soap's extended story line. It telescopes time and incidents; action jumps from one major scene to another. Also, various, distracting subplots, such as Joaquín's search for his sister, easily could have been cut.

Film's national b.o. success is due in part to its pre-existing small-screen fans and the support of co-producer Cine Colombia's domestic exhib and promotion clout. Also, its treatment of Colombian reality and plentiful music helped propel the pic to national blockbuster status.
— *Paul Lenti*

ZHAMGEDEH YOT OR
(DEADLINE IN SEVEN DAYS)
(ARMENIAN)

A Yerevan Kamerateatr production. Produced by Manvel Saribekian. Directed, written by Ara Ernjakian. Camera (color), Artiom Melkoumian; music, Ardashes Kartalian; art direction, Yevgenia Sarkissian. Reviewed at American Film Institute, L.A., June 9, 1992. (In AFI/L.A. FilmFest.) Running time: **98 MIN.**
With: Ashod Adamian, Nora Armani, Manana Melkonian.

"Deadline in Seven Days," a surreal noirish thriller with Kafkaesque overtones, is one of a kind. Scripter-helmer Ara Ernjakian's audacity and love of filmmaking reveal themselves in an onslaught of sparkling images. Stylized pic will not be to everyone's taste, but its originality should make its mark with fest and art house audiences.

Pic's hero is Khatchadour (Ashad Adamian), an idealistic and conscientious doctor whose trust in the system and human nature is challenged when he witnesses a bus accident that the government tries to hush up. His investigation of the incident entangles him in an all-encompassing political conspiracy, and he soon realizes that no one can be trusted in the corrupt totalitarian state.

Pic is also a tale of passionate romance. Khatchadour meets his love interest (the beautiful Nora Armani) at a bus stop by chance. She initially gets swept up in his strange courtship but soon tires of it, and when he tells her about the cover-up, she doesn't share his concern.

For long stretches, pic keeps its dialogue to a minimum. Language is often metaphorical but makes perfect sense in pic's allegorical context.

Strong in poetic imagery, pic is ambitious but not pretentious. Artiom Melkoumian's dark, atmospheric lensing, often permeated by rain and smoke, creates an ominous nightmare, reflecting the surreal vision of an increasingly paranoid state of mind.

Ernjakian's expert direction weaves the disparate images (some military, some religious) into a powerful and touching pic, alive with humanity and humor. His sustained inventiveness makes for a thoroughly unpredictable experience.

— *Emanuel Levy*

ARCHIVE REVIEW

LIMITE
(LIMIT)
(BRAZILIAN-B&W-SILENT)

A Museum of Modern Art release. Produced, directed, written by Mário Peixoto. Camera (b&w), Edgar Brazil; editor, Peixoto; Reviewed at 35th London Film Festival, Nov. 9, 1991. Running time: **95 MIN.** (at 19 f.p.s.)
Woman 1 . . . . Olga Breno
Woman 2 . . . . Taciana Rei
Man 1 . . . . Raul Schnoor
Man 2 . . . . D.G. Pedrera
Also with: Mário Peixoto, Carmen Santos, Yolanda Bernardes.

Much discussed at the time, but lost for decades afterwards, Mário Peixoto's 1931 silent "Limite" still has a mesmerizing power. Dubbed the "Chien Andalou" of Latino cinema and praised by Eisenstein in the '30s, surrealist pic isn't quite a major classic, but it's a hefty reminder of Brazil's filmmaking rep during the silent period.

Film was Peixoto's first and only completed project, made when helmer was in his late teens. "Limite" was first screened in Rio de Janiero in May 1931, but it led only to two other unfinished projects, some script work and a book. He's reported to be living in Copacabana.

Pic kicks off with some striking images of a man's handcuffed hands in front of a woman's face, a sparkling seascape and closeups of a girl's eyes. There's then the first of many shots of a man and two women adrift in a rowboat, dying of thirst and prey to fantasies. Rest of the action is their flashback memories.

Vague plot, set in a seaside town, has something to do with an escapee on the run, a man who works as an accompanist in a cinema, and two femmes. Relationships are vague at best, not helped by a short missing section and Peixoto's habit of showing only arms and legs of his protagonists.

Film's strength is its imagery rather than story or dialog (whole pic has only three intertitles). Offbeat angles, brattish displays of technique, massive closeups and stark landscapes create a despairing atmosphere of people on the edge (or "limit").

Clearly shot on an amateur basis, the film lacks the intellectual references and rigor of Bönuel's silent classics, but as an avant-garde elegy fully deserves its rep. Musical soundtrack (with extracts from works by Satie, Debussy, Borodin, Ravel, Stravinsky, Franck, Prokofiev) fits like a glove and helps to carry the picture during its more pedestrian stretches.

Print from the U.K.'s National Film Archive was shown at 19 frames per second, reckoned by restorers to be the most authentic speed. Quality is good, apart from a brief patch of nitrate decomposition 15 minutes in. Peixoto himself contributes a plot-crucial cameo as a weirdo in a graveyard. —*Derek Elley*

BED & BREAKFAST

A Hemdale Pictures release of a Jack Schwartzman production. Produced by Schwartzman. Co-producer, Marcus Viscidi. Directed by Robert Ellis Miller. Screenplay, Cindy Myers. Camera (color), Peter Sova; editor, John F. Burnett; music, David Shire; production design, Suzanne Cavedon; art direction, Ron Wilson; set decoration, Tracey Doyle; costume design, Jennifer Von Mayrhauser; sound (Dolby), Mike Rowland; casting, Dianne Crittenden. Reviewed at Beverly Center Cineplex, L.A., Aug. 11, 1992. MPAA Rating: PG-13. Running time: **98 MIN.**
Adam . . . . Roger Moore
Claire . . . . Talia Shire
Ruth . . . . Colleen Dewhurst
Cassie . . . . Nina Siemaszko
Amos . . . . Ford Rainey
Mitch . . . . Jamie Walters

Set on the breathtaking coast of Maine, "Bed & Breakfast" is an old-fashioned family melodrama about a charming stranger who descends on a household of squabbling women. Three-generational plot and the late Colleen Dewhurst's towering performance could have had some appeal among femme viewers, but pic is so predictable and sentimental that it will be quickly forgotten at the box office, making a fast route to video.

Claire (Talia Shire), the young widow of a Kennedy-like senator, runs a bed-and-breakfast owned by Ruth, her feisty mother-in-law (Colleen Dewhurst). The generational rift between the anxiety-ridden, repressed Shire and her rebellious adolescent daughter (Nina Siemaszko) occupies most of the narrative.

The depressingly stagnant tribe begins to change when the body of a mysterious stranger (Roger Moore), a con man pretending to have amnesia, washes ashore. Naming him Adam, the women hire him as a handyman. Soon his charismatic presence motivates them to renovate the run-down house and forces each woman to reassess her unfulfilled life and start afresh.

A theatrical sensibility permeates the film's conflicts, usually staged as confrontations between two characters. Cindy Myers' perfunctory script offers no narrative surprise; the few good bits are embedded in a schematic structure. Though scripted by a woman, film's sexual politics are a 1950s throwback reminiscent of William Inge's work.

It could have been fun to watch the always tanned and glamorous Moore in the midst of three bickering women, all attracted to him. But the film uses melodramatically conceived characters and situations without giving viewers the juicy satisfactions of the form.

Helmer Robert Ellis Miller, director of the deliciously bright comedy "Reuben, Reuben," has not done himself proud here. He handles the film gently, showing too much respect for the slight material. His generosity to the actors also has the unfortunate effect of exposing Myers' lackluster script.

Still, this the kind of small, intimate picture actors relish. The stunningly sensual Dewhurst dominates every scene she's in, making the lusty and down-to-earth Ruth at once credible and enchanting, and providing the only reason to see this amiable but timid film.

It's refreshing to see Shire, wife of producer Jack Schwartzman, in a different kind of role from those she played in the "Rocky" and "Godfather" films. Moore, gracefully aging in his post-James Bond era, gives one of his characteristically effortless but shallow performances.

Everything about the film is literal, from the women's coifs (pulled back before the stranger appears, down after his arrival), to the name they choose for him. Except for a few impressive Maine seascape shots, Peter Sova's camera observes with dispassionate efficiency. David Shire's music comments on the action and inflates the emotions the story attempts to arouse.

— *Emanuel Levy*

ALLEIN UNTER FRAUEN
(ALONE AMONG WOMEN)
(GERMAN)

A Scotia Film presentation of KF Kinofilm Sam Waynberg & SWF co-production. Produced by Dietrich Mack. Line producer, Wolfgang Bosken. Directed by Sonke Wortmann. Screenplay, Philipp Weinges. Camera (color), Hans-Jorg Allgeier; editor, Gudrun Bohl; music, Torsten Breuer; costume design, Katharina Von Martius. Reviewed at Famous Players Eaton Cinema, Aug. 8, 1992. (In Just For Laughs Comedy Festival.) Running time: **90 MIN.**
With: Thomas Heinze, Jennifer Nitsch, Carin C. Tietze, Meret Becker, Michael Schreiner.

Like its title, "Alone Among Women" is a provocative double-edged sword for both audience and target (a man). Much like previous German art house hit "Men," this comedy cleverly weaves feminism into a heterosexual mating dance. Predictable match should delight bran-and-fiber urbanites seeking politically correct foreign fare.

Unique premise is based on a trio of gorgeous feminists who set a trap for a gum-chewing, leather-clad swine, believing that if they can convert an "arrogant self-centered braggart" into a sensitive man, they've won the battle of the sexes. Unsuspecting of their experiment, unemployed Tom (smoothly played by Thomas Heinze) moves into the career women's basement and reluctantly accepts their job offer as househusband.

Treated as a sex object by sadistic physiotherapist Vio and ignored by battered Leah, sly Tom has his sights set on the fiesty, willowy blond electrician Annette (Jennifer Nitsch), who becomes increasingly confused about why she invited the fox into the hen house.

Annette's jealous fit when she finds out about Vio and Tom's basement rendezvous leads to childish pouting and turns this potential lesson into a typical boy-gets-girl scenario. Even when Annette funnels her energy back into raiding porn cinemas, there's never a moment's doubt the two will end up together.

Scripter Philipp Weinges cleverly works in lines such as "Porn films make men think women enjoy being humiliated," and male helmer Sonke Wortmann goes to great lengths to maintain the illusion his is a politically correct women's pic.

However, when Hans-Jorg Allgeier's camera starts lingering late in the film over Nitsch's voluptuous bathing suit-clad body, the p.o.v. has subtly shifted, as has the target. Ultimately, Tom has learned the new rules, and Annette gets beaten at her own game.

Also like "Men," pic deserves kudos for making a serious issue a light, highly entertaining and edifying romp, as it's impossible not to root for the brute during his metamorphosis.

This item requires an equally sly marketing strategy, but concept alone should spark some good word-of-mouth and press coverage. It would also provide a terrific alternative on homevid shelves.
— *Suzan Ayscough*

FAUX RAPPORTS
(FALSE REPORTS)
(SWISS)

A Tlaloc Films/Television Suisse Romande co-production. Produced, directed, written by Daniel Calderon. Camera (color), Yves Pouliquen; editor, Calderon; music, André Amrein; art direction, Pietro Musillo; sound, Laurent Barbey. Reviewed at Rex Cinema, Vevey, Switzerland, July 27, 1992. (Competing at Vevey Intl. Festival of Comedy Films). Running time: **75 MIN.**
Jim Goodis . . . . Andrew Moore
Charles-Albert Baer . . . . Teco Celio
Wife . . . . Karine Guex-Pierre
Mistress . . . . Sophie Paul
Berndt . . . . . Jean-Françoise Perrier
Garnier . . . . Howard Vernon

Upper echelon ties between money, sex and power are satirized in Swiss writer/helmer Daniel Calderon's first feature, "Faux Rapports." Pic has impressive visual flair, but absence of a defined story line will probably limit it to festivals and local wickets.

Set in "a big city in the '90s," pic evokes hard times in both high and low places. A swank industrial spy (Andrew Moore) is sleeping with his biz partner's wife but grows jealous when his own wife takes a lover. His files are rife with phony companies that serve as smokescreens for local pols and businessmen. Profoundly bored, he decides to blow the whistle on his own shady dealings.

Underdeveloped parallel intrigue concerns a nerdy cipher (Teco Celio) who latches on to public figures and mimics their personalities. The nebulous guy is made head of a phantom holding company, but he's not as harmless as he seems.

Film gets off to a snappy start only to peter out, but it has a clean, airy feel conveyed via nicely framed shots and offbeat imagery: Moore inserts a contact lens while looking in a mirror, and the room comes into focus. At another point, he tosses a poodle into a plate of hors d'oeuvres.

Englishman Moore, an established French-language performer in France, is frosty and ruthless as the hero. Thesping is good across the board, although not one character is the least bit sympathetic. Designer furnishings underscore the emotional distances between people.

The odd but appealing twang of an Afro-beat Jew's harp pops up in places. — *Lisa Nesselson*

TABLEAU D'HONNEUR
(HONOR ROLL)
(FRENCH)

An AFMD release of a CAPAC production in association with Investimage 3, Cofimage 3 & participation of Canal Plus. Produced by Paul Claudon. Directed by Charles Nemes. Screenplay, Nemes, Philippe Ferran. Camera (color), Etienne Fauduet; editor, Adeline Yoyotte-Husson; music, Marc-Olivier Dupin; sound, Alix Comte; costumes, Rose-Marie Melka; set design, Clorinde Méry. Reviewed at Club 13 screening room, Paris, Aug. 5, 1992. Running time: **95 MIN.**
With: Guillaume de Tonquédec, Claude Jade, Philippe Khorsand, Eric Elmosnino, François Berléand, Jean-Paul Roussillon, Evelyne Buyle.

The acting is adequate and the characters likable in "Tableau d'Honneur," but Charles Nemes' mildly diverting, middle-of-the-road comedy set in a private, suburban Paris high school plays more like a TV sitcom than a big-screen film.

Unsure as to what it's really about, pic is pleasant enough, but its characters intersect way too neatly to provide more than superficial commentary on "today's youth" or "hypocrisy in institutions." Co-scripter/helmer's third feature is just another competently executed but unlikely adolescent romance.

Handsome Jules (Guillaume de Tonquédec) has problems with school and girls. His domineering dad (Philippe Khorsand) doesn't make matters easier, although his mom (Claude Jade) is supportive of her only child. Contemplating an extramarital affair, Jade attempts to discreetly shop for condoms, a cute twist on what is traditionally a teenage boy's awkward ordeal.

Jules falls in with a playfully unscrupulous alum (Eric Elmosnino) who's launched a consumer rights crusade to get a tuition refund on the grounds that he can't hold a job so his education must have been faulty. Jules is also befriended by the school proctor (François Berléand), an unemployed actor who keeps Jules after school simply so he can collect overtime pay while practicing his lines.

Raspy-voiced Jean-Paul Roussillon is amusing as the principal, and Evelyne Buyle scores as his foul-mouthed secretary. Sparse score is perky, and all tech credits are okay.

— *Lisa Nesselson*

BOTTOM LAND

An Elephant Group presentation. Produced, directed by Edward A. Radtke. Screenplay, Radtke, M.S. Nieson. Camera (Duart color, 16m), John Inwood; editors, Suzanne Boucher, Radtke; music, Jim Young; sound, Neil Danziger; additional sound, Joe Romano; assistant director, Casi Pacillo; associate producers, Adriana Rivera, M.S. Nieson. Reviewed at WorldFest/Houston, April 25, 1992. Running time: **75 MIN.**
Bo Saunders . . . . . . Haskell Phillips
Stephen Saunders . . . . Richard Hyde
Wynn Saunders . . Bryan Shane Allen
Carl Richardson . . . . Ken West
Mrs. Richardson . . . . . . Eva Woods

"Bottom Land" is a no-frills, heartfelt drama that marks Edward A. Radtke as a filmmaker worth keeping an eye on. Technically rough-hewn, but dramatically sound pic deserves frequent exposure on the fest circuit, though its commercial prospects are iffy.

Radtke establishes his full control with the opening shot, a leisurely pan that initially appears to be a sunrise. As the camera glides along a stretch of highway, however, audience realizes the glow is an emergency flare at the site of a terrible car accident.

Crash seriously injures Ohio farmer Richard Hyde and kills his wife. Six months later, Hyde is released from a hospital following his nervous breakdown. His grizzled father (Haskell Phillips) offers a less than warm welcome home as he doesn't cotton much to psychiatry, and he sees his son as a weakling for being unable to stand the emotional devastation of his wife's death.

Meanwhile, Hyde's 8-year-old young son (Bryan Shane Allen) is seriously spooked, fearing his father and yet desperate for his love. The tentative rebirth of their relationship is delicately handled and deeply moving.

Pic basically is a three-hander, with Hyde anxious to regain his own father's respect, Phillips adamantly refusing to offer anything in the way of compassion, and Allen torn between both men. Climax is sound and satisfying without pandering to audience expectations.

Filmed on location in Ohio with partial funding from the state's arts council, pic has modest production values; sound quality in particular is annoyingly uneven. But the performances, especially Phillips' willfully hard-hearted grandfather, are first-rate.

Pic is the sort of commendable character-driven drama that regional filmmakers often strive for, but all too rarely pull off this well. — *Joe Leydon*

DOUBLE X:
THE NAME OF THE GAME
(BRITISH)

A Feature Film Co. (U.K.) release of a String of Pearls production. (Intl. sales: New World Intl.) Produced by Shani S. Grewal. Executive producer, Noel Cronin. Line producer, Edward Joffe. Directed, written by Grewal, based on David Fleming's short story "Vengeance." Camera (Fujicolor; Technicolor prints), Dominique Grosz; editor, Michael Johns; music, Raf Ravenscroft; production design, Colin Pocock; costume design, Andrew Edwards, John Cowell; sound (Dolby), Simon Clark, Cox; stunt coordinator, Terry Forrestal; assistant director, Quenton D. Annis. Reviewed at MGM Oxford Street theater, London, June 5, 1992. Running time: **96 MIN.**
Arthur Clutten . . . . Norman Wisdom
Michael Cooper . . . . . . William Katt
Jenny . . . . Gemma Craven
Edward Ross . . . . Simon Ward
Iggy Smith . . . . Bernard Hill
Sarah . . . . Chloe Annett

Veteran Brit pratfall comic Norman Wisdom makes an ill-advised return to the big screen in "Double X," an inept low-budget suspenser. Reliable cast is double-crossed by a laughable script and clumsy helming. Result, which hardly cuts it even as a TV pic, should expire fast.

A major U.K. b.o. draw during the 1950s and early '60s as a kind of homegrown Jerry Lewis, Wisdom last appeared in a film some 20 years ago. His aging fans will prefer to draw a veil over this belated attempt to play a straight dramatic role.

Pic is narrated by a former Chicago cop (William Katt) vacationing in Scotland. In the coastal village of Portpatrick, he befriends the nervous Wisdom, who, in a 40-minute flashback, tells how he's been on the run from a crime ring.

The bad guys have kidnapped Wisdom's daughter (newcomer Chloe Annett). An hour in, pic springs a major twist and veers off in another direction, with Katt trying to rescue the daughter. Silly finale pulls a cheap "Sunset Boulevard"-like script stunt.

Wisdom, sadly miscast, is dramatically wobbly and looks uneasy throughout; Bernard Hill, as a comic psycho, seems out of place; Simon Ward, looking like an overfed Christopher Walken, has fleeting moments as an oily crime boss; and Katt is solid as

the Yank.

Helming by Shani S. Grewal, in his feature bow, is routine in action segs and ham-fisted in dialog sequences. Tech credits are passable, with interiors shot at Bray Studios. Pic is the first feature made under the U.K.'s Business Expansion Scheme giving tax breaks to small investors. — *Derek Elley*

WILD WHEELS
(DOCU-16m)

A Tara release. Produced, directed by Harrod Blank. Narration written, directed by David Silberberg. Camera (color, 16m), Paul Cope, Harrod Blank, Les Blank; editor, Harrod Blank; sound, Silberberg; additional camera, Silberberg, Liz Zivic. Reviewed on videocassette, N.Y. No MPAA Rating. Running time: **64 MIN.**

A celebration of the work and personalities of those zanies who decorate their cars, "Wild Wheels" is a funny, deadpan documentary. Film, filmmaker and his decorated VW beetle will tour the country beginning Aug. 21.

Director Harrod Blank is a chip off the block of dad Les Blank, contriving a film that matches its subject matter. Decrying mass production, pic is strictly hand-made like the 45 weird cars it displays.

Blank traveled across the country to find and interview the owners. They emerge as free spirits, some flaky, some certifiable, but all exuding a '60s individualism. Nearly all are amateurs with the designation "car art" stressed by the more pretentious ones a hard concept to swallow. Most viewers will conclude that Blank and his soulmates are exhibitionists and/or entertainers.

Foremost in latter category are Jon Barnes, who sings and plays along in his "Ultimate Taxi" with an interior boasting a keyboard and nightclub lighting; and Dalton Stevens who plays guitar and obsessively covers his car and clothing with buttons.

A unique concept is presented by Gene Pool, whose "Grass Car" literally sprouts a lawn of grass to amuse and stimulate gawkers. Several of the owners make environmental statements with their autos, others are religious fanatics and the many nutcases include inevitable UFO spotters.

Blank doesn't push the film's message, but cumulatively a picture of Middle America emerges

with its pop/trash culture built around swap meets and flea markets (where the protagonists find their decorative materials).
— *Lawrence Cohn*

THE PAINT JOB

A Second Son Entertainment Co. presentation. Produced by Mark Pollard, Randall Poster. Executive producer, Marc Glimcher. Directed, written by Michael Taav. Camera (Alpha Cine color), Robert Yeoman; editor, Nancy Richardson; music, John Wesley Harding; production design, Mark Friedberg; costumes, Wendy A. Rolfe; art direction, Ginger Tougas; sound (Ultra Stereo), B. Warner; associate producers, Susan Dupre, Jennifer Vian Dennis, Lynn Goldner. Reviewed at WorldFest/Houston, April 27, 1992. MPAA rating: R. Running time: **96 MIN.**
With: Will Patton, Bebe Neuwirth, Robert Pastorelli, Casey Siemaszko, Mark Boone Jr.

If Joel and Ethan Coen had no talent, they might come up with "The Paint Job," an aggressively unfunny and over-played comedy that turns into a half-witted serial-killer thriller midway through. A couple of sitcom regulars in the cast may help vid sales, but theatrical prospects are nil.

Will Patton, a fine character actor overdue for a breakthrough, takes a few steps backward with his dim-bulb portrayal of a small-town housepainter in love with his boss' discontent, flaky wife (Bebe Neuwirth).

What the painter doesn't know might hurt him: Boss Robert Pastorelli has been killing drunken derelicts who remind him of his abusive father. Murder element, introduced relatively late in film, is cued by prologue sequence depicting one of Dad's drunken, macho rages.

Patton's tentative courtship of Neuwirth is played for broad laughs, as is the romance's frenetic consummation. But the comedy is too silly for words and brings out the actors' hammy worst. On the other hand, Pastorelli hits a few effective notes of menace and bottled-up rage.

Casey Siemaszko and Mark Boone Jr. are along for the ride as two fellow painters. Entire cast has been encouraged to speak in the kind of exaggerated nasal twang common to bad movies set in the U.S. heartland. (Pic was shot in and around Kenosha, Wisc.) Characters thus come across even more thick-headed than they are.

Director-screenwriter Michael Taav manages only a few mildly

amusing lines, most of them attempts at the deadpan humor. Tech credits are undistinguished, save for John Wesley Harding's pleasant musical score.
— *Joe Leydon*

MEET THE PARENTS

A CEM Prods. presentation. Produced by James Vincent. Executive producer, Emo Philips. Directed by Greg Glienna. Screenplay, Glienna, Mary Ruth Clarke. Camera (color), Bradley Sellers; editors, Glienna, James Vincent; music, Scott May; sound, Chris List; assistant director, James Vincent. Reviewed at Famous Players Eaton Cinema, Montreal, Aug. 6, 1992. (In Just For Laughs Comedy Festival.) Running time: **72 MIN.**
With: Greg Glienna, Jacqueline Cahill, Dick Galloway, Carol Whelan, Mary Ruth Clarke.

Who ever heard of a comedy where everyone gets shot, maimed, drowned or commits suicide? Welcome to the tragic world of Greg Glienna, whose wonderfully twisted black comedy turns a visit with the in-laws into a nightmare. Clearly not for mainstream auds, "Meet the Parents" could garner a cult following among anti-establishment urbanites.

Excessive and occasionally overdone, pic is a blatant attack on marriage, suburban indifference, Christian hypocrisy and the nuclear family.

Presented almost entirely in flashback, tale begins when a gas station attendant warns a client en route to meet the future in-laws to turn back while he still can. What follows is the tragic story of a previous future groom who didn't take the advice.

Enter inconspicuous and well-meaning Glienna, who innocently destroys everything he touches; he overflows the toilet and drops the dinner roast. After breakfast, Glienna blinds the mother with a fishing rod, ruins the family car, drowns the dog and accidentally climbs into bed with his fiancée's sister. Blackmail time leads to disaster.

Pic falls victim to predictability, as script desperately needed an objective eye and an occasional breather. As is, relentless theme leaves audience predicting the next catastrophe. Still, this low-budget indie is an amusing vehicle aptly displaying Glienna's multiple talents. Tech credits are raw.

— *Suzan Ayscough*

VERATARTS AVEDYATS YERGIR
(RETURN TO THE PROMISED LAND)
(ARMENIAN-DOCU-COLOR/B&W)

An Armenfilms Studios production. Directed by Haroutiun Katchatrian. Screenplay, Mikayel Stamboltsian, Katchatrian. Camera (color/b&w), Artiom Melkoumian; music, Avet Terterian; sound, Anahit Gessayan. Reviewed at Monica 4-Plex, Santa Monica, Calif., June 20, 1992. (In AFI/L.A. FilmFest.) Running time: **79 MIN.**

Relying exclusively on visual imagery and sound effects, this 1991 docudrama about a family trying to build a new home in harsh northern Armenia offers a powerful vision of a humanly rich but socially impoverished country. Wordless account and slow pace will restrict appeal of "Return to the Promised Land" to film fests and specialized venues.

Film begins with a black & white video of a mass demonstration in Yerevan following the devastating 1988 earthquake. Shot with a restless hand-held camera, sequence shows the casualties, wrecked buildings and thousands of homeless survivors crying in the streets.

Docudrama then switches to color as it chronicles the ordeal of Razmig, his pregnant wife and his young daughter as they transform barren land into green fields after months of excruciatingly hard work. Pic's cyclical approach follows the farming family through the four seasons.

The silent characters appear to be completely un-self-conscious in front of the unobtrusive camera. Sparing closeups of family members reveal expressionless faces; no melodramatics are imposed on the material. Viewers get an account of the tedium but also the beauty of routine life in the most primitive conditions.

Pic's major innovation is Avet Terterian's music approximating naturalistic sound. At one point, a whole symphony is created out of farm animal sounds. In another poignant scene, birth of a farmer's baby is depicted entirely via sound, sans visuals, as wife's screams during labor gradually segue to the baby's cries.

Although the pic focuses on one nuclear family, at the end the town becomes a community during a performance of a troupe of traveling musicians and acrobats. Yet just as the tone becomes peaceful and optimistic, director Haroutiun Katchatrian changes gears again and ends on a pessimistic note.

Though without dialogue or conventional drama, pic is not shapeless: Its specific form derives from the selectivity of the material and its editing.
— *Emanuel Levy*

LET'S KILL ALL THE LAWYERS

A Lighten Up Films presentation of a Dakota Jas production. Produced by Shannon Hamed. Executive producers, Hamed, Ron Senkowski, James A. Courtney, Brian C. Manoogian. Directed, written by Senkowski. Camera (color), Lou Stratton; editor, Christa Kindt; music, Martin Liebman; art direction, Tom Chaney; costumes, Scarlett Jade; sound, Al Rizzo; associate producers, Shannon Rain Berritt, David Monforton, Tom Tucker. Reviewed at WorldFest/Houston, April 27, 1992. Running time: **95 MIN.**
Foster Markul . . . . . Rick Frederick
Junior Rawley . . . . . . James Vezina
Satori Bunko . . . . Michelle DeVuono
Pops . . . . Lee Gusta
Larissa . . . . Cheryl Roy
Penelope . . . . Joanne Long
Crazy Mikey . . . . . . Ron Senkowski

Novice writer-director Ron Senkowski offers a few laughs in "Let's Kill All the Lawyers." Small-budget Michigan-filmed effort won't generate much b.o. coin but may find a few advocates on homevideo and cable.

Pic works best as a series of satirical comic blackouts. The gimmick is that a radical group called the Abe Lincoln Abductors is kidnapping dozens of lawyers throughout a large city. Each attorney has a few moments to demonstrate just how greedy, double-dealing or otherwise sleazy he or she is before being bagged. All that's missing at the end of each segment is the sound of a rim shot.

Trouble is, the weak plot uniting the blackouts is not half so funny. Rick Frederick plays a likable young law student shocked to learn that his mentor, a slick attorney played by Gene Siskel look-alike James Vezina, is corrupt.

Even as his disillusionment grows, Frederick is increasingly attracted to Michelle DeVuono, who operates a New Age retreat where lawyers can get in touch with their feelings. Not surprisingly, she's behind the kidnappings and has rigged a deadly booby trap for those lawyers who refuse to mellow out.

The kidnap-murder scheme is only sketchily developed and seems only an excuse to link the jokes. Best running gags have Senkowski playing Crazy Mikey, a wild-eyed attorney whose TV spots advise would-be litigants to "Give your case to Mikey — he'll try *anything.*"

Wit remains pretty much on the sophomoric level. But, then again, sophomores can be very funny sometimes. Performances are keyed to the pic's cartoonish level. Tech values are modest but more than adequate.
— *Joe Leydon*

LES ANNÉES CAMPAGNE
(THE COUNTRY YEARS)
(FRENCH)

An Ariane release of a Les Films Ariane/Baccara Prods./Films A2/Centre Européen Cinématographique Rhône-Alpes co-production. Produced by Chantal Perrin. Directed, written by Philippe Leriche. Camera (color), Etiene Fauduet; editor, Marie-Pierre Renaud; music, Georges Garvarentz; costumes, Marie-Claude Altot; set design, Dominique Maleret; sound, Paul Lainé. Reviewed at Parnassiens cinema, Paris, June 13, 1992. Running time: **88 MIN.**
Grandfather . . . . . Charles Aznavour
Jules . . . . Benoit Magimel
Evelyne . . . . Sophie Carle
Mother . . . . . . Clémentine Célarié
Grandmother . . . . Françoise Arnoul
Le Rouquin . . . Pierre-Olivier Mornas

"Les Années Campagne" adds nothing to the coming-of-age genre but first-time writer/helmer Philippe Leriche sensitively tells a somewhat banal tale with an eye for the pleasures and shortcomings of country life. Old-fashioned pic will fare best on TV and should lead to other roles for the young protagonist.

Fifteen-year-old Jules (Benoit Magimel) rarely sees his busy parents, who flit between Paris and Milan. A well-mannered only child who adores his mother and dislikes his businesslike father, he relishes rural life with his maternal grandparents (Charles Aznavour, Françoise Arnoul). When financial necessity obliges the retired couple to relocate to an apartment in a nearby town, Jules moves with them.

The fishing isn't nearly as good and the local youngsters are a cruel batch of losers and misfits, but Jules holds his own. A shapely young woman (Sophie Carle) initiates Jules into the pleasures of sex, which will be of some comfort to him when a twist of fate alters his family situation.

Aznavour is mellow and entertaining as Grandpa. All of the supporting players contribute to a believable atmosphere of boredom mitigated by the occasional prank or fight. Magimel, who resembles a young Sean Penn, is likable and convincing as the boy.

Lensing plays up the golden glow of summer in the French countryside. — *Lisa Nesselson*

LE RETOUR DES CHARLOTS
(THE CHARLOTS RETURN)
(FRENCH)

A Sirius release of a Films Christian Ardan/TF-1 Films/Prods. Belles Rives co-production with participation of Canal Plus. Produced by Christian Ardan. Directed, written by Jean Sarrus. Camera (color), C. Becognée; editor, M.J. Audiard; music, Patrick Ardan; costumes, C. Bourbigot; sound, G. Barra. Reviewed at Pathé Clichy cinema, Paris, June 26, 1992. Running time: **80 MIN.**
With: Luis Rego, Jezabelle Amato, Gérard Filipelli, Richard Bonnot, Jean Sarrus, Guy Montagné, Laurent Hilling, Jango Edwards, Gustave Parking.

Dumb sight gags, slapstick nonsense, wretched puns and a never more than perfunctory regard for lensing make "Le Retour des Charlots" a low-rent product that will garner a few cheap belly laughs on TV and video. Postsynchronizing is so approximate in places that this French pic (which dropped out of sight the week after its Paris release) may actually be improved by dubbing into other languages.

In the 10 years since shiftless Antonio returned to his native Portugal with his once svelte Parisian bride Amalia, she has taken on the proportions of a Macy's parade balloon. When she catches Antonio cheating on her with the sexy number who lives upstairs, she whacks him on the head. Rather than explain his infidelity, hubby feigns amnesia.

After a wacko doctor suggests Antonio's memory might be jarred by creating strong experiences from his past, Amalia calls on Antonio's three lifelong buddies in Paris, known collectively as "The Charlots," comprised of a wealthy dunce, a sneaky businessman, a giddy ladies' man and their one-time commanding officer. Pic revolves around their misguided efforts to remind their supposedly amnesiac pal of their many wild and woolly adventures gone by while getting into further difficulties in Lisbon.

At ease in her ample body, Jezebelle Amato anchors the silliness with her unaffected perf as Amalia. Rest of cast employs a casual toss-away style that suggests they just wanted a trip to Lisbon. Camerawork is completely rudimentary and gags are TV-skit fodder drawn out to feature length. After the first hour, script no longer even tries to make sense, but its crass humor keeps things moving along.

— *Lisa Nesselson*

HO SAP EL MINISTRE?
(DOES THE MINISTER KNOW?)
(SPANISH-CATALONIAN)

An Aura Films production & presentation. Produced by Richard Figueras. Directed by Josep M. Forn. Screenplay, Anna Laurado, Jaume Subirana, based on an original idea by Enrique Llovet, Diego Santillian. Camera (color), Xavier Cami; editor, Joana G. Saladie; music, Joan Vives; sound, Francisco Lopez; assistant director, Marcel Li Pares. Reviewed at Famous Players Eaton Cinema, Montreal, Aug. 5, 1992. (In Just for Laughs Comedy Festival.) Running time: 101 MIN.
With: Rosa Maria Sarda, Juango Puigcorbe, Juan Luis Galiardo, Jose Sazatornil, Muntsa Alcaniz, Ana Obregon, Peter Hortel, Francisco Carmana.

This politically charged sex farce found its ideal showcase at Montreal's Just for Laughs comedy fest and would please most audiences seeking escape with a lascivious twist. A slow tickler with a happy ending, "Does the Minister Know?" is light, gleefully adulterous fare for foreign film fans.

Two families from rivaling Catalonia and Andalusia vy for a $5 million contract to manufacture army uniforms. The pact is the McGuffin that draws frustrated and oversexed family members into countless hotel rooms in Madrid, where shenanigans unravel.

A dashing Peter Hortel plays a philanderer who married into the family for money. While he's regularly engaged in sex games with the company lawyer, his wife Marta pursues her lifelong mission to achieve orgasm by reading self-help books.

Meanwhile, clumsy sister Montse pines away about a long-lost anarchist love, who turns out to be the defense minister, while she's being pursued by the minister's assistant. Competitor Francisco Carmana falls for Marta thinking she's the compa-

ny lawyer.

Cute but predictable comedy unfolds like a TV soap, as all players wind up with new loves.

Low budget is not wasted: All tech credits are good, and wardrobe is exceptionally revealing of characters. The frustrated wife's transformation from plain Jane to tacky, overdressed blonde, and the company lawyer's radically different attire in boardroom and bedroom, superbly delineate characters.

Overly long pic could have used a final edit, as closing scenes drag when couples reorganize. Already knowing the outcome, audience is waiting for credits to roll. — *Suzan Ayscough*

NOCTURNO A ROSARIO
(NOCTURNE TO ROSARIO)
(MEXICAN)

A Mexican Film Institute (Imcine) release of an Imcine/Cooperativa José Revueltas/Fondo de Fomento a la Calidad Cinematográfica production. Produced, directed, written by Matilde Landeta. Camera (color), Henner Hoffman; editor, Carlos Savage; music, Amparo Rubín; sound, Oscar Mateos. Reviewed at 8th Muestra de Cine Mexicano, Guadalajara, Mexico, March 31, 1992. Running time: 86 MIN.
Manuel Acuña . . . . . Simón Guevara
Rosario de la Peña . . . . Ofelia Medina
Soledad . . . . Patricia Reyes Spíndola
Juan de Dios . . . . . . Andreas Pearce
Laura . . . . Evangelina Sosa

Although it is admirable that septuagenarian Mexican pioneer filmmaker Matilde Landeta has helmed a new film after a hiatus of over 40 years (her last film was the 1951 "Trotacalles"), results here are decidedly lackluster. Unfortunately, historical biopic comes off merely as a filmed script that seems ultimately destined for cultural TV fare.

Costumed drama is based on the life of national romantic poet Manuel Acuña, who committed suicide in 1873 at the age of 24. Acted by Spanish actor Simón Guevara, character lacks passion and fervor, generally looking like a wounded puppy.

Pic begins in contempo Mexico with a woman looking for a copy of Acuña's w.k. poem "Nocturne to Rosaurio," a paean to Rosario de la Peña (Ofelia Medina), a woman of questionable past who ran a fashionable arty salon.

Film flashbacks to 1867 when, as a student at the Academy of San Carlos, the 18-year-old poet behaves like a cad, first seducing his lowly maid (Patricia Reyes

Spíndola), later abandoning her for the orphaned strong-minded Laura (Evangelina Sosa).

When he meets the singular Rosario, stiffly played by Medina in yet another historical role, she is taken by his youthful literary reputation and basks in the poems that he dedicates to her, but she continually rejects his obsessive advances.

Tale is played out against a turbulent political backdrop that includes the deaths of Benito Juárez and Austrian prince/ex-emperor of Mexico Maximilian. But little insight is had on the period or Acuña's personality.

Period reconstruction is beautiful and tech work is above par, but camera placement lacks imagination or creativity. Pic strives for the right historical and reverential look, but script does little to penetrate the glossy surface.

— *Paul Lenti*

RAPID FIRE

A 20th Century Fox release of a Robert Lawrence production. Produced by Lawrence. Executive producers, Gerald Olson, John Fasano. Directed by Dwight H. Little. Screenplay, Alan McElroy, from story by Cindy Cirile, McElroy. Camera (Deluxe color), Ric Waite; editor, Gib Jaffe; music, Christopher Young; production design, Ron Foreman; art direction, Charles Butcher; set design, Natalie Richards; set decoration, Leslie Frankenheimer; costume design, Erica Edell Phillips; sound (Dolby), Rob Janiger; stunt coordinator, Jeff Imada; fight choreography, Brandon Lee, Imada; associate producer, Barry Berg; assistant director, Denis Stewart; 2nd unit director, Olson; casting, Richard Pagano, Sharon Bialy, Debi Manwiller. Reviewed at 20th Century Fox screening room, West L.A., Aug. 13, 1992. MPAA Rating: R. Running time: 95 MIN.
Jake Lo . . . . Brandon Lee
Mace Ryan . . . . Powers Boothe
Antonio Serrano . . . . . Nick Mancuso
Agent Stuart . . . . Raymond J. Barry
Karla Withers . . . . Kate Hodge
Kinman Tau . . . . Tzi Ma
Brunner Gazzi . . . . . . Tony Longo
Carl Chang . . . . . Michael Paul Chan

Brandon Lee, American-born son of the legendary chop-socky hero Bruce Lee, acquits himself well in his first lead role in a U.S. film, "Rapid Fire," as a pacifist college student forced to become a killing machine. Director Dwight H. Little expertly handles implausible but entertaining action sequences that keep the pic lively despite a schlocky plot and cardboard characterizations. The Fox release is a serviceable late-summer market entry.

Flashback memories of the Lee character's late father (not Bruce) being crushed by a tank at Bei-

jing's Tiananmen Square explain his underlying aversion to violence and political activity in Alan McElroy's script. Using such an event as backstory for this kind of pic is exploitive, but the character's obsession with his father's heroic memory does provide Lee with a shred of character to hang onto.

The lad's heritage naturally includes thorough martial arts training and a lithely muscular physique, both of which he's lucky to have after he witnesses a gangland rub-out. Thankfully devoid of standard hunk narcissism, young Lee manages to maintain audience sympathy despite having to surrender his ideals and annihilate hordes of bad guys (stock Mafia and Oriental types) on behalf of Chicago cop Powers Boothe.

Boothe, enjoyable as a lower-budget Clint Eastwood type, has moral ambiguities of his own; the audience realizes that because he never shaves, works out of an abandoned bowling alley, does illegal wiretapping and coldly uses Lee as bait in his 10-year vendetta against heroin-dealing bigwigs Tzi Ma and Nick Mancuso.

Aptly described in the advertising campaign as "unarmed and extremely dangerous," Lee mainly employs his fists and feet to survive the action set-pieces involving promiscuous expenditure of ammunition, shattering glass and smashing furniture. He has a seemingly superhuman ability to avoid being shot, but in a pinch will pick up a gun and fire it before dropping it with a grimace.

The script doesn't give the guy much choice about turning to a life of violence because he'd be a sitting duck otherwise. Boothe's macho female partner (is there any other kind these days?) Kate Hodge talks a lot about the idealism of the war on drugs, but it rings as hollow as most political rhetoric on that subject.

Little and his filmmaking team keep the pic moving rapidly until the script unwisely does away with Mancuso after only an hour. Since he's portrayed as even slimier than No. 1 bad guy Tzi Ma, who drops his impeccable manners only at the end, the tension slackens in the last section and even a budding sexual relationship between Lee and Hodge can't make up for it.

Kudos are due to Lee and Jeff Imada for their boisterous fight choreography. Imada also coor-

dinated the activities of 93 (count 'em) credited stunt people.
— *Joseph McBride*

CHRISTOPHER COLUMBUS:
THE DISCOVERY

A Warner Bros. release (U.S.) of an Alexander Salkind presentation of an Alexander & Ilya Salkind production. Produced by Ilya Salkind. Executive producer, Jane Chaplin. Co-producer, Bob Simmonds. Directed by John Glen. Screenplay, John Briley, Cary Bates, Mario Puzo, story by Puzo. Camera (Technicolor, Panavision), Alec Mills; editor, Matthew Glen; music, Cliff Eidelman; production design, Gil Parrondo; art direction, Terry Pritchard, Luis Koldo, Jose Maria Alarcon; costume design, John Bloomfield; sound (Dolby), Peter J. Devlin; ocean voyage unit director-camera, Arthur Wooster; assistant director, Brian Cook; casting, Michelle Guish. Reviewed at MGM screening room, Paris, Aug. 14, 1992. MPAA Rating: PG-13. Running time: **120 MIN.**
Torquemada . . . . . Marlon Brando
King Ferdinand . . . . . . Tom Selleck
Christopher Columbus
. . . . George Corraface
Queen Isabella . . . . . . Rachel Ward
Martin Pinzon . . . . Robert Davi
Beatriz . . . . . Catherine Zeta Jones
Harana . . . . Oliver Cotton
Alvaro . . . . Benicio Del Toro
King John . . . . . . Mathieu Carriere
Vicente Pinzon . . . . . Manuel de Blas
De La Cosa . . . . Glyn Grain
Fra Perez . . . . Peter Guinness
Roldan . . . . Nigel Terry

Advance word around the industry may have been that "Christopher Columbus: The Discovery" wasn't seaworthy, but then again, pundits laughed at Chris himself until he hit the Mother of All Wickets back in 1492. As it happens, John Glen's take on the Genovese explorer adds up to perfectly serviceable commercial entertainment: There are a few moments where Kirk Douglas or Charlton Heston would have felt right at home.

If public awareness of, and distrib confidence in, this Salkind production is indeed low, it may well sail out of theaters faster than it deserves to. But viewers who do turn out will not be bored by this fast-paced historical fiction and, whatever its shortcomings, general audiences worldwide are bound to like George Corraface in the title role. Marlon Brando's inimitable presence adds an extra touch of class.

Though swordplay, sabotage, mutiny, sharks and topless island maidens are plot elements of the PG-13-rated tale, pic may not grab Nintendo-conditioned youngsters as much as it will a slightly older crowd.

Using his James Bond-honed sense of expediency, Glen tells the story with broad strokes.

Columbus is quickly established as a lusty, playful and self-assured man-with-a-vision whose life, in time-honored biopic tradition, is an uninterrupted series of lively events.

Although script by John Briley, Cary Bates and Mario Puzo is certainly not devoid of clichés and corniness, good dialogue far outweighs the bad. The mix of accents is acceptable, there are few overt casting errors and the three working ship replicas are put to excellent use. In short, pic has sailed past most of the pitfalls that could have made it stodgy or laughable.

Leading man Corraface has the diction and charisma it takes to carry off his role. He is immensely likable — perhaps too much so for authenticity's sake. Although the cruel side of his personality is gradually revealed, thesp errs on the side of boyish charm. A member of Peter Brook's "Mahabharata" troupe and set for the lead in David Lean's ill-fated "Nostromo," Corraface should find attractive offers coming his way.

A combination of faith and ambition informs every move made by Torquemada, Columbus and Isabella. Brando makes a grand Grand Inquisitor. When he says, "Heresy by nature is insidious," one can't help but believe it. Tom Selleck's wry turn as King Ferdinand is a pleasant surprise, although a wan Rachel Ward could use more backbone in her evangelical enthusiasm.

Scenes aboard the three replica ships communicate the rigors of life at sea. A false land sighting after long weeks afloat is so moving that it steals some of the thunder from the actual landing on the Bahamian island of San Salvador, which Columbus believed to be in the Indies. Script neglects to clarify that "Cipango" is an ancient term for Japan.

Pic concentrates more on Columbus than on the indigenous peoples he conquered, but pic does boast a better-than-comic-book sensitivity to the initially docile locals, eventually shown to have minds of their own.

Two "interview" sequences are standouts: Columbus, using logic and nerve, convinces Torquemada that his navigational aspirations are not heretical, and the hopeful explorer's first audience with King Ferdinand in which Selleck's royal skepticism counters Corraface's determined enthusiasm. These are instances of verbal chess in which every move counts.

Columbus' explanation of his navigating theory using a large melon as the globe is fun and effective. One almost expects Corraface to burst into a Rogers & Hammerstein-style song about his love of adventure and the high seas. This and other peppy scenes nearly always taper off into forced back-slapping, cheery camaraderie and postsynched sounds of men's men, when a straight cut would have sufficed. While much of the language rings true, there are lines as dopey as, "He has the look of a man possessed."

Oliver Cotton is solid as Master at Arms Harana, but Benicio Del Torro as his errant son is a problem. His lines are among the most unpronounceable and his delivery does little to improve matters.

Robert Davi's urban menace translates well to the high seas, although his performance as captain of the Pinta is uneven. Nigel Terry is good as a murderous former convict. There's not enough time for Beatriz (Catherine Zeta Jones), Columbus' beloved, to be much more than too good to be true. Overall, supporting players have interesting faces and okay delivery.

In crossing the Atlantic from Spain to the Caribbean, the Special Ocean Voyages Unit, headed by Arthur Wooster, produced some fine images. Production design, especially aboard ship, is convincing. John Bloomfield's costumes suit the characters. Cliff Eidelman's score ranges from perfunctory to inspired.
— *Lisa Nesselson*

WATERLAND
(BRITISH-U.S.)

A Fine Line Features release of a Palace & Fine Line presentation in association with Pandora Cinema & Channel 4 Films with participation of British Screen of a Palace production. Produced by Katy McGuinness, Patrick Cassavetti. Executive producers, Nik Powell, Stephen Woolley, Ira Deutchman. Directed by Stephen Gyllenhaal. Screenplay, Peter Prince, based on Graham Swift's novel. Camera (Metrocolor, widescreen), Robert Elswit; editor, Lesley Walker; music, Carter Burwell; production design, Hugo Luczyc-Wyhowski; art direction, Helen Rayner; costume design, Lindy Hemming; sound (Dolby), Simon Okin; assistant director, David Brown; casting, Susie Figgis (U.K.), Deborah Aquila (U.S.). Reviewed at Culver Studios, Culver City, Calif., Aug. 20, 1992. MPAA Rating: R. Running time: **95 MIN.**
Tom Crick . . . . Jeremy Irons
Mathew Price . . . . . . Ethan Hawke
Mary Crick . . . . Sinead Cusack
Lewis Scott . . . . John Heard
Judy Dobson . . . . Cara Buono

Young Tom	Grant Warnock
Young Mary	Lena Headey
Dick Crick	David Morrissey
Freddie Parr	Callum Dixon
Henry Crick	Peter Postlethwaite

High school teacher Jeremy Irons walks his students through the physical and emotional landscapes of his troubled life in "Waterland," a talented but terminally parched piece of literary cinema. Decorous, academic treatment of bizarre and traumatic material makes for a merely unpleasant film rather than an insightful or genuinely disturbing one. Irons' name and possibility of some good notices will give this a foothold in the international art market, but audience appeal will be distinctly limited. Palace production opened in the U.K. over the weekend.

Graham Swift's recent novel attracted the attention of numerous filmmakers but invariably prompted the question of how it could possibly be adapted for the screen. Despite a tight and cleverly constructed time-jumping structure, it can't be said that scenarist Peter Prince has really solved the problem, since what's onscreen unfortunately creates the constant impression of a story that would be much more effectively told on the printed page.

This twisted, inbred yarn is not the sort of thing normally associated with British accents, scarfed pipe-smokers and memory flashbacks. At heart, tale is a Southern gothic of sordid family secrets.

Impetus for spilling the 30-year-old saga lies in the impulse that teacher Tom Crick (Irons) has to bring history alive by personalizing it. Seeing that his Pittsburgh students find little relevance in his lectures about the French Revolution, Crick begins telling them about his own upbringing in the odd area called the Fens, bleak, flat marshlands in East Anglia on the North Sea.

As pic cuts back and forth between the present (1974) and different moments in the past, Crick frequently dwells on the erotic: At 16, he and his sweetheart Mary used to have feverish sex in private train compartments and his pathetic "potato head" brother reacted violently and jealously to sexual knowledge and provocation.

Mary in the present is a barren woman in her 40s with a pathological desire for a child, someone clearly off the deep end who finally kidnaps a baby, insisting, "I got him from God" (she is named Mary, after all). The interlocking structure links her ongoing trauma to the ghastly illegal abortion she had to undergo in her teens.

To the extent that it concerns sex, the film has a certain pull. But on any grander dramatic or thematic levels, the pic fails to pull together in meaningful ways. When Tom's most insolent student (Ethan Hawke) challenges him to defend the teaching of history, one awaits the elaboration of the teacher's justification with reasonable expectation. Instead, we get superficial, borderline laughable scenes of the students riding through moments of British history in an open-air tour bus, and a summing-up by Tom that, in its fumbling sentimentality, seems like a portrait of the deterioration of teacher-student relations since the days of Mr. Chips.

In the service of the film's inability to achieve much of depth or substance, considerable skill is nevertheless on display. Irons does his best to carry the project through thick and thin, but he can't entirely break through its fundamental reediness. As his wife, Irons' real-life mate Sinead Cusack seems utterly possessed, beyond the care even of the man who has known her intimately for three decades.

Grant Warnock proves a reasonable teen facsimile of Irons, but most vivid impression is made by Lena Headey, who makes young Mary into a vibrant, lovely but sometimes inscrutable girl. Hawke and David Morrissey also have potent moments.

The desolate wet expanses of Britain's eastern coast comprise a haunting, unfamiliar setting for the wartime flashback sequences, and Robert Elswit's images have an appropriate soft moistness to them. Yank director Stephen Gyllenhaal, praised for last year's "Paris Trout," handles the often delicate subject matter with integrity on a scene-by-scene basis but can't transform what may simply be overly intractable material.

— Todd McCarthy

THE GUN IN BETTY LOU'S HANDBAG

A Buena Vista release of a Touchstone Pictures presentation of an Interscope Communications production in association with Nomura Babcock & Brown. Produced by Scott Kroopf. Executive producers, Ted Field, Robert W. Cort. Co-producer, Ira Halberstadt, Cynthia Sherman. Directed by Allan Moyle. Screenplay, Grace Cary Bickley. Camera (Astro Color Labs color, Technicolor prints), Charles Minsky; editors, Janice Hampton, Erica Huggins; music, Richard Gibbs; production design, Michael Corenblith; art direction, David J. Bomba; set design, Lori Rowbotham; set decoration, Merideth Boswell Charbonnet; costume design, Lisa Jensen; sound (Dolby), Douglas Axtell; associate producer, Sarah Bowman; assistant director, Tom Davies; casting, Billy Hopkins, Suzanne Smith. Reviewed at Avco Cinema Center, L.A., Aug. 19, 1992. MPAA Rating: PG-13. Running time: **89 MIN.**

Betty Lou	Penelope Ann Miller
Alex	Eric Thal
Ann	Alfre Woodard
Elinor	Julianne Moore
Herrick	Andy Romano
Frank	Ray McKinnon
Beaudeen	William Forsythe
Marchat	Xander Berkeley
Jergens	Michael O'Neill
Brown	Christopher John Fields
Reba	Cathy Moriarty

"The Gun in Betty Lou's Handbag," a clever premise that ends up being as bland as its put-upon title character, figures to fire a blank into the box office till. Director/co-writer Allan Moyle showed some flair with "Pump Up the Volume" and has his moments here, but not enough to rescue this one from a mundane existence in theaters and quick exile to homevid. Pic opened Aug. 21 on a regional basis.

Penelope Ann Miller has the title role as Betty Lou Perkins, a mousy librarian who seizes on a found gun (used in the motel-room slaying of an FBI informant) to shake up her pristine image and become a femme fatale. Her cop husband (Eric Thal) ignores her, her boss pushes her around and her friends can't picture her having an affair or shooting anyone. So why not use those library-honed storytelling skills to inject a little drama into her life and confess to the crime?

Her girl-who-cries-wolf plot has one deadly drawback, however, in the form of the sadistic mobster Beaudeen (William Forsythe), who fears Betty Lou possesses evidence that could convict him. After some gratuitous demonstrations of his hot temper, Beaudeen eventually nabs Betty Lou's attorney (Alfre Woodard) to set up a climactic showdown.

The idea of one happenstance discovery changing someone's life — and completely altering their public image — is a familiar one, but Moyle and writer Grace Cary Bickley don't lay enough groundwork to make Betty Lou as sympathetic as she needs to be, and the 89-minute production still has time for profound lapses in reason.

The lead character also loses some of her attraction by allowing the deception to drag on after she's clearly in over her head, causing her husband to lose his job and putting people around her in jeopardy.

The one area in which the film does excel is its occasionally sharp dialogue and supporting characters, with amusing moments from Woodard as the novice attorney, Julianne Moore as Betty Lou's hyperkinetic sister and Cathy Moriarty as a helpful hooker. In limited screen time, the reliable Forsythe also brings an uneasy sense of menace to his cajun-drawling heavy.

Miller finds herself properly cast again as the girl-next-door type, following her misuse as the high-powered attorney in "Other People's Money" and an equally disastrous turn in the recent romantic caper "The Year of the Comet." She's back on more comfortable terrain — closer to her roles in "Kindergarten Cop" and "Awakenings" — and it shows.

Thal, unrecognizable from his recent co-starring role in "A Stranger Among Us," is likable as well in the thinly written role as Betty Lou's husband, though the film presents a somewhat schizophrenic mix of feminist sentiments with the idea that hubby's approval — and his riding to the rescue — will make everything okay.

Like his last feature, Moyle saturates the film with music but it makes less sense here, to the point where it's hard not to be conscious of it. That score includes the song "Betty Lou's Gettin' Out Tonight," although based on the pic's limited appeal, she'll likely be all dressed up with no place to go.

Other tech credits are fine in the modestly scaled production.

— Brian Lowry

HONEYMOON IN VEGAS

A Columbia release of a Castle Rock Entertainment presentation in association with New Line Cinema of a Lobell/Bergman production. Produced by Mike Lobell. Executive producer, Neil Machlis. Directed, written by Andrew Bergman. Camera (CFI color, Technicolor prints), William A. Fraker; editor, Barry Malkin; music, David Newman; production design, William A. Elliott; art direction, John Warnke; set decoration, Linda De Scenna; costume design, Julie Weiss; sound (Dolby), David MacMillan, Tom Fleischman (N.Y.), Steve Maslow, Robert Beemer; stunt coordinator, Rick Barker; associate producer, Adam Mer-

ims; assistant director, Yudi Bennett; 2nd unit director, Mark Parry; casting, Mike Fenton, Valorie Massalas. Reviewed at AMC Century 14 Theater Complex, L.A., July 29, 1992. MPAA rating: PG-13. Running time: **95 MIN.**
Tommy Korman . . . . . . James Caan
Jack Singer . . . . Nicolas Cage
Betsy/Donna . . . Sarah Jessica Parker
Mahi Mahi . . . . Pat Morita
Johnny Sandwich . . . Johnny Williams
Sally Molars . . . . John Capodice
Sidney Tomashefsky . Robert Costanzo
Bea Singer . . . . Anne Bancroft
Chief Orman . . . . Peter Boyle
Roy . . . . Burton Gilliam

Writer-director Andrew Bergman has a rare talent for intelligently conceived farce, and he has plenty of fun with the premise of "Honeymoon in Vegas," an adult twist on Damon Runyon's "Little Miss Marker." Sarah Jessica Parker is the saucy, sympathetic prize in a poker game between her divorce-detective fiancé Nicolas Cage and sharkish Vegas gambler James Caan. Pic's a bit rough around the edges but should make merry at the B.O.

N.Y. shamus Cage's sleazy job has made him cynical about marriage, but he's tormented by his refusal to promise his mother (Anne Bancroft) on her deathbed that he'd never tie the knot. This background to Cage's skittishness about commitment is sketched in somewhat heavy-handedly, but pic starts to fly after it gets to Las Vegas.

Schoolteacher Parker has coerced Cage into marrying her, and they take a honeymoon suite at Bally's Casino Resort during the midst of a convention of Elvis impersonators, whose presence provides hilarious running gags throughout.

Parker's shabby emotional treatment by Cage lends her a sympathy that she and filmmaker Bergman deftly maintain while she succumbs to Caan's oily but masterful wiles. In an enjoyably manic, self-kidding performance, Caan plays a thug who for a while shows an unexpectedly gentlemanly streak, putting the hapless Cage to shame.

"If I was a medieval knight, I woulda jostled for ya," Caan tells Parker after winning a weekend with her in his poker game with Cage. Disgusted at first by her desperate fiancé's willingness to let her go, she becomes entranced with the idea of a Hawaiian fling with Caan, who toys with her emotions in captivating fashion.

William A. Fraker's lensing is cheesy-looking, but the Hawaiian locations compensate in this airy light entertainment.

Though the pacing seems haphazard in spots (the pic runs only 95 minutes), the likable characters and Bergman's knack for sustaining zany situations keep the film bouncing along.

Parker's natural, unforced charm and honest, strong-willed personality give the film a scintillating uncertainty after she begins taking Caan seriously. Bergman brings out a goofy "Everyman" appeal in Cage that never lets him alienate the audience even in the character's most obnoxious moments.

Cage's increasingly frantic attempts to win back Parker leave the audience torn between her two lovers, but the resolution is somewhat pat, requiring an unsatisfying turn of character from Caan.

Nevertheless, Bergman's staging of an aerial jump over Bally's by a squad of "Flying Elvises" led by toothsome Burton Gilliam sends the audience out laughing. The pic cleverly uses Elvis songs on the soundtrack to comment on the offbeat love triangle.

The director's penchant for parody also serves the film well in sendups of scenes from "Chinatown" and "Thunderball," as well as in his sly echoes of Caan's "The Gambler" and Cage's "Wild at Heart." Peter Boyle's off-the-wall Polynesian hippie character appears to be a wicked takeoff on Marlon Brando.

— *Joseph McBride*

UN VAMPIRE AU PARADIS
(A VAMPIRE IN PARADISE)
(FRENCH)

An Auramax & MC-4 release of a Les Films Auramax production with participation of Canal Plus & the CNC. Produced by Jean-Claude Patrice. Directed, written by Abdelkrim Bahloul. Camera (color), Jean-Francis Gondre; editor, Pierre Didier; sound, Alain Contrault; costumes, Catherine Siauvee-vausy; set design, Jean-Auguste Brunet. Reviewed at Rex cinema, Vevey, Switzerland, July 28, 1992. (In Vevey Intl. Festival of Comedy Film, noncompeting.) Running time: **90 MIN.**
Mr. Belfond . . . . Bruno Cremer
Mrs. Belfond . . . . . . Brigitte Fossey
Nosfer Arbi . . . . Farid Chopel
Nathalie . . . . Laure Marsac
Also with: Hélène Sugere, Abdel Kechiche, Jean-Claude Dreyfuss, Saïd Amadis, Benoît Giros, Mathieu Poirier, Abdelkrim Bahloul.

A bourgeois French businessman and an escaped lunatic who thinks he's a vampire form a surprisingly productive friendship in "Un Vampire au Paradis." Offbeat, cross-cultural comedy is crowd-pleasing entertainment with a tinge of mysticism and a message of tolerance. Good thesping and clever gags should give film a boost on the international art house market, although pic's use of ties between France and North Africa may not be an immediately accessible context for all audiences.

When a preppy 16-year-old French girl (Laure Marsac) begins throwing random fits in fluent Arabic, her parents (Bruno Cremer, Brigitte Fossey) are understandably perturbed. Daughter's unexplained condition took hold following the night she spotted a spectral man in a cape perched outside her window.

Fresh twist on vampire tales is peppered with both verbal and physical comedy. Lanky Farid Chopel's sunken features are perfect for the part of Nosfer Arbi, a Nosferatu stand-in who sinks his teeth into the good folk of Paris and Clichy in hopes of being killed and repatriated. Cremer and Fossey lend the necessary authority to a premise that might otherwise falter, and lovely Marsac handles both sides of her role with great skill.

Pic, winner of the Chamrousse Comedy Film Festival, pokes fun at notions of sanity and insanity, social class and respectability, while probing the strange forces at work to unite two youths from different cultures. Although the narrative does demand several leaps of faith, matter-of-fact mix of everyday life and supernatural concerns is deftly sustained.

Algerian-born French filmmaker Abdelkrim Bahloul plays a bit part as a grocer who summons a relative from North Africa to exorcise the girl.

The youth jury at the annual Paris Festival of Films for Children and Young People awarded the Grand Prix to "Un Vampire au Paradis" and voted best actress honors to Marsac.

— *Lisa Nesselson*

LITTLE NEMO:
ADVENTURES IN SLUMBERLAND
(JAPANESE-ANIMATED)

A Hemdale Pictures release of a Tokyo Movie Shinsha Co. Ltd. production. Produced by Yutaka Fujioka. Directed by Misami Hata, William T. Hurtz. Animation directors, Kazuhide Tomonaga, Nobuo Tomizawa. Screenplay, Chris Columbus, Richard Outten; story, Jean (Moebius) Giraud & Yukata Fujioka, based on characters by Winsor McCay; concept for the screen, Ray Bradbury. Camera (Tokyo Laboratories Color), Kenichi Kobayashi, Moriyuki Terashita, Takahisa Ogawa, Kazushige Ichinozuka, Atsuko Ito, Koji Asai, Takashi Nomura, Jin Nishiyama, Kiyoshi Kobayashi, Atsushi Yoshino, Kyoko Oosaki, Akio Saitoh, Hiroshi Kanai, Hitoshi Shirao, Hironori Yoshino, Mika Sakai, Rie Takeuchi, Kazushi Torigoe; editor, Takeshi Seyama; music, Thomas Chase, Steve Rucker; songs, Richard M. Sherman, Robert B. Sherman; conceptual design, Giraud; sound, Kunio Ando, Shizuo Kurahashi; assistant directors, Hiroaki Sato, Keiko Oyamada. Reviewed at Broadway Screening Room, N.Y., July 23, 1992. MPAA rating: G. Running time: **85 MIN.**
Voices:
Nemo . . . . Gabriel Damon
Flip . . . . Mickey Rooney
Prof. Genius . . . . . Rene Auberjonois
Icarus . . . . Danny Mann
Princess Camille . . . . Laura Mooney
King Morpheus . . . . Bernard Erhard
Nightmare King . . William E. Martin

The retro-technology of Jules Verne meets the dread of J.R.R. Tolkien in a superbly crafted tale of good and evil in a land of dreams. This slick steamroller can boast an impressive concept and imaginative design, even if a few scenes get too scary for a G rating. "Little Nemo" should be a hit with the kids and promises to have a long video shelf life after wide national late-summer release.

The title character, a boy in a Victorian-age-looking New York 'burb whose father ignores him, is carried off to Slumberland by a giant blimp to be the playmate of Princess Camille, daughter of kind King Morpheus. Moppet is made heir to the throne and given a key to all the doors in the realm. But the king makes Nemo swear never to open "that door," which leads to Nightmare Land.

Enter Flip, a mischievous trickster with Mickey Rooney's crackly voice, who dares the kid to open it. When Nemo and Flip rush back to make the coronation party, a dark demon slithers out and abducts the king.

Nemo must make up for his mistake by staging a rescue mission deep inside the evil kingdom, aided by his flying pet squirrel Icarus, the princess and the delicate Prof. Genius.

This universe was imagined from the ground up by French comic-book icon Jean (Moebius) Giraud, whose taste in design previously has ranged from the merely gigantic to the bellicose. Here, he has perfected the art of making even benevolent surroundings appear as if they might turn sinister at any moment, making "Nemo" more than standard fare in the genre.

Visually stunning scenes with massive structures and bizarre creatures floating through the air are welcome trademarks of this master of Verne sci-fi. Giraud's demons, black ooze and a one scene involving a splattered goblin recall his recent adult artwork, however, and may be a touch too much for the intended audience.

Overall production quality is as high as it gets. The score by Thomas Chase and Steve Rucker layers many moods, ranging from playful and brittle to swelling and loud, and is nicely punctured by a few catchy, funny themes by Richard and Robert Sherman reminiscent of their work for "Mary Poppins." The sound is rich and varied, with crisp little surprises to support the fun.

Animation itself is fluid and graceful, but occasionally it rushes ahead with a speed so dizzying even the MTV faithful will experience a sense of vertigo. A train chase in the opening sequence is one example of high-energy busyness that leaves the audience breathless and overwhelmed.

Eighteen camera credits on this film make for impressive multilevel sensations, especially during the many aerial shots combining the innocence of the tiny hero's design with the stark backdrop terror so typical of Japanese high-end products of this kind. — *Christian Moerk*

SVO Á JÖRDU SEM Á HIMNI
(AS IN HEAVEN)
(ICELANDIC)

A Tíu-Tíu Film Prods. production in association with Metronome Prods. (Denmark)/Norsk Film (Norway)/Suomen Elokuvasäätiö (Finland)/Svenska Filminstitutet (Sweden)/Nordic Film & TV Fund/Icelandic Film Fund. (Intl. sales: Seawell Films, Paris.) Produced by Sigurdur Pálsson. Directed, written by Kristín Jóhannesdóttir. Camera (Eastmancolor, widescreen), Snorri Thórisson; editor, Sigurdur Snaeberg Jónsson; music, Hilmar Örn Hilmarsson; art direction, Gudrún S. Haraldsdóttir; sound (Dolby), Kjartan Kjartansson. Reviewed at Cannes Film Festival market, May 16, 1992. Running time: **122 MIN.**
Dr. Charcot . . . . . . Pierre Vaneck
Mother . . . . . Tinna Gunnlaugsdóttir
Hrefna . . . . . Álfrún H. Örnólfsdóttir
Kristján . . . Valdimar Örn Flygenring
Grandmother . . . . . Sigrídur Hagalín
Grandfather . . . . . . Helgi Skúlason
Gonidec . . . . Christophe Pinon
Burte . . . . . . Christian Charmetant
(Icelandic & French dialogue)

After a decade in TV and legit, Icelandic director Kristín Jóhannesdóttir powers her way back to the big screen with "As in Heaven," an elemental mix of Nordic myth and superstition. Quality festival item will need a hard sell to make it theatrically, but pic's cinematic qualities only really bloom on the large sheet.

Setting is a remote farm on the west coast of Iceland in late summer 1936. While her family listens despondently to news of the Spanish Civil War raging in Europe, young Hrefna (Álfrún H. Örnólfsdóttir) gallivants alone by the seashore. Her fertile imagination is encouraged by her grandmother's (Sigrídur Hagalín) words that the area is under an ancient curse and by her foster brother Kristján's (Valdimar Örn Flygenring) bedtime yarns.

News comes that a French marine research ship is coming, led by the veteran Dr. Charcot (Pierre Vaneck). With her father still at sea on a fishing expedition, Hrefna soon starts mixing past and future in her imagination, traveling back to the origins of the 14th-century curse and projecting her thoughts into the destiny of the research ship.

Pic is highly assured and free of pretensions, from the atmospheric opening reels sketching the family's closed existence and reliance on the elements to the long close in which the lonely child finds herself powerless to alter the natural course of events.

As pic progresses, Jóhannesdóttir cuts increasingly freely between the '30s and the 14th century, with actors doubling. Details of plot and Nordic ritual, not made any clearer by the oblique narrative style, may tax some audiences' patience but the story's general thrust, helped by evocative music and lensing, is clear enough.

With thick specs and vacant gaze, young Örnólfsdóttir makes a suitably spooky Hrefna. Flame-haired Tinna Gunnlaugsdóttir ("Children of Nature") is good as both Hrefna's comforting mom and her wild medieval counterpart. French thesp Vaneck brings Charnot stature.

Tech credits are tip-top, with music, effects and seamless editing carrying the film through its more arcane moments. Pic was Iceland's contribution to the Nordic Co-production Year 1991-92, with additional coin from Eurimage and France's CNC.
— *Derek Elley*

STAY TUNED

A Warner Bros. release of a Morgan Creek production. Produced by James G. Robinson. Co-producer, Arne Schmidt. Executive producers, Gary Barber, David Nicksay. Directed, photographed (Alpha Cine color, Technicolor) by Peter Hyams. Screenplay, Tom S. Parker, Jim Jennewein, from story by Parker, Jennewein, Richard Siegel. Editor, Peter E. Berger; music, Bruce Broughton; production design, Philip Harrison; art direction, Richard Hudolin, David Willson; set decoration, Rose Marie McSherry, Daniel Bradette, Lin MacDonald, Annmarie Corbert; costume design, Joe Thompkins; sound (Dolby), Ralph Parker; animation supervised & mice characters designed by Chuck Jones; animation co-supervisor-storyboards, Jeffrey DeGrandis; visual effects, Rhythm & Hues; visual effects supervisor, John Nelson; stunt coordinator, Gary Combs; assistant director, Jack Sanders; casting, Lynn Stalmaster, Michelle Allen (Vancouver), Karen Hazzard (Toronto). Reviewed at Edwards' Atlantic Entertainment Complex, Alhambra, Calif., Aug. 14, 1992. MPAA Rating: PG. Running time: **87 MIN.**
Roy Knable . . . . John Ritter
Helen Knable . . . . Pam Dawber
Spike . . . . .Jeffrey Jones
Darryl Knable . . . . David Tom
Diane Knable . . . . Heather McComb
Murray Seidenbaum . . . . . Bob Dishy
Mrs. Seidenbaum . . . . Joyce Gordon
Crowley . . . . Eugene Levy
Pierce . . . . Erik King

Not diabolical enough for true black comedy, too scary and violent for kids lured by its PG rating and witless in its send-up of obsessive TV viewing, "Stay Tuned" is a picture with nothing for everybody. As a Seattle couple trapped in a hellish cable system run by the devil himself, John Ritter and Pam Dawber look glum for more than plot reasons. Pic was not trade-screened, had a weak opening and probably will soon be zapped from theaters.

Premise had some potential as an opportunity for a free-flowing satire of TV programming (à la "Tunnelvision" or "SCTV"), and with 666 channels to choose from in satanic emissary Jeffrey Jones' state-of-the-art cable system, director Peter Hyams had plenty of comedic options.

But the titles of the cable shows are the only (mildly) amusing things about them: "Sadistic Hidden Videos," "Three Men and Rosemary's Baby," "Autopsies of the Rich and Famous," "Driving Over Miss Daisy." The crudely executed skits tend to expire as soon as they're announced.

Ritter is introduced as the ultimate couch potato, a depressed plumbing-supplies salesman who's a sucker for the suave Jones' free cable-tryout offer. The

catch is that if he and Dawber don't survive 24 hours lost inside the alternate dimension, they forfeit (what else?) their souls.

An able farceur stuck in a thankless role, Ritter struggles with a variety of thin situations, including a nasty game show, a hideous wrestling match and a near-guillotining in a dull French Revolution program.

Saddled with a charmless part as couple's brighter half, strained-looking Dawber uses her wits to survive, but her (supposedly) clever idea to get them home is dismayingly simple-minded.

Intended as a satiric commentary on the dangers of excessive TV-watching, mechanical pic stays flatly on the surface of its subject, succumbing to the same kind of wretched, idiotic excess it intends to criticize.

One brief respite from the overall inanity is a six-minute cartoon interlude by the masterful Chuck Jones, with Ritter and Dawber portrayed as mice menaced by a robot cat. The animation has grace and depth.

Hyams' lensing and Philip Harrison's production design are slick, and Peter E. Berger's editing works hard to simulate the zapping effect of cable remote control, but technical cleverness can't overcome the deadly lack of intellectual invention on display.
— *Joseph McBride*

FREDDIE AS F.R.0.7
(BRITISH-ANIMATED)

A Rank (U.K.) & Miramax (U.S.) release of a Hollywood Road Films production. Produced by Norman Priggen, Jon Acevski. Directed by Acevski. Screenplay, Acevski, David Ashton. Camera (Fujicolor), Rex Neville; editors, Alex Rayment, Mick Manning; music, David Dundas, Rick Wentworth; songs, Dundas, Don Black, Wentworth, Acevski, Ashton, John Themis, George O'Dowd, Geoffrey Downs, Gregory Hart, John Payne, Holly Johnson; sung by George Benson, Patti Austin, Grace Jones, Barbara Dickson, Boy George, Asis, Johnson; art direction, Paul Shardlow; animation director, Tony Guy; sequence directors, Dave Unwin, Bill Hajee, Richard Fawdry, Stephen Weston, Roberto Casale, Alain Maindron; storyboard director, Denis Rich; visual effects supervisor, Peter Chiang; sound (Dolby SR), Gerry Humphreys, Dean Humphreys, John Bateman; casting, Marilyn Johnson. Reviewed at MGM Tottenham Court Road theater, London, Aug. 14, 1992. MPAA rating: PG. Running time: **90 MIN.**
Voices:
Freddie . . . . Ben Kingsley
Daffers . . . . Jenny Agutter
El Supremo . . . . Brian Blessed
Brigadier G . . . . . . Nigel Hawthorne
King . . . . Michael Hordern
Young Freddie . . . Edmund Kingsley
Nessie . . . . Phyllis Logan
Old Gentleman Raven . Victor Maddern
Trilby . . . . Jonathan Pryce

Queen	Prunella Scales
Scotty	John Sessions
Messina	Billie Whitelaw

A shake 'n' bake mixture of virtually every toon genre going, "Freddie As F.R.O.7" makes up in energy what it lacks in originality. Lumbered with an unattractive title, this likable enough saga of a super-agent frog looks unlikely to hop into the big time. Miramax releases wide Stateside Aug. 28.

London-based Hollywood Road Films deserves plaudits for indie-producing a full-length animated pic in the U.K. But somewhere during the three-year production period, they forgot about script. Story line lurches around like a paper cup in a storm.

Billing itself before the main title as "an amazing fantasy of a new kind," pic delivers plenty of the former but short-changes on the latter. Yarn starts out as a Never Never Land fairy tale, segues rapidly to Disney-like anthropomorphism and finally launches into a mix of James Bonderie and "Star Wars."

Plot kicks off with Freddie reminiscing about his origins as young Prince Frederic, turned into a frog by shape-shifting Aunt Messina and saved from her cobra alter ego by kindly Nessie, the Loch Ness monster. Growing up underwater, he later relocates to Paris as superagent F.R.O.7.

He battles the wicked Messina and megalomaniac El Supremo, who want to bring Blighty to its knees by shrinking its national monuments and unleashing a sleep-inducing ray.

In place of a properly developed plot line, director Jon Acevski busies the screen with characters and incident, every now and then breaking into pleasant enough musical numbers that don't advance the action a jot. Pic's other major flaw is its reliance on stereotypes reminiscent of vintage Disney — from toffee-nosed Brits to Freddie himself as a super-elegant Gallic dude. That may be okay for starters, but the filmmakers don't develop them into anything more substantial. Freddie's femme sidekick Daphne is introed as a martial arts specialist but largely left on the sidelines.

Voice cast features a heavyweight lineup of British talent, with Brian Blessed a standout as the booming El Supremo and Billie Whitelaw excellent as the hissing Aunt Messina. Ben Kingsley's Inspector Clouseau-like Freddie is surprisingly mild; Jenny Agutter's Daphne sounds mismatched to the character.

Technically, the picture suffers from distracting strobing in traveling sequences and loss of detail in action scenes. Still, the latter are fast and frequent, and pic can't be faulted for its antsy energy and dramatic play with perspective.

Yugoslavian-born Acevski, who worked Stateside as an actor before settling in the U.K., already has 10 minutes in the can of his next froggy outing, "Freddie Goes to Washington."

— *Derek Elley*

LOCARNO FEST

QIUYUE
(AUTUMN MOON)
(HONG KONG-JAPANESE)

A Right Staff Office & Eizo Tanteisha presentation of a Trix Films production. Produced by Clara Law, Fong Ling Ching. Directed by Law. Screenplay, Fong Ling Ching. Camera (color), Tony Leung; editor, Fong Ling Ching; music, Lau Yee Tat, Tats; art direction, Timmy Yip; makeup, Lee Wai Ming; sound, Tat Leung, Wai Wong. Reviewed at Locarno Film Festival (competition), Aug. 12, 1992. (Also in New York Film Festival.) Running time: **108 MIN.**

Tokio	Masatoshi Nagase
Wai	Li Pui Wai
Granny	Choi Siu Wan
Niki	Maki Kiuchi
Boyfriend	Sun Ching Hung

(Chinese, Japanese, English soundtrack)

More experienced than other Locarno competitors, Clara Law easily captured the Golden Leopard for her Antonioniesque tale of alienation in modern Hong Kong. Handsomely photographed and nicely blending humor and nostalgia, Law's fourth pic looms as a potential art house favorite for Western audiences, but its slow pace and contemplative mood may be considered obstacles on its home turf.

Tokio, a Japanese yuppie on leave in Hong Kong, can't find a decent restaurant to satisfy his palate. He meets and befriends Wai, a 15-year-old Chinese girl whose family has already left for Canada, where she's supposed to join them in a short while. She takes her new acquaintance home to her grandmother, the only person she knows who still masters the art of Chinese cooking.

Law follows two parallel affairs: the young girl's first dabbling in sexual infatuation, and the man's torrid encounter with the sister of a past adolescent sweetheart.

But Law's true interest is the face of a city that seems to have obliterated any traces of a past beyond the last 20 to 30 years, a spectacular city of concrete and glass in which McDonalds are already considered symbols of tradition, modern gadgets are obsessively accumulated and life is something to be observed through the video camera viewfinder. Typical of this new world is the use of three different languages throughout (Chinese, Japanese, English).

Via alternately moving and reflective approaches, Law uses to good effect Wai's youthful pouts and tantrums and Tokio's deadpan expressions which only strengthen the impact of his rare moments of crisis. At the same time, helmer addresses the 1997 Hong Kong trauma, as the already-evident danger of losing cultural roots threatens to become terminal. Emigration serves as the immediate solution for those who do not fancy submitting to Beijing rule.

One of the most touching moments comes toward pic's end, when the aged grandmother, about to part with her niece, delivers a long, painful monologue, eloquently putting the whole issue in the simplest, but also the most tragic, terms.

— *Dan Fainaru*

HUSBANDS AND WIVES

A TriStar release of a Jack Rollins & Charles H. Joffe production. Produced by Robert Greenhut. Executive producers, Rollins, Joffe. Co-producers, Helen Robin, Joseph Hartwick. Directed, written by Woody Allen. Camera (Duart color; Technicolor prints), Carlo Di Palma; editor, Susan E. Morse; production design, Santo Loquasto; art direction, Speed Hopkins; set decoration, Susan Bode; costume design, Jeffrey Kurland; sound (Dolby), James Sabat; associate producer-assistant director, Thomas Reilly; casting, Juliet Taylor. Reviewed at Sony Studios screening room, Culver City, Calif., Aug. 25, 1992. MPAA Rating: R. Running time: **107 MIN.**

Gabe Roth	Woody Allen
Rain's mother	Blythe Danner
Sally	Judy Davis
Judy Roth	Mia Farrow
Rain	Juliette Lewis
Michael	Liam Neeson
Jack	Sydney Pollack
Sam	Lysette Anthony
Shawn Grainger	Cristi Conaway
Paul	Timothy Jerome
Rain's analyst	Ron Rifkin
Dinner party guest	Jerry Zaks
Peter Styles	Bruce Jay Friedman
Judy's ex-husband	Benno Schmidt
Interviewer/narrator	Jeffrey Kurland

"Husbands and Wives" is major Woody. Preoccupied with the age-old but endlessly fascinating subject of the difficulty of relationships, and expressing perplexity at the way things work out between men and women, this sometimes comic drama stands with "Manhattan" and "Hannah and Her Sisters" as a richly satisfying ensemble piece about N.Y. neurotics falling in and out of love.

Had the recent Woody-Mia bomb never exploded, TriStar, with the help of a planned Allen junket, would no doubt have promoted the film to some of the best grosses the writer-director-star has ever achieved. As it stands, distrib has moved release up a week to Sept. 18 in 800 theaters, especially wide for Allen, and the attendant publicity will no doubt attract quite a few curious souls.

Many, of course, will come for the titillation of seeing Allen make out with a 21-year-old and go through a wrenching split from Farrow onscreen. Even those who enter in this frame of mind, however, probably will put these thoughts aside for the most part as they become involved in the romantic longings and verbal crossfire among interesting, difficult, intersecting characters.

Jarring opening scene gives a strong indication of things to come. Arriving to dine with their best friends Allen and Farrow, married couple Sydney Pollack and Judy Davis announce almost matter-of-factly that they're separating. While Allen drones in disbelief and offers reflex support, Farrow nearly goes into shock.

It quickly becomes apparent Allen and Farrow have their own troubles. They've never agreed upon having a child: She's for it, he's not. Farrow is also woefully insecure about her attractiveness and lovability, while Allen admits to daydreaming about sexy young things but never does anything about it, saying, "They don't want an old man."

Still, college English instructor Allen takes a special interest in a talented and provocative student, Juliette Lewis. Even though she has a history of dating middle-age men and pushes things with her admiring mentor, Allen steers clear of sexual involvement.

Indeed, subject of the attraction between older men and younger women is decidedly secondary here to the theme Allen's character is working out in his novel-in-progress: the conflicting desires to be married and live a single life, which also lie at the heart of "Husbands and Wives."

This concern is most thoroughly explored in the exploits of Pollack and Davis once they separate. After some initial philandering, Pollack takes up with knockout New Age bimbo Lysette Anthony.

Infuriated with how quickly Pollack has replaced her, the intense, seemingly eternally dissatisfied Davis goes out with Irish dreamboat Liam Neeson. When Neeson goes for Davis in a big way, Farrow becomes distraught, realizing the depth of her own feelings for him.

Allen creates a full-bodied gallery of hard-headed urbanites who more often than not operate out of self-destructive impulses. An "Annie Hall"-like coda reveals what happened to the characters a year-and-a-half later, with the expected bittersweet, melancholy results.

With the possible exception of Neeson's character, these people are unhappy and somewhat frustrated with their search for answers to life's impossible dilemmas. Allen's New York remains a romanticized construct, but those inhabiting it are angrier and more short-tempered than usual for him. The women, in particular, drink a lot, while the men are all defensive. This is definitely his edgiest, rawest

work in a good while.

While his subjects have remained much the same, Allen's style has undergone a radical change here. Although the color tones are still orangish and warm, Carlo Di Palma's lensing appears to be almost entirely hand-held, creating a look somewhere between early French New Wave and cinema vérité. The camera is as agitated and nervous as the characters, constantly prowling, hiding behind objects, zooming in to spy on the participants. The editing also frequently employs jump cuts to keep things off balance and unsettled.

Acting is of a very high caliber across the board, but Judy Davis, in a very meaty part compared to her previous walk-on for Allen's "Alice," is incandescent, revealing a whole new side to her onscreen personality. Her character does so many of the "wrong" things, making life much more difficult for herself and those around her than need be, yet people are compellingly drawn to her.

By contrast, Farrow seems terminally insecure, but she, too, is able to summon up strength and emerge stronger than before through luck and persistence. She and Allen, always a curious but endearing couple in their films together (this is their unlucky 13th), are first-rate.

Pollack, whose screen appearances until now have essentially been extended cameos, registers very strongly here as a man in classic mid-life crisis, while Neeson is vastly appealing as a too-good-to-be-true available man in Manhattan. Having replaced Emily Lloyd a ways into shooting, Lewis conveys an intriguing combination of precocious accessibility and elusiveness, while Anthony is hilarious in the ferocity of her stupid convictions.

As usual for Allen, score consists mostly of classic old tunes, most prominently Cole Porter's "What Is This Thing Called Love." In all respects, this is a full meal, as it deals with life with intelligence, truthful drama and rueful humor.

— *Todd McCarthy*

GLENGARRY GLEN ROSS

A New Line Cinema release of a Zupnick-Curtis production. Produced by Jerry Tokofsky, Stanley R. Zupnik. Executive producer, Joseph Caracciola Jr. Co-producers, Morris Ruskin, Nava Levin. Directed by James Foley. Screen-

play, David Mamet, based on his play. Camera (Duart color; Deluxe prints; widescreen), Juan-Ruiz Anchia; editor, Howard Smith; music, James Newton Howard; production design, Jane Musky; set decoration, Robert J. Franco; costume design, Jane Greenwood; sound (Dolby), Danny Michael; associate producer, Karen L. Oliver; assistant director, Thomas A. Reilly. Reviewed at Ocean screening room, Santa Monica, Calif., Aug. 21, 1992. MPAA Rating: R. Running time: **100 MIN.**

Ricky Roma	Al Pacino
Shelley Levene	Jack Lemmon
Blake	Alec Baldwin
Dave Moss	Ed Harris
George Aaronow	Alan Arkin
John Williamson	Kevin Spacey
James Lingk	Jonathan Pryce
Mr. Spannel	Bruce Altman
Detective	Jude Ciccolella
Policeman	Paul Butler

Fleshing out a tight, one- or two-set stage play for the big screen has always been a challenge not easily met, and the theatrical roots show rather clearly in the case of "Glengarry Glen Ross." A superb cast acting out one of David Mamet's major works yields quite a bit of promo ammo and will be enough to justify a look for many serious, upscale viewers. But it doesn't quite all come together here as it did onstage, and relentless scabrousness, heavy claustrophobia and vaguely dated feel will keep mainstream audiences away.

After runs in London and Chicago, Mamet's savage look at a group of slimy small-time real estate salesmen opened on Broadway in 1984 to strong reviews and went on to solid engagement of 378 performances. Producer Jerry Tokofsky has been trying to get his pic version off the ground almost ever since, and finally succeeded in rounding up a dream cast of big names to appear in what needed to be a modestly budgeted production.

In adapting his short two-act, two-set, seven-character piece, Mamet has moved the action around a bit to provide a few diverse settings, but the play's basic contours remain very much in place. Harsh story examines the underhanded, eventually criminal activities of the salesmen as they compete to outdo each other in hustling dubious properties to phone clients.

Key to their sales efforts are quality "leads," which have a lot to do with whether they satisfy their hard-driving bosses and are able to keep their jobs. Most in danger of getting the ax is, unsurprisingly, the oldest employe, Shelley Levene (Jack Lemmon), who begs, pleads and deals for better leads than the worthless ones he's been dealt.

By rote, he makes his time-worn sales pitches, both over the phone and in person, but in the high-powered sales world personified by Blake (Alec Baldwin), the terrorist from the head office, there's clearly no place for a dinosaur like Shelley.

Also in jeopardy and strategizing in different ways are George (Alan Arkin) and Dave (Ed Harris). Kevin Spacey plays the by-the-books office manager, while Jonathan Pryce plays a cowering customer.

But in contrast to all these drones is Ricky Roma (Al Pacino), a hotshot salesman who seems to know every trick in the book and how to play them. Unlike the others, Roma is nattily dressed, tan, and comes off like a guy who's going to use the system, not be used by it.

Action is divided into 50-minute halves, with the second act unfolding in the wake of an office robbery of the premium leads. While Shelley dominates the first section, Roma presides over the second, as Mamet propels things toward a startling, abrupt end.

Piece remains gripping in a way, but not in as captivating or edifying a way as it did onstage. Reasons for this have to do with the rhythms of the acting, the camera's magnification of artificial devices and director James Foley's mite fancy approach to stagebound material.

Playing a sad, desperate variation on Willy Loman, Lemmon hits many notes that ring painfully true. But it's also the case that he's been on this downtrodden road before, and be it the woefully pathetic character or the terrifying accuracy of the performance, something about seeing Shelley so close up makes one want to flee his presence.

An old Mamet hand, particularly by virtue of his stage work in "American Buffalo," Pacino knows his way around the territory and the language and comes up aces in Joe Mantegna's Tony-winning part. Also just right are Harris as a pugnacious younger agent, Arkin as a complaining, endangered veteran, and Spacey as the stony manager.

Baldwin's ferocious speech early on about the sanctity of the bottom line is scary, and it stands as a caustic indictment of 1980s business mentality. Mamet reveals his exceptional talent for writing almost poetic working class vernacular, scores his major implicit thematic thrusts against the nature of the way business-at-large is conducted, and generates a substantive argument against pure capitalism's brutal Darwinism.

But the viewer remains at a considerable remove, partly because Foley's attempts to keep the visuals lively and moving create distractions. While Juan-Ruiz Anchia's lighting is enormously inventive and colorful, there are a few too many camera moves, unnecessarily elaborate setups and attention-getting cutting tricks when a little simplicity would have been better.

Aside from those moments when it becomes obvious, Howard Smith's editing is extremely tight and propulsive, and James Newton Howard's jazzy score is a real plus. — *Todd McCarthy*

THE LAST OF THE MOHICANS

A 20th Century Fox release. (Intl. sales: Morgan Creek Intl.) Produced by Michael Mann, Hunt Lowry. Supervising producer, Ned Dowd. Executive producer, James G. Robinson. Directed by Mann. Screenplay, Mann, Christopher Crowe, based on James Fenimore Cooper's novel & the screenplay for 1936 United Artists version by Philip Dunne, with adaptation by John L. Balderston, Paul Perez, Daniel Moore. Camera (Deluxe color), Dante Spinotti; additional camera, Doug Milsome; editors, Dov Hoenig, Arthur Schmidt; music, Trevor Jones, Randy Edelman; additional music, Daniel Lanois; production design, Wolf Kroeger; art direction, Richard Holland, Robert Guerra; set design, Karl Martin, Masako Masuda; set decoration, Jim Erickson, James V. Kent; sound (Dolby), Simon Kaye, Paul Massey, Doug Hemphill, Mark Smith, Chris Jenkins; stunt coordinator, Mickey Gilbert; assistant director, Michael Waxman; 2nd unit directors, Gilbert, Gusmano Cesaretti; 2nd unit camera, Jerry G. Callaway; casting, Bonnie Timmerman, Susie Figgis (London). Reviewed at UGC Normandie Cinema, Paris, Aug. 11, 1992. MPAA rating: R. Running time: **122 MIN.**
Hawkeye . . . . Daniel Day-Lewis
Cora . . . . Madeleine Stowe
Chingachgook . . . . . Russell Means
Uncas . . . . Eric Schweig
Alice . . . . Jodhi May
Heyward . . . . . Steven Waddington
Magua . . . . Wes Studi
Col. Munro . . . . Maurice Roeves
Gen. Montcalm . . . . Patrice Chereau

Michael Mann's "The Last of the Mohicans" benefits from rich source material (James Fenimore Cooper's classic) and good performances. Film shouldn't have much trouble finding its audience, although viewers familiar with the Seven Years War will be better prepared to keep assorted alliances straight. Pic premiered in Paris, where literary lion Cooper lived from 1826 to '33, in advance of U.S. bow Sept. 25.

Adventure tale of life in the British colonies in America is a great ode to freedom and self-determination played out against codes of honor and loyalty, c. 1757. Lensed in South Carolina, pic blends pure adventure with a compelling central romance.

Sisters Alice (Jodhi May) and Cora (Madeleine Stowe) Munro are escorted through hostile country to join their colonel dad (Maurice Roeves), British commander of a fort under French siege. Rigid English soldier Duncan Heyward (Steven Waddington) is courting Cora sans success.

After an ambush leaves the Munro girls and Heyward unprotected, Hawkeye (Daniel Day-Lewis) and his adopted Mohican father (Russell Means) and brother (Eric Schweig) come to the rescue.

Lean and intense, with a dashing mane of hair, Day-Lewis brings his usual concentration to the role of the courageous woodsman at one with nature. The orphaned colonial child raised by Indians is a finely tuned human hybrid of America's original tenants and the population to come. Day-Lewis is all integrity and he thinks on his fleet feet.

Although at first seemingly incompatible, Day-Lewis and Stowe spark a convincing attraction arising from shared ideals and piqued by the excitement of life-and-death ordeals. And the actors' faces by candlelight are beautiful to behold.

Magua, a Huron scout allied with the French, is carrying out a deadly vendetta against the Munro family. When Magua, played with savage menace by Cherokee actor Wes Studi, swears to "cut out the heart of his enemy and eat it," it's not a figure of speech.

Native American activist Means is a wise bit of casting, as is French stage director Patrice Chereau as the French commander, the Marquis de Montcalm.

Modern lensing techniques allow the camera to run alongside Hawkeye and accompany the trajectory of a bullet or the flight of a spinning tomahawk. Well-staged battle sequences are brutal and bloody. Pacing is fluid, and pic successfully builds to action-packed finale on a majestic ridge.

—*Lisa Nesselson*

BITTER MOON
(FRENCH-BRITISH)

A Columbia TriStar Films (U.K.) release of an R.P. Prod.- Timothy Burrill Prods. production, in association with Les Films Alain Sarde-Canal Plus. Produced by Roman Polanski. Executive producer, Robert Benmussa. Co-producer, Alain Sarde. Directed by Polanski. Screenplay, Polanski, Gérard Brach, John Brownjohn, from Pascal Bruckner's novel "Lunes de fiel"; script collaboration, Jeff Gross. Camera (Eastmancolor), Tonino Delli Colli; editor, Hervé de Luze; associate editor, Glenn Cunningham; music, Vangelis; vocals, Sapho; production design, Willy Holt, Gérard Viard; costume design, Jackie Budin; sound (Dolby), Daniel Brisseau; choreography, Redha; assistant directors, Michel Cheyko, Eric Bartonio; casting, Bonnie Timmerman (U.S.), Mary Selway (U.K.), Françoise Menidrey (France). Previewed at Odeon Haymarket theater, London, Aug. 12, 1992. (In Edinburgh, San Sebastian film festivals.) Running time: **139 MIN.**
Oscar . . . . Peter Coyote
Mimi . . . . Emmanuelle Seigner
Nigel . . . . Hugh Grant
Fiona . . . . . . Kristin Scott Thomas
Mr. Singh . . . . Victor Bannerjee
Amrita . . . . Sophie Patel
Steward . . . . . . Patrick Albenque
Also with: Smilja Mihailovitch, Leo Eckmann, Luca Vellani.
(English dialogue)

Four years after "Frantic," Roman Polanski approaches rock bottom with "Bitter Moon," a phony slice of *huis clos* drama between two couples aboard a Euro liner. Strong playing by topliner Peter Coyote can't compensate for a script that's all over the map and a tone that veers from *outré* comedy to erotic game-playing. Pic, which world-preemed at Edinburgh, could excite initial interest on its sex content but looks headed for dry dock in English-speaking marts.

With its shipboard setting and emotional entanglements, pic would seem to recall Polanski's 30-year-old debut, "Knife in the Water." Instead, its misjudged tone and flowery prose (which may have worked in the original French novel) more often recall his loopy '70s comedy "What?"

Initial focus is on a couple of hoity-toity Brits (Hugh Grant, Kristin Scott Thomas) enjoying a seventh-anniversary Mediterranean cruise to Istanbul. Things immediately start to go awry when they help a distraught young femme, Mimi (Emmanuelle Seigner), whom Fiona finds on the floor of the ladies' john.

She turns out to be the ship's glamorous cabaret act, and when she later gives young Grant the cold shoulder in the bar, his interest is aroused. That night he's accosted by her American hubby (Peter Coyote), a wheelchair-bound misanthrope who lures the Englishman into a drinking session and insists on recounting his life story.

Thereon, pic settles into a series of long flashbacks detailing Coyote-Seigner's tempestuous love life. Coyote's scheme seems to be to lure Grant into Seigner's bed to perform the marital duties he's unable to perform.

Per flashbacks, Coyote was a typical Yank in Paris trying to become a second Henry Miller when smitten by dance student Seigner. Following a hotsy affair, they married; but when Coyote's fires cooled and his writing muse failed to arrive, he began to humiliate her to shake her off. Seigner's revenge was to cripple him for life, locking them together in love-hate hell.

Pic's structure soon starts to hit the reefs as the Coyote-Seigner story takes over. Given the length of the flashbacks (which would easily fill a normal feature), the present-day story becomes little more than a series of fillers marking time before the next boozy sesh between the men.

Grant is mostly reduced to bemused, stiff-upper-lip reactions as Coyote spills out the most intimate details about his wife. Scripters seem even more at a loss over what to do with the character of Scott Thomas, increasingly jealous of Coyote's grip on her husband's attentions.

Lopsided structure could have worked if Polanski had established a consistent visual style and dramatic approach. Instead, pic starts off as a romantic drama, dissolves into a Parisian *amour fou*, takes a left into kinky sex romps and winds up in sub-Pinterland. Ridiculous coda involving Scott Thomas and Seigner at a shipboard party is way over the top.

Despite its two-hour-plus length, pic holds a certain awful fascination as Polanski careens every which way with the material. But the sole real hook is finding out how Coyote ended up in a wheelchair. Thereafter it's downhill fast.

Coyote gives a scenery-chewing performance as both the younger lovestruck scribe and the whisky-soaked cripple, and deserves a medal for stone-facing ripe lines such as "her stomach was hungry, her organs in turmoil."

Seigner, matured since her "Frantic" days, is eye-popping in the sex scenes, but the helmer's wife often sounds as if she's reading her dialogue off cue cards. Scott Thomas is wasted in a sidelined part, and the bemused Grant looks like he's strayed off the set of a Merchant Ivory pic.

Tech credits are okay without being distinctive, with Vangelis' music adding a touch of gloss and Tonino Delli Colli's shadowy lensing at its best in the Billancourt Studios set of Coyote-Seigner's Paris apartment. Shipboard scenes were lensed aboard a real Mediterranean liner, credited in the final crawl. — *Derek Elley*

WUTHERING HEIGHTS
(BRITISH-U.S.)

A UIP (U.K.) release of a Paramount Pictures production. Produced by Mary Selway. Executive producer-2nd unit director, Simon Bosanquet. Directed by Peter Kosminsky. Screenplay, Anne Devlin, from Emily Brontë's novel. Camera (Eastmancolor; Technicolor prints), Mike Southon; editor, Tony Lawson; music, Ryuichi Sakamoto; production design, Brian Morris; art direction, Richard Earl; costume design, James Acheson; sound (Dolby SR), Peter Glossop; assistant director, Bill Westley; associate producer, Chris Thompson; casting, Sheila Trezise. Previewed at Edinburgh Intl. Film Festival, Aug. 25, 1992. Running time: **105 MIN.**
Cathy/Catherine . . . Juliette Binoche
Heathcliff . . . . Ralph Fiennes
Ellen Dean . . . . Janet McTeer
Isabella Linton . . . . . . Sophie Ward
Edgar Linton . . . . . Simon Shepherd
Hindley . . . . Jeremy Northam
Hareton . . . . Jason Riddington
Mr. Lockwood . . . . . . Paul Geoffrey
Mr. Earnshaw . . . . . John Woodvine
Mr. Linton . . . . Simon Ward

U.K.-lensed "Wuthering Heights" is a by-the-numbers telling of the Emily Brontë classic that's as cool as a Yorkshire moor, weakened by a wobbly central perf by Gallic thesp Juliette Binoche. Pic looks set to be a hard sell in English-speaking markets. Version world preemed at the Edinburgh film fest last week.

Third big-screen outing of the Brontë yarn lacks the visual stylization and intense performances of the 1939 Merle Oberon-Laurence Olivier classic, and the believability of the 1970 British remake (with Anna Calder-Mashall and a young Timothy Dalton). For the record, a talky Mexican reworking was directed by Luis Buñuel in 1954.

Present item, first out of the Paramount British Pictures hopper, serves up the full work (un-like the truncated 1939 version) but misses out on atmosphere and passion. Anne Devlin's script does a workmanlike job of compressing the novel into 105 minutes, inventing a female voiceover narrator and framing the story as one mega-flashback. But helming by Peter Kosminsky, in his feature bow after an award-winning string of political documentaries, doesn't add much to the narrative.

Controversial casting of Binoche as the Yorkshire lass is a major deficit. Fine in French-lingo pics, and even in the Czechoslovakia-set, English-language "The Unbearable Lightness of Being," she doesn't cut it in such British fare as this. Halting in her delivery, and with an accent that's every which way, she misses the spontaneity and feeling at the heart of the twin roles. Her dialogue also shows signs of having been trimmed: The Brit cast does most of the talking when she's around.

Screen newcomer Ralph Fiennes makes a good stab at the Heathcliff part, more successful in the later scenes as the embittered power player than in the early ones as the glowering bad boy. But it's a one-way contest with Binoche, and precious few sparks fly.

Pic begins promisingly with Lockwood (Paul Geoffrey), narrator in the novel but not here, arriving at Wuthering Heights and getting a cool reception from its owner, Heathcliff (Fiennes). That night, he thinks he sees a ghost resembling Catherine, daughter-in-law of Heathcliff.

Cue flashback to Heathcliff's youth when, as a mysterious orphan, he was brought to the house by its owner Earnshaw (John Woodvine). Treated as a servant, he grows up with Earnshaw's perky daughter Cathy, but when the adult Cathy (a brunette Binoche) marries into the family of neighboring rich folks, the Lintons, he plots long-term revenge.

Marrying and abusing Linton daughter Isabella (Sophie Ward), he still hangs round Cathy. When she dies, he later marries off his son to Cathy's grown-up daughter Catherine (a blonde Binoche), new sole heir to the Linton estate. Downbeat ending sees most main players dead, as per novel.

Sprawling story, set across two generations, moves at quite a clip to get everything in. Pacing, as well as look, is more akin to an edited-down TV miniseries than a developed feature. Filmmakers seem over-bound by fidelity to the novel and unwilling to take risks: a late-on fantasy sequence of Heathcliff reunited with the dead Cathy has some of the romantic panache badly missing elsewhere.

Fiennes plays up the unredeemed, social-outcast side of Heathcliff to good effect, when the script gives him a chance. Best of the supports is Janet McTeer, as the fully drawn servant Mrs. Dean. Ward is in only briefly as Isabella but is okay.

Production design by Brian Morris, and costuming by James Acheson, are both detailed but treated in unatmospheric style by Mike Southon's conservative lensing. Ryuchi Sakamoto's romantic main theme cries out for fuller development.

Exteriors were shot on authentic Yorkshire, north England locations, with studio work at Shepperton. —*Derek Elley*

MONTREAL FEST

EL LADO OSCURO DEL CORAZON
(HEART'S DARK SIDE)
(ARGENTINE)

A Transeuropa presentation of a CO3/Transeuropa production. Produced, directed, written by Eliseo Subiela. Camera (color), Hugo Colace; editor, Marcela Sáenz; music, Osvaldo Montes; art director, Margarita Jusid. Reviewed at Atlas Lavalle theater, Buenos Aires, May 21, 1992. (Competing at Montreal Film Festival.) Running time: **127 MIN.**
With: Darío Grandinetti, Sandra Ballesteros, Nacha Guevara, André Melançon, Jean Pierre Reguerraz, Inés Vernengo, Mónica Galán, Marisa Aguilera.

Eliseo Subiela's "El Lado Oscuro del Corazón" clicked at local box offices despite its being very unconventional. This surrealist story of a young poet tired of sex and hungry for love echoes Ingmar Bergman's metaphysics and Luis Buñuel's slyness and is colored with bits of Cocteauesque fantasy and Woody Allen wit. A feast for buff (but not mass) audiences, pic has a fresh, funny and candid approach to the complexities of a romantic soul.

Like Adolfo Aristarain's "Un Lugar en el Mundo," Subiela's pic looks at idealism quixotically trying to survive in a pragmatic environment. Young poet Oliv-erio eats by either declaiming his poems to motorists stopped at red lights or by exchanging them for steaks with a grill owner.

He has two cronies, a Canadian bohemian dazzled by the chaotic country and a sculptor who creates giant penises and buttocks. Oliverio seems to hate everybody else, including a chicken-hearted Death (Nacha Guevara) often pleading with him to get a good job. As for women, when he gets bored with one after sex, he simply ejects her down to oblivion from his bed.

His fate changes when he meets Ana, a whore in a cabaret. He falls so strongly that he accepts work in commercials to afford the $100 dates with her. Their lovemaking gets more and more furious, and they start levitating over the sheets, eventually reaching a full fly over the city. At one point he admits Ana has enlightened the dark side of his heart.

Dialogue includes poems or fragments of poems, but the words suit the feeling created by the enthralling photography, the often beautiful locations of Buenos Aires and Montevideo, the fine sets and a leisurely pace beefed up by astute cutting. A drawback is that the poems are sometimes difficult to hear.

Lively romantic music with fleeting tango touches is a plus, as are several cameos: writer Mario Benedetti dressed as a merchant navy captain, singer Dalila gives a bravura rendition in a subway station, María Martha Serra Lima and Trio Los Panchos are heard in boleros. Production values are first-rate.

Darío Grandinetti turns out the tenderness and learning Oliverio hides beneath his raptures, sardonic remarks and awkward look. Sexy newcomer Sandra Ballesteros is a convincing Ana, Jean Pierre Reguerraz shines as the racy sculptor, Canadian filmmaker André Melançon is fittingly cheerful, but his Spanish diction is difficult to understand. All other performances answer to Subiela's surefire helming.

In its second half, pic is less rich in creative fireworks, but it doesn't lose style, texture and insight. — *Domingo Di Nubila*

SÖNDAGSBARN
(SUNDAY'S CHILDREN)
(SWEDISH)

A Sandrew Film & Teater production in cooperation with Svenska Filminstitutet, Sweetland Films, Sveriges Television Kanal 1, Metronome Prods., Finlands Filmstiftelse, Islands Film Fond & Norsk Film with support of Nordic Film & TV fund & Eurimages/Europarådet. Executive producer, Klas Olofsson. Produced by Katinka Faragó. Directed by Daniel Bergman. Screenplay, Ingmar Bergman. Camera (color), Tony Forsberg; editor, Darek Hodor; music, Rune Gustafsson; costumes, Mona Theresia Forsén; production design, Sven Wichmann; sound, Klas Engström, Patrik Grede. Reviewed at Sandrews screening room, Stockholm, July 22, 1992. (Competing at Montreal Film Festival; also in Venice Film Festival Critics Week.) Running time: **120 MIN.**

With: Thommy Berggren, Henrik Linnros, Lena Endre, Jakob Leygraf, Anna Linnros, Malin Ek, Birgitta Valberg, Börje Ahlstedt.

With a screenplay by Ingmar Bergman telling a story from his youth, "Sunday's Children" could almost be a sequel to "The Best Intentions" (which Bergman also wrote) but stands on its own and should do well on the festival circuit. Box office results might be slim outside of Scandinavia.

Directed by Bergman's son Daniel, 30, in his feature debut, pic stems from a passage in Dad's autobio "The Magic Lantern." Story centers on the relationship between 10-year-old Pu (read: Ingmar) and his father.

The family stays at a summer house, and when Dad comes home for the weekend, he gives the Sunday sermon at a nearby church. Pu goes along, but during the day he sees his father's violent side as well as his caring, devoted moods. All in all, the experiences aid bonding.

Pic is another chapter in Ingmar Bergman's struggle to make up with his long-dead father, and though unintended, comparisons with "Best Intentions" are inevitable. Events here take place some 10 years after the latter ended, and some actors return. Lena Endre, mistress in the Bille August film, here plays Bergman's mother, and Börje Ahlstedt plays Uncle Carl as he did in both "Fanny & Alexander" and "Best Intentions."

"Sunday's Children" feels overlong, and it would have been more fulfilling if some of the other characters had been more developed. Put against "Best Intentions," this is the lesser film but still quite good, especially in capturing the moods of the father-son relationship and the poignantly shifting weather during the rides to and from the church.

Acting overall is very good. Thommy Berggren, known from several Bo Wilderberg films,

turns in one of his best performances in a long time, and Endre again proves she is one of Sweden's best young actresses. Young Henrik Linnros is also convincing in a difficult part that forces him to be in most scenes.

Tech credits are above par, with special merit earned by cinematographer Tony Forsberg and editor Darek Hodor.
— *Gunnar Rehlin*

LOCARNO FEST

QUARTIER MOZART
(CAMEROONIAN-FRENCH)

A Kola Case production. Produced, directed, written by Jean Pierre Bekolo. Camera (color), Regis Blondeau; editor, Bekolo; sound, Newton Aduaka; music, Philip Nikwe; sets-costumes, Maria Dubin. Reviewed at Locarno Film Festival (competition), Aug. 7, 1992. Running time: **80 MIN.**
Montype . . . . Serge Amougou
Samedi . . . . Sandrine Ola'a
Chien Mechant . . . . . Jimmy Biyong
Atango . . . . Essindi Mindja
Capo . . . . Atebass
Bon pour les morts
. . . . Timoleon Boyongueno
Sytsalla . . . Genevieve Ngo Ntamack
Kungassa . . . . Madeleine Messengue
Panka . . . . Sedou Abatcha
(French soundtrack)

A happy-go-lucky portrait of a Cameroonian suburb, Jean Pierre Bekolo's first feature evidences his past experience as a video editor and video director. Thin on plot but packed with upbeat musical selections commissioned by Bekolo, the pic has crowd-pleasing potential beyond specialized auds interested in African cinema.

Using several folk legends, Bekolo's story follows a naughty girl turned by a benevolent witch into a young man to satisfy her curiosity. In her new guise, she is challenged by other young men to court a tyrannical cop's daughter. Colorful characters bearing names like My Guy, Mad Dog, Saturday, Women's Sweetheart, Good for the Dead and Viper populate the pic, some of them blessed with uncanny gifts such as making a man's genitals disappear by shaking the person's hand.

While the courtship of the policeman's daughter is supposed to supply the main thrust of the story, Bekolo is mostly concerned with observations on moral and sexual customs of the carefree population, seemingly concerned only with having a good time or gossiping about those who do.

Thus, the cop has no objections to his offspring's affairs, as long as they are carried on out of his sight and a Catholic priest will bless a bigamous household if this will keep his congregation happy.

Using a cast that consists mostly of amateurs, Bekolo obtains some remarkably lively performances, as everyone gets into the spirit of this lighthearted spoof.

A rare film to come out of Cameroon, partly financed in France, pic should find auds both at home and abroad, if response at the Locarno film fest is any indication. — *Dan Fainaru*

EDDIE KING
(ISRAELI)

A Eddie King Ltd. production. Produced by Rafi Bukaee, Giddi Dar. Directed, written by Dar; dialogue, Dar, Ethan Blum. Camera (color)-art director, Ariel Semmel; editor, Danny Itzhaki; sound, Khen Harpaz. Reviewed at Locarno Film Festival (competition), Aug. 9, 1992. Running time: **92 MIN.**
With: Ethan Blum, Shuli Rand, Ronit Alkabetz, Shlomo Bassan, Albert Ilus, Gabi Shoshan, Fitcho Ben-Tzur.

First effort by Giddi Dar, a 27-year-old ex-jazz musician, is typical fare for fests and ambitious programmers looking for promising raw talent. Otherwise, pic's unlikely to find its way commercially.

Plot has unemployed actor Eddie King involved in an imaginary attempt by a shady U.S. tycoon to take over the second TV channel in Israel. Also figuring in are a gangster who intends to blackmail the tycoon, the gangster's brother with dubious allegiances, a driver who quotes philosophers, and the gangster's moll, who needs an unspecified medicine only the tycoon can get.

Far-fetched narrative gives Dar an excuse to explore notions pertaining to the uprooted Israelis' lack of cultural identity. Estranged from its old traditions and desperately trying to establish new ones, the new generation borrows from every possible source, from Euro-style alienation to U.S. film mythology. Classical and Oriental music get equal time on the soundtrack.

It doesn't always make sense, but to Dar's credit, his visual language is much richer and imaginative than most in Israeli films and he uses his musical background to advantage in the soundtrack. Shuli Rand as the gangster, Albert Iluz as his brother

and co-dialogue writer Ethan Blum as King fit in nicely with the general approach.

Inexperienced crew did surprisingly well considering the shoestring budget (bit more than $100,000). Still photographer Ariel Semmel (also art director) turned in commendable work in his first cinematography task.

Recipient of a Bronze Leopard in Locarno, pic will serve Dar as a useful calling card, but it's difficult to imagine it going much further than the next film fest.
— *Dan Fainaru*

OUT ON A LIMB

A Universal Pictures release of an Interscope Communications production. Produced by Michael Hertzberg. Executive producers, Ted Field, Scott Kroopf, Robert W. Cort. Directed by Francis Veber. Screenplay, Daniel Goldin, Joshua Goldin. Camera (Deluxe color), Donald E. Thorin; editor, Glenn Farr; music, Van Dyke Parks; production design, Stephen Marsh; assistant director, David Householter; production manager-line producer, Kelly Van Horn; sound (Dolby), Darin Knight; stunt coordinator-2nd unit director, Glenn Randall Jr.; 2nd unit camera, John Stephens; special visual effects, Introvision Intl.-supervisor, Tim Donahue; associate producer, James Moll; casting, Dianne Crittenden. Reviewed at Chelsea 7 theater, N.Y., Sept. 4, 1992. MPAA Rating: PG. Running time: **82 MIN.**

Bill Campbell	Matthew Broderick
Matt/Peter	Jeffrey Jones
Sally	Heidi Kling
Jim Jr.	John C. Reilly
Ann	Marian Mercer
Darren	Larry Hankin
Buchenwald	David Margulies
Marci	Courtney Peldon
Jim Sr.	Michael Monks
Cindy	Shawn Schepps

Matthew Broderick sinks with the ship in "Out on a Limb," a moronic comedy that leads the pack as worst film of the year so far.

In a very unwise career choice, Broderick stars in what's usually the Michael J. Fox role: a fish-out-of-water yuppie. Planning to finalize a $140 million company takeover over the weekend, he's drawn instead to the small California town of Buzzsaw to rescue his young sister Marci (Courtney Peldon) from the clutches of a mad villain played by Jeffrey Jones.

Evidently rewritten and reshot repeatedly, film makes no sense and develops not an iota of credibility. It's crudely framed as a "How I spent my summer vacation" tall tale told in school by Peldon, despite the fact that she's not present for 99% of the incidents she narrates in such great detail.

The picture's one clever gag is not original: Two young classmates of Peldon's are made up as a junior parody of Siskel & Ebert to periodically criticize her far-fetched story. In the real world, "Out on a Limb" was not screened for critics.

In the release version, the leading lady played by Heidi Kling is never given a character. Made up with red curly hair like a refugee from a 15 years-after reunion of stage "Annies," Kling enters the film on the run, kidnaps and torments Broderick for

several reels and finally wins him romantically with no explanation of who she is or why she's running.

Intervening segments consist of well-staged but pointless car chases and stunts from second unit director Glenn Randall Jr., as well as a boring story of Jones playing demented twin brothers who make John Lithgow in "Raising Cain" seem like a nice guy. One twin is the mayor of Buzzsaw, who happens to be Broderick and Peldon's stepdad. The other is just out of prison after a 15-year-stretch with revenge on his mind.

The screenwriters are twins Joshua and Daniel Goldin, who besides creating the Jones twins overemphasize a tedious running gag involving imbecilic, inbred hick brothers, both named Jim, whose slapstick is crucial to keeping the pot boiling.

The plot complications include that old wheeze of a corpse mistaken for a still-living drunk and Broderick's missing wallet containing a vital phone number.

By the time "Limb" (originally titled "Welcome to Buzzsaw") concludes with Peldon's most cynical classmates applauding her story, the unconvincing finish to that tale has Broderick suddenly chucking his millionaire financial career to settle down with Kling and run for mayor of Buzzsaw. It's as phony as what passed for entertainment in the preceding 75 minutes.

Broderick struggles to keep his poise in this shambles, and he's not aided by being saddled with an extended nude scene hitchhiking after Kling steals his BMW and clothing. Kling deserves another shot with some material to work with, while young Peldon proves to be a precocious scene stealer.

Director Francis Veber, known for his hit French farces, is out of luck here. Tech credits are adequate but except for the stunts give no indication of a big-budget film. — *Lawrence Cohn*

PET SEMATARY TWO

A Paramount Pictures release. Produced by Ralph S. Singleton. Directed by Mary Lambert. Screenplay, Richard Outten. Camera (Duart color), Russell Carpenter; editor, Tom Finan; music, Mark Governor; production design, Michelle Minch; art direction, Karen Steward; set decoration, Susan Benjamin; costume design, Marlene Stewart; sound (Dolby), Shirley Libby; assistant director, Jeffrey Wetzel; 2nd unit director/mechanical & special effects, Peter Chesney; special effects makeup & anima-

tronics, Steve Johnson; dead-animal effects, Bill (Splat) Johnson; casting, Richard Pagano, Sharon Bialy, Debi Manwiller. Reviewed at Paramount Studios screening room, Hollywood, Aug. 28, 1992. MPAA Rating: R. Running time: **100 MIN.**

Jeff Matthews	Edward Furlong
Chase Matthews	Anthony Edwards
Gus Gilbert	Clancy Brown
Clyde	Jared Rushton
Renee Hallow	Darlanne Fluegel
Amanda Gilbert	Lisa Waltz
Drew Gilbert	Jason McGuire
Marjorie Hargrove	Sarah Trigger

"Pet Sematary Two" is about 50% better than its predecessor, which is to say it's not very good at all. Pic still offers the requisite combination of tension and gore, and even tripping over some unintentional laughs, it's doubtful moviegoers will bury this latest outing deep enough to prevent a third trip to the graveyard.

Like the first installment, which was based on a truly scary Stephen King novel, the latest incarnation relies more on gore than genuine chills and is sorely lacking in subtlety, never the strong suit of this particular genre. That proves to be a problem here, however, because it's important to understand why someone would risk bringing a human corpse back to life, particularly after they've seen the process turn a run-of-the-mill dog into the Hound of the Baskervilles. The story opens with the accidental death of an actress (Darlanne Fluegel) in front of her teenage son (Edward Furlong). Mom is estranged from dad (Anthony Edwards), and father and son move to a small town, where the boy has to grapple with his loneliness and the obligatory school bully (Jared Rushton, much bigger than he was in "Big").

Jeff (Furlong) befriends another boy (Jason McGuire) whose tyrannical stepfather (Clancy Brown) guns down the kid's dog. Duo takes the beast to the "pet sematary," an ancient Indian burial ground rumored to revive the dead, subsequently repeating the process on the stepfather and setting up the inevitable question about tempting the forces of nature by awakening mom.

Director Mary Lambert (reprising her duties from the 1989 release) again errs by setting much of the action around the cemetery in daylight, although the pacing is significantly better than the first pic, and no source material means no deviations from the novel to gripe about. She and writer Richard Outten

nevertheless suffer several zombified lapses in logic.

After his impressive debut in "Terminator 2: Judgment Day," Furlong fares less well here, exhibiting essentially one posture under Lambert's guidance — surly adolescence. Rushton faces the same constraints as the one-note bully, while newcomer McGuire shows promise as the overweight friend.

Brown appears to have some fun with his "living dead" sheriff, but again, the performance is so over the top that everyone's matter-of-fact response to him borders on the absurd. Edwards is solid as the dad, though his own feelings about his wife are dealt with too sparingly to give the climax any resonance.

Makeup and special effects are topnotch, though Lambert tends to linger too long on gore shots, which should put off even the moderately squeamish.

Mark Governor's "Friday the 13th"-like score sets the proper mood, though it's still hard not to chuckle out loud at times as pic rots in the last act.

— *Brian Lowry*

POLICE STORY III:
SUPERCOP
(HONG KONG)

A Golden Way production of a Golden Harvest release. Produced by Willie Chan, Tang King-Sung. Executive producers, Leonard Ho, Jackie Chan. Directed by Stanley Tong (Tony Kwei Lai). Screenplay, Tang King-Sung, Ma Mei-Ping, Lee Wei-Yee. Camera (color), Lam Kwok-Wah; editors, Cheunng Yaeo-Chung, Cheung Kai Fei; music, Lee Chun Shing; art direction, Oliver Wong; costume design, Hung Wei-Chuk; stunt coordinator, Tong. Reviewed at Sun Sing Theater, N.Y., Aug. 20, 1992. Running time: **93 MIN.**

Chen Chia-chu	Jackie Chan
Director Yang	Michelle Yeaoh
May	Maggie Cheung
Big Brother Wei	Tsang Kong
Panther	Yuen Wah
The General	Lo Lieh
Also with: Tung Biao, Koo Kei-Wah.	
(In Cantonese with English & Chinese subtitles)	

Third installment in Jackie Chan's series of police thrillers is an okay adventure that should please his fans. While the story shifts in locales from Hong Kong to mainland China to the Thai-Malaysian border to Malaysia itself, plot basically adheres to the odd couple cops formula trusted in both East and West.

Story twist is that Chan, self-styled "supercop" Chen Chia-chu, must go to China to cooperate with the authorities in cracking an international drug ring. His partner turns out to be the beautiful but no-nonsense Director Wang (Michelle Yeoh). Aside from the contrast between the more disciplined Wang and the freewheeling Chen and some jokes about Hong Kong's upcoming return to Chinese control, differences between the two cultures are not exploited.

Plot takes a decidedly noirish turn when the supercop and Wang must go undercover to join the drug gang after helping one of its leading members, the "Panther," escape from prison. As members of the gang, they are even forced to kill cops to keep their cover. Somber side doesn't prevail too long and some comic complications occur when Chen's g.f. (Maggie Cheung) suddenly appears at a Malaysian resort unaware of his mission and assuming Chen is cheating on her.

Of course, Chen's cover is blown, but this just sets up an all-stops-out finale with a motorcycle catapulting onto a train and people dangling from car, train and helicopter.

All this is executed with a good deal of panache, if not originality, by stunt coordinator Stanley Tong, who also takes over directorial reins from Chan who helmed the first two "Police Story" films. Behind closing credits, outtakes show Chan being helped back on the train by smiling actors playing villains, good-naturedly demonstrating he's still doing his own stunts.

— *Fred Lombardi*

AITSU
(WAITING FOR THE FLOOD)
(JAPANESE)

A Ketty Film/Suntory/NHK Enterprises production. Produced by Kei Ijichi, Hirohisa Mukuju, Naonori Kawamura. Directed by Atsushi Kimura. Screenplay, Kimura, Ichiro Fujita. Camera (color), Akihiro Ito; editor, Nobuko Tomita; music, Seigen Ono; production design, Katsumi Nakazawa; sound, Mineharu Kitamura. Reviewed at Sydney Film Festival, June 16, 1992. Running time: **117 MIN.**
Hikaru . . . . Kenichi Okamoto
Yuki . . . . Hikari Ishida
Sadato . . . . Tadanobu Asano
Hikaru's father . . . . . Ittioku Kishibe
Hikaru's grandfather . . . Frankie Sato

Atsushi Kimura's first feature is a lethargic, self-important item about the alienation of a young asthmatic who dis-

covers he has mystical powers. Overlong and often obscure, the film looks like a tough sell in any situation.

Nerdy student Hikaru (Kenichi Okamoto) spends his time waiting for a Biblical-type flood and being bullied by his friend Sadato (Tadanobu Asano). After one beating from Sadato, Hikaru discovers he can bend spoons and break light bulbs without touching them. He also meets with Yuki (Hikari Ishida), a chirpy girl who lives on a barge.

Director's interesting use of locations and the bizarre activities of the protagonist are briefly engaging, but Kimura overworks his few ideas.

Technically, the pic is striking at times, but the characters become so maddening that audiences are likely to lose interest in the self-indulgent goings-on.

APRÈS L'AMOUR
(AFTER LOVE)
(FRENCH)

A UGC release of an Alexandre Films/ TF-1 Films/Prodeve co-production with participation of Canal Plus. Executive producer, Robert Benmussa. Directed by Diane Kurys. Screenplay, Kurys, Antoine Lacomblez. Camera (color), Fabio Conversi; editor, Hervé Schneid; music, Yves Simon; sound, Bernard Bats; costume design, Mic Cheminal; set design, Tony Egry; associate producer, Jean-Bernard Fetoux. Reviewed at Forum Horizon cinema, Paris, April 21, 1992. Running time: **104 MIN.**
Lola . . . . Isabelle Huppert
David . . . . Bernard Giraudeau
Tom . . . . Hippolyte Girardot
Marianne . . . . Lio
Romain . . . . Yvan Attal
Rachel . . . . Judith Reval

Diane Kurys' "Après l'Amour," in which attractive protagonists play sexual musical chairs, is somewhat sterile and aloof but still may lure upscale art house patrons.

Helmer Kurys, whose works are openly autobiographical, juggles a great many variations on the French theme of extramarital love. It's possible, if logistically tricky, to love two people at the same time, which is the complication confronting two couples with children and the childless "fifth wheel" who overlaps their lives.

All concerned could use a booker to keep their emotions straight and their private parts in the right bed at the right time. Since Kurys' definition of virtue is to give one's beloved total freedom, scenes of suitcases being packed are nearly as many as

scenes of lovemaking, including fervent coupling in a deserted lobby, on a bathroom counter and in the ruins at Pompeii.

Successful novelist Lola (Isabelle Huppert) lives with David (Bernard Giraudeau), a workaholic architect whom she has known and loved for 20 years. David, however, has two children with Marianne (Lio), a gorgeous firebrand who lives only for her family.

Lola's idea of acceptable behavior is to duck out of her own well-attended birthday party, thrown by her primary b.f., to neck with her most recent flame, a pop musician Tom (Hippolyte Girardot), who also has a beautiful and possessive wife (Laure Killing) and loving kids. Story, including subplots involving David's brother, sibling's g.f. and the antics of an unrepentent office tease, covers one year, ending on Lola's 35th birthday the following Christmas eve.

Ordinarily, the fun in eavesdropping on a screen affair comes from the sneaking around, the excuses, the likelihood of being found out. But Lola knows full well that both David and Tom have wives and children. And those wives know full well that their menfolk are in carnal cahoots with Lola. The women always know what's up; the men lie badly. Thesping is matter-of-fact and histrionic by turns. Characters who work for a living are too busy to suffer, and characters who don't work suffer full-time. By popular standards for pic heroines, Huppert is too glacial and blank to be sought after by two attractive men, although some viewers may interpret her stance as brave vulnerability.

Local scribes have praised helmer's keen eye for modern love as practiced by prosperous creative urbanites pushing 40. Kurys' film suggests that cheating on one's spouse or significant other can be a road to self-actualization. Or, at the very least, pregnancy.

Except for Giraudeau's nicely shaded perf, pic makes better use of Paris than of actors. Perhaps the characters are above conventional morality because they live and work high up over the city. A nice transitional gimmick involves panning up from Huppert's writing to colorized black & white scenes that bring her authorial fantasies to life.

—*Lisa Nesselson*

TOKYO DECADENCE
TOPAZ
(JAPANESE)

A Melsat Inc.-JVD Co. Ltd. production. (Intl. sales: JVD, Tokyo.) Produced, directed, written by Ryu Murakami, from his novel "Topaz." Camera (color), Tadashi Aoki; editor, Kazuki Katashima; music, Ryuichi Sakamoto; sound, Masami Usui, Akihiko Suzuki; production design, Murakami. Reviewed at Berlin Film Festival Panorama, Feb. 17, 1992. (At 22nd Taormina Film Festival, competition.) Running time: **111 MIN.**
Ai . . . . Miho Nikaido
Saki . . . . Sayoko Amano
Also with: Tenmei Kanou, Masahiko Shimada.

Chalk up another hotsy export by the Japanese. Arty "Tokyo Decadence Topaz," a lushly lensed hooker drama that should notch up plenty of tricks in late-night fest slots. With the right handling, pic could also rake in extra yen as an offshore cult item, ducking fire from feminist groups.

Work is the fourth feature of novelist-director Ryu Murakami. "Topaz" is a splicing of two stories from Murakami's own novel, focusing on young call-girl Ai (Miho Nikaido), an aimless beauty who works for an exclusive S&M agency.

Pic gets straight down to business with Ai strapped and gagged in a special chair and a honey-tongued client about to pump her full of drugs. But post-main title, she's just another sweet-looking girl.

On the way to a trick, she buys a topaz ring after being told by a clairvoyant that "a pink-colored ring will bring you luck." Following a sweaty session with a coke-sniffing mobster and his wife, she falls in with fellow call-girl Saki (Sayoko Amano), who's halfway to chemical hell.

Emboldened by Saki's advice and medicine cabinet, Ai trots off to visit a former lover. Final twist moves the goalposts like a switch from a Nicolas Roeg pic.

Murakami, with savvy skill, alternates heavy S&M numbers with workaday sequences of the demure Nikaido en route to assignments or just killing time. Look is highly controlled, with often long takes and static camera setups, giving an arty feel. Hardly coy in its visuals, pic still leaves more to the imagination than it flaunts on screen, though sensitive audiences may reckon that's plenty enough already.

The petite Nikaido is a zinger

in the central role, keeping a fixedly demure expression in the face of the most bizarre requests. She's neatly complemented by the darkly sexy Amano. Other roles are well cast, and all thesps play the script's black humor straight down the line.

Technically, pic's a treat for the eyes, with evocative use of color, costumes and noirish night scenes conjuring up a self-contained world. Music track played by Ryuichi Sakamoto adds the final coat of gloss. Like Just Jaeckin's 1975 version of the Gallic S&M classic "The Story of O," pic is a deluxe piece of highly charged nonsense that works well on its own terms. — *Derek Elley*

JOHN LURIE AND THE LOUNGE LIZARDS LIVE IN BERLIN
(DOCU-JAPANESE-U.S.)

A Telecom Japan Intl. presentation of a Japan Satellite Broadcasting, Telecom Japan Intl., Lagarto Prods. co-production. Produced by Valerie Goodman, Taku Nishimae. Executive producer, Kenji Okabe. Directed by Garret Linn. Concept, Robert Burden. Camera (color), Uta Badura, Andre Harris, Linn; editor, Caleb Oglesby; music, John Lurie; sound, Tom Lazarus. Reviewed on videocassette, N.Y. No MPAA Rating. Running time: **101 MIN.**
With: John Lurie, Michael Blake, Steven Bernstein, Jane Scarpantoni, Bryan Carrot, Michele Navazio, Billy Martin, Oren Bloedow, Grant Calvin Weston.

Actor-saxophonist John Lurie is captured in an enlightening, no-frills concert film shot at Berlin's Quartier Latin night club. Feature should serve to expand his musical audience rather than prove a b.o. attraction on its own.

Lurie, known for his roles in Jim Jarmusch's indie films, heads up a nonet that performs here in a jazz-fusion style refreshingly close to pure jazz. Main concession to fusion is the funky rhythms relying upon Oren Bloedow's bass guitar.

Soloing on both soprano and alto sax, Lurie shows a strong influence of the late John Coltrane, especially in several free jazz sections. His minor key compositions are quite varied here, ranging from a figure resembling Coltrane's "A Love Supreme" theme to near-pastiches of "St. James Infirmary" and even Bob Dylan's electric folk sound of "Rainy Day Women Nos. 12 & 35." Debuting feature director Garret Linn occa-

sionally overdoes the racking of focus or swish pan for effect but concentrates on recording the performance without audience shots or interview interruptions.

Lurie and company minimize the on-stage clowning. He provides direct contact to the audience with a droll recitation of a shaggy dog story that has a dynamite political punchline, setting the stage for a torrid drum solo (plus chanting) by Grant Calvin Weston.

Ensemble playing is emphasized, with the band members getting to show off as soloists during a final number when Lurie introduces each of them. Notable contributions by sidemen include vibraphonist Bryan Carrot, trumpet/cornetist Steven Bernstein and cellist Jane Scarpantoni, last-named fitting in well with the group's droning style.

—*Lawrence Cohn*

JERSEY GIRL

A Triumph Films release of an Electric Pictures/Interscope Communications production. Executive producers, Ted Field, Robert W. Cort. Produced by David Madden, Nicole Seguin, Staffan Ahrenberg. Directed by David Burton Morris. Screenplay, Gina Wendkos. Camera (Technicolor; Deluxe prints), Ron Fortunato; editor, Norman Hollyn; music, Misha Segal; production design, Lester Cohen; costume design, Claudia Brown; sound (Ultra-Stereo), Mark Weingarten; assistant director, Gary Sales; production manager-line producer, Amanda DiGiulio; casting, Jane Jenkins, Janet Hirshenson, Roger Mussenden. Reviewed at Sony Pictures screening room, N.Y., July 27, 1992. MPAA Rating: PG-13. Running time: **95 MIN.**
Toby Mastallone . . . . Jami Gertz
Sal . . . . Dylan McDermott
Tara . . . . Sheryl Lee
Jason . . . . Joseph Mazzello
Bennie Mastallone . . . Joseph Bologna
Angie . . . . Aida Turturro
Cookie . . . . Molly Price
Dottie . . . . Star Jasper

Jami Gertz gives a winning perf in "Jersey Girl," an unoriginal variation on such Italo-Yank romances as "Moonstruck." Not sharp enough to create much b.o. action, pic has the potential to warm the hearts of ancillary viewers, especially young women.

Just opened in England but not scheduled for U.S. release until '93, pic is an unusual low-budget entry backed by Interscope, which ordinarily delivers major product like the "Three Men and a Baby" pics.

It also marks a radical change of pace for indie director David Burton Morris ("Patti Rocks"),

who handles the romance well but is ultimately done in by too much corn in Gina Wendkos's script.

Gertz is the prototypical young woman from New Jersey, living with her dad Joe Bologna (who fears her becoming an old maid) and working in a day care center. She spends much of her time hanging out at the local Bendix Diner with her pals Aida Turturro, Molly Price and Star Jasper.

Wendkos's main theme is that old standby: Get out of your provincial rut and blossom. Instead of the "Working Girl" approach, Gertz takes a more old-fashioned route, trying to win some young hunk from Manhattan.

Staking her VW Beetle out in a Mercedes dealer lot, she "meets cute" with Dylan McDermott, a successful young graphics salesman. Gertz gets off on the wrong foot by causing a car accident that results in $6,300 damage to his new Mercedes, and she doesn't even have insurance. Her persistence pays off, however. When McDermott's blonde goddess g.f. (Sheryl Lee) dumps him, he calls Gertz for a date. They soon end up in the sack, but Gertz is soon given the brush-off.

At this point, what has been a heartwarming picture about Gertz's Pollyanna-esque search for love becomes formula filmmaking. McDermott, as an Italian guy from Queens, is interested only in the fast-track of wealth and status, so he drops Gertz, who represents what he's left behind.

Unlike Mike Nichols' "Working Girl," which embraced the '80s ethos of success, "Jersey Girl" unconvincingly opts out of the rat race. McDermott rather arbitrarily becomes fed up with snooty g.f. Lee and his back-stabbing boss, chucks his $100,000-plus job and wins back Gertz.

Movie audiences, especially women identifying with Gertz, might swallow some of this, but when McDermott proves his love to her by trashing his Mercedes, enough is enough.

Very attractively lensed by Ron Fortunato, Gertz shows a big talent in her first top-billed film appearance. McDermott certainly looks the part but operates a notch lower, unwisely using a vocal timber that recalls too closely Richard Gere in "Pretty Woman."

As tough-talking buddy Cookie, Price is a terrific scene-stealer, with good support from fellow gal pals Turturro and Jas-

per. Tech credits are good without any flamboyance or strong sense of style. A song score including tunes by local fave John Cafferty is effective.
— *Lawrence Cohn*

VENICE FEST

THE PLAGUE
(LA PESTE)
(FRENCH-ARGENTINE)

A Gaumont release of a Cyril de Rouvre/Pepper-Prince Co./Oscar Kramer co-production in association with Cinemania & with participation of Canal Plus. Produced by de Rouvre, Christian Charret, John R. Pepper, Jonathan Prince. Co-producer, Kramer. Executive producers, Christin Levraud, Larry Sugar. Directed, written by Luis Puenzo, adapted from Albert Camus' "The Plague." Camera (color), Felix Monti; editor, Juan Carlos Macias; sound, Jean-Pierre Ruh; costume design, Maria Julia Bertotto; production design, Jorge Sarundiansky, Juan Carlos Diana; assistant director, Rodrigo Furth. Reviewed at Club Gaumont screening room, Paris, Aug. 17, 1992. (Competing at Venice Film Festival; also in San Sebastian Film Festival.) Running time **146 MIN.**
Dr. Bernard Rieux . . . . William Hurt
Martine Rambert . Sandrine Bonnaire
Jean Tarrou . . . . . . Jean-Marc Barr
Joseph Grand . . . . . Robert Duvall
Cottard . . . . Raul Julia
Father Paneloux . . . . Lautaro Murua
Alicia Rieux . . . . . Victoria Tennant
Also with: Atilio Veronelli, Francisco Cocuzza, Laura Palmucci.
(English dialogue)

Luis Puenzo's "The Plague," in every way a valiant undertaking, sidesteps the obvious modern plague of AIDS to address the equally resonant scourge of military dictatorship. Eerie, uneven pic's message that the "plague" — literal or figurative — is never truly vanquished is a point worth making, but audiences for this lengthy, sober pic may prove as elusive as a cure for mankind's ills.

Oran, the seaport setting of Albert Camus' classic 1947 novel, has been updated and recast from Algeria to South America as a year identified as "199..." It works both visually and conceptually to have Buenos Aires serve as Oran.

Argentine-born Puenzo has an allegorical ax to grind with the dictators who long held brutal sway over his country. On the pretext of isolating the families of plague victims, sinister public health officials declare martial law and fill vast holding pens in the local stadium, ominously lensed by Felix Monti.

Pic is anchored in the overriding reality of deadly spreading bubonic plague and the surreal, suspended animation of normal human affairs brought on by loss of contact with the outside world. Episodic structure, foreboding music and era-confounding production design all conspire to create the disturbing impression that the audience is quarantined along with the entire population of Oran. Unsettling and claustrophobic atmosphere is as it should be, but will not correspond to many people's idea of a fun night out at the movies.

Dr. Rieux's (William Hurt) very deliberate, literary voiceover brackets the film, but body of pic is told in flashback. Opening sequence deftly tricks one into assuming what will happen to French TV cameraman-turned-medical-volunteer Jean Tarrou (Jean-Marc Barr). The range of moral choices possible in the face of potentially mortal adversity is treated with rigor, but this principled pic rarely soars as much as it might.

Hurt, as the devoted man of medicine who stands up to the plague and those who seek to profit by it, is weary, self-effacing and tightly wound. When he finally lets his rage and despair emerge, his emotions fly out like a spray of bullets. Tarrou's spiritual drifting and subsequent resolve prompt an occasionally rocky, not always convincing, performance from Barr.

Turning the book's Raymond Rambert into female TV reporter Martine Rambert (Sandrine Bonnarie) was a smart move. Having a professionally active woman on hand heightens the conflict and provides a welcome contrast to the otherwise masculine proceedings. Bonnaire pulls off some very tricky scenes, including one where she starts to masturbate in public. Her broad, strong face is never less than riveting.

Raul Julia injects playful nuances into the deceptively charming profiteer, but despite the thesp's skill, the script demands that he be too heavy a heavy at pic's tense denouement. As a retired statistician determined to write a perfect novel, Robert Duvall delivers every line with pure and gripping radiance, breathing life into the corridors of Death Row.

Although the narrative sticks close to the always interesting characters, some viewers will find the handling of issues too dogmatic. While not easy or conventionally entertaining, pic is accessible to any attentive, patient viewer. Pic runs long and could possibly be trimmed if distribs insist, but cutting too much could be risky since the pic's impact is very much cumulative.

Grayish-blue is the dominant color both inside and out. Smoggy pall over the city suggests that unchecked pollution is also a form of plague. Local faces and scenery give · film · much of its interest. Rougher edges might have boosted its power. Instead it is always smooth — almost glossy.

People on the brink of death can get away with a certain amount of lofty philosophizing, but there is a danger that English-speaking audiences will find much of the dialogue overly ponderous and arty. Certain ideas may come across best to those reading subtitles.

Pic seems unlikely to enthrall a large slice of mainstream U.S. audiences. It will probably fare better with viewers in Old World and Third World countries, where historical outbreaks of repression and fear lie closer to the surface. — *Lisa Nesselson*

UN COEUR EN HIVER
(A HEART OF STONE)
(FRENCH)

A Film Par Film/Cinea/Orly Films/DA Films/Paravision Intl./FR-3 Films production. (Intl. sales: Roissy Films.) Produced by Jean-Louis Livi, Philippe Carcassonne. Directed by Claude Sautet. Screenplay, Sautet, Jacques Fieschi. Camera (color), Yves Angelo; editor, Jacqueline Thiedot; music, Philippe Sarde; production design, Christian Marti; sound, Pierre Lenoir; assistant director, Yvon Rouve. Reviewed at Venice Film Festival (competing), Sept. 1, 1992. Running time: **104 MIN.**
Stephane . . . . Daniel Auteuil
Camille . . . . Emmanuelle Béart
Maxime . . . . André Dussolier
Hélène . . . . Elizabeth Bourgine
Mme. Amet . . . . Myriam Boyer
Regine . . . . Brigitte Catillon
Lachaume . . . . Maurice Garrel
Ostende . . . . Jean-Luc Bideau

"A Heart of Stone" is a cool, elegantly filmed triangular romance in which smiles and glances are used in place of dialogue and conventional action. Extremely subtle and intensely enjoyable, impressive pic deserves international art house attention and, with careful handling, could reach serious filmgoers around the world.**

Claude Sautet has an appreciative audience in France but has never really gained a following elsewhere. Yet his extremely subtle and realistic films about the French bourgeoisie are arguably more piercing than those of, say, Claude Chabrol.

In his new film, Sautet concentrates on Stephane (Daniel Auteuil) and Maxime (André Dussolier), friends since they studied music together and now partners in a small company that makes and repairs stringed instruments.

Maxim is married, but his wife is never seen; Stephane is single, though he has a platonic relationship with Hélène (Elizabeth Bourgine). One day at lunch, Maxime suddenly confesses that he's in love with Camille (Emmanuelle Béart), a beautiful young pianist who's dining with her possessive friend, Regine (Brigitte Catillon) at another table. Though he barely reacts to the news, Stephane is clearly taken aback, jealous of Camille's intrusion into his well-ordered world.

His response is to ingratiate himself with the interloper — not that he makes any moves, but with his looks, occasional words and very presence, he insinuates himself into her life. The ploy works, but not in the way Stephane had anticipated.

Sautet handles this material with great subtlety and is extremely well served by his actors who all give exceptional performances.

The picture unfolds against a background of achingly beautiful music (Maurice Ravel, used under the direction of Philippe Sarde), and Béart convincingly acquits herself on the violin. Yves Angelo's fine camerawork enhances the settings of rehearsal halls, recording studios, cafes and restaurants.

Because Sautet avoids overtly dramatic scenes (no sex, essentially no nudity, no violence), moments when passions boil to the surface (a slap in the face for instance) acquire unexpected power. — *David Stratton*

JAMON, JAMON
(SALAMI, SALAMI)
(SPANISH)

A Lolafilms & Ovideo TV production with collaboration of Sogepaq. Executive producer, Andrés Vicente Gómez. Directed by Bigas Luna. Screenplay, Luna, Cuca Canals; additional dialogue, Quim Monzo. Camera (color), José Luis Alcaine; editor, Teresa Font; music, Nicola Piovani; production design, Chu

Uroz, Noemi Campano; sound, Miquel Rejas; associate producers, Manuel Lombardero, Pepo Sol. Reviewed at Iberoamericana screening room, Mardrid, Aug. 27, 1992. (Competing at Venice Film Festival.) Running time: **93 MIN.**
Silvia . . . . Penelope Cruz
Conchita . . . . . . Stefania Sandrelli
Carmen . . . . Anna Galiena
Raúl . . . . Javier Bardem
José Luis . . . . Jordi Molla
Manuel . . . . Juan Diego
Also with: Tomas Penco, Armando del Rio, Diana Sassen, Chama Mazo, Isabel de Castro Oros, Nazaret Callao, Marianne Hermitte.

Good lensing, direction and a striking performance by newcomer Javier Bardem should garner interest in "Jamon, Jamon" in offshore markets, though the sex element is tame by standards of earlier Bigas Luna films.**

Luna's newie is a rural drama that stresses plot development and characterization more than kinky sex scenes. Using the sterile wastelands of Zaragoza as a backdrop, he deftly limns a mosaic of passion and sex among six characters who ultimately destroy each other. Symbolism abounds for those with a penchant for intellectualizing.

Pic's "Spanishness" seeps into every frame, from the opening sequence of the stud (Bardem) practicing with a toreador's cape, to the shoddy roadside cafe run by a prostitute, to the down-to-earth dialogue. Luna's skillful direction, with virtually no props, rivets aud interest throughout.

Some of Luna's outlandish scenes reveal a touch of wry humor: a fight to the death with two hams used as clubs; sex under a huge billboard in the shape of a bull, whose testicles later serve as an umbrella; a lineup of male models testing out bulging briefs for an underwear manufacturer.

The principals are a prostitute who runs a roadhouse, her daughter, a prosperous but bored married couple, their son, and a village tough used to break up the romance between the whore's daughter and the bourgeois boy.

None of the characters is especially likable, and, as the plot evolves, each interaction often evolves into sexuality: the young boy and the girl he has left pregnant; the stud and the respectable mother; the factory owner and the pregnant girl.

Script and dialogue are lively and well written, nicely mirroring lower tiers of modern Spain. Pic's build-up to a violent climax is fine, but when the blood boils at its hottest, the denouement is so melodramatic, it may strike many viewers as ludicrous.

— *Peter Besas*

MINBO NO ONNA
(THE ANTI-EXTORTION WOMAN)
(JAPANESE)

A Toho release of a Itami Films production. (Intl. sales: Intl. Creative Management.) Executive producers, Yukuo Takenaka, Nigel Sinclair. Produced by Yasushi Tamaoki. Directed, written by Juzo Itami. Camera (color), Yonezo Maeda; editor, Akira Suzuki; music, Toshiyuki Honda; production design, Shuji Nakamura; sound, Osamu Onodera; assistant director, Gen Yamakawa. Reviewed at Venice Film Festival (noncompeting), Sept. 1, 1992. Running time: **126 MIN.**
Mahiru Inoue . . . . Nobuko Miyamoto
Kobayashi . . . . Akira Takarada
Yuki Suzuki . . . . Yasuo Daichi
Taro Wakasugi . . . . Takehiro Murata
Hotel owner . . . . Hideji Otaki
Gang boss . . . . Noboru Mitani
Iriuchijima . . . . Shiro Ito
Ibagi . . . . Akira Nakao
Hanaoka . . . . Hosei Komatsu
Akechi . . . . Tetsu Watanabe

In an internationally publicized incident, writer-director Juzo Itami was attacked earlier this year by Japanese gangsters after the Tokyo opening of "The Anti-Extortion Woman," in which the filmmaker uses the same formula as his two "Taxing Woman" pics to shed light on yakuza operations. Clearly, the film made its mark in Japan, and it should travel well despite its length (about 20 minutes too long) and occasional overstatement.

Director's wife and muse, Noboku Miyamoto (the feisty tax investigator in the earlier films) plays a gutsy lawyer hired by a big international hotel to deal with extortionists. She forms an anti-yakuza task force, together with a pair of timid hotel employees (Yasuo Daichi and Takehiro Murata).

When the gangsters turn up at the hotel for routine collection of their extortion money, they're rebuffed. They counter with a blackmail plan putting the hotel manager (Akira Takarada) into a compromising situation with an under-age girl. The lawyer and her nervous assistants still refuse to buckle to the gangsters' increasing ire.

Most of the film is played as broad comedy, sometimes too broad for Western tastes. The gangsters are caricatured, and their buffoonish attempts to extort money are ridiculed. But an unexpected dramatic note is introed when the lawyer is brutal-

ly attacked by a knife-wielding man in a playground. This scene provides the film's most powerful moment.

Technically, this is up to the standard set by previous Itami films, with Miyamoto giving another confident performance as the resourceful heroine. Scenes in which the mobsters attempt to blacken the hotel's reputation (a cockroach "found" in the lasagne in one of the restaurants, for instance) are both amusing and revealing.

Pic would have benefited from some trimming, but otherwise is a fine addition to Itami's series of exposés of contemporary Japanese life. — *David Stratton*

EDINBURGH FEST

CONFESSIONS OF A SUBURBAN GIRL
(BRITISH-DOCU-COLOR/B&W-16m)

A BBC Scotland presentation of a Stonehedge production. Produced by Jonathan Brett. Executive producer, John Archer. Directed, written by Susan Seidelman. Camera (Duart color/b&w, 16m), Maryse Alberti; editor, Mona Davis; music, Joseph S. DeBeasi; production design, Jessica Lanier; costume design, Sharon Pinkerson; sound, Bruce Litecky; assistant director, Maureen Kelley McKenna. Reviewed at Edinburgh Intl. Film Festival, Aug. 19, 1992. (Also in Venice Film Festival.) Running time: **50 MIN.**
Young Susan . . . . . Cynthia Mullock
Young friends . . . . Ali Dibrino,
Kim Anastasi, Amy Learn,
Jessica Leiner
Tough girls . . . . Lissa Mogell,
Becky Vincenti
Naked lady . . . . Nancy Rommelman
Chemistry teacher . . . Michael Steven
Schultz
Female teacher . . . Sherry Greenberg
Also with: Susan Seidelman.

Third in the series of "A Director's Place" autobiographical docus commissioned by BBC Scotland, Susan Seidelman's "Confessions of a Suburban Girl" is a sparky, good-natured look at the helmer's teen years in '60s suburban Philly. More pointed and cohesive than previous entries by Nagisa Oshima and John Boorman, pic reps a strong buff item for film festivals and specialized webs.

Fronted and narrated by Seidelman herself as she returns to Huntingdon Valley, an "instant neighborhood" 20 minutes outside Philadelphia, the film mixes slick reportage, interviews with

old friends and '60s docu memorabilia with black & white recreations of teen memories. Result is a fascinating footnote to the helmer's career to date, as well as a perfect intro to her works.

Story starts with her family's move at age 9 to the safe, idealized suburb, where it was like living "inside a glass bubble." At age 14 an eye problem of blurry vision gave "a very weird twist to the world I was growing up in — American suburbia of the 1960s."

Main chunk of pic is Seidelman and old girlfriends lolling around in a bedroom and playing a mature version of truth or dare. There are lotsa confessions about growing up, boys, bowling, drive-ins and first sex, though Seidelman herself is coy on the last.

Per her school friends, SS for a time called herself the more gentile-sounding "Sue Seidel" and was considered "wild" by other parents. Helmer herself admits to lionizing "bad girls" in the neighborhood and becoming a director in New York to get actors to realize her suppressed fantasies.

Clips from "Desperately Seeking Susan," "Cookie" and "She-Devil" are slotted in to revealing effect, directly illustrating (per Seidelman) earlier teen incidents and fantasies. Movie buffs will get a big kick out of such juxtapositions, pure auteurist-theory stuff.

Beyond that, pic also lightly trawls the era's social changes: feminism, revolution, the changing perception of marriage and family. Seidelman keeps it light and humorous, with her friends saying most of the words. Focus, as dictated by the series, remains on the place she's evoking.

Tech credits are all excellent, with bright, clear 16m lensing by Maryse Alberti, sharp cutting, and a bouncy '60s-homage music track. — *Derek Elley*

LEON THE PIG FARMER
(BRITISH)

A Leon the Pig Farmer production. Produced by Gary Sinyor, Vadim Jean. Executive producer, Paul Brooks. Co-executive producers, David Altschuler, Howard Kitchner, Steven Margolis. Directed by Jean, Sinyor. Screenplay, Sinyor, Michael Norman. Camera (Rank color), Gordon Hickie; editor, Ewa J. Lind; music, John Murphy, David Hughes; production design, Simon Hicks; art direction, James Helps; sound (Dolby SR), Danny Hambrook; assistant director, Richard Lingard; associate producer, Simon Scotland. Reviewed at Edinburgh Intl. Film Festival, Aug. 26,

1992. (Also at Venice Film Festival Critics Week section.) Running time: **103 MIN.**
Leon Geller . . . . Mark Frankel
Judith Geller . . . . Janet Suzman
Brian Chadwick . . . . . Brian Glover
Yvonne Chadwick . . . . Connie Booth
Sidney Geller . . . . . David de Keyser
Madeleine . . . . Maryam D'Abo
Lisa . . . . Gina Bellman
Also with: Jean Anderson, Bernard Bresslaw, Annette Crosbie, Burt Kwouk, John Woodvine.

A London Jewish kid finds his real dad is in the bacon trade in "Leon the Pig Farmer," a good-humored riff on Jewish-gentile stereotypes. With further tightening and high-profile ad-pub, the pic could slice off some topside as a curio item.

Billing itself as "the first Jewish comedy feature film to come out of Britain," pic is very different in feel to Yank equivalents. Sitcom elements and British scatological humor keep peeking through the comic fabric. Pacing, too, is milder.

Opening has Leon (Mark Frankel) shocking his parents (Janet Suzman, David de Keyser) by chucking his job with an unprincipled North London realtor. Soon after, he finds he and his brothers are actually the products of artificial insemination, as Dad has a low sperm count.

Checking that the problem isn't hereditary, Leon discovers the medical center mixed up the test tubes years ago and his real father is gentile pig farmer Chadwick (Brian Glover) up north in the wilds of Yorkshire.

Surprised but delighted, Chadwick and his wife (Connie Booth) go 200% Jewish to make Leon feel at home. Twist comes when Leon, helping out on the farm, accidentally injects a pig with sheep's semen, producing the world's first kosher porker.

First hour, set in London, takes a while to get to the nut of the plot, with lotsa jokes about Jewish eating habits and sexual performance. Pic finds its feet in the Yorkshire scenes with Glover and Booth earnestly cooking chicken soup, planning vacations to Eilat and inviting two rabbis to check if the lamb-piglet (never shown on-screen) is kosher.

Playing of the uneven script is broad all round, with Glover dominating all his scenes and well supported by Booth. Suzman and De Keyser have less original material to chew on. Maryam D'Abo livens up the London segs as a horny gentile with the hots for Jewish boys. Franklin is okay as the bemused Leon.

Originally developed by U.K. indie Prominent Features, pic has a classy look way above its £155,000 budget, with cast and crew all working on deferment. Lensing by Gordon Hickie is bright and shapely. Editing, especially in the first hour, could be pacier.

First-time helmer Vadim Jean gets larger billing on the shared director credit, with co-director/ writer Gary Sinyor likewise on the producers' card. Pic has yet to get the nod from Blighty's Jewish authorities.

— *Derek Elley*

CREATURES OF LIGHT
(BRITISH-16m)

A National Film & Television School production. (Intl. sales: NFTS.) Produced by Katherine Hedderly. Directed, written by Bill Anderson. Camera (Kodak color, Technicolor prints, 16m), Pentti Keskimaki; editor, Melanie Adams; music, Robert Neufeld; production design, Ben Scott; costume design, Annie Symons; makeup, Louise Ricci; sound, Ron Bailey; assistant directors, Ian Henry, Ted Thornton. Reviewed at Edinburgh Intl. Film Festival, Aug. 27, 1992. Running time: **76 MIN.**
Eilidh . . . . Robin McCaffrey
Fionn . . . . Paul Higgins
Jean . . . . Jenny Lee
Minister . . . . Donald Douglas
Also with: Barbara Horne, Ralph Riach, Roy Sampson, Andy Barr, Billy Riddock.

Topnotch production and confident playing illuminate "Creatures of Light," a Celtic costumer about all-conquering love between a lame farmer and a strong woman. Beyond fests and tube playoff, pic could have limited theatrical potential as a quality drama in 35m blowup.

Pic's actually the graduation feature of mature NFTS directing student Bill Anderson, who has a track record in stage and TV scripting. But there's nothing film schoolish about the finished product with a pro feel.

Simple story is set in the 1850s on Scotland's remote Isle of Mull, though time and place are unspecified on screen. Young, partially lame Fionn (Paul Higgins) takes in the mysterious Eilidh (Robin McCaffrey), who one day washes up half-frozen in a boat with her hands bound.

Slowly recovering, she first tidies up his bachelor cottage and later invites him into her bed. The drama heightens as she corrals the womenfolk into building a "salmon ladder" to help the weaker fish survive the spawning journey, encountering the resistance of the local fishermen.

Economical script doesn't overdo the symbolism of femme support for nature's weaklings. Pic is more about the possibility of choice, of not accepting the inevitable.

Screen newcomers McCaffrey and Higgins make a confident pairing, in no way overshadowed by more experienced thesps Donald Douglas and Jenny Lee as the local minister and his wife.

Major plaudits, too, go to director Anderson and producer Katherine Hedderly for hewing such a good-looking pic from a modest £70,000 budget.

Tech credits are impressive, especially Robert Neufeld's assured symphonic score, Melanie Adams' smooth cutting and Finn Pentti Keskimaki's 16m lensing, which has a feel for spirit of place.

Pic shared the top Chaplin Award (with "Leon the Pig Farmer") at the recent Edinburgh fest.

— *Derek Elley*

LA VIE CREVÉE
(PUNCTURED LIFE)
(FRENCH)

A Fin de Siècle, Epithete, La Sept co-production. Produced by Jean Paul Alram. Directed, written by Guillaume Nicloux. Camera (color), Raoul Coutard; editor, Brigitte Benard; music, Hartman, performed by Alain Kremski; sound, Michel Laurent. Reviewed at Locarno Film Festival (competition), Aug. 8, 1992. Running time: **75 MIN.**
Raymond . . . . Michel Piccoli
Angele . . . . Arielle Dombasle
Alice . . . . Geraldine Danon
Georges . . . . Didier Abot
Jean . . . . Nicolas Jouhet
Postman . . . . Wadeck Stanczak

Vaguely reminiscent of shaky New Wave vagaries and surrealist explorations, Guillaume Nicloux's third film can only hope the presence of major French star Michel Piccoli will help find some kind of commercial release, denied his earlier efforts.

An older man living by himself in a country manor hosts two young couples stranded nearby when their car breaks down. During the next few days, he manipulates them at will, manages to sleep with one of the women and break up all the "guests'" relationships. His odd behavior could have made anyone hightail it early on, but the four stay on to take their punishment for no evident reason.

Hermetic at best and uncomprehensible for most of the time, pic will annoy anyone expecting it to make some sense. With all due respect to Piccoli's masterful presence, it's difficult to figure out why this film was made.

— *Dan Fainaru*

VIDEO BLUES
(HUNGARIAN)

A Cinemagyar presentation of a Hunnia Fils, Option Images, La Sept Cinemaco production. Directed by Arpad Sopsits. Screenplay, Sopsits, Sandor Fabri, Laszlo Garaczi. Camera (color), Sandor Kardos; editor, Katalin Kardebo; music, Laszlo Melis; sets, Csaba Stork, Zsolt Csenger; costumes, Janos Breckl; sound, Janos Reti; Reviewed at Locarno Film Festival (competition), Aug. 13, 1992. Running time: **100 MIN.**
Gabor . . . . Lajos Otto Horvath
Judit . . . . Judit Danyi
Janos . . . . Atila Epres
Eva . . . . Myriam Mezieres

A leading exponent of young Hungarian cinema, Arpad Sopsits has devised a vicious little game of make-believe which ultimately fails because it turns out to be mainly concerned with the rules of the game instead of the players.

Two brothers love the same woman. One marries her and stays in Budapest; the other goes to Paris and moves in with a rich woman. Latter bro pretends to be a success, hoping to make his brother envious. Instead of letters, they communicate via videotape, with the married one flaunting his happiness next to the woman they both love. The Parisian tries to disrupt this bliss with camera tricks intended to convince his sibling that his happiness is an illusion.

Sopsits packs "Video Blues" with intentional ambiguities: Who's the woman talking to when she addresses the camera pledging her love? Is it the man sitting next to her or the one who will be watching the tape at the other end of the continent? Helmer leaves the door open for many interpretations.

The film also could be a reflection on the difference between truth as it is and truth through the eye of the camera. It can also be taken as a kind of schizophrenic exercise, the two brothers repping opposite facets of the same person. If so, the perverse game is self-inflicted torture. But since the players themselves are so one-dimensional, it's difficult to care about the nature of the game.

— *Dan Fainaru*

CHAIN OF DESIRE

An Anant Singh & Distant Horizon presentation. Produced by Brian Cox. Executive producer, Singh. Directed, written by Temistocles Lopez. Camera (Technicolor), Nancy Schreiber; editor, Suzanne Fenn; music, Nathan Birnbaum; music supervisor, Jeffrey Kimball; production design, Scott Chambliss; art direction, Michael Shaw; set decoration, Judy Becker; costume design, Pilar Limosner; sound, Joe Romano; associate producers, Mickey Cottrell, Doug Lindeman, Sudhir Pragjee, Sanjeev Singh; assistant director, Tom Willey; casting, Andrea Stone Guttfreund, Laurel Smith. Reviewed at Ocean screening room, Santa Monica, Calif., Aug. 16, 1992. (Competing in Montreal World Film Festival). Running time: **107 MIN.**
Alma D'Angeli . . . . Linda Fiorentino
Jesus . . . . Elias Koteas
Ken . . . . Tim Guinee
Linda Bailey . . . . . . Grace Zabriskie
Cleo . . . . Assumpta Serna
Jerald Buckley . . . . Patrick Bauchau
Mel . . . . Seymour Cassel
Hubert Bailey . . . Malcolm McDowell
Isa . . . . Angel Aviles
Keith . . . . Jamie Harrold
David Bango . . . . Dewey Weber
Diana . . . . Holly Marie Combs
Joe . . . . Kevin Conroy
Angie . . . . Suzanne Douglas

A modern "La Ronde" played out under the shadow of AIDS, "Chain of Desire" is an uneven but alluringly sexy melodrama that gets better as it goes along. Enterprising, very handsome indie production boasts a strong cast of talented names and promising newcomers despite budget of well under $1 million, and should be quite promotable to sophisticated audiences by the right specialized distributor. World preem took place at Montreal.

A native Venezuelan with assorted theater and short film experience, writer-director Temistocles Lopez made one previous feature, the 1988 cult item "Exquisite Corpses." His new pic shows him to better advantage as a director than writer, but his sophisticated sensibility, talent with actors and implicit political commentary more than justify the presumption involved in refashioning Arthur Schnitzler's classic play, so beautifully filmed in 1950 by Max Ophuls.

Set in contempo New York, mostly downtown, Lopez's version introduces a somewhat jaded, bisexual perspective to the tale, but fortunately without the arch aestheticism often associated with self-consciously hip, quasi-European American filmmaking. No matter how many times these characters have been around the block, they remain vibrantly alive to life's possibilities, at least where the libido is concerned.

Opening has club chanteuse Linda Fiorentino repairing to the solitude of a church after breaking up with a b.f. But there she is approached by seductive building restorer Elias Koteas, with whom she begins a torrid affair.

Koteas' sexy wife, Angel Aviles, works as a maid for depraved millionaire Patrick Bauchau, who tries to get her into the bondage games in which he indulges with Grace Zabriskie. Latter has seen the passion disappear from her marriage to Malcolm McDowell, a TV commentator.

Up to this point, pic consists of cloistered encounters between two individuals in which nothing is fleshed out psychologically or dramatically. If it continued strictly in this vein, pic would quickly have become desultory.

But, coincidentally or not, the situations and incidents become more complex and intense once the pic switches into gay and bi territory. It turns out McDowell prefers boys these days, and his assignation with a corn-fed street hustler leads the film into the edgy subculture of druggies, the homeless and those who would help them, young kids who are just getting started and the art world.

On the lookout for the right man to take her into adulthood, tasty teen Holly Marie Combs meets eminent painter Seymour Cassel at a gallery opening, and the aging philanderer has the audacity to stand up his gorgeous wife, Assumpta Serna, while he gives Combs what he calls "the Lolita treatment."

In return, Serna gives super hunky worker Kevin Conroy a roll on a large canvas. Serna's overt approach to Conroy reps the film's hottest scene until the next one, a mini-classic of voyeuristic onanism involving three solo individuals that New York apartment dwellers will especially appreciate. The ultimate in safe sex proves, in this context, also to be the most exciting.

Although no issue is made of sexually transmitted diseases until the end, a climactic revelation provides an appropriately sobering and inescapable point to such a tale of serial sex in this day and age. Pic does not moralize or editorialize, but very effectively underlines how little one may know about one's sex partners.

Dialogue could have been considerably sharper, structure is sometimes lumpy, particularly in the early going, and tightening by five to 10 minutes would help. But Lopez has made the most of his assembled virtues, which most prominently include his very capable and sexy cast, and exceedingly strong production values for a low-budgeter.

Straight and gay viewers of both genders will have plenty to feast their eyes upon here, and thesps deliver with relaxed, humorous, knowing performances. The relish with which Serna attacks her role will attract everyone's attention. Conroy exudes considerable masculine authority, McDowell sensitively etches a man with a secret life, and Cassel is both amusing and pathetic as the veteran Lothario.

Nancy Schreiber's lensing superbly captures the colors and moods of Gotham both in lovely dockside exteriors and intimate chambers, while Scott Chambliss' production design outstandingly evokes many different strata of society. Composer Nathan Birnbaum and music supervisor Jeffrey Kimball have devised a largely effective soundtrack, although it needed a more vigorous, intoxicating tune over the end credits.
— *Todd McCarthy*

CONTRE L'OUBLI
(AGAINST OBLIVION)
(FRENCH-DOCU)

A Les Films du Paradoxe presentation of an Amnesty Intl. production in association with PRV. Directed by Chantal Akerman, Rene Allio, Denis Amar, Jean Becker, Jane Birkin, Jean-Michel Carre, Patrice Chereau, Alain Corneau, Costa-Gavras, Dominique Dante, Claire Denis, Raymond Depardon, Jacques Deray, Michel Deville, Jacques Doillon, Martine Franck, Gerard Frot-Coutaz, Francis Girod, Jean-Luc Godard (& Anne-Marie Mieville), Romain Goupil, Jean-Loup Hubert, Robert Kramer, Patrice Leconte, Sarah Moon, Philippe Muyl, Alain Resnais, Coline Serreau, Bertrand Tavernier, Nadine Trintignant. Various camera, editors; music, Mino Cinelli. Reviewed at Montreal World Film Festival, Aug. 30, 1992. Running time: **110 MIN.**
With: Catherine Deneuve, Philippe Noiret, Jane Birkin, Charlotte Gainsbourg, Sami Frey, Emmanuelle Béart, Henri Cartier-Bresson, Isabelle Huppert, Carole Bouquet, Marie Trintignant.

Despite the impressive bulk of heavyweight French talent on both sides of the camera, "Contre l'Oubli" faces an uphill battle to find audiences beyond fundraising affairs and narrow-niche specialty markets. Amnesty Intl., which produced the omnibus film for its 30th anni, would do better to bypass theatrical venues and simply sell videocassettes via an international direct-mail campaign.

Thirty French filmmakers each deliver a short plea on behalf of someone in the world who has disappeared, or been imprisoned or murdered, because of his or her political beliefs. Unfortunates range from a Palestinian wrongly detained in Israel to a human-rights activist imprisoned in Cuba, and from a mentally retarded African-American executed for murder in Louisiana to street urchins shot for sport by corrupt cops in Guatemala.

Most of the short films, such as Jean Becker's tersely effective bit with the great Philippe Noiret, simply have actors read letters of concern or outrage to the appropriate government leaders, while the words are illustrated with still photos, newsreel footage or dramatized re-creations.

A few others are more self-consciously imaginative. The best of this group is a lively rap-music number in support of South Korean activist Kim Song Man, directed by Costa-Gavras.

At least one segment is laugh-out-loud funny: Patrice Leconte's depiction of a surly blue-collar type (beautifully played by Guy Bedos) who's genuinely angry about the treatment of a Soviet Union dissident.

A few of the segments lurch into melodrama, or worse. Chantal Akerman badly miscalculates by having Catherine Deneuve wax eloquent about a murdered human-rights activist in El Salvador. Actress seems to say that the worst part of the tragedy is that the murdered woman won't be with her lover anymore.

Pic is an undeniably sincere effort graced with excellent production values. Unfortunately, but perhaps inevitably, even sympathetic audiences will wind up numbed to the horrors described. Midway through this well-intentioned but overlong pic, viewers will start concentrating more on film technique, or the actors, or anything else that will break the monotony of the relentless cavalcade of human misery.
— *Joe Leydon*

DIE SPUR DES BERNSTEINZIMMERS
(THE MYSTERY OF THE AMBER ROOM)
(GERMAN)

A Progress Film-Verleih release of a DEFA Studio in cooperation with WDR production. Produced by Horst Hartwig. Directed by Roland Gräf. Screenplay, Thomas Knauf; dramaturge, Christel Gräf. Camera (color), Roland Dressel; editor, Monika Schindler; production design, Dieter Döhl; costumes, Christiane Dorst; sound, Andreas Kaufmann; special effects, Toni Loeser, Gisela Schultze & FuturEffects. Reviewed at Börse screening room, Berlin, Aug. 18, 1992. (Competing at Montreal World Film Festival.) Running time: **107 MIN.**
Lisa Morbrink . . . . Corinna Harfouch
Max Buttstädt . . . . Kurt Böwe
Ludwig Kollenbey . . . Uwe Kockisch
Siegfried Emmler . . . . Ulrich Tukur
Costello . . . . . . Michael Gwisdek
Frau Ladenthin . . . . . Käthe Reichel
Dr. Kobler . . . . Horst Schultze
Morbrink . . . Joachim Tomaschewsky
Priest . . . . Arno Wyzniewski

A well-scripted and acted romantic thriller that's a cut above what's been coming out of Germany lately, "The Mystery of the Amber Moon" should do well at home and see some Euro biz. TV sales also look promising.

Film is based on the ongoing hunt for the actual Amber Room, a gift of the King of Prussia to Tsar Peter I. Stolen by the Nazis in 1944, the priceless 18th century mosaics have never resurfaced.

Lisa (Corinna Harfouch) is perplexed by the sudden death of her professor father who, she learns, was involved in the search for the Amber Room. Leaving her fiancé Ludwig (Uwe Kockisch), she drives to an eastern German town to talk to Dad's acquaintances about the possible cause of his death — she believes he could have been murdered. Her investigations suck her deeper into the search, involving her with sinister characters and near misses.

Ludwig, a music prof, is also bitten by the Amber Room bug when he realizes that certain clues to its location are buried in encoded Wagnerian texts. The two become involved with Siegfried, also seeking the treasure which his father was involved in stealing. But as the three hunt for the trove, they discover they're being hunted.

Script is well-wrought and suspenseful. Clever infusions of humor are used advantageously, especially to temper scenes of violence when items such as crucifixes or cakes are used as ersatz weapons. Roland Gräf infuses tongue-in-cheek comments about the fall of the German Democratic Republic (pic is set in pre-unification 1990), such as a scene in a drive-in bearing the communist slogan "Film art belongs to the people."

Overall, acting is solid, but veteran East German actor Michael Gwisdek's talents are underutilized, and his bad-guy costume consisting of dark sunglasses and a fedora come across as more ludicrous than menacing.

Tech credits are good, as is the use of eastern German landscapes and cities. Occasionally, post-dubbed sound rings a false note.

— *Rebecca Lieb*

BARAKA
(DOCU-70m)

A Magidson Films production. Produced by Mark Magidson. Directed by Ron Fricke. Concept-scenario, Fricke, Magidson, Bob Green. Camera (Todd-AO color, 70m), Fricke; editor, Fricke, Magidson, David E. Aubrey; music, Michael Stearns. Reviewed at Montreal World Film Festival, Aug. 30, 1992. Running time: **96 MIN.**

Words can't do justice to the visual masterpiece "Baraka," a smashingly edited, superbly scored, wild world tour that speaks volumes about the planet without uttering a word. Impossible concept will be a marketing nightmare, however.

Pic will need a distrib as focused as lenser-helmer Ron Fricke and as ruthless as its discerning editors to capitalize on inevitable word of mouth. A smash hit at its world preem in Montreal, the opus generated a buzz big enough for an additional screening.

Journey through urban jungles and civilized savagery in 24 countries is a "breath of life," or *baraka*, an ancient Middle Eastern Sufi word that translates as a blessing or as the breath/essence of life.

Nonfiction pic is a 96-minute Lear jet flight that takes timely breathers as filmmakers observe a passionate and destructive love/hate affair between woman and earth. If the name "Postcards From the Edge" hadn't already been used, this would be the film that lived up to the title.

Real-life snippets filmed in far-flung places such as Tanzania, Kuwait, Iran and Nepal are seamlessly woven, from intriguing "monkey chant" ceremonies in Bali to confining "sleep capsules" in Tokyo. Most are images never seen before. Pic stuns viewer with planet's vast diversity. Time-lapse subway sequence (edited to music score) is an ideal example of filmmakers' imaginative manipulation, as is a camera that occasionally lingers on curious or hard-boiled faces.

World beat soundtrack is an obvious marketing tool. Soundtrack artists include Dead Can Dance, Somei Satoh, the Harmonic Choir, Anugama & Sebastiano, Kohachiro Miyata, L. Subramaniam, Monks of the Dip Tse Ling Monastery, Ciro Hurtado and Brother.

Crackerjack editing also slips in tough images without moralizing. Stunning images speak for themselves. "Baraka" is an educational trip.

— *Suzan Ayscough*

JANA UND JAN
(JANA AND JAN)
(GERMAN)

A DEFA Studio Babelsberg production in association with ZDF. Produced by Uwe Kraft. Directed, written by Helmut Dziuba. Camera (color), Helmut Bergmann; music, Christian Steyer; editor, Monika Schindler; sound, Klaus Tolsdorf; costumes, Elke Hersman. Reviewed at Montreal World Film Festival, Aug. 29, 1992. Running time: **92 MIN.**
Jana . . . . Kristin Scheffer
Jan . . . . Rene Guss
Julia . . . . Julia Brendler
Lady . . . . Corinna Stockman
Sir . . . . Dirk Muller
Also with: Marco Neumann, Karin Gregorek, Peter Sodann, Harald Warmbrunn.

Helmut Dziuba's "Jana and Jan" is a morose, contrived drama that benefits greatly from its topicality. Set against a backdrop of the epochal changes in Germany, pic may attract the curious on the global fest circuit, but commercial prospects are doubtful.

Pic is a tale of star-crossed romance in a German Democratic Republic center for juvenile delinquents. Jana (Kristin Scheffer), a peroxided j.d. of 17, bets other bad girls that she can deflower a new inmate, sullen 15-year-old orphan Jan (Rene Guss).

She quickly wins the bet but falls in love with the guy, inspiring resentment among the other teen inmates, who aren't at all sympathetic when she winds up pregnant. When she tells Jan she's considering an abortion, Jan — who, surprisingly, really wants to be a father — punches her down a flight of stairs.

Drama unfolds as TV newscasts periodically report on progress of Germany's reunification. Evidently, Dziuba intends his lower-depths love story as a metaphor for the mixed blessings and new responsibilities that will come for the people of the former East Germany. Wisely, however, he doesn't harp on the issue.

Jana recovers and decides to have the baby. After suffering many indignities from her sister inmates, she is reunited with Jan, and they escape.

Dziuba comes awfully close to exploitation with scenes of bad girls taking lotsa showers, and he makes much too little of Jan's abuse of Jana. Worse, he strains credibility by making it very easy for the young lovers to repeatedly enjoy trysts in the dark corners of the juve prison.

Lead performances have a raw power and undeniable emotional impact. Supporting players are well cast. Christian Steyer's music is heavy-handed at times, but other tech credits are fine.

— *Joe Leydon*

DEUCE COUPE

An Airtight Filmworks production. Executive producers, Roland Hinz, Philip Magno. Produced by Robert Sloat. Directed by Mark Deimel. Screenplay, James Nichols. Camera (color), Stephen McNutt; editor, Paul White; music, Barry Ennis; production design, Mimi Cramatky, Shane Nelsen; sound, William Fiege, Chris Schwartz. Reviewed at Montreal World Film Festival, Aug. 28, 1992. Running time: **106 MIN.**
Eddie Fitzpatrick . . Kieran Mulroney
Ray Fitzpatrick . . . . . . Brian Bloom
Marie Vitelli . . . . . . Ashley Lauren
Virginia . . . . . Danielle Von Zerneck
Link Malone . . . . Cameron Dye
Slick Lowry . . . . Larry Hankin
Jean Fitzpatrick . . . . . Candy Clark
Sheriff . . . . Paul Le Mat

Competently made but thoroughly unremarkable, "Deuce Coupe" arrives too late to enjoy many happy days at the b.o. with its formulaic '50s nostalgia. By-the-numbers jalopy will doubtless be parked soon in vid and cable venues where it should benefit from casting of "American Graffiti" vets Candy Clark and Paul Le Mat in small but exploitable roles.

Kieran Mulroney stars as a small-town Virginia teen who worships older brother Brian Bloom, an aimless, hell-raising hot-rodder. The siblings have labored mightily to rev up Bloom's prized cherry-red deuce coupe, which Bloom races against the town's drag-race champ (Cameron Dye).

Bloom wins, but he quickly leaves town to join the Air Force. Enter Ashley Lauren, a bad-reputation babe who claims she's pregnant with Bloom's child. Mulroney is shocked, especially since he's sweet on the young woman himself, and is greatly upset when he sees her joyriding with Dye.

Mulroney rashly challenges Dye to a race that ends with the hero smashing up the deuce coupe. As he hustles to repair the damage before his brother returns on leave, Lauren copes with the kind of disapproval most small-town unwed mothers-to-be had to face in 1958.

Screenwriter James Nichols wants to say something profound about the dangers of hero worship and the wisdom that comes only with age. It's familiar territory, and Nichols fails to mine any new nuggets of insight.

Still, the period ambience is nicely evoked, and some of the performers find moments of emotional truth in stock roles, especially Dye as the bad guy who isn't so bad after all, and Danielle Von Zerneck as Bloom's very proper g.f.

Director Mark Deimel, yet another UCLA film school grad, takes a straightforward approach to the material and keeps the sentiment from getting too sticky. But he miscalculates by having a key dialogue exchange go on too long and too melodramatically in a heavy downpour. Scene winds up seeming comical, leaving the audience to wonder if the characters lack the good sense to come in out of the rain.

Reportedly, the occasionally overbearing score heard in the print shown at Montreal will be changed before the pic hits the marketplace. Other tech credits are standard. — *Joe Leydon*

OUR HOLLYWOOD EDUCATION
(SWISS-DOCU-16m)

An E-Motion Films production. Produced, directed, written by Michael Beltrami. Camera (color), Adrian Valicescu, Isham Abed, Leonard Myszynski; editor, Beltrami; music, Andre Knecht. Reviewed at Montreal World Film Festival, Aug. 28, 1992. Running time: **85 MIN.**
With: Oliver Stone, Krzysztof Zanussi, Charles Joffe, Glenn Ford, Sally Kirkland, Paul Bartel, Krzysztof Kieslowski.

"Our Hollywood Education" director Michael Beltrami flunks docu filmmaking with this amateur feature-length debut. Unrevealing interviews with solid Hollywood players like Oliver Stone or Charles Joffe don't rescue this pretentious slam of the "dream factory." Unfocused, unbalanced and virtually unedited, the picture totters between admiration and admonition of the Hollywood myth.

Voice-of-God narration doesn't reveal the questions put to directors, producers or actors interviewed. But given throwaway answers (such as in Hollywood, it's not what you know but who you know), audience can only assume queries are about success and failure.

Docu claims to address art vs. commerce, a premise that unearthed several notable remarks. Prophetic Polish director Krzysztof Zanussi declares that the term "film business sounds like a semantic contradiction."

Stone says anything can be a commercial hit, even a pic about starving Ethiopians, if the story "captures the human heart."

This docu doesn't even capture human interest.
— *Suzan Ayscough*

SNEAKERS

A Universal release of a Lawrence Lasker/Walter F. Parkes production. Produced by Parkes, Lasker. Executive producer, Lindsley Parsons Jr. Directed by Phil Alden Robinson. Screenplay, Robinson, Lasker, Parkes. Camera (Deluxe color), John Lindley; editor, Tom Rolf; music, James Horner; featured soprano sax, Branford Marsalis; production design, Patrizia von Brandenstein; art direction, Dianne Wager; set design, James J. Murakami, Keith B. Burns, James Tocci; set decoration, Samara Schaffer; costume design, Bernie Pollack; sound (Dolby), Willie D. Burton; associate producer-assistant director, William M. Elvin; 2nd unit director, Glenn H. Randall Jr.; casting, Risa Bramon Garcia, Juel Bestrop; Reviewed at AMC Santa Monica 7, Santa Monica, Calif., Aug. 23, 1992. MPAA Rating: PG-13. Running time: **125 MIN.**

Martin Bishop . . . . . Robert Redford
Mother . . . . Dan Aykroyd
Cosmo . . . . Ben Kingsley
Liz . . . . Mary McDonnell
Carl . . . . River Phoenix
Crease . . . . Sidney Poitier
Whistler . . . . David Strathairn
Dick Gordon . . . . . Timothy Busfield
Gregor . . . . George Hearn
Buddy Wallace . . . . . . Eddie Jones
Dr. Gunter Janek . . . . . Donal Logue
Dr. Elena Rhyzkov . . Lee Garlington
Dr. Brandes . . . Stephen Tobolowsky
Bernard Abbott . . . James Earl Jones
College-age Cosmo . . . . . Jojo Marr
College-age Bishop . Gary Hershberger

It's been awhile since the last slick, hip, liberal, hi-tech, all-star buddy spy comic caper pic, so there's no reason why this one shouldn't fit the bill for a good-sized public this fall. Until it becomes ludicrously far-fetched in the final reels, "Sneakers" serves up a breezy good time in the vein of some of toplined Robert Redford's 1970s hits, and the mainstream pleasures it affords should appeal to just about all audience segments, save perhaps ultra-sophisticates and lowbrow teens.

After floundering on the reefs of "Havana," Redford has returned to familiar territory in a role suiting his talents for flippancy, light comic irreverence, male bonding and mildly anti-establishment political comment.

"Field of Dreams" director Phil Alden Robinson demonstrates an agreeable flair for low-key comedy, changing tones and the orchestration of complicated logistics until falling into the black holes of gaping plot gaps and an insincere jokiness.

After a small-screen, black & white prologue set in 1969 in which one college student escapes arrest while his buddy is carted off to jail for some pioneer computer hacking, film gets off to a good start with a mock break-

in demonstrating the skill of Redford's company in cracking security systems.

Working out of a striking, glass-enclosed workshop in San Francisco, this gang of underpaid but fun-loving experts sports a full complement of shady backgrounds: Sidney Poitier was fired from the CIA, Dan Aykroyd is an ex-con, David Strathairn is a blind wiretapping and audio expert and River Phoenix changed his school grades by computer.

Redford's the kid who eluded authorities for more than 20 years. But then two alleged agents from the top-secret National Security Agency enlist his services to recover a mysterious black box that turns out to contain a device that can penetrate the computer systems of the Federal Reserve, the nation's electrical power grid, air traffic control and other vital services any government on earth would love to access.

For an hour, the script by Robinson and producers Lawrence Lasker and Walter F. Parkes ("WarGames") maintains a clever, knowing, devil-may-care tone. But when three characters are suddenly murdered (two onscreen), things turn darker and more dire. It turns out the boys are up against Redford's criminal college cohort Ben Kingsley, who now sees the box as a way to accomplish their student dream of changing the world, and to take revenge on Redford in the bargain.

Second half involves gunplay, Redford's abduction, an elaborate siege of Kingsley's seemingly impregnable h.q., two confrontations between the old college buddies, some elaborate computer calculations and a very hokey climactic getaway. It's all capped by government security honcho James Earl Jones bestowing, like some newfangled Wizard of Oz, what each member of the victorious crew most covets.

When the issues grow into matters of life and death, viewer can be expected to take matters more seriously as well. Unfortunately, script's second half can't support a more sober examination, as too many issues are ignored or glossed over.

Still, there are pleasures to be had, notably in Robinson's supremely confident, ultra-pro handling of filmmaking tools. He shows a strong grasp of how to direct the viewer's attention to what he wants to reveal, and the transitions between shots and be-

tween sequences are very well judged.

The film looks exceedingly expensive, and no doubt was. Helping Robinson achieve an air of technical mastery are John Lindley's richly textured lensing, Patrizia von Brandenstein's imaginative and varied production design keyed off of Bay Area locations, James Horner's sparkling score and Tom Rolf's alert editing, which lets out only a little slack toward the end.

Big-time cast provides sterling company, as the very casual demands put upon them allow the performers to convey the impression of enjoying a no-stress vacation. None of these mostly middle-aged actors has more than one level to act, but they all accomplish that with panache. — *Todd McCarthy*

SCHOOL TIES

A Paramount release of a Jaffe/Lansing production. Produced by Stanley R. Jaffe, Sherry Lansing. Executive producer, Danton Rissner. Directed by Robert Mandel. Screenplay, Dick Wolf, Darryl Ponicsan, from a story by Wolf. Camera (Technicolor dailies, Deluxe prints), Freddie Francis; editors, Jerry Greenberg, Jacqueline Cambas; music, Maurice Jarre; production design, Jeannine Claudia Oppewall; art direction, Steven Wolff; set decoration, Rosemary Brandenburg; set design, Marc Fisichella; costume design, Ann Roth; sound (Dolby), Keith Wester; stunt coordinator, Buddy Joe Hooker; associate producer, Michael Tadross; assistant directors, Steve Danton, Newton D. Arnold; 2nd unit director, Hooker; casting, Pat McCorkle, Lisa Beach. Reviewed at Mann Plaza Theater, West L.A., Sept. 10, 1992. MPAA Rating: PG13. Running time: **107 MIN.**

David Greene . . . . . Brendan Fraser
Charlie Dillon . . . . Matt Damon
Chris Reece . . . . . . Chris O'Donnell
Rip Van Kelt . . . . Randall Batinkoff
McGivern . . . . Andrew Lowery
Jack Connors . . . . Cole Hauser
Chesty Smith . . . . Ben Affleck
McGoo . . . . Anthony Rapp
Sally Wheeler . . . . Amy Locane
Headmaster Dr. Bartram . Peter Donat
Cleary . . . . Zeljko Ivanek
Coach McDevitt . . . . . . Kevin Tighe
Mr. Gierasch . . . . . Michael Higgins
Alan Greene . . . . Ed Lauter

A subject too rarely explored in movies — anti-Semitism — is treated forthrightly and intelligently in Paramount's 1955-set "School Ties." Brendan Fraser is superb in the lead role of a scholarship student painfully hiding his Jewishness to assimilate in an elite Eastern prep school. The handsome Jaffe/Lansing production, while somewhat overly studied in feeling, gives a multifaceted, nuanced look at the roots of prejudice and self-denial.

Pic's somber and uncompromising but could find some of the same audience that responded to the more flamboyant "Dead Poets Society."

Director Robert Mandel, lenser Freddie Francis and production designer Jeannine Claudia Oppewall conjure up alluring images of what appears on the surface to be an idealized prep school, the kind of place that reeks of tradition.

Fraser initially sees St. Matthew's as a dream come true, but the filmmakers cannily play off the audience's sense of nostalgia by gradually revealing the ugly underside of the school — the automatic anti-Semitic badinage the boys exchange as Fraser silently seethes and the even more viciously personal taunts and ostracism they inflict on him once his ethnic identity is unmasked.

Scripters Dick Wolf and Darryl Ponicsan explore the price Fraser pays for his attempt at assimilation in an era when ethnic pride was taboo. One boy scorns Harvard, Fraser's goal, as a place overrun by "Jews and Communists." Such remarks help capture the conformist ethos of '50s America.

Following the well-meaning but misguided advice of his father (Ed Lauter) to "fit in" among his gentile schoolmates, Fraser quickly becomes a big man on campus. Arriving as a senior, he has a maturity and reserve conspicuously lacking in the callow scions of privilege.

The filmmakers' strategy resembles the slyly satirical way the Sidney Poitier character was treated in "Guess Who's Coming to Dinner." Fraser is such a paragon — handsome, athletic, brainy, quick to defend himself with his fists, with a wry wit and buckets of charm — that anyone who could find anything to dislike in him could only be a bigot.

He's fully alive and aware, with a growing sense of irony, unlike the other boys, who struggle grimly under the burden of their families' often-unreasonable expectations. In one chilling episode, Andrew Lowery has a nervous breakdown when he realizes he won't make it into Princeton.

But Fraser's principal antagonist (Matt Damon) has it worse: He's doomed to a life of mediocrity and he knows it. Damon is a standout, the kind of believable villain who makes a film transcend melodrama by remaining human and understandable despite deep character flaws.

The cancerous growth of anti-Semitic reaction against Fraser, engendered by his rivalry with Damon for sweet but vapid shiksa Amy Locane, leads to a bitter split in the school, climaxing in a confrontation over the school's insidious "honor code," which compels the boys to inform on each other.

Though it stirs powerful feelings of anger and empathy, the film doesn't touch the heart as fully as it might, particularly in Fraser's relationship with Locane; her rejection of him might be truly heart-rending if the viewer weren't so aware he'll go on to better things.

Rather than neatly tying up the dramatic threads with a simple triumph-over-adversity ending, the filmmakers send the audience out thinking about the gray areas of life and sharing Fraser's bittersweet view of the society in which he finds his ambivalent place.

Francis' crisp, classical lensing gives the film a suitably '50s elegance, meshing beautifully with Mandel's subdued visual style, Ann Roth's tweedy costumes and the taut editing by Jerry Greenberg and Jacqueline Cambas. Maurice Jarre's score is appropriately melancholy and low-key. — *Joseph McBride*

WIND

A TriStar release of a Mata Yamamoto production, a co-production of Filmlink Intl. from American Zoetrope. Produced by Yamamoto, Tom Luddy. Executive producers, Francis Ford Coppola, Fred Fuchs. Directed by Carroll Ballard. Screenplay, Rudy Wurlitzer, Mac Gudgeon; story, Jeff Benjamin, Roger Vaughan, Kimball Livingston. Camera (Technicolor), John Toll; editor, Michael Chandler; music, Basil Poledouris; production design, Laurence Eastwood; art direction, Nick Bonham (Australia), Paul W. Gorfine (Newport), Roger S. Crandall (Utah); set decoration, Richard Hobbs (Australia), Bobbie Frankel (Newport), Brian Lives (Utah); costume design, Marit Allen; sound (Dolby), Drew Kunin; sound design, Alan Splet; associate producer, Betsy Pollack; assistant director, L. Dean Jones; 2nd unit camera, Gary Capo; casting, Linda Phillips Palo. Reviewed at Sheridan Opera House, Telluride, Colo., Sept. 3, 1992. MPAA Rating: PG-13. Running time: **125 MIN.**
Will Parker . . . . . . Matthew Modine
Kate Bass . . . . Jennifer Grey
Joe Heiser . . . . . . Stellan Skarsgard
Abigail Weld . . . . . . Rebecca Miller
Charley . . . . Ned Vaughn
Morgan Weld . . . . . Cliff Robertson
Jack Neville . . . . . . Jack Thompson

The elements prove far more stimulating than the people in "Wind," a sail-racing saga that could have used a great deal more dramatic rigging. Despite the sometimes striking images of expert crews guiding their beautiful boats through challenging waters, predictable story trajectory and bland human element will keep this physically ambitious picture in a b.o. stall.

In his two previous narrative pics ("The Black Stallion," "Never Cry Wolf"), maverick director Carroll Ballard had subjects that suited his tendency to make Mother Nature the main character. His talent for expressing and physicalizing the raw beauty of the planet and the impact of weather stands him in good stead for the extensive shipboard sequences that vividly display the rigors and discipline involved in mastering air and water currents.

Unfortunately, the crew members are stick figures of no emotional or psychological interest. It's disappointing for a director capable of expressing the metaphysical to concern himself with a text that says nothing more than, "To win is all."

Three-act script is credited to the distinctive writer Rudy Wurlitzer and Aussie scribe Mac Gudgeon, with three others receiving story credit. But several other scenarists reportedly had a hand in this unimaginatively fictional telling of the U.S. losing, for the first time, then winning back the America's Cup.

Uncompelling protagonists are Matthew Modine, a young sailor with a knack for choking when things get tough, and Jennifer Grey, his spunky g.f., who is seemingly a sailing genius but is kept off the crew due to sexism.

Set in tony Newport, R.I., first 40 minutes build to an apparent blunder by Modine causing millionaire skipper Cliff Robertson to allow sailing's Holy Grail to pass over to the upstart Aussies.

Things become rather more quirky and interesting during a spare central section. Having lost the race and his lady, Modine turns up six months later at Deadman's Flat, Nev., where Grey and new b.f./engineering whiz Stellan Skarsgard are designing aircraft.

Modine convinces them to develop a new yacht to compete in the next America's Cup race, more than three years hence and, with the help of Robertson's spoiled but rebellious daughter Rebecca Miller, they do so.

The appealingly odd, zig-zag manner in which this section proceeds, and Skarsgard's offbeat but undeveloped character, are the only imaginable traces of Wurlitzer's contribution.

Final 40 minutes go Down Under and downhill, with a "Rocky" underdog mood taking hold as the new challenger craft Geronimo goes head-to-head with the Aussie favorite piloted by Jack Thompson.

Given the by-the-numbers plotting and low-voltage perfs, one must be content with admiring the versatility and daring of John Toll's camerawork and the difficulty of maintaining continuity during the arduous water shooting. Physically, pic is splendid, though a widescreen format might have boosted impact.

Basil Poledouris' conventional score grows somewhat monotonous, where a more far-out, propulsive, Philip Glass-like soundtrack would have helped a lot.
— *Todd McCarthy*

HELLRAISER III:
HELL ON EARTH

A Dimension Pictures (division of Miramax Films) release of a Clive Barker presentation of a Fifth Avenue Entertainment/Lawrence Mortorff production. Produced by Mortorff. Executive producer, Barker. Directed by Anthony Hickox. Screenplay, Peter Atkins, from story by Atkins, Tony Randel, based on characters created by Barker. Camera (Foto-Kem color), Gerry Lively; supervising editor, Christopher Cibelli; editor, James D.R. Hickox; music, Randy Miller; additional music, Christopher Young; production design, Steve Hardie; costume design, Leonard Pollack; assistant director, Paul Martin; special effects coordinator-2nd unit director, Bob Keen; mechanical special effects coordinator, Ray Bivins; stunt coordinator, Bob Stephens; sound (Ultra-Stereo), Kim Ornitz; co-producer, Christopher Figg; associate producer, Olive McQueen; casting, Geno Havens (L.A.), Leonard Finger (N.Y.), Clayton D. Hill (N. Carolina). Reviewed at Murray Hill theater, N.Y., Sept. 11, 1992. MPAA Rating: R. Running time: **92 MIN.**
Joey Summerskill . . . . Terry Farrell
Pinhead/Elliott Spencer. Doug Bradley
Terri . . . . Paula Marshall
J.P. Monroe . . . . . . Kevin Bernhardt
Doc/Camerahead . . . . Ken Carpenter
Joey's father . . . . . . Peter Boynton
Sandy . . . . Aimee Leigh
Bum . . . . Lawrence Mortorff

"Hellraiser III" is a highly commercial horror entry inaugurating Miramax's Dimension label. Well-produced effort is an effective combination of imaginative special effects with the strangeness of author Clive Barker's conception.

Along with TriStar's upcoming Barker release "Candyman" this film helps restore an outré, fantastic flavor to the recently too-conventional horror genre.

Peter Atkins' script provides

enough background and exposition to initiate newcomers to the parallel world of the previous two "Hellraisers" (New World). All three films are set in New York, with the originals filmed in London while the latest was shot in North Carolina.

Terry Farrell toplines as an attractive TV newswoman summoned by the ghost of British World War I Capt. Elliott Spencer, who's contacted her via her recurring nightmares about her dad who was killed in Vietnam combat before she was born.

Spencer's experiments with the supernatural had unleashed evil on the world in the race of the Cenobites, led by Pinhead, whose adventures were limned in the prior pics. Pinhead is back, with a strange little box that's key to sending him back to Hell.

An okay subplot matches Pinhead's grisly rending of the flesh horrors with the more prosaic human variety, represented by evil young nightclub owner Kevin Bernhardt. Bernhardt buys a strange sculpture which includes the magical cube and is soon lured by Pinhead into becoming his henchman.

Bernhardt's retro-punk g.f. Paula Marshall becomes Farrell's first link to unraveling this strange story. With creepy music, morbid visuals and an overwhelming sense of dread film builds gradually to an extended setpiece of Farrell battling Pinhead.

Up until the final reels, helmer Anthony Hickox keeps tight control. Momentum dissipates with redundant violence and damsel-in-distress episodes that follow, but fadeout scene is elegant.

Farrell is a strong heroine binding the film together, and British thesp Doug Bradley is a commanding presence as Pinhead, while also doubling sans makeup as the good guy captain. Marshall has her moments as a sympathetic victim while Bernhardt is quite bland.

Film's extremely grotesque gore effects and negative tone will turn off mainstream viewers but hold a hypnotic appeal for hardcore horror afficianados.

— *Lawrence Cohn*

TELLURIDE FEST

THE CRYING GAME
(BRITISH)

A Miramax (U.S.)-Mayfair Entertainment (U.K.) release of a Palace & Channel Four Films presentation in association with Eurotrustees & Nippon Film Development & Finance Inc. (NDF) with participation of British Screen of a Palace/Stephen Woolley production. Produced by Woolley. Executive producer, Nik Powell. Co-producer, Elizabeth Karlsen. Directed, written by Neil Jordan. Camera (Metrocolor, Panavision widescreen), Ian Wilson; editor, Kant Pan; music, Anne Dudley; production design, Jim Clay; art direction, Chris Seagers; set decoration, Martin Childs; costume design, Sandy Powell; sound (Dolby), Colin Nicolson; associate producer, Paul Cowan; assistant director, Redmond Morris; casting, Susie Figgis. Reviewed at Telluride Film Festival, Sept. 7, 1992. (Also in Venice, Toronto, N.Y. film fests). Running time: **113 MIN.**

Fergus	Stephen Rea
Jude	Miranda Richardson
Jody	Forest Whitaker
Col	Jim Broadbent
Dave	Ralph Brown
Maguire	Adrian Dunbar
Dil	Jaye Davidson

An astonishingly good and daring film that richly develops several intertwined thematic lines, "The Crying Game" takes giant risks that are stunningly rewarded. Irish director Neil Jordan's seventh film is also his best, a work that may confound and put off the narrowminded but will mesmerize discriminating viewers.

This Miramax pickup presents one of the toughest marketing challenges in recent memory. Title is unenticing, cast has no certified stars and Irish Republican Army backdrop reps a turnoff for many. But more important, plot contains two major — and several minor — convulsive surprises that, if revealed, would considerably spoil a first-time viewing experience, making it nearly impossible to describe the film in advance in meaningful detail. Distrib's main hope lies in amassing a collection of rave reviews the likes of which will make attendance mandatory for specialized audiences.

The IRA's kidnapping in Northern Ireland of British soldier Forest Whitaker serves as the jumping off point for a fearlessly penetrating examination of politics, race, sexuality and human nature. The leading characters' normal affiliations, assumptions, tendencies and behavior are called into question as they face public and intimate events that leave them no room to hide and force them to act decisively under agonizing circumstances.

Jordan has placed several wild bumps in the road that the viewer must survive without falling off the dramatic wagon, but his writing is so skillful, and the relationships he establishes are so compelling, that one happily follows his lead into thoroughly unexpected territory.

First 40-minute act concerns Whitaker's country house incarceration by a small band of terrorists led by Maguire (Adrian Dunbar) and the sexy Jude (Miranda Richardson). Informing him that he will be killed within three days if the Brits don't release one of their senior officers, an unlikely proposition, they leave him mostly under the guard of Fergus (Jordan stalwart Stephen Rea), a sensitive recruit who develops an intense rapport with the good-natured, emotionally open Jody.

One somewhat expects Fergus' sympathy to be based, at least in part, on the fact that Jody is black and therefore a member of a similarly oppressed minority. But while race is mentioned (Jody observes that Northern Ireland is "the one place in the world where they'll call you nigger to your face"), they establish a more meaningful personal accord. If he dies, Jody says, Fergus is to look up his great love, Dil, in London.

Although the angst-ridden Fergus is ordered to execute Jody, chaos ensuing from an army raid pushes events in a different direction, and Fergus escapes to make his way to London, where he finds Dil (Jaye Davidson) working in a beauty salon. The very foxy and cool lady seems utterly in control except for the abuse she strangely takes from Dave (Ralph Brown), a tough guy who frequents the bar where Dil sometimes performs.

Refraining from telling Dil what happened with Jody, Fergus finds himself irresistably drawn to this fascinating creature with myriad contradictory traits. Hot and cold, petulant and seductive, needy and fiercely independent, Dil entices Fergus into a relationship that will definitely test just how far he's willing to go for love.

But the long arm of his radical cohorts reaches out to ensnare Fergus once again, forcing him to honor allegiances that he had hoped were put to rest. Climax provides the requisite action and suspense, but is informed with emotional and moral dimensions that resonate in the real world long after the deft coda and hilarious Lyle Lovett cover of "Stand By Your Man" over the end credits. Only a writer-director of tremendous confidence and skill could guide the viewer past the "Vertigo"-like transformation occurring about midway through the story, and Jordan shows he has as much talent as he has nerve. Writing for very different types of characters, this former novelist reveals the keenest of ears for dialogue and a knack for quickly developing deep relationships from scratch. Structure is as brilliant as it is unanticipated.

With such intimate subject matter, Jordan has made another surprising decision by shooting in widescreen, but he and cinematographer Ian Wilson create superb images and don't let any suspense leak out from the sides of the frame. Kant Pan's editing is taut, and the soundtrack outstandingly meshes numerous pop tunes (including an excellent Boy George-Pet Shop Boys cover of the 1960s title track) with Anne Dudley's moving, Delerue-ish original score.

Acting is uniformly superior. Long after he disappears from the scene, the force of Whitaker's big-hearted, hugely emotional performance is still being felt. He's simply terrific, and the Yank thesp has seemingly mastered a very specific British working-class accent.

As the vulnerable IRA henchman who wants to disappear into invisibility, Rea is intriguingly handsome-homely, decisive-passive, gentle-violent. In a very difficult part, actor remains just active and energetic enough to maintain audience interest, and walks a precise line between being accepting and closed-off.

Newcomer Davidson is almost impossibly right as the beautiful, mysterious Dil, while Richardson is equal parts fire and ice as the most resilient IRA member.

Just as "The Crying Game" tested the artistic limits of its key participants, so will it gauge the willingness of intelligent audiences to support a film that may not sound immediately appetizing, but is in fact satisfying and even thrilling in all the important ways. — *Todd McCarthy*

EL MARIACHI

A Columbia release of a Los Hooligans production. Produced, written by Robert Rodriguez, Carlos Gallardo. Di-

rected by Rodriguez. Story, camera (Technicolor), editing, sound (Dolby), Rodriguez; associate producers, Elizabeth Avellan, Carmen M. De Gallardo. Reviewed at Telluride Film Festival, Sept. 4, 1992. Running time: **82 MIN.**
El Mariachi . . . . Carlos Gallardo
Domino . . . . Consuelo Gomez
Azul . . . . Reinol Martinez
Moco . . . . Peter Marquardt
(Spanish language; English subtitles)

Almost certainly, at $7,000, the cheapest film ever released by a major Hollywood studio, Columbia's pickup "El Mariachi" is a fresh, resourceful first feature by 24-year-old Austin filmmaker Robert Rodriguez. Spanish lingo crime meller has a verve and cheekiness that will put it over with fest and sophisticated audiences that like to latch onto hot new talent, while distrib could also do well in the domestic Hispanic market.

Mainstream acceptance, however, will have to wait at least until the $6 million remake Rodriguez will reportedly do as part of his two-year deal at Col.

Lensed in two weeks in the Mexican border town of Acuna, the pic can edify and inspire aspiring filmmakers who complain about lack of coin. Even though he shot with a hand-held 16m camera and non-synch sound, Rodriguez has put a perfectly serviceable picture up on the screen (Col paid for the 35m blowup and Dolby sound add-on).

But Rodriguez has pulled off a good deal more than that, since he has created a solid genre piece with a sense of style that is partly original, partly dictated by economic necessity and partly a smart wedding of such influences as Sergio Leone, George Miller and south-of-the-border noir.

Simple tale is that of a lone stranger in town who stirs up trouble, although in this case the newcomer is a young, hapless mariachi singer looking for a gig. Unfortunately for him, also in town is a revenge-crazed drug dealer named Azul at war with his ex-partner Moco. Like El Mariachi, Azul wears black and carries a guitar case, although one loaded with heavy weaponry rather than a stringed instrument.

Cat-and-mouse plotting sees the earnest El Mariachi chased around town by Moco's henchmen, who themselves are being systematically mowed down by Azul. All El Mariachi wants is a job, which leads him to the cantina of the foxy Domino, a beauty who takes a shine to the kid but also happens to be a favorite of

murderous Moco.

Fortunately, Rodriguez doesn't take the well-worn plot elements too seriously, and instead has a high old time with his moments of mistaken identity, violent confrontations and numerous stylistic jokes, including speeded-up action and send-ups of genre conventions. Given pic's relative levity, amount of carnage at the climax comes as something of a surprise, and fade-out feels uncomfortably close to a set-up for a sequel.

For all the good will and likability Rodriguez generates by accomplishing so much on so little, there remains something a tad calculated about the film, a feeling that it was made almost entirely with the head, not with the heart. Pic feels like a technical exercise well executed, but one with little emotional conviction or p.o.v. behind it. Coupled with the thin plotting, this results in a work of marginal resonance.

Carlos Gallardo, who also cowrote and co-produced, makes for an affable Mariachi, if one a little green around the gills. Consuelo Martinez is suitably foxy as the barkeep caught in the middle, and Peter Marquardt is effective enough as a standard-issue drug baron, icy and gringoish. Tops in the cast is Reinol Martinez, whose football player build, relentlessness and amusing impassivity make Azul a memorable heavy.

Except for the repetitious chase scenes, Rodriguez has planned out his film exceedingly well visually, keeping the camera excitingly mobile and cutting expertly on action and within the frame. Even before the film's premiere here, Rodriguez was clearly a young director to watch on the basis of his unique career move. What's onscreen certainly displays enough talent to justify the interest.

— *Todd McCarthy*

QIU JU DA GUANSI
(THE STORY OF QIU JU)
(CHINESE-HONG KONG)

A Sil-Metropole Organization (Hong Kong)/Beijing Film Academy-Youth Film Studio (China) co-production. Executive producer, Ma Fung Kwok. Directed by Zhang Yimou. Screenplay,

Liu Heng, based on Chen Yuanbin's novel. Camera (color) Chi Xiaoning, Yu Xiaoqun; editor, Du Yuan; art direction, Cao Jiuping; music, Zhao Jiping. Reviewed at Venice Film Festival (competing), Sept. 7, 1992. Running time: **100 MIN.**
Qiu Ju . . . . Gong Li
Village head . . . . Lei Laosheng
Husband . . . . Liu Peiqi
Meizi . . . . Yang Liuchun
  Also with: Zhu Qanqing, Cui Luowen, Yang Huiqin, Wang Jianfa, Lin Zi.

Zhang Yimou, the Chinese director most accessible to the West thanks to his beautifully made "Ju Dou" and "Raise the Red Lantern," presents another jewel in a series linked by iron-willed heroines. Adapted from a novel set in rural China, "The Story of Qiu Ju" marks Zhang's first contempo story, and as such lacks the exotic visual pageantry that was a big attraction in his prior pics. Yet this simple, repetitive tale has a mesmerizing quality able to hook audiences from beginning to end, and it should have similar box office results.

Zhang leading lady Gong Li foregoes glamor to play a round, pregnant peasant, Qiu Ju. Her young husband (Liu Peiqi) is laid up after a fight with the village head (Lei Laosheng) over an insult regarding virility and sexism. The chief has four daughters, and Chinese law won't let him try again for a male heir. When the young husband reminds him of this in the heat of an argument, he receives a debilitating kick in the groin.

Qiu Ju makes up her mind that the village chief must apologize for the injury to her husband; this the old man, who's as stubborn as she, refuses to do. Qiu Ju thus embarks on a series of pilgrimages to get justice done. Local mediators and then the city court judges don't understand that it's a question of principles. They just rule the village chief must pay damages, which Qiu Ju couldn't care less about.

Her dogged determination to stand up for her rights continues even after it jeopardizes her marriage. In a final twist, Qiu Ju tastes a very bitter victory. Viewers are left to draw the line between a thirst for justice and obsession.

Portrayed with enormous humanity by Gong Li, Qiu Ju embodies the simple, honest spirit of Chinese country folk, adding a heroic willfulness all her own. Her trips to the city, toddling with her big belly beside her young sister-in-law, are imbued

with humorous grandeur. The two women are the center of Zhang's vast canvas of Chinese life. Many of the strikingly authentic crowd shots were snatched using a hidden camera.

Equally striking is the village folks' solidarity with each other. The quarrel between Qiu Ju and Lei Laosheng takes place alongside friendly offers of tea and food. For the Chinese, the film can be seen as criticizing the authorities' distance from the people's lives and concerns. At the same time, it publicizes a new Chinese law that allows citizens to appeal official decisions.

High-pitched songs punctuate the fable-like tale with authentic local music. Cinematography shifts from panoramas of majestic mountains and bustling cityscapes to intimate family scenes. Even without the stunning visuals of Zhang's earlier pics, "Qiu Ju" has much to look at.

— *Deborah Young*

ORLANDO
(BRITISH-RUSSIAN-FRENCH-DUTCH)

An Adventure Pictures (London)/Lenfilm (St. Petersburg)/Mikado Film (Rome)/Rio Film (Paris)/Sigma (Amsterdam) co-production, with the participation of British Screen. (Intl. sales: The Sales Co., London.) Produced by Christopher Sheppard. Directed, written by Sally Potter, from Virginia Woolf's book. Camera (Eastmancolor), Alexei Rodionov; editor, Herve Schneid; music, Bob Last; production design, Ben van Os, Jan Roelfs; costumes, Sandy Powell; sound, Jean-Louis Ducarme; production executives, Anna Vronskaya, Linda Bruce; line producer, Laurie Borg; assistant directors, Michael Zimbrich, Chris Newman. Reviewed at Venice Film Festival (competing), Sept. 7, 1992. Running time: **93 MIN.**
Orlando . . . . Tilda Swinton
Shelmerdine . . . . Billy Zane
The Khan . . . . Lothaire Bluteau
Archduke Harry . . . . . . John Wood
Sasha . . . . . . Charlotte Valandrey
Nick/publisher . . Heathcote Williams
Queen Elizabeth I . . . . Quentin Crisp
Mr. Pope . . . . Peter Eyre
William of Orange . . . Thom Hoffman
Falsetto/Angel . . . Jimmy Somerville
King James I . . . . . . Dudley Sutton

Overcoming European co-production pitfalls, "Orlando" provides exciting, wonderfully witty entertainment for discriminating auds. Glorious settings and costumes — and Tilda Swinton's sock performance in the title role — ensure that this inventive adaptation of Virginia Woolf's 1928 novel will be an international art house fave.

Woolf's novel is structured around the intriguing notion of a character who lived for 400 years, changing sex in the course of time. Via Orlando, a youth who, in 1600, becomes the favorite of the aging Queen Elizabeth I and lives to tell the tale well into the 20th century, Woolf was able to explore with great wit the role of women in British society over the ages.

Though she's really too feminine to pass for a man in pic's first half, Tilda Swinton is extraordinary as the eponymous Orlando, who frequently, in witty asides to the camera, takes the audience into his/her confidence.

Much of the credit for the success of this difficult material must go to writer-director Sally Powell, who battled for several years to get the project off the ground (credits acknowledge support she received from the late Michael Powell). Logistically, pic looks rich and expensive, with St. Petersburg locations standing in for medieval London in winter.

Pic also was shot in Uzbekistan, Middle East country where Orlando, anguished after being jilted by a beautiful Russian woman, spends 10 years as British ambassador at the court of the Khan (Lothaire Bluteau). The ageless hero then becomes a woman which, as Swinton says to the camera, makes "no difference at all — just a different sex." As a woman, however, Orlando is no longer entitled to her title and estates under English law. Nor is she taken seriously by the literary elite.

She discovers sex in 1850 in the arms of an American adventurer (Billy Zane) and as a result becomes pregnant. At the end of the film, set in present-day London, Potter adds some contempo irony with a scene in which a disdainful male publisher dismisses her autobiographical manuscript.

More than a feminist tract, pic is a sumptuous production with first-class production design by Ben van Os and Jan Roelfs, and gorgeous costumes by Sandy Powell. Peter Greenaway (especially "The Draughtman's Contract") is evoked at times, as is Derek Jarman, thanks to the casting of Swinton, but Potter has created a memorable film all her own.

The cast is uniformly strong, with Zane very effective as the manly Yank and Quentin Crisp looking exactly right as the aging Queen Elizabeth. Scenes of London in the grip of freezing winter are most beautiful.

Music is well used, with some clever mock-medieval songs written by Potter herself. Herve Schneid's editing has brought the film in at a sharp 93 minutes.

Woolf's distinctive literary style has proved daunting for filmmakers over the years, but this is by far the best screen adaptation of her work, and a credit to all concerned.

— David Stratton

L.627
(FRENCH)

An AMLF release of a Little Bear-Films Alaine Sarde production. (Intl. sales: WMF, Paris.) Produced by Sarde, Frédéric Bourboulon. Directed by Bertrand Tavernier. Screenplay, Tavernier, Michel Alexandre. Camera (color), Alain Choquart; editor, Ariane Boeglin; music, Philippe Sarde; production design, Guy-Claude François; sound, Michel Desrois, Gérard Lamps. Reviewed at Venice Film Festival (competing), Sept. 4, 1992. Running time: **145 MIN.**
Lucien Marguet (Lulu) . Didier Bezace
Dodo . . . . Jean-Paul Comart
Marie . . . . Charlotte Kady
Manu . . . . Jean-Roger Milo
Vincent . . . . Nils Tavernier
Antoine (Looping) . Philippe Torreton
Cécile . . . . Lara Guirao
Katy . . . . Cécile Garcia-Fogel
Adoré . . . . Claude Brosset

In his remarkable new film, Bertrand Tavernier takes an impassioned look inside the day-to-day activities of a small, ill-equipped branch of the Paris Drug Squad. With extraordinary documentary realism, the director has produced one of his best and most challenging films. International exposure seems assured.

Tavernier has said his interest in the police struggle against drug dealers stems from his son Nils' brief involvement in drugs. With the script collaboration of a 15-year veteran of the Paris police, Michel Alexandre, Tavernier takes a probing look at drug unit operations while avoiding cop film clichés.

His protagonist is Lulu (Didier Bezace), a dedicated cop posted to a drug squad run by Dodo (Jean-Paul Comart), a racist with a sick sense of humor, and the attractive Marie (Charlotte Kady), who copes amazingly well with her difficult job.

Without forcing the point, Tavernier reveals the constraints under which narcotics police operate. They are underequipped (old typewriters, too few vehicles), underpaid, overworked. Most of them are undereducated, racist, unnecessarily violent — and they make a lot of mistakes.

Yet there's a camaraderie here, and many, like Lulu, are determined against the odds to get drug dealers off the streets. Numerous scenes of stakeouts, raids and interrogations reveal both the routine and the awesome size of the problem. Most of the dealers arrested are blacks, or Arabs, but the film clearly harbors no racist attitude.

Because of the director's avoidance of generic shootouts and car chases and his deliberate depiction of this seedy Paris underworld (no sign of tourist spots here), he risks alienating audiences. But thanks to a grim sense of humor and astonishingly convincing detail, the film succeeds triumphantly.

Aside from his work, Lulu is involved with two women, his ex-wife (Cécile Garcia-Fogel) and a young prostitute/drug addict (Lara Guirao). He has a touching, though platonic, relationship with the the young woman (who is HIV positive), and their bond adds a further dimension to an already richly detailed film.

Spectacularly well shot by Alain Choquart on back streets, metro platforms and in rundown apartments, pic makes an impassioned plea for public support for police which, though riddled with incompetence and tainted by petty corruption, still is society's only defense against the drug scourge. The only real commercial drawback is the film's length, but precision pacing keeps it from seeming excessive. Philippe Sarde provides a fine, appropriate score.

Standouts in a generally fine cast are Bezace as Lulu, Kady as the femme cop and Nils Tavernier, to whom the film is dedicated, as a member of the squad. "L.627," titled after a French drug law, confirms Tavernier as one of Europe's most versatile and provocative filmmakers.

— David Stratton

OLIVIER OLIVIER
(FRENCH)

An Oliane Prods.-Films A-2 production. (Intl. sales: WMF, Paris.) Produced by Marie-Laure Reyre. Co-producer, Christian Ferry. Directed by Agnieszka Holland. Screenplay, Holland, Yves Lapointe, Régis Debray. Camera (Eastmancolor), Bernard Zitzermann; editor, Isabelle Lorente; music, Zbigniew Preisner; production design, Helene Bourgy; sound, Pierre Befve; assistant director, Kalinka Weiler. Reviewed at Venice Film Festival (competing), Sept. 4, 1992. (Also in Telluride, New York film fests.) Running time: **109 MIN.**
Serge . . . . Françoise Cluzet
Elisabeth . . . . Brigitte Roüan
Druot . . . . . Jean-Françoise Stevenin
Olivier . . . . Gregoire Colin
Nadine . . . . Marina Golovine
Marcel . . . . Frederic Quiring
Nadine (child) . . . . . . Faye Gatteau
Olivier (child) . . . Emmanuel Morozof

Before she made "Europa Europa," Polish exile Agnieszka Holland read a French newspaper story that inspired "Olivier Olivier," a seemingly simple but intriguing and ultimately powerful film about a provincial family. Very good international art house prospects loom for this one.

Early scenes establish the family of country veterinarian father (François Cluzet), mother (Brigitte Roüan) and their two children, Nadine and her younger, 9-year-old brother, Olivier. The mother dotes on her son, sometimes making his sister jealous; yet, the siblings are close.

One summer day, Olivier sets off on his bicycle to visit his sick grandmother and never returns. Police, led by Druot (Jean-François Stevenin), are baffled; the parents are distraught. Months go by, and eventually the marriage breaks up and the husband leaves to work in North Africa.

Six years later in Paris, Druot encounters a 15-year-old male prostie who fits the description of the missing Olivier. Under questioning, the youth seems to confirm his identity. He is reunited with his mother and sister, and soon his father returns from abroad. The family is together again, yet Nadine remains unconvinced that this youth really is her brother, especially when a sexual relationship develops between them. A final revelation adds a powerful string to the tale.

Working on a more restricted canvas than in her recent, large-scale films, though still dealing with real-life stories, Holland does some of her best work to date here. The film is not as simple as it seems, and is filled with ambiguities and insight into family relationships.

Thesping is first-rate down the line, with Roüan exceptional as the distraught mother who accepts a young stranger as her long-lost son. Pic's technically tops in every department.

— David Stratton

SOFIE
(DANISH-NORWEGIAN-SWEDISH)

A Pathe-Nordisk Film TV-Distribution presentation of a Danish-Norwegian-Swedish co-production between Nordisk Film & TV, Norsk Film, Svensk Filmindustri. Produced by Lars Kolvig. Directed by Liv Ullmann. Screenplay, Ullmann, Peter Poulsen based on Henri Nathansen's novel. Camera (color), Jorgen Persson; editor, Grete Moldrup; art direction, Peter Hoimark; costume design, Jette Termann; sound, Michael Dela; makeup, Cecilia Drott-Norlen. Reviewed at Montreal World Film Festival (competing), Aug. 30, 1992. Running time: **146 MIN.**
Sofie . . . . Karen-Lise Mynster
Sofie's father . . . . Erland Josephson
Sofie's mother . . . . Ghita Norby
Hans Hojby . . . . Jesper Christensen
Jonas . . . . Torben Zeller
Brother-in-law . . . . . Stig Hoffmeyer

Norwegian actress Liv Ullmann has made a Bergmanesque directorial debut with "Sofie," a stunningly beautiful, but overly long 19th century woman's tale which divided critics at its world preem at the Montreal festival.

A true art film in the classic sense, pic targets fans of Ingmar Bergman (who featured Ullmann in numerous of his films from 1966 to '78). His influence is strongly felt in style, pacing and detailed character development.

Pic's first hour is much like watching a female take on "Fanny and Alexander" as Ullmann meticulously intros a superb cast of characters. Story of Sofie's fun-free Jewish life begins in 1886 when the young woman is almost beyond marrying age at 29.

Sofie's tightly knit, traditional family stifle her budding love affair with a gentile painter Hans by effectively forcing her to marry a respectable Jewish suitor, Jonas, against her own better judgment.

The passionless marriage produces a son who eventually becomes Sofie's raison d'être and leads to a brief and tragic affair with her brother-in-law. Latter half of pic (which bogs down the pace) delves into Jewish traditions. She learns to embrace the very structure that ruined her one love.

Pic's last predictable 20 minutes drag as family members die one by one, and Sofie's sad life has come full circle.

Ullmann deserves kudos for selecting a superb cast led by Karen-lise Mynster, whose incredible range makes Sofie a rich, passionate lead. Ghita Norby ("Best Intentions") is witty and playful as Sofie's alternatingly sympathetic and dogmatic mother. Norby is perfectly paired with thesp Erland Josephson (as Sofie's father) whose devotion to wife and family is an on-screen inspiration. Jesper Christensen plays the artist to perfection, and Torben Zeller is ideal as the pathetic husband.

Ullmann and Peter Poulsen's screen adaptation resembles script's line: "My life is like a closed book where no one has ever opened the pages, only fumbled with them." Helmer fumbles in pic's latter scenes.

Jorgen Persson's divine camerawork is in league with Bergman's preferred cinematographer Sven Nykvist. Period costumes are gorgeous. Editing is weak in the last few reels.

At a press conference, Ullmann said the pic would not be cut, but a final edit would increase pic's art house potential.
— *Suzan Ayscough*

SINGLES

A Warner Bros. release of an Atkinson/Knickerbocker Films production. Produced by Cameron Crowe, Richard Hashimoto. Executive producer, Art Linson. Co-producer-2nd unit director-editor, Richard Chew. Directed, written by Crowe. Camera (Technicolor), Ueli Steiger; music, Paul Westerberg; production design, Stephen Lineweaver; art direction, Mark Haack; set design, Cosmas Demetriou; set decoration, Clay Griffith; costume design, Jane Ruhm; sound (Dolby), Art Rochester; associate producer, Kelly Curtis; assistant director, Jerry Ziesmer; 2nd unit camera, Billy O'Drobinak; casting, Marion Dougherty. Reviewed at Montreal World Film Festival, Sept. 6, 1992. MPAA rating: PG-13. Running time: **99 MIN.**
Janet Livermore . . . . Bridget Fonda
Steve Dunne . . . . . Campbell Scott
Linda Powell . . . . . Kyra Sedgwick
Debbie Hunt . . . . . . Sheila Kelley
David Bailey . . . . Jim True
Cliff Poncier . . . . Matt Dillon
Dr. Jamison . . . . Bill Pullman
Andy . . . . James Le Gros
Ruth . . . . Devon Raymond
Luiz . . . . Camilo Gallardo
Pam . . . . Ally Walker
Mime . . . . Eric Stoltz
Doug Hughley . . . . . Jeremy Piven
Mayor Weber . . . . . . Tom Skerritt
Boston doctor . . . . . . Bill Smillie

Warner Bros. appears to have a hit on its hands with the dynamite romantic comedy "Singles," which garnered great buzz after its Montreal fest world preem. Superbly scripted, cast and scored, pic is a natural for the partner-hunting twentysomething crowd and should easily cross over to thirtysomething singles or couples primed to laugh at the dating syndrome.

This younger version of "The Big Chill," with the Replacements frontman Paul Westerberg's hot sub-pop song tracks a great marketing tie-in, is a straightforward story about young adults who live separate and intertwined lives in a Seattle apartment building. They often share their secrets directly with the audience and their bodies with each other.

After an opening shot cruising through Seattle streets, writer-director-producer Cameron Crowe turns the camera on Linda (superbly played by Kyra Sedgwick) who faces the crowd with a "here's my life in a nutshell" vignette.

Surprisingly, Crowe's "interview" format works, and Linda becomes the link between the audience and parallel comedies. Her first romantic catastrophe sets the stage for the many hilarious horror stories — and feats of desperation — that follow.

Seduced by a Spanish university student who claims he has to leave the country in five days due to an expiring visa, Linda hops in the sack and dreams of marriage (so she'll always have a date) until she catches her cheating Casanova in a singles bar with another woman. Linda's been had and is determined not to be burned twice. She then begins a budding love story with honest, earnest, cool dude Steve (Campbell Scott).

Bridget Fonda turns in a stunning performance as dipsy Janet, in love with hopelessly bad guitar player Cliff (Matt Dillon, doing a great job as a brain-dead, self-centered, second-rate musician). Their story unfolds amidst various singles' crises, including Debbie Hunt's (Sheila Kelley) dating video search for a man. Any man.

There's no shortage of tender moments in this comedy, and former rock journalist Crowe cleverly transforms "real" problems into crackerjack material. However, scripter Crowe carefully sidesteps singles issues such as abortion, offering a too-convenient solution to one couple's accidental pregnancy, setting up crucial talks about crisis maintenance in relationships.

Richard Chew's editing is terrific. Tales are enhanced by a super soundtrack. Love songs are used to perfection and Westerberg's title track, "Dyslexic Heart," is a winner.
—*Suzan Ayscough*

LA ULTIMA SIEMBRA
(THE LAST HARVEST)
(ARGENTINE)

A Yacoraite Film & JEMPSA (Jorge Estrada Mora Prods.) production, in association with Television Espanola, Sociedad Estatal Quinto Centenario, Channel Four (London), the Sundance Institute, EUE & Portman Pictures (London). Produced by Julio Lencina, Ricardo Freixa. Directed, written by Miguel Pereira. Camera (color), Pablo Esteban Courtalon; editor, Miguel Perez; music, Ariel Petrocelli, Tukuta Gordillo-Isamara; production design, Mirta Spagarino; sound, Dante Amoroso. Reviewed at Montreal World Film Festival, Aug. 31, 1992. Running time: **91 MIN.**
Chauqui . . . . . . Patricio Contreras
Francisca . . . . Leonor Manso
Patricio . . . . Mario Pasik
Julian . . . . Alberto Benegas
Jose . . . . Gonzalo Morales
Don Carlos . . . . . . Antonio Paleari
Estela . . . . Ines Asfora

Miguel Pereira's "La Ultima Siembra" has been getting considerable exposure on the international fest circuit, and rightly so. North American commercial prospects are iffy, but the Argentine-produced pic might find an appreciative audience on the museum and film society circuit.

Drama is set on a cattle ranch in northwest Argentina, where an Indian from a distant province (Patricio Contreras) arrives in search of work. He left home after the accidental death of his son, for which he feels responsible, and he's immediately drawn to the illegitimate son of the ranch's housekeeper.

The boy's father (Alberto Benegas) is the ranch's chief gaucho who refuses to acknowledge the child as his. But he doesn't like the idea of the boy's being so friendly with the newcomer whom he immediately despises.

Tensions increase when the U.S.-educated son (Mario Pasik) of the ranch's aged owner returns armed with computer printouts and faxes. He turns Dad's ranch into a tobacco farm, and the employees who aren't fired are forced to drastically change their traditional ways of life. Nothing good comes of any of this.

Pic unfolds at a leisurely but engrossing pace. Chief interest is provided by the vivid clashes between tradition and progress, guilt and redemption. Acting is good across the board, with particularly fine work from Pasik as the ruthless entrepreneur and Benegas as the gaucho who pays dearly for his pride.

Ariel Petrocelli's music is evocative, and Pablo Esteban Courtalon's color lensing is first-rate. Pic partially financed by the Sundance Institute was showcased during a Latin American series at last January's Sundance Film Festival. — *Joe Leydon*

TORONTO FEST

MR. SATURDAY NIGHT

A Columbia release of a Castle Rock Entertainment in association with New Line Cinema presentation of a Face production. Produced, directed by Billy Crystal. Executive producers, Lowell Ganz, Babaloo Mandel. Co-producer, Peter Schindler. Screenplay, Crystal, Ganz, Mandel. Camera (Technicolor), Don Peterman; editor, Kent Beyda; music, Marc Shaiman; production design, Albert Brenner; art direction, Carol Winstead Wool; set design, Harold Fuhrman; set decoration, Kathe Klopp; costume design, Ruth Myers; sound (Dolby), Jeff Wexler; makeup-hair design, Peter Montagna, Bill Farley, Steve LaPorte; choreography, Lester Wilson; assistant director, Jim Chory; 2nd unit director, Schindler; 2nd unit camera, Gabor Kover; casting, Pam Dixon. Reviewed at AMC Century City 14, L.A., Sept. 8, 1992. (In Toronto Film Festival.) MPAA Rating: R. Running time: **119 MIN.**

Buddy Young Jr.	Billy Crystal
Stan Yankelman	David Paymer
Elaine	Julie Warner
Annie	Helen Hunt
Susan	Mary Mara
Phil Gussman	Jerry Orbach
Larry Meyerson	Ron Silver
Mom	Sage Allen
Abie (age 15)	Jason Marsden
Stan (age 18)	Michael Weiner
Gene	Jackie Gayle
Freddie	Carl Ballantine
Joey	Slappy White
Jerry Lewis	Himself

Bringing the fictional comedian he created eight years ago to the big screen, Billy Crystal — to use his favored baseball parlance — hits a double with "Mr. Saturday Night." By turns relentlessly jokey and shamelessly schmaltzy, the actor-writer's directorial debut charts a sometimes unpleasant funnyman's long career in choppy, two-dimensional fashion, but delivers enough laughs and heart-tugging to put this over as a solid, if not smashing, fall B.O. attraction.

Crystal's Buddy Young Jr. feels utterly like the genuine article, a Jewish New Yorker who's been an irrepressible entertainer since childhood, a master of insult humor weaned on late vaudeville, polished in the Catskills, spotlighted in Vegas and toplined on television who in his waning years trades barbs with other old timers at the Friars Club.

Clumsily structured screenplay by Crystal and the Lowell Ganz/Babaloo Mandel team resembles the latter's effort on "A League of Their Own" to an almost embarrassing degree. Both scripts feature the leading characters in old age looking back at the key moments of their lives with bittersweet nostalgia, and both feature a sibling rivalry tinged with resentment.

As a veteran who feels dead without an audience, Buddy says he's "got cancer of the career. It's inoperable." Flashbacks reveal that the stubborn comic was usually his own worst enemy, deliberately undercutting himself with his superiors and letting his emotions get the better of him, all of which prevent him from reaching the top levels of comedy superstardom.

Other than his career, the only thing of enduring importance to Buddy is his relationship with his brother Stan, a gentle, kind soul who is the ultimate second banana, a gofer-for-life who is self-sacrificing to a withering degree and always comes back for more, no matter how abusive Buddy might get.

The Buddy-Stan umbilical connection provides the emotional core of the picture, and David Paymer's standout performance as the weaker of the two puts the sentiment over more legitimately than it had any right to be, but scenes between the two go on and on making the same point ad infinitum. We get it, already.

Such prolonged concentration on the two men seriously subtracts from screen time that can be devoted to anyone else. Particularly affected are Julie Warner, whose Elaine virtually disappears after Buddy wins her in a cornball courtship scene, and Mary Mara, whose disaffected daughter pops in occasionally to spur Buddy's guilt. Negligibility of both characters, and total absence of Buddy's second child from the story, makes the nature of his family life a mystery and constitutes a major script oversight.

But Crystal has boundless affection for the old jokemaster and the world he came from, and he is perhaps second only to Robin Williams in spitting out the one-liners. No matter how serious the occasion (most notably his mother's funeral), Buddy can't resist the impulse to make wisecracks, and Crystal's timing and irrepressible funning make this a pleasure no matter how

clunky the storytelling becomes.

After Stan retires to Florida, Buddy decides to take on a new agent, Waspy blonde Helen Hunt, who has never heard of any of the old-time comedy greats but nevertheless gets Buddy a chance at some top jobs, such as a possible starring role in a film by megadirector Ron Silver.

A restaurant scene with Silver in which Buddy demonstrates dinner rolls as body adornments is particularly hilarious, but arguable high point is a priceless impromptu meeting at the Frairs between Buddy and Jerry Lewis, who plays himself as only he can.

Although no effort is made to evoke the neighborhood from which Buddy and Stan came, pic is bathed in a heavy ethnic sauce. Jewish traits and foibles are both kidded and embraced, with humor always as the forefront.

It's basically all Crystal and Paymer's show, and they age very convincingly through the years thanks to the expert makeup and hair designs of Peter Montagna, Bill Farley and Steve LaPorte. Albert Brenner's production design, Ruth Myers' costumes and Don Peterman's lensing nicely, but unemphatically, evoke the various periods.

— *Todd McCarthy*

THE PUBLIC EYE

A Universal release of a Robert Zemeckis production. Produced by Sue Baden-Powell. Executive producer, Zemeckis. Directed, written by Howard Franklin. Camera (Deluxe color), Peter Suschitzky; editor, Evan Lottman; music, Mark Isham; production design, Marcia Hinds-Johnson; art direction, Bo Johnson; Chicago art direction, Dina Lipton; set decoration, Jan Bergstrom; costume design, Jane Robinson; sound (Dolby), Stephan von Hase-Mihalik; special effects, Industrial Light & Magic; casting, Donna Isaacson. Reviewed at Universal Studios, Universal City, Calif., Aug. 19, 1992. (In Venice and Toronto film fests). MPPA Rating: R. Running time: **98 MIN.**

Leon (Bernzy) Bernstein	Joe Pesci
Kay Levitz	Barbara Hershey
Sal Minetto	Stanley Tucci
Arthur Nabler	Jerry Adler
Danny the Doorman	Jared Harris
Conklin	Gerry Becker
Spoleto	Dominic Chianese
H.R. Rineman	Del Close
Farinelli	Richard Foronjy
Agent Chadwick	Tim Gamble
Older agent	Bob Gunton
Spoleto's lieutenant	Joe Guzaldo
Federal watchman	Peter Maloney
Officer O'Brien	Richard Riehle

A down-and-dirty subject gets the velvet glove treatment in "The Public Eye." Playing a 1940s tabloid crime photographer who yearns for respecta-

bility and a little love, Joe Pesci creates an involving character, but almost everything about Howard Franklin's solo directorial debut is muted and moody where it should be bold and brash. Although it will probably receive critical endorsements from some quarters, b.o. outlook for this mid-October release looks subdued.

At least a half-dozen scenarios about the w.k. shutterbug Weegee floated around Hollywood in the 1980s, and Franklin wrote the present screenplay nine years ago, before making a name for himself with scripts to "Someone to Watch Over Me," "The Name of the Rose" and "Quick Change," which he co-directed last year with Bill Murray.

Weegee became celebrated for being the first to the scenes of many crimes, developing his pictures in the back of his car and capturing the human dimensions in tragic and/or grotesque situations. But the main challenge to anyone writing about him has been to create a compelling dramatic story featuring a schlumpy, unattractive central figure who was a social outcast, a man with few friends who spent midnight to dawn scouring the Big Apple for catastrophe.

After establishing that his fictionalized Leon Bernstein, "The Great Bernzini," has every other freelance photog in Gotham beat, Franklin concocts a story emphasizing the little man's emotional and artistic longings and testing his ability to remain an impartial outsider even in life-and-death circumstances.

Called in to do a favor for beauteous Kay Levitz (Barbara Hershey), a glamorpuss who has inherited an he exclusive nightclub from her wealthy late husband, Bernzy is flattered by her apparent serious interest in his book proposal. As a result, at her behest, he allows himself to get involved in a power struggle between two N.Y. mob factions when his whole career has been based on a philosophy of not playing favorites.

Bernzy plays spy for Kay to find out what's really going on. He's finally rewarded for his efforts when Kay visits his rattrap of an apartment and gives herself to him, an unlikely development given the cigar-chomping Bernzy's utter unkemptness and lack of sexuality.

Fulfilling the need for an action climax, it all ends with Bernzy witnessing and photographing a gangland massacre in an Italian restaurant and having greatness inadvertently thrust upon him.

In all respects, the film looks great, but that's the main problem. With terrific Marcia Hinds-Johnson production design evoking wartime N.Y. (location work was done in Cincinnati and Chicago) and gorgeous Peter Suschitzky lensing, pic approaches the physical beauty of a Coen Bros. or David Cronenberg film. Unfortunately, this is entirely counterproductive to the style that would have been appropriate for tabloid subject matter.

As displayed onscreen, Weegee/Bernzy's photos were all high-contrast exposés of real life caught in the raw. And so should the film have been. Instead of capturing a harsh, grubby, rough-and-tumble world full of vulgarity and vigor, Franklin and his team have turned out a clean, cool, elegant, extremely art-directed film that expresses nothing of the urban jungle that is his leading character's subject.

Even the soundtrack is curiously drained of the sounds of the city, and Mark Isham's rather mournful score pushes things even more in an introspective direction.

This would have been an ideal project for the likes of vet writer-director Samuel Fuller, whose Gotham journalistic background and bold, tabloid-like style would seem perfectly suited to a Weegee-like aesthetic.

Pesci, the best imaginable choice for the part of this feisty cock-of-the-walk always on the lookout for the telling shot, is more melancholy and brooding than one might have expected for the role, but he manages to carry the viewer through a series of only marginally believable incidents.

Decked out in fancy duds and accentuated décolletage, Hershey maintains an air of proper manners and poise throughout. Jared Harris has some potent moments as her status-conscious club doorman, and Stanley Tucci socks over his role as a duplicitous young mobster.

— *Todd McCarthy*

EDINBURGH FEST

A LITTLE BIT OF LIPPY
(BRITISH)

A BBC TV production. Produced by George Faber. Directed by Chris Bernard. Screenplay, Martyn Hesford, Camera (color, super 16m), Rex Maidment; editor, Sue Wyatt; music, Richard Blackford; production design, Chris Webster; costume design, Sarah Lubel; sound, Simon Wilson; assistant director, Alastair Duncan. Reviewed at Edinburgh Intl. Film Festival, Aug. 25, 1992. Running time: **75 MIN.**
Marian Fairley . . . . . Alison Swann
Rick Fairley . . . . Danny Cunningham
Reggie Titherington . Kenneth Cranham
Alma Titherington . . . Rachel Davies
Great Aunt Annie . Elizabeth Bradley
Venus Lamour . . . . . . Bette Bourne

A cross-dressing comedy with a mystical touch, "A Little Bit of Lippy" (lipstick) could drum up limited biz in theatrical clothes given careful handling. Popular Edinburgh fest hit reps a strong comeback for "Letter from Brezhnev" helmer Chris Bernard.

Marian (Alison Swann) and Rick (Danny Cunningham) are a young Liverpudlian working-class couple whose marriage has gone stale. In search of some sexual oomph, Marian surprises Rick one night in her scanties. Problem is, he's got to the make-up box first.

Rest of pic is a fruity melange of Marian discovering her hubby's parallel universe, much to the displeasure of her conservative father (Kenneth Cranham). Marian's acceptance of Rick's foible kickstarts the couple's sex life, as well as encouraging her own mother to branch out.

In their "fairytale for adults," Bernard and scripter Martyn Hesford have fashioned a joyous comedy on tolerance and sexual adventurism. Loopy tone, which rarely flags, recalls the '60s with its "Billy Liar"-like portrait of northern working-class life led by a grouchy Cranham. Sexy finale in a church setting could cause offense to Catholic groups.

Shot in super 16m with 35m blowup in mind, pic is pro in all departments. Swann is on the money as the dowdy wife transformed into a free-thinking swinger. Bright photography, lighting effects and Richard Blackford's magical score are all major assists in creating the pic's self-contained universe. Studio work was in nearby Manchester.

Pic airs Sept. 16 in the BBC's "Screen Play" series.

— *Derek Elley*

IMMACULATE CONCEPTION
(BRITISH)

A Feature Film Co. (U.K.) release of a Film Four Intl. presentation of a Dehlavi Films production. Produced, directed, written by Jamil Dehlavi. Camera (Agfacolor; Metrocolor prints), Nic Knowland; editor, Chris Barnes; music, Richard Harvey; production design, Mike Porter; art direction, Mohsin Mirza; costume design, Jane Moxson; sound (Dolby), Derek Williams, Godfrey Kirby; assistant director, Henry Tomlinson. Reviewed at Edinburgh Intl. Film Festival, Aug. 25, 1992. Running time: **122 MIN.**
Alistair . . . . James Wilby
Hannah . . . . Melissa Leo
Samira . . . . Shabana Azmi
Shehzada . . . . Zia Mohyeddin
Godfrey . . . . James Cossins
Dadaji . . . . Shreeram Lagoo
Kamal . . . . Ronny Jhutti
David . . . . Tim Choate
Also with: Bhaskar, Bill Bailey, Zafar Hameed.
(English & Urdu dialogue)

An ambitious culture-clash drama set in troubled 1988 Pakistan, "Immaculate Conception" tries to cover too many bases to score a solid hit. Handsome but distended pic toplining Merchant Ivory fave James Wilby may need a few miracles of its own to produce much in the B.O. department.

Wilby is Alistair, a wildlife conservationist based in Karachi with Jewish-American spouse Hannah (Melissa Leo), daughter of a powerful U.S. senator. Desperate to conceive a child, the couple visit a eunuch-run shrine reputed to have a cure for infertility.

In fact, the eunuchs slip them the local version of a Mickey and get teenager Kamal (Ronny Jhutti, from Brit soap "EastEnders") to do the business with a semicomatose Hannah. Sure enough, she later gives birth, but the marriage gradually falls apart from the strains of her conversion to Islam, her discovery of Alistair's affair with a close friend (Shabana Azmi) and the eunuchs' possessiveness of her baby.

Final turn of the screw is Kamal spilling the beans about what really happened when Hannah's brother (Tim Choate) hotfoots it from the States with instructions from Daddy.

There's a whole lot of different wheels grinding away in the script that need far better servicing than they get here. Leo's pantheistic desire to raise a Jewish-Muslim child; Wilby's philandering with well-connected Westernized photog Azmi; Jhutti's obsession with exiting to the West; and the background (on radio and TV) of the country's chaotic politics, with the junta leader Zia assassinated and Benazir Bhutto taking over.

For good measure, there's also the subplot of a gay Brit (James Cossins) who's in trouble with fundamentalists for importing banned books and photographing an ancient Koran. This briefly cross-fertilizes the main plot when Leo finds an incriminating snap of Wilby hidden in a copy of Salman Rushdie's "The Satanic Verses."

Franco-Pakistani helmer Jamil Dehlavi, whose 1980 feature "The Blood of Hussain" made him persona non grata with the Zia regime, can't be faulted for ambition or political objectivity (pic is often scathing on Pakistan's faults). But without a stronger central dramatic line, pic perpetually shifts in and out of focus, to overall mild emotional effect. Weak dialogue in several crucial scenes is a further minus.

Wilby, out of Edwardian white shirts and pants for a change, gives it his best shot but can't anchor the picture; Leo makes her best moves in the early going. Experienced Indian thesp Azmi is fine as the chic photog until her character is tossed overboard later on. Other playing is good within the script's limits, with an almost unrecognizable Zia Mohyeddin unctuous as the mascaraed chief eunuch.

Nic Knowland's richly hued photography is a major asset, neatly underscored by Richard Hartley's restrained music. All other credits are fine. Production shot in Pakistan in early 1991 during the Gulf War, with coin from TV web Channel Four. Urdu-dialogue segs are well subtitled. — *Derek Elley*

A RIVER RUNS THROUGH IT

A Columbia release. Produced by Robert Redford, Patrick Markey. Executive producer, Jake Eberts. Co-producers, Annick Smith, William Kittredge, Barbara Maltby. Directed by Redford. Screenplay, Richard Friedenberg, based on Norman Maclean's story. Camera (Technicolor), Philippe Rousselot; editors, Lynzee Klingman, Robert Estrin; music, Mark Isham; production design, Jon Hutman; art direction, Walter Martishius; set decoration, Gretchen Rau; costume design, Bernie Pollack, Kathy O'Rear; sound (Dolby), Hans Roland; assistant director, J. Stephen Buck; 2nd unit directors, Paul Ryan, Steve Perry, Patrick Markey; 2nd unit camera, Ryan; casting, Elisabeth Leustig. Reviewed at Toronto Festival of Festivals, Sept. 11, 1992. No MPAA rating. Running time: **123 MIN.**
Norman Maclean . . . . . Craig Sheffer
Paul Maclean . . . . Brad Pitt
Rev. Maclean . . . . Tom Skerritt
Mrs. Maclean . . . . . . Brenda Blethyn
Jessie Burns . . . . Emily Lloyd
Mrs. Burns . . . . Edie McClurg
Neal Burns . . . . Stephen Shellen
Mabel . . . . Nicole Burdette
Rawhide . . . . Susan Traylor
Young Norman . Joseph Gordon-Levitt
Young Paul . . . . Vann Gravage

A skilled, careful adaptation of a much-admired story, "A River Runs Through It" is a convincing trip back in time to a virtually vanished American West, as well as a nicely observed family study. Old-fashioned, literary and restrained, Robert Redford's third directorial outing should receive enough good reviews to propel it to respectable returns in limited platform release, but its concerns are too refined, gentle and, finally, unexciting to stir the masses. Pic had its world preem at the Toronto fest.

Published in 1976 and now in its 19th printing, the poetic, elegiac novella autobiographically traces author Norman Maclean's relationship with his wilder, younger brother in Montana against the backdrop of fly fishing, which is explored in all the necessary practical detail but is more importantly used as a metaphor for achieving a state of grace in life.

Story's concentration on the niceties of fly fishing made it an unlikely, possibly precious film prospect, and scenarist Richard Friedenberg has, of necessity, diminished the time accorded to the sport in favor of numerous invented, but appropriate, incidents (some drawn from the author's life) that beef up drama.

In some respects, the scrupulous reshaping has turned the material into an interesting companion piece to "Ordinary People," Redford's Oscar-winning first feature. Both stories focus on a small family whose members have great difficulty expressing emotions, although the new film lacks the convulsive psychological traumas and depth of the earlier one.

Arcing gracefully from 1910 to 1935, tale reveals the love and stability within the proud Maclean family, but also the inability to transform that love into the help younger brother Paul needs to save his life.

As rough-and-tumble boys, Norman and Paul are both imbued with a love of fly fishing by their father, a stern Scots Presbyterian minister. Although they always get along, they grow into very different young men, with Norman heading for college, an academic career and marriage, and Paul veering toward journalism, gambling and dissolute low life.

Narrative embraces several key life milestones, but these mostly occur off screen and are relayed though narration by Norman as an old man. Device heightens film's memory-play qualities but lessens the dramatic impact of the events and distances the viewer.

When Paul is in over his head with debt and in real danger, Norman tries, in his own way, to help, but Paul's nature puts him beyond reach. The beautiful son can only achieve grace and perfection in his life in fly fishing, but that is hardly enough.

Performances are thoughtful and well-judged. Craig Sheffer brings well-tempered nuances to Norman. With the showiest role, Brad Pitt shines, his smoldering James Dean-ish looks and recklessness encompassing both Paul's charm and doom.

Tom Skerritt discreetly reveals the loving core inside the reedy exterior of the boys' preacher father. Remainder of thesps have limited roles, but all are ideally cast.

Exquisitely lit and lensed by Philippe Rousselot, pic gives a strong physical sense of the majestic mountains and brilliant rivers of Montana, and production designer Jon Hutman, costume designers Bernie Pollack and Kathy O'Rear and other hands have helped Redford create a realistic yet heightened portrait of a very specific piece of American past. — *Todd McCarthy*

THE NUN AND THE BANDIT
(AUSTRALIAN)

A Greater Union Distributors release (Australia) of an Illumination Films/Film Victoria/Australian Film Finance Corp. production. Executive producer, William T. Marshall. Produced by Paul Ammitzboll, Paul Cox. Directed, written by Cox, from E.L. Grant Watson's book. Camera (Eastmancolor), Nino Martinetti; editor, Cox; music, Tom E. Lewis, Norman Kaye; production design, Neil Angwin; sound, James Currie, Craig Carter. Reviewed in Leura, Australia, Aug. 23, 1992. (In Toronto Film Festival.) Running time: **92 MIN.**
Sister Lucy . . . . . Gosia Dobrowolska
Michael Shanley . . . . Chris Haywood
Maureen . . . . Victoria Eagger
Julie . . . Charlotte Hughes Haywood
George Shanley . . . . . Norman Kaye
Bert Shanley . . . . Tom E. Lewis
Frankie . . . Scott Michael Stephenson
Also with: Robert Menzies, Eva Sitta, John Flaus, Tony Llewellyn-Jones.

Marking a departure for Aussie auteur Paul Cox, "The Nun and the Bandit" is adapted from a book and set in the primal Australian bush, far from the claustrophobic interiors of his earlier films. Still, this Toronto fest world preem is quintessential Cox, a leisurely, ambiguous moral tale in which concepts of good and evil blur.

Cox has updated E.L. Grant Watson's kidnap thriller set in the 1930s to what appears to be the '50s, playing down the thriller elements in favor of a brittle character study.

Cox's kidnappers are led by Michael Shanley (Chris Haywood), disaffected nephew of prominent citizen George Shanley (Norman Kaye). Michael is convinced he's been cheated of his father's interest in the family mine and wants compensation for himself, his simple-minded brother (Scott Michael Stephenson) and part-aboriginal half-brother (Tom E. Lewis).

When George refuses to pay up, Michael devises an impromptu, hare-brained scheme to hold the rich man's young granddaughter (played by the daughter of Haywood and actress Wendy Hughes, Charlotte Hughes Haywood) for ransom. The child is snatched when she's with her aunt, Sister Lucy (Gosia Dobrowolska), a Polish nun visiting her sickly sister (Eva Sitta), the girl's mother.

In a series of telling scenes, Cox contrasts Michael's ghastly, impoverished background with that of his wealthy, arrogant uncle. At the same time, he depicts this illiterate, but strangely charming ruffian's growing feeling for the helpless nun, first in terms of lust and later, growing love and need to be loved.

By this time, the plot's thriller aspects have been almost entirely abandoned, and the bulk of the film plays as a two-hander between the frightened, unworldly nun and the strange "bandit" who refuses to rape his victim but demands that she "be nice" to him. Cox leaves it up to the viewer to decide what happens between the two because, despite some scenes of nudity, the sexual relationship between kidnapper and victim apparently isn't consummated.

This ambiguity may irk some viewers, and the slow second half as Cox works out the spiritual relationship between his ill-matched protagonists, may also be an audience deterrent.

Cox regulars Dobrowolska and Chris Haywood give their usual standout performances, the former very touching as the nun who opts to sacrifice her chastity to guarantee the safety of the child in her care; and the latter bringing needed depth to the apparent villain who turns out to be more deserving of pity than hate. Among the supporting cast, Kaye excels as the charmingly unscrupulous capitalist.

Pic has very fine visuals and sound, with production values belying the modest budget. The bushland setting forms a crucial backdrop to the drama, its sites (shot by Nino Martinetti) and sounds (recorded by James Currie) evoking an almost primeval world. Music, much of it traditional aboriginal themes composed by thesp Lewis, while Kaye provides the Western elements) is subtly used throughout.

Pic will have to be carefully marketed since auds lured in by promises of a salacious melodrama will be disappointed. Feminists may also balk at scenes in which the nun shows affection for the man who has consistently threatened and humiliated her.

Yet, this is Cox's most spiritual film, and his fans will discover his familiar themes have been given new twists in this intriguing, surprisingly gentle saga.

— *David Stratton*

JUST ANOTHER GIRL ON THE I.R.T.

A Miramax release of a Truth 24 F.P.S. presentation. Produced by Erwin Wilson, Leslie Harris. Directed, written by Harris. Camera (color), Richard Connors; editor, Jack Haigis; music producer-supervisor, Eric Sadler; production design, Mike Green; set decoration, Robin Chase; costume design, Bruce Brickus; sound, Harrison Williams; casting, Tracey Moore. Reviewed at Toronto Festival of Festivals, Sept. 15, 1992. Running time: **92 MIN.**
Chantel . . . . Ariyan Johnson
Tyrone . . . . Kevin Thigpen
Natete . . . . Ebony Jerido
Paula . . . . Chequita Jackson
Cedrick . . . . William Badget
Gerard . . . . Jerard Washington

A debut effort by a young black woman filmmaker, "Just Another Girl on the I.R.T." is a crude but disturbing exposé of teenage ignorance and denial about the facts of life on the streets and in the bedroom. Shot independently in New York on a 17-day sked, Miramax pickup is probably too probing and critical to appeal widely to the minority adolescents that are its subject.

More upscale specialty house audiences could be lured in some numbers with a "female 'She's Gotta Have It'" pitch, but pic's quality is nowhere near that level, setting real limits on b.o. potential. Still, its novelty and distinctly different p.o.v. will attract attention.

In a raw, upfront style, writer-director Leslie Harris lays out a sad, brutal story. Plot's details may prove startling, even unbelievable at times, but there can be little doubt as to the veracity of Harris' take on the state of teen minds and attitudes. Pic's main value is as a report from a front that is largely ignored, at least in mainstream media and arts.

Harris deliberately creates a leading character who's pretty hard to take. Chantel, 17, is an arrogant Brooklyn h.s. student who mouths off to adults, imagines she's far smarter and hipper than her classmates and thinks nothing of dumping her regular b.f. for a hot guy with a Jeep. Determined to escape her community, she intends to finish high school in three years and make a beeline for med school.

Harris seems to be setting Chantel up for a fall, and fall she does, first into the arms of the Jeep man, fast-talking Tyrone, and consequently into unplanned, unwanted teen pregnancy. Chantel tells almost no one of her condition. First she procrastinates about what to do, then goes into denial, successfully hiding her size, and going on with her life as if nothing were different.

When Tyrone gives her $500 for an abortion, she shockingly spends it shopping. Finally, it's too late to do anything but have the child, and outcome is appalling and sobering.

Harris includes some pointed scenes existing solely to illustrate the extent of ignorance on birth control and the unpreparedness of teens to deal with adult responsibilities. That Chantel has medical aspirations doesn't quite jibe with her ignorance in this area, but her denial is so fearsomely all-encompassing rationality never enters the picture.

Although the film is punched up by some energetic cutting and hip-hop music, many dialogue scenes, particularly early on, are badly written and awkwardly staged. Things get marginally better as the material becomes more trenchant.

Performances possess vigor but are on the rough side. Ariyan Johnson creates a very abrasive character in Chantel, which can only be what Harris had in mind. Kevin Thigpen makes the most favorable impression as Tyrone, a slick operator who becomes gradually more humanized.

Technically, pic is similarly broad and unmodulated.

— *Todd McCarthy*

TELLURIDE FEST

PETER'S FRIENDS
(BRITISH)

A Samuel Goldwyn Co. release of a Renaissance Film production, produced in association with Film Four Intl. Produced, directed by Kenneth Branagh. Executive producer, Stephen Evans. Co-producer, Martin Bergman. Line producer, David Parfitt. Screenplay, Rita Rudner, Bergman. Camera (Technicolor), Roger Lanser; editor, Andrew Marcus; production design, Tim Harvey; art direction, Martin Childs; costume design, Susan Coates, Stephanie Collie; sound (Dolby), David Crozier. Reviewed at Telluride Film Festival, Sept. 6, 1992. Running time: **100 MIN.**
Andrew . . . . Kenneth Branagh
Sarah . . . . Alphonsia Emmanuel
Peter . . . . Stephen Fry
Roger . . . . Hugh Laurie
Vera . . . . Phyllida Law
Paul . . . . Alex Lowe
Carol . . . . Rita Rudner
Brian . . . . Tony Slattery
Mary . . . . Imelda Staunton
Maggie . . . . Emma Thompson
Paul . . . . Alex Scott

Already being called a British "Big Chill," Kenneth Branagh's third feature is a sometimes funny, often cloying entertainment about old friends who experience a year's worth of crises in two days. Glib humor and heavy emphasis on sex could put this over with the dating crowd and thirtysomething couples, but reaction to this Goldwyn Christmas release will be decidedly mixed.

Script by Rita Rudner and Martin Bergman confines the action almost entirely to the country estate of Peter (Stephen Fry), a witty, charmingly dissolute young aristocrat who invites his college theatrical friends and mates for a New Year's reunion. In a manner that smacks of both stage comedy and sitcoms, the various characters are paraded forward with their most humorous traits front and center.

Maggie (Emma Thompson) leaves photos of herself all over her home so her cat won't miss her; Roger and Mary (Hugh Laurie, Imelda Staunton) can barely tear themselves away from their infant son; Sarah and Brian (Alphonsia Emmanuel, Tony Slattery), lovers of two weeks, can't keep their clothes on or their hands off each other, and Andrew and TV star Carol (Branagh, Rudner) fly in from L.A., with Carol packing a gym's worth of workout equipment and Roger letting fly with rude remarks.

As the eating and drinking proceed, all manner of former relationships, emotional traumas and secret agendas are revealed into the wee hours of the new year, when a terrible announcement abruptly sobers up all the remaining revelers.

Scripters have loaded the plot down with an array of troubles and complications suitable to all-out farce, but not to semi-realistic character comedy. Many of the lines and the shadings brought to them by these expert performers are good for some laughs, and pic has plenty of energy, but it can't be taken as seriously as it wants to be.

The constant and boisterous horniness of Sarah and Brian is annoying and unfunny, but this is nothing compared to the running gag, if it actually is, of Mary calling home every other minute to see if her baby is okay. She and her laid-back husband are simply a drag.

Playing an insecure egotist and fitness freak who secretly raids the fridge, co-writer Rudner has given herself a lion's share of the good bits and she carries off the Joan Collins-ish role in high style.

As her tag-along hubby who has deserted the U.K. for L.A., Branagh is slyly humorous, but both his career and motivation for staying with an overbearing woman are unexplored, resulting in a hollow character.

Most appealing are the ditzy Thompson, whose sudden transformation into a glamorpuss by Carol and subsequent quickie affair are nevertheless jarring; Phyllida Law as the mansion's dignified, longtime housekeeper; and Fry as the affable host.

Stylistically, Branagh and lenser Roger Lanser have gone in for long, uninterrupted, roving takes that sometimes allow for good character interaction but at other times are merely show-offy. Branagh also has little feel for how to integrate pop tunes with the story.

— *Todd McCarthy*

SAN SEBASTIAN

EL MAESTRO DE ESGRIMA
(THE FENCING MASTER)
(SPANISH)

An Origen P.C. & Altube S.L. production. Executive producer, Antonio Cardenal. Directed by Pedro Olea. Screenplay, Antonio Larreta, Francisco Prada, Olea, Arturo Pérez Reverte, based on Reverte's novel. Camera (Eastmancolor), Alfredo Mayo; editor, José Salcedo; music, José Nieto; sets, Luis Valles; fencing master, Francisco Fuentes. (Opening pic at San Sebastian Film Festival.) Running time: **88 MIN.**
Astarloa . . . . Omero Antonutti
Adela . . . . Assumpta Serna
Ayala . . . . Joaquim de Almeida
Campillo . . . José Luis López Vázquez
Salanova . . . . Alberto Closas
Carceles . . . . Miguel Rellán
Also with: Elisa Matilla, Ramón Goyanes, Tomás Repila, Marcos Tizón, Miguel Angel Salomón.

Stellar performances by Omero Antonutti and Assumpta Serna, a distinguished and literate script, fine plot development, good sets and accomplished direction and lensing make "The Fencing Master" one of Spain's most winsome films this year.

Antonutti, who scored as leads in Victor Erice's "El Sur," Carlos Saura's "El Dorado" and other top Spanish films, here plays a fencing master in 1868 Madrid when the monarchy of Isabel II is being menaced by revolutionaries. With historical elements kept to a minimum, interest comes on one side from a conservative fencing master, for whom fencing is an art that eclipses all other human endeavors. On the other is a strikingly beautiful young woman who, for mysterious reasons, becomes his pupil.

Secondary characters include a pamphleteering revolutionary, a handsome aristocrat/fencing pupil and a police inspector. All interact in a well-constructed mystery. Good, histrionic swordplay is a plus.

Final whydunnit explanations leave various untied strings, and López Vázquez as the police chief is miscast, but these are minor objections in a superbly thesped film that should hold audiences from first to last frame.

— *Peter Besas*

BOSTON FEST

BANYA

A Zerkalo Prods. presentation. Executive producers, Sandra Forman, Jill Alman-Bernstein. Produced by Mark Donadio, Andrei Ustinov. Directed, written by Chris Schmidt. Camera (color), David Bernkopf; editor, Schmidt; music, Bevan Mason; art direction, Rauf Kashapov; sound, Bayard Carey; associate producers, Frank R. Steinfeild, Alexander Levashov, James V. Hoff. Reviewed at Copley Place Theater, Boston, Mass., Aug. 4, 1992. (In Boston Film Festival.) Running time: **110 MIN.**
Sabine . . . . Kathryn Mederos
Valera . . . . Vladimir Vashenko
Vitaly . . . . Valery Sergeev
Alyosha . . . . Mikhail Levchenko
Sasha . . . . Mikhail Zhedunov
Also with: Natalia Sherbovich, Tatiana Ivanova, Natalia Sergeeva.
(English, Russian dialogue)

"**B**anya" is a real curio: a film shot in Russia with an almost entirely Russian cast and a very Russian story, yet written, directed, produced and financed by American filmmakers. Pic doesn't entirely succeed largely due to the script, but it shows how a U.S. indie pic can be shot abroad and look as pro as homegrown product.

Four Russians summer in the countryside, supposedly to work on a small bathhouse/sauna ("banya"). But the men actually go so they can imagine they're Americans for a couple of weeks. They speak only English (more than two-thirds of the film is in English), listen and lip-synch to blues records and color their vodka with tea for "Jack Daniels." Unfortunately, the characters are not very well developed, and it's hard to empathize with them.

Plot thickens when they get involved with an American tourist (Kathryn Mederos, cast's only Yank) who's trying to smuggle icons out of the country. She is even less developed than the Russians, and her motivations remain obscure.

Instead of opting for a strong narrative spine, writer/director Chris Schmidt errs with an ensemble approach. At nearly two hours, the meandering story line (also including a stolen truck, one Russian's illegitimate son and a writer eating his typewriter) seem to go nowhere slowly.

Production values are crisp and can certainly stand comparison with modestly budgeted imports. Yaroslavl locations also have the benefit of seeming fresh and original, somewhat ironic since the town is over five centuries old.

— *Daniel M. Kimmel*

THE MINISTER'S WIFE

A Cinemabeam presentation of an Arturo Pictures production. Produced by Yoram Barzilai. Directed, written by Rob Spera. Camera (color), Rodrigo Garcia; editor, Olof Kollstrom; music, Steve Edwards; production design, Armandina Lozano, George Pierson; sound, Aletha Rogers; assistant director, Roberto Sneider; associate producer, Deborah Scott; casting, Lacy Bishop. Reviewed at Loews Copley Place Theater, Boston, Sept. 2, 1992. (In Boston Film Festival.) Running time: **83 MIN.**
Deborah Miles . . . . . . Susan Cash
Bobby Baline . . . . . . Blake Gibbons
James Miles . . . . . . Gregg Almquist
Hannah . . . . Evelyn Cole

A couple of topnotch performances grace this Kentucky-based production, but the last third of writer-director Robert Spera's script turns personal drama into hackneyed melodrama. Result disappoints.

Title character (Susan Cash) is facing a midlife crisis. Her husband (Gregg Almquist) is so wrapped up in his work, he can't even be bothered to come to bed anymore. Her daughter has left for college, and her best friend (Evelyn Cole) is one of the senior citizens she shepherds around as part of her volunteer church work.

Feeling old and used up at 40, the wife succumbs to the blandishments of a smooth young man (Blake Gibbons) who drives an ice cream truck, but whose darker side slowly becomes ap-

parent. First hour scores despite weakly written male characters; focus remains on the wife.

Newcomer Cash (who has done TV and stage work) is convincing as a woman who would risk an affair in order to bring some feeling back into her life. Cole ably supports but steals every scene she's in as an outspoken widow.

First hour is a finely etched portrait of a woman tired of just going through the motions. As a U.S. film with no stars, it could find a home on the Lifetime cable channel. But in the final third, pic turns more suitable for the USA channel's late-night schlock theater: Wife tries to break off the affair and her lover turns to blackmail and violence. Ending is cheap "Fatal Attraction"-style melodrama contradicting honest emotions earlier.

Tech credits are up to snuff, although using church choir music during love scenes comes across heavy-handedly.

— *Daniel M. Kimmel*

MONTREAL FEST

NORTH OF PITTSBURGH
(CANADIAN)

A Cinephile release of an Acme Motion Pictures production in association with Telefilm Canada & B.C. Film. Produced by Kim Steer, Cal Shumiatcher. Directed by Richard Martin. Screenplay, Jeff Schultz. Camera (Eastman Kodak color), Tobias A. Schliessler; editor, Bruce Lange; music, Graeme Coleman; production design, Brent Thomas; art direction, Doug Byggdin; costumes, Diane M. Widas, Gregory Mah; sound (Ultra Stereo), Patrick Ramsay; casting, Stuart Aikins. Reviewed at Montreal World Film Festival, Sept. 2, 1992. Running time: **98 MIN.**
Rosa Andretti . . . . . Viveca Lindfors
Tony Andretti . . . . Jeff Schultz
Also with: Bryon Lucas, John Cassini, Suzanne Ristic, Mario Sweet, Maria Gentile, Andrea Nemeth, Morgan Brayton, Jay Brazeau, Dick Martin.

Definite sleeper potential lies in "North of Pittsburgh," a beautifully acted and sharply written comedy-drama with enough cross-generational appeal to warm many of the same hearts captured by "Fried Green Tomatoes." Careful handling could pay off with nice box office coin.

This is a career-making breakthrough for actor Jeff Schultz, who also penned the episodic screenplay, and a notable credit for veteran Viveca Lindfors. Duo fuels this entertaining road movie

with heart, soul and vital give-and-take.

Pic is set in 1975, with Schultz cast as aimless young Ontario man who runs pot from Pittsburgh to the Canadian border. When he and his buddies bungle a delivery, Schultz finds himself in debt to a hot-headed hood who'd just as soon kill him.

Meanwhile, Schultz's beloved grandfather, a retired coal miner, rouses from his deathbed long enough to make Schultz promise to take care of the older man's wife (Lindfors). After the funeral, he moves in with Grandma, who neither trusts nor likes him very much.

Lindfors plans to file a claim for government compensation to black-lung victims like her late husband. Sensing a potential bonanza, Schultz offers to drive her to Pennsylvania to make the claim.

Bulk of pic has Schultz and Lindfors on the road in his clunky car, visiting kin and coping with mining-company officials. Grandson and grandmother squabble and talk a lot, eventually bringing out the best in each other. Finale relies on a healthy dose of feel-good Capra-corn, but it works.

Pic has slight similarities to Touchstone's "Crossing the Bridge," but the period flavor is evoked more strongly in "North of Pittsburgh," even though latter has cover versions of period tunes, not the originals. More to the point, "Pittsburgh" is the much better pic. Richard Martin directs with self-assurance and flawless pacing. He also gives a neat cameo part to his father, Dick Martin of "Laugh-In" fame. Other supporting players are first-rate.

Score by Graeme Coleman is exceptional. Other tech credits, including Tobias Schliessler's fluid lensing and Brent Thomas' evocative production design, are top of the line. — *Joe Leydon*

CROSSING THE BRIDGE

A Buena Vista release of a Touchstone Pictures presentation of an Outlaw production. Produced by Jeffrey Silver, Robert Newmyer. Co-producers, Caroline Baron, Jack Binder. Directed, written by Mike Binder. Camera (Panavision, Deluxe color), Tom Sigel; editor, Adam Weiss; music, Peter Himmelman; production design, Craig Stearns; costumes, Carol Ramsey; sound (Dolby Stereo), Ed Novick, Mark Goodermote; associate producers, Judd Apatow, Joel Madison; casting, Richard Pagano/Sharon Bialy, Debi Manwiller. Reviewed at Montreal World Film Festival, Sept. 3, 1992. MPAA rating: R. Running time: **103 MIN.**

Mort Golden . . . . .Josh Charles
Tim Reese . . . . .Jason Gedrick
Danny Morgan . . . .Stephen Baldwin
Carol Brockton . . . . .Cheryl Pollak
Kate Golden . . . . Rita Taggart
Manny Goldfarb . . . . . . .Hy Anzell
Mitchell . . . . Richard Edson
　Also with: Ken Jenkins, Abraham Benrubi, David Schwimmer, Bob Nickman, James Krag, Rana Haugen, Jeffrey Tambor.

"Crossing the Bridge,"

writer-director Mike Binder's autobiographical-flavored drama set in 1975 Detroit, should cross over to homevideo very quickly. Indie-produced pic won't remain long in theatrical tollbooths for Touchstone.

Three years after h.s. graduation, three buddies hang out and generally avoid thinking about the future. First hour or so plays like a retread of "Breaking Away," as the lads work at menial jobs, carouse with equally aimless buddies and consider themselves very superior to ex-classmates attending college.

Mort (Josh Charles), clearly intended as Binder's alter ego, is a budding writer and would-be comic whose chief ambition is to write sitcom. In that, he's much less aimless than hothead Tim (Jason Gedrick) and taciturn Danny (Stephen Baldwin).

Most of the episodic misadventures are played for laughs, including a stunningly bizarre sequence in which Mort's mother (Rita Taggart) and uncle (Jeffrey Tambor) have a famous New York Times writer (Hy Anzell) over for dinner. Mort listens in awe as the writer talks about wordsmithing; then the writer drops dead from a heart attack Uncle Alby thinks was caused by something Mort said. "This man survived the death camps of Nazi Germany!" Tambor cries, "only to succumb during an evening with you!"

It takes a colossal nerve to bring up the Holocaust for a cheap laugh, but, then again, Binder is quite shameless. His Mort is more sensitive and intelligent than everyone else on screen. Seldom has a cinematic self-portrait been so unabashedly celebratory.

Pic's final third has the three leads heading across the Ambassador Bridge to Canada, where they think they're going to pick up some hash from a hippie-scum supplier (Richard Edson). The guys find out they're really expected to smuggle heroin back to Detroit, triggering a three-part

crisis of conscience providing pic's only real suspense.

Pic relies heavily on well-chosen period tunes on the soundtrack and Carol Ramsey's evocative costume design. Cheryl Pollak is on hand so Mort can slow-dance to Tony Bennett's "The Shadow of Your Smile" with someone before he and his buddies drive off for the dope.

Performances are as good as they can be, given the circumstances. Baldwin in particular registers strong screen presence. Other tech credits are good.

— *Joe Leydon*

PRORVA
(MOSCOW PARADE)
(RUSSIAN-FRENCH)

A Project Campo (Moscow)/East West-Parimedia (Paris) co-production, with the participation of Canal Plus. Produced by Alexandre Shkodo, Pierre Rival, Claude Rosius. Directed by Ivan Dykhovichny. Screenplay, Dykhovichny, Nadejda Kojoushanaia. Camera (color), Vadim Jousov; editor, Eleonora Praksina; music, Joury Butsko, Alexandre Tsfasman; production design, Vladimir Aronin; sound, Ekaterina Popova. Reviewed at Venice Film Festival (noncompeting), Sept. 6, 1992. (Also in Toronto Film Festival.) Running time: **103 MIN.**

Anna . . . . Ute Lemper
Cultural commisar . . Alena Antonova
Gorbachevskaia . . Ekaterina Ryzkova
Ballerina . . . . . . Natalia Kalikanova
Anna's husband . Alexander Feklistov
Vassili . . . . Alexei Kortnev
　Also with: Vladimir Simonov, Evgeny Sidichin, Dimitri Dychovichny.

Late 1930s Moscow is given "Cabaret"-like treatment in this overheated extravaganza about an aristocratic woman married to a member of Josef Stalin's secret police. A cluttered screenplay results in a disjointed pic.

Instead of concentrating on the character of the masochistic Anna, who embarks on an affair with a baggage handler, director Ivan Dykhovichny fills the pic with bizarre subplots and a dozen characters, most of whom detract from the main story. German singer Ute Lemper gives a brave central performance but is unable to overcome script flaws.

Plot involves NKVD officers (later known as KGB) ordered to train a black stallion for the Red Army commander, Anna's sexual adventures, a poet who falls in love with a ballerina but is driven to suicide, a lawyer who falls for his client (a psychopath who

kills her sexual partners), and an NKVD officer who is a rapist.

It's all too much for the film to bear, yet pic is visually handsome, with location shooting on familiar Moscow landmarks. But it sorely lacks greater cohesion, resulting in a distinct lack of viewer involvement.

— *David Stratton*

ME AND VERONICA

A Columbia TriStar Homevideo presentation of a True One/True Pictures production. Produced by Mark Linn-Baker, Max Mayer, Nellie Nugiel, Leslie Urdang. Directed by Don Scardino. Screenplay, Leslie Lyles. Camera (color), Michael Barrow; editor, Jeffrey Wolf; music, David Mansfield; songs, Shawn Colvin. Reviewed at Venice Film Festival (competing), Sept. 9, 1992. Running time: **97 MIN.**

Fanny . . . . Elizabeth McGovern
Veronica . . . . Patricia Wettig
Michael . . . . Michael O'Keefe
Frankie . . . . John Heard
Boner . . . . Scott Renderer
Red . . . . Will Hare

This two-sisters drama set at the New Jersey shore struggles between cleverness and banality. Pic comes alive when dedicated duo Elizabeth McGovern and Patricia Wettig are on screen together, but when apart, pic reverts to yawning predictability. Venice film fest unwisely screened "Me and Veronica" in the thick of competition, instead of a sidebar where it could have shone in an honest light. Outing may pick up some European ancillary market interest for the U.S. homevid release.

After five years of feuding since new bride McGovern's caught sis Wettig in bed with her husband, vivacious troublemaker Wettig stops in to visit. The unwed mother and ne'er-do-well is on her way to prison for welfare fraud. The sensible sister is also on the skids, hiding from life and men in a rundown shack in a Jersey fishing town.

Pic's most sustained and convincing sequence has the two spending the night cruising bars and playing daredevil on a bridge in a carefree return to childhood. Then Wettig heads off to Rikers Island to serve her term. McGovern casually offers to take care of her children.

As the "bad" sister in a miniskirt, Wettig is a poetic foil to McGovern's bitter inwardness. But life sans Wettig is as dull for the viewer as it is for foster mom McGovern. Without arch Jersey dialogue that kept the sister

scenes lively and tense, screenplay falls into TV sameness.

Both actresses deliver finely calibrated performances which both attract and repel. In comparison, the men around them, including John Heard as a friendly bartender and Michael O'Keefe as Veronica's b.f., tend to interfere and disappear.

Pro cast is matched by solid, no-frills tech work. First feature directed by Don Scardino, artistic director of New York's off-Broadway Playwrights Horizons, shows no trace of staginess. Still, helmer's long experience directing TV remains a mantle harder to shake off. — *Deborah Young*

TANGO ARGENTINO
(SERBIAN)

A Singidunum Film production in cooperation with Vane & Belgrade TV. Produced by Dragana Ilic, Goran Paskaljevic. Directed by Paskaljevic. Screenplay, Gordan Mihic. Camera (color), Milan Spasic; art direction, Mile Nikolic; editor, Olga Skrigin, Olga Obradov; music, Zoran Simjanovic. Reviewed at Venice Film Festival (Window on Images section), Sept. 3, 1992. Running time: **93 MIN.**

Nikola . . . . Nikola Zarkovic
Father . . . . Miki Manojlovic
Mother . . . . Ina Gogalova
Julio Popovitch . . . . . Mija Aleksic
Mrs. Lakicevitch . . . . Rahela Ferari
Kerecky . . . . Mica Tomic
　Also with: Pepi Lekovic, Carna Manojlovic.

"Tango Argentino" is a

small film shot from the heart by Goran Paskaljevic, one of Yugoslavia's leading directors. Without ever directly touching on politics, it movingly conveys the sad, end-of-an-era climate in post-communist, pre-war Serbia. Premiered at the Munich fest, the film will play the major festivals and is a strong candidate for specialized theatrical and TV playoffs.

A smart 10-year-old boy, Nikola Zarkovic, lives with his quarrelsome young parents and sick sister. While Papa teaches music and Mama searches for her identity in a job, Nikola is left on his own. He finds the warmth and understanding that are missing at home in the company of the elderly people his mother shops and cleans for.

The old folks, in turn, are spurred to life by the boy's energy. He introduces them to each other and takes them on outings. Because of their advanced age, however, the old folks start disappearing. Faced with the pain of their loss, it isn't clear whether Nikola will grow up, or retreat into a world of pleasant dreams.

Largely a mood piece, pic is effective because it contrasts harshness and gentleness without going overboard on sentimentality. Death occurs behind doors, just off screen. The film also entertains with Nikola's schemes to earn money for his destitute family. He clearly has great potential — which circumstances may or may not allow him to develop.

As Nikola's father, Miki Manojlovic reprises the pathetic Don Juan character of "When Father Was Away on Business," locked in a tense marriage with the complex Ina Gogolova. One-time Argentine pop singer Mija Aleksic is a dignified charlatan as the main oldster.

Film's theme song is a catchy, omnipresent tango which, like the characters, goes through a dozen variations. Seductive and nostalgic when sung to the boy, the tango becomes rasping and shrill when the old man sings his way out of a psychiatric hospital.

Paskaljevic puts his scenes together with a masterful touch. Milan Spasic's camera creates a soft, gentle atmosphere that conveys the boy's view of the world.

— *Deborah Young*

FRATELLI E SORELLE
(BROTHERS AND SISTERS)
(ITALIAN)

A Filmauro relese of a Duea Film/ Filmauro production, in collaboration with RAI-1. (Intl. sales: Sacis, Rome.) Produced by Antonio Avati, Luigi & Aurelio De Laurentiis. Directed, written by Pupi Avati. Camera (color), Roberto D'Ettorre Piazzoli; editor, Amedeo Salfa; music, Riz Ortolani; production design, Carlo Simi; sound, Raffaele De Luca; casting, Angela Ricci. Reviewed at Venice Film Festival (competing), Sept. 3, 1992. Running time: **101 MIN.**
Franco . . . . Franco Nero
Lea . . . . Paola Quattrini
Gloria . . . . Anna Bonaiuto
Aldo . . . . Lino Capolicchio
Francesco . . . . . . Luciano Federico
Matteo . . . . Stefano Accorsi
Also with: Kelly Evinston, Barbara Wilder, Enrica M. Modugno, Consuelo Ferrara, Ciro Scalera, Lidia Broccolino.

Pupi Avati's follow-up to his disappointing American jazz film "Bix" is also set in the U.S., but "Brothers and Sisters" is an unhappy project for the director of fine and very Italian films ("Employees," "Story of Boys and Girls") as it comes across as phony, contrived and awkward. International prospects look slim.

Gloria, middled-aged mother of teen sons Matteo and Francesco, finds out her husband was cheating on her so she takes herself and her offspring to visit her sister in St. Louis. Stage is thus set for a promising exploration of culture shock as the two boys find themselves in a vastly different environment, but Avati's muddled, cluttered screenplay doesn't begin to address pic's most interesting theme.

The sister lives with a man who has two daughters, stereotypically introed as being respectively blonde, beautiful and wanton (Lillian) and brunette, plain and sympathetic (Gea). Matters are complicated by a film crew using the street where they live to make a very strange movie.

Avati has no ear for American language ("I envy those who get to see America through unsullied eyes" says Lillian) so that none of the Italo-Americans ring true. Nor is the writer-director interested in capturing the strangeness of America as seen through the eyes of the Europeans (à la Jim Jarmusch). Result instead is the most trite soap opera, a risible concoction network TV does with far more class. Unintentional laughs abound.

Performances are undistinguished, with top-billed Franco Nero saddled with a zero role as the father of the two American women. First-time thesps Stefano Accorsi and Luciano Federico are stuck with uninteresting characters.

Visually drab pic evidences problems with weather continuity in some scenes. A poorly staged boxing bout provides little relief from the talky, banal goings-on. One hopes Avati will return to the Italian themes and characters he has handled with success in the past.

— *David Stratton*

U.S. RELEASES

CAPTAIN RON

A Buena Vista Pictures release of a Touchstone Pictures presentation in association with Touchwood Pacific Partners I of a David Permut production. Produced by Permut, Paige Simpson. Executive producer, Ralph Winter. Coproducer, Ric Rondell. Directed by Thom Eberhardt. Screenplay, John Dwyer, Eberhardt; story by Dwyer. Camera (Rank Film Laboratories color), Daryn Okada; editor, Tina Hirsch; music, Nicholas Pike; production design, William F. Matthews; art direction, James F. Truesdale; set decoration, Jeff Haley, Irvin E. Jim Duffy Jr.; set design, Glenn Williams; costume design, Jennifer Von Mayrhauser; sound (Dolby), Mary H. Ellis; associate producers, Susanne Goldstein, Andy Cohen; assistant director, Marty Eli Schwartz; casting, Mary Gail Artz, Barbara Cohen. Reviewed at Avco Center Cinema, L.A., Sept. 14, 1992. MPAA Rating: PG-13. Running time: **100 MIN.**
Captain Ron . . . . Kurt Russell
Martin Harvey . . . . . Martin Short
Katherine Harvey . . . Mary Kay Place
Benjamin Harvey . Benjamin Salisbury
Caroline Harvey . . . . . Meadow Sisto

Kurt Russell and Martin Short find themselves trapped aboard a sinking ship in this highly derivative comedy, a sort of waterlogged knockoff of Touchstone's earlier "What About Bob?" Inoffensive but unexciting item could have some of "Bob's" appeal in homevideo after what promises to be a rather brief theatrical cruise.

The film can be boiled down to just enough amusing moments to produce a reasonably enticing trailer, coupled with the heartwarming, painfully predictable result that this peculiar outsider will bring a somewhat dysfunctional suburban family together.

Short plays a Chicago businessman whose dream of sailing the high seas becomes a reality when he inherits a yacht and decides to take the family to a remote Carribean island to fetch the boat, pilot it back to Miami and reap a wild windfall by selling it. Via a minor screw-up, he hires Captain Ron, a boozing lecher with a roving eye patch and poor sense of direction, to helm the ship.

What could make for a horror story (and in fact did in "Dead Calm") goes cruising for laughs here, as the boat washes up on a variety of obscure islands, with Short's family falling under Ron's spell even as Short becomes increasingly exasperated with him.

Working from a script he wrote with John Dwyer, director Thom Eberhardt's storytelling is as choppy as the high seas, enduring long, flat stretches between its loosely connected and sometimes over-the-top moments.

Even though playing for laughs, pic relies on some rather unfortunate xenophobia, with nearly all the Latin types either pirates, revolutionaries or trollops, a laziness that may hurt some feelings, if not tourism.

Short continues to suffer serious problems finding a way to tap his diverse "Saturday Night Live" talents on the big screen. Russell seems to have fun with this tattooed good-for-nothing, who bears a more than passing resemblance to his growling persona in "Escape From New York." Mary Kay Place is underutilized as the supportive wife, while Meadow Sisto is, like, pretty cool as the boy-crazed Valley girl (from Chicago?) of a daughter.

Pic's highlights come largely from travelogue scenery and a sprightly musical score mixing Calypso-like rhythms with more conventional strains. Other tech credits are relatively seaworthy, though not enough to keep the voyage on course.

— *Brian Lowry*

THE VAGRANT

A Metro-Goldwyn-Mayer release of a Brooksfilms production in association with Le Studio Canal. Produced by Gillian Richardson. Co-produced by Randy Auerbach. Executive producer, Mel Brooks. Directed by Chris Walas. Screenplay, Richard Jefferies. Camera (Deluxe color), Jack Wallner, John J. Connor; editor, Jay Ignaszewski; music, Christopher Young; production design, Michael Bolton; art direction, Eric A. Fraser; set decorator, Andrew Bernard; costume design, Katherine Dover; sound, Jennifer L. Ware; stunt coordinator, Robert King; casting, Bill Shepard. Reviewed at Chestnut Station Theaters, Chicago, Sept. 10, 1992. MPAA Rating: R. Running time: **91 MIN.**
Graham Krakowski . . . . . Bill Paxton
Lt. Ralf Barfuss . . . Michael Ironside
The Vagrant . . . . Marshall Bell
Edie Roberts . . . . Mitzi Kapture
Judy Dansig . . . . Colleen Camp
Doattie . . . . Patrika Darbo
Chuck . . . . Mark McClure
Mr. Feemster . . . . . . Stuart Pankin
Det. Lackson . . . Derek Mark Lochran
Mrs. Howler . . . . Mildred Brion

As psychological suspense thrillers go, "The Vagrant" should wind up pretty near the bottom of the barrel. Obviously made on a shoestring, the picture strives much too hard for its occasional moments of very broad, Mel Brooksian humor and then fails to deliver on the thrills and suspense it promised.

Director Chris Walas, the special effects makeup whiz, here displays little feeling for pacing and character development. Given pic's overall poor quality, it's readily apparent why this Brooksfilm production hasn't received wide distribution.

Richard Jefferies' script quickly introduces a nondescript, almost nerdy business exec Bill Paxton, who chooses to settle in a run-down house near what appears to be an urban wasteland where the hideous-looking Vagrant (Marshall Bell) is camped out. Though much about the film looks chintzy, no expense was spared on Bell's makeup.

Paxton soon discovers the menacing but clever vagrant has free and easy access to his new home, a revelation prompting the horrified businessman to transform his modest bungalow into a ridiculously overfortified fortress. The visual joke comes too early in the film and falls flat.

What ensues is a moderately grisly tale of murder and mayhem awkwardly suggesting the businessman could be turning into the film's psychopathic killer instead of the Vagrant. In the process of trying to get the Vagrant kept locked up, his life falls apart as he looses his best friend, girlfriend, job, house and sanity.

On the run from a dim-witted detective (Michael Ironside), Paxton signs on as the manager of a bizarre trailer park before confronting the Vagrant in a gruesome final encounter that tries with little success to tie up the story's psychological loose ends.

Limp pic's performances are generally of the caricature variety. Paxton seems at a loss as to how to play his character, while Bell's vagrant is mostly a series of well-executed grunts and groans. Cinematography is forgettable; ditto the lackluster music, editing and set decoration. —*Lewis Lazare*

HARD HUNTED

A Malibu Bay Films release. Produced by Arlene Sidaris. Directed, written by Andy Sidaris. Camera (Filmservice color), Mark Morris; editor, Craig Stewart; music, Richard Lyons; production design, Cher Ledwith; art direction, William Pryor; costume design, Miye Matsumoto; sound (Ultra-Stereo), Mike Hall; stunt coordinator, Christian Drew Sidaris; special effects, Eddie Surkin. Reviewed at Planet Hollywood screening room, N.Y., June 17, 1992. MPAA Rating: R. Running time: **97 MIN.**
Donna Hamilton . . . . . . Dona Speir
Nicole Justin . . . . . Roberta Vasquez
Bruce Christian . . . . . Bruce Penhall
Kane . . . . R.J. Moore
Lucas . . . . Tony Peck
Edy Stark . . . . . . Cynthia Brimhall
Raven . . . . Al Leong
Pico . . . . Rodrigo Obregon
Shane Abeline . . . . Michael J. Shane
　Also with: Ava Cadell, Skip Ward, Chu Chu Malave, Richard Cansino, Carolyn Liu, Buzzy Kerbox, Mika Quintard, Brett Baxter Clark, Paul Cody.

One of the better entries in the "Malibu Express" series of action films, "Hard Hunted" is a quality mix of stunts and T&A. Opening in Arizona where it was partially filmed, pic should score in pay cable and video.

Filmmaking team of writer-director Andy Sidaris and producer Arlene Sidaris have created a brand name with seven features concerning a team of Hawaii-based female secret agents. First of these, "Malibu Express" with Sybil Danning, has been playing almost continuously for seven years on pay-cable.

"Hard Hunted" benefits from return appearances by most of the actors from earlier films in the series, including star Dona Speir in her sixth straight assignment. Partnered once again with Roberta Vasquez, she's thrust into this adventure while on vacation in Arizona.

The duo become unwitting pawns in villain R.J. Moore's quest to retrieve a jade Buddha containing a device that's used in atomic bombs, stolen from a Chinese lab.

The feds supporting the women are summoned to Hawaii to battle Moore, but film ends in a stand-off with protagonists to settle the score in the next film in the series, "Fit to Kill."

Notwithstanding some campy dialogue and Sidaris' trademark gratuitous nude scenes featuring lovely models, "Hard Hunted" develops a more serious tone than its predecessor films.

Particularly engrossing is the first reel or so in which newcomer Mika Quintard teams with stunning Carolyn Liu (introduced in the last film "Do or Die") to steal the jade Buddha in action-packed, suspenseful footage.

Other highlights include well-staged stunts involving a miniature attack helicopter manned by Moore's chief henchman Al Leong, familiar as one of Brandon Lee's most imposing adversaries in the current release "Rapid Fire."

While initially used as alluring decoration, the women in Sidaris films are now quite convincing as action heroines, with both leads Speir and Vasquez solid in this department.

Roger Moore's son R.J. Moore makes a suave villain in his U.S. feature debut, while Gregory Peck's son Tony is also in the cast as head good guys.

Filming on numerous sites in Hawaii, Arizona and California belies pic's modest budget.
— *Lawrence Cohn*

HERO

A Columbia Pictures release of a Laura Ziskin production. Produced by Ziskin. Executive producer, Joseph M. Caracciolo. Directed by Stephen Frears. Screenplay by David Webb Peoples; story by Ziskin, Alvin Sargent, Peoples. Camera (Technicolor color), Oliver Stapleton; editor, Mick Audsley; music, George Fenton; production design, Dennis Gassner; art direction, Leslie McDonald; set decoration, Nancy Haigh; costume design, Richard Hornung; sound (Dolby), Jerry Ross; associate producer, Sandy Isaac; assistant director, Louis D'Esposito; casting, Howard Feuer, Juliet Taylor. Reviewed at Cineplex Odeon Century City Theaters, L.A., Sept. 18, 1992. MPAA Rating: PG-13. Running time: **116 MIN.**
Bernie Laplante . . . . Dustin Hoffman
Gale Gayley . . . . Geena Davis
John Bubber . . . . Andy Garcia
Evelyn . . . . Joan Cusack
Chucky . . . . Kevin J. O'Connor
Winston . . . . Maury Chaykin
Wallace . . . . . . Stephen Tobolowsky
Conklin . . . . . Christian Clemenson
Chick . . . . Tom Arnold
　Also with: James Madio, Chevy Chase, Fisher Stevens.

Third-act heroics help but can't rescue filmmaker Stephen Frears' most concerted mainstream push. Muddled effort cleverly skewering media and societal fascination with heroes doesn't create compelling characters for its big-name leads. Marquee value and a crowd-pleasing finale should salvage solid box office returns, however, although flabby narrative should soften "Hero's" bottom line.

The story centers on Bernie Laplante (Dustin Hoffman), a shiftless, small-time hood whose antics have cost him his wife and child, and he's due to be sentenced to jail for his latest misdemeanor. He stumbles onto a plane crash and ends up saving the people aboard.

No one gets a good look at him, and a TV reporter on the plane (Geena Davis) begins a search to find the unknown hero, dubbed "the angel of Flight 104." Eventually, that title falls to John Bubber (Andy Garcia), a homeless Vietnam veteran with movie-star looks under the dirt, who comes forward to claim the $1 million reward after giving Bernie a lift after the accident. Bubber, as a consequence, is hailed as the next coming of Jesus and Gandhi, even as Bernie's fortunes continue to sour.

Written by David Webb Peoples ("Unforgiven"), "Hero" is peppered with occasional gems but has to sift through a lot of wreckage to find them. Lacking focus, pic jumps back and forth

between Davis, probably pic's most marketable asset as the career-driven reporter attracted to her pseudo-savior, and the self-centered Bernie, who's hard-pressed to explain his act of selfless heroism.

Unfortunately, action tilts too heavily toward Hoffman, who simply mucks it up. Seemingly playing a bad version of Ratso Rizzo had he survived events in "Midnight Cowboy," his mumbling and poorly accented line readings are so annoying and put on that it takes roughly half the pic to acclimate to them.

Aside from being a first-rate example of talent packaging (made rather obvious by Garcia as a hilariously youthful Vietnam vet), the film at best offers several amusing, "Network"-esque observations about the media: Davis' station adopts a crashing plane as its logo and interviews a potential suicide live from the ledge.

Frears brings an approach to this potentially biting material that's too purposefully mundane, lacking the edginess that distinguished his earlier work.

The story, already long at nearly two hours, nevertheless feels choppy, since Davis is never really shown making the ethical or emotional leap her character needs. Garcia, in the same vein, arrives late as the made-for-TV hero and is never adequately fleshed out, particularly the gnawing self-doubt about his falsely acquired notoriety that spurs the climactic sequence.

Ultimately this mish-mash of media satire and cute throwaway lines (Bernie eschews credit for his deed because "I'm a cash kind of guy") should play okay with a Friday-night audience, but creatively, it's too little.

Tech contributions are superior, including almost irresistible score by George Fenton, clever crash-and-rescue sequence and dead-on TV pieces. Pic also benefits from nice perfs in smaller roles, including Kevin J. O'Connor as Davis' cameraman.
— *Brian Lowry*

INNOCENT BLOOD

A Warner Bros. release of a Lee Rich production. Produced by Rich, Leslie Belzberg. Executive producer, Jonathan Sheinberg. Directed by John Landis. Screenplay, Michael Wolk. Camera (Technicolor), Mac Ahlberg; editor, Dale Beldin; music, Ira Newborn; production design, Richard Sawyer; set design, Carl Stensel; set decoration, Peg Cummings; costume design, Deborah Nadoolman; sound (Dolby), Joseph Geisinger; special visual effects, Syd Dutton, Bill Tay-

lor; special makeup effects, Steve Johnson; stunt coordinator, Rick Avery; associate producer, Wolk; assistant director, Nicholas Mastandrea; casting, Sharon Howard-Field. Reviewed at Village Theater, L.A., Sept. 22, 1992. MPAA Rating: R. Running time: **112 MIN.**
Marie . . . . Anne Parillaud
Sal (The Shark) Macelli . Robert Loggia
Joe Gennaro . . . . . Anthony LaPaglia
Lenny . . . . David Proval
Emmanuel Bergman . . . Don Rickles
Tony . . . . Chazz Palminteri
Also with: Rocco Sisto, Kim Coates.

Teens and genre fans should eat up John Landis' latest mix of horror and camp comedy, which promises to tap a deep artery in the box office blood bank. Warner Bros. didn't fare terribly well with its first-to-the-beach Columbus pic but will do better with the fall's first vampire flick (though it's doubtful anyone will confuse this lightweight entry with "Bram Stoker's Dracula").

In fact, Landis doesn't even bother to follow most rules of films dealing with the undead or, for that matter, ever actually use the word "vampire." Neither does the film explain how the pic's comely protagonist (Anne Parillaud, last seen being sexy and deadly in "La Femme Nikita") got that way.

That won't matter much to fans, however, who will "ooh" at the various gross-out scenes and nifty special effects, "aah" at the film's sensuality and Parillaud's easy nudity, and savor the numerous in-jokes and horror references, from cameos by other goremeister directors to clips from various late-show staples.

Using a set-up (by first-time screenwriter Michael Wolk) that can best be described as "Fright Night" meets Landis' "The Blues Brothers," the director also benefits from a toothy performance by Robert Loggia as a mob boss who, endowed with vampiric powers by the mysterious Marie (Parillaud), goes on a rampage.

Marie ends up dining on several of Loggia's henchmen as well. She normally kills her "food" after draining it but doesn't get the chance in Loggia's case, forcing her to team up with a cop (Anthony LaPaglia) to stop him.

Eschewing fangs in favor of a nifty glowing-eye effect, Landis exhibits the fondness for the genre that characterized his "An American Werewolf in London," as well as some of the wretched excess that's plagued his work, as evidenced by the overblown, unspectacular finale.

Those who've sat through as many horror movies as Landis will also wonder why these particular vampires cast a reflection in mirrors, have no trouble going to church and die so easily, although the frenetic pace may keep less demanding moviegoers from pausing to ask.

Regardless, Landis' tendency toward overkill proves more muted here, and the director adds some adult appeal via the strong sexual element in the Parillaud-LaPaglia, vampire-human pairing, including one steamy encounter that may be the film's best and most original moment.

Making her U.S. film debut, Parillaud struggles a bit with enunciation and a quickly abandoned voiceover narration but nonetheless has charisma to spare, oozing sexuality, playfulness and menace all at once. With a little more vocal training for those stuffy Americans, the French actress has all the makings of a major star domestically in addition to internationally.

LaPaglia is likable and properly confused as the cop, while much of the rest of the cast provide a convincing gallery of "Godfather" rejects. Cameos include sci-fi/horror guru Forrest J. Ackerman, directors Frank Oz, Sam Raimi, Tom Savini and Michael Ritchie, plus Don Rickles as the mob boss' lawyer, suffering a fate lawyer-haters everywhere will doubtless relish.

Tech credits are top-notch, particularly the state-of-the-art (if overused) makeup effects and various stunts involving vampiric feats of strength. Landis again makes clever use of popular music to flesh out the comedy, in this case the appropriate Sinatra standards "I've Got You Under My Skin" and "That Old Black Magic." — *Brian Lowry*

RICH IN LOVE

An MGM release of a Zanuck Co. production. Produced by Richard D. Zanuck, Lili Fini Zanuck. Co-producers, David Brown, Gary Daigler. Directed by Bruce Beresford. Screenplay, Alfred Uhry, from Josephine Humphreys' novel. Camera (Deluxe color), Peter James; editor, Mark Warner; music, Georges Delerue; production design, John Stoddart; art direction; set design, Carl Copeland; set decoration, John Anderson; costume design, Colleen Kelsall; sound (Dolby), Hank Garfield, Steve Maslow, Gregg Landaker; assistant director, Katterli A. Frauenfelder; casting, Shari Rhodes. Reviewed at Filmland screening room, Culver City, Calif., Sept. 24, 1992. MPAA Rating: PG-13. Running time: **105 MIN.**
Warren Odom . . . . . . Albert Finney
Helen Odom . . . . Jill Clayburgh
Lucille Odom . . . . . Kathryn Erbe
Billy McQueen . . . . Kyle MacLachlan
Vera Delmage . . . . . . Piper Laurie
Wayne Frobiness . . . . Ethan Hawke
Rae Odom . . . . Suzy Amis
Rhody Poole . . . . . Alfre Woodard

The creative team that brought "Driving Miss Daisy" to the screen fails to conjure up similar magic with "Rich in Love." Despite a luminous performance by Kathryn Erbe, the story of a South Carolina teen's coming of age in a dysfunctional family seems overly familiar and dramatically diffuse. Bruce Beresford's direction is elegant and sensitive but doesn't bring out the poignancy the story demands. Commercial prospects appear modest.

"Daisy" playwright/scriptwriter Alfred Uhry, recruited by producers Richard Zanuck and Lili Fini Zanuck to adapt a novel by Josephine Humphreys, has a fine ear for Southern dialogue that's colorful but not too arch. But this languidly paced film follows a meandering narrative line that seems to have trouble coming to its point.

Is it a story about the shattering effect of divorce on Erbe and her aimless, recently retired father (Albert Finney)? Not really, since they eventually adapt quite well to life without mom (Jill Clayburgh), who briefly pops in and out of the film without making much of an impression.

A more central concern is the seemingly inevitable scattering of contemporary family relationships, with Erbe's strength of character providing the glue binding the various members of the eccentric Odom clan. Her maturation, signalled too abruptly at the end, gives film its meaning.

Finney fits into his Charleston accent like an old shoe, but he's working here with an unfocused character and using his technical virtuosity to carry it along. He confidently dominates pic's first half but virtually disappears from the second. The unglamorized but compellingly watchable Erbe occasionally puts the viewer in mind of Julie Harris in "The Member of the Wedding," yet Erbe plays the de facto head of the family, with her own peculiar blend of iron-butterfly Southern charm, girlish naiveté and blinkered earnestness.

Though the character's deepest feelings remain below the surface, it isn't Erbe's fault: She commendably avoids punching obvious emotional buttons. Pic's overly genteel, rather bloodless feeling seems more a function of its inability to come to grips with the girl's role in other lives.

A brief romantic interlude with Kyle MacLachlan, Yankee husband of her neurotic older sister (Suzy Amis), never develops into much of anything because his character is so amorphous.

Piper Laurie is hokey as Finney's blowsy new squeeze, Ethan Hawke is a cipher as Erbe's young friend, and Alfre Woodard is okay in a potentially interesting but ill-defined role as a family friend.

The Odoms' old white frame house, which visually echoes their mild decadence, is picturesquely placed next to the ocean outside Charleston. Though "Rich in Love" started production before the release of "The Prince of Tides," Beresford and lenser Peter James often visually echo the far superior Barbra Streisand picture.

Pic is dedicated to composer Georges Delerue, who died shortly after completing this score, which has his characteristic delicacy but can't pull the entire emotional weight placed upon it.
— *Joseph McBride*

THE MIGHTY DUCKS

A Buena Vista release of a Walt Disney presentation, in association with Touchstone Pacific Partners I of an Avnet/Kerner production. Produced by Jordan Kerner, Jon Avnet. Co-producers, Lynn Morgan, Martin Hubert. Directed by Stephen Herek. Screenplay, Steven Brill. Camera (Technicolor, Panavision), Thomas Del Ruth; editors, Larry Bock, John F. Link; music, David Newman; production design, Randy Ser; art direction, Tony Fanning; set design, Jack Ballance; set decoration, Julie Kay Fanton; costume design, Grania Preston; special effects supervisor, Paul Murphy; assistant director, Douglas E. Wise; casting, Renee Rousselot. Reviewed at Avco Center Cinema, L.A., Sept. 23, 1992. MPAA Rating: PG. Running time: **101 MIN.**
Gordon Bombay . . . . Emilio Estevez
Hans . . . . Joss Ackland
Coach Reilly . . . . Lane Smith
Casey . . . . Heidi Kling
Gerald Ducksworth . . . Josef Sommer
Charlie Conroy . . . . Joshua Jackson

Disney faces a marketing challenging in "The Mighty Ducks," a formulaic pic meant for children but actually focusing on a yuppie's struggle for redemption. Mildly entertaining but unexciting pic (with a blah title) will enjoy a short theatrical life before leaving stronger impact in videoland.

Emilio Estevez stars as an accomplished but arrogant lawyer who carelessly gets nailed on drunk driving charges. His stern boss cuts a deal for him to do community service instead of suffering the humiliation of court. Once Estevez meets the undisciplined, street-wise kids whom he must shape into a winning peewee hockey team, pic becomes predictable and mighty preachy.

Estevez is a driven workaholic who needs to regain his humanity and re-establish his self-worth. These tasks are fulfilled via his engrossing bond with a bright, fatherless kid (Joshua Jackson) who becomes his surrogate son. Male-dominated adventure also contains a contrived romance between Estevez and Heidi Kling, kid's tough but vulnerable mom.

Political correctness informs the film from the careful ethnic and gender composition of the hockey team to pic's value system: teamwork over aggressive individualism and concentration over strength.

Steven Brill's schematic script contains a few inspired one-liners, but not enough to distract attention from plot machinery.

Fortunately, the appealing Estevez holds the film together, credibly balancing the crude and compassionate dimensions of his character. As his big boss, great character actor Josef Sommer is underutilized; same with Lane Smith as Estevez' former coach and now rival. Of the kids, roles are not distinguishable enough to make individual impressions; save Jackson, who gives a natural, endearing performance.

Helmer Stephen Herek endows a familiar story with a crisp look and swift tempo, seldom allowing sanctimonious tale to linger too long or gags to get too tiresome. In pic's second part, the pace is accelerated by skillful montages of hockey games.

Thomas Del Ruth's proficient lensing of Minneapolis winter is handsome. David Newman's score has an appropriately bouncy sweep to it; pop tunes are well integrated into the narrative.

— *Emanuel Levy*

MR. BASEBALL

A Buena Vista release of a Walt Disney presentation, A Universal release of an Outlaw production in association with Pacific Artists produced in association with Dentsu. Produced by Fred Schepisi, Doug Claybourne, Robert Newmyer. Executive producers, John Kao, Jeffrey Silver. Executive producer-Japan, Susumu Kondoh. Japanese line producer, Tomoo Ito. Directed by Schepisi. Screenplay, Gary Ross, Kevin Wade, Monte Merrick, story by Theo Pelletier, John Junkerman. Camera (Deluxe color, Panavision widescreen), Ian Baker; editor, Peter Ho-

ness; music, Jerry Goldsmith; production design, Ted Haworth; art direction, Katsumi Nakazawa; set decoration, Yuuki Sato, Hirohide Shibata; costume design, Bruce Finlayson; sound (Dolby), David Kelson; assistant directors, Bruce Moriarty, Kazuto Kunishige (Japan); casting, Dianne Crittenden, Kenji Saitoh (Japan). Reviewed at the Hollywood Galaxy Theater, L.A., Sept. 24, 1992. MPAA Rating: PG-13. Running time: **109 MIN.**
Jack Elliot . . . . Tom Selleck
Uchiyama . . . . Ken Takakura
Hiroko Uchiyama . . . Aya Takanashi
Max (Hammer) . . . . Dennis Haysbert
Yoji Nishimura . . . . . . Toshi Shioya
Toshi Yamashita . . Kohsuke Toyohara
Ryoh Mukai . . . . . Toshizo Fujiwara
Shinji Igarashi . . . . Mak Takano
Hiroshi Kurosawa . . . Kenji Morinaga
Tomohiko Ohmae . . . . Joh Nishimura

In the opening scene of "Mr. Baseball," aging slugger Tom Selleck dreams he gets several extra swings past strike three. It doesn't matter, though, because he keeps swinging and missing, and it's the same with the film: A strikeout is a strikeout. Universal's $40 million-plus exercise in cross-cultural comedy will land in a b.o. league of its own — in the cellar.

Pic's a tame look at the cultural differences that erupt from a surly Yank trying to adjust his strapping frame and bad attitude to the rigid strictures of Japanese sport and society. Viewers who have been to Japan will appreciate many of the little observations and details, but these are the things of journalism, not dramatic narrative.

Given the central character of Jack Elliot, former Yankee World Series MVP who's traded off to Japan to make way for a young prospect (played by White Sox star Frank Thomas), there's only one direction in which the story can go, and it does, as if by prescription: He arrives in Nagoya to play for the Chunichi Dragons, hates it, looks down on all these little men who play such a safe, conformist brand of baseball, bristles at his stern manager, then finally starts getting it together as he begins to accept the virtues of the harmonic Japanese approach.

Also, an interracial romance between Elliot and the beautiful, Westernized Hiroko (Aya Takanashi), daughter of the Dragons' manager (Ken Takakura), stirs up prejudicial feelings within the family.

Selleck is utterly believable as the star who can't deal with his sudden demotion, but even his broad shoulders can't carry the weight of the entire pic. All the

Japanese remain one-dimensional, and while Selleck's character might have worked well as part of an ensemble, it doesn't begin to have to kind of depth needed when a character is going to be front-and-center in every scene.

Australian helmer Fred Schepisi is unable to bring his customary visual elegance or psychological penetration to this unwieldy production, which is rather messy visually. Ending is implausible, and U.S.-based coda is emotionally feeble. — *Todd McCarthy*

DRAGON INN
(HONG KONG)

A SeeYuen Film presentation of a Film Workshop (a Golden Harvest subsidiary) production. Produced by Tsui Hark. Presented by Ng See Yuen. Line producers, Cho King Man, Ng Chi Ming. Production supervisor, Ching Siu Tung. Directed by Raymond Lee. Screenplay, Tsui Hark, Carbon Cheung, Xiao Wu. Camera (color), Lau Moon Tong, Arthur Wong; editor, Poon Hung; music, Philip Chan; art direction, Willian Chang, Mark Chiu; set design, Leung Chi Hing, Chung Yee Fung; martial arts directors, Ching Siu Tung, Yuen Bun; special effects, Cinefex Workshop. Reviewed at Sung Sing Theater, N.Y., Sept. 16, 1992. Running time: **90 MIN.**
Jade King . . . . Maggie Cheung
Mo . . . . Brigitte Lin
Chow . . . . Tony Leung
Eunuch Tsao Yin . . . . . Donnie Yen
Also with: Xiong Xin Xin, Lau Shun, Yem Yee Kwan, Yuen Cheung Yan, Lawrence Ng Kai Wah.
(In Cantonese with English & Chinese subtitles)

At the very least, "Dragon Inn" will educate viewers that eunuchs were once potentates. This historical epic recounts the time during the Ming dynasty when a cabal of eunuchs seized power and a handful of patriots resisted them. Handsomely mounted and technically polished action feature should do well in areas where H.K. martial arts pics click. Despite strong thesping by the three leads, usual outrageous bits of fantasy hokum in the fight scenes will keep film from being taken seriously outside those markets.

Most of the plot takes place at an inn, a popular venue in past historical chopsocky pics, most notably King Hu's "The Fate of Lee Khan." In fact, current opus is a remake of Hu's "Dragon Gate Inn." Where "Khan" was praised for treating the inn as a dramatic stage, inn of this title is more like a labyrinth with swords coming out of walls and the building lined with chutes and secret passages.

Mo (Brigitte Lin) and her cohorts are trying to save a murdered minister's kids from the Eunuch Yin's forces when they stop at the inn, an oasis in the desert. A kind of malevolent Rick's Place, escapees from the empire seek safe passage through there, only to be undone by the seductive, spidery proprietor Jade King (Maggie Cheung) who sells her charges to the highest bidder. Her callousness is tested when she meets the handsome Chow (Tony Leung), Mo's accomplice in aiding escapees.

Mo and Jade, instant and appealing rivals, engage in a good bit of striptease combat (but not revealing enough for prurient interest.) Climactic desert battle with characters cavorting under the sands like moles has the evil despot battling the three principals assisted by a pugnacious

Original film
LUNG MUN KAR CHUAN
(DRAGON INN)
(HONG KONG)

A Shaw Bros. release (in Southeast Asia) of a Union Film production supervised by Chang Tao-jan. Stars Shangkuan Ling-feng, Shih Cheng, Pe Ying. Produced by Sha Yung-fong. Directed by Hu Chin-chuan. Camera (Uniscope Eastman Color), Hua Hui-ying; art director, Tsou Jyh-liang; production manager, Yang Shih-chin; unit manager, Chang Jou-ying. No other credits given. Reviewed at King's Theater, Hong Kong, Aug. 25, 1966. Running time: **108 MIN.**
Chu Hui . . . . . Shangkuan Ling-feng
Hsiao Shao-tzu . . . . Shih Cheng
Tsao Shao-chin . . . . Pe Ying
Yu Hsin . . . . Hsu Feng
Inn Keeper Wu . . . . Tsao Chien
Officer . . . . Li Chieh
Inn manager . . . . Kao Ming
Inn servant . . . . . . Ko Hsiao-pao
Qun Yu-chang . . . . Kao Fei
Chu Chi . . . . Hsieh Han

chef who can skin a human limb to the bone faster than you can say "jinsu."

Leung, who also starred in the European hit "The Lover," gives ample display of his charms but is more than matched by the femme leads.

Direction is credited to Raymond Lee, but big-name directors on board are Tsui Hark, as producer and co-writer, and Ching Siu Tung of "Chinese Ghost Story" as production supervisor and one of film's two able martial arts directors. Lee deserves plaudits for keeping the story taut and involving. Cinematography is accomplished and painterly. Film is purported to have been shot entirely in mainland China.
— *Fred Lombardi*

DOUBLE EDGE
(U.S.-ISRAELI)

A Castle Hill Prods. release. Produced by Amos Kollek, Rafi Reibenbach. Executive producer, Michael Steinhardt. Directed, written by Kollek. Camera (color), Amnon Salomon; editor, David Tour, Vicki Hiatt; music, Mira J. Spektor; set design, Zvika Aloni; costume design, Rakefet Levy, Bernardine Morgan; assistant director, Udi Yerushalmi. Reviewed at Magno Review 1 screening room, N.Y., Aug. 24, 1991. MPAA Rating: PG-13. Running time: **86 MIN.**
Faye Milano . . . . . . Faye Dunaway
David . . . . Amos Kollek
Mustafa Shafik . . . Mohammad Bakri
Ahmed Shafik . . . . . Makram Khouri
Max . . . . Michael Shneider
Moshe . . . . Shmuel Shiloh
Censor . . . . Anat Atzmon
Sarah . . . . Ann Belkin
Also with: Teddy Kollek, Abba Eban, Meir Kahane, Hanan Ashrawi, Ziad Abu Za'Yad, Naomi Altaraz.

Amos Kollek takes a fresh look at the ongoing Israeli/Palestinian crisis in the "Double Edge." Strong thesping by Faye Dunaway should focus attention on this interesting indie production.

Dunaway portrays a reporter for the fictional New York Herald who gets a three-week assignment in Israel. Determined to impress her bosses back home with front page stories, she hits the streets of Jerusalem and Arab towns on the West Bank in search of high-profile interviews and breaking news.

Befriended by a novelist (played by director Amos Kollek) in the Israeli army reserves, she gets her an interview with his uncle, Jerusalem mayor Teddy Kollek (director's real-life dad).

As an American disillusioned by Israeli policies of recent years, Dunaway takes a pro-Palestinian slant on several stories involving Israeli reprisals in Intefada incidents, running afoul of the government censor.

Episodic film contains interspersed interviews by the reporter with real-life figures, from the militant Rabbi Meir Kahane (murdered in New York shortly after filming here) to the familiar Palestinian spokeswoman Hanan Ashrawi. This "witnesses" technique adds verisimilitude and balance to the film but detracts from the forward narrative thrust.

Kollek's low-key lead role makes for an effective foil to Dunaway's hard-driving performance. Her casting is something of a coup, combining glamor, the otherness of a waspish American star and the gung-ho willfulness

she displayed in "Network."

Kollek unfortunately fumbles a key subplot in the final minutes. Dunaway finds out that she's gotten a story all wrong damning Kollek for hurting an Arab child he in fact aided as a Good Samaritan. It's too late to pull the story from her next edition. Film ends before Kollek's character discovers the trashing, and viewer is cheated out of the expected "Absence of Malice" Paul Newman/Sally Field-like confrontation.

Instead, the chilling finale literally thrusts the gut issues of the Arab/Israeli stand-off in the viewer's face. Blasé to danger, Dunaway finds herself alone on a remote road in a car being rocked back and forth by angry Arab kids. Pulling a gun out of the glove compartment, she's suddenly at ground zero, propelled by her own survival instincts.

Low-budget production benefits from on-location lensing and Kollek's decision to avoid thriller clichés and stage even the most violent scenes against idyllic, sunny day backdrops. Supporting cast, especially Arab actor Mohammad Bakri as a duplicitous militant for the Palestinian cause, is convincing.
— *Lawrence Cohn*

SOUTH CENTRAL

A Warner Bros. release of an Oliver Stone presentation of an Ixtlan production in association with Monument Pictures & Enchantment Films. Produced by Janet Yang, William B. Steakley. Line producer, Lowell D. Blank. Co-producer, Steve Anderson. Executive producer, Stone. Co-exec producers, Michael Spielberg, Brad Gilbert. Directed, written by Anderson, based on Donald Bakeer's novel "Crips." Camera (Deluxe color), Charlie Lieberman; editor, Steve Nevius; music, Tim Truman; production design, David Brian Miller, Marina Kieser; art direction, Andrew D. Brothers; set decoration, Caroline Stover; costume design, Mary Law Weir; sound (Dolby), Michael Florimbi, Rick Ash, Dean Zupancic; stunt coordinator, Julius LeFlore; assistant director, Phillip Christon; casting, Jaki Brown. Reviewed at Warner Bros. screening room, Burbank, Calif., Sept. 9, 1992. MPAA rating: R. Running time: **99 MIN.**
Bobby Johnson . . . . . Glenn Plummer
Ray Ray . . . . . . Byron Keith Minns
Bear . . . . Lexie D. Bigham
Loco . . . . Vincent Craig Dupree
Carole . . . . LaRita Shelby
Genie Lamp . . . . Kevin Best
Baby Jimmie . . . . . Allan Hatcher,
Alvin Hatcher
Jimmie (age 10) . . . Christian Coleman
Willie Manchester . . . . . Ivory Ocean
Nurse Shelly . . . . . Starletta Dupois
Ali . . . . Carl Lumbly

As a cautionary tale about the nihilistic life of street gangs, "South Central" speaks elo-

quently to black kids desperately in need of straight talk. A profoundly moving story of a father's attempt to save his son from his own mistakes, Steve Anderson's film has performances by Glenn Plummer and young Christian Coleman that will touch any viewer. Platform booking may need careful handling due to its subject matter but deserves widest possible release. It has the power to save lives.

With Oliver Stone exec producing for his Ixtlan banner, low-budget but polished pic benefits from authentic L.A. locations, a passionately convincing cast and a willingness not to flinch at hard truths. It's got the "ripped-from-today's-headlines" urgency of 1930s Warner Bros. social pics ("Wild Boys of the Road," "The Mayor of Hell")

Anderson's deep compassion for his characters, his ability to evoke the seething frustrations of the milieu and his sure-handed analysis of issues make this a film that should have a long life in schools, churches and other community venues beyond its theatrical run.

Based on a novel by an L.A. teacher, pic for the most part treats the symptoms of social breakdown without dealing directly with the root causes. But by using one man's story as a microcosm for the inner-city plagues of drugs, gang warfare and family distintegration, pic rings a loud alarm about the terrible price of society's indifference.

Starting in 1981, pic picks up Plummer as a hardened gang leader getting out of jail and drifting back into the clutches of charismatic Deuces boss Byron Keith Minns. Minns wants to make the nabe "safe for our kids and our bitches," but his way of doing so is to take over the local drug business from ruthless pusher/pimp Kevin Best.

To Plummer's surprise, he finds that he's become a father while in jail, but he's drawn instinctively to his infant son, carrying him everywhere. The director gets fascinating reactions from Alvin and Allan Hatcher, who alternate in the role, providing unspoken counterpoint amid omnipresent danger.

Since Best has appropriated Plummer's PCP-addict wife (LaRita Shelby), Plummer is easily manipulated into murdering the pusher, which sends him to prison for 10 years. While in the slammer, Plummer is trans-

formed into a man of reason and idealism by his Muslim cellmate (Carl Lumbly), who teaches him from a range of black leaders, including Booker T. Washington, W.E.B. DuBois, Martin Luther King Jr. and Jesse Jackson.

Lumbly urges Plummer to overcome the "cycle of hate" that society inflicts on black men by using the power of his fatherly love. He also educates Plummer about the evils of drugs, quoting Jackson's line, "We have allowed death to change his name from Southern rope to Northern dope."

Thus armed with new strength of character, Plummer goes forth from prison to a painful reunion with his son, who has a beatific look but is already a swaggering little Deuce. The powerful realization of what his example has done to his son, who's become the focus of his existence, gives Plummer all the more reason to risk everything to rescue him from "starting this whole thing all over again."

The direction is suitably unobtrusive and tech credits are pro, including Charlie Lieberman's grittily attractive lensing, Steve Nevius' taut editing and Tim Truman's somber symphonic music. — *Joseph McBride*

TORONTO FEST

PASSION FISH

An Atchafalaya Films production. Produced by Sarah Green, Maggie Renzi. Executive producer, John Sloss. Directed, written, edited by John Sayles. Camera (Duart color), Roger Deakins; music, Mason Daring; production design, Dan Bishop, Dianna Freas; costume design, Cynthia Flynt; sound (Dolby), John Sutton; assistant director, Steve Apicella; casting, Barbara Hewson Shapiro. Reviewed at Toronto Festival of Festivals, Sept. 19, 1992. Running time: **134 MIN.**
May-Alice Culhane . . Mary McDonnell
Chantelle . . . . Alfre Woodard
Rennie . . . . David Strathairn
Sugar LeDoux . . . Vondie Curtis-Hall
Ti-Marie . . . . Nora Dunn
Kim . . . . Sheila Kelley
Dawn/Rhonda . . . . . Angela Bassett
Reeves . . . . Leo Burmester
Precious . . . . Mary Portser
Denita . . . . Shauntisa Willis
Dr. Blades . . . . John Henry
Redwood Vance . . . . Michael Laskin

John Sayles charts the long road back from physical and emotional debilitation in "Passion Fish," a sympathetic if somewhat deliberate and overlong intimate study of two women emerging from their protective shells. Backed by some strong reviews and interest from upscale female audiences, this indie production could find a modest foothold in specialized theatrical release, but is too prosaic and telefilm-like in format to be the picture that breaks Sayles' b.o. jinx.

After the tumultuous urban problems and criss-crossing stories of "City of Hope," Sayles has turned to the interior struggles involved with battling afflictions, coping with unexpected life changes, letting down one's protective guard and developing friendships in middle age. Pic has a measure of charm, plenty of validity and some fine scenes, but lacks the intensity that would have made it galvanizing or transcendent.

Mary McDonnell plays May-Alice, a TV soap star who becomes paralyzed from the waist down in an accident she suffers en route to getting her legs waxed in New York. Retreating to her childhood womb, she installs herself in the deserted family home in Louisiana's Cajun Country and nastily rejects a succession of nurses until Chantelle (Alfred Woodard) comes along.

Understandably bitter, May-Alice sinks into a daily grind of drinking and nonstop TV watching. Not for long willing to tolerate maid status, Chantelle soon throws out the booze and forces her employer to shape up.

But Chantelle is fighting demons of her own. She used to live the high life in Chicago, but her drug addiction resulted in her daughter being placed in her father's custody. She needs to hold on to her job with May-Alice as much as the physically crippled woman requires help.

The slow emergence of trust and friendship between the two deeply inward women is enlivened considerably by the appearance on the scene of two local gentlemen. Dating back to high school, May-Alice always had a crush on good-looking wild man Rennie (David Strathairn) and, despite the fact that he's married with five kids and she believes she may be sexually dead, he begins hanging around more and more often.

At the same time, black Cajun cowboy Sugar LeDoux (Vondie Curtis-Hall) begins smoothly courting Chantelle. He has 10 children and a ladies' man manner that doesn't exactly inspire confidence in long-term possibilities, but his terrific friendliness slowly win her over.

Interludes with both men invigorate the picture and provide a way to introduce a welcome

dose of local color. Rennie knows every inch of the bayou backwater, and a boat excursion he leads with the two women makes for an agreeable, animal-filled travelogue. A blacksmith by trade, Sugar also plays guitar, and the live band performances of traditional, Zydeco and other tunes are rambunctious highlights.

Other relief, comic and otherwise, comes in the form of visits from a couple of bird-brained former schoolmates of May-Alice, three soap actresses from Gotham and the show's producer, who concocts a ratings-grabbing way for the paraplegic to return to the air.

More significantly, Chantelle's father turns up with her daughter to see if she might be approaching the day when she can assume her role as mother.

But mostly it's a story of the two women opening up to each other, something that happens with necessary but dramatically protracted slowness.

McDonnell's May-Alice is aware that she behaves like "a bitch on wheels," and this could have been pushed even further to humorous effect. But the actress has a constant air of over-earnestness that borders on smugness, and also an underlining prissiness that makes the many times she utters a dirty word ring false. Thesp effectively registers the thawing of her character, but doesn't exactly draw one in.

Woodard, who appeared in "Grand Canyon" with McDonnell but never in the same scene, is terrif as the fast-lane burn-out who must initially deal with her own pain by submerging it to that of her employer, and who finally finds the courage to begin embracing life again. In the end, her perf is the strongest reason to see the pic.

After his sterling work last year on "Barton Fink" and "Homicide," lenser Roger Deakins shows he's human with a decent but unremarkable visual turn. Sayles edited this one solo, and might have profited by advice to keep this small-scaled drama under two hours.

Title refers to some tiny fish that Strathairn's character finds in the belly of a large fish he catches.

—*Todd McCarthy*

TETSUO II: BODY HAMMER (JAPANESE)

An ICA Projects (U.K.) release of a Toshiba EMI presentation of a Kaijyu Theater production. Produced by Fuminori Shishido, Fumio Kurokawa. Executive producers, Hiroshi Koizumi, Shinya Tsukamoto. Directed, written by Tsukamoto. Camera (color), Tsukamoto, Fumikazu Oda, Katsunori Yokoyama; editor, Tsukamoto; music, Chu Ishikawa; art direction, Tsukamoto; special makeup-effects, Takashi Oda, Kan Takahama, Akira Fukaya. Reviewed at Century preview theater, London, Sept. 1, 1992. (In Toronto, London film fests.) Running time: **81 MIN.**
Taniguchi Tomoo . . Tomoroh Taguchi
Kana . . . . Nobu Kanaoka
Yatsu (The Guy) . . Shinya Tsukamoto
Minori . . . . Keinosuke Tomioka
Taniguchi's father . . . . . Sujin Kim
Taniguchi's mother . . . . Min Tanaka
Big skinhead . . . . . . Hideaki Tezuka
Young skinhead . . . . . Tomoo Asada
Mad scientist . . . Toraemon Utazawa

Nipponese enfant terrible Shinya Tsukamoto ladles on the cyberpunk culture in "Tetsuo II: Body Hammer," a brain-blowing follow-up to his cult hit "Tetsuo: The Iron Man." Beyond festivals, this gruesome gorefest looks to be a solid click with the midnight crowd and metal fetishists.

Pic, in color and 35m, boasts better production values than the no-budget 16m monochromer "Iron Man," but the one-man director/writer/lenser/co-exec producer/thesp still goes at it like a glorified home movie. Oriental buffs will groove on the *manga* (comic book) refs. To Western eyes, it weirdly melds Ridley Scott, David Cronenberg and "The Terminator" genre.

Though featuring several of the first pic's players, item is not a true sequel. This time out, the central character is a happily married Tokyoite, Taniguchi (Tomoroh Taguchi), whose young son is abducted in a shopping mall by psycho skinheads.

In major shock, Taniguchi sees his arm mutate into a cyber-gun. Later, when he's also kidnapped by the gang of bodybuilding skinheads, his whole body starts changing into a hideous killing machine, taking on the leader (also a mutant) and growing into a misshapen, tentacled block of metal.

Apart from a tinted, bloody flashback to Taniguchi's youth, pic is lighter on sex content than "Iron Man" and not without a wry sense of self-humor. Most of the repetitive action involves

metal monsters zapping the bejesus out of each other in a dingy warehouse. Overkill sets in early.

— *Derek Elley*

WILD WEST (BRITISH)

A Channel 4 Films presentation with the participation of British Screen of an Initial film. Produced by Eric Fellner. Co-producer, Nicky Kentish Barnes. Directed by David Attwood. Screenplay, Harwant Bains. Camera (Metrocolor), Nic Knowland; editor, Martin Walsh; music, Dominic Miller; production design, Caroline Hanania; art direction, Kave Naylor; costume design, Trisha Biggar; sound (Dolby), Chris Munro; assistant director, Chris Newman; casting, Suzanne Crowley, Gilly Poole. Reviewed at Toronto Festival of Festivals, Sept. 14, 1992. Running time: **85 MIN.**
Zaf . . . . Naveen Andrews
Rifat . . . . Sarita Choudhury
Kay . . . . Ronny Jhutti
Ali . . . . Ravi Kapoor
Gurdeep . . . . Ameet Chana
Jagdeep . . . . Bhasker
Mrs. Ayub . . . . Lalita Ahmed
Tony . . . . Shaun Scott

A charmingly picaresque comedy about a Pakistani country & western band in contempo London, "Wild West" is, as Woody Allen used to describe himself, thin but fun. Mangy and artless, this boisterous low-budgeter generates plenty of good laughs and gets lots of mileage from its comic, knowing observations about a vibrant British subculture. Novelty value and audience-pleasing qualities could make this a decent entry for limited specialized release Stateside.

First screenplay by playwright Harwant Bains and initial feature from TV director David Attwood appropriately trades in the kind of youthful dreams and determination to escape life's limitations normally associated with the U.S., not the U.K. immigrant and working classes, which have usually been portrayed as being stuck with their lot in life.

That the subjects here are young Asians living in Southall, west London, establishes the film's humorous incongruity. Zaf is an affably goofy young fellow who dresses like a cowboy, causes his mother endless grief by not being able to hold down a regular job and pursues dreams of Nashville stardom with his band the Honky Tonk Cowboys, a makeshift group comprised of himself, brothers Ali and Kay, and Sikh drummer Gurdeep.

Their crazy manager Jagdeep, who drives a Cadillac festooned with longhorns around the crime-ridden nabe, manages to get them a few gigs, but nothing clicks for the motley crew until beautiful young Rifat comes aboard as lead singer. Zaf has been pursuing her intermittently, and once she leaves her abusive white husband Tony, she's willing to try anything, including a brief roll in the hay with Zaf. Suddenly, the Cowboys are a hit, but when a record company wants to sign Rifat without the boys, it precipitates a crisis that leads to a bittersweet but optimistic fade-out.

Set in a neighborhood that seems all Asian except for some punk skinheads who, in a running gag, continually assault the brothers, pic makes lively use of a cultural backdrop that will be unfamiliar to most Yank and other international audiences.

Yet, Bains' script imaginatively exploits cross-cultural paradoxes, ironies and jokes with a glibness that keeps matters buoyant most of the time. Attwood's direction is scattershot and visually undistinguished, but it maintains a high energy level and an amiably eccentric tone.

Naveen Andrews, as the naively enthusiastic Zaf, and Bhasker, as the manic manager whose dream is to die in Beverly Hills, do everything they can to punch up the comedy, while Sarita Choudhury, so appealing in "Mississippi Masala," proves equally fetching here as the young woman who unintentionally trades marital misery for musical stardom.

Soundtrack is loaded with agreeable tunes by the likes of Steve Earle, Nanci Griffith, Garth Brooks and Dwight Yoakam. Pic was shot in Super 16m and blown up to 35m, with OK results.

— *Todd McCarthy*

EDINBURGH FEST

YOU, ME & MARLEY
(BRITISH–16m)

A BBC North production. Produced by Chris Parr. Executive producer, George Faber. Directed by Richard Spence. Screenplay, Graham Reid, from an idea by Spence. Camera (color, 16m), Graham Veevers; editor, Greg Miller; music, Stephen Warbeck; production design, David Wilson; costume design, Kayt Turner; sound, Malcolm Hill, Brian Saunders; assistant director, Nigel Taylor; associate producer, Ann Faggetter. Reviewed at Edinburgh Intl. Film Festival, Aug. 24, 1992. Running time: **86 MIN.**
Sean . . . . Marc O'Shea
Frances . . . . Bronagh Gallagher
Marley . . . . Michael Liebmann
Father Tom . . . . . . Lorcan Cranitch
Mr. Hagan . . . . Frank Grimes
Reggie Devine . . . . . Ian McElhinney
Hugh . . . . Michael Gregory
Mary . . . . Emma Moylan
Sarah . . . . Marie Jones
Rosaleen . . . . . Catherine Brennan
Mrs. Hagan . . . . . . Stella McCusker
Father Peter . . . . . . .James Greene

Full of rough, gutsy Belfast humor, "You, Me & Marley" is a powerful look at young Northern Irish no-hopers trapped in a society tearing itself apart. Politically charged pic, a prizewinner at Edinburgh, looks set to stir controversy in festival and tube outings. Theatrical chances look slimmer.

Bronagh Gallagher (the spunky young singer in "The Commitments") is one of five teens who joyride in stolen cars as an out for their frustrations. When local IRA-ites break the fingers of one of them, Marley (Michael Liebmann), to teach him a lesson in civic duty, the kids take their own revenge, setting off a vicious spiral of tit-for-tat.

Belfaster Graham Reid's tightly written script is a no-holds-barred portrait of a society populated by mobsters, drunks, nihilistic youth and endemic viciousness. "Even England would be better than this," says one kid. Their salty humor leavens pic's pessimistic tone without diluting the undercurrent of violence.

Like its central quintet, pic takes no political sides, with both Ulster police and IRA members portrayed as glorified thugs. Brit soldiers are shown as neutral peacekeepers. Violence is graphic but not lingered over.

Gallagher is excellent as the tomboyish schoolgirl with more guts than an Irish abattoir. Liebmann is a fine complement as the mercurial Marley, and there's a chilling performance from Ian McElhinney as the local IRA honcho. Thick Belfast accents, especially by the kids, could be a problem for North Americans.

For obvious reasons, pic was lensed entirely in mainland Britain, with Manchester locations convincingly repping suburban Belfast. Helmer Richard Spence brings the occasional cinematic flourish to a smooth package, neatly cut. Pic is part of the BBC's upcoming "Screen Play" series.

—*Derek Elley*

BOSTON FEST

THE RESTLESS GARDEN
(DOCU)

A Kino Eye presentation. Executive producer, Stas Namin, Andrei Kondrashin, Jim Steele. Produced by Phillip D'Arbanville. Directed by Victor Ginzburg. Camera (color), Sergei Kozlov, Ginzburg; editor, Lena Zabolotskaya; music, Sasha Lugin; sound, Misha Tikhonov. Reviewed at Copley Place Theater, Boston, Sept. 17, 1992. (In Boston Film Festival, N.Y. Independent Feature Film Market, Amsterdam Intl. Documentary Festival.) Running time: **86 MIN.**
With: Katya Rizjikova, Alexei Weitsler, Marina Shkinyova, Metal Korrosion, Natasha Kudryavtseva, LA-RE, Alla Segalova, Valery Baglai, Irini Kuznetsova, Nellie Yakovleva.

Victor Ginzburg, who left the USSR at age 14, returned in 1991 for this documentary about how political freedom had led to a new sexual frankness in pop and avant-garde culture there. Result is a one-of-a-kind film capturing the sexual revolution hitting the Soviet Union in the months before the fall.

Film uses a "happening" in Gorky Park (in the "Restless Garden" named by a 1917 Boris Pasternak poem) to introduce idea of a suddenly-liberated culture after decades of repression and government-imposed standards. Ginzburg records all the excesses without comment, as everyone from a magazine publisher to a heavy metal rock band to an absurdist stage director uses the new freedom largely to get Soviet women to take their clothes off.

The explanations for ubiquitous femme nudity are a cross between Hugh Hefner's "Playboy Philosophy" to artsy pretensiousness, with lots of claims about using eroticism as an aesthetic statement. These claims are neatly punctured by Ginzburg's images. Tellingly, the most erotic images are those of a male and female dancer, choreographed by Alla Segalova, who remain fully clothed the entire time.

Rejected by the Toronto film fest as an "exploitation film," pic bowed at the Boston fest. Viewers will need to be clued in that the film is not endorsing the rationalizations and banalities of the creators of Soviet erotica, but simply recording what was going on at a moment when everything seemed possible and no one knew how long it would last.

In many ways, "Restless Garden" brings to mind "Mondo Cane" and the other shockumentaries of the '60s. Ultimately the viewer is moved both to laughter at the naiveté and pomposity of interview subjects (a rock singer discussing porn stars clearly has no idea of what he is talking about) and to sadness about the exploitation of some Russo women. Ginzburg makes his clearest point when he interviews a young Moscow prostitute who plies her trade because she wants to afford the makeup and clothes she sees on other women.

Film should stir up interest on the fest circuit as well as in urban art houses. A November showing in Moscow is currently planned. — *Daniel M. Kimmel*

MONTREAL FEST

GOH-HIME
(BASARA — THE PRINCESS GOH)
(JAPANESE)

A Shochiku Co. presentation of a Shochiku Co. & Teshigahara Prods. co-production. Produced by Shigeyoshi Sugisaki, Yoshinobu Nishioka, Noriko Nomura. Executive producers, Kazuyoshi Okuyama, Ritsuo Isobe, Kyuemon Oda, Hiroshi Teshigahara. Co-producer, Eizo Kyoto Co. Directed by Teshigahara. Screenplay, Genpei Akasegawa, Teshigahara, based on Masaharu Fuji's novel. Camera (color), Fujio Morita; editor, Toshio Taniguchi; music, Toru Takemitsu; art direction, Yoshinobu Nishioka; costume design, Yoshiki Hishinuma; sound, Tetsuo Segawa; hair/makeup design, Shinichi Nomura; tea ceremony instructor, Tsuneo Yabe; ceramic art instructor, Yutaka Nakamura; tea ceremony production adviser, Jouchi Yabunouchi. Reviewed at Montreal World Film Festival (competition), Sept. 6, 1992. Running time: **147 MIN.**
Oribe Furuta . . . . . Tatsuya Nakadai
Princess Goh . . . . . . Rie Miyazawa
Usu . . . . Toshiya Nagasawa
Hideyoshi Toyotomi . . Katsuhiro Oida
Ieyasu Tokugawa . . . Hisashi Igawa
Ujisato Gamou . . . . Kei Suma
Toshitsune Maeda . . . Tetsuya Bessho
Ogin . . . . Kyoko Maya
Tadaoki Hosokawa . . . Kei Yamamoto

This gorgeous epic set in late 16th century Japan is ultimately a complex tale about freedom of expression and political oppression. Expressed almost entirely via sacred tea ceremonies, pic has little b.o. potential stateside but should fare well in its native Japan and continue to win raves on the fest circuit.

Director Hiroshi Teshigahara, best known for his 1963 Cannes prizewinner "Woman in the Dune," has engaged the same top-notch crew from his last picture "Rikyu" (1989), the previous chapter about warlords and tea masters.

"Basara" essentially picks up where "Rikyu" left off but works as a separate film. "Basara," which translates to "diamond" or "brilliance," here is a synonym for defiance, a quality the four principals share.

In the opening scene, tea master Rikyu is ordered to commit hari-kiri. Oribe (Tatsuya Nakadai of "Kagemusha" and "Ran") is appointed successor by new warlord Hideyoshi (thesp Katsuhiro Oida) and ordered to be "inventive."

The creative spin that Oribe puts on teacups thoroughly impresses the sassy and clever princess as well as her gardener Usu, who in turn defies the whole new political wave of samurai and an emerging cultural elite.

Notable acts of defiance include Oribe introducing the idea of esthetic imperfection into Japanese art (i.e. imperfectly shaped ceramic teacups), a crucial detail which leads to many closeups of pottery. (Helmer's also a famous potter.)

The defiant Princess challenges tradition several times throughout by holding her own forbidden tea ceremonies. Japan's leading actress Rie Miyazawa is a knockout as both the young fiesty rebel and the 40-year-old subdued revolutionary. Her complex relationship with Usu (thesp Toshiya Nagasawa) ranges from rape to collusion over pic's 30-year span.

All tech credits are superb. Like "Rikyu," pic sheds light on culture steeped in tradition (and tea), and is a must-see for anyone interested in Asian cinema or Japanese history.

— Suzan Ayscough

THE PORTRAIT
(CANADIAN)

A Raincoast release of One Prods. Ltd. presentation. Produced by Tom Braidwood. Directed, written by Jack Darcus. Camera (color), Tony Westman; editor, Jana Fritsch; music, Michael Conway Baker; production design, Michael Nemirsky, Garth Fleming; costumes, Lynn Kelly; sound, Michael McGee. Reviewed at Montreal World Film Festival, Aug. 28, 1992. Running time: **100 MIN.**
David Severn . . . . Alan Scarfe
Marguerite Chirac . . . Barbara March
Helen Schroeder . . . Gwynyth Walsh
John Schroeder . . . . . . Serge Houde
Lillian Severn . . . . . . Gabrielle Rose
Also with: Ty Haller, Tom Braidwood, Jessica Braidwood, Kate Braidwood, Stephen E. Miller, Alex Diakun.

Jack Darcus' "The Portrait" is a sharply witty and impressively acted drama that should appeal to moviegoers famished for works of nimble intelligence. With special handling, Vancouver-produced pic could click in urban markets. Video and cable prospects are bright.

Pic initially appears to be just another portrait of the artist as an aging rake. A robust art lecturer and little-known artist (Alan Scarfe) enjoys the financial support and sexual favors of an upscale married woman (Gwynyth Walsh) while avoiding child-support summonses from his embittered ex-wife (Gabrielle Rose). He spends at least as much time on self-indulgence and pontification as he does on painting.

But then a wealthy woman (Barbara March) shows up at his fashionably seedy loft. She wants a portrait done for her businessman husband, and she's very specific about how she wants to look in the painting.

The artist accepts the assignment — sort of. Something about painting the rich woman keys his basic artistic instincts, so he sets out to paint her the way he alone sees her. This cues a series of edgy, well-played verbal clashes in which artist and patron debate issues of life and death, art and immortality, inspiration and diligence, survival and self-respect.

Darcus, directing from his own pungent screenplay, offers a clever counterpoint to the lead's artistic (and personal) struggles in and out of his loft. The speeches are quite entertaining, and offer telling commentary on the action by suggesting that portrait painting — as art and as commerce — is a dying craft.

Scarfe is superb as the artist, bringing a touch of Denholm Elliott's mordant humor to his full-bodied performance. His scenes with March (who is excellent) emit a keen erotic undercurrent, but pic wisely stops short of a full-fledged affair. Darcus understands that sometimes the sexiest thing two people can do is have a meeting of the minds.

Fine support comes from Rose, Walsh and Serge Houde as Walsh's vaguely menacing husband. Tony Westman's fluid cinematography helps Darcus make inventive use of confined spaces. Other tech credits are good.

The terrific curtain line about an artist's ultimate act of self-

delusion is the perfect final touch for this vivid portrait of the artist as a hopeless romantic.

— Joe Leydon

HARD-BOILED
(HONG KONG)

A Golden Princess presentation of a Milestone Pictures production. Produced by Linda Kuk, Terence Chang. Directed by John Woo. Screenplay, Barry Wong, based on a story by Woo. Camera (color), Wang Wing-Heng; editor, David Wu, Kai Kit-Wai, John Woo; music, Michael Gibbs; production design, James Leung; action co-ordinator, Cheung Jue-Luh; associate producer, Amy Chin; assistant director. Reviewed at Toronto Festival of Festivals, Sept. 11, 1992. Running time: **126 MIN.**
Yuen (Tequila) . . . . . . Chow Yun-fat
Cop partner . . . . Bowie Lam
Chan . . . . Philip Chan
Tony . . . . Tony Leung
Mr. Hoi . . . . Kwan Hoi-shan
Johnny Wong . . . . . . Anthony Wong
Teresa . . . . Teresa Mo

Hong Kong splatter pic master John Woo has helmed yet another highly stylized gangster film with his trademark flare for superbly choreographed violence. Not quite as tight as his "Bullet in the Head" nor as slick as "The Killer," "Hard-Boiled" will likely have a better shot at Stateside b.o. after Woo's upcoming English-lingo debut "Hard Target" is released by Universal.

This pic emerges as an Asian "Die Hard" in a hospital with a dash of "Backdraft" and offers the usual clutch of graphic shoot-out scenes justified by a rigid code of ethics among killers on both sides of the law.

This time, Woo's favorite lead (Chow Yun-Fat) is on the right side of the law as an unappreciated cop (Tequila) who's trying to crack a futuristic gun-smuggling racket in 1997. Much to his inspector's dismay, trigger-happy Tequila blows an undercover operation, leading to pic's first bloodbath in a restaurant. Scene delivers Woo's usual Peckinpahesque slow-motion death shots propelled by rapid fire editing, gory closeups and occasional freeze frames.

Several shoot-outs later, Tequila hooks up with undercover cop Tony who's infiltrated the smuggling ring and discovered the mother of all ammo stockpiles is hidden in the hospital.

In the relentless final 30-minute showdown, the smugglers (dressed as cops) take and murder hostages amid dozens of explosions setting the screen ablaze. Meanwhile, the heros (dressed

as thugs) save the day, or at least the hospital babies.

Pic provides comic breathers, but unlike previous outings, "Hard-Boiled" often drags between shoot-out scenes as Woo tries a little too hard to humanize the killers. Pacing is also thwarted early in pic by numerous scenes in a jazz club, a connection which is never fleshed out (but the jazz track is great). These are minor flaws for hardcore Woo fans: Pic delivers ample ammunition with a good dose of humor.

— Suzan Ayscough

JUST LIKE A WOMAN
(BRITISH)

A Rank Film Distributors & LWT presentation, in association with British Screen, of a Zenith production. Produced by Nick Evans. Executive producers, Archie Tait, Fred Turner, Nick Elliott. Directed by Christopher Monger. Screenplay, Evans, based on Monica Jay's novel "Geraldine." Camera (color), Alan Hume; editor, Nicolas Gaster; music, Michael Storey; production design, John Box; costumes, Suzy Peters; sound, Neil Kingsbury. Reviewed at Montreal World Film Festival, Sept. 4, 1992. Running time: **106 MIN.**
Monica . . . . Julie Walters
Gerald . . . . Adrian Pasdar
Miles Millichamp . . . . Paul Freeman
C.J. . . . . Gordon Kennedy
Tom Braxton . . . . Ian Redford
Eleanor Tilson . . . Shelley Thompson
Akira Watanabe . . . . . . Togo Igawa

Except for Edward D. Wood's notorious "Glen or Glenda," which wasn't intentionally amusing, "Just Like a Woman" is the funniest plea for tolerance of transvestites ever made. Quirky British comedy could score in urban markets with inoffensively playful ad campaign.

The pic presents its naughty bits fairly innocuously, even more so than "La Cage aux Folles." Adrian Pasdar stars as a Yank financial whiz employed by a London investment firm. At first, he seems to have it all: a rewarding job, a wife, two children and all the lacy underwear a cross-dresser could want.

His world comes crashing down when his wife, finding some unfamiliar panties at home, figures her husband is unfaithful and kicks him out. Pasdar moves in to a roominghouse operated by the somewhat older (and appreciably wiser) Julie Walters, cast as a divorcée longing for excitement.

Pic is unexpectedly sweet as Pasdar and Walters fall in love, and he reveals his eccentricity. After her initial shock, she accepts it much like she would a passion for stamp collecting.

Pic briefly turns to heavy drama after Pasdar is stopped and humiliated by traffic cops, and the public embarrassment leads him to resign his job. He comes back — in drag, yet — to save a deal from snide boss Paul Freeman's sabotage.

This isn't quite as jarring as pic's occasionally heavy-handed efforts to preach that transvestites are people, too. Also jarring are indications that Walters gets some special kick from making love to a drag-bedecked Pasdar.

Director Christopher Monger and screenwriter-producer Nick Evans are much better dealing with humor, which is sharp here without being cutting, and too generous-spirited to be exploitative.

Walters offers a tasty mix of sauciness and common sense in her best big-screen turn since "Educating Rita." Pasdar is sympathetic and engaging in a tricky role, and he certainly looks androgynous enough for the basic gimmick to work. Supporting cast, including Gordon Kennedy as Pasdar's office buddy, is first-rate.

Special praise goes to Suzy Peters' costume designs, for obvious reasons. — *Joe Leydon*

PENSAVO FOSSE AMORE INVECE ERA UN CALESSE
(I THOUGHT IT WAS LOVE)
(ITALIAN)

A Penta Film production in association with Silvio Berlusconi Communications & Mario, Vittorio Cecchi Gori. Produced by Gaetano Danielle. Directed by Massimo Troisi. Screenplay, Troisi, Anna Pavignano. Camera (color), Camillo Bazzoni; editor, Angelo Nicolini; music, Pino Danielle; costumes, Christiana Lafayette. Reviewed at Montreal World Film Festival, Aug. 31, 1992. Running time: **113 MIN.**
Tommaso . . . . Massimo Troisi
Cecilia . . . . Francesca Neri
Also with: Angelo Orlando, Marco Messeri, Natalia Bizzi, Alessia Salustri, Nuccia Fumo, Anna Teresa Rossini.

Vet Italo comic actor Massimo Troisi gives himself most of the funny stuff in "I Thought It Was Love," a lightweight and amiable comedy, but one that isn't strong enough to attract much international attention.

In Troisi's fifth pic as director and star, he casts himself as a freewheeling restaurateur who just can't remain faithful to his beautiful fiancée (Francesca Neri). After several stormy quarrels over his infidelities, they break off their engagement, and she begins to date another man.

Troisi's jealous rages are quite funny, as are his reactions when a friend's younger sister declares her love for him by attempting to poison him. His performance is aptly broad and zestfully self-mocking.

Troisi works well with Neri, who proves to be his equal in the verbal and physical clashes. Unfortunately, pic lacks a strong third act, and the final scenes are a real letdown.

Tech credits are adequate. Naples looks picture-postcard lovely thanks to Camillo Bazzoni's lensing. — *Joe Leydon*

THE DONNER PARTY
(DOCU-COLOR/B&W)

A Steeplechase Films production in association with WGBH & WNET-13 for "The American Experience." Produced by Lisa Ades, Ric Burns. Executive producer, Judy Crichton. Directed, written by Burns. Narrated by David McCullough. Camera (Duart color/B&W), Buddy Squires, Allen Moore; editor, Bruce Shaw; music, Brian Keane; associate producer, Matthew Butcher. Reviewed at Telluride Film Festival, Sept. 5, 1992. Running time: **82 MIN.**
With: Harold Schindler, Joseph King, Wallace Stegner, Donald Buck.

The Donner Party catastrophe, which saw snowbound pioneers reduced to cannibalism in the Sierra Nevada during the bitter winter of 1846, has always made for one of the most gruesomely fascinating chapters in American history. Laced with dashed high hopes, tragic misjudgments, bad timing and misguided faith, this tale from the dark side of the continent's settling is a haunting yarn questioning every individual's possible behavior under such adverse circumstances.

A subject both ripe and dangerous for dramatization, it was on Roman Polanski's agenda before the Sharon Tate murders and inspired a lame Classics Illustrated telepic in 1978. This detailed account is by Ric Burns, co-writer of brother Ken's "The Civil War" and director of the '91 docu "Coney Island."

It's a great idea for a film, and story's gripping facts and multi-layered ironies are expressed in a torrent of nicely written narration and literary excerpts that create an almost unavoidably compelling docu. But Burns has duplicated the polite, elegiac, hushed style of "The Civil War" to such an extent it proves not only tiresomely familiar but counterproductive in expressing material's raw, shocking realities.

Still, want-to-see will be high among history buffs, and Burns' standing in the field will ensure major attention on PBS.

Researchers have come up with an astonishing array of photos and documents that help bring alive and personalize a distant time. Mixing these with maps, photographed letters and other writings, as well as original footage of Western landscapes, Burns has more to work with visually than one might have expected, although repetitions emerge.

With the help of sage commentary from historians, Burns deftly lays out the political realities of unprecedented westward immigration in 1846 before charting the progress of George Donner's party out of Springfield, Ill., that spring, and its nearly unimpeded journey across Indian territory as far as Fort Laramie. Unadvisably, the group turned off the normal route to try a short cut. About 2,500 miles and seven months later, the party was prevented by weather from crossing into safety by one day.

With virtually no food or supplies left, the group of 81 (out of an original 87) made camp. Some tried to leave and various rescue parties were launched, but as the area's worst-ever winter set in, people began to die and many of the starving survivors began to eat them. This continued until April, when the 46 remaining settlers were rescued.

Burns goes as far as he can with wonderful archival documents and has assembled stellar actors to read letters and diary entries. But the extensive new footage of plains, mountains, snowstorms and other manifestations of Mother Nature is simply too gorgeous.

These crucial images convey the beauty of the land but not the terror of the wilderness, so that the destructive elemental forces that doomed the party are not forcefully evoked.

Ultimately, the natural fascination created by the material is tempered by a growing irritation with the overly genteel style, a sense that the "Civil War" approach cannot be universally applied to all historical subjects with maximum effectiveness.
— *Todd McCarthy*

FEED
(DOCU)

A Video Democracy presentation. Produced, directed by Kevin Rafferty, James Ridgeway. Camera (Duart color), Rafferty, Jenny Darrow; editors, Sarah Durham, Rafferty; sound, Charles Arnot, Wolfgang Held. Reviewed at Telluride Film Festival, Sept. 5, 1992. (Also in Toronto Festival of Festivals.) Running time: **76 MIN.**

"Feed" is a cheap shot. A would-be incisive look at the 1992 presidential hopefuls courtesy of off-air satellite video feeds, thin docu encourages the viewer to laugh at people who are being caught unawares, and fact that these people happen to be political bigwigs doesn't prove anything. This will find a ready audience only among those eager to chortle at any and all pols, regardless.

Concentrating on "backhaul" TV material emanating from the February New Hampshire primary campaign, filmmakers Kevin Rafferty and James Ridgeway (who last year collaborated on the far more effective "Blood in the Face") begin with footage of George Bush boringly waiting to deliver a TV speech, then proceed to zing the field.

There's Bob Kerrey freezing at night while hanging on for some air time, Jerry Brown inhaling nasal spray and Hilary Clinton standing by her man in the wake of the Gennifer Flowers announcement. Ross Perot, Paul Tsongas, Tom Harkin and Bill Clinton himself receive more or less equal time, and Arnold Schwarzenegger puts in a guest appearance to cast aspersions at the Democratic aspirants.

But what is one supposed to learn from the spectacle of people waiting their turn at the microphone and camera? Much of the generally dull, unilluminating running time displays public figures sitting tight until technology is ready for them, and it doesn't figure that any civilian would react much differently to the glitches and patience-trying delays than these media-savvy pros do. This is "Candid Camera" without any stimulating provocation.

Fallacy that these video discards and outtakes would reveal the candidates' true character will be disproven to many by the fact that Pat Buchanan — ever polite and unruffled — makes the best impression under trying circumstances.

What "Feed" does reveal a bit of is the debilitating, circus-like atmosphere in which a campaign is conducted, and the circumstances surrounding the creation of sound bites. Pic adds a slightly different perspective to political coverage, but no additional depth.
— *Todd McCarthy*

AS YOU LIKE IT
(BRITISH)

A Buena Vista release (Squirrel Films in U.K.) of a George Reinhardt-Sands Films presentation of a Sands Films production, in association with Aim Prods. Executive producer, Richard Goodwin. Directed by Christine Edzard, from Shakespeare's play. Camera (Fujicolor; Metrocolor prints), Robin Vidgeon; editor, Edzard; music, Michel Sanvoisin; production design, Sands Films; costume design, Barbara Sonnex, Marion Weise; sound (Dolby), Anthony Sprung, Paul Carr. Reviewed at Sands Films studio, Rotherhithe, London, Aug. 13, 1992. (In Mill Valley, Calif., & Birmingham, England, film fests.) MPAA Rating: G. Running time: **117 MIN.**

Adam	Cyril Cusack
Jaques	James Fox
The Dukes	Don Henderson
Audrey	Miriam Margolyes
Rosalind	Emma Croft
Touchstone	Griff Rhys Jones
Orlando/Oliver	Andrew Tiernan
Celia	Celia Bannerman
Phebe	Valerie Gogan
Sir Oliver Martext	Murray Melvin

The Bard goes kitchen sink in Christine Edzard's "As You Like It," an updated version of the Shakespeare favorite that sacrifices sylvan whimsy for social edge. British low-budgeter, mostly shot on drab exteriors, will be limited to literary students and the very dedicated, given careful nursing.

Fourth feature of Edzard and producer husband Richard Goodwin was shot in five weeks at the couple's south-London studio, home of their earlier historical frescoes, "Little Dorrit" and "The Fool." Present item has none of those pics' elaborate production design but features a strong lineup of British thesps plus newer names.

Previous version of the play was the so-so Laurence Olivier-Elisabeth Bergner starrer (1936). Edzard's re-try is fuller and more faithful on text, longer on running time, and opts for modern dress and settings that play up the haves-and-have-nots political subtext for '90s Blighty.

Best known for its "all the world's a stage" soliloquy, play would seem to adapt well to modernization. Bad duke's castle becomes a classically pillored mansion of business wealth and power; Forest of Arden becomes an urban wasteland with the exiled duke a homeless dropout.

Pic starts uneasily in the first setting, not helped by Edzard's unadventurous camera style, clumsy cuts and variable sound quality. Things pick up in the wasteland exteriors, as the love story between Rosalind (Emma Croft, in boy's garb) and Orlando (Andrew Tiernan) gathers steam.

But by not supplying any bridging material, Edzard makes the pic a tough ride for the uncovered. Dialogue-heavy scenes make no concessions to the viewer, and modern dress blurs the differences between the double roles many thesps play. Talk of "doublet and hose" and "the forest" jars when characters walk around in jeans and eat fish and chips.

Performances are variable. Croft comes into her own halfway as the spunky Rosalind. Tiernan is stronger as the banker-type Oliver than the weedy, long-haired Orlando, object of Croft's hidden affections.

James Fox is okay, though subdued, as Jaques; Don Henderson mild as the two dukes; and TV comic Griff Rhys Jones often difficult to decipher as Touchstone the fool. Best playing among the supports is by Celia Bannerman, as Croft's friend, and Valerie Gogan, incisive as a miniskirted Phebe. Tech credits are average.
— *Derek Elley*

TOGETHER ALONE
(B&W)

A Frameline release of a P.J. Party production. (Intl. sales: Forefront Films, N.Y.) Produced, directed, written by P.J. Castellaneta. Camera (B&W), David Dechant; editors, Maria Lee, Castallaneta; music, Wayne Alabardo. Reviewed at Film Forum, N.Y., Sept. 26, 1992. Running time: **87 MIN.**

Bryan	Todd Stites
Brian	Terry Curry

Miraculously produced on a $7,000 budget, helmer P.J. Castellaneta pulls off a small wonder, producing a viable static pic that has captured both critical and public attention. Film has picked up prizes at film fests in the U.S., Canada and Germany.

Like "My Dinner With André," prolix gay-themed pic is roughly a 1½-hour filmed conversation. Despite a few exteriors, seen intermittently during opening credits, entire pic takes place in a loft apartment set in real time.

Set in the age of AIDS, "Together Alone" delves into conversations that pass through everyone's minds. Although the film's two characters have been educated in safe sex practices, wisdom had been thrown to the wind at the moment of passion.

Action picks up with blond Brian (Terry Curry) waking up and realizing that the bed-mate he had picked up had given him a false name. Rather than Bill, his partner (Todd Stites) turns out to be another Brian, but with a "y" (perhaps the inherent "why?" in the core of the film).

Brian is an open, if not practicing, gay man, while Bryan is a married bisexual. The whiny Brian has to deal with their engaging in unsafe sex, and suddenly the weight of the possible consequences bears hard and provokes a conversation with the usual issues of commitment, sexual identity, morality and the nature of relationships.

Schematic script doesn't take sides, and the low-key acting makes both men believable, albeit predictable. True kudos should go to David Dechant's imaginative and rich black & white camerawork, which makes good use of the confined space. It manages to maintain interest in what could have been an incredibly boring film.

There are some stylistic touches that don't ring true, such as the the duo's shared dream; cinematically, a nice moment but not credible. Wayne Alabardo's playful music slips into clichés (such as when it needs to suggest tension), but it works despite its self-consciousness.
— *Paul Lenti*

LOTTA PA BRAKMAKARGATAN
(LOTTA ON RASCAL STREET)
(SWEDISH)

A Svensk Filmindustri presentation of Svensk Filmindustri/SVT Kanal 1 Drama/Astrid Lindgrens production. Produced by Waldemar Bergendahl. Directed by Johanna Hald. Screenplay, Lindgren. Camera (color), Olof Johnson; editor, Jan Persson; music, Stefan Nilsson; costumes, Inger Pehrsson; production design, Lasse Westfelt; sound, Klas Dykhoff. Reviewed at Svensk screening room, Stockholm, Sept. 17, 1992. Running time: **73 MIN.**
With: Grete Haveskölд, Linn Gloppestad, Martin Andersson, Beatrice Järås, Claes Malmberg, Margreth Weivers.

Unabashedly nostalgic kidpic succeeds thanks to charming young thesps and low-keyed, gentle humor. Worldwide fame of author Astrid Lindgren should generate some interest in foreign markets.

"Lotta on Rascal Street" will be probably the last pic adaptation in a long series of Svensk-produced features based on the popular stories by the 80-year-old Lindgren. This item takes place in an unspecified past decade, probably the middle of the 1950s, and tells about 5-year-old Lotta who lives with her two older sisters and parents in a country town. She's a charming girl with a stubborn will.

Instead of high drama, pic revolves around Lotta's learning to ride a two-wheel bicycle, and whether she'll run away because she's been told she can't use a mild profanity. Grown-ups may be a little bored, but kids will identify with Lotta's exploits.

Depicting lovely days gone by of waffle-eating in the garden and visits with ever-loving grand-parents, pic will work perhaps because the unruly times call for this kind of nostalgia.

The kid actors are very good, especially young Grete Haves-köld who plays Lotta both with charm and integrity.

On the downside, dialogue post-looping leaves a lot to be desired, with its irritating and persistent lack of unity between the spoken words and lip movement. The choice to shoot the exteriors in the newly built "Astrid Lindgren World," a sort of minor theme park built around the author's works, was not a particularly good one. The town seen in the film looks as artificial as it is. — *Gunnar Rehlin*

CARRY ON COLUMBUS
(BRITISH)

A UIP (U.K.) release of an Island World presentation of a Comedy House production, in association with Peter Rogers Prods. Produced by John Goldstone. Executive producer, Peter Rogers. Directed by Gerald Thomas. Screenplay, Dave Freeman; additional material, John Antrobus. Camera (Eastmancolor), Alan Hume; editor, Chris Blunden; music, John Du Prez; production design, Harry Pottle; art direction, Peter Childs; costume design, Phoebe De Gaye; sound (Dolby), Chris Munro; special effects, Effects Associates; casting, Jane Arnell. Reviewed at Crown preview theater, London, Sept. 23, 1992. Running time: **91 MIN.**
Chris Columbus . . . . Jim Dale
Mort . . . . Bernard Cribbins
Countess Esmeralda . Maureen Lipman
Bart Columbus . . . Peter Richardson
Achmed . . . . Alexei Sayle
Sultan of Turkey . . . . . . Rik Mayall
Pontiac . . . . Charles Fleischer
Indian chief . . . . Larry Miller
Grand Wazir . . . . Nigel Planer
King Ferdinand . . . . Leslie Phillips
Queen Isabella . . . . . June Whitfield
Diego . . . . Julian Clary
Fatima . . . . Sara Crowe
Felipe . . . . Richard Wilson
Also with: Holly Aird, Keith Allen, Harold Berens, Allan Corduner, Jack Douglas, James Faulkner, Jon Pertwee, Tony Slattery, Sara Stockbridge.

"Carry On Columbus" is a whoopee cushion under the 1492 hoopla. Cheekily berthing its U.K. release between the Salkind and Ridley Scott blockbusters, pic resuscitates the bawdy, vaude-like humor of the original low-budget series with nary a nod to changing fashions. Fast playoff could reap rewards on home territory, but offshore chances will need careful nurturing.

"Columbus" is the 30th in the "Carry On" series that started in 1958 with "Sergeant" and halted 20 years later with "Emmannuelle." Vet director Gerald Thomas returns for behind-the-camera chores, with Peter Rogers, producer of the original, exec producing here.

Strength of the series, which coughed up its best titles in the first 10 years, was the core team of Brit household names like Sidney James, Kenneth Connor, Charles Hawtrey, Joan Sims and Kenneth Williams, whose ranks were augmented by guest players.

Current item continues the tradition of grafting on new comic talent but, with the trunk team now dead or absent, company feel is distinctly lacking. Oldest survivors Jim Dale (veteran of 10 titles), Jack Douglas (seven), Leslie Phillips, June Whitfield and Jon Pertwee (three each), and Bernard Cribbins (two). Effect, with newer names like Julian Clary, Alexei Sayle and Rik Mayall, is spotty, more a series of one-offs than a thoroughgoing company piece.

Script by Dave Freeman, responsible for "Carry On Behind" (1975), starts weakly with the Sultan of Turkey (Mayall, unfunny) sending two spies (Sayle, Sara Crowe) to spy on Chris Columbus (Dale), a mapmaker with dreams of finding a new sea route to the gold-rich Indies.

Financed by the king and queen of Spain (Phillips, Whitfield), Columbus sets sail with a motley crew and a map in Hebrew translated by a dumb mariner (Cribbins). Losing their way, they end up in the Americas, where the natives are streetwise Indians with Brooklyn accents.

Pic settles down during the central voyage, with plenty of the usual double entendres and pratfall comedy. But this by-the-numbers comedy lacks the conviction of old.

Best material is in the final half-hour, with Yank standup comics Larry Miller as a cigar-chewing chieftain and Charles Fleischer (voice of Roger Rabbit) as his sidekick.

There are some chuckles with Dale working hard as the bewildered Columbus and solid support from vet Cribbins. From the huge featured cast, Richard Wilson is waspish as a Spanish bookkeeper, and Phillips and Whitfield solid in their few scenes. Sayle and Clary (latter filling the camp Charles Hawtrey spot in the original team) are shadows of their TV persona.

Lensing by Alan Hume, who worked on 16 previous "Carry ons," is bright and handsome, garnished by John Du Prez's mock-heroic score. Thomas' direction is no-frills but helped along by tight cutting. Pic's £2.25 million budget is all on the screen in handsome costuming and authentically cheesy Pinewood sets. — *Derek Elley*

TOM AND JERRY:
THE MOVIE
(ANIMATED)

A Turner Pictures Worldwide release (Jugendfilm in Germany) of a Turner Entertainment Co. presentation in association with WMG of a Film Roman production. (U.S. rights: Live Entertainment.) Produced by Phil Roman. Co-producer, Bill Schultz. Executive producers, Roger Mayer, Jack Petrik, Hans Brockmann, Justin Ackerman. Directed by Roman. Sequence directors, John Sparey, Monte Young, Bob Nesler, Adam Kuhlman, Eric Daniels, Jay Jackson, Skip Jones. Screenplay, Dennis Marks, based on William Hanna & Joseph Barbera's cartoon characters. Creative consultants, Barbera, David Simone. In CFI Color. Supervising editor, Sam Horta; editor, Julie Ann Gustafson; music, Henry Mancini; songs, Mancini, Leslie Bricusse; art direction, Michael Peraza Jr., Michael Humphries; sound recording director (Dolby), Gordon Hunt; associate producer, James Wang; casting, Janet Hirshenson, Jane Jenkins, Roger Mussenden. Reviewed at Sunset Towers screening room, L.A., Sept. 30, 1992. No MPAA rating. Running time: **80 MIN.**
Voices:
Tom . . . . Richard Kind
Jerry . . . . Dana Hill
Robyn Starling . . . . . Anndi McAfee
Aunt Pristine Figg . . . Charlotte Rae
Lickboot . . . . Tony Jay
Capt. Kiddie . . . . Rip Taylor
Dr. Applecheek . . . . . Henry Gibson
Squawk . . . . Howard Morris

"Tom and Jerry talk!" won't go down in film history as a slogan to rival "Garbo Talks!" Though slickly animated, this first full-length pic featuring the vintage cat and mouse characters is misconceived from start to finish. Full of gooey sentimentality in a banal melodramatic plot, it's serviceable fare for TV and homevid, but theatrical potential is limited.

"Tom and Jerry: The Movie" opened last week in Germany and doesn't yet have a U.S. distrib. Live Entertainment has domestic rights.

Essence of the Tom and Jerry characters created by William Hanna and Joseph Barbera in 1940 was their endless cycle of conflict, their archetypal battle between malevolence and innocence. The most egregiously bad

idea in the pic is to turn them into buddies singing, dancing and doing battle together against the world.

Tom and Jerry's symbiotic relationship could have grounded an extended plot (their compulsive need for each other's antagonism), but changing their feud into fellowship is ridiculous. It's like a pic with the Roadrunner and Wile E. Coyote cuddling and starting housekeeping.

Making a full-lengther about Tom and Jerry had unusual creative perils. A cat chasing a mouse for 82 minutes would get repetitive, and keeping them mute, as they have been since birth, could mean making a silent movie. Even Chaplin had second thoughts about that issue.

Following an enjoyable, fast-paced 10-minute opening recalling the best of the old cartoons, pic does a screeching about-face when Tom and Jerry suddenly burst into words, surprising even each other. Though Tom is given the requisite wise-guy voice by Richard Kind, and Jerry is sweetly vocalized by Dana Hill, the feeling persists that the chatter should have been left to the human characters.

But the baddies in Dennis Marks' homiletic script are gratingly villainous, and their grasping designs on a child heiress friend of Tom and Jerry are cornball Saturday ayem cartoon stuff. Evil Miss Figg (voiced by Charlotte Rae) is a shameless knock-off of the villainous octopus Ursula in Disney's "The Little Mermaid," but without the wit and panache.

For long stretches of this item, cat and mouse simply vanish from the screen. Occasional slapstick passages, such as a scene in which Tom and Jerry wreck a kitchen, enliven the sluggish narrative, but viewers will find themselves longing for the old shorts.

Director Phil Roman has kept the animal sections supple and lively, and the art direction by Michael Peraza Jr. and Michael Humphries is attractive, but the human characters tend to look wooden. Henry Mancini and Leslie Bricusse contributed an energetic but mostly unmemorable score, aside from an amusing ditty about greed. — *Joseph McBride*

HEDD WYN
(BRITISH)

An S4C production. Produced by Shân Davies. Directed by Paul Turner.

Screenplay, Alan Llwyd. Camera (color), Ray Orton; editor, Chris Lawrence; music, John E.R. Hardy; production design, Jane Roberts, Martin Morley; sound, Jeff Matthews. Reviewed at Edinburgh Intl. Film Festival, Aug. 28, 1992. Running time: **125 MIN.**

Ellis Evans (Hedd Wyn) . Huw Garmon
Lizzie Roberts . . . . . . Sue Roderick
Jini Owen . . . . . .Judith Humphreys
  Also with: Nia Dryhurst, Gwen Ellis, Grey Evans, Emlyn Gomer, Arwel Gruffydd, Catrin Fychan, Llio Silyn, Gwyn Vaughan, Phil Reid.
  (Welsh dialogue; English subtitles)

"**H**edd Wyn" is a solidly crafted addition to the small ranks of Welsh-lingo pics, but the true story of a farmer bard whose life and literary career end in the killing fields of World War I is too studied to do much business beyond fest spots.

Huw Garmon toplines as Ellis Evans, a mercurial country boyo whose ambition is to win the ultimate Welsh literary prize. After achieving local reknown for his poetry, he romances singer Lizzie Roberts (Sue Roderick), who promptly ditches him when he refuses to sign up for the war in Europe.

Next g.f. is the more sympathetic Jini Owen (Judith Humphreys), but when the authorities finally force him to enlist, he's killed in the bloody massacre of the 1917 Battle of Passchendaele. Five weeks later, he's posthumously awarded the top literary prize for an epic poem written at the front.

Former BBC Wales editor Paul Turner creates a good-looking frame for the yarn, which in its emphasis on landscape and Celtic mysticism has an almost Nordic feel. Theme of the stupidity and waste of war sits comfortably with Evans' poetry, and the use of a black-veiled woman as a symbol of approaching death also plays well in the circumstances.

But with its emphasis on veracity and immaculate production design and costuming, pic lacks enough dramatic smarts to go the two-hour-plus distance. Darmon in his first leading film role makes a handsome and likable Evans, but it's essentially a one-note performance. Other playing is fine within script's limits.

John Hardy's discreet symphonic score (unwisely junked during the final battle scene for a chunk of Mahler's "Resurrection" symphony) reinforces the mystical atmosphere. Pic was produced by S4C, Wales' fourth channel. Title is Evans' bardic moniker.
— *Derek Elley*

GUMSHOE
(AUSTRALIAN-DOCU)

An M&A Film Prods. release of an M&A-Dakota Prods. production, with participation from the Australian Film Finance Corp. & Australian Broadcasting Corp. Produced by Tristram Miall, Malcolm McDonald. Directed, written by McDonald. Camera (color), Kim Batterham; editor, Suresh Ayyar; music, Peter Miller; sound, Leo Sullivan. Reviewed at Valhalla theater, Sydney, Aug. 5 1992. Running time: **60 MIN.**
  With: Warren Mallard, Peter Royle, Michael Oliver, Roy Montgomery, James Batman, Les, Chris Murphy.

"**G**umshoe" is a partly dramatized docu about the way a group of Sydney private eyes do their job. Some of the content is fascinating, but pic is basically a lightweight and overly ingratiating foray into a shady line of work.

Talking directly to the camera, four principal participants explain what they do and how. Warren and Les carry out insurance surveillance work. The camera crew accompanies Les as he stakes out a woman who was awarded a $400,000 compensation claim and is supposed to be unable to work. Les uses a video camera to tape her moving about her house and later follows her when she goes to work at her second job — as a belly dancer.

Missing persons expert Peter searches for a teen who turns out to have simply run away from home. Michael is a debt collector who stands up to a man he claims is involved in a scam involving a casino on a Pacific island. Also included in the film, presumably for balance, is prominent Sydney criminal lawyer Chris Murphy, who puts the case against the gumshoes.

Tone of Malcolm McDonald's film is jauntily humorous for much of its length, though the subject really is no laughing matter. While some sequences (Michael's confrontation with the suspect in the casino deal) appear to be genuine, others (Peter locating the runaway or the belly dancer sequence) appear to be staged for the camera. Mixture of fact and reconstruction gives the film an awkward structure, since McDonald doesn't make clear what's real and what isn't.

Technically, pic is rough but will pass muster at fests, on TV, or, in the Australian case, in limited theatrical exposure.
— *David Stratton*

LUMUMBA:
LA MORT DU PROPHETE
(LUMUMBA: DEATH OF A PROPHET)
(DOCU-GERMAN-SWISS)

A Velvet Film (Berlin) & Cinémamma (Zurich) production. Produced by Raoul Peck, Andreas Honegger. Directed by Peck. Camera (color), Matthias Kälin, Philippe Ros; editors, Eva Schlensag, Aïlo Auguste, Peck; sound, Martin Witz, Eric Vaucher. Reviewed at New York Film Festival, Sept. 24, 1992. Running time: **68 MIN.**

"**L**umumba: Death of a Prophet" mixes traditional docu techniques with snippets of a personal memoir, a filmmaking journal and a poetic tribute to its subject, managing to work successfully in a tight running time that will necessitate a companion piece for commercial playoff (it was paired with David Achar's "Allah Tantou" at the N.Y. film fest). Pic should be well received on the usual fest and public TV docu route.

As film makes clear, Patrice Lumumba, prime minister of the Congo (now Zaire) when it received its independence from Belgium in 1960, wanted to break all residual colonial control. He was executed by his African rivals, but it's generally believed the West played a key role in his downfall. (Though not mentioned in the documentary, perhaps because of the United Nations' suspect role, a U.N. investigating commission found that Lumumba was killed by a Belgian mercenary in the presence of Lumumba's enemy, Katangan secessionist Moishe Tshombe.)

Lumumba subsequently was mythologized as an African martyr to neo-colonialism. He was intended as the central figure in Italian director Valerio Zurlini's 1968 fiction film, "Seduto alla sua destra," a.k.a. "Black Jesus," starring Woody Strode.

Newsreel footage showing Lumumba being mocked and abused by soldiers only adds to the religious iconography. In archival interviews, Lumumba emerges not as a Malcolm X firebrand but a softspoken man who started studying revolutions when he saw that the values he was taught in Christian schools were not being practiced by Europeans.

Though some of the interviews with other participants are inci-
sive, as pic's title suggests, it is less an objective appraisal than a homage to the slain leader complete with poetic narration. The film is particularly fuzzy regarding Lumumba's ideological views, confining itself to one interviewee's opinion that Lumumba may have been a Marxist but could not have been a Communist because of his religious beliefs.

Aside from the American bribing of the army, the film's description of the U.S. role in undermining Lumumba is limited though it does note the value of uranium deposits in the Congo's Katanga province.

Director and co-producer Raoul Peck was born in Haiti but spent much of his childhood in the Congo when his parents were part of Lumumba's push to have the Haitian intelligentsia replace departing Europeans. Glimpses of his early life there and feelings about his African sojourn are briefly touched on. He also reveals some stories about the making of the docu.

Though helmer has stated his satisfaction with the length of the film, viewers may feel they might have been still better served with a more detailed portrait. — *Fred Lombardi*

TENGOKU NO TAIZAI
(HEAVENLY SIN)
(JAPANESE)

A Toei Co. production. Produced by Kyuemon Oda, Yusuke Okada. Directed by Toshio Masuda. Screenplay, Hiroo Matsuda. Camera (color), Daisaku Kimura; editor, Kiyoaki Saito; art direction, Hidetaka Ozawa; sound, Koichi Hayashi. Reviewed at Tokyo Intl. Film Festival (noncompeting), Sept. 25, 1992. Running time: **115 MIN.**

Roko Kinuhata . . . Sayuri Yoshinaga
Tsai Mang Hua . . . . . . .Omar Sharif
Huang Fung Foo . . Toshiyuki Nishida
Naramoto . . . . Koji Shimizu
Aoki . . . . . . Noriyuki Higashiyama
Kunio Tanabe . . . . Hiroki Matsukata

Omar Sharif's appearance is this xenophobic film's biggest claim to fame, but even his impressive language skills (English, Japanese, Cantonese and Spanish) don't compensate for melodramatic acting and a banal, predictable plot. Pic still may run fairly briskly in Japan because of its big-budget action look and famous Japanese stars, but laughable scenes in broken English give the pic a slim chance in the West.

A beautiful female district attorney (Sayuri Yoshinaga) ends a 10-year affair with her boss Tanabe (Hiroki Matsukata) and has their baby, later kidnapped by a criminal whose life she ruined. Big foreign-devil drug lord Sharif, Tanabe's nemesis, saves the baby and wins D.A.'s love.

Opening scenes show a Tokyo overrun by riots and hoods, drug users, illegal laborers, prostitutes — mainly Arabs, blacks, Southeast Asians and a few Caucasians thrown in for good measure. Interspersed are some steamy slow-mo sex shots of the D.A. and Tanabe.

The D.A. also is trying to get the conviction of a rapist, who is set free by Tanabe in exchange for info on drug pushers. Tanabe finds and arrests the No. 2 drug pusher, Huang Fung Foo (Toshiyuki Nishida playing Chinese). But big drug lord Sharif, depicted as an Arab-Chinese mix, tricks the D.A. into passing along message for Huang to kill himself rather than betray the ring.

After the unconvicted rapist kidnaps the D.A.'s baby as payback for hassling him, she turns to Sharif even though it was his trick that forced her to resign. He finds the baby and becomes surrogate father and husband-figure, until happy family life is interrupted by Tanabe's ongoing investigation into drug ring.

Poorly thought-out ending has the D.A. and Sharif, who have fallen in love, not-so-cleverly hiding out from Chinese mafia (who've put a price on Sharif's head) in western Canada not far from Vancouver, renowned for large Chinese gangster population. — *Karen Regelman*

SHINO FUNJATTA
(SUMO DO, SUMO DON'T)
(JAPANESE)

A Dalei Co. Ltd. release of a Dalei Co. Ltd. production. Produced by Shoji Masui. Executive producers, Yo Yamamoto, Izuru Hiraaki. Directed, written by Masayuki Suo. Camera (color), Naoki Kayano; editor, Junichi Kikuchi; music, Yoshikazu Suo. Reviewed at Montreal World Film Festival, Sept. 1, 1992. (Also in Tokyo Intl. Film Festival.) Running time: **105 MIN.**
Shushei . . . . Masahiro Motoki
Natsuko . . . . Misa Shimizu
Aoki . . . . Naoto Tanenaka
Anayama . . . . Akira Emoto
Tanaka . . . . Hiromasa Taguchi
Smiley . . . . Robert Hoffman
Haruo . . . . Masaaki Muroi

A funny and endearing workout of a classic teen-pic

formula, "Sumo Do, Sumo Don't" bears a bouncy resemblance to John Hughes' early high school comedies. Prospects are upbeat for appropriate specialty markets, but film's ultimate typing as an above-average genre pic won't facilitate crossover to Western auds.

Shushei, a handsome but lazy university student, has already secured a decent job through family connections. But first he must graduate, and his thesis professor, a former sumo champ, devises a bit of blackmail to release the necessary credits. Shushei must join the college's sumo "team" (which at present sports just one pathetic member) in order to secure its continued survival.

The other would-be wrestlers are recruited from the ranks of the obese, perilously skinny and otherwise athletically/socially unfit. An English rugby player and an enormous girl with a crush on a teammate complete the hapless group.

They're all prepared to throw in the towel after disastrous early matches. But the belligerence of wrestlers from the school's sumo glory days shames the boys into serious training.

Triumph-of-underdogs theme is hardly original, yet director Masayuki Suo makes the elements (save some gratuitous bathroom humor) work delightfully. The slapstick is well handled, the worm-turning successive climaxes exciting. Editing is tops throughout, photography bright and attractive. Performances are uncomplicatedly appealing. But sharp direction lets "Sumo Do" transcend its ordinary material. — *Dennis Harvey*

SAN SEBASTIAN

TITO I YA
(TITO AND I)
(YUGOSLAVIAN-FRENCH)

A Tramontana (Belgrade), Terra (Nova Sad) & Magda Prods. (Paris) co-production. Produced, directed, written by Goran Markovic. Co-producers, Zoran Masirevic, Michel Mavros, Zoran Tasic. Camera (color), Racoslav Vladic; editor, Snezana Ivanovic; music, Zoran Simjanovic; sets, Veljko Despotovic; costumes, Boris Caksiran. Reviewed at San Sebastian Film Festival, Sept. 19, 1992. Running time: **105 MIN.**
Zoran . . . . Dimitrie Vojnov
Raja . . . . Lazar Ristovski
Mother . . . . Anica Dobra
Father . . . . Pedrag Manojlovic
Aunt . . . . Ljiljana Dragutinovic
Zoran's uncle . . . . Bogdam Diklic
Also with: Olivera Markovic, Rade

Markovic, Vesna Trivalic.
(In Croatian)

The Marshal Tito years as seen through the eyes of a Belgrade boy are handled with wry and sometimes hilarious humor by Goran Markovic, yielding a pleasure to sit through. "Tito and I's" first half, set in a crowded apartment with the boy's bickering family, is especially funny; second half involves an excursion to the dictator's birthplace and could do with some cutting.

Story's 10-year-old boy narrator is a wonderfully offbeat anti-hero: Homely, short, overweight and clumsy, Zoran is apolitical despite the ideological rifts in his family. Still, newsreels and propaganda start to spur the boy's special feelings about Tito, whom he imagines giving him personal advice in his daily life.

When a tall, gangly 12-year-old girl Zoran likes tells him she's about to leave on a 10-day homage to Tito's birthplace, Zoran manages to join the trip by writing an adulatory poem to the leader.

Rest of pic covers the tour, punctuated by mishaps Zoran causes and a confrontation with his authoritarian and bumbling group leader. The delightful irony early in the pic turns to slapstick when the group takes shelter in a castle and the leader dresses up as a ghost. — *Peter Besas*

JACK AND HIS FRIENDS

An Arrow Entertainment production & release. Produced by Benjamin Gruberg, Karen Jaehne. Executive producer, Dennis Friedland. Co-exec producers, Barney Cohen, Kathryn Wallack. Associate producer, Elle Kamihira. Directed, written by Bruce Ornstein. Camera (color), Dan Stoloff; editor, Barbara Tulliver; production design, Ellen Caldwell; costume design, Ellen Ryba; line producers, Roberta Friedman, Mimi Bohbot; art direction, Roald Scott Lawson; sound, Bernard Hajdenberg. Reviewed at San Sebastian Film Festival, Sept. 23, 1992. Running time: **96 MIN.**
Jack . . . . Allen Garfield
Louie . . . . Sam Rockwell
Rosie . . . . Judy Reyes
Also with: Paul Hecht, Alison Fraser, Jeremy Roberts, Barry Snider.

This lightweight, low-budget comedy/farce might rack up some bucks in limited youth market playoffs. Sophomoric humor and Allen Garfield's histrionic performance do occasionally strike a funnybone, but

the story is too thin for a feature and good secondary characters are brought in too late.

Self-pitying, middle-aged overweight Jack has just caught his wife in bed with another man, and as he drives away on a rainy night, he is carjacked by a fugitive couple and forced to drive to his summer home on a virtually deserted island.

Jack is too devastated by his wife's infidelity to care much about the threats of his kidnappers, and doesn't even bother to call the cops when he can. His attitude towards the young delinquents varies from shock and opprobrium, such as when they break into a grocery story to steal food, to passive compliance.

The contrast between Jack, a shoe manufacturer with all the right middle-class virtues, and the two bland, bumbling kidnappers occasionally makes for droll interplay. Pic is given a lift when two cloying neighbors are brought into the act, as well as a local cop, who reveal that Jack's wife has been two-timing him with everyone from the ferry captain to the milkman. But Jack, unshakably uxorious to the end, decides to return to his spouse.

Nice perf by Garfield pushes slobbering self-pity to amusing limits, while Paul Hecht and Alison Fraser add a charming bit of class. Technical credits are okay. — *Peter Besas*

ZWOLNIENI Z ZYCIA
(DISMISSED FROM LIFE)
(POLISH)

A Zodiak Film & Jeck Film production. Executive producer, Pawel Rakowski. Directed, written by Waldemar Krzystek. Camera (color), Dariusz Kuc; editor, Krzysztof Osiecki; music, Zhigniew Preisner; production design, Tadeusz Kesarewicz. Reviewed at San Sebastian Film Festival, Sept. 23, 1992. Running time: **90 MIN.**
Marek . . . . Jan Frycz
Madwoman . . . . . . Krystyna Janda
Janek . . . . Wojcieh Wysocki
Also with: Suzel Goffre, Mariusz Benoit, Krzysztof Tyniec.

With a tighter story and less dialogue, this could have turned into a watchable political thriller about Poland in transition. As is, "Dismissed From Life" drags excessively and lacks dramatic emphasis. The final payoff is as exciting as a potato omelet.

Set in 1989, story concerns a man beat up by two ex-policemen and left for dead in a dump. Marek, however, survives after brain surgery that leaves him amnesiac. He wanders about the city, sought by his assailants who fear he will testify against them.

Marek finds shelter with a girlfriend/bagwoman who supposedly was once queen of the Paris boulevards. Marek regains his memory just as the villains are about to do him in, but there's no happy ending: He returns to his house only to find that his mother died, and his brother went to Australia, strange, since the brother's a highly-placed investigator who had been seeking him throughout the film.

— Peter Besas

LA REINA ANONIMA
(THE ANONYMOUS QUEEN)
(SPANISH)

A Ditirambo Films & Lola Films S.A. production, in collaboration with Sogepaq S.A. Executive producers, Andrés Vicente Gómez. Directed, written by Gonzalo Suárez. Camera (color), Carlos Suárez; editor, Pablo del Amo; sets, Wolfgang Burmann; costumes, Yvonne Blake; sound, Goldstein & Steinberg S.L.; music, Mario de Benito; associate producers, Ignacio Martinez, Manuel Lombardero. Reviewed at San Sebastian Film Festival, Sept. 21, 1992. Running time: **89 MIN.**
Ana Luz . . . . Carmen Maura
Neighbor . . . . Marisa Paredes
Husband . . . . . . Juanjo Puigcorbe
Also with: Jesús Bonilla, Cristina Marcos, Pepe López, Kiti Manver.

Veteran helmer Gonzalo Suárez has come up with a comedy in which scene after scene succeed each other without any discernible logic or reason. The humor will not get across to most audiences, and there's not much else in the film to redeem it. Commercial prospects seem dismal at best.

The non-story involves a housewife (Carmen Maura) visited by a zany, unexplained string of people who virtually take over her luxury apartment during her husband's absence. Mocking retinue includes a plumber whom Maura apparently kills with a screwdriver, a policeman shot by her neighbor, a troupe of actors, a TV repairman and a woman who claims to be her husband's lover.

The housewife at times thinks she is dreaming it all, but then apparently isn't. It all adds up to an incoherent, unfunny farce which at times is silly seemingly pointless and embarrassing.

— Peter Besas

DER ERDNUSSMAN
(THE PEANUT MAN)
(GERMAN)

A Kinowelt release of a Filmproduktion Berlin production under aegis of ZDF. Produced by Hartmut Jahn. Directed, written by Dietmar Klein. Camera (color), Michael Hammon; editor, Simone Bräuer, Andreas Herder; production design, Andreas M. Velten; costumes, Sibel Özer; sound, Sabine Hillmann, Georg Maas; assistant director, Lih Janowitz. Reviewed at Kurbel Cinema, Berlin, Aug. 12, 1992. (In San Sebastian Film Festival.) Running time: **80 MIN.**
Eddy . . . . Achim Grubel
Margot . . . . Franziska Troegner
Linda . . . . Ulrike Krumbiegel
Ralf . . . . Jürgen Watzke
Kasulke . . . . Ralf Holzhausen
Max . . . . Gerald Schaale
St. Just . . . . . . Alexander Schröder

Able but rather small comedy about an East German sucked into Western consumer culture could do well at homeland box offices with its combination of gentle humor and topical subject matter, but "The Peanut Man" is ultimately too local to travel far.

An East Berliner (Achim Grubel) ekes out a living posting billboards, spending his evenings in his modest apartment lounging and surfing channels. He quickly works his way up in the ad industry when, through a fluke, he becomes Shaky, the Peanut Man. Overnight, his smiling face is seen by millions on TV, in magazines and on the billboards he used to post, endlessly repeating vacuous slogans.

Stage vet Grubel plays the lead with the right note of subtle naiveté. Helmer Dietmar Klein should have extended his writing and directing skills to fleshing out supporting roles, especially Margot, Eddy's plump g.f. who sells sausages at a stand, and Linda, a sharklike creative director with a good heart.

Klein shows more talent in a game-show scene in which the Peanut Man, the diaper ad man, the pickle girl and the prototypical ad image of the East German compete. Sight gags are occasionally marred by slow tracking shots, enabling audiences to figure them out before seeing them.

Overall, pic strikes a nice comic tone and tech credits are quite good, but the idiom is too endemic to Berlin. *— Rebecca Lieb*

MORTE DI UN MATEMATICO NAPOLETANO
(DEATH OF A NEAPOLITAN MATHEMATICIAN)
(ITALIAN)

A Mikado release of a Teatri Uniti production in association with RAI-3, Banco di Napoli, Ministry of Entertainment. Produced by Angelo Curti. Associate producers, Antonietta De Lillo, Giorgio Magliulo (Angio Film). Directed by Mario Martone. Screenplay, Martone, Fabrizia Ramondino. Camera (color), Luca Bigazzi; editor, Jacopo Quadri; music, Michele Campanella; production design, Giancarlo Muselli. Reviewed at Venice Film Festival (competition), Sept. 6, 1992. Running time: **108 MIN.**
Renato Caccioppoli . . . . Carlo Cecchi
Wife . . . . Anna Bonaiuto
Brother . . . . . . Renato Carpentieri
Don Simplicio . . . . Antonio Neiwiller
Pietro . . . . Toni Servillo
Also with: Licia Maglietta, Fulvia Carotenuto, Roberto De Francesco.

It's probably better not to be acquainted with the charismatic historical figure on which "Death of a Neapolitan Mathematician" is loosely based. He's only a starting point for debuting helmer Mario Martone's subtle, dreamlike film about a hip intellectual who commits suicide in 1950s Naples.

Venice Special Jury awardwinner has done surprisingly well in homeland release, given its subject and rigor. More fest exposure could launch the pic into specialized distribution offshore. Martone does well to insist his Renato Caccioppoli is largely invented. In Italy, the film didn't go over as a portrait of the mathematician by those who had known him. Foreign viewers should be spared this problem.

Acclaimed stage thesp Carlo Cecchi has the stature to portray the grandson of a Russian anarchist and legendary university prof as a modern man full of erudite irony and lucid, existential torments. Brought low by chronic alcoholism but still a fascinating figure in trenchcoat and stubble, Caccioppoli spends his last week on earth taking account of his life.

He has cut the cord with the Communist Party after Stalin and the Soviet invasion of Hungary, but he still has old comrades. Between drinking bouts, he plays the piano like Mozart

and attends concerts at the Opera with Don Simplicio (Antonio Neiwiller, most lovable cleric in an Italian film this year).

"Death" remains firmly nonjudgmental of Caccioppoli's behavior, even when he holds exams on a binder and starts dancing around the lecture hall. Pietro, the bad student, judges him harshly; the good Don Simplicio, like director Martone, does not.

Stage director Martone draws resonant performances from the actors, who flesh out an elusive screenplay. Anna Bonaiuto is achingly sympathetic as the wife Caccioppoli has pushed out of his life, but who can't forget him. As the mathematician's brother, Renato Carpentieri is a perfect counterweight, all bourgeois virtues and condescending affection. Only student who stands out is black sheep Toni Servillo, a yuppie before his time. Not to be missed is Vera Lombardi as a sharptongued, lucid old aunt who wields tremendous academic power.

Views of a vanished Naples give this low-budget film a sensuous visual pleasure. Art director Giancarlo Muselli has done a splendid job catching the fading lights of architectural classicism, beautifully framed and lensed by cinematographer Luca Bigazzi.

— Deborah Young

LA CORSA DELL'INNOCENTE
(FLIGHT OF THE INNOCENT)
(ITALIAN-FRENCH)

An Artisti Associati release, produced by Cristaldifilm/Fandango in association with RAI-TV-3/Fildebroc. Produced by Franco Cristaldi, Domenico Procacci. Directed by Carlo Carlei. Screenplay, Carlei, Gualtiero Rosella. Camera (color), Raffaele Mertes; editor, Carlo Fontana, Claudio Di Mauro; music, Carlo Siliotto; art direction, Franco Ceraolo; visual consultant, Paolo Zeccara. Reviewed at Venice Film Festival, Sept. 9, 1992. Running time: **100 MIN.**
Vito . . . . Manuel Colao
Scarface . . . . Federico Pacifici
Police commissioner . . Nicola Di Pinto
Marta Rienzi . . . . . . Francesca Neri
Davide Rienzi . . . . . Jacques Perrin
Also with: Sal Borgese, Giusi Cataldo, Lucio Zagaria, Anita Zagaria.

Franco Cristaldi's final film, completed by Domenico Procacci after the producer's death, is a gutsy, exciting adventure about a small boy on the run for his life. Magnificently lensed and orchestrated, "Flight of the Innocent" is calculated to keep viewers on the edge of their seats. It could be a pickup for foreign audiences broader than art house habitués.

This isn't an art film at all, but a violent nightmarish fairy tale à la Grimm Bros. Like many recent Italo films, it tackles the theme of child abuse, but from an eerie Hansel and Gretel p.o.v.

Little Vito (Manuel Colao) is a smart, dreamy kid from Aspromonte, Italy's kidnapping center. His family is in the business, as Vito dimly perceives. He shudders when he sees blood on his father's shoe. It's the prelude to a terrifying massacre in which his family is shot to death in a feud between clans.

Vito flees and survives by wits — and with a good deal of help from the scriptwriters, who keep a departing train or streetcar within reach. Script is weak in realism but strong in American-style, breakneck pacing.

Pic's last third changes register as the boy makes his way to a luxurious home in northern Italy where he dreams of returning ransom money to kind Francesca Neri and Jacques Perrin, parents of one of the kipnapping family's hostages. Perrin is a good man but a little naive in dealing with kidnappers.

The film is so beautifully made, it's hard to believe it's director Carlo Carlei's feature debut. He gets a near-perfect performance from little Colao, a sweet boy with the loud, harsh voice of his people and never a whimper of self-pity.

Pic is breathtakingly visual; the cinematography of vast plains and threatening skies, work of Raffaele Mertes, is almost an end in itself. Carlo Siliotto's swelling musical score sweeps the audience away. Though the film doesn't go deep psychologically, it has very few nonentertaining moments.

— *Deborah Young*

LA CHASSE AUX PAPILLONS
(THE BUTTERFLY HUNT)
(FRENCH-GERMAN-ITALIAN)

A Pierre Grise Prods.-Sodaperaga-France 3 Cinema (Paris)/Metropolis Films (Munich)/Best Intl. Films (Rome) co-production (Intl. sales: Metropolis Film, Zurich.) Produced by Martine Marignac. Co-producers, Maurice Tinchant, Guy Seligman, Luciano Gloor, Ettore Rosboch, Lilia Smecchia. Directed, written by Otar Iosseliani. Camera (color), William Lubtchansky; editor, Iosseli-

ani; music, Nicolas Zourabichvili; production design, Emmanuel de Chauvigny; sound, Holger Gimpel, Alix Comte, Gerard Lamps, Axel Arft; artistic collaborators, Pierre André Boutang, Leila Naskidachvili; assistant director, Claire Lusseyrand. Reviewed at Venice Film Festival (competition), Sept. 5, 1992. Running time: **117 MIN.**

Solange . . . . Narda Blanchet
Marie-Agnes . . Thamar Tarassachvili
Henri de Lampadere
. . . . Alexandre Tcherkassoff
Helene . . . . . Alexandra Liebermann
Father Andre
. . . . . . Emmanuel de Chauvigny
Marie . . . . . Anne-Marie Eisenschitz
Caprice . . . . Maimouna N'Diaye
Valerie . Pierrette Pompom Bailhache
Olga . . . . Lilia Ollivier
Emir . . . . Sacha Piatigorsky
Yvonne . . . . . . Françoise Tsouladze
M. Carpentier . . . Yannick Carpentier
Ghost . . . . Otar Iosseliani
Drunk . . . . Alexander Askoldov
Quarrelsome man . . . . Pascal Aubier

Georgian writer-director Otar Iosseliani, long based in France, looks at a fast disappearing world of European aristocracy in "The Butterfly Hunt," a delightful, though somewhat extended comedy. Similar in mood to the helmer's '84 Venice success, "The Favorites of the Moon," pic could attract appreciative auds.

Setting is a picturesque French village dominated by two magnificent chateaux. In the dilapidated one, the owner, a very old lady of Russian extraction, lives with her equally elderly cousin. In the other chateau lives the old woman's lawyer, his son and the son's African wife. The lawyer is an entrepreneur who allows guided tours (mostly Japanese tourists) of his elegant home, and acts as real estate agent, offering stately homes to international buyers.

Life in the village and at the two chateaux is peaceful until the old lady suddenly dies. In a touchingly staged scene, the director appears as the ghost of a Russian officer who visits the woman at the moment of her death. Relatives are brought in from everywhere, including a sister and niece from Moscow, but an ironic coda reveals that Japanese buyers will soon own this prime French real estate.

Ioselliani's dry approach is very refreshing but may be a shade too elliptical for those who like their comedy more upfront. Scenes in Moscow, where the old woman's sister lives in a crowded apartment and the phone lines are still bugged, are very amusing, and buffs will note a cameo appearance by the director of "Commissar," Alexander Askoldov, as an unruly drunk.

Underlying it all is a melancholy feeling for the vanishing graceful homes and their elderly residents. Though references to the late Luis Buñuel abound, Iosseliani seems generally fond of these bourgeoisie.

Pic is exquisitely photographed by William Lubtchansky and has a lilting music score by Nicolas Zourabichvili. Editing, by the director himself, is a touch indulgent. The no-name actors play with an unforced naturalism.

— *David Stratton*

VALSI PECORAZE
(WALTZING ON THE RIVER PECORA)
(GEORGIAN-COLOR/B&W)

A Lileo Arts-J/V Co. production. Produced by Alexander Sharashidze. Directed by Lana Gogoberidze. Screenplay, Gogoberidze, Zaira Arsenisvili. Camera (color/B&W), Georgi Beridze; music, Georgi Tsintsadze; production design, Shota Cocolasvili, Salome Alexi-Meskhisvili. Reviewed at Venice Film Festival (competition), Sept. 9, 1992. (Also in Nouveau Cinema du Montreal Festival.) Running time: **106 MIN.**
With: Guram Pirtskhalava, Irina Kupchenko, Nino Surguladze, Mrika Chichinadze, Tamara Skhirtiadze, Ninely Chankuftadze, Dopo Chichinadze.

Repression in Josef Stalin's Soviet Union is the familiar theme of this sensitive autobiographical Georgian film, decently made but not striking enough to provoke international distrib interest.

Director Lana Gogoberidze, a figure on the Georgian film scene since the '60s, intercuts two stories, both drawn from her own experiences. In 1937, a 13-year-old Tbilisi girl has been sent to a state orphanage after her parents are arrested. She escapes and returns to her old apartment now occupied by a KGB officer. An uneasy relationship develops between the sensitive teen and the world-weary communist, who's eventually arrested for trying to help her.

The other story, shot mostly in black & white, centers on the wife of an "enemy of the people" sentenced to a prison camp in Siberia. But the camp is full, and she joins other femme prisoners on a trek through the icy wilderness, on the brink of starvation, looking for shelter.

Pic is sensitive but not very probing, and these personal stories, though well handled, underplay Stalinist horrors.

Elegant production design for

the Tbilisi scenes is counterpointed with the snowy vastness and eerie atmosphere of the Siberian sequences. Thesping is fine, with Russian actress Irina Kupchenko shining as the displaced woman in the Siberian scenes. — *David Stratton*

O ULTIMO MERGULHO
(THE LAST DIVE)
(PORTUGUESE)

A Radiotelevisao Portuguesa/La Sept/Madragoa Filmes co-production. Produced by Paulo Branco. Directed, written by João César Monteiro. Camera (color), Dominique Chapuis; editor, Stephanie Mahet; art direction, Isabel Branco; choreography, Mario Franco, Catarina Lourenco. Reviewed at Venice Film Festival (competition), Sept. 11, 1992. Running time: **85 MIN.**
Esperanca . . . . Fabienne Babe
Eloi . . . . . Henrique Babe e Castro
Samuel . . . . Dinis Neto Jorge
Also with: Francesca Prandi.

"The Last Dive," latest work by Portuguese cult helmer João César Monteiro, may disappoint fans. This episode (of four) of producer Paulo Branco's TV venture "The Elements" is a slight, disconnected film that starts out intriguing and ends up leaving the viewer cold. On the big screen, its unmotivated repetitions make it a tedious and mystifying tale.

Young Dinis Neto Jorge stands on a pier, ready to jump in the river and kill himself. He is interrupted by a retired sailor (Henrique Canto e Castro) also tired of living. The youth invites him to join, but the sailor instead takes the youth out on the town for two long, boisterous nights.

Though the boy remains a cipher throughout the film, the sailor is more fleshed out. His home life is hell, thanks to a bedridden wife who doesn't stop shrieking at him for the entire (real) time it takes the actors to eat a bowl of soup. They flee to a nightclub, where the sailor's mute daughter (the finely enigmatic Fabienne Babe) works as a hooker. The youth and daughter fall ecstatically in love.

Plot's promising irony (Monteiro at his best) is destroyed by director's reckless decision to try viewer patience with gratuitous avant-garde sequences. In a fancy outdoor restaurant, diners are treated to a 10-minute, fixed-camera version of Salome's dance performed by a professional dancer. Just as the viewer is recovering, Babe projects herself into the dance she has just seen, and the entire thing is repeated, without sound — maybe because Babe is deaf and mute?

The film works best as an offbeat tale of bars and hookers, embellished with long walks through colorful Lisbon. Many of the scenes, like Francesca Prandini's romp with the sailors on a Russian mercantile ship, have a pleasingly spontaneous, improvised quality. Otherwise, pic reps the kind of academic Portuguese cinema that makes a virtue of distancing the viewer.

— *Deborah Young*

TORONTO FEST

TWIST
(CANADIAN-DOCU-COLOR/B&W)

An Alliance Releasing release (Canada) of a Sphinx production. (Intl. sales: Films Transit, Montreal). Produced, directed by Ron Mann. Executive producer, Don Haig. Co-producer, Sue Len Quon. Camera (color), Bob Fresco; editor, Robert Kennedy; music, Keith Elliott, Nicholas Stirling; music consultant, Dave Booth; art direction, Gerlinde Scharinger; set design, Lynda Nakashima; sound, Brian Avery; dance consultant, Sally Sommer; dance & music research, David Segal, Wendy Rowland; associate producer, Ann Mayall. Reviewed at Toronto Festival of Festivals, Sept. 19, 1992. Running time: **78 MIN.**
With: Cholly Atkins, Hank Ballard, Chubby Checker, Joey Dee, Mama Lu Parks & the Parkettes, Dee Dee Sharp.

Ron Mann's "Twist" is an engaging dance docu about the gyratory craze that revolutionized pop culture during the darkest hour of the Cold War. Theatrical release will be limited to urban centers or special events (pic had the closing slot at the Toronto fest), but is a natural for cable and pubcasters.

Mann ("Comic Book Confidential") has again thoroughly researched and cleverly documented a subcultural phenomenon that exploded in the politically repressed '50s and strongly influenced the all-embracing '60s.

Whirling dance footage and revelatory talking head interviews (including the dance's popularizer Chubby Checker) are mixed to entertain both baby boomers, who were there, and curious young folk still hearing it on the radio 30 years later.

Structure is a bit clunky, as Mann breaks pic into "Seven Lessons." The first clarifies that Hank Ballard and the Midnights wrote and recorded the original

twist in an era where partners followed rigid steps to tunes like the jitterbug. It intros rare footage of Elvis Presley "rotating his pelvis," while a startled radio announcer tries to enunciate.

Another lesson addresses twist films and its tentacle reach into TV programs like "The Dick Van Dyke Show" or "The Flintstones."

The documentary avers that the twist paved the way for the Beatles and freestyle dancing in 1964 and after. Summarized by one twister on American Bandstand: "We were out there doin' our thing, and there's no goin' back now."

Editing is a bit sketchy (not surprising as final print arrived only hours before the fest unspooling), and pic bops — rather than twists — between crucial footage. But there's lots of lively dancing, plenty of groovy archival footage and a soundtrack of still familiar and inspiring tunes should provide a good marketing tool. — *Suzan Ayscough*

PRAYING WITH ANGER

A Crescent Moon Pictures production. Produced, directed, written by M. Night Shyamalan. Camera (Technicolor), Madhu Ambat; editor, Frank Reynolds; music, Edmund K. Choi; art direction, Krishnamurthy; sound (Dolby), Annette Danto; assistant director, K.V. Phanendra; associate producers, Jayalakshmi Shyamalan, Nelliate C. Shyamalan. Reviewed at Toronto Film Festival, Sept. 16. 1992. Running time: **107 MIN.**
Dev Raman . . . . M. Night Shyamalan
Sunjay Mohan . . . . Mike Muthu
Principal Balaji . Capt. K. Subramanian
Raj Kahn . . . . . . Arun Balachandran
Rupal Mohan . . . . Richa Ahuja
Sabitha . . . . Christabal Howie
Mrs. Mohan . . . . Sushma Ahuja
Mr. Mohan . . . . Apajit Singh
Swami . . . . S.K. Veeragavan

M. Night Shyamalan's impressively self-assured triple-threat debut as director, writer and star of "Praying With Anger," has, despite its technical polish, an endearingly ingenuous quality that could help it click with mainstream auds.

Indie comedy-drama was lensed in English on location in Madras, India, by Shyamalan, a 21-year-old New York University film school grad. He was born in India but moved with his parents to New York when he was 6 months old.

Not surprisingly, the picture has a strong autobiographical flavor in its depiction of a U.S.-born student who returns to his roots after being shipped off to college for a year in his parents' homeland.

Shyamalan makes a charismatic lead as Dev Raman, an exchange student less than thrilled about being a stranger in a strange land. Thinking himself 100% American, he chafes at the restraints imposed by Indian custom and tradition.

The episodic screenplay has Raman slowly learning to appreciate life in India and recognizing how much his late father, so aloof and demanding during their years together, really loved him. Emphasis is on the passionate approach Indians take to all facets of their life — particularly, but not exclusively, their worship of various gods — and pic doesn't shy away from depicting the religious intolerance of even seemingly intelligent people.

Entertaining fish-out-of-water story has Raman learning the hard way that, in India, professors do not tolerate questions from pupils, seniors are free to brutalize all other students and parents demand the final word in selecting spouses for their kid.

In a running gag, almost everyone Raman meets, including a holy man, asks if the visiting Yank has ever met Michael Jackson.

Shyamalan has a lot to learn about directing crowd scenes and fights, but his sense of dramatic pacing is sharp. Supporting players, all cast in India, are by and large fine, with Mike Muthu making the strongest impact as the son of the family hosting Raman.

Madhu Ambat's stunning color cinematography is among pic's strongest assets. Other tech credits are first-rate. — *Joe Leydon*

BOSTON FEST

LAIBACH:
POBEDA POD SUNCEM
(LAIBACH: VICTORY UNDER THE SUN)
(YUGOSLAVIAN-DOCU)

An Avala Film presentation. Executive producer, Gojko Kastraovic. Directed, written by Goran Gajic. Camera (color), Radan Popvic, Rade Vladic, Boris Gortinski, Predrag Bambic, Milorad Glusica, Gajic, Andrej Popovic; editor, Ana Milovanovic; music, Laibach; sound, Sinisa Jovanovic-Singer; narrator, Dusko Markovic. Reviewed at Copley Place Theater, Boston, Aug. 20, 1992. (In Boston Film Festival, Human Rights Watch sidebar.) Running time: **65 MIN.**

This 1988 docu is being

touted as a cross between "Triumph of the Will" and "A Hard Day's Night." That's not far from the truth.

Laibach is a rock group from Yugoslavia that uses fascist and Nazi imagery in their performances. Band takes its name from the German version of Ljubljana, the capital of Slovenia. Whether it's a put-on or serious is up to the viewer.

Pic mixes music video, documentary and staged footage with graphics of their European tour that look like they were lifted from a Third Reich newsreel. During the course of it, Laibach performs and makes pronouncements while commentators try to put their work in perspective.

In the wake of the break-up of Yugoslavia, and the charges of Serbian "ethnic cleansing" in Bosnia-Hercegovina, there's something a bit distasteful in the pseudo-fascist posturing of the group, which urges the "complete negation of one's identity" in favor of "the mass, collective ideology."

Writer-director Goran Gajic, who has previously made commercials for the Yugoslav office of Saatchi & Saatchi, saw this film temporarily banned by the Communist regime. Still, it remains a curious choice for the Boston fest's "Human Rights Watch" sidebar, and a disturbing film because it never answers the one question at the core of Laibach: If you can't tell the difference between the "performance" and the real thing, is there a difference?

— *Daniel M. Kimmel*

RAIN WITHOUT THUNDER

A TAZ Pictures production. Executive producers, Rich Callahan, Mike Mihalich. Produced by Nanette Sorenson, Gary Sorenson. Directed, written by Gary Bennett. Camera (Technicolor), Karl Kases; editor, Mallory Gottlieb, Suzanne Pillsbury; music, Randall Lynch, Alex Lynch; production design, Gail Bartley; associate producers, Nicole Myers, Judy Frey; casting, Susan Willett, Irene Schaeffer-Stockton. Reviewed at Loews Copley Place Theater, Boston, Sept. 8, 1992. (In Boston Film Festival.) Running time: **85 MIN.**
Reporter . . . . . Carolyn McCormick
Alison Goldring . . . . Ali Thomas
Beverly Goldring . . . . Betty Buckley
Andrea Murdoch . . . . . . Iona Morris
Jonathan Garson . . . . . Jeff Daniels
Warden . . . . . . Frederic Forrest
Atwood society director . . Linda Hunt
Jeremy Tanner . . . . Steve Zahn
Also with: Robert Earl Jones, Graham Greene, Austin Pendleton.

Slickly produced pro-abortion rights feature creates a world 50 years hence where abortions are banned in the U.S. and a kidnapping law punishes women who go overseas for the operation. A low budget enlisting some notable actors apparently for only a day of shooting apiece sinks pic's good intentions. Resulting pic with little drama but lots of talk will play the fest circuit and some art houses, gaining a strong cult following. Prospects beyond that are doubtful.

Premise is a reporter doing a docu on the first women prosecuted under a 2042 law meant to prevent well-heeled families from skirting the ban. Where seeing the ensuing battle might have made for a riveting dystopian drama, watching talking heads on the future wears thin.

Only time the film breaks out of the interviews mold is to show brief flashbacks that ironically couldn't have been filmed. Even with an impressive array of on-camera talent, pic's little more than a static propaganda piece.

Linda Hunt is quietly compelling as a women's rights leader who feels abortion on demand can't be argued; instead, they must fight for the more conservative goal of barring punishment for having abortions. Iona Morris is chilling as the crisp prosecutor who sees the kidnapping law as restoring equality to the system; previously, only poor women were punished.

Writer-director Gary Bennett has carefully worked out the ramifications of his brave new world, complete with a Catholic Church which strengthens its anti-abortion stand by reversing its ban on barrier contraceptives. Austin Pendleton has a nice turn as a priest explaining the "Messiah principle" — opposition to abortion because it might kill the coming of the Messiah.

Production values are crisp, with production design and costumes suggesting the mid-21st century world in swift and subtle strokes.
— *Daniel M. Kimmel*

PEEPHOLE

A Solomonness production. Produced by Jonny Solomon. Directed, written by Shem Bitterman. Camera (Fotokem color), Dermott Downs; editor, Peter Cohen; music, Christian Osborne; production design, Ted J. Crittenden; sound, Jack Lindauer; line producer, Bryan Azorsky. Reviewed at Loews Copley Place Theater, Boston, Sept. 8, 1992. (In Boston Film Festival.) Running time: **90 MIN.**

With: Patrick Husted, Rick Dean, Kristen Trucksess, Nancy Mette, William Dennis Hunt.

What may have worked as a psychodrama on a stylized stage set sputters to a halt on screen against a realistic background. Saga of an M.D. caught up in child molesting case is disjointed and confusing, resulting in lack of a convincing story to hold interest.

Patrick Husted plays a criminal psychiatrist who may not have all his marbles himself. He shares his house with his sister; maybe it's an incestuous relationship. He becomes involved with Sheena (Kristen Trucksess), a prostitute who knows his patient (Rick Dean), and ends up setting her up in her own house. He enjoys watching her with clients.

He parries with a detective (William Dennis Hunt) who maybe suspects Husted is guilty of a series of child murders. Ambiguity is apparently deliberate, but the point is lost because the filmmakers don't divulge enough details.

Performances add little to the mix. Writer/director Shem Bitterman, adapting his own play, keeps the settings dark and claustrophobic, but much of the film is just incident after incident — some unexplained — until thin story line emerges. Tech credits are low-key, low-budget, adequate. — *Daniel M. Kimmel*

ARCHIVE REVIEW

SPANISH DRACULA
(B&W)

A MCA/Universal release of a Universal City Studios production. Produced by Carl Laemmle Jr. Associate producer, Paul Kohner. Directed by George Melford. Screenplay, Garrett Fort, based on Bram Stoker's novel & Hamilton Deane, John Balderston's play; adapted in Spanish by B. Fernández Cue. Camera (B&W), George Robinson; editor, Arturo Tavares; art direction, Charles D. Hall. Reviewed on MCA/Universal videocassette, N.Y. Running time: **104 MIN.**

Dracula . . . . Carlos Villarias
Eva . . . . Lupita Tovar
Dr. Van Helsing . Eduardo Arozamena
Renfield . . . . . Pablo Alvarez Rubio
Juan Harker . . . . . . Barry Norton
Lucia . . . . Carmen Guerrero
Dr. Seward . . . . José Soriano Viosca
Marta . . . . Amelia Senisterra
Martin . . . . Manuel Arbó

When Tod Browning directed Bela Lugosi in "Dracu-

la" during the day in 1931, Spanish actor Carlos Villarias donned the cape in the evenings and a Spanish-lingo cast performed a simultaneous parallel version. Helmed by George Melford, using the same sets, locations and script, this curiosity (including recently discovered and archival footage) has been released as part of MCA/Universal Home Video's Classic Monsters Collection.

Contrasting the works, Dracula's entrance is more dramatic in the Spanish, beginning with a wide shot before going to a dolly and zoom, but in general the film is far less ambitious technically with fewer dolly or tracking shots. Images are more static with less tension, and shots tend to be wider with fewer closeups and less involvement in the individual characters.

Although both films share the same cutaways, the Spanish version lacks extras, making it look stagebound. The sea sequence has been reduced to just a few shots sans storm footage. Dialog has also been trimmed in the English version, picking up the pace.

Versions also differ in running time. While the Browning version clocks in at a brisk 75 minutes, Melford's creeps along to 104 minutes with ponderous pauses and plodding dialog.

While superior, Browning's version leaves some details unresolved: Lucy is forgotten in the former but lain to eternal rest in the Spanish rendition. Browning's film ends with Dr. Van Helsing saying he wants to remain at the Abbey, while Melford explains that the good doctor is going to "keep a promise" to Renfield.

Despite his scary looks, Villarias' Dracula lacks Lugosi's moth-to-the-flame allure and presence; his melodramatic pauses are almost comic. But the female characters, especially Lupita Tovar's Mina (Eva in the Spanish item), are more concupiscent, underlining the film's basic sexuality. In any language, Renfield's role is a gift to any ham actor, and the part of Martin has been expanded in Spanish from that of a Cockney skeptic to a genuine comic buffoon.

Tape begins with a short intro by Tovar, who in 1931 also played the title role in "Santa," Mexico's first talkie.

— *Paul Lenti*

1492:
CONQUEST OF PARADISE
(BRITISH-FRENCH-SPANISH)

A Paramount release of a Percy Main/Legende/Cyrk production. Produced by Ridley Scott, Alain Goldman. Executive producers, Mimi Polk Sotela, Iain Smith. Co-producers, Marc Boyman, Roselyne Bosch, Pere Fages. Directed by Scott. Screenplay, Bosch. Camera (Rank color; Panavision widescreen), Adrian Biddle; editors, William Anderson, Françoise Bonnot; music, Vangelis; production design, Norman Spencer; supervising art directors, Benjamin Fernandez, Leslie Tomkins; art direction, Raul Antonio Paton, Kevin Phipps, Martin Hitchcock, Luke Scott; set decoration, Ann Mollo; costume design, Charles Knode, Barbara Rutter; sound (Dolby), Pierre Gamet; associate producer, Garth Thomas; assistant director, Terry Needham; special effects supervisor, Kit West; 2nd unit director, Hugh Johnson; casting, Louis Digiaimo. Reviewed at Village Theater, L.A., Oct. 1, 1992. MPAA Rating: PG13. Running time: **150 MIN.**

Columbus . . . . . . Gérard Depardieu
Sanchez . . . . Armand Assante
Queen Isabel . . . . Sigourney Weaver
Older Fernando . . . . . Loren Dean
Beatrix . . . . Angela Molina
Marchena . . . . Fernando Rey
Moxica . . . . Michael Wincott
Pinzon . . . . Tcheky Karyo
Capt. Mendez . . . . . . Kevin Dunn
Santangel . . . . . . Frank Langella
Bobadilla . . . . . . Mark Margolis
Arojaz . . . . Kario Salem
Fernando (age 10) . . . . Billy Sullivan
Brother Buyl . . . . . . John Heffernan
Guevara . . . . Arnold Vosloo
Bartolome . . . . . Steven Waddington
Giacomo . . . . . . Fernando G. Cuervo
Alonso . . . . Jose Luis Ferrer
Utapan . . . . Bercelio Moya

All of Ridley Scott's vaunted visuals can't transform "1492" from a lumbering, one-dimensional historical fresco into the complex, ambiguous character study that it strives to be. Ambitious independent production often struggles to hold interest during the lengthy running time and, while the physical aspects of carving out a European presence in the New World are often vividly evoked, bombast and pretention are in greater evidence than real drama and psychological insight. Interest in Scott, Gérard Depardieu and seeing the "real" Columbus film may spark some initial box office, but pic looks to have a short commercial voyage.

In contrast to recent revisionist attacks on the explorer's character and leading role in launching the European subjugation of native Americans, French journalist and first-time screenwriter Roselyne Bosch offers up a humanistic pacifist driven by an enigmatic mix of motives to settle a new land. "They are not savages, and neither will we be," he announces to his crew.

At the outset, Columbus is presented as both a visionary and a man of logic, a man allied with monks but disgusted by the Inquisition, a rationalist in an age of religious superstition, an adventurer among timid conformists. Crucially, he is able to charm the Spanish queen into sending him into the unknown. After a remarkably uneventful voyage spurred by one little inspirational speech to his nervous crew, Columbus reaches his promised "earthly paradise" and establishes a relatively benign relationship with the natives.

After his triumphant return home, a new, 17-ship expedition is launched. Ultimately, Columbus administrates ineptly and tries ineffectually to promote a policy of peaceful coexistence. Minds dominated by military ambition, religious fervor and greed inevitably gain the upper hand and turn the lush tropical settlement into a living hell.

Bosch has imposed this basic dramatic arc upon a very unwieldy life story which actually encompassed four voyages over 10 years. Unfortunately, for all the visual impact Scott brings to the saga, his dazzling muralistic style has the effect of flattening things out to the point where they have all the dimensionality of a medieval painting.

Relationships in the movie barely exist. When Queen Isabel informs Columbus that he can embark on a third journey, but without his brothers, it's unclear that he's had brothers along with him before (a problem compounded by the fact that one is played by a Brit, the other by a Spaniard). And is Angela Molina the hero's wife or mistress?

Scott takes slightly greater interest in the political dynamics informing the yarn. The Crown's treasurer (Armand Assante) plays out an ambiguous relationship with Columbus throughout all of the latter's changing fortunes, while three of the hero's principal adversaries are cast so that the actors' nasty looks say it all about their villainy (e.g., Michael Wincott's saboteur).

Sigourney Weaver briefly suggests a sexual susceptibility to Columbus behind the queen's approval of his grand scheme. But no one is allowed the opportunity to develop a character.

As for Depardieu's Columbus, the great French actor does his best to get his mouth around the long speeches and harangues, and is comprehensible most of the time. His energy, passion and conviction are ideal for the role, but perhaps it remains beyond him at this point to act in English in depth.

In this Scott film, the visuals are expected to virtually do it all. As beautiful as some of the images are, helmer is mostly straining for effect here, injecting fog and smoke into the frame at every opportunity (even, implausibly, in open water under clear skies), and finally succumbs to total overkill in the gruesome, thunderous scenes of colonial calamity.

Still, there are striking moments that stick in the mind. Columbus' first glimpse of the New World comes, breathtakingly, as some fog breaks, revealing a verdant jungle looming close behind it.

Overall, dramatic pacing is ponderous and indulgent, accentuated by Vangelis' occasionally effective but mostly overbearing wall-to-wall score.

Adrian Biddle's lensing is marked by the contrast between gloomy interiors streaked with window and candle light, and blindingly sunny exteriors. Norman Spencer's wonderfully detailed production design abets the multitude of actual medieval locations in Spain, and creates a convincingly ratty initial colonial village (North American sections were shot in Costa Rica). Charles Knode and Barbara Rutter's costume contributions are first-rate, as are other behind-the-scenes efforts.

Three major pics, including the stodgy British 1949 Fredric March biopic and the recent Salkind flop, have proven Columbus' story difficult to dramatize or put over with the public (ironically, all have been undertaken by foreign, not U.S., producers). It should be a while until anyone tries again. — *Todd McCarthy*

UNDER SIEGE

A Warner Bros. release of an Arnon Milchan production, in association with Regency Enterprises, Le Studio Canal Plus & Alcor Films. Produced by Milchan, Steven Seagal, Steven Reuther. Executive producers, J.F. Lawton, Gary Goldstein. Co-producers, J. B. Bernstein, Peter Macgregor-Scott. Directed by Andrew Davis. Screenplay, Lawton. Camera (Technicolor, Panavision), Frank Tidy; editors, Robert A. Ferretti, Dennis Virkler, Don Brochu, Dov Hoenig; music, Gary Chang; production design, Bill Kenney; art direction, Bill Hiney, set design, Al Manzer; set decoration, Rick Gentz; costume design, Richard Bruno; special effects coordinator, Thomas L. Fisher; stunt coordinator, Conrad E. Palmisano; assistant director, Tom Mack; casting, Pamela Basker. Reviewed at Village Theater, L.A., Oct. 7, 1992. MPAA Rating: R. Running time: **102 MIN.**

Casey Ryback . . . . . . Steven Seagal
William Strannix . . Tommy Lee Jones
Commander Krill . . . . . Gary Busey
Jordan Tate . . . . Erika Eleniak
Capt. Adams . . . . . . Patrick O'Neal
Tom Breaker . . . . Nick Mancuso
Adm. Bates . . . . Andy Romano

Warners has the right stuff with "Under Siege," an immensely slick, if also old-fashioned and formulaic, entertainment. Steven Seagal fans and action buffs should eat this up — taut suspense, high production values, especially in cinematography and sound — guaranteeing a solid hit in a season that lacks competition from similar fare.

Seagal plays a cook on the USS Missouri, the Navy's largest and most powerful battleship, now reaching the end of a long line of service from World War II to the Gulf War. But en route to decommission, a quiet, calm journey turns out to be volatile and dangerous when two corrupt psychopaths, both top military experts, hijack the ship and steal its nuclear arsenal.

Scripter J.F. Lawton ("Pretty Woman") cleverly structures the suspenseful actioner around the three lead characters, all played by accomplished actors. Seagal's rebellious cook is actually a decorated Navy Seal. But his true identity is known only to his benevolent commander (Patrick O'Neal), who arranged the kitchen job for him to complete his tour of duty.

Seagal is contrasted with the lethal and hot-tempered William Strannix (Tommy Lee Jones), a former covert CIA operative, and Commander Krill (Gary Busey), a frustrated officer. Motivated by revenge, both men feel they have good reasons to execute their diabolical plot. An attractive actress (Playboy, "Baywatch" alum Erika Eleniak) hired to perform at a farewell party, is thrown into the all-male adventure, and later functions as Seagal's resourceful mate and quasi-romantic interest.

Regrettably, pic's broader political context is so superfluous and external to the core action that it becomes mere set decoration. Indeed, pic lacks an alert intelligence and a sense of immediacy that would charge up the story.

But the fun of such predictable fare is based in exhilarating action set pieces, of which the film has plenty. Moreover, in between battles, blasts and explosions, scripter Lawton has shrewdly placed funny one-liners, delivered by Seagal in his customary cool, tongue-in-cheek style.

Jones forcefully portrays a deranged villain in black leather jacket and sunglasses. In a smaller, but no less flashy, part, Busey also enlivens the otherwise simplistic narrative.

Pic stays completely within the conventions of the action genre, lacking any thematic turns or twists. The anticipated climax, a man-to-man fight between Seagal and Jones, is not only long in coming, but also too brief and disappointingly staged.

Director Andrew Davis' quick, by-the-numbers style and Frank Holgate's inventive lensing of the battleship's interior and exteriors build the necessary suspense. Bill Kenney's production design deftly sweeps viewers into the ship's inner, claustrophobic world. Editor Robert Ferretti and his crew enhanced the thrills with imaginative cutting.
— *Emanuel Levy*

AMERICAN FABULOUS
(DOCU)

A First Run Features presentation of a Dead Jeffe Prods. film. Produced, directed, edited by Reno Dakota. Written & performed by Jeffrey Strouth. Camera (color, video, 35m transfer), Travis Ruse, Dakota; song "Royal Cafe," written & performed by American Music Club. Reviewed in San Francisco, July 15, 1992. Running time: **105 MIN.**

Part Spalding Gray-type monologue, part cinéma-vérité Americana and 100% camp, "American Fabulous" is basically a forum for the distinctive chatter of its real-life subject. Pic's narrow focus and lack of visual interest will make it a tough sell in most markets.

Jeffrey Strouth (who died of AIDS last year) presents himself as a flamboyantly queeny, white-trash denizen of the Midwest — one whose saga would have worked well as an early John Waters pic. His bottomless well of lurid, often funny experiences constitute a kind of gay Jack Kerouac odyssey.

Holding forth from the backseat of an old car as it rolls around Ohio backroads and highways, Strouth says with some pride that "my very existence is a crime in most people's eyes." He's clearly reveled in being an outsider all his life, but his story has more than its share of brutality: beatings from an alcoholic father, poverty, a teenage prostitution stint, a bloody escape from a psycho and heroin addiction in NYC.

In his colorful oral history, though, even the bleakest episodes (like a sister's suicide and funeral) take on giddy comic hues. Drag queens, pathetic pickups and the Salvation Army are among the characters summoned up in various absurd/tragic tales.

Film is "spontaneously written and performed" by Strouth, resulting in a weird hybrid effect: His delivery is to an extent annoyingly calculated, but the material isn't neatly tied up into completed anecdotes or a full life's overview. Whether the stories are entirely true or not is an open question that comes with the tall-tale style.

Tech work is okay considering that the camera rarely does anything but point at the subject from the car's front seat, with primitive wipes between sequences. While hardly presenting a progressive gay image, docu does offer implicit respect for its hero's wild nonconformism.

Gus Van Sant and playwright Tony Kushner are acknowledged in end credits. — *Dennis Harvey*

NEW YORK FEST

NIGHT AND THE CITY

A 20th Century Fox release of a Tribeca production in association with Penta Entertainment. Produced by Jane Rosenthal, Irwin Winkler. Executive producers, Harry J. Ufland, Mary Jane Ufland, Rob Cowan. Co-producer, Rob Cowan. Directed by Winkler. Screenplay, Richard Price, based on the 1950 film directed by Jules Dassin; screenplay, Jo Eisinger, from Gerald Kersh's novel. Camera (Technicolor; Deluxe prints), Tak Fujimoto; editor, David Brenner; music, James Newton Howard; production design, Peter Larkin; art direction, Charley Beale; set decoration, Robert J. Franco; costume design, Richard Bruno; sound (Dolby), Tod Maitland; associate producer, Nelson McCormick; assistant director, Joseph Reidy; casting, Todd Thaler. Reviewed at CAA screening room, Beverly Hills, Calif., Aug. 12, 1992. MPAA Rating: R. Running time: **98 MIN.**
Harry Fabian . . . . . Robert De Niro
Helen Nasseros . . . . . Jessica Lange
Phil Nasseros . . . . Cliff Gorman
Boom Boom Grossman . . . Alan King
Al Grossman . . . . Jack Warden
Peck . . . . Eli Wallach
Tommy Tessler . . . . . . Barry Primus
Resnick . . . . Gene Kirkwood
Cuda Sanchez . . . . . . Pedro Sanchez

"Night and the City" is a

skilled, if not entirely psychologically convincing, remake of the 1950 film noir classic of the same name. Lively performances, pungent NYC atmosphere and abundance of dramatic incident keep this story of an irrepressible low-life hustler ripping along, although it will probably go down better with fresh audiences than those familiar with its predecessor.

Irwin Winkler's dark but energetic pic, which had its world premiere as the closing night item at the New York film fest Oct. 11, looks like a middle-range commercial entry.

Playing a frenetic, wired character right up his alley, Robert De Niro stars as Harry Fabian, a longtime ambulance-chasing lawyer who conceives the big-time scheme to promote "The Return of People's Boxing" with a night of fights featuring sharp locals.

Harry's timeworn methods, however, involve scamming and getting on the wrong side of people bigger than he is, such as boxing promoter Boom Boom Grossman (Alan King), a genial tough guy who doesn't take kindly to Harry horning in.

For help in putting on his card, Harry recruits Boom Boom's estranged brother Al (Jack Warden), a grizzled former prizefighter, and Eli Wallach's retired moneyman. He also counts on an investment from his good friend Phil (Cliff Gorman), a bar owner, but at the same time proceeds to lure away Phil's wife Helen (Jessica Lange), whom he then provides with a counterfeit liquor license for her own bar.

So not only does Harry display bad business sense, he seems in every way a loser, except for the eternal hope that keeps his hustle going. De Niro conveys splendidly the drive, naiveté and desperation that fuel Harry's ceaseless movement, as well as the enthusiasm necessary to convince people to do things against their better judgment. What doesn't quite click, though, is the idea that someone this compulsive wouldn't have gotten somewhere by this point.

Richard Widmark's Harry Fabian in the original film (set in London) was very credibly a young American who remained in Europe after the war and tried to con his way through a foreign, hostile system in which he was clearly an outsider. The way he pushed, he was either going to succeed quickly or die trying.

De Niro's Harry pushes just as brazenly, but fact that he's in

his late 40s creates a credibility gap never satisfactorily filled by biographical details. Such ballsiness in a man in his 20s can be written off to youthful audacity and nerve, but at Harry's age, it often looks like misguided foolishness.

Harry's chronic unreliability also makes it more than a bit farfetched that Helen, also in her 40s, would place her life in the hands of someone who has nothing to offer. No particular sexual spark is indicated between the two, nor does Lange's laid-back performance suggest any reasons for her understanding, forgiving behavior.

But these unsettling character factors aside, there's a lot going on here to grab the attention. Working territory he knows well, screenwriter Richard Price serves up lots of salty streetwise talk that fits snugly in pic's barrooms, gyms and back alleys.

Although much less of this film is set at night than is the original, director Winkler and lenser Tak Fujimoto keep their camera ever on the prowl, and always with an eye to the grungy, telling detail. Result is a vivid, rough, threatening view of life in Gotham today, even if the various techniques of quick cutting, long Steadicam shots and loads of vintage pop tunes inevitably recall the style of producer Winkler's frequent director partner, Martin Scorsese.

Character actors Gorman, King, Warden and Wallach have plenty of gritty dialogue and attitudes to sink their teeth into, and all come off extremely well. Gene Tierney's role in the first version, an add-on to the script at the behest of Darryl Zanuck, doesn't exist here. Story's ending has also been altered, to less powerful effect.

In a nice gesture, pic is dedicated to Jules Dassin, director of the original film.

— *Todd McCarthy*

IDIOT
(INDIAN)

A Doordarshan Television production. Directed by Mani Kaul. Screenplay, Anup Singh, based on Fyodor Dostoevsky's novel. Camera (color), Piyush Shah; editor, Lalitha Krishna; music, D. Wood, Vikram Joglekar; sound, Vikram Joglekar; costumes, Anuradha Chaubal. Reviewed at N.Y. Film Festival, Oct. 2, 1992. Running time: **185 MIN.**
Prince Miskin . . . . . Ayub Khan Din
Pavan Raghujan . . . Shah Rukh Khan
Nastassya . . . . Mita Vashisth
Amba Mehta . . . . . Navjot Hansra

Mathew . . . . Vasudeo Bhatt
Ganesh . . . . Deepak Mahan
Colonel . . . . Babulai Bora
Leelavati Mehta . Meenakshi Goswami
Mr. Mehta . . . . Zul Vellani
Shapit . . . . Amritlal Thulal

Director Mani Kaul has rendered an austere version of the Fyodor Dostoevsky classic that seeks to pare away all sentimentality. Although Kaul and scriptwriter Anup Singh have tried to shift the Russian author's concern for his homeland to a meditation on contemporary India, "Idiot" fails to develop the substance for an intellectual approach. Result is a turgid, lifeless three-hour film that will numb viewers and be a highly unlikely export.

Kaul's cerebral style manages to drain the screen of emotion while lacking the formal grace of a Robert Bresson that would keep the drama from lapsing into banality. Prince Miskin (Mishkin in the original novel) is shorn of some of his buffoonish traits and is portrayed as a slightly distracted saint. Ayub Khan Din plays the role with a disconcerting stoicism. Most of the other characters are also reduced to rhetorical mouthpieces who speak in declamatory tones.

Kaul, however, makes no attempt to tone down Dostoevsky's most wildly melodramatic character, Rogozhin, here called Raghujan. As played by Shah Rukh Khan, he starts most scenes with a sinister chuckle, as if he had prepared for his role by studying old Richard Widmark movies.

Kaul's moving camera weaves in and out among his players as if trying to penetrate some hidden truth, but little tension between the characters and their inner lives is ever signified. Annoying chime-like background sounds resound occasionally to underline a dramatic point.

The English subtitling, which may have been completed just in time for "Idiot's" premiere, is less helpful than it should be. Songs are heard untranslated, and among many spelling errors, one character is described as "teribly uneducated."

Of the several prior adaptations of this novel, perhaps the most famous is Akira Kurosawa's 1951 version. Georges Lampin directed a 1946 French adaptation starring Gerard Philipe, and Ivan Pyriev helmed a two-part 1959 Russian version.

— *Fred Lombardi*

IL GIARDINO DEI CILIEGI
(THE CHERRY ORCHARD)
(ITALIAN)

A DIAA production. Produced by Marco Donati & Pier Francesco Aiello. Directed by Antonello Aglioti. Screenplay, Aglioti, Bernardino Zapponi, based on an idea by Aglioti. Camera (Fujicolor), Luigi Verga; editor, Roberto Missiroli; music, Luigi Ceccarelli, Marco Ridolfi; sets, Nello Giorgetti; costumes, Carlo Poggioli; sound, Franco Borni. Reviewed at San Sebastian Film Festival, Sept. 23, 1992. Running time: **95 MIN.**
Livia . . . . Susan Strasberg
Vania . . . . Barbara de Rossi
Leo . . . . Gabriele Gori
Charlotte . . . . . . Marisa Berenson
Also with: Dado Rospoli, Valentina Forte, Aldo d'Amorocio, Fabrizio Mele.

"The Cherry Orchard" had the dubious (but justifiable) distinction of being the most lambasted by critics, both international and local, at San Sebastian. Vaguely based on the famous Anton Chekov play, dud pic is a seemingly endless succession of disjointed scenes. Original's poignancy and drama is totally missed.

The camera never remains on any character long enough for the viewer to get an inkling of who he or she is, and the story is lost amid period poses, clumsy cutting and inchoate dialogue.
— *Peter Besas*

VERLORENE LANDSCHAFT
(LOST LANDSCAPE)
(GERMAN-COLOR-B&W)

A Von Vietinghoff Filmproduktion film. Produced by Joachim von Vietinghoff. Directed, written by Andreas Kleinert. Camera (color, B&W), Sebastian Richter; editor, Helga Gentz; music, Brymmor Llewelyn Jones; sets, Paul Lehmann; costumes, Ulrike Stelzig; sound, Hans Henning Thölert. Reviewed at San Sebastian Film Festival, Sept. 21, 1992. Running time: **107 MIN.**
Elias . . . . Roland Schäfer
Mother (young) . Friedericke Kammer
Father (young) . . . . Sylvester Groth
Father (old) . . . . . . Christoph Engel
Mother (old) . . . . . . Christine Gloger
Laura . . . . Cornelia Schmaus

"Lost Landscape" is beautifully lensed, wonderfully thesped but considerably complex and laden with illusions that may be unknown to outsiders, making for a limited aud outside Germany.

Andreas Kleinert's film is a moving, symbol-laden, sensitive excursion into the memories of a German politician who grew up a stone's throw from the border.

Shot mostly in black & white, pic skillfully delves into the politico's childhood. He lived entirely within the confines of his parents' farm, a kind of expressionist world unto itself and a capsule of integrity within a corrupt world.

Most of pic is told as a long flashback when the politician receives an anonymous call that his parents have died. He returns to the small farm where he grew up, stopping at a shoddy hotel. Time frame moves back and forth between various periods of the pol's childhood. — *Peter Besas*

CANDYMAN

A TriStar release in association with Polygram Filmed Entertainment of a Propaganda Films production. Produced by Steve Golin, Sigurjon Sighvatsson, Alan Poul. Executive producer, Clive Barker. Line producer, Gregory Goodman. Directed, written by Bernard Rose, based on Barker's short story "The Forbidden." Camera (Deluxe color), Anthony B. Richmond; editor, Dan Rae; music, Philip Glass; production design, Jane Ann Stewart; art direction, David Lazan; set decoration, Kathryn Peters; costume design, Leonard Pollack; sound (Dolby), Reinhard Stergar; sound design, Nigel Holland; special makeup effects, Bob Keen; visual effects, Cruse & Company; special effects created by Martin Bresin; special makeup effects created by Image Animation; stunt coordinator, Walter Scott; assistant director, Thomas Patrick Smith; casting, Jason La Padura. Reviewed at Toronto Festival of Festivals, Sept. 12, 1992. MPAA rating: R. Running time: **93 MIN.**
Helen Lyle . . . . . . Virginia Madsen
Candyman . . . . Tony Todd
Trevor Lyle . . . . . Xander Berkeley
Bernadette Walsh . . . Kasi Lemmons
Anne-Marie McCoy . Vanessa Williams
Jake . . . . DeJuan Guy
Purcell . . . . Michael Culkin
Dr. Burke . . . . . . Stanley DeSantis
Det. Frank Valento . . . Gilbert Lewis

"Candyman" is an upperregister horror item that delivers the requisite shocks and gore but doesn't cheat or cop out. Premiered to appreciative screams and hoots at a Toronto fest midnight crowd, the picture should win theatrically in quick, wide playoff, as well as down the line on video.

TriStar released "Hook" last Christmas, but now it has the literal article: a mythical serial killer whose weapon is a ghastly hook where his right hand was.

Imaginatively setting the story between the physically proximate worlds of safe academia and threatening ghetto, writer-director Bernard Rose leads the audience into the mystery via doctoral candidate Virginia Madsen.

The wife of anthropology prof Trevor Lyle is studying neighborhood legends and learns that Candyman, the educated, talented son of a slave, had his hand cut off and was put to death by throwing him to a swarm of bees in revenge for impregnating a young upper-class woman.

Madsen's investigation leads her to the site of the century-old outrage, Cabrini Green, now crime-ridden housing projects in Chicago. Supposedly, Candyman has committed 21 murders thus far, and it doesn't take long for Madsen to discover his gruesome lair in the projects.

Both plot and the all-important psychological dimension are pulled together neatly and plausibly, and the usual horror coda proves emotionally satisfying for a change.

Film trades in an unspoken but troubling resonance between the racism that doomed the original Candyman and persistent polarity today, and is expressed in the unsettling Cabrini Green sequences. These raw urban realities bring an unusual dimension to this sort of genre piece.

Working from a story originally set in Liverpool by horrormeister Clive Barker, Brit helmer Rose provides plenty of jolts, both bogus and actual, along the way. Threat of Candyman bursting out from behind mirrors is ever-present, and his evisceration technique with his hook is particularly gruesome.

Performances are unusually credible for this sort of fare. Although Madsen behaves audaciously in the course of her research, she never stupidly wanders into harm's way like so many other horror heroines, and she registers as a strong lead. Vanessa Williams, as a bereaved mother, and little guy DeJuan Guy are notable as projects denizens, and Tony Todd, with his voice hugely amplified, is a suitably scary Candyman.

Philip Glass has delivered some highly effective backgrounding of piano, organ and chorus. Other tech credits are solid.
— *Todd McCarthy*

FATHER, SANTA KLAUS HAS DIED
(RUSSIAN-B&W)

A Lenfilm Studio Kinoassociation/ The Experimental Studio of the First Film production. Directed by Eugeny Yufit. Screenplay, Vladimir Maslov. Camera (B&W), Alexy Burov; editor, T. Shapiro; art direction, Yufit; sound, Mikhail Podtakui. Reviewed at Toronto Festival of Festivals, Sept. 18, 1992. (Also in Rimini Cinema fest.) Running time: **79 MIN.**
With: Anatoly Egorov, Ivan Ganzha, Ljudmila Kozlovskava, Valery Krishtapenco, Maxim Gribov.

Loosely based on Leo Tolstoy's short story "The Vampire's Family," "Father, Santa Klaus Has Died" works best as an almost silent horror film with poetic touches. Scripterhelmer Eugeny Yufit's impressive feature debut exemplifies the kind of art film perfectly suited for film fests.

Anatoly Egorov plays a serious biologist, bespectacled and intelligent. He is contrasted with his brother, an unshaven brute who lives in the country with his wife and son, to represent opposing philosophies of life.

Through the brothers' interaction, the narrative contrasts scientific rationality with the mystery of nature, socialized behavior with one dominated by biological instincts, and the power of living vs. the morbidity of death.

This is the work of a visionary director whose coherent concept and unique visual style show in every frame. Influenced by the late Russian master Andrei Tarkovsky, Yufit favors extreme long takes, stationery camera and slow pacing. Often mysterious film uses horror and sci-fi conventions, and the many standout tableaux depict S&M and bondage, the suicide of a young boy and a family funeral in the open fields. But the dark, moody film is not devoid of humor: After a lengthy sequence of sheer horror, a title card suddenly relates, "It was getting cold soon."

Yufit, who was a student of the great avant-garde director Aleksandr Sokhurov, also was art director of this feature. Pic's most prominent feature is its stark black & white cinematography which suitably conveys its heightened realism. As in most experimental Russo pics, dialogue

is extremely sparse, and there are long soundless stretches.
— *Emanuel Levy*

THE STONE
(RUSSIAN-B&W)

A Lenfilm Studio production. Directed by Aleksandr Sokhurov. Screenplay, Yuri Arabov. Camera (B&W), Andrey Bourov; editor, L. Semionova; sound, Vladimir Persov. Reviewed at Toronto Festival of Festivals, Sept. 15, 1992. (Also in New York Film Festival.) Running time: **87 MIN.**
With: Leonid Mozgovoy, Piotr Alexandrov, V. Semlonov.

"**The Stone**" reaffirms Aleksandr Sokhurov as one of the most innovative filmmakers in contempo avant-garde Russian cinema. In his extremely demanding new work, the prolific helmer continues to experiment with cinema language and its impact on the film experience. Lack of conventional story line and slow pacing here will prove difficult for mainstream moviegoers.

Set and actually lensed at the Anton Chekhov museum, pic is structured as a series of encounters between a young man who works as a museum guard and an older, mysterious man who may be the famous writer himself.

The film can be experienced as a reverie strong on ambiance and stunning visuals. There are many hidden messages in the interaction between the two men, who drift in and out of the story in an unpredictable, but always fascinating, manner. Freudian texture and tone suggests that the young man may relate to the older man as surrogate father.

Constructed like a symphony, this decidedly unconventional narrative film is an exploration of the two basic conventions of the medium, time and space, and the various ways they interact, fuse and collide.

For long periods, this quiet and hypnotic film relies on natural sounds. One can actually hear the men breathing. This stillness becomes particularly effective when it is violated by dialogue or broken with classical music.

Andrey Bourov's spellbinding lensing gives the mostly interior film a moody black & white stylization. Of the few outdoor scenes, one long take of a snowstorm is so magical, it gives the viewer the glowing feeling of being there. Almost every shot is startling with inventive mise en scene and unusual framing,

and because the camera stays at a chilling distance, the sparse use of closeups is most effective.

Provocative and always stimulating film forces the viewers to challenge and reexamine their own ways of reading films.
— *Emanuel Levy*

A FAIRY FOR DESSERT
(EINE TUNTE ZUM DESSERT)
(GERMAN)

A Wolfgang Krenz Filmproduktion. Produced by Krenz. Directed, written by Dagmar Beiersdorf. Camera (color), Christoph Gies; editor, Lothar Lambert; music, Pete Wyoming-Bender, Martine Felton, Albert Kittler; sound, Albert Kittler. Reviewed at Toronto Festival of Festivals, Sept. 19, 1992. Running time: **85 MIN.**
Julchen . . . . Lothar Lambert
Mascha . . . . Suzanne Gautier
Rajab . . . . Mustafa Iskandarani

Similar to, but less funny than "La Cage aux Folles," German feature "A Fairy for Dessert" aims at being an existential comedy about a modern family that defies easy labels. However, once the "deviant," nonconventional network is set and accepted, the narrative becomes conventional and the treatment sentimental.

Lothar Lambert, helmer Dagmar Beiersdorf's collaborator on other films, plays a good-natured transvestite and a mother figure to a half-Moroccan girl, via his relationship with her father. The daughter is told that her biological mother is dead, though she is very much around, observing her kid from afar. Narrative revolves around Lambert's strong desire and frustrating attempts to bring everybody together, which creates obvious complications.

Writer-director Beiersdorf's mild approach blends cynicism and sentimentality. Like "La Cage," the intermittently funny comedy attacks all facades and hypocrisies — gay or straight. Ultimately, what saves the comedy from overfamiliarity and banality is a gallery of warm and vulnerable characters who are treated sans prejudice or bias.

Beiersdorf's previous pic ("Dirty Daughters," also at the Toronto fest), showed tighter and more compelling direction. Fortunately, Lambert (also editor) gives a flamboyantly funny performance in the lead. He is ably supported by the rest, particularly Suzanne Gautier as the mother, who looks a bit like the older Simone Signoret.

Campy costume design uses pink and purple as dominant colors for Julchen's outrageous but tasteful outfits.

Pic is full of humanity but lacks comic energy; story often drags from one interfactional scene to another. And the happy ending is not only contrived but also unearned. — *Emanuel Levy*

TOKYO FEST

ANLIAN TAOHUAYUAN
(THE PEACH BLOSSOM LAND)
(TAIWANESE)

A production of Performance Workshop Films Ltd. Produced by Ding Nai-Chu. Directed, written by Stan Lai. Camera (color), Christopher Doyle; editor, Chen Bor-Wen; art direction, William Chang; sound, Du Du-Jih. Reviewed at Tokyo Intl. Film Festival (Young Cinema Competition), Sept. 29, 1992. Running time: **105 MIN.**
Yun Zhi-fan . . . . Li Ching-Hsia
(Brigitte Lin)
Jiang Bin-Liu . . . . Jin Shi-Jye
Old Tao . . . . Lee Li-Chun
Master Yuan . . . . Gu Bao-Ming
Spring Flower . . . . . . Ismeme Ding

This clever film about two plays accidentally booked into the same space for dress rehearsal is creative, beautifully filmed and always witty. Hottest pic out of Taiwan won the silver prize for director Stan Lai in the Tokyo fest's Young Cinema contest. Given the popularity of the play it's based on, as well as the pic's universal entertainment value, "The Peach Blossom Land" should be a real art house hit.

Pic opens with the rehearsal of a story centered around two lovers in Shanghai in 1949. Approach to humor is subtle as a touching scene between Yun Zhi-fan, played by major Asian star Brigitte Lin, and Jiang Bin-Liu (Jin Shi-Jye) is interrupted by second troupe wandering onstage.

That troupe performs a comical interpretation of a classical Chinese folk tale in which a cuckolded husband boats upstream and finds utopian Peach Blossom Land, which, unfortunately for him, is inhabited by lookalikes of his wife and her lover. Very physical and exaggerated humor transcends language and cultural barriers without being too schticky.

Following a tearjerking scene between the star-crossed lovers, the comedians again take over, but the pic reaches an hysterical climax when the troupes com-

promise and share the stage. Lines from the two scenes play off each other, altering or emphasizing meaning.

Throughout the play runs a dingbat stage manager who can't get anything right and a random crazy woman who comes to the theater looking for the unknown Liu Zi-ji. Her search wreaks even more havoc than already abounds.

First-ever Taiwanese pic to be made without Chinese subtitles, the film is mostly in Mandarin, with a bit of Taiwanese. Following in Chinese and with foreign-language subtitles will be easy.

Acting is skilled; photography slick and colorful. High-quality music for both plays is contrasting yet complementary.
— *Karen Regelman*

SLED DOZHDYA
(TRACES OF RAIN)
(RUSSIAN)

A Eguida production. Produced by Eskander Ametov. Directed by Vladimir V. Nakhabtsev. Screenplay, Sergei Veloshnikov, Nadezhda Smirnova. Camera (color), Nakhabtsev; editor, Valeria Belova; art direction, Andrei Modnikov; sound, Marina Nigmatulina. Reviewed at Tokyo Intl. Film Festival (Young Cinema Competition), Sept. 29, 1992. Running time: **85 MIN.**
Bergher . . . . Juosas Budraitis
Lisaveta . . . . . . Nadezhda Smirnova
Pavel . . . . Leonid Kuravlev
Tanya . . . . . . Ekaterina Vassilyeva

In this sweet and funny love story, a famous conductor tours homeland Russia after a long absence and ends up with a younger woman pianist who might be his daughter. With a touching script but slightly archaic technical prowess, pic is unlikely to be an international b.o. draw but is an encouraging sign from a promising young director and fledgling privatized Russian film industry.

Production company Eguida is a Russian acronym, first letter meaning "experimental," and the young, private company lives up to that compared to state-owned efforts. Lack of government coin shows, but pic is a sincere, artistic attempt to jump-start private Russo film industry.

Back in Russia after the fall of communism and 25 years of working in Germany, the conductor Bergher (Juosas Budraitis) catches up with old friend Pavel (Leonid Kuravlev).

Former wife Tanya (Ekaterian Vassilyeva) learns of Bergher's arrival and informs him he has a daughter — whereabouts unknown — born just after he left. Bergher befriends Lizaveta (Nadezhda Smirnova), Pavel's "ward." Pavel all but admits Lizaveta is his daughter and that he had had an affair with Tanya.

Bergher picks Lizaveta, a conservatory student, to take an absent piano soloist's place on tour. They eventually consummate romance on a train. When Tanya attends Bergher's concert, she sees her missing daughter at the piano and tells Bergher Lizaveta is his daughter.

The young woman threatens suicide and confronts Bergher and Pavel, who both claim to be her father. Very funny scene ensues when the two men, now understandably drunk, sit and figure out (mathematically) that only Pavel could be the dad.

Vladimir V. Nakhabtsev, 1989 film school grad and founder/owner of Eguida, makes his feature helming debut. That and the new private film industry's lack of funding and equipment may have caused costuming inconsistencies (some wardrobe is reused many times), inaccurate lighting and a few instances of shaky camerawork.

Overall, however, sweet pic sports a pleasing classical music soundtrack and treats the near-taboo relationship with humor.
— *Karen Regelman*

SHINO FUNJATTA
(SUMO DO, SUMO DON'T)
(JAPANESE)

A Dalei Co. Ltd. release of a Dalei Co. Ltd. production. Produced by Shoji Masui. Executive producers, Yo Yamamoto, Izuru Hiraaki. Directed, written by Masayuki Suo. Camera (color), Naoki Kayano; editor, Junichi Kikuchi; music, Yoshikazu Suo. Reviewed at Montreal World Film Festival, Sept. 1, 1992. (Also in Tokyo Intl. Film Festival.) Running time: **105 MIN.**
Shushei . . . . Masahiro Motoki
Natsuko . . . . Misa Shimizu
Aoki . . . . Naoto Tanenaka
Anayama . . . . Akira Emoto
Tanaka . . . . Hiromasa Taguchi
Smiley . . . . Robert Hoffman
Haruo . . . . Masaaki Muroi

A funny and endearing workout of a classic teen-pic formula, "Sumo Do, Sumo Don't" bears a bouncy resemblance to John Hughes' early high school comedies. Prospects are upbeat for appropriate specialty markets, but film's ultimate typing as an above-average genre pic won't facilitate a crossover move toward Western audiences.

Shushei, a handsome but lazy

university student, has already secured a decent job through family connections. But first he must graduate, and his thesis professor, a former sumo champ, devises a bit of blackmail to release the necessary credits. Shushei must join the college's sumo "team," which at present sports just one pathetic member, in order to secure its continued survival.

The other would-be wrestlers are recruited from the ranks of the obese, perilously skinny and otherwise athletically/socially unfit. An English rugby player and an enormous girl with a crush on a teammate complete the hapless group.

They're all prepared to throw in the towel after disastrous early matches. But the belligerence of wrestlers from the school's sumo glory days shames the boys into serious training.

Triumph-of-underdogs theme is hardly original, yet director Masayuki Suo makes the elements (save some gratuitous bathroom humor) work delightfully. The slapstick is well handled, the worm-turning successive climaxes exciting. Editing is tops; cinematography bright and attractive. Performances are uncomplicatedly appealing, but it's the sharp direction that lets "Sumo Do" transcend its ordinary material. — *Dennis Harvey*

VENICE FEST

KALKSTEIN
(THE VALLEY OF STONE)
(ITALIAN)

A Penta Film release of a Penta/Aura Film/Produzioni Sire co-production. Produced by Mario & Vittorio Cecchi Gori, Roberto Cicutto, Vincenzo De Leo, Marcello Siena. Directed by Maurizio Zaccaro. Screenplay, Ermanno Olmi, Zaccaro, based on Adalbert Stifter's novel. Camera (color), Pasquale Rachini; production design, Carlo Simi; music, Claudio Capponi, Alessio Vlad; editor, Paolo Cottignola. Reviewed at Venice Film Festival, Sept. 2, 1992. Running time: **103 MIN.**
Surveyor . . . . Charles Dance
Priest . . . . Aleksander Bardini
Assistant . . . . Fabio Bussotti
Also with: Klara Neroldova, Miroslav Kadic, Rudolf Hrusinsky, Milos Kopecky.

"Kalkstein," or "The Valley of Stone," is a tale capable of bringing tears to the eyes. Perfectly scripted by Ermanno Olmi and helmer Maurizio Zaccaro, the film radiates a pious simplicity that should appeal

not only to religious-minded audiences, but to all emotionally susceptible viewers. Essentially timeless and placeless, it ought to have a wide range of foreign markets.

Story of an honest old mountain priest is based on a novel by Austrian author Adalbert Stifter, and film retains German character and place names. There is little specifically Italian here, which may be an advantage for foreign sales. Technical work is very good.

The story is framed by Charles Dance's narration at a dinner table many years after the events occurred. Dance was a land surveyor assigned to draw up a map of particularly difficult terrain in rocky hills where the weather changes continually.

A friendship springs up between Dance and a meek parish priest (Aleksander Bardini) after he gives Dance shelter during a sudden storm. His bare home and frugal dinner, described through Dance's eyes in a beautifully sensitive scene, reflect an absolute spartan lifestyle. The only strange thing, discovers the surveyor, is that all the bedding is of the finest quality.

During an illness, the old priest reveals his secret origin: a wealthy family that has gone bankrupt. His fondness for fine linen dates back to a boyish infatuation with a washer woman's daughter. He entrusts the surveyor with a copy of his will.

After the priest dies, Dance returns to hear the will read: With his lifetime's savings, the priest wants a school built for the poor local children. His "savings" amount to nothing, but his humility was so great that the rich locals buy his few belongings for fabulous sums, and the school is built.

Zaccaro studied at Olmi's film school and made his first film, "Where the Night Begins," from a script by Pupi Avati. His directing has a rock-line solidity based more on suspenseful narrative than on originality. This hyper-classical approach to storytelling stacks brick on brick until "Kalkstein" reaches its moving climax.

Dance and Polish actor Bardini work superbly as a duo towards the final emotional payoff. Dance, a gentleman from the old school, finds an instant affinity for Bardini's ailing, eccentric parish priest.

— *Deborah Young*

KISNEVIJ GOLOD
(OXYGEN STARVATION)
(UKRAINIAN-CANADIAN)

A Kobza Joint Venture (Kiev)/Kobza Intl. (Toronto) co-production. Executive producer, Mykola Moros. Produced by Marko Stech, Andrij Doncik. Directed by Doncik. Screenplay, Doncik, Jurij Andruchovic. Camera (color), Igor Krupnov; editor, Veronika Arefeva; music, Jurij Saenko; production design, Volodimir Pancuk; sound, Sergij Vaci; associate producer, Andr Bennett; assistant director, Svitlana Osadca. Reviewed at Venice Film Festival (out of competition), Sept. 12, 1992. (Also in Toronto Film Festival.) Running time: **100 MIN.**
Roman Bilik . . . . . . Taras Denisenko
Kosacij . . . . Oleg Maslenkov
Gamalija . . . . Viktor Stepanov
Capt. Kapustin . . . . Oleksij Gordunov

"From Here to Eternity," Ukrainian-style, describes this grim item about a young conscript savagely treated at a Red Army training camp. This autobiographical horror pic makes its points forcefully but offers little other than a catalog of brutality and degradation.

Taking place only a couple of years ago, "Oxygen Starvation" is well made and uncompromising in its depiction of the dismal Russian camp. Lead character seems to be given a hard time simply because he's Ukrainian, not Russian, and he suffers many indignities and beatings until, in the not-unexpected climax, he turns to violence as a way out of his misery.

Forceful direction and impressive thesping make this tolerable, but it's a film for a limited audience. — *David Stratton*

MINDER DOOD
DAN DE ANDEREN
(LESS DEAD THAN THE OTHERS)
(BELGIAN)

A Films Lydia production. Produced, directed, written by Frans Buyens. Camera (color), Guido Van Rooy; editor, Lydia Chagoll; music, Brian Clifton. Reviewed at Venice Film Festival (out of competition), Sept. 8, 1992. Running time: **94 MIN.**
Mother . . . . Dora Van der Groen
Father . . . . Senne Rouffaer
Grandmother . . . . . . Mia Van Roy
Armand . . . . Koen De Bouw

In his grim little item, Frans Buyens directs actors to play late members of his family. The result may have been cathartic for the filmmaker, but it's hard to imagine an audience willing to sit through "Less Dead Than the Others."

Helmer's brother Armand died first as a result of a stupid accident: He was wearing a gorilla skin for a carnival when someone threw a lighted match at him. Pic shows Koen de Bouw as the severely burned and heavily bandaged Armand on his deathbed.

Top Flemish thesp Senne Rouffaer plays the father, a strong, vibrant man laid low by a terminal disease. After he suffers a long, painful death, the mother goes to live in an old people's home. The filmmaker (never seen in this dramatized docu) visits from time to time until she gets sick and is unable to persuade a doctor to help her die with dignity. Thus, for the filmmaker, she is "less dead than others."

This stark, somber film tackles an important subject, but few still would be willing to confront it in the cinema or even on TV, at least in Buyens' uncompromising form. Production values are minimal, but performances, especially Rouffaer's and Dora Van der Groen's as the mother, are very strong. — *David Stratton*

SABINE
(FRENCH)

A Ognon Pictures-La Sept production. (Intl. sales: Mercure Distribution, Paris.) Produced by Humbert Balsan. Directed by Philippe Faucon. Screenplay, Faucon, William Karel, based on Agnes L'Herbier & Françoise Huart's "La Vie Aux Trusses." Camera (color), Tomasz Cichawa; editor, Christian Dior; music, Benoit Schlosberg; production design, Nathalie Raoul, Marie-France Argentino; sound, Didier Sain. Reviewed at Venice Film Festival (out of competition), Sept. 4, 1992. Running time: **87 MIN.**
Agnes . . . . Catherine Klein
Jérôme . . . . Mark Saporta
Nicole . . . . Sylvia Haunetto
Liliane . . . . Corinne Debonniere
Fred . . . . Frank Paitel
Marco . . . . Salvatore Caputo
Agnes' father . . . . Reynald Lemarie

Inspired by the diary of a young woman who died of AIDS at 32, "Sabine" is a sober, delicate case history made with great sensitivity. Theatrical outings are possible for this touching but unsentimental contemporary tragedy.

Catherine Klein is outstanding as the high school dropout who walks out on her alcoholic father and forms a relationship with Jérôme. The teen moves into his tiny apartment, and soon she's pregnant and undergoes a difficult birth.

She drifts into heroin addic-

tion and abandons her son to Jérôme's mother so she can work as a prostitute to pay for drugs. A girlfriend ODs, and the hooker, who now calls herself Sabine, becomes HIV positive. She pulls herself together long enough to visit her 4-year-old son.

Philippe Faucon has constructed this simple but achingly sad story around a series of clipped scenes. Pacing is brisk, and the film covers a lot of ground during its short running time.
— *David Stratton*

CONSENTING ADULTS

A Buena Vista release of a Hollywood Pictures presentation in association with Touchwood Pacific Partners I. Produced by Alan J. Pakula, David Permut. Executive producer, Pieter Jan Brugge. Co-producer, Katie Jacobs. Directed by Pakula. Screenplay, Matthew Chapman. Camera (Technicolor color), Stephen Goldblatt; editor, Sam O'Steen; music, Michael Small; production design, Carol Spier; art direction, Alicia Keywan; set decoration, Gretchen Rau; set design, Thomas Minton, Kathleen Sullivan; costume design, Gary Jones, Ann Roth; sound (Dolby), James J. Sabat; assistant director, Alan B. Curtiss; casting, Alixe Gordin. Reviewed at Avco Cinema Center, L.A., Oct. 12, 1992. MPAA Rating: R. Running time: **100 MIN.**
Richard Parker . . . . . . Kevin Kline
Priscilla Parker . . . .
. . . . . . Mary Elizabeth Mastrantonio
Eddy Otis . . . . Kevin Spacey
Kay Otis . . . . Rebecca Miller
David Duttonville . . Forest Whitaker
George Gordon . . . . . E.G. Marshall
Lori Parker . . . Kimberly McCullough

Psychotic neighbors are the latest riff on the urban paranoia theme, to follow psychotic one-night stands, nannies, cops and roommates. "Consenting Adults" initially seems a little brainier than its brethren but soon gives way to the same cavernous lapses in logic and formula ending, though the cast and clear appeal of the genre could insure a strong opening and modest long-term box office life.

Most distinctive element here proves to be Kevin Spacey's over-the-top performance as the smarmy newcomer to the block, who ultimately lures his risk-aversive neighbor (Kevin Kline) into a proposed wife-swap that leads to the baseball-bat murder of Spacey's wife as part of an elaborate insurance scam.

Kline's character ends up framed for the murder, forcing him to try to decipher the mystery and win back his own wife (Mary Elizabeth Mastrantonio), who has conveniently and rather inexplicably fled to Spacey.

That's not all that's hard to figure out about this story, which, as constructed by director Alan J. Pakula and writer Matthew Chapman, provides no sense of the passage of time, making huge leaps from one narrative point to another with only the barest string connecting them.

For a long stretch, the audience is unsure just who was involved in the plot, an intriguing possibility that seems more by happenstance than design, based on the way the action plays out.

There are also lingering informational gaps, such as the extent of the other wife's involvement in the scheme.

Pic suffers from an absurdity level that somewhat undermines its chills as well as its few genuine laughs. The film also fails to explain what in Kline and Mastrantonio's marriage made them so susceptible to the wiles of this other couple — it's just a convenient plot device.

Pakula can't seem to decide whether this is a legitimate drama or conventional thriller — of the cheap scare variety — and finds himself caught in the same middle ground awkwardly straddled in "Single White Female."

Perhaps because of those narrative flaws, neither Kline nor Mastrantonio (reunited after teaming with more chemistry in another muddled effort, "The January Man") are particularly distinguished here. Rebecca Miller ("Regarding Henry") oozes sex appeal, but the real stand-out is Spacey, who established his inordinate skill playing psychopaths with a disarming sense of humor back during TV's "Wiseguy."

Among the supporting cast, Forest Whitaker and E.G. Marshall are underused as, respectively, an insurance investigator and Kline's attorney, in part because the authorities seem all too eager to buy the husband's story hook, line and sinker.

Tech credits are adequate, with thankfully little gore and particular kudos to the design of Spacey's bordello-like living room as well as the deftly shot love scene, which leaves ample room for speculation on what really happened. But in providing the answers, the filmmakers, unlike the murderer, end up with a low batting average. — *Brian Lowry*

THE WHOLE TRUTH

A Cinevista release of a WM production in association with Fast Films. Produced by Richard Bree. Executive producer, Dan Cohen. Directed by Cohen, Jonathan Smythe. Screenplay, Cohen. Camera (color), Dennis Michaels; editor, Rick Derby; music, Bill Grabowski; art direction, Christine Itle; costumes, Toni Karahalios, Aggy Toccket; sound, Doris Soraci. Reviewed at Preview 4, N.Y., Oct. 5, 1992. Running time: **85 MIN.**
Dan . . . . Dan Cohen
Vanessa . . . . Dyan Kane
Judge . . . . Jim Willig
Also with: Pat Lemay, Paul Kahane.

Indie feature "The Whole Truth" is a predictable and derivative romantic comedy that appears to take its cue from TV. Weak hybrid of "thirtysomething" and "L.A. Law" was written, exec produced, acted and co-helmed by Dan Cohen (with first-time director Jonathan Smythe).

This yuppie romance concerns two young professionals who meet via a dating service. Vanessa (Dyan Kane) is a community-minded architect while Dan (Cohen) runs a magic store and practices stand-up comedy in the evenings. Oddly, their incompatibility is the only thing that holds them together.

When she suddenly breaks off the relationship, he responds with scores of letters, myriad messages on her answering machine and visits to her home and work. Eventually, she brings him to court for harassment.

The U.S. court system may be overloaded, but the judge here gives both parties ample and unrestricted time to state their conflicting versions of the relationship. Pic's occasional self-conscious attempts at deconstruction via a TV reporter and flashback commentary is annoying rather than cute.

The abrupt ending indicates that the judge and others present in the courtroom have simply become bored with the story. If "The Whole Truth" be known, it seems like an apt comment about the entire film.

Except for Kane, who is always believable, acting is uniformly amateur. Tech credits are okay. — *Paul Lenti*

DEN DEMOKRATISKE TERRORISTEN
(THE DEMOCRATIC TERRORIST)
(SWEDISH-GERMAN)

A Sonet presentation of a Sonet/Multimedia Hamburg/Nordisk TV-4/Svensk Filmindustri/Filmteknik production. Executive producers, Gunnar Bergström, Wolfgang Esterer. Produced by Hans Iveberg. Directed by Per Berglund. Screenplay, Iveberg, from Jan Guillou's novel. Camera (color), Erling Thurmann-Andersen; editor, Sylvia Ingemarsson, Christin Loman; music, Björn Jason Lindh; production design, Rainer Schaper; costumes, Regina Bätz; sound, Mats Lindskog; co-producers, Mattias Wittich, Peter Hald. Reviewed at Rigoletto Cinema, Stockholm, Aug. 18, 1992. Running time: **100 MIN.**
With: Stellan Skarsgard, Katja Flint, Burkhard Driest, Ulrich Tukur, Rolf Hoppe, Gunter Maria Halmer, Karl Heinz Maslo, Heiko Deutschmann.
(In German & English)

Despite an uneven bal-

ance of talky sequences and too few action scenes, "The Democratic Terrorist" is a Swedish box office hit and stands to travel well to Germany, where most of the thriller was shot.

Journalist/author Jan Guillou's successful novels featuring Carl Hamilton, a Swedish secret agent with a conscience as well as a license to kill, have previously yielded the film "Coq Rouge" and TV series "Enemy of the Enemy." As in "Coq Rouge," the agent is played by lanky actor Stellan Skarsgard. Here he's assigned to infiltrate a terrorist group in Hamburg and prevent an attack on the U.S. embassy in Stockholm. Along the way, he falls in love with a beautiful female terrorist and tries to make her change her ways.

Set and lensed mainly in Hamburg, pic is mostly in German or English (with a German accent). This may sound strange to Swedes, and the film loses the local color that made the previous spy film an audience-pleaser in Sweden. Language track, however, may prove advantageous to foreign sales.

Technically handsome film's story line is disappointing, although a final confrontation between the terrorists and German soldiers has a raw, pulsating edge. — *Gunnar Rehlin*

YA HATIELLA OOVEEDIT ANGELOV
(I WANTED TO SEE ANGELS)
(RUSSIAN)

A Screen Angel Prods. & 12A Studio presentation. Produced by Carolyn Cavallero. Executive producers, A. Mihailov, L. Lev. Directed by Sergei Bodrov. Screenplay, Bodrov, Cavallero. Camera (color), Alosha Radionov, Sergei Taraskin; music, Mongol Shoodan; art direction, Valeri Kostrin. Reviewed at Telluride Film Festival, Sept. 5, 1992. Running time: **83 MIN.**
Bob . . . . Alexei Baranov
Nat . . . . Natasha Ginko
Mother . . . . Lea Akeojakova

A tough but poignant look at the bleak prospects faced by Russian youth today, "I Wanted to See Angels" feels like a late 1960s Yank disillusioned teen biker pic. Modest effort by prolific director Sergei Bodrov doesn't cut very deep but succeeds in effectively conveying a sense of place and state of mind. A more exciting, relevant title would help export chances.

Spare, low-key yarn charts the

eventful but desultory Moscow stay of 20-year-old Bob, a sturdy, pony-tailed, aimless kid in black leather from the provinces who rolls into town on his ancient chopper to collect some money owed by a gangster.

In a very Western-style after-hours hangout, he meets an inept young hustler, and Nat, a sullen 16-year-old who lives in a wet underground chamber that she claims was Ivan the Terrible's wine cellar. Warning her that he's only been with whores up to now, Bob stays over, and the two begin a romance made tentative by her disillusionment with people and his very American love of the open road ("Easy Rider" is his favorite film).

Misguided hustler meets a sorry fate when his mother turns him in to the cops, while shades of "Breathless" come into play as Bob allows his tender feelings for Nat to intrude on his professional, if criminal, activities.

Shot mostly at night and in interiors, pic creates a forbidding portrait of a gloomy, frigid Moscow in winter. A persistent rock score joins with the black outfits and tough attitudes in fashioning the impression of Russian teens aping Western behavioral styles.

Like many Russian films these days, this somber little tale is more compelling sociologically than artistically, but as such will interest anyone curious about life there at the moment. Acting is okay in the low-voltage vein, lensing is on the grainy side and subtitles are in poor English. — *Todd McCarthy*

DIE ABWESENHEIT
(THE ABSENCE)
(GERMAN-FRENCH-SPANISH)

A Road Movies (Berlin)/Gemini Films (Paris)/Marea Filmes (Madrid) co-production. (Intl. sales: Metropolis Film, Zurich.) Produced by Paolo Branco. Co-producers, Wim Wenders, Ulrich Felsberg, Adrian Lipp. Directed, written by Peter Handke. Camera (color), Agnes Godard; editor, Peter Przygodda; music, Leo Marino; production design, Maria-Jose Branco; sound, Jean-Paul Mugel; assistant director, Friedhelm Maye. Reviewed at Venice Film Festival (competition), Sept. 5, 1992. Running time: **109 MIN.**
With: Jeanne Moreau, Bruno Ganz, Alex Descas, Sophie Semin, Eustaquio Barjau.

Austrian-born novelist/playwright Peter Handke, who collaborated on early screenplays for Wim Wenders and

directed "The Left-Handed Woman" (1977), has come up with a precious, obscure effort in "The Absence." Audiences will apparently be limited.

Evoking classic pics such as "L'Avventura" and "The Searchers," in which protagonists spend their time searching for someone near to them who has disappeared, Handke has dreamed up an artificial, uninvolving plot line and five dreary characters.

What passes for a narrative simply intros an elderly, married Spaniard (Eustaquio Barjau), a German gambler (Bruno Ganz), a black soldier (Alex Descas) and a young Frenchwoman (Sophie Semin) who decide individually to drop out and roam Europe.

The old man later vanishes, and his place is taken by his wife, Jeanne Moreau. Handke never explains this, and his dialog is confined to abstract monologs, monotonously delivered by the cast in various languages.

Agnes Godard's camerawork is picture-postcard stuff, but there's no feeling for drama in this listless, uninvolving saga. Reaction in Venice appeared largely hostile, with mass walkouts at the screening caught.
— *David Stratton*

QUATTRO FIGLI UNICI
(FOUR ONLY CHILDREN)
(ITALIAN)

A Chance Film release of a Filmalpha/Nuova Dimensione co-production, with aid from Ministry of Entertainment. Produced by Mario Gallo, Enzo Giulioli, Gabriella Rebeggiani. Directed, written by Fulvio Wetzl. Camera (color), Erico Menczer, Renato Tafuri; editor, Antonio Siciliano; music, Fabrizio Siciliano; art direction, Bruno Nicola Rapisarda; associate producer, Lampo Calenda. Reviewed at Venice Film Festival, Sept. 9, 1992. Running time: **103 MIN.**
Virginia . . . . . . Mariella Valentini
Giorgio . . . . Roberto Citran
Ennio . . . . Ivano Marescotti
Micol . . . . . . Valentina Holtkamp
Paolo . . . . Fabio Iellini

Two kids who act like adults and two adults who act like kids add up to "Four Only Children," a delightfully light-hearted look at the parent-child gap. Fulvio Wetzl directs a cast of cutting-edge comedians with a knowing hand. With careful handling, the film could step beyond Italian borders, especially appealing to young TV audiences.

Mariella Valentini plays a hard-nosed reporter too busy with her job to pay much attention to her kids. Her 16-year-old son (Fabio Iellini) has been missing from the house for days, and Mom hasn't even noticed.

A search begins, aided by Valentini's b.f. Roberto Citran. The key to his disappearance is furnished by their 11-year-old daughter (Valentina Holtkamp), unhealthily engrossed in her computer world. Unbeknownst to the rest of the family, daughter has wired the house with hidden microphones, and she and Citran learn a few things from her secret tapes.

Not surprisingly, the son's flight turns out to be an elaborate game and an exasperated bid for parental attention.

Kid locales abound, from school to video game parlors, discos to cross-country motorbike trails. The daughter's amusing/amazing computer is practically a member of the cast. Another main ingredient is Bruno Nicola Rapisarda's apartment set, often lensed roofless from above to depict the family's separation into his or her ego-centered universe.

Wetzl has a light touch with a three-way emotional tangle between Valentini, Citran and ex-husband Ivano Marescotti. All are upcoming stage actors worth knowing, able to make their characters believable and appealing despite their individual egoism.

This unusually well-crafted film about contempo life quietly pleads for people to pay more attention to each other amid all professional and technological distractions. It is nobly lensed by Erico Menczer and Renato Tafuri. — *Deborah Young*

SITGES FEST

ARMY OF DARKNESS:
EVIL DEAD 3

A Universal release (in U.S.) of a Dino de Laurentiis Communications presentation of a Renaissance Pictures film. Produced by Robert Tapert. Co-producer, Bruce Campbell. Directed by Sam Raimi. Screenplay, Ivan & Sam Raimi. Camera (color), Bill Pope; editors, Bob Muraski, R.O.C. Sandstorm; music, Joe LoDuca, Danny Elfman; production design, Anthony Trembay; costumes, Ida Gearon; visual effects, Introvision Intl., William Mesa; makeup effects, Tony Gardner, Alterian Std., Kurtzman, Nicotero, Berber EFX Group; casting, Ira Belgrade. Reviewed at Sitges Film Festival, Oct. 9, 1992. MPAA Rating: R. Running time: **95 MIN.**
Ash . . . . Bruce Campbell
Sheila . . . . Embeth Davidtz
Arthur . . . . Marcus Gilbert
Wiseman . . . . Ian Abercrombie
Duke Henry . . . . . . Richard Grove
Gold Tooth . . . . . . Michael Earl Reid

Also with: Timothy Patrick Quill, Bridget Fonda, Patricia Tallman, Theodore Raimi, Deke Anderson, Bruce Thomas, Sara Shearer.

Blending almost nonstop violence with humorous parody, Sam Raimi's latest excursion into horror-kitsch should prove a crowd pleaser for the mall trade and perhaps a mite beyond. Cult thesp Bruce Campbell's ubiquitous presence performing outré antics and expert F/X are further come-ons for the under-30 crowd.

Although "Army of Darkness" is a loose continuation of the "Evil Dead" films, it seems more like an irreverent "A Connecticut Yankee in King Arthur's Court." The Yank, however, is equipped with a chainsaw for an arm and a '73 Oldsmobile instead of a steed. Using these, he helps Arthur slay an army of attacking skeletons. Those already inured to violence will cheer him on, and those who think nonstop gore is funny will be amused.

Whisked from his country cottage by some evil force, Campbell and his car are plunked down in the midst of an Arthurian war, where Campbell is posthaste thrown into chains. But thanks to his shotgun and chainsaw, he fights his way to freedom and ingratiates himself with Arthur.

The only way for him to get back to California is by retrieving a sacred book. On his quest he runs across various obstacles, including the evil dead (who turn the maiden he's sweet on into a witch). One amusing sequence has Campbell splintering into four or five clones of himself with whom he does battle.

Wizardry and special effects abound, but pic's most spectacular part is an enormous medieval battle between the attacking army of skeletons and Arthur's knights, helped by Campbell, defending a castle. The battle is finally won when a rival Scottish army arrives to help Arthur against the evil ones.

In the version shown at Sitges, the hero miscalculates the time he wants to travel ahead in space and arrives at the end of the 21st century only to see a planet in ruins.

Campbell said at the fest that this ending will be changed and the pic will lose 10 minutes for its U.S. release. Clipping the repetitive smashing of skulls and other mayhem will enhance, rather than dilute, pic's impact. — *Peter Besas*

SINNUI YAUMAN III:
DO DO DO
(A CHINESE GHOST STORY III)
(HONG KONG)

A Golden Princess presentation of a Film Workshop production. Executive producer, Tsui Hark. Directed by Ching Siu-tung. Screenplay, Tsui, Roy Szeto. Camera (color), Lau Moon-tong; editor, Mak Chi-seen; music-song, James Wong, Romeo Diaz (sung by Jacky Cheung); art direction, James Leung; costume design, William Cheung, Yu Ka-on, Ng Po-ling; sound, Sound Wave Film Prod.; martial arts directors, Ching, Ma Yuk-sing, Yuen Pan, Cheung Yiu-sing; assistant directors, To Wan, Wan Fat, Leung Pak-kin; line producer, Cho King-man. Reviewed in London. (In Sitges Film Festival.) Running time: **116 MIN.**
Fong . . . . Tony Leung Chiu-wai
Yin . . . . Jacky Cheung
Lotus . . . . Joey Wang
Butterfly . . . . Nina Li
Also with: Lau Siu-meng, Lau Seung, Lau Yuk-ting, Wong Kwong-leung.
(Cantonese dialogue;
Chinese & English subtitles)

Latest in the popular "A Chinese Ghost Story" series just about goes the distance on technique but lacks the knockout punch of its two predecessors. Asian movie buffs will want to add this one to their collection, but more general auds may feel it's one haunting too many.

Though again directed and exec produced by Ching Siu-tung and Tsui Hark, pic's flavor is noticeably different, diluting the slam-bang, effects-heavy style of "II" and stirring in some of the original's gentler romantic comedy.

Pic grossed a solid enough HK$15 million on local release in summer '91, but some way down in relative terms on the 1987 original's HK$18.8 million and the 1990 follow-up's handsome HK$21 million.

Like "II," pic opens with footage from the original: Star Leslie Cheung battles the giant tongue of the Tree Devil, who's promptly put in suspended animation for a century. Then follows the cheeky caption "A hundred years later . . . "

Central duo now are a bald scholar-monk (Tony Leung Chiu-wai) and his aged master, delivering a Golden Buddha across Kwan Bo County. Overnighting at the haunted Orchid Temple, they're soon prey to the sexy attentions of sister ghosts Lotus (Joey Wang) and Butterfly (Nina Li), cohorts of the resurrected androgynous Tree Devil.

Rest of yarn is a series of attempted seductions by the com-

petitive femmes, with comic inserts involving a moneygrabbing swordsman (Jacky Cheung) and incursions by the Tree Devil. Battles escalate to a final showdown, with the lapidary Mountain Devil lumbering in for good measure.

Humor this time round is explicitly satirical, sending up the swordplay genre and mixing in lotsa sexual jokes as Wang breaks down Leung's celibacy vows. Cheung, also in "II" but in a different role, steals all his scenes as a sword for hire. Leung is comically effective in offbeat casting, and Taiwanese actress Wang (the only principal in all three pics) does the business as the sultry ghost.

Director Ching, now an old hand at this stuff, lets the characters breathe between the cartoony action and special effects. Tech credits are pro for the genre. — *Derek Elley*

COLOGNE FEST

ABRACADABRA
(BELGIAN-FRENCH-LUXEMBOURGIAN)

A PDG & Partners production, Les Prods. Dussart, FR3 Films & SAMSA production in cooperation with RTL-TV & Canal Plus. (Intl. sales: Mainstream, Paris.) Produced by Pierre Drouot, Dany Geys. Co-produced by Catherine & Bertrand Dussart, Jani Thiltges. Directed, written by Harry Cleven. Camera (color), Remon Fromont; editor, Susanna Rossberg; music, Robbie Kelman, Brian James; sets, Yvan Bruyère; costumes, Nathalie du Roscoat; sound, Dominique Warnier, J.P. Loublier. Reviewed at Cologne Film Festival, Sept. 26, 1992. Running time: **90 MIN.**
Phil . . . . Philippe Volter
Martha . . . . Clémentine Célaré
Chris . . . . Thierry Frémont
Naze . . . . Thierry van Werveke
Rex . . . . Jean-Henri Compère
Lucie . . . . Sabrina Leurguin

A strong script and excellent performances distinguish this promising first feature that will bring helmer Harry Cleven deserved attention. A fest circuit natural, "Abracadabra" could conjure up respectable b.o. with intellectual Euro auds.

Phil (Philippe Volter), a petty criminal and amateur magician, is allowed out of prison for the weekend to attend his mother's funeral. Repentant and ready to go straight, he initially resists the temptation to pull off one final, sure-thing heist with his two brothers.

Wonderfully conceived and masterfully acted, the brothers are as different in disposition as they are devoted to one another. Chris, crippled since childhood, is fun-loving, docile and simple-minded, while Naze is volatile, impulsive and dangerous — and eager to win Phil's approval.

Scenes merge with a remarkable fluidity as Phil's brothers go all out to make his furlough memorable by getting him fed, drunk and laid. Gradually, it becomes apparent that sober Phil shares some of the more negative qualities of his brothers.

Slow to develop is the love story: Martha, the woman Phil still loves, married a local butcher after losing touch with Phil. All seems lost until a moving and humorous episode when Phil reclaims her love in front of her shop's customers.

Several plot twists later, the two make a break for it, and the film briefly loses its groundedness and goes over the top. By the end, things are firmly back on course.

All leading actors deliver commendable perfs, as does Sabrina Leurguin as a tart who grants sexual favors and coffee for money. Production design and camerawork are also good, although most of the pic is shot through a yellow filter which becomes distracting.

— *Rebecca Lieb*

SAN SEBASTIAN

DIE REISE VON ST. PETERSBURG NACH MOSKAU
(THE JOURNEY FROM ST. PETERSBURG TO MOSCOW)
(GERMAN-DOCU)

A Viola Stephan & Carsten Krüger Filmproduktion film in co-production with WDR, Cologne. Produced by Carsten Krüger. Executive producer, Renée Gundelach, Rainer Hoffmann. Directed, written by Viola Stephan. Camera (color), Pawel Lebeschew; editor, Yvonne Loquens; music, Peter Gordon; sound, Wolfgang Widner. Reviewed at San Sebastian Film Festival, Sept. 20, 1992. Running time: **115 MIN.**
(Russian soundtrack; English subtitles)

In March of 1991, a German camera crew and director drove the 400 miles from St. Petersburg to Moscow stopping along the way to film everything they thought to be of in-terest. Some of the footage (blown up to 35m) is fascinating and revelatory, but the film lacks cohesiveness and an underlying scheme.

As is bound to be the case, these are a traveler's chance impressions, which range interviews with gypsies and two ice fishermen to the organization of a marathon dance. Settings include markets, a roadside diner, amateur ballet and the naval academy of St. Petersburg.

Poverty, misery and hopelessness in much of Russia comes across poignantly. Unfortunately, subtitles are terribly inadequate, and sometimes people talk for a minute sans translation. Overindulgent camerawork dwells too long on some scenes, presumably trying to create a mood. Cut to an hour, pic could interest cultural TV channels.

— *Peter Besas*

SORRENTO FEST

DALL'ALTRA PARTE DEL MONDO
(FROM THE OTHER SIDE OF THE WORLD)
(ITALIAN-B&W)

An Axelotil Film production in association with Centro Sperimentale di Cinematografia & the Ministry of Tourism & Entertainment. Produced by Gianluca Arcopinto. Directed by Arnaldo Catinari. Screenplay, Michela Properzi, Catinari. Camera (B&W), Catinari; editor, Luca Benedetti; music, Raffaele Clemente; art direction, Paolo Bizzarri; costumes, Maria Giovanna Caselli; sound, Bruno Pupparo. Reviewed at Sorrento Intl. Film Festival (competition), Oct. 1, 1992. Running time: **88 MIN.**
Aureliano . . . . Massimo Girotti
Teresa . . . . Marina Berti
Muriel . . . . Kalubi Kabongo
Seydou . . . . Issa Seck
Phelix . . . . Jean Kian Mayala
Generoso . . . . Nanni Tamma
The German . . . . Lou Castel

Destiny cuts across generations and cultures, forcing two lives to intersect with grave repercussions in "From the Other Side of the World," a well-handled, visually striking first feature by Arnaldo Catinari. Modest but compellingly moody indie effort won the 28th Sorrento film fest's De Sica prize for young Italo cinema and should make a showing at new director showcases. But the pic could have traveled further with a wider view of the race and immigration issues it touches upon.

Veteran player Massimo Girotti makes a solemnly dignified pivotal figure as a retiring artist with a nostalgic fixation on his years spent in Africa. A persistent ex-lover (Marina Berti) also dwells on her past there and attempts to coax him back to her.

Girotti's staid, melancholy existence gets a jolt when a jaded hooker from the Ivory Coast (Kalubi Kabongo) and her feckless Senegalese protector (Issa Seck) turn up. Through a family connection of Seck's, they approach him for help after the hooker snatches a drug stash from a brutal prostitution ring.

Seck dies in a scuffle with their pursuers, and an affectionate but distanced rapport grows between Girotti and Kabongo which changes them both profoundly. Girotti resolves to reconcile with his ex and plan an African return. But in an effort to carve out a better future for the young femme, Girotti becomes the victim.

Pic is most exceptional when it covers the problems and attitudes of immigrants drawn into Italian underworld. Early on, it appears poised to be a well-honed meeting of drama and social documentary, but Catinari instead focuses on smaller concerns. Pic remains a powerful dramatic tract, though the characters' motives become less clear as events proceed.

Acting is solid all round, with convincing work from the mainly non-pro black cast, despite occasional dramatic limitations. Tech aspects are strong, including fluid editing and first-rate sound. Catinari's sharp black & white lensing gives a brooding, atmospheric look, keenly backed by Raffaele Clemente's exotic world-beat music.

— *David Rooney*

AMBROGIO
(ITALIAN)

An Istituto Luce-Italnoleggio Cinematografico release of a Cinelife production. Produced by Giuseppe Giovannini. Directed by Wilma Labate. Screenplay, Sandro Petragilia. Camera (color), Mauro Marchetti, Beppe Maccari; editor, Nino Baragli; music, Roberto Ciotti; art direction, Maurizio Leonardi; costumes, Sergio Ballo; sound, Raffaele De Luca. Reviewed at 28th Sorrento Intl. Film Festival (competition), Oct. 3, 1992. Running time: **90 MIN.**
Anna-Ambrogio . Francesca Antonelli
Leo . . . . Roberto Citran
Stefano . . . . Marco Galli
Zani . . . . Fabio Poggiali
Nino . . . . Antonello Scarano
Cicogna . . . . Enrico Brignani
Oreste . . . . Luciano Federico
Clarice . . . . Anita Ekberg
Anna's father . . . . . . Paolo Graziosi
Mute . . . . Carlos Gomez

"Ambrogio" is a well-acted, delicately told yarn about a teenage girl obstinately set on entering the all-male world of professional seamanship. Marking a plucky feature bow for Wilma Labate, pic should make a winning festival item, and proper handling could slip it into an art-house niche in selected markets.

With a love of the sea inherited from her father, Anna-Ambrogio (Francesca Antonelli) takes the advice of a genial seafarer (Roberto Citran) and enrolls in a school for aspiring sailors. After winning the battle against a "boys only" admission policy, she takes on a motley bunch of classmates and professors who dismiss her as an oddball, a manhunter or bad luck.

Labate and ace scripter Sandro Petraglia ("The Factotum," "The Stolen Children") allow her to win out without obvious tactics like coquettish charm or tomboyish force, but with cool, unwavering determination. Even with a dollop of good-natured hamming from some of the school's eccentric teachers, this midsection remains shrewdly judged and intelligently played, giving the film real momentum.

After a letdown in the love department, Ambrogio graduates and tale shifts to Lisbon, where she looks for a post aboard a ship. Turned down repeatedly, she prepares to throw in the towel, but Citran arrives to help out.

Set on the threshold of the 1960s, story quietly utilizes the birth of a decade of change as a backdrop for the realization of its spunky protagonist's dreams. The latter half becomes mildly overburdened with underexplored ideas, and plot complications eventually get tied up rather too neatly, but the script is full of disarming situations and snappy dialogue.

Performances are easy and unforced, with both Antonelli and Citran displaying charm to burn. Tech aspects are surefooted, opting for seamless simplicity over flashiness. Italo bluesman Roberto Ciotti's tunes are well-used, though some of the acoustic guitar compositions sound a little out-of-period.

— *David Rooney*

LETTERA DA PARIGI
(LETTER FROM PARIS)
(ITALIAN)

An Istituto Luce-Italnoleggio Cinematografico, Luciano Perugia presentation of a Telecinestar production in association with Studio EL, RAI-1, Istituto Luce. (Intl. sales: Sacis.) Produced by Perugia. Director of production, Giorgio Scotton. Directed by Ugo Fabrizio Giordani. Screenplay, Costanza De Palma, Giordani, Cristina Mecci. Camera (color), Paolo Carnera; editor, Franco Malvestito; music, Antonio Di Pofi; art direction, Luciano Ricceri; costumes, Annemarie Heinreich; sound, Roberto Forrest. Reviewed at Sorrento Intl. Film Festival (competition), Oct. 1, 1992. Running time: **97 MIN.**
Sergio . . . . . . Roberto De Francesco
Cristina . Lucrezia Lante della Rovere
Gina . . . . Irene Papas
Professore . . . . . . Felice Andreasi
Marco . . . . Stefano Dionisi
Also with: Barbara Scoppa, Adriana Russo.

Tracking emotional shifts within a fractured middle-class family, "Letter From France" gives classy but slightly antiseptic treatment to low-wattage material. A strong cast and clean, capable direction make for easy viewing, but the drama is too constricted to be really cinematic. Pic should find receptive addressees among quality European TV markets.

An aspiring opera singer (Lucrezia Lante della Rovere) lands in the directionless life of a university student (Roberto De Francesco), and a full-throttle love affair begins. Still struggling to forge a concrete bond with his own father (Felice Andreasi), the student is soon forced into early parenthood when he and the singer have a son.

Disgruntled with her partner's shirking of parental responsibility, the singer accepts an offer to work in Paris. In her four-year absence, De Francesco abandons his studies to take a lowly job, channeling his energies into creating the kind of father-son harmony he's missed.

Back from Paris to lay claim to her son, the opera singer comes up against a formidable family unit and claims she was pregnant when they met. Whether this is truth or a vicious blow is left ambiguous, as is a hint of reconciliation.

Carrying most of the dramatic weight, De Francesco gives a controlled, immensely likable performance, even if his perpetually adolescent features make him hard to accept as a father. Lante della Rovere wavers a little in her more dramatically challenging moments, but their early scenes together, in which love blossoms timidly, are a pleasure to watch. Supporting cast is uniformly good, with Irene Papas strongly sympathetic in an undemanding role as the loyal family housekeeper. — *David Rooney*

CHICAGO FEST

HUGH HEFNER:
ONCE UPON A TIME
(DOCU-COLOR/B&W)

An IRS release of a Lynch/Frost production. Produced by Gary H. Grossman, Robert Heath. Executive producer, Mark Frost. Coordinating producers, Denise Contis, Marijane Miller. Directed by Robert Heath. Written by Grossman, Michael Gross, Heath. Camera (color, B&W), Van Carlson, Dustin Teel, Tony Zapata; editor, Gross; music, Charlotte Lansberg, Reeves Gabrels, Tom Dube; executive in charge of production, Ken Scherer; research, Jerilynn Goodman. Reviewed at Chicago Intl. Film Festival, Oct. 14, 1992. No MPAA Rating. Running time: **90 MIN.**
Narrator: James Coburn.

This biographical documentary about Playboy Enterprises supremo Hugh Hefner is a beautifully produced, respectful look at a man who succeeded in living out many of the fantasies others only dream of. Though too fawning at times, the film (from the "Twin Peaks" production company) should amply satisfy audiences looking for an overview of Hef's wild life without much in-depth investigation of what also made it so controversial at times.

The playboy-to-be was raised in a strict, middle-class, sexually repressed Midwestern family, thereby setting the stage for his transformation into a party animal. Docu is filled with good detail, including his 1954 startup of Playboy magazine with a mere $8,000.

The magazine's unique mix of revealing pictorials and probing journalism was an instant success, and Hefner opted for the high life his lucrative magazine celebrated and which had eluded him as an adolescent and young adult.

In the rush to succeed, Hefner apparently became addicted to dexedrine. Things turned even darker with the dawn of the feminist era and charges that Hefner viewed women as sex objects. Close friend and personal assistant Bobbie Arnstein was arrested for cocaine possession and sentenced to prison. She subsequently committed suicide.

The burgeoning Playboy empire nearly collapsed in the mid-1970's during a federal drug probe within Hefner's company that ultimately turned up nothing. The pic tries to suggest the Feds were out to get Hefner at all costs.

Hefner's later problems in the casino biz are mostly glossed over, as is the decision to hand over day-to-day management of the company in the increasingly conservative 1980s to his daughter Christie because he wanted to make her happy.

Peter Bogdanovich figures prominently in the discussion of Playmate/actress Dorothy Stratten, who had an affair with the director before her murder. Hefner notes Stratten's death devastated Bogdanovich.

Despite many ugly moments in his life and career, docu leaves the mature Playboy magnate basking in the rosy glow of contented family life with his wife and children.

Interviews with Hefner's family, friends and business associates are expertly intercut with vintage video, film clips and TV footage. Heath, Michael Gross and Gary Grossman's eloquent script moves along well. Varied and interesting music by Charlotte Lansburg, Reeves Gabrels and Tom Dube also is a big plus. — *Lewis Lazare*

NEW YORK FEST

DELIVERED VACANT
(DOCU)

Produced, directed, edited by Nora Jacobson. Camera (color), Jacobson. Sound, Deb Augsberger, Doug Lindsay; editing consultant, Kathryn Barnier; sound editor, Lisa Prah. Reviewed at N.Y. Film Festival, Oct. 8, 1992. Running Time: **118 MIN.**

"Delivered Vacant" chronicles the 1980s gentrification battle in Hoboken, N.J.'s colorful "Naples-on-the-Hudson." Producer-director Nora Jacobson keeps this bit of social history vibrant with a lively assortment of characters and an involving battle over displacement of residents. Docu merits a commercial tryout at big-city art houses where it should be relevant to many urban dwellers.

With an eye for this working class community's ethnic diversity, Jacobson shows how the city was transformed and mobilized by the influx of developers, a trend that collapsed in the economic downturn of the '90s.

Tackling local politics, the film unflatteringly depicts incumbent mayor Steve Cappiello, heard endorsing the boom of development while expressing no concern for those displaced. Enter maverick politician Tom Vezetti, who in 1985 launched an anti-development campaign for mayor against Cappiello.

Vezetti's victory is seen uniting all the city's ethnic groups, but his administration is soon swamped by all the displaced residents asking for help. At first, it appears this will be another story of good intentions gone awry, but with the help of activist tenants, Vezetti finds resourceful ways to fight back.

The tide turns against the developers while Vezetti, proclaimed by the N.Y. Daily News as the "wackiest mayor in America," emerges as an oddball hero. In the midst of the tenant victories, however, he dies of a heart attack and a pro-devolpment pol becomes interim mayor. While jockeying between the factions ensues, both sides are soon undercut by hard times.

Although developers are given a chance to give their side of the story, the docu can be faulted for not discussing alternatives to reviving declining cities without gentrification and to what extent development should be permitted. An enormous amount of ground is covered in two hours; Hoboken could have provided enough material for many more. — *Fred Lombardi*

VANCOUVER FEST

MANUFACTURING CONSENT:
NOAM CHOMSKY AND THE MEDIA
(CANADIAN-DOCU)

A Necessary Illusions/NFB Studio C production. Produced by Mark Achbar, Peter Wintonik, Adam Symansky. Executive producers, Colin Neale, Dennis Murphy. Directed by Achbar, Wintonik. Camera (color), Francis Miquet, Achbar, Barry Perles, Norbert Bunge, Ken Reeves, Kirk Tongas, Antonin Lhotsky, Wintonik; videography, Achbar, Eddie Becker, Dan Garson, Michael Goldberg, William Turnley, Peter Walker,

Wintonik; editor, Wintonik; music, Carl Schultz; sound, Katharine Asals, Leigh Crisp, Jacques Drouin, Karen Glynn, Gary Marcuse, Hans Oomes, Robert Silverthorne, Deanne Snider. Reviewed at Toronto Festival of Festivals, Sept. 18, 1992. (Also in Vancouver Film Festival.) Running time: **168 MIN.**

With: Noam Chomsky.

Dedicated to the memory of distinguished documentarian Emile de Antonio and the people of East Timor, "Manufacturing Consent" details the mass media views of Noam Chomsky, distinguished linguistics prof, intellectual and activist. Unfortunately, excessive running time (95 minutes for part I; 73 minutes, part II) will restrict theatrical release. The documentary is otherwise insightful, informative, accessible and surprisingly entertaining.

Title derives from the influential media text Chomsky co-authored. In the first part, "Thought Control in Democratic Society," the Massachusetts Institute of Technology prof describes the necessity of every regime to create illusions and to control the public.

The mass media, he says, sets the general agenda, selecting, distorting and framing issues and the limits of debate — mechanisms promoting the interests of the ruling class. Mainstream media inevitably exclude dissenting voices and trivialize or marginalize controversial issues.

Docu offers two compelling case studies that illustrate the media's selective and distorted treatment of political issues. The East Timor genocide and the Cambodia invasion occurred at about the same time. Yet, the New York Times published 70 column inches about Timor, but 1,175 about Cambodia.

Another study, of what the linguist calls " 'Nightline's' usual suspects," analyzes 865 programs and finds that of the 1,530 appearances by Americans, 92% of the guests were white, 89% males and 80% professionals.

Filmmakers Mark Achbar and Peter Wintonik avoid voiceover narration and let charismatic Chomsky speak for himself. Archival footage, technical credits and production values are all very accomplished and make Chomsky's ideas accessible to the lay public.

Unfortunately, docu's skimpy personal and biographical info doesn't reveal the evolution of Chomsky's thought. Also missing is a discussion of his position in the New Left and his criticism of Zionism.

Pic celebrates Chomsky as a rare breed, a man of ideas and action. But too limited a time is given to Chomsky's opponents, among them popular novelist Tom Wolfe, who in a brief appearance describes the intellectual's views as "nonsense and rubbish."

Chomsky believes he helps people develop an intellectual self-defense, a critically independent mind. He's described as "the most important intellectual alive," but his actual influence within and outside academia isn't discussed.

Chomsky views the U.S. as "ideologically narrower" than other countries, and voices his strong opposition to the increasing cult of public personalities. Ironically, the docu will further his own reputation as a media star. — *Emanuel Levy*

THE SILENT TOUCH
(POLISH-BRITISH-DANISH)

A Mayfair Entertainment release of a Mark Forstater/TOR Film Group/Metronome production in association with British Screen Finance Corp. & European Co-Production Fund. Produced by Forstater. Executive producer, Ryszard Straszewski. Co-produced by Mads Egmont Christensen, Kryzsztof Zanussi. Directed by Zanussi. Screenplay, Peter Morgan, Mark Wadlow. Camera (color), Jaroslav Zamojda; editor, Marek Denys; music, Wojciech Kilar; production design, Ewa Braun; costume design, Dorota Roqueplo; sound, Wieslawa Dembinska; associate producer, Raymond Day, Michal Szczerbic; assistant directors, Marek Broszki, Magdalena Szwarcbart, Krzysztof Maj; translators, Barbara Maciejkowicz, Maria Czartoryska; casting, Tracey Seaward. Reviewed at Vancouver Intl. Film Festival, Oct. 11, 1992. Running time: **100 MIN.**

With: Max Von Sydow, Lothaire Bluteau, Sarah Miles, Sofie Grabol, Aleksander Bardini, Peter hesse Overgaard, Lars Lunoe.

After years of directing brilliant and complex Polish films, Krysztof Zanussi has helmed a simple and moving breakthrough pic about a crotchety old composer coaxed out of retirement by an inspired musicologist and a sweet young muse. "The Silent Touch" has serious potential Stateside if marketed to "Fried Green Tomatoes" fans as a glorious slice-of-life tale.

Max von Sydow delivers a definitive performance as a silenced classical composer and Holocaust survivor who re-blossoms from a miserable old drinker into a meticulous artist when Stefan (Lothaire Bluteau) arrives as "guardian angel." Casting is superb, though Sarah Miles' stiff delivery (in the wife role) is pic's drawback.

Bluteau ("Jesus of Montreal") does his usual low-key routine to perfection as the Polish music student who becomes obsessed with a melody he hears in his sleep (thesp's Quebecois accent is a non-issue in the film).

Stefan tracks down von Sydow in Copenhagen and, after much (believable) resistance, convinces him to compose a complex symphony on his neglected piano. Love interests take fascinating twists as loyal wife Miles reluctantly accepts her husband's music secretary (Danish thesp Sophie Grabol, a fresh screen presence) as his young lover.

Much like in "Amadeus," "The Silent Touch" is more comedy than musical. However, pic timely intros beautiful classical piano music and delivers the symphony scene right on cue after carefully structured suspense. No easy task for a pic about classical music.

Jaroslav Zamojda's remarkable camerawork uses many tight, well-lit closeups and lingering shots of Polish countryside, and Copenhagen's finer statues are carefully mixed with an array of warm, telling interiors.

Sound is also excellent, and tech credits in general indicate a much higher budget than Zanussi is accustomed to. Lack of action per se and beautifully structured, languid pace will be pic's major deterrent for general audiences and a draw for artier, "Driving Miss Daisy" crowds. Its deeply human appeal and adept storytelling also compare to the unlikely hits.

Fiesty, comical script allows its characters to indulge in the highs and lows of the human spirit. Von Sydow delivers lines like "I want to enjoy my senility and incontinence in private" as if he'd spent a lifetime rehearsing.

Another hook for the "On Golden Pond" crowd is the hero's summary of old age as "nature's way of anesthetizing us for death: You grow to look forward to it." And after such an enthralling story about a final artistic triumph, Zanussi cleverly wraps this lust-for-life pic with birth.

— *Suzan Ayscough*

LA VIE FANTOME
(PHANTOM LIFE)
(CANADIAN-COLOR)

A Max Films release of a Max Films. Produced by Roger Frappier. Associate producers, Suzanne Dussault, Doris Girard. Directed by Jacques Leduc. Screenplay, Leduc, Yvon Rivard. Camera (color), Pierre Mignot; editor, Yves Chaput; music, Jean Derome; art direction, Louise Jobin; costume design, Michele Hamel; sound, Richard Besse, Claude Beaugrand; casting, Lucie Robitaille. Reviewed at Montreal World Film Festival, Aug. 30, 1992. Running time: **98 MIN.**

Pierre . . . . Ron Lea
Laure . . . . Pascale Bussieres
Annie . . . . Johanne-Marie Tremblay
Ghislaine . . . . Elise Guilbault
Bruno . . . . Tobie Pelletier
Françoise . . . . Sarah Belanger
Lautier . . . . Gabriel Gascon

"Phantom Life" is Quebec's answer to the eternal triangle. Even-handed tale of a man who loves both mistress and wife offers neither eroticism nor insight into conundrums of the age-old passion play. While unlikely to survive in theatrical venues, pic could be a strong video rental with sexy marketing.

Only twist in helmer Jacques Leduc's version is that husband/lover Pierre (thesp Ron Lea giving subnormal Joe Average) isn't plagued by guilt and feels "whole" with each femme.

Both wife and lover are obliviously in love with the liar. It's the '90s, so wanton mistress Laure (superbly, subtly acted by Pascale Bussieres) isn't portrayed as a scheming homewrecker, but a respectable librarian, and career wife Annie (Johanne-Marie Tremblay, in a fine perf) isn't dismissed as a frigid mother.

Leduc aptly displays there is no reason, beyond passion, for a "happily married man" to lead a dual life, but he never convinces that passion is reason enough. Pic is beautifully shot but dutiful sex scenes are dull.

Pic's success or failure rests on the number of phantom folk who can relate to such a dilemma. It won't be the ladies' pick.

— *Suzan Ayscough*

PURE COUNTRY

A Warner Bros. release of a Jerry Weintraub production. Produced by Weintraub. Executive producer, R.J. Louis. Directed by Christopher Cain. Screenplay, Rex McGee. Camera (Technicolor), Richard Bowen; aerial concert camera, Jerry Holway; editor, Jack Hofstra; additional editing, Robin Katz; music, Steve Dorff; production design, Jeffrey Howard; set decoration, Derek R. Hill; costume design; sound (Dolby), Andy Wiskes; stunt coordinator, Bobby J. Foxworth; associate producer, Susan Ekins; assistant director, Cliff Coleman; 2nd unit director, Foxworth; casting, Sharon Howard-Field. Reviewed at United Artists Marketplace, Pasadena, Calif., Oct. 17, 1992. MPAA Rating: PG. Running time: **112 MIN.**

Dusty Wyatt Chandler . George Strait
Lula Rogers . . . . Lesley Ann Warren
Harley Tucker . . . . . . Isabel Glasser
Buddy Jackson . . . . . Kyle Chandler
Earl Blackstock . . . . John Doe
Ernest Tucker . . . . . . Rory Calhoun
Grandma Ivy Chandler . Molly McClure

Though this slick-looking paean to down-home values often undercuts its own message, "Pure Country" is an effective vehicle for amiable country star George Strait. Rex McGee's screenplay mingles corn with knowing satire of the hollowness of stardom, but the heartfelt romantic chemistry between Strait and Texas ranch gal Isabel Glasser carries the day. C&W fans should respond in okay numbers, but the pic may have limited B.O. appeal beyond its target audience.

Director Christopher Cain's overly busy camerawork and his grandiose staging of concert scenes make for an unambiguously glitzy effect at first, but when the disaffected singer escapes from his bus-and-truck caravan, the pic takes a more intriguing critical slant.

Debuting scripter and Billy Wilder protégé Rex McGee follows Wilder's favorite theme of fraudulent role-playing. Strait's Dusty feels like a sham in his gussied-up show and wants to get back to basics, while his desperate manager Lesley Ann Warren fools the public by having her new young stud (Kyle Chandler) lip-sync in his place.

Strait, who looks like a more wholesome version of the late Warren Oates, doesn't have much acting range, but he fits gently into his persona of good-natured cowboy angst. Though he doesn't seem all that different when he goes natural from the way he plays it earlier, Strait is convincing as someone who would just as soon chuck it all to settle down

on Glasser's ranch.

Glasser's freshly scrubbed, weatherbeaten beauty and forthright country charm stand in starkly loaded contrast to the twitchy, overheated neuroticism of Warren, who archly vamps in a role that cries out for Elizabeth Ashley to camp it up.

Supporting standouts include Rory Calhoun, amusing as Glasser's grizzled gramps who garrulously espouses the virtue of cowboy taciturnity; and John Doe, who solidly anchors the pic as Strait's drummer and best buddy.

Cain and cameraman Richard Bowen are too fond of fancy long-focus lenses that flatten out the images, but their Texas locations have windblown simplicity.

— *Joseph McBride*

ON THE BRIDGE
(DOCU-16m)

A Blackhawk Enterprises presentation. Produced, directed by Frank Perry. Executive producer, Emily Paine. Camera (Duart color, 16m), Kevin Keating; editor, Paine; music, Toni Childs; sound, Peter Tooke. Reviewed at Raleigh Studios, L.A., Aug. 31, 1992. (In Venice, Toronto film festivals). Running time: **95 MIN.**
With: Frank Perry.

"On the Bridge" is Frank Perry's up close, unflinching, quite upbeat filmed journal of his own battle with cancer. Clearly both a courageous and therapeutic endeavor for the veteran director, pic is not something everyone will want to see, but those who do will be impressed by the spirited way Perry has coped. Some specialized theatrical dates are possible, but widest audience will be reached via cable, public TV and video.

Shot in vérité style with the presence of the camera, cinematographer and sound man constantly acknowledged, film covers one year of Perry's life, beginning in December, 1990. Six months earlier, he was diagnosed with inoperable prostate cancer and, despite some predictions that he shouldn't have made it nearly this long, he's still going strong.

Perry's case provides a solid argument for the p.o.v. that one's attitude has a great deal to do with one's ability to arm-wrestle a disease. Not a religious man, Perry nevertheless warms to the teachings of Catholic philosopher Teilhard de Chardin regarding the holiness and sanctity of eve-

ryday life.

In this, as well as in sequences devoted to a New Age-type weekend cancer seminar and a Harvard speech by the Dalai Lama on the mind-body connection, tone becomes heavily touchy-feely. But balance is achieved by Perry's numerous visits to his New York doctor, of whom the patient demands explicit, concrete medical information, and by depiction of one of his 39 radiation treatments.

During the course of the year, prognosis flip-flops several times. In June, cancer appears on his ribs and, two months later, possibly in his lungs. But final sequence shows him happily pursuing his passion for skiing on the slopes of Aspen and expressing optimism about his prospects.

Far from static, pic shows Perry constantly on the move, attending to matters related to his disease but also visiting the offices of his defunct Corsair Pictures, working out and receiving a Guild Hall award in front of hundreds of people, including many celebs and doctors.

Only thing missing is any mention of his home life, if he has family or friends who have been particularly important in lending support during such a trying time.

Still, the honest, no-nonsense manner in which Perry tackles his condition will no doubt inspire and clarify things for many who either have cancer or know people who do, which means he has more than achieved his aims.

— *Todd McCarthy*

DR. GIGGLES

A Universal Pictures release of a Largo Entertainment presentation, in association with JVC Entertainment, of a Dark Horse production. Produced by Stuart M. Besser. Executive producer, Jack Roe. Directed by Manny Coto. Screenplay, Coto, Graeme Whifler. Camera (Otto Nemenz Widescreen, Deluxe color), Robert Draper; editor, Debra Neil; music, Brian May; production design, Bill Malley; art direction, Alan Locke; costume design, Sandy Culotta; sound (Dolby), Jim Stuebe; assistant director, Richard E. Espinoza; special makeup effects, (Robert) Kurtzman, (Greg) Nicotero & (Howard) Berger EFX Group; special effects, Phil Cory Special Effects; visual effects, Digital Fantasy Inc.; co-producer, Mike Richardson; casting, Karen Rea, L&M Casting (Oregon). Reviewed at Manhattan 1 theater, N.Y., Oct. 23, 1992. MPAA Rating: R. Running time: **95 MIN.**
Dr. Evan Rendell . . . . . Larry Drake
Jennifer Campbell . Holly Marie Combs
Tom Campbell . . . . . Cliff De Young
Max Anderson . . . . . . Glenn Quinn
Officer Joe Rietz . . . . Keith Diamond
Officer Hank Magruder

. . . . Richard Bradford
Tamara . . . . Michelle Johnson
Dr. Chamberlain . . . . . John Vickery
Elaine Henderson . . . . . Nancy Fish
Also with: Sara Melson, Zoe Trilling, Darin Heames, Deborah Tucker, Doug E. Doug, Denise Barnes.

Sick humor abounds in "Dr. Giggles," a wildly uneven horror film that's gory enough to give Universal the desired two weeks of Halloween business.

Boasting a strong central performance in the title role by Larry Drake (who was a convincing villain in Sam Raimi's "Darkman"), picture is aimed at the low-end of the shock audience. More care in scripting and fewer cheap yocks could have resulted in a viable new paranoid horror myth well-timed to America's ongoing crisis in health care.

Story premise has Drake escaping from a mental institution in a busy opening scene that dovetails neatly with a clever "Fantastic Voyage" inside the bloodstream credits sequence. He heads to his hometown seeking revenge, since a lynch mob in 1957 killed his doctor father.

Daddy's crime was killing seven people and cutting their hearts out in order to attempt the world's first heart transplant on his wife, who had a bum ticker. His son idolized him and emerges from stir at age 42 in the guise of a doctor with killing on his mind.

First half of the film degenerates into corny teen-slasher fare, with Drake quickly running up an impressive body count. At the halfway point he discovers potential victim Holly Marie Combs has a bad heart valve and he becomes obsessed with carrying on Dad's pioneering work using her as the guinea pig. With Drake spitting out a nonstop barrage of unfunny medical one-liners, "Dr. Giggles" works mainly on the level of watching him kill people grotesquely with medical instruments. Director Manny Coto manages some impressive set-pieces along the way, notably one of several homages to Orson Welles in a corridor of mirrors that's well-suited to film's Widescreen format.

Unfortunately these set-pieces, including a weird flashback of the full-grown boy cutting his way out of his dead mother's abdomen where he's been hiding, throw off the film's pacing and create a lengthy anticlimax out of the final reels. For every clever scene there's a groaner, particularly the staging of a Combs nightmare starring Drake that takes place *before* she's ever seen him.

Combs makes for a resourceful and vulnerable heroine, though how she indulges in so much strenuous action after her doctor warns her about her bad valve is an open question. Supporting cast is wasted, notably lovely Michelle Johnson as the girlfriend of Combs' dad.

Makeup effects by the KNB EFX Group are highly professional. — *Lawrence Cohn*

TRAVELLING LIGHT
(ITALIAN-DOCU)

An A.V. Arts presentation of a White Light production. Executive producer, Massimo Rendo. Produced, directed, written by Theo Eshetu. Camera (color), Robert Schaefer, Terry Flaxton, Emanuele Chiari; editor, Pierluici Caso, Catrina Bonavita; music, Joji Hirota; text-narration, David Haughton. Reviewed at Spoleto Film Festival, June 22, 1992. Running time: **60 MIN.**
With: The Lindsay Kemp Co., Jack Birkett, Jonathan Burnett, Steve Callen, Christian Flint, Sergio Flores, David Haughton, Marie Kemp, Attilio Lopez, David Bowie.

Videomaker Theo Eshetu uses dazzling mixed-media techniques in "Travelling Light," a rollicking portrait of British performer/mime Lindsay Kemp. Pic is animated by a continual visual invention that takes it far beyond the biopic genre and into the realm of pure art and rhythm. It should prove a widely sought item for experimental film and TV programs.

This ironic film begins with Kemp's conception in North Yorkshire where his parents wanted him to fill a void left by his dancing sister, who died as a child. Born with the "St. Vitus's dance" nervous disorder, he spent his first year in darkness and silence. But as soon as he was taken to the cabaret and movies, he found his vocation to imitate, "often in unrecognizable form," the culture of the age.

"Light" is interspersed with tiny gems from stage acts featuring Kemp and his most famous partners, from Jack Birkett (The Incredible Orlando) to David Bowie (Kemp reportedly invented his Ziggy Stardust character) and David Haughton, who also narrates Kemp's life.

Mini-sampler of Kemp's dreamlike plays includes "Salome," "Dream," "Mr. Punch," "Nijin-sky," "The Big Parade," "Alice" and his latest (which recently toured Japan) "Onnagata." In each, the director/writer/performer's inventiveness and originality are foregrounded, with no attempt to mask his narcissism.

This record of the life and work of a remarkable artist explores the possibility of film and video editing and special effects. Eshetu cuts and blends images, layering them thickly to create new meanings. In one sequence, a "shrunken" Kemp emerges from a real flower, on which electronic rain and butterflies play.

Visual and musical poem mirrors Kemp's art in its imaginative visualization of ideas as images — from a decomposing hedgehog to Grace Kelly sailing a model ship across a swimming pool. It is also an excellent introduction to Kemp's very literate gay theater, whose emotions and ideas range from amusing to tragic, from English variety shows and Spanish flamenco dancing, to vampires and self-immolation.

Pic's full of cleverly edited archive material culled from cinema, paintings and sculpture, docus and dance.
— *Deborah Young*

JOURNEY OF HONOR
(U.S.-JAPANESE)

A Rocket Pictures release of a Sanyo Finance Co. Ltd., Sho Kosugi Corp., Sho Prods. presentation of a Mayeda production. (Intl. sales: Blue Ridge/Filmtrust.) Produced by Sho Kosugi. Executive producers, Hiroshi Tscuchiya, Toshiaki Hamayashi. Directed by Gordon Hessler. Screenplay, Nelson Gidding, from story by Kosugi, Gidding. Camera (Deluxe color), John Connor; editor, Bill Butler; music, John Scott; production design, Adrian Gorton; production manager-2nd unit director-associate producer, Gene Kraft; sound (Dolby), Leon Citarella; assistant director, Petar Cvejic (Yugoslavia), Yoshihiro Hagiwara (Japan); stunt coordinator, John Stewart; narrator, Don Pedro Colley; line producer, Benni Korzen, Milos Antic (Yugoslavia); casting, Caro Jones, Hubbard Casting (U.K.). Reviewed on MCA/Universal vidcassette, N.Y. MPAA Rating: PG-13. Running time: **106 MIN.**
Mayeda . . . . Sho Kosugi
Don Pedro . . . . David Essex
Yorimune . . . . Kane Kosugi
King Philip . . . . . . Christopher Lee
Father Vasco . . . . . . Norman Lloyd
Capt. Crawford . . . . Ronald Pickup
El Zaidan . . . . . . John Rhys-Davies
Cecilia . . . . Polly Walker
Smitty . . . . Dylan Kussman
Lord Ieyasu . . . . . . Toshiro Mifune
Yadogimi . . . . Miwa Takada
Counselor . . . . . . Nijiko Kiyokawa

An enjoyable throwback to Saturday matinee movie fare,

"Journey of Honor" (a.k.a. "Shogun Mayeda") is a pleasant diversion that recently played regionally almost simultaneous with video release.

Brainchild of martial arts star Sho Kosugi, film cleverly mixes various genres of swashbucklers into an entertaining package as Kosugi gets to indulge in sword-fights on palace stairs reminiscent of vintage Errol Flynn/Basil Rathbone screen encounters.

Kosugi casts himself as chief warrior for an eastern kingdom lord (guest star Toshiro Mifune). He helps win a 1600 battle conquering Japan's western kingdom and is sent by Mifune to Spain in search of firearms.

On the trip is the lord's son (played by Sho's real-life son Kane Kosugi). Treachery's afoot as the Japanese heroes must contend with a self-serving Portuguese missionary (Norman Lloyd), a quick-tempered Spanish aristocrat (David Essex) and an Arab pirate (John Rhys-Davies).

Derring-do is excitingly staged on Yugoslavian and Japanese locations by vet Yank director Gordon Hessler. Essex (star of original London stage edition of "Evita") is a terrific dashing villain, and both Kosugis are bona fide action heroes.

Film, shot in 1990, introduces British actress Polly Walker, a very appealing blonde heroine, later to score (with different hair tints) in "Patriot Games" and "Enchanted April." Ronald Pickup as her sea captain dad and Christopher Lee as King Philip of Spain are solid in support.

Like "Christopher Columbus: The Discovery," "Journey of Honor" is very old-fashioned, but it delivers the panache and romance missing from the much more expensive Salkind epic.
— *Lawrence Cohn*

UN PARAGUAS PARA TRES
(AN UMBRELLA FOR THREE)
(SPANISH-FRENCH)

A Tornasol (Spain)-Gemini Films (French) production, in association with Esicma, ICAA, Canal Plus España, Canal Plus France. Produced by Gerardo Herrero. Directed, written by Felipe Vega. Camera (color), José Luis López-Linares; editor, Carmen Frias; music, Angel Muñoz; art direction, Ana Alvargonzález; sound, Goldstein & Steinberg. Reviewed at Walter Reade Theater (Spanish Cinema Now), N.Y., Oct. 12, 1992. Running time: **90 MIN.**
Daniel . . . . Juanjo Puigcorbé
Maía . . . . Eulalia Ramón
Alicia . . . . Iciar Bollain

Also with: Francis Lorenzo, Germán Cobos, Jean-François Stevenin.

The Spanish-French co-prod "An Umbrella for Three" is pleasant enough but unsuccessful commentary on the laws of chance. Helmer Felipe Vega inserts enough clever directorial bits to keep the film afloat despite its artificial premise.

Rather convoluted plot concerns Daniel (Juanjo Puigcorbé) and María (Eulalia Ramón), both formerly attached, who meet by chance at the Corte Inglés, Madrid's answer to Bloomingdale's.

Suddenly, they begin to run into each other in various other locations, and fate seems to present a star-crossed romance in the offing. Yet both are reticent: María dumps Daniel on various occasions while he beds her best friend and co-worker.

Underneath is repeated philosophical reflection on the theory of chance or luck. The ending reveals that chance is probably at work, but not in the way it first presents itself.

Vega adds nice imaginative bits to keep this romantic comedy just slightly off balance. The characters are not particularly sympathetic, though acting, and tech credits, are okay.
— *Paul Lenti*

CLAIRE OF THE MOON

A Demi-Monde production. Produced by Pamela S. Kuri. Executive producer, Nicole Conn. Co-executive producer, Nannette M. Troutman. Directed, written by Conn. Camera (Fotokem color), Randolph Sellars; editor, Michael Solinger; music, Michael Allen Harrison; sound, Brian Crain. Reviewed at Loews Copley Place Theater, Boston, Sept. 7, 1992. (In Toronto, Boston film festivals). Running time: **107 MIN.**
Claire Jabrowski . . . . . Trisha Todd
Dr. Noel Benedict . . . Karen Trumbo
Maggie . . . . Faith McDevitt
Tara O'Hara . . . . . . Caren Graham
BJ . . . . Shiela Dickinson
Brian . . . . Damon Craig

"Claire of the Moon" is a talky drama that plays like a lesbian version of "The Odd Couple." Dearth of pics dealing with lesbian romance (as opposed to "problem" films from "The Children's Hour" to "Personal Best") ensures that this will score with intended audience. But chances are slim of broadening its appeal beyond the fest and limited art house circuits, even to the modest level of "Desert Hearts."

Indie production looks polished, and leads are credible as two opposites who meet, repel and finally attract. Setting is a colony for women writers where novelist Claire Jabrowski (Trisha Todd) and psychiatrist Noel Benedict (Karen Trumbo) are forced to share accommodations when paired by Maggie (Faith McDevitt), the stereotypically "butch" proprietress. Indeed, all the supporting characters — lesbian and straight — are little more than caricatures.

Claire has been trading sex for intimacy and is generally unfulfilled. Noel is an open lesbian who has yet to meet Ms. Right. The novelist is a slob, the shrink is a neatnik. Like a distaff Felix and Oscar, they spend the first half of the film arguing.

Although it's patently obvious to everyone — including the other characters onscreen — that Claire and Noel belong together, it takes them almost the whole film to admit it. There are several false starts with one or the other pulling back. Climactic love scene is not so much of a release as a relief.

Nicole Conn's direction is adequate, and she brings a distinctly different perspective to scenes where leads share their fantasies. Tech credits are solid, if modest. — *Daniel M. Kimmel*

PERUMTHACHAN
(THE MASTER CARPENTER)
(INDIAN)

A Bhavachithra production. Produced by G. Jayakumar. Directed by Ajayan. Screenplay, M.T. Vasudevan Nair. Camera (color), Santhosh Sivan; editor, M.S. Money; music, Jhonson; art direction, P. Krishnamoorthy; sound, Sampath. Reviewed at Locarno Film Festival (competition), Aug. 11, 1992. Running time: **120 MIN.**
With: Thilakan, Nedumudi Venu, Prasanth, Manoj, M.S. Tripunithura, Babu Namboodri, Vinaya Prasad, Monisha.

An old Kerala legend about a master craftsman who cannot stand being eclipsed by his own son, enables first-time director Ajayan to explore themes of old vs. new and artist vs. society. Fans of Indian cinema will not mind the slow, deliberate pace and script's verbosity, though general auds might find it more difficult.

The master carpenter, who also works in stone, is the son of a Brahmin scholar and a low-caste woman, an artist of unsurpassed skill and inspiration who wanders the south of India building shrines and providing sculptures of deities to fill them up.

Pic compares the chaste, idealistic relationship he has with a wife of an admiring sponsor to that of his son, who, in a similar situation, dares the traditions and the laws of the land.

The difficulties encountered by a widowed prince consort who fails to control his daughter and the tragic outcome of her disobedience, indicate the generation gap is present at all social levels, even in a caste society.

Ajayan's point is that no progress can be made without traditions and that youthful impetuosity is too often destructive.

Spectacular Kerala landscapes and strong presence of actor Thilakan in the title role, help considerably to convey the story.

Already awarded several prizes at home, the film will find its own specialized niche.
— *Dan Fainaru*

CINECITTA ... CINECITTA
(ITALIAN)

A Massfilm, Studio EL production. Produced by Franco Committeri, Luciano Ricceri. Directed by Vincenzo Badolisani. Screenplay, Giovanna Caico, Maria Luigia Cafiero, Marco Cecconi, Costanza De Palma, Barbara Maccari, Maurizio Mandel, Francesca Panzarella, Leonardo Spina, Stefano Tummolini, Paoli Lasi. Camera (color), Massimiliano Sano; editor, Carla Simoncelli; music, Armando Trovajoli; art direction, Cinzia Lo Fazio; costumes, Delia De Angelis. Reviewed at Sorrento Intl. Film Festival (competition), Oct. 2, 1992. Running time: **100 MIN.**
With: Amanda Sandrelli, Corso Salani, Massimo Wertmüller, Fabio Traversa, Franco Trevisi, Saverio Vallone, Giovanni Pallavicino.

An ambling comedy loosely linking the paths of folks on the lot, "Cinecittà . . . Cinecittà" squanders a potentially intriguing idea on a script that's as bitty and uneven as its 10-writer team would suggest. Pic may play in Rome, where affection for the legendary studio runs high, but it will be tough making b.o. inroads elsewhere.

Shot on and around the mammoth set for Ettore Scola's costumer "Captain Fracassa's Journey," pic uses an aspiring screenwriter (Corso Salani) to thread together various characters. Having submitted his first script to an elusive producer, Salani spends days biding his time to get a reaction. A bittersweet microcosm of optimism, compromise and disillusionment emerges through the events he observes.

Up-and-comer Salani is an honest actor and makes an able guide through the multifarious plots. Amanda Sandrelli's scenes as a distracted young mother angling for an acting break have a relaxed appeal, and a pair of extras reminiscing while playing bloody corpses gets big laughs.

But ultimately pic is like "The Player" without bite, and without a central story thrust. The writing is too infrequently comic to be laugh-out-loud funny, and too unrealistic to work as human observation.

Tech contributions are functional. Vet film score composer Armando Trovajoli's work is effective in melancholy moments, but its more cheerful strains sound less nostalgic than old-fashioned. — *David Rooney*

ROSA NEGRA
(PORTUGUESE)

A Uniportugal presentation of a Companhia de Filmes do Principe Real production. Executive producer, Maria Joao Mayer. Directed, written by Margarida Gil. Camera (color), Sophie Matigneux; editor, Manuel Mozos; music, Joao Gil, Teresa Salgueiro; sound, Renee Lever, Antoine Bonfanti. Reviewed at Locarno Film Festival, Aug. 10, 1992. Running time: **90 MIN.**
With: Manuela de Freitas, Fernando Luis, Catarina C. Pinto, Dinis Neto Jorge.

Somewhere inside this lethargic chronicle of a small Portuguese town, a thriller is struggling to come out, along with perhaps a love story and political commentary on provincial corruption. But since director Margarida Gil is bent on moods, atmosphere and inconclusive images, none of these genres materializes.

Among the various characters in this ill-defined plot are an arson suspect who returns after many years and has a brief affair with a local girl, a high school teacher who tries to stage Sophocles' "Antigone" and is victimized by the town's thugs, a soldier on leave, a factory owner who may or may not be damaging his own property for the insurance and a barman who comments on the proceedings.

Precious little info is available to connect the characters or tie up loose ends. A lot seems to be going on under the surface, but director Gil doesn't try very hard to elucidate. — *Dan Fainaru*

SLEEPING BEAUTY

A Gemini Pictures production. Produced by Ralph Groemping. Executive producers, Francis O'Brien, Joan Sugerman. Directed, written by Sugerman. Camera (Duart color), Chris Li; editor, Deborah Peretz; music, Cracked Actor; production design, Richard Montgomery; costume design, Paul Tazewell; sound, Jim Gilchrist; associate producer, Willa Taylor; assistant director, Lindsey Evans-Thomas. Reviewed at Nova Plus screening room, L.A., July 16, 1992. (In Mifed market.) Running time: **99 MIN.**
Natalie Smith . . . . . . Ainsley Kellar
Tom Smith . . . . Fred Tietz
Uncle Bob Smith . . . Charlie Maloney
Mule . . . . David Marks

Inspired by the Grimm fairy tale, Joan Sugerman's "Sleeping Beauty" is a lame yuppie comedy about sexual repression. Outdated concept, tedious tempo and unimaginative direction restrict commercial appeal, but a video life is possible.

Tom and Natalie Smith have a mundane suburban life devoid of sensual pleasure. Determined not to have children, the couple shuns sex because it's dirty and requires showering afterwards.

But one night Natalie accidentally cuts her finger and, bingo, she begins to experience magic spells that liberate her repressed libido. Ensuing vignettes sketch the shocked husband's attempt to cure his wife of her sexual fantasies via therapy, acupuncture and surgery.

For the fable to work effectively, it needed to be erotic and funny, which it isn't. Sugerman approaches her material academically, failing to build gags. Viewed condescendingly, the two chief characters are so schematic they never come to life. Essentially an anecdote dragged out to feature-length, story is directed with little energy.

As Tom, Fred Tietz, who resembles the young Richard Benjamin, gives a forced, overemphatic performance. Attractive Ainsley Kellar comes off slightly better but is also misdirected. David Marks, as a brute who picks up the wife in a go-go bar, displays some vitality.

Tech credits are on the raw side. Chris Li's lensing of the film's few outdoor scenes in the Washington, D.C., vicinity, is grainy and rough, and some of the indoor scenes are ill-lit.
— *Emanuel Levy*

HORS SAISON
(OFF SEASON)
(SWISS-GERMAN-FRENCH)

Produced by Marcel Hoehn for T&C Film (Zurich)/Metropolis Filmproduktion (Berlin)/Pierre Grise Prods. (Paris) in association with ZDF/DRS/TSI/TSR/Beat Curti. Associate producers, Luciano Glor, Martine Marignac. Directed by Daniel Schmid. Screenplay, Schmid, Martin Suter. Camera (color), Renato Berta; editor, Daniela Roderer; music, Peer Raben; art direction, Raul Gimenez. Reviewed at Locarno Film Festival, Aug. 7, 1992. (In Mifed market.) Running time: **95 MIN.**
Narrator . . . . Sami Frey
Valentin . . . . Carlos Devesa
Lilo . . . . Ingrid Caven
Max . . . . Dieter Meier
Prof. Malini . . . . Ulli Lommel
Mlle. Gabriel . . . . . Andrea Ferreol
Mme. Studer . . . . . . Arielle Dobasle
Grandma . . . . . Maddalena Fellini
Sarah Bernhardt . . . . Marisa Paredes
Anarchist . . . . . . Geraldine Chaplin
Uncle Paul . . . . Vittorio Mezzogiorno

If Stanley Kubrick set nightmares in the Overlook Hotel, Daniel Schmid has only the happiest magical memories to animate his grand hotel nestled in the Swiss Alps. "Hors Saison" is an unabashed cinematic circus populated by a Fellini-like cast of caricatures. Its irony and good humor make it high-class entertainment for family audiences as well as the director's art house fans.

Middle-aged Valentin (Sami Frey) returns to the huge hotel his parents owned when he was a boy, which has long since been sold and is about to be torn down. As he wanders through the empty ballrooms and corridors, he remembers the incredible people he knew there.

Most of the film is told in flashback through the eyes of innocent young Valentin (Carlos Devesa). The central figure is his grandmother, played with boisterous naturalness by Maddalena Fellini (sister of Federico in her second acting role at 60). Grandma tells him improbable stories about the day a Russian anarchist (Geraldine Chaplin) assassinated an enemy of the people in the hotel, or how the capricious Sarah Bernhardt (a show-stopping Marisa Paredes) seduced his grandfather.

Ingrid Caven and Dieter Meier sing torch songs to keep the guests occupied (but actually one number too many for viewers). A magician (Ulli Lommel) hypnotizes guests into thinking they're crossing the Sahara. Arielle Dombasle dazzles Valentin with her beauty, as he watches

her slip into men's rooms with an enigmatic smile.

Schmid stresses the distortions, as well as the pleasures, of memories. Narrative structure is loose and unbinding, yet the film moves along gracefully with few snags. Renato Berta's cinematography and Raul Gimenez's sets underline the poignancy of lost boyhood in the empty shell of the hotel in contrast to the merry party atmosphere and bright colors when the hotel was in full swing.

Audiences who may leave the film wishing to spend a few weeks in that marvelous Swiss hotel would be disappointed: It's a pieced-together collage of hotels in Portugal. — *Deborah Young*

BLINKY BILL
(AUSTRALIAN-ANIMATED)

A Greater Union Distrubutors release of a Yoram Gross Film Studios production, in association with Australian Film Finance Corp. (Intl. sales: Beyond Films.) Executive producers, Sandra Gross, Tim Brooke-Hunt. Produced, directed by Yoram Gross. Screenplay, John Palmer, Leonard Lee, Yoram Gross, based on Dorothy Wall's "The Complete Adventures of Blinky Bill." In Eastmancolor; editors, G.Y. Jerzy, Lee Smith; music, Guy Gross; lyrics, John Palmer; animation directors, Sue Beak, Athol Henry, Ray Nowland; model construction, Robert Qiu; production supervisor, Robert Smit. Reviewed at Village Cinema, Sydney, Sept. 24, 1992. (In Mifed Market.) Running time: **97 MIN.**
Voices: Keith Scott, Robyn Moore.

Since his first appearance in Dorothy Wall's 1939 book, mischievous little koala Blinky Bill has become a favorite in Aussie children's fiction. This film version, Australia's most ambitious venture into animation, is likely to displease traditionalists who will find the character significantly altered, but the small fry probably won't mind much. Despite flaws, this cheerful entertainment for moppets could generate useful sales in most territories.

Wall's illustrated books were quintessentially Aussie yarns about the inhabitants of the bush: kangaroos, wombats, a platypus, various reptiles as well as koalas. Yoram Gross' pic gives the characters a contempo, environmental context in which evil loggers threaten to destroy the animals' homes to make woodchips.

Separated from his mother, Blinky (here rendered hairless, pink-cheeked and bland) sets out on an adventure that climaxes

when femme pal Nutsy is trapped inside the home of the lumbermen, one of whom has a daughter who prefers Nutsy to her teddy bear.

This is fare for the very young, and, at 97 minutes, pic is a bit long for its target audience. The animation is competent, with real-life backgrounds used (as in previous Gross outings). A handful of songs pad out the running time, but otherwise Guy Gross' music is jolly.

A continuing disappointment in Gross productions is unimaginative use of voices. Instead of employing a cast of character actors to supply the voices, "Blinky Bill" uses only two actors who voice dozens of creatures as well as the occasional human. If this was for cost-cutting, it was ill-advised.
— *David Stratton*

UN'ALTRA VITA
(ANOTHER LIFE)
(ITALIAN)

A DARC release of an Erre Produzioni production in association with RAI-2. Produced by Angelo Rizzoli. Directed by Carlo Mazzacurati. Screenplay, Franco Bernini, Mazzacurati. Camera (color), Alessandro Pesci; editor, Mirco Garrone; art direction, Massimo Spano; music, Ralph Towner. Reviewed at Venice Film Festival, Sept. 5, 1992. (In Mifed market.) Running time: **95 MIN.**
Saverio . . . . Silvio Orlando
Alia . . . . . . Adrianna Biedrzynska
Mauro . . . . Claudio Amendola
Vanni . . . . Giorgio Tirabassi
Rita . . . . Antonella Ponziani
Remo . . . . Antonella Fassari
Luisanna . . . . Monica Scattini

An Italian dentist falls unhappily in love with a Russian immigrant girl in "Another Life," a light, sensitive, bittersweet story by Carlo Mazzacurati. He turns the loneliness of city life into a quiet but ontarget film, graced by popular Italo comic Silvio Orlando, who should assure pic a good run domestically. Film is a strong candidate for specialized release offshore this season.

Orlando plays a nice-guy dentist living alone in a big apartment his parents left him. When Adrianna Biedrzynska turns up on his doorstep, beaten up and missing a tooth, the dentist works all night making her a new one.

They live together platonically until the girl leaves, mainly to keep from hurting the lovesick dentist's feelings. He can't forget her, and his search for her brings him into amusing contact with local hoods led by Claudio

Amendola, who's also in love with Biedrzynska and looking for her.

Despite a bleak conclusion, pic is constructed with an intelligently light-hearted spirit. Scripter Franco Bernini keeps the screenplay alive with plenty of soft, offbeat irony.

Orlando is sympathetic if one-note, passively letting himself go with the flow as he wistfully longs for emotional fulfillment. Since his faint Neapolitan accent is carefully noted in the film, one wonders about the casting of fine Polish actress Biedrzynska, who looks and sounds Russian only by suspension of belief. Her talent at portraying a complex, optimistic survivor of the East, however, amply makes up for the wrong nationality.

Alessandro Pesci's cool camerawork unveils a little-seen side of Rome: high-rise slums on the city outskirts and the unfashionable beach of satellite-city Ostia, where immigrants live in shacks.
— *Deborah Young*

FRIENDS AND ENEMIES
(FRENCH)

A Sideral Prods. presentation & production with Echo Rock Entertainment. Produced by Christine Purse, Dirk Blackman. Executive producer, Leonardo De La Fuente, Martin J. Frank. Directed by Andrew Frank. Screenplay, Mark Distefano, Tom McCluskey. Camera (color), Maximo Munzi; editor, Michele Lavigne; music, Gary Evanoff; production design, Walter Bambrick. Reviewed at Montreal World Film Festival (competition), Sept. 6, 1992. (In Mifed market.) Running time: **100 MIN.**
Dominick . . . . Roger Rignack
Paul . . . Steven Christopher Young
Nick . . . . Robert Restaino
Louis . . . . Todd Antony Bello
Rose-Ann . . . . . Rebecca Rocheford
Freddy . . . . Dean Stockwell
Cosmo . . . . Bob Frey
Barney . . . . . Anthony Caldareilla

This slice of Italian life should be called "Friends and Family" rather than "Friends and Enemies." Difficult, oddly structured film about unlikable characters marks an ambitious directorial debut for Andrew Frank.

Mafia-like credo suggests friends and family stick together even if murder is involved, but this cinéma vérité-style pic is no "Godfather."

Plausible story is about four overgrown beer-guzzling "boys" who enjoy babbling about baseball and broads. One evening at a sleezy pub after a big game, their lifelong friendship is challenged when Nick (Robert Restaino) picks a fight with a passive patron and almost kills him in the parking lot.

Local baseball hero Dominick (Roger Rignack) and dumb cousin Louis (Todd Antony Bello) want to call the cops, but buddy Paul (Steven Christopher Young) orchestrates a conspiracy of silence to save Nick's neck. They're counting on the victim to die.

Next four reels are predictable as conspirators wrestle with consciences, allegiances and laws. Hot on their trail is local detective Barney, part of the family clan (via Dominick's father who eventually approves his son's actions because he's protecting friends and family).

Helmer makes cover-up and ensuing friendship battles believable. Pic's main problem is that it's difficult to care about the main characters, depicted as redneck idiots. Story takes an interesting turn when the victim is recovering, but outcome is always predictable.

"Realistic" buddy pic may appeal to overgrown boys, but it's not mainstream fare for suburban or urban couples looking for a good time at the movies. Pic was completely overlooked by both jury and audience at its Montreal film fest preem.

— *Suzan Ayscough*

DESPUES DEL SUENO
(AFTER THE DREAM)
(SPANISH)

A Sogetel presentation. Executive producer, Fernando de Garcillan, Jose Luis Olaizola. Produced by Ricardo Garcia Arrojo. Directed, written by Mario Camus. Camera (color), Jaime Peracaula; editor, Jose Maria Biurrun; art direction, Rafael Palmero; costumes, Maria Jose Iglesias. Reviewed at Montreal World Film Festival (competition), Aug. 31, 1992. (In Mifed market.) Running time: **106 MIN.**
Amos Carro . . . . . . Carmelo Gomez
Antonio Blasco . . . . . Antonio Valero
Angeles Guiterrez . . . . . . Ana Belen
Ramiro Lanza . . . . . . Fernando Rey
Pepita . . . . Eulalia Ramon
Salud . . . . Judith Masco

"**A**fter the Dream," depicting a family's predictable search for a stolen Picasso, has neither surprises nor b.o. potential Stateside. Its future is as a TV movie for Spanish markets.

A mystery in which several romances bloom, plot revolves around a pilfered painting, which of course, is recovered after 106 painstaking minutes.

Solid cast does as much as can be expected with weak roles as scripted by helmer Mario Camus. Antonio Valero plays the womanizing lawyer coolly. Carmelo Gomez is shy as the trusting client who winds up with lawyer's gorgeous g.f. Judith Masco (a top-notch fashion model who reveals no hidden acting talent in this plodding vehicle).

— *Suzan Ayscough*

KAIVO
(THE WELL)
(FINNISH-SWEDISH-DANISH)

A KinoFinlandia (Helsinki)-Film Teknik (Stockholm)-Metronome Prods. (Copenhagen) co-production. (Intl. sales: Swedish Film Institute.) Produced, directed by Pekka Lehto. Screenplay, Outi Nyytaja, from Marja-Leena Mikkola's story. Camera (Scope, color), Esa Vuorinen; editor, Arturas Pozdniakovas; music, Anssi Tikanmaki; production design, Anu Maja; sound, Johan Hake, Oskari Viskari; line producer, Chuck Rowley; assistant director, Veikko Aaltonen. Reviewed at Venice Film Festival (competition), Sept. 12, 1992. (In Mifed market.) Running time: **109 MIN.**
Anna-Maija . . . . . Merja Larivaara
Matti . . . . Auvo Vihro
Taimi . . . . . Liisamaija Laaksonen
Merja . . . . Katariina Kaitue
Arvi . . . . Martti Suosalo

"**T**he Well," dazzlingly filmed but ultra-downbeat, was inspired by a real-life incident in which a farm woman was acquitted after throwing two of her children down a well. From this bleak subject matter, director Pekka Lehto has fashioned a visually and dramatically strong film which, unfortunately, not many people will want to see.

Pic opens with a flourish when Anna-Maija's husband, Matti, discovers his wife and children are missing. A large-scale search with police helicopters results in the safe discovery of the oldest boy, Marko, and his distraught mother, who has tried to drown herself in a lake. Her two young children have vanished.

Flashbacks reveal Anna-Maija's unhappy life with her domineering mother who gave her no help with the children and who was having an affair with a younger man. Anna-Maija's sister had left to live in Sweden some time earlier, and Matti was so absorbed with the farm he was unable to give his long-suffering wife attention and love.

Lehto's visceral approach to this material, with bravura widescreen camerawork and a soaring music score, doesn't disguise this farm's coldness. Thesping is fine, but audiences are likely to shy away from the unrelenting spiritual and mental desolation.

— *David Stratton*

CRAZY JOE

A 21st Century Film production. (Intl. sales: 21st Century.) Produced by Menahem Golan, Ami Artzi. Line producer, Nicholas Stamos. Directed by Steve Carver. Screenplay, Stephen Peters, from Joseph Goldman's story, Camera (DeLuxe color), Bernard Salzmann; editor, Irit Raz; music, Sasha Matson; production design, Scott Alan Buckwald; costumes, Tami Mor; sound (Ultra-Stereo), Bernard Cabral; stunt coordinator, Charlie Skeen; assistant director, Joseph Cowperthwaite; associate producer, Yael Golan. Reviewed at Cannes Film Festival market, May 15, 1992. (In Mifed market.) Running time: **87 MIN.**
Joe . . . . Justin Lazard
Mary . . . . Rachel York
Saunders . . . . Eb Lottimer
Carol . . . . Krista Shook
Chavez . . . . David Carradine
Also with: R.G. Armstrong, Frank McCarthy.

By the standards of current screen crazies, this "Crazy Joe" wouldn't scare the cassocks off a nuns' outing. Teasing but ultimately routine programmer about a street killer retrained by government goons is strictly for couch potatoes.

Aficionados of schlockmeister Steve Carver will slot this one several rungs below classics like "Lone Wolf McQuade," "Big Bad Mama" and "Capone," and a smidgeon above okay fare like "An Eye for an Eye." Pic delivers in some areas but never lives up to the promise of its opening.

Decidedly untough-looking Justin Lazard is the eponymous wasting machine, grabbed by the agency after nearly biting the big one in a shootout and assigned to blackbelt op Rachel York's less than tender care.

Early training scenes, where York and Lazard test each other's pain barriers by using their hands as ashtrays, don't develop into much once the plot hovers into view. And overtly jokey sequences include Lazard furnishing his apartment in speeded-up motion.

York acquits herself well in the slam-bang finale but otherwise is little more than statuesque. Lazard tries to look mean but signally fails. Pic is technically smooth but clearly shot on a budget. Co-prod Menahem Golan can be briefly spotted at an art-gallery pour.

— *Derek Elley*

ALBERT SOUFFRE
(ALBERT SUFFERS)
(FRENCH)

An AMLF release of a Les Films Alain Sarde/Spitz Prods./Renn Prods. co-production with participation of Canal Plus, CNC, Sofiarp, Investimage 3. Produced by Alain Sarde, Albert Koski. Executive producer, Catherine Mazières. Directed, written by Bruno Nuytten. Camera (color), Eric Gautier; editor, Jeanne Kef; music, Pixies; sound, Jean Minondo, Philippe Hessler; costumes, Virginie Viard; set design, Stefan Lubrina; casting, Tatiana Vialle. Reviewed at AMLF screening room, Paris, Aug. 6, 1992. (In Mifed market.) Running time: **105 MIN.**
Albert . . . . Julien Rassam
Jeanne . . . . Estelle Skornik
Jérôme . . . . . . Jean-Michel Portal
Charles . . . . . . Collin Obomalayat
Jo-Ann . . . . . . Kristen McMenamy

Helmer Bruno Nuytten takes the rowdy, aggressive approach to twentysomething angst in "Albert Souffre," a post-punk-inflected assault on the senses. Energetically lensed adventures of five interlocking characters will probably click with Gallic viewers over 25, but pic will be a harder sell for older auds.

Nuytten enlisted mostly first-time actors and technicians to make the retroactive "first" film he feels he should have made before tackling "Camille Claudel." "Albert Souffre" is just as relentless and wearing as the elaborate big-budget biopic but utterly contemporary.

Albert (Julien Rassam) suffers from too much energy, not enough affection and no career orientation. Some viewers may suffer from ringing ears and quizzical expressions after being bombarded with so many decibels (courtesy of a dozen cranked-up Pixies songs) and the free-wheeling protagonist's antics. He gathers ambient sounds and dictates his experiences into a tape recorder when he's not distracting more disciplined individuals from their appointed tasks.

Pic will be touching and exhilarating to those who take irksome imp Albert to heart; those who don't will endure the frequently obnoxious, irresponsible careening of a self-centered brat who cajoles everyone he meets into coming out to play.

Bordeaux hotel-dweller Jérôme (Jean-Michel Portal) is boning up for a crucial exam, as is his adorable g.f. Jeanne (Estelle Skornik). From Paris, Albert shows up the night before and, in the course of a weekend, will betray his friend, inspire the hotel's African desk clerk, meet a new love and begin to grow up. To its credit, pic feels like one long binge with the nonstop velocity of a continuous weekend.

In his maiden outing, Rassam is majestically annoying as Albert, who has an inability to grasp much of anything that isn't orbiting around his own navel. Other thesps are all convincing. In one brief shot, Portal exhibits a modified jockstrap after suffering an injury to his testicles.

Albert and Jérôme occasionally communicate in their own postsurrealist language which is translated with nonsensical subtitles. Subtitles are amusingly provided for Yank model-turned-actress Kristen McMenamy even when she's speaking French.

Tech credits are good, with special praise for thoughtful, evocative use of sound.

— Lisa Nesselson

MAX ET JEREMIE
(MAX AND JEREMY)
(FRENCH-COLOR)

An AMLF (France) release of a Les Films Alain Sarde/TF1 Film Prods./ Gruppo-Bema co-production with the participation of Canal Plus. Executive producer, Christine Gozlan. Produced by Sarde. Directed by Claire Devers. Screenplay, Devers, Bernard Stora, based on the novel "Max Trueblood and the Jersey Desperado" by Teri White. Camera (color), Bruno de Keyzer; editor, Marie Castro; music, Philippe Sarde; art direction, Carlos Conti; costume design, Catherine Leterrier; sound, Jean-Paul Mugel. Reviewed at Club Gaumont screening room, Paris, Oct. 1, 1992. Running time: **110 MIN.**
Max . . . . Philippe Noiret
Jeremie . . . . . . Christophe Lambert
Almeida . . . . . Jean-Pierre Marielle
Also with: Christophe Odent, Feodor Chaliapin Jr., Thierry Gimenez, Jean-Pierre Miquel, Jose Quaglio.

"**M**ax et Jeremie," the story of a novice hit man who bonds too closely with the seasoned killer he's supposed to bump off, approaches moral bankruptcy but entertains.

Local scribes have been singing the pic's praises since its mid-October release and Gallic audiences have warmed to Christophe Lambert's return to French-lingo fare after a five-year hiatus. The semi-comic thriller represents a commercially successful crossover into more mainstream territory for helmer Claire Devers, whose first two films were strictly arthouse.

Scruffy, emotionally needy Jeremie (Lambert) is an explosives expert who blows up people and things for Paris mobsters. He yearns for the kind of assignment that will improve his status and jumps at the chance to kill someone face to face.

But when his target, a dapper retired hit man named Max (Philippe Noiret), accepts one last contract (from the late Feodor Chaliapin Jr.) and lets Jeremie in on the lucrative deal, affection-starved Lambert can't bring himself to kill his benefactor.

Noiret, in a beautifully nuanced performance, is refined, meticulous and completely self-sufficient. Sometimes reminiscent of a young Brando, Lambert's streetsmart Jeremie is whiny and completely lacking in culture. Much of the humor stems from the contrast.

Max and soon-to-retire Inspector Almeida (Jean-Pierre Marielle, who is excellent) are cordial adversaries. Pic implies Noiret

and Marielle are the last of their breed, the new generation of cops and crooks lacking their ineffable class.

But after the suspense is resolved over whether Lambert will be able to eliminate Noiret, the pic switches gears and becomes tiresome. On the lam, Noiret runs through a series of tricks, but Lambert's clumsy, puppy-like devotion becomes a serious liability.

The dialogue is crisp, helming is assured and thesping is fine across the board. Only hitch is the actual subject matter: Two guys who commit grisly crimes are neither troubled by nor punished for their exploits and pull through with lots of luck.

Tech credits are all pro, although the score is way too insistent in several passages. Molotov cocktails, detonations and gunfire are skillfully deployed in violent action segments.

— Lisa Nesselson

DIE BLAUE STUNDE
(THE BLUE HOUR)
(GERMAN-SWISS)

A Wild Okapi release of a Marcel Gisler production. Produced by Gisler Filmproduktion & Transfilm in co-production with WDR & DRS. Directed by Marcel Gisler. Screenplay, Gisler, Andreas Herder, Rudolf Nadler. Camera (color, Super 16m), Ciro Cappellari; editor, Bettina Böhler; production design, Kirsten Johannsen; costume design, Beatrix Demleitner; sound, Klaus Klingler. Reviewed at Filmpalast Cinema, Berlin, Aug. 18, 1992. Running time: **87 MIN.**
Theo . . . . Andreas Herder
Marie . . . . Dina Leipzig
Paul . . . . Cyrille Rey-Coquis
Felix Baum . . . . . Anton Rattinger
Laszlo . . . . Christof Krix
First John . . . . Albert Kitzler
Second John . . . . . Wolfram Haack
Third John . . . . . Arne Bauer-Worch
Marie's Boss . . . . . Dagmar Cassens

Story of an unlikely friendship between a German callboy and his French neighbor in Berlin is a masterful study in character and extremely well structured and acted. "The Blue Hour" could break out of the fest circuit for art house showings to sophisticated urban auds.

Andreas Herder plays a prostitute whose movements are dictated by the telephone calls of his clients, coolly making appointments in apartments and hotel rooms with a variety of johns.

Across the hall lives a not-so-young-anymore woman (Dina Leipzig) alienated by her dreary job in a record store and exas-

perated with her b.f. (Cyrille Rey-Coquis), who lives off her meager earnings and spends his days chain-smoking instead of writing his all-important novel until she finally kicks him out for good. When the woman accidentally locks herself out one day, Herder helps her get back into her apartment, and, tentatively, the two begin a friendship. As they begin to trust each other, they even sleep together, Leipzig not uncomfortable with her new lover's profession.

Film is devoid of spectacle but distinguished by a fine script, excellent acting and Gisler's fine eye for character and slow, deliberate revelation of detail. Crosscutting between the disparate lives of the characters, he sensitively, subtly escalates fine tension in the drama. The film is on a very small scale, mainly shot in two apartments, but it satisfies on a much broader level.

— Rebecca Lieb

BLUE ICE

A Guild Film Distribution (U.K.) release of an M&M Prods. production, in association with HBO Pictures. (Intl. sales: Classico Entertainment.) Executive producer, Gary Levinsohn. Produced by Martin Bregman, Michael Caine. Directed by Russell Mulcahy. Screenplay, Ron Hutchinson, based on a character created by Ted Allbeury; Camera (Eastmancolor; Metrocolor & Technicolor prints), Denis Crossan; editor, Seth Flaum; music, Michael Kamen; production design, Grant Hicks; art direction, Lawrence Williams; costume design, Les Lansdown; sound (Dolby), Terry Elms, Dave Weathers; assistant director, John Watson; stunt coordinator, Alan Stuart; co-producer, Louis A. Stroller. associate producer, Barney Reisz; BBC producer, Peter Kendal; casting, Joyce Nettles. Reviewed at MGM Tottenham Court Rd. Theater, London, Oct. 9, 1992. Running time: **104 MIN.**
Harry Anders . . . . . . Michael Caine
Stacy Mansdorf . . . . . . Sean Young
Sir Hector . . . . Ian Holm
Osgood . . . . Alun Armstrong
George . . . . Sam Kelly
Stevens . . . . Jack Shepherd
Kyle . . . . Todd Boyce
Buddy . . . . Bobby Short
Sam Garcia . . . . Bob Hoskins

Michael Caine re-dons spy-catcher duds in "Blue Ice," a determinedly old-fashioned actioner that's terminally light on real thrills. Solid production values and star names may shake small change in undiscriminating markets but pic doesn't look like it will cut much ice in today's high-tech scene.

Caine is Harry Anders, a retired MI6 op who's whiling away his years running a London jazz bar. When a U.S. ambassador's wife (Sean Young) literally bumps into him at a red light, he gets drawn back into espionage when she asks him to find a former b.f. (Todd Boyce) who supposedly holds old love letters.

Problems (and pic's body count) start to mount when the b.f. and a cop friend of Caine's are found dead. When Young also disappears, the retired op plugs on alone to uncover dirty deeds by government highups.

The movie is a throwback to formula pics of the '60s, with transatlantic leads swanning around London tourist spots and an uncomplicated plot that has fewer twists than a cocktail spoon.

Aussie helmer Russell Mulcahy, who *can* turn on the suspense taps ("Ricochet"), settles on straight narrative with occasional touches of noirish atmosphere in night scenes and interiors.

As the retired cockney spy who cooks a mean langoustine provençale Caine skirts close to an aging Harry Palmer (his "Ipcress File"/"Funeral in Berlin" persona). His settled, effortless performance carries the pic, but there's a lack of real electricity with Young.

Tech credits are fine and production tab was a well-spent $7 million. Producers Caine and Martin Bregman are on record as hoping to launch a series of pics on the main character. Title refers to a chunk of ice falling off an airliner out of a clear blue sky and braining someone on the ground. — *Derek Elley*

VIELLE CANAILLE
(OLD RASCAL)
(FRENCH)

A Blue Dahlia production. (Intl. sales: President Films, Paris.) Produced by Michel Faure, Henri Vart. Directed by Gerard Jourd'hui. Screenplay, Dominique Roulet, Jourd'hui, based on Frederick Brown's novel "His Name Was Death." Camera (color), George Barsky; editor, Nicole Saunier; music, Bruno Coulais; art direction, Dominique Andre; sound, Yves Osmu. Reviewed at Toronto Festival of Festivals, Sept. 16, 1992. Running time: **97 MIN.**
Darius Caunes . . . . . Michel Serrault
Rose . . . . Anna Galiena
Charlie . . . . Pierre Richard
Claude . . . . Jean-Pierre Bouvier

"**O**ld Rascal" is a perky, impudent little comic crime story that serves as another showcase for the sublime thesping talents of Michel Serrault. Something of a French cousin to the mischievous old Ealing capers in Britain in the 1950s,

only with a nastier streak, pic is not a heavyweight entry but could stir a degree of interest in markets open to quirky foreign lingo fare.

Serrault plays a middle-aged bourgeois who happens to have killed his wife two years back and counterfeits impeccable 500 franc notes at his print shop. A walking definition of *sang froid*, he dines regularly with the police inspector (Pierre Richard), who failed to solve the wife's murder but became a good friend, and dons a disguise when he puts his phony money into circulation in the Lyon vicinity.

A deliciously corrupt and duplicitous villain who lives a life of fastidious regularity so that he might make an art of evil, Serrault's Darius is one of those unflappably arrogant characters whose increasing audacity in the face of all legal and moral norms creates its own source of fascination. One awaits his downfall with bated breath, all the while admiring his resourcefulness in eluding detection.

As long as everyone else falls in line with his plans, everything remains fine. However, when his attractive shop assistant (Anna Galiena, the leading lady of "The Hairdresser's Husband") unwittingly gives a former lover some of the 500 franc notes, Serrault is forced to begin improvising, right back into the murder business.

The small-scale thriller plot isn't much in itself, but provides an adequate platform from which director and co-writer Gerard Jourd'hui spins off a rib-tickling stream of black, mordant humor. Much of the mirth stems from Serrault's frustration when his diabolical deeds can't be executed as easily as intended, and more from his outrageously self-centered, callous attitude toward the rest of the world.

This wouldn't work nearly as well as it does without the impeccably controlled Serrault, who adds yet another jewel to his acting crown by creating such an insidiously likable killer. His economy of expression and precise conveyance of nuanced meanings and humor could serve as a lesson to even the best actors. Pierre Richard invests the hapless detective with welcome energy, while Galiena is once again a delight.

A former documentary and TV director, Jourd'hui tells his modest story with verve and an ingratiatingly wicked tone. Tech credits are very good.
— *Todd McCarthy*

BREAKING THE RULES

A Miramax Films release of a Sterling Entertainment presentation of a Jonathan D. Krane production. Produced by Krane, Kent Bateman. Executive producers, Larry Thompson, Deborah J. Simon. Directed by Neal Israel. Screenplay, Paul W. Shapiro. Camera (Technicolor), James Hayman; editor, Tom Walls; music, David Kitay; production design, Donald Light-Harris; costume design, Giovanna Ottobe-Melton; sound (Dolby), Ed White; assistant director, Matthew Carlisle; stunt coordinator-2nd unit director, Chris Howell; 2nd unit camera, Bob New; line producer, Elliot Rosenblatt; casting, Eliza Simons, Pam Rack. Reviewed at Manhattan 1 theater, N.Y., Oct. 9, 1992. MPAA Rating: PG-13. Running time: **100 MIN.**
Phil Stepler . . . . .Jason Bateman
Gene Michaels . . . .C. Thomas Howell
Rob Konigsberg . Jonathan Silverman
Mary Klinglitch . . . . . . Annie Potts
Rob's date . . . . . . .Krista Kesreau
Phil's dad . . . . Kent Bateman

"**B**reaking the Rules" is a stillborn road movie, way too maudlin to be touching or amusing. On the shelf for over three years, pic emerges as a poor entry in all markets.

Shot as "Sketches" in 1989 and one of since-defunct MCEG's final productions, pic bears all the marks of a TV movie. Yet unlike most other MCEG leftovers (such as the upcoming cable debuter "Chains of Gold"), it gets a lame-duck theatrical outing.

Cold storage hasn't helped. Gimmick of three 22-year-old guys from Cleveland trekking to Los Angeles for a final fling is old hat in the extreme.

Judging from a final dedication credit, Paul Shapiro's lame screenplay must have been a personal one for him. Topliner Jason Bateman suffers from leukemia and has a month to live. On the pretext of an engagement party (he has no girlfriend), he gets his boyhood pals Jonathan Silverman and C. Thomas Howell to come home, and then breaks the bad news to them.

Pic gets off on a bad foot when the trio decide to go to L.A. to get Bateman a dreamed-of shot on "Jeopardy," a gimmick subsequently well-used to set "White Men Can't Jump" into motion.

Pals pack into a van for uninteresting and unatmospheric adventures (Cleveland and other locales are poorly faked in Sacramento and environs). Film perks up a bit halfway with the entrance of waitress Annie Potts, who sort of adopts the trio.

A dull trip to Reno results in Bateman's whirlwind marriage to Potts, but she elects to sleep with Silverman instead. By the

time Bateman expires in Potts' arms in a California motel room in a poorly directed scene, any audience's patience will have been exhausted.

Working very hard, Silverman and Howell constantly upstage Bateman, a bad misstep for what is ostensibly a Bateman vehicle (his dad Kent Bateman co-produced and even appears as his on-screen dad). Potts is endearing though given a paper-thin role. Comedy helmer Neal Israel gets very few laughs for his efforts.
— *Lawrence Cohn*

CONFORTORIO
(ITALIAN)

An Andrea De Gioia for Arsenali Medicei production in association with Ministry of Entertainment & RAI-3. Directed, written by Paolo Benvenuti. Camera (color), Aldo Dimarcantonio; editor, Mario Benvenuti; art direction, Paolo Barbi; costumes, Marta Scarlatti. Reviewed at Locarno Film Festival (competition), Aug. 7, 1992. Running time: **85 MIN.**
Administrator . . . . . . Emidio Simini
Angeluccio . . . . Franco Pistoni
Abramo . . . Emanuele Carucci Viterbi

Incredible but true story of the Catholic Church's attempt to convert two Jewish thieves before hanging them is told with spartan rigor illuminated by dramatic moments in "Confortorio." Paolo Benvenuti's sarcasm for misguided ecclesiastical power is mirrored in his moving sympathy for the duo's plight. Locarno fest item should make further fest rounds and have some TV sales offshore.

During the reign of Pope Clement XII in 1736, criminals Abramo and Angeluccio were expelled by the rabbis from Rome's Jewish ghetto and handed over for punishment to the authorities, the Pontifical Tribunal, which judged the case and sentenced the housebreakers to hang.

But the church fathers realized afterwards that they had put themselves in a terrible moral bind: If they hanged a Jew, he would go to hell because of his guilt in killing Christ — and the Church would thus be an instrument of damnation instead of salvation. The only solution, then, was to convert the two before the hanging so they would die Christians and their souls would be saved.

In the course of one long night in the bowels of a Roman prison, the "confortorio" (whose role is to comfort those condemned to death) calls in every bigwig preacher in town to get the job done, including archbishops and converted rabbis. But instead of converting the terrified prisoners, the combined efforts backfire. The illiterate Abramo and Angeluccio become conscious of their forgotten cultural identity and die as real Jews.

The idea is terrific, and helmer Benvenuti makes the most of its curiosity potential. Sets are minimal, and all attention focuses on the intense faces of stage thesps Franco Pistoni and Emanuele Carucci Viterbi. Aldo Dimarcantonio's cinematography gives images a painterly essence.

Much of film's interest comes from the amazing details of the failed conversion, fruit of Simona Foa's historical research. The confortorio's administrator (Emidio Simini) painstakingly records the night's events, leaving a precious account behind him.

Another attraction is the arcane exoticism of the Castel Sant'Angelo prison (of "Tosca" fame). The shoestring production has a good laugh at its own lack of a budget in the final hanging scene, where the familiar outline of the prison appears as a cardboard cutout. Far from detracting, the theatricality of Paolo Barbi's set adds a solemn, ritual dimension. — *Deborah Young*

DEADLY CURRENTS
(CANADIAN)
(DOCU)

An Alliance release of an Associated Producers production, with participation of Telefilm Canada, Ontario Film Development Corp., in association with City TV. Executive producers, David Green, Jeff Sackman, Robert Topol. Produced by Simcha Jacobovici, Elliot Halpern, Ric Esther Bienstock. Directed by Jacobovici. Camera (color), Mark Mackay; editor, Steve Weslak; music, Stephen Price; sound, Chaim Gilud. Reviewed at Carnegie Hall Cinema, N.Y., Oct. 17, 1992. Running time: **115 MIN.**

Simcha Jacobovici's ambitious feature-length docu "Deadly Currents" illustrates that any answers to the Israeli-Palestinian problem will not be forthcoming in the near future. The incisive and complex pic has deservedly garnered awards at international fests including Houston and Nyon.

Starting with the premise — scrolled across the screen during the opening credits — that their animosity is approximately 4,000 years old, Jacobovici shows that both sides, claiming historical

rights, are intransigent about cohabitation in the Middle East. The film states that peace will only come after one side is expelled completely.

Rather than use voiceover, Jacobovici draws on images from many sources, presenting a highly textured mosaic punctuated by talking-head interviews with historians, political experts, soldiers, Palestinians and Israeli settlers. The crew is attacked by rocks and prohibited to enter some areas by street patrols.

The film also includes cultural expressions from both sides, showing how this situation is portrayed in dance, theater and by popular singers.

Jacobovici returns again and again to street performer Juliano Mor, son of a Palestinian father and an Israeli mother, who embodies the area's conflicting emotions. He is often inserted to demonstrate the anarchy of the situation: During an argument between two men, he mimics both, effectively showing that both sides are essentially the same and neither side wins.

Pic will probably irk some people for not taking sides. Yet, that is what makes this an important indictment of the continuing violence and inflexibility that continually stifle efforts for permanent peace in the area.
—*Paul Lenti*

THE MAGICAL WORLD OF CHUCK JONES
(DOCU)

A Warner Bros. release of a Magical World Pictures/IF/X Prods. presentation. Executive producer, Valerie Kausen. Produced by David Ka Lik Wong, George Daugherty. Directed by Daugherty. Camera (color), Peter Bonilla; editor, Peter E. Berger; music, Cameron Patrick; sound (Dolby), Robb Wenner. Reviewed at Mann's Westwood, L.A., Oct. 23, 1992. MPAA Rating: PG. Running time: **93 MIN.**
With: Steven Spielberg, Whoopi Goldberg, Ron Howard, Matt Groening, Leonard Maltin, Joe Dante, George Lucas, Steve Guttenberg, Chris Connelly, Danny Elfman, Gary Rydstrom, Friz Freleng, Roddy McDowall, June Foray, Kathleen Helppie-Shipley, Maurice Noble, Roger Mayer, Linda Jones Clough, Marian Jones, Valerie Kausen, Chuck Jones.

The great cartoon artist deserves much better than George Daugherty's "The Magical World of Chuck Jones," a tiresome documentary made in celebration of the animator's 80th birthday. The docu's tedious structure and lack of concern with the context of Jones'

work or his evolution as an artist provide little reward for the viewer's time. Following a very brief theatrical release, this is headed straight for TV, cable and video.

Jones' cartoons for Warner Bros., arguably some of the best and most entertaining ever made, have delighted generations, first on the big screen, then TV.

Daugherty's docu rightly applauds the man's creative personality and rich oeuvre. Unfortunately, "Magical World" consists for the most part of cursory, if laudatory, statements by directors and performers about the influence of Jones' work interspersed with all-too-brief clips from his half-century career.

Some of the more illuminating remarks come from self-described "cartoon freak" Whoopi Goldberg. The actress-comedian claims she has learned about classical music (heavily used by Jones), propaganda, characterization, storytelling techniques and delivery watching his cartoons.

Regrettably, some of the more revealing interviews, with Jones and his family, don't appear until the very end. Docu provides no information about Jones' background, training or career. Clips are presented without names or dates, thus failing to trace the evolution of his artistry.
— *Emanuel Levy*

WAX, OR THE DISCOVERY OF TELEVISION AMONG THE BEES
(COLOR/B&W)

A Jasmine T. Films release. Produced, directed, written by David Blair. Camera (color, B&W), Mark Kaplan; editor, Glorence Ormezzano; music and sound, Beo Morales, Brooks Williamson. Reviewed on videocassette, N.Y. Running time: **85 MIN.**
Jacob Maker . . . . David Blair
Melissa Maker . . . . Meg Savlov
Allellee Zillah . . . . . Florence Ormezzano
James (Hive) Maker . . William Burroughs
Father Bessarion . . . . Himself
Dr. Clyde Tombaugh . . . . Himself

In welding film to video, "Wax" provides an appropriate look for a visionary science fiction film, and while rejection of both conventional dialogue format and look will restrict exhibition to very specialized locales, pic has the potential to command a dedicated following.

"Wax" blends an avant-garde sensibility with mystical sci-fi and, save for one instance of synchro-

nous sound (from the real scientist who discovered Pluto), depends totally on off-screen narration. The plot moves through all kinds of bizarre turns, from excavations of the Tower of Babel to spirits of the future dead inhabiting the bodies of bees that implant a special form of television inside the head of the protagonist. There is enough mumbo-jumbo in the sprawling narrative to make the theories of Erich von Daniken sound like models of sound scientific deduction.

Fortunately, filmmaker David Blair's script and distinctive voice keep the narration's cacophony of associations fluid and almost mesmerizing as it lurches from semi-parody to surreal poetry. (Not inappropriately, William Burroughs has a cameo.)

Pic's visuals draw from old stock footage, location video and computer animation to evoke its world of the mind. There is also a sort of creative letter-boxing technique where Blair splits the screen in various ways with black spaces. Like much else in the film, this is done in adroit and expressive ways.

— *Fred Lombardi*

HONG 2 RUN 44
(CLASSMATES)
(THAI)

A Five Star Prod. Co. Ltd. production. Produced by Charoen Iamphungporn. Directed, written by Bandit Ritthakon. Camera (color), Phiphat Phayakkha; music, Charan Manophet, Damrong Thamphithak; art direction, Banphot Ritthakon. Reviewed at Tokyo Intl. Film Festival (noncompeting), Oct. 2, 1992. Running time: **123 MIN.**
Ramyong . . . . Chintara Sukkhaphat
Nathee . . . . Santisuk Phromsiri
Prungchat . . . Krit Sukkramongkhon
Khanthong . . Somratchanee Keerson
Latda . . . . Thip Thammasiri

A realistic portrayal of modern Thai society with a strong feminist message, pic is a rarity in usually violent Thai cinema. Screened at the recent Tokyo fest to two nearly full houses, pic is socially interesting but emotionally flat, and ultimately can't succeed outside Thailand or the sphere of Thai star Chintara Sukkhaphat's popularity in Asia.

Plot traces a group of women high school grads including heroine Ramyong (Sukkhaphat). She and friend Khanthong compete in a Miss Thailand contest, after which Ramyong turns down a wealthy man who wants to be her sugar daddy. She then watches in horror as Khanthong accepts, launching Ramyong's feminist stirrings against women selling their bodies.

Ramyong appears in "respectable" ads, studies journalism and begins work on a Bangkok TV news program. In the pic's last third, her problems and the plot begin in earnest. Ramyong researches and reports on young country girls who come to Bangkok hoping to sell themselves for wealth and material goods. One she meets dies of AIDS, setting her off on a one-woman crusade that causes a break-up with her handsome ad-man b.f., but is not powerful enough to feel emotionally involving. Also, she ends up betraying a classmate to get the story, nearly ruining the class' strong bonds.

Pic's photography is not quite up to Western standards, not infrequently blurry and shaky. Soundtrack is nearly agonizing, with severely low-key attempts at Western-style music.

— *Karen Regelman*

LUCRECIA:
CRONICA DE UN SECUESTRO
(LUCRECIA: CHRONICLE OF A KIDNAPPING)
(MEXICAN-SPANISH)

A Barr Imagen (Mexico)-Opal Films (Barcelona) production. Executive producer, Antonio Pérez Giner. Produced by Pérez Giner, Miguel Reyes Razo. Directed by Bosco Arochi C. Screenplay, Francisco Sánchez, Arochi, Josep Bras, Pérez Giner. Camera (color), Henner Hoffman; editor, Miguel Necoechea; music, Joan Vives, Joan Garde; sound, Servando Gaja. Reviewed at Cine Insurgentes, Mexico City, April 5, 1992. Running time: **95 MIN.**
Lucrecia . . . . Nuria Hosta
Zacarias . . . . Raúl Araiza
Gabriel . . . . . . Alberto Mayagoitia
Alex . . . . Arturo Meza
Hairdresser . . . . Claudia Fernández
Anselmo . . . . Sergio Jiménez

A sexist boyhood fantasy brought to the big screen, the Spanish-Mexican co-prod "Lucrecia" has little b.o. appeal despite a wide release in Mexico. At the screening attended, people left throughout, reflecting the wisdom of popular taste.

Directed by former head of Mexico's Churubusco Studios Bosco Arochi C., story chronicles the tale of a trio of adolescents who plot to kidnap a w.k. Spanish stripper hoping she'll find them attractive as bedmates. A weakly developed subplot has her involved in some nefarious activity concerning a cryptic package.

She believes her abduction is linked to the illegal venture and welcomely beds all three boys in exchange for her life. Later, she gladly accepts the truth as "sweet" and treats the boys to an elaborate dinner that goes on interminably, ending in a menage à quatre.

Both the police and silent villain (Sergio Jiménez) converge on the hideaway at the same time, and all hell breaks loose. The boys get their comeuppance and the stripper gains even more fame. Tech credits and thesping are passable. — *Paul Lenti*

MENIALY
(THE BIG EXCHANGE)
(RUSSIAN)

A 12-A Film Studios production with participation of Twelve L.A. Inc. & MP PRINC. Produced by Alexander Mikhailov, Leonard Lev. Directed by Georgi Shengelaya. Screenplay, Alexei Timm. Camera (color), Yakov Posselsky; editor, Vera Ostrinskaya; music, Georgi Movsesian; art director, Levan Shengelia. Reviewed at Rex cinema, Vevey, Switzerland, July 26, 1992. (Competing at Vevey Intl. Festival of Comedy Films.) Running time: **88 MIN.**
Babaskin . . . . Vladimir Ilyin
Jora Grakin . . . . Andrei Ponomarev
Prokhor . . . . . Vadim Zakharchenko
Beggar . . . . Youri Gorin
Zoya . . . . Valentina Telichkina

Muscovite helmer Georgi Shengelaya's "Menialy" is a two-character comic caper based on a true 1961 currency scam. Lively pic would fit in any Russian cinema program and should successfully make the rounds of international festivals. Irrepressible lead actor Vladimir Ilyin is a powerful talent who carries pic on his defiant, oddball shoulders.

Docu montage debut featuring black & white footage of triumphant Soviet cosmonauts segues into color shots of changing shop prices. Via currency reform, 100 old rubles will be worth only 10 new rubles.

Wily manager Prokhor (Vadim Zakharchenko) reasons that whereas paper money will sink in worth, copper coins will retain their face value. He assigns a trustworthy youngster (Andrei Ponomarev) to drive around the country exchanging 60,000 rubles worth of paper currency for 5-kopek copper coins. The kid can't speak so he requires the glib talents of a chubby, balding drunkard with a genius for improvisation (Ilyin).

Helmer, fond of wide-angle lenses with large objects or characters in the foreground, taps into a 1960s sensibility reinforced by color scheme and score. Energetic pace is maintained with time out for a nostalgic romantic reunion and the occasional vodka-soaked, philosophical monologue.

Viewers who equate Russian film with ponderous themes will be pleasantly surprised by this ultimately upbeat tale, from the same independent studio that produced "Cloud Paradise."

— *Lisa Nesselson*

AH-YING
(MING GHOST)
(TAIWANESE)

A COS Films Co. production. (Intl. sales: Anthex, Berlin.) Produced by Chou Nai-chung. Executive producers, Hsu T'ien-jung, Jenny. Directed by Ch'iu Kang-chien. Screenplay, Ch'iu, Ts'ai K'ang-yung. Camera (color), Bill Wong, Yang Wei-han; editor, Liao Ch'ing-sung; music, Shum Sing-tak; song, Frankie Wong, Ts'ai (sung by Jenny); production design, Yip Kam-tim; art direction, Silver Cheung; costumes, Ch'iu Wen-t'ing; sound, Hu Ting-yi; action coordinator, Su Yüan-feng; assistant directors, Chou Hui-k'un, Hsü Hsiang-hsi; associate producers, Stanley Kwan, Ts'ai. Reviewed on COS vidcassette, London, March 28, 1992. (In Rotterdam, Taormina, Haifa, Dunkirk film fests.) Running time: **142 MIN.**
Ah-ying . . . . Joey Wang
Huo-sang . . . . Kao Chieh
Hsiung-yen . . . . Shan Li-wen
Hsien Hsiao-chieh . . Huang Yao-ming
Ying-ming . . . . K'o Yi-cheng
Ta-ts'ai . . . . Ch'en Hui-lou
Mien-ko . . . . K'o Su-yün
Feng Ch'ing-yün . . . . Yü Han
(Mandarin dialogue;
Chinese & English subtitles)

An irreverent Chinese take on the Japanese classic "Rashomon," "Ming Ghost" is a treat for the eyes but often too knowing for its own good. Leisurely (and lengthy) costumer about four people's versions of a rape and murder is strictly a fest item. Camp subtext could win it extra friends at alternative events.

Pic has similarities to director Ch'iu Kang-chien's earlier "The Tang Concept of Play" (1986), an arty sex and swordplay number that had a critical following in East Asia.

Story opens with a paternalistic judge (K'o Yi-cheng) taking grisly retribution on his philandering wife (K'o Su-yün), who later dies. Fifteen years later, his daughter Ah-ying (Joey Wang) is supposedly raped and her husband (Yü Han) killed while travelling to see him.

Suspects are a bisexual weirdo (Shan Li-wen) who ambushed the couple and a young cosmetics salesman (Huang Yao-ming) who observed the deed. Both end up dead after testifying. Finale featuring the ghosts of past and present reveals the truth.

Some good ideas float around in the diffuse screenplay, particularly in the satire of Chinese costume pics and social conventions, but too often they get lost amid pervasive misogyny and self-conscious stylization (recalling the works of late Japanese helmer Shuji Terayama).

Taiwanese star Wang ("A Chinese Ghost Story") toplines strongly as the vengeful, seemingly demure Ah-ying. Real stars, however, are Hong Kong lenser Bill Wong and his Taiwan colleague Yang Wei-han. Other tech credits are solidly pro. Slangy subtitles are sometimes distracting.

— *Derek Elley*

MOHAMED BERTRAND-DUVAL
(FRENCH)

A Mercure Distribution release (France) of a Xandro Films presentation. Produced by Michel Cretel. Line producer, Nanou Metayer. Directed, written by Alex Metayer. Camera (color), Alain Choquart; editor, Roland Baubau; music, Babik Reinhardt; production design, Michel Lagrange; costumes, Monique Perrot; sound, Jean-Michel Chauvet; assistant director, Jacques Rebout; casting, Monique Perrot. Reviewed at Famous Players Eaton Cinema, Montreal, Aug. 4, 1992. (In Just For Laughs Comedy Festival.) Running time: **90 MIN.**
Maurice/Mohamed . . . . Alex Metayer
Gino . . . . Moussa Maskry
Fatima . . . . Netti
Abdelkader . . . . Mr. Bouzidi
Helene . . . . . Marie-Christine Adam
Zohra . . . . Chafia Boudraa
Catherine . . . . Anne Langlois

This zany comic adventure meets the mandate of its opening citation from Federico Fellini: "Show reality as if it were incredible." Delightful escapist fare should be especially appreciated in French lingo territories and, with careful marketing, could capture a marginal art house audience elsewhere. It's also natural family fare for homevid.

Helmer Alex Metayer scripted himself a terrific role as Maurice, a burned-out exec who leaves his bourgeois wife and winds up living a gypsy life with a happy gang of "honest" Arab thieves in the south of France.

Like other variations on the frustrated-rich-man-finds-happiness-in-poverty theme, pic plays heavily on escapism. However, in this wonderfully entertaining version, acute details and fiery chemistry among an exceptional cast allow audiences to make the necessary leap of faith.

In clever establishing scene, a translator from hell mangles Maurice's business pitch to the English boss, and Maurice finds himself jobless. His Valium-popping wife freaks, and he simply runs away with the camper.

Penniless, gas-less, depressed and destitute, he lands seaside in a makeshift village where Arabs promptly strip him of his appliances and naiveté. Dubbed Mohamed, he quickly learns the roots of the expression "as thick as thieves" and delights in the camaraderie. Harmless scams provide hilarious footage, especially as Mohamed and cohorts burglarize his own home with plans to open a restaurant.

Pic gleefully mocks racist attitudes about Arabs, depicting a community with strict morals, intense loyalty and a terrific sense of humor.

Moussa Maskry is perfect as swarthy guitar-strumming head thief. Anne Langlois is playful as the smart, sexy blonde in a wheelchair, and Netti masters her role as Fatima, an Arab girl who breaks all the rules and marries Mohamed.

Alain Choquart's camerawork is aces. Django Reinhardt's guitar music (arranged by his son Babik) establishes pic's playful rhythm and makes for a top-notch soundtrack.
— *Suzan Ayscough*

THE TURN OF THE SCREW
(BRITISH-FRENCH)

An Electric Pictures & Michael White production. Produced by Staffan Ahrenberg. Executive producers, Michael White, Pierre Spengler. Directed, written by Rusty Lemorande. Camera (color), Witold Stok; editor, John Victor Smith; production design, Max Gottlieb; costumes, Amy Roberts; sets, Trudie McCallum; sound, Alain Curvelier; associate producer, Steven Harding; casting, Liz Stoll. Reviewed at Sitges Film Festival, Oct. 9, 1992. Running time: **95 MIN.**
Jenny . . . . Patsy Kensit
Mrs. Gross . . . . . . Stephane Audran
Mr. Cooper . . . . Julian Sands
Flora . . . . Clare Szekores
Miles . . . . Joseph England
    Also with: Olivier Debray, Bryony Brind, Marianne Faithful, Mickey Monroe.

Certainly this is one screw that needed no further turning, especially when it's done in such a clumsy, pedestrian manner. Lame remake of the famous Henry James novella looks like TV fodder, lacking any flair or originality.

Set in some hard-to-determine postwar period, pic at first promises to update the familiar story, possibly adding some new twists. But soon it flounders into a retelling of the James classic.

Added are a sex scene between Quint and Miss Jessel, a few dream sequences for the new governess that add nothing and "ghosts" that have all the subtlety of Casper. A final death struggle between Miles and the governess and a freeze-frame end round off the inept trappings.
— *Peter Besas*

LAST SUPPER
(COLOR-16m)

A Vega Film AG/World Wide Intl. TV/BBC production. Produced by Ruth Waldburger. Directed by Robert Frank. Screenplay, Frank, Sam North, Michael Rovner. Camera (Duart color), Frank; editor, Jay Rabinow. Reviewed at Toronto Festival of Festivals, Sept. 17, 1992. Running time: **50 MIN.**
With: Zorah Lampert, Chris Parker, John Larkin, Taylor Mead.

"Last Supper" amounts to a report from that twilight outpost where intellectual pretension becomes artistic oblivion. Photographer Robert Frank's latest excursion into cinema manages to be both intensely boring and actively irritating, guaranteeing that few who sit down for this repast will by around for dessert.

The pic forces the viewer to spend nearly an hour with an inane group of mostly white New York twits who go to a party in a vacant Harlem lot for an author who never turns up. As the would-be revelers exchange dreadful witticisms and silly remarks during a singularly uneventful day, silent black neighbors look on with vague curiosity before converging after nightfall to devour the remaining comestibles.

Seemingly random characters interact in thoroughly meaningless, uninteresting ways, and whatever commentary Frank may have intended regarding black/white relations and the gap between art and life is simultaneously simplistic and obscure. When one of the party guests

ventures, "Are we just killing time?" the answer is the only affirmative thing about the picture. — *Todd McCarthy*

CHICAGO FEST

SEVILLANAS
(SPANISH)

An Unicaja presentation of a Juan Lebron production. Produced by Lebron. Directed by Carlos Saura. Camera (Fotofilm/Rank color), Jose Luis Alcaine; editor, Pablo del Amo; music supervisor, Manolo Sanlucar; choreography, Matilde Coral; sound (Dolby), Tim Bleckham. Reviewed at American Film Institute, L.A., Oct. 22, 1992. (In Chicago, Venice, Americas film festivals.) Running time: **53 MIN.**
With: Rocio Jurado, Paco de Lucia, Manolo Sanlucar, Camaron, Lola Flores, Manuel Pareja Obregon, Paco Toronjo.

A modest follow-up to his 1981-'86 flamenco trilogy of "Blood Wedding," "Carmen" and "El Amor Brujo," Carlos Saura's "Sevillanas" serves as a sort of primer on the Spanish dance form. Beautifully shot, recorded and performed, this one is more for aficionados than the earlier trio due to its non-narrative sequencing and more academic bent. Brief running time will also limit theatrical possibilities but marks it as a good candidate for hour slots on arts-oriented cable or TV outlets internationally.

Taking a cue from the rehearsal sequences of "Carmen," the best of his dance films, Saura casually moves his camera into a studio as a host of dancers warm up and practice.

First dance is enchantingly performed by some spry old-timers, who look like they could be pushing 80, the first of 11 titled sequences that illustrate different aspects of the Sevillanas, the best known form of flamenco. Each section lasts just four or five minutes, but even at this length the clockwork structuring is somewhat monotonous.

Inevitably, some of the performances are more striking than others, although Saura and his superb cameraman Jose Luis Alcaine have set many against pastel walls and lit them to approximate magic hour outdoors. Effect is invariably gorgeous, and with the boldly simple costumes and props creates an uninterrupted visual feast.

Despite the graceful, astutely planned camera moves across the

smooth dance floors and the dynamic cutting, pic never catches fire as "Carmen" did, although two sequences stand out.

First, entitled "Biblicas," features two rows of five black-garbed beauties dancing opposite each other in a sensual delight. Second, "A Dos Guitarras," is perhaps the simplest, featuring virtuoso guitarists Paco de Lucia and Manolo Sanlucar on a stunning and intricate duet that is a classical equivalent of "Duelling Banjos."

The songs and occasional utterances go untranslated, which is just as well since subtitles would clutter up the pristine images. Sound quality is exceptionally good. — *Todd McCarthy*

WILD BLUE MOON

A Quetzal Films production. Produced by Quetzal Films-Mexico. Executive producers, Taggart Siegel, Francesca Fisher. Line producer, Hector Lopez. Directed, written by Siegel, Fisher. Camera (color), Alex Phillips Jr.; editor, Dermott McNeillage; production design, Genevieve Desgagnes, Daniel Sirdey; sound, Fernando Camara; music, Lobo and Willie; assistant director, Rene Villarreal. Reviewed at Chicago Intl. Film Festival, Oct. 17, 1992. Running time: **107 MIN.**
Luna . . . . Maira Serbulo
Terrance . . . . Thom Vernon
Luz . . . . Zaide Silvia Gutierrez
Willie . . . . Greg Sporleder
Luna's mother . . . . . Malena Doria

A strong story line is this low-budget pic's major asset, but lackluster acting and sluggish editing diminishes overall impact and limits commercial appeal of "Wild Blue Moon."

Helmers Francesca Fisher and Taggart Siegel keep the suspense level fairly high in this erotic tale about an American painter (Thom Vernon) living in Mexico. He strikes up a fiery romance with a witch's daughter (Maira Serbulo), then abruptly drops her and returns to his fiancé Luz (Zaide Silvia Gutierrez) after his ex becomes pregnant.

The jilted Serbulo resorts to all manner of witchcraft to exact revenge. The Yank painter battles to maintain his sanity and save his life as the woman's machinations grow increasingly deadly. The pic builds reasonably well to its grim finale, but tighter editing would help.

Big problem is the weak thespian talent. Vernon is particularly bland in the key role of the libidinous artist. Still Alex Phil-

lips's camerawork adds mucho atmosphere throughout.
— *Lewis Lazare*

VANCOUVER FEST

FATHER AND SON
(CANADIAN-DOCU-16m)

A National Film Board of Canada production. Executive producer, Barbara Janes. Produced by Jennifer Torrance, Svend-Erik Eriksen. Directed, written by Colin Browne. Camera (color), Kirk Tougas; editor, John Kramer; music, Jean Piche; sound, Michael McGee; sound editor, Anke Bakker. Reviewed at Toronto Film Festival, Sept. 18, 1992. (Also in Vancouver Film Festival.) Running time: **85 MIN.**
With: Colin Browne, Michael Ignatieff, John Stoltenberg, Terence Davies, Samuel Osherson.

Vancouver filmmaker Colin Browne struggles to understand his father, and himself, in "Father and Son," a fitfully fascinating documentary that, ironically, works best when Browne turns his camera on other people. Pic is best suited for TV.

Browne's father, a retired Canadian Navy officer in his 70s, is depicted in family photos, stock footage and newly filmed interviews as representing an entire generation of fathers who put up brave, unemotional fronts while being dutiful providers and authority figures. Currently, the elder Browne lives in a full-care facility, and his fading memory makes a satisfying father-son reconciliation practically impossible.

Unfortunately, Browne is unable to make his father seem more than an imposing enigma. At the end, the filmmaker symbolically burns a Canadian Navy uniform, then goes swimming.

Pic's much more successful at contemplating Western culture's changing attitudes about the role of the father, and the nature of masculinity itself, in talking-head interviews with such notables as filmmaker Terence Davies ("Distant Voices, Still Lives") and author Samuel Osherson ("Finding Our Fathers").

Even better are interviews with a middle-aged construction worker admitting he's still not comfortable hugging his adult son, or the author speaking openly of his homosexuality in front of his sympathetic dad.

Unifying theme of memoirs and interviews appears to be that, even after a man becomes a father, he never stops being a son. Not exactly a novel insight, but here it's given a certain poignance, if not freshness. Tech credits are adequate. — *Joe Leydon*

GAUYAT SANDIU HAPLUI
(SAVIOUR OF THE SOUL)
(HONG KONG)

A Team Work Prod. House production. Executive producers, David Lai, Chan Pui-wa. Directed by Cory Yuen, David Lai. Screenplay, uncredited (Wong Kar-wai). Camera (color), Peter Pau; editors, Poon Hung-yiu, Hai Kit-wai; music, Leun Wing-leung (songs, sung by Andy Lau); art direction, Hai Tsung-man; costume design, Chan Ku-fong; sound (Dolby); martial arts director, Yuen Tak; assistant director, Yiu Man-kei. Reviewed at Metro Cinema, London, June 5, 1992. (In Toronto, Vancouver fests.) Running time: **104 MIN.**
Chin . . . . Andy Lau
Yiu May-kwan . . . . Anita Mui
Silver Fox . . . . Aaron Kwok
Ku Wai-heong . . . . Gloria Yip
Ku, her brother . . . . . . Kenny Bee
Pet Lady . . . . Carina Liu
*(Cantonese dialogue;
English & Chinese subtitles)*

Fresh twists to an old genre enliven "Saviour of the Soul," an inventive Hong Kong swordplay item that melds old and new to entertaining effect. Slick, visually resonant item should clock up a cult following among offshore Asian action buffs.

By standards of the genre, story is relatively straightforward. Wandering assassin Silver Fox (Aaron Kwok), member of Green Dragon Society, swears to avenge his dying master, rescued from a fortress penitentiary, by hunting down femme assassin Yiu (Anita Mui), now shacked up with b.f.s Chin and Ku (Andy Lau, Kenny Bee) and her crazy sister (Mui again).

When Ku cops it in a startling battle with Silver Fox, Yiu goes AWOL, leaving Chin to find her, in between looking after Ku's teen sis (Gloria Yip). Final series of duels see Chin and Yiu united.

Pic's Chinese title suggests an updated version of a famous 1959 novel by Hong Kong swordplay scribe Louis Cha. In fact, there are no plot parallels; but pic still melds modern city-warrior conventions with tried-and-true Chinese medieval actioners. Result is a bold take on the genre that works on many levels, with mucho boff appeal.

Hong Kong megastar Anita Mui, in her first swordplay role, acquits herself in style, with plenty of trademark leg-appeal. Less successful are Mui's falsetto turns as her loopy sister, clearly inserted as comic relief for Cantonese auds. Other players are all on the money, with matinee idol Lau fine as the tanktopped, insouciant hero and newcomer Kwok strong as the silver-haired killing machine.

Double teaming of vet action director Cory Yuen and journeyman helmer David Lai is smooth, with martial arts sequences inventive and interludes atmospheric. Lensing by top cameraman Peter Pau is tops. Uncredited script is actually by voguish director Wong Kar-wai.

Pic grossed a dandy HK$20.5 million on local release last December, as well as copping prizes for photography and art direction at this spring's Hong Kong Film Awards. — *Derek Elley*

HURT PENGUINS
(CANADIAN)

A Cinephile Ltd. release (Canada) of a Cold Feet Prods. & Lightshow Communications production. Produced by Robert Bergman, Myra Fried, Allan Levine. Directed by Bergman, Fried. Screenplay, Fried. Camera (color), Michael Storey; editor, Roushell Goldstein; music, Kim Deschamps; production design, Marian Wihak; costume design, Erika Larner Corbett; sound, Manse James; assistant director, Sheldon Inkol. Reviewed at Toronto Festival of Festivals, Sept. 14, 1992. (Also in Vancouver Film Festival.) Running time: **98 MIN.**
Harriet Swan . . . . Michele Muzzi
Nick Piccione . . . . Daniel Kash
Jeremy Finch . . . . George King
Robin Sommerfeld . . . . Myra Fried
Bilbo Roberts . . . . . Denny Doherty

"Hurt Penguins" doesn't quite match up to its quacky title, but this love triangle tale eventually delivers for patient festgoers who wade through the 40-minute set-up. Pic's destiny is Canadian TV or homevideo at best.

Myra Fried (as thesp) is superb as hopelessly cynical Robin, a user friendly pal of Harriet, a woman who loves her thick-headed rock 'n' roll b.f. Nick, and exploits her dry, wealthy love interest Jeremy.

Fried (as writer/director) needed an objective eye on the script. Initial pacing undermines comedy, but surprising twists late in pic confirm that she has latent scribe talent.

Pic's interesting twist on the triangle theme is that third party (Jeremy) is more of a sly killer whale than a hurt penguin: His supposed impotence turns out to be a tactical mating dance, a preplanned plot to indirectly seduce his wife to consummate their convenient marriage.

"Jules et Jim"-type scenario has a vague ending where Harriet wins both men's hearts and waltzes happily off-screen about eight months pregnant (an unnecessarily trite happy ending that doesn't work in context).

Problematic story line will hinder foreign sales but mini-budget pic ($C375,000 or $300,000 U.S) will undoubtedly launch Fried's Canadian career.

— *Suzan Ayscough*

ALADDIN

A Buena Vista release of a Walt Disney Pictures production. Produced, directed by John Musker, Ron Clements. Screenplay, Clements, Musker, Ted Elliott, Terry Rossio; Technicolor prints; editor, H. Lee Peterson; music, Alan Menken; songs, Howard Ashman, Tim Rice, Menken; production design, R.S. Vander Wende; art direction, Bill Perkins; sound (Dolby), Terry Porter, Mel Metcalfe, David J. Hudson; supervising animators, Glen Keane, Eric Goldberg, Mark Henn, Andreas Deja, Duncan Marjoribanks, Randy Cartwright, Will Finn, David Pruiksma; story supervisor, Ed Gombert; layout supervisor, Rasoul Azadani; background supervisor, Kathy Altieri; clean-up supervisor, Vera Lanpher; visual effects supervisor, Don Paul; computer graphics imagery supervisor, Steve Goldberg; artistic coordinator, Dan Hansen; co-producers, Donald W. Ernst, Amy Pell; casting, Albert Tavares. Reviewed at Avco Cinema Center, L.A., Nov. 2, 1992. MPAA Rating: G. Running time: **90 MIN.**
Voices of:
Aladdin . . . . Scott Weinger, Brad Kane (singing)
Genie . . . . Robin Williams
Jasmine . . . . Linda Larkin, Lea Salonga (singing)
Jafar . . . . Jonathan Freeman
Abu . . . . Frank Welker
Iago . . . . Gilbert Gottfried
Sultan . . . . Douglas Seale

Make way for another blockbuster from Disney's animation caravan, almost certain to join "Beauty and the Beast" as the only $100-million earners on the cel block. Floridly beautiful, shamelessly derivative and infused with an irreverent, sophisticated comic flair thanks to Robin Williams' vocal calisthenics, "Aladdin" probably won't equal its beastly predecessor but should still enjoy a magic carpet ride through the holiday season.

More an adventure-comedy than "Beauty" and less appealing in terms of its romantic component, "Aladdin" represents the ultimate synthesis of filmmaking and marketing, extracting winning elements from Disney's last two animated hits as well as more venerable sources, particularly the 1940 "The Thief of Baghdad."

Here, the studio has sought to expand the animated form's allure with Williams' hip humor as the Genie, whose lightning-fast references will, the filmmakers hope, bring in reluctant adults and teenagers.

"Aladdin" also includes some spectacular action sequences — among them a break-neck magic carpet ride through a cavern recalling "Indiana Jones and the Temple of Doom" — as well as an homage to the first Christopher Reeve "Superman" on the inherent romance of flight.

The film may lose a little something in the process, since Williams' high-energy performance — coupled with broad slapstick built around comic Gilbert Gottfried, voicing the villain's sputtering parrot — could raise the decibel-level too high for some adults, while the 90-minute length and few flat stretches may try the patience of the youngest children.

Still, that's ultimately nit-picking about an otherwise remarkable product from producer-directors John Musker and Ron Clements as well as composer Alan Menken and the late lyricist Howard Ashman. Lyricist Tim Rice ("Jesus Christ Superstar," "Evita") filled in seamlessly on three of the six songs after Ashman's death, and while Menken's score may not be as instantly hummable as "Beauty's," it's still impressive, with two show-stoppingly elaborate numbers.

Physically resembling "The Little Mermaid's" Prince Erik, Aladdin is a thief and street urchin who stumbles across the defiant and (again, like Belle in "Beauty") anachronistically liberated Princess Jasmine, who flees the palace to escape a law dictating that she must marry a prince.

The bad guy, functional if not one of the great Disney villains, is the Sultan's adviser Jafar, a sorceror who recruits Aladdin to help claim the magic lamp from a huge cave hidden in the desert. The narrative moves somewhat unevenly before the kid uncorks Williams, at which point things kick into another level.

Metamorphosing the Genie into whatever personality he adopts, from Jack Nicholson to William F. Buckley, Williams' talents yield a comedic feast and inspire a tour-de-force of animation. (There are also a couple of staggeringly funny Disney allusions, such as where the young lad would celebrate after winning a princess' heart.)

Showy as that performance is, "Aladdin" suffers no shortage of winning characters, and its most remarkable accomplishment may in fact be the magic carpet, which expresses a range of emotions not found in the entirety of a typical Joel Silver-type action yarn.

It may not equal the emotional wallop packed by "Beauty," but "Aladdin" certainly rivals it in many other respects and proves a worthy successor to the standard the new generation of Disney animators has established. With all that going for it, it doesn't take a magic lamp or crystal ball to foresee that it'll rub audiences the right way. — *Brian Lowry*

BRAM STOKER'S DRACULA

A Columbia release of an American Zoetrope/Osiris Films production. Produced by Francis Ford Coppola, Fred Fuchs, Charles Mulvehill. Executive producers, Michael Apted, Robert O'Connor. Directed by Coppola. Screenplay, Hart, based on Stoker's novel. Camera (Technicolor), Michael Ballhaus; editors, Nicholas C. Smith, Glen Scantlebury, Anne Goursaud; music, Wojciech Kilar; production design, Thomas Sanders; art direction, Andrew Precht; set decoration, Garrett Lewis; costume design, Eiko Ishioka; sound (Dolby), Robert Janiger; sound design, Leslie Shatz; visual effects-2nd unit director, Roman Coppola; special visual effects, Fantasy II Film Effects; makeup-hair design, Michele Burke; special makeup effects, Greg Cannom; associate producer, Susie Landau; assistant director, Peter Giuliano; 2nd unit camera, Steve Yaconelli; co-producers, James V. Hart, John Veitch; casting, Victoria Thomas. Reviewed at Ziegfeld Theater, N.Y., Oct. 30, 1992. MPAA Rating: R. Running time: **123 MIN.**
Dracula . . . . Gary Oldman
Mina/Elisabeta . . . . . Winona Ryder
Van Helsing . . . . . Anthony Hopkins
Jonathan Harker . . . . Keanu Reeves
Dr. Jack Seward . . . Richard E. Grant
Lord Arthur Holmwood . . Cary Elwes
Quincey P. Morris . . . . Bill Campbell
Lucy Westenra . . . . Sadie Frost
R.M. Renfield . . . . Tom Waits
Also with: Monica Bellucci, Michaela Bercu, Florina Kendrick, Jay Robinson.

Francis Ford Coppola's take on the Dracula legend is a bloody visual feast. Both the most extravagant screen telling of the oft-filmed story and the one most faithful to its literary source, this rendition sets grand romantic goals for itself that aren't fulfilled emotionally, and it is gory without being at all scary.

Grandiose production's main pleasures reside in its exceptional design and in seeing the original tale told in full. The Dracula name, such as it is, and a mighty promo push for its Friday the 13th bow should generate some strong early frame numbers, but pic's extreme adult nature will limit potential with younger auds, and reaction will be mixed.

Bram Stoker finally achieves title card billing à la Jackie Collins and Danielle Steele as James V. Hart is the first screenwriter with the good idea to fundamentally follow the wonderful 1897 novel. The considerably different 1927 Hamilton Deane-John Balderston stage play yielded the best known Dracula films, notably the 1931 Bela Lugosi version.

Hart sets epic parameters for his script with a prologue introducing Dracula's historical origins as Vlad the Impaler, a 15th century Romanian king who fought off Turkish invaders. As dramatically sketched here, the ruler's inamorata, Elisabeta, killed herself upon receiving false news of his death in battle, whereupon the monarch furiously renounced God and began his centuries-long devotion to evil.

In casting Winona Ryder as both Elisabeta and Mina Murray, the overarching story becomes Dracula's quest for recapturing his great love. Unfortunately, familiar plotting, Coppola's coldly magisterial style and Gary Oldman's plain appearance in the title role combine to prevent this strategy from working in more than theory.

But it does set a serious tone, and the director manages to steer a relatively steady course embracing dramatic conviction as well as the humor necessary to send up the vampire conventions that have inevitably become hoary with constant use. He also invests it with a primal sexuality and animalism consistent with the book.

Sent to the count's Transylvanian castle to advise him on London real estate, Jonathan Harker (Keanu Reeves) ends up being held prisoner there and being feasted upon by his host's three luscious concubines. Dracula, meanwhile, is plotting his unique conquest of Britain, which involves transporting coffins filled with fertile Transylvanian earth and infecting the populace via incarnations as wolf, bat and fog.

Mina awaits the return of her fiancé Harker in the company of her best friend, Lucy (Sadie Frost), a popular young lady whom Dracula soon seduces into the world of the undead. In a desperate bid to save her life, a beau, Dr. Jack Seward (Richard E. Grant), calls upon the eminent Dutch doctor/metaphysician Abraham Van Helsing (Anthony Hopkins), and they, along with Lucy's fiancé Lord Arthur Holmwood (Cary Elwes) and footloose Yank Quincey Morris (Bill Campbell) team to foil Dracula as he sets his sights on Mina.

Shot almost entirely on soundstages, film has the feel of an old-fashioned, 1930s, studio-enclosed production made with the benefit of '90s technology. From the striking, blood-drenched prologue on, viewer is constantly made aware of cinema artifice in its grandest manifestations.

Thomas Sanders' production design, Michael Ballhaus' lensing, Michele Burke's makeup and especially Eiko Ishioka's amazing costumes create a dark world of heightened irreality within a context both Gothic and Victorian. Linking all these elements together are many exceptional transitions — dissolves, superimpositions, juxtapositions and cuts that have been worked out with tremendous premeditation and imagination. Visual effects and second unit director Roman Coppola no doubt had a hand in all this, along with the three editors, and the threateningly turbulent score by Wojciech Kilar furthers the brooding mood.

Using a Romanian accent, Oldman comes up with a few unintelligible line readings, but enacts Dracula with wit, sophistication and proper seriousness. The problem may be, however, that the fundamentally fine young character actor and chameleon lacks the charisma and insinuating personality that would put across Coppola's conception of a highly sexualized vampire.

Other performances range from a bit stiff (the young male contingent) to playfully energetic (Hopkins) to compelling (Tom Waits as the insect-eating lunatic Renfield). Ryder has just the right combination of intelligence and enticing looks as Mina.

Coppola doesn't push it, but underlying everything here, as perhaps it must with any serious vampire story today, is an AIDS subtext involving sex, infected blood and the plague. Overall, this Dracula could have been less heavy and more deliciously evil than it is, but it does offer a sumptuous engorgement of the senses. — *Todd McCarthy*

JENNIFER EIGHT

A Paramount release of a Scott Rudin production. Executive producer, Rudin. Produced by Gary Lucchesi, David Wimbury. Directed, written by Bruce Robinson. Camera (Deluxe color), Conrad L. Hall; editor, Conrad Buff; music, Christopher Young; production design, Richard Macdonald; art direction, William Durrell Jr., John Willett; set design, Jim Bayliss, Louis M. Mann, Cosmos A. Demetriou; set decoration, Casey C. Hallenbeck, Elizabeth Wilcox; costume design, Judy Ruskin; sound (Dolby), Arthur Rochester; assistant directors, David B. Householter, Newton D. Arnold; associate producers, Grace Gilroy, Steve Lim; casting, Billy Hopkins, Suzan-

ne Smith. Reviewed at Village Theater, L.A., Oct. 29, 1992. MPAA Rating: R. Running time: **124 MIN.**

John Berlin	Andy Garcia
Helena Robertson	Uma Thurman
Freddy Ross	Lance Henriksen
Margie Ross	Kathy Baker
John Taylor	Graham Beckel
Citrine	Kevin Conway
St. Anne	John Malkovich
Travis	Perry Lang
Bisley	Nicholas Love
Serato	Michael O'Neill
Venables	Paul Bates
Blattis	Lenny Von Dohlen

"**Jennifer Eight**" is an unusually intelligent and unexploitative thriller, which probably won't help its box office chances. Involving but unexciting pic is notable for avoiding most standard suspense film contrivances, as well as for Conrad Hall's smashing cinematography.

Interesting cast and sober approach will mean more to critics and sophisticates than to general auds, resulting in okay results during brief release window before Christmas heavy hitters put this out to video pasture, where it might fare better.

British writer-director Bruce Robinson's script possesses all the elements for yet another product of the "Fatal Attraction"-"Basic Instinct" cookie cutter: A burned-out big-city homicide cop getting involved with a mysterious blonde, brutal attacks on women, gruff career cops who resent the probing maverick, an opportunity for female retribution and, in the bargain, a couple of unfortunate plot holes.

But Robinson proves to be almost as dogged as his hero in getting the job done, building a solid investigative and psychological case study around a disturbing series of crimes and an odd, muted love story.

Andy Garcia toplines as a wreck of a detective who joins a small-town Northern California police force after crashing and burning in the L.A. fast lane. His sister (Kathy Baker) lives there with cop hubby (Lance Henriksen), and Garcia becomes latter's partner in the search for a woman whose hand is found — in a stunningly shot nocturnal opening sequence — at a dump.

With little evidence to go on, Garcia postulates that the killing is just the latest in a string of murders. Next target could be Uma Thurman, who's blind like the most recent victim and was the last person to "see" her alive.

The dark visual scheme fashioned as a correlative to the murky, unfathomable depths in

which Garcia attempts to navigate provides the film with its most distinctive quality. Always noted for his superior night work, lenser Hall quite possibly surpasses himself here with a virtuoso job highlighted by numerous sequences lit only by flashlights or other single light sources.

Robinson manages to build up a fair degree of tension by playing scenes out to near-agonizing length. As a result, running time is a tad long, but one would be hard pressed to suggest where cuts could be made in this character-oriented piece.

Despite his dark good looks, Garcia once again displays a tendency toward character acting rather than leading-man posturing — fine for story plausibility, but it gives pic less weight than another actor might provide.

Henriksen is most engaging, and Baker thoroughly invigorates the potentially stock role of his smart wife. Surprisingly popping up well past halftime, John Malkovich deliciously chews over his extended cameo as a malicious FBI man who tries to pin the murders on Garcia.

But best of all is Thurman, who very touchingly conveys the vulnerability of the blind femme without for a moment begging for audience sympathy or indulging in undue hysterics, creating ongoing interest in a largely passive character.

At least one major plot development telegraphs itself well before it arrives, and circumstances under which Berlin cracks the case are a bit much. But climax is a corker both dramatically and emotionally, keeping this at least a cut or two above the usual Hollywood thriller.

— *Todd McCarthy*

TALONS OF THE EAGLE
(CANADIAN)

A Shapiro Glickenhaus Entertainment release of a Film One production. Produced by Jalal Merhi. Directed by Michael Kennedy. Screenplay, J. Stephen Maunder. Camera (color), Curtis Petersen; editor, Reid Dennison; music, VaRouje; art direction, Jasna Stefanovich; sound, Jack Buchanan; assistant director, Ian Robertson; fight choreography, Merhi, Billy Blanks; line producer, Dale Hildebrand; co-producers, Petersen, Hildebrand; associate producers, Maunder, Kevin Ward. Reviewed on MCA vidcassette, N.Y. MPAA Rating: R. Running time: **96 MIN.**

Tyler Wilson	Billy Blanks
Michael Reed	Jalal Merhi
Mr. Li	James Hong
Cassandra	Priscilla Barnes
Khan	Matthias Hues
Master Pan	Pan Qing Fu
Bodyguard	Eric Lee
Niko	Harry Mok
Tara	Kelly Gallant

No-frills martial arts action is displayed in "Talons of the Eagle," an acceptable B title that opened regionally Nov. 6 and is a Yule vid item.

With Steven Seagal and Jean-Claude Van Damme having successfully moved on to mainstream features, the martial arts vacuum is being filled by a number of interesting types, notably Don (The Dragon) Wilson and Cynthia Rothrock.

This feature teams muscular thesp Billy Blanks (usually a villain) with pony-tailed producer/star Jalal Merhi. Their moves are fine but actingwise they both need immediate and intensive sessions with Stella Adler.

Blanks plays a Drug Enforcement Agency operative sent from New York to Toronto to team with local agent Merhi on an undercover mission targeting local drug kingpin James Hong. They get to see the seamier side of Sin City, including a higher sexploitation quotient than usual for the genre.

With undercover agent Priscilla Barnes cast as Hong's g.f., the trio get the goods on him, but typical of genre plotting, it's mainly kicking, shooting and explosions that resolve matters.

Pic's main defect is deficient fight choreography, with missed kicks and pulled punches far more obvious than usual. Both leads are otherwise convincing in their roles and Barnes is appealing as a femme fatale.

Hong steals the show with his smooth villainy and a showy scene in which he uses a fan as a weapon. Oversized Matthias Hues is a worthy opponent in the climactic fights. — *Lawrence Cohn*

SOFT TOP
HARD SHOULDER
(BRITISH)

A Feature Film Co. (U.K.) release of a Gruber Bros. presentation of a Road Movies production. Produced by Richard Holmes. Co-producer, Georgia Masters. Directed by Stefan Schwartz. Screenplay, Peter Capaldi. Camera (Panavision, Fujicolor; Metrocolor prints), Henry Braham; editor, Derek Trigg; music, Chris Rea; production design, Sonja Klaus; costume design, Christopher Woods; sound, Matthew Harmer; assistant director, Giles Johnson; casting, Suzy Korel. Reviewed at Edinburgh Intl. Film Festival, Aug. 24, 1992. (In London Film Festival.) Running time: **93 MIN.**

Gavin Bellini	Peter Capaldi
Yvonne	Elaine Collins
Miss Trimble	Frances Barber
Eddie Cherdowski	Simon Callow
Karla	Phyllis Logan
Uncle Sal	Richard Wilson

Scotland gets its first road movie with "Soft Top Hard Shoulder," a wafer-thin but likable addition to the genre that may prove too mild to pull many paying passengers. But filmmakers clearly have talent to spare for future projects.

Pic starts off in high gear with a pacy main title segueing into the family history of Gavin Bellini (scripter Peter Capaldi), a crazy Italo-Scot trying to make it as an illustrator down south in London. Meeting his Uncle Sal (witty Richard Wilson) by chance, he learns he has 36 hours to make it to his father's surprise 60th birthday in Glasgow if he's to collect a chunk of family money.

Hitting the highways in a bronchial old auto, he quickly meets kooky hitchhiker Yvonne (Elaine Collins), a resourceful Glaswegian. Rest of pic follows the familiar route of the pair's love-hate relationship, stopovers and breakdowns, capped by a happy ending.

Capaldi's script comes up with plenty of incident, punctuated by cameos from Frances Barber (as an unctuous London publisher), Simon Callow (an eccentric ex-entertainer) and Phyllis Logan (a chatty mechanic). When it's good, it's very good, with plenty of dry Scots humor, but other sections lack zing.

Still, debuting director Schwartz and his crew, clearly working on a budget, have come up with a good-looking product. Confident use of wide screen, running visual gags and Chris Rea's bouncy score add up to a refreshingly different package.

Capaldi and Collins make a fine odd couple, the latter cool and collected in the face of the former's rants and raves. Much of the pic was in fact shot around London. Coin for the Gruber Bros. production (alias Schwartz and producer Richard Holmes, both 29-year-old ex-cabaret performers) was from a wealthy record producer. — *Derek Elley*

THERE GOES THE NEIGHBORHOOD

A Paramount Pictures release of a Kings Road production. Produced by Stephen Friedman. Directed, written by Bill Phillips. Camera (color, Panavision), Walt Lloyd; editor, Sharyn L. Ross; music, David Bell; production design, Dean Tschetter; casting, Mary Jo Slater. Reviewed at General Cinema Theater, Phoenix, Nov. 4, 1992. MPAA Rating: PG-13. Running time: **88 MIN.**
Willis Embris . . . . Jeff Daniels
Jessie . . . . Catherine O'Hara
Norman . . . . Hector Elizondo
Peedi . . . . Judith Ivey
Jeffrey . . . . Dabney Coleman
Lydia . . . . Rhea Perlman
Convict . . . . Harris Yulin

Though '92 isn't over yet, "There Goes the Neighborhood" is a top contender for the year's most outlandishly silly comedy. A TV-inspired high concept and inept production values combine for an unappealing film sans redeeming qualities. Lame pic is in limited run in the Phoenix area and will inevitably be rushed to video.

Jeff Daniels stars as a none-too-bright prison shrink, whose house is burglarized and bombed. Down on his luck, he decides to fulfill a dying convict's (Harris Yulin) last request to search for a huge amount of money stashed in the basement of a New Jersey home. Two other prisoners overhear the scheme and break out of jail to unearth the loot, only to get the address wrong.

Posing as a repairman, Daniels shows up at the suburban home of an attractive woman (Catherine O'Hara) in the middle of a nasty divorce. Jilted by his own g.f., he finds the perfect soulmate in the acerbic O'Hara.

Unfunny comedy's action shifts back and forth between Daniels and O'Hara feverishly digging up the basement, and the escaped criminals, who are holding captive next-door neighbors Hector Elizondo and Judith Ivey while desperately searching for the treasure.

The premise of the TV-like comedy is borrowed from the Humphrey Bogart vehicle "We're No Angels," in which a trio of genial escapees from Devil's Island descend on a family and soon form a happy, if lunatic, bond with their captors.

Writer-director Phillips can't sustain a consistent mood. Incoherent pic changes gears almost every scene, unsuccessfully blending conventions from screwball comedy, romantic comedy, sitcoms and campy spoof. David Bell's derivative and literal music tries but fails to reconcile the pic's various moods.

Under the misguided direction, a first-rate ensemble plays cartoonish roles and embarrassingly behaves like buffoons.

The inexplicable insertion of a sequence from Par's exciting action-comedy "48 HRS," which the captors and their tied-up hostages watch on TV like one big family, makes Phillips' film look even more preposterous and less enticing than it is.
— *Emanuel Levy*

PASSENGER 57

A Warner Bros. release of a Lee Rich production. Executive producer, Jonathan Sheinberg. Produced by Rich, Dan Paulson, Dylan Sellers. Directed by Kevin Hooks. Screenplay, David Loughery, Dan Gordon, story by Stewart Raffill, Gordon. Camera (Technicolor), Mark Irwin; editor, Richard Nord; music, Stanley Clarke; production design, Jaymes Hinkle; art direction, Alan Muraoka; set decoration, Don K. Ivey; costume design, Brad Loman; sound (Dolby), Robert Anderson, Jr.; assistant director, Gary Marcus; stunt coordinators, Glenn Wilder, Jeff Ward; co-producer, Robert J. Anderson; casting, Shari Rhodes. Reviewed at Bruin Theater, L.A., Nov. 3, 1992. MPAA Rating: R. Running time: **83 MIN.**
John Cutter . . . . Wesley Snipes
Charles Rane . . . . Bruce Payne
Sly Delvecchio . . . . . . Tom Sizemore
Marti Slayton . . . . Alex Datcher
Stuart Ramsey . . . . Bruce Greenwood
Dwight Henderson . . . . Robert Hooks
Sabrina Ritchie . . . Elizabeth Hurley
Forget . . . . Michael Horse
Vincent . . . . Marc Macaulay
Chief Biggs . . . . Ernie Lively

Warner Bros., already making a killing with "Under Siege," takes another stab at the "Die Hard" formula, this time aboard a jumbo jet that, unfortunately, runs out of gas before landing. Nevertheless, "Passenger 57" is a reasonably saucy action tale and could generate some early box office sparks — particularly in urban areas — if fueled by the right marketing approach.

Foremost, the pic should serve as a real test of the drawing power of star Wesley Snipes, cutting his teeth as a big-time action hero while surrounded by a largely unknown cast.

It also flags Kevin Hooks (actor-turned-TV director who made his feature debut on "Strictly Business") as another promising talent to watch among the current class of young African-American helmers. Here he shifts from comedy to utterly conventional actioner.

One of pic's major problems precedes take-off, due to the claustrophobic limitations of setting so much of the narrative on a jet and the numerous coincidences involved in the set-up. At least the filmmakers have the good sense to acknowledge the scenario's absurdity when an airline exec questions the logic, after the fact, of transporting a known hijacker (Bruce Payne) by air.

With his henchmen disguised as crew members, Payne seizes the jet, murdering the FBI agents and pilot. That leaves it to newly hired airline security expert Snipes to try and stop them, however burdened by the inconvenient emotional baggage of having watched his wife's murder under similar circumstances.

Snipes manages to force a landing, and the action moves to the ground, as he escapes but gets grief from the local redneck sheriff (Ernie Lively) before a helpful FBI man (Robert Hooks, the director's dad) shows up.

These take-offs and landings are indicative of the pic's uneven nature, with too little character development to maximize the nifty action sequences and solid tension.

Snipes seems to relish his opportunity to play this cross between John Shaft and "Die Hard's" John McClane, but David Loughery and Dan Gordon's script doesn't give him much room to operate. Still, his inherent likability and his physical presence establish him as a credible action star who could benefit from stronger material.

Payne's hissable villain contributes greatly to maintaining the film's intensity until the end, when an overdone payoff has about as much excitement as collecting luggage at LAX.

Tech credits are sound, including a jaunty Stanley Clarke score that helps keep tension going even when "Passenger 57" starts to run into some turbulence. — *Brian Lowry*

VERMONT IS FOR LOVERS

A Zeitgeist Film release of a Bellwether Films production. Produced, directed by John O'Brien. Camera (Duart color), O'Brien; editor, O'Brien; music, Tony Silbert; sound, Gordon Eriksen; associate producer, Molly O'Brien. Reviewed at Toronto Festival of Festivals, Sept. 13, 1992. (In Virginia Festival of American Film.) Running time: **86 MIN.**
With: George Thrush, Marya Cohn, Ann O'Brien, Euclid Farnham, Jeramiah Mullen, Ann Milliman.

Regional filmmaking heads further into the boonies with "Vermont Is for Lovers," a charmingly innocuous little romantic comedy about a New York couple getting married up among the cow pies and sheep farms of rural New England. Pic actually plays better than it sounds, but is too slight and inconsequential to draw many theatrical customers.

John O'Brien, co-director of urban low-budgeter "The Big Dis," blurs the lines between fiction and docu as he examines the trepidations of George and Marya, Gothamites planning to wed on her aunt's farm.

Although not nearly so complex or detailed, pic reminds at times of the recent "Slacker" in its attempt to paint a portrait of a community through the use of ordinary citizens in a quasi-fictional context. ("Slacker" was entirely scripted, however, while this was improvised and bears no screenplay credit.)

Pic could have taken a condescending, satiric attitude toward its villagers but happily does not. Instead, New Yorkers come off as, at worst, flaky and pretentious in their insecurities and desire to have a "different" wedding.

Film could have been richer had the N.Y. couple been given some depth and dimension. This is "True Love" out in the pasture, without any bite or angst.

Still, the film has its pleasant, aud-pleasing elements, including many cornball insert shots of animals reacting to the human nonsense around them. Typical of the locals' dry humor is the response of one old man who is asked if he has lived in the area all his life. "Not yet," he says.

There's plenty more where that came from, which makes "Vermont" an okay place for a visit. Like the leads, however, most viewers will be ready for a dose of the mean city streets afterward. — *Todd McCarthy*

GIANT STEPS
(CANADIAN)

A Cinephile (Canada) release of an O'B & D Films presentation. Produced by Greg Dummett, Tim O'Brien. Executive producer, O'Brien. Directed by Richard Rose. Screenplay, Dummett, Paul Quarrington. Camera (Medallion/PFA Lab color), Paul Sarossy; editor, Alan Collins; music, Eric Leeds; production design, Reuben Freed; sound (Dolby), Bryan Day. Reviewed at Toronto Festival of Festivals, Sept. 14, 1992. Running time: **94 MIN.**
Slate Thompson . . Billy Dee Williams
Arvo Lint . . . . Michael Mahonen
Leslie . . . . Robyn Stevan
Also with: Ted Dykstra, Ranee Lee, Nicu Branzea.

"**G**iant Steps" is a small contribution to the library of jazz in films. Despite colorful atmospherics and a resonant performance by Billy Dee Wil-

liams as a piano great, pic is hamstrung by coming-of-age conventions and lethargic, undramatic treatment. Prospects for export outside its native Canada look dim.

Michael Mahonen portrays a nerdy white high school trumpet whiz who manages to sneak into a private session of Williams and his band and, somewhat surprisingly, is allowed to jam with them. A jazz purist who has never gone commercial and demands the highest level of commitment from himself and his players, Williams exists to fill a mentor role for the uncouth youth and proceeds, unexcitingly, to do just that.

At home, Mahonen has to put up with the bitter rantings and discouragement of his misfit father, an Estonian emigré who does nothing but watch TV. He also hangs with his chubby gal pal Robyn Stevan and plays in the school band.

The real action he's interested in, however, is at night in the jazz clubs. The allure and glamor this world holds for the teen comes through clearly enough, but Greg Dummett and Paul Quarrington's script harbors virtually no surprises or unsuspected insights, and Richard Rose, an acclaimed young theater director making his feature debut, does little to stir more than casual interest.

Still, performances are solid, led by Williams' seasoned, nicely nuanced turn as a jazzman fully cognizant of his own legendary status. Speaking in a low, almost affectedly hushed voice, he seems to be having a great time playing a dude too cool for mass consumption, and the fun is contagious for awhile.

Mahonen and Stevan are thoroughly believable, but all the characters are rather narrowly conceived. Pic looks and sounds sharp. — *Todd McCarthy*

LE CAHIER VOLÉ
(THE STOLEN DIARY)
(FRENCH)

A Providence Films production, with the participation of SFPC, Scene Group, Canal Plus. (Intl. sales: Cinexport, Paris.) Produced by Yves Gasser. Directed by Christine Lipinska. Screenplay, Lipinska, Bernard Revon, from Régine Deforges' book. Camera (color), Romain Winding; editor, Marie-Claude Lacambre; music, Arie Dzierlatka; production design, Jean-Pierre Clech; sound, Alain Garnier; production executive, Jean-François Geneix. Reviewed at Venice Film Festival (out of competition), Sept. 9, 1992. Running time: **106 MIN.**
Virginie . . . . Elodie Bouchez
Anne . . . . Edwige Navarro

Maurice . . . . Benoit Magimel
Jacques . . . . Malcolm Conrath
Virginie's father . . . Serge Avedikian
Anne's mother . . . . Laurence Calame
Lucie . . . . Marie Riviere
Georgette . . . . . Anne-Marie Pisani

"**N**othing is more urgent than passion" is a line of dialog in "The Stolen Diary," but passion is mysteriously lacking in Christine Lipinska's new film. Based on a 1978 novel, this limpid tale of a teen lesbian romance in a postwar French village skirts its central theme and unconvincingly depicts schoolgirls in love.

In a mountain village, Anne (Edwige Navarro) and Jacques (Malcolm Conrath) are the handsome offspring of the district's richest family, but their father was killed in World War II. Lively, inquiring Virginie (Elodie Bouchez) is the daughter of the local barkeeper; an avid reader, she yearns to become a writer.

The rich girl makes the first advance, and soon Virginie is writing about their (off-screen) sapphic adventures in her diary, taking the precaution of naming her lover "Paul." Jacques, who also loves Virginie, is jealous of her strange behavior, and humiliates the writer by reading passages from the fateful diary aloud in the village square after Mass.

Given attractive, sensual performances from Bouchez and Navarro, helmer unfortunately can't convey liberating passion between the two. Not that sex scenes were necessarily called for, but something more could have been shown than the wan caresses that precede the lovers simply falling asleep.

Good production values and effective performances make the film watchable, but the downbeat finale is predictable and despite some qualities, pic is a lackluster affair. — *David Stratton*

TRACES OF RED

A Samuel Goldwyn Co. release. Executive producer, David V. Picker. Produced by Mark Gordon. Directed by Andy Wolk. Screenplay, Jim Piddock. Camera (Deluxe color), Timothy Suhrstedt; editor, Trudy Ship; music, Graeme Revell; production design, Dan Bishop, Dianna Freas; art direction, Richard Fojo; set decoration, Nancy Sivitz; costume design, Hilary Rosenfeld; sound (Dolby), Steve C. Aaron; assistant director, David Sardi; additional camera, Don Burgess; casting, Pam Dixon, Ellen Jacoby (Florida). Reviewed at Gramercy theater, N.Y., Oct. 27, 1992. MPAA Rating: R. Running time: **104 MIN.**
Jack Dobson . . . . . . James Belushi
Ellen Schofield . . . . Lorraine Bracco
Steve Frayn . . . . . . Tony Goldwyn
Michael Dobson . . . . . . William Russ
Beth Frayn . . . . Faye Grant
Morgan Cassidy . . . . Michelle Joyner
Lt. Hooks . . . . Joe Lisi
Susan Dobson . . . . . . Victoria Bass
Amanda . . . . Melanie Tomlin

Unintentional laughs and goofy plot twists make "Traces of Red" a dramatic failure but an entertaining exercise in camp. In the currently hot erotic thriller genre, it should be a strong video title but is miscast as far as the theatrical marketplace is concerned.

James Belushi brings his usual man of the people persona to a role that should have been a bit more uppercrust: a cop in Palm Beach, Fla., whose brother (William Russ) is running for Senate. Belushi is assigned to a murder case, and before long all of the principal characters (himself and brother included) are key suspects in the serial slayings of prostitutes and B girls.

With a nod to genre films like "Body Heat," "Traces of Red" initially holds the interest in a whodunit mode. Unfortunately, scripter Jim Piddock threw out all concern for character consistency in his desire to keep the pot boiling, so film becomes terminally silly.

Originally titled "Beyond Suspicion," pic includes so many traces of red herrings in its attempt to make every Palm Beach denizen a suspect, one fears that Ted Kennedy will eventually be dragged in as the killer. In particular, Lorraine Bracco, playing her femme fatale as a wannabe Melanie Griffith (right down to the voice), does many things for no reason other than to make the audience wonder about her.

A skeleton in the family closet proves to be key to unravelling a mystery that includes one satisfying, though phony, twist at the very end. To throw film buffs off the track, Belushi narrates the film as a corpse, a successfully misleading homage to Billy Wilder's "Sunset Boulevard" format.

Belushi has the edge to create a film noir antihero but hardly the sex appeal to follow in Michael Douglas' or William Hurt's genre footsteps. As his sidekick and adviser, Tony Goldwyn suffers from the lack of script logic.

Tech credits are okay but on the cheap side, missing the shadow play and lighting stylization a true film noir requires.

— *Lawrence Cohn*

KAIRAT
(KAZAKHSTANI-B&W)

A Kazakfilm Studio production. Produced by Saida Toursunova. Directed, written by Darezhan Omirabev. Camera (B&W), Aubakir Souleev. Reviewed at Toronto Festival of Festivals, Sept. 18, 1992. Running time: **68 MIN.**
Kairat . . . . Kairat Mahmetov
Indira . . . . . . Indira Jeksembaeva

In his second pic, writer-director Darezhan Omirabev explores the effects of big-city life on a young man from a small village, focusing on intertwined issues of disillusionment and maturity. With distinguished black & white cinematography, poetic film illuminates a coming-of-age tale that's both particular and universal. Using minimal dialogue, "Kairat" exemplifies art films that give festivals their raison d'être.

Not much happens by way of plot, but the crisp narrative lines up episodes depicting the boy's urban assimilation and its impact on his identity. Pic toys with a philosophical idea of how random events can dramatically change a person's life.

At the lyrical tale's center is a sweet-sour first romance launched when Kairat (Kairat Mahmetov) accidentally meets intriguing Indira (Indira Jeksembaeva) on a bus (although much of the pic is set on a train). A few days later, he sees her again at a cinema showing Werner Herzog's "Woyzeck." As expected, the story draws parallels between the film and the unfolding romance.

Aubakir Souleev's lensing is so precise and economical that he makes each and every long take consequential. In one of the film's visual highlights, Kairat dreams he returns to his village and goes to an amusement park where, all alone on a roller coaster, he is suspended in the air while his mother watches.

In the title role, the stunningly photogenic Mahmetov's strong screen presence enhances the effectiveness of Omirabev's highly personal and expressive film. —*Emanuel Levy*

AMAZING GRACE
(ISRAELI)

An Amazing Grace Films Ltd. presentation. Produced by Dagan Price. Directed, written by Amos Guttman. Camera (color), Amnon Zlayit; editor, Einat Glazer-Zarhin; music, Arkady Duchin; art direction, Shmuel Ma'oz; visual con-cept-costume design, Elimor Ziberman. Reviewed at Montreal World Film Festival, Sept. 4, 1992. (Also in Jerusalem, London film festivals.) Running time: **95 MIN.**
Judith . . . . Rivka Michaely
Thomas . . . . Sharon Alexander
Jonathan . . . . Gal Hoyberger
Also with: Hina Rozovska, Dvora Bertonov, Ada Valery-Tal, Aki Avni, Hasida Stolero, Karin Ofhir, Iggi Waxman.

Amos Guttman's "Amazing Grace" is a glum gay-themed drama that will have a hard time surviving commercially outside the international fest circuit, despite winning first prize at the 1992 Jerusalem Intl. Film Festival.

Guttman's script is an unfocused and rambling account of a 17-year-old homosexual (Gal Hoyberger) and his desperate search for love. Hoyberger shares a cramped apartment with a hunk (Aki Avni) who's much too hospitable to parasitical buddies and develops a crush on upstairs neighbor Rivka Michaely's son (Sharon Alexander), recently returned from New York.

Unfortunately, as Guttman makes very clear to everyone but Hoyberger early on, the 30ish Alexander is seriously ill. Pic is vague about whether he's HIV-positive or has full-blown AIDS, but the point is made strongly enough to provoke queasiness whenever the pair cozy up.

Intended story —of hope and love amid death, horror and day-to-day ennui —is not compelling enough, nor characters and perfs interesting enough to work as anything but a dour clinical study.

Lovemaking scenes are discreet but a fantasy scene of Jonathan imagining himself in a glossy homoerotic magazine photo is, unfortunately, funny. Arkady Duchin's music is too mournful by half; other tech credits are fair.—*Joe Leydon*

HUA PI ZHI YINYANG FAWANG
(PAINTED SKIN)
(HONG KONG)

A New Treasurer Films production and release. Produced by Wu Mingchai, Chow Kim Kwong, Tsai Song-lin. Directed by King Hu. Screenplay, Hu, Zhong Acheng, from Pu Songling's story. Camera (color), Stephen Yip; editors, Hu, Siku Lam; production design, James Leung, Wang Jixian. Reviewed at Venice Film Festival (out of competition), Sept. 12, 1992. Running time: **95 MIN.**
Wang Shunsheng . . . . . Adam Cheng
Yu Feng . . . . Joey Wong
Taiyi . . . . Samo Hung
Ghost . . . . Wu Ma

Yuqing . . . . Liu Xun

With epic Chinese action films like "A Touch of Zen" and "Dragon Gate Inn," King Hu two decades ago pioneered a whole school of exotic fantasies rooted in Chinese legends. But the director has recently been overtaken by the younger Hong Kong talents whose "Chinese Ghost Story" trilogy and others have become the yardstick by which to judge the genre. He seems to have been left behind in another era.

"Painted Skin," a ghost story along familiar lines, opens promisingly when a lecherous, married student discovers that the damsel in distress he'd tried to help is actually a ghost.

Much of the film is taken up with the efforts of mortals and a monk with a magic touch to overcome evil accompanied by the usual fights and balletic leaping.

Hu's heart doesn't seem to be in it; action scenes are lackluster, his shooting style surprisingly bland, actors unexciting.

Despite fest exposure, presumably based on Hu's past reputation, this pic will fade from sight as quickly as its ghosts.
— *David Stratton*

CUVSTVITEL'NYI MILICIONER
(THE SENTIMENTAL POLICEMAN)
(UKRAINIAN-FRENCH)

A Primodessa Film Odessa-Parimedia (Paris) co-production, with the participation of Canal Plus. Produced by Alexander Kononov, Daniel Delume. Directed by Kira Muratova. Screenplay, Muratova, Eugeny Goluvenko. Camera (color), Gennady Karjuk; editor, Valentina Olejnik; music, Petr Caikovsky; production design, Goluvenko, Alexei Vokatov; sound, Roger Di Penio. Reviewed at Venice Film Festival (competition), Sept. 7, 1992. Running time: **117 MIN.**
Kiriljuk . . . . Nikolai Satochin
Klava . . . . Irina Kovalenko
Zacharova . . . . . . Natalia Ralleeva

Odessa-based director Kira Muratova, whose pics were regularly shelved by Communist brass, has come up with a fresh, amusing comedy about a childless couple's attempts to adopt a baby. Slow pacing and a tendency to prolong and even repeat scenes works against the film, however, and finding an aud won't be easy.

It begins charmingly when an Odessa policeman (Nikolai Sato-chin) discovers an abandoned baby girl in a cabbage field. He takes the child to an orphanage, and later he and his easygoing wife (Irina Kovalenko) decide they want to adopt, which proves not to be simple.

Muratova's comedy style owes something to the Czech school of Milos Forman and Jiri Menzel, but she's also so in love with her material that the best scenes drag on too long. Opening scene with baby and cabbages is a delight at first, but the director seems reluctant to move on long after the point is made.

Similarly, the cop and his sweet, plump wife get up in the morning, bathe each other, share a towel and get dressed not once but twice. Unselfconscious nudity here is funny, but once was enough.

Only a small audience will have the patience to appreciate the director's good-natured jokes and incisive observations about the human condition, exemplified by the film's ending in which the main characters are forgotten as a man is seen on a busy street trying to juggle a baby and a large shopping bag. Apart from the overindulgent editing, the film is technically fine, with charming performances from the entire cast. — *David Stratton*

MAN TO MAN
(BRITISH)

A BBC Films presentation of a Basilisk production, in association with British Film Institute. (Intl. sales: BFI.) Produced by James Mackay. Executive producers, George Faber, Ben Gibson. Directed by John Maybury, from Manfred Karge's stage play "Jacke wie Hose," translated by Anthony Vivis. Camera (color-16m) Dominique Le Rigoleur; editor, John Maybury, Nigel Hadley; music, Nigel Holland; production design, Alan Macdonald; costume design, Annie Symons; makeup, Thelma Mathews; sound, Holland, Marvin Black; prosthetics, Graham High; assistant director, David Lewis. Reviewed at Edinburgh Intl. Film Festival, Aug. 26, 1992. Running time: **71 MIN.**
Ella/Max Gericke . . . . Tilda Swinton

Derek Jarman icon Tilda Swinton socks over her one-woman stage performance in "Man to Man," an inventive reworking of Manfred Karge's legiter about a woman who experiences German life of the past 50 years in the guise of a man. Beyond fests, pic could reap steady, small-scale biz on the strength of Swinton's rep and Karge's original.

Swinton first played the role

in an Edinburgh theater fest production in 1987, transferring to London's Royal Court theater the following year. Present production, mostly funded by BBC, is given a fresh spin by avant-garde filmmaker and musicvid director John Maybury, endorsed by Swinton as he hadn't seen the stage versions.

Pic is framed as a series of reminiscences by aged crone Ella Gericke (Swinton), who recalls taking her late husband's job as a crane-driver to earn a living in prewar Germany. Introduced to the beery, macho world of Teuton males, she sticks with her disguise, serving as a soldier during the war, falling briefly in love and working on a farm and in a high-tech factory during the country's postwar economic miracle. Ending returns to her solo in her dumpy apartment, awaiting death.

Potentially downbeat material is given a lift by Anthony Vivis' colloquial, salty translation and Swinton's tour de force perf. Latter will be a revelation to those accustomed to her generally more restrained playing in Jarman pics.

Sporting an incredible range of makeup and prosthetics, actress clearly has a lot of fun in her multiple disguises, revealing major comic as well as dramatic talent. Text's play with sexual role-playing and commentary on German socio-political history never subsumes the pic's entertainment values.

Shooting Swinton mostly in closeup, Maybury keeps things moving with an array of technical trickery ranging from integrated docu footage to multiple images (Swinton at one point kissing herself as her female lover). Nigel Holland's busy sound design and music are further pluses eked out of the peanuts £120,000 ($240,000) budget.

Bulk of pic was shot on 16m, with video effects added later. Version preemed at Edinburgh fest was some 10 minutes longer than the BBC's. A 35m transfer is planned for further fest screenings and theatrical outings.
— *Derek Elley*

ISRAELI FEST

AMERICAN CITIZEN
(ISRAELI)

A Guy Film Prods.-Transfax Film Prods. production. Produced by Marek Rozenbaum, Avi Kleinberger. Directed, written by Eitan Green. Camera (color), Danny Shneor; editor, Era Lapid; music, Adi Renhart; art direction, Ariel Roshko. Reviewed at Israeli Film Festival, N.Y., Oct. 25, 1992. Running time: **100 MIN.**
Michael . . . . Guy Garner
Yoel . . . . Icho Avital
   Also with: Eva Haddad, David Baruch.
(In English & Hebrew)

"American Citizen" is a male-bonding film chronicling the friendship between an aging pro basketball player (Guy Garner) and a young fan (Icho Avital). Pic's inspirational handling and basic English-lingo script might prove apt for cable.

American hoops star Garner, 31 and recovering from a knee injury, has been hired by a B-league in a small Israeli coastal town where he meets Avital, a young sportswriter who writes an article critical of him.

But Garney and Avital gradually become inseparable friends. While one is beginning his profession, the other is at the end of a career that demands youth.

Although Garner's team will get to and, inevitably, win the league finals, the focus on the characters lends interest. Acting is low key and tech credits are all right despite obvious low budget. — *Paul Lenti*

TEL AVIV STORIES
(ISRAELI)

A Udi Prods.-Dream Prods. production, in association with Fund for Promotion of Israeli Quality Films, Israel Broadcasting Authority & Tel Aviv Cinémathèque. Produced by Ehud Bleiberg, Yitzhak Ginsberg. Editor, Ayelet Menahemi; associate producer, Shuki Friedman. Reviewed at Israeli Film Festival, N.Y., Oct. 21, 1992. Running time: **107 MIN.**
SHARONA HONEY
Directed by Menahemi. Screenplay, Shemi Zarhin, Menahemi. Camera (color), Amnon Zlayet; music, Ari Frankel.
Sharona . . . . Yael Abecassis
OPERATION CAT
Directed, written by Ginsberg. Camera (color), Jorge Gurevitz; music, Shlomo Gronich.
Zofit . . . . Ruthi Goldberg
DIVORCE
Directed by Menahemi. Screenplay, Nirit Yaron. Camera (color), Zlayet; music, Frankel.
(In Hebrew, with English subtitles)

Taking their cue from "New York Stories," Israeli helmers Ayelet Menahemi and Yitzhak Ginsberg have compiled this commercial anthology, presenting a trio of comic tales that deal with three independent urban women in con-

tempo Tel Aviv. As with all anthologies, quality varies. Amusing, lightweight pic was a hit at native wickets and might find some international acceptance.

The strongest of the three stories, "Sharona Honey" chronicles the life of a model in the fast lane, who goes from one man to another. Even after she has grown tired of them, they continue to clutter her life the way a garbage strike piles debris around the city.

"Operation Cat" features poet and journalist Zofit, whose husband has left her for another woman. While her personal and professional life unravels, she suddenly fixates on the fate of a small kitten trapped in a storm drain — perhaps if she can rescue the cat, she can get everything else in order.

Final tale, "Divorce," receives the most apparent comic handling, with mixed results. It concerns a policewoman who goes crazy when she spots the husband who had abandoned her and the kids five years earlier. Under Israeli law, she is not free until either they divorce or he dies. She tries for both solutions, taking a group hostage while looking for him. It's amusing, but the overstated theme muddles tale's overall intention.

Tech credits and acting are okay throughout. — *Paul Lenti*

A FEW GOOD MEN

A Columbia release of a Columbia Pictures and Castle Rock Entertainment presentation of a David Brown production. Executive producers, William Gilmore, Rachel Pfeffer. Produced by Brown, Rob Reiner, Andrew Scheinman. Directed by Reiner. Screenplay, Aaron Sorkin, based on his play. Camera (Technicolor; Panavision widescreen), Robert Richardson; editor, Robert Leighton; music, Marc Shaiman; production design, J. Michael Riva; art direction, Dave Klassen; set design, Virginia Randolph, Rob Woodruff; set decoration, Michael Taylor; costume design, Gloria Gresham; sound (Dolby), Bob Eber; assistant director, Frank Capra III; 2nd unit camera, Gary Kibbe; co-producers, Steve Nicolaides, Jeffrey Stott; casting, Jane Jenkins, Janet Hirshenson. Reviewed at AMC Century 14, L.A., Nov. 9, 1992. MPAA Rating: R. Running time: **138 MIN.**
Lt. J.G. Kaffee . . . . Tom Cruise
Col. Jessep . . . . Jack Nicholson
Lt. Cdr. Galloway . . . . . Demi Moore
Capt. Ross . . . . Kevin Bacon
Lt. Kendrick . . . . Kiefer Sutherland
Lt. Weinberg . . . . Kevin Pollak
Pfc. Downey . . . . . James Marshall
Lt. Col. Markinson . . . . . J.T. Walsh
Dr. Stone . . . . . . Christopher Guest
Judge Randolph . . . . . . J.A. Preston
Lt. Spradling . . . . Matt Craven
Lance Cpl. Dawson . Wolfgang Bodison

"A Few Good Men" is a big-time, mainstream Hollywood movie par excellence. It's got all the elements for across-the-board acceptance: juicy parts for some of the top stars in the business, a Broadway pedigree, a riveting David vs. Goliath courtroom battle, serious attitudes that won't threaten or offend anyone, and skilled filmmaking hands at the top of their game. Fact that it covers such familiar ground and takes no risks will in no way constrain this Columbia/ Castle Rock entry from promotion to the top b.o. ranks.

Mass audiences will eat up this exposé of peacetime military malfeasance laced with the story of a bright young lawyer's struggle to get out from under the imposing shadow of an illustrious father. Expert story construction and compelling thesping and direction make all the narrative elements pay off.

Adapting his own 1989 play, which ran for 449 performances on Broadway, Aaron Sorkin has opened it up just enough to accommodate the requirements of the big screen and magnified the psychological father-son dilemma of the leading character.

Otherwise, the same histrionic fireworks that gripped theater audiences will prove even more compelling to filmgoers due to the star power and dramatic screw-tightening in the tale of the death of a private at the Guantanamo Bay, Cuba, naval base. Two young Marines, Dawson and Downey, are quickly charged with murder, as they appear to have gone too far in subjecting the victim to off-limits disciplinary action.

Chosen to defend them is Navy lawyer Lt. Kaffee (Tom Cruise), a hot dog who prefers baseball duds to military uniforms and enjoys an unblemished record of settling cases through plea bargains. Briefly alighting in Cuba to interview the base's commanding officer, Col. Nathan Jessep (Jack Nicholson), Kaffee barely goes through the motions of researching the case, but is goaded to press further by the driven special counsel, Lt. Cdr. Joanne Galloway (Demi Moore).

Basically, the defense team, which also includes Lt. Sam Weinberg (Kevin Pollak), has to show, against heavy odds, that Dawson and Downey were illegally ordered to inflict "Code Red" punishment on the victim, and by whom. Action ping-pongs back and forth between defense team strategy sessions, interrogations of the two perpetrators, man-to-mans between Kaffee and the friendly but fiercely competitive skilled prosecuting attorney Capt. Ross (Kevin Bacon), and raging exchanges in which Joanne won't let Kaffee off the hook, prodding and belittling him into rising to the occasion.

Kaffee's problem is that his late father was a celebrated Navy lawyer himself. Afraid to take on his paternal competition, he's putting himself, as well as his clients, at risk when he finally takes the floor — always good drama.

By the time of the climactic, 15-minute courtroom showdown between Kaffee and Jessep, the young man is in a hole so deep that viewers will be fairly drooling to find out how he's going to turn the tables on his adversary. Sorkin delivers the goods in potent fashion, and manages the nifty trick of making the audience feel as though it has experienced something considerably more sobering and profound than it really is.

Major values, such as honor, commitment, ethics, God and country, etc. are repeatedly invoked, and the dynamic way the narrative charges along makes it easy to overlook the fact that the text really doesn't have much to say about any of them.

But this is a well-made play well done in every respect. Director Rob Reiner hasn't missed a beat in extracting the most out the material and his actors.

Kaffee is a perfect part for Cruise, and he engages it totally in giving his most passionate, mature performance after "Born on the Fourth of July." Wearing tight-fitting military garb, Moore proves a good, challenging foil, standing up to Kaffee with fire and authority.

But the showiest turn is reserved for Nicholson, and the crafty old pro makes more than the most of it. Playing a Marine lifer who's worked his way almost to the top and long since mastered the art of pulling everyone's strings, he spellbinds the viewer. He's only got three major scenes, but they're all dynamite.

In fact, everyone registers strongly. Bacon scores as the snappy, intelligent prosecutor, and Sutherland's self-righteous good ol' boy is no one you'd want to meet in a dark alley. Acting newcomer Wolfgang Bodison and James Marshall are excellent as the defendants, while Pollak, Walsh, Christopher Guest and J.A. Preston all have moments.

Technically, film couldn't be better, as lenser Robert Richardson, working in widescreen, editor Robert Leighton, production designer J. Michael Riva, costume designer Gloria Gresham and composer Marc Shaiman have all made contributions of discreet excellence. At more than two-and-a-quarter hours, pic's not a minute too long.
— *Todd McCarthy*

MALCOLM X

A Warner Bros. release in association with Largo Intl. of a 40 Acres & a Mule Filmworks/Marvin Worth production. Produced by Worth, Spike Lee. Directed by Lee. Screenplay, Arnold Perl, Lee, based on "The Autobiography of Malcolm X" as told to Alex Haley. Camera (Duart color; Technicolor prints), Ernest Dickerson; editor, Barry Alexander Brown; music, Terence Blanchard; production design, Wynn Thomas; art direction, Tom Warren; costume design, Ruth Carter; sound (Dolby), Rolf Pardula; co-producers, Monty Ross, Jon Kilik, Preston Holmes; associate producer, Fernando Sulichin; assistant director, Randy Fletcher; casting, Robi Reed. Reviewed at Warner Bros. Studios, Burbank, Calif., Nov. 6, 1992. MPAA Rating: PG-13. Running time: **201 MIN.**
Malcolm X . . . . . Denzel Washington
Betty Shabazz . . . . . Angela Bassett
Baines . . . . Albert Hall
Elijah Muhammad . . . Al Freeman Jr.
West Indian Archie . . . Delroy Lindo
Shorty . . . . Spike Lee
Laura . . . . Theresa Randle
Sophia . . . . Kate Vernon
Louise Little . . . . . . Lonette McKee
Earl Little . . . . Tommy Hollis
Also with: Bobby Seale, Al Sharpton, Christopher Plummer, Karen Allen, Peter Boyle, William Kunstler, Ossie Davis.

Spike Lee has made a disappointingly conventional and sluggish film in "Malcolm X." Attempting to relate the extraordinary journey that was the black leader's life, Lee has set his sights much higher than ever before, and tribute must be paid to the way in which the filmmaker persevered and made the film his way. Nevertheless, the pic comes up short in several departments, notably in pacing and in giving a strong sense of why this man became a legend.

The "X" phenomenon reaches its natural climax with the release of the film, and the large number of people for whom this reps a "must see" guarantees heavy b.o. action for some time. Many critics and viewers might be respectful to the point of overindulgence, but the fact remains this is one long sit.

Despite Denzel Washington's forceful, magnetic and multilayered lead performance, the film clicks only sporadically, confirming the view that Lee has always been a much better director of individual scenes than of cohesive total works.

Where the film falters can best be seen simply by comparing it with its source. From beginning to end, "The Autobiography of Malcolm X" is a mesmerizing page-turner, an extraordinary glimpse into the political and spiritual transformations of one man during a tumultuous, tragically abbreviated lifespan.

Lee's account is loaded with speeches articulating Malcolm's Islamic and black nationalist perspective but, except for the American flag that, à la "Patton," backs the opening credits, none of it catches fire. Truly getting inside a character's head is never an easy task and, despite some first-person narration, Lee hasn't really managed it.

Still, the life itself is so compelling, and the issues it takes up so potent and relevant, the picture can't help but command a relatively strong degree of interest. Malcolm's progression from street hustler, burglar and convict to religious and political leader — and, now, to near-mythic figure — is unique in modern annals, and the period retains its own fascination, especially when seen from a black perspective.

The screenplay by the late Arnold Perl and Lee (James Baldwin's name, often invoked during production, is nowhere mentioned) tellingly begins during "the war years" with Lee's hipster character Shorty conking the hair of 16-year-old Malcolm Little, who has recently arrived in Boston. The initial hour chronicles Malcolm's misadventures in clubs and bars, his affair with a white woman, numbers running, involvement in drugs, and the burglary ring that eventually lands him in the pen.

The subsequent 25 minutes detail Malcolm's prison introduction to Islam and the beliefs of Elijah Muhammad, whose "white devil" racial theories and emphasis on black pride, discipline and separatism provide an all-embracing outlet for the anger and latent ideas that Malcolm's life experiences have given him.

The next hour presents Malcolm as the rising star of the Nation of Islam. Overwhelmed upon actually meeting Elijah Muhammad, he becomes a spellbinding street preacher in Harlem and, later, a minister at mosques. Countering the integrationist ideals of Martin Luther King and white liberals in the civil rights movement, Malcolm forecasts a "racial explosion" and espouses a "complete separation between the black race and the white race."

What comes across during this long stretch — devoted mostly to speeches and ideology with brief timeouts for Malcolm's courtship of his wife-to-be, Betty — is the resolve of a passionate believer and thinker: to speak his mind, tell the truth and go his own way.

But Malcolm's gradual break with Elijah Muhammad is handled in rather muddled fashion, and the final, short act of Malcolm's life — his realization that the world's races perhaps could be united, and his abortive solo attempt to merge his religious and political activities — isn't given the dramatic substance it deserves, despite the time lavished upon it.

Particularly desultory in this regard is Malcolm's momentous trip to Africa and the Middle East. What in life was a transforming experience becomes a second-unit travelogue in which Malcolm is hounded by presumed CIA cameramen.

Beginning, crucially, with Washington's, several of the performances are powerful enough to put the material over and provide continuity even when the script and storytelling sweep prove deficient. Washington convinces even as a hayseed teenager in the opening scenes and grows marvelously as Malcolm's character deepens and expands. Putting over the speeches with impressive power, he also makes very clear both the human, emotional roots of Malcolm's ideology and his humor.

Al Freeman Jr.'s wary reserve, self-satisfaction and halting, careful, high-pitched readings make Elijah Muhammad the unique, memorable figure he must have been. In addition to Albert Hall's commanding Baines, who becomes something of an adversary to Malcolm after having brought him to Islam, the other standout supporting turn comes from Delroy Lindo as West Indian Archie, who introduces young Malcolm to a life of crime. Angela Bassett is a warm, loving Betty Shabazz, and Lonette McKee has moments of high emotion as Malcolm's besieged mother.

Various periods from the 1940s through the mid-1960s have been elaborately evoked by production designer Wynn Thomas, cinematographer Ernest Dickerson, costume designer Ruth Carter and the multitude of behind-the-scenes craftspeople (the end credits last nine minutes). The score nicely mixes the eras' pop tunes with dramatic original compositions by Terence Blanchard.

But Lee has indulged himself and his subject by letting it run so long; even in one viewing, it is easy to see where he might have cut at least a half-hour and better served his artistic cause.

Beginning the film with one of Malcolm's more inflammatory speeches accompanied by the flag burning and footage from the Rodney King beating gets things off to a provocative start, while the final images are equally unusual but rather more benign — a series of shots of some of the celebs who helped Lee out during his financial problems — Michael Jordan, Tracy Chapman, Bill Cosby and others — all wearing "X" caps.

But it is a measure of how the film — as ambitious, right-minded and personal as it is — falls short of its goals that the climactic documentary montage of footage and stills of the real Malcolm prove infinitely more powerful than any of the drama that has preceded it.

— *Todd McCarthy*

HOME ALONE 2:
LOST IN NEW YORK

A 20th Century Fox release of a John Hughes production. Executive producers, Mark Radcliffe, Duncan Henderson, Richard Vane. Produced, written by Hughes. Directed by Chris Columbus. Camera (Kodak color), Julio Macat; editor, Raja Gosnell; music, John Williams; production design, Sandy Veneziano; art direction, Gary Lee; set decoration, Marvin March; set design, Stephen Berger; costume design, Jay Hurley; sound (Dolby), Jim Alexander; assistant director, James Giovannetti, Jr.; 2nd-unit director/stunt coordinator, Freddie Hice; visual effects supervisor, Craig Barron; casting, Janet Hirshenson, Jane Jenkins. Reviewed at the Avco Center Cinema, L.A., Nov. 8, 1992. MPAA Rating: PG. Running time: **120 MIN.**

Kevin	Macaulay Culkin
Harry	Joe Pesci
Marv	Daniel Stern
Kate	Catherine O'Hara
Peter	John Heard
Buzz	Devin Ratray
Concierge	Tim Curry
Pigeon Lady	Brenda Fricker
Mr. Duncan	Eddie Bracken
Uncle Frank	Gerry Bamman

Some day scholars will devote courses to the monstrous box office allure of the original "Home Alone," which, at the time, surprised even Fox. Still, you needn't be able to explain success to know not to tamper with it, so for a sequel the studio has simply remade the first movie, but with bigger pratfalls. Pic delivers on that level and will doubtless be another huge holiday draw, but the law of diminishing returns dictates its haul should fall well short of its predecessor.

For one thing, the filmmakers have made a minor miscalculation in terms of length, padding the screen time by nearly 20 minutes to two hours — not a great idea considering a big portion of the aud is young kids.

For another, one reason "Home Alone" became such an enormous hit — a lack of children's fare when it was released — isn't true this time out.

Finally, adults may be a bit less patient with the more saccharine aspects of the story as well as the absurd series of events/coincidences necessary to set up the cartoon-style payoff.

Aside from the lack of like-themed competition, as near as anyone can tell "Home Alone" became a monster blockbuster for three reasons: it represents the ultimate child's fantasy about out-smarting adults; all the grown-ups were cartoonishly broad, as was most of the humor; and it offered all the requisite

---

Christmas-time elements, down to the sentimental score.

Writer-producer John Hughes and director Chris Columbus thoroughly recycle that material, down to having Kevin (Macaulay Culkin, the child-turned-cottage-industry) overcome his fear and befriend a foreboding adult who provides his eventual salvation — in this case, a helpful homeless lady (Brenda Fricker) roaming Central Park.

Once again Culkin, provoked by his older brother, finds himself in the doghouse just before a family vacation, this time accidentally boarding the wrong plane and ending up in New York while the McCallister brood jets off to Florida. Meanwhile, the inept thieves from the first movie, Joe Pesci and Daniel Stern, have conveniently escaped from prison and caught a truck that arrives in New York about the same time Kevin does.

Using his dad's credit card, Kevin checks into a ritzy hotel, where he finds more adults to outwit, in this case a snooty concierge (Tim Curry) as well as the equally haughty staff. Ultimately, however, it's again Kevin versus the two bad guys, setting up elaborate traps at his uncle's being-remodeled home — the uncle naturally being out of town — which is of course loaded with pain-inflicting gadgets.

Hughes and company, too, are in the construction business, essentially rebuilding the same house with bigger windows and, if possible, a slightly sappier outlook. Under Columbus' careful direction, the wide-eyed Culkin again shows his skill at being an Everykid — cutely precocious, yet still vulnerable to childish whims such as running up a whopping room-service tab on chocolate sundaes.

Kevin's parents and relatives remain as cartoonish as the villains; as Wile E. Coyotes to Culkin's Road Runner, Pesci and Stern ham it up unabashedly. The action sequences are again well-choreographed, if, perhaps, more mean-spirited even in light of their cartoonish nature.

Tech credits are likewise sound, from the Kevin's-eye-view photography by Julio Macat to the amusing design of his family's nightmarish Florida motel. Even with their dubious travel record, the warm glow on Fox's balance sheet should inspire the McCallister clan to start planning their next trip fairly soon.

— *Brian Lowry*

OH, WHAT A NIGHT
(CANADIAN)

A Norstar Entertainment release of a Peter Simpson production. Produced by Simpson. Directed by Eric Till. Screenplay, Richard Nielsen. Camera (color), Brian R. Hebb; editor, Susan Shipton; music, Ian Thomas; art direction, David Moe; co-producers, Ray Sager, Ilana Frank; casting, Marsha Chesley. Reviewed at Chicago Intl. Film Festival, Oct. 21, 1992. Running time: **93 MIN.**

Eric	Corey Haim
Vera	Barbara Williams
Thorvald	Keir Dullea
Eva	Genevieve Bujold
Donald	Andrew Miller
Todd	Robbie Coltrane

Brimming with nostalgia for a more innocent past, the bittersweet "Oh, What a Night" is an only slightly cloying Canadian version of the coming-of-age pic. Though well made, it will be a hard sell to any but the hardcore Disney crowd.

With his winning smile, Corey Haim is an ideal choice for the role of a lonely 17-year-old who has moved with his father (Keir Dullea), stepmother and former housekeeper (Genevieve Bujold) to an uninviting chicken farm in 1955 Ontario.

Longing to fill a void created by the untimely death of his mother, Haim falls madly in love with an older woman (Barbara Williams) burdened with a boozing, common-law husband and two kids from a previous marriage.

Aware of the boy's feelings, Williams at first keeps her distance as Haim tries to distract himself with his teen buddies. But after several aborted encounters and blustery threats from Williams' husband, she and Haim finally make love in a beautifully moonlit barn loft, the film's touching high point.

Director Eric Till vamps for considerable amounts of time until the big, fleeting moment. But much of the filler — teens acting as sex-charged teens will — is not unentertaining. And in the big love scene, Till captures true romantic tenderness.

Most of the acting is strong, though distinguished thesps Bujold and Dullea have little to do. Brian Hebb's cinematography captures a lot of pretty Canadian countryside, but Susan Shipton's editing could be sharper. — *Lewis Lazare*

LOVE POTION NO. 9

A 20th Century Fox release. Executive producer, Thomas M. Hammel. Produced, directed, written by Dale Launer. Camera (CFI color), William Wages; editor, Suzanne Pettit; music, Jed Leiber; production design, Linda Pearl; art direction, Thomas Minton; set decoration, Sally Nicolaou; costume design, Timothy D'Arcy; sound (Dolby), Jim Hawkins; associate producer, Jeffrey Downer; assistant director, James Sbardellati; casting, Wendy Kurtzman. Reviewed at the Avco Center Cinema, L.A., Nov. 11, 1992. MPAA Rating: PG-13. Running time: **97 MIN.**
Paul Matthews . . . . . . Tate Donovan
Diane Farrow . . . . . Sandra Bullock
Marisa . . . . Mary Mara
Gary . . . . Dale Midkiff
Sally . . . . Hillary Bailey Smith
Prince Geoffrey . . . . . . Dylan Baker
Enrico Pazzoli . . . . Adrian Paul
Motorcycle Cop . . . . . . Blake Clark
Madame Ruth . . . . . . Anne Bancroft

Inspired by the 1959 hit song, Dale Launer's "Love Potion No. 9" is a light-hearted one-joke romantic comedy that tries too hard to be cute. Glib humor and emphasis on "feel good" values aim squarely at the dating crowd and twenty-something couples. But lack of real wit and comic vitality, absence of star names and sluggish pace make pic less appealing than it might have been.

Shot two years ago, the good-natured tale embraces a hopeful Capraesque belief: Under the right circumstances, every ordinary human being can gain confidence and transform into a beautiful, resourceful individual.

This variation on the Cinderella and ugly duckling fairytales focuses on Paul Matthews (Tate Donovan), a shy biochemist petrified of women, and Diane Farrow (Sandra Bullock), a repressed and lonely comparative psycho-biologologist.

The plain and mousy Donovan and Bullock are very similar: They live in unadorned apartments with posters of Einstein on their walls, listen to the same kind of music, and so on. But their quiet and boring lives are turned upside-down when gypsy Anne Bancroft gives Donovan a love potion that suddenly makes them physically attractive and sexually alluring.

There are, of course, complications and disastrous brushes with the potion to be overcome before the protagonists can reach a blissful union. Bullock has a manipulative b.f., and she is also courted by a British prince who, along with other men, falls under the spell of her magical charm.

Unfortunately, Launer's writing is not as rude and energetic as it was in "Ruthless People," and it lacks the clever one-liners that punctuated "My Cousin Vinny," two of the scripter's hit comedies. He points the action at a big, explosive climax that is lame and disappointing.

In his directorial debut, Launer exhibits a draggy, unmodulated style. His orchestration of sight gags is too leisurely and deliberate and he's not playful or loose enough to cash in on potentially hilarious situations. The construction feels contrived; isolated good pranks seldom build into an intricate clusters.

Linda Pearl's production design and Thomas D'Arcy's costumes are specifically detailed and deftly executed, underlining the progression of the leads' lifestyles. But William Wages' camera set-ups are uninventive, and Susan Pettit's editing is inconsistent; too many scenes run too long and don't flow together.

—*Emanuel Levy*

ANOTHER GIRL, ANOTHER PLANET
(B&W-16m)

A Nabu production. Produced by Michael Almereyda, Robin O'Hara, Bob Gosse. Directed, written by Almereyda (most of Nic's dialog, Nic Ratner). Camera (PXL-vision video; 16m blowup; Duart B&W), Jim Denault; editor, David Leonard; sound, Kirsten Smith; casting, Billy Hopkins. Reviewed at Toronto Festival of Festivals, Sept. 17, 1992. Running time: **56 MIN.**
Nic . . . . Nic Ratner
Bill . . . . Barry Sherman
Ramona . . . . Mary Ward
Prudence . . . . Lisa Perisot
Guy in Bar . . . . Thomas Roma
Mia . . . . Elina Lowensohn
Guy in Bar 2 . . . . Bob Gosse
Nabu . . . . Daisy

In a year of numerous no-budget pictures ("Laws of Gravity," "The Living Edge," "El Mariachi"), "Another Girl, Another Planet" may take the cake for economy of means. Shot on a plastic $45 "pixel vision" video camera designed for kids, and blown up to 16m, this intensely intimate drama of a young man's chaotic love life tries to make a virtue of its limitations and to a surprising degree succeeds. But short running time and technical crudeness will limit it to fringe venues with adventurous audiences.

Michael Almereyda, whose uneven 1989 feature "Twister" attracted some critical attention, packs a good deal into this hour-long chronicle of the comings and goings of several women into and out of the grungy East Village apartment of Bill (Barry Sherman).

Although he doesn't seem to have much going for him, Bill manages to bed some pretty attractive women. He kicks out one of them, but ultimately gets his when the gorgeous Mia (Elina Lowensohn) walks out on him.

The writing and storytelling have a lot to commend them and the relationships are amusing in their imbalance.

The film's tech aspect has a great deal to do with its effectiveness, pro and con. As it looks in the film transfer, at least, the black & white images have a smudged, atomized quality that approach the far extremes of Impressionist painting. This forces the viewer to respond to the ebb and flow of mood and feeling rather than to the niceties of style, resulting in a work of some resonance and lyricism.

Downside, however, is that the actors suffer from the simple fact of not being clearly seen. Watching the thesps through such a dense fog robs them of many of their most important tools: expressions, glances, subtle movements. The effect is akin to looking at a fifth-generation photocopy, although pic reportedly looks better on videotape.

The performances register with a degree of force on the soundtrack, which is perfectly clear, and pop tunes and source music are cleverly used.

— *Todd McCarthy*

DANDY
(GERMAN-B&W/COLOR)

A Pandora film production. Produced by Niko Brucher, Peter Sempel. Directed by Sempel. Camera (B&W/color), Frank Blasberg, Jonas Scholz, Norimichi Kasamatsu, Sempel; editor, Wolf Ingo Romer; sound, Drago Hari, Takashi Endo, Kai Wessel Reviewed at Vagabond Theater, L.A., Oct. 29, 1992. Running time: **91 MIN.**
With: Blixa Bargeld, Nick Cave, Dieter Meier, Kazuo Ohno, Yoshito Ohno, Nina Hagen, Lene Lovich, Rattenjenny.

"Dandy" is an intellectually pretentious, though never boring, meditation on decadence and anomie in the postindustrial world. Employing the logic of an extended musicvideo, it's an underground pic of extremely limited appeal. Though not a typical cult movie, Peter Sempel's purely imagistic and sensory work will still be best appreciated as a midnight movie experience.

Sempel claims Voltaire's "Candide" as his literary inspiration, with graftings of the anarchic and nihilistic philosophy of Wim Wenders, sans the humor and irony. Pic's title derives from the song "Death Is a Dandy on a Horse," which Blixa Bargeld sings with angst and gusto at the film's beginning and end.

Obsessed with alienation and the end of the world, "Dandy" is pregnant with heavy symbolism and simplistic allegories. Recurrent metaphoric closeups of a dead fish and a butterfly captured in a wine goblet are extended, as the real butterfly is crosscut with a human one, veteran Japanese performer Kazuo Ohno, who dances a *pas de deux* with his son Yoshito to Jessye Norman's exquisite rendition of "City Called Heaven."

Unfortunately, the continuous flow of inventive images and sounds is too often interrupted by a superfluous and unnecessary narration about the nuclear threat, violence and torture.

Brief philosophical assertions are made about the meaning of life and death, alienation and the dialectical relationship between life and art.

The intermittently entertaining pic features some of Germany's most eccentric underground figures, such as Nick Cave singing the blues and Nina Hagen making faces at the camera.

True to its postmodern, global, intercultural sensibility, the film contains stunning shots of Berlin, London, Cairo, the Himalayas, Marrakech and other exotic places. Pic's kaleidoscopic nature — West meets East — is also reflected in the blend of music and style.

Tech credits are only moderate, with original 16m images blown up to 35m.

— *Emanuel Levy*

LONDON FEST

ELENYA
(BRITISH-GERMAN)

A British Film Institute release of a Frankfurter Film/BFI production, in association with Ffilmiau Llifon for S4C, ZDF. (Intl. sales: BFI.) Executive producers, Ben Gibson, Michael Smeaton, Daffyd Huw Williams. Produced by Heidi

Ulmke. Directed, written by Steve Gough. Camera (Metrocolor), Patrick Duval; editor, Alan Smithee; music, Simon Fisher Turner; production design, Hayden Pearce; costume design, Aideen Morgan; sound, Simon Happ; assistant director, Dafydd Arwyn Jones; executives in charge of production, Angela Topping (BFI), Ian Jones (S4C), Brigitte Kramer (ZDF); associate producer, Gareth Lloyd Williams; line producer, Heike Richter-Karst. Previewed at BFI screening room, London, Oct. 28, 1992. (In London Film Festival.) Running time: **81 MIN.**

Old Elenya . . . . . . Margaret John
Young Elenya . Pascale Delafouge Jones
Glyn . . . . Seiriol Tomos
Maggie . . . . Sue Jones-Davies
Franz . . . . Klaus Behrendt
Sidney . . . . Iago Wynn Jones
Schoolteacher . . . . Llio Millward
Head teacher . . . . . . Catrin Llwyd
Phil . . . . Edward Elwyn Jones
Voiceover . . . . Pauline Yates
  Also with: Ioan Meredith, Eiry Palfrey.

(English soundtrack)

Welsh TV scripter Steve Gough makes an impressive debut with "Elenya," a slim but affecting vignette of a 12-year-old girl in wartime Wales who secretly cares for an injured German airman. Well-observed pic should gain plaudits on fest circuit, though tube sales loom more profitable than theatrical outings.

Pic is framed as a memory flashback by the middle-aged Elenya (Margaret John, voiced by Pauline Yates), recalling her youth in rural Wales, 1940. Daughter of an Italian mother she's never seen, 12-year-old Elenya (newcomer Pascale Delafouge Jones) is left alone with her aunt (Sue Jones-Davies) when her father is called to the front.

Ostracized by her classmates, she takes to wandering solo in the woods where one day she finds a wounded German pilot (Klaus Behrendt). The two strike up an edgy friendship as the girl nips clothing and supplies and tries to keep her secret. Finally, the village learns the truth, with tragic consequences.

Pic is slow to start, with the first 25 minutes sketching the girl's background, attachment to her father and school life before the German makes his entrance. Thereafter, it's largely a movie of looks and smiles, with more than a touch of Terence Davies in its portrait of a lonely child locked in a world of fantasies.

With Behrendt speaking only German, it's left to Delafouge Jones to carry the pic's emotional line. On screen virtually the whole time, the Franco-Welsh thespette hits just the right notes in understated but stalwart playing that mingles discreet edge-of-puberty emotions with an aching need for companionship.

In the only other substantial part, Jones-Davies is excellent as her embittered maiden aunt, similarly emotionally starved. Other roles are well cast.

Production design by Hayden Pearce and photography by Patrick Duval have a real '40s feel, with a desaturated look to the color achieved by the "bleach bi-pass" process. Discreet score by Derek Jarman composer Simon Fisher Turner is a further plus.

Bulk of pic was shot in Luxembourg (under the duchy's tax shelter scheme), convincingly repping the real thing. Version seen was lensed back-to-back with a Welsh-lingo version. Budget was a well-deployed £700,000 ($1.1 million).— *Derek Elley*

GOLEM, L'ESPRIT DE L'EXIL
(GOLEM, THE SPIRIT OF THE EXILE)
(FRENCH)

An Agav Films production in association with Allarts (Amsterdam), Nova Films (Rome), Friedlander Film (Hamburg), RAI-2, Groupe TSF, Channel 4, with participation of Canal Plus & the CNC, & financial aid from Eurimages Fund. Produced by Laurent Truchot. Directed, written by Amos Gitai. Camera (color), Henri Alekan; editor, Anna Ruiz; music, Simon & Markus Stockhausen; costume design, Marie Vernoux, Jean-Pierre Delifer; set design, Thierry François; sound, Antoine Bonfanti. Reviewed at L'Entrepot cinema, Paris, June 28, 1992. (In London Film Festival.) Running time: **112 MIN.**

With: Hanna Schygulla, Vittorio Mezzogiorno, Ophrah Shemesh, Samuel Fuller, Mireille Perrier, Sotigui Kouyaté, Fabienne Babe, Antonio Carallo, Bernard Levy, Marceline Loridan, Bernardo Bertolucci, Philippe Garel, Bernard Eisenschitz, Marisa Paredes, Pina Bausch Dancers.

Occasional patches of stunning lyricism and an international roll call of talent can't keep "Golem, l'Esprit de l'Exil" from turning into a well-meaning but heavy-handed exercise for committed viewers only.

Art films don't come any artier than this pic, in which Israeli filmmaker Amos Gitai tries to make the hardships of foreigners in an unwelcoming modern Paris fit a biblical mold.

By reciting a magical formula for the Cabala, Vittorio Mezzogiorno conjures Hanna Schygulla from earth and clay. She is the Golem, the spirit who protects and guides vagabonds and exiles. She has her work cut out for her as immigrant construction worker Samuel Fuller falls to his death, the first of many misfortunes for his widow, Ophrah Shemesh. Her sons are killed in a bias incident, and she is evicted from her meager home by Bernardo Bertolucci. Shemesh hits the road with her daughter-in-law, Mireille Perrier.

Gitai's visual sense outstrips his storytelling. At times practically a silent movie — complete with silent-era techniques such as multiple exposures — pic can also turn ponderously wordy. The superlative lensing of dean of French cinematographers Henri Alekan imparts real poetry to the images, but they are, by turns, too didactic or too obtuse.

Except for Schygulla, who achieves an other-worldly impact as she appears in a series of transformational get-ups, and Shemesh, who has the good bones and full lips befitting one who remains strong through untold suffering, the impressive cast is reduced to symbolic walk-ons.

Music, by Karlheinz Stockhausen's sons Markus and Simon, has an eerie, plaintive undercurrent blended with industrial clank. Though always nice to look at, pic becomes progressively less involving. The earthy Shemesh's hair grows shorter throughout the film, as does viewers' attention span. —*Lisa Nesselson*

THE HUMMINGBIRD TREE
(BRITISH)

A BBC Films production, in association with BBC Enterprises. (Intl. sales: BBC Enterprises, London.) Executive producer, Richard Broke. Produced by Gub Neal. Directed by Noella Smith. Screenplay, Jonathan Falla; from Ian McDonald's novel. Camera (color), Remi Adefarasin; editor, Mark Day; music, John Keane; production design, Tony Burrough; art direction, John Hill; costume design, Pat Godfrey; sound, Graham Ross; assistant director, Paul Judges; associate producer, Ian Hopkins. Reviewed at London Film Festival, Nov. 10, 1992. Running time: **85 MIN.**

Stephen Holmes . . . . Patrick Bergin
Marjorie Holmes . . . Susan Wooldridge
Alan Holmes . . . . . . Tom Beasley
Jaillin . . . . Desha Penco
Kaiser . . . . . . Sunil Y. Ramjitsingh
Alice . . . . . Valerie Laurent Stevens
Tom Ross . . . . Clive Wood
Judy Ross . . . . . . Rebecca Aldred

Former TV scripter-director Noella Smith brings big-screen values to feature bow "The Hummingbird Tree," an interracial puppy-love period piece set in Trinidad. The mild dramatic tone should cause only a gentle theatrical murmur, but the pic should reap solid tube and fest exposure.

Based on a semi-autobiographical novel by Trinidad-born Ian McDonald, pic opens in 1946 as the Brit Caribbean colony undergoes the first of the democratic stirrings that led to independence 16 years later.

Central character is Alan (Tom Beasley), 12-year-old son of well-off Catholic parents (Patrick Bergin, Susan Wooldridge). He's pals with two local East Indian kids, same-age Jaillin (Desha Penco) and her elder brother Kaiser (Sunil Y. Ramjitsingh). The friendship is tolerated by mom and dad but sneered at by Alan's white schoolmates.

There's precious little plot, but the telling is seductive enough. The parallel to Alan and Jaillin's prepubescent flirting — and his edgy relationship with the grousy Kaiser — are sketched against the preparations for an upcoming election, in which the black majority and sizable East Indian minority have the vote for the first time.

In a relatively small but telling role, Bergin resonates as the father who takes a determinedly liberal line toward his free-thinking son but finally comes down on the side of conservatism and realism. Wooldridge, in a less shaded part as the them-and-us mother, is solid.

Pic belongs, however, to the kids, all non-pros. Beasley, looking and sounding like an archetypal postwar middle-class Britisher, brings a likable naturalism to the part and handles his lines with ease. Trinidadians Penco (a real charmer) and Ramjitsingh play off well against the white "master," but their dialog would benefit from revoicing for greater clarity.

Though fenced in by the storyline, there's nothing boxy in Smith's direction, and luscious lensing by Remi Adefarasin and a balmy score by John Keane are bonuses. Period detail and Mark Day's editing are to the point.

Blowup from super-16m is impeccable. Pic is skedded by pubcaster BBC as the Christmas attraction in its "Screen One" series, with theatrical hopes elsewhere.

— *Derek Elley*

BECK
(BELGIAN-DUTCH)

A Filmcase and Prime Time presentation. Produced by Antonino Lombardo and Rolf Orthel. Directed, written by Jacob Bijl, based on Maj Sjowall and Per Wahloo's novel "The Locked Room." Camera (color), Tom Erisman; editor, Wim Louwrier; music, Lodewijk de Boer; art direction, Philippe Graff; costumes, Y. Tax; sound, B. Koops. Reviewed Sept. 2, 1992, at Montreal World Film Festival. (Also in London Film Festival.) Running time: **100 MIN.**

Martin Beck	Jan Decleir
Monita	Els Dottermans
Waterman	Warre Borgmans
Fisher	Jakob Beks

Classic French farce doesn't rely as heavily on coincidence as "Beck," a frankly contrived but entertaining thriller based on one of Sjowall & Wahloo's popular policiers that should enjoy modest success in international TV markets.

A Belgium-Netherlands coproduction, "Beck" has the title role, a middle-aged cop strongly played by Jan Decleir, returning to work as head of Antwerp's homicide unit after lengthy recovery from a gunshot wound.

Shaken by his brush with mortality, Beck remains a taciturn professional as he investigates the puzzling murder of a retiree found dead in a room locked from the inside.

As Beck plods through his solo queries, Monita (Els Dottermans), a divorced young mother, is paid to make a suspicious delivery for a photographer who's really a drug dealer and gun runner. Monita just happens to live in an apartment where the murder victim used to live, and the photographer just happens to be the old man's killer.

And Beck just happens to question Monita shortly before she's arrested during her delivery. He gets her freed, and they begin a brief affair.

Director-screenwriter Jacob Bijl takes a straightforward, no-frills approach to the convoluted plot, probably the best idea. Pic repeatedly strains credibility, but low-key performances by Decleir and Dottermans go a long way toward helping the audience accept the most jaw-dropping implausibilities, as does tone of witty, worldly-wise cynicism, and its suggestion that the best justice is of the ironic variety.

Tech credits are fine, especially Lodewijk de Boer's moody musical score. — *Joe Leydon*

AI NI TSUITE, TOKYO
(ABOUT LOVE, TOKYO)
(JAPANESE)

An About-Love-Tokyo Prod. Committee production. (Intl. sales: Shibata Films, Tokyo.) Executive producers, Minoru Tanaka, Masaaki Hagino. Produced by Masaru Koibuchi, Mitsuo Yanagimachi. Directed, written by Yanagimachi. Camera (color), Shohei Ando; editor, Nobuo Ogawa; music, Hajime Mizoguchi; production design, Takeo Kimura; sound, Soichi Inoue. Reviewed at Venice Film Festival (out of competition), Sept. 6, 1992. (In London, Tokyo and Hawaii film fests.) Running time: **109 MIN.**

Ho Jun	Wu Xiao Tong
Ailin	Asuka Okasaka
Endo	Hiroshi Fujioka
Zhang Linan	Qian Po
Li Baoguo	Gu Xiao Tong
Huang Li	Zeng Chun Hui
Pan Xiaomao	Ou Yang
Akiko	Jun Togawa

For much of its length, the new film by Mitsuo Yanagimachi ("Farewell to the Land," "Fire Festival") is an intriguing insight into Chinese students living in Japan and the way the two cultures relate to each other. Unfortunately, the writer-director allows the last third to degenerate into a routine crime story that, while well handled, is on a lower level than the rest of the pic.

Early scenes establish Ho Jun (Wu Xiao Tong), a Beijing student working in a cattle slaughterhouse in Tokyo. He lives in cheap lodgings with other Chinese friends and finds it hard to adapt himself to Japanese lifestyles; in turn, he's treated quite badly by the Japanese.

When he and a couple of friends devise a scheme to rip off a local pinball gambling house, the gangster who runs it (Hiroshi Fujioka) threatens to have Ho Jun exported back to China and, in an unlikely plot development, demands sexual favors from Ho Jun's Chinese/Japanese g.f. (Asuka Okasaka).

Although unable to make his plotting entirely convincing, Yanagimachi provides some fascinating insights into Sino-Japanese relationships on a grassroots level, with the Japanese generally coming across as domineering, arrogant and racist. These, and a scene in which the Chinese student and the Japanese gangster have to communicate in the writing they share and can understand, provide the best elements in an uneven film. — *David Stratton*

SENI SEVIYORUM ROSA
(ROSA, I LOVE YOU)
(TURKISH)

An Asya Film production. (Intl sales: Christa Saredi, Zurich.) Produced by Ali Ozgenturk. Directed, written by Isil Ozgenturk, based on Sevgi Soysal's novel. Camera (color), Ertunc Senkay; editor, Mevlot Kocak; music, Thesia Panayiotou; production design, Ismail Kundem; line producer, Ueli Selm; assistant director, Audin Sayman. Reviewed at Toronto Festival of Festivals, Sept. 16, 1992. (In Istanbul, London and Montpelier, France, film fests.) Running time: **93 MIN.**

Rosa	Sumru Yavrucuk
Violinist	Mahir Gunsiray
Cobbler	Ismet Ay
Husband	Mehmet Atak
Fortune-teller	Gulumser Gulhan
Mother	Guzin Ozyagcilar
Rosa (child)	Hande Mese

An ambitious, flawed first feature from female director Isil Ozgenturk, "Rosa, I Love You" traces the life of a woman who refuses to conform to male-dominated Turkish society. Based on a well-regarded novel, the film encapsulates a whole lifetime in a stylized, fairy tale manner, but Ozgenturk makes rather heavy weather of the difficult material, and an uncharismatic central performance doesn't help.

It begins with Rosa as a precocious, play-acting little girl who is expelled from convent school because she claims to have talked to Jesus. As a teenager, she becomes pregnant, marries and soon is an unhappy wife with two children. She leaves her family to live with a violinist, and later finds work in a brothel.

Finally, she becomes a homeless bag lady; her only companion is a parrot that she trains to say "Rosa, I love you," though she expires before she hears the bird speak the words.

This sad little biography unfolds with bold use of colors in decor and costumes, and dreams and imagined scenes (including appearances from Jesus Christ) alternating with realism. It's a heady mixture that doesn't always work, though more charismatic perf from Sumru Yavrucuk as Rosa would have helped.

The film won the special jury prize at this year's Istanbul film fest. — *David Stratton*

THE BODYGUARD

A Warner Bros. release of a Tig production in association with Kasdan Pictures. Produced by Lawrence Kasdan, Jim Wilson, Kevin Costner. Directed by Mick Jackson. Screenplay, Kasdan. Camera (Technicolor), Andrew Dunn; editor, Richard A. Harris, Donn Cambern; music, Alan Silvestri; production design, Jeffrey Beecroft; art direction, Wm Ladd Skinner; set decoration, Lisa Dean; set design, Antoinette J. Gordon, Roy Barnes; costume design, Susan Nininger; sound (Dolby), Richard Bryce Goodman; assistant director, Albert Shapiro; stunt coordinator, Norman L. Howell; casting, Elisabeth Leustig. Reviewed at Mann Village Theater, L.A., Nov. 17, 1992. MPAA Rating: R. Running time: **129 MIN.**

Frank Farmer	Kevin Costner
Rachel Marron	Whitney Houston
Sy Spector	Gary Kemp
Devaney	Bill Cobbs
Herb Farmer	Ralph Waite
Portman	Tomas Arana
Nicki	Michele Lamar Richards
Tony	Mike Starr
Henry	Christopher Birt
Fletcher	DeVaughn Nixon

No wonder this Lawrence Kasdan script has been on the shelf for more than a decade: In the custody of director Mick Jackson, it proves a jumbled mess with a few enjoyable moments but little continuity or flow. The intriguing romantic union of Kevin Costner and Whitney Houston should power strong initial box office curiosity before "The Bodyguard" fades into the holiday pack, but the closest this pic will get to an Oscar is in its overblown climax.

Considering its opulent trappings, the film is also surprisingly weak technically. From the first scene, with bodyguard-for-hire Frank Farmer (Costner) completing an earlier assignment, the story is a chore to follow —choppily edited with garbled sound that often demands some effort to sort out the dialogue.

Those shortcomings are puzzling since the pic's core is sheer simplicity: A bodyguard, who fears becoming too attached to his clients, takes a job protecting actress-singer Rachel Marron (Houston) and ends up falling for her. Someone is trying to kill her, and it seems possible that one of the members of her entourage may be involved.

Blame it on the setting, but the collaboration of Kasdan and Jackson (the one-time BBC director who helmed "L.A. Story") at times feels like a music video interrupted by a movie, but reinforces Costner's tough-guy charisma — as opposed to tough-sensitive guy — and provides

Houston a flattering showcase for her big-screen unveiling. In fact, the filmmakers seem more intent on featuring Houston musically—one half expects the cue "Insert video here"—than keeping the narrative moving, undercutting what could have been a crowd-pleasing finale simply because Jackson doesn't know when to say "cut."

For all that, pic isn't without its pleasures, from Costner silently drubbing his charge's testy security chief (Mike Starr) to his bluntly deflating a predatory partygoer. The problem is that those high points are spaced too far apart, with long meandering passages between the bursts of action, everything finally and predictably culminating in a payoff at the Academy Awards.

The chemistry between the leads stems more from their inherent appeal than anything the story develops. Houston makes a solid debut and looks glorious, snapping off saucy dialogue that may come as a jolt given her somewhat pristine image.

On the flip side, Costner dons his "No Way Out" look as a former Secret Service agent who fancies himself a modern-day samurai. Kasdan was inspired by Steve McQueen in "Bullitt" when he wrote the script in 1975, and Costner manages some of that quiet intensity in a pic that, if not an actual career setback, for the most part lets him down.

Other cast members are generally sound but too sparsely developed, the most notable of them being Michele Lamar Richards, a near ringer for Houston as her older sister, and Gary Kemp ("The Krays") as her unctuous publicist.

The sound is at times cranked up to absurd levels. The aural quality is better on the six new songs for Houston, although at times this item feels like a soundtrack in search of a movie.

— *Brian Lowry*

RESISTANCE
(AUSTRALIAN)

A Macau Light Film Corp. production, with the participation of Australian Film Finance Corp., produced in association with Wingjar & Workers Power. Produced by Christina Ferguson, Pauline Rosenberg, Jenny Day. Directed by Paul Elliott, Hugh Keays-Byrne. Screenplay, the Macau Collective. Camera (Panavision, Eastmancolor), Sally Bongers; editor, Stewart Young; music,

Davood A. Tabrizi; production design, Macgregor Knox; costumes, Sally Molineaux; sound design, Soundage; sound recording, Peter Clancy; creative consultant, Robyn Wells; stunts, Grant Page. Reviewed at Hoyts screening room, Sydney, Aug. 20, 1992. Running time: **109 MIN.**

Jean Skilling	Lorna Lesley
Natalie	Helen Jones
Wiley	Robyn Nevin
Strickland	Bogdan Koca
Col. Webber	Stephen Leeder
Peach	Harold Hopkins
Eric	Donal Gibson
Peter	Hugh Keays-Byrne
Ruth	Kris McQuade
Ruby	Jennifer Claire
Mr. Wilson	Jack Thompson

Also with: Arianthe Galani, Maya Sheridan, Gosia Dobrowolska, Tim Burns, Ralph Cotterill, Vincent Gill, Phillip Gordon, Bobby Noble, Danny Adcock, Sam Toomey, Lee Lin Chin.

"**R**esistance," produced by a collective of some 70 film people on a remote location (Narrabri in New South Wales), emerges as a visually handsome, action-packed thriller about a popular uprising against a military takeover in an unspecified country.

The film has a surfeit of principal characters and lacks a personal vision, but contains a generous amount of suspense and action, plus an upbeat ending. It should do decent mainstream theatrical business Down Under, and attract some distrib and video interest elsewhere, especially in territories where physical action pics don't have to be mindless.

One of the problems inherent in any collective situation is the impossibility of an individual p.o.v. being allowed to shape the material. The large cast of top-name Australian actors (some, like Jack Thompson and Gosia Dobrowolska, just in for pointless cameos) are forced to jostle to make their roles in the production clear. Simply too many characters vie for attention.

However, before long things settle down into a classical action formula in which working class types and native people combine to overthrow an oppressive military occupation. The role played by women in winning the struggle could spark female interest.

The time is the present, and the striking landscape, lushly photographed for the wide screen by Sally Bongers (whose previous work was on Jane Campion's acclaimed "Sweetie") is wheat country dominated by a mountain range. Most of the accents are decidedly Australian, but the native people are not Australian aborigines — they'd look more at home in Central America.

A Chinese newsreader reports that the country is on the verge

of collapse, that an "internal war" is taking place in the cities and a state of emergency has been declared. The trouble spreads to this remote part of the country when a military force arrives to establish law and order.

Technically, "Resistance" is fine, with convincingly cluttered sets, well-executed stunts and action scenes, and a solid score by Davood A. Tabrizi. Pic has a solid message about the dangers of a right-wing society out of control, and there's a timeless feel to the story, which could take place almost anywhere. But it's basically an action film, and will succeed or fail on that level.

— *David Stratton*

LA PETITE AMIE D'ANTONIO
(ANTONIO'S GIRLFRIEND)
(FRENCH)

An MKL Distribution release of a Cinq et Cinq Films/Ahora Film co-production with the participation of the Upper Normandy Regional Assn. for Cinema, Procirep, GAN, Canal Plus and the CNC. Produced by Jean-Christophe Colson. Directed, written by Manuel Poirier. Camera (color), Nara Keo Kosal; editor, Herve Schneid; music, CharlElie Couture; sound, Jean-Paul Bernard; mixing, Gerard Rousseau, Paul Bertault; associate producer, Anne Rusco. Reviewed at 14 Julliet Odeon cinema, Paris, Oct. 24, 1992. Running time: **101 MIN.**

Claudie	Hélène Foubert
Antonio	Sergi Lopez
Mother	Florence Giorgetti
Evelyn	Corine Darmon
Father	Guy Pierre Mineur
Marc	Laurent Arnal

Scripter-helmer Manuel Poirier's touching feature debut follows a floundering young woman gradually rescued from uncertainty and depression by a persistent boyfriend. Down-to-earth thesping and perfect narrative pitch rank the unassuming pic with the best of Gallic b.f./g.f. fare.

Deft structure lets the viewer learn about troubled Claudie (Hélène Foubert) at the same pace as does Antonio (Sergi Lopez), the Spanish immigrant construction worker who falls for her. Straightforward Antonio is willing to love Claudie, problems and all, but wants to understand how she ended up in residential mental therapy.

Pic captures the spontaneous joys and awkward pauses in male/female and familial relationships. Although Claudie's stepfather is a black man from Martinique, Antonio is a Catalonian immigrant, and her step-sister Bab-

ette is mulatto, the multiracial aspect of the family is put across with refreshing, matter-of-fact candor. Societal discrimation has little or nothing to do with Claudie's problems. Instead, the endearingly mopey kleptomaniac is haunted by an unresolved family incident.

Thesps, especially the young leads, are top-notch. Quirky folkster CharlElie Couture's thoughtful score is just right. Evocative lensing plays up dreary yet scenic overcast Normandy.

One modest feature isn't enough to say for sure, but Poirier, who made award-winning shorts in the mid-'80s, could do for working-class French people what Ken Loach and Mike Leigh have done in their tender and convincing portrayals of folks across the Channel.

— *Lisa Nesselson*

KRUMMERNE
(THE CRUMBS)
(DANISH)

A Krumme ApS production in collaboration with the Danish Film Institute. Produced by Regner Grasten. Directed by Sven Methling. Screenplay, John Olsen. Camera (color), Peter Roos; art direction, Viggo Bentzon; music, Michael Hardinger, Rasmus Schwenger. Reviewed at Palads multiplex, Copenhagen, March 6, 1992. Running time: **88 MIN.**

Krumme	Laus Höybye
Father	Dick Kaysöe
Mother	Karen-Lise Mynster
Boris	Peter Schröder
Ivan	Jarl Friis Mikkelsen

Also with: Line Kruse, Lukas Forchhammer, Buster Larsen, Elin Reimer, Sonja Oppenhagen, Kai Lövring.

This unassuming low-budget family film has become the "Home Alone" of Danish cinema; the exploits of the boy Krumme is similarly themed, good-natured fun.

The boy and his noisy but tightly knit family move into an old, ramshackle house where Krumme becomes entangled with a Laurel & Hardy-esque team of bankrobbers who have hidden their loot in the cellar. Pic contains a number of simple but appealing slapstick routines, and veteran helmer Sven Methling proves he can still turn out a nifty little comedy.

Young headliner Laus Höybye has become Denmark's Macauley Culkin and benefits from the solid support of the team of grown-up thesps on display. — *Peter Risby Hansen*

BUTTERSCOTCH AND CHOCOLATE

A Lange & Associates presentation of a Rickey Hendon production. Executive producer, Darlene Williams. Produced, written by Rickey Hendon. Directed by Nate Grant. Camera (color), Ron Courtney; editor, Rocco Labellarte; music, Hendon, Wayne Cannady; production design, Michael Greene; sound, Jack Burkhardt; associate producer, Carnell Garrett. Reviewed at Chestnut Station Theaters, Chicago, Nov. 4, 1992. MPAA Rating: PG-13. Running time: **87 MIN.**
Chocolate . . . . Rickey Hendon
Butterscotch . . . . Tony Alcantar
Big Mama . . . . E. Faye Butler
Sweetness . . . . Sheveta Carter
Lolita . . . . Adrian Green
Akbar . . . . Ernesto Borges Jr.

First feature from producer-writer Rickey Hendon is low-budget all the way, a hopeless prospect for b.o. success.

While Hendon displays some glimmers of talent as a writer, he needs to work on narrative coherence. Pic concerns two bumbling reporters named Butterscotch (Tony Alcantar) and Chocolate (Hendon) who are told to find a major scoop and deliver it to the newspaper within 24 hours or face dismissal.

From here, pic deteriorates into a chaotic jumble of plots. Among the key threads in Hendon's yarn is Butterscotch and Chocolate's efforts to get the story behind the abduction of the son of an African potentate.

Also thrown into the story are various romantic liaisons and criminal shenanigans that go nowhere and lend nothing of note. When the pic shines at all it is in the comedic scenes at Big Mama's Pork & Pea restaurant, a lively hangout for celebrity lookalikes, sequences full of wonderful, campy humor helmer Nate Grant does a good job of capturing.

Though pic concludes on an upbeat note, it is a struggle to remain involved to the end. Acting credits are uneven; Hendon should not have starred; Tony Alcantar is livelier, but can't get beyond the script's limitations.

Production values are poor all around.
— *Lewis Lazare*

LES AMIES DE MA FEMME
(MY WIFE'S GIRLFRIENDS)
(FRENCH)

A Pan-Européene release of a PCC Prods./TF-1 Films Prod./M-6 Films/FCC/PXP Prods. co-production with the participation of Canal Plus. Executive producer, François Galfré. Produced by Patrick Godeau. Directed, written by Didier Van Cauwelaert, from Philippe Adler's novel. Camera (color), Martial Thury; editor, Yann Dedet; music, Also Frank; set design, Valérie Grall; costumes, Sophie Marcou, Sylvie Marcou; sound, Gernard Bats. Reviewed at UGC Odeon cinema, Paris, Nov. 9, 1992. Running time: **84 MIN.**
Albert . . . . Michel Leeb
Victoire . . . . Christine Boisson
Marguerite . . . . Dominique Lavanant
Marie-Jean . . . . . . Catherine Arditi
Hélène . . . . Françoise Dorner
Béatrice . . . . Nadia Farès
Edmée . . . . Anne Kessler
Also with: Françoise Christophe, Bernard Alane, Fabienne Guyon.

An okay cast is wasted on contrived situations in an unsubtle comedy that never rises above TV sitcom caliber. First film helmed by novelist/playwright/screenwriter Didier Van Cauwelaert is tube fodder for undemanding viewers.

High-powered TV news exec Albert (Michel Leeb), 40, and his wife Victoire (Christine Boisson), 30, are stupendously compatible and deliriously happy. But Victoire is constantly on call for her five neurotic girlfriends, professionals fruitlessly searching for suitable male companionship.

When Albert loses his job, the five women — heretofore unwelcome intruders — keep his morale up and aid his job search.

The script sports an uncomfortably high quotient of jokes about gay men and shows scant compassion for Victoire's unlikely crew of female friends: an airline pilot subject to depression, a simultaneous translator who eats compulsively, a suicidal shrink, a frigid antique dealer and an easy-to-bed single mom who sells real estate.

There are a few laughs and shrewd observations along the way, but behavior is forced and improbable right up until the fairy tale happy ending. Helmer opts for frenetic pacing and broad caricatures where a lighter tough might have better conveyed the theme of generosity in friendship.
— *Lisa Nesselson*

JÖNSSON LIGAN & DEN SVARTA DIMANTEN
(THE JÖNSSON GANG & THE BLACK DIAMOND)
(SWEDISH)

A Sandrews presentation of a Sandrews & Tonefilm production. Executive producers, Klas Olofsson, Örjan Eström. Produced by Ingemar Ejve, Katinka Faragó. Directed by Hasåke Gabrielsson. Screenplay, Gabrielsson, Rolf Börjlind; story, Gabrielsson, Ejve. Camera (color), Rolf Lindström, Lars Karlsson; editor, Roger Sellberg; music, Thomas Lindahl; production design, Stig Boquist; costumes, Hedvid Andér; sound, Bo Persson, Lars Rechlin. Reviewed at Olympia Cinema, Stockholm, Oct. 26, 1992. Running time: **102 MIN.**
With: Ulf Brunnberg, Björn Gustafson, Peter Haber, Birgitta Andersson, Elias Ringquist, Björn Granath, Pontus Gustafson, Per Grunder.

Sixth entry in the popular comedy-series about a bumbling but always successful gang of crooks is entertaining enough to be a commercial hit in Sweden, but it has little chance of fumbling to similar success in other countries.

After the actor who previously played the gangleader ankled, the producers this time introduce a new character. As Dr. M.A. Busé, Peter Haber again shows why praise is heaped on him in Scandi circles: He makes the character work in the most outlandish circumstances.

The doc is forced to forsake medicine and become a crook, using the "criminal testament" — another nod to the character's Fritz Langian origins — of the now mentally deficient original leader. The other leading actors do their work flawlessly. Tech credits are okay; the action and chases are of the G-rated kind.
— *Gunnar Rehlin*

TO RENDER A LIFE
(DOCU)

A James Agee Film Project release. Produced by Ross Spears, Silvia Kersusan. Directed by Spears. Written by Kersusan. Camera (color), Spears. Reviewed at Film Forum, N.Y. Nov. 12, 1992. Running time: **88 MIN.**

"To Render a Life" succeeds as a portrait of a poverty-stricken rural family in present-day America. Director Ross Spears, by letting his film ruminate on the ethical issues involved, attempts to link his effort to the classic James Agee/Walker Evans 1930s photobook, "Let Us Now Praise Famous Men," an effort that is more provocative than accomplished. Despite limitations, pic should be welcome on public TV and in educational forums.

The subjects of the film, the Glass family of Virginia, labor to eke out a living on husband Obea's off-and-on work as a furniture refinisher. Wife Alice has left her job due to poor health, but to supplement Obea's wages does most of the work on the small family farm. Her own children grown, Alice also nurtures an adopted daughter, Anita. Although Obea's earnings are sub-minimum wage and his job offers no benefits, the family is not entitled to government aid.

Instead of commemorating the Glasses as symbols of the downtrodden, Spears lets the family cross the apparent cultural chasm, as Alice speaks earnestly about readily identifiable hopes and goals, and her resolve not to be felled by a bout with cancer and to raise her foster daughter.

Spears enlists commentary from such writers as Robert Coles, Howell Raines and filmmaker Frederick Wiseman both on the Agee/Evans book and the nature of documenting the plight of the poor, but the issue of exploiting the victim in such work is talked around rather than shown. — *Fred Lombardi*

COMPASSION IN EXILE:
THE LIFE OF THE 14th DALAI LAMA
(DOCU)

A Lemle Pictures production, in association with Central Independent Television, U.K. Produced, directed, written by Mickey Lemle. Camera (color), Buddy Squires; editor, Spiro C. Lampros; music, Philip Glass; associate producer, J. Michael Stremel. Reviewed on videcassette, L.A. Running time: **57 MIN.**

Mickey Lemle's intelligent, sensitive docu befits the noble stature and charismatic personality of Tibet's exiled spiritual leader, who won the 1989 Nobel Peace Prize. The devastating chronicle of the Chinese atrocities in Tibet since 1950 and the Western world's "conspiracy of silence" make this a timely item for film fests, public TV, cable and video.

"Compassion in Exile" provides a fascinating portrait of the peasant who at age 3 was recognized as the reincarnation of the 13th

Dalai Lama. Combining histori-cal and cultural footage of Tibet and interviews with the Dalai Lama's brothers and sisters, docu offers a somber look at a culture on the verge of extinction. Geno-cide, population transfers, steril-ization and other human rights violations have reduced Tibetans to an "ethnic minority" in their own land, destroying a religious heritage along with a people.

At the docu's center is an illu-minating interview with the Dalai Lama, who comes across as a compassionate, witty, even funny man who likes to giggle. Dressed in a red robe, he discusses his nonviolent doctrine. "Sometimes I lose my temper," he admits, "but afterwards I become more compassionate." His wish, after Tibet regains its freedom, is to become an "ordinary" monk and engage in "rigorous meditation."

Pic's production values are first-rate and overall effect is testi-mony to the indefatigable spirit of a leader. — *Emanuel Levy*

SEXES FAIBLES! (THE WEAKER SEXES!) (FRENCH)

A UGC release of a Gérard Mital Prods./TF-1 Films/M-6 Films co-pro-duction with the participation of Canal Plus & La Region Languedoc-Roussil-lon. Produced by Gérard Mital. Direct-ed, written by Serge Meynard, based on Tom Sharpe's novel "Blott on the Land-scape." Camera (color), Henri Habans, Jean-Paul Meurisse; editor, Philippe He-issler; music, Alexandre Desplat; set design, Emile Ghigo; costumes, Valen-tine Breton des Loys; sound, Roger Di Ponio, Gerard Lamps; assistant direc-tor, Pascal Chaumeil. Reviewed at George V cinema, Paris, Oct. 13, 1992. Running time: **87 MIN.**
Sébastien Sébastian . . François Cluzet
Maud Le Chesnay . Valerie Lemercier
Gilles Le Chesnay . . . . André Wilms
Blott . . . . Marc Berman
Mortheau . . . . Michel Aumont
Also with: Isabelle Nanty, Didier Be-nureau, Sarah Bertrand.

A crass one-joke comedy that shows traces of inventive-ness before lapsing into strained nonsense, this tale of property war between spouses whose marriage remains un-consummated after 10 years will yield a few yucks from mid-dle-aged TV and video auds after luring in big-screen view-ers, misled by an otherwise talented cast.

Faux-Hitchcock score, stop-action animation and closeup of mating snails in the opening cred-its promise a flippant, stylish pic. But the story, transposed to France from the novel's English

setting, quickly grows vulgar and tiresome.

Maud (Valerie Lemercier) has been married for a decade to Gilles (André Wilms), the town mayor, but they have never had sex. Their fabulous mansion has been in her family for centuries but, under French law, if she files for divorce he'll inherit eve-rything. As the French railways are about to pick a new route for a high-speed train line, Gilles is determined to have the house razed for the choo-choo, so he can collect a hefty sum in compensa-tion. Maud is determined to both save her property and get laid.

Dippy French rail official Sébas-tien Sébastian (François Cluzet) walks into this hornet's nest of mutual animosity and has to deal with horny Maud and venal hubby. Pic's only consistently amusing aspect is Alexandre Des-plat's score, which toys with classic suspense and film noir moods. Tech credits are all okay.
— *Lisa Nesselson*

LONDON FEST

LA CONTRE-ALLÉE (BOTH SIDES OF THE STREET) (FRENCH)

A Baccara Prods./Les Films Ariane/ TF1 Films production. (Intl. sales: Revcom, Paris.) Produced by Chantal Perrin. Directed by Isabel Sébastian. Screenplay by Sébastian, Jean-Paul Lilien-feld, Alain David. Camera (Eastmancol-or, Fujicolor), Willy Kurant; editor, Ray-monde Guyot; music, Didier Vasseur; art direction, Claude Lenoir; costume design, Florence Desouches, Frédéri-que Santerre; sound, Bernard Bats, Ber-nard Rochut; assistant director, Daniel Ravoux. Previewed at BFI screening room, London, Nov. 4, 1992. (In London Film Festival.) Running time: **83 MIN.**
Lilas . . . . Caroline Cellier
Marie . . . . Jennifer Covillault
Mme. Yvette . . . . Jacqueline Maillan
Pierre . . . . Massimo Ghini
Daniel . . . . Jacques Perrin
Véronique . . . Pénélope Schellenberg
Caroline . . . . Chantal Perrin
Manu . . . . . . Brigitte Chamarande
Lola . . . . Stéphanie Murat

Bright, light and easy on the eye, "Both Sides of the Street" handles a delicate theme with style and finesse: a Parisian pre-teen learning about the birds and the bees from a friendly hooker. Pic lacks the star power to score in foreign marts but makes an entertaining item for foreign-lingo tube slots.

Pic could hit trouble in territo-ries sensitive to the depiction of

underage sexuality. But there's nothing exploitative about the portrayal, and visually the film is always discreet.

The main character is Marie (Jennifer Covillault), a tomboy-ish moppet on the threshold of womanhood. When her photog father (Jacques Perrin) goes away on an assignment, she's left most-ly alone.

One day, she's knocked down in the road by Lilas (Caroline Cellier), a glamorous pro. Some time later, the two start to form a friendship when Marie spots her soliciting outside her apart-ment. The childless Lilas treats her like a niece and the kid learns an early thing or two about fe-male sexuality.

Helmer Isabel Sébastian, in her first feature after a career in spots and shorts, confidently walks the thin line between cute-ness and sleaze. The script's thin structure is kept afloat with witty and flavorsome dialogue and easy playing, especially by the two leads, especially young Covillault who, tomboyish to start with, handles the difficult role of the kid with a natural swagger. No-table are a tricky scene of her dressing like a hooker and solic-iting in the street, and an explor-atory attempt at seduction of her father's friend (Massimo Ghini).

Other roles are all in tune and tech credits are all A-class, with Willy Kurant's lensing and Didi-er Vasseur's pleasant score add-ing a final coat of gloss.
— *Derek Elley*

REDHEADS (AUSTRALIAN)

A Roxy Films production in associa-tion with Australian Film Finance Corp. Executive producer, Danny Vendram-ini. Produced by Richard Mason. Direct-ed, written by Vendramini, based on Rosie Scott's play. Camera (Eastman-color), Steven Mason; editor, Marc Van Buuren; music, Felicity Foxx; produc-tion design, Ross Wallace; sound, Max Bowring; assistant director, Bob How-ard; casting, Liz Mullinar. Reviewed at AFI Cinema, Sydney, Aug. 5, 1992. (In London Film Festival.) Running time: **100 MIN.**
Lucy . . . . Claudia Karvan
Diana Ferraro . Catherine McClements
Simon Dewhurst . Alexander Petersens
James Brewster . . . . Mark Henbrow
Terry Quigley . . . . Anthony Phelan
Jack McCoy . . . . Iain Gardiner
Zelda . . . . Sally McKenzie
Carolyn . . . . Jennifer Flowers

Danny Vendramini's first feature is a frustrating mix of good and bad, a fitfully intrigu-ing whodunit with a sock per-formance from Claudia Karvan

in the lead but an incoherent and illogical plot. Theatrical pro-spects look dull, but video shelf life's bright.

Karvan, the former child thesp who blossomed a couple of years ago in "The Big Steal," gives a strong portrayal as an amoral street kid who witnesses the mur-der of her lawyer lover (Mark Hembrow) and finds herself hunt-ed by the killer.

In the film's intriguing open-ing, she comes on to the appar-ently reluctant Hembrow and starts a video camera going as they have sex. She manages to hide when an intruder blasts the shyster, but doesn't see the kil-ler's face.

The terrified Karvan seeks help from a state-appointed at-torney, Catherine McClements, and the two women, both red-heads, team up to track down the murderer.

Vendramini and cinematogra-pher Steven Mason ("Strictly Ball-room") contribute some classy, inventive visuals to pump adre-naline into this initially promis-ing yarn and the two lead ac-tresses enter into the spirit of the thing.

Unfortunately, these quality elements are undermined by the ultimately creaky plot and some inadequate supporting perform-ances; neither Alexander Pe-tersens, as McClements' sleazy boyfriend, nor Anthony Phelan, as a slippery cop, seem comforta-ble in their roles, undermining what might have been an excit-ing thriller, with dubious box office returns the result.
— *David Stratton*

FROM HOLLYWOOD TO HANOI (DOCU-16M)

A Friendship Bridge Prods. produc-tion. (Intl. sales: Friendship Bridge, N.Y.) Produced, directed, written by Tiana Thi Thanh Nga. Camera (Duart color, 16m), Michael Dodds, Bruce Dorfman, Jamie Maxtone-Graham; supervising edi-tor, Pam Wise; editor, Roger Schulte; music, Allan Gus; sound, Gordon J. Grin-berg, Zeborah Tidwell. Reviewed at London Film Festival, Nov. 12, 1992. (Also in Telluride, Chicago, Hawaii fests.). Running time: **78 MIN.**

A rapid-fire blend of per-sonal odyssey and historical excavation, "From Hollywood to Hanoi" packs as many punch-es as it leaves questions unan-swered. Lively docu about an expatriate's return to her Viet-namese homeland is a natural for special-event screenings and cable outings.

The last time Hollywood visited Hanoi was in the Jane Fonda-Tom Hayden hour-long docu "Introduction to the Enemy," lensed in 1974 by Haskell Wexler. This time the Tinseltown rep is Saigon-born actress-entertainer Tiana Thi Thanh Nga, 31, who moved Stateside in 1966 and played chopsocky avengers in pics like "Catch the Heat" (with Rod Steiger) under the moniker Tiana Alexandra.

As the daughter of a former South Vietnamese press director and niece of a defense minister, she rates entrees to party bigwigs, including Le Duc Tho (Kissinger's counterpart at the Paris peace talks, also in Fonda's pic) and ex-premier Pham Van Dong. In a carefully graded snub, these two talk to her in French rather than Vietnamese.

Beyond loaded observations on the quality of life and a fleeting remark that the 20-year-old U.S. trade embargo seems to have been "not very effective," the pic steers clear of heavy-duty analysis. That's just as well, as Tiana's forte is more self-promo.

Tiana's search for her roots falls prey to the same unanswered questions and cultural head-butting as several other similar docus by Amerasians. But there's a brutal honesty in Tiana's camera-junkie approach that pays dividends both ways. She's unblinking in her choice of footage of the war itself, victims of Agent Orange, Eurasian flotsam left behind, and a Siamese twin in a Saigon hospital with whom she identifies. She's equally unblinking when, in full Hollywood gear, she meets up with a tearful, long lost aunt — and keeps the camera rolling and her own emotions under control.

Pic packs its biggest punches when the historical and personal collide in this way. During her visit to My Lai, site of the w.k. massacre of locals by G.I.s, Tiana asks a woman survivor why she can't look her in the face as she describes events. The woman replies, "When I told you the first time, I saw no one."

Technically, the film is okay, with excellently chosen archive footage. The single journey portrayed is actually a compilation of four trips from the 12 the filmer has so far made between Jan. '88 and late '91.

— Derek Elley

XUESE QINGCHEN
(BLOODY MORNING)
(CHINESE)

A Peking Film Studio production. (Intl. sales: Era Intl., Hong Kong.) Produced by Liao Xiaogeng, Tian Yuping. Directed by Li Shaohong. Screenplay, Xiao Mao, Li, from Gabriel García Márquez's novel "Chronicle of a Death Foretold." Camera (color), Zeng Nianping; editor, Zhou Xinxia; music, Meng Weidong; art direction, Shi Jiandu; costume design, Liu Fang; assistant director, Li Xiawan. Reviewed at London Film Festival, Nov. 11, 1992. (Also at Locarno, Toronto and Nantes fests.) Running time: **103 MIN.**
Li Hongxing . . . . Kong Lin
Qiangguo . . . . Gong Zhaohui
Mingguang . . . . Hu Yajie
Li Pingwa . . . . Zhao Jun
Li Gouwa . . . . Xie Yan

A slow-burning tale of rural Chinese passions and senseless murder, "Bloody Morning" is a clever reworking of Gabriel García Márquez's Colombian-set novel "Chronicle of a Death Foretold." Quality item could meet theatrical resistance due to a mass of earlier rural-set Chinese movies, but should slice off some specialized tube sales beyond the fest trail.

Compared with the lavish 1987 version by Francesco Rosi, this is a small-scale, visually bleak, connoisseur item. But story's transfer works well: Rural Chinese morality is a perfect mirror for macho Latin equivalents.

Opening has the investigator quizzing villagers about the death of young teacher Mingguang (Hu Yajie), found dead in an alley early one morning. Two brothers confess to the deed, and flashbacks interweaved with the present story limn the detailed truth.

Pic is a whydunit rather than a whodunit and, despite the complex relationships, turns on a simple nut: One of the brothers, Li Pingwa (Zhao Jun), reckoned the teacher deflowered their sister Hongxing (Kong Lin), who was best friends with the teacher's fiancée.

The movie is slow to establish a rhythm, and most viewers will spend the first half hour sorting out who's who in the complex web of relationships. The smoldering atmosphere starts to catch light during the middle section as the plot clears. The final 20 minutes are a tour de force of graded suspense and construction, as fate takes its inevitable course.

The themes of ignorance, pov-

erty and feudal morality —heightened by making the victim a teacher — combine powerfully in the final murder, as the villagers stand around like an impotent ancient Greek chorus as the teacher is hacked to death.

In only her second solo feature, femme helmer Li Shaohong, 37, turns in a class act. Performances are generally low-key and unaffected, with only pretty local starlet Kong bringing a touch of glamour to the proceedings. The soundtrack, including off-screen effects, is subtle and above average, with none of the usual hype. The English subtitles, vital to understanding motivations and relationships, could be improved.

The movie finished lensing in mid-'90 and was released locally in spring '91. Nervous Chinese authorities delayed its foreign release until this fall, by which time Li had already completed her third pic, "Family Portrait" (aka "A Man at Forty").

— Derek Elley

THE EXECUTION PROTOCOL
(BRITISH-DOCU-16M)

A Worldview Pictures/West End Films production, in association with Discovery Networks. (Intl. sales: Producers Services Group, London.) Executive producer, Paul Baker. Produced by Mitch Wood, Stephen Trombley. Directed by Trombley. Camera (color, 16m), Paul Gibson; editor, Peter Miller; music, Robert Lockhart; sound, John McCormack. Reviewed at London Film Festival, Nov. 11, 1992. Running time: **87 MIN.**

A chilling look at state execution procedures, Missouri-style, "The Execution Protocol" looks sure to raise debate on webs tough enough to take it. The morally confrontational pic is also a natural candidate for fests and special events.

N.Y.-born, U.K.-based docu-maker Stephen Trombley is best known Stateside for "Caffe Lena," which aired on PBS in 1990. Here he turns his unblinking lens on the maximum security Potosi Correctional Center, 65 miles southwest of St. Louis, and its lethal-injection system of capital punishment.

When Trombley visited, the jail housed 79 death row inmates, three of whom are featured in detail. Film's most disturbing aspect is its moral ambiguity that comes from placing both inmates and officials under a common umbrella: Both are responsible for

taking human lives.

The contradictions in Trombley's approach mount as the pic progresses. The trio of inmates interviewed emerge as reasoning, rational human beings (their crimes are, signally, not described); prison officials, however, come off mostly as robotic bureaucrats.

Trombley also serves up some cold cuts of background. Locals, it seems, petitioned for Potosi, as the area's mining industry was on the skids: One prison official proudly calls the center a "non-pollutive industry" providing valuable employment.

The most ghoulish sections feature the lethal injection machine's inventor — a self-styled expert in "execution technology" — who takes the viewer through the planning and operation of the death-dealing gizmo.

Visually, pic is always interesting, with a clinical feel to Paul Gibson's 16m photography and avoidance of talking-head setups. Robert Lockhart's atmospheric underscoring adds shape and cohesion.

At the screening caught, the pic drew frequent chuckles from the fest audience at prison officials' humorless self-importance and rotund vocabulary.

— Derek Elley

KUANG
(RIPPLES ACROSS STAGNANT WATER)
(CHINESE-HONG KONG)

A Skai Film Prods. (Hong Kong)/ Emei Film Studio (China) production. (Intl. sales: Shu Kei's Creative Workshop.) Produced by Skai Film, Emei Film Studio. Directed by Ling Zifeng. Screenplay, Han Lanfang. Camera, Sun Yongtian; editors, Pan Zufei, Li Yuanyuan. Reviewed at Vancouver Intl. Film Festival, Oct. 13, 1992. (In London Film Festival.) Running time: **91 MIN.**
With: Xu Qing, You Yong, Zhao Jun, Cheng Xi, Yao Jianguo.
(Mandarin dialogue; English and Chinese subtitles)

T here's something for almost everyone in "Ripples Across Stagnant Water": war, politics, religion, sex (steamy by Chinese standards) and turn-of-the-century feminism. Pic, rich in historical detail and emotional struggle, follows a young peasant woman whose rags-to-independence story will resonate with modern auds.

Enigmatic, strong-faced Xu Qing plays a young 1890s village woman who accepts an arranged marriage to a mildly retarded but well-connected shopkeeper who will take her to a larger town. Once there, she fancies her husband's cousin and benefactor, a powerful fellow with shady dealings around the province.

Eventually, they start living together, right under hubby's nose, but problems — the looming Boxer Rebellion, meddlesome Christian converts, and a vengance-minded business rival — overwhelm their shaky idyll.

Helmer Ling Zifeng, now 75, has made films since 1949, but his newest pic (based on a popular mid-'30s novel) is completely free of ideological taint. As in his '80s efforts "Border Town" and "Chun Tao," Ling is most interestd in depicting the struggle of small fry against major tides; the mix of period minutiae and universal passion is thoroughly engaging (although a few breaks in the storyline indicate more cutting than was necessary).

Tech values are fine, if not quite up to "Ju Dou"/"Raise the Red Lantern" standards. Still, same fans will enjoy "Ripples Across Stagnant Water" and women, in particular, should appreciate the finale: When the tale's travails wind down as the 20th century begins, the heroine is virtually the only character stronger than when she started.
— *Ken Eisner*

GROLLE D'ORO

GANGSTERS
(ITALIAN)

An Artisti Associati release of a Gianni Minervini, Silvio & Anna Maria Clementelli, Franco Cristaldi, Franco Committeri, RAI-2 presentation of an AMA Film, Clesi Cinematografica, Cristaldifilm, Massfilm production in association with RAI-2. (Intl. sales: Sacis.) Produced by Minervini. Directed by Massimo Guglielmi. Screenplay, Claudio Lizza, Federico Pacifici. Camera (Cinecittà color), Paolo Rossato; editor, Nino Baragli; music, Armando Trovajoli; art direction, Massimo Spano; costumes, Enrica Biscossi; sound, Tiziano Crotti. Reviewed at Grolle d'Oro Awards, Saint-Vincent (Italy), Nov. 1, 1992. Running time: **110 MIN.**
Giulio . . . . Ennio Fantastichini
Umberto . . . . . . Giuseppe Cederna
Evelina . . . . Isabella Ferrari
Enrico . . . . Giulio Scarpati
Franco . . . . Luca Lionello
Bava . . . . Ivano Marescotti
Nicola . . . . Claudio Bigagli
Also with: Maria Monti, Mattia Sbragia.

Seldom-covered deeds of vigilante resistance groups in post-World War II Italy pro-

vide engrossing fodder for "Gangsters," a well-played drama of moral dilemmas and tested loyalties. Pic has had a troubled path with local distribution, but it may prove more of a draw offshore and could work in markets not averse to solidly conventional Euro fare.

A trio of partisans led by unpredictably edgy black marketeer Giuseppe Cederna continue their anti-Fascist wartime exploits to the embarrassment of the once-supportive Communist Party. They lure their jaded ex-commander (Ennio Fantastichini) back into the fray with the prospect of eliminating a long-targeted Nazi official.

After the hit, Cerdena impulsively mows down two carabiniere officers who happen upon the scene and the heat is turned up. Increasingly entwined with a morphine-addicted floozy (Isabella Ferrari) at his seedy flophouse, Fantastichini grows fearful for the liberty he's just beginning to appreciate. With persistent Party messenger Ivano Marescotti breathing down his neck, Fantastichini is cornered into betraying his comrades.

Director Massimo Guglielmi's competent but anonymous storytelling lacks the dynamism a bolder helmer might have given it. Weaknesses are muffled, however, by able work from a fine crop of high-profile players.

Technically tidy pic's period feel is enhanced by Paolo Rossato's sharply sober lensing, and by good use of Armando Trovajoli's music and '40s tunes.
— *David Rooney*

ULTIMO RESPIRO
(FINAL BLOW)
(ITALIAN)

A CDI release of a Clemi Cinematografica production. Produced by Giovanni Di Clemente. Directed by Felice Farina. Screenplay, Sandro Veronesi, Farina, from Aurelio Grimaldi's story. Camera (Cinecittà color), Luca Bigazzi; editor, Roberto Schiavone; music, Tommaso Vittorini; art direction, Antonio Formica; costumes, Cinzia Lucchetti; sound, Hubrecht Nijhuis. Reviewed at Grolle d'Oro Awards, Saint-Vincent (Italy), Nov. 1, 1992. Running time: **104 MIN.**
Alfonso . . . . Francesco Benigno
Margherita . . . . . . Federica Moro
Tony . . . . Massimo Dapporto

"Final Blow" takes the bruising backdrop of Sicilian city life of a run of Italo pics and fuels it with film noirish emotional intrigue. Despite a

hard-to-swallow central relationship and a big casting miscalculation, it remains a persuasive mood piece thanks to Felice Farina's controlled directing. Pic's right for TV exposure.

A well-heeled, married counselor (Massimo Dapporto) turns up at his seaside villa for a latenight tryst with sleek Federica Moro and interrupts young street thug Francesco Benigno rummaging for cash. A menacing confrontation is cut short when Moro arrives, knocking Benigno out cold with some adroit wielding of household porcelain.

Unable to turn him in for fear of exposing their relationship, the lovers patch his wounds and pack him off with a palmful of cash next morning. Back in the grim confines of his seedy housing project, Benigno is goaded by his roughneck cohorts into returning to the scene.

Eavesdropping on the couple, he learns the reason for their lenience and begins making individual demands on each without the other's knowledge. A murky attraction binds the girl to silence, and his violent sexual impulses give way to romantic ambition. He attempts to go straight, taking a menial job teed up by Dapporto, but his hostile chums provide obstacles.

An improbable, but predictably rosy conclusion appears to loom, but the intelligent script pulls the rug out from under aud expectations, blocking Benigno with a cruel trick of fate.

Pic has minor problems aligning plot's romantic focus with the street-gang factor. Some scenes jar incongruously, and the ruffians' overacting doesn't help. But the insurmountable hurdle is Benigno's one-note tough boy characterization.

Other leads are fine, and tech aspects are smoothly executed, aside from some sound glitches which make dialogue occasionally hard to hear.
— *David Rooney*

SABATO ITALIANO
(ITALIAN SATURDAY)
(ITALIAN)

A Lucky Red Distribuzione release of a Numero Uno Intl. production. Produced by Claudio Bonivento. Directed by Luciano Manuzzi. Screenplay, Marco Tullio Giordana, Manuzzi. Camera (color), Fabio Cianchetti; editor, Osvaldo Bargero; music, Oscar Prudente; art direction, Luigi Pelizzo; costumes, Grazia Colombini; sound, Amadeo Casati. Re-

viewed at Grolle d'Oro Awards, Saint-Vincent (Italy), Oct. 31, 1992. Running time: **86 MIN.**
Marina . . . . Francesca Neri
Marzio . . . . Mauro Lorusso
Matteo . . . . Marco De Pasquale
Violante . . . . Ivonne Sciò
Angela . . . . Chiara Caselli
Enzo . . . . Massimo Di Cataldo
Ricky . . . . Stefano Dionisi
Danielle . . . . Isabelle Pasco
Boss . . . . Francesco Barilli

Attempting to give a human face to the alarming statistics of weekend revelry smash-ups plaguing Italo roads in recent years, "Italian Saturday" is a fast-paced pic with many prime moments, but it too often struggles due to weak script and poorly drawn characters. Undemanding markets and tube dates seem the way to go.

Contrary to the grave overlying mood, story's best track is the one with the lightest touch. Ignoring her better judgment, a cynical stripper (Francesca Neri) accepts big bucks to bump 'n' grind for a crowd of rowdy preteen boys. As she gets down to bare essentials, the kids' irate mothers arrive and threaten to call the cops. Aided by the show's two junior entrepreneurs, Neri escapes and makes a cross-country dash during which an innocent complicity embraces the unlikely trio. Accordingly padded, caper could have been winning feature material on its own.

Elsewhere, not-so-nuanced writing frequently succumbs to cliché-ridden premises, especially in the femme characters. Isabelle Pasco plays a French beauty whose life is reluctantly wagered by her lover (Francesco Barilli) after losing a poker game. Chiara Caselli and Ivonne Sciò figure as pill-popping thrill-seekers picked up in a disco by two greenhorns in pursuit of an estranged g.f.

Helmer/co-scripter Luciano Manuzzi ties the strands effectively in a conclusion that keeps casualties to a minimum but packs considerable emotional impact for its victims. But the build-up suffers from assembly-line editing that seemingly allocates fixed time slots to the various elements without fluidity.

Performances are uneven. Pasco limits herself to a sustained pout, and Caselli and Sciò are irritatingly one-dimensional. Barilli and Stefano Dionisi as his doomed lackey register as more sensitive presences.
— *David Rooney*

THROUGH THE VEIL OF EXILE
(ISRAELI-DOCU)

Produced by David Benchetrit, Sini Bar-David, Amos Mukadi. Directed by Benchetrit. Camera (color, 16m), Benchetrit; editor, Bar-David; music, Elias Taissir; sound, Shimon Fraiman, Shuki Besht, Shuki Zuta. Reviewed at Israel Film Festival, N.Y., Nov. 1, 1992. Running time: **86 MIN.**
(In English & Arabic with subtitles)

The sensitive feature docu "Through the Veil of Exile" examines the lives of three very different women living in refugee camps in the West Bank and Gaza, showing the personal effects of politics. Indie production by veteran news cameraman David Benchetrit, pic should have TV possibilities.

In contrast to the usual polarized attitudes, "Veil" spotlights individuals who are not only products of local politics but also victims of their own society and its attitudes toward women.

Dalal Abu-Kamar, an unmarried former political activist who spent 12 years in an Israeli prison, lives with a family who daily berate her as an "old maid." Per her mother, she should seek marriage with a wealthy Saudi to lift the family out of poverty.

Mary Khass, a 60-year-old Christian and former member of the Communist party, works to establish dialogue between Israelis and Palestinians and is a refugee by choice. One of her sons has been killed, while the other lives in exile in Egypt. A touching scene shows her shouting greetings to her banished son and grandchildren across a barbed-wire fence on the border.

Finally there is Um-Muhammed, a strikingly independent, illiterate widow who married an older man at age 13 and now supports herself by working for wealthy Palestinians. Bitter with her lot in life, she blames her parents and circumstances, and provides the contrast and texture to the film via her stark life.

Benchetrit's ambitious camera work captures the beauty of the grizzled landscape and frames these women's lives within a world of contrasts: ancient and modern, stark and fertile, crumbling slums and new highrises.

Three years in the making, "Veil" offers a different Israeli view of the Palestinians, not as terrorists, but individuals whose memory lingers long after the projector stops. — *Paul Lenti*

PRIDE AND JOY:
THE STORY OF ALLIGATOR RECORDS
(DOCU-16m)

A Mug-Shot production. Produced, directed, written by Robert Mugge. Camera (color, 16m), Mugge. Reviewed at Denver Intl. Film Festival, Oct. 17, 1992. Running time: **87 MIN.**
With: Bruce Iglauer, Katie Webster, Koko Taylor, Elvin Bishop, Lonnie Brooks, Ronnie Brooks, Bob Koester, Lil' Ed Williams.

With a high-powered stable of musicians, Alligator Records founding father Bruce Iglauer has become a major player among blues recorders. With this house-rockin' concert film, filmmaker Robert Mugge continues his explorations ("Deep Blues," "Saxophone Colossus," "Hawaiian Rainbow") of the U.S. music scene.

White-hot musical numbers demonstrate the versatility of Iglauer's house performers as they kindle fervent response on Alligator's 20th anniversary concert tour, all captured by Mugge's four cameras, focussing on the performers' extravagances.

Iglauer's career and determination are traced from a one-room apartment operation to his current success. Although Iglauer is not shown during concert performances, his enthusiasm is omnipresent.

Performers range from the slyly engaging Lil' Ed Williams to singer Koko Taylor, who makes up in intensity anything lacking in vocal range. Father Lonnie Brooks and son Ronnie Brooks provide generational contrasts.

Non-blues fans may find the numbers monotonous, but the film is completely engaged with its subject. The sound quality is outstanding, and the camerawork brings viewers into immediate contact with the performers.
— *Allen Young*

FEMALE MISBEHAVIOR
(GERMAN-U.S.-DOCU-16m)

A Hyena Films presentation of a Hyena Films production in association with Hamburger Filmburo and Kampnagelfabrik. Produced, directed by Monika Treut. Camera (16mm color), Elfi Mikesch; editor, Renate Merck; sound, Tonike Traum; Reviewed at Toronto Festival of Festivals, Sept. 14, 1992. Running time: **80 MIN.**
With: Carol, Camille Paglia, Annie Sprinkle, Max Valerio.

"Female Misbehavior" is an alternatingly hilarious and deadly serious docu that interviews four outspoken women on subjects ranging from lesbian bondage to "rock 'n' roll" testosterone injections. Pic is a natural for fests, special screenings, art houses and 42nd St.

No-budget political statement is a feature compilation of four shorts, beginning with "Bondage," a relatively dull interview with a self-proclaimed exhibitionist who's into S&M.

Next short, "Annie" is a glimpse into the mind and body parts of ex-porn queen, current performance artist Annie Sprinkle. Zoom and close-up shots of her cervix will (as intended) rile censor boards.

However, it is definitely motor-mouth professor "Dr. Paglia" who steals the film with her "crushing intellect" and taboo-shattering revelations in the third short. "Everyone in the world knows that women are the dominant sex. Everyone knows that, except feminists," per Paglia. Utterly captivating on celluloid, she gives the film an academic angle with a comical twist.

Paglia's a hard act to follow for Max (formerly Anita), a transsexual who rises to the occasion with witticisms about hormone horrors. Max claims testosterone stifles the occassional "good crying jag" and jokes that other men recommend "TV and junk food" as an alternative emotional release.

Candid revelations are attributable to helmer Monika Treut, whose track record includes such pics as "Seduction: The Cruel Woman," "Virgin Machine" and "My Father Is Coming." The two shorts in the latter half of "Female Misbehavior" are some of Treut's most provocative work to date. — *Suzan Ayscough*

OUR TWISTED HERO
· (SOUTH KOREAN)

A Dae Dong Heung Up Co. Ltd. production & presentation. Produced by Do Dong Hwan. Directed by Park Chong Won. Screenplay, Chang Hyun Soo, Rho Hyo Chung based on Yi Mun Yol's novel. Camera (color), Chung Kwang Seok; editor, Lee Kyung Ja; music, Song Byung-joon; production design, Do Yong Woo. Reviewed at Montreal World Film Festival (competition), Aug. 28, 1992. (In Hawaii Intl. Film Festival.) Running time: **119 MIN.**
Mr. Kim . . . . Choe Min-sik
Han Byung-tae . . . . Ko Jung-il
Um Suk-dae . . . . . Hong Kyung-in
Also with: Lee Jin-Sun, Shin Ku, Tae Min-Young.

A superb example of storytelling, "Our Twisted Hero" simplifies complex political structures via the eyes of children subjected to a tyrannical yet likable classmate during the Korean revolution in the early '60s. The plodding pace offers little b.o. potential Stateside, but pic works as a metaphor of twisted dictators and supposed revolutionary saviors.

Told largely in flashback, perspective unfolds via a 40-year-old teacher, Han, who reflects on his youth while en route to a funeral of his communist fifth grade teacher.

With his parents, young idealistic Han had moved from Seoul (where a democratic revolution was unfolding) to a countryside still ripe with hierarchical communist influence. A lazy old teacher permitted class "monitor" Um Suk-dae to rule the students.

After many fruitless attempts to "dethrone" the teen tyrant, star student Han succumbs to Um's control and helps him cheat. When a new teacher, Mr. Kim, "revolutionizes" the class, the new order offers only punishment.

Child actor Ko Jung-il displays depth as Han. His rival, Hong Kyung-in, is equally sweet and sour as the friendly tyrant.

Script and camera cleverly alternate between heroes' p.o.v.'s. Focus on straightforward narrative is a plus for the politically uninitiated. — *Suzan Ayscough*

DADDY AND THE MUSCLE ACADEMY
(FINNISH-DOCU)

A Filmitakomo production, in association with YLE TV2 Documentary. Produced by Kari Paljakka, Alvaro Pardo. Directed, written by Ilppo Pohjola. Camera (color, 16m), Kjell Lagerroos; editor, Jorma Höri; music, Elliot Sharp; sound, Kauko Lindfors, Pekka Karjalainen. Reviewed at Edinburgh Intl. Film Festival, Aug. 20, 1992. (In Toronto, Chicago film festivals.) Running time: **60 MIN.**
With: Tom of Finland, Bob Mizer, Nayland Blake, Durk Dehner, Etienne, Isaac Julien.
(Finnish & English soundtrack)

An exhaustive docu on late gay icon artist Tom of Finland, whose drawings of leather-clad musclebound males influenced names from Fassbinder to Robert Mapplethorpe, "Daddy and the Muscle Academy" should delight its target audience and do well in specialized situations. Tube sales will be limited by pic's graphic male nudity (actual and drawn) and unblinking approach to the fetishistic subject-matter.

Movie is anchored by a series of interviews with Tom of Finland (a.k.a. Touko Laaksonen) himself, prior to his death in Nov. '91, aged 71. The gravel-voiced illustrator talks dispassionately about his primary inspirations: an early obsession with uniforms during WW2 and growing love for the "living" quality of leather.

Influenced by Yank bodybuilding mags of the '50s, he first submitted drawings to Physique Pictorial in 1957, signing them simply "Tom." Mag editor Bob Mizer, knowing only the country they came from, dubbed the artist Tom of Finland. After growing demand during the '60s (especially for more exaggerated figures), in 1973 he finally visited the U.S., and was lionized by a section of the gay community.

Docu's tone is lively and varied, swinging from straightforward interviews with the ascetic figure of Laaksonen himself to plenty of examples of his graphic style, featuring heavily endowed trucker/biker types in fantastic homosexual couplings. Despite the material's explicitness, effect is strangely non-offensive, thanks to a strong vein of humor and the obvious cartoonishness.

More debatable is writer-director Ilppo Pohjola's admixture of footage with real musclebound leather fetishists, plus chintzy voiceovers by American gays declaring "I'm a Tom's man" at regular intervals. Personal testimonies by Yank art critics, and young British director Isaac Julien ("Young Soul Rebels"), are okay but add little.

Pic is technically fine, and immaculately researched on its subject. — *Derek Elley*

RIN
(THE LEGEND OF ICONS)
(RUSSIAN-JAPANESE)

A Will Prods. (Tokyo) co-production with Centaur, Leningrad Film Studio. Directed, written by Rodoh Seji. Camera (color), Vladimir Ilrin; editor, Rasisa Lasrowa; music, Daisaku Kume. Reviewed at San Sebastian Film Festival, Sept. 18, 1992. Running time: **120 MIN.**

With: Shoku Ijichi, Ivan Shivedov, Yuri Vilalainen, Yuri Jurian, Boris Romanov, Antonina Shranowa, Vladimir Asobik, Zinaida Sharko.

"The Icon" is an ambitious, overlong but beautifully crafted film that leaves auds as cold as St. Petersburg snow.

The filmmakers have obviously gone to great lengths to capture period locations in Russia and re-create historical events. Unfortunately, the rambling story of a young Japanese girl who travels to St. Petersburg in 1880 to study the art of painting icons in a convent soon becomes wearisome. Mixed into the yarn are the girl's brushes with revolutionaries, which give the pic repeated lifts but are always followed by stultifying returns to the nunnery or irrelevant twists.

The religious proselytizing is heavy-handed at times, and a sanctimonious ending worsens the arduous story.

Thesping and cinematography are good, but the editing is chaotic and direction often static. Most interesting are the views inside St. Petersburg churches and shots of Russian icons.
— *Peter Besas*

TSINIKI
(CYNICS)
(RUSSIAN)

A Lenfilm Studio Kinoassociation production. Produced by Mark Rudinstein. Directed by Dimitri Meskhiev. Screenplay, V. Todorovsky. Camera (color), Y. Shaigorodov; editor, Tamara Lipartia; music, Vladimir Glutuin; production design, B. Yushakov. Reviewed at Festival of Festivals, Toronto, Sept. 16, 1992. Running time: **110 MIN.**
With: I. Dapkunaite, N. Gundareva, I. Rosanova, A. Ilyn, Y. Belyayev, M. Pezhemsky.

In his second feature, 29-year-old Dimitri Meskhiev suggests that life in Petrograd 70 years ago had parallels with life in St. Petersburg today. It's a grim saga of love and betrayal that could spark limited international interest.

In once and future St. Petersburg in 1922, the euphoria that followed the Bolshevik Revolution of five years earlier has waned; everywhere there is poverty, food shortages, housing shortages. Against this is set a languid tale about a naive young man who marries a beautiful young woman who promptly betrays him with his best friend. The beauty's brother, meanwhile,

joins a unit of White Russians in the Civil War against the Bolsheviks and is killed. Time passes, and the wife becomes a virtual prostitute, selling her very considerable favors to the highest bidder while her ineffectual husband can only stand by.

This is a gloomy saga of deprivation, physical and spiritual suffering. Meskhiev handles it all rather listlessly, with slow pacing and faded color, but gets fine performances from his cast and the story covers an interesting period understandably ignored by filmmakers in Soviet era.

Technical credits are on the modest side. — *David Stratton*

EL MARIDO PERFECTO
(THE PERFECT HUSBAND)
(SPANISH-ARGENTINE-CZECHOSLOVAKIAN-BRITISH)

An Ion Films (Madrid)/Jempsa (Buenos Aires)/Barrandov Studios (Prague)/Portman Entertainment (London) co-production. Executive producers, Victor Manuel, Jorge Estrada Mora, Victor Glynn. Produced by Ricardo Freixa. Directed by Beda Docampo Feijóo. Screenplay, Docampo Feijóo, Juan Bautista Stagnare, based on Fyodor Dostoyevski's story. Camera (Eastmancolor), Frantisek Uldrich; editor, José Salcedo; music, pepe Nieto; production design, Jiri Hlupy; costumes, Vera Mirova. Reviewed at Valladolid Film Festival, Oct. 28, 1992. Running time: **92 MIN.**
Milan . . . . Tim Roth
Teresa . . . . Ana Belén
Franz . . . . Peter Firth
Klara . . . . . . Aitana Sánchez-Gijón
Also with: Carolina Estrada, Jennifer Lander, Jorge Marrale, Diego Leske, Juan Pedro Hernández.
(English soundtrack)

Superb acting by Tim Roth and Peter Firth, a tight, literate script, fine direction by Argentine helmer Beda Docampo Feijóo and good production values re-creating turn of the century Prague make this a thoroughly enjoyable version of a Dostoyevski original. But due to its very virtues, pic is probably limited to TV release on minority webs and pubcasters.

Story concerns Tim Roth's delightfully cynical rake, somewhat mysteriously visited in Prague by a former acquaintance (Firth) who had managed a luxury hotel in Marienbad, where Roth had known him. As pic skillfully moves back and forth between the two time frames we witness how Roth seduces the manager's wife (Ana Belén), almost at the connivance of Firth.

The twisted love-hate relationship between the two men, the

hidden taunts and feints, are part of an intricate background involving the faithless wife (clumsily played by Belén, who could use an English coach) in the earlier period and her sickly daughter, whose birth was fatal to Belén, in the latter. The daughter (strikingly miscast) becomes a pawn in the strategies of each of the men. The sex is kept soft.

Despite some casting flaws, pic holds audience interest, largely thanks to the two lead British thesps who provide a subtle but riveting *mano a mano*.
— *Peter Besas*

SIEMPRE FELICES
(HAPPY EVER AFTER)
(SPANISH)

A Siempre Felices production. Executive producer, Lola Respaldiza. Produced by Respaldiza, Joaquín Fonollá, Pedro Pinzolas. Directed, written by Pinzolas. Camera (color), Agustín Rodríguez; editor, Juan Alberto Jiménez; sound, Francisco García Minayo. Reviewed at Walter Reade Theater, N.Y., Oct. 17, 1992. (In Spanish Cinema Now series.) Running time: **85 MIN.**
Patricia . . . . Reyes Moleres
Alberto . . . . Carlos Montalvo
María . . . . Clara López
Also with: Carlos Iglesias, Fernando Algaba, Fonollá, Yolanda Robles, Olga Roig, Clara Pelico, Leticia Marco.

"Happy Ever After" is a quirky postmodern romance between two young professionals whose nauseatingly "idyllic" marriage must stand the test of modern thought. Off-beat comedy could find some interest on the art house circuit.

Script is a collage of juxtaposed scenes revolving around a group of characters and focused on the ups and downs in the relationship between Patricia (Reyes Moleres) and Alberto (Carlos Montalvo). Despite their insipid happiness together, Moleres thinks nothing of jumping into bed with clients for her bathroom fixtures and Montalvo also finds fidelity difficult, in spite of his constant declarations of love.

Later, Moleres and her friend María (Clara López) plot a Gidelian "gratuitous act" —murder for no reason — but the killing is never carried out.

Pic's literary posturing and basic lack of plot wears thin, as do some running gags such as a collapsing chair, but there is enough invention to keep the film moving. Despite its low budget (amplified from super 16m), tech credits are okay. Acting is also satisfactory. — *Paul Lenti*

RAAM KE NAAM
(IN THE NAME OF GOD)
(INDIAN-DOCU)

A First Run-Icarus Films release of a Patwardhan production. Produced, directed, written, camera (color), edited by Anand Patwardhan. Sound, Pervez Merwanji. Reviewed at Festival of Festivals, Toronto, Sept. 15, 1992. Running time: **95 MIN.**

This hard-hitting, provocative docu about religious clashes in India could spark interest on specialist TV networks worldwide. It's a revealing look at secularism in India under siege from militants on both sides.

The film, evidently a labor of love by Anand Patwardhan, focuses on the bitter, violent conflict over a 16th century Muslim mosque in the city of Ayodhya. Militant Hindis, most of them upper-caste, claim the mosque is built on the exact site of the birth of Lord Ram, whom they revere; but no one is able to confirm exactly where, or even when, Ram was, in fact, born. This does not deter the militants, however, who insist that the mosque be razed to the ground and replaced by a temple dedicated to Ram —though dozens of such temples already dot the city.

Naturally enough, the Muslims vigorously object to the Hindi demands and defend their mosque. Thus the stage is set for pointless, bloody religious violence in which the authorities seem to side with the Hindi extremists, and the poor people on both sides of the argument wind up the losers.

Patwardhan explores this tragedy in this lucid, courageous film that allows supporters of both positions to have their say. But tempers and feelings run high and at times it looks as though the filmmaker himself was taking a big risk obtaining his material. Climactic scenes in which the Hindis attack the mosque are vividly shot.

Though obviously of specialized appeal, "In the Name of God" is a docu well worth seeking out. — *David Stratton*

LANGER SAMSTAG
(LONGER SATURDAY)
(GERMAN)

A Scotia Films release of a Olga Film production, co-produced by ZDF. Directed, written, scored by Hanns Christian Müller. Idea, Müller, James Jacobs; camera, (color) Jacobs; editor, Helga Borsche; production design, Pit Janzen; costumes, Barbara Grupp, Barbara Winter; sound, Stanislav Litera; lighting, Manfred Klein. Reviewed at the Kurbel Cinema, Berlin, Oct. 13, 1992. Running time: **96 MIN.**
Susi Herzog . . . Gisela Schneeberger
Anton . . . . Campino (Andreas Frege)
Horst Schmude . . . . Dieter Pfaff
Markus . . . . Ottfried Fischer
Frau Dünskoven . . . . . Manuela Riva
Winkelhofer . . . . Hans Brenner
Herr Hässler . . . . Axel Milberg
Iris Meier . . . . Antje Späth
Theuerkauf . . . . Jürgen Hart
Sister Rotraut . . . . . Elisabeth Welz
Steindl . . . . Otto Grünmandl
Krebs . . . . Ludwig Wühr
Herr Uhl . . . . Jochen Busse
Charly . . . . Achim Grubel

This fast-moving comic strip of a film should do brisk local biz around holiday time. It could make a very respectable mark appealing to a broad German-lingo public.

Judging from reception at the screening — some were rolling in the aisles — auds will find this fast-moving, light-hearted and generally lightweight pic a corker. Action and gags are nonstop.

The time is the Saturday before Christmas at a mall. Fortyish Susi (Gisela Schneeberger) operates the gas station/snackbar in the parking lot and has more on her hands than she can handle from customers, her ex and her mum, when she learns that her lease is canceled effective end of the month.

Pic breaks loose when she unsuccessfully tries to get the head of the mall (Axel Milberg) to straighten things out, but is repeatedly foiled by a crooked exec with a hidden agenda (Dieter Pfaff). Susie is aided by a young punk (Campino, who fronts top German band the Töton Hosen), who literally yells "fire" in the crowded store — he's the only one besides Susi looking askance at the glut of consumerism.

Several hundred characters, chases and plot twists later, Susi and Anton prevail and are in love, although we don't glimpse a screen kiss or get much of an explanation for the May/December pairing.

Plot has some clever elements, and acting and tech credits are competent. — *Rebecca Lieb*

MOTHERS AND DAUGHTERS
(CANADIAN)

A Palama Films production. Produced by Pericles Creticos. Directed by Larry Kent. Screenplay, Kent, Linda Jarosiewicz, based on Aviva Ravel's play "Mother Variations"; additional dialogue, William Marsden. Camera (color), Daniel Villeneuve; editors, Mark Baxter, Kent; music, Fernand Martel, Robert Lauson; production design, Chris Brown; costumes, Roberto Cicirello. Reviewed at Montreal World Film Festival, Sept. 1, 1992. Running time: **90 MIN.**
Fay . . . . Mary Peach
Angela . . . . Clare Sims
Joan . . . . Rebecca Nelson
Also with: Gordon Day, Aaron Tager, Libby Barrett, Rachelle Glait, Ann Page.

Three fine lead performances and a few moments of resounding emotional truth lift "Mothers and Daughters" slightly above routine domestic drama. Even so, Canadian-produced pic will be a tough sell in theatrical markets.

Mary Peach stars as Fay, a sixtysomething widow just beginning to enjoy the independence of her golden years when she gets two unexpected visitors: fortyish daughter Joan (Rebecca Nelson), newly abandoned by her husband; and pregnant 18-year-old granddaughter Angela (Clair Sims), who's temperamentally ill-prepared to be an unwed mother. Both women want to remain long-term guests.

At first, Fay tries to make the best of the situation, spending most of her time preparing for a ballroom dancing contest with her gentleman friend (Gordon Day). Finally, however, she complains about her daughter's impractical lifestyle and her granddaughter's irresponsibility.

Revelation of a long-buried secret doesn't have as much dramatic impact as the often acrimonious cross-generational arguments. Pic appears headed toward an effective conclusion, but writer director Kent cops out.

Nelson gives a first-rate performance. Sims is persuasively self-absorbed, and Peach offers a vivid portrait of a matriarch who can't see why her offspring aren't as strong-willed as she is herself.

Most of the drama is set inside Fay's home, but smooth lensing keeps pic un-claustrophobic. Other tech credits are adequate.
— *Joe Leydon*

FAR FROM BERLIN
(FRENCH/GERMAN)

An ARP presentation of an ARP/Bebo Filmproduktion production. Produced by Michele Halberstadt, Laurent Petin. Directed, written by Keith McNally. Camera (color), Philippe Welt; editor, Joele Van Effentere; music, Juergen Knieper; production design, Olaf Schiefner; costume design, Angelika Huhn; sound, Michel Kharat; associate producer, Gary Marcus. Reviewed at the Toronto Festival of Festivals, Sept. 11, 1992. Running time: **95 MIN.**
Otto Linder . . . Armin Mueller-Stahl
Dieter Hausmann . . . Werner Stocker
Sonja Hausmann . . . Tatjana Blacher
Alex Hausmann . . . . . . Fritz Schaap
Georg Hausmann . . . . Nikolai Volev
Anna . . . . Nathalie Devaux
Anna's husband . . . Stefan Staudinger

Shot entirely in Berlin, "Far From Berlin" is an engaging little East meets West drama that works well until the overly melodramatic wrap scene. However, English-lingo French-German co-prod is fine TV fare, especially for Euro outlets.

German star Armin Mueller-Stahl superbly underplays the too-friendly stranger who insists on "helping" Dieter (Werner Stocker), an easterner who loses his menial factory job.

A family man whose child is stricken with an unusual and costly illness, Stocker reluctantly excepts Mueller-Stahl's job offer — and his request to spy on Mueller-Stahl's cheating "wife" Anna (Nathalie Devaux).

As the child grows sicker and requires special care from U.S. doctors, Stocker grows more dependent upon his "friend" whose demands turn deadly (murdering Devaux's lover). But plausible set-up is dashed in the finale.

Thesps are a plus. Philippe Welt's lensing highlights many Berlin landmarks. The low-budget tech credits are okay.
— *Suzan Ayscough*

ISHI:
THE LAST YAHI
(DOCU-COLOR/B&W-16m)

A Rattlesnake Prods. presentation. Produced, directed by Jed Riffe, Pamela Roberts. Screenplay, Anne Makepeace. Camera (color/B&W, 16m), Stephen Lighthill; editor, Jennifer Chinlund; script consultant-additional direction, Steven Okazaki; music, Mark Adler. Reviewed at Roxie Cinema, San Francisco, Sept. 21, 1992. (In Mill Valley Film Festival.) Running time: **60 MIN.**
Narrator: Linda Hunt.

This engrossing docu traces the life and times of California's "last wild Indian." Combining historical/anthropological interest with a revisionist view of relations between white settlers and Native Americans, the short feature should do well on fest circuit before planned PBS airing, with a likely educational shelf life to follow.

Ishi wandered out of the Northern California wilderness in 1911 after the last of his fellow Yahi tribe members perished due to hardship and "Indian hunters."

Shipped to San Francisco for "study" under the auspices of young Berkeley anthropologist Alfred Kroeber, the middle-aged man delighted in the wonders of the city. In turn, he captured the public's fancy, performing hunting skills and tribal practices at regular "exhibits." Not long after a return trip to his home terrain, Ishi died of tuberculosis.

The film pieces together the saga out of newsreel footage, period clippings and photos plus some handsome lensing of a recent expedition to Ishi's remote homelands. The result combines straightforward history with a fair-minded yet critical evaluation of white insensitivity to Native American culture then and now. Tech qualities are good throughout. — *Dennis Harvey*

FÜNFZIG JAHRE SCHWEIGEN: DEUTSCHE IN DER USSR
(50 YEARS OF SILENCE: THE VOLGA GERMANS)
(GERMAN-HUNGARIAN-DOCU-16m)

A Satellit Film production, in association with Hungarian TV. (Intl. sales: Satellit, Stamberg, Germany.) Produced, directed, written by Barna Kabay, Imre Gyöngyössy, Katalin Petényi. Camera (color), Péter Jankura, Andreas Gerö, György Kovács; editors, Karl Fugunt, Petényi; sound, Norbert Pries. Reviewed at Hungarofilm screening room, Budapest, Feb. 12, 1992. Running time: **76 MIN.**

(German & Russian soundtrack; English subtitles)

A timely and even-handed docu on the little-known Volga Germans, "50 Years of Silence" is a fascinating glimpse into a people doubly dispossessed by history. Pic should interest specialist webs hunting for ethnic material.

Item is a companion piece to the same filmmakers' "Homeless" (a.k.a. "Exiles"), a dramatized 35m look at a Volga German woman's search for her lost son. "50 Years" takes a broader, strictly docu approach to the subject.

Originally settled deep in the Russian steppes by Catherine the Great, in 1924 the Volga Germans got autonomous status as a republic based around Minsk. When Hitler broke with the Soviets in 1941, Stalin took revenge, deporting them to Kazakhstan

and Siberia where many died. Since mid-'70s, they've been returning to the Volga, where 6.5% of the population is German.

Trio of Hungarian filmers weave historical material into present-day footage of the Germans holding fast to their language and traditions. Some want to return to Germany proper; others hold the Volga region as their homeland. Russians interviewed just want them to go away.

Pic is technically okay within 16m limitations. — *Derek Elley*

AMER. INDIAN FEST

ACTS OF DEFIANCE
(CANADIAN-DOCU-16m)

A National Film Board of Canada production. Executive producer, Dennis Murphy. Produced by Mark Zannis. Directed by Alec G. MacLeod. Written, narrated, Zannis. Camera (color), Rene Sioui Labelle, Barry Perles, Roger Martin, Savas Kalogeras; music, Jean Derome. Reviewed at American Indian Film Festival, San Francisco, Nov. 5, 1992. Running time: **104 MIN.**

Like "Incident at Oglala," this Canadian docu charts a divisive, violent conflict between government and Native American interests: the 1990 standoff between two Quebec Mohawk communities and white authorities over ownership and use of traditional tribal lands. Lacking the editing zip of its U.S. counterpart, docu is good reportage unlikely to gain wide southern exposure.

When the municipality of Oka, Quebec, planned to develop a small tract into a golf course extension, local tribespeople blockaded bulldozers. Police attempted to remove the barricades; shots were exchanged and one policeman killed. In solidarity, the Kahnawake reservation on Montreal's South Shore blocked off all roads to their territory, including a major suburban bridge.

The tense 78-day standoff resulted in one more death (when reactionary whites stoned Indians fleeing in their cars), supply cutoffs, and deployment of Canadian Armed Forces. "We are about to become a nation which, forced to choose between a potential massacre and a long drive to work, chose the massacre," mourns one journalist.

Despite international attention and some national outrage at the excessive force employed, the conflict ended with no clear resolution in sight.

The result is strong but perhaps too exhaustive, sometimes dwelling on individual elements at ponderous length. Writer-producer Mark Zannis makes a somewhat stilted narrator, occasionally tilting from reportage to advocacy. — *Dennis Harvey*

MEDICINE FIDDLE
(DOCU-16m)

An Up North Films production. Produced, directed by Michael Loukinen. Camera (color), editor, Miroslav Janek; sound, Matt Quast. Reviewed American Indian Film Festival, San Francisco, Nov. 5, 1992. Running time: **81 MIN.**

A pleasant 20 minutes' worth of material dragged out to feature length, this docu charts the legacy of music and dancing introduced by Eurodescent trappers, traders and homesteaders to Native American peoples in the 17th and 18th centuries. Possible fest gigging aside, the repetitious flick will interest only music/ethnic academic auds.

Early immigrants from France, Ireland and Scotland brought the fiddle to tribes of the northern U.S. and Canada. Mixed-blood descendants still go "jigging," the bluegrassy music and step-dancing having long since intertwined with tribal customs and myths.

There's a lot of good (and some not-so-good) playing here for fans of downhome-style music, as well as a few superficial glimpses into the historical-cultural background. But the various reminiscences and anecdotes don't exactly dig deep most of the time (one old-timer's advice for young fiddlers is "Never try to play a tune you don't know"). And by the fifth or sixth view of people clomping around at fairs, rest homes, etc., it all begins to look the same.

The kind of palpable pleasure Les Blank routinely brings to similar musicological studies is lacking in this sluggish effort. Tech aspects are okay. — *Dennis Harvey*

THE RIDE TO WOUNDED KNEE
(DOCU-COLOR/B&W-16m)

A Ghost Dance production. Executive producer, Robert Clapsadle. Produced by Carol Wolman. Directed, written by Clapsadle. Camera (color/B&W), Frances Reid; editor, Greg Bezat; Lako-

ta music supervisor, Earl Bull Head; narrated by Mark White Bull, Jim Swan, Nancy Clapsadle, Rick Afraid of Hawk, Isaac Dog Eagle, Joe Walker. Reviewed at American Indian Film Festival, San Francisco, Nov. 2, 1992. Running time: **85 MIN.**

Taking a more cinematically imaginative approach to the same subject as the concurrent "Wiping the Tears of Seven Generations," this generally strong docu examines the 1890 massacre of 300 unarmed Lakota Indians. Fest dates should be followed by some specialty- house engagements and a long educational vid life.

Fleeing U.S. Cavalry after the killing of Sitting Bull, many of his followers journeyed 100 miles in subzero December weather from Standing Rock, N.D., to join Chief Big Foot's tribe at South Dakota's Cherry Creek. They, in turn, were captured, escaped, went another 150 miles to Pine Ridge, and were taken prisoner at Wounded Knee by Custer's old regiment, the 7th Cavalry.

On Dec. 29, the drunken and panicky troops opened fire; a blizzard froze the corpses, which were later dumped into a mass grave. Only four men and 45 women and children survived.

Impressionistic visual touches heighten the events prior to this tragic trek, supplemented by footage of silent Westerns, newsreels and contemporary newspapers and photos. The approach grows a bit more conventional as latter-day Lakotas retrace their ancestors' journey on horseback in 1989. But talking-head stuff is kept to a bare minimum.

Tech work (especially editing and outdoor photography) is excellent. — *Dennis Harvey*

VANCOUVER FEST

CHUGAKU KYOSHI
(THE GAMES TEACHERS PLAY)
(JAPANESE)

An Argo Projects (Japan) production. Produced by Koto Yamada, Koichi Furukawa. Directed by Hideyuki Hirayama. Screenplay, Hiroshi Saito. Camera (color), Kozo Shibazaki; editor, Shigeru Okuyama; music, Miyuki Otani. Reviewed at Vancouver Intl. Film Festival, Oct. 6, 1992. Running time: **105 MIN.**

With: Kyozo Nagatsuka, Kazuhiko Kaneyama, Toshiya Fujita, Atsuko Shimada.

Touted as a Japanese "Blackboard Jungle," pic is far headier stuff as it tackles not urban underprivileged but affluent, seemingly conformist junior high school kids drifting toward passive self-destruction. Powerhouse production and flawless acting puts this several cuts above the teens-in-trouble formula, with consumer culture and contemporary Japanese values coming under equally unflinching scrutiny.

Misleadingly titled pic isn't about coercive manipulation of students, but compares the responses of two diametrically opposed teachers to an increasingly out-of-control situation. Ultra-authoritarian Mr. Mikami (Kyozo Nagatsuka) takes a kamikaze approach toward students, parents, colleagues and his own family, reducing all activity to organized ritual.

Meanwhile, a sweet-tempered young art instructor (Toshiya Fujita) lets the kids run wild in an effort to instill individuality. The young woman takes an interest in three latchkey lads, with unfortunate — but non-sensationalized — consequences.

Uniformly superb tech credits, especially Kozo Shibazaki's bright lensing and Miyuki Otani's austere score, subtly support the gripping story, and Nagatsuka crams an amazing range of emotions into the stoical central character, who may stand for fading, patriarchal Japan.

But the greatest strength of "Games" is its even-handedness: As girls bully each other and boys sniff glue, the teachers each try, haltingly and with much sincerity, to reach them. In a show of solidarity after a student dies, the school agrees to Mikami's plan to stage an *ediken*, or intramural marathon.

The results, lensed in unfussy and surprisingly moving fashion, show the students rising to the challenge and exhibiting pride for the first time. But the effects are temporary, and everyone soon drifts back to their unspoken roles. — *Ken Eisner*

A DAI
(TAIWANESE-COLOR/B&W)

A Channel Film and Video Prod. Corp. (Taiwan) production. Produced by Li Jingxuan. Directed by Cai Yangming. Screenplay, Wu Nianzhen. Camera (B&W/color), Li Pingbin; editor, Chen Bo-wen; art direction, Chu Cha-ling; sound, Lin Sung-lan. Reviewed at Van-

couver Intl. Film Festival, Oct. 8, 1992. Running time: **120 MIN.**
With: Cheng Songyong, Cong Shan, Yu Tian, Yue Xun, Wu Ma, Fang Fang. *(Mandarin and Hokkien-dialect soundtrack)*

On the surface, "A Dai" looks like familiar gangster fare — interfamily disputes even follow the "Godfather" formula — but focus is on a rural teenager and his intimate relations with a well-depicted Taipei underworld. The philosophical undertone may surprise youth audiences expecting action, but older crowds will enjoy most of this, as well as pic's ultra-glamorous patina.

Gangly, dimpled Chen Songyong has tremendous appeal as Jen, nicknamed A Dai (some prints carry the title "Joe Goody"), a battered village youth who leaves his retarded mother and heads to the city for a life of crime. Introduced to powerful ganglord Mr. Lin (mustachioed Yu Tian, who comes on like a Chinese Ronald Colman), A Dai proves himself by tossing a passerby through a shop window, stabbing the man, then casually buying a soda from a machine.

The baddies are impressed, and make him Lin's personal chauffeur and bodyguard. He soon also becomes protector and confidante to Lin's small daughter and wife (ex-Mainland star Cong Shan, exuding sophisticated sexuality as the B-girl turned bizwoman who goes to A Dai for comfort when Lin leaves town).

In tale's best twist, only the audience knows A Dai is suffering from incapacitating headaches: The lad has an almost-inoperable brain tumor and it's clear that this symbol of corruption (and repressed anguish) will eventually overtake him.

Fresh lensing, especially early B&W scenes of A Dai's abuse at the hands of his brutal father, is a tip-off to pic's artful intent. Veteran genre helmsman Cai Yangming ("Taxi Dancer") is going for something deeper here, but pedestrian music and shaky plot sink its final quarter. After switching to Mrs. Lin's struggle for survival (and dwelling in too many beige-toned interiors), the thread of A Dai's journey is lost, and the story heads obediently for a predictable, not quite satisfying climax.

— *Ken Eisner*

GAGMAN
(SOUTH KOREAN)

A Tae Hung Prods. (Taiwan) production. (Intl. sales: Korean Motion Picture Promotion Corp.) Produced by Lee Tae-Won. Directed by Lee Myung-Se. Screenplay, Bae Chang-Ho, Lee Myung-Se. Camera, Yoo Young-Kil; editor, Kim Hyun; music, Kim Soo-Chul. Reviewed at Vancouver Intl. Film Festival, Oct. 11, 1992. (In Seoul Beauties series, N.Y.) Running time: **125 MIN.**
Lee Jong-Sae . . . . . . Ahn Sung-Ki
Mun Do-Sok . . . . . . Bae Chang-Ho
Oh Son-Yong . . . . . Hwang Shin-Hae
(Korean soundtrack; English subtitles)

Although this intermittently amusing tale of a would-be comic's delusionary rise and fall is tinged with universal humor, "Gagman" is finally too parochial and dragged-out to satisfy international auds.

Korean matinee idol Ahn Sung-Ki sports a Charlie Chaplin mustache as a small-time nightclub emcee who has cockeyed dreams of stardom. He never stops thanking people for their "continued support," even when they have no idea who he is.

To boost his would-be career, he enlists the aid of a dreamy, ever-hungry barber (actor-director Bae Chang-Ho, who co-scripted) and a fiercely independent ex-bargirl (Hwang Shin-Hae) to help him stage some mishapridden robberies in preparation for a projected crime spoof.

Helmsman Lee Myung-Se milks these situations with a clever nod to expectations (half the time, these star-struck crooks give more than they take), lensing is frequently imaginative, and references to Chaplin, Woody Allen, and Warner-style gangsterism are fun at first. But events are peppered with political twists and personal mannerisms that will only register with Korean auds and threadbare repetition sets in too soon.

This 1989 pic is primarily of interest to fest fans of Lee's more fully developed followup, the domestic comedy "My Love, My Bride." — *Ken Eisner*

BOWL OF BONE:
TALE OF THE SYUWE
(CANADIAN-DOCU-B&W/COLOR)

A Turtle Prods. (Canada) production in association with the National Film Board of Canada. Executive producers, Gillian Starling, Jack Silberman for Northern Lights Media Corp. Produced by Jan-Marie Martell. Producer for NFB, Barbara Janes. Directed, written by Martell. Camera (b&w/color),

Martell, with Kirk Tougas, Doug MacKay; editor, Martell, Shelly Hamer; music, J. Douglas Dodd; animation, Ruben Moller; set decoration, costume design, Barbara Clayden, Patrick Keating, Georgiana Chappell; associate producer, Betsy Carson. Reviewed at Vancouver Intl. Film Festival (on tape), Oct. 2, 1992. Running time: **114 MIN.**
With: Annie Zetko York, Jan-Marie Martell, Patti Fraser, Kirsten Paxton Judge, Art Urquhart, Kathleen York, Peg Campbell.

An unusual mix of docu footage, archival stills, stylized reenactment and personal ruminations, this bio of Northwest native healer and herbalist Annie York (subtitle's "Syuwe," pronounced *shuwa*, refers to shamanistic powers) took 16 years to assemble. The kaleidoscopic structure is striking, but helmer Jan-Marie Martell spends far more time on self than subject, an emphasis only intermittently rewarding.

A Michigan student who fled to Canada during the Vietnam War, Martell uses home movies, snapshots and dramatic devices to re-create events leading up to her 1976 encounter with York in rural Spuzzum, B.C. There is some humor generated by her confused, Carlos Castaneda-like attempts to comprehend her adopted teacher, and the quest is sometimes illuminated by spectacular, imaginative images.

York's doubts about her student and her own spiritual powers keep things from getting too sentimental, but pic is sunk by Martell's solemn narration — a droning, repetitive litany of neurotic conflicts and too-pat observations (which nonetheless won "Bowl" a Best Narration award at Canada's Atlantic Film Festival) — and dull music.

The most interesting aspects are found in the straight docu sections, but pic could find fans among ethnography students and still-searching baby boomers. For wider play, it needs a half-hour trim, new voiceover and score, and tighter structure (key to formlessness may be in the credit for "Concept Integrity," a list of 19 names!). — *Ken Eisner*

VERSO SUD
(TOWARD THE SOUTH)
(ITALIAN)

A Lucky Red release of a Kermit Smith, Andrea Occhipinti presentation of a Demian Film production in association with the Ministry of Tourism & Entertainment. Produced, directed, written by Pasquale Pozzessere. Camera (Technicolor), Bruno Cascio; editor, Carlo Valerio; music, Domenico Scuteri, Corrado Rizza; art direction, Cinzia Di Mauro; costumes, Anna Rita Piergotti; sound (Dolby), Mario Iaquone. Reviewed at Capranichetta Cinema, Rome, Sept. 29, 1992. (In Venice Film Festival.) Running time: **88 MIN.**

Paola	Antonella Ponziani
Eugenio	Stefano Dionisi
The priest	Tito Schipa Jr.
Teresa	Irene Grazioli
Franco	Lucio Zagaria

Also with: Luciano Curreli, Luigi Santamaria, Pierfrancesco Pergoli.

Sensitive performances and assured, unobtrusive direction hoist Pasquale Pozzessere's feature debut, "Toward the South," beyond the constraints of its familiar plot premise. The tale of two lost souls who find a sense of commitment through each other and turns midway into an ill-fated-drifters-on-the-road movie should benefit from critical attention in Italy. Further afield, pic should find festival slots, but it probably lacks universality to secure arthouse playdates.

Opening scenes parallel the lives of wanderers Antonella Ponziani and Stefano Dionisi as they drift around Rome's grimy Termini Station district. Fresh from a short prison stint, Ponziani looks for work and attempts to visit her young son, temporarily placed in state care. An alcoholic, Dionisi scrapes by stealing cash from church poor boxes. When they meet, a low-key affair begins and the couple shack up in a unused factory.

Given some pluck by her newfound luck in love. Ponziani makes a request to regain custody of her son. Turned down flat, she resorts to kidnapping, and the trio is forced to head south to evade police.

The narrative drags its feet before hitting the road, but Pozzessere effectively establishes a gradually strengthening bond between the lovers. Ponziani and Dionisi are a little scrubbed to be truly believable as desperados, but both actors turn in honest, moving performances. Dionisi is especially convincing, his intense gaze lending subtle credence to the determination and ultimate self-sacrifice.

Tech credits are simple and efficient. The story's harsh focus is matched by raw, unembellished lensing of both the bleak city locations and the southern Italy countryside. — *David Rooney*

GUELWAAR
(SENEGALESE-FRENCH)

A Film Domireew (Dakar)-Galatee Film (Paris) co-production, with the participation of FR-3. Produced by Ousmane Sembène, Jacques Perrin. Directed, written by Sembène. Camera (color), Dominique Gentil; editor, Marie Aimee; music, Baba Mall; production design, François Laurent Sulva; sound, Ndiouga Moctar Ba; assistant director, Clarence Delgado. Reviewed at Venice Film Festival (competition), Sept. 1, 1992. (Also in London Film Festival.) Running time: **115 MIN.**

Gora	Omar Seck
Barthelemy	Ndiawar Diop
Nogoy Marie Thioune	Mame Ndoumbe Diop
Veronique	Isseu Niang
Helene	Myriam Niang
Aloys	Mustapha Diop

An ironic race relations comedy-drama from one of Africa's most distinguished filmmakers, "Guelwaar" looks destined to play the fest circuit with specialized theatrical bookings in Europe possible.

The title is the name of an important man who stood against corruption, now murdered in a violent (offscreen) attack. When it's time for his funeral, his body has disappeared. Friends and relatives suspect the worst, but the solution turns out to be banal; the body of the Catholic Guelwaar was simply confused with the body of a Muslim man, and the dead hero has already been buried in a Muslim funeral.

Director Ousmane Sembène's dry approach to the subject is refreshing. He's well served by his cast, who give natural, unforced performances, and the fine camerawork of Dominique Gentil is a plus. Music by Baba Mall is used to advantage. The result of one of the more accessible African films to emerge in the last couple of years.

— *David Stratton*

KLAMEK JI BO BEKO
(A SONG FOR BEKO)
(GERMAN)

A Margarita Woskanian production with WDR. Produced by Woskanian. Directed by Nizamettin Aric. Screenplay, Aric, Christine Kernich. Camera (color), Thomas Mauch; editor, Gaby Wragge, Susann Lahaye; music, Aric; production design, Aric, Cemale Jora; sound, Ernst Marell; artistic and production adviser, Kernich. Reviewed at Venice Film Festival (out of competition), Sept. 7, 1992. Running time: **105 MIN.**

Beko	Nizamettin Aric
Zine	Bezara Arsen
Zeyno	Lusika Hesen
Cemal	Cemale Jora

(Kurdish language)

Said to be the first Kurdish-language film ever, "A Song for Beko" is a personal project for exiled Kurdish actor-poet Nizamettin Aric, who directed, co-scripted, composed the music and plays the leading role. Though a shade on the long side, pic is first class in every other tech department.

Pic is a fascinating insight into the Kurdish people, who live in parts of Iraq, Iran and Turkey. Pic begins in Turkey where Beko's brother Cemal skips the country to avoid being drafted into the Turkish army. Troops soon raid the village looking for him, beating and arresting Beko, who manages to escape and heads for the Syrian border, hoping to find his brother in Iraq.

In 1988 Iraq, as war with Iran is ending, Beko finds Kurds camping out in makeshift tents in the mountains, afraid to return to their ruined villages. While awaiting news of his brother, Beko befriends the children and discovers they have a strong feeling of Kurdish identity.

When the conflict ends, the Kurds return to the villages, which are subsequently sprayed with poison gas from Saddam Hussein's helicopters. Beko survives, as does a blind orphan girl. Eventually, Beko makes it to Germany and joins the community of Kurdish exiles. His brother was forced to serve as a Turkish soldier and was gunned down by his own people.

Aric, who was imprisoned in Turkey for his pro-Kurd activites, gives a forceful performance and has made a quietly effective film well shot on Armenian locations by top German lenser Thomas Mauch. Though breaking no new ground dramatically, the film rates attention as the firt feature to depict the plight of the Kurds from the inside. — *David Stratton*

CHAPLIN

A TriStar release of a Mario Kassar presentation of a Carolco/Le Studio Canal Plus/RCS Video production, produced in association with Japan Satellite Broadcasting. Produced by Richard Attenborough, Kassar. Co-producer, Terence Clegg. Directed by Attenborough. Screenplay, William Boyd, Bryan Forbes, William Goldman, from Charles Chaplin's "My Autobiography" and David Robinson's "Chaplin: His Life and Art"; story, Diana Hawkins. Camera (Technicolor), Sven Nykvist; editor, Anne V. Coates; music, John Barry; production design, Stuart Craig; supervising art director, Norman Dorme; art direction, Mark Mansbridge (L.A.), John King (London); set design, Stan Tropp, Don Woodruff (L.A.); set decoration, Chris A. Butler (L.A.), Stephenie McMillan (London); costume design, John Mollo, Ellen Mirojnick; sound (Dolby), Edward Tise; Chaplin prosthetic makeup created by John Gaglione Jr.; associate producer, Hawkins; assistant director, David Tomblin; L.A. 2nd unit director, Micky Moore; L.A. 2nd unit camera, Alex Witt; casting, Mike Fenton, Valorie Massalas, Susie Figgis. Reviewed at TriStar screening room, Culver City, Calif., Dec. 2, 1992. MPAA Rating: PG-13. Running time: **144 MIN.**

Charlie Chaplin	Robert Downey Jr.
Mack Sennett	Dan Aykroyd
Hannah Chaplin	Geraldine Chaplin
J. Edgar Hoover	Kevin Dunn
George Hayden	Anthony Hopkins
Mildred Harris	Milla Jovovich
Hetty Kelly/Oona O'Neill	Moira Kelly
Douglas Fairbanks	Kevin Kline
Paulette Goddard	Diane Lane
Edna Purviance	Penelope Ann Miller
Sydney Chaplin	Paul Rhys
Fred Karno	John Thaw
Mabel Normand	Marisa Tomei
Joan Berry	Nancy Travis
Lawyer Scott	James Woods

Also with: Michael Blevins, Tom Bradford, Francesca Buller, Matthew Cottle, Peter Crook, Hugh Downer, David Duchovny, Donnie Kehr, Karen Lewis, Deborah Maria Moore, Sean O'Bryan, Bill Paterson, Maria Pitillo, Gerald Sim, Graham Sinclair, John Standing, Robert Stephens, Norbert Weisser.

Like a stone skipping across the top of a deep, turbulent sea, "Chaplin" runs through the dramatic highs and lows in the life of the screen's foremost comic genius without stirring the waters much. Telling the entire story of Charles Chaplin's 88 years was probably a hopeless goal for a feature-length film, but Richard Attenborough's latest epic biopic does offer the saving grace of an uncanny, truly remarkable central performance by Robert Downey Jr. and a number of lovely moments along the way. Pic needs top reviews to help put it on the map, and their unlikelihood will make it hard to build mainstream audience interest in this difficult man.

Working within a relatively conventional running time of less than 2½ hours, Attenborough attempts to relate the whole of Chaplin's exceedingly eventful life — his impoverished London East End childhood, early success in vaudeville, quick rise to the top in movies, troubles with wives, young girls and the law, banishment from the U.S., European exile and eventual return to Hollywood in triumph.

Thematically, the filmmakers attempt to pinpoint the real life origins of some of his comic motifs, and plausibly argue that the source of his leftish political sympathies and antiauthoritarian attitudes in his films lay in painful personal experience.

The problem is that the life was just too rich and provides too much material to be adequately dealt with in the allotted time. Attenborough and his three eminent screenwriters haven't managed to find a proper dramatic focus or structure, so that after the picture's relatively satisfying first third, the film bolts along devoting a few minutes to each woman, motion picture or legal skirmish as it presents itself. Where Downey had been building towards a towering great performance, he soon gets very little to really play.

Arguably, then, "Chaplin" should have been a miniseries or, as a feature film, might have profitably limited itself to the silent period, ending, perhaps, with "City Lights" and Chaplin at the peak of his career. This would have allowed what works best here — the re-creation of silent film production, the development of Chaplin's characterizations, his total control over his work — to be played out at greater length. Individual scenes, such as a prolonged episode in which Chaplin begins feeling his oats as the Tramp on camera are, against considerable odds, totally successful.

Overwhelmingly responsible for this is Downey's dead-on impersonation. Even his vocal progression, from Cockney drawl to the careful enunciation of his later years, seems impeccable. Ultimately, the proof of Downey's convincingness is that Attenborough cuts actual footage from Chaplin films into his narrative with no adjustment necessary between real and reel figures.

But as time goes on, the story structure becomes a matter of connecting the historical dots. Douglas Fairbanks (Kevin Kline, perfect) and Mary Pickford are brought on, but not a word is said of United Artists; Chaplin offends J. Edgar Hoover at a

dinner party, and the FBI chief hounds him forever after (curiously, Hoover and his bureau are not even mentioned in the exhaustive Chaplin biography by David Robinson, who served as historical consultant); wives and girls come and go, sometimes causing Chaplin problems but never sticking around long enough to make a lasting impression, and the political climate becomes increasingly inhospitable, driving him into exile.

In a novel casting stroke, Geraldine Chaplin strongly etches her own grandmother's maternal love and incipient madness. Dan Aykroyd as comedy king Mack Sennett; Moira Kelly as both Chaplin's first love and last, Oona O'Neill; Penelope Ann Miller as his first leading lady, Edna Purviance; Paul Rhys as brother Sydney; John Thaw as music hall impresario Fred Karno; Nancy Travis as the unbalanced Joan Barry, who nearly destroys Chaplin with a paternity suit; Diane Lane, too voluptuous to be Paulette Goddard but just as saucy — all ring as true as actors can in this sort of enterprise.

Similarly, behind-the-scenes talents have contributed to a convincing portrait of both turn-of-the-century London and the details of early filmmaking techniques in Hollywood. Major credit here goes to production designer Stuart Craig, lenser Sven Nykvist and costume designers John Mollo and Ellen Mirojnick. John Barry's score is a bit thick with sentiment, but nicely incorporates Chaplin compositions.

It all ends, movingly, at the 1972 Academy Awards, with Chaplin welcomed back to the U.S. after 20 years to receive an honorary Oscar. Downey could find himself there next year due to his work here. — *Todd McCarthy*

DAMAGE
(BRITISH-FRENCH)

A New Line Cinema release of a Skreba/NEF/Le Studio Canal Plus production made with the assistance of the European Coproduction Fund in association with Channel Four Films/Canal Plus. (Intl. sales: Majestic Films Intl.). Produced, directed by Louis Malle. Coproducers, Vincent Malle, Simon Relph. Screenplay, David Hare, based on Josephine Hart's novel. Camera (Technicolor), Peter Biziou; editor, John Bloom; music, Zbigniew Preisner; production design, Brian Morris; art direction, Richard Earl; set decoration, Jill Quertier; costume design, Milena Canonero; sound (Dolby), Jean-Claude Laureux; assistant director, Michel Ferry; casting, Patsy Pollock. Reviewed at Warner Hollywood Studios, L.A., Nov. 30, 1992. MPAA Rating: R. Running time: **112**

MIN.
Dr. Stephen Fleming . . Jeremy Irons
Anna Barton . . . . . . Juliette Binoche
Ingrid . . . . Miranda Richardson
Martyn . . . . Rupert Graves
Edward Lloyd . . . . Ian Bannen
Elizabeth Prideaux . . . . Leslie Caron
Peter Wetzler . . . . . Peter Stormare
Sally . . . . Gemma Clark
Donald Lyndsaymp . . Julian Fellowes
Prime Minister . . . . . . Tony Doyle

A complex look at an illicit affair that ends in disaster for all concerned, "Damage" is a cold, brittle film about raging, traumatic emotions. Unjustly famous before its release for its hardly extraordinary erotic content, this veddy British-feeling drama from vet French director Louis Malle proves both compelling and borderline risible, wrenching and yet emotionally pinched, and reps a solid entry for arthouse auds worldwide. But mainstream Yank viewers led by publicity to expect a hot or romantic time are in for a dry two hours.

One of the most restrained and spare of well-known directors, Malle has been repeatedly drawn to stories of unconventional, sometimes taboo-breaking sexual relationships, notably in "The Lovers," "Murmur of the Heart" and "Pretty Baby." The latest addition to this list, "Damage" draws a clear-eyed perspective on an English MP whose secret liaison with a young beauty leads him to terribly betray both his wife and son.

The story engages weighty themes that are startling and disturbing but are sufficiently articulated to entice viewers in the right frame of mind. Most obviously, this is the portrait of a highly controlled middle-aged man who becomes unraveled by an unbridled, unprecedented passion. But the film also provocatively charts a father-son competition over a woman, pointing up how completely the libido can obliterate reason, and illustrates how living a lie can so easily become the norm that there seems nothing wrong with it.

As far as the sex goes, there are several sequences of abandon between Jeremy Irons and Juliette Binoche, but they are cut in so measured a way that their effect is far from being a turn-on. It was clearly not intended to be.

Original version, which was screened for critics while the battle over the initial NC-17 rating was played out, contains nothing that hasn't been seen in countless R-rated pics over the years;

specifications must now be considerably more rigorous than a few months ago.

Irons plays Stephen Fleming, a graying, very proper figure in the Tory establishment who has married into money and lives a carefully groomed and organized existence. His wife, Ingrid (Miranda Richardson), may be more intelligent than he; daughter Sally is going through the awkward stage; and son Martyn (Rupert Graves), has just embarked upon a promising journalism career.

At a boring political cocktail party, Stephen exchanges significant eye contact with his son's striking g.f., Anna Barton (Binoche), and destiny is written. In a scene that will do nothing for the reputation of British foreplay, at their next encounter Stephen is in Anna's pants in record time, and they embark on a reckless affair that heeds only the need for discretion, not for any of the other realities of their lives.

Instinctively attempting to order the wild impulses he is experiencing, Stephen takes the normal course of proposing to leave his wife and move in with Anna. But Anna, who has already confessed her dread of possessiveness and the tragic story of her brother's teenage suicide over love for her, tells him he has nothing to gain, as he already has as much of her as he could want, and always will.

No matter what they say or do, Stephen and Anna ultimately can't help themselves, which leads to catastrophe so devastating that "damage" represents a grievous understatement. The wrap-up is perhaps unnecessarily protracted, but the point is well made that none of the characters can possibly be the same after the string of lies, deceit, betrayals and cruelty.

Irons' character becomes more loathesome as he goes along, which will disaffect some viewers, but thesp's expertly calibrated performance makes utterly believable the notion that, from beginning to end, Stephen thinks he can get away with his outrageous behavior, even that he deserves to. As always, Malle refrains from judging or moralizing, but still makes very clear where Stephen goes wrong.

With parted short hair, black attire and an accent far more British than French, the beautiful Binoche comes off as rather severe, even masculine and delivers the critical idea that in sex with Stephen, Anna is able to reach a state of oblivion that momentarily wipes out the inescapable memory of her brother.

Malle's usual austerity is heightened by the clipped, sometimes constipated writing style of scripter David Hare. In his variably successful attempt to distill scenes to their essence, the celebrated playwright occasionally abbreviates them to the point where less actually is less.

The pitiable, in-the-dark wife for most of the running time, Richardson puts frightening force behind her rage when all hell finally breaks loose and Graves ultimately lends some nice shadings to the basically agreeable, somewhat green Martyn.

Awash with ironies and implicit parallels between political and emotional bankruptcy, pic has a frosty handsomeness entirely in keeping with its subject. Zbigniew Preisner's score is full of foreboding and mournfulness.
— *Todd McCarthy*

FOREVER YOUNG

A Warner Bros. release of an Icon production in association with Edward S. Feldman. Executive producers, Feldman, Jeffrey Abrams. Produced by Bruce Davey. Directed by Steve Miner. Screenplay, Abrams. Camera (Technicolor), Russell Boyd; editor, Jon Poll; music, Jerry Goldsmith; production design, Gregg Fonseca; art direction, Bruce A. Miller; set decoration, Jay R. Hart; set design, Jann K. Engel, Richard Yanez, Steve Jeffrey Wolff; costume design, Aggie Guerard Rogers; sound (Dolby), Jim Tanenbaum; assistant director, Matt Earl Beesley; creative makeup design, Dick Smith; special makeup created, applied by Greg Cannom; casting, Marion Dougherty. Reviewed at the Plaza Theater, L.A., Dec. 1, 1992. MPAA Rating: PG. Running time: **102 MIN.**
Daniel . . . . Mel Gibson
Claire . . . . Jamie Lee Curtis
Nat . . . . Elijah Wood
Helen . . . . Isabel Glasser
Harry . . . . George Wendt
Cameron . . . . Joe Morton
John . . . . Nicholas Surovy
Wilcox. . . . . . David Marshall Grant
Felix . . . . Robert Hy Gorman
Susan Finley . . . . Millie Slavin

While it's hard to call a film with Mel Gibson "a sleeper," Warner Bros. has a big, rousing, old-fashioned romance on its hands if it can just get people to take the ride. A perfect "women's picture" alternative to action fare and kid-oriented sequels, "Forever Young" may be one of those slow-building hits, à la "Fried Green Tomatoes," that brings 'em in well after some of the holiday's boom/bust films have exhausted themselves.

The picture would seem to be a tough sell conceptually (no one beat down the door to see similarly themed "Late for Dinner") and the title probably doesn't help. Still, the script by Jeffrey Abrams and Steve Miner's direction seldom strike a false chord— even when they're tugging shamelessly at the heartstrings in almost "E.T."- like fashion — and WB should build word of mouth with two weekends of sneaks prior to the wide opening.

The action begins in 1939, as test pilot Daniel (Gibson) can't bring himself to propose to Helen (Isabel Glasser), right up until the moment she walks in front of a speeding truck.

Helen ends up in a coma, and the distraught Daniel volunteers for an experiment in which his best friend Harry (George Wendt) is to freeze him for a year in an early test of cryogenics.

Cut to 1992, when Daniel is thawed out by two mischievous 10-year-olds and, through a series of circumstances, moves in with one of the boys (Elijah Wood of "Radio Flyer" and "Avalon" renown) and his single mom (Jamie Lee Curtis).

To elaborate would spoil much of the fun, but with the Army in pursuit of their long-forgotten experiment gone awry, the film takes some clever and extremely satisfying turns — tinged with poignance and plenty of humor stemming from Daniel's Rip Van Winkle-like slumber.

Miner, who's directed TV's "The Wonder Years" and "Elvis" in addition to the modest feature "Wild Hearts Can't Be Broken," brings the same dreamy quality to this production, augmented by sumptuous '30s sets and a lush setting for the climax. Remarkably, the director manages to toe the line of melodrama without ever slipping over into camp, balancing those elements with humor and suspense to carry "Forever Young," if not over the moon, at least into the clouds.

The cast is equally splendid, and Gibson — for all the talk of his breakthrough into "serious" roles by doing "Hamlet" — demonstrates his versatility here with a performance that captures the best, less-lethal elements of his onscreen persona.

Curtis conveys a great deal with her limited role as the caring mom, while Wood proves far more engaging than another moppet who stays home alone. Wendt and Morton appear in what amount to cameos as sympathetic scientists of different eras.

"Forever Young" also shines technically, as Russell Boyd's camera adoringly captures Gibson's boyish charms in the manner of an old matinee idol, and Jerry Goldsmith delivers yet another tremendous score tinged with adventure, romance and melancholy. Kudos also to Dick Smith, et al., for the terrific makeup, which, like the movie, should wear extremely well. — *Brian Lowry*

THE DISTINGUISHED GENTLEMAN

A Buena Vista release of a Hollywood Pictures presentation in association with Touchwood Pacific Partners I of a Leonard Goldberg production. Executive producer, Marty Kaplan. Produced by Goldberg, Michael Peyser. Directed by Jonathan Lynn. Screenplay, Kaplan; story by Kaplan, Jonathan Reynolds; camera (Technicolor), Gabriel Beristain; editors, Tony Lombardo, Barry B. Leirer; music, Randy Edelman; production design, Leslie Dilley; art direction, Ed Verreaux; set decoration, Dorree Cooper; costume design, Francine Jamison-Tanchuck; sound (Dolby), Russell Williams II; assistant director, Frank Capra III; casting, Mary Goldberg. Reviewed at Avco Center Cinema, L.A., Nov. 30, 1992. MPAA Rating: R. Running time: **113 MIN.**
Thomas Jefferson Johnson
. . . . Eddie Murphy
Dick Dodge . . . . Lane Smith
Miss Loretta . . . . Sheryl Lee Ralph
Olaf Andersen . . . . . Joe Don Baker
Celia Kirby . . . . Victoria Rowell
Arthur Reinhardt . . . . . Grant Shaud
Terry Corrigan . . . . Kevin McCarthy
Elijah Hawkins . . . Charles S. Dutton
Armando . . . . Victor Rivers
Homer . . . . Chi
Van Dyke . . . . . . Sonny Jim Gaines
Zeke Bridges . . . . Noble Willingham
Iowa . . . . Gary Frank

Mr. Murphy goes to Washington and the big winner is Mickey Mouse, as Disney figures to cash in with a hefty honorarium from this uneven but occasionally quite funny political satire. Those tired of Eddie Murphy Classic — down to the over-used wheezing laugh — may not line up to shake hands with this gentleman, but fans will get a chance to see the comic (as opposed to actor) strut his stuff more amiably than in his last several outings for Paramount.

Coming out of a national election, the movie starts with a very funny premise but doesn't sustain it once the action shifts to the nation's capital: What if a con man was swept into Washington by using the same name as a recently deceased congressman — playing on the notion most people don't know if their rep is dead or alive anyway.

The twist, of course, is that the biggest scams of all go on legally in Washington. Yet while the con artist arrives intent on cashing in from a sea of political action committees and interest groups, his better nature takes over and prompts him to do the ethical thing.

The screenplay by Marty Kaplan (a former speechwriter for Walter Mondale) certainly has its fun with the depraved ins and outs of politics, even if there are no new wrinkles beyond the genuine indignation of "Mr. Smith Goes to Washington."

Where Kaplan ends up looking like a political novice is in the way he structures his main character. The transformation of Jeff Johnson (Murphy shares the name with a philandering senator cameoed by James Garner) into a caring sort is never convincing, other than his understandable desire to woo the niece (Victoria Rowell) of a principled rep (Charles S. Dutton).

Instead of oratorical fire and brimstone, however, Jeff goes on the offensive by setting out to stage a sting against Dick Dodge (Lane Smith), an amoral senior congressman from his state.

"The Distinguished Gentleman" is an amalgam of past Murphy roles but most closely resembles "Trading Places," down to the broad humor, the pleasure of seeing Murphy as a fish-out-of-water among the upper crust and the idea of a con man who exacts vengeance on his one-time benefactors.

Here he reverts to his stand-up talents. Several scenes, in fact, seem to have been added solely for use in the movie's trailer.

Where the film excels, actually, is in the supporting roles, with Smith wonderfully smarmy and the likes of "Murphy Brown's" Grant Shaud, Dutton, Joe Don Baker and Kevin McCarthy as other D.C. archetypes, as well as Sheryl Lee Ralph as the most fetching member of Murphy's entourage.

Director Jonathan Lynn ("My Cousin Vinny") maintains a steady pace but can't avoid arid stretches, and the film drags whenever it ventures too far into propping up Murphy's shallow character. There's an affecting moment, for example, when the congressman encounters a young cancer victim, but it's so incongruous it feels like a cheap ploy to generate instant sympathy.

Tech credits get an "aye" vote, from Randy Edelman's lively score to the costume and set

designs underscoring the heights of Washington largess.
— *Brian Lowry*

SCHULD UND GEDÄCHTNIS
(GUILT AND REMEMBRANCE)
(AUSTRIAN-DOCU)

A Prisma Film production in association with Austrian Ministry for Education & Art. Executive producers, Michael Seeber, Heinz Stussak. Produced by Stussak. Directed, written by Egon Humer. Camera (color), Peter Freiss; editor, Karina Ressler; sound, Hans Eder. Reviewed at Vienna Film Festival, Oct. 18, 1992. Running time: **87 MIN.**

Possibly the most devastating documentary ever made about Nazis who survived the war, "Schuld und Gedächtnis" is a restrained but shocking portrait of blindness, arrogance and hatred. Four former Nazi officers recount their experiences and feelings under Hitler and the reasons they still think that way. Pointing his camera at these white-haired, pleasant-looking men in suits, director Egon Humer proves the unthinkable is reality: The Nazi past is not over.

It's worth watching not only to see the new freedom these old Nazis feel to share their views in 1992, but to chronicle the reality of a politics most people only know from newsreels or distorted Hollywood bad-guy portrayals. These four men, all doctors and lawyers, were high-ranking Nazi officials (one served as a doctor in a concentration camp) sentenced at Nuremberg but freed after a few years.

Until recently, they had lain low. All are respected and one has even since been awarded the "Distinguished Service Medal." Their reasons for speaking out now? One says: "I'm 83 years old — I don't care what happens now." Another reasons: "We are reunified and Germany is the World Soccer Champion. It's time we spoke out again."

And speak out they do. Director Humer calmly places questions and lets his four subjects say what they have to say without any attempt to trap them or contradict them (though he does sparingly intercut the interviews with newsreel footage).

Though they declare the innocence of their cause (if Jews were ever slaughtered, it was only an isolated case here and there, people working on their own), they adamantly defend fascism ("The war, well, that was hardly avoidable. And even then [when we were pushed into it], we went in with joy in our hearts."), racism ("[The Gypsies] were asocial! The parents would perform their sexual intercourse before the eyes of the children, and the children, they would start participating in sexual intercourse at the ages of 14 or 15. That's un-European and asocial!"), even anti-Semitism ("I became an anti-Semite because I saw how the Jews infiltrated our people and dirtied and weakened them. But I was never against individual Jews.") and doubts that the Holocaust really happened ("Despite the World War and despite the alleged killing of 6 million Jews, there are still enough Jews around, aren't there?").

In defending their "cause," they betray not only their ignorance and naïveté, they show a fanatic hatred one fears can never be cured. — *Eric Hansen*

ICH BIN MEINE EIGENE FRAU
(I AM MY OWN WOMAN)
(GERMAN-DOCU)

A Rosa von Praunheim production in association with Renee Perraudin/Scala Z Film. Produced, directed by von Praunheim. Screenplay, Valentin Passoni, from Charlotte von Mahlsdorf's book. Camera (color), Lorenz Haarmann; editor, Mike Shepard; music, Joachim Litty; production design, Peter Kothe; costumes, Joachim Voeltzke; sound, Shepard; assistant director, Passoni, Florian Bodenschweger. Reviewed at the Intl. Hof Film Days, Oct. 31, 1992. Running time: **90 MIN.**
Charlotte (15-17) . . . . Jens Taschner
Charlotte (20-40) . . Ichgola Androgyn
Charlotte von Mahlsdorf . . . . Herself
Also with: Beate Jung, Sylvia Seelow.

To tell this fascinating story, gay, self-styled "bad boy" director Rosa von Praunheim has chosen a mixture of documentary and drama. Though pic is sloppy and suffers from mediocre production values, it will do well in festivals and on the gay circuit simply because of the power, originality and spectacular drama of its subject, Charlotte von Mahlsdorf, the best-known transvestite of East Germany.

Von Mahlsdorf, 64, (whose real name is Lothar Berfelde) has been a soft- and outspoken "woman" almost exclusively since escaping from her macho Nazi father. Her life has been a game of resistance and survival, and, for German homosexuals, a model of bravery and idealism.

Von Praunheim tells the story using dramatized sequences of Charlotte at different ages, interspersed with interviews in which the actual Charlotte often walks into a scene to be asked by the actor: "What did you feel when that happened? How should I play that scene?"

Though theoretically interesting, tech aspects are not as professional as expected from a filmmaker with more than 25 productions to his name. The actors seem to be playing at scenes from the life of a good friend at a birthday party, and the interviews lack imagination.

What is fascinating is Charlotte herself. Episodes from her early life, her brushes with death under the Nazis and with the twisted authority of the Communist regimes are thought-provoking and full of potential, unfortunately not realized as well as it might. — *Eric Hansen*

1991: THE YEAR PUNK BROKE
(DOCU-COLOR/B&W-16m)

A Tara release of a Geffen/DGC presentation of a Sonic Life/We Got Power production. Directed, edited by Dave Markey. Camera (color/B&W, Super 8m to 16m), Markey; Sonic Youth live sound, Terry Parson; Nirvana live sound, Craig Montgomery. Reviewed at Red Vic Movie House, San Francisco, Nov. 20, 1992. Running time: **99 MIN.**
With: Sonic Youth, Nirvana, Dinosaur Jr., Babes in Toyland, Gumball, the Ramones.

Formless, endless and technically crude, "The Year Punk Broke" is the sloppiest rock-doc to win actual release in some time. Only the alternative-market popularity of headliners Sonic Youth and massive success (subsequent to this shoot) of Nirvana will keep it from instant vid oblivion. Negative fan word of mouth should mean short urban playdates.

Following veteran NYC noise band Sonic Youth around Europe for a two-week tour, director Dave Markey manages an amazing level of tedium. The nonstop stage performances are padded with largely nonsynched, clumsy, fast-mo/quick-cut zoom shots, all shakily hand-held.

Audio qualities aren't much better than visuals. A vocally ragged version of Nirvana's eventual monster hit "Smells Like Teen Spirit" is hardly definitive.

Title implies some overview of how and why such alternative, and often raucous, bands have finally broken from underground to mainstream status. But film offers no insight.

Onstage hijinks (knocking over drum sets — wow!) are none too charismatic here, nor is aimless footage of band members. While some of these musicians have been fairly articulate in print, they come off as moronic here.

This depressing snore comes as a surprise from Markey, whose 1980s fiction featurettes "Desperate Teenage Lovedolls" and "Lovedoll Superstar" were hilarious punk parodies of rock mythology. — *Dennis Harvey*

DIE ZWEITE HEIMAT:
LEAVING HOME
(GERMAN-COLOR/B&W)

An Edgar Reitz production, in association with WDR/HR/NDR/BR/SFB/SWF/BBC/TVE/TV-1/YLE/DR/NRK/ORF. Produced, directed, written by Reitz. Camera (color/B&W), Gernot Roll (parts 1-5), Gerard Vandenberg (6-8), Christian Reitz (9-13); editor, Susanne Hartmann; music, Nikos Mamangakis; production design, Franz Bauer; costumes, Bille Brassers, Nikola Hoeltz; sound, Heiko Hinderks, Haymo Heyder, Manfred Banach, Reiner Wiehr; makeup, Mia Schoepke; assistant director, casting, Robert Busch. Reviewed at the Prinz Regenten Theater, Munich, Sept. 5 to 8, 1992. (In London Film Festival) Running time: **1,532 MIN.**
Hermann . . . . Henry Arnold
Clarissa . . . . Salome Kammer
Schnüsschen . . . . . . Anke Sevenich
Juan . . . . Daniel Smith
Alex . . . . Michael Schönborn
Renate . . . . Franziska Traub
Elisabeth Cerphal . . Hannelore Hoger
Frau Moretti . . . . . . Hanna Köhler
Evelyne . . . . Gisela Müller
Ansgar . . . . Michael Seyfried
Volker . . . . Armin Fuchs
Jean-Marie . . . . . Martin Maria Blau
Olga . . . . Lena Lessing
Rob . . . . Peter Weiss
Stefan . . . . Frank Röth
Reihhard . . . . Laszlo I. Kish
Esther . . . . Susanne Lothar
Dorli . . . . Veronika Ferres
Frau Ries . . . . Franziska Stömmer
Gerold Gattinger . . . Manfred Andrae

A 25 1/2-hour movie is not just a movie, it is a commitment. Half of the merit of "Die Zweite Heimat: Leaving Home" is that it miraculously convinces the audience to stay for all 13 two-hour installments. Though length is unwieldy, this accessible, human epic about a bunch of kids growing up in Munich in the '60s is bound to

be the hit of any festival.

Edgar Reitz co-wrote and directed the 1984 16-hour "Heimat" and for this sequel takes on both chores (sans co-scripter) again, now following a character from the first film, Hermann (musician Henry Arnold), as he bitterly abandons his home town and goes to Munich to study music composition.

There, Arnold slowly becomes involved with a group of fellow music and film students centering on the house of a rich, immature publisher's daughter, who acts as a patron. Many are recognizable as Munich figures of the '60s/'70s, including members of the New German Cinema.

Arnold's Hermann is alternately awkward and in control. Mentally tough, he loves, but is afraid of loving, Clarissa (singer-cellist Salome Kammer), a sometimes angry, self-destructive enigma over the script's 2,143-pages.

Watching these characters for more than 25 hours has a strange effect. Unlike in a soap opera, where the characters remain largely the same over years, the finely tuned, personal script and dedicated, convincing thesping lets the characters evolve naturally. When the film ends, the usual feeling of closure is missing, leaving instead a sense that the characters have simply gone on living, but somewhere else.

Most roles are taken by inexperienced actors (at least when the 552-day shoot began), mostly young musicians, as they had to perform their own music. But their performances are almost miraculous, especially Daniel Smith as the magical, world-weary and wise Chilean Juan.

Only toward the the end of the film does Reitz lose track. Where the early '60s are depicted with humor and warmth, his comedic sense falters in the latter half of the decade; perhaps (as one viewer suggested) he is still too close to it to see the humor.

Reitz also has problems tying the loose ends together, finally sending Arnold off on a surreal train trip in which he meets most of the main characters again. Seeing how much they have changed, how his family of peers has split into a series of individuals, Arnold realizes that, as he had left home, he now must leave Munich. The solution is functionally correct, but feels inelegant and even false.

Reitz's manner is unlike his New German Cinema colleagues; "Die Zweite Heimat" is a mas-

terpiece in realistic storytelling, beautifully photographed — day sequences are in realistic B&W, night and evening sequences shot in warm colors. It comes much closer to Dostoevsky's tangled human relationships than Wim Wenders' unpeopled land- and think-scapes, a difference perhaps summed up by a young director in the film: "Life is always there where the filmmakers aren't." —*Eric Hansen*

LUNGO IL FIUME
(DOWN THE RIVER)
(ITALIAN-DOCU)

A RAI presentation of a Cinemaundici/RAI Uno production. Executive producer, Giampietro Bonamigo. Produced by Giuseppe Cereda (for RAI). Directed, written by Ermanno Olmi. Camera (Eastmancolor), Olmi, Fabio Olmi; editors, E. Olmi, Paolo Cottignola; sound (Dolby), F. Olmi. Reviewed at London Film Festival, Nov. 8, 1992. Running time: **81 MIN.**
Voice: Francesco Carnelutti.

A poetic meditation on Italy's giant Po, "Down the River" finds veteran director Ermanno Olmi traveling back to his roots as a documaker. Commercial chances are zip beyond tube sales, but the film will appeal to connoisseurs and buffs eager to keep up with Olmi's slim output.

Despite the title, the film is not a travelogue. Beyond a vague winter-to-winter timescale, the journey is more philosophical than geographical, a reverie on mankind's relationship with nature that picks up themes from Olmi's earlier features.

Starting with a powerful eco-message — the polluted river runs through Italy's industrialized north — the pic settles down into a series of exquisite images of the Po in all its moods, backed by biblical quotations (mostly from Isaiah) and extracts from Handel's "Messiah" (conducted by Trevor Pinnock). The general awed, hushed tone imparts an autumnal feel.

Dramatic gearshifts are rare. One moment, two-thirds in, when the tranquility of a solo fisherman is shattered by speedboats, shocks with its power.

Olmi's viewpoint is consciously naïve: the simplicity and perfection of creation vs. the vanity and rapaciousness of man. His religioso outlook may pall with nonbelievers when he gets specific, with refs to Christ's trial and crucifixion, at the end.

Technically, pic is first-rate, and benefits from big screen viewing. Trimming by some 15 minutes would tighten pacing.

Supporting bill at London fest was Michelangelo Antonioni's striking 11-minute, 35m docu "Volcanoes and Carnival" ("Noto — Mandorli — Vulcano — Stromboli — Carnevale"), funded by Italian electricity company ENEL and debuted at Expo '92, Seville. Divided into five segs, sans narration, the Sicilian-lensed pic is a visually robust footnote to the career of the semi-paralyzed octogenarian, here assisted by his wife, Enrica.
— *Derek Elley*

EL SUR
(THE SOUTH)
(SPANISH)

An Iberoamericana Films/Quinto Centenario production, for Televisión Española. (U.S. sales: Televisión Española, Madrid; rest of world: Quinto Centenario, Madrid.) Executive producer, Andres Vicente Gómez. Directed, written by Carlos Saura, from Jorge Luis Borges' story "El Sur." Camera (Eastmancolor), Jose Luis Alcaine; editor, Pablo G. del Amo; music, Ariel Ramirez, Hamlet Lima Quintana; production design, Victor Albarran, Alejandro Arando; art direction, Emilio Basaldua; costume design, Beatriz Di Benedetto; sound, Alfonso Pino, Jose Luis Diaz. Reviewed at London Film Festival, Nov. 15, 1992. Running time: **60 MIN.**
Juan Dahlman . . . . . Oscar Martínez
Carlos . . . . Gerardo Romano
Doña Rosario Flores . . . Nini Gambler
Alejandro . . . . Villanueve Cosse
Pastor Guillermo Brige . Jorge Narrale
Casiano . . . . Arturo Bonin
Doctor/Patron . . . . Luis Tasca
Sergio . . . . Juan Legrado

Carlos Saura's "The South" is top-flight cinematic storytelling. Hourlong TV movie, about a Buenos Aires librarian's obsession with his family home in the south, should rate festival exposure on the strength of the Spanish director's name and makes a perfect dualer with his subsequent "Sevillanas" dance docu for arthouse payoffs.

Saura has updated the two-page short story by late Argentinian scribe Jorge Luis Borges from the '30s to spring 1990, and played up its autobiographical elements, such as the protagonist's strong mother. Helmer sees it as "a bit of an experimental film," though its precision mounting and dream-like ending echo elements in his work from the past 20 years.

Central character is shy, time-serving librarian Juan Dahlman

(Oscar Martínez) who dreams he's stabbed to death at the family's beautiful southern ranch, a place he's wanted to revisit since childhood. One day, after injuring his head in a fall, he undergoes surgery and is ordered to rest. And so he finally journeys south, to his appointment with destiny . . .

Pic is basically a slowly-paced mood piece — a study of a man emotionally (and later, physically) between life and death — but Saura keeps plenty of emotion bubbling away beneath the surface to prevent the pic becoming an academic exercise.

The quirky classical/Hispanic soundtrack and Jose Luis Alcaine's visuals keep ears and eyes engaged.

Performances are all neatly etched and highly focused. Buenos Aires locations are used with economy. — *Derek Elley*

TALE OF A VAMPIRE
(JAPANESE-BRITISH)

A State Screen (U.K.) release of a Tsuburaya/State Screen Prods. production. (Intl. sales: State Screen, London.) Executive producer, Noriko Shishikura. Produced by Simon Johnson. Directed by Shimako Sato. Screenplay, Sato, Jane Corbett, from Sato's story; camera (Technicolor), Zubin Mistry; editor, Chris Wright; music, Julian Joseph; production design, Alice Normington; art direction, Tom Burton; costume design, Margaret Miller; sound (Dolby), Ronald Bailey; special effects coordinator, David Watkins; assistant directors, Ray Corbett, Charlie Watson; production manager, Mark Matthews; stunt cooordinator, Terry Forrestal; 2nd unit director, Chris Wright; 2nd unit camera, Martyn Bray; co-producer, Linda Kay. Reviewed at London Film Festival, Nov. 17, 1992. Running time: **102 MIN.**
Alex . . . . Julian Sands
Anne/Virginia . . . . Suzanna Hamilton
Edgar . . . . Kenneth Cranham
Denise . . . . Marian Diamond
Also with: Michael Kenton, Catherine Blake, Mark Kempner.

Elegant to a fault, "Tale of a Vampire" is nailed to the floor by anemic perfs from its two leads and a script that's all tease and no bite. Pic may build a small cult following among genre buffs but won't score many general converts.

Original story by Japanese-born, London-trained director Shimako Sato goes the familiar route of love across the ages. Here, the lonesome fangster in modern-day London is Alex (Julian Sands). The plot starts to move forward when the mysterious Edgar (Kenneth Cranham) arranges for a young woman, Anne (Suzanna Hamilton), to be hired as an assistant at the library where Alex researches martyrs. Alex realizes she's his 19th-century mistress reincarnate and the stage is set (slowly) for the trio to work out their destiny.

Sato's evident ambition to ring the changes on the genre is torpedoed by duff dialogue and a spartan storyline. Her keen designer's eye is no substitute, finally, for original content, though her potential is clear.

Sands and Hamilton make a bloodless couple; Cranham is fine within the script's limitations and with a larger part would have stolen the movie.

Despite a hasty four-week shoot and peanuts budget, tech credits are stylish, Zubin Mistry's light-play lensing rating a special bow.— *Derek Elley*

A CSALÁS GYÖNYÖRE
(RAPTURE OF DECEIT)
(HUNGARIAN)

A Dialóg Studió/Cinema F/Hungarian Motion Picture Foundation production. (Intl. sales: Hungarian Television.) Produced by Ferenc András. Executive producer, András Elek. Directed by Lívia Gyarmathy. Screenplay, Géza Böszörményi, from Gyarmathy's short story; camera (Agfacolor), Gábor Balog; editor, Mária Nagy; music, Ennio Morricone; art direction, Csaba Stork, Zsolt Csengeri; costume design, Márta Jánoskuti; sound (Dolby), István Wolf; assistant director, István Albrecht. Reviewed at London Film Festival, Nov. 22, 1992. Running time: **96 MIN.**
Dora Tas . . . . Rita Tushingham
Júlia . . . . Anikó Für
Feri . . . . Péter Andorai
Joe . . . . György Dörner
Adam . . . . Gábor Reviczky
Adam's wife . . . . .Judit Pogány

Despite its overheated title, "Rapture of Deceit" is a likable study of changes in contempo Hungary vis-à-vis two women groping for their own kind of independence. Curious casting of U.K. actress Rita Tushingham is more off-putting than advantageous, but may work in pic's favor for offshore tube sales.

Top-billed Tushingham in fact plays second fiddle to the movie's true star, the striking Anikó Für. Latter plays Júlia, 30, an electrical engineer who gets pinkslipped in the new economy and finds herself on the job market.

After discovering her careerist husband (Péter Andorai) in the sack with his boss' daughter, she moves in with a widowed, 40-year-old lawyer friend (Tushingham). Júlia finally lands a job as a waitress, but gets entangled in the struggles of her young boss (György Dörner) against

local hoods after his eaterie.

The picture works on several levels at the same time: parallels between the new independence of Hungary and the two women; people's ability (or inability) to adapt; and the country's move from institutionalized party violence to market-driven, dog-eat-dog violence.

Pic is more accessible than many recent Hungarian items, with leavening humor and more attention paid to commercial values. Its broader-based storyline points to a potentially profitable avenue for Magyar moviemaking.

Für's sensitive performance anchors the movie. The casting of Tushingham is more problematic: She looks the part but, totally revoiced by Hungarian actress Erika Kiss, adds little a local thesp couldn't. Other roles are all solid.

Lívia Gyarmathy brings an easy rhythm to the piece in the style of her previous relationship pics ("Every Wednesday," etc.). Gábor Balog's lensing and Ennio Morricone's pleasant (if unmemorable) score are smooth pluses.
— *Derek Elley*

AILEEN WUORNOS:
THE SELLING OF A
SERIAL KILLER
(BRITISH-DOCU-16m)

A Lafayette Films production for Channel 4. (Intl. sales: Lafayette, London.) Executive producer, Peter Moore. Produced, directed, written by Nick Broomfield. Camera (Duart color, 16m), Barry Ackroyd; editors, Richard M. Lewis, Rick Vick; music, David Bergeaud; sound, Broomfield; co-producer, Rieta Oord. Reviewed at London Film Festival, Nov. 17, 1992. Running time: **82 MIN.**

Brit documaker Nick Broomfield adds another quality pic to his canon with "Aileen Wuornos," a quizzical, horrorshow look at the hyping of the "world's first female serial killer," now awaiting the chair in a Florida. pen. Verbally explicit item will be limited to special outings and possibly hardnosed webs.

Michigan-born Wuornos, now 36, was arrested Jan. 9, 1991, in Daytona Beach, Fla., and charged with shooting seven men. Dubbed "The Angels of Death," she and her lesbian lover had worked central Florida highways as hitchhiking prostitutes until her lover decamped and became the prosecution's chief witness.

Broomfield's docu unites his

interest in social outsiders and oversize personalities evident in previous works, ranging from "Soldier Girls" to "Lily Tomlin" and the hooker docu "Chicken Ranch." Here, the focus is on the hard sell, the book/movie deals and other alleged dirty dealing surrounding Wuornos — rather than Wuornos per se.

Main players in the film are Arlene Pralle, a ranch-owning born-again Christian who adopted Wuornos in '91, and Steven Glazer, Wuornos' self-promoting, guitar-strumming, singing lawyer. Pralle demands $25,000 before she'll be interviewed by Broomfield, and Glazer spends most of the time ferrying the director around in circles and crooning homespun ditties.

Broomfield cannily makes his own quest for the truth the pic's central motor. The sight of the dogged Brit doorstopping locals with his boom mike, and only at the last moment meeting Wuornos herself (who appears a sympathetic interviewee), puts a blackly humorous spin on it all.

Though it doesn't get even close to the tangled truth, the docu raises enough questions to justify its running time. Emotionally charged court videos of Wuornos pack quite a punch, and pic's rough technical edges fit its fly-on-the-wall approach.
—*Derek Elley*

ELECTRIC MOON
(BRITISH-INDIAN)

A Winstone Films (U.K.) release of a Grapevine Media production for Channel 4 in association with Times Television. (Intl. sales: Film Four Intl., London.) Produced by Sundeep Singh Bedi. Directed by Pradip Krishen. Screenplay, Arundhati Roy. Camera (Technicolor), Giles Nuttgens; editor, Krishen; music, Simeon Venkov; production design, Roy; sound (Dolby), Robert Taylor, Ernest Marsh; assistant directors, Tigmanshu Dhulia, Habib Faisal. Reviewed at London Film Festival, Nov. 18, 1992. Running time: 103 MIN.
Ranveer . . . . Roshan Seth
Rambuhj Goswami . Naseeruddin Shah
Sukanya ("Socks") . . . . . Leela Naidu
Boltoo . . . . Raghubir Yadav
Bikram ("Bubbles") . Gerson Da Cunha
Louise Robinson . . . . . Alice Spivak
Emma Lamp . . . . Frances Helm
Simon Lidell . . . . James Fleet
Phoebe Fenton . . . . . Francesca Brill
Also with: Gareth Forwood, Surendra Rajan, Malcolm Jamieson, Barbara Lott.
(English & Urdu soundtrack)

"Electric Moon" loses its shine early on. This amiable, good-humored satire on cultural stereotypes on both sides of the Indian tourist fence is

too low-voltage to create much of a theatrical buzz.

Setting is modern-day central India, where a trio of penurious aristocrats peddle "traditional" local culture for gullible foreigners. Their ritzy lodge, in the middle of a national park, is a time capsule of Raj India, complete with elephants, afternoon tea, cut-glass colonial accents and the marketing tag "Nobody gives you the jungle like we do." All goes well until a bureaucratic new park director cracks down on the rules, drying up bookings.

The idea has plenty of potential but, after a promising start, characters come and go, the humor loses its edge, and pacing slows to a dawdle.

The playing, especially by Roshan Seth as the entrepreneurial Ranveer and Leela Naidu as aristocratic "Socks," is generally fine. The tourist types, including Louise Robinson as a lonesome Yank, are okay but tighter cutting would have helped all perfs.

Photography and design are attractive, and the £400,000 ($600,000) budget is well spent. More of Simeon Venkov's music would have helped move things along. — *Derek Elley*

LES NUITS FAUVES
(SAVAGE NIGHTS)
(FRENCH-ITALIAN)

A Pan Européenne release of a Nella Banfi presentation of a Banfilm Ter/La Sept Cinema/Erre Produzioni/SNC co-production in association with Sofinergie 2/CNC/Canal Plus/Procirep. (Intl. sales: UGC). Executive producer, Jean-Frédéric Samie. Directors of production, Olivier Ramon, Agnès Berthola. Produced by Banfi. Directed by Cyril Collard. Screenplay, Collard, Jacques Fieschi, based on Collard's novel. Camera (color), Manuel Teran; editor, Lise Beaulieu; music, René-Marc Bini, Collard; art direction, Jacky Macchi, Katja Kosenina; costumes, Régine Arniaud; sound (Dolby), Michel Brethez, Dominique Hennequin. Reviewed at Turin Intl. Festival of Young Cinema (competition), Nov. 19, 1992. (In Sarasota French Film Festival.) Running time: **126 MIN.**
Jean . . . . Cyril Collard
Laura . . . . Romane Bohringer
Samy . . . . Carlos Lopez
Laura's mother . . . . . . Corine Blue
Jean's mother . . . . . Claude Winter
Marc . . . . René-Marc Bini
Noria . . . . Maria Schneider
Also with: Clémentine Célarié, Laura Favali, Denis D'Archangelo.

As feature debuts go, Gallic *enfant terrible* Cyril Collard's film of his autobiographically tinged novel "Les Nuits

Fauves" is the kind of electrifying, angry, attention-getting, high-energy entrée most young hopefuls only dream about. But as a sprint across the sexual minefield, with Collard as the drama's HIV-positive-ly lit fuse, it's abrasively off-key. Pic should find as many staunch defenders as violent attackers and potential to make sparks fly should help crack the Euro market in a big way. Yank pickup looks less certain.

In a seemingly deliberate move to shut out audience sympathy, Collard's character is a narcissistic, sexually omnivorous hedonist with a static expression of knowing smugness, who beds down first with intense nymphette Romane Bohringer and next with hunky footballer Carlos Lopez without forewarning either of his precarious condition. The script almost endorses his irresponsibility with reckless, poetic notions about passion being its own protection, and when the triangle's two rival sides both forgive Collard's reprehensible bedside manner and consciously opt for unsafe sex, it takes on the queasy arrogance of a demented vanity exercise.

Reservations about the basic concept aside, Collard maps the volatile path of each relationship with an unflagging tension that never loosens its grip. Punctuating the main action are Collard's nocturnal cruises through a Paris given such menacing allure by Manuel Teran's camera that the central trio turns into a quartet.

As Collard's health starts showing danger signs, pic's hard-edged vitality becomes violently edgy. A succession of slamming doors, phones and bodies, together with Teran's bravura hand-held work and Lise Beaulieu's dizzying editing becomes both wearing and exhilarating, especially the crescendo of answering machine messages conveying Bohringer's growing hysteria.

Where the script's imbalance really surfaces is in the triangle's deterioration. The male-female bond dissolves with kid-glove handling, but Collard's link with Lopez is dismissed flippantly, ultimately serving no purpose.

The controversy the pic is bound to stoke with safe sex crusaders will equal the heckling it stands to bear for its extremely negative gay p.o.v. Images presented are invariably loveless and self-punishing, and a superfluous coda showing Lopez's involvement in neo-Nazi antics and Collard threatening to use his bleeding hand as a weapon is a grating miscalculation.

Despite fundamental story flaws, Collard's limitations as an actor, and an excess of ideas, pic remains a boldly confidant directing bow laced with touches of stylistic brilliance. Equally impressive is Bohringer, who registers strongly and looks set to join the ranks of France's top new-generation thesps. Tech aspects are right on target, lensing ably serving pic's in-your-face attitude. — *David Rooney*

VERSAILLES RIVE-GAUCHE
(A NIGHT IN VERSAILLES)
(FRENCH)

A CTV Intl. presentation of a Flagrant Delit production. Directed by Bruno Podalydes. Screenplay, Podalydes, Denis Podalydes; camera (color), Pierre Stoeber; editor, Marie-France Cuenot; music, Dominique Paulin. Reviewed at Sarasota French Film Festival, Nov. 12, 1992. Running time: **47 MIN.**
Claire . . . . Isabelle Candelier
Arnaud . . . . Denis Podalydes
The Neighbor . . . . . Philippe Uchan
Jean-Claude . . . . . Michel Vuillermoz

Bruno Podalydes gets 47 minutes of comic mileage from a single gag in "A Night in Versailles," a comedy just short enough to keep the variations on a theme from becoming labored. Pic has been surprisingly popular with Paris audiences, and doubtless will continue its well-received tour of the global fest circuit. North American theatrical prospects are doubtful, however.

Denis Podalydes, the director's brother and co-scriptwriter, plays a mild-mannered young man who has invited a pretty Parisian woman to his small Versailles apartment for dinner. Unfortunately, his brother (and neighbor) also is interested in his guest. Even more unfortunately, the brother's arrival triggers the arrival of several more unwelcome (and inconvenient) guests.

That, by and large, is the plot. The subtle comedy springs from sly construction of steadily escalating complications.

Director Podalydes fails to cap everything off with a satisfying finale, or even a funny curtain line. But "Night in Versailles" showcases a bright young cast (Isabelle Candelier is a standout as the dinner guest), and is an altogether pleasant, if not hilarious, diversion. — *Joe Leydon*

CONFESSIONS D'UN BARJO
(CONFESSIONS OF A CRAP ARTIST)
(FRENCH)

A Pan Européenne release of a PCC Prods./Aliceleo/FR-3 Films/Centre Européen Cinematographique Rhône-Alpes co-production with participation of Sofinergie 2/Investimage 3/CNC/Canal Plus. Executive producer, Françoise Galfré. Produced by Patrick Godeau. Directed by Jérôme Boivin. Screenplay, Jacques Audiard, Boivin, based on Philip K. Dick's novel "Confessions of a Crap Artist." Camera (color), Jean-Claude Larrieu; editor, Anne Lafarge; music, Hugues Le Bars; costumes, Caroline de Vivaise; set design, Dominique Malaret; sound, François Waledisch. Reviewed at Forum Horizon cinema, Paris, June 16, 1992. (In Sarasota French Film Festival.) Running time: **85 MIN.**
Charles . . . . Richard Bohringer
Fanfan . . . . Anne Brochet
Barjo . . . . Hippolyte Girardot
Mme. Hermelin . Consuelo de Haviland

Jérôme Boivin's relentlessly stylish "Confessions of a Crap Artist" leaves an odd impression that will amuse some but irk others. There's certain to be a core audience for this strangely touching mix of memories, impulsive behavior, black comedy and misfortune, but offbeat pic is a category-defying marketing challenge.

Boivin has made Philip K. Dick's '50s American characters into modern French archetypes. Hippolyte Girardot, introduced via aggressive voiceover, is geeky perfection as Barjo, an exasperatingly naïve four-eyed nerd whose cheerful questioning and note-taking drive others batty. He indiscriminately records all info coming his way and randomly redispenses it, with sometimes disastrous results.

After a fire destroys his house and most of his fetishistic quasi-scientific collectibles, Girardot moves in with his whim-driven twin sister, Fanfan (Anne Brochet), and her long-suffering husband (Richard Bohringer).

Brochet, in a radical departure from the maidens she played in "Cyrano" and "Tous les Matins du Monde," is utterly wacko, vulgar, obnoxious and selfish. Her awkward, compulsive pursuit of a young couple is both disturbing and believable.

Pic is a weird blend of comedy and melancholy. Lensing and art direction are perfectly in keeping with the rapid-fire tale of emotional cripples oblivious to their own peculiarities.

Helmer keeps vestiges of a 1950s sensibility down to a catchy-but-silly '50s-style theme song and the Bohringer home is one that the Jetsons might rent; Brochet's wardrobe underlines space-age foolishness.

Viewers not irritated by the demanding, kvetchy characters may warm to pic's view of an extremely dysfunctional family. In a subplot concerning the imminent end of the world, Consuelo de Havilland scores as a psychic. — *Lisa Nesselson*

NOVEMBRE
(FRENCH-POLISH)

A Motion Media presentation of a Jeck Films (Paris)/Studio Indeks (Lodz)/TV Varsovie (Poland) co-production in association with CNC/Canal Plus, with the participation of the Region Languedoc-Roussillon. Directed by Lukasz Karwowski. Screenplay, Karwowski, Pawel Edelman. Camera (color), Edelman; sound, Piotr Domaradzki; art direction, Andrzej Przedworski, Ursula Szubert, Slawomir Witczak; costumes, Elzbieta Radke. Reviewed at Sarasota French Film Festival, Nov. 14, 1992. Running time: **90 MIN.**
Sara . . . . Marine Delterme
Nowak . . . . Judith Henry
Piotr . . . . Bartek Topa
Fr. Andre . . Aleksander Kajdanowski
Also with: Michel Vitold, Zbigniew Zapasiewicz, Myriam David and Jean-Yves Gautier.

Lukasz Karwowski's "Novembre" is a mind-numbingly, jaw-droppingly pretentious piece of high-toned rubbish. French-Polish co-production has no commercial potential whatsoever, and serves only to prove that Karwowski, a Lodz film school grad making his feature directing debut, has a bright future ahead of him in music videos. Or perfume ads.

The plot, at once simplistic and obscure, deals with the mental disintegration of a beautiful med school student (Marine Delterme). At first, all she has to worry about are fits and blackouts. But she knows she's really in bad shape when she single-handedly attacks and kills several customers in a dingy bar. Her med school classmate (Judith Henry of "La Discrète," totally wasted) decides Delterme must be possessed by the devil. But when exorcism fails, Delterme chains herself inside a car, pours gasoline over herself and lights a match. Yes, she really does.

Technically, "Novembre" is a dazzler, with many MTV-worthy shots of smoky, bluish-gray, rain-slicked streets and interiors, but it's almost as though Karwowski wanted to re-create every striking image he's ever seen — in movies, on album covers, during dreams, whatever — without any regard for disciplining them with anything resembling a story. — *Joe Leydon*

LOIN DU BRESIL
(FAR FROM BRAZIL)
(FRENCH)

A Les Films Pelléas/Olivier Masclet release of a Flash Film/FR-3 Films Prods./SGGC/Limbo Film AG (Zurich) co-production with the participation of Canal Plus and the CNC. Produced by Philippe Martin. Directed, written by Tilly. Camera (color), Benoit Delhomme; editor, Martin Barraqué; music, Gégard Barreaux; set design, Michèle Abbe Vannier; costume design, Florence Emir; sound, Florian Eidenbenz; co-producers, Luciano Gloor, Isabelle Fauvel; associate producers, Jean Bernard Feytoux, Jean François Lepetit. Reviewed at the Luxembourg cinema, Paris, Oct. 13, 1992. (In Sarasota French Film Festival.) Running time: **98 MIN.**
Juliette . . . . Emmanuelle Riva
Honorie . . . . Jenny Cleve
Benoit . . . . . . Christophe Huysman
Kim . . . . Eric Doyle
Isabelle . . . . Charlotte Clamens
Also with: Gilles Treton, Jérôme Chappatte, Marylin Even, Alexandra Kazan, Michèle Gleizer, Jean Marc Roulot.

French playwright Tilly's first film takes a perceptive look at a vivacious matriarch whose five grown children make an eventful weekend visit. Biting comedy steers clear of conventions as an top cast parlays Tilly's trenchant dialogue into an involving and affecting pic.

It's been 22 years since Juliette's (Emmanuelle Riva) husband ran off to Brazil with another woman, leaving her to raise their brood. Riva now lives alone in her country manor near Deauville with long-suffering cook Honorine (Jenny Cleve). Although obviously accustomed to bourgeois comforts and society, Riva stirs up gossip by consorting with a much younger man and slumming with a fun-loving neighbor.

Family members arrive at their big childhood home for a rare reunion, starting with 24-year-old Benoit (Christophe Huysman) and his male companion, Kim. Riva is oblivious to her youngest son's sexual preference; the others make their contempt known.

Pregnant daughter Isabelle (Charlotte Clamens) dislikes mom, but remains close to her obnoxious twin brother Laurent (Jérôme Chappatte) who has brought along his hip, vulgar g.f. Daughter Sophie (Alexandra

Kazan), a glamorous globe-trotting TV news reporter with an annoyingly take-charge demeanor, is the only sibling to visit wayward dad in Brazil. Eldest and dutiful son Philippe (Jean-Marc Roulot) completes the clan with his no-nonsense wife and three wholesome daughters.

Riva gets on everyone's nerves and is not sincerely loved by anyone but the gay son. Scripter-helmer draws viewers into family relationships as funny as they are cruel. Large ensemble cast is all wonderfully distinct and memorable. Riva, especially, shines as the frivolous, self-centered woman who remains wounded by her husband's betrayal.

Intelligent lensing makes Riva's spacious house into a character in its own right. Biting dialogue demands equally sharp subtitles. — *Lisa Nesselson*

UN ÉTÉ SANS HISTOIRES
(FRENCH SUMMER)
(FRENCH)

A Rezo Film presentation of a Le Jour/Le Nuit production. Produced by Annie Madeleine Gonzalez. Directed by Philippe Harel. Screenplay, Harel, Dodine Herry. Camera (color), Olivier Raffet; editors, Benedicte Teiger, Frederique Oger; music, Philippe Eidel; sound, Christophe Lamby; assistant director, Catherine Herbert. Reviewed at Sarasota French Film Festival, Nov. 12, 1992. Running time: **65 MIN.**
Claudine . . . . Dodine Herry
Henri . . . . Philippe Harel
Titia . . . . Brigitte Bemol
Also with: Mathieu Kassovitz, Philippe Rostand, Claude Mondor, Jean-Pierre Hutinet, Claudie Chainet, François Toumarkine, Pierre Yvernault, Christiane Yvernault, Germaine Demars.

Anyone seeking proof that brevity is the soul of wit need look no further than "Un Été Sans Histoires," a richly amusing French featurette that may find a cult following in specialized markets.

Pic marks the feature directing debut of Philippe Harel, who co-stars with co-writer Dodine Herry and proves himself a master of deadpan comedy of manners. Subtle oddball humor is reminiscent of the works of U.S. indie Hal Hartley, but has an engaging charm all its own.

Herry plays a summer vacationer pulling a trailer with a rattletrap Citroen DS en route to join her boyfriend in the south with Harel, her boyfriend's indefatigably grumpy brother, along

for the ride.

They can barely tolerate each other and it looks like an edgy situation will only get worse when Herry's car breaks down on a country road. But while they're camped out in the trailer, waiting for the car to be repaired, the pair begin a gradual (albeit platonic) thawing-out.

One of the joys of "Été" is that hardly anything really "happens," in conventional movie terms, but everything is at least mildly amusing, and some things are downright hilarious. Perhaps the funniest bits are those involving Harel's growing obsession with Herry's video camera. His transformation from tiresome crank into amateur auteur turns out to be both daffy and endearing.

Brigitte Bemol wanders by as a lovely country lass fleeing her boorish boyfriend, and gracefully slides into the comic rhythms of the two leads.

"Été" looks as though it were a lark for all involved, but there is nothing self-indulgent about it. Tech credits are adequate, all pic really needs. — *Joe Leydon*

USED PEOPLE

A 20th Century Fox release from Largo Entertainment of a Lawrence Gordon presentation, in association with JVC Entertainment. Executive producers, Lloyd Levin, Michael Barnathan. Produced by Peggy Rajski. Directed by Beeban Kidron. Screenplay, co-producer, Todd Graff, from his "The Grandma Plays"; camera (Duart color; Deluxe prints), David Watkin; editor, John Tintori; music, Rachel Portman; sound (Dolby), Doug Ganton, Dennis & Tod Maitland (N.Y.); production design, Stuart Wurtzel; costume design, Marilyn Vance-Straker; assistant director, Tony Lucibello; production manager, David Coatsworth, Diana Pokorny (N.Y.); choreography, Pat Birch; casting, Mary Colquhoun. Reviewed at 20th Century Fox screening room, N.Y., Dec. 7, 1992. MPAA Rating: PG-13. Running time: **115 MIN.**
Pearl Berman . . . . Shirley MacLaine
Bibby . . . . Kathy Bates
Freida . . . . Jessica Tandy
Joe Meledandri . Marcello Mastroianni
Norma . . . . . . Marcia Gay Harden
Becky . . . . Sylvia Sidney
Frank . . . . Joe Pantoliano
Swee' Pea . . . . . . Mathew Branton
Jack Berman . . . . Bob Dishy
Paolo . . . . Charles Cioffi
Normy . . . . Louis Guss
Also with: Helen Hanft, Irving Metzman, Doris Roberts, Lee Wallace.

A modern, absurdist sensibility informs the soap opera "Used People," making this Fox release an unusual and problematic entry in the crowded holiday sweepstakes. Terrific cast should ensure a hefty audience sample.

Peopled with an eye toward the growing market segment that patronized its stars' hits "Steel Magnolias," "Driving Miss Daisy" and "Fried Green Tomatoes," the Largo film actually harks back to '50s weepies. With Shirley MacLaine as its spine, the film updates the type of picture that Shirley Booth (e.g., in "About Miss Leslie") or Jane Wyman routinely used to make.

Actor Todd Graff has scripted an actors' showcase, with heightened performances by the ensemble eschewing the naturalism favored by mainstream fare. Whether viewers will get with the program is another matter; film's trailer emphasizes its comedic elements (and sight gags) while hiding its more ambitious melodramatic segments.

Set in 1969 in the Sunnyside section of Queens, N.Y., film limns the colorful family life of a Jewish matriarchy centered around MacLaine, whose husband (Bob Dishy) has just died. Key characters include her protective mom (Jessica Tandy), dysfunctional children (Kathy Bates and Marcia

Gay Harden), both of whom have been divorced, and Tandy's best friend (Sylvia Sidney).

Enter Marcello Mastroianni, MacLaine's secret admirer who uses the family's sitting shiva after Dishy's funeral as his occasion to make his platonic affection for her manifest. As shown in flashbacks, he met Dishy in his brother Charles Cioffi's bar 23 years ago and encouraged him to continue his marriage to Shirley rather than leave her.

The family's rejection of Mastroianni and cross-cultural antics between them and Mastroianni's Italian-American clan make for some effective comedy in the middle reels but Graff's work is built around highly dramatic confrontation scenes. In particular, a heart-rending fight between MacLaine and daughter Bates becomes the film's emotional core, marred only by Graff's frequently obvious dialogue.

As demonstrated in her previous picture, "Antonia & Jane," British director Beeban Kidron is fond of injecting caricature and satire, here personified by Harden's character who keeps imitating movie icons like Marilyn Monroe and Anne Bancroft in "The Graduate." Latter motif digresses at length as she and Mastroianni's brother-in-law (Joe Pantoliano) engage in a Dustin Hoffman/Bancroft sex scene that segues to light bondage.

Least successful element of black humor involves Harden's young son (Mathew Branton), who believes grandpa Dishy's spirit is protecting him. Throughout the film he places himself in suicidal situations only to be saved by luck. Like Graff's other subplots, this yields a heart-warming resolution but is tough sledding along the way.

MacLaine's precise acting is laudatory and balanced by a very sympathetic turn by twinkle-eyed Mastroianni, in his best English-language role by far. The support ensemble is excellent, with Sylvia Sidney, perfectly matched opposite Tandy, stealing most of her scenes adroitly. Harden's work, as it was in "Miller's Crossing," is promising but brittle compared with the ease shown by her vet co-stars.

Both Tandy and Bates have essentially supporting assignments but fans will appreciate their lack of showboating here. David Watkin, who covered similar territory in lensing "Moonstruck," photographs the action unobtrusively while capturing some memorable images, such as Harden visiting a cemetery or MacLaine dancing in her apartment. Rachel Portman's score handily supports the film's serious mood and helps avoid risibility. — *Lawrence Cohn*

LOVE FIELD

An Orion release of a Sanford/Pillsbury production. Executive producers, George Goodman, Kate Guinzburg. Produced by Sarah Pillsbury, Midge Sanford. Directed by Jonathan Kaplan. Screenplay, Don Roos. Camera (Technicolor; Deluxe prints), Ralf Bode; editor, Jane Kurson; music, Jerry Goldsmith; production design, Mark Freeborn; art direction, David Willson, Lance King; set decoration, Jim Erickson; costume design, Peter Mitchell; Michelle Pfeiffer's costume design, Colleen Atwood; sound (Dolby), Glen Anderson; co-producer, Roos; associate producer, Sulla Hamer; assistant director, Tom Davies; 2nd unit director, Bode; casting, Julie Selzer, Sally Dennison. Reviewed at Orion screening room, L.A., Nov. 12, 1992. MPAA Rating: PG-13. Running time: **104 MIN.**
Lurene Hallett . . . . Michelle Pfeiffer
Paul Cater . . . . . Dennis Haysbert
Jonell . . . . . . Stephanie McFadden
Ray Hallett . . . . Brian Kerwin
Mrs. Enright . . . . . Louise Lathan
Mrs. Heisenbuttal . . . . . Peggy Rea
Hazel . . . . Beth Grant

After sitting on the shelf for well over a year during Orion's bankruptcy woes, "Love Field" emerges as a bittersweet reminder of the company's knack for nurturing interesting, thoughtful character pieces without necessarily having a strong marketing angle. Strong marketing, however, is exactly what this sincere, not fully realized 1960s drama will need. Pic is being slipped into year-end L.A. and N.Y. release in hopes of snaring an Academy Award nomination for Michelle Pfeiffer's flashy performance, but failing an Oscar score, film should have only a modest theatrical run, if a pleasant video and cable life.

Yet another variation on the "where were you when you heard JFK was shot" theme, story introduces Lurene Hallett (Pfeiffer), a rather dim Dallas hairdresser with a 100-watt platinum coif who imagines a kinship with Jacqueline Kennedy, since both lost infant children.

After failing to shake the first lady's hand at the eponymous Dallas airport, Lurene heads off to work while tragic history unfolds. The film spares viewers the assassination footage, moving quickly to the oft-repeated but always wrenching footage of Walter Cronkite reporting Kennedy's death.

Against her husband's (Brian Kerwin) wishes, Lurene hops a Greyhound north to attend the state funeral. On board she meets and gradually befriends a "Negro" man, Paul (Dennis Haysbert), with something to hide. With Paul is his traumatized young daughter, Jonell (Stephanie McFadden). Through a series of blunders sparked by the hapless Lurene, the three are thrown together and must fend for themselves in the all-too-predictable American South.

The growing attraction between Lurene and Paul, while no surprise, is delicately handled. But it defies reason that any black man on the run would hook up with a woman with a beacon for a hairdo. The third act disintegrates into a series of unbelievable plot turns, one of which requires the long-suffering husband to suddenly emerge as a full-fledged redneck.

Don Roos' screenplay struggles to tie together some of the loose strands of mid-'60s American history — the fall of Camelot, the nascent civil rights movement, the birth of feminism — but never quite coalesces. The parts are, however, more rewarding than the whole. Jonathan Kaplan's direction is careful and well-paced, but lacks an essential tension — too many scenes are given equal weight. Jane Kurson's superior, unobtrusive editing never lets pic drag.

Pfeiffer notches yet another memorable characterization, although her attempt at defining a not terribly bright woman skirts condescension. Haysbert, in a role that Denzel Washington relinquished over "creative differences," is solid and likable, but the part needed more gradation — he's asked to pluck the same, quietly exasperated chord one too many times.

The real find is 6-year-old McFadden, in her acting debut. With only a few lines, she heartbreakingly telegraphs volumes of emotional distress. Kaplan deserves credit for never letting her lapse into an animated Keane painting.

Technically the film is aces. Ralf Bode's cinematography is rich and evocative yet realistic. Colleen Atwood deserves special mention for Pfeiffer's Jackie Kennedy-style outfits. Jerry Goldsmith did the astutely judged score. — *Richard Natale*

THAT NIGHT

A Warner Bros. release of a Regency Entertainment/Alcor Films/Le Studio Canal Plus presentation of an Arnon Milchan production. Produced by Milchan, Steven Reuther. Executive producers, Elliot Lewitt, Julie Kirkham. Co-producer, Llewellyn Wells. Directed, written by Craig Bolotin, based on Alice McDermott's novel. Camera (Technicolor), Bruce Surtees; editor, Priscilla Nedd-Friendly; music, David Newman; production design, Maher Ahmad; costume design, Carol Ramsey. Reviewed at Village Roadshow screening room, Sydney, Nov. 12, 1992. Running time: **89 MIN.**
Rick . . . . C. Thomas Howell
Sheryl O'Connor . . . . Juliette Lewis
Ann O'Connor . . . . . . Helen Shaver
Alice Bloom . . . . Eliza Dushku
Larry Bloom . . . . John Dossett
Carol Bloom . . . . . J. Smith-Cameron
Also with: Katherine Heigl, Benjamin Terzulli, Thomas Terzulli, Sarah Joy Stevenson.

"That Night" is a modestly affecting romantic drama set in the Long Island suburbs 30 years ago. The familiar nostalgia evoked in Craig Bolotin's first feature, backed by a potent soundtrack of hits from 1961, could generate OK initial response, with interest in Juliette Lewis' first starring role, adding to the appeal. However, soft b.o. looms in the long term for this lightweight pic, which is being world-preemed in Australia to gauge reactions.

Bolotin, co-scripter of Ridley Scott's "Black Rain," hasn't stretched himself in his directorial debut, either in his screenplay, based on an autobiographical novel by Alice McDermott, or in his careful helming.

He seems to have pinned his faith on casting and performances, and concentrates on his actors, eschewing a strong visual imprint, despite the good work of lenser Bruce Surtees.

Bolotin is particularly well-served by 12-year-old Eliza Dushku who, as Alice, is really the focus of the story.

A shy, imaginative child, she lives with her parents across the street from her idol, Sheryl (Juliette Lewis), the seemingly sophisticated high school beauty who has everything Alice yearns for, including a close relationship with her father.

When the father suddenly dies, Sheryl reacts by dating Rick (C. Thomas Howell), a boy from the wrong side of the tracks, despite her mother's strong disapproval.

The affair ends in Sheryl's pregnancy, and she's sent to a home for unwed mothers. Only the concerned and observant Alice can guide Rick to the place where his girl has been sent.

This isn't exactly riveting material, and the film's modest production values seem more suited to the small screen. Nevertheless, Dushku makes the hero-worshipping moppet an engaging character, and Howell is just right as every suburban mom's idea of a daughter's undesirable boyfriend. Lewis is more than adequate as the lively Sheryl, though she made more impact in smaller roles in "Cape Fear" and "Husbands and Wives."

Pic will be up against some heavyweight summer blockbusters in its Australian release; if it works in this territory it could have chances for international success. — David Stratton

LA CRISE
(CRISIS-GO-'ROUND)
(FRENCH)

An AMLF release of a Les Films Alain Sarde/TF1 Films Prod./Eniloc/ Leader Cinematografica/RAI 2 co-production with the participation of Canal Plus. Produced by Alain Sarde. Directed, written by Coline Serreau. Camera (color), Robert Alazraki; editor, Catherine Renault; music, Sonia Wieder-Atherton; set design, Guy Claude François; costumes, Karen Muller; sound, Guillaume Sciama, Dominique Dalmasso; assistant director, Elizabeth Parniere. Reviewed at UGC Odeon Cinema, Paris, Dec. 7, 1992. Running time: 92 MIN.
Victor . . . . Vincent Lindon
Michou . . . . Patrick Timsit
With: Zabou, Maria Pancome, Yves Robert, Annick Alane, Gilles Privat, Michelle Laroque, Catherine Wilkening.

Coline Serreau's new comedy, "La Crise," is one of the most satisfying French films in recent memory. Smartly paced, hilarious and wise, this compact tale of compound crises should delight arthouse audiences in most major markets.

The same compassionate perceptivity that made "Three Men and a Cradle" and "Mama, There's a Man in Your Bed" very French yet universal also suggest U.S. remake potential.

When corporate lawyer Vincent Lindon loses his wife and job on the same day, he goes in search of a sympathetic ear only to find that everyone he knows is a ticking time bomb of stress.

Although most of Lindon's peers and relatives are blessed with ritzy property, good jobs, attractive spouses and healthy children, they're mad as hell and not gonna take it anymore, human

geysers of seamless rants. Pic is a mile-a-minute cavalcade of honest, believable emotions deftly disguised as comical complaints.

Scripter-helmer sharply conveys societal lunacy via precise individual examples. After winning a megabuck case for his firm, Lindon is fired because "This kind of windfall won't happen again for 20 years, so we won't require anyone as brilliant as you for awhile."

While drowning his sorrows in a bar, Lindon meets scruffy, good-hearted simpleton Patrick Timsit, who has no home, no job and no prospects but seems content to tag along with his reluctant benefactor.

With Timsit in tow, Lindon visits his parents, only to discover that his 50-year-old mother is leaving her husband for a lover 10 years her junior. Mom's personal liberation speech to son, daughter and spouse is a gem.

Wherever Lindon, his sister (Zabou) and their sidekick turn, couples are splitting, children are rebelling, friends and lovers are overreacting. In the course of a few hectic days, Lindon sheds his blinders and learns valuable lessons. Serreau's humanism is heartening but never cloying.

Thesps are terrific across the board. Rapid-fire litanies of grievances are delivered with smooth-tongued righteous fury. A possible drawback for foreign auds is the necessity of condensing luxuriant raving into terse subtitles. Thanks to intelligent editing, the frantic proceedings are easy to follow. The plaintive score is used sparingly. — Lisa Nesselson

THE MUPPET CHRISTMAS CAROL

A Buena Vista release of a Walt Disney Pictures presentation from Jim Henson Prods. Executive producer, Frank Oz. Produced by Brian Henson, Martin G. Baker. Directed by Henson. Screenplay, Jerry Juhl, based on Charles Dickens' novella. Camera (Technicolor), John Fenner; editor, Michael Jablow; music, Miles Goodman; songs, Paul Williams; production design, Val Strazovec; supervising art director, Alan Cassie; art direction, Dennis Bosher; set decoration, Michael Ford; costume design, Polly Smith; sound (Dolby), Bobby Mackston; choreography, Pat Garrett; Muppet electro/mechanical effects supervisor, Larry Jameson; co-producer, Jerry Juhl; line producer, David Barron; assistant director, Crispin Reece; 2nd unit director, Nick Willing; 2nd unit camera, Ivan Bartos; miniatures unit director, Paul Gentry; miniatures unit camera, Paul Wilson; casting, Suzanne Crowley, Gilly Poole, Mike Fenton. Reviewed at Cinerama Dome, L.A., Dec. 5, 1992. MPAA Rating: G. Running time: 85 MIN.

Scrooge . . . . Michael Caine
The Great Gonzo/Robert Marley/Bunsen Moneydew/Betina Cratchit
. . . . Dave Goelz
Rizzo the Rat/Bean Bunny/Kermit the Frog/Beaker/Belinda Cratchit
. . . . Steve Whitmire
Tiny Tim Cratchit/Jacob Marley/Ma Bear
. . . . Jerry Nelson
Miss Piggy/Fozzie Bear/Sam Eagle/ Animal . . . . Frank Oz
Peter Cratchit/Old Joe/Swedish Chef
. . . . David Rudman
Ghost of Christmas Present
. . . . . . Donald Austen, Jerry Nelson
Ghost of Christmas Yet To Come
. . . . . . Donald Austen, Rob Tygner
Ghost of Christmas Past
. . . . Karen Prell, Rob Tygner, William Todd Jones, Jessica Fox.

This latest adaptation of Charles Dickens' Christmas classic is not as enchanting or amusing as the previous entries in the Muppet series. With too much Scrooge and not enough Muppets, pic's tone may be a shade dark and somber for what is basically a children's entertainment. But nothing can really diminish the late Jim Henson's irresistibly appealing characters. The new incarnation will yield solid b.o. returns for Disney through the holiday season and possibly beyond.

Closely following the Dickens story, "The Muppet Christmas Carol" is structured around Scrooge's encounters with the Ghosts of Christmas Past, Present and Yet to Come.

Michael Caine is perfectly cast as the nasty Scrooge, though his role is too dominant. Muppets take the other roles: Kermit the Frog becomes abused bookkeeper Bob Cratchit, Miss Piggy is his wife Emily, and the Great Gonzo is transformed into Dickens himself. The latter's narration is often obtrusive, creating unnecessary distance between the viewer and the tale.

Unfortunately, the new Muppet film, lacks the charm of "The Muppet Movie" (1979) or the fun of "The Muppets Take Manhattan" (1984). Still, the production values here are high as ever. Brian Henson does a fluid, if not spectacular, job of direction. Lenser John Fenner gives the studio-shot film the luminous feel of a holiday celebration, stressing its wintery look. The sight of Scrooge flying over London's rooftops will inevitably be magical for children.

Henson and editor Michael Jablow effectively contrast mega-closeups of Caine with Kermit the Frog and the other tiny Muppets. However, Paul Williams' pedestrian songs are repetitious, failing to endow the tale with the sort of bouncy score that marked

the other Muppet films.
— Emanuel Levy

LA FILLE DE L'AIR
(THE GIRL IN THE AIR)
(FRENCH)

An AMLF release of a Ciby 2000/TF-1 Films Prod. co-production with the participation of Investimage 4 & Canal Plus. Produced by Jean-Claude Fleury. Directed by Maroun Bagdadi. Screenplay, Florece Quentin, Dan Franck, Bagdadi from Nadine Vaujour's book. Camera (color), Thierry Arbogast; editor, Luc Barnier; music, Gabriel Yared; set design, Michel Vandestien; sound, Jean-Pierre Duet, Stéphanie Granel; helicopter stunts, Yann Le Bouar. Reviewed at Club Gaumont screening room, Paris, Nov. 12, 1992. Running time: 106 MIN.
Brigitte . . . . Béatrice Dalle
Daniel . . . . Thierry Fortineau
Philippe . . . . Hippolyte Girardot
Marcel . . . . . Jean-Claude Dreyfus
Mr. Lefort . . . . Roland Bertin
The mother . . . . . . Liliane Rovere
Also with: Jean-Paul Roussillon, Catherine Jacob.

Girl marries imprisoned boy. Girl learns to fly helicopter. Girl flies over Paris into prison yard and rescues jailbird hubby in broad daylight. Based on a well-publicized true story, Maroun Bagdadi's "La Fille de L'Air" delivers on action and suspense, even though Gallic viewers know the ending. Punchy retelling of how an ordinary woman was driven to an offbeat feat of daring should spark plenty of TV sales and could fly on the big screen and in video in territories where Béatrice Dalle has fans.

Helmer Bagdadi, whose previous films include 1991 Cannes jury prize-winner "Hors la Vie" and dealt with harrowing circumstances in his native Lebanon, again masters the theme of seeking freedom against the odds.

In 1986, Nadine Vaujour stunned France with her bold helicopter rescue of longtime convict Michel Vaujour. Michel and Nadine have here been renamed Daniel (Thierry Fortineau) and Brigitte (Dalle). Although it seems unlikely that Brigitte, in her fervor to marry an incarcerated criminal, would fail to comprehend that her husband is in the joint for another 36 years, Dalle pulls it off.

Outside prison and in, lensing accentuates the contrast between liberty informed by a sense of purpose and the numbing dead end of captivity. Flight sequences are invigorating and the actual rescue is nail-biting fare.

The carefully calibrated pic is

bracketed by two impressive bursts of raw action. Characters are never romanticized, although the fact that Daniel's crimes remain vague helps the viewer to root for his eventual escape.

Some supporting characters, including Dalle's brother (Hippolyte Girardot), are underdeveloped, compared with Dalle's full, determined perf. Fortineau paces his cell like a caged tiger and effectively conveys his frustration, although his head-bashing despair verges on cliché.

The exploit, had it transpired in the U.S., would quickly have been turned into a telefilm rather than a full-blown theatrical pic. Some local critics, who would have preferred more psychological probing, have accused d.p. Thierry Arbogast of "American-style" lensing, but the complaint is misplaced since the forceful visuals give the film its strength.
— *Lisa Nesselson*

NERO
(ITALIAN)

A Titanus Distribuzione Intl. release of a Titanus Distribuzione/Intersound production. Executive producer, Claudio Argento. Produced by Giovanna Romagnoli, Argento. Director of production, Emanuele Emiliani. Directed by Giancarlo Soldi. Screenplay, Tiziano Sclavi, Soldi, from Sclavi's novel. Camera (Telecolor), Luca Bigazzi; editor, Mauro Bonanni; music, Mau Mau; art direction, Mauro Radaelli; costumes, Paola Artioli; sound (Dolby), Hubrecht Nijhuis. Reviewed at Esperia Cinema, Rome, Sept. 28, 1992. (In Venice Film Festival, Window on Italian Cinema.) Running time: **100 MIN.**
Federico . . . . Sergio Castellitto
Francesca . . . . . . Chiara Caselli
 Also with: Carlo Colnaghi, Luis Molteni, Hugo Pratt.

A curious mélange of absurd humor, casual gore and nightmarish surrealism, "Nero" takes a bold stab at the kind of dauntless, amoral lunacy that propelled pics like "Basket Case" to notoriety. But despite frequent flashes of inspiration and a hipper-than-thou attitude, this offbeat thriller flounders without settling into a definite tone.

Scripter Tiziano Sclavi, author of megaselling Italo cult comic "Dylan Dog," should furnish a ready-made teen audience at home and pic is reportedly selling well to prime Euro territories, but needs kid-glove marketing to work as an offshore item.

On an errand to the apartment his g.f. Chiara Caselli has just fled, neurotic daydreamer Sergio Castellitto stumbles on her

ex-lover with his throat cut. Believing her to be the murderer, he mops up and stashes the corpse in his trunk. A botched burial and more deaths follow.

Peppered with a grotesque assortment of comic strip characters and an energetic pop culture sensibility, the film should be a lot more fun than it actually is. Part of the problem lies in a series of overlong scenes that too often mistake incoherence for darkly inspired idiocy. Giancarlo Soldi has an uneven grip on the proceedings and things keep hovering on the edge of the cartoon world he seems to want to enter.

With his cartoonish features and goggle-eyed expression, Castellitto is emphatically on-target as the anguished goon. Caselli, however, doesn't fit. The fragile intensity that worked for her in pics like "My Own Private Idaho" is wasted and out of place here, and she never quite delivers the wickedly sensual irresponsibility that's required.

Mauro Bonanni's rhythmic, musicvideo-style cutting and a frenetic music score by Mau Mau are well-harnessed to keep the exercise in motion. Luca Bigazzi's muscular camerawork also helps, despite murky lighting that gives the film a somewhat flat, colorless look.
— *David Rooney*

SVART LUCIA
(BLACK LUCIA)
(SWEDISH)

A Svensk Filmindustri presentation of a SF/SVT Kanal 1 Drama/Nordisk Film & TV/Svenska Filminstitutet/Det Danske Filminstitut/Nordisk Film & TV Fund production. Produced by Waldemar Bergendahl. Directed by Rumle Hammerich. Screenplay, Carina Rydberg. Camera (color), Jens Fischer; sound, Jan Brodin, Jan Alvermar; production design, Gert Wibe; costumes, Malin Birch-Jensen, Kersti Vitali; music, Jacob Groth; editor, Camilla Skousen. Reviewed at Riviera cinema, Stockholm, Nov. 24, 1992. Running time: **115 MIN.**
 With: Tova Magnusson-Norling, Figge Norling, Björn Kjellman, Malin Berghagen, Niklas Hjulström, Liv Alsterlund, Lars Green, Agneta Ekmanner, Marie Göranzon, Reine Brynolfsson.

This muddled attempt to make a psycho-thriller confuses style with content. Pic might do initial business in Sweden, but will not become the success producers hope for.

First-time scripter Carina Rydberg is an acclaimed author and here deals with a gang of boys and girls in their later teens, all going to the same school. Mi-

kaela has a crush on a teacher, using him as the subject of her erotic essays. The teacher, in turn, uses the essays as sex scripts with the women he meets.

Mikaela begins spying on him and starts believing he has killed one of the women. At the same time, she feels herself spied upon by someone unknown. Tensions arise and at a party on Lucia Day, a Swedish holiday, one of her classmates is murdered.

The basics of a good thriller are here but Danish director Rumle Hammerich indulges in an exercise in style rather than straightforward storytelling.

Technically, the film is very well made, and there are some brilliant set pieces, but in the end, you get tired of pans, long walks through dark rooms and corridors, flashing lights, heightened sound effects, sex- and blood-symbolism, etc. In the end, you don't care who was murdered or who did it.

Acting by the mostly unknown young actors is very good overall; Hammerich obviously knows how to work with them. A special mention to Liv Alsterlund, whose insecure young girl has real depths. — *Gunnar Rehlin*

THE LEGEND OF WOLF MOUNTAIN

A Hemdale release of a Majestic Entertainment presentation in association with Wolf Mountain Prods. Produced by Bryce Fillmore. Executive producers, Eric Parkinson, Charles A. Lund. Directed by Craig Clyde. Screenplay, Clyde, James Hennessy. Camera (color), Gary Eckert; editor, Michael Amundsen; music, Jon McCallum; art direction, Michael Klint; sound (Dolby), Michael McDonough; assistant director, Tony Rohovit; casting, Billy DaMota. Reviewed at Directors Guild of America, L.A., Aug. 18, 1992. MPAA Rating: PG. Running time: **91 MIN.**
Ranger Haynes . . . . Bo Hopkins
Jensen . . . . Mickey Rooney
Jocko Painter . . . . Robert Z'Dar
Dewayne Bixby . . . . . . David Shark
Simcoe . . . . Don Shanks
Kerrie Haynes . . . . Nicole Lund
Maggie Haynes . . . . . . Natalie Lund
John Page . . . . Jonathan Best
Casey James . . . . . . Matthew Lewis
Sheriff Page . . . . Frank Magner

Based on folklore, "The Legend of Wolf Mountain" is a lukewarm attempt to make a children's adventure in the mold of the old Disney movies. Pic's target audiences, children and adolescents, may enjoy the moderately entertaining tale, but it will strain the patience of adults, who may look at their watches instead of the screen.

The Hemdale release is in sporadic regional distribution in warmup for video.

Film begins and ends at a school. Ranger Bo Hopkins tries to excite the students about the natural wonders of nearby Wolf Mountain National Park. Sure enough, three kids — Nicole Lund, Matthew Lewis and Jonathan Best — are enjoying the park when they're abducted by prison escapees Robert Z'Dar and David Shark.

The intermittently amiable pic crosscuts between the children's "adventures" with their vicious kidnappers and parents' attempts to rescue them. In no time, the children outsmart the stereotypical villains, disabling their stolen car, grabbing their money, then surviving in the wilderness, relying on their instincts.

The politically correct film tries hard to punch across universal messages about environmental issues, Native Americans as whites' noble victims, generation gaps and camaraderie among youth. But these undoubtedly worthy causes are bluntly stated rather than shaded into characterization. Moreover, a crucial dream sequence, in which a wolf is transformed into an Indian warrior who protects the kids, lacks the requisite magic.

Helmer Craig Clyde, who has a TV background, establishes a slow, brooding tempo. The one refreshing twist is that the trio's smart leader is a girl, and 10-year-old Nicole Lund gives the film's most assured performance. Mickey Rooney appears in the small part of a ranger. Tech values are unimpressive. — *Emanuel Levy*

TURIN FEST

THE PROM
(16m)

An American Film Institute presentation. Produced by Felicity Cockram. Directed by Steven Shainberg. Screenplay, Shainberg, Denis Johnson. Camera (color, 16m), Carlos Montaner; editor, Donn Aron; music, Kevin Haskins; production design, Majid Falamaki; art direction, Kuladee Suchartanun; set decoration, Ellen Zuckerman, Paul Morse; costume design, Colby Bart; special effects makeup, Dean Jones; sound, Andy Adams; casting, Mali Finn, Megan McConnell. Reviewed at Turin Intl. Festival of Young Cinema, Nov. 19, 1992. Running time: **50 MIN.**
Marty . . . . Andras Jones
Lana . . . . Jennifer Jason Leigh
Grover Dean . . . . J.T. Walsh
Healer . . . . . . Natalija Nogulich
Cherry . . . . Nada Despotovich

Jennifer Jason Leigh adds memorable entry to her bulging gallery of wayward waifs in Steven Shainberg's quirky romantic outing "The Prom." Concise, visually snappy treatment of a highschooler's skin discoloration stigma and the open-hearted bad girl who helps him overcome it will be candy to hip young auds, especially the sensitive dating set. Brief running time, however, makes pic a challenge to place outside of tube dates.

Opening title sequence flips through a photobook of physically deformed subjects caught in sensitive, human-contact moments, and pic's focus is on self-acceptance via compassionate understanding.

A top scholarship student (Andras Jones) shies away from gym class showers and de rigueur heavy petting sessions at his swanky boarding school, prompting a bad attitude rep. His shame-faced, solitude-seeking nature contrasts with the preppy good-looker's outward appearance (Jones is stamped from the Tom Cruise mold), and stems from large crimson blotches covering his body, which neither hi-tech medicine nor faith healers have managed to cure.

Jones wanders into a peep show parlor advertising face-to-face encounter booths. Kevin Haskins' ominously brooding soundtrack creates an otherworldly atmosphere as Jones chooses between the fantasies on offer — dungeon, nursery, office, boudoir — before settling on "The Prom." A shutter reveals Leigh, a tatty corsage strapped to her wrist, painting her nails.

The set-up has been previously exploited (notably in "Paris, Texas" and "Hardcore") but Leigh's remarkable, intuitive work keeps it fresh and compelling. The dimly lit anonymity lets Jones loosen up and Leigh initially pretends not to see his blotchy flesh as they take on the squeaky-clean prom personas of an average couple. Without resorting to hidden heart-of-gold tacks, Leigh's strictly business attitude gives way to a warmer side that allows Jones to emerge from his shell.

Pairing with another medium-length feature might facilitate limited theatrical and video exposure. Pic has been making fest rounds in tandem with fellow AFI alumnus William Chartoff's "Colored Balloons," a livewire comedy about a trio of junkies on a wild ride through La La Land, literally trying to cough up a drug haul. — *David Rooney*

HIGHWAY 66 REVISITED
(GERMAN-DOCU-16m-B&W)

A Thomas Repp/Munich Television & Film School/Bayerischer Rundfunk/Factory Entertainment production. Produced, directed by Repp. Camera (B&W, 16m), Rudolf Barmettler; editor, Patricia Loncle; sound, Karl Michael, Tomas Bastian. Reviewed at Turin Intl. Festival of Young Cinema, Nov. 16, 1992. Running time: **110 MIN.**

German documaker Thomas Repp motors west on the largely unused two-lane highway between Chicago and L.A. and steps into the atmospheric lost world of Nowheresville, U.S.A. At nearly two hours, "Highway 66 Revisited" is a leisurely trip that could improve mileage with further editing, but Repp's affectionate, almost reverential feel for the charm of the American sticks and its colorful habitués should steer pic to wide public TV and cable exposure.

Docu is dedicated to Jack D. Rittenhouse, who penned a guidebook to the 2,200-mile stretch in 1946. Repp retraces Rittenhouse's journey, quickly leaving behind the opening cacophony of Chicago traffic to take in a slew of ghostly towns and forgotten townsfolk, chronicling the killing blow dealt backroads tradespeople when the more efficient Interstate system took through-traffic elsewhere.

Repp's subjects range from doddering old-timers to local yokels to harmless eccentrics. He alternates between sober accounts of hardship (a drive-in theater owner struggling to pull in customers; union workers protesting the use of scab labor; the owner of a pool hall straight out of "The Last Picture Show" lamenting the passing of time-honored meeting places) and lighter encounters milking the natural humor of rural Americana.

At times (particularly in the slow opening reel) Repp overplays the somber poetry of the road, holding long, static shots that give pic a halting rhythm. A surfeit of painstaking attention to workaday detail (road workers refilling surface cracks, etc.) also creates a sporadic lag. But pacing quibbles aside, pic is an engagingly reflective sociological tract that benefits from an outsider's uncritical admiration for smalltown American ways and touches gently on the road's passage through Native American and Old West tradition.

Rudolf Barmettler's clean B&W lensing gives a spectral quality to the abandoned highway and its desolate surrounding landscape. Other tech credits are modest but effective, and the occasionally uneven sound recording doesn't jar in the pic's no-frills docu context.
— *David Rooney*

SHINDE MO II
(ORIGINAL SIN)
(JAPANESE)

An Argo Project/Suntory production. (Intl. sales: INEX Inc.) Produced by Kei Ijichi. Directed, written by Takashi Ishii, from Bo Nishimura's novel "Hi no Ga." Camera (color), Yasushi Sasakihara; editor, Yoshio Sugano; music, Gorou Yasakawa; art direction, Terumi Hosoichi; sound, Tsutomu Honda. Reviewed at Turin Intl. Festival of Young Cinema (competition), Nov. 17, 1992. Running time: **117 MIN.**
Nami Tsuchiya . . . . Shinobu Ohtake
Makoto Hirano . . . Masatoshi Nagase
Hideki Tsuchiya . . . . . Hideo Murota
   Also with: Kouen Okumura, Naoto Takenaka.

Passion runs riot, love packs a punch and tragedy erupts in "Original Sin," a steamy romantic triangle saga that plays like an Eastern "The Postman Always Rings Twice." Violently sensual pic offers the acute pleasure of experiencing a Japanese take on classic Yank film noir material and should travel far as a superior curio item for festival and quality tube programming.

After a slam-bang collision under pouring rain, drifter Masatoshi Nagase is stung by an obsessive desire for prim office girl Shinobu Ohtake. He follows her into the real estate agency where she works and, despite her protests to husband/boss Hideo Murota, wangles a job.

Furtive, heated glances segue into an unceremonious pouncing when he rapes her on the floor of a display home. Recognizing the pang of genuine love behind his wham-bam approach, Ohtake consents to a further tryst, and pretty soon they're punishing the futon on a regular basis.

Where the story (taken from a Japanese novel based on a tabloid crime of 10 years back) differs fundamentally from James M. Cain's 1934 classic is that all three principals are treated redemptively, driven by nothing less noble than love. There's no spitfire slut lurking beneath Ohtake's good-wifely exterior and, though she's confused, she truly loves both hubby and lover. Murota might be a boozing philanderer, flaunting his bar floozies, but he's kept humane, reduced to tears by a syrupy love song. When the lovers discuss killing Murota, the scene is treated not as an illicit scheme, but an inexorable last resort.

Cartoonist-turned-director Takashi Ishii draws the yarn to a resonantly tragic conclusion with an invigorating audacity, mixing Japanese rigor with the often clumsily explosive violence of Hong Kong actioners. Murota's murder is bloody and grueling, leaving a hollow visceral impact in its wake. Sound is used effectively, especially the pounding footsteps on wooden floors giving events a harsh urgency. Yasushi Sasakihara's camerawork revels in its own raw edges, careening in for tight closeups then wheeling off again at high speed.

Performances are grade A. Ohtake takes on the conflicting choices of her character with supreme subtlety, and Nagase (known to Western auds as the Elvis fan in Jim Jarmusch's "Mystery Train") is a dynamo of blindly passionate intensity.
— *David Rooney*

CHICKPEAS

A Tri-Ark Films presentation. Produced by Nigol Bezjian, John Ohanessian. Co-producer, Bedo Ben Manoukian. Directed, written by Bezjian. Camera (color), Ara Madzounian; editor, Manoukian; music, Milcho Leviev; sound, Pierre Desire. Reviewed at Boston Film Festival, Sept. 17, 1992. (In Turin Intl. Festival of Young Cinema.) Running time: **128 MIN.**
Elizabeth . . . . . . Arsinee Khanjian
Raffi . . . . Nazareth Kurdoghlian
Paul . . . . Raffi Bekmezjian
Pierre . . . . . . Shavarsh Manoukian
Father . . . . Koko Satamian
Maro . . . . Anna Nshanian
Anahid . . . . Nelly Saatchian
Ohan . . . . Khoren Ekmekjian

First feature by Nigol Bezjian focuses on L.A.'s Armenian community, which apparently comes mostly from Lebanon. The story, centering on three friends trying to straighten out family and romantic problems while starting a business together, manages to depict a particular people while reaching for wider appeal.

The film, enacted mostly by film novices (except Arsinee Khanjian), depicts situations that every immigrant to the U.S. has endured: homesickness, family squabbles, conflict between "old ways" and an American lifestyle. Soundtrack mixes Armenian (with subtitles) and English to underscore the conflict.

The closest parallel might be Wayne Wang's "Dim Sum" in showing a culture clash that resonates both for a particular group and society at large. Bezjian's canvas is large enough to cover a lot of ground, as each of the three friends must relate not only to each other, but to girlfriends, relatives and the community.

The pic's greatest strength is in casting, especially the supporting roles, where characters with rich histories beyond the frame of the film are quickly sketched in. Most of the principals are more on the order of talented amateurs, but their occasional awkwardness in front of the camera plays well with the theme of their characters' awkwardness in a strange society.

Bezjian also gets good mileage out of his locations, giving us a feel for the world of his story far beyond the limitations of his budget. Participation of jazz composer Milcho Leviev on the soundtrack is a plus as well.

Already cut to its current 128 minutes, the pic can easily handle additional trims.

— Daniel M. Kimmel

ANO NATSU, ICHIBAN SHIZUKANA UMI
(A SCENE AT THE SEA)
(JAPANESE)

An Office Kitano production. (Intl. sales: Toho Intl.) Director of production, Yukio Tate. Produced by Masayuki Mori. Directed, written, edited by Takeshi Kitano. Camera (color), Katsumi Yanagishima; music, Hisaishi Jo; art direction, Osamu Sasaki; sound, Senji Horiuchi. Reviewed at Turin Intl. Festival of Young Cinema (competition), Nov. 15, 1992. Running time: **101 MIN.**
Shigeru . . . . Kurodo Maki
Takako . . . . Hiroko Oshima
    Also with: Sabu Kawahara, Nenzo Fujiwara, Keiko Kagimoto, Katsuya Koiso, Matsui Toshio.

Fast-rising cult director Takeshi Kitano opts for a surprising change of pace and delivers winning results with his third feature, "A Scene at the Sea." Swapping the muscular, frequently screwy mayhem of previous outings for a delicate balance of poignant human drama and casually hip humor, he tracks the disarming story of a young deaf couple's passion for surfing. Pic is sure to accelerate the quirky Japanese helmer's international emergence and it could be an appealingly low-key arthouse item for discerning markets.

A garbage collector (Kurodo Maki) finds a broken surfboard among the trash, and is instantly gripped by a coolly focused obsession with riding the waves. A similar determination embraces g.f. Hiroko Oshima as she watches attentively from the beach, fetching drinks and meticulously folding his clothes. Both are revealed, gradually and almost incidentally, to be deaf.

Action follows Maki's progress from botched initial forays on the patched-up board to competition-level feats on a deluxe model. But Kitano has only a passing interest in the spectacle of surfing. Instead, he patiently tails the couple through the ritualistic repetitiveness of their rise to surfing excellence — trips to and from the beach; pricing and purchase of a new board; participation in surf carnivals. Melding together the regimented poise of a tea ceremony with the wild spontaneity that characterized his earlier pics, Kitano establishes and sustains an irresistibly seductive rhythm in perfect alignment with the incoming waves.

The soothing, feel-good sentimentality of the underdog couple's fulfillment is sharply interrupted by a tragic surfing accident, presented not with jolt-inducing shockwaves, but a gentle touch combining cruel cynicism with melancholy sweetness.

Incidental pleasures are countless. The duo's almost unwitting assimilation into the surfing subculture introduces a funny lineup of supporting characters, from a dim pair of novice surfers to a blundering lunkhead striving to impress his fickle beach babe. The deaf couple's unity is touching without being mawkish, and their reconciliation scene after a tiff is a small jewel. Kitano plays sly games with traditional Eastern notions of male-female roles. The custom of Japanese women walking two paces behind men is wryly acknowledged by having Oshima haul the back end of the board.

Maki and Oshima are multidimensional and warmly sympathetic in their nonspeaking roles. His stern inexpressiveness partially masks a tenderness within, and she comes across as unquestioningly dutiful with an assertive streak bubbling underneath.

Technical backup never falters. Kitano's editing and Hisaishi Jo's insistent, melodic score work dazzlingly together to tap out a lilting, hypnotic tempo. Katsumi Yanagishima's camera pays sharp service to the eye-catching compositions, many of them shot from behind, giving pic an almost passively observant quality. The surfing scene's lurid hues (iridescent wet suits, vividly painted surfboards) are used inventively as slashes of color across the cool blue background of sky and sea.

— David Rooney

GITO, L'INGRAT
(GITO THE UNGRATEFUL)
(BURUNDI-SWISS-FRENCH)

A Jaques Sandoz Film (Switzerland)/ Capital Entertainment (France)/Productions Cinematographiques du Burundi co-production. Produced by Sandoz. Directed by Léonce Ngabo. Screenplay, Ngabo, Patrick Herzig. Camera (color), Matthias Kaelin; editor, Dominique Roy; music, Pierre-Alain Hoffman; art direction, Joseph Kpobly; costumes, Salika Wenger; sound, Ricardo Castro. Reviewed at Turin Intl. Festival of Young Cinema (competition), Nov. 18, 1992. Running time: **90 MIN.**
Gito . . . . Joseph Kumbela
Christine . . . . Marie Bunel
Flora . . . . Aoua Sangare
André . . . . Louis Kamatari
Hotelier . . . . Paul Favier
Gito's father . . . . . Eraste Bishenga
Gito's mother . . . . . Léa Nyakuruike

First 35m feature from the African republic of Burundi is a lightweight but likable comic fable chastising the sins of vanity and hauteur. The frontierless sisterhood of story's appealing, feminist-flavored comeuppance should help "Gito the Ungrateful" strut into limited dates in French-lingo territories before primping for a wider public on small screens.

Armed with ostentatiously sharp threads, a hard-earned diploma and a conquering attitude, Gito (Joseph Kumbela) heads home to Burundi confident of becoming a big wheel in the ministry. He leaves behind French flame Marie Bunel in Paris, planning to send for her when he's set up. Cold-shouldering his distinctly uncitified parents, Kumbela launches a dogged bid for success, but finds his culturally superior posturing isn't the door-opener he expected.

Romance is rekindled with childhood sweetheart Aoua Sangare, but things get tricky when Bunel turns up unexpectedly and, spelling trouble for future family lineage, is a big hit with Kumbela's folks. Adapting easily to field work and village mores, she partially closes the African-European cultural chasm Kumbela has opened.

When the rival consorts collide, animosity soon gives way to conspiratorial fury at their mutual humiliation, and they turn the tables on the hapless poseur.

Kumbela is a sprightly, sympathetic lead, never pushing Gito's arrogance over unforgivable boundaries, and he's handsomely flanked by breezy turns from Bunel and Sangare.

Debuting director Léonce Ngabo (also a musician, conductor, poet, singer and director of the Ecole de Telecommunications in Burundi's capital, Bujumbura) takes a straightforwardly slick approach to the spirited yarn that makes for engaging if unexceptional fare. Pierre-Alain Hoffman's music is sometimes overly zealous in setting a goofy Gallic comedy tone, but tech work is otherwise smooth.

— David Rooney

LONDON FEST

O DIA DO DESESPERO
(THE DAY OF DESPAIR)
(PORTUGUESE)

A Madragoa Filmes/Gemini Films production. (Intl. sales: Metropolis Film, Zürich.) Produced by Paulo Branco. Executive producer, Camilo Joao. Directed, written by Manoel de Oliveira, from Camilo Castelo Branco's novel "Amor de Perdicao." Camera (Eastmancolor), Mário Barroso; editors, Oliveira, Valérie Loiseleux; art direction, Isabel Branco; costume design, Jasmin de Matos; sound, Gita Cerveira; assistant director, José Maria Vaz da Silva. Reviewed at London Film Festival, Nov. 18, 1992. Running time: **76 MIN.**
Ana Plácido . . . . . Teresa Madruga
Camilo Castelo Branco . Mário Barroso
Freitas Fortuna . . Luís Miguel Cintra
Dr. Edmundo Magalhaes . Diogo Dória

Latest offering by festival icon Manoel de Oliveira, 84, is a slow-moving, crisply lensed study of a last-century Portuguese writer that's for connoisseurs and Oliveira converts only. Uncharacteristically short running time still won't be short enough for those unattuned to the vet's uncompromising style.

Writer in question is Camilo Castelo Branco (1825-90) — "one of the greatest figures of 19th century Portuguese literature," per pic — who scandalized society with a succession of mistresses and finally shot himself. Oliveira, who's already filmed one of his novels (the "Romeo and Juliet"-like "Love of Perdition") and featured him in another pic ("Francisca"), aims to "bring to life" the writer in a stylized docu.

The film presupposes knowledge of Branco's work and molto sympathy for a character who emerges as self-obsessed and melancholy. The precise, painterly compositions, and heavily metaphysical voiceovers, are reinforced by chunks of "Parsifal" and "Tristan und Isolde" on the soundtrack. For a film about passion and internal conflict, it's all remarkably uninvolving.

Performances by the small band of Oliveira regulars are okay, with Mário Barroso reprising his Branco role from "Francisca" and Teresa Madruga solid as the mistress. Pic is Portugese entry in foreign film Oscar stakes. — *Derek Elley*

BLUE BLACK PERMANENT
(BRITISH)

A BFI Distribution (U.K.) release of a Channel 4/British Film Institute presentation of a Viz Permanent production, in association with Scottish Film Prod. Fund/Orkney Islands Council/Edinburgh District Council/Grampian TV/British Screen Finance. Produced by Barbara Grigor. Executive producers, Ben Gibson, Rod Stoneman, Kate Swan. Executive in charge of production (BFI), Angela Topping. Co-producer, Swan. Directed, written by Margaret Tait. Camera (color), Alex Scott; editor, John MacDonnell; music, John Gray; production design, Andrew Semple; costume design, Lynn Aitken; sound (Dolby), Colin Nicolson; associate producer, Christine Maclean; casting, Susie Bruffin. Reviewed at Edinburgh Intl. Film Festival, Aug. 28, 1992. (Also in London Film Festival.) Running time: **84 MIN.**
Philip Lomax . . . . . . Jack Shepherd
Barbara Thorburn . . . . . Celia Imrie
Greta Thorburn . . . Gerda Stevenson
Jim Thorburn . . . . James Fleet
Andrew Cunningham . . Sean Scanlan
Wendy . . . . Hilary Maclean
Sam Kelday . . . . Walter Leask
Also with: Sheana Marr, Eoin Macdonald, Jimmy Moar, Liz Robertson, Bobby Bews, Keith Hutcheon.

Most of the ideas bustling around in "Blue Black Permanent" don't survive the move from page to screen. Pretentious pic about a woman's memories of her poet mother's life and death looks like a fast fader at specialized wickets.

Film is the feature debut of Orkney-born Margaret Tait, 73, who's steadily built a rep with over 30 shorts since the early '50s. Main problem with the present item is that it simply doesn't play on screen.

The story, based in present-day Edinburgh, yo-yos back and forth between the '50s and '30s (in Edinburgh and the Orkney isles) as Barbara (Celia Imrie) tries to exorcize memories about her mother Greta (Gerda Stevenson), a poet-writer who died young 40 years ago.

Flashbacks sketch Greta's troubled years; back in the present, Barbara, a photog, links up with Greta's old pal Andrew (Sean Scanlan), now a w.k. artist, at a modern-day exhibition. A final flashback limns Greta's watery fate in the Orkneys.

A stronger dramatic line might have held all this together. The movie works best when the arty types shut up and Tait lets her camera play on the beauties of the Orkneys and the young Greta's fascination with the sea.

Imrie and Stevenson, both experienced thesps, can't do much with their mix of meaningful and exposition-laden dialogue. Stevenson is okay as the forlorn poetess; Scanlan comes over weakly as the artist. Alex Scott's lensing is the real star, aided by John Gray's evocative score.
—*Derek Elley*

UZLASMA
(THE CONSENSUS)
(TURKISH)

A Belge Film production. (Intl. sales: Belge Film, Istanbul.) Produced by Sabahattin Çetin. Directed by Oguzhan Tercan. Screenplay, Çetin, Tercan; camera (color), Aytekin Çakmakçi; editor, Ismail Kalkan; music, Zülfü Livaneli; production design, Rauf Ozangli; art direction/costume design, Zeyner Tercan; sound, Ercan Okan. Reviewed at London Film Festival, Nov. 10, 1992. Running time: **97 MIN.**
Abdi Ipekçi . . . . Halil Ergün
Mehmet Ali Agca . . . . Berhan Simsek
Sema . . . . Nur Sürer
Also with: Bülent Ecevit, Süleyman Demiret, Alpaslan Türkes, Hasan Fehmi Günes.

"The Consensus" is a Turkish political thriller with over-arty pretensions. Rewinding real-life events through the eyes of an actor cast in a movie reconstruction, the pic is too specific to travel well but will be of interest to those familiar with the territory.

Background is the murder of prominent Istanbul newspaper editor Abdi Ipekçi by terrorist Mehmet Ali Agca, who later tried to waste the Pope in 1981. The death of Ipekçi, a high-level mediator in Turkish politics of the time, led to the right-wing coup by the country's military.

Berhan Simsek plays an actor researching the role of Agca for a movie. After meeting a journalist (Nur Sürer) on a trip to the late editor's newspaper, he strikes up a friendship but begins to research too seriously, imagining himself in past events.

For those unfamiliar with the politics and personalities of the period, the movie demands close attention as first-time feature director Oguzhan Tercan increasingly blurs the line between fiction and reality. Latter reels even include docu interviews with past politicos like p.m. Bülent Ecevit who emerge bland and evasive.

Technically the pic is okay, with a moody synth score by well-known composer Zülfü Livaneli that keeps the atmosphere simmering. — *Derek Elley*

MISSA ON MUSETTE?
(WHERE IS MUSETTE?)
(FINNISH-DOCU-COLOR-16m)

A Kuvaruukki Oy production. Produced, directed, written by Veikko Nieminen, Jarmo Vesteri. Camera (color), editor, Nieminen; sound, Vesteri. Reviewed at London Film Festival, Nov. 22, 1992. Running time: **50 MIN.**
With: Aki Kaurismäki, Matti Pellonpaa, Kari Vaananen, Andre Wilms, Evelyne Didi, Christine Murillo, Jean-Pierre Leaud, Samuel Fuller, Timo Salminen, Jacques Cheuriche, Jouko Lumme, Timo Linnasalo, John Ebden, Gilles Charmant, Simon Murray, Peter Hoffman, Kari Pulkkinen, Erkki Lahti, Irneli Debarle, Mark Lavis, Ansii Tinanmakii.

This docu peek at Finnish auteur Aki Kaurismäki at work in Paris on his latest film, "La Vie de Boheme," is for fans only, but sympathetically parallels the young director's highly independent, even anarchic working methods with the attitudes of his fictional characters. Transferred in just passable fashion from video to film, pic is a highly specialized entry for fests, foreign rep houses and, possibly, arts cable TV.

Only somewhat less prolific than Fassbinder and Godard in the first stages of their careers, Kaurismäki has developed a limited international following with his minimalist, often humorously deadpan studies of disenfranchised characters.

Given the personal excess for which is he known, the Kaurismäki interviewed here is striking for his extreme sobriety, as he carefully positions himself far outside "the dead monster" of Hollywood, where a director is just "an errand boy in a big machine" in which producers and actors are far more powerful.

Helmer acknowledges that, "Since my shoots always turn out to be chaotic, a nine-to-five crew just won't do." The behind-the-scenes team he has carefully assembled over the years appears virtually interchangable with the troupe portraying Henry Murger's fictional characters on suburban Paris locations.

The many collaborators who get their two cents in lend a strong "one for all, all for one" impression, but docu is far from being analytical or critical, and even comes dangerously close to feeling like a promo at times. Another constricting factor is many of the participants' limited expressiveness in the language — usually English or French —in which they are interviewed.

Still, buffs will be grateful for this gently humorous look at an individualistic rebel filmmaker, and the best is saved for last. Prevented from shooting at the Gare d'Austerlitz, Kaurismäki makes do in the best B-movie fashion, with cut-outs of a departing train silhouetted against a garage door. Many Hollywood "errand boys" could benefit from this sort of resourcefulness.
— *Todd McCarthy*

NIIWAM
(SENEGALESE-FRENCH)

An SNPC/Emmanuel Films/Les Ateliers de l'Arche production. (Intl. sales: Les Ateliers de l'Arche, Paris.) Directed by Clarence Thomas Delgado. Screenplay, Delgado, Fidele Dieme, Yves Diagne, from Ousmane Sembéne's novel; camera (Eastmancolor), Guy Chanel; editor, Rose Evans Decraene; music, Aziz Dieng; sound, Maguette Salla; assistant director, Fidele Dieme. Reviewed at London Film Festival, Nov. 8, 1992. Running time: **74 MIN.**
With: Samba Wane, Rama Thiam, Abou Carara, Ablaye Diop Dany, Soukayna Diayne.
(Wolof soundtrack)

"Niiwam" is a well-made, accessible item that could find wider distribution than most sub-Saharan fare. Slim but ironic tale of a poor Senegalese's bus journey to bury his dead kid has enough broad-based humor and observation to appeal to limited arthouse auds if properly sold.

Story is based on a novel by w.k. local filmer Ousmane Sembéne, with whom debuting director Clarence Thomas Delgado has worked as an assistant (most recently on Sembene's "Guelwaar"). Well-turned script shows its quality origins.

After taking his sickly baby daughter to a hospital in the capital only to have her die, penniless fisherman Thieno takes a bus to a cemetery on the outskirts, with the baby's body (pic's Wolof title means "The Corpse") swaddled in his lap.

The journey is the heart of the movie, with a rich assortment of passengers introduced en route. Characters range from the poor to the wealthy, the truculent to the inconsiderate, the blind to the grasping. Thieno remains a largely mute observer of this microcosm. Final payoff is neat.

After a dramatically unsteady start, the picture starts to deliver in the lengthy bus section. Use of the limited space (without resort to studio work) is assured, with no problems of mismatching. Overall tone is light, but always pointed.

The picture, budgeted at 3.5 million French francs ($650,000), shot for seven weeks and was then shelved for a year after initial editing. Production later resumed under a different producer. Tech credits are fine, and the mixed pro/non-pro cast is okay. — *Derek Elley*

VIENNA FEST

DEAD FLOWERS
(AUSTRIAN)

A Wega Film production. Executive producer, Veit Heiduschka. Produced by Gebhard Zupan, Michael Katz. Directed by Peter Ily Huemer. Screenplay by Huemer. Camera (color), Walter Kindler; editor, Eliska Stibrova; sound, Thomas Szabolcs; music, Peter Scherer; production design, Tommy Vögel; costumes, Heidi Melinc. Reviewed at Vienna Film Festival, Oct. 23, 1992. Running time: **98 MIN.**
Alice . . . . Kate Valk
Alex . . . . Thierry van Werveke
Grandmother . . . . . Tana Schanzara
Willy de Ville . . . Dominique Horwitz

Though it seems all basic love-conquers-death stories have been told by now, the concept of "Dead Flowers" is truly original. Though weird and mysterious in concept, however, it is structured and played so flatly that it fails to generate more than 10 minutes worth of interest and the result is just another cheap subsidy quickie.

Unlike other such stories, in this one, love begins after death. Due to sloppy paperwork (Death is a huge, incompetent bureaucracy), a certain Alice (sloppily played by Kate Valk) is allowed to cross into life. There she meets Alex (played with a cute smile but little else by Thierry van Werveke), who falls for her.

Only when the mistake is corrected and the mysterious Alice is dragged back into the realm of death, does van Werveke — and the audience — realize something very strange is going on.

Alex's journey to hell and his confrontation with "The Boss," an amiable clerk-ish woman (Mara Mattuschka) is run of the mill, however. The twist ending (Alex trades the life of a criminal for Alice's) is not dramatic enough to be a surprise.

Though their situation is full of potential for suspense and mystery, at no time does scripter-director Peter Ily Huemer take advantage of it, and the careless production design, poor lighting and indifferent acting only make matters worse. A waste of such good material is a minor creative tragedy. — *Eric Hansen*

RUNNING WILD
(AUSTRIAN-DOCU)

A Prisma production in association with the Austrian Ministry for Education and Art. Executive producers, Michael Seeber, Heinz Stussak. Produced by Curd M. Abdalla. Directed, written by Egon Humer. Camera (color), Wolfgang Lehner; editor, Karina Ressler; music, Muttertag, Krüppelschlag; sound, Alexander Biedermann, Hans Eder, Jörg Priesner. Reviewed at Vienna Film Festival, Oct. 26, 1992. Running time: **90 MIN.**

In "Running Wild," Egon Humer overestimates his subject. The street gangs of Vienna are neither as interesting nor as dramatic as he would like us to think. Despite a good sense of pacing and an aggressive soundtrack, he has little to show. Though it generated a lot of interest at the Vienna Film Festival, it will have little life outside an obligatory TV run.

Humer gives his film a powerful start: close-ups of switchblades snapping open in shadowy blue light, overlaid with rap music. We know what's going to happen here: street gangs, fights and wasted youth. Alas, Humer never cashes in on the promise. The opening remains the most exciting image in the film.

Though he gets a number of Viennese kids to talk (and practice kung fu) in front of the camera, they don't say anything one wouldn't expect from countless other documentaries on potentially violent European youth.

To get the kids to cooperate, Humer let them decide themselves how they wanted to be protrayed on film. One of the gang members, though filmed hanging around with kids flipping knives and carrying pistols, asks Humer to cut out any scene showing him smoking. If his father saw him smoke, he'd get into trouble. But anything more incriminating is edited out. What's left is a bunch of kids hanging out in parks playing with knives and practicing martial arts; the audience doesn't get any real sense of them or their situation. — *Eric Hansen*

HOFFA

A 20th Century Fox release presented in association with Jersey Films of an Edward R. Pressman production. Executive producer, Joseph Isgro. Produced by Pressman, Danny DeVito, Caldecot Chubb. Directed by DeVito. Screenplay, David Mamet. Camera (color; Panavision widescreen), Stephen H. Burum; editors, Lynzee Klingman, Ronald Roose; music, David Newman; production design, Ida Random; art direction, Gary Wissner; visual consultant, Harold Michelson; set design, Charles Daboub Jr., Robert Fechtman; costume design, Deborah L. Scott; sound (Dolby), Thomas D. Causey; co-producer, Harold Schneider; associate producers, Mamet, William Barclay Malcolm; assistant director, Ned Dowd; casting, David Rubin, Debra Zane. Reviewed at 20th Century Fox Studios, L.A., Dec. 8, 1992. MPAA Rating: R. Running time: **140 MIN.**
James R. Hoffa . . . . . Jack Nicholson
Bobby Ciaro . . . . . . Danny DeVito
Carol D'Allesandro . Armand Assante
Fitzsimmons . . . . J.T. Walsh
Pete Cponnelly . . . . . John C. Reilly
Young Kid . . . . Frank Whaley
Robert Kennedy . . . Kevin Anderson
Red Bennett . . . . John P. Ryan
Billy Flynn . . . . Robert Prosky
Jo Hoffa . . . . Natalija Nogulich
Hoffa's Attorney . . . . Nicholas Pryor
Ted Harmon . . . . Paul Guilfoyle
Young Woman at RTA . Karen Young
Solly Stein . . . . Cliff Gorman

"Hoffa" presents the controversial labor leader as public icon, a man of iron, granite and *cojones* who bullies his way across the union and political landscape of the mid-century all for the good of the working man. Unfortunately, this grimly ambitious biopic goes no deeper than that, offering hardly a trace of psychology, motivation or inner life. Jack Nicholson's powerhouse lead performance will command attention and respect, assuring a measure of critical and public interest, but approach is too one-dimensional and chilly to put this in the winner's circle.

A portrait of thuggery as a way of life for people on all sides of the law and an elevation of David Mamet's favorite Anglo-Saxon expletive to the level of a philosophy, "Hoffa" is the second biographical drama of the Christmas season devoted to a feverishly ideological firebrand whose favorite activity was making speeches, who didn't carouse or fool around with women, and who was eventually done in by former allies. But at least Malcolm X had a private life. From all the evidence offered here, Jimmy Hoffa was only at home with a fight on his hands.

First section of Danny DeVito's dark look at American economic and business dealings consists almost entirely of Hoffa's harangues and agitations on behalf of the union. Jumping into the truck of fictitious everyman Bobby Ciaro (DeVito) one night, Hoffa preaches the gospel of the Teamsters, expressing it with almost mathematical logic.

Hoffa's further disruptions at a loading dock cost Ciaro his job, upon which the rising organizer takes the little man on as his full-time flunky and sounding board. Unfortunately, Ciaro is never given any dimension besides loyal lackey, and the amount of screen time director DeVito gives to his own cardboard character quickly becomes annoying.

As soon as Hoffa achieves some stature, he is abducted by a few fellows whose native language is Italian. In response, and given little choice, Hoffa talks turkey with them, and is thereby permanently corrupted and compromised very early in his career. But it's all for the good of the working man, he says, without the filmmakers offering any further analysis or critique.

So Hoffa continues his rise, recruiting and negotiating with the single-minded fervor of a religious proselytizer, mixing it up with company goons when he feels like it, finally ascending to the Teamster presidency.

But mixed in with the roots of his success are the seeds of his downfall. Some of the film's few fireworks are supplied when a young "punk" named Robert Kennedy squares off with a testy Hoffa in public hearings and promises him he'll eventually be convicted. Hoffa has no qualms about telling RFK what he and his brother can do to themselves and, when a reporter informs him of an incriminating story, Hoffa's response is so explicitly threatening the story is killed.

Hoffa gets sent up the river anyway — which finally occasions the first scene with Hoffa and his wife — and is eventually pardoned by Nixon but barred from holding union office again.

Intercut with the flow of historical action are scenes of the aging Hoffa and Ciaro waiting for unknown associates at a roadside cafe. With his boss waiting in a parked car, Ciaro gets chatting with a young fellow driver inside and, as the events on parade gradually become more contemporaneous, it's not hard to see what lies in store for the two old pals. Matter of Hoffa's fate is neatly wrapped up without being too specific.

Mainly because of Nicholson's

galvanizing performance and Mamet's peppery, confrontational dialogue, all this is not exactly dull, but it is very dry and uninvolving. Seemingly set during a bleak, uninterrupted Eastern industrial winter, film views Hoffa's life — all life — as constant combat, an unending series of screw or be screwed situations.

Decked out in an entirely acceptable hairpiece and built-up nose, Nicholson meets everything here head-on, shrugs and rights himself whenever he takes a hit, and charges ahead as fearlessly as Joe Frazier or Mike Tyson in the ring. In a rare tackling of a real-life character (Eugene O'Neill in "Reds" was another), Nicholson triumphs again.

Strong supporting cast, notably including J.T. Walsh as Frank Fitzsimmons, Frank Whaley as the roadside stranger and Robert Prosky as an early Hoffa cohort, contributes a rough-and-ready working class feel, though locations are oddly mixed with obvious sets for some exterior scenes, giving the film the insular look of a studio picture of the 1930s or '40s. Tech contributions waver between strong and heavy.

DeVito's direction tends toward the over-busy, with plenty of crane shots and imaginative but fussy scene transitions. As is so often the case with biopics that attempt to convey decades, something gets sacrificed. Here, it's a human drama one can relate to. — *Todd McCarthy*

LORENZO'S OIL

A Universal Pictures release of a Kennedy Miller film. Executive producer, Arnold Burk. Produced by Doug Mitchell, George Miller. Directed by Miller. Screenplay, Miller, Nick Enright. Camera (Atlab Australia; Technicolor), John Seale; editors, Richard Francis-Bruce, Marcus D'Arcy, Lee Smith; production design, Kristi Zea; art direction, Dennis Bradford; set decoration, Karen A. O'Hara; costume design, Colleen Atwood; sound (Dolby), Ben Osmo; sound design, Lee Smith; associate producers, Johnny Friedkin, Daphne Paris, Lynn O'Hare; assistant director, Steven E. Andrews; casting, John Lyons. Reviewed at AMC Century 14 Theaters, L.A., Dec. 3, 1992. MPAA Rating: PG-13. Running time: **135 MIN.**
Augusto Odone . . . . Nick Nolte
Michaela Odone . . . . Susan Sarandon
Professor Nikolais . . . . Peter Ustinov
Deirdre Murphy . . . Kathleen Wilhoite
Doctor Judalon . . . . . Gerry Bamman
Wendy Gimble . . . Margo Martindale
Ellard Muscatine . . . James Rebhorn
Loretta Muscatine . . . . . Ann Hearn
Omouri . . . . Maduka Steady
Lorenzo Odone
. . . . . . Zack O'Malley Greenburg
Comorian Teacher . . . . . Mary Wakio
Don Suddaby . . . . Don Suddaby

"Lorenzo's Oil" is as grueling a medical case study as any audience would ever want to sit through. A true-life story brought to the screen intelligently and with passionate motivation by George Miller, pic details in a very precise way how a couple raced time to save the life of their young son after he contracted a rare, always fatal disease. A one-of-a-kind film that will devastate some viewers and prove too overbearing and clinical for others, it is as obsessive and relentless as its leading characters. Universal release will likely develop a limited loyal following, but is no doubt too strong a prescription for the general public.

A practicing physician himself before forging his filmmaking career with the "Mad Max" actioners, Miller has, from all accounts, scrupulously adhered to the facts in relating the harrowing but inspiring tale of Augusto and Michaela Odone.

In 1984, their 5-year-old son Lorenzo was diagnosed with adrenoleukodystrophy (ALD), a condition occurring only in boys that results in the deterioration of the myelin coating around the nerves and leads to seizures, paralysis and, within two years, certain death.

Despite its seriousness, the disease was so obscure few doctors were working on it, and the only therapy involved experimental diets. Advised to just try to make their son's remaining days as comfortable as possible and faced with a slowly grinding medical establishment, the Odones took it upon themselves to research the subject from scratch and try to find a cure for Lorenzo.

Given that the resourceful couple succeeded to the extent that they curbed their son's deterioration, kept him alive — he is now 14 — and enabled many other boys with the disease to avoid its symptoms through the use of the oil they identified until a cure is found, the Odones' story had the makings of an illness-of-the-week TV movie, complete with nobly suffering child and inspirational music.

Instead, Miller has fashioned an emotionally gritty, medically dense portrait of undeterrable parental devotion that ranks as the most unflinching look at a disease and its consequences since the little-seen 1980 Dutch film "In for Treatment."

First section, which details the discovery of Lorenzo's ailment, is the most effective and visually striking. Employing a succession of brief scenes, Miller keeps tracking in on characters in ways more normally associated with action films than intimate dramas. His use of blackouts allows the emotional impact and meaning of scenes to sink in, and his exceptionally imaginative camera moves make even a laborious research expedition to the library a visually vital experience.

As the film progresses, however, its single-mindedness is such one is not surprised to see an 800 number for ALD info on the end credits, and some other elements have gotten out of hand or lost in the shuffle.

Among the irritants is an acting style that is generally cranked up to full throttle or beyond. As Augusto, Nick Nolte sports an accent unrecognizable until being identified as Italian; playing this nationality has encouraged him to furrow his brow and gesticulate most of the time. An appealing humanity comes through as well, but the mannerisms and accent get in the way more often than not.

As Michaela, Susan Sarandon fares better, as she convincingly conveys a fierceness and tenacity that is almost frightening. The character never lets up, and neither does the film, which makes for an intense, exhausting, unmodulated experience. This is arguably appropriate to the story of a child for whom concern and care cannot be put on hold even for an instant, but dramatically it has its downside.

Further, Miller introduces a spiritual element that is not at all satisfactorily resolved. After an early, striking sequence of the couple praying in church, Michaela seems to turn her back on faith in favor of pragmatic action. And yet the director continues to use religious music, slips in an unexplained taste of African mysticism and mysteriously concludes matters with a view of the Sistine Chapel ceiling.

To the great credit of Miller and co-writer Nick Enright the complicated medical matters are expressed with admirable clarity, and the fact that complex concepts can be made comprehensible to the viewer makes it credible that the Odones, as laymen, could have made the discoveries they did.

It also helps that young Zack O'Malley Greenburg makes Lorenzo so clearly a bright, spirited child. Lorenzo's condition is viewed without sentimentality, and the film refuses to condescend to the audience. But the terrible suffering Lorenzo endures will be more than some people want to watch.

Peter Ustinov nicely understates his role as an eminent M.D. who develops an ambivalent relationship with the protagonists. Lensed largely in Pittsburgh but with numerous side trips, pic is technically prodigious.

Very clearly hand-crafted in every respect rather than machine-tooled, pic is a troubling experience, as much for the subject matter as for the ambitious, accomplished but ultimately somewhat offputting way in which it was made. — *Todd McCarthy*

TOYS

A 20th Century Fox release of a Baltimore Pictures production. Produced by Barry Levinson, Mark Johnson. Directed by Levinson. Screenplay, Valerie Curtin, Levinson. Camera (CFI color), Adam Greenberg; editor, Stu Linder; music, Hans Zimmer, Trevor Horn; production design, Ferdinando Scarfiotti; art direction, Edward Richardson; set decoration, Linda DeScenna; costume design, Albert Wolsky; sound (Dolby), Ron Judkins; sound design, Richard Beggs; special effects coordinator, Clayton Pinney; visual effects supervisor, Mat Beck; co-producers, Charles Newirth, Peter Giuliano; assistant director, Giuliano; casting, Ellen Chenoweth. Reviewed at the 20th Century Fox Little Theater, L.A., Dec. 4, 1992. MPAA Rating: PG-13. Running time: **121 MIN.**

Leslie Zevo . . . . Robin Williams
The General . . . . . Michael Gambon
Alsatia Zevo . . . . Joan Cusack
Gwen . . . . Robin Wright
Patrick . . . . LL Cool J
Kenneth Zevo . . . . Donald O'Connor
Owens Owens . . . . . . Arthur Malet
Zevo, Sr. . . . . Jack Warden
Nurse Debbie . . . . Debi Mazar

Only a filmmaker with Barry Levinson's clout would have been so indulged to create such a sprawling, seemingly unsupervised mess as "Toys," a painful exercise that makes "Hudson Hawk" look like a modest throwaway. Once word gets out, even Robin Williams fans will pass in favor of another trip to "Aladdin." It will be hard to top as the season's major clunker.

Williams appeared in the very funny trailer for the movie last summer, in which there was an early giveaway: no actual footage was shown. As it is, the trailer provided Williams almost as much screen time as he gets in the movie, a reunion of the actor-director pairing that yielded

"Good Morning, Vietnam."

There's a bomb here, too, but what Levinson has really done is "frag" himself — erecting a staggering array of sets to present a "Willie Wonka"-like fantasy world that's so loud, droning and unpleasant those unmoved by graphic splendor for its own sake will be stampeding for the exits.

The slow-developing story has aging toymaker Kenneth Zevo (a cameo by Donald O'Connor) leave his factory to his army-general brother (Michael Gambon), fearing that his two children (Williams and Joan Cusack) are too immature for the job.

Rendered obsolete by the end of the Cold War, the General goes about converting the plant into a factory producing war toys and machines of war, sinisterly training toddlers to operate them through the use of videogames.

Levinson, a director most at home with slice-of-life portraits relating to his Baltimore roots, tries his hand here at a darkly satiric fable and ends up doing an extremely poor impression of Terry Gilliam. Even the movie's messages — war is bad, joy and innocence are good — are so simplistic one has to wonder at whom the film is aimed.

Certainly not kids, who will be either bored or scared by the dour tone despite the splendid visual flourishes and nonstop barrage of gadgetry. Yet even the filmmaking techniques are derivative and almost abusive.

Against the fantastic backdrop are uneven, over-the-top performances that provide no one to root for or against. Gambon, as the Snidely Whiplash in the piece, proves a rather toothless villain — a cross between a mad scientist and the animated Commander McBragg.

On the flip side, Williams and Cusack, the supposed spirits of innocence, are for the most part annoying — particularly Cusack's adult-as-child antics. Through sheer energy Williams generates a few laughs, but the movie gets so preoccupied with gimmickry it pays little heed to the actors and only underscores how much better used Williams' gifts were in "Aladdin."

"Toys" shines technically in a number of areas, though the more magnificent the sets, the more resentment the script's weakness engenders. The movie's real star, production designer Ferdinando Scarfiotti ("The Last Emperor"), nevertheless deserves enormous credit, as do art director Edward Richardson and the

many designers and effects personnel involved.

In the production notes, Levinson's longtime collaborator, producer Mark Johnson, notes that "Toys" was a dozen years in the making and expresses gratitude to "everyone who didn't or wouldn't make the movie." Fox will no doubt wish it could have been on that thank-you list.

— *Brian Lowry*

TRESPASS

A Universal release of a Canton/Zemeckis/Gale production. Executive producers, Robert Zemeckis, Bob Gale. Produced by Neil Canton. Directed by Walter Hill. Screenplay, Gale, Zemeckis. Camera (Deluxe color), Lloyd Ahern; editor, Freeman Davies; music, Ry Cooder; production design, Jon Hutman; art direction, Charles Breen; set design, Kathleen Sullivan; set decoration, Beth Rubino; costume design, Dan Moore; sound (Dolby), Charles M. Wilborn; co-producer, Michael S. Glick; assistant director, Barry K. Thomas; 2nd unit director, Allan Graf; casting, Reuben Cannon. Reviewed at Universal Studios, Universal City, Calif., Dec. 7, 1992. MPAA Rating: R. Running time: **101 MIN.**

Vince . . . . Bill Paxton
King James . . . . Ice T
Don . . . . William Sadler
Savon . . . . Ice Cube
Bradlee . . . . Art Evans
Lucky . . . . De'voreaux White
Raymond . . . . Bruce A. Young
Luther . . . . Glenn Plummer
Wickey . . . . Stoney Jackson
Video . . . . T.E. Russell
Cletus . . . . Tiny Lister
Goose . . . . John Toles-Bey
Moon . . . . Byron Minns
Davis . . . . Tico Wells

Throw together "The Treasure of the Sierra Madre" and "Rio Bravo," bring in the Ice crew, inject a noxious dose of racial hatred and stir in some sharp action direction and you've got "Trespass." From a strictly filmmaking point of view, this is Walter Hill's best work in some years, but the rehashed story elements and violence for violence's sake leave this feeling like a rather empty exercise. Not exactly one's idea of a Christmas release, this bearer of bad will toward men should generate decent biz on the action circuit.

Originally called "Looters," pic underwent a title change, a delay and some alterations after the L.A. riots this spring. Understandably so: Even if the story explicitly involves criminals rather than normal citizens, the level of racial tension depicted here is way past the boiling point.

Although less stylized than some of the director's earlier films,

"Trespass" has even more compression. After a brief prologue, it is entirely set in one location, a huge abandoned factory in East St. Louis, Ill. Learning that a huge stash of gold is supposedly buried somewhere in the bombed-out building, good ol' boy firemen Bill Paxton and William Sadler drive to the eerily under-populated area with the idea of uncovering the loot.

Unfortunately for them, the two Arkansas crackers stumble onto a gangland murder and instantly become marked men. Pursued by some tough, well-armed blacks led by a resplendent Ice T (playing a crime lord named King James), Paxton and Sadler manage to nab T's brother, De'voreaux White. Holed up in one room, the white guys squabble between themselves about what to do about the gold, how to use the hostage as their ticket out, and what to do about a sassy old derelict (Bruce A. Young) who claims the building, and the gold, as his own.

For the black gang members' part, Ice T wants to continue negotiating in hopes of getting his brother out alive; hothead subordinate Ice Cube keeps insisting that force is the only answer. The disagreements on both sides inevitably lead to heavy carnage, which is as senseless on a human level as it is desirable to those hungry for high body counts in action pics. Ending is both predictable and contrived.

Borrowing the nihilistic greed angle from "Sierra Madre" and the stand-off in tight quarters over a hostage brother from "Rio Bravo," script generates a certain amount of tension from its bluntly dramatic situation. Hill's handling of the action is more fluid and kinetic than in a long while, making the film a pleasure to watch purely for the expertness of its craft.

But the hatred based on race and turf and imagined threats steadily escalates throughout, to the point that all the shouting sounds hollow and the shooting seems futile. The central role of the gold treasure has a hokey, hoary aspect to it after all this time, and the borrowings from old movies and other fictions don't comfortably match up with the brutal realities of inner city crime and racial tensions. To say the least, this is quite unlike anything the mainstream commercial team of Bob Gale and Robert Zemeckis has written, or at least had produced, to date.

Ice T and Ice Cube strut their stuff in impressively forceful, if one-dimensional, fashion. To balance them off, pic could have used some bigger, more resonant names on the white side, rather than the little-known Paxton and Sadler, who come off as decent but unremarkable. What about two country-western singers, or maybe sports figures? A little mythic or cultural weight up against the Ice team would have helped.

Young gets off a few amusingly rude remarks in the Walter Brennan part. Remainder of the mostly black cast is essentially called upon to deliver hostile attitude, and does so effectively.

Technically, film is tops. Stunts and explosions are extensive and expertly done, lenser Lloyd Ahern creates rich-looking images out of shadows, smoke and dingy locations (buildings in Atlanta and Memphis were employed for the single location), and Ry Cooder has cranked out a tense score to accompany nearly a dozen rap-oriented tunes for the soundtrack.

Editor Freeman Davies is to be complimented, not only for the dynamic pacing he maintains, but for being at least partly responsible for one of the only films of the Christmas season that is not a moment too long.
— *Todd McCarthy*

INTO THE WEST
(BRITISH-U.S.)

A Miramax Films (U.S.)/Entertainment Film Distributors (U.K.) release of a Majestic Film Intl./Miramax/Film Four Intl./Newcom presentation of a Little Bird Prods. production in association with Parallel Films and with participation of British Screen. Executive producer, James Mitchell. Produced by Jonathan Cavendish, Tim Palmer. Directed by Mike Newell. Screenplay, Jim Sheridan, from Michael Pearce's story; additional writing, David Keating. Camera (Eastmancolor; Technicolor prints), Tom Sigel; editor, Peter Boyle; music, Patrick Doyle; production design, Jamie Leonard; art direction, Mark Geraghty; costume design, Consolata Boyle; sound (Dolby), Peter Lindsay; stunt coordinator, Tony Smart; co-producers, Susan Slonaker, Jane Doolan; co-executive producers, Guy East, Bob & Harvey Weinstein; associate producer, Gabriel Byrne; assistant director, Simon Moseley; 2nd unit director, Barry Blackmore; casting, Ros & John Hubbard. Reviewed at Odeon Haymarket theater, London, Dec. 15, 1992. Running time: **102 MIN.**
Papa Reilly . . . . Gabriel Byrne
Kathleen . . . . Ellen Barkin
Ossie . . . . Ciaran Fitzgerald
Tito . . . . Ruaidhri Conroy
Grandpa Ward . . . . . . David Kelly

"Into the West" is a likable but modest pic about two Dublin moppets who take to the hills on a beautiful white stallion. Offbeat casting of Gabriel Byrne and Ellen Barkin as two hobos in pursuit could spark initial interest, but pic will prove a marketing challenge thanks to its complex mix of kiddies' adventure and grown-up Gaelic myth. Now in U.K. distribution, film is opening night attraction at Sundance fest in January.

Scripter Jim Sheridan, whose "My Left Foot" and "The Field" showed outsiders coping inspiringly with the real world, works with thinner material this time round. Result is a wispy yarn that has some fine moments (such as when kids and hoss overnight at a village movie theater and watch "Back to the Future Part III"), plenty of Gaelic charm (recalling Brit pics of the '40s and '50s), but takes a while to sort out where it's headed.

Byrne is Papa Reilly, a modern-day gypsy "traveller" (hobo) who's finally settled in a grim, high-rise nabe of Dublin with his two kids, Tito (Ruaidhri Conroy) and Ossie (Ciaran Fitzgerald). His fanciful old father-in-law (David Kelly) captures the brats' imagination with elaborate fairy tales woven around a white horse he's brought back.

When the kids move the equine into their ramshackle apartment, the law moves in and sells it to a rich farmer. The kids promptly steal it back and set out for the "wild" west of Ireland, fired by grandpa's stories and cowboy movies. Byrne, joined by fellow "traveller" Kathleen (Barkin), sets out in hot pursuit, closely followed by the authorities.

Pic's antiauthoritarian subtext isn't labored, with the forces of law and order mostly portrayed (aside from an unsettling scene of Dublin cops browbeating Byrne) as johnny-come-lately bumblers. With the children rather than the adults in the dramatic driver's seat, the movie is often similar in feel to the 1989 Paul Scofield-Helen Mirren starrer, "When the Whales Came," another mix of myth and kidpic.

Director Mike Newell ("Enchanted April") gives the material his best shot, paring dialogue to a minimum, keeping the camera mobile (with jolting, handheld stuff at moments of emotional drama), and further aided by Peter Boyle's pacey cutting.

A major asset throughout is the omnipresent symphonic score by Patrick Doyle, who's done yeoman service on Kenneth Branagh pics as well as the recent Gallic big-budgeter "Indochine." It's often Doyle's rich, Gaelic-flavored scoring that carries the movie's emotional line and fairy tale atmosphere.

Byrne (who also scores an associate producer credit among the mass of production honchos) gives a credible, if low-key, rendering of the weak, illiterate father, scarred by the death of his wife. Barkin, who appears halfway through and is mostly consigned to a supporting role, downplays her looks and carries off an Irish accent with aplomb. The script features no bonding between the two, aside from a brief nocturnal chat.

The real stars are the two kids, notably Ciaran Fitzgerald as the younger bro, whose desire to commune with his late mother fuels the pic's latter stages as the horse leads them to their destiny on the west coast. Some of the dialogue is hard to disentangle from their rich Irish brogue but they make a winning combo.

Other credits are pro, although Tom Sigel's lensing of the rugged Irish landscape is often ill-served by less-than-sharp processing. Studio work was done at Ireland's Ardmore complex, with postproduction in London.
— *Derek Elley*

SCENT OF A WOMAN

A Universal release of a City Light Films production. Executive producer, Ronald L. Schwary. Produced, directed by Martin Brest. Screenplay, Bo Goldman, suggested by Dino Risi's film "Profumo Di Donna" written by Ruggero Maccari, Risi, from Giovanni Arpino's novel "Il Buio E Il Miele." Camera (Duart color; Deluxe prints), Donald E. Thorin; editors, William Steinkamp, Michael Tronick, Harvey Rosenstock; music, Thomas Newman; production design, Angelo Graham; art direction, W. Steven Graham; set decoration, George DeTitta Jr.; costume design, Aude Bronson-Howard; sound (Dolby), Danny Michael; associate producer, G. Mac Brown; assistant director, Amy Sayres; casting, Ellen Lewis. Reviewed at Universal Studios, Universal City, Calif., Dec. 4, 1992. MPAA Rating: R. Running time: **157 MIN.**
Lt. Col. Frank Slade . . . . . Al Pacino
Charlie Simms . . . . . Chris O'Donnell
Mr. Trask . . . . James Rebhorn
Donna . . . . Gabrielle Anwar
George Willis Jr. . . . Philip S. Hoffman
W.R. Slade . . . . . . Richard Venture
Randy . . . . Bradley Whitford
Officer Gore . . . . Ron Eldard
Christine Downes . . . Frances Conroy
Karen Rossi . . . . Sally Murphy
Harry Havemeyer . . . Nicholas Sadler
Manny . . . . Gene Canfield

Of note for Al Pacino's theatrical, virtuoso star turn as a blind ex-military officer who introduces a greenhorn to the things of life, "Scent of a Woman" indulgently stretches a modest conceit well past the breaking point. Essentially a two-character piece that goes on nearly an hour too long, Martin Brest's latest boasts good writing, filmmaking and performances, but far too much of each. Story's unusual incidents and ultimate sentimentality will please audiences up to a point, resulting in decent b.o., but this is decidedly a case where more is less.

Universal release is based on a 1974 Italian film directed by Dino Risi that Fox distributed with some success Stateside, but while the central premise remains similar, screenwriter Bo Goldman has so thoroughly reworked, nay, overworked the story it stands more as a reconceptualization than a remake. Oddly, original title was kept when it has next to nothing to do with anything.

Script takes the p.o.v. of teenager Charlie Simms (Chris O'Donnell), a straight-arrow student at a snooty Eastern boarding school. A poor kid from Oregon, O'Donnell inadvertently lands in hot water when he and a well-heeled buddy witness three other kids setting up a prank in which the headmaster and his new Jaguar get doused in paint.

But punishment has to wait until after Thanksgiving vacation. While the other boys head for Vermont to ski, O'Donnell is obliged to earn a few bucks by caring for a sightless lieutenant colonel (Pacino) whose family is leaving for the long weekend.

Frank Slade is a feisty, combative, irascible, remarkably insightful character who drinks all day but never gets drunk and holds on to a genuine, if embittered, lust for life. No sooner have his relatives departed than he whisks the reluctant Charlie into a first-class cabin of a plane for New York City, where he intends to savor some of his favorite things one last time.

Setup takes a leisurely 35 minutes, whereupon the mismatched pair indulge in some relatively mild pleasures and pranks — zipping around Gotham in a limo, taking a test drive in a Ferrari, and disrupting some other relatives, who reveal aspects of Pacino's checkered past.

Otherwise, most of the action is confined to the pair's suite at the Waldorf-Astoria. Sometimes frightening and bluntly cruel, Pacino hectors the young man into growing up and seizing what life has to offer. These scenes are reasonable, if a bit hokey, but they are nothing compared to the cornball finale.

To a significant extent, this is Pacino's show, and he's got much to work with here, responding with one of his most energetic, emotionally open performances. It stands almost as an antithesis of some of his earlier, inward, brooding work. At the same time, there is an element of theatrical grandstanding, a sense in which all the scenes have been created to put the character center stage, emoting to maximum effect while dominating everyone around him. It's a part John Barrymore would have loved playing.

O'Donnell does pretty well holding his own, although for dramatic purposes the character stays the same and protests too long when one knows he's stuck for the long haul.

Goldman's screenplay and director Brest's handling of it evince integrity and intelligence, and the film indisputably has a distinctive character and finely crafted contours all its own. But for what the picture has to offer —detailed characterizations, an agreeable if conventional philosophical stance, moderately absorbing and amusing incidents — there's just far too much of it to sustain unflagging interest. Reportedly, two shorter versions of the film were tested at previews but went over less well with auds than the release cut.

Tech credits are ultra-professional, and Thomas Newman's score stands out for its appealing, varied textures.

— *Todd McCarthy*

LEAP OF FAITH

A Paramount Pictures release of a Michael Manheim/David V. Picker production. Executive producer, Ralph S. Singleton. Produced by Manheim, Picker. Directed by Richard Pearce. Screenplay, Janus Cercone. Camera (Deluxe color), Matthew F. Leonetti; editors, Don Zimmerman, Mark Warner, John F. Burnett; music, Cliff Eidelman; production design, Patrizia Von Brandenstein; art direction, Dennis Bradford; set decoration, Gretchen Rau; costume design, Theadora Van Runkle; sound (Dolby), Petur Hliddal; associate producers, Cercone, Burt Bluestein, Roger Joseph Pugliese; assistant directors, Doug Metzger, Anthony Brand; casting, Gretchen Rennell. Reviewed at the Paramount Studio Theater, L.A., Dec. 2, 1992. MPAA Rating: PG-13. Running time: **108 MIN.**
Jonas . . . . Steve Martin
Jane . . . . Debra Winger
Marva . . . . Lolita Davidovich
Will . . . . Liam Neeson
Boyd . . . . Lukas Haas
Hoover . . . . Meat Loaf
Matt . . . . . Philip Seymour Hoffman
Tiny . . . . M.C. Gainey

Steve Martin's showy but sober performance as a phony faith healer won't be enough to part the b.o. heavens for this earnest effort, which may be best remembered as the only holiday release to follow Brandon Tartikoff's exit from Paramount. Well-made but muddled in its aims, "Leap of Faith" should have a tough time luring customers into the tent.

The foremost problem, ultimately, is that the film waffles as to what it's about, never embarking on a full-scale indictment of charlatans and TV ministries (à la Genesis' scathing song/video "Jesus He Knows Me") and never unabashedly embracing any higher power, despite its cryptic ending.

Like the rubes in the tent, the spirituality surrounding the denouement may leave some feeling as if they've seen somethin', when it mostly boils down to smoke and mirrors.

Martin's latest "serious" role isn't as dour as "Pennies From Heaven" but has the same joyless quality that seems to permeate many comics' dramatic work. For all his on-stage antics preaching, Martin and director Richard Pearce ("The Long Walk Home") never expose the underbelly of this hard-shelled con man.

There are also too many hackneyed elements within the story, which begins when, as minister Jonas Nightengale, Martin's traveling motorcade is forced to make an unscheduled stop-over in a small, depressed Kansas town. The entourage includes Martin's assistant (Debra Winger), and an assortment of roadies and singers intent on finding marks to help make their $3,500-a-day production nut.

The act starts to unravel, however, as Winger becomes enamored with the local sheriff (Liam Neeson), who isn't fooled by Martin's act, while the ersatz preacher gets entangled with a pretty waitress (Lolita Davidovich) and her crippled brother (Lukas Haas), who were previously victimized by one of his brethren.

First-time writer Janus Cercone's script proves intriguing at first as it goes about debunking the faith-healing mystique (the credits even include a "cons & fraud consultant"), and the gospel music and stage-show elements provide an energy that almost seems to endorse Martin's point, made to the sheriff, that whether he's preaching the gospel or not he at least endeavors to "give my people a good show."

Still, not enough groundwork is laid to grasp why Winger begins to sour on the routine, or to understand Martin's own ambivalence about the crippled youth. There's also little insight into Martin and Winger's relationship, a problematic oversight when their playful sparring later becomes more serious.

His character may capture his share of fool's gold, but despite early buzz that Martin's perf will be an Oscar contender, it seems a long shot. The character is such a consummate fraud he proves impenetrable, and the preaching scenes show only that Martin still has a way with fancy footwork and makes a nifty-looking human mirror ball.

Most other roles are equally under-developed, and the budding romance between Winger and Neeson is reduced to scenes that rely more on schmaltzy settings than character.

Tech credits are solid, with a strong musical score and clever staging of the numerous revival sequences, from sets and costumes to cinematography. Still, "Leap's" ultimate reward should come on a different plane — namely, homevideo. — *Brian Lowry*

KILLER IMAGE
(CANADIAN)

A Groundstar Entertainment release of a Malofilm Group/Groundstar Entertainment/Storia Films production. (Intl. sales: Image Organization.) Executive producer, Jim Murphy. Produced by David Winning, Rudy Barichello, Bruce Harvey. Directed by Winning. Screenplay, Winning, Stan Edmonds, Jaron Summers. Camera (Fuji color), Dean Bennett; editor, Alan Collins; music, Stephen Foster; sound, George Tarrant; art direction, Bruce Sinski; assistant director, David MacLeod; line producer, Les Kimber; associate producer, André Lauzon; casting, Leslie Swan. Reviewed on Paramount vidcassette, N.Y., Dec. 11, 1992. MPAA Rating: R. Running time: **96 MIN.**
Sam Kane . . . . . . M. Emmet Walsh
Max Oliver . . . John Pyper-Ferguson
Shelly . . . . Krista Errickson
Luther . . . . Michael Ironside
Stacey . . . . Barbra Gajewskia
Ric Oliver . . . . Paul Austin
Lori . . . . Chantelle Jenkins
Carrie . . . . Kristie Baker

"Killer Image" is a well-made Canadian suspense feature that has inexplicably opened at year's end in Los Angeles to qualify for Oscar consideration. Its natural home is homevideo, where Paramount Home Video released it this past summer.

M. Emmet Walsh toplines as a corrupt senator whose brother, perennial screen baddie Michael Ironside, is shown dumping a body in film's opening.

Incriminating photos of Walsh with a prostitute, snapped by Paul Austin, cost the shutterbug his life. Austin's brother Max (John Pyper-Ferguson) is out to set things right, but Ironside frames him for the murder of another hooker and discredits him with the police as a "boy who cried wolf."

Filmmaker David Winning, in his second feature assignment, has a plot that becomes increasingly far-fetched as Ironside's complicated schemes keep going awry. Pyper-Ferguson teams up with his brother's g.f., lovely U.S. thesp Krista Errickson, and of course a romance develops.

Storyline resolves itself with Pyper-Ferguson turning Walsh and Ironside against each other. The symmetry of brothers vs. brothers is not fully developed since Austin's role is minor.

Though the film is set in the U.S., its Calgary area locations are attractive, including a cliffhanger finale above surging water rapids. Cast is okay.

— *Lawrence Cohn*

L'ACCOMPAGNATRICE
(THE ACCOMPANIST)
(FRENCH)

An AMLF release of a Film Par Film/Les Films de la Boissiere/Orly Films/Sedif/France 3 Cinema co-production in association with Paravision Intl. and with the participation of Canal Plus/Sofiarp. Produced by Jean-Louis Livi. Directed by Claude Miller. Screenplay, Miller, Luc Beraud, from Nina Berberova's novel. Camera (color), Yves Angelo; editor, Albert Jurgenson; musical direction, Alain Jomy; set design, Jean-Pierre Kohut Svelko; costume design, Jacqueline Bouchard; sound, Paul Laine, Gerard Lamps. Reviewed at Max Linder Cinema, Paris, Nov. 16, 1992. Running time: **111 MIN.**
Charles Brice . . . . Richard Bohringer
Irene Brice . . . . Elena Safonova
Sophie Vasseur . . Romane Bohringer
Singer's voice . . . Laurence Monteyrol
Also with: Samuel Labarthe, Julien Rassam, Bernard Verley, Nelly Borgeaud, Niels Dubost, Sacha Briquet, Claude Rich.

Despite the irresistably radiant Elena Safonova and promising first-time pairing of talented father-daughter thesps Richard and Romane Bohringer, the delicate emotional entanglements in Claude Miller's "L'accompagnatrice" are rendered with too heavy a hand.

Tragic drama of a privileged singer and her self-effacing piano accompanist during the German Occupation of France strives to be touching and haunting but comes across as dour and bleak.

Transposed from a novel set in St. Petersburg and Paris at the time of the Russian Revolution, pic's WWII portrait of misplaced loyalty and heartbreak is never completely believable.

In Paris during the brutal winter of 1943, 20-year-old pianist Sophie (Romane Bohringer) leaves constant hunger and deprivation behind when she is hired as accompanist to beautiful and gifted classical singer Irene Brice (Safonova, Anna in "Dark Eyes"), a Russian émigré married to successful French businessman Charles Brice (Richard Bohringer). A gruff wheeler-dealer who has continued to profit from the Germans, Charles adores his wife and keeps her in high style. But Irene's heart secretly belongs to a dashing Resistance fighter. Story is told from Sophie's p.o.v., complete with sometimes jarring voiceovers.

Tortured by her desire to serve a talent greater than her own, Sophie is a self-effacing martyr who develops a love-hate relationship with Irene and, in always deferring, misses her own chance for happiness.

Romane Bohringer, whose recent breakthrough performance in "Les Nuits Fauves" has been widely acclaimed, brings the right blend of stunted ambition and longing to her role, but remains an unlikable character whose increasingly bitter outlook is an obstacle to audience sympathy.

Richard Bohringer projects manly devotion and love-prompted sacrifice, but seems an unlikely spouse for so elegant a woman as Safonova.

Miller, whose knack for exploring the world of young girls was amply demonstrated in "L'effrontee" and "La Petite Voleuse," captures the ambiguous symbiosis between the two women only to water it down with travel, politics and other distractions.

Helmer is fond of closeups, while lenser Yves Angelo gets the most out of stately, lingering shots in concert halls. Period production design is fine and tech credits are all smooth, with a special nod to the score.
— *Lisa Nesselson*

DAS SOMMERALBUM
(THE SUMMER ALBUM)
(GERMAN-UKRAINIAN)

A Basis-Film release of an Ottokar Runze production. Co-produced by DOM Film Prod./Odessa/NDR. Directed by Kai Wessel. Screenplay, Beate Langmark. Camera, (color) Achim Poulheim; editor, Sabine Jagiella; production design, Langmark; costumes, Susanne Witt, Daiwa Petrulité; sound, Sergei Dubkow. Reviewed at Filmbühne am Steinplatz Cinema, Berlin, Dec. 9, 1992. Running time: **91 MIN.**

Mother . . . . Eva Mattes
Josefine . . . . Hanna Mattes
Zacharias . . . . Wanja Mues
Bartholomus . . . . . . Jan Hinrichsen
Father . . . . Micha Lampert
Otto . . . . Gustav Peter Whler
Dascha . . . . Janna Arsenyeva
Vesper . . . . Valery Kuksin
Frau von Wahl . . . . Brigitte Janner
Herr von Wahl . Aurostunas Venskunas
Marie-Alice . . . . . Charlotte Oszkinat
Doctor . . . . Benjamin Kleiner
Miss Krusenstern . . . Galina Pavlova

Well-intentioned, good-looking pic about a young girl's discovery of photography is much too slow for children and too kid-oriented for grownups, making both theatrical and TV prospects dim.

On vacation in the summer of 1905 in Latvia, 11-year-old Josefine is bored silly. Her brothers ignore her and there's no one to play with. The gift of a camera from her father awakens a passion in her that saves the summer. Hanna Mattes, daughter of vet German thesp Eva who also plays her screen mom, proves she can carry a film in the role of Josefine.

Her perf and splendid costume design are not quite enough to compensate for an unbalanced script. Josefine spends the first two thirds of the film being lonely, until she gets the camera. The character of her mother is erratic: loving and sympathetic when it serves the momentary needs of the plot; cold, aloof and unfeeling when Josefine's solitude must be emphasized.

At times, the dialogue seems inappropriate to certain characters, who speak above or below class or national expectations, especially minor Russian characters. — *Rebecca Lieb*

A DEMAIN
(SEE YOU TOMORROW)
(FRENCH)

An AMLF release of a Ciby 2000/M-6 Films co-production with the participation of Investimage 3/Sofiarp/Valor 2/Canal Plus/CNC. Produced by Florence Quentin, Romain Brémond, Jean-Claude Fleury. Directed by Didier Martiny. Screenplay, Martiny, Yasmina Reza. Camera (color), Emmanuel Machuel; editor, Sylvie Quester; music, Anne-Marie Fijal; costume design, Christian Gasc; set design, Michel Vandestien; sound, Philippe Lioret, François Groult. Reviewed at George V cinema, Paris, Dec. 3, 1992. Running time: **95 MIN.**

Tété . . . . Jeanne Moreau
Gilles . . . . François Cluzet
Bouddha . . . . François Perrot
Hélène . . . . Yasmina Reza
Amé . . . . Margot Capelier
Pierre . . . . Laurent Lavergne

"A Demain" is a harmless, uneven childhood memoir whose cumulative effect is endearing. Aided by pleasant perfs and convincing period detail, it's the sort of story that's been told before but can always be told again. Presence of Jeanne Moreau may help with offshore sales.

In voiceover, grown Pierre presides over extended flashbacks of his reasonably happy childhood in Paris in the early 1960s. Ace production designer Michel Vandestien has built a wonderful set of the family apartment-cum-doctor's office, through which a Steadicam snakes in a lengthy and carefully choreographed early shot.

Young Pierre (Laurent Lavergne, in a likable performance) lives there with his younger sister, mother, father, a grandfather who is married to Jeanne Moreau, and Moreau's 94-year-old mother, pluckily played by veteran casting director Margot Capelier. Dad (François Cluzet) and granddad (François Perrot) are general practitioners; Moreau's an acupuncturist.

Visual and narrative bravado of opening sequence is soon undercut by a static and strained scene of a family lunch. Pic continues to lurch between lyrical and stalled sequences.

Nice bits include the household fuss over an acupuncture appointment for late thesp Anthony Perkins, the purchase of a mink coat in Switzerland followed by tense anticipation of a customs check, and radical efforts to disinfect comic books after a sick classmate borrows them.

Pierre adores Moreau, who introduces him to the concept of mortality, first via carefully chosen words (spoken while seated on a park bench that is sometimes arbitrarily plunked into outrageous dream landscapes), and then by dying when Pierre is 9 years old. Moreau's deftly handled death takes place 48 minutes into the pic, which adds a melancholy twist to subsequent flashbacks in which she continues to appear. Moreau is delightful in her low-key way, but her scraggly wig-like hairdo detracts.

The title refers to Pierre's nightly ritual of repeating "See you tomorrow," which his parents (of whom, co-scripter Yasmina Reza gives a buoyant perf as Pierre's mom) must echo in reply. Evocative kiddie schtick paves the way for a poignant final shot.
— *Lisa Nesselson*

BELLE EPOQUE
(SPANISH)

A Fernando Trueba P.C. S.A. (Madrid)/Lola Films (Barcelona) Anematografo (Lisbon)/French Prod. (Paris) co-production with the cooperation of Sogepaq, Euroimages. Executive producer, Andrés Vicente Gómez. Directed by Fernando Trueba. Screenplay, Trueba, Rafael Azcona, José Luis Sánchez; camera (color), José Luis Alcaine; editor, Carmen Frías; sets, Juan Botella; sound, Georges Prat; music, Antoine Duhamel; costumes, Lala Huete. Reviewed at Cine Gran Via, Madrid, Nov. 26, 1992. Running time: **108 MIN.**

Luz . . . . Penelope Cruz
Clara . . . . Miriam Díaz-Aroca
Jacinto . . . . Gabino Diego
Manolo . . . . Fernando Fernán Gómez
Violeta . . . . Ariadna Gil
Fernando . . . . Jorge Sanz
Rocío . . . . Maribel Verdú
Also with: Michel Galabru, Chus Lampreave, Mary Carmen Ramirez, Juan José Otegui, Jesús Bonilla, María Galiana.

Reversing the trend of rural Spanish stories set in 1930s that emphasize grim oppressiveness, scripters Azcona, Luis Sánchez and Trueba do an about-face in this tongue-in-cheek yarn about an army deserter's friendship with a village paterfamilias.

The dialogue is perky and thesping vivacious, but the plot is wafer-thin and opening and closing sequences seem gratuitous. Though pic is filled with references to the local politics of the time — Carlists, Monarchists, Republicans — the amorous antics of the deserter (presented with no nudity) and the clever sarcasm of the script, could win over some viewers outside Spain.

This being a comedy, it matters little that none of the characters is believable; the usual stereotypes are given a ironic twist. The local priest talks like a freethinker; the Civil Guards are buffoons; the villager dad is so liberal he doesn't seem to object to a young, handsome stranger bedding down with his four daughters. It is a story that would be dubious even in 1992 Spain and totally contrary to what Spain was in 1931.

The bouffe thesping is handled well and some of the lines and droll situations provide an occasional laugh. — *Peter Besas*

BEAU FIXE
(SET FARE)
(FRENCH)

A Pan-Europeenne release of a Les Productions Lazennec/Les Films Alain Sarde/France 3 Cinema/Pan-Europeenne/CMV Prods. co-production with the participation of Canal Plus/Investimage. Produced by Alain Rocca. Directed by Christian Vincent. Screenplay, Vincent, Philippe Alard. Camera (color), Denis Lenoir; editor, François Ceppi; art direction, Sylvie Olive; sound, Claude Bertrand; associate producers, Adeline Lecallier, Christophe Rossignon; assistant director, Marianne Fricheau. Reviewed at Gaumont Hautefeuille Cinema, Paris, Nov. 30, 1992. Running time: **92 MIN.**
Valerie . . . . Isabelle Carre
Carine . . . . Judith Remy
Frederique . . . . . . Elsa Zylberstein
Armelle . . . . Estelle Larrivaz
Francis . . . . Frederic Gelard

"**B**eau Fixe," in which a bland, minimalist premise is diligently pursued to a bland conclusion, points up how difficult it is to pull off a Rohmerish film if one is not Eric Rohmer. A good showcase for its cast but a dull spell for audiences, this one is unlikely to raise much interest beyond French-lingo territories.

Helmer Christian Vincent's first film was the surprise 1990 critical and popular success "La Discrète." For the script to his sophomore outing, Vincent has teamed up with Philippe Alard, whose Super 8m feature "Villa Beausoleil" traced virtually the same lame theme and featured the same gangly male lead as this item. Together, they've cornered the market on a wispy premise heretofore underexploited, and for good reason.

Four female pre-med students decide to spend two weeks in a seaside villa, studying for their final exams. All goes relatively well until a gawky, somewhat dim male cousin (Frederic Gelard) shows up to paint the shutters. As the days go by and the guy putters around, the girls grow less studious and less compatible. The end.

Only saving grace is the thesping by talented, carefully cast newcomers. The helmer says in the production notes, "Life is mostly made up of encounters that lead nowhere." True enough — but that's hardly a recipe for an engaging film.

— *Lisa Nesselson*

BAJARSE AL MORO
(GOING SOUTH SHOPPING)
(SPANISH)

An Ion Films/Lola Films production, in association with RTVE. Executive producers, Carles Durán, José Luis García Sánchez. Directed by Fernando Colomo. Screenplay, José Luis Alonso de Santos, Joaquín Oristell, Colomo, based on de Santos' play. Camera (color), Javier Salmones; editor, Miguel Angel Santamaría; sound, Migel Polo; art direction, Alberto Gutiérrez. Reviewed at Joseph Papp Theater, N.Y., Nov. 27, 1992. Running time: **86 MIN.**
Chusa . . . . Verónica Forqué
Alberto . . . . Antonio Banderas
Jaimito . . . . Juan Echanove
Elena . . . . Aitana Sánchez-Gijón
Also with: Chus Lampreave, Miguel Rellán, Francisco Merino.

An outrageous comedy with something of the sensibility of Pedro Almodóvar, fellow Spanish helmer Fernando Colomo's "Bajarse al Moro" follows the misadventures of an indie drug dealer in her quest for a good time. Although pic loses some steam in the last 20 minutes, there is enough offbeat fun here to tap into the international arthouse market.

Title refers to Madrileños who go to Morocco to score illegal hashish. Forever trendy Chusa (Verónica Forqué) is an old hand who smuggles the drug into the country through various body orifices. When she enlists the aid of her friend Elena, she is confronted by a problem: Elena is a virgin and thus won't be able to carry much hash.

Wanting to make a really big score, Chusa convinces her policeman b.f. Alberto (Antonio Banderas) to "help" Elena. Although at first he refuses, Alberto eventually does the job so well Chusa loses both friend and boyfriend.

In counterpoint to pic's unconventional humor, pic inserts several conventional messages: A heroin addict overdoses and, while in Morocco, Chusa finds her hashish-crazed former b.f. Nazario cannot even remember who she is. In context, they come off gratuitous at best.

The rock trio Pata Negra, featured as Chusa's rooftop neighbors, provide an upbeat musical score. — *Paul Lenti*

WALLS & BRIDGES

A Cold Grey Entertainment Corp. production. Executive producer, Albert R. Murray Jr. Produced, directed, written by Uzo. Camera (color), John R. Rosnel; editor, Jack Haigis; music, Teo Macero; sound, Bernie Hajdenberg; associate producers, Karen Jaehne, Link Blake. Reviewed at VI Americas Film Festival, AFI, Washington, D.C., Oct. 14, 1992. Running time: **87 MIN.**
Trent Ubard . . . . . Mark D. Kennerly
Camille Kelly . . . Ellen Tina Landress
Carol . . . . Vanessa Shaw
Uncle John . . . . Al Jones
Also with: Jack Howell, Muriel Wickes, Christopher Cooke, Jane Reibel.

Delving into the theme of interracial relationships, indie "Walls & Bridges" comes off as a TV version of "Jungle Fever." Lacking Spike Lee's larger vision and sense of hyperbole, inspirational pic is a quiet, rather limp statement with little pace or drive.

The debut effort of Nigerian-born helmer Uzo, the film chronicles the life of young black commercial artist Trent (Mark Kennerly), who one day meets an offbeat white nun (Ellen Tina Landress), who teaches art at a religious children's center. Both are undergoing changes: Kennerly is dissatisfied with his relationship with his boss and g.f. Vanessa Shaw, who doesn't understand his artistic concerns, while Landress has been questioning her vocation.

When the inevitable happens — they fall in love and marry — problems come from family and friends, who refuse to accept their relationship. Eventually, Kennerly, preparing for an exhibit of his paintings, is blinded by a stray bullet. Metaphor is a bit hackneyed.

Acting is okay, especially Vanessa Shaw, but overall tone is flat. Uzo is also responsible for the impressive Miró-inspired paintings seen in the film.

— *Paul Lenti*

SIEMPRE DE DIFICIL
VOLVER A CASA
(IT'S ALWAYS HARD
TO RETURN HOME)
(ARGENTINE)

An Argentina Sono Film production. Executive producers, Salvador D'Antonio, GArlos Mentasti, Luis Mentasti, Víctor Bo. Produced by Bo. Directed by Jorge Polaco. Screenplay, Graciela Speranza, Polaco, from Antonio Dal Massetto's novel. Camera (color), Esteban Courtaló; editors, Eduardo López, Miguel López; music, Lito Vitale; art direction, María Julia Bertoto. Reviewed at VI Americas Film Festival, AFI, Washington, D.C., Oct. 9, 1992. Running time: **83 MIN.**
With: Miguel Torres del Sel, Dady Brieva, Daniel Miglioranza, Rubén Stella, Cristina Benegas, Carolina Papaleo, Ignacio Quiros, Juan Manuel Tenuta, Sabina Olmos, Héctor Malamud.

Fourth feature by helmer Jorge Polaco, "It's Always Hard to Return Home" is a caper film run awry. Frenetic handling and basic slapstick humor make premise a bit too broad for wide play, but pic might find limited appeal.

Rambling storyline concerns a quartet of friends who attempt a bank robbery in a small town. When their getaway car gets stuck behind a funeral procession, they abandon it and flee on foot, the police in hot pursuit. The rest of the film involves their disparate and oftentimes illogical attempts to escape.

With escaped criminals on the loose, the townsfolk use their presence for their own purposes: An unfaithful husband kills his wife and blames them; a firearms aficionado finds an opportunity to use his specialty rifles; local kids play cops and robbers.

The slapstick approach to humor and forced situations wear thin as gags are given preference over the logic of situations. The individual characters are also too sketchy to arouse audience sympathy to their plight.

Although drawing from preexisting source material, pic bears Polaco's characteristic camerawork — frequent tracking shots and offbeat angles that often pit quirky characters against the stylized sets; his brusque editing techniques also counterpoint and disorient individual scenes.

— *Paul Lenti*

INTL. HOF DAYS

TERROR 2000 —
INTENSIVSTATION
DEUTSCHLAND
(TERROR 2000 — INTENSIVE
STATION GERMANY)
(GERMAN)

A Dem Film production in association with Norddeutscher Rundfunk/Westdeutscher Rundfunk. Executive producer, Renee Gundelach. Produced by Christian Fürst. Directed by Christoph

Schlingensief. Screenplay, Oskar Roehler, Schlingensief, Uli Hanisch. Camera, Reinhard Köcher; editor, Bettina Boehler; sound, Eki Kuchenbecker; music, Jaques Arr; production design, Uli Hanisch; line producer, Fürst; costumes, Tabea Braun, Julia Koep; makeup, Heide Hass. Reviewed at Intl. Hof Film Days, Oct. 30, 1992. Running time: **79 MIN.**
With: Margit Carstensen, Peter Kern, Susanne Bredehöft, Alfred Edel.

A political spoof in slasher style, "Terror 2000" takes a whack at everything from famous German crimes to neo-Nazis, and its star is a whirlwind of tongue-in-cheek screams, blood and perversity. The low-budget satire shocker will please Christoph Schlingensief fans and do at least as well as his last film, "German Chainsaw Massacre," but it is not meant to break out of cult circles, and won't.

Schlingensief's style is not for the weak-stomached and tedious for those who like a little more meat. His method is simple: Take every quotable event in recent years and make it even more tasteless. This film starts with a weakling leftist social worker taking a Polish family to political asylum in Germany. When they are attacked and killed by crazed rightists, a secret sevice agent (played by art film director Peter Kern) and his sexually frustrated partner (Margit Carstensen) are sent to investigate, à la "Mississipi Burning."

From there, the plot is largely ignored. The bad guys go around raping and pillaging, and soon the good guys join them. Schlingensief's world view: Those who don't rape like to be raped. Those who don't scream like to be screamed at. The crazed rightists are spoofed as much as the wimpy leftists. No one is mentally healthy. Schlingensief keeps the pace as fast, the adrenalin as high and the tastelessness as extreme as possible.

On one hand, this method of parody is as adolescent politically as it is aesthetically. Taking everything to the same extreme makes it all seem the same. Reducing socio-political events like German reunification or the outburst of racism to "tastelessness" is making things simpler than they are.

But the film's audience is adolescent as well, and what they want is less an analysis of the situation than to intellectually (or anti-intellectually) bang their heads against posts. Schlingensief, 32, is rightly thought of as one of Germany's top cult film-

ers, though his movies are only coherent to Germans and only enjoyed by a young, left-intellectual crowd. Soon, his fans will grow up. If he wants to keep them, he will have to start diversifying. — *Eric Hansen*

PROBEFAHRT INS PARADIES
(TEST RUN TO PARADISE)
(GERMAN-SWISS)

A Calypsofilm production in association with Bernard Lang, with the support of Filmstiftung NRW/WDR/Filmbüro NW of the Ministry of Science and Art of Baden-Württemburg. Produced by Werner Possardt, Hans-Christian Hess. Directed by Douglas Wolfsperger. Screenplay, Wolfsperger, Franz Bielefeld with Tobias Engelsing, Luisa de Martin. Camera, Jörg Schmidt-Reitwein; editor, Corinna Dietz; music, Jürgen Nieper; production design, Gerald Damovsky; costumes, Bea Gossmann; sound, Michael Loeken; makeup, Sylvia Tommasi, Marianne Halter; assistant director, Evi Esser. Reviewed at Intl. Hof Film Days, Nov. 1, 1992. Running time: **83 MIN.**
Theresa . . . . Barbara Auer
Sister Ursula . . . Christiane Hörbiger
Freddie . . . . . . Mathias Gnädinger
Father Strobel . . . . . . Axel Milberg

Right on target thematically, this modest road movie about a group of Catholics pilgriming to Lourdes is meant to ridicule all that is holy for orthodox Catholics, from common decency to celibacy. Unfortunately, a limp script and uninspired cast and crew insure that it doesn't live up to its promise.

Conceived as a modern Catholic Ship of Fools, "Probefahrt ins Paradies" follows a group of pilgrims in a dangerous-looking black tourist bus on their way from Lake Constance to the shrine of Mary at Lourdes. The characters divide into two sides. On the one hand, there's Sister Ursula (played well by one of Germany's best character actresses, Christiane Hörbiger) as the hard-nosed super-orthodox keeper of the flame. On the other, there's liberal Father Strobel (a drab Axel Milberg), uncomfortable with all this Mary worship and superstition.

There is plenty of room for conflict, but writers Douglas Wolfsperger and Franz Bielefeld can't find it. When they throw in the priest's pregnant girlfriend, Theresa (a stone-faced Barbara Auer), the whole ensuing story becomes lopsided in favor of a single issue: celibacy.

Though there is an attempt at

satire, in the end director Wolfsperger is only capable of lamely repeating the w.k. precepts of liberal Catholics: celibacy/orthodoxy bad, love/liberalism good.

"Probefahrt ins Paradies" is another one of those projects that must have sounded so wonderful as an idea that no one bothered to put any extra thought into the execution. Though the black bus looks devilishly threatening, no other technical credits are worth mentioning. — *Eric Hansen*

LONDON FEST

TAHADER KATHA
(THEIR STORY)
(INDIAN)

A National Film Development Corp. production. (Intl. sales: NFDC, Bombay.) Executive producer, Ravi Malik, D. Majumdar. Directed, written by Buddhadeb Dasgupta, from Kamalkumar Maumdar's short story. Camera (Eastmancolor), Venu; editor, Ujjal Nandi; music, Biswadeb Dasgupta; sound, Durga Mitra; art direction, Nikhill Sengupta; costume design, Kuntala Dasgupta. Reviewed at London Film Festival, Nov. 12, 1992. Running time: **97 MIN.**
With: Mithun Chakraborty, Anasua Majumdar, Deborshi Bhattacharyay, Bidisha Chakraborty.
(Bengali dialogue)

"Their Story" is a sincere but ultimately uninvolving attempt at interior cinema. Thoughtfully made but dramatically underdeveloped study of a former political prisoner in newly independent India is strictly a hardcore buff item.

Three years after the country's partition, Shibnath (Mithun Chakraborty) returns to his village following 11 years in lockup, including three in a loony bin. He once made passionate anti-British speeches; now he's a broken man.

His wife and two children are initially supportive, but soon the former gets fed up with his perpetual mooning around. Friends who try to persuade him to take a job as a teacher and "shake off this madness" also get nowhere. In the end he's carted off in chains whence he came.

The script has something to say about the lack of revolutionary zeal in post-independence India but it says it early on and thereafter simply constructs elaborate philosophical circles. Pic's rondo-like structure, with Shibnath revisiting the same locations and people, will either delight or

infuriate viewers.

Hindi megastar Chakraborty, in a startlingly different role (and Bengali-language movie), is a neutral center, difficult to empathize with. Main character interest comes from the lively two children and small number of concerned friends.

Visually, pic is a treat, cutting is precise, and Biswadeb Dasgupta's lazy, woodwind-flavored score is an atmospheric plus. Helmer Buddhadeb Dasgupta's previous alienation-themed movie, "The Tiger Dancer," did the fest rounds two years ago to some acclaim. —*Derek Elley*

DHARAVI
(CITY OF DREAMS)
(INDIAN)

A National Film Development Corp./Doordarshan production. (Intl. sales: NFDC, Bombay.) Executive producers, Ravi Mallick, N.P. Mukane. Directed, written by Sudhir Mishra. Camera (Eastmancolor), Rajesh Joshi; editor, Renu Saluja; music, Rajat Dholakia; art direction, Subash Sinha Roy; costume design, Vandana Khanna; sound design, Dholakia; sound, Hitendra Ghosh; assistant director, Rajesh Singh. Reviewed at Mr. Young's preview theater, London, Nov. 16, 1992. (In London Film Festival.) Running time: **100 MIN.**
Rajkaran . . . . Om Puri
Kumud . . . . Shabana Azmi
Chandu . . . . Raghubir Yadav
Pareshan . . . . Chandu Parkhi
Chaskar . . . . Veerendra Saxena
Chaurasia . . . . Deepak Qazir
Mother . . . . Pramod Bala
Dada Sarkar . . . . . Satish Khopker
Shanker . . . . Mushtaq Khan
Fantasy film star . . . . Madhuri Dixit
(Hindi soundtrack)

Good intentions aren't enough to make "City of Dreams" rise above its melodrama foundations. Slice-of-life drama about an ambitious cab driver in a Bombay shantytown stirs in too many commercial elements to attract paying passengers on the foreign arthouse circuit.

Rajkaran (Om Puri) is a penurious cabbie who dreams of his own business but is permanently in hock to moneylenders. Borrowing more from the local slumlord, he sets up an illegal dye shop with some partners; when it's pulled down, he gets sucked into a vicious spiral of gang wars.

In his third feature, director Sudhir Mishra, shooting mainly on location, brings a real feel for place to an essentially by-the-numbers rise-and-fall story. But what starts as a pacey variation on Indian social realist dramas takes a sideturn halfway into crime yarn with echoes of commercial Hindi moviemaking.

The pic's often oblique narrative style, only explaining itself after the event, is also problematic, and not helped by so-so subtitling. Dream sequences, featuring pretty Bombay musical star Madhuri Dixit, are colorful but unlikely to resonate fully with non-Indian auds.

Puri, a commanding presence in Indian pics, here shows a lack of shading necessary for the central role. As the woman who's deserted her husband to share Puri's dream, Shabana Azmi (last seen alongside Puri in Roland Joffé's "City of Joy") is as reliable as ever but hindered by a shallow script.

Tech credits are average, with typically forward post-synching. Version at London fest was some 15 minutes shorter than the original, with some scenes reportedly reordered. The Hindi title, the name of the actual Bombay slum, literally means "Quicksand."

— *Derek Elley*

L'ILE FLOTTANTE
(L'ISOLA ALLA DERIVA)
(FLOATING ISLAND)
(ITALIAN)

A Spectre Film production. (Intl. sales: Spectre, Rome.) Executive producers, Lanfranco Secco Suardo, Alessandro Azzano. Directed by Tommaso Mottola. Screenplay, Luca D'Alisera, Mottola, Vassilis Vassilikos, from a Mottola's story. Camera (Eastmancolor), José Luis Garcia, Giorgio Bottos; editor, Alessandra Perpignani; music, Rosanna Santa Maria; art direction, Patrizia Pernia, Giuseppe Maria Gaudino; costume design, Marisa Urruti; assistant directors, Stella Leonetti, Horacio Guisado. Reviewed at London Film Festival, Nov. 22, 1992. Running time: **109 MIN.**
Mademoiselle . . . . . . Delia Boccardo
Ferdinando . Bernardo Olivieri Passeri
The Commander . . . . William James
Arianna/Aurora
. . . . Marina Moreso Cascales
Rolando . . . . Victor Proncet
The Captain . . . . . . Enrique Kossi
Marta . . . . Susana Mayo
Donna Anna . . . . Sara Krell

"**F**loating Island" sinks with all hands early on, leaving a trail of confused ideas and images. Pretentious Italo fantasy about two kids lured to an island of the afterlife looks set to disappear swiftly.

Sole cast name Delia Boccardo plays the mysterious "Mademoiselle" who pals up with two moppets in a derelict house. One night she shows them a meringue-and-baked-custard dish called a "floating island" and their hyperactive imaginations transform

this into the real thing, populated by a bunch of ranting crazies. After some kind of apocalypse strikes the island (powered by a huge engine, like a ship), Boccardo and the boy try to swim for it.

Pic recalls other continental European kid fantasies with its collection of eccentrics and cute imagery. But despite good tech credits (including sharp lensing of the Patagonian locations, and a dreamy score), the movie quickly takes on the shape of an allegory headed nowhere. Boccardo goes through the motions, and the rest of the cast make up in energy what the script lacks in comprehension. Pic's principal title is in French with an Italo translation underneath.

— *Derek Elley*

AVETIK
(ARMENIAN-GERMAN)

A Margarita Woskanian/NDR (Germany)/FIAF (Armenia) co-productio with assistance from Filmbüro NW. Produced by Woskanian. Directed, written, edited by Don Askarian. Camera (color), Gagik Avakian, Martin Gressmann, Andreas Sinanos; music, Woskanian; art direction, Askarian; costumes, Woskanian; sound, Rudolph Schwarz, Oliver Grafe. Reviewed at Turin Intl. Festival of Young Cinema (competition), Nov. 14, 1992. Running time: **84 MIN.**
Avetik . . . . Alik Assatrian
Young Avetik . . . Mikhael Stephanian
Refugee . . . . . . Karen Ganibekian
Poet-Kuchak . . . . Eduard Saribekian
Armenian king . . . Samvel Ovasapian
Journalist . . . . Geno Lechner

In "Avetik," Berlin-based Armenian auteur Don Askarian takes a tough stand against traditional narrative conventions, using dreamlike recollections and poetic visions to conjure a disquieting portrait of his afflicted homeland and its disappearing culture. Arresting visuals and a formidable overlying mood make this a commanding festival entry, but only half compensate for a barrage of paralyzing symbolism that makes pic all but impenetrable without preparatory decoding or multiple viewings.

Around the central figure of an Armenian forging an alienated existence in the West, Askarian lays a mosaic of impressions of his country's history and people, from bygone kings to 1989 earthquake victims. Ruminations of love, death, childhood, sexual awakening and the corruption of

film as an art form surface along with some bitter observations on being a foreigner in Germany.

Dialogue is oblique and sparse, and use of the brief stretches of classical and Armenian folk music is only slightly less so. Askarian instead constructs a film poem out of loosely connected lyrical passages, often recalling both the visionary trailblazing and the obscurantism of neighbors like Andrei Tarkovsky and Sergei Paradjanov.

Superior artistry and technical craftsmanship are consistently on view, but moments of lucidity and clues to aid viewer access are so rare that pic remains admirable almost wholly for the icy beauty of its surreal imagery, and not for its heavily veiled heart. Still, Askarian's uncompromising views on audience-pandering commercial cinema surface repeatedly. His artistic integrity in sticking to his guns command respect, and stand to stoke the international rep he carved out with his first feature, "Komitas." — *David Rooney*

JIGI — L'ESPOIR
(JIGI — THE HOPE)
(BURKINA FASO-16m)

A Sanou Kollo/Direction de la Production Cinématographique/Centre National d'Equipment Agricole du Burkina Faso presentation. Produced, directed, written by Kollo. Camera (color, 16m), Sékou Ouedraogo; editor, Alphonse Sanou; music, Jacob Soubeiga; sound, Issa Traore, Joahny Traore. Reviewed at Turin Intl. Festival of Young Cinema, Nov. 16, 1992. Running time: **60 MIN.**
With: Honoré Compaore, Simone Tapsoba, Joséphine Ouedraogo, Mady Pafadnam, Serge Zongo, Daniel Kabore.

Captivatingly simple rural hardship tale, "Jigi — The Hope" is another beautifully made parable of basic human values from economically bereft but filmically rich Burkina Faso. Sanou Kollo's gentle, controlled film is ideal for cultural education forums, public TV and further festival spots.

Story chronicles a run of misfortune afflicting poor cotton farmer Nikiema, struggling to hold his family together and placate debt collectors after a mule he borrowed from a shady villager is stolen — later revealed to be the owner's crooked stunt. One dissatisfied son wants to flee the remote village and find a city job; another is progressively weaker from untreated measles.

Final straw comes when Nikiema's cart is swiped outside the hospital as he learns of the son's death. Sticking a rifle barrel in his mouth, Nikiema prepares to shoot just as a third son turns up with money earned in the city, and another cycle of hope begins.

Kollo steadily amplifies the well-written story's solemn tone as fate's cruel blows multiply, and understated use of modern and traditional music further enhances the delicate, melancholy momentum. Pic is technically accomplished in all quarters, with Sékou Ouedraogo's crisp lensing giving rich visual rewards.

— *David Rooney*

MUSS DENKEN
(GOTTA THINK)
(AUSTRIAN-DOCU)

A Wega Film production. Executive producer, Veit Heiduschka. Produced by Christa Polster. Directed by Niki List. Screenplay, Christa Polster, List. Camera, Peter Roehsler; editor, List, sound, Mohsan Nasiri; music, Martin Lichtenwallner. Reviewed at Vienna Film Festival, Oct. 17, 1992. Running time: **90 MIN.**
With: Christian Polster, Christa and Robert Polster.

"**M**uss Denken" is a loving, dedicated portrait of a victim of Down's syndrome. It portrays a happy life, but lacks a critical or analytical eye. The result is mentally handicapped but charming Christian Polster coming and going, telling stories and dancing. Though it reveals the dignity and joy of a life many may not have suspected worth living, that alone does not justify 90 minutes.

Eight years ago, Austria's foremost director, Niki List, made his first documentary about Christian Polster, called "Mama Lustig . . . ?" Now, he has made a second part showing Christian at 24. His declared purpose is to show a largely ignorant world how handicapped people live.

But he succeeds in this only nominally. All he shows are scenes of Christian in pleasant situations — in his apartment, with friends, in a good mood; nor does he hint at the political or social climate in Vienna regarding the handicapped.

It even leaves a negative aftertaste: Christian's life seems so wonderful and conflict-free, List seems to be advertising for it, as if the life of handicapped persons were some kind of secret utopia. Polster deserves to be taken more seriously. — *Eric Hansen*

ARCHIVE REVIEW

TIGRES DE PAPEL
(PAPER TIGERS)
(SPANISH)

A La Salamandra production. Executive producer, Alicia Mora. Produced by Miguel Angel Bermejo. Directed, written by Fernando Colomo. Camera (color), Angel Luis Fernández; editor, Miguel Angel Santamaría; music, Tomasso Albinoni; sound, Miguel Angel Polo. Reviewed at the Joseph Papp Public Theater, N.Y., Nov. 2, 1992. Running time: **89 MIN.**
Alberto . . . . Miguel Arribas
Carmen . . . . Carmen Maura
Juan . . . . Joaquín Hinojosa
Also with: Pedro del Corral, Cocha Gregori, Félex Rotaeta, Juan Lombardero, Aurora Pastor, Jaime Lizaur, Guillermo Vallejo, Enma Cohen.

Spanish director Fernando Colomo's 1977 debut pic, "Paper Tigers," is a time-piece chronicling a country trying to find its feet after the death of Franco. Low-key comedy is interesting as a historical curiosity, showing a Spain about to awaken after a long sleep.

Featuring the first film appearance of Carmen Maura, pic revolves around a friendly love triangle, whose fragile interpersonal relationships mirror the larger political picture.

Alberto, Carmen and Juan drink and use drugs, attend political rallies, discuss philosophical options, and live in a milieu of dysfunctional friends, all attempting to define who they are and what they want but not knowing how to adapt to a changing world where the line between friendship and love blurs.

The dialogue is natural and ensemble acting style — with a large cast of bit actors — gives the film a slice-of-life texture. Title comes from Mao's condemnation of society's reactionary forces, which pose as illusory threats to real change. — *Paul Lenti*

ADDENDUM

DICE RULES

A Seven Arts release of a Fleebin Dabble production. Produced by Fred Silverstein. Co-producer, Tim Clawson. Executive producers, J.R. Guterman, Jana Sue Memel. Directed by Jay Dubin. Concert material written by Andrew Dice Clay; "A Day In The Life" screenplay by Lenny Shulman; story by Clay. Camera (Foto-Kem color), Michael Negrin; editor, Mitchell Sinoway; production design, Jane Musky; sound (Dolby), Ron Bartlett; line producer, Loucas George; associate producer, Robert J. Degus; assistant directors, George, Tony Adler; associate director, Christine Rae Clark; "A Day In The Life" crew: assistant directors, Michael Alan Kahn, Gregory K. Simmons; camera, Charlie Lieberman; editor, John K. Currin; production design, Robert L. Smith; art direction, Scott A. Ault; set decoration, Francesca Root; casting, Pagano/Bialy/Manwiller, Mary Margiotta. Reviewed at the UA Egyptian Theater, Hollywood, May 16, 1991. MPAA Rating: NC-17. Running time: 83 MIN.

With: Andrew Dice Clay, Eddie Griffin, Sylvia Harman, Lee Lawrence, Noodles Levenstein, Maria Parkinson, Michael (Wheels) Parise, Sumont, Hot Tub Johnny West, Fred Silverstein.

The controversy surrounding the film's release and the urge to vilify its namesake may conceal the fact that "Dice Rules" isn't terribly well done.

Pic should roll snake-eyes at the b.o. once fans chip in their opening-weekend coin. All the hoopla could have the effect of turning the pic into a curiosity, but pic's reign should be confined to home-vid.

Even devotees may not feel terribly compelled to catch the film, since it largely rehashes routines that many fans will have undoubtedly committed to memory — thanks to a long-in-release recording of the same Madison Square Garden concert.

Pic kicks off with a thud: The 20-minute "A Day In The Life" segment, narrated by Clay, recounts how a leather jacket transformed the comedian from Abner Milquetoast into "Dice."

If nothing else, the sequence demonstrates that Clay's controversial persona saved him from an otherwise undistinguished career as a poor man's Pee-wee Herman — his original standup act before evolving into the misogynistic Dice.

Needless to say, it's the concert footage that is at the center of the controversy surrounding the film.

Visually, the film suffers from rapid-fire editing and director Jay Dubin's insistence on following every joke with a shot of the howling audience. Some reaction shots even appear to be lifted from other portions of the film, and the soundtrack often carries muted eruptions of laughter at puzzling moments.

As a result, the onscreen audience appears to be having a better time than the most sympathetic viewer will — though Clay's nursery rhyme routine may qualify this as the first audience-participation concert film.

Nevertheless, "Dice Rules" is a pretty accurate snapshot of the comic's standup act — crude, sexist, racist, homophobic and designed to shock.

Clay would argue, with some justification, that Dice is simply a character delivering jokes. Some of material even betrays self-deprecating humor.

But critics would be fair in saying that such humor can often encourage just the sort of opinions and behavior it may be poking fun at. There's little subtlety, to be sure, in the racial epithets aimed at the Japanese. Dice's harsher barbs targeting gays are notably absent.

Some aspects of Clay's act can reach beyond his ostensible core audience of beer-drinking louts and schoolboys, as he propels male stereotypes into the realm of caricature.

Clay also exhibits a lesser-known talent as he impersonates several w.k. actors and then launches into a musical number.

Suffice it to say, Fox probably didn't make a major mistake in deciding not to release "Dice Rules." However, as with the stir surrounding his appearance on "Saturday Night Live," Clay has proven that those intent on denying him a stage generally succeed only in giving him a more prominent podium. — *Bril.*

PURE LUCK

A Universal Pictures presentation of a Sean Daniel Co. production. Produced by Lance Hool, Sean Daniel. Executive producer, Francis Veber. Directed by Nadia Tass. Screenplay, Herschel Weingrod, Timothy Harris; camera (Deluxe color), David Parker; editor, Billy Weber; music, Jonathan Scheffer; main title theme, Danny Elfman; sound (Dolby), Fernando Camara; production design, Peter Wooley; costume design, Grania Preston; art direction, Hector Romero Jr.; set design, Arturo Brito; assistant director, Matt Beesley; associate producer, Conrad Hool; stunt coordinator, Joe Dunne; 2nd unit directors, Lance Hool, Parker, Dunne; casting, Nancy Nayor. Reviewed at Avco Cinema Center, Westwood, Calif., Aug. 7, 1991. MPAA rating: PG. Running time: 96 MIN.

Proctor	Martin Short
Campanella	Danny Glover
Valerie	Sheila Kelley
Highsmith	Sam Wanamaker
Grimes	Scott Wilson
Monosoff	Harry Shearer

Also with: Jorge Russek, Rodrigo Puebla, John H. Brennan, Jorge Luke.

Purely lucky pairing of Martin Short and Danny Glover creates a sprinkling of good laughs in this light, likable comedy remake of the French film "La Chevre," but audiences are likely to find "Pure Luck" more tempting at video rental prices than in theaters.

Nonetheless, this banana-peel soufflé enjoys more *bon chance* in the hands of director Nadia Tass, whose flair for offbeat comedy ("Rikky & Pete") keeps the one-joke premise afloat, than did the earlier, less amusing "Three Fugitives" from Touchstone, also a French remake starring Short and exec produced by Francis Veber.

Here, Short plays a disastrously unlucky accountant who's hired by his wealthy boss (Sam Wanamaker) to lead an investigation to find the boss' extraordinarily klutzy daughter (Sheila Kelley), who's disappeared during a Mexican vacation.

Harry Shearer plays a psychiatrist who has sold the corporate chief on his theory that behavior patterns of calamity-prone individuals are remarkably similar. Boss buys into it and puts the hapless Short on the job.

He's paired with Glover, a logic-driven, hardbitten P.I. who's gravely unamused at the prospect of being subordinate to the jinxed accountant. Pair sets out for Acapulco and Puerto Vallarta on the trail already trodden unsuccessfully by Glover, but this time mishaps keep leading them into the same pitfalls the daughter stumbled into.

Premise generates a fair share of comedy as the disbelieving Campanella starts setting little traps for Short, just to test the behavioral theory. But most of the antics are just creative stalling to draw out the plot out for pic's 96-minute running time.

Hard-working Short keeps the energy up with mugging and temper tantrums, while the ultra-low-key Glover strikes a nice

LA CHEVRE
(THE GOAT)

Gaumont release of a Gaumont Intl./Fideline production. Produced by Alain Poire. Written and directed by Francis Veber. Camera (color), Alex Philips; editor, Albert Jurgenson; music, Vladimir Cosma; sound, Bernard Rochut; art direction, Jacques Bufnoir; production managers, Marc Goldstaub, Jacques Bourdon. Reviewed at Gaumont Ambassade theater, Paris, Feb. 2, 1982. Running time: 91 MIN.

Perrin	Pierre Richard
Campana	Gérard Depardieu
Marie	Corynne Charbit
Bens	Michel Robin
Meyer	Andre Valardy

contrast as he struggles to adapt to the weird dynamic by which things come together in Short's world.

Pic falls flat in places, such as in a jailhouse seg where the bad luck inexplicably shifts to Campanella's side, the string of calamities grows redundant despite many attempts to vary the theme, and there's not a glimmer of deeper meaning to trip up the stumbling protagonists.

Nonetheless, this first offering under former Universal production prez Sean Daniel's banner is amiable and well-mounted, and the ending as directed by Tass is certainly cute, if cute is one's cup of tea.

Shearer aids the momentum of film's setup with his focused and funny performance. Production design in the Mexican locales has the apropos whimsical, colorful tone. — *Amy Dawes*

FRANKIE AND JOHNNY

A Paramount release. Produced and directed by Garry Marshall. Executive producers, Alexandra Rose, Charles Mulvehill. Screenplay, Terrence McNally, based on his play "Frankie And Johnny In The Clair De Lune"; camera (Technicolor), Dante Spinotti; editor, Battle Davis, Jacqueline Cambas; music, Marvin Hamlisch; sound (Dolby), Keith A. Wester, John Carter III (2nd unit), James Sabat (N.Y.); co-producer-2nd unit director, Nick Abdo; assistant directors, Ellen H. Schwartz, Bettiann Fishman (N.Y.); 2nd unit camera, Steve Yaconelli; casting, Lynn Stalmaster. Reviewed at Paramount Studios, L.A., Oct. 3, 1991. MPAA rating: R. Running time: **118 MIN.**

Johnny . . . . Al Pacino
Frankie . . . . Michelle Pfeiffer
Nick . . . . Hector Elizondo
Tim . . . . Nathan Lane
Cora . . . . Kate Nelligan
Nedda . . . . Jane Morris
Tino . . . . Greg Lewis
Also with: Al Fann, Ele Keats, Fernando Lopez, Glenn Plummer, Tim Hopper, Harvey Miller, Sean O'Bryan.

"**F**rankie And Johnny" is an all-star, high-gloss, feel-good romantic feature sitcom. Amiably written and performed but fearsomely predictable, this middle-of-the-road adaptation of Terrence McNally's Off Broadway hit invites audiences to indulge in watching beautiful movie stars play lonely little people struggling to find love, a time-tested ploy that should result in a fall b.o. winner.

Ultra-Hollywood take on this slowly evolving but inevitable affair between two wounded souls is best reflected in the casting of Al Pacino and Michelle Pfeiffer in the roles originated onstage by Kathy Bates and F. Murray Abraham (after that Manhattan Theater Club workshop, Kenneth Welsh joined Bates at its main stage premiere). No one's going to mind looking at these two appealing performers hold centerscreen for two hours, but the switch does transform a realistic portrait of emotional isolation into fanciful playacting.

In his first outing since his monster hit "Pretty Woman," director Garry Marshall sprinkles a little of his Cinderella dust on this story of an ex-con who takes a job as a short order chef in Manhattan and instantly falls for a hard-case waitress. Although middle-aged and cut off from his ex-wife and kids, Johnny still is determined to get something out of life, and he has undertaken a self-improvement campaign of reading Shakespeare and learning a new word everyday.

Frankie, who may once have aspired to something more, feels safe within the confines of the cafe, which is patronized mostly by oldtimers, but she hasn't been on a date in years and passes the time spying on the residents of nearby apartments before making the big move to buy a VCR.

He is as persistent as she is resistant, and at one point during his efforts to woo Frankie, Johnny breaks down and takes a tumble with a brassy waitress (Kate Nelligan). But he is otherwise singleminded in his pursuit, coming on to Frankie over the counter, turning up on her bowling night and pestering her at home until these two with the legendary names become lovers.

As it's inconceivable the principal characters aren't going to wind up together despite considerable emotional handicaps, only points of interest are the reasons behind his flawed life and her dismal self-esteem. What crime sent him to prison at a relatively advanced age? Why is this lovely woman so withdrawn and down on men? The answers are hardly exciting or surprising, but are somehow enough to sustain mild interest.

Like a warm, slobbering dog who can't leave people alone, Pacino's Johnny comes on real strong, and his pronounced neediness is too much at times. But his appeal and desire to give are genuine, and the actor gives the film a real boost of energy.

No one's going to believe that Pfeiffer hasn't had a date since Ronald Reagan was president, and no matter how hard she tries to look plain, there is no disguising that she just gets more beautiful all the time. But she gives a performance filled with many

Original play
FRANKIE AND JOHNNY IN THE CLAIR DE LUNE

Manhattan Theater Club presentation of a comedy in two acts by Terrance McNally. Staged by Paul Benedict. Setting, James Noone; costumes, David Woolard; lighting, David Noling; sound, John Gromada; stage manager, Pamela Singer; casting, Lyons/Isaacson; artistic director, Lynne Meadow; managing director, Barry Grove; publicity, Helene Davis. Opened Oct. 7, '87 at the Manhattan Theater Club/City Center, N.Y. $26 top.
With: Kathy Bates, Kenneth Welsh.

moods and numerous affecting moments. Her pairing with Pacino serves as a reminder of the incredible distance the actress has come since they first appeared together in "Scarface" eight years ago.

Frequent McNally actor Nathan Lane has the best low comedy lines as Frankie's gay best friend, and the normally patrician Nelligan gets way down to play the libidinous waitress. Acting is pretty broad across the boards.

Although McNally has packed some acute emotional observations into his script at times, pic remains a romantic confection and optimistic life lesson, one that can charm but doesn't convince. Behind-the-scenes contributions are on the money.

— *Todd McCarthy*

RICOCHET

A Warner Bros. release of an HBO in association with Cinema Plus L.P. presentation of a Silver Pictures production. Produced by Joel Silver, Michael Levy. Executive producer, Barry Josephson. Directed by Russell Mulcahy. Screenplay, Steven de Souza, based on a story by Fred Dekker, Menno Meyjes; camera (color), Peter Levy; editor, Peter Honess; music, Alan Silvestri; sound (Dolby), Ed Novick; production design, Jaymes Hinkle; costume design, Marilyn Vance-Straker; art direction, Christiaan Wagener; set decoration, Richard Goddard, Sam Gross; assistant director, David Sardi; co-producers, James Herbert, Suzanne Todd; casting, Robin Lippin, Fern Cassel. Reviewed at Mann Westwood theater, Westwood, Calif., Oct. 3, 1991. MPAA rating: R. Running time: **97 MIN.**
Nick Styles . . . . Denzel Washington
Blake . . . . John Lithgow
Odessa . . . . Ice T
Larry . . . . Kevin Pollak
Brimleigh . . . . . . Lindsay Wagner
Alice . . . . Victoria Dillard
Farris . . . . John Cothran Jr.
Kim . . . . Josh Evans

A taut, twisty urban suspenser powered by the spring-loaded performance of Denzel Washington in his first major action role, "Ricochet" might have been a real b.o. contender were it not for a nasty streak and a tendency toward implausible excess. As is, pic should be a frontrunner for a few good weekends.

Washington plays an ambitious young cop who nails a vicious hitman (John Lithgow), putting him behind bars just as his own career begins an upward spiral. The pathological killer plots his revenge for seven years, watching the gifted cop become district attorney and acquire a loving family and a promising political future. When Lithgow finally breaks out of jail, he's armed with a diabolical plan to wreak havoc on everything his nemesis has attained.

Tension is sustained by skillful cutting between the two opposite lives and full-bore performances on both ends of the seesaw. Plot kicks into high gear once the killer gets loose to pursue his prey. It's yet another videotape-driven plot, as the ubiquitous medium is a pivotal tool in exposing the lawman at his best and worst, and yet another pic in which the press corps gets bashed.

Steven de Souza's screenplay offers unusually good dialog for the smooth-talking Washington and a number of scenes to savor, including one in which the cocksure d.a. reads the riot act to a den full of crack dealers, then makes an audacious exit.

But pic's charms, which also include winning supporting perfs by Kevin Pollak as Washington's law enforcement buddy and Ice T as the homeboy who runs the streets, are undercut by an abundance of mean-spirited violence. Too many people die with their guts splattered or impaled on a spike, and the clanging, banging, over-miked action veers into degrading ugliness often enough to be numbing. There's a cruel sensibility afoot, and it's a turnoff.

Pic threatens to become truly absorbing as Lithgow's brilliant revenge scheme unfolds, but "Ricochet" soon abandons cleverness in favor of spectacle. Washington rallies to his own defense with outsized tactics including a "Die Hard"-style building explosion and tower-top duel to the death, à la "Batman." Believability is left behind.

Washington does much to elevate the material in a charismatic, highly energetic performance, and Lithgow powerfully conveys a murderous mood that undercuts the d.a.'s occasional smugness.

Peter Levy's punchy, hyperactive camera style and the abrasive street soundtrack (including several Ice T numbers) effectively turn up the energy. Kudos to whoever staged the empty swimming poool scene, one of pic's great strokes of inspiration. — *Amy Dawes*

THE SUPER

A 20th Century Fox release of a Largo Entertainment presentation in association with JVC Entertainment of a Charles Gordon production. Produced by Gordon. Executive producer, Ron Frazier. Directed by Rod Daniel. Screenplay, Sam Simon; camera (Deluxe color), Bruce Surtees; editor, Jack Hofstra; music, Miles Goodman; sound (Dolby), Tom Brandau; production design, Kristi Zea; art direction, Jeremy Conway; set decoration, Leslie Pope; costume design, Aude Bronson-Howard; stunt coordinator, Jery Hewitt; associate producer, Steven Felder; assistant director, Henry Bronchtein; 2nd unit director, David Lux; casting, Avy Kaufman. Reviewed at GCC Beverly Connection Theaters, L.A., Sept. 30, 1991. MPAA Rating: R. Running time: **86 MIN.**

Louie Kritski	Joe Pesci
Big Lou Kritski	Vincent Gardenia
Naomi	Madolyn Smith Osborne
Marlon	Ruben Blades
Heather	Stacey Travis
Irene Kritski	Carole Shelley
Tito	Kenny Blank
Gilliam	Paul Benjamin
Leotha	Beatrice Winde

Visually, "The Super" succeeds all too well in creating a believable image of an urban hellhole. Comedically, "The Super" is a hellhole. Aside from Joe Pesci's Dickensian caricature of a N.Y. slumlord ordered to live among his miserable tenants, pic is almost unrelentingly depressing and unbelievably schmaltzy to boot. Boxoffice prospects are grim.

To do justice to the horrors of the subject in a black comedy vein would have required the talents of a Buñuel, and director Rod Daniel is no Luis Buñuel. Daniel's sitcom roots are constantly evident in his sledgehammer direction of Sam Simon's overly jokey script, and the tone seems grotesque in light of the subject matter.

Pesci adds another flamboyantly vile character to his gallery. While providing what is euphemistically termed "affordable housing for the underprivileged," he's the kind of landlord who gleefully snaps "Get a man!" when a matron complains that her apartment is freezing.

But he seems like Gandhi next to his father (Vincent Gardenia), a raging racist whose ultimate solution to Pesci's problems with tenants and the Housing Authority is to hire an arsonist to torch the building.

Bruce Surtees' extremely dark lensing and Kristi Zea's repulsively accurate production design magnify the unfunny elements. Their work is admirable but belongs in a different film, one with the heart to make the surroundings bearable, as Hal Ashby did in "The Landlord."

The sentimental turnabout in Pesci's character, while predictable, is done so abruptly it seems utterly false. A lecture on human rights by an adorable black kid (Kenny Blank) is enough to turn this Scrooge into a neighborhood Santa Claus.

So brilliant in supporting roles, Pesci plays the slumlord's evil side with relish and manages a goofy charm in the Mr. Warmth parts, but he can't carry a whole picture by himself, particularly one with an artificial heart.

Pic's worst failing is that it portrays Pesci's black and Hispanic tenants as benign caricatures rather than flesh-and-blood human beings. Besides Blank, there's the wise hustler (Ruben Blades), the earth mother (Beatrice Winde) and the religious seer (Paul Benjamin).

Rather than tearing Pesci and Gardenia limb from limb, these victims improbably shower their tormentors with kindness. By robbing the tenants of their anger, the pic robs them of their dignity and robs the story of its bite. — *Joseph McBride*

THIS IS MY LIFE

A 20th Century Fox release. Produced by Lynda Obst. Executive producers, Patricia K. Meyer, Carole Isenberg. Co-producer, Michael R. Joyce. Directed by Nora Ephron. Screenplay, Nora Ephron & Delia Ephron, based on Meg Wolitzer's novel "This Is Your Life." Camera (Deluxe color), Bobby Byrne; editor, Robert Reitano; music, Carly Simon; costume design, Jeffrey Kurland; art direction, Barbra Matis; set decoration, Hilton Rosemarin, Jaro Dick; sound, Goug Ganton; assistant director, Henry Bronchtein; casting, Juliet Taylor. Reviewed at Sundance Film Festival, Salt Lake City, Utah, Jan. 16, 1992. MPAA rating: R. Running time: **105 MIN.**

Dottie Ingels	Julie Kavner
Erica Ingels	Samantha Mathis
Opal Ingels	Gaby Hoffmann
Claudia Curtis	Carrie Fisher
Arnold Moss	Dan Aykroyd
Jordan	Danny Zorn

A schlepper turns star but finds that when your kids still need you, success is all very complicated in "This Is My Life," a deftly accomplished directorial debut from scripter Nora Ephron that should turn a modest profit. Intimate, honestly rendered film looks likely to score some emotional points with the working parents it speaks to, but a funny but frank teen sex scene may somewhat erode its potential as family fare.

Glib urban sensibility that informed Ephron's screenplay for "When Harry Met Sally" is toned down this time in favor of humbler, texture-of-life comedy in this pic co-scripted with sister Delia Ephron.

Julie Kavner stars as a New Jersey divorcee who hams it up in her cosmetics counter job selling placenta extract and exfoliating wax to Jewish mavens, then shares her excess comic energy with her 16- and 10-year-old daughters (Samantha Mathis, Gaby Hoffmann) as they dream of her comedy breakthrough.

When an aunt leaves Kavner some start-up money, she packs the kids up for Manhattan, and before long her dreams do start to come true. It's a lot of fun at first, until snowballing success takes her away from them for weeks at a time, and it's more than the teenage daughter, who's introverted and dependent, can handle.

With some slyness and wit and a few sharp edges, pic addresses the tough reality that some kids would rather have their mother handy than happy. After years of devotion, Mom chafes at the short leash they're giving her, while the kids fear they're losing her and aren't ready.

Based on a novel by Meg Wolitzer, pic moves along quite briskly under Ephron's direction and succeeds within its modest parameters at dealing with some difficult family issues honestly and with spirit, and with an ending that smartly avoids being too neat.

Comedienne Kavner gives a zesty and touching perf as the mom coming into her own, and both girls, particularly Mathis as the confused, hypercritical teen, are quite skillful.

Carrie Fisher contributes a deft and savory turn as a glib and chummy agent who cheerfully bemoans her romantic involvement with Mr. Wrong, while Dan Aykroyd stays out of the spotlight — perhaps due to a startling weight gain — in a well-tuned but undemanding turn as a talent agent important to Kavner's growth.

Music composed and sung by Carly Simon is sometimes overobvious, sometimes on-target and delightful, and in the ukelele-backed gem "Back The Way."

Made at Fox with considerable creative latitude (per producer Lynda Obst in introductory remarks at the Sundance fest), pic's production values do very well by the $10 million budget. Film went over quite pleasantly with the first-night crowd in its world premiere at the film fest. — *Amy Dawes*

WHERE THE DAY TAKES YOU

A New Line Cinema release of a Cinetel Films production. Produced by Paul Hertzberg. Executive producers, Lisa M. Hansen, Marc Rocco. Co-producer, Phil McKeon. Co-executive producer, Don McKeon. Directed by Rocco. Screenplay, Michael Hitchcock, Kurt Voss, Rocco. Camera (color), King Baggot; editor, Russell Livingstone; production design, Kirk Petrucelli; set decoration, Greg Grande; sound, Bill Fiege; assistant director, Scott Javine. Reviewed at Palm Springs (Calif.) Intl. Film Festival, Jan. 11, 1992. Running time: **92 MIN.**

King	Dermot Mulroney
Heather	Lara Flynn Boyle
Little J	Balthazar Getty
Greg	Sean Astin
Crasher	James LeGros
Brenda	Ricki Lake
Ted	Kyle MacLachlan
Tommy Ray	Peter Dobson
Charles	Stephen Tobolowsky
Manny	Will Smith
Black	Adam Baldwin
Interviewer	Laura San Giacomo

Attempting a hard-hitting pic on the grimy realities of Hollywood Boulevard street life with the temptations and distortions of Hollywood itself so close is tricky business. Blessed with a cast bursting with up-and-comer names and a technically adept cameraman, "Where the Day Takes You" inevitably winds up giving the runaway's life the kind of romantic-tragic scope that appeals to troubled teens.

Skewed intentions or not, pic has the potential to garner more than a little spare change from the Guns N' Roses crowd if handled carefully.

A goateed and tatooed Dermot Mulroney, in a very charismatic turn, plays King, a 21-year-old parolee who returns to his position as natural leader of street-dwellers who sleep under a freeway embankment in a den they call the Hole.

A tough but compassionate big-brother type who keeps "the family" together, he has his hands full watching a gun-happy youth (Balthazar Getty) with an itch for violence and a middle-class runaway (Sean Astin) who stays totally "tweaked" on speed.

In between profiling himself in social work sessions with a sultry-voiced interviewer (Laura San Giacomo), King takes up with the newest and prettiest chick off the bus from Chicago (a braless Lara Flynn Boyle), and shows her around the streets.

Teen protagonists also include a long-haired James LeGros as King's reluctant first lieutenant, and Ricki Lake, who deserves better than this minor role, in which she's the butt of fat jokes. They find various ways of surviving — panhandling, stealing car stereos, selling drugs, turning tricks.

At their best, this gang is having a whooping good time down at the railroad yard at midnight, jumping onto moving trains while sweeping camerawork sets a romantic tone that begs for a Jon Bon Jovi soundtrack.

At their worst, they're in big trouble after tempers and guns go off, and the cops, right or wrong, start looking for King.

Drugs are nowhere, says this pic, and turning tricks is creepy, but a couple as attractive as Mulroney and Boyle still makes running like wolves look like a lot more fun than high school.

Director Mark Rocco shapes some very fine performances, particularly from Mulroney, Boyle and Getty, while Steven Tobolowsky turns in a memorably chilly perf as a wealthy gay man who pays Getty for titillation. An uncredited Christian Slater turns up in a brief cameo as a social worker.

Cinematography is excellent, with camera always placed for maximum effect — if edgy, lyrical drama and adventure are indeed the goals here.

World premiered at the Palm Springs Intl. Film Festival fresh from the editing bays, pic was screened in a print still lacking end credits and some scoring, but score it had, notably a chilling remix of the '60s anthem "For What It's Worth," added plenty of punch. — *Amy Dawes*

CLAUDE

A JJ Films presentation. Produced by Mark Evan Jacobs, Cindy Lou Johnson. Co-producer, Diana Phillips. Directed, written by Johnson. Camera (color), Bernd Heinl; editor, Camilla Toniolo; music, Stanley Myers; art direction, Philip Messina; production design, Cynthia Kay Charette; costume design, Isis Mussenden; set decoration, Robert Kensinger; sound, Mark Weingarten; casting, Simon & Kumin. Reviewed at Palm Springs (Calif.) Intl. Film Festival, Jan. 11, 1992. Running time: **91 MIN.**
Claude . . . . Mark Evan Jacobs
Beatrice . . . . Irene Jacob
Mrs. Dewey . . . . . Charlotte Moore
Al Dewey . . . . Pat McNamara
Daddy V.J. . . . . . . Leonard Cimino

French actress Irene Jacob is stuck giving a high-pitched screwball comedy performance in director Cindy Lou Johnson's hazily executed debut. European-tinged indieprod about a daffy immigrant (Jacob), her Cambodian child and their dependence on a barely competent young man, Claude (Mark Evan Jacobs), unfolds at a snail's pace and is unlikely to shake loose any distribution dollars.

This ambling, low-key art pic's main problem is a shaky premise involving Claude's accidental torching of the rented house he lives in on the same day Jacob has become a tenant there. Claiming she has lost everything, the waiflike Jacob adopts the malleable Claude as her protector just hours after she's seen moving in with nothing but her child and a few items in a red wagon.

Dramatic tension, hinging on her inevitable discovery that the terrible arsonist was the hapless Claude, is slight, since little was actually lost.

As for pic's direction, pacing is too slack and its goals too vague for script's occasional good lines to become zingers, while the family portrait of Claude's catatonic grandfather, diffident father and confused mother is not as funny as it might have been under a more definite hand.

Film's comedy is muted as director's timing and camera placement always seem to be just shy of maximum effect.

Actress Jacob displays ample ability, but her heavy French accent is a bit much over the course of a film in which she has most of the lines, while her daffily exuberant yet cloyingly helpless act seems dated.

Actor Jacobs gives a low-key, reactive perf that's a bit short on technique. Shot in Providence, R.I., pic establishes a lilting visual tone at first, with beguiling photography by German lenser Bernd Heinl, while overall production values are competent.
— *Amy Dawes*

WHITE MEN CAN'T JUMP

A Twentieth Century Fox release. Produced by Don Miller, David Lester. Executive producer, Michelle Rappaport. Written and directed by Ron Shelton. Camera (DeLuxe color), Russell Boyd; editor, Paul Seydor; music, Bennie Wallace; production design, Dennis Washington; art direction, Robert Fortune; set decoration, Robert Benton; costume design, Francine Jamison-Tanchuck; assistant director, Richard Wells; sound (Dolby), Kirk Francis; stunt coordinator, Julius LeFlore; casting, Victoria Thomas. Reviewed at Mann Village Theater, Los Angeles, March 25, 1992. MPAA Rating: R. Running time: **114 MIN.**
Sidney Deane . . . . . . Wesley Snipes
Billy Hoyle . . . . . . Woody Harrelson
Gloria Clemente . . . . . . Rosie Perez
Rhonda Deane . . . . Tyra Ferrell
Robert . . . . Cylk Cozart
Junior . . . . Kadeem Hardison
George . . . . Ernest Harden Jr.
Walter . . . . John Marshall Jones
Raymond . . . . Marques Johnson
T.J. . . . . David Roberson
Zeke . . . . Kevin Benton

Fox has the right stuff with this immensely entertaining comedy, which should cross over and score big in all quarters — with black and white, basketball fans and those who think the Final Four refers to remaining presidential aspirants. That broad appeal should light up the b.o. scoreboard, keeping auds jumping through the NBA playoffs.

Writer-director Ron Shelton ("Bull Durham") has taken a one-note premise — a self-proclaimed "ebony and ivory" pair of playground hustlers who depend on their black dupes to assume that white guys are deficient when it comes to basketball — and structured a story of relationships, friendship and ample humor.

Billy (Woody Harrelson), a compulsive gambler, is the lam with his "Jeopardy!"-obsessed girlfriend, Gloria (Rosie Perez of "Do the Right Thing"). Two basketball fixers want $8,000 or Billy's life.

Sidney (Wesley Snipes) is a sometime salesman, part-time hustler and family man whose tolerant wife (Tyra Ferrell) is yearning for more stability and a move out of their perilous neighborhood.

After Billy hustles Sidney on the playground with an impressive display of long-range marksmanship, Sidney schemes to cash in on Billy as a ringer. He challenges playground pairs to a little two-on-two and allows them to pick his partner — inevitably the goofy-looking white guy conveniently standing by.

Wisely, Shelton has avoided the obvious "Rocky" elements to which most sports films fall victim, instead using the context to explore broader issues about relationships and life. The setup proves primarily a device to bring the two grudgingly together, even as it threatens to drive them from their respective significant others.

Shelton has crafted a first-rate film that happens to be sports-related. "Bull Durham," for all its poetic speeches about baseball as myth, was about two people getting together. And "White Men Can't Jump" picks up where that film leaves off — namely, how do two people stay together when so many outside pressures can pull them apart?

Shelton nevertheless delivers ample basketball-as-ballet showmanship while exhibiting a wonderful ear for playground bravado. The basketball footage shines thanks to the skills of Snipes and Harrelson, both of whom are credible as athletes.

Hoop enthusiasts will also get a kick out of seeing some former NBA and college players talking trash on the courts — among them former UCLA stars Marques Johnson and Nigel Miguel and prolific scorer Freeman Williams. Shelton elicits perfectly natural performances from these bench players.

For all the film's male bonding, Shelton again has provided a wonderful, wildly eccentric female character (remember "Durham's" Annie Savoy?) in the form of Perez's Gloria, whose own fantasy fulfillment may provide the film's most jarring laughs.

Perez has a grating voice, but she's extremely sexy and appealing. And under Shelton's guidance, she shows a real comic flair. Ferrell, memorable for a small part in "Jungle Fever," provides another strong presence in a less showy role.

Snipes will solidify his film-star credentials with his effortless performance, while Harrelson has his first breakthrough movie role after six years of stupefying splendor on "Cheers."

Shelton capitalizes on the language-induced R rating with steamy sex scenes that feel neither forced nor gratuitous.

Tech credits are another slam dunk, from the jamming score to high-flying basketball choreography. Southern California locations are put to good use.

The marketing campaign, which has blanketed the areas where couch potatoes gather better than a tough man-to-man defense, should lift "White Men" to a strong tipoff. — *Brian Lowry*

1991
INDEX

The following feature films were reviewed in Variety in 1991. A film's title or English-translation title is not only listed in parentheses, but also alphabetically listed as a duplicate entry. Title is followed by director and review date. (The director's name is included only with the original-language listing.)

A

(A Beating Heart) Un Coeur Qui Bat June 24
A Brighter Summer Day d. Edward Yang Sept. 2
A Captive In The Land d. John Berry May 13
(A Crazy Couple) Eine Wahnsinnesehe Mar. 11
(A Day To Remember) Aujourd'hui Peut-tre Apr. 22
A Divina Comedia (The Divine Comedy) d. Manoel de Oliveira Sept. 23
(A Dream In The Abyss) Un Sueño En El Abismo Dec. 2
A Karim Na Sala (Karim And Sala) d. Idrissa Ouedraogo June 17
A Kiss Before Dying d. James Dearden Apr. 29
(A Little Bit Of Soul) Ovo Malo Duse May 13
A Little Stiff d. Greg Watkins Feb. 11
(A Man And Two Women) Un Homme Et Deux Femmes Nov. 4
(A Paradise Without Billiards) Ett Paradis Utan Biljard Jan. 28
(A Peaceful Air Of The West) L'Aria Serena Dell'Ouest Apr. 1
A Rage In Harlem d. Bill Duke May 6
A Row Of Crows d. J.S. Cardone June 17
A Royal Hunt) Narskar Oxota Nov. 4
(A Simple Story) Una Storia Semplice Sept. 16
A Small Dance d. Alan Horrox Dec. 16
A Távollét Hercege (The Prince Of Absence) d. Tams Tolmr Nov. 4
A Woman's Tale d. Paul Cox Apr. 22
Abraxus, Guardian Of The Universe d. Damien Lee Apr. 15
Absolutely Positive d. Peter Adair Mar. 25
Accidental Golfer, The (Den Ofrivillige Goldfaren) d. Lasse Aberg Dec. 23
(Adam's Rib) Rebro Adama Sept. 23
Addams Family, The d. Barry Sonnenfeld Nov. 18
Adjuster, The d. Atom Egoyan May 27
Afghan Breakdown d. Vladimir Bortko May 27
Afraid Of The Dark d. Mark Peploe Nov. 25
(After All ...) Es Megis ... June 10
Agantuk (The Stranger) d. Satyajit Ray Oct. 21
Agnes Cecilia d. Anders Grnros Aug. 19
Ah Fei Zheng Zhuan (Days Of Being Wild) d. Wong Kar-wai Apr. 1
Al Moaten Al Myssri (War In The Land Of Egypt) d. Salah Abou Seif July 22
Alambrado (Fenced In) d. Marco Bechis Nov. 4
(Alan And Eric Between Hello And Goodbye) Seung Sing Gusi July 1
Alas De Mariposa (Butterfly Wings) d. Juanma Bajo Ulloa Oct. 7
(Alice In Wonder Town) Alicia En El Pueblo De Maravillas Mar. 18
Alicia En El Pueblo De Maravillas (Alice In Wonder Town) d. Daniel Diaz
 Torres Mar. 18
All I Want For Christmas d. Robert Lieberman Nov. 18
(All Jews Out!) Alle Juden Raus! Mar. 11
All Of Me d. Betinna Wilhelm Apr. 1
All Out d. Thomas Koerfer Apr. 1
Alle Juden Raus! (All Jews Out!) d. Emanuel Rund Mar. 11
Allemagne Neuf Zero (Germany Nine Zero) d. Jean-Luc Godard Sept. 16
Alta Marea (High Tide) d. Lician Segura Nov. 11

✱ Reviews for film titles marked with an asterisk are found in the Addendum.

B

Behind The Mask d. Frank Martin Sept. 16
Beijing Nizao (Good Morning Beijing) d. Zhang Nuanxin Sept. 23
Bekhatere Hameh Chiz (For Everything) d. Rajab Mohammadin Mar. 18
(Benjamin's Woman) La Mujer De Benjamin Mar. 25
Berdel d. Atif Yilmaz Apr. 8
(Beyond The Seven Seas) Bak Sju Hav July 8
Bian Zhou Bian Chang (Life On A String) d. Chen Kaige May 27
Bienvenue A Bord! (Welcome Aboard!) d. Jean-Louis Leconte July 8
Big Slice, The d. John Bradshaw Aug. 5
Bikini Island d. Anthony Markes July 22
Biletas Iki Taj Mahal (Ticket To Taj Mahal) d. Algimantas Puipa July 15
Bill & Ted's Bogus Journey d. Peter Hewitt July 22
(Billions) Miliardi Mar. 25
Billy Bathgate d. Robert Benton Nov. 4
Bingo d. Matthew Robbins Aug. 19
Bix d. Pupi Avati May 13
Black Demons d. Umberto Lenzi June 3
(Black Lizard) Kurotakage Aug. 12
Black Magic Woman d. Deryn Warren Apr. 8
Black Robe d. Bruce Beresford Sept. 9
Blade Runner (Director's Version) d. Ridley Scott Sept. 30
Blobermouth d. Kent Skov Apr. 15
Blonde Fist d. Frank Clarke Sept. 30
Blood And Concrete d. Jeffrey Reiner Jan. 21
Blood In The Face d. Anne Bohlen Feb. 11
Bloodfist II d. Andy Blumenthal Apr. 15
Blowback d. Marc Levin July 29
(Blown Kiss) Vozdusniy Potzelui July 29
Blue Desert d. Brad Battersby Jan. 14
(Blue Note) La Note Bleue Aug. 5
Body Parts d. Eric Red Aug. 12
Bokura No Nanoka-Kan Senso (Seven Days' War) d. Hiroshi Sugawara Nov. 4
(Border, The) Granica May 6
Börn Náttúrunnar (Children Of Nature) d. Fridrik Thr Fridriksson Aug. 12
Borrower, The d. John McNaughton Sept. 9
Boy Who Cried Bitch, The d. Juan Jose Campanella June 17
Boyz N The Hood d. John Singleton May 20
Brain Twisters d. Jerry Sangiuliano June 3
Bratan (Brother) d. Bachtjar Chudojnazarov Nov. 25
Breathing Under Water d. Susan Murphy Dermody Nov. 18
(Bride, The) Arus Apr. 15
Bride Of Re-Animator d. Brian Yuzna Feb. 25
Bridge, The d. Syd Macartney May 27
(Broken Youth) Slomjena Mladost July 8
(Brother) Bratan Nov. 25
Buddy's Song d. Claude Whatham Mar. 11
Bugsy d. Barry Levinson Dec. 9
(Buick, The) Buicken Oct. 7
Buicken (The Buick) d. Hans Otto Nicolayssen Oct. 7
Bullseye! d. Michael Winner July 29
(Burial Of Potatoes) Pogrzeb Kartofla May 27
Buster's Bedroom d. Rebecca Horn Apr. 15
Butcher's Wife, The d. Terry Hughes Oct. 28
(Butterfly Wings) Alas De Mariposa Oct. 7
By The Sword d. Jeremy Kagan Oct. 14

C

Cabeza De Vaca d. Nicolas Echevarria Mar. 4

Csapd Le Csacsi! (Slap-Jack) d. Pter Timr Aug. 5
(Cup Final) G'mar Giviya July 29
Curly Sue d. John Hughes Oct. 28
(Cyclist, The) Der Radfahrer Apr. 1

D

Da Nacht Van De Wilde Ezels (The Night Of The Wild Donkeys) d. Pim de la
 Parra Feb. 18
Da Taijian Li Lianying (Li Lianying, The Imperial Eunuch) d. Tian
 Zhuangzhuang Mar. 11
Dahong Denglong Gaogao Gua (Raise The Red Letter) d. Zhang Yimou Oct. 7
Dakota Road d. Nick Ward Mar. 11
Dali d. Antoni Ribas Apr. 8
Dames Galantes (Gallant Ladies) d. Jean-Charles Tacchella Mar. 18
Damned In The USA d. Paul Yule Sept. 23
Dana Lech d. Frank-Guido Blasberg Mar. 11
(Dance On The Dump) Tanz Auf Der Kippe Apr. 22
Dance To Win d. Ted Mather Nov. 4
Dandan-E Mar (Snake Fang) d. Masoud Kimiai Feb. 25
Danzon d. Mara Novaro Apr. 29
Dar Kuche-Haye Eshgh (In The Alleys Of Love), d. Khosro Sinai Apr. 1
Darbe (The Stroke) d.Ümit Efekan Apr. 8
Dark Backward, The d. Adam Rifkin Mar. 18
Dark City d. Chris Curling Aug. 12
Dark Wind, The d. Errol Morris Nov. 25
Das Deutsche Kettensägenmassaker (The German Chainsaw Massacre) d.
 Christoph Schlingensief Mar. 11
Das Heimweh Des Walerjan Wrobel (Walerjan Wrobel's Homesickness) d. Rolf
 Schbel July 29
Das Lachen Der Maca Daracs (The Laughter Of Maca Daracs) d. Dieter Berner
 July 8
Das Mädchen Aus Dem Fahrstuhl (The Girl In The Lift), Hermann Zschoche
 Mar. 11
Das Serbische Mädchen (The Serbian Girl) d. Peter Sehr Apr. 1
Daughters Of The Dust d. Julie Dash Feb. 11
(Day, The) DGE Mar. 18
(Days Of Being Wild) Ah Fei Zheng Zhuan Apr. 1
De Hollywood A Tamanrasset (From Hollywood To Tamanrasset) d. Mahmoud
 Zemmouri June 17
De Laatste Sessie (Last Date) d. Hans Hylkema Dec. 23
De Onfatsoenlijke Vrouw (The Indecent Woman) d. Ben Verbong June 10
De Provincie (The Province) d. Jan Bosdriesz Oct. 7
De Zondagsjongen (The Sunday Boy) d. Pieter Verhoeff Oct. 7
Dead Again d. Kenneth Branagh Aug. 26
Dead Sleep d. Alec Mills Feb. 18
Dead Space d. Fred Gallo June 24
Dead To The World d. Ross Gibson June 17
Deadly d. Esben Storm Apr. 29
Deadly Currents d. Simcha Jacobovici Oct. 28
(Death Of A Schoolboy) Gavre Princip Himmel Unter Steinen Jan. 21
Deceived d. Damian Harris Sept. 30
December d. Gabe Torres Dec. 9
December 7th: The Movie d. Gregg Toland, John Ford Dec. 2
Deep Blues d. Robert Mugge June 24
Defending Your Life d. Albert Brooks Mar. 18
Defenseless d. Martin Campbell Aug. 12
Delicatessen d. Jean-Pierre Jeunet, Marc Caro May 27

E

F

G

H

J

K

Kafka d. Steven Soderbergh Dec. 9
(Karim And Sala) A Karim Na Sala June 17
Kasba d. Kumar Shahani Nov. 4
Kashti-e Angelica (The Ship Angelica) d. Mohammad Reza Bozorgnia Mar. 18
(Katya's Autumn) Muuttolinnun Aika Apr. 15
Ked Hviezdy Boli Cervene (When The Stars Were Red) d. Dusan Trancik Apr.29
Kedulo Urichurum (The, Like Us) d. Park Kwang-su June 17
Kei Wong (The King Of Chess) d. Yim Ho Dec. 2
KGB Agents Also Fall In Love) Los De La KGB Tambien Se Enamoran Dec. 16
Kickboxer 2: The Road Back d. Albert Pyun Feb. 11
Kikuchi (Tokyo Cleaning Man) d. Kenchi Iwamoto Apr. 15
(The King Of Chess) Kei Wong Dec. 2
King Ralph d. David S. Ward Feb. 18
Kiss Me A Killer d. Marcus DeLeon Apr. 15
Kleisti Strophi (U-Turn) d. Nikos Grammatikos Oct. 21
Knot In The Necktie, The) Il Nodo Alla Cravatta Sept. 2
K2 d. Franc Estrin, Hal Weiner Dec. 2
Komm In Den Garten (Come Into The Garden) d. Heinz Brinkman Mar. 4
Kurotakage (Black Lizard) d. Kinji Fukasaku Aug. 12
Kuutamosonaatti 2: Kadunlakaisijat (Moonlight Sonata 2: The Street
 Sweepers) d. Olli Soinio Apr. 15

L

L'Amico Arabo (The Arab Friend) d. Carmine Fornari Oct. 21
L'Amore Necessario (Necessary Love) d. Fabio Carpi Sept. 16
L'Année De L'Eveil (The Year Of Awakening) d. Grard Corbiau Sept. 2
L'Aria Serena Dell'Ouest (A Peaceful Air Of The West) d. Silvio Soldini
 Apr. 1
L'Autre (The Other) d. Bernard Giraudeau June 24
L'Entrainement Du Champion Avant La Course (The Training Of The Champion
 Before The Race) d. Bernard Favre June 3
L'Homme Qui A Perdu Son Ombre (The Man Who Lost His Shadow) d. Alain
 Tanner Sept. 2
L'Opration Corned Beef (Operation Corned Beef) d. Jean-Marie Poir Apr. 29
La Belle Noiseuse d. Jacques Rivette May 20
La Carne (The Flesh) d. Marco Ferreri May 20
La Casa Del Sorriso (House Of Smiles) d. Marco Ferreri Mar. 4
* La Chevre (The Goat) d. Francis Veber Aug. 12
La Condanna (The Judgment) d. Michele Placido, Pietro Valsecchi Mar. 11
La Desenchantée (The Disenchanted) d. Benoit Jacquot Aug. 12
La Domenica Specialmente (Especially On Sunday) d. Giuseppe Tornatore,
 Marco Tullio Giordana, Giuseppe Bertolucci, Francesco Barilli Oct. 21
La Double Vie De Veronique (The Double Life Of Weronika) d. Krzysztof
 Kieslowski May 20
La Femme Fardee d. Jos Pinheiro July 15
La Gloire De Mon Pre (My Father's Glory) d. Yves Robert Jan. 14
La Blanca Paloma (The White Dove) d. Juan Minon May 27
La Leyenda De Una Mascara (The Legend Of A Mask) d. Jos Buil Apr. 22
La Mujer De Benjamin (Benjamin's Woman) d. Carlos Carrera Mar. 25
La Mujer Del Puerto (Woman Of The Port) d. Arturo Ripstein June 10
La Neige Et Le Feu (Snow And Fire) d. Claude Pinoteau Nov. 25
La Niña En La Palomera (The Girl In The Dovecote) d. Alfredo Rates Feb. 4
La Noche Ms Larga (The Longest Night) d. Jos Luis Garca Oct. 7

M

O

P

Q

R

S

T

U

V

W

Y

Z

1992
INDEX

The following feature films were reviewed in Variety in 1992. A film's title or English-translation title is not only listed in parentheses, but also alphabetically listed as a duplicate entry. Title is followed by director and review date. (The director's name is included only with the original-language listing.)

A

A Dai d. Cal Yangming Nov. 30
A Demain (See You Tomorrow) d. Didier Martiny Dec. 21
A Harom Nover (Three Sisters) d. Andor Lukats Feb. 24
A Idade Major (Alex) d. Teresa Villaverde Jan. 6
A Korpio Megeszi az Kreket Reggelire (Scorpio Eats Gemini for Breakfast)
  d. Pter Grdos Feb. 24
A Nyaralo (The Summer Guest) Feb. 24
(About Love, Tokyo) Ai Ni Tsuite, Tokyo Nov. 16
(Above the Mountains) Boven de Bergen Feb. 24
Abracadabra d. Harry Cleven Oct. 19
(Absence, The) Die Abwesenheit Oct. 19
(Accompanist, The) L'Accompagnatrice Dec. 21
Aces: Iron Eagle III d. John Glen June 8
(Acquitted for Having Committed the Deed) Assolto per Aver Commesso il
  Fatto May 4
Acts of Defiance d. Alec G. MacLeod Nov. 30
Adorable Lies d. Gerardo Chijona Mar. 23
(Adventures of Kalle Stropp and the Frog Ball, The) Kalle Stropp och Gro-
  dan Boll Pa Svindlande ventyr Feb. 24
Affengeil (Life Is Like a Cucumber) d. Rosa von Praunheim June 29
(After Love) Apres l'Amour Sept. 7
(After the Dream) Despues del Sueno Oct. 26
Afureru Atsui Namida (Swimming With Tears) d. Koichi Sakuma Apr. 6
(Against Oblivion) Contre l'Oubli Sept. 7
(Age Isn't Everything) Life in the Food Chain d. Douglas Katz Aug. 10
Ah-Ying (Ming Ghost) d. Ch'iu Kangchien Nov. 2
Ai Ni Tsuite, Tokyo (About Love, Tokyo) d. Mitsuo Yanagimachi Nov. 16
Aileen Wuornos: The Selling of a Serial Killer d. Nick Broomfield Dec. 7
Aitsu (Waiting for the Flood) d. Atsushi Kimura Sept. 7
Aladdin d. John Musker, Ron Clements Nov. 9
Alan & Naomi d. Sterling VanWagenen Feb. 3
Albert Souffre (Albert Suffers) d. Bruno Nuytten Oct. 26
(Albert Suffers) Albert Souffre Oct. 26
(Alex) A Idade Major Jan. 6
Alias `La Gringa' d. Alberto Durant Jan. 13
Alien 3 d. David Fincher May 25
(All Lies) Alles Lge Apr. 6
All My Husbands d. Andr Farwagi June 22
All-American Murder d. Anson Williams Mar. 30
Allein Unter Frauen (Alone Among Women) d. Sonke Wortmann Aug. 17
Alles Lge (All Lies) d. Heiko Schier Apr. 6
Almost Blue d. Keoni Waxman June 15
(Alone Among Women) Allein Unter Frauen Aug. 17
Am Ende der Nacht (At the End of the Night) d. Christoph Schaub May 18
Amar y Vivir (To Love and Live) d. Carlos Duplat Sanjuan Aug. 10
Amazing Grace d. Amos Guttman Nov. 9
Amazon d. Mika Kaurismki Mar. 2

* Reviews for film titles marked with an asterisk are found in the Addendum.

B

Boomerang d. Reginald Hudlin June 29
Border Line d. Danile Dubroux Mar. 30
(Borges Tales, Part I) Cuentos de Borges I Jan. 13
Born to Ski d. Don Brolin Jan. 20
(Both Sides of the Street) La ContreAlle Nov. 23
Bottom Land d. Edward A. Radtke Aug. 17
Boven de Bergen (Above the Mountains) d. Digna Sinke Feb. 24
Bowl of Bone: Tale of the Syuwe d. Jan-Marie Martell Nov. 30
(Boys From St. Petri, The) Drengene fra Sankt Petri Jan. 27
Brain Donors d. Dennis Dugan Apr. 27
Braindead d. Peter Jackson May 25
Bram Stoker's Dracula d. Francis Ford Coppola Nov. 9
Brandnacht (Night on Fire) d. Markus Fischer July 13
(Brats) Felalom Feb. 24
Breaking the Rules d. Neal Israel Nov. 2
Brief History of Time, A d. Errol Morris Jan. 20
Brother's Keeper d. Joe Berlinger, Bruce Sinofsky Feb. 10
(Brothers and Sisters) Fratelli e Sorelle Sept. 21
Buffalo Jump d. Chris Johnstone June 8
Buffy the Vampire Slayer d. Fran Rubel Kuzui Aug. 3
Bullets for Breakfast d. Holly Fisher Mar. 16
(Butterfly Hunt, The) La Chasse aux Papillons Oct. 5
Butterscotch and Chocolate d. Nate Grant Nov. 23

C

C'Est Arriv Prs de Chez Vous (Man Bites Dog) d. Rmy Belvaux May 25
Candyman d. Bernard Rose Oct. 12
Captain America d. Albert Pyun June 8
Captain Ron d. Thom Eberhardt Sept. 21
Caravana d. Julio Csar Rodrguez, Rogelio Paris May 4
Careful d. Guy Maddin May 18
Carry On Columbus d. Gerald Thomas Oct. 5
(Casanova's Return) Le Retour de Casanova May 18
(Cash Academy) Sup de Fric Aug. 10
Cline d. Jean-Claude Brisseau Mar. 9
(Censorship Has No Access to My Memory) Senzuru K Pamjati Ne Dopuskaju
  Apr. 27
Center of the Web d. David A. Prior May 4
(Center Stage) Ruan Ling-Yu Mar. 9
Cerni Baroni (The Black Barons) d. Zdenek Sirovy July 27
Chain of Desire d. Temistocles Lopez Sept. 7
Changing Our Minds: The Story of Dr. Evelyn Hooker d. Richard Schmiechen
  July 13
Chaplin d. Richard Attenborough Dec. 7
Charlie's Ear d. Gary Chason May 11
(Charlots Return, The) Le Retour des Charlots Aug. 17
(Chekist, The) Tchekiste June 1
Cheongsonguro Ganunkil (The Way to Cheong Song)
  d. Lee Doo-yong June 29
(Cherry Orchard, The) Il Giardino dei Ciliegi Oct. 12
Chickpeas d. Nigol Bezjian Dec. 14
(Child of Man, The) Cilveka Berns Mar. 2
(Child of the Open Road) Kinder der Landstrasse June 22
(Child's Play) Kinderspiele July 27
Children of the Night d. Tony Randel May 18
(Children Thief, The) Le Voleur d'Enfants Apr. 13
(Chinese Ghost Story III, A) Sinnui Yauman III: Do Do Do Oct. 19

D

E

F

G

Gumshoe d. Malcolm McDonald Oct. 5
Gun in Betty Lou's Handbag, The d. Allan Moyle Aug. 24
Guncrazy d. Tamra Davis June 1

H

Ha Ett Underbart Liv (Have a Wonderful Life) d. Ulf Malmoros Feb. 10
Haimwee Naar de Dood (Nostalgia for Death) d. Ramon Gieling Feb. 24
Hak Mau (Black Cat) d. Stephen Shin June 22
Hand That Rocks the Cradle, The d. Curtis Hansen Jan. 6
(Happily Ever After) Siempre Felices Nov. 30
(Happy Birthday!) Happy Birthday, Turke! Mar. 2
Happy Birthday, Turke! (Happy Birthday!) d. Doris Dorrie Mar. 2
(Happy Days) Stchastlivye Dni June 29
Hard Hunted d. Andy Sidaris Sept. 21
Hard-Boiled d. John Wood Sept. 28
(Have a Wonderful Life) Ha Ett Underbart Liv Feb. 10
Hay Que Zurrar a los Pobres (Let's Trash the Poor) d. Santiago San Miguel
  May 25
(Hayfever) Hofeber Apr. 20
(Heart of Stone, A) Un Coeur en Hiver Sept. 7
(Heart's Dark Side) El Lado Oscuro del Corazon Aug. 31
(Heartbreakers) Rompecorazones Apr. 13
(Heaven or Hell) Himmel Oder Holle July 20
(Heavenly Sin) Tengoku no Taizai Oct. 5
Hedd Wyn d. Paul Turner Oct. 5
Hello Hemingway d. Fernando Prez Jan. 6
Hellraiser III: Hell on Earth d. Anthony Hickox Sept. 14
Hero d. Stephen Frears Sept. 28
(Heroes) Bayani Apr. 27
(Hidden Lens) Obiettivo Indiscreto Apr. 27
(Hideaway, The) Mv og Funder July 13
Highway 66 Revisited d. Thomas Repp Dec. 14
(Highway Patrolman) El Patrullero May 25
Highway to Hell d. Ate de Jong Mar. 23
Hikarigoke (Luminous Moss) d. Ken Kumai Feb. 24
Himmel Oder Holle (Heaven or Hell) d. Wolfgang Murnberger July 20
Hit the Dutchman d. Menahem Golan June 1
Ho Sap el Ministre? (Does the Minister Know?) d. Josep M. Forn Aug. 17
Hochzitsnuecht (Wedding Night-End of the Song) d. Pol Cruchten June 8
Hofeber (Hayfever) d. Annelise Hovmand Apr. 20
Hoffa d. Danny DeVito Dec. 21
Hold Me, Thrill Me, Kiss Me d. Joel Hirshman June 8
(Hollywood) Joligud Apr. 6
Holod 33 (Famine '33) d. Oles Yanchuk Aug. 10
Home Alone 2: Lost in New York d. Chris Columbus Nov. 16
Home Fires Burning d. L.A. Puopolo June 8
Honey, I Blew Up the Kid d. Randal Kleiser July 20
Honeymoon in Vegas d. Andrew Bergman Aug. 24
Hong 2 Run 44 (Classmates) d. Bandit Ritthakon Nov. 2
(Honor Roll) Tableau d'Honneur Aug. 17
Hors Saison (Off Season) d. Daniel Schmid Oct. 26
Hostage d. Robert Young May 25
Hours and Times, The d. Christopher Munch Jan. 27
Housesitter d. Frank Oz June 8
Howards End d. James Ivory Feb. 24
Hua Pi Zhi Yinyang Fawang (Painted Skin) d. King Hu Nov. 9
Hugh Hefner: Once Upon a Time d. Robert Heath Oct. 19
Human Shield, The d. Ted Post June 8

Hummingbird Tree, The d. Noella Smith Nov. 16
Hurricane Smith d. Colin Budd May 4
Hurt Penguins d. Robert Bergman Nov. 2
Husbands and Lovers d. Mauro Bolognini May 4
Husbands and Wives d. Woody Allen Aug. 31
(Hyenas) Hyenes May 25
Hyenes (Hyenas) d. Djibril Diop Mambety May 25

I

(I Am My Own Woman) Ich Bin Meine Eigene Frau Dec. 7
(I Am Twenty) Mne Dvadstat Let Mar. 9
I Don't Buy Kisses Anymore d. Robert Marcarelli Feb. 24
I Love Vienna d. Houchang Allahyari Apr. 13
(I Thought It Was Love) Pensavo Fosse Amore Invece Era Un Calesse Sept. 28
(I Wanted to See Angels) Ya Hatiella Ooveedit Angelov Oct. 19
I Was on Mars d. Dani Levy Jan. 20
(I've Heard the Ammonite Murmur) Anmonaito No Sasayaki Wo Kiita June 1
Ich Bin Meine Eigene Frau (I Am My Own Woman) d. Rosa von Praunheim Dec. 7
(Identification of Desire) Identifikatsia Zhelanii Mar. 2
Identifikatsia Zhelanii (Identification of Desire) d. Tolib Khamidov Mar. 2
Idiot d. Mani Kaul Oct. 12
Il Giardino dei Ciliegi (The Cherry Orchard) d. Antonello Aglioti Oct. 12
Il Ladro di Bambini (The Stolen Children) d. Gianni Amelio May 11
(Images of the World and the Inscription of War) Bilder der Welt und In-
  schrift des Krieges Jan. 6
Immaculate Conception d. Jamil Dehlavi Sept. 14
(In Heaven As on Earth) Sur la Terre Comme au Ciel Feb. 17
In Search of Our Fathers d. Marco Williams Feb. 10
(In the Country of Juliets) Au Pays des Juliets May 18
In the Heat of Passion d. Rodman Flender Feb. 10
(In the Name of God) Raam Ke Naam Nov. 30
(In the Name of the Father and the Son) Au Nom de Pre et du Fils Apr. 20
In the Soup d. Alexandre Rockwell Jan. 27
Incident at Oglala d. Michael Apted Feb. 3
(Independent Life, An) Samostoiatelnaia Jizn May 18
(Indochina) Indochine May 11
Indochine (Indochina) d. Rgis Wargnier May 11
Infinitas d. Marlen Chuziev Mar. 9
Ingal d. sds Thoroddsen May 25
Inland Sea, The d. Lucille Carra Feb. 10
Innocent Blood d. John Landis Sept. 28
Innocents Abroad d. Les Blank Jan. 27
Inside Monkey Zetterland d. Jefery Levy July 27
Intimate Stranger d. Alan Berliner Feb. 10
Into the Sun d. Fritz Kiersch Jan. 27
Into the West d. Mike Newell Dec. 21
IP5: L'Ile aux Pachydermes (IP5: The Island of Pachyderms) d. Jean-Jacques
  Beineix June 15
(IP5: The Island of Pachyderms) IP5: L'Ile aux Pachydermes June 15
Ir Ten Krantai Smeleti (There Are Sandy Beaches Too) d. Algimantas Puipa
  July 27
Ishi: The Last Yahi d. Jeff Riffe, Pamela Roberts Nov. 30
Isimeria (Equinox) d. Nikos Cornilios May 25
(It's Always Hard to Return Home) Siempre de Dificil Volver a Casa Dec. 21
(Italian Saturday) Sabato Italiano Nov. 23

J

K

L

M

N

O

P

Q

R

S

T

W

X

Y

Z